Fourteenth Edition

Blue Book of Gun Values™

By S.P. Fjestad

FRONT COVER

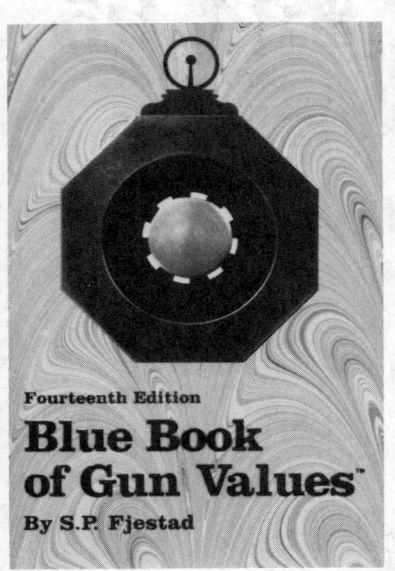

Fourteenth Edition

Blue Book of Gun Values™

By S.P. Fjestad

Perhaps many of you have already noticed the 14th Edition cover graphics are a little different than the images you have seen on past editions. The swirl pattern background is a reproduction of a "marbled" paper design that has been classically used to formally separate the hardbound cover from the inside main text on finer quality publications. The different colored inks are literally poured in layers on heavy paper stock, followed by a very precise series of mechanical fingered "combings" that produce the unique and imperfect geometrical patterns and color arrays (some marbled paper designs are so precise and consistent that once the inks dry, the final image can be copyrighted for future reproduction).

Once printed in four-color, the cover sheets were transported onto the next production stop which specialized in high-tech foil stamping/embossing, which allowed 10X bullet accuracy (you be the judge). After the covers were foil stamped (two separate press runs requiring perfect die registration), the cover sheets were again transported from St. Paul back to the printer in Minneapolis for laminating (a clear, protective laminate which after heating adheres to the cover paper stock). The laminating process now completed, the already tired sheets made the trip back across the river again where the "2-up" sheets went through the embossing stage, a critical phase where the images are punched up in multi-levels by using state-of-the-art custom dies. Once embossed, it was back to the printer one last time for final trimming and the final destination - the bindery.

These five separately critical operations allowed the 14th Edition covers to cumulatively put on over 8,000,000 miles before they ever left our warehouse! Hopefully, all your shots this year can be as true as the copper bullet just clearing the muzzle end of this 14th Edition's Model 1886 Deluxe in the *ultra rare* .310 Cadet caliber.

After recently looking at Ivana's paint-by-numbers credit listing in a recent *Lears* magazine, I decided the following may be appropriate for the good image we share. The following vendor and art direction credits made this cover possible:

Cover Design and Final Layout - S.P. Fjestad
Art Director - Doreen Pomije
Back Cover Photography - G. Allan Brown - Photographer
Back Cover Colt's and Case - courtesy of H. Greeley
Color Separations and Final Stripping - Leslie, Roger, and Dick from Northwoods Color
Printing - Jack, Steve, Dave, and "Beam-Him-Up" Scotty from Viking Press
Foil Stamping and Embossing - Duane, Pat, and Crew from Modernistic Die

BACK COVER

The guns pictured on the 14th Edition's back cover are a pair of Colt Single Action Army Pistols, consecutively serial numbered SA 73,26X and SA 73,26X+1 and are engraved by Dennis Kies. Both pistols have one-piece ivory stocks which have been scrimshawed and have full metal butt caps. The American style engraving is accentuated with a Florentine background as opposed to the punch dot pattern normally found on this type of pistol. The blue pistol has gold inlaid barrel and cylinder bands as well as a gold outline of the frame.

The artist responsible for the case illustrated on the rear cover is Jeffrey Brundege of Rogersville, MO. He is a cross between expert woodworker and artist - he sometimes refers to himself as a functional artist.

The case was fashioned after the bar room nudes of the Old West. Brundege's client wanted to case an engraved pair of Colt Single Action Army pistols and felt something with a western flair would be appropriate. Pushing the tassel on the right-hand side of the case slowly lowers the door while playing the Blue Danube Waltz.

Settling on the design took some 18 months - questions about which side she would recline on, her hair, type of settee, etc., all were sorted out with lengthy telephone calls. Finally, Brundege settled on the design and preparations for the construction began. A clay model of the case was constructed first showing most of the details. Many of the smaller points were corrected or changed at this state - a model was photographed and used as a guide to help with the smaller details. When the clay was as close to what Brundege believed to be the idea he and the client had in mind, a rubber mold was made. From this mold a plaster cast was made and sent to the client - who gave immediate approval. At this point, some three hundred hours of work had already been devoted to this project. This can be easily seen when one considers the time involved in placing arms, hands, etc., finalizing the design. At this point the real work began!!

The next step was preparation of the wood which entailed matching and gluing the wood. With the wood and plaster cast at hand a rough carving using a Dupli Carver (a machine similar to a key maker) was made and the piece was ready for carving and finishing. The final carving took some 640 hours followed by 80 hours on the mechanisms (three were tried) used to lower the door and play the music. To top it all off, about 80 additional hours of work went into finishing. All together, Brundege put well over 1,100 hours into the project - far more than the original estimate, which was about one third of that time.

The publisher wishes to express thanks to Mr. Horace Greeley for allowing this unique cased set of Colt Single Actions a 4-color appearance on the back cover.

Fourteenth Edition

Blue Book
of Gun Values ™

Publisher's Note:

This book is the result of nonstop and continual firearms research obtained by attending gun shows communicating with gun dealers and collectors throughout the country each year. This book represents an analysis of prices for which collectible firearms have actually been selling for during that period at an average retail level.

Although every reasonable effort has been made to compile an accurate and reliable guide, gun prices may vary significantly depending on such factors as the locality of the sale, the number of sales we were able to consider, and economic conditions.

Accordingly, no representation can be made that the guns listed may be bought or sold at prices indicated, nor shall the author or publisher be responsible for any error made in compiling and recording such prices.

Blue Book of Gun Values Order Form
One Appletree Square
Minneapolis, MN 55425 U.S.A.
Phone No. 612-854-5229

-To Order Domestically-

Call : **TOLL FREE 1-800-877-GUNS (4867)** or FAX (612) 853-1486 to use your **VISA, MASTERCARD** or **DISCOVER** charge cards, or send in this order form with payment.

MN residents please include 6.5% sales tax - $1.62 per book.

OFFICE HOURS: 8:30 AM - 5:00 PM (CST), Monday - Friday. Answering machine services available 5:00 PM - 8:30 AM, Monday - Friday and weekends. FAX service available 24 hours per day. All FAX and phone message orders (if information is complete) will be shipped within 2 business days.

☐ **14th Edition is $29.95** (includes $5 s/h- 4th class U.S. Mail)

> **Expedited Shipping Costs:** *in the continental U.S.* ; 1st class U.S. Mail or UPS ground service add $2.00; UPS 2nd day air add $5.00; Next Day - add $15.00
>
> *Alaska and Hawaii* - 2nd day air - add $10.00; Next Day - add $20.00
>
> **International Shipping** - *Canada and Mexico* add $5.00
>
> *Europe* - air mail - add $15.00, to *Africa, Asia,* or *Pacific Rim* - add $20.00.
>
> *International* Surface Rate add $5.00

☐ **14th & 15th Edition is $49.95** (includes 4th class U.S. Mail delivery)

SORRY, NO C.O.D.'s.
This offer expires March 1, 1994

Company Name _____

Name_____

Address_____

Phone _____

City _____ **State** _____ **Zip** _____

VISA/MASTERCARD/DISCOVER # _____

Expiration Date of Card _____

Signature _____

(Personal or cashiers check, money order, etc. are also considered good funds. All orders are shipped within 2 working days after receiving good funds).

Or Send Payment To:

Blue Book of Gun Values
Department 522
One Appletree Square #1391
Minneapolis, MN 55425 U.S.A.

☐ *CADA Gun Journal,* **1 year subscription** (3rd class U.S. mail)
only $29.95 (please inquire for other delivery options)

   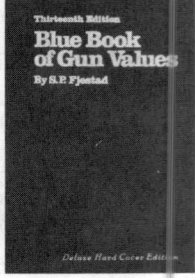

Pictured are soft cover Editions 1 through 13, also hard cover Editions 11-13. Older editions in mint condition have become very collectible. Inventory permitting, we occasionally can offer older editions at the following prices:

Editions 1-6	$25.00 to $50.00 each *(depending on condition)*
Editions 7-13	$24.95 each.
Hard Covers	$50.00 each *(when available)*

Please call 1-800-877-4867 (USA) for availability and pricing on these older editions.

CONTENTS

Cover Introduction 2-3

Title Page..4

Blue Book Order Form 5

Blue Book Pictorial History...6

How to Use the Blue Book 8-10

Acknowledgements..11-12

A Word About Pricing 13

Correspondence Inquiries 14

Diarrhea of an Edition..15-17

A Unique Concept...18

Introduction 19-23

Trash or Treasure? 24-27

Glossary..28-30

Abbreviations 31

CADA Subscription Form 32

Photo Percentage Grading System 33-64

Cartridge Interchangeability 65

Firearms Associations..66-68

Meet the Staff...69-71

Firearms Publications...72-81

Grading Criteria 82

NRA Condition Standards 83

References 84

Periodicals 85

Modern/Antique Firearms Text 87-1,080

Modern Airguns 1,081-1,104

Modern Black Powder Firearms 1,105-1,174

Trademark Index 1,175-1,184

Serialization...1,185-1,205

Proofmarks 1,206-1,211

Index 1,212-1,216

How to Use This Book

The prices listed in the 14th Edition of the *Blue Book of Gun Values* are based on national average retail prices for both antique and modern firearms. This is not a wholesale pricing guide (I doubt if there could be such a thing). Percentages of original condition (with corresponding prices) are listed between 10%-100% for most antiques (unless configuration, rarity, and age preclude upper conditions) and 60%-100% on modern firearms since condition below 60% is seldom encountered (or purchased). Please consult our expanded 32-page color grading insert (pages 33-64) to learn more about the condition of your firearm. This is the first time, to my knowledge, that color plates have been utilized to accurately illustrate the firearms percentage grading system. Since condition is the overriding factor in price evaluation, study these photos carefully to learn more about the condition of your specimen(s).

New for this edition are line-art graphics depicting specified models that should assist you with the visual identification of that model. Long guns are typically pictured over their model name and description - hand guns are typically pictured beside their model name and description. When looking up information in this text remember, it reads just like a good *National Enquirer* article — turn the page to see if there is another good sentence waiting for you.

For your convenience, the N.R.A. condition standards and grading criteria have been included to make the conversion to percentages easier (see pages 82 and 83). This will especially be helpful when evaluating antiques.

For sake of simplicity the following organizational framework has been adopted throughout this publication.

1. Trademark manufacturer, brand name, or importer is listed in bold face type alphabetically, i.e.,

ANSCHUTZ, BROWNING, WINCHESTER.

2. Manufacturer information is listed directly beneath the trademark heading, i.e.,

Manufacturer Located In New Haven, CT. Mfg. Began In 1866.

3. Next classification is a category name (inside a gray box) referring mostly to a firearm's configuration, i.e.,

PISTOLS, REVOLVERS, RIFLES, SHOTGUNS

4. Model names appear flush left, are bold faced, and capitalized in chronological (normally) order grouped under either pistol, rifle, or shotgun subheadings, i.e.,

SINGLE ACTION ARMY, MODEL 29, MODEL 12.

5. barrel lengths, calibers, gauges and other descriptive data are further categorized adjacent to both models and sub-models in this type face. This is where most of the information is listed for each specific model including identifiable features and possibly some production data (including quantity and circa of manufacture if known).

6. Variations within a model appear as sub-models - they are differentiated from model names by an artistic "bullet" prefix, are indented, and in upper and lower case, i.e.,

 ⇥ **PPK/S Durgarde, Mannlicher Type Full Stock, Engraved Carbine.**

7. Manufacturer and other notes/information appear in smaller type and should be read since they contain both important and other critical, up-to-date information, last manufacturer's suggested retail price (if known), i.e.,

This model was also available with No. 3 factory engraving on a very limited special order basis. Watch for fakes!

8. Extra cost features/special value orders and other added/subtracted features (add-ons for currently manufactured guns reflect retail) are placed directly under individual price lines and appear bolder than other descriptive typeface, i.e.,

Add 15% for nickel finish (disc. 1989) - add 10% for 8⅜ in. barrel.

9. Grading lines will appear at the top of each page and in the middle if pricing lines change. The most commonly encountered grading line in this text is from 100%-60%, i.e.,

Grading		100%	98%	95%	90%	80%	70%	60%
		$795	$650	$600	$525	$495	$475	$450

Antique grading lines have values listed for 100%-10%, or 80%-10%, i.e.,

100%	98%	95%	90%	80%	70%	60%	50%	40%	30%	20%	10%
$1,900	$1,650	$1,375	$1,075	$950	$875	$800	$725	$650	$575	$525	$450

Grading				80%	70%	60%	50%	40%	30%	20%	10%
				$2,365	$1,925	$1,650	$1,430	$1,210	$990	$770	$605

Commemorative/limited edition grading and pricing lines will appear as follows:

Grading	100%	issue price	qty made
	$1,800	$1,500	$500

10. Price lines have been changed to allow the following - when the price line shown below is encountered,

Mfg.'s Sug. Retail	$170		$150	$130	$115	$105	$95	$85	$80

it automatically indicates the gun is currently manufactured and the manufacturer's retail price is shown left of the 100% column. Following are the 100%-60% values. The 100% price is what you can typically expect to pay for that model in NIB condition (must include box, warranty card, owner's manual, and packing materials) with normal discounting (if any). The 98%-60% remaining values represent actual retail selling prices - simply find the correct column and refer to the price listed. 100% specimens without boxes, warranties, etc., that are currently manufactured must be discounted slightly (5%-15%, depending on the desirability of make and model).

11. A currently manufactured gun without a retail price published by the manufacturer/importer (becoming more common every year) will appear as follows:

No Mfg.'s Retail	$495	$450	$400	$350	$310	$280	$250

Obviously, the 100% price is the national average price a consumer will pay for a gun in new condition. The same situation for a stainless steel or limited mfg./special edition firearm without retail pricing will appear as follows.

No Mfg.'s Retail	$240	$185	$160	$145

12. A price line with 7 values listed (represented below) indicates a

$715	$660	$605	$550	$440	$385	$330

discontinued, out of production model with values shown for 100%-60% conditions. Obviously, no "Mfg.'s Sug. Retail" will appear in the left margin, but a model note may appear below the price line indicating what the last Mfg.'s Sug. Retail was.

13. A 4-value price line indicates a current production gun, and

Mfg.'s Sug. Retail	$822	$665	$545	$465

prices are not shown in 90% or less conditon since the specimen (notice model description) is either stainless steel, a commemorative, or limited production. Because these types of firearms are almost never encountered in 90% or less condition, values for lower conditions are not listed.

14. New for the 14th Edition are grading and price lines that incorporate price ranges on certain configurations

Below Average	Average	Above Average

of firearms that preclude accurate percentage evaluation. Price ranges appear as follows:

$400 - $850	$850 - $1,400	$1,400 - $2,100

An explanation of condition factors to look for in these three ranges will precede this information in that section.

To find a particular gun in this book, first look under the name of the manufacturer, importer, or brand name. Next find the correct subdivision (either pistols, rifles, shotguns, etc.). When applicable, antiques will appear before modern guns and are subdivided like modern weapons. Once you find the correct model or sub-model under its respective subheading, determine the weapon's percentage of *original* condition (see the Photo Percentage Grading System starting on page 33) and find the corresponding percentage column showing the price.

Commemoratives will appear last under a manufacturer's heading.

Enlarged in the 14th Edition are sections on Trademark Index, Modern Black Powder Guns, Modern Airguns, and Model Serialization breakdown of major trademarks. Three or four prices will be listed for both Black Powder and Airgun Models. When using the Model Serialization section make sure your model is listed and find the serial number within the yearly range listings.

Acknowledgements

Many of you who have followed this project have seen the listing of names on this page grow somewhat in proportion to the size of the book. I would like to thank all of you who have written, FAX'ed, or called me on potential revisions, additions, and corrections. This is the best tool I know of to make this publication more up-to-date and complete every year. To the people listed below, a special thanks is in order, as they have been critical in providing more information annually. Stand up and take a bow.

Dr. Leonardo Antaris
LeRoy Merz
Evan Whildin
Robert Rayburn
Lowell Pauli
Richard Bauter
of Browning
Thomas Koessl
Gurney Brown
Joyce Gentilo
of Beretta U.S.A. Corp.
Bob Jones
Gary Brown
Charles E. Carder
Stephen McCarthy
Rudy Etchen
Rick Crosier
Keith Rolf
Robert White
Leon Wier, Jr.
Jack Heath
of Remington Arms Co.
Charles Semmer
Bill Allen
Dr. Robert Beeman

Patrick Lucking
A. O. Salvo
Roy Jinks
of Smith & Wesson
Lynn Oliver
Jim Supica, Jr.
Jim Jasken
Kevin Cherry
Hal Hamilton
Dean Rinehart
John Lacy
Jeff Faintich
F. E. "Pete" Wall
Joe Gillenwater
T. Rees Day
James Goergen
Les Hovenkamp
Rick Kennerknecht
William Larkin Moore
Tommy Rholes
Martin J. Lane
David Noll
John Boyd
Harrison Carroll

John Picchietti

Felix Bedlan

David Buehn

Ray Saign

Damon Mills

Robert Saunders
of American Derringer Corp.

Larry Del Greco

Jeff Brooks

Jack Skeuse
of Parker Reproductions

Louis Yearout

Gary Green

Tom Gibbons

Larry Orr

Daniel Sheil, Jr.

Brian Bunkowsky

Jim Ronaghan

Pat Redmond

Larry Baer

Don Criswell

Norm Carroso

Cody Firearms Museum

R. L. Wilson

Joe Prather
of Griffin & Howe

S. Hallock Du Pont, Jr.

Horrace Greeley

Jim and Carol Wimer

Gerry Landskron

Morris Hallowell IV

Danny Fontaine

John Gyde

Marty Huber & Kathleen Hoyt
of Colt's Firearms

Richard Alexander
of Interarms

Patrick McKune

Mims Reed

Mossberg Collector's Association

Ruger Collector's Association

Colt Collector's Association

Remington Society of America

Steve Weston
of The Computer Source

and to

"Diamond" Dave Kosowski who helped make this 14th Edition a real gem. Thanks, Dave, for dotting all the "t's" and crossing all the "i's".

Dedication

This 14th Edition of the *Blue Book of Gun Values* is dedicated to my Mom, Dad, and Brother, for never allowing me to take too long a nap after lunch while on our farm. Putting that first bale of first crop alfalfa on the back of the hay rack has always reminded me of beginning the "A section" each edition.

An Overview of *Blue Book of Gun Values*
Pricing and Information

In order of call frequency, these are the heavyweights: "How did you come up with this price?" "Where did you get this information?" "Are you sure that this was the last year of manufacture?" "Why isn't my gun in your book?" "Looks pretty good to me, it shoots, it's got a hammer, barrel, and trigger, so it must be in excellent condition." "I can't find it."

"Steve, how do you come up with all this stuff?" That could be a separate book in itself. The intake volume of materials and resultant data precipitant is a job that, if taken seriously, will put you at the edge. Certainly, those people listed on the Acknowledgements page have been responsible for a lot of the information that has been previously unpublished and they deserve a lot of the credit. But, the final insertion onto the WordStar computer files is reserved for me, and we must live with those results for 10 months.

Remember, when the Achy-Breaky Byte-Master finished this year's 14th Edition, it had over 421,000,000 publishing bytes of computer information. If the right 10 bytes in a row are wrong, I could get 100 letters. This is another way of saying that this book has never been perfect, and never will be. It simply can't. As much as we try to groom every numeral and letter, Murphy will find his way in someplace. For this reason, if you feel some price is out of line or I have omitted or misrepresented a particular model, by all means contact me and let's discuss it. I would like to thank all of you who have already pointed out typo's, errors, and possible questions on information/prices in past editions. It is the best way I know to squelch mistakes from one edition to the next.

For those of you who may have some confusion on how to extract all the information published from this most recent edition, please refer to the "How to Use This Book" section on pages 8-10. They are very helpful.

We'd like to encourage all of you to fill up Bernie's mailbag here at One Appletree Square - keep sending those comments, observations, criticisms, and other ideas our way. Direct technical and pricing correspondence to me at:

Blue Book of Gun Values
Research - Attn: S. P. Fjestad
One Appletree Square
Minneapolis, MN 55425 USA
Phone No.: **612-854-5229**
FAX No.: **612-853-1486**
Once again, please allow 2-4 weeks normally for a reply.

One last thing, and it'll just take a second. For those people who are convinced that the Blue Book of Gun Values is no different than their American Express card (don't leave home without it), we are offering a lifetime subscription. The cost is $399 (non-refundable), we'll send you the new edition every year, and we don't care how old you are. This offer is not transferable and it must be deliverable to you "above ground". It's that easy. You may send your payment in full, or in two separate installments within six months of each other. This offer expires March 15, 1994. It could be the best $399 you spend this year.

Blue Book Publications, Inc.

One Appletree Square, Minneapolis, Minnesota 55425 U.S.A.

CORRESPONDENCE INQUIRIES

January 1, 1993 was a day to be remembered at One Appletree Square. For the first time ever, I didn't bring a backlog of older correspondence into a new calendar year! However, this 1,200+ page project has stacked us up again temporarily.

With the addition of new personnel, correspondence under normal circumstances takes us between 3-7 working days, one of the fastest turn-around times in the industry. To make sure we can assist you with any correspondence, please include good quality photos of the specimen in question, any information available about that particular specimen, including caliber, barrel length, finish, stocks, barrel markings, other potentially significant gun marks that would assist us with identifying your gun, and special order features. In addition, be sure to include both your address and phone number, giving us an option of how to contact you for best service. To keep up with this constant onslaught of U.S. mail/FAXes, we have a large network of both dealers and collectors who can answer most of your questions within this time frame.

Because of the flood of mail and phone calls we get yearly, we can no longer perform free evaluations. The charge for this comprehensive research service is $20.00 per gun and payment must accompany your correspondence.

Your letters/FAXes will be answered in a FIFO system (first in — first out). Again, make sure to include a detailed description with all pertinent information about the gun(s) in question in your letter/FAX with good quality photos of the receiver, special markings, etc. would also be appreciated. Correspondence sent in without payment will be returned. Phone calls regarding firearms related questions will be taken between 2-5 pm daily, during most weekdays, unless we are absent. We appreciate your patience if you can not reach us by phone immediately, since our ringy-dingy never stops.

Time permitting, pink slip calls will be returned but paid correspondence and FAXes will receive first priority. We are hoping our turnaround time for research will improve significantly, and the only way to achieve this is to limit phone access time. We hope you will appreciate these measures taken towards delivering more reliable service on the thousands of questions submitted annually. It's a big job!

All correspondence should be directed to:

Blue Book Publications, Inc.
ATTN: Research Department
One Appletree Square
Minneapolis, MN 55425
Phone: 612-854-5229
FAX#: 612-853-1486

SORRY - No order or request for research paid by credit card will be processed without a credit card expiration date.

DIARRHEA OF AN EDITION

At the summit, FINALLY. Sunrise, March 3rd. Only a few thoughts, and then prepare for the dangerous descent. The exhilaration, the exhaustion, the discipline, the pain, the pride, the release, the apprehensiveness, the frustration, the sacrifice, the dedication, and the upcoming metamorphosis. It was all there - the final trek to this Edition's summit took 25 hours of continuous climbing. But who cares, not too many people read this section anyway. Talk is cheap, and since I have an upset stomach, this is it. We'll let the pictures do the talking in this Edition.

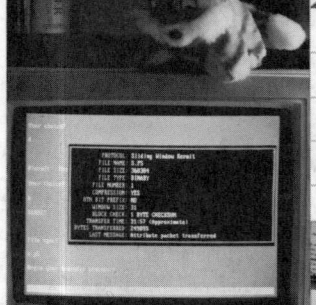

Paul finally got what he wanted, while it's just punching through zero on the outside, the Knight-Byte-Rider blurs the camera with his speed again.

Kernbit, overseeing The Monster flowing through the lines properly. Occasionally, he'll take a couple of bytes out of you.

It's round-up time in the bunker. Members of the staff are seen trying to recreate the bucking geometry of bull writing. John, as seen through the eyes of one of our other copiers.

Below, Paul and Tom seen trying to figure out how Clinton's new tax bill could effect them.

A well earned nap, taken while the author spits out another 280K on the telephone.

Tom, A) looking relaxed,
   B) needing a laxative,
   C) taking a laxidasical attitude,
   D) laxing discipline to do his job.
      (Vote for one only).
To the right is our customer service
department, ready with the hardware
necessary to serve you.

An upside-down
Anne Marie, in a
holding pattern on
yet another order.

Above, Michelle, taking another
shot at Rocky Squirrel (it's a tough
shot across the gutter).
(Left) It can be your best friend and
your worst enemy, all in two phone
calls. This wide ribbon producer never
stops.

I know what you're thinking, but it did happen.
On her third shot, Michelle shot off the branch that
Rocky was perched on (you would have laughed too
after watching a fat squirrel fall 20 feet into a cold
snowbank).

Steven, trying to re-boot after shaving
cream clogged his ports.

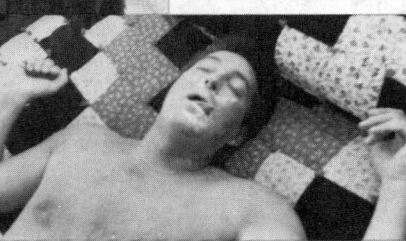

Doreen will do
anything to save
money on
   tanning sessions.

Fully re-booted, the author attempts to perform a task without a phone interruption.

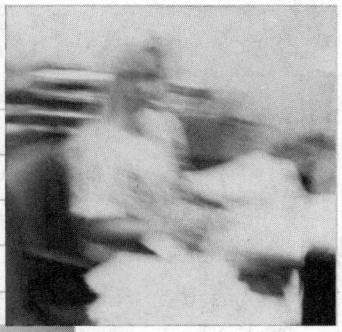

Above, Lisa, caught in a whirlwind of activity. Doing operational tasks this fast requires superspeed film and superhuman endurance.

Rocky Squirrel, looking somewhat scared after three close calls. Another white knuckled trip about a half an hour behind.

The Art Director seen below, giving the finger to someone on her way to another press check.

Below, Die Maestro, directing all the 486 bytes up to the screen for a curtain call, making sure (see the loaded .45 in back of his head?) that all the computer choreography is going smoothly.

One of the new series of flexible neck 6-strings currently being manufactured for serious string benders.

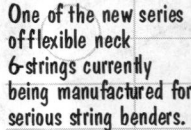

A Unique Concept

The Blue Book of Gun Values is the only book that:

✓ Utilizes the professionals' grading system of percentage of original finish remaining. (Eliminates confusing descriptions such as "Good", "Excellent", "Fair".)

✓ Is updated annually and expeditiously providing the freshest information available!

✓ Is based on actual selling prices. (These are the prices you can expect to pay — not artificial list prices or some "expert's" opinion.)

✓ Offers you personal consultation by mail on special questions you may have! (No book can cover everything.)

We also have an earlier edition's Photo Percentage Grading System available under separate cover (includes 60 high resolution color plates). Originally priced at $10, they are now available for $5 each (includes shipping and handling). Please use the address/phone number listed below to order.

In the past I have offered one free consultation per book order. With the growth of this project (not to mention the hundreds of letters and phone calls I am already behind on), this is no longer possible. Individual appraisals and/or additional research can be performed for $20.00 per gun (see the "Correspondence Inquiries" section for more information on this service). Please include a detailed description with all pertinent information about the gun(s) in question in your letter/fax. Good quality photos of the receiver, special markings, etc. would also be appreciated.

BUYING OR SELLING?

Interested in buying or selling a particular firearm(s)? Or maybe hesitating because you are unsure of what a fair market price should be? Depending on what you are interested in, a referral will be made that will enable you to be sure that you are getting what you paid for (or getting paid a fair price). This service is designed to help all those people who are worried or scared about purchasing a potentially "bad gun" or getting "ripped off" when selling. There is no charge for this referral service - we are simply connecting you with the best person(s) possible within your field of collecting ensuring that you get a fair deal. This hybrid matchmaking can make 25%-50% worth of difference on potentially buying or selling a gun. Please phone or write the Blue Book of Gun Values for both availability and dealer referrals that can be relied upon for both buying and selling. All replies are treated strictly confidential. Replies should be directed to:

Blue Book of Gun Values ™
    Attn: Steven Fjestad
    One Appletree Square
    Minneapolis, MN 55425
    Phone No. 612-854-5229
    FAX NO. 612-853-1486

If we're not available, please leave a message.

Introduction

How to Start Gun Collecting

In every part of this country, there are firearms collecting associations. You can benefit from membership/affiliation in such an association, since you can use it to meet other collectors and firearms experts who are excellent sources of information, help, guidance and invaluable education. In most major cities, there are regularly scheduled firearms shows where you can buy, sell or swap your weapons and gain insight into general prices and values. Also, at the larger national shows, you'll find many prominent and reputable dealers who usually have high-quality merchandise for sale.

I personally recommend that you attend at least one major weapons show each year. When you do, you'll be able to see everything from ultra-rare antiques to modern commemoratives. This will help you to determine where your interest lies. You can also make price comparisons. Shows are a place to meet collectors, investors and dealers from all over the nation. Once you have decided what you want to collect, we recommend you talk to everyone who could have any knowledge and provide you with information in this area. You must do the homework.

Recently, I wrote a dealer friend of mine on what a beginning collector should do to start this fascinating hobby. His comments were: collect what you really like, buy books and read, get out and look with a magnifying glass, be involved in a collecting fraternity, know your dealer(s)— pick them carefully, listen to them and knowledgeable others, avoid speculation, and get a receipt. These are good measures to follow.

For your benefit, we've included a mini-directory of recommended reading material and reference works as well as trade publications that will further assist you in gathering the knowledge needed for your chosen area(s) of interest.

Starting Tips

My advice would be to pick out an area where knowledge or interest already exists. Once you have found an area that you find interesting and want to collect, formulate a plan on what you would like to purchase as an overall collection. Expand this established base with additional knowledge. Buy the necessary books, magazines, and trade periodicals to make yourself as informed as possible in the niche you've chosen.

Most advanced collectors and dealers have expansive reference libraries for fast, fingertip accessibility. Don't worry about the price for reference material — one book can easily pay for itself in one gun trade. And the books themselves become investments as they go out of print and command increased prices. No one individual can know everything about every gun — reference works are a must.

Once you're "book trained" the next step is to start looking at — not buying — guns in the field you've chosen. Attend a few gun shows or visit dealers that have inventories of items you're looking for. *Don't* get side-tracked by other fascinating merchandise. Pay close attention to the coloration of bluing, crispness of metal markings (proof marks, barrel address, etc.), wood to metal fit, bore condition, and possible non-factory alterations.

In this business, the experience gained in running guns through your hands has no substitute. I have known people who would quote from memory every gauge, choke, barrel, and stock variation available for the Model 12 Winchester, yet these sample people can't spot a reblued gun. Knowing the correct factory bluing color, style of wood, and finish, production variation, etc., does not come overnight. It takes experience and a well-trained eye. If in doubt about "original finish" someone claims, consult a dealer or collector who does know the difference. Only after you've taken these steps are you ready to become a buyer. Anything less could result in a "long-term" investment.

Where and How to Buy and Sell Guns

This "Art" has changed drastically over the last 30 years. Dealer showrooms, gun shows, and local advertising were the only means of buying or selling guns for many years. Trading was more localized and regional price differences were more evident. Many fine weapons stayed in one locality for long periods of time. With the advent of the 5 second long distance telephone call and overnight express mail, the firearms marketplace now reaches coast to coast. International marketing is even possible where regulations permit. All this means increased merchandise exposure, more universal grading standards, and higher levels of competition in pricing firearms fairly.

Buying

It's been said that good guns are wherever you find them. Nothing could be truer. The following listing will give an idea of where to purchase collector guns:

A) Gun shows — these shows exist throughout the United States and are usually well-attended. With hundreds of shows being held yearly (check your gun shop or trade publications for dates), it is possible to take in two shows on a single weekend — locations permitting.

Advantages include:

1. Physically inspecting potential purchases.

2. Comparing prices against other similar items at the same show.

3. Having a large selection from which to choose.

4. Providing unequaled opportunity to meet fellow collectors and other experts in the field to exchange information.

5. Displaying the broadest base of firearms, accessories, and memorabilia from which to develop new interests.

6. Haggling for better prices, especially for items still unsold late in the show.

7. Offering "trade-in" potential with prices established at the show — rather hard and lengthy to do by mail.

Disadvantages include:

1. A good chance of running into fakes, reblued items, and non-factory alterations or conversions. Higher prices over the last 5 years have resulted in many common models being "upgraded" to a model much rarer. Be careful on purchases where this type of activity might exist.

2. Most sales are final. Once the cash has been transferred, your inspection is over. A collector pays for his "mistakes" in this business. If a sale is contingent on a yet-to-come factory letter, part(s), or additional accessories, make sure the seller includes them in his bill-of-sale. It's simply good business for both parties. When contemplating a purchase, ask the seller what he/she knows about the specimen(s) you are considering, including finish condition (and if original), possible alterations, and how it was obtained. If those answers pass your screening test, then you are ready to ask what the seller would take in payment for the gun OR if they would be interested in trading. Asking a seller what their lowest cash price would be and then offering a "pretty good old 12 ga. double barrel" in trade will not put you on the Christmas card list of your average firearms dealer.

3. "Show Pressure" forces you into decisions that have to be made in a few minutes — oftentimes with 2 other people simultaneously bargaining for the same gun.

4. Being side-tracked into other areas. Know what you want, what you want to pay for it, and don't impulse buy. Keep a level head, and stick to the areas you're familiar with. This is important with merchandise ranging from stuffed animal heads to Browning .50 calibers.

Remember — most good gun show "buys" occur during the gun show's opening hours, or the night previous to opening before the public is admitted. An apparent bargain found on Sunday afternoon sounds skeptical at best, although many dealers will "negotiate" a price very late in the show, depending on their cash flow and desire to haul a potential sale to yet another gun show. Get to the show at the opening, walk the aisles with orderly precision, avoid back tracking, and when you find a specimen that meets *all* of your criteria *and* is on your shopping list: Buy it. Too many times I've walked back to a table ready to buy and an empty spot is all that remains. Truly good guns that are fairly priced sell fast because dealers are competing with collectors. One last item — don't interrupt an exhibitor engaged in selling (even if it's one you want). It's not in the gun circuit code of ethics. Be patient.

B) Gun Shops — Many modern gun shops have good selections of collector guns in stock. Take one gun at a time here — and make sure that gun is within your field of expertise. Sometimes dealers selling mostly new guns get items in on trade that they know very little about — including trade-ins that "aren't right". Be able to know the difference before you buy. Again, don't get sidetracked. While you are likely to get a fair deal at a gun shop, you may find an item in your field once every five years.

C) Auctions — While not as major as gun shows or gun shops in the marketplace, auctions can be used to your advantage in buying. Large auction houses such as Christie's and Sotheby's deal in only extremely fine and rare specimens that carry big price tags. Know what you want and your monetary limit before conducting business at this level. Some auction guns are "dogs" with hidden defects that preclude their sale through reputable dealers. Estate, household, and farm auctions can be used with some success if you know previously which guns will be sold. Frequently, no "gun" dealers will be in attendance and prices could be quite low. Make sure that condition is at par with your standards. With all auctions, attend the preliminary exhibition and be sure you make a careful inspection of all guns you might bid on. Mail order bids are sometimes an option to being at the auction. Before bids are submitted, know everything about what you're potentially purchasing.

D) Other Collectors — Buying from other collectors is dependent on how comfortable you are with his knowledge, expertise, honesty, and previous dealings. Serious collectors usually sell their finest guns last. Make sure the gun you're considering isn't a poor duplicate in the collection or one of his "mistakes". Obviously, it is to a collector's advantage to sell to another collector and thereby avoid the "middleman" dealer markup. Find out if the guns were carefully chosen originally, part of an estate settlement, or other important past history. Also, big collections don't necessarily guarantee good collections. More than a few "collections" are gathered around poor quality, high quantity odds and ends.

E) Mail Order Dealer — This area has really grown in the past 10 years. These dealers send out regular inventory listings to previous customers and much business is out-of-state. It is to the dealer's advantage to accurately grade his guns very carefully to avoid misrepresentation and eliminate customer fears in not being able to see the gun. Good mail-order dealers *always* give an inspection period. Returned guns don't make anyone happy so the dealer is always faced with selling as good a gun as possible for a competitive price. Anything less results in stagnating inventory levels. Many of these dealers specialize in specific areas. Their specialization usually ensures the buyer of good condition original guns made possible by the dealer's thorough "screening" used before buying. Getting as many dealer inventory listings as possible will give you a chance to "shop" around and check prices. A dealer's reputation is a big factor in this area. Deal with those you're comfortable with and will listen when you want to trade in something previously purchased.

F) Classified Ads — Rarely anymore do good quality, collector guns show up under the "Guns for Sale" Ad in the local newspaper. The "steals" of the '60s and '70s are mostly gone. Still, keep your eyes open and follow every lead. These wild goose chases can sometimes be very rewarding. An "advertised" WWII Luger for $485.00 is certainly worth buying if it turns out to be a Krieghoff. Be fast — don't hesitate when real "buys" do pop up.

G) Trade Periodicals — Magazines, such as *Shotgun News, Gun Report, Gun List, CADA Gun Journal, American Rifleman, Guns and Ammo, Man at Arms,* and others, contain valuable firearms information. Some listed firearms are good buys — others are out and out rip-offs. Know who you are buying from, insist on an inspection period covering all purchases, and get a receipt. See References/Periodicals Section for addresses and subscription costs.

Selling

Certainly as many considerations confront the potential seller as the potential buyer. Different approaches must be used when selling a single gun, a few guns, or an extensive collection. Locality, modern or antique status, and proper grading all have to be studied. No standard format is applicable to every situation here.

Knowing the market and prices should be an advantage in selling. The collector is familiar with gun values, knows dealers that handle his type of guns, and has established contact with fellow collectors of similar merchandise. These potential buyers increase the liquidity base.

When selling more than one gun and similar items are involved, either the piecemeal or "sold only as a group" method should be determined first. Selling a collection intact is certainly cleaner than taking one-at-a-time. More money can be extracted selling individually — if you have the patience.

In 1981, when gold and silver were fluctuating large amounts daily, a woman called in and asked me, "What's the spot price of Winchesters today?" After my initial laugh, I told her collector gun values have always been dictated by marketplace supply and demand. Just as a spot price for a Winchester will never appear in the *Wall Street Journal*, a fair market price tag on your 98% P.38 will not necessarily guarantee you instant liquidity. Lack of inflation has caused a drop in asking prices for many collector guns that are available in good supply.

When selling, use the same general headings listed under "Buying" as possibilities. Certainly, an obvious place to sell a valuable gun is to the dealer who might have originally sold you the item. Since he considered it worthy of ownership previously, restocking the gun should be in his scope of interest. How much will you get? This will depend on length of ownership, any change of condition, that gun's increased market appeal (if any), and the dealer's current inventory levels. Unless the funds generated in selling a gun are needed immediately, never be in a rush to sell a nice gun. Patience will reward you over panic. When that right person shows genuine interest, offer the gun professionally and stick close to your asking price — you'll probably get it.

Many major trade publications offer national exposure — and larger exposure generally means higher prices. It makes sense that 75,000 people reading *Shotgun News* will generate more interest than 300 tire-kickers at a hometown gun show. While results may take more time (3-6 weeks), the added dollars on the sale price usually justify the wait.

Trends to be Aware Of

Collecting firearms as a hobby originally started because of nostalgia over antique firearms and their place in history. Modern collectible firearms are today the fastest-growing area. If you spend time studying these modern guns, you will see there are many excellent choices to be made from Colt's, Lugers, Mausers, Smith & Wessons and Winchesters. Much interest is also developing in .22-caliber pistols from antiques through modern variations. Another area showing increasing collector interest is high-grade quality Damascus-barreled shotguns.

What to Collect —
The Answers Depend on You

Firearms offer something for everyone. There are different-purpose firearms with many designs. Some have historical value and are quite fascinating. History has often been changed because some faction or culture had superior firearms to influence or force its culture and politics on another.

To a certain extent, there is no right or wrong area in which to collect. Pick the category you prefer and then do some studying before you make a choice and begin buying. Be sure you're comfortable with the area you ultimately decide to go with.

I would suggest that you keep your collection orderly and coherent. Collect one maker or one model in all its variations (if possible). You could also base a collection on type, such as Kentucky dueling pistols or military automatic handguns. Collections have been based on firearms of one caliber, such as the 9mm Parabellum or .22-caliber Rim Fire. The variations are numerous, but the collection will have greater appeal if there is a visible purpose to it. This should not stop you from purchasing something outside your collection if you like it — and it is a genuine bargain.

When buying for your collection, you will be much better off if you purchase quality items. Owning only one extremely high-quality collector firearm is preferable to owning two or three lesser ones. The greatest demand and appreciation will always be with the highest-quality pieces. Guns in poor condition may show smaller increases in value. Current production firearms and those just out of production have collector value only if in close to new condition or in the original box. The corresponding ratings shown herein would be 95%, 98% or 100%. See section "How to Use and Apply Grading System." Commemoratives, for example, must be new (100%) or they have lost much of their collector value. If a commemorative is no more than the standard-issue firearm but with minor trim added, its chance of appreciating is about nil. At the other extreme, an antique or possibly a military firearm may be found with no remaining finish, and if there is demand because of rarity, it could be an excellent addition to a collection. The main consideration is how they are normally found and collector demand. Study my price value guidelines for a better indication of rarity and values.

A shrewd collector may look for a firearm not actively collected but with growing interest.

What Dictates Value —
A Combination of Factors

Condition, rarity, demand, special features and historical significance determine current value. All values are based on the premise that the firearm is authentic and original. The value of a collector arm is always in relation to the condition of other examples of the same make, model and variation. Condition is the amount of overall original finish remaining on all parts of the firearm and condition of wood, if stocked, which can run from 0% to 100%. The collector is encouraged to acquire the better examples of what is available. If you find one better than the norm and it can be purchased at a fair price, you have had a stroke of luck. Most modern arms should be in the premium class, 95% to 100%, for collector purposes and definitely for maximum appreciation.

Restoration

Restoration occurs mainly in antiques but can be found with any popular arms. In most cases, a restored or refinished firearm does not deserve the status of a collectible firearm. Once a firearm has been restored, it can never be returned to its original condition. Restoration of antiques is accepted by many people because of the scarcity of good original arms. Such guns should be so marked and explicitly sold as restored pieces. Unfortunately, as they pass through several owners, this information tends to be lost. Replacement or repair done with current original parts should not affect the value.

Modification and Conversion

Many collector arms have been modified for personal taste and not with the intent to defraud or produce a fake. Often, it was done before a collector demand developed. Usually, it was done to copy a much scarcer variation of the same firearm. At a recent gun show, I found offered for sale as the genuine item six of the same rare variations of a modern handgun. All were priced in the correct range, were they authentic. Each was a fake made from a more common model. Their true value was about 20% of the asking price. Upgrading can take place in most firearms but can cost the most with engraved guns. Most often a low-grade shotgun is engraved to simulate a much-scarcer, higher-grade gun. Conversions are most common with antiques. Disagreement exists on whether it is permissible to reconvert guns such as Percussions back to their original Flintlock condition. Guns so converted should be noted as such and sold on that basis.

TRASH OR TREASURE?

A Study of Firearms Desirability vs. Rarity - Facts vs. Fiction

by S.P. Fjestad

It usually starts when the person on the other end of the telephone asks, "I have this old damascus shotgun that Uncle Mortimer used to own - what's it worth?" After I tell them to please hold this rare artifact closer to the microphone so that I can "see" it better, their next sentence is usually devoted to establishing the rarity factor since they haven't been able to find out anything about it in any gun book. At this point in the conversation I typically ask them to identify the trademark (or barrel/frame markings), and about 50% of the time, I haven't heard of the name(s). Unfortunately, the automatic implication at this juncture is that their rare gun is an expensive, desirable specimen that most gun collectors would gladly overpay for in order to get in their gun cabinets immediately. In this whole process, it seems like rarity is usually mistaken for desirability rather than understand that a firearms rarity factor is only one component when determining desirability.

To understand any gun's desirability factor, one has to understand this word's definition fully. To be desirable is to be demanded, but to be rare does not guarantee anything. Desirability insures demand - rarity does not. In fact, in some cases, the only thing rarer than a particular gun is the guy who will spend money to own it. Why is this? Ever gone to a garage sale and seen a home brewed painting under the card table that the owner was pumping up for $20? You would have probably pulled out an "Andy Jackson" rather fast if you would have seen an authentic Picasso signature at the bottom right. Why? Because the demand factor became much larger once the collectible's trademark/status became accurately established.

Let's break down each firearm's desirability into individual elements enabling us to understand both the demand and supply economics one gun at a time. The following components will always come into play (even though any gun's unique "mix" of these properties is usually different) when determining a specimen's overall desirability. The key factors when determining a gun's demand factor (desirability) are as follows:

1. Trademark Recognition/Acceptance/Importance. How popular or collected is the maker's name? Having a Colt, Winchester, Parker, Remington, Holland & Holland is going to be a lot different than having a Crescent Firearms, Lars Johnson, Western Field, or any one of the thousands of trademarks nobody has heard of or cares about. Most of these guns were manufactured to undercut the competition at the time, and while many were (some still are) fair quality, inexpensively made, utilitarian shooting/hunting pieces, their value today must be based on their shooting value only since in most cases, there is little or no collector interest. Many of these turn of the century companies (or subcontractors) were in business for only a brief time and little history remains on their shoe-string operations. One of the big reasons that Colt, Winchester, Remington, and others have a large collector following today is because these factories are still in business and company records/documents are also available to prove the authenticity of their older manufactured guns. Without this important factory documentation, many important specimens would

be forced to sell for a fraction of today's prices (i.e. if you can't prove it, who's going to buy it?)

2. Condition. In most cases a firearm's original condition is what is rare, not the model itself. Original condition for many collectors is the most important factor in determining a gun's desirability. Many collectors simply will not purchase a gun below a certain condition factor, regardless of price. Original condition is Polar North for most firearms collectors today. Once condition decreases on most specimens, the "shooting value" comes more into play than "collector's value" on more recently made models. Major trademark antiques that are older retain collector interest down to a "no finish left" condition factor since they are collectible regardless of their "shootability." Refinished or reblued guns in commonly encountered models with good supply are not as desirable as original condition specimens. In other words, a common World War II P.38 pistol that has been professionally refinished will never be as desirable as an original specimen, since all things considered, collectors would rather concentrate on original condition (if it is available in the marketplace).

However, a properly restored firearm in a model/variation that is seldomly seen (or offered for sale) in mint, original condition is gaining popularity every year. During the past several months, a new pattern has been established for selling top-shelf condition cream puffs in major trademarks. Some major auction houses have set new records on many of these minty jewels. Recently, a highly embellished Winchester Model 1876 Deluxe in mint condition that was presented to a famous Canadian military officer sold for over a half a million dollars - a new record for a single specimen! This is what can happen to price when you hook up condition, trademark importance, historical documentation/ acceptance, and rarity - then let the top dealers, collectors, and investors turbocharge the price tag in the fast and furious atmosphere of an auction house.

3. Historical Recognition/Notarized Provenance. In other words, if you can prove by historical documentation that the firearm(s) you own belonged to a Teddy Roosevelt, Andy Jackson, Billy the Kid, etc., the price tag will escalate tremendously. The sale price will be contingent on how well the personality/organization is known. Very few people will care (or pay) for a local personality's "main squeeze." A specimen owned by a regionally famous person will command a regional price. If the gun belonged to Buffalo Bill Cody and you can prove it in front of a judge and jury, then, in most cases, an auction may be the only way of assessing the correct value. In some cases, whoever presented the gun as a gift will make at least as much difference as whom the gun was presented to.

4. Price. Any gun becomes a value at the right price. At some subterranean low price, regardless what kind of firearm is being sold, many of us will buy it (justified by becoming more diversified in our collecting). As you would expect, pricing is more predictable as your sampling ratio increases. In other words, the correct price will be much easier to determine on a S&W Model

27 than on an inscribed Civil War Henry rifle. While there are literally thousands of Model 27's that are sold nationally every year, only a very few Henry's will exchange hands during the same time period. If the price seems like it's at the summit, see if it can be budged into the price range you are looking for. If not, give it up and wait until the next opportunity. If the price is close to what you would like to pay, perhaps light "chiseling" may be used with some effectiveness. Veterans in this business, however, will tell you to pay a little extra to get something that is a little bit better. The worst feeling at a gun show is when you walk back to that table with the nice Remington Model 12C on it (that you tried to buy a half hour ago for $75 off) and all that remains is an empty spot on the table. Does the price make the gun more desirable or does it detract from it to the point that you can't possibly buy it? These are questions you have to ask yourself on every potential purchase. My advice on this subject is to do your homework before you get tested under "combat conditions." Map out your area of collecting and buy the necessary pricing guides and reference books that will give you the information that you are going to need. In addition, attend a few gun shows annually (including at least one big show). Get to know a few reputable dealers in your field and make sure you get their inventory listings and pricing information. Last, but certainly not least, BUY SOMETHING! It's good for the economy and your collection.

5. Rarity. Most guns are not rare. Rather, their condition can make them rare. Again, while it is true that many firearms may be relatively hard to find, sometimes the potential purchaser for these off-brand trademarks can be rarer than the gun. Literally, there are thousands of trademarks/brand names both domestically and internationally that nobody cares about. I have 5 books in my office that provide a "grocery listing" of approximately 50,000 obscure makers/trademarks that most dealers have never heard of or are hesitant to own as inventory. The configuration of these guns becomes much more important than the barrel address/markings. Also remember that because a gun belonged to a great-uncle or family relative does not make it any rarer (or desirable) in the eyes of the next potential purchaser.

Many people think that some popular guns are rare. As an example, most Winchester Model 12's are not rare - they made almost 2 million of them. A Model 12 in 28 ga. with a 26 inch improved cylinder, matted rib barrel and No. 5 factory engraving is rare. Sometimes, the most commonly encountered features in a particular model end up being the most desirable (i.e., most Winchester collectors prefer octagon barrels, even though the round barrels are substantially rarer). Colt people still like the .44-40 and .45 cal.'s - cowboy calibers - despite the fact that others are rarer. Be careful when letting rarity control your pocketbook - the other factors listed in this article are considerably more important. Exercise caution on those unknown specimens commonly described as, "I don't think I've ever seen another one like it." While a fortunate few have been lucky when adding these rarities to their collections, more have "damaged their estates" by basing value on rarity only.

6. Special Order Features/Embellishments/Accessories/Accouterments. Many firearms have been special ordered with optional accessories including different sights, barrel lengths, embellishments, wood carving or checkering, special metal finishes, personalized inscriptions, etc. A Winchester rifle could be ordered with over 20 different special order features alone! All of these special orders/options act both independently and interdependently to determine the correct value for a particular firearm. On major trademark specimens it is important that these features

were done at the factory, not by someone outside the factory at a later date. On modern customized guns, the resale is hard to predict since a customized gun was originally created to fit a particular individual's shooting requirements, not someone else's at a later date.

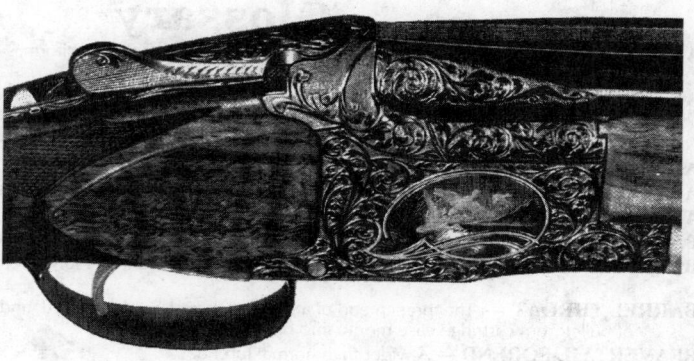

Many times on a customized gun involving resale, "the whole is not the sum of its parts." In other words, the total cost of the gun and customizing will be more than what it will bring in the used marketplace. On some military specimens, the original accouterments can get to be more expensive than the gun itself since they are often times considerably rarer. Many of these firearms accessories and accouterments can be very hard to predict accurate pricing since very few are bought/sold during the coarse of each year. Most of the time, a knowledgeable dealer or advanced collector should be consulted on the difference these special orders/options can make on the price of a firearm.

7. Regional Demand Differences. In 1862 a Henry rifle with a retail price of $40 was being sold for as high as $100 in California due to lack of supply. With the advent of expedited shipping services (overnight delivery is now a way of life) many firearms that were previously "stuck" in one geographical area have now been sold and shipped thousands of miles away. Yet it is no secret that a Kentucky Flintlock rifle will command more money under normal circumstances in Pennsylvania than in Northern Wyoming. Also, a more recent stainless steel handgun will be more desirable in Miami than in Boise, Idaho. This especially comes into play with special editions/commemoratives manufactured to commemorate a city, state, or organization. A Smith & Wesson Model 19 Oregon State Police Commemorative will not bring much of a premium in southern Kentucky. Shotguns used to have some regional demand differences due to configuration. With the coming of age of steel shot for hunting, however, smaller gauge, shorter barrel, open choked specimens have become a lot more desirable than a 12 gauge, 30 inch, full choke variation.

In closing, I would like you to remember that when purchasing firearms for storing value, consider overall desirability first, condition second, price third, and rarity last. Since the supply of most out-of-production firearms is fixed (or slightly decreasing), it is the demand side of the marketplace that determines what is desirable, regardless of rarity. Most collectors like trademarks backed by historical provenance having many models/variations (and existing information) from which to choose and build into an orderly collection. Once a gun's overall desirability factor has been accurately determined, you will have a much better idea if that next potential firearms purchase deserves a spot in your gun cabinet.

Publisher's note: This article is an edited re-print taken from the April 1993 issue of *Guns & Ammo*, published by Petersen Publishing Co. located in Los Angeles, CA.

Glossary

ACCOUTERMENT — All equipment carried by a soldier on outside of uniform, such as buckles, belts, or canteens, but not including weapons.

ACTION — The heart of the gun, receiver, bolt or breech block feeding and firearm mechanism - see Box Lock, Rolling Block, or Side Lock.

ADJUSTABLE CHOKE -- A device built into the muzzle of a shotgun to change from one choke to another.

AIR GUN—A gun which utilizes compressed air or gas to launch the projectile.

APERTURE SIGHT—A rear sight consisting of a hole or aperture through which the front sight and target are aligned.

AUTO LOADING— See semi-automatic.

BACKSTRAP — That part of the revolver or pistol frame that is exposed at the rear of the grip.

BARREL BAND — A metal band, either fixed or adjustable, around the forend of a gun that holds the barrel to the stock.

BARREL THROAT — The breech end of a revolver barrel is chambered and somewhat funneled for passage of bullet from cartridge case mouth into barrel.

BEAVERTAIL FOREND — A wider than normal forend.

BLUING — The blue or black finish of the metal parts of a gun. The process is actually one of controlled rusting and brushing and is usually created with an acid bath. Bluing minimizes light reflection, gives a "finish" to the bare metal, and protects somewhat against rust.

BORE — Inside of a barrel. Also the diameter of the barrel as measured across the lands of a rifled barrel.

BOX LOCK ACTION —typified by Parker shotgun in U.S. and Westley Richards in England. Generally considered not to be as strong as the side lock. Developed by Anson & Deeley, the box lock is hammerless. It has two disadvantages: Hammer pin must be placed directly below knee of action, which is its weakest spot, and action walls must be thinned out to receive locks. These are inserted from below into large slots in action body, which is then closed with a plate. Greener crossbolt, when made correctly, overcomes many of the box lock weaknesses.

BREECH — That portion of a gun which contains the action, the trigger or firing mechanism, the magazine, and the chamber portion of the barrel(s). An imprecise term generally including all the essential working parts of a gun.

BUCKHORN SIGHT — An open, metallic rear sight with sides that curl upward and inward.

BULL BARREL — A heavier, thicker than normal barrel with little or no taper.

BUTT PLATE — A protective plate attached to the butt.

CALIBER — The diameter of the bore.

CHAMBER — Rear part of the barrel that has been reamed out so that it will contain a cartridge. When the breech is closed, the cartridge is supported in the chamber, and the chamber must align the primer with the firing pin, the bullet with the bore.

CHAMBER THROAT — Also called THROAT, is that area in the barrel that is directly forward of the chamber and that tapers to bore diameter.

CHECKERING — A functional decoration applied to pistol grips and forends consisting of pointed pyramids cut into the wood.

CHOKE — The muzzle constriction on a shotgun to control spread of the shot.

COCKING INDICATOR — Any device which the act of cocking a gun moves into a position where it may be seen or felt in order to notify the shooter that the gun is cocked. Typical examples are the pins found on some high-grade hammerless shotguns which protrude slightly when they are cocked, and also the exposed cocking knobs on bolt-action rifles. Exposed hammers found on some rifles and pistols are also considered cocking indicators.

COLOR CASEHARDENING — A method of hardening steel and iron while imparting to it colorful swirls as well as surface figure. Metal is heated by means of animal charcoal to 800°-900° C, then plunged into cold water.

COMB — The portion of the stock on which the shooter's cheek rests.

COMBINATION GUN — Generally a break-open shotgun configuration fitted with at least one shotgun barrel and one rifle barrel. Such guns may be encountered with either two or three barrels, and less frequently with as many as four or five, and have been known to chamber for as many as four different calibers.

COMPENSATOR — A recoil-reducing device which mounts on the muzzle of a gun to deflect part of the powder gases up and rearward. Also called a "muzzle brake".

CRANE — In a modern solid-frame, swing-out revolver, the U-shaped yoke on which the cylinder rotates, and which holds the cylinder in the frame.

CROWNING —The rounding or chamfering normally done to a barrel muzzle to insure that the mouth of the bore is square with the bore axis and that the edge is countersunk below the surface to protect it from impact damage. Traditionally, crowning was accomplished by spinning an abrasive-coated brass ball against the muzzle while moving it in a figure-eight pattern until the abrasive had cut away any irregularities and produced a uniform and square mouth.

CYLINDER — A rotating cartridge container in a revolver. The cartridges are held in chambers and the cylinder turns, either to the left or the right, depending on the gunmaker's design, as the hammer is cocked.

DAMASCENE — The decorating of metal with another metal, either by inlaying or attaching in some fashion. Damascene is often confused with Damaskeening or engine turning.

DAMASCUS BARREL — A barrel made by twisting, forming and welding thin strips of steel around a mandrel.

DERRINGER — A small, usually large-caliber pistol.

DOUBLE ACTION — The principle in a revolver or auto-loading pistol wherein the hammer can be cocked and dropped by a single pull of the trigger. Most of these actions also provide capability for single action fire. In auto-loading pistols, double action normally applies only to the first shot of any series, the hammer being cocked by the slide for subsequent shots.

DOUBLE-BARRELED — A gun consisting of two barrels joined either side by side or one over the other.

DOUBLE-SET TRIGGER — A device which consists of two triggers — one to cock the mechanism that spring-assists the other trigger, substantially lightening trigger pull.

DOVETAIL — A flaring machined or hand cut slot that is also slightly tapered toward one end. Cut into the upper surface of barrels and sometimes actions, the dovetail accepts a corresponding part on which a sight is mounted. Dovetail slot blanks are used to cover the dovetail when the original sight has been removed or lost; this gives the barrel a more pleasing appearance and configuration.

DRILLING — German for "triple", which is their designation for a three-barrel gun.

EJECTOR — Mechanical device used to eject empty cartridges from chamber(s).

ENGINE TURNING — Overlapped spots of circular polishing.

ENGLISH STOCK — A very straight, slender-gripped stock.

ENGRAVING — The art of carving metal in decorative patterns. Scroll engraving is the most common type of hand engraving encountered. Much of the factory engraving is roll-on engraving; this is done mechanically. Hand engraving is a tedious and costly job.

ETCHING — A method of decorating metal gun parts.

EXTRACTOR — A device that withdraws the fired case from the chamber.

FALLING BLOCK — A single-shot action where the breech block drops straight down when the lever is actuated.

FIT AND FINISH — Terms used to describe over-all firearm workmanship.

FLOATING BARREL — A barrel bedded to avoid contact with any point on the stock.

FLOOR PLATE — The piece which closes the bottom of the magazine body.

FORCING CONE — Forward part of the chamber in a shotgun where the chamber diameter is reduced to bore diameter. The forcing cone aids the passage of shot into the barrel.

FOREND — The forward portion of a rifle or shotgun stock.

FREE RIFLE — A rifle designed for international-type target shooting. The only restriction on design is weight — maximum 8 kilograms (17.6 lbs.).

FRONT STRAP — That part of the revolver or pistol grip frame that faces forward and often joins with the trigger guard. In target guns, notably the .45 ACP, the front strap is often stippled to give shooter's hand a slip-proof surface.

GAUGE — The bore diameter of a shotgun.

GROOVES — The spiral cuts in the bore of a rifle or handgun barrel that give the bullet its spin or rotation as it moves down the barrel.

HAMMERLESS — Some "hammerless" firearms do in fact have hidden hammers, which are located in the action housing. Truly hammerless guns, such as the Savage M99, have a firing mechanism that is based on a spring-activated firing pin.

HEEL — Back end of the upper edge of the buttstock at the upper edge of the buttplate or recoil pad.

LAMINATED STOCK — A gunstock made of many layers of wood glued together under pressure. They are very resistant to warpage.

LANDS — Portions of the bore left between the grooves of the rifling in the bore of a firearm. In rifling, the grooves are usually twice the width of the land. Land diameter is measured across the bore, from land to land.

MAGAZINE — The container which holds cartridges under spring pressure to be fed into the gun's chamber.

MAGNUM — A modern cartridge with a higher-velocity load or heavier projectile than standard.

MAINSPRING —The spring that delivers energy to the hammer or striker. The recoil or operating spring in semiautomatic guns is a part of the breech closing system; is not the same as the mainspring.

MANNLICHER STOCK — A full-length slender forend extending to the muzzle.

MICROMETER SIGHT — A finely adjustable target sight.

MONTE CARLO STOCK — A stock with an elevated comb used primarily for scoped rifles.

MUZZLE — The forward end of the barrel where the projectile exits.

MUZZLE BRAKE — A recoil-reducing device attached to the muzzle.

OVER-UNDER — A two-barrel gun in which the barrels are stacked one on top of the other.

PARALLAX — Occurs in telescopic sights when the primary image of the objective lens does not coincide with the reticle. In practice, parallax is detected in the scope when, as the viewing eye is moved laterally, the image and the reticle appear to move in relation to each other.

PARKERIZING — A matted rust-resistant oxide finish, usually gray or gray-green in color, found on military guns.

PEEP SIGHT — A rear sight consisting of a hole or aperture through which the front sight and target are aligned.

PEPPERBOX — An early form of revolving repeating pistol in which a number of barrels were bored in a circle in a single piece of metal resembling the cylinder of a modern revolver. Functioning was the same as a revolver, the entire cylinder being revolved to bring successive barrels under the hammer for firing. Though occurring as far back as the 16th century, the pepperbox did not become practical until the advent of the percussion cap in the early 1800s. Pepperboxes were made in a wide variety of sizes and styles, and reached their popularity peak during the percussion period. Few were made after the advent of practical metallic cartridges. Both single- and double-action pepperboxes were made. Single-barreled revolvers after the 1840s were more accurate and easier to handle and soon displaced the rather clumsy and muzzle-heavy pepperbox.

POPE RIB — A rib integral with the barrel. Designed by Harry M. Pope, famed barrel maker and shooter, the rib made it possible to mount a target scope low over the barrel.

PROOF MARK — On European guns, is quite specific, indicating proof house and all proofs performed, sometimes also date of proof. Proof marks are applied to all parts actually tested, usually on the barrel, and that in the white - that is, not blued, and without sights. In the U.S., there is no federalized or government proof house, only the manufacturer's in-house proof mark indicating that a firearm has passed their internal quality control standards per government specifications.

RECEIVER — That part of a rifle or shotgun (excluding hinged frame guns) that houses the bolt, firing pin, mainspring, trigger group, and magazine or ammunition feed system. The barrel is threaded into the somewhat enlarged forward part of the receiver, called the receiver ring. At the rear of the receiver, the butt or stock is fastened. In semiautomatic pistols, the frame or housing is sometimes referred to as the receiver.

RELEASE TRIGGER — A trap shooting trigger that fires the gun when the trigger is released.

RIB — A raised sighting plane affixed to the top of a barrel.

RIFLING — The spirally cut grooves in the bore of a rifle or handgun. The rifling stabilizes the bullet in flight. Rifling may rotate to the left or the right, the higher parts of the bore being called lands, the cuts or lower parts being called the grooves. Many types exist, such as oval, polygonal, button, Newton, Newton-Pope, parabolic, Haddan, Enfield, segmental rifling, etc. Most U.S.-made barrels have a right-hand twist, while British gunmakers prefer a left-hand twist. In practice, there seems to be little difference in accuracy or barrel longevity.

ROLLING BLOCK ACTION — Single shot action, designed in the U.S. and widely used in early Remington arms. Also known as the REMINGTON-RIDER action, the breechblock, actuated by a lever, rotates down and back from the chamber. Firing pin is contained in block and is activated by hammer fall.

SCHNABEL FOREND — Erroneously also called shnobel or schnobel. A curved and sometimes carved shape at the forend that resembles the beak of a bird (*Schnabel* in German). This type of forend is common on Austrian and German guns; was popular in the U.S., but the popularity of the schnable forend comes and goes with the seasons. A schnabel forend is often seen on custom stocks and rifles.

SHORT ACTION — A rifle designed for shorter cartridges.

SIDE LOCK — A type of action, usually shotgun, where the moving parts are located on the lock plates inletted in the stock. Usually found only on high-quality shotguns and rifles.

SIDE PLATES — Ornamental additions to simulate a side lock gun on a boxlock.

SINGLE ACTION — A revolver design which requires the hammer to be manually cocked for each shot. Also an auto-loading pistol design which requires manual cocking of the hammer for the first shot only.

SINGLE TRIGGER — One trigger on a double-barrel gun. It fires both barrels singly by successive pulls.

SLING SWIVELS — Metal loops affixed to the gun on which a carrying strap is attached.

SPUR TRIGGER — A trigger mounting system that housed the trigger in an extension of the frame in some old guns. The trigger projected only slightly from the front of the extension or spur, and no trigger guard was used on these guns.

SUICIDE SPECIAL — A mass-produced variety of inexpensive rimfire single action revolvers, usually with a spur trigger. These guns carried many fancy names; those in good condition have become true collector's items.

TAKE DOWN — A gun which can be easily taken apart for carrying or shipping.

TANG — An extension of the receiver into the stock.

TOP STRAP — The upper part of a revolver frame, which often is either slightly grooved - the groove serving as rear sight - or which carries at its rearward end a sight that may be adjustable.

TRAP STOCK — A shotgun stock with greater length and less drop for trap shooting.

TWIST BARRELS — A process in which a steel rod (called a mandrel) was wrapped with "skelps" - ribbons of iron. The skelps were then welded in a charcoal fire to form one piece of metal, after which the rod was driven out to be used again. The interior of the resulting tube then had to be laboriously bored out by hand to remove the roughness. Once polished, the outside was smoothed on big grinding wheels, usually turned by water power.

VENTILATED RIB — A sighting plane affixed along the length of a shotgun barrel with gaps or slots milled for cooling purposes.

ABBREVIATIONS

ACP	Automatic Colt Pistol	O&U	Over and Under
ADJ	Adjustable	OA	Overall
AE	Automatic Ejectors	OB	Octagon Barrel
BR	Bench Rest	OBFM	Octagon Barrel w/full mag.
BPE	Black Power Express	OBO	Or Best Offer
B	Blue	OCT	Octagon
BAC	Browning Arms Company	ODB	Or Don't Bother
BBL	Barrel	PG	Pistol Grip
BP	Butt Plate	PPD	Post Paid
BT	Beavertail	P.O.R.	Price on Request
CAL	Caliber	QD	Quick Detachable
CB	Crescent Buttplate	RB	Round Barrel/Round Butt
CCA	Colt Collectors Association	REC	Receiver
CC	Case Colors	REM	Remington
CF	Centerfire	RF	Rimfire
CH	Cross Hair	RFM	Rim Fire Magnum
COMP	Compensated/Competition	RK	Round Knob
CYL	Cylinder	RKLT	Round Knob Long Tang
DSL	Detachable Side Locks	RR	Red Ramp
DISC	Discontinued	SA	Single Action
DA	Double Action	SAA	Single Action Army
DB	Double Barrel	SAE	Selective Automatic Ejectors
DST	Double Set Triggers	SB	Shotgun Butt
DTs	Double Triggers	S.G.	Straight Grip
DWM	DeutscheWaffen and Munitions Fabrik	SK	Skeet
		SMG	Sub Machine Gun
EXC	Excellent	SMLE	Short Magazine Lee Enfield Rifle
EXT	Extractors	S/N	Serial Number
FBT	Full Beavertail Forearm	SNT	Single Non-Selective Trigger
FA	Forearm	SPEC	Special
F&M	Full & Modified	SPG	Semi-Pistol Grip
FE	Fore End	SPL	Special
FFL	Federal Firearms License	SR	Solid Rib
FK	Flat Knob	S.R.C.	Saddle Ring Carbine
FKLT	Flat Knob Long Tang	SS	Single Shot or Stainless Steel
FM	Full Mag	SST	Single Selective Trigger
FN	Fabrique Nationale	ST	Single Trigger
HB	Heavy Barrel	S&W	Smith & Wesson
HC	Hard Case	SxS	Side by Side
H&H	Holland & Holland	TD	Take Down
HP	Hollow Point	TGT	Target
IC	Improved Cylinder	TH	Target Hammer
LC	Long Colt	TT	Target Trigger
LPI	Lines Per Inch	UMC	Union Metallic Cartridge Co.
LT	Long Tang or Light	VG	Very Good
LTRK	Long Tang Round Knob	VR	Ventilated Rib
MAG	Magnum Caliber	WC	Wad Cutter
mag.	Magazine or Clip	WD	Wood
MC	Monte Carlo	WBY	Weatherby
MFG.	Manufactured/manufacture	WIN	Winchester
MK	Mark	WCF	Winchester Center Fire
M&P	Military & Police	WFF	Watch For Fakes
MR	Matted Rib	WO	White Outline
MSR	Manufacturer's Suggested Retail	WRA	Winchester Repeating Arms Co.
NM	National Match	WRF	Winchester Rim Fire
N	Nickel	WRM	Winchester Rimfire Magnum
NIB	New in Box	WW	World War

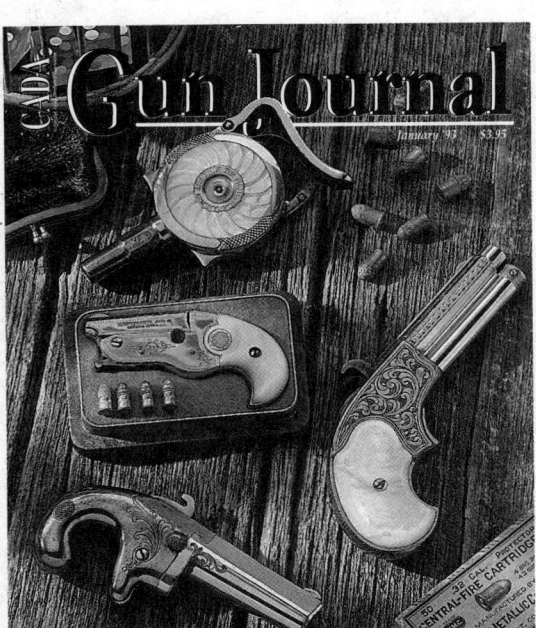

THE BLUE BOOK OF GUN VALUES™
PHOTO PERCENTAGE GRADING SYSTEM ©

Three editions ago, I stated, "Hopefully, this might be the end of an era." Unfortunately, I am still in the process of trying to end it. While the voices and the minds are different (some are extremely polite, some are rude, some are Alzheimerish, and some rattle off facts like a runaway BATF computer) - the question finally remains the same, "How much is it worth?" The answer lies in accurately ascertaining the correct condition factor for the specimen(s) in question. This problem is not unique to the area of collectible firearms - try calling up a coin, car, stamp, baseball card, or antique furniture dealer and ask him/her what they will pay you in C-notes for your deceased Uncle Mortimer's up-to-this-point previously unknown mother-lode stash of "good stuff." Again, the answer is pretty standard, "I'm going to have to see it before I can make a determination on how much it's worth." In other words, talk is cheap because condition is usually over-described. In the end, the merchandise always speaks for itself better than any verbal description.

If there is a harder subject to write about than trying to explain a collectible's unique condition factor via the pen-and-ink mode, I'm glad I haven't had a chance to write about it. As with most other collectibles (including firearms), value is usually determined by a variety of factors, the most critical usually being realistically determining the original condition of the specimen in question. Once the condition question has been answered, monetary evaluation will get much easier.

As in the past, three categories of guns are represented in these photo grading illustrations: Rifles, Shotguns, and Handguns. Chosen category representative models are as follows: Rifles – various Winchester lever actions; Shotguns - Winchester Model 12 and Browning A-5; Handguns - German P.38's and various Colt's . Each photo has its own caption. Simply compare your guns against these photos to find out the corresponding condition in percentages. If your particular configuration is not pictured, try to interpolate areas of wear to the closest category shown (i.e., a Zimmerschuetzen should be compared to the rifles pictured).

It is extremely important when examining wear in any firearm to think about how that wear occurred after a period of normal (and possibly abnormal) use. You will notice in the following Winchester grading photographs that regardless of the amount of receiver bluing, the barrel (magazine tube also if rifle) usually retains over 90% finish. This is because when the owner(s) carried this gun their hand(s) came in contact with the receiver metal just in front of the lever or trigger guard – in other words, where the rifle/shotgun naturally balances when holding it. You don't carry a gun in the field by its barrel or stock, and that explains why they typically show wear last. For these reasons, the receiver on a rifle or shotgun is the king pin when ascertaining condition. A long gun with only 30% barrel blue and 95% receiver finish with crisp checkering simply doesn't add up, unless either the barrel has been replaced or the frame/wood have been refinished/replaced.

On a handgun, wear also starts where it is held when shooting or carrying – on the front and rear grip straps and grips themselves. Worn finish on the sides accumulates after holster use, rubbing or movement against hard, abrasive surfaces, corrosion from gun powder residue, cleaning, etc. On any firearm, the first areas to show wear are the sharp corners and places of mechanical movement or contact (i.e., breech block "primer rings" and striations, lockup notches on cylinders, gun powder corrosion in the breech area, etc.). I have examined many guns that have been fired very little but are in 95%-98% condition because the proud owner(s) has worn off 2%-5% over-zealously cleaning his/her pride and joy every month for the last ten years! Thinking about how a gun accumulates wear naturally is critical when examining any specimen for condition and originality – I cannot emphasize this point enough. On every gun you examine, ask yourself, "Is the cumulative condition overall the sum of its individual parts?"

On older antique firearms, several other factors must be taken into consideration. The amount of heavy finish remaining (Winchester purveyors describe this phenomenon as "bright bluing"), may override the condition factor. To illustrate this, study photo's #4 and #5. #4 has more blue remaining than #5, even though the receiver metal finish is turning brown (on its way to patina) while #5 exhibits a brighter blue finish that is closer to how the gun appeared originally when new. For that reason, #5 is more desirable (and expensive) than #4. In lower condition factors, another variable enters the equation. Long guns with no receiver finish remaining (photo #11) but exhibit overall smooth metal surfaces, average wood, and good internals will be more in demand than a better condition gun with metal pitting, a dark bore, and average wood. Therefore, in many cases, a 0%-10% finish gun will sell at a higher price than a 30%-50% item with oxidized metal surfaces (including pitting) and thinning blue or patina. Also, on most antiques in average condition the bore factor may be overlooked, but on high quality specimens the bore is usually expected to be at least as good as the overall exterior finish.

Remember, for most guns in good supply, original condition is Polar North to the serious collector or investor. Not even a professionally refurbished gun that could otherwise be readily purchased in mint original condition will approach the price of an original. Interestingly enough, however, a newer Browning higher grade Superposed in 80% original condition could have its value increased by having the Browning Service Dept. restore the gun to 100%. Also, on important English shotgun trademarks, top-quality refinishing has been "kosher" for decades, and prices are effected very little. The key to value in situations like this is the desirability factor **after** the restoration in relation to the value of an original. While most Winchester collectors frown on a restored gun (regardless how good the job), a classic American shotgun collector in most cases would rather have a professionally refinished gun than an original in 40% or less overall condition (**if** the restoration process is performed at a level of quality that equals or surpasses that of the original factory work). Knowing how and why these condition factors can override others becomes critical to an accurate price. Pro-rating these condition factors in their proper pecking order is not a job for amateurs and professional advice should be obtained from several sources before multiple C-notes change hands.

We are lucky that the consistency and uniformity of firearms grading standards have not changed. In the coin business, just when you thought those easy, short-term profits were in your sights, the coin industry changed the grading system, making your numismatics fall (not to mention profits) a grade or two. A 98% gun from 1960 is still a 98% gun today. Nothing has changed except for the values going up considerably and the really good stuff has never been harder to find because gun collectors usually dispose of their firearms as their last financial alternative. The first thing an investor sells after 4 or 5 years is his worst investment. The last thing a gun collector will sell is his/her best specimen(s) — unless a cash offer gets tendered that can't be refused.

Always try to buy as much original condition as you can afford. Remember, however, that you can overpay for those last couple of percentage points of a firearm's condition. During the past twelve months, some of the gavel drops that sounded during major gun auctions seem to be linked to some very unpredictable, high price tags. Some dealers have recently indicated that if they priced their better merchandise along-side auction values, not only would they get laughed at on the expensive items, but some potential buyers may think the rest of their merchandise is overpriced as well. Don't forget about those crazed investment (non-collector) diamond buyers who purchased 1-Carat, D-Flawless certified stones (the best quality) for over $80,000 in the early 1980's and flushed them down their portfolio toilets several years later for $12,000. As in any other area of collecting, it is typically wise to stay away from a model, area, or category that has gone up faster than the Space Shuttle in an alarmingly short time. While it's true that these short-term boomers may continue to rise and take you with them, chances are you may be dropped off at the summit of Mt. Everest with no oxygen for the way down. Inflationary or non-inflationary domestic economics occurring within the next 3-5 years will have the final say on whether today's price tags constitute a value or a long-term tax loss.

If you have any questions regarding either the photos or accompanying captions, please contact me. While no grading system is perfect, hopefully this Photo Percentage Grading System© will enable you to ascertain the approximate grade of your individual firearms. Only after learning the correct condition of a firearm can you accurately determine its true value.

Steven P. Fjestad   Author & Publisher
Blue Book of Gun Values

P.S. - I would like to thank LeRoy Merz and Richard Ellis for their firearms, contributions, and expertise in helping with this improved Photo Percentage Grading System©. Also, Martin Mandall (Mandall's Shooting Supplies), Patrick McKune, and Robert White get a free ride at The Mall of America's Camp Snoopy (exempt Thanksgiving through Christmas) for supplying some of the firearms pictured in this section.

All photos in this section were taken by Paul Goodwin and S. P. Fjestad.

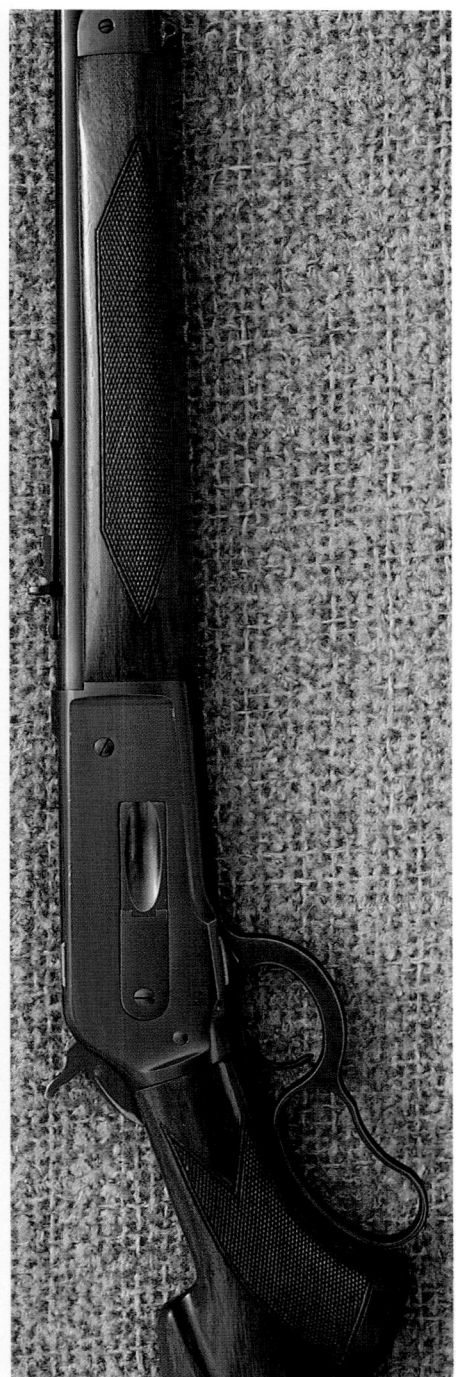

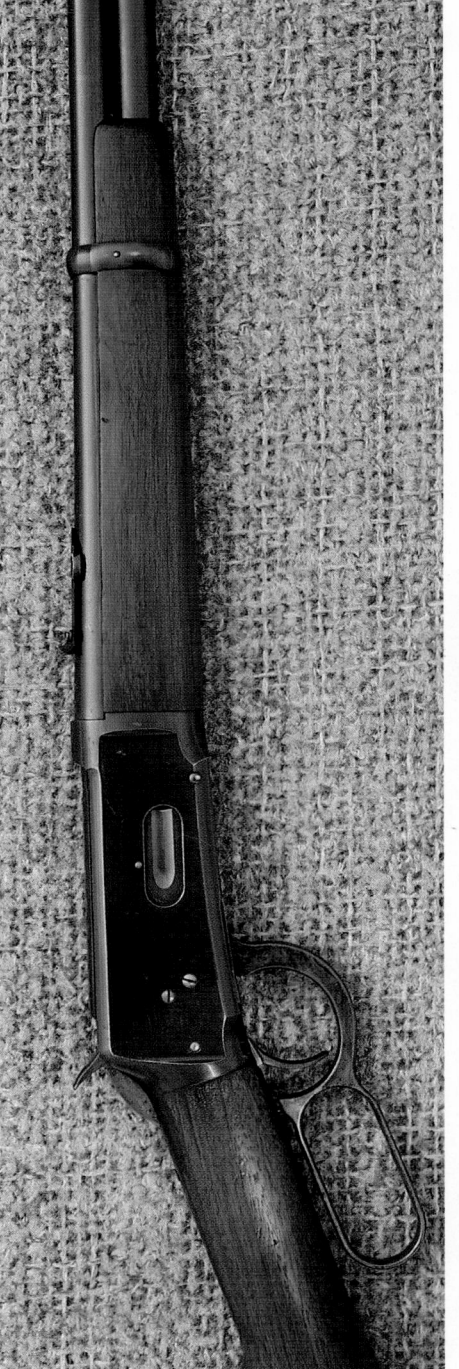

Photo No. 1 - Model 71 Deluxe Rifle with 98%+ bright shiny original blue overall. Most dealers would consider this a mint specimen. Note how sharp the points of the checkering are. While this gun is not 100%, it is close. Observe the slight wear on rear hammer curvature and corners of frame.

Photo No. 2 - Model 1894 Carbine with 95%+ bright shiny original receiver finish and 100% barrel/mag. bluing. Winchester collectors will recognize this as a very fine early gun by the bright vivid case colors still intact on the lever and hammer. This is an extremely desirable specimen - many dealers would call this mint, but corners of frame/loading gate and wood show a little wear.

Rifle Photo Percentage Grading System

Photo No. 3 - Model 1894 Rifle with 90%+ bright shiny original blue on receiver and 98% barrel/mag. blue. Compare almost faded case colors on lever and hammer to Photo No. 2 - again indicating an early gun. Wood is also excellent with perfect fit to metal.

Photo No. 4 - Model 1892 Rifle with 85%-90% original bluing with some light handling and storage marks. Note the darkness of the wood and the mostly shiny forearm cap. Also, observe the color of the bluing is turning a light patina (oxidized bluing which turns a plum-brown color after aging) compared to Photo No. 5. Overall, a nice original specimen.

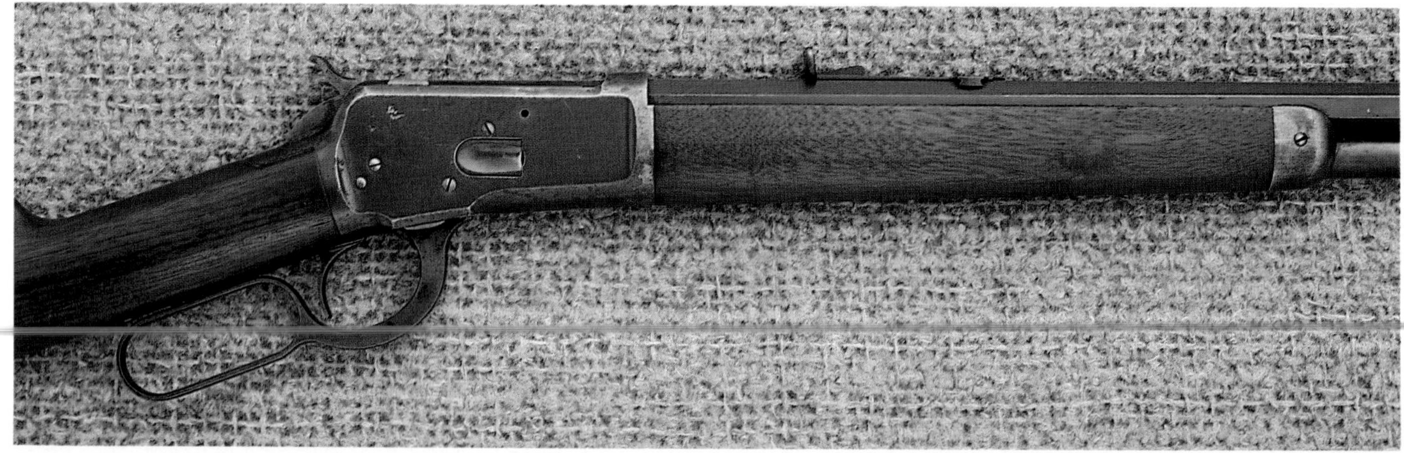

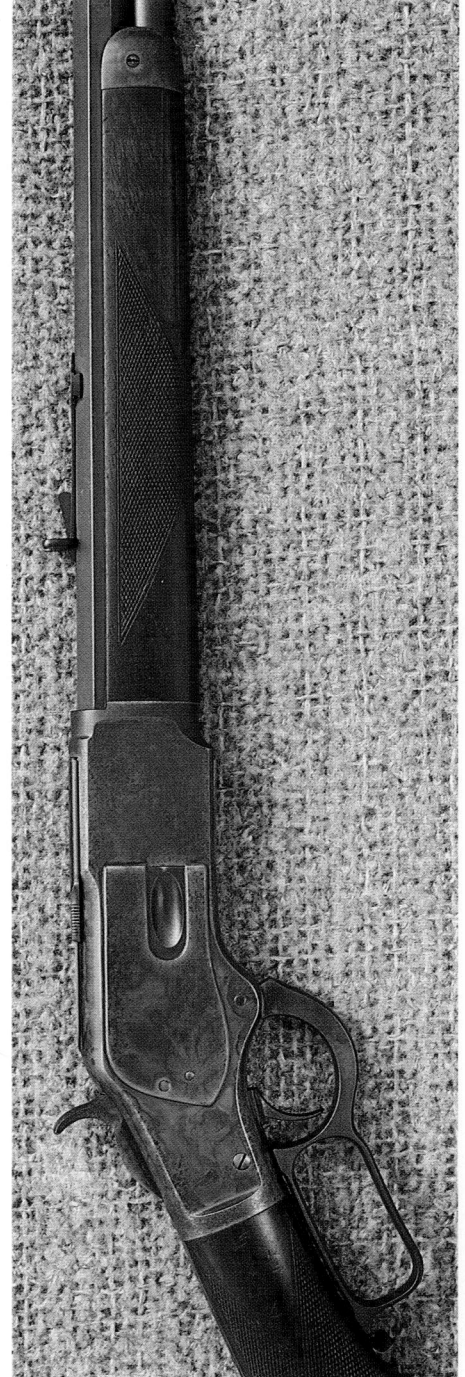

Photo No. 5 - Model 1892 Pistol Grip Takedown Rifle with 75%-80% original receiver bluing. This is a clean sharp gun showing no abuse - only normal wear. Notice that the checkering shows wear on the stock and forearm, and the lever has turned shiny due to use. Note the receiver metal condition compared to Photo No. 4 - while retaining less finish this rifle is more valuable than No. 4 because of the bright bluing factor.

Photo No. 6 - Model 1873 Deluxe Rifle with 60%-70% vivid receiver case colors and 95% barrel blue. Observe the natural color mottling on sideplate and receiver rear - also some small brown rust spots from improper storage can be seen on receiver front. Original bright case colors are extremely desirable on any older firearm.

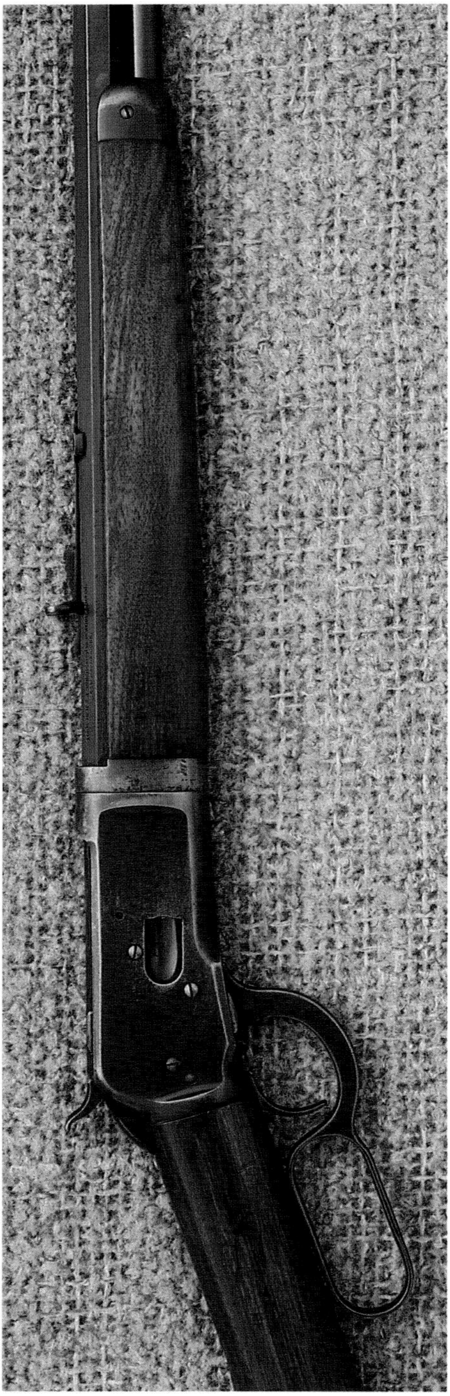

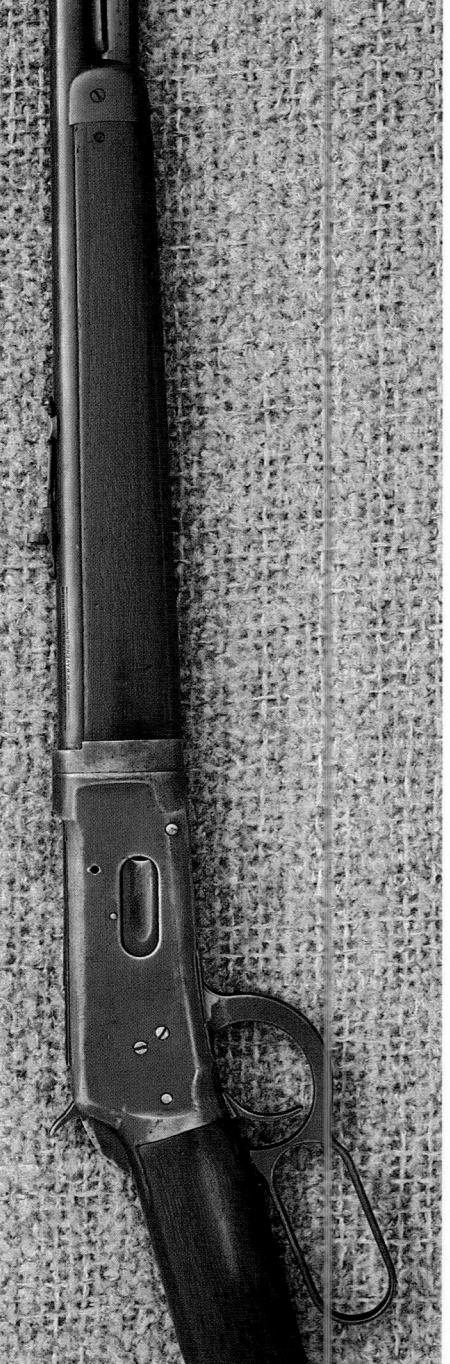

Photo No. 7 - Model 1892 Takedown Rifle showing approximately 60% receiver finish and 95% barrel blue. Notice that the balance of the receiver has flaked and turned brown. Also, close observation indicates that the frame screws have never been damaged by a screwdriver.

Photo No. 8 - Model 55 Takedown Rifle retaining 40%- 50% of what appears to be an older reblued finish (note how frame corners are rounded due to excessive polishing). The dark wood is generally in good condition. Notice that the top frame screw shows damage and that the lever has been bent (is not flush against lower tang) due to older abuse.

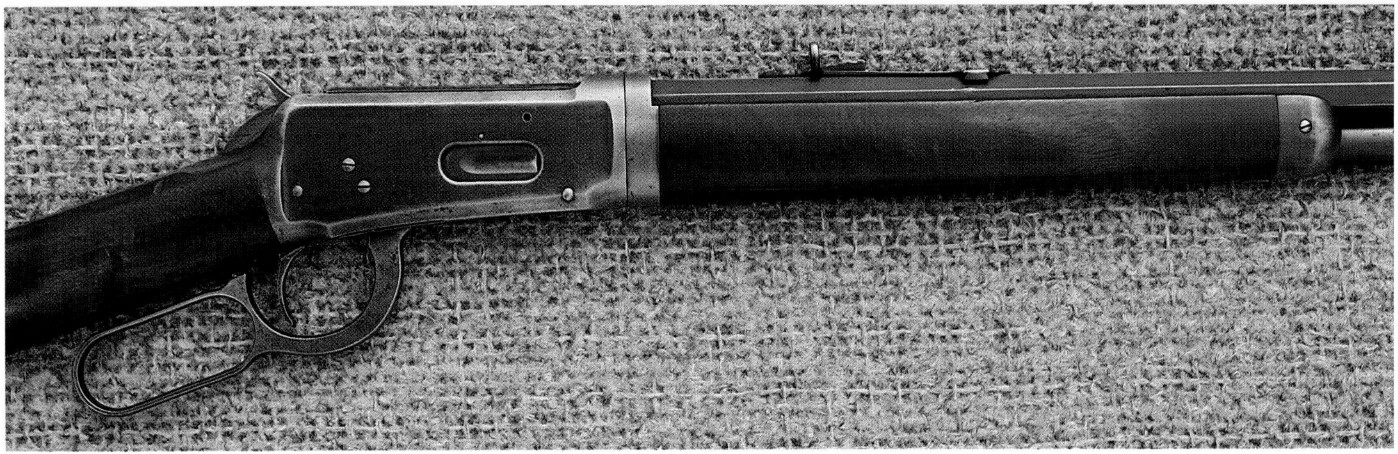

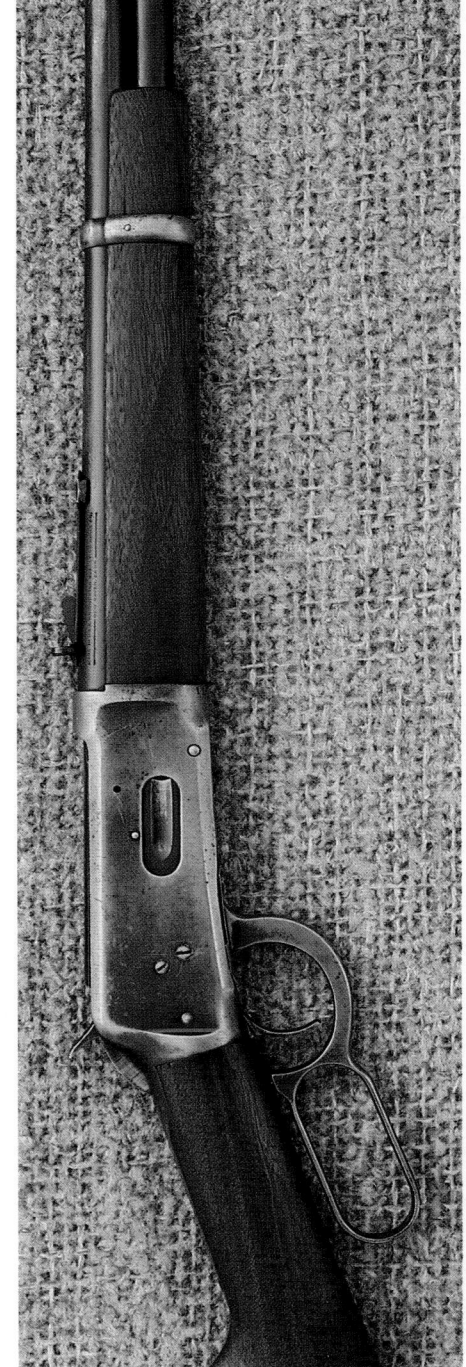

Photo No. 9 - Model 1894 Takedown Rifle with 40% original blue turning brown on frame and 90% barrel blue. The bottom and top of receiver and takedown ring have turned silvery from handling. This is normal wear and consistent with the rest of the gun's condition.

Photo No. 10 - Model 1894 Carbine depicting 20% receiver blue and 90% barrel/mag. blue. Notice the pattern of wear and how the balance of finish is turning a gun metal gray, including the barrel band. This carbine's condition is typical of many older Winchesters. A well used specimen showing no abuse.

Photo No. 11 - Model 55 Takedown Rifle with no receiver blue remaining (it has flaked off) and 50% barrel/mag. blue. The wood is in very good condition. This is commonly referred to as a "shiny gun". While this gun appears in poor condition due to flaking, it is still a lot more desirable than the Model 1892 pictured in Photo No. 12.

Photo No. 12 - Model 1892 Rifle showing a lot of wear with all metal surfaces having turned a dark brown heavy patina due to much use, some abuse (note nails in front of forearm), and neglect. In the business, this is called a "brown gun" and is the least desirable from a condition standpoint.

Photo No. 13 - Winchester Model 42 in mint condition. Collectors will note the VR, subcontracted to Simmons even though it was a factory option. Winchester then assembled the completed barrels - note sharp features and condition of wood. Factory VR's on Model 42's (and 12's) should have the definitive Winchester proofmark offset on rear top of barrel assembly.

Photo No. 14 - Winchester Model 12 in 96%-98% original condition. Observe wear on receiver corners and horizontal striation on magazine tube where slide action contacts metal. Nice original older dark wood (notice that stock is slightly oversized where it meets frame metal indicating not sanded) with "corncob" forearm.

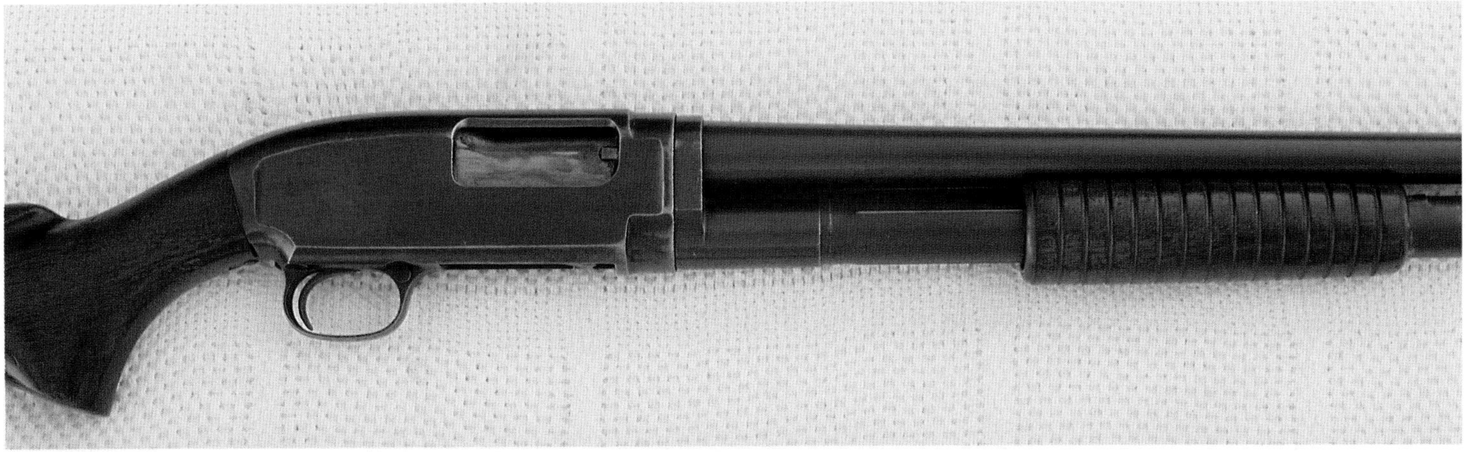

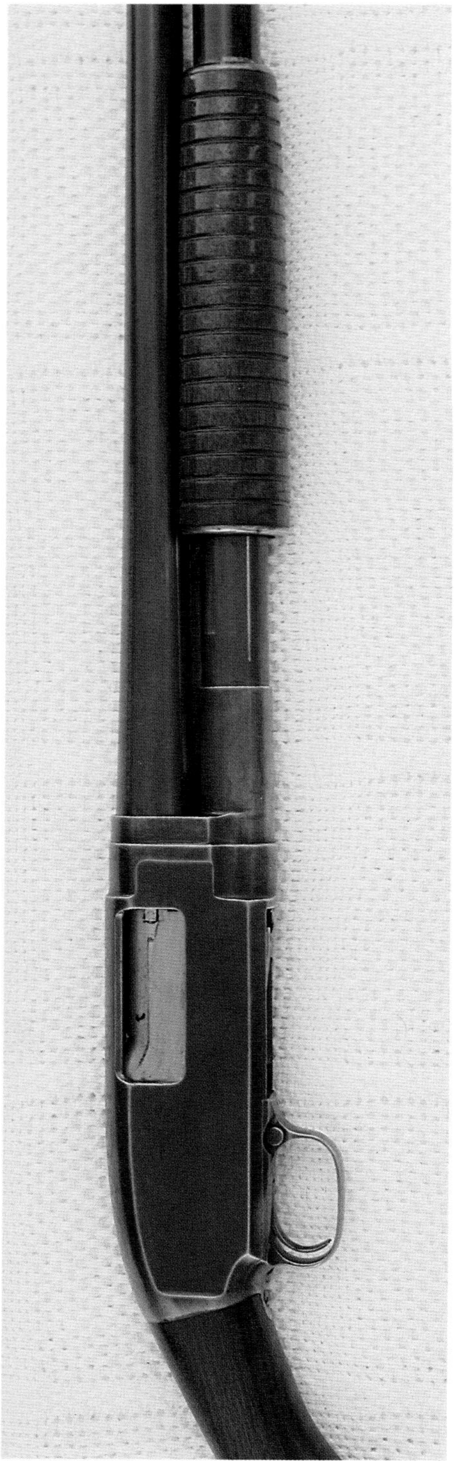

Photo No. 15 - Winchester Model 12 in 90% original condition. Notice more wear on metal than Photo No. 14 - especially on rear rounded frame contour and magazine tube where it disassembles from receiver. The bottom of frame and trigger guard also are turning silvery indicating normal hunting wear.

Photo No. 16 - Winchester Model 12 in 80% overall condition. Metal indicates additional wear than depicted in Photo No. 15. Barrel is starting to visibly show wear and magazine tube has accumulated shininess indicating much usage. You will notice that the stock shows little wear (and is a different color) compared to the forearm indicating refinishing.

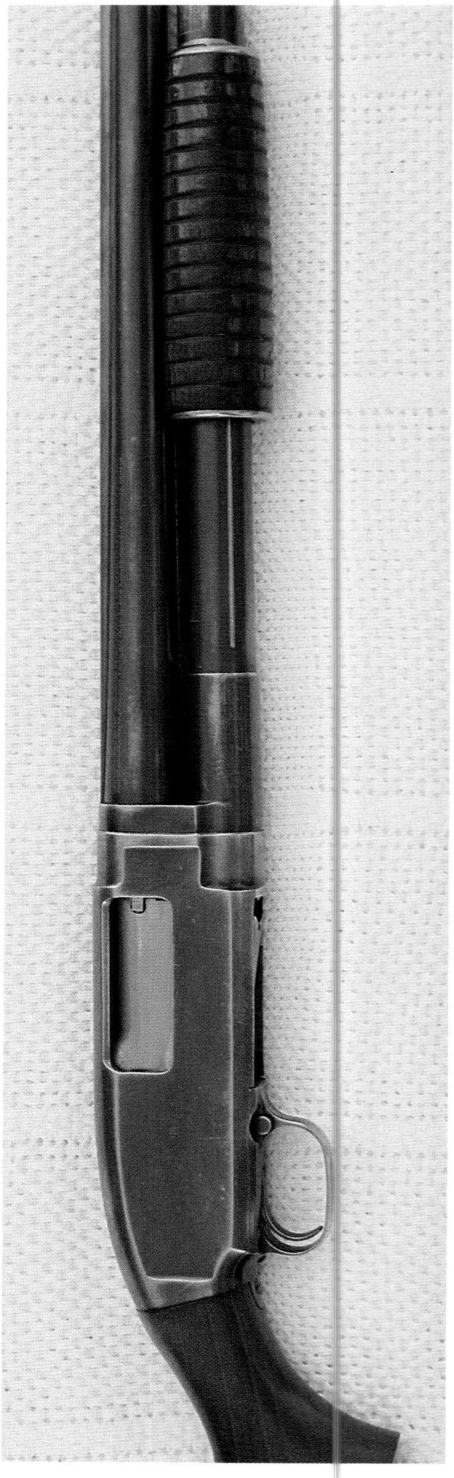

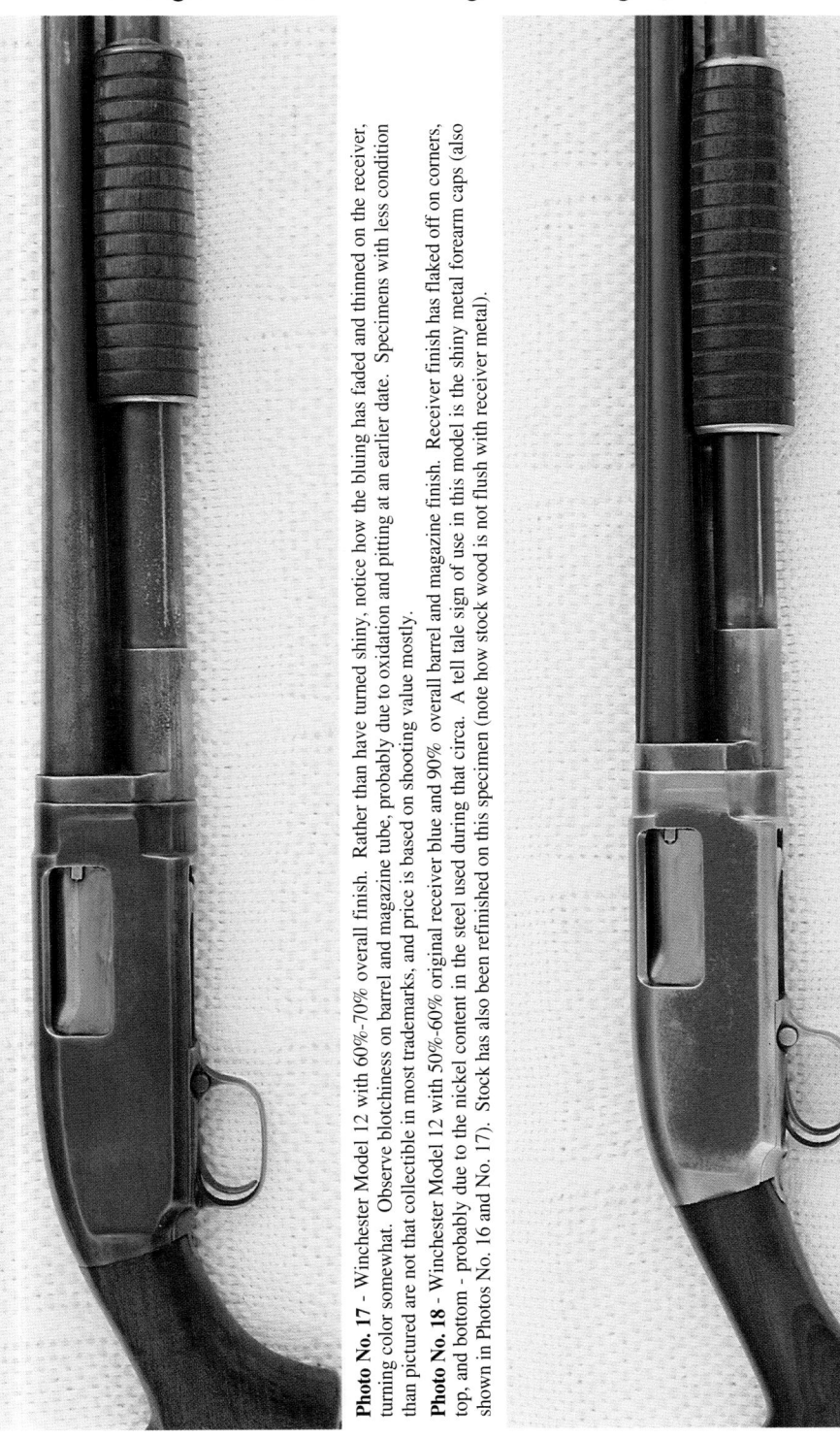

Photo No. 17 - Winchester Model 12 with 60%-70% overall finish. Rather than have turned shiny, notice how the bluing has faded and thinned on the receiver, turning color somewhat. Observe blotchiness on barrel and magazine tube, probably due to oxidation and pitting at an earlier date. Specimens with less condition than pictured are not that collectible in most trademarks, and price is based on shooting value mostly.

Photo No. 18 - Winchester Model 12 with 50%-60% original receiver blue and 90% overall barrel and magazine finish. Receiver finish has flaked off on corners, top, and bottom - probably due to the nickel content in the steel used during that circa. A tell tale sign of use in this model is the shiny metal forearm caps (also shown in Photos No. 16 and No. 17). Stock has also been refinished on this specimen (note how stock wood is not flush with receiver metal).

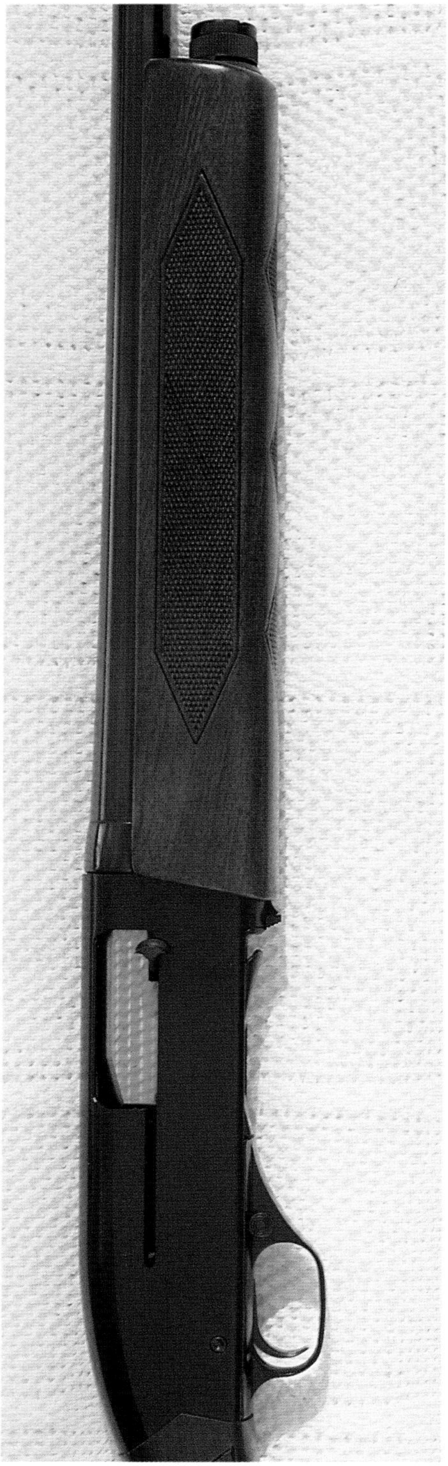

Photo No. 19 - Winchester Model 1400 in new condition or 100%. Notice no wear on any visible part. Close examination will show checkering is pressed in rather than hand-cut. Swirl marks on breech block indicate engine-turning. Receiver appears black because it is an alloy and takes bluing differently than the steel barrel.

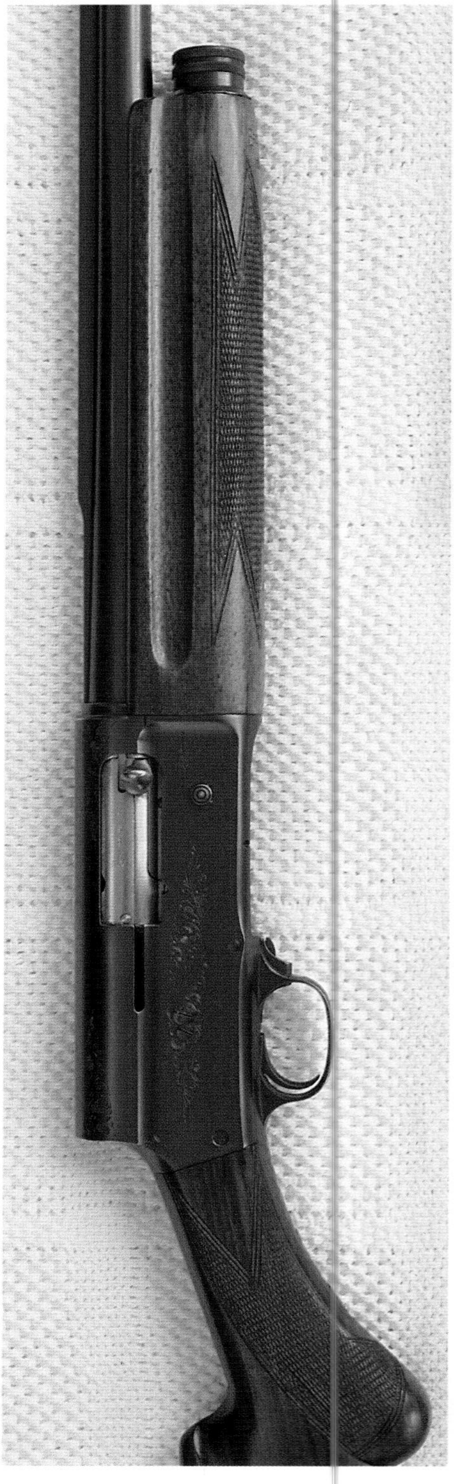

Photo No. 20 - Browning A-5 in mint condition (over 99%+ original condition). Note round knob pistol grip and safety location (indicative of an early gun). Checkering is sharp on pistol grip but slightly worn on forearm. Close inspection will reveal a dark hairline crack on bottom of forearm next to frame (common in this model).

Photo No. 21 - Bottom view of L.C. Smith Field Grade with hammers. No argument about this gun's condition - it's mint! A Field Model hammer gun with all the original case colors and bluing remaining is ultra rare. Notice exact wood to metal fit around sideplates and trigger guard.

Photo No. 22 - L.C. Smith Field Grade (hammerless). Again, another mint specimen of an L.C. Smith. Notice the way the case colors on frame top are mottled, wood to metal fit, and the checkering without points (common in most domestically manufactured field grade models).

Photo No. 23 - L.C. Smith Ideal Grade with approximately 30% original case colors remaining. Notice the stock cracks around the sideplate (somewhat common with older, well- used L.C. Smiths) and case colors next to frame shoulder.

Photo No. 24 - This is the bottom view of Photo 23. Notice the shininess on the front and bottom of frame indicating much usage. Also note the "LONGRANGE" and "HUNTER ONE TRIGGER" markings on receiver bottom, nail alterations to forearm, and visible stock cracking (these problems lower this specimen's value over 40%).

Photo No. 25 - Another L.C. Smith in Specialty Grade with traces of case colors barely remaining. Observe light pitting around bottom front of receiver, noticeable crack in forearm, and slight wood splinters missing around sideplate area (normal).

Photo No. 26 - Older Parker Brothers D-Grade hammer gun with fluid steel barrels. While appearing original, this shotgun has been professionally refurbished (somewhat distinguishable by faint game scene engraving in front of hammer indicative of older use or over-polishing). Note the light scroll engraving and scalloped shoulders of frame.

Photo No. 27 - Colt Series 80 National Match Model in new condition (100%). No observable wear on any visible part. Note how roll-die stamp put the slide logo at different depths along the length of the legend. Compare color difference in bluing to Photos No. 33 and No. 41, indicating the differences in metallurgy, machining, polishing, and bluing solvents.

Photo No. 28 - Walther Post-War P1 (commercial variation of the P.38) in 98% original condition. Observe wear on slide edges, top of trigger, and hold-open lever. The color difference between frame and slide bluing is normal since the frame is an alloy and the upper slide is steel, and each metal reacts to the bluing differently.

Photo No. 29 - Walther Post-War P1 in 95%+ original condition. Note more wear than Photo No. 28 on slide edges. Barrel, trigger guard, safety, takedown lever and bottom of grips also show additional usage. Silvery scratching above serial number remains where some "craftsman" tried to "erase" an operation ID number - this decreases value 30%+.

Photo No. 30 - Walther WWII ac-44 Model in 90% condition. While it appears to be original, close inspection reveals a refinished gun (note how tops of slide serial numbers and P.38 logo have disappeared when the gun was over-polished during refinishing). Because P.38's are in good supply in 90%+ original condition, this lowers the value to shooting status.

Photo No. 31 - Mauser WWII byf-43 Model in 70% original condition. This specimen shows dark areas of blotchiness from older oxidation on slide and frame. While this pistol offers little collector value (most commonly available handguns in this condition are the same), it still maintains a minimum "spot price" as a shooter.

Photo No. 32 - Korth Revolver (W. German mfg.) in new condition (100%). This revolver has been included to show the exceptional metal machining, polishing, and translucent-like bluing. Metal parts almost resemble polished black marble. This is perhaps the finest (and most expensive) new revolver available in today's marketplace.

Photo No. 33 - Model 1911 Springfield Armory in 96%-97% original condition. Notice markings and trigger wear. Also note scratch from top of trigger guard to slide stop lever indicating careless reassembly.

Photo No. 34 - Model 1911 Springfield Armory in 60% original condition. As wear has accumulated, the metal has become a duller grayish color. Notice martial markings next to trigger and rear of slide on both guns.

Photo No. 35 - Model 1911A1 manufactured by Singer for WWII contract. This pistol is ultra-rare in this condition factor - 98%. A very "crisp" specimen, considering only 500 were manufactured in 1942.

Photo No. 36 - Model 1911 manufactured by North American Arms Co. Limited. In this condition (99% overall) it can be considered one of the "Holy Grails" of Colt semi- auto collecting. Prices can be very non-predictable, and auctions continue to set the "high-water" mark on prices for any gun with major trademark acceptance in this type of condition.

Photo No. 37 - Another Model 1911 North American Arms in approximately 85%-90% original condition. Observe pitting on slide top and great condition of frame. Despite the pitting and upper slide wear, this variation's rarity still makes this specimen very desirable.

Photo No. 38 - Model 1911 manufactured by North American Arms in approximately 75% original condition. Compare this pistol against Photo No. 37 and notice this specimen's additional wear on front grip strap and grip safety.

Photo No. 39 - North American Arms Model 1911 in approximately 60% original condition. Again, notice the additional bluing wear compared to Photo No. 38.

Photo No. 40 - Another Model 1911 manufactured by North American Arms in approximately 20%-30% original condition. This pistol's rarity factor, despite its condition, still makes it very desirable.

Photo No. 41 - Model 1911 manufactured under military contract by Remington U.M.C. in 98% original condition. Notice ordnance proofing, crispness of slide/frame markings, and condition of walnut grips.

Photo No. 42 - Colt Model 1911 Military manufactured in 1913. This gun is in mint (99%+) condition overall. Note the difference in the coloration of bluing compared to the Remington U.M.C. Model 1911 in Photo No. 41.

Photo No. 43 - Pre-War Colt commercial in .38 Super cal. (very desirable). This "creampuff" is in mint condition. This pristine specimen (and gun in Photo No. 42) dictate the most demand for collectors/investors.

Photo No. 44 - Colt Pre-War Government Model .45 that has been reblued. Note thinning of "patent legend" on slide side with slight corner rounding on bottom of slide and other originally sharp corners.

Photo No. 45 - Colt Model 1911A1 with correct darker parkerized finish in mint condition. Observe dark plastic grips.

Photo No. 46 - A.J. Savage slide Model 1911 with almost all the original finish worn off. This pistol would grade approximately 5%-10%.

Handgun Photo Percentage Grading System

Photo No. 47 - Colt Pre-War New Service revolver in mint overall original condition. Notice the grip condition and barely distinguishable vertical striation between cylinder lock-up notches.

Photo No. 48 - Colt Model 1917 Army in 98% original condition. Note direction of polishing by front sight blade.

Photo No. 49 - Colt New Service in 98%+ overall original condition. Notice how fine the metal has been polished, high luster bluing, and fire blued frame and grip screws.

Photo No. 50 - Colt Model 1909 U.S.M.C. in 95% original condition with "light freckling". Observe polishing and coloration of bluing.

Handgun Photo Percentage Grading System

Photo No. 51 - Model 1917 Army "in the white" from the factory. This gun was never blued, notice vertical striations in polishing.

Photo No. 52 - Colt Model 1909 U.S.M.C. in 90% overall original condition. Note holster wear on barrel tip, striations between cylinder cutouts, and shininess on frame edges.

Photo No. 53 - Colt Early Officer's Model with factory engraving and Mother-of-Pearl grips. This specimen is in approximately 80% original condition. Note adjustable front sight and light pitting at barrel muzzle.

Photo No. 54 - Colt Model 1889 Double Action in approximately 60% original condition. Notice amount and location of wear.

Photo No. 55 - Colt Model 1851 U.S. Army contract in approximately 90% overall condition. Note case colors remaining on frame, perfect frame screws, and brass grip straps.

Photo No. 56 - Colt Model 1851 U.S. Navy contract in approximately 70%-80% original condition. Note the oxidized brownish splotches on barrel and areas of frame.

Photo No. 57 - Colt Model 1851 U.S. Navy contract in 30%-40% original condition. Note thinning and grayish patina color of bluing. Overall, a very clean original specimen showing honest wear.

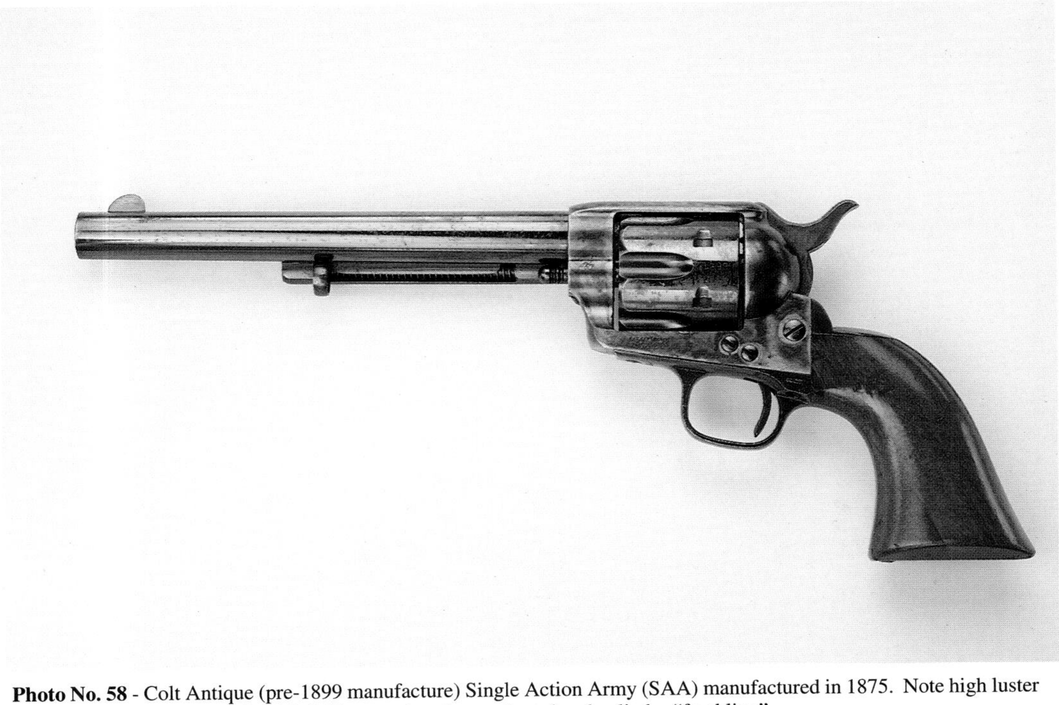

Photo No. 58 - Colt Antique (pre-1899 manufacture) Single Action Army (SAA) manufactured in 1875. Note high luster finish and case colors on this 90%-95% gun, also observe barrel and cylinder "freckling".

Handgun Photo Percentage Grading System

Photo No. 59 - Colt 3rd Model Dragoon in approximately 80% overall condition. A beautiful specimen considering 1851 manufacture. As in some other Colt's, note the fire bluing on frame screws and trigger. Also notice the still visible cylinder scene indicating careful use.

Photo No. 60 - Colt 2nd Model Dragoon with no finish remaining. While appearing original, this pistol has been artificially aged giving it an older appearance. Fakes in rarer Colt models have become more elaborate. Always get a receipt indicating condition (original or otherwise) when purchasing older guns such as this specimen.

Cartridge Interchangeability

This section is for the shooter whose motto is "If it fits, I'll shoot it". Many apparent "fits" are not adapted for a shorter round, and either immediate or future damage can occur to the firearm by firing ammunition not specifically adapted to the chambering of a particular gun. As an example, many people think that shooting .22 Shorts in a barrel marked for .22 Long Rifle is acceptable. In fact, repeated firing can cause erosion of the chamber to the point that shell extraction can become difficult in addition to experiencing velocity loss in extreme cases. Below is a listing of recommended caliber interchangeability. No other cartridge switching is recommended nor does this chart work vise-versa. For shotguns, there is no interchangeability for gauges. Only shells that are shorter than the specified chamber length in the same gauge may be used (ie. 2-3/4 in. 12 ga. ammunition may be used in a 12. ga. gun with a 3 in. chamber).

RIMFIRE INTERCHANGEABILITY

Firearm marked for:	Can also be used with:
.22 Short	.22 BB Cap, .22 CB Cap, .22 Short Blank, 22 CB Short
.22 Long	.22 BB Cap, .22 CB Cap, .22 Short Blank, .22 Short, .22 CB Short, .22 CB Long
.22 Long Rifle	.22 BB Cap, .22 CB Cap, .22 Short Blank, .22 CB Short, .22 CB Long, .22 Long, .22 L.R. Shot
.22 Win. Mag. R.F	..22 Win. R.F., .22 Rem. Spl.
.22 Rem. Spl	.22 Win. R.F.
.22 Win. R.F.	.22 Rem. Spl.
.25 Stevens	.25 Stevens Short
.32 Long	.32 Short

CENTERFIRE HANDGUN INTERCHANGEABILITY

Firearm marked for:	Can also be used with:
.32 Smith & Wesson Long	.32 Smith & Wesson, .32 Smith & Wesson Blank, .32 Colt New Police
.32 Colt New Police	.32 Smith & Wesson, .32 Smith & Wesson Blank, .32 Smith & Wesson Long
.32 Long Colt	.32 Short Colt
.38 Long Colt	.38 Short Colt
.38 Smith & Wesson	.38 Colt New Police, .38 Smith & Wesson Blank
.38 Colt New Police	.38 Smith & Wesson, .38 Smith & Wesson Blank
.38 Special	.38 Short Colt, .38 Long Colt, .38 Special Blank
.357 Magnum	.38 Short Colt, .38 Long Colt, .38 Special Blank, .38 Special, .38 Special +P
.38-40 Winchester	5 in 1 Blank
.38 Super Auto	.38 Auto Colt
.44 S&W Special	.44 S&W Russian
.44 Remington Magnum	.44 S&W Special
.44-40 Winchester	5 in 1 Blank
.45 Colt	5 in 1 Blank

GUNS ALSO CALLED CENTERFIRE PISTOLS

Full name:	Also called:
.25 Automatic	.25 Auto, .25 ACP, .25 C.A.P., 6.35mm Auto, 6.35mm Browning (Auto)
.30 Luger	7.65 Luger, 7.65 Parabellum
.32 Automatic	.32 Auto, .32 ACP, .32 C.A.P., 7.65 Auto, 7.65mm Browning (Auto)
9mm Luger	9mm Parabellum
380 Automatic	9mm Corto, 9mm Kurtz
.38-40 Winchester	.38-40, .38 W.C.F., .38 Winchester, .38-40 Remington, .38-40 Marlin
.44-40 Winchester	.44-40, .44 W.C.F., .44 Winchester, .44-40 Remington, .44-40 Marlin

CENTERFIRE RIFLES

Full name:	Also called:
6mm Remington	(formerly) .244 Remington
.25-20 Winchester	.25-20, .25 W.C.F., .25-20 Marlin
.30-30 Winchester	.30-30, .30 Winchester, .30 Marlin, .30 Savage, .30 W.C.F.
.32-20 Winchester	.32-20, .32 Winchester, .32 Marlin, .32 Remington, .32 W.C.F., .32 Colt L.M.R.
.38-40 Winchester	.38-40, .38 W.C.F., .38 Winchester, .38-40 Remington, .38-40 Marlin
.44-40 Winchester	.44-40, .44 W.C.F., .44 Winchester, .44-40 Remington, .44-40 Marlin
.45-70 Government	.45-70, .45-70 Marlin, .45-70-405, .45-70-500

Firearms Associations

Alabama Gun Collectors
P.O. Box 59606
Birmingham, AL 35259

Alaska Gun Collectors Association
c/o Wayne Anthony Ross, President
P.O. Box 101522
Anchorage, Alaska 99510

Ark - La - Tex - Gun Collectors
Thomas L. Baird, President
9601 Blom Blvd.
Shreveport, LA 71118

Bay Colony Weapons Collectors, Inc.
Ronald B. Santurjian
47 Homer Road
Belmont, MA 02178

Boardman Valley Collectors Guild
Secretary Jack Johnson
County Road 600
Manton, MI 49663

Browning Collectors Assn.
Mrs. Bobbie Hamit
P.O. Box 526
Aurora, NE 68818

C.A.D.A.(Collector Arms Dealer Association)
P.O. Box 427
Thomson, IL 61285

California Rifle & Pistol Association, Inc.
James H. Erdman, Executive Director
12062 Valley View St., Suite 107
Garden Grove, CA 92645

Central Illinois Gun Collectors Assn. Inc.
Russ Gardner Sec.- Treas.
P.O. Box 875
Jacksonville, IL 62651-0875

Central Penn Antique Arms Association
John E. Holman Jr.
978 Thistle Road
Elizabethtown, PA 17022

Chisholm Trail Antique Gun Association
E.D. Stone
1906 Richmond
Wichita, KS 67203

Civil War Round Table of North New Jersey
James F. Elliott
124 Conover Lane
Red Bank, NJ 07701

Colt Collectors Association
Sydna Guest, Secretary
3200 Westminster
Dallas, TX 75205
Annual Membership $35

Delaware Weapons Association
97 Johnson Rd.
Bangor, PA 18013

Derringer Collectors Association
Mr. J. Michael Hall
500 E. Old 66
Shamrock, TX 79079

Ducks Unlimited
One Waterfowl Way
Memphis, TN

Florida Gun Collectors Association, Inc.
1621 South Drive
Sarasota, FL 34239

Golden Eagle Collectors Association
11144 Slate Creek Rd.
Grass Valley, CA 95945

Gun Owners Civil Rights Alliance
Mr. Joseph E. Olson, President
P.O. Box 131254
St. Paul, MN 55113

Gun Owners of America
8001 Forbes Pl., Suite 102
Springfield, VA 22151

Hawaii Historic Arms Association
Box 1733
Honolulu, HI 96806

Hopkins & Allen Arms & Memorabilia Society
1309 Pamela Circle
Delphos, OH 45833

Houston Gun Collectors Association
P.O. Box 741429
Houston, TX 77274-1429

Hunter Education Association
Box 525
Draper, UT 84020
Phone No.: 801-571-9461

Indianhead Firearms Assn.
R#9 Box 186
Chippewa Falls, WI 54729

Indian Territory Gun Collectors Association
Box 4491
Tulsa, OK 74159

Iroquois Arms Collectors Association
Kenneth Keller-sec.
Susann Keller-show sec.
214 70th St.
Niagara Falls, NY 14304

Jersey Shore Antique Arms Collectors
Joe Sisia
P.O. Box 100
Bayville, NJ 08721

Kansas Cartridge Collectors Association
Vic Suetter
Route 1
Lincoln, KS 67455

Kentuckiana Arms Collectors Assoc.
Cindi Higgins, Secretary
P.O. Box 1776
Louisville, KY 40201

Kentucky Gun Collectors Association
Ruth Johnson, Exec. Sec.
P.O. Box 64
Owensboro, KY 42302

Lancaster Muzzle Loading Rifle Association
James H. Frederick, Jr.
779 Prospect Road
Columbia, PA 17512

Long Island Antique Gun Collectors Assoc.
Frederick R. Wilkens
35 Beach Street
Farmingdale, L.I., NY 11735
$20 Annual Dues

The Mannlicher Collectors Association
Don L. Henry, Executive Secretary
P.O. Box 7144
Salem, OR 97303

Marlin Firearms Collectors Association, Ltd.
Mr. Dick Paterson, Secretary/Treasurer
407 Lincoln Bldg.
44 Main Street
Champaign, IL 61820
$7 annual dues

Maryland Arms Collectors Assoc. (MACA)
Mr. D. Kuzemchak, Secretary
33 S. Main Street
P.O. Box 206
Loganville, PA 17342-0206
$25 annual membership fee

Memphis Antique Weapons Association
Lonnie Griffin
108 Clark Place
Memphis, TN 38104

Minnesota Rifle and Revolver Association
Karin A. Ostrand, President
10 Pheasant Ln.
North Oaks, MN 55127

Minnesota Weapons Collectors Association
Gail Foster, Executive Secretary
P.O. Box 662
Hopkins, MN 55343

Miniature Arms Collectors/Makers Society, Ltd.
104 White Sand Lane
Racine, WI 53402

Missouri Valley Arms Collectors Association, Inc.
L.P. Brammer, Membership Secretary
P.O. Box 33033
Kansas City, MO 64114
(816) 333-6509
Annual membership $17.50– ages 21+; $7.50– under 21

Montana Arms Collectors Association
Dean E. Yearout
1516 - 21st Ave. S.
Great Falls, MT 59405
$20 Annual Membership Fee

Mossberg Collectors Association
Victor Havlin
P.O. Box 22156
St. Louis, MO 63116
$10 Annual Membership Fee

Mule Deer Foundation
1005 Terminal Way, Ste. 110
Reno, NV 89502
$25 Annual Memberhsip Fee

N.A.P.C.A.
c/o Automag
Box 15738 TGS
St. Louis, MO 63163

National Alliance of Stocking Gun Dealers
P.O. Box 187
Havelock, NC 28532

National Rifle Association (NRA)
1600 Rhode Island Avenue N.W.
Washington, D.C. 20036
Membership dues $25 a year
$68 for 3 years
$100 for 5 years

New Hampshire Arms Collectors, Inc.
Warren Thayer
P.O. Box 6
Harrisville, N.H. 03450

North Eastern Arms Collectors Assoc., Inc.
Thomas J. Mulligan, President
P.O. Box 185
Amityville, NY 11701

Northwest Montana Arms Collectors Association
Paul C. Beckstrom
P.O. Box 653
Kalispell, MT 59901

Ohio Gun Collectors Association
P.O. Box 24170
Cincinnati, OH 45224-0170

Old Fort Gun Collectors Association
No current address

Oregon Arms Collectors
Ted Dowd
P.O. Box 25103
Portland, OR 97225

Pelican Arms Collectors Association
Bob Thompson
P.O. Box 747
Clinton, LA 70722

Pennsylvania Antique Gun Collectors Assoc.
Mrs. Kathleen Beyer Secy./Treas.
28 Fulmer Avenue
Havertown, PA 19083
$10 annual membership fee

Potomac Arms Collectors Association
Bruce D. Feinberg
P.O. Box 2676
Laurel, MD 20811

Quail Unlimited
Rt. #3 - Box 29B
Edgefield, SC 29824
$20 Annual Membership includes
bimonthly subscription to Quail Unlimited

Remington Society of America
Marv Adams, Secretary-Treasurer
130 W. South Boundary
Perrysburg, OH 43551-1754
Annual Membership $30
Life Membership $300

Ruger Collectors Association, Inc.
P.O. Box 1778
Chino Valley, AZ 86323
$25 annual membership fee

Safari Club International
4800 W. Gates Pass Rd.
Tucson, AZ 85745
Phone: 602-620-1220
$30 Annual Membership USA/CAN/MEX

Sako Collectors Association, Inc.
Mims C. Reed
1725 Woodhill Lane
Bedford, TX 76021
$20 annual membership fee
$200 life membership

Santa Barbara Historical Arms Coll. Assoc.
P.O. Box 6291
Santa Barbara, CA 93160-6291
$25 annual membership fee
$15 initiation fee

San Bernardino Valley Arms Collectors
Robert Walter
18710 Cajon Blvd.
San Bernardino, CA 92407

San Fernando Valley Arms Coll. Assoc.
Harold Ball
P.O. Box 65
North Hollywood, CA 91603

Second Amendment Foundation/Gun Week
12500 Northeast 10 Pl.
Bellevue, WA 98005

Smith & Wesson Collectors Association
R.D. Kolesar, Secretary
P.O. Box 321
Bellevue, WA 98009

The Stark Gun Collectors, Inc.
Pat F. McDonald
602 Summerdale N.W.
Massillon, OH 44646

Tampa Bay Arms Collectors Association
John J. Tuvell, Secretary
2461-67th Avenue South
St. Petersburg, FL 33712

Texas Gun Collectors Association
13201 Wells Fargo Trail
Austin, TX 78737
(512) 288-5039

The Thompson Center Association
Hilary Wright, Secretary
P.O. Box 792
Northboro, MA 01532
$25 annual membership fee

Tri-State Gun Collectors, Inc.
P.O. Box 1201
Lima, OH 45801

Washington Arms Collectors, Inc.
J. Dennis Cook
P.O. Box 7335
Tacoma, WA 98407

Weapons Collectors Society of Montana
3100 Bancroft
Missoula, MT 59801

Weatherby Collectors Association, Inc.
P.O. Box 128
Moira, NY 12957

Williamette Valley Arms Collectors Association, Inc.
Murry Brooks, Executive Secretary
P.O. Box 5191
Eugene, OR 97405

Winchester Arms Collectors Association, Inc.
Richard A. Berg, Exec. Sec.
P.O. Box 6754
Great Falls, MT 59406

Winchester Club of America
Larry Jones
3070 S. Wyandot
Englewood, CO 80110

Ye Connecticut Gun Guild
Robert L. Harris
U.S. Route 7-Kent Road
Cornwall Bridge, CT 06754

Zumbro Valley Arms Collectors, Inc.
Box 6621
Rochester, MN 55901

Meet the Staff

Chances are you have already "seen" one or more of these faces on the other end of one of our ever-increasing telephone lines (we probably have the only business in Bloomington with two incoming WATTS lines trying deep fry eight phones and the people attached to them) - all in less than 1,500 square feet! As in any successful small business, key people always make the difference. The individuals pictured and described below have earned their stripes, one scar at a time.

S. P. Fjestad

Seen trying to uncover himself after another near fatal 8½ x 11 in. glossy avalanche, the author is trying to make an attempt to right himself before the next potential paperslide occurs. Once again, this publication was written within the protective confines of "The Ranch" bunker, still sans snowblower (thanks Cal).

Tom Gagnon

He might be the smartest guy in Suite 1391, but that still doesn't mean he gets any respect. Having recently become part owner, Tom does the numbers (photo was taken after seeing the Holiday Inn food/beverage total for the staff at the end of "Power Weak" production), and oversees the ever- increasing bookkeeping tasks.

Patrick Lucking

Patrick, about to pull up a bead on the next unwanted photographer. No newcomer (except for his picture this edition), he has been responsible for the Airguns and Black Powder sections this past decade. Patrick has an avid interest in these two fields, and accompanies the *Blue Book* staff on their annual pilgrimage to the SHOT Show.

Paul Wichtendahl

The Achy-Breaky Bite-Master with his soon-to-be-over-exposed Chernobyl complexion, Paul truly is the Bite-Master, compressing more computer bytes per page in the 14th Edition than any previous *Blue Book*. He took this manuscript from unspecified typefaces to 1,216 corrected pages totaling over 18,000,000 computer bytes in 10 days. "Paul, one last thing, and it will only take ...".

Doreen Pomije

Doreen cuts it up around the office - literally. As Art Director, she is constantly carving up something, if not 4-color seps for the CADA Gun Journal, then maybe designing a guitar body on the computer. Doreen's goal is to get the publisher to tell her about deadlines at least 24 hours before the artwork is due.

Michelle Schroeder

The Wizard of WordStar really got leaned on this year (how many 3 AM mornings were there?). In this photo, Michelle is attempting a long shot at Rocky Squirrel (see photo on page 17). As usual, her Type A manuscript aggressiveness was responsible for your reading these 1,216 pages earlier than any other edition.

Lisa Winkels

Buffalo Bill's favorite blonde is busier than ever. In addition to being Operations Manager, Lisa also supervises distributor accounts, generates a couple of thousand new computer files each month, and rides herd on the office spread, making sure nobody is "milking" a job.

Jeff Perkins

Mr. Bandana (the Tambourine Man?) is currently working on the upcoming 1st Edition of the *Blue Book of Guitar Values*, due to be published in June of this year. The "Sweeties King" also helps in operations and with special order shipping and handling.

John Allen

John is new to the Blue Book Publications staff, and as of yet, has accumulated only light scar tissue. John also is the manager of customer research and number one talkshow host of the always- popular Dear Abby Hour (2-5 PM weekdays, now in its tenth consecutive year at One Appletree Square). All this, and he still got his deer!

Staff Photo

How can you go wrong dealing with a staff like this? Thanks for all your business in the past - we have enjoyed serving you. Hope to see you all again in print next year.

Anne Marie Jones

Anne Marie was recently hired for hazardous pay qualified switch board duty and operational assistance. Her rigid discipline on the job, how- ever, makes her almost too boring to work with. Maybe she'll get excited next year!

FIREARMS PUBLICATIONS

When people ask me how I have learned so much about firearms, much of the credit goes to the extensive library I have accumulated. Recently, I took an inventory of these gun related publications with current replacement values. The total came to over $30,000.00! Once I got over that shock, I wanted to know what I had approximately paid for them originally and how they had performed as an investment. The results are impressive - many of my books are rarer than the guns inside and each time they are reprinted (some are not) the price usually goes up substantially.

If you are a firearms collector or investor, quality reference works in the area(s) you are interested in are a must. Not only will they probably pay for themselves by saving you money (not to mention mistakes), but as stated above, they also perform as solid investment. It's like getting paid to get educated. I always chuckle when I hear someone complain about the "high price" of a particular book when it could have saved him hundreds of dollars on the non-original gun he bought several weeks before. Unless you like to learn by making expensive mistakes, good quality firearms publications will give you the knowledge needed to make intelligent choices when buying or selling.

I would encourage you to look through the following book listing for many of the best reference works available today on many important trademarks. To order, simply call us **TOLL-FREE at 1-800-877-4867**, to use your **VISA/MASTER-CARD or DISCOVER** or use the enclosed order form. Remember, books also make great gifts for any shooter or firearms enthusiast.

If I had to make one book recommendation this year, it would be R.L. Wilson's new Winchester Engraving book. This is the second edition of this publication, and while the retail price is $115.00, it is worth every penny (both as a reference and an investment). I paid $45.00 fifteen years ago for a first edition - today it is very liquid at $300.00+. I'm sure the second edition will perform the same way.

Having these reference works at fingertip accessibility will make you a better firearms buyer/seller, and sooner or later, they will pay for themselves. When people ask me how to start collecting firearms, my reply is to go out and buy a 2'x4' bookcase and do not stop buying firearms related publications until it is full. One last thing, if you are interested in publications not listed on the following pages, please call/FAX/write us with your request(s).

Steven P. Fjestad

A01 **African Rifles & Cartridges** by Taylor (HC) 431 pgs., Illus. 2 lbs. 35.00

A02 **American Gunsmiths** by Sellers (HC) 349 pgs., 3 lbs. 39.95

A03 **American Knives** by Peterson (HC) 178 pgs., 2 lbs. 19.95

A04 **Astra Automatic Pistols** by Antaris (HC) 248 pgs., Illus., B&W & Color photos, 4 lbs.. 40.00

A05 **American Socket Bayonets and Scabbards** by Reilly .... (HC) 269 pgs., Illus. 3 lbs. 40.00

A06 **The American Eagle Pommel Sword** by Mowbray (HC), 244 pgs., Illus., B&W photos, 3 lbs...45.00

A07 **The AK 47 Story** by Ezell (SC) 256 pgs., B&W photos,2 lbs. 16.95

A08 **American Premium Guide to Knives & Razors Identification and Values** by Sargent (SC) 474 pgs., Color & B&W photos, 3 lbs. 22.95

A09 **The American Sword 1775-1945** by Peterson(HC) 345 pgs., Illus. 2 lbs.............. 45.00

A10 **Axis Pistols** by Still (HC) 360 pgs., B&W photos. 3 lbs. 55.00

A11 **Arsenal of Freedom, The Springfield Armory, 1890-1948** by Brophy (SC) 400 pgs., 3 lbs. 29.95

A12 **American West, A Historical Chronology** by Keith Cochran(HC) 464 pgs., B&W photos, 3 lbs. 35.00

A13 **Arms Makers of Lancaster County, PA** by Wood Jr. & Whisker (HC) 142 pgs., Illus. 2 lbs.. 35.00

A14 **The Story of Allen & Wheelock Firearms** by Thomas (SC) 125 pgs., Illus. 2 lbs. 9.00

B02 **Big Bore Rifles & Cartridges** by Wolfe (SC) 360 pgs., Illus., 3 lbs. 26.00

B03 **Book of the Garand** by Hatcher (HC) 292 pgs., Illus., 2 lbs. 26.95

B04 **Bullard Arms** by G. Scott Jamieson (HC) 244 pgs., Illus. 3 lbs. 35.00

B06 **Breech-Loading Carbines, U.S. Civil War Period** by Pitman (HC) 94 pgs., line drawings, 2 lbs. 29.95

B07 **Browning Dates of Manufacture** by Madis (SC) 48 pgs., under 1 lb............. 5.00

B08 **The Browning Guide and Handbook 1924-1985** (now updated through 1987) (SC) under 1 lb. 8.95

B09 **The History of Browning Guns From 1931** by Browning (SC) under 1 lb. 14.95

B10 **The Guide to Browning Serial Numbers** (SC) under 1 lb. 7.95

B11 **The Browning High Power Automatic Pistol** by Stevens (HC), 297 pgs., Illus. 3 lbs. 47.50

B12 **The Breech-Loading Single-Shot Rifle** by Roberts & Waters (HC) 333 pgs., B&W photos, 3 lbs.. 32.95

B13 **The Black Rifle M16 Retrospective** by Stevens & Ezell (HC), 400 pgs., Illus. B&W photos 3 lbs. 59.95

B14 **Boy's Single Shot Rifle** by Grant (HC), 597 pgs., Illus., 3 lbs. 36.00

B15 **Book of the Springfield** by Crossman (HC), 567 pgs., B&W photos, 2 lbs. 36.00

B16 **Big Game Rifles & Cartridges** by Keith (HC), 161 pgs. Illus. 1 lb. 29.95

B17 **Badges of the United States Marshals** by Sherrard & Stumpf (SC), B&W photos 2 lbs. 20.00

B18 **The Big Bore Rifle** by McIntosh (HC), 224 pgs., B&W photos, 2 lbs. 39.50

B19 **Best Guns** by McIntosh (HC) 288 pgs., Color & B&W photos, 2 lbs. 39.50

C01 **Colt, An American Legend** by Wilson (HC) 406 pgs., Illus. Color photos, 5 lbs. 29.98

C02 **Colt Dates of Manufacture** by Wilson (SC) 61 pgs. under 1 lb. 5.00

C04 **Colt Peacemaker Encyclopedia, Vol. I** by Cochran .... (HC) 434 pgs., B&W photos, 4 lbs. 60.00

C05 **Colt Peacemaker British Model** by Cochran (HC) 159 pgs., B&W photos, 2 lbs. 35.00

C06 **Colt Peacemaker Yearly Variation** by Cochran (SC) 96 pgs., B&W photos, 1 lb. 15.00

C07 **Colt Peacemaker Yearly Variaton** by Cochran (HC) 96 pgs., B&W photos, 1 lb. 20.00

C08 **Cartridges of the Gras System** by Ramio & Mention.... (HC) 147 pgs., B&W photos, 3 lbs. 37.95

C09 **Cartridges of the World** by Barnes (SC) 448 pgs., Illus. 3 lbs. 19.95

C10 **Collecting Military Headgear of the First World War** by Calkins (SC) 104 pgs., Illus. 1 lb. 20.00

C11 **Collector's Guide to the '03 Springfield** by Canfield (HC), 160 pgs., Illus. 2 lbs. 35.00

C13 **Civil War Breechloading Rifles** by McAulay (SC) 128 pgs., Illus., 1 lb. 15.00

C14 **Colt's SAA Post War Models** by Garton (HC) 166 pgs., B&W photos, 2 lbs. 29.95

C16 **Colt Peacemaker Collector Pocket Compendium** by Cochran (SC) 48 pgs., under 1 lb. 7.50

C17 **Cowboy Collectibles and Western Memorabilia** by Ball and Vebell (with price guide) (SC), 157 pgs., color photos, 2 lbs. 29.95

C18 **Colt Firearms** by Serven (HC), 393 pgs., Illus. 4 lbs. 45.00

C19 **Colt Peacemaker Encyclopedia, Vol. II** by Cochran (HC), 416 pgs., Illus., B&W photos, 3 lbs. 60.00

C20 **Collector's Guide to the M1 Garand & M1 Carbine** by Canfield (SC) 144 pgs., Illus. 2 lbs. 22.00

C21 **Cowboy Culture: The Last Frontier of American Antiques** by Friedman (with price guide) (HC), 298 pgs., color photos, 6 lbs. 79.95

C22 **Collecting Antique Bird Decoys and Duckcalls, An Identification & Value Guide, 2nd Edition** by Luckey (SC), 232 pgs., color & B&W photos, 2 lbs......... 22.50

C23 **Colt's .38 Automatic Pistols** by Douglas G. Sheldon (SC) 185 pgs., Illus., 1 lb.. 19.95

C24 **Colt .45 Service Pistol Models of 1911 & 1911A1** by Clawson (HC), 429 pgs., B&W photos, 3 lbs............................ 65.00

C25 **Cowboys** by Eggen (SC) 129 pgs., B&W photos, 2 lbs. 19.95

C26 **Civil War Pistols** by McAulay (SC), Illus., B&W photos, 2 lbs. 24.00

C27 **Collector's Guide to United States Combat Shotguns by Canfield** (SC), Illus., 2 lb. 24.00

C28 **'51 Colt Navies** by Swayze (HC), 243 pgs., Illus., photos, 5 lbs. 59.95

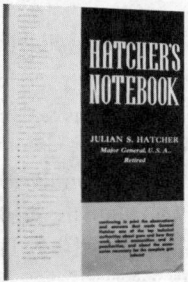

D01 **The Derringer in America** by Wilson & Eberhart (HC), 271 pgs., color & B&W photos, 3 lbs. 48.00

D02 **Death from Above: The German FG42 Paratroop Rifle** by Dugelby & Stevens (HC), 147 pgs., Illus., 2 lbs. 39.95

F01 **Flayderman's Guide (5th Edition)** (SC) 624 pgs., Illus., 3 lbs.................... 27.95

F02 **Firearms & Tackle Memorabilia, A Collector's Guide** by Delph (HC), 141 pgs., color photos, 3 lbs............................. 39.95

F03 **A.H. Fox** by McIntosh (HC), 390 pgs., Illus., color & B&W photos, 3 lbs.......... 49.50

G01 **German Pistols and Holsters 1934/1945, Military-Police- NSDAP, Vol. I** by Whittington III (HC), 224 pgs., Illus. B&W photos of pistols & holsters, 2 lbs............. 30.00

G02 **German Pistols and Holsters, Vol. II** by Whittington III (HC), 312 pgs., Illus. & B&W photos of pistols only, 3 lbs. 55.00

G03 **German Pistols and Holsters, Vol. III** by Whittington III (HC) 312 pgs., Illus. & B&W photos of holsters only, 3 lbs. .. 55.00

G04 **The German Military Pistols 1909-1930 (The Luger Pistol, Its History & Development from 1893-1945)** by Datig (SC) 88 pgs. 1 lb.................................... 14.95

G06 **German Pistols and Holsters, Vol. IV** by Whitting III (HC) 208 pgs., Tells where & to whom pistols & holsters were issued, 2 lbs.. 30.00

G07 **The Gun that Made the Twenties Roar** by Helmer (HC) 294 pgs., Illus., 2 lbs. 24.95

G08 **The Golden Age of Shotgunning** by Hinman (HC), 175 pgs., B&W photos, 2 lbs. 17.95

G09 **German Military Rifles and Machine Pistols (1871-1945)** by Gotz (HC), 245 pgs., Illus. & B&W photos, 4 lbs. 35.00

G10 **Gunsmiths of Virginia** by Whisker (HC), 127 pgs., Illus. 2 lbs. 40.00

G11 **Gunsmiths of Adams, Franklin & Cumberland Counties, PA** by Whisker (HC) 126 pgs., Illus., 2 lbs. 35.00

G12 **Gunsmiths of Bedford, Somerset & Fulton Counties** by Whisker (HC), 152 pgs., Illus., 2 lbs. 35.00

G13 **Gunsmiths of York County, PA** by Whisker (SC), 100 pgs., Illus. 1 lb. 15.00

H01 **High Standard Automatic Pistols (1932-1950)** by Petty (HC), 125 pgs., B&W photos, 1 lb...................................... 19.95

H02 High Standard, A Collector's Guide to the Hamden & Hartford Target Pistols by Dance (SC), 191 pgs., Illus. & B&W photos, 2 lbs................................. 24.00

H03 Hatcher's Notebook by Hatcher (HC), 640 pgs., Illus. B&W photos, 3 lbs...... 29.95

H04 History of Smith & Wesson by Jinks (HC), 290 pgs., Illus., 2 lbs. 27.95

H06 Home Guide to Cartridge Conversion by Nonte.. (HC), 404 pgs., Illus. 2 lbs. 24.95

H07 Hell, I Was There by Keith (HC), 308 pgs., Illus., 3 lbs............................. 24.95

H08 Hiram Berdan, Civil War Chief of Sharpshooters, Military Commander & Firearms Inventor by Marcot (HC), 342 pgs., Illus.& B&W photos, 4 lbs.......... 59.95

I01 The Ithaca Gun Co. by Snyder (HC), 246 pgs., Color & B&W photos, 3 lbs........ 59.95

I02 Imperial Lugers by Still (HC), 219 pgs., color photos, 3 lbs................................. 55.00

I03 Iver Johnson Arms & Cycle Works Handguns 1871-1978 by Goforth (SC), 164 pgs., Illus., 2 lbs. 14.95

J01 James Reid and His Catskill Knuckledusters by Bowen (HC), 288 pgs., Illus., 2 lbs. 24.95

K01 The Krag Rifle by Brophy (HC), 258 pgs., Illus.,3 lbs................................. 35.00

K02 Know Your Colt .45 Auto Pistols Models 1911 & A1 by Hoffschmidt (SC), 65 pgs., photos under 1 lb. 9.95

K03 Know Your M1 Garand Rifles by Hoffschmidt (SC), 80 pgs., photos under 1 lb................................. 9.95

K04 Know Your Broomhandle Mausers by Berger (SC), 95 pgs.,Illus., under 1 lb. . 9.95

K05 Know Your Walther P38 Pistols by Hoffschmidt (SC), 77 pgs., Illus. under 1 lb................................. 9.95

K06 Know Your Walther PP & PPK Pistols by Hoffschmidt (SC), 87 pgs., Illus., under 1 lb. 9.95

K07 Know Your Czechoslovakian Pistols by Berger (SC), 96 pgs., Illus. under 1 lb. . 9.95

K08 Keith's Rifles for Large Game by Keith (HC), 406 pgs., Illus., 2 lbs.................. 39.95

K09 Kentucky Rifle Patchboxes, All New Vol. 2 by Chandler & Whisker (HC), 430 pgs., Illus., 3 lbs. 40.00

L01 L.C. Smith Shotguns by Brophy (HC), 244 pgs., Illus., 3 lbs. 35.00

L02 Lugers at Random by Kenyon (Revised format edition, 1990) (HC), 416 pgs., Illus. B&W photos, 4 lbs............................. 39.95

L03 **Luger, The Multi-National Pistol** by Kenyon 6(HC), 185 pgs., Illus. color photos, 3 lbs. 9.95

L04 **Lee Enfield Number 4 Rifles** by Petrillo (SC) 64 pgs., Ullus. B&W photos, 1 lb............. 10.95

L05 **Lee Enfield Number 1 Rifles** by Petrillo (SC), 64 pgs., Illus. B&W photos, under 1 lb. 10.95

L06 **1990 Luger, U.S. Test Trials by Reese II** (SC), Illus., under 1 lb. 4.95

L07 **Luger Tips** by Reese II (SC) 120 pgs., Illus. under 1 lb............................... 10.95

M01 **Marlin Firearms** by Brophy (HC) 696 pgs., Illus. & B&W photos, 6 lbs. 59.95

M02 **More Single Shot Rifles** by Grant (HC) 322 pgs., Illus. 2 lbs............................ 29.95

M03 **Mauser Rifles and Pistols** by Smith (HC) 334 pgs., Illus. 2 lbs. 30.00

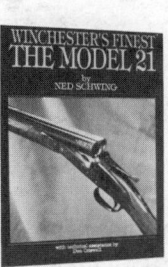

M04 **Mauser Bolt Rifles** by Olson (Third Edition, Updated 9th Printing) (HC) 360 pgs., B&W Illus. 5 lbs. 47.25

M06 **The 336 (Marlin)** by Murray (SC) 90 pgs., Illus. 1 lb. 17.00

M07 **The Mountain Men** by Lacock(HC) 308 pgs., color & B&W photos, 3 lbs. 29.95

M08 **The History & Development of the M16 Rifle & Cartridge** by Hughes (HC) 294 pgs., Illus., B&W photos, 3 lbs..... 49.95

M09 **Merwin Hulbert Book** by Phelps (HC) 218 pgs., Illus., 3 lbs............................. 56.00

M10 **Militaria, A Study of German Helmets & Uniforms (1729-1918)** by Kube (HC) 235 pgs., color & B&W photos, 3 lbs. 29.95

M11 **The Military Remington Rolling Block Rifle** by Layman (SC) 107 pgs., Illus., 1 lb. 21.00

M12 **The Muzzle-Loading Cap Lock Rifle** by Roberts ..... (HC) 432 pgs., Illus., 2 lbs. 30.00

M13 **Modern Shotguns and Loads** by Askins (HC) 416 pgs., Illus., 2 lbs.................... 30.00

M14 **M1 Carbine: Design, Development & Production** by Ruth (SC) 291 pgs., Illus., 2 lbs....................................... 19.95

N01 **The Navy Luger** by Gortz & Walter (HC) 128 pgs., Illus. B&W photos, 2 lbs. 24.95

N02 **The Ninety-Nine, Revised Third Edition, A History of the Savage** by Murray (SC) Illus., 1 lb......................... 23.00

N03 **North American Indian Ornamental & Ceremonial Artifacts** by Hothem (SC) 133 pgs., B&W photos, 2 lbs................. 19.95

N04 **L. D. Nimschke Firearms Engraver** by Wilson (reprint) (HC) 109 pgs., B&W drawings, 3 lbs. 100.00

N06 **9mm Parabellum, A History of the World's 9mm Pistols & Ammunition** by Konig and Hugo (HC) 301 pgs., Illus. B&W photos, 4 lbs.............................. 39.95

O01 **Outdoor Pastimes of an American Hunter** by Roosevelt (SC) 369 pgs., 2 lbs. 16.95

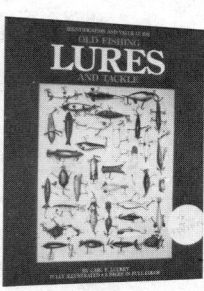

O02 The Old Man and the Boy & the Old Man's Boy Grows Older by Ruark (SC) 630 pgs., 3 lbs. 17.95

O03 Old Fishing Lures & Tackle Identification and Values (No. 3) by Luckey (SC) 466 pgs., Illus. color photos, 3 lbs....... 22.95

O04 Ohio Long Rifles, Vol. II by Whisker 124 pgs., Illus., 3 lbs. 35.00

P01 The Parker Gun by Baer (HC) 196 pgs., Illus., B&W photos, 3 lbs......................... 35.00

P02 Pet Loads (set of Vol. 1 & 2) by Waters (SC) 5 lbs. 29.50

P03 The Powder Flask Book by Riling (reprint) (HC) 495 pgs., Illus., B&W photos, 5 lbs. 69.95

P04 Pawnee Bill's Historic Wild West, A Photo Documentary of the 1901-1905 Show Tours (SC) 126 pgs., B&W photos, 2 lbs.. 19.95

P05 The Peacemakers, Arms and Adventure in the American West by R.L. Wilson (HC) 391 pgs., Illus., color photos & B&W photos, 5 lbs. 65.00

R02 Ruger, NRA Publication edited by Roberts, Jr. (SC) 109 pgs., 1 lb. 14.95

R03 Remington Rolling Block Firearms by Schreier, Jr. (SC) 61 pgs., Illus., 1 lb. 6.95

R04 Remington Tips by Larson (SC) 99 pgs., Illus., 1 lb. 4.95

R05 Encyclopedia of Ruger Rimfire Semi-Automatic Pistols by Hiddleson (HC) 288 pgs., Illus., B&W photos, 3 lbs. 29.95

S01 Single Shot Rifles by Grant (HC) 395 pgs., Illus., 4 lbs. 29.95

S02 Sharps Firearms by Sellers 358 pgs., Illus., 4 lbs......................................45.00

S03 The Springfield 1903 Rifles by Brophy (HC) 616 pgs., Illus. B&W photos, 5 lbs... 49.95

S05 The Shooting Field - 150 Years with Holland & Holland by King (HC) 184 pgs., Illus. color & B&W photos, 3 lbs. 49.95

S07 The Standard Directory of Proofmarks by Wirnsberger (SC) 192 pgs., Illus. 1 lb. 14.95

S08 The SPIW, The Deadliest Weapon that Ever Was by Stevens & Ezell (HC) 138 pgs., Illus., 2 lbs. 29.95

S09 Six Guns, The Standard Reference Work by Keith (1992) (HC) 335 pgs., Illus., 3 lbs.. 35.00

S10 Sixgun Cartridges & Loads by Keith (reprint) (HC) 151 pgs., 1 lb..................... 24.95

S11 Single Shot Rifle Finale by Grant (HC) 133 pgs., Illus., 2 lbs............................. 36.00

S12 Sporting Collectibles by Karsnitz (SC) 160 pgs., color photos, 2 lbs. 29.95

S13 Soviet Russian Postwar Military Pistols & Cartridges 1945- 1986 (Vol. 16) by Datig (HC) 152 pgs., Illus., B&W photos, 3 lbs...34.95

S14 Soviet Russian Tokarev "TT" Pistols & Cartridges 1929-1953 (Vol. 13) by Datig (HC) 168 pgs., Illus., B&W photos, 3 lbs. 34.95

S15 Swiss Variations 1897-1947 (The Luger Pistol, Its History and Development from 1893-1947) by Datig (SC) 88 pgs., Illus., B&W photos, 3 lbs. 14.95

T01 Trapdoor Springfield by Waite & Ernst (HC) 213 pgs., Illus. B&W photos, 3 lbs. 39.95

T02 Third Reich Lugers by Still (HC) 291 pgs., Illus., B&W photos, 4 lbs. 55.00

T03 Twenty-two Caliber Varmint Rifles by Landis (HC) 531 pgs., Illus., 2 lbs. 32.00

U01 U.S. Military Arms Dates of Manufacture by Madis (SC) 62 pgs., under 1 lb. 5.00

U02 U.S. Military Small Arms (1816-1865) by Reilly (HC) 275 pgs., Illus., 3 lbs...........39.95

U03 U.S. Martial Flintlocks by Reilly (HC) 263 pgs., Illus., 4 lbs. 39.50

U04 U.S. Rifle M14 - from John Garand to the M21 (Vol. One) by Stevens (HC) 340 pgs., Illus., 3 lbs....................... 47.50

U05 U.S. Military Holsters & Pistol Cartridge Boxes by Meadows (HC) 432 pgs., Illus., B&W photos, 5 lbs. 45.00

W01 Winchester Book by Madis (HC) 654 pgs., Illus. B&W photos, 5 lbs. 45.00

W02 Winchester Dates of Manufacture by Madis (SC) 59 pgs.,under 1 lb. 5.00

W03 Winchester Model Twelve by Madis (HC) 174 pgs., Illus.B&W photos, 2 lbs.. 19.95

W04 Winchester Handbook by Madis (HC) 267 pgs., B&W photos,2 lbs................. 19.95

W05 Winchester Era by Madis (HC) 180 pgs., Illus. 1 lb.......................................14.95

W06 Winchester Engraving by Wilson color photos, (HC) 512 pgs.,6 lbs. 115.00

W08 Winchester Model 94 by Renneberg (HC) 208 pgs., Illus. B&W photos, 3 lbs.. 34.95

W09 History of Winchester Firearms 1866-1980 by Barnes (HC) 237 pgs., Illus., 2 lbs.. 19.95

W10 Winchester Model 42 by Schwing (HC) 160 pgs., Illus.,B&W photos, 3 lbs....... 34.95

W11 Winchester Model 21 by Schwing (HC) 360 pgs., Illus., color & B&W photos, 4 lbs.. 49.95

W13 Winchester, An American Legend by Wilson (HC) 404 pgs., color photos, 5 lbs.. 65.00

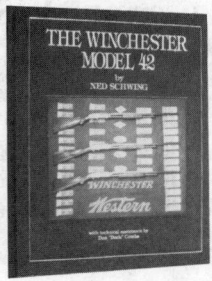

W14 Collector's Guide to Winchester in the Serice by Canfield (HC) 184 pgs., Illus., B&W photos, 2 lbs. 38.00

W15 The Eighty-Eight (Collector's Reference on the Winchester Model 88 Lever Action) by Murray (SC) 90 pgs., 1 lb. 20.00

W16 Sequence of Takedown and Assembly for Winchester Model 42 (SC) 102 pgs., drawings, 1 lb. 14.95

W17 Sequence of Takedown and Assembly for Winchester Model 70 (SC) 58 pgs., drawings, 1 lb. 14.95

W18 Sequence of Takedown and Assembly for Winchester Model 61 (SC) 94 pgs., drawings, 1 lb. 14.95

W19 Sequence of Takedown and Assembly for Winchester Model 63 (SC) 88 pgs., drawings, 1 lb. 14.95

W20 Sequence of Takedown and Assembly for Winchester Model 12 (SC) 116 pgs., drawings, 1 lb. 14.95

W23 Sequence of Takedown and Assembly for Winchester Model 94 (SC) 63 pgs., drawings, 1 lb. 14.95

W24 War Baby! The U.S. Caliber .30 Carbine by Larry L. Ruth (HC) 495 pgs., Illus., 4 lbs.. 69.95

W25 Weatherby, The Man, The Gun, The Legend by Gresham & Gresham (HC) 290 pgs., Illus., 3 lbs. 24.95

W26 Winchester Slide-Action Rifles, Vol. I: Model 1890 & 1906 by Schwing (HC) 400 pgs., Illus. B&W photos, 4 lbs. 39.95

W27 Webley & Scott Automatic Pistols by Bruce (HC) 304 pgs., B&W photos, 3 lbs. 58.00

W28 War Baby, Comes Home, The U.S. Caliber .30 Carbine, Vol. II by Larry Ruth (HC) 366 pgs., Illus. 3 lbs..................... 49.95

W29 To the Dreams of Youth: The .22 Caliber Single Shot Winchester Rifle by Houze (HC) 208 pgs., Illus. B&W photos, 3 lbs... 34.95

W30 Winchester Slide-Action Rifles, Vol. II, Model 61 & 62 by Schwing (HC) 208 pgs., Illus. B&W photos, 3 lbs. 34.95

Mail your payment
or
for faster results
Call TOLL FREE 1-800-877-4867
International 1-612-854-5229
and use your VISA, MASTERCARD or DISCOVER

SHIPPING COSTS: (Use this chart when you order)

From	To	Ship Cost	From	To	Ship Cost
.25 lb	1 lb	$ 4.00	6 lbs	8 lbs	$ 8.00
1 lb	2 lbs	$ 5.00	9 lbs	11 lbs	$ 9.00
3 lbs	5 lbs	$ 7.50	12 lbs	15 lbs	$10.50

Add $0.50 for each additional pound over 15 lbs. Out of the continental USA add an additional $3.00

BLUE BOOK PUBLICATIONS ORDER FORM
One Appletree Square
Minneapolis, MN 55425

- To Order Domestically -

Call: **TOLL FREE 1-800-GUNS** (4867) or FAX (612) 853-1486 to use your **VISA, MASTERCARD or DISCOVER** charge cards. (**MN residents** call (612) 854-5229) or send in this order card with payment.

Company Name _____

Name _____

Address _____

Phone _____

City _____ **State** _____ **Zip** _____

VISA/MASTERCARD/DISCOVER# _____

Expiration Date of Card _____

Signature _____

Catalog #	Qty	Title	Author	Weight	Price
		Total from above			
		Shipping & Handling			
		MN Res. add 6½% Sales Tax			
		TOTAL AMOUNT DUE			

To calculate your cost for shipping and handling, total the weight of the books you are ordering and compare that total to the chart on the facing page.

Grading Criteria for Firearms

The old, NRA method of firearms grading — by relying upon adjectives such as "Excellent" or "Fair" — served the firearms fraternity for a long time. Today's collectors, however, are turning away from such a subjective system. One man's "Fair" is another man's "Good!"

The leading professionals in the grading of firearms now utilize what is essentially an objective method for deciding the price range of a gun: THE PERCENTAGE OF ORIGINAL FACTORY BLUING REMAINING ON THE GUN. After looking critically at a few firearms, and carefully studying the Photo Percentage Grading System (starts after page 32), even the novice can soon tell whether a piece has 100%, 98%, 95%, or less bluing remaining.

Of course, factors such as "depth" and quality of the bluing, engraving and embellishment, historical significance, and even the condition of the stock can and do affect the price. But the basic "condition" — and therefore the price — is best determined by the percentage of original bluing remaining. The key word here is "original," for if anyone other than the factory has reblued the gun, its value as a collector's item is greatly diminished, with the exception of rare and historical pieces that have been properly restored.

Study the photographs on these pages. Note how the bluing in certain areas of the firearm wears off first. These are usually places where the gun rubs against the holster, hand or body. We have chosen a Luger and a Winchester as examples, but the principles apply to almost any firearm.

It should be noted that the older a collectible firearm is, the smaller the percentage of original bluing one can expect to find. Some very old and/or very rare firearms are acceptable to collectors in almost any condition! The average collector, however, will probably never have the opportunity to purchase such a specimen.

For your convenience, NRA Condition Standards are shown below. Converting from this grading system to percentages can now be done accurately.

CONVERTING TO NRA MODERN STANDARDS

**When converting from NRA Modern Standards,
the following rules generally apply:**

Perfect — 100% with or without box. Not mint - new. 100% on currently manufactured firearms assumes NIB condition.

Excellent — 95%+ - 99% (typically).

Very Good — 80 - 95% - all original.

Good — 60 - 80% - all original.

Fair — 20 - 60% - May not be original (shootable, not very collectible).

Poor — Under 20%.

NRA Condition Standards

MODERN CONDITIONS —

New — not previously sold at retail, in same condition as current factory production.

Perfect — in new condition in every respect

Excellent — new condition, used but little, no noticeable marring of wood or metal, bluing perfect (except at muzzle or sharp edges).

Very Good — in perfect working condition, no appreciable wear on working surfaces, no corrosion or pitting, only minor surface dents or scratches.

Good — in safe working condition, minor wear on working surfaces, no broken parts, no corrosion or pitting that will interfere with proper functioning.

Fair — in safe working condition, but well worn, perhaps requiring replacement of minor parts or adjustments which should be indicated in advertisement, no rust, but may have corrosion pits which do not render article unsafe or inoperable.

ANTIQUE CONDITIONS —

Factory New — all original parts; 100% original finish; in perfect condition in every respect, inside and out.

Excellent — all original parts; over 80% original finish; sharp lettering, numerals and design on metal and wood; unmarred wood; fine bore.

Fine — all original parts; over 30% original finish; sharp lettering, numerals and design on metal and wood; minor marks in wood; good bore.

Very Good — all original parts; none to 30% original finish; original metal surfaces smooth with all edges sharp; clear lettering, numerals and design on metal; wood slightly scratched or bruised; bore disregarded for collectors firearms.

Good — some minor replacement parts; metal smoothly rusted or lightly pitted in places, cleaned or reblued; principal lettering, numerals and design on metal legible; wood refinished, scratched, bruised or minor cracks repaired; in good working order.

Fair — some major parts replaced; minor replacement parts may be required; metal rusted, may be lightly pitted all over, vigorously cleaned or reblued; rounded edges of metal and wood; principal lettering, numerals and design on metal partly obliterated; wood scratched, bruised, cracked or repaired where broken; in fair working order or can be easily repaired and placed in working order.

Poor — major and minor parts replaced; major replacement parts required and extensive restoration needed; metal deeply pitted; principal lettering, numerals and design obliterated, wood badly scratched, bruised, cracked or broken; mechanically inoperative, generally undesirable as a collectors firearm.

These NRA conditions have been used by the author as the guidelines for the value ranges in this work. In order to use this book correctly, the reader is urged to constantly consult these condition standards when assessing a gun before applying a value to it. They stand as the crux of the valuation matter.

References

Antaris, Leonardo, Dr., *Astra Automatic Pistols*. Sterling, Co: FIRAC Publishing Co., 1988.

Bady, Donald B., *Colt Automatic Pistols*. Los Angeles, Ca: Borden Publishing Co., 1973.

Baer, Larry L., *The Parker Book* North Hollywood, Ca: Beinfeld Publishing Co., 1974.

Belford, James N. and Dunlap, Jack, *Mauser Self Loading Pistol*. Alhambia, Ca: Borden Publishing Co., 1969.

Bender, Roy G. III, *Mauser*. Houston, Tx: Collector's Press, 1971.

Breathed and Schroeder, *System Mauser*. Chicago, Il: Handgun Press, 1967.

Brophy, William S., *L.C. Smith Shotguns*. North Hollywood, Ca: Beinfeld Publishing Co., 1977.

Butzer, David F., *The American Shotgun*. Middlefield, Ct: Lyman Publications, 1973.

Buxton, Warren H., *The P-38 Pistol: Volume I*. Los Alamos, Nm: U.C. Ross Books, 1978.

Costanza, Sam, *World of Lugers: Volume I*. Mayfield Heights, Oh: World of Lugers, 1977.

Hill and Anthony, *Confederate Long Arms and Pistols*. Charlotte, Nc: Confederate Arms, 1978.

Jinks, Roy G., *History of Smith & Wesson*. North Hollywood, Ca: Beinfeld Publishing Co., 1977.

Karr and Karr, Jr., *Remington Handgun*. Stackpole Co., Second Edition, 1951.

Kenyon, Charles Jr., *Lugers at Random*. Chicago, Il: Handgun Press, 1969.

Kopel, Graham, and Moore, *A Study of the Colt Single Action Army Revolver*. La Puente,CA: Kopel, Graham, and Moore Publishers, 1978.

Krasne, Jerry A. *Enyclopedia and Reference Catalog for Auto Loading Guns*. San Diego, CA: Triple K Manufacturing, 1989.

Leithe, Frederick, *Japanese Handguns*. California: Borden Publishing Co., 1968.

Madis, George, *The Model 12*. Lancaster, TX: Published by Author, 1981.

Madis, George, *The Winchester Book*. Lancaster, TX: Privately Published by Author, 1975.

Maxwell, Samuel L., Sr., *Lever Action Magazine Rifles*. Published by Author, 1978.

Murray, Douglas, *The Ninety-Nine*. Published by Author, 1985.

Nonte, Jr., George C. *Firearms Encyclopedia*. Outdoor Life: New York, NY, 1973.

Olson, Ludwig, *Mauser Bolt Action Rifles*. Montezuma, IA: F. Brownell & Son Publishers, Inc., 1976.

Rankin, James L., *Walther*, Vol.'s I, II, III. Coral Gables, FL: Published by Author, 1976.

Sellers, Frank, *Sharp's Firearms*. North Hollywood, Ca: Beinfeld Publishing Co., 1978.

Serven, editor, *The Collecting of Guns*. Bonanza Books, 1964.

Sharpe, Phillip B., *The Rifle in America*. Funk and Wagnalls, 1947.

Shooter's Bible. S. Hackensack, NJ: Published annually by Stoeger Industries.

Steindler, *Steindler's New Firearms Dictionary*. Phoenix, AZ: Stackpole Books, 1985.

Tanner, Hans, *Guns of the World*. Bonanza Books, 1972, 1977.

West, Bill, *Browning Arms & History*. Santa Fe Springs, Ca: Stockton Trade Press, Inc., 1972.

West, Bill, *Marlin and Ballard Firearms & History*. Norwalk, Ca: Stockton Trade Press, Inc., 1977.

West, Bill, *Remington Arms & History*. Whittier, Ca: Stockton Trade Press, Inc., 1970.

West, Bill, *Savage and Stevens Arms & History*. Whittier, Ca: Stockton Trade Press, Inc., 1971.

Whitaker, Dean H., *Model 70 Winchester 1937-1964*. Dallas, Tx: Taylor Publishing Co., 1978.

Wilkerson, Don, *Post War Colt Single Action Army*. Published by Author, 1978.

Wilkerson, Don, *Post-War Colt Single-Action Revolver, 1976-1986*. Dallas, TX: Taylor Publishing, 1986.

Wilson, R.L., *Colt Commemorative Firearms*. Geneseo, Il: Robert E.P. Cherry Publishing Co., 1973.

Wilson, R.L., *The Colt Heritage*. New York, NY: Simon and Schuster.

PERIODICALS LISTINGS

American Firearms Industry 2455 E. Sunrise Blvd., Ft. Lauderdale, FL 33304. Phone No.: 305-561-3505. Membership is $25 per year. Trade publications and related material.

American Rifleman Published by the NRA, 1600 Rhode Island Ave. NW, Washington, DC 20036. Phone No.: 800-368-5714 or 202-828-6279. Subscription included in price of NRA Membership ($25). Published monthly

CADA Gun Journal Published monthly by Blue Book Publications, 1 Appletree Square, Minneapolis, MN 55425. Phone 1-800-368-2232. Subscription is $29.95 per year (12 issues). Trade Publication for buying & selling.

Field & Stream Magazine 2 Park Ave., New York, NY 10016. Phone No.: 800- 289-0639 or 212-779-5000. Subscription rate $15.94 annually. Published monthly (12 issues).

Gun Report P.O. Box 38, Aledo, IL 61231 Phone No.: 309-582- 5311. $29.95 per year (USA), published monthly.

Guns and Ammo 8490 Sunset Blvd., Los Angeles, CA 90069. Phone No. 310-854-2222. $21.94 per year (USA), published monthly.

Gun Week P.O.Box 488, Station C, Buffalo, NY 14209. Annual Subscription - $32. Published weekly. Phone No.: 716- 885- 6408

Man at Arms P.O. Box 460, Lincoln, RI 02865. Published bi- monthly ($24 yearly). Phone No. 401-726-8011

National Alliance of Stocking Gun Dealers P.O. Box 187, Havelock, NC 28532. Phone No.: 919-447-1313. Members, dealers, and gun dealers $25, others $200. Published monthly.

North American Hunter 12301 Whitewater Dr., Minnetonka, MN 55343. Phone No.: 612-936-9333. Published monthly (included in membership).

Outdoor Life Magazine Two Park Ave., New York, NY 10016. Phone No.: 800- 365-1580 or 212-779-5000. $15.94 per year (USA).

Publishers Development Corportation 591 Camino De La Reina #200, San Diego, CA 92108. Publisher of: Shooting Industry, American Handgunner and Guns magazines. Phone No.: 800-537-3006, call for subscription rates

Shotgun News P.O. Box 669, Hastings, NE 68902. Subscription - $20 yearly (36 issues). 402-463-4589

Safari Club International 4800 W. Gates Pass Rd., Tucson, AZ 85745. Phone No.: 602-620-1220. Publications: Safari magazine, Safari Africa, Deer of the World, Sheep of the World, International Record Book of Trophy Animals, Record Book Field Edition.

Shooting Sportsman Magazine P.O. Box 149 Oldwick, NJ 08858. Phone No.: 908-439- 2445. $29.95 per year (USA).

Sporting Clays Magazine 5211 S. Washington Ave., Titusville, FL 32780. Phone No.: 800-677-5212 or 803-681-2219. $26 per year (USA). Published bi-monthly

The Sporting Goods Dealer 1212 N. Lindbergh Blvd., St. Louis, MO 63132. Phone No.: 314-997-7111

Sporting Goods Business 1515 Broadway, New York, NY 10036. Phone No.: 212- 869-1300. (60 issues) $82.80.

Sports Afield Magazine 250 W. 55th St., New York, NY 10019. Phone No.: 212-649-4300. (12 issues) $13.97.

Women & Guns Published by Second Amendment Foundation, P.O. Box 488, Station C, Buffalo, NY 14209. $24.95 annual subscription. Published weekly.

86

A section

A.A.

Previously manufactured by Azanza & Arrizablaga located in Eibar, Spain.

Grading	100%	98%	95%	90%	80%	70%	60%

A.A. — semi-auto pistol, 7.65mm, slide marked Azanza & Arrizablaga Model 1916, A.A. in oval on frame.

	100%	98%	95%	90%	80%	70%	60%
	$130	$105	$85	$65	$55	$50	$45

REIMS — semi-auto pistol, 6.35mm or 7.65mm, copies of M1906 Browning, marked 1914 Model.

	100%	98%	95%	90%	80%	70%	60%
	$120	$100	$75	$65	$55	$50	$45

A.A.A.

Previously manufactured by Aldazabal located in Spain.

M1919 — semi-auto pistol, 7.65mm.

	100%	98%	95%	90%	80%	70%	60%
	$110	$100	$85	$70	$65	$60	$55

A & R SALES

Previous manufacturer located in South El Monte, CA.

HANDGUN — .45 ACP cal., semi-auto patterned after Colt Model 1911 Gov.'t, less weight than normal Colt .45.

	100%	98%	95%	90%	80%	70%	60%
	$225	$205	$175	$155	$145	$135	$125

RIFLE: MARK IV SPORTER — semi-auto, .308 Winchester, M-14 action-clip fed, adj. sights.

	100%	98%	95%	90%	80%	70%	60%
	$295	$260	$225	$200	$175	$155	$140

A F C

Previously manufactured by Auguste Francotte located in Liege, Belgium, 1912-1914.

SEMI-AUTO PISTOL — 6.35mm, 6 shot mag., frame marked "Francotte Liege".

	100%	98%	95%	90%	80%	70%	60%
	$275	$250	$220	$165	$140	$110	$85

A. J. ORDNANCE

THOMAS — .45 double action, .45 ACP, 6 shot, 3½ in. barrel, fixed sights, checkered plastic grips, delayed blowback action, each shot double action, stainless steel barrel. Disc.

	100%	98%	95%	90%	80%	70%	60%
	$470	$415	$385	$360	$330	$275	$220
Chrome	$525	$470	$440	$415	$385	$330	$275

A K S (AK-47s)

Semi-auto paramilitary design rifle originally designed in Russia (1947). Currently manufactured by several arsenals in China including Norinco and Poly Technologies, Inc. Also manufactured in other countries including Yugoslavia, Czechoslovakia, and Hungary.

Grading	100%	98%	95%	90%	80%	70%	60%

Originally, U.S. importation was discontinued for commercial sales in 1989 due to federal legislation (in original configuration with either fixed or folding stocks). "Sporterized" stock configurations have recently been responsible for this rifle to meet import regulations, once again making it eligible for importation.

Since the Federal ban on this type of paramilitary designed rifle, demand initially surged (summer and fall of 1989) and currently the supply/demand factors are conducive to more predictable prices. AK-47s are not rare - over 700 million have been manufactured in China alone since WW II.

AK-47 MODELS

Also refer to separate listings under Poly Technologies, Inc., Norinco, Federal Ordnance, American Arms, Inc., and others who imported this configuration until March, 1989. Values below are for generic imports with average quality in mfg.

AK-47 STANDARD MILITARY RIFLE — 7.62mm x 39mm (standard Russian military cal.) or .223 cal., semi-auto Kalashnikov action, 16½ in. barrel, 5 or 30 shot mag., wood stock and forearm except on folding stock model, recent importation has newer "sporterized" (most with thumb holes) fixed stocks only, may be supplied with bayonet, sling, cleaning kit, standard military production rifle of China and Russia.

$550	$495	$450	$395	$350	$300	$265

Folding stock models are now commanding a 10-15% premium.
Yugoslavian, Czechoslovakian, or Hungarian manufactured AK-47s will command a $100-$200 premium over Norinco mfg. rifles. Poly Technologies mfg. (see separate heading) also command a premium. Presently, the .223 cal. is more desirable than 7.62 x 39mm. Values may change significantly due to regional demand for this rifle configuration (i.e. values will be less in Montana than in California).

A M A C

See Iver Johnson section in this text. AMAC stands for American Military Arms Corporation manufactured in Jacksonville, AR.

A M T

Manufactured by Arcadia Machine & Tool located in Irwindale, CA. Also see Auto-Mag for discontinued models. Distributor and dealer sales.

PISTOLS: SEMI-AUTO

LIGHTNING — .22 LR, semi-auto, stainless steel only, 5 (bull only), 6½, 8½, 10½, or 12½ (disc. 1987) in. bull or tapered barrels, adj. sights and trigger, pistol based on semi-auto Ruger action, tapered barrels. Mfg. 1984-87.

$240	$200	$150

Last Mfg.'s Sug. Retail was $289.
This model features a frame grooved for scope mounts, Clarke trigger, Millett sights, and either Pachmayr rubber or Wayland wood grips as standard equipment.

Bull's Eye Regulation Target — similar to 6½ in. Lightning with bull barrel, except has vent. rib, wooden grips, extended rear sight. Mfg. 1986 only.

$350	$285	$220

Last Mfg.'s Sug. Retail was $436.

BABY AUTOMAG — .22 LR, semi-auto, stainless steel only, 8½ in. vent. rib barrel, Millett adj. sights, smooth walnut grips, 1,000 mfg.

$450	$400	$350

AUTOMAG II — .22 Mag., stainless steel only, 3⅜ (Compact Model), 4½, or 6 in. barrel, gas assisted action, Millett adj. sights with white outline, grooved Lexan grips, 7 (Compact) or 9 shot mag., 24-32 oz. New 1987.

Mfg.'s Sug. Retail	$376		$295	$230	$195

Grading	100%	98%	95%	90%	80%	70%	60%

AUTOMAG III — .30 Carbine or 9mm Win. Mag. (new 1993) cal., stainless steel, $6^3/_8$ in. barrel, patterned after Colt Gov't Model, white outline Millett adj. sights, grooved Lexan grips, 8 shot mag., 43 oz. New 1992.

Mfg.'s Sug. Retail	$466		$395	$300	$245		

AUTOMAG IV — 10mm or .45 Win. mag. cal., $6^1/_2$ (.45 Win. Mag. only) or $8^5/_8$ in. barrel, 7 shot mag., Millett adj. sights, stainless steel, 46 oz. New 1992.

Mfg.'s Sug. Retail	$680		$560	$460	$360		

JAVELINA — 10mm cal., semi-auto, 7 in. barrel, 8 shot mag., Millett adj. sights, wrap-around Neoprene grips, wide adj. trigger, long grip safety, 48 oz. Mfg. 1992 only.

			$560	$460	$360		

Last Mfg.'s Sug. Retail was $676.

BACKUP PISTOL — .22 LR (disc. 1987) or .380 ACP cal., semi-auto, choice of traditional double action (disc. 1992) or double action only (new 1992), $2^1/_2$ in. barrel, stainless steel, Lexan grips, formerly TDE, 5 shot mag. in .380, 8 shot mag. in .22 LR, 18 oz. Older disc. walnut grip models are worth a slight premium.

Mfg.'s Sug. Retail	$296		$220	$170	$135		

In 1992, AMT re-engineered this model and removed all external levers.

BACKUP PISTOL II — .380 ACP cal., single action semi-auto, stainless steel, $2^1/_2$ in. barrel, 5 shot finger extension mag., black carbon fiber grips, 18 oz. New 1993.

Mfg.'s Sug. Retail	$296		$220	$170	$135		

.45 ACP STANDARD GOVERNMENT MODEL — .45 ACP, similar to Colt semi-auto Gov't model, stainless steel, 5 in. barrel, fixed rear sight, loaded chamber indicator, adj. trigger, wrap-around neoprene grips.

Mfg.'s Sug. Retail	$476		$385	$295	$250		

HARDBALLER — .45 ACP, similar to Colt Gold Cup Model, stainless steel, 5 in. barrel, adj. Millett rear sight, serrated rib, loaded chamber indicator, adj. trigger, wrap-around neoprene grips.

Mfg.'s Sug. Retail	$530		$420	$325	$275		

Add $280 for 5 in. Hardballer conversion kit.

⚞ **Hardballer Long Slide** — similar to Hardballer, except 7 in. barrel and longer slide assembly.

Mfg.'s Sug. Retail	$575		$445	$340	$295		

Add $300 for 7 in. Long Slide conversion kit.

SKIPPER — similar to Hardballer, except approx. 1 in. shorter slide on pre-'84 mfg, re-released in 1991 with choice of .40 S&W or .45 ACP cal., $4^1/_4$ in. barrel, checkered walnut grips, matte finish stainless steel, Millett adj. rear sight, 7 shot mag., 33 oz. Disc. 1991.

			$350	$285	$250		

Last Mfg.'s Sug. Retail was $450.

COMBAT SKIPPER — similar to Skipper, only with fixed sights. Disc. 1984.

			$375	$330	$295		

BULL'S EYE TARGET MODEL — .40 S&W, similar to Hardballer with 5 in. barrel, 8 shot mag., adj. Millett sights, wrap around Neoprene grips, 38 oz. Mfg. 1991 only.

			$400	$340	$295		

Last Mfg.'s Sug. Retail was $500.

Grading	100%	98%	95%	90%	80%	70%	60%

"ON DUTY" DOUBLE ACTION — 9mm Para., .40 S&W, or .45 ACP (new 1992) cal., stainless steel slide and barrel, 4½ in. barrel, 15 (9mm Para.), 11 (.40 S&W), or 9 (.45 ACP) shot mag., 3-dot sighting system, anodized aluminum frame, trigger disconnect safety with inertia firing pin, carbon fiber grips, 32 oz. New 1991.

Mfg.'s Sug. Retail	$470	$385	$295	$250

Add $60 for .45 ACP cal.

In 1992, this model became available with either traditional double action with decocking lever or double action only with safety.

RIFLES

LIGHTNING (25/22) — .22 LR, semi-auto based on Ruger 10-22 action, stainless steel, 30 shot mag., 17½ in. bull or tapered barrel, nylon pistol grip handle and forearm, folding stock with recoil pad or youth stock, fixed sights, 6 lbs. New 1986.

Mfg.'s Sug. Retail	$296	$220	$175	$150

SMALL GAME HUNTER (SGH) — .22 LR, same mechanical action as Lightning, except has matte black nylon stock with checkered forearm and grip, 22 in. barrel, 10 shot mag., no sights, removable recoil pad allows storage in stock, 6 lbs. New 1986.

Mfg.'s Sug. Retail	$300	$230	$190	$160

SMALL GAME HUNTER II — similar to Small Game Hunter, except has match grade 22 in. heavyweight full-floating barrel, 10 shot rotary mag., black fiberglass nylon stock, no sights, 6 lbs. New 1993.

Mfg.'s Sug. Retail	$300	$230	$190	$160

Add $70 for 17½ in. stainless steel barrel.
Add $150 for 22½ in. stainless steel match grade barrel.

HUNTING RIFLE — .22 Mag., semi-auto, 22 in. barrel, stainless steel construction, black synthetic stock with Monte Carlo cheekpiece, 10 shot rotary mag., grooved for scope, removable recoil pad provides storage for ammo., cleaning rod, and survival knife, 6 lbs. Mfg. 1992 only.

	$275	$225	$185

Last Mfg.'s Sug. Retail was $360.

MAGNUM HUNTER — .22 Mag., semi-auto, 22 in. match grade free-floating barrel, synthetic stock with removable recoil pad, 10 shot rotary mag., no sights, grooved receiver, 6 lbs. New 1993.

Mfg.'s Sug. Retail	$450	$375	$295	$250

A-SQUARE

Manufacturer located in Bedford, KY. Previously manufactured until 1991 in Madison, IN. Direct sales only.

A-Square also offers at extra cost different grades of walnut, different metal finishes, and various sights/scope rings. Custom calibers are also available upon special order. Values of these special order options can be obtained by contacting A-Square directly.

RIFLES: BOLT ACTION

Add $200 for A-Grade walnut.
Add $400 for AAA-Grade fancy walnut.
Add $400 for English walnut.
Add $250 for black synthetic stock.
Add $150 for 3-leaf steel express sights.
Add $300 for royal high gloss blue finish.
Add $150 for high gloss polymer wood finish.

Grading	100%	98%	95%	90%	80%	70%	60%

HANNIBAL MODEL — .270 Win. (disc. 1990), .30-06, .300 Wby. Mag., .300 Win. Mag., .300 H&H (new 1988), .308 Norma Mag. (disc. 1987), .338 Win. Mag., .338 A-Square, .340 Wby. Mag., .375 Wby. Mag., .375 H&H, .375 JRS (1990 mfg. only), .375 A-Square, .378 Wby. Mag., .404 Jeffrey, .416 Wby. Mag. (new 1989), .416 Hoffman, .416 Taylor (new 1988), .416 Rem Mag. (new 1989), .425 Express (new 1989), .450 Ackley Mag., .458 Win. Mag., .458 Lott (new 1989), .460 Short A-Square, .460 Long A-Square (disc. 1987), .460 Wby. Mag., .470 Ruark (1990 mfg. only), .495 A-Square, .500 A-Square, 7mm Rem Mag., 7mm STW (1990 mfg. only), 8mm Rem. Mag. (new 1988), or 9.3 x 64 (new 1988), or 9.3 x 64 (new in 1988) cal. Bolt action built on a P-17 Enfield receiver, various cals., 22-26 in. barrel, 9 - 11¼ lbs., select walnut wood with pistol grip and recoil pad. New 1986.

Mfg.'s Sug. Retail	$2,495		$2,495	$2,050	$1,850	$1,500	$1,225	$1,100	$995

CAESAR MODEL — .270 Win. (disc. 1990), .30-06, .300 Win. Mag., .300 Wby. Mag., .300 H&H (new 1988), .308 Norma Mag. (disc. 1987), .338 Win. Mag., .340 Wby. Mag., .375 Wby. Mag., .375 H&H, .375 JRS (1990 mfg. only), .404 Jeffrey (new 1991), .416 Hoffman, .416 Taylor (new 1988), .416 Rem Mag. (new 1989), .425 Express (new 1989) .450 Ackley Mag., .458 Win. Mag., .458 Lott (new 1989), .470 Ruark (1990 mfg. only), 7mm Rem Mag., 7mm STW (1990 mfg. only), 8mm Rem. Mag. (new 1988), or 9.3 x 62 (new 1988), or 9.3 x 64 (new in 1988) cal. Bolt action built on a Remington M-700 receiver, various cals., 22-26 in. barrel, 9 - 10¾ lbs., select walnut with pistol grip and recoil pad. Also available in left-hand action at no extra charge. New 1986.

Mfg.'s Sug. Retail	$2,550		$2,550	$2,075	$1,875	$1,500	$1,225	$1,100	$995

A T C S A
Maker: Armas De Tiro Y Casa.

COLT POCKET PISTOL COPY — revolver, .38 cal., 6 shot.

	$155	$140	$110	$100	$90	$75	$65

SINGLE SHOT REVOLVER — target pistol.

	$195	$165	$145	$110	$100	$90	$75

AYA (AGUIRRE Y ARANZABAL)
Manufacturer located in Eibar, Spain. Currently imported and marketed by Armes De Chasse (starting 1992) located in Chadds Ford, PA. Recent manufacture was by Diarm located in Eibar, Spain. Previously imported (1990-91) by Scotia Group Ltd., located in Maryland and American Arms, Inc. located in North Kansas City, MO. Retail sales by importer and AYA select dealers.

SHOTGUNS: O/U
Add 10% on current models listed below if other than 12 ga.

AUGUSTA — 12 ga. only, deluxe O/U sidelock, arabesque engraving in deep relief, select walnut. Importation disc. 1985, resumed in 1991-92.

	$7,900	$6,850	$5,500	$4,950	$4,250	$3,500	$3,150

Last Mfg.'s Sug. Retail was $24,446.

CORAL "A" — 12 or 16 ga., boxlock action with Kersten cross bolt, vent. rib, ejectors, double triggers. Disc. 1985.

	$1,275	$1,050	$875	$775	$695	$625	$560

Last Mfg.'s Sug. Retail was $2,195.

CORAL "B" — similar to Coral A, except for coin-wash engraved receiver. Disc. 1985.

	$1,395	$1,100	$925	$820	$720	$650	$595

Last Mfg.'s Sug. Retail was $2,450.

Grading	100%	98%	95%	90%	80%	70%	60%

MODEL 37 SUPER — 12, 16, or 20 ga., various barrel lengths and chokes, vent. rib, sidelock, auto ejector, elaborate engraving, high grade wood. Merkel style action. Prices below reflect older models.

	100%	98%	95%	90%	80%	70%	60%
12 ga.	$2,600	$2,350	$2,100	$1,900	$1,700	$1,500	$1,250
16 ga.	$2,550	$2,200	$2,000	$1,700	$1,500	$1,350	$1,150
20 ga.	$3,000	$2,500	$2,200	$1,900	$1,700	$1,600	$1,475

✄ **New Model 37 Super A** — game scene engraved, detachable sidelock action, nickel steel receiver. Importation disc. 1985, resumed 1991-92.

	100%	98%	95%	90%	80%	70%	60%
	$6,450	$5,250	$4,300	$3,750	$3,250	$2,650	$2,175

Last Mfg.'s Sug. Retail was $13,932.

✄ **New Model 37 Super B** — fine scroll engraved, detachable sidelock action, nickel steel receiver. Disc. 1985.

	100%	98%	95%	90%	80%	70%	60%
	$5,250	$4,750	$4,300	$3,720	$3,350	$2,650	$2,175

Last Mfg.'s Sug. Retail was $7,795.

79 "A" — 12 ga. only, boxlock with double locking lugs, sel. trigger, ejectors. Disc. 1985.

	100%	98%	95%	90%	80%	70%	60%
	$1,275	$1,075	$965	$880	$790	$705	$640

Last Mfg.'s Sug. Retail was $1,595.

79 "B" — similar to 79 "A", only more elaborate engraving. Disc. 1985.

	100%	98%	95%	90%	80%	70%	60%
	$1,395	$1,200	$1,085	$990	$890	$790	$695

Last Mfg.'s Sug. Retail was $1,795.

79 "C" — similar to 79 "B", only more elaborate engraving, double triggers on request. Disc. 1985.

	100%	98%	95%	90%	80%	70%	60%
	$2,050	$1,825	$1,605	$1,460	$1,315	$1,165	$1,000

Last Mfg.'s Sug. Retail was $2,650.

77 — 12 ga. only, Merkel style O/U sidelock with Greener crossbolt, deluxe engraving-checkering. Disc. 1985.

	100%	98%	95%	90%	80%	70%	60%
	$3,100	$2,750	$2,500	$2,255	$2,030	$1,805	$1,600

Last Mfg.'s Sug. Retail was $4,100.

SHOTGUNS: SxS

Armes De Chasse should be contacted directly regarding special order options on the models listed below.

On current models listed below, add 10% to values if other than 12 ga.

Values on currently imported AYA shotguns have increased considerably, while prices for used specimens (98% or less original condition) have not increased proportionately, and in some cases, have changed very little.

BOLERO — similar to Matador, with non-selective single trigger and extractors. Disc. 1984.

	100%	98%	95%	90%	80%	70%	60%
	$440	$360	$330	$305	$275	$250	$220

IBERIA — 12 or 20 ga., 3 in., boxlock, double triggers, plain walnut. Disc. 1984.

	100%	98%	95%	90%	80%	70%	60%
	$566	$440	$370	$315	$285	$255	$230

IBERIA II — 12 or 16 ga., 28 in. barrels, 2¾ in. chamber only, double triggers, plain walnut. Mfg. 1984-1985 only.

	100%	98%	95%	90%	80%	70%	60%
	$515	$430	$370	$315	$285	$255	$230

Last Mfg.'s Sug. Retail was $570.

Grading	100%	98%	95%	90%	80%	70%	60%

MATADOR — 12, 16, 20, 28, or .410 ga., 26, 28, or 30 in. barrel, various chokes, Anson & Deeley boxlock, auto ejectors, beavertail forearm, SST, checkered pistol grip stock. Mfg. 1955-1963.

	100%	98%	95%	90%	80%	70%	60%
	$475	$375	$325	$275	$225	$200	$180

Add 20% for .410 or 28 ga.

MATADOR II —similar to Matador, with vent. rib, 12 or 20 ga. only. Disc.

	$525	$425	$360	$315	$265	$225	$200

MATADOR III — 12 or 20 ga., 3 in. chamber in 20 ga. only, boxlock, vent. rib, ejectors, SST. Disc. 1985.

	$750	$650	$550	$495	$440	$385	$335

Last Mfg.'s Sug. Retail was $1,235.

SENIOR — 12 ga. only, self-opener, engraved sidelock action, select walnut. Top-of-the-line-quality, made to special order only. Lighter up-land version also available. Disc. 1987.

	$15,500	$12,000	$10,000	$8,000	$6,500	$5,500	$4,500

Last Mfg.'s Sug. Retail was $21,000.

NO. 1 — 12 or 20 ga., full sidelock action with third lever fastener, straight grip, ejectors, DTs, elaborate fine scroll engraving. Importation disc. 1987, resumed in 1991.

Mfg.'s Sug. Retail	$6,500	$5,750	$2,750	$2,250	$1,800	$1,500	$1,200	$950

Add $2,562 for extra set of barrels.

NO. 2 — 12, 16, 20, 28 or .410 ga., 3 in. chambers, English-style sidelock, ejector, cocking indicators, DTs, third lever fastener. Importation disc. 1987, resumed 1991.

Mfg.'s Sug. Retail	$3,380	$2,950	$1,250	$950	$750	$600	$500	$425

Add $1,328 for extra set of barrels.

NO. 3-A — 12, 16, 20, 28, or .410 ga., boxlock, extractors, double triggers. Disc. 1985.

	$640	$540	$495	$450	$400	$375	$350

Add 25%-35% for 28 or .410 ga.
Last Mfg.'s Sug. Retail was $850.

NO. 4-A — 12, 16 (disc. 1985), 20, 28, or .410 ga., 3 in. chambers, English-style straight stock, boxlock action, ejectors, double trigger, straight grip. Importation disc. 1987, resumed 1991.

Mfg.'s Sug. Retail	$1,770	$1,575	$600	$500	$450	$410	$365	$325

4-A DELUXE — English-style, boxlock ejector. Stock, forearm, trigger to order. Importation disc. 1985, resumed 1991.

Mfg.'s Sug. Retail	$3,115	$2,750	$1,100	$900	$800	$740	$680	$625

XXV BOXLOCK (BL) — 12 or 20 ga. only, similar to 4-A Deluxe, except 25 in. barrels, Churchill rib. Importation disc. 1986, resumed 1991.

Mfg.'s Sug. Retail	$3,100	$2,850	$1,200	$975	$875	$800	$740	$680

Add $2,013 for extra set of barrels.

XXV SIDELOCK (SL) — 12, 16, 20, 28 or .410 ga., sidelock ejector, 25 in. barrels, Churchill rib. Stock, forearm, trigger to order. Importation disc. 1986, resumed 1991.

12, 16, or 20 ga.

Mfg.'s Sug. Retail	$4,000	$3,750	$1,650	$1,350	$975	$850	$750	$650

Add $2,097 for extra set of barrels.

NO. 53 — 12, 16, or 20 ga., engraved sidelock ejector, sideclips, third lock. Stock, forearm, trigger to order. Importation disc. 1986, resumed 1991.

Mfg.'s Sug. Retail	$4,900	$4,550	$1,950	$1,500	$1,100	$950	$850	$750

AYA cont.

Grading	100%	98%	95%	90%	80%	70%	60%

NO. 56 — 12, 16, or 20 ga., sidelock action-engraved, ejectors, sel. trigger. Importation disc. 1985, resumed 1991.

Mfg.'s Sug. Retail	$7,570	$6,950	$3,250	$2,650	$2,250	$1,950	$1,650	$1,400

NO. 106 — 12, 16, or 20 ga., English-style boxlock, double trigger, pistol grip, 28 in. barrels. Disc. 1985.

$530	$440	$400	$360	$320	$300	$275

Last Mfg.'s Sug. Retail was $585.

107-LI — 12 or 16 ga., English-style boxlock, double trigger, straight grip, light English scroll engraving. Disc. 1985.

$675	$560	$520	$480	$425	$400	$360

Last Mfg.'s Sug. Retail was $745.

MODEL 116 — 12, 16, or 20 ga., 27-30 in. barrels, any choke, hand detachable H&H sidelocks, double triggers, engraved, select checkered walnut pistol grip stock. Disc. 1985.

$1,000	$845	$795	$750	$675	$600	$500

Last Mfg.'s Sug. Retail was $1,125.

MODEL 117 — 12, 16 or 20 ga., 3 in. chambers, 26-30 in. barrels, any choke, hand detachable H&H sidelocks, ejectors, SST, engraved, select checkered walnut pistol grip stock. Disc. 1986.

$835	$715	$660	$620	$585	$545	$500

Last Mfg.'s Sug. Retail was $1,075.

QUAIL UNLIMITED MODEL 117 — 12 ga. only, 26 in. barrels choked IC/M with 3 in. chambers, upgraded wood and checkering, high gloss bluing, gold colored ST, engraved by Baron Technologies in PA, only 42 mfg. for Quail Unlimited of North America.

$1,650	$1,400	$1,150	$975	$875	$800	$725

This model had a retail price of $1,700 but was made available to Quail Unlimited members for approx. $1,200.

MODEL 210 — 12 or 16 ga., boxlock, exposed hammers, double triggers, plain walnut, light engraving. Disc. 1985.

$795	$675	$550	$475	$435	$395	$350

Last Mfg.'s Sug. Retail was $900.

711 BOXLOCK — 12 ga. only, boxlock, selective trigger, ejectors, vent. rib. Disc. 1984.

$880	$680	$575	$490	$445	$395	$350

⁑ 711 Sidelock — sidelock action. Mfg. 1985 only.

$995	$850	$775	$695	$625	$550	$475

Last Mfg.'s Sug. Retail was $1,250.

ABADIE
Maker: Several Belgian makers for Portuguese Military.

MODEL 1878 (OFFICER'S MODEL) — 9.1mm, solid frame revolver, 6 shot, ejector rod, officer's issue A.

$220	$195	$165	$130	$120	$110	$100

MODEL 1886 (TROOPER'S MODEL) — similar to 1878, but larger, trooper issue A.

$195	$175	$160	$120	$110	$100	$90

ABBEY, GEORGE T.
Utica, NY from 1845-1852. Chicago, Il from 1852-1874. Percussion and breechloading firearms.

100%	98%	95%	90%	80%	70%	60%	50%	40%	30%	20%	10%

PERCUSSION RIFLE

⚞ **.44 cal.** — 32 in. octagon barrel.

100%	98%	95%	90%	80%	70%	60%	50%	40%	30%	20%	10%
$605	$550	$470	$415	$370	$340	$305	$275	$250	$220	$195	$165

⚞ **.44 cal.** — octagon barrel, brass trimmed.

$770	$735	$695	$605	$550	$485	$450	$405	$365	$330	$275	$220

⚞ **.44 cal.** — 31 in. double barrel.

$1,210	$1,100	$880	$770	$715	$650	$595	$550	$515	$475	$430	$360

⚞ **.44 cal.** — double barrel O/U, brass trimmed.

$1,485	$1,295	$1,130	$990	$910	$855	$770	$715	$660	$605	$495	$330

ABBEY, F.J. & COMPANY
Chicago, IL, 1858-1878. Muzzle and breechloading shotguns and rifles.

PERCUSSION RIFLE — several variations.

$605	$550	$470	$415	$360	$305	$275	$250	$210	$175	$145	$110

PERCUSSION SHOTGUN — several variations.

$800	$715	$635	$550	$470	$415	$360	$320	$285	$250	$210	$155

ABBIATICO & SALVINELLI (FAMARS)
Manufacturer located in Gardone, Italy. Imported exclusively in the U.S. by Mr. Joe Bojalad located in Pittsburgh, PA.

A & S Famars manufactures some of the world's finest rifles and shotguns - only 50-60 are fabricated yearly. Values listed below are for base models with no extra embellishments or special orders. Because every A & S Famars longarm is an individual custom order, each Famars firearm must have its value ascertained on an individual appraisal basis.

RIFLES: CUSTOM MANUFACTURE

Boxlock and sidelock rifles are all best quality and range in calibers between .22 LR and .600 Nitro Express. Each gun is manufactured per individual customer special order, and values below reflect base model pricing with no additional special features. Further information and price quotations are available by contacting the above listed U.S. agent directly.

Grading		100%	98%	95%	90%	80%	70%	60%
AFRICA EXPRESS								
Mfg.'s Sug. Retail	$15,650	$15,650	$12,000	$10,000	$8,750	$7,500	$6,250	$5,950
VENUS EXPRESS PROFESSIONAL								
Mfg.'s Sug. Retail	$26,000	$26,000	$22,000	$19,000	$16,000	$14,000	$12,000	$9,950

VENUS EXPRESS EXTRALUSSO — top-of-the-line model.
   Prices are quoted per individual order.

SHOTGUNS: CUSTOM MANUFACTURE

HAMMER SHOTGUN — double barrel, SxS only, hammers, double triggers, various gauges.
   Prices usually start in the $11,000 range and go up according to options.

Grading		100%	98%	95%	90%	80%	70%	60%

BOXLOCK SHOTGUN — SxS only, available with Anson-Deeley boxlock action, scalloped or rounded frame, various engraving patterns available.

⚞ **Zeus**

Mfg.'s Sug. Retail	$11,500	$11,500	$10,000	$8,750	$7,500	$6,250	$5,000	$4,750

⚞ **Tribute**

Mfg.'s Sug. Retail	$12,600	$12,600	$10,800	$9,250	$7,900	$6,500	$5,250	$4,750

⚞ **Venere**

Mfg.'s Sug. Retail	$12,600	$12,600	$10,800	$9,250	$7,900	$6,500	$5,250	$4,750

⚞ **Castore**

Mfg.'s Sug. Retail	$12,600	$12,600	$10,800	$9,250	$7,900	$6,500	$5,250	$4,750

⚞ **Highline**

Mfg.'s Sug. Retail	$13,700	$13,700	$11,500	$9,750	$8,350	$6,750	$5,450	$4,850

⚞ **Venus**

Mfg.'s Sug. Retail	$20,850	$20,850	$17,250	$14,250	$11,750	$9,750	$8,350	$6,750

JOREMA SIDELOCK — 12 or 20 ga.

Mfg.'s Sug. Retail	$20,850	$20,850	$17,250	$14,250	$11,750	$9,750	$8,350	$6,750

EXCALIBUR SIDELOCK — 12 or 20 ga., top-of-the-line model.
Prices are quoted per individual order.

ROMBO QUATTROCANNE — .410 ga. only.

Mfg.'s Sug. Retail	$23,000	$23,000	$19,500	$16,000	$13,000	$10,500	$9,250	$7,750

ACCU-TEK
Manufacturer located in Chino, CA. Distributor sales only.

PISTOLS: SEMI-AUTO

MODEL AT-9 — 9mm Para. cal., double action only, 3.2 in. barrel, 7 shot mag., firing pin block with no external safeties, black or brushed stainless finish, 3 dot sights adj. for windage, 28 oz. New 1993.

Mfg.'s Sug. Retail	$270		$230	$195	$160			

Add $5 for black finish.

MODEL AT-40 — .40 S&W cal., double action only, 3.2 in. barrel, 7 shot mag., firing pin block with no external safeties, black or brushed stainless finish, 3 dot sights adj. for windage, 28 oz. New 1993.

Mfg.'s Sug. Retail	$270		$230	$195	$160			

Add $5 for black finish.

MODEL AT-25 — .25 ACP cal., single action, 2½ in. barrel, 7 shot mag. with finger extension, similar design to AT-32, stainless steel, aluminum, or alloy construction with choice of stainless, satin aluminum, or black finish, 11 (Model AT-25AL) or 18 (Model AT-25B) oz. New 1992.

Mfg.'s Sug. Retail	$147		$130	$115	$100	$90	$80	$70	$60

Add $5 for satin aluminum (Model AT-25AL) or black (Model AT-25SSB) finish.

Grading	100%	98%	95%	90%	80%	70%	60%

MODEL AT-32SS — .32 ACP cal., single action design, 2½ in. barrel, 5 shot mag. with finger extension, alloy (disc. 1991) or stainless steel (new 1992) construction, manual hand safety with firing pin block and trigger disconnect, side mag. release, exposed hammer, satin aluminum finish (disc. 1991), 16 oz. Mfg. in U.S. New 1990.

Mfg.'s Sug. Retail	$164	$150	$130	$115	$100	$90	$80	$70

Add $5 for black finish (Model AT-32SSB).

MODEL AT-380SS — .380 ACP cal., similar to Model AT-32, except has 2¾ in. barrel, alloy (disc. 1991) or stainless steel construction, 20 oz. New 1990.

Mfg.'s Sug. Retail	$170	$155	$135	$115	$100	$90	$80	$70

Add $5 for black finish (Model AT-380SSB).

MODEL HC-380SS — .380 ACP cal., single action semi-auto, 2½ in. barrel, 13 shot mag., manual safety with firing pin block and trigger disconnect, exposed hammer. New 1993.

Mfg.'s Sug. Retail	$230	$195	$160	$130

ACHA

Maker: Domingo Acha, Spain.

MODEL 1916 — semi-auto pistol, 7.76mm, 7 shot mag., 1903 Browning copy.

	$220	$165	$100	$85	$65	$55	$45

ATLAS — semi-auto pistol, 6.35mm, 6 shot mag., slide marked ATLAS, 1906 Browning copy.

	$165	$140	$125	$95	$75	$65	$50

LOOKING GLASS — semi-auto pistol, 6.35mm, 6 shot mag., blued or nickel, 1906 Browning copy, side marked "Looking Glass", many variations.

	$220	$165	$130	$100	$85	$70	$55

LOOKING GLASS — semi-auto pistol, 7.65mm, exposed hammer.

	$220	$165	$140	$105	$90	$75	$65

ACME

Trade name of Davenport Arms Company Shotguns, Maltby Henley & Co. Revolvers, and Merwin Hulburt & Co. Owl Head Revolvers.

100%	98%	95%	90%	80%	70%	60%	50%	40%	30%	20%	10%

SEVEN SHOT REVOLVER — single action, .22 Short rimfire.

$360	$310	$240	$185	$165	$150	$120	$110	$100	$90	$65	$55

FIVE SHOT REVOLVER — single action, .32 Short rimfire.

$360	$320	$255	$200	$175	$160	$120	$110	$100	$90	$65	$55

ACME ARMS

Trade name for Cornwall Hardware Co., NY.

REVOLVERS

SEVEN SHOT — single action, .22 Short rimfire.

$275	$250	$210	$185	$165	$155	$140	$120	$100	$90	$85	$75

FIVE SHOT — single action, .32 Short rimfire.

$285	$255	$215	$195	$175	$165	$145	$125	$110	$90	$85	$75

100%	98%	95%	90%	80%	70%	60%	50%	40%	30%	20%	10%

SHOTGUN

SIDE-BY-SIDE — 12 ga., damascus barrel.

100%	98%	95%	90%	80%	70%	60%	50%	40%	30%	20%	10%
$275	$240	$195	$165	$145	$125	$110	$95	$65	$60	$50	$45

ACME HAMMERLESS
Maker: Hopkins & Allen, for Hulbert Brothers, 1893.

REVOLVERS

FIVE SHOT — double action, top break, .32 centerfire, non-ejecting.

100%	98%	95%	90%	80%	70%	60%	50%	40%	30%	20%	10%
$145	$125	$100	$90	$80	$70	$60	$50	$40	$30	$20	$15

Also known as Forehand Model 1891, can be hammer or hammerless.

FIVE SHOT — double action, top break, .38 centerfire, non-ejecting.

100%	98%	95%	90%	80%	70%	60%	50%	40%	30%	20%	10%
$145	$125	$100	$90	$80	$70	$60	$50	$40	$30	$20	$15

Also known as Forehand Model 1891, can be hammer or hammerless.

ACTION (M.S.)
Maker: Modesto Santos, Eibar, Spain.

Grading	100%	98%	95%	90%	80%	70%	60%

MODEL 1915 — semi-auto pistol (French Military), 7.65mm.

Grading	100%	98%	95%	90%	80%	70%	60%
	$175	$145	$110	$85	$70	$60	$45

MODEL 1920 — semi-auto pistol (action), 6.35mm.

Grading	100%	98%	95%	90%	80%	70%	60%
	$195	$150	$120	$90	$75	$65	$45

ACTION ARMS LTD.
Importer and distributor located in Philadelphia, PA. Mostly distributor direct.

Only Action Arms Models AT84S and AT88S will be listed under this heading. Galil, Timberwolf, and Uzi trademarks can be located in their respective sections.

PISTOLS

AT-84S — 9mm Para., selective double action design, patterned after the CZ-75, 4.8 in. barrel, 15 shot mag., originally introduced in 1985.

100%	98%	95%	90%	80%	70%	60%
$470	$415	$385	$360	$330	$275	$220

The AT-84S Series was mfg. in Switzerland by Industrial Technology & Machines A.G. and was sold by Action Arms between June of 1987 and 1989. Serial number range is 01201-06000. No P or H models were ever mfg. in this series (2 or 3 prototypes only).

AT-88S — 9mm or .41 Action Express (available early 1990) cal., selective double action design patterned after CZ-75, 4.8 in. barrel, 15 shot (9mm) or 10 shot (.41 AE) mag., can be "cocked and locked", fixed sights, blued metal, walnut grips, 35.3 oz. Introduced in 1987 with limited production samples being imported in 1989.

100%	98%	95%	90%	80%	70%	60%
$500	$450	$395	$360	$330	$275	$220

A very small quantity of AT-88Ss (various configurations) was made by I.T.M. of Switzerland and finishes included all blue, all chrome, or 2-tone. These pistols may exhibit both I.T.M. and A.A.L. markings. More recent manufacture was performed by Sphinx-Muller of Switzerland. These pistols are still mfg. by Sphinx-Muller, renamed the AT-2000 Series and imported by Sile Distributors.

RIFLES

TIMBERWOLF — see separate listing in T section.

ADAMS
Maker: Deane, Adams, & Deane, located in London, Eng.

PERCUSSION REVOLVERS

100%	98%	95%	90%	80%	70%	60%	50%	40%	30%	20%	10%

MODEL 1851 — double action, .38 cal., 4½ in. barrel.

100%	98%	95%	90%	80%	70%	60%	50%	40%	30%	20%	10%
$1,375	$1,265	$1,100	$990	$855	$745	$690	$605	$550	$440	$385	$330

MODEL 1851 — double action, .44 cal., 6 in. barrel.

100%	98%	95%	90%	80%	70%	60%	50%	40%	30%	20%	10%
$935	$880	$800	$690	$550	$495	$440	$395	$340	$305	$275	$255

MODEL 1851 — Dragoon, double action, .50 cal., 8 in. barrel.

100%	98%	95%	90%	80%	70%	60%	50%	40%	30%	20%	10%
$1,375	$1,265	$1,100	$990	$855	$715	$690	$605	$550	$385	$360	$340

MODEL 1851 — .38 cal., cased with accessories.

100%	98%	95%	90%	80%	70%	60%	50%	40%	30%	20%	10%
$1,760	$1,595	$1,375	$1,100	$990	$910	$825	$745	$660	$605	$550	$525

MODEL 1851 — .44 cal., cased with accessories.

100%	98%	95%	90%	80%	70%	60%	50%	40%	30%	20%	10%
$1,295	$1,155	$990	$880	$770	$690	$635	$550	$440	$385	$360	$330

MODEL 1851 — Dragoon, .50 cal., cased with accessories.

100%	98%	95%	90%	80%	70%	60%	50%	40%	30%	20%	10%
$1,680	$1,485	$1,210	$1,185	$990	$880	$800	$715	$635	$550	$495	$470

ADAMS, JOSEPH
Birmingham, England.

OFFICER MODEL — flintlock pistol, musket caliber .65, Brown Bess.

100%	98%	95%	90%	80%	70%	60%	50%	40%	30%	20%	10%
$2,850	$2,500	$2,250	$2,000	$1,800	$1,600	$1,400	$1,100	$900	$825	$725	$600

ADAMY, GEBRUDER
Suhl, Germany, 1920's and 1930's.

Grading	100%	98%	95%	90%	80%	70%	60%

SHOTGUN — O/U, double trigger, engraved, cased.

100%	98%	95%	90%	80%	70%	60%
$1,815	$1,650	$1,375	$1,155	$990	$880	$770

ADIRONDACK ARMS COMPANY
Plattsburgh, NY, 1870-1874.

Magazine loaded repeating rifle, .44 cal., brass or iron frame, later model, may also be marked A.S. Babbitt, Plattsburgh, N.Y., absorbed by Winchester in 1874, then disc.

This rifle was designed in 1870 and patented by Orvill M. Robinson in Upper Jay, NY. It was available in .38 and .44 cal. rimfire rifles without a wooden forend and had a high cyclic rate of fire. Original models were made in Plattsburgh, NY at which time A.S. Babbitt became one of several additional partners. In 1872, Robinson was granted a patent for a second model rifle. It was similar to the 1870, except a wooden forend was added and the operating mechanism was changed considerably. Following these improvements, Mr. Oliver Winchester contacted Mr. Robinson and purchased the entire Robinson company, discontinuing manufacture.

100%	98%	95%	90%	80%	70%	60%	50%	40%	30%	20%	10%

EARLY MODEL — finger holds on hammer.

100%	98%	95%	90%	80%	70%	60%	50%	40%	30%	20%	10%
$2,400	$2,100	$1,750	$1,450	$1,325	$1,200	$1,075	$975	$875	$775	$675	$600

LATE MODEL — action worked by buttons top of receiver mid-section.

100%	98%	95%	90%	80%	70%	60%	50%	40%	30%	20%	10%
$2,200	$1,950	$1,675	$1,300	$1,200	$1,100	$975	$875	$775	$675	$550	$495

ADLER
Maker: Engelbrecht & Wolff located in Blasii, Germany, 1905-1907.

Grading	100%	98%	95%	90%	80%	70%	60%

SEMI-AUTO PISTOL — 7mm Adler, 8 shot mag., cocking lever on top of frame, not competitive in its price range.

100%	98%	95%	90%	80%	70%	60%
$2,200	$1,925	$1,540	$1,045	$770	$495	$330

ADVANTAGE ARMS USA, INC.
Previous manufacturer located in St. Paul, MN. Advantage Arms USA, Inc. was distributed by Wildfire Sports, Inc. also located in St. Paul.

MODEL 422 — .22 LR and Mag., 4 barrel double action derringer, rotating firing pin, this model is patterned after the Mossberg "Brownie", 2½ in. barrel, high grade alloy frame and barrel, 4 shot, available in blue, nickel, or QPQ (heat treated but appears blued) finish, 15 oz. Mfg. 1986-87 only.

100%	98%	95%	90%	80%	70%	60%
$150	$135	$115	$105	$95	$85	$75

Add $10 for .22 Mag. cal.
Add $6 for nickel finish.
Add $11 for QPQ finish.
Last Mfg.'s Sug. Retail was $166.

AETNA
Previously manufactured by Harrington & Richardson located in Worchester, MA.

Type: single action revolvers, all of the same general size and configuration, solid frame, spur trigger, so called "Suicide Specials" during their day.

100%	98%	95%	90%	80%	70%	60%	50%	40%	30%	20%	10%

AETNA NO. 2 — .32 rimfire, 5 shot.

100%	98%	95%	90%	80%	70%	60%	50%	40%	30%	20%	10%
$330	$275	$215	$185	$170	$155	$145	$120	$100	$85	$75	$55

AETNA NO. 2½ — .32 rimfire, 5 shot.

100%	98%	95%	90%	80%	70%	60%	50%	40%	30%	20%	10%
$330	$275	$215	$185	$170	$155	$145	$120	$100	$85	$75	$55

MODEL 1876 — .22 rimfire, 7 shot.

100%	98%	95%	90%	80%	70%	60%	50%	40%	30%	20%	10%
$330	$275	$210	$195	$175	$165	$155	$130	$110	$95	$90	$65

MODEL 1876 — .32 rimfire, 5 shot.

100%	98%	95%	90%	80%	70%	60%	50%	40%	30%	20%	10%
$330	$275	$210	$175	$165	$155	$145	$120	$105	$90	$75	$55

MODEL 1876 — .38 rimfire, 5 shot.

100%	98%	95%	90%	80%	70%	60%	50%	40%	30%	20%	10%
$330	$275	$220	$205	$195	$175	$165	$145	$120	$105	$95	$85

AETNA ARMS COMPANY
Manufacturer located in New York, 1869-1883.

Single action pocket revolver, blued or nickel, birdshead grip, copy of S&W models 1-3, models marked ALLING are worth a slight premium.

100%	98%	95%	90%	80%	70%	60%	50%	40%	30%	20%	10%

SEVEN SHOT — .22 rimfire.

100%	98%	95%	90%	80%	70%	60%	50%	40%	30%	20%	10%
$250	$235	$210	$195	$175	$165	$155	$130	$110	$95	$90	$65

FIVE SHOT — .32 rimfire.

$230	$220	$205	$175	$165	$155	$145	$120	$105	$90	$75	$55

AGNER

Manufactured by Saxhoj Products Inc. in Denmark. Imported until 1986 by Beeman Arms, Inc. located in Santa Rosa, CA.

PISTOL: SEMI-AUTO

Grading	100%	98%	95%	90%	80%	70%	60%

M 80 — .22 LR only, stainless steel, semi-auto target pistol, new design features unique security key safety feature, adj. French walnut grips, dry fire mechanism, 5.9 in. barrel, 5 shot mag., limited production, 2.4 lbs. Imported 1981-1986.

			100%	98%	95%
			$1,125	$1,040	$950

Add $100 for left-hand action.
Last Mfg.'s Sug. Retail was $1,295.

AIR MATCH

Previously imported by Kendall International, located in Paris, KY.

AIR MATCH 500 — .22 cal. match single shot pistol, target grips, adj. front counterweight, 10½ in. barrel. Imported 1984-86.

100%	98%	95%	90%	80%	70%	60%
$550	$495	$450	$425	$395	$360	$330

Last Mfg.'s Sug. Retail was $788.

AJAX ARMY

Distributed by E.C. Meacham Co., maker unknown, circa 1880s.

100%	98%	95%	90%	80%	70%	60%	50%	40%	30%	20%	10%

SINGLE ACTION — .44 rimfire, spur trigger, solid frame.

$550	$440	$360	$315	$275	$255	$230	$210	$185	$170	$155	$140

AKRILL, E.

French, 1800's.

FLINTLOCK RIFLE — breech loaded, .69 cal., damascus octagon barrel.

$3,300	$2,750	$2,200	$1,980	$1,460	$1,320	$1,240	$1,075	$935	$800	$745	$660

ALAMO RANGER

Grading	100%	98%	95%	90%	80%	70%	60%

REVOLVER — .38 cal., Spanish copy of Colt Model 1929.

100%	98%	95%	90%	80%	70%	60%
$140	$120	$110	$100	$90	$85	$75

ALASKA

Maker: Hood Firearms Company, Norwich, CT, 1873-1884.
Dubbed "Suicide Specials" in their day.

REVOLVERS

100%	98%	95%	90%	80%	70%	60%	50%	40%	30%	20%	10%

SINGLE ACTION — .22 rimfire, 7 shot, spur trigger, solid frame.

100%	98%	95%	90%	80%	70%	60%	50%	40%	30%	20%	10%
$275	$220	$195	$145	$140	$125	$110	$100	$90	$75	$70	$65

FIVE SHOT — .32 Short rimfire.

100%	98%	95%	90%	80%	70%	60%	50%	40%	30%	20%	10%
$220	$195	$160	$155	$150	$140	$125	$105	$95	$85	$75	$70

ALASKAN COMMEMORATIVES

The following is a complete chronological listing of special and limited editions manufactured for the state of Alaska.

Grading	100%	Issue Price	Qty. Made

1967 ALASKAN PURCHASE CENTENNIAL WINCHESTER 94 CARBINE — see listing under Winchester Commemoratives.

1967 ALASKA PURCHASE CENTENNIAL CONTENDER — Thompson Contender with 2 barrels chambered for .22 Hornet and .357 Mag., Ser. no. C0001.
Issue price is unknown and rarity precludes accurate secondary market pricing.

1976 ALASKA PIPELINE COMMEMORATIVE — Colt SAA in .45 cal., cased with Kershaw knife.

100%	Issue Price	Qty. Made
$1,200	$800	801

1981 ALASKA STATE TROOPER 40TH ANNIVERSARY — Smith & Wesson Model 19-5, .357 Mag., 4 in. barrel, cased with belt buckle and patch.

100%	Issue Price	Qty. Made
$850	$500	250

1984 STATE OF ALASKA SILVER ANNIVERSARY EDITION — Smith & Wesson Model 29-3, .44 Mag., 6 in. barrel, cased with bronze brown bear and ivory grips with scrimshaw AK state seal and silver engraving.

100%	Issue Price	Qty. Made
$15,000	$10,000	10

1984 ALASKA SILVER ANNIVERSARY — Smith & Wesson Model 29-3, .44 Mag., 6 in. barrel, cased with gold engraving.

100%	Issue Price	Qty. Made
$1,500	$1,195	300

1984 ALASKA STATEHOOD 25TH ANNIVERSARY — Winchester Model 70XTR, .338 Win. Mag. cal., sterling silver engraving.

100%	Issue Price	Qty. Made
$1,350	$1,080	500

1984 ALASKA 25TH ANNIVERSARY — Colt Python, .357 Mag., 6 in. barrel, engraved brown bear with gold lettering and numbers, cased.

100%	Issue Price	Qty. Made
$1,000	$500	200

1988 IDITAROD "1 OF 1,000" — Smith & Wesson Model 629-1, .44 Mag., 6 in. barrel, cased with laser-etched box, while a thousand were planned, only 500 were mfg.

100%	Issue Price	Qty. Made
$1,250	$775	500

1988 ALASKA SERIES "TOKLAT" SPECIAL — LAR mfg. Grizzly Mag., .45 Win. Mag., mfg. for Great Northern Guns in Anchorage, AK, cased with plaque.

100%	Issue Price	Qty. Made
$1,500	$1,195	20

ALDAZABAL
Maker: Aldazabal, Leturiondo & Cia.

Grading	100%	98%	95%	90%	80%	70%	60%
SEMI-AUTOMATIC PISTOL — 7.65mm, 7 shot, Eibar style.							
	$195	$165	$110	$100	$90	$75	$65

ALERT
Maker: Hood Firearms Company, Norwich, CT, 1873-1881.
These revolvers were dubbed "Suicide Specials" in their day.

REVOLVERS

100%	98%	95%	90%	80%	70%	60%	50%	40%	30%	20%	10%
SINGLE ACTION — .22 rimfire, 7 shot, spur trigger, solid frame.											
$220	$195	$165	$145	$130	$125	$110	$100	$90	$75	$70	$65
FIVE SHOT — .32 Short rimfire.											
$170	$165	$160	$155	$150	$140	$125	$105	$95	$85	$75	$70

ALEXIA
Maker: Hopkins & Allen, Norwich, CT, 1867-1915.

Also known as: Blue Jacket, Captain Jack, Chichester, Defender, Dictator, Monarch, Mountain Eagle, Hopkins & Allen, Towers Police Safety, and Universal.

Description: single action revolver, solid frame, spur trigger, inexpensive vest pocket pistol issued under numerous names for private companies, octagon barrel.

REVOLVERS

100%	98%	95%	90%	80%	70%	60%	50%	40%	30%	20%	10%
.22 RIMFIRE — 7 shot.											
$165	$160	$155	$145	$130	$125	$110	$100	$90	$75	$70	$65
.32 SHORT RIMFIRE — 5 shot.											
$170	$165	$160	$155	$150	$140	$125	$105	$95	$85	$75	$70
SINGLE ACTION .38 SHORT RIMFIRE — 5 shot.											
$195	$180	$170	$165	$160	$145	$140	$120	$110	$100	$90	$85
.41 SHORT RIMFIRE — 5 shot.											
$220	$210	$205	$195	$180	$170	$160	$145	$125	$110	$100	$90

ALFA
Maker: Armero Especialistas Reunidas, located in Eibar, Spain, 1920's.
All revolvers are marked Alfa on grips.

Grading	100%	98%	95%	90%	80%	70%	60%
EARLY MODEL — .32, .38, or .44 cal., copies of S&W No. 2 by O. Hermanos.							
	$145	$130	$120	$110	$105	$95	$75
LATE MODEL — .22 LR, .32 S&W, or .38 S&W cal., copies of Colt Police Positive and S&W Military and Police.							
	$160	$150	$130	$120	$110	$100	$90

ALKARTASUNA FABRICA DE ARMAS, S.A.
Manufacturer located in Guernica, Spain.

Grading	100%	98%	95%	90%	80%	70%	60%

ALKARTASUNA RUBY AUTOMATIC — 7.65mm, 9 shot, $3\frac{5}{8}$ in. barrel, blue, fixed sights, checkered wood or hard rubber grips, used by French Army in WWI and WWII. Mfg. 1917-1922.

	100%	98%	95%	90%	80%	70%	60%
	$220	$195	$165	$110	$65	$55	$45

ALLEN & THURBER
Note: Ethan Allen started many plants to keep up with expanding business after 1832. Listed below is a chronological order of the firms constituting the family dynasty founded by Ethan Allen.

E. Allen — Grafton, Mass. 1832-1837
Allen & Thurber — Grafton, Mass. 1837-1842
Allen & Thurber — Norwich, Conn. 1842-1847
Allen & Thurber — Worcester, Mass. 1847-1854
Allen, Thurber, & Co. — Worcester, Mass. 1854-1856
Allen & Wheelock — Worcester, Mass. 1856-1865
E. Allen & Co. — Worcester, Mass. 1865-1871
Forehand & Wadsworth — Worcester, Mass. 1871-1890
Forehand Arms Co. — Worcester, Mass. 1890-1902

No other 19th century American firm produced a wider variety of firearms than did Ethan Allen & subsidiaries.

ALLEN FIREARMS
Previous importer located in Santa Fe, NM importing A. Uberti Firearms until early in 1987. After Allen Firearms closed, Cimarron F.A. Mfg. Co. located in Houston, TX purchased the remaining inventory (in addition to ordering new products under their name).

Allen Firearms was formerly called Western Arms and manufactured both modern and black powder reproduction firearms and accessories patterned after famous older models. Only modern cartridge guns will be shown in this section. Black powder guns will appear under Modern Black Powder Guns.

Rather than provide a complete listing of Allen Firearms models, the following rules usually apply. Since Allen Firearms imported A. Uberti firearms, the Uberti section in this text should be referenced for current values regarding models with similar configurations. Collectibility to date has been limited on most Allen Firearms models, and as a rule, up-to-date values on this trademark are established by current importation prices of Uberti firearms. A complete listing of older Allen Firearms models can be found in Blue Book editions Eleven and Twelve. The models listed below are provided since Uberti is not currently manufacturing them.

SHARPS/GEMMER SPORTING RIFLE — .45-70 cal. only, copy of the famous Sharps rifle. New 1985.

	100%	98%	95%	90%	80%	70%	60%
	$575	$515	$430	$375	$320	$295	$270

Last Mfg.'s Sug. Retail was $599.

1979 JUSTIN CENTENNIAL COMMEMORATIVE — includes specially engraved 1866 sporting rifle and 1873 single action revolver ($7\frac{1}{2}$ in. barrel) with gold plated parts and inlay. Both guns are chambered for .44-40 cal. Also includes special hand signed pair of Justin boots, serial numbered belt buckle and presentation oak case. All serial numbers are matching.

Grading	100%	Issue Price	Qty. Made

MODEL 1873 1 of 1,000 — .44-40 cal, special wood, only 1,000 manufactured. Disc. 1985.

	100%	Issue Price	Qty. Made
	$1,350	$1,500	1,000

ALPHA ARMS INC.
Previous manufacturer located in Flower Mound, TX from 1983-87.
Retail price included custom hard case.

Grading	100%	98%	95%	90%	80%	70%	60%

RIFLES: BOLT ACTION

Many special order options including an octagonal barrel, various finishes, and special sights were available at extra cost on the models listed below. These options, while not listed separately by price, will add value to the prices shown below.

ALPHA JAGUAR — available in most calibers from .222 Rem. through .338 Win., Mauser-type barreled action, Alphawood laminate stock, 20 to 24 in. barrel lengths, approx. 6 lbs. New 1987.

Grade I Jaguar — slide safety, supplied with luggage case.

	$900	$800	$700	$625	$560	$500	$425

Last Mfg.'s Sug. Retail was $995.

Grade II Jaguar — similar to Grade I Jaguar, except has Douglas premium barrel.

	$995	$900	$800	$700	$625	$560	$500

Last Mfg.'s Sug. Retail was $1,095.

Grade III Jaguar — similar to Grade II Jaguar, except has Model 70-type 3-position safety, honed trigger and action.

	$1,125	$995	$900	$800	$700	$625	$560

Last Mfg.'s Sug. Retail was $1,395.

Grade IV Jaguar — similar to Grade III Jaguar, except has fully lightened action & installed swivel studs.

	$1,250	$1,050	$930	$825	$725	$640	$560

Last Mfg.'s Sug. Retail was $1,595.

ALPHA CUSTOM — available in most calibers from .222 Rem. through .338-284, many other calibers available on special order, 20 to 24 in. barrel lengths, limited production, right or left-hand, approx. 6 lbs. New 1984.

	$1,525	$1,200	$975	$850	$725	$640	$560

Last Mfg.'s Sug. Retail was $1,735.

ALPHA GRAND SLAM — same general specifications as the Alpha Custom, except comes standard with laminated wood stock, fluted bolt and non-glare matte finished metal parts, right or left-hand, approx., 6½ lbs. New 1985.

	$1,200	$950	$875	$750	$650	$600	$525

Last Mfg.'s Sug. Retail was $1,465.

ALPHA ALASKAN — .308 Win., .350 Rem. Mag., .358 Win., or .458 Win. cal. Action is similar to Alpha Grand Slam, except barrel, receiver, bolt and safety are stainless steel, right or left-hand, approx. 6¾ - 7½ lbs. New 1985.

	$1,525	$1,200	$975	$850	$725	$640	$560

Last Mfg.'s Sug. Retail was $1,735.

ALPHA BIG-FIVE — .300 H&H thru .375 H&H or .458 Win. cal., action is similar to Alpha Jaguar Grade IV, except has reinforced stock and decelerator recoil pad. Mfg. 1987 only.

	$1,575	$1,250	$1,050	$895	$750	$640	$560

Last Mfg.'s Sug. Retail was $1,795.

AMERICAN ARMS
Previous manufacturer located in Garden Grove, CA.

EAGLE 380 — .380 ACP only, stainless steel semi-auto, copy of Walther PPK/S, 6 shot mag., 3¼ in. barrel, 20 oz.

	$295	$250	$215				

Add $25 for black teflon finish (disc. 1985).
Last Mfg.'s Sug. Retail was $289.

AMERICAN ARMS CO.

Manufacturer located in Boston, MA from 1870-1901. 1893 to 1904 at Milwaukee, WI. Acquired by Marlin In 1901.

100%	98%	95%	90%	80%	70%	60%	50%	40%	30%	20%	10%

HANDGUNS

O/U DESIGN — Wheeler Pat. Action, brass frame, spur trigger, .22 Short R.F., .32 Short R.F., .41 Short R.F.

100%	98%	95%	90%	80%	70%	60%	50%	40%	30%	20%	10%
$800	$750	$700	$650	$575	$500	$420	$360	$300	$225	$160	$110

SHOTGUNS

HAMMERLESS MODEL — 12 ga., semi-hammerless.

100%	98%	95%	90%	80%	70%	60%	50%	40%	30%	20%	10%
$600	$550	$500	$450	$350	$275	$225	$175	$150	$125	$100	$75

WHITMORE PATENT — 10 or 12 ga., hammerless, checkering, SxS. Add 10% for 10 ga. (2⅞ in. chambers).

100%	98%	95%	90%	80%	70%	60%	50%	40%	30%	20%	10%
$685	$625	$575	$520	$460	$400	$340	$270	$200	$150	$125	$100

SINGLESHOT — 12 ga., semi-hammerless, damascus barrel.

100%	98%	95%	90%	80%	70%	60%	50%	40%	30%	20%	10%
$260	$225	$200	$175	$150	$125	$90	$70	$50	$40	$30	$20

AMERICAN ARMS, INC.

Importer/manufacturer located in North Kansas City, MO. American Arms imports various Spanish shotguns (Grulla, Indesal, Lanber, Norica, and Zabala Hermanos), Italian shotguns including F. Stefano and Luigi Franchi, several European pistols and rifles, and exclusively imports Sites handguns (new 1990) mfg. in Torino, Italy. This company also manufactures several pistols in North Kansas City, MO. American Arms previously imported (1988-89 only) Norica Airguns that may be found under the Norica heading in the Modern Airguns section in the back of this publication.

AMERICAN ARMS ALSO IMPORTS FRANCHI O/U AND SEMI-AUTO SHOTGUNS WHICH CAN BE FOUND UNDER THE FRANCHI LISTING IN THIS TEXT.

Grading	100%	98%	95%	90%	80%	70%	60%

PISTOLS

MODEL TT-9MM TOKAREV — 9mm Para., semi-auto single action, 4½ in. barrel, 9 shot mag., hammer block external safety, 31 oz. Imported 1988-89 only.

	100%	98%	95%	90%	80%	70%	60%
	$250	$230	$210	$195	$180	$170	$160

Last Mfg.'s Sug. Retail was $289.
This model is patterned after the Tokarev action and is made from machined steel parts in Yugoslavia.

MODEL EP-380 — .380 ACP, semi-auto double action, stainless steel, 3½ in. barrel, 7 shot mag., wood checkered grips, adj. rear sight, 25 oz. Imported 1988-90 only.

	100%	98%	95%	90%	80%	70%	60%
	$375	$325	$250				

This model was made in West Germany.
Last Mfg.'s Sug. Retail was $449.

MODEL PK-22 CLASSIC — .22 LR, semi-auto double action, styled after Gov't .45 ACP, 3⅓ in. barrel, 8 shot finger extension mag., black polymer grips, 22 oz. New 1988.

	100%	98%	95%	90%	80%	70%	60%
Mfg.'s Sug. Retail	$198	$170	$145	$125	$110	$100	$90	$80

This model is made in North Kansas City, MO. It has patented safety features such as external hammer block and internal blocking of the firing pin until the trigger is pulled.

American Arms, Inc., cont.

Grading	100%	98%	95%	90%	80%	70%	60%

MODEL CX-22 CLASSIC — .22 LR, style patterned after Walther PPK, 3⅓ in. barrel, 8 shot finger extension mag., 22 oz. New 1990.

Mfg.'s Sug. Retail	$198	$170	$145	$125	$110	$100	$90	$80

This model is made in North Kansas City, MO. It has patented safety features such as external hammer block and internal blocking of the firing pin until the trigger is pulled.

⚵ CXC-22 — similar to CX-22 Classic, except has chrome slide. Mfg. in 1990 only.

		$170	$150	$125	$110	$100	$90	$80

Last Mfg.'s Sug. Retail was $189.

MODEL PX-22/25 CLASSIC — .22 LR or .25 ACP (mfg. 1991 only) cal., compact variation of the Model CX-22, 2¾ in. barrel, 7 shot finger extension mag., 15 oz. New 1989, PX-25 was mfg. 1991 only.

Mfg.'s Sug. Retail	$193	$170	$145	$125	$110	$100	$90	$80

Add $10 for .25 ACP cal.

This model is made in North Kansas City, MO. It has patented safety features such as external hammer block and internal blocking of the firing pin until the trigger is pulled.

MODEL P-98 CLASSIC — .22 LR, semi-auto double action patterned after Walther P.38, 5 in. barrel, 8 shot mag., blue/black finish, grooved wrap around grips, 26 oz. New 1990.

Mfg.'s Sug. Retail	$213	$185	$165	$140	$120	$110	$100	$90

SABRE — while this model was advertised, it was never mfg.

SPECTRE — 9mm Para., .40 S&W (mfg. 1991 only), or .45 ACP (new 1993) cal., semi-auto double action, 6 in. barrel with polygonal rifling, 30 shot mag., ambidextrous safety, decocking lever, adj. sights, 4½ lbs., mfg. in Italy by Sites. New in 1990.

Mfg.'s Sug. Retail	$429	$370	$325	$275	$240	$200	$185	$170

Add $28 for .45 ACP cal.

This model was previously imported by F.I.E. located in Hialeah, FL (1989-1990).

REVOLVERS: SAA

REGULATOR MODEL — .357 Mag., .44-40, or .45 cal., 4¾, 5½ (new 1993), or 7½ in. barrel, reproduction of the Colt Peacemaker, featuring brass trigger guard and back strap, fixed sights, half-cock and hammer block safeties, blade front, grooved rear sights, color case hardened frame, walnut grips 35 oz. Importation began 1992.

Mfg.'s Sug. Retail	$305	$265	$225	$200	$185	$170	$160	$150

Add $44 for dual cylinder set (.44-40/.44 Spl. or .45 LC/.45 ACP).

⚵ Regulator Deluxe — similar to Regulator Model, except has case hardened steel trigger guard and back strap. Importation disc. 1992.

		$295	$250	$225	$200	$185	$170	$160

Add $30 for dual cylinder set (.44-40/.44 Spl. or .45 LC/.45 ACP).
Last Mfg.'s Sug. Retail was $369.

⚵ Buckhorn — .44 Mag cal., 4¾, 6, or 7½ in. barrel, otherwise similar to Regulator Model, 44 oz. Importation began 1993.

Mfg.'s Sug. Retail	$320	$275	$235	$200	$185	$170	$160	$150

RIFLES

MODEL ZCY 308 — .308 cal., gas operated semi-auto AK-47 type action, Yugoslavian mfg. Imported 1988 only.

		$775	$650	$550	$450	$400	$375	$350

Last Mfg.'s Sug. Retail was $825.

Grading	100%	98%	95%	90%	80%	70%	60%

MODEL AKY 39 — 7.62 x 39mm cal., gas operated semi-auto AK-47 type action, Teakwood fixed stock and grip, flip up Tritium night front sight and rear, Yugoslavian mfg. Imported 1988-89 only.

	$550	$495	$440	$395	$350	$300	$270

Last Mfg.'s Sug. Retail was $559. This model was supplied with sling and cleaning kit.

Model AKF 39 Folding Stock — 7.62 x 39mm cal., folding stock variation of the Model AKY-39. Imported 1988-89 only.

	$575	$500	$450	$400	$350	$300	$270

Last Mfg.'s Sug. Retail was $589.

EXP-64 SURVIVAL RIFLE — .22 LR, semi-auto, takedown rifle stores in oversize synthetic stock compartment, 21 in. barrel, 10 shot clip mag., open sights, receiver grooved for scope mounting, cross bolt safety, 40 in. overall length, 7 lbs. Imported 1989-90 only.

	$150	$135	$125	$115	$105	$95	$85

Last Mfg.'s Sug. Retail was $169.

MINI-MAX — .22 LR, semi-auto, 18¾ in. barrel, wood or black synthetic stock, 10 shot mag., adj. rear sight, 4⅓ lbs. Imported in 1990 only.

	$85	$75	$65	$55	$45	$40	$35

Add $6 for wood stock.
Last Mfg.'s Sug. Retail was $99.

SM 64 TD SPORTER — .22 LR, semi-auto, takedown barrel, 21 in. barrel, checkered walnut finished hardwood stock and forend, hooded front sight and adj. rear sight, 7 lbs. Imported 1989-90 only.

	$130	$115	$105	$95	$85	$75	$65

Last Mfg.'s Sug. Retail was $149.

SHOTGUNS: OVER AND UNDER

American Arms is currently importing Spanish shotguns manufactured by Zabala Hermanos, Lanber, and Indesal. Italian shotguns are also imported mfg. by Stefano Fausti (Models Silver, Waterfowl, and Turkey Special). American Arms imported Franchi Black Magic semi-auto and O/U shotguns will appear under the Franchi section in this text. Older Diarm models have been listed below.

LINCE — 12 or 20 ga., 3 in. chambers, boxlock with Greener crossbolt, various barrel lengths and chokings, available in either blue or shiny chrome finish, SST, VR, ejectors. Imported 1986 only.

	$510	$400	$380	$360	$340	$320	$300

Add $70 for choke tubes.
Last Mfg.'s Sug. Retail was $610.

SILVER MODEL — 12 or 20 ga. only, similar to Lince Model, except has brushed aluminum finished receiver, no engraving. Imported 1986-87 only.

	$495	$450	$390	$360	$330	$300	$285

Add $50 for multi-chokes.
Last Mfg.'s Sug. Retail was $545.

SILVER I — similar to Silver Model, except also available in 28 or .410 ga. (both new 1988), single selective trigger became standard in 1988, extractors, engraved frame, fixed chokes, recoil pad. New 1986.

Mfg.'s Sug. Retail	$549	$450	$390	$345	$300	$285	$270	$255

Add $60 for 28 or .410 ga.
Engraved frame became standard in 1987.

Grading	100%	98%	95%	90%	80%	70%	60%

SILVER II — similar to Silver Model, except is supplied with choke tubes, deluxe walnut, and ejectors. New 1987.

Mfg.'s Sug. Retail	$699	$600	$535	$465	$395	$360	$330	$300

Add $20 for 28 and .410 ga. (fixed chokes only).

Small Gauge Combo — includes 28 and .410 ga. barrels bored IC/M. New 1989.

Mfg.'s Sug. Retail	$1,199	$1,025	$895	$750	$625	$550	$495	$450

SILVER LITE — 12 or 20 ga., 2¾ in. chambers, boxlock action, 26 in. vent. barrels with VR and choke tubes, blued alloy receiver, SST, ejectors, gold trigger, checkered walnut stock and forearm, 5 lbs. 14 oz. or 6 (12 ga.) lbs., mfg. by Lanber. Imported 1990-92.

		$625	$535	$460	$400	$360	$330	$300

Last Mfg.'s Sug. Retail was $749.

SILVER SPORTING — 12 ga. only, Sporting Clay model, boxlock action, 28 or 30 (new 1993) in. ported vent. barrels with channelled broadway VR and choke tubes, nickel finished engraved receiver, SST, ejectors, figured walnut stock and forearm with handcut checkering, 7 lbs. 6 oz., mfg. by Lanber. Importation began 1990. 1993 manufacture by Pettersoli.

Mfg.'s Sug. Retail	$899	$790	$685	$575	$495	$450	$400	$360

SILVER SKEET — 12 ga. only, similar appearance to Silver Sporting, 26 or 28 (new 1993) in. ported vent. barrels with raised VR, 4 choke tubes, recoil pad, 7 lbs. 6 oz. Importation began 1992.

Mfg.'s Sug. Retail	$899	$790	$685	$575	$495	$450	$400	$360

SILVER TRAP — similar appearance to Silver Sporting, 30 in. ported barrels with raised VR, 4 choke tubes, recoil pad, trap stock dimensions, 7¾ lbs. Importation began 1992.

Mfg.'s Sug. Retail	$899	$790	$685	$575	$495	$450	$400	$360

STERLING/BRISTOL — 12 or 20 ga., 3 in. chambers, boxlock with Greener crossbolt and false side plates, various barrel lengths and choke tubes, chrome finished receiver with moderate game scene engraving, SST, VR, ejectors. Imported 1986-89.

		$695	$550	$495	$450	$400	$375	$350

Last Mfg.'s Sug. Retail was $825.
Until 1989, this model was designated the Bristol. In 1988, the engraving pattern was changed from game scene to elaborate scroll type.

SIR — 12 or 20 ga., 3 in. chambers, sidelock with Greener crossbolt, various barrel lengths and chokings, chrome finished receiver with game scene engraving, ST, VR, ejectors, deluxe checkered pistol grip stock and forearm. Imported 1986 only.

		$900	$725	$660	$610	$565	$520	$485

Add $75 for choke tubes.
Last Mfg.'s Sug. Retail was $1,090.

ROYAL — 12 or 20 ga., 3 in. chambers, sidelock with Greener crossbolt, various barrel lengths and chokings, chrome finished receiver with elaborate scroll engraving, ST, VR, ejectors, oil finished deluxe checkered pistol grip and forearm. Imported 1986-87 only.

	$1,595	$1,310	$1,080	$960	$850	$750	$675

Add $65 for choke tubes.
Last Mfg.'s Sug. Retail was $1,730

Grading	100%	98%	95%	90%	80%	70%	60%

EXCELSIOR — 12 or 20 ga., 3 in. chambers, sidelock with Greener crossbolt, various barrel lengths and chokings, chrome finished receiver with elaborate deep relief engraving and multiple gold inlays, ST, VR, ejectors, oil finished deluxe checkered pistol grip and forearm. Imported 1986-87 only.

	$1,775	$1,510	$1,250	$1,100	$975	$885	$780

Add $70 for choke tubes.
Last Mfg.'s Sug. Retail was $1,925.

O/U 12 WATERFOWL/TURKEY SPECIAL — 12 ga. only, Mag. chambers (3½ in. was added in 1989), 24 (Turkey) or 28 (Waterfowl) in. barrels with choke tubes, SST, ejectors, parkerized metal finish, matte finished stock and forearm, sling swivels, recoil pad, approx. 7 lbs. New 1987.

Mfg.'s Sug. Retail	**$719**	$615	$545	$465	$395	$360	$330	$300

⁜ **10 ga. Waterfowl** — 10 ga. Mag., double triggers, extractors, matte finishes similar to 12 ga. Waterfowl, beavertail forearm. Imported 1988-89 only.

	$750	$625	$550	$495	$450	$390	$360

Last Mfg.'s Sug. Retail was $829.

WT-O/U10 TURKEY SPECIAL — 10 ga., 3½ in. Mag., 26 in. barrels with choke tubes, SST (became standard in 1990), extractors, recoil pad, non-glare metal finish, 9 lbs. 10 oz. New 1988.

Mfg.'s Sug. Retail	**$945**	$840	$650	$540	$500	$450	$390	$360

F.S. 200 — 12 ga., trap or skeet model, 26 or 32 in. separated barrels only, SST, ejectors, boxlock with Greener crossbolt, black or chromed receiver, checkered walnut stock and forearm. Imported 1986-87 only.

	$690	$560	$500	$450	$410	$375	$350

Last Mfg.'s Sug. Retail was $835.

F.S. 300 — 12 ga., trap or skeet model, 26, 30, or 32 in. separated barrels only, SST, ejectors, boxlock with Greener crossbolt and false side plates lightly engraved, chromed receiver, checkered walnut stock and forearm. Imported 1986 only.

	$825	$675	$610	$555	$510	$470	$440

Last Mfg.'s Sug. Retail was $995.

F.S. 400 — 12 ga., trap or skeet model, 26, 30, or 32 in. separated barrels only, ST, ejectors, sidelock with Greener crossbolt, lightly engraved chromed receiver, checkered walnut stock and forearm. Imported 1986 only.

	$1,145	$945	$860	$800	$740	$680	$620

Last Mfg.'s Sug. Retail was $1,360.

F.S. 500 — same specifications as FS 400. Importation disc. 1985.

	$1,175	$950	$860	$795	$730	$660	$595

Last Mfg.'s Sug. Retail was $1,360.

SHOTGUNS: SIDE-BY-SIDE

American Arms is currently importing Spanish shotguns manufactured by Zabala Hermanos and Grulla. Older discontinued Diarm models will also be shown in this section.

GENTRY/YORK — 12, 16 (disc. 1990), 20, 28, or .410 ga., 3 in. chambers, boxlock, ejectors (extractors after 1986), double or SST (became standard in 1992), chromed receiver features fine scroll engraving, fixed chokes, pistol grip stock with recoil pad and beavertail forearm. New 1986.

Mfg.'s Sug. Retail	**$625**	$515	$425	$350	$300	$280	$260	$240

Add $30 for 28 or .410 ga.
Before 1988 this model was designated York (case coloring began 1988, silver finish began 1993). A SST is available on the 20 and 12 ga. model. DTs have been supplied with 28 or .410 ga. since 1990.

Grading	100%	98%	95%	90%	80%	70%	60%

BRITTANY — 12 or 20 ga., boxlock action, 25 (20 ga.), 26, or 27 (12 ga.) in. barrels, SST, ejectors, matted solid rib, choke tubes, engraved case colored frame, checkered walnut straight grip stock with recoil pad and semi-beavertail forearm, 6½ or 7 lbs. New 1989.

Mfg.'s Sug. Retail	$763	$640	$550	$475	$435	$400	$375	$350

The wood finish was changed in this model from oil to semi-gloss in 1991.

SHOGUN — 10 ga., 3½ in. chambers, boxlock, ejectors, double triggers, chromed receiver features fine scroll engraving. Imported 1986 only.

	$440	$350	$325	$300	$280	$260	$240

Last Mfg.'s Sug. Retail was $525.

DERBY — 12, 20, 28 (disc. 1991), or .410 (disc. 1991) ga., 3 in. chambers, sidelock, ejectors, double (disc. 1989) or SNT, chromed receiver features fine scroll engraving, fixed chokes, straight grip walnut stock and forearm. New 1986.

Mfg.'s Sug. Retail	$999	$860	$740	$625	$500	$425	$385	$350

Add 10% for 28 or .410 ga. (disc. 1991).
Subtract 10% for DT.
Add approx. 40% for 2-barrel set (20 and 28 ga.) - disc. 1990.

This model featured a case-colored receiver between 1988-90 and was changed to coin finish in late 1991. At the same time, the wood finish was changed from oil to semi-gloss.

GRULLA NO. 2 — 12, 20, 28, or .410 ga., hand fitted sidelock action, 26 or 28 in. bbls., DTs, ejectors, fixed chokes, concave rib, case color. receiver with elaborate engraving, deluxe English style straight stock and splinter forearm (checkered and hand rubbed), between 5¾ - 6¼ lbs. New 1989.

Mfg.'s Sug. Retail	$2,943	$2,500	$2,175	$1,725	$1,350	$1,050	$900	$800

This model is individually handcrafted with less than 800 mfg. each year.

Small Gauge Set — includes choice of 20/28 ga. or 28/.410 ga. barrel combination (26 in. fixed choke barrels). New 1989.

Mfg.'s Sug. Retail	$4,089	$3,525	$2,975	$2,375	$2,000	$1,650	$1,325	$1,150

WS/SS 10 WATERFOWL SPECIAL — 10 ga. only, 3½ in. chambers, 32 in. barrels, DTs, parkerized finish, sling swivels and camouflaged sling, extractors, fixed chokes, recoil pad, 11 lbs. 3 oz. New 1987.

Mfg.'s Sug. Retail	$639	$560	$500	$450	$400	$375	$350	$325

TS/SS 10/12 TURKEY SPECIAL — 10 or 12 ga., Mag. chambers (3½ in. 12 ga. introduced in 1989), 26 in. barrels only, double triggers, parkerized finish, dull finish stock and forearm, sling swivels, recoil pad, choke tubes, 7 lbs. 6 oz. or 10 lbs. 13 oz. (10 ga.). New 1987.

Mfg.'s Sug. Retail	$639	$560	$500	$440	$400	$375	$350	$325

This model in 12 ga. is supplied with a SST.

COMBINATION GUNS

RS COMBO — choice of .222 Rem. or .308 rifle barrel under 12 ga. barrel, engraved boxlock frame with antique silver finish, DTs, 24 in. VR barrels with shotgun choke tubes, rifle sights, grooved for scope mounting, Monte Carlo stock, 7 lbs. 14 oz. Imported 1989 only.

	$675	$595	$550	$495	$450	$420	$385

Last Mfg.'s Sug. Retail was $749.

SHOTGUNS: SINGLE SHOT

SINGLE SHOT MODEL — 12, 20, or .410 ga., 3 in. Mag., non-exposed hammer, pistol grip stock, non-reflective finish. Imported 1988-89 only.

	$90	$80	$70	$60	$55	$50	$45

Last Mfg.'s Sug. Retail was $99.

Grading	100%	98%	95%	90%	80%	70%	60%

Camper Special — 12, 20, or .410 ga., 3 in. Mag., folding design, 21 in. barrel, pistol grip. Imported 1988-89 only.

	100%	98%	95%	90%	80%	70%	60%
	$95	$80	$70	$60	$55	$50	$45

Last Mfg.'s Sug. Retail was $107.

Slugger — 12 or 20 ga., 24 in. Slug shotgun barrel with adj. rear sight and blade front, recoil pad. Imported 1989 only.

	100%	98%	95%	90%	80%	70%	60%
	$100	$85	$75	$65	$55	$50	$45

Last Mfg.'s Sug. Retail was $115.

Youth — 20 or .410 ga., 26 in. barrel, 12½ in. stock dimensions, recoil pad. Imported 1989 only.

	100%	98%	95%	90%	80%	70%	60%
	$100	$85	$75	$65	$55	$50	$45

Last Mfg.'s Sug. Retail was $115.

Combo — interchangeable rifle and shotgun barrels, choice of .22 Hornet/12 ga. with 28 in. barrel or .22 LR/20 ga. with 26 in. barrel, includes fitted hard case. Imported 1989 only.

	100%	98%	95%	90%	80%	70%	60%
	$195	$165	$130	$115	$100	$90	$80

Last Mfg.'s Sug. Retail was $235.

10 Ga. Model — 10 ga. only, 3½ in. chambers, 26 in. multi-choke or 32 in. full fixed choke barrel, non-exposed hammer, non-reflective finish. Imported 1988-89 only.

	100%	98%	95%	90%	80%	70%	60%
	$135	$115	$95	$80	$70	$60	$55

Add $30 for multi-chokes (26 in. barrel).
Last Mfg.'s Sug. Retail was $149.

AMERICAN BARLOCK WONDER
Manufactured by Crescent Arms for Sears Roebuck & Co.

SHOTGUNS

SIDE-BY-SIDE — various gauges, hammerless or outside hammer, damascus or steel barrels. Add 15% for steel barrels, smaller gauges.

	100%	98%	95%	90%	80%	70%	60%
	$240	$225	$200	$175	$140	$100	$75

SINGLE SHOT — various gauges, hammer, steel barrel. Add 35% for smaller gauges.

	100%	98%	95%	90%	80%	70%	60%
	$125	$115	$100	$90	$75	$60	$50

AMERICAN DERRINGER CORPORATION
Manufacturer located in Waco, TX 1980-present. Distributor and dealer sales.

DERRINGERS: STAINLESS STEEL

MODEL 1 — available in over 55 cals. including .22 LR through .45-70, also 2½ in. .410 shot shell, O/U stainless steel derringer, 3 in. barrels, automatic barrel selection, "hammer block" type safety, 15 oz., spur trigger, rosewood grips. New 1980.

Regular Cal.'s — most cals. between .22 LR and .38 Spl.

Mfg.'s Sug. Retail	$215		$180	$160	$130		

Add approx. $165 for .22 Hornet (disc. 1989), .223 Rem., or .30-30 cal.

Larger Cal.'s — typically .41 cal. and larger.

Mfg.'s Sug. Retail	$320		$270	$220	$180		

Subtract approx. $75 for .357 Mag. or .45 ACP cal.
Add approx. $65 for .41 - .45 Mag. cals.
This model can be ordered with special ser. no.'s and other custom features at additional cost(s).

American Derringer Corp., cont.

Grading	100%	98%	95%	90%	80%	70%	60%

⚞ **Model 1 Engraved** — limited mfg., mostly special ordered.
   Mfg.'s Sug. Retail $855 · $725 · $600 · $495

LADY DERRINGER — .32 Mag. or .38 Spl. standard cals., also available in .22 LR, .22 Mag., .357 Mag., .380 ACP, 9mm Para., .45 ACP, or .45 LC/.410 shotshell cal. at a small premium, high polished finish with synthetic ivory grips, handfitted action allowing easy cocking, cased in French styled jewelry box. New 1990.

⚞ **Standard Grade** — standard model as described above, 1990 mfg. only.
   $215 $185 $160
   Last Mfg.'s Sug. Retail was $250.

⚞ **Deluxe Grade** — similar to Standard Grade, except synthetic grips are scrimshawed in a cameo or rose design, choice of walnut case or French jewelry box.
   Mfg.'s Sug. Retail $235 · $205 · $180 · $160

⚞ **Deluxe Engraved** — similar to Deluxe Grade, except hand engraved with circa 1880 patterns.
   Mfg.'s Sug. Retail $750 · $650 · $515 · $400
   Mother-of-pearl grips and personalized engraving are available as extra cost options on this model.

⚞ **14 KT. Gold Engraved** — entire Derringer manufactured out of a 14 KT. gold bar (contains approx. 20 oz. of 14 KT. gold and 3 oz. of stainless steel), custom engraved with diamond sights, special order only.
   Mfg.'s Sug. Retail $110,000 · $110,000 $70,000 $49,500

MODEL 1 TEXAS COMMEMORATIVE — .38 Spl., .44-40, or .45 LC cal., similar to Model 1 except has brass frame, stainless steel barrel, and stag grips. 500 mfg. in each cal. starting in 1986.

Grading	100%	Issue Price	Qty. Made
.44-40 cal. (current mfg.)	$280	$320	500
.45 cal. (current mfg.)	$285	$320	500
.32 Mag. (disc.)	$185	$200	500
.38 Spl. (current mfg.)	$185	$215	500
.22 LR (mfg. 1991-92)	$200	$238	500
.41 Rimfire (not shootable)	$235	$295	500
Fully engraved model	$875	$875	limited

125TH ANNIVERSARY — special edition 125th anniversary variation with pistol case.

	100%	Issue Price	Qty. Made
.44-40 or .45 cal. (current mfg.)	$285	$320	500
.38 Spl. (current mfg.)	$185	$215	500
Deluxe engraved model	$650	$750	limited

Grading	100%	98%	95%	90%	80%	70%	60%

MODEL 3 — .32 Mag. (new 1990 - limited availability) or .38 Spl. cal., single shot, 2½ in. barrel, 8½ oz., spur trigger, rosewood grips.
   Mfg.'s Sug. Retail $120 · $95 · $70 · $55

MODEL 4 — .357 Mag., .357 Max., .44 Mag., .45 ACP, or .45 LC cal on upper barrel, 3 in. .410 shot shell lower barrel, O/U derringer combination pistol, $4^1/_{10}$ in. barrel, rosewood grips, $16^1/_2$ oz. New 1985.

Mfg.'s Sug. Retail	$352	$310	$250	$210

Add $30 for oversized grips.
Add $70 for .44 Mag. cal.
Add $143 for .45-70 cal. in both barrels.
Add $17 for .357 Mag., .357 Max., or .45 ACP cal.
This model is also available on special order in either .50-70 or .50 Saunders cal. (new 1989 - single shot only). Retail is $395.

⅜ **Alaskan Survival Model** — similar to Model 4, except choice of .45-70 or .44 Mag. cal. upper or lower barrel.

Mfg.'s Sug. Retail	$388	$340	$295	$260

MODEL 6 — .45 Colt/.410 ga. O/U, 6 in. barrel, 21 oz. Available in high polish, satin, or gray matte finish (standard). New 1986.

Mfg.'s Sug. Retail	$350	$295	$260	$220

Add $13 for satin finish.
Add $38 for high polish finish.
Add $35 for oversized grips.

MODEL 7 — .22 LR, .22 Mag. (new 1992), .32 Mag., .38 Spl., .38 S&W (disc. 1989), .380 ACP, or .44 Spl. cal., O/U, same basic specifications as Model 1, except ultra lightweight ($7^1/_2$ oz.).

Mfg.'s Sug. Retail	$200	$165	$140	$115

Add $15 for .22 Mag. cal.

⅜ **.44 Special Cal.** — .44 Spl. cal. only.

Mfg.'s Sug. Retail	$500	$445	$410	$350

MODEL 10 — .45 ACP or .45 LC, O/U, 3 in. barrels, aluminum frame, matte finish, 10 oz. New 1988.

Mfg.'s Sug. Retail	$250	$215	$175	$145

Add $70 for .45 LC cal.

MODEL 11 — .38 Spl. only, same basic specifications as Model 1, matte gray finish, only 11 oz.

Mfg.'s Sug. Retail	$205	$170	$145	$125

HIGH STANDARD DOUBLE ACTION — .22 LR or .22 Mag. cal., $3^1/_2$ in. O/U barrels, double action trigger, dual extraction, hammerless, blue finish with black synthetic grips, 11 oz. New 1990.

Mfg.'s Sug. Retail	$170	$145	$115	$95

This O/U Derringer duplicates the original High Standard design.

DA 38 DOUBLE ACTION — .357 Mag. (new 1991), .38 Spl., 9mm Para., or .40 S&W (new 1993) cal., 3 in. O/U barrels, satin stainless steel with aluminum grip frame, double action trigger design, hammerblock thumb safety, choice of checkered rosewood, walnut, or other hardwood grips, 14.5 oz. New 1990.

Mfg.'s Sug. Retail	$244	$205	$170	$145

Add $31 for 9mm Para. cal.
Add $6 for .38 Spl. cal.
Add $56 for .40 S&W cal.
Add $20 for Lady Derringer Model (scrimshawed synthetic ivory grips, .38 Spl. only. New 1992.)

Grading	100%	98%	95%	90%	80%	70%	60%

MINI-COP — .22 Mag. cal., 4 shot double action design, stainless steel construction, patterned after the original Mini-Cop mfg. in Torrance, CA. New 1990.

Mfg.'s Sug. Retail	$313	$250	$220	$185			

COP STAINLESS — .357 Mag. cal., double action, similar design to Mini-Cop. New 1991.

Mfg.'s Sug. Retail	$375	$315	$265	$200			

CUSTOM TARGET MODELS — .38 Spl. Wadcutter or 9mm Federal (disc.) cal., mfg. for End of Trail Derringer Match, limited production. Mfg. 1990-92.

		$695	$575	$475			

Last Mfg.'s Sug. Retail was $750.

PISTOLS: PEN DESIGN

MODEL 2 PEN PISTOL — .22 LR, .25 ACP, or .32 ACP cal., unique hinged action allows pen to be converted into a legal pistol within two seconds, folding design, 2 in. barrel, cocks on opening action, firing pin block grip safety, brushed stainless finish, 5 oz. New 1993.

Mfg.'s Sug. Retail	$180		$145	$120	$100		

Add $8 for .32 ACP cal.

PISTOLS: SEMI-AUTO

STANDARD MODEL

.25 Mag. Cal. — .25 Mag., semi-auto single action, less than 100 manufactured in stainless steel only.

		$500	$400	$300			

.25 ACP Cal. — .25 ACP, semi-auto single action, less than 400 manufactured in stainless steel, less than 50 in blued steel.

Stainless		$400	$300	$250			
Blue		$550	$400	$325			

LM-4 — see separate listing under Semmerling.

AMERICAN FIREARMS MANUFACTURING COMPANY, INC.
Previous manufacturer located in San Antonio, TX between 1972-1974.

AMERICAN .25 AUTOMATIC — .25 auto, 8 shot, $2\frac{1}{10}$ in. barrel, smooth walnut grips, mfg. 1966-74.

Stainless		$195	$180	$165			
Blue		$165	$150	$140	$120	$100	$90	$85

AMERICAN .38 SPL. — .38 Spl., O/U configuration, approx. 3,000-4,000 mfg. between 1972-74.

		$200	$165	$135			

AMERICAN .380 AUTOMATIC — .380 auto, 8 shot, $3\frac{1}{2}$ in. barrel, stainless steel, smooth walnut grips. Mfg. 1972-1974.

		$700	$500	$300			

This model is extremely rare — only 10 were manufactured. Prices hard to evaluate.

Grading	100%	98%	95%	90%	80%	70%	60%

AMERICAN GUN CO.

Manufactured by Crescent Firearms Co. distributed by H. & D. Folsom Co.

HANDGUNS

REVOLVER — .32 S&W, 5 shot, double action, top break-open action.

	100%	98%	95%	90%	80%	70%	60%
	$175	$160	$140	$120	$95	$65	$50

SHOTGUNS

SxS — various gauges, hammer or hammerless, damascus or steel barrels.

	100%	98%	95%	90%	80%	70%	60%
	$240	$225	$200	$175	$140	$100	$75

Add 15% for small gauges or steel barrels.

AMERICAN HISTORICAL FOUNDATION, THE

A private organization which privately commissions historical commemoratives in conjunction with leading manufacturers and craftsmen around the world. The AHF is located in Richmond, VA. Direct retail sales only.

AHF limited edition models are not necessarily all manufactured at one time. Rather, guns are fabricated as demand dictates.

COMMEMORATIVE ISSUES

Values listed below reflect AHF's original issue prices and the last published retail price. No other values are listed since AHF limited edition firearms do not appear that frequently in the secondary marketplace. This is because the AHF has always sold to consumers directly, without involving normal gun dealers and distributors. Most AHF members are veterans, who keep these items as family collectibles and usually do not resell them. Because of this consumer direct sales program, many gun dealers do not have a working knowledge about what AHF firearms are currently selling for. The publisher suggests that those people owning AHF Commemorative Issue firearms contact the AHF (See Trademark Index) for current information, including prices as they are involved in this marketplace daily.

PISTOLS

Values listed below do not include original display cases (typically priced between $85 and $180).

Grading	Most Recent Issue Price

ARMED FORCES MODEL 1911A1 SERIES — .45 ACP cal., consists of four Model 1911A1s (one for each U.S. armed service branch), custom designed artwork with selective etchings, grips are finished in different woods and medallions, 1,911 mfg. for each branch by Auto Ordnance Corp. Original issue price was $995.

$1,095

AIRBORNE JUBILEE MODEL 1911A1 — .45 ACP cal., high polished bluing with etched commemorative inscriptions, 24 Kt. gold plated selected parts, 500 mfg. by Auto Ordnance Corp. Original issue price was $995.

$1,095

D-DAY COMMEM. M1911A1 — .45 ACP cal., serial numbered DDAY 0001 - DDAY 1,000. Introduced 1989. Original issue price was $995.

$1,095

VIETNAM WAR LIMITED EDITION M1911A1 — .45 ACP cal., ser. numbered VN001-VN2500. Issued in 1990.

$1,095

Grading	Most Recent Issue Price

40TH ANNIVERSARY COMMEM. RUGER MARK II — .22 LR cal., ser. numbered 40th 1-40th 950. Issued 1990. Original issue price was $995.
$1,095

ARMED FORCES RUGER — .22 LR, Ruger Gov.'t Model, bulled barrel variation of the Ruger MK II, available in Army, Navy, Marine, and Air Force variations, high polish blue finish with 24 Kt. gold foliate motif covering barrel and receiver, various gold plated small parts, cloisonne medallion in wooden grips, 250 mfg. for each service branch.
$1,095

ALLIED VICTORY BROWNING HI-POWER — 9mm cal., 24 Kt. highlights, 500 mfg.
$1,795

ETO LUGER COLLECTORS EDITION — 9mm cal., original WWII P.08 with gold high-lights, 750 mfg.
$1,795

⊰ **ETO Luger Deluxe Edition** — 10 mfg.
$3,995

FIVE-STAR GENERAL SERIES — .45 ACP, Auto-Ordnance M15. Ongoing series, first of series features Gen. Eisenhower, second depicts Gen. MacArthur, 500 of each mfg.
$1,295

S & W TACTICAL COMPETITION — .40 S&W cal., 40 mfg. of Collector's Edition, 10 mfg. of Deluxe Edition. All are match grade.

Collector's Edition	**$2,795**
Deluxe Edition	**$3,795**

The Deluxe Edition is sold out.

UZI PISTOL — 9mm Para., 100 mfg. by IMI in Israel.
$2,495

This edition is sold out.

WWII COLT .45 SERIES — .45 ACP cal., 12 variations commemorating the major campaigns of WWII, each variation is limited to 250 mfg.
$995

This price includes display case.

REVOLVERS

Values listed below do not include original display cases (typically priced between $179 and $395).

TEXAS PATERSON — .36 cal., limited edition of 950, mfg. by D. Pedersoli of Italy. Original issue price was $1,495. 1st issue of the Single Colt Gold Tribute Collection.
$2,195

1847 MODEL WALKER — .44 cal., limited edition of 950, mfg. by A. Uberti, located in Italy. Original issue price was $1,895. 2nd issue of the Single Colt Gold Tribute Collection.
$2,195

CIVIL WAR COLT DRAGOONS — .44 cal., available as either Union (hand engraved and 24 Kt. gold plating) or Confederate Model (hand engraved and silver plated). 125 mfg. of each, entire edition is sold out. Original issue price was $2,495.
$2,495

American Historical Foundation, cont.

JEFFERSON DAVIS MODEL 1851 NAVY — .36 cal., patterned after the Colt 1851 Navy presented to J. Davis in 1858, limited edition of 250, mfg. by A. Uberti.

$2,995

WILD BILL HICKOCK MODEL 1851 NAVY — .36 cal., features reproduction of Wild Bill Hickock motifs, limited edition of 500, mfg. by A. Uberti.

$1,995

COL. J. S. MOSBY MODEL 1860 ARMY — .44 cal., limited edition of 150, mfg. by Colt Firearms, entire edition is sold out. Original issue price was $2,495.

$2,495

J.E.B. STUART LEMAT — .44 cal., 9 shot, includes single shot .65 cal. shotgun barrel, limited edition of 500, mfg. by Navy Arms beginning 1987. Original issue price was $2,195.

$2,695

200TH CONSTITUTION COMMEMORATIVE REVOLVER — .44 Mag., Dan Wesson manufactured revolver, Collector's edition serial numbered CC001-CC950 (950 mfg.), Deluxe edition serial numbered CD001-CD500 (500 mfg.), 4 lbs. Released 1987. Original issue price for Collector's Edition was $995 (sold out), Deluxe Museum Edition was $1,595 (sold out).

Collector's Edition   **$1,295**
Deluxe Museum Edition   **$1,595**

2ND AMENDMENT COMMEM. REVOLVER — .44 Mag., 10 in. barrel, mfg. by Dan Wesson to AHF specifications, 2 different models, walnut grips with medallions. Released 1989.

Collector's Edition — 1,500 mfg., serial numbered 2AC0001 - 2AC1500. Original issue price was $1,295.

$1,695

Deluxe Museum Edition — 750 mfg., serial numbered 2AD001 - 2AD750. Original issue price was $1,595.

$1,895

AMERICAN DEER HUNTER COMMEMORATIVE — .44 Mag., mfg. by Dan Wesson, 10 in. barrel, 4 lbs. Issued 1990.

Sportsman's Edition — field grade version, 750 mfg., serial numbered 001S-750S with "DEER" prefix. Original issue price was $995.

$1,095

This variation is also available in a bear, moose, elk, or sheep edition.

Deluxe Trophy Edition — 250 mfg. serial numbered 001T-250T with "DEER" prefix.

$1,995

This variation is also available in a bear, moose, elk, or sheep edition.

GENERAL PATTON SAA — .45 LC, 5½ in. barrel, 2500 mfg. in limited edition beginning 1988, serial numbered P0001-P2500. Mfg. by A. Uberti in Italy. The entire edition is sold out. Original issue price was $1,495.

$1,895

TEDDY ROOSEVELT SAA — .44-40 cal., reproduction of Teddy Roosevelt's famous Colt engraved SAA, 750 mfg. by A. Uberti.

$1,995

Grading	Most Recent Issue Price

OLD WEST SHERRIF'S MODEL COLT — .45 LC Colt SAA, limited edition of 10, mfg. by AHF Custom Shop. Price includes display case.
$10,995

WWII BRITISH COMMANDO ENFIELD — .38 Enfield No. 2 Mark I revolver, 250 mfg.
$995
This price includes display case and Commando Knife mfg. by H.G. Long & Co.

RIFLES AND CARBINES

Values listed below do not include original display cases (typically priced between $249 and $499).

50 STATES HENRY — .44-40 cal., Uberti mfg. Henry repeating rifle, 100 mfg. by AHF Custom Shop, with two commemorating each state, sets are marked with state's outline and motto.
$11,995

1885 DEER HUNTER — .45-70 cal., Browning mfg., grayed receiver, 100 mfg. in Collector's edition, 10 mfg. in Deluxe edition, which has extensive gold inlay on blued finish.
Collector's Edition   **$2,975**
Deluxe Edition   **$5,995**

MODEL 1861 SPRINGFIELD MUSKET — .58 cal., issued to commemorate 125th anniversary of the Civil War, 125 mfg. by Ezechiele and Rino Chiappa.
$3,495

CONSTITUTION COMMEMORATIVE HENRY — .44-40 cal., patterned after the famous Henry rifle, brass frame, hand engraved with 24 Kt. gold plating, 200 mfg. by A. Uberti. Entire edition is sold out.
$2,395

CIVIL WAR COMMEMORATIVE HENRY — similar to Constitution Commemorative Henry, choice of either Abraham Lincoln (hand engraved brass frame with gold plating and blued barrel) or Jefferson Davis (hand engraved brass frame with silver plating and brown barrel), 250 of each model mfg. by A. Uberti. Original issue price was $3,495.
$3,995

WINCHESTER MODEL 94 — .30-30 cal., issued to commemorate the closing of the American West, mfg. by Winchester.

Collector's Edition — 750 mfg. Original issue price was $1,795.
$1,895

Deluxe Museum Edition — 250 mfg. Original issue price was $2,495.
$2,895

WWII M1 GARAND RIFLE — .30-06 cal., mfg. from original WWII Garands, serial numbered WW0001-WW2500, 9½ lbs. Original issue price was $1,695.
$1,895

AIRBORNE GOLDEN JUBILEE M1A1 CARBINE — .30 carbine, mfg. from original circa WWII carbines with folding stock, 500 unit limited edition.
$1,295

AIRBORNE GOLDEN JUBILEE THOMPSON — .45 ACP, issued to commemorate 50th anniversary of the Airborne, special commemorative etchings and medallions, 500 mfg. by Auto Ordnance Corp.
$1,995

Grading	Most Recent Issue Price

KOREAN WAR THOMPSON RIFLE — .45 ACP, semi-auto (also fully auto with class III license) reproduction of the famous military Thompson sub-machine gun, mfg. by Auto-Ordnance Corp., 2,000 mfg. 1984 serial numbered KW0001-KW3000. This edition is sold out.
$995

⚜ **Thompson Engraved Model** — similar to above, except has full engraving coverage. 25 available within the edition limit. This edition is sold out.
$4,995

ARMED FORCES SEMI-AUTO THOMPSON — .45 ACP, semi-auto reproduction of the Thompson sub-machine gun, four models commemorating the four U.S. service branches (Air Force, Army, Marine Corps. and Navy), 750 manufactured for each U.S. service branch. Original issue price was $1,895.
$1,995

VIETNAM M14 RIFLE — .308 cal., manufactured by Federal Ordnance, mfg. limited to 500 of each edition. Released 1987. Original issue price for Collector's Edition was $2,195, Deluxe Edition was $2,495.

Collectors Edition	$2,495
Deluxe Museum Edition	$2,895

M16 VIETNAM WAR COMMEMORATIVE — .223 cal., semi-auto version of the M16, includes hand engraving, 24 Kt. gold plated small parts and stock medallions, 1,500 mfg. by B.F.I., serial numbered VN0001-VN1000. This edition is sold out.
$1,995

ARMED FORCES M16's — four models commemorating the four U.S. service branches (Air Force, Army, Marine Corps., and Navy), hand engraved, 24 Kt. gold plated small parts, medallions in stock, bipod included, 100 mfg. for each branch. This set is now sold out.
$2,995

M16 AIRBORNE — .223 cal., carbine variation, 950 mfg. by B.F.I. Original issue price was $2,495.
$2,795

AMERICAN ARMED FORCES UZI — 9mm, semi-auto, carbine variation, 1,500 were ordered in 1988, but approx. 400 were delivered by IMI, serial numbered UZI001 - UZI1,500, mfg. by I.M.I., includes fixed (serialized approx. UZI-001 through UZI-950) wooden stock. This model is sold out.
$2,195
A large portion of this variation was returned to Action Arms, who in turn sold them to R.S.R. Wholesalers.

SPECIAL FORCES MAC-10 — .45 ACP, issued to commemorate 25th anniversary of the MAC-10, semi-auto, special etching and engraving, 1,500 mfg. by Military Armament Corporation. Original issue price was $1,195.
$1,595

LAW ENFORCEMENT THOMPSON — .45 ACP, available in a policeman and sheriff model, 1,500 of each mfg. by Auto Ordnance Corp. Original issue price was $1,595.
$1,795

ETO/PTO THOMPSON — .45 ACP cal., 24 Kt. plated small parts, includes Cutts compensator, 500 mfg. of each theater of operation.
$1,595

Grading	Most Recent Issue Price

WWII '03 SPRINGFIELD — .30-06 cal., 500 mfg. Original issue price was $1,495.

$1,695

SHOTGUNS

Values listed below include original display cases.

FEDERAL DUCK STAMP BROWNING EDITIONS (SUPERPOSED AND A-5) — 12 ga., 3 different grades include Citori (Japanese - 200 mfg.), B-125 (Belgium - 100 mfg.), and B-25 (Belgium - 50 mfg.), features multiple 24 Kt. gold inlays, special custom order only, 250 mfg. of A-5 Mag.

Citori	$5,495
B-125 (12 or 20 ga.)	$10,495
B-25 (12 or 20 ga.)	$14,995
A-5	$2,495

Original issue prices were (Citori) $4,995, (B-125) $9,995, and (B-25) $14,500.

FRENCH REVOLUTION SHOTGUN — hand engraved, signed by Cesare Giovanelli, left side of receiver depicts the storming of Bastille, right side shows the March on Versailles, 200 mfg. by Renato Gamba.

$10,995

VIETNAM WAR COMBAT SHOTGUN — 12 ga., hand engraved receiver with 24 Kt. gold plated small parts, serial numbered VN001 - VN750, 750 mfg. 1988 by Savage Industries, this edition is entirely sold out.

$1,595

Add $249 for optional case.

AMERICAN INDUSTRIES
Please refer to the Calico section in this text.

AMERICAN INTERNATIONAL
Austria.

Grading	100%	98%	95%	90%	80%	70%	60%
AMERICAN 180 AUTO CARBINE — a specialized .22 LR, designed for para military use, 177 round drum mag., 16½ in. barrel, aperture sight, high impact plastic stock.	$660	$550	$440	$360	$330	$305	$275

Add $550 for Laser Lok System.
Add $125 for Extra Drum Mag. and Winder.
Note: This gun was available in a selective fire version for law enforcement only. The gun also was available with a laser assisted sighting system which, when affixed to the weapon, projects a beam to point of impact.

ANCIENS ETABLISSEMENTS PIEPER
Please refer to the Bayard section in this text for Bayard Models 1908, 1923, and 1930. In addition, Bergmann-Bayard Models 1908 and 1910 mfg. in Gaggenau, Germany will appear under the Bergman heading.

ANSCHUTZ
Manufacturer located in Ulm, Germany. Imported and distributed exclusively in the U.S. by Precision Sales International Inc., located in Westfield, MA. Dealer direct sales only.

Grading	100%	98%	95%	90%	80%	70%	60%

PISTOLS

EXEMPLAR — .22 LR, bolt action, Match 64 left-hand action (for right-hand shooters), 10 in. barrel, 5 shot mag., two stage trigger, adj. rear sight, receiver grooved for scope, contoured grip and forestock are stippled, 3⅓ lbs., also available for left-hand shooters. New 1987.

Mfg.'s Sug. Retail	$500	$410	$350	$285	$250	$225	$200	$180

Exemplar Magnum — while advertised in 1987, the .22 Mag. was never manufactured.

Exemplar XIV — .22 LR, similar to Exemplar, except has 14 in. barrel, 4.15 lbs. New 1988.

Mfg.'s Sug. Retail	$522	$445	$370	$300	$250	$225	$200	$180

Exemplar Hornet — .22 Hornet cal., 5 shot mag., Match 54 left hand-action, 10 in. barrel, no sights - tapped and grooved, 4.35 lbs. New 1988.

Mfg.'s Sug. Retail	$822	$745	$650	$575	$525	$475	$415	$365

RIFLES: BOLT ACTION, DISC.

In the early 1960's, Anschutz rifles were imported directly by Sile Distributors located in New York. Savage imported Anschutz rifles were available from 1963-1981. While some of those models might not be listed below, refer to models of similar caliber and quality that are listed to ascertain values.

During the period when Savage was importing Anschutz rifles, certain models in the Anschutz line were designated "Savage-Anschutz" for sales by Savage in the U.S. Conversely, certain models manufactured by Savage were designated "Anschutz-Savage" for sale by Anschutz in Europe. Some of these models did not have any modifications but others were restocked, supplied with different sights, and had other different features from their original counterparts. In most cases, the original model numbers were used. Some "Anschutz-Savage" rifles have made their way into the U.S. While somewhat rare, these rifles are typically based on the Savage Model 110 action. They are not as desirable as those "Savage-Anschutz" marked rifles utilizing the superior Anschutz action. Anschutz also manufactured between 1,000-2,000 rifles utilizing SAKO actions in .222 Rem. cal. in the late 50's-early 60's. These guns will approximate values shown on the discontinued centerfire models listed below.

MARK 10 TARGET RIFLE — .22 LR cal., single shot, 26 in. heavy barrel, adj. sights, globe front, target stock with full pistol grip, adj. palm stop, mfg. 1963-1981.

	$350	$320	$290	$260	$230	$210	$195

MODEL 1407 — .22 LR cal. "I.S.U." model, heavy barrel, no sights, disc.

	$375	$340	$300	$260	$230	$210	$195

MODEL 1408 — .22 LR cal., heavy barrel, no sights. Disc.

	$375	$340	$300	$260	$230	$210	$195

Add $150 for 1408 ED Model.

MODEL 1411 — .22 LR cal., prone position target model, heavy barrel, no sights. Disc.

	$360	$320	$290	$260	$230	$210	$195

MODEL 1413 MATCH — .22 LR cal., adj. cheek piece, heavy target barrel with no sights, competition model. Disc.

	$550	$475	$420	$375	$325	$285	$240

MODEL 1418 MANNLICHER — .22 LR cal., hunting model, fine checkering, clip mag.

	$650	$575	$500	$450	$365	$315	$275

MODEL 1418/19 — .22 LR cal., sporter variation, previous importation by Savage Arms.

	$300	$260	$225	$200	$175	$150	$125

Grading	100%	98%	95%	90%	80%	70%	60%

MODEL 1450 — .22 LR cal., Sporter, 5 shot mag.

	100%	98%	95%	90%	80%	70%	60%
	$275	$225	$200	$175	$150	$125	$110

MODEL 1518 MANNLICHER — deluxe model of Model 1418.

	$700	$595	$540	$485	$430	$375	$325

MODEL 1574 SPORTER — .22 Mag., .222 Rem., .22-250 Rem., .223 Rem., .243 Win., or .308 Win. cal., mfg. by Krico (Kreigeskorte) located at Stuttgart and distributed by Anschutz, approx. 1,000 imported during 1970-73.

	$795	$695	$595	$540	$485	$430	$375

MODEL 153 — .222 Rem., 24 in. barrel, folding leaf rear sight, French walnut stock, rosewood forend tip and pistol grip cap. Mfg. 1963-1981.

	$550	$475	$400	$375	$350	$300	$280

MODEL 153-S — similar to Model 153, .222 Rem., 24 in. barrel, double set triggers.

	$600	$525	$450	$425	$385	$330	$305

MODEL 184 — .22 LR, 21½ in. barrel, Monte Carlo combination, checkered pistol grip, Schnabel forend, folding leaf sight. Mfg. 1963-1981.

	$350	$320	$290	$260	$230	$210	$195

MODEL 54 SPORTER — .22 LR, 5 shot clip, 24 in. round tapered barrel, Monte Carlo roll over combination, folding leaf sight, checkered pistol grip. Mfg. 1963-1981.

	$675	$595	$525	$450	$400	$360	$330

MODEL 54M — similar to Sporter, except .22 Win. Mag.

	$725	$625	$550	$475	$425	$395	$350

MODEL 141 — .22 LR, 5 shot clip, 23 in. round tapered barrel, Monte Carlo stock, folding leaf sight. Disc.

	$345	$280	$240	$200	$180	$160	$140
Model 141M (Mag.)	$365	$300	$265	$225	$200	$180	$160

MODEL 164 — .22 LR, 5 shot clip, 23 in. round tapered barrel, Monte Carlo stock, folding leaf sight. Mfg. 1963-1981.

	$345	$280	$240	$200	$180	$160	$140

MODEL 164M — similar to 164, only .22 Win. Mag.

	$365	$300	$265	$225	$200	$180	$160

SPORTER RIFLES: RECENT MANUFACTURE

Prices below reflect the recent devaluation of the U.S. dollar against some foreign currencies. While the manufacturer's suggested retails have gone up considerably, prices for used specimens (98% or less original condition) have not increased proportionately, and in some cases, have changed very little.

THE KADETT — .22 LR, bolt action, 22 in. barrel, 5 shot clip mag., folding leaf rear sight, single stage trigger, grooved receiver, checkered hard-wood stock, 5½ lbs. Mfg. 1987 only.

	$235	$200	$180	$165	$150	$135	$120

Last Mfg.'s Sug. Retail was $265.

THE ACHIEVER — .22 LR, bolt action, 19½ in. barrel, single shot, folding leaf rear sight, two stage trigger, grooved receiver, stippled hard-wood stock with vented forearm and adj. length of pull, 5¼ lbs. New 1987.

Mfg.'s Sug. Retail	$395	$340	$280	$230	$205	$185	$165	$150

Grading	100%	98%	95%	90%	80%	70%	60%

MODEL 1449D YOUTH

— .22 LR, bolt action design, 16¼ in tapered barrel with adj. rear sight, receiver is grooved for scope mounting, 5 shot clip mag. with single shot clip adapter available, European hardwood stock, 12¼ in. trigger pull, 3½ lbs. Imported 1990-91 only.

| | | **$210** | **$185** | **$165** | **$150** | **$135** | **$120** | **$110** |

Last Mfg.'s Sug. Retail was $249.

Model Woodchucker — .22 LR, similar to Model 1449D Youth, sold exclusively by R.S.R. Wholesale.

| | | **$210** | **$185** | **$165** | **$150** | **$135** | **$120** | **$110** |

MODEL 1416D CUSTOM

— .22 LR, bolt action, 22½ in. barrel, 5 or 10 shot mag., Monte Carlo walnut stock, folding leaf sight.

| Mfg.'s Sug. Retail | **$690** | **$580** | **$475** | **$400** | **$350** | **$295** | **$240** | **$225** |

This model utilizes the Match 64 action, similar to the Anschutz Model 1403 Target.

Model 1416D Fiberglass — similar to Model 1416D Custom, except has McMillan fiberglass stock in hunter brown color and includes roll-over cheekpiece and checkered Wundhammer swell pistol grip, 5¼ lbs. Imported 1991 only.

| | | **$755** | **$650** | **$575** | **$525** | **$475** | **$415** | **$365** |

Last Mfg.'s Sug. Retail was $842.

1416DCL Classic — same specifications as 1416D Custom, except regular stock.

| Mfg.'s Sug. Retail | **$678** | **$590** | **$475** | **$400** | **$350** | **$295** | **$240** | **$225** |

Add $33 for left-hand action.

MODEL 1418D

— .22 LR, Mannlicher full stock, skipline checkering, 19¾ in. barrel, same action as Model 1416D.

| Mfg.'s Sug. Retail | **$1,053** | **$895** | **$750** | **$650** | **$550** | **$495** | **$425** | **$360** |

Add $40 for set trigger (mfg. 1985-89).

MODEL 1700D CUSTOM - .22 LR

— .22 LR, bolt action, 5 shot mag., 24 in. barrel, iron sights, heavy barrel, Monte Carlo stock with skipline checkering, 7¼ lbs.

| Mfg.'s Sug. Retail | **$1,258** | **$1,100** | **$895** | **$750** | **$650** | **$550** | **$450** | **$375** |

Add $199 for Meistergrade (select walnut and gold etched trigger guard).
This model was designated 1422D until 1989 when it was changed to the Model 1700D with some modifications. The Model 1400D Meistergrade was disc. 1987 - the last advertised retail price was $930.
This rifle employs the Anschutz Match 54 action.

1700D Graphite — similar to Model 1700D Custom, except has McMillan black graphite reinforced stock with Monte Carlo roll-over cheekpiece, includes sling and swivels, 22 in. barrel, 7¼ lbs. New 1991.

| Mfg.'s Sug. Retail | **$1,183** | **$1,050** | **$850** | **$750** | **$650** | **$550** | **$450** | **$375** |

1700D Classic — same general specifications as 1700D Custom, except smaller diameter barrel and regular stock.

| Mfg.'s Sug. Retail | **$1,228** | **$1,095** | **$860** | **$750** | **$650** | **$550** | **$450** | **$375** |

Add $199 for Meistergrade (select walnut and gold etched trigger guard).
This model was designated 1422DCL Classic until 1989 when it was changed to the Model 1700D Classic with some modifications. The Model 1422DCL Classic Meistergrade was disc. 1987 - the last advertised retail price was $875.

1700D FEATHERWEIGHT

— similar to Model 1700D Custom, except has matte black McMillan fiberglass stock configured like the Custom Model, 22 in. barrel, no sights, 6¼ lbs. New 1989.

| Mfg.'s Sug. Retail | **$1,118** | **$995** | **$850** | **$750** | **$650** | **$550** | **$450** | **$375** |

Grading	100%	98%	95%	90%	80%	70%	60%

1700D Featherweight Deluxe — similar specification to the 1700D Featherweight, except has skip-line checkered Fibergrain synthetic stock with realistic wood grain. New 1990.

Mfg.'s Sug. Retail	$1,327	$1,150	$995	$875	$775	$650	$550	$450

DIE MEISTERMACHER — .22 LR, similar action and specifications as Model 1422D Custom, limited edition of 25 guns, select wood, extra polish on metal parts, hand-lapped barrel, with numerous gold inlays including Olympic wreath. Mfg. 1985.

	$2,500	$2,000	$1,600

Last Mfg.'s Sug. Retail was $2,475. This variation sold out in late 1988.

MODEL 1700D CUSTOM - .22 HORNET — .22 Hornet, 24 in. barrel, folding leaf sight, Monte Carlo stock with skipline checkering and rosewood grip cap, 4 shot mag., 7¾ lbs. Model 1432D was disc. 1987, and the Model 1700D was introduced 1989.

Mfg.'s Sug. Retail	$1,416	$1,225	$1,050	$875	$775	$650	$550	$450

Add $199 for Meistergrade variation (select walnut).
This model was designated 1432D until 1987 and then reintroduced 1989 as the Model 1700D with some modifications. The Model 1432D Custom Meistergrade was disc. 1986 - the last advertised retail price was $770.
This model comes standard with the Anschutz Match 54 action.

Model 1700D Classic — same general specifications as 1700D Custom, except regular stock and 23½ (1432DCL) or 24 (1700D) in. barrel.

Mfg.'s Sug. Retail	$1,387	$1,195	$995	$835	$735	$615	$500	$400

Add $199 for Meistergrade variation (select walnut).
This model was designated 1432D until 1987 and then reintroduced 1989 as the Model 1700D with some modifications. This model comes standard with the Anschutz Match 54 action.
Last Mfg.'s Sug. Retail was $849 on the Model 1432DCL.

MODEL 1733D — .22 Hornet cal., Mannlicher full stock featuring skipline checkering, European walnut, and rosewood Schnabel tip. New 1993.

Mfg.'s Sug. Retail	$1,537	$1,275	$1,075	$895	$750	$650	$550	$475

MODEL 1433D — .22 Hornet, special order only, Match 54 target action, Mannlicher full stock, 4 shot mag. Set trigger new 1985 — add $15. Disc. 1986.

	$995	$840	$740	$640	$525	$425	$350

Last Mfg.'s Sug. Retail was $826.

MODEL 1516D CUSTOM — similar to Model 1416D, except .22 Mag., 4 shot mag.

Mfg.'s Sug. Retail	$716	$600	$495	$400	$350	$295	$240	$225

This model utilizes the Match 64 action, similar to the Anschutz Model 1403 Target.

1516DCL Classic — same specifications as 1516D Custom, except regular stock.

Mfg.'s Sug. Retail	$704	$595	$490	$400	$350	$295	$240	$225

MODEL 1518D — .22 Mag. otherwise similar to Model 1418D (Mannlicher stock), 4 shot mag, 5½ lbs.

Mfg.'s Sug. Retail	$1,073	$915	$750	$625	$525	$440	$375	$325

Add $40 for set trigger (disc.).

MODEL 1700D CUSTOM - .22 MAG. — .22 Mag., bolt action, 5 shot mag., 24 in. barrel, iron sights, heavy barrel, Monte Carlo stock with skipline checkering, 7¼ lbs. Importation disc. 1991.

	$1,095	$895	$750	$650	$550	$450	$375

Add $195 for Meistergrade variation (select walnut).
This model was designated 1522D until 1989 and then reintroduced as the Model 1700D with some modifications. The Model 1522D Custom Meistergrade was disc. 1985 - last advertised retail price was $678.
Last Mfg.'s Sug. Retail was $1,229 for Model 1700D.

Grading	100%	98%	95%	90%	80%	70%	60%

1700D Classic — same general specifications as 1700D Custom, except smaller diameter barrel and regular stock. Importation disc. 1991.

	100%	98%	95%	90%	80%	70%	60%
	$1,075	$875	$725	$625	$525	$425	$350

Add $195 for Meistergrade variation (select walnut).

This model was designated 1522DCL until 1989 and then reintroduced as the Model 1700D with some modifications. The Model 1522DCL Classic Meistergrade was disc. 1985 - the last advertised retail price was $660.

Last Mfg.'s Sug. Retail was $1,199 for Model 1700D Classic.

MODEL 1700D BAVARIAN — .22 LR, .22 Mag., .22 Hornet, or .222 Rem. cal., 24 in. barrel, clip mag., checkered European style stock with European Monte Carlo cheek piece and schnabel forend, 7½ lbs. New 1988.

Mfg.'s Sug. Retail	$1,258	$1,100	$895	$750	$650	$550	$450	$375

Add $158 for .22 Hornet or .222 Rem. cal.
Add $199 for Meistergrade variation (select walnut).

MODEL 1700D CUSTOM - .222 REM. — .222 Rem., otherwise similar to Model 1700D Custom.

Mfg.'s Sug. Retail	$1,416	$1,225	$1,050	$875	$775	$650	$550	$450

Add $199 for Meistergrade variation (select walnut).
Last Mfg.'s Sug. Retail was $909 on the Model 1532D.

This model was designated 1532D until 1987 and then reintroduced 1989 as the Model 1700D with some modifications. The Model 1532D MG Custom Meistergrade was disc. 1986 - the last advertised retail price was $770.

1700D Classic — similar to Model 1700D Custom, except regular stock.

Mfg.'s Sug. Retail	$1,387	$1,195	$995	$835	$735	$615	$500	$400

Add $199 for Meistergrade variation (select walnut).
This model was designated 1532DCL until 1987 and then reintroduced 1989 as the Model 1700D with some modifications.
Last Mfg.'s Sug. Retail was $849 on Model 1532DCL.

RIFLES: SINGLE SHOT SILHOUETTE

MODEL 64S RIFLE — single shot, .22 LR, 26 in. round barrel, beavertail forearm, adj. single stage trigger, aperture sights, target stock with Wundhammer grip and adj. butt plate, checkered pistol grip, mfg. 1963-1981.

	$475	$425	$375	$325	$285	$240	$220

Subtract 15% if without sights (Model 64).
This model was available in left or right hand action.

MODEL 64MS — .22 LR, single shot silhouette target model, 21¼ in. barrel, no sights, Wundhammer swell stippled pistol grip stock, adj. trigger, 8 lbs.

Mfg.'s Sug. Retail	$912	$785	$640	$525	$450	$375	$350	$285

Add $45 for left-hand action.
This variation employs the Model 1403 action.

Model 64MS - FWT — similar to Model 64MS, except single stage trigger, 6¼ lbs. Disc. 1988.

	$550	$475	$425	$350	$325	$260	$230

Last Mfg.'s Sug. Retail was $596.

MODEL 54.18MS — .22 LR, silhouette target model, 22 in. barrel, match 54 single shot action, walnut Wundhammer stock is stippled on pistol grip and entire forearm, no sights, 8 lbs. 6 oz.

Mfg.'s Sug. Retail	$1,488	$1,235	$1,050	$875	$750	$650	$550	$475

Add $106 for left-hand action.
This model employs the Super Match 54 action.

Grading	100%	98%	95%	90%	80%	70%	60%

Model 54.18MS ED — same action as Model 54.18MS, except has 19¼ in. barrel (⅞ in. diameter) with 14¼ in. extension tube, 3 removable muzzle weights. Disc. 1988.

	100%	98%	95%	90%	80%	70%	60%
	$1,075	$900	$775	$675	$575	$485	$410

Add $100 for left-hand action.
Last Mfg.'s Sug. Retail was $1,215.

MODEL 54.18MS REP — similar to Model 54.18MS, except has repeating action, 5 shot mag., thumbhole wood stock with vented forestock, 7¾ lbs. This model was introduced in 1989 with a wood stock and a retail price of $1,650. In 1990, the stock was changed to a synthetic McMillan fiberglass finished in grey.

	100%	98%	95%	90%	80%	70%	60%
Mfg.'s Sug. Retail $1,766	$1,525	$1,250	$1,000	$895	$785	$695	$595

Add 10% for wood stock (1989 mfg. only).
This model features a 54 Super Match action with clip mag.

Model 54.18MS REP Deluxe — deluxe version of the Model 54.18MS REP featuring Fiber-grain McMillan stock with advanced thumbhole design and stippled checkering. New 1990.

	100%	98%	95%	90%	80%	70%	60%
Mfg.'s Sug. Retail $2,055	$1,775	$1,475	$1,200	$1,000	$895	$785	$695

MATCH RIFLES: BOLT ACTION · RECENT PRODUCTION

MODEL 2000 MK — .22 LR, single shot match, 26 in. barrel, aperture sights, 7½ lbs. Disc. 1988.

	100%	98%	95%	90%	80%	70%	60%
	$340	$290	$250	$210	$180	$160	$145

Last Mfg.'s Sug. Retail was $400.

MODEL 1403D — .22 LR, improved Model 64S match rifle, single shot, no sights, adj. trigger, 8 lbs. 6 oz. Importation disc. in 1990.

	100%	98%	95%	90%	80%	70%	60%
	$600	$525	$450	$360	$300	$260	$225

Add $50 for left-hand action (disc. 1988).
Last Mfg.'s Sug. Retail was $700.

MODEL 1803D — .22 LR, Match 64 action, 25½ in. target barrel, single stage adj. trigger, blond finished wood with dark stippling on pistol grip and forearm, adj. cheek piece and butt plate, 8.6 lbs. New 1987.

	100%	98%	95%	90%	80%	70%	60%
Mfg.'s Sug. Retail $1,012	$850	$725	$625	$525	$430	$365	$310

Add $70 for left-hand action (disc. 1989).

MODEL 1808D RT (RUNNING TARGET) — .22 LR, single shot running target model, 32½ in. barrel, adj. stock, cheek piece, trigger, heavy beavertail forend, no sights, muzzle barrel weights, 9¼ lbs.

	100%	98%	95%	90%	80%	70%	60%
Mfg.'s Sug. Retail $1,759	$1,490	$1,225	$950	$800	$695	$580	$500

Add $50 for left-hand action (disc. 1991).
This model was previously designated the Model 1808 ED Super during 1990 and earlier mfg.

MODEL 1903D — .22 LR, similar specifications to the Model 1803D, except has new improved target stock and adj. cheekpiece made from walnut finished European hardwood, full length stippled checkering on forend and contoured pistol grip, fully adj. new style butt plate, 8.6 lbs. New 1990.

	100%	98%	95%	90%	80%	70%	60%
Mfg.'s Sug. Retail $1,070	$875	$725	$625	$525	$430	$365	$310

Add $73 for left-hand action.

MODEL 1907 ISU — .22 LR, single shot match "I.S.U." model, 26 in. barrel, prone and position shooting, removable cheek piece, adj. butt plate, hand stippled stock with ventilated forearm and blond wood finish, 11 lbs.

	100%	98%	95%	90%	80%	70%	60%
Mfg.'s Sug. Retail $1,780	$1,525	$1,250	$995	$825	$695	$580	$500

Add $108 for left-hand action.
This variation was designated Model 1807 before 1989.

Grading	100%	98%	95%	90%	80%	70%	60%

MODEL 1910 SUPER MATCH II — .22 LR, single shot, 27¼ in. barrel, diopter sights, thumbhole stock is fully adj., 12 lbs., model down from 1813 (or 1913), special order only.

Mfg.'s Sug. Retail	$2,660	$2,225	$1,825	$1,400	$1,050	$875	$725	$625

Add $153 for left-hand action.
This variation was designated as Model 1810 before 1988.

MODEL 1911 PRONE MATCH — .22 LR, single shot match prone rifle, 27¼ in. barrel, adj. cheek piece, butt plate, no sights.

Mfg.'s Sug. Retail	$2,086	$1,795	$1,475	$1,175	$1,000	$895	$785	$695

Add $113 for left-hand action.
This variation was designated Model 1811 before 1988.

MODEL 1913 SUPER MATCH — .22 LR single shot, top-of-the-line match rifle, every possible refinement, international diopter sights, 27¼ in. barrel, hand and palm rest, 13.9 lbs.

Mfg.'s Sug. Retail	$2,980	$2,550	$1,800	$1,400	$1,050	$875	$725	$625

Add $168 for left-hand action.
This variation was designated Model 1813 before 1988.

MODEL 2007 ISU STANDARD — .22 LR, ISU model featuring 19¾ in. barrel and new heavy receiver, detachable tube in front of barrel providing for different sights and counterweights, adj. cheekpiece and rubber butt plate, grooved and vented forearm, Match 54 action, 10.8 lbs. New 1992.

Mfg.'s Sug. Retail	$2,650	$2,325	$1,825	$1,400	$1,050	$875	$725	$625

Add $86 for left-hand action (new 1993).

MODEL 2013 SUPER MATCH — .22 LR, top-of-the-line international target rifle featuring 19¾ in. barrel with detachable front tube allowing for different sights and counter-weights, top grain walnut stock with adj. hand rest, palm rest, cheekpiece, and elaborate metal butt plate, Match 54 action, 12½ lbs. New 1992.

Mfg.'s Sug. Retail	$3,700	$3,275	$2,825	$2,400	$2,125	$1,895	$1,650	$1,400

Add $205 for left-hand action (new 1993).

BIATHLON RIFLES

MODEL 1450B — .22 LR bolt action, Mark 2000 action, 19½ in. barrel, European hardwood with vent. forearm and adj. butt plate, aperture sights, 5 lbs. New 1993.

Mfg.'s Sug. Retail	$765	$650	$550	$450	$375	$300	$260	$230

MODEL 1403B — .22 LR bolt action, Match 64 action, 21½ in. barrel, blonde finished European hardwood with stippled pistol grip, Biathlon design allows 4 mags. to be stored in a housing attached to the forend on right side, entry level Biathlon gun, 8½ lbs. Mfg. 1990-92.

		$850	$730	$660	$525	$450	$375	$335

Last Mfg.'s Sug. Retail was $998.

MODEL 1827B — .22 LR bolt action, biathlon rifle, carries four 5 shot mags. in stock, special biathlon features, 21½ in. barrel, limited production.

Mfg.'s Sug. Retail	$2,233	$1,895	$1,475	$1,175	$1,025	$895	$785	$695

Add $120 for left-hand action (disc. 1989).
In 1990, the stock design was changed permitting 8 mags. to be stored in two housings attached to both the stock and forend on right side.

Model 1827BT Fortner — same general specifications as Model 1827B, except has Fortner straight pull-through bolt action, 9 lbs. New 1986.

Mfg.'s Sug. Retail	$3,449	$3,075	$2,725	$2,375	$2,125	$1,895	$1,650	$1,400

Add $345 for left-hand action.
In 1990, the stock design was changed permitting 8 mags. to be stored in two housings attached to both the stock and forend on right side.

Grading	100%	98%	95%	90%	80%	70%	60%

RIFLES: SEMI-AUTO

MODEL 520/61 — .22 LR, semi-auto, 24 in. barrel, 10 shot mag., Monte Carlo stock, 6½ lbs. Disc. 1983.

	$260	$205	$185	$155	$145	$130	$120

MARK 525 SPORTER RIFLE — .22 LR, semi-auto, 24 in. barrel, 10 shot mag., adj. rear sight, Monte Carlo stock, 6½ lbs. New 1984.

Mfg.'s Sug. Retail	$528	$460	$385	$350	$295	$250	$215	$175

⚐ **Mark 525 Carbine** — similar to Mark 525 Rifle, except has 20 in. barrel. Disc. 1986.

	$385	$310	$260	$220	$195	$160	$145

ANSCHUTZ SHOTGUNS

Anschutz marked O/U shotguns that were manufactured by Miroku of Japan were distributed previously in Europe. Several grades of these shotguns were manufactured and while rarely seen in the U.S., values approximate other Miroku O/Us of similar quality and features ($650 - $1,000 assuming 95% or better condition).

APACHE
Previous importer, mfg. by Ojanguren Y Vidosa, Eibar, Spain.

HANDGUN

SEMI-AUTO — 6.35mm., clip fed.

	$190	$175	$160	$140	$120	$95	$75

ARLINGTON ORDNANCE
Importer located in Weston, CT. Distributor sales only.

M1 GARAND RIFLE — .30-06 cal., these Garands are being imported from Korea in used condition, various manufacturers, with import stamp. Importation began 1991.

No Mfg.'s Retail	$335	$295	$250	$200	$180	$160	$140

Add $35 for stock upgrade (better wood).

.30 CAL. CARBINE — .30 Carbine, 18 in. barrel, these Carbines are being imported from Korea in used condition, various manufacturers, with import stamp. Importation began 1991.

No Mfg.'s Retail	$225	$190	$170	$150	$125	$115	$100

Add $30 for stock upgrade (better wood).

ARMALITE INCORPORATED
Costa Mesa, CA.

RIFLES

AR-7 EXPLORER — semi-auto, .22 LR, 16 in. aluminum barrel with steel liner, aperture sight, gun takes down and can be stored in hollow plastic stock, gun will float, mfg. 1959-1973 by Armalite, 1974-1990 by Charter Arms, and currently mfg. by Survival Arms located in Cocoa, FL from 1990-present.

	$101	$90	$80	$75	$70	$65	$60

AR-7 CUSTOM — similar to AR-7 Explorer, only with custom walnut stock including cheek piece, pistol grip. Mfg. 1964-1970.

	$165	$140	$120	$100	$90	$80	$70

Grading	100%	98%	95%	90%	80%	70%	60%

AR-180 — .223 Rem. cal., semi-auto, gas operated, 18¼ in. barrel, folding stock. Manufactured by Armalite in Costa Mesa, CA, 1969-1972, Howa Machinery Ltd., Nagoya, Japan 1972 and 1973. Since 1976 the AR-180 has been made by Sterling Armament Co. Ltd., Dagenham, Essex, England.

⚔ **Sterling Mfg.**

| | $850 | $775 | $695 | $625 | $550 | $495 | $450 |

⚔ **Costa Mesa Mfg.**

| | $995 | $875 | $750 | $675 | $600 | $550 | $500 |

⚔ **Howa Mfg.**

| | $1,350 | $1,110 | $995 | $875 | $795 | $725 | $650 |

SHOTGUN

AR-17 — 12 ga., semi-auto, 24 in. barrel, interchangeable choke tubes, gas operated, high strength aluminum barrel and receiver, plastic stock and forearm, either gold anodized or black finish. Only 2000 mfg. between 1964-1965.

| | $575 | $460 | $420 | $360 | $310 | $260 | $220 |

ARMAMENT TECHNOLOGY CORP.
Previous manufacturer located in Las Vegas, NV between 1972-1978.

RIFLES

In addition to the models listed below, ATC also manufactured a fully auto pistol named "Firefly II".

MODEL 4 POCKET RIFLE — .22 LR, semi-auto action (supplied by Mossberg), 5 in. barrel, shortened rifle (18½ in. overall length) with cut stock, 7 shot mag., approx. 450 mfg., approx. 3 lbs.

| | $350 | $295 | $260 | $230 | $195 | $175 | $150 |

MODEL 6 — full length variation of the Model 4, Mossberg Model 453-T with ATC trademarks, approx. 12 mfg., approx. 5½ lbs.

| | $125 | $100 | $85 | $75 | $65 | $55 | $45 |

M-2 FIREFLY — 9mm Para., featured a unique gas delayed blowback action, paramilitary configuration, collapsible stock, very limited mfg., 4¾ lbs.

| | $475 | $395 | $350 | $295 | $250 | $225 | $195 |

ARMES DE CHASSE
Importer/distributor/retailer located in Chadds Ford, PA.

Armes de Chasse exclusively imports AYA shotguns from Spain and A. Francotte shotguns/rifles from Belgium.

ARMI TECNICHE OF EMILIO RIZZINI
Manufacturer located in Brescia, Italy.

This trademark has had limited importation to date and currently, there is no exclusive U.S. importer/distributor. Most Armi Tecniche of E. Rizzini O/U shotguns that have been imported recently have sold in the $475-$695 range. Please contact the factory directly (see listing in Trademark Index) for more information on this trademark or how to order directly from the manufacturer.

ARMINEX LTD.
Previous manufacturer located in Scottsdale, AZ.

Grading	100%	98%	95%	90%	80%	70%	60%

TRI-FIRE — .45 ACP, 9mm Para., and .38 Super cals., single action auto, interchangeable barrels allow caliber conversion. Available in 5, 6, or 7 (disc. 1984) in. stainless barrel lengths, no grip safety, steel frame construction, ambidextrous thumb safety (on Target and Presentation only), smooth walnut grips, 38 oz. Approx. 250 mfg. between 1981-85.

	100%	98%	95%	90%	80%	70%	60%
	$525	$475	$425	$400	$375	$350	$325

Add $50 if presentation cased.
Add approx. $130/conversion unit.
Last Mfg.'s Sug. Retail was $396.

Target Model — same specifications as Tri-Fire, except has 6 or 7 (disc. 1984) in. barrel, very limited mfg.

	100%	98%	95%	90%	80%	70%	60%
	$595	$550	$495	$450	$400	$360	$320

Last Mfg.'s Sug. Retail was $448.

ARMINIUS

Zella-Mehlis, Germany 1922-present. Currently imported by FIE Corp. in Hialeah, FL. — see the FIE section for current production models.

HANDGUNS: SINGLE SHOT

MODEL 1 — .22 LR Target, adj. sights.

	100%	98%	95%	90%	80%	70%	60%
	$275	$210	$195	$165	$155	$140	$110

MODEL 2 — similar to Model 1, except has set trigger.

	100%	98%	95%	90%	80%	70%	60%
	$340	$255	$225	$190	$170	$155	$140

HANDGUNS: REVOLVER

MODEL 3 — .25 ACP, folding trigger, hammerless.

	100%	98%	95%	90%	80%	70%	60%
	$175	$135	$125	$105	$100	$90	$80

MODEL 8 — .320 Revolver, folding trigger, hammerless.

	100%	98%	95%	90%	80%	70%	60%
	$175	$135	$125	$105	$100	$90	$80

MODEL 9 — .32 ACP.

	100%	98%	95%	90%	80%	70%	60%
	$185	$140	$130	$115	$105	$95	$85

MODEL 10 — .32 ACP, hammerless.

	100%	98%	95%	90%	80%	70%	60%
	$165	$125	$120	$100	$95	$85	$75

TARGET — .22 LR.

	100%	98%	95%	90%	80%	70%	60%
	$90	$70	$65	$55	$50	$45	$45

ARMITAGE INTERNATIONAL, LTD.

Previous manufacturer until 1990 located in Seneca, SC.

SCARAB SKORPION — 9mm Para., paramilitary design patterned after the Czech Model 61, direct blow back action, 4.63 in. barrel, matte black finish, 12 shot (standard) or 32 shot (optional) mag., 3.5 lbs. Mfg. in U.S. 1989-90 only.

	100%	98%	95%	90%	80%	70%	60%
	$375	$330	$295	$260	$240	$220	$200

Add $45 for threaded flash hider or imitation suppressor.
Only 602 Scarab Skorpions were manufactured during 1989-90.
Last Mfg.'s Sug. Retail was $400.

ARMS CORPORATION OF THE PHILIPPINES

Manufacturer located in Manila, Philippines since 1980. Imported until 1991 by Armscorp Precision Inc. located in San Mateo, CA.

In 1991, the importation of Arms Corporation of the Philippines firearms was changed to Ruko Products, Inc. located in Buffalo, NY. Barrel markings on firearms imported by Ruko Products, Inc. state "Ruko-Armscor" (see Ruko listing) instead of the older "Armscorp Precision" barrel markings. All Armscorp Precision, Inc. models were discontinued in 1991.

REVOLVERS

Many of the current models listed below will have limited availability initially because of an existing military contract which is consuming most of the hand gun production.

Grading	100%	98%	95%	90%	80%	70%	60%

MODEL M100 — .22 LR, .22 Mag., or .38 Spl., double action revolver, 6 shot, 4 in. vent. rib barrel, blued finish only, adj. sights, checkered hardwood grips, 33 oz. Imported 1985-1989.

| | $185 | $150 | $125 | $115 | $105 | $95 | $85 |

Formerly designated as M100TC or Special Edition. .22 LR and .22 Mag. cals. were disc. 1988.

MODEL 200 P (POLICE) — .38 Spl., 6 shot, double action, 4 in. half shroud barrel, fixed sights, rubber or wood grips, 26 oz. New 1990.

| | $185 | $160 | $145 | $130 | $120 | $110 | $100 |

MODEL 200 TC (THUNDER CHIEF) — .38 Spl., 6 shot, double action, 4 in. full shroud barrel, adj. rear sight, checkered wood grips, 28 oz. New 1990.

| | $210 | $185 | $160 | $145 | $130 | $120 | $110 |

RIFLES

Older Arms Corp. of the Philippines models that are duplicated by Ruko firearms have been omitted from this section. Please refer to the Ruko section of this text for information and prices on these older Arms Corp. rifles.

M1600C RIFLE — similar to Ruko M1600, except has 20 in. barrel, fiberglass stock, barrel enclosing forearm, 7½ lbs. Mfg. 1986 only.

| | $135 | $115 | $95 | $85 | $75 | $65 | $55 |

Last Mfg.'s Sug. Retail was $150.

M1600W — similar to 1600C, except has wood stock. Mfg. 1986 only.

| | $135 | $115 | $95 | $85 | $75 | $65 | $55 |

Last Mfg.'s Sug. Retail was $150.

M1800 — .22 Hornet, bolt action, 5 shot clip mag., 23 in. barrel, checkered mahogany stock with Monte Carlo cheek piece, 6½ lbs. A few samples mfg. 1986 only.

| | $165 | $145 | $125 | $110 | $100 | $90 | $85 |

Last Mfg.'s Sug. Retail was $176.

SHOTGUNS

Older Arms Corp. of the Philippines models that are duplicated by Ruko firearms have been omitted from this section. Please refer to the Ruko section of this text for information and prices on these older Arms Corp. shotguns.

MODEL M30 D — 12 ga. only, slide action, 28 or 30 in. plain barrel, 6 shot mag., all steel receiver, checkered mahogany stock and forearm, 7.3 lbs. Imported 1986-89.

| | $185 | $155 | $135 | $115 | $95 | $85 | $80 |

Grading	100%	98%	95%	90%	80%	70%	60%

MODEL M30 K (COMBAT) — 12 ga., 21 in. barrel, 7 shot mag., combat olive green butt stock and forearm, 7.4 lbs. New 1990.

	$150	$130	$105	$95	$80	$70	$60

MODEL M30 FS (FOLDING STOCK) — 12 ga., 20 in. barrel, 5 shot mag., features 3 piece matte black folding stock and grooved forearm, grooved pistol grip, 7 lbs. New 1990.

	$175	$155	$135	$115	$100	$90	$80

Last Mfg.'s Sug. Retail was $210.

ARMS RESEARCH ASSOCIATES

Previous manufacturer located in Stone Park, IL.

Arms Research Associates stopped manufacturing firearms in 1991. They do repair their older guns (on a non-warranty basis) and have an inventory of parts.

KF SYSTEM — 9mm, paramilitary design carbine, 18½ in. barrel, vent. barrel shroud, 20 or 36 shot mag., matte black finish, 7½ lbs., select fire-class III transferable only.

	$340	$295	$275	$250	$230	$210	$195

Last Mfg.'s Sug. Retail was $379.

ARMSCORP USA, INC.

Manufacturer/importer located in Baltimore, MD. Dealer direct sales only.

PISTOLS: SEMI-AUTO

HI POWER — 9mm, patterned after Browning design, 4⅔ in. barrel, military finish, 13 shot mag., synthetic checkered grips, spur hammer, 2 lbs. Imported 1989-90 only, mfg. in Argentina.

	$300	$250	$230	$215	$200	$185	$170

Add $15 for round hammer.
Add $50 for hard chrome finish w/combat grips (disc. 1989).
Last Mfg.'s Sug. Retail was $450.

Compact Detective HP — similar to Hi Power, except has 3½ in. barrel, 1.9 lbs. Mfg. 1989 only.

	$325	$275	$240	$220	$200	$185	$170

Last Mfg.'s Sug. Retail was $475.

SD-9 — 9mm Para., double action only, blowback mechanism, 3.07 in. barrel, 6 shot mag., frame is fabricated mostly of heavy gauge sheet metal stampings, chamber indicator, Israeli mfg., 1½ lbs. Imported 1989-90 only.

	$295	$250	$230	$210	$195	$180	$170

This pistol has also been manufactured by Sirkus Industries - refer to their section in this text.
Last Mfg.'s Sug. Retail was $350.

P22 — .22 LR, patterned after the Colt Woodsman, 4 or 6 in. barrel, 10 shot mag., checkered wooden grips, mfg. in Argentina. Imported 1989-90 only.

	$190	$150	$130	$115	$100	$95	$85

Last Mfg.'s Sug. Retail was $225.

RIFLES: SEMI-AUTO

M-14 RIFLE (NORINCO PARTS) — .308 cal., 20 shot mag., newly mfg. M-14 using Norinco parts, wood stock. Mfg. 1991-92 only.

	$600	$525	$475	$425	$375	$325	$275

Last Mfg.'s Sug. Retail was $688.

Grading	100%	98%	95%	90%	80%	70%	60%

M-14 RIFLE (USGI PARTS) — .308 cal., 20 shot mag., newly manufactured M-14 using original excellent condition forged G.I. parts including used fiberglass stock with rubber recoil pad. New 1986.

Mfg.'s Sug. Retail	$940	$835	$700	$600	$525	$465	$420	$375

Add $68 for G.I. buttplate.
Add $135 for new walnut stock (Model M-14RNS).

M-14 BEGINNING NATIONAL MATCH — .308 cal., mfg. from hand selected older USGI parts, except for new receiver and new USGI air gauged premium barrel, guaranteed to shoot 1¼ in. group at 100 yards. New 1993.

Mfg.'s Sug. Retail	$1,550	$1,325	$1,050	$950	$875	$795	$695	$575

M-14 NATIONAL MATCH — .308 cal., built in accordance with A.M.T.U. mil. specs., 3 different barrel weights to choose from, national match rear sight system, calibrated mag., leather sling, guaranteed 1" MOA. New 1987.

* **AMTU Model**

Mfg.'s Sug. Retail	$1,850	$1,675	$1,300	$1,050	$950	$875	$795	$700

* **M21 Match Rifle**

Mfg.'s Sug. Retail	$2,375	$2,050	$1,675	$1,200	$1,050	$900	$825	$725

T-48 FAL ISRAELI PATTERN RIFLE — .308 (7.62 NATO) cal., mfg. in the U.S. to precise original metric dimensions (parts are interchangeable with original Belgium FAL), forged receiver, hammer forged chrome lined mil.spec. 21 in. barrel (standard or heavy) with flash suppressor, adj. front sight, aperture rear sight, 10 lbs. Imported 1990-92.

$1,075	$900	$775	$625	$525	$465	$425

This model was guaranteed to shoot within 2.5 MOA with match ammunition.
Last Mfg.'s Sug. Retail was $1,244.

* **T-48 FAL L1A1 Pattern** — .308 cal., fully enclosed forend with vents, 10 lbs. Imported 1992 only.

$995	$875	$775	$625	$525	$465	$425

Add $122 for wooden handguard sporter model (limited supply).
Last Mfg.'s Sug. Retail was $1,181.

T-48 BUSH MODEL — similar to T-48 FAL, except has 18 in. barrel, 9¾ lbs. Mfg. 1990 only.

$1,100	$925	$800	$650	$525	$465	$425

Last Mfg.'s Sug. Retail was $1,250.

FRHB — .308 (7.62 NATO) cal., Israeli mfg. with heavy barrel and bipod. Imported 1990 only.

$1,725	$1,450	$1,150	$975	$875	$795	$725

Last Mfg.'s Sug. Retail was $1,895.

FAL — .308 cal., Armscorp forged receiver, 21 in. Argentinian rebuilt barrel, manufactured to military specs., supplied with one military 20 shot mag., aperture rear sight, 10 lbs. Mfg. 1987-89.

$850	$750	$600	$540	$465	$420	$375

Subtract $55 if without flash hider.
Add $75 for heavy barrel with bipod (14 lbs.).
Add $400 (last retail) for .22 LR conversion kit.
This model is guaranteed to shoot within 2.5 MOA with match ammunition.
Last Mfg.'s Sug. Retail was $875.

* **FAL Bush Model** — similar to FAL, except has 18 in. barrel with flash suppressor, 9¾ lbs. Mfg. 1989 only.

$875	$760	$625	$550	$465	$420	$375

Last Mfg.'s Sug. Retail was $900.

Armscorp USA, Inc., cont.

135

Grading	100%	98%	95%	90%	80%	70%	60%

⚔ FAL Para Model – similar to FAL Bush Model, except has metal folding stock, leaf rear sight. Mfg. 1989 only.

| | $900 | $775 | $635 | $550 | $465 | $420 | $375 |

Last Mfg.'s Sug. Retail was $930.

⚔ FAL Factory Rebuilt – factory (Argentine) rebuilt FAL without flash suppressor in excellent condition with Armscorp forged receiver, 9 lbs. 10 oz. Disc. 1989.

| | $695 | $625 | $560 | $520 | $450 | $400 | $360 |

Last Mfg.'s Sug. Retail was $675.

M36 ISRAELI SNIPER RIFLE – .308 cal., gas operated semi-auto, Bullpup configuration, 22 in. free floating barrel, Armscorp M14 receiver, 20 shot mag., includes flash suppressor and bipod, 10 lbs. Civilian offering 1989 only.

| | $2,900 | $2,500 | $2,275 | $2,050 | $1,900 | $1,775 | $1,600 |

Last Mfg.'s Sug. Retail was $3,000.

EXPERT MODEL – .22 LR, semi-auto, 20.9 in. barrel, 10 shot mag., wood stock with one-screw takedown, iron sights with grooved receiver, 5.1 lbs. New 1989.

| | $195 | $150 | $125 | $115 | $105 | $95 | $85 |

Last Mfg.'s Sug. Retail was $225.

ARMSPORT

Current importer and distributor located in Miami, FL specializing in European manufacturers. Distributor preferred but dealer direct sales also. Beginning 1993, Armsport discontinued importation of all modern firearms, and has chosen to specialize instead in air rifle and black powder importation (refer to individual headings in back of book).

COMBINATION GUNS

2781 AND 2782 – 12 ga./.222 cal., O/U turkey gun, blued receiver. Model 2782 has chrome receiver. Model 2782 was imported 1985 only. Model 2782 new 1985. Disc. 1989.

| | $650 | $550 | $495 | $440 | $395 | $350 | $300 |

Last Mfg.'s Sug. Retail on Model 2781 was $650.
Last Mfg.'s Sug. Retail on Model 2782 was $750 (disc. 1989).

2783 – similar to Model 2782, except is deluxe model with lateral rib. Imported 1986-1988.

| | $1,350 | $1,075 | $925 | $820 | $750 | $680 | $600 |

Last Mfg.'s Sug. Retail was $1,600.

2784 – same action as Model 2783, except is chambered for .243 Win. Imported 1986-1988.

| | $1,350 | $1,075 | $925 | $820 | $750 | $680 | $600 |

Last Mfg.'s Sug. Retail was $1,600.

2785 – same action as Model 2783, except is chambered for .270 Win. Imported 1986-1988.

| | $1,350 | $1,075 | $925 | $820 | $750 | $680 | $600 |

Last Mfg.'s Sug. Retail was $1,600.

2786 – 20 ga./.222 cal., O/U turkey gun, otherwise same specifications as Model 2783. Mfg. 1986 only.

| | $1,350 | $1,075 | $925 | $820 | $750 | $680 | $600 |

Last Mfg.'s Sug. Retail was $1,350.

2787 – similar to Model 2786, except is chambered for .243 Win. Mfg. 1986 only.

| | $1,350 | $1,075 | $925 | $820 | $750 | $680 | $600 |

Last Mfg.'s Sug. Retail was $1,350.

Grading	100%	98%	95%	90%	80%	70%	60%

2788 — similar to Model 2786, except is chambered for .270 Win. Mfg. 1986 only.

| | $1,350 | $1,075 | $925 | $820 | $750 | $680 | $600 |

Last Mfg.'s Sug. Retail was $1,350.

4043 — 12, 16, or 20 ga./rifle O/U combination gun, choice of caliber, select walnut, 23½ in. barrels, relief engraved. Disc. 1983.

| | $1,675 | $1,260 | $1,090 | $925 | $840 | $755 | $670 |

4651 — Tikka deluxe O/U shotgun/rifle, exposed hammers, combo. 12 ga./.222. 12 ga. is chambered for 3 in. shells. Disc. 1984.

| | $750 | $565 | $490 | $415 | $375 | $340 | $300 |

4690 — Tikka deluxe O/U shotgun/rifle, hammerless, combo 12 ga./.222. 12 ga. is chambered for 3 in. shells. Disc. 1984.

| | $1,095 | $820 | $750 | $700 | $650 | $575 | $500 |

RIFLES: BOLT-ACTION

2801 — .30-06 cal., 24 in. barrel, iron sights, checkered walnut stock and forearm. Imported 1986 only.

| | $725 | $600 | $495 | $430 | $380 | $335 | $285 |

Last Mfg.'s Sug. Retail was $895.

2802 — similar to Model 2801, except chambered for .308 cal.

| | $725 | $600 | $495 | $430 | $380 | $335 | $285 |

Last Mfg.'s Sug. Retail was $895.

2803 — similar to Model 2801, except chambered for .270 Win. cal.

| | $725 | $600 | $495 | $430 | $380 | $335 | $285 |

Last Mfg.'s Sug. Retail was $895.

2804 — similar to Model 2801, except chambered for .243 Win. cal.

| | $725 | $600 | $495 | $430 | $380 | $335 | $285 |

Last Mfg.'s Sug. Retail was $895.

2805 — similar to Model 2801, except chambered for 7mm Rem. Mag.

| | $725 | $600 | $495 | $430 | $380 | $335 | $285 |

Last Mfg.'s Sug. Retail was $895.

2806 — similar to Model 2801, except chambered for .300 Win. Mag.

| | $725 | $600 | $495 | $430 | $380 | $335 | $285 |

4601, 4603, 4605, & 4606 — Tikka deluxe, .30-06 cal., bolt action. Model 4603 is .270 Win. Model 4605 is 7mm Rem. Model 4606 is 300 Win. Mag. Disc. 1984.

| | $725 | $545 | $450 | $380 | $340 | $295 | $260 |

4602, 4604, & 4607 — Tikka deluxe .308 Win. bolt action. Model 4604 is .243 Win. Model 4607 .222 Rem. Disc. 1983.

| | $675 | $510 | $450 | $420 | $390 | $350 | $310 |

RIFLES: DOUBLE & COMBINATION

4020 — Express set O/U double rifle with ejectors plus an extra set of O/U shotgun barrels. Disc. 1986.

| | $3,850 | $3,300 | $2,860 | $2,420 | $2,200 | $1,980 | $1,760 |

Last Mfg.'s Sug. Retail was $4,400.

Grading	100%	98%	95%	90%	80%	70%	60%

4021 — same combination as Model 4020, except rifle has extractors. Disc. 1986.

$3,400 $2,910 $2,520 $2,135 $1,940 $1,745 $1,550

Last Mfg.'s Sug. Retail was $3,875.

4022 — Express O/U rifle only with ejectors, choice of calibers. Disc. 1986.

$3,450 $2,945 $2,555 $2,160 $1,965 $1,770 $1,570

Last Mfg.'s Sug. Retail was $3,925.

4023 — similar to Model 4022, except has extractors. Disc. 1986.

$2,925 $2,515 $2,180 $1,845 $1,675 $1,510 $1,340

Last Mfg.'s Sug. Retail was $3,350.

4010 — Emperor SxS, double rifle with extra set of 20 ga. barrels and forearm. Completely hand made and finished using the best materials and craftsmen, choice of caliber, leather fitted case. Disc. 1983.

$16,300 $12,225 $10,595 $8,965 $8,150 $7,335 $6,520

4011 — similar to Model 4010, except rifle only, 9.3 x 74R cal. Disc. 1984.

$12,750 $9,565 $8,290 $7,015 $6,375 $5,740 $5,100

4012 — Emperor "One-of-a-Kind" SxS rifle/shotgun set. Special engraving finishing per individual customer order, choice of gauges, calibers. Leather fitted case. Rare. Disc. 1983.

$26,000 $19,500 $16,900 $14,300 $13,000 $11,700 $10,400

4013 — similar to Model 4012, but SxS double rifle only. Disc. 1983.

$22,850 $17,140 $14,855 $12,570 $11,425 $10,285 $9,140

RIFLES: LEVER-ACTION

4500 & 4501 — .44-40 cal., deluxe copy of Winchester Model 1873 Rifle, engraved. Model 4501 is .357 Mag. Model 4500 (.44-40) disc. in 1984. Model 4501 (.357 Mag.) disc. 1986.

$1,135 $975 $845 $715 $650 $585 $520

Last Mfg.'s Sug. Retail was $1,296.

4502 & 4503 — .44-40 cal., deluxe copy of Winchester Model 1873 Carbine, engraved. Model 4503 is .357 Mag. Model 4502 (.44-40) disc. in 1984. Model 4503 (.357 Mag.) disc. 1986.

$960 $825 $715 $605 $550 $495 $440

Last Mfg.'s Sug. Retail was $1,095.

4504 — .357 Mag., standard copy of Winchester Model 1873 carbine. Disc. 1986.

$555 $470 $410 $345 $315 $285 $250

Last Mfg.'s Sug. Retail was $625.

RIFLES: SEMI-AUTO

2785 & 2786 — .22 LR cal., semi-auto, 10 shot mag. Model 2786 is military type with 15 shot mag. Imported 1985 only.

$150 $125 $100 $90 $80 $70 $60

Last Mfg.'s Sug. Retail was $170.

Grading	100%	98%	95%	90%	80%	70%	60%

SHOTGUNS: O/U

Armsport choking codes (on rear left of barrels) designate the following: *indicates full choke, ** *identifies improved modified choking,* *** *refers to modified,* **** *is improved cylinder,* ***** *indicates cylinder bore.*

The models listed below that have -3 suffixes indicate 1988 importation. *All models listed below were discontinued in 1993, unless otherwise indicated.*

2528 — 12 ga., 3 in. Mag., 28 in. barrels, single trigger with auto ejectors. Disc. 1983.

| | $595 | $450 | $390 | $330 | $300 | $270 | $240 |

2626 — 20 ga., 3 in. Mag., 26 in. barrels, single trigger with auto ejectors. Disc. 1983.

| | $595 | $450 | $390 | $330 | $300 | $270 | $240 |

2697 & 2698 — 10 ga., 3½ in. Mag., similar to Models 2699 & 2700 except have 3 screw-in choke tubes, Model 2698 has 32 in barrels. New 1989.

| | $1,100 | $850 | $675 | $575 | $520 | $495 | $475 |

Last Mfg.'s Sug. Retail was $1,299.

2699/2700C & 2700 — 10 ga., 3½ in. Mag., 27 (2699 - new 1989), 28 (2700C), or 32 (2700) in. barrels with 12mm vent. rib, extractors, DTs. New 1986.

| | $995 | $775 | $625 | $550 | $475 | $430 | $395 |

Last Mfg.'s Sug. Retail was $1,190.

2700B — similar to Model 2700, except has deluxe walnut (32 in. barrels only). Mfg. 1987 only.

| | $660 | $575 | $480 | $430 | $395 | $370 | $350 |

Last Mfg.'s Sug. Retail was $795.

2701/2702 & 2703/2704 — 12 and 20 ga., 3 in. Mag., 26 and 28 in. barrels, double triggers, extractors. Disc. 1985, and reintroduced 1989. Current models are 2702 and 2704.

| | $570 | $450 | $375 | $295 | $265 | $230 | $200 |

Last Mfg.'s Sug. Retail was $685.

2705 — .410 ga., double triggers, 26 in. barrels, bored F & F, extractors. Importation began 1986.

| | $670 | $525 | $425 | $350 | $300 | $275 | $235 |

Last Mfg.'s Sug. Retail was $785.

2706 — 12 ga. only, law enforcement model, 20 in. barrels, double triggers, extractors. Imported 1986 only.

| | $330 | $280 | $260 | $240 | $220 | $200 | $185 |

Last Mfg.'s Sug. Retail was $375.

2707 — 28 ga., otherwise similar to Model 2705. New 1990.

| | $670 | $525 | $425 | $350 | $300 | $275 | $235 |

Last Mfg.'s Sug. Retail was $785.

2708 — 12 ga. only, slug gun, 23 in. barrels, single trigger, ejectors. Importation began 1986.

| | $685 | $550 | $450 | $385 | $325 | $300 | $280 |

A Model 2708-3 was mfg. 1986-1989. This variation had 20 in. barrels, double triggers, and extractors. Values of this earlier variation will be approx. 30-40% less than listed above.
Last Mfg.'s Sug. Retail was $840.

Grading	100%	98%	95%	90%	80%	70%	60%

2711, 2713-3, 2721, & 2723 — 12 or 20 ga., 3 in. Mag., 26 or 28 in. barrels, extractors. Models 2721 and 2723 have ejectors and were disc. 1985. Models 2711 and 2713-3 were disc. 1989.

| | $445 | $385 | $340 | $310 | $275 | $250 | $230 |

Add 25% with ejectors.
Last Mfg.'s Sug. Retail was $375 on Models 2721/2723.
Last Mfg.'s Sug. Retail was $535 on Models 2711/2713-3.

2717, 2719, 2720, & 2725 — 12 (Model 2717), 20 (Model 2719), 28 (Model 2725 - new 1990), or .410 (Model 2720) ga., 3 in. Mag. (except Model 2725), 26 or 28 in. barrels, SST.

| | $645 | $525 | $450 | $385 | $325 | $300 | $280 |

Add $70 for 28 or .410 ga.
Last Mfg.'s Sug. Retail was $765.

2712, 2714-3, 2722, & 2724 — 12 or 20 ga., 3 in. Mag., 26 or 28 in. barrels. Models 2712 and 2722 are 12 ga., engraved with 12mm vent. rib. Models 2722 and 2724 have ejectors. Importation of Models 2712, 2722, and 2724 were disc. 1986. Model 2714-3 was disc. 1988.

| | $500 | $395 | $350 | $300 | $275 | $235 | $200 |

Last Mfg.'s Sug. Retail was $615 on Model 2714-3.
Last Mfg.'s Sug. Retail was $395 on Models 2712/2722/2724.

2715-3 & 2716-3 — 12 ga. only, 28 in. barrels with 3 choke tubes, auto ejectors, single trigger. Imported 1988 only.

| | $575 | $465 | $400 | $350 | $295 | $265 | $245 |

Last Mfg.'s Sug. Retail was $680.

2718, 2733, & 2735 — 12 and 20 ga., 3 in. Mag., 26 and 28 in. barrels, SST, extractors. Models 2733/2735 have deluxe Boss actions. Model 2718 was disc. 1985.

| | $650 | $540 | $450 | $385 | $325 | $300 | $280 |

Last Mfg.'s Sug. Retail was $390 on Model 2718.
Last Mfg.'s Sug. Retail was $790 on Model 2733 and 2735.

2734 & 2736 Sporting Clays — 12 (2734) or 20 (2736) ga., similar to Models 2733 and 2735, except has 3 choke tubes.

| | $695 | $560 | $450 | $385 | $325 | $300 | $280 |

Last Mfg.'s Sug. Retail was $840.

2745, 2746 & 2747 — 12 ga., 3½ in. chambers, 24 (2745), 27/28 (2746) or 31/32 (2747) in. barrels with wide rib and 3 choke tubes, auto extractors, Boss type action. New 1989.

| | $715 | $575 | $450 | $385 | $325 | $300 | $280 |

These models are mfg. by Armi Techniche of Emilio Rizzini located in Italy.
Last Mfg.'s Sug. Retail was $880.

2726, 2728, 2742, & 2744 — 12 and 20 ga., 3 in. Mag., 26 and 28 in. barrels, SST, ejectors. Models 2726 & 2728 were disc. 1985.

| | $740 | $595 | $475 | $400 | $350 | $315 | $290 |

Last Mfg.'s Sug. Retail on Models 2726 & 2728 was $440.
Last Mfg.'s Sug. Retail on Models 2742 & 2744 was $930.

2727-3 & 2729-3 — 1986 designations for Models 2726 & 2728 respectively. -3 suffixes indicate 1988 designations. Importation disc. 1988.

| | $550 | $450 | $385 | $330 | $295 | $265 | $245 |

Last Mfg.'s Sug. Retail was $615.

Armsport, cont.

Grading	100%	98%	95%	90%	80%	70%	60%

2727 & 2729 — 12 (Model 2727) or 20 (Model 2729) ga., field model, boxlock action, 26 or 28 in. barrels with wide rib and fixed chokes. New 1990.

	$660	$550	$450	$385	$325	$300	$280

These models have evolved from Models 2726/2728 and Models 2727-3 and 2729-3. Last Mfg.'s Sug. Retail was $800.

2730 — 12 ga., skeet gun, 27 in. barrel, has six interchangeable chokes, Boss-type action.

	$775	$650	$550	$495	$450	$425	$395

These models are mfg. by Armi Techniche of Emilio Rizzini located in Italy. Last Mfg.'s Sug. Retail was $975.

2731 — similar to Model 2730, except is 20 ga. and has 26 in. barrels.

	$795	$675	$565	$525	$465	$435	$400

Last Mfg.'s Sug. Retail was $975.

2732 & 2732/3 — 12 ga. only, competition trap model, 30 in. barrel. New 1990.

	$930	$700	$600	$525	$470	$440	$415

Add $110 for Model 2732/3 (includes choke tubes).
These two models are mfg. by Emilio Rizzini located in Italy. Last Mfg.'s Sug. Retail was $1,165.

2741 & 2743 — 12 (Model 2741) or 20 (Model 2743) ga., field model, 26 or 28 in. barrels with wide rib and fixed chokes, Boss type action. New 1990.

	$665	$550	$450	$385	$325	$300	$280

These models are mfg. by Armi Techniche of Emilio Rizzini located in Italy. Last Mfg.'s Sug. Retail was $825.

2750 & 2751 — 12 (Model 2750) or 20 (Model 2751) ga., Sporting Clays configuration, 26 or 28 in. barrels with 5 choke tubes, includes engraved sideplates. New 1990.

	$830	$675	$575	$525	$475	$445	$400

Last Mfg.'s Sug. Retail was $1,050.

2760 — 12 ga., tournament trap model with choke tubes. Mfg. by Ferlib beginning 1991.

	$1,475	$1,200	$995	$800	$675	$600	$540

Last Mfg.'s Sug. Retail was $1,700.

2763 — 12 ga., sporting clays configuration, includes 5 choke tubes, mfg. by Ferlib in Italy - importation began in 1991.

	$1,525	$1,225	$1,000	$800	$675	$600	$540

Last Mfg.'s Sug. Retail was $1,775.

2765 — similar to Model 2763, except is 20 ga. with 26 in. barrels. Imported 1991 only.

	$1,700	$1,350	$1,100	$850	$700	$625	$550

Last Mfg.'s Sug. Retail was $2,000.

4014 — Emperor Grade SxS. Individually fitted per customer H&H type action, engraved, fitted leather case, choice of gauge, barrel lengths, etc. Completely hand finished.

	$9,175	$6,885	$5,965	$5,050	$4,590	$4,130	$3,670

Emperor Grade models are disc. Limited availability.

4015 — Emperor "One-of-a-Kind" SxS. Similar to Model 4014, except that every part of the gun is made per customer order. Specifications including style of engraving, dimensions, wood configuration, special requests, etc. No expense spared. Disc. 1984.

	$18,000	$13,500	$11,700	$9,900	$9,000	$8,100	$7,200

Grading	100%	98%	95%	90%	80%	70%	60%

4016 — Emperor SxS with outside hammers, fitted leather case, extensively engraved, any gauge. Disc. 1983.

| | $4,550 | $3,415 | $2,960 | $2,505 | $2,275 | $2,050 | $1,820 |

4017 — Emperor "One-of-a-Kind" SxS with outside hammers. Flexibility of options is similar to Model 4015. Disc. 1984.

| | $12,750 | $9,565 | $8,290 | $7,015 | $6,375 | $5,740 | $5,100 |

4030 & 4031 — 12 ga. SxS, Holland-style detachable locks, English walnut, ejectors, engraved. Model 4031 is 20 ga. Disc. 1983.

| | $3,950 | $2,965 | $2,570 | $2,175 | $1,975 | $1,780 | $1,580 |

4032 & 4033 — 12 ga. Premier Mono Trap Gun, 32 in. barrel, ejector. Model 4033 is same, except for 34 in. barrel. Disc. 1986.

| | $1,810 | $1,560 | $1,350 | $1,145 | $1,040 | $935 | $830 |

Last Mfg.'s Sug. Retail was $2,075.

4034 & 4035 — 12 ga. Premier Mono Trap Set, 32 in. single, 30 in. O/U. Model 4035 is same, except has 34 in. single, 32 in. O/U. Disc. 1986.

| | $2,565 | $2,215 | $1,920 | $1,625 | $1,475 | $1,330 | $1,180 |

Last Mfg.'s Sug. Retail was $2,950.

4040 — 12 ga. Slug Special SxS, 23 in. barrels. Disc. 1984.

| | $1,325 | $995 | $865 | $730 | $665 | $600 | $530 |

4046 & 4047 — 12 ga. trap gun, 34 in. barrel, extra trigger mechanism. Model 4047 is 32 in. Disc. 1986.

| | $2,860 | $2,460 | $2,100 | $1,850 | $1,700 | $1,500 | $1,300 |

Last Mfg.'s Sug. Retail was $3,275.

4050 — Pigeon Grade O/U, 12 ga., engraved. Disc. 1986.

| | $2,375 | $2,025 | $1,755 | $1,485 | $1,350 | $1,215 | $1,080 |

Last Mfg.'s Sug. Retail was $2,700.

4055 & 4056 — Premier Skeet 12 ga., selective trigger, ejectors, engraved, select wood. Model 4056 is 20 ga. Disc. 1983.

| | $2,000 | $1,500 | $1,300 | $1,100 | $1,000 | $900 | $800 |

4061 & 4062 — .410 ga. SxS, single trigger, selective ejectors. Model 4062 is 28 ga. Disc. 1983.

| | $995 | $750 | $650 | $550 | $500 | $450 | $400 |

4063 & 4064 — .410 ga. O/U, single trigger, selective ejectors. Model 4064 is 28 ga. Disc. 1983.

| | $995 | $750 | $650 | $550 | $500 | $450 | $400 |

SHOTGUNS: REPEATING

2755 — 12 ga., 7 shot, Atis mfg., black anodized receiver, 24 or 28 in. barrel with VR. Mfg. 1985-87 only.

| | $335 | $260 | $225 | $195 | $180 | $160 | $145 |

Last Mfg.'s Sug. Retail was $395.

2755A — similar to Model 2755, except has 30 in. barrel. Mfg. 1986-87 only.

| | $335 | $260 | $225 | $195 | $180 | $160 | $145 |

Grading	100%	98%	95%	90%	80%	70%	60%
2756 — 12 ga., 28 in. VR barrel, 3 interchangeable chokes. Mfg. 1986-87 only.							
	$390	$335	$280	$230	$205	$190	$175
Last Mfg.'s Sug. Retail was $465.							
⁂ **2756A** — similar to Model 2756, except has 30 in. vent. rib barrel. Mfg. 1986-87 only.							
	$390	$335	$280	$230	$205	$190	$175
Last Mfg.'s Sug. Retail was $465.							
2757 — 12 ga. only, law enforcement model, 20 in. barrel, black receiver. Mfg. 1986-87 only.							
	$310	$250	$205	$190	$175	$155	$140
Last Mfg.'s Sug. Retail was $375.							
2766, 2767, & 2768 — 12 ga., Fabarms mfg., 25 in. barrel. Model 2768 has 20 in. barrel. Imported 1985 only.							
	$260	$220	$200	$180	$160	$140	$120
Last Mfg.'s Sug. Retail was $300.							

SHOTGUNS: SEMI-AUTO

Grading	100%	98%	95%	90%	80%	70%	60%
2751 — 12 ga., 3 in. Mag., semi-auto, Atis mfg., black anodized receiver, 28 in. barrel. Mfg. 1985-87 only.							
	$430	$340	$310	$285	$255	$230	$200
Last Mfg.'s Sug. Retail was $575.							
⁂ **2751A** — similar to Model 2751, except has 30 in. full choke barrel. Mfg. 1986-87 only.							
	$430	$340	$310	$285	$255	$230	$200
Last Mfg.'s Sug. Retail was $575.							
2752 — same action as Model 2751, except chrome receiver and engraving. Mfg. 1986-87 only.							
	$440	$345	$310	$285	$255	$230	$200
Last Mfg.'s Sug. Retail was $600.							
⁂ **2752A** — similar to Model 2752, except has 30 in. barrel. Mfg. 1986-87 only.							
	$440	$345	$310	$285	$255	$230	$200
Last Mfg.'s Sug. Retail was $600.							
2753 — same action as Model 2751, except has 28 in. barrel with 3 interchangeable chokes. Mfg. 1986-87 only.							
	$460	$355	$315	$285	$255	$230	$200
Last Mfg.'s Sug. Retail was $650.							
⁂ **2753A** — similar to Model 2753, except has chrome receiver and engraving. Mfg. 1986-87 only.							
	$470	$365	$320	$285	$255	$230	$200
Last Mfg.'s Sug. Retail was $675.							
2761 & 2762 — 12 ga., black or chrome receiver, Fabarms made, engraved action, 27 in. barrel. Add $75 for interchangeable choke tubes. Imported during 1985 only.							
	$410	$360	$315	$295	$270	$245	$215
Last Mfg.'s Sug. Retail was $475.							

SHOTGUNS: SINGLE AND SIDE-BY-SIDE

Grading	100%	98%	95%	90%	80%	70%	60%
1033 — 10 ga. SxS, 3½ in. Mag., 32 in. full and full chokes. Disc. 1985.							
	$395	$340	$315	$275	$250	$225	$200
Last Mfg.'s Sug. Retail was $450.							

Grading	100%	98%	95%	90%	80%	70%	60%

1050-1 — 1986 designation for the Model 1051. -1 suffix designates 1988 and later importation.

| | $650 | $540 | $450 | $385 | $325 | $300 | $280 |

Last Mfg.'s Sug. Retail was $785.

1051 & 1052 — 12 ga. SxS, 3 in. Mag., 28 in. mod. & full chokes. Model 1052 is 20 ga., 3 in. Mag., 26 in. Imp. & Mod. Disc. 1985.

| | $330 | $280 | $260 | $240 | $225 | $205 | $180 |

Last Mfg.'s Sug. Retail was $375.

1053-1 — 1986 designation for the Model 1052. -1 suffix designates 1988 and later importation.

| | $650 | $540 | $450 | $385 | $325 | $300 | $280 |

Last Mfg.'s Sug. Retail was $785.

1054-1 & 1055-1 — .410 (1054) or .28 (1055) ga. -1 suffix designates 1988 and later importation.

| | $700 | $600 | $500 | $450 | $400 | $365 | $330 |

Last Mfg.'s Sug. Retail was $860.

1055 & 1057 — 28 and .410 ga. SxS, 3 in. Mag., 26 in. barrel, Imp. and Mod. chokes. Model 1057 is 28 ga., 3 in. Mag., 26 in. Imp. & Mod. Disc. 1985.

| | $330 | $280 | $260 | $240 | $225 | $205 | $180 |

Last Mfg.'s Sug. Retail was $375.
Model 1057 was redesignated 1055 in 1985 and Model 1055 was changed to 1054.

1101, 1102, 1103, & 1104 — 12 ga., folding single barrel w/vent. rib. Model 1102 is 20 ga. Model 1103 is .410 ga. Model 1104 is 28 ga. Disc. 1985.

| | $125 | $105 | $90 | $75 | $70 | $65 | $60 |

Last Mfg.'s Sug. Retail was $140.

1107 & 1108 — 12 ga., folding single barrel 19 in., pistol grip. Model 1108 is 20 ga. Disc. 1983.

| | $135 | $105 | $95 | $85 | $75 | $70 | $65 |

1125, 1126, & 1127 — 12 or 20 ga., single barrel, 3 in. chamber, bottom lever opening, Model 1127 is 20 ga. New 1987.

| Mfg.'s Sug. Retail $90 | $75 | $55 | $50 | $45 | $40 | $35 | $30 |

The Model 1125 was disc. 1989.

1128 — .410 ga., otherwise similar to Models 1125/1126/1127. Importation disc. 1990.

| | $75 | $55 | $50 | $45 | $40 | $35 | $30 |

Last Mfg.'s Sug. Retail was $90.

1212 & 1213 — 12 ga., SxS, outside hammers, engraved action, 20 in. barrels. Model 1213 is 20 ga. Disc. 1983.

| | $450 | $340 | $295 | $250 | $225 | $205 | $180 |

1225 — 12 ga. only, O/U configuration, folding action, top lever break. Mfg. 1986-87 only.

| | $275 | $235 | $200 | $185 | $170 | $165 | $150 |

Last Mfg.'s Sug. Retail was $345.

1226 — 20 ga. only, O/U configuration, folding action, top lever break. Mfg. 1986-87 only.

| | $275 | $235 | $200 | $185 | $170 | $165 | $150 |

Last Mfg.'s Sug. Retail was $345.

Grading	100%	98%	95%	90%	80%	70%	60%

SHOTGUNS: TRI-BARREL

MODEL 2900 TRILLING — 12 ga., 3 barrel shotgun with 28 in. barrels bored F & M or choke tubes over IC/choke tubes. Importation began 1986-87 and was resumed in 1990.

| | **$2,900** | **$2,375** | **$2,000** | **$1,650** | **$1,400** | **$1,200** | **$995** |

Subtract 25% for fixed chokes (1986-87 mfg.).
This model was re-introduced in 1990 and includes choke tubes on all 3 barrels.
Last Mfg.'s Sug. Retail was $3,400.

ARRIETA, S.L.

Manufacturer located in Elgoibar, Spain. Currently imported by several importers including Quality Arms, New England Arms, Hi-Grade Imports, Orvis (catalog sales - see Orvis listing), Hi-Grade Imports, and Jack Jansma.

More information can be obtained on Arietta by either contacting the above listed importers or the factory.

SHOTGUNS: CURRENT SxS

The models listed below are essentially custom ordered per individual specifications - delivery time is approx. 9 months (12 months for small gauges).

All Arrieta shotguns have frames scaled to individual guages. Various special options are available by custom order, and a few are listed below. On the models listed below, there are 4 qualities of action. Fourth quality is used on the Model 550. Third quality is used on Models 557-588. Second quality is used on Models 590 and 595 (designed for heavy use). First quality is used on Models 600-903, except for Model 900 (557 action).

ADD THE FOLLOWING AMOUNTS FOR CURRENTLY MANUFACTURED SHOTGUNS.
Add 10% for small gauges (20, 28, or .410).
Add approx. $750 for single trigger depending on action.
Add 10% for matched pair.
Add 10% for rounded action on standard models.
Extra barrels are priced from $975-$1,600/set depending on model.

557 STANDARD — 12, 16, or 20 ga., Demi-Bloc steel barrels, detachable engraved sidelocks, double triggers, ejectors.

| Mfg.'s Sug. Retail | $2,795 | | $2,700 | $1,850 | $1,425 | $1,100 | $900 | $750 | $640 |

570 LIEJA — 12, 16, or 20 ga., similar to 560, except has non-detachable sidelocks.

| Mfg.'s Sug. Retail | $3,275 | | $3,275 | $2,250 | $1,725 | $1,325 | $1,075 | $850 | $750 |

575 SPORT — 12, 16, or 20 ga., similar to 560, except is more elaborately engraved.

| Mfg.'s Sug. Retail | $3,300 | | $3,300 | $2,275 | $1,725 | $1,325 | $1,075 | $850 | $750 |

578 VICTORIA — 12, 16, or 20 ga., similar to 570, except is fine English scrollwork engraved.

| Mfg.'s Sug. Retail | $3,600 | | $3,600 | $2,425 | $1,775 | $1,375 | $1,100 | $925 | $850 |

585 LIRIA — 12, 16, or 20 ga., similar to 575, except has profuse engraving.

| Mfg.'s Sug. Retail | $4,100 | | $4,100 | $2,775 | $2,200 | $1,875 | $1,550 | $1,250 | $1,025 |

590 REGINA — 12, 16, or 20 ga., similar to 570, except has more profuse engraving.

| Mfg.'s Sug. Retail | $4,350 | | $4,350 | $2,900 | $2,275 | $1,925 | $1,600 | $1,275 | $1,050 |

595 PRINCIPE — all gauges, sidelock action, relief engraved hunting scenes, ejectors, DTs.

| Mfg.'s Sug. Retail | $6,600 | | $6,600 | $4,700 | $3,950 | $3,400 | $2,925 | $2,500 | $2,000 |

600 IMPERIAL — 12, 16, or 20 ga., top-of-the-line self-opening action, very ornate engraving throughout.

| Mfg.'s Sug. Retail | $5,800 | | $5,800 | $4,100 | $3,700 | $3,150 | $2,750 | $2,400 | $1,950 |

Grading	100%	98%	95%	90%	80%	70%	60%

600-1 IMPERIAL — 12, 16, or 20 ga., similar to 600 Imperial, except has light border engraving around sidelocks, tangs, trigger guard. Importation disc. 1988.

		100%	98%	95%	90%	80%	70%	60%
		$4,600	$3,825	$3,500	$3,175	$2,835	$2,460	$2,000

Last Mfg.'s Sug. Retail was $5,380.

601 TIRO — all gauges, sidelock action with nickle plating, ejectors, SST, self-opening action, border engraving.

		100%	98%	95%	90%	80%	70%	60%
Mfg.'s Sug. Retail	$6,850	$6,850	$4,825	$4,000	$3,400	$2,950	$2,500	$2,000

801 — all gauges, Holland-style detachable sidelocks, self-opening action, ejectors, coin-wash finish, finest Churchill style engraving.

		100%	98%	95%	90%	80%	70%	60%
Mfg.'s Sug. Retail	$9,800	$9,800	$7,100	$6,000	$5,100	$4,600	$4,000	$3,450

Model's 801 through 875 are also available with self-opening actions as an option — add $800.

802 — 12, 16, or 20 ga., similar to 801 only non-detachable sidelocks, finest Holland-style engraving.

		100%	98%	95%	90%	80%	70%	60%
Mfg.'s Sug. Retail	$9,800	$9,800	$7,100	$6,000	$5,100	$4,600	$4,000	$3,450

803 — all gauges, similar to 801, finest Purdey-style engraving.

		100%	98%	95%	90%	80%	70%	60%
Mfg.'s Sug. Retail	$6,600	$6,600	$4,700	$3,950	$3,400	$2,925	$2,500	$2,000

871 — all gauges, rounded frame sidelock action with Demi-Bloc barrels, scroll engraved, ejectors, DTs.

		100%	98%	95%	90%	80%	70%	60%
Mfg.'s Sug. Retail	$4,750	$4,700	$3,200	$2,650	$2,150	$1,750	$1,450	$1,275

872 — all gauges, rounded frame sidelock action with Demi-Bloc barrels, elaborate scroll engraving with third lever fastener.

		100%	98%	95%	90%	80%	70%	60%
Mfg.'s Sug. Retail	$11,400	$11,400	$8,500	$7,250	$5,950	$5,200	$4,400	$3,600

873 — all gauges, sidelock action with Demi-Bloc barrels, game scene engraving, ejectors, SST.

		100%	98%	95%	90%	80%	70%	60%
Mfg.'s Sug. Retail	$7,200	$7,000	$4,825	$4,000	$3,400	$2,950	$2,500	$2,000

874 — all gauges, sidelock action with Demi-Bloc barrels, action is gold line engraved.

		100%	98%	95%	90%	80%	70%	60%
Mfg.'s Sug. Retail	$8,500	$8,500	$6,100	$4,750	$3,850	$3,425	$3,000	$2,600

875 — all gauges, top-of-the-line quality, built to individual customer specs. only, elaborate engraving with gold inlays.

		100%	98%	95%	90%	80%	70%	60%
Mfg.'s Sug. Retail	$14,250	$12,650	$10,000	$8,950	$7,850	$6,850	$5,900	$4,950

ARRIZABLAGA

Manufacturer located in Eibar, Spain since 1940. Currently imported and distributed by New England Arms located in Kittery Point, ME.

Arrizablaga manufactures best quality guns only, carefully made to individual customer specifications. The models listed below are essentially custom ordered per individual specifications - delivery time is approx. 9 months (12 months for small gauges).

ADD THE FOLLOWING AMOUNTS ON ARRIZABLAGA SHOTGUNS:

All Arrizablaga shotguns have self-opening (assisted) actions.
Add 10% for matched pair.
Add $2,000 (retail) for extra barrels.
Add $500 for 28 ga.
Add $1,000 for .410 ga.
Add $1,000 for single trigger.
Add $250 for pistol grip stock.

Grading	100%	98%	95%	90%	80%	70%	60%

HEAVY SCROLL MODEL — 12, 16, or 20 ga., sidelock action, elaborate engraving, deluxe oil finished stock and forearm.

Mfg.'s Sug. Retail	$9,000	$9,000	$6,250	$5,400	$4,750	$4,300	$3,850	$3,325

ENGLISH SCROLL MODEL — 12, 16, or 20 ga., sidelock action, English scroll engraving, deluxe oil finished walnut stock and forearm.

Mfg.'s Sug. Retail	$9,500	$9,500	$6,700	$5,650	$4,950	$4,500	$4,000	$3,450

SPECIAL MODEL — 12, 16, or 20 ga., sidelock top of the line model, best quality wood and engraving.

Mfg.'s Sug. Retail	$12,500	$12,500	$8,800	$8,200	$7,400	$6,600	$5,900	$4,950

ASP

Customized variation of a S&W Model 39-2 semi-auto pistol (or related variations) mfg. by Armament Systems and Procedures located in Appleton, WI.

PISTOLS

ASP — 9mm Para., compact double action semi-auto, features see-through grips with cut-away mag. making cartridges visible, Teflon coated, re-contoured lightened slide, combat trigger guard, spurless hammer, and mostly painted Guttersnipe rear sight (no front sight), 24 oz. loaded, approx. 1,000 mfg. until approx. 1990.

		$1,600	$1,450	$1,350	$1,250	$1,150	$1,050	$950

Add $200 for Tritium filled Guttersnipe.
This pistol is marked ASP on the magazine extension. There were also 100 mfg. as a special edition marked "Quest for Excellence", and included buffalo horn grips, presentation book case and letter opener.

ASP REVOLVER — .44 Spl., conversion from a Ruger Speed or Security Six, 5 shot, less than 100 mfg., unmarked.

		$1,150	$1,000	$925	$850	$775	$700	$650

ASTRA

Manufactured by Unceta Y Cia., Guernica, Spain. Currently imported by European American Armory located in Hialeah, FL. Previously imported until 1992 by Interarms located in Alexandria, VA. Distributor sales only.

PISTOLS: RECENT MANUFACTURE

CONSTABLE — double action, .22 LR (10 shot, disc. in 1990.), .32 auto (8 shot, disc. 1984), .380 ACP (7 shot), exposed hammer, 3½ in. barrel, fixed sight, blue or chrome (disc.) finish, plastic grips. Imported 1965-91.

		$310	$250	$210	$180	$165	$150	$135

Add $10 for chrome finish or wood grips (disc. in 1990).
Last Mfg.'s Sug. Retail was $380.

Constable Stainless — .380 ACP only, stainless version of the Constable. Mfg. 1986 only.

		$350	$300	$240	$220	$200	$175	$150

Last Mfg.'s Sug. Retail was $345.

Constable Sport — similar to Constable, except has 6 in. barrel, blue finish only, 35 oz. Mfg. 1986-87 only.

		$325	$245	$210	$180	$165	$150	$135

Last Mfg.'s Sug. Retail was $330.

Grading	100%	98%	95%	90%	80%	70%	60%

⭐ Blue Engraved Constable — blue engraved. Importation disc. 1987.

	$375	$295	$250				

Add $20 for .22 LR or checkered wood grips.
Last Mfg.'s Sug. Retail was $375.

⭐ Chrome Engraved Constable — chrome engraved. Importation disc. 1987.

	$350	$295	$250				

Add $20 for .22 LR or checkered wood grips.
Last Mfg.'s Sug. Retail was $390.

CONSTABLE A-60 — .380 ACP, double action, $3\frac{1}{2}$ in. barrel, 13 shot mag., ambidextrous safety, adj. rear sight, blue finish only. Imported 1986-91.

	$395	$325	$280	$245	$220	$185	$160

Last Mfg.'s Sug. Retail was $475.

MODEL A-70 — 9mm Para. or .40 S&W cal., single action, $3\frac{1}{2}$ in. barrel, steel frame and slide, 7 (.40 S&W) or 8 (9mm Para.) shot mag., compact design, dual safeties, 3-dot sights, matte blue or nickel (new 1993) finish, $25\frac{3}{4}$ oz. Importation began 1991.

Mfg.'s Sug. Retail	$495	$395	$350	$275	$230	$200	$180	$160

Add $30 for nickel finish.

MODEL A-75 — action similar to Model A-70, except has selective double action with a decocking lever. Importation began 1993.

Mfg.'s Sug. Retail	$575	$475	$395	$325	$275	$230	$200	$180

Add $30 for nickel finish.

MODEL A-80 — 9mm Para, .38 Super (disc.) or .45 ACP cal., double action, semi-auto, 15 shot mag. (9 for .45 ACP), $3\frac{3}{4}$ in. barrel. Imported 1982-89.

	$370	$320	$285	$265	$240	$210	$185

Add $35 for chrome finish (disc.).
.38 Super cal. in chrome finish will command a premium (10%-20%).
Last Mfg.'s Sug. Retail was $425.

MODEL A-90 — 9mm Para. or .45 ACP cal., 1986 designation for Model A-80 with updated slide mounted safety and pushbutton mag. release, $3\frac{3}{4}$ in. barrel, 14 shot mag. (9mm) or 8 shot (.45 ACP), blue only, approx. 48 oz. Imported 1986-90, replaced by Model A-100.

	$400	$340	$300	$275	$245	$225	$200

Last Mfg.'s Sug. Retail was $500.

MODEL A-100 — 9mm Para., .40 S&W, or .45 ACP cal., replaced the Model A-90 in 1990, with similar specifications, re-engineered 1993 incorporating increased mag. capacity (17 shot mag. - 9mm, 12 shot mag. - .40 S&W, 9 shot mag. - .45 ACP), approx. 29 oz. Importation began 1990.

Mfg.'s Sug. Retail	$590	$495	$400	$325	$275	$230	$200	$180

Add $40 for .45 ACP cal.

MODEL 4000 FALCON — .22 LR, .32 ACP, or .380 ACP cal., 4 in. barrel, fixed sights, blue, plastic grips, exposed hammer. Mfg. 1956-1986.

	$450	$400	$330	$260	$235	$200	$150

Add 50% for .22 cal.
Add 100% for engraved M-4000.
Last Mfg.'s Sug. Retail was $340.

Grading	100%	98%	95%	90%	80%	70%	60%

⚞ **Model 4000 Tri-cal. Kit** — includes .22 LR, .32 ACP, and .380 ACP cals., either rust blued or salt blued finish, less than 200 mfg. Boxed.

	$1,100	**$875**	**$750**				

PISTOLS: DISCONTINUED

MODEL 1911 — .25 ACP or .32 ACP cal., semi-auto, may have external or internal hammer.

	$325	$225	$165	$135	$115	$100	$85

Add 20% if with external hammer.

MODEL 1915/1916 — .32 ACP cal., semi-auto.

	$275	$200	$165	$135	$115	$100	$85

Note: Models 1915/1916 were later referred to as Model 100 Special.

CAMPO GIRO 1913 — mfg. 1913.

	$2,750	$2,250	$1,750	$1,250	$800	$600	$400

CAMPO GIRO 1913-16 — mfg. 1913-16.

	$1,750	$1,350	$900	$675	$550	$450	$300

MODEL 200 FIRECAT AUTOMATIC PISTOL — .25 ACP cal., 2¼ in. barrel, 6 shot, blue, plastic grips, mfg. 1920-present, U.S. importation stopped by GCA 68.

	$240	$190	$165	$145	$125	$110	$100

Add 50% for engraved M-200.

MODEL 300 — .32 ACP or .380 ACP cal., semi-auto.

	$450	$350	$270	$240	$210	$180	$150

Add 20% if Nazi-proofed.
Add 200% for engraved M-300.

MODEL 400 AUTOMATIC PISTOL — 9mm Bayard long, 9 shot, 6 in. barrel, blue, fixed sights, plastic grips, mfg. 1921-1945.

	$400	$325	$230	$200	$170	$135	$100

Add 200% for Navy variation.
Add 100% for Nazi accepted specimens.
Approx. serial range of Nazi accepted specimens (no markings) is S/N 92,851 - 98,850.

⚞ **"F. Ascaso" Marked Model 400 Copies** — close copy of the Astra Model 400, produced by the Spanish Republican forces during the later part of the Spanish Civil War, F. Ascaso marked (un-numbered) mags., salt blued, estimated production is 5,000 to 8,000 (approx. end of ser. range), has identifying logo on slide and grip panels.

	$600	$475	$325	$250	$200	$175	$150

⚞ **R.E. (Republica Espagnola) Marked Model 400 Copies** — ser. range to approx. 15,000, has identifying logo on forward slide and grip panels.

	$475	$400	$295	$240	$210	$170	$125

MODEL 600 MOD. AUTOMATIC — 9mm Luger, 8 shot, 5¼ in. barrel, blue, fixed sights, wood or plastic grips, mfg. 1944-1945.

	$300	$250	$200	$175	$155	$140	$130

Add a 100%+ premium for Nazi Waffenamt proofing (approx. serial range 1 - 10,500).

Grading	100%	98%	95%	90%	80%	70%	60%

MODEL 700 SPECIAL — .32 ACP cal., semi-auto.

	$600	$500	$425	$350	$275	$215	$170

MODEL 800 CONDOR AUTOMATIC — similar to 600, except has exposed hammer, 9mm, mfg. 1958-1965.

	$1,650	$1,250	$950	$650	$550	$450	$350

Add 20% if NIB with accessories.

MODEL 900 — 7.63 Mauser cal., Broomhandle copy, parts non-interchangeable with Mauser. Mfg. from 1928-1936.

	$2,500	$1,850	$1,350	$850	$700	$525	$425

Add $500 for non-matching stock.
Add $650 for matching detachable stock.
Add 50% for early Bolo grip variation.
Add 20% for specimens with Japanese characters.

MODEL 902 — 7.63 Mauser cal., semi-auto, similar to 900 except 20 shot mag.

	$9,500	$7,250	$5,000	$3,000	$2,500	$2,100	$1,700

Add $1,250 for original "booted" stock.
Deduct 50% for selective fire version.

MACHINE PISTOLS — class III, transferrable only, 10 or 20 shot detachable mag., several variations.

	$3,500	$2,750	$1,900	$1,600	$1,250	$900	$600

MODEL 3000 POCKET AUTOMATIC — .32 auto or .380 auto, 4 in. barrel, fixed sights, blue, plastic grips, mfg. 1947-1956.

	$450	$325	$240	$210	$180	$150	$120

Add 100% for engraved M3000.

MODEL 1000 OR 1000 SPECIAL —semi-auto, .32 ACP.

	$600	$475	$365	$310	$280	$255	$225

MODEL 2000 CUB — .22 Short or .25 auto cal., $2\frac{1}{4}$ in. barrel, fixed sights, blue, plastic grips, also chrome finish, mfg. 1954-present, U.S. importation stopped by GCA 68. Astra also made 2000 Cubs for Colt called Jr. Model {see Colt section}.

	$200	$170	$140	$115	$95	$85	$75

Add 25% for chrome finish.
Add 50% for engraved M-2000.

MODEL 2000 CAMPER — similar to Cub, .22 Short only, with 4 in. barrel, mfg. 1955-1960.

	$350	$275	$200	$160	$125	$90	$70

ASTRA CADIX DOUBLE ACTION REVOLVER — .22 LR, 9 shot, .38 Spl., 5 shot, 4 or 6 in. barrel, adj. sights, blue, plastic grips, mfg. 1960-1968.

	$165	$155	$140	$120	$110		$85	$55

REVOLVERS

.357 D/A REVOLVER — .357 Mag., 6 shot, 3, 4, 6 or $8\frac{1}{2}$ in. barrel (add $10), adj. sights, blue, checkered wood grips, mfg. 1972-1988.

	$250	$215	$185	$170	$155	$140	$125

Last Mfg.'s Sug. Retail was $295.

Grading	100%	98%	95%	90%	80%	70%	60%

⚹ **Stainless Steel** — 4 in. barrel only. Disc. 1987.

	100%	98%	95%	90%	80%	70%	60%
	$285	$245	$205				

Last Mfg.'s Sug. Retail was $330.

.44/.45 CAL. D/A REVOLVER — .41 Mag. (disc. 1985), .44 Mag. or .45 ACP (disc. 1987), 6 shot, 6 or 8½ in. (.44 Mag. only) barrels. Mfg. 1980-87.

	100%	98%	95%	90%	80%	70%	60%
	$280	$235	$210	$190	$180	$170	$160

Last Mfg.'s Sug. Retail was $315.

⚹ **Stainless Steel** — .44 Mag. only, 6 in. barrel only, 2½ lbs.

	Mfg.'s Sug. Retail	98%	95%	90%
	$450	$370	$300	$265

CONVERTIBLE REVOLVER — 9mm with extra .357 Mag. cylinder, 6 shot, 3 in. barrel, blue only, checkered walnut grips, 2¼ lbs. Mfg. 1986 - present.

Mfg.'s Sug. Retail		98%	95%	90%	80%	70%	60%
$395		$335	$275	$250	$225	$200	$180	$160

TERMINATOR — .44 Mag. or .44 Spl. (disc.) cal., 6 shot, adj. rear sight, Roberts rubber grips, 2¾ in. shrouded barrel only. Inventories were depleted in 1989.

⚹ **Blue finish**

	100%	98%	95%	90%	80%	70%	60%
	$250	$225	$190	$175	$160	$150	$140

Last Mfg.'s Sug. Retail was $250.

⚹ **Stainless steel**

	100%	98%	95%
	$275	$235	$190

These models were distributed by Sile Distributors, Inc. located in New York, NY. Last Mfg.'s Sug. Retail was $275.

AUSTRALIAN AUTOMATIC ARMS PTY. LTD.

Manufacturer located in Tasmania, Australia. Previously imported and distributed by California Armory, Inc. located in San Bruno, CA. Dealer direct sales only.

Since the Australian government has banned the exportation of firearms to other countries, Australian Automatic Arms is in the process of trying to relocate their factory in the U.S. Until this transition period is complete, there will be no further importation of this trademark. Retail prices listed below reflect 1992 information - currently, there are no guns for sale domestically.

SAR — .223 cal., semi-auto paramilitary design rifle, 16¼ or 20 in. (new 1989) barrel, 5 or 20 shot M-16 style mag., fiberglass stock and forearm, 7½ lbs. Imported 1986-89.

	100%	98%	95%	90%	80%	70%	60%
	$725	$625	$550	$510	$465	$410	$370

Add $25 for 20 in. barrel.
Also available in fully auto version (AR) — same values as shown above.
Last Mfg.'s Sug. Retail was $663.

SAC — .223 cal., semi-auto paramilitary design carbine, 10½ in. barrel, 20 shot mag., fiberglass stock and forearm, 6.9 lbs. New 1986.
This model is available to class III dealers and law enforcement agencies only.

SAP — .223 cal., semi-auto paramilitary design pistol, 10½ in. barrel, 20 shot mag., fiberglass stock and forearm, 5.9 lbs. New 1986.

Mfg.'s Sug. Retail		98%	95%	90%	80%	70%	60%
$799		$725	$650	$575	$525	$495	$475	$450

SP — .223 cal., semi-auto, sporting configuration, 16¼ or 20 in. barrel, wood stock and forearm, 5 or 20 shot M-16 style mag., 7.5 lbs. Importation began late 1991.

Mfg.'s Sug. Retail		98%	95%	90%	80%	70%	60%
$879		$795	$675	$575	$525	$495	$475	$450

Add $40 for wood stock.

AUTO MAG

Previously manufactured by Auto Mag. Corp. and TDE Corp.

Short recoil rotary bolt system made entirely of stainless steel. Most pistols were sold in .44 AMP cal. although .357 AMP was also a popular factory option. Several other calibers and variations were marketed through Lee Jurras including exotics like the .44 Condor (16 in. barrel and scoped - one of a kind). Also, a .30 cal. Cougar with 12 in. barrel and highly polished metal was a one of a kind item. Other limited Jurras variations include The Custom 100 Series (.44 cal., custom tuned, magna ported, special serialization), The Grizzly (.41 cal.), The Backpacker (.357 cal.), in addition to the Metallic Silhouette.

A unique handgun, the Auto Mag has never been a commercial success due to high manufacturing costs and initial functioning problems (mostly attributed to hand loading all the ammo - once factory ammo became available, reliability improved significantly). Initial reaction to Dirty Harry's use of this weapon in the movie "Sudden Impact" made prices escalate considerably, but most values appear to have stablized since 1986. Be aware of fakes - especially of the XP variety (re-serialized, re-stamped, location of markings, etc.). Also, the ease of barrel swapping should be considered when deciding on a potential purchase. Auto Mags were never magna ported from the factory (only The Custom 100 Series). Non-original magna porting actually detracts from the values listed below, since it is a non-factory alteration.

Serial number ranges for the various models are as follows: Pasadena mfg. - A0000 through A03700. TDE North Hollywood - mostly A02500 through A05015 although some were marked with very low ser. no.'s. TDE El Monte mfg. - A05016 through A08300. High Standard guns were originally marked with "H" prefix serial numbers (only 132 made), after which they carried standard "A0" prefix serial numbers. The "H" prefix guns remain a collectors item and command a 25% premium over values listed below. TDE/OMC marked pistols - B00001 through B00370 are known as the "B" series or solid bolt models (only 370 manufactured). This "B" series also commands collector premiums.

AMT manufactured the last two lots of Auto Mags; the first was the "C" series and was basically the same as the "B" except that only 50 guns were fabricated. The last Auto Mags made by AMT were appropriately serial numbered LAST 1 through LAST 50. These guns had the reputation of being the poorest quality but do carry collector premiums. One interesting variation is the North Hollywood "two-line" model. Also, the first .357 cal. pistols manufactured did not have the words AUTO MAG appearing on the gun. These are also collectors items.

In addition to the above calibers, a very few non-factory .22 and .25 cal. prototypes were fabricated by Kent Lomont. These specimens will usually demand a premium over the values listed below. Also, some barrels and pistols were made in Covina, CA.

LESS THAN 10,000 AUTO MAGS WERE PRODUCED BY ALL MANUFACTURERS. ALL PISTOLS ORIGINALLY HAD ALL STAINLESS STEEL MAGS.

Grading	100%	98%	95%	90%	80%	70%	60%

ORIGINAL PASADENA — .44 AMP only, 6½ in. VR barrel.

$2,500 $2,300 $1,995

This model is generally regarded as having the most quality, as all components were milled from Carpenter 455 stainless steel stock.

TDE NORTH HOLLYWOOD

.44 AMP — 6½ in. VR barrel, initial guns were mfg. from existing Pasadena parts, later mfg. required new components made by TDE.

$2,500 $2,300 $1,995

Quality on this model goes down in later mfg. (some small parts are not stainless). Because of this, higher serial numbered guns in this model are less desirable.

.357 AMP — two line address.

$2,500 $2,300 $1,995

There are no factory records verifying this caliber.

TDE EL MONTE

.44 AMP — 6½ VR, 8, or 10 in. tapered barrel.

$2,100 $1,800 $1,600

Grading	100%	98%	95%	90%	80%	70%	60%

.357 AMP — 6½ VR, 8, or 10 in. tapered barrel.

| | $1,800 | $1,600 | $1,500 |

HIGH STANDARD — "H" prefixed serial numbers, mfg. by TDE with High Standard markings.

| | $2,500 | $2,300 | $1,995 |

TDE/OMC "B" SERIES — 6½ VR or 10 in. barrel.

| | $2,500 | $2,300 | $1,995 |

AMT "C" SERIES — 6½ VR or 10 in. barrel.

| | $2,500 | $2,300 | $1,995 |

Add 50%+ for L.E. Jurras Custom 100 Series.
Add 10% for Jurras Lion marked models.
Lee Jurras added his Lion's head logo (from 1977 on) on TDE manufactured guns. There were also a very limited quantity of original shoulder stocks (perhaps less than 5) - extreme rarity precludes accurate price evaluation.
Note: guns were cased (plastic attache style) with accessories. Original Auto-Mag ammo (only original mfg. by CDM in Mexico and Norma in Sweden) is currently selling for approx. $85 a box.

AUTO-ORDNANCE CORP.
Manufacturer located in West Hurley, NY. Distributor sales only.

Auto-Ordnance Corp. manufactures an exact reproduction of the original 1927 Thompson machine gun. They are currently available in semi-auto only since production ceased on fully automatic variations in 1986 (mfg. 1975-1986).

CARBINES: SEMI-AUTO

1927 A1 STANDARD — .45 ACP, 16 in. plain barrel, solid steel construction, standard military sight, walnut stock and horizontal forearm. Disc. 1986.

| | $570 | $490 | $430 | $360 | $315 | $290 | $270 |

Last Mfg.'s Sug. Retail was $575.

1927 A1 DELUXE — 10mm (new 1991) or .45 ACP cal., 16 in. finned barrel, solid steel construction, adj. rear sight, walnut stock and hand grips.

| Mfg.'s Sug. Retail | $735 | $610 | $515 | $440 | $370 | $320 | $295 | $275 |

Add $10 for 10mm cal.
Add $140 (retail) for 50 shot drum mag. or $345 for 100 shot drum mag. (new in 1990) on this model and other 1927 variations. Also add $105 (retail) for Thompson hard case (violin type).

THOMPSON M1 — .45 ACP, combat model, 16½ in. smooth barrel, side-cocking lever, flat black finish, walnut stock, pistol grip, and grooved forearm, 11½ lbs. New 1986.

| Mfg.'s Sug. Retail | $713 | $600 | $505 | $435 | $360 | $310 | $285 | $265 |

1927 A1C LIGHTWEIGHT — .45 ACP, similar to 1927 A-1 Deluxe, except receiver made of a lightweight alloy. 20% weight reduction. New 1984.

| Mfg.'s Sug. Retail | $707 | $595 | $500 | $430 | $350 | $310 | $285 | $265 |

1927 A5 PISTOL/CARBINE — .45 ACP, 13 in. finned barrel, alloy construction, overall length 26 in., 30 shot mag., 7 lbs.

| Mfg.'s Sug. Retail | $704 | $595 | $495 | $425 | $350 | $300 | $275 | $260 |

1927 A3 - .22 CAL. — .22 LR, 16 in. finned barrel, alloy frame and receiver, walnut stock, pistol grip, and forearm pistol grip, 7 lbs.

| Mfg.'s Sug. Retail | $488 | $425 | $365 | $320 | $285 | $260 | $230 | $200 |

Grading	100%	98%	95%	90%	80%	70%	60%

PISTOLS: SEMI-AUTO

1911 A1 — .38 Super, 9mm Para., .40 S&W (new 1991), 10mm (new 1991), or .45 ACP cal., 4½ (.40 S&W cal. only) or 5 in. barrel, single action, parts interchange with the original Colt Gov't Model, blue only, checkered plastic grips, 39 oz.

Mfg.'s Sug. Retail $389	$325	$275	$250	$235	$225	$215	$200

Add $39 for .40 S&W cal.
Add $26 for .38 Super, 9mm Para. cal.
Add $32 for 10mm cal.
Add $16 for satin nickel (new 1990) or duo-tone (new 1992) finish (.45 ACP only).

1911 A1 Deluxe — .45 ACP only, 5 in. barrel, 3 dot sights, wraparound grips, 39 oz. New 1991.

Mfg.'s Sug. Retail $405	$340	$295	$250	$235	$225	$215	$200

1911 A1 General — .45 ACP, 4½ in. barrel with full length recoil guide system, 7 shot mag., blued finish, 3 dot fixed Millett sights, black rubber wrap-around grips, Commander styling, 37 oz. New 1992.

Mfg.'s Sug. Retail $428	$365	$300	$250	$235	$225	$215	$200

Parkerized 1911 A1 — .45 ACP, no frills variation of the Model 1911 A1, military parkerizing, checkered walnut grips. New 1992.

Mfg.'s Sug. Retail $379	$315	$270	$250	$235	$225	$215	$200

This model is distributed exclusively by RSR Wholesale Guns, Inc.

Competition 1911 — .45 ACP cal., competition features include compensated barrel, commander hammer, flat mainspring housing, white 3-dot sighting system, beavertail grip safety, black textured wrap-around grips. New 1993.

Mfg.'s Sug. Retail $575	$485	$390	$365	$330	$300	$285	$270

MODEL ZG-51 "PIT BULL" — .45 ACP only, compact variation of the 1911 A1, 3½ in. barrel, 7 shot mag., 36 oz. New 1988.

Mfg.'s Sug. Retail $421	$345	$290	$250	$235	$225	$215	$200

AUTO - POINTER

Manufactured by Yamamoto Co. Formerly imported by Sloans.

SEMI-AUTO SHOTGUN — 12 or 20 ga., gas operated. Disc.

$275	$240	$220	$195	$180	$160	$145

B section

BSA GUNS LIMITED

Birmingham Small Arms, located in Birmingham, England. Manufactured 1861-current in England. Imported until 1985 by Precision Sports, from Ithaca, NY and 1986 by BSA Guns Ltd., located in Grand Prairie, TX. Imported and distributed until 1989 by Samco Global Arms, Inc., located in Miami, FL (small quantities of certain models still remain). Currently, BSA firearms are not being imported. BSA airguns may be found under the Airgun section of this text.

RIFLES: RECENT IMPORTATION

Importation of all BSA rimfire and centerfire rifles were disc. 1987.

Grading	100%	98%	95%	90%	80%	70%	60%
CF-2 ACTION							
Sporter/Classic	$325	$275	$250	$225	$210	$195	$180
Classic Varminter	$325	$275	$250	$225	$210	$190	$175
Heavy Barrel Model	$375	$300	$260	$240	$225	$210	$180
Carbine Model	$350	$325	$295	$270	$250	$225	$200
Stutzen Rifle	$450	$375	$325	$300	$275	$250	$225
Regal Custom	$875	$795	$685	$590	$550	$500	$450
CFT TARGET RIFLE	$675	$590	$550	$500	$450	$400	$360

CF-2 ACTION – .222 R., .22-250, .243 Win., 6.5 x 55mm, 7 x 57, 7 x 64mm, 7mm Rem. Mag., .270 Win., .308 Win., .30-06, or .300 Win. Mag. cal., bolt action, barrel length 23-26 in., 7½ -8 lbs. CF-2 nomenclature designates an action rather than a model. CF-2 actioned models are listed below. Add $70 for double set trigger option on the below listed models. Limited quantities of English mfg. models remain.

Sporter/Classic – same cals. as above, checkered oil finished walnut stock. Imported 1986-87. Sporter Model features Monte Carlo stock, rosewood capped forearm and pistol grip stock, and swivels. Last Mfg.'s Sug. Retail was $360.

Classic Varminter – available in .222R-.243 W. cals. only, heavy barrel, matte finish, with swivels. Imported 1986 only. Last Mfg.'s Sug. Retail was $345.

Heavy Barrel Model – .222R, .22-250, or .243W cal., approx. 9 lbs., no sights. Last Mfg.'s Sug. Retail was $410.

Carbine Model – 20 in. barrel. Disc. 1985. Last Mfg.'s Sug. Retail was $480.

Stutzen Rifle – Mannlicher style full length stock, same general specifications as Sporter/Classic, 20½ in. barrel. Not available in 7mm Rem. Mag. or .300 Win. Mag cal. Last Mfg.'s Sug. Retail was $385.

Regal Custom – similar to Sporter Model, except has slim classic European style stock with Schnabel forend, deluxe walnut with extra checkering, ebony forend cap, engraved action and floorplate. Limited importation (1986 only). Last Mfg.'s Sug. Retail was $950. This model was custom made by special order only.

CFT TARGET RIFLE – 7.62mm, single shot, bolt action, globe front and aperture rear sights, 26½ in. barrel, 11 lbs. Disc. 1987. Last Mfg.'s Sug. Retail was $780.

Grading	100%	98%	95%	90%	80%	70%	60%

RIFLES: DISCONTINUED, SINGLE SHOT

NO. 12 MARTINI — .22 LR, 29 in. barrel, target sights, straight stock, pre-WWII.

	100%	98%	95%	90%	80%	70%	60%
	$360	$275	$250	$210	$175	$155	$130

MODEL 15 — similar to 12, except pistol grip stock, better grade target sights, pre-WWII.

	$385	$305	$275	$240	$200	$175	$155

CENTURION MATCH RIFLE — similar to 15, except Centurion guarantee — 1½ in. grouping at 100 yards, 24 in. barrel, pre-WWII.

	$440	$385	$330	$275	$240	$220	$175

MATCH 12/15 — similar to 15, except made after WWII.

	$385	$305	$275	$240	$200	$175	$155

MODEL 12/15 — heavy barrel.

	$415	$330	$305	$270	$230	$195	$165

MODEL 13 — lighter version of 12.

	$340	$265	$235	$200	$165	$150	$125

MODEL 13 SPORTER — similar to 13, except has sport sights.

	100%	98%	95%	90%	80%	70%	60%
	$330	$240	$220	$175	$155	$140	$120
.22 Hornet	$385	$305	$275	$240	$200	$175	$155

MARTINI INTERNATIONAL MATCH — .22 LR, 29 in. heavy barrel, international sights, mfg. 1950-1953.

	$415	$360	$320	$275	$255	$230	$200

INTERNATIONAL LIGHT — 26 in. lightweight barrel.

	$415	$360	$320	$275	$255	$230	$200

INTERNATIONAL MKII — improved trigger, ejectors and stock design, mfg. 1953-1959.

	$425	$375	$340	$315	$285	$255	$220

INTERNATIONAL MKIII — longer action, floating barrel, mfg. 1959-1967.

	$495	$430	$385	$360	$330	$305	$265

INTERNATIONAL ISU — modeled to meet ISU standards, 28 in. barrel, mfg. 1968-disc.

	$495	$430	$385	$360	$330	$305	$265

INTERNATIONAL MARK V — similar to ISU, but heavier barrel, mfg. 1976-disc.

	$525	$460	$430	$375	$350	$330	$305

RIFLES: DISCONTINUED, BOLT ACTION

MAJESTIC FEATHERWEIGHT DELUXE — .243, .270, .308, or .30-06 cal., bolt action, 22 in. barrel, folding sight, checkered European style stock, mfg. 1959-1965.

	100%	98%	95%	90%	80%	70%	60%
	$330	$250	$220	$195	$180	$165	$145
.458 Mag.	$445	$375	$305	$275	$220	$210	$200

MAJESTIC DELUXE — .222, .22 Hornet, .243, 7 x 57, .308, or .30-06 cal., heavier barrel.

	$330	$250	$220	$195	$180	$165	$145

Grading	100%	98%	95%	90%	80%	70%	60%

MONARCH DELUXE — similar to Majestic Deluxe, but American design stock, mfg. 1965-1974.

	$350	$275	$250	$220	$195	$180	$165

MONARCH DELUXE VARMINT — similar to Monarch Deluxe, except .222 or .243 cal., 24 in. heavy barrel. Disc.

	$370	$305	$275	$250	$210	$195	$180

MARTINI ISU MATCH .22 — single shot, bolt action, .22 cal. only, similar to CFT Model. Add $100 for Mk. V.H.B. Model. Disc. 1985.

	$825	$700	$600	$530	$475	$435	$400

Last Mfg.'s Sug. Retail was $1,000.

BAFORD ARMS, INC.
Manufactured by Baford Arms, Inc. located in Bristol, TN. Distributed by C.L. Reedy & Associates, Inc. located in Melbourne, FL.

MODEL 35 FIRE POWER — 9mm Para., semi-auto single action, patterned after the Browning Hi-Power, total stainless steel construction, 4¾ in. barrel, combat hammer and safety, Pachmayr grips, removable barrel bushing, Millett Mk. II sights, 14 shot mag., 32 oz. Introduced late 1988 with limited mfg. until 1991, and was resumed September, 1992.

Mfg.'s Sug. Retail	$550	$500	$425	$350			

THUNDER DERRINGER — .44 Spl./.410 shotshell, single shot, tip out action, 3 in. barrel, blued steel finish, spur trigger, wood grips. Introduced late 1988 with limited mfg. until 1991, when production temporarily ceased.

	$130	$110	$95	$90	$85	$80	$75

Add $90 for interchangable barrel kit.
Interchangeable pistol barrels are chambered in various calibers between .22 Short and 9mm Para. There are two types: one fits flush while the other facilitates a scope mounting. Last Mfg.'s Sug. Retail was $130.

BAIKAL
Manufactured in the U.S.S.R. since approx. WWII. Current importer is KBI, Inc. located in Harrisburg, PA. Distributor and dealer sales.

Baikal shotguns have had limited importation into the U.S. 1993 marks the first year that Baikal's have officially (and legally) been imported into the U.S. because of Russia's previous export restrictions domestically. In prior years, however, a few O/Us have been seen for sale and have no doubt been "imported" into this country one at a time. Quality is in the intermediate level and collector interest is not particularly great. Most older O/U shotguns fall into the $400 - $1,000 range if quality is at par with other more famous trademarks.

PISTOLS

IJ-70 — 9 x 18 Makarov cal., double action semi-auto, all steel blued construction, fully adj. target sights, inlcudes two 8 shot mags., holster and cleaning rod.

Mfg.'s Sug. Retail	$249	$225	$195	$180	$165	$150	$135	$120

SHOTGUNS: RECENT IMPORTATION

With the break-up of the Soviet Union in 1991, this Russian trademark will see more U.S. importation in the future as trade barriers continue to be taken down on previous Soviet bloc countries.

IJ-18M SINGLE BARREL — 12, 16, 20, or .410 ga., 26 or 28 in. barrel.

Mfg.'s Sug. Retail	$89	$75	$60	$50	$40	$35	$30	$30

Grading	100%	98%	95%	90%	80%	70%	60%

IJ-43 SXS FIELD MODEL — 12 or 20 ga., double triggers, extractors, 26 or 28 in. barrels.

Mfg.'s Sug. Retail	$379	$295	$235	$200	$160	$130	$95	$75

IJ-27 O/U FIELD MODEL — 12 or 20 (new 1992) ga., double triggers, extractors, 26 or 28 in. barrels.

Mfg.'s Sug. Retail	$459	$355	$290	$260	$225	$195	$180	$165

Add $30 for single trigger and automatic ejectors (Model IJ-27EIC).

BAILONS GUNMAKERS LIMITED

Manufacturer and refurbisher located in Birmingham, England. Limited exportation into the U.S. (see Trademark Index in back for more information).

Bailons also makes to special order, both boxlock and sidelock shotguns in most popular gauges. Prices are subject to negotiation and dependent upon the amount and type of engraving specified as well as quality of the wood. Also, Bailons repairs and refurbishes English shotguns using original materials and old world finishing techniques.

HUNTING RIFLE — various cals., modified Mauser bolt action, barrel length to suit from 18 to 30 in., set triggers or match, Habicht Telescope sight (magnification and reticle to suit), engraving, and types of finishes are at optional cost, prices below reflect standard rifle with no options. New 1986.

Mfg.'s Sug. Retail	$2,750	$2,750	$2,350	$2,050	$1,800	$1,675	$1,475	$1,350

BAKER GUN & FORGING CO.

Previous manufacturer located in Batavia, NY. 1889-1933.

SHOTGUNS: SIDE BY SIDE

Note: Original damascus guns in 80% or better condition with bright case colors will approach the values of steel barrel counterparts.

THE NEW BAKER — 10 or 12 ga., exposed hammers, damascus barrels, extractors.

	$350	$300	$260	$225	$195	$175	$150

BATAVIA SPECIAL — 12, 16, or 20 ga., 26, 28, 30, or 32 in. barrels, any standard choke, checkered pistol grip stock, sidelock, extractors.

	$385	$305	$275	$260	$250	$220	$200

BATAVIA LEADER — similar to Special, except has deluxe finish.

	$440	$360	$335	$305	$285	$265	$220
Auto ejectors	$525	$440	$415	$385	$370	$330	$305

BLACK BEAUTY SPECIAL — similar to Leader, except has engraved, select wood.

	$745	$650	$615	$590	$550	$525	$495
Auto ejectors	$855	$760	$725	$700	$660	$635	$605

BATAVIA EJECTOR — similar to Leader, but finer finish.

	$880	$770	$745	$715	$690	$660	$635
Damascus barrels	$440	$330	$305	$275	$250	$220	$165

BAKER S GRADE — similar to Leader, but finer finish, better grade wood.

	$880	$775	$745	$715	$690	$650	$635
Auto ejectors	$1,100	$990	$965	$935	$910	$880	$745

Grading	100%	98%	95%	90%	80%	70%	60%

BAKER R GRADE — similar to Leader, except scroll and game scene engraved, Krupp barrels, fancy wood.

	100%	98%	95%	90%	80%	70%	60%
	$1,100	$990	$965	$935	$910	$880	$745
Auto ejectors	$1,320	$1,210	$1,155	$1,100	$1,075	$1,045	$965
Damascus barrel	$550	$415	$385	$360	$330	$275	$230

PARAGON GRADE — custom order only to customer specifications.

	100%	98%	95%	90%	80%	70%	60%
	$1,650	$1,430	$1,320	$1,210	$1,155	$1,045	$770
Auto ejectors	$1,815	$1,595	$1,485	$1,375	$1,210	$1,100	$990

EXPERT GRADE — auto ejectors standard, overall finer grade wood and engraving.

	100%	98%	95%	90%	80%	70%	60%
	$2,500	$2,100	$1,850	$1,500	$1,250	$1,000	$750

DELUXE GRADE — best quality.

	100%	98%	95%	90%	80%	70%	60%
	$3,750	$3,250	$2,950	$2,650	$2,300	$2,000	$1,600

Add $200 for single trigger.

⚞ **Damascus barrels** — also known as Early Paragon Grade. If condition is 50% or less subtract 50% or more. If 90% original condition or better, prices will be the same as for damascus L.C. Smith guns.

SHOTGUNS: SINGLE BARREL TRAP

Baker single barrel trap guns, although more rare than their side by side counterparts, are not as desirable as those models listed above. Typically, values will be 50%-75% of a side by side model of equal grade.

BARRETT FIREARMS MANUFACTURING, INC.
Manufacturer located in Murfreesboro, TN. Dealer direct sales.

MODEL 82 RIFLE — .50 Browning machine gun cartridge, semi-auto recoil operation, 33-37 in. barrel, 11 shot mag., 2,850 FPS muzzle velocity, scope sight only, parkerized finish, 35 lbs. Mfg. 1985-87.

	100%	98%	95%	90%	80%	70%	60%
	$4,350	$3,950	$3,450	$2,700	$2,150	$1,800	$1,500

Last Mfg.'s Sug. Retail for consumers was $3,180 in 1985.
This model underwent design changes since initial production. Only 115 were mfg. starting with ser. no. 100.

MODEL 82A1 — .50 BMG, current military configuration, variant of the original Model 82, available to civilians, back-up iron sights provided, 2 mags., and fitted hard case, 29 (new late 1989) or 33 (disc. 1989) in. barrel, 10 shot mag., 32½ lbs. for 1989 and older mfg., 28½ lbs. for 1990 mfg.

	Mfg.'s Sug. Retail	$6,750		98%	95%	90%	80%	70%	60%
			$6,350	$4,950	$4,250	$3,650	$3,150	$2,650	$2,200

Add $275 for camo backpack carrying case.
Add $1,150 for new 10X scope and mounts.
This model boasts official U.S. rifle status following government procurement during Operation Desert Storm. In 1992, a new "arrowhead" shaped muzzle brake was introduced to reduce recoil.

MODEL 90 — .50 BMG, bolt action design, 29 in. match grade barrel with muzzle brake, 5 shot detachable box mag., includes extendible bi-pod legs, Sorbothane recoil pad, scope optional, 22 lbs. New 1990.

	Mfg.'s Sug. Retail	$3,650		98%	95%	90%	80%	70%	60%
			$3,450	$2,950	$2,400	$2,150	$1,875	$1,600	$1,500

Add $1,150 for new 10X scope and mounts.

BAR-STO
Previous manufacturer of semi-auto pistols.

Grading	100%	98%	95%	90%	80%	70%	60%

BAR-STO .25 ACP — .25 ACP, patterned after the Baby Browning, brushed stainless steel finish, walnut grips, approx. 250 manufactured in circa 1974.

$195 $165 $125

BAUER FIREARMS CORPORATION
Previous manufacturer located in Fraser, MI.

BAUER .25 AUTOMATIC — .25 auto, 2½ in. barrel, 6 shot, fixed sights, checkered walnut or pearlite grips, mfg. 1972-1984.

$150 $130 $110

Note: These guns are identical to the Baby Browning, except stainless steel.

THE RABBIT — combination gun, all metal construction, .22 cal. and .410 ga., O/U configuration. Mfg. 1982-1984.

$125 $100 $90 $80 $70 $60 $50

BAYARD
Previously manufactured by Anciens Etablissements Pieper located in Herstal, Belgium.

Even though Bayard Models 1908, both 1923s, and 1930 were manufactured only by Anciens Etablissements Pieper of Herstal, Belgium these pistols are listed under this heading as they are most commonly referred to by this trademark designation.

.25 and .380 cals. are more rare than the .32's and will command a 20%+ premium above values listed below unless indicated differently.

MODEL 1908 POCKET AUTOMATIC — .25 auto, .32 auto, .380 auto, 6 shot, 2¼ in. barrel, fixed sights, blue, hard rubber grips.

$220 $195 $165 $100 $85 $70 $55

MODEL 1923 POCKET AUTOMATIC — .25 auto, 2½ in. barrel, blue, fixed sights, checkered hard rubber grips.

$220 $195 $140 $100 $85 $70 $55

BAYARD 1923 POCKET AUTOMATIC — .32 auto, .380 auto, 6 shot, 3⁵⁄₁₆ in. barrel, fixed sights, blue, checkered hard rubber grips.

$250 $200 $170 $145 $120 $95 $75

Add 100% for .380 cal.

BAYARD 1930 POCKET AUTOMATIC — slight modification of 1923.

$250 $200 $170 $145 $120 $95 $75

BEEMAN PRECISION ARMS, INC.
Importer and distributor located in Santa Rosa, CA.

Beeman is a large importer, primarily specializing in high quality European rifles and pistols. Trademarks currently being distributed in the U.S. are manufactured by: Agner (disc. 1986), Erma (disc. 1985), FAS, Fabarm, Feinwerkbau, Korth, Krico, Unique, and Weihrauch. These trademarks will appear under their respective alphabetical headings. Air rifles, pistols, and/or black powder firearms will appear under those headings in the back of the book.

Grading	100%	98%	95%	90%	80%	70%	60%

Below listed firearms were manufactured to Beeman specifications, and are therefore listed under the Beeman Heading.

PISTOLS: SEMI-AUTO

BEEMAN MP-08 — .380 ACP, Luger type toggle action, 3½ in. barrel, 6 shot mag., blue, 1.4 lbs. Mfg. 1968-1990.

	$335	$275	$240	$185	$145	$115	$95

In 1988, Beeman took over importation of these two models (MP-08 and P-08). These revised models have new Luger style checkered walnut grips and 3½ in. barrel. Previous variations had plastic grips.
Last Mfg.'s Sug. Retail was $390.

BEEMAN P-08 — .22 LR, Luger type toggle action, 8 shot mag., 3.8 in. barrel, blue, checkered walnut grips, 1.9 lbs. Mfg. 1969-1990.

	$335	$275	$240	$185	$145	$115	$95

Last Mfg.'s Sug. Retail was $390.

PISTOLS: SINGLE SHOT

MODEL SPX — .22 LR cal., designed for silhouette shooting, 10 in. heavy bull barrel, blued metal parts, birchwood stocks and forearm, aperture sights, 3.9 lbs. New 1993.

Mfg.'s Sug. Retail	$700	$625	$550	$475	$425	$375	$330	$295

Model SPX Deluxe — similar to Model SPX, except has matte chrome metal finish, hand stippled walnut grips, and Anschutz rear sight. New 1993.

Mfg.'s Sug. Retail	$900	$800	$725	$650	$575	$500	$425	$350

SP STANDARD — .22 LR cal., sidelever action, 8, 10, 12, or 15 in. barrel, adj. sights and walnut grips, single shot. Made in W. Germany. Imported 1985-86 only.

	$250	$220	$180	$170	$160	$150	$140

Add $10 or $30 for 12 or 15 in. barrel respectively.
Last Mfg.'s Sug. Retail was $250.

SP DELUXE — similar to SP Standard, except has forearm, about 3½ lbs. Made in W. Germany. Imported 1985-86 only.

	$275	$240	$200	$185	$170	$155	$145

Add $10 or $30 for 12 or 15 in. barrel respectively.
Last Mfg.'s Sug. Retail was $300.

BEHOLLA PISTOL
Previously manufactured by Becker & Hollander located in Suhl, Germany.

BEHOLLA POCKET AUTOMATIC — .32 auto, 7 shot, 2.9 in. barrel, blue, serrated wood or rubber grips, mfg. 1915-1920, from 1920-1925 the same gun was mfg. by Stenda-Werke.

	$225	$170	$150	$135	$120	$100	$90

BENELLI
Manufacturer located in Urbino, Italy. Shotguns currently imported by Heckler And Koch, Inc. located in Chantilly, VA (dealer sales only). Handguns currently imported by European American Armory, located in Hialeah, FL and Sile Distributors, Inc., located in New York, NY (dealer sales only). Previously imported by Saco, located in Arlington, VA.

Grading	100%	98%	95%	90%	80%	70%	60%

PISTOLS

Models B-77, B-80, and MP3S are imported by Sile Distributors. Model MP-90S is imported by EAA.

MODEL B-76 — 9mm Luger, selective double action, all steel, 4¼ in. barrel, 8 shot mag., 34 oz. Importation disc. in 1990.

	$390	$340	$295	$245	$225	$210	$190

Last Mfg.'s Sug. Retail was $428.

MODEL B-76S TARGET — 9mm, similar to B-76, except has 5½ in. barrel, target grips, and adj. rear sights. Importation disc. 1990.

	$475	$425	$395	$350	$325	$300	$280

Last Mfg.'s Sug. Retail was $595.

MODEL B-77 — .32 ACP, selective double action, all steel, 4¼ in. barrel, 8 shot mag.

Mfg.'s Sug. Retail	$399	$275	$245	$225	$200	$180	$170	$160

MODEL B-80 — .30 Luger, selective double action, all steel, 4¼ in. barrel, 8 shot mag., 34 oz.

Mfg.'s Sug. Retail	$385	$275	$245	$225	$200	$180	$170	$160

MODEL B-80S TARGET — similar to B-80, except has 5½ in. barrel, target grips, and adj. rear sights.

Mfg.'s Sug. Retail	$572	$395	$350	$325	$295	$275	$250	$225

MODEL MP3S — .32 Smith & Wesson Long Wadcutter, target variation with 5½ in. barrel, high gloss bluing, target grips, and adj. rear sights.

Mfg.'s Sug. Retail	$785	$450	$375	$325	$295	$275	$250	$225

MODEL MP90S — .22 S, .22 LR, or .32 WC cal., 4⅓ in. barrel, target pistol featuring forward assisted breach bolt mechanism, anatomic grips, and adj. weight, 5 shot mag., 2.4 lbs. Importation began 1992.

Mfg.'s Sug. Retail	$1,995	$1,500	$1,250	$1,050	$925	$800	$700	$600

Conversion kits are also avail. for this model at an extra charge. This model is imported exclusively by EAA.

SHOTGUNS: SEMI-AUTO

Older models (disc. before 1986) may have a parts availability problem if repairs are needed. Approx. 50,000 SL-80 series shotguns were mfg. before discontinuance.

SL80 SERIES MODEL SL-121V — 12 ga., mechanically like SL-123V, various barrel lengths, black receiver finish, 3 in. Mag.— no extra charge. Disc. 1985.

	$360	$295	$260	$245	$215	$190	$175

Last Mfg.'s Sug. Retail was $397.

SL80 SERIES MODEL SL-121 SLUG — 12 ga., mechanically like SL-123V, only 21¹¹⁄₁₆ in. cylinder bore barrel, approx. 7 lbs. 3 oz. Disc. 1985.

	$395	$315	$275	$250	$220	$195	$175

Last Mfg.'s Sug. Retail was $434.

SL80 SERIES MODEL SL-122 SLUG — 12 ga. only, SL80 Series action, includes premium grade checkered walnut with Monte Carlo cheek piece and flat bottomed trap style forearm, solid rubber recoil pad, limited importation.

	$495	$425	$350	$325	$295	$275	$250

Grading	100%	98%	95%	90%	80%	70%	60%

SL80 SERIES MODEL SL123V AND DELUXE — 12 ga. fast "3rd generation" action, lower receiver Ergal special aluminum alloy, various chokes, approx. 6 lbs. 13 oz. Disc. 1985.

	$400	$325	$285	$255	$225	$200	$180

Last Mfg.'s Sug. Retail was $464.

SL80 SERIES MODEL 123V SPECIAL TRAP AND SKEET — 12 ga., choice of photo-engraving and frame finish, 32 in. barrel, approx. 7 lbs. 10 oz. Disc. 1985.

	$500	$425	$365	$330	$300	$275	$245

Add $115 for Skeet Model.
Last Mfg.'s Sug. Retail was $584.
Very limited quantities of the EXL Trap were mfg. (similar to 123 Trap Model, except has hand engraved receiver).

MODEL 80 SPECIAL SKEET — 12 ga. only, skeet variation, nickel plated receiver, limited importation, disc. 1989.

	$450	$350	$315	$275	$250	$225	$195

Last Mfg.'s Sug. Retail was $531.

MODEL 80 SPECIAL TRAP — 12 ga only, supplied with nickel plated receiver, disc. 1989.

	$425	$335	$300	$265	$240	$215	$185

SL80 SERIES MODEL SL201 — 20 ga., 26 in. barrel bored imp. mod., approx. 5 lbs. 10 oz. Disc. 1985.

	$375	$300	$260	$240	$215	$190	$165

Last Mfg.'s Sug. Retail was $399.

BRI-BENELLI SLUG — 12 ga. only, premium slug gun featuring SL80 Series action and drilled and tapped rifle barrel by E. R. Shaw Barrel Co., assembled by BRI in the U.S., trap grade stock with high cheek piece, approx. 25 guns total mfg. 1986-1987.

	$1,395	$1,175	$995	$850	$725	$600	$495

Original issue price on this model was $750-$850. These specimens are marked "BRI-Benelli". No warranties exist on this model.

M1 SUPER 90 SLUG — 12 ga. only, 3 in. Mag., semi-auto, incorporates improvements on the Benelli action, including rotating Montefeltro bolt system, 19¾ in. cyl. bore barrel with iron sights, 7 shot mag., fiberglass stock and forearm, 6.7 lbs. New 1986. Imported exclusively by H&K.

Mfg.'s Sug. Retail	$724	$600	$475	$350	$315	$280	$260	$240

Add $40 for ghost-ring sighting system.

M1 SUPER 90 DEFENSE — similar to Super 90 Slug, except has pistol grip stock, 7.1 lbs.

Mfg.'s Sug. Retail	$764	$625	$500	$375	$315	$280	$260	$240

Add $50 for ghost-ring sighting system.

M1 SUPER 90 TACTICAL — 12 ga. only, 18½ in. barrel, includes ghost ring sighting system, available with synthetic pistol grip or standard butt stock, includes 3 choke tubes, 7 shot mag., 6½ lbs. New 1993.

Mfg.'s Sug. Retail	$829	$675	$525	$400	$350	$300	$270	$240

M1 SUPER 90 ENTRY — 12 ga. only, includes 14 in. barrel, choice of pistol grip or standard stock, 5 shot mag. (2 shot extension), 6.7 lbs. New 1992.

Mfg.'s Sug. Retail	$814	$665	$525	$395	$350	$300	$270	$240

Add $45 for ghost ring sights.
This model requires special licensing (Class III transfer).

M1 SUPER 90 FIELD — similar to M1 Super 90, except has 21 (new 1990), 24 (new 1990), 26, or 28 in. vent. rib barrel and 3-shot mag., includes 3 screw in choke tubes, approx. 7.3 lbs.

Mfg.'s Sug. Retail	$799	$650	$450	$375	$330	$295	$275	$260

This model is available with either a short or extended magazine tube. The short tube is available in all barrel lengths - an extended mag. tube is available in 26 or 28 in. barrel only.

M1 SUPER 90 SPORTING SPECIAL — 12 ga., 18½ in. barrel, black matte finish, includes ghost ring sighting system, 6½ lbs. New 1993.

Mfg.'s Sug. Retail	$829	$675	$525	$400	$350	$300	$270	$240

MONTEFELTRO SUPER 90 STANDARD HUNTER — 12 or 20 (new 1993, 21 in. barrel only) ga., 3 in. chamber, 21, 24, 26, or 28 in. VR barrel with 3 choke tubes, matte black metal finish, checkered walnut stock and forearm with choice of high gloss or satin finish, 5 shot mag., 7¼ lbs. New 1988.

Mfg.'s Sug. Retail	$824	$675	$525	$400	$350	$300	$270	$240

Add $20 for left-hand action (26 or 28 in. barrel only).

✄ **Montefeltro Turkey Gun** — similar to Montefeltro Standard Hunter except has 24 in. VR barrel with 3 choke tubes, satin finish wood only, 7 lbs. Imported 1989 only.

		$575	$440	$370	$330	$295	$275	$260

Last Mfg.'s Sug. Retail was $675.

✄ **Montefeltro Uplander** — similar to Montefeltro Turkey Gun except has 21 or 24 in. VR barrel with 3 choke tubes, satin finish wood only, 7 lbs. Mfg. 1989-92.

		$650	$450	$375	$330	$295	$275	$260

Last Mfg.'s Sug. Retail was $799.

✄ **Montefeltro Slug Gun** — deer gun configuration with 19¾ in. slug barrel. Disc. 1992.

		$650	$450	$375	$330	$295	$275	$260

Last Mfg.'s Sug. Retail was $799.

BLACK EAGLE — 12 ga., Montefeltro action, similar to Montefeltro Super 90 Standard Hunter except has black synthetic stock and forearm, 21, 24, 26, or 28 (new 1990) in. VR barrel with 3 choke tubes, right hand only. Imported 1989-90, configuration changed to competition in 1991 (see Black Eagle Competition Model).

		$675	$575	$475	$395	$340	$300	$275

Last Mfg.'s Sug. Retail was $807.

✄ **Black Eagle Competition Model** — 12 ga. only, designed for competition shooting with action adj. for lighter loads, silver finished etched lower receiver, 26 or 28 in. VR barrel with 5 choke tubes and wrench provided, includes buttstock drop adjustment kit. New 1991.

Mfg.'s Sug. Retail	$1,099	$925	$750	$625	$500	$395	$340	$300

✄ **Black Eagle Slug Gun** — 12 ga., 24 in. rifled barrel with receiver scope mount. Imported 1990-91 only.

		$735	$625	$475	$395	$340	$300	$275

Last Mfg.'s Sug. Retail was $859.

SUPER BLACK EAGLE — 12 ga. only, 3½ in. chamber, updated Montefeltro action accepts all 12 ga. loads, 24, 26, or 28 in. VR barrel with 5 choke tubes and wrench provided, choice of matte finish and satin stock or blued finish and high gloss wood finish (26 in. barrel only), black synthetic stock and forearm with matte metal finish became optional 1993, vent. recoil pad, includes buttstock drop adjustment kit, approx. 7.1 lbs. New 1991.

Mfg.'s Sug. Retail	$1,079	$900	$775	$640	$525	$400	$340	$300

Grading	100%	98%	95%	90%	80%	70%	60%

Super Black Eagle Slug Gun — includes 24 in. E.R. Shaw rifle barrel with matte metal finish and choice of black polymer (new 1993) or satin finished wood. New 1992.

Mfg.'s Sug. Retail	$1,079	$900	$775	$640	$525	$400	$340	$300

M3 SUPER 90 — 12 ga. only, defense configuration incorporating convertible (fingertip activated) pump or semi-auto action, 19¾ in. cyl. bore barrel with rifle sights, choice of standard polymer stock or integral pistol grip, 7½ lbs. New 1989.

Mfg.'s Sug. Retail	$919	$785	$625	$475	$395	$340	$300	$275

Add $30 for ghost-ring sighting system.
Add $110 for folding stock (new 1990) - only available as a complete gun.
Add $340 for Model 200 Laser Sight System with bracket (disc.).

BENSON FIREARMS LTD.

Manufactured by Aldo Uberti in Italy. Previously imported and distributed from 1987-1989 by Benson Firearms Ltd. located in Seattle, WA. Benson Firearms Ltd. combined with A. Uberti USA Inc. in early 1989 and discontinued importation.

Benson Firearms can be differentiated from other A. Uberti imports by the "Benson Firearms Seattle, WA" barrel marking. Many of the models listed below are similar to those models imported by Allen Firearms (disc. 1987) and A. Uberti USA, Inc., (current importer).

Rather than provide a complete listing of Benson Firearms models, the following rules usually apply. Since Benson Firearms imported A. Uberti firearms, the Uberti section in this text should be referenced for current values regarding models with similar configurations. Collectibility to date has been limited on most Benson Firearms models, and as a rule, up-to-date values on this trademark are established by current importation prices of Uberti firearms. A complete listing of older Benson Firearms models can be found in Blue Book editions Eleven and Twelve.

BERETTA, DR. FRANCO

Current manufacturer located in Concesio (Brescia), Italy. Currently imported and distributed by Nevada Cartridge Co. located in San Francisco, CA beginning 1993. Previously distributed exclusively through Double M Shooting Sports located in Guilford, CT until 1988.

SHOTGUNS: O/U - BLACK DIAMOND SERIES

Black Diamond target guns were imported exclusively by Double M Shooting Sports until 1988.

FIELD MODEL — 12, 16, 20, 28, or .410 ga., variety of chokes, coin finish receiver.

		$595	$550	$495	$450	$395	$365	$335

Last Mfg.'s Sug. Retail was $960.

GRADE ONE — 12, 16, 20, 28, or .410 ga., variety of chokes, coin finish receiver with acid etched engraving, French walnut. Trap or skeet model also available, except in 16 ga.

		$1,020	$900	$810	$720	$630	$570	$525

Last Mfg.'s Sug. Retail was $1,440.

GRADE TWO — 12, 16, 20, 28, or .410 ga., variety of chokes, coin finish receiver with moderate engraving, French walnut. Trap or skeet model also available, except in 16 ga.

	$1,475	$1,320	$1,200	$1,080	$930	$815	$750

Last Mfg.'s Sug. Retail was $2,040.

GRADE THREE — 12, 16, 20, 28, or .410 ga., variety of chokes, coin finish receiver with scrollwork engraving, French walnut. Trap or skeet model also available, except in 16 ga.

	$2,100	$1,920	$1,775	$1,560	$1,410	$1,200	$1,035

Last Mfg.'s Sug. Retail was $3,000.

Grading	100%	98%	95%	90%	80%	70%	60%

GRADE FOUR — 12, 16, 20, 28, or .410 ga., variety of chokes, coin finish receiver with elaborate engraving, French walnut. Trap or skeet model also available, except in 16 ga.

	$2,500	$2,250	$1,950	$1,650	$1,375	$1,125	$995

Last Mfg.'s Sug. Retail was $3,960.

SKEET SET — includes 12, 20, 28, and .410 ga. barrels, available in Grades One through Four.
Multiply values on Grades One - Four by 275% for 4 ga. Skeet sets.

SHOTGUNS: O/U, S X S, & SINGLE BARREL RECENT MFG.

GAMMA STANDARD O & U — 12, 16, or 20 ga., 26 or 28 in. barrels, coin finish receiver with extensive engraving, Italian walnut. Add $83 with single trigger and ejectors. Imported 1984-1988.

	$400	$360	$330	$300	$275	$260	$240

Last Mfg.'s Sug. Retail was $445.

Gamma Standard — with interchangeable choke tubes, importation disc. 1988, resumed 1993.

Mfg.'s Sug. Retail	$1,000	$825	$695	$525	$425	$325	$250	$195

Add 20% for auto ejectors.
Add $100 for single trigger.
Add 36% for Gamma Trap or Skeet variation (ST).

GAMMA DELUXE O & U — 12, 16, or 20 ga., 26 or 28 in. barrels, coin finish receiver with extensive engraving, Italian walnut. Add $84 with single trigger and ejectors. Imported 1984-1988.

	$445	$405	$370	$350	$325	$300	$275

Last Mfg.'s Sug. Retail was $480.

Gamma Deluxe — with interchangeable choke tubes. Importation disc. 1988.

	$635	$570	$530	$490	$450	$420	$390

Last Mfg.'s Sug. Retail was $685.

GAMMA TARGET O & U — 12 ga. only, SST, ejectors, Wundhammer swell pistol grip, English walnut stock and beavertail forearm. Imported 1986-1988.

	$550	$505	$455	$410	$370	$350	$325

Last Mfg.'s Sug. Retail was $595.

ALPHA STANDARD O & U — 12, 16, or 20 ga., 26 or 28 in. barrels, coin finish receiver with extensive engraving, Italian walnut. Imported 1984-1988, resumed 1993.

Mfg.'s Sug. Retail	$780	$720	$650	$525	$450	$375	$300	$250

Add 18% for auto ejectors.
Add $100 for single trigger.

ALPHA DELUXE O & U — 12, 16, or 20 ga., 26 or 28 in. barrels, coin finish receiver with extensive engraving, sling swivels, Italian walnut. Add $75 with single trigger and ejectors, $80 for interchangeable choke tubes (disc. 1985). Imported 1984-1988.

	$395	$355	$330	$300	$275	$250	$230

Last Mfg.'s Sug. Retail was $435.

AMERICA STANDARD O & U — .410 ga. only, 26 or 28 in. barrels, coin finish receiver with extensive engraving, Italian walnut. Add $85 for Deluxe model. Imported 1984-1988.

	$305	$280	$265	$240	$215	$205	$190

Last Mfg.'s Sug. Retail was $335.

Grading	100%	98%	95%	90%	80%	70%	60%

EUROPA O & U — .410 ga. only, 26 in. barrels, coin finish receiver with some engraving, Italian walnut. Add $95 for Deluxe model (disc. 1985). Imported 1984-1988.

	100%	98%	95%	90%	80%	70%	60%
	$275	$250	$235	$220	$210	$200	$185

Last Mfg.'s Sug. Retail was $295.

FRANCIA STANDARD SXS — .410 ga. only, double triggers, extractors, checkered walnut. Imported 1986-1988. Add $19 for Deluxe Model.

	100%	98%	95%	90%	80%	70%	60%
	$235	$220	$210	$200	$185	$175	$160

Last Mfg.'s Sug. Retail was $255.

OMEGA STANDARD SXS — 12, 16, or 20 ga., 26 or 28 in. barrels, coin finish receiver with extensive engraving, Italian walnut. Imported 1984-1988, resumed 1993.

Mfg.'s Sug. Retail	$880	$780	$695	$550	$450	$375	$300	$250

Add 32% for auto ejectors.
Add 10% for single trigger (disc. 1985).

MILANO O/U — 9mm Flobert, folding design. Importation began 1993.

Mfg.'s Sug. Retail	$420	$380	$330	$295	$250	$210	$180	$150

VERONA/BERGAMO SxS — 9mm Flobert, folding design, Bergamo model has hammers, Verona model is hammerless. Importation began 1993.

Mfg.'s Sug. Retail	$300	$270	$225	$180	$140	$115	$95	$75

BRESCIA SINGLE BARREL — 9mm Flobert, folding design. Importation began 1993.

Mfg.'s Sug. Retail	$200	$175	$150	$130	$110	$90	$70	$55

BETA SINGLE BARREL — single barrel field gun, available in 12, 16, 20, 24, 28, 32, or .410 ga., VR, chrome finish receiver, folding design. Imported 1985-1988, resumed 1993.

Mfg.'s Sug. Retail	$240	$215	$185	$160	$145	$135	$125	$115

Add 10% for VR.

SHOTGUNS: SEMI-AUTO

ARIETE STANDARD — 12 ga. only, gas operated, 2¾ or 3 in. chamber, various barrel lengths, with or without choke tubes, aluminum receiver, checkered stock and forearm, approx. 6.9 lbs. Importation began 1993.

Mfg.'s Sug. Retail	$1,180	$995	$795	$525	$425	$325	$250	$195

Add $20 for 3 in. mag. variation.

SHOTGUNS: SLIDE ACTION

ARIETE — 12 ga. only, 3 in. chamber, various barrel lengths without VR, twin action bars, matte finish, recoil pad. Importation began 1993.

Mfg.'s Sug. Retail	$880	$780	$695	$550	$450	$375	$300	$250

BERETTA, PIETRO

Manufactured in Brescia, Italy 1526-present and Accokeek, MD 1978 to date. Beretta U.S.A. Corp. was formed in 1977 and is located in Accokeek, MD. Beretta U.S.A. Corp. has been importing Beretta Firearms exclusively since 1980. 1970-1977 manufacture was imported exclusively by Garcia. Distributor sales only.

PISTOLS: SEMI-AUTO, DISC.

MODEL 1910 — .25 ACP cal., single action, 7 shot, fixed sights, wood grips, mfg. 1910-1934.

	100%	98%	95%	90%	80%	70%	60%
	$300	$275	$250	$195	$165	$145	$110

Grading	100%	98%	95%	90%	80%	70%	60%

MODEL 1915 — .32 ACP, 8 shot, 3.3 in. barrel, fixed sights, blue, wood grips, mfg. 1915-1919.

| | $350 | $315 | $275 | $250 | $195 | $165 | $110 |

MODEL 1915 — 9mm Glisenti, second variation - larger version, mfg. 1915.

| | $450 | $385 | $330 | $275 | $220 | $195 | $140 |

9mm Para. is not interchangeable and potentially dangerous if interchanged with 9mm Glisenti.

MODEL 1923 — 9mm, 8 shot, 4 in. barrel, fixed sights, steel grips, mfg. 1923-1935.

| | $750 | $600 | $475 | $350 | $300 | $250 | $200 |

Add 25% for slotted rear grip strap.

MODEL 1934 — .380 ACP (9mm Kurz), 3⅜ in. barrel, fixed sights, blue, plastic grips. Italy's service weapon in WWII, military models have poorer finish, mfg. 1934-1959.

| | $290 | $275 | $250 | $195 | $165 | $140 | $110 |
| Commercial model | $365 | $320 | $275 | $220 | $195 | $165 | $140 |

MODEL 1935 — .32 ACP, 3½ in. barrel, fixed sights, blue, plastic grips, the wartime model had poor finish, mfg. 1935-1959.

| | $250 | $225 | $200 | $180 | $160 | $140 | $120 |
| Commercial model | $275 | $250 | $215 | $185 | $165 | $145 | $125 |

MODEL 318 — .25 ACP, 2½ in. barrel, fixed sights, blue, plastic grips, mfg. 1934-1939.

| | $275 | $250 | $220 | $195 | $165 | $140 | $110 |

MODEL 418 — .25 ACP, fixed sights.

| | $220 | $190 | $170 | $145 | $125 | $110 | $100 |

MODEL 420 — .25 ACP, chrome finish, small coverage engraving.

| | $350 | $300 | $260 | $230 | $200 | $175 | $160 |

MODEL 421 — .25 ACP, gold plated, elaborate engraving.

| | $475 | $430 | $400 | $360 | $320 | $280 | $230 |

PISTOLS: POST WWII MFG.

100% values on below listed models assume NIB condition.

MODEL 948 — .22 LR, 3½ or 6 in. barrel, fixed sights, hammer.

| | $175 | $150 | $125 | $100 | $75 | $60 | $50 |

MODEL 949 OLYMPIC TARGET — .22 S or LR, 8¾ in. barrel, target sights, adj. barrel weights, blue, muzzle brake, checkered wood grips with thumbrest, limited mfg. 1959-1964.

| | $660 | $550 | $495 | $385 | $305 | $250 | $195 |

MODEL 950CC MINX M2 — .22 Short, hinged 2⅜ in. barrel, fixed sights, blue, plastic grips. Mfg. 1955-disc.

| | $135 | $115 | $105 | $95 | $85 | $75 | $70 |

MODEL 950CC SPECIAL MINX M4 — similar to M2, with 4 in. barrel.

| | $135 | $115 | $105 | $95 | $85 | $75 | $70 |

Grading	100%	98%	95%	90%	80%	70%	60%

MODEL 950B JETFIRE — similar to M2, in .25 ACP.

	$135	$115	$105	$95	$85	$75	$70

MODEL 951 BRIGADIER — 9mm, 4½ in. barrel, fixed sights, blue, plastic grips, current Italian service pistol. Mfg. 1952-present.

	$250	$215	$195	$175	$150	$130	$115

Add $350 for "Brigadier" or "Israeli" Model.

MODEL 20 — .25 ACP, double action, alloy frame, 9 shot, 2½ in. barrel, plastic or walnut grips, 10.9 oz. Disc. 1985.

	$160	$140	$125	$115	$95	$85	$75

Last Mfg.'s Sug. Retail was $214.

MODEL 70 PUMA OR COUGAR — .32 ACP or .380 ACP cal., 3½ in. barrel, fixed or adj. sights, blue, plastic grips, .32 Puma alloy frame, .380 Cougar steel frame. Disc.

	$200	$180	$165	$150	$130	$110	$90

This model is more desirable in .380 ACP cal.

MODEL 70T — similar to 70, .32 ACP, target sights. Disc.

	$275	$250	$220	$195	$165	$150	$140

MODEL 70S — .22 LR or .380 ACP cal., single action, 3½ in. barrel, 9 shot, blued finish, plastic grips, weight .22 cal. — 18 oz., .380 ACP — 23 oz., steel frame, .22 LR has adj. rear sight. Disc. 1985.

	$240	$210	$185	$170	$155	$140	$125

Last Mfg.'s Sug. Retail was $295.

MODEL 71 JAGUAR — alloy frame, .22 LR version of 70. Disc.

	$220	$195	$180	$160	$150	$140	$110

MODEL 72 JAGUAR — similar to 71, with 6 in. barrel. Disc.

	$220	$195	$180	$160	$150	$140	$110

MODEL 76P-76W TARGET PISTOL — .22 LR, single action, 11 shot, steel frame, 6 in. barrel, adj. sights, blued finish, thumbrest plastic grips (76-P). Disc. 1985.

	$345	$300	$275	$245	$220	$195	$170

Add $40 for thumbrest wood grips (Model 76-W).
Last Mfg.'s Sug. Retail was $395.

MODEL 80 — .22 Short cal., target pistol with limited importation into the U.S.

	$750	$675	$595	$550	$495	$450	$395

MODEL 81P-81W — .32 ACP, double action, 13 shot, 3.8 in. barrel, fixed sights, blue. Imported 1976-1984.

	$300	$250	$225	$195	$175	$155	$135

Add $90 for nickel finish.
Add $20 for wood grips (W Suffix).

MODEL 82W — .32 ACP, double action, more compact than Model 81, 10 shot, walnut grips, 17 oz. Importation disc. 1984.

	$300	$250	$225	$195	$175	$155	$135

Add $75 for nickel finish.

Grading	100%	98%	95%	90%	80%	70%	60%

MODEL 84W-EL — similar to Model 84 only specially engraved, select walnut grips. Presentation case. Disc. 1984.

	$1,025	$770	$720	$615	$565	$520	$460

MODEL 86P-86W — .380 ACP only, double action, tip-up 4⅓ in. barrel, 8 shot mag., plastic or walnut grips, 23 oz. Add $80 for walnut grips (86-W). This model was advertised, but never released.
Mfg.'s Sug. Retail was $480 in 1986.

MODEL 90 DOUBLE ACTION AUTOMATIC — .32 ACP, 3⅝ in. barrel, fixed sights, blue, plastic grips. Mfg. 1969-1983.

	$275	$195	$175	$155	$130	$110	$95

MODEL 92 (FIRST SERIES) — same general specifications as current Model 92SB, originally mfg. 1976 until disc.

	$400	$350	$315	$280	$255	$240	$220

Early production Model 92s had a frame mounted safety and mag. release button at base of pistol grip in addition to a serial number suffix. The Model 92's design evolved from the Beretta Model 951.

MODEL 92S (SECOND SERIES) — similar to Model 92, except has firing pin safety. Disc.

	$375	$325	$260	$230	$200	$180	$165

MODEL 92SB-P (THIRD SERIES) — 9mm Luger, double action, 16 shot, 4.92 in. barrel, fixed sights, alloy frame, high-polish blued finish, plastic grips (Model 92SB-P), 34½ oz. Mfg. 1980-1985.

	$475	$425	$385	$345	$310	$285	$260

Last Mfg.'s Sug. Retail was $600.

Model 92SB-W — similar to above, only with wooden grips. Disc. 1985.

	$495	$430	$390	$355	$330	$290	$260

Last Mfg.'s Sug. Retail was $620.

MODEL 92SB-P COMPACT — similar to Model 92SB, except has 4.3 in. barrel, 14 shot, plastic grips (Model 92SB-P), 31 oz. Disc. 1985.

	$500	$440	$385	$345	$310	$285	$260

Add $60 for nickel finish.
Last Mfg.'s Sug. Retail was $620.

Model 92SB-W Compact — similar to above only with wooden grips. Disc. 1985.

	$525	$465	$395	$355	$335	$300	$280

Last Mfg.'s Sug. Retail was $635.

MODEL 100 — .32 ACP, fixed sights. Disc.

	$250	$220	$195	$165	$150	$140	$130

MODEL 101 — similar to 70T, in .22 LR. Disc.

	$250	$220	$195	$165	$150	$140	$130

PISTOLS: SEMI-AUTO, RECENT MFG.

On Beretta's large frame pistols, alphabetical suffixes refer to the following: F Model - double/single action system with external safety decocking lever, G Model - double/single action system with external decocking only lever, D Model - double action only without safety lever, DS Model - double action only with external safety lever.

Grading	100%	98%	95%	90%	80%	70%	60%

MODEL 21(A)-W — .22 LR or .25 ACP, double action, alloy frame, 7 shot mag. (.22 LR) or 8 shot mag. (.25 ACP), 2.4 in. barrel, walnut grips, 11½ oz.

⚰ **Blue/Nickel Finish**

Mfg.'s Sug. Retail	$235	$190	$155	$140	$130	$115	$95	$85

Add $25 for nickel finish.
Add $50 for engraving.

⚰ **Matte Finish** — matte finished metal, plastic grips. Introduced 1992.

Mfg.'s Sug. Retail	$185	$160	$140	$130	$115	$95	$85	$80

This model is manufactured by Beretta U.S.A. Corp. in Accokeek, MD.

⚰ **Lady Beretta** — .22 LR only, similar to Model 21-W, except is specially serial numbered and has gold etching on top of frame and slide sides. Supplied with a blue velvet drawstring bag. 1990 issue.

		$245	$185	$160	$140	$130	$115	$100

This model was sold exclusively by Lew Horton Distributing Co.
Last Mfg.'s Sug. Retail was $285.

MODEL 71 — .22 LR, single action, 8 shot, 6 in. barrel, plastic grips with thumbrest, finger extension mag. Imported 1987 only.

		$190	$160	$140	$130	$115	$95	$85

Last Mfg.'s Sug. Retail was $215.

MODEL 84P-84W — .380 ACP cal., double action semi-auto, 3.82 in. barrel, alloy frame, steel slide, 13 shot mag., firing pin block, ambidextrous manual safety (also used as a decocking lever), low dot profile sights, curved trigger guard, plastic or wood grips, blue or nickel finish, 23 oz.

Mfg.'s Sug. Retail	$525	$410	$335	$300	$270	$240	$210	$190

Add $30 for wooden grips (Model 84W).
Add $75 for nickel finish (includes checkered wooden grips).

⚰ **Model 84F** — similar specifications to the Model 84P-84W, except patterned after the Model 92F Govt. Model, matte black Bruniton finish, squared off trigger guard, plastic or wood grips, 23 oz. Mfg. 1990 only.

		$395	$330	$300	$270	$240	$210	$190

Last Mfg.'s Sug. Retail was $479.

MODEL 85P-85W — same general specifications as the Model 84, except slimmer profile because of 8 shot straight line mag., Model 85P has plastic grips, 22 oz.

Mfg.'s Sug. Retail	$485	$385	$310	$270	$240	$210	$190	$175

Add $65 for nickel finish.
Add $25 for wooden grips (Model 85W).

⚰ **Model 85F** — similar specifications to the Model 85P-85W, except patterned after the Model 92F Govt. Model, matte black Bruniton finish, squared off trigger guard, plastic or wood grips, 21.8 oz. Mfg. in 1990 only.

		$375	$300	$270	$240	$210	$190	$175

Add $25 for wooden grips.
Last Mfg.'s Sug. Retail was $440.

MODEL 86 — .380 ACP, double action semi-auto with 4.4 in. tip-up barrel, 8 shot mag., checkered walnut grips, matte finish, fixed sights, gold trigger, 23.3 oz. Importation began 1991.

Mfg.'s Sug. Retail	$510	$425	$350	$295	$250	$225	$190	$175

Grading	100%	98%	95%	90%	80%	70%	60%

MODEL 87 — .22 LR, double action semi-auto, 7 shot mag., 3.82 or 6 in. target barrel with counterweight, wood grips, 20 oz. (3.82 in. barrel). Importation began 1986.

Mfg.'s Sug. Retail	$490	$395	$330	$280	$245	$210	$190	$175

⚮ **Model 87 Target** — single action only target variation of the Model 87 with 6 in. barrel, 23.3 oz.

Mfg.'s Sug. Retail	$510	$415	$350	$285	$245	$210	$190	$175

MODEL 89 — .22 LR, single action target semi-auto, matte black finish on metal parts, 10 shot mag., anatomical wood grips, adj. sights, 41 oz. Importation began 1988.

Mfg.'s Sug. Retail	$735	$585	$485	$400	$350	$300	$275	$250

MODEL 92D — 9mm Para., double action only, otherwise similar to Model 92F, except does not have a manual safety lever, black plastic grips, 3 dot sights, 33.8 oz. Introduced 1992.

Mfg.'s Sug. Retail	$585	$460	$360	$300	$250	$210	$190	$175

Add $65 for Trijicon sight system.

⚮ **Model 92D Deluxe** — deluxe model featuring gold plating and elaborate engraving. New 1993.

Mfg.'s Sug. Retail	$5,430		$4,950	$3,750	$2,500

MODEL 92F — 9mm Para., official U.S. military variation of 92 Series, 4.9 in. barrel, alloy frame, steel slide, 15 shot mag., chamber loaded indicator, matte black Bruniton finish, squared off trigger guard to facilitate two-hand shooting, extended mag. base, choice of regular or 3 dot sights (new 1991). Model 92F-P has plastic grips. Model 92F-W has wood grips. New 1984.

Mfg.'s Sug. Retail	$625	$545	$445	$410	$375	$335	$300	$275

Add $20 for checkered wood grips.
Add $65 for Trijicon sight system.
Add $165 for gold engraving/accenting (Model 92F-W only).
Add $500 for 9mm Competition Conversion Kit (new 1992).

Plastic grips are currently as desirable as wood, even though wood adds $25 to the retail price.

Older Italian mfg. Model 92s if in 98%+ condition are commanding slight premiums in some areas.

The U.S. military on January 15, 1985 announced that the Model 92F (M9) would replace the Colt Govt. Model .45 ACP as the standard government issue sidearm. Because of domestic political pressures, Congress requested that a new sidearm competition be conducted again in 1988. The result of this second trial was that the Department of the Army announced on May 22, 1989 that Beretta had won again. This military contract with Beretta U.S.A. Corp. involves over 320,000 Model M9 (military designation for the commercial Model 92F) being manufactured for U.S. military consumption in the 1990's. Actual delivery of commercial Model 92s began in January of 1986. Actual M9 delivery to U.S. Armed Forces has exceeded 250,000 units to date.

⚮ **Model 92F (Stainless)** — similar to Model 92F, except is mfg. from stainless steel, satin finish with plastic grips, 3 dot sights, initially released to law enforcement agencies only, a limited amount have found their way into the commercial market (usually with premiums being asked).

Mfg.'s Sug. Retail	$755	$625	$525	$450

Add $20 for wood grips.
Add $70 for Trijicon sight system (new 1993).
Add $485 for barrel engraving and gold trim (Model 92F-EL).

⚮ **Model 92F Centurion** — similar to Model 92F, except has compact barrel slide unit with full size frame, 4.3 in. barrel, choice of plastic or wood grips, 3 dot sight system, same length as Model 92F Compact, 15 shot mag., 33.2 oz. Introduced 1992.

Mfg.'s Sug. Retail	$625	$550	$450	$415	$375	$335	$300	$275

Add $20 for checkered walnut grips (Model 92F Wood).
Add $65 for Trijicon sight system.

Grading	100%	98%	95%	90%	80%	70%	60%

🗲 **Model 92EL** — deluxe variation of the Model 92F featuring high polish, bright blue with gold highlights on trim, frame etchings, and small parts, special ergonomic walnut grips. Importation began 1992.

Mfg.'s Sug. Retail	$790		$685	$550	$425		

MODEL 92F COMPACT — similar to Model 92F, except has 4.3 in. barrel and 13 shot mag., plastic or wood grips, 31½ oz. While temporarily suspended in 1986, production was resumed in 1989.

| Mfg.'s Sug. Retail | $625 | $550 | $450 | $415 | $375 | $335 | $300 | $275 |

Add $20 for checkered walnut grips (Model 92F Wood).
Add $65 for Trijicon sight system.

🗲 **Model 92F Compact "M"** — similar to Model 92F Compact, except has 8 shot straight line mag., plastic grips only. Imported 1990-93.

| | | $550 | $450 | $415 | $375 | $335 | $300 | $275 |

Add $65 for Trijicon sight system.
Last Mfg.'s Sug. Retail was $625.
Approx. 1,200 92SBM Models were imported in the 1980s.

MODEL 92G — 9mm Para., identical to the Model 92F, except features a spring loaded decocking lever that safely lowers the hammer allowing fire-ready when unholstering the pistol. New 1990.
The Model 92G is sold to law enforcement agencies only and no commercial prices are available. This pistol has been used by French Gendarmes since 1987.

MODEL 96F — .40 S&W cal., similar to Model 92F, 4.9 in. barrel, plastic grips only, flared grip with grip strap serrations, Bruniton matte black finish, 3 dot sight system, 10 shot mag., 33.4 oz. Introduced 1992.

| Mfg.'s Sug. Retail | $640 | $560 | $450 | $415 | $375 | $335 | $300 | $275 |

Add $70 for Trijicon sight system.

🗲 **Model 96F Compact** — while advertised, this model was never mfg. (suggested retail was $640).

🗲 **Model 96F Centurion** — similar to Model 96F, except has 4.3 in. barrel and 10 shot mag., 33.2 oz. New 1992.

| Mfg.'s Sug. Retail | $640 | $560 | $450 | $415 | $375 | $335 | $300 | $275 |

🗲 **Model 96D** — double action only variation of the Model 96F, no safety, 3 dot sight system, 33.8 oz. New 1992.

| Mfg.'s Sug. Retail | $605 | $540 | $450 | $415 | $375 | $335 | $300 | $275 |

Add $65 for Trijicon sight system.

MODEL 950 BS — .22 Short (disc. 1992) or .25 ACP cal., single action, alloy frame, 8 shot (.25 cal. only) or 6 shot mag., tip-up 2½ and 4 in. (.22 only) barrel, plastic grips, thumb safety, 8-10 oz.

| Mfg.'s Sug. Retail | $180 | $150 | $125 | $110 | $100 | $90 | $80 | $70 |

Add $30 for nickel finish.
Add $80 for engraved variation.
Subtract $30 for matte finish (new 1992), plastic grips only.
This model is manufactured by Beretta U.S.A. Corp. in Accokeek, MD.

🗲 **Model 950 EL** — same general specifications as Model 950 BS, only with wooden grips and gold plated parts. Mfg. disc. 1988.

| | | $190 | $175 | $150 | $140 | $130 | $115 | $105 |

Last Mfg.'s Sug. Retail was $210.

Grading	100%	98%	95%	90%	80%	70%	60%

RIFLES: BOLT ACTION, RECENT MFG.

MODEL 500 CUSTOM — .222 Rem., .223 Rem., .243 Win., .270 Win., .30-06, or .308 Win. cal., 3 action lengths, 24 in. barrel, iron sights, checkered walnut stock with recoil pad. Importation was resumed 1988 only.

	$595	$530	$450	$395	$350	$315	$275

Last Mfg.'s Sug. Retail was $725.

⚔ **Model 500S** — similar to Model 500, except is equipped with iron sights. Imported 1986 only.

	$615	$560	$460	$400	$350	$315	$275

Last Mfg.'s Sug. Retail was $700.

⚔ **Model 500 DL** — same specifications as Model 500, only better walnut and light engraving. Disc. 1986.

	$1,395	$1,260	$1,000	$875	$795	$725	$650

Last Mfg.'s Sug. Retail was $1,595.

⚔ **Model 500 DLS** — similar to Model 500 DL, except is equipped with iron sights. Imported 1986 only.

	$1,420	$1,285	$1,020	$875	$795	$725	$650

Last Mfg.'s Sug. Retail was $1,625.

⚔ **Model 500 EELL** — same specifications as Model 500 DL, only select walnut and more engraving. Disc. 1986.

	$1,550	$1,260	$1,150	$1,000	$875	$800	$725

Last Mfg.'s Sug. Retail was $1,745.

⚔ **Model 500 EELLS** — similar to Model 500 EELL, except is equipped with iron sights. Imported 1986 only.

	$1,575	$1,425	$1,200	$1,120	$875	$800	$725

Last Mfg.'s Sug. Retail was $1,785.

MODEL 501 — available in either .243 or .308 Win. cal., medium bolt action, 6 shot, 23 in. barrel, no sights, checkered walnut stock. Disc. 1986.

	$595	$530	$465	$395	$350	$315	$275

Last Mfg.'s Sug. Retail was $665.

⚔ **Model 501 S** — similar to Model 501, except is equipped with iron sights. Imported 1986 only.

	$615	$560	$460	$400	$350	$315	$275

Last Mfg.'s Sug. Retail was $700.

⚔ **Model 501 DL** — same specifications as Model 501, only better walnut and light engraving. Disc. 1986.

	$1,395	$1,260	$1,000	$875	$795	$725	$650

Last Mfg.'s Sug. Retail was $1,575.

⚔ **Model 501 DLS** — similar to Model 501 DL, except is equipped with iron sights. Imported 1986 only.

	$1,420	$1,285	$1,020	$875	$795	$725	$650

Last Mfg.'s Sug. Retail was $1,625.

⚔ **Model 501 EELL** — same specifications as Model 501 DL, only select walnut and more engraving. Disc. 1986.

	$1,550	$1,260	$1,150	$1,000	$875	$800	$725

Last Mfg.'s Sug. Retail was $1,745.

Grading	100%	98%	95%	90%	80%	70%	60%

⚔ **Model 501 EELLS** — similar to Model 501 EELL, except is equipped with iron sights. Imported 1986 only.

	$1,575	$1,425	$1,200	$1,120	$875	$800	$725

Last Mfg.'s Sug. Retail was $1,785.

MODEL 502 — available in either .30-06, .270 or 7mm Rem. Mag. cal., long bolt action, 5 or 6 shot, 24 in. barrel, no sights, checkered walnut stock. Disc. 1986.

	$625	$565	$490	$440	$395	$360	$330

Last Mfg.'s Sug. Retail was $710.

⚔ **Model 502 S** — similar to Model 502, except is equipped with iron sights. Imported 1986 only.

	$650	$595	$525	$460	$395	$360	$330

Last Mfg.'s Sug. Retail was $745.

⚔ **Model 502 DL** — same specifications as Model 502, only better walnut and light engraving. Also available in .375 H&H Mag. Disc. 1986.

	$1,495	$1,310	$1,175	$1,025	$900	$775	$695

Last Mfg.'s Sug. Retail was $1,640.

⚔ **Model 502 DLS** — similar to Model 502, except is equipped with iron sights. Imported 1986 only.

	$1,410	$1,325	$1,175	$1,025	$900	$775	$695

Last Mfg.'s Sug. Retail was $1,660.

⚔ **Model 502 EELL** — same specifications as Model 502 DL, only select walnut and more engraving. Also available in .375 H&H Mag. Disc. 1986.

	$1,575	$1,425	$1,200	$1,120	$875	$800	$725

Last Mfg.'s Sug. Retail was $1,785.

⚔ **Model 502 EELLS** — similar to Model 502 EELL, except is equipped with iron sights. Imported 1986 only.

	$1,575	$1,425	$1,200	$1,120	$875	$800	$725

Last Mfg.'s Sug. Retail was $1,785.

RIFLES: SEMI-AUTO, RECENT MFG.

AR 70 — .222 or .223 cal., semi-auto paramilitary design rifle, 5, 8 or 30 shot mag.'s, Diopter sights, epoxy finish, 17.72 in. barrel, 8.3 lbs.

	$1,050	$875	$725	$600	$500	$450	$400

Last Mfg.'s Sug. Retail was $1,065. 1989 Federal legislation banned the importation of this model into U.S.

RIFLES: CUSTOM, RECENT MFG.

Current high grade Beretta O/U and SxS rifles are sold only by premium grade franchised Beretta dealers. For a listing of these dealers, contact the Beretta Gallery at 1-800-528-7453.

Older specimens in this SO series (not custom ordered within the last several years) could have values considerably lower than those listed below since new gun prices have escalated considerably recently due to the devaluation of the American dollar.

MODEL S689 O/U — 9.3 x 74R or 30-06 cal., boxlock action, nickel (disc. 1985) or case hardened (new 1986) receiver, double triggers, 23 in. barrels, auto ejectors, sling swivels, 7.7 lbs. Importation disc. in 1990.

	$3,700	$2,600	$2,200	$1,850	$1,550	$1,275	$1,050

Add $1,000 for scope and claw mounts.
Last Mfg.'s Sug. Retail was $4,907.

🔫 Beretta cont.

Grading	100%	98%	95%	90%	80%	70%	60%

SSO EXPRESS O/U — .375 H&H or .458 Win. Mag. cal., sidelock action, case hardened receiver, double triggers, 23 in. barrels, auto ejectors, 11 lbs., cased. Importation disc. 1989.

	100%	98%	95%	90%	80%	70%	60%
	$12,500	$9,500	$8,250	$6,950	$6,100	$5,600	$4,875

Add $425 for claw mounts.
Last Mfg.'s Sug. Retail was $17,533.

SSO5 EXPRESS O/U — similar to SSO Express except has more elaborate engraving and better walnut.

	100%	98%	95%	90%	80%	70%	60%
	$14,250	$11,750	$8,750	$7,500	$6,750	$6,100	$5,600

Last Mfg.'s Sug. Retail was $19,600.

SSO6 EXPRESS O/U — 9.3 x 74R, .375 H&H, or .458 Win. Mag. cal., next to top-of-the-line sidelock double rifle, individually built to the customers specifications, cased. New 1990.

Mfg.'s Sug. Retail	$20,000	$18,250	$15,350	$12,250	$10,000	$8,450	$7,150	$6,000

Add $2,750 for gold inlays.
Add $5,450 for extra set of barrels.

MODEL 455 SIDE-BY-SIDE — .375 H&H, .416 Rigby, .458 Win. Mag., .470 NE, or .500 3 in. NE cal., top of the line sidelock double rifle, individually built to the customers specifications, cased. New 1990.

Mfg.'s Sug. Retail	$36,250	$33,000	$28,500	$23,750	$19,000	$16,000	$13,000	$10,000

Model 455 EELL — similar cals. as Model 455 SxS, top-of-the-line custom sidelock double rifle featuring every refinement of the gunmaker's art, cased.

Mfg.'s Sug. Retail	$46,500	$42,750	$36,950	$32,750	$27,500	$23,000	$19,000	$16,000

SHOTGUNS: O/U, DISC.

BL-1 — 12 ga., 26, 28, or 30 in. barrels, various chokes, boxlock, extractors, double triggers, checkered pistol grip stock. Mfg. 1968-1973.

	100%	98%	95%	90%	80%	70%	60%
	$385	$330	$275	$220	$190	$175	$160

BL-2 — similar to BL-1, with single selective trigger, more engraving.

	100%	98%	95%	90%	80%	70%	60%
	$420	$385	$360	$305	$265	$225	$185

BL-2 STAKE-OUT — riot configuration with 18 in. barrels, DT.

	100%	98%	95%	90%	80%	70%	60%
	$385	$330	$275	$220	$190	$175	$160

BL-2/S — similar to BL-2, with vent. rib and speed trigger. Mfg. 1974-1976.

	100%	98%	95%	90%	80%	70%	60%
	$440	$385	$330	$305	$265	$225	$185

BL-3 — O/U, similar to BL-2, with more engraving, vent. rib and ejectors, also available in 20 ga. Mfg. 1968-1976.

	100%	98%	95%	90%	80%	70%	60%
	$595	$550	$525	$470	$440	$385	$350

BL-3 SKEET

	100%	98%	95%	90%	80%	70%	60%
	$660	$605	$580	$525	$470	$415	$370

BL-3 TRAP

	100%	98%	95%	90%	80%	70%	60%
	$580	$520	$495	$450	$415	$375	$335

BL-4 — deluxe version of BL-3, more engraving, better wood.

	100%	98%	95%	90%	80%	70%	60%
	$695	$650	$595	$550	$495	$450	$395

BL-4 SKEET

	100%	98%	95%	90%	80%	70%	60%
	$745	$690	$635	$550	$495	$450	$395

Grading	100%	98%	95%	90%	80%	70%	60%

BL-4 TRAP

	100%	98%	95%	90%	80%	70%	60%
	$675	$625	$580	$525	$475	$425	$360

BL-5 — higher grade version of BL-4.

	$910	$855	$800	$715	$650	$575	$475

BL-5 SKEET

	$960	$910	$855	$760	$675	$600	$500

BL-5 TRAP

	$850	$820	$775	$695	$595	$525	$430

BL-6 — auto ejectors, sidelock, elaborate engraving.

	$1,250	$1,100	$990	$935	$850	$765	$680

BL-6 SKEET

	$1,295	$1,100	$990	$935	$850	$765	$680

BL-6 TRAP

	$1,100	$950	$885	$810	$755	$670	$580

MODEL S55B — 12 or 20 ga., O/U, 26, 28, or 30 in. barrels, various chokes, boxlock, extractors, selective trigger, checkered pistol grip stock. Disc.

	$550	$495	$440	$385	$330	$300	$280

MODEL S56 E — similar to S55B, with engraved receiver and auto ejectors. Disc.

	$605	$555	$515	$460	$415	$365	$330

MODEL S58 SKEET — similar to S56E, with 26 in. Bohler steel barrels, skeet bore, wide vent. rib, skeet.

	$770	$695	$630	$550	$495	$445	$395

MODEL S58 TRAP — similar to S58 Skeet, with 30 in. barrels, imp. mod. and full choke, Monte Carlo stock with pad.

	$700	$625	$550	$495	$450	$410	$365

SILVER SNIPE — 12 or 20 ga., 26, 28, or 30 in. barrels, boxlock, extractors, trigger optional, checkered pistol grip stock. Mfg. 1955-1967.

	$450	$415	$370	$330	$295	$265	$230

⌇ **Silver Snipe SST** — with vent. rib and SST.

	$550	$495	$440	$415	$360	$330	$295

Add 25% for ejectors.

GOLDEN SNIPE — similar to Silver Snipe, with auto ejectors and vent. rib standard.

	$660	$605	$550	$525	$470	$430	$385

⌇ **Golden Snipe SST** — with SST.

	$715	$660	$605	$580	$525	$465	$410

MODEL 57 E — higher quality version of Golden Snipe. Mfg. 1955-1967.

	$825	$770	$660	$635	$550	$495	$450

⌇ **Model 57 E SST** — with single selective trigger.

	$880	$825	$715	$690	$605	$540	$495

Grading	100%	98%	95%	90%	80%	70%	60%

ASEL MODEL — 12 or 20 ga., 26, 28, or 30 in. barrels, various chokes, single trigger, checkered pistol grip stock, auto ejectors. Mfg. 1947-1964.

	100%	98%	95%	90%	80%	70%	60%
12 ga.	$1,600	$1,375	$1,100	$990	$880	$800	$720
20 ga.	$2,750	$2,475	$2,050	$1,650	$1,375	$1,100	$895

GRADE 100 — 12 ga., 26, 28, or 30 in. barrels, any choke, sidelock, double trigger, auto ejectors, checkered pistol grip or straight stock.

	100%	98%	95%	90%	80%	70%	60%
	$1,820	$1,550	$1,300	$1,100	$900	$775	$695

MODEL 200 — similar to 100, with chrome lined bores and action parts, higher quality engraving.

	100%	98%	95%	90%	80%	70%	60%
	$2,310	$2,000	$1,870	$1,650	$1,375	$1,100	$875

MODEL 680 — competition trap and skeet model, 12 ga. only, boxlock, various chokes. Mono-trap model available. Silver finish receiver, hand engraved, premium walnut. Disc.

	100%	98%	95%	90%	80%	70%	60%
	$1,215	$1,030	$870	$790	$715	$635	$550

Add $60 for 2 barrel combo. package.

SHOTGUNS: FIELD O/U, RECENT MFG.

BERETTA CHOKES AND THEIR CODES (ON REAR LEFT-SIDE OF BARREL)
*   designates full choke (F).
**   designates improved modified choke (IM).
***   designates modified choke (M).
****   designates improved cylinder choke (IC).
FK   designates skeet (SK).
***** designates cylinder bore (CYL).

MODEL 685 — 12 or 20 ga. 2¾ or 3 in. chambers, matte chromed receiver, extractors, single trigger. Disc. 1986.

	100%	98%	95%	90%	80%	70%	60%
	$595	$525	$460	$420	$360	$320	$295

Last Mfg.'s Sug. Retail was $875.

MODEL 686L — 12 (disc. 1990), 20 (disc. 1990), or 28 ga., field model, boxlock action, various barrels/chokes, ejectors, single trigger, engraved silver finished receiver, special walnut, pistol or straight grip stock. Fixed-chokes disc. 1987.

	100%	98%	95%	90%	80%	70%	60%
Mfg.'s Sug. Retail	$1,355	$1,100	$850	$650	$575	$525	$460	$415

Subtract $100 with fixed chokes.

MODEL 686 ONYX — 12 or 20 ga., 3 in. chambers, boxlock action, 26 or 28 in. barrels with multi-chokes, matte finish on metal parts, choice of standard pistol grip or English straight stock, single trigger, ejectors. New 1988.

	100%	98%	95%	90%	80%	70%	60%
Mfg.'s Sug. Retail	$1,355	$1,100	$850	$675	$595	$550	$480	$425

⚞ **Model 686 Onyx Ultralight** — 12 ga. only, 2 ¾ in. chambers, Ergal alloy receiver reinforced with titanium plate, matte black finish on receiver and barrels, checkered walnut stock and forearm, choke tubes, gilded lettering and logo, gold SST, ejectors, very light weight, 5 lbs. 11 oz. Importation began 1992.

	100%	98%	95%	90%	80%	70%	60%
Mfg.'s Sug. Retail	$1,525	$1,300	$975	$775	$625	$575	$525	$475

⚞ **Model 686 Silver** — 12 or 20 ga., 3 in. chambers, 26 or 28 VR barrels with choke tubes, silvered receiver with scroll engraving, gold trigger, checkered walnut stock and forearm. New 1992.

	100%	98%	95%	90%	80%	70%	60%
Mfg.'s Sug. Retail	$1,385	$1,150	$925	$800	$700	$650	$575	$525

⚞ **Model 686 Onyx Magnum** — 12 ga. only, similar to Model 686 Onyx, except has 3½ in. chambers. New 1990.

	100%	98%	95%	90%	80%	70%	60%
Mfg.'s Sug. Retail	$1,355	$1,125	$925	$800	$700	$650	$575	$525

Grading	100%	98%	95%	90%	80%	70%	60%

⚜ **Model 686 Onyx Combo** — similar to Model 686 Field, except is supplied with 1 set each of 20 ga. (28 in.) and 28 ga. (26 in.) barrels. Introduced 1986.

Mfg.'s Sug. Retail $2,085	$1,675	$1,325	$1,150	$950	$875	$820	$775

MODEL 686 EL FIELD — 12 or 20 ga., 3 in. chambers, boxlock action with engraved sideplates, silver receiver finish, 26 or 28 VR barrels with choke tubes, gold SST, checkered walnut stock and forearm, cased, approx. 6¼-6¾ lbs, cased. New 1992.

Mfg.'s Sug. Retail $2,200	$1,800	$1,375	$1,150	$950	$875	$820	$775

MODEL 687 L — 12 or 20 ga., 3 in. chambers, boxlock, various barrels/chokes, ejectors, floral engraved nickel finished receiver, select walnut, fitted case is optional.

Mfg.'s Sug. Retail $1,870	$1,475	$1,100	$850	$700	$635	$575	$525

Subtract $100 without multi-chokes.

MODEL 687 DU — 12 (1990 release) or 28 (1992 release) ga., mfg. for DU dinner gun auctions and membership, prices may vary significantly from region to region.

	$1,950	$1,700	$1,450	$1,175	$895	$725	$575

MODEL 687 L ONYX — 12 or 20 ga., 3 in. chambers, same game scene engraving as standard Model 687 L, except has Onyx blackened receiver, multi-chokes standard. Mfg. 1990 only.

	$1,250	$995	$825	$700	$635	$575	$525

Last Mfg.'s Sug. Retail was $1,590.

MODEL 687 GOLDEN ONYX — 12 or 20 ga., 3 in. chambers, similar to Model 686 Onyx, except has more engraving, better walnut, and several gold inlays. Imported 1988-89 only.

	$1,375	$1,075	$875	$775	$685	$635	$575

Last Mfg.'s Sug. Retail was $1,800.

MODEL 687 EL — same general specifications as Model 687L Field, except available in 20, 28 (new 1990), or .410 (new 1990) ga. also, 2¾ or 3 in. chambers, boxlock with sideplates, better walnut, and more engraving.

Mfg.'s Sug. Retail $3,180	$2,650	$2,100	$1,775	$1,500	$1,350	$1,150	$1,000

Add $140 for .410 ga.

⚜ **Model 687 EL DU** — small frame 28 ga., released 1992 for DU auctions and membership.

	$2,850	$2,200	$1,800	$1,550	$1,400	$1,200	$1,050

MODEL 687 EL ONYX — 12 or 20 ga., 3 in. chambers, simulated sidelock plates with classic scroll engraving. Mfg. 1990 only.

	$2,295	$2,000	$1,725	$1,500	$1,350	$1,150	$1,000

Last Mfg.'s Sug. Retail was $2,660.

MODEL 687 EELL — 12, 20, or 28 ga., same general specifications as Model 687EL, except has extra select walnut, game scene engraving, 3 in. chambers and gold plated trigger, cased, multi-chokes introduced 1988.

Mfg.'s Sug. Retail $4,625	$3,875	$2,950	$2,400	$2,000	$1,725	$1,500	$1,250

Subtract 10% if without multi-chokes.
This model is also available with a straight grip English stock at no extra charge (20 ga. only).

⚜ **Model 687 EELL Combo** — includes one set of 28 ga. (26 in. barrels with multi-chokes) and one set of 20 ga. (choice of 26 or 28 multi-choke) barrels, cased.

Mfg.'s Sug. Retail $5,130	$4,350	$3,250	$2,600	$2,050	$1,725	$1,500	$1,250

Subtract 10% for fixed chokes.
Multi-chokes became standard in 1991.

Grading		100%	98%	95%	90%	80%	70%	60%

MODEL ASE 90 PIGEON — 12 ga. only, 28 in. fixed choke (IM/F) vent. barrels with VR, new design features nickel-chrominum-molybdenum receiver with special hardening and cross bolt engaging 2 monobloc lugs, detachable trigger grouping, V-shaped main springs, cold hammered barrels, choice of silver or blued receiver with gold etching and no engraving, top quality checkered walnut stock and forearm with vent recoil pad, choke tubes, 7 lbs. 13 oz., cased. New 1992.

Mfg.'s Sug. Retail $8,070 $7,100 $5,950 $4,850 $3,950 $3,300 $2,850 $2,500

⚡ **ASE Top Combo** — includes choice of 32 or 34 in. top single barrel with VR and multi-chokes. New 1993.
This model did not have formalized pricing as this edition went to press.

SHOTGUNS: SKEET O/U, RECENT MFG.

MODEL 682 SKEET — competition skeet model, 12, 20 (disc. 1991), 28 (disc. 1988), or .410 ga. (disc. 1988), 26 or 28 in. barrels, boxlock, skeet chokes, silver finish receiver, hand engraved, premium walnut, cased. New 1984.

Mfg.'s Sug. Retail $2,520 $2,100 $1,650 $1,300 $1,050 $950 $895 $800

⚡ **Model 682 Super Skeet** — 12 ga. only, 28 in. VR barrels bored SK/SK featuring factory porting, stock has separate adj. comb cheekpiece. New 1991.

Mfg.'s Sug. Retail $2,915 $2,500 $1,900 $1,650 $1,475 $1,275 $1,050 $950

⚡ **Model 682 Skeet Deluxe** — similar to Model 682, except deluxe walnut and elaborate engraving. Disc. 1986.

$2,650 $2,300 $2,100 $1,850 $1,600 $1,400 $1,200

Last Mfg.'s Sug. Retail was $3,000.

⚡ **Model 682 2-Barrel Skeet Set** — 12 ga. only, two barrel set bored for skeet and sporting clays competition. Imported 1988 only.

$4,950 $4,200 $3,675 $3,175 $2,850 $2,500 $2,175

Last Mfg.'s Sug. Retail was $6,650.

⚡ **Model 682 4-Ga. Skeet Set** — four barrel skeet set comes with interchangeable barrels (28 in.) in 12, 20, 28, and 410 ga.'s. New 1985.

Mfg.'s Sug. Retail $5,860 $4,875 $3,950 $3,300 $2,850 $2,500 $2,175 $1,900

MODEL 687 EELL SKEET — 12 ga. only, fixed chokes, 28 in. barrels, cased.

Mfg.'s Sug. Retail $4,230 $3,650 $2,800 $2,400 $2,000 $1,800 $1,500 $1,250

⚡ **Model 687 EELL 4-Ga. Skeet Set** — four ga. skeet set, cased. New 1988.

Mfg.'s Sug. Retail $8,040 $7,000 $6,000 $4,750 $3,950 $3,400 $3,000 $2,700

MODEL ASE 90 SKEET — 12 ga. only, 28 in. fixed choke vent. barrels with VR, similar action and specifications as the Model ASE 90 Pigeon, 7 lbs. 13 oz., cased. New 1992.

Mfg.'s Sug. Retail $8,070 $7,100 $5,950 $4,850 $3,950 $3,300 $2,850 $2,500

SHOTGUNS: SPORTING CLAYS O/U, RECENT MFG.

These variations have been specifically designed for sporting clay target shooting. All models listed below have 3 in. chambers, unless specified otherwise.

MODEL 682 SPORT — 12 ga. only, 2¾ in. chambers, 28 or 30 in. VR barrels with multi-chokes, designed for English Sporting Clays courses, previously was Model Super Sport with tapered rib. New 1993.

Mfg.'s Sug. Retail $2,715 $2,250 $1,725 $1,300 $1,050 $950 $895 $800

Grading	100%	98%	95%	90%	80%	70%	60%

MODEL 682 SPORTING — 12 or 20 (new 1992) ga., similar specifications to Model 682, 23/4 in. chambers, 28 or 30 (new 1989) in. VR barrels, except over-field stock dimensions and hand engraved silver finished receiver. Multichokes are standard.

| Mfg.'s Sug. Retail | $2,605 | $2,175 | $1,700 | $1,300 | $1,050 | $950 | $895 | $800 |

Add $45 for 20 ga.
Add $865 for extra set of 12 ga. barrels (combo. package - new 1990).

MODEL 682 SUPER SPORTING — 12 ga. only, 2¾ in. chambers, 28 or 30 in. VR ported (new 1993) barrels with multi-chokes and tapered rib, otherwise similar to Model 682 Sporting, cased. New 1989.

| Mfg.'s Sug. Retail | $2,925 | $2,450 | $1,950 | $1,425 | $1,050 | $950 | $895 | $800 |

Beginning 1993, this model features a special fully adj. stock and length of pull.

MODEL 686 SPORTING — 12 ga. only, 3 in. chambers, deluxe checkered walnut stock and forearm with over-field dimensions, 28 or 30 (new 1991) in. barrels only, multi-chokes standard. Mfg. 1987-92.

| | | $1,600 | $1,300 | $1,050 | $925 | $875 | $775 | $695 |

Last Mfg.'s Sug. Retail was $1,940.

Model 686 Sporting Combo — includes extra set of 30 in. barrels. New 1991.

| Mfg.'s Sug. Retail | $2,600 | $2,200 | $1,725 | $1,300 | $1,000 | $925 | $850 | $775 |

Model 686 Hunter Sport — 12 or 20 ga., 28 or 30 (12 ga. only) in. VR barrels with multi-chokes. New 1993.

| Mfg.'s Sug. Retail | $1,425 | $1,150 | $875 | $675 | $575 | $525 | $460 | $415 |

Model 686 Onyx Sporting — 12 ga. only, 28 or 30 in. vent. barrels with VR, high luster blue finish with gold lettering on receiver sides. Mfg. 1992 only.

| | | $1,600 | $1,300 | $1,050 | $925 | $875 | $775 | $695 |

Last Mfg.'s Sug. Retail was $1,940.

Model 686 Onyx Hunter Sport — 12 ga. only, 28 or 30 in. VR barrels with multi-chokes. New 1993.

| Mfg.'s Sug. Retail | $1,385 | $1,125 | $850 | $650 | $575 | $525 | $460 | $415 |

Model 686 English Course — 12 ga. only, features 28 in. VR barrels and special reverse tapered VR with special sighting plane designed for English courses. Mfg. 1991-92.

| | | $1,675 | $1,350 | $1,050 | $925 | $875 | $775 | $695 |

Last Mfg.'s Sug. Retail was $2,015.

MODEL 687 SPORTING — 12 or 20 ga. only, deluxe checkered walnut stock and forearm with over-field dimensions, 28 or 30 (12 ga. only) in. barrels, multi-chokes standard. New 1987.

| Mfg.'s Sug. Retail | $2,285 | $1,950 | $1,500 | $1,175 | $975 | $875 | $775 | $675 |

Add $1,120 for extra set of 12 ga. barrels (combo. package - new 1991).

Model 687 English Course — 12 ga. only, features 28 in. VR barrels and special reverse tapered VR with special sighting plane designed for English courses. Mfg. 1991-92.

| | | $2,225 | $1,750 | $1,325 | $1,050 | $950 | $895 | $800 |

Last Mfg.'s Sug. Retail was $2,630.

MODEL 687 EL SPORTING — 12 ga. only, 28 or 30 in. VR barrels with multi-chokes. New 1993.

| Mfg.'s Sug. Retail | $3,225 | $2,675 | $2,100 | $1,475 | $1,075 | $950 | $895 | $800 |

 **Beretta** cont.

Grading	100%	98%	95%	90%	80%	70%	60%

MODEL 687 EELL SPORTING — 12 or 20 (disc. 1992) ga. only, deluxe checkered walnut stock and forearm with over-field dimensions, 28 in. barrels only, multi-chokes standard, cased. New 1987.

Mfg.'s Sug. Retail	$4,700		$3,950	$3,100	$2,450	$2,000	$1,725	$1,500	$1,250

Add $875 for extra set of barrels (combo. package - 1990 mfg. only).

MODEL ASE 90 SPORTING — 12 ga. only, 28 or 30 in. vent. barrels with VR, similar action and specifications to Model ASE 90 Pigeon, 7 lbs. 11 oz., cased. New 1992.

Mfg.'s Sug. Retail	$8,140		$7,175	$6,000	$4,850	$3,950	$3,300	$2,850	$2,500

SHOTGUNS: TRAP O/U, RECENT MFG.

MODEL 682 TRAP O/U — 12 ga. only, competition trap model, silver or Bruniton finish (matte black), 30 or 32 in. barrels, adj. trigger, supplied with case. New 1985.

Mfg.'s Sug. Retail	$2,495		$1,950	$1,575	$1,250	$1,050	$950	$895	$800

Add $75 for multi-chokes.
Add $75 for 32 in. barrels.

Model 682 Mono — single under-barrel trap model, high post vent. rib, 32 or 34 in. barrel. No extra charge for multi-chokes. Imported 1985-1988.

			$1,530	$1,400	$1,200	$1,025	$925	$875	$775

Last Mfg.'s Sug. Retail was $1,890.

Model 682 Pigeon Trap — 12 ga. only, includes features for international style pigeon and competition shooters including international style stock, flat VR, and mid-rib sights, silver (new 1991) or matte black (disc.) metal finish, semi-gloss American walnut stock, light scroll engraving, sliding trigger, includes multi-chokes, cased. New 1990.

Mfg.'s Sug. Retail	$2,760		$2,225	$1,725	$1,375	$1,075	$950	$895	$800

Model 682 Top Single — 12 ga. only, single over-barrel trap model, 32 or 34 in. barrel. New 1986.

Mfg.'s Sug. Retail	$2,650		$2,225	$1,750	$1,325	$1,050	$950	$895	$800

Subtract 5% if without multi-chokes.
Multi-chokes became standard in 1989.

Model 682 Unsingle — 12 ga. only, single under barrel trap model with 32 in. high post VR, choke tubes. New 1992.

Mfg.'s Sug. Retail	$2,650		$2,225	$1,750	$1,325	$1,050	$950	$895	$800

Model 682 Mono/Top Combo — 12 ga. only, supplied with mono under or upper single barrel and O/U barrel sets. Otherwise same specifications as Model 682 Trap. Cased.

Mfg.'s Sug. Retail	$3,400		$2,750	$2,175	$1,800	$1,525	$1,375	$1,200	$1,000

Subtract $60 if without multi-chokes.

MODEL 682 SUPER TRAP O/U — 12 ga. only, competition trap model, 30 in. barrels, step tapered rib, factory porting, length of pull and separate stock cheekpiece are adjustable, cased. New 1991.

Mfg.'s Sug. Retail	$2,820		$2,250	$1,775	$1,400	$1,075	$950	$895	$800

Add $65 for multi-chokes.

Model 682 Top Single Super Trap — 12 ga. only, single over-barrel trap model, 32 or 34 in. barrel with choice of fixed or multi-chokes. New 1991.

Mfg.'s Sug. Retail	$2,990		$2,425	$1,825	$1,400	$1,095	$975	$900	$800

Add $70 for multi-chokes.

Model 682 Top Combo Super Trap — 12 ga. only, supplied with upper single barrel and O/U barrel sets. Otherwise same specifications as Model 682 Super Trap. Cased.

Mfg.'s Sug. Retail	$3,790		$3,100	$2,300	$1,875	$1,600	$1,375	$1,200	$1,000

Add $75 for multi-chokes on both barrels.

Grading	100%	98%	95%	90%	80%	70%	60%

MODEL 687 EELL O/U — 12 ga. only, boxlock action with engraved black (new 1992) or silver (disc. 1991) finished side plates, Monte Carlo stock with recoil pad, 30 in. barrels with choke tubes, cased.

Mfg.'s Sug. Retail $4,610	$3,900	$3,100	$2,450	$2,000	$1,725	$1,500	$1,250

MODEL 687 EELL TOP SINGLE TRAP — 12 ga. only, single over-barrel trap model, 32 or 34 in. barrel. Mfg. 1988-92.

$4,150	$3,250	$2,575	$2,250	$1,775	$1,500	$1,250

Add $55 for multi-chokes.
Last Mfg.'s Sug. Retail was $4,835

⚖ **Model 687 EELL Top Trap Combo** — 12 ga. only, supplied with 30 or 32 in. O/U barrels and a mono trap upper barrel, multi-chokes standard. New 1988.

Mfg.'s Sug. Retail $5,770	$4,850	$3,950	$3,300	$2,850	$2,500	$2,175	$1,900

Add $45 for multi-chokes.

⚖ **Model 687 EELL Mono Trap Combo** — 12 ga. only, supplied with 30 or 32 in. O/U barrels and a mono trap bottom barrel. Imported 1986-1988.

$4,175	$3,725	$3,395	$3,000	$2,775	$2,550	$2,250

Add $140 for multi-chokes.
Last Mfg.'s Sug. Retail was $4,900.

MODEL ASE 90 TRAP — 12 ga. only, 30 in. vent. barrels with VR, similar action and specifications to Model ASE 90 Pigeon, 8 lbs. 6 oz., cased with extra trigger group. New 1992.

Mfg.'s Sug. Retail $8,070	$7,100	$5,950	$4,850	$3,950	$3,300	$2,850	$2,500

Add $70 for multi-chokes.

SHOTGUNS: CUSTOM GRADE O/U, RECENT MFG.

Current high grade Beretta O/U and SxS shotguns are sold only by premium grade franchised Beretta dealers. For a listing of these dealers, contact the Beretta Gallery at 1-800-528-7453.

Older specimens in this SO series (not custom ordered within the last several years) could have values considerably lower than those listed below since new gun prices have escalated considerably recently due to the devaluation of the American dollar.

SO-2 — 12 ga., 26-30 in. barrels, sidelock, any chokes, vent. rib, auto ejectors, SST, checkered stock in various configurations (field, skeet, or trap), grades differ in wood, engraving, and finish, cased. Mfg. 1948-present.

$4,900	$4,200	$3,000	$2,600	$2,200	$1,900	$1,675

SO-3 — 2nd grade of the SO series. Disc. 1987.

$7,850	$6,800	$4,900	$4,450	$3,875	$3,400	$2,950

Last Mfg.'s Sug. Retail was $8,250.

SO-3 EL — grade-up from SO-3 with better wood and engraving. Disc. 1985.

$8,250	$6,900	$6,000	$5,500	$4,450	$3,900	$3,500

Last Mfg.'s Sug. Retail was $8,100.

SO-3 EELL — best quality model, custom specifications, choice of engraving motifs. Disc. 1987.

$8,995	$7,975	$6,700	$5,750	$5,000	$4,500	$3,950

Add $1,375/set of O/U barrels.
Last Mfg.'s Sug. Retail was $11,625.

 **Beretta** cont.

Grading	100%	98%	95%	90%	80%	70%	60%

SO-4 — 12 ga., sidelock, available in field, skeet, or trap configurations, custom specs., fluorescent sights, wide rib, cased. Disc. 1987.

	$8,350	$6,500	$5,900	$5,250	$4,500	$3,850	$3,250

Add $2,300 for extra set of O/U barrels.
Last Mfg.'s Sug. Retail was $8,700.

SO-5 COMPETITION — best quality O/U, extensively engraved, top quality checkered walnut stock (semi-pistol grip) and forearm, available in either Trap, Skeet, or Sporting configurations, limited importation, cased.

Mfg.'s Sug. Retail	$12,000		$10,750	$8,800	$7,950	$6,750	$5,950	$5,200	$4,500

Add $4,000 for extra set of barrels.
Add $3,460 for Trap Combo set.

SO-5 EELL — next to top-of-the-line model, available in either Trap, Skeet, or Sporting configurations, custom built to customer dimensions. Importation disc. 1988.

	$12,750	$10,000	$8,500	$7,500	$6,500	$5,500	$4,500

Last Mfg.'s Sug. Retail was $21,750.

SO-6 COMPETITION — high quality O/U, extensively engraved, top quality checkered walnut stock (semi-pistol grip) and forearm, choice of trap, skeet, or sporting clays configuration (older mfg. included field models), built to customer specifications, limited importation, cased.

Mfg.'s Sug. Retail	$16,300		$15,000	$12,000	$10,000	$8,000	$7,250	$6,250	$5,500

Add $4,000 for extra set of barrels.

SO-6 EELL — 12 ga., current next to top-of-the-line model, field dimensions, custom built to customer specifications, cased.

Mfg.'s Sug. Retail	$26,000		$24,250	$20,500	$17,250	$13,950	$11,250	$8,750	$6,450

Add $4,000 for extra set of barrels.

SO-9 — 12, 20, 28, or .410 ga., top-of-the-line sidleock model, 1990 was the first time the SO series was offered in smaller gauges, 28 or .410 ga. models have smaller proportionate frames. New 1990.

Mfg.'s Sug. Retail	$28,500		$25,750	$21,750	$17,750	$14,250	$11,500	$8,950	$6,750

Add $4,000 for extra set of barrels.

SHOTGUNS: SxS, DISC.

MODEL 409 PB — 12, 16, 20, or 28 ga., 27, 28, and 30 in. barrels, various chokes, double triggers, plain extractors, checkered pistol grip stock. Mfg. 1934-1964.

	$770	$660	$605	$550	$495	$440	$385

MODEL 410 E — higher quality, auto ejector version of 409PB.

	$880	$770	$715	$660	$605	$550	$495

MODEL 410 — similar to 410 E, except 10 ga. Mag., 32 in. barrel, full choke, heavier construction, mfg. 1934. Disc.

	$1,200	$995	$880	$795	$700	$625	$550

MODEL 411 E — similar to 409 PB, with false sideplates and finer finishing. Mfg. 1934-1964.

	$1,210	$1,100	$1,045	$990	$880	$825	$770

MODEL 424-426 — 12 and 20 ga. (Model 426 only), 26 and 28 in. barrels, various chokes, boxlock, extractors, double triggers, light engraving, checkered straight stock. Add $115 for Model 426.

	$900	$715	$660	$635	$550	$495	$415

Grading	100%	98%	95%	90%	80%	70%	60%

MODEL 426 E — similar to 424, with auto ejectors, SST, select wood and more intricate engraving, silver pigeon inlay. Disc. 1983.

| | $1,115 | $935 | $880 | $855 | $770 | $715 | $635 |

MODEL 625 — 12 or 20 ga., 26-30 in. barrels, various chokes, boxlock, extractors, double triggers, light engraving, checkered straight stock. Imported 1984-1986.

| | $795 | $745 | $660 | $580 | $530 | $485 | $440 |

Last Mfg.'s Sug. Retail was $835.

MODEL GR-2 — 12 and 20 ga.'s, 26 and 28 in. barrels, various chokes, boxlock, extractors, double triggers, checkered pistol grip stock. Mfg. 1968-1976.

| | $660 | $605 | $550 | $495 | $385 | $330 | $275 |

MODEL GR-3 — similar to GR-2, with select wood and more engraving. Mfg. 1968-1976.

| | $770 | $715 | $640 | $560 | $475 | $425 | $375 |

MODEL GR-4 — similar to GR-3, with auto ejectors. Mfg. 1968-1976.

| | $880 | $750 | $675 | $600 | $500 | $450 | $395 |

SILVER HAWK — 12 ga. Mag. & 10 ga. Mag. with double triggers and extractors. Disc. 1967.

| | $495 | $380 | $325 | $275 | $250 | $225 | $200 |

Add $100 for 10 ga.

SILVER HAWK FEATHERWEIGHT — 12, 16, 20, or 28 ga., 26-32 in. barrels, high solid rib, various chokes, single or double triggers, checkered pistol grip stock, beavertail forearm. Disc. 1967.

| | $495 | $440 | $415 | $385 | $360 | $330 | $275 |
| Single trigger | $550 | $495 | $440 | $415 | $385 | $360 | $330 |

SO-6 DOUBLE BARREL — same general specifications and embellishments as the SO series O/U guns, but S x S. Mfg. 1948-1982.

| | $5,900 | $5,500 | $5,280 | $5,060 | $4,840 | $4,400 | $3,850 |

SO-7 DOUBLE BARREL — top of the line S x S, finest quality wood, more elaborate engraving. Disc.

| | $8,250 | $7,700 | $7,150 | $6,600 | $6,050 | $5,500 | $4,620 |

SHOTGUNS: SxS, RECENT MFG.

MODEL 626 FIELD — 12 or 20 (disc. 1987) ga., 2¾ in. chambers, 26 and 28 in. barrels, various chokes, boxlock, ejectors, single trigger, moderate engraving, pistol grip or straight checkered stock. Imported 1984-1988.

| | $895 | $800 | $740 | $685 | $595 | $540 | $490 |

Last Mfg.'s Sug. Retail was $995.

MODEL 626 ONYX — 12 or 20 ga., 3 in. chambers, 26 or 28 (new 1990) in. VR barrels with multi-chokes, matte finished metal parts, select checkered walnut stock and forearm. New 1988.

| Mfg.'s Sug. Retail | $1,870 | $1,425 | $1,125 | $850 | $750 | $685 | $595 | $540 |

Model 626 Onyx Magnum — 12 ga. only, 3½ in. chambers. Mfg. 1990-92.

| | $1,425 | $1,175 | $900 | $800 | $700 | $600 | $550 |

Last Mfg.'s Sug. Retail was $1,870.

MODEL 627 EL FIELD — 12 and 20 (disc. 1987) ga., 2¾ (disc. 1990) or 3 in. (became standard in 1991) chambers, 26 and 28 in. barrels, various chokes, boxlock, ejectors, single trigger, extensive engraving, pistol grip or straight checkered stock, cased. New 1985.

Mfg.'s Sug. Retail	$3,270	$2,725	$2,150	$1,775	$1,500	$1,350	$1,150	$1,000

Subtract 5% for fixed chokes and 2¾ in. chambers.

⁑ **Model 627 EL Sport** — similar to Model 627 EL Field, except 12 ga. only, knurled rib, sporting clays dimensions. Importation disc. 1988.

	$1,800	$1,625	$1,500	$1,300	$1,100	$925	$795

Last Mfg.'s Sug. Retail was $1,995.

MODEL 627 EELL — 12 or 20 (disc. 1987) ga., 2¾ (disc.) or 3 (12 ga. only) in. chambers, 26 or 28 in. barrels, various chokes, boxlock, ejectors, single trigger, elaborate engraving, pistol grip or straight English checkered stock, cased. New 1985.

Mfg.'s Sug. Retail	$5,405	$4,600	$3,850	$3,300	$2,850	$2,500	$2,175	$1,900

Subtract 5% if fixed chokes only.
Multi-chokes became standard in 1991.

SHOTGUNS: SxS, CUSTOM GRADE

Current high grade Beretta O/U and SxS shotguns are sold only by premium grade franchised Beretta dealers. For a listing of these dealers, contact the Beretta Gallery at 1-800-528-7453.

Older specimens in this SO series (not custom ordered within the last several years) could have values considerably lower than those listed below since new gun prices have escalated considerably recently due to the devaluation of the American dollar.

MODEL 451 SERIES — 12 ga., totally hand-made, sidelock action, ejectors, scroll engraving. Custom made to order with fitted luggage case, various grades have increasing embellishments in EL Models.

⁑ **Model 451** — disc. 1987.

	$6,000	$5,200	$4,875	$4,600	$4,300	$3,995	$3,600

Last Mfg.'s Sug. Retail was $12,375.

⁑ **Model 451 E** — 12 ga. only, double triggers, specifications furnished by individual customer. Imported 1989 only.

	$14,650	$10,950	$9,750	$8,500	$7,800	$6,750	$5,800

Add $4,000 for extra set of barrels.
Add $750 for SST.
Last Mfg.'s Sug. Retail was $20,467.

⁑ **Model 451 EL** — disc. 1984.

	$6,450	$5,400	$4,875	$4,600	$4,300	$4,000	$3,600

⁑ **Model 451 EELL** — previous top-of-the-line model, choice of engraving motifs per customer specifications. Disc. 1987, reintroduced 1989 only.

	$17,500	$12,950	$11,000	$8,500	$7,800	$6,750	$5,950

Last Mfg.'s Sug. Retail in 1989 was $24,367.
Last Mfg.'s Sug. Retail in 1987 was $14,925.

MODEL 452 — 12 ga. only, next to top-of-the-line side-by side shotgun featuring H&H style detachable locks, cased. New 1990.

Mfg.'s Sug. Retail	$22,000	$19,950	$16,750	$13,500	$10,250	$8,750	$6,650	$5,500

Add $4,000 for extra set of barrels.

Grading	100%	98%	95%	90%	80%	70%	60%

Model 452 EELL — 12 ga. only, top-of-the-line custom sidelock model featuring every refinement, cased. Importation began 1992.

Mfg.'s Sug. Retail	$30,500	$27,450	$22,750	$18,250	$14,500	$11,500	$8,950	$6,750

Add $4,000 for extra set of barrels.

SHOTGUNS: SINGLE BARREL, DISC.

MARK II TRAP — 12 ga., 32 or 34 in. wide vent. rib, full choke, boxlock with auto ejector, Monte Carlo stock, recoil pad. Mfg. 1972-1976.

	$495	$450	$400	$360	$330	$295	$260

MODEL FS-1 SINGLE BARREL — 12, 16, 20, 28, or .410 ga., 26 or 28 in. barrels, full choke, checkered semi-pistol grip, under lever break open, folds to length of barrel (also known as Companion).

	$175	$150	$125	$110	$100	$90	$80

TR-1 TRAP — 12 ga., 32 in. full choke barrel, under lever break open, Monte Carlo pistol grip stock with pad, engraved. Mfg. 1968-1971.

	$275	$250	$220	$195	$140	$110	$100

TR-2 TRAP — similar to TR-1, with high rib, mfg. 1969-1973.

	$290	$260	$230	$205	$150	$120	$110

MODEL 412 — 12, 20, 28, or .410 ga., monobloc construction, folding action, sling swivels, checkered walnut stock and forearm, 5 lbs. Importation disc. 1988.

	$190	$170	$125	$100	$85	$70	$60

Last Mfg.'s Sug. Retail was $215.

SHOTGUNS: SLIDE ACTION, DISC.

MODEL SL-2 — 12 ga., 26, 28, or 30 in. barrels, various chokes, vent. rib, checkered pistol, grip stock. Mfg. 1968-1971.

	$300	$275	$250	$220	$195	$165	$140

SILVER PIGEON — 12 ga., various chokes, light engraving.

	$250	$200	$175	$160	$150	$140	$130

GOLD PIGEON — 12 ga., various chokes, vent. rib, engraved. Add $200 for deluxe models.

	$475	$375	$310	$275	$240	$215	$195

RUBY PIGEON — 12 ga., various chokes, vent. rib, elaborately engraved, special deluxe walnut.

	$600	$475	$395	$350	$295	$260	$230

SHOTGUNS: SEMI-AUTO, DISC.

SILVER LARK — 12 ga., various chokes.

	$295	$260	$240	$220	$200	$185	$170

GOLD LARK — 12 ga., vent. rib, light scroll engraving, select walnut.

	$480	$400	$325	$260	$230	$210	$195

RUBY LARK — 12 ga., vent. rib, heavy engraving, deluxe walnut.

	$675	$550	$475	$395	$350	$295	$260

 **Beretta** cont.

Grading	100%	98%	95%	90%	80%	70%	60%

MODEL AL-1 — 12 and 20 ga., semi-auto gas operated, 26, 28, and 30 in. plain barrel, various chokes, checkered pistol grip stock. Mfg. 1971-1973.

	$385	$360	$330	$305	$250	$195	$165

MODEL AL-2 — 12 or 20 ga., 26, 28, or 30 in. barrels, vent. rib, various chokes, gas operated, checkered pistol grip stock. Mfg. 1973-1975.

	$330	$305	$275	$250	$220	$195	$165

MODEL AL-2 SKEET — similar to AL-2, with 26 in. wide rib skeet bored barrel, mfg. 1973-1975.

	$395	$360	$320	$275	$220	$200	$185

MODEL AL-2 TRAP — similar to AL-2, with 30 in. full choke barrel, wide rib, Monte Carlo stock, with recoil pad. Mfg. 1973-1975.

	$375	$345	$315	$285	$250	$195	$165

MODEL AL-2 MAGNUM — 12 ga., 28 and 30 in. mod. or full choke, 3 in. chambers. Mfg. 1973-1975.

	$415	$385	$330	$275	$250	$230	$210

MODEL AL-3 — continuation of the AL-2 series. Mfg. 1975-1976.

	100%	98%	95%	90%	80%	70%	60%
Field grade	$395	$360	$330	$260	$240	$220	$190
Magnum grade	$425	$385	$330	$275	$250	$230	$210
Skeet grade	$400	$360	$330	$260	$240	$220	$190
Trap grade	$385	$350	$295	$250	$225	$210	$185

MODEL AL-3 DELUXE TRAP — similar to AL-3, with fully engraved receiver, premium grade wood. Mfg. 1975-1976.

	$770	$715	$660	$605	$550	$495	$440

SHOTGUNS: SEMI-AUTO, RECENT MFG.

It is possible on some of the models listed below to have production variances occur including different engraving motifs, stock configurations and specifications, finishes, etc. These have occurred when Beretta has changed from production of one model to another. Also, some European and English distributors have sold their excess inventory through Beretta U.S.A., creating additional variations/configurations that are not normally imported domestically. While sometimes rare, these specimens typically do not command premiums over Beretta's domestic models.

MODEL 1200 FIELD — 12 ga., inertia recoil system, 28 in. VR barrels with multi-chokes, checkered European walnut stock and forearm (pre-1989), matte black polymer stock and forearm (starting 1989), recoil pad, 4 shot mag., approx. 8 lbs. Imported 1984-1989.

	$475	$415	$350	$295	$250	$225	$200

Last Mfg.'s Sug. Retail was $580.

Model 1200 Riot — 12 ga. only, 2¾ or 3 in. chamber, 20 in. cyl. bore barrel with iron sights, extended mag. Imported 1989-90 only.

	$525	$425	$350	$295	$250	$225	$200

Last Mfg.'s Sug. Retail was $660.

MODEL 1201 FIELD MAGNUM — 12 ga., 3 in. chamber, 24, 26, 28 in. VR barrel with multi-chokes (2), matte black polymer stock and forearm. New 1989.

Mfg.'s Sug. Retail	$625	$500	$395	$340	$285	$250	$225	$200

The Model 1201 can be differentiated from the Model 1200 by stock spacers to adjust length.

Grading	100%	98%	95%	90%	80%	70%	60%

Model 1201 FP3 — 12 ga., riot configuration featuring 20 in. cylinder bore barrel, adj. rifle sights, matte finish. New 1991.

Mfg.'s Sug. Retail	$660	$525	$425	$350	$295	$250	$225	$200

Add $45 for pistol grip configuration (Model 1201 FPG3).

MODEL 300/301 — continuation of the AL-3 series, scroll engraved receiver. Mfg. 1977-1982.

	100%	98%	95%	90%	80%	70%	60%
Field grade	$395	$360	$330	$260	$240	$220	$190
Magnum grade	$425	$385	$330	$275	$250	$230	$210
Skeet grade	$400	$360	$330	$260	$240	$220	$190
Trap grade	$385	$350	$295	$250	$225	$210	$185

Beretta changed model nomenclature rapidly during the Model 300 Series. In approx. 10 months, the evolution of this model had progressed from the 300 to 303 Series. Beginning with the Model 303, all receivers were milled with a 3 in. ejection port window.

MODEL 301 SLUG GUN — 22 in. barrel, with sights. Disc.

	$395	$360	$330	$305	$265	$230	$190

MODEL 302 — 12 or 20 ga., self-compensating gas operation semi-auto, designed for both 2¾ and 3 in. shells, available with interchangeable chokes, slug barrel, trap and skeet models (disc.), VR, mag. cut-off. Mfg. 1982-1987. This model was superceded by the Model 303.

	$395	$365	$340	$310	$280	$255	$225

Add $30 for multi-choke set.
Last Mfg.'s Sug. Retail was $480.

Model 302 Super Lusso — same specifications as Model A302, but includes hand engraved receiver, many gold plated parts, and stock and forearm made from presentation grade walnut. Disc. 1986.

	$2,150	$1,950	$1,750	$1,550	$1,300	$1,050	$895

Last Mfg.'s Sug. Retail was $2,500.

MODEL A-303 FIELD — 12 or 20 ga., 2¾ or 3 in. chambers, same gas operation as the Model 302, 26 or 28 in. VR barrel, high-strength alloy receiver, select wood with choice pistol grip or straight English stock, beavertail forearm, multi-chokes became standard 1987.

Mfg.'s Sug. Retail	$755	$625	$450	$375	$335	$300	$270	$240

Subtract 10% without multi-chokes.
Subtract $20 for straight grip English stock.

A-303 Upland — 12 or 20 ga., 24 in. VR barrel with multi-chokes, English style straight stock. New 1989.

Mfg.'s Sug. Retail	$735	$615	$450	$395	$350	$300	$270	$240

A-303 Waterfowl/Turkey — 12 ga. only, 3 in. chamber, choice of 24, 26, 28, or 30 in. VR barrel, matte finished wood and metal, multi-chokes are standard. Imported 1991 only.

	$540	$450	$395	$350	$300	$270	$240

Last Mfg.'s Sug. Retail was $665.

A-303 Sporting — 12 or 20 (new 1991) ga. only, 2¾ in. chambers, sporting clay dimensions, 28 or 30 (12 ga. only) in. VR barrel with multi-chokes. New 1988.

Mfg.'s Sug. Retail	$835	$695	$525	$450	$375	$325	$300	$275

A-303 Skeet — 12 or 20 ga., 26 in. VR barrel with fixed skeet choking.

Mfg.'s Sug. Retail	$735	$615	$440	$375	$335	$300	$270	$240

A-303 Super Skeet — 12 ga. only, 28 in. VR fixed choke barrel, features factory porting, adj. length of pull, and adj. separate cheekpiece on stock. Mfg. 1991-92.

	$975	$750	$625	$500	$425	$365	$300

Last Mfg.'s Sug. Retail was $1,160.

Grading	100%	98%	95%	90%	80%	70%	60%

A-303 Trap — 12 ga. only, 30 or 32 in. VR barrel with fixed choking or multi-chokes.

Mfg.'s Sug. Retail	$735	$615	$425	$360	$325	$280	$250	$220

Add $40 for multi-chokes (with Monte Carlo stock).

A-303 Super Trap — 12 ga. only, 30 or 32 in. VR multi-choke barrel with step tapered rib, features factory porting, adj. length of pull, and adj. separate cheekpiece on stock. Mfg. 1991-92.

	$1,025	$775	$625	$500	$425	$365	$300

Last Mfg.'s Sug. Retail was $1,210.

A-303 Slug — 12 or 20 ga., 3 in. chamber (12 ga. only), 22 in. cylinder bore barrel, iron sights. Importation disc. 1991.

	$540	$425	$360	$325	$295	$265	$240

Last Mfg.'s Sug. Retail was $665.

A-303 Youth — 20 ga. only, 2¾ or 3 in. chamber, 24 in. VR barrel with multi-chokes, shortened stock. New 1988.

Mfg.'s Sug. Retail	$735	$615	$435	$370	$330	$300	$270	$240

MODEL 390 FIELD — 12 ga. only, 3 in. chamber, features new gas system that will accept all 2¾ and 3 in. shotshells, single stainless steel piston with self regulating valve, mag. cut-off on left side of receiver, 24, 26, 28, or 30 in. VR barrel with Mobilchoke system, standard field or matte finish on lightly engraved receiver, adj. checkered walnut stock, gold trigger, approx. 7 lbs. New 1992.

Mfg.'s Sug. Retail	$775	$650	$475	$395	$350	$300	$270	$240

Model 390 Field Deluxe — similar to Model 390 Field, except has gold accents on receiver frame, including a gold filled snipe, setter, and P. Beretta signature, deluxe walnut. New 1993.

Mfg.'s Sug. Retail	$935	$775	$550	$450	$400	$360	$320	$285

Model 390 Super Trap — 12 ga. only, 30 or 32 in. VR multi-choke ported barrels, adj. stock comb and length of pull. New 1993.

Mfg.'s Sug. Retail	$1,210	$1,000	$800	$600	$550	$495	$460	$425

Model 390 Super Skeet — 12 ga. only, 28 in. skeet choke VR ported barrels, includes adj. stock comb and length of pull. New 1993.

Mfg.'s Sug. Retail	$1,160	$975	$775	$575	$525	$475	$440	$400

MODEL VITTORIA — 12 ga., 3 in. chamber, uses Montefeltro short action, 24 or 26 in. VR barrel, matte finish, includes sling swivels. New 1993.

Mfg.'s Sug. Retail	$700	$595	$425	$360	$325	$280	$250	$230

Vittoria Slug — 12 ga. only, 24 in. slug barrel, includes rifle sights and rifle choke tubes. New 1993.

Mfg.'s Sug. Retail	$700	$595	$425	$360	$325	$280	$250	$230

COMMEMORATIVES

MODEL A-303 DUCKS UNLIMITED — 12 or 20 ga., D.U. serialization, 5,500 mfg. in 12 ga. 1986-87, 3,500 mfg. in 20 ga. 1987-88.

12 ga.	$575	$450	$350
20 ga.	$675	$475	$375

These D.U. Models had no retail pricing from Beretta. Rather, they were auctioned off at D.U. dinners, and as a result, prices could vary substantially from region to region.

Grading	100%	98%	95%	90%	80%	70%	60%

MODEL 687 O/U SHOTGUN TERCENTENNIAL — 12 ga., comes with S.S.T. and ejectors. Limited production, only 300 manufactured.

		$2,500	$1,950	$1,400			

MODEL 84 PISTOL TERCENTENNIAL — commemorative, only 300 manufactured. Fully engraved with gold inlays. Presentation case. Only 100 imported to U.S.

		$1,450	$1,100	$850			

BERGMANN

Manufacturer located in Gaggenau, Germany 1892-1944. Re-established in 1931 under Bergmann Erben.

100%	98%	95%	90%	80%	70%	60%	50%	40%	30%	20%	10%

SEMI-AUTO

Prices established are for original guns with matching parts.

MODEL 1894 (ANTIQUE) — 5mm or 8mm. Extremely rare. Add 50% for 5mm.

$4,500	$3,750	$3,350	$2,860	$2,550	$2,200	$1,900	$1,600	$1,250	$995	$925	$850

MODEL 1896-NO. 2 — 5mm, smaller type frame.

$2,100	$1,900	$1,600	$1,300	$1,100	$895	$715	$660	$610	$565	$515	$450

MODEL 1896-NO. 3 — 6.5mm - 80mm barrel.

$2,200	$1,950	$1,650	$1,350	$1,125	$925	$750	$700	$665	$630	$600	$565

MODEL 1896-NO. 4 — 8mm, military contract.

$2,275	$2,000	$1,650	$1,350	$1,125	$925	$750	$700	$665	$630	$600	$565

MODEL 1897-NO. 5 — 7.8mm, commercial manufacture.

$2,600	$2,275	$2,000	$1,650	$1,350	$1,125	$925	$750	$700	$665	$630	$600

MODEL 2 — .25 cal., small frame. Add $100 for Model 2A.

$300	$285	$260	$240	$215	$180	$160	$135	$115	$95	$80	$65

MODEL 3 — .25 cal., small frame. Add $100 for Model 3A.

$300	$285	$260	$240	$215	$180	$160	$135	$115	$95	$80	$65

ERBEN — Models I, II, and Special, .25 Cal. except Special .32 Cal.

$335	$300	$285	$260	$240	$215	$180	$160	$135	$115	$95	$80

BERGMANN-BAYARD PISTOLS

Even though the below listed Bergmann-Bayard models were manufactured only by Anciens Etablissements Pieper of Herstal, Belgium, these pistols are listed under this heading as they are most commonly referred to by this trademark designation.

MODEL 1908 STANDARD COMMERCIAL — 9mm Bergmann, identified by a mounted knight on the left magazine housing and is without finger cuts at base of magazine housing.

$1,500	$1,250	$1,000	$750	$600	$500	$400	$360	$335	$310	$285	$260

Add 25% if backstrap is slotted for shoulder stock.
Add $2,500 for excellent original leather/wood shoulder stock.

MODEL 1908 SPANISH CONTRACT — 9mm Bergmann, total contract was for 3,000 pistols, can be identified from standard commercial pistols by the Spanish military acceptance stamp struck on the receiver.

$1,350	$1,100	$900	$750	$600	$450	$400	$360	$335	$310	$285	$260

100%	98%	95%	90%	80%	70%	60%	50%	40%	30%	20%	10%

MODEL 1910 STANDARD COMMERCIAL — 9mm Bergmann, mechanically similar to Model 1908 Standard Commercial except has finger cuts in bottom of magazine housing, circular grooves are present on each side of magazine base.

| $1,100 | $900 | $700 | $600 | $500 | $400 | $350 | $315 | $280 | $265 | $245 | $225 |

MODEL 1910 DANISH GOVERNMENT CONTRACT — 9mm Bergmann, Trolit grips were used for the original conversion, followed later by wood replacements, total contract was for 4,840 pistols with delivery mfg. 1911-1914. This variation can be identified from the usual commercial pistols by the Danish proof mark on the left receiver side and Danish inventory number on right side of receiver.

| $1,350 | $1,100 | $900 | $750 | $600 | $450 | $400 | $360 | $335 | $310 | $285 | $260 |

Deduct 20% if converted and overstamped M.1910/21.

MODEL 1910/21 TOJHUS — 9mm Bergmann, these pistols are marked "Haerens Tojhus" and are numbered from 1-900, original grips were black Trolit, replacement grips are either all smooth or with checkered circles above and below grip screw.

| $1,500 | $1,250 | $1,000 | $750 | $600 | $500 | $400 | $360 | $335 | $310 | $285 | $260 |

This contract was manufactured by the Danish Royal Arsenal located in Copenhagen.

MODEL 1910/21 RUSTKAMMER — 9mm Bergmann, pistols are marked "Haerens Rustkammer", and numbered 901-2204, grip replacements are the same as noted for Haerens Tojhus.

| $1,350 | $1,100 | $900 | $750 | $600 | $450 | $400 | $360 | $335 | $310 | $285 | $260 |

This contract was manufactured by the Danish Royal Arsenal located in Copenhagen.

BERNARDELLI, VINCENZO

Manufactured since 1721 in Brescia, Italy. Bernardelli did not have a domestic importer as this edition went to press. Previously imported and distributed by Magnum Research, Inc. located in Minneapolis, MN (1989-92), Quality Arms, Inc. located in Houston, TX, Armes De Chasse located in Chadds Ford, PA, Stoeger located in New York, NY, and Action Arms, Ltd. located in Philadelphia, PA.

Rather than show a discontinuance of all models recently imported by Magnum Research listed below, manufacturer's suggested retails from 1992 have been retained for reference information.

There is some confusion on the Bernardelli trademark as there have been three different companies (Pietro Bernardelli, Vincenzo Bernardelli, and Santini Bernardelli) that have produced firearms. Several years ago, there was quite a lot of Pietro Bernardellis that were "dumped" in the American marketplace - these guns do not have the quality of Vincenzo Bernardelli and are not covered within the scope of this text. The only company that is currently manufacturing firearms is Vincenzo Bernardelli - only models from this company will be listed within this section.

Grading	100%	98%	95%	90%	80%	70%	60%

COMBINATION GUNS

MODEL 190 — combination rifle/shotgun chambered for 12, 16, or 20 ga. under .243, .30-06, or .308 cal., boxlock action, DTs, extractors. Imported 1989 only.

| | | | $1,295 | $1,025 | $895 | $800 | $700 | $600 | $525 |

Add $700 for extra set of 12 ga. O/U barrels.
Mfg.'s Sug. Retail was $1,393.

MODEL COMB 2000 — 12, 16, or 20 ga. under choice of rifle cals., ejectors, set trigger. Importation began 1990.

| Mfg.'s Sug. Retail | $2,441 | | $2,075 | $1,775 | $1,550 | $1,350 | $1,100 | $925 | $800 |

Add $621 for extra set of O/U shotgun barrels (Model COMB 2000S).

Grading	100%	98%	95%	90%	80%	70%	60%

MODEL 120 — 12 ga. over choice of 12 cals., deluxe checkered walnut stock and forearm, iron sights, double triggers, vent. recoil pad, coin washed receiver with light engraving.

	100%	98%	95%	90%	80%	70%	60%
	$1,950	$1,585	$1,300	$1,050	$850	$760	$650

Add $130 for extra set of shotgun barrels.
Last Mfg.'s Sug. Retail was $2,411.

PISTOLS: SEMI-AUTO, DISCONTINUED

VEST POCKET MODEL — .25 auto, 2⅛ in. barrel, fixed sights, blue, bakelite grips. Mfg. 1945-1948.

	$250	$195	$165	$140	$110	$90	$65

BABY SEMI-AUTO — .22 S or L, 2⅛ in. barrel, fixed sights, blue, bakelite grips. Mfg. 1949-1968.

	$250	$175	$150	$130	$100	$90	$80

SPORTER MODEL — .22 LR, 6, 8, or 10 in. barrels, target sights, blue, wood grips. Mfg. 1949-1968.

	$305	$275	$220	$165	$140	$110	$85

MODEL 60 — .22 LR, .32 auto, or .380 auto cal., 3½ in. barrel, fixed sights, blue, bakelite grips. Mfg. 1959-present.

	$220	$195	$180	$165	$155	$135	$120

This model is not imported domestically.

MODEL 68 — .22 Short or .22 LR cal., vest pocket model, 6 shot, bakelite grips, 8½ oz. Current mfg.

	$140	$120	$110	$100	$90	$80	$70

This model is not imported domestically.

PISTOLS: SEMI-AUTO, RECENT MFG.

Prices could differ from values shown below because of the fluctuating U.S. dollar.

MODEL 80 — .22 LR or .380 auto cal., 3½ in. barrel, adj. sights, blue, thumbrest plastic grips. Imported 1968-1988.

	$185	$160	$150	$140	$130	$115	$100

Add $5 for .380 ACP.
Note: This model was produced to conform to import regulations of GCA 1968. Importation of this model was disc. 1988.

MODEL USA — .22 LR, .32 (disc.), or .380 ACP. cal., semi-auto, single action, steel frame, loaded chamber indicator, adj. sights, target bakelite grips, 7 shot (.380 ACP) or 10 shot (.22 LR) mag.

Mfg.'s Sug. Retail	$289	$265	$240	$220	$195	$175	$150	$130

This model has the same technical specifications as the Model 60.

MODEL AMR — .22 LR, .32 (disc.), or .380 ACP cal., similar action to USA Model except has 6 in. barrel and adj. rear sight.

Mfg.'s Sug. Retail	$309	$290	$245	$225	$195	$175	$150	$130

MODEL 90 SPORT TARGET — similar to 80, only .32 ACP or .22 LR, with 6 in. barrel. Imported 1968-1988.

	$210	$185	$170	$155	$140	$120	$110

Last Mfg.'s Sug. Retail was $245.

Grading	100%	98%	95%	90%	80%	70%	60%

MODEL 69 TARGET — .22 LR, target semi-auto, single action, 5.9 in. heavy barrel, 10 shot mag., wrap-around checkered wooden grips, 38 oz.

Mfg.'s Sug. Retail	$459	$420	$360	$320	$285	$240	$200	$185

This model was previously designated Model 100.

MODEL 100 TARGET — .22 LR, 5.9 in. barrel, adj. sight, blue, checkered wood, thumbrest grips, cased. Imported 1968-1988.

		$395	$325	$295	$260	$225	$190	$175

Last Mfg.'s Sug. Retail was $360.

MODEL P010 TARGET — .22 LR, single action, 5.9 in. barrel, adj. sights and trigger, matte black finish, large anatomic walnut stippled grips with thumbrest, 10 shot mag., 40.5 oz. New 1989.

Mfg.'s Sug. Retail	$519	$475	$395	$350	$320	$285	$260	$240

Add $60 for wooden case.

MODEL P018 — 7.65mm (disc. 1988) or 9mm Luger, double action, semi-auto, steel construction, 4⅞ in. barrel, 16 shot mag., plastic (standard) or walnut checkered grips, 36 oz. Imported 1985-present.

Mfg.'s Sug. Retail	$499	$450	$385	$340	$300	$275	$250	$230

Add $40 for walnut grips.
Add $30 for carrying case w/combination lock (disc. 1989).

This model was extensively redesigned in 1989 and includes a " cocked and locked" feature, thumb mag. release, loaded chamber indicator, as well as other improvements.

P018 Compact — similar to Model P018 except has 4 in. barrel and 14 shot mag., approx. 2 lbs. New 1989.

Mfg.'s Sug. Retail	$519	$465	$395	$345	$300	$275	$250	$230

This model was also redesigned in 1989 to incorporate the same features as the Model P018.

DOUBLE RIFLES

EXPRESS VB — various cals., side-by-side sidelock action, ejectors, double triggers. Importation began 1990.

Mfg.'s Sug. Retail	$7,033	$6,150	$5,100	$4,675	$4,100	$3,600	$3,100	$2,650

Add $207 for single trigger (Model Express VB M).

RIFLES: SEMI-AUTO

SEMI-AUTO .22 — .22 LR, blow back action. Importation began 1990.

Mfg.'s Sug. Retail	$438	$385	$295	$250	$210	$170	$150	$135

SHOTGUNS: SIDE-BY-SIDE, DISCONTINUED

MODEL 110 — 12 ga., trap or skeet model, separated barrels, high post rib.

		$2,000	$1,500	$1,300	$1,100	$1,000	$900	$800

MODEL 110 EXTRA — similar to Model 110, except engraved.

		$3,021	$2,265	$1,970	$1,665	$1,510	$1,360	$1,210

S. UBERTO 1 GAMECOCK — 12, 16, 20, or 28 ga., 25¾ in. imp. cyl. and mod., 27½ in. full and mod., hammerless, boxlock, extractors, two triggers, English style stock, checkered.

		$853	$635	$605	$550	$495	$440	$415

Add 20% for ejectors.

Grading	100%	98%	95%	90%	80%	70%	60%

SHOTGUNS: SIDE-BY-SIDE, CURRENT MFG.

Bernardelli side-by-side shotguns are manufactured with straight grip, English-style stocks with pistol grip available as a special order. Importation of Bernardelli shotguns has been inconsistent in the past and current dealer inventories of older merchandise might be priced less than similar models currently imported.

A wide variety of special order options is available on these shotguns. Individual price quotations are available by contacting Magnum Research, Inc. in Minneapolis, MN directly.

Barrel choke markings for V. Bernardelli shotguns are as follows; Full: *, Impr. Mod: **, Mod: ***, Impr. Cyl: ****, Cylinder: CL.

BRESCIA HAMMER DOUBLE BARREL — 12, 16, or 20 ga., 25¾, 27½ and 29½ in. mod. and full, 12 ga., 25½ in. imp. cyl. and mod., sidelock, extractors, two triggers, straight English stock, splinter forearm, checkered.

Mfg.'s Sug. Retail	$2,482	$2,050	$795	$600	$450	$425	$395	$375

Sudden drop in values reflects desirability factor in today's marketplace.

ITALIA HAMMER DOUBLE BARREL — similar to Brescia, except higher grade engraving and wood.

Mfg.'s Sug. Retail	$2,844	$2,275	$1,200	$900	$735	$650	$600	$550

Sudden drop in values reflects desirability factor in today's marketplace.

ITALIA EXTRA HAMMER — hammer double, 12, 16, or 20 ga. Top-of-the-line hammer model.

Mfg.'s Sug. Retail	$7,861	$6,400	$3,150	$2,200	$1,650	$1,375	$1,050	$800

Sudden drop in values reflects desirability factor in today's marketplace.

MODEL 112 — 12 ga., entry-level model with extractors and DTs. Imported 1989 only.

		$850	$750	$675	$625	$550	$495	$450

Add $64 for single trigger (Model 112 M - disc.).
Last Mfg.'s Sug. Retail was $998.

MODEL 112E — 12 ga., Anson & Deeley action, light engraving. Importation disc. 1989.

		$995	$850	$775	$695	$625	$550	$495

Last Mfg.'s Sug. Retail was $1,108.

MODEL 112 EM — similar to Model 112E, except has single trigger.

Mfg.'s Sug. Retail	$1,798	$1,475	$950	$825	$725	$650	$540	$495

Model 112 EM - MC — similar to Model 112 EM, except has 3 in. chambers and 5 choke tubes. Importation began 1990.

Mfg.'s Sug. Retail	$1,971	$1,600	$1,000	$850	$775	$675	$575	$495

Model 112 EM-MC-WF — includes 3½ in. chambers, waterfowl model with matte finish, single trigger and 3 choke tubes. Importation disc. 1990.

		$1,275	$975	$850	$775	$675	$575	$495

Last Mfg.'s Sug. Retail was $1,444.

S. UBERTO 1 — 12, 16, 20, or 28 ga., Anson & Deeley action, Purdey locks, light engraving, case hardened receiver, double triggers, extractors.

		$1,050	$900	$800	$700	$625	$550	$495

Add $65 for single trigger (Model S. Uberto 1M).
Last Mfg.'s Sug. Retail was $1,164.

S. Uberto 1E — similar to S. Uberto 1, except with ejectors. Importation disc. 1990.

		$1,175	$950	$850	$740	$650	$565	$495

Add $65 for single trigger (Model S. Uberto 1EM).
Last Mfg.'s Sug. Retail was $1,357.

Grading	100%	98%	95%	90%	80%	70%	60%

S. UBERTO 2 — 12, 16, 20, and 28 ga.'s, Anson & Deeley action, Purdey locks, light scroll engraving, silver finished receiver, double triggers, extractors. Importation disc. 1989.

	$1,075	$925	$820	$720	$650	$540	$495

Add $35 for single trigger (Model S. Uberto 2M).
Last Mfg.'s Sug. Retail was $1,260.

⚔ **S. Uberto 2E** — similar to S. Uberto 2, except with ejectors.

Mfg.'s Sug. Retail	$1,924	$1,575	$975	$850	$750	$665	$550	$500

Add $81 for single trigger (Model S. Uberto 2EM).

S. UBERTO FS — 12, 16, 20, or 28 ga., Purdey locks, relief engraved with hunting scenes on silver finished receiver, double triggers, extractors. Importation disc. 1989.

	$1,275	$1,025	$900	$775	$670	$560	$500

Add $65 for single trigger (Model S. Uberto FSM - disc. 1989).
Last Mfg.'s Sug. Retail was $1,421.

⚔ **S. Uberto FSE** — similar to S. Uberto F.S., except with ejectors. Importation disc. 1989.

	$1,375	$1,100	$975	$850	$750	$625	$550

Add $65 for single trigger (Model S. Uberto FSEM).
Last Mfg.'s Sug. Retail was $1,537.

ROMA 3 — similar to S. Uberto, double triggers, extractors, false sideplates, case hardened receiver. Importation disc. 1989.

	$1,150	$950	$850	$740	$650	$565	$475

Add $65 for single trigger (Model Roma 3M).
Last Mfg.'s Sug. Retail was $1,274.

⚔ **Roma 3E** — similar to Roma 3, except with ejectors.

Mfg.'s Sug. Retail	$1,986	$1,625	$1,000	$850	$775	$675	$575	$495

Add $81 for single trigger (Model Roma 3EM).

ROMA 4 — more deluxe model than Roma 3, false sideplates, scroll engraved, silver finished receiver. Importation disc. 1989.

	$1,250	$1,025	$900	$800	$700	$625	$550

Add $65 for single trigger (Model Roma 4M).
Last Mfg.'s Sug. Retail was $1,439.

⚔ **Roma 4E** — similar to Roma 4, except with ejectors.

Mfg.'s Sug. Retail	$2,276	$1,825	$1,225	$950	$850	$750	$650	$595

Add $78 for single trigger (Model Roma 4EM).

ROMA 6 — 12, 16, 20, or 28 ga., fully engraved sideplates with hunting scenes, Purdey locks, silver finish receiver, single trigger, finely figured English walnut. Importation disc. 1989.

	$1,395	$1,150	$975	$875	$775	$675	$600

Add $175 for single trigger (Model Roma 6M).
Last Mfg.'s Sug. Retail was $1,619.

⚔ **Roma 6E** — similar to Roma 6, except with ejectors, 16 ga. was disc. 1989.

Mfg.'s Sug. Retail	$2,482	$1,975	$1,325	$1,050	$950	$810	$720	$630

Add $81 for single trigger (Model Roma 6EM).

ELIO — 12 ga. only, lightweight, extractors, fine English style scroll engraving on silver finish receiver. Importation disc. 1989.

	$1,125	$925	$850	$740	$650	$565	$475

Add $65 for single trigger (Model Elio M).
Last Mfg.'s Sug. Retail was $1,238.

Bernardelli, Vincenzo, cont.

Grading	100%	98%	95%	90%	80%	70%	60%

Elio E — similar to Elio, except with ejectors. Importation disc. 1989.
$1,200 / $1,000 / $895 / $795 / $695 / $595 / $500
Add $65 for single trigger (Model Elio EM).
Last Mfg.'s Sug. Retail was $1,353.

SLUG GUN — 12 ga. only, 23¾ in. slug bored barrels, extractors, Anson & Deeley action, Purdey locks, lightly engraved, silver finish receiver. Importation disc. 1990.
$1,325 / $1,000 / $895 / $795 / $695 / $595 / $500
Add $65 for single trigger (Model Slug M).
Last Mfg.'s Sug. Retail was $1,575.

SLUG LUSSO — 12 ga. only, 23¾ in. slug bored barrels, sideplates, with extensive engraving featuring hunting scenes, cheek piece, ejectors, silver finished receiver.
Mfg.'s Sug. Retail $2,793 / $2,325 / $1,550 / $1,200 / $995 / $875 / $750 / $650
Add $80 for single trigger (Model Slug Lusso M).
This model was previously designated Slug Deluxe (1988 or earlier).

HEMINGWAY — 12, 20, or 28 (new 1992) ga., boxlock action, coin finished receiver with game scene engraving, 23½ in. barrels, DTs, deluxe checkered walnut stock and forearm, 6¼ lbs.
Mfg.'s Sug. Retail $2,172 / $1,750 / $1,250 / $950 / $850 / $750 / $650 / $600
Add $81 for single trigger (Model Hemingway M).

HEMINGWAY DE LUXE — similar to Hemingway, except is also available in 16 ga. and has sideplates, better wood, and more engraving.
Mfg.'s Sug. Retail $2,482 / $2,025 / $1,400 / $1,000 / $925 / $810 / $720 / $630
Add $81 for single trigger (Model Hemingway De Luxe M).

LAS PALOMAS PIGEON — 12 ga. live pigeon gun, single trigger, special dimensions for live pigeon shooting.
Mfg.'s Sug. Retail $3,930 / $3,375 / $2,400 / $1,850 / $1,625 / $1,500 / $1,375 / $1,195
Add $81 for single trigger (Model Las Palomas M).

HOLLAND V.B. LISCIO — 12 ga. only, Holland type sidelocks, light engraving, silver finish receiver, single trigger, ejectors, select walnut.
Mfg.'s Sug. Retail $10,757 / $8,700 / $5,000 / $4,450 / $3,900 / $3,350 / $2,850 / $2,400

HOLLAND V.B. INCISO — 12 ga. only, H&H sidelock action, Purdey locks, various barrel lengths, single trigger, ejectors, straight or pistol grip stock, 100% engraved on coin finished receiver.
Mfg.'s Sug. Retail $12,929 / $10,700 / $7,000 / $5,500 / $4,700 / $4,200 / $3,500 / $3,000

HOLLAND V.B. LUSSO — 12 ga. only, H&H sidelock action, Purdey locks, various barrel lengths, single trigger, ejectors, straight or pistol grip stock, same features as Holland V.B. Inciso, only extra select wood and game scene engraving.
Mfg.'s Sug. Retail $14,377 / $8,900 / $7,900 / $6,500 / $5,200 / $4,750 / $4,000 / $3,450

HOLLAND V.B. EXTRA — 12 ga. only, H&H style action, any barrel length and choke, double triggers, auto ejectors, straight or pistol grip stock, 100% engraved on coin finished receiver. Prices are completely dependent upon individual customer specifications. Values listed below are for engraving pattern No. 3.
Mfg.'s Sug. Retail $16,549 / $13,250 / $9,700 / $7,450 / $6,150 / $5,200 / $4,600 / $3,950
Add $1,034 for engraving pattern No. 4.
Add $4,551 for engraving pattern No. 12.
Add $8,895 for engraving pattern No. 20.
Add $621 for single trigger.
Older specimens (not custom ordered within the last 2 years) could have values considerably lower than those listed above.

Grading	100%	98%	95%	90%	80%	70%	60%

HOLLAND V.B. GOLD — top-of-the-line model, made to individual order. Very limited production and ultra-rare.

		100%	98%	95%	90%	80%	70%	60%
Mfg.'s Sug. Retail	$57,922	$47,500	$32,500	$24,000	$18,500	$13,000	$11,500	$9,950

Older specimens (not custom ordered within the last 2 years) could have values considerably lower than those listed above.

SHOTGUNS: OVER & UNDER, RECENT MFG.

A wide variety of special order options is available on these shotguns. Individual price quotations are available by contacting Magnum Research, Inc. in Minneapolis, MN directly.

MODEL 115 HUNTING — 12 ga. only, boxlock action, monobloc frame, inclined plane lockings, blued receiver, single trigger, ejectors. Importation disc. 1989.

100%	98%	95%	90%	80%	70%	60%
$1,770	$1,425	$1,225	$1,000	$895	$750	$650

Last Mfg.'s Sug. Retail was $1,915.

Model 115S — similar to 115, except moderate engraving.

100%	98%	95%	90%	80%	70%	60%
$2,150	$1,925	$1,745	$1,500	$1,250	$1,025	$950

Last Mfg.'s Sug. Retail was $2,500.

Model 115L — similar to 115S, except extensive scroll engraving on silver finish receiver.

100%	98%	95%	90%	80%	70%	60%
$2,600	$2,375	$2,050	$1,750	$1,450	$1,100	$850

Last Mfg.'s Sug. Retail was $3,170.

Model 115E — sideplate, boxlock action, ejector, bulino game scene engraving.

100%	98%	95%	90%	80%	70%	60%
$4,650	$4,125	$3,600	$3,100	$2,650	$2,200	$1,800

Last Mfg.'s Sug. Retail was $5,200.

MODEL 115 TARGET — 12 ga. only, same specifications as Model 115, except trap dimensions. Importation disc. 1989.

100%	98%	95%	90%	80%	70%	60%
$1,800	$1,595	$1,375	$1,175	$1,000	$895	$750

Last Mfg.'s Sug. Retail was $2,160.

Model 115S — same specifications as 115 Target, except light engraving.

		100%	98%	95%	90%	80%	70%	60%
Mfg.'s Sug. Retail	$3,920	$3,275	$2,425	$1,825	$1,500	$1,250	$1,025	$895

This model is available in either Pigeon, Skeet, Sporting Clays, or Trap configuration.

Model 115L — similar to 115S, except extensive scroll engraving on silver finish receiver. Importation disc.1990.

100%	98%	95%	90%	80%	70%	60%
$3,700	$2,995	$2,600	$2,375	$2,050	$1,750	$1,450

Last Mfg.'s Sug. Retail was $4,201.

Model 115E — same specifications as 115S, except with extensively engraved sideplates. Importation disc. 1990.

100%	98%	95%	90%	80%	70%	60%
$5,950	$4,800	$4,125	$3,600	$3,100	$2,650	$2,200

Last Mfg.'s Sug. Retail was $6,827.

Model 115S Monotrap — 12 ga. only, single barrel. Imported 1989 only.

100%	98%	95%	90%	80%	70%	60%
$2,600	$2,150	$1,900	$1,700	$1,500	$1,250	$1,025

Add $1,000 for extra trap barrel.
Last Mfg.'s Sug. Retail was $2,976.

Grading	100%	98%	95%	90%	80%	70%	60%

MODEL 190 TARGET — 12 ga, SST, ejectors, engraved silver receiver, select checkered walnut stock and forearm. Imported 1986-1989.

| | $1,425 | $1,095 | $925 | $800 | $700 | $600 | $525 |

Last Mfg.'s Sug. Retail was $1,572.

Model 190 MC — similar to Model 190 Target except has Monte Carlo stock. Imported 1989 only.

| | $1,000 | $825 | $700 | $600 | $525 | $475 | $450 |

Last Mfg.'s Sug. Retail was $1,155.

Model 190 Special — 12 ga. only, similar to Model 190 Target, except has better walnut and engraving. Imported 1988-1989.

| | $1,335 | $1,000 | $895 | $800 | $700 | $600 | $525 |

Add $75 for single trigger (Model 190 Special MS).
These variations are hunting models.
Last Mfg.'s Sug. Retail was $1,456.

MODEL 192 MS COMPETITION — 12 ga. only, ejectors, selective or non-selective triggers, multi-chokes standard on Sporting Clays Model. New 1990.

| Mfg.'s Sug. Retail | $2,307 | $1,925 | $1,400 | $1,075 | $900 | $825 | $725 | $625 |

This model is available in either Pigeon, Skeet, Sporting Clays, or Trap configuration.

MODEL 192 MS-MC HUNTING — 12 ga. only, boxlock action with engraved coin finished receiver, 3 in. chambers, ejectors, SST, 26¾ or 28 in. VR barrels with choke tubes, steel shot compatible. Importation began 1990.

| Mfg.'s Sug. Retail | $1,833 | $1,400 | $995 | $825 | $700 | $600 | $525 | $475 |

Model 192 MS-MC-WF — waterfowler variation which includes 3½ in. chambers, 3 choke tubes, and SST. Imported 1990 only.

| | $1,275 | $950 | $875 | $775 | $675 | $575 | $500 |

Last Mfg.'s Sug. Retail was $1,444.

MODEL 200 LIGHTWEIGHT MS — 12 ga. only, silver gray finished receiver with game scene engraving. Imported 1988-1989.

| | $1,075 | $895 | $800 | $700 | $600 | $525 | $475 |

Last Mfg.'s Sug. Retail was $1,211.

MODEL 220 MS HUNTING — 12 (disc. 1989) or 20 ga., silver gray finished receiver with engraving. New 1988.

| Mfg.'s Sug. Retail | $1,812 | $1,395 | $975 | $825 | $700 | $600 | $525 | $475 |

Add $700 for extra set of 12 ga. barrels (disc. 1990).
This model is available with either a pistol grip or English grip (straight) stock.

SATURNO MS-MC COMPETITION — 12 ga. only, sporter configuration, boxlock action with lightly engraved side plates. Importation began 1991.

| Mfg.'s Sug. Retail | $2,927 | $2,475 | $1,650 | $1,150 | $975 | $810 | $720 | $630 |

This model is available in either Pigeon, Skeet, Sporting Clays, or Trap configuration.

SATURNO MS-MC HUNTING — 12 ga. only, boxlock action with lightly engraved side plates, ejectors, SST, includes multi-chokes. Importation began 1991.

| Mfg.'s Sug. Retail | $2,609 | $2,275 | $1,525 | $1,050 | $875 | $750 | $695 | $600 |

Bernardelli, Vincenzo, cont.

Grading	100%	98%	95%	90%	80%	70%	60%

ORIONE — 12 ga., double Purdey lock, vent. rib, case hardened receiver, double triggers, extractors. Importation disc. 1989.

	$1,150	$995	$850	$750	$640	$555	$495

Last Mfg.'s Sug. Retail was $1,380.

ORIONE S — similar to Orione, except ejectors, engraved nickel finish receiver. Importation disc. 1989.

	$1,175	$1,025	$860	$760	$650	$560	$510

Last Mfg.'s Sug. Retail was $1,425.

ORIONE L — similar to Orione S, single trigger, finer engraving, English or pistol type select walnut stock. Importation disc. 1989.

	$1,285	$1,125	$950	$840	$750	$650	$550

Last Mfg.'s Sug. Retail was $1,550.

ORIONE E — top-of-the-line, deep relief engraving. Importation disc. 1989.

	$1,375	$1,200	$1,020	$900	$820	$710	$650

Last Mfg.'s Sug. Retail was $1,660.

SHOTGUNS: SEMI-AUTO

MODEL 9MM FLOBERT — 9mm rimfire shot cartridge, 24.4 in. smooth bore barrel, 3 shot mag., steel receiver, walnut stock and forearm with sling and swivels, 5 lbs. 3 oz.

Mfg.'s Sug. Retail	$393	$325	$225	$175	$150	$125	$105	$95

SHOTGUNS: FOLDING MODELS

SINGLE BARREL — 12, 16, 20, 24, 28, 32 or .410 ga., gun folds in half. Importation disc. 1990.

	$230	$185	$150	$135	$125	$115	$100

Last Mfg.'s Sug. Retail was $265.

DOUBLE BARREL — 12 and 16 ga., gun folds in half, double triggers. Current manufacture, but available in Europe only.

	$570	$430	$370	$315	$285	$260	$230

BERSA

Manufacturer located in Argentina. Currently imported and distributed exclusively by Eagle Imports, Inc. located in Ocean, NJ. Previously imported and distributed before 1988 by Rock Island Armory located in Geneseo, IL and Outdoor Sports Headquarters, Inc. located in Dayton, OH. Distributor sales only.

THUNDER 9 — 9mm Para., double action semi-auto, 3½ in. barrel, 14 shot mag., ambidextrous manual safety and decocking lever, automatic firing pin safety, 3-dot sights, aluminum frame, wrap-around matte black polymer grips, link-free locked breech design, non-glare matte blue finish. Importation began 1993.

Mfg.'s Sug. Retail	$415	$365	$310	$285	$260	$235	$210	$190

MODEL 23 — .22 LR, double action semi-auto, 9 shot mag., 3½ in. barrel, walnut grips, 24½ oz. New 1988.

Mfg.'s Sug. Retail	$282	$230	$180	$150	$125	$115	$105	$95

Add $33 for satin nickel finish.

Grading	100%	98%	95%	90%	80%	70%	60%

MODEL 83 — .380 ACP, double action semi-auto, 3½ in. barrel, blued finish, custom walnut grips, 6 shot mag., 24½ oz. New 1988.

Mfg.'s Sug. Retail	$282	$230	$180	$150	$125	$115	$105	$95

Add $33 for satin nickel finish.

MODEL 85 — .380 ACP, similar specifications to Model 83 except has 12 shot mag., 30½ oz. New 1988.

Mfg.'s Sug. Retail	$332	$280	$245	$220	$195	$170	$150	$130

Add $60 for satin nickel finish.

MODEL 86 — .380 ACP cal., matte finish, undercover model, wrap around rubber grips, 12 shot mag. Importation began 1991.

Mfg.'s Sug. Retail	$367	$310	$265	$225	$200	$170	$150	$130

Add $33 for nickel finish.

MODEL 90 — 9mm Para., single action, semi-auto, steel frame, checkered walnut grips, 13 shot mag., deep blue finish. Imported 1990-91 only.

		$325	$280	$250	$220	$195	$170	$150

Last Mfg.'s Sug. Retail was $384.

MODEL 223 — .22 LR, single action semi-auto, 10 shot mag., 3½ in. barrel, squared-off trigger guard, nylon grips, blued action. Importation disc. 1987.

		$200	$170	$150	$125	$115	$105	$95

Last Mfg.'s Sug. Retail was $239.

MODEL 224 — similar to Model 223, except has 4 in. barrel. Imported 1987 only.

		$200	$170	$150	$125	$115	$105	$95

Last Mfg.'s Sug. Retail was $239.

MODEL 225 — similar to Model 223, except has 5 in. barrel and 10 shot mag. Disc. 1987.

		$155	$135	$125	$115	$105	$95	$85

Last Mfg.'s Sug. Retail was $170.

MODEL 226 — similar to Model 225, except has 6 in. barrel. Importation disc. 1987.

		$200	$170	$150	$125	$115	$105	$95

Last Mfg.'s Sug. Retail was $239.

MODEL 323 — .32 ACP, single action semi-auto, 8 shot mag., thumbrest plastic grips, 25 oz. Disc. 1987.

		$105	$95	$85	$75	$65	$55	$45

Last Mfg.'s Sug. Retail was $125.

MODEL 383 — .380 ACP, single action semi-auto, 3½ in. barrel, blued finish, nylon grips, 7 shot mag. Importation disc. 1988.

		$120	$95	$90	$80	$70	$60	$50

Last Mfg.'s Sug. Retail was $188.

MODEL 383 — .380 ACP, double action semi-auto, 3½ in. barrel, blued finish, custom wood grips, 7 shot mag. Importation disc. 1988.

		$135	$105	$95	$85	$75	$65	$55

Last Mfg.'s Sug. Retail was $239.

BERTUZZI
Manufacturer located in Brescia, Italy since 1886. Imported and distributed by New England Arms Co. located in Kittery Point, ME. Direct from importer.

SHOTGUNS: S X S

MODEL ORIONE — 12 ga., scalloped Anson & Deeley boxlock action, beavertail forearm, single trigger, auto ejector. This model is available on special order only — contact the distributor listed above for availability, prices, and options. Prices start at $4,500.

BEST QUALITY SIDELOCK — various gauges, best quality sidelock model with extensive engraving. Prices start at $9,500.

HAMMER GUN — all gauges, upper tang safety, double triggers, fine quality engraving. Prices start at $8,500 and approach $10,000 with ejectors and single trigger. The self-cocking mechanism is popular in this model and prices can vary between $9,500-$20,000.

SHOTGUNS: O/U

ZEUS — 12 ga., sidelock, auto ejector, deluxe engraving, deluxe wood checkering, SST. This model is available on special order only — contact the distributor listed above for availability, prices, and options. Prices generally range from $18,500-$27,500.

ZEUS EXTRA LUSSO — 12 ga., sidelock, auto ejector, deluxe wood, deluxe checkering and engraving, SST. This model is available on special order only — contact the distributor listed above for availability, prices, and options. Prices generally range $25,000+.

BIG BEAR
Current importer and distributor since 1992 located in Dallas, TX specializing in Russian shotguns manufactured by the Tula Arsenal located in Russia. Dealer direct sales only.

PISTOLS

Grading	100%	98%	95%	90%	80%	70%	60%
TOZ-35M — .22 LR, single shot, Olympic Free Pistol, adj. palm rest, firing pin cocked with cocking lever, fitted case with necessary tools. Importation began 1992.							
No Mfg.'s Retail	$895	$750	$625	$500	$425	$350	$295

SHOTGUNS

	100%	98%	95%	90%	80%	70%	60%
MODEL MZ 20-01 — 20 ga., standard model with blued finish. Importation disc. 1992.	$175	$155	$130	$115	$100	$85	$75

Add $35 for Souvenir Model (includes engraving).

	100%	98%	95%	90%	80%	70%	60%
MZ-21 SEMI-AUTO FIELD GRADE — 12 ga. only, 4 shot mag., 28 in. bbl.							
No Mfg.'s Retail	$695	$595	$500	$425	$350	$295	$225
MZ-21 SEMI-AUTO SOUVENIR — 12 ga. only, Souvenir Model, 4 shot mag., extensive hand engraving and stock carving. Importation disc. 1992.	$1,995	$1,750	$1,400	$1,200	$995	$795	$595
TOZ-34 O/U FIELD GRADE — 12 ga. only, boxlock action, blued, DTs, extractors, 28 in. bbls., extensive engraving.							
No Mfg.'s Retail	$795	$650	$500	$400	$350	$300	$260

Grading	100%	98%	95%	90%	80%	70%	60%

TOZ-34E O/U PRESENTATION GRADE — 12 ga. only, boxlock action, blued, DTs, extractors, 28 in. bbls., extensive engraving.

No Mfg.'s Retail — $2,700 $2,200 $1,800 $1,500 $1,300 $1,100 $850

TOZ-91 O/U FIELD GRADE — 12 or 20 ga., boxlock action, blued, DTs, extractors, 28 in. bbls.

No Mfg.'s Retail — $1,000 $825 $700 $600 $500 $400 $300

TOZ-91 O/U PRESENTATION GRADE — 12 or 20 ga., boxlock action, blued, DTs, extractors, 28 in. bbls., extensive engraving.

No Mfg.'s Retail — $4,150 $3,150 $2,800 $2,400 $1,950 $1,500 $1,200

BIG HORN ARMS CORP.
Previous manufacturer located in Watertown, SD.

TARGET PISTOL — .22 Short only, unique action permitting auto. ejection, ambidextrous stock made of molded Tufflex with carvings, 26 oz. Approx. 1,200 mfg. Disc. in the late 60's.

$175 $150 $135 $125 $115 $105 $95

LIL' MAGNUM SHOTGUN — .410 diameter reloadable shot cartridge, single shot open bolt operation, included reloading equipment, approx. 2,000 mfg. in the late 60's.

$125 $100 $75 $65 $55 $50 $45

BIGHORN RIFLE CO.
Previous manufacturer located in Orem, UT.

BIGHORN RIFLE — Mauser action, choice of calibers, custom made bolt action of high quality, interchangeable barrels (gun is supplied with 2 barrels), adj. trigger, deluxe walnut stock, many custom options. Mfg. 1984 only.

$2,100 $1,800 $1,600 $1,400 $1,200 $1,000 $850

BIGHORN PISTOL — .22 LR, bolt action design, research is underway to gather more information concerning this model.

BINGHAM, LTD.
Manufacturer located in Norcross, GA 1976-1985.

RIFLES

PPS 50 — .22 LR only, blowback action, 50 round drum mag., standard model has Beechwood stock. Add $20 for deluxe model with walnut stock. Duramil model has chrome finish and walnut stock — add $30. Disc. 1985.

$195 $160 $145 $135 $125 $110 $100

This model was styled after the Soviet WWII Model PPSh Sub Machine Gun. Last Mfg.'s Sug. Retail was $230.

AK-22 — .22 LR only, blowback action, styled after AK-47, 15 shot mag. standard, 29 shot mag. available. Standard model has Beechwood stock. Deluxe model has walnut stock — add $20. Disc. 1985.

$225 $195 $160 $145 $135 $125 $110

Last Mfg.'s Sug. Retail was $230.

BANTAM — .22 LR or 22 Mag., bolt action single shot, 18½ in. barrel. Disc. 1985.

$110 $90 $75 $65 $55 $45 $40

Last Mfg.'s Sug. Retail was $120.

Grading	100%	98%	95%	90%	80%	70%	60%

FG-9 — 9mm only, blowback action, semi-auto paramilitary design carbine, 20½ in. barrel. New design for 1984. While advertised this model was never manufactured.

BITTNER
Manufactured by Gustav Bittner located in Vieprty, Bohemia, (Austria, Hungary).

BITTNER MODEL 1893 — 7.7mm Bittner cal., pistol with hand activated repeater mechanism, box magazine, checkered grips, limited manufacture in circa 1893.

	$5,500	**$4,500**	**$3,500**	**$2,700**	**$2,300**	**$1,900**	**$1,500**

BLAND, THOMAS & SONS GUNMAKERS LTD.
English manufacturer located in England since 1840. This firm was purchased in 1990 by Woodcock Hill located in Benton, PA. Manufacturer direct sales only.

Woodcock Hill should be contacted directly (address listed in Trademark Index) for more information (including current models and prices) regarding Thomas Bland & Sons firearms. Prices will vary depending on the exchange rate between the pound/dollar.

SHOTGUNS

Both boxlock and sidelock best quality shotguns are available in all gauges with prices ranging between $5,000 - $40,000 depending upon type, finish, and accessories.

RIFLES

Double rifles are available in almost all calibers and specifications. Prices vary between $12,000 - $45,000 depending upon type, finish, and accessories. Bolt action rifles are available in any type of action, most calibers, and other special options. The bolt action models are not manufactured in England. Prices range between $1,100 - $11,000.

BLASER
Manufactured by Blaser Jagdwaffen Gmbh in Isny/Allgau, Germany. Currently imported and distributed in the U.S. by Autumn Sales Inc. located in Fort Worth, TX. Direct sales from the importer only.

Prices could differ from values shown below because of the fluctuating U.S. dollar.
Blaser Jagdwaffen manufactures a large variety of rifles, drillings, and combination guns for the European market. The models below have been selected for domestic sales. More information is available on the European models by contacting Autumn Sales (see Trademark Index).

MODEL R-84 — .22-250, .243 Win., 6mm Rem., .25-06 Rem., .270 Win., .280 Rem., or .30-06 standard cals., .257 Wby. Mag., .264 Win. Mag., 7mm Rem. Mag., .300 Win. Mag., .300 Wby. Mag., .338 Win. Mag., or .375 H&H Magnum cal., 23 or 24 (Mag. cals. only) in. interchangeable barrel, scroll engraving on receiver, short bolt action with 60 degree rotation, checkered Turkish walnut stock and forearm, approx. 7 lbs. Introduced 1988.

Mfg.'s Sug. Retail	$2,250	$2,075	$1,575	$1,275	$1,050	$950	$850	$775

Add $50 for left-hand action.
Add $575 per interchangeable barrel.
This model features the scope being mounted directly to the barrel (and not the receiver). Since the scope mounts are on the barrel extension, this takedown rifle is unique in that it does not require re-zeroing when the rifle is reassembled, regardless of caliber change.

Model R84 Deluxe — features a better grade of Turkish walnut with a North American game scene engraved on receiver, silver pistol grip cap with animal scene engraving.

Mfg.'s Sug. Retail	$2,500	$2,325	$2,000	$1,650	$1,200	$1,000	$925	$825

Add $50 for left hand action.

Grading	100%	98%	95%	90%	80%	70%	60%

⚔ **Model R84 Super Deluxe** — best grade Turkish walnut with receiver featuring African game scene engraving (animals are in gold and silver), and silver pistol grip cap with gold animal engraving.

Mfg.'s Sug. Retail	**$2,850**	**$2,625**	**$2,200**	**$1,775**	**$1,300**	**$1,100**	**$975**	**$895**

Add $50 for left hand action.

ULTIMATE BOLT ACTION — .22-250, .243, .25-06, .270, .308, .30-06, 7 x 57, 7 x 64, .264 Win. Mag., 7mm Rem. Mag., 300 Win. Mag., .338 Win. Mag., or .375 H&H cal., unique bolt action design with 60 degree bolt throw, interchangeable barrel capability, 3 locking lugs, safety lever cocks and uncocks the firing pin spring, exposed hammer, aluminum receiver, 22 or 24 in. barrel, single set trigger, silver finished receiver has light engraving, select checkered walnut stock and forearm, 6¾ lbs. Extra interchangeable barrels are $545 each, extra bolt heads are $175 each. Mfg. 1985-1989.

	$1,350	**$1,100**	**$975**	**$925**	**$825**	**$750**	**$675**

All models were available in left-hand version at no extra charge.
Last Mfg.'s Sug. Retail was $1,495.

MODEL K77 A SINGLE SHOT — .22-250, .243 Win., 6.5 x 55mm, .270 Win., 7 x 57R, 7 x 65R, or .30-06 standard cals., 7mm Rem. Mag., .300 Win. Mag. or .300 Wby. Magnum cal., break open action, 23 or 24 in. barrel, 3 piece take down, upper tang safety, checkered walnut stock and forearm, engraved silver finished receiver, sling swivels, 5½ lbs. Imported 1988-90.

	$2,000	**$1,675**	**$1,475**	**$1,300**	**$1,100**	**$925**	**$800**

Add $50 for Mag. calibers.
Add $730-$778 per interchangeable barrel.
Last Mfg.'s Sug. Retail was $2,280.

ULTIMATE: SPECIAL ORDER

All of the below listed models may have been ordered with a butt stock cartridge trap — add $250-$500 depending on model. Special order guns required 3 to 9 months to hand fabricate. Mfg. was disc. 1989 on all models.

⚔ **Ultimate Deluxe** — similar to Ultimate, except better wood and game scene engraving.

	$1,425	**$1,175**	**$1,000**	**$950**	**$850**	**$775**	**$700**

Last Mfg.'s Sug. Retail was $1,595.

⚔ **Ultimate Deluxe Carbine** — .243 Win. or .308 Win. cal. only, 19½ in. barrel with full length forearm. New 1986.

	$1,600	**$1,375**	**$1,150**	**$1,000**	**$900**	**$825**	**$750**

Last Mfg.'s Sug. Retail was $1,800.

⚔ **Ultimate Super Deluxe** — similar to Ultimate Deluxe, except features better wood and game scene engraving. New 1986.

	$3,750	**$3,250**	**$2,900**	**$2,600**	**$2,300**	**$2,100**	**$1,850**

Last Mfg.'s Sug. Retail was $4,030.

⚔ **Ultimate Exclusive** — similar to Ultimate Super Deluxe, except features better wood and game scene engraving. New 1986.

	$4,850	**$4,300**	**$3,500**	**$2,975**	**$2,600**	**$2,275**	**$1,975**

Add $700 per interchangeable barrel.
Last Mfg.'s Sug. Retail was $5,655.

⚔ **Ultimate Super Exclusive** — similar to Ultimate Exclusive, except features better wood and game scene engraving. New 1986.

	$7,700	**$6,800**	**$5,750**	**$4,700**	**$3,950**	**$3,450**	**$2,950**

Add $950 per interchangeable barrel.
Last Mfg.'s Sug. Retail was $8,905.

Grading	100%	98%	95%	90%	80%	70%	60%

⌐ **Ultimate Royal** — best quality Ultimate, featuring Bavarian cheek piece and checkering/carving on stock and forearm, elaborate game scene engraving, gold plated hammer. New 1986.

	100%	98%	95%	90%	80%	70%	60%
	$9,000	$7,500	$6,750	$6,000	$5,375	$4,600	$4,000

Add $1,200 per interchangeable barrel.
Last Mfg.'s Sug. Retail was $11,500.

BOITO
Manufacturer located in Brazil. Previously imported by F.I.E. Corp. located in Hialeah, FL.

Boito shotguns were inexpensive, utilitarian shotguns that are shootable, but not collectible. Because of this, prices typically range between $100 - $225, depending on the gauge and condition.

BORCHARDT
Manufacturer located in Germany from 1894 - 1897.

PISTOL: SEMI-AUTO

These prices are established with matching parts and original finish guns.

MODEL 1893 — 7.65mm, with accessories, cased. Subtract 40% if uncased and without accessories.

⌐ **Ludwig Loewe mfg.** — serial numbered 1-1104.

	100%	98%	95%	90%	80%	70%	60%
	$18,500	$15,000	$12,500	$10,000	$8,000	$6,500	$5,000

⌐ **DWM mfg.** — starting approx. 1895, serial numbered 1105-3000.

	100%	98%	95%	90%	80%	70%	60%
	$17,500	$15,000	$12,500	$10,000	$8,000	$6,500	$5,000

BOSS & CO., LTD.
Manufacturer located in London, England 1812 to date. Direct sales from the manufacturer only.

Boss manufactures some of the world's finest shotguns (best quality guns only). They have always been custom built per individual order. Less than 10,000 have been manufactured to date. We will list the basic models with approximate values, but should the opportunity for purchase or sale arise, competent appraisals should be secured.

The values below are based on a 50 pounds = $100 currency exchange rate.

SHOTGUNS

BOSS SIDE-BY-SIDE — all gauges, barrel lengths and chokes to specifications, bar-action sidelock, easy-open action (not self-opening), square or round action, checkered stock, pistol grip (optional) or straight grip stock, single or double triggers, splinter or beavertail (optional) forearm, traditional English rose & scroll engraving.

	Mfg.'s Sug. Retail	100%	98%	95%	90%	80%	70%	60%
	$37,250	$37,250	$31,750	$22,500	$18,750	$15,000	$13,000	$11,000

Add $2,980 for 20 ga. Other gauges are quoted per individual request.
Add $1,490 for ST. Patented "3 pull" system.
Add 10% for opening assist.
Add appropriate price ($500 on up) if properly cased.

BOSS O/U — 12 ga. standard, other ga.'s available, barrel lengths and chokes to specifications, shell-framed sidelock, auto ejectors, double triggers or single non-selective, English straight grip stock standard to specifications, VR or pistol grip stock optional, traditional English rose & scroll fine engraving.

	Mfg.'s Sug. Retail	100%	98%	95%	90%	80%	70%	60%
	$59,600	$59,600	$49,500	$37,500	$32,500	$27,500	$22,500	$18,000

Smaller gauges on current mfg. are quoted per individual request.
Add 30% for 20 ga. on older mfg.
Add 65% for 28 ga. on older mfg.
Add 75%+ for .410 ga. on older mfg.
Add 10% for opening assist. Add appropriate price ($500 on up) if properly cased.
Note: above values represent base gun only. Any additional engraving (traditional rose and scroll) and/or special orders will add considerably to the above prices.

BOSWELL, CHARLES

Previously manufactured in London, England. In 1988, Charles Boswell was purchased by U.S. interests and Cape Horn Outfitters located in Charlotte, NC has been retained to sell and manufacture the Boswell Guns in the U.S. In addition to aquiring their entire inventory of English manufactured firearms, Charles Boswell is currently fabricating new shotguns and double rifles in the U.S. using the best materials including English lock mechanisms and will retain the Charles Boswell Co. Trademark. Every gun will be custom ordered to an individual client's requirements/specifications. Previously imported by Saxon Arms, Ltd., located in Clearwater, FL.

SHOTGUNS: SIDE-BY-SIDE

Current manufacture is very limited.

Grading	100%	98%	95%	90%	80%	70%	60%

BOXLOCK SXS — made to individual order, choice of engraving - including game scenes with gold, Anson & Deeley boxlock actions, select European hybrid walnut, double triggers, leather cased, currently mfg. While each shotgun is priced per individual special order, the below listed prices represent standard features and embellishments.

Best Quality
Mfg.'s Sug. Retail $9,500 | $9,500 $7,750 $6,500 $5,650 $4,800 $4,200 $3,750

Deluxe Grade — game scene engraved.
Mfg.'s Sug. Retail $10,500 | $10,500 $8,350 $7,250 $6,000 $5,000 $4,400 $3,750
Add $900 for single trigger.
Add $2,800 for extra set of barrels.
Add $2,200 for smaller gauges.

FEATHERWEIGHT MONARCH GRADE — lavishly engraved with gold game scenes, lightweight model, specifications per individual customer special order. Mfg. began 1989.

Boxlock Model
Mfg.'s Sug. Retail $12,500 | $12,500 $9,750 $7,350 $6,000 $5,000 $4,400 $3,750

Sidelock Model
Mfg.'s Sug. Retail $25,000 | $25,000 $18,750 $15,000 $12,750 $10,000 $7,950 $6,250

SIDELOCK SXS — made to individual order, choice of game scene engraving, H&H sidelock action, select European hybrid walnut, double triggers, leather cased, currently mfg. While each shotgun is priced per individual special order, the below listed values represent standard features and embellishments.
Mfg.'s Sug. Retail $17,500 | $17,500 $15,000 $12,750 $10,000 $9,000 $8,500 $7,750
Add $4,000 for smaller gauges except .410 — add $5,000.
Add $2,800 for extra set of barrels.
Add $2,800 for extra set of .410 ga. barrels.

DOUBLE RIFLES

BOXLOCK SXS RIFLE — made to individual order, .300 Express, .375 H&H, .458 Win. Mag., or .500 NE cal., choice of game scene engraving, Anson & Deeley boxlock actions, select European hybrid walnut, double triggers, leather cased.
Mfg.'s Sug. Retail $35,000 | $35,000 $27,500 $23,000 $19,000 $16,500 $15,000 $13,250

.600 Nitro Express
This model is priced by quotation only. A recently built .600 NE sold for $123,000 in 1991.

Grading	100%	98%	95%	90%	80%	70%	60%

SIDELOCK SXS RIFLE — made to individual order, .300 Express, .375 H&H, or .458 Win. Mag. cal., choice of game scene engraving, H&H sidelock action, select European hybrid walnut, double triggers, leather cased.

Mfg.'s Sug. Retail	$65,000	$65,000	$49,500	$40,000	$35,000	$31,000	$25,000	$21,500

⚔ **.600 Nitro Express**

Mfg.'s Sug. Retail	$125,000	$125,000	$95,000	$70,000	$54,500	$43,500	$37,500	$31,000

Premiums are often times paid for these models due to extreme rarity and slow fabrication time.

BREDA, ERNESTO

Manufacturer located in Milan, Italy. Previous importation by Diana Imports Co., located in San Francisco, CA.

SHOTGUNS: SEMI-AUTO

GOLD SERIES SEMI-AUTO — 12 or 20 (lightweight) ga., semi-auto, 2¾ in., 25 or 27 in. barrels, gas operated. Current model has interchangeable choke tubes, vent. rib is standard. Add $26 for choke tubes (each).

⚔ **Antares Standard** — all steel construction. Importation disc. 1988.

	$440	$375	$340	$310	$285	$260	$240

Last Mfg.'s Sug. Retail was $495.

⚔ **Argus** — lightweight standard, weighs only 6.6 lbs. Importation disc. 1988.

	$450	$380	$340	$310	$285	$260	$240

Last Mfg.'s Sug. Retail was $510.

⚔ **Aries** — Magnum, 3 in. chambers, 7.9 lbs. Importation disc. 1988.

	$460	$395	$350	$320	$295	$270	$250

Last Mfg.'s Sug. Retail was $525.

STANDARD — 12 ga., semi-auto, 2¾ in., 25 or 27 in. barrels, recoil operated, lightly engraved. Current model has interchangeable choke tubes. Add $35 for vent. rib, $20 for choke tubes (each). Disc.

	$300	$275	$255	$230	$215	$200	$180

GRADE 1 — 12 ga., similar to standard, except with fancier wood and engraving.

	$575	$530	$485	$440	$410	$380	$350

GRADE 2 — 12 ga., exceeds Grade 1 on embellishments.

	$685	$620	$560	$500	$460	$420	$375

GRADE 3 — 12 ga., top-of-the-line semi-auto.

	$850	$790	$700	$640	$590	$540	$480

MAGNUM MODEL — 12 ga. only, chambered for 3 in. shells. Add $20 for vent. rib.

	$470	$415	$380	$350	$315	$290	$265

ALTAIR SPECIAL — 12 ga. semi-auto, 2¾ in., 25 or 27 in. barrels, gas operated, alloy construction. Current model has interchangeable choke tubes, vent. rib is standard. Add $25 for choke tubes (each). Choice of blued or chromed receiver.

	$440	$375	$340	$310	$285	$260	$240

Last Mfg.'s Sug. Retail was $495.

Grading	100%	98%	95%	90%	80%	70%	60%

SHOTGUNS: OVER AND UNDER

VEGA SPECIAL — 12 ga. only, boxlock action, 26 or 28 in. barrels, single trigger, ejectors, blue only.

	$575	$495	$460	$440	$400	$375	$350

Last Mfg.'s Sug. Retail was $650.

VEGA SPECIAL TRAP — 12 ga. only, boxlock action, triggers and locks designed for competition shooting, 30 or 32 in. barrels, single trigger, ejectors, blue only.

	$885	$820	$760	$720	$675	$635	$575

Last Mfg.'s Sug. Retail was $1,114.

SIRIO STANDARD — 12 ga. only, boxlock action, 26 or 28 in. barrels, single trigger, ejectors, blue only, action extensively engraved. Also available in skeet model (28 in. barrels).

	$2,000	$1,850	$1,630	$1,480	$1,320	$1,200	$1,050

Last Mfg.'s Sug. Retail was $2,225.

SHOTGUNS: SIDE-BY-SIDE

ANDROMEDA SPECIAL — 12 ga. only, single trigger, ejectors, select checkered walnut, satin finish receiver with elaborate engraving.

	$640	$550	$480	$420	$365	$300	$250

Last Mfg.'s Sug. Retail was $685.

BREN

Manufactured 1983-86 by Dornaus & Dixon Ent., Inc., located in Huntington Beach, CA.

Note: the Bren 10 shoots a Norma factory loaded 10mm auto. cartridge. Ballistically, it is very close to a .41 Mag. Bren pistols also have unique power seal rifling, with five lands and grooves.

Since the discontinuance of the Bren pistol in 1986, collector interest has accelerated, driving prices up substantially.

Bren 10 magazines played an important part in the failure of these pistols to be accepted by consumers. Originally, Bren magazines were not shipped in some cases until a year after the customer received his gun. The complications arising around manufacturing a reliable magazine domestically lead to the downfall of this company. For this reason, ORIGINAL BREN 10 MAGAZINES ARE CURRENTLY SELLING FOR $150-$175 IF NEW (WATCH FOR FAKES).

PISTOLS

While in production, Bren pistols underwent 4 engineering changes, the most important probably being re-designing the floorplate of the magazine, thus preventing mag. shifting while undergoing recoil.

100% values in this section assume NIB condition. Subtract 10% without box/manual.

BREN 10 STANDARD MODEL — 10mm only, semi-auto selective double action design, brushed satin finish, 5 in. barrel, 11 shot, stainless steel frame, usually supplied with two mags. "83SM" ser. no. prefix. Mfg. 1984-86.

	$1,450	$1,150	$975

Add $500 for .45 conversion unit.
Last Mfg.'s Sug. Retail for this pistol was $500.

BREN 10 MILITARY/POLICE MODEL — 10mm only, identical to standard model, except has all black finish, "MP" ser. no. prefix. Mfg. 1984-86.

	$1,400	$1,100	$900

Last Mfg.'s Sug. Retail was $550.

Grading	100%	98%	95%	90%	80%	70%	60%

BREN 10 SPECIAL FORCES MODEL — 10mm only, commercial version of the military pistol submitted to the U.S. gov't. Model D has dark finish. Model L has light finish, "SFD" ser. no. prefix on Model D, "SFL" ser. no. prefix on Model L. Disc. 1986.

Dark finish - Model D	$1,500	$1,275	$900				
Light finish - Model L	$1,850	$1,600	$1,500				

Last Mfg.'s Sug. Retail was $600.

BREN 10 DUAL-MASTER PRESENTATION MODEL — 10mm and .45 ACP, supplied with extra slide and barrel (numbered to gun) to accommodate the .45 ACP, same Mag. for both cals., extra fine finish, light scroll engraving, with wood presentation case, "83DM" ser. no. prefix, less than 50 mfg. Disc. 1986.

$2,875 $2,300 $2,000

Last Mfg.'s Sug. Retail was $800.

BREN 10 JEFF COOPER COMMEMORATIVE — 10mm only, while 2,000 were announced for mfg., sources believe less than 30 were actually made, 22Kt. gold plated detailing, laser engraved stocks, special presentation chest. Disc. 1986.

$4,000 $3,425 $2,950

Last Mfg.'s Sug. Retail was $2,000.

MARKSMAN MODEL — .45 ACP, 250 mfg. (in its own ser. range) for a retail shop in Chicago called "The Marksman", action similar to Bren 10 Standard Model, "MSM" ser. no. prefix.

$1,200 $975 $750

Add $550 for 10mm conversion unit.

BRETTON

Manufactured in Saint-Etienne, France. Imported and distributed by Mandall Shooting Supplies, Inc. located in Scottsdale, AZ.

SHOTGUNS: OVER AND UNDER

All Bretton shotguns are extremely lightweight and well balanced because of their unique design (permitting total disassembly including barrels) and use of various composition alloys.

BABY STANDARD (SPRINT MODEL) — 12 or 20 ga. only, sliding breech action allows barrels to move straight forward, 27½ in. separated barrels, double triggers, side opening lever, blued action and barrels, recoil pad, checkered walnut stock and forearm, 4.8 lbs.

Mfg.'s Sug. Retail	$865	$815	$700	$625	$575	$475	$430	$395

Available from Mandall Shooting Supply, Inc. only.

SPRINT DELUXE — 12, 16 (disc.), or 20 ga., action similar to Baby Standard, engraved coin finished receiver, 27½ in. separated barrels, deluxe checkered walnut stock and forearm, extremely lightweight, 4.8 lbs.

Mfg.'s Sug. Retail	$975	$895	$750	$675	$600	$550	$500	$460

Available from Quality Arms, Inc. and Mandall Shooting Supply, Inc.

FAIR PLAY MODEL — 12 or 20 ga., differs from Sprint Models in that action pivots like normal O/U, 27½ in. separated barrels, lightweight construction, 4.8 lbs.

Mfg.'s Sug. Retail	$1,025	$925	$775	$695	$600	$550	$500	$460

BRITARMS

Manufactured by Berdan Gunmakers Ltd. located in England. Currently imported and distributed by Mandall Shooting Supplies, Inc. located in Scottsdale, AZ and Action Arms Ltd. (1982-83) located in Philadelphia, PA.

Britarms Target Pistols have had very limited importation to date in the U.S. While Britarms has manufactured other models, only the Model 2000 is listed since it has been formally imported through a U.S. firms.

Grading	100%	98%	95%	90%	80%	70%	60%

Model 2000 (MK II) — .22 LR, standard fire target semi-auto pistol, adj. trigger and rear sight, anatomical adj. grips, 5.82 in. barrel, 5 shot mag., without hold-open device, 3 lbs., limited importation, including approx. 200 through Action Arms Ltd.

Mfg.'s Sug. Retail	$1,295	$995	$825	$700	$625	$550	$495	$450

Limited quantities of this model are still available from Mandall Shooting Supplies, Inc. Most Action Arms specimens have a "BA9" serial number prefix.

BRNO ARMS

Manufactured in Brno & Uherski Brod, Czechoslovakia since 1936. Brno rifles and CZ firearms produced at the CZ factory are currently imported and distributed exclusively by Action Arms Ltd. located in Philadelphia, PA. Bohemia Arms, located in Fountain Valley, CA, imports Brno manufactured O/U and SxS shotguns in addition to some rifles. Previously imported by T.D. Arms located in New Baltimore, MI. Pragotrade located in Ontario, Canada also imports this trademark for Canada currently (and exclusively).

While little history is known about this important European trademark, the following biographical sketch will provide some information. In approximately 1916, some military personnel took over the controlling interest of the Austro-Hungarian armament shop in Brno, Czechoslovakia, renaming it The State Armament and Engineering Works. Approximately a year later, the name was changed to Czechoslovak State Armament Works. Prior to 1924, this firm was involved mainly with Mauser Model 98 type rifles (both assembly and mfg.). In 1924, the name was again changed to Ceskoslovenska Zbrojovka A.Z. (Czechoslovakian Arms Factory Ltd.) - commonly known as the CZ firm. CZ manufactured the VZ-24 Mauser rifle for Czechoslovakia as well as other M-98 military rifles and carbines for other countries, including many which Germany used during WWII. After WWII, the name was again changed to Zbrojovka Brno (Brno Arms Works), or ZB for short. With the iron curtain descending on Europe after WWII, communist bloc countries had little exportation to the U.S., including Czechoslovakia. In the early '50s, Brno rifles were imported by Continental Arms Corp. located in New York City. With the sudden decline in communism during the past year, more and more products (including firearms from Czechoslovakia) will see their way into the U.S. without the 65% importation tax previously levied on goods from older communist bloc countries.

CZ PISTOLS

See separate listing under CZ in this text.

RIFLES: BOLT ACTION

The Brno Lightweight Sporter was introduced in the late 1930's. A small quantity was manufactured during pre-war and WWII. Most production occured between 1946-1955. Total production of this model was approx. 40,000+ units. A design change was implemented at approximatly serial number 23,000, at which time the receiver was changed to a double square bridge dovetailed to accept scope mounts. Earlier mfg. had a rounded receiver and some had claw type scope mounts installed. These guns were referenced as Models 21 and 22 domestically, but no model designation appears on the gun. Available cals. were 6.5 x 57, 7 x 57, 7 x 64, 8 x 57, or 8 x 60mm. Configuration was small ring Mauser 98 receiver with double set trigger(s), butterknife bolt, checkered walnut pistol grip stock (half or full length), with cheekpiece and sling swivels, late production incorporated four variations and two barrel lengths (20.5 or 23.6 in.).

BRNO RIFLES MAY BE DATED BY THE 2-DIGIT DATE BESIDE THEIR PROOF-MARKS.

HORNET SPORTER (MODEL ZKW 465) — miniature Mauser action, .22 Hornet, $22\frac{3}{4}$ in. barrel, 5 shot clip mag., 3-leaf express sight, double set trigger(s), checkered pistol grip stock, also called Z-B Mauser, serial range noted is 02,901-37,393, approx. 40,000 mfg. between 1949-1973.

	$875	$700	$600	$470	$385	$305	$220

There are few examples in .218 Bee and .222 Rem. cal. - premiums can be added. This model was redesigned with a subsequent designation of ZKB 680 Fox in approx. 1975.

Grading	100%	98%	95%	90%	80%	70%	60%

MODEL ZG-47 — .270 Win., .30-06, 7 x 57, 7 x 64, 8 x 64S, 8 x 57mm, 9.3 x 62, or 10.75 x 68mm cal., large ring Mauser 98 action with 20mm dovetails on receiver ring and bridge, single trigger, hinged floorplate, rollover type safety and bolt handle designed for low scope mounting, 23½ in. barrel, checkered pistol grip walnut stock with sling swivels and Schnabel forend, serialization noted is 02,702 (1956) - 16,931 (1962), approx. 20,000 mfg. and exported world-wide between 1956-1962 (approx.).

	$995	$875	$700	$600	$470	$385	$305

Early specimens of this model are marked "BRNO MADE IN CZECHOSLOVAKIA". This model is generally regarded as being one of the finest rifles that Brno has manufactured.

MODEL 21H — 6.5 x 57, 7 x 57, 7 x 64 (scarce), or 8 x 57 cal., featherweight style design of the small ring Mauser type action, with (post-1949) or without 20mm dovetails on receiver ring and bridge, 20½ or 23 in. barrel, butterknife style bolt handle, double set triggers, 2-leaf rear sight, checkered pistol grip walnut stock with cheekpiece and plastic buttplate/grip cap, small Schnabel forend, sling swivels included, noted serialization is 14,410-40,098, mfg. approx. 1946-1955.

	$850	$675	$575	$470	$385	$305	$220

This model was available in 4 different variations: short barrel/short stock, short barrel/full length stock, long barrel/short stock, long barrel/full length stock. The left receiver rail on these models is marked "ZBROJOVKA BRNO, NARODINI PODNIK".

MODEL 22F — similar to 21H, with full length stock. Disc.

	$1,050	$900	$700	$525	$440	$360	$275

MODEL 1 — .22 LR, 22¾ in. barrel, 3-leaf sight, 5 shot clip mag., checkered pistol, 6 lbs. Mfg. 1946-1957.

	$595	$540	$485	$405	$375	$320	$265

MODEL 2 — similar to Model 1, with checkered deluxe walnut stock.

	$635	$570	$515	$430	$405	$350	$295

MODEL 3 — .22 LR, target rifle model with 27½ in. heavy barrel, adj. click target sights, 5 shot clip mag., plain target style stock with large swivels, 9½ lbs. Mfg. 1949-1956.

	$635	$570	$515	$430	$405	$350	$295

MODEL 4 — similar to Model 3, except has improved trigger design and safety. Mfg. 1957-1962.

	$700	$635	$570	$515	$430	$405	$350

MODEL 5 — similar to Model 1, except has improved trigger design and safety. Mfg. 1957-1973.

	$650	$570	$515	$430	$405	$350	$295

MODEL ZKM-452 — .22 LR, bolt action, 5 or 10 shot mag., 23.6 or 25 (disc.) in. barrel, uncheckered hardwood stock, 4.9 lbs. Importation disc. 1986, resumed in 1992 with changes.

Mfg.'s Sug. Retail	$305	$265	$220	$185	$170	$155	$140	$130

This model and its variations are imported exclusively by Action Arms.

Model ZKM-452D (Deluxe) — similar to ZKM-452 only with checkered walnut stock.

Mfg.'s Sug. Retail	$349	$295	$240	$195	$175	$160	$145	$130

MODEL ZKM-456 LUX — .22 LR cal., bolt action, 5 or 10 shot mag., 24.4 in. barrel, folding rear sight, blued finish, Beech wood stock with pistol grip, 6.8 lbs. Importation began 1992.

No Mfg.'s Retail	$295	$260	$215	$175	$155	$135	$120

This model and its variations are imported exclusively by Bohemia Arms International.

Grading	100%	98%	95%	90%	80%	70%	60%

Model 456 L Target — .22 LR cal., Target variation of the ZKM-456 Lux featuring 27½ in. barrel with adj. front and rear sights, 10.1 lbs. Importation began 1992.

No Mfg.'s Retail		$265	$235	$190	$160	$140	$120	$100

Model 456 Match Single Shot — .22 LR cal., designed for UIT competition at 50 M, features 27½ in. barrel, adj. cheekpiece and buttplate, aperture sights, 9.9 lbs. Importation began 1992.

No Mfg.'s Retail		$375	$335	$280	$250	$215	$175	$155

CZ-527 — .22 Hornet, .222 Rem., or .223 Rem. cal., scaled down receiver with claw extractor and Mauser type bolt, detachable 5 shot mag., double triggers, adj. rear sight, grooved receiver, thumb safety, synthetic (new 1993) or checkered walnut stock, 6.2 lbs. Importation began 1992.

Mfg.'s Sug. Retail	$599	$515	$430	$385	$340	$310	$285	$260

Add $66 for walnut stock.

This model is imported exclusively by Action Arms.

CZ-537 — .243 (new 1993), .270 Win., .30-06, or .308 (new 1993) cal., single set trigger, adj. rear sight with hooded front, forged one-piece bolt, cocking indicator, 5 shot internal mag., synthetic (new 1993) or checkered walnut stock with recoil pad and sling swivels, 7.3 lbs. Importation began 1992.

Mfg.'s Sug. Retail	$599	$515	$430	$385	$340	$310	$285	$260

Add $70 for walnut stock.

This model and its variations are imported exclusively by Action Arms.

ZKK 600 — .270 Win., .30-06, 7 x 57mm, or 7 x 64mm (disc.) cal., improved Mauser type action, 23½ in. barrel, synthetic (new 1993) or checkered walnut stock, 5 shot internal mag., thumb safety, 7.2 lbs.

Mfg.'s Sug. Retail	$559	$485	$410	$365	$330	$300	$275	$250

Add $50 for walnut stock.

This model is imported exclusively by Action Arms.

ZKK 601 — .223 Rem. (importation disc. 1991), .243 Win. or .308 Win. cal., otherwise similar to ZKK 600.

Mfg.'s Sug. Retail	$559	$485	$410	$365	$330	$300	$275	$250

This model is imported exclusively by Action Arms.

ZKK 602 — .300 Win. Mag., .375 H&H, 8 x 68mm (disc.), .416 Rigby (disc. 1986), or .458 Win. Mag. (disc. 1986) cal., similar to ZKK 600, except has 25.2 in. barrel and 3 leaf express rear sight, 9.3 lbs.

Mfg.'s Sug. Retail	$745	$660	$560	$495	$450	$395	$350	$310

Add $90 for walnut stock (not available in .375 H&H or .458 Win. Mag. cal.).

This model is imported exclusively by Action Arms.

ZKB 680 (FOX II) — .22 Hornet or .222 Rem. (disc.) cal., 23½ in. barrel, 5 shot mag., set triggers, 5 lbs. 12 oz. Importation disc. 1991.

		$445	$380	$340	$295	$255	$230	$200

Last Mfg.'s Sug. Retail was $499.

RIFLES: SEMI-AUTO

CZ-511 — .22 LR, semi-auto, select walnut stock, adj. sights. Disc. 1986.

		$280	$250	$230	$215	$200	$190	$180

Last Mfg.'s Sug. Retail was $310.

Grading	100%	98%	95%	90%	80%	70%	60%

ZKM-611 — .22 Mag. cal., 20 ½ in. barrel, 6 or 12 shot mag., black metal finish, walnut stock and forend, grooved receiver, 6.2 lbs. Importation began 1992.

No Mfg.'s Retail $560 $425 $375 $325 $290 $260 $230

This model is imported exclusively by Bohemia Arms International.

MODEL 581 — .22 LR, semi-auto, select walnut stock, adj. sights, 5 shot mag. Disc.

$600 $540 $495 $440 $395 $350 $295

RIFLES: O/U

SUPER EXPRESS — 7 x 65R, 9.3 x 74R, .375 H&H, or .458 Win. Mag. (disc.) cal., sidelock action with Kersten breech crossbolt, hand engraved, skipline checkering, approx. 9 lbs. Importation disc. 1992.

$3,450 $2,875 $2,300 $1,875 $1,600 $1,375 $1,200

This model previously could be ordered with 6 different types of engraving options. They were: Grade I — add $2,060, Grade II — add $1,030, Grade III — add $1,545, Grade IV — add $1,030, Grade V — add $620, Grade VI — add $660.
Last Mfg.'s Sug. Retail was $3,900.

SUPER SAFARI — 7 x 64R, .375 H&H Mag., or 9.3 x 74R cal., action derived from the Super Express, sidelock, DT with set trigger built in, adj. point of impact, 23.6 in. barrels with open sights, deluxe skipline checkered walnut stock and forearm with vent. recoil pad, approx. 9 lbs. Importation began 1992.

No Mfg.'s Retail $2,375 $1,975 $1,675 $1,450 $1,225 $1,000 $900

This model is imported exclusively by Bohemia Arms International.

SHOTGUNS/COMBINATIONS GUNS: O/U

The current models listed below are being imported and distributed by Bohemia Arms International located in Fountain Valley, CA.

ZH-SERIES

ZH series over and unders are unique in that they permit 8 different interchangeable barrels including rifle and shotgun sets, interrupter on double trigger, blued action, engraved, diamond checkered walnut.
Add $25 for Monte Carlo stock (disc.).
Add for $45 for set triggers (disc.).

ZH-300 — 12 ga. only, double triggers with rear trigger doubling as single trigger, 27½ in. barrels, 7 lbs. Imported 1986-92.

$530 $430 $395 $360 $330 $300 $275

This model is available in skeet, trap, or field configuration.
Last Mfg.'s Sug. Retail was $599.

ZH-301 FIELD — 12 ga. field, 27½ in. barrels, optional Monte Carlo stock.

No Mfg.'s Retail $510 $415 $335 $275 $225 $195 $175
Add $20 for Monte Carlo stock.

ZH-302 SKEET — 12 ga., skeet model, 26 in. barrels, optional Monte Carlo stock.

No Mfg.'s Retail $515 $425 $350 $295 $245 $205 $185
Add $20 for Monte Carlo stock.

ZH-303 TRAP — 12 ga., trap model, 30 in. barrels, optional Monte Carlo stock.

No Mfg.'s Retail $515 $425 $350 $295 $245 $205 $185
Add $20 for Monte Carlo stock.

Grading	100%	98%	95%	90%	80%	70%	60%

ZH-304 COMBINATION GUN — 7 x 57R mm x 12 ga., combination rifle/shotgun, optional adj. trigger and Monte Carlo stock.

| No Mfg.'s Retail | $595 | $500 | $450 | $395 | $360 | $330 | $300 |

Add $35 for adj. trigger.
Add $20 for Monte Carlo stock.

ZH-305 — 5.6 x 52R mm x 12 ga., combination rifle/shotgun. Disc.

| | $685 | $640 | $585 | $520 | $460 | $415 | $360 |

ZH-306 — 5.6 x 50mm Mag. x 12 ga., combination rifle/shotgun. Disc.

| | $685 | $640 | $585 | $520 | $460 | $415 | $360 |

ZH-321 — 16 ga. field, 27 in. barrels. Disc. 1986.

| | $570 | $505 | $460 | $435 | $410 | $390 | $370 |

Last Mfg.'s Sug. Retail was $605.

ZH-324 — 7 x 57R mm x 16 ga., combination rifle/shotgun. Disc. 1986.

| | $640 | $570 | $530 | $495 | $475 | $450 | $420 |

Last Mfg.'s Sug. Retail was $685.

MODEL ZH-300 COMBO SET — Model ZH-300 style engraving and features, equipped with 8 interchangeable barrels that include various O/U configurations including shotgun/shotgun and shotgun/rifle configurations in various ga.'s and cals. Imported 1986-91.

| | $2,950 | $2,600 | $2,250 | $2,000 | $1,800 | $1,600 | $1,450 |

Last Mfg.'s Sug. Retail was $3,500.

MODEL 500/501 SERIES O/U COMBINATION GUN — 12 ga. only, ejectors, O/U shotgun or as combination shotgun/ rifle available in a wide variety of cals. (only 6 x 52R is available currently), field tubes, acid etched engraving, skipline checkering and cheekpiece. New 1986.

| No Mfg.'s Retail | $785 | $650 | $575 | $525 | $475 | $425 | $395 |

Add $50 for combination gun.

Model 500 Combo Set — shotgun/rifle set comprised of 4 barrels including 12 ga. over barrels with choice of 5.6 x 52R (disc.), 7 x 57R, 7 x 65R mm, or 12 ga. under barrels (in either field, skeet, or trap chokings), sling swivels, set trigger on rifle/shotgun combo, chemically engraved, about 7½ lbs. Imported 1987-91.

| | $1,925 | $1,625 | $1,400 | $1,200 | $1,075 | $950 | $825 |

This model is available in limited quanitity.
Last Mfg.'s Sug. Retail was $2,169.

BS-571/572 SHOTGUN/COMBINATION GUN — 12 ga. only, boxlock action with ejectors, 6 x 65R (disc.) or 7 x 65R rifle cal. only. Importation began 1992.

| No Mfg.'s Retail | $995 | $825 | $700 | $600 | $550 | $475 | $425 |

Add approx. $115 for rifle/shotgun (12 ga. only) combination (Model 572).

CZ-581 — 12 ga., boxlock with Greener crossbolt, Poldi steel action, 28 in. barrels, vent. rib, sel. ejectors, sling swivels. Importation disc. 1991.

| | $525 | $440 | $400 | $370 | $355 | $340 | $320 |

Add $30 for single trigger (disc.)
Last Mfg.'s Sug. Retail was $649.

CZ-584 — 12 ga. and 7 x 57R mm rifle/shotgun combination , .222 Rem. and .308 Win. cals. also available, 24½ in. barrels, ejectors. Disc. 1986.

| | $920 | $820 | $750 | $700 | $650 | $600 | $550 |

Last Mfg.'s Sug. Retail was $999.

Grading	100%	98%	95%	90%	80%	70%	60%

SUPER SERIES — available in 12 ga. field, skeet, and trap configuration as well as combination shotgun/rifle in 12 ga. x 7 x 57R or 7 x 65R cal. Importation disc. 1991.

	$800	$700	$640	$590	$550	$515	$475

Add $70 for single trigger or trap/skeet configuration (disc.).
Add $700 for extra set of 12 ga. field barrels.
Add $1,101 for hand engraving.
Last Mfg.'s Sug. Retail was $899.

⚡ **Super Combo** — 3 barrel set including 12 ga., 7 x 57R mm, and 7 x 65R mm barrels. Imported 1987-90.

	$1,925	$1,640	$1,425	$1,250	$1,100	$1,000	$925

Last Mfg.'s Sug. Retail was $2,169.

SHOTGUNS: SIDE-BY-SIDE

ZP-49 — 12 ga. only, ejectors, double triggers, true sidelock, Purdey-type top bolt, cocking indicators, walnut stock, swivels. Imported since 1986, but importer is currently out of stock. Imported 1986-91.

	$535	$460	$420	$385	$350	$320	$290

Add $20 for engraving.
Last Mfg.'s Sug. Retail was $589.

ZP-149 — similar to ZP-49, except has game scene engraving on sideplates, choice of English or pistol grip stock. Imported 1986-1989, and 1992.

	$550	$460	$420	$385	$350	$320	$290

Add $50 for pistol grip stock.

ZP-349 — 12 ga. only, extractors, double triggers, true sidelock, Purdey-type top bolt, cocking indicators, walnut stock with cheek piece, beavertail forearm, swivels, 7.3 lbs. Imported 1986 only.

	$450	$390	$360	$325	$300	$270	$250

Add $20 for engraving.
Last Mfg.'s Sug. Retail was $520.

BRONCO
Echave Y Arizmendi, Eibar, Spain.

MODEL 1918 POCKET AUTOMATIC — 7.65mm, 6 shot, 2½ in. barrel, fixed sights, blue, hard rubber grips. Mfg. 1918-1925.

	$175	$150	$100	$80	$70	$60	$50

VEST POCKET AUTOMATIC — 6.35mm, small frame. Disc.

	$160	$125	$110	$95	$80	$60	$40

BROWN PRECISION, INC.
Manufacturer located in Los Molinos, CA since 1967.

Brown Precision Inc. manufactures primarily rifles using Remington or Winchester actions and restocks them using a combination of Kevlar, Fiberglass and Graphite (wrinkle finish) to save weight. Stock colors are green, brown, gray, black, camo brown, camo green, or camo gray.

PISTOLS

CUSTOM XP-100 HIGH COUNTRY — includes highly tuned XP-100 single shot action with Shilen stainless match grade barrel, electroless nickel or Teflon finish, fiberglass stock. New 1993.

Mfg.'s Sug. Retail	$1,575		$1,475	$1,325	$1,125	$950	$775	$650	$525

Grading	100%	98%	95%	90%	80%	70%	60%

RIFLES: BOLT ACTION

STANDARD HIGH COUNTRY BOLT ACTION RIFLE — various cals. within those factory barreled actions, choice of 700 ADL/BDL, Ruger 77, or Win. Model 70 action, brown fiberglass/Kevlar stock (various colors), sling swivels and pad. Mfg. 1975-present.

Mfg.'s Sug. Retail	$1,085	$995	$875	$725	$625	$525	$440	$400

Add $110 for left hand BDL, Ruger 77, or Win. M 70 action.
Add $40 for Mag. cals.

⚔ **Custom High Country** — similar to High Country, except many custom features can be added. Prices available per individual work order.

HIGH COUNTRY YOUTH RIFLE — various cals., choice of Rem. Model 7 or 700 factory barreled action, fiberglass stock. New 1993.

Mfg.'s Sug. Retail	$1,165	$1,050	$925	$775	$675	$550	$495	$440

MODEL 7 SUPER LIGHT — .223, .243, 6mm, 7mm-08 Rem., or .308 Win. cal., Model 7 action, 18 in. factory barrel, no sights, 5 lbs. 4 oz. Disc. 1992.

		$995	$900	$750	$650	$575	$500	$450

This model can be special ordered with similar options from the Custom High Country Model, with the exception of left-hand action.
Last Mfg.'s Sug. Retail was $1,059.

LAW ENFORCEMENT SELECTIVE TARGET — .308 cal., Model 700 Varmint action with 20, 22, or 24 in. factory barrel, O.D. green camouflage treatment. Disc. 1992.

		$995	$900	$750	$650	$575	$500	$450

This model can be special ordered with similar options from the Custom High Country Model, with the exception of left-hand action.
Last Mfg.'s Sug. Retail was $1,086.

PRO VARMINTER — various cals., includes custom tuned Rem. Model 700 ADL action, Shilen match stainless steel barrel. New 1993.

Mfg.'s Sug. Retail	$1,625	$1,500	$1,350	$1,125	$950	$775	$650	$525

Add $110 for left-hand action.
Add $974 for optional Rem. Model 40-XB action.

PRO-HUNTER — available in over 25 cals., Model 700 ADL or Model 70 action, match grade stainless steel barrel, dull electroless nickel, blue, or teflon finish, express sights, synthetic stock (four different colors). New 1988.

Mfg.'s Sug. Retail	$2,147	$1,975	$1,800	$1,525	$1,350	$1,175	$995	$825

Add $110 for left-hand action.

⚔ **Pro Hunter Elite** — various cals., includes many custom order features. New 1993.

Mfg.'s Sug. Retail	$3,170	$2,950	$2,550	$2,200	$1,975	$1,700	$1,525	$1,250

In late 1991, improvements were made including decelerator recoil pad, barrel band swivel, and speed lock firing pin spring.

BROWN PRECISION WINCHESTER 70 — .270 or .30-06 cal., 22 in. featherweight barrel, camo stock in four colors with black recoil pad, 6¼ lbs. Mfg. 1989-92.

		$650	$575	$475	$425	$385	$325	$300

Add $20 for 7mm Rem. Mag. (24 in. sporter barrel).
Last Mfg.'s Sug. Retail was $750.

BLASER BOLT ACTION RIFLE — standard Camex Blaser cals. and action, fiberglass stock and nickel plated barrel. Disc. 1989.

	$1,395	$1,150	$995	$875	$750	$675	$600

Last Mfg.'s Sug. Retail was $1,395.

BROWNING ARMS

Browning guns originally were manufactured in Ogden, UT, circa 1880. Current BAC headquarters (not manufacturing) are located in Morgan, UT. Browning firearms are manufactured by Fabrique Nationale in Herstal and Liege, Belgium. Since 1976, Browning has also contracted Miroku of Japan and A.T.I. in Salt Lake City, UT to manufacture both long arms and handguns. During 1992, Browning (including F.N.) was acquired by GIAT of France.

The Browning section in this text has been arranged in the following order—PISTOLS, RIFLES, SHOTGUNS: SEMI-AUTO, SHOTGUNS: O/U, OTHER SHOTGUNS, LIMITED EDITIONS-COMMEMORATIVES.

The Browning firm, first known as J.M. Browning & Bro., was established in Ogden, Utah about 1880. Later known as Browning Brothers and Browning Arms Company (BAC), the firm actually manufactured only one gun — the Model 1878 Single Shot which was John M.'s first patent. Winchester bought the production and distribution rights to this gun in 1883, bringing it out as the Winchester M1885. From that time until 1900, Mr. Browning sold Winchester the exclusive rights to 31 rifles and 13 shotguns, of which Winchester produced only 7 rifles (M1885SS: the lever actions M1886, 1892, 1894 and 1895: and the slide action .22s M1890 and 1906) and 3 shotguns (M1887, M1893 and M1897). The other models were bought from Browning simply to keep them out of the hands of other arms makers.

John M. Browning, perhaps the greatest firearms inventor the world has ever known, was directly responsible for an estimated 80 separate firearms that evolved from his 128 patents. During his most prolific period from 1894 to 1910, Browning sold the rights to his rifles, semi-auto pistols, shotguns and machine guns to Winchester, Remington, Colt and Stevens in this country and to Fabrique Nationale for sale outside the U.S. Every Colt and FN semi-auto pistol is based on a Browning patent. In 1902, Browning broke off relations with Winchester when the company refused to negotiate a royalty arrangement for his new semi-auto shotgun(A-5). Browning took the prototype to FN where it became the most commercially successful of all his inventions. FN has produced 6 automatic pistols, 3 rifles and 2 shotguns designed by John M. Browning and is still a major producer of arms sold by Browning in the U.S. and by FN distributors world wide.

Our American military was armed for many years with Browning designed weaponry, not the least of which is the venerable "Old Slabside" 1911 Gov't Model .45 ACP. Today, the firm that bears the Browning name still stands at the forefront with the other makers of fine sporting weapons.

Note: Between 1966-1971 Browning used a salt-curing process to speed the drying time needed for their walnut stock blanks. Unfortunately, the salt would be released from the wood and oxidize the metal surface(s) after a period of time. These guns, especially bolt action rifles in all grades, some BARs, Superposed shotguns, and T-bolt models should be examined carefully around the edges of the wood for signs of freckling and rust. Discount guns that show evidence of salt corrosion 15-50%, depending on how bad rusting has occurred. Check screws and wood under butt plate as well.

Editor's Note: It is important to note the differences in values of Browning weapons manufactured in Belgium by F.N. and those made recently in Japan by Miroku. We feel that these values are somewhat higher because of collector interest in Browning guns made in Belgium and not as the result of any inferiority of the quality of Browning guns made anywhere else.

AS A FINAL NOTE: Most post-war Brownings are collectible only if in 95% or better condition as most models have relatively high mfg. and are not that old. Condition under 95% is normally very shootable, but not as collectible and values for 95% or less condition could be lower than shown in some areas.

Since the inception and standardization of steel shot for hunting purposes, the desirablility factor of shotguns has changed considerably. Any shorter barreled, open choked Belgian Browning shotgun is currently quite a bit more desirable than its 30 in., full choked barrel counterpart. Premiums do exist for this shorter barreled configuration, especially on the Belgian Superposed and A-5 Models. On newer manufacture, choke tubes have become very desirable, and specimens without choke tubes (especially guns with longer barrels) must be discounted somewhat. Browning does not recommend using steel shot in any Superposed (B-25) or older Belgian Auto-5 barrels.

Most 100% values in this section assume N.I.B. condition. Subtract 10% without box/manual. Also, all add-ons or deductions in this section reflect retail pricing without any discounting. On higher grade Browning firearms that are engraved, signed specimens by FN's master engravers Funken, J. Baerten, Vrancken, and Watrin will command premiums over the values listed below.

BROWNING SERIALIZATION

In addition to the Browning serialization listed in the back of this text, the following codes will determine the year and origin of those guns made from 1975 to date. The 2 letters in the middle of the serial number are the code designations for year of manufacture. They represent the following: RV - 1975, RT - 1976, RR - 1977, RP - 1978, RN - 1979, PM - 1980, PZ - 1981, PY - 1982, PX - 1983, PW - 1984, PV - 1985, PT -1986, PR - 1987, PP - 1988, PN - 1989, NM - 1990, NZ - 1991, NY - 1992, NX - 1993. Since most Brownings use a 3-digit model identification code (appearing first on European or U.S. mfg. guns and last on Japanese mfg.), both where and when the specimen was made can easily be determined (i.e. Ser. No. 611RP2785 would be a Model B-2000 made in either Belgium or Portugal in 1978 with 2785 being the Ser. No.— Ser. No. 1479PX368 indicates a BSS 20 ga. mfg. in Japan in 1983 with Ser. No. 1479).

PISTOLS: SEMI-AUTO, F.N. PRODUCTION UNLESS OTHERWISE NOTED

Grading	100%	98%	95%	90%	80%	70%	60%

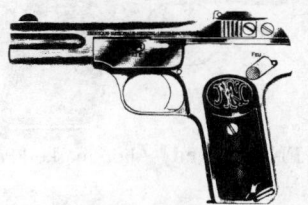

MODEL 1900-FN — 7.65mm cal., first Belgium Browning, 4 in. barrel. 724,500 mfg. 1899-1910.

	100%	98%	95%	90%	80%	70%	60%
	$350	$295	$240	$200	$160	$130	$100

Add 30% for early pistols with "pistol logo" grips.

MODEL 1903-FN — 9mm Browning Long cartridge, 5 in. barrel. 58,400 mfg. 1903-1939.

	100%	98%	95%	90%	80%	70%	60%
	$500	$425	$350	$300	$260	$220	$180

Add 50% if slotted to accept shoulder stock.
This variation was also manufactured with a detachable shoulder stock — this accessory is rare and can add as much as $2,000 to values listed above.

MODEL 1903-SWEDISH CONTRACT — 9mm cal., manufactured by Husqvarna and Swedish Arsenal (so marked), many were imported into U.S. and converted to .380 ACP from original Browning 9mm Long.

	100%	98%	95%	90%	80%	70%	60%
	$300	$260	$230	$200	$180	$150	$125

Deduct 25% for .380 ACP conversion.

MODEL 1905-FN (VEST POCKET) — 6.35mm (.25 ACP), dubbed "Vest Pocket" model, manufactured by Fabrique Nationale, Herstal, Belgium. 1,086,133, mfg. 1906-1959.

First Variation — no slide lock/safety lever.

	100%	98%	95%	90%	80%	70%	60%
	$375	$325	$300	$280	$225	$195	$150

Add 10% for nickel finish.

Second Variation — post 1908, with slide lock/safety lever.

	100%	98%	95%	90%	80%	70%	60%
	$325	$295	$275	$250	$225	$195	$150

Add 10% for nickel finish.

MODEL 1910-FN (MODEL 1955) — 7.65mm (.32 ACP) and Browning 9mm short (.380 ACP) 4 in. barrel. FN manufacture. 701,266 mfg. 1912-1980.

	100%	98%	95%	90%	80%	70%	60%
	$325	$300	$275	$250	$225	$195	$150

Add 20% if BAC marked and .380 ACP cal.
Add 30% if BAC marked and 7.65mm cal.
This model is also referred to as the Model 1955. BAC marked pistols were imported 1954-1968.

Grading	100%	98%	95%	90%	80%	70%	60%

MODEL 1922 OR 10/22 FN — 7.65mm (.32 ACP) or .380 ACP cal., modified Model 1910 with 4½ in. barrel, longer grip frame and mag., made for commercial sale as well as military contracts. Several hundred thousand made by Nazis during the occupation of Liege, Belgium 1940-1944. Mfg. between 1912-1959.

	100%	98%	95%	90%	80%	70%	60%
	$240	$215	$195	$175	$150	$125	$110

Add 10% for Waffenampt proofing.
Add 20% for foreign contracts.
Add 20% if .380 ACP Waffenampt proofed.

The Model 10/22 and M1922 are the same pistol. The Model 1910 was modified by FN technicians for sale to Serbian armed forces in 1923. Also sold to France, Holland, Yugoslavia, and other countries. Also made by the German military 1940-1944.

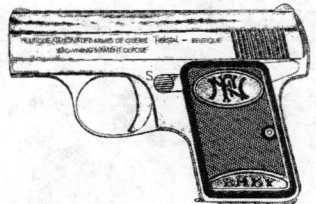

FN "BABY" MODEL — 6.35mm (.25 ACP) cal., lighter, smaller modification of Browning Model 1905 Vest Pocket .25, without grip safety or slide lock, imported under BAC trademark from 1954-1970 in standard blue finish, lightweight nickel and engraved Renaissance models. Mfg. 1931-1983. Total production is over 510,000.

FN Marked — slide marked Fabrique Nationale, blued finish standard.

	$395	$350	$310	$280	$245	$225	$200

BAC Marked — slide marked Browning Arms Co., blued finish standard.

	$300	$265	$225	$195	$180	$165	$150

Lightweight model — nickel frame, with pearl grips.

	$395	$350	$310	$280	$245	$225	$200

Renaissance model — engraved, satin grey finish.

	$875	$725	$550

Add 20% if coin finished.

FN/BROWNING MODEL 10/71 — 4½ in. barrel, modified version of Model 1922 (10/22) in .380 ACP cal., grip safety, includes target sights and grips in addition to incorporating a magazine finger tip extension designed to comply with GCA of 1968. Sold in U.S. by BAC 1970-1974 as the "Standard .380", still mfg. by FN as Model 125.

	$375	$295	$250	$220	$205	$190	$160

Renaissance Model

	$1,050	$850	$775

Gold Line Model

	$1,500	$1,250	$995

MODEL 1935 HI-POWER — 9mm, 13 shot mag., 4⅝ in. barrel, Browning's last pistol design, millions made 1927 to date in variations for commercial, military, and police use in over 68 countries, first imported under BAC trademark in 1954.

Please refer to the Fabrique Nationale section of this book for pre-1954 variations (including WWII and earlier commercial models).

Grading	100%	98%	95%	90%	80%	70%	60%

HI-POWER: POST-1954 MFG. — 9mm, similar to FN model 1935, has BAC slide marking, 13 shot mag., 4⅝ in. barrel, polished blue finish, checkered walnut grips, fixed sights, molded grips were introduced in 1986, ambidextrous saftey was added to all models in 1989. Mfg. 1954-present.

Polished Blue Finish — includes fixed sights.

Mfg.'s Sug. Retail	$525	$455	$370	$325	$300	$280	$260	$240

Subtract $31 for molded grips (disc. 1990).

This model has been produced with both a spur (disc.) or round (current mfg.) hammer configuration. The round cone hammer variation is more desirable but does not necessarily command a higher value. Older specimens in original black pouches (especially with gold metal zipper) will command slight premiums over boxed guns.

Adj. sights

Mfg.'s Sug. Retail	$572	$495	$395	$350	$325	$300	$280	$255

Matte Blue Finish — non-glare matte finish, ambidextrous safety, fixed sights only. New 1985.

Mfg.'s Sug. Retail	$494	$450	$345	$300	$280	$260	$240	$225

Recently, Hi-Powers that appear to have a "black" finish have been noticed. These guns are painted rather than blued and some parties have been selling them as original military FNs. Do not confuse these painted specimens for original pistols and remember, original guns will be worth more than refinished pistols.

Silver Chrome Finish — entire gun finished in silver chrome, includes adj. sights and Pachmayr rubber grips. New 1991.

Mfg.'s Sug. Retail	$582	$495	$395	$350	$325	$300	$280	$255

Practical Model — features blued slide, silver - chromed frame finish, wrap around Pachmayr rubber grips, round style serrated hammer, and choice of adj. sights (new 1993) or removable front sight, 36 oz. New 1990.

Mfg.'s Sug. Retail	$566	$485	$395	$350	$325	$300	$280	$255

Add $47 for adj. sights.

Capitan Polished Blue Finish — features 50-500 meter tangent rear sight, blued finish with walnut grips, 32 oz. New 1993.

Mfg.'s Sug. Retail	$620	$525	$450	$375	$335	$300	$280	$260

Nickel/Silver Chrome finish — not to be confused with stainless steel (never offered in the Hi-Power). Also, this finish is different from the silver chrome finish released in 1991. Disc. 1985.

	$550	$475	$415	$375	$360	$340	$315

Last Mfg.'s Sug. Retail was $525.

.30 Luger Hi-Power — .30 Luger cal., mfg. for European sales 1986-87 (most are marked F.N. on slide), approx. 1,500 imported late 1986-89, similar specifications as 9mm model.

	$650	$575	$500	$450	$400	$360	$330

This model was never cataloged for sale by BAC in the U.S. A few specimens have been noted with B.A.C. slide markings and are more desirable than F.N. marked pistols.

Grading	100%	98%	95%	90%	80%	70%	60%

GP Competition — 9mm, competition model with 6 in. barrel, detent adj. rear sight, rubber wrap-around grips, front counterweight, improved barrel bushing, decreased trigger pull, approx. 36½ oz.

	100%	98%	95%	90%	80%	70%	60%
	$650	$550	$475	$425	$395	$350	$325

The original GP Competition came in a black plastic case w/accesories and is more desirable than later imported specimens which were computer serial numbered and came in a styrofoam box. Above prices are for older models — deduct 10% if newer model (computer serial numbered).

This model was never cataloged for sale by BAC in the U.S.

Tangent Rear Sight Model — manufactured from 1965-1978. Adj. rear sight to 500 meters. A total of approx. 7,000 were imported by Browning Arms Co. Early pistols are designated by "T" prefix and were mfg. 1964-69, later pistols had spur hammers.

	100%	98%	95%	90%	80%	70%	60%
	$700	$600	$525	$440	$400	$370	$340
Renaissance Model	$1,950	$1,600	$1,175				

Tangent Rear Sight Slotted — variation with grip strap slotted to accommodate shoulder stock. Early pistols had "T" prefixes. Later pistols had spur hammers and are in the serial range 73CXXXX-74CXXXX.

	100%	98%	95%	90%	80%	70%	60%
	$1,100	$950	$775	$650	$525	$440	$400

Add $150 if with "T" prefix.

This variation will command a premium; beware of fakes, however (carefully examine slot milling).

BCA EDITION HI-POWER — limited edition made specifically for the Browning Collectors Association in 1980.

	100%	98%	95%
	$600	$495	$400

GOLD LINE HI-POWER — blued finish with gold line perimeter engraving.

	100%	98%	95%
	$1,195	$950	$675

RENAISSANCE HI-POWER — extensive scroll engraving on gray silver receiver, synthetic pearl grips, gold plated trigger. Disc. 1980.

	100%	98%	95%
Round Hammer/fixed sights	$1,250	$900	$725
Spur Hammer/adj. sights	$1,050	$860	$700
Spur Hammer/fixed sights	$975	$825	$650

Add 5% for adj. sights.

CASED RENAISSANCE SET — one each .25 auto, .380 auto, and Hi-Power Renaissance models in walnut case, non-matching serial numbers. Offered 1955-1969.

	100%	98%	95%
	$3,500	$2,750	$2,100

CENTENNIAL MODEL HI-POWER — similar to fixed sight Hi-Power, chrome plated with inscription "Browning Centennial/1878-1978", engraved on side, cased, 3,500 mfg. in 1978. Original issue price was $495.

	100%	98%	95%
	$650	$500	$425

LOUIS XVI MODEL — 9mm, chemically etched throughout in leaf scroll patterns, satin finish, checkered grips, walnut case. Disc. 1984.

	100%	98%	95%
	$850	$675	$525

Add 5% for adj. sights.

9 MM CLASSIC SERIES - PISTOL — 9mm, Hi-Power action, less than 2,500 manufactured in Classic model and under 350 manufactured in Gold Classic. Both editions feature multiple engraved scenes, and a special silver grey finish, presentation grips, cased. Mfg. 1984-86.

	100%	98%	95%
	$850	$675	$495

Last Mfg.'s Sug. Retail was $1,000.

Grading	100%	98%	95%	90%	80%	70%	60%

⚞ Gold Classic — 5 gold inlays, select walnut grips are both checkered and carved. Mfg. 1984-86.

		$1,800	$1,450	$1,150			

Last Mfg.'s Sug. Retail was $2,000.

HI-POWER DOUBLE ACTION — this model was first listed in the Browning catalog in 1985 but was never manufactured. The proposed 1985 retail price was $494.

BDM DOUBLE ACTION — 9mm Para., new double mode design featuring slide selector allowing choice between pistol (true double action operation) or revolver mode (full hammer decocking after each shot), dual purpose decocking lever/safety, 4.73 in. barrel, 15 shot mag., matte blue finish, black molded wrap around grips, unique breech block allows visible cartridge inspection, adj. rear sight, 31 oz. New 1991-mfg. in U.S.A.

Mfg.'s Sug. Retail	$560	$485	$395	$360	$325	$300	$280	$260

This model features hammer block and firing pin block safeties.

BDA-380 — .380 ACP, double action, 14 shot, 3$^{13}\!/_{16}$ in. barrel, fixed sights, smooth walnut grips, 23 oz., introduced 1982-current production, mfg. by Beretta.

Mfg.'s Sug. Retail	$593	$445	$335	$265	$240	$220	$200	$180

⚞ Nickel finish

Mfg.'s Sug. Retail	$625	$475	$350	$275	$250	$225	$205	$185

BDA MODEL — 9mm (9 shot) — 2,740 mfg., .38 Super — 752 mfg., .45 ACP (7 shot), mfg. from 1977-1979 by Sig-Sauer of W. Germany (same as Sig-Sauer 220).

9mm	$425	$375	$300	$275	$250	$225	$200
.38 Super	$650	$575	$495	$450	$390	$350	$320
.45 ACP	$425	$375	$300	$275	$250	$225	$200

NOMAD MODEL — .22 LR, 10 shot, 4$^1\!/_2$ and 6$^3\!/_4$ in. barrels, steel frame, adj. sights, blued finish, black plastic grips. Mfg. 1962-1974 by FN.

	$280	$225	$170	$140	$125	$100	$85

CHALLENGER MODEL — .22 LR, 10 shot, 4$^1\!/_2$ and 6$^3\!/_4$ in. barrels, steel frame, adj. sights, checkered wrap-around walnut grips, gold plated trigger. Mfg. 1962-1975 by FN.

	$350	$295	$250	$215	$190	$170	$155

⚞ Renaissance — engraved satin nickel finish.

	$1,150	$800	$400				

⚞ Gold Line — blued finish, gold lining on perimeter of frame surfaces.

	$1,150	$800	$400				

CHALLENGER II — .22 cal., Salt Lake City mfg., 6$^3\!/_4$ in. barrel, alloy frame, plastic impregnated hardwood grips, 38 oz. Mfg. 1975-1982.

	$230	$180	$170	$145	$135	$120	$110

⚞ Challenger II BCA Commemorative — mfg. to commemorate BCA's fourth anniversary.

	$295	$240	$175				

CHALLENGER III — .22 cal., Salt Lake City mfg., 5$^1\!/_2$ in. bull barrel, 11 shot, alloy frame, adj. sights, 35 oz. Mfg. 1982-1985.

	$220	$190	$170	$145	$135	$120	$110

Last Mfg.'s Retail was $240.

Grading	100%	98%	95%	90%	80%	70%	60%

CHALLENGER III SPORTER — similar to Challenger III, except 6¾ in. round barrel, wide trigger, 29 oz. Mfg. 1982-85.

	$220	$190	$170	$145	$135	$120	$110

Last Mfg.'s Sug. Retail was $240.

Challenger II BCA Commemorative — mfg. to commemorate BCA's fourth anniversary.

	$295	$240	$175				

BUCK MARK STANDARD .22 — .22 LR, 11 shot, 5½ in. bull barrel, composite grips with skipline checkering (disc. 1990) or molded rubber grips (new 1991), adj. sights, gold trigger, matte blued finish, 36 oz. New 1985.

Mfg.'s Sug. Retail	$235	$180	$150	$130	$120	$110	$100	$90

Add $40 for nickel finish (new 1991).
Buck Mark models are manufactured in Salt Lake City, UT.

Micro Buck Mark — similar to Buck Mark Standard, except has 4 in. barrel, choice of standard or nickel finish, 32 oz. New 1992.

Mfg.'s Sug. Retail	$235	$180	$150	$130	$120	$110	$100	$90

Add $40 for nickel finish.
Add $50 for for Micro Buck Mark Plus (includes laminated wood grips).

Buck Mark Plus — similar to Buck Mark, except has uncheckered laminated wooden grips and high polish blue. New 1987.

Mfg.'s Sug. Retail	$285	$225	$180	$145	$135	$120	$110	$100

Buck Mark 5.5 Target — same action as Buck Mark, 5½ in. barrel with serrated top rib allowing adj. sight positioning, target sights, matte blue finish, choice of contoured walnut or walnut wrap-around finger groove grips (new 1992), 35 oz. New 1990.

Mfg.'s Sug. Retail	$375	$290	$245	$210	$180	$160	$140	$125

Buck Mark 5.5 Gold Target — similar to 5.5 Target, except has gold anodized frame and top rib. Introduced in 1991.

Mfg.'s Sug. Retail	$400	$310	$255	$215	$180	$160	$140	$125

Buck Mark 5.5 Field — same action and barrel as the Target 5.5, except sights are designed for field use, anodized blue finish, contoured walnut grips, choice of contoured walnut or walnut wrap-around finger groove grips (new 1992), 35 oz. New 1991.

Mfg.'s Sug. Retail	$375	$295	$245	$210	$180	$160	$140	$125

Buck Mark Varmint — same action as Buck Mark, 9⅞ in. barrel with serrated top rib allowing adj. sight positioning, laminated wood grips, choice of contoured walnut or walnut wrap-around finger groove grips (new 1992), optional detachable forearm, matte blue, 48 oz. New 1987.

Mfg.'s Sug. Retail	$355	$285	$240	$200	$175	$155	$135	$120

Buck Mark Silhouette — silhouette variation of the Buck Mark, 9⅞ in. bull barrel with serrated top rib allowing adj. sight positioning, hooded target sights, laminated wood stocks and forearm, choice of contoured walnut or walnut wrap-around finger groove grips (new 1992), matte blue, 53 oz. New 1987.

Mfg.'s Sug. Retail	$395	$325	$270	$225	$195	$170	$150	$135

Buck Mark Unlimited Silhouette (Match) — similar to Silhouette Model featuring 14 in. barrel with set back front sight, choice of contoured walnut or walnut wrap-around finger groove grips (new 1992), 64 oz. New 1991.

Mfg.'s Sug. Retail	$470	$390	$320	$265	$225	$195	$170	$150

Grading	100%	98%	95%	90%	80%	70%	60%

MEDALIST TARGET MODEL — .22 LR, 6¾ in. barrel, vent. rib, adj. target sights and barrel weights (3 supplied), blued finish, target walnut grips with thumbrest, dry-fire mechanism, 46 oz., cased. Mfg. 1964-1975 by FN.

	100%	98%	95%	90%	80%	70%	60%
	$695	$625	$575	$495	$425	$375	$325

Deduct 15% if without case and accessories.

	100%	98%	95%
Gold Line (407 mfg. 1963)	$1,700	$1,000	$650
Renaissance Model	$2,100	$1,400	$900

A total of 337 were mfg. by FN 1964-82.

	100%	98%	95%
BCA Edition Engraved (60 mfg.)	$2,350	$1,900	$1,400

INTERNATIONAL MEDALIST — target variation model manufactured 1977-80, 5.9 in. barrel, only 681 made with BAC markings and blued finish. Currently manufactured by FN in the parkerized international configuration.

	100%	98%	95%	90%	80%	70%	60%
	$615	$535	$475	$410	$350	$300	$275
Early Model	$700	$625	$550	$425	$360	$330	$280

RIFLES: SINGLE SHOT

100%	98%	95%	90%	80%	70%	60%	50%	40%	30%	20%	10%

MODEL 1878 STANDARD — various cals., J.M. Browning's first patent, fewer than 600 made by Browning Brothers in Ogden, Utah between 1878-1883, octagon barrel marked "Browning Bros. Ogden, Utah USA" plain wood stock and forearm with and without pistol grips, crescent steel buttplate, with or without ramrod, several receiver configurations, a very few were made in the deluxe model, seldom found in better than average used condition.

100%	98%	95%	90%	80%	70%	60%	50%	40%	30%	20%	10%
$20,000	$18,500	$15,000	$13,500	$12,000	$11,000	$10,000	$9,000	$8,000	$7,000	$6,000	$5,000

Add 50% for Deluxe Rifle (checkered stock and forearm).
Add 10% for Early Rifle with Sharps Borchardt type lever.
Add 40% for Early Rifle stamped "Ogden, U.T.".
Add 20% for any caliber other than .40-70 SS or .45-70 Govt.
Deduct 20% if stock and/or forearm have been replaced.
Deduct 20% if the original sights have been removed or replaced incorrectly.
Add 25% for Late Model with rammer rod under barrel held by two thimbles (known as "Montana Model").
Add 10% minimum for any non-standard feature, such as single or double set trigger asssemblies, removable lower stock tang, round barrel, with Ballard type stock bolts, fore-end caps of silver or pewter or other metal.
Calibers in this model are listed from rarest to most commonly encountered: .50-70 Govt., .45 Sharps, .44 Rem., .40-90 Sharps, .44-77 Sharps, .45-70 Govt., and .40-70 Sharps Straight. This model is rare since approx. only 550 were mfg. (approx. ser. range 1-550). This patent was sold to Winchester, which became their Model 1885 single shot. To date, less than 100 original Model 1878s have been encountered indicating a high mortality rate (most remaining specimens are in poor original condition). An inherent weakness of the original design was the way the stock attached to the action - Winchester later corrected this design flaw. A few remaining examples are not serial numbered. Barter guns are rifles that have Browning stamped actions and barrels of an older gunsmith's identity.

Grading	100%	98%	95%	90%	80%	70%	60%

MODEL 78 — .22-250, 6mm, .243, .25-06, 7mm Mag., .30-06, or .45-70 cal., 24 or 26 in. round or octagon barrel, lever activated falling block, no sights except .45-70, checkered walnut stock, approx. 24,000 mfg. 1973-1982.

	100%	98%	95%	90%	80%	70%	60%
	$550	$425	$365	$325	$295	$275	$250
.45-70 cal.	$600	$450	$375	$325	$295	$275	$250

The Model 78 was reintroduced as the Model 1885 in 1985.

Grading	100%	98%	95%	90%	80%	70%	60%

MODEL 1885 — .22-250 Rem., .223 Rem., .270 Win., .30-06, 7mm Rem. Mag., or .45-70 cal., falling block action, sear safety, 28 in. octagonal barrel, adj. trigger, no sights, checkered walnut stock and Schnabel forearm, exposed hammer, gold trigger, 8¾ lbs. Introduced 1985.

Mfg.'s Sug. Retail	$810	$635	$525	$425	$360	$330	$295	$275

This model in .45-70 cal. is equipped with open sights.

RIFLES: SEMI-AUTO .22 LR

GRADES I - III — .22 LR or .22 Short, takedown design, 11 shot (16 for .22 Short) tube mag. in butt stock, 19¼ in. barrel in LR, 22¼ in. barrel in short (rare), checkered pistol grip stock, semi-beavertail forearm, stock has hole machined halfway to allow partial filling of tube mag., adj. folding rear sight, grades differ in finish, amount of engraving, and grade of wood, 4¾ lbs. Mfg. 1914-1976 by FN, 1976-present by Miroku in Japan.

Grade I — FN

	$450	$350	$275	$225	$195	$165	$150

Add 10-15% for "Shorts only" or thumb wheel rear sight older models if in 95% or better condition.

FN Grade I's have a lightly engraved blued steel receiver, checkered walnut, blued trigger, and a variety of rear sights.

Grade I — Miroku

Mfg.'s Sug. Retail	$345	$280	$230	$200	$175	$160	$150	$140

Miroku manufactured .22s can be determined by year of manufacture in the following manner: RV suffix - 1975, RT - 1976, RR - 1977, RP - 1978, RN - 1979, PM - 1980, PZ - 1981, PY - 1982, PX - 1983, PW - 1984, PV - 1985, PT - 1986, PR - 1987, PP - 1988, PN - 1989, NM - 1990, NZ - 1991, NY - 1992, NX - 1993.

Grade II — FN

	$850	$600	$450	$360	$325	$295	$260

FN Grade IIs have gray chromed receiver, deluxe wood with finer checkering, gold plated trigger, and engraving depicting two squirrels and two prairie dogs. Signed or unsigned by engraver.

Grade II — Miroku — disc. 1984.

	$425	$350	$295	$225	$200	$180	$160

Grade III — FN

	$1,550	$1,150	$875	$825	$770	$715	$605

FN Grade IIIs have coin finish or gray chromed receiver, extra deluxe walnut with skipline checkering, gold plated trigger, and more elaborate game scene engraving usually featuring a dog flushing ducks or upland game. Signed or unsigned by engraver (Funken, J. Baerten, Vrancken, and Watrin will command premiums over values listed above). A few were also special ordered with blued finish and special engraving — these command an extra premium.

Grade III — Miroku — disc. 1983.

	$750	$650	$540	$495	$450	$400	$360

Grade VI — Miroku — game scene engraved with gold plating, choice of blued or grayed receiver, deluxe walnut. New 1987.

Mfg.'s Sug. Retail	$709	$600	$500	$400	$360	$325	$295	$260

BAR-22 — .22 LR, 20¼ in. barrel, 15 shot tube mag., folding leaf sight, high polish alloy receiver, checkered pistol grip stock, 5 lbs. 13 oz. Mfg. 1977-1985 by Miroku.

	$235	$205	$185	$170	$155	$140	$125

Last Mfg.'s Sug. Retail was $245.

Grading	100%	98%	95%	90%	80%	70%	60%

BAR-22 GRADE II — engraved model of BAR-22 featuring game scenes on silver greyed alloy receiver, select French walnut. Disc. 1985.

| | $350 | $275 | $245 | $210 | $195 | $175 | $160 |

Last Mfg.'s Sug. Retail was $350.

RIFLES: BAR SERIES

BROWNING PATENT 1900 — .35 Rem. only, manufactured by FN from 1910-1931, only 4,913 made in standard and deluxe grades, similar to Remington Model 8 auto-loading rifle.

| | $650 | $575 | $495 | $440 | $385 | $340 | $300 |

Deluxe model — with checkered walnut stock and adj. sights on solid rib barrel.

| | $750 | $650 | $550 | $525 | $470 | $440 | $415 |

THE BAR MK II SAFARI — .243 Win., .270 Win., .30-06, .308 Win., .270 Wby. Mag., 7mm Rem. Mag., .300 Win. Mag., or .338 Win. Mag. cal., improved BAR action featuring redesigned bolt release, new gas operational system, and reduced recoil, removable trigger assembly, 22 or 24 (Mag. cals. only) in. barrel with (adj. for windage and elevation) or without sights, blued finish with engraved receiver, checkered walnut stock and forearm, gold trigger, detachable box mag., 7 lbs. 6 oz. - 8 lbs. 6 oz. New 1993.

| Mfg.'s Sug. Retail | $648 | $565 | $475 | $425 | $375 | $350 | $330 | $310 |

Add $17 for open sights.
Add $50 for Mag. cals.
The new BAR MK II Safari does not have interchangeable magazine capability with the older pre-1993 BAR's.

BAR SEMI-AUTO — .243, .270, .280 Rem. (new 1990), .308, or .30-06 cal. available in standard model, Mag. cals. include 7mm Rem., .300 Win., and .338 Win. (reintroduced 1990), gas operated, blued receiver, 22 or 24 (Mag. only) in. barrel, rotary bolt with seven lugs, folding leaf sight, walnut stock. Grades differ in engraving, finish, and grade of wood, approx. 7 lbs. 6 oz. Mfg. 1967-present. In 1993, to celebrate the 25th Anniversary of the BAR, Browning introduced the BAR MK II Safari (See model listed above).
Add 15% for FN mfg. and assembled BARs (marked "FN manufactured and assembled").
Add 10% for .338 Win. Mag. cal. (FN mfg. only).
Note: Original .338s were limited production, mostly seen in the deluxe Grade II only. During the last year of FN .338 production, several were delivered in a Grade I by FN. Although being rarer than the Grade II, it is not as desirable. The following prices are for Portugese assembled guns, manufactured by FN, and are so stamped on the barrel.

Grade I — standard grade without engraving, blued finish. Ordering this model without sights became an option in 1988. Disc. 1992.

| | $540 | $450 | $395 | $350 | $325 | $300 | $280 |

Subtract $16 without sights.
FN mfg. and assembled Grade I's can be denoted by light scroll engraving on the receiver. Last Mfg.'s Sug. Retail was $633.

Grade I Magnum — standard grade without engraving, with recoil pad, 8 lbs. 6 oz. Disc. 1992.

| | $575 | $495 | $425 | $375 | $350 | $330 | $310 |

Subtract $16 without sights.
Ordering this gun without sights became an option in 1988.
Last Mfg.'s Sug. Retail was $680.

Grade II — blued receiver, engraved with big game heads. Mfg. 1967-1974.

| | $725 | $625 | $550 | $525 | $470 | $440 | $415 |

This model was previously designated Deluxe.

Grading	100%	98%	95%	90%	80%	70%	60%

⚞ **Grade II Magnum** — magnum version of Grade II. Mfg. 1967-1974.

	100%	98%	95%	90%	80%	70%	60%
	$795	$675	$595	$550	$510	$460	$430

⚞ **Grade III** — features elk and sheep game scenes etched on greyed steel receiver, select checkered stock and forearm. Disc. 1984.

	$925	$800	$660	$620	$580	$560	$540

⚞ **Grade III Magnum** — magnum version of Grade III. Disc. 1984.

	$1,025	$850	$700	$660	$620	$595	$580

⚞ **Grade IV** — engraved satin finish greyed receiver depicts big game animal scenes and trigger guard, carved borders on checkering. Disc. 1989.

	$1,475	$1,300	$1,150	$1,000	$900	$825	$750

Last Mfg.'s Sug. Retail was $1,670.

⚞ **Grade IV Magnum** — magnum version of Grade IV. Disc. 1984.

	$1,675	$1,495	$1,225	$1,050	$950	$850	$775

Last Mfg.'s Sug. Retail was $1,720.

⚞ **Grade V** — more elaborate engraving than Grade IV, with gold inlays. Mfg. 1971-1974.

	$3,000	$2,600	$2,250	$1,850	$1,600	$1,450	$1,250

⚞ **Grade V Magnum** — magnum version of Grade V.

	$3,650	$2,900	$2,400	$1,950	$1,700	$1,595	$1,400

BAR NORTH AMERICAN DEER RIFLE ISSUE — .30-06 cal. only, BAR style action with silver grey finish and engraved action, 600 total production, walnut cased with accessories. Disc. 1983 but were sold through 1989.

	$2,650	$2,100	$1,700

Last Mfg.'s Sug. Retail was $3,550.

RIFLES: FAL

The following semi-auto FALs were imported by BAC in limited numbers. Current production FALs can be found under the Fabrique Nationale heading.

FAL G SERIES STANDARD — 7.62mm, paramilitary design rifle, wood butt stock, wood or nylon forearm, milled receiver.

	$3,200	$2,850	$2,300	$1,950	$1,650	$1,350	$1,040

⚞ **G Series Heavy Barrel** — wood furniture, milled receiver with special bipod.

	$6,000	$5,250	$4,700	$4,160	$3,600	$3,100	$2,650

⚞ **G Series Lightweight** — lightweight variation of the FAL.

	$4,000	$3,500	$3,000	$2,500	$2,100	$1,875	$1,600

The Lightweight Model had the trigger frame, magazine, and return spring tube made out of aluminum.

⚞ **Browning Arms Co. Import** — milled receiver, wood or nylon furniture.

	$2,400	$2,000	$1,700	$1,550	$1,400	$1,275	$1,150

⚞ **CAL Prototype** — originally imported in 1980, prototype to the current FN FNC, at first declared illegal but later given amnesty, only 20 imported.

	$6,000	$5,250	$4,700	$4,160	$3,600	$3,100	$2,650

G series FALs were imported between 1959-1962 by Browning Arms Co. This rifle was declared illegal by the GCA of 1968 and was exempted 5 years later. Total numbers exempted are: Standard model-1822, Heavy Barrel model-21, Paratrooper model-5.

Grading	100%	98%	95%	90%	80%	70%	60%

RIFLES: LEVER ACTION

BL-22 GRADE I — .22 S, L, and LR, 20 in. barrel, short throw lever, folding leaf sight, 15 shot (LR) mag., exposed hammer, Western style stock and forearm, 5 lbs. Mfg. 1970-present by Miroku.

Mfg.'s Sug. Retail	$302	$245	$205	$175	$150	$125	$110	$100

*⚔ **BL-22 Grade II** — same general specifications as BL-22, except scroll engraved blue receiver and checkered select walnut.

Mfg.'s Sug. Retail	$344	$285	$235	$195	$165	$140	$125	$115

MODEL 53 DELUXE LIMITED EDITION — .32-20 cal. (round nose or hollow point bullets only), patterned after the original Winchester Model 53 (redesigned Model 1892), 7 shot tube mag., high polished blued metal, open sights, 22 in. tapered barrel, high grade checkered walnut stock featuring full pistol grip cap and shotgun style metal butt plate, 6½ lbs. Only 5,000 mfg. in 1990.

$450 $400 $375

Last Mfg.'s Sug. Retail was $675.

MODEL 65 GRADE I LIMITED EDITION — .218 Bee, patterned after the Winchester Model 65, round tapered 24 in. barrel, open sights (hooded front), blued metal finish, 7 shot tube mag., uncheckered pistol grip stock and semi-beavertail forearm, metal butt plate, 6¾ lbs. 3,500 total mfg. for Grade I in 1989 only, inventory depleted in 1990.

$475 $400 $375

Last Mfg.'s Sug. Retail was $550.

*⚔ **Model 65 High Grade** — grayed receiver (and lever) with scroll engraving and gold plated animals, gold plated trigger, deluxe checkered walnut stock and semi-beavertail forearm. 1,500 total mfg. in 1989, inventory depleted in 1990.

$850 $775 $700

Last Mfg.'s Sug. Retail was $850.

MODEL 71 LIMITED EDITION CARBINE — .348 Win., reproduction of the Winchester Model 71 carbine, 20 in. barrel, open sights, 4 shot mag., 8 lbs. New 1987 with inventory depleted in 1990.

*⚔ **Grade I** — uncheckered satin finished walnut stock and forearm. 4,000 mfg. 1986-87 only.

$450 $400 $365 $340 $320 $300 $275

Last Mfg.'s Sug. Retail was $600.

*⚔ **High Grade** — deluxe checkered walnut stock and forearm with high gloss finish, scroll engraved-gray receiver with gold inlays and trigger. 3,000 mfg. 1986-87 only.

$750 $600 $500

Last Mfg.'s Sug. Retail was $980.

MODEL 71 LIMITED EDITION RIFLE — .348 Win. reproduction of the Winchester Model 71 rifle, 24 in. barrel, open sights, 4 shot mag., 8 lbs. 2 oz. Mfg. 1986-87 only with inventory depleted in 1990.

*⚔ **Grade I** — uncheckered satin finished walnut stock and forearm. 3,000 mfg. 1986-87 only.

$495 $425 $375 $350 $325 $300 $275

Last Mfg.'s Sug. Retail was $600.

Grading	100%	98%	95%	90%	80%	70%	60%

High Grade — deluxe checkered walnut stock and forearm with high gloss finish, scroll engraved-gray receiver with gold inlays and trigger. 3,000 mfg. 1986-87 only.

	100%	98%	95%
	$795	$625	$525

Last Mfg.'s Sug. Retail was $980.

MODEL 81 BLR — .22-250 Rem., .222 Rem. (disc. 1989), .223 Rem., .243 Win., .257 Roberts (disc. 1992), 7mm-08 Rem., .284 Win., .308 Win., or .358 Win. (disc. 1992) cal., rotary bolt locking lugs, 20 in. barrel, 4 shot detachable mag., adj. sight, checkered stock, recoil pad, 1971 mfg. in Belgium, 1972-present by Miroku. No sights optional 1988-89.

Mfg.'s Sug. Retail	$510	$400	$330	$285	$250	$220	$195	$165

Add 15%+ for Belgium mfg. (1971 only, designated the BLR).
Subtract $15 without sights.
.243 Win., .308 Win. and 7mm-08 Rem. cals. are the most popular in this model.
This model was also manufactured by TRW in Cleveland, OH for a very limited production in .243 and .308 cals. This variation has a 2-line legend on the right side marked "MADE IN USA" and "PATENT PENDING". While they are rare, they are not widely collected and are more of an oddity than anything else.

Model 81 BLR Long Action — .270 Win., .30-06, or 7mm Rem Mag. cal., 22 or 24 in. barrel, approx. 8½ lbs. New 1991.

Mfg.'s Sug. Retail	$540	$430	$350	$300	$270	$240	$220	$200

MODEL 1886 LIMITED EDITION GRADE I RIFLE — .45-70 Gov't. only, patterned after the Winchester Model 1886, blued receiver, 26 in. octagon barrel, full mag., crescent butt plate, open sights. 7,000 mfg. 1986 only.

	100%	98%	95%
	$875	$695	$575

Last Mfg.'s Sug. Retail was $578.

Model 1886 Limited Edition High Grade Rifle — same general specifications as Model 1886, except has checkered high grade walnut stock and forearm, greyed steel receiver, with game scene engraving including elk and American Bison, gold accenting with "1 of 3,000" engraved on top of barrel. 3,000 mfg. 1986 only.

	100%	98%	95%
	$1,350	$925	$725

Last Mfg.'s Sug. Retail was $935.

Model 1886 Montana Centennial Rifle — similar to Model 1886 High Grade. 2,000 mfg. 1986 only to commemorate Montana Centennial.

	100%	98%	95%
	$1,350	$925	$725

Last Mfg.'s Sug. Retail was $935.

MODEL 1886 LIMITED EDITION GRADE I CARBINE — .45-70 Gov't. only, saddle ring carbine, patterned after the Winchester Model 1886 Carbine, blued receiver, 22 in. round barrel, 8 shot full mag., crescent butt plate, open sights. 7,000 total mfg. beginning 1992.

Mfg. Sug. Retail	$750	$750	$575	$450

Model 1886 Limited Edition High Grade Carbine — same general specifications as Model 1886, except has checkered high grade walnut stock and forearm, greyed steel receiver, with game scene engraving including bear and elk, gold accenting, 3,000 total mfg. beginning 1992.

Mfg.'s Sug. Retail	$1,175	$1,175	$850	$675

B-92 CARBINE — .357 Mag. or .44 Rem. Mag. cal., 20 in. barrel, patterned after the Winchester Model 92, 11 shot mag. (tubular), blued finish. Disc. 1986.

	100%	98%	95%	90%	80%	70%	60%
	$395	$300	$225	$200	$175	$160	$150

Last Mfg.'s Sug. Retail was $342.

Grading	100%	98%	95%	90%	80%	70%	60%

B-92 Centennial — .44 Mag., 6,000 mfg. in 1978.

	$425	$325	$275				

Last Mfg.'s Sug. Retail was $220.

B-92 BCA Commemorative — mfg. to commemorate BCA's third anniversary.

	$395	$325	$275				

MODEL 1895 LIMITED EDITION GRADE I — .30/40 Krag or .30-06 cal. only, patterned after the Winchester Model 1895, blued receiver, 24 in. barrel, 4 shot mag.(box type), select walnut, rear buckhorn sight, 8 lbs. Mfg. 1984 only.

	100%	98%	95%	90%	80%	70%	60%
.30/40 Krag	$550	$475	$375	$325	$300	$280	$260
.30-06	$650	$525	$400	$350	$325	$300	$280

Production totaled 6,000 in the .30-06 cal. and 2,000 in .30/40 Krag for this model.

Model 1895 Limited Edition High Grade — same general specifications as Model 1895, except gold plated game scenes on satin finish receiver, gold trigger, and finely checkered select French walnut.

	$995	$895	$795				

Production totaled 1,000 in the .30-06 cal. and 1,000 in .30/40 Krag for this model.

RIFLES: BOLT ACTION

A-BOLT HUNTER MODEL — available in .25-06 Rem., .270 Win., .280 Rem. (new 1988), .30-06, 7mm Rem. Mag., .300 Win. Mag., or .338 Win. Mag. cal. in long action, short action available in .223 Rem. (new 1988), .22-250 Rem., .243 Win., .257 Roberts, .284 Win. (new 1989), 7mm-08 Rem., or .308 Win. cal., matte blue finish, 3 lug rotary bolt locking, 22 (short action only), 24 in. (disc. 1987), or 26 in. barrel (new 1988 - long action Mag. cals. only), 60 degree bolt throw, adj. trigger, hidden detachable mag., with or without sights, top tang thumb safety, checkered pistol grip stock, 6 lbs. 3 oz. - 7 lbs. 11oz. Mfg. since 1985 by Miroku.

Mfg.'s Sug. Retail	$510	$415	$340	$295	$265	$240	$225	$210

Add $65 for open sights.

Medallion Model — same A-Bolt specifications, except also available in .375 H&H cal., features better grade walnut stock with rosewood pistol grip and forend cap, synthetic floor plate, high lustre bluing, no sights.

Mfg.'s Sug. Retail	$597	$475	$385	$330	$290	$265	$250	$235

Add $25 for left-hand action (avail. in long action cals. only).
Add $100 for .375 H&H cal. (open sights only).
Left hand action available in .25-06 Rem., .270 Win., .280 Rem., .30-06, 7mm Rem. Mag., .300 Win. Mag., .338 Win. Mag., or .375 H&H cal.

Micro Medallion Model — .223 Rem. (new 1988), .22-250 Rem., .243 Win., .257 Roberts, .284 Win., .308 Win., or 7mm-08 Rem. cal., scaled down variation of the A-Bolt Hunter Model, 20 in. barrel, short action only, $13\frac{5}{16}$ in. length of pull, 3 shot mag., no sights, 6 lbs. 3 oz. for short action. Introduced 1988.

Mfg.'s Sug. Retail	$597	$475	$385	$330	$290	$265	$250	$235

Gold Medallion Model — .270 Win., .30-06, .300 Win. Mag. (new 1993), or 7mm Rem. Mag. cal., similar to Medallion Model, except has extra select walnut stock with continental style cheek piece, gold lettering and light engraving, no sights. New 1988.

Mfg.'s Sug. Retail	$810	$670	$535	$430	$360	$330	$300	$265

Grading	100%	98%	95%	90%	80%	70%	60%

Euro-Bolt — .22-250 Rem., .243 Win., .270 Win., .30-06, .308 Win., or 7mm Rem. Mag. cal., features European styling including Schnabel style forearm, rounded rear receiver, Mannlicher style bolt, European cheekpiece on satin finished checkered stock, low-luster bluing, hinged floor plate with removable mag., cocking indicator, upper tang thumb activated safety, 6 lbs. 14 oz. - 7 lbs. 6 oz. (Mag.). New 1993.

Mfg.'s Sug. Retail	$700	$600	$475	$395	$350	$300	$265	$250

Stainless Stalker — .22-250 Rem. (left-hand only, new 1993), .25-06 Rem., .270 Win., .280 Rem., .30-06, 7mm Rem. Mag., .300 Win. Mag., .338 Win. Mag. or .375 H&H (new 1990) cal., action and barrel are stainless steel, matte black graphite fiberglass composite stock, dull stainless finish, no sights, 6 lbs. 11 oz. - 7 lbs. 3 oz. New 1987.

Mfg.'s Sug. Retail $665 $575 $430 $350

Add $100 for .375 H&H cal.
Add $20 for left hand action.
Originally, this model was offered in .270 Win., .30-06, or 7mm Rem. Mag. cal. only.

Camo Stalker — .270 Win., .30-06, or 7mm Rem. Mag. cal., laminated black and green wood stock, matte finish on metal parts, no sights. Mfg. 1987-1989.

$400 $340 $310 $285 $250 $230 $215

Last Mfg.'s Sug. Retail was $483.

Composite Stalker — .25-06 Rem., .270 Win., .280 Rem., .30-06, 7mm Rem. Mag., .300 Win. Mag., or .338 Win. Mag. cal., black graphite fiberglass composite stock, matte non-glare metal finish, 6 lbs. 11 oz. - 7 lbs. 3 oz. New 1988.

Mfg.'s Sug. Retail $525 $410 $340 $295 $265 $240 $225 $210

A-BOLT BIGHORN SHEEP ISSUE — .270 Win. only, 22 in. barrel, high grade walnut stock with gloss finish and skipline checkering, deep relief engraving on receiver barrel, floorplate, and trigger guard, two 24Kt. inlays depicting bighorn sheep. 600 mfg. 1986-87 only.

$850 $725 $600

Last Mfg.'s Sug. Retail was $1,365.

A-BOLT PRONGHORN ISSUE — .243 Win., presentation grade walnut with skipline checkering and pearl borders, receiver and barrel engraving, multiple gold inlays on receiver top and floor plate. 500 mfg. 1987 only.

$795 $675 $550

Last Mfg.'s Sug. Retail was $1,302.

A-BOLT GRADE I RIMFIRE — .22 LR or .22 Mag. (new 1989), 60 degree bolt throw, 22 in. barrel, checkered walnut stock and forearm or laminated stock (approx. 142 were mfg. 1986), 5 or 15 (optional) shot mag., adj. trigger, available with or without open sights, 5 lbs. 9 oz. New 1986.

.22 LR cal.
Mfg.'s Sug. Retail $375 $290 $235 $190 $175 $160 $145 $130
Add $10 for open sights.
A 15 shot mag. is also available for this model at $30 retail.

.22 Win. Mag. cal.
Mfg.'s Sug. Retail $430 $335 $270 $215 $190 $175 $160 $150
Add $10 for open sights.

MODEL 52 LIMITED EDITION — .22 LR cal., virtually identical to the original Winchester Model 52C Sporter, except for minor safety enhancements, bolt action, 24 in. drilled and tapped barrel, 5 shot detachable mag., pistol grip walnut stock with oil style finish, deep blue finish, adj. trigger, two position safety, 7 lbs. 5,000 mfg. 1991-92.

$575 $475 $400

Last Mfg.'s Sug. Retail was $500.

Grading	100%	98%	95%	90%	80%	70%	60%

GOLD MEDALLION .22 A-BOLT — similar to A-Bolt, except has high grade select walnut stock checkered 22 lines per inch, rosewood pistol and forend cap, high gloss finish, gold filled lettering and moderate engraving, solid recoil pad. New 1988.

Mfg.'s Sug. Retail	$497	$415	$340	$300	$265	$240	$225	$210

MODEL BBR — .25-06, .270, .30-06, 7mm Mag., .300 or .338 Win. Mag. cal., short action available in .22-250, 243 W., 257 Roberts, 7mm-08 Rem., or 308 Win. cal., 24 in. barrel, 60 degree throw, fluted bolt, adj. trigger, hidden detachable mag., no sights, checkered pistol grip, Monte Carlo stock. Mfg. 1978-1984 by Miroku.

	$470	$360	$330	$305	$250	$220	$200

Some rare production calibers will add premiums to the values listed above (i.e., add 50% for .243 Win. cal.).

BBR RIFLE ELK ISSUE — 7mm Rem. Mag., bolt action rifle, 1,000 manufactured, deeply blued receiver which has multiple animals gold inlaid, high grade walnut stock and forearm feature skipline checkering. Disc. 1986.

	$1,195	$950	$795

Last Mfg.'s Sug. Retail was $1,395.

T-BOLT T-1 — .22 LR, straight pull bolt action, 5 shot mag., 22 in. barrel, adj. rear sight, 5½ lbs., plain pistol grip stock. Mfg. 1965-1974 by FN.

	$375	$350	$295	$255	$210	$180	$160

An aperture rear sight was standard for the first nine years of production.

T-BOLT T-2 — similar to T-1, only with select checkered walnut stock (lacquer finished), 24 in. barrel, 6 lbs.

	$450	$375	$330	$295	$240	$200	$180

‡ **Late production T-2** — features oil finished stock, plastic front sight, and Browning computerized serialization.

	$350	$295	$255	$210	$180	$160	$140

FN HIGH-POWER BOLT ACTION MODEL — .222 R. (Sako action), .22-250 (Sako action), .243 Win., .257 Roberts, .264 Win. Mag., .270, .284 Win. (Sako action), .30-06, .308 Win., 7mm Mag., .300 Win. Mag., .308 Norma Mag., .300 H&H, .338 Mag., .375 H&H, or .458 Win. Mag. cal., standard Mauser type action with either short or long (more desirable) extractor, 22 or 24 in. (heavy available) barrel, folding leaf sight (except on .222 R. and .22-250), checkered pistol grip stock. Mfg. 1959-1974 by FN.

The .243 and .308 Win. cals. were built on the small ring Mauser action prior to using the Sako medium action. The .222 Rem. Mag. was also furnished without sights.

Note: Grades differ in engraving, finish, checkering, and grade of wood. It should be noted that the salt wood problem is more common in these high powered models. Guns should be checked carefully for rust below wood surfaces.

‡ **Safari Grade** — basic model with blued finish.

Standard cals.	$795	$675	$550	$450	$400	$350	$325
Mag. cals.	$900	$750	$650	$595	$525	$450	$400
.257 Roberts	$1,295	$1,050	$825	$700	$600	$525	$450
.284 Win.	$1,550	$1,200	$950	$800	$700	$600	$500
.308 Norma Mag.	$1,050	$850	$700	$600	$525	$450	$400
.338 Win. Mag.	$1,150	$950	$850	$735	$650	$595	$525
.375 H&H	$1,300	$1,000	$800	$700	$600	$525	$450
.458 Win. Mag.	$1,095	$995	$895	$750	$625	$525	$450

Add 15% for Magnum long extractor models.

Between 1963 and 1974, Browning also offered short and medium barrelled actions in the Safari, Medallion and Olympian Grades. These models have Sako barrelled actions and were stocked by FN. Medium weight barrels could also be ordered.

Grading	100%	98%	95%	90%	80%	70%	60%

⚔ **Safari Grade - Short Sako Action** — short action, .222 Rem. or .222 Rem. Mag. cal.

	100%	98%	95%	90%	80%	70%	60%
	$800	$675	$550	$450	$400	$350	$325

⚔ **Safari Grade - Medium Sako Action** — medium action, .22-250, .243, .284 or .308 cal.

	100%	98%	95%	90%	80%	70%	60%
	$800	$675	$550	$450	$400	$350	$325

Add 50% for .284 cal.
Only 192 rifles (in Safari, Medallion, and Olympian grades) were mfg. in .284 cal. between 1965-1976.

⚔ **Medallion Grade** — features select figured walnut with skipline checkering, rosewood grip and forearm caps, blue/black lustre bluing, receiver and barrel portion scroll engraved, ram's head engraved on floor plate.

	100%	98%	95%	90%	80%	70%	60%
	$1,450	$1,195	$1,000	$925	$830	$700	$575

Add 10%-50% for rare calibers.
Add 20% for pencil barrel in Sako actions. Add 15% for Mag. cals. with long extractor.
This model was also available with a Sako short or long action - cals. are the same as listed for the Sako Safari.

⚔ **Olympian Grade** — top-of-the-line model featuring highly figured walnut stock that is both checkered and carved. Receiver, floor plate, and trigger guard are chrome plated in a satin finish that have deep relief animal scenes engraved, as well as deep scroll work on other metal parts.

	100%	98%	95%	90%	80%	70%	60%
	$2,350	$2,050	$1,875	$1,700	$1,550	$1,350	$1,175

Add 10%-50% for rare calibers (.284 is among the rarest).
Add 20% for pencil barrel in Sako actions. Add 15% for Mag. cals. with long extractor.
This model was also available with a Sako short or long action - cals. are the same as listed for the Sako Safari.

RIFLES: SLIDE ACTION

BPR-22 — .22 LR or .22 Mag., short-stroke action, 20¼ in. barrel, 11 shot tube mag., mfg. 1977-1982.

	100%	98%	95%	90%	80%	70%	60%
	$275	$195	$170	$160	$140	$130	$100

⚔ **BPR-22 Grade II** — similar to BPR-22, only engraved action, select walnut.

	100%	98%	95%	90%	80%	70%	60%
	$400	$350	$295	$260	$230	$200	$175

TROMBONE MODEL — .22 LR only, slide action with tube mag., fixed sights, takedown, 24 in. barrel, hammerless, similar to Win. Model 61, with either F.N. or U.S. (rare) barrel address.

⚔ **FN Barrel Address**

	100%	98%	95%	90%	80%	70%	60%
	$595	$495	$395	$350	$295	$260	$225

⚔ **BAC Barrel Markings**

	100%	98%	95%	90%	80%	70%	60%
	$750	$625	$495	$425	$350	$295	$250

Over 150,000 "Trombones" were mfg. by FN from 1922-1974. About 3,200 were imported by BAC in late 1960's. Very rare with factory engraving.

BCA GRADE III FN TROMBONE — only 60 manufactured for the Browning Collectors Association 1985-86, silver engraved frame with deluxe walnut.

	100%	98%	95%
	$2,350	$1,995	$1,600

RIFLES: O/U

EXPRESS RIFLE — .270 Win., .30-06 cal., or 9.3 x 74R cal., superposed style action. 24 in. barrels, auto ejectors, Fleur-de-lis engraving, single trigger, folding leaf rear sight, 6 lbs. 14 oz., cased. Disc. 1986.

	100%	98%	95%	90%	80%	70%	60%
	$2,200	$1,850	$1,600	$1,475	$1,300	$1,100	$900

Last Mfg.'s Sug. Retail was $3,125.

Grading	100%	98%	95%	90%	80%	70%	60%

SHOTGUNS: SEMI-AUTO, DISC.

BROWNING CHOKES AND THEIR CODES (ON REAR LEFT-SIDE OF BARREL)
* designates full choke (F).
*- designates improved modified choke (IM).
** designates modified choke (M).
**- designates improved cylinder choke (IC).
**$ designates skeet (SK).
*** designates cylinder bore (CYL).
INV. designates barrel is threaded for Browning Invector choke tube system.

AUTO-5 STANDARD - 1903-1939 MFG. — 12 or 16 ga.(introduced in U.S. in 1923), 26-32 in. barrel, recoil operated, various chokes, checkered pistol grip stock, mfg. 1903-1939 by FN, grades differ in engraving, inlays, and grade of wood. Approx. ser. range 1-229,000 (12ga.), 1-128,000 (16 ga.).

	100%	98%	95%	90%	80%	70%	60%
Grade 1	$475	$425	$375	$325	$285	$250	$200
Solid matte rib	$575	$495	$425	$375	$325	$275	$250
With vent. rib	$695	$500	$450	$400	$350	$300	$250
Grade 2.(disc.1940)	$1,250	$1,000	$875	$750	$625	$550	$495
Solid matte rib	$1,450	$1,150	$1,000	$875	$750	$625	$575
With vent. rib	$1,625	$1,300	$1,200	$1,000	$850	$750	$650
Grade 3.(disc. 1940)	$2,500	$2,200	$1,975	$1,775	$1,500	$1,250	$995
Solid matte rib	$2,700	$2,400	$2,100	$1,850	$1,650	$1,375	$1,100
With vent. rib	$2,950	$2,550	$2,250	$2,000	$1,775	$1,500	$1,225
Grade 4.(disc. 1940)	$3,995	$3,655	$3,300	$2,995	$2,550	$2,050	$1,600
Solid matte rib	$4,150	$3,885	$3,450	$3,175	$2,700	$2,200	$1,800

Pre-WWII 16 ga. A-5s are chambered for 2⁹⁄₁₆ in. shells. These shotguns are considerably less desirable than 16 ga. A-5s chambered for 2¾ in. modern shotshells. Since some guns have been modified to 2¾ in., careful inspection is advised before purchasing or shooting.

"AMERICAN BROWNING" AUTO-5 — 12, 16, or 20 ga., Remington-produced model of the Auto 5, very similar to the Remington Model 11, except with Browning logo, mag. cut-off, and different engraving, over 45,000 mfg. in 12 ga., over 25,000 in 16 ga., and 20,000 in 20 ga., stocks have Remington style round knob pistol grips with black plastic caps. Mfg. 1940-1942 and ser. numbered approx. 229,000-346,000, 12 ga. has "B" prefix on left side of receiver, "A" denotes 16 ga., and "C" denotes 20 ga.

	100%	98%	95%	90%	80%	70%	60%
	$395	$345	$295	$225	$200	$185	$170

Add 10% for vent. rib and/or 20 ga.

AUTO-5 STANDARDWEIGHT — 12, 20, or 16 ga., recoil operation, 26-32 in. barrels, standard production gun between 1952-1969, various chokes, checkered walnut stock and forearm, synthetic Browning marked butt plate, lacquer (until approx. 1966) or polyurethane finish, butt stock has either round knob pistol grip (1952-1976) or flat knob (introduced 1967), watch for cracked forearms on all A-5s (due to barrel recoil), between 7⅓-8 lbs.

	100%	98%	95%	90%	80%	70%	60%
Plain barrel	$425	$375	$325	$295	$270	$240	$210
Matted Rib	$525	$450	$400	$350	$300	$275	$245
Vent Rib	$550	$460	$410	$370	$325	$300	$265

Add 10% for N.I.B. condition.
Barrel addresses appeared as follows: 1952-1958 "St. Louis, Missouri", 1959-1968 "St. Louis, Missouri and Montreal P.Q.", 1969-1975 "Morgan, Utah and Montreal, P.Q.". Make sure barrel address date matches year of mfg. (see listings in the back of this text). Standardweight models had H or M prefixes.

Grading	100%	98%	95%	90%	80%	70%	60%

SHOTGUNS: SEMI-AUTO RECENT MFG.

Miroku manufactured A-5s can be determined by year of manufacture in the following manner: RV suffix - 1975, RT - 1976, RR - 1977, RP - 1978, RN - 1979, PM - 1980, PZ - 1981, PY - 1982, PX - 1983, PW - 1984, PV - 1985, PT - 1986, PR - 1987, PP - 1988, PN - 1989, NM - 1990, NZ - 1991, NY - 1992, NX - 1993.

NOTE: Barrels are interchangeable between older Belgium A-5 models and recent Japanese A-5s mfg. by Miroku. A different barrel ring design might necessitate some minor sanding of the inner forearm on the older model, but otherwise, these barrels are fully interchangeable.

NOTE: The use of steel shot is recommended ONLY in those recent models manufactured in Japan incorporating the Invector choke system - NOT in the older Belgium variations.

Add 10-15% for the round knob (rounded pistol grip knob on stock) variation on FN models only.

AUTO-5 LIGHTWEIGHT (LIGHT 12) — 12 or 20 ga., recoil operated, 26, 28, and 30 in. barrels, various chokes, scroll engraved receiver, checkered pistol grip stock, approx. 10 oz. lighter than Standardweight, mfg. 1952-1976 by FN, mfg. 1976-present by Miroku in Japan. Over 2,750,000 A-5s were mfg. by FN in all configurations between 1902-1976.

FN model	$450	$400	$375	$325	$295	$270	$240
FN-vent. rib	$650	$475	$410	$370	$330	$295	$260

Add 10% for N.I.B. condition.
Add 10% for 20 ga. with VR.

Light 12 Miroku — 12 ga. only, now standard with vent. rib (1986) and Invector choke system.

Mfg.'s Sug. Retail	$725	$580	$450	$400	$350	$300	$280	$260

Subtract $40 without Invector chokes.

Light 20 Miroku — 20 ga. only, 2¾ in. chamber, similar to original Belgium Light 20, VR, Invector choke standard. New 1987.

Mfg.'s Sug. Retail	$720	$580	$475	$420	$380	$340	$300	$270

AUTO-5 MAGNUM — 12 or 20 ga., 3 in. chamber, 26, 28, 30, or 32 in. barrels, various chokes, VR, similar to Standard. Mfg. 1958-1976 by FN, mfg. 1976-present by Miroku.

FN model.	$550	$450	$400	$350	$320	$260	$240
FN, vent. rib.	$675	$575	$525	$480	$430	$340	$315

Add 10% for N.I.B. condition.
Add 15% for 20 ga. with VR if NIB.

Between 1976-1985 approx. 2,000 Belgian 12 ga. A-5 Mag.'s were imported into the U.S. These late models can be differentiated by serialization — also, slight premiums may be asked. The 20 ga. Mag. was not introduced until 1967.

A-5 Mag. Miroku — 12 or 20 ga., VR barrel with Invector choke system.

Mfg.'s Sug. Retail	$743	$620	$510	$430	$385	$350	$325	$290

Subtract $40 without Invector chokes.

AUTO-5 STALKER — 12 ga. only, 2¾ (Light-12) or 3 (Mag. Stalker) in. chamber, 26, 28, or 30 in. VR barrel with Invector chokes, black matte finish graphite- fiberglass stock and forearm, matte finished metal, recoil pad, 8 lbs. 1 oz. - 8 lbs. 13 oz. New late 1992.

Mfg.'s Sug. Retail	$735	$590	$460	$400	$350	$300	$280	$260

Add $22 for Mag. Stalker (28 or 30 in. barrel only).

AUTO-5 LIGHT 12 BUCK SPECIAL — similar to Standard only with 24 in. barrel, slug bore, adj. sight, mfg. 1958-1976 by FN, mfg. 1976-1984 and 1989 again by Miroku. Between 1985-1988, Buck Special barrels were available at extra cost.

FN Mfg.

	$675	$475	$410	$370	$330	$295	$240

Grading	100%	98%	95%	90%	80%	70%	60%

⚔ Miroku model
Mfg.'s Sug. Retail

	100%	98%	95%	90%	80%	70%	60%
Mfg.'s Sug. Retail	$725	$585	$465	$400	$360	$320	$290	$260

Add $22 for Buck Special on 3 in. Mag. receiver.

AUTO-5 SKEET — similar to Standard Light, only with 26 or 28 in. skeet bored, vent. rib barrel. Pre-1976 mfg. by FN, 1976-1983 mfg. by Miroku.

⚔ FN Mfg.

	100%	98%	95%	90%	80%	70%	60%
	$550	$425	$375	$325	$295	$270	$240

Add 20% for vent. rib.

⚔ Standard Miroku

100%	98%	95%	90%	80%	70%	60%
$460	$420	$380	$340	$300	$270	$250

AUTO-5 TRAP MODEL — similar to Standard, 12 ga. only, 30 in. full vent. rib barrel, 8½ lbs., mfg. by FN until 1971.

100%	98%	95%	90%	80%	70%	60%
$595	$525	$465	$410	$335	$320	$295

AUTO-5 SWEET 16 — similar to Standardweight Model, except 16 ga. (2¾ in. chamber) only and approx. 10 oz. lighter, gold plated trigger. Mfg. 1950-1976 by Fabrique Nationale.

⚔ Plain Barrel

100%	98%	95%	90%	80%	70%	60%
$525	$415	$350	$295	$250	$220	$195

⚔ Solid Matte Rib

100%	98%	95%	90%	80%	70%	60%
$695	$575	$465	$375	$295	$250	$225

⚔ Vent. Rib

100%	98%	95%	90%	80%	70%	60%
$875	$695	$575	$425	$375	$325	$275

⚔ Sweet 16 Miroku — 16 ga. only, similar to original Belgium Sweet 16, VR, invector choke standard. Mfg. 1987-92.

100%	98%	95%	90%	80%	70%	60%
$580	$475	$420	$380	$340	$300	$270

Last Mfg.'s Sug. Retail was $720.

AUTO-5 2-MILLIONTH COMMEMORATIVE — 12 ga., 2,500 mfg., 1971-74 mfg., special walnut, engraving, high-luster bluing, cased with Browning book. Issue price — $550-$700.

100%	98%	95%
$1,195	$900	$750

A-5 CLASSIC SERIES SHOTGUN — 12 ga., 5,000 mfg. in Classic model, 500 mfg. in Gold Classic. Both editions feature game scenes, John M. Browning's profile, and other inscriptions, special silver grey finished receiver. Introduced 1984.

⚔ Classic Model — no inlays. Factory inventories were depleted in 1987.

100%	98%	95%
$950	$750	$600

Last Mfg.'s Sug. Retail was $1,260.

⚔ Gold Classic Model — features 5 inlays depicting duck hunting scenes. Mfg. 1986 with inventory depleted 1989.

100%	98%	95%
$3,500	$2,750	$1,950

Last Mfg.'s Sug. Retail was $6,500.

A-5 BCA COMMEMORATIVE — 12 ga., 3 in. Mag., round knob, Belgian mfg., issue price was $595.

100%	98%	95%
$650	$575	$450

A-5 DU 50TH ANNIVERSARY

A-5 DU Light 12 — 12 ga. only, 5,500 mfg. in 1987 only for Ducks Unlimited chapters throughout North America. Prices will fluctuate greatly from chapter to chapter as these guns were auctioned to the highest bidder. Receiver is specially engraved and has "Fiftieth year" depicted on right side of receiver, deluxe checkered stock and forearm, high gloss blue.

	100%	98%	95%
	$1,195	$950	$750

A-5 DU Sweet Sixteen — 16 ga. only, companion 1988-89 DU auction gun, 4500 mfg. 1988 only.

	$1,195	$950	$750

A-5 DU Light 20 — 20 ga. only, companion 1990 DU auction gun, 4500 mfg. 1990 only.

	$1,195	$950	$750

DOUBLE AUTOMATIC SHOTGUN — short recoil action, 12 ga. only, 2 shot, 26, 28, or 30 in. barrel, various chokes, checkered pistol grip stock, blued steel receiver. Mfg. 1952-1971.

	100%	98%	95%	90%	80%	70%	60%
	$475	$400	$350	$300	$260	$220	$195
w/vent. rib	$650	$495	$420	$375	$325	$295	$245

TWELVETTE DOUBLE AUTO — similar to Double Auto, except hiduminum (aircraft alloy) frame and color anodized in blue, silver, brown, green, and black, approx. 7 lbs. without rib. Approx. 67,000 (all variations) mfg. 1952-1971.

	$475	$400	$350	$295	$250	$220	$200
w/vent. rib	$650	$495	$425	$395	$340	$280	$250

Add 20-25% for dark red, royal blue, brown, or gold colored receivers (rare).

TWENTYWEIGHT DOUBLE AUTO — similar to Twelvette, but ¾ pound lighter, 26½ in. barrel only. Mfg. 1952-1971.

	$575	$450	$375	$295	$235	$220	$200
w/vent. rib	$725	$625	$525	$450	$400	$350	$295

B/2000 STANDARD — 12 or 20 ga., 26, 28, or 30 in. barrel, various chokes, vent. rib, gas operated, checkered pistol grip stock, Belgium manufactured but assembled in Portugal, approx. 115,000 imported into the U.S. between 1974-1983.

	$360	$325	$295	$275	$250	$225	$195

B/2000 MAGNUM — similar to B/2000 Auto Shotgun, with 3 in. chambers, recoil pad, vent. rib.

	$385	$340	$310	$280	$260	$230	$200

B/2000 SKEET — similar to Standard, with 26 in. skeet bored barrel, floating vent. rib, skeet stock, pad.

	$375	$325	$295	$275	$250	$225	$195

B/2000 TRAP — similar to Standard, with 30 or 32 in. barrel bored F or IM, floating rib, Monte Carlo trap stock.

	$375	$325	$295	$275	$250	$225	$195

B/2000 BUCK SPECIAL — 12 or 20 ga., barrel sights on 24 in. barrel.

	$375	$325	$295	$275	$250	$225	$195

Grading	100%	98%	95%	90%	80%	70%	60%

1976 CANADIAN OLYMPICS B2000 — 12 ga., 100 manufactured in 1976 for Canadian sales only, high polish blue with multiple gold inlays including Olympic crest, 30 in. barrel, cased. Issue price was $1,295.

			$1,395	$995	$695		

MODEL B-80 — 12 or 20 ga., 3 in. capability by changing barrel, gas operation, 4 shot, hunting models use choice of steel or aluminum receiver, anodized aluminum was used in the Superlight (12 ga. mfg. 1984 only), 6 to 8 lbs. 1 oz. Buck special disc. 1984. Components manufactured by Beretta of Italy and finished and assembled FN's plant in Portugal. Mfg. 1981-late 1988, final inventory was sold in 1991. Invector chokes became standard in 1985.

	$450	$375	$325	$295	$275	$250	$230

Steel frames were reintroduced into production again in 1988.
Last Mfg.'s Sug. Retail was $562.

⋇ **Model B-80 Upland Special** — 12 or 20 ga., 2¾ in. chamber, 22 in. vent. rib barrel, straight grip stock, invector chokes. Mfg. 1986-1988.

	$475	$390	$340	$305	$280	$260	$240

Last Mfg.'s Sug. Retail was $562.

MODEL B 80 DU COMMEMORATIVE — mfg. for American DU Chapters (The Plains and others), price fluctuates greatly as collector support is sometimes limited. Unless new, this model's values approximate those of the regular Model B-80. If NIB, values recently have been in the $700-$995 range.

A-500 — 12 ga. only, recoil operation self adjusting for any load, 3 in. chamber, 26, 28, or 30 in. invector choked barrel with vent. rib, checkered walnut stock and forearm with recoil pad, rotary bolt lock-up, magazine cut-off, high polished blue, light engraving, approx. 7 lbs. 5 oz. Mfg. 1987-1989.

	$465	$390	$345	$305	$280	$260	$240

This model was renamed the A-500R (see listing below) with the introduction of the A-500G.
Last Mfg.'s Sug. Retail was $560.

A-500G HUNTING — similar to A-500, except is gas operated, distinguishable by "A-500G" in gold accents on receiver, capable of shooting all 2¾ or 3 in. shells interchangeably, approx. 8 lbs. New 1990.

Mfg.'s Sug. Retail	$653	$555	$425	$375	$325	$295	$275	$250

A Buck Special variation was mfg. until 1992. No premiums currently exist.

⋇ **A-500G Sporting Clays** — 12 ga. only, Sporting Clays variation with 30 in. VR barrel, 8 lbs. 2 oz. New 1992.

Mfg.'s Sug. Retail	$653	$555	$425	$375	$325	$295	$275	$250

A-500R — 12 ga. only, 3 in. chamber, new design utilizing short recoil system with a four-lug rotary bolt design, capable of shooting all 12 gauge loads interchangeably, magazine cut-off, 26, 28, or 30 in. VR barrel with Invector chokes standard, 24 in. barrel on Buck Special (fixed choke), high polished blued finish with red accents on receiver sides, gold trigger, checkered semi-pistol grip walnut stock with vent. recoil pad, 7 lbs. 11 oz. - 8 lbs. 1 oz. New 1990.

Mfg.'s Sug. Retail	$560	$475	$425	$375	$325	$295	$275	$250

Add $33 for Buck Special variation (Invector chokes).
This model features fewer moving parts than many other semi-auto shotguns due to the short recoil operating system.

Grading	100%	98%	95%	90%	80%	70%	60%

BSA 10 — 10 ga. only, $3\frac{1}{2}$ in. chamber, short stroke gas operation, solid steel fabrication, 26, 28, or 30 in. VR Invector choked barrel, choice of gloss blue or dull finish (Stalker Model), checkered walnut or black graphite - fiberglass (Stalker Model) stock and forearm, trigger guard safety, 4 shot mag., approx. $10\frac{1}{2}$ lbs. New 1993.

Mfg.'s Sug. Retail	$900	$795	$675	$575	$495	$425	$375	$325

SHOTGUNS: O/U

SUPERPOSED SHOTGUN: 1931-1976 MANUFACTURE — 12, 20, 28, or .410 ga., $26\frac{1}{2}$, 28, 30, or 32 in. barrels, various chokes, boxlock, auto ejectors, SST, DT, or twin single triggers (early mfg.), checkered pistol grip stock, mfg. 1931-1940 and 1949-1976 by FN, grades differ in amount of engraving, inlay, general quality of workmanship and wood. Currently, shorter barrel ($26\frac{1}{2}$ in.) superposed models are bringing a small premium over a 30 in. F & M model. Prices below assume vent. rib models, earlier matted rib guns will be 5-10% less, depending on condition.

NOTE: The use of steel shot is NOT recommended in any Superposed Series manufactured in Belgium (B-25 variations).

BROWNING CHOKES AND THEIR CODES (ON BARREL)

* designates full choke (F).

*- designates improved modified choke (IM).

** designates modified choke (M).

**- designates improved cylinder choke (IC).

**$ designates skeet (SK).

*** designates cylinder bore (CYL).

SKEET MODELS were available in every ga. and grade - values are 15% less than prices listed below.

TRAP MODELS were available in every grade in 12 ga. only - DEDUCT 5-10% from values shown below. BROADWAY TRAP MODELS with $\frac{5}{8}$ in. wide vent. rib were also available in every grade - DEDUCT 10-15%.

Add 15%-20% for 20 ga. on all grades.

Add 70-100% for 28 ga. on Grade I, 30% on higher grades.

Add 30% for .410 ga. on Grade I models.

Add 15% for round knob, long tang stock variations.

Deduct 25% for early DT models.

Grade I Standard — the Grade I has a blued steel frame with hand engraved scroll and rosette patterns, checkered walnut stock and forearm. Grade I Standard was disc. 1973.

	$1,395	$1,075	$925	$840	$775	$650	$550

Grade I Lightning — similar to Grade I Standard. Disc. 1976.

	$1,650	$1,175	$975	$870	$810	$690	$600

Grade I Magnum — 3 in. chambers with standard Browning recoil pad. Disc. 1976.

	$1,395	$1,075	$900	$825	$760	$635	$525

Because of the mandatory use of steel shot in recent years, values for 12 ga. Magnum and Lightning models have gone down (these models are not compatible with steel shot).

Pigeon Grade — designated Grade II after WWII and renamed Pigeon in October, 1959. This grade featured a silver grey receiver with 2 flying pigeons surrounded by fine scroll engraving on each side of the frame. The receiver bottom and tangs also exhibit fine scroll work. The Pigeon Grade was disc. 1974.

	$2,650	$2,250	$1,950	$1,825	$1,650	$1,570	$1,485

Grade III — satin finished receiver with game scene engraving featuring pheasants and fighting cocks on receiver, receiver bottom has a retriever and pheasant. Disc. October, 1959.

	$2,500	$2,150	$2,000	$1,815	$1,650	$1,570	$1,485

Grading	100%	98%	95%	90%	80%	70%	60%

Pointer Grade — also designated Grade III, manufactured post-war only until renamed Pointer in early October, 1959. Features engraved silver grey receiver with a Pointer depicted on each frame side, select walnut. Disc. 1966, except for special orders.

	$3,500	$2,850	$2,450	$2,050	$1,850	$1,700	$1,625

Grade IV — limited manufacture between 1950-1959, engraving usually featured a dog and bird scene in deep relief.

	$3,650	$3,100	$2,700	$2,175	$1,875	$1,750	$1,650

Diana Grade — also designated Grade V in post-war manufacture until renamed Diana in October, 1959. Pre-WWII Grade Vs featured more delicate scroll engraving with deer adorning the right side and wild boar shown on the left. Post-WWII guns exhibit deep relief engraving with duck and pheasant game scenes on each frame side, select checkered walnut stock and forearm. Disc. 1976.

	$3,875	$3,150	$2,650	$2,150	$1,900	$1,800	$1,700

Midas Grade — also designated Grade VI during post-war manufacture until renamed Midas in October, 1959. Pre-WWII Midas Grades featured an inlaid pigeon with outstretched wings on blued frame sides and bottom plus trigger guard. This earlier Midas also exhibited multiple gold escutcheons and gold lining. Post-war models feature deep relief scroll engraving with gold inlaid ducks and pheasants on frame sides and a quail on the bottom. Ejector trip rods, ejector hammers and firing pins are also 18Kt. gold plated. Finest checkered walnut. Disc. 1976.

	$5,500	$3,950	$3,450	$2,950	$2,600	$2,250	$1,900

Grade VI — 12 or 20 ga. only, offered from 1955-October, 1959 only. Elaborate deep relief scroll engraved with multiple gold inlays.

	100%	98%	95%	90%	80%	70%	60%
12 ga.	$5,500	$4,500	$4,000	$3,500	$3,200	$3,000	$2,600
20 ga.	$7,500	$6,500	$5,750	$4,950	$4,250	$3,500	$2,750

SUPERPOSED WITH EXTRA BARREL(S) OR SUPER-TUBES

Could be ordered from the factory in the following combinations: 12 or 20 ga. with one extra set of barrels in same ga. 12 ga. with one extra set in 20 ga. 12 or 20 ga. with two extra barrel sets of same ga. 20 ga. with one extra set in either 28 or .410 ga. 20 ga. with both 28 and .410 ga. barrel sets. 28 ga. with extra set of .410 barrels. Super-Tubes were adaptable on 12 ga. guns only; came from the factory cased with accessories, 16½ in. long, factory installation.

Grade I extra barrel set(s) — add 40-50% of the gun's value for each extra set. Add approx. $1,500 per barrel set in higher grades.

Super-Tubes — available for 12 ga. only, single ga. — add $250.

Super-Tube Set — 3 ga. set (20, 28 and .410 ga.'s) — add $400.

EXPOSITION/EXHIBITION MODEL

This specially manufactured Superposed saw limited production from the late 60's through 1976. This model had its own serial range (usually 3 digit) with a "C" prefix. Grades A through G ranged from fairly simple scroll designs without gold inlays up to extremely ornate designs featuring multi-colored gold inlaid game figures. Most of these guns were produced by FN for display purposes, potential production models, or potential engraving standardization. Many of these Exhibition/Exposition superposed models were consigned to Browning Arms Co. during the 1970's because of the depressed market conditions of that time. Prices are determined by the embellishments and engraving per individual gun (A Grade being the lowest, G Grade with gold being the highest). Prices usually start at around $5,000, while a G Grade with extensive gold inlays could reach 5 digits.

BICENTENNIAL SUPERPOSED SUPERLIGHT SHOTGUN — specially engraved limited edition Model, 51 mfg. — one for each state and Washington, D.C. Left side has U.S. Flag, bald eagle and state emblem inlaid in gold. Right side has gold inlaid hunter and turkey. Blued receiver, fancy checkered English stock, Schnabel forend, velvet lined wood case. Made 1976 by FN.

	$14,000	$10,000	$8,750

Grading	100%	98%	95%	90%	80%	70%	60%

WATERFOWL SUPERPOSED SHOTGUN SERIES — 12 ga., 500 made of each issue. Gold inlays with extensive engraving, lightning action, 28 in. barrels, walnut cased, factory depleted Mallard, Pintail, and Black Duck Issues in 1989.

⚮ **1981 Mallard Issue**

$4,150 $3,250 $2,250

Last Mfg.'s Sug. Retail was $7,000. This issue was sold out in 1988.

⚮ **1982 Pintail Issue**

$3,995 $3,150 $2,150

Last Mfg.'s Sug. Retail was $8,800.

⚮ **1983 Black Duck Issue**

$3,995 $3,150 $2,150

Last Mfg.'s Sug. Retail was $8,800.

OVER/UNDER CLASSIC SERIES SHOTGUN — 20 ga. only, 26 in. barrels, less than 2,500 manufactured in Classic model and under 350 manufactured in Gold Classic. Both editions feature multiple engraved scenes and a special silver grey finish. Select American walnut featuring oil finish. Available 1986 only.

$1,750 $1,500 $1,200

Last Mfg.'s Sug. Retail was $2,000.

⚮ **Gold Classic** — 8 gold inlays, select walnut forearm and stock are both checkered and carved, many were shipped back to Belgium due to poor sales domestically. Available 1986 only.

$5,500 $4,150 $3,150

Last Mfg.'s Sug. Retail was $6,000.

SUPERPOSED SUPERLIGHT — 12 or 20 ga., 26½ in. solid or VR barrels, lightened slimmer forearm and straight grip stock. Mfg. 1967-1976 by FN.

	100%	98%	95%	90%	80%	70%	60%
12 gauge	$1,795	$1,475	$1,225	$1,110	$1,025	$925	$800
20 gauge	$2,400	$1,925	$1,575	$1,350	$1,250	$1,000	$850

For Pigeon, Diana, and Midas grade Superlight 12 ga. models use previous values on standard model high-grades and add approx. 25% (plus gauge premiums).
There is also a Quail Unlimited limited edition in the Superlight series. Values are somewhat higher but difficult to ascertain because so few are bought and sold each year.

SUPERPOSED SHOTGUN: 1983-86 MANUFACTURE — 12 or 20 ga. In 1983, Browning announced renewed production of the famous Belgium "Superposed" O/U in Grade I only. Available in Lightning or Superlight models, 3 in. chambers in Lightning 20 ga., 26½ or 28 in. barrels. Belgium manufactured from 1983-86.

⚮ **Grade I** — limited availability.

$1,850 $1,375 $1,100 $975 $850 $725 $595

Last Mfg.'s Sug. Retail was $1,995.

SUPERPOSED CONTINENTAL — 20 ga. O/U shotgun w/extra set of .30-06 O/U rifle barrels. Shotgun barrels are 26½ in., rifle barrels are 24 in., SST, ejectors, elaborate scroll engraved receiver, special oil finish walnut, cased. 500 mfg. Disc. 1986.

$3,600 $3,150 $2,750 $2,400 $2,100 $1,865 $1,700

Last Mfg.'s Sug. Retail was $4,375.

Grading	100%	98%	95%	90%	80%	70%	60%

SUPERPOSED PRESENTATION MODELS (P1-P4) — custom made versions of the Lightning Field, Super Light, Trap, and Skeet guns, specifications the same as Standard models, with differences in finish, engraving and inlay(s), and grade of wood and checkering. These guns were introduced by FN in 1977 and were disc. after 1984. Add $1,775 for extra set of barrels, add $3,600 for 2 sets of extra barrels.

P Series Trap — deduct 10% from values listed below.
P Series Broadway Trap — deduct 10-15% from values listed below.
P Series Skeet 12 and 20 ga. — deduct 10-15% from values listed below.

Since P Series Superposed were disc. 1985, collector interest will undoubtedly increase and prices might be increased somewhat. BAC has no remaining inventory of this model. Interestingly, the P series models are rarer than most of the pre-1976 high grade Superposed models.

Add 20% for 20 ga.
Add 30% for 28 ga.
Add 20% for .410 ga.

Presentation 1 — silver grey or blued receiver, oak leaf and fine scroll engraved, choice of 6 different animal scenes.

	$2,850	$2,350	$1,995	$1,750	$1,500	$1,250	$1,000

Presentation 1 w/gold inlays — similar to Presentation 1, only with gold inlays.

	$3,450	$2,800	$2,350	$2,050	$1,825	$1,700	$1,500

Presentation 2 — silver grey or blued receiver, high relief engraving, choice of 3 different sets of game scenes.

	$3,400	$2,750	$2,300	$2,050	$1,825	$1,700	$1,500

Presentation 2 w/gold inlays — similar to Presentation 2, only with gold inlays.

	$3,950	$3,250	$2,550	$2,150	$1,925	$1,750	$1,550

Presentation 3 — silver grey or blued receiver, more elaborate high relief engraving with choice of partridges, mallards or geese depicted on frame sides in 18Kt. gold.

	$5,450	$4,700	$4,100	$3,600	$3,200	$2,875	$2,300

Presentation 4 — features engraved side plates in either silver grey or blued finish, engraved game scenes include waterfowl on right frame side, 5 pheasants on left frame side, 2 quail on receiver bottom, and a retriever's head on trigger guard. Extra figure walnut stock and forearm.

	$6,000	$4,950	$4,350	$3,825	$3,350	$2,950	$2,375

Presentation 4 w/gold inlays — similar to Presentation 4, only with game scenes inlaid in 18Kt. gold.

	$7,200	$6,500	$5,265	$4,750	$4,250	$3,650	$2,950

P SERIES SUPERLIGHT — available in various configurations including multi-barrel sets. Typically, add 20-25% onto the values listed for the regular P series as shown above. Also add 20-40% for the 28 ga.

LIEGE O/U — 12 ga., 26½, 28 or 30 in. barrels, various chokes, boxlock, auto ejectors, non-selective single trigger, vent. rib, checkered pistol grip stock. Approx. 10,000 mfg. 1973-1975 by FN.

	$750	$625	$575	$500	$425	$400	$375

This model is also known as the B-26.

B-26 — with BAC markings. Mfg. 1973-75.

	$750	$625	$575	$500	$425	$400	$375

Grading	100%	98%	95%	90%	80%	70%	60%

B-27 — F.N. manufactured modified B 26, imported into the U.S. in 1984, same action as Liege (B 26), blued or satin finished receiver with light engraving, no BAC markings and never cataloged.

⚜ **Standard Game** — 28 in. barrels, $\frac{9}{32}$ in. vent. rib, pistol grip stock, Schnabel forearm, SST, blued receiver, choking M/F only.

	$650	$575	$525	$475	$425	$400	$375

Also available in Skeet model with gold "Browning" logo on blued receiver. Prices are the same.

⚜ **Deluxe Game (Grade II)** — similar to Standard Grade, except has 30 in. barrels, better wood and English scroll engraved satin finished receiver, choking M/F only.

	$875	$725	$625	$575	$510	$475	$445

⚜ **Grand Deluxe Game** — 28 in. IC/IM & M/F choked barrels, game scene engraved, signed by the engraver, 90% receiver coverage.

	$1,100	$850	$775	$700	$640	$580	$520

This model was also available in a Trap configuration — values are about the same as above.

⚜ **Deluxe Skeet** — similar to Deluxe, except is designed for skeet shooting.

	$850	$725	$625	$575	$510	$475	$445

International Skeet is also available at same price; hand fit pistol grip with stippling and International Type recoil pad.

⚜ **Deluxe Trap** — similar to Deluxe, except is configured for trap shooting.

	$750	$650	$560	$530	$500	$475	$445

⚜ **City of Liege Commemorative** — limited edition of 250 units manufactured to commemorate the 1,000th anniversary of the city of Liege, cased. Only 29 imported into the U.S.

	$1,125	$975	$910	$850	$775	$700	$600

ST-100 — 12 ga., Belgian mfg., O/U trap configuration with separated barrels and adj. point of impact, manufactured 1979-1983 for European sale mostly, floating VR, ST, deluxe checkered walnut stock and forearm, non-B.A.C. model.

	$2,375	$1,950	$1,700	$1,400	$1,200	$975	$825

SUPERPOSED HIGH GRADES: 1985-PRESENT

Browning, in 1985, resumed production of the Superposed in Pigeon, Pointer, Diana, and Midas grades. They are available in 12 and 20 ga. only, in either a Lightning or Superlight configuration. These higher grades are custom ordered from the factory with delivery ranging from 8 to more than 12 months. Custom options can be special ordered on each grade with corresponding prices being higher than shown below. B-25 engraving patterns on these various grades will nearly duplicate those styles manufactured before 1976. Skeet models are not available.

B-25 — 12 or 20 ga. only, original Superposed Model manufactured entirely from parts fabricated in Herstal, Belgium. Also available in Superlight configuration.

⚜ **Pigeon Grade**

Mfg.'s Sug. Retail	$7,100	$5,950	$5,250	$4,250	$2,450	$1,950	$1,800	$1,650

Add $2,900 for an extra set of barrels.

⚜ **Pointer Grade**

Mfg.'s Sug. Retail	$8,500	$7,000	$6,150	$5,000	$2,750	$2,250	$1,950	$1,750

Add $3,100 for an extra set of barrels.

⚜ **Diana Grade**

Mfg.'s Sug. Retail	$9,100	$7,400	$6,350	$5,250	$2,850	$2,250	$1,950	$1,750

Add $4,400 for an extra set of barrels.

Grading	100%	98%	95%	90%	80%	70%	60%

Midas Grade
Mfg.'s Sug. Retail $12,500	$10,750	$8,950	$7,500	$3,400	$2,850	$2,450	$2,000

Add $5,000 for an extra set of barrels.

B-125 — 12 or 20 ga. only, retains all the features of the original Superposed, except parts are subcontracted worldwide to decrease production costs and are assembled "in the white" at Herstal's Custom Gun Shop in Belgium, choice of three different engraving styles and two receiver finishes. Introduced 1988.

Hunting Model — available in either Lightweight or Superlight configuration.
A STYLE ENGRAVING - blued receiver with border engraving featuring Browning logo engraved on each side.

Mfg.'s Sug. Retail $4,150	$3,650	$2,850	$2,100	$1,700	$1,450	$1,275	$1,050

B STYLE ENGRAVING - coined finished receiver with smaller game scene engravings.

Mfg.'s Sug. Retail $4,450	$3,850	$2,950	$2,150	$1,750	$1,500	$1,300	$1,100

C STYLE ENGRAVING - coined finished receiver with elaborate scroll work and game scene engraving.

Mfg.'s Sug. Retail $4,850	$4,100	$3,200	$2,350	$1,900	$1,600	$1,400	$1,200

Sporting Clays Model — 12 ga. only, designed for sporting clays competition and includes Invector plus choke tube system.
A STYLE ENGRAVING - blued receiver with border engraving featuring Browning logo engraved on each side.

Mfg.'s Sug. Retail $4,250	$3,725	$2,900	$2,125	$1,700	$1,450	$1,275	$1,050

B STYLE ENGRAVING - coined finished receiver with smaller game scene engravings.

Mfg.'s Sug. Retail $4,550	$3,975	$3,000	$2,175	$1,750	$1,500	$1,300	$1,100

C STYLE ENGRAVING - coined finished receiver with elaborate scroll work and game scene engraving.

Mfg.'s Sug. Retail $4,900	$4,125	$3,225	$2,350	$1,900	$1,600	$1,400	$1,200

Trap Model — standard F-1 style engraving.
Mfg.'s Sug. Retail $4,350	$3,800	$2,950	$2,150	$1,700	$1,450	$1,275	$1,050

SHOTGUNS: O/U CITORI HUNTING SERIES

All Citori shotguns which incorporate the Invector choke tube system may be used with steel shot.
On some Citori models, the retail value for a currently manufactured 28 or .410 ga. is less than for a 12 ga. When evaluating these smaller gauges in used condition, values will generally be higher than those listed below.

CITORI HUNTING MODELS — 12, 20, 28 or .410 ga., 26, 28, or 30 in. barrels, various chokes, boxlock, auto ejectors, SST, vent. rib, features checkered semi-pistol grip stock with grooved semi-beavertail forearm, grades differ in amount of engraving, finish, and wood. Mfg. 1973-present by Miroku.

Grade I
Mfg.'s Sug. Retail $1,165	$885	$685	$575	$495	$450	$395	$350

Subtract $10 for 28 or .410 ga.
Subtract $100 without Invector chokes.
Invector chokes became standard on this model in 1988.

3½ in. Magnum Model — 12 ga., 3½ in. chambers, 28 or 30 in. VR barrels with back-bored Invector plus choke tubes, with recoil pad, 8 lbs. 9 oz. New 1989.
Mfg.'s Sug. Retail $1,240	$1,025	$865	$775	$700	$625	$575	$525

Grading	100%	98%	95%	90%	80%	70%	60%

⚔ **Upland Special** — 12, 16 (mfg. 1989 only), or 20 ga., checkered straight grip stock, 24 in. barrels, Invector chokes standard. New 1984.

Mfg.'s Sug. Retail $1,215	$865	$685	$575	$495	$450	$425	$395

⚔ **Grade II** — 12, 20, 28, or .410 ga. Disc. 1983.

	$995	$810	$740	$685	$610	$570	$540

⚔ **Grade III** — 12, 20, 28, or .410 ga., greyed steel with engraved game scenes, Invector chokes standard. New 1985.

Mfg.'s Sug. Retail $1,715	$1,300	$995	$825	$725	$625	$585	$550

Add 15-25% for .410 or 28 ga. (disc. 1989).

⚔ **Grade V** — 12, 20, 28, or .410 ga., extensive deep relief engraving with game scenes on satin grey receiver. Disc. 1984.

	$1,550	$1,265	$1,100	$990	$880	$795	$695

⚔ **Grade VI** — 12, 20, 28, or .410 ga. (disc. 1989), blued or grayed receiver with extensive engraving including 8 gold inlays.

Mfg.'s Sug. Retail $2,485	$1,850	$1,375	$1,150	$1,000	$895	$795	$695

Add 15-25% for 28 ga. (disc. 1992).

CITORI SUPERLIGHT MODELS — 12, 20, 28, or .410 ga., 2¾ in. chambers except for .410, English stock, 6 lbs. 9 oz., oil finish, Invector chokes became standard in 1988. Mfg. 1983-present.

⚔ **Grade I**

Mfg.'s Sug. Retail $1,215	$865	$685	$575	$495	$450	$425	$395

Subtract $100 without Invector chokes.
Add $5 for 28 or .410 ga.

⚔ **Grade III** — same gauges as Grade I, Invector chokes standard on 12, 16, or 20 ga. New 1986.

Mfg.'s Sug. Retail $1,750	$1,350	$1,050	$850	$725	$625	$585	$550

Add $170 for 28 or .410 ga.

⚔ **Grade V** — sideplate available. Disc. 1984.

	$1,550	$1,265	$1,100	$990	$880	$795	$695

⚔ **Grade VI** — Invector chokes standard, except not available on 28 or .410 ga.

Mfg.'s Sug. Retail $2,540	$1,930	$1,475	$1,175	$1,000	$895	$795	$695

Add $160 for 28 or .410 ga.

CITORI SPORTER MODELS — similar to Citori Field, only with 3 in. chambers, 26 in. barrels, various chokes, straight grip stock, Schnabel forearm. Disc. 1983.

	$875	$740	$600	$550	$495	$440	$385

Add $50 for 28 or .410 ga.

⚔ **Sporter Grade II** — 12, 20, 28, or .410 ga.

	$1,250	$1,075	$1,020	$965	$880	$770	$715

⚔ **Sporter Grade V** — 12, 20, 28, or .410 ga.

	$1,575	$1,395	$1,225	$1,100	$990	$880	$825

Grading	100%	98%	95%	90%	80%	70%	60%

CITORI LIGHTNING MODELS — 12, 16 (disc. 1989), 20, 28, or .410 ga., (3½ in. 12 ga. was introduced 1989), 26, 28, or 30 in. barrels, Invector chokes standard in 12, 16, or 20 ga., boxlock, auto ejectors, SST, vent. rib, features checkered round knob pistol grip stock and slimmer forearm, grades differ in amount of engraving, finish, and quality of wood. Introduced 1988.

Grade I
Mfg.'s Sug. Retail	$1,198	$865	$695	$575	$495	$450	$425	$395

Add 15% for 16 ga.
Add $2 for 28 or .410 ga.

Grade III — 12, 16 (disc. 1989), 20, 28, or .410 ga., greyed steel receiver with engraved game scenes, Invector chokes standard. New 1988.
Mfg.'s Sug. Retail	$1,745	$1,350	$1,025	$825	$725	$625	$585	$550

Add 15% for 16 ga.
Add $175 for 28 or .410 ga.

Grade VI — 12, 16 (disc. 1989), 20, 28, or .410 ga., blued or greyed receiver with extensive engraving including 8 gold inlays.
Mfg.'s Sug. Retail	$2,530	$1,930	$1,475	$1,175	$1,000	$895	$795	$695

Add 15% for 16 ga.
Add $165 for 28 or .410 ga.

GRAN LIGHTNING MODEL — 12 or 20 ga. only, 3 in. chambers, similar to Lightning Model, except has higher grade walnut stock and forearm with satin/oil finish, includes recoil pad, 26 or 28 in. barrels, 6¾ - 8 lbs. New 1990.
Mfg.'s Sug. Retail	$1,630	$1,325	$1,025	$850	$725	$625	$585	$550

MICRO LIGHTNING — 20 ga. only, 2¾ in. chambers, 24 in. Invector choked barrels, 6 lbs. 3 oz. New 1991.

Grade I
Mfg.'s Sug. Retail	$1,228	$925	$750	$625	$525	$450	$425	$395

Grade III — 20 ga. only. New 1993.
Mfg.'s Sug. Retail	$1,775	$1,365	$1,035	$825	$725	$625	$585	$550

Grade VI — 20 ga. only. New 1993.
Mfg.'s Sug. Retail	$2,515	$1,915	$1,475	$1,175	$1,000	$895	$795	$695

SHOTGUNS: O/U SPORTING CLAYS

MODEL 325 — 12 or 20 ga., 28, 30, or 32 (12 ga. only) in. 10mm VR barrels, ported with Invector Plus chokes in 12 ga. only, European styling featuring checkered walnut stock and Schnabel forearm, grayed nitrous finished receiver, top tang safety, SST, ejectors, 6 lbs. 12 oz. - 7 lbs. 15 oz. New 1993.
Mfg.'s Sug. Retail	$1,470	$1,295	$925	$825	$700	$575	$495	$450

Add $70 for 12 ga. variation (includes ported barrels and Invector chokes).

GTI — 12 ga. only, 28 or 30 in. barrel with 13 mm vent. rib and barrels, red lettering on receiver during 1989 only - changed to gold lettering and borders with Browning logo in 1990, checkered stock and semi-beavertail forearm, Invector chokes standard, back-bored Invector plus chokes became standard in 1990, approx. 8 lbs. New 1989.
Mfg.'s Sug. Retail	$1,380	$1,195	$875	$700	$600	$525	$495	$450

Subtract $75 without ported barrels (disc. 1992).
Add $30 for Signature Painted Model (includes special paint treatment on stock and forearm, new 1993).
Ported barrels were new in 1990 and became standard in 1992.

Grading	100%	98%	95%	90%	80%	70%	60%

GTI Golden Clays — 12 ga. only, 28, 30, or 32 in. ported VR barrels, Invector Plus choking, GTI features, satin grey receiver with Grade VI level of engraving and gold inlays depicting a transitional hunting to clay birds scene. New 1993.

Mfg.'s Sug. Retail	$2,750	$2,250	$1,725	$1,425	$1,125	$975	$875	$825

GRADE I SPECIAL SPORTING — target dimensions, high post tapered rib, 28, 30, or 32 in. barrels, full pistol grip with palm swell, approx. 8 lbs. 3 oz. New 1989.

Mfg.'s Sug. Retail	$1,360	$1,145	$850	$700	$600	$525	$495	$450

Subtract $75 without ported barrels (disc. 1992).
Add $30 for Signature Painted Model (includes special paint treatment on stock and forearm, new 1993).
Add $800 for 2 barrel set (28 and 30 in. barrels), disc. 1990.
Ported barrels were new in 1990 and became standard in 1992.
In 1990, the Grade I designation was added to this model. Changes include back-bored barrels with Invector plus choke tubes.

Special Sporting Golden Clays — 12 ga. only, 28, 30, or 32 in. ported barrels with high-post VR, Invector Plus choking, Special Sporting features, satin grey receiver with Grade VI level of engraving and gold inlays depicting a transitional hunting to clay birds scene. New 1993.

Mfg.'s Sug. Retail	$2,750	$2,250	$1,725	$1,425	$1,125	$975	$875	$825

GRADE I SPECIAL SPORTING PIGEON GRADE — 12 ga. only, higher grade model featuring higher grade walnut and gold line receiver accents. New 1993.

Mfg.'s Sug. Retail	$1,550	$1,350	$950	$850	$700	$575	$495	$450

GRADE I LIGHTNING SPORTING — features rounded pistol grip, Lightning style forearm, high or low post vent. rib, "Lightning Sporting Clays Edition" inscribed and gold-filled on receiver, 30 in. barrels. New 1989.

Mfg.'s Sug. Retail	$1,300	$1,095	$815	$700	$600	$525	$495	$450

Add $60 for high-post rib.
Subtract $75 if without ported barrels.
Add $90 for Signature Painted Model (includes special paint treatment on stock and forearm, new 1993).
Ported barrels were new in 1990 and became standard in 1992.
In 1990, the Grade I designation was added to this model. Changes include back-bored barrels with Invector plus choke tubes.

Lightning Sporting Golden Clays — 12 ga. only, 28, 30, or 32 in. ported barrels with choice of low or high-post VR, Invector Plus choking, Lightning Sporting features, satin grey receiver with Grade VI level of engraving and gold inlays depicting a transitional hunting to clay birds scene. New 1993.

Mfg.'s Sug. Retail	$2,750	$2,250	$1,725	$1,425	$1,125	$975	$875	$825

Subtract $100 for low-post VR.

GRADE I LIGHTNING SPORTING PIGEON GRADE — 12 ga. only, higher grade model featuring higher grade walnut and gold line receiver accents. New 1993.

Mfg.'s Sug. Retail	$1,550	$1,350	$950	$850	$700	$575	$495	$450

Subtract $62 for low profile VR barrel.

SHOTGUNS: O/U CITORI SKEET

CITORI SKEET MODELS — 12, 20, 28, or .410 ga., same action as Citori Field, only with high post target rib (standard 1985), 26 and 28 in. skeet barrels, recoil pad, Invector chokes became standard in 1990 in 12 and 20 ga., Invector Plus chokes with ported barrels became an option in 1992.

Mfg.'s Sug. Retail	$1,315	$1,050	$825	$675	$600	$525	$495	$450

Add $65 for Invector Plus chokes and ported barrels (12 ga. only).
Subtract $100 if without Invector chokes.
Earlier mfg. skeet guns had a low profile, wide VR.

Grading	100%	98%	95%	90%	80%	70%	60%

Grade II — 12, 20, 28, or .410 ga., high rib. Disc. 1983.

	100%	98%	95%	90%	80%	70%	60%
	$1,000	$850	$800	$740	$690	$650	$600

Grade III — 12, 20, 28, or .410 ga., Invector chokes in 12 and 20 ga. only. New 1986.

	Mfg.'s Sug. Retail	$1,860	98%	95%	90%	80%	70%	60%
			$1,450	$1,075	$850	$725	$625	$550	$495

Add $36 for Invector Plus chokes and ported barrels (12 ga. only).

Grade V — 12, 20, 28, or .410 ga., high rib. Disc. 1984.

	100%	98%	95%	90%	80%	70%	60%
	$1,495	$1,265	$1,100	$990	$880	$795	$650

Grade VI — Skeet gauges, choice of blue or grey finished receiver with multi gold inlays, deluxe walnut.

Mfg.'s Sug. Retail $2,520

	98%	95%	90%	80%	70%	60%
	$2,000	$1,600	$1,325	$1,100	$960	$875	$825

Add $170 for ported barrels (12 ga. only).
Add $130 for 20, 28, or .410 ga.

Skeet Golden Clays — 12 ga. only, 26 or 28 in. ported VR barrels, Invector Plus choking, Skeet features, satin grey receiver with Grade VI level of engraving and gold inlays depicting a transitional hunting to clay birds scene. New 1993.

Mfg.'s Sug. Retail $2,690 $2,220 $1,700 $1,400 $1,125 $975 $875 $825

CITORI 3 GAUGE SKEET SETS — 12 ga. only, comes with 1 removable forearm and 3 sets of barrels consisting of 20, 28 and .410 ga.'s, cased. New 1987.

Grade I — with high post target rib.
Mfg.'s Sug. Retail $2,960 $2,450 $2,025 $1,650 $1,450 $1,275 $1,050 $975

Grade III — with high post target rib.
Mfg.'s Sug. Retail $3,560 $2,775 $2,225 $1,850 $1,550 $1,395 $1,250 $1,125

Grade VI — with high post target rib.
Mfg.'s Sug. Retail $4,200 $3,550 $2,700 $2,225 $1,875 $1,700 $1,675 $1,495

CITORI 4 GAUGE SKEET SETS — 12 ga. only, comes with 1 removable forearm and 4 sets of barrels consisting of 12, 20, 28 and .410 ga.'s, cased. New 1985.

Grade I — with high post target rib.
Mfg.'s Sug. Retail $4,250 $3,650 $2,775 $2,375 $1,975 $1,800 $1,775 $1,600

Grade III — with high post target rib.
Mfg.'s Sug. Retail $4,860 $4,100 $2,995 $2,550 $2,100 $1,900 $1,800 $1,700

Grade VI — with high post target rib.
Mfg.'s Sug. Retail $5,500 $4,600 $3,350 $2,775 $2,300 $2,100 $2,000 $1,900

SHOTGUNS: O/U CITORI TRAP

CITORI TRAP MODELS — similar to Standard Citori, with 12 ga., 30 and 32 in. barrels, trap chokes, Monte Carlo stock, recoil pad. Invector chokes became standard in 1988, Invector Plus chokes with ported barrels became an option in 1992, and were made standard in 1993.

Mfg.'s Sug. Retail $1,380 $1,150 $875 $700 $600 $525 $495 $450
Subtract $75 without Invector chokes or high rib.

Trap Combination Set — Grade I only, 32 in. O/U and 34 in. single barrel, cased. Disc.

	100%	98%	95%	90%	80%	70%	60%
	$1,185	$1,100	$1,045	$990	$910	$855	$800

Grading		100%	98%	95%	90%	80%	70%	60%

Grade I Plus Trap — features adj. rib and stock, back-bored barrels, Invector Plus choke system. New 1990.

Mfg.'s Sug. Retail	$1,925	$1,500	$1,150	$925	$800	$700	$600	$500

Add $25 for ported barrels.

In 1991 this model included a travel vault gun case at no extra charge. Subtract $50 for older mfg. without travel case.

Grade I Plus Trap Combo — includes ported barrels with Invector Plus choking and extra standard single ported barrel, luggage case. New 1992.

Mfg.'s Sug. Retail	$3,300	$2,775	$2,400	$2,100	$1,900	$1,700	$1,500	$1,250

Plus Trap Golden Clays — 12 ga. only, 30 or 32 in. ported VR barrels, Invector Plus choking, Trap features, satin grey receiver with Grade VI level of engraving and gold inlays depicting a transitional hunting to clay birds scene. New 1993.

Mfg.'s Sug. Retail	$3,300	$2,775	$2,250	$1,900	$1,600	$1,400	$1,200	$995

Plus Trap Golden Clays Combo — includes O/U ported barrels with Invector Plus choking and extra standard single ported barrel, luggage case. New 1993.

Mfg.'s Sug. Retail	$5,000	$4,300	$3,250	$2,750	$2,250	$1,925	$1,800	$1,700

Pigeon Grade — 12 ga. only, features extra deluxe walnut, Invector Plus ported barrels, and receiver gold accents. New 1993.

Mfg.'s Sug. Retail	$2,140	$1,650	$1,225	$950	$800	$700	$600	$500

Signature Painted — 12 ga. only, features painted red/black stock with Browning logos on stock and forearm, Invector Plus ported barrels. New 1993.

Mfg.'s Sug. Retail	$1,985	$1,540	$1,175	$925	$800	$700	$600	$500

Grade II — high post rib. Disc. 1983.

		$1,000	$850	$800	$740	$690	$650	$600

Grade III — 12 ga. only, high post rib. New 1986.

Mfg.'s Sug. Retail	$1,896	$1,475	$1,075	$850	$725	$625	$550	$495

Add $35 for Invector Plus chokes with ported barrels.

Grade V — high post rib. Disc. 1984.

		$1,475	$1,150	$990	$880	$795	$710	$620

Grade VI — 12 ga. only, Invector chokes became standard in 1985.

Mfg.'s Sug. Retail	$2,520	$1,900	$1,500	$1,225	$1,100	$960	$875	$825

Add $170 for Invector Plus chokes with ported barrels.

Trap Golden Clays — 12 ga. only, 30 or 32 in. ported VR barrels, Invector Plus choking, Trap features, Monte Carlo or regular stock, satin grey receiver with Grade VI level of engraving and gold inlays depicting a transitional hunting to clay birds scene. New 1993.

Mfg.'s Sug. Retail	$2,690	$2,220	$1,700	$1,400	$1,125	$975	$875	$825

SHOTGUNS: SINGLE BARREL

BT-99 STANDARD TRAP GUN — 12 ga., 32 or 34 in. vent. rib barrel, mod., imp. mod., or full choke, boxlock, auto ejector, checkered pistol grip with Monte Carlo or conventional style stock, beavertail forearm, mfg. 1968-present by Miroku. Invector chokes became standard in 1986 and ported barrel with Invector Plus chokes became standard in 1992. Values below assume Invector Plus choking with ported barrel.

Mfg.'s Sug. Retail	$1,225	$950	$700	$550	$460	$400	$360	$330

Subtract $125 without Invector chokes or ported barrels.

Grading	100%	98%	95%	90%	80%	70%	60%

BT-99 Stainless — features all stainless construction with Invector Plus ported 32 or 34 in. black VR barrel. New 1993.

Mfg.'s Sug. Retail	$1,650	$1,425	$995	$875	$700	$575	$495	$450

Pigeon Grade — features higher grade walnut and gold receiver accents, Invector chokes and ported barrels. New 1993.

Mfg.'s Sug. Retail	$1,430	$1,175	$875	$700	$600	$525	$495	$450

Signature Painted — features painted red/black stock with Browning logos on stock and forearm, Invector Plus ported barrels. New 1993.

Mfg.'s Sug. Retail	$1,260	$975	$700	$550	$460	$400	$360	$330

GRADE I BT-99 PLUS — same action as BT-99 except has adj. rib to control point of impact and new recoil reduction system that reduces felt recoil by 50%, stock has adj. comb and butt plate (recoil pad), back-bored barrel, Invector chokes, 8¾ lbs. New 1989.

Mfg.'s Sug. Retail	$1,765	$1,425	$1,100	$925	$775	$675	$595	$550

Add $15 for ported barrel.

In 1990, the Grade I designation was added to this model. Changes include back-bored barrels with Invector plus choke tubes. In 1991, this model was supplied with a travel vault gun case as standard equipment. Older mfg. will not have these cases as an original accessory.

BT-99 Plus Stainless — features all stainless construction with Invector Plus ported 32 or 34 in. black VR barrel. New 1993.

Mfg.'s Sug. Retail	$2,150	$1,650	$1,225	$950	$800	$700	$600	$500

BT-99 Plus Pigeon Grade — features higher grade walnut and gold receiver accents, Invector chokes and ported barrels. New 1993.

Mfg.'s Sug. Retail	$1,985	$1,540	$1,175	$925	$800	$700	$600	$500

BT-99 Plus Signature Painted — features painted red/black stock with Browning logos on stock and forearm, Invector Plus ported barrels. New 1993.

Mfg.'s Sug. Retail	$1,815	$1,450	$1,125	$900	$800	$700	$600	$500

BT-99 MICRO PLUS — similar to Grade I BT-99 Plus, except has youth dimensions and choice of 28 or 30 in. barrel, 8 lbs. 6 oz. New 1991.

Mfg.'s Sug. Retail	$1,765	$1,425	$1,100	$925	$775	$675	$595	$550

Add $15 for ported barrel.

BT-99 Micro Plus Stainless — features all stainless construction with Invector Plus ported 32 or 34 in. black VR barrel. New 1993.

Mfg.'s Sug. Retail	$2,150	$1,650	$1,225	$950	$800	$700	$600	$500

BT-99 Micro Plus Pigeon Grade — features higher grade walnut and gold receiver accents, Invector chokes and ported barrels. New 1993.

Mfg.'s Sug. Retail	$1,985	$1,540	$1,175	$925	$800	$700	$600	$500

BT-99 Micro Plus Signature Painted — features painted red/black stock with Browning logos on stock and forearm, Invector Plus ported barrels. New 1993.

Mfg.'s Sug. Retail	$1,815	$1,450	$1,125	$900	$800	$700	$600	$500

BT-99 2 Barrel Set — disc. 1983.

		$1,030	$880	$825	$750	$700	$650	$600

BT-99 Pigeon Grade — satin grey receiver with deep relief, engraved pigeons in fleur-de-lis background. Disc. 1984.

		$1,300	$950	$800	$700	$600	$525	$440

BROWNING cont.

Grading	100%	98%	95%	90%	80%	70%	60%

RECOILLESS SINGLE BARREL TRAP — 12 ga., special bolt action design that elimi-nates 72% of felt recoil, 27 (Micro Model) or 30 in. high-post vent. rib Invector Plus choked back-bored barrel, rib adjusts for 3 points of impact, stock has adj. pull (2 sizes) and comb height, approx. 8½ lbs.

	100%	98%	95%	90%	80%	70%	60%
Mfg.'s Sug. Retail $1,670	$1,425	$995	$875	$700	$575	$495	$450

SHOTGUNS: SxS, DISC.

BSS MODEL — 12 or 20 ga., 26, 28, or 30 in. barrels, various chokes, boxlock, auto ejectors, checkered pistol grip stock, beavertail forearm, selective single trigger. Mfg. 1971-1988 by Miroku.

	100%	98%	95%	90%	80%	70%	60%
	$595	$495	$450	$400	$365	$330	$300

Add 10%-15% for 20 ga.
Last Mfg.'s Sug. Retail was $775.
Early guns had a single non-selective trigger (silver plated) — subtract 10%.

⚞ **Grade II** — satin greyed steel receiver featuring an engraved pheasant, duck, quail and dogs. Disc. 1983.

	100%	98%	95%	90%	80%	70%	60%
	$1,100	$950	$800	$700	$600	$525	$450

⚞ **Sporter Model** — has straight grip stock and slim forearm, oil finish, 26 or 28 in. barrels. Disc. 1988.

	100%	98%	95%	90%	80%	70%	60%
	$700	$625	$545	$500	$445	$410	$370

Add 10%-15% for 20 ga.
Last Mfg.'s Sug. Retail was $775.

BSS SIDELOCK — 12 or 20 ga., engraved sidelock action in satin grey finish, ST, 26 or 28 in. barrels, English select walnut stock, splinter forend. Mfg. 1983-1988 in Miroku in Japan.

	100%	98%	95%	90%	80%	70%	60%
12 ga.	$1,995	$1,450	$1,125	$975	$825	$750	$675
20 ga.	$2,400	$1,750	$1,375	$1,100	$900	$800	$700

Last Mfg.'s Sug. Retail was $2,000.

SHOTGUNS: SLIDE ACTION

BPS MODELS — 12 or 20 ga., gauges are chambered for Mag. ammunition. Invector option (standard for 1985) allows 6 screw-in choke tubes to be interchanged, Invector Plus chokes became standard in 1993, bottom ejection, double action bars, top tang safety, 5 shot capacity, vent. rib, all steel receiver. Mfg. by Miroku 1977-to-date.

⚞ **Hunting Model** — 12 or 20 ga., 3 in. chambers.

	100%	98%	95%	90%	80%	70%	60%
Mfg.'s Sug. Retail $443	$355	$295	$250	$225	$200	$185	$175

Add $20 for Invector Plus chokes.

⚞ **Stalker Model** — 12 ga. only, 3 in. chamber, all metal parts have a dull matte finish, non-glare black synthetic composite stock and forearm. New 1987.

	100%	98%	95%	90%	80%	70%	60%
Mfg.'s Sug. Retail $463	$365	$295	$250	$225	$200	$185	$175

⚞ **Magnum Hunting or Stalker 3½ in.** — 10 or 12 ga., 3½ in. chamber, 12 ga. 3½ in. chamber was new 1989, 26 (10 ga. only), 28 or 30 in. barrel with Invector chokes and vent. rib, 4 shot mag., 8¾ (12 ga.) or 9½ (10 ga.) lbs.

	100%	98%	95%	90%	80%	70%	60%
Mfg.'s Sug. Retail $585	$500	$440	$410	$375	$340	$310	$290

In 1990, the back-bored Invector plus choke tube system became standard in 12 ga. 3½ in. chamber only.

Grading	100%	98%	95%	90%	80%	70%	60%

Magnum Hunting Waterfowl — 10 ga., 3½ in. Mag. with choice of 28 or 30 in. matte finished VR barrel with standard Invector choking, features higher grade walnut and gold trimmed receiver with Waterfowl outlined, approx. 9 lbs. 6 oz. New 1993.

Mfg.'s Sug. Retail	$750	$625	$525	$450	$395	$350	$325	$300

Pigeon Grade — 12 ga. only, 3 in. chamber, features high grade walnut and gold trimmed receiver, 26 or 28 in. VR barrel with Invector chokes, 7 lbs. 10 oz. New 1992.

Mfg.'s Sug. Retail	$620	$520	$450	$425	$375	$340	$310	$290

Upland Special — 12 or 20 ga., 22 in. barrel, straight grip stock with Schnabel forearm, 6½ - 7½ lbs. New 1985.

Mfg.'s Sug. Retail	$463	$365	$295	$250	$225	$200	$185	$175

Turkey Special — 12 ga. only, 3 in. chamber, 20½ in. lightened barrel, non-glare walnut stock, matte finished barrel and receiver, receiver is drilled and tapped for scope base, rifle-style stock dimensions, sling swivels, new extra-full Invector choke tube, 7 lbs. 7 oz. New 1992.

Mfg.'s Sug. Retail	$500	$395	$310	$250	$225	$200	$185	$175

Deer Special — 12 ga. only, 3 in. chamber, 20½ in. barrel with 5 in. rifled choke tube, iron sights, scope mount base, gloss finished checkered stock with recoil pad and forearm, sling swivels, matte finished metal, 7 lbs. 7 oz. New 1992.

Mfg.'s Sug. Retail	$528	$415	$310	$250	$225	$200	$185	$175

Youth and Ladies Model — 20 ga. only, 22 in. vent. rib barrel, straight grip shortened stock, 6¾ lbs. New 1986.

Mfg.'s Sug. Retail	$443	$355	$295	$250	$225	$200	$185	$175

Buck Special — 12 or 20 (disc. 1984) ga., 3 in. chamber, 24 in. barrel with Invector chokes, iron sights. Reintroduced 1988.

Mfg.'s Sug. Retail	$449	$365	$300	$250	$225	$200	$185	$175

3½ in. Buck Special — 10 or 12 ga., 3½ in. chambers, 24 in. barrel. New 1990.

Mfg.'s Sug. Retail	$590	$510	$430	$400	$360	$330	$310	$290

Trap Model — 12 ga., 30 in. barrel. Disc. 1984 but trap barrels were available separately for several years.

	$360	$300	$270	$230	$210	$190	$170

Wild Turkey Federation Commemorative — only 500 manufactured. Disc. 1991.

	$495	$395	$325

Pacific Edition DU — limited mfg., DU serialization, cased.

	$595	$475	$350

The Coastal DU — limited mfg., DU serialization, cased.

	$595	$475	$350

Waterfowl Deluxe — 12 ga. Mag., gold trigger and etching, invector chokes, limited mfg.

	$625	$525	$450

MODEL 12 LIMITED EDITION SERIES

Grade I 20 Ga. — 20 ga. only, 2¾ in. chamber only, reproduction of the famous Winchester Model 12 with slight design improvements, 26 in. VR barrel bored modified, 5 shot mag., high post floating rib, walnut stock and forearm with semi-gloss finish, take down, 7 lbs. 1 oz. 8,000 mfg. in 1988 with inventory depleted 1990.

	$625	$500	$400

Last Mfg.'s Sug. Retail was $735.
Browning Arms Company is limiting manufacture to 8,000 Grade I 20 Ga.'s.

⚮ **Grade V 20 Ga.** — similar specifications to Grade I, except has select walnut checkered 22 lines per inch with high gloss finish, extensive game scene engraving including multiple gold inlays. mfg. 1988 only.

| | $1,000 | $800 | $575 |

Last Mfg.'s Sug. Retail was $1,187.
Browning Arms Company is limiting manufacture to 4,000 Grade V 20 Ga.'s.

⚮ **Grade I 28 Ga.** — 28 ga. only, similar to Grade I 20 Ga., except in 28 ga., 26 in. VR modified choke barrel. 7,000 mfg. 1991-92.

| | $675 | $550 | $425 |

Last Mfg.'s Sug. Retail was $772.

⚮ **Grade V 28 Ga.** — 28 ga. only, similar to Grade V 20 Ga., except in 28 ga., 26 in. VR modified choke barrel. 5,000 mfg. 1991-92.

| | $1,095 | $850 | $675 |

Last Mfg.'s Sug. Retail was $1,246.

MODEL 42 LIMITED EDITION

⚮ **Model 42 Grade I** — .410 ga., 3 in. chamber, reproduction of the Winchester Model 42 with slight design improvements, 26 in. VR full choke barrel, select walnut stock, 6 lbs. 12 oz. New in late 1991.

| Mfg.'s Sug. Retail | $800 | $695 | $600 | $525 |

Browning Arms Company is limiting manufacture to 6,000 Grade I Model 42s.

⚮ **Model 42 Grade V** — engraving and embellishments similar to the Model 12 Grade 5 in .410 ga. Introduced in late 1991.

| Mfg.'s Sug. Retail | $1,360 | $1,100 | $925 | $750 |

Browning Arms Company is limiting manufacture to 6,000 Grade V Model 42s.

LIMITED EDITION SETS INCLUDING BLACK POWDER

BICENTENNIAL 1876-1976 SET — .45-70 Model 78 rifle with specially engraved receiver, silver finish, fancy wood, cased, with engraved knife and medallion, 1,000 sets mfg. in 1976. Issue price — $1,500.

| | $1,750 | $1,300 | $850 |

CASED RENAISSANCE SET — one each .25 auto, .380 auto, and Hi-Power Renaissance models in walnut case. Mfg. 1955-1969.

| | $3,500 | $2,750 | $2,100 |

JONATHAN BROWNING MOUNTAIN RIFLE — 50 cal., percussion, 30 in. octagon barrel, single set trigger, engraved lock plate, select walnut stock, cased with medallion, 1,000 mfg. in 1978. Issue price — $650.

| | $650 | $475 | $275 |

MOUNTAIN RIFLE — similar to Jonathan Browning Mountain Rifle, without Centennial embellishments, not cased. Also in .45 or .54 cal.

| | $375 | $275 | $200 | $170 | $150 | $135 | $125 |

CENTENNIAL O/U RIFLE/SHOTGUN — superposed 20 ga. action fitted with .30-06, 24 in. barrels, folding leaf sight, 26½ in. mod. and full, 20 ga. barrels, auto ejectors, SST, elaborately engraved, gold inlaid, high grade checkered walnut stock, deluxe walnut case, 500 mfg. to commemorate Browning Centennial — 1878-1978.

| | $4,000 | $3,500 | $3,000 | $2,550 | $2,100 | $1,725 | $1,500 |

Last Mfg.'s Sug. Retail was $7,000.

Grading	100%	98%	95%	90%	80%	70%	60%

CENTENNIAL SET — complete Browning set mfg. in 1978, includes the Centennial O/U Rifle/Shotgun, 9mm Hi-Power, B92 .44 Mag., Mountain Rifle, and a set of three knives.

$5,950 $3,750 $2,100

1 OF 50 BICENTENNIAL RIFLE — .30-06 cal., Model 78 single shot with 26 in. octagon barrel, includes special engraving by Neil Hartliep (non-factory), extra fine walnut, 4X wide angle scope, special luggage case. 50 mfg. (one for each state) during 1976 only and sold by silent mail order bidding (minimum bid was $3,100 in 1976).

As very few specimens are bought or sold each year, pricing is rather unpredictable. A few specimens have been sold in the $3,250 - $5,000 range recently. Remember, the work on this gun was subcontracted by Centennial Guns (division of Frigon Guns located in Clay Center, KS).

BRUCHET

Manufacturer located in Saint Etienne. Distributed exclusively from 1982-1989 by Wes Gilpin located in Dallas, TX. In 1989, Bruchet was able to get permission to use the older Darne trademark and all new manufacture will be entered under the Darne listing.

Paul Bruchet has been manufacturing his shotguns patterned after the Darne action since 1981, following his tenure at Darne as line foreman until 1979 (at which time the Darne plant closed). These new Bruchet Models were designated "A" or "B". All shotguns were totally hand made with approx. 50 guns being mfg. each year.

Since Paul Bruchet was able to retain the Darne trademark in 1989, please refer to the Darne section in this text for all manufacture after 1989 (current prices will also be listed).

MODEL A — 12, 16, 20, 28, or .410 ga., small key opening, ejectors, double triggers only, basically 4 variations (1, 1A, 2, and 2A), wide assortment of customer specified special orders.

Retail values are as follows: Model 1A starts at under $2,000, the Model 2 starts at $3,000, and the Model 2A starts at $3,500. Each additional grade represents more embellishments and better grade of walnut. Magnum chambers can be ordered at a small surcharge. Importation began 1982, values above represent the last published retail prices from 1989.

MODEL B — 12, 16, 20, 28, or .410 ga., large key opening, self-opening (assisted) action, ejectors, double triggers only, basically special ordered to individual customer specifications.

Retail values are as follows: Model B starts at $5,800 and includes deluxe carrying case. Each additional upgrade represents more embellishments and a better grade of walnut. Magnum chambers can be ordered at a small surcharge. Importation began 1982, values above represent the last published retail prices from 1989.

BRYCO ARMS

Manufacturer located in Irvine, CA. Distributed by Jennings Firearms, Inc. located in Carson City, NV. Distributor sales only.

Pistols listed below are single action design.

BRYCO 38 — .32 ACP or .380 ACP cal., semi-auto, 2.8 in. barrel, choice of nickel, chrome, or black teflon finish, alloy receiver, 16 oz. New 1988.

Mfg.'s Sug. Retail	$90	$80	$65	$60	$55	$50	$45	$40

Add $10 for .380 ACP cal.

BRYCO 48 — .22 LR (late 1992), .380 ACP cal., semi-auto, black or chrome finish, black grips, 4 in. barrel, 24 oz. New 1989.

Mfg.'s Sug. Retail	$110	$95	$85	$75	$60	$55	$50	$45

BUDISCHOWSKY
Previous manufacturer located in Mt. Clemens, MI.

PISTOLS: SEMI-AUTO

Grading	100%	98%	95%	90%	80%	70%	60%

TP-70 — .22 LR, double action, 2½ in. barrel, stainless steel, fixed sights, plastic grips. Mfg. 1973-1977.

	$440	$385	$330				

TP-70 — similar to TP-70, except .25 ACP cal. Mfg. 1973-1977.

	$330	$275	$220				

Note: In 1977, Norton Arms marketed this pistol. Quality of workmanship is not on a par with the early Budischowsky and values are approx. 35% less.

SEMI-AUTO PISTOL — .223 cal., 11⅝ in. barrel, 20 or 30 shot mag., fixed sights, a novel paramilitary designed type pistol.

	$470	$415	$385	$360	$305	$250	$220

PARAMILITARY DESIGN RIFLE — .223 cal., semi-auto, 18 in. barrel, wooden paramilitary stock.

	$505	$440	$415	$385	$330	$275	$250

PARAMILITARY DESIGN RIFLE FOLDING STOCK

	$525	$470	$440	$415	$360	$305	$275

BUSHMASTER FIREARMS, INC.
Originally manufactured by Gwinn Arms Co., Winston-Salem, N.C. 1972-1974. Previously manufactured by Bushmaster Firearms, Inc. located in North Windham, ME 1974-1993. The Quality Parts Co. gained control in 1986 and the Bushmaster pistol and rifle are now discontinued.

Bushmaster pistols and rifles had limited mfg. until production ceased in 1986. Further information can be obtained on this trademark by contacting Quality Parts Co. (see Trademark Index).

BUSHMASTER PISTOL — .223 Rem., semi-auto., top bolt (older models with aluminum receivers) or side bolt (current mfg.) operation, steel frame (current mfg.), 11½ in. barrel, parkerized finish, adj. sights, wood stock, 5¼ lbs.

	$350	$280	$250	$225	$180	$140	$120

Add $40 for electroless nickel finish (disc. 1988).
This model uses a 30 shot M-16 mag. and the AK-47 gas system.
Last Mfg.'s Sug. Retail was $375.

BUSHMASTER RIFLE — .223 Rem., semi-auto., top bolt (older models with aluminum receivers) or side bolt (current mfg.) operation, steel frame (current mfg.), 18½ in. barrel, parkerized finish, adj. sights, wood stock, 6¼ lbs., base values are for folding stock model.

	$325	$280	$250	$225	$180	$140	$120

Add $40 for electroless nickel finish (disc. 1988).
Add $65 for fixed rock maple wood stock.
This model uses a 30 shot M-16 mag. and the AK-47 gas system.
Last Mfg.'s Sug. Retail was $350.

Rifle Combination System — includes rifle with both metal folding stock and wood stock with pistol grip.

	$400	$360	$330	$300	$275	$250	$230

Last Mfg.'s Sug. Retail was $450.

C section

CETME

Grading	100%	98%	95%	90%	80%	70%	60%

AUTOLOADING RIFLE — .308 cal., 17¾ in. barrel, gas operated, roller cam action, similar to HK-91 in appearance, wood military style stock, aperture rear sight.

	100%	98%	95%	90%	80%	70%	60%
	$715	$660	$605	$550	$440	$385	$330

C Z (CESKA ZBROJOVKA)

Current manufacturer located in Uhersky Brod, Czechoslovakia, 1921-current. Previous mfg. was in Strakonice, Czechoslovakia. CZ pistols are currently imported exclusively by Action Arms located in Philadelphia, PA.

While little history is known about this important European trademark, the following biographical sketch will provide some information. In approximately 1916, some military personnel took over the controlling interest of the Austro-Hungarian armament shop in Brno, Czechoslovakia, renaming it The State Armament and Engineering Works. Approximately a year later, the name was changed to Czechoslovak State Armament Works. Prior to 1924, this firm was involved mainly with Mauser Model 98 type rifles (both assembly and mfg.). In 1924, the name was again changed to Ceskoslovenska Zbrojovka A.Z. (Czechoslovakian Arms Factory Ltd.) - commonly known as the CZ firm. CZ manufactured the VZ-24 Mauser rifle for Czechoslovakia as well as other M-98 military rifles and carbines for other countries, including many which Germany used during WWII. After WWII, the name was again changed to Zbrojovka Brno (Brno Arms Works), or ZB for short. With the iron curtain descending on Europe after WWII, communist bloc countries, including Czechoslovakia, had little exportation to the U.S.. Currently, CZ handguns are made at the plant in Uhersky Brod and Brno long arms are made in both Uhersky Brod and Brno. With the sudden decline in communism during the past years, more and more products (including firearms from Czechoslovakia) will see their way into the U.S. without the 65% importation tax previously levied on goods from older communist bloc countries.

PISTOLS: DISC. SEMI-AUTO

"DUO" POCKET AUTOMATIC — .25 auto, 6 shot, 2⅛ in. barrel, fixed sights, blue or nickel, plastic grips. Mfg. 1926-present (current Z pistol by Brno).

$200	$185	$170	$150	$125	$100	$75

Add 40% for WWII years.
This model was manufactured by Dushek and is similar to the Z pistol equivalent by Brno.

CZ 22 — .380 cal., derived from Mauser Nickel Pistol and manufactured under license from Mauser. Mfg. 1923 only.

$400	$350	$320	$300	$275	$235	$200

CZ 24 — .380 cal.

✦ **Standard Frame** — 8 shot mag. Over 175,000 mfg. 1924-38. Over half issued to Czech Army. Same general design as CZ 22 except no gap between trigger and frame. Add $50 if Nazi proofed. Production continued to 1941.

$350	$320	$290	$260	$230	$195	$150

A small number were Kriegsmarine proofed. Add 200%. Beware of counterfeit markings.

✦ **Long Frame** — 9 shot mag.

$600	$550	$500	$450	$375	$300	$225

Add $750 if fit with stock slot (either standard frame or long frame).

Grading	100%	98%	95%	90%	80%	70%	60%

CZ 27 — .32 cal.

⚔ **"CESKA" Slide Legend Variation** — slanted slide grooves, high polish. Ser. range 16,000-21,500

	100%	98%	95%	90%	80%	70%	60%
Prewar Commercial	$450	$400	$350	$300	$250	$200	$150
DR Proofed	$450	$400	$350	$300	$250	$200	$150
Nazi Proofed	$450	$400	$350	$300	$250	$200	$150

⚔ **"BOHMISCHE" Slide Legend Variation** — vertical slide grooves, high or medium polish. Ser. range 21,500-261,000. Nazi proofed.

100%	98%	95%	90%	80%	70%	60%
$225	$200	$175	$150	$135	$120	$110

Nazi Police pistols dated 1941, 1942, or 1943 marked with Eagle/K on left trigger guard web, add 125% for 1941 date, add 100% for 1942 and 1943 date.
A small number were Kriegsmarine proofed. Add 200%. Beware of counterfeit markings.

⚔ **"fnh" Slide Legend Variation** — Medium polish or phosphate. Ser. range 261,000-476,000.

100%	98%	95%	90%	80%	70%	60%
$200	$175	$150	$125	$100	$85	$70

⚔ **"Phosphate" finish** — a small number of phosphate pistols were fit with an extended barrel for silencer attachment. Usually in 450,000-460,000 Ser. range.

100%	98%	95%	90%	80%	70%	60%
$550	$500	$450	$400	$375	$350	$325

⚔ **Post WWII mfg.** — dated 1945, 1946, 1947, 1948, 1949, 1950, 1951. These models will have the "NARODNI PODNIK" inscription on slide.
Currently, these variations average $250 in 95%+ condition while reworks (very common) average under $200.

VZ 38 DOUBLE ACTION AUTOMATIC — .380 auto, 9 shot, double action only, $4\frac{5}{8}$ in. barrel, fixed sights, blue, plastic grips. Mfg. 1938-1939.

100%	98%	95%	90%	80%	70%	60%
$350	$300	$250	$200	$170	$140	$125

For Waffenampt proofed (E/WaA76 on barrel and left frame), usually phosphate finished and either unnumbered or in B291,000-B293,000 Ser. range — add $1,000.
Changed to Model 39T after 1939.

VZ 38 "BULGARIAN CONTRACT" — .380 auto, 9 shot, single or double action, prominent safety on left frame. Usually in 420,000-423,000 range.

100%	98%	95%	90%	80%	70%	60%
$1,350	$1,100	$900	$750	$600	$500	$400

MODEL 1945 DOUBLE ACTION
AUTOMATIC — .25 auto, 8 shot, $2\frac{1}{2}$ in. barrel, fixed sights, blue, plastic grips. Double action only. Mfg. between 1945-1952.

100%	98%	95%	90%	80%	70%	60%
$200	$175	$165	$150	$140	$130	$120

NEW MODEL .006 DOUBLE ACTION AUTOMATIC — .32 auto, 8 shot, $3\frac{3}{8}$ in. barrel, fixed sight, blue, plastic grips, called VZ-50 in Czechoslovakia, used by National Police.

100%	98%	95%	90%	80%	70%	60%
$500	$425	$350	$300	$265	$230	$190

C Z, cont.

CZ HANDGUNS: RECENT MFG.

CZ-50/70 — .32 ACP cal., double action, blowback action, 3¾ in. barrel, loaded chamber indicator, 8 shot mag.

Mfg.'s Sug. Retail	$205	$165	$150	$135	$125	$115	$95	$85

This model is imported by Century International Arms, Inc. located in St. Albans, VT.

CZ-52 — 7.62 Tokarev, single action semi-auto, roller locking breech system, 4.9 in. barrel, 8 shot mag.

| Mfg.'s Sug. Retail | $180 | $150 | $135 | $125 | $115 | $95 | $85 | $75 |

This model is imported by Century International Arms, Inc. located in St. Albans, VT.

CZ-70 — 7.65mm, double action, similar to Walther PP, 8 shot mag., 1 lb. 9 oz. Disc.

| | | $400 | $350 | $300 | $275 | $250 | $225 | $200 |

A very limited quantity of this model was imported.

CZ-75 — 9mm Para., Poldi steel, selective double action, thumb safety, 4¾ in. barrel, 15 shot mag., currently available in black polymer (standard), matte blue, or high polish blue finish, black plastic grips, 35 oz.

| Mfg.'s Sug. Retail | $459 | $415 | $375 | $350 | $325 | $295 | $275 | $250 |

Add $20 for matte blue finish.
Add $36 for high polish blue finish.
Add 15% for earlier non-import marked specimens.
"First Model" variations, mostly imported by Pragotrade of Canada, are identifiable by short slide rails, no half-cock feature, and were mostly available in high polish blue only. These early pistols sell for $1,000 if N.I.B. condition; chrome engraved $1,500 (N.I.B.); factory competition $1,350 (N.I.B.)

CZ-75 Compact — similar to CZ-75, except has 3.9 in. barrel, 13 shot mag., checkered walnut grips, choice of black polymer, matte blue, or high polish blue finish, 32 oz. New 1993.

| Mfg.'s Sug. Retail | $495 | $435 | $385 | $360 | $330 | $300 | $275 | $250 |

Add $21 for matte blue finish.
Add $40 for high polish blue finish.

Model CZ-75 Special Editions — similar to CZ-75, except has optional special edition finishes including all matte nickel, bright nickel frame, matte chrome, all brushed chrome, bright chrome, or gold frame, choice of matching finish slide, master blue slide, gold appointments, or master blue slide with gold appointments. Importation began 1993.

| Mfg.'s Sug. Retail | $629 | $545 | $475 | $400 | $365 | $335 | $310 | $285 |

Add $100 for gold appointments (new 1993).
Add $150 for gold frame/blue slide variation (new 1993).
Add $150 for all gold edition (new 1993).

CZ-82 — 9 x 18mm Makarov, current Czech military sidearm, recent exportation to W. Germany in Makarov chambering.
This model is similar to the CZ-83 except for cal. Prices are similar to the model CZ-83.

CZ-83 — .32 ACP (importation disc. 1991) or .380 ACP (new 1986) cal., modern design, 3 dot sights, choice of carry modes, blue only with black synthetic grips, 13 shot mag. Mfg. began 1985, but U.S. importation started in 1992.

| Mfg.'s Sug. Retail | $369 | $325 | $280 | $240 | $210 | $185 | $165 | $150 |

Grading	100%	98%	95%	90%	80%	70%	60%

CZ-83 Special Editions — similar to CZ-83, has optional special edition finishes including all matte nickel, bright nickel frame, matte chrome, all brushed chrome, bright chrome, or gold frame, choice of matching finish slide, master blue slide, gold appointments, or master blue slide with gold appointments.

Mfg.'s Sug. Retail	$509	$450	$385	$335	$285	$250	$225	$200

Add $156 for gold appointments (new 1993).
Add $156 for gold frame/blue slide variation (new 1993).
Add $156 for all gold edition (new 1993).

CZ-85 — 9mm Para. or 9 x 21mm (new 1993) cal., variation of the CZ-75 with ambidextrous controls, new plastic grip design, sight rib, available in black polymer, matte blue, or high-gloss blue (9mm Para. only) finish, includes firing pin block and finger rest trigger, plastic grips.

Mfg.'s Sug. Retail	$490	$440	$385	$360	$330	$300	$275	$250

Add $16 for matte blue finish.
Add $43 for high polish blue.

CZ-85 Combat — similar to CZ-85, except has fully adj. sights, walnut grips, extended mag. release, and free dropping mag. Importation began 1992.

Mfg.'s Sug. Retail	$595	$525	$460	$395	$365	$335	$310	$285

Model CZ-85 Special Editions — similar to CZ-85, has optional special edition finishes including all matte nickel, bright nickel frame, matte chrome, all brushed chrome, bright chrome, or gold frame, choice of matching finish slide, master blue slide, gold appointments, or master blue slide with gold appointments. Importation began 1993.

Mfg.'s Sug. Retail	$675	$575	$485	$400	$365	$335	$310	$285

Add $104 for gold appointments (new 1993).
Add $104 for gold frame/blue slide variation (new 1993).
Add $104 for all gold edition (new 1993).

PAV — .22 LR, single shot, 9¾ in. barrel, all steel construction. Imported 1986 only.

	$95	$85	$75	$65	$60	$55	$50

Last Mfg.'s Sug. Retail was $105.

DRULOV 70 — .22 cal., single shot. Add $30 for set trigger. Disc. 1986.

	$105	$95	$85	$75	$70	$65	$60

Last Mfg.'s Sug. Retail was $115.

DRULOV 75 — .22 cal., single shot with set trigger & micrometer sights. Also available in left-hand. Importation disc. 1991.

	$300	$250	$215	$185	$155	$140	$120

Last Mfg.'s Sug. Retail was $349.

DRULOV 78 — .22 cal., similar to Drulov 75. Imported 1986 only.

	$275	$240	$200	$175	$150	$130	$110

Last Mfg.'s Sug. Retail was $180.

RIFLES: MILITARY

G 33-40 — 8mm, mfg. between 1940-42, most have been sporterized.

	$350	$295	$260	$230	$200	$175	$150

This model is Brno mfg., not CZ.

Grading	100%	98%	95%	90%	80%	70%	60%

CZ-M52 (1952) — 7.62x45mm Czech cal., semi-auto, 20⅔ in. barrel, 10 shot detachable mag., tagent rear sight, recently imported again by Samco Global Arms, Inc. located in Miami, FL, limited quantities.

	100%	98%	95%	90%	80%	70%	60%
	$350	$295	$260	$230	$200	$175	$150

CZ-M52/57 (1957) — 7.62 x 39mm, later variation of the CZ-M52.

	100%	98%	95%	90%	80%	70%	60%
	$250	$215	$185	$160	$140	$125	$110

CZ RIFLES: CURRENT MFG.

Note: modern commercial Czeskoslovenska rifles are located in the Brno section of this book.

CABANAS

Manufactured by Industrias Cabanas, S.A. in Aguilas, Mexico since 1949. Imported and retailed by Mandall Shooting Supplies, Inc. located in Scottsdale, AZ.

.22 BLANK POWERED RIFLE — shoots oversize .177 pellets/BBs powered by .22 blanks, 1,150 fps, single shot bolt action operation, iron sights, models vary in barrel lengths, stock configurations, etc. Transfer requires FFL.

⚔ Mini-82 Youth Pony

	100%	98%	95%	90%	80%	70%	60%
Mfg.'s Sug. Retail	$70	$70	$65	$55	$50	$45	$40	$35

⚔ R-83 Larger Youth

Mfg.'s Sug. Retail	$80	$80	$75	$65	$55	$45	$40	$35

⚔ Safari

		$100	$90	$80	$70	$60	$50	$40

Last Mfg.'s Sug. Retail was $100 (disc. 1990).

⚔ Varmint

Mfg.'s Sug. Retail	$120	$100	$90	$80	$70	$60	$50	$40

⚔ Espronceda IV

Mfg.'s Sug. Retail	$135	$120	$110	$100	$90	$80	$70	$60

⚔ Leyre

Mfg.'s Sug. Retail	$150	$150	$120	$110	$100	$90	$80	$70

⚔ Master — top-of-the-line model, 19⅔ in. barrel, adj. iron sights. Disc. 1990.

		$135	$120	$110	$100	$90	$80	$70

Blanks (6mm) and BBs (4.5mm) are available at $3.50 for 50 of each.
Last Mfg.'s Sug. Retail was $150.

⚔ Phaser — features thumb hole stock with Monte Carlo cheek piece and finger contoured pistol grip, automatic latch, barrel weight compensator. Importation began 1991.

Mfg.'s Sug. Retail	$160	$160	$125	$110	$100	$90	$80	$70

CABELA'S INC.

Sporting goods dealer located in Sidney, NB.

SHOTGUNS: SIDE BY SIDE

HEMINGWAY MODEL — mfg. for Cabela's by V. Bernardelli located in Italy, ST, ejectors.

Mfg.'s Sug. Retail	$975	$925	$775	$700	$640	$575	$525	$465

Grading	100%	98%	95%	90%	80%	70%	60%

AYA GRADE II CUSTOM — mfg. for Cabela's by AYA located in Eibar, Spain, ST, ejectors, similar to AYA Model II with Model 53 engraving and trim. Disc. and sold out.

	$1,295	$1,150	$895	$775	$700	$640	$575

CALICO

Manufacturer located in Bakersfield, CA. Distributor sales only.

Calico also makes select-fire machine gun pistols and carbines that are mfg. for military or law enforcement use only. These models do not appear in this publication.

A complete line of accessories is available for all Calico carbines and pistols.

CARBINES

M-100 — .22 LR, semi-auto carbine, paramilitary design with folding butt stock, 100 shot helical feed mag., alloy frame, ambidextrous safety, 16.1 shrouded barrel with flash suppressor/muzzle brake, 4.2 lbs. empty. New 1986.

Mfg.'s Sug. Retail	$347	$290	$240	$210	$190	$175	$160	$150

M-101 — while advertised, this model was never mfg.

M-105 SPORTER — similar to M-100, except has walnut distinctively styled butt stock and forend, 4¾ lbs. empty. New 1989.

Mfg.'s Sug. Retail	$377	$315	$250	$225	$200	$175	$160	$150

M-106 — while advertised, this model was never mfg.

M-900 — 9mm Para., retarded blowback action, paramilitary design with collapsible butt stock, cast aluminum receiver with stainless steel bolt, static cocking handle, 16 in. barrel, fixed rear sight with adj. post front, 50 (standard) or 100 shot helical feed mag., ambidextrous safety, black polymer pistol grip and forend, 3.7 lbs. empty. Mfg. 1989-1990, reintroduced 1992.

Mfg.'s Sug. Retail	$618	$560	$475	$350	$300	$285	$270	$255

M-900S — similar to M-900, except has non-collapsible shoulder stock.

Mfg.'s Sug. Retail	$632	$575	$485	$360	$300	$285	$270	$255

M-901 Canada Carbine — 9mm Para. cal., similar to M-900, except has 18½ in. barrel and sliding stock. Disc. 1992.

	$575	$475	$350	$300	$285	$270	$255

This model is also available with solid fixed stock (Model 901S).
Last Mfg.'s Sug. Retail was $643.

M-951 TACTICAL CARBINE — 9mm Para., 16.1 in. barrel, similar appearance to M-900 Carbine, except has muzzle brake and extra pistol grip on front of forearm, 4¾ lbs. New 1990.

Mfg.'s Sug. Retail	$662	$570	$460	$375	$325	$300	$285	$270

M-951S — similar to M-951, except has synthetic buttstock. New 1991.

Mfg.'s Sug. Retail	$675	$580	$465	$375	$325	$300	$285	$270

PISTOLS: SEMI-AUTO

M-110 — .22 LR, same action as M-100 Carbine, 6 in. barrel with muzzle brake, 100 round helical feed mag., includes notched rear sight and adj. windage front sight, 10½ in. sight radius, ambidextrous safety, pistol grip storage compartment, 2.21 lbs. empty. New 1989.

Mfg.'s Sug. Retail	$302	$255	$210	$185	$165	$150	$140	$130

Grading	100%	98%	95%	90%	80%	70%	60%

M-950 — 9mm Para., same operating mechanism as the M-900 Carbine, 6 in. barrel, 50 (standard) or 100 shot helical feed mag., 2¼ lbs. empty. New 1989.

Mfg.'s Sug. Retail $573	$495	$400	$350	$300	$285	$270	$255

Many accessories are also available for this model.

CAMEX-BLASER USA, INC.

Previous importer/distributor of Blaser Jagwaffen Gmbh rifles.

Previously imported Camex-Blaser rifles can be located in the Blaser section in this text.

CARTRIDGE FIREARMS

Unknown maker.

Many models of pistols, rifles, and shotguns — antique and modern. Many poor quality copies in addition to a few high quality, nicely engraved guns. Most of these firearms that are average quality, trade in the $100-$300 area. Engraved models can add as much as 150%. High mfg.

CASARTELLI, CARLO

Manufactured in Brescia, Italy. Imported and distributed by New England Arms Co. located in Kittery Point, ME.

Casartelli rifles and shotguns are available through special order only. Virtually any custom gun can be constructed to the customer's exact specifications and requirements. More information can be obtained by writing the above importer/distributor.

RIFLES

AFRICA MODEL — BOLT ACTION — various heavy and Mag. cals., action is square bridge type Mauser, full coverage game scene engraving appropriate to caliber, takedown, limited production.

Mfg.'s Sug. Retail $12,000	$12,000	$10,200	$7,500	$5,900	$5,300	$4,700	$4,100

SAFARI MODEL — BOLT ACTION — standard cals., regular Mauser action, full coverage game scene engraving, limited production.

Mfg.'s Sug. Retail $8,250	$8,250	$6,250	$5,900	$5,250	$4,950	$4,150	$3,650

KENYA — DOUBLE RIFLE — most standard and Mag. cals., sidelock action, elaborate game scene and/or scroll engraving, limited production.

Mfg.'s Sug. Retail $35,000	$35,000	$24,250	$21,500	$17,750	$14,750	$12,000	$9,950

SHOTGUNS

SIDELOCK MODEL — various ga.'s, elaborate game scene and/or scroll engraving, limited production.

Mfg.'s Sug. Retail $17,000	$17,000	$11,500	$9,200	$7,900	$6,500	$5,200	$4,250

CASPIAN ARMS, LTD.

Current manufacturer located in Hardwick, VT. Dealer direct sales only.

Caspian Arms currently fabricates both steel and alloy high quality, high capacity frames and related small parts for the Colt Government Model 1911-A1.

VIETNAM COMMEMORATIVE — .45 ACP, total production is 1,000, hand engraved by J.J. Adams, nickel plated, branch service medallion installed in grips. Mfg. began 1986, limited quantities remain.

Mfg.'s Sug. Retail $1,500	$1,450	$995	$795

Add $350 for gold plating. Add $200 for serial numbers below RVN100.
This Vietnam Commemorative is also available in 24Kt. gold hand inlay edition for $14,000 — very limited production.

CENTURY GUN DISTRIBUTING, INC.

Manufactured by Century Manufacturing, Inc. located in Greenfield, IN. Distributed by Century Gun Distributing Inc., located in Greenfield, IN. Consumer direct and/or dealer direct sales only.

This revolver-design was originally manufactured in 1972 by Russell Wilson, who sandcasted the bronze frame (cloned after the Colt SAA configuration) in Evansville, IN. Gene Phelps purchased the manufacturing rights for this gun and formed a partnership with Earl Keller to produce a redesigned frame, also using sandcast bronze.

The original Century revolver was made in Evansville, IN beginning in 1973 (1973 was the 100th anniversary of the .45-70 Gov.'t cartridge - hence the term Century) and production was halted in 1976 at ser. no. 524. In late 1976, Phelps and Keller (the 2 original partners on the venture) disolved their partnership and each began manufacturing their own version of the .45-70 revolver. Gene Phelps completely redesigned the gun's interior and began manufacturing the Heritage I, with an investment-cast steel frame, and without the Century's novel cross-bolt safety. Keller's Century Manufacturing, Inc. continued to produce the original Century, with some design refinements, and in 1985 the company was purchased by Dr. Paul Majors. The current Century revolver features a manganese bronze frame and other components in addition to having a cross-bolt safety. They are produced in .45-70 and various other cals., in Greenfield, IN. Earl Keller died in 1986. The second series is being made in Greenfield, IN with limited production resuming in 1986. Earlier handmade "Evansville" Model 100s (disc.) are currently selling for between $2,500-$3,500, depending on the region.

REVOLVERS

Less than 1,200 Model 100s have been manufactured since 1976. Values below are for .45-70 cal. Other calibers are priced from $1,500 on up.

Grading	100%	98%	95%	90%	80%	70%	60%

MODEL 100 — .30-30 (new 1987), .375 Win. (new 1986), .444 Marlin (new 1986), .45-70, .50-70 Gov't (new 1987), or .50-110 cal., single action 6 shot, manganese bronze frame, steel cylinder, 6½, 8, 10, or 12 in. round or octagon barrel, unique crossbolt safety that locks the hammer, adj. sights, walnut grips, 5 lbs. 14 oz.

	100%	98%	95%	90%	80%	70%	60%
Mfg.'s Sug. Retail $1,250	$1,100	$875	$775	$675	$595	$550	$495

Add $750 for .50-70 cal.
Add $110 for normal octagon barrel.
Add $150 for stainless steel fabrication.

CENTURY INTERNATIONAL ARMS, INC.

Importer and distributor located in St. Albans, VT.

Century Arms imports a variety of used military rifles and pistols, including various Mauser rifle contract models, French Lebels and MAS models, Mannlichers, F.N. Model 49s, Lee Enfields, Hakims, Moisin-Nagants, Egyptian Rashids, Swedish Ljungman Model 46Bs, Chinese SKS-56s, arsenal refinished M-1 carbines/Garands and various WWI and WWII used military pistols (including Mauser Broomhandles, Argentine mfg. M1911s, and French PA 35s). Because most of these items range in the $95-$200 price range, individual listings are not listed in this text. Most of these models are in good to like new condition overall. In addition, surplus and currently manufactured ammunition is available at very competitive prices. Generally, these models offer good values to the shooter and a few are collectible.

PISTOLS

HI-POWER — 9mm Para. cal., copy of the FN Browning Hi-Power, mfg. in Argentina by Fabrica Militar under license from FN, matte finish, 13 shot mag., 4.6 in barrel, 32 oz. Importation began 1991.

No Mfg.'s Retail	$330	$275	$240	$210	$185	$160	$145

FP9 — 9mm Para. cal., patterned after the FN Browning Hi-Power, with 5 in. VR barrel, mfg. in Hungary, fixed sights, 14 shot mag., 2 lbs. 3 oz.

No Mfg.'s Retail	$285	$225	$195	$175	$160	$150	$140

Grading	100%	98%	95%	90%	80%	70%	60%

PA63 — 9mm Makarov cal., patterned after the Walther PP, aluminum frame, European mfg., 3.8 in. barrel, thumbrest grips, hammer block safety, 7 shot mag., 22 oz.

No Mfg.'s Retail	$160	$140	$125	$115	$100	$90	$85

HUNGARIAN T-58 — 7.62 Tokarev or 9mm Para. cal., improved Tokarev pistol, is supplied with both 7.62 and 9mm barrels and mags., wraparound grips, thumb safety, 4½ in. barrel, 8 shot mag., 31 oz.

No Mfg.'s Retail	$195	$160	$145	$130	$115	$100	$90

P9R — 9mm Para. cal., patterned after the FN Browning Hi-Power, except is double action and has slide mounted safety/decocking lever, all steel, 4⅔ in. barrel, 15 shot mag., 2 lbs. 3 oz.

No Mfg.'s Retail	$275	$220	$195	$175	$160	$150	$140

B9R — .380 ACP cal., mfg. by FEG, double action, 4 in. barrel, walnut grips, hammer drop safety, 15 shot mag., 1 lb. 9 oz.

No Mfg.'s Retail	$325	$270	$235	$205	$185	$160	$145

AP9 — .380 ACP cal., patterned after the Walther PP, developed by Hungary, alloy construction, 3.94 in. barrel, double action, thumbrest grips, 7 shot mag., 1.31 lbs.

No Mfg.'s Retail	$175	$145	$130	$115	$100	$90	$85

R-61 — .380 ACP cal., patterned after the Walther PPK with aluminum alloy frame, 6 shot mag., mfg. in Hungary.

No Mfg.'s Retail	$175	$145	$130	$115	$100	$90	$85

RIFLES

CBC MODEL N66 — .22 LR, semi-auto design patterned after the Remington Nylon 66, 14 shot tube mag., 19½ in. barrel. Imported 1989-91.

	$95	$80	$70	$60	$55	$50	$45

NORINCO JW-8 — .22 LR, bolt action, 5 shot mag., 23 in. barrel, sling swivels. Imported 1989-91.

	$95	$80	$70	$60	$55	$50	$45

JW-27 — .22 LR, updated JW-8, importation began 1991.

No Mfg.'s Retail	$145	$110	$75	$65	$60	$55	$50

CENTURION P14 SPORTER — .300 Win. Mag., .303 British (disc.), or 7mm Rem. Mag. cal., P-14 action with sporterized stock and 24 in. barrel, checkered beechwood stock, tapped and drilled for scope mounts. New 1987.

No Mfg.'s Retail	$275	$240	$220	$190	$170	$150	$125

Beginning 1993, this model features a new fiberglass stock with steel recoil lug and recoil pad.

CENTURION 98 SPORTER — .270 Win., .30-06, or .308 Win. cal., mfg. from military Mauser 98 actions, turned down bolt handles, black Rynite stock with integral blind mag., 22 in. barrel, 7 lbs. 6 oz.

No Mfg.'s Retail	$300	$250	$220	$190	$170	$150	$125

MAS 36 SPORTER — 7.5mm, MAS 36 action with shorter barrel, military stock has been sporterized, reblued metal, positive safety. Importation disc.

	$135	$115	$95	$85	$80	$75	$70

Grading	100%	98%	95%	90%	80%	70%	60%

SWEDISH CONTRACT M38 — 6.5 X 55mm, Swedish Mauser M38 with new Monte Carlo stock, 24 in. barrel, 5 shot fixed mag.

No Mfg.'s Retail	$195	$150	$135	$125	$115	$105	$95

FAL SPORTER RIFLE — .308 Win. cal., sporter version of the FAL rifle, features new black synthetic or camo thumbhole stock and new semi-auto receiver, flash hider and bayonet lug removed, 20¾ in. barrel, refurbished in matte finish, 10 lbs. 2 oz.

No Mfg.'s Retail	$650	$525	$475	$425	$375	$325	$295

ARGENTINE 1909 SPORTER — 7.65mm or .30-06 cal., sporterized version of Argentine 1909 carbine, 22¼ in. barrel, checkered beechwood European sporter stock, original military sights, 5 shot mag. Importation began 1991.

No Mfg.'s Retail	$215	$180	$150	$135	$120	$110	$100

BRAZILIAN MODEL 08/34 SPORTER — .30-06, Brazilian Mauser refinished with new barrel and European Monte Carlo stock, 23 in. drilled and tapped barrel, refinished condition. Importation began 1991.

No Mfg.'s Retail	$225	$190	$160	$140	$125	$110	$100

ENFIELD SPORTER NO. 4 MARK II — .303 British, new checkered stock with Monte Carlo cheek piece, 25.2 in. barrel, 10 shot detach. mag.

No. Mfg.'s Retail	$210	$175	$140	$125	$115	$105	$95

TOZ-17-1 — .22 LR cal., modified TO3-17 action, checkered pistol grip stock, rear tangent adj. sight, grooved receiver, 21 in. barrel, 5 shot detachable mag., 5.3 lbs.

No Mfg.'s Retail	$110	$90	$70	$60	$50	$40	$35

JUNGLE SPORTER NO. 5 — .303 British, 20.5 in.barrel with flash eliminator, new checkered Monte Carlo stock and forearm, detach. mag. Importation disc.

	$190	$150	$135	$125	$115	$105	$95

MAS .223 — .223 cal., civilian version of the FAMAS 5.56mm paramilitary design rifle, made by Giat in France, switchable ejection port, rubber covered cheek piece, bullpup configuration, protected sights, with bipod, 20 shot mag. Less than 25 imported 1986-89.

	$2,750	$2,250	$1,850	$1,600	$1,400	$1,200	$1,000

This model has been banned from domestic importation due to 1989 Federal legislation.

MAK 90 — 7.62 x 39mm cal., AKS variation, mfg. by Norinco, thumbhole stock has recoil pad, 16½ in. barrel, two 5-shot mag.'s.

No Mfg.'s Retail	$375	$325	$275	$250	$225	$200	$180

M-1 GARAND — .30-06, 24 in. barrel, arsenal repaired stocks, good to very good condition. Importation disc.

	$350	$275	$250	$235	$215	$200	$190

M-14 SPORTER — .308 Win., sporterized M-14 with modified stock, 22 in. barrel, flash suppressor and bayonet lug have been removed, 8¼ lbs. Importation began late 1991.

No Mfg.'s Retail	$495	$450	$375	$325	$280	$240	$200

SHOTGUNS: O/U

CENTURION — 12 ga. only, boxlock action, 26 or 28 in. VR barrels, DTs, extractors, blued receiver with Century logo.

No Mfg.'s Retail	$365	$295	$240	$220	$190	$170	$150

CHAMPLIN FIREARMS, INC.

Custom manufacturer/gunsmith located in Enid, OK. Champlin Firearms was established In 1966. Direct sales only.

Champlin Firearms, Inc. manufactures handcrafted rifles built around a patented bolt action of their own design and manufacture. Most guns are built per individual customer order and specifications. Values will vary greatly depending on the configuration, desirability, and special order specifications. All Champlin rifles are built along classic lines with best quality wood and exemplary workmanship. They have been used successfully on safaris and have shot dangerous game throughout the world.

Champlin Firearms, Inc. also inventories a wide selection of high grade, top quality shotguns and rifles (especially top trademark doubles and bolt actions). Contact George Caswell (owner) directly for a current listing. Additional services include a complete gunsmithing service for all grades of English double rifles and shotguns. Custom stocks are also built to individual customer specifications. All double rifles are test fired and checked thoroughly upon completion of manufacture or repair. Again, Champlin Firearms should be contacted for consultation and quotation regarding this additional work.

Grading		100%	98%	95%	90%	80%	70%	60%

BOLT ACTION RIFLE — standard, all calibers, round or octagon barrel, adj. trigger, each rifle is built to customer specifications. Values below represent base gun with standard wood, no options, and no engraving.

Mfg.'s Sug. Retail	$8,500		$8,500	$8,000	$7,000	$6,750	$6,000	$5,250	$4,500

Many additional special order options are available on this model and Champlin Firearms should be contacted directly for price quotations.

CHAPUIS ARMES

Manufacturer located in St. Bonnet Le Chateau, France. Currently, Chapuis Armes has no importer, but guns are available direct by contacting the factory (see Trademark Index for current information). Imported until 1993 by Armes De Chasse located in Chadds Ford, PA. Factory direct.

Chapuis rifles and shotguns are manufactured on a limited basis. Most of their emphasis is on high quality double rifles and shotguns. For further information regarding this respected French trademark, please contact the importer listed above. The below listed models are imported exclusively by Armes de Chasse.

RIFLES/COMBINATION GUNS

RGEX EXPRESS MODEL SXS DOUBLE RIFLE — .30-06, .300 Win. Mag., 7 X 65R, 8 X 57JRS, 8 X 75RS, or 9.3 X 74R cal., double rifle, ejectors, boxlock action, 23.6 in. barrels, deluxe checkered walnut stock with cheek piece, full line of options are available, 7 lbs. 6 oz. Importation began 1989.

Mfg.'s Sug. Retail	$5,938		$5,938	$5,300	$4,750	$4,150	$3,650	$2,995	$2,450

Add approx. $700 for .300 Win. Mag. cal.
Subtract approx. $300 for 8 x 75RS cal.
Add approx. 60% for HGEX Express Supreme Model (engraved, not avail. in .300 Win. Mag. cal.).
Add 110% for HGEX Express Imperial Model (scroll engraved, not avail. in .300 Win. Mag. cal.).
Above values assume metric or .30-06 cal.

EXPRESS AGEX BROUSSE SxS DOUBLE RIFLE — same cals. as AGEX Savanna, notched boxlock action with English scroll engraving, selective ejectors, deluxe walnut.

Mfg.'s Sug. Retail	$8,438		$8,438	$7,850	$7,000	$6,200	$5,400	$4,200	$3,500

Add $2,812 for .470 NE cal.
Add $5,062 for .416 R Chapuis cal.

Grading	100%	98%	95%	90%	80%	70%	60%

EXPRESS AGEX SAVANNA SxS DOUBLE RIFLE—.375 H&H, .416 R Chapuis, or .470 NE cal. only, deluxe version of the Agex Jungle, except has hand engraved leaves on action sides and Cape Buffalo head on floorplate of action.

Mfg.'s Sug. Retail $10,125	$10,125	$9,100	$8,250	$6,850	$5,500	$4,600	$3,850

Add $2,919 for .470 NE cal.
Add $3,375 for .416 R Chapuis cal.

EXPRESS AGEX JUNGLE SxS DOUBLE RIFLE — .375 H&H, .416 R Chapuis (new 1993), or .470 NE (new 1992) cal., boxlock action, special reinforced receiver with double underbites, $25\frac{5}{8}$ in. barrels, fine English scroll engraving, ejectors, select French walnut with compartment in pistol grip cap.

Mfg.'s Sug. Retail $15,962	$15,962	$12,750	$10,750	$8,750	$6,750	$5,600	$4,775

Add $2,810 for .470 NE cal.
Add $5,062 for .416 R Chapuis cal.

EXPRESS AGEX AFRICA SxS DOUBLE RIFLE — same cals. as AGEX Jungle, notched boxlock action, master signed scroll engraving and African game scenes, selective ejectors, cased.

Mfg.'s Sug. Retail $20,954	$20,954	$17,750	$15,250	$13,500	$11,250	$10,000	$9,000

Add $2,896 for .470 NE cal.
Add $5,626 for .416 R Chapuis cal.

EXPRESS AGEX SAFARI SxS DOUBLE RIFLE — similar to AGEX Africa, except has top-of-the-line engraving and wood.

Mfg.'s Sug. Retail $30,375	$30,375	$26,550	$22,350	$19,150	$16,950	$14,000	$12,000

Add $2,040 for .470 NE cal.
Add $5,134 for .416 R Chapuis cal.

RIFLES: SINGLE SHOT

OURAL EXEL — .270 Win., .300 Win. Mag., 7mm Rem. Mag. cal., notched boxlock action, English scroll engraving, extractors, $23\frac{5}{8}$ in. barrel, fitted and engraved scope mounts.

Mfg.'s Sug. Retail $5,204	$5,204	$4,625	$4,150	$3,650	$2,995	$2,450	$1,950

Add $281 for .300 Win. Mag. cal.
Add $854 for 7mm Rem. Mag. cal.
Add approx. 41% for Oural Luxe Model (features better engraving and wood).
Add approx. 84% for Oural Elite Model (features game scene engraving and presentation walnut).

SHOTGUNS

Chapuis Armes is also capable of manufacturing high quality SxS and O/U shotguns. The manufacturer should be contacted directly for a price quotation regarding these configurations.

CHAPUIS, P. ARMES ET FILS
Manufacturer located in Saint-Bonnet le Chateau, France.

Paul Chapuis specializes in custom order rifles and shotguns. Currently, this manufacturer has no U.S. importer and should be contacted directly (see Trademark Index) for more model information and current pricing. This is a different company than Chapuis Armes.

CHARLIN ARMS
Previously manufactured in France.

Charlin Arms previously made shotguns which were patterned after Darne firearms. Typically, they are very high quality and values seem to approximate the Darne guns. Once you have determined the comparable model in Darne, please refer to the Darne section in this book.

CHARLES DALY
See Daly, Charles.

CHARTER ARMS
Manufactured by Charco, Inc. located in Stratford, CT beginning 1992. Previously manufactured by Charter Arms located in Stratford, CT. Distributor sales only.

REVOLVERS: DOUBLE ACTION

All Charter Arms revolvers have a hammer block safety system, 8 groove rifling, unbreakable beryllium copper firing pin, triple safety features, no sideplate, steel frames, and lifetime warranty to the original owner.

Grading	100%	98%	95%	90%	80%	70%	60%
BONNIE & CLYDE SET — .32 H&R Mag. (Bonnie) and .38 Spl. (Clyde), matched pair, 6 shot, 2½ in. fully shrouded barrel, wood laminate grips (color coordinated), blued finish, pistols individually marked Bonnie or Clyde on barrels, supplied with gun rugs. Mfg. 1989-91.	$425	$365	$335	$295	$260	$240	$220
PATHFINDER — .22 LR or .22 Mag. (disc. 1989), 6 shot, 2, 3, or 6 (disc. 1985) in. barrels, round butt, adj. sights, walnut grips, wide trigger and spur hammer. Disc. 1990.	$185	$150	$125	$110	$90	$70	$50
⚞ **Pathfinder — Square Butt** — .22 LR or 22 Mag. (disc. 1989), 6 in. barrel, square butt, otherwise similar to Pathfinder. Disc. 1990.	$190	$155	$125	$110	$90	$70	$50
⚞ **Pathfinder Stainless** — stainless variation, .22 LR or .22 Mag. (disc. 1989), 3½ in. shrouded barrel. Disc. 1990.	$185	$150	$130				
UNDERCOVER — .32 S&W (disc. 1989) or .38 Spl. cal., 5 shot in .38 Spl., 6 shot in .32 S&W, 2 (.38 Spl.) or 3 in. barrel, wide trigger and spur hammer, fixed sights, .38 Spl. can also be ordered with pocket hammer. Disc. 1991.	$175	$145	$115	$100	$90	$85	$80
⚞ **Undercover Stainless** — 2 in. shrouded barrel only. **Mfg.'s Sug. Retail** $304	$260	$195	$140				
UNDERCOVERETTE — similar to Undercover, in .32 S&W long, 6 shot, 2 in. barrel, blue. Disc.	$155	$140	$110	$100	$90	$70	$55
BULLDOG — .44 Spl., 5 shot, 2½ or 3 (disc. 1988) in. barrels, wide trigger and spur or pocket hammer, checkered bulldog grips (walnut or neoprene). Disc. 1991.	$190	$155	$125	$110	$90	$70	$50
⚞ **Bulldog Stainless** — 2½ in. bull or 3 (disc. 1989) in. regular barrel. Disc. 1991.	$195	$155	$125				
⚞ **Target Bulldog** — .357 Mag. or .44 Spl. cal., 5 shot, 4 in. shrouded barrel, adj. sights, square butt only, blued finish. Mfg. 1986-1988.	$225	$150	$125	$110	$100	$90	$80

Subtract $10 for .357 Mag. cal.
Last Mfg.'s Sug. Retail was $255.

Grading	100%	98%	95%	90%	80%	70%	60%

Target Bulldog Stainless — 9mm Federal, .357 Mag. or .44 Spl. cal., 5 shot, 5½ in. shrouded VR barrel, adj. sights, square butt target grips only, matte finished, 28 oz. Mfg. 1989-91.

		$250	$175	$125			

BULLDOG PUG — .44 Spl., 5 shot, 2½ in. shrouded barrel, fixed sights, walnut or neoprene grips. New 1986.

Mfg.'s Sug. Retail	$279	$240	$195	$160	$130	$110	$100	$90

Bulldog Pug Stainless — 2½ in. shrouded barrel. New 1987.

Mfg.'s Sug. Retail	$334	$300	$235	$175			

BULLDOG TRACKER — .357 Mag. (.38 Spl.), 5 shot, 2½, 4 (disc. 1989), and 6 (disc. 1989) in. bull barrels, adj. sights, blue only, checkered bulldog grips, square butt on 4 or 6 in. barrel only. Disc. 1986, - reintroduced 1989-91.

	$185	$150	$125	$110	$100	$90	$80

POLICE BULLDOG — .32 H&R Mag., .38 Spl. or .44 Spl. cal., 5 (.44 Spl. only) or 6 shot, fixed sights, blue only, 3½ or 4 in. barrel, Neoprene grips or square butt (.44 Spl. only). Disc. 1991.

	$175	$140	$120	$105	$95	$85	$75

Add $20 for either .44 Spl. cal or 3½ in. shrouded barrel.

Stainless Police Bulldog — .32 Mag., .357 Mag. (new 1989), .38 Spl. (disc. 1988 - reintroduced 1990) or .44 Spl. (new 1989), 5 (.357 Mag. or .44 Spl.) or 6 (.32 Mag. or .38 Spl.) shot, square butt, 3½ or 4 in. shrouded barrel. Mfg. 1987-91.

	$195	$160	$150	$140			

Add $20 for .357 Mag. or .44 Special cal.
Neoprene grips are standard on these models except for the .357 Mag. (square butt).

POLICE UNDERCOVER — .32 H&R Mag. or .38 Spl. cal., 6 shot, spur or pocket hammer, 2 in. shrouded barrel, checkered walnut grips, fixed sights, blue only.

Mfg.'s Sug. Retail	$250	$215	$175	$145	$120	$100	$85	$75

Stainless Police Undercover — similar to Police Undercover.

Mfg.'s Sug. Retail	$276	$240	$185	$150			

OFF DUTY — .22 LR (new 1990) or .38 Spl. cal., 5 (.38 Spl.) or 6 (.22 LR) shot, 2 in. barrel, fixed sights, blue only, matte black finish.

Mfg.'s Sug. Retail	$209	$180	$150	$120	$105	$90	$85	$80

Stainless Off Duty — similar to Off Duty.

Mfg.'s Sug. Retail	$268	$235	$180	$145			

PIT BULL — 9mm Federal, .357 Mag. (disc. 1989), or .38 Spl. (disc. 1989) cal., 5 shot, 2½, 3½, or 4 (disc. 1989) in. full shrouded barrel, Neoprene grips, approx. 26 oz. Mfg. 1989-91.

	$230	$180	$150	$125	$115	$100	$90

Stainless Pit Bull — 2½ or 3½ in. shrouded barrel. Disc. 1991.

	$240	$190	$155				

PISTOLS: SEMI-AUTO

MODEL 40 — .22 LR only, double action semi-auto., 3.3 in. barrel, 8 shot mag., 21½ oz., fixed sights, stainless steel. Mfg. 1984-86.

	$265	$240	$220				

Last Mfg.'s Sug. Retail was $319.

Grading	100%	98%	95%	90%	80%	70%	60%

MODEL 79K — .32 or .380 ACP cal., double action semi-auto., 3.6 in. barrel, 7 shot mag., 24½ oz., fixed sights, stainless steel. Mfg. 1984-86.

	100%	98%	95%				
	$325	$300	$280				

Last Mfg.'s Sug. Retail was $390.

EXPLORER II & S II PISTOL — .22 LR, semi-auto survival pistol, barrel unscrews, 8 shot mag., black, gold (disc.), silvertone, or camouflage finish, 6, 8, or 10 in. barrels, simulated walnut grips. Disc. 1986.

	100%	98%	95%	90%	80%	70%	60%
	$90	$80	$70	$60	$55	$50	$45

Last Mfg.'s Sug. Retail was $109.
This model uses a modified AR-7 action.
Manufacture of this model is by Survival Arms located in Cocoa, FL.

TARGET PISTOLS

MODEL 42T (COMPETITION II TARGET) — .22 LR only, single action, 5.9 in. barrel, target model with checkered walnut grips, adj. sights, blue finish only. Mfg. 1984-1985 only.

	100%	98%	95%	90%	80%	70%	60%
	$490	$450	$395	$350	$300	$260	$220

Last Mfg.'s Sug. Retail was $599.

RIFLES

AR-7 EXPLORER RIFLE — .22 LR cal., takedown, barreled action stores in Cycolac sythetic stock, 8 shot mag., adj. sights, 16 in. barrel, black finish on AR-7, silvertone on AR-7S. Camouflage finish new 1986 (AR-7C). Mfg. until 1990.

	100%	98%	95%	90%	80%	70%	60%
	$125	$100	$85	$75	$65	$55	$50

In 1990, the manufacturing of this model was taken over by Survival Arms located in Cocoa, FL. Current mfg. AR-7 rifles will be found under the Survival Arms heading in the "S" section.
Last Mfg.'s Sug. Retail was $146.

CHINESE FIREARMS

Most Chinese firearms for U.S. export are currently being manufactured by two companies: Poly Technologies, Inc. and Norinco. Poly Technologies, Inc. is currently being imported by Keng's Firearms Specialty located in Riverdale, GA and is distributed by Ptk International, Inc. in Atlanta, GA. Norinco is imported and distributed by China Sports, Inc. located in Dallas, TX. Please refer to the Poly Technologies, Inc. and Norinco sections in this text to find out more about these firearms. In addition to these two trademarks, other Chinese models have been manufactured under various subcontracts with the Chinese Arsenals. These guns (typically AKS copies) are generally unmarked and quality can vary greatly.

CHIPMUNK MANUFACTURING INC.

Currently manufactured by Oregon Arms Co. located in Medford, OR since 1988. Previously manufactured by Chipmunk Manufacturing located in Medford, OR until 1988.

CHIPMUNK SINGLE SHOT RIFLE — .22 LR or .22 Mag. (disc. 1987) cal., manually cocked single shot, 16⅛ in. barrel, iron sights (adj. aperture rear), 30 in. overall length, 2½ lbs.

Mfg.'s Sug. Retail	$150	$125	$110	$90	$80	$70	$60	$50

⚡ **Deluxe Rifle** — similar to standard rifle, except has deluxe hand checkered walnut stock. New 1987.

Mfg.'s Sug. Retail	$200	$165	$145	$125	$105	$85	$75	$65

Grading	100%	98%	95%	90%	80%	70%	60%

SILHOUETTE PISTOL — .22 LR, bolt action design with $14\frac{7}{8}$ in. barrel, iron sights, rear grip walnut stock. Mfg. 1984-88.

	100%	98%	95%	90%	80%	70%	60%
	$135	$115	$95	$80	$70	$60	$50

Last Mfg.'s Sug. Retail was $150.

CHURCHILL, E.J., (GUNMAKERS) LTD.

Previously manufactured in London, England. The company underwent various trading forms until Churchill, Atkin, Grant & Lang Ltd. closed in 1981. Currently, E.J. Churchill side by side shotguns are manufactured in Surrey, England and while they are not imported into the U.S., these models are shown with U.S. prices if purchased in England. Prices are subject to fluctuating U.S. dollar.

Churchill Guns are among the world's finest with many custom features. We will list both discontinued and current models and approximate values, but strongly urge competent appraisal if purchase or sale is contemplated.

Prices could differ from values shown below because of the fluctuating U.S. dollar.

SHOTGUNS AND RIFLES

All below models were built or finished to customer specifications pertaining to choking, chambers, barrel lengths, stock measurements, weight, engraving patterns. Standardized patterns did exist, however, for each model. The "XXV" designation referred to the 25 in. barrel length which was a Churchill specialty and was also a registered trademark.

PREMIER QUALITY SXS — all ga.'s, best quality, easy opening or standard opening, 25, 28, 30, or 32 in. barrels, any choke, sidelock, auto ejectors, standard with double triggers, engraved, checkered, straight or pistol grip stock. Also mfg. in some double rifles. Disc.

	100%	98%	95%	90%	80%	70%	60%
	$17,000	$15,000	$12,000	$10,000	$9,000	$7,500	$6,500

20 ga. — add 20%.
28 ga. — add 40%.
SST — add $1,000.
16 ga. — deduct 10%.
Double rifle — add 35%.

Premier Grade — 12 ga. only, sidelock, assisted opening, limited current mfg.

	Mfg.'s Sug. Retail	$18,750	98%	95%	90%	80%	70%	60%
			$16,000	$14,000	$12,000	$10,000	$9,000	$7,500	$6,500

IMPERIAL SXS — all ga.'s, most barrel lengths, second quality sidelock model, ejectors, mostly standard opening, a few made as easy opening. Also mfg. in some double rifles. Disc.

	$13,500	$11,500	$9,500	$7,500	$6,500	$5,250	$4,000

20 ga. — add 20%.
28 ga. — add 40%.
SST — add $1,000.
16 ga. — deduct 10%.
Double rifle — add 35%.

Imperial Grade — 12 or 20 ga., second quality sidelock model, ejectors, standard opening, limited current mfg.

Mfg.'s Sug. Retail $14,250

	$12,000	$9,950	$7,700	$6,600	$5,600	$4,500	$3,500

FIELD MODEL — 12 ga. only, most barrel lengths, third quality sidelock model. Disc.

	$9,000	$8,000	$7,000	$6,000	$5,000	$4,500	$3,500

20 ga. — add 20%.
28 ga. — add 40%.
SST — add $1,000.
16 ga. — deduct 10%.

Grading	100%	98%	95%	90%	80%	70%	60%

HERCULES MODEL — all ga.'s, 25-30 in. barrels, best quality boxlock model, ejectors, easy opening or standard opening. Also made in some double rifles in .22 Hornet and similar cals.

	$9,000	$8,000	$7,000	$6,000	$5,000	$4,500	$3,500

20 ga. — add 20%.
28 ga. — add 40%.
SST — add $1,000.
16 ga. — deduct 10%.
Double rifle — add 35%.

UTILITY MODEL — mostly 12 ga., 25-30 in. barrels, second quality boxlock model, ejectors, checkered straight or pistol grip stock. Disc.

	$6,250	$4,500	$3,500	$3,000	$2,500	$2,000	$1,800

20 ga. — add 20%.
28 ga. — add 40%.
.410. — add 60%.
SST — add $500.
16 ga. — deduct 10%.

CROWN MODEL — 12, 16, 20, or .410 (rare) ga., third quality boxlock model, various barrel lengths. Disc.

	$4,500	$3,500	$3,000	$2,500	$2,000	$1,600	$1,200

20 ga. — add 20%.
28 ga. — add 40%.
.410 — add 60%.
SST — add $500.
16 ga. — deduct 10%.

REGAL — 12, 16, 20, 28, or .410 ga., second quality boxlock model introduced after WWII, released after Utility Model was disc. Premium for 28 or .410 ga.

	$6,000	$4,300	$3,750	$3,100	$2,500	$2,000	$1,800

20 ga. — add 20%.
28 ga. — add 40%.
.410 ga. — add 60%.
SST — add $500.
16 ga. — deduct 10%.

Regal Grade — 12, 20, 28, or .410 ga., best quality boxlock model, ejectors, standard opening, limited current production.

Mfg.'s Sug. Retail	$5,625	$4,800	$4,000	$3,500	$3,000	$2,500	$2,000	$1,800

PREMIER QUALITY O/U — 12, 16, 20, or 28 ga., same barrel and bore as Premier Double, engraved, sidelock, auto ejectors, checkered pistol grip or straight stock. Disc.

	$17,000	$15,000	$12,000	$10,000	$9,000	$7,500	$6,500

20 ga. — add 20%.
28 ga. — add 40%.
SST — add $1,000.
Vent. rib — add $500.
16 ga. — deduct 10%.

RIFLES

"ONE OF ONE THOUSAND RIFLE" — Mauser type bolt action, .270, 7mm Rem. Mag., .308, .30-06, .300 Win. Mag., .375 H&H Mag., or .458 Win. Mag. cal., 5 shot standard, 3 shot mag. Magnum, 24 in. barrel, classic French walnut stock, swivel recoil pad with trap, trap pistol grip cap. Mfg. 1973 for Interarms 20th Anniversary, limited, 100 mfg.

	$1,400	$1,250	$1,000	$900	$750	$700	$600

Churchill

CHURCHILL

Ellett Brothers located in Chapin, SC imported and distributed Churchill shotguns until 1993. There will be no current manufacture for this trademark for 1993-94. Previously imported (until 1988) by Kassnar Imports, Inc. located in Harrisburg, PA. Not affiliated with E.J. Churchill Gunmakers, Ltd.

In late 1988, the Churchill trademark was sold to Ellett Brothers located in Chapin, SC.

RIFLES

Grading	100%	98%	95%	90%	80%	70%	60%

HIGHLANDER — .25-06 Rem., .243 Win., .270 Win., .308 Win., .30-06, 7mm Rem. Mag., or .300 Win. Mag. cal., bolt action, 22 in. barrel, thumb safety, no sights, 3 or 4 shot mag., checkered walnut stock, 7½ lbs. Importation disc. 1991.

	100%	98%	95%	90%	80%	70%	60%
	$395	$350	$330	$300	$270	$240	$215

Add $30 for iron sights (disc).
Last Mfg.'s Sug. Retail was $460.

REGENT — same cals. as Highlander, deluxe checkered walnut with Monte Carlo comb and cheek piece. Last imported by Kassner in 1988.

	100%	98%	95%	90%	80%	70%	60%
	$555	$455	$385	$340	$300	$280	$260

Add $30 for iron sights.
Last Mfg.'s Sug. Retail was $610.

ROTARY 22 — .22 LR, beginners rifle, bolt hold-open device, adj. rear sight, 10 shot rotary mag. Imported 1989 only.

	100%	98%	95%	90%	80%	70%	60%
	$120	$105	$95	$85	$75	$65	$55

Last Mfg.'s Sug. Retail was $130.

SHOTGUNS: SIDE BY SIDE

WINDSOR I — 10 (disc. 1988), 12, 16, 20, 28, or .410 ga., double barrel, 23-32 in. barrels, Anson and Deeley boxlock, antique silver finish receiver with fine scroll engraving, extractors, double triggers, checkered pistol grip and forend. Importation disc. 1991.

	100%	98%	95%	90%	80%	70%	60%
	$550	$465	$450	$385	$300	$250	$230

Add $150 for 10 ga.
Add $55 for 28 or .410 ga.
Add $30 for Flyweight Models (25 in. barrels - disc. 1988).
Last Mfg.'s Sug. Retail was $653.

WINDSOR II — 12 or 20 ga., double barrel, 26-30 in. barrels, Anson and Deeley boxlock, antique silver finish receiver with fine scroll engraving, ejectors, double triggers, checkered pistol grip and forend. Add $100 for 10 ga. (disc.). Importation disc. 1987.

	100%	98%	95%	90%	80%	70%	60%
	$595	$485	$415	$350	$315	$270	$240

Last Mfg.'s Sug. Retail was $638.

WINDSOR VI — 12 or 20 (disc.) ga., double barrel, 25 or 28 in. barrels, sidelock, antique silver finish receiver with fine scroll engraving, ejectors, double triggers, checkered pistol grip and forend. Disc. 1987.

	100%	98%	95%	90%	80%	70%	60%
	$840	$700	$600	$550	$510	$460	$420

Last Mfg.'s Sug. Retail was $900.

ROYAL — available in 10, 12, 20, 28, or .410 ga., DTs, extractors, checkered walnut stock and forearm, case hardened receiver. Imported late 1988-1991.

	100%	98%	95%	90%	80%	70%	60%
	$485	$405	$370	$310	$275	$250	$230

Add $20 for 28 ga.
Add $74 for .410 ga.
Last Mfg.'s Sug. Retail was $540.

Grading	100%	98%	95%	90%	80%	70%	60%

SHOTGUNS: OVER/UNDER

MONARCH — 12, 20, 28 (disc.), or .410 (disc.) ga., 25 (disc.), 26, or 28 in. vent. rib barrels, SST, extractors, boxlock action, DT, silver finish receiver with fine scroll engraving, checkered European walnut stock and forearm, 6½-7½ lbs.

	$460	$370	$340	$300	$250	$230	$210

Add $67 for .410 ga. with 26 in. barrels (disc.).
Deduct $40 without SST.
Last Mfg.'s Sug. Retail was $520.

Monarch Turkey Gun — 12 ga. only, 24 in. barrels with matte finish. Imported 1990-1991 only.

	$460	$370	$340	$300	$250	$230	$210

Last Mfg.'s Sug. Retail was $529.

SPORTING CLAYS MODEL — 12 ga. only, designed for sporting clays competition with 28 in. VR ported barrels with choke tubes, ejectors, raised target style VR, checkered high gloss finish stock and forearm, 7 lbs. 6 oz. Imported 1992 only.

	$800	$725	$650	$575	$500	$450	$395

Last Mfg.'s Sug. Retail was $900.

WINDSOR III — 12, 20, or .410 ga. (disc.), double barrel, 27 or 30 in. barrels, double bottom lock, antique silver finish receiver with fine scroll engraving, extractors, SST, vent. rib, checkered pistol grip and forend. Importation disc. 1991.

	$550	$495	$450	$380	$340	$300	$280

Add $140 for Flyweight Model or choke tubes (disc.).
Add $75 for .410 ga.
Last Mfg.'s Sug. Retail was $625.

NEW WINDSOR IV — 12 or 20 ga., 3 in. chambers, boxlock action, silver receiver with full scroll engraving, 26 or 28 in. (12 ga. only) VR barrels with choke tubes, ejectors, SST, checkered walnut pistol grip stock with black rubber vent. recoil pad, finger grooved forearm, gloss finish, gold trigger, 5 year warranty. Mfg. 1992 only.

	$625	$525	$450	$375	$325	$295	$275

Last Mfg.'s Sug. Retail was $690.

WINDSOR IV - DISC. — 12, 20, 28, or .410 ga., double barrel, 26-30 in. barrels, double bottom lock, antique silver finish receiver with fine scroll engraving, ejectors, SST, vent. rib, checkered pistol grip and forend. Interchangeable chokes became standard in 1989. Importation disc. 1991.

	$725	$640	$530	$470	$430	$395	$360

Deduct $52 for 28 or .410 ga.   Deduct $100 if without choke tubes.
Last Mfg.'s Sug. Retail was $852.

REGENT V — 12 or 20 ga., double barrel, 27 in. barrels, double bottom lock, antique silver finish receiver with extra fine scroll engraving, ejectors, single trigger, vent. rib, checkered pistol grip and forend. Interchangeable choke tubes standard. Disc. 1986, reintroduced 1990. Limited quantities still available.

	$895	$795	$700	$620	$560	$510	$470

This model was previously designated Regent VII until 1989 when it changed to the Regent V.
Last Mfg.'s Sug. Retail was $1,100.

REGENT TRAP AND SKEET — 12 or 20 ga., double barrel, 26 or 30 in. barrels, double bottom lock, antique silver finish receiver with sideplates engraved in fine scroll, ejectors, SST, vent. rib, checkered pistol grip and forend. Importation disc. 1991.

	$795	$650	$575	$540	$485	$440	$390

Add $40 for trap variation.
Last Mfg.'s Sug. Retail was $963.

Grading	100%	98%	95%	90%	80%	70%	60%

REGENT GRADE SHOTGUN/RIFLE COMBINATION — 12 ga. over either .222 Rem., .223, .243 Win. (disc.), .270 Win., .30-06, or .308 Win. cal., double barrel, 25 in. barrels, double bottom lock, antique silver finish receiver with extra fine scroll engraving, ejectors, single trigger, vent. rib, checkered pistol grip and forend. Importation disc. 1991.

	$800	$700	$635	$560	$510	$475	$440

Last Mfg.'s Sug. Retail was $927.

SHOTGUNS: SEMI-AUTO

STANDARD MODEL — 12 ga. only, gas operated and shoots different loads interchangeably without alterations, 24, 26, 28 in. VR barrel, magazine cut-off, hand checkered walnut with satin finish, matte metal finish, includes ICT choke tubes. New 1990.

	$495	$415	$375	$310	$275	$250	$230

Last Mfg.'s Sug. Retail was $550.

✴ **Turkey Model** — similar to Standard Model, except has 24 in. barrel only. New 1990.

	$510	$425	$380	$315	$275	$250	$230

Last Mfg.'s Sug. Retail was $570.

WINDSOR GRADE — 12 ga. only, 26, 28, or 30 in. barrels, gas operation, anodized alloy receiver, vent. rib, checkered pistol grip and forend, 7½ lbs. Deluxe model includes polished receiver with etching.

	$380	$320	$300	$275	$250	$225	$200

Add $35 for choke tubes.
Add $55 for Deluxe model.
Last Mfg.'s Sug. Retail was $420.

REGENT GRADE — 12 ga. only, 26, 28, or 30 in. barrels, gas operation, anodized alloy receiver, vent. rib, checkered pistol grip and forend, 7½ lbs. Deluxe model includes polished receiver with etching. Disc. 1986.

	$440	$365	$340	$320	$300	$285	$270

Add $35 for choke tubes.
Add $55 for Deluxe model.
Last Mfg.'s Sug. Retail was $495.

SHOTGUNS: SLIDE ACTION

WINDSOR GRADE — 12 ga. only, 26, 27, 28, or 30 in. barrels, double slides, anodized alloy receiver, vent. rib, checkered pistol grip and forend, 7½ lbs. Disc. 1986.

	$385	$330	$310	$275	$250	$225	$200

Last Mfg.'s Sug. Retail was $430.

CIMARRON F.A. MFG. CO.

Importer/distributor/retailer located in Houston, TX. Currently importing Aldo Uberti Modern and Black Powder Firearms. Black Powder reproductions can be located in the Black Powder section under Cimarron Arms in the back of this text. Previously named Old-West Guns Co. Dealer direct sales only.

REVOLVERS & CARBINES: SINGLE ACTION REPRODUCTIONS

The Cimarron Arms reproduction of the 1873 Colt Peacemaker is available in two configurations listed below. These pistols are extremely accurate reproductions of the original Colt pre-war Peacemaker and are marked (and machined) the same as the originals including serial numbers on frames, backstrap, trigger guard, and cylinder. Barrels are radiused and cylinders are beveled. Frames are color case hardened, stocks are walnut - choice of 4¾, 5½, or 7½ in. barrel. All Cimarron SAAs are barrel marked "- CIMARRON F.A. MFG. Co. HOUSTON, TX. U.S.A. -".

Grading	100%	98%	95%	90%	80%	70%	60%

The "Old Model" configuration has the older style black powder frame, screw in cylinder pin retainer, and circular "bullseye" ejector head.

The Standard Model includes the post-1890 style frame with spring loaded cross-pin cylinder retainer and "half-moon" ejector head.

Only the Old Model is available in the authentic old style "charcoal blue" finish (sometimes referred to as fire-bluing).

Add $350 for "A" style engraving (30% coverage) on SAAs listed below.
Add $425 for "B" style engraving (50% coverage) on SAAs listed below.
Add $750 for "C" style engraving (100% coverage) on SAAs listed below.
Add $800 for "Texas Cattlebrands" engraving pattern.

CIMARRON SAA & VARIATIONS — available in .22 LR, .22 Mag, .357 Mag., .38 Spl., .44-40, or .45 LC cal., 4¾, 5½, and 7½ in. barrel lengths, steel backstraps and trigger guard.

Standard or Old Model

Mfg.'s Sug. Retail	$430		$370	$285	$250	$220	$195	$175	$160

Sheriff's Model — .44-40 or .45 LC cal., 3 or 4 (disc. 1992) in. barrel, steel backstraps and trigger guard.

Mfg.'s Sug. Retail	$430		$370	$285	$250	$220	$195	$175	$160

Target Model — similar to Standard Model, except has fully adj. target rear sight, brass or steel backstrap. Importation disc. 1991.

	$355	$280	$255	$220	$195	$175	$160

Add $40 for .357 Mag. cal.
This variation is available in the Standard Model configuration only and with standard finish.
Last Mfg.'s Sug. Retail was $400.

BUNTLINE MODEL — .357 Mag., .44-40, or .45 LC cal., 18 in. barrel, brass or steel backstrap cut for shoulder stock. Disc. 1989.

	$355	$280	$255	$220	$195	$175	$160

Add $10 for target sights.
Last Mfg.'s Sug. Retail was $400.

BUNTLINE CARBINE — similar cals. to Buntline Model, except also includes .22 LR/.22 Mag. (convertible cylinders), 18 in. barrel, includes non-detachable shoulder stock with brass hardware and finger extension trigger guard. Importation disc. 1991.

	$380	$295	$260	$225	$195	$175	$160

Add $20 for target sights.
Add $20 for .22 LR/.22 Mag. combo.
Last Mfg.'s Sug. Retail was $440.

BUCKHORN — .44 Spl. or .44 Mag., reinforced variation of the Cimarron SAA designed for more powerful cartridges, 4¾, 6 or 7½ in. barrel, brass or steel backstap.

Mfg.'s Sug. Retail	$400		$355	$285	$260	$220	$195	$175	$160

Buckhorn Convertible Model — includes .44 Mag./.44-40 cylinders, 4¾, 6 or 7½ in. barrel. Disc. 1989.

	$375	$295	$265	$220	$195	$175	$160

Add $12 for target sights.
Last Mfg.'s Sug. Retail was $427.

Buckhorn Target Model — .44 Spl. or .44 Mag. cal., 4¾, 6 or 7½ in. barrel, adj. rear sight. Importation disc. 1991.

	$370	$290	$265	$225	$195	$175	$160

Last Mfg.'s Sug. Retail was $420.

Grading	100%	98%	95%	90%	80%	70%	60%

Buckhorn Buntline — .44-40, .44 Spl., or .44 Mag. cal., 18 in. barrel, fixed or target sights. Disc. 1989.

	$370	$285	$265	$220	$195	$175	$160

Add $30 for target sights.
Last Mfg.'s Sug. Retail was $419.

Buckhorn Carbine — .44-40, .44 Spl., or .44 Mag. cal., 18 in. barrel, includes non-detachable shoulder stock with brass hardware and lanyard ring. Disc. 1990.

	$375	$290	$265	$220	$195	$175	$160

Add $30 for target sights.
Last Mfg.'s Sug. Retail was $429.

SPECIAL EDITION SAA'S

U.S. 7TH CAVALRY CUSTER MODEL — authentic reproduction of original Colt military cavalry contract, 7½ in. barrel, marked U.S. on lower left frame, one piece walnut grips with military cartouche.

Mfg.'s Sug. Retail	$459	$400	$330	$300	$280	$260	$240	$220

U.S. ARTILLERY MODEL — Renaldo A. Carr 1895 U.S. Artillery Model Commemorative, limited mfg.

Mfg.'s Sug. Retail	$459	$400	$330	$300	$280	$260	$240	$220

7TH CAVALRY CASED SET — U.S. Cavalry Model in case with accessories. Disc. 1990.

	$695	$625	$550	$500	$460	$420	$385

Last Mfg.'s Sug. Retail was $780.

JUDGE ROY BEAN COMMEMORATIVE — mfg. to commemorate Judge Roy Bean's Texas cattlebrand.

Mfg.'s Sug. Retail	$1,695	$1,500	$1,175	$995	$875	$750	$625	$550

REMINGTON REPRODUCTIONS

These guns are reproductions of the Models 1875 and 1890.
Add $90 for nickel plating, $10 for charcoal blue finish on models listed below.

MODEL 1875 — available in .357 Mag., .44-40, or .45 LC cal., 7½ barrel.

Mfg.'s Sug. Retail	$390	$340	$250	$200	$170	$155	$140	$120

Model 1875 Carbine — same cals. as Model 1875, 18 in. barrel, includes non-detachable shoulder stock with brass hardware and lanyard ring. Importation disc. 1990.

	$410	$340	$300	$265	$230	$200	$180

Last Mfg.'s Sug. Retail was $460.

MODEL 1890 — .357 Mag., .44-40, or .45 LC cal., 5½ or 7½ in. barrel.

Mfg.'s Sug. Retail	$390	$340	$250	$210	$175	$160	$145	$125

1871 ROLLING BLOCK TARGET PISTOL — .22 LR, .22 Hornet (new 1990), .22 Mag., or .357 Mag. cal., 9½ in. barrel. Importation disc. 1990.

	$250	$200	$180	$160	$140	$125	$110

Last Mfg.'s Sug. Retail was $280.

1871 Rolling Block Baby Carbine — same cals. as Target Pistol, has 22 in. barrel and walnut stock and forearm, brass trigger guard and butt plate. Importation disc. 1990.

	$310	$245	$205	$170	$155	$140	$120

Last Mfg.'s Sug. Retail was $340.

Cimarron F. A. Mfg. Co., cont.

Grading	100%	98%	95%	90%	80%	70%	60%

ROLLING BLOCK SPORTING RIFLE — .45-70 cal., 30 in. barrel, walnut stock and forearm. Imported 1989-1990 only.

| | $565 | $430 | $395 | $350 | $320 | $300 | $275 |

Last Mfg.'s Sug. Retail was $620.

⚰ **Deluxe Rolling Block Sporting Rifle** — similar to standard model, except has select wood. Importation disc. 1990.

| | $640 | $485 | $450 | $375 | $340 | $320 | $295 |

Last Mfg.'s Sug. Retail was $720.

RIFLES: WINCHESTER REPRODUCTIONS

Add $25 for Charcoal Blue finish for below listed models.

HENRY RIFLE/CARBINE — .44-40, .44 Spl. (new 1993), or .45 LC (new 1993) cal., brass frame, 24 in. barrel on rifle, 22 (.44-40 cal. only) in. barrel on carbine.

| Mfg.'s Sug. Retail | $875 | $740 | $600 | $465 | $415 | $360 | $325 | $295 |

Can also be special ordered with Grade A engraving ($425 extra), Grade B engraving ($550 extra), and Grade C engraving ($725 extra).

CIVIL WAR HENRY RIFLE — .44-40 cal., 24 in. barrel, exact copy of the U.S. issue original inspected by Chas. G. Chapman (C.G.C.) with military inspector's marks and cartouche. Importation began 1993.

| Mfg.'s Sug. Retail | $899 | $775 | $635 | $500 | $425 | $360 | $325 | $295 |

Add $25 for military sling swivels.

1866 SPORTING RIFLE — .22 LR, .22 Mag., .44-40, or .45 LC (new 1993) cal., brass receiver, 24 in. octagon barrel.

| Mfg.'s Sug. Retail | $725 | $600 | $500 | $400 | $340 | $275 | $240 | $200 |

Add $425 (retail) for A engraving, $595 for B engraving, $940 for C engraving.

1866 YELLOWBOY CARBINE — includes .38 Spl. cal., otherwise similar to Model 1866 Sporting Rifle, features 19 in. round barrel with 2 bands, saddle ring, uncheckered walnut stock and forearm.

| Mfg.'s Sug. Retail | $725 | $600 | $500 | $400 | $340 | $275 | $240 | $200 |

⚰ **1866 Trapper Carbine** — .44-40 cal., 16 in. round barrel. Importation disc. 1990.

| | $465 | $385 | $340 | $320 | $275 | $240 | $200 |

Last Mfg.'s Sug. Retail was $538.

⚰ **1866 Yellowboy Indian Carbine** — .22 LR, .22 Mag., .38 Spl., or .44-40 cal., 19 in. round barrel. Disc. 1989.

| | $575 | $475 | $400 | $350 | $300 | $260 | $220 |

This model has a photo engraved brass frame and has brass tacks in stock and forearm. Last Mfg.'s Sug. Retail was $649.

⚰ **Red Cloud Commemorative Carbine** — same cals. as Yellowboy Indian Carbine, includes special engraving representing Oglalla Indian tribe symbols, brass tacks in forearm and stock. Disc. 1989.

| | $575 | $475 | $400 | $350 | $300 | $260 | $220 |

Last Mfg.'s Sug. Retail was $649.

1873 SPORTING RIFLE — .22 LR, .22 Mag., .357 Mag., .44-40, or .45 LC cal., 24 in. octagon barrel, case hardened reciever, full mag., iron sights.

| Mfg.'s Sug. Retail | $875 | $740 | $600 | $500 | $425 | $360 | $325 | $295 |

Add $425 (retail) for A engraving, $595 for B engraving, $940 for C engraving, or $1,300 for "1 of 1000" engraving.

Grading	100%	98%	95%	90%	80%	70%	60%
1873 Short Rifle — .44-40 or .45 LC cal., features 20 in. octagon barrel, case hardened receiver, iron sights. New 1990.							
Mfg.'s Sug. Retail $875	$740	$600	$500	$425	$360	$325	$295
1873 Long Range Rifle — .44-40 or .45 LC cal., includes 30 in. octagon barrel with full mag., case hardened receiver, iron sights. New 1990.							
Mfg.'s Sug. Retail $899	$760	$615	$515	$425	$395	$370	$345
1873 Saddle Ring Carbine — .22 LR, .22 Mag., .357 Mag., .44-40, or .45 LC cal., blued steel receiver, saddle ring, 19 in. round barrel.							
Mfg.'s Sug. Retail $875	$740	$600	$500	$425	$360	$325	$295
Add $90 for nickel plating (disc.).							
1873 Trapper Carbine — .357 Mag. (new 1990), .44-40, or .45 LC (new 1990) cal., 16 in. barrel, blue finish only. Importation disc, 1990.							
	$575	$475	$400	$350	$300	$260	$220

Last Mfg.'s Sug. Retail was $650.

CLARIDGE HI-TEC INC.

Manufacturer located in Northridge, CA since 1990. Distributor sales only except for law enforcement.

In 1990, Claridge Hi-Tec, Inc. was created - this new company took over Goncz Armament, Inc. Warranties from Goncz Armament, Inc. are not transferable to Claridge Hi-Tec, Inc.

All Claridge Hi-Tec firearms utilize match barrels mfg. in-house that are button-rifled. The Claridge action is an original design and does not copy other actions. All guns feature a lifetime repair policy. Claridge Hi-Tec models can be altered (Law Enforcement Companion Series) to accept Beretta 92F or Sig Model 226 magazines.

PISTOLS & CARBINES

Add $40 for polished stainless steel frame construction.

L-9 PISTOL — 9mm Para., .40 S&W, or .45 ACP cal., semi-auto paramilitary design, $7\frac{1}{2}$ (new 1992) or $9\frac{1}{2}$ (disc. 1991) in. shrouded barrel, aluminum receiver, choice of black matte, matte silver, or polished silver finish, one piece grip, safety locks firing pin in place, 10 (disc.), 17, or 30 shot double row mag., adj. sights, $3\frac{3}{4}$ lbs. New 1991.

Mfg.'s Sug. Retail $598	$525	$375	$300	$265	$225	$200	$175

A trigger activated laser sighting scope is available in Models M, L, C, and T - add $395 for new mfg.

S-9 PISTOL — similar to L-9, except has 5 in. non-shrouded threaded barrel, 3 lbs. 9 oz.

Mfg.'s Sug. Retail $535	$475	$350	$280	$250	$225	$200	$175

T-9 PISTOL — similar to L-9, except has $9\frac{1}{2}$ in. barrel. New 1992.

Mfg.'s Sug. Retail $598	$525	$375	$300	$265	$225	$200	$175

M PISTOL — similar to L Model, except has $7\frac{1}{2}$ in. barrel, 3 lbs. Disc. 1991.

	$500	$375	$300	$265	$225	$200	$175

Last Mfg.'s Sug. Retail was $720.

C-9 CARBINE — same cals. as L and S Model pistols, 16.1 in. shrouded barrel, choice of composite or uncheckered walnut stock and forearm, 5 lbs. 12 oz. New in 1991.

Mfg.'s Sug. Retail $675	$595	$525	$450	$395	$350	$300	$275

Add $74 for black graphite composite stock.
Add $474 for integral laser model (with graphite stock).
This model is available with either gloss walnut, dull walnut, or black graphite composite stock.

Grading	100%	98%	95%	90%	80%	70%	60%

LAW ENFORCEMENT COMPANION (LEC) — 9mm, .40 S&W, or .45 ACP cal., 16¼ button rifled barrel, black graphite composition buttstock and foregrip, buttstock also provides space for an extra mag., available in either aluminum or stainless steel frame, matte black finish, available with full integral laser sighting system. New 1992.

Mfg.'s Sug. Retail	$749	$650	$575	$495	$425	$375	$325	$295

Add $400 for integral laser sighting system.

CLARK CUSTOM GUNS, INC.

Clark Custom Guns, Inc. has been customizing various configurations of both handguns and rifles since 1950. It would be impossible to list within the confines of this text the many conversions this company has performed. It is recommended to contact this company (see Trademark Index) to learn more about their current model line-up and prices.

CLASSIC DOUBLES

Previously manufactured in Tochigi City, Japan. Previously imported and distributed by Classic Doubles International, Inc. located in St. Louis, MO. The factory closed in 1987, and all Classic Doubles remaining in inventory were sold to GU Wholesalers located in Omaha, NE in 1990. While a few models are still available through GU Wholesalers (call for availability), all values listed below reflect discontinuance of mfg. to date, there has been little collectibility in the Classic Doubles trademark. As a result, values are determined by the shooting value each model has to offer against other competing models in the same configuration. Also, in some regions of the country, 98% condition or less specimens may be priced lower than values shown in this section.

In late 1987, Winchester/Olin discontinued importation of their Japanese shotgun models (Models 101 and 23). At that point, Classic Doubles International, Inc. became the sole importer of these shotguns. There have been very few changes made during this changeover of importation. However, the new Classic Double shotguns (Models 101 and 201) do not have the Winchester trademark or definitive Winchester proofmark stamped on the barrels. The Model 201 is a new model designation.

SHOTGUNS: O/U - MODEL 101

All newly imported Classic Doubles have an interchangeable choke tube system compatable with the older Winchester manufatctured models. Prices listed include a luggage style carrying case.

CLASSIC FIELD GRADE I — 12 or 20 ga., 3 in. chambers, vent. rib, 25½ or 28 in. vent. barrels with choke tubes, blued receiver with moderate scroll engraving, ejectors, checkered pistol grip or English stock and forearm, 6¼ - 7 lbs.

$1,400	$1,250	$1,100	$1,000	$900	$825	$750

Last Mfg.'s Sug. Retail was $1,905.

WATERFOWL MODEL — 12 ga. only, 3 in. chambers, 30 in. barrels with vent. rib and choke tubes, matte blued receiver with moderate engraving, low gloss walnut stock with vent. recoil pad, 7 ¾ lbs.

$1,150	$995	$895	$800	$700	$600	$500

Last Mfg.'s Sug. Retail was $1,520.

CLASSIC SPORTER — 12 ga. only, made for Sporting Clays competition, 28 or 30 in. vent. barrels and rib with choke tubes, quick detachable stock system, border engraved coin finished receiver with non-reflective matte surface on top frame and lever, checkered walnut stock and forearm, 7¾ lbs.

$1,500	$1,295	$1,150	$1,000	$900	$825	$750

Add $965 for extra barrel.
Last Mfg.'s Sug. Retail was $1,980.

Grading	100%	98%	95%	90%	80%	70%	60%

CLASSIC FIELD GRADE II — 12, 20, 28 or .410 ga., 28 in. VR barrels with choke tubes, deluxe walnut with round knob pistol grip stock and forearm with fine fleur-de-lis checkering, coin finished receiver (different sizes) with game scene engraving featuring hunting motifs on receiver sides and bottom, .410 ga. bored M/F only, 6¼ - 7lbs.

	$1,675	$1,425	$1,245	$1,100	$1,000	$900	$795

The .410 and 28 ga.'s are more desirable in this model.
Last Mfg.'s Sug. Retail was $2,190.

CLASSIC FIELD GRADE II TWO BARREL SET — 12 and 20 ga. barrels, both with Winchokes, 26 in. barrels - 20 ga., 28 in. barrels - 12 ga., coin finished receiver with game scene engraving and borders, 6½ (20 ga.) or 7 (12 ga.) lbs.

	$2,500	$2,100	$1,825	$1,550	$1,375	$1,200	$1,075

Last Mfg.'s Sug. Retail was $3,420.

TARGET GUNS

CLASSIC TRAP SINGLE — 12 ga. only, over single 32 or 34 in. VR barrel with choke tubes, blued receiver with light engraving, choice of Monte Carlo or regular stock, recoil pad, 8½ lbs.

	$1,425	$1,250	$1,100	$1,000	$900	$825	$750

Last Mfg.'s Sug. Retail was $2,070.

CLASSIC TRAP O/U — 12 ga. only, 30 or 32 in. vent. barrels and rib with choke tubes, finish and engraving similar to Classic Trap Single, choice of Monte Carlo or standard stock with recoil pad, 8¾ or 9 lbs.

	$1,300	$1,125	$1,000	$900	$825	$750	$675

Last Mfg.'s Sug. Retail was $1,905.

CLASSIC TRAP COMBO — includes one set of O/U barrels (30 or 32 in.) and one over single barrel (32 or 34 in.), choke tubes, choice of Monte Carlo or standard stock, 8¾ or 9 lbs.

	$2,125	$1,875	$1,600	$1,475	$1,300	$1,175	$995

Last Mfg.'s Sug. Retail was $2,825.

CLASSIC SKEET — 12 or 20 ga., 27½ in. vent. barrels and rib, choke tubes on 12 ga. only, smaller ga.'s are bored SK/SK, similar metal finish to Classic Trap models, 7¼ or 7¾ lbs.

	$1,450	$1,275	$1,125	$1,000	$900	$825	$750

Last Mfg.'s Sug. Retail was $1,905.

Classic Skeet 4 ga. Set — similar to Classic Skeet except has 4 barrels (12, 20, 28, or .410 ga.), 12 ga. has choke tubes, smaller ga.'s are bored SK/SK.

	$3,900	$3,500	$3,100	$2,875	$2,600	$2,300	$1,995

Last Mfg.'s Sug. Retail was $4,765.

SHOTGUNS: SIDE BY SIDE

MODEL 201 CLASSIC — 12 or 20 ga., 3 in. chambers, forged steel monobloc with improved lug design, 26 in. choke tube barrels with vent. rib, high lustre bluing, no engraving, SST, ejectors, premium walnut stock and beavertail forearm with fancy checkering pattern, solid red rubber recoil pad, 6¾ - 7 lbs.

	$1,400	$1,200	$995	$775	$650	$575	$495

Add $120 for 20 ga.
The 12 ga. could be ordered with choke tubes at no extra charge. Only 63 were mfg. with choke tubes and slight premiums are being asked.
Last Mfg.'s Sug. Retail was $2,190.

Grading	100%	98%	95%	90%	80%	70%	60%

Model 201 Classic Small Bore Set — 28 and .410 ga. two barrel set, similar to Model 201 Classic except has smaller frame and overall dimensions, 28 in. VR barrels only bored IC/M on 28 ga. and M/F on .410 ga., 6 or 6½ lbs

$2,650	$2,250	$1,900	$1,700	$1,550	$1,350	$1,150

Last Mfg.'s Sug. Retail was $3,675.

CLERKE PRODUCTS
Santa Monica, CA.

DOUBLE ACTION REVOLVER — .22 RF or .32 S&W Long cal., inexpensive double action revolvers that sold to dealers for $15 in 1971.

HI-WALL — single shot rifle, falling block replica of Winchester 1885 High Wall, lever operated, case hardened receiver, 26 in. barrel, available in most modern calibers, no sights, checkered walnut pistol grip stock, Schnabel forearm. Mfg. 1972-1974.

$250	$225	$185	$175	$150	$140	$125

DELUXE HI-WALL — similar to Hi-Wall, except half octagon barrel, select wood and recoil pad.

$300	$275	$235	$210	$180	$160	$145

CLIFTON ARMS
Manufacturer and retailer of Custom Rifles located in Grand Prairie, TX. Clifton Arms mostly specializes in composite stocks (with or without integral, retractable bipod). Manufacturer direct sales only.

Clifton Arms mostly manufactures composite, hand laminated stocks that are patterned after the Dakota 76 stock configuration. However, custom rifles can be ordered by contacting the company and specifying the type of action, caliber, barrel and stock configuration and/or color. Price quotations vary per individual, special order rifle.

RIFLES: BOLT ACTION

CLIFTON SCOUT RIFLE — .243 Win., .30-06, .308, .350 Rem. Mag. (Super Scout), 7mm-08 Rem., .35 Whelen, or .416 Rem. cal., choice of BRNO 602, regular Sako, or Ruger 77 MK II (standard) stainless action with bolt face altered to controlled round feeding, Shilen stainless premium match grade barrel, Clifton synthetic stock with bipod, many other special orders are available, mfg. began 1992.

Mfg.'s Sug. Retail	$2,600		$2,600	$2,100	$1,500		

COBRAY INDUSTRIES
See listing under S.W.D. in the S section of this text.

COGSWELL & HARRISON, LIMITED
Previous manufacture located in London, England, 1770-approx. WWII.

SHOTGUNS

REGENCY — 12, 16, or 20 ga., double barrel, 26, 28, or 30 in. barrels, any choke combination, hammerless Anson & Deeley system, boxlock, double triggers, auto ejectors, straight English stock.

$2,750	$2,500	$2,250	$2,000	$1,800	$1,600	$1,375

Last Mfg.'s Sug. Retail was $3,200.

Grading	100%	98%	95%	90%	80%	70%	60%

AMBASSADOR MODEL — double barrel, same gauges and barrels as Regency, boxlock with false sideplates, auto ejectors, double triggers, engraved game scene or scroll rose motif, English stock.

	100%	98%	95%	90%	80%	70%	60%
	$3,650	$3,100	$2,850	$2,700	$2,500	$2,250	$1,995

Last Mfg.'s Sug. Retail was $4,000.

MARKOR — 12, 16, or 20 ga., double barrel, 27½ or 30 in. barrel and choke, boxlock, double trigger, English stock. Disc.

	100%	98%	95%	90%	80%	70%	60%
	$1,500	$1,350	$1,200	$1,000	$950	$825	$700
Auto ejectors	$1,750	$1,500	$1,350	$1,200	$1,100	$900	$700

HUNTIC MODEL — 12, 16, or 20 ga., double barrel, 25, 27, or 30 in. barrels, any choke, sidelock, auto ejectors, English style stock. Disc.

	100%	98%	95%	90%	80%	70%	60%
	$3,500	$3,200	$3,000	$2,800	$2,500	$2,175	$1,850

SST — add $400.

AVANT TOUT SERIES — 12, 16, or 20 ga., double barrel, 25, 27½, or 30 in. barrels, boxlock, false sideplates, straight English stock, auto ejectors, series disc.

	100%	98%	95%	90%	80%	70%	60%
	$2,250	$1,925	$1,700	$1,495	$1,350	$1,200	$1,075

REX OR AVANT TOUT III — no sideplates.

	100%	98%	95%	90%	80%	70%	60%
	$1,800	$1,650	$1,500	$1,350	$1,200	$1,075	$895

SANDHURST OR AVANT TOUT II

	100%	98%	95%	90%	80%	70%	60%
	$2,500	$2,300	$2,150	$2,000	$1,750	$1,500	$1,225

KONOR OR AVANT TOUT I

	100%	98%	95%	90%	80%	70%	60%
	$2,850	$2,700	$2,500	$2,250	$2,000	$1,775	$1,500

SST — add $400.
20 ga. — add 20%.
16 ga. — deduct 10%.

BEST QUALITY — 12, 16, or 20 ga.'s, double barrel, 25, 26, 28, or 30 in. barrels, any choke, hand detachable sidelock, auto ejectors, double triggers standard, English stock.

⇄ **Primic Model** — disc.

	100%	98%	95%	90%	80%	70%	60%
	$5,750	$4,650	$4,150	$3,650	$3,050	$2,500	$1,950

⇄ **Victor Model**

		100%	98%	95%	90%	80%	70%	60%
Mfg.'s Sug. Retail	$10,000	$8,600	$6,250	$5,000	$4,350	$3,740	$3,000	$2,375

SST — add $400.
20 ga. — add 20%.
16 ga. — deduct 10%.
Note: Degree of engraving and grade of wood are the basic differences among models.

COLT'S MANUFACTURING COMPANY, INC.
Manufacturer located in Hartford, CT.

Manufactured from 1836-1841 in Paterson, NJ; 1847 to 1848 in Whitneyville, CT; 1854 to 1864 in London, England; and from 1848 to date in Hartford, CT. Colt Firearms became a division of Colt Industries in 1964. In March, 1990, the Colt Firearms Division was sold to C.F. Holding Corp. located in Hartford, CT. The new company is called Colt's Manufacturing Company, Inc. Colt's plans to close the original Hartford plant in 1993, moving operations to the W. Hartford plant.

PERCUSSION REVOLVERS

Prices shown for percussion Colt's are for guns only. Original cased guns with accessories will bring a healthy premium over non-cased models (200-350% over a gun only is common). Be very careful when buying an "original" cased gun, as many fake cases have shown up in recent years.

100%	98%	95%	90%	80%	70%	60%	50%	40%	30%	20%	10%

Prices shown on the following pages for extremely rare Colt's firearms might not include values in the 90%, 95%, 98%, and 100% condition columns. Prices are very hard to establish since these excellent to mint specimens are seldomly seen or sold.

POCKET MODEL PATERSON NO. 1 — also known as "Baby Paterson", .28 cal., 5 shot, 2½ in. to 4¾ in. octagon barrels, blued metal, varnished walnut grips. Serial range 1 to approx. 500. Standard bbl. marking "Patent Arms M'g Co. Paterson N.J.-Colt's Pt.". Centaur scene with four horse head trademark and "COLT" on 1¹⁄₁₆ in. cylinder of round or square type. Mfg. 1837-1838.

This and all other Paterson models have 5 shot cylinders and serial numbers are not commonly in evidence externally. Disassembly of the arm is usually necessary to determine the serial number.

The Pocket Model Paterson No. 1 (Baby Paterson) is the first production made handgun in its Paterson, N.J. facility. It is very small in size, almost appearing as a toy or miniature.

Standard Production Model — without attached loading lever.

100%	98%	95%	90%	80%	70%	60%	50%	40%	30%	20%	10%
N/A	N/A	$27,500	$23,000	$20,000	$17,500	$15,000	$13,250	$11,750	$10,250	$9,000	$8,000

Late Production Ehlers Model — with attached loading lever, 3¹⁄₃₂ round back cylinder and recoil shield milled for ease of capping. Barrel marked "Patent Arms Paterson N.J.-Colt's Pt.". Approx. 500 mfg. including the Ehlers Model under Belt Model No. 2 Mfg. 1840-1843.

100%	98%	95%	90%	80%	70%	60%	50%	40%	30%	20%	10%
N/A	N/A	$31,000	$25,500	$21,500	$18,000	$15,500	$13,750	$12,250	$10,750	$9,500	$8,500

BELT MODEL PATERSON NO. 2 — .31 or .34 cal., 5 shot, 2½ in. to 5½ in. octagon barrels, blued metal, varnished walnut grips. Serial range 1- approx. 850 which includes the Belt Model No. 3. All standard production Belt Models No. 2 have straight bottom style grips. Standard bbl. markings "Patent Arms M'g Co. Paterson N-J. Colt's Pt.". Centaur scene with four horse head trademark and "COLT" on cylinder of round or square backed type. Mfg 1837-1840. Somewhat heavier than the Pocket No. 1 revolver.

Standard Production Model — without attached loading lever.

100%	98%	95%	90%	80%	70%	60%	50%	40%	30%	20%	10%
N/A	N/A	$28,000	$23,750	$20,500	$18,000	$15,750	$13,750	$12,250	$11,000	$9,500	$8,500

Ehlers Model — with attached loading lever, 1¹⁄₁₆ in. round back cylinder, recoil shield milled for ease of capping. Barrel marked "Patent Arms Paterson N-J. Colt's Pt.". Approx. 500 mfg. including the Ehlers Model under Pocket Model No. 1. Mfg. 1840-1843.

100%	98%	95%	90%	80%	70%	60%	50%	40%	30%	20%	10%
N/A	N/A	$33,500	$28,500	$24,500	$21,000	$18,000	$15,500	$13,500	$12,000	$10,600	$9,500

BELT MODEL PATERSON NO. 3 — .31 or .34 cal., 5 shot, 3½ in. to 5½ in. octagon barrels, blued metal, a few having case hardened hammers. Varnished walnut grips. Serial range 1- approx. 850 which includes the Belt Model No. 2. All standard production Belt Models No. 3 have the flared bottom style grips. Standard barrel markings "Patent Arms M'g Co. Paterson N-J. Colt's Pt.". The square backed cylinder is seen less often than the more common round back, both bearing the Centaur scene with four horse head trademark and "COLT". With both Belt Models, revolvers exhibiting attached loading levers are less common than those without a lever. Mfg. 1837-1840.

Standard Model W/O Lever — without attached loading lever.

100%	98%	95%	90%	80%	70%	60%	50%	40%	30%	20%	10%
N/A	N/A	$31,000	$27,000	$23,000	$19,500	$17,000	$15,000	$13,500	$11,750	$10,500	$9,250

COLT **cont.**

100%	98%	95%	90%	80%	70%	60%	50%	40%	30%	20%	10%

Standard Model With Lever — with attached loading lever and recoil shield milled for ease of capping (scarce).

| N/A | N/A | $34,000 | $29,500 | $25,500 | $22,500 | $19,750 | $17,500 | $15,250 | $13,500 | $12,000 | $10,750 |

HOLSTER MODEL NO. 5 — also known as "Texas Paterson" - .36 cal., 5 shot, 4 in. to 12 in. octagon barrels, blued metal with case hardened frame and hammer. All cylinders bear the stage coach hold-up scene. Varnished walnut grips of flared bottom style. Serial range 1 to approx. 1,000. As with all models of Patersons, the serial number usually cannot be seen without disassembly of the revolver. Very large and heavy compared to the other Paterson models. Enjoys more popularity with collectors because of its military and frontier use. Mfg. 1838-1840.

Many specimens encountered in this variation show extreme use. Consequently, fine to mint specimens are quire rare and highly prized by collectors. Values are given for non-military marked specimens. Any specimen bearing an authenticated martial marking is truly a rarity and should be appraised individually. NOTE: Watch for fakes here. There are now many times more faked martial markings, often times on non-original Patersons, than there are originals.

Standard Production Model W/O Lever — without attached loading lever, round or square backed cylinder.

| N/A | N/A | $125,000 | $95,000 | $78,000 | $66,500 | $57,000 | $49,000 | $42,000 | $37,000 | $32,500 | $28,000 |

Standard Production Model With Lever — with attached loading lever, round backed cylinder and recoil shield milled for ease of capping.

| N/A | N/A | $138,000 | $105,500 | $87,500 | $73,500 | $63,500 | $55,000 | $47,500 | $41,500 | $37,000 | $32,500 |

WALKER MODEL REVOLVER — .44 cal., 6 shot, 9 in. part round, part octagon barrel, blued metal with case hardened frame, lever and hammer. Cylinder left without finish, brass trigger guard. One piece walnut grips. Mfg. 1847; total production approx. 1,100. Ser. numbers beginning with no. 1 were applied for each of five different military companies (A,B,C,D, & E). The total for the military issue Walkers was approx. 1,000 revolvers; the remaining approx. 100 revolvers were produced for civilian distribution. Barrels marked "Address SamL Colt New-York City". Found on right side of barrel lug is "US" over "1847". Cylinder bears Texas Ranger/Indian fight scene. Various metal parts and walnut grips stamped with Gov't. Inspectors' marks.

Because of these arms being subjected to great extremes of use, they will exhibit high degrees of wear, often to the extent that most or all markings will be worn off. Replaced parts are common and many badly worn and damaged specimens have been extensively rebuilt and restored. NOTE: Use great caution when contemplating the purchase of a Walker. A multitude of out-and-out fakes and "antiqued" reproduction Walkers have been fed into the market over the past few decades. Some of these are old enough (and have aged enough naturally) to almost resemble an authentic specimen. Enlist the services of a qualified expert before your dollars are spent. Only 10-12% of the original production of approx. 1,100 specimens have been accounted for. The acquisition of an authenticated Walker revolver is the ultimate goal of serious Colt collectors.

Standard Military Issue Model

| N/A | N/A | N/A | $235,000 | $175,000 | $139,500 | $118,000 | $90,000 | $74,500 | $61,000 | $48,500 | $37,500 |

Limited Civilian Issue Model — serial range 1001 to approx. 1100. Similar to military model except Gov't inspectors' marks were not applied. Pricing is difficult on the civilian issue arms. They tend to be in considerably better condition than the much more common military specimens. The factors of scarcity and condition will often bring higher prices from the advanced collector of means, especially in the finer grades of condition. On the other hand, the collector appreciating military usage will pay more for military marked examples. This publication tries to reflect the latest trends on purchase of civilian models.

| N/A | N/A | N/A | $245,000 | $180,000 | $138,000 | $115,000 | $88,500 | $73,000 | $59,500 | $47,000 | $36,000 |

100%	98%	95%	90%	80%	70%	60%	50%	40%	30%	20%	10%

WHITNEYVILLE HARTFORD DRAGOON — .44 cal., 6 shot, 7½ in. part octagon, part round barrel, some of the left-over Walker parts were used in Dragoons, blued metal with casehardened frame, lever, hammer, brass trigger guard and steel cylinder bears Texas Ranger and Indian battle scene. Mfg.'d 1847. Total production approx. 240. Serial range approx. 1,100 to 1,340 in sequence following civilian Walkers.

⚔ Rear frame cut out for grips

100%	98%	95%	90%	80%	70%	60%	50%	40%	30%	20%	10%
N/A	N/A	$129,000	$104,000	$84,000	$70,000	$60,000	$53,000	$47,000	$42,000	$38,000	$35,000

⚔ Straight rear frame

100%	98%	95%	90%	80%	70%	60%	50%	40%	30%	20%	10%
N/A	N/A	$82,000	$62,500	$48,500	$39,000	$32,500	$28,500	$25,000	$22,000	$20,000	$18,500

FIRST MODEL DRAGOON — .44 cal., 6 shot, 7½ in. round and octagon barrel, blued metal with case hardened frame, lever, hammer, brass grip straps, silvered straps for civilian market, serial range numbered after Hartford Dragoon, 1341 to around 8000. Mfg. 1848-1850. Total production approx. 7,000. Oval cyl. slots, square back trigger guard, Texas ranger and indian fight scene on cylinder.

⚔ Military model

100%	98%	95%	90%	80%	70%	60%	50%	40%	30%	20%	10%
N/A	N/A	$36,000	$27,500	$21,250	$17,500	$15,000	$12,500	$10,500	$8,750	$7,500	$6,500

⚔ Civilian model

100%	98%	95%	90%	80%	70%	60%	50%	40%	30%	20%	10%
N/A	N/A	$33,500	$24,500	$18,500	$15,000	$12,000	$9,500	$7,500	$5,500	$4,250	$3,400

FLUCK MODEL DRAGOON — basically a First Model Dragoon, with 7½ in. altered Walker barrels and fully martially marked, should be extensively checked over, used to replace defective Walkers. Mfg. 1848. Total production 300. Serial range approx. 2,216 to 2,515.

100%	98%	95%	90%	80%	70%	60%	50%	40%	30%	20%	10%
N/A	N/A	$42,000	$33,000	$27,000	$22,500	$19,000	$16,000	$13,500	$11,000	$10,000	$9,500

SECOND MODEL DRAGOON — .44 cal., 6 shot, 7½ in. round and octagon barrel, serial range following the First Model Dragoon 8000-10,700. Mfg. 1850-1851. Texas ranger and indian fight scene on cylinder.

⚔ Military model

100%	98%	95%	90%	80%	70%	60%	50%	40%	30%	20%	10%
N/A	N/A	$39,000	$30,500	$23,500	$18,000	$14,750	$12,000	$10,000	$8,500	$7,500	$6,500

⚔ Civilian model

100%	98%	95%	90%	80%	70%	60%	50%	40%	30%	20%	10%
N/A	N/A	$34,500	$25,750	$20,000	$16,750	$13,250	$11,500	$9,500	$7,750	$6,500	$5,500

⚔ New Hampshire or Massachusetts — notice state markings on front portion of trigger guard.

100%	98%	95%	90%	80%	70%	60%	50%	40%	30%	20%	10%
N/A	N/A	$42,500	$31,750	$24,750	$19,500	$15,750	$13,250	$11,250	$9,500	$8,500	$7,750

THIRD MODEL DRAGOON — .44 cal., 6 shot, 7½ in. round or octagon barrel, same basic features as earlier models, but with round trigger guard and rectangular cylinder slots, serial range approx. 10,200-19,600, some overlapping of numbers, with approx. 10,500 mfg. from 1851-1861. Texas ranger and indian fight scene on cylinder.

⚔ Third model Dragoon

100%	98%	95%	90%	80%	70%	60%	50%	40%	30%	20%	10%
N/A	N/A	$27,500	$19,500	$14,500	$12,000	$10,250	$8,900	$7,800	$6,900	$6,250	$5,750

⚔ Martially marked U.S.

100%	98%	95%	90%	80%	70%	60%	50%	40%	30%	20%	10%
N/A	N/A	$30,000	$22,000	$17,000	$14,750	$12,750	$11,000	$9,500	$8,250	$7,250	$6,500

⚔ Third model — 8 in. barrel.

100%	98%	95%	90%	80%	70%	60%	50%	40%	30%	20%	10%
N/A	N/A	$42,500	$33,000	$27,000	$23,000	$19,500	$16,500	$14,000	$11,500	$9,500	$8,000

⚔ First and second variation — shoulder stock model.

100%	98%	95%	90%	80%	70%	60%	50%	40%	30%	20%	10%
N/A	N/A	$37,500	$29,000	$23,000	$19,000	$16,350	$14,000	$11,750	$9,750	$8,250	$7,250

	100%	98%	95%	90%	80%	70%	60%	50%	40%	30%	20%	10%

Third Variation

	100%	98%	95%	90%	80%	70%	60%	50%	40%	30%	20%	10%
	N/A	N/A	$36,000	$28,500	$21,750	$18,500	$15,750	$13,250	$11,000	$9,000	$7,500	$6,500

C.L. Dragoon

	N/A	N/A	$48,500	$36,750	$28,000	$23,700	$20,250	$17,250	$14,750	$12,500	$10,500	$8,500

ENGLISH HARTFORD DRAGOON — basically a Third Model Dragoon, assembled at Colt's London factory, with unique serial range 1-700, some were assembled from earlier parts inventories, easy to spot with British proofs of crown over V and crown over GP, the blue was of the English type, many were engraved.

	N/A	N/A	$29,000	$21,000	$15,250	$12,750	$10,500	$9,100	$8,000	$7,150	$6,500	$6,000

Recently, several 10-20% condition factory engraved English Dragoons have auctioned off at between $6,000-$8,500, depending on the amount of engraving.

1848 BABY DRAGOONS — .31 cal., 5 shot, 3, 4, 5, or 6 in. octagon barrels, most without loading lever, serial range 1-15,500, a scaled down version of the .44 caliber Dragoons, early ones with Texas Ranger scene and later ones with the holdup scene.

Type I — left hand barrel stamping, Texas Ranger and Indian scene, approx. serial range 1-150.

	N/A	N/A	$20,000	$15,000	$11,750	$9,850	$8,650	$7,500	$6,500	$5,750	$5,250	$4,850

Type II — with Texas Ranger and Indian scene, 11,600 serial range, without loading lever.

	N/A	N/A	$15,000	$11,500	$8,250	$7,100	$5,750	$4,750	$3,950	$3,300	$3,000	$2,800

Type III — with Stagecoach scene and oval cylinder slots, serial range 10,400-12,000.

	N/A	N/A	$14,500	$11,500	$8,450	$6,800	$5,450	$4,500	$3,800	$3,200	$2,800	$2,500

Type IV — with Stagecoach holdup scene, rectangle cylinder slots, serial range 11,000-12,500.

	N/A	N/A	$15,750	$12,000	$9,000	$7,250	$5,900	$5,000	$4,250	$3,600	$3,250	$3,000

Type V — with Stagecoach holdup scene, rectangle cylinder slots and loading lever, serial range 11,600-15,500.

	N/A	N/A	$14,500	$11,000	$8,450	$6,800	$5,450	$4,500	$3,800	$3,200	$2,850	$2,550

1849 POCKET MODEL — .31 cal., 5 or 6 shot, 3, 4, 5, and 6 in. octagon barrels, most with loading levers, blued metal with case hardened frame, lever and hammer, grip straps of brass (silver plated), or steel (silver plated or blued), stagecoach hold-up scene on cylinder, serial range 12,000 to 340,000. Mfg. 1850-1873.

First Type — 4, 5, or 6 in. barrel, loading lever and small or large brass trigger guard.

	N/A	N/A	$4,475	$3,375	$2,625	$2,050	$1,650	$1,350	$1,000	$750	$600	$550

Second Type — 4, 5, or 6 in. barrel, loading lever and steel grip straps.

	N/A	N/A	$5,500	$4,075	$3,175	$2,450	$1,950	$1,650	$1,150	$850	$700	$650

Wells Fargo Model — 3 in. barrel, without loading lever and with small round trigger guard.

	N/A	N/A	$15,500	$10,750	$7,650	$5,350	$3,750	$2,650	$2,000	$1,700	$1,550	$1,450

1849 LONDON POCKET MODEL — London pistols were of the same general configuration, but of better finish, serial range 1-11,000. Mfg. 1853-1857.

Early Type — serial numbered under 1500, with small trigger guard and brass grip straps.

	N/A	N/A	$6,750	$5,450	$4,450	$3,650	$2,950	$2,350	$1,850	$1,450	$1,150	$1,000

Late Type — oval trigger guard and steel grip straps.

	N/A	N/A	$4,500	$3,500	$2,750	$2,250	$1,850	$1,475	$1,175	$950	$825	$775

100%	98%	95%	90%	80%	70%	60%	50%	40%	30%	20%	10%

1851 NAVY — .36 cal., 6 shot, 7½ in. octagon barrel and loading lever, blued metal with casehardened frame, lever and hammer, one piece walnut finished grips, cylinder scene of Texas Navy battle with Mexico, serial range 1-highest recorded number was 215,348, three barrel addresses 1-74,000 (ADDRESS SAM COLT, HARTFORD, CT.), 74,000-101,000 (ADDRESS SAM COLT, HARTFORD, CT.) 101,000-215,348 (ADDRESS COL. SAM COLT, NEW YORK, U.S. AMERICA). Mfg. 1850-1873.

⚜ **First Model** — square back trigger guard, bottom wedge screw, serial range 1-1,250.

| N/A | N/A | $25,000 | $19,500 | $16,000 | $13,000 | $10,500 | $8,500 | $7,000 | $5,750 | $4,750 | $4,000 |

⚜ **Second Model** — square back trigger guard, top wedge screw, serial range 1,250-4,000.

| N/A | N/A | $16,000 | $12,000 | $9,750 | $7,700 | $6,450 | $5,450 | $4,600 | $3,900 | $3,300 | $2,800 |

⚜ **Third Model** — small round brass trigger guard, serial range 4,200-85,000.

| N/A | N/A | $8,400 | $6,600 | $5,250 | $4,100 | $3,400 | $2,800 | $2,300 | $1,900 | $1,550 | $1,250 |

⚜ **Fourth Model** — large round brass trigger guard, serial range 85,000-215,348.

| N/A | N/A | $7,400 | $5,875 | $4,775 | $3,975 | $3,175 | $2,600 | $2,125 | $1,750 | $1,425 | $1,175 |

⚜ **Iron Gripstrap Model** — most often seen in fourth model.

| N/A | N/A | $9,300 | $7,400 | $6,000 | $4,925 | $4,175 | $3,425 | $2,750 | $2,200 | $1,750 | $1,375 |

⚜ **Martially Marked U.S. Navies** — brass or iron gripstrap.

| N/A | N/A | $11,450 | $9,200 | $7,500 | $6,000 | $4,750 | $3,750 | $2,900 | $2,325 | $1,875 | $1,500 |

⚜ **Cut for shoulder stock** — first and second type (like third model Dragoon).

| N/A | N/A | $15,750 | $11,750 | $9,000 | $7,000 | $5,500 | $4,500 | $3,750 | $3,000 | $2,450 | $1,950 |

⚜ **Third Type** — four screw frame.

| N/A | N/A | $10,500 | $8,650 | $7,250 | $6,000 | $4,850 | $3,850 | $3,100 | $2,500 | $2,000 | $1,650 |

51 NAVY LONDON MODEL — basically the same gun as the Hartford piece with London barrel address, with British proof marks in serial range 1-42,000. Mfg. 1853-1857.

⚜ **Early First Model** — serial range below 2000, brass grip straps and small trigger guard.

| N/A | N/A | $11,625 | $7,500 | $6,000 | $5,025 | $4,225 | $3,475 | $2,800 | $2,250 | $1,800 | $1,475 |

⚜ **Late Second Model** — balance of production, large round trigger guard, steel grip straps, all London parts.

| N/A | N/A | $8,825 | $6,925 | $5,625 | $4,725 | $3,975 | $3,275 | $2,575 | $2,000 | $1,650 | $1,375 |

1855 SIDEHAMMER POCKET MODEL — .28 cal., had 3½ in. octagon barrels, all .31 cal. usually had 3½ in. or 4½ in. round barrels. Blued with case hardened lever and hammer, one piece wrap around style walnut grips.
Commonly called the "Root" model by collectors, manufactured 1855 through 1870. The .28 cal. model serial numbered 1 through approx. 30,000. The .31 cal. round barrel model serial numbered 1 through approx. 14,000. Total production approx. 44,000.
Easily recognizable by its side mounted hammer and cylinder rotation ratchet at rear of frame.

⚜ **Model 1 and 1A** — 3⁷⁄₁₆ in. octagonal bbl., oct. load lever, .28 cal., Indian/cabin cyl. scene, Hartford barrel address. Serial range 1 to 384.

| N/A | N/A | $5,350 | $4,050 | $3,250 | $2,700 | $2,325 | $2,075 | $1,925 | $1,825 | $1,750 | $1,700 |

⚜ **Model 2** — 3½ in. oct. bbl., .28 cal., Indian/cabin cyl. scene, Hartford barrel address with pointed hand. Serial range 476 to 25,000.

| N/A | N/A | $2,350 | $1,750 | $1,290 | $1,040 | $890 | $765 | $665 | $590 | $540 | $500 |

	100%	98%	95%	90%	80%	70%	60%	50%	40%	30%	20%	10%

⚔ **Model 3** — 3½ in. oct. bbl., .28 cal., full fluted cylinder, Hartford barrel address with pointed hand. Serial range 25,001 to 30,000.

N/A	N/A	$2,475	$1,825	$1,355	$1,105	$955	$830	$730	$650	$585	$535

⚔ **Model 3A** — 3½ in. oct. bbl., .31 cal., full fluted cylinder, Hartford barrel address. Serial range 1 to 1,350.

N/A	N/A	$2,750	$1,425	$1,250	$1,100	$975	$875	$800	$735	$700	$675

⚔ **Model 4** — 3½ in. oct. bbl., .31 cal., full fluted cylinder, Hartford barrel address. Serial range 1,351 to 2,400.

N/A	N/A	$2,750	$1,425	$1,250	$1,100	$975	$875	$800	$735	$700	$675

⚔ **Model 5** — 3½ in. round bbl., .31 cal., full fluted cylinder, "COL. COLT NEW-YORK" barrel address. Serial range 2,401 to 8,000.

N/A	N/A	$2,475	$1,825	$1,355	$1,105	$955	$830	$730	$650	$585	$535

⚔ **Model 5A** — 4½ in. round bbl., included in same serial range as Model 5.

N/A	N/A	$3,250	$2,600	$2,100	$1,750	$1,350	$1,200	$1,075	$975	$900	$850

⚔ **Model 6** — 3½ in. round bbl., .31 cal., stage coach hold-up cylinder scene, "COL. COLT NEW-YORK" barrel address. Serial range 8,001 through 11,074.

N/A	N/A	$2,475	$1,825	$1,355	$1,105	$955	$830	$730	$650	$585	$535

⚔ **Model 6A** — 4½ in. round bbl., included in same serial range as Model 6.

N/A	N/A	$2,550	$1,935	$1,470	$1,195	$1,030	$895	$785	$700	$625	$575

⚔ **Model 7** — 3½ in. round bbl., .31 cal., stage coach hold-up cylinder scene, "COL. COLT NEW-YORK" barrel address. Cylinder pin retained by screw-in cylinder. Serial range 11,075 through 14,000.

N/A	N/A	$3,400	$2,400	$1,650	$1,325	$1,200	$1,110	$1,035	$975	$925	$875

⚔ **Model 7A** — 4½ in. round bbl., included in same cylinder scene, barrel address and serial range as Model 7.

N/A	N/A	$4,000	$2,650	$1,750	$1,375	$1,250	$1,150	$1,085	$1,025	$975	$925

1860 MODEL ARMY — .44 cal., 6 shot, 7½ and 8 in. round barrels with loading lever, blued metal with case hardened frame, lever and hammer, one piece walnut grips, normally blued steel back strap and brass trigger guard, barrel markings were (ADDRESS SAM COLT, HARTFORD, CT.) on early productions and (ADDRESS COL. SAM COLT, NEW YORK, U.S. AMERICA) on balance, serial range 1-about 200,500, Texas Navy scene on round cylinder model. Mfg. 1860-1873.

⚔ **Fluted Cylinder Model** — Fluted Cylinder Model, full length cylinder flutes and no cylinder scene, 7½ or 8 in. barrel, grips of Navy (very rare) or Army size, usually 4 screw frames.

N/A	N/A	$16,500	$12,250	$9,900	$7,750	$6,450	$5,400	$4,550	$3,850	$3,250	$2,750

⚔ **Round Cylinder Model** — roll engraved Texas Navy scene, some with early Hartford address, Army grips, four screw frame to about 50,000 range, most were sold to the U.S. Government and will be martially marked.

N/A	N/A	$10,500	$8,650	$7,250	$6,000	$4,850	$3,850	$3,100	$2,500	$2,000	$1,650

⚔ **Civilian Model** — same general configurations as Round Cylinder Model, but with 3 screw frame, no shoulder stock cuts and better blue finish than military pieces, late New York barrel address.

N/A	N/A	$9,450	$8,025	$6,625	$5,375	$4,375	$3,525	$2,825	$2,275	$1,850	$1,500

100%	98%	95%	90%	80%	70%	60%	50%	40%	30%	20%	10%

1861 MODEL NAVY — .36 cal., 6 shot, 7½ in. round barrel with loading lever, blued metal with case hardened frame, lever and hammer, silver plated brass grip straps, the barrel address was (ADDRESS COL. SAM COLT, NEW YORK, U.S. AMERICA), serial range 1 - 38,843, cylinder scene of Texas Navy and Mexico Battle, mfg. 1861-1873.

Fluted Cylinder Navy — in serial range 1-100, with fluted cylinder and without rolled cylinder scene.

100%	98%	95%	90%	80%	70%	60%	50%	40%	30%	20%	10%
N/A	N/A	$36,000	$26,750	$19,750	$16,250	$13,250	$10,750	$8,750	$7,250	$6,250	$5,750

Regular production model

100%	98%	95%	90%	80%	70%	60%	50%	40%	30%	20%	10%
N/A	N/A	$10,200	$8,450	$7,000	$5,750	$4,600	$3,700	$3,000	$2,450	$2,000	$1,650

Martially Marked Navies — will bear the U.S. stamp and inspector's marks, those marked U.S.N. on butt were of a 650 piece order for the Navy.

100%	98%	95%	90%	80%	70%	60%	50%	40%	30%	20%	10%
N/A	N/A	$14,000	$11,000	$8,600	$6,600	$4,950	$4,050	$3,350	$2,775	$2,300	$1,900

London Mark Navy — with (ADDRESS COL. COLT, LONDON), for barrel address.

100%	98%	95%	90%	80%	70%	60%	50%	40%	30%	20%	10%
N/A	N/A	$11,750	$9,450	$7,525	$5,925	$4,775	$3,900	$3,225	$2,675	$2,225	$1,850

Shoulder Stock Cut Navy — 4 screw frames in serial range 11,000-14,000, made for third style stock (see Dragoon stocks).

100%	98%	95%	90%	80%	70%	60%	50%	40%	30%	20%	10%
N/A	N/A	$19,750	$14,250	$10,500	$8,000	$6,500	$5,500	$4,650	$3,950	$3,350	$2,850

1862 POLICE MODEL — .36 cal., 5 shot half fluted and rebated cylinder, 4½, 5½, and 6½ in. round barrels (also 3½ in. bbl. but quite rare) and loading lever. Mfg. 1861 to 1873. Serial numbered with Model 1862 Pocket Navy, approx. 28,000 1862 Police Models were produced. Blued with case hardened frame, lever and hammer, grip straps silver plated, one piece walnut grips.

Serial range 1 through approx. 47,000. Standard barrel marking "ADDRESS COL. SAML COLT NEW-YORK U.S. AMERICA". "COLTS/ PATENT" on left side of frame, "PAT SEPT. 10TH 1850" stamped in cyl. flute.

Many models 1862 Police and 1862 Pocket Navy revolvers were converted to cartridge with the advent of the metallic cartridge. Consequently these models in their original cap and ball chambering are quite desirable to collectors.

Early Model — "ADDRESS SAM COLT/HARTFORD CT" barrel address, silvered iron grip straps.

100%	98%	95%	90%	80%	70%	60%	50%	40%	30%	20%	10%
N/A	N/A	$11,500	$8,250	$6,500	$5,100	$4,250	$3,450	$2,750	$2,200	$1,750	$1,375

Early Model — same but silvered brass grip straps.

100%	98%	95%	90%	80%	70%	60%	50%	40%	30%	20%	10%
N/A	N/A	$10,950	$8,100	$6,150	$4,750	$3,850	$3,000	$2,300	$1,875	$1,535	$1,235

Standard Production Model — with New York barrel address.

100%	98%	95%	90%	80%	70%	60%	50%	40%	30%	20%	10%
N/A	N/A	$8,500	$6,100	$4,200	$3,100	$2,400	$1,975	$1,675	$1,400	$1,175	$925

Export Production Model — with "L" below serial numbers (for export to England), steel grip straps. Most often but not always bearing British proofs.

100%	98%	95%	90%	80%	70%	60%	50%	40%	30%	20%	10%
N/A	N/A	$9,000	$6,370	$4,470	$3,320	$2,585	$2,135	$1,810	$1,525	$1,275	$1,050

London Marked Model — similar to above, except with "ADDRESS, COL. COLT/LONDON" address on barrel.

100%	98%	95%	90%	80%	70%	60%	50%	40%	30%	20%	10%
N/A	N/A	$16,000	$11,500	$8,500	$6,500	$5,100	$4,050	$3,250	$2,750	$2,400	$2,150

100%	98%	95%	90%	80%	70%	60%	50%	40%	30%	20%	10%

1862 POCKET MODEL NAVY — .36 cal., 5 shot rebated cylinder, $4\frac{1}{2}$ in., $5\frac{1}{2}$ in., and $6\frac{1}{2}$ in. octagonal barrels with loading lever. Mfg. 1861 to 1873. Serial numbered with Model 1862 Police Model, approx. 19,000 Model 1862 Pocket Navy Revolvers produced. Blued with case hardened frame, lever and hammer, grip straps silver plated brass, one piece walnut grips.

Serial range 1 through approx. 47,000. Standard barrel markings "ADDRESS COL. SAML COLT NEW-YORK U.S. AMERICA". "COLTS/ PATENT" on left side of frame, stage coach hold-up scene on cylinder.

Known to collectors for many years as the Model 1853, this model has finally been correctly identified through diligent combing of factory ledgers.

Because of being produced during the advent of the metallic cartridge, the number remaining in the original cap and ball state is rather few; scarce with any serial number, but particularly so in numbers over approx. 19,800.

Standard Model — $4\frac{1}{2}$, $5\frac{1}{2}$ and $6\frac{1}{2}$ barrel lengths.

100%	98%	95%	90%	80%	70%	60%	50%	40%	30%	20%	10%
N/A	N/A	$10,950	$8,100	$6,175	$4,775	$3,850	$3,000	$2,300	$1,875	$1,535	$1,235

Export Production Model — with "L" below serial numbers (for export to England), steel grip straps. Often found with British proofs.

100%	98%	95%	90%	80%	70%	60%	50%	40%	30%	20%	10%
N/A	N/A	$12,000	$9,000	$7,500	$6,000	$4,750	$3,775	$3,025	$2,475	$2,000	$1,650

London Marked Model — similar to above but "ADDRESS COL. COLT/LONDON" address on barrel.

100%	98%	95%	90%	80%	70%	60%	50%	40%	30%	20%	10%
N/A	N/A	$19,400	$14,175	$10,650	$8,250	$6,550	$5,500	$4,650	$3,950	$3,350	$2,850

2ND GENERATION BLACK POWDER SERIES

Please refer to this heading under Colt's Firearms in the Modern Black Powder section in the back of this book for current information and values on this 2nd Generation Colt Black Powder Series (including serialization).

DERRINGERS

FIRST MODEL DERRINGER — .41 rimfire, single shot, $2\frac{1}{2}$ in. barrel, scroll engraving standard, blued, nickel, or silver plated barrel, downward pivoting barrel, no grips, serial numbered 1-6,500. Mfg. approx. 1870-1890.

100%	98%	95%	90%	80%	70%	60%	50%	40%	30%	20%	10%
$3,100	$2,350	$2,050	$1,825	$1,625	$1,425	$1,250	$1,075	$875	$750	$675	$650

SECOND MODEL DERRINGER — .41 rimfire or centerfire, single shot, $2\frac{1}{2}$ in. barrel, scroll engraving standard, blued, nickel, or silver plated barrel, downward pivoting barrel, checkered and varnished walnut grips, "No 2" marked on top of barrel, serial numbered 1-9,000. Mfg. approx. 1870-1890.

100%	98%	95%	90%	80%	70%	60%	50%	40%	30%	20%	10%
$1,650	$1,400	$1,200	$1,060	$935	$835	$730	$630	$585	$535	$500	$475

.41 Centerfire — add 100%.

THIRD MODEL DERRINGER (THUER MODEL) — .41 rimfire or centerfire (rare), single shot, side pivoting $2\frac{1}{2}$ in. barrel, varnished walnut grips, blued barrels, bronze frames were either nickel or silver plated, engraving optional, Colt-barrel address, spur trigger, serial numbered approx. 1-45,000. Mfg. approx. 1875-1910.

100%	98%	95%	90%	80%	70%	60%	50%	40%	30%	20%	10%
$1,175	$1,015	$890	$790	$700	$620	$550	$495	$450	$415	$385	$360

.41 centerfire is worth an additional 30-50% and early models are worth considerably more.

Grading	100%	98%	95%

FOURTH MODEL DERRINGER — .22 Short, single shot similar in appearance to the 3rd Model, $2\frac{1}{2}$ in. barrel, approx. 112,000 mfg. between 1959-1963 with either D or N suffix. A few were put in books, picture frames, penholders, bookends, etc. (these will command premiums).

100%	98%	95%
$100	$85	$65

LORD DERRINGER — .22 Short only, side pivoting Thuer action, gold plated with black chrome barrel and walnut grips. Mfg. approx. 1959-1963 by Colt, cased.

$175 $140 $100

LADY DERRINGER — .22 Short only, side pivoting Thuer action, full gold plated finish with pearlite grips. Mfg. approx. 1959-1963 by Colt, cased.

$175 $140 $100

LORD & LADY CASED SET — one each of the Lord & Lady derringers or combinations, consecutive serial numbers.

$350 $275 $200

LADY CASED SET — cased pair of Lady Derringers.

$350 $275 $200

LORD CASED SET — cased pair of Lord Derringers.

$350 $275 $200

BOOKCASE DERRINGER PAIR — includes consecutively numbered .22 Short derringers with synthetic ivory grips and nickel finish, cased inside unique hard cover "Colt Derringers" labeled book with red velvet lining, limited mfg. in early 60's.

$350 $275 $200

POCKET PISTOLS

100%	98%	95%	90%	80%	70%	60%	50%	40%	30%	20%	10%

CLOVERLEAF HOUSE PISTOL — .41 Short or long rimfire, cloverleaf configured 4 shot cylinder, spur trigger, 1½ or 3 in. barrel, approx. 7,500 mfg. in ser. no. range 1-8,300 during 1871-1876.

| $2,150 | $1,750 | $1,510 | $1,310 | $1,160 | $1,030 | $915 | $815 | $730 | $660 | $610 | $575 |

This model is sometimes referred to as the Jim Fisk model as he was murdered by Edward Stokes with a Cloverleaf.
Add 80% for 1½ in. barrel.

5-shot Cloverleaf — similar to 4-shot model, except has round 5-shot cylinder and 2⅝ in. barrel only, approx. 2,500 mfg. in ser. no. range 6,160-9,950 during 1871-1876.

| $1,825 | $1,480 | $1,260 | $1,085 | $940 | $820 | $720 | $640 | $580 | $535 | $500 | $475 |

OPEN TOP REVOLVER (OLD LINE) — .22 Short or long rimfire, 2⅜ or 2⅞ in. barrel, without topstrap on frame, with or without integral ejector, blued or nickel plated, varnished walnut grips, approx. 114,200 mfg. 1871-1877.

| $1,175 | $1,000 | $900 | $825 | $750 | $700 | $600 | $550 | $450 | $375 | $325 | $275 |

Add 120% for Early Model with ejector and high hammer spur.

NEW LINE REVOLVER AND VARIATIONS

1ST MODEL — .22, .30, .32, .38, or .41 cal. rim and centerfire, mfg. 1873-1876, 7 (.22 cal. only) or 5 shot, short cylinder flutes, cylinder stop slots cut on exterior of cylinder, 1¾, 2¼, or 4 in. barrel, full nickel or blue/case hardened finish, spur trigger, many thousands mfg. 1873-1884.

| $1,150 | $990 | $875 | $810 | $740 | $685 | $580 | $540 | $425 | $355 | $300 | $250 |

2ND MODEL — similar to 1st Model, except has longer cylinder flutes and cylinder stop slots are on the back of cylinder, may or may not have loading gate. Mfg. 1876-1884.

| $1,050 | $935 | $845 | $775 | $705 | $645 | $540 | $500 | $390 | $320 | $270 | $235 |

Caliber rarity on both models from highest mfg. to lowest is: .22, .32, .30, .41, and .38.

	100%	98%	95%	90%	80%	70%	60%	50%	40%	30%	20%	10%

NEW HOUSE MODEL — .38 or .41 cal. centerfire, 5 shot, 2¼ in. barrel, spur trigger, checkered hard rubber grips. Approx. 4,000 mfg. 1880-1886 starting at ser. no. 10,300.

| $1,375 | $1,075 | $950 | $850 | $760 | $675 | $600 | $485 | $425 | $360 | $325 | $310 |

NEW POLICE MODEL — .32, .38, or .41 cal. centerfire, 5 shot, 2¼, 4½, 5, or 6 in. barrel, spur trigger, with or without ejector, stamped or etched "NEW POLICE" on barrel. Approx. 4,000 mfg. 1882-1886.

| $1,675 | $1,425 | $1,225 | $1,050 | $900 | $785 | $700 | $635 | $585 | $550 | $520 | $495 |

PERCUSSION CONVERSIONS

Research is currently underway to categorize the many variations (including Thuer) that exist on Percussion revolvers which were converted for centerfire capability. Over 46,000 conversions were made on the following models listed in order of highest mfg. to lowest: 1862 Police and Pocket Navy, Model 1860 Army Richards, Thuer's patent conversions, Model 1851 Navy, Model 1861 Navy, Model 1860 Army Richards-Mason. Out of these, the Models 1862 Police and Pocket Navy accounted for slightly over 50%. Be wary of "2nd" generation alterations. Prices generally are in the $650-$2,500+ range with rarer variations selling for considerably more. Cased models will command 175-300%+ premiums.

"OPEN TOP" REVOLVERS

1871-72 OPEN TOP MODEL RIMFIRE — .44 cal. rimfire, 6 shot, 7½ in. barrel, without frame topstrap, blued metal with casehardened hammer, serial range 1-approx. 7000, barrel address (ADDRESS COL. SAM COLT, NEW YORK, U.S. AMERICA), forerunner of the single action Army, quite desirable. Mfg. 1871-1872.

Regular Production Model — 7½ in. barrel, New York address, Navy grips.

| N/A | N/A | $11,500 | $9,250 | $7,500 | $6,000 | $5,300 | $4,850 | $4,250 | $4,075 | $3,875 | $3,750 |

Regular Production — with Army grips.

| N/A | N/A | $12,750 | $10,500 | $8,650 | $6,600 | $5,900 | $5,400 | $4,500 | $4,250 | $4,050 | $3,900 |

Late Production — with address (COLT PT. F. A. MANUFACTURING CO., HARTFORD, CT. U.S.A.).

| N/A | N/A | $9,950 | $7,950 | $6,300 | $5,375 | $4,725 | $4,300 | $3,975 | $3,750 | $3,575 | $3,450 |

Add 40% for models with 8 in. barrel or COLTS/PATENT frame markings.

REVOLVERS: SAA – 1873-1940 MFG. (SER. NO.'S 1 - 357,000)

Note: The Colt SAA was produced in over 30 Calibers with just about any special order feature or combination of special orders available directly from the factory. All of these special orders act independently and interdependently to determine a correct value for a particular Colt SAA. Single action Colt's rank at the top for revolver collectors. When contemplating a purchase in the 4 digit plus price range, several professional opinions should be secured. Caliber rarities make a major difference in pricing single actions.

It is advisable to procure a factory letter when buying or selling older or recently manufactured Colt Single Actions (hence guaranteeing authenticity and value credibility). These watermarked letters are available by writing Colt Firearms in Hartford, CT, with a charge of $45 per serial number - if Colt cannot provide you with proper documentation after conducting research, they will refund you $10. Include your name and address, Colt model name, serial number, and check to: COLT HISTORIAN, P.O. BOX 1868, HARTFORD, CT 06101. Please allow adequate time for proper response.

Values shown below are for guns without special order features. Factory engraving, ivory grips, very rare special order barrel lengths, and special finishes would add considerably to the values shown below. One final word on single action Colts: Black Powder Colts (pre 182,000 serial range) should be scrutinized carefully for restamped serial numbers on various parts. This makes a major difference in pricing the SAA, as a true, original collector's gun differs greatly in value from a restamped "parts gun". .44-40 and .45 cals. in the pre 182,000 serial range will bring premiums over other calibers, especially in shorter barrel lengths. The .44-40 caliber is very collectible since this ammunition at inception was interchangeable with the most popular rifle/carbine of its era - the Winchester Model 1873.

100%	98%	95%	90%	80%	70%	60%	50%	40%	30%	20%	10%

EARLY MODEL SAA (PINCH FRAME) — serial range 1-100, with frame pinched to make rear sight, .45 cal., 7½ in. barrel. Mfg. 1873.

100%	98%	95%	90%	80%	70%	60%	50%	40%	30%	20%	10%
N/A	N/A	$38,500	$31,000	$25,200	$21,200	$17,900	$15,000	$12,600	$10,600	$9,250	$8,250

Watch for fakes! In this variation there are more counterfeits than original specimens.

MARTIALLY MARKED U.S. CAVALRY SAA — .45 LC cal., 7½ in. barrel, U.S. marked on left lower frame, one-piece walnut grips with military cartouche.

100%	98%	95%	90%	80%	70%	60%	50%	40%	30%	20%	10%
N/A	$15,000	$13,250	$10,750	$8,725	$7,175	$6,025	$5,150	$4,475	$3,950	$3,550	$3,250

Early examples with low serial numbers and desirable inspector markings will command premiums over prices listed above.

.22 RIMFIRE SAA — .22 LR cal.

⚞ Conversion (converted from .44 cal.)

100%	98%	95%	90%	80%	70%	60%	50%	40%	30%	20%	10%
N/A	N/A	$11,250	$8,750	$7,175	$6,600	$5,500	$4,400	$3,300	$2,750	$2,425	$2,050

⚞ Original Mfg.

100%	98%	95%	90%	80%	70%	60%	50%	40%	30%	20%	10%
N/A	N/A	$18,000	$15,250	$13,350	$10,750	$8,725	$7,175	$6,025	$5,150	$4,475	$3,950

.44 RIMFIRE SAA — mostly in .44 Henry rimfire, 7½ in. barrel, serial numbered in own range 1-1863, mfg. 1875-1880, most specimens were shipped to Mexico and saw hard use, rare in any original condition.

100%	98%	95%	90%	80%	70%	60%	50%	40%	30%	20%	10%
N/A	N/A	$17,950	$14,650	$12,000	$9,900	$8,150	$6,750	$5,750	$4,850	$4,100	$3,600

This variation is one of the most frequently faked Colt revolvers — be careful (and get a receipt).

SINGLE ACTION ARMY (SAA) — single action, 6 shot revolver, over 30 calibers, 3 in. (Sheriff's model), 4¾, 5½, 7½, and 12 in. (Buntline model) barrels. Blue, nickel, or case hardened frame, walnut or hard rubber grips, total production 357,000. Mfg. 1873-1940.

EARLY CIVILIAN MFG. SAA — standard production model commonly referred to as the Black Powder SAA, script barrel address, stops at serial range approx. 22,000.

100%	98%	95%	90%	80%	70%	60%	50%	40%	30%	20%	10%
N/A	$15,250	$13,350	$10,750	$8,500	$6,950	$5,850	$4,850	$3,900	$3,100	$2,250	$1,750

Considerable premiums should be added for rare cals.

LATER CIVILIAN MFG. SAA — black powder frames, serial number range is approx. 22,000 - 164,000.

100%	98%	95%	90%	80%	70%	60%	50%	40%	30%	20%	10%
N/A	$10,000	$9,150	$8,250	$7,175	$6,600	$5,500	$4,400	$3,450	$2,650	$2,050	$1,500

Considerable premiums should be added for rare cals.

SMOKELESS FRAME SAA (1896-1940 MFG.) — mfg. 1896-1940, approx. serial range of smokeless frames is 164,000 - 182,000.
ADD 25% FOR PRE-1899 MFG.

⚞ .45 cal.

100%	98%	95%	90%	80%	70%	60%	50%	40%	30%	20%	10%
$5,950	$4,950	$4,200	$3,675	$3,275	$2,950	$2,675	$2,375	$2,100	$1,800	$1,550	$1,350

⚞ .44-40 cal. — roll-die "Colt Frontier Six Shooter" marking on left side of barrel.

100%	98%	95%	90%	80%	70%	60%	50%	40%	30%	20%	10%
$6,650	$5,400	$4,375	$3,825	$3,425	$3,100	$2,800	$2,500	$2,225	$1,925	$1,675	$1,475

Colt changed from the etched barrel marking to a roll die in approx. 1881.

⚞ .41 cal.

100%	98%	95%	90%	80%	70%	60%	50%	40%	30%	20%	10%
$5,675	$4,650	$3,950	$3,550	$3,175	$2,875	$2,575	$2,275	$2,000	$1,700	$1,450	$1,250

100%	98%	95%	90%	80%	70%	60%	50%	40%	30%	20%	10%

.38-40 cal.

100%	98%	95%	90%	80%	70%	60%	50%	40%	30%	20%	10%
$5,575	$4,600	$3,900	$3,500	$3,125	$2,825	$2,550	$2,275	$1,975	$1,675	$1,445	$1,235

.38 Special Cal.

$5,100	$4,400	$3,850	$3,450	$3,150	$2,825	$2,550	$2,250	$1,975	$1,675	$1,450	$1,250

This cal. was mfg. pre-war only and 82 were mfg., plus 7 in. target variation.

.32-20 cal.

$4,850	$4,100	$3,625	$3,300	$2,950	$2,625	$2,325	$2,000	$1,700	$1,400	$1,175	$975

ARTILLERY MODEL SAA — .45 Colt, 5½ in. barrel, marked U.S. on left lower frame. With one piece walnut grips, military cartouche. These guns are the original artillery model Colts returned to the factory or Springfield Armory. Barrels were shortened to 5½ in. and the guns were refinished and reissued to the military. Very seldom do the serial numbered parts on these guns match. Not all factory letters will indicate refurbishing as Colt did not do all of them.

$9,000	$7,500	$6,500	$5,750	$4,700	$3,850	$3,200	$2,750	$2,400	$2,100	$1,850	$1,650

ETCHED BARREL .44-40 SAA — Colt Frontier, "Colt Frontier Six Shooter" acid etched into barrel instead of stamped, 21,000-65,000 ser. no. range.

$10,250	$7,875	$6,900	$5,950	$4,900	$4,025	$3,475	$3,025	$2,650	$2,325	$2,050	$1,850

This variation was only mfg. from 1876-1881. Watch for fake, replaced, or re-etched barrels.

SHERIFF'S MODEL SAA — 2½ (rare), 3, 4, 4¾ (rare), or 7½ (rare) in. barrel, without ejector housing, this model's most distinguishable feature is the lack of an ejector housing. Mfg. stopped 1927. Watch For Fakes.

N/A	N/A	$15,350	$13,600	$12,000	$10,400	$8,900	$7,400	$6,000	$4,950	$4,250	$3,750

Add 50% for black powder frame.

Fakes can be detected on this model by re-welded frames. While 2½, 4¾, or 7½ in. barrels in this variation do exist, be careful, get a second opinion, and ask for a receipt.

FLAT-TOP TARGET SAA — various calibers from .22 to .476 Eley, approx. 925 mfg., 1888-1896.

N/A	N/A	$13,625	$11,900	$10,450	$9,000	$7,750	$6,500	$5,400	$4,550	$3,950	$3,450

Note: Different calibers make a substantial difference in pricing for this model.

BISLEY MODEL SAA — differs from single action Army by hump backed grip frame and raked hammer, approx. 44,350 mfg., 1894-1915.

.455 Eley — mfg. for the International Revolver contests held in Bisley, England.

$6,350	$5,400	$4,750	$4,150	$3,700	$3,300	$2,900	$2,525	$2,200	$1,925	$1,675	$1,450

.45 cal.

$4,500	$4,025	$3,675	$3,325	$3,000	$2,675	$2,350	$2,025	$1,725	$1,425	$1,200	$1,000

.44-40 cal.

$5,350	$4,650	$4,200	$3,750	$3,300	$2,850	$2,450	$2,125	$1,850	$1,625	$1,425	$1,250

.41 cal.

$4,250	$3,750	$3,350	$3,000	$2,675	$2,375	$2,075	$1,800	$1,550	$1,325	$1,125	$975

.38-40 cal.

$4,150	$3,650	$3,300	$2,950	$2,625	$2,350	$2,050	$1,775	$1,525	$1,300	$1,100	$950

.32-20 cal. — mfg. for the international revolver contests held in Bisley, England.

$3,950	$3,450	$3,125	$2,800	$2,500	$2,225	$1,975	$1,750	$1,475	$1,250	$1,050	$900

BISLEY TARGET FLAT-TOP — flat top frame, removable target sights, 976 mfg., 1894-1913.
Values are 200% greater than respective Standard Bisley Models.

POST-WAR 1ST GENERATION SAA — approx. 860 manufactured in various configurations after 1945. These specimens in 98%+ condition will approximate values on the pre-war models. Ser. no. range 357,000-357,860.

2ND GENERATION SINGLE ACTION ARMY: 1956-1975 MFG.

Popular demand brought back the Single Action Army in 1956 with minor modifications, most not noticeable except to experts. Serial numbers began at 0001SA and continue to 73,000SA before the "New Model" was introduced in 1976 (ser. no. 80000 SA). Premiums are paid for rare production variances if NIB condition. Prices stated assume 7½ barrel length. It should be noted that many "premium niches" exist in this model as collectors are establishing premiums paid for rarer production variances (the interrelation of barrel length, caliber, frame type, finish quality, year of manufacture, and other special features).

The order of desirability on standard 2nd generation SAASs is as follows: 4¾ barrels are the most desirable, followed by 5½ in., and then 7½ in. Caliber desirability is as follows: .45 LC has the most demand followed by .44 Spl., .38 Spl., and then .357 Mag. It follows that desirable calibers found with desirable barrel lengths will command healthy premiums — especially if production was unusually low in a particular combination. Reference books specifically on the post-war SAA are a must when determining the rarity factors (or if they exist) on these multiple production combinations. Buntlines, Sheriff's models, and special orders through the Custom Gun Shop are in a class by themselves and have to be evaluated one at a time.

It is advisable to procure a factory letter when buying or selling older or recently manufactured Colt Single Actions (hence guaranteeing authenticity and value credibility). These watermarked letters are available by writing Colt Firearms in Hartford, CT, with a charge of $45 per serial number - if Colt cannot provide you with proper documentation after conducting research, they will refund you $10. Include your name and address, Colt model name, serial number, and check to: COLT HISTORIAN, P.O. BOX 1868, HARTFORD, CT 06101. Please allow adequate time for proper response.

Grading	100%	98%	95%	90%	80%	70%	60%

SINGLE ACTION ARMY — SA suffix, .357 Mag., .38 Special, .44 Special., or .45 LC cal., 3 (Sheriff's Model), 4¾, 5½, 7½, or 12 in. (Buntline) barrel lengths, all blue, blue/case hardened, or nickel finishes, hard rubber stocks (standard until 1970).
Because SAAs are a complex field in themselves, values below have been separated by calibers first, barrel lengths second, and finishes third (CH designates color case hardening).

.357 Mag. cal.

	100%	98%	95%	90%	80%	70%	60%
4¾ in. CH frame	$2,195	$1,825	$1,550	$1,250	$950	$825	$695
5½ in. CH frame	$1,695	$1,425	$1,200	$995	$850	$725	$595
7½ in. CH frame	$1,995	$1,700	$1,400	$1,100	$895	$775	$650
4¾ in. Blue frame	$1,995	$1,700	$1,400	$1,100	$895	$775	$650
5½ in. Blue frame	$1,995	$1,700	$1,400	$1,100	$895	$775	$650
4¾ in. Nickel	$2,295	$1,875	$1,600	$1,275	$975	$850	$725
5½ in. Nickel	$2,095	$1,775	$1,450	$1,125	$900	$775	$650
7½ in. Nickel	$2,195	$1,825	$1,550	$1,250	$950	$825	$695

Grading	100%	98%	95%	90%	80%	70%	60%
.38 Spl. cal.							
4¾ in. CH frame	$2,195	$1,825	$1,550	$1,250	$950	$825	$695
5½ in. CH frame	$1,695	$1,425	$1,200	$995	$850	$725	$595
7½ in. CH frame	$1,995	$1,700	$1,400	$1,100	$895	$775	$650
5½ in. Blue frame	$1,995	$1,700	$1,400	$1,100	$895	$775	$650
4¾ in. Nickel	$2,395	$1,950	$1,650	$1,325	$1,025	$895	$775
5½ in. Nickel	$2,395	$1,950	$1,650	$1,325	$1,025	$895	$775
7½ in. Nickel	$2,395	$1,950	$1,650	$1,325	$1,025	$895	$775
.44 Spl. cal.							
5½ in. CH frame	$1,850	$1,550	$1,300	$1,050	$875	$750	$625
7½ in. CH frame	$1,850	$1,550	$1,300	$1,050	$875	$750	$625
5½ in. Blue frame	$1,850	$1,550	$1,300	$1,050	$875	$750	$625
7½ in. Blue frame	$1,850	$1,550	$1,300	$1,050	$875	$750	$625
5½ in. Nickel	$2,395	$1,950	$1,650	$1,325	$1,025	$895	$775
7½ in. Nickel	$2,995	$2,550	$2,100	$1,775	$1,425	$1,100	$900
.45 LC cal.							
4¾ in. CH frame	$2,250	$1,850	$1,575	$1,250	$950	$825	$695
5½ in. CH frame	$1,850	$1,550	$1,300	$1,050	$875	$750	$625
7½ in. CH frame	$1,650	$1,400	$1,200	$995	$850	$725	$595
4¾ in. Blue frame	$1,650	$1,400	$1,200	$995	$850	$725	$595
5½ in. Blue frame	$1,650	$1,400	$1,200	$995	$850	$725	$595
7½ in. Blue frame	$1,650	$1,400	$1,200	$995	$850	$725	$595
4¾ in. Nickel	$2,250	$1,850	$1,575	$1,250	$950	$825	$695
5½ in. Nickel	$1,850	$1,550	$1,300	$1,050	$875	$750	$625
7½ in. Nickel	$1,650	$1,400	$1,200	$995	$850	$725	$595

Add $200+ for original ivory grips.
Add $50-$75 for those pistols with original "black box".
100% assumes NIB condition for this model.
Earlier 2nd generations with the Rampant Colt grips (serial numbered under 50,000 approx.) are a little more desirable than those SAAs with Eagle grips (serial numbered over 50,000 approx.).
Early 2nd generation SAAs in 98%+ original condition with the black box (pre-1965) will command a premium over values listed above. "Stagecoach" boxes were used approx. 1965-1973 and are not quite as desirable as the one piece black box. Original "Stagecoach" boxes in excellent condition are currently selling for approx. $50.

Factory Engraved 2nd Generation SAAs — since approx. only 350 SAAs were factory engraved (with almost 90% being in .45 LC cal.), accurate pricing with this degree of rarity factor is difficult to ascertain with any degree of certainty. Prices overall will be at least 50% higher than their 3rd generation engraved counterparts.
Factory engraved 2nd generation SAAs are at least 10 times rarer than 3rd generation engraved pistols.

Sheriff's Model (1961 Model) — SM suffix, .45 cal., 3 in. barrel without ejector rod housing, casehardened finish, many custom options were ordered in this variation. Approx. 1,000 mfg. 1961.

	100%	98%	95%	90%	80%	70%	60%
	$1,995	$1,725	$1,375	$995	$800	$750	$695

Add 300% for nickel finish.
Add $200 for ivory grips.

Grading	100%	98%	95%	90%	80%	70%	60%

Buntline Special — .45 Colt only, 12 in. barrel, case hardened frame, hard rubber (rarer) or walnut grips. Over 3,900 mfg. between 1957-1975.

	100%	98%	95%	90%	80%	70%	60%
	$950	$825	$700	$635	$600	$575	$550

Add 50% for nickel finish (rare).

NEW FRONTIER — "NF" suffix, flat-top frame, adj. rear sight, .357 Mag., .38 Spl. (rare), .44 Spl., or .45 cal., 4¾ (rare), 5½ (rare) or 7½ (common) in. barrel, uncheckered walnut grips, case-hardened frame, over 4,200 mfg. 1961-1975.

	100%	98%	95%	90%	80%	70%	60%
	$850	$775	$675	$600	$550	$500	$475

Nickel or full-blue finish is very rare in this model.

New Frontier Buntline Special — .45 Colt only, 12 in. barrel, flat-top frame, adj. rear sight. Approx. 70 mfg. 1962-1967.

	100%	98%	95%	90%	80%	70%	60%
	$1,750	$1,450	$995	$850	$725	$600	$500

3RD GENERATION SINGLE ACTION ARMY: 1976-1985 MFG.

For a listing of Colt's 'P-Codes' (referring to the factory's model number designations specifying caliber, finish, and barrel length), please refer to 'COLT SINGLE-ACTION MODEL NUMBERS' on page 1,191.

The order of desirability on standard 3nd generation SAAs is as follows: 4¾ barrels are the most desirable, followed by 5½ in., and then 7½ in. Caliber desirability is as follows: .44-40 and .45 LC have the most demand followed by .44 Spl., .38 Spl., and then .357 Mag. It follows that desirable calibers found with desirable barrel lengths will command healthy premiums — especially if production was unusually low in a particular combination. Reference books specifically on the post-war SAA are a must when determining the rarity factors(or if they exist) on these multiple production combinations. Buntlines, Sheriff's models, and special orders through the Custom Gun Shop are in a class by themselves and have to be evaluated one at a time.

SINGLE ACTION ARMY — .357 Mag., .44 Spl., .44-40, or .45 LC cal., 3 (Sheriff's Model), 4¾, 5½, 7½, or 12 in. (Buntline) barrel lengths, all blue, blue/case hardened, or nickel finishes, walnut or rubber stocks.

3rd model production began in 1976 with ser. no. 80000SA and reached no. 99999SA in 1978. At this point the SA suffix changed to a prefix (beginning with SA01001).

It is advisable to procure a factory letter when buying or selling older or recently manufactured Colt Single Actions (hence guaranteeing authenticity and value credibility). These watermarked letters are available by writing Colt Firearms in Hartford, CT, with a charge of $45 per serial number - if Colt cannot provide you with proper documentation after conducting research, they will refund you $10. Include your name and address, Colt model name, serial number, and check to: COLT HISTORIAN, P.O. BOX 1868, HARTFORD, CT 06101. Please allow adequate time for proper response.

Because SAAs are a complex field in themselves, values below have been separated by calibers first, barrel lengths second, and finishes third (CH designates color case hardening).

.357 Mag. cal.

	100%	98%	95%	90%	80%	70%	60%
4¾ in. CH frame	$895	$775	$695	$650	$600	$550	$495
5½ in. CH frame	$795	$675	$625	$575	$525	$495	$450
7½ in. CH frame	$795	$675	$625	$575	$525	$495	$450
4¾ in. Blue frame	$850	$725	$650	$620	$565	$525	$475
5½ in. Blue frame	$795	$675	$625	$575	$525	$495	$450
7½ in. Blue frame	$795	$675	$625	$575	$525	$495	$450
4¾ in. Nickel	$895	$775	$695	$650	$600	$550	$495
5½ in. Nickel	$795	$675	$625	$575	$525	$495	$450
7½ in. Nickel	$795	$675	$625	$575	$525	$495	$450

Grading	100%	98%	95%	90%	80%	70%	60%
.38 Spl. cal. — this cal. is hard to find in a 3rd Generation SAA.							
4³⁄₄ in. CH frame	$1,495	$1,225	$1,050	$950	$825	$750	$675
5¹⁄₂ in. CH frame	$1,295	$1,095	$925	$825	$750	$695	$625
7¹⁄₂ in. CH frame	$1,295	$1,095	$925	$825	$750	$695	$625
4³⁄₄ in. Nickel	$1,495	$1,225	$1,050	$950	$825	$750	$675
5¹⁄₂ in. Nickel	$1,295	$1,095	$925	$825	$750	$695	$625
7¹⁄₂ in. Nickel	$1,295	$1,095	$925	$825	$750	$695	$625
.44 Spl. cal.							
4³⁄₄ in. CH frame	$895	$775	$695	$650	$600	$550	$495
5¹⁄₂ in. CH frame	$850	$725	$650	$620	$565	$525	$475
7¹⁄₂ in. CH frame	$795	$675	$625	$575	$525	$495	$450
4³⁄₄ in. Blue frame	$850	$725	$650	$620	$565	$525	$475
5¹⁄₂ in. Blue frame	$795	$675	$625	$575	$525	$495	$450
7¹⁄₂ in. Blue frame	$795	$675	$625	$575	$525	$495	$450
4³⁄₄ in. Nickel	$895	$775	$695	$650	$600	$550	$495
5¹⁄₂ in. Nickel	$850	$725	$650	$620	$565	$525	$475
7¹⁄₂ in. Nickel	$795	$675	$625	$575	$525	$495	$450
.44-40 cal.							
4³⁄₄ in. CH frame	$1,195	$1,025	$895	$795	$725	$675	$595
5¹⁄₂ in. CH frame	$995	$850	$750	$695	$650	$595	$525
7¹⁄₂ in. CH frame	$950	$825	$725	$675	$625	$575	$500
4³⁄₄ in. Blue frame	$995	$850	$750	$695	$650	$595	$525
5¹⁄₂ in. Blue frame	$895	$775	$695	$650	$600	$550	$495
7¹⁄₂ in. Blue frame	$895	$775	$695	$650	$600	$550	$495
4³⁄₄ in. Nickel	$1,195	$1,025	$895	$795	$725	$675	$595
5¹⁄₂ in. Nickel	$995	$850	$750	$695	$650	$595	$525
7¹⁄₂ in. Nickel	$950	$825	$725	$675	$625	$575	$500
.45 LC							
4³⁄₄ in. CH frame	$1,195	$1,025	$895	$795	$725	$675	$595
5¹⁄₂ in. CH frame	$1,095	$950	$825	$750	$695	$650	$575
7¹⁄₂ in. CH frame	$950	$825	$725	$675	$625	$575	$500
4³⁄₄ in. Blue frame	$995	$850	$750	$695	$650	$595	$525
5¹⁄₂ in. Blue frame	$895	$775	$695	$650	$600	$550	$495
7¹⁄₂ in. Blue frame	$895	$775	$695	$650	$600	$550	$495
4³⁄₄ in. Nickel	$1,195	$1,025	$895	$795	$725	$675	$595
5¹⁄₂ in. Nickel	$1,095	$950	$825	$750	$695	$650	$575
7¹⁄₂ in. Nickel	$950	$825	$725	$675	$625	$575	$500

Add $200 for ivory grips.
Add $100 for nickel finish.
100% assumes NIB condition for this model. Most of the buying/selling activity with 3rd Generation SAAs involves NIB specimens.

Grading	100%	98%	95%	90%	80%	70%	60%

Buntline Special — .45 Colt only, 12 in. barrel, case hardened frame.

	$795	$675	$625	$600	$575	$535	$500

Add 10% for nickel finish.

New Frontier — "NF" suffix, flat-top frame, adj. rear sight, .44 Spl., .44-40 (rare), or .45 cal., 4¾ (rare), 5½ (rare) or 7½ (common) in. barrel, uncheckered walnut grips, case hardened frame. Mfg. 1978-1981.

	$675	$525	$450	$425	$410	$395	$380

3rd generation NF serialization can be differentiated from 2nd by 5 digits (starting with 0) followed by the NF suffix. 2nd generation guns had 4 digit numbers.
For factory engraved New Frontier Models, refer to above SAA engraved listing and subtract 25%.

New Frontier Buntline Special — .45 Colt only, 12 in. barrel, flat-top frame, adj. rear sight. Rare.

	$795	$675	$575	$550	$525	$500	$485

Sheriff's Model — .44-40 or .45 LC cal., 3 in. barrel without ejector rod housing, casehardened, nickel, or royal blue finish, approx. 4,560 guns mfg. 1980-85.

	$795	$695	$650	$575	$535	$495	$460

Add 10% for extra convertible cylinder.
Add 10% for nickel finish.
Add $200 for ivory grips.
This model was also available with two cylinders (.45 LC & .45 ACP or .44 Spl. & .44-40) — add $200. The .45 LC/.45 ACP is perhaps more desirable.

Storekeepers Model — .45 LC cal. only, black powder frame, 4 in. barrel, without ejector rod, casehardened, royal blue, or nickel finish, approx. 280 mfg. 1984-85.

	$1,195	$900	$795	$700	$650	$575	$535

Premiums will exist for nickel finish.

FACTORY ENGRAVED 3RD GENERATION SAA'S

3rd generation factory engraved SAAs were produced in much greater numbers than their 2nd generation counterparts. As a result, pricing is also more predictable - especially on .45 LC cal. Since over 80% of all engraved 3rd generation SAAs are in .45 LC, values listed below represent this caliber. Engraved specimens encountered in other calibers (especially .44-40, approx. 2% of engraved production) will be considerably more expensive. Most specimens encountered are in 7½ in. barrel length. Pistols with 4¾ (most desirable) or 5½ in. barrels will add additional premiums (15%-30%).

SAA Class A Engraved — with class A engraving (25% coverage on gun).

	$1,395	$1,000	$875	$800	$725	$650	$575

Add 10% for nickel finish.

SAA Class B Engraved — with class B engraving (50% coverage on gun).

	$1,495	$1,150	$1,050	$975	$880	$760	$650

Add 10% for nickel finish.

SAA Class C Engraved — with class C engraving (75% coverage on gun).

	$1,700	$1,325	$1,125	$1,025	$925	$825	$725

Add 10% for nickel finish.

SAA Class D Engraved — with class D engraving (100% coverage on gun).

	$2,100	$1,625	$1,300	$1,125	$995	$875	$795

Add 15% for nickel finish.

SINGLE ACTION ARMY: CURRENT MFG. (1985-PRESENT)

Most collector interest in recently manufactured SAAs is for either mint or NIB specimens.

STANDARD SINGLE ACTION ARMY — .38-40, .44-40, or .45 cal., 3 (special order only), 4 (disc. 1988), 4¾, 5 (disc. 1987), 5½, 7½ or 10 (special order only) in. barrel, blue, royal blue, color case hardened (reintroduced 1989), or nickel finish, blackpowder frame, 3 line patent date, custom order only.

Mfg.'s Sug. Retail   **$1,274**   **$1,125**   **$895**   **$695**

Popular SAA Special Order Options:
Add $160 for nickel finish.
Add $160 for royal blue finish.
Add $185 for color case hardening.
Add $200 for mirror brite finish.
Add $39 (per part) to $337 for heat blued small parts.
Add $404 for gold or silver plating.
Add $207 for optional walnut/rosewood/ebony grips.
Add $269 for stag grips.
Add $759 for ivory grips.
Add $115 for consecutive serial numbers (pair).
Add $306 for individual unique serial number.
Add $230 for custom barrel shortening.
Many other options are available from the Colt Custom Shop - simply contact them for availability and a price quotation.

CUSTOM ENGRAVED MODELS

European Model — 9mm Para., nickel finish only, 4¾, 5½, or 7½ in. barrel, rosewood grips with silver medallions, 40-43 oz. Mfg. 1991-92 only.

                    $1,395 **$1,195**   **$995**

Last Mfg.'s Sug. Retail was $1,990.

U.S. Model — .45 ACP, royal blue finish only, 4¾, 5½, or 7½ in. barrel, walnut grips, 40-43 oz. Mfg. 1991-92 only.

                    $1,295 **$1,095**   **$875**

Last Mfg.'s Sug. Retail was $1,960.

CUSTOM SHOP ENGRAVING — Values below reflect published 1993 Custom Shop, Master Quality engraving options. SAA values are determined by the optional engraving shown below plus the base price of the gun (including any other special order features).
Add $1,163 for Class "A" engraving (¼ metal coverage).
Add $2,324 for Class "B" engraving (½ metal coverage).
Add $3,486 for Class "C" engraving (¾ metal coverage).
Add $4,647 for Class "D" engraving (full metal coverage).
Add an additional 13% (approx.) for buntline engraving.

Additional SAA Custom Order Options — the Colt Custom Shop will perform additional work (special orders including engraving, custom stocks, non-standard barrel lengths, gold or silver plating, and other custom features) if the individual work order totals over $1,274 retail. Quotations are supplied at $25/each for these special order guns. Please contact the Colt Custom Gun Shop for this written estimate regarding these custom built SAAs. Their address is: Colt Customer Service Dept., Attn: SAA Quotation, P.O. Box 1868, Hartford, CT 06101.

Grading	100%	98%	95%	90%	80%	70%	60%

SCOUT MODEL SAA

FRONTIER SCOUT (Q or F SUFFIX) — .22 LR or .22 Mag. (introduced after 1960) cal., "Q" or "F" suffix, blue with bright alloy frame, all blue, or duotone ("Q" models only) finish (rare), 4¾ or 9½ (Buntline) barrel, available with interchangeable cylinders after 1964, black composition or walnut grips, approx. 246,000 mfg. 1957-1970.

	$375	$325	$275	$225	$175	$150	$140

Add 10% for extra cylinder.
Add 20% for Buntline model.
Add 25% for "Q" suffix - mfg. 1957-58 only.

FRONTIER SCOUT (K SUFFIX) — Zamac alloy frame version of "Q" Model with "K" suffix, blue or nickel finish with walnut stocks, approx. 44,000 mfg. 1960-1970.

	$395	$350	$295	$250	$200	$175	$150

Add 25% for nickel finish.
This model used the alloy Zamac for manufacture (as opposed to aluminum in the "Q" and "F" suffix models), and specimens are 6 oz. heavier as a result.

FRONTIER SCOUT '62 (P SUFFIX) — blue finish version of "K" Model, except has "P" suffix, staglite grips, approx. 68,000 mfg. 1962-1970.

	$395	$350	$295	$250	$200	$175	$150

PEACEMAKER — .22 LR/.22 Mag., color casehardened steel frame, 4⅜, 6, or 7½ (nicknamed Buntline Model but may be marked Peacemaker or Buntline) in. barrel, black composition grips, furnished with interchangeable .22 LR/.22 Mag. cylinders, approx. 190,000 mfg. 1970-1977.

	$300	$260	$225	$185	$160	$140	$130

Add 20% for Buntline model or 4¾ in. barrel.
Subtract $35 if without extra cylinder.
This model can be denoted by a "G" or "L" prefix.

G 18711
6" 6.

NEW FRONTIER — similar features as Peacemaker Model, except with flat top frame, ramp front and adj. rear sight, mfg. 1970-1977. Reintroduced in 1982 without convertible .22 Mag. cylinder and added cross bolt safety, available in Coltguard finish, all blue finish became standard in 1985, mfg. disc. 1986.

	$280	$240	$200	$175	$155	$140	$130

Add 15% for Buntline model or 4¾ in. barrel.
This model can be denoted by a "G" or "L" prefix.
Last Mfg.'s Sug. Retail was $181.

PISTOLS: SEMI-AUTO

Until several years ago, the Single Action Army revolver commanded the most attention among Colt handgun collectors. Since 1987, Colt Semi-Autos have been in tremendous demand and have out-accelerated many other areas of Colt collecting. Because condition and originality play such a key role in determining Colt Semi-Auto prices, many variations have had their values pushed upward to the point where it is difficult to accurately determine a realistic price - especially on those models in 98% original condition or better. As a result, some of the rarer models seldomly encountered in true 100% original condition have had their values deleted in the 13th edition since extreme rarity precludes accurate price evaluation in this 100% condition category. As always, the hardest prices to ascertain when firearms market conditions are bullish are the 98-100% values.

MODEL 1900 — .38 ACP, 6 in. barrel, blue, fixed sights, plain walnut grips - checkered hard rubber grips after S/N 2,450, high spur hammer, sight safety. Mfg. 1900-1903.

	N/A	$5,500	$4,200	$3,000	$1,850	$1,300	$1,000

Add 60%+ for USN marked.
Add 50% for US marked with inspector initials.
Deduct 30%-50% for sight safety altered (factory refinished).
This model is serial numbered approx. between 1-4,274.

Grading	100%	98%	95%	90%	80%	70%	60%

MODEL 1902 SPORTING — .38 ACP, 6 in. barrel, blue, fixed sights, checkered hard rubber grips, no safety, high spur hammer and round hammer. Mfg. 1902-1908.

	N/A	$2,600	$1,500	$1,100	$850	$650	$550

This model is serial numbered approx. 4,275-11,000 and 30,000-30,190.

MODEL 1902 MILITARY — .38 ACP, 6 in. barrel, blue, similar to 1902 Sporting, hammer changed to spur type in 1908, checkered black hard rubber grips, Lanyard swivel on bottom rear of left grip. Mfg. 1902-1929.

	N/A	$2,000	$1,200	$900	$750	$625	$500

Add 30% for front slide checkering.
This model is serial numbered approx. 11,000-16,000 and 30,200-43,266.

MODEL 1902 MILITARY-U.S. ARMY MARKED — similar specifications to 1902 Military, only serial number range 15,001-15,200.

	N/A	$6,500	$5,000	$4,000	$3,500	$2,750	$1,950

MODEL 1903 POCKET (MODEL M 38 ACP) — .38 ACP, 4½ in. barrel, blue finish, checkered black hard rubber grips, similar to 1902 Sporting, but 4½ in. barrel, 7½ in. overall. Mfg. 1903-1929.

	N/A	$1,100	$850	$700	$525	$475	$425

Add 10% for early round hammer.
This model is serial numbered approx. 16,000-47,226.

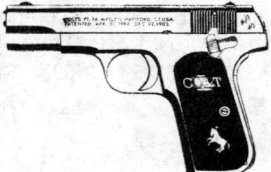

MODEL 1903 POCKET (MODEL M 32 ACP) — .32 ACP, 4 in. barrel, wood blue, checkered hard rubber grips, hammerless, slide lock and grip safety, barrel lock bushing. Mfg. 1903-1940.

$500	$400	$350	$300	$275	$250	$200

Add $50 for nickel finish (mostly w/pearl grips).
Add 20% for first model (Type I) mfg. 1903-1911.
Type I - 32 ACPs have a 4 in. barrel, barrel bushing, no magazine safety, and are serial numbered 1-71,999.
Type II - 32 ACPs still retain their barrel bushing but have a 3¾ in. barrel and were mfg. from 1908-1910. They are serial numbered 72,000-105,050.
Type III - 32 ACPs do not have a barrel bushing and were mfg. from 1910-1926. They are serial numbered 105,051-468,096.
Type IV - 32 ACPs have the added magazine safety (of which there are both the commercial and "U.S. Property" variations). They are serial numbered 468,097-554,446.

Model 1903 Parkerized — U.S. property, 3¼ in. barrel, no barrel bushing, magazine safety, serial numbered 554,447-572,214.

$925	$750	$625	$475	$375	$320	$275

Add 15% for blue U.S. Property S/N 554,447 - approx. 562,000.
The 100% value on this model assumes NIB condition.

MODEL 1905 — .45 ACP, 5 in. barrel, blue fixed sights, checkered walnut stocks, similar to 1902 .38 ACP. Mfg. 1905-1911.

	N/A	$3,500	$2,500	$1,500	$1,100	$850	$700

Add 150% for 1907 U.S. Military Contract variation.
The shoulder stock option for this pistol is exceedingly rare. Depending on the condition, this accessory can add $5,000-$10,000 to the price of the gun.

Grading	100%	98%	95%	90%	80%	70%	60%

MODEL 1908 POCKET (MODEL M 380 ACP)

MODEL 1908 POCKET (MODEL M 380 ACP) — .380 ACP, first issue, 3¾ in.barrel only, similar to Pocket Model .32 ACP (32 ACP), except chambered for .380 ACP. Mfg. 1908-1940.

	100%	98%	95%	90%	80%	70%	60%
	$750	$600	$425	$350	$300	$250	$225

Add 15% for Type II (see explanation below).
Add $50 for nickel finish (mostly w/pearl grips).
100% values assume NIB condition. Deduct 15% if without cardboard box. Pearl grips are normally encountered with nickel finish on this model.
Type II - 380 ACPs with barrel bushing and were mfg. 1908-1910 (6,251 mfg.). They are serial numbered 1-6,251.
Type III - 380 ACPs do not have a barrel bushing and were mfg. 1910-1926. They are serial numbered 6,252-92,893.
Type IV - 380 ACPs have the added magazine safety (of which there are both the commercial and "U.S. Property" variations). They are serial numbered 92,894-134,499.

Model 1908 "U.S. Property" — blue finish only, U.S. property. Serial numbered 134,500-138,000.

	100%	98%	95%	90%	80%	70%	60%
	$1,500	$1,250	$925	$750	$650	$500	$350

VEST POCKET MODEL 1908-

HAMMERLESS — .25 ACP, 2 in. barrel, fixed sights, checkered hard rubber grips on early models, walnut on later, magazine disconnect added on guns made after 1916. Mfg. 1908-1941.

	100%	98%	95%	90%	80%	70%	60%
Blue finish	$500	$400	$315	$270	$240	$200	$155
Nickel finish	$575	$425	$325	$285	$240	$200	$155

100% values assume NIB condition. Deduct 15% if without cardboard box. Pearl grips are normally encountered with nickel finish on this model.

MODEL 1909

MODEL 1909 — .45 ACP, straight handle design, 5 in. barrel, checkered walnut grips, approx. 22 mfg., ultra rare.
Extreme rarity factor precludes accurate price evaluation by individual condition factors. Specimens that are original and over 90% have sold for over $35,000 recently.

GENERAL OFFICER'S PISTOL

GENERAL OFFICER'S PISTOL — issued not only to Generals, but also, many were issued to the OSS, U.S. Navy, and other government agencies, .32 U.S. Properties were blued until 1942, after which the parkerized finish became standard (most went to England and exhibit British proofmarks), .380 U.S. Properties were always blued, 1911A1 WWII specimens have standard military finish, and the Rock Island Arsenal .45s were all issued to Generals.

	100%	98%	95%	90%	80%	70%	60%
.32 cal. parkerized	$1,800	$1,550	$1,275	$1,100	$975	$875	$775
.32 cal. blue	$2,500	$2,250	$1,975	$1,725	$1,500	$1,300	$1,100
.380 ACP cal.	$2,700	$2,400	$2,100	$1,850	$1,600	$1,400	$1,200
.45 ACP cal. (WWII mfg.)	$1,500	$1,250	$1,050	$875	$775	$675	$595
M15 (Rock Island Arsenal Mfg.)	$4,000	$3,500	$3,150	$2,650	$2,250	$1,850	$1,500

Values above assume issue to a General (i.e., except for the Rock Island Arsenal .45 ACP cal. variation, there must be paperwork to link up the gun to the recipient).

GOVT. MODEL 1911 COMMERCIAL VARIATIONS

MODEL 1911 — .45 ACP, 5 in. barrel, fixed sights, 7 shot mag., flat main spring housing, polished blue finish only (commercial and original military), checkered walnut grips. Colt licensed other companies to manufacture under government contracts, 39 oz. Mfg. 1912-1925. Most M1911 variations listed below are not as collectible if under 60% original condition. However, they are still very desirable as shooters and values (if in original condition) will approximate the 60% prices if in good mechanical condition.

Add 20% for 4-digit ser. no., 40% for 3-digit, 60%+ for 2-digit.

Colt Model 1911s are enjoying high demand as of this writing and prices have increased the most in the 95%-100% condition factors. Be careful on the 98%+ condition specimens, especially the rarer variations. Some collectors are now requiring a potential high-dollar Model 1911 to pass an X-ray examination metallurgically before purchasing.

⚔ **Model 1911 Commercial** — denoted by "C" preceding serial number, approx. ser. number range C1-C138,532. Watch for fakes.

	100%	98%	95%	90%	80%	70%	60%
1912-1914 mfg.	$2,800	$1,850	$1,200	$875	$695	$550	$425
1914-1925 mfg.	$2,600	$1,600	$1,100	$850	$650	$525	$400

Approx. 138,532 were mfg. between 1912-1925.

100% values assume NIB condition. Deduct 15% if without cardboard box. Pearl grips are normally encountered with nickel finish on this model.

GOVT. MODEL 1911 .45 ACP MILITARY VARIATIONS

COLT MFG. MODEL 1911 MILITARY — right side of slide marked "MODEL OF 1911 U.S. ARMY", blue finish only (NOT parkerized unless reworked).

	100%	98%	95%	90%	80%	70%	60%
1912-1913 mfg.	$2,000	$1,500	$895	$675	$475	$450	$400
1914-1925 mfg.	$1,600	$1,200	$850	$595	$540	$425	$375

Over 2,550,000 M1911 pistols were ordered during WWI by U.S. Government but approx. 650,000 were mfg. between 1911-1925. Those pistols with a parkerized finish will indicate post-WWI reworking, usually marked with an arsenal code (ie. AA-AUGUSTA ARSENAL, SA-SPRINGFIELD ARSENAL, etc.). These reworks do not have the same values as original, unaltered specimens and prices generally are in the $295-$475 range.

NORTH AMERICAN ARMS COMPANY — less than 100 mfg. in Quebec, Ontario during 1918 only, blued finish. Be very wary of fakes as this variation is perhaps the most desirable Colt WWI Govt. semi-auto.

100%	98%	95%	90%	80%	70%	60%
$12,500	$9,950	$8,750	$7,850	$6,750	$6,000	$5,000

REMINGTON - UMC — over 21,500 mfg. (ser. numbered 1-21,676) in 1918-1919 only, blued finish.

100%	98%	95%	90%	80%	70%	60%
$2,250	$1,500	$1,000	$750	$600	$550	$500

SPRINGFIELD ARMORY — approx. 30,000 mfg. between 1914-1915, blued finish.

100%	98%	95%	90%	80%	70%	60%
$2,000	$1,325	$850	$675	$550	$500	$475

Serialization is 72,751-83,855, 102,597-107,596, 113,497-120,566, and 125,567-133,186.

U.S. NAVY — over 31,000 mfg. for U.S. Navy contract between 1911-1914 in defined serial ranges, blued finish. Marked "MODEL OF 1911 U.S. NAVY" on right slide side.

100%	98%	95%	90%	80%	70%	60%
$3,000	$2,400	$1,800	$1,500	$1,200	$995	$750

U.S. Navy specimens are seldomly found in over 80% original condition because of the corrosive factor encountered while at sea.

Grading	100%	98%	95%	90%	80%	70%	60%

U.S. MARINE CORPS. — approx. 13,500 mfg. between 1911-1913 and 1916-1918 in defined serial ranges, blued finish, right side of slide marked "MODEL OF 1911 U.S. ARMY".

	$2,750	$2,200	$1,800	$1,500	$1,200	$995	$750

WWI BRITISH SERIES — .455 cal., serialized W10001-W21000, marked "CALIBRE 455", blued finish, proofed with broad arrow British Ordnance punch Mfg. 1915-1916.

	$1,995	$1,600	$1,150	$900	$795	$600	$475

Add 25% for variations with either Navy or Marine markings. Many WWI British-series M1911s were exported back to the U.S. following WWI and were converted to .45 ACP. Usually, a "5" has been crossed-out of the original cal. designation. These reworks are not as collectible and prices range from $350-$500.

BRITISH RAF REWORK — this variation is the WWI British series re-issued to RAF officers in the early 1920's, blued finish, differentiated by hand-stamped "RAF" or "R.A.F." on left side of frame.

	$975	$875	$825	$675	$575	$495	$460

A.J. SAVAGE MUNITIONS CO. — mfg. slides only, blued finish, marked in middle on left side of slide with flaming ordnance bomb with "S" in center.

	$1,600	$1,200	$850	$750	$675	$600	$525

NORWEGIAN TRIAL MODEL 1911 COLT — 11.25mm cal., approx. 300 mfg. with "C" prefix in 1913-14 only, usually encountered in 90% or less condition.

	$1,350	$1,100	$975	$850	$750	$595	$495

These guns were ordered for Norwegian service evaluation and were mfg. by Colt's in Hartford, CT.

NORWEGIAN MODEL 1912 11.25MM — 11.25mm cal., mfg. under license from Colt's between 1917-1919, "M1912" slide designation, approx. 500 mfg.

	$1,650	$1,300	$975	$850	$750	$595	$495

NORWEGIAN 1914 11.25MM — This model has a distinctive extended slide release, approx. 20,000 mfg. between 1919-1932.

	$950	$725	$600	$525	$475	$425	$375

Add 100% for Waffenamt Nazi mfg. (mfg. 1945 only).
Nazi production of the M1914 began in 1941, with serialization beginning where 1932 mfg. left off (approx. 21,000 range). Between 1941-42, approx. 7,000 pistols were mfg. without Waffenamt stampings. Nazi stamped guns (all 1945 dated) began in the mid-29,000 serial range and existing specimens indicate that approx. 1,000 were mfg. with the Nazi Eagle.

ARGENTINE CONTRACT — mfg. 1917-1925, ser. no.'s are in C20,001-21,000 and C110,000-130,000 range, slide marked "Pistola Automatica Sistema Colt, Calilbre 11.25 mm, Modelo 1916", usually marked with Argentine seal.

	$1,250	$900	$625	$575	$450	$410	$350

This variation is not to be confused with the Ballestar Molina Model with integral grip strap (.45 ACP or .22 LR) that resembles a Colt 1911, but was not licensed or mfg. by Colt. 100% value for the .45 ACP is $400 - add 100% for .22 LR Target Model.

RUSSIAN CONTRACT — approx. 50,000 mfg. with frame marked "ANGLO ZAKAZIVAT", blued finish. Mfg. 1915-1917, seldomly encountered - watch for fakes.

	$2,450	$2,000	$1,600	$1,400	$1,250	$1,100	$1,000

Grading	100%	98%	95%	90%	80%	70%	60%

GOVT. MODEL 1911A1 & VARIATIONS

MODEL 1911 A1 — .45 ACP, blue or parkerized, checkered walnut grips, plastic on later military guns, checkered arched mainspring housing and longer grip safety spur. As in the Model 1911, Colt licensed other companies to produce under govt. contract during WWII. Mfg. 1925-1970.

Inspect carefully for arsenal reworks (so marked by proofing, normally on left side of frame above or behind trigger), and reparkerizing.

Most M1911 A1 variations listed below are not as collectible if under 60% original condition. However, they are still very desirable as shooters and values (if in original condition) will approximate the 60% prices if in good mechanical condition.

PRE-WWII COLT COMMERCIAL — "C" preceding serial number, mfg. 1925-1942. Approx. ser. no. range C138,533-C215,000.

	$1,450	$975	$750	$620	$575	$495	$400

1946-1969 COLT COMMERCIAL — "C" prefix until 1950 when changed to "C" suffix, approx. 196,000 mfg. 1946-1970.

	$750	$600	$550	$425	$375	$330	$295

Add 20% for "C" prefix models after ser. no. 221,000.

SUPER .38 AUTOMATIC PISTOL — identical to Govt. Model .45, except chambered for .38 Super automatic. Mfg. 1928-1970.

	100%	98%	95%	90%	80%	70%	60%
Pre-War	$2,600	$2,200	$1,500	$1,200	$950	$850	$750
Post-War	$850	$750	$575	$500	$450	$400	$375

Add 15% to post-war if with heavy barrel (under approx. 115,000 ser. no.).
Pre-war variations are serialized below approx. 37,000.

SUPER MATCH .38 — similar to Super .38, but hand honed action, match grade barrel. Mfg. 1935-1941. Examine carefully for fakes.

	100%	98%	95%	90%	80%	70%	60%
Fixed sights	$4,750	$3,950	$3,000	$2,200	$1,450	$1,150	$1,000

Add 20% for adj. sights.

SUPER MATCH .38 AMU — .38 rimless Spl. cal. (cartridges were mfg. by Win.), this variation was mfg. by Colt from a .38 Super frame (and has .38 Super serialization) with a .38 AMU conversion kit slide, the Army took .45 frames and assembled their guns using .38 AMU kits, blued finish.

	100%	98%	95%	90%	80%	70%	60%
Colt mfg. (unmodified)	$2,500	$2,200	$1,900	$1,675	$1,400	$1,175	$975
Army modified	$1,400	$1,200	$995	$800	$650	$550	$495
AMU kit only	$550	$475	$425	$385	$350	$325	$295

On this configuration, the barrel, slide, and mag. were marked ".38 AMU".

SUPER MATCH .38 MS — .38 Super cal., 1961 mfg., serial numbered 101MS - 855MS, 754 total manufactured, same configuration as the .38 Midrange.

	$2,800	$2,500	$1,750	$1,495	$1,375	$1,175	$1,000

1968-1969 BB TRANSITIONAL

	$800	$695	$600	$550	$495	$425	$375

Grading	100%	98%	95%	90%	80%	70%	60%

.45 ACP TO .22 LR CONVERSION UNIT — consists of slide assembly, barrel, bushing, floating chamber, ejector, recoil spring and guide, fitted with Stevens adj. rear sight, mfg. 1938 to 1947. Colt Master adj. sight 1947-54.

		$375	$325	$225	$175	$150	$140	$120

Add 100% for prewar mfg. (u-prefix S/N on top of slide).

.22 LR TO .45 ACP CONVERSION UNIT — converted service Ace .22 to .45 ACP. Mfg. 1938-1942. Very rare — 112 mfg.

	$3,500	$2,500	$1,750	$1,000	$800	$700	$600

These units are serial numbered on top of slide.

GOVT. MODEL 1911A1 MILITARY VARIATIONS

COLT MFG. MODEL 1911A1 MILITARY — approx. 1,643,068 mfg. between 1924-1945, ser. nos. 700,000 - on up, right side of frame marked "M1911A1 U.S. ARMY".

		$850	$675	$525	$425	$375	$350	$325

On early 1911 A1 military models with bright blue finish — add 100% if condition is 98% or better.

A large grouping of over 7,000 Commercial 1911A1s was transferred to the U.S. government - these pistols had their commercial serial numbers crudely removed (in ser. range 860,000 - 866,000) and renumbered with a new military serial number. Some of these guns are unusual as the frames and slides have been cut for the Schwartz safety. This variation is rare, and premiums exist depending on the condition.

DRAKE NATIONAL MATCH — Drake made slides only for use by U.S. Army Marksman Unit to allow assembly of match guns.

	$1,150	$995	$850	$700	$585	$510	$450

GOVERNMENT NATIONAL MATCH REWORKS — assembled by government armorers, all parts marked "NM", parkerized finish. Most will be S.A. marked.

	$1,100	$950	$800	$675	$585	$510	$450

These pistols were made specifically for the U.S. shooting team at Camp Perry.

ITHACA — approx. 369,129 mfg. 1943-1945 in Ithaca, NY, ser. no. ranges 856,101 - 916,404, 1,208,674 - 1,279,673, 1,441,431 - 1,471,430, 1,816,642 - 1,890,503, and 2,619,014 - 2,693,613. Parkerized finish.

	$695	$575	$495	$450	$375	$350	$325

UNION SWITCH AND SIGNAL — approx. 55,000 mfg. 1943 only in Swissvale, PA, ser. no. range 1,041,405 - 1,096,404. Parkerized finish.

	$1,150	$895	$675	$550	$475	$425	$395

REMINGTON RAND — approx. 1,086,624 mfg. 1943-1945 in Syracuse, NY, ser. no. ranges 916,405 - 1,041,404, 1,279,649 - 1,441,430, 1,471,431 - 1,609,528, 1,743,847 - 1,816,641, 1,890,504 - 2,075,103, 2,134,404 - 2,244,803, and 2,380,014 - 2,619,013. Parkerized finish.

	$650	$550	$475	$425	$370	$350	$325

SINGER MFG. CO. — 500 mfg. 1942 in Elizabeth, NJ, ser. no. range S800,001 - S800,500. Blued finish with plastic grips.

	$13,250	$10,950	$9,150	$8,375	$7,500	$6,750	$5,875

The Singer 1911A1 variation is one of the most sought after Colt models. In recent years, values have increased significantly and as a result, many fakes have emerged. Most specimens are now recognized by ser. no. and be very cautious when contemplating a purchase. Some collectors unsure of authenticity are now requiring X-ray testing to determine originality (slide restampings, ser. no. changes, etc.).

Grading	100%	98%	95%	90%	80%	70%	60%

MEXICAN CONTRACT — mfg. approx. 1921-1927 with "C" prefix ser. nos., frames marked "EJERCITO MEXICANO", most surviving examples show much use.

| | $1,500 | $1,100 | $825 | $700 | $625 | $550 | $495 |

BRAZILIAN

| | $1,500 | $1,100 | $825 | $700 | $625 | $550 | $495 |

ARGENTINE CONTRACT — mfg. 1927-early 30's, ser. nos. are in low C140,000 range, slide marked "EJERCITO ARGENTINO COLT.CAL.45 MOD.1927" checkered walnut grips. This variation has recently been imported again.

| | $1,200 | $995 | $825 | $700 | $625 | $550 | $495 |

ARGENTINE MFG. — in 1927, the Argentina Arsenal began manufacturing the Model 1911A1. The slide marking is two lines and reads "EJERCITO ARGENTINO SIST.COLT.CAL. 11.25 mm MOD.1927".

| | $750 | $650 | $500 | $450 | $400 | $350 | $325 |

ACE MODELS: PRE-WWII

COMMERCIAL ACE — .22 LR, similar to Government .45 ACP, but in .22LR cal., 4¾ in. barrel, blue, adj. sights, checkered walnut grips, almost 11,000 mfg. (ser. no. range 1-10,935) 1931-1941 and 1947.

| | $1,950 | $1,675 | $1,250 | $900 | $700 | $550 | $450 |

SERVICE MODEL ACE — .22 LR, 5 in. barrel, blue or parkerized finish, similar to .45 ACP National Match except for caliber, has floating chamber to simulate .45 ACP recoil, limited mfg. 1935-1945.

| | $2,250 | $1,850 | $1,375 | $1,000 | $775 | $600 | $525 |

This variation is marked "SERVICE MODEL" on left frame, serial numbers have "SM" prefix and have ranges to approx. 13,800. Parkerized finish is less desirable.

PRE-WWII NATIONAL MATCH MODELS

NATIONAL MATCH — .45 ACP, similar to Government Model, except has hand honed action, match grade barrel, blue. Mfg. 1933-1941 within ser. no. range C164,800 - C215,000.

✠ **Fixed sights**

| | $2,200 | $1,600 | $1,250 | $850 | $625 | $550 | $500 |

✠ **Adj. sights**

| | $2,950 | $2,200 | $1,750 | $1,475 | $1,200 | $995 | $750 |

POST-WWII NATIONAL MATCH MODELS

GOLD CUP NATIONAL MATCH — .45 ACP, match grade barrel, new design bushing, flat mainspring housing, long adj. stop trigger, hand fitted slide with enlarged ejection port, adj. target sights, gold medallions in grips, "NM" suffix. Mfg. 1957-1970.

| | $825 | $675 | $550 | $450 | $405 | $380 | $350 |

Note: This model was the first National Match Model manufactured following WW II.

GOLD CUP MKIII NATIONAL MATCH — .38 Spl., similar to Gold Cup National Match, except chambered for .38 Spl., mid-range wadcutter. Mfg. 1961-1974.

| | $875 | $775 | $695 | $625 | $575 | $475 | $435 |

Grading	100%	98%	95%	90%	80%	70%	60%

MKIV/SERIES 70 GOLD CUP NATIONAL MATCH — .45 ACP, flat mainspring housing, accurizer barrel and bushing, adj. trigger, target hammer, solid rib, Colt Elliason sight. Mfg. 1970-1983.

		$650	$595	$525	$465	$435	$395	$360

MKIV/SERIES 70 GOLD CUP 75TH ANNIVERSARY NATIONAL MATCH — similar to Gold Cup except for commemorative aspect for Camp Perry, 1978, 200 made.
Add 100% to standard Mark IV/Series 70 Gold Cup prices.

GOLD CUP MKIV SERIES 80 NATIONAL MATCH — .45 ACP, 5 in. barrel, 7 or 8 (new 1992) shot mag., 39 oz., Colt-Elliason adj. rear sight, wide grooved adj. target trigger, under cut front sight, flat mainspring housing, critical internal parts are hand honed. Mfg. 1983-present.

Mfg.'s Sug. Retail	$861	$685	$540	$450	$400	$380	$350	$325

In 1992, this model was updated to accept an 8 shot mag.

* **Stainless Gold Cup National Match** — similar to Gold Cup, only manufactured from stainless steel, matte finish, released late in 1986.

Mfg.'s Sug. Retail	$921	$725	$565	$450

Add $69 for "Ultimate" bright stainless steel finish.

* **.38 Super Elite National Match** — two-tone gun (stainless slide and blued frame), special edition by Accu-Sports.

	$1,100	$925	$825

* **Bullseye National Match** — .45 ACP cal., hand built, tuned, and adjusted by Colt's custom gunsmiths for precise match accuracy, includes factory installed Bomar sights, equipped with carrying case and 2 extra mag.'s. Mfg. 1991-92.

	$1,325	$1,075	$895	$800	$725	$650	$600

Last Mfg.'s Sug. Retail was $1,500.

* **Presentation Gold Cup** — .45 ACP cal., similar to regular Gold Cup Series 80 National Match, except has a deep blue-mirror bright finish accented by custom jeweled hammer, trigger, and barrel hood. Supplied with oak and velvet custom case. Mfg. 1991-92.

	$1,075	$895	$800	$725	$650	$600	$550

Last Mfg.'s Sug. Retail was $1,195.

PISTOLS: SEMI-AUTO, RECENT MFG.

The values listed below are the last published factory engraving prices - factory specified "Class A - Class D" pricing was discontinued late 1990. Beginning in 1991, factory engraving on the models listed below is done per individual price quotation. Quotations from Colt are available at $25 each (deductible from work order). These prices (disc. 1990) should be added to the cost of each engraved production gun (NIB condition only) to determine an approximate value.

MODELS MUSTANG, .380 ACP GOVERNMENT, DETECTIVE SPECIAL, AND DIAMONDBACK
CLASS "A" ENGRAVING (¼ METAL COVERAGE) — ADD $587.
CLASS "B" ENGRAVING (½ METAL COVERAGE) — ADD $793.
CLASS "C" ENGRAVING (¾ METAL COVERAGE) — ADD $1,026.
CLASS "D" ENGRAVING (FULL METAL COVERAGE) — ADD $1,203.
MODELS .45 ACP GOLD CUP, GOVERNMENT MODEL, OFFICER'S ACP, PYTHON, COMBAT COMMANDER, KING COBRA, TROOPER MKV, LAWMAN MKV, AND DELTA ELITE.
CLASS "A" ENGRAVING (¼ METAL COVERAGE) — ADD $734.
CLASS "B" ENGRAVING (½ METAL COVERAGE) — ADD $997.
CLASS "C" ENGRAVING (¾ METAL COVERAGE) — ADD $1,231.
CLASS "D" ENGRAVING (FULL METAL COVERAGE) — ADD $1,495.
Beginning in 1991, Colt began shipping all models in a distinctive blue plastic carrying case/shipping container.

COLT cont.

Grading	100%	98%	95%	90%	80%	70%	60%

SPECIAL ENGRAVING/OPTIONS — Also available: inlays, seals, custom grips, lettering, prices quoted on request. Smooth ivory grips are $215 extra (1990 retail).

JUNIOR POCKET MODEL — 2¼ in. barrel, blue, checkered walnut grips, made by Astra in Spain from 1958-1968.

	100%	98%	95%	90%	80%	70%	60%
.22 Short	$350	$300	$240	$210	$180	$160	$140
.25 ACP	$300	$275	$200	$180	$150	$140	$130

Add 10% for nickel finish.

A very few conversion kits were offered for this model. They are rare and asking prices are $250-$325 if in mint condition.

COLT AUTOMATIC CALIBER .25 — .25 ACP cal., mfg. by Firearms International for Colt between 1970-1973.

	100%	98%	95%	90%	80%	70%	60%
	$300	$275	$225	$185	$150	$140	$130

COMMANDER (PRE-70 SERIES) — 9mm Para, .38 Super, or .45 ACP cal., 4¼ in. barrel, full size grips, steel or alloy (Lightweight Model) variations. Mfg. 1950-1969.

	100%	98%	95%	90%	80%	70%	60%
9mm	$525	$450	$400	$350	$325	$300	$275
.38 Super/.45 ACP	$625	$550	$475	$425	$375	$325	$295

MKIV/SERIES 70 GOVERNMENT MODEL — .45 ACP, .38 Super, 9mm, or 9mm Steyr, 5 in. barrel, checkered walnut grips/medallion. A slight premium might be asked for the Series 70 models if NIB. Series 70 models were mfg. 1970-1983 and were serial numbered with with "70G" prefixes 1970-1976, "G70" suffixes 1976-1980, "B70" suffixes 1979-1981, and "70B" prefixes 1981-1983.

	100%	98%	95%	90%	80%	70%	60%
Blue finish	$575	$495	$435	$380	$350	$300	$275
Nickel finish	$625	$525	$450	$400	$375	$325	$295

9mm Steyr was made for European exportation only. However, a few specimens have found their way into the United States. Prices for NIB specimens usually start in the $595+ range.

⚔ **Series 70 Combat Govt.** — .45 ACP cal., bluish-black metal finish, features modifications for combat shooting, forerunner to the Combat Elite.

	100%	98%	95%	90%	80%	70%	60%
	$575	$500	$425	$395	$365	$325	$285

⚔ **Series 70 Lightweight Commander** — 9mm Para, .38 Super, or .45 ACP cal., 4¼ in. barrel, full size grips. Mfg. 1970-1983.

	100%	98%	95%	90%	80%	70%	60%
9mm	$525	$465	$415	$350	$325	$300	$275
.38 Super/.45 ACP	$575	$525	$465	$425	$375	$325	$295

⚔ **Series 70 Combat Commander**

	100%	98%	95%	90%	80%	70%	60%
	$575	$500	$425	$395	$365	$325	$285

⚔ **Conversion Unit** — converts .45 ACP to .22 LR, mfg. 1954-84 with either Accro adj. rear sight or fixed sight.

	100%	98%	95%	90%	80%	70%	60%
Adj Sight	$350	$300	$240	$210	$190	$165	$140
Fixed Sight	$300	$275	$210	$190	$170	$155	$140

POST-WAR ACE SERVICE MODEL — .22 LR, similar specifications to previous Pre-WWII manufacture, "SM" prefix, approx. 30,000 mfg. between 1978-1982.

	100%	98%	95%	90%	80%	70%	60%
	$650	$595	$500	$450	$425	$395	$375

This model is serial numbered approx. SM14,001-SM43,830.

Grading	100%	98%	95%	90%	80%	70%	60%

MKIV/SERIES 80 GOVERNMENT MODEL — .38 Super, 9mm Para. (disc. 1992), or .45 ACP cal., single action, 5 in. barrel, 7 or 8 (new 1992) shot mag. in .45 ACP, approx. 38 oz., action has firing pin safety, checkered walnut (pre-1991 mfg.) or rubber combat style grips with medallion (new 1991). Production started in 1983 with ser. no. FG01000.

※ **Blue Finish**

Mfg.'s Sug. Retail $674	$540	$460	$385	$340	$315	$295	$275

Add $11 for 9mm Para. (disc. 1992) or .38 Super cal.

※ **Nickel Finish** — available in .45 ACP (disc. 1986) or .38 Super (disc. in 1987) cal.

$525	$465	$380	$350	$315	$285	$260

Last Mfg.'s Sug. Retail was $600.

※ **Satin Nickel/Blue** — is supplied with Colt-Pachmayr grips. Disc. 1986.

$510	$445	$370	$345	$310	$280	$255

Last Mfg.'s Sug. Retail was $557.

※ **Stainless Steel** — 9mm Para. (mfg. 1991-92), .38 Super (new 1990), .40 S&W (new 1992) or .45 ACP cal.

Mfg.'s Sug. Retail $718	$585	$490	$425

Add $9 for 9mm Para. (disc. 1992) or 38 Super cal.

※ **"Ultimate" Bright Stainless Steel** — .38 Super (new 1991) or .45 ACP cal., high polish stainless finish. New 1986.

Mfg.'s Sug. Retail $791	$635	$500	$450

Add $5 for .38 Super cal.

※ **Combat Government** — .45 ACP cal., dark matte metal finish, features modifications for combat shooting, successor to the Series 70 Combat Govt. Disc.

$550	$475	$400	$345	$310	$280	$255

※ **Special Combat Government** — .45 ACP, competition model featuring skeletized trigger, custom tuning, polished ramp, throated barrel, flared ejection port, and cut-out hammer. Supplied with two 8 shot mag.'s, hard chrome slide and receiver, Bowmar rear and Clark dovetail front sight, flared mag. well, shipped with certified target. New 1992.

Mfg.'s Sug. Retail $1,450	$1,250	$995	$895	$775	$650	$575	$495

※ **Special Combat Government (Carry Model)** — similar to Special Combat Government, except has royal blue finish, bar-dot night sights, and ambidextrous safety. New 1992.

Mfg.'s Sug. Retail $1,250	$995	$875	$750	$650	$575	$495	$400

※ **Combat Elite** — .38 Super or .45 ACP cal., similar to Gold Cup, only with wrap-around rubber grips, beveled magazine well, stainless steel receiver with carbon steel slide, and Accro adj. sighting system.

Mfg.'s Sug. Retail $816	$675	$595	$450	$400	$360	$330	$300

Add $10 for .38 Super cal.

※ **Conversion Unit - Series 80** — converts Series 80 Govt. Model only to .22 LR or 9mm, mfg. 1984-86 with Accro adj. rear sight.

9mm Para.	$325	$300	$250	$200	$170	$155	$140
.22 LR	$400	$350	$300	$240	$200	$175	$155

Last Mfg.'s Sug. Retail was $305.

LIGHTWEIGHT COMMANDER SERIES 80 — .45 ACP, 4 1/4 in. barrel, similar to Government Model, except shorter and lighter alloy frame, 27 1/2 oz., round spur hammer. Mfg. 1983-present, fixed sights.

Mfg.'s Sug. Retail $674	$575	$500	$425	$395	$360	$330	$295

Add 10% for .38 Super or 9mm Para. (disc.) cals.

Grading	100%	98%	95%	90%	80%	70%	60%

COMBAT COMMANDER SERIES 80 — .38 Super (disc.), 9mm Para. (disc. 1992), or .45 ACP cal., similar to Lightweight, except has steel frame.

⚔ **Blued Finish**

Mfg.'s Sug. Retail	$674	$540	$460	$390	$350	$300	$265	$240

Add $20 for 9mm Para. (disc.) or .38 Super (disc.) cal.

⚔ **Stainless Steel** — .38 Super (new 1992) or .45 ACP cal. only. New 1990.

Mfg.'s Sug. Retail	$728	$590	$485	$430

⚔ **Satin Nickel** — disc. 1986.

		$500	$450	$410	$365	$310	$275	$250

Last Mfg.'s Sug. Retail was $550.

⚔ **Gold Cup Commander** — .45 ACP cal., features custom shop alterations including heavy duty adj. target sights, beveled mag. well, serrated front strap, checkered mainspring housing, wide grip safety, and Palo Alto wood grips. 1991 release.

Mfg.'s Sug. Retail	$936	$865	$715	$595	$550	$495	$440	$395

⚔ **Gold Cup Commander Stainless** — stainless variation of the Gold Cup Commander. New 1992.

Mfg.'s Sug. Retail	$949	$870	$715	$595

OFFICER'S ACP SERIES 80 — .45 ACP only, 3½ in. barrel, 34 oz., 6 shot mag., short version of the Government Model. New 1985.

⚔ **Blued Finish**

Mfg.'s Sug. Retail	$674	$540	$460	$390	$350	$300	$265	$240

⚔ **Matte Blued Finish**

		$525	$440	$370	$330	$280	$250	$225

Last Mfg.'s Sug. Retail was $625 (disc. 1991).

⚔ **Officer's Stainless Steel** — matte stainless steel finish. New 1986.

Mfg.'s Sug. Retail	$718	$585	$490	$420

Add $73 for "Ultimate" bright stainless steel finish (new 1987).

⚔ **Officer's Lightweight** — similar to Officer's ACP, except has alloy frame and weighs 24 oz. New 1986.

Mfg.'s Sug. Retail	$674	$545	$460	$395	$350	$300	$265	$240

⚔ **Officer's Satin Nickel** — disc. 1985.

		$470	$410	$370	$320	$280	$260	$235

Last Mfg.'s Sug. Retail was $513.

⚔ **General Officer's Model** — bright stainless steel with rosewood grips, special edition.

Mfg.'s Sug. Retail	$750	$650	$550	$450

MKIV/SERIES 80 GOLD CUP NATIONAL MATCH — .45 ACP, flat mainspring housing, 8 shot mag., accurizer barrel and bushing, adj. trigger, target hammer, solid rib, Colt-Elliason sight, made 1983-present.

Mfg.'s Sug. Retail	$861	$685	$540	$450	$400	$380	$350	$325

In 1992, this model was updated to accept an 8 shot mag.

⚔ **Stainless Gold Cup National Match** — similar to Gold Cup, only manufactured from stainless steel, matte finish, released late in 1986.

Mfg.'s Sug. Retail	$921	$725	$565	$450

Add $69 for "Ultimate" bright stainless steel finish.

Grading	100%	98%	95%	90%	80%	70%	60%

MODEL M1991 A1 — .45 ACP only, similar to original WWII issue pistols with government issue parkerized finish, fixed sights, and black composite grips, 5 in. barrel, 7 shot mag., 38 oz., includes brown molded case. New 1991.

Mfg.'s Sug. Retail	$500	$425	$360	$330	$295	$275	$250	$225

This model is serialized consecutively with the last batch of Govt. models manufactured during 1945.

⚔ **Model M1991 A1 Compact** — similar to Model M1991 A1, except has 3½ in. barrel, 6 shot mag, 34 oz. New 1992.

Mfg.'s Sug. Retail	$500	$425	$360	$330	$295	$275	$250	$225

⚔ **Model M1991 A1 Commander** — .45 ACP cal., 4¼ in. barrel, full size grip, 7 shot mag, 36 oz. New 1993.

Mfg.'s Sug. Retail	$500	$425	$360	$330	$295	$275	$250	$225

DELTA ELITE — 10mm Norma, 5 in. barrel, black neoprene grips, high profile 3 dot sights, blue finish, 8 shot mag., 38 oz. Introduced 1987.

Mfg.'s Sug. Retail	$744	$630	$520	$460	$390	$350	$330	$310

⚔ **Stainless Steel** — matte stainless steel finish, new 1989.

Mfg.'s Sug. Retail	$754	$640	$520	$455

Add $78 for "Ultimate" brite stainless steel finish.

DELTA GOLD CUP STAINLESS — 10mm Norma, target variation, includes Accro adj. rear sight and trigger (serrated also), wrap around combat grips. New 1989.

Mfg.'s Sug. Retail	$948	$790	$640	$525

⚔ **Delta Gold Cup Blue** — similar to Delta Gold Cup Stainless, except has blue finish. Mfg. 1991 only.

	$730	$600	$500	$450	$400	$360	$330

Last Mfg.'s Sug. Retail was $870.

DOUBLE EAGLE SERIES 90 — 9mm Para. (mfg. 1991 only), .38 Super (mfg. 1991 only), .45 ACP, or 10mm cal., double action semi-auto that operates on the Browning/Colt short recoil, link pivot locking system used by the Govt. Model, 5 in. barrel, matte stainless steel only, 3 dot sighting system, checkered synthetic Xenoy grips, 8 shot mag. (9 shot in 9mm Para. or .38 Super cal.), decocking lever, squared off combat trigger guard, 39 oz. New 1990.

Mfg.'s Sug. Retail	$696	$585	$495	$425

Add $25 for 9mm Para. or .38 Super cal. (disc. 1991).
Add $20 for 10mm cal.
Add $30 for Accro adj. rear sight (new 1991).
The first edition on this model did not have a decocking lever.

⚔ **Double Eagle Combat Commander** — .40 S&W (new 1992) or .45 ACP cal., 4¼ in. barrel, 8 shot mag., white dot sights, 36 oz. New 1991.

Mfg.'s Sug. Retail	$696	$585	$495	$425

⚔ **Officers Model** — .45 ACP cal., 3½ in. barrel, 8 shot mag., 35 oz. New 1991.

Mfg.'s Sug. Retail	$696	$585	$495	$425

⚔ **Officers Lightweight Model** — .45 ACP cal. only, 3½ in. barrel, alloy frame with blue finish only, white dot sights, 25 oz. New 1991.

Mfg.'s Sug. Retail	$696	$585	$495	$425	$400	$360	$330	$295

ALL AMERICAN MODEL 2000 — 9mm Para. only, double action semi-auto, new design features roller-bearing mounted trigger allowing double action only trigger pull every shot, utilizes a recoil operated rotary action featuring integral locking lugs similar to the military M-16 rifle, hammerless, 4½ in. barrel, matte finished steel slide and polymer receiver, 15 shot mag., 3-dot sighting system, ambidextrous mag. release, black synthetic checkered grips, internal striker block safety, checkered trigger guard and front grip strap, 29 oz. New 1991.

Model 2000 - Polymer Frame

Mfg.'s Sug. Retail	$575	$525	$460	$425	$390	$350	$325	$300

Also available for this model is a 3¾ in. barrel/bushing kit allowing rapid conversion, since no tools or other components are needed (new 1993) - retail is $75.

Model 2000 - Aluminum Frame — similar specifications to polymer frame, available 1993. A first edition serial numbered RK00001-RK03000 to commemorate the designer (Reed Knight) will be released in 1993.
No retail had been established on this model as this publication went to press.

.380 SERIES 80 GOVERNMENT MODEL — .380 ACP only, single action, 3¼ in. barrel, 7 shot mag., fixed sights, composition stocks, 21¾ oz. New 1985.

Blue Finish

Mfg.'s Sug. Retail	$420	$335	$290	$235	$215	$200	$190	$180

Nickel Finish — bright polish nickel finish with white composite grips.

Mfg.'s Sug. Retail	$470	$385	$320	$270	$240	$220	$210	$200

Coltguard Finish — employs a high strength electroless matte nickel finish. Mfg. 1986-1989.

		$325	$300	$260	$235	$210	$200	$185

Last Mfg.'s Sug. Retail was $406.

Stainless Steel — new 1989.

Mfg.'s Sug. Retail	$450	$360	$320	$270				

GOVT. POCKETLITE — similar to .380 Series 80 Govt. Model, except frame is mfg. with alloy, blue or nickel/stainless (new 1992) finish only, black composition grips, 14¾ oz. New 1991.

Mfg.'s Sug. Retail	$420	$350	$300	$250	$215	$200	$190	$180

Add $30 for nickel/stainless finish.

MUSTANG — similar to .380 Series Govt., except has 2¾ in. barrel, 5 or 6 (new 1992) shot mag., blue finish only, 18½ oz. New 1986.

Mfg.'s Sug. Retail	$420	$330	$290	$235	$215	$200	$190	$180

Nickel finish — bright polish nickel finish with white composite grips. New 1987.

Mfg.'s Sug. Retail	$470	$385	$320	$270	$240	$220	$210	$200

Stainless Steel — stainless steel variation of the Mustang. New 1990.

Mfg.'s Sug. Retail	$450	$365	$320	$270				

Coltguard finish — employs a high strength electroless matte nickel finish. Mfg. 1987.

		$330	$300	$260	$235	$210	$200	$185

Last Mfg.'s Sug. Retail was $406.

MUSTANG PLUS II — .380 ACP only, 2¾ in. barrel, blued finish, black composition grips, 7 shot mag., 20 oz. New 1988.

Mfg.'s Sug. Retail	$420	$330	$290	$235	$215	$200	$190	$180

This model has the full grip length of the .380 Government Model.

Grading	100%	98%	95%	90%	80%	70%	60%

⚞ **Stainless Steel** — stainless steel variation of the Mustang Plus II. New 1990.

Mfg.'s Sug. Retail	$450	$365	$320	$270			

MUSTANG POCKETLITE — similar to Mustang, except has aluminum alloy receiver, blue only, black composite grips, 12½ oz. Introduced 1987.

Mfg.'s Sug. Retail	$420	$330	$290	$235	$215	$200	$190	$180

⚞ **Nickel/Stainless Steel Finish** — similar to Mustang Pocketlite, except has nickel finish frame and stainless steel slide. New 1991.

Mfg.'s Sug. Retail	$450	$375	$325	$275	$230	$200	$190	$180

PISTOLS: SEMI-AUTO .22 CAL. (WOODSMAN SERIES)

The publisher wishes to express his thanks to Major Robert J. Rayburn for his generous contributions of information regarding the Colt Woodsman Series, some of which has been published for the first time.

The Colt Woodsman was made for 62 years, and included a multitude of variations/options in models, sights, barrels, grips, markings, etc. Many of the variations are quite scarce and desirable, but generally known only to specialized collectors. The following price guidelines are for standard production models, and only for those specimens in unmodified, factory original condition.

Note: *All 100% condition Woodsmans with the original serial numbered box, test target, instruction folder, hang tag, and screw driver command a 10-25% premium, depending on the model's age and rarity.*

Over 690,000 Woodsmans with variations were mfg. between 1915-1977.

PRE-WOODSMAN — .22 LR, 6½ in. barrel. Mfg. 1915-1927, production totaled about 54,000, this model was officially named "COLT .22 Automatic Target Pistol" (and so stamped on mag. base).

$895	$695	$500	$400	$325	$275	$250

This model was manufactured to use standard velocity ammunition only (not high speed). Colt did offer a conversion kit for high velocity ammo after the transition to high velocity in 1932. Woodsmans mfg. between 1915-1922 had a lightweight pencil barrel (approx. serial range 1-31,000). The medium barrel was introduced approx. 1922 and was retained until the 90,000 serial range (approx. mfg. 1922-1934).

WOODSMAN 1ST SERIES — .22 LR, 10 shot Mag., blue only, bottom mag. release, checkered wood grips, marked "The Woodsman" on receiver, adj. sights, mfg. from 1927-1947, total production was approx. 112,000.

Note: Guns made prior to 1932 were designed for standard velocity .22 LR ammunition only. The new style main spring housing, designed for high velocity ammunition, began appearing at approx. ser. no. 80,000 and was completely phased in by approx. ser. no. 85,000. Later guns, INCLUDING ALL PISTOLS MADE AFTER WWII, were designed for high velocity ammunition.

Between 1934 and 1947 a tapered barrel was standard production (approx. ser. range 90,000-187,423).

⚞ **Sport Model** — 4½ in. barrel, this model was introduced in 1933.

$950	$750	$550	$450	$375	$325	$300

Approx. serial range on this variation is 86,105 - 187,423. Sport Model was disc. 1947.

⚞ **Target Model** — 6½ in. barrel.

$800	$600	$475	$400	$325	$275	$250

Note: Colt discontinued the 1st Model series in 1947. These guns are quite different from the 2nd Model series started in 1948.

Grading	100%	98%	95%	90%	80%	70%	60%

WOODSMAN 1ST SERIES MATCH TARGET — .22 LR only, 6½ in. heavy barrel, commonly called "Bullseye" Match Target, mfg. 1938-1944, production totaled around 16,000. Difficult to find in mint condition. Values listed assume original one-piece extended walnut grips.

	100%	98%	95%	90%	80%	70%	60%
	$1,850	$1,275	$975	$750	$575	$475	$400

⚔ **"U.S. Property" Marked** — approx. 4,000 Match Target Woodsmans were sold to the U.S. Army and U.S. Navy during WWII. Most have serial numbers above MT12500, although some were shipped out of sequence with lower numbers. The wartime guns had elongated plastic stocks and standard blue finish, although many of them are now parkerized as the result of arsenal refinishing. They are marked with either "US PROPERTY" or the ordnance wheel with crossed cannon, as well as the initials of the govt. inspector. Some also have additional markings.

	100%	98%	95%	90%	80%	70%	60%
	$2,100	$1,700	$1,400	$1,150	$925	$750	$575

WOODSMAN 2ND SERIES — .22 LR only, slide stop and hold open, push button mag. release on this model is located on the top side of frame, Coltwood plastic grips (mfg. 1948-1950) or brown plastic grips (mfg. 1950-1955), mfg. between 1948-1955, total production on all 2nd Series was approx. 146,000.

⚔ **Sport Model** — 4½ in. barrel.

	100%	98%	95%	90%	80%	70%	60%
	$650	$500	$450	$400	$350	$295	$250

⚔ **Target Model** — 6 in. barrel.

	$600	$450	$400	$350	$325	$275	$225

⚔ **Match Target Model** — 4½ in. heavy barrel. This variation will command a premium over the 6 in. barrel.

	$795	$675	$550	$450	$425	$400	$375

⚔ **Match Target Model** — 6 in. heavy barrel.

	$650	$575	$475	$400	$350	$325	$300

WOODSMAN 3RD SERIES — .22 LR only, slide stop and hold open, mfg. between 1955-1977, black plastic grips (mfg. 1955-1960) or walnut grips (1960-1977), 3rd Models can be differentiated from 2nd Models by their bottom mag. release.

⚔ **Sport Model** — 4½ in. barrel.

	$550	$450	$375	$325	$300	$275	$250

⚔ **Target Model** — 6 in. barrel.

	$500	$400	$325	$275	$250	$235	$225

⚔ **Match Target Model** — 4½ in. heavy barrel.

	$695	$625	$525	$450	$400	$375	$350

⚔ **Match Target Model** — 6 in. heavy barrel.

	$595	$550	$450	$400	$350	$325	$295

CHALLENGER MODEL — similar to Woodsman 2rd Series, only with fixed sights, without hold open, and bottom mag. release, 4½ and 6 in. barrels, mfg. between 1950-1955 with total production reaching approx. 77,000.

	$395	$325	$275	$250	$225	$210	$180

HUNTSMAN MODEL — .22 LR only, fixed sights and no hold open, 4½ and 6 in. barrels, black plastic grips to serial number 1411940C - walnut grips after that cutoff, mfg. between 1955-1977 with total production reaching over 100,000.

	$350	$295	$250	$225	$200	$180	$160

The Huntsman is very similar to the Challenger Model, except is built on a 3rd series frame.

Grading	100%	98%	95%	90%	80%	70%	60%

⚞ **Huntsman Model S Master Series** — approx. 400 Model S Masters were sold in 1983. This was a parts clean up by Colt, using Huntsman frames left over from the last days of production. They were equipped with automatic slide stop and Elliason rear sight, gold etching on the slide, and a French fitted walnut case marked "1 of 400". Approx. 285 had straight, non-tapered Huntsman barrel, while the remainder had the tapered Woodsman Sport barrel with pinned front sight.

	100%	98%	95%	90%	80%	70%	60%
Huntsman	$700	$600	$500	$425	$350	$325	$295
Woodsman	$800	$700	$600	$500	$425	$350	$325

Above values assume original walnut case included.

TARGETSMAN MODEL — similar to the Huntsman, except has adj. rear sight and thumbrest on left grip, 6 in. barrel only, approx. 65,000 mfg. 1959-1977.

	100%	98%	95%	90%	80%	70%	60%
	$450	$350	$280	$260	$240	$220	$200

REVOLVERS: DOUBLE ACTION

100%	98%	95%	90%	80%	70%	60%	50%	40%	30%	20%	10%

MODEL 1877 LIGHTNING — .38 Colt or .32 Colt (very rare), 2, 2½, 3½, 4½, or 6 in. barrels without ejector. 4½, 5, 6, 7, or 7½ in. barrels with ejector, 6 shot double action, long cylinder fluting, blued finish with case hardened frame and hammer, full nickel plating also available. Over 166,000 mfg. from 1877-1910.

100%	98%	95%	90%	80%	70%	60%	50%	40%	30%	20%	10%
$1,495	$1,350	$1,175	$900	$795	$690	$575	$465	$375	$295	$255	$235

MODEL 1877 THUNDERER — .41 Colt cal. only, otherwise same general specifications as Model 1877 Lightning.

100%	98%	95%	90%	80%	70%	60%	50%	40%	30%	20%	10%
$1,575	$1,275	$1,150	$1,010	$900	$775	$635	$500	$410	$315	$285	$265

MODEL 1878 FRONTIER — .32-20 WCF, .38-40 WCF, .44-40 WCF, .45 Colt, or .450-.455-.476 Eley cal., 3½ or 4 in. barrels without ejector, 4¾, 5½, or 7½ in. with ejector. 6 in. is 1902 U.S. Revolver. 6 shot cylinder with long flutes, pinched frame, removable trigger guard, early guns have checked walnut stocks, later guns have hard black rubber. Mfg. 1878-1905. Over 51,000 made.

100%	98%	95%	90%	80%	70%	60%	50%	40%	30%	20%	10%
$3,500	$3,000	$2,500	$1,750	$1,500	$950	$850	$750	$650	$550	$435	$375

MODEL 1889 "NAVY" — .38 Short and Long Colt, and .41 Short and Long Colt, 3, 4½, and 6 in. barrel, wood or rubber grips, blue or nickel finish, the first solid frame, swing out cylinder (counter-clockwise rotation) Colt produced, approx. 28,000 made 1889-1894, 1st 5,000 were ordered by U.S. Navy - hence name.

⚞ **Blue finish**

100%	98%	95%	90%	80%	70%	60%	50%	40%	30%	20%	10%
$1,050	$950	$850	$735	$610	$525	$450	$395	$350	$315	$275	$250

⚞ **U.S. Navy Contract (S.N. 1-5,000), U.S.N. on butt - add 40%.**

MODEL 1892 "NEW ARMY & NAVY" (2ND ISSUE) — similar to 1889 Navy, but double cylinder notches, double locking bolt, and shorter flutes, square cyl. release thumb catch, .38 Special added in 1904, .32-20 added in 1905, mfg. 1892-1907.

100%	98%	95%	90%	80%	70%	60%	50%	40%	30%	20%	10%
$895	$800	$700	$595	$475	$375	$310	$265	$235	$225	$210	$195

Add $100 for U.S.N. markings.
This model also had sub-variations that included Models 1894, 1895, 1896, 1901, & 1903. Values will approximate those shown above.

OFFICER'S MODEL TARGET FIRST ISSUE — .38 Spl., 6 in. barrel, adj. sights, high luster blue, flat-top. Mfg. 1904-1908.

100%	98%	95%	90%	80%	70%	60%	50%	40%	30%	20%	10%
$925	$825	$725	$600	$475	$375	$310	$265	$235	$225	$210	$195

100%	98%	95%	90%	80%	70%	60%	50%	40%	30%	20%	10%

OFFICER'S MODEL TARGET (SECOND ISSUE)

— .32 Colt or .38 Spl. cal., 4, 4½, 5, 6, or 7½ in. barrel, 7½ in. barrel in .38 Spl. only, high luster blue, adj. sights, checkered walnut grips, deep set medallions in grips were standard from 1913-1923. Mfg. 1908-1926.

100%	98%	95%	90%	80%	70%	60%	50%	40%	30%	20%	10%
$950	$825	$795	$600	$515	$450	$395	$330	$290	$250	$225	$210

Add 60% for .32 Colt cal.

This model was also produced in "single action only" in limited numbers with wide hammer - add a 25%-40% premium, depending on condition.

OFFICER'S MODEL TARGET (THIRD ISSUE)
— similar design to the Second Issue, .22 cal. was added beginning 1930. Mfg. 1927-1949.

100%	98%	95%	90%	80%	70%	60%	50%	40%	30%	20%	10%
$675	$625	$560	$500	$450	$375	$325	$295	$265	$245	$225	$205

Add 10% for .22 LR cal. (mfg. started 1930).

MODEL 1905 MARINE CORPS
— similar to New Navy Second Issue, except has a round butt, in .38 short, long, and special, only 6 in. barrel. Mfg. 1905-1909 in approx. ser. no. range 10,000-10,925, about 925 mfg.

100%	98%	95%	90%	80%	70%	60%	50%	40%	30%	20%	10%
$2,250	$1,975	$1,750	$1,500	$1,350	$1,150	$1,000	$875	$725	$625	$550	$495

Add 30% for Military issue marked "USMC" on butt.

ARMY SPECIAL MODEL
— .32-20, .38 (various), and .41 Colt, 4, 4½, 5, and 6 in. barrels, hard rubber grips standard through 1923 - checkered wood with medallions after 1923, fixed sights, rounded cylinder release thumb catch, has heavier frame than New Navy, approx. ser. no. range 291,000-540,000, mfg. 1908-1927.

Blue finish

100%	98%	95%	90%	80%	70%	60%	50%	40%	30%	20%	10%
$550	$450	$375	$335	$295	$265	$245	$230	$215	$200	$185	$175

Add 15% for nickel finish.

NEW SERVICE MODEL
— .38 Spl., .357 Mag., .38-40, .44-40, .44 Russian, .44 Spl., .45 ACP, .45 Colt, .450 Eley, .455 Eley, or .476 Eley, 4, 5, or 6 in. barrels in .357 Mag. and .38 Spl., 4½, 5½, and 7½ in. barrel in all others, blue or nickel finish, originally hard rubber (until approx. late '20s), with later guns having walnut grips. Mfg. 1898-1942. Rare cals. (.450 and .476 Eley cals.) will command premiums over values listed below.

Commercial

100%	98%	95%	90%	80%	70%	60%	50%	40%	30%	20%	10%
$1,500	$1,375	$1,175	$1,000	$925	$850	$775	$650	$500	$425	$375	$295

1909 Army Model

100%	98%	95%	90%	80%	70%	60%	50%	40%	30%	20%	10%
$1,275	$1,125	$1,000	$925	$850	$775	$680	$590	$510	$435	$375	$325

1909 Navy Model
— shortest production run of the Model 1909 variations.

100%	98%	95%	90%	80%	70%	60%	50%	40%	30%	20%	10%
$2,450	$2,100	$1,825	$1,450	$1,150	$1,000	$895	$775	$600	$500	$450	$395

1909 - USMC

100%	98%	95%	90%	80%	70%	60%	50%	40%	30%	20%	10%
$2,850	$2,400	$2,100	$1,775	$1,500	$1,250	$975	$825	$700	$600	$500	$450

1917 Army

100%	98%	95%	90%	80%	70%	60%	50%	40%	30%	20%	10%
$875	$795	$735	$670	$610	$525	$455	$390	$335	$295	$250	$200

100%	98%	95%	90%	80%	70%	60%	50%	40%	30%	20%	10%

New Service Target — similar to New Service Model, flat-top frame, hand-honed action and adj. sights, 6 (scarce-less than 50 mfg.) or 7½ in. barrel, square butt, blue or nickel (scarce) finish. Mfg. 1900-1940.

| $2,000 | $1,775 | $1,550 | $1,325 | $1,185 | $1,050 | $895 | $795 | $675 | $550 | $450 | $375 |

Add 40% for 6 in. barrel.

Shooting Master — various cals. from 38 Spl. through .45 LC, 6 in. barrel, checkered walnut grips with Colt Medallion, machined grip straps, trigger, hammer, and ejector rod head, round butt, approx. ser. no. range 333,000 - 350,000.

| $1,250 | $1,100 | $975 | $900 | $825 | $755 | $665 | $575 | $500 | $435 | $395 | $375 |

Add 35% for .357 Mag.
Add 100% for .44 Spl., .45 ACP, or .45 LC cal.
The Shooting Master could be ordered with a square butt after 1933.

OFFICIAL POLICE PRE-WAR — .32-20 (disc. 1942), .41 long (disc. 1930), .38 Spl., or .22 LR (introduced 1930 - 6 in. barrel only), 6 shot, square butt, 4, 5, or 6 in. barrels, 2 in. barrel (scarce) in .38 Spl., checkered walnut grips, fixed sights. Mfg. 1927-1946.

Blue finish

| $495 | $425 | $375 | $325 | $295 | $265 | $235 | $210 | $185 | $165 | $145 | $135 |

Add 15% for nickel finish.
Add 15% for .22 LR cal.

OFFICIAL POLICE POST-WAR — .22 LR or .38 Spl. cal., 2, 4, or 6 in. barrel, Coltwood plastic grips 1947-1954 - checkered walnut thereafter, fixed sights mfg. 1947-1969.

| $425 | $375 | $325 | $295 | $265 | $235 | $210 | $185 | $165 | $145 | $135 | $125 |

Add 15% for nickel finish.
Add 15% for .22 cal.
On this model, the 2 in. barrel in .38 Spl. cal. is scarce. .22 cal. was available with 4 or 6 in. barrel only.

MARSHAL MODEL — .38 Special, 2 (less common) or 4 in. barrel, round butt, differentiated by "M" suffix and "COLT MARSHAL" on barrel, about 2,500 mfg. 1954-1956 in approx. ser. no. range 833350-M through 845320-M.

| $800 | $700 | $600 | $475 | $395 | $335 | $305 | $275 | $245 | $215 | $180 | $160 |

COMMANDO MODEL — .38 Special, 2 in. (scarce), 4 in. (common), or 6 in. (rare) barrel, parkerized finish, about 50,000 mfg. between 1942-1945, 32 oz., marked "COLT COMMANDO" on barrel.

| $550 | $400 | $315 | $265 | $225 | $205 | $190 | $175 | $160 | $150 | $140 | $120 |

Add 15% for 2 in. barrel.

OFFICIAL POLICE MKIII — .38 Spl., 4, 5, or 6 in. barrels. Mfg. 1969-1975.

Blue finish

| $325 | $235 | $180 | $150 | $135 | $125 | $115 | $105 | $100 | $95 | $90 | $85 |

Nickel finish

| $350 | $250 | $195 | $175 | $165 | $155 | $145 | $135 | $125 | $115 | $105 | $100 |

METROPOLITAN MK III — .38 Spl., similar to Official Police, except heavier and 4 in. heavy barrel only, blue finish. Mfg. 1969-1972.

| $400 | $300 | $240 | $190 | $175 | $165 | $150 | $140 | $130 | $120 | $110 | $100 |

100%	98%	95%	90%	80%	70%	60%	50%	40%	30%	20%	10%

OFFICER'S MODEL SPECIAL (FOURTH ISSUE) — .22 LR or .38 Spl., 6 in. barrel, blue, similar to Second Issue, only heavier non-tapered barrel, new style hammer and "Coltmaster Sight", checkered plastic grips. Mfg. 1949-1953.

$575	$500	$450	$375	$325	$295	$265	$245	$225	$205	$190	$175

Add $75 for .22 LR cal.

OFFICER'S MODEL MATCH (FIFTH ISSUE) — .22 LR, .22 Mag, or .38 Spl., 6 in. barrel, tapered heavy barrel, wide spur hammer, Accro sight, large target grips (walnut). Mfg. 1953-1970.

$475	$425	$375	$325	$300	$275	$250	$225	$200	$185	$170	$155

Add $75 for .22 LR cal.
Add 100% for .22 Mag. cal. (approx. 850 mfg.).
This model was also produced in "single action only" in limited numbers - add a 25%-40% premium, depending on condition.

OFFICER'S MODEL MATCH MK III (SIXTH ISSUE) — .38 Spl. only, 6 in. shrouded VR barrel, wide spur hammer, Accro sights, target grips, 496 mfg. 1969-70 only.

$1,200	$1,100	$995	$925	$850	$775	$700	$650	$600	$550	$475	$425

NEW POCKET — .32 S and LC, 2½, 3½, or 6 in. barrel, rubber grips. Mfg. 1895-1905.

◦ **Blue finish**

$495	$450	$395	$325	$300	$275	$250	$225	$200	$185	$170	$155

Add 15% for nickel finish.

POCKET POSITIVE — similar to New Pocket, except has positive lock feature, also chambered for .32 Colt, .32 S&W, and .32 Colt New Police. Mfg. 1905-1940.

◦ **Blue finish**

$495	$440	$385	$350	$325	$295	$265	$235	$210	$185	$165	$145

Add 15%-20% for nickel finish.

NEW POLICE — .32 Colt and .32 Colt New Police, 2½, 4, and 6 in. barrels, fixed sights, same frame as New Pocket, except larger grips, rubber grips. Mfg. 1896-1905.

◦ **Blue finish**

$495	$395	$295	$255	$230	$215	$200	$185	$170	$160	$150	$145

Add 10% for nickel finish.

NEW POLICE TARGET — .32 cal. only, 6 in. barrel, blue, approx. 5,000 mfg. 1897-1905.

$750	$675	$595	$525	$450	$395	$335	$300	$275	$250	$220	$195

POLICE POSITIVE — .32 Colt, .32 New Police, .38 New Police, or .38 S&W, 2½ in. (.32 only), 4, 5, or 6 in. barrels, improved "positive lock" version of the New Police, walnut or rubber grips. Mfg. 1905-1947.

◦ **Blue finish**

$435	$385	$335	$295	$275	$250	$225	$205	$185	$170	$160	$150

Add 15% for nickel finish.

POLICE POSITIVE TARGET MODEL — .22 LR, .22 WRF, .32 Colt, or .32 New Police, 6 in. barrel, blue, adj. sight, checkered walnut grips. Mfg. 1905-1940.

$695	$625	$575	$525	$475	$425	$390	$360	$325	$285	$250	$210

Add 10% for .22 WRF cal.

100%	98%	95%	90%	80%	70%	60%	50%	40%	30%	20%	10%

POLICE POSITIVE SPECIAL (FIRST ISSUE) — .32-20, .32 New Police, .38 New Police, or .38 Spl., 4, 5, or 6 in. barrels, fixed sights, frame longer to permit longer cylinder, wood, rubber, or plastic grips. Mfg. 1907-1946.

100%	98%	95%	90%	80%	70%	60%	50%	40%	30%	20%	10%
$495	$450	$395	$325	$300	$275	$250	$225	$200	$185	$170	$155

CAMP PERRY MODEL — .22 LR, 8 in. (scarce) or 10 in., Officer's Model frame modified to accept a flat single shot chamber. The model name was stamped on the left side of the chamber, the only single shot Colt on a revolver frame. 2,488 mfg. between 1926-1941.

100%	98%	95%	90%	80%	70%	60%	50%	40%	30%	20%	10%
$1,250	$1,050	$950	$885	$835	$775	$715	$645	$575	$495	$425	$365

Add 25% for 8 in. barrel.

BANKER'S SPECIAL — 2 in. barrel, blue, rounded butt. Mfg. 1926-1940.

✷ .38 cal.

100%	98%	95%	90%	80%	70%	60%	50%	40%	30%	20%	10%
$695	$595	$525	$450	$380	$340	$315	$275	$235	$205	$185	$165

✷ .22 cal.

100%	98%	95%	90%	80%	70%	60%	50%	40%	30%	20%	10%
$1,200	$1,000	$875	$750	$650	$550	$475	$425	$385	$355	$325	$290

COURIER — .22 S, L, & LR, .32 New Police, double action, 6 shot, 3 in. barrel, approx. 3,053 mfg. 1953-1956.

100%	98%	95%	90%	80%	70%	60%	50%	40%	30%	20%	10%
$895	$825	$775	$675	$550	$450	$395	$350	$325	$295	$260	$230

Add 10% for .22 cal.
Even though fewer .22 cal. Couriers were mfg. than Banker's Specials, the Banker's Specials are still more desirable as they are less frequently encountered in 95-100% condition.

AIRCREWMAN SPECIAL — .38 Spl., double action, aluminum frame, 2 in. barrel, 11 oz., fixed sights, checkered walnut grips, mfg. 1951 mostly.

100%	98%	95%	90%	80%	70%	60%	50%	40%	30%	20%	10%
$3,500	$3,100	$2,550	$2,100	$1,700	$1,350	$1,075	$950	$850	$750	$675	$595

Approx. 1,200 mfg. within ser. no. range 2,900LW - 7,775LW. Perhaps less than 25 have survived.

BORDER PATROL — .38 Spl., double action, 6 shot, 4 in. heavy barrel, 400 mfg. during 1952 only in 823,000 ser. no. range.

100%	98%	95%	90%	80%	70%	60%	50%	40%	30%	20%	10%
$2,895	$2,475	$2,175	$1,775	$1,400	$1,125	$995	$875	$775	$675	$595	$525

This model is built on the Official Police Model frame.

DETECTIVE SPECIAL PRE-WAR (FIRST ISSUE) — .38 Spl. cal., 2 or 3 (scarce) in. barrel, blue, wood grips. Mfg. 1927-1946.

100%	98%	95%	90%	80%	70%	60%	50%	40%	30%	20%	10%
$600	$525	$475	$425	$375	$325	$275	$250	$225	$205	$190	$175

Add 15% for nickel finish.

DETECTIVE SPECIAL POST-WAR (SECOND ISSUE) — .32 New Police, .38 New Police, or .38 Spl. cal., 2 or 3 (scarce) in. barrel, plastic grips 1947-1954 - wood grips thereafter, wrap-under wood grips started in 1966. Mfg. 1947-1972.

100%	98%	95%	90%	80%	70%	60%	50%	40%	30%	20%	10%
$395	$350	$295	$250	$225	$200	$185	$170	$160	$150	$140	$120

Add 15% for nickel finish.

COBRA ROUND BUTT — first issue, 2, 3, or 4 in. barrel, blue or nickel finish, similar to Detective Special, only alloy frame and available in .22 LR.

100%	98%	95%	90%	80%	70%	60%	50%	40%	30%	20%	10%
$395	$350	$295	$250	$225	$200	$185	$170	$160	$150	$140	$120

Add 20% for .22 LR cal.
Add 15% for nickel finish.
The .22 LR cal. is available in 3 in. barrel only.

	100%	98%	95%	90%	80%	70%	60%	50%	40%	30%	20%	10%

COBRA SQUARE BUTT — blue, similar to Cobra Round Butt, only 4 in. barrel, round or square butt. Mfg. 1951-1973.

| | $450 | $375 | $325 | $250 | $225 | $200 | $185 | $170 | $160 | $150 | $140 | $120 |

AGENT (FIRST ISSUE) — .38 Spl., similar to Cobra first issue, except shorter grip frame. Mfg. 1955-1973.

| | $375 | $265 | $215 | $190 | $175 | $165 | $150 | $140 | $130 | $120 | $110 | $100 |

AGENT L.W. — .38 Spl., similar to First Issue, except shrouded ejector rod, alloy frame, matte finish since 1982. Mfg. 1973-86.

| | $325 | $285 | $250 | $200 | $175 | $160 | $145 | $135 | $125 | $115 | $105 | $100 |

Last Mfg.'s Sug. Retail was $260.

COBRA (SECOND ISSUE) — .38 Spl., similar to Cobra first issue, except shrouded ejector rod. Mfg. 1973-1981.

| | $375 | $325 | $275 | $250 | $225 | $200 | $190 | $175 | $160 | $150 | $140 | $120 |

DETECTIVE SPECIAL (THIRD ISSUE) — .38 Spl., similar to Second Issue, shrouded ejector rod, 2 or 3 (scarce) in. barrel, fixed sights, wrap-around wood grips. Mfg. 1973-86.

| | $375 | $325 | $275 | $250 | $225 | $200 | $190 | $175 | $160 | $150 | $140 | $120 |

Add $50 for nickel.
Last Mfg.'s Sug. Retail was $429.
Also available with class A engraving - add $590 if in 98% condition or better.

COMMANDO SPECIAL — .38 Spl., similar to Detective Special with steel frame, shrouded ejector rod, 2 in. barrel, matte parkerized finish, rubber grips. Mfg. 1984-86.

| | $325 | $285 | $250 | $200 | $175 | $160 | $145 | $135 | $125 | $115 | $105 | $100 |

Last Mfg.'s Sug. Retail was $260.

POLICE POSITIVE SPECIAL (SECOND ISSUE) — .38 Spl., similar to Detective Special Second Issue, except 4, 5 or 6 in. barrel. Mfg. 1947-76.

| | $325 | $285 | $250 | $200 | $175 | $160 | $145 | $135 | $125 | $115 | $105 | $100 |

POLICE POSITIVE SPECIAL (THIRD ISSUE) — .38 Spl. cal., 4 in. shrouded barrel, steel frame, blue or nickel finish. Mfg. 1977-78 only.

| | $350 | $310 | $265 | $220 | $185 | $170 | $150 | $135 | $125 | $115 | $105 | $100 |

Add 10% for nickel finish.

DIAMONDBACK — .22 LR or .38 Spl., 2½ (very scarce in .22 LR), 4, or 6 in. VR barrel, adj. sights, steel frame, checkered walnut grips, made 1966-86.

| | $395 | $340 | $300 | $265 | $245 | $225 | $205 | $190 | $175 | $160 | $150 | $140 |

Add $55 for nickel finish.
Add 20% for .22 LR cal.
Last Mfg.'s Sug. Retail was $461.
Note: Approx. 2,200 Diamondbacks were made with 6 in. barrels and nickel finish in .22 cal. - made 1979. Add additional $150 for 100% specimens.

VIPER MODEL — .38 Spl., similar to Cobra Model, alloy frame, 4 in. shrouded barrel. Mfg. 1977 only.

| | $375 | $325 | $275 | $250 | $225 | $200 | $190 | $175 | $160 | $150 | $140 | $120 |

COLT .357 MAG — 4 in. or 6 in. barrel, heavy frame, Accro sight, blue or nickel finish, checkered walnut grips. Later guns marked Trooper. Mfg. 1953-1961.

Standard hammer

| | $425 | $350 | $300 | $285 | $270 | $260 | $250 | $240 | $230 | $220 | $210 | $200 |

100%	98%	95%	90%	80%	70%	60%	50%	40%	30%	20%	10%

Wide hammer w/target grips

100%	98%	95%	90%	80%	70%	60%	50%	40%	30%	20%	10%
$475	$400	$350	$300	$285	$265	$255	$245	$235	$225	$215	$205

TROOPER — .22 LR (scarce) or .38 Spl., 4 or 6 in. barrel, blue, quick draw ramp front sight, adj. rear sight, checkered walnut grips. Mfg. 1953-1969.

Standard hammer

100%	98%	95%	90%	80%	70%	60%	50%	40%	30%	20%	10%
$325	$275	$225	$210	$200	$190	$180	$170	$165	$160	$155	$150

Wide hammer and target grips

100%	98%	95%	90%	80%	70%	60%	50%	40%	30%	20%	10%
$375	$325	$275	$225	$210	$200	$190	$180	$170	$165	$160	$155

Add $75-$125 for .22 LR cal. (4 in. barrel only), depending on condition.

Grading	100%	98%	95%	90%	80%	70%	60%

TROOPER MK III — .22 LR, .22 Mag., or .357 Mag. cal., 4, 6, or 8 in. solid rib barrel, adj. sights, walnut target grips, redesigned lock work to reduce amount of hand fitting needed on earlier predecessors. Mfg. 1969-1983.

	100%	98%	95%	90%	80%	70%	60%
Blue finish	$325	$275	$190	$180	$170	$160	$150
Nickel finish	$345	$275	$200	$190	$180	$170	$160

Officer's Model Match MK III — .38 Spl. cal. only, 6 in. VR barrel, similar to Trooper MK III in appearance, 450 mfg. 1969-70 only.

	100%	98%	95%	90%	80%	70%	60%
	$1,200	$1,000	$800	$600	$400	$300	$200

TROOPER MK V — .357 Mag., 4 or 6 in. barrel, adj. sights, walnut target grips, improved version of Mark III action, vent. rib barrel, redesigned 1982. Disc. 1986.

Blue finish

	100%	98%	95%	90%	80%	70%	60%
	$330	$290	$250	$215	$185	$170	$160

Last Mfg.'s Sug. Retail was $362.

Nickel finish

	100%	98%	95%	90%	80%	70%	60%
	$365	$315	$285	$235	$200	$185	$170

Last Mfg.'s Sug. Retail was $396.

LAWMAN MK III — .357 Mag., 2 in. and 4 in. barrel, unshrouded or shrouded ejector rod for 2 in. barrel, fixed sights, checkered walnut grips. Mfg. 1969-1983.

	100%	98%	95%	90%	80%	70%	60%
Blue finish	$295	$240	$190	$180	$170	$160	$150
Nickel finish	$315	$250	$200	$190	$180	$170	$160

LAWMAN MK V — .357 Mag., 2 or 4 in. barrel, shrouded ejector rod for 2 in. barrel, fixed sights, checkered walnut grips, improved version of MK III action. Mfg. 1984 and 1985 only.

Blue finish

	100%	98%	95%	90%	80%	70%	60%
	$295	$250	$200	$175	$160	$150	$140

Last Mfg.'s Sug. Retail was $309.

Nickel finish

	100%	98%	95%	90%	80%	70%	60%
	$325	$280	$225	$200	$180	$170	$160

Last Mfg.'s Sug. Retail was $328.

BORDER PATROL (SECOND ISSUE) — .357 Mag., 4 in. heavy barrel, Mark III Trooper frame, limited mfg. in 1970-75.

Blue Finish — 5,356 mfg.

	100%	98%	95%	90%	80%	70%	60%
	$450	$375	$325	$275	$235	$200	$180

Grading	100%	98%	95%	90%	80%	70%	60%

✦ **Nickel Finish** — 1,152 mfg.

	100%	98%	95%	90%	80%	70%	60%
	$550	$495	$425	$375	$325	$275	$235

PEACEKEEPER — .357 Mag. cal., similar to Trooper MK V, 4 or 6 in. barrel, matte blue finish, rubber combat grips, adj. rear sight, about 42 oz. Mfg. 1985-1987.

	$320	$275	$245	$205	$195	$180	$165

Last Mfg.'s Sug. Retail was $330.

BOA — .357 Mag., deep blue polish, full length ejector shroud with Mark V action, 600 each mfg. in 4 and 6 in. barrel lengths. Entire production run was purchased by Lew Horton Distributing Co., Inc. located in Southboro, MA. 1985 retail was $525.

	$595	$525	$450	$415	$375	$350	$325

✦ **Boa Set** — 100 sets mfg. including 4 and 6 in. barrels with fully shrouded ejector rod housing, consecutive serial numbers, and cherry wood presentation case. 1985 retail was $1,200.

	$1,450	$1,100	$875

DETECTIVE SPECIAL — .38 Spl. cal., 6 shot, 2 in. barrel, alloy steel, blue finish, black composition grips with gold medallions, 21 oz. Reintroduced 1993.

Mfg.'s Sug. Retail	$384	$335	$285	$250	$225	$195	$180	$165

COMBAT COBRA — .357 Mag., 2½ in. barrel, special edition for Lew Horton with CC prefix and stainless steel construction.

	$475	$440	$395	$350	$315	$280	$250

KING COBRA — .357 Mag., blued metal, black neoprene round butt grips, 2 ½ (new 1990), 4 or 6 in. solid rib barrel only, outline sights, approx. 42 oz. (4 in. barrel). Mfg. 1988-92.

	$335	$295	$260	$235	$210	$200	$185

Last Mfg.'s Sug. Retail was $410.

KING COBRA STAINLESS — .357 Mag., stainless steel construction, black neoprene round butt grips, 2 (disc. 1987), 2½ (new 1988), 4, 6, or 8 (new 1990) in. solid rib barrel, outline sights, approx. 36 oz. (2½ in. barrel). Mfg. late 1987-92.

	$370	$325	$265

Last Mfg.'s Sug. Retail was $435.

✦ **King Cobra "Ultimate" Bright Stainless** — similar to King Cobra, except for bright stainless steel, 2 ½ (new 1990), 4, 6, or 8 (new 1991) in. barrel. Mfg. 1988-92.

	$400	$340	$280

Last Mfg.'s Sug. Retail was $470.

PYTHON — .357 Mag., 2½, 3 (disc.), 4, 6, or 8 in. barrel with vent rib, royal blue finish, full shrouded ejector rod, checkered walnut grips (prior to 1991), rubber combat (2½ or 4 in. barrel), or target (6 or 8 in. barrel) stocks. Mfg. 1955-present.

✦ **Blue or royal blue finish**

Mfg.'s Sug. Retail	$776	$550	$415	$350	$325	$300	$275	$250

Early 2½, 4 or 6 in. Pythons without letter prefix before ser. no. will bring a small premium if in 100% condition or N.I.B., as well as the disc. 3 in. barrel.

Also available with Class A, B, C, or D engraving — prices are the same as the .45 ACP Government Models listed previously under the Pistols: Semi-Auto, Recent Manufacture.

Grading	100%	98%	95%	90%	80%	70%	60%

⚔ **Nickel finish** — available in polished or satin nickel, disc. 1985.

		$550	$460	$415	$365	$325	$300	$275

Last Mfg.'s Sug. Retail was $693.

⚔ **Stainless Steel Python** — stainless steel construction, matte finish, neoprene target or combat stocks, 2½, 4, 6 or 8 (new 1989) in. barrel. Introduced 1983.

Mfg.'s Sug. Retail	$865	$660	$565	$450

The 6 in. barrel includes neoprene target stocks.

⚔ **"Ultimate" Stainless Steel** — deluxe, highly polished stainless model. New 1985.

Mfg.'s Sug. Retail	$895	$675	$575	$450

ULTIMATE PYTHON — .357 Mag., specially tuned by the custom gun shop, supplied with both Elliason target and Accro white outline sighting systems, walnut and rubber grips also included, choice of Colt Royal Blue or Ultimate Stainless finish, 6 in. barrel only. 1991 release.

Mfg.'s Sug. Retail	$1,140	$1,025	$850	$775	$695	$625	$550	$475

Add $120 for Ultimate Stainless Model.

PYTHON HUNTER — .357 Mag., 8 in. barrel, includes EER Leupold 2X scope, Halliburton aluminum case and accessories. Mfg. 1981 only.

	$1,050	$900	$750	$650	$595	$540	$495

Last Mfg.'s Sug. Retail was $995.

PYTHON .38 SPECIAL — 8 in. barrel, blue or nickel finish. Disc.

	$595	$500	$425	$375	$350	$325	$300

WHITETAILER — .357 Mag. cal., 8 in. barrel, matte stainless finish, aluminum hard shell cased with 2X scope.

	$995	$850	$750	$650	$595	$540	$495

⚔ **Whitetailer II** — similar to Whitetailer, except has high polish finish.

	$1,050	$875	$750	$650	$595	$540	$495

ANACONDA — .44 Mag. or .45 LC (new 1992) cal., double action, 4 (new 1991), 6 (.45 LC only, 500 mfg. 1992) or 8 (new 1991) in. VR barrel, transfer bar safety system, 6 shot, matte stainless steel only, black neoprene combat grips with Colt medallion, red ramp front sight, full length ejector rod housing, white outline rear adj. sight, approx. 53 oz. New 1990.

Mfg.'s Sug. Retail	$570	$480	$400	$350

⚔ **Anaconda Hunter** — .44 Mag. cal., supplied with Leupold 2X scope, carrying case, cleaning accessories, and both walnut and rubber grips, 8 in. barrel only. 1991 release.

Mfg.'s Sug. Retail	$1,200	$1,095	$895	$725

⚔ **Custom Anaconda** — .44 Mag.cal., features Magna-ported barrel and Elliason rear sight, contoured trigger, and Pachmayr rubber grips, brushed stainless steel. New 1992.

Mfg.'s Sug. Retail	$800	$625	$525	$425

RIFLES: DISCONTINUED

100%	98%	95%	90%	80%	70%	60%	50%	40%	30%	20%	10%

FIRST MODEL RING LEVER — .34, .36, .38, .40, or .44, 8 or 10 shot revolving cylinder, 32 in. octagon barrel, walnut stock, no forend, 200 mfg., Percussion. Mfg. 1837-1838.

⚔ **Standard Model**

100%	98%	95%	90%	80%	70%	60%	50%	40%	30%	20%	10%
N/A	N/A	N/A	$37,500	$28,000	$21,500	$16,500	$13,500	$11,000	$9,000	$7,500	$6,500

100%	98%	95%	90%	80%	70%	60%	50%	40%	30%	20%	10%

Improved Model — attached loading lever.

100%	98%	95%	90%	80%	70%	60%	50%	40%	30%	20%	10%
N/A	N/A	N/A	$41,000	$29,650	$22,750	$17,500	$14,500	$12,000	$10,000	$8,500	$7,500

SECOND MODEL RING LEVER — similar to First Model, without top strap over cylinder, .44 caliber only, Percussion, 5000 mfg., 1838-1841.

Standard Model

100%	98%	95%	90%	80%	70%	60%	50%	40%	30%	20%	10%
N/A	N/A	N/A	$33,500	$24,500	$17,000	$13,000	$11,000	$8,780	$7,200	$6,300	$5,650

Improved Model

100%	98%	95%	90%	80%	70%	60%	50%	40%	30%	20%	10%
N/A	N/A	N/A	$34,750	$26,000	$17,750	$13,300	$11,200	$8,900	$7,325	$6,390	$5,725

MODEL 1839 CARBINE — .525 smooth bore, 6 shot cylinder, 24 in. barrel, exposed hammer for cocking, blued, walnut stock, Percussion, approx. 950 mfg., 1838-1841.

Early Model

100%	98%	95%	90%	80%	70%	60%	50%	40%	30%	20%	10%
N/A	N/A	N/A	$38,500	$29,000	$22,000	$17,500	$14,750	$11,500	$9,350	$7,750	$6,750

Standard Model — no loading lever.

100%	98%	95%	90%	80%	70%	60%	50%	40%	30%	20%	10%
N/A	N/A	N/A	$31,000	$22,500	$17,000	$13,500	$11,250	$9,000	$7,500	$6,600	$6,000

MODEL 1855 REVOLVING — .36, .44, or .56 cal., various barrel lengths and stock styles, 5 or 6 shot cylinder, blued with walnut butt stock, no forend, percussion. Mfg. 1856-1864.

½ Stoc k Sporter — 24, 27, or 30 in. barrel, approx. 1500 mfg.

100%	98%	95%	90%	80%	70%	60%	50%	40%	30%	20%	10%
N/A	N/A	N/A	$11,500	$9,000	$7,850	$7,000	$6,500	$6,000	$5,500	$5,100	$4,750

Full Stock Sporter — 21, 24, 27, 30, or 31 in. barrel, approx. 2000 mfg.

100%	98%	95%	90%	80%	70%	60%	50%	40%	30%	20%	10%
N/A	N/A	N/A	$13,500	$11,275	$9,150	$8,250	$7,500	$6,950	$6,500	$6,100	$5,750

Military Model, U.S. — marked, 21-37 in. barrel, 9310 mfg.

100%	98%	95%	90%	80%	70%	60%	50%	40%	30%	20%	10%
N/A	N/A	N/A	$17,500	$14,650	$11,900	$10,500	$9,800	$9,050	$8,450	$7,900	$7,475

.36 Caliber Carbine Model — 15, 18, or 21 in. barrel, 4400 mfg.

100%	98%	95%	90%	80%	70%	60%	50%	40%	30%	20%	10%
N/A	N/A	N/A	$17,150	$14,350	$11,660	$10,525	$9,600	$8,875	$8,275	$7,750	$7,300

.56 Caliber Artillery Carbine — 24 in. barrel.

100%	98%	95%	90%	80%	70%	60%	50%	40%	30%	20%	10%
N/A	N/A	N/A	$19,000	$16,500	$13,500	$10,875	$10,125	$3,300	$9,450	$9,000	$8,400

Shotgun Model — .60 or .75 cal., smooth bore, 27, 30, 33, or 36 in. barrels, 1100 mfg.

100%	98%	95%	90%	80%	70%	60%	50%	40%	30%	20%	10%
N/A	N/A	N/A	$12,750	$11,000	$9,000	$8,000	$7,250	$6,750	$6,300	$6,000	$5,600

MODEL 1861 MUSKET — .58 cal., Percussion, muzzle loader, 40 in. barrel, with 3 bands, metal parts, white walnut stock, 75,000 mfg., 1861-1865.

100%	98%	95%	90%	80%	70%	60%	50%	40%	30%	20%	10%
$2,100	$1,875	$1,675	$1,500	$1,225	$1,125	$1,050	$985	$935	$900	$875	$850

COLT-BURGESS LEVER ACTION — .44-40 cal., 25½ in. barrel, 15 shot tube mag., blue with case hardened lever and hammer, walnut stock, 6400 mfg., 1883-1885.

100%	98%	95%	90%	80%	70%	60%	50%	40%	30%	20%	10%
$8,750	$7,450	$6,350	$5,500	$4,900	$4,465	$4,170	$3,930	$3,700	$3,525	$3,350	$3,100

COLT-BURGESS CARBINE — similar to Rifle, with 20 in. barrel.

100%	98%	95%	90%	80%	70%	60%	50%	40%	30%	20%	10%
$11,500	$9,950	$8,750	$7,900	$7,300	$6,725	$6,250	$5,850	$5,500	$5,200	$4,950	$4,750

COLT-BURGESS BABY CARBINE — similar to Carbine, with lightened frame.

100%	98%	95%	90%	80%	70%	60%	50%	40%	30%	20%	10%
$14,000	$12,250	$10,750	$9,720	$8,975	$8,275	$7,695	$7,200	$6,765	$6,395	$6,100	$5,850

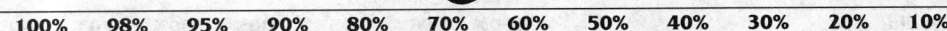

100%	98%	95%	90%	80%	70%	60%	50%	40%	30%	20%	10%

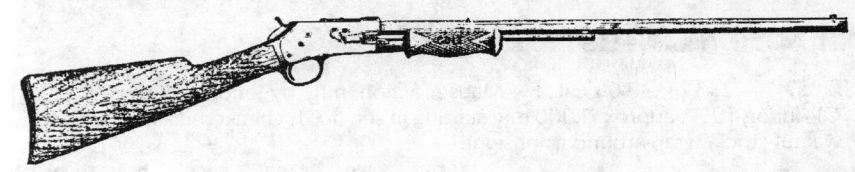

LIGHTNING SLIDE ACTION - SMALL FRAME — small frame, .22 cal., 24 in. barrel, open sights, walnut straight stock, round or octagon barrel, 90,000 mfg. Mfg. 1887-1904.

100%	98%	95%	90%	80%	70%	60%	50%	40%	30%	20%	10%
$1,650	$1,350	$1,075	$850	$725	$650	$575	$535	$495	$450	$400	$375

LIGHTNING SLIDE ACTION - MEDIUM FRAME — medium frame, similar to small frame, in .32-20, .38-40, or .44-40, with larger frame.

$3,250	$2,550	$2,150	$1,775	$1,475	$1,175	$950	$775	$650	$550	$495	$450

LIGHTNING CARBINE MEDIUM FRAME — similar to Rifle, with 20 in. barrel.

$5,250	$3,850	$3,250	$2,850	$2,450	$2,150	$1,950	$1,750	$1,450	$1,175	$1,050	$950

LIGHTNING BABY CARBINE MEDIUM FRAME — lightened version of Carbine.

$7,000	$5,500	$4,750	$4,000	$3,450	$2,950	$2,450	$2,100	$1,850	$1,650	$1,425	$1,350

LIGHTNING SLIDE ACTION - LARGE FRAME — large frame, .38-56 - .50-95, express, large version of previously described Lightnings, 6500 mfg. Mfg. 1887-1894.

$6,250	$4,750	$3,850	$3,250	$2,750	$2,250	$1,850	$1,650	$1,450	$1,325	$1,250	$1,175

LIGHTNING CARBINE LARGE FRAME — 22 in. barrel.

$8,650	$7,350	$6,250	$5,400	$4,800	$4,375	$4,100	$3,865	$3,650	$3,460	$3,285	$3,125

BABY CARBINE LARGE FRAME — lightened version.

$11,000	$9,450	$8,250	$7,450	$6,850	$6,300	$5,825	$5,425	$5,075	$4,775	$5,225	$4,350

Note: .50-95 express will bring premium of 20%.

DOUBLE RIFLE SXS — Various cals. in the .45 range, hammers, very limited production between 1878-1880. Most guns were owned by friends of Caldwell Colt — Sam Colt's son, the original designer. Colt Double Rifles are extremely rare and desirable, and should be examined carefully. Prices typically range between $15,000-$25,000, if all original.

.22 CAL RIFLES

Grading	100%	98%	95%	90%	80%	70%	60%

COLTEER 1-22 — .22 LR and Mag., single shot bolt action, 20 or 20 in. round barrel, adj. rear sight, plain walnut stock. Approx. 50,000 mfg. 1957-1966.

	100%	98%	95%	90%	80%	70%	60%
	$275	$215	$175	$140	$110	$95	$80

STAGECOACH — .22LR, semi-auto, 16½ in. barrel, 13 shot mag. deluxe walnut, saddle ring w/leather thong, roll-engraved hold-up scene. Over 25,000 mfg. 1965-mid 70's.

	100%	98%	95%	90%	80%	70%	60%
	$325	$275	$215	$175	$140	$110	$90

COURIER — similar to Colteer semi-auto, except pistol-grip stock and enlarged forearm. Mfg. 1970-mid 70's.

	100%	98%	95%	90%	80%	70%	60%
	$275	$215	$175	$140	$110	$95	$80

COLTEER — .22 LR, similar to Stagecoach, except 19 3/8 in. barrel, 15 shot mag., no engraving and plain walnut. Over 25,000 mfg. 1965-mid 70's.

	100%	98%	95%	90%	80%	70%	60%
	$275	$215	$175	$140	$110	$95	$80

COLT cont.

Grading	100%	98%	95%	90%	80%	70%	60%

BOLT ACTION CENTERFIRE RIFLES

COLT "57" — .243 or .30-06 cal., FN Mauser action, mfg. by Jefferson Mfg. Co. in N. Haven, CT during 1957, approx. 5,000 mfg starting at ser. no. 1, checkered American Monte Carlo walnut stock, wrap-around front sight.

	100%	98%	95%	90%	80%	70%	60%
	$550	$450	$400	$350	$300	$265	$230

This model was also available in a deluxe version with deluxe hand checkered walnut stock — add 15%.

COLTSMAN STANDARD RIFLE — .243 Win., .30-06, .300 Mag., or .308 cal., mfg. by Kodiak, Mauser or Sako-action, 22 in. or 24 in.(.300 Mag.), 5 or 6 shot mag. Approx. 10,000 (both models) mfg. 1958-1966.

	100%	98%	95%	90%	80%	70%	60%
	$475	$400	$350	$300	$265	$230	$210

COLTSMAN CUSTOM RIFLE — deluxe variation including deluxe walnut with skipline checkering and rosewood forearm cap.

	100%	98%	95%	90%	80%	70%	60%
	$700	$600	$500	$450	$390	$340	$300

COLT SAUER RIFLE (STANDARD ACTION) — non-rotating bolt action, manufactured in Germany by J. P. Sauer & Son, .25-06, .270 Win. or .30-06, 24 in. barrel, 4 round mag., no sights, checkered walnut stock with rosewood forend tip and pistol grip cap, recoil pad. Disc. 1985.

	100%	98%	95%	90%	80%	70%	60%
	$1,150	$975	$800	$700	$660	$620	$575

Last Mfg.'s Sug. Retail was $1,257.

COLT SAUER SHORT ACTION — similar to the standard except in .22-250, .243 Win. or .308 Win. Disc. 1985.

	100%	98%	95%	90%	80%	70%	60%
	$1,200	$975	$800	$700	$660	$620	$575

Last Mfg.'s Sug. Retail was $1,257.

COLT SAUER MAGNUM — similar to the standard except in 7mm Rem. Mag., 300 Win. Mag., or 300 Weatherby Mag. Disc. 1985.

	100%	98%	95%	90%	80%	70%	60%
	$1,250	$1,000	$800	$700	$660	$620	$575

Last Mfg.'s Sug. Retail was $1,300.

COLT SAUER GRAND ALASKAN — heavier version in .375 H&H Mag., adj. sights.

	100%	98%	95%	90%	80%	70%	60%
	$1,375	$1,125	$995	$900	$820	$740	$690

COLT SAUER GRAND AFRICAN — .458 Win. Mag., 4 round capacity, 9 lb. 12 oz. Disc. 1985.

	100%	98%	95%	90%	80%	70%	60%
	$1,450	$1,150	$995	$900	$820	$740	$690

Last Mfg.'s Sug. Retail was $1,400.

DRILLINGS

COLT SAUER DRILLING — 12 ga./.30-06 or .243 Combo gun, 25 in. barrels, engraved, 8 lbs. Disc. 1985.

	100%	98%	95%	90%	80%	70%	60%
	$2,950	$2,500	$2,100	$1,800	$1,500	$1,250	$1,000

Last Mfg.'s Sug. Retail was $4,228.

RIFLES: SINGLE SHOT CENTERFIRE

COLT-SHARPS RIFLE — .17 Bee, .22-250, .243, .25-06, 7mm Rem. Mag., .30-06, or .375 H&H cal., Sharps falling block action, high-gloss bluing, deluxe checkered walnut stock and forearm. Approx. 500 mfg. 1970-1977.

	100%	98%	95%	90%	80%	70%	60%
	$2,295	$1,950	$1,650	$1,200	$1,000	$800	$650

Grading	100%	98%	95%	90%	80%	70%	60%

RIFLES: RECENT MFG. (INCLUDES OLDER AR-15A2'S AND CURRENT SPORTERS)

SPORTER LIGHTWEIGHT (R6430, R6530, or R6830) — .223 Rem. (R6530), 7.62 x 39mm (R6830, new 1992), or 9mm Para. (R6430, new 1992) cal., features 16 in. barrel and shorter stock and handguard, adj. rear sight for windage and elevation, includes 2 detachable 5 shot mag's., approx. 7½ lbs. New 1991.

Mfg.'s Sug. Retail	$878	$825	$750	$675	$595	$525	$475	$425

Subtract $18 for 7.62 x 39mm cal.
Add $172 for .22 LR conversion kit.

TARGET GOVT. MODEL RIFLE (R6550/6551) — .223 Rem. (5.56mm), semi-auto version of the M-16 rifle with forward bolt assist, gas operated, 20 in. barrel, straight line black nylon stock, aperture rear, post front sight, 5, 20 (disc.), or 30 (disc.) shot detachable box mag. (supplied with two 5 shot mag.'s starting in 1989), 7½ lbs.

Mfg.'s Sug. Retail	$898	$835	$750	$675	$595	$525	$475	$425

Add $168 for .22 LR conversion kit (new 1990).
Subtract $70 for older field-style rear sight assembly (pre-1987).
In 1987, Colt replaced the AR-15A2 Sporter II Rifle with the AR-15A2 Govt. Model. This new model has the 800 meter rear sighting system housed in the receiver's carrying handle (similar to the M-16 A2).
The original AR-15A1 (AR-15 SP1) did not have a forward bolt assist and was mfg. 1963-84. Finishes included parkerizing and electroless nickel. Some dealers are asking premiums for this earlier variation.

SPORTER COMPETITION H-BAR RIFLE (R6700) — .223 Rem., features flat top upper receiver for scope mounting, 20 in. barrel, quick detachable carry handle with rear sight assembly, counterbored muzzle, dovetailed upper receiver is grooved to accept Weaver style scope rings, supplied with two 5-shot mag's, cleaning kit, and sling, matte black finish, 8 lbs. New 1992.

Mfg.'s Sug. Retail	$990	$910	$795	$725	$650	$600	$550	$495

SPORTER COMPETITION H-BAR RIFLE RANGE SELECTED (R6700CH) — similar to Sporter Competition I, except has been range selected for optimal accuracy, includes Cordura nylon case, 3-9X rubber armored variable scope, and cleaning kit, 10½ lbs. New 1992.

Mfg.'s Sug. Retail	$1,490	$1,325	$1,100	$995	$895	$795	$695	$595

SPORTER MATCH H-BAR (R6600/6601) — similar to AR-15A2 Govt. Model Rifle, except has heavy 20 in. barrel that has been range selected for optimal accuracy, includes Cordura-nylon soft-side carrying case, 8 lbs. New 1986.

Mfg.'s Sug. Retail	$939	$885	$795	$725	$650	$600	$550	$495

Add $172 for .22 LR conversion kit (new 1990).

Sporter Match Delta H-Bar (M6600DH/6601DH) — similar to AR-15A2 H-Bar, except has 3-9X rubber armored variable scope, removable cheek piece, adj. scope mount, and leather sling. Aluminum cased. Mfg. 1987-1991.

		$1,300	$1,100	$995	$825	$750	$695	$650

Add $160 for .22 LR conversion kit (new 1990).
Last Mfg.'s Sug. Retail was $1,460.

AR-15A2 Sporter II — standard 20 in. barrel, rear sight adj. for windage only, 7½ lbs. Disc. 1989.

		$995	$900	$800	$700	$600	$525	$470

Last Mfg.'s Sug. Retail was $740.

Grading	100%	98%	95%	90%	80%	70%	60%

AR-15A2 CARBINE — similar to older AR-15A2 Sporter II Rifle, except has collapsible butt stock, field sights, 16 in. barrel, shortened forearm, 5 lbs. 13 oz. Disc. 1988.

	$995	$900	$800	$700	$600	$525	$470

Last Mfg.'s Sug. Retail was $770.

AR-15A2 GOVT. MODEL CARBINE (R6520) — similar to AR-15A2 Govt. Model Rifle, except has collapsible butt stock, 800 meter adj. rear sight, 16 in. barrel, 5 lbs. 13 oz., shortened forearm. Mfg. 1988-1990 (civilian sales disc. because of Federal/State regulations).

	$995	$895	$800	$700	$600	$525	$470

Last Mfg.'s Sug. Retail was $880.

⚔ **AR-15 9mm Carbine** — similar to 5.56mm Carbine, except 9mm with 20 shot Mag., 6 lbs. 5 oz. Mfg. 1985-86 only.

	$1,100	$975	$850	$775	$675	$595	$550

Last Mfg.'s Sug. Retail was $696.

AR-15 SCOPE (4X) AND MOUNT

Mfg.'s Sug. Retail	$296	$220	$175	$160			

SHOTGUNS: DISCONTINUED

Strong, original case colors and vivid damascus barrel patterning will make the difference when determining values on the Models 1878 and 1883. Remember, these are black powder shotguns.

100%	98%	95%	90%	80%	70%	60%	50%	40%	30%	20%	10%

MODEL 1878 HAMMER SHOTGUN SXS — 10 or 12 ga., 28-32 in. blued or browned damascus barrels, double triggers, sideplates, case hardened breech, non-automatic ejectors, semi-pistol grip stock, 22,683 mfg. between 1878-1889. Many of these guns were ordered with special features - these original guns command premiums above the prices listed below.

$3,750	$3,250	$2,950	$2,675	$2,200	$1,925	$1,650	$1,485	$1,100	$990	$880	$725

MODEL 1883 HAMMERLESS SXS — 8, 10 or 12 ga., 28-32 in. damascus barrels, many deluxe custom orders occur in this model. Mfg. from 1883-1895. Approx. serial range is No. 1-3,050 and 4,055-8,365. Seldom encountered in mint condition.

$4,250	$3,750	$3,350	$2,995	$2,675	$2,200	$1,925	$1,650	$1,485	$1,100	$990	$875

This model was generally a custom order gun with no standard grades being designated. Quality was extremely high, and the high cost of manufacture is a large reason why the gun never sold in large numbers commercially. The Model 1883 was discontinued after only 12 years of manufacture (it was one of the most expensive shotguns during its day). Values above assume moderate engraving and above average walnut.

Grading	100%	98%	95%	90%	80%	70%	60%

STANDARD AUTO SHOTGUN — 12 or 20 ga. (also available in Mag.'s), mfg. by Franchi of Italy, aluminum frame, 26, 28, 30, or 32 in. plain or VR barrel, almost 5,300 mfg. (both models) 1962-1966.

	$375	$350	$325	$295	$260	$230	$200

Add $50 for VR barrel.

CUSTOM AUTO SHOTGUN — similar to Standard Model, except deluxe walnut, hand engraved receiver. Mfg. 1962-1966.

	$475	$425	$375	$350	$325	$295	$260

Grading	100%	98%	95%	90%	80%	70%	60%

COLTSMAN PUMP SHOTGUN — 12, 16, or 20 ga., Franchi frame assembled by both Kodiak and Montgomery Wards, 26 or 28 in. plain barrel, aluminum frame. Approx. 2,000 mfg. 1961-1965.

	100%	98%	95%	90%	80%	70%	60%
	$325	$295	$260	$230	$200	$180	$165

COMMEMORATIVES, SPECIAL EDITIONS, & LIMITED MFG.

During the course of a year, I receive many phone calls and letters on special editions and limited editions that do not appear in this section. It should be noted that a commemorative issue is a gun that has been manufactured, marketed, and sold through the auspices of the specific trademark (in this case Colt). There have literally been hundreds of special and limited editions which, although mostly made by Colt (some were subcontracted), were not marketed or retailed by Colt. These guns are not Colt commemoratives and for the most part, do not have the desirability factor that the factory commemoratives have. Typically, special and limited editions are made for an organization, state, special event, personality, etc. and are sold and marketed through a company/individual to those people who want to purchase them. These special editions may or may not have a retail price and oftentimes, since demand is regional, values decrease rapidly in other areas of the country. Desirability is the key to determining values on these editions. More information on these special and limited editions not listed in the following pages can be obtained by contacting the factory. The fee for this research is $45 per serial number ($10 refunded if no information is found). Please send name and address, Colt model name, serial number, and check to: COLT HISTORIAN, P.O. BOX 1868, HARTFORD, CT 06101. Allow adequate time for proper response.

As a reminder on commemoratives, I would like to repeat a few facts, especially for the beginning collector, applicable to all manufacturers of commemoratives. Commemoratives are current production guns designed as a reproduction of an historically famous gun model, or as a tie-in with historically famous persons or events. They are generally of very excellent quality and often embellished with select woods and finishes such as silver, nickel, or gold plating. Obviously, they are manufactured to be instant collectibles and to be pleasing to the eye. As with firearms in general, not all commemorative models have achieved collector status, although most enjoy an active market. Consecutive-numbered pairs as well as collections based on the same serial number will bring a premium. Remember that handguns usually are in some type of wood presentation case, and that rifles may be cased or in packaging with graphics styled to the particular theme of the collectible. The original factory packaging and papers should always accompany the firearm as they are necessary to realize full value at the time of sale. All commemorative firearms should be absolutely new, unfired, and as issued since any obvious use or wear removes it from collector status and lowers its value significantly. Many owners have allowed their commemoratives to sit in their boxes for years without inspecting them for corrosion or oxidation damage. Periodic inspection should be implemented to insure no damage occurs - this is important, since even light "freckling" created from touching the metal surfaces can reduce values significantly. A fired gun with obvious wear or without its original packaging can lose as much as 50% of its normal value.

Until recently, commemoratives in general have experienced poor liquidity and an overall reduction of prices. Commemorative production in some trademarks has totalled well over 250,000 units, and some collectors are weighing the "limited production" factor on each model before paying a premium over the standard production model of that particular commemorative. The following values reflect average purchase prices made in various areas of the U.S. In some regions it is possible to purchase an SAA commemorative made in substantial quantity for almost no premium over a standard production SAA. Because of this, prices could fluctuate over 25% depending on the geographic location of purchase or sale.

A final note on commemoratives: As a rule, what determines the bottom of the market in commemoratives is the top of the market for their standard model production relatives. A problem with limited editions is that over the years of ownership, most of the original amount manufactured stays in the same N.I.B. condition. Thus, if supply always is constant and in one condition, demand has to increase before price appreciation can occur. Taking into consideration the inflation factor during the past 2 decades, many older, high manufacture commemoratives/limited editions have not performed very well as investments. Yet, others have. Many commemorative dealers have told me that recent changes in overseas currency rates have made domestic guns less expensive to own, especially for Europeans. For this reason, many commemoratives are being sold overseas resulting in less supply for the domestic market. This secondary demand factor has strengthened commemorative prices. After 29 years of special edition production, many models' performance record can be accurately analyzed and any appreciation (or depreciation) can be compared against other purchases of equal vintage. You be the judge.

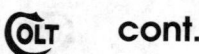
LEW HORTON SPECIAL EDITIONS — some Lew Horton Special Editions appear within the Colt section by individual model name. In addition, the following special editions have been issued by Lew Horton.

Editions include: Ultimate Officer's .45 ACP - 500 mfg. 1989 - $777 retail; Lt. Commander .45 ACP - 800 mfg. 1985 - $590 retail; Combat Cobra 2½ in. - 1,000 mfg. - $500 retail; The Lady Colt (MKIV .380 ACP) - 1,000 mfg. 1989 - $547 retail; Night Commander .45 ACP - 250 mfg. 1989 - $725 retail; El Presidente .38 Super Stainless Govt. - 350 mfg. 1990 - $800 retail.

Grading	100%	Issue Price	Qty. Made
1961 GENESEO, ILLINOIS 125TH ANNIVERSARY DERRINGER			
	$650	$28	104
1961 SHERIFF'S MODEL — blue and case hardened.			
	$1,995	$130	478
1961 SHERIFF'S MODEL — nickel.			
	$5,000	$140	25
1961 125TH ANNIVERSARY MODEL SAA			
	$895	$150	7,390
1961 KANSAS STATEHOOD SCOUT			
	$350	$75	6,201
1961 PONY EXPRESS CENTENNIAL SCOUT			
	$450	$80	1,007
1961 CIVIL WAR CENTENNIAL PISTOL .22 SHORT			
	$175	$33	24,114
1962 ROCK ISLAND ARSENAL CENTENNIAL SCOUT			
	$250	$39	550
1962 COLUMBUS, OHIO SESQUICENTENNIAL SCOUT			
	$550	$100	200
1962 FORT FINDLAY, OHIO SESQUICENTENNIAL SCOUT			
	$650	$90	110
1962 FORT FINDLAY CASE PAIR — .22 LR - .22 Mag.			
	$2,500	$185	20
1962 NEW MEXICO GOLDEN ANNIVERSARY SCOUT			
	$375	$80	1,000
1962 FORT MCPHERSON, NEBRASKA CENTENNIAL DERRINGER			
	$395	$29	300
1962 WEST VIRGINIA STATEHOOD CENTENNIAL SCOUT			
	$350	$75	3,452
1963 WEST VIRGINIA STATEHOOD CENTENNIAL SAA .45			
	$950	$150	600

Grading	100%	Issue Price	Qty. Made
1963 ARIZONA TERRITORIAL CENTENNIAL SCOUT			
	$350	$75	5,355
1963 ARIZONA TERRITORIAL CENTENNIAL SAA .45			
	$950	$150	1,280
1963 CAROLINA CHARTER TERCENTENARY SCOUT			
	$395	$75	300
1963 CAROLINA CHARTER TERCENTENARY 22/45 COMBO			
	$1,195	$240	251
1963 H. COOK "1 TO 100" 22/45 COMBO			
	$1,595	$275	100
1963 FORT STEPHENSON, OHIO SESQUICENTENNIAL SCOUT			
	$550	$75	200
1963 BATTLE OF GETTYSBURG CENTENNIAL SCOUT			
	$350	$90	1,019
1963 IDAHO TERRITORIAL CENTENNIAL SCOUT			
	$350	$75	902
1963 GEN. JOHN HUNT MORGAN INDIANA RAID SCOUT			
	$650	$75	100
1964 CHERRY'S SPORTING GOODS 35TH ANNIVERSARY 22/45 COMBO			
	$1,595	$275	100
1964 NEVADA STATEHOOD CENTENNIAL SCOUT			
	$350	$75	3,984
1964 NEVADA STATEHOOD CENTENNIAL SAA .45			
	$950	$150	1,688
1964 NEVADA STATEHOOD CENTENNIAL 22/45 COMBO			
	$1,295	$240	189
1964 NEVADA ST. CENT. 22/45 COMBO W/EXTRA ENGR. CYLS.			
	$1,395	$350	577
1964 NEVADA "BATTLE BORN" SCOUT			
	$350	$85	981
1964 NEVADA "BATTLE BORN" SAA .45			
	$1,195	$175	80
1964 NEVADA "BATTLE BORN" 22/45 COMBO			
	$2,595	$265	20
1964 MONTANA TERRITORIAL CENTENNIAL SCOUT			
	$375	$75	2,300
1964 MONTANA TERRITORIAL CENTENNIAL SAA .45			
	$950	$150	851

Grading	100%	Issue Price	Qty. Made
1964 WYOMING DIAMOND JUBILEE SCOUT			
	$350	$75	2,357
1964 GENERAL HOOD CENTENNIAL SCOUT			
	$350	$75	1,503
1964 NEW JERSEY TERCENTENARY SCOUT			
	$350	$75	1,001
1964 NEW JERSEY TERCENTENARY SAA .45			
	$950	$150	250
1964 ST. LOUIS BICENTENNIAL SCOUT			
	$350	$75	802
1964 ST. LOUIS BICENTENNIAL SAA .45			
	$950	$150	200
1964 ST. LOUIS BICENTENNIAL 22/45 COMBO			
	$1,295	$240	250
1964 CALIFORNIA GOLD RUSH SCOUT			
	$375	$80	500
1964 PONY EXPRESS PRESENTATION SAA .45			
	$1,095	$250	1,004
1964 CHAMIZAL TREATY SCOUT			
	$395	$85	450
1964 CHAMIZAL TREATY SAA .45			
	$1,295	$170	50
1964 CHAMIZAL TREATY 22/45 COMBO			
	$1,995	$280	50
1964 COL. SAM COLT SESQUICENTENNIAL PRESENTATION SAA .45			
	$950	$225	4,750
1964 COL. SAM COLT SESQUICENTENNIAL DELUXE PRES. SAA .45			
	$1,950	$500	200
1964 COL. SAM COLT SESQUICENTENNIAL SPEC. DELUXE PRES. SAA .45			
	$2,950	$1,000	50
1964 WYATT EARP BUNTLINE SAA .45			
	$1,795	$250	150
1965 OREGON TRAIL SCOUT			
	$350	$75	1,995
1965 JOAQUIN MURIETTA 22/45 COMBO			
	$1,595	$350	100
1965 FORTY-NINER MINER SCOUT			
	$350	$85	500

Grading	100%	Issue Price	Qty. Made
1965 OLD FT. DES MOINES RECONSTRUCTION SCOUT			
	$375	$90	700
1965 OLD FT. DES MOINES RECONSTRUCTION SAA .45			
	$995	$170	100
1965 OLD FT. DES MOINES RECONSTRUCTION 22/45 COMBO			
	$1,595	$290	100
1965 APPOMATTOX CENTENNIAL SCOUT			
	$350	$75	1,001
1965 APPOMATTOX CENTENNIAL SAA .45			
	$950	$150	250
1965 APPOMATTOX CENTENNIAL 22/45 COMBO			
	$1,295	$240	250
1965 GENERAL MEADE CAMPAIGN SCOUT			
	$350	$75	1,197
1965 ST. AUGUSTINE QUADRACENTENNIAL SCOUT			
	$350	$85	500
1965 KANSAS COWTOWN SERIES — Wichita Scout.			
	$350	$85	500
1966 KANSAS COWTOWN SERIES — Dodge City Scout.			
	$350	$85	500
1966 COLORADO GOLD RUSH SCOUT			
	$375	$85	1,350
1966 OKLAHOMA TERRITORY SCOUT			
	$350	$85	1,343
1966 DAKOTA TERRITORY SCOUT			
	$350	$85	1,000
1966 GENERAL MEADE SAA .45			
	$950	$165	200
1966 ABERCROMBIE & FITCH "TRAILBLAZER" — New York.			
	$995	$275	200
1966 KANSAS COWTOWN SERIES — Abilene Scout.			
	$350	$95	500
1966 INDIANA SESQUICENTENNIAL SCOUT			
	$350	$85	1,500
1966 PONY EXPRESS .45 SAA 4-SQUARE SET (4 GUNS)			
	$4,250	$1,400	unknown
1966 CALIFORNIA GOLD RUSH SAA .45			
	$1,195	$175	130

Grading	100%	Issue Price	Qty. Made
1966 ABERCROMBIE & FITCH "TRAILBLAZER" — Chicago.			
	$995	$275	100
1966 ABERCROMBIE & FITCH "TRAILBLAZER" — San Francisco.			
	$995	$275	100
1967 LAWMAN SERIES — Bat Masterson Scout.			
	$350	$90	3,000
1967 LAWMAN SERIES — Bat Masterson SAA .45.			
	$1,200	$180	500
1967 ALAMO SCOUT			
	$350	$85	4,250
1967 ALAMO SAA .45			
	$950	$165	750
1967 ALAMO 22/45 COMBO			
	$1,295	$265	250
1967 KANSAS COWTOWN SERIES — Coffeyville Scout.			
	$350	$95	500
1967 KANSAS TRAIL SERIES — Chisolm Trail Scout.			
	$350	$100	500
1967 WWI SERIES — Chateau Thierry .45 Auto.			
	$650	$200	7,400
1967 WWI SERIES — Chateau Thierry Deluxe.			
	$1,350	$500	75
1967 WWI SERIES — Chateau Thierry Spec. Deluxe.			
	$2,750	$1,000	25
1968 NEBRASKA CENTENNIAL SCOUT			
	$350	$100	7,001
1968 KANSAS TRAIL SERIES — Pawnee Trail Scout.			
	$350	$110	501
1968 WWI SERIES — Belleau Wood.			
	$650	$200	7,400
1968 WWI SERIES — Belleau Wood Deluxe.			
	$1,350	$500	75
1968 WWI SERIES — Belleau Wood Special Deluxe.			
	$2,750	$1,000	25
1968 LAWMAN SERIES — Pat Garrett Scout.			
	$350	$110	3,000

Grading	100%	Issue Price	Qty. Made
1968 LAWMAN SERIES — Pat Garrett .45 SAA.			
	$995	$220	500
1969 GEN. NATHAN BEDFORD FOREST SCOUT			
	$350	$110	3,000
1969 KANSAS TRAIL SERIES — Santa Fe Trail Scout.			
	$350	$120	501
1969 WWI SERIES — Battle of 2nd Marne .45 Auto.			
	$650	$220	7,400
1969 WWI SERIES — Battle of 2nd Marne Deluxe.			
	$1,350	$500	75
1969 WWI SERIES — Battle of 2nd Marne Spec. Deluxe.			
	$2,750	$1,000	25
1969 ALABAMA SESQUICENTENNIAL SCOUT			
	$350	$110	3,001
1969 ALABAMA SESQUICENTENNIAL .45 SAA			
	$15,000	unknown	1
1969 GOLDEN SPIKE SCOUT			
	$350	$135	11,000
1969 KANSAS TRAIL SERIES — Shawnee Trail Scout.			
	$350	$120	501
1969 WWI SERIES — Meuse-Argonne .45 Auto.			
	$650	$220	7,400
1969 WWI SERIES — Meuse-Argonne .45 Deluxe.			
	$1,350	$500	75
1969 WWI SERIES — Meuse-Argonne Spec. Deluxe.			
	$2,750	$1,000	25
1969 ARKANSAS TERRITORIAL SESQUICENTENNIAL SCOUT			
	$350	$110	3,500
1969 LAWMAN SERIES — .45 SAA Wild Bill Hickock.			
	$995	$220	500
1969 LAWMAN SERIES — Wild Bill Hickock Scout.			
	$350	$117	3,000
1969 CALIFORNIA BICENTENNIAL SCOUT			
	$350	$135	5,000
1970 KANSAS FORT SERIES — Ft. Larned Scout.			
	$350	$120	500

Grading	100%	Issue Price	Qty. Made
1970 WWII SERIES — European Theatre.			
	$650	$250	11,500
1970 WWII SERIES — Pacific Theatre.			
	$650	$250	11,500

Note: A complete set of the WWI and WWII Series standard grade models (6 guns) with matching serial numbers in NIB condition is currently selling in the $4,000 range.

Grading	100%	Issue Price	Qty. Made
1970 TEXAS RANGER SAA .45			
	$1,795	$650	1,000
1970 TEXAS RANGER GRADE II			
	$3,995	$2,250	unknown
1970 TEXAS RANGER GRADE III			
	$4,500	$2,950	unknown
1970 KANSAS FORTS — Ft. Hays Scout.			
	$350	$130	500
1970 MAINE SESQUICENTENNIAL SCOUT			
	$350	$120	3,000
1970 MISSOURI SESQUICENTENNIAL SCOUT			
	$350	$125	3,000
1970 MISSOURI SESQUICENTENNIAL .45 SAA			
	$795	$220	900
1970 KANSAS FORTS — Ft. Riley Scout.			
	$350	$130	500
1970 LAWMAN SERIES — Wyatt Earp Scout.			
	$395	$125	3,000
1970 LAWMAN SERIES — Wyatt Earp .45 SAA.			
	$1,650	$395	500
1971 NRA CENTENNIAL .45 SAA			
	$895	$250	5,000
1971 NRA CENTENNIAL .357 SAA			
	$695	$250	5,000
1971 NRA CENTENNIAL GOLD CUP .45 ACP			
	$750	$250	2,500
1971 1851 NAVY — U.S. Grant.			
	$595	$250	4,750
1971 1851 NAVY — Robert E. Lee.			
	$595	$250	4,750
1971 1851 NAVY — Lee-Grant Set.			
	$1,350	$500	250

Grading	100%	Issue Price	Qty. Made

1971 KANSAS SERIES — Ft. Scott Scout.

| | $350 | $130 | 500 |

1972 FLORIDA TERRITORY SESQUICENTENNIAL SCOUT

| | $350 | $125 | 2,001 |

1972 ARIZONA RANGER SCOUT

| | $350 | $135 | 3,001 |

1975 PEACEMAKER CENTENNIAL .45

| | $950 | $300 | 1,500 |

1975 PEACEMAKER CENTENNIAL 44.40

| | $950 | $300 | 1,500 |

1975 PEACEMAKER CENT. CASED PAIR

| | $1,995 | $625 | 500 |

USS TEXAS BATTLESHIP SPECIAL EDITION (1975) — .45 ACP, Model 1911A1 with special embellishments, nickel finish, this model is not a factory commemorative.

| | $895 | unknown | 500 |

USS ARIZONA BATTLESHIP SPECIAL EDITION (1975) — .45 ACP, Model 1911A1 with special embellishments, nickel finish, this model is not a factory commemorative.

| | $895 | unknown | 500 |

1976 U.S. BICENTENNIAL SET — includes SAA .45, Python .357 Mag., and black powder Dragoon in walnut display case with drawers.

| | $1,895 | $1,695 | 1,776 |

1976 BICENTENNIAL SAA FREEDOM COLTS — consisted of A, B, and C sets, set As were engraved, Bs had gold work and accessories, Cs were similar to B's, but had shoulder stock.   Set A prices averaged $1,500-$3,000 in 1976, set B prices varied between $3,500-$20,000, and set C prices started at $5,000. Total mfg. was 4 set As, 6 set Bs, and 1 set C. These sets in today's marketplace are too rare to accurately evaluate and pricing is literally "what the market will bear".
These guns were all manufactured by Dwain Wright located in Sisters, OR.

1977 2ND AMENDMENT .22

| | $325 | $195 | 3,020 |

1977 U.S. CAVALRY 200TH ANNIVERSARY SET

| | $1,250 | $995 | 3,000 |

1978 STATEHOOD 3RD MODEL DRAGOON

| | $6,995 | $12,500 | 52 |

1979 NED BUNTLINE .45 SAA

| | $795 | $895 | 3,000 |

OHIO PRESIDENT'S SPECIAL EDITION (1979) — .45 ACP, Model 1911A1 with special Ohio embellishments, this is not a factory commemorative.

| | $850 | unknown | 250 |

COLT cont.

Grading	100%	Issue Price	Qty. Made

1979 TOMBSTONE CENTENNIAL .45 SAA — .45 LC cal., 7½ in. barrel, nickel finish, two-piece walnut stocks, P-1876 Model, etched with scroll engraving and Western scenes. 300 mfg. (200 singles and 50 pairs).

	$950	$550	300

A pair of the above would sell in the $2,000 price range.
This model was not sold retail through the auspices of Colt.

1980 DRUG ENFORCEMENT AGENCY (DEA) .45 AUTO

	$1,100	$550	910

This model was not sold retail through the auspices of Colt.

1980 OLYMPICS ACE MODEL SPECIAL EDITION

	$1,150	$1,000	200

This model was not sold retail through the auspices of Colt.

1980 HERITAGE-WALKER .44 PERCUSSION

	$950	$1,475	1,847

1981 "JOHN M. BROWNING" .45 ACP SEMI-AUTO

	$795	$1,100	3,000

1980-81 .45 ACP GOVT. SIGNATURE SERIES — .45 ACP cal., blue finished Govt. slide with gold auroplated slide or nickel finish. 250 mfg. in both finishes.

	$750	$833	250

Add $50 for blue finish.

1980-81 ACE SIGNATURE SERIES — .22 LR cal., featured Cocobolo grips with medallions, blued finish with photo engraving, cased. 1,000 mfg.

	$900	$955	1,000

1982 JOHN WAYNE SAA STANDARD

	$1,995	$2,995	3,100

While advertising literature indicated 3,100 were mfg., 3,041 were sold.

1982 JOHN WAYNE SAA DELUXE

	$5,500	$10,000	500

While advertising literature indicated 500 were mfg., only 90 were sold.

1982 JOHN WAYNE SAA PRESENTATION

	$12,000	$20,000	100

While advertising literature indicated 100 were mfg., only 47 were sold.
Note: Each grade of the above John Wayne commemoratives has its own serial number range.

1983 BUFFALO BILL WILD WEST SHOW CENTENNIAL SAA .45

	$1,100	$1,350	500

1983 CCA LIMITED EDITION SAA — .44-40 cal., 4¾ in. barrel, nickel finish, fleur-de-lis checkered wood grips, 250 mfg. in 1983 to commemorate Colt Collector's Assn.

	$1,295	$825	250

This model was not sold retail through the auspices of Colt.

Grading	100%	Issue Price	Qty. Made

1983 "ARMORY MODEL" SAA .45 ACP — this model had limited production, and should not be confused as being a commemorative. So called because was shipped with extra .45 long Colt cylinder and the "Colt Armory Edition" book by E. Grant, presentation cased.

| | $1,395 | $1,125 | 500 |

Armory model commemoratives available with class A engraving — $2,062, B engraving — $2,395, C engraving — $2,995, D engraving — $3,500. 20 total available.

1983 PYTHON SILVER SNAKE SPECIAL EDITION — .357 Mag., 6 in. barrel, black chrome stainless steel, Pachmayr grips with custom shop pewter medallions, etched engraving, includes custom gun pouch.

| | $1,225 | $1,150 | 250 |

1984 1ST EDITION GOVT. MODEL .380 ACP

| | $425 | $425 | 1,000 |

Serial range RC00000-01000.

1984 JOHN WAYNE "DUKE" FRONTIER .22

| | $450 | $475 | 5,000 |

1984 COLT/WINCHESTER SET — 1 ea. of the Model 1894 Winchester carbine and Colt Peacemaker, serial numbered 1WC-4440WC, .44-40 cal., elaborate gold etching, cased. Pistol became available for sale individually in 1986 - see individual listing below for values.
Please refer to 1984 Winchester/Colt Set in the Winchester Commemorative section in this text.

WINCHESTER/COLT SAA — .44-40 cal., 7½ in. barrel, gold etching, this commemorative was originally made as part of the 1984 Winchester/Colt rifle-pistol set but now can be purchased individually. Originally mfg. 1984.

| | $795 | N/A | 4,000 |

1984 USA EDITION SAA — .44-40 cal., 7½ in. barrel, old style black powder frame, bullseye ejector rod head, 3 line patent date, high polished blue with gold line engraving. 100 guns total mfg. — 1 for each state and its capitol.

| | $2,500 | $4,995 | 100 |

1984 KIT CARSON .22 NEW FRONTIER — 6 in. barrel, color case hardened frame, gold artwork, serial numbered KCC0001-KCC1000, cased.

| | $350 | $550 | 1,000 |

1984 SECOND EDITION GOVT. MODEL .380 ACP — serial numbered 00000-01000RC.

| | $495 | $525 | 1,000 |

1984 OFFICER'S COMMENCEMENT ISSUE — Officer's ACP with Marine Corps emblem, rosewood grips, silver plated oak leaf scroll, cased.

| | $650 | $700 | 1,000 |

This model was not sold retail through the auspices of Colt.

1984 THEODORE ROOSEVELT COMMEMORATIVE SAA — .44-40 cal., 7½ in. barrel, black powder frame, case colored receiver, factory "B" hand engraving, ivory stocks, cased.

| | $1,495 | $1,695 | 500 |

1984 NORTH AMERICAN OILMEN SAA BUNTLINE — .45 Long Colt, 12 in. barrel, non-fluted cylinder, elaborate gold etching, ebony grips with ivory inlays, stand-up glass case, ser. nos. 1-100 mfg. for Canada, 101-200 for the U.S.

| | $3,250 | $3,900 | 200 |

This model was not sold retail through the auspices of Colt.

1985 TEXAS 150th SESQUICENTENNIAL SAA — .45 cal., Sheriff's model, 4 ¾ in. barrel, mirror bright blue, gold etching, 24 Kt. gold plated backstrap and trigger guard, smooth ivory grips, French fit oak presentation case. Mfg. 1985 only.

Premier Model — elaborate engraving, 75 mfg.

	100%	Issue Price	Qty. Made
	$4,995	$7,995	75

Standard Model — 1,000 mfg.

	100%	Issue Price	Qty. Made
	$995	$1,836	1,000

1986 150th ANNIVERSARY SAA — .45 Long Colt, 10 in. barrel, 50% engraved, royal blue finish, Goncalo Alves smooth grips, 150th anniversary logo in stocks, cherrywood case. 490 mfg. 1986 only.

	100%	Issue Price	Qty. Made
	$1,395	$1,595	490

1986 150th ANNIVERSARY ENGRAVING SAMPLER SAA — various cals., 4 different engraving styles on metal surfaces, 75% coverage, ivory grips, signed by the engraver, available with either blue or nickel finish. New 1986.

	100%	Issue Price	Qty. Made
	$2,000	$1,613	unknown

Add $120 for nickel.

1986 150th ANNIVERSARY ENGRAVING SAMPLER .45 M1911 A1 — .45 ACP, 4 different engraving styles on metal surfaces, 75% coverage, ivory grips, signed by the engraver, available with either blue or nickel finish. New 1986.

	100%	Issue Price	Qty. Made
	$1,095	$1,155	unknown

Add $60 for nickel.

1986 MUSTANG FIRST EDITION — .380 ACP, 1,000 manufactured serialized MU00001-MU01000 (the first thousand of production), rosewood stocks, walnut presentation case. Mfg. 1986 only.

	100%	Issue Price	Qty. Made
	$450	$475	1,000

OFFICER'S ACP HEIRLOOM EDITION — .45 ACP, personalized with individual's choice for serial number (ie. John Smith 1), mirror brite bluing, jeweled barrel, hammer, and trigger, ivory grips, with historical letter and mahogany case. New 1986.

	100%	Issue Price	Qty. Made
	$1,550	$1,643	open

1986 DOUBLE DIAMOND SET — set is comprised of a Python Ultimate .357 Mag. revolver and Officer's Model .45 ACP, both guns in stainless steel, smooth rosewood grips, presentation cased. 1,000 sets mfg. 1986 only, serial numbered 1-1,000 (matched).

	100%	Issue Price	Qty. Made
	$1,595	$1,575	1,000

DELTA MATCH H-BAR RIFLE — AR-15 A2 H-Bar rifle selectively chosen and equipped with 3 x 9 variable power rubber armored scope, leather sling, shoulder stock cheek piece, cased. Mfg. 1987.

	100%	Issue Price	Qty. Made
	$1,500	$1,425	open

12TH MAN-'SPIRIT OF AGGIELAND' — .45 ACP, mfg. to commemorate Texas A & M University, serial numbered TAM001-TAM999, 24Kt gold plating including wreaths on left frame and inscription on right, cherrywood glass top presentation case, includes personalized class graduation inscription. Available 1987 only.

	100%	Issue Price	Qty. Made
	$950	$950	999

This model was not sold retail through the auspices of Colt.

Grading	100%	Issue Price	Qty. Made

KLAY-COLT 1851 NAVY – .36 cal., cased reproduction of the 3rd Model 1851 Navy, special fabrication insuring old world quality, charcoal bluing, heat treated screws and accessories, cased. Introduced 1986.

⚔ **Standard Edition** – no engraving.

	100%	Issue Price	Qty. Made
	$1,850	$1,850	150

⚔ **Engraved Edition** – choice of engraving.

	$3,150	$3,150	50

Optional engraving patterns with or without gold inlays available at extra cost.

COMBAT ELITE CUSTOM EDITION – .45 ACP, with ambidextrous thumb safety, wide grip safety, hand honed action, and carrying case, ser. numbered CG00001 - CG00500. Mfg. 1987.

	$900	$900	500

1987 SHERIFF'S EDITION – set of 5 SAA Sheriff's configuration pistols in .45 LC cal., barrel lengths include 2, 2½, 3, 4, and 5½ in., royal blue finish, smooth rosewood grips with medallions, supplied with glass top display case which displays the revolvers in a circle around a brass sheriff's badge. Serialization has 3 numeral prefix (which is the same in each set), followed by the letters "SE", followed by 1 or 2 numerals (indicating barrel length) - i.e. serial number 002SE25 indicates the second set built, Sheriff's Edition (SE), and a barrel length of 2½ inches).

	$4,200	$7,500	100 sets

1989 SNAKE EYES LIMITED EDITION – includes two Python revolvers (2½ in. barrels), one finished in brite stainless steel and the other in royal blue finish, grips are ivory like with scrimshaw "snake eyes" dice on left side and royal flush poker hand on right, includes chips and playing cards, 500 sets only of consecutive serial numbers. New 1989.

	$1,950	$2,950	500

1990 SAA HEIRLOOM II EDITION – .45 LC cal., 7 ½ in. barrel, color case hardened frame and hammer, balance of metal finished in Colt Royal Blue, one piece American Walnut grips with cartouche on lower left side, personalized inscription on backstrap, walnut cased. Available 1990 only.

	$1,395	$1,600	open

1990 JOE FOSS LIMITED EDITION .45 ACP GOVT. MODEL – .45 ACP cal., first limited edition in Colt's All American Hero Series, commemorates Joe Foss, famous American WWII Marine Fighter Pilot, gun features gold etched scenes on slide sides, smooth walnut grips, 2,500 mfg. serial numbered JF 0001 - JF 2,500, French fitted walnut presentation case, 38 oz. Mfg. 1990 only.

	$1,200	$1,375	2,500

COMMANDO ARMS
Manufactured previously in Knoxville, TN.
Commando Arms became the new name for Volunteer Enterprises in the late 1970's.

Grading	100%	98%	95%	90%	80%	70%	60%

MARK 45 – .45 ACP, carbine styled after the Thompson sub-machine gun, 16½ in. barrel.

	100%	98%	95%	90%	80%	70%	60%
	$350	$315	$280	$225	$195	$175	$160

COMPETITOR

Manufactured by Competitor Corporation, Inc. located in West Groton, MA beginning 1988. Manufacturer, dealer direct, or distributor sales.

PISTOLS

Grading	100%	98%	95%	90%	80%	70%	60%

COMPETITOR — available in over 180 cals., ranging from small rimfire to large belted Magnums, rotary cannon action, cocks on opening, dual sliding thumb and trigger safety, rotary style ejector, click adj. sights, choice of synthetic, laminated, or natural wood grips (ambidextrous). New 1988.

Mfg.'s Sug. Retail	$365	$335	$300	$275	$250	$225	$200	$185

Add $133 for extra 14 in. standard cal. barrel with sights.
Add $163 for extra 10½ - 16 in. standard cal. barrel with sights.
Add $60 for factory installed muzzle brake.

CONNECTICUT VALLEY ARMS, INC.

Manufacturer located in Norcross, GA.

CVA manufactures mostly percussion/flintlock/finished and kit guns in either rifle or shotgun configurations. Black powder firearms can be found in the back of this text.

CONNECTICUT VALLEY CLASSICS

Manufacturer located in Westport, CT since 1993. Dealer direct sales.

SHOTGUNS: O/U

The models listed below have receiver dimensions built to the exact specifications as the original Classic Doubles Model 101. The only difference is that the tang spacer has been made an integral part of the frame.

CLASSIC 101 SPORTER — 12 ga. only, boxlock action, monoblock, 28, 30, or 32 in. VR barrels with multi-chokes, SST, ejectors, nickel finished receiver with light engraving, checkered American black walnut stock and forearm with low luster finish. New 1993.

Mfg.'s Sug. Retail	$2,195	$1,875	$1,550	$1,225	$1,000	$825	$700	$600

⚸ **Classic 101 Sporter Stainless** — similar to Classic 101 Sporter, except has stainless steel receiver. New 1993.

Mfg.'s Sug. Retail	$2,395	$2,000	$1,650	$1,250	$1,000	$825	$700	$600

⚸ **Classic Field Waterfowler** — 12 ga. only, 30 in. barrels, non-reflective surfaces. New 1993.

Mfg.'s Sug. Retail	$1,895	$1,700	$1,400	$995	$825	$700	$600	$525

CONTENTO/VENTURA

Previously imported by Ventura Imports in Seal Beach, CA. Ventura also imported Bertuzzi and Piotti.

SHOTGUNS

CONTENTO O/U — 12 ga., 32 in. barrels, boxlock, optional screw in choke tubes, high vent. rib, SST, auto ejectors, hand checkered Monte Carlo trap stock.

	$1,045	$990	$935	$880	$770	$690	$635

MK 2 — 2 barrel, O/U, with extra single barrel.

	$1,375	$1,320	$1,265	$1,210	$1,100	$1,020	$965

MK 2 — leather cased, combination set.

	$1,705	$1,650	$1,595	$1,540	$1,430	$1,350	$1,295

Grading	100%	98%	95%	90%	80%	70%	60%

MK 3 — engraved, O/U.

| | $1,650 | $1,570 | $1,485 | $1,375 | $1,295 | $1,185 | $1,100 |

MK 3 — 2 barrel, O/U, with extra single barrel.

| | $2,200 | $2,035 | $1,925 | $1,815 | $1,650 | $1,595 | $1,515 |

MK 3 — leather cased, combination set.

| | $2,750 | $2,420 | $2,200 | $2,090 | $1,955 | $1,815 | $1,760 |

MODEL 51 SXS — 12, 16, 20, 28, or .410 ga., 26-32 in. barrels, various chokes, extractors, boxlock, double triggers, checkered straight stock.

| | $385 | $360 | $330 | $305 | $250 | $220 | $165 |
| Auto ejectors | $495 | $440 | $385 | $360 | $305 | $275 | $220 |

MODEL 52 SXS — 10 ga., double triggers only, otherwise similar to 51.

| | $525 | $495 | $470 | $415 | $360 | $305 | $250 |

MODEL 53 SXS — deluxe version of 51, scalloped frame, auto ejectors.

| | $470 | $440 | $415 | $385 | $330 | $275 | $220 |

SST

| | $605 | $550 | $525 | $495 | $440 | $385 | $330 |

MODEL 61 SXS — 12 or 20 ga., 26, 27, 28, or 30 in. barrels, H&H sidelocks, various chokes, floral engraved, hand detachable locks, cocking indicators, select walnut pistol grip stock, auto ejectors.

| | $880 | $825 | $770 | $745 | $690 | $605 | $550 |

SST

| | $1,020 | $965 | $910 | $855 | $800 | $715 | $660 |

MODEL 65 SXS — similar to 61, with elaborate engraving and quality hand finishing.

| | $1,100 | $1,045 | $990 | $965 | $880 | $825 | $770 |

CONTINENTAL ARMS CORPORATION
Previous importer located in New York, mfg. in Belgium.

DOUBLE RIFLE — .270, .303, .30-40, .348, .30-06, .375 H&H, .400 Jeffreys, .465, .475, .500, or .600, Nitro Express cal., 24 or 26 in. barrels, Anson & Deeley boxlock system, double triggers, checkered stock.

| | $5,500 | $4,620 | $3,850 | $3,300 | $2,970 | $2,750 | $2,420 |

COOEY MACHINE & ARMS CO. LTD.
Previous manufacturer located in Cobourg, Ontario - Canada. Winchester acquired Cooey sometime in the 70's, at which time, production ceased.

There is limited information available on the variety of shotguns and rifles manufactured by this company (most distribution occurred in Canada). To date, there is limited collector demand for this trademark and values should be based on the shooting utility rather than collector premiums due to rarity. Most values will range between $75-$150.

COONAN ARMS, INC.
Manufacturer located in St. Paul, MN. Distributor sales only.

PISTOLS

Grading	100%	98%	95%	90%	80%	70%	60%

COONAN .357 MAG. MODEL B — .357 Mag. only, stainless steel and alloy construction, single action, semi-auto, design based on the Colt Model 1911, 7 shot mag., 5 in. barrel, smooth walnut grips, 42 oz. New 1983.

Mfg.'s Sug. Retail	$720	$675	$530	$425

Add $35 for 6 in. barrel (new 1989).
Add $125 for Millett adj. rear sight.
Add $140 for BoMar sight.
Add $45 for .38 Spl. conversion kit (new 1986).
This model can be differentiated from the Model A in that it has an extended grip safety lever, linkless barrel system, trigger bar slot is enclosed, and recontoured rear grip strap. This model became standard in 1985.

‡ **Coonan .357 Cadet Model** — similar to .357 Mag. Model B, except is compact variation with 3.9 in. barrel and 6 shot mag., 39 oz. New 1993.

Mfg.'s Sug. Retail	$841	$775	$625	$500

‡ **Model B Compensated** — 6 in. barrel with compensator, new 1990.

Mfg.'s Sug. Retail	$999	$895	$795	$650

COONAN .357 MAG. MODEL A — original model without above listed improvements, special order only, inventory depleted in 1991. Serialization is under 2,000 for this model (less than 1,200 were mfg.). No further production is being planned.

$995	$775	$550

This variation will also shoot .38+P loads.
Last Mfg.'s Sug. Retail was $625.

COOPER ARMS
Manufacturer located in Stevensville, MT. Dealer direct sales only.

RIFLES: BOLT ACTION

MODEL 36 SPORTER — .22 LR cal., 4 shot mag., 24 in. stainless steel barrel, AA Claro walnut with 22 LPI checkering, 45 degree bolt, sling swivels, hand rubbed oil finish, 8 lbs. New 1992.

Mfg.'s Sug. Retail	$995	$895	$725	$625	$550	$495	$450	$400

Add $200 for Custom Grade.
The custom grade includes choice of AAA Claro or AA French walnut with Monte Carlo cheek piece.

‡ **Model 36 TRP-1** — target variation of the Model 36 with ISU synthetic stock and adj. cheek piece, 23 in. Wiseman/McMillan stainless steel or chrome moly barrel, single shot, fully adj. single staged trigger, vent forearm. New 1992.

Mfg.'s Sug. Retail	$1,095	$950	$795	$625	$525	$475	$425	$375

‡ **Model MS-36 (TRP-1S)** — silhouette variation of the Model 36 TRP-1, clear epoxy finish, silhouette style stock, Pachmayr buttpad. New 1992.

Mfg.'s Sug. Retail	$995	$895	$725	$625	$550	$495	$450	$400

Grading	100%	98%	95%	90%	80%	70%	60%

MODEL 38 SPORTER — .22 CCM or .17 CCM cal., 3 shot mag., 24 in. stainless steel barrel, AA Claro walnut with 22 LPI checkering, 45 degree bolt, sling swivels, hand rubbed oil finish, 8 lbs. New 1992.

	Mfg.'s Sug. Retail	$995		$895	$725	$625	$550	$495	$450	$400

Add $100 for Standard Grade (AA Claro walnut).
Add $300 for Custom Grade.
The custom grade includes choice of AAA Claro or AA French walnut with Monte Carlo cheek piece.
The .17 CCM and .22 CCM cartridges designate Cooper Centerfire Magnum. Basically, the .22 CCM is a centerfire derivative of the .22 Mag. cal., and the .17 CCM is simply a necked down variation.

MODEL BR-50 — .22 LR cal., benchrest variation featuring black synthetic stock and heavy stainless barrel. New 1993.

	Mfg.'s Sug. Retail	$995		$895	$725	$625	$550	$495	$450	$400

COP

Previous manufacturer located in Torrance, CA.

COP DERRINGER — .357 Mag., 4 shot, 3 in. barrel, stainless steel mfg., single action, wood grips, 28 oz. COP stands for Compact Off-Duty Police. Disc.

			$350	$325	$285	$260	$240	$220	$200

COSMI, AMERICO & FIGLIO

Manufactured in Torrette, Italy since 1930. Imported and distributed by New England Arms Co. located in Kittery Point, ME.

Approximately 6,800 Cosmi shotguns have been manufactured since 1930.

SHOTGUNS: SEMI-AUTO

SEMI-AUTO MODEL — 12 or 20 ga., 2¾ or 3 in. chamber, semi-auto, unique pivoting break open action loads cartridges into stock chamber from inside of receiver, 8 shot mag. with 3 shot option, Boehler Antinit steel barrel available with or without choke tubes, all internal parts are mfg. from special chrome-nickel steel, custom order gun only with dimensions specified by individual customer (approx. 4-6 month delivery time).

⁂ **Standard Grade** — barrel and attatched receiver assembly are blued, frame is chromed-nickel steel. In 1991, Cosmi introduced a new variation with solid titanium frame - more information can be obtained by contacting New England Arms Co.

	Mfg.'s Sug. Retail	$6,750		$6,750	$6,000	$5,000	$4,500	$4,000	$3,500	$2,000

Add $2,000 for titanium fabrication.
Add $10,500 for De Luxe Model with #3 engraving.
Add $12,000 for Extra De Luxe Model with #2 engraving.
Add $14,000 for Extra De Luxe Model with #4 engraving.
Add $14,000 for Extra De Luxe Model with #1 engraving.
Add $15,000 for Extra De Luxe Model with #5 engraving.
Cosmi also manufactures an Extra Series with more elaborate engraving. Series C specimens start at $17,000, Series B start at $15,000, and Series A (top-of-the-line) start at $23,000.

⁂ **Extra Luso Models** — available with various styles and amounts of engraving. Prices are quoted individually and can be obtained by contacting New England Arms Co.

CRESCENT FIRE ARMS COMPANY

Manufactured 1888-1893 in Norwich, CT. Sold to H&D Folsom in 1893 and became a division of Stevens Arms & Tool in 1926.

Values below assume standard models with double triggers, extractors, original finish, and 100% working order. Sidelock actions were also available and will command premiums from prices listed below. Shotguns with exposed hammers can equal their hammerless counterparts if condition is 80% or better.

Grading	100%	98%	95%	90%	80%	70%	60%
SXS SHOTGUN							
12 ga.	$195	$175	$150	$125	$100	$85	$65
16 ga.	$195	$175	$150	$125	$100	$85	$65
20 ga.	$295	$265	$230	$200	$170	$150	$125
28 ga.	$375	$325	$280	$250	$200	$150	$100
.410 ga.	$400	$350	$300	$250	$200	$150	$100

Inexpensive, but hard to duplicate at today's prices. Later bought out by Folsom and became maker of "house" guns for various companies.

CUSTOM GUN GUILD

Manufactured in Doraville, GA.

WOOD'S MODEL IV SINGLE SHOT — Various cals., custom manufactured, falling block type single shot, lightweight, only 5½ lbs. Mfg. 1984 only.

$2,975	$2,500	$2,250	$2,000	$1,850	$1,700	$1,050

D section

D W M

Deutsche Waffen And Munitions Fabriken. Berlin, Germany 1900 -1930.

Grading	100%	98%	95%	90%	80%	70%	60%

POCKET AUTOMATIC — 7.65mm, $3\frac{1}{2}$ in. barrel, blue, hard rubber grips. Mfg. 1921-1931.

$700	$630	$580	$500	$420	$380	$330

DAEWOO

Manufacturer located in Korea. Currently imported and distributed by KBI, Inc. and Firstshot, Inc. both located in Harrisburg, PA.

Daewoo makes a variety of firearms, most of which are not imported into the U.S.

PISTOLS

DP51 — 9mm Para., double action, 4 in. barrel, 3-dot sighting, tri-action mechanism, ambidextrous controls, alloy receiver, polished or sand-blasted black finish, 28 oz., includes lockable carrying case with accessories. Importation began 1991.

Mfg.'s Sug. Retail	$500	$450	$375	$325	$295	$275	$250	$225

This model is imported exclusively by Firstshot, Inc.

RIFLES

MAX II (K2) — 5.56 cal. (.223), paramilitary design rifle, 18 in. barrel, gas operated rotating bolt, folding fiberglass stock, interchangeable mag.'s with the Colt M16, 7 lbs. Importation disc. 1986.

$495	$425	$375	$350	$325	$295	$270

Last Mfg.'s Sug. Retail was $609.

MAX I (K1A1) — similar to above, except has retractable stock. Importation disc. 1986.

$475	$395	$375	$350	$325	$295	$270

Last Mfg.'s Sug. Retail was $592.

DAISY

Manufacturer located in Rogers, AR. Also see Daisy section under Modern Air Rifles & Pistols. Distributor sales only.

RIFLES: DISCONTINUED

In addition to the models listed below, in 1987, Daisy assembled approximately 30,000 guns using left-over Iver Johnson parts. This model carried the Daisy trademark and was designated the '08 - it was an inexpensive bolt action single shot private labeled for Walmart. Secondary values on these rifles range from $25-$65.

V/L STANDARD RIFLE — single shot, .22 V/L, a caseless air ignited cartridge, 1,100 FPS, 18 in. barrel, plastic stock, 19,000 mfg., 1968-1969.

$110	$90	$75	$65	$55	$45	$30

Grading	100%	98%	95%	90%	80%	70%	60%

V/L PRESENTATION — similar to Collector's Kit, except does not have owner's name inscribed on butt plate, walnut stock, 4,000 mfg. for dealers.

	100%	98%	95%	90%	80%	70%	60%
	$165	$130	$110	$90	$70	$55	$45

Last Mfg.'s Sug. Retail was $125.

V/L COLLECTOR'S KIT — comes with case, gun cradles, 300 rounds of ammo, and a gold plated brass butt plate with owner's name and serial number of gun, approx. 4,000 mfg., available only by direct factory order.

	100%	98%	95%	90%	80%	70%	60%
	$275	$165	$130	$110	$90	$70	$55

Last Mfg.'s Sug. Retail was $125.

Note: The Daisy .22 V/L is the only commercial caseless ammo system. It was discontinued because the BATF ruled that the gun constituted a firearm, and since Daisy is federally licensed to manufacture air weapons only, the factory decided to discontinue manufacture.

LEGACY RIFLES: RECENT MFG.

All Legacy models have a removable trigger, slings and swivels, takedown barrel, dovetail receiver for scope mounting, rifled inner steel barrel with 12 lands and grooves, and an adj. rear sight. Weight is between 6½ - 7 lbs.

MODELS 2201/2211 — .22 LR cal., single shot, bolt action, plastic (2201) or walnut finished hardwood (2211) stock, models vary in features, prices range from $80-$130. Mfg. 1988-91.

MODELS 2202/2212 — .22 LR cal., bolt action repeater, 10 shot rotary mag., plastic (2202) or walnut finished hardwood (2212) stock, models vary in features, prices range from $90-$135. Mfg. 1988-91.
Model 2202 has copolymer stock with adj. butt plate.

MODELS 2203/2213 — .22 LR cal., semi-auto, 7 shot clip mag., models vary in features, prices range from $95-$140. Mfg. 1988-91.
Model 2203 has copolymer stock with adj. butt plate. Model 2213 has American hardwood stock.

DAKIN GUN CO.
San Francisco, CA. 1960's.

SHOTGUNS

MODEL 100 SXS — 12 or 20 ga., boxlock, engraved, double trigger.

	100%	98%	95%	90%	80%	70%	60%
	$425	$350	$275	$240	$205	$190	$170

MODEL 147 SXS — 12 or 20 ga., boxlock, engraved, vent. rib, double trigger.

	100%	98%	95%	90%	80%	70%	60%
	$495	$385	$300	$265	$235	$215	$195

MODEL 160 SXS — 12 or 20 ga., boxlock, single trigger, ejectors, vent. rib.

	100%	98%	95%	90%	80%	70%	60%
	$825	$700	$595	$495	$450	$395	$360

MODEL 215 SXS — 12 or 20 ga., sidelock, heavy engraving, special walnut, single trigger, ejectors, vent. rib.

	100%	98%	95%	90%	80%	70%	60%
	$2,250	$1,900	$1,675	$1,300	$1,100	$925	$775

MODEL 170 O&U — 12, 16, or 20 ga., boxlock, light engraving, double triggers, vent rib.

	100%	98%	95%	90%	80%	70%	60%
	$495	$400	$325	$275	$245	$220	$195

DAKOTA ARMS, INC.
Manufacturer located in Sturgis, SD. Direct sales through
manufacturer only.

DAKOTA ARMS
INC

RIFLES

*Dakota Arms models listed below are also available with
many custom options. Actions (barreled or unbarreled) may also be purchased separately. Please contact
the manufacturer directly for individual quotations.*

Grading	100%	98%	95%	90%	80%	70%	60%
DAKOTA 22 RIFLE Mfg.'s Sug. Retail	$1,500	$1,325	$995	$850	$775	$695	$625	$550
DAKOTA 76 CLASSIC GRADE Mfg.'s Sug. Retail	$2,300	$2,125	$1,675	$1,375	$1,150	$990	$880	$770
DAKOTA 76 SAFARI GRADE Mfg.'s Sug. Retail	$3,000	$2,750	$2,375	$2,150	$1,850	$1,600	$1,350	$1,050
DAKOTA 76 AFRICAN GRADE Mfg.'s Sug. Retail	$3,500	$3,300	$2,925	$2,600	$2,300	$1,950	$1,675	$1,400
DAKOTA 76 ALPINE GRADE		$1,850	$1,495	$1,300	$1,075	$925	$800	$700
DAKOTA 10 SINGLE SHOT MODEL Mfg.'s Sug. Retail	$2,300	$2,125	$1,675	$1,375	$1,150	$990	$880	$770

DAKOTA 22 RIFLE — .22 LR or .22 Hornet cal., combines features of the Win. Model 52 Sporter and Dakota 76, full sized receiver, trigger and striker block safety similar to Dakota 76, 5 shot mag., 22 in. chrome moly barrel, checkered walnut stock, no sights, 6½ lbs. New 1992.

DAKOTA 76 CLASSIC GRADE — available in various cals. (short, standard, or long action), custom frame incorporating many Win. Model 70 features, 21 or 23 in. barrel, Mauser type extractor, checkered X English walnut stock, 7½ lbs. Left-hand action available at no extra charge. New 1987.
This Model is also available with a composite stock at no extra charge.

DAKOTA 76 SAFARI GRADE — available in various cals., 23 in. barrel, one-piece drop trigger guard assembly with hinged floor plate, checkered XXX English walnut stock with ebony forearm tip. Left-hand action available at no extra charge, 8½ lbs. New 1987.
Subtract $400 (retail) if ordered with composite stock.

DAKOTA 76 AFRICAN GRADE — .404 Jeffery, .416 Dakota, .416 Rigby, or .450 Dakota cal., 4 shot mag., select wood with cross bolts in the stock, other features similar to Safari Grade Model, 24 in. barrel, "R" prefix on serial number, 9½ lbs. New 1989.

DAKOTA 76 ALPINE GRADE — .22-250, .243 Win., 6mm Rem., .250-3000, 7mm/08, .308, or .358 cal., short action variation of the Classic Grade, 21 or 23 in. barrel, lighter weight model featuring a blind 4 shot mag., checkered X English walnut slimmer stock and barrel, serial numbered with a "K" prefix, 6½ lbs. Mfg. 1989-92.
Other calibers were available on a special order basis.
Last Mfg.'s Sug. Retail was $1,995.

DAKOTA 10 SINGLE SHOT MODEL — available in most rimmed and rimless commercially loaded cals., Farquharson action, 23 in. round barrel, removable trigger plate, top tang safety, deluxe checkered X English walnut stock and forearm, 6 lbs. New 1990.

DAKOTA SINGLE ACTION REVOLVERS
Manufactured in Italy, imported and distributed by E.M.F. Co., Inc. located in Santa Ana, CA. Dealer direct sales only.
Note: Other firearms imported by E.M.F. Co., Inc. will be found in the E section of this book.

Dakota Single Action Revolvers, cont.

Grading	100%	98%	95%	90%	80%	70%	60%

SAA VARIATIONS

Old Model — .22 LR, .32-20, .357 Mag., .38-40, .44 Spl., .44-40, or .45 LC cal., copy of the Colt S.A.A., 4⅝, 5½, or 7½ in. barrels, blue finish, case hardened frame, 1-piece walnut grips, solid brass backstrap and trigger guard. Importation disc. 1991.

	$325	$250	$200	$175	$150	$135	$120

Add $100 for nickel finish (disc.).
Add $110 for convertible cylinders.
Last Mfg.'s Sug. Retail was $600.

New Model — .357 Mag., .44-40, or .45 LC cal., features forged steel frame, black nickel backstrap and trigger guard, 4¾, 5½, or 7½ in. barrel, choice of case hardened or nickel frame, one piece walnut grips, original Colt type hammer (without transfer bar safety). Importation began 1991.

Mfg.'s Sug. Retail	$460	$320	$260	$225	$175	$150	$135	$120

Add $125 for nickel finish.

Dakota Premier — .45 LC cal., black powder frame, initial mfg. was with 4⅝ or 5½ in. barrel, set screw cylinder pin release, steel backstrap and trigger guard, one-piece grips. This model was the predecessor to the New Hartford Model.

	$375	$295	$250	$190	$170	$160	$150

Last Mfg.'s Sug. Retail was $520.

New Hartford Model — .22 LR (disc. 1992), .32-20, .357 Mag., .38-40, .44-40, .44 Spl. or .45 LC cal., features forged steel frame, backstrap, and trigger guard, exact reproduction of Colt's 1st or 2nd generation SAA, choice of black powder (with base pin frame set screw) or 2nd generation (push button cylinder pin release) frame, case hardened frame, original Colt markings, 4¾, 5½ or 7½ in. barrel. Importation began 1991.

Mfg.'s Sug. Retail	$600	$425	$350	$275	$225	$175	$150	$130

Add $160 for nickel finish.

Engraved Old Model — .32-20, .357, .38-40, .44-40, or .45 cal., 4¾, 5½ or 7½ in. barrel.

Mfg.'s Sug. Retail	$840	$695	$500	$425	$350	$325	$300	$275

Add $160 for nickel finish.

Cattlebrand Engraved — .44-40 or .45 LC cal., 5½ or 7½ in. barrel, patterned after the famous Colt Cattlebrand variation (features various cattlebrands engraved on the barrel, frame and cylinder). Importation began 1992.

Mfg.'s Sug. Retail	$1,150	$925	$625	$550	$495	$450	$400	$350

Cavalry Model — .45 LC cal., 7½ in. barrel, faithful reproduction of the original Colt Cavalry Model, one-piece walnut grips with inspector cartouche, case hardened frame and hammer. Importation began 1991.

Mfg.'s Sug. Retail	$655	$425	$325	$275	$220	$185	$160	$150

Artillery Model — .45 LC cal., similar to Cavalry Model, except has 5½ in. barrel. Importation began 1991.

Mfg.'s Sug. Retail	$655	$425	$325	$275	$220	$185	$160	$150

Texas Sesquicentennial — .45 LC cal., 4¾ in. barrel, 50 mfg. for Texas Sesquicentennial with special engraving, includes numbered belt buckle and presentation case. Disc. 1991.

	$1,200	$925	$725

Original list price was $4,550.

Grading	100%	98%	95%	90%	80%	70%	60%

❁ **Target Model** — .357 Mag., .44-40, or .45 LC cal., 5½ or 7½ in. barrel, case hardened frame, brass backstrap. Imported 1987-90.

	$325	$240	$185	$150	$140	$130	$120

Last Mfg.'s Sug. Retail was $500.

❁ **Buntline Model** — 12 in. barrel, .357, .44-40, or .45 LC cal., blue only. Importation disc. 1990.

	$300	$250	$175	$160	$150	$140	$130

Last Mfg.'s Sug. Retail was $520.

❁ **Buckhorn Model** — 16¼ in. barrel, otherwise similar to Buntline. Importation disc. 1987.

	$295	$250	$180	$170	$160	$150	$140

Last Mfg.'s Sug. Retail was $495.

❁ **Sheriff's Old Model** — .357 Mag., .44-40, or .45 cal., 3½ in. barrel only. Importation disc. 1991.

	$295	$225	$165	$150	$135	$125	$110

Last Mfg.'s Sug. Retail was $450.

❁ **U.S. Army** — variety of cals., premium quality construction. Disc. 1985.

	$300	$205	$180	$165	$155	$145	$135

Last Mfg.'s Sug. Retail was $395.

❁ **Convertible Model** — available with .22 LR/.22 Mag., .32-20/.32 H & R Mag., .357 Mag./9mm, or .44-40/.44 Spl. cal., .45 LC/.45 ACP double cylinders. Imported 1986-90.

	$380	$310	$260	$220	$195	$170	$150

Last Mfg.'s Sug. Retail was $580.

❁ **Fast Draw Model** — .22 LR, .22 Mag., .32-20, .32 H & R Mag., .357 Mag., .38-40, 9mm, .44 Spl., .44-40, .45 ACP, or .45 LC cal., case hardened frame, 4⅝ in. barrel. Importation disc. 1990.

	$300	$225	$165	$150	$135	$125	$110

Last Mfg.'s Sug. Retail was $480.

❁ **Bisley Model** — .22 LR, .22 Mag., .32-20, .32 H & R Mag., .38-40, .357 Mag., 9mm, .44 Spl., .44-40, .45 ACP, or .45 LC (current) cal., 4¾, 5½, or 7½ in. barrel lengths. Imported 1986-91, re-introduced 1993.

Mfg.'s Sug. Retail	$600	$495	$425	$350	$275	$225	$195	$175

Add $30 for nickel finish (disc.).
This model is currently available in .45 LC cal. only.

❁ **Engraved Bisley** — .32-20, .38-40, .357 Mag., .44-40, or .45 LC cal. (disc. 1990), 4¾, 5½ or 7½ in. barrel, action engraved throughout. Imported 1987-91.

	$425	$350	$275	$250	$225	$200	$180

Add $100 for nickel finish.
Last Mfg.'s Sug. Retail was $570.

❁ **U.S. Army Commemorative** — .45 cal., 7½ in. barrel, serial numbered 1-500, blue finish, case hardened frame, steel backstrap and trigger guard, 1-piece walnut grips. Importation disc. 1987.

	$350	$265	$185	$170	$160	$150	$135

Last Mfg.'s Sug. Retail was $495.

DALY, CHARLES: PRUSSIAN MFG.

Charles Daly was an importer whose goal was to give the U.S. shotgun consumer a European manufactured gun of similar quality to the premier American shotguns of the same era. In that behalf, he had various European firms fabricate shotguns with American shooting features and preferences. Many "Prussian" Dalys were built by various firms in Suhl, Germany. Importation ceased prior to WWII. These Prussian Charles Dalys utilized the finest materials and best workmanship of their time.

SHOTGUNS

In the higher grade Prussian Daly variations, there is quite a bit of difference in their manufacture, including engraving options, levels of wood embellishment, and other extra cost features at the time. H. A. Linder produced approx. 2,500 guns (ser. numbered accordingly), and many of the higher grades show a noticeable difference in the amount of engraving (from minimal to considerable game scene engraving), can be either case colored only or have gold inlaid birds and animals (the number of which can also vary), barrels can have various levels of engraving on both the breech and muzzle ends - all of these factors have considerable impact on the overall value of a particular specimen. It is estimated that it took three craftsmen one year to produce a single Diamond Regent gun.

Grading	100%	98%	95%	90%	80%	70%	60%

EMPIRE O&U — 12, 16, or 20 ga., various barrel lengths, Anson & Deeley boxlock, ejectors and double triggers, fine engraving, deluxe walnut. Disc. 1933.

	100%	98%	95%	90%	80%	70%	60%
	$4,000	$3,400	$2,750	$2,375	$2,000	$1,825	$1,625

DIAMOND O&U — similar to Empire model, only finer workmanship and materials.

	100%	98%	95%	90%	80%	70%	60%
	$5,000	$4,300	$3,475	$3,000	$2,600	$2,300	$2,000

SUPERIOR SXS — 10, 12, 20, 28, or .410 ga., Anson & Deeley boxlock, various barrel lengths, ejectors (except superior model). Disc. 1933.

	100%	98%	95%	90%	80%	70%	60%
	$1,050	$790	$690	$580	$525	$475	$420

EMPIRE SXS — similar to Superior, only more engraving and better wood.

	100%	98%	95%	90%	80%	70%	60%
Linder mfg.	$5,000	$4,400	$3,900	$3,500	$2,800	$2,200	$1,500
Sauer mfg.	$4,200	$3,500	$3,100	$2,800	$2,200	$1,800	$1,400

DIAMOND SXS — similar to Empire model, only more elaborate and with gold inlays.

	100%	98%	95%	90%	80%	70%	60%
Linder mfg.	$10,000	$9,000	$8,500	$8,000	$7,000	$6,000	$4,500
Sauer mfg.	$7,000	$6,200	$5,500	$5,000	$4,000	$3,000	$2,000

Deduct 20%-25% if without gold inlays.

REGENT DIAMOND SXS — top-of-the-line Prussian side-by-side and with gold inlays.

	100%	98%	95%	90%	80%	70%	60%
Linder mfg.	$16,000	$13,500	$12,000	$11,000	$8,500	$7,000	$5,000
Sauer mfg.	$8,500	$7,700	$7,000	$6,500	$5,000	$4,000	$3,000

EMPIRE SINGLE BARREL TRAP — 12 ga., 30-34 in. barrel, Anson & Deeley boxlock, ejector, vent. rib, finely engraved with select walnut, chopper lump extension, top quality. Disc. 1933.

	100%	98%	95%	90%	80%	70%	60%
	$2,150	$1,675	$1,375	$1,100	$960	$850	$750

SEXTUPLE SINGLE BARREL TRAP — 12 ga., 30-34 in. barrel, six locking bolts, ejector, vent. rib, elaborately engraved and checkered. Regent Diamond Model has better engraving and wood.

⅜ **Empire Quality**

	100%	98%	95%	90%	80%	70%	60%
	$2,600	$2,100	$1,700	$1,400	$1,100	$900	$750

⅜ **Regent Diamond Quality**

	100%	98%	95%	90%	80%	70%	60%
	$3,300	$2,850	$2,400	$1,950	$1,650	$1,350	$995

Grading	100%	98%	95%	90%	80%	70%	60%

DRILLING MODEL — 3 barrel combination gun, available in 12, 16 or 20 ga.'s and .25-20, .25-35, and .30-30 cals., extractors, double triggers, engraved action, select walnut, mfg. by both Linder and Sauer. Linder mfg. guns are extremely rare - very few specimens are to be found domestically. Sauer guns were not marked for grade, but rather had three levels of engraving which determined the grade. Most Sauer guns had a tang mounted aperture rear sight and a separate rifle cock and were sidelocks. Disc. 1933.

Superior Quality — borderline engraving only.

	100%	98%	95%	90%	80%	70%	60%
Sauer mfg.	$3,000	$2,600	$2,300	$2,000	$1,700	$1,500	$1,200

Diamond Quality — full scroll engraving.

	100%	98%	95%	90%	80%	70%	60%
Sauer mfg.	$5,500	$4,800	$4,400	$4,000	$3,500	$3,000	$2,200

Regent Diamond Quality — top-of-the-line model featuring full game scene coverage.

	100%	98%	95%	90%	80%	70%	60%
Linder mfg.	$12,000	$11,000	$10,000	$9,000	$7,000	$6,000	$5,000
Sauer mfg.	$8,000	$7,000	$6,700	$6,000	$5,000	$4,000	$3,000

COMMANIDER O&U — 12, 16, 20, 28, or .410 ga., Anson & Deeley boxlock action, single or double triggers, ejectors. Mfg. in Belgium circa 1939.

Model 100

	100%	98%	95%	90%	80%	70%	60%
	$500	$375	$325	$275	$250	$225	$200

Add $100 for single trigger.

Model 200 — similar to Model 100, except has deluxe walnut.

	100%	98%	95%	90%	80%	70%	60%
	$650	$490	$425	$360	$325	$300	$260

For 28 and .410 ga.'s — add 10% - 30%.

RIFLES

BOLT ACTION GRADE I — .22 Hornet, mfg. by F. Jaeger & Co. of Suhl, Germany, 5 shot mag., 24 in. barrel, miniature Mauser bolt action, deluxe walnut. Disc.

	100%	98%	95%	90%	80%	70%	60%
	$820	$615	$535	$455	$410	$370	$330

DALY, CHARLES: JAPANESE MFG.
Manufactured by B.C. Miroku, Japan.

SHOTGUNS

In the early sixties, C. Daly guns were manufactured by the firm of B.C. Miroku in Tokyo, Japan. This Japanese gun manufacturing company has produced guns for many companies, Browning being the biggest current customer. Miroku guns are high quality with excellent fit and finish. Many of them are highly engraved and are fine examples of the gunmaker's art. Charles Daly Miroku Guns are becoming quite collectible in some areas (smaller gauges with open chokes). Their production ceased in 1976.

O/U SHOTGUN — 12, 20, 28, or .410 ga., 26, 28, or 30 in. vent. rib barrels, various chokes, boxlock, auto ejectors, SST, select walnut checkered pistol grip stock, Superior and Diamond Grade Trap have Monte Carlo stocks, the grades differ in amount of engraving and wood. Mfg. 1963-1976 by Miroku.
Add 10% for 20 ga. on models listed below.
Add 30% for 28 ga. on models listed below.
Add 40% for .410 ga. on models listed below.
Less than 500 28 ga. guns were built on .410 frames. These guns are worth a premium of add-ons listed above.

VENTURE GRADE

	100%	98%	95%	90%	80%	70%	60%
	$550	$495	$470	$440	$415	$360	$305

Grading	100%	98%	95%	90%	80%	70%	60%
VENTURE SKEET — 26 in. skeet and skeet.							
	$575	$525	$495	$470	$440	$385	$330
VENTURE TRAP — 30 in. imp. mod. and full.							
	$530	$495	$470	$415	$360	$330	$300
FIELD GRADE — 12 or 20 ga., field gun.							
	$625	$550	$525	$500	$450	$400	$375
SUPERIOR GRADE							
	$725	$660	$635	$605	$550	$495	$440
SUPERIOR TRAP							
	$640	$590	$550	$500	$460	$425	$390

This model had an optional selective ejection system enabling the shooter to deactivate the ejectors.

Grading	100%	98%	95%	90%	80%	70%	60%
DIAMOND GRADE FIELD							
	$1,070	$990	$935	$880	$770	$715	$660
DIAMOND GRADE SKEET							
	$1,095	$990	$910	$800	$745	$690	$635
DIAMOND GRADE TRAP							
	$925	$885	$800	$740	$685	$620	$560
WIDE RIB DIAMOND GRADE FLAT-TOP TRAP							
	$960	$920	$840	$815	$760	$700	$640

DIAMOND REGENT GRADE — mostly 12 ga., extensive frame engraving with gold inlays, rare.

	100%	98%	95%	90%	80%	70%	60%
	$2,000	$1,700	$1,425	$1,275	$1,100	$990	$880

EMPIRE DOUBLE BARREL SHOTGUN — 12, 16, or 20 ga., 26, 28, or 30 in. barrels, various chokes, boxlock, extractors, single trigger, checkered pistol grip stock. Mfg. 1968-1971.

	100%	98%	95%	90%	80%	70%	60%
	$545	$495	$470	$415	$360	$305	$250
Vent. rib	$595	$535	$500	$450	$400	$350	$300

SUPERIOR GRADE SINGLE BARREL TRAP — 12 ga., 32 or 34 in. vent. rib, full choke barrel, auto ejector, Monte Carlo stock with recoil pad. Mfg. 1968-1976.

	100%	98%	95%	90%	80%	70%	60%
	$550	$525	$495	$440	$385	$330	$305

1974 WILDLIFE COMMEMORATIVE — duck scene engraved, Diamond grade, Trap, or Skeet, limited to 500 guns. Mfg. 1974.

	100%	98%	95%	90%	80%	70%	60%
	$1,650	$1,430	$1,320	$1,100	$990	$880	$770

DALY, CHARLES: 1976 TO PRESENT

Currently imported by Outdoor Sports Headquarters, Inc. located in Dayton, OH. Italian manufacturer.

Note: The Charles Daly "Noramatic" shotguns were produced in 1968 by Breda in Italy. Current production shotguns have been manufactured in Italy since 1976 by Breda in Milan.

SHOTGUNS: SEMI-AUTO

The Noramatic series was not imported by Outdoor Sport Headquarters, Inc.

Grading	100%	98%	95%	90%	80%	70%	60%

NORAMATIC LIGHTWEIGHT MODEL — 12 ga., 26 or 28 in. barrel, various chokes, available with quick choke interchangeable tubes, checkered pistol grip stock, similar to the Breda shotgun. Mfg. 1968 only.

	100%	98%	95%	90%	80%	70%	60%
	$305	$275	$250	$220	$195	$165	$140

Add $25 for vent. rib.
Add $15 for quick choke.

NORAMATIC SUPER LIGHTWEIGHT — 12 or 20 ga., similar to Lightweight, except approx. 1/2 lb. lighter.

	100%	98%	95%	90%	80%	70%	60%
	$330	$305	$275	$250	$220	$195	$165

Add $25 for vent. rib.
Add $15 for quick choke.

NORAMATIC MAGNUM — similar to Lightweight, with 3 in. 12 or 20 ga. chambers, 28 or 30 in. vent rib barrel, full choke.

	100%	98%	95%	90%	80%	70%	60%
	$330	$305	$275	$250	$220	$195	$165

NORAMATIC TRAP — similar to Lightweight, with 30 in. full vent. rib barrel, Monte Carlo stock.

	100%	98%	95%	90%	80%	70%	60%
	$360	$330	$305	$275	$250	$220	$195

CHARLES DALY AUTOMATIC — 12 ga., 2 3/4 or 3 in. chambers, gas operation, alloy frame, pistol grip (high gloss) or English stock, vent. rib, 5 shot mag. Also available as slug gun with iron sights. Invector chokes became standard in 1986. Disc. 1988.

	100%	98%	95%	90%	80%	70%	60%
	$320	$275	$235	$205	$190	$170	$150

Add $15 for oil finished English stock.
Last Mfg.'s Sug. Retail was $365.

MULTI-XII — 12 ga. only, 3 in. chamber, 27 in. vent. rib multichoke barrel, self adjusting gas operation, deluxe checkered walnut stock with recoil pad and forearm. Imported 1987-88 only.

	100%	98%	95%	90%	80%	70%	60%
	$425	$360	$320	$285	$250	$225	$195

Last Mfg.'s Sug. Retail was $498.

SHOTGUNS: O/U

Indesol from Spain currently manufactures the new models listed below.

PRESENTATION MODEL — 12 or 20 ga., with choke tubes, Purdey double underlug locking action with decorative engraved sideplates, French walnut, single trigger, ejectors. Disc. 1986.

	100%	98%	95%	90%	80%	70%	60%
	$995	$840	$750	$670	$615	$560	$520

Last Mfg.'s Sug. Retail was $1,165.

LUXE MODEL — 12, 20, 28, or .410 ga., boxlock with self adj. crossbolt, 26 or 28 chrome lined VR barrels with internal choke tubes, SST, ejectors, antique silver finish on receiver, deluxe hand checkered walnut stock and forearm. New 1989.

	100%	98%	95%	90%	80%	70%	60%
Mfg.'s Sug. Retail	$699	$595	$500	$460	$425	$400	$375	$350

FIELD MODEL — similar to Luxe Grade except has fixed chokes, extractors, machine stock checkering, and blued receiver, not available in 28 or .410 ga. New 1989.

	100%	98%	95%	90%	80%	70%	60%
Mfg.'s Sug. Retail	$475	$400	$370	$340	$315	$285	$260	$230

DIAMOND FIELD — 12 or 20 ga. (disc. 1986) Mag.'s, with choke tubes. Same action as Presentation Model without sideplates, engraved, select walnut, single trigger, ejectors. Disc. 1986.

	100%	98%	95%	90%	80%	70%	60%
	$695	$600	$550	$510	$460	$420	$380

Last Mfg.'s Sug. Retail was $895.

Grading	100%	98%	95%	90%	80%	70%	60%

⚜ Diamond Trap or Skeet — 12 ga. only, 26 or 30 in. barrels only. Disc. 1986.

	100%	98%	95%	90%	80%	70%	60%
	$850	$700	$550	$500	$475	$450	$425

Deduct $50 for Skeet Model.
Last Mfg.'s Sug. Retail was $1,050.

SUPERIOR II — 12 or 20 ga., various chokes, boxlock action, single trigger, ejectors, engraved. Disc. 1988.

	100%	98%	95%	90%	80%	70%	60%
	$675	$575	$475	$425	$395	$375	$350

Add $35 for 12 ga. Mag. (disc. 1987).
Last Mfg.'s Sug. Retail was $875.

FIELD III — 12 or 20 ga., various chokes, boxlock action, single trigger. Disc. 1989.

	100%	98%	95%	90%	80%	70%	60%
	$395	$370	$340	$315	$285	$260	$230

Last Mfg.'s Sug. Retail was $450.

SHOTGUNS: SIDE-BY-SIDE

SUPERIOR — 12 or 20 ga., boxlock action, various chokes, single trigger. Disc. 1985.

	100%	98%	95%	90%	80%	70%	60%
	$550	$470	$405	$345	$315	$280	$250

Last Mfg.'s Sug. Retail was $624.

LUXE MODEL — 12 (disc. 1991) or 20 ga., boxlock action, SST, ejectors, 26 in. barrels with choke tubes, checkered pistol grip walnut stock with semi-beavertail forearm, recoil pad. New 1990.

	Mfg.'s Sug. Retail						
	$650	$575	$450	$395	$350	$315	$285	$260

This model is manufactured by Hermanos located in Spain.

DAN ARMS OF AMERICA

Manufactured in Italy by Silma. Previously imported by Dan Arms of America located in Allentown, PA and by Dan Arms of North America (previously called Sportsman's Emporium Ltd.) located in Ft. Washington, PA.

All shotguns listed below were discontinued in early 1988.

SHOTGUNS: OVER AND UNDER

LUX GRADE I — 12 or 20 ga., 3 in. Mag. chambers, 26, 28, or 30 in. barrels, vent rib, extractors, pistol grip, double trigger, European walnut.

	100%	98%	95%	90%	80%	70%	60%
	$280	$220	$210	$200	$190	$180	$170

Last Mfg.'s Sug. Retail was $350.

LUX GRADE II — 12 ga. only, 3 in. Mag. chambers, 26, 28, or 30 in. barrels, vent. rib, extractors, pistol grip, single trigger, European walnut.

	100%	98%	95%	90%	80%	70%	60%
	$320	$250	$240	$230	$215	$200	$190

Last Mfg.'s Sug. Retail was $395.

LUX GRADE III — 12 or 20 ga., 3 in. Mag. chambers, 26, 28, or 30 in. barrels, vent rib, ejectors, pistol grip, single trigger, checkered European walnut.

	100%	98%	95%	90%	80%	70%	60%
	$375	$300	$285	$270	$255	$240	$220

Last Mfg.'s Sug. Retail was $450.

LUX GRADE IV — 12 ga. only, 3 in. Mag. chambers, 28 in. barrels, vent. rib, ejectors, pistol grip, single trigger, checkered European walnut, multi-choked with 5 tubes.

	100%	98%	95%	90%	80%	70%	60%
	$460	$390	$350	$310	$285	$265	$245

Last Mfg.'s Sug. Retail was $550.

Grading	100%	98%	95%	90%	80%	70%	60%

SKEET MODEL — 12 ga. only, 26½ in. barrels, 10mm vent. rib, anatomical pistol grip.

	100%	98%	95%	90%	80%	70%	60%
	$550	$450	$400	$355	$320	$300	$285

Last Mfg.'s Sug. Retail was $650.

TRAP MODEL — 12 ga. only, 30 in. barrels, 10mm vent. rib, anatomical pistol grip.

	100%	98%	95%	90%	80%	70%	60%
	$550	$450	$400	$355	$320	$300	$285

Last Mfg.'s Sug. Retail was $650.

SILVERSNIPE — 12 or 20 ga., made to customer specifications, sideplates, select high grade walnut, name engraving upon request.

	100%	98%	95%	90%	80%	70%	60%
	$1,300	$1,200	$1,050	$900	$800	$700	$600

Last Mfg.'s Sug. Retail was $1,475.

SHOTGUNS: SIDE-BY-SIDE

FIELD MODEL — 12, 16, 20, 28, or .410 ga., double triggers, extractors, 26 or 28 in. barrels.

	100%	98%	95%	90%	80%	70%	60%
	$285	$220	$210	$200	$190	$180	$170

Last Mfg.'s Sug. Retail was $350.

DELUXE FIELD MODEL — 12 or 20 ga., single triggers, ejectors, 26 or 28 in. barrels.

	100%	98%	95%	90%	80%	70%	60%
	$440	$375	$340	$310	$290	$260	$230

Last Mfg.'s Sug. Retail was $500.

DARDICK
Previously manufactured in Hamden, CT.

PISTOLS

SERIES 1100 — .38 Dardick Tround, double action, 10 shot mag.

	100%	98%	95%	90%	80%	70%	60%
	$560	$420	$365	$310	$255	$225	$200

Dardick ammunition in itself is collectible - currently, individual rounds are selling in the $5-$10 range.

SERIES 1500 — .22, .30, or .38 Dardick Tround, double action.

	100%	98%	95%	90%	80%	70%	60%
	$875	$660	$570	$490	$440	$395	$350

Subtract $400 for .30 cal.
Note: carbine conversion units (.22 or .38 cal) add $175 - $400.

DARNE S.A.
Manufactured between 1881-1979 and 1990 to date in Saint Etienne, France. Currently imported by Wes Gilpin located in Dallas, TX.
Please refer to the Bruchet section for 1982-1990 mfg. utilizing the Darne action.

SHOTGUNS: PRE-1980 MFG.

DARNE SLIDING BREECH SHOTGUN — 12, 16, 20, or 28 ga., double barrel, SxS, unique action utilizes sliding breech lock-up, high quality mfg., 27½ in. barrel standard with other lengths available, any choke combination, either straight grip or pistol grip stock, checkered, models differ in amount of engraving and grade of wood.

Bird Hunter Model R11

	100%	98%	95%	90%	80%	70%	60%
	$1,000	$715	$635	$550	$495	$440	$360

Darne S. A., cont.

Grading	100%	98%	95%	90%	80%	70%	60%
Pheasant Hunter Model R15							
	$2,300	$1,950	$1,750	$1,625	$1,500	$1,425	$1,300
Magnum Model R16							
	$1,650	$1,450	$1,350	$1,250	$1,125	$1,000	$900
Quail Hunter Model V19							
	$3,350	$2,750	$2,500	$2,250	$2,000	$1,800	$1,650
Model V22							
	$3,750	$3,300	$3,000	$2,600	$2,300	$2,050	$1,850
Hors Series No. 1 Model V							
	$4,400	$3,850	$3,575	$3,300	$3,080	$2,750	$2,200

SHOTGUNS: 1989 TO DATE MFG.

In 1990, Paul Bruchet (the old Darne plant superintendent) obtained permission to once again use the Darne trademark. Hence, all 1990 and later mfg. has been produced by Paul Bruchet.

All new mfg. Darnes can be choked to the customer's choice. All models listed below have automatic ejectors, are oil finished by hand, and may be barreled to any length (except for Models R 11, 12, and 13). All prices are subject to change without notice.

R 11 — 12 or 16 ga., half pistol grip stock, light engraving.

		100%	98%	95%	90%	80%	70%	60%
Mfg.'s Sug. Retail	$2,875	$2,625	$2,175	$1,870	$1,760	$1,650	$1,375	$1,225

R 12 — similar to above, except with better engraving.

		100%	98%	95%	90%	80%	70%	60%
Mfg.'s Sug. Retail	$4,460	$3,225	$2,550	$2,100	$1,870	$1,760	$1,650	$1,375

R 13 — 12, 16, or 20 ga., straight or pistol grip stock, traditional action with bouquet engraving.

		100%	98%	95%	90%	80%	70%	60%
Mfg.'s Sug. Retail	$3,950	$3,675	$2,950	$2,450	$2,100	$1,870	$1,760	$1,500

R 14 — 12, 16, or 20 ga., slug gun, choice of forends, light engraving, and optional cheek rest pistol grip stock is also available.

		100%	98%	95%	90%	80%	70%	60%
Mfg.'s Sug. Retail	$3,625	$3,350	$2,375	$2,100	$1,870	$1,760	$1,650	$1,375

R 15 — 12, 16, 20, 24, or 28 ga., select walnut stock and forearm with fine checkering, large scroll engraving, obturator disks.

		100%	98%	95%	90%	80%	70%	60%
Mfg.'s Sug. Retail	$4,350	$3,950	$3,100	$2,575	$2,300	$2,000	$1,775	$1,475

R 17 — 12 or 20 ga., Magnum model (3 in. chambers), customer's choice of full coverage engraving, superior quality walnut and checkering.

		100%	98%	95%	90%	80%	70%	60%
Mfg.'s Sug. Retail	$5,400	$4,900	$3,625	$2,950	$2,575	$2,250	$1,925	$1,600

V 19 — all gauges, easy opening large key action, top quality walnut and checkering, full coverage rose and scroll engraving with chiseled fences.

		100%	98%	95%	90%	80%	70%	60%
Mfg.'s Sug. Retail	$8,025	$7,450	$6,500	$5,150	$4,700	$3,500	$2,950	$2,575

V 21 — similar to V 19, except has large scroll rosace engraving and chiseled fences.

		100%	98%	95%	90%	80%	70%	60%
Mfg.'s Sug. Retail	$8,500	$7,900	$6,950	$5,475	$4,950	$3,675	$3,100	$2,675

V 22 — similar to V 21, except has bulino style engraving featuring hunting scenes, ornamental borders, and gold inlays (if specified).

		100%	98%	95%	90%	80%	70%	60%
Mfg.'s Sug. Retail	$10,750	$9,800	$8,250	$6,300	$5,400	$4,000	$3,475	$3,000

Grading	100%	98%	95%	90%	80%	70%	60%

VHS — all gauges, top of the line model incorporating customers choice of engraving style, type of inlays, and checkering pattern, best quality wood. The values below represent base prices without options.

Mfg.'s Sug. Retail $12,200	$11,000	$9,000	$7,000	$6,100	$4,800	$3,950	$3,375

DAVIDSON FIREARMS
Maker: Fabrica De Armas, Eibar, Spain.

MODEL 63B — 12, 16, 20, 28, or .410 ga., double barrel, 25, 26, 28, or 30 in. barrels, Anson & Deeley boxlock, engraved and nickel plated frame, various chokes, walnut checkered stock. Mfg. 1963-disc.

$275	$260	$220	$200	$175	$165	$155

Model 63B Magnum — similar to 63B, except 10 ga. Mag., 12, or 20 ga. Mag., 32 in. barrel.

12 or 20 ga. $360	$340	$310	$275	$230	$195	$165
10 ga. $385	$370	$340	$305	$250	$220	$195

MODEL 69SL — 12 or 20 ga., true detachable sidelock action, engraved nickel plated action, 26 in. and 28 in. barrels, imp. cyl. and mod., mod. and full, checkered walnut stock. Mfg. 1963-1976.

$415	$395	$375	$340	$320	$290	$260

MODEL 73 STAGECOACH — 12 or 20 ga., detachable sidelock exposed hammers, 3 in. chambers, 20 in. mod. and full barrels, checkered walnut stock. Mfg. 1976-disc.

$275	$260	$220	$200	$175	$165	$155

DAVIS INDUSTRIES
Manufacturer located in Mira Loma, CA. Distributor sales only.

Davis Industries provides a lifetime warranty to the original purchaser of all models listed below.

D-22/D-25/D-32/D-38 SERIES DERRINGER — .22 LR, .22 Mag., .25 ACP, .32 ACP, or .38 Spl. (new 1992) cal., O/U steel construction, 2.4 or 2¾ (.38 Spl. only) in. vent. rib barrel, 9½ or 11½ oz., black Teflon or chrome finish.

Mfg.'s Sug. Retail $65	$55	$50	$45	$40	$35	$30	$30

Add $25 for .38 Spl. cal.
In this series, the .25 ACP cal. is the Model D-25 and the .32 ACP cal. is the Model D-32.

P-32 — .32 ACP, single action semi-auto, 6 shot mag., 2.8 in. barrel, black Teflon or chrome finish, laminated wood grips, 22 oz. New 1987.

Mfg.'s Sug. Retail $88	$75	$65	$55	$45	$40	$35	$30

P-380 — .380 ACP, single action semi-auto, similar to P-32, 5 shot mag., 2.8 in. barrel, 22 oz., bright chrome or black Teflon finish, internal shock resister for recoil, wood (disc.) or black synthetic grips. New 1989.

Mfg.'s Sug. Retail $98	$85	$75	$65	$55	$45	$40	$35

DEMRO
Manufacturer located in Manchester, CT.

T.A.C. MODEL 1 RIFLE — .45 ACP or 9mm Luger, blow back operation, 16⅞ in. barrel, also available in carbine model and fully auto.

$360	$310	$260	$220	$200	$180	$165

Grading	100%	98%	95%	90%	80%	70%	60%

XF-7 WASP CARBINE — .45 ACP or 9mm Luger, blow back operation, 16⅞ in. barrel, also available in fully auto.

| | $360 | $310 | $260 | $220 | $200 | $180 | $165 |

Add $45 for case.

DESERT INDUSTRIES, INC.

Manufacturer located in Las Vegas, NV beginning 1991. Distributor and dealer direct sales. See listing under STEEL CITY ARMS, INC. for older models.

In 1990, Desert Industries, Inc. was created - this new company took over Steel City Arms, Inc. To date, manufacture has consisted of a parts clean-up using older Steel City Arms marked components. More recently manufactured guns will have the Las Vegas slide address.

PISTOLS

THE DOUBLE DEUCE — .22 LR, double action, 2½ in. barrel, matte stainless steel construction, 6 shot mag., rosewood grips, 15 oz. New 1991.

| Mfg.'s Sug. Retail | $400 | $350 | $295 | $275 | $250 | $225 | $200 | $175 |

TWO BIT SPECIAL — .25 ACP, double action, 2½ in. barrel, similar to Double Deuce, except has 5 shot mag., 15 oz. New 1991.

| Mfg.'s Sug. Retail | $400 | $350 | $295 | $275 | $250 | $225 | $200 | $175 |

WAR EAGLE — 9mm Para., 10mm, or .45 ACP cal., double action, 4 in. barrel, matte stainless steel construction, fixed sights, rosewood grips, 13, 14, or 15 shot mag. New 1991.

| Mfg.'s Sug. Retail | $625 | $550 | $475 | $400 | $350 | $300 | $250 | $225 |

RIFLES

G-90 — various cals., single shot rifle with interchangeable barrels (light, medium, or heavy), drilled and tapped, no sights. New 1993.

| Mfg.'s Sug. Retail | $525 | $450 | $375 | $325 | $275 | $250 | $225 | $200 |

SHOTGUNS

BIG TWENTY — 20 ga. only, single shot, collapsible stock with wooden forend. New 1993.

| Mfg.'s Sug. Retail | $190 | $170 | $140 | $115 | $95 | $80 | $70 | $60 |

DETONICS FIREARMS INDUSTRIES

Detonics Firearms Industries was a previous manufacturer located in Bellevue, WA 1976 -1988. Detonics was sold in early 1988 to the New Detonics Manufacturing Corporation, a wholly owned subsidiary of "1045 Investors Group Limited".

Please refer to the New Detonics Manufacturing Corporation in the "N" section of this text for complete model listings of both companies.

DIARM S.A.

Previous manufacturing conglomerate (25 companies) located in Deba, Spain 1986 -1989. Previously imported and distributed by American Arms, Inc. located in North Kansas City, MO. Older Diarm models can be found under the American Arms, Inc. heading in this publication.

DIXIE GUN WORKS

See "Modern Black Powder Guns" Section.

DOMINGO ACHA

Manufactured in Spain.

Grading	100%	98%	95%	90%	80%	70%	60%

LOOKING GLASS — .25 and .32 cal. auto pistol.

	100%	98%	95%	90%	80%	70%	60%
	$150	$125	$105	$85	$75	$60	$50

DOMINO, IGI

Previously imported from Italy by Mandall Shooting Supplies located in Scottsdale, AZ. This firm was absorbed by FAS (see separate listing in F section) in 1990. Limited quantities of Domino pistols are still available from Mandall Shooting Supplies.

MODEL OP 601 MATCH PISTOL — .22 Short, 5 shot, 5.6 in. barrel, match sights, full target grips, vent barrel and slide to reduce recoil, adj. and removable trigger.

	100%	98%	95%	90%	80%	70%	60%
	$1,300	$1,000	$715	$635	$550	$495	$440

Last Mfg.'s Sug. Retail was $1,495.

MODEL SP 602 MATCH PISTOL — .22 LR, 5½ in. barrel, similar to 601, but .22 LR and slightly different trigger.

	100%	98%	95%	90%	80%	70%	60%
	$1,300	$1,100	$800	$700	$600	$550	$495

Last Mfg.'s Sug. Retail was $1,495.

DREYSE PISTOL

Manufactured by Rheinische Metallwaren and Machinenfabrik, located in Sommerda, Germany.

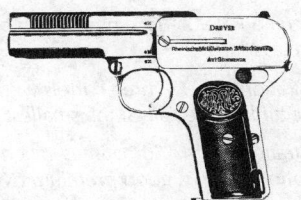

MODEL 1907 AUTOMATIC — 7.65mm, 8 shot, 3½ in. barrel, blue, fixed sights, hard rubber grips. Mfg. 1907-1914.

	100%	98%	95%	90%	80%	70%	60%
	$200	$170	$150	$120	$95	$75	$50

MODEL 1910 — 9mm Luger, 3½ in. barrel. Mfg. 1912-1915.

	100%	98%	95%	90%	80%	70%	60%
	$760	$570	$495	$420	$380	$345	$305

VEST POCKET AUTOMATIC — .25 ACP, 6 shot, 2 in. barrel, blue, fixed sights, hard rubber grips. Mfg. 1912-1915.

	100%	98%	95%	90%	80%	70%	60%
	$225	$190	$165	$130	$100	$75	$50

DRILLINGS

A Drilling is a three-barrel combination gun (two shotgun barrels and a rifle barrel, vice versa, or three shotgun barrels). Normally, two triggers fire the shotgun barrels and one of them activates the rifle barrel when the barrel selector is moved forward (usually located on the upper tang). Most well made Drillings in above average condition are surprisingly accurate when using the rifle barrel(s).

Please refer to illustrations below depicting the most commonly encountered Drilling configurations.

Drillings, cont.

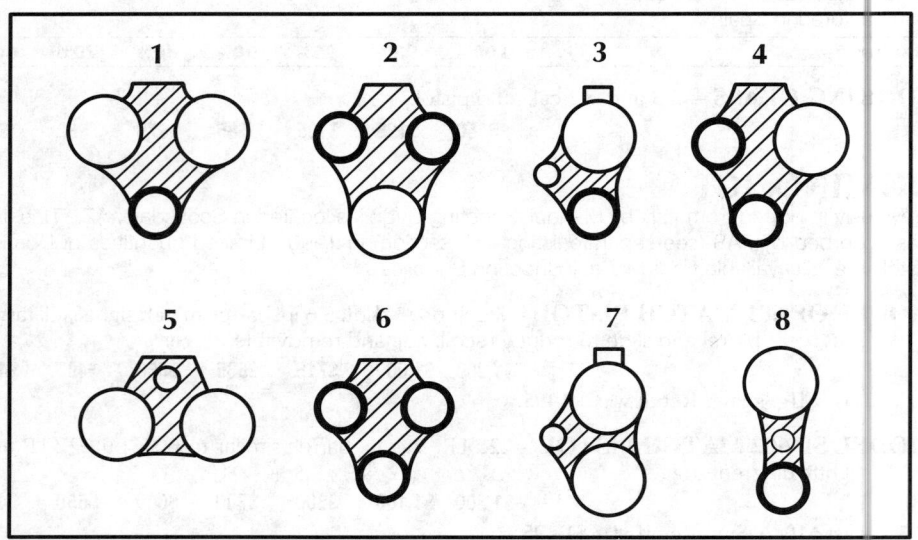

Illustration No. 1 - Normal Drilling configuration with 2 shotgun barrels over a rimmed, centerfire rifle (most are 16 ga. x 16 ga. by either 9.3 x 72R or 8 x 57JR cal.).

Illustration No. 2 - Two rifle barrels over a shotgun. This configuration will normally command twice the price as No. 1.

Illustration No. 3 - Three barrels with no two being the same gauge or caliber. This configuration is very collectible, especially if the smallest caliber is .22LR. Again, price will be double of No. 1.

Illustration No. 4 - Sometimes called a "cross-eyed" Drilling with one shotgun and two rifle barrels. This variation brings a good premium over No. 1.

Illustration No. 5 - Rib Drilling with rifle caliber generally small (.22LR or .22 Hornet).

Illustration No. 6 - Three shotgun barrels with the same gauge. This configuration is quite rare and healthy premiums are charged over No. 1.

Illustration No. 7 - A variation of No. 3, this configuration features shotgun O/U barrels with a rifle barrel on the side.

Illustration No. 8 - Very unusual - a 3 barrel drilling in vertical design - 2 rifle barrels under a shotgun barrel. This configuration is seldomly encountered.

For over 125 years Drillings have been the classic hunting gun of many European countries, especially Germany and Austria. Because a single hunting trip may require shooting both wildfowl and animals (oftentimes within several hours), Europeans have long favored a single long-arm that could afford both rifle and shotgun shooting, be reliable, and not wear the hunter out while transporting it in the field. Americans, on the other hand, have not placed as much emphasis on this combination gun principle, and more often than not, have chosen to buy both a rifle and shotgun for each specific hunting application. Since Drillings generally have not been as popular in the U.S., collectibility has been somewhat limited in this country, except for those who see the utility and functionality of these mostly hand assembled weapons. Very few Drillings manufactured before WWII are alike today in configuration and condition.

Some people may be confused as to how the European metric calibers compare to domestic cartridges in terms of overall performance. This comparison has been added to assist you when contemplating what type of field performance, velocity, and killing power you can expect in these European calibers: 9.3 x 74 is similar to .375 Win. Mag., 9.3 x 72 is similar to .44 Mag. or .44-40, 8 x 57 JRS is similar to .30-06, 8 x 57 JR is similar to .30-06, 7 x 65 R is similar to .280 Rem., 7 x 57 R is similar to .257 Roberts, 6.5 x 57 R is similar to .243 Win., 5.6 x 52 R is a .22 Savage Hi-Power, 5.6 x 34 R is similar to .22 Hornet.

DRILLING VALUES

Rather than list the various manufacturers of Drillings (there are hundreds), it should be noted that guns with major trademarks and established provenances (i.e. Charles Daly, Colt Sauer, Ferlach addressed, Heym, Krieghoff, J.P. Sauer, Suhl addressed, etc.) will be more collectible than other lesser known brands - even if the quality of workmanship is similar. Pre-war specimens are generally more desirable to collectors (even though less expensive than post-war variations) and to date, have outperformed post-war specimens in price appreciation. Many older pre-war specimens were designed for rimmed cartridges with lower breech pressures and should not be re-bored or reloaded for the "hotter" cartridges/loads available today. It should be noted that since Drillings are more complex than a typical shotgun, most of the manufacture has been done by hand - some guns have taken individual craftsmen over a year to fabricate! Ordering a new Drilling today would be a very expensive proposition, and buying a good used specimen will save you thousands of dollars (and maybe a year wait). For these reasons, many collectors feel Drillings today are under-priced since they can be purchased at a fraction of the cost for a new one (and may well be better quality also).

GENERAL OBSERVATIONS CONCERNING DRILLING COLLECTIBILITY:

Subtract approx. 50% for exposed hammers (as opposed to hammerless).

Nitro-proofed Drillings are worth twice that of blackpowder or damascus barrel specimens.

Drillings with original claw-mounted scopes are worth 30-40% premiums.

Many post-war variations are valued for their hunting use only, and do not have the collectibility of the pre-war guns.

FEATURES THAT ADD VALUE TO DRILLINGS:

Drillings with American calibers and smaller gauges will be more desirable (and expensive) than the European metric calibers (i.e. a gun configured 20 ga. x 20 ga. by .243 Win. will outperform a similar gun in 16 ga. x 16 ga. by 9.3 x 72R cal.). The most commonly encountered gauges and calibers are 16 ga. (most pre-war guns are chambered for $2^{9}/_{16}$ in. and would have to be re-chambered for $2^{3}/_{4}$ in. to be shootable today). In addition, a sidelock action will be more desirable than a boxlock, and alot more expensive if the locks are also detachable.

Features and embellishments become very critical in ascertaining Drilling values also - a gun with deep relief engraving, carved stock, claw mounts w/scope, buffalo horn trigger guard and butt plate, cocking indicators, two position front sight (i.e. night sight), middle set of express sights, adj. trigger, concealed upper tang peep sight, a non-Greener safety system, lightweight (under $6^{1}/_{2}$ lbs.), separate rifle cocking, shotgun barrel inserts in .22LR or .22 Mag. cal. (approx. 8 or 11 in. long), cartridge trap, etc. is going to be ALOT more collectible than a plain-Jane hammer model with a loose action.

FEATURES THAT DETRACT VALUE FROM DRILLINGS:

These include exposed hammers, damascus or blackpowder only guns, bottom lever break, calibers for which ammo is not readily available or cannot be easily made from other more common brass, loose action, mechanical problems which hinder shooting, etc.

CONDITION FACTORS:

Condition is another major consideration - a gun that shows much use and is not operationally intact/correct may bring several thousand dollars less than another similar specimen showing little wear and excellent original finish (including the case colors). Most good boxlock Drillings in the above mentioned trademarks start in the $1,750 range and can go to $4,000 and higher if the configuration, features, and condition are all desirable. Average Drillings usually sell in the $725 - $1,850 range assuming worn condition, metric calibers and few features. For these reasons, Drillings have to be evaluated one at a time and a COMPETENT appraisal/evaluation should be procured before buying or selling a specimen.

DUBIEL ARMS COMPANY

Previous manufacturer located in Sherman, TX. Dubiel Arms made custom bolt action rifles from 1973-approx. 1990.

Grading	100%	98%	95%	90%	80%	70%	60%p

BOLT ACTION RIFLE — custom made bolt action, .22-250-.458 Win. Mag. cal's available, barrel length and weight to order, no sights, Canjar trigger, all steel parts, custom made rifle stocks available in five styles. Disc.

100%	98%	95%	90%	80%	70%	60%p
$2,000	$1,750	$1,500	$1,275	$1,125	$975	$825

Last Mfg.'s Sug. Retail was $2,500.

DUMOULIN, ERNEST

Manufacturer located in Herstal, Belgium. Previously imported (until 1990) and retailed on a very limited basis by Midwest Gun Sport located in Zebulon, NC (formerly from Ellisville, MO.). Older importation was by Abercrombie & Fitch located in New York, NY.

Note: Most Ernest Dumoulin rifles and shotguns are essentially custom ordered firearms with a long list of options available which, in some cases, can easily double the values of models shown below. Because of this, these options are not listed individually. To determine the exact price on a specific model with certain options, Ernest Dumoulin (see Trademark Index) should be contacted directly to obtain a firm price (dependent on the fluctuation of the U.S. dollar and other domestic and foreign regulations). Written correspondence should include a SASE (a FAX will be faster).

RIFLES: BOLT ACTION

E. Dumoulin has had very limited importation since 1989 and all discontinued retail values reflect 1989 information.

Grading	100%	98%	95%	90%	80%	70%	60%
BAVARIA DELUXE — .243 Win. through .458 Win. cals., 21½, 24, or 25½ in. octagonal barrel, French walnut stock with rosewood forend tip and pistol grip cap, no sights, custom made essentially with Sako (disc.) or Mauser action. Many engraving options available from $510-$1,900. Disc. 1985.							
Series I	$995	$890	$775	$650	$575	$530	$460

Add 15% for .375 H&H or .458 Win. Mag. cal. Last Mfg.'s Sug. Retail was $1,080.

	100%	98%	95%	90%	80%	70%	60%
RIFLE MOUSQUETON — .240 Win. through .338 Win. cals., 20 in. barrel, Mannlicher style, French walnut stock and pistol grip cap, no sights, custom made essentially with Sako or Mauser action. Many engraving options available from $510 - $1,900. Disc.	$720	$620	$560	$510	$470	$420	$360
CENTURION MODEL — .270 Win. through .458 Win. cals., 21½, 24, or 25½ in. barrels, French walnut stock with rosewood forearm tip and pistol grip cap, no sights, custom made essentially with Sako or Mauser action. Many engraving options available from $510 - $1,900. Importation disc. 1986.	$660	$590	$535	$480	$425	$390	$360

Last Mfg.'s Sug. Retail was $740.

	100%	98%	95%	90%	80%	70%	60%
CENTURION CLASSIC — similar to Centurion, standard cals. only, Mauser 98 action only and has better wood.	$1,525	$1,375	$1,175	$975	$800	$700	$600

These models are also available in Mag. cals. that are divided into 4 groups — 1, 2, 3, and 4 Mag. Series. These options retail in the $50 - $300 price range.
Last Mfg.'s Sug. Retail was $1,525.

	100%	98%	95%	90%	80%	70%	60%
Diane — grade up from Centurion Classic, 22 in. barrel, Mauser 98 action, M-70 safety, adj. steel trigger.	$1,450	$1,250	$1,000	$825	$700	$600	$500

Above values represent base price with no options.
Last Mfg.'s Sug. Retail was $1,450.

	100%	98%	95%	90%	80%	70%	60%
Amazone — grade up from Diane, 20 in. barrel, full stock.	$1,750	$1,525	$1,325	$1,075	$865	$750	$600

Above values represent base price with no options.
Last Mfg.'s Sug. Retail was $1,750.

Grading	100%	98%	95%	90%	80%	70%	60%

Bavaria Deluxe — .243 Win. through .458 Win. cals., 21½, 24, or 25½ in. octagonal barrel, French walnut stock with rosewood forend tip and pistol grip cap, no sights, custom made essentially with Sako (disc.) or Mauser action. Many engraving options available from $510 - $1,900.

	100%	98%	95%	90%	80%	70%	60%
	$1,900	$1,675	$1,450	$1,200	$995	$775	$650

Above values represent base price with no options.
Last Mfg.'s Sug. Retail was $1,900.

Safari — Mag. cals. only.

	100%	98%	95%	90%	80%	70%	60%
	$2,350	$1,775	$1,475	$1,200	$995	$775	$650

Above values represent base price with no options.
Last Mfg.'s Sug. Retail was $2,350.

MANNLICHER MODEL — Mauser type bolt action, various cals., full stocked. Disc. 1985.

	100%	98%	95%	90%	80%	70%	60%
	$730	$660	$580	$520	$470	$430	$395

Last Mfg.'s Sug. Retail was $825.

Mannlicher Classic — similar to basic Mannlicher, except has better walnut. Disc. 1985.

	100%	98%	95%	90%	80%	70%	60%
	$995	$890	$775	$650	$575	$530	$460

Last Mfg.'s Sug. Retail was $1,065.

MATCH MODEL — match target rifle, adj. sights and stock. Disc. 1985.

	100%	98%	95%	90%	80%	70%	60%
	$1,640	$1,490	$1,300	$1,050	$900	$800	$700

Last Mfg.'s Sug. Retail was $1,860.

Match NATO — 7.62 cal. match rifle. Disc. 1985.

	100%	98%	95%	90%	80%	70%	60%
	$2,640	$2,400	$2,175	$1,850	$1,595	$1,400	$1,195

Last Mfg.'s Sug. Retail was $3,000.

ST. HUBERT MODEL — Sako action, various cals. and barrel lengths. Disc. 1985.

	100%	98%	95%	90%	80%	70%	60%
	$1,900	$1,700	$1,495	$1,300	$1,150	$995	$850

Last Mfg.'s Sug. Retail was $2,125.

SAFARI SPORTSMAN — Mauser 98 action, .416 Rigby, .375 H&H, .505 Gibbs, or .404 Jeffreys cal., 4 shot mag., limited availability in 1986.

	100%	98%	95%	90%	80%	70%	60%
	$4,000	$3,550	$3,250	$2,800	$2,400	$2,000	$1,750

Add $300 for .505 Gibbs cal.
Above values represent base price with no options.
Last Mfg.'s Sug. Retail was $4,000.

AFRICAN PRO — similar to Safari Sportsman except has ebony or buffalo horn forearm tip, tilting hood for the front sight, multiple folding rear sight.

	100%	98%	95%	90%	80%	70%	60%
	$4,800	$4,000	$3,550	$3,250	$2,800	$2,400	$2,000

Above values represent base price with no options.
Last Mfg.'s Sug. Retail was $4,800.

DOUBLE RIFLES

EUROPA I — .22 Hornet, .222 Rem., .222 Rem. Mag., 6mm Rem., .243 Win., .25-06, .30-06, 6.5 X 57R, 7 X 57R, 8 X 57JRS, or 9.3 X 74R cal., Anson & Deeley boxlock action, moderate engraving. New 1989.

	100%	98%	95%	90%	80%	70%	60%
	$4,800	$4,200	$3,800	$3,500	$3,250	$2,995	$2,700

Above values represent base price with no options.
Last Mfg.'s Sug. Retail was $4,800.

Dumoulin, Ernest, cont.

Grading	100%	98%	95%	90%	80%	70%	60%

CONTINENTAL I — same calibers as Europa I, sidelock action, 12 engraving options to choose from, many options available on special order. New 1989.

	$8,600	$7,700	$6,995	$6,400	$5,600	$4,750	$4,150

Above values represent base price with no options.
Last Mfg.'s Sug. Retail was $8,600.

"PIONNIER" JUXTAPOSED EXPRESS RIFLES — assorted cals. from .22 Hornet through .600 Nitro Express, SxS configuration, heavily engraved, select walnut. Limited production, Anson & Deeley triple lock action, sideplates available at extra charge.

P-I and P-II — English style scroll or bouquet (P-II) engraving.

	$7,850	$6,500	$5,825	$5,200	$4,650	$4,160	$3,700

Add $400 for P-II engraving.
Last Mfg.'s Sug. Retail was $7,850.

P III — English style lace engraving (tapestry style).

	$8,640	$7,750	$7,000	$6,400	$5,600	$4,750	$4,150

Last Mfg.'s Sug. Retail was $8,640.

P-IV through P-VIII — various styles of royal engraving with or without hunting scenes.

	$9,100	$7,995	$7,450	$6,800	$6,000	$5,000	$4,350

Add $400 for gold inlays.
Last Mfg.'s Sug. Retail was $9,100.

P-IX through P-XII — Louis XVI style engraving.

	$9,540	$8,600	$7,800	$7,250	$6,400	$5,250	$4,500

Last Mfg.'s Sug. Retail was $9,540.

Pionnier Magnum — .338 Win. Mag., .375 H&H, .416 Rigby, .416 Hoffman, .458 Win. Mag., .577 Nitro Express, or .600 Nitro Express. Boxlock action with Greener crossbolt.

	$10,900	$9,400	$8,650	$7,800	$7,000	$6,450	$5,825

Above values represent base price with no options.
Last Mfg.'s Sug. Retail was $10,900.

ARISTOCRATE MODEL — available in all cals. up to .375 H&H (also in 20 ga.), single shot action with low profile, exhibition oil finished walnut stock and forearm. Values below assume standard model (12 engraving options available). Imported 1987-1988 only.

	$9,100	$8,450	$7,775	$7,000	$6,450	$5,825	$5,275

Last Mfg.'s Sug. Retail was $10,400.
Above values represent base price with no options.

PRESTIGE RIFLE (SIDELOCK) — best quality sidelock, various cals., triple locking, 10 different presentation options available, values below reflect standard model without options. Custom order only, 1 year waiting period. New 1986.

	$17,900	$15,000	$12,500	$9,995	$8,000	$7,000	$6,000

Add $600 for Mag. cals. over .416 Rigby.
Last Mfg.'s Sug. Retail was $17,900.

SHOTGUNS

EUROPA MODEL — 12, 20, 28, or .410 ga., Anson & Deeley boxlock action, single or double trigger, moderately engraved, oil finished stock and forearm, choice of 6 engraving options. New 1989.

	$3,300	$2,750	$2,350	$2,000	$1,800	$1,575	$1,400

Last Mfg.'s Sug. Retail was $3,300.

Grading	100%	98%	95%	90%	80%	70%	60%

LEIGE JUXTAPOSED SHOTGUN (SxS) — 12, 16 (disc. 1986), 20, or 28 ga., Anson & Deeley locking action, elaborate engraving, deluxe walnut. New 1986.

Luxe Model

| | $5,300 | $4,600 | $3,900 | $3,300 | $2,900 | $2,600 | $2,300 |

Last Mfg.'s Sug. Retail was $5,900 (disc. 1988).

Grand Luxe

| | $6,900 | $6,000 | $5,000 | $4,300 | $3,600 | $3,200 | $2,875 |

Add 15% for 28 ga.
Add 15% for sideplates.
Many engraving options and other special order features can be added to the above models.
Last Mfg.'s Sug. Retail was $6,900.

CONTINENTAL MODEL — 12, 20, 28, or .410 ga., sidelock action, double or single trigger, deluxe oil finished walnut stock, choice of 6 engraving options. New 1989.

| | $7,400 | $6,250 | $5,200 | $4,400 | $3,700 | $3,200 | $2,875 |

Above values represent base price with no options.
Last Mfg.'s Sug. Retail was $7,400.

ETENDART JUXTAPOSED SHOTGUN (SxS) — 12, 20 and 28 ga., full sidelock, exhibition grade walnut, double triggers, top-of-the-line quality, built to special order. Values listed assume standard gun (12 engraving options available). New 1987.

| | $14,400 | $12,250 | $9,995 | $9,100 | $8,450 | $7,775 | $7,000 |

Add 6% for 28 ga.
Last Mfg.'s Sug. Retail was $14,400.

BOSS ROYAL SUPERPOSED (O/U) — 12, 20 or 28 ga., full sidelock, exhibition grade walnut, double triggers, top-of-the-line quality, built to special order. Values listed assume standard gun (12 engraving options available). New 1987.

| | $18,500 | $16,000 | $13,750 | $11,000 | $9,775 | $8,000 | $6,950 |

Add 6½% for 28 ga.
Last Mfg.'s Sug. Retail was $18,500.

SUPERPOSED EXPRESS "INTERNATIONAL" — O/U shotgun, includes extra set of rifle barrels, 20 ga., 7 choices of rifle cals., deluxe walnut. Elaborate engraving patterns available at extra charge, limited production. Disc. 1985.

| | $2,400 | $2,000 | $1,800 | $1,575 | $1,400 | $1,200 | $1,050 |

Last Mfg.'s Sug. Retail was $2,490.

COMBINATION GUNS

EAGLE MODEL — O/U configuration (shotgun barrel on bottom), 12 or 20 ga., .22 Hornet, .222 Rem., .222 Rem. Mag., 6mm Rem., .243 Win., .25-06, .30-06, 6.5 X 57R, 7 X 57R, 8 X 57JRS, or 9.3 X 74R cal., boxlock action. New 1989.

| | $2,700 | $2,400 | $2,175 | $1,850 | $1,595 | $1,400 | $1,195 |

Above values represent base price with no options.
Last Mfg.'s Sug. Retail was $2,700.

DUMOULIN, HENRI & FILS

Manufacturer located in Herstal, Belgium. Imported and distributed by New England Arms, Co. located in Kittery Point, ME.

H. Dumoulin has manufactured quality firearms in Liege/Herstal, Belgium since 1947. They have specialized in bolt action rifles, generally built on Mauser 98 or commercial Mauser actions. The Imperial Magnum action was developed and introduced in 1987.

Grading	100%	98%	95%	90%	80%	70%	60%

RIFLES

GRAND LUXE BOLT ACTION — .300 Wby., .338 Win. Mag., .375 H&H, .378 Wby., .404 Jeffrey, .416 Rigby, .460 Wby., or .505 Gibbs cal., 24, 25.6, or 26 in. barrel, European walnut stock with ebony forend tip and pistol grip cap, folding leaf sights with hooded front, custom made on the Dumoulin Imperial Magnum double square bridge action. Many engraving options available.

Mfg.'s Sug. Retail	$7,000		$6,850	$6,200	$5,500	$4,950	$4,300	$3,600	$3,200

Add $500 for left hand action.
Add $850 for extended top and bottom tang.
Add $800 for claw mounts.
Add $700 for .505 Gibbs cal.

SOVEREIGN — available in same cals. as Grand Luxe Bolt Action, except with a higher quality finish, knurled bolt handles, gold inlayed lettering. Many engraving options available. Pricing on this model depends on engraving, wood and other options. Imperial Magnum is also available in various stages of completion, barreled actions, actions in the white, etc. Please contact New England Arms, Co. directly for quotation.

SXS BOXLOCK RIFLE — boxlock action, best quality double rifle, highly figured European walnut, finely hand checkered with standard scroll engraving. Custom ordered to customer's dimensions. Prices start at $11,000.

SXS SIDELOCK RIFLE — sidelock action, best quality hand detachable locks, top quality European walnut, finely hand checkered with standard scroll engraving. Additional engraving or deluxe wood quoted on request. Prices start at $15,000.

SHOTGUNS

BOXLOCK MODEL — available in most ga.'s, individually built per customer special order. The importer should be contacted directly for more information and a price quotation.

SIDELOCK MODEL — available in most ga.'s, individually built per customer special order. The importer should be contacted directly for more information and a price quotation.

E section

E.M.F. CO., INC.

Current importer and distributor located in Santa Ana, CA.

Grading		100%	98%	95%	90%	80%	70%	60%

PISTOLS: REPRODUCTIONS

REMINGTON ROLLING BLOCK PISTOL — .357 Mag. cal., rolling block design. Disc. 1992.

		$300	$225	$185	$165	$155	$145	$135

Last Mfg.'s Sug. Retail was $395.

1875 REMINGTON OUTLAW — .357 Mag., .44-40, or .45 LC cal., copy of the Rem. Model 1875 SA, 7½ in. barrel only, case hardened frame, walnut grips, blue only.

Mfg.'s Sug. Retail	$465	$325	$250	$185	$165	$155	$145	$135

Add $85 for nickel plating.
Add $135 for engraving.

1890 REMINGTON POLICE SINGLE ACTION — .357 Mag., .44-40, or .45 LC cal., 5½ in. barrel, lanyard ring in butt stock, blue frame, walnut grips. New 1986.

Mfg.'s Sug. Retail	$470	$330	$255	$185	$165	$155	$145	$135

Add $90 for nickel plating.
Add $150 for engraving.

DERRINGERS: REPRODUCTIONS

STANDARD MODEL — .22 Short, copy of Colt Model Lord or Lady Derringer, blue, gold, or silver gold finish. Disc. 1992.

		$100	$80	$70	$60	$55	$50	$45

Last Mfg.'s Sug. Retail was $125.

RIFLES: MODERN REPRODUCTIONS

These models are authentic shooting reproductions mfg. in Italy.

AP 74 — .22 LR or .32 ACP cal., copy of the Colt AR-15, semi-auto, 15 shot mag., 20 in. barrel, 6¾ lbs. Importation disc. 1989.

		$295	$250	$200	$175	$155	$145	$135

Add $25 for .32 cal.
Last Mfg.'s Sug. Retail was $295.

Sporter Carbine — wood sporter stock, .22 LR only. Importation disc. 1989.

		$320	$275	$225	$195	$175	$160	$140

Last Mfg.'s Sug. Retail was $320.

Paramilitary Paratrooper Carbine — .22 LR only, folding wire stock, black nylon on paramilitary design model. Importation disc. 1987.

		$260	$190	$175	$165	$155	$145	$135

Add $10 for wood folding stock.
Last Mfg.'s Sug. Retail was $325.

"Dressed" Military Model — with Cyclops scope, Colt bayonet, sling, and bipod. Disc. 1986.

		$330	$265	$240	$220	$200	$185	$170

Last Mfg.'s Sug. Retail was $450.

Grading	100%	98%	95%	90%	80%	70%	60%

ISRAELI GALIL — .22 LR only, reproduction of the Israeli Galil, semi-auto. Importation disc. 1989.

	100%	98%	95%	90%	80%	70%	60%
	$295	$250	$200	$175	$155	$145	$135

Last Mfg.'s Sug. Retail was $295.

KALASHNIKOV AK-47 — .22 LR only, reproduction of the Russian AK-47, semi-auto. Importation disc. 1989.

	100%	98%	95%	90%	80%	70%	60%
	$295	$250	$200	$175	$155	$145	$135

Last Mfg.'s Sug. Retail was $295.

FRENCH M.A.S. — .22 LR only, reproduction of the French Bull-Pup Combat Rifle, semi-auto with carrying handle, 29 shot mag. Importation disc. 1989.

	100%	98%	95%	90%	80%	70%	60%
	$320	$265	$240	$220	$200	$185	$170

Last Mfg.'s Sug. Retail was $320.

M1 CARBINE — .30 cal. only, copy of the U.S. Military M1 Carbine. Disc. 1985.

	100%	98%	95%	90%	80%	70%	60%
	$175	$150	$140	$130	$120	$110	$100

Add $43 for Paratrooper variation.
Last Mfg.'s Sug. Retail was $205.

RIFLES: REMINGTON REPRODUCTIONS

ROLLING BLOCK CARBINE — .45-70 cal., authentic reproduction of the Remington Rolling Block Carbine. Importation began 1991.

	Mfg.'s Sug. Retail	$820	95%	90%	80%	70%	60%
			$585	$400	$325	$250	$235	$220	$200

BABY ROLLING BLOCK CARBINE — .357 Mag. Mfg. 1992 only.

	100%	98%	95%	90%	80%	70%	60%
	$395	$300	$260	$220	$185	$160	$140

Last Mfg.'s Sug. Retail was $490.

REVOLVING CARBINE — .357 Mag., .44-40, or .45 LC cal., 18 in. barrel, Model 1875 Army Single Action design, 5 lbs.

	Mfg.'s Sug. Retail	$880					
			$660	$525	$425	$325	$295	$260	$230

TEXAS CARBINE — .22 LR, action patterned after Remington revolving carbine, 21 in. octagon barrel, wood stock and forearm, brass frame. Also available with extra .22 Mag. cylinder.

	Mfg.'s Sug. Retail	$420					
			$250	$210	$165	$150	$135	$125	$110

RIFLES: SHARPS REPRODUCTIONS

SHARPS SPORTING OR MILITARY RIFLE — .45-70 cal., copy of the Sharps Single Shot, 28 in. octagonal barrel, case hardened frame, single or double set triggers.

	Mfg.'s Sug. Retail	$860					
			$650	$525	$425	$325	$295	$260	$230

Add $90 for double set triggers.

Carbine Model — saddle-ring carbine with 22 in. round barrel, single trigger.

	Mfg.'s Sug. Retail	$860					
			$650	$525	$425	$325	$295	$260	$230

RIFLES: WINCHESTER REPRODUCTIONS

DELUXE HENRY RIFLE — .44-40 cal. only, deluxe walnut, reproduction of New Haven Arms Co.'s Henry Rifle. New 1987.

	Mfg.'s Sug. Retail	$1,111					
			$850	$600	$450	$330	$295	$260	$230

Grading	100%	98%	95%	90%	80%	70%	60%

Engraved Henry Rifle — similar to deluxe Henry Rifle except has hand engraved receiver. Imported 1987-90.

	100%	98%	95%	90%	80%	70%	60%
	$1,200	$975	$700	$525	$400	$340	$295

Last Mfg.'s Sug. Retail was $1,598.

1866 YELLOWBOY CARBINE — .22 LR (disc.), .38 Spl., .44-40, or .45 LC (new 1993) cal., 19 in. barrel, saddle-ring carbine, brass frame.

Mfg.'s Sug. Retail	$825	$595	$400	$325	$250	$235	$220	$200

1866 Rifle — same cals. as 1866 Yellowboy Carbine, 24¼ in. barrel.

Mfg.'s Sug. Retail	$848	$600	$400	$325	$250	$235	$220	$200

Engraved Yellowboy Carbine — .38 Spl., or .44-40 cal. only. Importation disc. 1990.

	$800	$575	$440	$330	$295	$260	$230

Last Mfg.'s Sug. Retail was $1,080.

1873 CARBINE — .22 Mag. (disc.), .357 Mag., .44-40, or .45 LC cal., 19 in. barrel, copy of the Winchester Model 1873, case hardened receiver.

Mfg.'s Sug. Retail	$1,020	$780	$575	$440	$330	$295	$260	$230

1873 Rifle — 24¼ in. barrel, available only in .357 Mag. or .44-40 cal.

Mfg.'s Sug. Retail	$1,050	$795	$595	$450	$330	$295	$260	$230

Engraved Rifle — available in .357 Mag. or .44-40 cal. only. Importation disc. 1987.

	$895	$635	$500	$450	$400	$360	$325

Last Mfg.'s Sug. Retail was $850.

PREMIER 1873 CARBINE & RIFLE — .45 LC cal., case hardened frame, uncheckered walnut stock and forearm, full mag., rifle has 24¼ in. barrel, carbine has 19 in. barrel. Imported 1988-1989 only.

	$850	$595	$450	$330	$295	$260	$230

Add $38 for rifle variation.
Last Mfg.'s Sug. Retail was $1,160.

84 GUN CO.
Previous manufacturer located in Eighty Four, PA. Circa-early 1970's.

RIFLES

CLASSIC RIFLE — Bolt action, various calibers. Grades 1-4.

	100%	98%	95%	90%	80%	70%	60%
Grade 1	$420	$315	$275	$235	$210	$190	$170
Grade 2	$780	$585	$512	$430	$390	$355	$315
Grade 3	$860	$645	$560	$475	$430	$390	$345
Grade 4	$1,580	$1,185	$1,030	$870	$790	$715	$640

LOBO RIFLE — bolt action, various calibers. Grades standard, 1-4.

	100%	98%	95%	90%	80%	70%	60%
Standard	$415	$315	$270	$230	$210	$190	$170
Grade 1	$540	$405	$355	$300	$270	$245	$220
Grade 2	$795	$600	$520	$440	$400	$360	$320
Grade 3	$1,600	$1,200	$1,040	$880	$800	$720	$640
Grade 4	$2,350	$1,765	$1,530	$1,295	$1,175	$1,060	$940

Grading	100%	98%	95%	90%	80%	70%	60%

PENNSYLVANIA RIFLE — bolt action, various calibers. Grades standard, 1-4.

	100%	98%	95%	90%	80%	70%	60%
Standard	$420	$315	$275	$235	$210	$190	$170
Grade 1	$540	$405	$355	$300	$270	$245	$220
Grade 2	$795	$600	$520	$440	$400	$360	$320
Grade 3	$1,600	$1,200	$1,040	$880	$800	$720	$640
Grade 4	$2,350	$1,765	$1,530	$1,295	$1,175	$1,060	$940

EAGLE ARMS, INC.
Manufacturer located in Coal Valley, IL.

RIFLES

On the models listed below, E-1 accessories include collapsible carbine type buttstock and forward bolt assist mechanism. E-2 accessories are similar, except have National Match sights also.

MODEL EA-15 E-1 RIFLE — .223 cal., patterned after the Colt AR-15A2, 20 in. barrel, forward bolt assist, 7 lbs. New 1990.

Mfg.'s Sug. Retail	$800	$750	$650	$575	$475	$400	$365	$325

EA-15 E-1 Carbine — similar to EA-15 E-1 Rifle, except has sliding butt stock and 16 in. barrel, 5 lbs. 14 oz. New 1990.

Mfg.'s Sug. Retail	$895	$825	$725	$600	$525	$450	$400	$375

Beginning 1993, the E-2 accessory kit became standard on this model.

EA-15 E-2 H-BAR Rifle — similar to Model EA-15 E-1, except has heavy barrel, 8 lbs. 14 oz., includes E-2 accessories. New 1990.

Mfg.'s Sug. Retail	$895	$825	$725	$600	$525	$450	$400	$375

Subtract $5 for National Match sights.

EA-15 Eagle Spirit — includes 16 in. premium air gauge national match barrel and fixed stock, full length tubular aluminum hand guard, designed for IPSC shooting, includes match grade accessories, 8 lbs. 6 oz. New 1993.

Mfg.'s Sug. Retail	$1,075	$975	$850	$725	$600	$525	$450	$400

EA-15 Golden Eagle — similar to EA-15 H-BAR, except has (N.M.) National Match accessories, 20 in. extra heavy barrel, 12 lbs. 12 oz. New 1991.

Mfg.'s Sug. Retail	$1,075	$975	$850	$725	$600	$525	$450	$400

EA-15 Eagle Eye — includes 24 in. free floating 1 in. barrel with tubular aluminum hand guard, weighted buttstock, designed for silhouette matches, 14 lbs. New 1993.

Mfg.'s Sug. Retail	$1,495	$1,325	$1,075	$875	$725	$600	$525	$450

EA-15 Action Master — match rifle, solid aluminum handguard tube that allows for free floating 20 in. Douglas premium fluted barrel with compensator, N.M. accessories, fixed stock, 8 lbs. 5 oz. New 1992.

Mfg.'s Sug. Retail	$1,075	$975	$850	$725	$600	$525	$450	$400

EGO ARMS, S.A.
Manufacturer located in Eibar, Spain. No current U.S. importation.

Ego Armas manufactures high quality sidelock double rifles ranging in price from $4,000-$14,000. Calibers include .375 H&H Mag. and .416 Rigby in their high quality deluxe models. Mounted scopes are also available. Boxlock and sidelock shotguns are also available ranging in price from $400-$4,000. More information, including current models and approximate U.S. pricing, can be obtained by writing this manufacturer directly (see Trademark Index).

ENFIELD
Royal Small Arms Factory, Middlesex, England.

Grading	100%	98%	95%	90%	80%	70%	60%

NO. 2 MK. I REVOLVER — .380 British Service (based on .38 S&W with a 200 grain bullet), double action, 6 shot, 5 in. barrel, fixed sights, blue, composition grips, top break, issued to British army 1932.

	100%	98%	95%	90%	80%	70%	60%
	$235	$195	$175	$140	$130	$120	$110

RIFLES

SMLE stands for Rifle, Short, Magazine, Lee-Enfield. The SMLE rifles served the British Military from 1902-1954.

NO. 1 MK. III SMLE — .303 British, bolt action, 10 shot mag., 25.2 in. barrel, open sights, long range volley sights, magazine cut-off, adopted by British Army in 1907.

	$225	$190	$150	$125	$100	$90	$75

NO. 1 MK. III SMLE — a simplified rifle adopted by the British during WWI, volley sights and magazine cut-off deleted, the most common variation of SMLE.

	$225	$190	$150	$125	$100	$90	$75

NO. 2 MK. IV — .22 LR cal., single shot, recently imported from Australia.

	$495	$425	$375	$315	$260	$215	$160

NO. 3 MK. I PATTERN 14 RIFLE — modified Mauser type bolt action, .303 British, issued as substitute standard by British Army during WWI, manufactured in U.S. (the later U.S. 1917 Enfield is identical except for caliber and sights).

	$225	$190	$150	$125	$100	$90	$75

NO. 3 MK. I — .22 cal., single shot military training model.

	$350	$300	$275	$250	$225	$200	$175

NO. 4 MK. I — an improved SMLE with aperture rear sight, stronger receiver and more easily manufactured parts, adopted in 1939 by the British Army.

	$215	$185	$145	$120	$95	$75	$55

This model was manufactured during WWII in Canada, England, and the U.S. To determine which armory manufactured this model, the following information should be studied. Savage-Stevens mfg. is denoted by "US Property S" with a C in ser. no., Canadian mfg. (Long Branch, Ontario) is indicated by "Long Branch" - no code, British mfg. was by B.S.A., Shirley and marked "M.47C"., Royal Ordnance Factory (near Liverpool) marked "ROF(F)", or Royal Ordnance Factory (near Sheffield) marked "ROFM" or "RM" or "M".

Sniper Model — cased, with or without scope.

	100%	98%	95%	90%	80%	70%	60%
Cased	$1,250	$1,000	$800	$595	$540	$480	$420
Uncased	$750	$600	$535	$480	$420	$350	$295

NO. 5 MK. I JUNGLE CARBINE — a shorter, lighter version of the No. 4 MK. I with a 20.5 in. barrel, flash hider, recoil pad and shortened forend and hand guard, 7.2 lbs., developed during WWII.

	$350	$275	$200	$150	$125	$100	$85

ENFIELD AMERICA, INC.
Manufacturer located in Atlanta, GA.

Grading	100%	98%	95%	90%	80%	70%	60%

MP-45 — .45 ACP, semi-auto paramilitary design pistol, 4½, 6, 8, 10, or 18½ in. shrouded barrel, Parkerized finish, 10, 30, 40, or 50 shot mag., 6 lbs. Mfg. 1985 only.

	100%	98%	95%	90%	80%	70%	60%
	$350	$295	$260	$240	$220	$200	$185

Last Mfg.'s Sug. Retail was $350.

ERA
Manufacturer located in Brazil.

ERA O/U SHOTGUN — 12 or 20 ga., 28 in. vent. rib barrel, full and mod., double triggers, extractors, checkered hardwood stock.

	100%	98%	95%	90%	80%	70%	60%
	$275	$250	$225	$200	$170	$150	$125
Trap version	$300	$275	$250	$225	$200	$175	$150
Skeet version	$300	$275	$250	$225	$200	$175	$150

ERA DOUBLE BARREL — 12, 20, or .410 ga., 26, 28, or 30 in. barrels, various chokes, double triggers, extractors, checkered pistol grip stock.

	100%	98%	95%	90%	80%	70%	60%
	$165	$150	$135	$125	$110	$100	$85

ERA DOUBLE RIOT MODEL — similar to Double Barrel, except 12 or 20 ga., 18 in. barrel.

	100%	98%	95%	90%	80%	70%	60%
	$185	$175	$150	$140	$125	$110	$95

ERA QUAIL MODEL — similar to Standard, except 12 or 20 ga., 20 in. barrel.

	100%	98%	95%	90%	80%	70%	60%
	$185	$175	$150	$140	$125	$110	$95

ERMA-WERKE

Manufacturer located in Dachau, Germany. Currently, pistols and revolvers are imported and distributed by Mandall's Shooting Supplies, Inc. located in Scottsdale, AZ and Precision Sales International, Inc. located in Westfield, MA. Previously distributed by Excam located in Hialeah, FL.

Erma-Werke rifles are not currently imported into the U.S. Erma-Werke also private labels handguns for American Arms Inc. (refer to their section for listings).

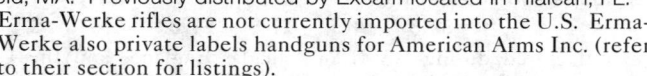

PISTOLS: SEMI-AUTO

MODEL LA 22 — .22 LR, semi-auto, action patterned after the Luger, mfg. 1964-1967.

	100%	98%	95%	90%	80%	70%	60%
	$395	$335	$275	$240	$200	$175	$140

ERMA KGP68A/BEEMAN MP-08 — Luger type toggle action, .32 ACP (disc. 1987) or .380 ACP, 3½ (Beeman) or 4 in. barrel, 6 shot mag., blue, 1.4 lbs. Mfg. 1968-present.

	100%	98%	95%	90%	80%	70%	60%
	$335	$275	$240	$185	$145	$115	$95

Last Mfg.'s Sug. Retail was $390.
From 1988-90, Beeman took over importation of this model in .380 ACP cal. only with new Luger style checkered walnut grips and 3½ in. barrel. Previous models had plastic grips.

ERMA KGP69/BEEMAN P-08 — Luger type toggle action, .22 LR, 8 shot mag., 3¾ in. barrel, blue, plastic (disc.) or checkered walnut grips. Mfg. 1969-present.

	100%	98%	95%	90%	80%	70%	60%
	$335	$275	$240	$185	$145	$115	$95

Last Mfg.'s Sug. Retail was $390.
Beeman was the sole importer of this model between 1988-90.

Grading	100%	98%	95%	90%	80%	70%	60%

MODEL ESP 85A SPORTING/MATCH PISTOL — .22 LR or .32 S&W Long Wadcutter, blow back semi-auto, 6 in. barrel, 5 or 8 (.32 S&W only) shot mag., choice of sporting or adj. stippled match grips with thumbrest, fully adj. and interchangeable sights, gun is supplied with 1 extra weight, extra mag., sights, disassembly tools, and attache style case ($134 option) with foam rubber cut-outs, 2½ lbs. Importation began 1989.

Mfg.'s Sug. Retail $1,228	$1,030	$900	$800	$700	$625	$550	$495

Add $56 for .32 S&W cal.
Add $117 for Match Model (with anatomical grips).
Add $746 for conversion unit.
Add approx. $221 for chrome finish.
Add $30 for left-hand action (Match Model only).
This model is distributed by Precision Sales International, Inc. and Mandall's Shooting Supplies, Inc.

Model ESP 85A Complete Set — includes both .22 LR and .32 S&W Long Wadcutter barrels and mag.'s, cased with accessories, complete set was disc. 1991.

	$1,775	$1,525	$1,350	$1,125	$950	$825	$750

Last Mfg.'s Sug. Retail was $1,995.

ET-22 LUGER CARBINE — .22 LR, 11¾ in. barrel, blue rear ramp sight, checkered walnut grips and uncheckered forearm, adj. artillery type rear sight, rarely seen.

	$395	$335	$275	$240	$200	$175	$140

Add 20% for leatherette case.

REVOLVERS: DOUBLE ACTION

These models are distributed by Precision Sales International, Inc. only.

ER 772 STANDARD/MATCH — .22 LR, standard or match gun with special adj. contoured grips with stippling, 6 in. barrel, action similar to ER 777, fully adj. and extended rear sight, interchangeable front sight, 3 lbs. Importation began 1990.

Mfg.'s Sug. Retail $1,265	$1,025	$840	$700	$625	$550	$495	$450

Add $80 for Match Model.

ER 773 STANDARD/MATCH — .32 S&W Long, otherwise similar to ER 772 Match, 2.9 lbs. Importation began 1990.

Mfg.'s Sug. Retail $1,265	$1,025	$840	$700	$625	$550	$495	$450

Add $80 for Match Model.

ER-777 STANDARD — .357 Mag., 6 shot, 4 or 5½ in. barrel, solid rib and full barrel shroud, adj. target rear sight, blued steel, checkered sport grips, 2¾ lbs. Importation began 1990.

Mfg.'s Sug. Retail $1,200	$1,050	$825	$700	$625	$550	$495	$450

RIFLES

Models listed below are available from Mandall's Shooting Supplies.

EM1 .22 CARBINE — M1 copy .22 LR cal., 10 or 15 shot mag., 18 in. barrel, rear adj. aperature sight, 5.6 lbs. Mfg. 1966-current.

Mfg.'s Sug. Retail $400	$365	$295	$250	$215	$190	$175	$160

EGM-1 — similar to EM1 except for unslotted butt stock, 5 shot mag.

Mfg.'s Sug. Retail $295	$260	$230	$195	$175	$150	$125	$100

EG72 PUMP — outside hammer, .22 LR cal., 15 shot mag., 18½ in. barrel. Mfg. 1970-1976.

	$125	$95	$90	$75	$70	$65	$60

Grading	100%	98%	95%	90%	80%	70%	60%

EG712 LEVER-ACTION — Win. Model 94 copy, .22 LR cal., tube mag., 18½ in. barrel. Mfg. 1976 to date.

Mfg.'s Sug. Retail	$295	$260	$230	$195	$175	$150	$125	$100

EG-73 — similar to EG712 except .22 Mag. cal., 12 shot mag. Mfg. 1973 to date.

Mfg.'s Sug. Retail	$300	$265	$230	$195	$175	$150	$125	$100

EUROPEAN AMERICAN ARMORY CORP.
Importer/distributor located in Hialeah, FL beginning late 1990.

EAA imports their handguns from Atis, Sabatti, Tanfoglio located in Italy, and H. Weihrauch located in Germany. All guns are covered by EAA's lifetime limited warranty.

EAA rifles & shotguns are manufactured by Sabatti in Italy (est. 1674). Importation began 1992.

PISTOLS: D/A EUROPEAN SERIES

EUROPEAN 380 D/A — .380 ACP cal., double action design, 3.2 in. barrel, blue, brushed chrome, or matte blue/chrome finish, 7 shot bottom release mag., steel construction, firing pin safety, external hammer, smooth wood grips, 26 oz. Importation began 1992.

Mfg.'s Sug. Retail	$270	$235	$175	$140	$115	$105	$95	$85

Add $22 for brushed chrome or matte blue/chrome finish.
This model employs a unique patent pending magazine gun lock system.

PISTOLS: SEMI-AUTO - WITNESS SERIES

EA 9 SERIES — 9mm Para. cal., action patterned after the CZ-75, selective double action, 4½ in. barrel, steel frame, 16 shot mag., choice of stainless steel or blue, blue/chrome, or brushed chrome finish, combat sights, black neoprene grips, 33 oz. Importation began late 1990.

Mfg.'s Sug. Retail	$595	$450	$375	$325	$275	$250	$225	$200

Add approx. $40 for blue/chrome or brushed chrome finish.

⚔ **Model EA 9 Stainless** — similar to EA 9, except is stainless steel. Importation began 1992.

Mfg.'s Sug. Retail	$695	$575	$450	$350

⚔ **Model EA 9 Compact** — similar to EA 9, except has 3½ in. barrel and 13 shot mag.

Mfg.'s Sug. Retail	$595	$450	$375	$325	$275	$250	$225	$200

Add approx. $40 for blue/chrome or brushed chrome finish.

⚔ **Model EA 9 Long Slide Ported Sport** — ported variation of the Model EA 9, except has 4¾ in. ported barrel and slide, Duo-Tone finish, competition sights, 34½ oz.

Mfg.'s Sug. Retail	$950	$795	$675	$595	$550	$495	$450	$395

EA 40 SERIES — .40 S&W cal., action patterned after the CZ-75, selective double action, 4½ in. barrel, steel frame, 12 shot mag., choice of stainless steel or blue, blue/chrome, or brushed chrome finish, combat sights, black neoprene grips, 33 oz. Importation began late 1990.

Mfg.'s Sug. Retail	$625	$495	$425	$375	$325	$295	$260	$230

Add approx. $40 for blue/chrome or brushed chrome finish.

⚔ **Model EA 40 Stainless** — similar to EA 40, except is stainless steel. Importation began 1992.

Mfg.'s Sug. Retail	$725	$600	$525	$425

⚔ **Model EA 40 Compact** — similar to EA 40, except has 3½ in. barrel and 9 shot mag.

Mfg.'s Sug. Retail	$625	$495	$425	$375	$325	$295	$260	$230

Add approx. $40 for blue/chrome or matte chrome finish.

Grading	100%	98%	95%	90%	80%	70%	60%

Model EA 40 Long Slide Ported Sport — ported variation of the Model EA 40, except has 4¾ in. ported barrel and slide, Duo-Tone finish, competition sights, 34½ oz.

Mfg.'s Sug. Retail	$950	$795	$675	$595	$550	$495	$450	$395

EA 41 SERIES — .41 Action Express cal., action patterned after the CZ-75, selective double action, 4½ in. barrel, steel frame, 11 shot mag., blue, blue/chrome, or brushed chrome finish, combat sights, black neoprene grips, 33 oz.

Mfg.'s Sug. Retail	$595	$450	$375	$325	$275	$250	$225	$200

Add $40 for blue/chrome or brushed chrome finish.

Model EA 41 Compact — similar to EA 41, except has 3½ in. barrel and 8 shot mag.

Mfg.'s Sug. Retail	$625	$495	$425	$375	$325	$295	$260	$230

Add $40 for blue/chrome or brushed chrome finish.

Model EA 41 Long Slide Ported Sport — compensated variation of the Model EA 41, except has 4¾ in. ported barrel and slide, Duo-Tone finish, competition sights, 34½ oz.

Mfg.'s Sug. Retail	$950	$795	$675	$595	$550	$495	$450	$395

EA 45 SERIES — .45 ACP cal., action patterned after the CZ-75, selective double action, 4½ in. barrel, steel frame, 11 shot mag., choice of stainless steel or blue, blue/chrome, or brushed chrome finish, combat sights, walnut grips, 35 oz. Importation began late 1990.

Mfg.'s Sug. Retail	$750	$600	$525	$450	$375	$325	$295	$260

Add approx. $40 for blue/chrome or matte chrome finish.

Model EA 45 Stainless — similar to EA 45, except is stainless steel. Importation began 1992.

Mfg.'s Sug. Retail	$850	$700	$600	$495				

Model EA 45 Long Slide Ported Sport — ported variation of the Model EA 45, except has 4¾ in. ported barrel and slide, Duo-Tone finish, competition sights, 35 oz.

Mfg.'s Sug. Retail	$1,095	$895	$795	$675	$595	$550	$495	$450

WITNESS CARRY COMP GUN — 9mm Para. or .40 S&W cal., full size frame with compact slide and 1 in. compensator, blue or Duo-Tone finish. Importation began 1992.

Mfg.'s Sug. Retail	$795	$650	$525	$450	$375	$325	$295	$260

Add approx. $40 for Duo-Tone finish.

Witness Combo Pakcage — includes one built up frame and 9mm Para./.40 S&W complete conversion kits, blue, chrome, or Duo-Tone finish, compact or full size variation. Importation began 1992.

Mfg.'s Sug. Retail	$825	$660	$525	$450	$375	$325	$295	$260

Add approx. $40 for chrome or Duo-Tone finish.

Witness Tri-Caliber Package — includes one built up frame and caliber conversions (9mm Para., .40 S&W, and .41 AE) that include slide, barrel, recoil guide, and spring, matte blue or chrome finish, compact or full size variations, includes carry case. Importation began 1992.

Mfg.'s Sug. Retail	$1,195	$975	$825	$700	$575	$495	$425	$375

Add $40 for chrome finish.

WITNESS SILVER TEAM — .38 Super, 9mm Para., 9 x 21mm, 10mm Norma, .40 S&W, or .45 ACP cal., dual comp. chambers, S/A trigger, super sight and/or drilled and tapped for scope mount, competition features include hammer, extended safety, paddle mag. release, checkered walnut grips, double-dip blue finish, high capacity mag. Importation began 1992.

Mfg.'s Sug. Retail	$1,350	$1,050	$875	$725	$595	$500	$425	$375

European American Armory Corp., cont.

Grading	100%	98%	95%	90%	80%	70%	60%

WITNESS GOLD TEAM — .38 Super, 9mm Para., 9 x 21mm, 10mm Norma, .40 S&W, or .45 ACP cal., triple comp. chambers, S/A trigger, super sight and/or drilled and tapped for scope mount, top-of-the-line competition model featuring hand-fitted major components and 25 LPI checkering, hard chrome finish. Importation began 1992.

Mfg.'s Sug. Retail $2,495	$2,100	$1,750	$1,475	$1,225	$995	$825	$700

This model is also avail. as a frame only - retail is $325.

PISTOLS: D/A FAB 92 SERIES

F.A.B. 92 — 9mm Para. or .40 S&W cal., features hammer drop safety and decocker (Witness style), 4½ in. barrel, 16 (9mm Para.) or 12 (.40 S&W) shot mag., all steel construction, blue, chrome, or Duo-Tone finish, smooth wood grips, 33 oz. Importation began 1992.

Mfg.'s Sug. Retail $550	$450	$350	$275	$225	$200	$185	$170

Add $40 for chrome or Duo-Tone finish.
Add $50 for .40 S&W cal.
F.A.B. designates Foreign American Brands.

F.A.B. 92 Compact — similar to F.A.B. 92, except has 3⅔ in. barrel, 13 (9mm Para.) or 9 (.40 S&W) shot mag., 30 oz. Importation began 1992.

Mfg.'s Sug. Retail $550	$450	$350	$275	$225	$200	$185	$170

Add $40 for chrome or Duo-Tone finish.
Add $50 for .40 S&W cal.

PISTOLS: SINGLE ACTION - EUROPEAN SERIES

MODEL EA220 — .22 LR cal., 3.88 in. barrel, 10 shot mag., single action, steel frame, 26 oz., blue, chrome or blue/chrome, wooden grips. Importation disc. 1992, but limited quantities are still avail. from the importer.

Mfg.'s Sug. Retail $225	$185	$150	$120	$100	$95	$85	$75

Add approx. $20 for chrome or blue chrome finish.

MODEL EA22-T — .22 LR cal., 6 in. barrel, 12 shot mag., single action, steel frame, target model, 40 oz. Importation began 1991.

Mfg.'s Sug. Retail $450	$375	$295	$260	$220	$185	$165	$150

MODEL EA32 — .32 ACP cal., 3.88 in. barrel, 7 shot mag., single action, steel frame, 26 oz., blue, chrome or blue/chrome, wooden grips. Importation began 1991.

Mfg.'s Sug. Retail $225	$185	$150	$120	$100	$95	$85	$75

Add approx. $20 for chrome or blue chrome finish.

MODEL EA380 — .380 ACP cal., single action, 3.88 in. barrel, 7 shot mag., steel frame, blue, chrome or blue/chrome, wooden grips, 26 oz. Importation began 1991.

Mfg.'s Sug. Retail $225	$185	$150	$120	$100	$95	$85	$75

Add $40 for blue/gold finish.
Add approx. $20 for chrome or blue chrome finish.

Model EA380 Lady — .380 ACP cal., single action, 3.2 in. barrel, features 24 Kt. gold plated slide, ivorytex grips with laser etchings, 26 oz. New 1993.

Mfg.'s Sug. Retail $325	$260	$220	$190	$160	$130	$110	$100

REVOLVERS: SAA BOUNTY HUNTER SERIES

MODEL EASAB — .22 LR, single action revolver, 6 shot, 4¾ in. barrel, blued or chrome (disc. 1991) finish, wood grips.

Mfg.'s Sug. Retail $120	$95	$80	$65	$55	$50	$45	$40

Add $20 for chrome finish.

Grading	100%	98%	95%	90%	80%	70%	60%

MODEL EASAMB COMBO — includes .22 LR and .22 Mag. cylinders, 4¾ (standard), 6, or 9 in. barrel, blue finish, wood grips.

Mfg.'s Sug. Retail	$150	$115	$95	$85	$75	$60	$55	$50

Add $25 for 6 or 9 in. barrel.
Add $40 for gold backstrap and trigger guard.

BIG BORE BOUNTY HUNTER — .357 Mag., .44 Mag., or .45 LC cal., 5½ or 7½ in. barrel, 6 shot, choice of blue, case color, gold trigger guard/backstrap, or gold finish, 32-41 oz. New 1992.

Mfg.'s Sug. Retail	$450	$375	$295	$260	$220	$185	$165	$150

Add approx. $25 for case colored frame.
Add approx. $40 for gold plated grip strap and trigger guard.
Add approx. $100 for gold plated finish.

REVOLVERS: WINDICATOR SERIES

STANDARD GRADE — .22 LR, .22LR/.22 Mag. combo., .22 Mag., .32 H&R, or .38 Spl. cal., 2 (.32 H&R and .38 Spl. only), 4, or 6 in. squared off barrel, blue finish only, 6 (.38 Spl.), 7 (.32 H&R), or 8 (.22 LR/.22 Mag.) shot, finger grooved rubber grips, double or single action. Importation began 1992.

Mfg.'s Sug. Retail	$275	$200	$175	$150	$135	$125	$115	$105

Add approx. $25 for longer barrel lengths.
Add $100 for .22 LR/.22 Mag. combo.

TACTICAL GRADE — .38 Spl. only, fixed sights, 6 shot, 2 in. (bobbed hammer) or 4 in. compensated barrel, blue finish only. Importation began 1992.

Mfg.'s Sug. Retail	$295	$220	$190	$165	$145	$130	$115	$105

Add $80 for 4 in. compensated barrel.

TARGET GRADE — .22 LR, .357 Mag., or .38 Spl. cal., 6 or 8 (.22 LR) shot, 6 in. squared off barrel, finger grooved hardwood stocks, adj. trigger pull and rear sight, blue finish only, 3.1 lbs. Importation began 1992.

Mfg.'s Sug. Retail	$550	$425	$325	$260	$220	$200	$185	$170

RIFLES

In addition to the models listed below, EAA also imports Herman Weihrauch Target Rifles (See separate listing in the H. Weihrauch section).

ROVER 870 — .22-250 Rem., .243 Win., .25-06 Rem., .270 Rem., .30-06, .308 Win., 7mm Rem. Mag., .300 Win. Mag., or .338 Win. Mag. cal., bolt action rifle featuring all-steel construction with 22 in. hammer-forged rifled barrel, staggered 5 shot internal mag., open sights. Importation began 1993.

Mfg.'s Sug. Retail	$995	$795	$695	$600	$550	$495	$450	$395

SHOTGUNS: O/U

FALCON — 12, 20, or .410 ga., 3 in. chambers, 26, 28, or 30 in. fixed choke VR barrels, boxlock action, single or double trigger, extractors or ejectors, checkered pistol grip and fore-end. Importation began 1993.

Mfg.'s Sug. Retail	$795	$650	$525	$450	$375	$325	$295	$260

Add $80 for .410 ga.
Add $100 for SST and ejectors.

SPORTING CLAYS — 12 ga. only, 3 in. chambers, 28 in. fixed choke wide VR barrels, boxlock action, SST, extractors, blued receiver with engraving. Importation began 1993.

Mfg.'s Sug. Retail	$995	$750	$650	$575	$525	$475	$425	$375

Grading	100%	98%	95%	90%	80%	70%	60%

Sporting Clays Pro — similar to Sporting Clays, except has ejectors, recoil pad, six screw-in chokes, and is cased. Importation began 1993.

Mfg.'s Sug. Retail $1,495	$1,100	$950	$825	$700	$575	$495	$425

SHOTGUNS: SIDE-BY-SIDE

SABA —12, 20, 28, or .410 ga., 3 in. chambers, boxlock action with scrolled nickel finish, DT or SST, 26 or 28 in. fixed choke barrels with raised matted rib, ejectors, checkered stock and forearm with sling swivels. Importation began 1993.

Mfg.'s Sug. Retail $1,195	$950	$825	$700	$575	$495	$425	$375

Add $100 for SST.

SHOTGUNS: SLIDE ACTION

MODEL PM2 — 12 ga. only, slide action, unique 7 shot detachable mag., 20 in. barrel, black wood stock and composite forearm, dual action bars, cross trigger safety, available in matte blue or chrome finish, 6.81 lbs. Importation began 1992.

Mfg.'s Sug. Retail $695	$550	$450	$395	$335	$295	$260	$230

Add $200 for night sights.
Add $75 for matte chrome finish.

EXCAM

Previous importer and distributor located in Hialeah, FL that went out of business late 1990. Excam distributed Dart, Erma, Tanarmi, Targa, & Warrior exclusively for the U.S. These trademarks will appear under Excam only in this book. All importation of Excam firearms ceased in 1990.

All Targa and Tanarmi pistols were manufactured in Gardone V.T., Italy. All Erma and Warrior pistols and rifles were manufactured in W. Germany. Senator O/U shotguns were manufactured by A. Zoli located in Brescia, Italy.

ERMA PISTOLS

RX 22 — .22 LR only, double action-Walther copy, $3\frac{1}{4}$ in. barrel, 8 shot mag., blue only, plastic grips, 17 oz. Assembled in the U.S. Disc. 1986.

	$140	$125	$105	$95	$90	$85	$80

Last Mfg.'s Sug. Retail was $139.

KGP 22 — .22 LR only, Luger type toggle action, 3.78 in. barrel, 8 shot mag., blue only, plastic grips, 29 oz. Importation disc. 1986.

	$220	$195	$175	$155	$135	$120	$105

Last Mfg.'s Sug. Retail was $220.

KGP 380 — .380 ACP only, Luger type toggle action, $3\frac{1}{2}$ in. barrel, 5 shot mag., blue only, plastic grips, 23 oz. Disc. 1986.

	$250	$215	$185	$160	$145	$135	$125

Last Mfg.'s Sug. Retail was $230.

ERMA RIFLES

EG 712 — .22 LR only, lever action copied after the Win. Model 92, $18\frac{1}{2}$ in. barrel, 15 shot, iron sights. Disc. 1985.

	$180	$160	$140	$125	$115	$100	$90

Last Mfg.'s Sug. Retail was $204.

Grading	100%	98%	95%	90%	80%	70%	60%

EG 712L — .22 LR only, lever action copied after the Win. Model 92, 18½ in. octagonal barrel, deluxe walnut silver plated receiver and barrel bands, 15 shot, iron sights. Disc.

	$300	$241	$220	$180	$150	$130	$115

EG 73 — .22 Mag. only, lever action copied after the Win. Model 92, 19¼ in. barrel, 12 shot, iron sights, blue only. Disc. 1985.

	$205	$185	$160	$140	$130	$120	$105

Last Mfg.'s Sug. Retail was $229.

EG 722 — .22 LR only, slide action, 18½ in. barrel, 15 shot, iron sights, blue only. Disc. 1985.

	$180	$160	$140	$125	$115	$100	$90

Last Mfg.'s Sug. Retail was $204.

EM 1 CARBINE — .22 LR or .22 Mag., gas semi-auto, copy of the original M1 carbine, 19½ in. barrel, 15 shot, iron sights, blue only. ESG 22 is 22 Mag. (12 shot) — add $100. Disc. 1985.

	$175	$155	$140	$125	$115	$100	$90

Last Mfg.'s Sug. Retail was $195.

SENATOR OVER/UNDER SHOTGUNS

SENATOR MODEL — 12, 20, or .410 ga., 3 in. chambers, 26 or 28 in. F/M barrels, folding action, double triggers, extractors, vent. barrels and rib, checkered walnut stock and forearm, engraved silver finished receiver. Imported 1986-1987.

	$235	$200	$180	$165	$150	$140	$130

Last Mfg.'s Sug. Retail was $275.

TANARMI HANDGUNS

MODEL TA 22 — .22 LR, 6 shot, 4¾ in. barrel, brass trigger guard and grip straps, blued finish, wood grips, 34 oz.

	$85	$70	$60	$55	$50	$45	$40

Last Mfg.'s Sug. Retail was $99.

MODEL TA 76 S.A.A. — .22 LR, single action revolver, 4¾ in. barrel, 6 shot, blue finish only, wood grips, 32 oz.

	$85	$65	$55	$50	$45	$40	$35

Add $4 for chrome finish or brass backstrap and trigger guard.
Last Mfg.'s Sug. Retail was $95.

Model TA 76M Combo — includes .22 LR and .22 Mag. cylinders, 4¾ (standard), 6, or 9 in. barrel, blue finish, wood grips.

	$95	$75	$65	$60	$55	$50	$45

Add $6 for chrome plated finish (4¾ in. barrel only).
Add $10 for 6 (Model TA 766) or 9 (Model TA 769) in. barrel.
Add $16 for brass backstrap and trigger guard (N/A in 9 in. barrel).
Last Mfg.'s Sug. Retail was $105.

TA 38SB O/U DERRINGER — .38 Spl. only, O/U Derringer-copy of Rem. Model 41, 3 in. barrels, 14 oz., with safety, blue finish only, checkered nylon grips. Importation disc. 1985.

	$90	$75	$65	$55	$50	$45	$40

Last Mfg.'s Sug. Retail was $80.

Grading	100%	98%	95%	90%	80%	70%	60%

TA 41 SERIES SEMI-AUTO — .41 Action Express cal., action similar to TA 90 Series, 11 shot mag., matte blue (Model TA 41B) or matte chrome (Model TA 41C) finish, combat sights, black neoprene grips, 38 oz. Importation began 1989.

	$450	$390	$360	$330	$295	$265	$240

Add $70 for adj. target sights (Model TA 41BT).
Last Mfg.'s Sug. Retail was $490.

⚮ **Model TA 41C** — matte chrome finish.

	$485	$430	$395	$360	$330	$295	$270

Add $50 (retail) for adj. target sights (Model TA 41CT).
Last Mfg.'s Sug. Retail was $550.

⚮ **Model TA 41 SS** — .41 AE, compensated variation of the Model TA 41 except has 5 in. ported barrel and slide, blue/chrome finish, competition sights, 40 oz. Importation began 1989.

	$575	$450	$420	$385	$350	$325	$300

Last Mfg.'s Sug. Retail was $650.

TA 90 SERIES SEMI-AUTO — 9mm, double action, copy of the CZ-75, 4¾ in. barrel, steel frame, 15 shot mag., matte blue (Model TA 90B) or matte chrome finish (Model TA 90C), combat sights, wood (disc. 1985) or neoprene grips, 38 oz. New 1985.

	$365	$300	$260	$225	$205	$190	$180

Add $85 for adj. target sights (TA 90BT).
Earlier models featured a polished blue finish and nickel steel alloy frame (35 oz.).
Last Mfg.'s Sug. Retail was $415.

⚮ **Model TA 90C** — matte chrome finish.

	$380	$315	$270	$235	$210	$190	$180

Add $95 for adj. target sights (TA 90CT).
Last Mfg.'s Sug. Retail was $430.

⚮ **Model BTA 90B and C** — 9mm, smaller version of TA 90, 3½ in. barrel, 12 shot mag., neoprene grips. New 1986.

	$380	$315	$270	$235	$210	$190	$180

Add $20 for chrome finish (BTA 90C).
Last Mfg.'s Sug. Retail was $430.

⚮ **Model TA 90 SS** — 9mm, compensated variation of the Model TA 90 except has 5 in. ported barrel and slide, blue/chrome finish, competition sights, 40 oz. Importation began 1989.

	$575	$450	$420	$385	$350	$325	$300

Last Mfg.'s Sug. Retail was $650.

⚮ **TA 90BK** — convertible kit including 2 barrels (9mm and .41 AE) and 2 mag.'s. While advertised, this combination never saw production.

TARGA PISTOLS

GT 22 SERIES — .22 LR, 3.88 in. barrel, 10 shot mag., single action 26 oz., steel frame, either satin chrome (GT 22C) or standard blue (GT 22B) finish, wooden grips became standard in 1986. GT 22T is 6 in. barrel target version (12 shot mag.).

	$170	$140	$125	$110	$95	$80	$70

Add $15 for chrome finish (Model GT 22C).
Last Mfg.'s Sug. Retail was $200.

Grading	100%	98%	95%	90%	80%	70%	60%

GT 26 and GT 27B OR C — .25 ACP, 2½ in. barrel, 6 shot mag., single action, 13 oz., available in standard blue alloy, satin chrome alloy (GT 27B or C), or steel frame (GT 26S), wooden grips became standard in 1986.

	$50	$45	$35	$30	$30	$25	$25

Add $59 for steel frame (Model GT 26S).
Add $13 for chrome alloy (Model GT 27C).
Last Mfg.'s Sug. Retail was $56.

GT 28 SERIES — .25 ACP, 2½ in. barrel, 5 shot mag., single action, blue alloy, wood grips. New 1990.

	$45	$35	$30	$30	$25	$25	$20

Add $18 for chrome finish (Model GT 28C).
Last Mfg.'s Sug. Retail was $51.

GT 32 SERIES — .32 ACP, 3.88 in. barrel, 7 shot mag., single action, steel frame, 26 oz., either satin chrome (GT 32C) or standard blue (GT 32B), wooden grips became standard in 1986.

	$170	$140	$125	$110	$95	$80	$70

Add $15 for chrome finish (Model GT 32C).
Last Mfg.'s Sug. Retail was $200.

GT 380 ACP SERIES — .380 ACP, 3.88 in. barrel, 6 shot mag., single action, steel frame, 26 oz., either satin chrome (GT 380C) or standard blue (GT 380B), wooden grips became standard in 1986.

	$175	$145	$135	$125	$115	$105	$95

Add $8 for chrome finish (Model GT 380C).
Last Mfg.'s Sug. Retail was $212.

GT 380 LW — similar to GT 380 Series except has light alloy receiver and 3¼ in. barrel.

	$100	$85	$70	$60	$55	$50	$45

Last Mfg.'s Sug. Retail was $119.

GT 380 BE or CE — engraved models, either blue (BE) or chrome (CE) finish, wood grips. Importation disc. 1989.

	$180	$155	$145	$135	$125	$115	$105

Add $25 for chrome finish (Model GT 380 CE).
Last Mfg.'s Sug. Retail was $220.

GT 380 XE — .380 ACP, 3.88 in. barrel, 11 shot mag., blue only, wood grips, 28 oz.

	$190	$165	$155	$145	$135	$125	$115

Last Mfg.'s Sug. Retail was $235.

GT 32 XEB — similar to GT 380 XE, only .32 ACP, 12 shot mag. Disc. 1985.

	$165	$145	$135	$125	$115	$100	$95

Last Mfg.'s Sug. Retail was $189.

REVOLVERS: CURRENT MFG.

RX 38 B — .38 Spl., double action, 6 shot, 2 in. barrel, blue finish only. Importation began 1990.

	$85	$65	$55	$50	$45	$40	$35

Last Mfg.'s Sug. Retail was $95.

Grading	100%	98%	95%	90%	80%	70%	60%

UBERTI REVOLVERS

Importation of these revolvers by Excam was stopped in 1986.

ALDO UBERTI CATTLEMAN SA REVOLVER — .375 Mag., .44 Mag., or .45 LC cal., 6 shot, single action, 5½, 6, or 7½ in. barrels, target sights, wood grips, blued finish. New 1985. Disc. 1986.

	$295	$250	$195	$165	$150	$140	$130

Add $10 for .44 Mag. cal.
Last Mfg.'s Sug. Retail was $222.

ALDO UBERTI DA INSPECTOR — .38 Spl., double action, 3 or 4 in. barrel, blue finish, wood grips, 6 shot. Disc. 1986.

	$325	$250	$200	$180	$165	$150	$140

Add $17 for adj. sights.
Last Mfg.'s Sug. Retail was $240.

WARRIOR REVOLVERS

Importation of these revolvers by Excam was stopped in 1986.

WARRIOR DOUBLE ACTION MODEL W 722 (B) — .22 LR or .22 Mag. only, double action, 6 in. barrel, 8 shot, blue only, plastic grips, 35 oz. Disc. 1986.

	$100	$80	$70	$65	$60	$55	$50

Add $50 for .22 Mag. extra cyl.
Last Mfg.'s Sug. Retail was $98.

WARRIOR DOUBLE ACTION MODEL W 384 (B) — .38 Spl. only, double action, 4 or 6 in. barrels, 6 shot, blue only, plastic grips, 30 oz. Vent. rib standard. Disc. 1986.

	$135	$110	$100	$90	$80	$70	$65

Add $5 for 6 in. barrel (W 386 B).
Last Mfg.'s Sug. Retail was $125.

WARRIOR DOUBLE ACTION MODEL W 357 — .357 Mag. only, double action, 4 or 6 in. barrels, 6 shot, blue only, plastic grips, 36 oz. Vent. rib standard. 6 in. barrel (W 3576). Disc. 1986.

	$190	$165	$145	$135	$130	$125	$120

Last Mfg.'s Sug. Retail was $185.

EXEL ARMS OF AMERICA, INC.

Previous importer located in Gardener, MA. Exel Arms previously imported Lanber (Series 100), Ugartechea (Series 200), and Laurona (Series 300) shotguns. Lanber, Ugartechea, and Laurona, are listed alphabetically below.

LANBER SHOTGUNS: OVER AND UNDER

Lanber shotguns are not being imported currently. The last Mfg.'s Sug. Retail on all models listed below reflects 1987 pricing, the last year they were imported. Any future importation could reflect pricing changes.

EXEL SERIES 100: MODELS 101 THROUGH 104 — 12 ga., boxlock action, vent. rib, extractors, single trigger. Add $16 for 103 Mag., $92 for ejectors (Model 104 only).

	$400	$350	$310	$270	$240	$225	$200

Last Mfg.'s Sug. Retail was $451.
These models were previously designated the 844ST Series.

Grading	100%	98%	95%	90%	80%	70%	60%

EXEL MODEL 105 — 12 ga., boxlock action, single trigger, ejectors, Lanber screw-in chokes, deluxe wood, engraved satin finish action.

| | $575 | $495 | $440 | $405 | $370 | $345 | $310 |

Last Mfg.'s Sug. Retail was $644.
This model was previously designated the Model 2004LCH.

EXEL MODELS 106 AND 107 — 12 ga., similar to 105, only more deluxe version with vent. barrels and rib, blued receiver only, interchangeable Lanber screw-in chokes. Trap model is Model 107.

| | $725 | $625 | $550 | $500 | $475 | $450 | $425 |

Last Mfg.'s Sug. Retail was $845.
These models were previously designated 2008LCH and 2009LCH respectively.

UGARTECHEA SHOTGUNS: SIDE-BY-SIDE

Ugartechea shotguns are not being imported currently. The last Mfg.'s Sug. Retail on all models listed below reflects 1986-87 pricing, the last years they were imported. Any future importation could reflect pricing changes.

EXEL 200 SERIES — these side-by-sides are available in 12 or 20 ga. (3 in.) only. Model 201 is basic gun with 213 being the highest grade.

Model 201, 202, and 203 — double triggers, extractors, straight grip, matted rib, various chokes and barrel lengths.

| | $375 | $325 | $260 | $240 | $215 | $180 | $165 |

Last Mfg.'s Sug. Retail was $429.
Previously designated Model 30.

Model 281 — similar to 201 series, except 28 ga.

| | $420 | $325 | $275 | $250 | $235 | $210 | $195 |

Last Mfg.'s Sug. Retail was $472.
Previously designated Model 30.

Model 240 — similar to 201 series, except .410 ga.

| | $450 | $355 | $295 | $270 | $250 | $235 | $210 |

Last Mfg.'s Sug. Retail was $472.
Previously designated Model 30.

Models 204, 205, and 206 — single trigger optional, ejectors, straight grip, silver finish, various chokes and barrel lengths. Importation disc. 1986.

| | $550 | $470 | $415 | $370 | $340 | $315 | $280 |

Last Mfg.'s Sug. Retail was $627.

Models 207 and 207A — 12 ga. only, sidelock, case hardened action. 207A is deluxe model with ejectors. Model 201 disc. 1986.

| | $725 | $650 | $580 | $515 | $465 | $400 | $345 |

Deduct 33% without ejectors (Model 207).
This model was previously designated the Milano EX.
Last Mfg.'s Sug. Retail was $836.

Models 208 and 208A — similar to 207/207A, only engraved coin finished receiver. 208A is deluxe model with ejectors. Model 208 disc. 1986.

| | $775 | $695 | $625 | $550 | $485 | $420 | $360 |

Deduct 33% without ejectors (Model 208).
This model was previously designated the Model 75 EX.
Last Mfg.'s Sug. Retail was $925.

Grading	100%	98%	95%	90%	80%	70%	60%

Models 209 and 210 — better engraving and walnut than 207/207A. Model 210 is 20 ga. Importation disc. 1986.

| | $580 | $505 | $450 | $415 | $375 | $340 | $310 |

Last Mfg.'s Sug. Retail was $672.

Models 211, 212, and 213 — top-of-the-line model, best quality engraving and walnut. Special order only.

| | $2,350 | $2,000 | $1,780 | $1,475 | $1,200 | $1,000 | $850 |

Last Mfg.'s Sug. Retail was $3,100. Previously designated Model 110.

MODEL 251 — .410-3 in. ga., folding design, 26 in. barrels only, DTs, extractors, walnut stock and forearm. New 1987.

| | $185 | $165 | $140 | $120 | $105 | $95 | $85 |

Last Mfg.'s Sug. Retail was $215.

LAURONA SHOTGUNS: OVER AND UNDER

Laurona shotguns are no longer being imported by Exel Arms of America, Inc. Laurona shotguns were imported by Galaxy Imports located in Victoria, TX until 1991 and these recent models can be located in the Laurona section of this text. Model nomenclature has changed from the discontinued Exel 300 Series below.

EXEL 300 SERIES — These over and unders are available in 12 or 20 ga. only. Model 301 is basic gun with 310 being the highest grade.

Models 301 and 302 — 12 ga., double selective trigger system, ejectors, pistol grip, vent. rib, lightly engraved chrome finish receiver, various chokes and barrel lengths. Importation disc. 1986.

| | $485 | $415 | $380 | $340 | $300 | $275 | $250 |

Last Mfg.'s Sug. Retail was $553.

Models 303 and 304 — 12 ga., similar to 301/302, except has better engraving on coin finish receiver, vent. barrels. Importation disc. 1987.

| | $545 | $470 | $430 | $385 | $340 | $315 | $270 |

Last Mfg.'s Sug. Retail was $623.
Previously designated Model 82G Super.

Models 305(A) and 306(A) — 12 or 20 ga., similar to 303/304, except has better engraving on coin finish receiver, screw-in choke tubes. Importation disc. 1987.

| | $625 | $535 | $470 | $430 | $390 | $350 | $315 |

Last Mfg.'s Sug. Retail was $711.
Previously designated Models 83MG and 85MS.

Models 307 and 308 — 12 ga., trap model, 29 in. barrels, extensive engraving, Monte Carlo stock. Importation disc. 1987.

| | $580 | $500 | $460 | $420 | $380 | $340 | $300 |

Last Mfg.'s Sug. Retail was $668.
Previously designated Model 82U Trap.

Models 309 and 310 — super trap model, 29 in. vent. barrels, more extensive engraving than Models 307/308. Importation disc. 1987.

| | $630 | $545 | $495 | $460 | $415 | $385 | $340 |

Last Mfg.'s Sug. Retail was $726. Previously designated Model 82 S. Trap.

Model 82 — double selective trigger system, ejectors, pistol grip, vent. rib, various chokes and barrel lengths. Disc.

| | $549 | $410 | $380 | $340 | $300 | $275 | $250 |

F section

FAS

Manufacturer located in Italy. Currently imported and distributed by Nygord Precision located in La Crescenta, CA and Mandall's Shooting Supplies Inc. located in Scottsdale, AZ. Previously imported by Beeman Precision Arms, Inc. located in Santa Rosa, CA and Osborne's located in Cheboygan, MI.

Grading	100%	98%	95%	90%	80%	70%	60%

PISTOLS: SEMI-AUTO

MODEL 601 — .22 Short only, semi-auto competition pistol, 5½ in. barrel, 5 shot mag., wrap-around match wood grips, 41½ oz.

Mfg.'s Sug. Retail	$1,200	$995	$875	$695	$640	$565	$500	$450

MODEL 602 — .22 LR only, semi-auto competition pistol, 5.6 in. barrel, 5 shot mag., wrap-around match wood grips, 40 oz.

Mfg.'s Sug. Retail	$1,100	$895	$800	$625	$600	$525	$475	$425

MODEL 603 — .32 S&W Wadcutter only, semi-auto competition pistol, 5.6 in. barrel, 5 shot mag., wrap-around adj. or non-adj. match wood grips, 40 oz.

Mfg.'s Sug. Retail	$1,200	$995	$875	$695	$640	$565	$500	$450

FEG

Manufacturer located in Hungary (FEG stands for Fegyvergyan) since the turn of the century. Currently imported and distributed by KBI, Inc. located in Harrisburg, PA.

Some older, disc. models can be found under the Interarms section in this text.

PISTOLS

All FEG pistols are supplied with two mags.

MODEL PMK-380 — .380 ACP cal., patterned after Walther PP, alloy frame, double action, 4 in. barrel, plastic grips with thumbrest, blued finish, 21 oz. Importation began 1992.

Mfg.'s Sug. Retail	$249	$220	$195	$180	$165	$150	$135	$115

MODEL SMC-380 — .380 ACP cal., double action semi-auto, patterned after Walther PPK, alloy frame, 3½ in. barrel, 6 shot mag., plastic grips with thumbrest, blue finish, 18½ oz. Importation began 1993.

Mfg.'s Sug. Retail	$299	$265	$235	$210	$195	$175	$160	$145

MODEL MBK-9HP — 9mm Para., patterned after Browning Hi-Power, double action, 4⅔ in. barrel, 14 shot mag., blued finish, steel construction, checkered wood grips, 36 oz. Imported 1992 only.

	$315	$270	$250	$225	$200	$185	$170

Last Mfg.'s Sug. Retail was $349.

Model MBK-9HPC — compact variation of the Model MBK-9HP with 4 in. barrel, 34 oz. Imported 1992 only.

	$325	$275	$250	$225	$200	$185	$170

Last Mfg.'s Sug. Retail was $359.

FEG, cont.

Grading	100%	98%	95%	90%	80%	70%	60%

MODEL PJK-9HP — 9mm Para., patterned after Browning Hi-Power, all steel construction, 4¾ in. barrel, thumb safety, 13 shot mag. and cleaning rod, 32 oz. Importation began 1992.

Mfg.'s Sug. Retail	$329	$285	$255	$230	$215	$195	$180	$165

Add $65 for industrial hard chrome finish (includes Uncle Mike's rubber grips).

MODEL GKK-92C — 9mm Para., double action semi-auto, 4 in. barrel, 14 shot mag., improved variation of MBK models, includes same accessories as PJK-9H, 34 oz.

Mfg.'s Sug. Retail	$369	$315	$280	$255	$230	$200	$185	$170

MODEL GKK-45 — .45 ACP cal., double action semi-auto, all steel, 4¼ in. barrel, checkered walnut grips, 8 shot mag., approx. 37 oz. Importation began 1993.

Mfg.'s Sug. Retail	$379	$330	$300	$275	$250	$220	$200	$180

RIFLES

MODEL SA-85M — 7.62 x 39mm K. cal., semi-auto, sporter rifle utilizing semi-auto AKM action, 16.3 in. barrel, 6 shot detachable mag., thumb hole stock, 7 lbs. 10 oz. Importation began 1991.

Mfg.'s Sug. Retail	$499	$415	$370	$335	$300	$280	$260	$240

F.I.E.

Firearms import & export previously located in Hialeah, FL.

F.I.E. filed bankrupcy in November of 1990 and all models are discontinued. Parts and service for these older firearms may be obtained through Quality Firearms, Inc. (see Trademark Index), even though all warranties on F.I.E. guns are void.

ARMINIUS REVOLVERS: DOUBLE ACTION

All pistols under this heading are manufactured in W. Germany under the trademark Arminius. .22 cal. is 8 shot, .32 S&W is 7 shot, all others 6 shot.

MODEL 522TB — .22 LR, blue finish, 4 in. barrel, 8 shot.

	$130	$100	$85	$75	$70	$65	$60

Add $23 for walnut grips.
Last Mfg.'s Sug. Retail was $174.

722 SERIES — .22 LR, blue (standard) or chrome finish (disc. 1985), 6 in. barrel, 8 shot.

	$125	$100	$90	$80	$70	$65	$60

Add $23 for walnut grips.
Add $49 for .22 LR/.22 Mag. combo.
Add $15 for chrome finish.
Last Mfg.'s Sug. Retail was $161.

STANDARD REVOLVER — .22 LR, .22 Mag., .32 Mag. or .38 Spl., 2 or 4 in. barrel, blued finish, fixed sights, without ejector assembly. Mfg. in U.S. starting 1989.

	$80	$70	$65	$60	$55	$50	$45

Add $19 for chrome finish (2 in. barrel only).
Add $38 for gold plated finish (2 in. barrel only).
Add $23 for .22 Combo package (2 cylinders - 4 in. barrel only).
Models with 4 in. barrels are available in blued finish only.
Last Mfg.'s Sug. Retail was $101.

MODEL 532TB — .32 S&W, blue (standard) or chrome finish (disc. 1985), adj. sights, 4 in. barrel, 7 shot.

	$145	$120	$100	$80	$75	$70	$65

Add $23 for walnut grips.
Add $15 for chrome finish.
Last Mfg.'s Sug. Retail was $183.

Grading	100%	98%	95%	90%	80%	70%	60%

MODEL 732B — similar to Model 532TB, except has 6 in. barrel and fixed sights. Imported 1988 only.

	100%	98%	95%	90%	80%	70%	60%
	$120	$100	$90	$80	$70	$65	$60

Last Mfg.'s Sug. Retail was $140.

MODEL N-38 (TITAN TIGER) — .38 Spl., blue (standard) or chrome finish (disc. 1985), 2 or 4 in. barrel, fixed sights. Mfg. in U.S.

	100%	98%	95%	90%	80%	70%	60%
	$130	$110	$95	$80	$75	$65	$60

Add $23 for walnut grips.
Add $15 for chrome finish.
Last Mfg.'s Sug. Retail was $176.

ZEPHYR — .38 Spl., 5 shot, aluminum construction, 2 in. barrel, blue finish, checkered grips, 14 oz. New 1990.

	100%	98%	95%	90%	80%	70%	60%
	$145	$120	$100	$80	$75	$70	$65

Last Mfg.'s Sug. Retail was $189.

Lady Zephyr — similar to Zephyr, except has gold trimmed parts, scrimshawed red rose on ivory polymer grips, and gold case. New 1990.

	100%	98%	95%	90%	80%	70%	60%
	$250	$210	$180	$155	$135	$115	$95

Last Mfg.'s Sug. Retail was $295.

MODEL 384TB — .38 Spl., blue (standard) or chrome finish (disc. 1985), 6 shot, 4 in. barrel.

	100%	98%	95%	90%	80%	70%	60%
	$150	$125	$105	$85	$80	$70	$65

Add $23 for walnut grips.
Add $13 for chrome finish.
Last Mfg.'s Sug. Retail was $195.

MODEL 386TB — .38 Spl., blue (standard) or chrome finish (disc. 1985), 6 shot, 6 in. barrel.

	100%	98%	95%	90%	80%	70%	60%
	$150	$125	$105	$85	$80	$70	$65

Add $23 for walnut grips.
Add $13 for chrome finish.
Last Mfg.'s Sug. Retail was $195.

.357 MAG. SERIES — .357 Mag., blue (standard) or chrome finish (disc. 1985), 6 shot, 3 (Model 3573TB), 4 (Model 3574TB), or 6 (Model 3576TB) in. barrels.

	100%	98%	95%	90%	80%	70%	60%
	$200	$170	$135	$120	$110	$100	$90

Add $23 for walnut grips.
Add $15 for chrome finish.
Last Mfg.'s Sug. Retail was $255.

REVOLVERS: DISCONTINUED SNUB-NOSE

Currently manufactured 2 in. snub-nosed revolvers are listed in the previous category under Standard Revolver, Titan Tiger, and Zephyr.

222 SERIES — .22 LR & .22 Mag. cal., blue (standard) or chrome finish, 2 in. snub-nose barrel. Disc. 1985.

	100%	98%	95%	90%	80%	70%	60%
	$135	$115	$90	$85	$75	$65	$60

Add $15 for walnut grips.
Add $45 for .22 LR/.22 Mag. combo.
Last Mfg.'s Sug. Retail was $120.

222B SERIES — .22 LR only starting 1989, similar to 222 Series, reintroduced 1987-1989.

	100%	98%	95%	90%	80%	70%	60%
	$150	$120	$105	$85	$80	$70	$65

Add $45 for .22 LR/.22 Mag. combo (disc. 1988).
Last Mfg.'s Sug. Retail was $185.

Grading	100%	98%	95%	90%	80%	70%	60%

232 SERIES — .32 S&W, blue (standard) or chrome finish, 2 in. barrel. Disc.

	100%	98%	95%	90%	80%	70%	60%
	$120	$90	$85	$75	$65	$60	$55

Add $15 for walnut grips.
Add $14 for adj. sights.
Add $28 for chrome finish.

232B SERIES — similar to 232 Series, 2 in. barrel. Reintroduced 1987-1989.

	100%	98%	95%	90%	80%	70%	60%
	$150	$125	$110	$95	$85	$75	$70

Add $5 for adj. sights.
Last Mfg.'s Sug. Retail was $185.

MODEL 382TB — .38 Spl., blue (standard) or chrome finish, 2 in. barrel. Disc. 1985.

	100%	98%	95%	90%	80%	70%	60%
	$125	$110	$100	$90	$80	$75	$65

Add $15 for walnut grips.
Add $16 for chrome finish.
Last Mfg.'s Sug. Retail was $145.

MODEL 3572 — .357 Mag., blue (standard) or chrome finish, 2 in. barrel. Disc. 1984.

	100%	98%	95%	90%	80%	70%	60%
	$223	$170	$160	$135	$125	$115	$100

Add $15 for walnut grips.
Add $17 for chrome finish.

REVOLVERS: SINGLE ACTION

Combo designations on below listed models indicate 2 cylinders (.22 LR/.22 Mag.).

COWBOY — .22 LR or .22 LR/Mag. combo, 3¼ or 6 in. barrel, blued finish, square butt grip, without ejector tube, fixed sights. Mfg. in the U.S. starting 1989.

	100%	98%	95%	90%	80%	70%	60%
	$75	$65	$50	$45	$40	$35	$30

Add $23 for combo.
Last Mfg.'s Sug. Retail was $95.

GOLD RUSH — .22 LR or .22 LR/Mag. combo, 3¼, 4¾, or 6½ in. barrel, round (3¼ in. barrel only) or square butt grip, gold band on barrel and cylinder, ivory-tex grips. Mfg. in U.S. starting 1989.

	100%	98%	95%	90%	80%	70%	60%
	$155	$125	$110	$95	$85	$75	$70

Add $47 for combo.
Last Mfg.'s Sug. Retail was $189.

TEXAS RANGER (TEX 22 SERIES) — .22 LR or .22 Mag. (combo only), 3¼ (new 1986), 4¾, 6½ (new 1989), 7, or 9 in. barrel, 6 shot, blue only. Mfg. U.S.

	100%	98%	95%	90%	80%	70%	60%
	$80	$70	$60	$50	$45	$40	$35

Add $23 for combo.
Add $6 for 9 in. barrel.
This model with a 3¼ in. barrel is called the Little Ranger.
Last Mfg.'s Sug. Retail was $108.

BUFFALO SCOUT (E15 SERIES) — .22 LR or .22 Mag., blue (standard) or chrome finish, 4¾ in. barrel. Mfg. Brescia, Italy.

	100%	98%	95%	90%	80%	70%	60%
	$75	$55	$45	$35	$35	$30	$30

Add $23 for walnut grips.
Add $23 for combo.
Add $9 for chrome or blue/gold finish.
Last Mfg.'s Sug. Retail was $98.

Grading	100%	98%	95%	90%	80%	70%	60%

The Yellow Rose Combo — all metal parts 24 Kt. gold plated, smooth walnut grips. New 1986.

	100%	98%	95%
	$130	$110	$95

Add $151 for scrimshawed ivory polymer grips - walnut cased (new 1989).
Last Mfg.'s Sug. Retail was $161.

LEGEND S.A.A. (PL-22 SERIES) — .22 LR or .22 Mag., blue only. Mfg. Brescia, Italy. Disc. 1984.

100%	98%	95%	90%	80%	70%	60%
$120	$90	$85	$75	$65	$60	$55

Add $3 for walnut grips.
Add $17 for combo.

HOMBRE MODEL — .357 Mag., .44 Mag., or .45 cal., color case hardened receiver, 5½ (disc. 1985), 6, or 7½ in. barrel, 45 oz., smooth walnut grips. Mfg. W. Germany.

100%	98%	95%	90%	80%	70%	60%
$220	$180	$145	$130	$120	$110	$100

Add $25 for brass back strap and trigger guard (disc.).
Last Mfg.'s Sug. Retail was $265.

Golden Hombre — same general specifications as Hombre, except all metal surfaces are plated in 24Kt. gold.

100%	98%	95%
$300	$210	$145

Add $65 for ivory polymer grips (new 1989).
Last Mfg.'s Sug. Retail was $350.

TITAN PISTOLS: SEMI-AUTO

TITAN II (E32 SERIES) — .32 ACP (disc. 1988), or .380 ACP, single action, blue (standard) or chrome finish. Mfg. USA.

100%	98%	95%	90%	80%	70%	60%
$195	$160	$135	$120	$105	$95	$85

Add $25 for walnut grips.
Add $10 for chrome finish.
This series was redesigned in 1988 to be shorter and more compact. Older series Titans are worth approx. $50 less than values shown above.
Last Mfg.'s Sug. Retail was $220.

SUPER TITAN II — .32 ACP (disc. 1988), or .380 ACP, single action, 12 shot mag. in .32 ACP, 11 for .380 cal., walnut grips, standard blue only. Mfg. U.S.

100%	98%	95%	90%	80%	70%	60%
$215	$185	$155	$135	$120	$105	$95

Last Mfg.'s Sug. Retail was $260.

.22 TITAN II (E22) — .22 LR, single action, 10 shot mag., blue finish only. Walnut grips standard.

100%	98%	95%	90%	80%	70%	60%
$130	$105	$90	$80	$70	$65	$60

Last Mfg.'s Sug. Retail was $161.

Lady .22 — similar to .22 TITAN II except has combination blue/gold finish with scrimshawed red rose on ivory polymer grips. New 1990.

100%	98%	95%	90%	80%	70%	60%
$185	$155	$130	$120	$105	$95	$85

Last Mfg.'s Sug. Retail was $208.

THE BEST (A27) — .25 ACP, single action, blue only, deluxe finish, walnut grips, steel frame, 6 shot mag. Mfg. in Spain by Astra. Importation disc. 1988.

100%	98%	95%	90%	80%	70%	60%
$125	$105	$90	$80	$70	$65	$60

Last Mfg.'s Sug. Retail was $155.

Grading	100%	98%	95%	90%	80%	70%	60%

.25 TITAN (E27 SERIES) — .25 ACP, single action, blue (disc. 1989) or Dyna-chrome finish (standard 1990).

| | $60 | $50 | $45 | $40 | $35 | $30 | $30 |

Subtract $5 for blued finish.
Add $26 for gold trim (new 1986).
Add $62 for Misty Gold finish (1988 only).
Last Mfg.'s Sug. Retail was $77.

⚹ **Titan Tigress** — similar to .25 Titan except is entirely gold plated and cased, ladies pistol. Importation began 1989.

| | $130 | $110 | $95 |

Last Mfg.'s Sug. Retail was $153.

.25 TITAN (E38 SERIES) — .25 ACP, similar to E27 series except has standard blue finish. New 1990.

| | $50 | $45 | $40 | $35 | $30 | $30 | $25 |

Add $9 for Dyna-chrome finish.
Last Mfg.'s Sug. Retail was $59.

SSP SERIES — .32 ACP or .380 ACP cal., single action semi-auto, 3⅛ in. barrel, 5 shot mag., blue or chrome finish, composition grips, 25 oz. Mfg. U.S. New 1990.

| | $120 | $95 | $85 | $75 | $65 | $60 | $55 |

Add $19 for chrome finish.
Last Mfg.'s Sug. Retail was $146.

⚹ **Lady SSP** — similar to SSP except has gold trimmed parts, scrimshawed red rose on ivory polymer grips, and gold case. New 1990.

| | $210 | $180 | $155 | $135 | $120 | $105 | $95 |

Last Mfg.'s Sug. Retail was $250.

TZ-75 — 9mm Para., double action, 4.72 in. barrel, steel frame and slide, 15 shot mag., patterned after the CZ-75 action, 35 oz. Imported 1982-1989. This model was updated in 1988 (Series 88).

| | $375 | $325 | $290 | $270 | $250 | $235 | $220 |

Add $20 for satin chrome finish (new 1986).
Add $20 for black rubber grips.
Last Mfg.'s Sug. Retail was $440.

TZ-75 SERIES 88 — 9mm Para. or .41 Action Express cal., improved TZ-75 action, 4.72 in. barrel, steel frame and slide, 11 (.41 AE) or 17 (9mm) shot mag., fixed removable rear sight, choice of matte blue, satin chrome, or blue slide/chrome frame finish, updated CZ-75 action, 35 oz. New 1988.

| | $435 | $360 | $330 | $295 | $280 | $260 | $240 |

Add $97 for .41 Action Express cal.
Add $20 for satin chrome on 9mm, $29 on .41 AE.
Add $14 for black rubber grips.
This model is also available with a blue slide/chrome frame (I.P.S.C. configuration) at no extra charge.
The TZ-75 Series 88 was re-engineered in 1988 to include: frame mounted sear locking safety (cocked and locked), Colt style firing pin safety block, improved recessed slide serrations, muzzle barrel swell, bobbed hammer design, elongated combat style slide stop, new mag. release, and removable rear sight. Last Mfg.'s Sug. Retail was $519.

⚹ **TZ-75 Combo** — includes both .41 Action Express cal. and 9mm Para. barrels. New 1990.

| | $615 | $535 | $475 | $430 | $395 | $370 | $350 |

Add $29 for satin chrome or blue slide/chrome frame finish.
Last Mfg.'s Sug. Retail was $709.

Grading	100%	98%	95%	90%	80%	70%	60%

⚮ **TZ-75 Series 88 Govt. Model** — 9mm Para. only, compact variation of the TZ-75 Series 88, 3⅗ in. barrel, 12 shot mag., checkered walnut grips, 33½ oz. New 1990.

	$435	$360	$330	$295	$280	$260	$240

Add $20 for satin chrome or blue slide/chrome frame finish.
Last Mfg.'s Sug. Retail was $519.

⚮ **TZ-75 Series 88 with ported barrel** — similar to the TZ-75 Series 88 except has 5 in. ported barrel and slide. New 1990.

	$615	$535	$475	$430	$395	$370	$350

Last Mfg.'s Sug. Retail was $709.

⚮ **Compensated TZ-75 Series 88** — similar to the TZ-75 Series 88 except has 5¾ in. compensated barrel, 42 oz. New 1990.

	$700	$615	$535	$475	$430	$395	$370

Last Mfg.'s Sug. Retail was $804.

MODEL 722 TP SILHOUETTE PISTOL — .22 LR, bolt action target pistol, 10 in. free-floating barrel, 4-way adj. trigger, micro adj. rear sight, 6 or 10 shot mag., stippled pistol grip and forearm, supplied with 2-piece scope mount, 3.4 lbs. New 1990.

	$220	$190	$160	$140	$125	$115	$100

Last Mfg.'s Sug. Retail was $263.

SPECTRE PISTOL — 9mm Para. or .45 ACP cal., double action, unique triple action blowback system with two piece bolt, 6 in. barrel, military style configuration, adj. sights, 30 or 50 (opt.) shot mag. (unique 4 column configuration), 4.8 lbs. New 1989.

	$375	$325	$275	$240	$200	$185	$170

Add $14 for mag. loading tool.
Last Mfg.'s Sug. Retail was $718.

KG-99 — 9mm, paramilitary design pistol, 36 shot mag. Mini-99 also available with 20 shot mag. and 3 in. barrel. Disc. 1984.

	$425	$340	$300	$250	$225	$210	$180

This model was not manufactured but sold by F.I.E.

DERRINGERS

MODEL D38 — .38 Spl., O/U, chrome finish only, no transfer bar. Disc. 1985.

	$70	$60	$55	$45	$40	$35	$30

Add $17 for walnut grips.
Last Mfg.'s Sug. Retail was $82.

MODEL D86 — .38 Spl., single shot, 3 in. barrel, internal transfer bar safety, ammo storage compartment, blue or Dyna-chrome finish, 11 oz. New 1986.

	$80	$65	$55	$50	$45	$40	$35

Add $9 for Dyna-chrome finish.
Add $25 for deluxe model (walnut stocks).
Add $60 for Misty Gold finish (disc.).
Last Mfg.'s Sug. Retail was $95.

RIFLES: SEMI-AUTO

GR-8 BLACK BEAUTY — .22 cal. only, 14 shot, 19½ in. barrel, 64 oz., tubular feed, black nylon stock, patterned after Rem. Nylon 66. Mfg. by C.B.C. of Brazil. F.I.E. Importation disc. 1988, now imported by K.B.I.

	$90	$75	$70	$65	$60	$55	$50

Last Mfg.'s Sug. Retail was $100.

Grading	100%	98%	95%	90%	80%	70%	60%

PARA RIFLE — .22 LR, paramilitary designed rifle with case, takedown, 11 shot, matte black receiver finish. Mfg. by L. Franchi between 1979-1984. Imported into the U.S. from 1985-88.

	100%	98%	95%	90%	80%	70%	60%
	$225	$195	$155	$140	$130	$120	$110

8,000 of this model were manufactured by L. Franchi. 5,000 went to the Italian Government and were used as training rifles (with German scopes). The remainder has been imported by F.I.E. (without scopes).
Last Mfg.'s Sug. Retail was $225.

SPECTRE CARBINE — 9mm Para., same action as Spectre pistol, paramilitary design carbine, collapsible metal butt stock, 30 or 50 (opt.) shot mag., adj. rear sight, with pistol and forearm grip. New 1989.

	100%	98%	95%	90%	80%	70%	60%
	$450	$395	$340	$295	$260	$230	$200

Last Mfg.'s Sug. Retail was $700.

RIFLES: BOLT-ACTION

MODEL 122 — .22 LR, 6 or 10 shot clip mag., 21 in. tapered barrel, Monte Carlo walnut stock, adj. sights. Mfg. by Hamilton & Hunter. New 1986.

	100%	98%	95%	90%	80%	70%	60%
	$100	$80	$70	$60	$55	$50	$45

Last Mfg.'s Sug. Retail was $115.

MODEL 322 — .22 LR, competition model, 26.2 in. floating barrel, adj. trigger, 6 or 10 shot mag., stippled pistol grip, 7 lbs. New 1990.

	100%	98%	95%	90%	80%	70%	60%
	$580	$425	$380	$340	$295	$260	$230

Last Mfg.'s Sug. Retail was $665.

MODEL 422 — similar to Model 322 except has heavy barrel, 9 lbs. New 1990.

	100%	98%	95%	90%	80%	70%	60%
	$580	$425	$380	$340	$295	$260	$230

Last Mfg.'s Sug. Retail was $665.

SHOTGUNS

All Franchi shotguns can be located in the Franchi section of this text.

S.O.B. — 12, 20, or .410 ga., 18½ in. single barrel, pistol grip only. Disc. 1984.

	100%	98%	95%	90%	80%	70%	60%
	$100	$90	$80	$70	$60	$55	$50

COMPETITOR SEMI-AUTO — 12 or 20 ga., gas operated semi-auto, various barrel lengths with screw-in chokes standard. Mfg. in the U.S. New 1990.
Pricing on this model was not available before publication release.

THE STURDY O/U — 12 or 20 ga., 3 in. chambers, 28 in. barrels, vent. rib and barrels, engraved silver finish receiver, double triggers, extractors, manufactured by Maroccini of Italy. Imported 1985-1988.

	100%	98%	95%	90%	80%	70%	60%
	$300	$275	$250	$235	$220	$205	$190

Last Mfg.'s Sug. Retail was $350.

Sturdy Deluxe Priti — similar to The Sturdy model except has deluxe walnut. Importation disc. 1988.

	100%	98%	95%	90%	80%	70%	60%
	$325	$290	$260	$240	$225	$205	$195

Add $70 for ejectors, SST, and choke tubes.
Last Mfg.'s Sug. Retail was $380.

Grading	100%	98%	95%	90%	80%	70%	60%

⚹ Model 12 Deluxe — 12 ga. only, SST, auto ejectors, multi-choked barrels, select walnut. Imported 1988 only.

	100%	98%	95%	90%	80%	70%	60%
	$320	$290	$260	$240	$225	$205	$195

Last Mfg.'s Sug. Retail was $380.

THE BRUTE — 12, 20, or .410 ga., 19 in. barrels, 30 in. overall length. Side-by-side action, disc. 1984.

	100%	98%	95%	90%	80%	70%	60%
	$195	$150	$140	$120	$110	$100	$90

SPAS-12 — this model appears under the Franchi heading in the F section.

SAS-12 — this model appears under the Franchi heading in the F section.

LAW-12 — this model appears under the Franchi heading in the F section.

FABARM

Manufacturer located in Brescia, Italy. Previously imported and distributed (1988-90) by St. Lawrence Sales, Inc. located in Lake Orion, MI. Previously imported until 1986 by Beeman Precision Arms, Inc. located in Santa Rosa, CA.

The information below represents the last published retail values afforded this publication (1990). Fabarm guns have had almost no recent importation since 1990.

SHOTGUNS: DISC. O/U

The Field Model and Skeet/Trap Combination Set listed below were previously imported by Beeman Precision Arms, Inc.

FIELD MODEL — 12 ga. only, 29⅛ in. barrels, VR, single trigger ejectors, silver finished receiver, also available in Skeet and Trap models. Disc. 1985.

	100%	98%	95%	90%	80%	70%	60%
	$695	$595	$550	$500	$460	$420	$390

Last Mfg.'s Sug. Retail was $795.

SKEET/TRAP COMBINATION SET — 12 ga. only, is supplied with both skeet and trap barrel assemblies, cased. Disc. 1986.

	100%	98%	95%	90%	80%	70%	60%
	$1,050	$900	$840	$780	$720	$670	$600

Last Mfg.'s Sug. Retail was $1,195.

Models below have boxlock actions with coin finished receivers and light engraving. A high gloss wood finish is also available at $39 extra, and auto safety is an additional $30.

GAMMA SPORTING COMPETITION — 12 ga. only, designed for sporting clays competition, SST, 29 in. VR, (10mm) and barrels supplied with 5 innerchokes, special recoil pad, ejectors, checkered walnut stock and forearm. Importation began 1989.

	100%	98%	95%	90%	80%	70%	60%
Mfg.'s Sug. Retail $961	$850	$775	$725	$650	$575	$495	$400

Add $17 for stock and forend trap (includes 28 in. barrels with 5 choke tubes).

GAMMA SKEET — 12 ga. only, 27½ in. VR barrels, SST, ejectors, supplied with 5 innerchokes, special recoil pad, checkered walnut stock and forearm. Importation began 1989.

	100%	98%	95%	90%	80%	70%	60%
Mfg.'s Sug. Retail $921	$825	$750	$700	$635	$550	$450	$375

GAMMA TRAP — 12 ga. only, 29 in. VR barrels with special trap chokes, SST, ejectors, checkered Monte Carlo stock and forearm, 7½ lbs. Importation began 1989.

	100%	98%	95%	90%	80%	70%	60%
Mfg.'s Sug. Retail $921	$825	$700	$650	$600	$525	$425	$350

EURALFA TRAP — 12 ga. only, 3 in. chambers, 30 in. barrels bored IM/F. New 1990.

	100%	98%	95%	90%	80%	70%	60%
Mfg.'s Sug. Retail $636	$550	$495	$460	$430	$400	$360	$320

Grading	100%	98%	95%	90%	80%	70%	60%

SHOTGUNS: SPORTING O/U

Models below have boxlock actions with coin finished receivers and light engraving.

GAMMA FIELD — 12 or 20 ga., SST, ejectors, 26, 28, or 29 in. VR barrels (fixed chokes), checkered walnut stock and forearm, 6½ lbs. Importation began 1989.

Mfg.'s Sug. Retail	$913	$840	$695	$625	$550	$475	$400	$325

Add $40 for 5 innerchokes with wrench (3 in. chambers in 12 ga.).
Add $48 for 20 ga. (3 in. chambers).

⚞ **Gamma AL Superlight** — 12 ga. only, similar to Gamma Field except receiver is made from Ergal light alloy, 6 lbs. Importation began 1989.

Mfg.'s Sug. Retail	$970	$875	$760	$695	$625	$550	$450	$375

Add $41 for 5 innerchokes with wrench.
Add $66 for 20 ga. with 3 in. chambers. New 1990.
This model is chambered for 2¾ in. shells only.

GAMMA PARADOX — 12 ga. only, 25 in. VR barrels with top barrel rifled and lower barrel supplied with 3 innerchokes, SST, ejectors, checkered walnut stock and forearm, 6 lbs. 6 oz. Importation began 1989.

Mfg.'s Sug. Retail	$945	$850	$750	$695	$625	$550	$450	$375

⚞ **Gamma Paradox AL Superlight** — similar to Gamma Paradox except receiver is made from Ergal light alloy, 5 lbs. 7 oz. Importation began 1989.

Mfg.'s Sug. Retail	$960	$875	$760	$695	$625	$550	$450	$375

EURALFA — 12 ga., 2¾ in. chambers, 26 or 28 in. VR barrels with fixed chokes, DT or SNT, extractors, blued receiver with photo engraving, 6½ lbs. Importation began 1989.

Mfg.'s Sug. Retail	$571	$495	$460	$420	$390	$350	$310	$275

⚞ **Euralfa AL Superlight** — 12 ga., similar to Euralfa except receiver is made from Ergal light alloy, 6 lbs. Importation began 1989.

Mfg.'s Sug. Retail	$603	$515	$475	$430	$400	$360	$320	$285

⚞ **Euralfa Magnum** — 12 ga., 3 in. chambers, 26, 28, or 29 in. VR (10mm wide) barrels with fixed chokes, rubber recoil pad. Importation began 1989.

Mfg.'s Sug. Retail	$587	$515	$475	$430	$400	$360	$320	$285

⚞ **Euralfa Innerchoke** — 12 ga. only, 3 in. chambers, 28 in. barrels. New 1990.

Mfg.'s Sug. Retail	$652	$560	$500	$460	$430	$400	$360	$320

⚞ **Euralfa Slug** — 12 ga. only, 24 in. barrels bored cyl./cyl. New 1990.

Mfg.'s Sug. Retail	$571	$500	$475	$430	$400	$360	$320	$285

EURALFA PARADOX — 12 ga. only, similar to Euralfa except 25 in. VR barrels with top barrel rifled and lower barrel supplied with 3 innerchokes, 6 lbs. 6 oz. Importation began 1989.

Mfg.'s Sug. Retail	$636	$550	$495	$460	$430	$400	$360	$320

⚞ **Euralfa Paradox AL Superlight** — similar to Euralfa Paradox except receiver is made from Ergal light alloy, 5 lbs. 7 oz. Importation began 1989.

Mfg.'s Sug. Retail	$636	$550	$495	$460	$430	$400	$360	$320

SHOTGUNS: SEMI-AUTO

The models listed below are gas operated self compensating, have 4 shot mag.'s, aluminum receivers, twin action bars, blued receiver with photo etched game scene engraving, and checkered walnut stock and forearm. Add $25 for De Luxe engraving or camouflage wood finish.

Grading	100%	98%	95%	90%	80%	70%	60%

ELLEGI STANDARD — 12 ga. only, 28 in. VR barrel with fixed choke, blued receiver, gold trigger, 6 lbs. 9 oz. Importation began 1989.

Mfg.'s Sug. Retail	$619	$525	$450	$375	$325	$300	$275	$250

⅜ **Ellegi Multichoke** — similar to Ellegi Standard except 5 different choke tubes extend length of barrel up to 6 in., average weight is 6 lbs. 9 oz. Importation began 1989.

Mfg.'s Sug. Retail	$644	$540	$475	$395	$350	$325	$300	$265

The standard barrel length on this model is 24½ in. (30½ in. with full extra-long choke tube).

⅜ **Ellegi Innerchoke** — 12 ga. only, 3 in. chamber, 28 in. VR barrel with 5 innerchokes supplied, 7 lbs. Importation began 1989.

Mfg.'s Sug. Retail	$644	$540	$475	$395	$350	$325	$300	$265

⅜ **Ellegi Magnum** — 12 ga. only, 3 in. chamber, 30 in. VR barrel with fixed choke, recoil pad, 7¼ lbs. Importation began 1989.

Mfg.'s Sug. Retail	$619	$525	$450	$375	$325	$300	$275	$250

⅜ **Ellegi Super Goose** — 12 ga. only, 3 in. chamber, 35½ in. VR (12mm wide) barrel with fixed choke, adj. rifle rear sight, supplied with rail for mounting scope rings, rubber recoil pad, designed especially for long range shooting, 7½ lbs. Importation began 1989.

Mfg.'s Sug. Retail	$734	$625	$495	$425	$375	$340	$315	$280

⅜ **Ellegi Slug** — 12 ga. only, 24½ in. barrel, adj. rear sight and bead front, 6 lbs. 9 oz. Importation began 1989.

Mfg.'s Sug. Retail	$652	$545	$475	$395	$350	$325	$300	$265

Add $200 for combo set (includes innerchoked 28 in. barrel).

⅜ **Ellegi Police** — 12 ga. only, 20 in. cylinder bored barrel, matte black receiver, non-glare stock and forearm. Importation began 1989.

Mfg.'s Sug. Retail	$587	$495	$425	$360	$300	$275	$250	$225

SHOTGUNS: SIDE X SIDE

The models listed below have boxlock actions with added sideplates.

BETA MODEL — 12 ga. only, 2¾ in. chambers, standard model with checkered walnut stock and forearm, ST, ejectors. Imported 1989 only.

	$695	$625	$550	$450	$375	$300	$250

Last Mfg.'s Sug. Retail was $920.
This model was replaced by the Beta Lux in 1990.

BETA LUX — 12 ga. only, 3 in. chambers, 28 in. barrels bored F/M, 6.6 lbs. New 1990.

Mfg.'s Sug. Retail	$913	$840	$695	$625	$550	$475	$400	$325

Add $114 for competition trap/pigeon model.

BETA EUROPE — 12 ga. only, deluxe model with coin finished game scene engraved sideplates, 26½ or 27½ in. barrels with fixed chokes, ejectors, DT or SST, checkered English stock and splinter forearm, 6 lbs. 6 oz. Importation began 1989.

Mfg.'s Sug. Retail	$1,711	$1,400	$1,100	$850	$700	$575	$495	$450

Add $33 for semi-beavertail forend.
Add $130 for competition trap/pigeon model.

Grading	100%	98%	95%	90%	80%	70%	60%

SHOTGUNS: SLIDE ACTION

The models listed below are variations of the same action based on a twin bar slide system, alloy receiver with anti-glare finish (including barrel), rear trigger guard safety, and 2¾ or 3 in. shell interchangeability.

Add $25 for camouflage wood finish on the models listed below.

MODEL S.D.A.S.S. — 12 ga. only, 3 in. chamber, originally designed for police and self defense use, 8 shot tube mag., 20 or 24½ in. barrel threaded for external choke tubes, approx. 6 lbs. 6 oz. Importation began 1989.

Mfg.'s Sug. Retail	$415	$325	$285	$260	$230	$195	$160	$140

This model with 24½ in. barrel is threaded for external multi-chokes which can add up to 6 in. to the barrel length - available for a $17 extra charge.

⚡ **Special Police** — similar to Model S.D.A.S.S. except has special heavy 20 in. cylinder bored barrel VR, cooling jacket, 6 shot mag., rubber recoil pad. Importation began 1989.

Mfg.'s Sug. Retail	$440	$340	$295	$265	$230	$195	$160	$140

⚡ **Martial** — 12 ga. only, 18, 20, 28, 30, or 35½ (disc. 1989) in. barrel, fixed sights and choke, approx. 6¼ lbs. Importation began 1989.

Mfg.'s Sug. Retail	$424	$330	$290	$260	$225	$190	$160	$140

Add $41 for VR.
Add $20 for 35½ (disc. 1989) in. barrel.
Add $33 for multi-choke (plain rib with 1 choke and wrench).
Add $65 for innerchoke (includes 1 choke and wrench - VR barrel only).

SHOTGUNS: SINGLE BARREL

The models listed below have receivers made out of aluminum alloy, rear trigger guard safety, and matte black finish metal surfaces.

OMEGA STANDARD — 12, 20, or .410 ga., 3 in. chamber, 26 or 28 (12 ga. only) in. barrel, checkered beech stock and forearm, approx. 5 lbs. 5 oz. Importation began 1989.

Mfg.'s Sug. Retail	$139	$120	$95	$80	$70	$60	$55	$50

⚡ **Goose Gun** — similar to Omega Standard except is 12 ga. only with a 35½ in. barrel, 6 lbs. Importation began 1989.

Mfg.'s Sug. Retail	$156	$135	$115	$90	$80	$70	$60	$55

FABBRI, ARMI

Manufacturer located in Gardone V.T., Italy. No current importer - the factory should be contacted directly (see Trademark Index) for more information regarding current information and prices on the models listed below.

SIDE BY SIDE SHOTGUN — 12 or 20 ga., one of the world's best current production guns, highest-quality sidelock, ejectors, full engraving.

O/U SHOTGUN — 12 or 20 ga., top-of-the-line quality with any combination of engraving, wood, and other options.

FABRIQUE NATIONALE

Manufacturer located in Herstal and Liege, Belgium. Established a contract with John M. Browning in 1902 for exclusive manufacture of various Browning Patent Firearms. In 1992, FN was acquired by GIAT of France.

Also See: Browning Arms under Rifles, Shotguns, and Pistols.

Grading	100%	98%	95%	90%	80%	70%	60%

PISTOLS: SEMI-AUTO

For FN models 1900, 1903, 1905, 1910, 1922 (10/22), Baby Model, and the Model 10/71, please refer to the Browning Pistol section in this text.

PISTOLS: HI-POWERS

The F.N. Hi-Power (also known as P-35) was Browning's last pistol design. A single action semi-auto 9mm pistol, it was the first to incorporate a staggered high capacity magazine. It has a $4^{21}/_{32}$ in. barrel, 13 shot mag., hammer and mag. safeties, a wide variety of finishes and sight options. It's probably the most widely used military pistol in the world.

PRE-WAR COMMERCIAL HP — semi-auto pistol, 9mm, blue, wood grips, fixed or tangent rear sight, 13 shot mag., slotted for stock.

	100%	98%	95%	90%	80%	70%	60%
Fixed sight	$650	$575	$500	$450	$400	$350	$300
Tangent sight	$1,000	$850	$750	$600	$500	$400	$375

Add $300 for wooden holster stock.

PRE-WAR MILITARY CONTRACT — mfg. under military contract for various European countries.

	100%	98%	95%	90%	80%	70%	60%
Lithuanian Crest	$1,300	$1,175	$950	$750	$600	$450	$375
Latvian Contract	$1,550	$1,325	$1,150	$950	$800	$550	$400
Estonian Contract	$1,200	$1,000	$850	$700	$600	$500	$400

Since so many variations have been manufactured for military contract, the listing above represents a few of the more interesting (and collectable) models.

WWII Production: Waffenamt Proofed

There is a range of finishes during Nazi production that varies from the excellent pre-war commercial finish on early guns assembled from captured parts to the roughly milled, poorly finished specimens mfg. late in the war. Values below assume all major parts (slide, barrel, and frame) are matching.

In recent years, many Nazi production Hi-Powers have had the rear grip strap milled out and slotted to accept a shoulder stock. Careful observation is advised before purchasing a "rare" (and expensive) slotted and tangent sight specimen.

Type I: Tangent sights — slotted — assembled from existing pre-war Belgian army parts, quality is excellent, correct ser. range is quite limited, approx. 48,000-52,000. All are proofed WaA 613.

100%	98%	95%	90%	80%	70%	60%
$1,750	$1,450	$1,200	$1,000	$800	$600	$500

Type II — tangent rear sight only, approx. 50,000 mfg. with generally good quality finish.

100%	98%	95%	90%	80%	70%	60%
$1,000	$800	$620	$475	$450	$400	$325

Type III Standard Fixed Sights

100%	98%	95%	90%	80%	70%	60%
$490	$445	$410	$350	$310	$275	$240

POST-WAR COMMERCIAL CONTRACT — not manufactured until 1950, first imported with BAC markings in 1954 (see Browning HP section).

Add $50 if round hammer.

Tangent sight only

100%	98%	95%	90%	80%	70%	60%
$725	$670	$645	$590	$535	$425	$350

Tangent sight — slotted for stock.

100%	98%	95%	90%	80%	70%	60%
$1,200	$950	$835	$780	$725	$500	$450

Fixed sight — ring hammer.

100%	98%	95%	90%	80%	70%	60%
$450	$400	$375	$350	$325	$300	$275

Add $50 for pre-1970 models with round hammer.

Grading	100%	98%	95%	90%	80%	70%	60%

POST-WAR MILITARY CONTRACT — mfg. from 1946-present, early models are identifiable by an "A" serial number prefix and are not fitted with a magazine safety. In 1947 the rear slide bushing became hardened by a new heat treatment process. Other design modifications were added in 1950 making post 1950 barrels not interchangeable with earlier frames. Many thousands manufactured under various government contracts.

⁂ Tangent sight and slotted

	$1,200	$950	$890	$725	$650	$600	$525

⁂ Tangent sight only

	$780	$725	$670	$550	$525	$500	$475

⁂ Fixed sight

	$550	$450	$425	$325	$300	$275	$250

MUSCAT AND OMAN CONTRACT

⁂ First Model — 9 guns.

	$4,500	$2,750	$1,495

⁂ Second Model — 27 guns.

	$3,000	$1,700	$995

INGLIS MANUFACTURED HI-POWERS — SEE INGLIS SECTION.

RIFLES

MODEL 1949 — semi-auto, 7mm, 7.65mm, 7.92mm, or .30-06 cal., gas operated 10 shot mag., 23 in. barrel, military rifle, tangent rear sight, military stock. Mfg. 160,000.

	$425	$350	$275	$250	$225	$185	$155

Add 10% for .30-06 cal.
Add 100% for sniper variation.

FN SNIPER RIFLE (MODEL 30 - BOLT ACTION) — .308 cal., this model was a Mauser actioned Sniper Rifle equipped with 20 in. extra heavy barrel, flash hider, diopter sights, Hensoldt 4X scope, hard case, bipod, and sling. 51 were imported into the U.S. with the last retail price (1988) being $2,950. When encountered today, values will range from $3,500 and higher (depending on condition).

RIFLES: FAL/LAR/FNC SERIES

After tremendous price increases between 1985-1988, Fabrique Nationale decided in 1988 to discontinue this series completely. Not only are these rifles not exported to the U.S. any longer, but all production has ceased in Belgium as well. The only way FN will produce these models again is if they are given a large military contract - in which case a "side-order" of commercial guns may be built. 1989 Federal legislation regarding this type of paramilitary design also helped push up prices to their current level. FAL rifles were also mfg. in Israel by I.M.I.

F.N. FAL — semi-auto, French designation for the FN L.A.R. (light automatic rifle), otherwise similar to LAR. See values for LAR model listed below.

F.N. L.A.R. COMPETITION (LIGHT AUTOMATIC RIFLE) — .308 Win. (7.62 x 51), semi-auto, competition rifle with match flash hider, 21 in. barrel, adj. 4 position fire selector on automatic models, wood stock, aperture rear sight adj. from 100-600 meters, 9.4 lbs. Mfg. 1981-83.

	$2,000	$1,750	$1,600	$1,450	$1,300	$1,175	$1,000

This model was designated by the factory as the 50.00 Model.
Mid-1987 retail on this model was $1,258. The last Mfg.'s Sug. Retail was $3,179 (this price reflected the last exchange rate and special order status of this model).

Grading	100%	98%	95%	90%	80%	70%	60%

Heavy barrel rifle — barrel is twice as heavy as standard LAR, includes wood or synthetic stock, short wood forearm, and bi-pod, 12.2 lbs. Importation disc. 1988.

	100%	98%	95%	90%	80%	70%	60%
	$2,500	$2,150	$1,850	$1,500	$1,350	$1,200	$1,050

Add $400 for walnut stock.

There were 2 variations of this model. The Model 50.41 had a synthetic butt stock while the Model 50.42 had a wood butt stock with steel butt plate incorporating a top extension used for either shoulder resting or inverted grenade launching.

Mid-1987 retail on this model was $1,497 (Model 50.41) or $1,654 (Model 50.42). The last Mfg.'s Sug. Retail was $3,776 (this price reflected the last exchange rate and special order status of this model).

Paratrooper rifle — similar to LAR model, except has folding stock, 8.3 lbs. Mfg. 1950-1988.

	100%	98%	95%	90%	80%	70%	60%
	$1,200	$1,000	$850	$750	$650	$575	$500

There were 2 variations of the Paratrooper LAR Model. The Model 50.63 had a stationary aperture rear sight and 18 in. barrel. The Model 50.64 was supplied with a 21 in. barrel and had a rear sight calibrated for either 150 or 200 meters. Both models retailed for the same price.

Mid-1987 retail on this model was $1,310 (both the Model 50.63 and 50.64). The last Mfg.'s Sug. Retail was $3,239 (this price reflected the last exchange rate and special order status of this model).

FNC MODEL — .223 Rem. (5.56mm), lightweight combat carbine, 18½ in. barrel, NATO approved, 30 shot mag., 8.4 lbs. Disc. 1987.

	100%	98%	95%	90%	80%	70%	60%
	$1,100	$975	$825	$725	$625	$550	$500

Add $50 for Paratrooper model (16 or 18½ in. barrel).

While rarer, the 16 in. barrel model incorporated a flash hider that did not perform as well as the flash hider used on the standard 18½ in. barrel.

Mid-1987 retail on this model was $749 (Standard Model) and $782 (Paratrooper Model). The last Mfg.'s Sug. Retail was $2,204 (Standard Model) and $2,322 (Paratrooper Model) - these prices reflected the last exchange rate and special order status of these models.

F.N. MAUSER SPORTER DELUXE — available in popular American and European calibers, 24 in. barrel, adj. sight, checkered pistol grip stock. Mfg. 1947-1963.

	100%	98%	95%	90%	80%	70%	60%
	$650	$550	$495	$460	$300	$275	$250

F.N. PRESENTATION GRADE — similar to Deluxe, except engraved and select wood.

	100%	98%	95%	90%	80%	70%	60%
	$1,150	$935	$855	$770	$500	$475	$450

F.N. SUPREME BOLT ACTION — .243, .270, 7mm, .308, or .30-06, 24 in. barrel, peep sight, checkered pistol grip stock. Mfg. 1957-1975.

	100%	98%	95%	90%	80%	70%	60%
	$650	$550	$495	$460	$300	$275	$250

F.N. SUPREME MAGNUM — similar to Bolt Action, .264 Mag., 7mm Mag., or .300 Win. Mag.

	100%	98%	95%	90%	80%	70%	60%
	$675	$575	$540	$495	$325	$275	$250

FALCON FIREARMS

Previous manufacturer located in Northridge, CA from 1986-90.

PORTSIDER — .45 ACP, patterned after Colt M 1911 A-1, stainless steel, fixed sights, 5 in. barrel, 7 shot mag., available in left-hand only. Mfg. 1986-90.

	100%	98%	95%
	$500	$425	$375

Last Mfg.'s Sug. Retail was $580.

Grading		100%	98%	95%	90%	80%	70%	60%

Portsider Set — features right and left hand models with matching serial numbers. Only 100 sets mfg. 1986-1987.

		$1,300	$1,100	$895				

Last Mfg.'s Sug. Retail was $1,400.

GOLD FALCON — .45 ACP, machined receiver made from solid 17 Kt gold alloy, stainless steel slide, diamond sighting system, choice of grips, standard or personalized engraving options. Only 50 mfg.

		$25,000	$17,500	$11,500				

Last Mfg.'s Sug. Retail was $30,500.

FAMARS, ABBIATICO & SALVINELLI
Please refer to the Abbiatico & Salvinelli listing in this text.

FAUSTI, STEFANO
Manufacturer located in Marcheno, Italy.

S. Fausti manufactures shotguns in O/U, SxS, and single shot configurations. To date there has been little importation, but American Arms is private labeling a .410 and 10 gauge O/U (please refer to American Arms section in this text).

FEATHER INDUSTRIES, INC.
Manufacturer located in Boulder, CO.

DERRINGERS

GUARDIAN ANGEL 9mm/.38 Spl. — 9mm Para., O/U design, stainless steel, double action backup derringer. Mfg. 1988-1989 only.

		$130		$95	$75			

Last Mfg.'s Sug. Retail was $140.
This model has interchangeable loading blocks that allow shooting 9mm Para. or .38 Spl. There is no exposed hammer and trigger is totally enclosed.

GUARDIAN ANGEL .22 LR/.22 MAG. — .22 LR or .22 Mag., design is similar to 9mm/.38 Spl. model, 2 in. barrel, fixed sights, 12 oz. New in 1990.

Mfg.'s Sug. Retail		$120		$90	$75	$60		

Add $30 for individual extra loading blocks.
This model has interchangeable loading blocks that allow shooting .22LR or .22 Mag. There is no exposed hammer and the trigger is totally enclosed.

PISTOLS

MINI-AT — .22 LR, pistol variation of the AT-22, $5\frac{1}{2}$ in. shrouded barrel, 20 shot mag., approx. 2 lbs. Mfg. 1986-1989.

		$195	$165	$145	$135	$130	$125	$115

Last Mfg.'s Sug. Retail was $220.

RIFLES

AT-22 — .22 LR, semi-auto blowback action, 17 in. detachable shrouded barrel, collapsible metal stock, adj. rear sight, with sling and swivels, 20 shot mag., $3\frac{1}{4}$ lbs. New 1986.

Mfg.'s Sug. Retail		$250	$225	$175	$155	$145	$135	$125	$115

F2 — similar to AT-22, except is equipped with a fixed polymer buttstock. New in 1992.

Mfg.'s Sug. Retail		$280	$245	$190	$165	$150	$135	$125	$115

Grading	100%	98%	95%	90%	80%	70%	60%

AT-9 — 9mm Para., semi-auto blowback action, 16 in. barrel, paramilitary design, available with either 32 or 100 (optional) mag., 5 lbs. New 1988.

Mfg.'s Sug. Retail	$500	$440	$375	$310	$280	$260	$240	$200

Add $80 for 100 round drum mag (disc. 1989).

F9 — similar to AT-9, except is equipped with a fixed polymer buttstock. New in 1992.

Mfg.'s Sug. Retail	$535	$465	$385	$325	$285	$260	$240	$200

SATURN 30 — 7.62 x 39mm Kalashnikov cal., semi-auto, gas operated, 19½ in. barrel, composite stock with large thumbhole pistol grip, 5 shot detachable mag., drilled and tapped for scope mounts, adj. rear sight, 8½ lbs. Mfg. in 1990 only.

$625	$525	$450	$375	$325	$280	$260

Last Mfg.'s Sug. Retail was $695.

KG-9 — 9mm Para., semi-auto blowback action, 25 or 50 shot mag., assault configuration. Mfg. 1989 only.

$495	$425	$375	$325	$275	$240	$200

Last Mfg.'s Sug. Retail was $560.

SAR-180 — .22 LR, semi-auto blowback action, 17½ in. barrel, 165 shot drum mag., fully adj. rear sight, walnut stock with combat style pistol grip and forend, 6¼ lbs. Mfg. 1989 only.

$450	$395	$350	$295	$260	$240	$200

Add $105 for retractable stock.
Add $395 for laser sight.
Last Mfg.'s Sug. Retail was $500.

KG-22 — .22 LR, similar to KG-9 except is .22 LR and has 20 shot mag. Mfg. 1989 only.

$295	$250	$200	$175	$155	$145	$135

Last Mfg.'s Sug. Retail was $300.

FEDERAL ENGINEERING CORPORATION

Previous manufacturer located in Chicago, IL.

Values below represent changes due to 1989 Federal legislation regarding this paramilitary configuration of firearm. Mfg. of these models has been disc.

XC-220 — .22 LR semi-auto paramilitary design rifle, 16⁵⁄₁₆ in. barrel length, 28 shot mag., machined steel action, 7½ lbs. New 1984.

$395	$350	$300	$275	$250	$230	$210

XC-450 — .45 ACP only, semi-auto paramilitary design carbine, 16½ in. barrel length, 30 shot mag., fires from closed bolt, machined steel action, 8½ lbs. New 1984.

$950	$825	$750	$675	$600	$550	$500

XC-900 — 9mm only, semi-auto paramilitary design carbine, 16½ in. barrel length, 32 shot mag., fires from closed bolt, machine steel action, 8 lbs. New 1984.

$950	$825	$750	$675	$600	$550	$500

FEDERAL ORDNANCE, INC.

Previous manufacturer/importer/distributor located in South El Monte, CA from 1966-1992. Brickley Trading Co. bought the remaining assets of Federal Ordnance, Inc. in late 1992, and are resuming business using the old Federal Ordnance location.

Federal Ordnance imported and distributed both foreign and domestic military handguns and rifles until 1992. In addition, they also fabricated firearms using mostly newer parts. Listed below are those models which were recently manufactured or remanufactured.

In addition to the models listed below, Fed. Ord. also distributed used M-1 Carbines, AK-47s, SKSs, Finnish 39s, Lee Enfields, Baby Carbines, P-14s, M-1 Garands, Hakims, Mauser 98s, and other rifles. Most of these, if they are in good to excellent overall condition, typically sell in the $165-$400 range (except the M-1 Garand), depending on the model and quality.

CARBINES

Grading	100%	98%	95%	90%	80%	70%	60%

MODEL 713 DELUXE MAUSER CARBINE — 7.63 Mauser or 9mm Para. cal. 16 in. barrel, detachable stock, one 10 shot and one 20 shot detachable mag., deluxe walnut, leather case with accessories, adj. sights to 1,000 meters, 5 lbs. 1,500 mfg. 1986-92.

	100%	98%	95%	90%	80%	70%	60%
	$1,775	$1,450	$1,050				

Last Mfg.'s Sug. Retail was $1,986.

Field Grade Mauser Carbine — 7.63 Mauser or 9mm Para. (new 1989) cal., 16 in. barrel, 10 shot fixed mag., nondetachable walnut stock. Mfg. 1987-92.

	100%	98%	95%	90%	80%	70%	60%
	$995	$795	$695	$595	$500	$450	$400

Last Mfg.'s Sug. Retail was $1,200.

PISTOLS

In addition to the Broomhandle models listed below, Federal Ordnance also manufactured other special editions. These models include the British Model, Cut-Away, Cartridge Counter, Para La Guerra, and others. Prices are in the $800-$950 price range (retail).

MODEL 714 BROOMHANDLE — 7.63 Mauser or 9mm Para. cal., 5½ in. barrel, new frame, exterior completely refinished, 10 shot detachable mag., "fair" bore, adj. rear sight. Mfg. 1986-1991.

	100%	98%	95%	90%	80%	70%	60%
	$750	$595	$500	$440	$400	$375	$350

Add $100 for new barrel.
Last Mfg.'s Sug. Retail was $820.

Model 714 Para La Guerra — 7.63 Mauser or 9mm Para., remanufactured to duplicate Spanish Civil War configuration Broomhandle, includes 10 in. barrel with "Para La Guerra" engraved on side. Mfg. 1990-91 only.

	100%	98%	95%	90%	80%	70%	60%
	$775	$625	$525	$450	$400	$375	$350

Last Mfg.'s Sug. Retail was $890.

Model 714 Bolo — similar to Model 714 Broomhandle, except has smaller grips, 3.9 in. barrel, 10 shot mag. standard. Mfg. 1988 only.

	100%	98%	95%	90%	80%	70%	60%
	$775	$600	$500	$440	$400	$375	$350

Last Mfg.'s Sug. Retail was $890.

STANDARD BROOMHANDLE — 7.63 Mauser or 9mm Para. cal., refurbished (new barrels, completely refinished, etc.) C-96 pistols, replaced springs, includes original Chinese shoulder/holster stock. Disc. 1991.

	100%	98%	95%	90%	80%	70%	60%
	$625	$500	$460	$430	$400	$375	$350

Subtract $195 without shoulder/holster stock.
Last Mfg.'s Sug. Retail was $735.

Grading	100%	98%	95%	90%	80%	70%	60%

⚡ **Standard Bolo** — similar to Standard Broomhandle, except Bolo configuration (3.9 in. barrel and smaller grips). Mfg. 1990-91 only.

	$480	$385	$350	$310	$280	$260	$240

Last Mfg.'s Sug. Retail was $530.

RANGER 1911A1 GI — .45 ACP, 5 in. barrel, 7 shot mag., steel construction throughout, checkered walnut grips, 40 oz. Mfg. 1988-92.

	$385	$350	$310	$280	$260	$240	$200

Add $20 for Ranger Extended Model (40 oz. - new 1990).
Add $40 for Ranger Ambo (ambidextrous safety, 40 oz. - new 1990).
Add $15 for lightweight Ranger Lite Model (32 oz. - new 1990).
These pistols are patterned after the Colt 1911A1 Govt. Model.
Last Mfg.'s Sug. Retail was $440.

⚡ **Ranger Ten** — 10mm cal., otherwise similar to regular Ranger 1911A1. Mfg. 1990-91 only.

	$675	$525	$475	$450	$420	$395	$370

Last Mfg.'s Sug. Retail was $780.

RANGER SUPERCOMP — .45 ACP or 10mm cal., compensated variation of the Ranger 1911A1 with 6 in. compensated barrel, slide, tuned trigger, and other competition features, 42 oz. Mfg. 1990-91 only.

	$1,250	$875	$775	$675	$600	$550	$495

Add $10 for 10mm cal.
Last Mfg.'s Sug. Retail was $1,390.

THE RANGER ALPHA — .38 Super, 10mm, or .45 ACP cal., 5 or 6 in. barrel, patterned after the Colt Govt. Model. Mfg. 1990-91 only.

	$895	$775	$675	$575	$475	$425	$380

Add $16 for 10mm cal.
Add $16 for 6 in. barrel.
Add $9-$25 for ported 5 or 6 in. barrel depending on cal.
Last Mfg.'s Sug. Retail was $1,000.

PETERS STAHL PS-07 — 10mm or .45 ACP cal., mfg. by Peters Stahl of W. Germany to exacting standards, 6 in. barrel with polygonal rifling, top-of-the-line competition model with compensated barrel and other advanced competition features, 45 oz. Mfg. 1990-91 only.

	$2,350	$1,800	$1,500	$1,200	$995	$825	$700

Add $51 for 10mm cal.
Last Mfg.'s Sug. Retail was $2,600.
This model was imported in very limited quantities.

RIFLES

ALL AMERICAN SPORTER — .30-06 cal., Springfield M1903 receiver, new sporter stock, drilled and tapped for scope base (included), blued finish. Mfg. late 1991-92.

	$165	$145	$120	$100	$90	$80	$75

M-14 S.A. — .308 cal., legal for private ownership (no selector), 20 shot mag., refinished original M-14 parts, available in either filled fiberglass, G.I. fiberglass, refinished wood, or new walnut stock. Mfg. 1986-91.

	$625	$550	$495	$450	$395	$335	$285

Add $50 for filled fiberglass stock.
Add $110 for refinished wood stock.
Add $190 for new walnut stock with handguard.
Last Mfg.'s Sug. Retail was $700.

Grading	100%	98%	95%	90%	80%	70%	60%

TANKER GARAND — .30-06 or .308 Win. cal., original U.S. GI parts, 18 in. barrel, new hardwood stock, parkerized finish. Mfg. began late 1991.

As this edition went to press, prices had yet to be formalized on this model.

CHINESE RPK 86S-7 — 7.62 X 39mm cal., semi-auto version of the P.R.C.-RPK light machine gun, 75 shot drum mag., 23¾ in. barrel, with bipod. Imported 1989 only.

	100%	98%	95%	90%	80%	70%	60%
	$1,000	$875	$725	$650	$575	$525	$475

Last Mfg.'s Sug. Retail was $500.

FEINWERKBAU

Manufacturer located in Oberndorf, West Germany. Currently imported exclusively by Beeman Precision Arms located in Santa Rosa, CA.

Feinwerkbau manufactures some of the world's finest quality target rifles and pistols (.22 LR rimfire and airgun).

Prices below reflect the recent devaluation of the U.S. dollar against some foreign currencies. While the manufacturer's suggested retails have gone up considerably, prices for used specimens (98% or less original condition) have not increased proportionately, and in some cases, have changed very little.

MODEL 2000 — .22 LR only, single shot, match target bolt action rifle, fully adj. trigger, walnut stocks, four variations featuring different specifications. Importation disc. 1988.

⚞ **Universal Model** — 26⅜ in. barrel, aperture sights, stippled pistol grip and forearm, 9¾ lbs.

	100%	98%	95%	90%	80%	70%	60%
	$1,150	$925	$850	$735	$650	$595	$550

Add $350 for electronic trigger.
Add $160 for left-hand variation.
Last Mfg.'s Sug. Retail was $1,395.

⚞ **Mini 2000 (Junior)** — 22 in. barrel, aperture sights, stippled pistol grip, 9⅛ lbs.

	100%	98%	95%	90%	80%	70%	60%
	$1,025	$875	$825	$700	$625	$575	$525

Add $350 for electronic trigger.
Add $150 for left-hand variation.
Last Mfg.'s Sug. Retail was $1,225.

⚞ **Match Model** — 26¼ in. barrel, adj. cheek piece on stock, stippled pistol grip and forearm, aperture sights.

	100%	98%	95%	90%	80%	70%	60%
	$1,075	$895	$825	$700	$625	$575	$525

Add $390 for electronic trigger.
Add $113 for left-hand variation.
Last Mfg.'s Sug. Retail was $1,285.

⚞ **Running Target** — adj. cheek piece on stock, thumbhole stippled pistol grip, no sights, for running boar competition.

	100%	98%	95%	90%	80%	70%	60%
	$1,150	$925	$850	$735	$650	$595	$550

Add $142 for left-hand variation.
Last Mfg.'s Sug. Retail was $1,398.

MODEL 2600 UNIVERSAL — .22 LR only, similar design to Model 600 air rifle, single shot, 26.3 in. barrel, aperture sights, 10.6 lbs. New 1986.

		100%	98%	95%	90%	80%	70%	60%
Mfg.'s Sug. Retail	$1,695	$1,425	$1,125	$925	$850	$735	$650	$595

Add $160 for left-hand variation.

MODEL 2600 ULTRA MATCH FREE RIFLE — .22 LR, single shot match gun based on Model 2600 action, 26.1 in. barrel, laminate stock with thumbhole, fully adj. aperture sights, 14 lbs. 1 oz. New 1986.

		100%	98%	95%	90%	80%	70%	60%
Mfg.'s Sug. Retail	$2,498	$2,175	$1,750	$1,400	$1,150	$925	$850	$735

Add $250 for electronic trigger (disc. 1988).
Add $152 for left-hand variation.

FEMARU

Previously manufactured by Femaru-Febyver-Es Gepgyar R.T. located in Budapest, Hungary.

Grading	100%	98%	95%	90%	80%	70%	60%

MODEL 1910 — 7.65mm Roth/Steyr cal., rare and only infrequently encountered.

	100%	98%	95%	90%	80%	70%	60%
	$1,750	$1,550	$1,350	$1,150	$975	$850	$725

MODEL 1937 — 7.65mm, 3.93 in. barrel, 8 shot mag., commercial blue finish, 2-piece walnut grips, Nazi marked jhv 41-jhv 44.

	$275	$240	$215	$190	$175	$160	$145

Add 35% for Waffenamt proofing.

FROMMER STOP POCKET AUTO — .32 ACP, .380 ACP, 6 or 7 shot, $3\frac{7}{8}$ in. barrel, fixed sights, blue, rubber grips, locked breech, outside hammer. Mfg. 1912-1920.

	$150	$135	$125	$110	$90	$75	$50

FROMMER BABY POCKET AUTO — similar to Stop Pocket Auto, except 2 in. barrel, 5 or 6 shot.

	$175	$165	$150	$135	$100	$85	$65

FROMMER LILIPUT AUTO — blowback action, .25 auto, 6 shot, 2.14 in. barrel, blue, hard rubber grips. Mfg. in early twenties.

	$225	$200	$175	$145	$115	$90	$75

FERLACH GUNS

Includes those firearms manufactured in Ferlach, Austria from 1558 to present. Currently imported and sold by Adler Arms located in Pittsburgh, PA (a complete Ferlach catalog is available for $10 - see Adler Arms listing in the Trademark Index).

Many people are confused that Ferlach is a trademark - it is not. Rather, it is a small village in Austria where a gun guild was started as early as 1558. At that time, it was absolutely necessary that all the people involved in fabricating a firearm were located together in close proximity. This enabled the barrel maker, the stock maker, and the lock mechanism maker to work together closely to ensure that everyone was performing their task(s) correctly, effectively and efficiently. As the individual skills became better and more refined, more and more firearms were manufactured. Eventually, individual gunsmiths began to put their name on the barrel or frame of those guns which they had either manufactured solely or with the help of their fellow Ferlach craftsmen. Since all Ferlach firearms are essentially hand made per individual special order, very few are exactly alike. In the past, the gunsmiths of Ferlach have produced almost every type of shoulder arm imaginable including such modern weapons as superposed and juxtaposed rifles and shotguns, hammerless drillings, repeating rifles, 3 barrel rifles, combination guns, 4 barrel rifles/shotguns/combination guns (called Vierlings), hammer guns of every type, etc. Some of these specimens represent the highest refinement in the gunmakers trade. Because of the almost unlimited variety of Ferlach variations, it is recommended that a COMPETENT appraisal is procured before buying or selling a specimen.

As is the case with many other European weapons, those models with desirable American features will generally outperform those with European specifications (i.e. a Ferlach sidelock combination gun that is 20 ga. x .243 Win. will be more valuable than a similar specimen chambered for 16 ga. x 5.6 by 50R mm with sling swivels). Original condition and overall beauty are the primary factors to consider when contemplating buying or selling a Ferlach longarm. Other considerations include: type of action, difficulty of fabrication (Vierlings are very complicated to construct), caliber/gauge desirability, notoriety of gunsmith on barrel legend, elaborateness of embellishments, condition, rarity, accessories, and any provenance a specimen might have.

Today's master gunsmiths of Ferlach carry on the old world tradition of quality in every respect. Most guns manufactured today are by individual special order with a wide range of calibers/gauges and other special features and options. As of this writing, these gunsmiths in alphabetical order are: *LUDWIG BOROVNIK, JOHANN FANZOJ, WILFRIED GLANZNIG, JOSEF HAMBRUSCH, KARL HAUPTMANN, GOTTFRIED JUCH, JOSEF JUST, JAKOB KOSCHAT, JOHANN MICHELITSCH, WALTER OUTSCHAR, HERBERT SCHEIRING, BENEDIKT WINKLER, AND JOSEF WINKLER.* Anyone wishing to contact these master gunmakers should either write to the guild or address them individually at: Ferlach, Waagplatz, 6, A-9170 Ferlach, AUSTRIA. Please allow at least 4-6 weeks for a response.

FERLIB

Manufacturer located in Gardone V.T., Italy. Distributed by Quality Arms located in Houston, TX, W.L. Moore & Company located in Westlake Village, CA, and New England Arms Co. located in Kittery Point, ME.

SHOTGUNS: SIDE-BY-SIDE

Models listed below are available in 10, 12, 16, 20, 24, 28, 32, or .410 ga. Also available for an additional charge are extra quality wood and upgraded engraving.

Add 10% for 24, 28, 32, or .410 ga.
Add $250 for single trigger.
Add $650 for leather case.

Grading	100%	98%	95%	90%	80%	70%	60%

HAMMER GUN — boxlock action, exposed hammers, deluxe checkered walnut stock and forearm, blued action. Disc. 1989.

	100%	98%	95%	90%	80%	70%	60%
	$4,250	$3,500	$3,175	$2,850	$2,350	$2,100	$1,800

Last Mfg.'s Sug. Retail was $4,500.

MODEL F.VI — 12, 16, 20, 28, or .410 ga., Anson & Deeley scalloped boxlock action, ejectors, double triggers, case hardened frame, select checkered stock and forearm. Disc. 1992.

	100%	98%	95%	90%	80%	70%	60%
	$2,950	$2,275	$1,975	$1,600	$1,250	$1,000	$750

Last Mfg.'s Sug. Retail was $3,250.

MODEL F.VII — 12, 16, 20, 28, or .410 ga., Anson & Deeley scalloped boxlock action, ejectors, double triggers, coin finish, full coverage English scroll or game scene engraving, select checkered stock and forearm.

Mfg.'s Sug. Retail	$7,500	$6,000	$5,250	$4,950	$4,275	$3,675	$3,000	$2,600

Add 10% for 28 or .410 ga.

MODEL F.VII/SC — 12, 16, 20, 28, or .410 ga., Anson & Deeley scalloped boxlock action, ejectors, double triggers, coin finish, game scene with scroll accent engraving with gold inlays, select checkered stock and forearm.

Mfg.'s Sug. Retail	$9,000	$7,200	$6,500	$5,700	$5,000	$4,350	$3,600	$3,000

Add 10% for 28 or .410 ga.

MODEL F.VII SIDEPLATE — 12, 16, 20, 28, or .410 ga., Anson & Deeley boxlock action with sideplates, ejectors, single trigger, coin finish, extensive game scene and scroll accent engraving, select checkered stock and forearm.

Mfg.'s Sug. Retail	$9,600	$7,700	$6,800	$6,000	$5,200	$4,450	$3,700	$3,100

Add 10% for 28 or .410 ga.

F.VII/SC Gold — similar to F.VII Sideplate, except with gold inlays.

Mfg.'s Sug. Retail	$13,000	$10,400	$9,250	$8,100	$7,275	$6,350	$5,300	$4,350

Add 10% for 28 or .410 ga.

Ferlib, cont.

F.V. SIDELOCK — various ga.'s, full sidelock action, special order to customer specifications. Values start in the $15,000 range and go up.

FIALA OUTFITTERS INCORPORATED
New York City, NY.

Grading	100%	98%	95%	90%	80%	70%	60%

FIALA REPEATING PISTOL — .22 LR, 10 shot, 3, 7½, or 20 in. barrels, blue, plain wood grips, resembles an auto loader, but is actually hand operated by moving the slide to eject, load and cock. Mfg. 1920-1923.

	100%	98%	95%	90%	80%	70%	60%
	$475	$400	$340	$280	$230	$200	$175

Add 50% for 3-barrel set.
Add $150 for original case.
Add $250 for stock.
Add $300 for canvas holster stock.

FIAS
Manufacturer located in Brescia, Italy.
See listings under the KBI section of this text.

FINNISH LION
Manufactured by Valmet (now Tikka) located in Sweden. Limited importation into the U.S by Mandall's Shooting Supplies, Inc. Scottsdale, AZ.

RIFLES

MATCH RIFLE — .22 LR, bolt action, single shot, 29 in. barrel, extended aperture sight, globe front sight, thumbhole stock, adj. hook butt. Mfg. 1937-1972.

	$495	$415	$360	$305	$250	$210	$195

CHAMPION FREE RIFLE — .22 LR, bolt action, single shot, 29 in. barrel, double set trigger, full target stock and accessories. Mfg. 1965-1972.

	$580	$495	$440	$385	$330	$290	$265

STANDARD ISU TARGET RIFLE — .22 LR, bolt action, single shot, 27 in. barrel, full target stock and accessories. Mfg. 1966-1977.

	$330	$275	$250	$205	$180	$165	$150

TARGET RIFLE — .22 LR, target rifle with adj. stock and trigger, bolt action, single shot, aperture sights.

Mfg.'s Sug. Retail	$795	$725	$595	$495	$440	$385	$340	$295

FIOCCHI OF AMERICA, INC.
Importer and distributor located In Ozark, MO.

Fiocchi of America imports Pardini target pistols and manufactures a wide variety of ammunition domestically. Until 1988, Fiocchi imported Antonio Zoli shotguns. These trademarks can be found in their respective sections of this text.

FIREARMS INTERNATIONAL (F I)
Previous importer/assembler located in Washington, D.C.

F.I. imported various shotguns and pistols including the Star D and Iver Johnson Pony handguns. F.I. sold less than 100 .380 ACPs that were marked Colt before the Mustang was introduced - these are rare. While some models are relatively rare, collectability to date has been minimal and most models sell in the $125-$250 range.

FOX, A. H.

Previously manufactured in Philadelphia, PA 1903-1930. Manufactured by Savage since 1930.

Mr. Ansley H. Fox first started manufacturing shotguns in circa 1896. This first company was called the Fox Gun Co. located in Baltimore, MD. Relatively few guns were made and surviving specimens today are very rare. After this venture, he was employed by the Baltimore Gun Co. for several years (circa 1900-1903). Following this period, he formed the Philadelphia Gun Co. where the predecessors to the A.H. Fox Gun Co. models were manufactured. These Philadelphia Gun Co. models (circa 1904) were the same as the newer Fox shotguns except that the hinge pin was removed. Sources indicate that the lowest grade was an "A" with the highest being an "E" (fully engraved and ultra rare). Following this tenure, Mr. Fox went on to form the A.H. Fox Gun Co. that was started approx. 1905. In addition to being an entrepreneur and trend setter, Mr. Fox also had the reputation of being an expert shot in his own right, winning more than a few events on the East Coast around the turn of the century.

The A.H. Fox Gun Company of Philadelphia, Pennsylvania, began production in 1905 and produced high quality double barrel shotguns until 1930. The Savage Arms Company, then of Utica, New York, acquired the Fox Company and produced these guns until 1942, when all but the utilitarian model B series guns were discontinued.

A.H. Fox guns are rapidly being considered an American classic as is the L.C. Smith and Parker. Collector interest is high and will undoubtedly grow. The guns do not command quite as high a price as the Smith and Parker guns, but represent a fine investment collectible value.

The Savage made guns from 1930-1942 usually are valued at about 25% less than the early A.H. Fox guns. The current production B series are just not in the same class and are obviously not intended to be. They are lower priced by today's standards and are designed as a utility grade hunting gun.

FOX COMPANY CHRONOLOGY

1906 - Company formed January 1906, A, B & C Grades introduced in 12 ga. only. D and F Grades introduced in 12 ga. in 1907. Ejector guns introduced in 1908. 1910 saw the introduction of the 12 ga. Sterlingworth - William H. Gough takes over as Chief of Engraving. Ansley Fox resigns in 1911 - first catalog showing Sterlingworth Model (called Model 1911). A-F Grades released in 16 and 20 ga. during 1912, as well as the addition of a 20 ga. Sterlingworth. 16 ga. Sterlingworth introduced in 1913. Fox/Kautsky single trigger introduced in 1914 - engraving 000.sition complete. During 1915, the XE Grade was introduced. The B Grade was dropped in 1918. Single barrel trap guns (J, K, and L Grades) were introduced in 1919. 1920 saw the introduction of the M Grade single barrel trap. In 1922, both the G and HE Grades were released. Beavertail forend and vent. rib were introduced in 1927. 1929 was the Savage buy-out (November), GE Grade dropped. Company moved from Philadelphia, PA to Utica, NY in 1930. Skeeter Grade introduced in 1931 while the 20 ga. HE Grade was disc. 1932 saw the introduction of both the Trap Grade Double and SP Grade. Wildfowl Grade was introduced in 1934. 1935 was the last year of the K and L single barrel trap guns. 1937 was the last year for the J Grade single barrel trap gun. The last 16 and 12 ga. Sterlingworths were built in 1939. The outbreak of the war in 1940 saw the last FE Grade shipped, the Wildfowler Grade dropped, and the introduction of the Model B. 1942 was the last retail catalog. Factory records indicate that the last 12 ga. was shipped in 1945 and the last 20 ga. was shipped during 1946 (SP Grade shipped in December, 1946). However, guns continued to be assembled from left-over parts and were shipped to customers as late as the 1960s.

FOX SERIAL NUMBER ASSIGNMENTS

The publisher wishes to express his thanks to Mr. Gurney Brown for providing the model serialization and years of mfg. in this section.

Ser. # range 50,000-200,000 — 12 ga. Sterlingworth — 111,556 mfg.
Ser. # range 350,000-400,000 — 16 ga. Sterlingworth — 28,481 mfg.
Ser. # range 250,000-300,000 — 20 ga. Sterlingworth — 21,304 mfg.
Ser. # range 1-50,000 — 12 ga. A-F Grades — 35,280 mfg.
Ser. # range 300,000-350,000 — 16 ga. A-F Grades — 3,875 mfg.
Ser. # range 200,000-250,000 — 20 ga. A-F Grades — 3,974 mfg.
Ser. # range 400,000-400,568 — 12 ga. Single Barrel Traps — 568 mfg.

Fox, A. H., cont.

FOX MODELS BY YEARS IN MFG.

Model	Years	
Sterlingworth	1910-1942 mfg.	32 years.
Wildfowler	1934-1940 mfg.	6 years.
Trap Double	1932-1942 mfg.	10 years.
Skeeter	1931-1942 mfg.	11 years.
SP	1932-1946 mfg.	14 years.
A	1906-1942 mfg.	36 years.
B	1906-1919 mfg.	13 years.
C	1906-1942 mfg.	36 years.
D	1907-1942 mfg.	35 years.
F	1907-1940 mfg.	33 years.
G	1922-1929 mfg.	7 years.
J	1919-1937 mfg.	18 years.
K	1919-1935 mfg.	16 years.
L	1919-1935 mfg.	16 years.
M	1920-1937 mfg.	17 years.
H	1922-1939 mfg.	17 years.
X	1915-1942 mfg.	27 years.

100%	98%	95%	90%	80%	70%	60%	50%	40%	30%	20%	10%

STERLINGWORTH SXS — 12, 16, or 20 ga., 26, 28, or 30 in. barrels, various chokes, boxlock, extractors, double trigger, checkered pistol grip stock. Mfg. 1905-1930.

100%	98%	95%	90%	80%	70%	60%	50%	40%	30%	20%	10%
$1,495	$1,250	$1,050	$875	$750	$650	$500	$450	$400	$365	$325	$275

Add 33% for auto ejectors.
Add 50% for 20 ga.
A single trigger is a very desirable option on this model.
Ser. no. range on 12 ga. Sterlingworths is 50,000-200,000, 16 ga. is 350,000-400,000, and 20 ga. is 250,000-300,000.

STERLINGWORTH DELUXE — similar to Sterlingworth, with recoil pad and ivory bead, 32 in. barrel available.

100%	98%	95%	90%	80%	70%	60%	50%	40%	30%	20%	10%
$1,875	$1,500	$1,200	$995	$900	$825	$725	$650	$550	$475	$425	$395

Add $200 for auto ejectors.
Add 50% for 20 ga.
A single trigger was not an option on this model.

STERLINGWORTH SKEET — similar to Sterlingworth, with 26 or 28 in. skeet boring, straight grip stock.
This model is very scarce (only several are known) and the extreme rarity factor precludes accurate price evaluation.

SUPER HE GRADE — 12 ga., 2¾ (very rare) or 3 in. chambered long range gun, 30 and 32 in. full choke, auto ejectors, otherwise similar to Sterlingworth.

100%	98%	95%	90%	80%	70%	60%	50%	40%	30%	20%	10%
$3,150	$2,675	$2,100	$1,750	$1,400	$1,100	$995	$900	$825	$750	$675	$600

Add $300 for SST.
Original 3 in. chambered HE grades are marked "not warranteed, see instruction tag" on barrel flats. The HE grade was also manufactured in 20 ga. but is extremely rare. 2¾ in. chambers are rarer than 3 in. guns in this model.

HIGHER GRADE MODELS (A-F) — the following higher grade Fox shotguns are similar to the Sterlingworth in configuration. The grades differ in engraving and inlays, grade of wood and general workmanship. The E designation means auto ejectors.
Early A and B grades have very little engraving and are much less desirable than later models. Values below are for later guns.
Values below are for 12 ga.
Add 30% for 16 ga. (made on same frame as 20 ga.). Add 60% for 20 ga.
Subtract 25% for Savage mfg.
Add $200-$1,000 for vent. rib, depending on grade.
Add $200-$1,000 for SST, depending on grade.
Add $200-$1,000 for beavertail forearm, depending on grade.
Note: These guns were disc. in 1942 by Savage Arms after they mfg. them for 12 years. Pre-1930 guns were made by A.H. Fox Company.

100%	98%	95%	90%	80%	70%	60%	50%	40%	30%	20%	10%

⚞ A Grade

100%	98%	95%	90%	80%	70%	60%	50%	40%	30%	20%	10%
$1,950	$1,675	$1,375	$1,075	$900	$825	$725	$650	$550	$475	$425	$395

⚞ AE Grade (ejectors)

| $2,475 | $2,075 | $1,675 | $1,250 | $1,000 | $900 | $800 | $725 | $650 | $575 | $500 | $450 |

⚞ BE Grade (ejectors)

| $3,800 | $3,350 | $2,675 | $2,250 | $1,850 | $1,500 | $1,150 | $995 | $900 | $825 | $750 | $675 |

This model is rarely encountered.

⚞ CE Grade (ejectors)

| $3,800 | $3,350 | $2,675 | $2,250 | $1,850 | $1,500 | $1,150 | $995 | $900 | $825 | $750 | $675 |

⚞ XE Grade (ejectors)

| $6,750 | $5,500 | $4,500 | $3,250 | $2,500 | $2,200 | $1,800 | $1,500 | $1,150 | $995 | $900 | $825 |

⚞ DE Grade (ejectors)

| $10,500 | $8,950 | $7,500 | $6,500 | $5,500 | $4,500 | $3,500 | $2,500 | $2,200 | $1,800 | $1,500 | $1,250 |

⚞ FE Grade (ejectors) — top-of-the-line model, only infrequently encountered.

| $25,000 | $20,000 | $15,000 | $12,000 | $10,000 | $9,000 | $8,000 | $7,250 | $6,500 | $5,800 | $5,250 | $4,500 |

SINGLE BARREL TRAP — 12 ga., 30 or 32 in. vent. rib barrel, full choke, boxlock, auto ejector, checkered trap style stock and recoil pad. The grades differ in wood, engraving, and overall quality. ME grade is custom built and extremely high quality with gold inlays. These models were disc. 1942. 568 single barrel trap guns were mfg. between 1932-1942 and have a ser. range of 400,000-400,568, with Monte Carlo stock.

Even though trap guns may be rarer than their SxS counterparts, to date their desirability is less since there are simply fewer collectors.

⚞ JE Grade

| $1,800 | $1,600 | $1,450 | $1,300 | $1,150 | $995 | $900 | $825 | $750 | $675 | $595 | $525 |

⚞ KE Grade

| $2,500 | $2,250 | $1,975 | $1,750 | $1,500 | $1,300 | $1,100 | $925 | $825 | $725 | $650 | $600 |

⚞ LE Grade

| $3,350 | $2,995 | $2,650 | $2,300 | $2,000 | $1,750 | $1,500 | $1,300 | $1,100 | $900 | $750 | $650 |

⚞ ME Grade

| $8,250 | $7,700 | $7,150 | $6,600 | $6,000 | $5,500 | $4,950 | $4,500 | $3,950 | $3,500 | $3,000 | $2,500 |

Grading	100%	98%	95%	90%	80%	70%	60%

MODEL B DOUBLE BARREL — 12, 16, 20, or .410 ga., 24-30 in. barrels, various chokes, vent rib on newer models, boxlock, extractors, double triggers, checkered pistol grip stock. Mfg. 1940-1986.

	100%	98%	95%	90%	80%	70%	60%
	$230	$210	$205	$185	$165	$145	$120

Last Mfg.'s Sug. Retail was $250.

Grading	100%	98%	95%	90%	80%	70%	60%

MODEL B-ST — similar to model B, with single trigger. Mfg. 1955-1966.

	$275	$250	$220	$195	$165	$140	$120

MODEL B-DL — similar to model B-ST, with satin chrome receiver, select wood. Mfg. 1962-1965.

	$315	$275	$240	$220	$195	$165	$140

MODEL B-DE — similar to B-DL, with less checkering. Mfg. 1965-1966.

	$295	$255	$230	$210	$180	$155	$125

MODEL B-SE — 12, 20, or .410 ga., single trigger, selective ejectors, vent. rib, beavertail forend, select walnut. Mfg. 1966-88.

	$415	$370	$325	$280	$240	$210	$180

Add 20% for .410 ga.
Last Mfg.'s Sug. Retail was $525.
Even though there were multiple series designations assigned to this model, there seems to be little difference in desirability. For that reason, other designations will be priced similarly to values shown above.

FRANCHI, LUIGI

Manufacturer located in Brescia, Italy. Currently imported exclusively by American Arms, Inc. located in North Kansas City, MO. Some models were previously imported by FIE firearms located in Hialeah, FL.

Also see Sauer/Franchi heading in the S section.

RIFLES

CENTENNIAL SEMI-AUTO — .22 LR, 21 in. barrel, open sight to commemorate Franchi's 100th anniversary. Mfg. 1968 only.

	$330	$250	$220	$195	$165	$150	$140

⚞ **Engraved deluxe model**

	$415	$330	$305	$275	$240	$200	$165

⚞ **Gallery model**

	$220	$195	$160	$120	$100	$80	$60

SHOTGUNS: SEMI-AUTO

BLACK MAGIC GAME — 12 ga. only, 3 in. chamber with gas metering system, interchangeable shell handling without adjustments, two-tone black alloy receiver with gold accents and trigger, 24, 26, or 28 in. VR barrel with Franchokes, checkered walnut stock and forearm, 7 lbs. Imported 1989-91.

	$550	$450	$395	$330	$300	$270	$240

Last Mfg.'s Sug. Retail was $659.

⚞ **Black Magic Skeet** — skeet variation of the Black Magic Game, 2¾ in. chamber, 26 in. ported VR barrel with fixed Tula skeet choke, skeet dimensioned stock, 7¼ lbs. Imported 1989-91.

	$580	$475	$425	$350	$325	$295	$265

Last Mfg.'s Sug. Retail was $699.

⚞ **Black Magic Trap** — trap variation of the Black Magic Game, 2¾ in. chamber, 30 in. VR barrel with Franchoke system, trap dimensioned stock, 7½ lbs. Imported 1989-91.

	$615	$495	$430	$350	$325	$295	$265

Last Mfg.'s Sug. Retail was $739.

Grading	100%	98%	95%	90%	80%	70%	60%

STANDARD MODEL (48/AL) — 12 or 20 ga., 24, 26, 28, or 30 (disc. in 1990) in. VR barrel, recoil operated, alloy frame, checkered pistol grip stock, VR standard, Franchokes became available in 1989, 12 ga., 6 lbs. 9 oz. and 20 ga., 5 lbs. 6 oz. Mfg. 1950-present.

Mfg.'s Sug. Retail	$609	$485	$380	$300	$270	$250	$230	$210

Add 10% for 12 ga. 24 in. slug barrel.
Subtract $40 if without Franchokes.
Starting in 1990, this model comes standard with black receiver and gold accents. Franchokes became standard in 1990.

STANDARD MAGNUM (48/AL) — similar to Standard, except 28 in. (disc. 1988) or 32 in. VR barrel, Mag. chamber, recoil pad, Mfg. 1954-1990.

	$415	$360	$300	$270	$250	$230	$210

Last Mfg.'s Sug. Retail was $482.
This model was replaced by the Combo S/T currently imported by American Arms, Inc. located in North Kansas City, MO.

COMBO S/T — while advertised, this model was never developed.

HUNTER MODEL (48/AL) — similar to Standard, except etched receiver, better wood, VR standard, Franchokes became available in 1989. Mfg. 1950-1990.

	$415	$360	$300	$270	$250	$230	$210

Add $35 for internal Franchokes (3).
Last Mfg.'s Sug. Retail was $482.
This model was imported exclusively by FIE Firearms located in Hialeah, FL.

HUNTER MAGNUM — mfg. 1954-1973.

	$430	$380	$370	$340	$315	$290	$275

PRESTIGE MODEL — 12 ga. only, gas operated, vent. rib, various barrel lengths, alloy receiver, Franchokes became available in 1989. Imported 1985-1989.

	$575	$475	$395	$325	$310	$295	$275

Add $40 for internal Franchokes (3).
Last Mfg.'s Sug. Retail was $720.
This model was imported exclusively by FIE Firearms located in Hialeah, FL.

Turkey Model — similar to Prestige Model except has dull matte black finish, Franchokes standard. Imported 1989 only.

	$615	$515	$425	$350	$320	$300	$280

Last Mfg.'s Sug. Retail was $760.
This model was imported exclusively by FIE Firearms located in Hialeah, FL.

ELITE MODEL — same general specifications as the Prestige Model, only etched receiver, Franchokes became available in 1989. Imported 1985-1989.

	$595	$500	$425	$350	$320	$300	$280

Add $45 for internal Franchokes (3).
Last Mfg.'s Sug. Retail was $740.
This model was imported exclusively by FIE Firearms located in Hialeah, FL.

SPAS-12 — 12 ga., $2\frac{3}{4}$ in. chamber, combat shotgun that offers pump or semi-auto operation, 5 (new 1991) or 8 (disc.) shot tube mag., alloy receiver, synthetic stock with built-in pistol grip, one-button switch to change from semi-auto to slide action operation, $21\frac{1}{2}$ in. barrel, $8\frac{3}{4}$ lbs.

Mfg.'s Sug. Retail	$713	$560	$485	$400	$360	$320	$300	$280

This model was imported exclusively by FIE Firearms located in Hialeah, FL until 1990.

Grading	100%	98%	95%	90%	80%	70%	60%

SPAS-15 — 12 ga. only, 2¾ in. chamber, operates as either semi-auto or slide action that is convertible with a one-button switch, 6 shot detachable box mag., 21½ in. barrel, lateral folding skeleton stock, carrying handle, 10 lbs. Limited importation 1989 only.
This model had very limited importation (less than 200) as the BATF disallowed further importation almost immediately. Even though the retail was in the $700 range, demand and rarity has pushed prices past the $2,000 level already.

SAS-12 — 12 ga. only, 3 in. chamber, slide action only, synthetic stock with built-in pistol grip, 8 shot tube mag., 21½ in. barrel, 6.8 lbs. Imported 1988-90 only.

	$415	$360	$300	$270	$250	$230	$210

Last Mfg.'s Sug. Retail was $473.
This model was imported exclusively by FIE Firearms located in Hialeah, FL.

LAW-12 — 12 ga. only, 2¾ in. chamber, gas operated semi-auto, synthetic stock with built-in pistol grip, 5 (new 1991) or 8 (disc.) shot tube mag., 21½ in. barrel, 6¾ lbs. Importation began 1988.

Mfg.'s Sug. Retail	$686	$550	$475	$400	$360	$320	$300	$280

TURKEY GUN — similar to Standard Mag., 12 ga., 3 in. barrel only, turkey scene engraved. Mfg. 1963-1965.

	$415	$385	$370	$340	$315	$290	$275

SLUG GUN — 22 in. plain barrel, and rifle sights.

	$360	$330	$315	$295	$275	$255	$240

SKEET GUN — 26 in. skeet choke, vent. rib, select wood. Mfg. 1972-1974.

	$385	$370	$350	$330	$310	$285	$265

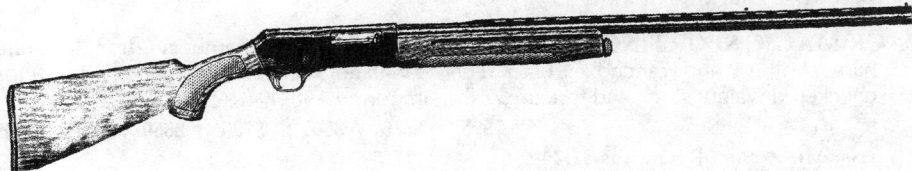

ELDORADO — fancy wood and gold filled engraved receiver. Mfg. 1954-1975.

	$450	$420	$395	$380	$360	$340	$320

CROWN GRADE — engraved hunting scene. Mfg. 1954-1975.

	$1,540	$1,320	$1,210	$1,045	$965	$910	$855

DIAMOND GRADE SILVER INLAID SCROLL — mfg. 1954-1975.

	$1,980	$1,735	$1,540	$1,430	$1,210	$1,045	$965

IMPERIAL GRADE — gold inlaid hunting scene.

	$2,420	$2,090	$1,925	$1,760	$1,595	$1,485	$1,320

Note: Standard, Skeet and Slug with steel frame mfg. 1965-1972, designated "Dynamic" 12 ga., values are the same.

MODEL 500 STANDARD — 12 ga, 26 or 28 in. barrel, various chokes, vent. rib, gas operated, checkered pistol grip stock. Mfg. 1976-disc.

	$330	$310	$305	$265	$230	$195	$165

MODEL 520 DELUXE — engraved receiver.

	$385	$365	$330	$290	$260	$220	$195

Grading	100%	98%	95%	90%	80%	70%	60%

MODEL 520 ELDORADO GOLD — fine wood, engraved gold, inlaid receiver. Mfg. 1977-present.

	$990	$770	$715	$660	$580	$525	$470

MODEL 530 AUTO TRAP — similar to 500, except 30 in. and 32 in. full, very high rib, special trap stock, pad.

	$660	$550	$525	$440	$415	$385	$330

SHOTGUNS - O/U

DE LUXE MODEL PRITI — 12 or 20 ga., boxlock action, ST, ejectors, 26 or 28 in. VR barrels with fixed chokes. Imported 1988-1989 only.

	$395	$350	$315	$285	$240	$215	$185

Last Mfg.'s Sug. Retail was $460.
This model was imported exclusively by FIE Firearms located in Hialeah, FL.

ALCIONE MODEL — 12 ga., 28 in. barrels, less engraving than Alcione SL, separated barrels. Importation disc. 1989.

	$675	$550	$495	$460	$430	$380	$335

Last Mfg.'s Sug. Retail was $800.
Previously designated Diamond Model.
This model was imported exclusively by FIE Firearms located in Hialeah, FL.

ALCIONE SL — 12 ga., 27 or 28 in. barrels, 6 lbs. 13 oz., separated barrels, ejectors, single trigger, silver finished receiver engraved with luggage case. Importation disc. 1986.

	$1,150	$995	$875	$800	$725	$640	$550

Last Mfg.'s Sug. Retail was $1,595.

BLACK MAGIC SPORTING HUNTER — 12 ga. only, 3 in. chambers, 28 in. separated barrels with VR and Franchokes, black receiver with gold accents and trigger, SST, ejectors, checkered walnut stock and forearm, 7 lbs. Imported 1989-91.

	$995	$875	$800	$725	$650	$575	$495

Last Mfg.'s Sug. Retail was $1,249.
The Black Magic Model Series was imported exclusively by American Arms, Inc. located in North Kansas City, MO.

Black Magic Lightweight Hunter — similar to Black Magic Sporting Hunter except 2¾ in. chambers only, 26 in. separated barrels with VR and Franchokes, alloy receiver, 6 lbs. Imported 1989-91.

	$975	$850	$775	$700	$625	$550	$475

Last Mfg.'s Sug. Retail was $1,209.

SPORTING 2000 — 12 ga. only, design for sporting clays or hunting, 28 in. vent. ported barrels with target VR and choke tubes, SST, ejectors, select walnut with checkering, solid pad, 7¾ lbs. Importation began 1992.

Mfg.'s Sug. Retail	$1,619		$1,450	$1,250	$995	$850	$725	$650	$575

ARISTOCRAT FIELD — 12 ga., 26, 28, or 30 in. barrels, various chokes, vent. rib, auto ejectors, boxlock, selective single trigger, checkered pistol grip stock. Mfg. 1960-1969.

	$660	$470	$440	$395	$375	$340	$310

Grading	100%	98%	95%	90%	80%	70%	60%

ARISTOCRAT MAGNUM — similar to Field, except 32 in. barrel, 3 in. chamber, full choke, pad. Mfg. 1962-1965.

	$660	$470	$440	$395	$375	$340	$310

ARISTOCRAT SKEET — similar to Field, but 26 in. vent. rib, bored skeet no. 1 and no. 2. Mfg. 1960-1969.

	$715	$525	$495	$450	$430	$395	$365

ARISTOCRAT TRAP — 30 in. vent. rib barrel, bored mod. and full, trap stock Mfg. 1960-1969.

	$745	$550	$525	$480	$455	$415	$380

ARISTOCRAT SILVER KING — select wood, engraved coin finished receiver. Mfg. 1962-1969.

	$750	$560	$535	$485	$470	$430	$400

ARISTOCRAT DELUXE — finer wood, more engraving. Mfg. 1960-1966.

	$990	$870	$835	$810	$770	$715	$660

ARISTOCRAT SUPREME — gold inlaid game birds. Mfg. 1960-1966.

	$1,430	$1,265	$1,155	$1,075	$990	$935	$880

ARISTOCRAT IMPERIAL — high grade wood, more engraving. Mfg. 1967-1969.

	$2,640	$2,200	$2,090	$1,925	$1,815	$1,650	$1,430

ARISTOCRAT MONTE CARLO — highest grade wood, elaborate engraving and inlay, mfg. 1967-1969.

	$3,520	$3,080	$2,915	$2,640	$2,420	$2,090	$1,870

FALCONET S — 12 ga., lightweight model of the Alcione SL, 27 or 28 in. barrels, 6 lbs. 1 oz., separated barrels, moderate engraving on silver finish receiver. Disc. 1985.

	$895	$765	$660	$560	$510	$460	$410

Last Mfg.'s Sug. Retail was $1,015.

FALCONET FIELD — 12, 16, 20, 28, or .410 ga., 24-30 in. barrels, various chokes, auto ejectors, select single trigger, engraved alloy receiver, checkered walnut stock. Mfg. 1968-1975.

	100%	98%	95%	90%	80%	70%	60%
Buckskin (light)	$550	$495	$470	$440	$415	$385	$360
Ebony (black)	$550	$495	$470	$440	$415	$385	$360
Silver	$605	$550	$525	$495	$470	$415	$385

28 ga. and .410 — add 25%.

FALCONET SKEET — 26 in. barrels, bored skeet no. 1 and no. 2, wide vent. rib, case hardened steel receiver. Mfg. 1970-1974.

	$935	$855	$825	$770	$715	$690	$650

FALCONET INTERNATIONAL SKEET — higher grade wood, more engraving. Mfg. 1970-1974.

	$1,045	$935	$865	$825	$770	$745	$700

FALCONET STANDARD TRAP — 12 ga., 30 in. mod. and full, wide vent. rib, trap stock, pad. Mfg. 1970-1974.

	$935	$855	$825	$770	$715	$690	$650

Grading	100%	98%	95%	90%	80%	70%	60%

FALCONET INTERNATIONAL TRAP — higher grade wood, more engraving. Mfg. 1970-1974.

	$1,045	$935	$865	$825	$770	$745	$700

FALCONET 2000— 12 ga. only, boxlock with alloy receiver featuring silver finish with gold plated game scenes, 26 in. separated barrels with VR and choke tubes, SST, ejectors, select checkered walnut stock and forearm, 6 lbs. Importation began 1992.

Mfg.'s Sug. Retail	$1,419	$1,260	$995	$850	$725	$650	$575	$500

PEREGRINE MODEL 451 — 12 ga., 26-28 in. barrels, various chokes, vent. rib, auto ejectors, alloy receiver, selective single trigger, checkered pistol grip stock. Mfg. 1975.

	$605	$550	$525	$495	$440	$415	$360

PEREGRINE MODEL 400 — similar to 451, except steel receiver. Mfg. 1975.

	$660	$605	$570	$540	$495	$460	$385

MODEL 2003 TRAP — 12 ga., 30 or 32 in. barrels, imp. mod. and full, or full and full, boxlock, auto ejectors, single selective trigger, high vent. rib, trap style stock, pad, cased. Mfg. 1976. Disc.

	$1,205	$1,090	$1,045	$910	$855	$770	$660

MODEL 2004 TRAP — similar to 2003, except single barrel, cased. Mfg. 1976. Disc.

	$1,205	$1,090	$1,045	$910	$855	$770	$660

MODEL 2005 COMBINATION TRAP — two sets of barrels, one single, one O/U, cased. Mfg. 1976. Disc.

	$1,815	$1,595	$1,515	$1,320	$1,210	$1,075	$935

MODEL 2005/3 COMBINATION TRAP — three sets of barrels, cased. Mfg. 1976. Disc.

	$2,420	$2,090	$1,980	$1,705	$1,515	$1,485	$1,320

UNDERGUN MODEL 3000 — radical competition trap, very high rib separated barrels, single and O/U, set cased. Disc.

	$2,750	$2,530	$2,310	$2,090	$1,980	$1,870	$1,760

SHOTGUNS: SIDE-BY-SIDE

AIRONE — 12 ga., double barrel, choice of barrel length and chokes, box lock, Anson & Deeley, auto ejectors, double triggers, checkered English style stock, engraved. Mfg. 1940-1950.

	$1,320	$1,100	$935	$825	$745	$715	$660

ASTORE — double barrel, similar to Airone, except less engraving, extractors. Mfg. 1937-1960.

	$990	$910	$770	$715	$635	$580	$550

ASTORE 5 — similar to Astore, except higher grade wood, more engraving, auto ejectors. Disc.

	$2,200	$1,925	$1,650	$1,540	$1,460	$1,375	$1,320

ASTORE II — similar to Astore 5, except less elaborate, currently mfg. in Spain for Franchi.

	$1,210	$1,045	$935	$880	$800	$715	$660

Grading	100%	98%	95%	90%	80%	70%	60%

SIDELOCK DOUBLE BARREL — 12, 16, or 20 ga., barrels and choke custom order, stock to order, hand detachable side lock, self-opening action, auto ejectors, six grades offered, they differ only in overall quality and ornamentation, and grade of wood used.

	100%	98%	95%	90%	80%	70%	60%
Condor	$7,700	$6,600	$6,050	$5,720	$5,500	$4,620	$3,960
Imperial	$10,450	$9,350	$8,800	$8,250	$7,480	$6,600	$5,720
Imperiales	$10,670	$9,570	$9,020	$8,470	$7,700	$6,820	$5,940

SIDE-LOCK DOUBLE BARREL

	100%	98%	95%	90%	80%	70%	60%
✹ No. 5 Imperial Monte Carlo	$15,400	$13,200	$11,000	$9,900	$9,350	$8,250	$7,150
✹ No. 11 Imperial Monte Carlo	$16,500	$14,300	$12,100	$11,000	$10,450	$9,350	$8,250
✹ Imperial Monte Carlo Extra	$19,800	$17,050	$14,300	$13,200	$12,650	$11,000	$9,900

Note: Imperial Monte Carlo Extra is currently being mfg. on special order only; the other models are disc.

FRANCOTTE, AUGUSTE & CIE. S.A.

Manufacturer located in Liege, Belgium since 1805. Currently imported by Armes De Chasse located in Chadds Ford, PA. Previously imported by VL&O between 1900-1930's, Abercrombie & Fitch until approx. 1962.

Prices below reflect the recent devaluation of the U.S. dollar against some European currencies. While the manufacturer's suggested retails have gone up considerably, prices for used specimens (98% or less original condition) have not increased proportionately, and in some cases, have changed very little.

REVOLVERS

Francotte manufactured Pryse-type revolvers at the end of the previous century, and these revolvers bore the name of the well-known British retailer. Encountered only infrequently domestically, these specimens found overseas are usually priced in the $150-$650 range.

SHOTGUNS

All newly manufactured shotguns in this section are custom made to purchaser's individual specifications. Basic types listed below are also available in 24 or 32 ga. upon special order. Auguste Francotte does not manufacture guns by model - all guns are custom order.

BOXLOCK SXS — premium grade Belgium side-by-side, double triggers standard, auto ejectors. Available in 12, 16, 20, 28, or .410 ga., with English scroll engraving, Anson & Deeley boxlock action.

		100%	98%	95%	90%	80%	70%	60%
Mfg.'s Sug. Retail	$15,642	$14,850	$11,000	$8,000	$6,250	$5,000	$4,000	$3,250

Add 10% for 28 or .410 ga.
Add $1,449 for sideplates with engraving.

✹ **Deluxe Anson & Deeley** — gold inlaid game scenes, and engraving is by customer's personal preference.
Prices and options are quoted per individual request.

SIDELOCK SXS — true sidelock action, available in 12, 16, 20, 28, or .410 ga., Arabesque scroll engraving, various chokes and barrel lengths, custom order only.

		100%	98%	95%	90%	80%	70%	60%
Mfg.'s Sug. Retail	$27,310	$26,000	$21,500	$18,500	$15,000	$12,000	$9,000	$7,750

Add 10% for 28 or .410 ga.

Grading	100%	98%	95%	90%	80%	70%	60%

⚞ **Deluxe sidelock** — gold inlaid game scenes and engraving are by customer's personal preference.
Prices and options are quoted per individual request.

JUBILEE

	100%	98%	95%	90%	80%	70%	60%
	$1,595	$1,430	$1,265	$1,100	$990	$825	$715
No. 14	$2,000	$1,900	$1,800	$1,650	$1,500	$1,450	$1,200
No. 18	$2,500	$2,400	$2,250	$2,000	$1,800	$1,600	$1,300
No. 20	$3,000	$2,600	$2,350	$2,100	$1,900	$1,700	$1,500
No. 25	$3,500	$3,000	$2,500	$2,200	$2,100	$1,900	$1,700
No. 30	$5,000	$4,500	$4,000	$3,500	$2,500	$2,200	$2,000

KNOCKABOUT — disc. circa 1975.

	100%	98%	95%	90%	80%	70%	60%
	$1,265	$1,100	$935	$825	$715	$635	$550

Add 20% for 20 ga.
Add 30% for 28 ga.
Add 40% for .410 ga.

NO. 45 EAGLE GRADE — disc. circa 1977.

	100%	98%	95%	90%	80%	70%	60%
	$5,850	$4,950	$4,250	$3,800	$3,000	$2,650	$2,250

RIFLES

All newly mfg. rifles in this section are custom made to the purchaser's individual specifications.

BOLT ACTION MODEL — many calibers available between .18 Bee and .505 Gibbs Mag., select checkered walnut stock, engraved mag. floor plate, gold inlay and special engraving is available by special order only.

⚞ **Short Bolt Action** — cals. with shorter cartridges.

	Mfg.'s Sug. Retail	100%	98%	95%	90%	80%	70%	60%
	$10,173	$9,100	$7,250	$6,000	$4,950	$4,100	$3,300	$2,700

⚞ **Standard Model** — cals. with medium cartridge lengths.

	Mfg.'s Sug. Retail	100%	98%	95%	90%	80%	70%	60%
	$8,173	$7,575	$6,000	$4,950	$4,100	$3,300	$2,700	$2,000

⚞ **Magnum Action** — cals. with longer cartridge lengths.

	Mfg.'s Sug. Retail	100%	98%	95%	90%	80%	70%	60%
	$14,068	$13,150	$10,650	$9,250	$7,750	$6,400	$4,950	$3,950

SINGLE SHOT MOUNTAIN RIFLE — available in a variety of cals., boxlock or sidelock action, custom order only.

⚞ **Boxlock Mountain Rifle** — 6.5x50R, 7x57R, or 7x65R.

	Mfg.'s Sug. Retail	100%	98%	95%	90%	80%	70%	60%
	$14,482	$13,400	$10,850	$9,350	$7,850	$6,500	$5,000	$4,000

Add 10% for optional sideplates.

⚞ **Sidelock Mountain Rifle** — 7x65R or 7mm Rem. Mag. cal.

	Mfg.'s Sug. Retail	100%	98%	95%	90%	80%	70%	60%
	$26,275	$24,000	$20,000	$16,500	$13,000	$10,500	$9,000	$8,000

STANDARD SXS BOXLOCK RIFLE — available in a variety of cals., custom order only.

	Mfg.'s Sug. Retail	100%	98%	95%	90%	80%	70%	60%
	$19,103	$18,000	$15,250	$11,250	$8,750	$6,950	$5,750	$5,000

Add $1,449 for optional sideplates.
Add 15% for .375 H&H, .458 Win. Mag. cal., or other larger calibers upon request.

STANDARD SXS SIDELOCK RIFLE — available in a variety of cals., custom order only.

	Mfg.'s Sug. Retail	100%	98%	95%	90%	80%	70%	60%
	$30,034	$28,250	$24,500	$20,000	$16,500	$13,000	$10,500	$9,000

FRASER, DANL. & CO.
Manufacturer located in Europe. Limited importation into the United States.
Danl. Fraser & Co. has been building rifles since 1873 (originally in Edinburgh, Scotland).

Grading	100%	98%	95%	90%	80%	70%	60%

HIGHLANDER SINGLE SHOT — .22 LR or .22 Hornet cal., underlever falling block action (color case hardened), 24 in. (½ round, ½ octagon) barrel, folding express-style sights, pistol grip walnut stock with fine checkering. Disc.

	$415	$335	$300	$280	$260	$240	$220

Last Mfg.'s Sug. Retail was $475.

⚁ **Royal Highlander** — .22 LR or .22 Hornet cal., mfg. in Scotland, rose and scroll engraving with 18 Kt. inlays. Special order only — prices available upon request.

FRASER FIREARMS CORP.
Previously manufactured by R.B. Industries, Ltd. until 1990. Previously distributed by Fraser Firearms Corp. located in Fraser, MI.

FRASER 25 CAL. — .25 cal. only, copy of the Bauer semi-auto pocket model, 6 shot mag., 2¼ in. barrel, stainless steel construction.

	$120	$100	$90

Add $17 for Model 2 (black nylon grips).
Add $115 for Model 3 (24 Kt. gold plated).
Last Mfg.'s Sug. Retail was $133.

FREEDOM ARMS
Manufacturer located in Freedom, WY.
Percussion mini-revolvers can be found in the Blackpowder Section of this text.

MINI-REVOLVERS: STAINLESS STEEL

Because Freedom Arms' manufacturing capacity has been maximized due to the success of the .454 Casull revolver, the mini-revolver series has been temporarily discontinued starting in 1989. As a result, prices have escalated on these models due to no production and normal demand.

FA-S-22LR (PATRIOT) — .22 LR cal., 5 shot, 1, 1¾ (disc. 1988), or 3 (disc. 1988) in. barrel, Hi-Gloss finish.

	$175	$125	$95

Add $15 for 3 in. barrel model (FA-BG-22LR, Minute-Man, disc. 1988).
Last Mfg.'s Sug. Retail was $153.

FA-S-22M (IRONSIDES) — .22 Mag. cal., 4 shot, 1, 1¾ (disc. 1988), or 3 in. barrel, Hi Gloss finish.

	$190	$150	$110

Add $43 for 3 in. barrel model (Bostonian).
Last Mfg.'s Sug. Retail was $177.

FA-S-22-LR BUCKLE/REVOLVER COMBINATION — .22 LR, 1 in. barrel, pistol is housed in belt buckle.

	$210	$165	$135

Last Mfg.'s Sug. Retail was $193.

⚁ **.22 Mag. cal.**

	$240	$185	$150

Last Mfg.'s Sug. Retail was $216.

Grading	100%	98%	95%	90%	80%	70%	60%

CASULL SA REVOLVERS: STAINLESS STEEL

Freedom Arms also offers a complete line of accessories and factory installed options. The factory should be contacted directly for an up-to-date listing and prices.

MODEL 252 — .22 LR cal., 5 shot, unique two point firing pin, choice of $7\frac{1}{2}$ (Varmint Class Model with express sights, black/green laminated hardwood grips) or 10 in. (Silhouette Class Model with competition sights and black micarta grips), approx. $3\frac{3}{4}$ lbs. New 1991.

Mfg.'s Sug. Retail $1,248 $1,075 $850 $725

Add $213 for extra .22 Mag. cylinder.

Model 252 Silhouette — silhouette shooting features, 10 in. barrel only, black micarta grips.

Mfg.'s Sug. Retail $1,318 $1,125 $895 $675

MODEL 353 FIELD GRADE — .357 Mag., $4\frac{3}{4}$, 6, $7\frac{1}{2}$, or 9 in. barrel on non-glare field grade finish, Pachmayr grips, adj. sights, $3\frac{3}{4}$ lbs. New 1992.

Mfg.'s Sug. Retail $1,115 $995 $825 $695

Model 353 Premium Grade — similar to Field Grade, except has premier grade finish and impregnated hardwood grips. New 1992.

Mfg.'s Sug. Retail $1,385 $1,175 $895 $750

Model 353 Silhouette — includes silhouette competition sights, 9 in. barrel, field grade finish, Pachmayr grips and trigger overtravel screw. New 1992.

Mfg.'s Sug. Retail $1,214 $1,050 $850 $675

.44 REM. MAG. FIELD GRADE — .44 Rem. Mag., $4\frac{3}{4}$, 6, $7\frac{1}{2}$, or 10 in. barrel.

Mfg.'s Sug. Retail $1,115 $995 $825 $675

.44 Rem. Mag. Silhouette — field grade finish with silhouette competition sights, 10 in. barrel only, includes Pachmayr grips.

Mfg.'s Sug. Retail $1,214 $1,050 $850 $675

.454 CASULL FIELD GRADE — .44 Mag. (new 1991) or .454 Casull cal., 5 shot, $4\frac{3}{4}$ (fixed sight only), 6, $7\frac{1}{2}$, or 10 in. barrel, stainless steel matte finish with Pachmayr presentation grips. New 1988.

Mfg.'s Sug. Retail $1,035 $900 $775 $650

Add $80 for adj. sights.

Add $213 for extra .45 LC or .45 ACP (new 1990) cylinder.

Silhouette Model — .44 Mag. or .454 Casull, includes 10 in. barrel, Pachmayr grips, field grade finish, silhouette competition sights, and trigger overtravel screw. Mfg. 1992 only.

                     $995 $825 $675

Last Mfg.'s Sug. Retail was $1,132.

Silhouette Pak — .44 Mag., includes 10 in. barrel revolver, silhouette competition sight, honed action with 3 lb. trigger pull, plastic grips, locking aluminum carrying case with cleaning kit and tool. Mfg. 1990 only.

                     $1,000 $850 $750

Last Mfg.'s Sug. Retail was $1,180.

Grading	100%	98%	95%	90%	80%	70%	60%

.454 CASULL PREMIER GRADE — .44 Rem. Mag., .44 Win. Mag. (disc. 1989), .45 LC (disc. 1990), or .454 Casull cal., 5 shot, stainless steel with brushed finish, single action revolver, the .454 Casull shoots 225 grain bullet at over 2000 fps., 4¾, 6, 7½, 10, and 12 (disc. 1988) in. barrels, walnut (older mfg.) or impregnated hardwood grips. Mfg. 1983-present.

Mfg.'s Sug. Retail $1,298 $1,095 $825 $650
Add $87 for .44 Mag. cal.
The no sights model was available in 7½ in. barrel only - receiver is drilled and tapped for scope base - mfg. 1990-91.

⚔ **Adj. sights**
Mfg.'s Sug. Retail $1,385 $1,175 $895 $750
Add $88-$114 for Mag-na-porting.
Add $127 for SSK Industries T'SOB 3-ring scope mount.

⚔ **Silhouette Pak** — .44 Mag., includes 10 in. barrel revolver, silhouette competition sight, honed action with 3 lb. trigger pull, hardwood grips, locking aluminum carrying case with cleaning kit and tool. Mfg. 1990 only.
    $1,275 $995 $850
Last Mfg.'s Sug. Retail was $1,395.

HUNTER PAK FIELD GRADE — .357 Mag., .44 Rem. Mag., or .454 Casull cal., 7½ in. barrel, plastic grips, field grade low profile adj. sight or no front sight base, sling and studs, locking aluminum carrying case with cleaning kit and tool. New 1990.
Mfg.'s Sug. Retail $1,333 $1,075 $925 $775
Add $76 for low profile adj. sight and Pachmayr grips.

⚔ **Hunter Pak Premier Grade** — .357 Mag., .44 Rem. Mag., or .454 Casull cal., 7½ in. barrel, ebony micarta grips, no sights or premier grade adj. sight, sling and studs, locking aluminum carrying case with cleaning kit and tool. New 1990.
Mfg.'s Sug. Retail $1,611 $1,395 $1,025 $850
Add $100 for adj. sights.

U.S. DEPUTY MARSHALL — 3 in. barrel only with no ejector, fixed sights, U.S. Marshall medallion in left hardwood grip. New 1990.
Mfg.'s Sug. Retail $1,558 $1,325 $900 $750
Add $83 for adj. sights.

SIGNATURE EDITION — .454 Casull, high polish stainless steel, 7½ in. barrel only, rosewood grips, cased with accessories, only 93 of 100 were actually mfg.
    $2,300 $1,750 $1,300
Last Mfg.'s Sug. Retail was $2,684.

PRIMUS INTER PARES — 1 of every 100 guns is made in this variation, includes octagonal barrel, ivory grips, 7½ in. barrel, and cased. Contact the factory directly for prices on this model.

FRENCH MILITARY
Manufactured in various locations In France.

MODEL 1886 LEBEL — bolt action, 8mm Lebel, 32 in. barrel, adj. sight, military stock. Mfg. 1886 - WWII.
    $125 $100 $75 $65 $50 $40 $25

1936 MAS MILITARY RIFLE — bolt action, 7.5mm MAS, 22 in. barrel, adj. sight, military stock, bayonet in forearm. Mfg. 1936-1940.
    $125 $100 $75 $65 $50 $40 $25

French Military, cont.

MODEL 1935A AUTO PISTOL — 7.65mm long, 8 shot, 4.3 in. barrel, fixed sights, blue, checkered wood grips, French service sidearm. Mfg. 1935-1945.

	100%	98%	95%	90%	80%	70%	60%
	$195	$175	$150	$125	$110	$100	$90

M.A.B. MODEL C — 7.65mm, design based on FN Browning Model 1910, 6.1 in. barrel. Introduced 1933.

	100%	98%	95%	90%	80%	70%	60%
	$250	$220	$190	$170	$150	$125	$110

M.A.B. MODEL D — 7.65mm, 7 in barrel, single action, similar to Model C, mfg. commercially 1933-1940, many thousands mfg. for the German military during WWII (marked "Pistole MAB Kaliber 7.65mm")

	100%	98%	95%	90%	80%	70%	60%
	$275	$225	$200	$175	$150	$125	$110

MODEL M.A.B. PA - 15 — 9mm, single action semi-auto, 16 shot, currently used by French military.

	100%	98%	95%
	$700	$595	$450

MODEL M.A.B. PA - 15 TARGET — rare target variation of PA-15, adj. sight, 6 in. barrel, cased.

	100%	98%	95%
	$1,600	$1,200	$750

FRIGON

Manufactured by Marocchi in Italy. Imported and distributed by Frigon Guns located in Clay Center, KS.

FT I — 12 ga. only, single barrel trap gun, blued finish, 32 or 34 in. VR barrel, quick-change stock. New 1986.

	Mfg.'s Sug. Retail	$1,100	$925	$675	$525	$435	$375	$350	$295

FTC — 12 ga. only, quick-change stock, trap combination gun includes 1 single barrel and 1 set of O/U barrels, cased. New 1986.

	Mfg.'s Sug. Retail	$1,975	$1,700	$1,325	$1,050	$875	$775	$685	$620

FS-4 — 4-barrel skeet set including 12, 20, 28, or .410 ga., individual forearms, quick-change stock, vent. barrels (except for .410 ga.), cased. New 1986.

	Mfg.'s Sug. Retail	$2,890	$2,575	$1,975	$1,675	$1,475	$1,350	$1,250	$1,150

FROMMER PISTOLS

Femaru-Febyver-Es Gepgyar R.T., Budapest, Hungary.

Please refer to the Femaru listing in this section.

FURR ARMS

Manufacturer located in Orem, UT.

Please refer to the Gatling Gun Company listing in this text.

G section

GALEF SHOTGUNS

Previous importer of Zabal Hermanos (Spanish) and Antonio Zoli (Italian) shotguns.

Grading	100%	98%	95%	90%	80%	70%	60%

COMPANION FOLDING SINGLE BARREL — 12, 16, 20, 28, or .410 ga., 28 in. barrel, full choke, 30 in. full, 12 ga. only, hammerless, underlever, checkered pistol grip stock.

	100%	98%	95%	90%	80%	70%	60%
	$125	$100	$90	$80	$70	$60	$55

MONTE CARLO TRAP — 12 ga., single barrel, 32 in. full vent. rib, hammerless, underlever, recoil pad, checkered pistol grip Monte Carlo stock, disc.

	$225	$185	$175	$150	$135	$125	$100

SILVER SNIPE — 12 or 20 ga., O/U, 3 in. chambers, 26, 28, or 30 in. barrels, imp. cyl. and mod. or full and mod. vent. rib, checkered pistol grip stock, boxlock, extractors, single trigger, mfg. by Angelo Zoli, disc.

	$450	$400	$350	$295	$275	$250	$220

GOLDEN SNIPE — O/U, similar to Silver Snipe, except auto ejectors.

	$525	$475	$425	$375	$325	$300	$275

SILVER HAWK — 12 or 20 ga., SxS, 3 in. chambers, 26, 28, or 30 in. barrels, imp. cyl. and mod. or mod. and full, boxlock, extractors, checkered pistol grip and beavertail forearm. Mfg. by Angelo Zoli, 1968-1972.

	$425	$395	$350	$295	$255	$225	$200

GALEF ZABALA DOUBLE — 10, 12, 16, or 20 ga., SxS, 22, 26, 28, or 30 in. barrels, boxlock, extractors.

	100%	98%	95%	90%	80%	70%	60%
10 gauge	$250	$230	$200	$175	$150	$140	$125
Other gauges	$200	$175	$150	$130	$120	$110	$100

GALIL

Manufactured by Israel Military Industries (IMI). Currently imported by Action Arms, Ltd. located in Philadelphia, PA. Previously imported by Springfield Armory located in Geneseo, IL and Magnum Research, Inc., located in Minneapolis, MN.

The Models AR, ARM, and Sniper Outfit have not been imported since the federal ban on this semi-auto configuration was implemented. Magnum Research importation can be denoted by a serial number prefix "MR", while Action Arms imported rifles have either "AA" or "AAL" prefixes.

RIFLES: SEMI-AUTO

Models 329, 330 (Hadar II), 331, 332, 339 (sniper system with 6/40 mounted Nimrod scope), 361, 372, 386 and 392 all refer to various configurations of the Galil rifle.

MODEL AR — .223 cal. or .308 cal., semi-auto paramilitary design rifle, gas operated - rotating bolt, 16.1 in. (.223 only) or 19 in. (.308 only) barrel, parkerized, folding stock. Flip-up Tritium night sights. 8.6 lbs.

	$1,050	$900	$775	$650	$575	$500	$425

Last Mfg.'s Sug. Retail was $950.

GALIL SPORTER — similar to above, except has one-piece thumbhole stock, 4 (.308 Win.) or 5 (.223 Rem.) shot mag., choice of wood (disc.) or polymer hand guard, 8½ lbs. Importation began 1991.

	100%	98%	95%	90%	80%	70%	60%
Mfg.'s Sug. Retail $950	$875	$725	$600	$525	$475	$425	$395

Grading	100%	98%	95%	90%	80%	70%	60%

MODEL ARM — similar to Model AR, except includes folding bipod, vented hardwood handguard, and carrying handle.

	100%	98%	95%	90%	80%	70%	60%
	$1,150	$950	$825	$700	$600	$525	$450

Last Mfg.'s Sug. Retail was $1,050.

HADAR II — .308 cal., gas operated, hunting rifle configuration, 1 piece walnut thumbhole stock with pistol grip and forearm, 18½ in. barrel, adj. rear sight, recoil pad, 4 shot (standard) or 25 shot mag., 10.3 lbs. Imported 1989 only.

	100%	98%	95%	90%	80%	70%	60%
	$950	$850	$750	$650	$600	$540	$475

Last Mfg.'s Sug. Retail was $998.

SNIPER OUTFIT — .308 cal., semi-auto, limited production, sniper model built to exact I.D.F. specifications for improved accuracy, 20 in. heavy barrel, hardwood folding stock (adj. recoil pad and adj. cheek piece) and forearm, includes Tritium night sights, bipod, detachable 6 X 40mm Nimrod scope, two 25 shot mag.'s, carrying/storage case, 14.1 lbs. Imported 1989 only.

	100%	98%	95%	90%	80%	70%	60%
	$4,000	$3,500	$3,000	$2,650	$2,150	$1,750	$1,300

Last Mfg.'s Sug. Retail was $3,995.

GAMBA, RENATO

Manufacturer located in Gardone V.T., Italy. Gamba shotguns are currently imported by Giacomo Sporting, Inc. located in Rome, NY, and New England Arms located in Kittery Point, ME. Pistols were previously imported and distributed (until 1990) by Armscorp of America, Inc. located in Baltimore, MD. Shotguns were previously (until 1992) imported by Heckler & Koch, Inc. located in Sterling, VA.

Renato Gamba firearms have had limited importation since 1986. In 1989, several smaller European firearms companies were purchased by R. Gamba and are now part of the Renato Gamba Group. The importation of R. Gamba guns changed in 1990 to reflect their long term interest in exporting firearms to America. Earlier imported models may be rare but have not enjoyed much collectability to date.

PISTOLS

R. Gamba pistols are currently not being imported into the U.S. Importation was discontinued in 1990.

SAB G90 STANDARD — 7.65 P (disc.), 9 x 18mm Ultra (disc.), or 9mm Para. cal., double action, 4.72 in. barrel, 15 shot side release mag., blue or chrome (disc.) finish, hammer drop safety on frame, smooth walnut grips, 2.2 lbs.

	100%	98%	95%	90%	80%	70%	60%
	$375	$325	$295	$275	$250	$225	$200

Add $65 for chrome finish (disc.).
Last Mfg.'s Sug. Retail was $475.

SAB G90 Competition — 9mm Para., similar to SAB G90 Standard, except has adj. rear sight, "cocked and locked" operation, and checkered walnut grips. Imported 1990 only.

	100%	98%	95%	90%	80%	70%	60%
	$425	$375	$325	$300	$275	$250	$225

Last Mfg.'s Sug. Retail was $550.

SAB G91 COMPACT — similar to SAB G90, except has 3.54 in. barrel, 12 shot mag., 1.87 lbs.

	100%	98%	95%	90%	80%	70%	60%
	$395	$350	$315	$285	$250	$225	$200

Add $65 for chrome finish (disc.).
Last Mfg.'s Sug. Retail was $500.

SAB G91 Competition — 9mm Para., similar to SAB G91 Compact, except has adj. rear sight, "cocked and locked" operation, and checkered walnut grips. Imported 1990 only.

	100%	98%	95%	90%	80%	70%	60%
	$450	$395	$330	$300	$275	$250	$225

Last Mfg.'s Sug. Retail was $575.

Grading	100%	98%	95%	90%	80%	70%	60%

REVOLVERS

R. Gamba revolvers have not been imported since 1986.

TRIDENT FAST ACTION — .32 S&W or .38 Spl. cal., 2½ or 3 in. barrel, double action, blued receiver with checkered walnut grips, 6 shot, 23 oz.

	$495	$395	$360	$330	$295	$270	$245

Last Mfg.'s Sug. Retail was $595.

TRIDENT SUPER — .32 S&W or .38 Spl. cal., 4 in. vent. rib barrel, 6 shot, double action, checkered walnut grips, 25 oz.

	$530	$425	$380	$345	$300	$270	$245

Last Mfg.'s Sug. Retail was $645.

TRIDENT MATCH 900 — .32 W.C. or .38 Spl. cal., match gun featuring 6 in. heavy barrel and anatomically compatible checkered walnut grips, target sights, 2.2 lbs.

	$750	$660	$590	$525	$475	$430	$390

Last Mfg.'s Sug. Retail was $995.

Trident Match 901 — similar to Trident Match 900.

	$750	$660	$590	$525	$475	$430	$390

Last Mfg.'s Sug. Retail was $995.

RIFLES

SAFARI EXPRESS SxS — 7 x 65R, 9.3 x 74R, or .375 H&H cal., 25 in. barrels with open sights, underlug locking with Greener crossbolt, ejectors except on .375 H&H, coin finished receiver with scroll work and game scene engraving, DTs, deluxe checkered walnut stock with cheek piece and recoil pad, 9.9 lbs.

	$5,685	$4,575	$3,950	$3,575	$3,175	$2,850	$2,500

Last Mfg.'s Sug. Retail was $6,630.

EXPRESS MAXIM SxS — .375 H&H, .458 Win. Mag., or .470 N.E. cal., sidelock action, fine engraving with big game scenes signed by the master engraver, includes leather case. R. Gamba should be contacted directly regarding values on this model as each individual special order is quoted upon request.

MUSTANG EXTRA SINGLE SHOT — 5.6 x 50 (disc.), 5.6 x 57R, 6.5 x 57R (disc.), 7 x 65R, .222 Rem. (disc.), .243 Win., .270 Win. (disc.), or .30-06 cal., single 25½ in. barrel configuration with highly engraved sidelock action featuring triple-bite double Purdey locking system with Greener crossbolt, extra fine vine leaf Renaissance engraving (game scene upon request), double-set triggers, best quality checkered walnut stock and forearm, 6.17 lbs.

Mfg.'s Sug. Retail	$14,575	$13,250	$10,750	$8,950	$8,000	$7,500	$7,000	$6,650

RGZ 1000 BOLT ACTION — 7 x 64, .270 Win., 7mm Rem. Mag., .300 Win. Mag., modified Mauser K-98 action, 20½ in. barrel, pistol grip stock with cheek piece, 7 lbs.

	$1,100	$885	$825	$760	$700	$640	$575

Last Mfg.'s Sug. Retail was $1,310.

RGX 1000 Express — similar to RGZ 1000, except has 23¾ in. barrel and double set triggers, 7.7 lbs.

	$1,255	$960	$875	$795	$725	$650	$575

Last Mfg.'s Sug. Retail was $1,475.

Grading	100%	98%	95%	90%	80%	70%	60%

SHOTGUNS: OVER AND UNDER

Most O/U models (except for the Daytona Trap Model) listed below were discontinued in 1990 when H&K became the exclusive importer for R. Gamba shotguns.

EUROPA 2000 — 12 ga. only, engraved, silver finished boxlock action with sideplates, vent. rib, single trigger, ejectors, deluxe checkered stock and forearm, 6.84 lbs.

| | $1,250 | $995 | $895 | $835 | $775 | $715 | $650 |

Last Mfg.'s Sug. Retail was $1,475.

EDINBURGH SUPER SLUG — 12 ga. only, trap model, SST, ejectors, engraved action, deluxe checkered stock and forearm.

| | $1,225 | $980 | $895 | $835 | $775 | $715 | $650 |

Last Mfg.'s Sug. Retail was $1,425.

GRIFONE SPORTING TRAP — 12 ga. only, trap model, SST, ejectors, moderately engraved action, deluxe checkered stock and forearm.

| | $1,225 | $980 | $895 | $835 | $775 | $715 | $650 |

Last Mfg.'s Sug. Retail was $1,425.

GRINTA TRAP/SKEET — 12 ga. only, trap/skeet model, SST, ejectors, medium engraving coverage.

| | $1,460 | $1,250 | $995 | $895 | $835 | $775 | $715 |

Last Mfg.'s Sug. Retail was $1,710.

VICTORY TRAP/SKEET — similar to Grinta Model, except has better walnut and more engraving.

| | $1,620 | $1,295 | $1,100 | $995 | $895 | $835 | $775 |

Last Mfg.'s Sug. Retail was $1,905.

EDINBURG MATCH — similar to Victory Model, except has different style of engraving.

| | $1,630 | $1,300 | $1,100 | $995 | $895 | $835 | $775 |

Last Mfg.'s Sug. Retail was $1,930.

MONTREAL MODEL 81 — 12 ga. only, boxlock, interchangeable trigger assembly, select walnut, vent. rib. Available in International Trap, American Skeet, Sporting, and Field models. Add $50 for adj. single barrel.

| | $1,995 | $1,500 | $1,300 | $1,100 | $1,000 | $900 | $800 |

MONTREAL 81 AMERICAN TRAP COMBO — 12 ga. only, 32 in. barrels and adj. impact, single 34 in. barrel, interchangeable trigger assembly.

| | $2,800 | $2,100 | $1,820 | $1,540 | $1,400 | $1,260 | $1,120 |

SINGLE BARREL TRAP-MODEL 496 — 12 ga. only, boxlock, vent. rib.

| | $1,150 | $865 | $750 | $635 | $575 | $520 | $460 |

S. VINCENT 580 EXTRA DELUXE SXS — 12 ga. only, custom made to individual preferences, very high quality, sidelock action, engraving coverage 100%.

| | $3,250 | $2,440 | $2,115 | $1,790 | $1,625 | $1,465 | $1,300 |

DAYTONA MODEL — 12 ga. only, monolithic boxlock action, SST, ejectors, detachable trigger group, available in either Hunting, Skeet, Pigeon, Sporting Clays, Olympic Trap, or American Trap configuration, deluxe walnut with fine English scroll engraving with game scenes. Importation began 1990.

| Mfg.'s Sug. Retail | $4,995 | $4,500 | $3,850 | $3,300 | $2,800 | $2,350 | $1,900 | $1,500 |

Add $400 for American Trap configuration.
Add $2,100 for extra set of O/U barrels.
The Hunting O/U Daytona is available in 12 ga. only.

Grading	100%	98%	95%	90%	80%	70%	60%

⚞ **Grade 4 Daytona Model** — most elaborately engraved Daytona model.

Mfg.'s Sug. Retail	$13,195	$11,250	$9,250	$7,950	$6,500	$5,000	$4,250	$3,750

⚞ **Grade 5 Daytona Model** — one grade below Grade 4.

Mfg.'s Sug. Retail	$10,390	$9,350	$7,950	$6,500	$5,000	$4,250	$3,750	$3,250

⚞ **Grade 6 Daytona Model** — one grade below Grade 5.

Mfg.'s Sug. Retail	$9,950	$8,950	$7,950	$6,500	$5,000	$4,250	$3,750	$3,250

⚞ **Grade 7 Daytona Model** — introductory engraved model.

Mfg.'s Sug. Retail	$9,390	$8,500	$7,650	$6,250	$4,750	$3,950	$3,350	$2,950

DAYTONA SL — deluxe variation of the Daytona Model, except has sideplates with extensive engraving, available in the same configurations as the Daytona Model, includes case. Importation began 1990.

Mfg.'s Sug. Retail	$11,500	$10,250	$8,750	$7,250	$5,400	$4,450	$3,950	$3,500

Add $400 for American Trap configuration.

DAYTONA SLHH — 12 or 20 ga., H&H style sidelock action with Boss improved lock-up, top of the line model, includes leather case. Importation began in 1990.

⚞ **Grade 1** — similar to Grade 2, except has better engraving.

Mfg.'s Sug. Retail	$26,995	$23,750	$20,500	$17,500	$13,000	$10,750	$8,950	$6,950

⚞ **Grade 2** — available in either Hunting (12 ga. only), Skeet, Trap, Pigeon, or Sporting Clays configuration.

Mfg.'s Sug. Retail	$23,995	$21,500	$17,750	$14,750	$11,000	$9,000	$7,500	$5,950

BAYERN 88 COMBINATION GUN — 12 ga. over same cals. listed for Mustang Model, coin finished boxlock action with game scene engraving, double DTs, extractors, deluxe checkered walnut stock with recoil pad, 7½ lbs.

			$1,365	$1,050	$950	$860	$775	$715	$665

Last Mfg.'s Sug. Retail was $1,595.

SHOTGUNS: SIDE X SIDE

Previous to 1989, most of the models listed below were available in 28 ga. on a 28 ga. frame by option. These 28 ga. guns will command 15%+ premiums over values listed below.

HUNTER SUPER — 12 ga. only, Anson & Deeley engraved boxlock action with silver finish, DTs, extractors, 6.84 lbs.

			$1,395	$1,100	$865	$760	$630	$575	$525

Last Mfg.'s Sug. Retail was $1,506.

PRINCIPESSA — 12 or 20 ga., similar to Hunter Super except has English straight grip stock and better engraving, 6.62 lbs.

Mfg.'s Sug. Retail	$2,495	$2,195	$1,650	$1,400	$1,200	$995	$800	$625

Add $200 for single trigger.

OXFORD 90 — 12 or 20 ga., boxlock action with Purdey locking system, DTs, ejectors, scroll engraving on sideplates, deluxe checkered straight grip walnut stock with recoil pad or checkered butt, 6.84 lbs.

Mfg.'s Sug. Retail	$2,595	$2,295	$1,900	$1,625	$1,300	$1,050	$825	$650

Add $155 for single trigger.

OXFORD EXTRA — 20 ga. only, includes elegantly engraved sideplates, ejectors, and better quality hand checkered stock and forearm. Importation began 1992.

Mfg.'s Sug. Retail	$3,500	$3,225	$2,700	$2,295	$1,900	$1,625	$1,300	$1,050

Add $175 for single trigger.

Grading	100%	98%	95%	90%	80%	70%	60%

PRINCE — 12 or 20 ga., boxlock action, ejectors, hand checkered walnut stock and forearm. Importation began 1992.

Mfg.'s Sug. Retail	$3,575	$3,250	$2,725	$2,295	$1,900	$1,625	$1,300	$1,050

Add $200 for single trigger.

LONDON — 12 or 20 (disc.) ga., H&H side-lock system, ejectors, DT or SST, chopper lump barrels, English scroll engraving, deluxe checkered straight grip stock and forearm, 6.84 lbs.

Mfg.'s Sug. Retail	$7,500	$6,850	$4,500	$3,950	$3,500	$3,100	$2,700	$2,250

Add $250 for single trigger.

LONDON ROYAL — similar to London Model except has less extensive game scene engraving.

		$5,250	$4,350	$3,750	$3,300	$3,050	$2,800	$2,500

Last Mfg.'s Sug. Retail was $6,730.

AMBASSADOR MODEL — 12 or 20 ga., H&H side-lock system, available with either gold-line engraving on barrels and receiver with blued receiver (Gold and Black Model) or English scroll engraving (English Engraved Model), single trigger, ejectors, deluxe checkered walnut stock and forearm, cased, 6.4 lbs.

Mfg.'s Sug. Retail	$17,550	$15,500	$11,750	$9,000	$7,850	$6,700	$5,600	$4,500

This model is also available in either Field or Sporting versions upon special request.

AMBASSADOR EXECUTIVE — 12 or 20 ga. only, top-of-the-line model, made to individual order only, every possible refinement.

Mfg.'s Sug. Retail	$27,950	$24,750	$19,995	$16,250	$12,750	$10,000	$8,750	$7,400

SHOTGUNS: SLIDE ACTION

MODEL 2100 — 12 ga. Mag., 19½ in. barrel, 7 shot mag., law enforcement configuration with matte black metal and wood, 6.62 lbs. Limited importation.

		$610	$480	$390	$330	$275	$220	$195

Last Mfg.'s Sug. Retail was $715.

GARBI

Manufacturer located in Eibar, Spain. Imported and distributed exclusively by W.L. Moore & Co. located in Westlake Village, CA.

SHOTGUNS: DISCONTINUED SIDE-BY-SIDE

Currently, Garbi is mfg. 400-500 shotguns per year.

MODEL 51 A — 12 ga. only, extractors, case hardened finish, straight grip.

		$450	$350	$325	$300	$280	$260	$240

MODEL 51 B — 12, 16, or 20 ga., ejectors, case hardened or coin finish receiver, straight grip.

		$850	$650	$590	$540	$500	$460	$420

MODEL 60 A — 12 ga. only, extractors, case hardened finish, true sidelock, large scroll engraving, cocking indicators, hand checkered butt, choice of grip.

		$725	$575	$530	$475	$440	$400	$360

MODEL 60 B — 12, 16, or 20 ga., ejectors, case hardened or coin finish receiver, extensive engraving, straight grip.

		$1,200	$850	$790	$735	$680	$630	$575

Grading	100%	98%	95%	90%	80%	70%	60%

MODEL 62 A — 12 ga. only, extractors, case hardened finish, true sidelock, light engraving, cocking indicators, hand checkered butt, choice of grip.

	$725	$575	$530	$475	$440	$400	$360

MODEL 62 B — 12, 16, or 20 ga. only, ejectors, case hardened or coin finish receiver, extensive engraving, straight grip.

	$1,200	$850	$790	$735	$680	$630	$575

SHOTGUNS: SXS RECENT MFG.

Garbi currently manufactures between 400 - 500 shotguns yearly.

For the following models — add 5% for 28 ga., $750 for single trigger, $120-$250 for beavertail forearm, $1,125-$2,300 per extra set of barrels (depending on grade), and $250 for Churchill style level file-cut rib.

MODEL 71 — 12, 16, or 20 ga., Holland-pattern detachable sidelock ejector double, fine English scroll engraving, oil finish, select walnut, articulated trigger. Importation disc. 1988.

	$2,250	$1,825	$1,500	$1,300	$1,075	$980	$900

Last Mfg.'s Sug. Retail was $2,600.

MODEL 100 — 12, 16, or 20 ga., Holland-pattern detachable sidelock ejector double, Purdy style scroll engraving, chopper lump barrels, oil finish, select walnut, articulated trigger.

Mfg.'s Sug. Retail	$4,500	$3,600	$2,750	$2,100	$1,650	$1,450	$1,200	$1,025

MODEL 101 — 12, 16, or 20 ga., Holland-pattern sidelock ejector double with chopper lump barrels, Continental style floral and scroll engraving, selected walnut stock.

Mfg.'s Sug. Retail	$5,750	$4,600	$3,600	$2,800	$2,300	$1,900	$1,650	$1,400

MODEL 102 — 12, 16, 20, or 28 ga., Holland-pattern sidelock ejector double with chopper lump barrels, Holland-type large scroll engraving, selected walnut stock.

Mfg.'s Sug. Retail	$7,100	$5,700	$4,500	$3,450	$2,700	$2,350	$2,000	$1,750

MODEL 103A — 12, 16, 20, or 28 ga., Holland-pattern sidelock ejector double with chopper lump barrels, Purdey-type fine scroll and rosette engraving, selected walnut stock.

Mfg.'s Sug. Retail	$7,100	$5,700	$4,500	$3,450	$2,700	$2,350	$2,000	$1,750

MODEL 103B — 12, 16, 20, or 28 ga., Holland-pattern sidelock ejector double with chopper lump barrels of nickel-chrome steel, H&H type easy opening mechanism, Purdey-type fine scroll and rosette engraving, well figured walnut stock.

Mfg.'s Sug. Retail	$9,900	$7,900	$6,200	$5,150	$4,250	$3,500	$2,750	$2,250

MODEL 120 — 12, 16, 20, or 28 ga., Holland-pattern sidelock ejector double with chopper lump barrels of nickel-chrome steel, H&H type easy opening mechanism, game scene engraving-3 patterns available. Well figured walnut stock.

Mfg.'s Sug. Retail	$9,400	$7,500	$6,000	$4,875	$4,125	$3,375	$2,600	$2,200

MODEL 200 — 12, 16, 20, or 28 ga., Holland-pattern sidelock ejector double with chopper lump barrels of nickel-chrome steel, heavy-duty locks, magnum proofed, very fine Continental style floral and scroll engraving, well figured walnut stock.

Mfg.'s Sug. Retail	$9,400	$7,500	$6,000	$4,875	$4,125	$3,375	$2,600	$2,200

SPECIAL WLM — 12, 16, 20, or 28 ga., top-of-the-line Holland-pattern sidelock ejector double with chopper lump barrels, full coverage large scroll engraving, fancy-figured walnut stock.

Mfg.'s Sug. Retail	$9,400	$7,500	$6,000	$4,875	$4,125	$3,375	$2,600	$2,200

Grading	100%	98%	95%	90%	80%	70%	60%

SPECIAL AG — 12, 16, 20, or 28 ga., top-of-the-line Holland-pattern sidelock ejector double with chopper lump barrels, large scroll engraving patterned after Labeau-Courally, fancy figured walnut stock.

Mfg.'s Sug. Retail	$9,000	$8,000	$6,350	$5,200	$4,300	$3,550	$2,750	$2,300

GASTINNE RENETTE
Manufacturer and retailer located in Paris, France.

Currently being manufactured with limited importation and distribution. No Manufacturer's list price is shown in this section. Gastine Renette should be contacted directly (see Trademark Index) for an up-to-date quotation or information on their current model line-up.

RIFLES: BOLT ACTION

Values listed below are base prices for each model - since all guns are made to individual order, the customer can choose the wood, level of engraving, and other special features, all at additional cost. Gastinne Renette should be contacted directly (see Trademark Index) for an individual price quotation.

STANDARD MODEL MAUSER ACTION

Mfg.'s Sug. Retail	$5,200	$5,200	$4,650	$4,150	$3,650	$3,050	$2,550	$1,900

DELUXE MAUSER ACTION

Mfg.'s Sug. Retail	$10,800	$10,800	$7,500	$6,750	$5,650	$4,800	$3,900	$2,950

RIFLES: SINGLE SHOT

FALLING BLOCK MODEL

Mfg.'s Sug. Retail	$14,000	$14,000	$12,000	$9,750	$8,250	$6,750	$5,900	$5,000

SIDELOCK MODEL — features breakdown action. New 1993.

Mfg.'s Sug. Retail	$34,000	$34,000	$29,500	$25,750	$21,250	$18,000	$14,750	$11,350

RIFLES: DOUBLE SxS

BOXLOCK MODEL — variety of cals., features Anson & Deeley boxlock mechanism, color case hardened receiver. New 1993.

Mfg.'s Sug. Retail	$10,000	$10,000	$7,750	$6,950	$5,850	$4,950	$4,100	$3,200

EUROPEAN SIDELOCK

Mfg.'s Sug. Retail	$36,000	$36,000	$31,000	$27,000	$22,500	$18,750	$15,000	$12,500

AFRICAN SIDELOCK — various Mag. cals. New 1993.

Mfg.'s Sug. Retail	$40,000	$40,000	$33,000	$28,750	$23,500	$19,250	$15,500	$12,750

STANDARD TYPE G — 9.3 x 74R, 7.65R, .30-06, or .375 H&H cal., double bolt action, ejectors, reinforced stock, 23¾ in. barrels, bouquet style engraving with deluxe walnut stock and forearm, 7lbs. 6 oz.

	$2,995	$2,500	$2,150	$1,700	$1,560	$1,480	$1,340

DELUXE TYPE R — 9.3 x 74R, 7.65R, .30-06, or .375 H&H cal., double bolt action, true sideplates, ejectors, reinforced stock, 23¾ in. barrels, animal engraving with deluxe walnut stock and forearm, 7 lbs. 6 oz.

	$3,875	$3,325	$2,700	$2,175	$1,850	$1,700	$1,525

PRESIDENT TYPE PT — 9.3 x 74R, 7.65R, .30-06, or .375 H&H cal., double bolt action, true sideplates, ejectors, reinforced stock, 23¾ in. barrels, light engraving with gold line inlays, best quality walnut, 7 lbs. 6 oz.

	$4,250	$3,725	$3,200	$2,650	$2,250	$1,825	$1,600

Grading	100%	98%	95%	90%	80%	70%	60%

SHOTGUNS SXS

MODEL 105 — 12 or 20 ga., Anson and Deeley type triple bolt action, ejectors, double triggers, case hardened frame, 6 lbs. 8 oz.

| | $2,250 | $1,800 | $1,400 | $1,250 | $1,125 | $1,000 | $900 |

MODEL 98 — 12 and 20 ga., Purdey type triple bolt action, ejectors, double triggers, case hardened frame, 6 lbs. 8 oz.

| | $2,995 | $2,500 | $2,000 | $1,850 | $1,580 | $1,430 | $1,260 |

MODEL 202 — 12 or 20 ga., Purdey type triple bolt action, sidelocks, fine English engraving, first grade French walnut, ejectors, double triggers, coin finished receiver, 6 lbs. 10 oz.

| | $5,250 | $4,500 | $3,950 | $3,250 | $2,500 | $2,175 | $1,875 |

MODEL 353 — 12 or 20 ga., Purdey type triple bolt action, hand detachable sidelocks, Chopper lump barrels, fine English engraving, first grade French walnut, ejectors, double triggers, case hardened receiver, best quality, 6 lbs. 10 oz.

| | $19,950 | $17,500 | $13,650 | $11,000 | $8,900 | $6,700 | $6,250 |

GATLING GUN COMPANY

Manufactured since 1961 by Furr Arms located in Orem, UT. Distributed by J & G Sales, Inc. located in Prescott, AZ.

The Gatling Gun Company manufactures high quality 1/6, 1/3, 1/2, 3/4 and full scale brass reproductions of famous, antique machine guns and cannons. Models include the 1874 Gatling Gun on carriage (includes 225 round Broadwell feed drum and 10 exposed barrels), 1876 Camel Gun (includes 225 round Broadwell feed drum), 1883 Gatling Gun on carriage (Accles feed drum, 10 enclosed barrels), 1893 Police, British Naval Cannon, and the James Six Pounder. Prices vary according to the complexity of each model, and are available by contacting the distributor.

Except for Models 1876 Carriage Gatling (1/2 scale) and 1876 Camel Tripod (1/2 scale), all the models listed below may be purchased on a special order basis from the factory. 100% values represent the current manufacturer's suggested retail.

1874 Carriage 1/2	$5,000	$4,000	$3,500
1874 Carriage Gatling 1/3	$6,500	$5,250	$4,250
1876 Carriage Gatling 1/2	$12,000	$9,000	$7,500
1876 Carriage Gatling 3/4	$19,000	$15,000	$12,000
1874 Camel Tripod 1/6	$4,000	$3,000	$2,500
1874 Camel Tripod 1/3	$4,500	$3,500	$2,800
1876 Camel Tripod 1/2	$8,000	$6,500	$5,250
1876 Camel Tripod 3/4	$12,000	$9,000	$7,500
1876 Camel Tripod (Full)	$18,000	$14,500	$11,500
1893 Police Gatling 1/6	$2,500	$2,100	$1,650
1893 Police Gatling 1/3	$3,200	$2,550	$2,000
1883 Carriage Gatling 1/6	$5,000	$4,000	$3,500
1883 Carriage Gatling 1/3	$6,500	$5,250	$4,250
James Six Lb. Cannon 1/6	$900	$750	$575
James Six Lb. Cannon 1/5	$2,200	$1,850	$1,400
James Six Lb. Cannon 1/3	$3,200	$2,550	$2,000

H.M.S. Victory Naval Cannon 1/10

| | $500 | $375 | $325 |

Grading	100%	98%	95%	90%	80%	70%	60%

H.M.S. Victory Naval Cannon $^{1}/_{10}$ — this cannon is mounted on an oak ship deck section complete with planking, port lid, and working block and tackle.

	$900	$750	$575

H.M.S. Victory Naval Cannon $^{1}/_{3}$

	$3,200	$2,550	$2,000

GAUCHER

 *Gaucher* **Armes**

Manufacturer located in St. Etienne, France. Currently imported and distributed by Mandall's Shooting Supplies located in Scottsdale, AZ.

PISTOLS: TARGET

MODEL GN1 — .22 LR cal., single shot silhouette pistol featuring 10 in. barrel, adj. sights, anatomically shaped grips, monobloc lever cocking, 2.42 lbs. Importation began 1991.

Mfg.'s Sug. Retail	$380	$360	$325	$290	$260	$230	$200	$185

MODEL GP — similar to Model GN1, except has forearm integrated into grip. Importation began 1991.

Mfg.'s Sug. Retail	$323	$300	$275	$250	$225	$200	$185	$160

GAVAGE

Previous manufacturer located in Liege, Belgium between 1936-1943 approximately.

GAVAGE PISTOL — 7.65mm, patterned after the "Clement", fixed barrel, limited mfg.

	$375	$325	$250	$200	$175	$150	$125

This pistol is very rare if encountered with Waffenamt proofmarks - healthy premiums are being asked.

GENTRY, DAVID

Custom rifle gunmaker located in Belgrade, MT.

David Gentry is a current custom rifle builder who usually fabricates rifles to individual custom order requests. In addition to special orders, he also builds the Rough Rider Model ($995 base price), Outfitter's Rifle ($2,400 base price), in addition to top quality muzzle brakes and stainless steel Featherlight scope rings (1 in. and 30mm). Mr Gentry should be contacted directly (see Trademark Index) for more information on options/prices.

GERMAN WWII MILITARY PISTOLS

Also See: Fabrique Nationale, Luger, Mauser, and Walther for other military pistols.

P.38 — double action, 9mm, 5 in. barrel, 8 shot mag., fixed sights, brown or black composite grips, blued finish. Many variations exhibiting a variety of metal finishes and codings, 34 oz. Over 1,000,000 manufactured during WW II.

Note: This model was adopted as the standard service pistol of the German Military in 1938. The P.38 was manufactured by Walther - code "ac" (mfg. 1939-1945), Mauser - code "byf" (mfg. Nov. of 1942-1945), and Spreewerke - code "cyq." (mfg. 1943-1945). The finish on most WWII 1942 and later P.38s is not of the same quality as the pre and early war Walther guns with the Spreewerke (cyq) models being the poorest. Pre-war Walther commercial manufactured P.38s command a 10-35% premium (models MP, AP, and Walther Banner HPs) over Zero-series prices listed below.

Grading	100%	98%	95%	90%	80%	70%	60%

ZERO-SERIES HP — "Heeres Pistole", with Mauser banner, high polish finish. Mfg. 1939 and 1940. 5-digit number without suffix. Add 10% for matching mag.

⚁ **Zero Series - 1st Issue** — internal extractor, square firing pin.

| | $3,500 | $3,000 | $2,250 | $1,800 | $1,500 | $1,200 | $1,000 |

⚁ **Zero Series - 2nd Issue** — external extractor, square firing pin.

| | $2,750 | $2,200 | $2,000 | $1,700 | $1,400 | $1,100 | $900 |

⚁ **Zero Series - 3rd Issue** — external extractor, round firing pin.

| | $1,800 | $1,400 | $1,000 | $800 | $700 | $600 | $500 |

⚁ **480 code** — "480" appears on slide.

| | $1,850 | $1,400 | $1,100 | $850 | $725 | $625 | $525 |

ac-40 CODE — indicates 1940 mfg., the 480 code was dropped in October of 1940, and the "ac" code was started.

| | $1,100 | $800 | $700 | $600 | $500 | $430 | $380 |

Add 20% for matching mag.

ac-41 OR ac-42 CODE — indicates 1941 or 1942 mfg.

| | $650 | $500 | $425 | $380 | $340 | $300 | $275 |

Add 20% for matching mag.

"ac" OR "byf" CODED 43-45 — letters are followed by two digit code corresponding to year of mfg. 1943-1945. Two line codes are more desirable than single line models. Highest P.38 production occurred in 1943 and 1944.

| | $495 | $395 | $325 | $250 | $225 | $200 | $175 |

Add 20% for "dual tone" (phosphate finish — byf-44 date).

"cyq" CODE AND "ac-45" MISMATCH — cyq variation typically exhibits rough machining with visible circular milling marks, mismatched slide and frame on ac-45 model.

| | $425 | $350 | $275 | $240 | $210 | $190 | $165 |

Deduct 20% for ac-45 mismatch.

LATE WAR (1945) — Zero Series with rough milled finish.

| | $700 | $600 | $500 | $425 | $350 | $300 | $250 |

1945 "svw" CODE — Mauser mfg. after January, 1945.

| | $350 | $300 | $260 | $230 | $200 | $180 | $165 |

Recent importation has decreased values substantially in the last several years.

1946 "svw" CODE — Mauser mfg. 1946.

| | $425 | $365 | $285 | $250 | $210 | $190 | $165 |

GEVARM
Ste. Etienne, France.

E-1 AUTOLOADING RIFLE — .22 LR, 19 in. barrel, open sights, walnut pistol grip stock.

| | $165 | $130 | $110 | $100 | $85 | $65 | $55 |

GIB

10 GAUGE MAGNUM SHOTGUN — 10 ga., 3½ in. chambers, 32 in. full choke barrel, case hardened receiver, matted rib, rubber pad, checkered pistol grip walnut stock. Disc.

| | $275 | $250 | $235 | $220 | $200 | $175 | $150 |

GIBBS GUNS, INC.

Previously manufactured by Volunteer Enterprises in Knoxville, TN and previously distributed by Gibbs Guns, Inc. located in Greenback, TN.

Grading	100%	98%	95%	90%	80%	70%	60%

MARK 45 CARBINE — .45 ACP only, based on TS M6 Thompson machine gun, 16½ in. barrel, 5, 15, 30, or 90 shot clip, U.S. mfg. Disc. 1988.

	$315	$275	$225	$180	$165	$155	$145

Add $60 minimum for nickel plating.
Last Mfg.'s Sug. Retail was $279.

GIBBS RIFLE COMPANY

Manufacturer located in Martinsburg, WV beginning 1991. Dealer direct sales.

In addition to manufacturing rifles in its new facility located in Martinsburg, WV, Gibbs Rifle Co. also imports a variety of older firearms including English military rifles and handguns (both original and refurbished condition), a wide variety of used military contract pistols and rifles, in addition to other shooting products and accessories. Gibbs Rifle Co. blackpowder reproductions are located in the back of this text under their own separate heading. Gibbs also imports W.W. Greener Ltd. shotguns which is located under its own trademark heading.

RIFLES: BOLT ACTION

Gibbs Guns bolt action rifles utilize the Mauser K-98 action and are offered in a variety of configurations.

GIBBS ECONOMY SPORTER — 8mm Mauser, sporterized military action with good barrel and sporting sights, walnut finished checkered hardwood stock. New 1993.

Mfg.'s Sug. Retail	$205	$185	$150	$135	$120	$100	$85	$70

GIBBS MAUSER SPORTER — .243 Win., .270 Win., .30-06, or .308 Win. cal., features M-98 action, walnut finished checkered hardwood stock, action is drilled and tapped, flip-up rear sight and ramp front. New 1993.

Mfg.'s Sug. Retail	$295	$250	$220	$195	$175	$150	$135	$120

MODEL 81 CLASSIC — available in 11 cals. between .22-250 and 7mm Rem. Mag., 24 in. barrel, open sights, 4 shot mag., select checkered walnut with sling swivels, 7¾ lbs.

Mfg.'s Sug. Retail	$900	$795	$595	$475	$395	$340	$300	$280

Model 81 African — .375 H&H or 9.3 x 62mm cal., similar specifications as Model 81 Classic with quarter rib and express sights, engraved action, Pachmayr recoil pad, 9 lbs.

Mfg.'s Sug. Retail	$1,050	$925	$725	$600	$500	$425	$360	$330

MODEL 85 SNIPER RIFLE — .308 cal., bolt action, 24 in. extended heavy barrel, 10 shot mag., camo green synthetic McMillan stock with stippling, built in adj. bipod and recoil pad, enlarged contoured bolt, adj. sights, 12 lbs. 6 oz.

Mfg.'s Sug. Retail	$2,050	$1,825	$1,450	$1,275	$1,050	$875	$750	$625

MODEL 87 TARGET — .243, 6.5 x 55, .308, .30-06, or .300 Win. Mag. cal., target stock, aperture sights. Mfg. disc. 1992.

	$1,375	$1,100	$900	$775	$650	$550	$495

Last Mfg.'s Sug. Retail was $1,500.

MODEL 1000 STANDARD — .22-250, .243 Win., 6mm Rem., 6.5 x 55mm, 7 x 57mm, 7 x 64mm, .270 Win., .30-06, or .308 Win. cal., 22 in. barrel, 4 shot built in mag., checkered walnut stock with cheek piece, open sights, 7¼ lbs.

Mfg.'s Sug. Retail	$495	$425	$375	$325	$290	$260	$240	$220

Grading	100%	98%	95%	90%	80%	70%	60%

Model 1000 Clip — similar to Model 1000 Standard, except has detachable 4 shot mag.

Mfg.'s Sug. Retail	$535	$460	$395	$350	$300	$270	$240	$220

MODEL 1100 LIGHTWEIGHT — available in 9 cals. between .22-250 and .308 Win., 22 in. barrel, open sights, 4 shot mag., 6½ lbs.

Mfg.'s Sug. Retail	$510	$435	$380	$325	$290	$260	$240	$220

Model 1100M African — .375 H&H, or .458 Win. Mag. cal., 24 in. barrel, 4 shot mag., 9½ lbs.

Mfg.'s Sug. Retail	$930	$825	$650	$575	$500	$450	$425	$400

MODEL 1200 SUPER — bolt action, Mauser type action, .22-250, .243, 6mm, 6.5 x 55mm, 7 x 64mm, .270, .30-06, or .308 cal., 24 in. barrel, folding sight, skip checkered walnut stock, pad swivels, rosewood pistol grip cap and forend tip.

Mfg.'s Sug. Retail	$595	$495	$400	$350	$325	$285	$270	$255

Model 1200 Super Clip — similar to Model 1200 Super, except has detachable 4 shot box mag.

Mfg.'s Sug. Retail	$640	$525	$425	$375	$350	$300	$280	$265

MODEL 1300S SCOUT — .243 Win. or .308 Win., 20 in. barrel with muzzle brake, internal 5 shot or detachable 5/10 shot mag., laminated checkered birchwood stock, sling swivels, 8½ lbs.

Mfg.'s Sug. Retail	$495	$425	$375	$325	$290	$260	$240	$220

Add $30 for detachable mag. (Model 1300C)

MODEL 1500S SURVIVOR — .308 Win. cal., bolt action, matte stainless construction, black composite (Kevlar/fiberglass) stock, 22 in. barrel, 4 shot mag., 7 lbs. Mfg. began 1993.

Mfg.'s Sug. Retail	$450	$395	$350	$300	$270	$240	$210	$185

Add $30 for detachable clip (Model 1500C).
This model is made for the Gibbs Rifle Co. by Bell & Carlson, Inc.

RIFLES: MIDLAND BOLT ACTION SERIES

MODEL 2100 MIDLAND DELUXE — similar to Model 2600 Midland, except has checkered walnut stock and pistol grip cap.

Mfg.'s Sug. Retail	$390	$335	$280	$235	$210	$190	$180	$170

MODEL 2600 MIDLAND — .22-250, .243 Win., 6mm Rem., 6.5 x 55mm, 7 x 57mm, 7 x 64mm, .270 Win., .30-06, or .308 Win. cal., 22 in. barrel, 4 shot mag., checkered hardwood stock with Monte Carlo cheekpiece, open sights, drilled and tapped action, 7 lbs.

Mfg.'s Sug. Retail	$375	$320	$270	$225	$200	$180	$165	$150

MIDLAND 2700 LIGHTWEIGHT — lightweight variation of the Model 2100 Midland Deluxe featuring tapered barrel, anodized aluminum trigger housing and lightened stock with full pistol grip and recoil pad, Schnabel forend, 6½ lbs.

Mfg.'s Sug. Retail	$415	$350	$285	$245	$225	$200	$190	$180

MIDLAND 2800 — similar to Model 2600 Midland, except has laminate birchwood stock, 7 lbs.

Mfg.'s Sug. Retail	$405	$340	$280	$240	$210	$190	$180	$170

SHOTGUNS

MIDLAND STALKER — 12 ga., trigger bar safety, unique squeeze break open action and cocking system, 28½ in. barrel bored F, hardwood stock and forearm, 6 lbs.

Mfg.'s Sug. Retail	$110	$90	$65	$55	$45	$35	$30	$25

GLOCK
Manufactured by Glock Ges.m.b.H. in Austria since 1983. Exclusively imported and distributed by Glock, Inc., located in Smyrna, GA.

All Glock pistols have a "safe action" safety system (double action only) which includes trigger safety, firing pin safety, and drop safety. Glock pistols have only 35 parts for reliability and simplicity in operation.

PISTOLS: SEMI-AUTO

Most of the models below are available in a cutaway configuration for sale to law enforcement agencies. The current retail price is $690.

Grading	100%	98%	95%	90%	80%	70%	60%

MODEL 17 SPORT/SERVICE — 9mm, double action, unique polymer frame, mag., trigger and other pistol parts. Steel barrel, slide, and springs, 17 or 19 shot mag., 4.49 in. barrel with hexagonal rifling, adj. (Sport Model) or fixed (Service Model) rear sight, hammerless, includes extra mag., case, and spare rear sight, 24 oz. empty. Importation began late 1985.

Mfg.'s Sug. Retail $580 $490 $385 $300
Add $135 for factory installed fixed night sights.
Adj. rear sight available at no extra charge (Sport Model).

⚱ **Model 17L Competition Model** — competition version of the Model 17, includes internally compensated 6.02 in. barrel, recalibrated trigger pull (3½ lb. pull), adj. rear sight, 25.4 oz. New 1988.

Mfg.'s Sug. Retail $768 $650 $525 $425

⚱ **Glock 17 Desert Storm Commemorative** — 9mm Para., features coalition forces listing on top of barrel, inscription on side of slide "NEW WORLD ORDER", 1,000 mfg. in 1991 only.

                $995 $825 $600

Last Mfg.'s Sug. Retail was $795.

MODEL 19 COMPACT SPORT/SERVICE — similar to Model 17, except has scaled down dimensions with 4.02 in. barrel and serrated grip straps, 15 or 17 shot mag, fixed (Service Model) or adj. (Sport Model) rear sight, 23 oz. New 1988.

Mfg.'s Sug. Retail $580 $490 $385 $300

MODEL 20 SPORT/SERVICE — 10mm Norma cal., similar action to Model 17, features 4.6 in. barrel, 15 shot mag., thicker trigger guard, fixed (Service Model) or adj. (Sport Model) rear sight, 28.4 oz. New 1990.

Mfg.'s Sug. Retail $639 $560 $485 $425

MODEL 21 SPORT/SERVICE — .45 ACP cal., otherwise similar to Model 20, 13 shot mag., 27.2 oz. Introduced May, 1991.

Mfg.'s Sug. Retail $639 $560 $485 $425

The Sport Model has adj. sights and the Service Model has fixed sights.

MODEL 22 SPORT/SERVICE — .40 S&W cal., similar to Model 20, except has 4.49 in. barrel, 15 shot mag., 24 oz. Introduced 1990.

Mfg.'s Sug. Retail $580 $490 $385 $300

The Sport Model has adj. sights and the Service Model has fixed sights.
200 Model 22s were originally shipped with consecutive serial numbers "NY-1 - NY-200". Somehow, they probably were erroneously numbered at the factory (probably thinking that they somehow were part of the New York State Troopers shipment of Model 17s) during 1990. Premiums will occur on this variation.

Grading	100%	98%	95%	90%	80%	70%	60%

MODEL 23 COMPACT SPORT/SERVICE — compact variation of the Model 22 with 4.02 in. barrel and 13 shot mag., 22.4 oz. New 1990.

Mfg.'s Sug. Retail	$580	$490	$385	$300			

The Sport Model has adj. sights and the Service Model has fixed sights.

GOLDEN EAGLE
Trademark of rifles/shotguns produced by Nikko Limited located in Tochigi, Japan.

Please refer to the Nikko Limited listing in this text for a complete chronological history of Nikko - Japan's previous long gun manufacturer.

RIFLES

MODEL 7000 GRADE I — bolt action, all popular American calibers, including .270, and .300 Wby., 24 or 26 in. barrels, select skipline checkered walnut stock, rosewood forend tip, golden eagle head engraved in pistol grip cap, recoil pad. Mfg. 1976-1981.

	$525	$460	$375	$315	$280	$225	$195

MODEL 7000 GRADE I AFRICAN — similar to 7000, except .375 H&H and .458 Win. Mag., open sights.

	$575	$485	$385	$325	$285	$230	$200

MODEL 7000 GRADE II — scroll engraving, better grade wood.

	$640	$525	$415	$360	$310	$250	$225

SHOTGUNS

MODEL 5000 GRADE I — O/U shotgun, 12 or 20 ga., 26, 28, or 30 in. barrels, various chokes, vent. rib, engraved receiver, gold eagle head inlay, auto ejectors, SST, checkered pistol grip beavertail stock. Mfg. 1975-1981.

	$850	$775	$695	$625	$550	$475	$395

MODEL 5000 GRADE I SKEET — similar to 5000, except 26 or 28 in. skeet bored, wide rib.

	$925	$850	$750	$660	$550	$475	$395

MODEL 5000 GRADE I TRAP — similar to Field, except 30 or 32 in. barrel, mod. and full, imp. mod. and full, or full and full choke, wide rib, trap stock with pad.

	$950	$875	$775	$660	$550	$475	$395

MODEL 5000 GRADE II — available in Field, Trap, and Skeet, more engraving, better grade wood, with screaming eagle on receiver in gold.

	$995	$895	$825	$750	$650	$550	$450
Skeet	$1,000	$900	$830	$750	$675	$595	$525
Trap	$995	$895	$825	$750	$650	$550	$450

GRANDEE GRADE III — similar to 5000 Grade II, except elaborate engraving, inlays, and better grade wood.

	$2,500	$2,150	$1,750	$1,300	$1,125	$1,000	$850

GOLDEN STATE ARMS
Previous importer located in Pasadena, CA. Golden State Arms both imported and subcontracted various firearms constructed by European and Japanese manufacturers - achieving private label status on some guns. More research is underway to learn more about this company that imported firearms circa 1960-74.

GONCZ ARMAMENT, INC.
Previous owner/manufacturer located in North Hollywood, CA 1984-1990.

While advertised, records indicate very few Goncz pistols or carbines were actually produced. All of these guns were prototypes or individually hand-built and none were ever mass produced through normal fabrication techniques.

In 1990, Claridge Hi-Tec, Inc. purchased Goncz Armament, Inc. Although all warranties for Goncz pistols/carbines are now void, Claridge Hi-Tec does offer parts and service for these older weapons (please see information in Trademark Index).

Any consumer wishing to know more about any Goncz firearm should contact Claridge Hi-Tec, Inc. directly. While advertised, so few models were manufactured that a listing of these has been omitted to avoid confusion and speculation.

GRANGER, G.
Manufacturer located in Saint Etienne, France since 1902.

G. Granger manufactures high quality, limited production side-by-side boxlock and sidelock shotguns in 12, 16, or 20 ga. All guns are made on a custom order basis with prices ranging between $20,000 - $37,800. Prices will vary per customer specifications and appointments.

G. Granger should be contacted directly (see Trademark Index) regarding up-to-date model information (including current pricing).

GRANT, STEPHEN
Previously manufactured in London, England.

Manufacturer specializing in custom order only SxS rifles and shotguns. Shotguns (12, 16, or 20 ga.) can be top or side lever and are equipped with sidelocks and a self-opening mechanism. Very limited production making values hard to establish. Prices are at par with similar quality H&H firearms.

GREAT WESTERN ARMS COMPANY
Great Western Arms Co. was located at 9001-9007 Miner Street, Los Angeles, CA. Founded through the efforts of Mr. Hy Hunter, with William R. Wilson as President.

Originated probably in early 1953, when Colt Firearms Company ceased production of what is known today as "First Generation Single Action Army Revolvers," Mr. Hunter could see the public's continued demand of such a revolver. After several trips to the Colt factory to ascertain Colt's intent of reviving their production of the S.A. Army, and being assured it would never be revived, he founded the G.W. Arms Co. The main change between the Colt S.A. and the G.W. Frontier was removing the firing pin from the hammer and the design of a rebounding firing pin inserted in the revolver frame. This firm also redesigned the Remington 2 shot derringer and designed a derringer in 2 cals., .38 S&W and .38 S&W Special. Approx. 2,000 of these were mfg. Production of the Frontier probably did not exceed 23,000. When the Colt Company resumed production of their 2nd Generation S.A. 1873 Revolver, it rang the death knell of Great Western Arms Co. products, and the G.W. Arms Co. soon disappeared with its last sales of their "Frontier" being sold as unassembled "Kit Guns" to be assembled by the purchaser.

100%	98%	95%	90%	80%	70%	60%	50%	40%	30%	20%	10%

SINGLE ACTION REVOLVER: FRONTIER — .45 Colt, .44-40, .44 Mag., .44 Spl., .357 Atomic, .357 Mag., .38 S&W Spl., .32-20 WCF, or .22 Rimfire cal., 7½, 5½, or 3½ in. barrel, blue with case hardened colors on frame, gate and hammer, all blue, satin blue, nickel, black nickel, copper plated black oxide, gold, silver, gold and silver and parkerizing, grips were imitation stag (plastic), wood, pearl, ivory and sterling silver on special order. Unfinished "Kit Guns" were also sold, allowing buyer to assemble and finish.

$650	$625	$600	$575	$550	$500	$450	$350	$325	$295	$270	$250

Add 50% for Special .22 Target Model with micro sights.
Add 100% for Fast Draw Model.
Add 25% for electroplated barrels.
Add 25% for electroplated cylinder.
Add minimum 5% for any finish other than parkerized or blue with case hardened frame.
Add 20% for consecutive ser. no. sets.
Add 50% if with factory original presentation case.

Add 60% if with factory original letter.
Add 25% for .44 Mag. or .357 Atomic cal.
Add 50% for factory original cals. not listed above.
Add 60% for Sheriff Model (called Deputy Model).
Add 80% for any barrel length above 7½ in.
Add minimum 100% for original factory engraving.
Add minimum 300% for original factory engraving with silver and gold.
Add 75% for factory sterling silver grips.
Add 20% for factory pearl or ivory grips.
Add 10% for factory wood grips.
Add 30% for any gun with a longer than factory standard or shorter than standard barrel.
Deduct 25% for assembled kit guns.
Values for unassembled kit gun in original box are same as above.

100%	98%	95%	90%	80%	70%	60%	50%	40%	30%	20%	10%

GREAT WESTERN DERRINGER — .38 S&W or .38 S&W Spl. cal. (not interchangeable). Basically an improved version of the Remington 2 shot derringer frame.

100%	98%	95%	90%	80%	70%	60%	50%	40%	30%	20%	10%
$395	$375	$350	$325	$300	$250	$200	$175	$150	$125	$100	$90

Add 10% for consecutive ser. no. sets.
Add 20% for factory pearl or ivory grips.
Add 25% for factory original casing.
Add minimum 200% for factory original engraving.

GREENER, W.W., LIMITED

Manufacturer located in Birmingham, England since 1829. Gibbs Rifle Co. located in Martinsburg, WV is the agent for W.W. Greener Ltd. in the U.S.

W.W. Greener manufactures best quality rifles and shotguns only. Approximately 20-50 guns are made annually.

Values below are based on a $100 = 67.1 English pounds exchange rate.

RIFLES: SxS · CURRENT MFG.

Boxlock and sidelock rifle quotations may be obtained by writing the company directly (see Trademark Index). A complete choice of calibers, engraving options, and walnut selection are available on a special order basis only.

SHOTGUNS: SINGLE SHOT

Grading	100%	98%	95%	90%	80%	70%	60%

GP MK II — 12 ga. only, famed general purpose (GP) English shotgun configuration featuring Greener Martini action, 28 or 30 in. barrel, walnut stock and forearm. Mfg. resumed in 1991.

	100%	98%	95%	90%	80%	70%	60%
Mfg.'s Sug. Retail $522	$522	$450	$400	$350	$300	$250	$195

SHOTGUNS: SxS · CURRENT MFG.

Various hard and soft cases are available for the models listed below with prices ranging from $500 up to $3,200.

NO. 5 NEEDHAM EJECTOR—12, 16, 20, or .410 ga., scalloped boxlock action, DT, any barrel length.

	100%	98%	95%	90%	80%	70%	60%
Mfg.'s Sug. Retail $4,470	$4,470	$3,750	$3,175	$2,750	$2,250	$1,825	$1,475

This model has been re-introduced to commemorate the takeover of J. V. Needham by W.W. Greener in 1874.

DH 40 —similar to No. 5 Needham Ejector, except has better engraving and deluxe walnut stock and forearm.

	100%	98%	95%	90%	80%	70%	60%
Mfg.'s Sug. Retail $6,705	$6,705	$5,900	$5,000	$4,250	$3,500	$2,850	$2,100

Greener, W.W., Limited, cont.

Grading		100%	98%	95%	90%	80%	70%	60%

DH 75—12 ga. only, 2¾ in. chambers, Greener "Facile Princeps" scalloped boxlock action 27, 28, or 30 in. barrels, case hardened receiver, choice of engraving (game scene or fine scroll work).

Mfg.'s Sug. Retail	$11,175	$11,175	$9,950	$8,450	$7,250	$6,000	$4,950	$3,875

DOH 90—12, 16, 20, or .410 ga., 2½, 2¾ or 3 in. Mag. chambers, best boxlock featuring Anson & Deeley scalloped boxlock action with Greener easy-opening device, French walnut stock, DT.

Mfg.'s Sug. Retail	$14,900	$14,900	$12,500	$9,750	$8,250	$7,000	$5,850	$4,675

L 120—12, 16, 20, or .410 ga., best sidelock ejector model with dovetail lump barrels, fine scroll engraving with choice of bright or color case hardened frame finish.

Mfg.'s Sug. Retail	$22,350	$22,350	$19,500	$16,000	$13,000	$10,000	$7,850	$6,000

L 150—12, 16, 20, or .410 ga., 2½ or 3 in. chambers, very best sidelock ejector model with chopper lump barrels and easy-opening device, bright or color case hardened frame finish.

Mfg.'s Sug. Retail	$29,800	$29,800	$24,000	$21,000	$17,000	$14,000	$11,000	$8,500

L 500—12, 16, 20, or .410 ga., new St. George sidelock ejector model incorporating top-of-the-line carved engraving, walnut, and workmanship.
Because this model is entirely custom ordered per individual choice, a price quotation is necessary on every order.

SHOTGUNS: DISCONTINUED

FARKILLER GRADE F35 — double barrel, 12 ga., 28, 30, or 32 in. barrels, hammerless boxlock, checkered straight or semi-pistol grip stock.

		$2,420	$2,200	$2,090	$1,870	$1,760	$1,650	$1,540
Auto ejectors		$3,300	$3,025	$2,750	$2,475	$2,035	$1,925	$1,650

FARKILLER GRADE F35 LARGE BORE — similar to F35 above, except 8 or 10 ga.

		$2,750	$2,585	$2,310	$2,090	$1,980	$1,815	$1,650
Auto ejectors		$3,575	$3,300	$3,080	$2,860	$2,640	$2,090	$1,925

HAMMERLESS EJECTOR MODELS — 12, 16, 20, 28, or .410 ga., 26, 28, or 30 in. barrels supplied with any choke combination, auto ejectors, single or double triggers, straight or semi-pistol grip stock, grades differ as follows:

Jubilee Grade DH35

		$2,420	$2,255	$2,090	$1,925	$1,650	$1,540	$1,375

Sovereign Grade DH40

		$2,860	$2,695	$2,420	$2,200	$1,980	$1,815	$1,595

Crown Grade DH55

		$3,300	$3,080	$2,915	$2,750	$2,420	$2,035	$1,760

Royal Grade DH75

		$4,400	$4,180	$3,850	$3,300	$3,080	$2,915	$2,640

Add $400 for SST.
Note: Degree of engraving and grade of wood are the basic differences between models.

EMPIRE — double barrel, 12 ga. only, 2¾ or 3 in., any choke, 28, 30, or 32 in. barrel, hammerless, boxlock, straight stock or semi pistol grip.

		$1,760	$1,540	$1,320	$1,100	$935	$825	$770
Auto ejectors		$1,980	$1,760	$1,540	$1,320	$1,155	$1,045	$990

Grading	100%	98%	95%	90%	80%	70%	60%

EMPIRE DELUXE — double barrel, similar to Empire, only better grade wood.

	$1,980	$1,760	$1,540	$1,320	$1,155	$1,045	$990
Auto ejectors	$2,200	$1,980	$1,760	$1,540	$1,375	$1,265	$1,100

GENERAL PURPOSE — 12 ga., improved Martini action, single shot, 26, 30, or 32 in. barrel, full or mod., auto ejectors, straight checkered stock.

	$330	$305	$275	$220	$195	$165	$160

GREIFELT AND COMPANY
Suhl, Germany.

SHOTGUNS: SIDE-BY-SIDE

MODEL 22 — 12 or 20 ga., 28 or 30 in. mod. and full, hammerless, boxlock, false sideplates, extractors, checkered pistol grip or English style stock, post-WWII.

	$2,200	$1,760	$1,595	$1,320	$1,100	$990	$825

MODEL 22E — similar to Model 22, except has auto ejectors.

	$2,750	$2,200	$1,980	$1,760	$1,540	$1,430	$1,265

MODEL 103 — 12 or 16 ga., 28 or 30 in. mod. and full, extractors, double triggers, checkered pistol grip or English stock, post-war.

	$1,980	$1,650	$1,485	$1,210	$990	$880	$715

MODEL 103E — similar to Model 103, except has auto ejectors.

	$2,200	$1,760	$1,595	$1,320	$1,100	$990	$825

SHOTGUNS: OVER/UNDER & DRILLING

GRADE NO. 1 — O/U, 12, 16, 20, 28, or .410 ga., any barrel 26-32 in., choke, vent. or solid rib, Anson & Deeley boxlock, auto ejectors, checkered pistol grip or English stock, pre-war.

12 or 20 ga.	$3,600	$3,200	$2,850	$2,500	$2,100	$1,750	$1,500

Deduct 10% for 16 ga.
Add 30% for 28 or .410 ga.
Add $300 for vent. rib.
Add $400 for SST.

GRADE NO. 3 — similar to No. 1, except less elaborate engraving, pre-WWII.

12 ga.	$2,850	$2,500	$2,200	$2,000	$1,650	$1,350	$1,200

Deduct 10% for 16 ga.
Add 20% for 28 or .410 ga.
Add $300 for vent. rib.   Add $400 for SST.

MODEL 143E — O/U, similar to model 1, except not as high quality as pre-war model, not available in 28 or .410 ga. Mfg. post-WWII.

	$2,400	$2,150	$1,850	$1,550	$1,350	$1,175	$1,000

Add 10% for vent. rib and SST.

O/U COMBINATION GUN — 12, 16, 20, 28, or .410 ga., shotgun barrel, rifle in any rimmed caliber, 24 or 26 in. solid rib barrel, pre-WWII.

	$5,200	$4,800	$4,400	$4,000	$3,600	$3,150	$2,800

Add $700 for auto ejectors.
Deduct 10% for 16 ga.
Add 20% for 28 or .410 ga.
Deduct 40-50% for obsolete rifle caliber.
Above values for 12 or 20 ga. over obtainable rifle cartridge.

Grading	100%	98%	95%	90%	80%	70%	60%

DRILLING — 12, 16, or 20 ga., SxS over any rimmed rifle caliber, 26 in. barrels, boxlock, extractors, double triggers, rifle sight activated by barrel selector, pre-WWII.

	100%	98%	95%	90%	80%	70%	60%
	$3,500	$3,000	$2,750	$2,550	$2,300	$2,000	$1,750

Deduct 10% for 16 ga.
Deduct 40-50% for obsolete cals.
Previous values for 12 and 20 ga. over available caliber.

GRENDEL, INC.
Manufacturer located in Rockledge, FL since 1984. Dealer direct sales.

Grendel firearms are noted for their precision manufacture, outstanding accuracy, and lightweight characteristics.

PISTOLS

MODEL P-10 SERIES — .380 ACP, semi-auto, blowback double action, 10 shot mag., small dimensions, hammerless, matte blue finish, 15 oz. Mfg. disc. 1991.

	100%	98%	95%	90%	80%	70%	60%
	$140	$125	$115	$105	$95	$90	$85

Add $15 for electroless nickel finish.
Add $15 for nickel green finish.
Green finish is available at no extra charge.
Last Mfg.'s Sug. Retail was $155.

MODEL P-12 — .380 ACP, semi-auto, double action only, 3 in. barrel, steel construction with polymer grip area, no external safety, 11 shot Zytel mag., blue or electroless nickel finish, 11 lb. trigger pull, 13 oz. New 1992.

		100%	98%	95%	90%	80%	70%	60%
Mfg.'s Sug. Retail	$175	$155	$135	$120	$110	$100	$90	$80

Add $20 for nickel finish.
Add $50 for threaded barrel with muzzle brake parts option.

MODEL P-30 — .22 Mag. cal., blowback similar action to P-12, 5 in. barrel, hammerless, matte black finish, 30 shot mag., 21 oz. New 1990.

		100%	98%	95%	90%	80%	70%	60%
Mfg.'s Sug. Retail	$225	$200	$175	$155	$140	$125	$115	$105

Add $25 for electroless nickel finish (disc. 1991).
Add $35 for scope mount (Weaver base).

Model P-30M — similar to Model P-30, except has 5.6 in. barrel with removable muzzle brake. New 1990.

		100%	98%	95%	90%	80%	70%	60%
Mfg.'s Sug. Retail	$235	$205	$180	$160	$140	$125	$115	$105

Add $25 for electroless nickel finish (disc. 1991).

MODEL P-30L — similar to Model P-30, except has 8 in. barrel with removable muzzle brake, 22 oz. Mfg. 1991-92.

	100%	98%	95%	90%	80%	70%	60%
	$240	$200	$180	$160	$140	$125	$110

Add $15 for Model P-30LM that allows for fitting various accessories.
Last Mfg.'s Sug. Retail was $280.

MODEL P-31 — .22 Mag., same action as P-30, except has 11 in. barrel, enclosed synthetic barrel shroud and flash hider, 48 oz. New 1990.

		100%	98%	95%	90%	80%	70%	60%
Mfg.'s Sug. Retail	$345	$285	$240	$215	$185	$160	$145	$130

RIFLES/CARBINES

MODEL R-31 — similar design to Model P-31, except has 16 in. barrel and telescoping stock, 64 oz. New 1991.

		100%	98%	95%	90%	80%	70%	60%
Mfg.'s Sug. Retail	$385	$315	$260	$235	$210	$185	$165	$150

Grading	100%	98%	95%	90%	80%	70%	60%

SRT-20F COMPACT — .243 Win. or .308 cal., bolt action based on the Sako A-2 action, 20 in. match grade finned barrel with muzzle brake, folding synthetic stock, integrated bipod rest, no sights, 9 shot mag., 6.7 lbs. Disc. 1989.

	100%	98%	95%	90%	80%	70%	60%
	$575	$525	$475	$395	$365	$340	$320

Grendel previously manufactured the SRT-16F, SRT-20L, and SRT-24 - all were disc. 1988. Values are approx. the same as the SRT-20F.
Last Mfg.'s Sug. Retail was $525.

GRIFFIN & HOWE

Custom gunsmith/manufacturer located in New York, NY and Bernardsville, NJ.

Founded in 1923 by Seymour Griffin and James Howe, Griffin & Howe continues to build its custom rifles as well as providing the full spectrum of gunsmithing services.

Griffin & Howe has been building custom rifles since 1923. They also perform a variety of custom gunsmithing services. Prices may vary greatly depending on configuration, desirability, condition and special features. Most used Griffin & Howe Custom Rifles in average condition and without special engraving start at $2,500+ and rise according to condition and nature of the individual gun. Since 1923, fewer than 2,800 have been made. In 1930, Grifin & Howe became a subsidiary of Abercrombie & Fitch and remained with them until 1976 when it became a privately held company. Because all Griffin & Howe rifles are essentially special ordered, accurate pricing can be ascertained only by examining each individual gun. Elaborate specimens by this maker trademark will command over $10,000. Engraving by Joseph Fugger, Winston Churchill, Bob Swartley or Kornbrath will add considerably to the value.

Pricing on new custom rifles, with a wide selection of options, is available directly from Griffin & Howe.

RIFLES

Values below represent a base gun with normal wood and no options.

WIN M70 STANDARD ACTION — for .243, .270, .30-06, or .308 cal.

	100%	98%	95%	90%	80%	70%	60%
	$5,000	$4,250	$3,450	$3,150	$2,750	$2,500	$2,250

WIN M70 MEDIUM — for .300, 7mm, or .338 cal.

	$5,300	$4,500	$3,600	$3,350	$2,950	$2,750	$2,350

WIN M70 MAGNUM — for .375, or .416 Rem. cal.

	$5,500	$4,750	$3,850	$3,500	$3,000	$2,850	$2,450

WIN M52 — for .22 LR cal.

	$2,500	$2,250	$1,750	$1,650	$1,450	$1,300	$1,150

WIN HIGHWALL

	$1,850	$1,650	$1,250	$1,150	$1,000	$950	$850

SPRINGFIELD 1903

	$2,450	$2,150	$1,750	$1,550	$1,350	$1,250	$1,100

SPRINGFIELD 1922

	$2,450	$2,150	$1,750	$1,550	$1,350	$1,250	$1,100

MAUSER STANDARD

	$3,200	$2,850	$2,250	$2,000	$1,750	$1,650	$1,450

MAUSER MAGNUM

	$7,500	$6,500	$5,250	$4,750	$4,250	$3,850	$3,350

Grading	100%	98%	95%	90%	80%	70%	60%
SAVAGE 99							
	$1,850	$1,650	$1,250	$1,150	$1,025	$950	$850

GRULLA ARMAS
Manufacturer located in Eibar, Spain.

Grulla Armas manufactures a complete line of quality SxS shotguns. To date, there has been limited U.S. importation and most shotguns have been special ordered directly from the manufacturer. To obtain more information about this manufacturer's quality SxS shotguns, please contact per address/FAX number listed under the Grulla heading in the "Trademark Index" located in the back of this text. The factory will accept individual special orders.

GUNWORKS, LTD.
Previously manufactured and distributed in Buffalo, NY. Early guns were made in Tonawanda, NY.

MODEL 9 — O/U derringer, .357 Mag., 9mm or .38 Super, or .38 Spl. cal., electroless nickel finish, 2½ in. barrel, wood grips, Millett sights, 15 oz. Disc. 1986.

		$135	$120	$105	$95	$65	$55	$50

Last Mfg.'s Sug. Retail was $149.

GUSTAF, CARL
Manufacturer located in Eskilstuna, Sweden. Imported and distributed into the U.S. starting in 1991 by Precision Sales International located in Westfield, MA.

MODEL CG 2000 — 6.5 x 55mm, 7 x 64mm, 9.3 x 62mm, .243 Win., .270 Win., .30-06, .308, 7mm Rem. Mag., or .300 Win. Mag. cal., bolt action, Monte Carlo walnut stock with checkering and Wundhammer grip, 24 in. barrel, detachable 3 or 4 shot mag., open sights, cold-swaged barrel and receiver, 60 degree bolt, 3-way slide safety, 7½ lbs. Importation resumed late 1991.

Mfg.'s Sug. Retail $1,875 | $1,650 | $1,300 | $1,050 | $895 | $750 | $600 | $500
Add $110 with adj. iron sights.

This model is supplied with individual 80 meter signed test targets.

STANDARD BOLT ACTION RIFLE — 6.5 x 55, 7 x 64, .270, 7mm Mag., .308, .30-06, or 9.3 x 62 cal., 24 in. barrel, folding rear sight, checkered classic style stock. Mfg. 1970-1977.

	$375	$325	$300	$275	$250	$225	$200

※ **Monte Carlo stock**

	$450	$395	$350	$300	$275	$250	$225

GRADE II — similar to Monte Carlo Standard, in .22-250, .25-06, 6.5 x 55, .270, 7mm Mag., .308, .30-06, or .300 Win. Mag. cal., select stock and rosewood pistol grip cap, and forearm tip.

	$500	$425	$375	$325	$295	$275	$250

GRADE III — similar to Grade II, except fancy wood, deluxe high gloss finish.

	$575	$475	$425	$350	$325	$300	$275

DELUXE — similar to Grade III, except engraved floorplate and trigger guard, Deluxe French walnut, and jeweled bolt.

	$675	$575	$475	$400	$375	$350	$325

VARMINT TARGET MODEL — bolt action, fast lock time, .222, .22-250, .243, or 6.5 x 55 cal., 27 in. barrel, no sights, large bakelite bolt knob, target type stock. Mfg. 1970. Disc.

	$550	$495	$440	$385	$360	$320	$290

Grading	100%	98%	95%	90%	80%	70%	60%

GRAND PRIX SINGLE SHOT TARGET — fastest lock time bolt action, .22 LR, 27 in. heavy barrel with adj. weight, no sights, target stock, adj. butt plate. Mfg. 1970. Disc.

$550	$495	$440	$385	$360	$320	$290

GYROJET

See MBA Gyrojet listing in the M Section of this text.

H section

H.J.S. INDUSTRIES, INC.
Brownsville, TX.

Grading	100%	98%	95%	90%	80%	70%	60%

FRONTIER FOUR DERRINGER — 4 shot derringer, .22 LR cal. only, stainless steel construction, 5½ oz.

	100%	98%	95%
	$115	$90	$80

LONE STAR DERRINGER — single shot derringer, .38 S&W only, stainless steel construction, 6 oz.

	100%	98%	95%
	$137	$105	$95

H & R 1871, INC. (Harrington & Richardson)
Holding company located in Gardner, MA since 1991.

H & R 1871 Inc. is a new company utilizing the older H & R trademark and does not accept warranty work for older (pre-1986 mfg.) Harrington & Richardson, Inc. firearms. Distributor sales only.

The use of the original Harrington & Richardson trademark was permitted in 1991. All new manufacture will use this trademark, but older H & Rs manufactured by Harrington & Richardson, Inc. are not the responsibility of H & R 1871, Inc.

REVOLVERS

Additional revolvers using the New England Firearms trademark may be located in the N section of this text.

SPORTSMAN 999 — .22 LR cal., single or double action, 9 shot, 4 or 6 in. barrel with fluted solid rib, top break action with auto shell ejection, smooth hardwood stocks, transfer bar safety, blue finish, adj. sights, 30-34 oz. Mfg. began 1991.

	100%	98%	95%	90%	80%	70%	60%
Mfg.'s Sug. Retail $280	$225	$180	$145	$125	$115	$100	$90

RIFLES

ULTRA SINGLE SHOT — .22-250 Rem. or .223 Rem. cal., single shot break-open action, heavy 22 in. barrel with scope mount rail, checkered curly maple Monte Carlo stock with black lined recoil pad, sling swivel studs. New 1993.

	100%	98%	95%	90%	80%	70%	60%
Mfg.'s Sug. Retail $250	$210	$170	$135	$115	$105	$95	$85

SHOTGUNS: TOPPER SERIES

TOPPER 098 — 12, 16 (new 1992), 20, 28 (new 1992), or .410 ga., 3 in. chamber, 26 or 28 in. barrel, break open side lever release action, transfer bar safety, ejector, satin nickel frame with blue barrel, black finish hardwood stock and forearm, 5-6 lbs. Mfg. began 1991.

	100%	98%	95%	90%	80%	70%	60%
Mfg.'s Sug. Retail $110	$90	$80	$70	$60	$50	$40	$35

⚡ **Topper Deluxe** — 12 ga. only, 3½ in. chamber, satin nickel frame with blue barrel, 28 in. barrel with 1 choke tube, black finish hardwood stock and forearm, 5-6 lbs. New 1991.

	100%	98%	95%	90%	80%	70%	60%
Mfg.'s Sug. Retail $125	$100	$90	$80	$70	$60	$50	$40

⚡ **H & R NWTF Turkey Mag.** — 12 ga., 3½ in. chamber, 24 in. drilled and tapped barrel with 1 choke tube, entire gun is covered in mossy oak camo, 6 lbs. New 1991.

	100%	98%	95%	90%	80%	70%	60%
Mfg.'s Sug. Retail $160	$130	$115	$100	$85	$75	$65	$55

This model is part of the National Wild Turkey Federation (NWTF) sponsorship program.

Grading		100%	98%	95%	90%	80%	70%	60%

Topper Jr. — 20 or .410 ga., smaller variation of the Topper 098 with youth dimensions including 22 in. barrel and shortened stock with recoil pad, satin nickel frame with blue barrel. Mfg. began 1991.

Mfg.'s Sug. Retail	$115	$95	$80	$70	$60	$50	$40	$35

Topper Jr. Classic — 20, 28, or .410 ga., checkered American walnut stock and forearm, recoil pad. Mfg. began 1991.

Mfg.'s Sug. Retail	$140	$115	$90	$80	$70	$60	$50	$40

H-S PRECISION, INC.
Custom rifle manufacturer located in Rapid City, SD. H-S Precision, Inc. also manufactures synthetic stocks and custom machines barrels as well.

In addition to the models listed below, H-S Precision, Inc. will also build rifles using a customer's action (Remington 700 ADL or 700 BDL, Sako, Weatherby, or Winchester). These models will be approx. 1/3 less expensive than values listed below (not available in Sniper Model).

RIFLES: CUSTOM MFG. BOLT ACTION

All H-S Precision rifles feature Kevlar/graphite laminate stocks, cut rifle barrels, and other high tech innovations including a molded in aluminum bedding block system.

PRO SERIES SPORTER/VARMINT — .223 Rem., .22 PPC, .22-250 Rem., .243 Win., 6mm PPC, 7mm-08 Rem., or .308 Win. cal. are available in short action, .270 Win., .30-06, 7mm Rem. Mag., .300 Win. Mag., or .338 Win. Mag. cal. are available in long action, Remington ADL action only, each rifle is built per individual specifications. New 1990.

Mfg.'s Sug. Retail	$1,625	$1,625	$1,350	$1,150	$895	$750	$650	$575

Add $155 for left hand action.
Add $880 for extra stainless barrel.

PRO SERIES TACTICAL MARKSMAN — .223 Rem., .243 Win., .30-06, .308, 7mm Rem. Mag., or .300 Win. Mag. cal., stainless fluted barrel standard, Remington BDL action. New 1990.

Mfg.'s Sug. Retail	$1,800	$1,800	$1,475	$1,225	$925	$775	$675	$575

Add $155 for left hand action.

TAKEDOWN PRO SERIES SPORTER/VARMINT — .22-250, .243 Win., 7mm-08 Rem., or .308 Win. cal. in short action, .25-06 Rem., .270 Win., .30-06, 7mm Rem. Mag., .300 Win. Mag., or .338 Win. Mag. cal. in long action, stainless steel barrel, Remington BDL takedown action, matte blue finish. New 1990.

Mfg.'s Sug. Retail	$2,640	$2,640	$2,000	$1,570	$1,225	$900	$800	$700

Add $1,000 for extra barrel.

TAKEDOWN PRO SERIES TACTICAL MARKSMAN — .223 Rem., .243 Win., .30-06, .308 Win., 7mm Rem. Mag., .300 Win. Mag., or .338 Win. Mag. cal., includes "kwik klip" and stainless fluted barrel. New 1990.

Mfg.'s Sug. Retail	$2,920	$2,920	$2,225	$1,675	$1,350	$995	$850	$750

A complete rifle package consisting of 2 calibers (.308 Win. and .300 Win. Mag.), scope and fitted case is available for $5,200 retail.

HWP INDUSTRIES
Previous manufacturer located in Milwaukee, WI.

THE SLEDGEHAMMER — .500 HWP Mag. cal., 5 shot revolver, double action, stainless steel, full shrouded 4 in. barrel (quick change), Pachmayr grips. Limited mfg. 1989 only.

			$1,150	$895	$750

Last Mfg.'s Sug. Retail was $1,295.

HAENEL, C.G.

Previous manufacturer located in Suhl, Germany. Mfg. between 1925-1940.

RIFLES

Grading	100%	98%	95%	90%	80%	70%	60%
MAUSER-MANNLICHER SPORTING RIFLE — M/88 Mauser type action, 7 x 57, 8 x 57, or 9 x 57 cal., 22 or 24 in. octagon barrel, Mannlicher box mag., double set triggers, raised rib on barrel leaf sight, sporter stock.	$440	$360	$330	$275	$250	$220	$165
88 MAUSER SPORTER — similar to Mauser-Mannlicher, with Mauser 5 shot mag.	$525	$450	$375	$325	$275	$240	$200

PISTOLS

	100%	98%	95%	90%	80%	70%	60%
SCHMEISSER MODEL 1 & 2 — .25 ACP cal., similar to Baby Browning.	$385	$340	$300	$275	$230	$200	$180

MODELS 200-205 — See Hammerli-Walther

HAMBRUSCH JAGDWAFFEN GmbH

Manufacturer located in Ferlach, Austria since 1782.

SHOTGUN — boxlock or sidelock SxS, various ga.'s, most specimens exhibit game scene engraving, ejectors, SST or DT. Not many specimens are encountered in this trademark - please contact Mr. Hambrusch directly (see Trademark Index) for current model information and price quotations. Please allow 4-6 weeks for a reply.

HAMMERLI

Manufacturer located in Lenzburg, Switzerland. Currently imported and distributed by Mandall Shooting Supplies, Inc. located in Scottsdale, AZ and Beeman Precision Arms located in Santa Rosa, CA. Previously imported by Osborne's located in Cheboygan, MI.

PISTOLS

	100%	98%	95%	90%	80%	70%	60%
MODEL 100 FREE PISTOL — .22 LR cal., 11½ in. octagon barrel, blue, martini action single shot, set trigger, micro rear sight, walnut stock and forearm. Mfg. 1933-1949.	$880	$660	$605	$550	$470	$440	$385
Deluxe model — carved stock.	$990	$770	$715	$660	$580	$550	$495
MODEL 101 — similar to Model 100, but heavy round barrel, improved action and sights, matte finish. Mfg. 1956-1960.	$880	$660	$605	$550	$470	$440	$385
MODEL 102 — similar to Model 101, except high polished finish. Mfg. 1956-1960.	$880	$660	$605	$550	$470	$440	$385
Deluxe model.	$990	$770	$715	$660	$580	$550	$495

Grading	100%	98%	95%	90%	80%	70%	60%

MODEL 103 FREE PISTOL — similar to Model 101, except lighter octagon polished barrel. Mfg. 1956-1960.

	100%	98%	95%	90%	80%	70%	60%
	$935	$715	$660	$605	$580	$550	$495

MODEL 104 MATCH PISTOL — similar to Model 103, except lighter round barrel, redesigned stock, mfg. 1961-1965.

	$760	$660	$550	$495	$470	$440	$385

MODEL 105 MATCH PISTOL — similar to Model 103, except redesigned action and stock. Mfg. 1962-1965.

	$935	$715	$660	$605	$580	$550	$495

MATCH PISTOL — similar to Model 105, except improved trigger.

	$910	$690	$580	$525	$495	$470	$415

MODEL 107 MATCH PISTOL — similar to Model 105, except improved trigger.

	$990	$770	$660	$550	$525	$495	$440

⚒ **Deluxe model** — engraved and carved wood.

	$1,320	$990	$880	$660	$635	$605	$550

MODEL 120-1 SINGLE SHOT FREE PISTOL — .22 LR cal., bolt action, 9.9 in. barrel, blue barrel and receiver, side lever operated, anodized aluminum lever and frame, walnut checkered grips.

	$440	$360	$305	$275	$220	$200	$175

MODEL 120-2 — similar to 120-1, except stocks hand contoured.

	$470	$385	$330	$305	$250	$220	$195

MODEL 120 HEAVY BARREL — similar to 120-1, with 5.7 in. bull barrel.

MODEL 150 FREE PISTOL — .22 LR cal., 11.3 in. barrel, improved Martini-type action, set trigger, innovative design incorporating many unusual features. Disc. 1989.

	$1,850	$1,495	$1,275	$1,120	$980	$900	$850

Add $113 for left-hand variation.
Last Mfg.'s Sug. Retail was $1,980. The Model 150 has been replaced by the Model 160.

MODEL 151 FREE PISTOL — replacement for the Model 150 Free Pistol. New 1990.

Mfg.'s Sug. Retail	$1,980	$1,850	$1,495	$1,275	$1,120	$995	$900	$800

MODEL 152 FREE PISTOL — .22 LR cal., 11.3 in. barrel. improved Martini-type action, electronic trigger release, innovative design incorporating many unusual features. State of the art target pistol. Disc. 1992.

	$1,995	$1,600	$1,350	$1,195	$1,090	$990	$895

Add $57 for left-hand variation.
Last Mfg.'s Sug. Retail was $2,105.

MODEL 160 — .22 LR cal., similar to Model 150, except has poly-carbon fiber grips and forend. New 1993.

Mfg.'s Sug. Retail	$2,300	$2,100	$1,850	$1,600	$1,350	$1,125	$900	$800

MODEL 162 — .22 LR cal., replacement for the Model 152 Free Pistol, includes poly-carbon fiber grips and forend. New 1993.

Mfg.'s Sug. Retail	$2,400	$2,150	$1,850	$1,600	$1,350	$1,125	$900	$800

Grading	100%	98%	95%	90%	80%	70%	60%

MODELS 200-205 — See Hammerli-Walther

	$440	$360	$305	$275	$220	$200	$175

INTERNATIONAL MODEL 206 — .22 LR cal., .22 S, semi-auto, 7$^1/_{16}$ in. barrel with muzzle brake, adj. sights, walnut grips, blue. Mfg. 1962-1969.

	$690	$605	$495	$470	$385	$360	$330

INTERNATIONAL MODEL 207 — similar to 206, except adj. grip heel.

	$705	$635	$505	$480	$395	$370	$340

INTERNATIONAL MODEL 208 — .22 LR cal., semi-auto, 9 shot, 6 in. barrel, blue, adj. sights, checkered walnut grips with adj. heel. Mfg. 1966-1988.

Mfg.'s Sug. Retail	$1,755	$1,600	$1,300	$1,050	$950	$880	$835	$770

Limited quantities of this model are still available. This model was replaced by the Model 208S.

Model 208S — similar to Model 208, except has redesigned trigger guard and interchangeable rear sight element. Importation started 1988.

Mfg.'s Sug. Retail	$1,755	$1,600	$1,300	$1,050	$950	$880	$835	$770

This model is distributed by Mandall Shooting Supplies located in Scottsdale, AZ.

Model 208 Deluxe — similar to Model 208, except has carved grips and elaborate engraving. Importation disc. 1988.

	$2,995	$2,500	$1,995

Last Mfg.'s Sug. Retail was $3,250.

Model 208C (Commemorative) — limited edition commemorative. Disc. 1987.

	$2,100	$1,750	$1,400

Last Mfg.'s Sug. Retail was $2,225.

INTERNATIONAL MODEL 209 — .22 Short, semi-auto, 5 shot, 4$^3/_4$ in. barrel, muzzle brake, adj. sights, blue, walnut stock. Mfg. 1966-1970.

	$800	$690	$635	$550	$525	$485	$440

INTERNATIONAL MODEL 210 — similar to 209, but grips have adj. heel. Mfg. 1966-1970.

	$800	$715	$660	$590	$540	$525	$495

MODEL 211 — .22 LR cal., semi-auto, 9 shot, 6 in. barrel, adj. sights, blue, similar to Model 208 except non-adj. walnut stocks. Importation disc. 1990.

Mfg.'s Sug. Retail	$1,669	$1,550	$1,275	$1,050	$950	$880	$835	$770

MODEL 212 HUNTER — .22 LR cal., semi-auto, hunter's pistol, 9 shot, 5 in. barrel, adj. sights, blue, walnut stocks.

	$1,500	$1,250	$975	$875	$820	$760	$600

Last Mfg.'s Sug. Retail was $1,650.

MODEL 215 — .22 LR cal., semi-auto, Model 208 specs on commercial target model, 9 shot, 5 in. barrel, adj. sights, blue, walnut stocks. Importation disc. 1990.

	$1,395	$1,050	$895	$775	$695	$650	$600

Last Mfg.'s Sug. Retail was $1,505.

MODEL 230 RAPID FIRE PISTOL — .22 S, semi-auto, 5 shot, 6.3 in. barrel, blue, adj. sights, smooth walnut grips. Mfg. 1970-1983.

	$705	$635	$580	$530	$485	$450	$415

Grading	100%	98%	95%	90%	80%	70%	60%

MODEL 230-2 — similar to 230, except checkered grips with adj. heel. Mfg. 1970-1983.

	$735	$655	$605	$570	$515	$485	$470

MODEL 232-1 RAPID FIRE PISTOL — .22 S, semi-auto, 6 shot, 5.1 in. barrel, blue, adj. sights, contoured walnut grips.

Mfg.'s Sug. Retail	$1,505	$1,395	$1,125	$950	$850	$750	$700	$650

Add $25 for wrap-around grips sizes S-M-LG (Model 232-2).

MODEL 280 — .22 LR or .32 S&W Long, new modular pistol design utilizing carbon fiber synthetic material to replace frame and other critical parts, adj. grips, trigger, and rear sight, 4.6 in. barrel, 5 or 6 shot mag., approx. 2.2 lbs. New 1988.

Mfg.'s Sug. Retail	$1,995	$1,750	$1,400	$1,100	$950	$850	$750	$700

Add $1,005 for .22 LR or .32 Wadcutter conversion.

A package is also available with both calibers, magazines, and hard case for $3,000.

MODEL P-240 — see S.I.G.- HAMMERLI for this model.

RIFLES: TARGET

OLYMPIC 300 METER — .30-06 or .300 H&H Mag., bolt action, single shot free rifle, U.S.A. import, 7 x 57mm overseas, $20\frac{1}{2}$ in. heavy barrel, double set trigger, aperture rear sight, globe front, free rifle stock with thumbhole pistol grip, beavertail forearm, Swiss style target butt. Mfg. 1945-1959.

	$880	$745	$605	$550	$470	$440	$415

HAMMERLI-TANNER 300 METER FREE RIFLE — similar to Olympic 300 , except 7.5mm standard, can be ordered in other calibers. Mfg. 1962-disc.

	$895	$825	$770	$715	$660	$580	$520

Last Mfg.'s Sug. Retail was $935.

MODEL 45 SMALLBORE MATCH RIFLE — .22 LR cal., bolt action, single shot, $27\frac{1}{2}$ in. heavy barrel, same sights and stock type as Hammerli-Tanner. Mfg. 1945-1957.

	$660	$550	$470	$440	$385	$360	$330

MODEL 54 SMALLBORE MATCH RIFLE — similar to 45 Smallbore, except adj. butt. Mfg. 1954-1957.

	$670	$560	$480	$450	$395	$370	$340

MODEL 503 SMALLBORE FREE RIFLE — similar to 54 Smallbore, except free style stock.

	$660	$550	$470	$440	$385	$360	$330

MODEL 505 MATCH RIFLE — match stock with aperture sights.

	$690	$580	$495	$470	$415	$385	$360

MODEL 506 SMALLBORE MATCH RIFLE — similar to 503 Smallbore. Mfg. 1963-1966.

	$690	$580	$495	$470	$415	$385	$360

SPORTING RIFLE — various calibers, set triggers. Hunting Model-single shot.

	$725	$650	$490	$425	$360	$325	$300

HAMMERLI-WALTHER
Target Pistols manufactured under joint effort.

Grading	100%	98%	95%	90%	80%	70%	60%

PISTOLS: SEMI-AUTO

MODEL 200 OLYMPIA — .22 Short or LR, 7½ in. barrel, 1952 type, adj. sights, barrel weight, blue, checkered walnut grips. Mfg. 1952-1958.

	100%	98%	95%	90%	80%	70%	60%
	$660	$605	$550	$440	$415	$385	$360

MODEL 200 OLYMPIA — 1958 type, similar to 1952 type, except has muzzle brake. Mfg. 1958-1963.

	$715	$605	$550	$495	$470	$415	$385

MODEL 201 — similar to 200, 1952 type, except 9½ in. barrel. Mfg. 1955-1957.

	$660	$605	$550	$440	$415	$385	$360

MODEL 202 — similar to 201, except adj. heel grips. Mfg. 1955-1957.

	$715	$605	$550	$495	$470	$415	$385

MODEL 203 — similar to 200, except has adj. heel grip.

1955 Type — no muzzle brake.

	$715	$605	$550	$495	$470	$415	$385

1958 Type — muzzle brake.

	$770	$660	$605	$550	$525	$470	$440

MODEL 204 — similar to 200, except .22 LR cal. only.

1956 Type — no muzzle brake.

	$745	$635	$580	$525	$495	$470	$440

1958 Type — muzzle brake.

	$800	$690	$635	$550	$525	$495	$470

MODEL 205 — .22 LR cal., similar to 204, except adj. heel grips.

	100%	98%	95%	90%	80%	70%	60%
1956 type	$800	$690	$635	$550	$525	$495	$470
1958 type, M.B.	$855	$745	$715	$635	$580	$525	$495

HARRINGTON & RICHARDSON, INC.

Previous manufacturer located in Gardner, MA - formerly from Worchester, MA. Successors to Wesson & Harrington, manufactured from 1871 until January 24, 1986. In 1991, H & R 1871, Inc. was formed (see their listing in the front of this section) and several new Topper shotgun models and the Sportsman 999 revolver were reintroduced. H & R 1871, Inc. is not responsible for the warranties or safety of older pre-1986 H & R firearms.

A manufacturer of utilitarian firearms for over 115 years, H & R ceased operation on January 24, 1986. Even though new manufacture (under H & R 1871, Inc.) is utilizing the H & R trademark, the discontinuance of older models in either N.I.B. or mint condition may command slight asking premiums, but probably will not affect values on those handguns only recently discontinued.

Most H & R firearms are still purchased for their shooting value rather than collecting potential.

PISTOLS: PRE-1942

MODEL 4 — .32 S&W Long 6 shot, or .38 S&W Long 5 shot, (1904), double action, 2½, 4½, and 6 in. barrels, blued or nickel, hard rubber grips, solid frame, fixed sights.

	$95	$85	$70	$55	$45	$35	$30

Grading	100%	98%	95%	90%	80%	70%	60%

MODEL 5 — .32 S&W Long, 5 shot only, (1905), double action, same as Model 4.

	100%	98%	95%	90%	80%	70%	60%
	$95	$85	$70	$55	$45	$35	$30

MODEL 6 — .22 LR, 7 shot only, (1906), double action, similar to Model 4.

	$95	$85	$70	$55	$45	$35	$30

AMERICAN — .32 S&W, 6 shot, .38 S&W, 5 shot, double action, 2½, 4, or 6 in. barrels, fixed sights, blue or nickel.

	$95	$85	$70	$55	$45	$35	$30

YOUNG AMERICAN — .22 Long, 7 shot, .32 S&W, 5 shot, double action, 2, 4½, or 6 in. barrel, fixed sights, blue or nickel.

	$95	$85	$70	$55	$45	$35	$30

VEST POCKET — double action, 1⅛ in. barrel, blue or nickel, solid frame, spurless hammer.

	$95	$85	$70	$55	$45	$35	$30

HUNTER — .22 LR, double action, 10 in. octagon barrel, 9 shot, checkered walnut grips.

	$140	$110	$100	$85	$65	$55	$45

TRAPPER — .22 LR, double action, 7 shot, 6 in. octagon barrel, checkered walnut stocks.

	$140	$120	$100	$85	$65	$55	$45

MODEL 922 — .22 LR, first issue, 9 shot, 10 in. octagon barrel on early models, 6 in. round barrel on later models, checkered walnut grips.

	$140	$120	$100	$85	$65	$55	$45

AUTOMATIC EJECTING — .32 S&W, 6 shot, .38 S&W, 5 shot, double action, 3¼, 4, 5, or 6 in. barrels, hinged break open, fixed sights, black rubber grips.

	$160	$150	$105	$90	$75	$65	$55

PREMIER — .22 LR, 7 shot, .32 S&W, 5 shot, double action, break open, small frame.

	$95	$85	$70	$55	$45	$35	$30

HAMMERLESS — .22 LR, 7 shot, .32 S&W, 5 shot, double action, 2, 3, 4, 5, or 6 in. barrels, small frame, break open, blue or nickel, black rubber grips.

	$125	$110	$100	$85	$65	$55	$45

HAMMERLESS — .32 S&W, 6 shot, .38 S&W, 5 shot, double action, 3¼, 4, 5, or 6 in. barrels, large frame, break open.

	$125	$110	$100	$85	$65	$55	$45

TARGET MODEL — .22 LR, .22 WRF, 7 shot, double action, 6 in. barrel, fixed sights, break open, small frame, blue only, walnut grips.

	$140	$120	$100	$85	$70	$60	$50

.22 SPECIAL — .22 LR, .22 WRF, 7 shot, double action, 6 in. barrel, break open, large frame, blue only, gold plated front sight, walnut grips.

	$165	$140	$120	$100	$85	$70	$60

EXPERT — double action, similar to .22 Special, except 10 in. barrel.

	$150	$140	$120	$100	$85	$70	$60

Grading	100%	98%	95%	90%	80%	70%	60%

SPORTSMAN NO. 199 — .22 LR, 9 shot, single action, 6 in. barrel, adj. target sights, break open, blue only, checkered walnut grips.

	$195	$165	$140	$110	$90	$75	$65

DEFENDER — .38 S&W, double action, 4 or 6 in. barrel, fixed sights, blue, break open, black plastic grips, made during WWII for police reserves and major corporation guards.

	$140	$120	$110	$100	$85	$65	$55

ULTRA SPORTSMAN — .22 LR, 9 shot, single action, 6 in. barrel, blue, break open, adj. sights, walnut grips, short cylinder action, wide hammer spur.

	$220	$200	$180	$150	$120	$100	$85

NEW DEFENDER — .22 LR, 9 shot, double action, 2 in. barrel, break open, adj. sights, blue, round butt, checkered walnut grip.

	$220	$200	$180	$150	$120	$100	$85

USRA SINGLE SHOT TARGET — .22 LR, 7, 8, or 10 in. barrel, blue, hinged break open, adj. sights, walnut grips. Mfg. 1928-1941.

	$440	$415	$385	$330	$290	$250	$195

Add 10% for nickel finish.

.25 CAL. SELF LOADING PISTOL — .25 ACP, 6 shot, 2 in. barrel, blue, black rubber grips.

	$330	$305	$250	$195	$165	$140	$110

.32 CAL. SELF LOADING PISTOL — .32 ACP, 8 shot, 3½ in. barrel, fixed sights, black rubber grips.

	$330	$305	$250	$195	$165	$140	$110

Add 20% for type I models if in 90%+ original condition.
Type I models with 12 slide pull grooves are serialized 1-3,025. Type II (more common) are serialized 3,026 - 35,000.

HANDY GUN — shotgun (mfg. 1920-1934) or rifle (mfg. 1931-1933) pistol mfg. between 1921-1933, available in either 8 or 12¼ in. choked or unchoked shotgun barrel, in either .410 or 28 ga., 12¼ in. barrel for rifle, rifle cals. (.22 LR or .32-20) also were available, although not as common. Guns were either case hardened (in Tiger stripe colors), or blued. Case hardened frames have "Handy Gun" stamped on side. Serial numbers on barrel lug and back of frame-numbers should match. .410 ga in 12¼ in. barrel length is most common. These guns had to be registered during the Amnesty period pre-1968. The legality of the Handy Gun may be obtained by contacting a local BATF branch.

Shotgun

	$795	$675	$575	$475	$425	$375	$300

Rifle

	$550	$475	$400	$350	$300	$325	$275

Add $50-75 for original box or $75-175 for original H & R holster.
The serialization range of the H & R Handy Gun is approximatley 1-53,637, but only 20,000-25,000 guns were originally mfg. This is because the H & R Model 1915 (also called the No. 5) single shot shotgun also shared the same serial range.
It should be noted that over 20 variations of the Handy Gun have been documented. Many of these rarer configurations are more valuable than the prices listed above for the more frequently encountered models.
A detachable wire stock was available on the rifles and optional on the shotguns. Most shotgun models were not drilled for a shoulder stock. In 1934, a .410 model with an 18 in. choke barrel was mfg. These are extremely rare with no more than 50 being mfg.

Grading	100%	98%	95%	90%	80%	70%	60%

REVOLVERS: RECENT PRODUCTION

MODEL 504 SQUARE BUTT — .32 H&R Mag., 5 shot, 4 or 6 in. bull barrels, adj. rear sight, swing out cylinder, blue, black plastic and walnut grips. Mfg. 1984 and 1985.

	100%	98%	95%	90%	80%	70%	60%
	$165	$145	$135	$120	$110	$100	$90

Last Mfg.'s Sug. Retail was $185.

⚞ **Model 504 Round Butt** — compact design available with 3 or 4 in. barrel only. Disc. 1985.

	$165	$145	$135	$120	$110	$100	$90

Last Mfg.'s Sug. Retail was $185.

MODEL 532 — .32 H&R Mag., 5 shot, 2½ and 4 in. barrels, solid frame revolver, blue, pull pin cylinder, black plastic and walnut grips. Mfg. 1984 and 1985.

	$100	$90	$80	$70	$60	$50	$45

Last Mfg.'s Sug. Retail was $115.

MODEL 586 — .32 H&R Mag., 5 shot, Western-style revolver, double action, 4½, 5½, 7½, or 10 in. barrels, adj. rear sight, fixed cylinder, antique finish, black plastic or walnut grips. Made 1984 and 1985.

	$175	$155	$135	$120	$110	$100	$90

Last Mfg.'s Sug. Retail was $195.

MODEL 603 — .22 Mag. cal., 6 in. barrel, double action. Disc.

	$159	$120	$110	$95	$90	$80	$70

MODEL 604 — same specifications as the Model 603, only has 6 in. bull barrel.

	$170	$130	$115	$95	$90	$80	$70

MODEL 622 — .22 Short, long, or LR, solid frame, 6 shot, 2½, 4, or 6 in. barrels, blue, plastic grips. Mfg. 1957-1985.

	$95	$82	$70	$60	$55	$50	$45

Last Mfg.'s Sug. Retail was $104.

MODEL 623 — same basic specifications as the Model 622, only nickel finish. Disc.

	$115	$95	$75	$60	$55	$50	$45

MODEL 632 GUARDSMAN — .32 S&W, 6 shot, 2½ or 4 in. barrel, solid frame, checkered tenite grips, blue. Mfg. 1953-1984.

	$104	$82	$70	$60	$55	$50	$45

MODEL 633 — same basic specifications as the Model 632, only nickel finish. Disc.

	$115	$95	$75	$60	$55	$50	$45

MODEL 642 — .22 Mag cal., 2½ or 4 in. barrel. Disc.

	$95	$70	$65	$60	$50	$45	$40

MODEL 649 CONVERTIBLE — .22 LR or .22 Mag. cal., furnished with extra cylinder, Western style, double action, side loading, 5½ or 7½ in. barrel, 6 shot, walnut grips, blued finish. Mfg. 1976-1985.

	$140	$120	$110	$95	$90	$80	$70

Last Mfg.'s Sug. Retail was $160.

Grading	100%	98%	95%	90%	80%	70%	60%

MODEL 650 CONVERTIBLE — similar to Model 649, except with nickel finish and only available with 5½ in. barrel. Disc. 1985.

| | $150 | $130 | $115 | $100 | $90 | $80 | $70 |

Last Mfg.'s Sug. Retail was $175.

MODEL 666 — .22 LR or .22 Win. Mag. cal., 6 shot, 6 in. barrel, blue, plastic grips, convertible. Mfg. 1976-1982.

| | $100 | $90 | $70 | $50 | $45 | $35 | $30 |

MODEL 676 — .22 LR or .22 Win. Mag. cal., 6 shot, 4½, 5½, 7½, or 12 in. barrel, side load and eject, convertible (includes .22 LR/.22 Mag. cylinders), blue, case hardened frame, one piece walnut stock. Mfg. 1976-1982.

| | $140 | $120 | $100 | $85 | $60 | $45 | $35 |

MODEL 686 CONVERTIBLE — .22 LR or .22 Mag. cal., furnished with extra cylinder, Western style, double action, side loading, 5½, 7½, 10 or 12 in. barrel, 6 shot, walnut grips, color case hardened frame, adj. rear sight, 12 in. barrel. Disc. 1984.

| | $185 | $160 | $140 | $125 | $110 | $90 | $80 |

MODEL 732 — .32 S&W or .32 H&R Mag. cal., 6 shot, 2½ and 4 in. barrels, fixed sights, swing out cylinder, blue, black plastic grips. Add $15 for .32 H&R Mag. cal. Mfg. 1958-disc.

| | $127 | $100 | $85 | $75 | $65 | $55 | $45 |

MODEL 733 — same specifications as the Model 732, only nickel finish and available only with 2½ in. barrel. Add $15 for .32 H&R Mag. cal.

| | $140 | $125 | $110 | $85 | $75 | $60 | $50 |

MODEL 900 — .22 S, L, or LR, 9 shot, 2½, 4 or 6 in. barrels, snap out cylinder, blue, black plastic grips. Mfg. 1962-1973.

| | $90 | $85 | $70 | $55 | $50 | $40 | $30 |

MODEL 901 — similar to 900, but chrome with white tenite grips. Mfg. 1962-1963.

| | $110 | $100 | $90 | $70 | $50 | $40 | $30 |

MODEL 904 — .22 cal., double action, 4 or 6 in. bull barrel, target grade, 9 shot. Disc. 1985.

| | $150 | $135 | $120 | $105 | $95 | $80 | $70 |

Last Mfg.'s Sug. Retail was $168.

MODEL 905 — similar to Model 904, except with nickel finish and 4 in. barrel only. Disc. 1985.

| | $160 | $140 | $125 | $105 | $95 | $80 | $70 |

Last Mfg.'s Sug. Retail was $185.

MODEL 922 — Second Issue, .22 LR cal., 9 shot, 2½, 4 or 6 in. barrels, solid frame, blue, plastic grips. Mfg. 1950-1982.

| | $85 | $70 | $60 | $45 | $40 | $30 | $25 |

MODEL 923 — similar to 922, only nickel.

| | $90 | $75 | $65 | $50 | $45 | $35 | $30 |

MODEL 925 DEFENDER — .38 S&W cal., 5 shot, 2½ in. barrel, blue, break open, adj. sight, wrap-around one piece grip. Mfg. 1964-1984.

| | $130 | $120 | $100 | $85 | $70 | $60 | $50 |

Model 935 — similar to Model 925, except with nickel finish.

| | $145 | $135 | $115 | $100 | $70 | $60 | $50 |

Grading	100%	98%	95%	90%	80%	70%	60%

MODEL 926 — .22 LR cal., 9 shot, or .38 S&W, 5 shot, 4 in. barrel, blue, adj. rear sight, break open, walnut grips. Mfg. 1968-1982.

	100%	98%	95%	90%	80%	70%	60%
	$130	$120	$100	$85	$70	$60	$50

⚛ **Model 926 Abilene Kansas Centennial** — .22 LR cal., barrel is marked "Abilene Kansas" and "1869 Centennial 1969", mfg. 1969 only.

	100%	98%	95%	90%	80%	70%	60%
	$175	$155	$125	$105	$90	$80	$70

MODEL 929 SIDEKICK — .22 LR cal., 9 shot, 2½, 4 or 6 in. barrels, swing out cylinder, plastic grips, blue. Mfg. 1956-1985.

	100%	98%	95%	90%	80%	70%	60%
	$115	$100	$70	$55	$45	$35	$30

Last Mfg.'s Sug. Retail was $127.

MODEL 930 SIDEKICK — similar to 929 Sidekick, only nickel finish and not available with 6 in. barrel. Disc. 1985.

	100%	98%	95%	90%	80%	70%	60%
	$125	$110	$80	$65	$55	$45	$40

Last Mfg.'s Sug. Retail was $140.

MODEL 939 ULTRA SIDEKICK — .22 S, L or LR, 9 shot, 6 in. barrel, swing out cylinder, vent rib, adj. sights, blue. Mfg. 1958-1982.

	100%	98%	95%	90%	80%	70%	60%
	$110	$100	$85	$70	$55	$45	$30

MODEL 940 ULTRA SIDEKICK — similar to 939, only round barrel. Disc.

	100%	98%	95%	90%	80%	70%	60%
	$105	$95	$75	$65	$50	$40	$30

MODEL 949 "FORTY NINER" — .22 S, L or LR, 5½ in. barrel, double action, solid frame, 9 shot, side load and Western style ejection, adj. rear sight, walnut grips. Mfg. 1960-1985.

	100%	98%	95%	90%	80%	70%	60%
	$115	$100	$85	$70	$55	$50	$45

Last Mfg.'s Sug. Retail was $127.

MODEL 950 — similar to Model 949, except with nickel finish. Disc. 1985.

	100%	98%	95%	90%	80%	70%	60%
	$125	$105	$90	$70	$55	$50	$45

Last Mfg.'s Sug. Retail was $145.

MODEL 976 — similar to 949, only color case hardened frame. Disc.

	100%	98%	95%	90%	80%	70%	60%
	$100	$90	$85	$70	$60	$50	$35

MODEL 999 SPORTSMAN — Second Issue, .22 LR cal., 9 shot, 4 or 6 in. vent. rib barrel, top-break action, adj. sights, walnut grips. Mfg. 1950-1985.

	100%	98%	95%	90%	80%	70%	60%
	$195	$170	$155	$140	$125	$110	$95

This model was also made in a Sportsman Centennial Commemorative. Add 15%-25% if NIB.

MODEL 999 ENGRAVED — similar to 999, only engraved throughout, 6 in. barrel only. Disc. 1985.

	100%	98%	95%	90%	80%	70%	60%
	$425	$375	$300	$260	$225	$190	$175

Last Mfg.'s Sug. Retail was $525.

RIFLES

REISING MODEL 60 — semi-auto, .45 ACP cal., 12 or 20 shot, 18¼ in. barrel, detachable mag. Mfg. 1944-1946.

	100%	98%	95%	90%	80%	70%	60%
	$360	$340	$310	$275	$220	$200	$175

Grading	100%	98%	95%	90%	80%	70%	60%

MODEL 65 MILITARY — .22 LR cal., 10 shot mag., 23 in. barrel, Redfield aperture rear sight. Mfg. 1944-1946 for USMC.

| | $250 | $230 | $200 | $165 | $145 | $130 | $110 |

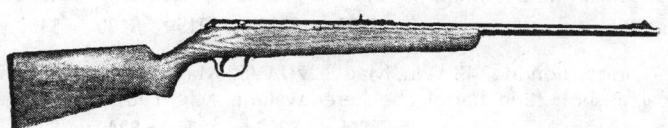

MODEL 150 — semi-auto, .22 LR cal., 5 shot. Mfg. 1949-1953.

| | $95 | $85 | $70 | $55 | $40 | $35 | $30 |

MODEL 155 — single shot, .44 Mag. or .45-70 cal., break open. Mfg. 1972-disc.

| | $150 | $130 | $115 | $95 | $75 | $55 | $45 |

MODEL 157 — single shot, .22 Mag., .22 Hornet or .30-30 cal., break open. Mfg. 1976-disc.

| | $135 | $110 | $100 | $80 | $65 | $45 | $35 |

MODEL 158 — .22 Jet, .22 Hornet, .30-30, .357 Mag or .44 Mag. cal., single shot break open, 22 in. barrel, side lever action release, ejector, case hardened frame. Disc. 1985.

| | $120 | $105 | $90 | $80 | $60 | $50 | $40 |

Last Mfg.'s Sug. Retail was $115.

Model 158 Combination — supplied with rifle barrel and 20 ga., 26 in. barrel. Disc. 1985.

| | $195 | $175 | $150 | $135 | $115 | $100 | $90 |

Last Mfg.'s Sug. Retail was $145.

MODEL 165 — .22 LR, 10 shot. Mfg. 1945-1961.

| | $120 | $110 | $95 | $85 | $70 | $55 | $50 |

MODEL 171 — .45-70 Model 1873 Trapdoor copy, 22 in. barrel, Model 174 is the deluxe model. Disc.

| | $350 | $300 | $270 | $250 | $230 | $210 | $195 |

MODEL 171-DL — single shot, .45-70 govt. cal., Springfield copy, 22 in. barrel. Mfg. 1984 and 1985.

| | $400 | $350 | $295 | $250 | $225 | $200 | $185 |

Last Mfg.'s Sug. Retail was $385.

MODEL 300 ULTRA — bolt action, .22-250, .243 Win., .270 Win., .30-06, .308 Win., 7mm Mag., or .300 Win. Mag. cal., 22 or 24 in. barrel. Mfg. 1965-1978.

| | $440 | $415 | $360 | $305 | $250 | $210 | $195 |

MODEL 301 CARBINE — similar to 300, but 18 in. barrel, full length Mannlicher stock, N/A .22-250.

| | $440 | $415 | $360 | $305 | $250 | $220 | $195 |

MODEL 317 ULTRA WILDCAT — short action Sako, .17 Rem., .17-223, .222 Rem., or .223 Rem. cal., 20 in. barrel, no sights. Mfg. 1968-1976.

| | $485 | $440 | $415 | $360 | $305 | $275 | $220 |

Grading	100%	98%	95%	90%	80%	70%	60%

MODEL 317P PRESENTATION — similar to 317, but deluxe wood basketweave checkering. Mfg. 1968-1976.

	$625	$550	$495	$440	$400	$360	$305

MODEL 333 — similar to 300, in 7mm Mag. cal., plainer version. Mfg. 1974 only.

	$250	$230	$215	$180	$160	$140	$120

MODEL 340 — bolt action in .243 Win. Mag., .270 Win. Mag., .30-06, .308 Win. Mag., 7mm Mauser cal., 5 shot, 22 in. barrel, checkered walnut. Mfg. 1982-1984.

	$395	$300	$275	$240	$220	$200	$180

MODEL 360 ULTRA AUTOMATIC — .243 Win. or .308 Win. cal., 3 shot, 22 in. barrel. Mfg. 1965-1978.

	$350	$330	$315	$275	$240	$220	$200

MODEL 370 ULTRA MEDALIST TARGET — Varmint Rifle, .22-250, .243 Win., or 6mm Rem. cal., 24 in. varmint weight barrel, semi-beavertail forearm. Mfg. 1968-1973.

	$440	$415	$360	$305	$275	$220	$195

MODEL 422 — slide action, .22 S, L or LR cal. Mfg. 1956-1958.

	$110	$100	$85	$65	$45	$40	$30

MODEL 451 MEDALIST — bolt action, .22 LR cal., 5 shot, 26 in. barrel. Mfg. 1948-1961.

	$165	$150	$140	$110	$100	$85	$55

Model 450 — similar to Model 451, only no sights.

	$150	$140	$120	$110	$95	$70	$55

MODEL 700 — .22 Win. Mag. cal., semi-auto, 5 shot, clip mag., 22 in. barrel. Mfg. 1977-1985.

	$200	$175	$150	$130	$110	$90	$75

Last Mfg.'s Sug. Retail was $210.

MODEL 700DL — similar to Model 700, except deluxe checkered walnut. 4-power scope is standard, recoil pad. Disc. 1985.

	$315	$270	$230	$195	$175	$150	$135

Last Mfg.'s Sug. Retail was $360.

MODEL 750 — .22 cal. single shot bolt action, 22 in. barrel, open sights, youth stock dimensions. Disc. 1985.

	$85	$75	$60	$50	$45	$40	$35

Last Mfg.'s Sug. Retail was $95.

MODEL 865 — .22 cal. bolt action. 5 shot mag., 22 in. barrel. Disc. 1985.

	$90	$80	$65	$55	$50	$45	$40

Last Mfg.'s Sug. Retail was $105.

MODEL 5200 TARGET — .22 cal. target rifle, heavy 28 in. barrel, adj. trigger, no sights, single shot. 11 lbs. Disc. 1985.

	$435	$395	$350	$295	$260	$230	$200

Last Mfg.'s Sug. Retail was $450.

MODEL 5200 SPORTER — .22 cal., bolt action, 5 shot, 24 in. barrel, adj. sights, checkered walnut. Disc. 1983.

	$475	$425	$400	$375	$350	$325	$295

Grading	100%	98%	95%	90%	80%	70%	60%

SHOTGUNS

HARRICH NO. 1 — single barrel Trap Gun, 12 ga., 32 or 34 in. full choke, high quality, engraved, vent. rib. Mfg. by Ferlach of Austria from 1971-1975.

	$1,650	$1,595	$1,485	$1,320	$1,100	$880	$770

MODEL 3 HAMMERLESS — similar to Model 8, but no visible external hammer. Mfg. 1908-1942.

	$85	$75	$70	$55	$45	$40	$30

MODEL 5 LIGHTWEIGHT — 24, 28, or .410 ga. only. Mfg. 1908-1942.

	$95	$90	$75	$65	$55	$40	$35

MODEL 6 HEAVY BREECH — similar to Model 8, only 10 ga. - 20 ga., heavier barrels. Mfg. 1908-1942.

	$95	$85	$75	$60	$50	$45	$35

MODEL 7 OR 9 BAY STATE — similar to Model 8, only 12, 16, 20 or .410 ga., rounded pistol grip. Mfg. 1908-1942.

	$85	$75	$70	$55	$45	$40	$30

MODEL 8 STANDARD — single shot, 12, 16, 20, 24, 28, or .410 ga., 26-32 in. barrels, plain pistol grip stock, auto ejector, break open. Mfg. 1908-1942.

	$150	$125	$95	$75	$65	$60	$55

Add 100% for 28 or .410 ga.

FOLDING GUN — hinged frame, barrel folds against stock. Mfg. 1908-1942.

	$95	$90	$75	$65	$55	$40	$35

TOPPER — single shot, break open, 10 different models of this shotgun, all are very similar and values run too close to differentiate. Mfg. 1946-disc.

	$145	$125	$100	$85	$70	$55	$45

MODEL 088 — 12, 16, 20, 28, or .410 ga., single shot, hammer model, ejector, blue barrel finish with case hardened frame, Disc. 1985.

	$85	$75	$55	$50	$45	$40	$35

Last Mfg.'s Sug. Retail was $95.

MODEL 099 — 12, 16, 20, or .410 ga., similar to Model 088, only electroless nickel finish, ejector. Disc. 1984.

	$95	$80	$60	$55	$50	$45	$40

MODEL 162 — 12 or 20 ga., single shot, 24 in. slug barrel with rifle sights, case hardened frame, 20 ga. Disc. 1984.

	$115	$105	$90	$80	$65	$55	$45

MODEL 176 — 10 (3½ in.), 12, or 20 ga., Mag., single shot, 32-36 in. heavy barrel, break open. Mfg. 1977-1985.

	$110	$95	$80	$70	$60	$50	$45

Last Mfg.'s Sug. Retail was $125.

MODEL 400 PUMP ACTION — 12, 16, or 20 ga., 28 in. full choke. Mfg. 1955-1967.

	$155	$145	$125	$110	$90	$75	$55

Grading	100%	98%	95%	90%	80%	70%	60%

MODEL 401 PUMP — similar to 400, but H&R variable choke. Mfg. 1956-1963.

| | $165 | $155 | $140 | $120 | $100 | $90 | $65 |

MODEL 402 PUMP — similar to 400, only .410 ga., lightweight. Mfg. 1959-1967.

| | $175 | $165 | $150 | $140 | $110 | $100 | $85 |

MODEL 403 AUTOLOADER — .410 ga., 26 in. full choke, takedown. Mfg. 1964 only.

| | $195 | $180 | $165 | $155 | $120 | $100 | $85 |

MODEL 404 — double barrel, SxS, 12, 20, or .410 ga., 26 or 28 in. barrel, boxlock, extractors, double triggers. Mfg. by Rossi of Brazil 1969-1972.

| | $185 | $175 | $165 | $145 | $110 | $90 | $70 |

MODEL 404C — similar to 404, only checkered stock.

| | $200 | $185 | $175 | $155 | $120 | $100 | $85 |

MODEL 440 — pump action, 12, 16, or 20 ga., 26, 28, or 30 in. barrels, available in various chokes, plain pistol grip and slide. Mfg. 1968-1973.

| | $145 | $130 | $110 | $100 | $85 | $70 | $55 |

MODEL 442 — pump action, similar to 440, only vent. rib, checkered stock. Mfg. 1969-1973.

| | $175 | $165 | $155 | $140 | $100 | $85 | $65 |

MODEL 490 — 20 or .410 ga., made for junior shooters, Greenwing finish — add $10. Disc. 1984.

| | $85 | $65 | $60 | $50 | $45 | $40 | $40 |

MODEL 1212 — O/U, Field, 12 ga., 2¾ in., 28 in. vent. rib barrels, various chokes, checkered walnut stocks. Mfg. by Lanber Arms, Spain, from 1976-disc.

| | $310 | $295 | $275 | $250 | $200 | $175 | $155 |

MODEL 1212 WATERFOWL — similar to 1212, except 3 in. 12 ga., 30 in. barrel.

| | $320 | $310 | $285 | $260 | $210 | $185 | $165 |

SINGLE SHOT COMBINATION GUNS

MODEL 058 — 20 ga./.30-30, .22 Hornet, .44 Mag., .357 Mag. combination — 2 separate barrels supplied, blue only. Disc. 1985.

| | $130 | $110 | $95 | $85 | $75 | $65 | $60 |

Last Mfg.'s Sug. Retail was $145.

MODEL 258 COMBINATION HANDY GUN II — supplied with 20 ga., 22 in. barrel and 22 in. rifle barrel in .22 Hornet, .30-30 Win., or .357 Mag. cal., electroless, matte nickel finish, side lever action release, cased, 6½ lbs. Disc. 1985.

| | $175 | $155 | $140 | $130 | $120 | $100 | $95 |

Last Mfg.'s Sug. Retail was $195.

COMMEMORATIVES & REPLICAS

ABILENE ANNIVERSARY .22 REVOLVER — 300 mfg. 1967.

| | $150 | $115 | $75 |

Last Mfg.'s Sug. Retail was $83.50 (1967).

Grading	100%	98%	95%	90%	80%	70%	60%

H&R 100TH ANNIVERSARY OFFICER'S MODEL — 1871-1971, Commemorative Officer's Model, Springfield 1873 Replica, Trapdoor, .45-70 cal., engraved metal work, 26 in. barrel, anniversary plaque on stock, 10,000 mfg. in 1971.

	$450	$350	$275				

Last Mfg.'s Sug. Retail was $250 (1971).

MODEL 171 AND 171 DELUXE — listed in previous rifle section.

MODEL 173 RIFLE — .45-70, similar to Officer's Model, no plaque on stock. Mfg. 1972-1983.

	$495	$425	$325				

MODEL 174 CARBINE (LITTLE BIG HORN) — .45-70, Little Big Horn Commercial Carbine. Quantity unknown.

	$395	$325	$250				

Last Mfg.'s Sug. Retail was $220 (1972).

MODEL 178 — .45-70, Infantry Musket Replica, 32 in. barrel. Mfg. 1973-1984.

	$350	$295	$195				

1873 SPRINGFIELD TRAPDOOR — .45-70 cal., unknown quantities mfg. 1973.

	$450	$350	$275				

Last Mfg.'s Sug. Retail was $250.

CUSTER MEMORIAL ISSUE — .45-70 cal., limited production, deluxe walnut stock, highly engraved, gold inlaid, mahogany display case and two volumes on Custer history. Each weapon bears the name of one who fell at Little Big Horn.

⚔ **Officer's Model** — 25 mfg., must be new with original box/accessories.

	$3,995	$3,150	$2,400				

Last Mfg.'s Sug. Retail was $3,000 (1973).

⚔ **Enlisted Men's Model** — 243 mfg., must be new with original box/accessories.

	$1,995	$1,400	$900				

Last Mfg.'s Sug. Retail was $2,000 (1973).

HK4 COMMEMORATIVE — .22 LR and .380 ACP cals. with conversion kits, mfg. by H & K of West Germany, cased, limited mfg. in 1971 only.

	$495	$375	$295				

HARTFORD ARMS & EQUIPMENT COMPANY

Hartford Arms was the forerunner of High Standard Arms Co., who acquired them in 1932.

HARTFORD AUTOMATIC TARGET — .22 LR, 10 shot, 6¾ in. barrel, blue, black rubber grips. Mfg. 1929-1930.

	$650	$575	$500	$450	$375	$300	$275

HARTFORD REPEATING PISTOL — .22 cal., similar in appearance to Automatic, except a hand operated repeater. Mfg. 1929-1930.

	$495	$425	$360	$310	$260	$250	$225

HARTFORD SINGLE SHOT TARGET — similar in appearance to Automatic, .22 LR cal., 6¾ in. barrel, target sights, case colored frame and slide, blue barrel, rubber or wood grips. Mfg. 1929-1930.

	$475	$390	$350	$310	$260	$250	$225

HASKELL MANUFACTURING

Manufacturer located in Lima, OH. Distributed by MKS Supply located in Mansfield, OH. Distributor sales only.

Refer to listing under Hi-Point Firearms.

HATFIELD GUN CO., INC.

Manufacture by Hatfield Gun Co., Inc. (designated Hatfield Rifle Works until 1986) located in St. Joseph, MO.

Hatfield also manufactures flintlock and percussion black powder rifles which can be located in the Modern Black Powder Guns section of this text.

SHOTGUNS: UPLANDER SERIES S X S

In addition to Grades I and II listed below, Hatfield also offers custom order shotguns built per individual special order - prices start at $3,000.

Grading	100%	98%	95%	90%	80%	70%	60%

GRADE I — 20 or 28 ga., 3 in. chambers, 26 in. IC/M, matted rib barrels, case hardened boxlock action, single trigger, ejectors, deluxe checkered straight grip maple stock and forearm, 5¾ lbs, cased. New 1987.

Mfg.'s Sug. Retail $1,995	$1,775	$1,525	$1,325	$1,150	$900	$725	$575

Add $600 for extra 28 ga. barrels.

Collector's Grade I — mfg. 1990-92.

	$1,475	$1,200	$1,000	$875	$700	$550	$475

Add $400 for extra 28 ga. barrels.
Last Mfg.'s Sug. Retail was $1,625.

GRADE II PIGEON — similar to Grade I, except has scroll engraving on top lever, sides, floor plate, and trigger guard, cased. New 1987.

Mfg.'s Sug. Retail $2,595	$2,250	$1,675	$1,350	$1,050	$900	$775	$675

Add $800 for extra 28 ga. barrels.

Collector's Grade II — mfg. 1990-92.

	$2,675	$2,000	$1,600	$1,250	$1,050	$875	$775

Add $400 for extra 28 ga. barrels.
Last Mfg.'s Sug. Retail was $3,025.

GRADE III SUPER PIGEON — includes heavy relief scroll engraving (total coverage) on frame, top lever, floor plate, and trigger guard, leather cased. Mfg. 1987-disc.

	$2,350	$1,900	$1,495	$1,200	$1,025	$900	$775

Add $900 for extra 28 ga. barrels.
Last Mfg.'s Sug. Retail was $3,500.

Collector's Grade III — mfg. 1990-disc.

	$3,000	$2,500	$2,000	$1,750	$1,400	$1,175	$995

Add $900 for extra 28 ga. barrels.
Last Mfg.'s Sug. Retail was $4,375.

GRADE IV GOLDEN QUAIL — more extensive engraving including six 24 Kt. gold inlays on frame and floor plate, 2 gold barrel bands, leather cased. Mfg. 1987-disc.

	$3,995	$3,575	$2,900	$2,350	$1,900	$1,600	$1,300

Add $900 for extra 28 ga. barrels.
Last Mfg.'s Sug. Retail was $5,500.

Collector's Grade IV — mfg. 1990-disc.

	$4,475	$3,900	$3,300	$2,650	$2,175	$1,800	$1,500

Add $1,350 for extra 28 ga. barrels.
Last Mfg.'s Sug. Retail was $6,625.

Grading	100%	98%	95%	90%	80%	70%	60%

GRADE V WOODCOCK — previous top-of-the-line model with best quality engraving and multiple gold inlays, leather cased. Mfg. 1987-disc.

| | $4,600 | $4,400 | $3,350 | $2,700 | $2,175 | $1,800 | $1,500 |

Add $1,500 for extra 28 ga. barrels.
Last Mfg.'s Sug. Retail was $6,900.

‡ **Collector's Grade V** — mfg. 1990-disc.

| | $6,200 | $5,700 | $4,475 | $3,900 | $3,300 | $2,650 | $2,200 |

Add $2,000 for extra 28 ga. barrels.
Last Mfg.'s Sug. Retail was $8,500.

GRADE VI BLACK WIDOW — mfg. 1990-disc.

| | $5,200 | $4,875 | $3,700 | $3,000 | $2,500 | $2,100 | $1,800 |

Last Mfg.'s Sug. Retail was $7,900.

GRADE VII ROYALE — mfg. 1990-disc.

| | $5,200 | $4,875 | $3,700 | $3,000 | $2,500 | $2,100 | $1,800 |

Last Mfg.'s Sug. Retail was $7,900.

GRADE VIII TOP HAT — top-of-the-line model with best quality wood and extensive engraving with gold inlays. Built to individual customer specifications. Mfg. 1990-disc.

| | $12,000 | $9,750 | $8,750 | $7,500 | $6,500 | $5,500 | $4,500 |

Last Mfg.'s Sug. Retail was $17,500.

HAWES FIREARMS

Manufactured by J.P. Sauer & Sohn in Eckernforde, W. Germany. Imported by Hawes Firearms in Van Nuys, CA.

Rather than give an individual listing of the various single action revolvers that have been imported, a generalized price range is as follows: centerfire single actions usually are in the $130 - $250 range while .22 rimfire models are typically valued between $60 - $140.

HECKLER & KOCH

Manufacturer located in Oberndorf/Neckar, Germany. Imported and distributed by Heckler & Koch, Inc. (U.S. headquarters) located in Sterling, VA (previously located in Chantilly, VA). In early 1991, H & K was absorbed by Royal Ordnance, a division of British Aerospace located in England.

PISTOLS: SEMI-AUTO, RECENT MANUFACTURE

HK4 — double action auto, .380, .32 auto, .25 auto, and .22 LR, available with all caliber conversion units, 3⅓ in. barrel, blue, plastic grips. In recent years, used HK 4s have been imported into the U.S. at discount prices - thus affecting used HK 4 prices. Disc. 1984.

	100%	98%	95%	90%	80%	70%	60%
.25 or .32 ACP cal.	$295	$260	$230	$215	$180	$150	$130
.22 or .380 cal.	$430	$345	$300	$250	$195	$160	$140

‡ **.380 with .22 conversion**

| | $480 | $385 | $350 | $325 | $310 | $290 | $280 |

‡ **.380 with all conversions**

| | $590 | $475 | $450 | $420 | $390 | $375 | $360 |

This model was also mfg. in a French model in .22 LR and/or .32 ACP (about 500 imported).

Grading	100%	98%	95%	90%	80%	70%	60%

P9S — .45 ACP or 9mm Para., double action combat model, 4 in. barrel, phosphated finish, sculptured plastic grips, fixed sights. Although production ceased in 1984, limited quantities were available until 1989.

	$600	$480	$400	$360	$320	$290	$265

Last Mfg.'s Sug. Retail was $1,299.

P9S TARGET — .45 ACP or 9mm Para., 4 in. barrel, phosphated finish, adj. sights and trigger. Although production ceased in 1984, limited quantities were available until 1989.

	$850	$700	$600	$540	$500	$465	$430

Last Mfg.'s Sug. Retail was $1,382.

P9S COMPETITION KIT — 9mm Para only, similar to P9S Target, except extra 5$\frac{1}{2}$ in. barrel and weight, competition walnut grip, 2 slides. Disc. 1984.

	$1,150	$950	$875	$800	$720	$640	$550

Last Mfg.'s Sug. Retail was $2,250.

P7 PSP — 9mm Para., older variation of the P7 M8, without extended trigger guard, ambidextrous mag. release (European style), or heat shield. Standard production ceased 1986.

Mfg.'s Sug. Retail	$1,059	$795	$625	$525	$460	$410	$390	$370

This model is available in limited quantities only. A re-issue of this model was mfg. in 1990 with approx. 150 mfg.

P7 M8 — 9mm Para., unique squeeze cocking single action, extended square combat type trigger guard with heat shield, 4.13 in. fixed barrel with polygonal rifling, 8 shot mag., ambidextrous mag. release, fixed 3-dot sighting system, stippled black plastic grips, black phosphate or nickel (new 1992) finish, includes 2 mags., 28 oz.

Mfg.'s Sug. Retail	$1,059	$825	$700	$600	$525	$450	$410	$390

Add $59 for Tritium sights (various colors, new 1993).

P7 M13 — similar to P7 M8, only with staggered 13 shot mag., 30 oz.

Mfg.'s Sug. Retail	$1,284	$950	$775	$700	$630	$580	$530	$480

Add $59 for Tritium sights (various colors, new 1993).

P7 M10 — .40 S&W cal., similar specifications as P7 M13, except has 10 shot mag., 29 oz. New 1991.

Mfg.'s Sug. Retail	$1,314	$975	$800	$725	$650	$600	$550	$495

Add $59 for Tritium sights (various colors, new 1993).

P7 K3 — .22 LR or .380 ACP cal., uses unique oil-filled buffer to decrease recoil, 3.8 in. barrel, 8 shot mag. (includes 2), 26$\frac{1}{2}$ oz. New 1988.

Mfg.'s Sug. Retail	$1,059	$825	$700	$600	$525	$450	$410	$390

Add $524 for .22 LR conversion kit.
Add $228 for .32 ACP conversion kit.
Add $59 for Tritium sights (various colors, new 1993).

Grading	100%	98%	95%	90%	80%	70%	60%

USP 9 — 9mm Para., semi-auto, available in regular DA/SA mode or DA only, 4.13 in. barrel, Browning-type action with H&K recoil reduction system, polymer frame, all metal surfaces specially treated, can be carried cocked and locked, stipled synthetic grips, bobbed hammer, 3-dot sighting system, multiple safeties, 16 shot polymer mag., 26½ oz. New 1993.

	100%	98%	95%	90%	80%	70%	60%
Mfg.'s Sug. Retail $624	$560	$475	$425	$385	$350	$325	$295

Add $20 for control lever (safety/decocking lever on right side).
Add $59 for Tritium sights (various colors, new 1993).

USP 40 — .40 S&W, similar to USP 9, 13 shot mag., 27¾ oz. New 1993.

	100%	98%	95%	90%	80%	70%	60%
Mfg.'s Sug. Retail $624	$560	$475	$425	$385	$350	$325	$295

Add $20 for control lever (safety/decocking lever on right side).
Add $59 for Tritium sights (various colors, new 1993).

SP 89 — 9mm Para., semi-auto, recoil operated delayed roller-locked bolt system, 4.5 in. barrel, 15 shot mag., rotated aperture adj. rear sight (accepts HK claw-lock scope mounts), 4.4 lbs. New 1990.

	100%	98%	95%	90%	80%	70%	60%
Mfg.'s Sug. Retail $1,324	$985	$800	$725	$650	$600	$550	$495

Add $129 for adj. target grip.

VP 70Z — 9mm, 18 shot, double action only, 4½ in. barrel, parkerized finish, plastic receiver/grip assembly. Disc. 1984.

	100%	98%	95%	90%	80%	70%	60%
	$375	$320	$275	$250	$230	$210	$195

RIFLES: SEMI-AUTO

The models listed below, being of a paramilitary design, were disc. 1989 due to Federal legislation as a result of the controversy with this type of firearms configuration.

In 1991, the HK-91, HK-93, and HK-94 were discontinued. Last published retail prices (1991) were $999 for fixed stock models and $1,199 for retractable stock models.

In the early 70's, S.A.C.O. importers located in Virginia sold the Models 41 and 43 which were the predecessors to the Model 91 and 93, respectively. Values for these earlier variations will be higher than values listed below.

MODEL 41 — 7.62mm cal., predecessor to the Model 91 A-2, originally imported by Golden State Arms.

	100%	98%	95%	90%	80%	70%	60%
	$1,100	$995	$895	$795	$695	$600	$500

SR-9 — .308 cal. (7.62mm), semi-auto sporting rifle, 19.7 in. barrel, Kevlar reinforced fiberglass thumbhole stock and forearm, 5 shot mag., Diopter adj. rear sight, accepts HK claw-lock scope mounts. New 1990.

	100%	98%	95%	90%	80%	70%	60%
Mfg.'s Sug. Retail $1,369	$1,150	$995	$850	$725	$650	$575	$500

SR-9T — .308 cal., precision target rifle with adj. MSG 90 buttstock and PSG-1 trigger group, 5 shot mag. New 1992.

	100%	98%	95%	90%	80%	70%	60%
Mfg.'s Sug. Retail $1,799	$1,550	$1,150	$995	$850	$750	$650	$575

SR-9TC — .308 cal., similar to SR-9T, except has PSG-1 adj. butt stock. New 1993.

	100%	98%	95%	90%	80%	70%	60%
Mfg.'s Sug. Retail $1,946	$1,675	$1,250	$1,050	$900	$800	$650	$575

PSG-1 — .308 cal. only, high precision marksman's rifle, 5 shot mag., adj. buttstock, includes accessories and case (Hensholdt illuminated 6 x 42 power scope), 17.8 lbs.

	100%	98%	95%	90%	80%	70%	60%
Mfg.'s Sug. Retail $9,325	$7,750	$6,750	$5,875	$5,100	$4,500	$3,850	$3,400

Grading	100%	98%	95%	90%	80%	70%	60%

MODEL 91 A-2 — .308 cal. (7.62mm), semi-auto paramilitary design rifle, delayed roller lock bolt system, antennuated recoil, black cycolac stock, 17.7 in. barrel, 20 shot mag., 9.7 lbs. Importation disc. 1989.

⚔ **Fixed stock model**

	100%	98%	95%	90%	80%	70%	60%
	$1,275	$1,100	$995	$895	$795	$695	$600

Add $200 for desert camo finish.
Add $275 for NATO black finish.
Last Mfg.'s Sug. Retail was $999.

⚔ **Model 91 A-3** — with retractable metal stock.

	100%	98%	95%	90%	80%	70%	60%
	$1,750	$1,500	$1,300	$1,100	$950	$850	$725

Add $400 for .22 LR conversion kit.
Last Mfg.'s Sug. Retail was $1,114.

⚔ **Model 91 A-2 Package** — includes A.R.M.S. mount, B-Square rings, Leupold 3 x 9 compact scope with matte finish. Importation disc. 1988.

	100%	98%	95%	90%	80%	70%	60%
	$1,850	$1,575	$1,375	$1,175	$995	$875	$750

Add $150 for retractable stock.
Last Mfg.'s Sug. Retail was $1,285.

MODEL 93 A-2 — .223 cal. (5.56mm), smaller version of the H&K 91, 25 shot mag., 16.14 in. barrel, 8 lbs.

⚔ **Fixed stock model**

	100%	98%	95%	90%	80%	70%	60%
	$1,100	$995	$900	$800	$700	$625	$550

Add $200 for desert camo finish.   Add $275 for NATO black finish.
Last Mfg.'s Sug. Retail was $946.

⚔ **Model 93 A-3** — with retractable metal stock.

	100%	98%	95%	90%	80%	70%	60%
	$1,250	$1,075	$975	$850	$750	$675	$595

Last Mfg.'s Sug. Retail was $1,114.

⚔ **Model 93 A-2 Package** — includes A.R.M.S. mount, B-Square rings, Leupold 3 x 9 compact scope with matte finish. Importation disc. 1988.

	100%	98%	95%	90%	80%	70%	60%
	$1,850	$1,575	$1,375	$1,175	$995	$875	$750

Add $150 for retractable stock.
Last Mfg.'s Sug. Retail was $1,285.

MODEL 94 CARBINE A-2 — 9mm, semi-auto carbine, 16.54 in. barrel, aperture rear sight, 15 shot mag. New 1983.

⚔ **Fixed stock model**

	100%	98%	95%	90%	80%	70%	60%
	$1,450	$1,250	$1,075	$925	$800	$725	$625

Last Mfg.'s Sug. Retail was $946.

⚔ **Model 94 Carbine A-3** — retractable metal stock.

	100%	98%	95%	90%	80%	70%	60%
	$1,595	$1,375	$1,100	$975	$875	$795	$675

Last Mfg.'s Sug. Retail was $1,114.

⚔ **Model 94 A-2 Package** — includes A.R.M.S. mount, B-Square rings, Leupold 3 x 9 compact scope with matte finish. Importation disc. 1988.

	100%	98%	95%	90%	80%	70%	60%
	$1,850	$1,575	$1,375	$1,175	$995	$875	$750

Add $150 for retractable stock.
Last Mfg.'s Sug. Retail was $1,285.

Grading	100%	98%	95%	90%	80%	70%	60%

⚔ **Model 94 SGI** — 9mm, semi-auto, target rifle, aluminum alloy bipod, Leupold 6X scope, 15 or 30 shot mag. Imported 1986 only.

	$2,150	$1,750	$1,475	$1,250	$1,075	$900	$795

Last Mfg.'s Sug. Retail was $1,340.

MODEL 270 — .22 LR cal. semi-auto, sporting rifle, 19.7 in. barrel with standard or polygonal rifling, 5 or 20 shot mag., high luster blue, plain walnut stock, approx. 5.7 lbs. Disc. 1985.

	$400	$350	$300	$275	$250	$225	$200

Last Mfg.'s Sug. Retail was $200.

MODEL 300 — .22 Mag. cal., semi-auto, 5 or 15 shot, polygonal rifling standard, otherwise similar to H&K 270 with checkered walnut stock. Importation disc. 1989.

	$575	$525	$450	$400	$375	$350	$325

Add $150-$175 for factory H&K scope mount system.
Last Mfg.'s Sug. Retail was $608.

⚔ **Model 300 Package** — includes A.R.M.S. mount, B-Square rings, Leupold 3 x 9 compact scope with matte finish. Importation disc. 1988.

	$750	$700	$650	$600	$550	$500	$460

Last Mfg.'s Sug. Retail was $689.

MODEL 630 — .223 cal., semi-auto, delayed roller lock bolt system, 17.7 in. barrel, reduced recoil, checkered walnut, 4 or 10 shot mag., 7.04 lbs. Importation disc. 1986.

	$725	$650	$550	$495	$460	$430	$400

Add $150-$175 for factory H&K scope mount system.
Last Mfg.'s Sug. Retail was $784.
Because of the significant price increases since 1986 triggered by the devaluation of the American dollar, the importation of this model was stopped. Above values are indicative of current market prices, which could fluctuate due to regional supply and demand.

MODEL 770 — .308 cal., 3 or 10 shot mag., 19.7 in. barrel, 7.92 lbs., otherwise similar to model 630. Importation disc. 1986.

	$750	$675	$600	$560	$530	$500	$485

Add $150-$175 for factory H&K scope mount system.
Last Mfg.'s Sug. Retail was $797.
Significant price increases stopped the importation of this model.
Approx. 6 Model 770s were imported in .243 Win. cal. during 1984. Values for the .243 cal. will be considerably higher than listed above for the .308 cal.

MODEL 940 — .30-06 cal., 21.6 in. barrel, 8.62 lbs., otherwise same as model 770. Importation disc. 1986.

	$800	$695	$625	$565	$500	$465	$430

Add $150-$175 for factory H&K scope mount system.
Last Mfg.'s Sug. Retail was $917.
Significant price increases stopped the importation of this model.

⚔ **Model 940K** — Similar to Model 940, except has 16 in. barrel and higher cheekpiece. Imported 1984 only.

	$950	$825	$725	$625	$565	$500	$465

MODELS SL6 & SL7 CARBINE — .223 or .308 cal., 17.71 in. barrel, semi-auto, delayed roller lock bolt system, reduced recoil, vent. wooden hand guard, 3 or 4 shot mag, 8.36 lbs., matte black metal finish, HK-SL6 is .223 cal., HK-SL7 is .308 cal. Disc. in 1986.

	$675	$595	$550	$495	$460	$430	$400

Grading	100%	98%	95%	90%	80%	70%	60%

RIFLES: BOLT ACTION

BASR — .22, .22-250, 6mm PPC, 300 Win. Mag., .30-06, or .308 cal., Kevlar stock, stainless steel barrel, limited production. Special order only. Mfg. 1986 only.

	$8,500	$7,500	$6,500	$5,750	$5,000	$4,500	$4,000

Less than 135 of this variation were manufactured and they are extremely rare. Contractual disputes with the U.S. supplier stopped H&K from receiving any BASR models.

SHOTGUNS

H & K imported Benelli shotguns can be found under their own heading.

HELWAN

This model is currently being imported by Interarms and Navy Arms Co.

BRIGADIER — 9mm Para., single action, 4.5 in. barrel, all steel construction, 8 shot mag. with finger extension, black plastic grips, 32.6 oz. Importation began 1988.

Mfg.'s Sug. Retail	$235	$185	$145	$125	$115	$105	$95	$85

This model is patterned after the Beretta Model 1952. They were manufactured at the Helwan arsenal in Egypt.

HENRY RIFLE

Please refer to the Winchester section in this text.

HEROLD RIFLE

Franz Jaeger, Suhl, Germany.

BOLT ACTION SPORTING RIFLE — miniature Mauser action, .22 Hornet, 24 in. barrel, leaf sight, double set trigger, select checkered stock, imported by Daly & Stoeger, pre-WWII.

	$990	$880	$825	$770	$660	$550	$495

HERTERS

Previous importer/distributor/retailer headquartered in Waseca, MN from early 1960's - 1979.

Herters subcontracted various manufacturers (mostly European) to fabricate revolvers, rifles, and shotguns which were mostly patterned after more famous original models. Most of these copies were designed to undersell the competition at the time and while quality in most cases was quite good, consumer sales were not strong enough to continue production. While many Herters models are relatively rare, collectability to date has been minimal. Herters model values are usually under the original trademarks from which they were derived and to date have been based more on the shooting utility than the collector potential.

HEYM, FRIEDRICH WILH.

Originally founded in 1865 by F.H. Heym with location in Suhl. Currently manufactured in Muennerstadt, Germany. As this edition went to press, Heym did not have a current importer for the U.S. Previously imported and distributed by Heckler & Koch, Inc. (until 1993) located in Sterling, VA. Previously imported and distributed by Heym America, Inc. (subsidiary of F.W. Heym of W. Germany) located in Fort Wayne, IN.

Rather than discontinue all the models listed below, 1992 retail prices continue to be published for reference information.

Pre-war guns will bring a premium over values listed below.

Grading	100%	98%	95%	90%	80%	70%	60%

OVER AND UNDERS

MODEL 22 S2 — rifle/shotgun combination, 12, 16, or 20 ga. (3 in.), under rifle (17 cals. available), single set trigger, takedown feature (standard 1990), coin finish with engraving, 5½ lbs.

Mfg.'s Sug. Retail $4,125	$3,675	$3,000	$2,450	$1,875	$1,575	$1,325	$1,100

Subtract $380 **without engraving.**

This model features a dampened rifle barrel which prevents the "climbing" of groups, thereby enhancing accuracy.

MODEL 55 BF — rifle/shotgun combination, popular U.S. and European cals., shotgun barrels interchangeable in 12 (disc.), 16, or 20 ga., 25 or 28 in. barrels, boxlock, auto ejectors, silver finish, fine German engraving, folding leaf sight, checkered pistol grip stock. Extra barrels — add $3,250 for O/U rifle and $2,250 for O/U shotgun or shotgun/rifle combination.

Mfg.'s Sug. Retail $7,485	$6,500	$5,400	$4,950	$4,525	$3,950	$3,615	$3,210

⚞ **Model 55 B** — O/U rifle only, various cals., engraving similar to Model 55 BF.

Mfg.'s Sug. Retail $10,100	$8,750	$7,500	$6,875	$5,925	$5,100	$4,650	$3,975

⚞ **Model 55 BS** — O/U rifle only with different caliber for each barrel, double set triggers, "Bergstutzen" design.

Mfg.'s Sug. Retail $10,435	$9,000	$7,750	$6,950	$5,950	$5,125	$4,650	$3,975

⚞ **Model 55 F** — O/U shotgun, ejectors, 20 or 16 ga., engraved, 6.6 lbs. Importation disc. 1992.

	$5,100	$4,525	$3,950	$3,615	$3,200	$2,775	$2,300

Last Mfg.'s Sug. Retail was $5,500.

⚞ **Model 55 SS** — sidelock version of Model 55 F, large engraved hunting scenes.

Mfg.'s Sug. Retail $4,890	$4,500	$3,825	$3,300	$2,850	$2,400	$2,000	$1,700

MODEL 200 — 20 ga., 3 in. chambers, boxlock action, DTs, 28 in. VR barrels, light engraving, previous importation.

$895	$795	$700	$650	$600	$550	$500

DRILLINGS

MODEL 33 BOXLOCK STANDARD — 16 or 20 ga., boxlock, Arabesque engraving, shotgun barrels over popular European cals., and .222, .243, .270, .308, and .30-06 rifle barrel, 25 in. full and mod. barrels, set trigger on rifle, checkered pistol grip stock.

Mfg.'s Sug. Retail $8,700	$7,400	$5,950	$4,950	$4,525	$3,950	$3,615	$3,210

The Model 33 will be discontinued when existing parts are depleted and current inventory is limited.

⚞ **Model 33 Deluxe** — same specifications as Standard Model, only hunting scene engraved.

Mfg.'s Sug. Retail $9,080	$7,600	$6,000	$5,000	$4,600	$4,025	$3,700	$3,300

MODEL 37 SIDELOCK STANDARD — shotgun barrels (12, 16, or 20 ga.) over rifle, detachable sidelocks, select French walnut, border engraving, 8 lbs.

Mfg.'s Sug. Retail $11,815	$10,400	$8,800	$7,750	$6,650	$5,700	$4,900	$3,950

⚞ **Model 37 Deluxe** — similar to Model 37 Standard, except has large engraved hunting scenes.

Mfg.'s Sug. Retail $13,750	$12,000	$9,950	$8,200	$7,475	$6,500	$5,650	$4,600

Grading	100%	98%	95%	90%	80%	70%	60%

MODEL 37 B STANDARD — rifle barrels over shotgun (20 ga.), sidelock, border engraved, about 8.6 lbs.

Mfg.'s Sug. Retail $15,065	$13,250	$10,875	$9,500	$8,400	$7,550	$6,500	$5,650

⚔ **Model 37 B Deluxe** — similar to Model 37 B Standard, except has large hunting scene engraving.

Mfg.'s Sug. Retail $17,620	$15,600	$12,750	$10,700	$9,450	$8,200	$7,050	$5,750

RIFLES: BOLT ACTION

On the models listed below, a "N" suffix in the model denotes standard calibers whereas "G" refers to Mag. cals.

MODEL SR 20N CLASSIC SPORTER — available in 18 cals., Mauser type bolt action, single trigger, French walnut, 24 in. Krupp steel barrel except Mag. (25 in.).

Mfg.'s Sug. Retail $2,120	$1,825	$1,425	$1,100	$900	$800	$700	$600

Subtract $70 without iron sights.
Add $430 for left-hand variation.
Add $115 for Mag. cals. (G suffix).

⚔ **Model SR 20 Hunter** — similar to Model SR 20N, except has classic style fiberglass stock with either matte blue or parkerized metal finish. Imported 1988-90.

	$1,500	$1,225	$1,050	$900	$800	$700	$600

Last Mfg.'s Sug. Retail was $1,750.

⚔ **Model SR 20L** — Mannlicher style stock, European configuration, 18 in. barrel, 7 lbs.

Mfg.'s Sug. Retail $1,700	$1,475	$1,225	$985	$895	$785	$720	$650

SR 20 TROPHY — available in all SR 20 cals., bolt action, 22 or 24 (Mag. cals. only) in. octagonal barrel, classic stock configuration with cheek piece and recoil pad. Importation began 1989.

Mfg.'s Sug. Retail $2,815	$2,550	$2,100	$1,800	$1,500	$1,250	$985	$895

Add $120 for Mag. cal's.
This model is available with either right hand or left hand action.

SR 20G CLASSIC SPORTER — available in various cals., bolt action, 22 or 24 in. round barrel, steel grip cap. Importation began 1989.

Mfg.'s Sug. Retail $2,235	$1,875	$1,600	$1,300	$1,050	$900	$785	$720

Subtract $70 without iron sights.
This model is available with either right hand or left hand action.

SR 20 ALPINE — available in standard cals. between .243 Win. and 9.3 X 62, mountain style rifle with Mannlicher forend and classic buttstock, supplied with mounted open sights. Importation began 1989.

Mfg.'s Sug. Retail $2,165	$1,900	$1,650	$1,325	$1,075	$925	$800	$750

This model is available with either right hand or left hand action.

SR 20 MATCH — .308 cal. only, 24 in. heavy barrel, target stock with accessory rail, large bolt handle, supplied without sights, 9 lbs. New 1991.

Mfg.'s Sug. Retail $2,200	$1,860	$1,600	$1,300	$1,050	$900	$785	$720

SR 20 CLASSIC SAFARI — .375 H&H, .404 Jeffries (disc.), .425 Express, or .458 Win. Mag., 24 in. barrel only, express rear sight and large front post sights, tight grained walnut. Importation began 1989.

Mfg.'s Sug. Retail $2,530	$2,150	$1,650	$1,250	$1,050	$875	$800	$700

This model is available with either right hand or left hand action.

Grading	100%	98%	95%	90%	80%	70%	60%

EXPRESS SERIES RIFLE — .338 Lapua Mag., .375 H&H, .378 Wby. Mag., .404 rimless Jeffries, .416 Rigby, .450 Ackley, .460 Wby. Mag., or .500 A-Square, express sights, Timney single trigger. Importation began 1989.

Mfg.'s Sug. Retail	$6,245	$5,500	$4,375	$3,750	$3,000	$2,350	$2,000	$1,750

Add $555 for left-hand action.

.600 NE Rifle — .600 NE cal., 24 in. barrel, reinforced action, 2 shot mag., importation began 1991.

Mfg.'s Sug. Retail	$10,900	$9,250	$7,850	$6,950	$5,950	$5,125	$4,650	$3,975

RIFLES: SINGLE SHOT

MODEL HR 30N SINGLE SHOT — available in many cals., Ruger No. 1 falling block action, 24 in. barrel, French walnut with Bavarian cheek piece, round barrel, Sporter or full length carbine style French walnut stock, engraved coin finished receiver, 6.6 lbs.

Mfg.'s Sug. Retail	$4,040	$3,500	$2,975	$2,350	$1,950	$1,675	$1,350	$1,175

Add $440 for Mag. cals.
Add $1,710 for Mannlicher stocked Carbine Model.
Add $850 for hunting scene engraving (minimum extra charge).

MODEL HR 38 N — available in many cals., Ruger No. 1 falling block action 24 in. barrel, octagon barrel, French walnut with Bavarian cheek piece, Sporter or full length carbine style French walnut stock, engraved coin finished receiver, 6.6 lbs.

Mfg.'s Sug. Retail	$4,835	$4,150	$3,450	$2,875	$2,300	$1,950	$1,675	$1,350

Add $235 for Mag. cal's.
Add $2,400 for sideplates with engraved large game hunting scenes.

SIDELOCK RIFLE SHOTGUN

MODEL 35 STANDARD — 3 barrels, (two rifle and one shotgun), choice of cal's with top barrel either 16 or 20 ga., light border engraving, 8¼ lbs.

Mfg.'s Sug. Retail	$15,100	$13,650	$11,000	$9,250	$8,000	$6,850	$5,700	$4,600

Add $2,430 for hunting scene engraving.

RIFLES: SIDE-BY-SIDE

MODEL 88 B — available in various cals. up to .375 H&H, SxS double rifle, boxlock action, Krupp steel barrels, double underlocking lugs with Greener crossbolt, ejectors, checkered circassian walnut, built to customer specifications, 7½ lbs.

Mfg.'s Sug. Retail	$13,860	$11,800	$9,950	$8,450	$6,950	$6,125	$5,420	$4,575

Model 88 BSS — sidelock model with interceptor sears.

Mfg.'s Sug. Retail	$15,820	$13,750	$11,500	$9,950	$8,450	$7,175	$6,000	$5,000

Model 88 B Safari — available in .375 H&H, .458 Win. Mag., .470 Nitro Express, or .500 Nitro Express cal., 24 in. barrels, 9.9 lbs.

Mfg.'s Sug. Retail	$15,639	$13,600	$11,250	$9,850	$8,300	$7,000	$5,950	$4,950

MODEL 88 BF RIFLE-SHOTGUN — 2 barrel set with 20 ga. barrels and an extra set of rifle barrels available in cals. .375 H&H Mag., .458 Win. Mag., .470 N.E., or .500 N.E.

Mfg.'s Sug. Retail	$15,060	$13,100	$10,750	$9,600	$8,150	$6,900	$5,850	$4,850

This model is a larger frame variation of the Model 88 B.

Model 88B/F Safari — includes set of rifle and shotgun barrels, choice of .375 H&H, .458 Win. Mag., .470 NE, or .500 NE cal. and extra set of 20 ga. 3 in. chamber barrels.

Mfg.'s Sug. Retail	$18,530	$16,150	$14,100	$11,950	$10,250	$8,950	$6,750	$5,250

Grading	100%	98%	95%	90%	80%	70%	60%

MODEL 88 F SIDE-BY-SIDE SHOTGUN — available in cals. 20 ga. with 2¾ or 3 in. chambers.

Mfg.'s Sug. Retail	$14,650	$13,300	$11,250	$10,100	$9,400	$8,000	$6,950	$5,800

HI-POINT FIREARMS

Distributed by MKS Supply, Inc. located in Mansfield, Ohio.

Prior to 1993, trademarks sold by MKS Supply, Inc. (including Beemiller, Inc., Haskell Manufacturing, Inc., Iberia Firearms, Inc., and Stallard Arms, Inc.) had their own separate manufacturers' markings. Beginning in 1993, Hi-Point Firearms eliminated these indivualized markings and chose instead to have currently manufactured guns labelled Hi-Point Firearms.

JS-9 — 9mm Para. cal., semi-auto single action, 4½ in. barrel, thumb safety, fixed sights, 8 shot mag., non-glare military blue finish (early mfg.) or satin black finish (new 1991), copolymer synthetic grips, 41 oz. New 1990.

Mfg.'s Sug. Retail	$140	$125	$100	$85	$75	$70	$65	$60

Add $10 for nickel finish.
This model is manufactured by Stallard Arms, Inc. located in Mansfield, OH.

JS-9 Compact — compact variation of the Model JS-9 with 3¾ in. barrel and 7 shot mag. New 1993.

Mfg.'s Sug. Retail	$125	$100	$85	$75	$70	$65	$60	$55

This model is manufactured by Beemiller, Inc. located in Mansfield, OH.

JS-.40 — .40 S&W cal., semi-auto single action, black finish, 4¾ in. barrel, 8 shot mag. New 1992.

Mfg.'s Sug. Retail	$130	$105	$90	$75	$70	$65	$60	$55

Add $7 for nickel finish.
This model is manufactured by Iberia Firearms, Inc. located in Iberia, OH.

JS .45 — .45 ACP cal., semi-auto single action, similar to Stallard Arms JS-9mm, except has 7 shot mag. and 4¾ in. barrel, 44 oz. New 1991.

Mfg.'s Sug. Retail	$149	$135	$110	$100	$90	$80	$75	$70

Add $10 for nickel finish.
This model is manufactured by Haskell Mfg., Inc. located in Lima, OH.

HIGGINS, J.C.

Trademark used on Sears & Roebuck rifles and shotguns manufactured between 1946-1962.

The J.C. Higgins trademark has appeared literally on hundreds of various models (shotguns and rifles) sold through the Sears & Roebuck retail network. Most of these models were manufactured through subcontracts with both domestic and international firearms manufacturers. Typically, they were "spec." guns made to sell at a specific price to undersell the competition. Most of these models were derivatives of existing factory models with less expensive wood and perhaps missing the features found on those models from which they were derived.

To date, there has been very little interest in collecting J.C. Higgins guns, regardless of rarity. Rather than list J.C. Higgins models, a general guideline is that values generally are under those of their "1st generation relatives". The Ranger trademark was also used by Sears & Roebuck - it is not any more desirable than those guns marked J.C. Higgins. As a result, prices are ascertained by the shooting value of the gun, rather than its collector value.

HIGH STANDARD

High Standard Mfg. Co. was founded in 1926. They purchased Hartford Arms and Equipment Co. in 1932. The original plant was located in New Haven, CT from 1932-1950 until they moved to a larger facility at Hamden, CT from 1951-1977. A final move was made to East Hartford, CT in 1978 where they remained until the doors were closed in January, 1984. In 1992, Mitchell Arms, located in Santa Ana, CA, began manufacturing certain High Standard models using the Mitchell Arms logo above the model number. These new pistols may be found under the Mitchell section in this text.

The approximate serial number cut-off for Hamden, CT manufacture is 2,300,000.

The High Standard section in this edition has changed extensively to reflect a more complete chronological grouping of the various models.

High Standard values have risen dramatically over the past several years. Many collectors have realized the rarity and quality factors this trademark has earned (Models C, A, D, E, H-D, H-E, H-A, H-B First Model, G-380, GB, GD, GE, GO - 13 different variations had a total production of less than 48,000 pistols). For these reasons, top condition High Standard pistols are getting more difficult to find each year.

SEMI-AUTO PISTOLS

PRE-WAR HIGH STANDARD SEMI-AUTOMATIC PISTOLS HAD 3 DIFFERENT TAKEDOWN TYPES.

I-A TYPE MFG. 1932-38. Takedown lever on left side of frame next to safety. Round retracting rod on rear of slide. This takedown was used on Models B & C.

I-B TYPE MFG. 1938. Similar to I-A Type except has strengthened rectangular rod on rear of slide.

TYPE II MFG. 1939. Takedown lever located on right side of frame. Round pick-up rod on top of slide.

HAMMERLESS FIXED BARREL SERIES

This series consists of the 5 original pistols mfg. in 1932-1942. All serial numbers are located on forestrap of frame.

Grading	100%	98%	95%	90%	80%	70%	60%

MODEL B — original High Standard pistol, basically the same gun as Hartford Arms 1925 Automatic, .22 LR, small frame, 4½ or 6¾ in. light weight barrel, fixed Partridge type front and rear sights, checkered hard rubber grips with or without H.S. monogram, 10 shot mag. Beginning ser. no. 5,000. Approx. 65,000 mfg. 1932-42.

	$600	$495	$375	$325	$260	$220	$200

Add $75 for I-B Type takedown.
Less than 14,000 pistols with this takedown were mfg.

MODEL S — essentially a Model B with a 6¾ in. smooth bore barrel only without choke, chambered for .22 LR shot shell cartridge, left side of slide is stamped "HI-STANDARD MODEL S .22 LR SHOT ONLY", this variation was never a production model with approx. 5-10 guns mfg. total, 10 shot mag. Mfg. 1939 only.
Because of the extreme rarity factory of this model, a specimen in almost any condition will bring $3,000. This model was used primarily for pest control.

MODEL C — identical to Model B in appearance, except .22 Short only, small frame, 4½ or 6¾ in. light weight barrel, fixed rear sight, checkered hard rubber grips with or without H.S. monogram, this action was adapted for the decreased power of the .22 Short cartridge. Beginning ser. no. 500 to 31XX, later beginning ser. no. 42XXX. Approx. 4,700 mfg. 1936-42.

	$795	$625	$450	$345	$275	$230	$200

Add $100 for I-A takedown.
Add $250 for I-B takedown.
This model was used primarily for plinking and gallery shooting. The Model C was made in all 3 variations of takedowns - I-A, I-B, and Type 2 (but less than 100 were mfg. in I-B).

High Standard, cont.

Grading	100%	98%	95%	90%	80%	70%	60%

MODEL A — similar to Model B, except enlarged frame, squared-off butt, .22 LR, 4½ or 6¾ in. light weight barrel, adj. rear sight, checkered walnut grips, automatic slide lock, trigger stop, 10 shot mag. Beginning ser. no. 33XXX. Approx. 7,300 mfg. 1938-42.

	$725	$595	$430	$345	$260	$220	$200

MODEL D — identical to Model A except 4½ or 6¾ in. medium weight barrel, .22 LR, adj. sights, walnut grips, slide lock trigger stop, 10 shot mag. Beginning ser. no. 33XXX. Approx. 2,500 mfg. 1938-42.

	$795	$625	$450	$365	$265	$250	$215

MODEL E — high quality, deluxe model of the hammerless series, .22 LR, adj. sight, 4½ or 6¾ in. heavy bull barrel, checkered walnut target grips with thumbrest, automatic slide lock, 10 shot mag. Beginning ser. no. 34XXX. Approx. 2,600 mfg. 1938-42.

	$1,075	$875	$650	$500	$375	$325	$295

EXPOSED HAMMER–FIXED BARREL SERIES

This series consists of 4 pistols that were introduced in 1940. Frame and slide modified to accommodate external hammer. All ser. no.'s located on forestrap of frame. Prefix "H" added to standard model designation with the exception of Model C. Mfg. 1940-42. This series has very low production numbers.

MODEL H-D — first exposed hammer model, similar to Model D, .22 LR, 4½ or 6¾ in. medium weight barrel, adj. sight, target or standard walnlut grips, no external safety, 10 shot mag. High quality pistol. Beginning ser. no. 51XXX. Approx. 2,000 mfg. 1940-42.

	$950	$750	$575	$475	$275	$245	$220

This variation is infrequently encountered.

MODEL H-E — high quality, deluxe model of exposed hammer series, .22 LR, 4½ or 6¾ in. heavy barrel, adj. sight, deluxe hand checkered walnut grips with thumbrests, no external safety, 10 shot mag. Rarest of the H.S. pistols. Beginning ser. no. 51XXX. Approx 1,000 mfg. 1941-42.

	$1,650	$1,325	$1,050	$800	$625	$450	$395

MODEL H-A — similar to Model A, .22 LR, 4½ or 6¾ in. light weight barrel, adj. sight, plain checkered walnut grips, no external safety, 10 shot mag. Very rare gun. Beginning ser. no. 53XXX. Approx. 1,000 mfg. 1940-42.

	$850	$675	$525	$425	$300	$250	$225

MODEL H-B — duplicate of Model B with external hammer, .22 LR, 4½ or 6¾ in. light weight barrel, fixed sight, checkered hard rubber grips with or without H.S. monogram, no external safety, 10 shot mag. This first Model H-B had beginning ser. no. 52XXX. Approx. 2,200 mfg. 1940-42.

	$775	$625	$495	$375	$325	$265	$245

Model H-B Second Model — H.S. reintroduced a H-B second model similar to first model, except with external safety. Beginning ser. no. 308XXX. Approx. 25,000 mfg. 1949-1954.

	$675	$550	$400	$325	$240	$215	$200

U.S. MILITARY SERIES

These models are earlier H.S. pistols adapted as training guns during WWII. They were the sole suppliers of the .22 cal. pistol for military training. Ser. no.'s located on forestrap of frame.

MODEL B-US — adapted Model B with minor changes, .22 LR, available in 4½ in. barrel only, checkered hard rubber grips, fixed sight, marked "Property of U.S." on right side of frame and on top of barrel. Ordnance acceptance crossed cannon stamped on right side of frame above trigger guard, 10 shot mag. Beginning ser. no. 95XXX. Approx. 14,000 mfg. 1942-43.

	$795	$625	$450	$325	$265	$245	$215

Grading	100%	98%	95%	90%	80%	70%	60%

MODEL USA-HD — the government needed a training pistol similar to the Colt Model 1911 .45 ACP. The result was a Model HD with external safety and fixed sight, 4½ in. medium weight barrel, .22 LR only. The barrel is marked "Property of USA", black checkered hard rubber grips. First models mfg. had high gloss blue finish, changed to a Parkerized finish near ser. no. 130XXX. Beginning ser. no. 109XXX-153XXX. Approx. 44,000 mfg. 1943-46.

| | $695 | $550 | $400 | $300 | $230 | $210 | $200 |

Add 20% for early blue finish.

MODEL USA-HD-MS — variation of the Model USA-HD with attached silencer, mfg. for U.S. Government covert operations, original ownership required NFA transfer, approx. 2,000 mfg.

| | $3,500 | $3,150 | $2,750 | $2,500 | $2,250 | $1,995 | $1,750 |

MODEL H-D MILITARY — though called H-D Military, this model was not mfg. for the government. Essentially a USA-HD with the addition of adj. sights, .22 LR, 4½ or 6¾ in. barrel, checkered walnut grips, external safety, 10 shot mag. Beginning ser. no. 147XXX. Approx. 150,000 mfg. 1946-55.

| | $650 | $500 | $375 | $285 | $220 | $210 | $200 |

MODEL G-380 — this is H.S.'s only in-house production of a center-fire pistol other than a .22 cal. A transition model to the G-series using a lever takedown. Has exposed hammer, fixed sights, .380 cal., checkered black plastic grips, external safety, 5 in. barrel only, 6 shot mag. Beginning ser. no. 100. Approx. 7,400 mfg. 1947-50.

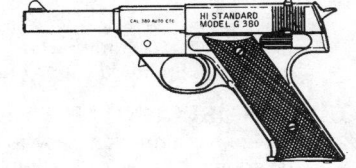

| | $750 | $595 | $450 | $400 | $295 | $265 | $230 |

THE G-SERIES

This series is hammerless with interchangeable target barrel, 6¾ in. and plinking barrel, 4½ in., consists of 4 pistols, all using lever takedown. An adaptation of the G-380 design. Ser. no.'s on right side of slide and rear right side of frame. Mfg. 1948-50.

MODEL GB — similar to Model B with light barrel, small frame, .22 LR, external safety, fixed sight, checkered brown plastic grips, interchangeable 4½ or 6¾ in. barrel with lever takedown, 10 shot mag. Beginning ser. no. 311XXX. Approx. 4,900 mfg. 1949-50.

| | $700 | $575 | $425 | $350 | $275 | $225 | $200 |

Add 15-20% for both barrels.

MODEL GD — large frame with medium weight with interchangeable 4½ or 6¾ in. barrel with lever takedown, .22 LR, featured new adj. "Davis" sight, named for designer G.F. Davis. Grips avail. in plain checkered walnut or deluxe with thumbrest grips, 10 shot mag. Beginning ser. no. 311XXX. Approx. 3,300 mfg. 1949-50.

| | $795 | $650 | $475 | $360 | $275 | $225 | $200 |

Add 15-20% for both barrels.
This sight is adjustable for both windage and elevation.

MODEL GE — deluxe top-of-the-line quality .22 LR pistol, large frame with interchangeable 4½ or 6¾ in. heavy "bull" barrel with lever takedown, "Davis" sight adj. sight, deluxe walnut hand checkered grips with thumbrest, 10 shot mag. Beginning ser. no. 312XXX. Approx. 2,900 mfg. 1949-50.

| | $1,175 | $975 | $750 | $575 | $450 | $350 | $300 |

Add 15-20% for both barrels.
This model has a grooved fore and rear strap.

MODEL G-O — also known as First Model Olympic. First fired in Olympic competition in 1948. Adaptation of Model GE in .22 cal. short. Deluxe top-of-the-line quality, interchangeable 4½ or 6¾ in. heavy "bull" barrel with lever takedown, "Davis" adj. sight, deluxe hand checkered walnut grips with thumbrests. First High Standard large production gun with aluminum slide. Has unique curved magazine, flat milled surface on top of barrel. Rare. Beginning ser. no. 307XXX. Approx. 1,200 mfg. 1949-50.

	100%	98%	95%	90%	80%	70%	60%
	$1,250	$995	$775	$595	$475	$375	$325

Add 15-20% for both barrels.
This model has a grooved fore and rear strap.

THE SUPERMATIC SERIES

All of this series were mfg. at the Hamden, CT plant from 1951-53. Consisted of 4 guns, featuring the lever takedown introduced in the G-Series. Hammerless, new positive lock safety, use of one screw to attach grips, no production figures available. Approximate serial range of this series is 340,000- 440,000.

SUPERMATIC (FIRST MODEL) — .22 LR, 10 shot mag., 4½ or 6¾ in. interchangeable barrel with lever takedown, "Davis" adj. sight, slide lock, front and back straps grooved, serrated rib between front and rear sight, adj. 2 oz. and 3 oz. weights which dovetail into and beneath barrel.

	$725	$575	$400	$345	$275	$220	$200

Add 15-20% for both barrels.
The High Standard catalog number for this model was 9070-71.

OLYMPIC (SECOND MODEL) — .22 cal. short, identical in all respects to the Supermatic, except has aluminum slide for rapid recoil, interchangeable 4½ or 6¾ in. barrel with lever takedown, "Davis" adj. sight, adj. 2 oz. and 3 oz. weights, 10 shot mag.

	$850	$675	$525	$375	$285	$230	$200

Add 15-20% for both barrels.
The High Standard catalog number for this model was 9043-44.

FIELD-KING (FIRST MODEL) — plain version of Supermatic, .22 LR, 10 shot mag., interchangeable 4½ or 6¾ in. barrels with lever takedown, "Davis" adj. sight, 10 shot mag.

	$675	$495	$375	$275	$220	$210	$200

Add 10-15% for both barrels.
The High Standard catalog number for this model was 9090-91.

SPORT-KING (FIRST MODEL) — .22 LR, 10 shot mag., similar to Field-King but has fixed sight and light weight interchangeable 4½ or 6¾ in. barrel featuring lever takedown.

	$625	$475	$350	$275	$220	$210	$200

Add 10-15% for extra barrel.
This model was available with or without slide lock.
The High Standard catalog number for this model was 9080-81.

QUICK CHANGE CONVERSION KIT — avail. in 1951 to let you shoot both .22 LR or .22 Short in the Supermatic, Olympic, or Field-King models. Featured factory fitted barrel, slide, barrel weights and magazine included in this kit.

	$500	$400	$350

This kit featured all components fitted neatly into a small maroon and yellow box. At this time, .22 LR Conversion kits are also available for the Olympic Model.

THE M-100 AND M-101 SERIES

All of this series were mfg. at the Hamden, CT plant from 1954-57. Hammerless design consisting of 5 pistols featuring a new push-button type takedown. The beginning ser. no. for .22 LR pistols only in this series was 443,611. This series featured slanted plastic grips as standard issue. The serial range for this series was 443,XXX-770,XXX.

Grading	100%	98%	95%	90%	80%	70%	60%

SUPERMATIC (SECOND MODEL) — S 100 or S 101 stamped on right side of slide, .22 LR, 10 shot mag., 4½ or 6¾ in. interchangeable barrel with push-button takedown, adj. 2 oz. or 3 oz. weights. Integral slotted stabilizer with 6¾ in. target barrel was an option. Adj. rear sight.

	$650	$575	$395	$300	$220	$210	$200

The High Standard catalog number for this model was 9118-19.

OLYMPIC (THIRD MODEL) — 0-100 or 0-101 stamped on right side of alloy slide, .22 Short, 10 shot mag., 4½ or 6¾ in. interchangeable barrel with push-button takedown,adj. 2 oz. or 3 oz. weights. Integral slotted stabilizer 6¾ in. target barrel was an option. Adj. rear sight.

	$800	$625	$475	$375	$275	$230	$200

The High Standard catalog number for this model was 9121-22.

FIELD-KING (SECOND MODEL) — FK 100 or FK 101 stamped on right side of slide, .22 LR, 10 shot mag. 4½ or 6¾ in. interchangeable barrel with push-button takedown, front and rear grip straps on this model are smooth. Slotted stabilizer 6¾ in. target barrel was an option. Adj. rear sight.

	$625	$475	$350	$275	$220	$210	$200

The High Standard catalog number for this model was 9115-16.

FLITE-KING (FIRST MODEL) — LW 100 or LW 101 stamped on right side of slide, .22 Short, 10 shot mag., 4½ or 6¾ in. interchangeable light weight barrel with push- button takedown, alloy slide, front and rear grip straps on this model are smooth. First commercial use of aluminum alloy for frame. Fixed rear sight. Mfg. until 1960.

	$625	$475	$350	$275	$220	$210	$200

Add 15-20% for both barrels.
The High Standard catalog number for this model was 9103-04.

SPORT-KING (SECOND MODEL) — SK 100 or SK 101 stamped on right side of slide, .22 LR, similar to Flite-King but with steel slide and frame, front and rear grip straps on this model are smooth. This model was also avail. in nickel. Fixed rear sight.

	$575	$435	$300	$250	$220	$210	$200

Add 15-20% for both barrels.
Add 20% for nickel finish.
The High Standard catalog number for this model was 9100-01.

SPORT-KING LIGHTWEIGHT — .22 LR, similar to standard Sport-King, except has forged aluminum alloy frame. The word "Lightweight" is inscribed in script on the left side of frame. Also avail. in nickel. Mfg. began 1956.

	$550	$425	$295	$250	$220	$210	$200

Add 20% for nickel finish (H.S. number 9166-67).
The High Standard catalog number for this model was 9156-57.

DURAMATIC — .22 LR, 4½ or 6¾ in. barrels, fixed sight, oversized plastic grips. M-100 or M-101 stamped on right side of slide. Mfg. 1954-70. The Duramatic was sold by Sears Roebuck & Co. as the J. C. Higgins Model 80. This Sears variation had some minor exterior differences, but mechanically it was the same. Unique thumb screw takedown, push button mag. release and oversized trigger guard.

	$525	$395	$295	$230	$220	$210	$200

Add 20% for extra barrel.
The High Standard catalog number for this model was 9124-25.

MODEL 102 AND 103 SERIES

This series included the following and were mfg. in Hamden, CT. The words "Model 102" or "Model 103" and the serial number were inscribed on the right side of slide, and the serial number was duplicated on the right side of the new and longer frame. A new and larger push-button takedown enabling easier use was another improvement. A grooved and wider trigger in addition to a new rear sight were also added on the target models. The 102 Series was mfg. from 1957-1960 and the serial range was approx. 770,XXX-1,100,XXX. The 103 Series was mfg. between 1960-1963 and the approximate serial range was 1,100,XXX-1,300,XXX. Plastic grips were standard and checkered walnut grips with thumbrest were optional.

Grading	100%	98%	95%	90%	80%	70%	60%

SPORT-KING — similar to the Series 100/101, but stamped Model 102 or Model 103, the lightweight Sport King was still available but was disc. in 1964. This basic Sport-King was mfg. from 1958-77.

	$475	$365	$275	$240	$220	$210	$200

Add 20% for nickel finish (introduced 1974, H.S. number 9208-09).
The High Standard catalog number for this model was 9200-9201.

FLITE-KING — similar to Series 100/101, this variation of the Flite-King featured an all steel frame with an alloy slide. Mfg. 1958-1965.

	$475	$375	$275	$240	$220	$210	$200

The High Standard catalog number for this model was 9220-21.

SUPERMATIC TOURNAMENT — .22 LR, 10 shot, 4½, 5½ bull (avail. 1963), or 6¾ in. straight barrel, brown diamond checkered plastic slant grips, adj. sight, push-button takedown, this model featured smooth front and back grip straps. The gov.'t ordered a quantity of Mod. 102 Tournament for training. These were marked "US" on right side of frame. Mfg. 1958-1965.

	$700	$575	$450	$375	$250	$240	$230

The High Standard catalog number for this model was 9270-71.

SUPERMATIC CITATION — .22 LR, 10 shot, 6¾ in., 8 in. and 10 in. tapered barrels, diamond checkered plastic slant grips, adj. sight, push-button takedown, one grade above Tournament. Grooved front and back grip straps. Sight located on 8 and 10 in. barrel (a 5½ in. target bull barrel became avail. in 1962). Detachable stabilizer and 2 or 3 oz. barrel weights available. Mfg. 1958-65.

	$775	$625	$495	$395	$295	$275	$250

The High Standard catalog number for this model was 9260-61.

SUPERMATIC TROPHY — .22 LR, 10 shot, 6¾ in., 8 in. and 10 in. tapered barrels, 5½ bull and 7¼ in. fluted barrels became avail. in 1962, detachable barrel weights and stabilizer were also available, walnut checkered grips. Features gold trigger, gold safety button and gold inlaid lettering, adj. sight and push-button takedown. Mfg. 1958-63.

	$775	$625	$495	$395	$295	$275	$250

This variation was High Standards Top-of-the-Line Target pistol.
The High Standard catalog number for this model was 9250-51.

ISU OLYMPIC — this is the model which brought the 33rd Gold Medal in the Rome Olympics in 1960. .22 Short, 10 shot, 6¾ in. barrel with integral stabilizer, checkered walnut grips, high luster finish, alloy slide. Top-of-the-line Olympic model. Complies with all rapid-fire International Shooting Union regulations. Mfg. 1961-66.

	$875	$700	$525	$425	$300	$275	$250

The High Standard catalog number for this model was 9289-9299.

Grading	100%	98%	95%	90%	80%	70%	60%

OLYMPIC — same basic gun as ISU Olympic, but it is of lesser quality finish. Adj. sight located on 8 in. barrel. Mfg. 1958-65.

| | $850 | $650 | $475 | $375 | $275 | $250 | $225 |

This model has also been observed with markings "OLYMPIC CITATION".
The High Standard catalog number for this model was 9280-81.

MODEL 104 SERIES

This series was mfg. from 1964-1972. This is the last series to feature the slant grip pistol. Serial No. range is approx. 1,300,000-2,300,000.

SUPERMATIC TOURNAMENT — similar to Model 102/103 series. Mfg. 1964-65.

| | $525 | $465 | $395 | $350 | $300 | $260 | $230 |

The High Standard catalog number for this model was 9275.

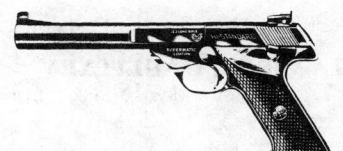

SUPERMATIC CITATION — similar to Model 102/103 series, brown plastic grips or walnut checkered grips, 5½ in. bull, 7¼ in. fluted barrel available in 1965, grooved front and back straps. Mfg. 1964-65.

| | $775 | $625 | $475 | $395 | $295 | $275 | $250 |

The High Standard catalog number for this model was 9263.

SUPERMATIC TROPHY — similar to Model 102/103 series, Top-of-the-line target, 5½ in. bull, 7¼ in. fluted barrel available, muzzle brake and wts. optional, grooved front and back straps, checkered walnut grips.

| | $850 | $675 | $525 | $425 | $375 | $325 | $290 |

The High Standard catalog number for this model was 9254-55.

ISU OLYMPIC — .22 Short, similar to Model 102/103 Olympic series, grooved front and back straps, 6¾ in. barrel with det. muzzle brake & wts. avail., brown plastic grips standard or walnut checkered grips optional.

| | $850 | $675 | $525 | $425 | $375 | $325 | $290 |

The High Standard catalog number for this model was 9237-9299.

HIGH STANDARD DID NOT HAVE A MODEL 105 SERIES

MILITARY MODEL 106 SERIES

This series was mfg. 1965-1968. This new military model features a walnut checkered grip and a frame that has the exact heft and feel of the famous Military 45. This military model features a new slide and a new rear bridge or saddle type sight, adjustable permanently fixed to the frame. Front and rear grip straps are stippled and a new design magazine has an extension foot. Removeable stabilizer and wts. available on all models. Beginning serial no. for 106 series was approx. 1,400,000-2,000,000.

SUPERMATIC TOURNAMENT MILITARY — bottom of the line .22 long rifle target pistol, smooth front & back straps, slide mounted rear sight instead of bridge sight, 5½ in. bull or 6¾ in. straight barrel with military grips.

| | $525 | $450 | $395 | $350 | $300 | $260 | $230 |

The High Standard catalog number for this model was 9230-31.

Grading	100%	98%	95%	90%	80%	70%	60%

SUPERMATIC CITATION MILITARY — middle of the line .22 long rifle target pistol, stippled front & back straps, 5½ in. bull barrel or 7¼ in. fluted barrel, new rear bridge or saddle type sight.

	$725	$595	$475	$395	$295	$275	$250

The High Standard catalog number for this model was 9240-41.

SUPERMATIC TROPHY MILITARY — top-of-the-line .22 long rifle target pistol, stippled front and back straps, 5½ bull or 7¼ in. fluted barrel avail., gold plated trigger, safety and magazine release, gold filled lettering.

	$825	$675	$575	$475	$395	$295	$275

The High Standard catalog number for this model was 9245-46.

OLYMPIC MILITARY — .22 Short target pistol, 5½ in. bull barrel, back & front straps, stippled alloy slide, bridge rear sight, military grips.

	$850	$695	$575	$475	$395	$295	$275

The High Standard catalog number for this model was 9235.

OLYMPIC ISU MILITARY — .22 Short target pistol, 6¾ in. tapered barrel with integral stabilizer and wts., back & front straps stippled, rear bridge or saddle type sight, military grips.

	$850	$695	$575	$475	$395	$295	$275

The High Standard catalog number for this model was 9236.

MILITARY MODEL 107 SERIES

The Military 107 Series was mfg. 1968-1972. They are basically identical to the Military Model 106 Series. Serial no. range is approx. 2,000,000-2,300,000. In 1968 the company was sold to the Leisure Group, Inc.

SUPERMATIC TOURNAMENT MILITARY — similar to Model 106 series, this was the last of the Tournament pistols, adj. sight replace the bridge sight, 6¾ in. bull barrel. Disc. 1971.

	$525	$450	$395	$350	$300	$260	$230

The High Standard catalog number for this model was 9232-33.

SUPERMATIC CITATION MILITARY — similar to Model 106 series, middle of the line target pistol, 7¼ fluted and 5½ in. bull barrel available.

	$725	$575	$475	$395	$295	$275	$250

The High Standard catalog number for this model was 9242-43.

SUPERMATIC TROPHY MILITARY — similar to Model 106 series, Top-of-the-Line target pistol.

	$825	$675	$575	$475	$395	$295	$275

The High Standard catalog number for this model was 9247-48.

OLYMPIC ISU MILITARY — .22 short target pistol for Olympic Style Rapid Fire Events. 6¾ in. fluted barrel with integral stabilizer & two det. wts.

	$825	$675	$575	$475	$395	$295	$275

The High Standard catalog number for this model was 9238.

Grading	100%	98%	95%	90%	80%	70%	60%

THE VICTOR — introduced in 1972. Newest and most expensive production target pistol, had all steel vented rib running length of barrel, early adj. sight located on rear of barrel on rib. A bridge sight was utilized later, .22 long rifle built on a military frame, walnut grips, available in 4½ or 5½ in. barrel, push-button takedown, stippled front and rear straps, 10 shot mag., barrel slab sided, wts. are rectangular. Mfg. in Hamden, CT. Stamped "THE VICTOR" on left side of barrel.

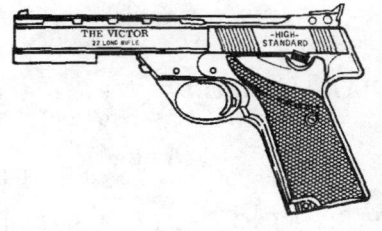

	100%	98%	95%	90%	80%	70%	60%
	$825	$675	$575	$475	$395	$295	$275

The High Standard catalog number for this model was 1916-17.

SEVEN-NUMBER SERIES

After the 107 series, High Standard began using a seven-digit serial number. This was used from 1972-1975 and were assigned to pistols as they were manufactured. These pistols included the following: The serial numbers approx. 2,300,000-2,500,000.

SHARPSHOOTER — .22 LR, successor to the Tournament, introduced in 1971 as part of the Model 107 series, new model using the slant model grip frame, 5½ in. bull barrel only.

	100%	98%	95%	90%	80%	70%	60%
	$495	$385	$295	$250	$220	$210	$200

The High Standard catalog number for this model was 9205.

PLINKER — .22 long rifle, introduced in 1971-73. Successor to Duramatic and identical in almost all aspects. Thumb screw takedown.

	100%	98%	95%	90%	80%	70%	60%
	$495	$385	$295	$250	$220	$210	$200

The High Standard catalog number for this model was 9214-15.

SPORT KING — .22 long rifle, this was a nickel plated Sport King with black slanted plastic grips with silver medallion insert on grip. Mfg. 1974-77.

	100%	98%	95%	90%	80%	70%	60%
	$450	$350	$275	$240	$220	$210	$200

The High Standard catalog number for this model was 9208-09.

SUPERMATIC CITATION MILITARY — .22 long rifle similar to 107 series.

	100%	98%	95%	90%	80%	70%	60%
	$725	$575	$475	$395	$295	$275	$250

The High Standard catalog number for this model was 9242-43.

SUPERMATIC TROPHY MILITARY — .22 long rifle similar to 107 series.

	100%	98%	95%	90%	80%	70%	60%
	$775	$650	$595	$495	$350	$250	$225

The High Standard catalog number for this model was 9247-48.

ISU OLYMPIC MILITARY — .22 short pistol, identical to 107 series with 6¾ in. integral stabilizer in barrel.

	100%	98%	95%	90%	80%	70%	60%
	$775	$650	$595	$495	$350	$250	$225

The High Standard catalog number for this model was 9238.

THE VICTOR — .22 LR cal., similar to 107 series, Hamden mfg., military grips, in 1974 an aluminum vent. rib was used to lighten this variation, a solid rib was also available, a slant grip Victor was mfg. in 1973-74.

	100%	98%	95%	90%	80%	70%	60%
	$595	$495	$395	$345	$300	$250	$220

Add $150 for solid rib (military grips).   Add $250 for rare slant grip Victor.
The High Standard catalog number for the solid rib with military grips was 9206-11. The vent. rib model was catalog number 9218-19, and the solid rib model was cataloged at 9226-29.

Grading	100%	98%	95%	90%	80%	70%	60%

ML PREFIX SERIES

In 1975, High Standard again revised their numbering system. This was a five digit serial number with and ML prefix. Mfg. 1975-1981. ML serial number range from 25,000 to 87,000.

SHARPSHOOTER – .22 long rifle similar to seven number series, some of the Sharpshooters with military grips were labeled "SHARPSHOOTER-M".

	$475	$385	$295	$250	$220	$210	$200

The High Standard catalog number for this model was 9210.

SPORT KING – .22 LR cal., similar to previous Sport Kings, but they now use military grips. Some of these Sport Kings were labeled "SPORT KING-M".

	$450	$350	$275	$240	$220	$210	$200

The High Standard catalog number for this model was 9258-59.

SUPERMATIC CITATION MILITARY – .22 LR cal., similar to previous model.

	$695	$575	$475	$395	$295	$275	$250

The High Standard catalog number for this model was 9242-43.

SUPERMATIC TROPHY MILITARY – .22 LR cal., similar to previous series.

	$750	$650	$595	$495	$350	$250	$225

The High Standard catalog number for this model was 9247-48.

SUPERMATIC ISU OLYMPIC MILITARY – .22 short target pistol similar to previous model. Disc. 1981.

	$750	$650	$595	$495	$350	$250	$225

The High Standard catalog number for this model was 9238.

THE VICTOR – .22 long rifle similar to previous model, military grip, vent. or solid rib. Last solid rib mfg. in 1977. Later Victors in this series were stamped simply "VICTOR" above trigger guard.

	$750	$650	$595	$495	$350	$250	$225

The High Standard catalog number for this model was 9216-17.
The High Standard catalog number for the solid rib model was 9206-9211.

10-X – specifically designed for top flight shooting, 5½ in. bull, 7¼ in. fluted barrel, or 5½ in. vented barrel, push-button takedown. This model used hand-picked parts and was precisely assembled by a High Standard Master Gunsmith (with his initials under the left grip of each gun). Black matte finish, black painted walnut grips, stippled front and back straps. Mfg. 1981.

Push Button Barrel Release

	$2,200	$1,850	$1,475	$1,250	$1,050	$825	$695

The High Standard catalog number for this model was 9234-9249-9372.

G PREFIX SERIES

In 1975, some of the High Standard pistols had a five digit serial number with a G prefix (assigned to slant grip models only).

SH SERIES

This was the last of the High Standard series. Mfg. from 1982-84. Serial Nos. ranged approx. 10,000-35,000 prefixed with SH. Features a new barrel release in place of the push button takedown. An allenhead screw attached the frame to the barrel.

Grading	100%	98%	95%	90%	80%	70%	60%

SPORT KING — .22 long rifle, SH prefix serial no. with allen screw takedown, military grips with new electroless nickel model available. Mfg. 1982-84.

	$450	$350	$275	$240	$220	$210	$200

This model was also called the "SPORT KING-M".
The High Standard catalog number for this model was 9450-51.

SHARPSHOOTER — .22 long rifle, SH prefix serial no. with allen screw takedown, military grips with new electroless nickel model available. Mfg. 1982.

	$495	$385	$295	$250	$220	$210	$200

This model was also sometimes called "SHARPSHOOTER-M".
The High Standard catalog number for this model was 9210-9424.

SUPERMATIC CITATION MILITARY — .22 long rifle, SH prefix, similar to previous Citation model with allen screw takedown, military grips. Disc. May 1982.

	$695	$575	$475	$395	$295	$275	$250

The High Standard catalog number for this model was 9242-43.

CITATION II — .22 LR, 10 shot, new variation of the Supermatic Citation, 5½ and 7¼ in. barrels, checkered military-type wood grips, allen screw takedown, SH prefix serial no. Slabbed sided barrel, electroless nickel model also available. Mfg. 1982-84.

	$695	$575	$475	$395	$295	$275	$250

The High Standard catalog number for this model was 9348-49.

VICTOR — .22 LR similar to previous Victor, new allen screw takedown, SH prefix, military grips, 5½ in. vent. barrel only mfg. in this Victor Series, some Victor serial no.'s had a "V" suffix.

	$750	$650	$595	$495	$350	$250	$225

The High Standard catalog number for this model was 9217.

10X — .22 LR, high quality gun similar to previous 10X, but with allen screw takedown, a High Standard 10X Victor was also offered. These had a 5½ in. vented victor rib; only a few were mfg.

* **Allen Screw Barrel Release**

	$2,000	$1,725	$1,475	$1,250	$1,050	$825	$695

The High Standard catalog number for this model was 9234-9249-9372.

SURVIVAL PACK — introduced in 1982, Sharpshooter "M" or Citation II electroless nickel, allen screw takedown, packaged in canvas carrying case with extra nickel magazine. Disc. 1984.

	$595	$525	$425	$350	$250	$230	$210

The High Standard catalog number for this model was 9424.

COMMEMORATIVE MODELS

1972 OLYMPIC COMMEMORATIVE — a highly engraved version of a Supermatic Trophy Military, Model 107, in .22 LR, has 5 Olympic gold rings on right side of receiver, Ser. no. has a "T" prefix, blue finish, 5½ in. bull barrel, lined presentation case avail. Limited edition of 1,000 guns, but it is believed only about half of these were manufactured due to their high price, issue price was $550. Mfg. 1972-1974 only.

	$2,500	$2,000	$1,500

Early models were marked "MODEL 107".
The High Standard catalog number for this model was 9207.

Grading	100%	98%	95%	90%	80%	70%	60%

1980 OLYMPIC COMMEMORATIVE — .22 Short, an ISU Olympic Military with $6\frac{3}{4}$ in. tapered barrel with integral stabilizer and weights. Has 5 Olympic gold rings on right side of receiver. Produced in a limited edition of 1,000 guns. Ser. no. has a "USA" prefix, blue finish, lined presentation case avail. Mfg. 1980 only.

	$1,175	$950	$800

The High Standard catalog number for this model was 9239.

CONVERSION KITS

These kits convert .22 LR to .22 Short, contain an alloy slide with vent. rib, barrel weight, and two Short mag.'s, kit comes in "gun size box" set in styrofoam. These kits were designated either #9370 or #9371 when mfg., depending on the pistol to be converted.

VICTOR KIT — this model was designated #9370 when in mfg.

	$500	$400	$350

TROPHY/CITATION KIT — this kit also includes a stabilizer. This model was designated #9371 when in mfg.

	$500	$400	$350

DERRINGERS

FIRST MODEL — double action only O/U, .22 S, L, or LR, or .22 WMR, 2 shot, $3\frac{1}{2}$ in. barrels, blue or nickel. Black or white grips. D-100, D-101, DM-101 appears on left side of gun. The first derringer was mfg. about 1962 in Hamden, CT.

	$225	$195	$175	$145	$125	$100	$90

Add $30 for nickel finish.

LATE MODELS — double action only O/U, .22 S, L, or LR, or .22 WMR 2 shot, $3\frac{1}{2}$ in. barrels, blue or nickel, plastic grips. Mfg. in E. Hartford 1978-84.

⚔ **Blue Finish** — .22 LR or .22 Mag. This model was designated #9193 and #9194 when in mfg.

	$225	$195	$175	$145	$125	$100	$90

⚔ **Nickel Finish** — .22 Mag.

	$250	$220	$195	$170	$140	$110	$100

⚔ **Electroless Nickel** — included walnut grips. This model was designated #9420-21.

	$275	$235	$185

⚔ **Silver plated** — includes presentation case. 500 mfg. This model was designated #9341. Ser. no. has "SP" prefix.

	$450	$395	$300

⚔ **Gold plated** — introduced in 1965. Includes presentation case. This model was designated #9195 Ser. No. has "GP" prefix.

	$450	$395	$300

Add 120% for a cased, matched set with consecutive serial numbers.

REVOLVERS

SENTINEL — .22 LR, 9 shot, swing out cylinder, 3, 4, or 6 in. barrel, aluminum frame, made 1955-1956.

	100%	98%	95%	90%	80%	70%	60%
Blue finish	$120	$110	$100	$95	$85	$70	$55
Nickel finish	$130	$120	$110	$105	$95	$85	$65
Pink finish	$150	$135	$120	$110	$100	$95	$85
Yellow finish	$150	$135	$120	$110	$105	$95	$85

Grading	100%	98%	95%	90%	80%	70%	60%

SENTINEL IMPERIAL — similar to Sentinel, with adj. sights, walnut grips, made 1962-1965.

	100%	98%	95%	90%	80%	70%	60%
Blue finish	$140	$125	$115	$110	$100	$90	$75
Nickel finish	$150	$140	$125	$120	$110	$100	$90

SENTINEL DELUXE — similar to Sentinel, except adj. sights, wide trigger, 4 and 6 in. barrel, square butt, made 1957-1974.

	100%	98%	95%	90%	80%	70%	60%
Blue finish	$140	$125	$115	$110	$100	$90	$75
Nickel finish	$150	$140	$115	$120	$110	$100	$90

SENTINEL SNUB — similar to Deluxe, except checkered bird's-head grip, $2\frac{3}{8}$ in. barrel.

	100%	98%	95%	90%	80%	70%	60%
Blue finish	$145	$140	$130	$120	$110	$90	$85
Nickel finish	$155	$150	$145	$130	$120	$100	$95

DURANGO — .22 LR, double action, steel frame, $4\frac{1}{2}$ and $5\frac{1}{2}$ in. barrel, wood grips, made 1971-1973.

	100%	98%	95%	90%	80%	70%	60%
Blue finish	$145	$130	$120	$95	$85	$70	$55
Nickel finish	$150	$140	$125	$105	$95	$85	$65

HOMBRE DOUBLE ACTION — similar to Double Nine steel frame, but no ejector rod housing, $4\frac{1}{2}$ in. barrel, made 1971-1973.

	100%	98%	95%	90%	80%	70%	60%
Blue finish	$125	$120	$110	$105	$95	$85	$65
Nickel finish	$140	$130	$120	$115	$105	$95	$75

LONGHORN STEEL FRAME — similar to Double Nine, except $9\frac{1}{2}$ in. barrel.

	100%	98%	95%	90%	80%	70%	60%
Fixed sights	$210	$170	$150	$120	$110	$105	$85
Adj. sights	$165	$155	$150	$130	$120	$115	$95

HIGH SIERRA — similar to Double Nine steel frame, except 7 in. octagon barrel, gold plated grip frame. Discontinued in 1984. Add $10 for adj. sights.

	100%	98%	95%	90%	80%	70%	60%
Fixed sights	$235	$175	$150	$130	$120	$105	$90

KIT GUN — .22 LR, swing out cylinder, 9 shot, 4 in. barrel, adj. sights, blue, walnut grips, made 1970-1973.

	100%	98%	95%	90%	80%	70%	60%
	$155	$145	$140	$125	$115	$105	$85

DOUBLE NINE — .22 LR, Western style double action, $5\frac{1}{2}$ in. barrel, aluminum frame, simulated stag, ebony or ivory grips, made 1959-1984.

	100%	98%	95%	90%	80%	70%	60%
Blue finish	$235	$180	$160	$140	$120	$105	$90
Nickel finish (disc. in 1982)	$245	$190	$170	$150	$130	$115	$100

POSSE — similar to Double Nine aluminum, except $3\frac{1}{2}$ in. barrel, blue, brass grip frame, walnut grips, made 1961-1966.

	100%	98%	95%	90%	80%	70%	60%
	$120	$110	$95	$90	$85	$70	$55

NATCHEZ — similar to Double Nine aluminum, except has bird's-head grip, made 1961-1966.

	100%	98%	95%	90%	80%	70%	60%
	$120	$110	$100	$90	$85	$70	$55

Grading	100%	98%	95%	90%	80%	70%	60%

LONGHORN ALUMINUM FRAME — similar to Natchez, but 4½, 5½, and 9½ in. barrel, longhorn hammer spur, made 1961-1966.

	100%	98%	95%	90%	80%	70%	60%
	$145	$130	$110	$100	$85	$70	$55

9½ in. model — Discontinued in 1984.

	$250	$190	$160	$140	$120	$100	$90

CAMP GUN DOUBLE ACTION — .22 LR or .22 Win. Mag., 6 in. barrel, blue, adj. rear sight, checkered walnut grips, made 1976-1984.

	$250	$185	$165	$145	$125	$110	$100

SENTINEL 1 DOUBLE ACTION — .22 LR, 2, 3, and 4 in. barrel, 9 shot, smooth walnut grips, made 1974-present.

	100%	98%	95%	90%	80%	70%	60%
Blue finish	$235	$180	$160	$140	$120	$105	$90
Nickel finish	$250	$195	$175	$150	$130	$110	$95

Blue w/adj. sights — add $15 to above prices.

SENTINEL MARK IV DOUBLE ACTION — similar to Sentinel 1, except .22 WRM.

	100%	98%	95%	90%	80%	70%	60%
Blue finish	$145	$140	$125	$120	$115	$95	$90
Nickel finish	$155	$150	$140	$130	$125	$105	$100

Adj. sights

	$160	$155	$150	$145	$125	$115	$100

SENTINEL MARK II DOUBLE ACTION — .357 Mag., 6 shot, double action, 2½, 4, and 6 in. barrel, blue, fixed sights, wood grips, made 1974-1976.

	$225	$190	$165	$155	$150	$140	$130

SENTINEL MARK III DOUBLE ACTION — similar to Mark II, except adj. sights.

	$250	$220	$185	$175	$170	$160	$150

CRUSADER — .357 Mag., .44 Mag. or .45 LC, double action employing gear assembly, swing-out cylinder, unique action, adj. sights, limited mfg. starting 1976 because of expensive fabrication.

	$575	$495	$440	$395	$360	$320	$295

Add 10% for NIB condition.

LIMITED EDITIONS

GRISWOLD & GUNNISON — copy of Confederate Revolver, 7½ in. barrel, 500 mfg. in 1974.

	$250	$195	$150

Last Mfg.'s Sug. Retail was $175.

LEECH & RIGDON — black powder commemorative, 500 mfg. in 1974.

	$250	$195	$150

Last Mfg.'s Sug. Retail was $175.

PRESIDENTIAL DERRINGER — limited mfg. in 1974 only.

	$250	$195	$150

Last Mfg.'s Sug. Retail was $150.

SCHNEIDER & GLASSICK — 1,000 mfg. in 1975 only.

	$325	$250	$175

Last Mfg.'s Sug. Retail was $325.

Grading	100%	98%	95%	90%	80%	70%	60%

CRUSADER 50TH ANNIVERSARY — .44 Mag. or .45 LC cal., approx. 50 mfg. for each cal. in 1977 only.

	$1,250	$995	$775				

Limited availability might affect asking prices considerably. Two gun sets with matching serial numbers were also available - current asking prices are over $3,250.

BICENTENNIAL BLACK POWDER — .36 cal., 1776-1976 bicentennial edition with belt buckle.

	$525	$395	$300				

RIFLES

SPORT KING FIELD MODEL — .22 S (hi-speed), .22 L, .22 LR, semi-auto, tube mag., 22 in. barrel, open sight, plain pistol grip stock, made 1960-1966.

	$100	$90	$85	$75	$65	$55	$45

SPORT KING SPECIAL — similar to Field, except beavertail forearm and Monte Carlo stock.

	$140	$120	$95	$90	$75	$65	$55

SPORT KING CARBINE — similar to Field, except 18 in. barrel, straight grip, barrel band and sling, made 1964-1973.

	$170	$150	$120	$110	$100	$90	$85

SPORT KING DELUXE — similar to Special, but stock checkered, made 1966-1975.

	$185	$160	$140	$115	$90	$75	$65

HI-POWER FIELD BOLT ACTION — Mauser type action, .270, .30-06, 4 shot mag., 22 in. barrel, folding rear sight, plain stock, made 1962-1966.

	$295	$230	$210	$195	$180	$165	$150

HI-POWER DELUXE — similar to Field, except checkered Monte Carlo stock, swivels, made 1962-1966.

	$350	$285	$240	$220	$205	$195	$165

FLITE KING SLIDE ACTION — .22 S, L, or LR, 24 in. barrel, tube mag., hammerless, patridge sight, Monte Carlo stock with pistol grip, semi beavertail forearm, made 1962-1975.

	$120	$105	$95	$85	$65	$60	$50

SHOTGUNS

SUPERMATIC FIELD GRADE — 12 ga., 28 and 30 in. barrel, mod. or full, gas operated semi-auto, plain pistol grip stock, made 1960-1966.

	$205	$185	$175	$160	$145	$140	$120

SUPERMATIC SPECIAL — 12 ga., similar to Field, 27 in. barrel, adj. choke, made 1960-1966.

	$210	$195	$180	$165	$150	$145	$125

SUPERMATIC DELUXE — similar to Field, except vent. rib, checkered stock and forearm, made 1961-1966.

	$265	$225	$200	$175	$160	$155	$140

SUPERMATIC TROPHY — similar to Deluxe, except 27 in. barrel, adj. choke.

	$235	$215	$205	$180	$165	$160	$145

High Standard, cont.

Grading	100%	98%	95%	90%	80%	70%	60%

SUPERMATIC DUCK — similar to Field, except 3 in. Mag., 30 in. full barrel, recoil pad, made 1961-1966.

| | $275 | $235 | $190 | $160 | $145 | $125 | $110 |

SUPERMATIC DUCK VENT RIB — similar to Duck, vent. rib, checkered stock and forearm, made 1961-1966.

| | $295 | $250 | $210 | $175 | $150 | $130 | $115 |

SUPERMATIC DEER GUN — similar to Field, except 22 in. cylinder bore barrel, rifle sights, checkered stock and forearm, recoil pad, made 1965.

| | $230 | $210 | $200 | $185 | $165 | $155 | $140 |

SUPERMATIC SKEET — similar to Deluxe Rib, except 26 in. barrel, skeet bore, made 1962-1966.

| | $300 | $260 | $225 | $195 | $175 | $160 | $150 |

SUPERMATIC TRAP — similar to Skeet, except 30 in. full barrel, trap stock with pad, made 1962-1966.

| | $245 | $230 | $220 | $205 | $185 | $170 | $160 |

Note: All preceding models, except Deer and Trap, chambered only for 20 ga., 3 in. Mag. values are $10 higher.

High Standard restyled the Supermatic Autoloader in 1966. The new model Supermatics are recognized by the new checkering pattern and jeweled bolt. All models previously listed are offered, 12 and 20 ga. values are $25 higher per model. All are considered deluxe models. They were discontinued in 1975.

FLITE KING PUMP FIELD GRADE — 12, 20, 28, or .410 ga., slide action, 26, 28, or 30 in. barrel, imp. cyl., mod., or full choke, plain pistol grip stock and slide, made 1960-1966.

| | $165 | $150 | $140 | $130 | $120 | $110 | $100 |

FLITE KING SPECIAL — 12, 20, 28, or .410 ga., similar to Pump Field, except 27 in. barrel, adj. choke, made 1960-1966.

| | $185 | $160 | $150 | $145 | $130 | $120 | $110 |

FLITE KING DELUXE RIB — 12, 20, 28, or .410 ga., similar to Pump Special, except vent. rib, checkered stock, made 1961-1966.

| | $195 | $175 | $170 | $165 | $155 | $140 | $125 |

FLITE KING TROPHY — 12, 20, 28, or .410 ga., similar to Deluxe Rib, except 27 in. vent. rib barrel, adj. choke, made 1960-1966.

| | $200 | $180 | $175 | $170 | $160 | $145 | $130 |

FLITE KING BRUSH — 12 ga. only, similar to Field, except 18 or 20 in. cylinder bore barrel, rifle sights, made 1962-1964.

| | $185 | $170 | $165 | $160 | $150 | $140 | $120 |

FLITE KING BRUSH DELUXE — 12 ga. only, similar to Brush, except adj. aperture rear sight, checkered stock, recoil pad, swivels and sling, 20 in. barrel only, made 1964-1966.

| | $265 | $230 | $195 | $170 | $155 | $145 | $130 |

FLITE KING SKEET — 12, 20, 28, or .410 ga. only, similar to Deluxe Rib, except 26 in. vent. rib, skeet bore, made 1962-1966.

| | $265 | $230 | $195 | $170 | $155 | $145 | $130 |

Grading	100%	98%	95%	90%	80%	70%	60%

FLITE KING TRAP — 12 ga. only, similar to Deluxe Rib, except 30 in. vent. rib, full choke and pad, made 1962-1966.

	$250	$220	$195	$165	$150	$140	$125

Note: Flite King is available in 16 ga. also, except for the Brush, Skeet, and Trap models. Values are about $20 less per model. A .410 bore was offered in all models that were offered in 20 ga., except the Special and Trophy models. Values are generally the same per model.

High Standard restyled the Flite King in 1966. The new models have a jeweled bolt and new checkering pattern. These new guns were available as Deluxe, Deluxe Rib, Brush, Brush Deluxe, Skeet Deluxe, and Trap Deluxe. Their values are about $20 higher per model.

The new redesigned Flite King was also offered in Deluxe, Deluxe Rib, and Deluxe Skeet, in 20, 28, and .410 ga.'s. The 28 and .410 ga.'s will bring an additional 10-40%.

MODEL 10B — 12 ga. combat shotgun, 18 in. barrel, semi-auto, unique design incorporates raked pistol grip in front of receiver and metal shoulder pad attached directly to rear of receiver, black cycolac plastic shroud and pistol grip, folding carrying handle, provisions made for attaching a small flashlight to receiver top, extended blade front sight, very compact size (28 in. overall). Discontinued.

	$650	$575	$500	$425	$375	$325	$275

The predecessor to this model was the 10A. This variation had the flashlight built in.

RIOT SHOTGUN — 18 or 20 in. barrel, police riot gun was also offered until 1975. This was a reliable weapon available with or without rifle sights, 12 ga. only on the Flite King Action.

	$195	$165	$155	$140	$130	$120	$115

SUPERMATIC INDY O/U — This model was made in Japan and imported in 1974 and 1975, boxlock, fully engraved receiver, selective auto ejectors and single trigger, 12 ga., 27½ sk & sk, 29½ imp. mod. and full, or full and full, air flow vent. rib, checkered (skipline) pistol grip stock with pad and vent. forearm.

	$815	$720	$635	$590	$550	$495	$440

SUPERMATIC SHADOW SEVEN O/U — similar to Indy O/U, except less elaborate engraving, unvented forearm, standard vent. rib, regular checkering, no recoil pad, imported 1974-1975.

	$670	$590	$540	$495	$470	$425	$385

SUPERMATIC SHADOW AUTO — 12 and 20 ga., 2¾ or 3 in. chambers in 12 ga., air flow rib, 26 in. imp. cyl. or skeet, 28 in. mod., imp. mod. or full and 30 in. full or trap, checkered walnut stock, gas operated, imported 1974-1975.

	$340	$285	$240	$210	$180	$165	$155

HOFER-JAGDWAFFEN, PETER

Master gunsmith located in Ferlach, Austria. Custom order only, best quality rifles (over 100 cals. available) and shotguns (O/U and SxS) made per individual order — prices typically start at $20,000+. Information can be obtained by writing to Mr. Hofer directly at: Peter Hofer-Jagdwaffen, Kirchgasse 24, A-9170 Ferlach, Austria.

HOLLAND & HOLLAND LTD.

Manufacturer located in London, England since 1835. All H&H long guns are built per individual special order. Orders may be placed directly with the factory in England. Please refer to their listing in the Trademark Index for address, telephone, telex, or FAX information.

HOLLAND & HOLLAND
— *Established 1835* —

Holland & Holland over the years has justly earned the reputation of producing some of the finest firearms ever manufactured. Their Double Rifles chambered for the Large Black Powder Express Cartridges are still among the most powerful rifles ever made, while exhibiting outstanding quality and superior craftsmanship. Most of these fine arms were made to order for the famous, wealthy, or royalty of their day. Because of the individual nature of each firearm, these early guns, as with any high grade item, must be individually appraised.

The early Double Rifles were proofed and regulated with the Black Powder of their day. These exposed hammer rifles were almost exclusively sold cased with accessories by Holland & Holland. They are seldom found on the market, and then not in the best of condition. Purchase of these as well as any high grade firearm should include trusted appraisal.

RIFLES: MODERN

ROOK RIFLE — various cals., single shot, break-open action, various levels of embellishment - most were base models with few extra features. Values today range from $295 (average condition, small cal.) to $995 (larger cal., better wood, perhaps cased). Disc.

Grading	100%	98%	95%	90%	80%	70%	60%

BEST QUALITY MAGAZINE RIFLE — Mauser 98 (current mfg.) or Enfield (disc.) action, various cals., incl. .300 H&H Mag., .375 H&H Mag., 4 shot mag., 24 in. barrel, folding leaf sight, checkered French walnut stock available in traditional configuration or with Monte Carlo pattern.

Mfg.'s Sug. Retail $14,528 $14,528 $10,250 $7,500 $5,300 $4,250 $3,600 $3,250

The values above represent the standard model without additional options (of which there are a wide array). Mfg. to customer specifications.

DE LUXE MAGAZINE RIFLE — similar to Best Quality, except with deluxe grade walnut and various engraving options, very limited mfg.
There is no standard base price on this model - rather, individual options are custom ordered and are individually priced.

NO. 2 MODEL DOUBLE RIFLE S x S — various British and American cals., 24-28 in. barrels, sidelock, folding leaf sight, checkered French walnut stock, auto ejectors.

$15,000 $13,000 $11,000 $10,000 $9,000 $7,000 $6,500

ROYAL DOUBLE S x S RIFLE — available in most popular cals. between .300 and .577, similar to No. 2, except has deluxe finish and more engraving.

.300 or .375 cal.
Mfg.'s Sug. Retail $68,242 $68,242 $45,000 $31,500 $25,500 $19,000 $16,000 $13,500

.465 cal.
Mfg.'s Sug. Retail $71,371 $71,371 $47,250 $32,750 $26,000 $20,000 $17,000 $14,000

.577 cal.
Mfg.'s Sug. Retail $77,927 $77,927 $52,250 $34,750 $27,000 $21,500 $18,000 $15,000

ROYAL DE LUXE S x S RIFLE — same cals. as the Royal Double SxS, top-of-the-line model, every refinement, built to individual order only with almost any option possible.

Grading		100%	98%	95%	90%	80%	70%	60%
⚜ **.300 or .375 cal.**								
Mfg.'s Sug. Retail	$74,500	$74,500	$48,750	$33,250	$27,000	$20,750	$17,750	$14,250
⚜ **.465 cal.**								
Mfg.'s Sug. Retail	$78,523	$78,523	$53,250	$35,500	$27,500	$21,500	$18,500	$15,500
⚜ **.577 cal.**								
Mfg.'s Sug. Retail	$84,930	$84,930	$58,250	$38,750	$29,500	$22,750	$19,250	$16,000

H&H .700 BORE DOUBLE RIFLE — .700 H&H cal., 1,000 grain jacketed bullet, approx. 19 lbs. with 26 in. barrels chambered 3½ in. This is the largest caliber rifle available in the world today.

		100%	98%	95%	90%	80%	70%	60%
⚜ **Royal Model**								
Mfg.'s Sug. Retail	$107,280	$107,280	$95,000	$85,000	$77,500	$70,000	$62,500	$55,000
⚜ **Royal De Luxe Model**								
Mfg.'s Sug. Retail	$115,475	$115,475	$100,000	$90,000	$81,500	$73,000	$65,000	$57,500

SHOTGUNS: SINGLE SHOT AND SIDE BY SIDE

Holland & Holland currently manufactures the Royal De Luxe Game Gun and Royal Game Gun models in sidelock configuration (and are listed below). In addition to the sidelock models, H&H also manufactures the boxlock models Cavalier, Cavalier De Luxe, Northwood, and Northwood De Luxe. The values below assume standard model with double triggers, game rib, standard walnut, or casing. Additional special order features will add considerable value to the price of a new custom order.

In 1988, Holland & Holland absorbed W & C Scott and manufactured the Chatsworth, Bowood, and Kinmount boxlock models until they were discontinued in late 1990. H&H has phased this trademark out, and more information can be found in the W & C Scott section of this text.

SINGLE BARREL TRAP GUN — 12 ga., 30 or 32 in. full choke barrel, vent. rib, boxlock, auto ejector, Monte Carlo pistol grip stock, pad. Disc. 1992.

				90%	80%	70%	60%
	$23,500	$18,750	$14,750	$11,750	$8,750	$6,750	$4,950

Last Mfg.'s Sug. Retail was $28,420.

⚜ **Trap Guns - Older Mfg.**

	100%	98%	95%	90%	80%	70%	60%
Standard Grade	$5,000	$4,500	$4,000	$3,250	$2,500	$2,250	$2,000
De Luxe Grade	$8,250	$7,000	$6,250	$5,000	$4,500	$3,750	$3,000
Exhibition Grade	$10,500	$8,950	$7,500	$6,000	$5,500	$5,000	$4,250

NORTHWOOD S x S BOXLOCK — 12, 16 (disc. 1992), 20, or 28 (disc. 1992) ga., 28 or 30 in. barrels, scalloped-case colored receiver, boxlock, auto ejectors, double triggers, border engraving, checkered pistol grip or straight stock. The values shown below are for standard model.

		100%	98%	95%	90%	80%	70%	60%
Mfg.'s Sug. Retail	$6,705	$6,705	$5,950	$5,200	$4,450	$3,850	$3,300	$2,800

Add approx. 10% for 28 ga. (disc.).

⚜ **Northwood De Luxe** — 12, 16, 20, or 28 ga., scalloped-case colored receiver with moderate engraving and select walnut, double triggers. Current mfg.

		100%	98%	95%	90%	80%	70%	60%
Mfg.'s Sug. Retail	$7,450	$7,450	$6,375	$5,450	$4,600	$3,950	$3,350	$2,850

Add approx. 10% for 28 ga. (disc.).

CAVALIER S x S BOXLOCK — 12, 20, or 28 (disc. 1992) ga., best quality model boxlock with scalloped frame, double triggers, ejectors, and case colored receiver. Current mfg.

		100%	98%	95%	90%	80%	70%	60%
Mfg.'s Sug. Retail	$11,175	$11,175	$9,500	$7,750	$6,350	$5,500	$4,850	$4,100

Add approx. 10% for 28 ga. (disc.).

Grading	100%	98%	95%	90%	80%	70%	60%

Cavalier De Luxe — similar to Cavalier Model, except has deluxe walnut and better engraving. Current mfg.

Mfg.'s Sug. Retail	$11,920	$11,920	$9,950	$8,000	$6,500	$5,600	$4,950	$4,200

Add approx. 10% for 28 ga. (disc.).

DOMINION SIDELOCK — 12, 16, or 20 ga., 25-30 in. barrels, any choke, sidelock, auto ejectors, double triggers, checkered straight grip stock.

		$7,500	$6,250	$5,000	$4,000	$3,500	$3,250	$3,000

20 gauge — add 20%.

Above values are for older, previously manufactured specimens.

Dominion Game Gun — 12 ga. only, single or double triggers. Disc. 1989.

	$20,000	$17,000	$14,500	$12,250	$10,000	$8,500	$6,750

Last Mfg.'s Sug. Retail was $28,000.

ROYAL HAMMERLESS EJECTOR SIDELOCK — 12, 16, 20, 28, or .410 ga., customer specifications as to barrel length and chokes, hand detachable sidelocks and a self opening action, stocked in pistol grip or straight style to specifications. Mfg. 1885-disc.

	$14,500	$11,500	$8,750	$7,750	$6,950	$6,350	$5,250

20 gauge — add 20%.
28 gauge — add 40%.
.410 gauge — add 60%.
Without SST — subtract $1,000.

Above values are for older, previously manufactured specimens.

ROYAL GAME GUN — 12, 16, 20, 28 or .410 ga., best quality sidelock game gun. Mfg. per individual customer specifications. Current production.

Mfg.'s Sug. Retail	$44,477	$44,477	$29,750	$21,500	$16,500	$12,750	$10,500	$9,000

Add $4,693 for 28 or .410 ga.
Add $4,135 for ST.
Add $3,100 for VR (disc.).

DE LUXE MODEL — similar to Royal Hammerless Ejector, except with more elaborate engraving and exhibition wood, self-opening gun. Older mfg.

	$18,750	$15,500	$13,000	$11,000	$9,000	$7,500	$6,500

Add 20% for 20 gauge.
Add 40% for 28 gauge.
Add 60% for .410 gauge.
Subtract $1,000 if without SST.

Above values are for older, previously manufactured specimens.

ROYAL DE LUXE GAME GUN — 12, 16, 20, 28, or .410 ga., top-of-the-line sidelock shotgun. Mfg. per individual customer specifications. Current production.

Mfg.'s Sug. Retail	$52,672	$52,672	$33,750	$23,500	$17,750	$14,000	$11,250	$9,000

Add $4,693 for 28 or .410 ga.
Add $4,135 for ST.
Add $3,100 for VR (disc.).

BADMINTON SIDELOCK — similar to Royal model, without self opening action. Mfg. 1902-disc.

	$10,500	$9,000	$8,000	$7,000	$6,000	$5,000	$4,000

20 gauge — add 20%.
28 gauge — add 40%.
.410 gauge — add 60%.
SST — add $1,000.

Above values are for older, previously manufactured specimens.

Grading	100%	98%	95%	90%	80%	70%	60%

Badminton Game Gun — 12 or 20 ga., double or single trigger. Disc. 1988.

	$20,000	$17,000	$14,500	$12,250	$10,000	$8,500	$6,750

Last Mfg.'s Sug. Retail was $28,000.

RIVIERA SIDELOCK — similar to Badminton model, with two sets of barrels. Mfg. until 1967.

	$15,000	$11,500	$9,500	$7,950	$7,100	$6,350	$5,600

20 gauge — add 20%.
28 gauge — add 40%.
.410 gauge — add 60%.

CENTENARY SIDELOCK — 12 ga., 2 in. chambers, lightened version of Royal, Badminton, and Dominion grades. The values would be the same as for the standard models, mfg. until 1962.

SHOTGUNS: O/U

H&H has finalized the design elements of their new O/U shotguns. The descriptions and prices listed below reflect the most current information on these new models.

ROYAL MODEL O/U SHOTGUN OLD MODEL — 12 ga., customer specifications as to barrel length and choke, hand detachable sidelocks, auto ejectors, checkered straight grip stock. Mfg. until 1951. Rare, fewer than 30 made.

	$32,000	$28,000	$23,500	$20,000	$18,000	$16,500	$15,000

Single trigger — add $1,000.

ROYAL NEW MODEL O/U — similar to Old Model, with improved narrow action. Mfg. until 1960.

	$27,500	$24,000	$22,000	$19,500	$18,500	$17,000	$15,500

ROYAL O/U SIDELOCK GAME GUN — 12 or 20 ga., somewhat similar to New Model, with improved cocking, striking and ejection, slimmer action body, 25 to 30 in. game or VR barrels, 2¾ in. chambers, finest checkered walnut straight hand or pistol grip stock, scroll engraved receiver with color case hardened or bright finish, prototype testing has finished and guns are available for demonstration, 5 lbs. 1 oz - 7 lbs. 8 oz. Written quotations on this re-released model are available by contacting H&H directly (see Trademark Index). Values listed below are for base models only.

Mfg.'s Sug. Retail	$55,875	$55,875	$30,000	$25,000	$21,000	$19,500	$18,250	$16,000

28 and .410 ga. variations are scheduled for release in 1997.

ROYAL DE LUXE MODEL — similar to Royal O/U Sidelock Game Gun, except choice of more elaborate engraving and exhibition wood.

Mfg.'s Sug. Retail	$64,815	$64,815	$40,000	$32,500	$26,500	$22,500	$20,000	$18,000

28 and .410 ga. variations are scheduled for release in 1997.

SPORTING O/U MODEL — 12 ga. only, 2¾ in. chambers, designed with a trigger plate action, Game or Sporting Clays configuration featuring detachable SST mechanism, 28 to 32 in. game or VR barrels. Options on specifications to include screw-in chokes. New 1993.

Mfg.'s Sug. Retail	$26,448	$26,448	$22,500	$18,750	$15,250	$12,750	$10,750	$8,750

A 20 ga. variation is scheduled for release in 1995.

SPORTING DE LUXE MODEL — similar to Sporting O/U Model, except with choice of more elaborate engraving and exhibition wood. New 1993.

Mfg.'s Sug. Retail	$31,290	$31,290	$25,750	$20,750	$17,000	$13,750	$11,500	$9,500

A 20 ga. variation is scheduled for release in 1995.

HOLLOWAY ARMS CO.

Manufactured In Fort Worth, TX.

Holloway firearms did not make many rifles or carbines before operations ceased. While rare, they still are not particularly collectible at this point.

Grading	100%	98%	95%	90%	80%	70%	60%

HAC MODEL 7 — 7.62mm NATO (.308), gas operated semi-auto paramilitary design rifle, 20 in. barrel, adj. front and rear sights, 20 shot mag., side folding stock. Mfg. 1984-1985 only. Also available in fully auto (class III dealers only) — add $80. Add $50 for left-hand variation.

	$995	$895	$795	$695	$595	$525	$465

Last Mfg.'s Sug. Retail was $675.

Model 7C — 16 in. carbine, same general specifications as Model 7. Disc. 1985.

	$995	$895	$795	$695	$595	$525	$465

Last Mfg.'s Sug. Retail was $675. Also available from the manufacturer were the models 7S and 7M (Sniper and Match models).

HOLMES FIREARMS

Manufacturer located in Wheeler, AR. Distributed by D.B. Distributing, Fayetteville, AR.

These pistols were mfg. in very limited numbers, most were in prototype configuration and exhibit changes from gun to gun.

MP-83 — 9mm or .45 ACP cal., paramilitary design pistol, 6 in. barrel, walnut stock and forearm, blued finish, 3½ lbs. Add $75 for deluxe package and $220 for conversion kit. Mfg. 1985 only.

	$595	$550	$500	$450	$400	$375	$350

Last Mfg.'s Sug. Retail was $450.

MP-22 — .22 LR cal., 2½ lbs., steel and aluminum construction, 6 in. barrel, similar appearance to MP-83. Mfg. 1985 only.

	$395	$360	$320	$285	$250	$230	$210

Last Mfg.'s Sug. Retail was $400.

COMBAT 12 — 12 ga., riot configuration, cylinder bore barrel. Disc. 1983.

	$795	$720	$650	$595	$550	$500	$450

Last Mfg.'s Sug. Retail was $750.

HOPKINS & ALLEN ARMS COMPANY, 1902-1914

H&A started their firearms business in 1867, manufacturing percussion revolvers. Before 1870, they were producing rimfire cartridge guns and eventually centerfire handguns and long guns. Prior to 1896, H&A guns were marked "HOPKINS & ALLEN MANUFG. CO. NORWICH CONN." or other private tradenames, including Merwin, Hulbert & Company. Hopkins & Allen guns are about equally priced with Stevens, N.R. Davis, Crescent Firearms Co., etc. There are many exceptions due to the numerous limited production guns, examples are the AA GRADE double shotgun and the "PARROT BEAK" Derringer. Hopkins & Allen also manufactured firearms which were not described in their catalogs.

Compiled from Hopkins & Allen catalogs by Charles E. Carder.

SHOTGUNS: SxS

Hopkins & Allen purchased Forehand Arms Co. and continued to produce their line of firearms and after a few years, dropped the Forehand name. In 1902, they offered the Forehand double boxlocks with or without outside hammers. Most models were offered in 12, 16 & 20 gauge. Sidelocks were added 1906-09. In 1902, the AA GRADE, a very high quality boxlock, was offered for $100 to $125. It had fine Damascus barrels, straight grip, plain or automatic ejectors, fine wood and engraving and was competitive with some Remingtons, L.C. Smiths, Bakers and other fine guns of that era. This gun was very short lived and today is rare. One feature found on all H&A double barrel guns is the "rib extension" or "doll's head".

BOXLOCK – Anson & Deeley type frame, damascus, twist, and steel barrels. Values range from $75-$250.

BOXLOCK – similar to above, except with outside hammers. Values range from $75-$250.

SIDELOCK – hammerless, damascus, twist, and steel barrels. Values range from $90-$250.

SIDELOCK – similar to above, except with outside hammers. Values range from $75-$250.

SINGLE BARREL SHOTGUNS

H&A produced a "falling block" shotgun in most gauges circa 1887 - early 1900s. Falling Blocks (FBs) in 12 ga. were built on heavy frames with the 20 and 16 gauges sharing a medium frame. Prior to 1902, some FBs were chambered for .45-70 shotshells and, today, these are rare if in good condition. From the 1890s through 1914, 38XL, 44XL shotshell guns were periodically offered in the Junior frame. After 1902, "tip-over" single shotguns were offered in Forehand designs and, later, the Davenport designs.

FALLING BLOCK – lever operated, outside hammer. Values range from $100-$275.

BOXLOCK – with outside hammer, damascus, twist, and steel barrels. Values range from $65-$150.

BOXLOCK – hammerless, top safety. Values range from $65-$150.

BOXLOCK – hammerless, top safety. Values range from $65-$150.

GOOSE GUNS – outside hammer, 8, 10, or 12 ga., were offered with barrels up to 40 inches long. Values range from $90-$200.

"SAFETY SINGLE GUN" – engraved with outside hammer and top safety. (Was offered in 1911 and recommended for trap shooting for $15.00). Values range from $100-$200.

RIFLES

Hopkins & Allen started building "falling block" rifles circa 1887-1914 with the buy-out of the Baystate Arms Company. Most commonly seen is the "Junior" model, known after 1902 as 922, 925, and 932. These numbers were in reference to the catalog numbers, not model numbers. In the very late 1890s or early 1900s, the Number 722, 822 and 832 rifles were added. In 1906, a "bolt action" repeater was added to their line, followed in 1909 by a "bolt action" single shot "military". Lyman tang sights were an option for many H&A rifles - add $60-$75.

NUMBER 922 – falling block, lever operated, .22 cal. rimfire, with round bbl. Values range from $70-$200.

NUMBER 925 – similar to above in .25 cal. rimfire. Values range from $70-$200.

NUMBER 932 – similar to above in .32 cal. rimfire. Values range from $70-$200.

NUMBER 938 – similar to above in .38 S&W centerfire. Values range from $120-$250.

NUMBER 1922 – similar to above in .22 cal. with octagon bbl. Values range from $85-$225.

NUMBER 1932 – similar to above in .32 cal. Values range from $85-$225.

NUMBER 2922 – similar to above in .22 cal., with checkering. Values range from $100-$250.

NUMBER 2932 – similar to above in .32 caliber. Values range from $100-$250.

NUMBER 3922 – similar to above in .22 rimfire, " SCHUETZEN RIFLE", nickeled Swiss butt plate, octagon barrel. (Schuetzen rifles in good cond. are somewhat rare.) Values range from $250-$590.

NUMBER 3925 — similar to above in .25-20 centerfire. (This caliber rifle is more rare than the .22 rimfire). Values range from $300-$645.

NUMBER 44XL — similar to Number 922, except has smooth bore, chambered for the 44XL shotshell. (Referred to as, "TAXIERMIST'S" or "LADIES GUN"). Values range from $150-$325.

NUMBER 722 — rolling block, thumb operated, .22 cal. rimfire. Values range from $70-$200.

SCOUT MILITARY RIFLE — similar to above with military style stock and a "Bonneted Indian" stamped on the left side of frame. (These are somewhat rare). Values range from $100-$265.

NUMBER 822 — rolling block, lever operated, .22 cal. rimfire. Values range from $80-$215.

NUMBER 832 — similar to above in .32 cal. rimfire. (This model was offered first with "pig tail" type levers and later with "loop" type levers. The "loop levers" are somewhat rare.) Values range from $80-$215.

NUMBER 4922 — .22 rimfire cal., bolt action, repeater. Values range from $100-$200.

NUMBER 5022 — similar to above with deluxe checkering. Values range from $120-$240.

MILITARY RIFLE — similar to above, except single shot with military style stock and sling. (In good condition, these are somewhat rare.) Values range from $120-$240.

NOISELESS — .22 rimfire, similar to the Number 922, except for checkered wood and the addition of a noise suppressor attached to the muzzle, by means of mating threads inside of suppressor and outside of barrel. The job is so well fitted, that it is difficult to recognize the suppressor. The front sight is attached to a dovetail slot in the suppressor. (These rifles are listed under the National Firearms Act of 1934 and must have proper licensing. Very rare.) Values range from $250-$550.

HANDGUNS

Most H&A handguns are nickel plated, with blue finish costing $.50 extra, grips are hard rubber, wood or pearl. Some have engraving from low to very good quality. Revolver barrel lengths vary from 1¾-6 in. Calibers are .22 rimfire to .38 centerfire.

FOREHAND MODEL — breaktop, double action, five shot, .32 caliber. Values range from $60-$190.

FOREHAND MODEL — similar to above except hammerless. (This model was offered in large and small frame). Values range from $60-$190.

FOREHAND MODEL — large frame as above in .32 and .38 centerfire with full hammer or "bobbed" hammer. Values range from $60-$190.

FOREHAND MODEL — solid frame and hard rubber grips, otherwise as above in small frame. Values range from $50-$160.

FOREHAND MODEL — similar to above models, with "folding hammer". .22 rimfires were seven shot, while .32 and .38 centerfires were five shot. By 1909, the Forehand logo was dropped from these revolvers. Values range from $50-$160.

H&A NEW MODEL AUTOMATIC HAMMER REVOLVER — similar to breaktop with hammer, produced in small and large frame, in .22 rimfire, .32 and .38 centerfire. Values range from $50-$165.

H&A SOLID FRAME — .32 and .38 centerfire, five shot, double action, hammer or "bobbed" hammer. Values range from $40-$140.

H&A XL MODEL — similar to above in .22, .32 and .38 calibers. Values range from $40-$140.

H&A RANGE MODEL — .22, .32 and .38 caliber, solid frame, loading gate on right side, wood target style grips, single or double action. (Two models, large and small frames.) Values range from $50-$165.

H&A TRIPLE ACTION SAFETY POLICE REVOLVER — breaktop with newly design locking mechanism, .22, .32 and .38 caliber, hard rubber or pearl grips. (Considered to be one of the best designed breaktops on the market. Other options for this model, include hammerless, engraved, wood target or pearl grips.) Values range from $70-$190.

H&A NEW VEST POCKET DERRINGER — .22 short rimfire, single shot, tip up, single action, 3½ in. overall length, folding trigger, blue or nickel finish, wood or pearl grips with golden monograms. This model was first listed about 1910 and known as the "Parrot Beak". An estimate of less than one thousand were produced and they are very rare. Values range from $550-$1900.

H&A NEW MODEL TARGET PISTOL — .22 rimfire, single shot breaktop with the same new locking mechanism as the Safety Police Revolver, wood target grips with golden monograms, blue finish and 6, 8 or 10 in. barrels. Values range from $200-$450.

H&A NEW MODEL SKELETON STOCK TARGET PISTOL — similar to above, with rounded hard rubber grips with logo, detachable "skeleton metal stock", 18 in. barrel and blue finish. Values range from $250-$525.

HOWA
Manufacturer located in Japan.
Recently, Howa rifles have been imported by both Smith & Wesson (pre-1985) and Mossberg (1986-87). Currently, Howa sporting rifles are being imported by Interarms and this trademark will appear in the Interarms section in this text. Older Howa models will appear in both the S&W and Mossberg sections of this text.

HUNTER ARMS COMPANY
Manufacturer located in Fulton, NY between 1891 and 1945.
The Hunter Arms Company was formed to manufacture L.C. Smith shotguns. Please refer to the L.C. Smith section in this text for further information regarding this manufacturer (including Fulton, Fulton Special, and Hunter Special models.)

HUSQVARNA
Previous manufacturer located in Husqvarna, Sweden.
Also see: Lahti Pistols

RIFLE: BOLT ACTION

Grading	100%	98%	95%	90%	80%	70%	60%
HI-POWER — Mauser type action, .220 Swift, .270, or .30-06 cal., open sight, checkered beech wood. Mfg. 1946-1951, early models found in 6.5 x 55, 8 x 57, 9.3 x 57 cals.	$395	$365	$330	$295	$265	$235	$200
MODEL 1951 — similar to Hi-Power, except high profile stock.	$425	$385	$340	$300	$270	$240	$210
SERIES 1100 DELUXE — similar to Model 1951, except has European walnut and jeweled bolt. Mfg. 1952-1956.	$440	$360	$330	$310	$290	$275	$250
SERIES 1000 SUPER GRADE — similar to Model 1951, has walnut Monte Carlo stock. Mfg. 1952-1956.	$440	$360	$330	$310	$290	$275	$250

Grading	100%	98%	95%	90%	80%	70%	60%

SERIES 3100 CROWN GRADE — improved HVA Mauser action, .243, .270, .30-06, 7mm, or .308 cal., 24 in. barrel, walnut stock, black forend tip and pistol grip cap. Mfg. 1954-1972.

| | $470 | $385 | $360 | $330 | $315 | $305 | $275 |

SERIES 3000 CROWN GRADE — similar to 3100, except has Monte Carlo stock.

| | $470 | $385 | $360 | $330 | $315 | $305 | $275 |

SERIES 4100 LIGHTWEIGHT — HVA Mauser action, calibers same as 3100, 20½ in. barrel, open sights, lightweight walnut stock, pistol grip, Schnabel forend. Mfg. 1954-1972.

| | $470 | $385 | $360 | $330 | $315 | $305 | $275 |

SERIES 4000 LIGHTWEIGHT — similar to 4100, except has Monte Carlo stock, no sights.

| | $470 | $385 | $360 | $330 | $315 | $305 | $275 |

MODEL 456 LIGHTWEIGHT — similar to 4000/4100, except full length stock. Mfg. 1959-1970.

| | $495 | $415 | $385 | $360 | $330 | $310 | $290 |

SERIES 6000 IMPERIAL GRADE — similar to 3100, except has select wood, 3 leaf folding sight. Mfg. 1968-1970.

| | $580 | $495 | $470 | $440 | $395 | $365 | $330 |

SERIES 6000 IMPERIAL LIGHTWEIGHT — similar to 6000 Imperial, except 20½ in. barrel, lightweight stock.

| | $580 | $495 | $470 | $440 | $395 | $365 | $330 |

SERIES P-3000 PRESENTATION — similar to Crown, except engraved action, special wood. Mfg. 1968-1970.

| | $770 | $660 | $635 | $605 | $550 | $510 | $485 |

MODEL 9000 CROWN GRADE — Husqvarna action, .300 Win. Mag. added to line, 23½ in. barrel, adj. trigger, adj. sight, walnut stock. Mfg. 1971-1972.

| | $470 | $385 | $360 | $330 | $315 | $305 | $275 |

MODEL 8000 IMPERIAL — similar to 9000, but jeweled bolt, engraved floor plate, no sights and deluxe stock. Mfg. 1971-1972.

| | $605 | $525 | $495 | $470 | $415 | $385 | $350 |

HY-HUNTER INC. FIREARMS MANUFACTURING CO.
Previous manufacturer located in W. Germany, imported by Hy-Hunter Inc.

Previous importer of single action revolvers in various calibers. Typically, prices are determined by their shooting value rather than their collector value. Prices generally range from $100-$175 depending on caliber and finish.

HYPER
Previous manufacturer located in Jenks, OK.

SINGLE SHOT RIFLE — all calibers, all standard lengths and contours, falling block trigger guard lever activated, adj. trigger, no sights, stocked to customer specifications, in AA grade walnut. Disc. 1984.

| | $2,200 | $1,980 | $1,925 | $1,870 | $1,650 | $1,540 | $1,375 |

Add $75 for stainless barrel.
Add $85 for octagon barrel.

I section

I A B SHOTGUNS

Manufactured by Industria Armi Bresciane, Italy. Previously distributed by Sporting Arms International, Inc. located in Indianola, MS.

I A B manufactures high quality competition (O/U and single barrel trap or skeet) shotguns in various styles and configurations including combo sets. These guns employ a boxlock action, have ejectors, and various amounts of engraving. Prices for 100% condition usually start in the $550-$900 price range. I A B shotguns are not being imported currently - values for older models will be determined by the prices shooters, not collectors, are willing to pay for them.

I A I

Please refer to the Irwindale Arms, Inc. heading in this section.

I G A SHOTGUNS

Manufacturer located in Veranopolis, Brazil. Currently imported by Stoeger Industries located in South Hackensack, NJ.

Grading	100%	98%	95%	90%	80%	70%	60%
UPLANDER SxS — 12, 20, 28, or .410 ga., 3 in. chambers, underlug lockup, double triggers, extractors.							
Mfg.'s Sug. Retail $383	$285	$200	$170	$145	$130	$115	$100
Add $42 for choke tubes (all gauges).							
COACH GUN SxS — 12, 20, or .410 (new 1991) ga., similar to standard grade, only 20 in. barrels.							
Mfg.'s Sug. Retail $367	$270	$190	$165	$140	$125	$110	$100
CONDOR O/U — 12 ga. only, single trigger, ejectors, presentation walnut, chrome lined bores. Disc. 1985.							
	$580	$500	$450	$410	$375	$350	$325
Last Mfg.'s Sug. Retail was $667.							
CONDOR I SINGLE TRIGGER O/U — 12 or 20 ga., 3 in. chambers, sliding underlug action, VR, deluxe checkered walnut, separated barrels.							
Mfg.'s Sug. Retail $540	$405	$330	$250	$225	$210	$195	$180
Add $42 for choke tubes (new 1992).							
CONDOR II DOUBLE TRIGGER O/U — 12 or 20 (disc.) ga., sliding underlug action, VR, checkered walnut, separated barrels.							
Mfg.'s Sug. Retail $432	$340	$290	$260	$240	$220	$195	$170
ERA 2000 — 12 ga. only, 26 or 28 in. VR barrels with choke tubes, single trigger. Importation began 1992.							
Mfg.'s Sug. Retail $665	$555	$365	$310	$250	$215	$195	$180
REUNA SINGLE BARREL — 12, 20, or .410 ga., exposed hammer with half-cock, extractor.							
Mfg.'s Sug. Retail $115	$90	$70	$60	$50	$45	$40	$35
Add $17 for choke tubes (12 ga. new 1992, 20 ga. new 1993).							
Reuna Single Barrel Youth — 20 or .410 ga., 22 in. barrel, features rubber recoil pad. Importation began 1993.							
Mfg.'s Sug. Retail $127	$95	$70	$60	$50	$45	$40	$35

IBERIA FIREARMS

Manufacturer located in Iberia, OH.   Distributed by MKS Supply located in Mansfield, OH. Distributor sales only.

Please refer to the Hi-Point section in this text.

INDIAN ARMS

Previously manufactured by Indian Arms Corporation located in Detroit, MI.

Grading	100%	98%	95%	90%	80%	70%	60%

INDIAN ARMS .380 SEMI-AUTO — .380 ACP, patterned after Walther PPK, stainless steel, 3¼ in. barrel, 6 shot mag., natural or blue finish, with (early specimens) or without key lock safety, with or without VR barrel, walnut grips, 20 oz. Mfg. 1975-1977.

	$350	$275	$225				

This model had limited manufacture with approx. 1,000 guns being made.

INDUSTRIA ARMI GALESI

Previous manufacturer located in Brescia, Italy.

PISTOL: SEMI-AUTO

GALESI MODEL 6 POCKET AUTO — .22 LR, .25 ACP, 6 shot, 2¼ in. barrel blue, fixed sights, plastic grips. Mfg. 1930-disc.

	$130	$120	$105	$90	$75	$65	$55

GALESI MODEL 9 POCKET AUTO — .22 LR, .32 ACP, .380 ACP, 8 shot, 3¼ in. barrel, blue, fixed sights, plastic grips. Mfg. 1930-disc.

	$140	$125	$110	$100	$85	$65	$55

INFALLIBLE

Mfg. by Warner Arms Corp. located in Norwich, CT and Davis-Warner Arms Corp. located in Assonet, MA.

INFALLIBLE PISTOL — .32 ACP cal., 3.2 in. barrel, 7 shot mag., 24.7 oz.

 Type I — mfg. and marked "Warner Arms Corp., Norwich, Conn.", serial range is 501-2,299.

	$325	$295	$270	$250	$225	$200	$180

 Type II — marked "Davis-Warner Arms Corporation, Assonet, Massachusetts ", serial range is 2,300-5,299.

	$295	$270	$250	$225	$195	$170	$150

 Type III — marked "Warner Arms Corporation, Norwich, Connecticut", serial range is 5,300-7,400.

	$295	$270	$250	$225	$195	$170	$150

INGLIS HI-POWERS

Manufactured by John Inglis Co. Limited of Toronto, Canada. Over 151,000 Inglis hi-powers were manufactured between February 1944 and September 1945 under military contractual agreement.

CHINESE CONTRACT PATTERN 35

 Chinese No. 1 — with markings, slotted for stock and tangent sights.

	$1,775	$1,475	$1,100	$995	$900	$800	$700

Add $200 for wooden holster stock.

Grading	100%	98%	95%	90%	80%	70%	60%

CH SERIES CHINESE CONTRACT — recently being imported again, market is currently somewhat flooded.

⚔ **MK 1-slotted** — tangent sights.

	$1,200	$1,000	$900	$800	$700	$600	$500

CANADIAN MILITARY

⚔ **MK 1-No. 1 Inglis** — tangent sight, slotted.

	$1,150	$975	$850	$725	$650	$550	$450

Add $200 for wooden holster stock.

⚔ **MK 1-No. 2 Inglis** — fixed sight, no slot.

	$550	$475	$450	$425	$400	$350	$275

⚔ **MK 1-No. 2 Inglis** — fixed sight, slotted. Inspect slot carefully.

	$1,150	$975	$850	$725	$650	$550	$450

Add $200 for wooden holster stock.

T SERIES CANADIAN MILITARY

	100%	98%	95%	90%	80%	70%	60%
1 T	$725	$600	$550	$500	$450	$400	$350
2 T	$600	$500	$450	$395	$345	$295	$275
3 T	$550	$450	$400	$350	$300	$260	$240
4 T	$550	$450	$400	$350	$300	$260	$240
5 T	$550	$450	$400	$350	$300	$260	$240
6 T	$550	$450	$400	$350	$300	$260	$240
7 T	$550	$450	$400	$350	$300	$260	$240
8 T	$800	$695	$595	$550	$530	$460	$395
9 T	$860	$750	$650	$550	$530	$460	$395

INGRAM

Military Armament Corp. (Mac), previously located in Atlanta, GA. Disc. late 1982.

MAC 10 — .45 ACP or 9mm cal., semi-auto, open bolt, pistol version of the sub machine gun, 16 and 32 shot mag., compact construction, all metal construction, rear aperture and front blade sight. Disc. 1982.

	$850	$775	$700	$650	$600	$550	$495

Add approx. $160 for accessories (barrel extension, case, and extra mag).

MAC 10A1 — similar to MAC 10 except fires from a closed bolt.

	$295	$275	$250	$230	$215	$200	$190

MAC 11 — similar to MAC 10 except in .380 ACP cal.

	$650	$595	$550	$525	$500	$480	$460

INTERARMS

Manufacturer/importer/distributor located in Alexandria, VA.

Interarms has imported a multitude of trademarks and models since the early 1960s. Most of the models shown below are recent imports, and specific information on older, limited import models can be obtained by contacting Interarms directly. The Astra, Rossi, Star, and Walther trademarks will be found in their own sections listed alphabetically in this text.

INTERARMS

Grading	100%	98%	95%	90%	80%	70%	60%

FEG PISTOLS

FEG pistols were imported by Interarms from Hungary during 1986-87 only.

FEG MODEL R-9 — 9mm Para., patterned after Browning Hi-Power, double action, 13 shot mag., blued finish, steel construction, checkered wood grips. Imported 1986-87 only.

	$275	$230	$200	$180	$165	$155	$145

Last Mfg.'s Sug. Retail was $375.

FEG MODEL PPH — .380 ACP, patterned after Walther PP, alloy frame, double action, plastic grips with thumbrest, blued finish. Imported 1986-87 only.

	$200	$170	$140	$125	$115	$105	$95

Last Mfg.'s Sug. Retail was $225.

HELWAN PISTOLS

Please refer to the Helwan section in this text.

NORINCO PISTOLS

MODEL 93 SPORTSMAN — .22 LR, semi-auto single action, patterned after the Colt Woodsman, 4.6 in. barrel, 10 shot mag., blue finish only with checkered plastic grips, loaded chamber indicator, new safeties include firing pin block and mag. release, 26 oz. Importation began 1992.

Mfg.'s Sug. Retail	$238	$180	$150	$125	$115	$105	$95	$85

VIRGINIAN REVOLVERS: SINGLE ACTION

Virginian Revolvers were previously imported from Europe by various manufacturers (including Hammerli of Switzerland). They were also manufactured in Midland, VA from 1976-1984. Older models with exceptional quality (including Hammerli guns) are worth a premium over values listed below.

VIRGINIAN DRAGOON STANDARD — improved action patterned after Colt S.A. design, 6 shot, .44 Mag. cal. only, 6, 7½, 8⅜, or 12 (Buntline) in. barrel, blue finish, smooth walnut grips, adj. rear sight, 51 oz. with 7½ in. barrel.

	$255	$225	$205	$190	$180	$170	$160

Add 15% for Buntline Model.
Last Mfg.'s Sug. Retail was $315.

Dragoon Standard Stainless — .44 Mag., 6 (disc.), 7½ (disc.), or 8⅜ in. barrel, same general specifications as Standard Dragoon.

	$265	$230	$210

Last Mfg.'s Sug. Retail was $315.

DRAGOON SILHOUETTE — .357 or .44 Mag. cal., stainless steel, 7½, 8⅜, or 10½ in. (standard on .357 Mag.) barrel, special sights and grips.

	$365	$320	$275

Last Mfg.'s Sug. Retail was $425.

DRAGOON ENGRAVED — .44 Mag. only, choice of stainless steel or blue finish, 6 or 7½ in. barrel.

	$545	$470	$430	$395	$360	$320	$285

Add $75 for presentation case.
Last Mfg.'s Sug. Retail was $625.

Grading	100%	98%	95%	90%	80%	70%	60%

DRAGOON "DEPUTY" — .357 or .44 Mag. cal., blued barrel, case hardened frame, 5 in. barrel only.

	100%	98%	95%	90%	80%	70%	60%
	$250	$215	$195	$180	$165	$155	$145

Last Mfg.'s Sug. Retail was $295.

⚞ Stainless Deputy — similar to above, except .44 Mag. available in 6 in. barrel only, stainless steel.

	100%	98%	95%
	$255	$225	$205

Last Mfg.'s Sug. Retail was $295.

VIRGINIAN .22 CONVERTIBLE — .22 LR/.22 Mag. cylinders, 5½ in. barrel only, adj. rear sight, 38 oz.

	100%	98%	95%	90%	80%	70%	60%
	$185	$155	$145	$135	$125	$115	$105

Last Mfg.'s Sug. Retail was $219.

⚞ Virginian .22 Convertible Stainless — stainless steel fabrication, otherwise similar to above.

	100%	98%	95%
	$200	$170	$155

Last Mfg.'s Sug. Retail was $239.

RIFLES: HOWA MFG.

MODEL 1500 HUNTER — .22-250, .223, .243, .270, .308, .30-06, .300 Win. Mag., or 7mm Rem. Mag. cal., 3 (Mag. cals. only) or 5 shot, 22 or 24 in. barrel, adj. rear sight and trigger, checkered walnut stock. Importation with Interarms 1988 only.

	100%	98%	95%	90%	80%	70%	60%
	$360	$310	$285	$260	$240	$225	$205

Add $15 for 7mm Rem. Mag./.300 Win. Mag. cal.
Last Mfg.'s Sug. Retail was $440.

⚞ Model 1500 Lightning — .270, .30-06, .300 Win. Mag., or 7mm Rem. Mag. cal., lightweight variation of the Model 1500 Hunter featuring lightweight Carbolite (synthetic) stock, 7 lbs. Imported 1988-91.

	100%	98%	95%	90%	80%	70%	60%
	$415	$335	$290	$260	$240	$225	$205

Add $20 for Mag. cals.
Last Mfg.'s Sug. Retail was $539.

MODEL 1500 TROPHY — .22-250, .223, .243, .270, .308, .30-06, .300 Win. Mag., .338 Win. Mag. or 7mm Rem. Mag. cal., 3 (Mag. cals. only) or 5 shot, 22 or 24 in. barrel, adj. rear sight and trigger, select Monte Carlo stock with skipline checkering. Imported 1988-92.

	100%	98%	95%	90%	80%	70%	60%
	$528	$410	$335	$290	$260	$240	$225

Add $20 for Mag. cals.
Last Mfg.'s Sug. Retail was $528.

⚞ Model 1500 Varmint — .22-250, .223, or .308 (new 1990) cal., 24 in. heavy barrel without sights, 5 shot mag., 7 lbs. 1 oz. Imported 1988-92.

	100%	98%	95%	90%	80%	70%	60%
	$435	$350	$300	$275	$255	$230	$210

Last Mfg.'s Sug. Retail was $565.

LIGHTNING RIFLE — .22-250, .223, .243, .270, .30-06, .308, 7mm Mag., .300 Win. Mag., or .338 Win. Mag. cal., 22 or 24 in. barrel, black synthetic Carbolite stock with cheekpiece and pressed checkering, no sights, 3 or 5 shot mag., high luster bluing, approx. 7 ½ lbs. Importation began 1993.

	100%	98%	95%	90%	80%	70%	60%
Mfg.'s Sug. Retail $498	$400	$350	$300	$250	$225	$200	$195

Add $19 for Mag. cals.

Grading	100%	98%	95%	90%	80%	70%	60%

REALTREE CAMO RIFLE — .270 or .30-06 cal., 22 in. barrel, 5 shot mag., monobloc receiver, drilled and tapped, thumb safety, entire rifle is coated with a Realtree brown leaf camo pattern, no sights, 8 lbs. Importation began 1993.

Mfg.'s Sug. Retail	$620	$495	$400	$350	$325	$300	$280	$260

RIFLES: MAUSER ACTIONS

Whitworth rifles are mfg. in England. Mark X rifles are currently mfg. in Yugoslavia by Zastava Arms.

MARK X VISCOUNT — .22-250, .243, .25-06, .270, 7 x 57mm, 7mm Mag., .308, .30-06, or .300 Win. Mag. cal., 5 shot, 3 shot mag., 24 in. barrel, adj. rear sight and trigger, classic style Monte Carlo stock. Disc. 1983, re-introduced 1985.

Mfg.'s Sug. Retail	$568	$440	$350	$300	$265	$240	$225	$205

Add $22 for 7mm Rem. Mag. or .300 Win. Mag. cal.

This model is often referred to as the Viscount. Early manufacture was done in Manchester, England. Recent manufacture is in Yugoslavia. Earlier Manchester guns (before approx. 1980) will bring a slight premium over the values listed above.

Mini Mark X — .223 or 7.62 X 39mm (new in 1990) cal., miniature M98 Mauser System action, 20 in. barrel with iron sights, checkered hardwood stock, 5 shot mag., adj. trigger, 6.35 lbs. New 1987.

Mfg.'s Sug. Retail	$527	$415	$355	$300	$250	$225	$200	$185

Lightweight Mark X — .270, .30-06, or 7mm Rem. Mag. cal., similar to Mark X Viscount, except has Carbolite (synthetic) stock and 20 in. barrel, 7 lbs. Mfg. in 1988-90.

		$435	$385	$340	$300	$270	$240	$215

Add $20 for 7mm Rem. Mag. cal.
Last Mfg.'s Sug. Retail was $519.

MARK X WHITWORTH — same cals. as Mark X Rifle, Mauser action, 24 in. barrel, open sights, 5 shot mag.(.300 Win. Mag. is only 3), checkered deluxe walnut with ebony forearm tip, thumb safety with sling swivels, adj. trigger, rubber recoil butt plate, 7 lbs. Imported since 1984.

Mfg.'s Sug. Retail	$700	$535	$425	$360	$320	$275	$250	$225

Add $22 for 7mm Rem. Mag. or .300 Win. Mag. cal.
This model was the Whitworth American Field Series until 1987. Early manufacture was done in Manchester, England. Recent manufacture is by Zastava located in Yugoslavia. Earlier Manchester guns (before approx. 1980) will bring a slight premium over the values listed above.

WHITWORTH MANNLICHER STYLE CARBINE — .243, .270, .308, 7 x 57mm, or .30-06 cal., bolt action with full length walnut Mannlicher style stock, open sights, sling swivels, thumb safety, 20 in. barrel, 5 shot mag., 7 lbs. Imported 1984-87.

		$570	$495	$455	$410	$375	$340	$310

Last Mfg.'s Sug. Retail was $675.

WHITWORTH EXPRESS RIFLE — .375 H&H or .458 Win. Mag. cal., 3 shot, 24 in. barrel, 3 leaf express sight, English style stock of walnut, checkered pistol grip forearm, 8½ lbs. Mfg. 1974-present.

Mfg.'s Sug. Retail	$870	$700	$615	$535	$465	$425	$395	$375

Grading	100%	98%	95%	90%	80%	70%	60%

RIFLES: BOLT-ACTION

MODEL JW-15 — .22 LR, 5 shot detachable mag., 23.8 in. barrel, open sights, blued finish, Model 70 style safety, patterned after the Brno Model ZKM, 5.5 lbs. Importation began 1990.

Mfg.'s Sug. Retail	$118	$95	$70	$60	$50	$40	$35	$30

This model is mfg. by Norinco in China.

ENFIELD NO. 4 — .303 British cal.

Mfg.'s Sug. Retail	$108	$85	$60	$50	$40	$35	$30	$30

RIFLES: SEMI-AUTO

22-ATD — .22 LR only, patterned after the Browning Semi-Auto, 19.4 in. barrel, 11 shot mag. in stock, blued finish, checkered hardwood stock, take-down design, adj. rear sight, 4.6 lbs. New 1987.

Mfg.'s Sug. Retail	$168	$140	$110	$100	$90	$80	$75	$70

Add $16 for camo case (disc.).
This model is mfg. by Norinco in China.

RIFLES: DISCONTINUED

CAVALIER — similar to Viscount, except modern style stock, roll-over cheek piece, rosewood pistol grip cap and forend tip, recoil pad. Disc.

	$365	$330	$305	$290	$265	$230	$195

MANNLICHER STYLE CARBINE — similar to Cavalier, except 20 in. barrel, full length stock, no Magnum or varmint calibers. Disc.

	$365	$330	$305	$290	$265	$230	$195

CONTINENTAL CARBINE — similar to Mannlicher Style, except with double set trigger. Disc.

	$395	$365	$330	$310	$285	$255	$220

THE MARQUIS — .243, .270, .308, 7x51mm, or .30-06 cal., 20 in. barrel, adj. trigger. Mannlicher style carbine. Disc. 1984.

	$430	$325	$300	$275	$250	$230	$215

ALASKAN — similar to Mark X, except .375 H&H or .458 Win. Mag. cal., recoil pad and extra stock crossbolt. Disc. 1984.

	$460	$350	$330	$310	$290	$250	$210

INTERDYNAMIC OF AMERICA, INC.
Previously distributed 1981-84 under the above heading out of Miami, FL.

KG-9 — 9mm Para., 3 in. barrel, open bolt, semi-auto paramilitary design pistol. Disc. approx. 1983.

	$750	$700	$650	$600	$575	$550	$525

KG-99 — 9mm Para., 3 in. barrel, semi-auto paramilitary design pistol, closed bolt, 36 shot mag, 5 in. vent. shroud barrel, blue only, also available in fully auto version (Class III only — add $140), a stainless steel version of the KG 99. Mfg. by Interdynamic 1984 only.

	$260	$200	$180	$160	$145	$130	$120
KG-99M, mini pistol	$213	$165	$155	$145	$135	$125	$115

INTRATEC
Manufacturer located in Miami, FL. Distributor sales only.

PROTECTOR SERIES PISTOLS

Grading	100%	98%	95%	90%	80%	70%	60%

PROTEC-22 — .22 LR cal., double action semi-auto, 2½ in. barrel, 10 shot mag., fixed sights, choice of black, satin, or Tec-Kote finish, black, grey, or driftwood colored wraparound grips, 13 oz. New 1993.
Prices had not been formalized on this model as this edition went to press.

PROTEC-25 — .25 ACP., double action only semi-auto, 2½ in. barrel, 8 shot mag., otherwise similar to Protec-22. New 1991.

	100%	98%	95%	90%	80%	70%	60%
Mfg.'s Sug. Retail	$100	$85	$65	$55	$40	$35	$30	$25

Add $5 for satin, Tec-Kote finish, or black slide/frame finish.

TEC-SERIES PISTOLS

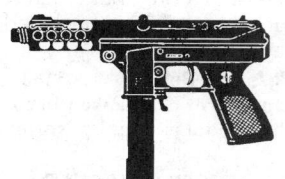

TEC-9 — 9mm Para., semi-auto paramilitary design pistol, 5 in. shrouded barrel, matte black finish, 32 shot mag. New 1985.

	100%	98%	95%	90%	80%	70%	60%
Mfg.'s Sug. Retail	$260	$225	$175	$155	$140	$130	$120	$110

⚡ **TEC-9K** — similar to TEC-9, except has new durable Tec-Kote finish with better protection than hard chrome. New 1991.

Mfg.'s Sug. Retail	$290	$245	$185	$160	$140	$130	$120	$110

⚡ **TEC-9S** — matte stainless version of the TEC-9.

Mfg.'s Sug. Retail	$353	$295	$240	$185

For above TEC-9 with accessory package (deluxe case, 3-36 shot mag.'s, paramilitary design grip, and recoil compensator), add $178.

TEC-9M — mini version of the Model TEC-9, including 3 in. barrel and 20 shot mag.

Mfg.'s Sug. Retail	$239	$200	$165	$150	$140	$130	$120	$110

⚡ **TEC-9MK** — similar to TEC-9M, except has Tec-Kote rust resistant finish. New 1991.

Mfg.'s Sug. Retail	$270	$235	$180	$155	$140	$130	$120	$110

⚡ **TEC-9MS** — matte stainless version of the TEC-9M.

Mfg.'s Sug. Retail	$330	$280	$225	$180

TEC-9C — 9mm, carbine variation with 16½ in. barrel, 36 shot mag. Only 1 gun mfg. 1987 - extreme rarity precludes pricing.

TEC-22 "SCORPION" — .22 LR, semi-auto pistol, paramilitary design, 4 in. barrel, ambidextrous safety, military matte finish, or electroless nickel, 30 shot mag., adj. sights, 30 oz. Mfg. 1988-90.

	$190	$165	$150	$135	$120	$100	$90

Add $20 for Tec-Kote finish.
Last Mfg.'s Sug. Retail was $202.

⚡ **TEC-22N** — similar to TEC-22, except has nickel finish. Mfg. 1990 only.

	$200	$175	$160	$140	$125	$105	$95

Add $16 for threaded barrel (Model TEC-22TN).
Last Mfg.'s Sug. Retail was $226.

Grading	100%	98%	95%	90%	80%	70%	60%

TEC-22T — threaded barrel variation of the TEC-22 "Scorpion". New 1991.

Mfg.'s Sug. Retail	$157	$145	$125	$110	$100	$90	$80	$70

Add $22 for Tec-Kote finish.

TEC-38 DERRINGER — .38 Spl., O/U, derringer, 3 in. barrel, blue frame, double action, 13 oz. Mfg. 1986-1988.

	$110	$95	$85	$75	$65	$60	$55

Last Mfg.'s Sug. Retail was $125.

PISTOLS: DOUBLE ACTION

CATEGORY 9 — 9mm Para. cal., double action only, black finish, polymer frame with top sight channel, only 27 parts, 7 shot mag., 21 oz. New 1993.
Prices have yet to be formalized on this model as this edition went to press.

IRWINDALE ARMS, INC. (IAI)
Previous manufacturer located in Irwindale, CA 1988-1991.

PISTOLS

In June, 1991, AMT retained manufacture of all IAI models.

AUTOMAG III — .30 Carbine or 9mm Win. Mag. (mfg. 1990-92), stainless steel only, 6⅜ in. barrel, patterned after Colt Gov.'t Model, Millett adj. sights with white outline, grooved Lexan grips, 8 shot mag., 43 oz. Mfg. 1989-91.

	$550	$475	$395

Last Mfg.'s Sug. Retail was $606.

AUTOMAG IV — .45 Win. Mag. or 10mm cal., semi-auto, 6½ or 8⅝ (mfg. 1991) in. barrel, 7 shot mag., Millett adj. sights, stainless steel only, 46 oz. Mfg. 1990-91.

	$565	$485	$500

Last Mfg.'s Sug. Retail was $630.

JAVELINA — 10mm, semi-auto, 5 (disc. 1991) or 7 in. barrel, 8 shot mag., Millett adj. sights, wraparound Neoprene grips, stainless steel, wide adj. trigger, long grip safety, 48 oz. Mfg. 1990-91.

	$525	$450	$375

Last Mfg.'s Sug. Retail was $570.

BACKUP PISTOL — .380 ACP cal., semi-auto action, 2½ in. barrel, stainless steel, Lexan grips, 5 shot mag. in 380, 18 oz. Older disc. walnut grip models are worth a slight premium. Disc. 1989.

	$200	$165	$135

Last Mfg.'s Sug. Retail was $243.

ISRAEL ARMS LTD.
Manufacturer located in Petah-Tikva Israel. Imported exclusively by J.O. Arms, Inc. located in Houston, TX.

KAREEN MK II — 9mm Para., semi-auto double action, 4.64 in. barrel, blue, matte, or chrome finish, 13 shot mag. New 1993.

Mfg.'s Sug. Retail	$350	$320	$285	$250	$225	$200	$185	$170

Add $40-$60 for special order chrome finish.

ISRAELI MILITARY INDUSTRIES (IMI)
Manufacturer located in Israel.

IMI manufactured guns (Galil, Magnum Research, Uzi, and others) can be located in their respective sections of this text.

ITALIAN MILITARY ARMS

Grading	100%	98%	95%	90%	80%	70%	60%

MODEL 1891 MANNLICHER-CARCANO — bolt action, 6.5mm, 6 shot, 31 in. barrel, straight handle, adj. sight, military stock.

	$120	$100	$85	$70	$55	$40	$30

MODEL 38 TERNI MILITARY RIFLE — 7.35mm, similar to 1891, except turned down bolt handle, 21 in. barrel and folding bayonet.

	$120	$100	$85	$70	$55	$40	$30

GLISENTI MODEL 1910 — 9mm Glisenti cal., 4 in. barrel, 7 shot mag., checkered wooden grips, official Italian service pistol of both WWI and WWII, 32 oz.

	$550	$400	$285	$250	$225	$200	$185

Warning: 9mm Parabellum ammunition cannot be used in this pistol - only 9mm Glisenti, as it is approx. 25% less powerful than the 9mm Para.

BRIXIA — similar to Glisenti Model 1910, except utilizes simplified mfg. techniques, mostly sold to civilians.

	$500	$400	$275	$240	$215	$190	$175

ITHACA GUN
Manufactured in Ithaca, NY, 1886 to Nov. of 1986. Re-opened in early 1987 as Ithaca Acquisition Corp. using the old trademark. In the past, Ithaca also absorbed companies including Syracuse Arms Co., Lefever Arms Co., Union Fire Arms Co., Wilkes-Barre Gun Co., as well as others.

On March 6, 1987 the Ithaca Gun Company was sold to Ithaca Acquisition Corporation doing business as Ithaca Gun Company. Currently, Ithaca is manufacturing the Model 87 slide action shotgun (previously designated the Model 37). While warranties do not apply from one company to the other, non-warranty repairs will be performed by Ithaca Gun at specified shop rates. Currently, Ithaca will perform repair services on Models 37, 51, 87, and Mag-10 only.

HANDGUNS

X-CALIBER SINGLE SHOT — .22 LR or .44 Mag. cal., break open action with contoured wooden grip and forearm, 10 or 15 in. barrel, unique dual firing pin detonates both rimfire and centerfire cartridges. Model 20 is target model (blued finish with Goncalo Alves wood grips), or Model 30 Hunting (sandblasted teflon finish with American walnut grips). Frames and barrels can be purchased separately. While advertised in 1988, this gun was only manufactured in .22 cal. with approx. 300 units being produced before production ceased due to unsolvable production problems. Mfg.'s Sug. Retail was $270.

RIFLES: BOLT ACTION

LSA-55 STANDARD — Mauser type action, .222, .22-250, 6mm, .243, or .308 cal., 22 in. barrel, leaf sight, 3 shot clip mag., checkered Monte Carlo stock. Mfg. in Finland by Tikka from 1969 to 1977.

	$400	$375	$350	$310	$275	$250	$230

Grading	100%	98%	95%	90%	80%	70%	60%

LSA-55 DELUXE — similar to Standard, except rollover cheekpiece, rosewood pistol grip cap and forend tip, skipline checkering, no sights, scope mounts furnished.

	$475	$415	$385	$350	$300	$280	$260

LSA-55 HEAVY BARREL — similar to LSA-55, except .222 or .22-250 only, target heavy barrel, special beavertail stock 8½ lbs.

	$450	$400	$375	$340	$295	$275	$255

LSA-65 — similar to LSA-55, except long action for calibers .25-06, .270, or .30-06. Mfg. 1969 to 1977.

	$400	$375	$350	$310	$275	$250	$230

LSA-65 DELUXE — similar to LSA-55 Deluxe, except .25-06, .270, or .30-06.

	$475	$415	$385	$350	$300	$280	$260

COMBINATION GUNS

LSA-55 TURKEY GUN — O/U shotgun-rifle combo, 12 ga., .222 Rem., 24½ in. ribbed barrel, exposed hammer, folding rear sight, checkered Monte Carlo stock. Mfg. by Tikka, Finland 1970-1981.

	$605	$550	$415	$495	$425	$385	$330

RIFLES: SEMI-AUTO

MODEL X5-C — .22 LR cal., 7 shot Mag., semi-auto action. Mfg. 1958-1964. Model X5-T has tube mag.

	$135	$110	$95	$80	$70	$60	$55

MODEL X-15 — .22 LR cal., similar to X5-C only forearm is not grooved. Mfg. 1964-1967.

	$135	$110	$95	$80	$70	$60	$55

RIFLES: LEVER ACTION

MODEL 49 SADDLEGUN — .22 LR cal., lever action, single shot. Mfg. 1961-1978. Martini-style action Mag. — add $15, deluxe model — add $45.

	$150	$115	$75	$60	$50	$45	$40

MODEL 49 PRESENTATION — like model 49, except gold-plated trigger, hammer, engraved receiver, fancy walnut. Mfg. 1962-1974.

	$220	$165	$155	$130	$120	$110	$100

MODEL 49 ST. LOUIS BICENTENNIAL — like deluxe model 49, except inscription on receiver, 200 mfg. 1964.

	$195	$160	$125

Last Mfg.'s Sug. Retail was $35.

Grading	100%	98%	95%	90%	80%	70%	60%

MODEL 72 SADDLEGUN — .22 or .22 mag., lever action, 18½ in. barrel, hooded front sight. Mfg. 1973-1978 by Erma Werke, W. Germany.

	100%	98%	95%	90%	80%	70%	60%
	$185	$140	$130	$110	$100	$90	$85

MODEL 72 DELUXE — similar to Model 72, except has silver finished engraved receiver, deluxe walnut, octagon barrel. Mfg. 1974-1976.

	100%	98%	95%	90%	80%	70%	60%
	$260	$195	$185	$155	$145	$130	$120

SHOTGUNS: SIDE X SIDE - EARLY PRODUCTION

ITHACA HAMMERLESS DOUBLE BARREL — 12, 16, 20, 28 or .410 ga., 26-32 in. barrels, boxlock, extractors, double triggers, any standard choke, checkered pistol grip stock and forearm, grades shown differ in overall quality, ornamentation, grade of wood, and style of checkering.

Values below are for guns mfg. between 1925-1948. Newer models can be found later in this section.
Add $200 for SST.
Add $150 for SNT.
Add $350 for VR on Grades 4, 5, 7, and $2,000 Grade.
Add $200 for VR - lower grades.
Add $175 for beavertail forearm.
Add 33% for auto ejectors on Grades No. 1, 2, and 3.
Subtract 33% if without ejectors on Grades 4E-7E.

NOTE: In 1925, the rotary bolt and stronger frame were adapted (ser. no.'s after 400,000 - commonly referred to as NID or New Ithaca Double). It is recommended that these guns (pre-400,000 ser. range) are not shot with modern ammo as their mechanisms are not as strong as the rotary bolt.

Early hammer doubles in average condition are approx. valued between $175-$450. However, if 60% condition remains (including original case colors), values can approximate those listed below.

100%	98%	95%	90%	80%	70%	60%	50%	40%	30%	20%	10%

FIELD GRADE

⚷ **10 ga. Mag.**

100%	98%	95%	90%	80%	70%	60%	50%	40%	30%	20%	10%
$2,000	$1,800	$1,500	$1,400	$1,300	$1,200	$1,100	$950	$825	$700	$575	$495

3½ in. chambered 10 ga. Mag.'s are serial numbered over 500,000. Total production was approx. 850 guns. 2⅞ in. chambered 10 ga.'s are priced the same as a 12 ga. A 12 ga., 3 in. model was also made on the 10 ga. frame - only 87 were mfg. and specimens are noted in the 500,000 serial range.

⚷ **12 ga.**

100%	98%	95%	90%	80%	70%	60%	50%	40%	30%	20%	10%
$1,000	$800	$600	$550	$500	$450	$415	$380	$350	$325	$300	$265

⚷ **16 ga.**

100%	98%	95%	90%	80%	70%	60%	50%	40%	30%	20%	10%
$1,000	$800	$600	$550	$500	$450	$415	$380	$350	$325	$300	$265

⚷ **20 ga.**

100%	98%	95%	90%	80%	70%	60%	50%	40%	30%	20%	10%
$1,200	$1,000	$800	$675	$575	$500	$450	$415	$380	$350	$325	$300

⚷ **28 ga.**

100%	98%	95%	90%	80%	70%	60%	50%	40%	30%	20%	10%
$2,000	$1,800	$1,500	$1,400	$1,300	$1,200	$1,100	$1,000	$925	$850	$775	$695

⚷ **.410 ga.**

100%	98%	95%	90%	80%	70%	60%	50%	40%	30%	20%	10%
$2,000	$1,800	$1,500	$1,400	$1,300	$1,200	$1,100	$1,000	$925	$850	$795	$750

	100%	98%	95%	90%	80%	70%	60%	50%	40%	30%	20%	10%

GRADE NO. 2

10 ga. Mag.
$2,400 $2,000 $1,800 $1,600 $1,400 $1,300 $1,200 $1,100 $950 $825 $700 $575

3½ in. chambered 10 ga. Mag.'s are serial numbered over 500,000. Total production was approx. 850 guns. 2⅞ in. chambered 10 ga.'s are priced the same as a 12 ga.

12 ga.
$1,500 $1,200 $1,000 $800 $600 $550 $500 $450 $415 $380 $350 $325

16 ga.
$1,500 $1,200 $1,000 $800 $600 $550 $500 $450 $415 $380 $350 $325

20 ga.
$1,800 $1,500 $1,200 $1,000 $800 $600 $550 $500 $450 $415 $380 $350

28 ga.
$2,500 $2,000 $1,800 $1,500 $1,400 $1,300 $1,200 $1,100 $1,000 $925 $850 $775

.410 ga.
$2,500 $2,000 $1,800 $1,500 $1,400 $1,300 $1,200 $1,100 $1,000 $925 $850 $795

GRADE NO. 3

10 ga. Mag.
$3,000 $2,500 $2,100 $1,800 $1,600 $1,400 $1,300 $1,200 $1,100 $950 $825 $700

3½ in. chambered 10 ga. Mag.'s are serial numbered over 500,000. Total production was approx. 850 guns. 2⅞ in. chambered 10 ga.'s are priced the same as a 12 ga.

12 ga.
$1,850 $1,500 $1,200 $1,000 $800 $600 $550 $500 $450 $415 $380 $350

16 ga.
$1,850 $1,500 $1,200 $1,000 $800 $600 $550 $500 $450 $415 $380 $350

20 ga.
$1,800 $1,500 $1,200 $1,000 $800 $600 $550 $500 $450 $415 $380 $350

28 ga.
$3,200 $2,800 $2,400 $2,100 $1,800 $1,500 $1,400 $1,300 $1,200 $1,100 $1,000 $925

.410 ga.
$3,400 $2,950 $2,500 $2,150 $1,800 $1,500 $1,400 $1,300 $1,200 $1,100 $1,000 $925

GRADE NO. 4E — auto ejectors.

10 ga. Mag.
$4,000 $3,500 $3,000 $2,500 $2,100 $1,800 $1,600 $1,400 $1,300 $1,200 $1,100 $950

3½ in. chambered 10 ga. Mag.'s are serial numbered over 500,000. Total production was approx. 850 guns. 2⅞ in. chambered 10 ga.'s are priced the same as a 12 ga.

12 ga.
$3,000 $2,500 $2,200 $1,850 $1,500 $1,200 $1,000 $800 $600 $550 $500 $450

16 ga.
$3,000 $2,500 $2,200 $1,850 $1,500 $1,200 $1,000 $800 $600 $550 $500 $450

	100%	98%	95%	90%	80%	70%	60%	50%	40%	30%	20%	10%

⚞ 20 ga.

	100%	98%	95%	90%	80%	70%	60%	50%	40%	30%	20%	10%
	$4,000	$3,500	$3,000	$2,500	$2,200	$1,850	$1,500	$1,200	$1,000	$800	$600	$550

⚞ 28 ga.
Extreme rarity factor precludes accurate pricing evaluation.

⚞ .410 ga.
Extreme rarity factor precludes accurate pricing evaluation.

GRADE NO. 5E — auto ejectors.

⚞ 10 ga. Mag.

	100%	98%	95%	90%	80%	70%	60%	50%	40%	30%	20%	10%
	$5,000	$4,500	$4,000	$3,500	$3,000	$2,500	$2,100	$1,800	$1,600	$1,400	$1,200	$1,000

3½ in. chambered 10 ga. Mag.'s are serial numbered over 500,000. Total production was approx. 850 guns. 2⅞ in. chambered 10 ga.'s are priced the same as a 12 ga.

⚞ 12 ga.

	100%	98%	95%	90%	80%	70%	60%	50%	40%	30%	20%	10%
	$4,250	$3,250	$2,600	$2,200	$1,850	$1,500	$1,200	$1,000	$800	$600	$550	$500

⚞ 16 ga.

	100%	98%	95%	90%	80%	70%	60%	50%	40%	30%	20%	10%
	$4,250	$3,250	$2,600	$2,200	$1,850	$1,500	$1,200	$1,000	$800	$600	$550	$500

⚞ 20 ga.

	100%	98%	95%	90%	80%	70%	60%	50%	40%	30%	20%	10%
	$4,800	$4,100	$3,500	$3,000	$2,500	$2,200	$1,850	$1,600	$1,400	$1,200	$1,000	$895

⚞ 28 ga.
Extreme rarity factor precludes accurate pricing evaluation.

⚞ .410 ga.
Extreme rarity factor precludes accurate pricing evaluation.

GRADE NO. 6E — auto ejectors.

⚞ 10 ga. Mag.

	100%	98%	95%	90%	80%	70%	60%	50%	40%	30%	20%	10%
	$5,600	$5,000	$4,500	$4,000	$3,500	$3,000	$2,500	$2,100	$1,800	$1,600	$1,400	$1,200

3½ in. chambered 10 ga. Mag.'s are serial numbered over 500,000. Total production was approx. 850 guns. 2⅞ in. chambered 10 ga.'s are priced the same as a 12 ga.

⚞ 12 ga.

	100%	98%	95%	90%	80%	70%	60%	50%	40%	30%	20%	10%
	$4,750	$4,000	$3,250	$2,600	$2,200	$1,850	$1,500	$1,200	$1,000	$800	$600	$550

⚞ 16 ga.

	100%	98%	95%	90%	80%	70%	60%	50%	40%	30%	20%	10%
	$4,750	$4,250	$3,250	$2,600	$2,200	$1,850	$1,500	$1,200	$1,000	$800	$600	$550

⚞ 20 ga.

	100%	98%	95%	90%	80%	70%	60%	50%	40%	30%	20%	10%
	$5,350	$4,675	$4,100	$3,500	$3,000	$2,500	$2,200	$1,850	$1,600	$1,400	$1,200	$995

⚞ 28 ga.
Extreme rarity factor precludes accurate pricing evaluation.

⚞ .410 ga.
Extreme rarity factor precludes accurate pricing evaluation.

GRADE NO. 7E — auto ejectors.

⚞ 10 ga. Mag. — extreme rarity factor precludes accurate pricing evaluation.
3½ in. chambered 10 ga. Mag.'s are serial numbered over 500,000. Total production was approx. 850 guns. 2⅞ in. chambered 10 ga.'s are priced the same as a 12 ga.

	100%	98%	95%	90%	80%	70%	60%	50%	40%	30%	20%	10%

⚔ 12 ga.

100%	98%	95%	90%	80%	70%	60%	50%	40%	30%	20%	10%
$9,250	$8,300	$7,400	$6,500	$5,650	$4,750	$4,000	$3,250	$2,600	$2,100	$1,600	$1,150

⚔ 16 ga.

100%	98%	95%	90%	80%	70%	60%	50%	40%	30%	20%	10%
$9,250	$8,300	$7,400	$6,500	$5,650	$4,750	$4,000	$3,250	$2,600	$2,100	$1,600	$1,150

⚔ 20 ga.

100%	98%	95%	90%	80%	70%	60%	50%	40%	30%	20%	10%
$10,400	$9,250	$8,300	$7,400	$6,500	$5,650	$4,750	$4,000	$3,250	$2,600	$2,100	$1,600

⚔ 28 ga.
   Extreme rarity factor precludes accurate pricing evaluation.

⚔ .410 ga.
   Extreme rarity factor precludes accurate pricing evaluation.

$2,000 GRADE — 12 ga., top-of-the-line model, auto ejectors, single selective trigger.

100%	98%	95%	90%	80%	70%	60%	50%	40%	30%	20%	10%
$11,000	$9,500	$8,450	$7,400	$6,500	$5,650	$4,750	$4,000	$3,250	$2,600	$2,100	$1,600

   Rarity on 16 or 20 ga. precludes accurate pricing.

PRE-WAR $1,000 GRADE — 12 ga., top-of-the-line models, auto ejectors, single selective trigger.

100%	98%	95%	90%	80%	70%	60%	50%	40%	30%	20%	10%
$13,000	$11,000	$9,500	$8,450	$7,400	$6,500	$5,650	$4,750	$4,000	$3,250	$2,600	$2,100

   Rarity on 16 or 20 ga. precludes accurate pricing.

SOUSA GRADE — has mermaids on trigger guard in gold, only 11 manufactured (including one .410 ga.). This model is very rare and prices are hard to establish. Recently, the price range has been approx. $15,000-$40,000, depending on original condition.
   This model had help in development by the famous band director and composer, John Phillip Sousa.

SHOTGUNS: SINGLE BARREL TRAP

Grading	100%	98%	95%	90%	80%	70%	60%

CENTURY TRAP — 12 ga., 32 or 34 in. VR barrel, engraved, auto ejector, full choke, checkered walnut stock. Mfg. 1973 and 1976 by SKB.

100%	98%	95%	90%	80%	70%	60%
$550	$525	$470	$440	$385	$360	$320

CENTURY II TRAP — improved trap stock version of Century, Monte Carlo stock.

100%	98%	95%	90%	80%	70%	60%
$600	$550	$495	$470	$415	$385	$350

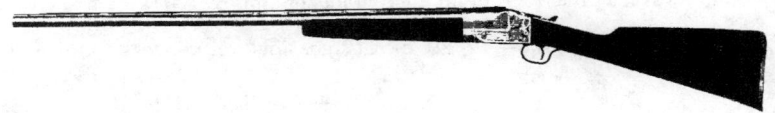

SINGLE BARREL TRAP — 12 ga., 30, 32, or 34 in. barrels, VR, boxlock, auto ejector, checkered pistol grip and forearm, grades differ in engraving, overall workmanship, and grade or wood and checkering. Values on these models sometimes vary greatly depending on originality of finish, customer alterations, and other variations trap shooters might use to alter dimensions for their particular shooting requirements. Below values represent trap guns in original, unaltered condition.
   Note: Flues model mfg. prior to 1921 with serial numbers under 400,000 generally have better engraving than NID models. It is recommended that shotguns serial numbered under 400,000 should not be fired using modern ammunition.

   Trap guns under 60% original condition will be within 25% of the value shown in the 60% column.

Grading	100%	98%	95%	90%	80%	70%	60%

Knick Model — mfg. 1921-disc. Serial numbered above 400,000. Can be distinguished by triple underbolt locking.

	$1,395	$1,000	$900	$800	$675	$600	$550

Victory Grade — disc. 1938.

	$995	$850	$775	$675	$575	$495	$440

No. 4E — disc. 1976.

	$1,500	$1,200	$1,000	$875	$750	$650	$595

No. 5E — 12 ga., 32 or 34 in. barrel, custom order only, elaborate engraving, quality workmanship throughout. Originally mfg. 1925-1986, mfg. resumed 1988-91.

	$2,950	$2,550	$2,175	$1,900	$1,725	$1,495	$1,300

Last Mfg.'s Sug. Retail was $7,500.

No. 6E — this model was available by special order only. Rarity factor precludes accurate pricing.

No. 7E — disc. 1964.

	$3,950	$3,450	$3,000	$2,750	$2,475	$2,225	$1,995

Dollar Grade — 12 ga., 32 or 34 in. barrel. Top-of-the-line model custom built to customer specifications. Original mfg. was stopped 1986 and resumed 1988-91.

	$5,950	$5,200	$4,600	$3,850	$3,250	$2,775	$2,250

Last Mfg.'s Sug. Retail was $10,000.

$5,000 Grade — similar to Pre-War $1,000 grade.

	$9,500	$8,900	$8,175	$7,650	$6,725	$5,825	$4,950

Sousa Grade — extremely rare.
Extreme rarity factor precludes accurate pricing evaluation. Prices will be higher than the $5,000 Grade.

SHOTGUNS: MISCELLANEOUS

AUTO & BURGLAR S X S — 20 ga., 10 or 14 in. barrels, with or without cocking indicators, blue finish, pistol grip, classified as Curio (short barreled shotgun status) in 1977 - must be registered, offered in Model A (has grip spur on back of pistol grip) or B (squared grips). Approx. 4,500 mfg. 1922-1933.

	$1,050	$925	$775	$725	$675	$650	$575

This model was manufactured in production lots of approx. 100 (as demand dictated).

MODEL 66 LEVER ACTION — 12, 20, or .410 ga. single shot lever action, field gun only. Mfg. 1963-1978.

	$125	$95	$90	$75	$70	$65	$55

Add 33% to .410 ga.
Add 25% for VRs that were also available on special order.

Model 66 RS — 20 ga. slug gun with 22 in. barrel and rifle type sights, recoil pad.

	$150	$130	$110	$90	$80	$70	$60

Note: Ventilated ribs were also available on special order — add 25%.

SKB SHOTGUNS: PREVIOUSLY IMPORTED BY ITHACA

Note: Can be found under SKB heading.

Grading	100%	98%	95%	90%	80%	70%	60%

SHOTGUNS: SLIDE ACTION

In 1987, Ithaca Acquisition Corp. reintroduced the Model 37 as the Model 87. New Model 87s are listed below and also include pre-1986 mfg. (Model 37s). Unless a particular Model 37 specimen has rare features, special wood, or was a deluxe order, values will approximate most older models as well.

MODEL 37 TRENCH AND RIOT GUNS — see separate listing under Trench Guns in the T Section.

MODEL 37 FEATHERLIGHT STANDARD — 12, 16, or 20 ga., bottom ejection, 4 shot mag., 26, 28, or 30 in. barrel, hammerless, take down, any standard choke. Mfg. 1937-disc.

	$260	$225	$205	$185	$165	$150	$135

MODEL 37V — similar to 37, except VR. Mfg. 1962-disc.

	$315	$260	$240	$195	$180	$170	$165

All currently manufactured Model 37s have the Featherlight designation. Prices above are for older manufactured Model 37's.

MODEL 37D — similar to 37, except recoil pad, beavertail forearm, checkered. Mfg. 1954-1981.

	$360	$275	$255	$205	$195	$185	$175

MODEL 37DV — similar to 37D, except VR. Mfg. 1962-1981.

	$395	$320	$295	$245	$225	$200	$185

MODEL 37 FIELD GRADE MAGNUM — 12 or 20 ga., 3 in. chambers, VR, walnut stock and corncob forearm, supplied with three choke tubes. Mfg. 1984-1986.

	$300	$240	$195	$180	$170	$165	$150

Last Mfg.'s Sug. Retail was $428.

MODEL 37 FIELD GRADE STANDARD — 12 or 20 ga., economy model, corncob forearm, 26, 28, or 30 in. barrel. Mfg. 1983-1985 only.

	$260	$225	$205	$180	$165	$150	$135

Last Mfg.'s Sug. Retail was $298.

MODEL 37 ENGLISH ULTRALITE — 12 or 20 ga., 25 or 26 in. barrels, world's lightest pump, 20 ga. weighs 4¾ lb., 12 ga. weighs 5½ lbs., checkered straight stock. Mfg. 1983-1986.

	$350	$310	$275	$250	$225	$200	$180

Last Mfg.'s Sug. Retail was $522.

MODEL 37R — solid rib. Mfg. 1937-1967.

	100%	98%	95%	90%	80%	70%	60%
Plain stock	$340	$200	$175	$145	$130	$110	$90
Checkered stock	$380	$220	$200	$175	$165	$145	$120

MODEL 37R DELUXE — similar to 37R, except fancy wood. Mfg. 1937-1955.

	$440	$275	$255	$230	$210	$195	$165

MODEL 37S SKEET GRADE — similar to 37, except Knicker VR, large forearm, fancy wood. Mfg. 1937-1955.

	$475	$425	$375	$335	$300	$275	$250

MODEL 37T TRAP GRADE — similar to 37S, except trap stock, select walnut, recoil pad. Mfg. 1937-1955.

	$475	$425	$375	$325	$295	$275	$250

Add 20% for early models with Fleur-de-lis checkering.

Grading	100%	98%	95%	90%	80%	70%	60%

MODEL 37T TARGET GRADE — replaced 37S and 37T. Mfg. from 1955-1961.

	100%	98%	95%	90%	80%	70%	60%
	$475	$425	$375	$325	$295	$275	$250

MODEL 37 SUPER DELUXE DEERSLAYER — similar to Model 37 (87) Deerslayer, except fancy wood. Mfg. 1962-1985.

	100%	98%	95%	90%	80%	70%	60%
	$390	$335	$300	$270	$235	$210	$185

Last Mfg.'s Sug. Retail was $447.

MODEL 37 BICENTENNIAL — 12 ga., engraved, fancy wood, cased with pewter buckle, 1,776 mfg. 1976, 100% value assumes NIB condition with case and belt buckle.

	100%	98%	95%	90%	80%	70%	60%
	$425	$375	$340	$315	$295	$270	$250

MODEL 37 2500 SERIES CENTENNIAL — 12 ga., customized version of the Model 37 commemorating Ithaca's 100th year anniversary, silver plated, etched antique finish receiver, deluxe walnut. Mfg. 1980-1984.

	100%	98%	95%	90%	80%	70%	60%
	$850	$690	$600	$505	$460	$415	$370

Last Mfg.'s Sug. Retail was $919.

MODEL 37 PRESENTATION — 12 ga., blued, engraved, gold mounted receiver with extra-fancy walnut, cased, limited production. Mfg. 1981-86.

	100%	98%	95%	90%	80%	70%	60%
	$1,475	$1,245	$1,080	$915	$830	$745	$665

Last Mfg.'s Sug. Retail was $1,658.

MODEL 37 DUCKS UNLIMITED — 12 ga., VR.

	100%	98%	95%
	$385	$305	$275

MODEL 37 $1000 GRADE — all gauges, deluxe engraving and checkering, gold inlaid, select figured walnut, hand-finished parts. Mfg. 1937-1940.

	100%	98%	95%	90%	80%	70%	60%
	$5,750	$5,200	$4,750	$4,250	$3,750	$3,250	$2,650

MODEL 37 $5000 GRADE — similar to $1000 Grade, post-war designation. Mfg. 1947-1967.

	100%	98%	95%	90%	80%	70%	60%
	$5,250	$4,850	$4,250	$3,850	$3,250	$2,850	$2,250

MODEL 87 FIELD GRADE — 12 or 20 ga., 3 in. chamber, economy model, walnut stock and forearm with pressed checkering, 26, 28, or 30 in. barrel with 3 choke tubes standard. Reintroduced 1989, disc. 1992.

	100%	98%	95%	90%	80%	70%	60%
	$350	$300	$275	$240	$210	$185	$165

Last Mfg.'s Sug. Retail was $427.

⚔ **Model 87 Basic Field Combo** — 12 or 20 ga., includes 20/25 in. deer barrel with special bore and 28 in. VR multi-choke field barrel, unchecked walnut stock and corncob forearm, 7 lbs. Mfg. 1989-92.

	100%	98%	95%	90%	80%	70%	60%
	$360	$290	$250	$200	$175	$160	$145

Add $32 for rifled bore barrel.
Add $104 for laminated wood (includes rifle bored barrel).
Last Mfg.'s Sug. Retail was $459.

⚔ **Model 87 Camo Field** — 12 ga. only, 3 in. chamber, 24, 26, or 28 in. VR barrel, camo-seal rust resistant finish on exterior parts. Available in either green or brown, includes sling and swivels. Mfg. began 1986, resumed 1988.

Mfg.'s Sug. Retail	$458		98%	95%	90%	80%	70%	60%
			$360	$290	$250	$200	$175	$160	$145

Grading	100%	98%	95%	90%	80%	70%	60%

Model 87 Turkey Field — 12 ga. only, 24 in. VR barrel with choice of fixed full choke or full choke tube, camo or matte blue finish. New 1989.

Mfg.'s Sug. Retail	$380	$310	$265	$225	$190	$170	$160	$145

Add $43 for camo finish.
Add $14 for full choke tube.

Model 87 Deluxe — similar to Model 87 Field Grade except has cut checkering, high gloss lacquer finish, and gold trigger, newer mfg. includes 3 choke tubes. New 1989.

Mfg.'s Sug. Retail	$463	$395	$350	$295	$245	$220	$190	$170

Add $54 for combo package (includes 20 in. special bore deer barrel, disc. 1992).
Add $87 for combo package with 20 or 25 in. rifled bore deer barrel, disc. 1992.

Model 87 Deluxe Magnum — 12 or 20 ga., 3 in. chambers, VR, deluxe wood with checkered forearm. Mfg. 1981-1986, production resumed 1988 only.

	$320	$270	$230	$210	$200	$185	$165

Add $77 for Combo package (extra 28 in. barrel).
Last Mfg.'s Sug. Retail was $395.
New mfg. 20 ga. shotguns were available with a 25 in. barrel only (with choke tubes).

MODEL 87 ULTRALITE FIELD
— 12 or 20 ga., 3 in. chamber, aluminum receiver, 20 (disc. 1988), 24, 25 (disc. 1988), or 26 in. barrel. 20 ga. weighs 5 lbs., 12 ga. weighs 5¾ lbs, multi-chokes (3) became standard in 1989. Originally mfg. 1988-86, reintroduced 1988-90.

	$400	$340	$285	$240	$210	$190	$170

Add $50 for slim grip model (12½ in. stock - disc. 1985).
Subtract $42 if without multiple choke feature.
The 20 and 25 in. barrels were disc. when mfg. was resumed 1988.
Last Mfg.'s Sug. Retail was $481.

Model 87 Ultra Deluxe — similar to Ultralite Field except has cut checkering, high gloss lacquer finish, and gold trigger. Mfg 1989-91.

	$425	$360	$300	$250	$220	$190	$170

Last Mfg.'s Sug. Retail was $514.

ENGLISH 87
— 20 ga. only, 3 in. chamber, 24 or 26 in. VR barrel with 3 choke tubes, steel receiver, checkered walnut stock and forearm, recoil pad, 6¾ lbs. New 1991.

Mfg.'s Sug. Retail	$463	$395	$350	$295	$245	$220	$190	$170

MODEL 87 SUPREME GRADE
— 12 or 20 ga., presentation walnut, high luster blue, limited production, previously available in either trap, skeet, or field models, fixed chokes. Originally manufactured 1967-86, reintroduced 1988.

Mfg.'s Sug. Retail	$668	$525	$425	$380	$320	$295	$270	$250

BASIC DEERSLAYER
— 12 ga. only, 20 or 25 in. special bore barrel, oil finished stock and corncob forearm with no checkering, iron sights, matte metal finish, 7 lbs. New 1989.

Mfg.'s Sug. Retail	$391	$320	$265	$230	$195	$175	$160	$145

MODEL 87 FIELD DEERSLAYER
— 12 or 20 ga., rifle slug barrel, 20 or 25 in. special bore barrel, open sights. Mfg. 1959-86, reintroduced 1988.

Mfg.'s Sug. Retail	$364	$300	$250	$210	$180	$160	$150	$140

Model 87 Deluxe Deerslayer — similar to Field Deerslayer except has cut checkering, high gloss lacquer finish, and gold trigger. New 1989.

Mfg.'s Sug. Retail	$400	$325	$275	$235	$195	$175	$160	$145

Add $33 for rifled bore.
Add $120 for combo package (28 in. multi-choke barrel).

Grading	100%	98%	95%	90%	80%	70%	60%

Model 87 Ultra Deerslayer — similar to Deluxe Deerslayer except has aluminum frame. Mfg. 1989-90 only.

		$350	$285	$245	$200	$175	$160	$145

Last Mfg.'s Sug. Retail was $444.

MONTE CARLO DEERSLAYER II — 12 ga. only, 25 in. barrel with rifling, Monte Carlo stock and forearm with cut checkering, receiver is drilled and tapped for scope mounting, 7 lbs. New 1989.

Mfg.'s Sug. Retail	$489	$400	$350	$300	$250	$220	$190	$170

DEERSLAYER II BRENNEKE — 12 ga. only, 25 in. rifled permanently fixed barrel, Monte Carlo stock with checkering, receiver is drilled and tapped. Mfg. began 1992.

Mfg.'s Sug. Retail	$550	$440	$385	$325	$275	$235	$200	$180

MODEL 87 MILITARY & POLICE — 12 or 20 (new 1989) ga., short barrel Model 37 w/normal stock or pistol grip only, 18½ or 20 in. barrel, 5 or 8 shot. Originally disc. 1983, reintroduced 1988.

Mfg.'s Sug. Retail	$323	$265	$230	$200	$180	$170	$160	$150

Add $104 for nickel finish (mfg. 1991-92 only).
Subtract $35 without parkerizing (disc.).

SHOTGUNS: SEMI-AUTO

MODEL 51A FEATHERWEIGHT STANDARD — 12 or 20 ga., 30 in. full, 28 in. full or mod., 26 in. imp. cyl., gas operated, autoloading, checkered pistol grip stock. Mfg. 1970-1985. Vent. rib became standard during late production.

Older models (no VR)		$285	$230	$200	$180	$165	$150	$130

Recent production — with VR.

		$325	$295	$275	$250	$225	$195	$165

Last Mfg.'s Sug. Retail with VR was $477.

MODEL 51A MAGNUM — similar to 51 Standard, except 3 in. shells only, blue finish, recoil pad, VR became standard in 1984. Disc. for 1985.

Older models with no VR		$295	$255	$220	$205	$180	$165	$150
Vent. rib		$350	$310	$280	$255	$230	$200	$170

MODEL 51A MAGNUM WATERFOWLER — similar to 51 Standard, except 3 in. shells only, matte finished metal & flat finished walnut, recoil pad. Vent. rib standard. Mfg. 1984-1986.

		$365	$325	$280	$255	$230	$200	$180

Add $40 for camouflaged exterior finish (mfg. 1986 only).
Last Mfg.'s Sug. Retail was $625.

MODEL 51A SUPREME TRAP — similar to 51 Standard, except 12 ga. only, 30 in. barrel, 7 post rib, full choke, select wood, pad, trap style stock. Add $36 for Monte Carlo. Mfg. 1970-1986.

		$425	$365	$315	$295	$270	$250	$230

Last Mfg.'s Sug. Retail was $869.

MODEL 51A SUPREME SKEET — similar to 51 Standard, except 26 in. VR barrel, skeet choke, select wood. Mfg. 1970-present. 20 ga. was available 1983. Disc. 1986.

		$465	$395	$340	$300	$280	$260	$240

Last Mfg.'s Sug. Retail was $858.

Grading	100%	98%	95%	90%	80%	70%	60%

MODEL 51A DEERSLAYER — similar to 51 Standard, with 24 in. slug barrel, rifle sights, recoil pad, no rib. Mfg. 1972-1983.

	$350	$300	$260	$230	$195	$180	$165

Last Mfg.'s Sug. Retail was $477.

MODEL 51A TURKEY GUN — .12 ga. Mag. only, 26 in. barrel, matte finish, sling and swivels included. Mfg. 1984-1986.

	$360	$305	$275	$265	$250	$230	$210

Last Mfg.'s Sug. Retail was $625.

MODEL 51 DUCKS UNLIMITED — similar to 51 Deluxe, with D/U emblem on receiver.

	$425	$375	$335	$300	$280	$260	$230

MODEL 51 PRESENTATION — 12 ga., blued, engraved, gold engraved receiver with deluxe walnut. Mfg. 1984-1986.

	$1,250	$1,000	$875	$700	$575	$450	$325

Last Mfg.'s Sug. Retail was $1,658.

SEMI-AUTO: MAG-10 SEMI-AUTO

All Ithaca Mag-10s were disc. 1986.

MAG-10 — 10 ga., 3½ in. Mag., semi-auto, various barrel lengths, stainless steel breech block assembly, gas operated, various chokes, plain barrel, 11 lb. Mfg. 1975-1986.
100% values assume NIB condition - if without, subtract 10%.

Standard Grade — no checkering, ribless barrel, dull finished wood.

	$600	$550	$500	$460	$430	$395	$375

Last Mfg.'s Sug. Retail was $726.

Standard Grade with VR — available in 22, 26, 28, or 32 in. barrel lengths - otherwise similar to Standard grade. Add $60 for camouflaged exterior finish.

	$675	$625	$575	$525	$480	$440	$395

Interchangeable choke tubes (3) became available in 1986 — add $60.
Last Mfg.'s Sug. Retail was $781.

Deluxe Vent — select checkered walnut stock and forearm, 22, 26, 28, or 32 in. barrels, high lustre wood finish.

	$750	$675	$600	$550	$495	$450	$400

Last Mfg.'s Sug. Retail was $924.

Supreme Grade — extra-select checkered walnut stock and forearm, otherwise similar to Deluxe Vent.

	$895	$800	$725	$675	$595	$550	$495

Last Mfg.'s Sug. Retail was $1,124.

Mag. 10 Roadblocker — 22 in. cylinder bored ribless barrel, parkerized finish.

	$625	$575	$500	$460	$430	$400	$375

Last Mfg.'s Sug. Retail was $741.

National Wild Turkey Fed. Special Edition — mfg. in 1985 only.

	$950	$795	$625

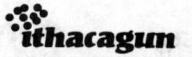 **cont.**

MAG-10 PRESENTATION OR CENTENNIAL — 10 ga. Mag., blued, engraved, gold inlaid receiver, extra fancy walnut. Limited production. Approx. 200 mfg. in Presentation Grade 1983-1986.

	100%	98%	95%	90%	80%	70%	60%
	$1,875	$1,550	$1,300	$1,050	$915	$830	$745

Last Mfg.'s Sug. Retail was $1,727.

PERAZZI SHOTGUNS

NOTE: Ithaca was sole importer for Perazzi in the 70s. All new and used models will be in the P section under Perazzi. Perazzi today distributes their own firearms.

J section

JSL (HEREFORD)

Manufacturer located in Hereford, England. Currently imported by Specialty Shooters Supply, Inc. located in Fort Lauderdale, FL. Direct sales only.

Grading	100%	98%	95%	90%	80%	70%	60%

SPITFIRE (G1) — 9mm Para. or 9 x 21mm cal., patterned after the Czech CZ-75/85, 3.7 in. barrel, ambidextrous safety, commander style hammer, black non-slip rubberized grip panels, investment cast stainless steel fabrication, 15 shot mag., 2.2 lbs. Importation began 1992.

 ⚔ **Spitfire Standard** — includes fixed rear sight, 2 mags., presentation case, and allen key.
 Mfg.'s Sug. Retail $1,332 $1,332 $1,100 $925
 Add $81 for adj. rear sight (Sterling Model).

 ⚔ **Super Sterling** — 9mm Para. or 9 x 21mm cal., 4.29 in. barrel with single port compensator, adj. rear sight.
 Mfg.'s Sug. Retail $1,640 $1,640 $1,325 $1,075

 ⚔ **Competition** — features slide with tapered rib, dual port compensator, match hammer, adj. rear sight and trigger stop.
 Mfg.'s Sug. Retail $1,854 $1,854 $1,525 $1,275

 ⚔ **Master** — features dual port compensator and fitted stainless steel bridge mount to accept aimpoint sight.
 Mfg.'s Sug. Retail $2,145 $2,145 $1,700 $1,475

 ⚔ **Squadron** — deluxe model with compensated barrel and other features including 4 mags., fitted leather case, and other premium accessories.
 Mfg.'s Sug. Retail $6,000 $6,000 $4,750 $3,250

 ⚔ **Battle of Britain 50th Anniversary Commemorative** — 9mm Para., 1,056 mfg. to commemorate aircraft Spitfire mfg. during WWII, special logos, checkered walnut grips, presentation cased.
 Mfg.'s Sug. Retail $1,927 $1,927 $1,575 $1,275

JACKSON HOLE FIREARMS

Previous manufacturer located in Jackson Hole, WY during the mid-70's.

RIFLES

BOLT ACTION RIFLE — various cals., Mauser 98 action utilizing patented system for interchangeable barrels, checkered walnut stock.

	$1,050	$875	$800	$725	$650	$575	$495

Jackson Hole Firearms manufactured a limited quantity of their unique interchangeable barrel bolt action rifles. Collectibility to date has been minimal, and values are affected by the J.P. Sauer Models 90 and 200 which also feature the interchangeable barrel design.

JAGD-UND SPORTWAFFEN SUHL GmbH

Manufacturer located in Suhl, Germany since 1535.

Currently, the famous Merkel trademark (mfg. by Jagd-Und Sportwaffen Suhl GmbH) is imported by Gun South Inc. located in Trussville, AL. Please refer to the Merkel listing in this text for current information regarding this older European trademark. See the Trademark Index in this text for current factory information.

JAPANESE MILITARY RIFLES

WWII manufacture in Tokyo, Japan.

NOTE: All Japanese rifles: deduct 20% if National Crest (chrysanthemum flower) has been ground off front receiver ring, deduct 20% if serial numbers are not matching, deduct 10-40% for training rifles of each type.

Grading	100%	98%	95%	90%	80%	70%	60%
MODEL 38 ARISAKA RIFLE — Jap. Mauser type action, 6.5mm, 31 in. barrel, adj. sight, adapted 1905.	$165	$135	$105	$95	$75	$65	$50
MODEL 38 CAVALRY CARBINE — similar to T38 Rifle, except shorter barrel. Mfg. 1911.	$175	$140	$110	$100	$80	$70	$55
MODEL 44 CAVALRY ARISAKA CARBINE — similar to T38 Carbine, 6.5mm with 19 in. barrel, folding bayonet.	$275	$235	$210	$190	$170	$155	$135
MODEL 99 SERVICE RIFLE — WWII version of 38, 7.7mm.	$165	$135	$110	$100	$80	$70	$55

Add 20% for monopod.

PARATROOPER TAKEDOWN VERSION — adopted 1940, crossbolt barrel lock.

	100%	98%	95%	90%	80%	70%	60%
Type 2	$395	$325	$265	$220	$190	$165	$135

NAMBU PISTOLS — See Nambu section in this text.

JARRETT RIFLES, INC.

Manufacturer located in Jackson, SC since 1979. Direct custom order sales only.

PISTOLS

CUSTOM XP-1 HUNTER — various cals., re-machined Remington XP-100 action, Jarrett match grade stainless steel barrel, McMillan fiberglass stock, various options.

	Mfg.'s Sug. Retail						
Mfg.'s Sug. Retail	$2,450	$2,450	$2,100	$1,800	$1,500	$1,250	$995	$850

RIFLES: BOLT ACTION

A wide variety of options is available for Jarrett custom rifles (holders of 16 world records in rifle accuracy). The factory should be contacted directly (see Trademark Index for info.) for pricing and availability regarding these special order options. Custom gunsmithing services are also available and again, the manufacturer should be contacted directly for gunsmith quotations. Custom gunsmithing requires individuals to supply receivers.

STANDARD HUNTING RIFLE — various cals., Remington Model 700 right hand or left hand action, McMillan fiberglass stock, blued receiver, Jarrett match grade barrel, sling studs and leather sling, rings and base, weights vary.

Mfg.'s Sug. Retail	$2,850	$2,850	$2,300	$1,850	$1,500	$1,250	$995	$850

ACCURACY LEGEND SERIES — similar to Standard Hunting Rifle, except has many accuracy tune-ups incorporated as well as muzzle brake, 100 mfg. Disc.

	$3,495	$2,850	$2,300	$1,850	$1,500	$1,250	$995

Last Mfg.'s Sug. Retail was $3,495.

PRIVATE COLLECTION — similar quality as the Standard Hunting Rifle, except many extra cost, special order options are included, ser. numbered 1-100. New 1993.

Mfg.'s Sug. Retail	$3,495	$3,495	$2,850	$2,300	$1,850	$1,500	$1,250	$995

Grading		100%	98%	95%	90%	80%	70%	60%

PROFESSIONAL HUNTER — .338 Win. Mag., .375 H&H, or .416 Rem. Mag. cal., features pre-64 Winchester Super Grade receiver with claw extractor and 3 position bolt shroud safety, Jarrett match grade stainless steel barrel, McMillan stock, quarter rib, includes 2 sets of detachable rings and two 1.5X-5X Leupold scopes, break down construction.

Mfg.'s Sug. Retail	$6,000	$6,000	$5,000	$4,250	$3,500	$2,850	$2,300	$1,850

SHOTGUNS

JARRETT ULTIMATE SHOTGUN — 12 ga., Remington Model 870 action with 21 in. hand lapped barrel with interchangeable chokes, 8 shot mag. extension, matte black or olive drab green finish.

Mfg.'s Sug. Retail	$1,450	$1,450	$1,175	$975	$850	$725	$600	$525

JEFFERY, W.J. & CO. LTD

Previously manufactured in London, England.

In addition to making a complete line of their own shotguns and rifles, W.J. Jeffery also was subcontracted by many other exporters, distributors, and retailers (including London's famous Army & Navy department store). Many models were produced and rather than list them individually, a generalized format has been adopted for determining values on both rifles and shotguns.

RIFLES

SINGLE SHOT — various cals., falling block action, checkered walnut stock and forearm, usually multiple folding leaves rear sight (also tangent), excellent quality. Prices start in the $600 range for poor condition specimens in obsolete or undesirable cals. and can go up to $5,000 for 100% condition in .600 Nitro Express.
Subtract substantially for the Martini action variation.

BOXLOCK DOUBLE RIFLE — many cals., various engraving patterns, top or under (usually large cals.) lever opening, multiple folding leaves rear sight, checkered walnut stock and forearm. Prices usually start in the $1,500 range for poor condition in undesirable cals. and can exceed $8,000 if encountered with elaborate engraving in .475 Express or larger cals.
Subtract approx. 40% if with hammers, over 50% if with damascus barrels.

SIDELOCK DOUBLE RIFLE — various cals., available in No. 1 or No. 2 grade, top-lever opening, best quality engraving, deluxe checkered walnut stock and forearm, almost any custom order could be filled. Prices start in the $3,250 range for 60% condition in smaller cals. and can easily go to $12,000+ when found in excellent condition in the larger cals.
Subtract approx. 40% if with hammers, over 50% if with damascus barrels.

SHOTGUNS

BOXLOCK SHOTGUN — most ga.'s, many combinations of options available, top-lever opening, many ranges of engraving, high quality and worksmanship. Values usually start in the $650 range if in poor condition and can go to $4,500+ if in a small ga. in near new condition ($1,750 for 12 ga.).
Subtract approx. 40% if with hammers, over 50% if with damascus barrels.

SIDELOCK SHOTGUN — most ga.'s, many combinations of options available, top-lever opening, many ranges of engraving, high quality and worksmanship. Values usually start in the $1,250 range if in poor condition and can go to $8,500+ if in a small ga. in near new condition ($3,950 for 12 ga.).

JENNINGS FIREARMS, INC.

Manufactured by Bryco Arms located in Irvine, CA. Distributed by Jennings Firearms, Inc. in Carson City, NV. Previously manufactured by Calwestco located in Chino, CA. Distributor sales only.

Grading	100%	98%	95%	90%	80%	70%	60%

PISTOLS: SEMI-AUTO

Bryco Arms will appear under the B section. All pistols below are single action.

MODEL J-22 — .22 LR cal., 6 shot, semi-auto single action, 2½ in. barrel, positive safety locks sear, satin nickel, bright chrome or black teflon finish, 13 oz.

Mfg.'s Sug. Retail	$76	$65	$50	$40	$35	$30	$30	$30

MODEL J-25 — .25 cal., aluminum alloy frame, 2.5 in. barrel, single action, synthetic ivory, walnut, or black combat grips, positive safety, 11 oz. New 1988.

Mfg.'s Sug. Retail	$66	$55	$40	$35	$30	$30	$30	$30

This model is available in either satin nickel, bright chrome, or black teflon finish.

MODEL M-38 — .22 LR, .32 ACP, or .380 ACP cal., semi-auto single action, 2.8 in. barrel, pressure cast fabrication using non-ferrous alloy, chrome or blue finish, black combat grips, 16 oz. New 1991.

Mfg.'s Sug. Retail	$90	$75	$60	$50	$45	$40	$35	$30

Add $10 for .380 ACP cal.

MODEL M-48 — .22 LR, .32 ACP, or .380 ACP cal., semi-auto single action, 4 in. barrel, larger frame variation of the M-38, chrome or blue finish, black combat grips, 24 oz. New 1991.

Mfg.'s Sug. Retail	$110	$95	$70	$60	$50	$40	$35	$30

MODELS M-49 & M-50 — while these 9mm Para. semi-auto pistols were advertised in 1991, they have yet to go into production.

JERICHO
Trademark of Israeli Military Industries (I.M.I.). Previously imported by K.B.I., Inc. located in Harrisburg, PA.

JERICHO 941 — 9mm Para., .41 Action Express (by conversion only), or .40 S&W cal. (new 1991), semi-auto double action or single action, 4.72 in. barrel with polygonal rifling, all steel fabrication, 3 dot Tritium sights, 11 or 16 (9mm) shot mag., ambidextrous safety, polymer grips, decocking lever, 38½ oz. Imported 1990-92.

	$550	$475	$425	$375	$325	$295	$260

Add $299 for .41 AE conversion kit.
Industrial hard chrome or nickel finishes are also available for all Jericho pistols. Contact K.B.I. for current pricing/availability.
Last Mfg.'s Sug. Retail was $649.

Jericho 941 Pistol Package — includes 9mm Para. and .40 S&W barrels, also includes .41 AE conversion kit, cased with accessories. Mfg. 1990-91 only.

	$695	$625	$550	$495	$450	$400	$360

Last Mfg.'s Sug. Retail was $775.

JERICHO 945 COMPACT — while advertised, this model was never mfg. Suggested retail was $629.

JOHNSON AUTOMATICS, INC.
Previous manufacturer located in Providence, RI.

MODEL 1941 — .30-06 or 7mm cal., semi-auto, 22 in. removable air cooled barrel, recoil operated, perforated metal handguard, aperture sight, military stock. Most were made for Dutch military, some used by Marine Paratroopers, during WWII all .30-06 and 7mm were ordered by South American governments.

	$850	$770	$720	$650	$600	$550	$500

Grading	100%	98%	95%	90%	80%	70%	60%

⚡ **7mm caliber** — subtract $50 because not original U.S. Military cal. Also deduct 10% if ser. no.'s don't match.

IVER JOHNSON ARMS, INC.

Manufactured in Fitchburg, MA, 1883-1984 and Jacksonville, AR 1984 to date. Formerly Johnson Bye & Co. 1871-1883. Renamed Iver Johnson & Co. in 1871 until 1891. Renamed Iver Johnson's Arms & Cycle Works in 1891 with manufacturing moving to Fitchburg, MA. In 1975 the name changed to Iver Johnson's Arms, Inc., and two years later, company facilities were moved to Middlesex, MA. In 1982, production was moved to Jacksonville, AR under the trade name Iver Johnson Arms, Inc. In 1983, Universal Firearms, Inc. was acquired by Iver Johnson Arms, Inc. Distributor sales only.

Iver Johnson Arms was sold in March of 1987 and was acquired by American Military Arms Corporation (AMAC). Currently, AMAC has reintroduced some older I. Johnson models, mostly using previously existing parts. In addition, AMAC has also introduced some newly designed models.

REVOLVERS

MODEL 1900 — .22, .32 S&W, or .38 S&W cal., double action, 2½, 4½, or 6 in. barrel, fixed sights, blue or nickel, rubber grips. Mfg. 1900-1947.

	$125	$80	$70	$60	$55	$45	$40

MODEL 1900 TARGET — .22 LR, 6 shot, 6 or 9½ in. barrel, blue, fixed sights. Mfg. 1925-1942.

	$140	$90	$80	$70	$65	$55	$50

TARGET SEALED 8 — .22 LR, 8 shot, 6 or 10 in. barrel, blue, fixed sights, rubber grips. Mfg. 1931-1957.

	$150	$100	$95	$80	$75	$65	$60

TARGET 9 SHOT — similar to Target Sealed 8, except 9 shot. Mfg. 1929-1946.

	$145	$90	$80	$70	$65	$55	$50

SAFETY HAMMER MODEL — .22 LR, .32 S&W, or .38 S&W cal., 2 or 3 in. barrel standard, 4, 5, or 6 in. available at extra cost, fixed sights, blue (standard) or nickel, break open. Mfg. 1892-1950.

	$150	$80	$70	$60	$55	$45	$40

SAFETY HAMMERLESS — .32 S&W or .38 S&W cal., 2, 3 (.32 only), or 3¼ in. barrel, double action only, break open, fixed sights, rubber grips, blue or nickel. Mfg. 1895-1950.

	$145	$100	$95	$80	$75	$65	$60

.22 SUPERSHOT — .22 LR, 6 in. barrel, blue, fixed sights, checkered wood grips, break open, no counterbore. Mfg. 1929-1949.

	$150	$80	$70	$60	$55	$45	$40

TRIGGER COCKING SINGLE ACTION — .22 LR, 8 shot, 6 in. barrel, break open, counterbored, blue, checkered wood grips, first pull on trigger cocks, second fires. Mfg. 1940-1947. Rare in 100% condition.

	$175	$120	$110	$95	$80	$75	$65

.22 TARGET SINGLE ACTION — .22 LR, 8 shot, 6 in. barrel, break open, counterbored, checkered wood, adj. grips and sights. Mfg. 1938-1948.

	$160	$120	$110	$95	$80	$75	$65

Iver Johnson Arms, Inc., cont.

Grading	100%	98%	95%	90%	80%	70%	60%

SUPERSHOT SEALED 8 — .22 LR, 8 shot, break open, blue, adj. sights, checkered wood grips. Mfg. 1931-1957.

	100%	98%	95%	90%	80%	70%	60%
	$175	$130	$120	$110	$90	$85	$75

SUPERSHOT 9 — similar to Sealed 8, only 9 shot, not counterbored. Mfg. 1929-1949.

	$135	$90	$80	$75	$60	$50	$40

PROTECTOR SEALED 8 — .22 LR, 8 shot, 2½ in. barrel, break open, fixed sights, blue, wood grips. Mfg. 1933-1949.

	$175	$135	$125	$110	$90	$80	$75

SUPERSHOT MODEL 844 — .22 LR, 8 shot, 4½ or 6 in. barrel, adj. sights, break open, blue, wood grips. Mfg. 1955-1956.

	$100	$90	$85	$80	$75	$60	$50

ARMSWORTH MODEL 855 — .22 LR, single action, 8 shot, 6 in. barrel, break open, blue, adj. sights, wood grips, adj. finger rest. Mfg. 1955-1957.

	$135	$125	$120	$110	$90	$80	$75

MODEL 55A TARGET — .22 LR, 8 shot, 4½ or 6 in. barrel, solid frame, blue, fixed sights, wood grips, loading gate. Mfg. 1955-1984.

	$75	$65	$55	$45	$35	$30	$15

CADET — .22 LR, .22 WRM, .32 S&W, .38 S&W, or .38 Spl. cal., 2½ in. barrel, blue, fixed sights, plastic grips. Mfg. 1955-1984.

	$110	$90	$80	$75	$65	$55	$50

MODEL 57A TARGET — .22 LR, 8 shot, 4½ or 6 in. barrel, solid frame, blue, adj. sights, wood grips. Mfg. 1955-1975.

	$100	$80	$75	$65	$55	$45	$40

MODEL 66 TRAILSMAN — .22 LR, 6 in. barrel, break open, blue, adj. sights, rebounding hammer, wood grips. Mfg. 1958-1975.

	$110	$90	$85	$75	$65	$55	$50

SIDEWINDER — .22 LR, 6 or 8 shot, 4¾ or 6 in. barrel, solid frame, blue, nickel, or case hardened plastic grips, wood on case color model. Mfg. 1961-present, 8 shot pre-1975.

	$110	$90	$85	$75	$65	$55	$50

SIDEWINDER S — similar to Sidewinder, except .22 WMR, interchangeable cylinder.

	$125	$100	$95	$85	$75	$65	$60

MODEL 67 VIKING — .22 LR, 8 shot, 4½ or 6 in. barrel, break open, blue, adj. sights, wood grips with thumbrest. Mfg. 1964-1975.

	$135	$110	$100	$95	$85	$75	$65

MODEL 67S VIKING — .22 LR, .32 S&W, or .38 S&W cal., 8 shot in .22, 5 shot in .32 or .38, 2¾ in. barrel, break open, adj. sights, plastic grips. Mfg. 1964-1975.

	$130	$100	$95	$85	$75	$60	$50

Grading	100%	98%	95%	90%	80%	70%	60%

AMERICAN BULLDOG — .22 LR, .22 WRM, or .38 Spl. cal., 6 shot in .22, 5 shot in .38, 2½ or 4 in. barrel, blue or nickel, adj. sights, plastic grips. Mfg. 1974-1976.

	$135	$110	$100	$90	$80	$65	$60

ROOKIE — .38 Spl., 5 shot, 4 in. barrel, solid frame, blue or nickel, plastic grips. Mfg. 1975-1984.

	$100	$80	$75	$65	$55	$45	$35

SPORTSMAN — .22 LR, 6 shot, 4¾ or 6 in. barrel, solid frame, blue, fixed sights, plastic grips. Mfg. 1974-1976.

	$100	$80	$75	$65	$55	$45	$35

DELUXE TARGET — similar to Sportsman, adj. sights. Mfg. 1975-1976.

	$110	$90	$85	$75	$65	$55	$40

SWING OUT — .22 LR, .22 WRM, .32 S&W, or .38 S&W cal., 6 shot in .22, 5 shot in .32 or .38, 2, 3, or 4 in. barrel, VR, 4 or 6 in., blue or nickel, fixed or adj. sights. Mfg. 1977-1984.

	$130	$110	$100	$90	$80	$75	$65

⚔ **VR Barrel** — 4 or 6 in. VR barrel, adj. sights.

	$170	$150	$140	$130	$125	$120	$100

PISTOLS: SEMI-AUTO

AMAC also manufactures a Super Enforcer .30 cal., Delta 786 9mm (disc. 1989), and a M-2 machine gun which are not listed in this text.

MODEL 9 — 9mm, double action, 6 shot mag., 3 in. barrel, blue or matte blue only, ambidextrous safety, smooth hardwood grips, 26 oz. Has not been released to date.

TRAILSMEN PISTOL — .22 LR only, semi-auto, all steel construction, 4½ or 6 in. barrel, blue finish, black checkered composition grips, 10 shot mag., approx. 30 oz. Mfg. 1985-86 and reintroduced 1990 only.

	$200	$165	$145	$130	$120	$110	$100

Add $20 for hardwood stocks and high polish blue (disc. 1990).
Last Mfg.'s Sug. Retail was $230.

PONY PISTOL (PO380 SERIES) — .380 ACP only, semi-auto single action, 3 in. barrel, 6 shot mag., all steel construction, blue or matte blue finish, 20 oz. Mfg. 1985-1986 (by Firearms International) and reintroduced 1990 only.

	$290	$245	$210	$185	$170	$155	$140

Last Mfg.'s Sug. Retail was $330.

⚔ **Pony .380 Stainless** — similar to Pony Pistol, except is stainless steel construction. New 1990 only.

	$315	$280	$240				

Last Mfg.'s Sug. Retail was $365.

⚔ **Nickel Pony** — with nickel finish. Mfg. 1985 only.

	$260	$230	$215	$200	$185	$170	$160

Last Mfg.'s Sug. Retail was $290 for nickel finish.

Grading	100%	98%	95%	90%	80%	70%	60%

POCKET PISTOL (TP SERIES) — .22 LR or .25 ACP cal., semi-auto, double action, 3 in. barrel, 7 shot finger tip extension mag., black plastic grips, fixed sights, blue or matte finish, 15 oz. Previously mfg. 1985-86, reintroduced 1988-90.

		$145	$125	$110	$100	$90	$80	$70

Add $15 for nickel finish (disc. 1989).
Last Mfg.'s Sug. Retail was $165.

AMAC-22/25 COMPACT — .22 Short (disc.) or .25 ACP cal., semi-auto, single action, 5 shot mag., 2 in. barrel, all steel construction, plastic grips, 9.3 oz.

Mfg.'s Sug. Retail	$200	$165	$135	$115	$100	$90	$80	$70

Add $10 for nickel finish (disc. 1990).

⚞ **Compact Elite Engraved** — similar to .25 ACP Compact, except has extensive engraving. New 1991.

Mfg.'s Sug. Retail	$1,000	$850	$600	$475

SILVER HAWK — .22 LR or .25 ACP cal., double action semi-auto, similar to TP-22 Series, except is stainless steel. New 1990.

Mfg.'s Sug. Retail	$250	$215	$185	$160

SUPER ENFORCER (MODEL 3000) — .30 cal. only, pistol version of the Carbine with 11 in. shrouded barrel. Add $40 for stainless steel (disc. for 1986). Mfg. 1985-1986 only.

		$285	$250	$225	$200	$175	$160	$145

Last Mfg.'s Sug. Retail was $255.

⚞ **Enforcer** — similar to Super Enforcer model, except has 10½ in. barrel. Reintroduced 1988.

Mfg.'s Sug. Retail	$417	$325	$275	$240	$200	$175	$160	$145

CATTLEMAN MAGNUM — .357 Mag., .44 Mag., or .45 Colt, single action, 6 shot, Colt replica, 4¾, 5½, or 7½ in. barrel, case color frame, blue barrel, and brass grip frame, smooth walnut grips, fixed sights. Disc. 1984.

		$190	$175	$150	$140	$130	$125	$110
.44 Mag.		$220	$190	$175	$165	$145	$135	$125

BUCKHORN MAGNUM — similar to Cattleman, except flat top, adj. sights.

		$210	$190	$175	$165	$145	$140	$125

BUNTLINE BUCKHORN MAGNUM — similar to Buckhorn, only 18 in. barrel, detachable stock.

		$345	$310	$295	$275	$260	$250	$225
.44 Mag.		$375	$325	$310	$295	$280	$275	$250

TRAIL BLAZER — .22 LR, or .22 Mag. cal., interchangeable cylinder, 5½ or 6½ in. barrel, blue.

		$175	$145	$130	$120	$110	$100	$80

RIFLES

AMAC also manufactures a full-auto M2 Carbine that is not listed in this text.

MODEL X — .22 Short, Long, or LR, bolt action, single shot, 22 in. barrel, open sight, pistol grip with knob forend. Mfg. 1928-1932.

		$90	$60	$50	$40	$35	$30	$25

MODEL 2X — improved Model X, 24 in. heavy barrel larger stock, adj. sights. Mfg. 1932-1955.

		$120	$95	$75	$50	$40	$35	$30

Grading	100%	98%	95%	90%	80%	70%	60%

LI'L CHAMP — .22 LR only, single shot bolt action, 16¼ in. barrel, black molded stock, nickel plated bolt, youth dimensions, (32½ in. overall length), 3 lbs. Introduced 1986, reintroduced 1988 only.

	100%	98%	95%	90%	80%	70%	60%
	$75	$60	$50	$45	$40	$35	$35

Last Mfg.'s Sug. Retail was $92.

LONG RANGE RIFLE — .308 (new 1991) or .50 BMG cal., bolt action design, single shot, 29 in. stainless steel fluted barrel with muzzle brake, adj. trigger pull, built in bipod, adj. rail stock, includes Leupold M-1 Ultra 20X scope, 36 lbs. New 1988.

	100%	98%	95%	90%	80%	70%	60%
Mfg.'s Sug. Retail $5,000	$4,350	$3,500	$3,150	$2,750	$2,400	$2,100	$1,800

Custom rifles in either military or sporting configuration are also available in the AMAC 338/416 cal.

9MM CARBINE (JJ9MM SERIES) — 9mm only, copy of U.S. military M1, 16 in. barrel, blue finish only, 20 shot mag. Mfg. 1985-86 only.

⇇ **Hardwood Stock Model** — disc. 1986.

	100%	98%	95%	90%	80%	70%	60%
	$230	$200	$180	$170	$160	$150	$140

Last Mfg.'s Sug. Retail was $255.

⇇ **Standard Model** — with plastic stock. Disc. 1985.

	100%	98%	95%	90%	80%	70%	60%
	$225	$200	$180	$170	$160	$150	$140

Last Mfg.'s Sug. Retail was $250.

⇇ **Folding Plastic Stock Model** — disc. 1985.

	100%	98%	95%	90%	80%	70%	60%
	$255	$225	$200	$180	$170	$160	$150

Last Mfg.'s Sug. Retail was $281.

DELTA-786 — 9mm Para., semi-auto, patterned after the U.S. military M1, 16 in. barrel, matte black finish. Mfg. 1989 only.

	100%	98%	95%	90%	80%	70%	60%
	$575	$425	$360	$325	$295	$260	$230

Last Mfg.'s Sug. Retail was $665.

.30 CAL. CARBINE — .30 M1 or 9mm Para. (new 1991) cal., semi-auto, 18 or 20 (new 1991) in. barrel, available in various stock configurations, hardwood stock. Mfg. 1985-1986, reintroduced 1988.

	100%	98%	95%	90%	80%	70%	60%
Mfg.'s Sug. Retail $350	$285	$215	$190	$165	$150	$140	$130

Add $16 for 9mm Para. cal.
Add $35 for walnut stock, Parkerized finish (disc. 1990), or 20 in. barrel (new 1991).

⇇ **Paratrooper Model** — similar to standard model, except has folding synthetic stock.

	100%	98%	95%	90%	80%	70%	60%
Mfg.'s Sug. Retail $433	$345	$270	$225	$195	$165	$150	$140

⇇ **Stainless Steel Variation** — disc. 1985.

	100%	98%	95%	90%	80%	70%	60%
	$230	$200	$180				

Last Mfg.'s Sug. Retail was $250.

⇇ **5.7mm Johnson (Spitfire) Cal.** — remilled, add $30 for stainless steel.

	100%	98%	95%	90%	80%	70%	60%
	$195	$175	$165	$155	$145	$135	$125

Last Mfg.'s Sug. Retail was $219.

.22 CAL. U.S. CARBINE — .22 LR or .22 Mag. cal., 18½ in. barrel, except for Mag. (19.3 in.), 5.8 lbs., 15 shot mag., sling swivels. Mfg. 1985-1986, reintroduced 1988 only.

	100%	98%	95%	90%	80%	70%	60%
	$150	$120	$110	$100	$90	$85	$80

Add $120 for .22 Mag. model (gas operated — disc. 1986).
Last Mfg.'s Sug. Retail was $183 for .22 Mag. cal.
Last Mfg.'s Sug. Retail was $166 for .22 LR cal.

Grading	100%	98%	95%	90%	80%	70%	60%

TARGETMASTER SLIDE ACTION — .22 LR or Mag. (disc. 1986) cal., 18½ in. barrel, 12 shot (LR) tube mag., 5¾ lbs. Mfg. 1985 only, reintroduced 1988-90.

	$175	$140	$125	$115	$100	$90	$80

This model was designated EW.22 HBP previously.
Last Mfg.'s Sug. Retail was $209.

MODEL EW.22 HBL LEVER ACTION (WAGONMASTER) — .22 S, L, and LR or .22 Mag. cal., 18½ in. barrel, walnut finish, hardwood stock, blue finish, 5¾ lbs., grooved for scope mounts. Mfg. 1985-1986, reintroduced 1988-90.

	$175	$140	$125	$115	$100	$90	$80

Add $23 for .22 Mag. cal. (19 in. barrel).
This model was designated EW.22 HBL previously. It was also available in a Junior model featuring smaller dimensions; values same as listed above.
Last Mfg.'s Sug. Retail was $209.

TRAIL BLAZER SEMI-AUTO (MODEL IJ.22 HB) — .22 LR only, 10 shot clip mag., 18½ in. barrel, 5.8 lbs. Mfg. 1985 only.

	$115	$100	$90	$85	$80	$75	$70

Last Mfg.'s Sug. Retail was $125.

SHOTGUNS

CHAMPION — 10, 12, 16, 20, 24, 28, 32, or .410 ga., also available in .44, .45, 12mm, or 14mm rifle cal., single barrel shotgun or rifle, 26-32 in. full barrel, exposed hammer, auto ejector, plain pistol grip stock. Mfg. 1909-1956.

	$145	$100	$80	$60	$40	$35	$25

Values on both smaller gauge shotguns and rifles would be considerably higher than those listed above. A mint .410 ga. might command 400% more than the above values.

MATTED RIB GRADE — similar to Champion, except in 12, 16, or 20 ga. only, solid rib, checkered stock. Mfg. 1909-1948.

	$165	$115	$95	$70	$50	$45	$40

This model has either a semi-octagon (with top matted) or jacketed breech.

TRAP GRADE — similar to Matted Rib, except 32 in. full barrel, 12 ga., vent rib. Mfg. 1909-1942.

	$275	$165	$140	$120	$100	$90	$80

HERCULES GRADE — 12, 16, 20, 28, or .410 ga., double barrel, 26-32 in. barrels, hammerless, boxlock, various chokes, extractors and double triggers standard, checkered pistol grip or straight stock. Mfg. 1918-1943.

	$600	$400	$375	$365	$335	$310	$290

Add $100 for auto ejectors.
Add $100 for SST.
Add 10% for 16 ga.
Add 20% for 20 ga.
Add 200% for 28 ga.
Add 100% for .410 ga.
The Hercules Model was mfg. in both USA and Canada. The Hercules name was dropped in 1936 and became known as the "Iver Johnson Hammerless" until the end of production. Case colored frames were standard until 1936, blued frames were standard 1937-1943. A special run of Hercules Doubles was built in the 1930s for Montgomery Ward under the "Western Field" name. All Western Field guns had a beavertail forearm, twin ivory sights, and recoil pad. Hercules 28 ga. SxS's are extremely rare.

Grading	100%	98%	95%	90%	80%	70%	60%

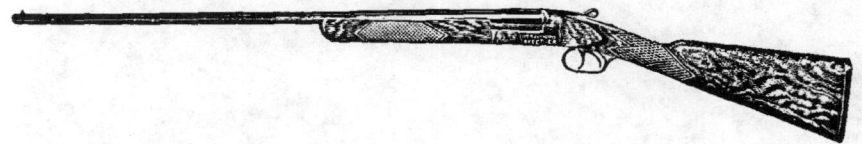

SKEET-ER MODEL — 12, 16, 20, 28, or .410 ga., similar to Hercules Model, except has blued receiver, super select wood and beavertail forearm, many Skeet-ers were special order guns with options including selective or non-selective Miller trigger, custom stock, barrel chokes, chamber lengths, checkering and wood finishes, sling swivels, recoil pad, checkered butt, VR, and various engraving patterns. Approx. 1,800 mfg. 1933-1942.

	$1,095	$800	$600	$525	$450	$410	$390

Add 20% for auto ejectors.
Add 20% for SST.
Add 50% for factory VR.
Add 20% for 16 or 20 ga.
Add 100% for 28 or .410 ga.
Add 200% for rare factory engraving.

.410 ga. is the most commonly encountered gun and was made on a special small frame. This model was probably responsible for more Skeet records than any other American .410 ga. SxS shotgun.

SUPER TRAP — 12 ga. only, 32 in. full VR, boxlock, extractors, checkered pistol grip stock, beavertail forend and recoil pad. Mfg. until 1942. Scarce.

	$1,095	$750	$550	$475	$415	$395	$370

Add $100 for auto ejectors.
Add $100 for SST.

SILVER SHADOW — O/U, 12 ga., 26 or 28 in. barrels, various chokes, extractors, vent rib, checkered pistol grip stock, Italian mfg. Disc.

	$375	$325	$300	$275	$225	$185	$175

Add $100 for ST.

JURRAS

Custom pistolsmith located in Prescott, AZ. Previously distributed by J & G Sales located in Prescott, AZ.

Ammunition for Jurras pistols is exclusively manufactured by Robert Davis, Jr. located in Athens, TN.

PISTOLS

Lee E. Jurras manufactures custom pistols in larger calibers. Almost any caliber is available by special order and the listings below represent a few of his more standard items. Special order inquiries may be directed to Mr. Jurras, in Prescott, AZ.

HOWDAH — available in .375, .416, .460, .475, .500, or .577 cal., action based on Thompson/Center Contender receiver, 12 in. bull barrel, nitex finish, adj. rear sights, limited mfg. (100).

Custom Grade

	$1,150	$925	$800	$725	$650	$575	$500

Presentation Grade — .375 Jurras or .460 Jurras, deluxe Claro walnut stock and forearm.

	$2,000	$1,750	$1,500	$1,250	$1,050	$950	$825

.416, .475, .500, or .577 calibers command a premium on this model.

K section

KBI, INC.

Importer/manufacturer located in Harrisburg, PA. Distributor and dealer sales.

KBI Inc. imports C.B.C. from Brazil and the Jericho pistol manufactured by I.M.I. from Israel. The Jericho pistol may be found under it's own heading in this text.

Grading	100%	98%	95%	90%	80%	70%	60%

PISTOLS

PSP-25 — .25 ACP, semi-auto, single action, patterned after the Baby Browning, all steel construction with high polish finish, dual safety system. New 1989.

Mfg.'s Sug. Retail	$249	$220	$190	$175	$160	$150	$140	$130

Add $50 for industrial hard chrome finish.

This pistol is mfg. in the U.S. under license from Fabrique Nationale.

PSP Signature Editions — similar to above, except has "Michael B. Kassnar" signature on left slide top in gold. Mfg. 1989-91.

	$325	$295	$260	$230	$200	$175	$160

Also available in this series is a Limited Edition that is serial numbered 00011-00100 and includes partial engraving and pearlite grips - retail price $900. Also available is a Limited Edition (serial numbers 00001-00010) with full engraving and gold lining around slide sides - retail price is $1,500.

Last Mfg.'s Sug. Retail was $385.

RIFLES

KASSNAR BOLT ACTION GRADE I — available in 9 cals., thumb safety that locks trigger, with or without deluxe sights, 22 in. barrel, 3 or 4 shot mag., includes swivel posts and oil finished standard grade European walnut with recoil pad, 7½ lbs. Importation started 1989.

Mfg.'s Sug. Retail	$499	$445	$385	$325	$275	$225	$195	$175

NYLON 66 — .22 LR, patterned after the Remington Nylon 66. Imported until 1990 from C.B.C. in Brazil, South America.

	$125	$110	$95	$85	$75	$70	$65

Last Mfg.'s Sug. Retail was $134.

MODEL 122 — .22 LR, bolt action design with clip mag. Imported from South America until 1990.

	$125	$110	$95	$85	$75	$70	$65

Last Mfg.'s Sug. Retail was $136.

MODEL 522 — .22 LR, bolt action design with tube mag. Imported from South America until 1990.

	$130	$115	$100	$85	$75	$70	$65

Last Mfg.'s Sug. Retail was $142.

BANTAM SINGLE SHOT — .22 LR, youth dimensions. Imported 1989-90 only.

	$110	$90	$85	$75	$70	$65	$60

Last Mfg.'s Sug. Retail was $120.

Grading	100%	98%	95%	90%	80%	70%	60%

SHOTGUNS

GRADE I O/U — 12, 20, 28, or .410 ga., gold plated SST, extractors, vent. rib, checkered walnut stock and forearm. Importation started 1989.

Mfg.'s Sug. Retail	$599	$525	$425	$350	$295	$265	$240	$220

Add $70 for 28 or .410 ga.
Add $50 for choke tubes (12 and 20 ga. only).
Add $150 for automatic ejectors (with choke tubes only).

GRADE II SXS — 10, 12, 16, 20, 28, or .410 ga., boxlock action, case hardened receiver, English style checkered European walnut stock with splinter forearm, chrome barrels with concave rib, extractors, double hinged triggers. Imported 1989-90 only.

$515	$435	$375	$325	$275	$250	$225

Add $95 for 28 or .410 ga.
Add $85 for 10 ga.
Last Mfg.'s Sug. Retail was $575.

KDF, INC.

Manufacturer located in Sequin, TX. Previously, KDF rifles were manufactured by Voere (until 1986) in Vohrenbach, W. Germany. Manufacture in 1987 was absorbed by Mauser-Werke in Oberndorf, W. Germany.

Older KDF rifles were private labeled by Voere and were marked KDF. Since Voere was absorbed by Mauser-Werke in 1987, model designations changed. Mauser-Werke does not private label (i.e. newer guns are marked Mauser-Werke), and these rifles can be found under the Mauser-Werke heading in this text.

RIFLES: U.S. MFG.

In 1989, KDF announced the release of a new American built redesigned Model K15 with many improvements. While advertised, approximately 25 were manufactured in various cals.

K15 — .22-250 (disc. 1992), .243 Win., 6mm Rem., .25-06 Rem., .270 Win., .280 Rem., .30-06 cal. or .308 Win. cal., 60 degree short lift bolt action with 3 lugs, Kevlar composite or laminate walnut stock, adj. single stage competition trigger, box magazine, thumb activated slide safety, satin blue finish, 24 in. match grade barrel, deluxe checkered walnut stock with ebony accents and Pachmayr Decelerator recoil pad, approx. 8 lbs. Limited mfg. in U.S. starting 1989.

Mfg.'s Sug. Retail	$1,950	$1,750	$1,375	$1,150	$950	$750	$650	$575

K15 Magnum — .270 Wby., .300 Win. Mag., .300 Wby., 7mm Rem. Mag., .338 Win. Mag., .340 Wby. (disc.), .375 H&H, .411 KDF, .416 Rem. Mag. (disc.), or .458 Win. Mag. cal., similar to K15, except has 26 in. barrel. Mfg. in U.S. starting in 1989.

Mfg.'s Sug. Retail	$2,000	$1,795	$1,400	$1,175	$975	$775	$675	$600

RIFLES: OLDER VOERE MFG. (PRE-1988)

TITAN SPORTER SERIES — various cals., bolt action, 24 or 26 in. barrel length, select walnut, pistol grip stock.
This series is available with either European Monte Carlo high-luster stock or in classic featherweight configuration with Schnabel forend — add $50-$200.

Titan Menor — .222 or .223 cal. Importation disc. 1987.

$675	$615	$560	$495	$450	$395	$350

Add $100 for Match or Competition model (.223 cal.).
Last Mfg.'s Sug. Retail was $765.

Grading	100%	98%	95%	90%	80%	70%	60%

Titan II Standard — many cals., between .243 and .30-06. Disc. 1988.

| | $950 | $825 | $725 | $625 | $550 | $500 | $450 |

Add $100 for Match or Competition model (.308 cal.).
Last Mfg.'s Sug. Retail was $1,075.

Titan II Magnum — available in cals. between 7mm Rem. and .375 H&H. Disc. 1988.

| | $995 | $875 | $750 | $650 | $575 | $520 | $475 |

Last Mfg.'s Sug. Retail was $1,125.

Titan .411 KDF Mag. — .411 KDF cal., 26 in. barrel with recoil arrestor, 3 shot mag., blue or electroless nickel finish, 9¼ lbs. Imported 1986-1988.

| | $1,175 | $965 | $810 | $725 | $650 | $575 | $520 |

Last Mfg.'s Sug. Retail was $1,300.

MODEL 2005 — .22 LR only, semi-auto, 19½ in. barrel, Monte Carlo stock, 5 shot clip mag., iron sights, 6 lbs. Imported 1986 only.

| | $135 | $115 | $100 | $90 | $85 | $80 | $75 |

Last Mfg.'s Sug. Retail was $165.
This model was ruled no longer importable by the BATF.

Model 2005 Deluxe — similar to Model 2005, except has deluxe checkered walnut. Mfg. 1986-87 only.

| | $160 | $135 | $110 | $95 | $85 | $80 | $75 |

Last Mfg.'s Sug. Retail was $185.

MODEL 2107 — .22 LR or .22 Mag. cal., bolt action, 19½ in. barrel, 5 shot clip mag., adj. iron sights, 6 lbs. Imported 1986-87 only.

| | $175 | $150 | $125 | $105 | $95 | $85 | $80 |

Add $42 for .22 Mag. cal.
Last Mfg.'s Sug. Retail was $197.

Model 2107 Deluxe (Mauser 107) — similar to Model 2107, except has deluxe checkered walnut. Imported 1986-1988.

| | $185 | $165 | $140 | $125 | $110 | $105 | $100 |

Add $50 for .22 Mag. cal.
This model has been redesignated KDF-Mauser Model 107 since current distributer/dealer inventories have been depleted.
Last Mfg.'s Sug. Retail was $219.

MODEL 2112 — .22 LR or .22 Mag. cal., similar to Model 2107, except has extra select walnut. Imported 1988 only.

| | $235 | $200 | $180 | $160 | $145 | $135 | $125 |

Add $50 for .22 Mag. cal.
Last Mfg.'s Sug. Retail was $279.

K-14 INSTA FIRE RIFLE — .22-250, .458 Win. Mag., .270, or .300 Wby. Mag. cal., 24 or 26 in. barrel, no sights, ultra fast lock time, hidden detachable mag., checkered Monte Carlo stock, recoil pad.

| | $725 | $650 | $575 | $525 | $475 | $425 | $375 |
| K15 (.22 cal.) | $235 | $205 | $175 | $150 | $135 | $120 | $105 |

K-15 (MODEL 225) — available in 13 cals. between .243 Win. and .300 Wby. Mag., bolt action, 60 degree bolt lift with 3 locking lugs, ultra fast lock time, adj. trigger, 24 or 26 (Mag. only) in. barrel, 3 or 5 shot mag., no sights, guaranteed ½ in. accuracy at 100 yards, many stock options available at extra cost. Left-handed action available in certain cals. at a $50 charge.

KDF, Inc., cont.

Grading	100%	98%	95%	90%	80%	70%	60%

⚔ **Deluxe Standard Sporter** — standard model available in 6 regular cals. and 9 Mag. cals. Disc. 1988.

	$1,075	$950	$810	$700	$625	$550	$495

Add $50 for Magnum action.
Add $525 for .411 KDF cal.
In addition to the 15 regular cals., it is also possible to order various other factory cals. as a $200 option.
This model has been redesignated KDF-Mauser Model 225 (standard cals.) since current distributer/dealer inventories have been depleted.
Last Mfg.'s Sug. Retail was $1,275.

⚔ **K-15 Fiberstock Pro-hunter** — similar to the K-15, except is supplied with fiberglass stock (various colors), choice of parkerized, matte blue, or electroless nickel metal finish, and recoil arrestor installed. Imported 1986-1988.

	$1,420	$1,200	$950

Add $50 for Magnum action.
This model has been redesignated KDF-Mauser Model 225 (standard cals.) since current distributer/dealer inventories have been depleted.
Last Mfg.'s Sug. Retail was $1,680.

⚔ **K-15 Dangerous Game** — .411 KDF Mag. (new cartridge 1985), choice of finishes, oil finished deluxe American walnut stock. Imported 1986-1988.

	$1,895	$1,500	$1,150

This model has been redesignated KDF-Mauser Model 225 since current distributer/dealer inventories have been depleted.
Last Mfg.'s Sug. Retail was $2,100.

⚔ **K-15 Swat Rifle** — .308 cal. standard, 24 or 26 in. barrel, parkerized metal, oil finished target walnut stock, 3 or 4 shot detachable mag., 10 lbs. Importation disc. 1988.

	$1,475	$1,250	$1,000	$850	$725	$650	$575

Last Mfg.'s Sug. Retail was $1,725.

K-16 — available in 6 standard cals. between .243 Win. and .300 Win. Mag. in addition to optional cals., modified Remington Model 700 action, standard features include KDF accurizing and instant fire ignition, single stage adj. trigger, Dupont Rynite stock (camel or grey), choice of finishes (high-gloss blue standard), recoil pad and quick detachable sling swivels, many options available. Imported 1988 only.

	$765	$675	$615	$560	$495	$450	$395

Add $120 for KDF muzzle brake.
Add $250 for optional cals.
Add $350 for .411 KDF Mag. cal.
Last Mfg.'s Sug. Retail was $876.

K-22 (MAUSER 201) — .22 LR cal., bolt action, free floating 21 in. barrel, clip 5 shot mag., adj. trigger, scaled down version of the K-15, unusual action incorporates two front-located locking lugs on bolt face that engage Stellite inserts on the front receiver portion, guaranteed 1 in. groupings at 100 yards, blue only, no sights, select walnut stock with cheek piece, standard model disc. 1987. Add $50 for .22 Mag. cal. on the K-22 models listed below.

	$310	$285	$260	$240	$225	$210	$195

Last Mfg.'s Sug. Retail was $345.

⚔ **K-22 Deluxe (Mauser 201)** — better walnut and stock options. Model notation changed in 1988.

	$410	$360	$295	$275	$250	$235	$210

This model has been redesignated KDF-Mauser Model 201 since current distributer/dealer inventories have been depleted.
Last Mfg.'s Sug. Retail was $495.

Grading	100%	98%	95%	90%	80%	70%	60%

K-22 Deluxe Custom — richly layered walnut and stock options. Importation disc. 1987.

	$655	$595	$550	$495	$450	$395	$350

Last Mfg.'s Sug. Retail was $725.

K-22 Deluxe Special Select — top-of-the-line bolt action, double set triggers. Importation disc. 1987.

	$1,060	$950	$850	$750	$695	$650	$595

Last Mfg.'s Sug. Retail was $1,225.

SHOTGUNS

CONDOR O/U — 12 ga., 28 in. barrel, various chokes, selective single trigger, auto ejectors, wide VR, boxlock, checkered pistol grip stock, Italian made.

	$660	$635	$605	$580	$525	$470	$415

BRESCIA S X S — 12 ga., 28 in. barrel, full and mod., double triggers, engraved, checkered pistol grip stock.

	$330	$305	$275	$250	$195	$165	$140

K.F.C.

Formerly manufactured by Kawaguchiya Firearms Co., Ltd. Previously imported and distributed by La Paloma Marketing, Inc. located in Tucson, AZ.

SHOTGUNS

MODEL 250 — 12 ga. only, semi-auto incorporating a patented, cushioned piston assembly, 26, 28, or 30 in. barrel, matte blue finish, vent. rib standard, checkered premium walnut, 7 lbs. Manufactured 1980-86.

	$360	$290	$270	$250	$235	$220	$205

Add $60 for multi-chokes.
Last Mfg.'s Sug. Retail was $485.

Model 250 Deluxe — same specifications as Model 250, except has scrolled acid etching panels on both sides of normally black receiver. Disc. 1986.

	$395	$310	$290	$270	$250	$225	$210

Last Mfg.'s Sug. Retail was $520.

FIELD GUN O/U — 12 ga. only, VR, premium grade walnut, semi pistol grip stock, F&IC chokes. Disc. 1986.

	$645	$565	$530	$495	$470	$445	$410

Last Mfg.'s Sug. Retail was $748.

E-1 TRAP OR SKEET O/U — 12 ga. only, VR, oil finished premium grade walnut, semi pistol grip stock, engraved. Disc. 1986.

	$935	$800	$750	$700	$625	$550	$495

Last Mfg.'s Sug. Retail was $1,070.

E-2 TRAP OR SKEET O/U — 12 ga. only, VR, oil finished premium grade walnut, semi pistol grip stock, detailed engraving. Disc. 1986.

	$1,450	$1,250	$1,075	$950	$850	$750	$650

Last Mfg. Sug. Retail was $1,660.

KASSNAR IMPORTS, INC.

Previous importer and distributor (operations ceased April, 1989) located in Harrisburg, Pa.

Kassnar also imported Omega shotguns which can be found in their individual section.

PISTOLS

Grading	100%	98%	95%	90%	80%	70%	60%

PJK-9HP — 9mm, single action, patterned after the Browning Hi-Power, 4¾ in. barrel, 13 shot mag., cone hammer, checkered walnut grips, 32 oz.

	$225	$200	$185	$175	$165	$155	$145

Add $15 for VR barrel.

This pistol was imported from Hungary. Approx. 18,000 (including the MBK-9HP) were imported until importation was disc. because of Federal ramifications.

MBK-9HP — 9mm, double action, patterned after the Browning Hi-Power, 4⅔ in. barrel, spur hammer, blued metal, checkered walnut grips, 14 shot mag., 36 oz. Limited importation was stopped in late 1985.

	$295	$260	$230	$190	$175	$165	$155

PMK-380 — .380 ACP, double action, patterned after the Walther PP, plastic grips with thumbrest, 4 in barrel, 7 shot mag., 21 oz. Limited importation.

	$275	$235	$200	$185	$175	$165	$155

This model was imported in very limited quantities before Interarms began exclusive importation.

KEBERST INTERNATIONAL

Previously manufactured and distributed by Kendall International located in Paris, KY.

KEBERST MODEL 1A — .338 Lapua Mag., .338-416 Rigby, or .338-06 cal., bolt action, muzzle brake and unique recoil pad, camouflaged synthetic stock, package includes 3-9 power Leupold scope, stainless steel cleaning rod, custom designed case, built to special order only. Mfg. 1987-1988 only.

	$3,475	$2,850	$2,475	$2,100	$1,750	$1,400	$1,150

Add $275 for 10X Ultra scope.

Last Mfg.'s Sug. Retail was $3,750.

KENDALL INTERNATIONAL

Previous importer/distributor located in Paris, KY. Kendall International also imported Australian Automatic Arms, the Keberst Rifle, and several air rifles that can be found in their respective sections in this text.

KEPPELER, DIETER

Manufacturer located in Langenau, West Germany. No current domestic importer.

Keppeler rifles are typically centerfire and target configured. Both metric and domestic calibers are available as well as a variety of special order options.

Price quotations are available upon request by writing Dieter Keppeler at the following address: DIETER KEPPELER, Postfach 1106, D-7907, Langenau, W. Germany.

KEPPLINGER, ING. HANNES

Manufacturer located in Kufstein, Austria. No current importer.

RIFLES

Kepplinger rifles are essentially built per individual order. In addition to his unique bolt action, he also makes other bolt action designs and O/U rifles as well.

Grading	100%	98%	95%	90%	80%	70%	60%

3-S SYSTEM RIFLE — various cals., unique short action allows for straight-on cartridge loading, high strength alloy main parts, grip safety on lower pistol grip, unique uncocking device allowing manual cocking/decocking of the firing pin spring, 23.6 in. standard barrel, 3 shot detachable mag., iron sights, receiver drilled for scope mounts, best quality wood, available in either Schnabel forearm or Mannlicher configuration, many styles of engraving are optional, 7.14 lbs.

Price quotations are available upon request by writing Mr. Kepplinger at the following address: ING. HANNES KEPPLINGER, Carl-Wagner-Strabe 1, A-6330 Kufstein, AUSTRIA.

KESSLER ARMS CORPORATION

Manufacturer located in Silver Creek, NY.

LEVERMATIC SHOTGUN — lever action, 12, 16, or 20 ga., 26 or 28 in. full choke, takedown, plain pistol grip stock. Disc. 1953.

	100%	98%	95%	90%	80%	70%	60%
	$125	$75	$60	$50	$45	$45	$45

BOLT ACTION SHOTGUN — 12, 16, or 20 ga., 26 or 28 in. full, takedown, plain stock. Mfg. 1951-1953.

	100%	98%	95%	90%	80%	70%	60%
	$90	$65	$50	$45	$35	$35	$35

J. KIMBALL ARMS CO.

Previous manufacturer located in Detroit, MI.

AUTOMATIC PISTOL — .30 U.S. Carbine or .22 Hornet (very rare) cal., semi-auto, 7 shot, 3 in.(Combat Model) or 5 in. (Target Model) barrel, approx. 32 oz. Less than 300 mfg. in 1958 only.

	100%	98%	95%	90%	80%	70%	60%
	$950	$850	$725	$600	$500	$395	$300

Functional weaknesses of this pistol caused discontinuance. Surviving specimens should be checked carefully for slide failures and other potential problems. Values above assume no operational damage to the pistol. .22 Hornet cal. rarity factor precludes accurate price evaluation.

KIMBER OF OREGON, INC.

Previous manufacturer located in Clackamas, OR between 1980-1991.

Kimber of Oregon had its final sale in 1991, and is now out of business. Rare models are starting to attract premiums already. In some models, magazines for these fine quality rifles are getting extremely hard to find with healthy premiums being asked.

RIFLES: BOLT ACTION

Note: No suffix in Kimber models denotes pre-1986 action design, "A" suffix models refer to the new action in right or left-hand, "B" suffix models also incorporate the new action with improved cocking system, faster lock time, swept-back bolt design, improved recoil lug, and are right handed.

Add $150 for skeleton grip cap on models listed below.
Add $250 for skeleton buttplate on models listed below.
Add $80 for checkered bolt handle on models listed below.

Grading	100%	98%	95%	90%	80%	70%	60%

MODEL 82 RIMFIRE SERIES

STANDARD MODEL 82 — .22 LR, .22 Mag., or .22 Hornet cal., Mauser type rear locking bolt action, 3 (.22 Hornet), 4 (.22 Mag.), or 5 (.22 LR) shot mag., 22 in. (Sporter) or 24 in. (Varmint) barrel, deluxe claro walnut, steel butt plate, rocker style safety, 6½ lbs. Add $45 for .22 Hornet or .22 Mag. cal. for all variations of this model.

⚔ **Classic Model** — disc. 1988.

$600	$500	$400	$350	$295	$250	$225

Add $55 for disc. Cascade Model (Monte Carlo cheek piece).
Last Mfg.'s Sug. Retail was $750.

⚔ **Custom Classic Model** — higher grade claro walnut, ebony forearm tip, Niedner style steel butt plate. Disc. 1988.

$795	$675	$550	$475	$395	$340	$295

Also previously available in the .218 Bee or .25-20 (single shot only) cals. These cals. may bring a slight premium. Mfg. 1985 only (retail price was $695).
Last Mfg.'s Sug. Retail was $995.

⚔ **Deluxe Grade** — .22 LR only, similar to Custom Classic Model, AA walnut, 5 or 10 (optional) shot mag., 6½ lbs. Mfg. 1989-90 only.

$995	$895	$700	$595	$525	$450	$395

A left-hand variation is also available at no extra charge, but had limited mfg. in 1990.
Last Mfg.'s Sug. Retail was $1,195.

SPORTER MODEL — .22 LR, includes Model 82A action, 22 in. sporter weight barrel, 4 shot mag., round top receiver with bases, checkered stock and forend, 6½ lbs. Mfg. 1991 only.

$895	$750	$650	$550	$495	$450	$395

Last Mfg.'s Sug. Retail was $995.

RIMFIRE VARMINTER — .22 LR only, Model 82A action, free floating 25 in. medium heavy barrel, laminated stock, 5 or optional 10 shot mag., rubber butt pad, 8¼ lbs. Mfg. 1990-91 only.

$675	$550	$475	$425	$375	$325	$280

Last Mfg.'s Sug. Retail was $795.

HUNTER GRADE — .22 LR only, similar to Rimfire Varminter with Super America configured barrel and action with low glare metal finish. Mfg. 1990 only.

$750	$600	$525	$450	$395	$340	$295

Last Mfg.'s Sug. Retail was $895.

MINI CLASSIC — .22 LR only, Model 82 action, 18 in. barrel, steel butt plate, sling swivels. Mfg. 1988 only.

$550	$475	$415	$375	$340	$300	$275

Last Mfg.'s Sug. Retail was $795.

GOVERNMENT MODEL 82A TARGET — .22 LR only, specifically designed for U.S. Army training, 25 in. heavy target barrel including scope blocks, oversized stock, 10¾ lbs. Mfg. 1987-91.

$540	$480	$440	$400	$365	$325	$295

20,000 rifles were mfg. 1987-1989 to fill the initial U.S. government contract. Commercial guns were manufactured for the private sector with values listed above.
Last Mfg.'s Sug. Retail was $595.

Grading	100%	98%	95%	90%	80%	70%	60%

ALL AMERICAN MATCH — .22 LR only, precision rifled 25 in. free floating target grade barrel, stock is adj. both vertically and for length of pull, fully adj. single stage trigger, approx. 9 lbs. Mfg. 1990-91 only.

	$750	$600	$525	$450	$395	$340	$295

Last Mfg.'s Sug. Retail was $895.

CONTINENTAL — .22 LR, .22 Mag., or .22 Hornet cal., Sporter action only, full length Mannlicher stock, open sights, deluxe walnut. New 1987.
This model was only available as a special order with prices on request from the factory.

⚄ **Super Continental** — similar to Continental, except has AAA claro walnut with 22 lines/in. checkering. Mfg. 1987-1988.

	$1,250	$1,000	$875	$795	$740	$680	$620

Last Mfg.'s Sug. Retail was $1,465.

SUPER AMERICA — top-of-the-line model, includes detachable scope mounts, Niedner checkered steel butt plate and best quality walnut, available in Sporter configuration only. This model was disc. 1988, and reintroduced 1990-91.

	$1,075	$950	$775	$625	$550	$475	$425

Last Mfg.'s Sug. Retail was $1,295.

⚄ **Super Grade** — similar to Super America, AAA walnut, beaded cheek piece, 5 or 10 (optional) shot mag., 6½ lbs. Mfg. 1989 only.

	$950	$775	$625	$550	$475	$425	$375

Last Mfg.'s Sug. Retail was $1,095.

CUSTOM MATCH — .22 LR or .22 Mag. cal., limited edition of 500 rifles, match dimension chamber, french walnut stock with 22 L.P.I. checkering, rust blued finish, other custom rifle features. Introduced 1984.

	$1,675	$1,350	$1,000	$875	$795	$725	$650

Add $200 for .22 Mag. cal.

BROWNELL — .22 LR, only 500 mfg. to commemorate the late Leonard Brownell, Mannlicher style extra deluxe claro walnut stock. Mfg. 1986 only.

	$1,250	$1,000	$800

Last Mfg.'s Sug. Retail was $1,500.

CENTENNIAL — .22 LR only, limited edition (100 rifles) to commemorate centennial of .22 LR cal., includes hand-picked checkered walnut, moderate engraving, special Wilson Arms match barrel, skeleton butt plate and other refinements, serial numbered C1-C100. Mfg. 1987 only.

	$2,600	$2,350	$1,900

Last Mfg.'s Sug. Retail was $2,950.

TENTH ANNIVERSARY ISSUE — .22 LR, limited edition, french walnut stock featuring slim forend design with shadowed cheekpiece, Neidner steel buttplate and other refinements. Mfg. 1989 only.

	$1,495	$1,200	$975

Add $100 for matte finish.

Grading	100%	98%	95%	90%	80%	70%	60%

MODEL 84 CENTERFIRE SERIES

Add $250-$300 for 3-position safety in this series.

STANDARD MODEL 84 — .17 Rem., .17 Mach IV (disc. 1987), 6 x 45 or 47mm (disc. 1987), 5.6 x 50mm (disc. 1987), .221 Fireball, .222 Rem., .222 Rem. Mag. (disc. 1987), or .223 Rem. cal., "Mini-Mauser" type head locking bolt action, 5 shot mag., 22 (Sporter) or 24 (Varmint) in. barrel, deluxe claro walnut, steel butt plate, rocker style safety, 6½ lbs.

* **Classic Model** — disc. 1988.

		$705	$625	$540	$450	$375	$300	$260

Add $55 for disc. Cascade Model (Monte Carlo cheek piece).
Last Mfg.'s Sug. Retail was $885.

CUSTOM CLASSIC MODEL — higher grade claro walnut, ebony forearm tip, Niedner style steel butt plate. Disc. 1988.

		$970	$825	$720	$595	$500	$440	$365

Last Mfg.'s Sug. Retail was $1,130.

* **Deluxe Grade Sporter** — .17 Rem., .221 Rem., or .223 Rem. cal., Mauser action, AA walnut, similar to Custom Classic Model, 6¼ lbs. Mfg. 1989-90.

		$1,075	$950	$775	$625	$550	$475	$425

Also available in left-hand action (.223 cal. only), limited mfg.
Last Mfg.'s Sug. Retail was $1,295.

CONTINENTAL — .221 Fireball (new 1988), .222 Rem. or .223 Rem. cal., Sporter action only, full length Mannlicher stock, open sights, deluxe walnut. New 1987.
This model was only available as a special order with prices on request from the factory.

* **Super Continental** — similar to Continental (same cals.), except has AAA claro walnut with 22 lines/in. checkering. Mfg. 1987-1988.

		$1,325	$1,060	$920	$830	$740	$680	$620

Last Mfg.'s Sug. Retail was $1,600.

HUNTER GRADE — .17 Rem., .222 Rem., or .223 Rem. cal., laminated stock, Super America configured action and barrel with low glare metal finish. Mfg. 1990 only.

		$825	$650	$550	$475	$425	$375	$325

Last Mfg.'s Sug. Retail was $995.

SPORTER — .17 Rem., .22 Hornet, .222 Rem., .22-250 Rem., or .223 cal., 22 in. sporter weight barrel, "A" grade Claro walnut, round top receiver with bases, 4 shot mag., hand checkering. Mfg. 1991 only.

		$975	$800	$700	$600	$550	$500	$495

This model was available in either right or left hand action.
Last Mfg.'s Sug. Retail was $1,095.

* **Big Bore Sporter** — .250 Savage or .35 Rem. cal., similar action to Sporter Model, except has ¾ in. red Pachmayr Decelerator recoil pad. Mfg. 1991 only.

		$975	$800	$700	$600	$550	$500	$495

This model was available in either right or left hand action.
Last Mfg.'s Sug. Retail was $1,095.

Grading	100%	98%	95%	90%	80%	70%	60%

SUPER AMERICA — .17 Rem., .22 Hornet, .222 Rem., .22-250 Rem., or .223 Rem. cal., 22 in. sporter weight barrel, top-of-the-line, with detachable scope mounts, available in Sporter configuration only, 4 shot mag., right or left hand action. Disc. 1988, reintroduced 1990-91.

	$1,250	$975	$850	$725	$600	$500	$450

Last Mfg.'s Sug. Retail was $1,495.

Big Bore Super America — .250 Savage or .35 Rem., similar action to Super America Model, except has ¾ in. red Pachmayr Decelerator recoil pad. Mfg. 1991 only.

	$1,250	$975	$850	$725	$600	$500	$450

Last Mfg.'s Sug. Retail was $1,495.

SUPER GRADE — .17 Rem., .221 Rem., or .223 Rem. cal., Mauser action, AAA walnut, similar to Super America, 6¼ lbs. Mfg. 1989 only.

	$995	$850	$695	$600	$500	$450	$395

Last Mfg.'s Sug. Retail was $1,250.

CUSTOM MATCH — .222 Rem. or .223 Rem. cal., limited edition of 200 rifles, match dimension chamber, french walnut stock with 22 L.P.I. checkering, rust blued finish, other custom rifle features. Introduced 1986.

	$1,995	$1,600	$1,350	$995	$850	$750	$650

TENTH ANNIVERSARY ISSUE — .223 Rem. cal., limited edition, french walnut stock featuring slim forend design with shadowed cheekpiece, 22 in. barrel, roundtop receiver with mounts, Neidner steel buttplate and other refinements. Mfg. 1989 only.

	$1,650	$1,425	$1,150				

ULTRA VARMINTER — .17 Rem., .22 Hornet (new 1991), .221 Rem. (disc. 1990), .222 Rem., .22-250 Rem., or .223 Rem. cal., 24 in. medium weight stainless steel barrel, laminated birch stock, plain butt stock, right or left hand action, 7¾lbs. Mfg. 1989-91 only.

	$1,075	$950	$775	$625	$550	$475	$425

Last Mfg.'s Sug. Retail was $1,295.

Super Varminter — similar to Ultra Varminter except has steel barrel, AAA walnut stock with beaded cheek piece, 7¼ lbs. Mfg. 1989-91 only.

	$1,250	$975	$850	$725	$600	$500	$450

Last Mfg.'s Sug. Retail was $1,495.

MODEL 89 BIG GAME RIFLE SERIES

MODEL 89 BGR — .270 Win., .280 Rem., 7mm Rem. Mag., .30-06, .300 Win. Mag., .338 Win. Mag., or 375 H&H cal., new action incorporates features from both Mauser 98 and Win. pre-64 Model 70, three position safety, 22 or 24 in. barrel. While advertised in 1987, this model was not mfg. until 1989.

Classic Model — deluxe claro walnut checkered 18 lines/in. with steel butt plate. Disc. 1988.

	$790	$675	$550	$475	$395	$340	$295

Add $200 for .375 H&H cal.
Last Mfg.'s Sug. Retail was $985.

Custom Classic Model — higher grade claro walnut, ebony forearm tip, Niedner style steel butt plate. Disc. 1988.

	$1,025	$865	$750	$625	$500	$440	$365

Add $200 for .375 H&H cal.
Last Mfg.'s Sug. Retail was $1,230.

Grading	100%	98%	95%	90%	80%	70%	60%

DELUXE GRADE — similar to Custom Classic Model, round top receiver with Model 70 hole space configuration, AA walnut stock with ebony forend tip and rubber recoil pad (no cheek piece), 22 or 24 in. barrel, 7½-8½ lbs. New 1989.

⚞ **Featherweight Barrel Model** — .257 Roberts, .25-06 Rem., 7 x 57mm (disc. 1990), .270 Win., .280 Rem., or .30-06 cal., 5 shot mag., 22 in. Featherweight barrel, right hand action only, 7½ lbs. Disc. 1990.

	$1,525	$1,175	$975	$825	$700	$600	$525

Add $470 for Super America Grade with square bridge, dovetail receiver (current mfg.).
The Super America Grade will accept Kimber double lever scope mounts and has one grade better wood than the Deluxe Grade with beaded cheek piece.
Last Mfg.'s Sug. Retail was $1,795.

⚞ **Medium-weight Barrel Model** — .300 Win. Mag., .300 H&H (disc. 1990), .300 Wby. (new 1991), .338 Win. Mag., .35 Whelen (disc. 1990), or 7mm Rem. Mag. cal., 3 shot mag., 24 in. medium-weight barrel, right hand action only, 7¾-8½ lbs. Disc. 1990.

	$1,600	$1,225	$1,000	$850	$725	$625	$550

Add $495 for Super America Grade with square bridge, dovetail receiver (current mfg.).
The Super America Grade will accept Kimber double lever scope mounts and has one grade better wood than the Deluxe Grade with beaded cheek piece.
Last Mfg.'s Sug. Retail was $1,895.

⚞ **Heavy-weight Barrel Model** — .375 H&H Mag. or .458 Win. Mag. (new 1991) cal., 3 shot mag., 24 in. heavy-weight barrel, right hand action only, 9 lbs. Disc. 1990.

	$1,700	$1,275	$1,050	$900	$775	$700	$650

Add $495 for Super America Grade with square bridge, dovetail receiver (current mfg.).
The Super America Grade will accept Kimber double lever scope mounts and has one grade better wood than the Deluxe Grade with beaded cheek piece.
Last Mfg.'s Sug. Retail was $1,995.

SPORTER MODEL — same cals. as Deluxe/Super America Models, 22 in. featherweight or 24 in. medium or heavy barrel, double square bridge dovetail receiver, "A" grade Claro walnut stock with ¾ red Pachmayr Decelerator recoil pad. Mfg. 1991 only.

	$1,325	$1,000	$875	$750	$625	$500	$450

Add $100 for medium magnum action.
Add $200 for heavy magnum action (.375 H&H and .458 Win. Mag. cals.).
Last Mfg.'s Sug. Retail was $1,595.

HUNTER GRADE — .270 Win., .30-06, .300 Win. Mag., .338 Win. Mag., or 7mm Rem. Mag. cal., laminated stock, Super America configured action and barrel with low glare metal finish. Mfg. 1990-91 only.

	$1,250	$975	$850	$725	$600	$500	$450

Add $100 for Mag. cals.
Last Mfg.'s Sug. Retail was $1,495.

SUPER GRADE — similar to Super America Model, square top frame, AAA walnut, 22 or 24 in. barrel, plain butt stock, 7½-8½ lbs. Mfg. 1989 only.

	$1,500	$1,275	$995	$825	$695	$550	$500

Add $100 for .375 H&H cal.
Add $100 for matte blue metal finish.
Last Mfg.'s Sug. Retail was $1,495.
The 24 in. barrel was available in Mag. cals. only.

Grading	100%	98%	95%	90%	80%	70%	60%

LIMITED WILDLIFE EDITION SERIES — series of 5 guns, includes .257 Roberts (Whitetail Deer Edition), .270 Win. (Mule Deer Edition), .338 Win. Mag. (Rocky Mt. Elk Edition), 7mm Rem. Mag. (Big Horn Sheep Edition), and .375 H&H (Grizzly Bear Edition) cals. included, hand select walnut, special Shilen Rifle barrel, gold plated trigger, receivers are stamped "Wildlife Edition", special prefix serialization, only 25 sets were to be manufactured in 1991 only, includes rings, swivels, and hard case.
While advertised, there is no record that this model was ever mfg. Retail price was scheduled to be $3,595.

MODEL 89 AFRICAN SERIES

MODEL 89 AFRICAN — .375 H&H, .416 Rigby, or .505 Gibbs cal., magnum action, 24 in. heavy barrel, AA English walnut stock with beaded cheek piece and rubber recoil pad, includes twin recoil cross bolts, express sights on quarter rib, drop box magazine, 10-10½ lbs. Mfg. 1990-91 only.

	$3,100	$2,575	$2,050	$1,725	$1,525	$1,275	$1,100

Last Mfg.'s Sug. Retail was $3,595.

PISTOLS

PREDATOR MODEL — .221 Fireball, .223 Rem., 6mm TCU (disc. 1987), 7mm TCU, or 6 x 45mm (disc. 1987) cal., single shot Model 84 action with shortened 14⅞ in. barrel, scope use only, one piece deluxe walnut stock with contoured pistol grip, 5¼ lbs. Approx. 200 mfg. 1987-1988 only.

⚔ **Hunter Grade** — AA claro walnut without checkering. Disc. 1988.

	$1,500	$1,250	$1,000	$875	$750	$675	$600

Last Mfg.'s Sug. Retail was $995.

⚔ **Super Grade** — similar to Hunter Grade, except has select French walnut with ebony forend tip and 22 lines/in. checkering. Disc. 1988.

	$1,950	$1,750	$1,500	$1,300	$1,100	$950	$800

Last Mfg.'s Sug. Retail was $1,195.

KIMEL

Manufactured by AAArms located in Mint Hill, NC. Distributed by Kimel Industries, Inc. located in Matthews, NC. Distributor and dealer sales.

AP-9 PISTOL — 9mm Para., semi-auto paramilitary design, blowback action with bolt knob on left side of receiver, 5 in. barrel with vent. shroud, front mounted 20 shot detachable mag., black matte finish, adj. front sight, 3 lbs. 7 oz. New 1989.

Mfg.'s Sug. Retail	$279	$245	$185	$155	$135	$120	$110	$100

Add $10 for nickel finish.

⚔ **Mini AP-9** — compact variation of the AP-9 Model with 3 in. barrel, blue or nickel finish. New 1991.

Mfg.'s Sug. Retail	$273	$240	$180	$155	$135	$120	$110	$100

Add $10 for nickel finish.

⚔ **Target AP-9** — target variation of the AP-9 with 12 in. match barrel with shroud, blue finish only. New 1991.

Mfg.'s Sug. Retail	$294	$255	$190	$160	$140	$120	$110	$100

Grading	100%	98%	95%	90%	80%	70%	60%

⊰ **P-95** — similar to AP-9, except without barrel shroud and is supplied with 5 shot mag., parts are interchangeable with AP-9. Mfg. 1990-91 only.

	100%	98%	95%	90%	80%	70%	60%
	$225	$175	$155	$135	$120	$110	$100

Last Mfg.'s Sug. Retail was $250.

AR-9 Carbine — 9mm Para., carbine variation of the AP-9 with 16½ in. barrel, 20 shot mag., and steel rod folding stock. New 1991.

Mfg.'s Sug. Retail	$384	$335	$255	$220	$195	$175	$155	$135

KLEINGUENTHER FIREARMS CO.

Manufacturer located in Seguin, TX. The original KDF Co. was started by Mr. Robert Kleinguenther and sold in the early 1980's. At this juncture, Mr. Kleinguenther started a new company called Kleinguenther Firearms Co. Direct custom order sales only.

RIFLES: BOLT ACTION

Values listed below are for base model only with no additional customer special order options.

BOLT ACTION RIFLE — various cals., individual customer special order rifle with a variety of options, guns are guaranteed to shoot ½ M.O.A., choice of actions, various weights.

⊰ **Winchester Model 70 Custom**

Mfg.'s Sug. Retail	$975	$975	$800	$675	$575	$500	$450	$400

⊰ **Sako Action**

Mfg.'s Sug. Retail	$1,100	$1,100	$950	$800	$675	$575	$500	$450

⊰ **K-15**

Mfg.'s Sug. Retail	$1,375	$1,375	$1,100	$950	$800	$675	$575	$500

KODIAK CO.

Previous manufacture located in North Haven, CT - circa 1965.

Kodiak Co. was in business for only a short time in the mid-1960's. They produced the first .22 Mag. semi-auto rifle (Model 260), as well as a center fire bolt action (Model 158 Deluxe), and a slide action shotgun (Model 458). While Kodiak long guns are rare and extremely well made, collectability to date has been minimal with most specimens selling at a slight premium over similar quality trade name counterparts of that era.

KOLIBRI

Manufactured 1914-1925 by H. Grabner located in Krems/Donau, Austria.

KOLIBRI SEMI-AUTO PISTOL — 2.7 or 3mm centerfire, unrifled barrel, 5 shot box mag., world's smallest semi-auto centerfire pistol.

			$1,200	$1,000	$875	$740	$600	$520	$440

Individual rounds of 2.7 or 3mm (rarer) ammunition are currently trading in the $75 range as it has the distinction of being the world's smallest centerfire shell (shooting a 3 grain bullet).

KORRIPHILA

Previous manufacturer located in Germany. Previously imported and distributed by Osborne's located in Cheboygan, MI.

This trademark had very limited U.S. importation, and the information listed below reflects the last information received (1988).

Grading	100%	98%	95%	90%	80%	70%	60%

HSP 701 TYPE I — 7.65 Luger, .38 Spl., 9mm Luger, 9mm Police, 9mm Steyr, .45 ACP, or 10mm auto cal., semi-auto, double action, 40% stainless steel parts, 4 in. barrel, blue or satin finish, very limited production.

	100%	98%	95%	90%	80%	70%	60%
	$2,000	$1,675	$1,375	$1,100	$995	$820	$740

Last Mfg.'s Sug. Retail was $2,395.

Type II — similar to Type I, except has 5 in. barrel.

	100%	98%	95%	90%	80%	70%	60%
	$2,150	$1,750	$1,475	$1,200	$1,075	$850	$760

Last Mfg.'s Sug. Retail was $2,615.

Type III — similar to Type II, except single action trigger.

	100%	98%	95%	90%	80%	70%	60%
	$2,200	$1,800	$1,550	$1,200	$1,075	$850	$760

Last Mfg.'s Sug. Retail was $2,785.

KORTH

Manufacturer located in Ratzeburg, Germany. Currently imported by various companies, including Mandall Shooting Supplies, Inc. located in Scottsdale, AZ. Previously imported by Beeman Precision Arms, located in Santa Rosa, CA and by Osborne's in Cheboygan, MI.

Korth handguns are very high quality and are literally manufactured one-at-a-time, resulting in limited mfg. and importation.

REVOLVERS

Currently, Mandall Shooting Supplies, Inc. is stocking these guns with extra cylinders (.22 LR/.22 Mag. or .357 Mag./9mm Para.). This is because both cylinders are cut from the same billet of steel, and for metallurgical reasons, once a gun is made with a single cylinder, the extra convertible cylinder cannot be ordered at a later date.

SPORT/COMBAT RIMFIRE — .22 LR or .22 Mag. cal., 3, 4 (Combat only), 5¼, or 6 in. barrel (VR available on 4 in. or longer barrel only), 6 shot, micro adj. sights (Sport), Combat sights fully adj., full length shrouded ejector rod, adj. trigger, checkered and oil finished walnut grips, 2.6 lbs. Introduced 1967.

	100%	98%	95%	90%	80%	70%	60%
Mfg.'s Sug. Retail　$3,300	$3,100	$2,650	$2,250	$1,850	$1,600	$1,325	$1,050

Add $400 for stainless steel (limited mfg.).
Add $200 for ISU Match Model.
Add $670 for special order 8 in. barrel.
Subtract $475 if without extra .22 LR cylinder.

SPORT/COMBAT CENTERFIRE — .22 Rem. Jet, .32 S&W Long, .32 H&R Mag., .38 Spl., .357 Mag., or 9mm Para. cal., 3, 4 (Combat only), 5¼ or 6 in. barrel, 6 shot, otherwise similar specs. as Sport/Combat Rimfire Model, 2.1-2.6 lbs.

	100%	98%	95%	90%	80%	70%	60%
Mfg.'s Sug. Retail　$3,500	$3,300	$2,675	$2,250	$1,850	$1,600	$1,325	$1,050

Add $400 for stainless steel (limited mfg.).
Add $200 for ISU Match Model.
Add $200 for .22 Rem. Jet.
Add $670 for special order 8 in. barrel.
Subtract $475 if without extra 9mm Para. cylinder.
This model is available in additional rimmed and rimless calibers on special order. Most importation has occurred in either .357 Mag. or 9mm Para. cal.

PRESENTATION MODEL — deluxe variation of the Sport/Target Model.
This variation is available with etching, engraving, and other special options that are priced per individual quotation from the importer.

Grading	100%	98%	95%	90%	80%	70%	60%

PISTOLS: SEMI-AUTO

KORTH SEMI-AUTO — 9mm Para. or 9 x 21mm IMI (special order only), double action, 4, 5, or 6 in. barrel, all steel construction, 10 shot mag., adj. sights, checkered walnut stocks, very limited production and special order only. Introduced 1986 with first guns shipped 1988.

Mfg.'s Sug. Retail	$3,295		$2,995	$2,250	$1,750		

Add $500+ for interchangeable barrels.

KRAG-JORGENSEN

U.S. magazine military rifle. First small caliber (.30-40) military repeating rifle to shoot smokeless powder ammunition. Manufactured 1892-1902.

There have been many conversions of Krag-Jorgensen rifles - many of which are hard to identify. As a rule, these conversions are not as desirable as these specific models listed below.

M1892-DATED 1894, 1895, OR 1896 — Springfield Armory, with cleaning rod. Note: designated Type I, has wide, solid upper barrel band.

	100%	98%	95%	90%	80%	70%	60%
	$4,180	$3,960	$3,740	$3,575	$3,300	$3,000	$2,600

Dated 1894 or 1895 — designated Type II. Upper band has double strap instead of being solid as in Type I.

	$1,870	$1,705	$1,540	$1,210	$880	$720	$595

FACTORY — ALTERED TO M1896 STYLE

	$250	$220	$195	$165	$140	$125	$105

M1896 — Dated 1896, 1897, 1898, Springfield Armory.

	$470	$440	$330	$250	$220	$185	$155

M1896 CARBINE

	$660	$580	$495	$385	$360	$320	$280

M1895 CARBINE — This is a variant that was dated 1895 and 1896 and omits the word "Model".

	$880	$800	$660	$550	$440	$385	$330

M1896 CADET RIFLE

	$3,025	$2,750	$2,530	$2,200	$1,815	$1,500	$1,200

M1898 RIFLE

	$440	$360	$330	$250	$220	$190	$160

M1898 CARBINE

	$1,450	$1,225	$950	$800	$660	$580	$525

M1899 CARBINE

	$635	$525	$495	$470	$440	$395	$360

M1899 CARBINE, PHILIPPINE CONSTABULARY

	$1,100	$990	$825	$715	$550	$480	$400

KRICO

Manufactured in Stuttgart, Germany by Sportwaffenfabrik Kriegeskorte Gmbh. Currently imported by Mandall Shooting Supplies, Inc. located in Scottsdale, AZ. Previously imported (until 1988) by Beeman Precision Firearms Inc. located in Santa Rosa, CA.

Between 1983-86, Krico was imported/distributed by over ten U.S. companies/individuals. Beeman Precision Arms imported these rifles 1986-1988 in limited quantities. Krico manufactures a high quality rifle and to date, has had limited domestic distribution.

RIFLES: BOLT ACTION

Values below reflect 1992 information, as this publication was not afforded the necessary 1993 information.

Grading	100%	98%	95%	90%	80%	70%	60%

SPORTING RIFLE — .22 Hornet or .222 Rem. cal., miniature Mauser action, 4 shot, 22, 24, or 26 in. barrel, single or double set triggers, open sights, checkered walnut stock, pistol grip. Mfg. 1956-1962.

	100%	98%	95%	90%	80%	70%	60%
	$605	$550	$495	$440	$400	$360	$305

CARBINE — similar to Sporting Rifle, except 20 or 22 in. barrel, full length stock.

	100%	98%	95%	90%	80%	70%	60%
	$635	$580	$415	$470	$420	$375	$320

SPECIAL VARMINT RIFLE — similar to Sporting Rifle, except heavy barrel, no sights.

	100%	98%	95%	90%	80%	70%	60%
	$605	$550	$495	$440	$400	$360	$300

MODEL 300 SPORTER — .22 LR, .22 Mag., or .22 Hornet cal., select walnut with straight, checkered stock and fuller forearm, 23½ in. barrel, 5 shot mag., grooved receiver, 6½ lbs.

	100%	98%	95%	90%	80%	70%	60%
Mfg.'s Sug. Retail $595	$550	$495	$450	$410	$380	$350	$320

Add $30 for .22 Mag. cal.
Add $155 for .22 Hornet cal.
This model was designated Model 302 Sporter until 1986.

Model 300 Deluxe — similar to Model 300 Standard, except has deluxe wood and checkering. Importation began 1991.

	100%	98%	95%	90%	80%	70%	60%
Mfg.'s Sug. Retail $695	$625	$550	$480	$430	$385	$350	$320

Add $25 for .22 Mag. cal.
Add $200 for .22 Hornet cal.

MODEL 311 SMALL BORE RIFLE — .22 LR only, bolt action, 5 or 10 shot, 22 in. barrel, single or double set trigger, open sights, checkered stock. Disc.

	100%	98%	95%	90%	80%	70%	60%
	$330	$275	$250	$220	$195	$165	$155

Add 30% for Kaps 2½ power scope.

MODEL 320 MANNLICHER SPORTER — .22 LR, .22 Mag., or .22 Hornet cal., full stock sporter, 19½ in. barrel, 5 shot mag., double set triggers, 6 lbs.

	100%	98%	95%	90%	80%	70%	60%
Mfg.'s Sug. Retail $750	$650	$575	$500	$460	$430	$395	$370

Add $25 for .22 Mag. cal.
Add $150 for .22 Hornet cal.
This model was designated Model 304 Mannlicher Sporter until 1986. In 1991 it was redesignated the Model 320 Stutzen.

MODEL 340 S ST — .22 LR only, silhouette model, 21 in. bull barrel, match trigger, no sights, 5 shot mag., stippled pistol grip and forearm, 7½ lbs.

	100%	98%	95%	90%	80%	70%	60%
Mfg.'s Sug. Retail $795	$750	$625	$550	$500	$450	$375	$325

Grading	100%	98%	95%	90%	80%	70%	60%

Model 340 Kricotronic — similar to above, except with Krico electronic trigger. Importation disc. 1988.

		100%	98%	95%	90%	80%	70%	60%
		$1,295	$995	$900	$800	$690	$600	$550

Last Mfg.'s Sug. Retail was $1,450.

Model 340 Mini-Sniper — non-glare wood and metal finish, military style barrel with muzzle brake, vent. forearm, no sights, match trigger (interchangeable), 5 shot, raised cheek piece. Importation disc. 1988.

	100%	98%	95%	90%	80%	70%	60%
	$1,050	$825	$725	$600	$550	$500	$450

Last Mfg.'s Sug. Retail was $1,200.

BIATHLON MODEL 360 S — .22 LR cal., standard biathlon configuration with conventional straight pull bolt.

Mfg.'s Sug. Retail	$1,695	$1,375	$1,075	$925	$750	$625	$550	$500

BIATHLON MODEL 360 S2 — .22 LR cal., biathlon competition rifle featuring unique pistol grip operated rapid fire action, includes 5 mag.'s, aperture sights, snow guards, and black stock.

Mfg.'s Sug. Retail	$1,595	$1,300	$1,050	$900	$750	$625	$550	$500

MODEL 400 SPORTER — .22 LR or .22 Hornet cal., 23½ in. barrel, select checkered walnut with European style curved cheek piece, 5 shot mag., open sights, 6.8 lbs.

Mfg.'s Sug. Retail	$895	$840	$750	$625	$550	$500	$450	$375

Add $55 for .22 Hornet cal.

Model 400 Match Single Shot — .22 LR only, match rifle configuration.

Mfg.'s Sug. Retail	$950	$875	$750	$625	$550	$500	$450	$375

Model 400 Silhouette — .22 LR only, designed for silhouette shooting, no sights.

Mfg.'s Sug. Retail	$775	$725	$615	$550	$500	$450	$375	$325

MODEL 420 L ST MANNLICHER SPORTER — .22 Hornet only, full stock sporter, 19½ in. barrel, double set triggers, 5 shot, 6½ lbs.

	$875	$750	$625	$550	$500	$450	$375

MODEL 440 — .22 Hornet, otherwise similar to Model 340. Importation disc. 1988.

	$900	$725	$575	$525	$450	$400	$360

Last Mfg.'s Sug. Retail was $1,025.

MODEL 600 HUNTING — .222 Rem., .223 Rem., .22-250 Rem., .243 Win., .308 Win., or 5.6 x 50 Mag. cal., 23½ in. barrel, select checkered walnut with curved European style cheek piece and vent. forend, 3 or 4 shot mag., open sights, single set trigger, 7 lbs.

Mfg.'s Sug. Retail	$1,295	$1,100	$975	$850	$750	$625	$550	$500

Add $55 for Model 600 SC.
Add $300 for Model 600 Benchrest.
Add $355 for Model 600 in sniper configuration.
This model is also available in single shot configuration at no extra charge as well as in a Match Model Group I & II - add $100 for Group II.

MODEL 620 MANNLICHER SPORTER — same cals. as Model 600, full stock sporter, 20¾ in. barrel, double set triggers, 3 shot mag., 6.8 lbs. Importation disc. 1988.

	$1,165	$965	$875	$760	$695	$650	$590

Last Mfg.'s Sug. Retail was $1,300.

Grading	100%	98%	95%	90%	80%	70%	60%

MODEL 640 S ST VARMINT — .22-250, .222 Rem., or .223 Rem. cal., 23¾ in. heavy barrel, high Monte Carlo comb and full cheek piece, rosewood forearm tip and grip cap, Wundhammer hand swell, double set triggers, 4 shot mag., 9.6 lbs. Importation disc. 1990

	$875	$750	$625	$550	$500	$450	$375

Last Mfg.'s Sug. Retail was $950.

⚔ **Model 640 Sniper** — similar to Model 640, except has non-adj. cheek piece. Importation disc. 1988.

	$1,325	$1,075	$965	$875	$760	$695	$650

Last Mfg.'s Sug. Retail was $1,500.

MODEL 640 DELUXE/SUPER SNIPER — .223 Rem. or .308 Win. cal., 23 in. barrel, select walnut stock has stippled hand grip, adj. cheek piece and vent. forearm, engine turned bolt assembly, 3 shot mag., match trigger, 10 lbs. Importation disc. 1988.

	$1,495	$1,175	$1,025	$875	$760	$695	$650

This model was known as the 650 Sniper/Match until 1986.
Last Mfg.'s Sug. Retail was $1,725.

MODEL 700A ECONOMY — .222 Rem., .243 Win., or .308 Win. cal. (Group I) or 6.5 x 55mm, 7 x 64mm, .270 Win., or .30-06 cal. (Group II), without sights, single trigger. Importation began 1991.

Mfg.'s Sug. Retail	$995	$900	$775	$650	$550	$500	$450	$375

Add $70 for Group II cals.

MODEL 700 SERIES — .17 Rem., .22-250 Rem., .222 Rem., .222 Rem. Mag., .223 Rem., 5.6 x 50mm Mag., .243 Win., .308 Win., or 5.6 x 57 RWS cal. (Group I), 6.5 x 55mm, 7 x 57mm, .270 Win., 7 x 64mm, .30-06, or 9.3 x 72 cal. (Group II), or 6.5 x 68mm, 7mm Rem. Mag., .300 Win. Mag., 8 x 68S, 7.5mm Swiss, or 6 x 62mm Freres cal. (Group III), matte black metal finish, open sights, approx. 7 lbs. Importation began 1991.

⚔ **Model 700 Hunting** — available in Group I or II cals. only, walnut hunting stock with Bavarian cheek piece, recoil pad, and palm swell grip.

Mfg.'s Sug. Retail	$1,249	$1,075	$950	$850	$750	$625	$550	$500

Add $50 for Group II cals.

⚔ **Model 700 DeLuxe** — similar to Model 700 Hunting, except has better grade walnut and is available in Group III cal's also.

Mfg.'s Sug. Retail	$1,379	$1,150	$1,000	$875	$750	$625	$550	$500

Add $20 for Group II cals.
Add $71 for Group III cals.
Add $150 for left-hand action.
Add $346-$516 for repeating variation in Groups I-III.

⚔ **Model 700 Stutzen** — full stock variation (Mannlicher) of the Model 700 DeLuxe.

Mfg.'s Sug. Retail	$1,450	$1,200	$1,025	$895	$750	$625	$550	$500

Add $39 for Group II cals.
Add $160 for Group III cals.
Add $275 for DeLuxe variation (includes better wood and finish).

MODEL 700 DL R SPORTER — .270 or .30-06 cal., 23½ in. barrel, curved European cheek piece, select walnut, 3 shot Mag., single set trigger, open sights, 7 lbs. Importation disc. 1990.

	$925	$800	$650	$575	$500	$450	$375

Subtract $30 for Model 700 DM ST.
Add $470 for Model 700 DLM.
Last Mfg.'s Sug. Retail was $1,025.

Grading	100%	98%	95%	90%	80%	70%	60%

MODEL 720 MANNLICHER SPORTER — similar to Model 700, only has 20¾ in. barrel, double set triggers, 6.8 lbs. Importation disc. 1990.

	100%	98%	95%	90%	80%	70%	60%
	$1,100	$975	$850	$750	$625	$550	$500

Last Mfg.'s Sug. Retail was $1,295.

⚒ **Model 720 Limited Edition** — .270 cal. only, 24Kt. gold scroll work on bolt handle, receiver, barrel and mounts. Trigger and front side are gold plated. Serial numbered in gold. Disc. 1986.

	100%	98%	95%	90%	80%	70%	60%
	$2,310	$1,990	$1,700	$1,450	$1,200	$1,050	$950

Last Mfg.'s Sug. Retail was $2,659.

RIFLES: SEMI-AUTO

MODEL 260 SPORTER — .22 LR only, semi-auto action, standard features. Importation began 1991.

	Mfg.'s Sug. Retail	98%	95%	90%	80%	70%	60%
	$595	$550	$495	$450	$410	$380	$350	$320

H. KRIEGHOFF GUN CO. (SHOTGUNS OF ULM)

Current manufacturer located in Ulm, Germany. Previous manufacture was in Suhl, Germany, 1886-1948. Currently imported and distributed by Krieghoff International Inc. located in Ottsville, PA. Dealer direct sales only.

WWII Krieghoff Lugers appear in the Luger section of this text.

SHOTGUNS: OVER AND UNDER

MODEL 32 STANDARD — O/U, 12, 20, 28, or .410 ga., 26½ - 32 in. barrels, auto ejector, boxlock, single trigger, select wood. Disc. 1980.

	100%	98%	95%	90%	80%	70%	60%
	$1,995	$1,795	$1,600	$1,450	$1,300	$1,175	$1,000

⚒ **Low Rib** — 28 or .410 ga., two-barrel set, 50% premium.

	100%	98%	95%	90%	80%	70%	60%
	$3,520	$2,860	$2,640	$2,200	$1,980	$1,870	$1,540

MODEL 32 4-BARREL SKEET SET — O/U, 12, 20, 28, or .410 ga., matched barrels in case, grades differ in engraving and wood quality, available as follows:

	100%	98%	95%	90%	80%	70%	60%
Standard	$5,500	$4,400	$3,960	$3,300	$3,080	$2,970	$2,750
Munchen Grade	$7,920	$6,820	$6,050	$5,720	$5,500	$5,225	$4,950
San Remo Grade	$9,020	$7,920	$7,150	$6,820	$6,600	$6,325	$6,050
⚒ Monte Carlo Grade	$16,500	$14,300	$12,650	$11,000	$9,900	$9,350	$8,800
Crown Grade	$19,800	$16,500	$14,300	$13,200	$12,100	$10,340	$9,680
⚒ Super Crown Grade	$24,200	$19,800	$16,500	$15,400	$14,300	$12,650	$11,000
Exhibition Grade	$39,500	$33,000	$27,500	$24,750	$22,000	$19,800	$16,500

MODEL 32 SINGLE BARREL TRAP — same action as O/U, 12 ga., 32-34 in. barrel, VR, mod., imp. mod., or full choke.

	100%	98%	95%	90%	80%	70%	60%
	$1,850	$1,400	$1,200	$1,000	$895	$795	$695

Grading	100%	98%	95%	90%	80%	70%	60%

KS-5 SINGLE BARREL TRAP — 12 ga. only, 32 or 34 in. barrel, adj. point of impact, innovative trigger configuration, optional choke tubes, redesigned streamlined receiver (new 1993). New 1985.

Mfg.'s Sug. Retail	$3,575		$3,050	$2,175	$1,700	$1,350	$1,100	$925	$850

Add $1,875 per additional barrel.
Add $400 for screw-in choke option.
Add $395 for factory adj. comb stock.
Add $375 for aluminum case.

Adj. point of impact on this model is achieved by means of different, optional fronthangers.

⚞ **KS-5 Special** — 12 ga. only, 32 or 34 in. barrel, features adj. rib and comb stock, cased. New 1990.

Mfg.'s Sug. Retail	$4,450		$3,750	$2,875	$2,400	$1,875	$1,575	$1,275	$1,075

Add $2,525 per additional barrel.
Add $400 for screw-in choke option.

Adj. point of impact on this model is achieved by an adj. rib and comb stock at no extra charge.

K-80 TRAP — 12 ga. only, available in O/U, Unsingle, Top Single (single top barrel), and Combo (O/U with extra trap barrel) configurations, standard model has silver finished receiver, adj. rib allowing variable points of impact (new 1993). In O/U configuration the barrels are separated, about 8½ lbs. A wide variety of custom order options can be ordered on this model.

For the Model K-80 Trap, extra barrels cost $2,385 for O/Us, $3,250 for top single, and $3,250 for unsingle barrel. Add $375 for single release trigger, $625 for double release trigger. Add $400 for 3 screw-in chokes (single barrel guns only), $590 for O/U screw-in chokes (5 tubes).

⚞ **Standard Model O/U** — special order only for Top Single, add 9% for Unsingle, or 40% for Combo Standard K-80 variations.

Mfg.'s Sug. Retail	$6,695		$5,800	$4,850	$4,250	$3,550	$3,000	$2,600	$2,295

⚞ **Bavaria Model O/U** — game scene engraved silver receiver with light scroll perimeter scroll work, select walnut. Special order only for Top Single, add 5% for Unsingle, or 24% for Combo Bavaria variations.

Mfg.'s Sug. Retail	$11,195		$9,650	$7,450	$6,200	$5,000	$4,375	$3,950	$3,300

⚞ **Danube Model O/U** — fine English scrollwork on receiver sides and floorplate. Special order only for Top Single, add 4.5% for Unsingle, or 20% for Combo Danube variations.

Mfg.'s Sug. Retail	$13,395		$11,750	$9,250	$7,925	$6,950	$5,950	$5,250	$4,800

⚞ **Gold Target Model** — deep chiseled scroll engraving with gold line accents, 100% coverage finest quality walnut. Special order only for Top Single, add 3% for Unsingle, and 14% for Combo Gold Target variations.

Mfg.'s Sug. Retail	$19,695		$16,650	$13,000	$10,350	$8,950	$7,150	$6,570	$5,850

⚞ **Centennial Model** — 12 ga. only, available in combo configuration only, 100 only mfg. 1986 to commemorate Krieghoff's centennial year, ser. no. 14501-14600. H. Krieghoff's signature inlaid in gold on frame sides. Add $150 for screw-in interchangeable chokes, $1,755 for 4-barrel set.

				$6,000	$5,000	$4,400			

Last Mfg.'s Sug. Retail was $5,995.

H. Krieghoff Gun Co., cont.

Grading	100%	98%	95%	90%	80%	70%	60%

K-80 SKEET O/U — 12 ga. only, available in Lightweight (8mm rib), Standardweight (8mm rib), or International (12mm rib) configurations, factory porting on both barrels, 28 in. barrels only, 8.2 lbs.

For the Model K-80 Skeet, add $705 for International Model, $300 for 30 in. light barrels, $260 for Tula choking (even choking), $605 for Skeet Special (choke tubes & tapered flat rib).

International Skeet models are supplied with hard case. Standardweight and Lightweight models include soft case.

⚮ **Standard Model** — available with either lightweight (Dural aluminum) or standardweight frame. Hard case optional.

	100%	98%	95%	90%	80%	70%	60%
Mfg.'s Sug. Retail	$6,290	$5,425	$4,275	$3,300	$2,850	$2,450	$2,125	$1,900

Add $605 for Skeet Special (includes 2 choke tubes & tapered flat rib).

⚮ **Bavaria Model O/U** — game scene engraved silver receiver with light perimeter scroll work, select walnut. Available in either Standardweight or Lightweight configuration.

	100%	98%	95%	90%	80%	70%	60%
Mfg.'s Sug. Retail	$10,790	$9,225	$6,300	$5,500	$4,950	$4,375	$3,950	$3,300

⚮ **Danube Model O/U** — fine English scrollwork on receiver sides and floorplate. Available in either Standardweight or Lightweight configuration.

	100%	98%	95%	90%	80%	70%	60%
Mfg.'s Sug. Retail	$12,990	$10,950	$9,000	$7,850	$7,000	$6,100	$5,250	$4,800

⚮ **Gold Target Model** — deep chiseled scroll engraving with gold line accents, 100% coverage finest quality walnut. This model is available in Standardweight frame only.

	100%	98%	95%	90%	80%	70%	60%
Mfg.'s Sug. Retail	$19,290	$16,450	$12,950	$10,350	$8,950	$7,150	$6,570	$5,850

⚮ **Centennial Skeet** — available in skeet configuration — special features as noted above on Centennial Model description listed under K-80 Trap. Mfg. 1986 only.

	95%	90%	80%
	$3,675	$3,150	$2,700

Last Mfg.'s Sug. Retail was $3,980.

K-80 2-BARREL LIGHTWEIGHT SKEET SET — 12 ga. Tula and tubing barrel, 8mm rib, hard case standard. New 1988.

⚮ **Standard Grade**

	100%	98%	95%	90%	80%	70%	60%
Mfg.'s Sug. Retail	$10,935	$8,875	$6,750	$5,050	$4,275	$3,875	$3,300	$3,000

Subtract $1,760 for heavy barrel variation, which does not include sub-gauge tubes. Retail price for 2 barrel heavy set with choke tubes is $9,175.

⚮ **Bavaria Model O/U** — game scene engraved silver receiver with light perimeter scroll work, select walnut. Importation began 1988.

	100%	98%	95%	90%	80%	70%	60%
Mfg.'s Sug. Retail	$15,435	$13,800	$10,400	$8,300	$7,100	$6,200	$5,250	$4,800

Subtract $1,760 for heavy barrel variation, which does not include sub-gauge tubes. Retail price for 2 barrel heavy set with choke tubes is $13,675.

⚮ **Danube Model O/U** — fine English scroll work on receiver sides and floorplate. Importation began 1988.

	100%	98%	95%	90%	80%	70%	60%
Mfg.'s Sug. Retail	$17,635	$14,200	$11,100	$9,350	$7,750	$6,700	$5,850	$5,450

Subtract $1,760 for heavy barrel variation, which does not include sub-gauge tubes. Retail price for 2 barrel heavy set with choke tubes is $15,875.

⚮ **Gold Target Model** — deep chiseled scroll engraving with gold line accents, 100% coverage finest quality walnut.

	100%	98%	95%	90%	80%	70%	60%
Mfg.'s Sug. Retail	$23,000	$18,950	$13,850	$11,900	$9,100	$7,750	$7,000	$6,650

Subtract $1,760 for heavy barrel variation. Retail price for 2 barrel heavy set with choke tubes is $21,175.

H. Krieghoff Gun Co., cont. 563

Grading	100%	98%	95%	90%	80%	70%	60%

K-80 4-BARREL SKEET SET — 1 barrel each of 12, 20, 28, and .410 ga., 12 ga. is Tula choked (even patterning), 8mm VR., includes hard case.

⚞ **Standard Grade** — satin finished receiver with skeet scroll engraving.
Mfg.'s Sug. Retail $14,200 $11,300 $9,500 $8,300 $7,100 $6,100 $5,250 $4,500

⚞ **Bavaria Model O/U** — game scene engraved silver receiver with light perimeter scrollwork, select walnut.
Mfg.'s Sug. Retail $18,700 $15,750 $12,950 $11,000 $9,250 $7,975 $6,900 $5,400

⚞ **Danube Model O/U** — fine English scroll work on receiver sides and floorplate.
Mfg.'s Sug. Retail $20,950 $17,600 $14,300 $12,100 $9,950 $8,600 $7,725 $6,900

⚞ **Gold Target Model** — deep chiseled scroll engraving with gold line accents, 100% coverage finest quality walnut.
Mfg.'s Sug. Retail $27,200 $22,800 $18,775 $15,650 $12,250 $9,950 $8,700 $7,500

K-80 PIGEON O/U — 12 ga. only, available with 28, 29, or 30 in. barrels, standard tapered step rib, IM/SF choking, available in Lightweight or Standardweight configuration (no extra charge).
Beginning 1992, the K-80 Pigeon Model is available by special order only. Values will be approximately the same as the K-80 Trap Models in the various grades. Values for the models listed below reflect the last factory retail pricing of this variation (1991).

⚞ **Standard Grade** — satin finished receiver with no engraving.
Mfg.'s Sug. Retail $5,950 $5,250 $4,600 $4,200 $3,550 $3,000 $2,600 $2,295

⚞ **Bavaria Model O/U** — game scene engraved silver receiver with light scroll perimeter scroll work, select walnut.
Mfg.'s Sug. Retail $9,775 $8,700 $6,950 $5,975 $5,000 $4,375 $3,950 $3,300

⚞ **Danube Model O/U** — fine English scroll work on receiver sides and floorplate.
Mfg.'s Sug. Retail $12,100 $10,875 $8,800 $7,675 $6,950 $6,000 $5,250 $4,800

⚞ **Gold Target Model** — deep chiseled scroll engraving with gold line accents, 100% coverage finest quality walnut.
Mfg.'s Sug. Retail $15,870 $13,700 $11,500 $9,995 $8,700 $5,675 $6,570 $5,850

K-80 SPORTING CLAYS O/U — 12 ga. only, 28, 30 (new 1991), or 32 (new 1993) in. barrels with 5 choke tubes, choice of 8mm VR Skeet, tapered flat (broadway) or step rib (special order), sporting clay stock dimensions. New 1988.
Add $2,975 for extra set of O/U barrels.

⚞ **Standard Grade** — satin finished receiver with sporting scroll engraving.
Mfg.'s Sug. Retail $7,350 $6,200 $5,100 $4,350 $3,650 $3,000 $2,600 $2,100

⚞ **Bavaria Model O/U** — game scene engraved silver receiver with light scroll perimeter scroll work, select walnut.
Mfg.'s Sug. Retail $11,850 $9,800 $7,850 $6,350 $5,350 $4,450 $3,950 $3,300

⚞ **Danube Model O/U** — fine English scroll work on receiver sides and floorplate.
Mfg.'s Sug. Retail $14,050 $11,600 $9,500 $8,150 $7,150 $6,200 $5,250 $4,400

⚞ **Gold Target Model** — deep chiseled scroll engraving with gold line accents, 100% coverage finest quality walnut.
Mfg.'s Sug. Retail $20,350 $16,200 $12,550 $10,100 $8,100 $6,950 $5,950 $4,950

VANDALIA TRAP — high rib, two barrel combination.
$4,180 $3,520 $3,300 $2,860 $2,640 $2,530 $2,200

H. Krieghoff Gun Co., cont.

Grading	100%	98%	95%	90%	80%	70%	60%

O/U SHOTGUN OR COMBINATION GUN

Add $550 for hand detachable sidelocks (Ulm only).
Add $1,100 for 4-claw scope mount system.

TECK MODEL — O/U shotgun or rifle/shotgun combo., 12 and 16 ga., various cals. (7 x 57R, 7 x 64mm, 7 x 65R, .30-06, or .308 Win.), boxlock action, Kersten double crossbolt, auto ejectors, 7½ lbs.

Mfg.'s Sug. Retail	$7,400	$6,400	$5,000	$4,350	$3,550	$3,000	$2,600	$2,295

Teck Dural — Dural aluminum frame variation of the Teck, 6.8 lbs.

Mfg.'s Sug. Retail	$7,730	$6,625	$5,100	$4,350	$3,550	$3,000	$2,600	$2,295

ULM — similar to Teck, except sidelock and fully engraved with leaf arabesques.

Mfg.'s Sug. Retail	$12,900	$10,550	$8,525	$7,350	$6,250	$5,250	$4,400	$3,500

Ulm Dural — Dural aluminum frame variation of the Ulm.

Mfg.'s Sug. Retail	$12,900	$10,550	$8,525	$7,350	$6,250	$5,250	$4,400	$3,500

ULM PRIMUS — similar to Ulm, except game scene engraved with English arabesques.

Mfg.'s Sug. Retail	$18,790	$15,100	$11,100	$8,500	$6,850	$5,975	$5,450	$4,995

Ulm Primus Dural — Dural aluminum frame variation of the Ulm Primus.

Mfg.'s Sug. Retail	$18,790	$15,100	$11,100	$8,500	$6,850	$5,975	$5,450	$4,995

ULTRA — combination O/U, 12 ga. only, various calibers (lower barrel), 25 in. barrels, "Kickspannar" mechanism allows manual cocking from thumb safety, satin finish receiver, VR, 6 lbs. New 1985.

Mfg.'s Sug. Retail	$4,450	$3,675	$2,425	$1,800	$1,400	$1,200	$1,050	$900

Ultra-B — similar to Ultra, except features a selector to switch the front set trigger to the top shotgun barrel.

Mfg.'s Sug. Retail	$4,990	$4,050	$2,675	$1,925	$1,550	$1,350	$1,150	$1,000

SHOTGUNS: O/U

ULM-P — 12 ga. only, live pigeon gun with hand detachable sidelocks, standard grade has light scrollwork engraving.

Mfg.'s Sug. Retail	$15,900	$12,950	$10,200	$8,375	$7,100	$5,850	$5,450	$4,995

Bavaria Grade — similar to Ulm-P, only with elaborate game scene engraving.

Mfg.'s Sug. Retail	$20,500	$16,000	$12,500	$10,000	$8,250	$6,600	$5,700	$5,300

KS-2 SERIES — any ga., full H&H type sidelocks, priced by individual special order. Prices start at $24,000. Custom order only with substantial wait.

DOUBLE RIFLES

Various grades differ in style and amount of engraving, choice of walnut and various options that can be special ordered.

TECK O/U — .30-06, .300 Win. Mag., .308 Win., 7 X 56R, 8 X 57JRS, 9.3 X 74R, .375 H&H (disc. 1988), or .458 Win. Mag. cal., 25 in. barrels, boxlock action, cocking indicators.

Mfg.'s Sug. Retail	$9,200	$7,800	$6,150	$4,975	$4,150	$3,650	$3,300	$3,000

Add $700 for 7 x 56R, 8 x 57 JRS, .375 H&H (disc. 1988), or .458 Win. Mag. cal.
Add $950 for DTs with front set trigger.

Grading	100%	98%	95%	90%	80%	70%	60%

⚞ **Teck-Handspanner** — manual cocking, 7 x 65R, .30-06, or .308 Win. on 16 ga. receiver frame.

	100%	98%	95%	90%	80%	70%	60%
Mfg.'s Sug. Retail $10,970	$9,150	$7,500	$6,400	$5,175	$4,375	$3,950	$3,200

ULTRA O/U — various cals. up to 9.3 x 74R, features unique manual cocking/self cocking device and interchangeable muzzle wedge for adjustable point of impact. New 1993.

	100%	98%	95%	90%	80%	70%	60%
Mfg.'s Sug. Retail $6,875	$6,200	$5,600	$4,950	$4,250	$3,500	$2,950	$2,250

ULM O/U — similar to Teck Double Rifle, except has any combination of cals., with sidelocks and more elaborate engraving.

	100%	98%	95%	90%	80%	70%	60%
Mfg.'s Sug. Retail $14,580	$12,200	$9,200	$8,000	$6,775	$6,100	$5,500	$4,950

Add $550 for hand detachable sidelocks.
Add $1,775 with single/double trigger.

⚞ **Ulm Dekor** — sidelock with light scroll engraving. Importation disc. 1991.

100%	98%	95%	90%	80%	70%	60%
$10,450	$9,150	$8,000	$6,750	$5,600	$5,000	$4,400

Last Mfg.'s Sug. Retail was $12,500.

⚞ **Ulm Primus** — deluxe sidelock.

	100%	98%	95%	90%	80%	70%	60%
Mfg.'s Sug. Retail $20,500	$16,250	$11,400	$9,400	$7,700	$6,450	$5,700	$5,300

TRUMPF SxS — boxlock action, similar to Teck model, except in .30-06, 8 x 57JRS, or 9.3 X 74R cal.

	100%	98%	95%	90%	80%	70%	60%
Mfg.'s Sug. Retail $16,150	$13,200	$9,700	$8,350	$6,900	$6,100	$5,500	$4,950

NEPTUN SxS — sidelock double rifle, same features as the Ulm model. Importation disc. 1991.

100%	98%	95%	90%	80%	70%	60%
$12,750	$10,400	$8,700	$7,350	$6,000	$5,450	$4,995

Last Mfg.'s Sug. Retail was $15,500.

DRILLINGS

H.Krieghoff drillings can be ordered with a variety of cals. (.222 Rem., .243 Win., .270 Win., or .30-06) and special order features. Prices shown below are for standard guns with no options. Better models will have a finer grade walnut and exhibit more elaborate deep relief engraving.

Add $425 for free floating rifle barrels on Trumpf and Neptun Models listed below (both regular steel frame and Dural variations).

PLUS MODEL — 12 or 20 ga. over rifle barrel (.222 Rem., .243 Win., .270 Win., or .30-06 cal.), boxlock action, light engraving. New 1988.

	100%	98%	95%	90%	80%	70%	60%
Mfg.'s Sug. Retail $5,245	$4,400	$3,375	$2,700	$2,150	$1,825	$1,525	$1,200

TRUMPF MODEL — 12, 16, or 20 ga. O/U, or rifle shotgun combo., various cals., boxlock, 25 in. barrels, 7½ lbs.

	100%	98%	95%	90%	80%	70%	60%
Mfg.'s Sug. Retail $9,450	$7,925	$6,125	$5,250	$4,250	$3,300	$2,750	$2,200

Add $2,580 for single trigger.

⚞ **Trumpf Dural** — Dural aluminum frame variation of the Trumpf, 6.8 lbs., cased.

	100%	98%	95%	90%	80%	70%	60%
Mfg.'s Sug. Retail $9,450	$7,925	$6,125	$5,250	$4,250	$3,300	$2,750	$2,200

Add $2,580 for single trigger.

NEPTUN MODEL — 12 or 20 ga., variety of cals., elaborate engraving, sidelocks.

	100%	98%	95%	90%	80%	70%	60%
Mfg.'s Sug. Retail $14,950	$12,250	$9,925	$8,550	$7,350	$6,100	$5,100	$4,150

⚞ **Neptun Dural** — Dural aluminum frame variation of the Neptun, cased.

	100%	98%	95%	90%	80%	70%	60%
Mfg.'s Sug. Retail $14,950	$12,250	$9,925	$8,550	$7,350	$6,100	$5,100	$4,150

NEPTUN PRIMUS MODEL — similar to Neptun Model, only hand detachable sidelocks and elaborate deep relief engraving.

	100%	98%	95%	90%	80%	70%	60%
Mfg.'s Sug. Retail $19,950	$15,550	$12,100	$9,950	$8,200	$7,000	$5,850	$4,950

H. Krieghoff Gun Co., cont.

Grading	100%	98%	95%	90%	80%	70%	60%

⚡ **Neptun Primus Dural** — Dural aluminum frame variation available at no extra charge.

	100%	98%	95%	90%	80%	70%	60%
Mfg.'s Sug. Retail	$19,950	$15,550	$12,100	$9,950	$8,200	$7,000	$5,850	$4,950

L section

L.A.R. MANUFACTURING, INC.
Manufacturer located in West Jordan, UT.

Grading	100%	98%	95%	90%	80%	70%	60%

GRIZZLY WIN. MAG. MARK I — .357 Mag., 357/45 Grizzly Win. Mag. (new 1990), .45 ACP, 10mm, or .45 Win. Mag., single action, semi-auto based on the Colt 1911 design, 5.4 in. (new 1986), 6½ in., 8 in. (new 1987), or 10 in. (new 1987) barrel, parkerized finish, 7 shot mag., ambidextrous safeties, checkered rubber grips, adj. sights, 48 oz. empty. Also can be converted to .45 ACP, 10mm (new 1988), .357 Mag., or .30 Mauser (disc.). New 1984.

⚐ **Short Barrel Lengths** — 5.4 or 6.5 in. barrel.

Mfg.'s Sug. Retail	$920	$795	$650	$600	$525	$495	$475	$450

Add $13 if purchased in .357 Mag.
Add $138 for hard chrome frame.
Add $240 for full hard chrome.
Add $214-$228 for cal. conversion units.
Conversion units include .357 Mag., 10mm, .40 S&W (new 1991), and .45 ACP cals.

⚐ **Long Barrel Lengths** — .357 Mag., .45 Win. Mag., or 357/45 Grizzly Win. Mag. (new 1990), 8 or 10 in. barrel, extended slides.

Mfg.'s Sug. Retail	$1,313	$1,195	$975	$895	$800	$725	$650	$575

Add $62 for 10 in. barrel.
Add $25 if purchased in .357 Mag.
Add $143 for scope mounts (disc.).
Add $110 for muzzle compensator.

GRIZZLY .44 MAG. MARK 4 — .44 Mag., choice of lusterless blue or parkerized finish, 5.4 or 6.5 in. barrel, adj. sights. New 1991.

Mfg.'s Sug. Retail	$933	$800	$665	$600	$525	$495	$475	$450

GRIZZLY .50 MARK 5 — .50 Action Express, single action semi-auto, 5.4 or 6.5 in. barrel, 6 shot mag., checkered walnut grips, 56 oz. New 1993.

Mfg.'s Sug. Retail	$1,060	$950	$825	$700	$600	$525	$495	$475

GRIZZLY WIN. MAG. MARK II — similar to Mark I, except has fixed sights, standard safeties, and different metal finish. Mfg. 1986 only.

		$625	$550	$525	$495	$475	$450	$425

Add $25 for .357 Mag.
Last Mfg.'s Sug. Retail was $550.

L E S INCORPORATED
Previous manufacturer located in Morton Grove, IL.

PISTOL: SEMI-AUTO
The Steyr Model GB is patterned after this action.

P-18 ROGAK DOUBLE ACTION — 9mm Para., double action, 18 shot, 5½ in. barrel, stainless steel, black plastic grips with partial thumb rest. Disc.

				$350	$295	$265		

⚐ **High polish finish**

				$395	$330	$295		

Approx. 2,300 P-18s were mfg. before being disc.

LAHTI PISTOL

Previous manufacturer located in Husqvarna, Sweden & Vkt (state rifle factory in Jyvaskyla), Finland.

Grading	100%	98%	95%	90%	80%	70%	60%

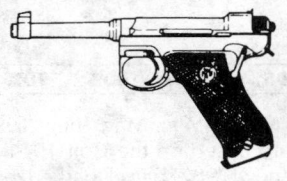

SWEDISH MODEL 40 — 9mm Para., 4¾ in. barrel, blued finish, fixed sights, plastic grips, mfg. 1940-1944.

	100%	98%	95%	90%	80%	70%	60%
	$395	$350	$300	$275	$260	$250	$240

Add 10% for Holster-Rig.

FINNISH L-35 — mfg. 1935-1944.

	100%	98%	95%	90%	80%	70%	60%
	$1,250	$1,050	$900	$760	$680	$620	$575

Note: It is important to note that there are diversely marked variations of this pistol, such as RPLT (Danish State Police); such police markings reduce value by about 10%.

LAKE FIELD ARMS LTD.

Manufacturer located in Ontario, Canada. Distributor sales only through most major U.S. distributors.

MARK I — .22 LR, single shot bolt action, 20½ in. choked or smooth bore barrel, adj. rear sight, thumb rotary safety, walnut finish hardwood stock, 5½ lbs.

Mfg.'s Sug. Retail	$120	$100	$75	$65	$55	$50	$40	$30

This model is also available in youth dimensions at no extra charge (Model Mark I-Y).

MARK II — .22 LR, bolt action, 10 shot clip mag., 20½ in. barrel, adj. rear sight, thumb rotary safety, walnut finish hardwood stock, 5½ lbs.

Mfg.'s Sug. Retail	$125	$110	$80	$70	$60	$50	$40	$30

Add $15 for left-hand variation (new 1993).
This model is also available in youth dimensions at no extra charge (Model Mark II-Y).

MODEL 64B — .22 LR, semi-auto, side ejection, 10 shot clip mag., 20½ in. barrel, adj. rear sight, thumb rotary safety, walnut finish hardwood stock, 5½ lbs.

Mfg.'s Sug. Retail	$133	$115	$85	$75	$65	$55	$45	$40

MODEL 90B (BIATHLON) — .22 LR, biathlon rifle, includes five 5-shot mag.'s, 21 in. barrel, aperture sights, one piece natural finish hardwood stock, 8¼ lbs. New 1991.

Mfg.'s Sug. Retail	$535	$410	$295	$225	$195	$170	$150	$130

Add $55 for left-hand variation (new 1993).

MODEL 91T — .22 LR, target rifle available as either single shot or 5-shot repeater, 25 in. barrel with aperture sights, dark hardwood finished stock, 8 lbs. New 1991.

Mfg.'s Sug. Retail	$425	$325	$250	$215	$175	$150	$135	$115

Model 91TR — repeater version of the Model 91T, 5 shot mag.

Mfg.'s Sug. Retail	$455	$345	$260	$215	$175	$150	$135	$115

Add $45 for left-hand variation (new 1993).

MODEL 92S — .22 LR, 5 shot detachable mag., 21 in. barrel, hardwood stock with Monte Carlo cheekpiece, 8 lbs. New 1993.

Mfg.'s Sug. Retail	$365	$285	$235	$200	$175	$160	$150	$135

Add $35 for left-hand variation.

LAMES

Previous manufacturer located In Italy.

Grading	100%	98%	95%	90%	80%	70%	60%

SHOTGUNS

FIELD MODEL O/U — 12 ga., 26, 28, or 30 in. barrels, various chokes, VR, engraving, SST, auto ejectors, checkered pistol grip stock with pad.

	$400	$380	$365	$350	$325	$300	$275

Separated barrels

	$500	$480	$465	$450	$425	$400	$375

STANDARD TRAP O/U — similar to Field, 30 or 32 in. various trap bore barrels, with wide VR, trap style Monte Carlo stock.

	$600	$575	$550	$525	$425	$400	$450

CALIFORNIA TRAP O/U — similar to Standard Trap, with separated barrels.

	$700	$675	$650	$625	$525	$500	$450

SKEET MODEL — similar to Field, with 26 in. skeet bore barrels, skeet stock and separated barrels.

	$600	$575	$550	$525	$425	$400	$350

LANBER SHOTGUNS

Manufacturer located in Zaldbar, Spain. Previously imported by Exel Arms of America, Inc., located in Gardener, MA and by Lanber Arms of America located in Adrian, MI.

Lanber makes a wide range of quality O/U and semi-auto shotguns. Currently, they do not have a U.S. agent/importer, and the factory should be contacted directly (see Trademark Index) for more information or to special order their shotguns.

SHOTGUNS: O/U RECENT MFG.

Also, refer to disc. Exel Models 101-104 and 105-107 in the "E" section of this text previously manufactured by Lanber.

The following models were imported by Lanber Arms of America, Inc. located in Adrian, MI until business ceased in late 1986.

844 ST — 12 ga. only, boxlock, 26 or 28 in. barrels, choked IC/IM, extractors, SST, automatic safety, VR, European walnut with hand checkering, blued finish with engraved receiver, $7\frac{1}{8}$ lbs. Importation disc. 1986.

	$395	$340	$320	$300	$285	$270	$255

Last Mfg.'s Sug. Retail was $450.

844 MST — 12 ga. only, 3 in. chambers, 30 in. F & M barrels, otherwise similar to 844 ST. Importation disc. 1986.

	$405	$350	$335	$320	$310	$300	$295

Last Mfg.'s Sug. Retail was $470.

2004 LCH — 12 ga. only, boxlock action, 28 in. barrels, SST, ejectors, supplied with 5 screw-in choke tubes, engraved satin finish receiver, checkered European walnut, $7\frac{3}{8}$ lbs. Importation disc. 1986.

	$575	$485	$460	$440	$420	$395	$380

Last Mfg.'s Sug. Retail was $650.

2004 LCH SKEET — 12 ga. only, 28 in. barrels supplied with 5 choke tubes, blued finish, moderately engraved, select checkered walnut, $7\frac{3}{8}$ lbs. Importation disc. 1986.

	$740	$635	$585	$560	$540	$520	$495

Last Mfg.'s Sug. Retail was $845.

Grading	100%	98%	95%	90%	80%	70%	60%

2004 LCH TRAP — 12 ga. only, 30 in. barrels supplied with 3 choke tubes, European walnut has trap dimensions, blued finish. Importation disc. 1986.

		100%	98%	95%	90%	80%	70%	60%
		$675	$625	$585	$560	$540	$520	$495

Last Mfg.'s Sug. Retail was $845.

LASALLE
Previous manufacturer located in France.

SLIDE ACTION SHOTGUN — 12 or 20 ga., 26, 28, or 30 in. barrels, various chokes, alloy frame, checkered pistol grip stock.

	100%	98%	95%	90%	80%	70%	60%
	$250	$225	$200	$175	$150	$125	$100

AUTOMATIC SHOTGUN — 12 ga., 26, 28, or 30 in. barrels, various chokes, gas operated, checkered pistol grip stock.

	100%	98%	95%	90%	80%	70%	60%
	$300	$275	$250	$225	$200	$175	$150

LASERARMS
Manufactured in Thermopolis, WY. Marketed and distributed by Laserarms, Inc. located in Little Rock, AR, a division of Emerging Technologies, Inc. Direct or limited dealer sales only.

PISTOLS: STAINLESS STEEL

SERIES I — .40 S&W, .45 ACP, or 10mm cal., semi-auto single action, $5\frac{1}{2}$ in. barrel with compensator, Millett adj. sights, ambidextrous safety, all metal parts Teflon coated, beveled mag. well, integral accessory mounts, 7 (.45 ACP) or 8 (10mm or .40 S&W) shot mag., 52 oz. New 1993.

Mfg.'s Sug. Retail $599 $525 $450 $395
Add $40 for Nightowl configuration (includes Millett adj. Tritium sights).

⚸ **Series I Compact** — .40 S&W or .45 ACP cal., compact variation of the Series I with $3\frac{7}{8}$ in. barrel, 46 oz. New 1993.
Mfg.'s Sug. Retail $599 $525 $450 $395
Add $40 for Nightowl configuration (includes Millett adj. Tritium sights).

SERIES I ILLUSION — similar to Series I, except includes 1 in. Illusion red-dot optical scope, scope rings, and accessories. New 1993.
Mfg.'s Sug. Retail $769 $675 $550 $450

SERIES I DREAM TEAM — .40 S&W, .45 ACP, or 10mm cal., similar configuration as the Series I, except includes Laseraim sight mounted on front trigger guard and mounting system. New 1993.
Mfg.'s Sug. Retail $835 $725 $595 $495
This model is available in Standard Model ($5\frac{1}{2}$ in. barrel) or Compact Model ($3\frac{7}{8}$ in. barrel, not available in 10mm cal.).

SERIES II — .40 S&W, .45 ACP, or 10mm cal., similar technical specs. as the Series I, except has non-reflective stainless steel finish, fixed or adj. sights, and 5 in. non-compensated barrel, 43 oz. New 1993.
Mfg.'s Sug. Retail $529 $460 $375 $300
Add $27 for adj. sights.
Add $50 for Nightowl configuration (includes adj. Tritium sights).

⚸ **Series II Compact** — .40 S&W or .45 ACP cal., $3\frac{3}{8}$ in. barrel, 37 oz. New 1993.
Mfg.'s Sug. Retail $529 $460 $375 $300

Grading	100%	98%	95%	90%	80%	70%	60%

SERIES II ILLUSION — similar to Series II, except includes 1 in. Illusion red-dot optical scope, scope rings, and accessories. New 1993.

Mfg.'s Sug. Retail	$699		$625	$525	$425		

SERIES II DREAM TEAM — .40 S&W, .45 ACP, or 10mm cal., similar configuration as the Series II, except includes Laseraim sight mounted on front trigger guard and mounting system. New 1993.

Mfg.'s Sug. Retail	$770		$675	$550	$450		

LAURONA

Manufacturer located in Eibar, Spain. Available factory direct only (see Trademark Index for Laurona information). Previously imported and distributed by Galaxy Imports located in Victoria, TX until 1991.

Laurona manufactures high quality O/U shotguns and O/U express rifles/combination guns. Beginning 1992, Laurona switched from a one-piece, demi-block type of fabrication to a monobloc system which has improved strength characteristics while reducing weight in their X-Series line of shotguns and express rifles. Since this trademark has no current U.S. importer/agent, the factory should be contacted directly (see Trademark Index) for more information or to special order their quality firearms. Current values below are quoted WITHOUT U.S. importation shipping charges and domestic excise tax (in other words, FOB Spanish seaport or airport - export packing included).

Laurona long guns come standard with a black chrome metal finish that is extremely resistant to oxidation. Left hand stocks are available for the 83 MG Super Game, 85 MS Super Game, Trap, and Super Skeet, Silhouette Trap models, and Silhouette Sporting Clays.

Suffix designations on Laurona shotguns refer to the following: G - twin single triggers, S - selective single trigger, M - multi-chokes, T - Tulip, BV - beavertail.

All Super Game Models were available with a deluxe package which includes a recoil pad, mid-bead sight, and select wood for an additional $250. Special order dull matte finished barrels (with multi-chokes) were available for an additional $200 - extra barrels were priced between $635 (20 ga.) or $800 (12 ga.) per set.

If more information is required on an older Laurona model not listed in this publication, it is advisable to do the following. Please send/FAX an accurate description of your specimen (including Laurona model name, serial number, and other pertinent data - include photos if possible) to Galaxy Imports located at P.O. Box 3661, Victoria, TX 77903, phone: 512-573-4867, FAX: 512-576-9622. The charge for this service is $25 per serial number.

RIFLES: O/U CURRENT MFG.

MODEL 2000X EXPRESS RIFLE — .30-06, 8 x 57 JRS, 8 x 75 RS, 9.3 x 74 R, or .375 H&H Mag. cal., monobloc construction, 24 in. separated barrels featuring quarter rib sight and convergency adjustment at muzzle, matte black chrome finish, open sights, ejectors or extractors, SST or DT, approx. 8.1 lbs. New 1992.

Mfg.'s Sug. Retail	$1,808		$1,808	$1,525	$1,375	$1,100	$995	$895	$795

Add $242 for .375 H&H Mag. cal.

This model accepts Leupold or European styled ring mounts.

Model 2000X Combo — includes choice of cals. listed above, except for .375 H&H Mag. with 12 ga. under-barrel. New 1992.

Mfg.'s Sug. Retail	$1,356		$1,356	$1,100	$925	$825	$725	$625	$525

SHOTGUNS: O/U DISC. MFG.

Please refer to the Exel 300 Series in the "E" section.

SHOTGUNS: O/U RECENT MFG.

MODEL 82 — double selective trigger system, ejectors, pistol grip, vent rib, various chokes and barrel lengths. Disc.

	100%	98%	95%	90%	80%	70%	60%
	$549	$410	$380	$340	$300	$275	$250

This model was imported by Exel Arms of America, Inc.

SUPER GAME MODELS — 12 or 20 ga., boxlock, 28 in. barrels, unique twin single triggers, ejectors, extensive fine scroll engraving on a satin finished receiver, anti-rust black chrome barrel finish, VR, elongated forcing cones, checkered walnut stock and forearm.
Twin single triggers can function as conventional double triggers in addition to either trigger functioning as a non-selective single trigger. For example, each trigger can fire both barrels - the back trigger fires from top to bottom and the front trigger uses the bottom to top sequence.

82 G Super Game — new designation for 82 Super Game, with T forend, 2¾ in. chambers, 28 in. separated barrels choked F/M or IC/IM with 8mm VR, twin single triggers. Importation disc. 1989.

	$975	$875	$795	$675	$625	$550	$495

This model was previously designated 82 Super Game.
Last Mfg.'s Sug. Retail was $1,100.

82 Pigeon Competition — similar to 82 Trap Competition, except 28 in. barrels with different chokings. Importation disc. 1986.

	$545	$465	$440	$420	$405	$390	$375

Last Mfg.'s Sug. Retail was $630.

82 Trap Combo — trap model, 8mm VR, non-selective single trigger. Importation disc. 1986.

	$485	$390	$375	$360	$350	$340	$330

Last Mfg.'s Sug. Retail was $566.

82 Trap Competition — 29 in. barrels, oil finished Monte Carlo stock, 13mm VR, non-selective single trigger, motif engraving, rubber recoil pad, 8.1 lbs. Importation disc. 1986.

	$540	$460	$435	$420	$405	$390	$375

Last Mfg.'s Sug. Retail was $625.

83 MG SUPER GAME — 12 or 20 ga., similar to 82 G Super Game except has multi-chokes, 2¾ or 3 in. Mag. chambers.

	$1,275	$1,025	$895	$795	$675	$625	$550

Last Mfg.'s Sug. Retail was $1,540.

83 MG Super Game 2 Barrel Set — includes 2 sets of barrels (12 and 20 ga.).

	$1,775	$1,500	$1,275	$1,000	$875	$775	$700

Last Mfg.'s Sug. Retail was $2,180.

83 M Puma Hunting — importation disc. 1986.

	$485	$445	$425	$410	$395	$380	$375

Last Mfg.'s Sug. Retail was $529.

84 S SUPER GAME — similar to 82 G Super Game except has SST and available with 3 in. Mag. chambers. Importation disc. 1989.

	$925	$840	$775	$675	$625	$550	$495

Last Mfg.'s Sug. Retail was $1,100.

Grading	100%	98%	95%	90%	80%	70%	60%

84 S SUPER TRAP — 29 in. barrels, extensive fine scroll engraving, separated barrels with 13mm aluminum VR, rubber recoil pad, full pistol grip stock with orthopedic grip, beavertail forearm, single selective trigger, elongated forcing cones, choked IM/F or M/F, 7¾ lbs.

| | $1,650 | $1,250 | $995 | $875 | $750 | $625 | $495 |

Last Mfg.'s Sug. Retail was $1,920.

85 MS SUPER GAME — available in 12 or 20 ga., similar to 83 MG Super Game, except has SST.

| | $1,295 | $1,025 | $895 | $795 | $675 | $625 | $550 |

Last Mfg.'s Sug. Retail was $1,575.

85 MS Super Game 2 Barrel Set — includes 2 sets of barrels (12 and 20 ga.).

| | $1,800 | $1,500 | $1,275 | $1,000 | $875 | $775 | $700 |

Last Mfg.'s Sug. Retail was $2,215.

85 MS SUPER TRAP — similar to 84 S Super Trap, except chokes are full over multi-choke.

| | $1,675 | $1,250 | $995 | $875 | $750 | $625 | $495 |

Last Mfg.'s Sug. Retail was $1,970.

85 MS Super Pigeon — similar to 85 Super Trap, except choked IM/choke tube with 28 in. barrels and 13mm aluminum rib, stocked for live pigeon shooting, 7¼ lbs.

| | $1,625 | $1,250 | $995 | $875 | $750 | $625 | $495 |

Add $60 for left hand stock.
Last Mfg.'s Sug. Retail was $1,890.

85 S SUPER SKEET — 12 ga. only, 28 in. barrels, 2¾ in. chambers with elongated forcing cones, extensive fine scroll engraving, rust resistant black chrome finish, separated barrels, 13mm aluminum VR, mechanical triggers with 5 lb. pull, 7¼ lbs.

| | $1,550 | $1,225 | $995 | $875 | $750 | $625 | $495 |

Last Mfg.'s Sug. Retail was $1,810.

85 MS Special Sporting — 12 ga. only, similar to 85 MS Super Pigeon except with field stock designed for upland game, SST, 28 in. barrels choked IM over multi-choke, 7¼ lbs. Importation began 1988-90.

| | $1,575 | $1,225 | $995 | $875 | $750 | $625 | $500 |

Last Mfg.'s Sug. Retail was $1,850.

MODEL 85X/NEW CLASSIC X GAME — 12 ga. only, 28 or 29 (Trap only) in. VR separated barrels, monobloc construction, underbolt locking, choice of SST or twin single triggers, ejectors, deluxe checkered wood with horizontal grooves carved in upper forearm, satin nickel upper receiver with engraving, available in Game (8mm VR), Trap (11mm VR), or Sporting (11mm VR) configuration. New 1992.

| Mfg.'s Sug. Retail | $685 | $685 | $595 | $525 | $475 | $425 | $375 | $325 |

Add $56 for 2 multi-chokes.

New Classic Trap/Sporting — available with fixed or screw-in chokes, special high competition stock. New 1992.

| Mfg.'s Sug. Retail | $879 | $879 | $725 | $650 | $575 | $500 | $450 | $395 |

Add $18 for screw-in chokes (standard on Sporting).

MODEL 92X GAME — 12 ga. only, similar technical specs. as the Model 600X Game, except has red outlined motifs on black receiver sides, available in Game (8mm VR), Trap (11mm VR), or Sporting (11mm VR) configuration. New 1992.

| Mfg.'s Sug. Retail | $641 | $641 | $560 | $500 | $460 | $410 | $370 | $320 |

Add $56 for 2 multi-chokes.

Laurona, cont.

Grading	100%	98%	95%	90%	80%	70%	60%

Model 92X Sporting/Trap — available with fixed or screw-in chokes, special high competition stock. New 1992.

Mfg.'s Sug. Retail	$886	$886	$725	$650	$575	$500	$450	$395

Subtract $15 for Sporting configuration.

Model 92X Olympic Trap — features extra deluxe high competition configured walnut stock, complete set of choke tubes, adj. trigger with two shoes, case. New 1993.

Mfg.'s Sug. Retail	$1,262	$1,262	$1,050	$900	$800	$700	$600	$500

GTO/GTU TRAP COMBO SILHOUETTE SERIES — 12 ga. only, 2¾ in. chamber, features black and silver striped receiver, 29 in. O/U barrels with multi-F chokes and 34 in. top single barrel with multi-F chokes. Importation began 1990.

	$2,175	$1,650	$1,300	$1,050	$900	$800	$725

Add $110 for GTU Model (bottom single barrel).
Last Mfg.'s Sug. Retail was $2,660.

SILHOUETTE GAME — 12 ga. only, 3 in. chambers, 28 in. barrels, multi-K chokes. Although advertised, this model was never imported (similar specifications as the Model 85 MS Super Game).

SILHOUETTE 300 SPORTING CLAYS — 12 ga. only, 3 in. chambers, 28 in. barrels with 11mm VR, field stock with special recoil pad designed for dropped stock style shooting, 7¼ lbs. New 1988.

	$1,495	$1,200	$975	$875	$750	$625	$500

Last Mfg.'s Sug. Retail was $1,760.
Available with either flush or knurled multi-chokes.

SILHOUETTE 300 TRAP — 12 ga. only, similar to 85 MS Super Trap except has 29 in. steel barrels with 11mm VR, flush or knurled multi-chokes, black chrome finish, distinctive silver striped receiver (similar to Silver Sporting Clays), 8 lbs. New 1988.

	$1,525	$1,200	$975	$875	$750	$625	$500

Last Mfg.'s Sug. Retail was $1,790.

MODEL SILHOUETTE 600X GAME — similar technical specs. as the Model 85X, except receiver has horizontal nickel striping over black background, available in Game (8mm VR), Trap (11mm VR), or Sporting (11mm VR) configuration. New 1992.

Mfg.'s Sug. Retail	$641	$641	$560	$500	$460	$410	$370	$320

Add $56 for 2 multi-chokes.

Silhouette 600X Sporting/Trap — available with fixed or screw-in chokes, special high competition stock. New 1992.

Mfg.'s Sug. Retail	$886	$886	$725	$650	$575	$500	$450	$395

Subtract $15 for Sporting configuration.

SILHOUETTE SINGLE BARREL TRAP — 34 in. barrel only with 7/16 in. VR, choice of either top single or bottom single barrel. Importation began 1991.

	$1,725	$1,275	$995	$875	$750	$625	$495

Add $110 for bottom single barrel.
Last Mfg.'s Sug. Retail was $2,030.

SILHOUETTE ULTRA-MAGNUM — 12 ga., 3½ in. chamber, 28 in. barrels, single trigger, ejectors, checkered walnut stock and forearm. Importation began 1990.

	$1,495	$1,200	$975	$875	$750	$625	$500

Last Mfg.'s Sug. Retail was $1,760.

Grading	100%	98%	95%	90%	80%	70%	60%

Waterfowler Ultra-Magnum — similar to Silhouette Ultra-Magnum, except has non-glare finish and 29 in. barrels. New 1990.

	$1,495	$1,200	$975	$875	$750	$625	$500

Last Mfg.'s Sug. Retail was $1,760.

LAW ENFORCEMENT ORDNANCE CORPORATION

Previous manufacturer located in Ridgeway, PA until 1990.

STRIKER-12 — 12 ga. Mag., paramilitary design shotgun featuring 12 shot rotary mag., 12 or 18¼ in. barrel, semi-auto, alloy shrouded barrel with PG extension, folding or fixed paramilitary design stock, 9.2 lbs., limited mfg. 1986-1990.

	$725	$650	$575	$500	$475	$450	$425

Add $100 for Marine variation ("Metal Life" finish).

Earlier variations were imported and available to law enforcement agencies only. In 1987, manufacture was started in PA and these firearms could be sold to individuals (18 in. barrel only). This design was originally developed in South Rhodesia.
Last Mfg.'s Sug. Retail was $725.

LEBEAU-COURALLY

Manufactured since 1865 in Liege, Belgium. Currently imported by New England Arms Co. located in Kittery Point, ME.
Lebeau-Courally manufactures only best quality rifles and shotguns. Approximately 50 are manufactured annually.

RIFLES: SINGLE SHOT

SINGLE SHOT — 6.5 x 57 R or 9.3 x 74 R cal., best quality, boxlock or sidelock action.
The importers should be contacted directly (see Trademark Index) for current information and prices regarding this model.

RIFLES: SIDE-BY-SIDE

BOXLOCK EJECTOR — 8 x 57 JRS or 9.3 x 74 R cal., Anson & Deeley boxlock, ejectors, select French walnut stock, quarter rib with ramp front sight, about 8 lbs. Importation disc. 1988, resumed 1993.

Mfg.'s Sug. Retail	$19,100		$17,500	$15,750	$13,250	$11,500	$9,250	$7,500	$6,250

Add $1,400 for standard cals.

SIDELOCK EJECTOR — 8 x 57 JRS, 9.3 x 74 R, .375 H&H, .458 Win. Mag., .470 NE (new 1991), or .577 NE (new 1992), chopper lump barrels, reinforced action, select French walnut stock, quarter rib with ramp front sight, approx. 8 lbs.

Mfg.'s Sug. Retail	$38,000		$34,000	$29,000	$24,500	$20,750	$17,500	$14,500	$11,850

SHOTGUNS

For currently manufactured shotguns — add $2,250 for single trigger. Older mfg. Lebeau-Courally shotguns have a completely different action and locking system than the newer models. These older models are typically seen priced in the $750-$2,500 range.

SOLOGNE SXS — 12, 16, or 20 ga., Anson & Deeley boxlock action, various chokes and barrel lengths, select walnut, no engraving. Add $850 for false sideplates.

Mfg.'s Sug. Retail	$14,650		$13,250	$11,250	$9,350	$7,500	$6,250	$5,150	$4,350

GRAND RUSSE MODEL — grade up from Sologne Model.

Mfg.'s Sug. Retail	$18,820		$16,480	$13,000	$10,750	$8,475	$7,375	$5,250	$4,450

Grading	100%	98%	95%	90%	80%	70%	60%

BOXLOCK EJECTOR SXS — 12, 16, or 20 ga., choice of classic or rounded action, with or without sideplates, select French walnut stock, choice of numerous engraving patterns (optional), 26, 28, or 30 in. barrels, double trigger.

Mfg.'s Sug. Retail	$14,650	$13,250	$11,250	$9,350	$7,500	$6,250	$5,150	$4,350

¾ **Boxlock with sideplates**

Mfg.'s Sug. Retail	$15,500	$13,850	$11,650	$9,650	$7,700	$6,250	$5,150	$4,350

SIDELOCK EJECTOR SXS — 12, 16, 20, 28, or .410 ga., choice of classic or rounded action, chopper lump barrels, select French walnut stock, choice of numerous engraving patterns (optional), 26, 28, or 30 in. barrels, double triggers.

Mfg.'s Sug. Retail	$31,100	$26,500	$22,750	$18,750	$14,750	$11,000	$8,750	$7,000

Add 10% for 28 or .410 ga.

SIDELOCK O/U — similar to Boss Model, except less engraving, and different quality wood.

Mfg.'s Sug. Retail	$37,600	$33,800	$29,000	$24,500	$20,750	$17,500	$14,500	$11,850

BOSS MODEL O/U — 12 only, Boss pattern sidelock with low profile action, top-of-the-line O/U individually made to customer specifications.

Mfg.'s Sug. Retail	$60,500	$54,000	$48,000	$39,500	$31,750	$24,500	$16,500	$12,000

LEFEVER ARMS COMPANY
Previous manufacturer located in Syracuse, NY.

SHOTGUNS

The Lefever was the first commercially successful hammerless double barrel shotgun made in America. They were made in Syracuse, NY from 1885-1916, at which time the company was acquired by Ithaca Gun Company. Ithaca made the Lefever until 1916. In 1921 the Box Lock Nitro Special was introduced and in 1934 the Lefever Grade A was introduced. Production of Lefever guns ceased in 1948.

The following is a percentage breakdown of gauges made between 1885-1916 (totaling 100%): 8 ga.—$\frac{1}{2}$%, 10 ga.—25%, 12 ga.—60%, 14 ga.—$\frac{1}{2}$%, 16 ga.—8%, 20 ga.—6%. Total manufacture was approx. 72,000 during this period. Damascus specimens of this trademark are worth approximately the same if in 60% or better original condition as their fluid steel barrel counterparts because of the rarity and desirability factors. Prices shown below for 90% and up condition are very difficult to evaluate and are meant as a guide only - any Lefever shotgun is rare and hard to evaluate if in over 95%.

SIDELOCK DOUBLE BARREL SHOTGUN — 10, 12, 16, or 20 ga., 26-32 in. barrels, any choke, cocking indicators on all but DS and DSE grades, double triggers standard, checkered straight or pistol grip stock, auto ejectors designated by letter E after grade. Mfg. 1885-1919.

Deduct 10% for 16 ga.
Add 20% for 20 ga.
Add 10% for SST.

	100%	98%	95%	90%	80%	70%	60%
I grade	$1,250	$1,000	$800	$700	$525	$470	$415
DS grade	$1,250	$1,000	$800	$700	$525	$470	$415
DSE grade	$1,650	$1,300	$1,100	$950	$700	$575	$500
H grade	$1,400	$1,100	$950	$800	$625	$580	$525
HE grade	$1,825	$1,650	$1,450	$1,200	$900	$775	$625
G grade	$1,550	$1,425	$1,200	$1,000	$800	$700	$595
GE grade	$1,950	$1,800	$1,575	$1,325	$1,175	$1,000	$800
F grade	$1,700	$1,550	$1,325	$1,125	$925	$800	$750
FE grade	$2,200	$1,950	$1,750	$1,475	$1,250	$1,100	$1,045
E grade	$2,000	$1,675	$1,500	$1,325	$1,100	$975	$950

Grading	100%	98%	95%	90%	80%	70%	60%
EE grade	$2,700	$2,200	$1,875	$1,600	$1,400	$1,250	$1,155
D grade	$2,400	$2,000	$1,750	$1,500	$1,430	$1,375	$1,265
DE grade	$3,200	$2,750	$2,400	$2,000	$1,750	$1,595	$1,485
C grade	$4,000	$3,400	$2,950	$2,400	$2,000	$1,815	$1,705
CE grade	$6,000	$5,500	$5,000	$4,200	$3,200	$2,200	$1,750
B grade	$5,750	$5,100	$4,600	$3,850	$2,750	$2,300	$1,900
BE grade	$10,000	$9,000	$7,500	$5,500	$3,500	$2,875	$2,310

⚸ **A grade** — auto ejectors standard.

	100%	98%	95%	90%	80%	70%	60%
	$20,000	$15,000	$11,000	$8,000	$5,000	$3,650	$2,530

⚸ **AA grade** — auto ejectors standard.

	100%	98%	95%	90%	80%	70%	60%
	$30,000	$20,000	$15,000	$11,000	$7,750	$5,500	$3,500

⚸ **Optimus Grade** — auto ejectors standard. Extreme rarity precludes accurate percentage pricing.

⚸ **Thousand Dollar Grade** — auto ejectors standard. Extreme rarity precludes accurate percentage pricing.

NITRO SPECIAL DOUBLE BARREL SHOTGUN — 12, 16, 20, or .410 ga., 26-32 in. barrels, various chokes, boxlock, extractors, checkered pistol grip stock. Mfg. 1921-1948.

	100%	98%	95%	90%	80%	70%	60%
	$400	$375	$350	$300	$250	$225	$200

Add $75 for ST.
Deduct 10% for 16 ga.
Add 20% for 20 ga.
Add 100% for .410 ga.

GRADE A DOUBLE BARREL SHOTGUN — 12, 16, 20, or .410 ga., 26-32 in. barrels, various chokes, boxlock, checkered pistol grip stock. Mfg. 1934-1942.

	100%	98%	95%	90%	80%	70%	60%
	$880	$770	$715	$660	$550	$495	$440

Add 33% for auto ejectors.
Add $75 for ST.
Add $75 for beavertail forearm.
Deduct 10% for 16 ga.
Add 20% for 20 ga.
Add 100% for .410 ga.

GRADE A SKEET MODEL — similar to Grade A, with 26 in. skeet bore barrels, auto ejector, single trigger and beavertail forearm standard.

	100%	98%	95%	90%	80%	70%	60%
	$1,155	$1,045	$990	$935	$825	$770	$715

Deduct 10% for 16 ga.
Add 20% for 20 ga.
Add 100% for .410 ga.

SINGLE BARREL TRAP GUN — 12 ga. only, 30 or 32 in. VR barrel, full choke, boxlock, auto ejector, checkered pistol grip stock. Disc. 1942.

	100%	98%	95%	90%	80%	70%	60%
	$550	$440	$385	$330	$275	$250	$195

LONG RANGE SINGLE BARREL FIELD — 12, 16, 20, or .410 ga., 26-32 in. barrel, boxlock, extractor, checkered pistol grip stock. Disc. 1942.

	100%	98%	95%	90%	80%	70%	60%
	$330	$275	$250	$220	$165	$140	$120

LEFEVER, D.M. & SON
Previous manufacturer located in Bowling Green, OH.

SHOTGUNS

   "Uncle Dan" Lefever, founder of Lefever Arms, designed and manufactured the first breech loading double hammerless shotgun made in the U.S. Production started in 1872 and continued in the Syracuse, NY plant until he sold his interest in the Lefever Arms Company during the early 1900's. He then moved to Ohio and started another factory under the name D.M. Lefever & Son. After his death a few years later the Ohio factory was closed, while his old company (Lefever Arms Co.) continued manufacturing Lefevers until being sold to Ithaca Gun Company in the early 20's. From that point, Lefever Arms Co. was a branch of Ithaca and continued to make shotguns until shortly after WWII.

   Total production on D.M. Lefever shotguns between 1901-1904 totaled less than 1,200. Because of their inherent rarity, values listed below show only 10%-80% condition specimens. D.M. Lefever specimens are so rare in 80%+ condition that prices cannot be accurately ascertained.

Grading	80%	70%	60%	50%	40%	30%	20%	10%

NEW LEFEVER DOUBLE BARREL SHOTGUN — 12, 16, or 20 ga., any length barrel and choke on order, auto ejectors standard on all grades except O Excelsior, double triggers standard on all except Uncle Dan grade, optional single triggers available, checkered walnut pistol grip or straight stock, grades differ as to engraving, wood, checkering and overall quality. Mfg. 1904-1906.
Deduct 10% for 16 ga.
Add 20% for 20 ga.
Add 10% for SST.

O Excelsior Grade

	$2,365	$1,925	$1,650	$1,430	$1,210	$990	$770	$605

Excelsior Grade w/ejectors

	$2,640	$2,310	$1,925	$1,595	$1,320	$1,045	$825	$660

F Grade, No. 9

	$3,000	$2,640	$2,310	$1,925	$1,595	$1,320	$1,045	$825

G Grade — 10 ga., sidelock, damascus barrels.

	$3,450	$2,950	$2,500	$2,000	$1,650	$1,375	$1,100	$875

E Grade, No. 8

	$4,000	$3,350	$2,875	$2,300	$1,980	$1,650	$1,320	$990

D Grade, No. 7

	$4,400	$4,125	$3,850	$3,300	$2,750	$2,475	$2,200	$1,650

C Grade, No. 6

	$4,950	$4,400	$4,125	$3,850	$3,300	$2,750	$2,420	$2,050

B Grade, No. 5

	$6,600	$5,500	$4,400	$4,125	$3,850	$3,300	$3,000	$2,600

AA Grade, No. 4

	$8,800	$7,700	$6,600	$5,500	$4,400	$3,630	$3,250	$2,850

UNCLE DAN GRADE — too rare to accurately determine values.

SINGLE BARREL TRAP GUN — 12 ga., 26-32 in. full choke, auto ejector, boxlock, checkered pistol grip stock. Mfg. 1904-1906. Too rare to accurately determine values.

LE FORGERON

Manufacturer located in Belgium. Previously imported and distributed by Midwest Gun Sport in Zebulon, NC.

SHOTGUNS

Prices below reflect circa 1989 information as this was the last year they were formally imported.

Grading	100%	98%	95%	90%	80%	70%	60%
BOXLOCK EJECTOR SXS	$3,975	$3,650	$3,325	$2,995	$2,600	$2,250	$1,900

BOXLOCK EJECTOR SXS — 20 or 28 ga. only, with or without sideplates, select French walnut stock, choice of engraving patterns (optional), single trigger.

Add $1,000 for sideplates.
Last Mfg.'s Sug. Retail was $4,400.

SIDELOCK EJECTOR SXS — 20 or 28 ga. only, select French walnut stock, choice of engraving patterns (optional), rounded action, single trigger.

	100%	98%	95%	90%	80%	70%	60%
	$10,200	$9,250	$8,500	$7,900	$7,100	$6,300	$5,500

Last Mfg.'s Sug. Retail was $11,600.

RIFLES

MODEL 6020 — 9.3 x 74R cal., boxlock action, beavertail forearm, pistol grip stock.

	100%	98%	95%	90%	80%	70%	60%
	$4,450	$4,025	$3,750	$3,475	$3,100	$2,800	$2,550

Add $700 for sideplates (Model 6040).
Last Mfg.'s Sug. Retail was $4,900.

MODEL 6030 — sidelock action, engraved action with deluxe French walnut stock and forearm.

	100%	98%	95%	90%	80%	70%	60%
	$8,475	$7,900	$7,100	$6,300	$5,500	$4,700	$4,000

Last Mfg.'s Sug. Retail was $8,950.

LE FRANCAIS PISTOLS

Manufactured by Francais D'armes Et Cycles located in Ste. Etienne, France.

STAFF OFFICER MODEL AUTOMATIC — .25 auto, 2½ in. barrel, blue, fixed sights, rubber grips, no visible cocking piece. Mfg. 1914-disc.

	100%	98%	95%	90%	80%	70%	60%
	$275	$230	$200	$165	$140	$115	$80

POLICEMAN MODEL AUTOMATIC — .32 auto, double action, 7 shot, 3½ in. barrel, hinged finned barrel, blue, fixed sights, rubber grips. Mfg. 1950's.

	100%	98%	95%	90%	80%	70%	60%
	$850	$800	$700	$575	$435	$350	$275

ARMY MODEL AUTOMATIC — 9mm Browning, 8 shot, 5 in. barrel, blue, fixed sights, checkered walnut grips. Mfg. 1928-1938. Early model with tapered barrel, later model with finned barrel.

	100%	98%	95%	90%	80%	70%	60%
	$1,400	$1,100	$850	$700	$550	$425	$350

Liberator

LIBERATOR

Mfg. by the Guide Lamp Corporation (division of General Motors) in 1942 Only.

Grading	100%	98%	95%	90%	80%	70%	60%

LIBERATOR PISTOL — .45 ACP cal., single shot, simplistic design and action utilizing nonstrategic WWII materials, mfg. for European resistance movement during WWII (most were issued or air-dropped in Europe), each gun was individually packaged in a paraffin-coated cardboard box which included the gun, a graphics only (no English) instruction sheet, wooden ram rod, and 10 rounds of .45 ACP ammo stored in the gun's butt, 4 in. smooth bore barrel, sheet steel stamping mfg. with welds, 1 million mfg. 1942 only.

	$650	$525	$465	$415	$380	$340	$300

Even though 1 million of these pistols were mfg., remaining specimens brought into the U.S. with the above listed accessories are rare since all were delivered overseas. While the Liberator's appearance is crude, remember that the entire production run (1 million) was mfg. and ready for overseas shipment in 13 weeks.

LIBERTY ARMS WORKS, INC.

Manufacturer located in West Chester, PA. Dealer direct sales only.

L.A.W. ENFORCER — .22 LR, 9mm Para., 10mm, or .45 ACP cal., patterned after the Ingram MAC 10, single action semi-auto, 6¼ in. threaded barrel, closed bolt operation, manual safety, 30 shot mag., 5 lbs. 1 oz. New 1991.

Mfg.'s Sug. Retail	$445	$385	$335	$295	$275	$250	$225	$200

LIEGEOISE D'ARMES

Manufacturer located in Belgium.

Small manufacturer specializing in boxlock shotguns, normally engraved and with ejectors. Prices usually start in the $600+ range.

LIGNOSE (BERGMAN)

Manufacturer located in Suhl, Germany.

EINHAND MODEL 2A POCKET AUTOMATIC — .25 auto, 6 shot, 2 in. barrel, blue, rubber grips, can be cocked by rearward pressure on trigger guard.

	$220	$205	$195	$165	$140	$110	$85

MODEL 3 POCKET AUTOMATIC — similar to 3A, except without one hand cocking trigger guard.

	$220	$205	$195	$165	$140	$110	$85

MODEL 3A POCKET AUTOMATIC — similar to 2A, except longer grip, 9 shot capacity.

	$220	$205	$195	$165	$140	$110	$85

MODEL 2 POCKET AUTOMATIC — similar to 2A, without one hand cocking trigger guard.

	$165	$155	$140	$110	$90	$75	$55

LILIPUT

Previous mfg. by August Menz, located in Suhl, Germany.

PISTOLS: SEMI-AUTO

4.25mm CAL. — 4.25mm centerfire Liliput cal. (shoots 12 grain bullet), blue or nickel finish, limited 1920's mfg.

	$550	$495	$425	$385	$340	$300	$280

Grading	100%	98%	95%	90%	80%	70%	60%

6.35mm CAL. — .25 ACP cal., mfg. in large quantities pre-WWII.

	$165	$155	$140	$110	$90	$75	$55

LJUNGMAN
Previous manufacture by Carl Gustaf, located in Eskilstuna, Sweden.

AG 42 — semi-auto rifle, 6.5mm, 10 shot mag., wood stock, tangent rear sight, hooded front, bayonet lug, designed in 1941. This was the first mass produced, direct gas operated rifle. This weapon was also used by the Egyptian armed forces and was known as the Hakim.

	$925	$850	$715	$660	$580	$525	$440

LJUTIC INDUSTRIES, INC.
Manufacturer located in Yakima, WA. Dealer direct sales only.

Prior to 1960, Ljutic was doing business as Ljutic Gun Co.

TRAP SHOTGUNS

To date approx. 12,500 target shotguns have been manufactured total (all models).

DYNATRAP SINGLE BARREL SHOTGUN — 12 ga., 33 in. barrel, full choke, push button opening, extractor, trap stock.

	$2,500	$2,150	$1,600	$1,475	$1,300	$1,200	$1,100

Add $400 for release trigger.
Add $500 for custom stock.
Add $750 for extra release trigger.
Add $550 for extra pull trigger.

MODEL X-73 SINGLE BARREL — 12 ga., 33 in. full, push button opening, high rib fancy Monte Carlo stock.

	$2,500	$2,250	$2,000	$1,850	$1,700	$1,600	$1,500

Add $1,995 for extra barrel.
Add $550 for extra pull trigger.
Add $750 for extra release trigger.

MONO GUN SINGLE BARREL — 12 ga., 34 in. barrel, custom choked, custom stocked, pull or release trigger, a "built to customers specifications" trap gun. Also known as Standard Rib or Medium Rib.

Standard, Medium, or Olympic Rib Model

Mfg.'s Sug. Retail	$4,495	$4,495	$3,500	$2,950	$2,775	$2,500	$2,200	$1,900

Add $100 for medium rib.
Add $200 for screw-in choke tubes.
Approximately 3,000 Mono Guns have been manufactured to date.

LTX (Deluxe Mono Trap) — similar to Mono Gun except has 33 in. medium rib barrel and exhibition wood and checkering.

Mfg.'s Sug. Retail	$5,595	$5,250	$4,250	$3,750	$3,300	$2,950	$2,500	$2,250

Add $500 for pull trigger.
Add $400 if with release trigger.
Add $400 for choke tube barrel with 3 chokes.
Add $1,400 for Pro Package (includes Laib adj. comb, adj. alum. base plate with 2 pads, and Pro barrel with special bore).
Add $750 for extra release trigger.
Add $2,195 for extra standard rib barrel.

Grading	100%	98%	95%	90%	80%	70%	60%

SPACE GUN — 12 ga. only, single barrel, unusual design permits in-line round stock with recoil pad, circular forearm wraps around barrel, high post rib on muzzle half of barrel.

Mfg.'s Sug. Retail	$4,595	$4,595	$3,400	$3,000	$2,600	$2,200	$1,950	$1,750

Add $1,400 for stainless steel mfg.
Add $1,400 for Monte Carlo stock, 2 pads, and adj. rib.
Add $1,900 for SLE Pro Package (similar to LTX special order, except is cased).

LM 6 O/U — 12 ga. only, supplied with one set of O/U barrels, deluxe wood and checkering, separated barrels on O/U.

Mfg.'s Sug. Retail	$14,995	$14,995	$12,000	$9,250	$8,000	$6,950	$6,250	$5,600

Add $5,000 for extra set of O/U barrels.
Add $7,000 for top single barrel (includes 2 pull trigger groups, and 2 forearms).

BI MATIC AUTO LOADER — 12 ga., 2 shot, 26-32 in. barrels, low recoil, trap or skeet models available, stock and choking to customer specifications.

Mfg.'s Sug. Retail	$5,995	$5,995	$4,450	$3,850	$3,400	$3,000	$2,500	$2,250

Add $2,000 for extra barrel.
Add $750 for extra release trigger.

LLAMA HANDGUNS

Manufacturer located in Gabilondo Y Cia, Victoria, Spain. Currently imported and distributed by Stoeger Industries located in South Hackensack, NJ.

PISTOLS: SEMI-AUTO

MODEL IIIA — .380 auto, 7 shot, 3 in. barrel, adj. sights, blue, plastic grips. Mfg. 1951-disc.

	$235	$200	$180	$160	$140	$120	$110

MODEL XA — similar to Model IIIA, except .32 auto.

	$235	$200	$180	$160	$140	$120	$110

MODEL XV — similar to Model XA, except .22 LR.

	$235	$200	$180	$160	$140	$120	$110

MODELS C-IIIA, C-XA, C-XV — similar to Model C, except engraved chrome.

	$305	$260	$230	$205	$180	$155	$140

MODELS BE-IIIA, BE-XA, BE-XV — similar to Model CE, except engraved, blue.

	$290	$250	$220	$195	$165	$140	$125

Deluxe Models, all blue or chrome engraved with simulated pearl grips, add $20.

MODEL G-IIIA — similar to IIIA, except gold engraved, simulated pearl grips.

	$1,515	$880	$825	$660	$550	$440	$330

MODEL VIII — .38 Super, 9 shot, 5 in. barrel, fixed sights, wood grips. Mfg. 1952-disc.

	$305	$255	$220	$195	$180	$165	$140

MODEL IXA — similar to Model VIII, except .45 ACP.

	$305	$255	$220	$195	$180	$165	$140

Grading	100%	98%	95%	90%	80%	70%	60%

MODEL XI — similar to Model IXA, except 9mm.

	100%	98%	95%	90%	80%	70%	60%
	$305	$255	$220	$195	$180	$165	$140

MODELS C-VIII, C-IXA, C-XI — similar to Model VIII, except satin chrome.

	$360	$315	$285	$260	$220	$195	$165

MODELS CE-VIII, CE-IXA, CE-XI

	$425	$350	$310	$285	$265	$220	$195

MODELS BE-VIII, BE-IXA, BE-XI — similar to Model CE, except blue, engraving.

	$425	$350	$295	$275	$250	$210	$180

Deluxe Models, similar to above, except simulated pearl grips - add $20.

OMNI — .45 ACP or 9mm, double action, all steel construction, 2 sear bars, 3 safeties, 4¼ in. barrel, 7 shot mag. in .45 cal., 13 shot mag. in 9mm, blue finish. Importation disc. 1986.

9mm Caliber

	$440	$380	$330	$295	$260	$225	$200

Last Mfg.'s Sug. Retail was $546.

.45 ACP Caliber

	$395	$360	$320	$285	$250	$220	$195

Last Mfg.'s Sug. Retail was $500.

SMALL FRAME MODEL — .22 LR, .32 ACP, or .380 ACP cal., Colt 1911 A1 design, semi-auto, single action, 3¹¹⁄₁₆ in. barrel, 7 shot mag, 23 oz. Also available in satin chrome, optional engraving patterns.

Mfg.'s Sug. Retail	$325	$250	$200	$155	$130	$120	$110	$100

Add $60 for duo-tone finish (.380 ACP only, new 1991).
Add $74 for chrome finish (not avail. in .32 ACP cal.).

COMPACT FRAME MODEL — 9mm (disc.) or .45 ACP cal., scaled down variation of the Large Frame Model, 4¼ in. barrel, 7 or 9 shot mag., 34 or 37 oz. New 1986.

Mfg.'s Sug. Retail	$385	$280	$235	$190	$170	$160	$155	$150

Add $114 for satin chrome finish.
Add $90 for duo-tone finish (new in 1990).

LARGE FRAME MODEL — 9mm (disc.), .38 Super (new 1988), or .45 ACP cal., similar to small-frame model, 5⅛ in. barrel, 36 oz., 9 shot mag. in 9mm, 7 shot mag. in .45 ACP. Engraved and deluxe models available also.

Mfg.'s Sug. Retail	$385	$280	$235	$190	$170	$160	$155	$150

Add $114 for satin chrome finish (.45 ACP only).
Add $90 for duo-tone finish (.45 ACP only, new 1991).

MODEL 82 — 9mm Para., double action, 4¼ in. barrel, blue finish, 3-dot sighting system, 15 shot mag., ambidextrous safety, loaded chamber indicator, black polymer grips, 39 oz. New 1988.

Mfg.'s Sug. Retail	$975	$850	$675	$550	$495	$450	$395	$365

Grading	100%	98%	95%	90%	80%	70%	60%

MODEL 87 COMPETITION — 9mm Para., competition variation of the Model 82, includes built in ported compensator, oversize magazine and safety release, fixed barrel bushing, beveled rapid load magazine well, 14 shot mag., extended and serrated trigger guard, and adj. trigger. New 1989.

Mfg.'s Sug. Retail $1,450	$1,275	$995	$850	$750	$650	$575	$500

REVOLVERS

MARTIAL DOUBLE ACTION REVOLVER — .22 LR, .38 Spl., 6 shot, 4 and 6 in. barrels, target sights, blue, checkered wood grips. Mfg. 1969-1976.

	$220	$200	$180	$165	$140	$120	$100

DELUXE MARTIAL — similar to Martial, except finish as follows:

	100%	98%	95%	90%	80%	70%	60%
Satin chrome	$275	$250	$220	$195	$165	$140	$120
Chrome, engraved	$305	$275	$250	$220	$195	$165	$140
Blue, engraved	$290	$265	$235	$210	$180	$155	$120
Gold, engraved	$1,430	$880	$770	$660	$550	$495	$415

COMANCHE I — similar to Martial .22, double action. Mfg. 1977-1982.

	$255	$220	$195	$165	$155	$140	$110

COMANCHE II — similar to Martial .38, double action. Mfg. 1977-1982 and 1986 in .22 LR and .22 Mag. only.

	$240	$220	$195	$165	$155	$140	$110

Last Mfg.'s Sug. Retail was $272.

COMANCHE III — .22 LR (disc.) or .357 Mag., double action, 6 shot, 4, 6, or 8½ (disc. 1986) in. barrel, blue, adj. sights, checkered walnut grips. Mfg. 1975-present. Before 1977, it was called "Comanche".

Mfg.'s Sug. Retail $339	$280	$245	$200	$165	$155	$140	$130

⅜ **Satin Chrome Finish**

Mfg.'s Sug. Retail $395	$330	$270	$230	$205	$185	$170	$160

⅜ **Gold Finish (disc.)**

	$1,100	$880	$825	$660	$550	$440	$330

SUPER COMANCHE IV — .44 Mag., double action, 6 or 8½ in. VR barrel, adj. sights, blue only.

Mfg.'s Sug. Retail $440	$350	$285	$235	$220	$205	$185	$175

SUPER COMANCHE V — .357 Mag., double action, 6 shot, 4, 6, or 8½ in. VR barrel, adj. sights, blue only. Importation disc. 1988.

	$335	$275	$230	$210	$200	$190	$180

Last Mfg.'s Sug. Retail was $414.

LORCIN ENGINEERING CO., INC.
Manufacturer located in Mira Loma, CA. Distributor sales only.

PISTOLS

L-22 MODEL — .22 LR cal., similar to L-25 Model, except 2.55 in. barrel and 9 shot mag., black or chrome finish, 16 oz. New 1992.

Mfg.'s Sug. Retail $79	$70	$60	$50	$45	$40	$35	$35

Grading	100%	98%	95%	90%	80%	70%	60%

L-25 MODEL — .25 ACP cal., semi-auto single action, 6 shot mag., 2.4 in. barrel, anatomically designed grips to fit hand better, choice of black and gold, chrome and pearl, satin chrome and pearl, teflon camo finish (new 1992), or black and pearl finish, 13.5 oz. New 1989.

Mfg.'s Sug. Retail	$69	$60	$50	$45	$40	$35	$35	$35

Add $20 for lightweight frame (Model L—25 LT, new in 1990).

Lady Lorcin — same specifications as the L-25 Model, except is available in chrome, satin chrome, or black exterior finish with pink grips. Values are the same as the L-25 Model. New 1990.

Mfg.'s Sug. Retail	$79	$70	$60	$50	$45	$40	$35	$35

L-32 — .32 ACP cal., semi-auto single action, 6 shot mag., 3.2 in. barrel, available in black or chrome finish, 20 oz. New 1992.

Mfg.'s Sug. Retail	$89	$80	$70	$60	$50	$45	$40	$35

L-380 — .380 ACP cal., semi-auto single action, 6 shot mag., 3.2 in. barrel, available in black or chrome finish, 20 oz. New 1992.

Mfg.'s Sug. Retail	$110	$90	$80	$70	$60	$50	$45	$40

LUGERS WITH VARIATIONS

Note: The Luger section in this book is arranged chronologically by year of manufacture (1900 models to Post-War production), under individual manufacturer headings.

Often times, year of production can be hard to nail down, especially on commercial models. An easier way to initially identify your Luger is to categorize by toggle marking first - then by chamber marking within groups (chronologically for dated chambers). Once you know period of manufacture, simply refer to the appropriate subheading in this section. While some rare variations will be excluded in this generalized overview, it will be very helpful to establish correct, basic knowledge about your particular Luger.

While many recently imported Lugers would make workable shooters, they have in no way lowered prices on 90%+ condition specimens due to normal collector activity in top quality only pistols. Recently imported Lugers should have the importer's name visibly stamped on an exterior surface. Most of these imports are in the 9mm - 4 in. barrel configuration.

Every year more and more reblued, restrawed, regripped, reframed, rebarreled Lugers are sold to unknowing military handgun collectors as rare variations. On any expensive contract variation, careful inspection on all parts must be made before potentially purchasing. If in doubt, secure 2 or 3 additional appraisals/observations from qualified individuals. Lugers are a field in themselves and an experienced Winchester dealer would not be qualified to guesstimate the originality of these German handguns.

A final note on Lugers: Original pistols in 98%-100% condition have not been affected by the influx of recent imports as these newly imported guns are usually in 80% and lower condition or have been reblued.

It seems that every year the prices of top quality (98%+ condition) original Lugers get more expensive and less predictable - FOR THIS REASON, THE 100% VALUES ON SOME VINTAGE LUGERS HAVE BEEN OMITTED INTENTIONALLY SINCE RARITY PRECLUDES ACCURATE PRICE EVALUATION IN THIS CONDITION FACTOR. Please contact this publication for current estimated 100% values on Lugers.

REFERENCE GUIDE BY TOGGLE MARKING

DWM TOGGLE IDENTIFICATION

DWM MODELS — mfg. from 1900 to 1930 in Berlin, Germany.

⇉ **1900 Models** — grip safety and "Dished" Toggles, ser. no.'s 1-24,999.

⇉ **1906 Models** — grip safety, many chamber markings, ser. no.'s 25,000-74,000.

⇉ **1908 Commercial Models** — no grip safety, 9mm, ser. no.'s 39,000-74,000.

⇉ **1908 Military Models** — no stock lug.

⇉ **1914 Military Models** — stock lug, dated 1913-1918.

⇉ **1920 Commercial Models** — no grip safety, usually 3⅞ in. barrel. Most common Luger, undated chamber, 7.65 mm or 9mm.
Note: Lugers with 4 inch barrels are most frequently encountered in military and commercial models. 6 in. barrels usually denote "Navy" models. 8 in. barrels usually denote "Artillery" models. Guns with barrels over 8 inches are rare and should be checked carefully for originality.

DWM COMMERCIAL LUGERS

DWM MEANS DEUTSCHE WAFFEN & MUNITIONS FABRIKEN
These are models manufactured from 1900-1923 found in the five digit serial range.

MODEL 1900 — serial range 1-20,000. Configuration: 4¾ in. x .30 Commercial, American Eagle, Swiss.

MODEL 1900 — serial range 20,001-21,000. Configuration: 4¾ in. x .30 Bulgarian.

MODEL 1902 — serial range 21,001-25,000. Configuration: 9 mm x 4 in. "fat barrels" and 11¾ in. x .30 Carbine models, intermixed with 4¾ x .30 American Eagles and Commercials.

MODEL 1906 — serial range 25,001-39,000. Configuration: Commercial American Eagle, Navy Commercial and Swiss, both 4¾ in. x .30 and 9 mm x 4 in. grip safety models.

MODEL 1908 — serial range 39,001-71,000. Configuration: First 9 mm x 4 in. without grip safety, M1908 Commercials were interspersed with .30 and 9 mm Eagles, Commercials, Navy Commercials, and a few Carbines and Swiss.

MODEL 1914 — serial range 71,001-74,000. Configuration: Last pre-WWI Commercial Lugers, made with stock lug, with a few 9mm Commercials mixed in.

MODEL 1923 — serial range 74,001-89,000. Configuration: Post-WWI Commercials, mostly 3⅞ in. x .30 cal.

MODEL 1923 — serial range 89,001-91,000. Configuration: The last thousand or so made have "safe" on lever and "loaded" on the extractor, 3⅞ in. x .30 barrels.

ERFURT TOGGLE IDENTIFICATION

ERFURT MODELS

Produced from 1911-1914 and 1916-1918 in Erfurt, Germany. Military Model - Chamber dated 1911-1914 and 1916-1918. Erfurt models exhibit the most proof marks and individual parts numbering. Walnut grips.

SIMSON & CO. TOGGLE IDENTIFICATION

SIMSON & CO.

Manufactured 1922 to 1934 in Suhl, Germany. Most Simson Lugers are military models (9mm - 4 in. barrels). During this 10 year period, Simson supplied the German Army Lugers exclusively. Can be dated 1925-1928. Many reworks of WWI DWM Military Lugers were refurbished by Simson, and can be detected by the Simson "Eagle-over-6" proof on repaired parts. A very few Simsons made in 1934 have just an "S" on the toggle (very rare).

SWISS TOGGLE IDENTIFICATION

SWISS BERN MODELS

Manufactured 1924 to 1929 by WAFFENFABRIK Bern, Switzerland. Relatively rare - these Swiss models have "improved" changes (flat and curved front grip strap), 4¾ in. barrels, walnut or plastic grips, grip safety. 1929 model has Geneva Cross in shield on front link.

MAUSER TOGGLE IDENTIFICATION

MAUSER VARIATIONS

Manufactured 1934-1942 in Oberndorf, Germany. Between 1930 and 1934 Mauser Werke was primarily engaged in reworking older Lugers, since transfer of machinery and personnel to the DWM plant in Berlin was completed in 1931. Mauser "Banner" models were made from 1934 to 1942, many are dated from 1939-1942 on the chamber. S/42 models are MOSTLY MILITARY contract guns manufactured between 1934 and 1940, usually chamber marked. "42" toggle marked guns (Mauser code) were mfg. 1939 and 1940 and are dated. "byf" marked toggles indicate guns made for German military use after 1940 and are more common than other military models. The Mauser Werke trademark also appears on those Lugers made in the 1970's.

Lugers with Variations, cont.

KRIEGHOFF TOGGLE IDENTIFICATION

KRIEGHOFF MODELS

Manufactured between 1934-1946 in Suhl, Germany. Early Krieghoffs are side frame inscribed. The German Luftwaffe contracted with Krieghoff for military guns in 1935. Early military Krieghoffs have "S" marked chambers, most are chamber dated between 1936 and 1945. Krieghoff Lugers are prized for their quality fit and finish and command higher prices because of their rarity factor.

VICKERS TOGGLE IDENTIFICATION

VICKERS

Manufactured by Vickers, Ltd., circa 1921, in England from DWM parts for military contract sale to the Netherlands. Added barrel date is a date of arsenal refinish or refurbishing. Distinguishable by Vickers toggle and "rust" marked safety. Serial range is 1-10,100. Grips can be finely checkered with shallow contour or very coarsely checkered. Configuration is 9mm, 4 in. barrel, and grip safety.

PRE-1900 AND 1900 DWM MANUFACTURED LUGERS

Values on most 100% Lugers have been omitted intentionally since rarity precludes accurate price evaluation in this condition factor.

Grading	100%	98%	95%	90%	80%	70%	60%

1898/99 BORCHARDT LUGER TRANSITIONAL — 7.65mm, 5 in. barrel, this is perhaps one of the most desirable Lugers, only few mfg. Examples scarce, no reported sales, an original example would command a price in the 5-figure range.

1899/1900 SWISS TEST MODEL — 7.65mm, 4¾ in. barrel, 100 or less mfg., the very first true Luger. Engraved "Swiss Cross" chamber marking.

	100%	98%	95%	90%	80%	70%	60%
	N/A	$15,000	$10,000	$7,500	$6,500	$6,000	$5,000

This variation is serial numbered in the 1-50 range approx.

1900 COMMERCIAL DWM — 7.65mm, 4¾ in. barrel, 5,500 mfg.

	100%	98%	95%	90%	80%	70%	60%
	N/A	$2,350	$1,600	$1,000	$750	$600	$500

1900 SWISS COMMERCIAL DWM — 7.65mm, 4¾ in. barrel, 2,000 commercially mfg. and 3000 military mfg.

	100%	98%	95%	90%	80%	70%	60%
	N/A	$3,500	$2,000	$1,200	$800	$600	$500

Add 15% for wide trigger (found only in ser. no. range 4000).

1900 AMERICAN EAGLE DWM — 7.65mm, 4¾ in. barrel, approx. 12,000 mfg.

	100%	98%	95%	90%	80%	70%	60%
	N/A	$2,600	$1,500	$1,000	$700	$600	$500

Add 30% for U.S. Test Model (approx. ser. no. range 6200-7400).

Grading	100%	98%	95%	90%	80%	70%	60%

1900 BULGARIAN DWM — 7.65mm, 4¾ in. barrel, 1,000 mfg., very rare in U.S., most often seen in the 60% and lower condition.

| | N/A | $7,500 | $4,500 | $3,500 | $2,700 | $2,200 | $1,800 |

Deduct 30% if rebarreled.

LUGERS: 1902-DWM MFG.

1902 COMMERCIAL — 9mm, 4 in. barrel, serial number range 22,300-22,400 and 22,900-23,500 (500-600 mfg.). Commonly called "Fat Barrel" model.

| | N/A | $5,500 | $4,250 | $3,400 | $3,000 | $2,500 | $2,000 |

1902 AMERICAN EAGLE — 9mm, 4 in. barrel, 600-700 mfg., commonly called the "fat barrel". Same ser. range as 1902 Commercial Model.

| | N/A | $6,250 | $4,250 | $3,400 | $3,000 | $2,500 | $2,000 |

1902 CARTRIDGE COUNTER AMERICAN EAGLE — 9mm, only 50 mfg. with the Powell Indication Device; be extremely wary of fakes. ser. no. range 22,401-22,450.

| | N/A | $20,000 | $13,500 | $9,500 | $7,500 | $6,000 | $5,000 |

1902 DANZIG TEST — 7.65 or 9mm, blank toggle, 4 in. barrel, Crown D proofs.

| | N/A | $4,600 | $3,700 | $3,000 | $2,200 | $1,800 | $1,500 |

1902 CARBINE — 7.65mm, 11¾ in. barrel, approx. 2500 mfg.

		100%	98%	95%	90%	80%	70%	60%
Gun w/matching stock		N/A	$9,500	$7,500	$5,500	$4,000	$3,000	$2,000
Gun only		N/A	$4,995	$4,000	$3,200	$2,700	$2,200	$1,800

1902/06 TRANSITIONAL CARBINE — 11¾ in. barrel, 50-100 mfg., may have new model frame. Ser. no.'s start at 50,000.

| | N/A | $7,500 | $5,500 | $4,500 | $4,200 | $4,000 | $3,800 |

Deduct 30% if without matching stock.

1903 COMMERCIAL — 7.65mm, 4 in. barrel, 50 mfg., extractor marked "charge". Ser. No. Range (25,000-25,050).

| | N/A | $6,500 | $6,000 | $5,500 | $5,000 | $3,000 | $2,500 |

LUGERS: 1904-DWM MFG.

1904 NAVY DWM — 9mm, 6 in. barrel, 1200-1500 mfg., a Transitional Navy.

| | N/A | $12,000 | $9,000 | $6,000 | $4,600 | $3,800 | $3,200 |

LUGERS: 1906-DWM MFG.

1906 COMMERCIAL 7.65mm W/"GESICHERT" MARKED SAFETY — 7.65mm, 4¾ in. barrel, "GESICHERT" marked safety, long frame. Approx. 750 mfg.

| | N/A | $1,700 | $1,300 | $1,100 | $900 | $750 | $600 |

Grading	100%	98%	95%	90%	80%	70%	60%

1906 COMMERCIAL 9mm PARA. — 9mm, 4 in. barrel, 3500-4000 mfg. Scarcer than 7.65mm.

| | N/A | $1,900 | $1,400 | $1,000 | $800 | $650 | $500 |

1906 COMMERCIAL 7.65mm — 7.65mm, 4¾ in. barrel, area under safety polished bright, 5000 mfg.

| | N/A | $1,700 | $1,250 | $800 | $600 | $500 | $400 |

1906 AMERICAN EAGLE - 9MM — 9mm, 4 in. barrel, American Eagle stamped in front of breech, 3000 mfg.

| | N/A | $2,350 | $1,500 | $1,100 | $700 | $550 | $450 |

1906 AMERICAN EAGLE - 7.65MM — 7.65mm, 4¾ in. barrel, 7,500-8,000 mfg. Add 40% for long frame.

| | N/A | $1,900 | $1,400 | $750 | $600 | $475 | $400 |

1906 NAVY COMMERCIAL — 9mm, 6 in. barrel, approx. 2,500 mfg. Add 50% for 7.65 cal. with 6 in. barrel.

| | N/A | $3,250 | $2,500 | $1,800 | $1,600 | $1,200 | $950 |

1906 NAVY MILITARY — 9mm, 6 in. barrel, first issue, 19,000 mfg., mostly altered safety marking - "GESICHERT" in lower position. Ser. no. range 1-9,000a.

| | N/A | $3,000 | $2,250 | $1,600 | $1,200 | $875 | $600 |

Add 25% for unaltered safety variation.

1906 NAVY MILITARY — 9mm, 6 in. barrel, second issue, 2,000 mfg. Ser. range 9,000a-1,000b.

| | N/A | $2,750 | $1,900 | $1,600 | $1,300 | $1,075 | $900 |

LUGERS: 1906-1918 DWM AND ERFURT MFG.

Most common variations in good supply within this section in 50% or less condition will approximate the 60% value. This reflects its value as a representative shooter rather than a higher priced collector's gun.

1906 SWISS COMMERCIAL — 7.65 or 9mm, 4¾ in. barrel, less than 1,000 mfg., Swiss "Cross in Sunburst," short frame.

| | N/A | $2,000 | $1,750 | $1,500 | $1,350 | $1,200 | $1,100 |

1906 SWISS MILITARY — 7.65mm, 4¾ in. barrel, long frame, Swiss Police has Cross in Shield. Either "Cross in Shield" or "Cross in Sunburst".

| | N/A | $2,000 | $1,600 | $1,200 | $900 | $800 | $700 |

1906/23 DUTCH — 9mm, 4 in. barrel, approx. 4,000 mfg., often seen as arsenal rework. Deduct 30% if arsenal reblued and/or rebarreled.

| | N/A | $1,600 | $1,400 | $900 | $750 | $600 | $525 |

1906 BRAZILIAN — 7.65mm, 4¾ in. barrel, 5,000 mfg., extremely rare in fine condition.

| | N/A | $1,950 | $1,400 | $900 | $850 | $700 | $650 |

1906 BULGARIAN — 7.65mm, 4¾ in. barrel, 1,500 mfg., most rebarrelled to 9mm (deduct 30%).

| | N/A | $4,200 | $3,500 | $3,500 | $2,000 | $1,850 | $1,450 |

1908 BULGARIAN — 9mm, 4 in. barrel, DWM on chamber, 10,000 mfg., extremely rare in mint condition.

| | N/A | $2,000 | $1,500 | $900 | $825 | $750 | $675 |

Grading	100%	98%	95%	90%	80%	70%	60%

1906 PORTUGUESE ARMY — 7.65mm, 4¾ in. barrel, Manuel II crest on chamber. Approx. 5000 mfg.

	N/A	$1,450	$950	$600	$525	$450	$350

1906 ROYAL PORTUGUESE NAVY — 9mm, 4 in. barrel, Anchor & Crown on chamber, very rare.

	N/A	$7,000	$4,500	$3,000	$2,500	$2,000	$1,500

1906 REPUBLIC OF PORTUGAL NAVY — Anchor R.P. on chamber, very rare.

	N/A	$7,000	$4,500	$3,000	$2,500	$2,000	$1,500

1906 RUSSIAN — 9mm, 4 in. barrel, approx. 1,000 mfg., only 6 reported.

	N/A	$8,500	$7,000	$4,300	$3,200	$2,600	$2,000

1906 VICKERS DUTCH — 9mm, 4 in. barrel, approx. 10,000 assembled by Vickers Ltd. from DWM supplied parts.

	N/A	$1,700	$1,200	$750	$650	$600	$495

1906 FRENCH COMMERCIAL — 7.65mm, 4¾ in. barrel. Add 30% if cased with accessories.

	N/A	$2,350	$1,800	$1,575	$1,400	$1,200	$995

1908 COMMERCIAL AND MILITARY — DWM, 9mm, 4 in. barrel, Test/Acceptance Model, approx. 500 mfg. Ser. no. range 69,000-71,200.

	N/A	$1,200	$800	$700	$575	$475	$400

1908 NAVY COMMERCIAL — 9mm, 6 in. barrel. Add 50% for 7.65mm with 6 in. barrel.

	N/A	$3,500	$2,700	$2,200	$1,800	$1,500	$1,300

1908 DWM MILITARY — 9mm, 4 in. barrel, approx. 95,000 mfg. Each year, undated 1st issue or dated 1910-1913, no stock lug, except for a few late 1913 mfg. guns.

	N/A	$795	$650	$450	$400	$350	$300

Add 20% for undated or for 1913 date w/stock lug.
Approx. 25,000 1st issue pistols were mfg., 20,000 dated 1910, 15,000 dated 1911, 10,000 dated 1912, 25,000 dated 1913.

1908 DWM COMMERCIAL — 9mm, 4 in. barrel, no stock lug or hold open, blank chamber.

	N/A	$800	$600	$450	$400	$350	$300

1911-1914 DATED 1908 ERFURT MILITARY — 9mm, 4 in. barrel (dated 1911-1914), 1911, 1912, and most 1913 chamber dates do not have stock lugs.

	N/A	$700	$550	$475	$400	$350	$295

Add 20% for 1913 chamber date with stock lug.

1908 NAVY — 9mm, 6 in. barrel, scarce. Ser. no. range 1,000b-10,000b, 9,000 manufactured.

	N/A	$2,950	$1,700	$1,300	$1,100	$950	$800

1908 BOLIVIAN CONTRACT — 9mm, 4 in. barrel.

	N/A	$3,000	$2,500	$1,700	$1,300	$1,100	$900

1913 COMMERCIAL DWM — 9mm, 4 in. barrel, grip safety and stock lug, horizontal "N" proof mark, 71,000 ser. no. range, rare.

	N/A	$2,250	$1,500	$1,050	$900	$780	$700

Grading	100%	98%	95%	90%	80%	70%	60%

1914 COMMERCIAL DWM — 9mm, 4 in. barrel, undated, stock lug, horizontal crown-N proofed.

	N/A	$1,000	$800	$550	$450	$400	$350

1914 NAVY — 9mm, 6 in. barrel, scarce. Dated 1916 and 1917.

	N/A	$2,750	$2,000	$1,500	$1,050	$950	$800

1916-1918 DATED ERFURT MILITARY — 9mm, 4 in. barrel, dated 1916-1918 - there are no known 1915 chamber dated Erfurts.

	N/A	$700	$550	$450	$400	$350	$300

Add 20% for 1914 date.
Add $75 for original holster in average+ condition.
Add 10% for matching mag.
Add 50% for 2 matching mag.'s.
Note: Date stamped on top frame is date of production; thus dates could be 1914, 1915, 1916, 1917, or 1918. All are Military P.08s, however. 99%-100% Erfurts are rare.

1914 ERFURT ARTILLERY — 9mm, 1914 date is only one seen, 8 in. barrel.

	N/A	$1,500	$1,150	$850	$675	$550	$425

1913-1918 DATED WWI DWM MILITARY — 9mm, 4 in. barrel. 1913-1918 dated. Most frequently encountered WWI military Luger, stock lug.

	N/A	$750	$550	$475	$400	$350	$295

Add $75 for original holster in average+ condition.
Add 10% for matching mag.
Add 50% for 2 matching mag.'s.
Note: Date stamped on top frame is date of production; thus dates could be 1914, 1915, 1916, 1917, or 1918. All are Military P.08s, however.

1914-1918 DATED DWM ARTILLERY — 9mm, 8 in. barrel. Dated 1914-1918.

	N/A	$1,500	$1,000	$800	$600	$500	$400

Add $350 for matching stock.
Add $200 for proper non-matching stock.
Add $200 for original leather holster with shoulder strap.
Add 40% for rare 1914 chamber date.

LUGERS: 1920-1930 DWM

Most common variations in good supply within this section in 50% or less condition will approximate the 60% value. This reflects its value as a representative shooter rather than a higher priced collector's gun.

1920 DWM OR ERFURT — 9mm, 4 in. barrel, military and police, reworked and issued to police units, many thousand reworked, double date also, 1920 and 1921 dated.

	N/A	$700	$540	$450	$375	$300	$250

1920 COMMERCIAL — 7.65mm or 9mm cal., 3⅞-4 in. barrel, many thousand produced.

	$675	$525	$425	$385	$335	$285	$250

Add 25% for 9mm cal.

1920 NAVY COMMERCIAL — 9mm, 6 in. barrel, very rare rework, Navy rear sight. Add 20% for 7.65mm with 6 in. barrel.

	N/A	$2,000	$1,400	$1,000	$900	$800	$700

Grading	100%	98%	95%	90%	80%	70%	60%

1920 COMMERCIAL ARTILLERY — 9mm, 8 in. barrel, very rare rework.

	N/A	$1,350	$950	$800	$600	$500	$400

While this variation is undoubtedly rarer than the 1914-1918 military Artillery models, it is less desirable.

1920 "LONG BARREL" COMMERCIAL — 7.65mm or 9mm, 10-20 in. barrel, extremely rare.

	N/A	$1,400	$1,100	$1,000	$750	$655	$600

Watch for fakes - these guns have to be evaluated one at a time.

1920 NAVY CARBINE — 7.65mm, 11¾ in. barrel, long frame (if short frame, be wary of fakes, very few produced). Navy rear sight, no forearm under barrel.

	N/A	$2,000	$1,600	$1,100	$1,025	$950	$850

1920 CARBINE — 7.65mm, 11¾ in. barrel, very rare.

	100%	98%	95%	90%	80%	70%	60%
Gun only	N/A	$5,450	$4,750	$4,000	$3,000	$2,500	$2,000
Gun with stock	N/A	$9,250	$7,250	$6,400	$5,500	$4,650	$3,650

1920 SWISS REWORK — 7.65mm 3⅝-6 in. barrel, several hundred produced.

	N/A	$1,400	$1,100	$1,000	$750	$655	$600

ABERCROMBIE & FITCH COMMERCIAL — 7.65mm or 9mm, long frame, 4¾ in. barrel, 100 mfg., total for both cals. A few 6 in. barrels - add 30%.

	N/A	$4,250	$3,500	$3,000	$2,500	$2,100	$1,850

Inspect barrel legend very carefully (as in beware of fakes).

1920/21-DWM — 9mm, 4 in. barrel.

	N/A	$700	$600	$450	$400	$350	$300

Deduct 20% of arsenal reworked.

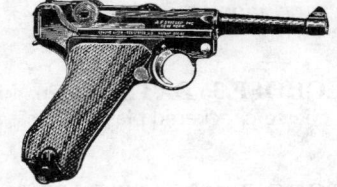

1920/23 STOEGER EAGLE — 7.65mm or 9mm, 3⅝-24 in. barrels, less than 1000 mfg., made by DWM for Stoeger, sold in USA, longer barrel models have higher value.

	100%	98%	95%	90%	80%	70%	60%
3⅞ - 6 in. barrels	N/A	$2,750	$1,450	$1,200	$1,050	$950	$825
8 in. barrel	N/A	$4,500	$2,300	$2,000	$1,650	$1,200	$995

Add 50% for Mauser mfg.

Be extremely careful when examining the frame markings on this variation as there are many fakes in the marketplace.

1923 DWM COMMERCIAL — 7.65mm, 3⅝ in. barrel, 14,000 mfg. (Ser. No. Range 74,000-89,000).

	N/A	$695	$525	$435	$375	$330	$275

1923 DWM "SAFE AND LOADED" COMMERCIAL — "safe and loaded" marked on frame and ejector, 7.65mm, 3⅞ in. barrel, safety and extractor marked in English, 2000 mfg. (Ser. No. Range 89,000-91,000).

	N/A	$1,000	$850	$600	$500	$420	$350

Grading	100%	98%	95%	90%	80%	70%	60%

1923 FINNISH LUGER — 7.65mm, approx. 5,000-7,000 units made for Finnish military contract (Army and Navy), marked "SA" surrounded by a rectangle, most have been recently imported into the U.S.

| | N/A | $550 | $450 | $375 | $325 | $300 | $275 |

LUGERS: KRIEGHOFF MFG.

1923 DWM/KRIEGHOFF COMMERCIAL — 7.65mm x 3⅞ in. or 9mm x 4 in. barrels, few made, reworked by Krieghoff, chamber dated 1921 or unmarked, most in "in" range, Krieghoff stamped on back-frame. Be wary of fakes.

| | N/A | $1,425 | $1,210 | $1,100 | $880 | $770 | $660 |

DWM/KRIEGHOFF COMMERCIAL — 7.65mm or 9mm, 4 in. barrel, a few hundred made, side frame marked Krieghoff. Be wary of fakes.

| | N/A | $2,400 | $2,000 | $1,650 | $1,300 | $1,000 | $800 |

KRIEGHOFF COMMERCIAL SIDE FRAME — 7.65mm or 9mm, 4 or 6 in. barrel, 1500 mfg., 1000 with side frame marked, and 500 without. "P" prefix ser. no.'s. Add 30% for side frame marked 7.65mm.

| | N/A | $2,100 | $1,600 | $1,200 | $995 | $800 | $700 |

KRIEGHOFF S CODE EARLY — 9mm, 4 in. barrel, 1800 mfg., German Luftwaffe. Has fat walnut grips, "H-K Suhl" toggle.

| | N/A | $2,350 | $1,750 | $1,200 | $995 | $895 | $775 |

KRIEGHOFF S CODE MID SERIES — 9mm, 4 in. barrel, 500-700 mfg., Luftwaffe, ser. no. range 1600-2500, fine-checkered plastic grips.

| | N/A | $2,650 | $1,950 | $1,500 | $995 | $800 | $700 |

KRIEGHOFF S CODE LATE — 9mm, 4 in. barrel, 1800 mfg., Luftwaffe, ser. no. range 2300-4200.

| | N/A | $2,500 | $1,800 | $1,200 | $750 | $600 | $500 |

KRIEGHOFF 36 DATE — 9mm, 4 in. barrel, 500-700 made, Luftwaffe military, 2 digit date, coarse checkered plastic grips.

| | N/A | $2,800 | $2,000 | $1,650 | $1,300 | $1,000 | $800 |

KRIEGHOFF 1936-1945 DATED — 9mm, 4 in. barrel, approx. 9,000 mfg., 4 digit chamber date, 1936, 1937 and 1940 most common; 1938 and 1941 through 1945 dates command 70-200% premiums. 1945 is extremely rare - add 500%.

| | N/A | $2,500 | $1,825 | $1,550 | $1,320 | $1,225 | $1,100 |

The 1941 "large date" is very rare - watch for fakes (re-dated frames) on this model in general.

POST-WAR KRIEGHOFF TYPE I — 9mm, 4 in. barrel, 150 mfg. for occupation forces, H-K marked toggle link.

| | N/A | $1,550 | $1,300 | $1,200 | $1,100 | $995 | $875 |

POST-WAR KRIEGHOFF TYPE II — 9mm, 4 in. barrel, 150 mfg., unmarked toggle link, many parts proofed "Eagle-over-2".

| | N/A | $1,200 | $1,100 | $1,000 | $900 | $800 | $775 |

POST-WAR KRIEGHOFF COMMERCIAL — 7.65mm, 4 in. barrel, 100-200 mfg., unmarked toggle, many parts proofed "Eagle-over-2".

| | N/A | $1,200 | $1,100 | $1,000 | $900 | $800 | $775 |

Grading	100%	98%	95%	90%	80%	70%	60%

LUGERS: MAUSER MFG.

Most common variations in good supply within this section in 50% or less condition will approximate the 60% value. This reflects its value as a representative shooter rather than a higher priced collector's gun.

1935-06 PORTUGUESE GNR — 7.65mm, 4¾ in. barrel, 564 mfg., GNR on chamber, Portuguese marked safety and extractor.

	N/A	$1,750	$1,200	$900	$700	$650	$425

1934/06 MAUSER SWISS COMMERCIAL — 7.65mm, 4¾ in. barrel, a few hundred produced, cross in sunburst or blank chamber, grip safety.

	N/A	$2,800	$2,400	$2,000	$1,500	$1,250	$850

1934 MAUSER BANNER COMMERCIAL — 7.65mm or 9mm, 4 in. barrel, hundreds produced, unmarked chamber, "v" suffix to ser. no.

	N/A	$1,800	$1,600	$1,400	$1,150	$950	$725

Add 15% for "Kal. 7.65" barrel marking.

S/42 K DATE — mfg. 1934 only, 9mm, 4 in. barrel, approx. 10,000 mfg., military.

	N/A	$2,450	$1,800	$900	$800	$700	$550

Add 50% for "large eagle over M Navy" proofmark.

S/42 G DATE — mfg. 1935 only, 9mm, 4 in. barrel, many thousand produced.

	N/A	$950	$650	$500	$450	$400	$375

Add 20% for Navy markings.

S/42 DATED CHAMBER — 9mm, 4 in. barrel, many thousands produced, "S/42" stamped rear toggle, chamber dated 1936-1939. One of the most frequently encountered WWII military Lugers.

	N/A	$795	$625	$500	$425	$375	$350

Add $75 for original holster in average+ condition.
Add 10% for matching mag.
Add 50% for 2 matching mag.'s.
Add 20% for Navy markings.
The last regular production S/42 Models were mfg. approx. April of 1939.

MAUSER PERSIAN (IRANIAN) CONTRACT — 9mm, 4 and 8 in. barrels, 1,000 — 8 in. mfg., and 1,000 — 4 in. mfg., Farsi numerals.

	100%	98%	95%	90%	80%	70%	60%
4 in. barrel	N/A	$3,750	$3,200	$2,750	$2,250	$2,000	$1,750
Artillery (8 in.)	N/A	$2,400	$2,000	$1,800	$1,650	$1,475	$1,200

Add 50% for Artillery with matching rig.
This variation became less desirable after the U.S. hostage situation occurred in Iran.

1936-1942 DATED MAUSER BANNER — 9mm, 4 in. barrel, over 1,000 mfg., commercial and contract sales. No sear safety, often have strawed small parts.

	N/A	$1,500	$1,050	$800	$700	$600	$500

MAUSER BANNER DUTCH CONTRACT — 9mm, 4 in. barrel, 1,000 mfg., safety marked "Rust". Dated 1936-1940.

	N/A	$1,500	$1,000	$695	$600	$500	$400

Add 10% for 1936, 1937, or 1938 chamber date.

MAUSER BANNER SWEDISH CONTRACT — 275 mfg. in 9mm, 4¾ in. barrels, dated 1938, 25 mfg. in 9mm, dated 1939, 30 mfg. in 7.65mm, dated 1939, very rare in 7.65mm dated 1940.

	N/A	$1,850	$1,300	$750	$695	$600	$500

Add 15% for 7.65 mm cal.

Lugers with Variations, cont.

Grading	100%	98%	95%	90%	80%	70%	60%

CODE "S/42" COMMERCIAL CONTRACT — 9mm, 4 in. barrel, a few hundred produced, dated 1938. Commercial proof marks only.

	N/A	$1,200	$975	$750	$650	$550	$500

CODE "42" — 9mm, 4 in. barrels, dated 1939-1940, rear toggle marked "42". One of the most frequently encountered WWII military Lugers. Add 40% for Navy markings.

	N/A	$750	$550	$375	$325	$275	$250

Add $75 for original holster in average+ condition.

MAUSER BANNER POLICE — approx. 30 thousand mfg., dated 1939-1942, police contract, have sear safeties, blued small parts. A few observed dated 1938 —.

	N/A	$1,500	$1,000	$600	$500	$400	$350

Add 30% with 1938 chamber date (rare).

CODE "41-42" — 9mm, 4 in. barrel, 2-digit date, approx. 7,000 mfg. in January of 1941, "41" dated chamber, "42" code, most 42 dates are reworks.

	N/A	$1,000	$750	$500	$425	$375	$350

Add $75 for original holster in average+ condition.

CODE "byf" — 9mm, 4 in. barrel, thousands made, chamber dated 41 and 42. Rear toggle is stamped "byf", standard magazine was "fxo" marked and had an un-numbered plastic bottom. One of the most frequently encountered WWII military Lugers.

	N/A	$850	$700	$500	$425	$375	$350

Add 20% for original black bakelite grips.
Add $75 for original holster in average+ condition.
Code "byf" Lugers with black bakelite grips are referred to as the "Black Widow" variation.

AUSTRIAN BUNDES HEER — 9mm, 4 in. barrel, several hundred produced, Austrian Federal Army, no serial letter suffix-same ser. placement as KU. Rarely encountered in mint condition.

	N/A	$1,400	$1,000	$950	$825	$750	$650

MAUSER 1934 CODE BYF, S/42 AND 42 KU — 3,500 mfg. Post-1942 Luftwaffe subcontract.

	N/A	$1,700	$1,300	$950	$825	$750	$650

LUGER: REWORKS

DEATH'S HEAD REWORK — 9mm, 4 in. barrel, very rare, possible early SS unit issue. Watch for fakes.

	N/A	$1,800	$995	$850	$700	$600	$450

SIMSON REWORK — 9mm, 4 in. barrel, DWM toggles, Simpson Eagle proofs on reworked parts.

	N/A	$750	$550	$450	$375	$325	$295

DOUBLE DATED DWM/ERFURT — 9mm, 4 or 8 in. barrel, very scarce. 1920 over 1910-1918 chamber dates. Often with sear safety and mag. safety remnant.

	N/A	$795	$500	$300	$275	$250	$225

Add 30% for intact mag. safety.
Add 40% for 8 in. barrel.

KONZENTRATION LUGER REWORK — 9mm, 4 in. barrel, 200-300 marked "Kl 1933" and issued to guards working in the first concentration camps - most went to Dachau.

	N/A	$1,100	$850	$600	$475	$400	$350

Grading	100%	98%	95%	90%	80%	70%	60%

LUGERS: SIMSON MFG.

SIMSON & COMPANY — 7.65mm or 9mm, $3\frac{7}{8}$ or 4 in. barrel, military and limited commercial sales, many thousands produced, but rarely found.

	N/A	$1,300	$800	$650	$500	$450	$375

SIMSON GRIP SAFETY — 9mm, $3\frac{7}{8}$ in. barrel, very rare, production unknown. Be wary of fakes.

	N/A	$1,800	$1,600	$1,200	$975	$675	$475

SIMSON MILITARY DATED — 9mm, 4 in. barrel, 2,000 mfg., dated 1925-1928.

	N/A	$2,000	$1,500	$1,000	$800	$675	$550

This model is most commonly encountered with a 1925 chamber date.

SIMSON S CODE — 9mm, 4 in. barrel, less than 1,000 mfg. Rare.

	$1,600	$1,200	$975	$675	$550	$475

LUGERS: SWISS BERN

1906 BERN — 7.65mm, $4\frac{3}{4}$ in. barrel, "Waffenfabrik Bern" on toggle, Swiss military, bordered checkered walnut grips, exactly 17,874 mfg.

	N/A	$1,950	$1,400	$1,000	$800	$600	$500

1929 SWISS BERN — 7.65mm, $4\frac{3}{4}$ in. barrel, 29,857 mfg., many machining changes to simplify production, straight front grip strap, P prefix designates commercial model, brown or black plastic grips.

	N/A	$1,500	$1,100	$900	$800	$600	$500

LUGERS: KDF, INTERARMS, STOEGER, & RECENT IMPORT

Note: These Lugers have been manufactured by Mauser Werke in Oberndorf, W. Germany in the 1970's and again recently. Earlier importation was by Interarms of Alexandria, VA (and so marked on these guns). Currently, Mauser Werke 7.65 and 9mm Lugers are available in various configurations - including the Karabiner (Carbine), Cartridge Counter, and special order variations (4 in. standard barrel and Artillery).

Currently, only Precision Imports, Inc. located in San Antonio, TX, is importing the Mauser manufactured P.08 (on a special order basis only). Prices start at $3,210 for the standard model. Engraved or limited production models typically start at approx. $7,200 and go up according to the amount of workmanship needed to complete the fabrication.

Prices below for 100% condition Lugers assume N.I.B. status. If without box and accessories, deduct 25%.

Prices below reflect the recent devaluation of the U.S. dollar against some foreign currencies. While the manufacturer's suggested retails have gone up considerably, prices for used specimens (98% or less original condition) have not increased proportionately, and in some cases, have changed very little.

MAUSER P.O8 — imported by KDF in various configurations including engraved models. Prices start in the $3,210 range (4 in. barrel) and vary substantially depending on model, type(s) of finish, and amount of engraving.

INTERARMS MAUSER P.O8 — 7.65 and 9mm, 4 or 6 in. barrel, fully-contoured front grip strap.

	$795	$525	$450	$400	$375	$350	$300

INTERARMS "SWISS-STYLE" MAUSER EAGLE — 9mm or 7.65mm, "straight" front grip strap, American eagle logo on top of frame.

	$695	$475	$425	$375	$350	$325	$275

Add 10% for 6 in. barrel in 9mm.

Grading	100%	98%	95%	90%	80%	70%	60%

STOEGER .22 CAL. LUGER — .22 LR cal., toggle action, all steel construction, 4½ in. barrel, 10 shot mag. capacity, previously mfg. in the U.S. until 1985.

	$150	$125	$100	$85	$70	$60	$50

Last Mfg.'s Sug. Retail was $200.

"1 of 1,000" — 1,000 mfg. in 1984-85, includes wooden box and extra mag.

	$295	$225	$175

NEW MODEL CARBINE WITH STOCK — 9mm Para., authentic reproduction of the original Luger Carbine complete with matching stock, accessories, and case.

Mfg.'s Sug. Retail	$7,895		$3,375	$2,250	$1,500

Manufacture has been disc. but limited quantities are still available through Interarms.

CARTRIDGE COUNTER — left grip is slotted and contains a numbered metal strip. Introduced 1983.

Mfg.'s Sug. Retail	$4,107		$2,000	$1,400	$800

Manufacture has been disc. but limited quantities are still available through Interarms.

COMMEMORATIVE BULGARIAN — 100 available on U.S. market.

	$1,800	$1,200	$800

COMMEMORATIVE RUSSIAN — 100 available on U.S. market.

	$1,800	$1,200	$800

Matched pair of each

	$4,000	$2,550	$1,850

MAUSER SPORT PARABELLUM — 10 each, 7.65mm and 9mm, imported target barrel and adj. sights.

	$2,500	$2,000	$1,250

MAUSER SPORT PARABELLUM

Consecutive pair — 7.65mm or 9mm.

	$4,250	$3,175	$1,950

LUGERS: SPECIAL INTEREST

SPANDAU LUGER — 200 mfg. as prototype in 1918, 10 known. Controversial.
Prices vary substantially on this "variation" and are not predictable.

1945 CHAMBER DATED KRIEGHOFF — 100 mfg., 3 known.

	N/A	$10,000	$7,500	$4,500	$2,900	$2,400	$1,850

MO4/05 G.L. BABY LUGER — 7.65mm or 9 mm, 3¼ in. barrel, G.L. proofed, hand-made under Georg Luger's supervision, two known to exist. Made with shortened barrel, mag., and grip frame.

BABY LUGER 1925/26 — Prototype, 380/32 ACP, 4 mfg., only 1 known is .380. Only Luger documented by the manufacturer.

VONO REWORK — 7.54mm or 9mm, 4 in. barrel, commercial, rework by W.P. Von Nordheim, extremely rare variation.

	$1,500	$1,275	$1,050	$900	$800	$700	$600

1900 DWM CARBINE — 7.65mm, 11¾ in. barrel, 100 mfg., only one known to exist. Characterized by "Ski slope" sight on rear toggle.

Grading	100%	98%	95%	90%	80%	70%	60%

1907 U.S. ARMY TEST TRIAL — .45 cal., at least four mfg., three known to exist. BIG bucks.

KRIEGHOFF GRIP SAFETY — 9mm, 4 in. barrel, extremely rare, test trial gun.

$3,800	$3,500	$3,000				

1906/29 SWISS SPECIAL ASSEMBLY — 7.65mm, 4¾ in. barrel.

$2,200	$1,650	$1,200				

1929 SWISS 9MM PROTOTYPE — 4¾ in. barrel.

$4,200	$3,000	$2,100				

CONVERSIONS: JOHN MARTZ — John Martz of CA has converted P.38s and WWI or WWII Lugers into various configurations since 1968. These conversions are known for their quality workmanship and functional accuracy. Below is a generalized listing of variations he has fabricated and their values to date with production totals.

.380 ACP Baby Luger — 6 mfg. (disc.).

$3,500	$3,000	$2,400				

7.65mm Baby Luger — 10 mfg.

$4,500	$3,750	$3,000				

9mm Baby Luger — 105 mfg., 2 to 3 in. barrel.

$2,500	$2,000	$1,500				

Navy Model — .45 ACP, 4 or 8 in. barrel, adj. rear Navy sight, 27 mfg.

$4,500	$3,750	$3,000				

Add 10% for Navy Model with 100-200 meter rear sight.

Navy Model Ltd. Edition — .38 Super, 6 in. barrel, adj. rear Navy sight, 10 mfg. (disc.).

$5,000	$3,950	$3,250				

Subtract 10% for fixed rear sight (standard model with 4 in. barrel).

Standard Model — .38 Super, 4 to 8 in. barrel, fixed sight, 2 mfg.

$4,500	$3,750	$3,000				

Target Luger — .22 Mag., 6 or 8 in. barrel, fixed sight, 5 mfg. (disc.).

$5,000	$3,950	$3,250				

Luger Carbines (with shoulder stock) .22 Mag., 7.65mm Para., 9mm Para., or .38 Super cal., 11-18 in. barrel with adj. rear sights.

$5,000	$3,950	$3,250				

Add 20% for .22 Mag. cal.

Experimental Lugers — experimental pistols have been made in .40 S&W, .41 AE, and .357 Mag. Most have 8 in. barrels (except for .40 S&W cal.). Extreme rarity (and not for sale status) precludes accurate price evaluation.

LUGERS: ACCESSORIES

.22 CALIBER CONVERSION UNITS:

ERMA — (POSTWAR-GREEN CARD BOARD BOX)

$350	$320	$295	$275	$250	$225	$200

Grading	100%	98%	95%	90%	80%	70%	60%
ERMA-PREWAR IN WOODEN BOX — Pre-war in wooden box - deduct 20% for mismatched. Add 20% for Nazi Navy property numbered.							
	$650	$600	$550	$550	$430	$400	$360

DETACHABLE STOCKS:

	100%	98%	95%	90%	80%	70%	60%
ARTILLERY TYPE FLAT BOARD							
	$250	$200	$165	$135	$120	$110	$100
NAVAL-TYPE FLAT BOARD							
	$750	$625	$550	$500	$450	$410	$350
CARBINE CONTOURED (ORIGINAL)							
	$1,500	$1,200	$900	$850	$750	$700	$600
HOLLOW ARTILLERY HOLSTER TYPE — hollow wood broomhandle type-very rare (watch for fakes).							
	$6,000	$5,500	$5,000	$4,500	$4,000	$3,500	$3,000
IDEAL TELESCOPING WITH GRIPS — mfg. U.S. by Ideal Corp.							
	$1,200	$750	$675	$625	$575	$530	$500

"SNAIL" DRUM MAGAZINE:

	100%	98%	95%	90%	80%	70%	60%
1ST ISSUE							
	$550	$500	$450				
2ND ISSUE							
	$450	$400	$350				
LOADING TOOL OR UNLOADING TOOL (2 TYPES)							
	$425	$375	$350				
ARTILLERY HOLSTER RIG, COMPLETE							
	$450	$400	$350				
If shoulder strap is missing — deduct 20%.							
NAVAL HOLSTER RIG, COMPLETE							
	$1,500	$1,200	$900	$750	$700	$650	$600

LUNA
Germany.

SINGLE SHOT

	100%	98%	95%	90%	80%	70%	60%
SINGLE SHOT TARGET RIFLE — falling block action, .22 LR and .22 Hornet, 20 in. barrel, adj. sights, target type stocks, pre-WWII.							
	$990	$880	$800	$690	$605	$550	$495
MODEL 200 FREE PISTOL — .22 LR, 11 in. barrel, blue, target sights, checkered target grips, pre-WWII.							
	$1,100	$990	$855	$770	$660	$605	$525

M section

MAC (MILITARY ARMAMENT CORP.)
Please refer to the Ingram section in this text.

MAS
Manufacture D'Armes St. Etienne (MAS) located in France.

Grading	100%	98%	95%	90%	80%	70%	60%

MODEL 1935S — 7.65mm French Long cal., 4⅓ in. barrel, enamel finish, Colt Govt. Model locking system, 26 oz.

	100%	98%	95%	90%	80%	70%	60%
	$325	$295	$260	$225	$195	$170	$150

MBA GYROJET
Previous manufacturer (1966-1969) located in San Ramon, CA.

MARK I GYROJET PISTOL — 12 or 13mm (no cartridge case), uses spin-stabilized rocket projectiles that accelerate to 1,250 FPS in .12 seconds, 2 in. (rare) or 5 in. barrel, 6-shot semi-auto action drives rocket projectile (primer activated) into fixed firing pin, smooth walnut grips, black or antique nickel finish, 13 or 16 oz. Not particularly accurate.

	$550	$495	$450	$400	$360	$330	$300

The rocket ammunition for this model is rare and reports of $20+/round are not uncommon. Plans are underway to manufacture a new batch of rocket ammunition.

Mark I Presentation Model — cased with 10 dummy rounds and bronze medal honoring rocket pioneers Robert H. Goddard and Joseph J. Stubbs.

	$2,250	$1,600	$995

MARK I CARBINE — 13mm, same action as Mark I pistol, full stock with pistol grip extension, 18 in. barrel, nickel finish, 4½ lbs. Limited mfg.

	$1,050	$850	$750	$650	$595	$550	$500

MK ARMS INC.
Manufacturer located in Irvine, CA.

MK 760 — 9mm Para., semi-auto, paramilitary design carbine configuration, steel frame, 16 in. shrouded barrel, fires from closed bolt, 14, 24, or 36 shot mag., parkerized finish, folding metal stock, fixed sights. Mfg. in CA since 1983.

Mfg.'s Sug. Retail	$575		$525	$450	$375	$340	$310	$280	$250

MKE
Manufacturer located in Ankara, Turkey. Currently distributed by Mandall Shooting Supplies, Inc., located in Scottsdale, AZ.

KIRIKKALE DOUBLE ACTION AUTOMATIC — 7.65mm (disc.), or .380 ACP, 7 shot, blue, fixed sights, checkered plastic grips, this is a close copy of Walther's PP and the Turkish Army's standard service pistol. Disc. 1987.

	$365	$295	$240	$215	$185	$170	$155

Although disc. by the Turkish Government in 1987, Mandall Shooting Supplies still has limited amounts of inventory on this model.
Last Mfg.'s Sug. Retail was $395.

M.O.A. CORPORATION
Manufacturer located in Eaton, OH. Dealer direct sales only.

PISTOLS

Approx. 500-600 maximum pistols are produced annually.

Grading	100%	98%	95%	90%	80%	70%	60%

MAXIMUM — available in 28 standard chamberings between .22 Rimfire and .44 Mag., additional custom calibers are also available upon special order, single shot lever action pistol, falling block action, Chromoly receiver (disc. 1991), Armoloy coated Chromoly (disc. late 1992), or stainless steel (new 1991, standard 1992) receiver, 8¾ (new 1989), 10¾, or 14 in. interchangeable barrel, transfer bar safety, adj. open sights, walnut grips and forearm. New 1986.

Mfg.'s Sug. Retail	$622	$565	$500	$460	$430	$395	$375	$350

Add $52 for scope mount.
Subtract $85 for steel receiver.
Add $55 for stainless steel barrel on either receiver.
Add $164 per extra steel barrel.
Add $222 per extra stainless steel barrel.
Barrels must be fitted to individual receivers at the factory initially. Afterwards, they can be changed by the customer with the spanner wrench (included with extra barrels).

Carbine Model — similar to Maximum, except has 18 in. barrel. Mfg. 1986-87 only. This model will be reintroduced shortly.

	$495	$430	$365	$330	$300	$275	$250

Last Mfg.'s Sug. Retail was $575.

MAGNUM RESEARCH, INC.
Manufactured by Israeli Military Industries. Exclusively imported and distributed by Magnum Research, Inc., in Minneapolis, MN. Dealer and distributor sales.

In addition to the models listed below, Magnum Research can also provide a variety of special order options through their custom shop. Prices can be obtained by contacting Magnum Research directly.

PISTOLS

THE MOUNTAIN EAGLE — .22 LR cal., semi-auto single action, 6½ in. polymer and steel barrel, features alloy receiver and polymer technology, matte black finish, adj. rear sight, 15 or 20 shot mag. 21 oz. New 1992.

Mfg.'s Sug. Retail	$239	$195	$150	$135	$120	$105	$95	$85

PISTOLS: DESERT EAGLE SERIES

Magnum Research also offers a Collector's Edition Presentation Series. Special models include a Gold Edition (serial numbered 1-100), a Silver Edition (serial numbered 101-500), and a Bronze Edition (serial numbered 501-1,000). Each pistol from this series is supplied with a walnut presentation case, 2 sided medallion, and certificate of authenticity. Prices are available upon request by contacting Magnum Research directly.

Alloy frames on the Desert Eagle Series of Pistols were discontinued in 1992. However, if sufficient demand warrants, these models will once again be available to consumers at the same price as the steel frames.

THE BABY EAGLE — 9mm Para., .40 S&W, or .41 AE cal., double action, all steel construction, short barrel recoil operation, polygonal rifling, combat styled trigger guard, decocking safety, blued, matte hard chrome, or brushed chrome finish, 16 (9mm Para.), 11 (.41 AE), or 10 (.40 S&W) shot mag., 38½ oz. New 1991.

Mfg.'s Sug. Retail	$569	$495	$425	$375	$335	$300	$275	$250

Add $149 for matte hard chrome or brushed chrome finish.
Add $239 for conversion kit (9mm to .41 AE or .41 AE to 9mm, includes barrel, spring, and mag.).

Grading	100%	98%	95%	90%	80%	70%	60%

MARK VII .357 MAG. DESERT EAGLE — .357 Mag., gas operated, semi-auto pistol, 6, 10, or 14 in. barrel lengths, steel (58.3 oz.) or alloy (47.8 oz.) frame, adaptable to .44 Mag with optional kit, 9 shot mag. (8 for .44 Mag.). New 1983.

Mfg.'s Sug. Retail	$789	$685	$575	$500	$455	$415	$380	$355

Add $169 for choice of finishes.
Add approx. $150 for 10 or 14 in. barrel.
Add $495 for .357 Mag. to .41 Mag./.44 Mag. conversion kit (6 in. barrel).
Add $685 for .357 Mag. to .44 Mag. conversion kit (10 or 14 in. barrel).
Choice of finishes includes nickel, polished blue, or hardchrome (matte, polished, or brushed).

Whitetail Special .357 Mag. 14 in. barrel, includes scope mount, target walnut grips, and Desert Eagle premiums. Mfg. 1990-1992.

		$925	$750	$650	$550	$450	$400	$375

Add $50 for stainless steel frame.
Last Mfg.'s Sug. Retail was $1,088.

Stainless Steel .357 Mag. — similar to .357 Mag. Desert Eagle, except has stainless steel frame, 58.3 oz. New 1987.

Mfg.'s Sug. Retail	$839		$750	$650	$550			

Add approx. $150 for 10 or 14 in. barrel.

MARK VII .41 MAG. DESERT EAGLE — .41 Mag., similar to .357 Desert Eagle, 6 in. barrel only, 8 shot mag., steel (62.8 oz.) or alloy (52.3 oz.) frame. New late 1988.

Mfg.'s Sug. Retail	$799	$690	$575	$510	$460	$415	$390	$365

Add $395 for .41 Mag. to .44 Mag. conversion kit (6 in. barrel only).
Add $169 for choice of finishes.
Choice of finishes includes nickel, polished blue, or hardchrome (matte, polished, or brushed).

Stainless Steel .41 Mag. — similar to .41 Mag. Desert Eagle, except has stainless steel frame, 58.3 oz. New late 1988.

Mfg.'s Sug. Retail	$849		$755	$650	$550			

MARK VII .44 MAG. DESERT EAGLE — .44 Mag., similar to .357 Desert Eagle, 8 shot mag., steel (62.8 oz.) or alloy (52.3 oz.) frame. Introduced late 1986.

Mfg.'s Sug. Retail	$899	$785	$675	$565	$500	$465	$420	$390

Add $169 for choice of finishes.
Add approx. $200 for 10 or 14 in. barrel.
Add $475 for .44 Mag. to .357 Mag. conversion kit (6 in. barrel).
Add $675 for .44 Mag. to .357 Mag. conversion kit (10 or 14 in. barrel).
Add $395 for .44 Mag. to .41 Mag. conversion kit (6 in. barrel).
Choice of finishes includes nickel, polished blue, or hardchrome (matte, polished, or brushed).

Stainless Steel .44 Mag. — similar to .44 Mag. Desert Eagle, except has stainless steel frame, 58.3 oz. New 1987.

Mfg.'s Sug. Retail	$949		$825	$700	$550			

Add approx. $210 for 10 or 14 in. barrel.

HUNTER EDITION MARK VII — .357 or .44 Mag., 6 in. barrel with extra 14 in. hunting barrel, includes Simmons 2 x 20 compact scope, scope mount, cherry hardwood presentation case. New late 1987.

Mfg.'s Sug. Retail	$1,239	$1,125	$925	$800	$675	$550	$475	$425

Add $62 for .44 Mag. cal.
Add $159 for choice of finishes.
Choice of finishes includes nickel, polished blue, or hardchrome (matte, polished, or brushed).

Grading	100%	98%	95%	90%	80%	70%	60%

MARK VII .50 MAG. DESERT EAGLE — .50 AE cal., 6 in. barrel only, steel only, 7-shot mag., 72.4 oz. New 1991.

Mfg.'s Sug. Retail	$1,249	$1,125	$950	$825	$675	$550	$475	$425

This new cartridge utilizes the same rim dimensions as the .44 Mag. Currently there is a choice between a 300 and 325 grain (both are available in either soft or hollow point) bullet. The .50 Mag. Action Express cal. has 60% more stopping power than the .44 Mag., with a minimal increase in felt recoil. And yes, the software has finally arrived (ammo is now available).

PISTOLS: SINGLE SHOT

MODEL LONE EAGLE (SSP-91) — .22 LR (disc. 1992), .22 Win. Mag. (disc. 1992), .22 Hornet, .22-250, .223, .243, .30-30, .30-06, .308, 6mmBR (disc. 1992), 7mm-08, 7mmBR, .35 Rem., .357 Max., .358 Win., .44 Mag., or .444 Marlin cal., circular rear breech action, quick change 14 in. barrels (drilled and tapped), synthetic Lexan stock with pistol grip, 4 lbs. 3 oz. - 4 lbs. 7 oz. New in 1991.

Mfg.'s Sug. Retail	$254	$230	$185	$170	$150	$135	$120	$110

Add $35 for adj. sights.

This model is designed and manufactured by Ordnance Technology, Inc.

MALIN, F.E.

Manufacturer located in England. Currently sold on a limited basis by Cape Horn Outfitters located in Charlotte, NC. Previously imported by Saxon Arms, Inc. located in Clearwater, FL.

SHOTGUNS: OVER-AND-UNDER AND SIDE-BY-SIDE

BOXLOCK — made to individual order, choice of game scene engraving, Anson & Deeley boxlock actions, select European hybrid walnut, double triggers, leather cased, current manufacture. Prices start at $3,750 and each shotgun is priced per individual special order.

SIDELOCK — made to individual order, choice of game scene engraving, H&H sidelock action, select European hybrid walnut, double triggers, leather cased, current manufacture. Prices start at $5,000 and each shotgun is priced per individual special order.

MAGTECH

Importer/distributor located in Las Vegas, NV. Manufactured by CBC located in Brazil. Distributor sales only.

RIFLES

MODEL 122 — .22 LR, bolt action, 6 shot detachable clip, safety lever disconnects trigger from firing mechanism, un-checkered hardwood stock, 5.7 lbs. Imported 1992 only.

			$115	$95	$80	$70	$60	$50	$40

Last Mfg.'s Sug. Retail was $131.

SHOTGUNS

MODEL 151 SINGLE SHOT — 12, 16, 20, or .410 ga., 26, 28, or 30 in. barrel, exposed hammer, ejector, front trigger guard opening mechanism, 5 - 6½ lbs. Imported 1992 only.

			$95	$80	$70	$60	$50	$40	$35

Last Mfg.'s Sug. Retail was $109.

Grading	100%	98%	95%	90%	80%	70%	60%

MODEL MT-586 — 12 ga. only, 3 in. chamber, standard Field model shotgun, 28 in. barrel with fixed chokes, hardwood stock and forearm, double slide bars. Importation began 1993.

Mfg.'s Sug. Retail	$229	$190	$175	$160	$140	$130	$120	$110

⚞ **Model MT-586-VR** — similar to Model MT-586, except has choice of 26 or 28 in. VR barrel with interchangeable chokes. Importation began 1993.

Mfg.'s Sug. Retail	$259	$220	$185	$170	$155	$140	$130	$120

MODEL MT-586 SLUG — 12 ga. only, slug gun featuring 24 in. cylinder bore barrel with rifle sights, matte finished metal parts, and special Monte Carlo stock. Importation began 1993.

Mfg.'s Sug. Retail	$239	$195	$180	$165	$145	$130	$120	$110

MODEL MT-586P — 12 ga. only, 3 in. chamber, slide action, 19 in. cylinder bored barrel, 7 shot mag., double slide bars, steel construction, hardwood stock, 7.3 lbs. Importation began 1992.

Mfg.'s Sug. Retail	$219	$185	$170	$155	$140	$130	$120	$110

MAKAROV

Pistol design originating from Russia. Russian mfg. Makarovs may be found under "Russian Service Pistol and Rifle" heading in this text. Pistols listed below have recently been imported by Century International Arms, Inc. located in St. Albans, VT.

PISTOLS

GERMAN MAKAROV — 9mm Makarov cal., patterned after the Soviet Makarov and made in E. Germany, double action semi-auto, blowback design, all steel, slide mounted safety that doubles as a decocking lever, 3.6 in. barrel, 8 shot mag., 25 oz.

Mfg.'s Sug. Retail	$185	$150	$135	$125	$115	$95	$85	$75

The importation of this type of pistol has been increased beginning 1992, since import restrictions have been lowered due to changes in eastern bloc politics and domestic import laws regarding previous communist bloc countries.

MAMBA

Previously mfg. by Viper Mfg. Co. (a division of Sandock Austral Boksburg) located in South Africa.

AUTO PISTOL — 9mm Para., less than 80 imported into the U.S.

Rarity factor precludes accurate pricing, values vary greatly in different regions.

MANDALL SHOOTING SUPPLIES, INC.

Importer/distributor/retailer located in Scottsdale, AZ.

Mandall Shooting Supplies distributes/imports various firearms including pistols, revolvers, rifles, shotguns, as well as other models. Most of these firearms can be located under their individual trademark headings and include Bretton, Britarms, Cabanas, Erma-Werke, FAS, Gaucher, Hammerli, Domino, Korth, Krico rifles, Mandall private label shotguns, Sig, Sig-Hammerli, Tanner rifles, Techni-Mec, Zanardini, and A. Zoli shotguns and rifles.

Due to the fluctuation of the U.S. dollar against the currencies of other countries, the above trademarks can change price during the course of a year. For this reason, Mandall Shooting Supplies, Inc. should be contacted directly for current pricing and special order questions.

COACH SHOTGUN — 12, 16, or 20 ga., SxS sidelock shotgun with either external hammers or hammerless, 18, 26, 28, or 30 in. barrels, DT, sling swivels, mfg. in Spain.

Mfg.'s Sug. Retail	$500	465	$390	$365	$330	$300	$270	$240

MANNLICHER SCHOENAUER SPORTING RIFLES

Manufactured by Steyr, Daimler, Puch, in Austria from 1850s - present. Please refer to Steyr-Mannlicher in this text for current manufactured rifles.

The publisher apologizes for the Mannlicher Schoenauer prices in the 13th Edition due, in part, to some materials sent in by the Mannlicher Collector's Association. Values listed below reflect new information.

RIFLES: PRE-WWII BOLT ACTIONS

Models 1903, 1905, and 1908 may be encountered in calibers different than described. These re-chamberings were performed by gunsmith at a later date and are not original Mannlicher cals. Early Mannlichers are encountered in carbine, half-stock rifle, takedown half stock carbine, and takedown rifle configurations. Approx. 25%-40% of pre-war rifles were in takedown configuration. Steyr tang sights were also a factory option.Since there are no remaining factory records, rarity must be based on observation rather than hard facts.

The following add-ons apply on models listed below.
Add 5% for original ribbed barrel.
Deduct 60% for non-original barrel.
Add 5% for double set triggers - Deduct 5% for single trigger.
Add 15% for factory installed scope and mounts (metric threads on pre-war, metric rear threads on post war).
Deduct 40%-60% for non-factory installed mounts or holes resulting from modifications.
Add 10% for anti-coro or anti-nit barrel if so marked and original.

Grading	100%	98%	95%	90%	80%	70%	60%

MODEL 1903 CARBINE — 6.5 x 54mm Mannlicher Schoenauer cal., bolt action, 5 shot, 17.7 in. barrel, rotary mag., two leaf rear sight, double set trigger, full length stock.

	$1,050	$875	$770	$550	$470	$385	$330

This caliber is also referred to 6.5 x 53mm.
This model is normally encountered in poor condition.

MODEL 1905 CARBINE — similar to Model 1903, except 9 x 56mm Mannlicher Schoenauer cal., 19.7 in. barrel.

	$1,200	$950	$825	$660	$580	$495	$415

This model is normally encountered in poor condition. It is perhaps the least desirable of pre-war models because of the wide variation in bore diameters.

MODEL 1908 CARBINE — similar to Model 1905, except in 8 x 56mm Mannlicher Schoenauer cal.

	$1,050	$875	$770	$550	$470	$385	$330

This model is frequently noticed in better condition factors. Some exceptional takedown variations also exist within this model.

MODEL 1910 CARBINE — similar design to the Model 1905, except originally chambered for 9.5 x 56mm Mannlicher, .375 Express, or 9.5 x 57mm Mauser, this model was the predecessor of the post-war Model 1924.

	$1,050	$875	$770	$550	$470	$385	$330

MODEL 1924 CARBINE — similar to 1905, except .30-06.

	$1,200	$1,050	$990	$770	$715	$605	$525

HIGH VELOCITY SPORTING RIFLE — bolt action, 7 x 64 Brenneke, .30-06, 8 x 60 Mag., 9.3 x 62mm, 10.75 x 68mm, 23.6 in. barrel, 3 leaf sight, half stock.

	$1,320	$1,100	$825	$660	$580	$495	$415

Takedown Model

	$2,200	$1,980	$1,650	$1,320	$880	$715	$635

Add 10%-25% for Takedown Model, depending on rarity and condition.

Grading	100%	98%	95%	90%	80%	70%	60%

RIFLES: POST-WWII BOLT ACTION

Values below represent standard models with no engraving. Original engraving will add at least $200 to prices listed below with some heavily engraved "Alpine" models selling for large premiums.

A variation of the 1950-1952 Series is called the "GK" because of its traditionally styled European stock - which is a variant of the pre-war style and approaches the design of the Model 1961 MCA.

MODEL 1950 — various cals. including .243 Rem., .257 Roberts, .270 Win., .280 Rem., .30-06, .358 Win., 6.5 x 54mm (very desirable), 7 x 57mm, 8 x 57mm Mauser, or 9.3 x 62mm Mauser, bolt action, 5 shot rotary mag., 24 in. barrel, low bolt handle, half length stock, ebony forearm. Mfg. 1950-1952.

MODEL 1950 CARBINE — similar to 1950, except 20 in. barrel, full length stock. Mfg. 1950-1952.

	$1,000	$875	$770	$675	$580	$525	$440

MODEL 1950 CARBINE 6.5 — similar to 1950 Carbine, except 6.5 x 54mm cal., 18½ in. barrel. Mfg. 1950-1952.

	$1,000	$875	$770	$675	$580	$525	$440

Deduct 50% if encountered with oversized bore (over .265 in.).

IMPROVED MODEL 1952 — same specifications as 1950, except swept back bolt handle. Mfg. 1952-1956.

	$795	$725	$650	$575	$500	$460	$420

IMPROVED MODEL 1952 CARBINE — .257 Roberts, .270 Win., 7 x 57mm, or .30-06 cal., swept bolt handle, otherwise similar to 1950 Carbine.

	$1,000	$875	$770	$675	$580	$525	$440

IMPROVED MODEL 1952 6.5 CARBINE — similar to 1952 Carbine, except 6.5mm, 18½ in. barrel. Mfg. 1952-1956.

	$1,000	$875	$770	$675	$580	$525	$440

MODEL 1956 RIFLE — similar to 1952, except .243 and .30-06 cals., new high comb stock design, 22 in. barrel, half length stock. Mfg. 1956-1960.

	$850	$750	$650	$575	$500	$460	$420

‡ **Model 1956 Magnum** — includes .257 Wby., .458 Win. mag., 6.5 x 68mm, or 8 x 68mm cal.

	$925	$850	$750	$650	$575	$500	$460

MODEL 1956 CARBINE — similar to 1956 Rifle, except .243, 6.5 x 53mm, .257 Roberts, .270, 7mm, .30-06, or .308 cal., 20 in. barrel, full length stock. Mfg. 1956-1960.

	$1,000	$875	$770	$675	$580	$525	$440

MODEL 1961 MCA RIFLE — similar to Model 1956, except Monte Carlo stock. Mfg. 1961-1971.

	$795	$725	$650	$575	$500	$460	$420

MODEL 1961 MCA CARBINE — similar to 1956 Carbine, except Monte Carlo stock. Mfg. 1961-1971.

	$1,000	$875	$770	$675	$580	$525	$440

RIFLES: CURRENT MANUFACTURE

Current production guns are now called Steyr-Mannlicher models and can be located under this trademark in the S section.

MANUFRANCE
Manufacturer located in St. Etienne, France since 1902.

Manufrance currently manufactures many models in both rifles and shotguns that are not being imported in the U.S. at this time. These models are not covered in this book.

Grading	100%	98%	95%	90%	80%	70%	60%
AUTO SHOTGUN — 12 ga., 26, 28, or 30 in. imp. cyl., mod. and full, 2¾ or 3 in. chamber, gas operated, walnut stock, black matte receiver, vent rib.							
	$330	$305	$290	$275	$255	$240	$220
FALCOR — O/U, 12 ga., VR, 26 in. imp. cyl. and mod., 28 in. mod. and full, SST, auto ejector, chrome lined barrel, walnut checkered stock.							
	$715	$665	$635	$605	$550	$495	$470

MANURHIN
Manufacturer located in Mulhouse, France by Matra Manurhin Defense. Currently imported and distributed exclusively in the U.S. by ABO Industries located in San Diego, CA (previously Atlantic Business Organization located in New York, NY until 1992). Previously imported (1984-86) directly by Matra-Manurhin International, Inc., located in Fort Lauderdale, FL.

Manurhin in France has been manufacturing models PP, PPK, and PPK/S since 1952. Previously, they were imported by Interarms out of Alexandria, VA. In 1984, Manurhin imported their new models directly and they were marked Manurhin on the left front slide assembly. This differs from the previous Walther stamped guns. Also, no Interarms logo appears on the right side.

HANDGUNS: CURRENT IMPORTATION

All models listed below are imported exclusively through Atlantic Business Organizations, Inc., located in New York, NY.

MODEL PP — .380 ACP cal., 3⅞ in. barrel, 7 shot mag. blue only, 24 oz., all steel construction, double action with positive steel hammer block safety. Importation resumed 1988.

Mfg.'s Sug. Retail	$415	$360	$320	$275	$230	$205	$185	$170

MODEL PPK/S — .380 ACP cal., 3¼ in. barrel, 7 shot mag. blue only, all steel construction, double action with positive steel hammer block safety, 23 oz. Importation resumed 1988.

Mfg.'s Sug. Retail	$415	$360	$320	$275	$230	$205	$185	$170

MODEL 73 DEFENSE REVOLVER — .357 Mag./.38 Special, 6 shot, 2½, 3, or 4 in. barrel, checkered wood stocks, mfg. to precise tolerances, 31-33½ oz. Importation began 1988.

Mfg.'s Sug. Retail	$1,122	$1,000	$850	$725	$600	$500	$425	$350

MODEL 73 GENDARMERIE — .357 Mag./.38 Special, 6 shot, similar to Model 73 Defense except has adj. sighting components and also is offered in 5¼, 6, or 8 in. barrel lengths. Manufactured for police requirements. Importation began 1988.

Mfg.'s Sug. Retail	$1,220	$1,075	$900	$750	$625	$525	$450	$375

MODEL 73 SPORT — .357 Mag./.38 Special, 6 shot, sport shooting features include minimized hammer stroke, micrometer rear sight, and free release trigger with fitted adj. Importation began 1988.

Mfg.'s Sug. Retail	$1,220	$1,075	$900	$750	$625	$525	$450	$375

MODEL 73 CONVERTIBLE — includes choice of .22 LR/.38 Special or .22 LR/.32 cal. cylinders and barrels (5¾ in. for .38 Spl. and 6 in. for .22 LR/.32). Importation began 1988.

Mfg.'s Sug. Retail	$1,847	$1,675	$1,325	$1,125	$950	$800	$700	$600

3 Cylinder Model 73 Convertible — similar to Model 73 Convertible except includes 3 calibers (.22 LR, .32, and .38 Special). Importation began 1988.

Mfg.'s Sug. Retail	$2,230	$1,950	$1,700	$1,375	$1,150	$975	$850	$750

Grading	100%	98%	95%	90%	80%	70%	60%

MODEL 73 SILHOUETTE — .22 LR or .357 Mag. cal., Silhouette variation with fully adj. rear sight and either 10 (.22 LR) or 10¾ (.357 Mag.) in. heavy barrel with full shroud, contoured wooden target grips, approx. 4 lbs. Importation began 1988.

Mfg.'s Sug. Retail	$1,189	$1,050	$875	$735	$615	$525	$450	$375

Add $13 for .357 Mag. cal.

PISTOLS: PREVIOUS IMPORTATION

P-1 — 9mm, similar to W. German P-38, double action, 5 in. barrel.

	$440	$380	$325	$275	$230	$205	$185

MODEL P4 — 9mm, P.38 variation issued to the French Police when in Berlin during post-WWII.

	$495	$440	$380	$325	$275	$230	$200

MODEL PP — .22 LR, .32 ACP, or .380 ACP cal., 3⅞ in. barrel, 10 shot mag.-.22 LR, 8 shot mag.-.32 ACP, 7 shot mag.-.380 ACP, blue only, all steel construction, double action with positive steel hammer block safety, 24 oz. Add $10 for .22 LR cal., $46 for Durgarde finish. Imported 1984-86.

	$360	$320	$275	$230	$205	$185	$170

Last Mfg.'s Sug. Retail was $419.

⚔ **Collector Model** — blue finish, special engraving. Imported 1986 only.

	$465	$415	$350

Last Mfg.'s Sug. Retail was $529.

⚔ **Presentation Model** — blue finish, special ornamentation. Imported 1986 only.

	$720	$650	$500

Last Mfg.'s Sug. Retail was $819.
Also available with various engraving options in either blue, nickel, or gold finish - prices range from $222 - $540.

MODEL PPK/S — .22 LR, .32 ACP, or .380 ACP cal., 3¼ in. barrel, 10 shot mag.-.22 LR, 8 shot mag.-.32 ACP, 7 shot mag.-.380 ACP, blue only, all steel construction, double action with positive steel hammer block safety, 23 oz. Add $10 for .22 LR cal. Imported 1984-86.

	$360	$320	$275	$230	$205	$185	$170

Last Mfg.'s Sug. Retail was $419.

⚔ **PPK/S Durgarde** — similar to above, only with bonded brushed chrome finish. Add $14 for .22 LR cal.

	$410	$365	$325	$290	$265	$250	$240

Last Mfg.'s Sug. Retail was $465.

⚔ **Collector Model** — blue finish, special engraving. Imported 1986 only.

	$465	$415	$350

Last Mfg.'s Sug. Retail was $529.

⚔ **Presentation Model** — blue finish, special ornamentation. Imported 1986 only.

	$720	$650	$500

Last Mfg.'s Sug. Retail was $819.
Also available with various engraving options in either blue, nickel, or gold finish - prices range from $222 - $540.

Grading	100%	98%	95%	90%	80%	70%	60%

PP SPORT — .22 LR cal. only, double action, 6.1 or 8.1 in. barrel, blue finish only, precision adj. sights, contoured plastic grips with thumb rest, 25 oz. New Manurhin design for 1985. Imported 1984-86.

| | $545 | $485 | $430 | $385 | $325 | $290 | $270 |

Last Mfg.'s Sug. Retail was $635.

⭒ **PP Sport-C** — similar to PP Sport, except has single action with softened trigger.

| | $540 | $475 | $415 | $370 | $310 | $280 | $260 |

Last Mfg.'s Sug. Retail was $635.

MARATHON PRODUCTS, INC.

Previously manufactured by Santa Barbara Armaments exclusively for Marathon Products, Inc. Most of the below listed models were also available in kit form but are not shown in this book.

.22 FIRST SHOT — .22 cal., single shot bolt action, 16½ in. barrel, hardwood stock, open sights, 31 in. total length, 3.8 lbs. Mfg. 1985-87.

| | $55 | $45 | $40 | $35 | $35 | $30 | $30 |

Last Mfg.'s Sug. Retail was $60.

⭒ **.22 Super Shot** — similar to First Shot, except with 24 in. barrel and regular dimension stock. Mfg. 1985-87.

| | $55 | $45 | $40 | $35 | $35 | $30 | $30 |

Last Mfg.'s Sug. Retail was $60.

⭒ **.22 Hot Shot Pistol** — .22 LR only, bolt action, single shot, fixed sights, 14¾ in. barrel, hardwood stock with target grip configuration. Mfg. 1986-87.

| | $55 | $45 | $40 | $35 | $35 | $30 | $30 |

Last Mfg.'s Sug. Retail was $60.

CENTERFIRE MODEL — .243, .270 Win., 7 x 57, 7mm Rem. Mag., .30-06, .300 Win. Mag., or .308 Mag. cal., Mauser type bolt action, 5 shot fixed box mag., 24 in. barrel, select walnut with recoil pad, adj. trigger, open sights, 7.9 lbs. Available 1985-86 only.

| | $295 | $240 | $215 | $195 | $180 | $170 | $160 |

Last Mfg.'s Sug. Retail was $320.

MARBLE'S GAME GETTER

Manufacturer located in Lansing, MI.

In addition to axes and compasses, Marble's also manufactured their Game Getter O/U combination gun from approx. 1907 to the late 1920's. During this period of production, the gun underwent quite a few changes including sights (an aperture sight mounted on the rear backstrap was standard until changed to a top frame sight), different configuration folding metal stock, and other changes.

GAME GETTER MODEL — .22 S, L, or LR cal., upper rifled barrel over choice of .44-40 Game Getter/.410 ga. (2 in.) or .410 ga. (2½ in.) smooth bore lower barrel, choice of 12, 15, or 18 in. separated barrels, folding steel skeleton attached stock, pivoting hammer striker mechanically selects upper or lower barrel, tip-up barrels are opened by pulling trigger guard back, gutta percha or walnut stocks, approx. 3½ lbs.

| | $795 | $725 | $650 | $600 | $550 | $520 | $480 |

Add $100 for original leather holster in good condition.

Above values assume 18 in. barrels or correct registration on 12 or 15 in. models. Those 12 or 15 in. barreled Game Getters not registered during the 1968 BATF amnesty program are not legally transferable today. If not a legal configuration, values will drop considerably.

The lower barrel of this model was capable of shooting .410 ga. 2 in. paper or brass shotshells, .410 ga. 2½ in. paper shotshell (standard configuration), and .410 or .44 cal. round ball cartridges.

MARGOLIN
Russian Target Pistol manufacturer located in the U.S.S.R.

TARGET MODEL — .22 LR, semi-auto, manufactured to precise tolerances, used by some members of the Russian shooting team, basically individually made to shooters specifications, seldomly encountered in the U.S.A., while rare, desirability to date has been limited, current mfg.

Margolin pistols are typically priced in the $475-$750 range, depending on features and assuming 95%+ original condition. While currently imported Chinese copies are considerably less expensive, they do not have the quality (or accuracy) of the Russian Margolins.

MARLIN FIREARMS COMPANY
Marlin has been manufacturing firearms since 1870. From 1969- present manufacture has been located in North Haven, CT. Previously, Marlin was manufactured (1870-1969) in New Haven, CT. Distributor sales only.

PISTOLS: DERRINGERS AND REVOLVERS

Research is underway to gather more information on the variety of derringers and revolvers that Marlin mfg. between 1863-1901. While many of these variations sell in the $150-$250 range (average condition), rarer specimens with 90% original condition will be priced higher.

RIFLES: ANTIQUE MANUFACTURE

Values below are for standard models only without special order features.

100%	98%	95%	90%	80%	70%	60%	50%	40%	30%	20%	10%

MODEL 1881 LEVER ACTION — .32-40, .38-55, .40-60, .45-70, or .45-85 cal., tube mag., 28 in. octagonal barrel standard, top ejection, blued finish with case hardened hammer, lever, and butt plate. First models (pre ser. no. 600) are rare, add 200-300% premium. Approx. 20,000 mfg. between 1881-1892.

100%	98%	95%	90%	80%	70%	60%	50%	40%	30%	20%	10%
N/A	N/A	N/A	$900	$825	$725	$625	$550	$500	$450	$400	$350

This model came in 2 or 3 frame thicknesses for various calibers.

MODEL 1888 LEVER ACTION — .32-20, .38-40, or .44-40 cal., 24 in. octagonal barrel most frequently encountered, top ejection, blued finish with case hardened hammer, lever, and butt plate, short throw lever action principle. Approx. 4,800 mfg. between 1888-1889. Ser. range approx. 19,560 - 27,850.

100%	98%	95%	90%	80%	70%	60%	50%	40%	30%	20%	10%
$2,650	$2,375	$2,075	$1,825	$1,625	$1,400	$1,200	$1,000	$875	$750	$625	$500

MODEL 1889 LEVER ACTION — .25-20 (very rare), .32-20, .38-40, or .44-40 cal., 24 in. octagonal barrel most frequently encountered, side ejection with solid top frame, blued finish with case hardened hammer, lever, and butt plate, short throw lever action principle. Approx. 55,000 mfg. between 1889-1899. Ser. range approx. 25,000-100,000. Also available as Carbine (15 in. barrel-add 50%) or Musket (30 in. barrel-add 300-500%, very rare).

100%	98%	95%	90%	80%	70%	60%	50%	40%	30%	20%	10%
$995	$875	$700	$550	$465	$425	$385	$340	$295	$260	$230	$200

MODEL 1891 LEVER ACTION — .22 Rimfire and .32 Rimfire/Centerfire, 24 in. octagonal barrel most often encountered, blued finish with case hardened hammer, lever, and butt plate, sear safety system on lever action. Approx. 18,650 mfg. between 1891-1897. Ser. No. range is approx. 37,500-118,000.

100%	98%	95%	90%	80%	70%	60%	50%	40%	30%	20%	10%
$1,800	$1,625	$1,450	$1,150	$995	$925	$850	$775	$695	$625	$550	$475

MODEL 1892 LEVER ACTION — .22 S, L, or LR, .32 S or L, 16, 24, 26, or 28 in. barrel, tubular mag., open sight, plain straight stock. Mfg. 1892-1916.

100%	98%	95%	90%	80%	70%	60%	50%	40%	30%	20%	10%
$1,350	$1,175	$875	$725	$675	$600	$525	$475	$425	$385	$340	$300

.22 cals. will bring a premium in this model.

100%	98%	95%	90%	80%	70%	60%	50%	40%	30%	20%	10%

MODEL 1893 LEVER ACTION — .25-36 Marlin, .30-30, .32 Spl., .32-40, or .38-55 cal., 20-32 in. round or octagonal barrels, 10 shot tube mag., straight or pistol grip stock. Mfg. 1893-1936. Musket model also mfg. - 30 in. barrel and military style forearm.

| $1,475 | $1,175 | $895 | $750 | $675 | $600 | $525 | $475 | $425 | $385 | $340 | $300 |

MODEL 1893 CARBINE — .30-30, .32 Spl., .32-40 cal., or .38-55 cal., 20 in. round barrel, 7 shot tube mag., straight or pistol grip stock. Mfg. 1893-1936.

| $1,495 | $1,200 | $900 | $775 | $695 | $625 | $525 | $475 | $425 | $385 | $340 | $300 |

MODEL 1894 LEVER ACTION — .25-20, .32-20, .38-40, or .44-40 cal., 10 shot tube mag., 24 in. round or octagon barrel, straight or pistol grip stock. Mfg. 1894-1934.

| $1,350 | $1,175 | $875 | $725 | $675 | $600 | $525 | $475 | $425 | $385 | $340 | $300 |

MODEL 1895 LEVER ACTION — .33 WCF, .38-56, .40-65, .40-70, .40-82, or .45-70 cal., 9 shot tube mag., 24 in. round or octagon barrel standard, other lengths were available, open sights, plain straight or pistol grip stock. Mfg. 1895-1915.

| $1,575 | $1,275 | $975 | $850 | $750 | $650 | $550 | $475 | $425 | $385 | $340 | $300 |

MODEL 1897 LEVER ACTION — .22 S, L, or LR, tube mag., 16, 24, 26, or 28 in. barrel, takedown, open sights, plain straight or pistol grip stock. Mfg. 1897-1922.

| $2,250 | $1,875 | $1,500 | $1,200 | $900 | $850 | $725 | $600 | $500 | $400 | $350 | $300 |

RIFLES: MODERN PRODUCTION

Year of manufacture can be determined from 1946-1968 by the following letter prefix: 1946-C, 1947-D, 1948-E, 1949-F, 1950-G, 1951-H, 1952-J, 1953-K, 1954-L, 1955-M, 1956-N, 1957-P, 1958-R, 1959-S, 1960-T, 1961-U, 1962-V, 1963-W, 1964-Y,Z, 1965-AA, 1966-AB, 1967-AC, 1968-AD.

The models below are listed in numerical sequence to assist quick access.

Grading	100%	98%	95%	90%	80%	70%	60%

MODEL 9 CAMP CARBINE SEMI-AUTO — 9mm only, 16½ in. barrel, 12 and 20 shot mag. disc. 1989, 4 shot clip mag. became standard in 1990, sand blasted steel receiver, open sights, last shot automatic hold-open, 6¾ lbs. New 1985.

| Mfg.'s Sug. Retail | $374 | $295 | $210 | $170 | $150 | $140 | $130 | $125 |

Add $48 for nickel plating (new 1991, Model 9N).
A new high visibility orange front sight post with cutaway hood was added in 1989.

MODEL 18 SLIDE ACTION — .22 S, L, or LR, tube mag., 20 in. round or octagon barrel, open sight, exposed hammer, plain straight grip stock. Mfg. 1906-1909.

| | $330 | $250 | $195 | $140 | $110 | $100 | $85 |

MODEL 20 SLIDE ACTION — .22 S, L, or LR, 24 in. octagon barrel, open sight, exposed hammer, takedown, plain straight grip stock. Mfg. 1907-1922.

| | $330 | $250 | $195 | $140 | $110 | $100 | $85 |

MODEL 25 SLIDE ACTION — .22 Short, tube mag., 23 in. barrel, open sight, exposed hammer, takedown, plain straight grip stock. Mfg. 1909-1910.

| | $360 | $275 | $220 | $165 | $140 | $120 | $95 |

Grading	100%	98%	95%	90%	80%	70%	60%

MODEL 25MB — .22 Mag. cal., bolt action, $16\frac{1}{4}$ in. micro-groove barrel, 7 shot clip mag., hardwood stock, takedown action, 6 lbs. Mfg. 1987-88 only.

	100%	98%	95%	90%	80%	70%	60%
	$145	$115	$95	$85	$75	$70	$65

This model included both a scope and gun case.
Last Mfg.'s Sug. Retail was $173.

MODEL 25MN — .22 Mag. cal., bolt action, 7 shot clip mag., 22 in. barrel, walnut finished hardwood stock, grooved receiver, 6 lbs. New 1989.

Mfg.'s Sug. Retail	$181	$140	$110	$90	$80	$75	$70	$65

Add $8 for 4X scope.

MODEL 27 SLIDE ACTION — .25-20 or .32-20 cal., $\frac{2}{3}$ tube mag., 7 shot, 24 in. octagon barrel, open sight, plain straight grip stock. Mfg. 1910-1916.

	$330	$250	$195	$140	$110	$100	$85

MODEL 27S — similar to 27, with round or octagonal barrel.

	$330	$250	$195	$140	$110	$100	$85

MODEL 29 SLIDE ACTION — similar to 20, with 23 in. round barrel, $\frac{1}{2}$ tube mag. Mfg. 1913-1916.

	$330	$250	$195	$140	$110	$100	$85

MODEL 30/30A LEVER ACTION — .30-30 cal., 20 in. barrel, promotional model mfg. 1964-1983.

	$220	$185	$160	$135	$120	$110	$100

MODEL 30 AS LEVER ACTION — .30-30 cal. only, 20 in. barrel, walnut finish hardwood, open sights, no frills version of the 336 CS, 7 lbs. New 1985.

Mfg.'s Sug. Retail	$344	$260	$200	$145	$130	$125	$120	$115

Add $55 for 4X scope.

MODEL 32 SLIDE ACTION — .22 S, L, or LR, $\frac{2}{3}$ tube mag., 24 in. octagon barrel, open sight, plain pistol grip stock, hammerless. Mfg. 1914-1915.

	$330	$250	$195	$140	$110	$100	$85

MODEL 1936 RIFLE/CARBINE LEVER ACTION — .30-30 or .32 Spl. cal., 6 shot, 20 or 24 in. barrel, tubular mag., open sights, pistol grip stock, barrel band. Mfg. 1936-1937.

	$275	$220	$195	$165	$140	$110	$95

MODEL 36A RIFLE — similar to 1936 Rifle, 24 in. barrel, $\frac{2}{3}$ tube mag. Mfg. 1938-1947.

	$275	$220	$195	$165	$140	$110	$95

MODEL 36A-DL — similar to 36A, with deluxe checkered stock, sling and swivels. Mfg. 1940-1947.

	$305	$250	$220	$195	$165	$140	$110

MODEL 36RC — .30-30 or .32 Spl. cal., regular carbine variation with 20 in. barrel. Mfg. 1938-1947.

	$275	$220	$195	$165	$140	$110	$95

Grading	100%	98%	95%	90%	80%	70%	60%

MODEL 36SC — similar to Model 36RC, except has ⅔ length magazine tube. Mfg. 1938-1947.

	$295	$235	$200	$170	$140	$110	$95

MODEL 37 SLIDE ACTION — similar to Model 29, with 24 in. barrel, full length tube mag. Mfg. 1913-1916.

	$330	$250	$195	$140	$110	$100	$85

MODEL 38 SLIDE ACTION — .22 S, L, or LR, ⅔ tube mag., 24 in. octagon barrel, open sights, hammerless, takedown, plain pistol grip stock. Mfg. 1920-1930.

	$330	$250	$195	$140	$110	$100	$85

MODEL 39 LEVER ACTION — .22 S, L, or LR, 24 in. octagon barrel with tube mag., open sights, takedown, case hardened receiver and lever, S-shaped pistol grip stock, bluing on barrel, forend tip, mag. tube, bolt, hammer, and screws, various qualities of walnut (X, 2X, or 3X), hard rubber buttplate. Approx. 40-50,000 mfg. 1922-1938.

	$1,950	$1,700	$1,400	$1,150	$895	$625	$450

Excellent original condition in this model is extremely hard to find since most specimens were well used due to the 16/25 shell mag. capacity, reliability, and the fact that the balance point of the gun (the receiver) normally wore first due to carrying wear. Earlier guns without a prefix or with an S prefix are noted for their superior workmanship and fine finish - 2X or 3X wood on these early guns will really add a premium. Later HS prefix (High Speed) are not quite as valuable as these earlier guns.

MODEL 39A — similar to 39, with blued or color case hardened (1 year only) receiver, round barrel. Mfg. 1938-1940.

	100%	98%	95%	90%	80%	70%	60%
Blue Finish	$475	$425	$375	$335	$295	$250	$200
Case Hardened Finish	$1,500	$1,250	$995	$875	$750	$625	$495

GOLDEN 39A — similar to 39A, with gold plated trigger, sling swivels. Mfg. 1960-1987.

	$225	$195	$175	$150	$135	$115	$90

MODEL 39A "MOUNTIE" — straight grip stock, slim forearm, otherwise similar to 39A. Mfg. 1953-1972.

	$225	$195	$175	$150	$135	$115	$90

90TH ANNIVERSARY 39A — similar to 39A, with chrome barrel and action, select checkered walnut stock, carved squirrel on side of butt stock. 500 mfg. in 1961.

	$795	$695	$550	$400	$350	$300	$250

Last Mfg.'s Sug. Retail was $100.

90TH ANNIVERSARY MODEL 39M MOUNTIE CARBINE — similar to 90th Anniversary 39A, except 20 in. barrel, straight stock. 500 mfg. in 1960.

	$795	$695	$550	$400	$350	$300	$250

Last Mfg.'s Sug. Retail was $100.

MODEL 39A-DL — similar to 90th Anniversary, with blue barrel and action, regular production. Mfg. 1960-1963.

	$250	$195	$165	$140	$110	$100	$85

MODEL 39A OCTAGON — similar to Golden 39A, with octagon barrel, no pistol grip cap. Mfg. 1972-73.

	$275	$235	$200	$185	$165	$150	$135

MODEL 39 CARBINE — similar to 39M, with light barrel, ¾ tube mag. Mfg. 1963-1967.

	$225	$195	$175	$150	$135	$115	$90

Grading	100%	98%	95%	90%	80%	70%	60%

MODEL 39D — similar to 39M, with pistol grip stock. Mfg. 1971-1973.

		$225	$195	$175	$150	$135	$115	$90

MODEL 39AS — .22 LR cal., current production model, lever action, tube mag., 19 shot, 24 in. barrel, walnut stock, open sights, gold trigger, takedown, 6½ lbs.

Mfg.'s Sug. Retail	$405	$315	$225	$165	$145	$130	$110	$100

This model was previously designated the Model 39A. In 1988, the Model 39AS became the standard production model and included a rebounding hammer and hammer block safety.

MODEL 39TDS — .22 LR cal., carbine variation of the Model 39AS, 16½ in. barrel with open sights, 5¼ lbs. New 1988.

Mfg.'s Sug. Retail	$419	$325	$230	$175	$155	$135	$120	$110

MODEL 39M — carbine version of Model 39A, 20 in. lightweight barrel, 16 shot tube mag., squared finger lever, 6 lbs. Disc. 1987.

		$225	$180	$155	$145	$130	$110	$100

Last Mfg.'s Sug. Retail was $304.

MODEL 39M OCTAGON — similar to 39M, with octagon barrel. Mfg. 1973.

		$225	$175	$165	$150	$135	$115	$105

MODEL 39 CENTURY LTD — Marlin Centennial 1870-1970 Commemorative, 20 in. octagon barrel, select walnut straight stock, brass forearm cap and butt plate, name plate in butt. 35,388 mfg. 1970.

		$395	$340	$275	$195	$180	$155	$140

MODEL 39A ARTICLE II — NRA Centennial Commemorative 1871-1971, "Right to Bear Arms" medallion in receiver, 24 in. octagon barrel, fancy pistol grip stock, brass butt plate and forearm cap. Mfg. 6,244 1971.

		$265	$180	$165	$150	$120	$100	$85

MODEL 39M ARTICLE II CARBINE — similar to 39A Article II, with 20 in. barrel, straight grip stock. Mfg. 3,824.

		$275	$195	$175	$160	$130	$110	$95

MODEL 45 CARBINE — .45 ACP only, 7 shot clip mag., sandblasted steel receiver, 16½ in. barrel, last shot hold open device, adj. rear sight, 6¾ lbs. New 1986.

Mfg.'s Sug. Retail	$374	$295	$210	$170	$150	$140	$130	$125

A new high visibility orange front sight post with cutaway hood was added in 1989.

MODEL 56 — similar to 57, with clip mag. Mfg. 1955-1964.

		$130	$100	$85	$70	$55	$40	$30

MODEL 57 LEVERMATIC — .22 S, L, or LR, tube mag., 22 in. barrel, open sight, Monte Carlo pistol grip stock. Mfg. 1959-1965.

		$175	$160	$145	$130	$110	$100	$80

MODEL 57M — Mag. version of Model 57 Levermatic.

		$210	$185	$165	$150	$135	$125	$110

MODEL 60SS SEMI-AUTO STAINLESS — .22 LR, 14 shot tube mag., stainless steel construction with laminated black/gray birch stock with Monte Carlo cheekpiece, Mar-Shield finish, 22 in. barrel, open sights with adj. rear, 5½ lbs. New 1993.

Mfg.'s Sug. Retail	$222	$185	$160	$140

Grading	100%	98%	95%	90%	80%	70%	60%

MODEL 62 LEVERMATIC — .256 Mag. or .30 Carbine cal., 4 shot clip mag., 23 in. barrel, open sight, pistol grip Monte Carlo stock. Mfg. 1963-1969.

	100%	98%	95%	90%	80%	70%	60%
.256 Mag.	$250	$225	$200	$185	$170	$150	$135
.30 Carbine	$225	$200	$180	$165	$150	$135	$120

MODEL 70P (PAPOOSE) — .22 LR cal. only, semi-auto, takedown carbine with 16¼ in. barrel, 7 shot clip mag., rustproof receiver, bolt hold open, is supplied with floating nylon carrying case. New 1986.

		100%	98%	95%	90%	80%	70%	60%
Mfg.'s Sug. Retail	$196	$155	$120	$85	$70	$65	$60	$55

Subtract $25 if without 4X scope.
The 4X scope became standard on this model in 1993.

MODEL 322 BOLT ACTION VARMINT — Sako Mauser type action, .222 Rem., 3 shot clip mag., 24 in. medium weight barrel, 2 position aperture sight, checkered stock. Mfg. 1954-1957.

100%	98%	95%	90%	80%	70%	60%
$385	$305	$275	$220	$195	$165	$140

MODEL 336A RIFLE — improved 36A, .30-30, .35 Rem., or .32 Spl. cal., round breech bolt, 24 in. barrel with ⅔ mag. Mfg. 1948-1962, re-introduced 1973-1980.

100%	98%	95%	90%	80%	70%	60%
$225	$185	$165	$150	$135	$125	$115

Add 10%-15% for pre-62 mfg.
The .35 Rem. cal. was added in 1953, .32 Spl. was disc. in 1962.

⚐ **Model 336A-DL Rifle** — similar to Model 336A Rifle, except has deluxe checkered walnut stock and forearm. Mfg. 1948-1962.

100%	98%	95%	90%	80%	70%	60%
$285	$250	$215	$185	$170	$155	$145

MODEL 336 RC CARBINE — .30-30, .32 Spl., or .35 Rem. cal., standard model carbine with 20 in. barrel. Mfg. 1948-68.

100%	98%	95%	90%	80%	70%	60%
$275	$220	$195	$165	$155	$140	$120

MODEL 336C CARBINE — .30-30, .32 Spl., or .35 Rem. cal., standard model carbine with 20 in. barrel. Mfg. 1969-1983.

100%	98%	95%	90%	80%	70%	60%
$235	$210	$185	$160	$150	$135	$115

MODEL 336SC SPORTS CARBINE — similar to Model 36SC, with 20 in. barrel and ⅔ length mag. tube. Mfg. 1948-1963.

100%	98%	95%	90%	80%	70%	60%
$235	$210	$185	$170	$150	$135	$120

MODEL 336SC .219 ZIPPER — similar to Model 336SC, in .219 Zipper cal., 5 shot mag. Mfg. 1955-1960.

100%	98%	95%	90%	80%	70%	60%
$495	$415	$360	$330	$275	$250	$220

MODEL 336SD CARBINE — .30-30, .32 Spl., or .35 Rem. cal., deluxe sporting carbine with 20 in. barrel. Mfg. 1954-1962.

100%	98%	95%	90%	80%	70%	60%
$275	$225	$195	$165	$155	$140	$120

MODEL 336 CS CARBINE LEVER ACTION — .30-30 Win., or .35 Rem. cal., 6 shot tube mag., 20 in. barrel, hammer block safety, American black walnut pistol grip stock, 7 lbs. Introduced 1984.

		100%	98%	95%	90%	80%	70%	60%
Mfg.'s Sug. Retail	$404	$315	$225	$165	$145	$130	$110	$100

MODEL 336 LTS CARBINE — .30-30 cal. only, 16¼ in. barrel, 5 shot tube mag., 6½ lbs. Mfg. 1988-89 only.

100%	98%	95%	90%	80%	70%	60%
$275	$215	$175	$150	$140	$130	$120

Last Mfg.'s Sug. Retail was $346.

Grading	100%	98%	95%	90%	80%	70%	60%

MODEL 336 ER (EXTRA RANGE) — .307 (disc. 1984) or .356 Win. cal., 5 shot tube mag., 20 in. barrel, walnut pistol grip stock, open sights, 7 lbs. Mfg. 1983-86.

	$275	$250	$225	$200	$185	$160	$145

Last Mfg.'s Sug. Retail was $350.

MODEL 336T CARBINE "TEXAN" — .30-30, .35 Rem., or .44 Mag. cal., similar to 336C, with straight stock, 18½ (1983 only) or 20 in. barrel. Mfg. 1954-1983.

	$275	$220	$195	$165	$155	$140	$120

Add 15% for .44 Mag. cal.

MODEL 336DT CARBINE "TEXAN" — select stock version of 336T, longhorn and map of Texas carved on butt stock. Mfg. 1962-1963.

	$325	$300	$275	$225	$175	$150	$135

MODEL 336 TS TEXAN — similar to 336 CS, except is .30-30 cal., 18½ in. barrel, straight grip stock and squared finger lever, crossbolt safety. Mfg. 1984-87.

	$240	$185	$160	$150	$140	$130	$120

Last Mfg.'s Sug. Retail was $314.

MODEL 336 OCTAGON RIFLE — .30-30 cal. only, with 22 in. octagon barrel, standard model. Mfg. 1973.

	$275	$235	$210	$185	$175	$165	$150

MODEL 336 MARAUDER CARBINE — .30-30 or 35 Rem. cal., 16¼ in. barrel. Mfg. 1963-1964.

	$265	$225	$190	$175	$160	$150	$140

MODEL 336 MAGNUM CARBINE — .44 Mag. cal., 20 in. standard carbine configuration. Mfg. 1963-1967.

	$275	$235	$200	$185	$170	$160	$150

MODEL 336 ZANE GREY CENTURY CARBINE — .30-30 cal., similar to 336 Octagon, 22 in. octagon barrel, Zane Grey medallion inlaid in receiver, select walnut stock, pistol grip, brass butt plate and forearm cap. Approx. 10,000 mfg. in 1971.

	$295	$250	$220

This model was mfg. to commemorate the 100th anniversary of the birth of Zane Grey.

MODEL 336 PRESENTATION RIFLE — .30-30 cal., 22 in. octagon barrel, engraved action, sold with Model 37 Presentation. Mfg. 1970 only.

	$295	$240	$215

MARLIN CENTENNIAL MATCHED PAIR — Model 336 and Model 339 serial numbered the same, .30-30 or .22 LR cal., engraved, deluxe wood, inlaid medallions, cased. 1,000 mfg. sets in 1971.

	$1,150	$875	$695

Last Mfg.'s Sug. Retail was $750.

MODEL 375 — similar to 336 CS, except is .375 Win. cal. Mfg. 1980-83.

	$230	$200	$180	$165	$155	$145	$135

MODEL 444 LEVER ACTION — .444 Marlin cal., 4 shot tube mag., 24 in. barrel, open sights, straight grip, Monte Carlo stock, recoil pad, swivels, sling. Mfg. 1965-1971.

	$250	$225	$200	$185	$165	$150	$135

Model 444 S — similar to Model 444, except has pistol grip stock. Mfg. 1972-1983.

	$250	$225	$200	$185	$165	$150	$135

Marlin Firearms Company, cont.

Grading	100%	98%	95%	90%	80%	70%	60%

MODEL 444 SS SPORTER — similar to 444 Rifle, with 22 in. barrel and hammer block safety, pistol grip stock without Monte Carlo configuration, 7½ lbs. Mfg. 1984-present.

Mfg.'s Sug. Retail	$490	$400	$330	$275	$230	$195	$180	$170

MODEL 455 BOLT ACTION SPORTER — FN Mauser action with Sako trigger, .30-06, or .308 cal., 24 in. barrel, stainless steel barrel, Lyman aperture sight, checkered Monte Carlo pistol grip stock. Mfg. 1957-1959.

	$415	$330	$305	$250	$220	$195	$165

MODELS 780, 781, 782, and 783 BOLT ACTION — .22 LR or .22 Mag. (Models 782 and 783) cal., tube or clip mag., 22 in. barrel. Disc. 1988.

	$110	$85	$75	$70	$65	$55	$50

Add $17-$25 for Models 782 and 783.
Last Mfg.'s Sug. Retail was $162.

MODELS 880/881 BOLT ACTION — .22 LR or .22 Mag. cal., replacements for Models 780, 781, Model 880 is .22 LR with 7 shot clip mag. and 22 in. barrel, Model 881 is .22 LR with 17 shot tube mag. and 22 in. barrel, 6 lbs. New 1989.

Mfg.'s Sug. Retail	$218	$170	$130	$100	$85	$75	$70	$65

Add $9 for Model 881.

MODELS 882/883 BOLT ACTION
— .22 Win. Mag., 7 shot clip (Model 882) or 12 shot tube mag. (Model 883), checkered black walnut Monte Carlo stock with Mar-Shield finish, adj. semi-buckhorn rear sight and hooded front, thumb safety, 6 lbs. New 1989.

Mfg.'s Sug. Retail	$240	$185	$140	$110	$95	$85	$75	$70

Add $9 for Model 883.
Add $35 for nickel finish on Model 883 (883N).
The Models 882 and 883 are the replacements for Models 782 and 783.

Model 882L — similar to Model 882, except has laminated hardwood stock. New 1992.

Mfg.'s Sug. Retail	$255	$195	$150	$115	$95	$85	$75	$70

Model 883SS — .22 Win. Mag., similar to Model 883, except is stainless steel and stock is laminated two-tone brown birch with Monte Carlo cheekpiece. New 1993.

Mfg.'s Sug. Retail	$264	$210	$165	$120

MODEL 990 SEMI-AUTO — .22 LR cal. only, 18 shot tube mag., 22 in. barrel, last shot automatic bolt hold-open, Monte Carlo American black walnut stock with pistol grip, 5½ lbs. Disc. 1987.

	$115	$90	$75	$65	$60	$55	$50

Last Mfg.'s Sug. Retail was $159.

MODEL 990L SEMI-AUTO — .22 LR cal., 14 shot tube mag., 22 in. barrel, laminated two-tone brown Monte Carlo stock, gold trigger, adj. rear sight, grooved receiver, 5¾ lbs. New 1993.

Mfg.'s Sug. Retail	$216	$175	$160	$145	$130	$120	$110	$100

MODEL 992 SEMI-AUTO — .22 Win. Mag. cal., 7 shot detachable mag., 20½ in. barrel, Grand style safety, alloy receiver, hold-open device, uncheckered walnut stock with solid pad, blued steel (hard coated on receiver), 6½ lbs. New 1993.

Mfg.'s Sug. Retail	$363	$300	$265	$230	$200	$185	$175	$165

MODEL 995 SEMI-AUTO — .22 LR cal. only, 7 shot clip mag., 18 in. barrel, Monte Carlo walnut stock, 5 lbs.

Mfg.'s Sug. Retail	$199	$155	$120	$85	$70	$65	$60	$55

Grading	100%	98%	95%	90%	80%	70%	60%

MODEL 1894 — .44 Spl. or .44 Mag. cal., 20 in. bbl., 10 shot tube mag., adj. sights, straight grip walnut stock and forearm, 6 lbs. Mfg. 1969-1984.

| | $400 | $300 | $250 | $195 | $165 | $145 | $130 |

MODEL 1894 C — without hammer block safety, mfg. 1979-1984.

| | $375 | $275 | $225 | $180 | $160 | $145 | $130 |

MODEL 1894 SPORTER — .44 Mag. only, 6 shot half mag. tube, crescent shaped hard rubber buttplate, 1,398 mfg. 1973 only.

| | $575 | $475 | $375 | $300 | $250 | $200 | $175 |

MODEL 1894 CS (CARBINE) — copy of original Model 1894, .357 Mag./.38 Spl., 9 shot mag., 18½ in. round barrel, open sights, straight grip stock, squared finger lever, 6 lbs. Mfg. 1984-present.

| Mfg.'s Sug. Retail | $455 | $365 | $265 | $195 | $170 | $150 | $140 | $130 |

MODEL 1894 S (SPORTER) — .41 Mag. (disc. 1991), .44 Mag./.44 Spl., or .45 LC (mfg. 1988-91) cal., Model 1894 with addition of hammer block safety, 20 in. barrel, 10 shot tube mag., adj. sights, 6 lbs., straight grip walnut stock and forearm.

| Mfg.'s Sug. Retail | $455 | $365 | $265 | $195 | $170 | $150 | $140 | $130 |

MODEL 1894 M (.22 MAG.) — .22 Mag. cal., with 20 in. barrel, 11 shot tube mag., straight grip walnut stock and forearm, 6¼ lbs. Disc. 1989.

| | $275 | $210 | $180 | $150 | $135 | $125 | $115 |

Last Mfg.'s Sug. Retail was $358.

MODEL 1894 CL — .218 Bee (new 1990), .25-20 or .32-20 cal., 6 shot (two-thirds length) tube mag., 22 in. barrel, 6¼ lbs. New 1988.

| Mfg.'s Sug. Retail | $488 | $375 | $285 | $210 | $175 | $155 | $140 | $130 |

MODEL 1894 OCTAGON — similar to 1894 Carbine, with octagon barrel. Mfg. 1973.

| | $300 | $275 | $250 | $235 | $215 | $200 | $185 |

MODEL 1895 LEVER ACTION — .45-70 Govt., 4 shot tube mag., 22 in. barrel, open sights, straight grip stock with curved buttplate, forearm cap, sling and swivels. Mfg. 1972-1984.

| | $265 | $210 | $185 | $175 | $165 | $150 | $140 |

Model 1895 S — similar to Model 1895, except has pistol grip stock and straight buttpad.

| | $265 | $210 | $185 | $175 | $165 | $150 | $140 |

MODEL 1895 SS — similar to Model 1895 S only with hammer block safety. New 1983.

| Mfg.'s Sug. Retail | $490 | $385 | $285 | $210 | $175 | $155 | $140 | $130 |

MODEL 2000 TARGET BOLT ACTION — .22 LR cal., single shot (can be converted), 22 in. heavy barrel with Lyman adj. sights, 2 stage target trigger, molded synthetic stock made from fiberglass and Kevlar with twice baked blue enamel, adj. buttplate, aluminum forearm rail, 8 lbs. New 1991.

| Mfg.'s Sug. Retail | $560 | $475 | $395 | $350 | $300 | $275 | $250 | $225 |

Add $32 for 5-shot clip conversion unit (for summer biathlon competition).

MARLIN PROMOTIONAL MODELS — Models 15 (disc.), 15Y (disc.), 15YN (Youth Model - new 1989), 25 (disc.), 25M (disc.), 25N (new 1989), 60, 70 (disc.), 70HC (new 1989), and 75C (disc.) are inexpensive, utilitarian .22 LR or .22 Mag. cal. (Model 25M only), rifles meant for shooting, not for collecting. All the above models retail for approx. $149-$169, but can be purchased for less, depending on discounting.
Series 15 and 25 Models designate bolt action, Series 60 and 70 designate semi-auto design.

Marlin Firearms Company, cont.

RIFLES: BOLT ACTION, SINGLE SHOT

Between 1930 and the present, Marlin made a number of .22 cal. rimfire rifles, bolt action single shots, bolt action repeaters and auto loaders. These were good quality, low priced weapons. In 1960 the name Glenfield was also used in connection with these guns. They are valued from a high of about $100 for a 100% gun to about $25 for a 60% or less gun that is still in working order. We will list these models for reference purposes.

Model 65 _____ 1932-1938.
Model 65E _____ 1932-1938.
Model 100 _____ 1936-1941.
Model 100S Tom Mix Special — disc. ($250 if N.I.B.).
Model 100SB ____ 1936-1941.
Model 101 _____ 1951-disc.
Model 101 DL ___ disc.
Model 101G _____ 1960-1965, Marlin Glenfield.
Model 10 _____ 1966-disc., Marlin Glenfield.
Model 122 _____ 1966-disc.

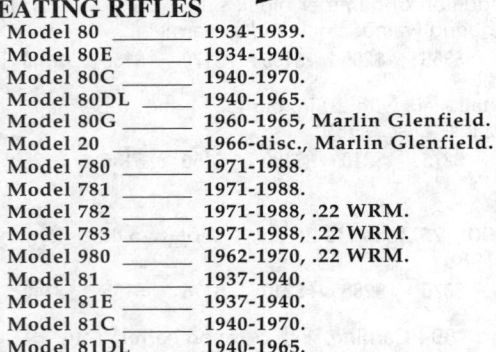

BOLT ACTION:
REPEATING RIFLES

Model 80 _____ 1934-1939.
Model 80E _____ 1934-1940.
Model 80C _____ 1940-1970.
Model 80DL _____ 1940-1965.
Model 80G _____ 1960-1965, Marlin Glenfield.
Model 20 _____ 1966-disc., Marlin Glenfield.
Model 780 _____ 1971-1988.
Model 781 _____ 1971-1988.
Model 782 _____ 1971-1988, .22 WRM.
Model 783 _____ 1971-1988, .22 WRM.
Model 980 _____ 1962-1970, .22 WRM.
Model 81 _____ 1937-1940.
Model 81E _____ 1937-1940.
Model 81C _____ 1940-1970.
Model 81DL_____ 1940-1965.
Model 81G _____ 1960-1965 Marlin Glenfield.

AUTOLOADING RIFLES

Model 50 _____ 1931-1935.
Model 50E _____ 1931-1934.
Model A-1 _____ 1936-1940.
Model A-1E _____ 1935-1946.
Model A-1C _____ 1941-1946.
Model A-1DL ____ 1941-1946.
Model 88-C _____ 1948-1956.
Model 88-DL ____ 1953-1956.
Model 89-C _____ 1948-1961.
Model 89-DL ____ 1950-1961.
Model 98 _____ 1957-1959.
Model 99 _____ 1959-1960.
Model 99C _____ 1961-1978.
Model 99G _____ 1960-1965, Marlin Glenfield.
Model 60 _____ 1960-present, Marlin Glenfield.
Model 99DL _____ 1960-1964.
Model 49 _____ 1968-1970.
Model 49DL _____ 1971-1978.
Model 99M1 _____ 1964-1978.
Model 989M2 ____ 1966-disc.
Model 989 _____ 1962-1965.
Model 70 _____ 1966-present, Marlin Glenfield.
Model 989G _____ 1962-1964, Marlin Glenfield.
Model 990 _____ disc.
Model 995 _____ present.

Grading	100%	98%	95%	90%	80%	70%	60%

SHOTGUNS

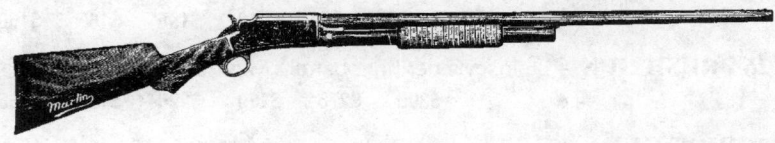

MODEL 1898 SLIDE ACTION — 12 ga., 5 shot tube mag., 26-32 in. barrels, various chokes, exposed hammer, pistol grip stock, grades differ in quality of wood and engraving on C and D. Mfg. 1898-1905.

	100%	98%	95%	90%	80%	70%	60%
Grade A	$495	$385	$330	$305	$250	$195	$165
Grade B	$580	$495	$440	$415	$360	$305	$275
Grade C	$880	$715	$635	$580	$525	$495	$440
Grade D	$1,760	$1,540	$1,320	$1,210	$1,045	$965	$880

MODEL 16 — 16 ga. only, 26 or 28 in. barrel, various chokes, takedown, pistol grip stock. Mfg. 1904-1910.

	100%	98%	95%	90%	80%	70%	60%
Grade A	$385	$305	$250	$220	$195	$165	$140
Grade B	$495	$415	$360	$330	$305	$275	$250
Grade C	$635	$525	$495	$440	$415	$385	$330
Grade D	$1,320	$1,100	$990	$825	$715	$635	$550

MODEL 17 SLIDE ACTION — 12 ga., 30 or 32 in. full choke barrel, solid frame, straight stock. Mfg. 1906-1908.

	100%	98%	95%	90%	80%	70%	60%
	$440	$330	$305	$250	$220	$180	$150

MODEL 17 BRUSH GUN — similar to 17, with 26 in. cylinder bore barrel. Mfg. 1906-1908.

	100%	98%	95%	90%	80%	70%	60%
	$470	$360	$330	$275	$250	$220	$165

MODEL 17 RIOT GUN — similar to 17, with 20 in. barrel. Mfg. 1906-1908.

	100%	98%	95%	90%	80%	70%	60%
	$415	$330	$275	$250	$195	$180	$160

MODEL 19 SLIDE ACTION — improved lightened version of 1898, matte top surface on barrel. Mfg. 1906-1907.

	100%	98%	95%	90%	80%	70%	60%
Grade A	$385	$305	$250	$220	$195	$165	$140
Grade B	$495	$415	$360	$330	$305	$275	$250
Grade C	$635	$525	$495	$440	$415	$385	$330
Grade D	$1,320	$1,100	$990	$825	$715	$635	$550

MODEL 21 SLIDE ACTION — straight grip version of 19.

	100%	98%	95%	90%	80%	70%	60%
Grade A	$385	$305	$250	$220	$195	$165	$140
Grade B	$495	$415	$360	$330	$305	$275	$250
Grade C	$635	$525	$495	$440	$415	$385	$330
Grade D	$1,320	$1,100	$990	$825	$715	$635	$550

MODEL 24 — improved 21, takedown, automatic recoil lock on slide, solid matte rib. Mfg. 1908-1915.

	100%	98%	95%	90%	80%	70%	60%
Grade A	$330	$305	$275	$250	$220	$195	$165
Grade B	$525	$440	$385	$360	$330	$305	$275
Grade C	$660	$550	$525	$470	$440	$415	$360
Grade D	$1,375	$1,155	$1,045	$880	$770	$660	$580

Grading	100%	98%	95%	90%	80%	70%	60%

MODEL 26 — similar to 24 Grade A, with solid frame, 30 or 32 in. full choke barrel. Mfg. 1909-1915.

	100%	98%	95%	90%	80%	70%	60%
	$275	$230	$210	$195	$165	$150	$140

MODEL 26 BRUSH GUN — 26 in. cylinder bore barrel. Mfg. 1909-1915.

	$305	$275	$250	$220	$195	$165	$150

MODEL 26 RIOT GUN — 20 in. cylinder bore barrel. Mfg. 1909-1915.

	$250	$195	$180	$165	$150	$140	$120

MODEL 28 HAMMERLESS — 12 ga., 26-32 in. barrels, various chokes, takedown, matte top barrel, pistol grip stock. Mfg. 1913-1922.

	100%	98%	95%	90%	80%	70%	60%
Grade A	$385	$305	$250	$220	$195	$165	$140
Grade B	$495	$415	$360	$330	$305	$275	$250
Grade C	$635	$525	$495	$440	$415	$385	$330
Grade D	$1,320	$1,100	$990	$825	$715	$635	$550

MODEL 28TS TRAP GUN — similar to 28, with 30 in. matte rib barrel, full choke, high comb straight grip stock. Mfg. 1915.

	$415	$330	$275	$250	$220	$195	$165

MODEL 28T — similar to 28TS, with fancy wood, checkering, better finish. Mfg. 1915.

	$605	$525	$495	$470	$415	$360	$305

MODEL 30 — similar to 16, with automatic recoil lock on slide. Mfg. 1910-1914.

	100%	98%	95%	90%	80%	70%	60%
Grade A	$385	$305	$250	$220	$195	$165	$140
Grade B	$495	$415	$360	$330	$305	$275	$250
Grade C	$635	$525	$495	$440	$415	$385	$330
Grade D	$1,320	$1,100	$990	$825	$715	$635	$550

MODEL 30 FIELD GRADE — similar to 30 Grade B, with 25 in. mod. barrel, straight stock. Mfg. 1913-1914.

	$360	$275	$220	$180	$160	$130	$115

MODEL 31 — scaled down small ga. (16 and 20 ga.) version of the Model 28, has 26 and 28 in. barrels, various chokes. Mfg. 1915-1922.

	100%	98%	95%	90%	80%	70%	60%
Grade A	$385	$305	$250	$220	$195	$165	$140
Grade B	$495	$415	$360	$330	$305	$275	$250
Grade C	$636	$525	$495	$440	$415	$385	$330
Grade D	$1,320	$1,100	$990	$825	$715	$635	$550

MODEL 31F FIELD GUN — 25 in. mod. barrel. Mfg. 1915-1917.

	$495	$415	$360	$330	$305	$275	$250

MODEL 42A — similar to 24, but lesser quality finishing. Mfg. 1922-1934.

	$250	$220	$195	$165	$140	$120	$100

MODEL 43 HAMMERLESS — similar to 28, with lesser quality finish. Mfg. 1923-1930.

	$330	$250	$220	$195	$165	$140	$110

MODEL 43TS — similar to 28T, lower quality.

	$525	$440	$415	$385	$360	$305	$275

Marlin Firearms Company, cont.

Grading	100%	98%	95%	90%	80%	70%	60%

MODEL 44A — similar to 31A, 20 ga. only. Mfg. 1923-1935.

	$360	$275	$250	$220	$195	$165	$140

MODEL 44S — select checkered stock.

	$470	$385	$360	$330	$195	$165	$140

MODEL 49 — lower priced version of 42A. They were given to purchasers of 4 shares of Marlin stock. 3,000 mfg. in 1925-1928.

	$440	$360	$305	$275	$220	$195	$165

MODEL 53 — similar to 43A. Mfg. 1929-1930.

	$330	$275	$250	$220	$195	$165	$140

MODEL 63 — similar to 43, later model. Mfg. 1931-1935.

	$330	$250	$220	$195	$165	$140	$110

MODEL 63TS — similar to 43TS, with trap style stock.

	$385	$305	$250	$220	$195	$165	$140

MODEL .410 LEVER ACTION — .410 ga., 22 or 26 in. barrel, full choke, lever action, similar to 1893, exposed hammer, plain pistol grip stock. Mfg. 1929-1932 as a stockholders promotional firearm.

	$550	$525	$495	$475	$450	$425	$395

Model .410 Deluxe — includes deluxe checkered walnut stock and forearm.

	$750	$650	$625	$595	$570	$535	$500

MODEL 60 SINGLE BARREL — 12 ga., 30 or 32 in. barrel, full choke, top lever, break open, exposed hammer, pistol grip stock. Approx. 3,000 mfg.

	$195	$165	$140	$120	$110	$100	$90

MODEL 90 O/U — 12, 16, 20, or .410 ga., 26, 28, or 30 in. barrels, boxlock, extractors, checkered pistol grip stock. Mfg. 1937-1958. Guns made from 1937-1949 had vent. separated barrels, after 1949, solid barrels.

	$495	$385	$360	$330	$290	$265	$230

With single trigger

	$605	$495	$470	$440	$400	$375	$340

Add 25% for .410 ga.

MODEL 120 MAGNUM — slide action, 12 ga., 3 in. chamber, 26-38 in. barrel, various chokes, checkered pistol grip stock. Mfg. 1971-1985.

	$290	$225	$215	$205	$195	$180	$165

Subtract $35 if without VR.
Last Mfg.'s Sug. Retail was $370.

MODEL 778 — 12 ga. Mag. slide action, 20-38 in. barrels, 7¾ lbs. Disc. 1984.

	$225	$190	$175	$155	$140	$125	$110

PREMIER MARK I SLIDE ACTION — 12 ga. only, aluminum receiver, takedown, manufactured in France for Marlin.

	$200	$180	$160	$150	$140	$120	$95

PREMIER MARK II — similar to Mark I, except with engraved receiver and checkering. Mfg. 1960-1963 in France.

	$260	$205	$170	$155	$145	$125	$100

Grading	100%	98%	95%	90%	80%	70%	60%

PREMIER MARK IV — similar to Mark II, only deluxe grade with better wood, more engraving. Mfg. 1960-1963 in France.

	100%	98%	95%	90%	80%	70%	60%
	$305	$250	$220	$195	$165	$140	$110
With VR	$330	$275	$250	$220	$195	$165	$140

SHOTGUNS: BOLT ACTION

MODEL 55 — 12, 16, or 20 ga., 2 shot detachable mag., 26 and 28 in. full choke barrel, plain pistol grip stock. Mfg. 1950-1965.

	100%	98%	95%	90%	80%	70%	60%
	$90	$70	$55	$40	$35	$30	$25

With adj. choke

	100%	98%	95%	90%	80%	70%	60%
	$100	$85	$65	$50	$45	$40	$30

MODEL 55 GOOSE GUN — similar to 55, except 12 ga. only, 36 in. full choke barrel, 3 in. chamber, 2 shot clip mag., leather carrying strap and detachable swivels, rubber recoil pad, 8 lbs. Mfg. 1962-present.

		100%	98%	95%	90%	80%	70%	60%
Mfg.'s Sug. Retail	$275	$210	$175	$145	$125	$115	$100	$90

MODEL 55 SWAMP GUN — similar to 55, 12 ga., 20 in. adj. choke barrel, 3 in. mag. Mfg. 1963-1965.

	100%	98%	95%	90%	80%	70%	60%
	$105	$90	$70	$55	$50	$45	$35

MODEL 55S SLUG GUN — 24 in. barrel, cylinder bore, rifle sights. Mfg. 1974-1983.

	100%	98%	95%	90%	80%	70%	60%
	$140	$120	$110	$95	$85	$55	$40

MODEL 5510 — 10 ga., 3½ in. mag., 2 shot clip mag., 34 in. barrel, leather carrying strap and detachable swivels, rubber recoil pad, 10½ lbs. Mfg. 1976-1985.

	100%	98%	95%	90%	80%	70%	60%
	$220	$170	$160	$150	$140	$130	$120

Last Mfg.'s Sug. Retail was $282.

MAROCCHI

Manufactured since 1922 by Armi Marocchi in Brescia, Italy. Currently imported and distributed by Precision Sales International, Inc. located in Westfield, MA and Sile Distributors Inc., located in New York, NY.

Marocchi makes a wide variety of quality shotguns and O/U rifles. Many of their models however, are not being imported currently. Frigon guns (manufactured by Marocchi) appear under the F section in this text.

SHOTGUNS: AVANZA SERIES

This model is imported exclusively by Precision Sales International, Inc.

AVANZA — 12 or 20 ga., 3 in. chambers, monobloc boxlock action, 26 or 28 in. vent. barrels with VR (with or without choke tubes), SST, ejectors, deluxe checkered walnut stock and forearm with vent. recoil pad, high polish bluing with gold accents, all steel lightweight mfg., 6 lbs. 5 oz. - 6 lbs. 13 oz. Importation began 1990.

		100%	98%	95%	90%	80%	70%	60%
Mfg.'s Sug. Retail	$725	$660	$575	$525	$475	$425	$375	$325

Add $43 for 20 ga.
Add $44 for choke tubes (3).

Avanza Sporting Clays — 12 ga. only, 3 in. chambers, built on 20 ga. frame, 28 in. vent. barrels with VR and choke tubes, select checkered walnut stock with deluxe recoil pad and forearm, gold plated trigger, 7 lbs. New 1991.

		100%	98%	95%	90%	80%	70%	60%
Mfg.'s Sug. Retail	$839	$750	$600	$550	$500	$450	$400	$350

Add $99 for Premier Grade (includes select walnut and gold etched trigger guard).
This model features a trigger that is adjustable for length and pull without special tools.

Grading	100%	98%	95%	90%	80%	70%	60%

SHOTGUNS & COMBO GUNS

The following models are imported exclusively by Sile Distributors, Inc. Other Marocchi models are also imported by Sile Distributors on a limited basis and Sile should be contacted directly regarding dealer pricing/inventory.

FIELD MASTER I O/U — 12 ga. only, 26 or 28 in. VR barrels and rib with choke tubes, engraved coin finished receiver, extractors, SNT, checkered walnut stock and forearm.

Mfg.'s Sug. Retail	$476	$395	$325	$275	$240	$215	$200	$185

⚡ Field Master II — similar to Field Master I except has SST and choke tubes.

Mfg.'s Sug. Retail	$550	$475	$350	$295	$260	$225	$210	$190

SKEET MODEL — 12 ga. only, 26 in. barrels bored SK/SK.

Mfg.'s Sug. Retail	$392	$340	$300	$275	$240	$215	$200	$185

TRAP MODEL — 12 ga. only, 30 in. barrels bored M/F, ejectors.

Mfg.'s Sug. Retail	$560	$475	$385	$340	$300	$275	$240	$215

MODEL 2000 SINGLE SHOT — 12 ga. only, 3 in. chamber, hammer, 28 in. barrel, ejector, lightly engraved receiver. Importation disc. 1991.

	$80	$70	$60	$50	$45	$40	$35

Last Mfg.'s Sug. Retail was $94.

VALLEY COMBO — 12 ga. over .222 Rem. cal., 23½ in. separated barrels with VR, 3 in. chamber, fold down rear sight and will accept claw scope mounts, fixed cylinder choke, DTs, engraved silver receiver, satin finish walnut Monte Carlo stock with checkering and recoil pad, 8¼ lbs.

Mfg.'s Sug. Retail	$680	$575	$475	$415	$375	$325	$295	$275

MASQUELIER S.A.

Manufacturer located in Belgium. Previously distributed (until 1986) by Ambel Ltd., Inc. located in Sugar Land, TX.

SHOTGUNS

BOXLOCK SxS — 12 ga. only, 2¾ in. chambers, Anson & Deeley boxlock action, ejectors, fine scroll engraving with French walnut. Importation disc. 1986.

	$4,400	$4,000	$3,650	$3,300	$2,995	$2,600	$2,200

Last Mfg.'s Sug. Retail was $4,780.

SIDELOCK SxS — 12 ga. only, 2¾ in. chambers, H&H style sidelocks, auto ejectors, English style fine scroll engraving with French walnut. Importation disc. 1986.

	$12,500	$10,000	$8,750	$7,600	$6,700	$5,800	$5,000

Last Mfg.'s Sug. Retail was $15,850.

RIFLES

CARPATHE — .243, .270, .30-06, 7 x 57R, or 7 x 65R cal., single shot, hair trigger, push-down cocking system. Importation disc. 1986.

	$3,500	$3,200	$2,900	$2,600	$2,300	$2,100	$1,850

Last Mfg.'s Sug. Retail was $3,850.

Grading	100%	98%	95%	90%	80%	70%	60%

EXPRESS — .270, .30-06, 8 x 57JRS, or 9.3 x 74R cal., O/U configuration, SST, ejectors. Add $800 for extra set of 20 ga. barrels. Importation disc. 1986.

	$3,300	$3,000	$2,800	$2,600	$2,300	$2,100	$1,850

Last Mfg.'s Sug. Retail was $3,600.

ARDENNES MODEL — top-of-the-line model, custom order only. Importation disc. 1986.

	$6,600	$6,000	$5,400	$4,800	$4,300	$3,900	$3,450

Last Mfg.'s Sug. Retail was $7,250.

MATIBA

Manufactured by Macchine Termo Balistiche located in Italy. To date, this trademark has had little importation domestically.

REVOLVERS

MATIBA REVOLVER — various cals., 6, 7, or 8 shot, unique design permits barrel to fire lowest shell in cylinder (6 o'clock position), mechanism to rear of cylinder, interchangeable barrels.
Depending on features, standard variations of this model usually sell in the $300-$650 range.

MATRA MANURHIN DEFENSE

Please refer to the Manurhin heading in this section.

MAUSER-WERKE

Manufacturer located in Oberndorf, Germany 1812 to date. Rifles and handguns are currently imported by Precision Imports, Inc. located in San Antonio, TX. Previously imported by KDF located in Seguin, TX (1987-89). Luger pistols are also imported by Precision Imports, Inc. on a custom order basis and may be found in the back of the Luger section in this text.

PISTOLS: SEMI-AUTO

The Models 1906-08, 1912-14, and HSv are very rare and only infrequently encountered. A competent appraisal is advisable before buying or selling these models.

MODEL 1906-08 — 9mm Export (9 x 25mm), detachable mag., incorporates features of both the pocket pistols and Model 1896 Broomhandle. Serial range 1-100 (est.).

	$39,500	$35,000	$29,500	$25,000	$19,500	$15,000	$9,950

MODEL 1912-14 — generally chambered for 9mm Para., similar to pocket pistol configuration, but considerably larger, earliest specimens have inscribed slide legend. Those under serial number 100 (approx.) are not slotted for shoulder stock while those over 100 are generally slotted. Serial range 1-175 (est.).

	$25,000	$20,000	$16,000	$12,000	$10,000	$8,000	$6,000

Add 50% if slotted with matching shoulder stock.
This variation is very rare in .45 ACP cal. or with a tangent rear sight.

WTP MODEL I VEST POCKET AUTOMATIC — 6.35mm, 6 shot, 2½ in. barrel, blue, rubber grips. Mfg. 1922-1937.

	$495	$325	$250	$200	$160	$140	$100

Grading	100%	98%	95%	90%	80%	70%	60%

WTP MODEL II — similar to Model I, but 2 in. barrel. Mfg. 1938-1940.

	$650	$525	$450	$350	$250	$200	$150

POCKET MODEL 1910 — 6.35mm, 9 shot, 3 in. barrel, blue fixed sights, checkered walnut or hard rubber grips. Mfg. 1910-1934.

	$395	$275	$180	$165	$150	$140	$130

POCKET MODEL 1914 — similar to 1910, but 7.65mm, 3.4 in. barrel. Mfg. 1914-1934.

	$395	$275	$175	$165	$150	$145	$135

Add 10% for Eagle WWI proofs.
Add 500% for the "humpback" model.

POCKET MODEL 1934 — similar to 1914, but one piece grip. Mfg. 1934-1939.

	$450	$325	$210	$175	$160	$150	$140

Add 15% for Waffenamt.
Add 100% for Nazi Navy marked.

MODEL HSv — 9mm Para. cal., limited mfg., similar features to HSc, except has larger dimensions.

	$19,500	$15,000	$10,000	$8,500	$7,000	$6,500	$5,500

MODEL HSc DOUBLE ACTION — 7.65mm (8 shot) or .380 ACP (7 shot), 3.4 in. barrel, blue or nickel, fixed sights, checkered walnut grips. Mfg. 1938-present (current mfg. is by R. Gamba in Italy).

* **Early Commercial** — standard pre-war Commercial Model. Most frequently encountered variation.

	$450	$340	$300	$265	$225	$200	$185

* **Transitional** — exhibits features of both early and late models.

	$425	$320	$290	$250	$215	$195	$175

WWII MILITARY VARIATIONS

* **Early Nazi Army** — proofed 655 and 135.

	$425	$340	$300	$265	$225	$200	$185

* **Early Nazi Navy** — marked on front grip strap.

	$750	$595	$540	$500	$440	$395	$350

* **Early Nazi Police** — Eagle L proof only.

	$475	$395	$360	$320	$285	$245	$200

* **Wartime Nazi Army** — proof 135 and WaA 135. Eagle N proofed also

	$375	$325	$290	$250	$200	$180	$150

* **Wartime Nazi Navy** — proofed on left side of trigger guard.

	$550	$450	$400	$340	$295	$260	$230

* **Wartime Nazi Police** — proofed Eagle L. Add 10% if Eagle F.

	$475	$395	$360	$320	$285	$245	$200

Grading	100%	98%	95%	90%	80%	70%	60%
Wartime Commercial — standard WWII Commercial Model.							
	$375	$325	$290	$265	$200	$180	$150
Swiss Commercial — ser. range 800,000-900,000. Very rare.							
	$1,400	$1,250	$1,125	$995	$900	$850	$600
Low Grip Screw — very rare, less than 2,000 mfg.							
	$2,750	$2,100	$1,600	$1,200	$1,000	$800	$650
Add 20% if Navy marked.							
Cutaways — mfg. to visibly show mechanism. Should not be proofed.							
	$1,495	$1,000	$900	$850	$800	$750	$700

POST-WWII VARIATIONS

	100%	98%	95%	90%	80%	70%	60%
French Manufacture — frequently encountered in poor condition — post-WWII production.							
	$325	$275	$245	$220	$180	$155	$130
Mauser Production — .32 or .380 cal., 15 shot, mfg. 1968-1981.							
	$350	$295	$260	$225	$180	$150	$130
Deduct 20% if not boxed or in .32 cal.							
Interarms Import — imported by Interarms from 1983-1985 (Italian mfg. by Gamba).							
	$325	$275	$250	$220	$180	$150	$125
Last Mfg.'s Sug. Retail was $415.							
One of Five Thousand Edition — American Eagle edition (marked on gun), 5,000 total mfg. (serial numbered 1-5000).							
	$375	$300	$250				
Armes de Chasse Import — previously imported by Armes De Chasse located in Chadds Ford, PA on a limited basis. For G15 variation (9 shot) add $58.							
	$475	$425	$330	$300	$260	$240	$220

Add $195 for Limited Series.
Last Mfg.'s Sug. Retail was $695.

MAUSER LUGERS

Both pre-war and post-war Mauser manufactured Lugers will be found in the Luger section of this book (including those variations currently imported by Precision Imports, Inc. located in San Antonio, TX).

PISTOLS: CURRENT MFG.

MODEL 80 SA — 9mm Para., semi-auto single action patterned after the Browning Hi-power, 4⅔ in. barrel, blue finish with checkered walnut grips, round hammer, steel construction, 13 shot mag., 1.95 lbs. Importation began 1992.

Mfg.'s Sug. Retail	$372	$330	$295	$270	$240	$215	$185	$165

MODEL 90 DA — similar to Model 80 SA, except is double action, spur hammer, and has 14 shot mag., 2.15 lbs. Importation began 1992.

Mfg.'s Sug. Retail	$399	$350	$315	$285	$250	$225	$190	$170

Model 90 DAC — similar to Model 90 DA, except is compact model with 4⅛ in. barrel, 2.05 lbs. Importation began 1992.

Mfg.'s Sug. Retail	$425	$375	$325	$295	$260	$230	$195	$175

Grading	100%	98%	95%	90%	80%	70%	60%

MODEL 1896 BROOMHANDLES

Note: Manufactured in Oberndorf, Germany between 1897 & 1938.

While many variations of the famous 1896 Broomhandle exist, most common Broomhandles are pre-war Commercials, Model 1930 Commercials, Red 9s, and Bolos. They can be found in chronological order in this section. Holster stocks are a very popular accessory in this model. Commercial stocks may be matching or may not be serial numbered to gun (proper stock). Add $300+ for stock depending on overall original condition and if matching/non-matching.

In 1984, Federal legislation once again allowed importation of non-domestic WWI and WWII military handguns. As a result, many Bolo and various commercial Banner models have been seen at gun shows in some quantity. Condition on most of these recent imports is 25% or lower (with pitting on many) and prices typically start in the $150 range. While many of these newer imports would make workable shooters, they have in no way lowered prices on 90%+ condition specimens due to normal collector activity in top quality only pistols. Recently imported Broomhandles should have the importer's name visibly stamped on an exterior surface.

CONEHAMMER VARIATIONS

STANDARD CONEHAMMER — 7.63 Mauser, distinguishable by circular machined upper hammer with concentric rings. 5.5 in. barrel, 23 groove wooden grips, rear adjustable sight available in 1-10, 50-500, 100-300, 50-300, 50-700 meter configurations, 10 shot mag.

	$3,200	$2,500	$1,850	$1,200	$1,050	$925	$700

Add 40% for matching stock.

FIXED SIGHT CONEHAMMER — 7.63 Mauser, similar to Standard Conehammer, except has fixed rear sight.

	$3,750	$2,700	$1,600	$1,300	$1,100	$925	$700

6 SHOT CONEHAMMER - FIXED SIGHT — 7.63 Mauser, 4¾ in. barrel, 6 shot mag., rare.

	$6,000	$5,200	$4,200	$3,500	$3,000	$2,500	$2,000

6 Shot Conehammer w/adjustable sight — 7.63 Mauser, 5.5 in. barrel, very rare.

	$11,000	$8,500	$6,000	$5,000	$4,000	$3,000	$2,500

Sales of this variation are extremely limited.

TURKISH CONEHAMMER — 7.63 Mauser, 5.5 in. barrel, 10 shot mag. Approx. 1,000 mfg. for Turkey in 1898, Farsi serial numbers.

	$4,500	$3,600	$2,800	$2,400	$2,100	$1,800	$1,500

"SYSTEM MAUSER" CONEHAMMER — 7.63 Mauser, "SYSTEM MAUSER" marked on top of chamber, improved 5.5 in. tapered barrel, 10 shot mag.

	$12,500	$9,500	$6,000	$5,000	$4,000	$3,500	$3,000

Add 40% for "SYSTEM MAUSER" stock.

Stepped barrel variation — similar to System Mauser variation, except has older 5.5 in. stepped barrel with no taper.

	$20,000	$15,000	$10,000	$8,000	$7,000	$6,000	$5,000

20 SHOT CONEHAMMER — 7.63 Mauser, 20 shot non-detachable mag., frame can either be flatside or have milled panels, 5.5 in. tapered barrel, extremely rare.

	$27,500	$22,000	$15,000	$12,000	$9,000	$8,000	$7,000

Add 20% for milled panel variation.
Add 40% for matching stock cut for 20 shot mag.

Grading	100%	98%	95%	90%	80%	70%	60%

EARLY TRANSITIONAL LARGE RING HAMMER — 7.63 Mauser, distinguishable by large, open centered ring, 10 shot mag., 5.5 in. barrel.

	$3,000	$2,250	$1,550	$1,200	$1,050	$925	$700

This variation is normally found in the 12,000-15,000 serial range only.

FLATSIDE VARIATIONS

Add approximately $500 for a matching shoulder stock on the following models, $350 for non-matching.

ITALIAN CONTRACT FLATSIDE — 7.63 Mauser, distinguishable by flatside frame and DV/AV proofmarks, 10 shot mag., 5.5 in. barrel.

	$3,500	$2,500	$1,600	$1,300	$1,100	$900	$700

This variation is found in the 1-5,000 serial range only.

FLATSIDE COMMERCIAL — 7.63 Mauser, 5.5 in. barrel, 23 groove walnut grips, adj. rear sight typically marked 1-10 or 50-1000.

	$2,700	$2,000	$1,500	$1,000	$800	$600	$400

Early specimens may have pinned rear sights. Found in serial range 20,000-30,000.

POST 1900 VARIATIONS

Add approximately $400 for a matching shoulder stock on the following models, $325 for non-matching.

PRE-WAR LARGE RING BOLO — 7.63 Mauser, 3.9 in. barrel, floral grips, usually found in 29,000 and 40,000 serial range.

	$4,250	$3,000	$2,000	$1,450	$1,000	$700	$450

Add $850 for short pre-war bolo stock.

LARGE RING SHALLOW MILLING — 7.63 Mauser, 5.5 in. barrel, 23 groove walnut or hard rubber grips, normally found in the 30,000-33,000 ser. range.

	$2,500	$1,600	$1,000	$750	$625	$500	$400

LARGE RING DEEP MILLING — 7.63 Mauser, 5.5 in. barrel, 35 groove walnut or hard rubber grips, normally found in the 34,000 ser. range.

	$2,650	$1,650	$1,000	$750	$625	$500	$400

PRE-WAR SMALL RING BOLO — 7.63 Mauser, 3.9 in. barrel, floral/checkered rubber or 31-36 groove walnut grips, usually found in 40,000-44,000 serial range.

	$3,250	$2,300	$1,600	$1,200	$800	$575	$400

6-SHOT BOLO — 7.63 Mauser, distinctive 6 shot mag., 3.9 in. barrel, either fixed rear sight (more common) or adjustable, could have either large ring or small ring hammer.

	$6,500	$5,000	$3,500	$3,000	$2,600	$2,200	$1,500

STANDARD PRE-WAR COMMERCIAL — 7.63 Mauser, 5.5 in. barrel, 10 shot mag., 34 groove walnut or checkered black rubber grips, typically 50-1,000 meter adj. rear sight.

	$1,600	$1,200	$850	$725	$600	$500	$400

This variation is the most commonly encountered of all M1896 broomhandles. It can be encountered in the 39,000-274,000 serial range. Early guns below serial no. 100,000 are often Von Lengerke and Detmold marked and can be encountered with hard rubber grips. Rifling changed from 4 groove to 6 groove at approx. serial no. 100,000.

Note: This model is once again being imported by domestic distributors/dealers. Condition is somewhat poor, and prices usually start in the $250 range. These specimens usually have been reblued in addition to other reworking because the original condition has generally been very poor.

Grading	100%	98%	95%	90%	80%	70%	60%

MAUSER BANNER CHAMBER MARKED — 7.63 Mauser or 9mm export (rare), 5.5 in. barrel, distinguishable by Mauser banner trademark on top of chamber, 32 groove walnut grips. Approx. 10,000 mfg. in serial range 84,000-94,000.

	$2,700	$1,900	$1,250	$850	$725	$600	$500

This model is very similar in appearance to the Pre-War Commercial.

PERSIAN CONTRACT — 7.63 Mauser, 5.5 in. barrel, distinguished by Persian lion crest in left rear frame panel, must be in the 154,000 serial range, 50-1,000 meter adj. rear sight.

	$3,750	$2,800	$2,200	$1,600	$1,100	$850	$700

This variation is frequently faked - pay close attention to serial no. and Persian crest.

STANDARD WARTIME COMMERCIAL — 7.63 Mauser, 5.5 in. barrel, 10 shot mag., 30 groove walnut grips, adj. 50-1,000 meter rear sight.

	$1,400	$1,000	$750	$650	$550	$450	$350

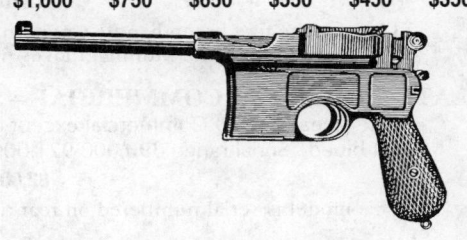

This variation is encountered almost as frequently as the Standard Pre-War Commercial. It is usually found in the 290,000-440,000 serial range. It was the first model to utilize the "new safety" design, and can be noticed by the "NS" marking on the back of hammer. Similar features as the Pre-War Commercial, except finish and polishing exhibit more machine and tooling marks.

Note: This model is once again being imported by domestic distributors/dealers. Condition is somewhat poor, and prices usually start in the $250 range. These specimens usually have been reblued in addition to other reworking because the original condition has generally been very poor.

RED-9 ADJ. SIGHT — 9mm P, 5.5 in. barrel, 10 shot mag., 24 groove walnut grips usually marked with large red no. 9, adj. 50-500 meter rear sight, standard WWI military contract model with separate serial range 1-150,000, generally poorly finished. Mfg. 1916-1918.

	$1,650	$1,250	$1,000	$850	$750	$650	$550

Add $600 for matching stock.
Add $350 for non-matching stock.
Add $200 for original leather.
Add 10% if Prussian Eagle proofed on front of magazine well.
Note: Be cautious for originality since metal refinishing is prevalent in this model. The last 10,000 guns of this German military contract are not military proofed, are better polished, and will command a slight premium.

RED-9 FIXED SIGHT — 9mm P, 3.9 in. barrel, this is a 1920 commercial rework of the Red-9 military, may be dated 1920 and/or have police markings on front grip strap.

	$925	$750	$650	$550	$475	$400	$350

Because of the Treaty of Versailles following WWI, barrels had to be shortened to less than 4 inches and the adj. rear sight removed.

FRENCH GENDARME — 7.63 Mauser, 3.9 in. barrel, distinguished by Bolo barrel length on large frame, hard rubber or walnut (rare) grips, found in the serial range 431,000-434,000, adj. 50-500 meter rear sight.

	$2,850	$2,000	$1,250	$850	$700	$550	$400

EARLY POST-WAR BOLO — 7.63 Mauser, 3.9 in. barrel, shot extractor, small ring hammer, usually found in the 440,000-500,000 serial range.

	$2,350	$1,650	$925	$725	$600	$500	$375

Add 50% for long barrel Bolos in approx. the 475,000 serial range.

Grading	100%	98%	95%	90%	80%	70%	60%

LATE POST-WAR BOLO — 7.63 Mauser, 3.9 in. barrel, similar features of Early Post-War Bolo except has Mauser banner trademark on left rear frame panel, usually encountered in the 500,000-700,000+ serial range.

	$2,600	$1,750	$1,250	$800	$625	$500	$375

POST 1930 VARIATIONS

Add approximately $500 for a matching shoulder stock on the following models, $350 for non-matching.

EARLY MODEL 1930 COMMERCIAL — 7.63 Mauser, 5.2 (common) or 5.5 in. stepped barrel, 12 groove walnut grips, adj. 50-1,000 meter rear sight, usually found in the 800,000-890,000 serial range.

	$2,100	$1,500	$950	$750	$625	$500	$375

This was the first broomhandle variation to have a high polish, salt blue finish. Small parts are still fire blued and milling grooves were machined in receiver rails.

LATE MODEL 1930 COMMERCIAL — 7.63 Mauser, 5.5 in. stepped barrel, similar appearance to early 1930 Commercial except has solid receiver rails and various small parts are salt blued. Serial range 890,000-921,000 with production ending in late 1930's.

	$2,000	$1,400	$950	$750	$625	$500	$375

This model is serial numbered on rear top of breech bolt assembly.

MODEL 1930 REMOVABLE MAG. — 7.63 Mauser, 5.5 in. stepped barrel, 12 groove walnut grips, adj. 50-1,000 meter rear sight, very rare.

	$13,000	$11,000	$8,000	$5,000	$4,000	$3,200	$2,500

Original specimens of this variation have frames without the extra cuts required for the selector switch. Fakes are usually welded up Schnellfeuers made to look original. Only a very few are known in the 84,000-88,000 serial range. They are not slotted for the shoulder stock. Also known as the Model 711.

SCHNELLFEUER (MODEL 712) — 7.63 Mauser, 5.5 in. stepped barrel, 12 groove walnut grips, adj. 50-1,000 meter rear sight, switchable full auto variation generally with selector switch, separate serial range 1-100,000, 10 or 20 shot detachable mag. 712 stock is internally grooved for selector switch.

	$3,750	$3,150	$2,600	$2,200	$1,800	$1,500	$1,200

Add $750 for correct stock.
Deduct 60% if Class III transferable only (dealer sample).
The Model 712 is classified as a machine gun and is subject to registration and payment of a $200 transfer tax.

BROOMHANDLE CARBINES: SEMI-AUTO

FLUTED BARREL MODEL — marked "July 1897".

	$20,000	$16,000	$12,000	$8,000	$6,000	$5,000	$4,000

FLATSIDE CONE HAMMER — 7.63mm, 11¾ in. barrel, experimental variation.

	$15,000	$13,000	$10,000	$7,000	$6,000	$5,000	$4,000

FLATSIDE TRANSITIONAL — 7.63mm, 11¾ in. barrel.

	$13,000	$11,000	$8,000	$7,000	$6,000	$5,000	$4,000

LARGE RING HAMMER TRANSITIONAL — 7.63mm, 11¾ in. barrel.

	$13,000	$11,000	$8,000	$7,000	$6,000	$5,000	$4,000

Grading	100%	98%	95%	90%	80%	70%	60%

LARGE RING HAMMER — 7.63mm, 14½ in. barrel.

	100%	98%	95%	90%	80%	70%	60%
	$13,000	$11,000	$8,000	$7,000	$6,000	$5,000	$4,000

SMALL RING HAMMER — 7.63mm, 14½ in. barrel.

	100%	98%	95%	90%	80%	70%	60%
	$10,000	$7,000	$6,000	$5,500	$5,000	$4,500	$4,000

BROOMHANDLE COPIES FROM OTHER COUNTRIES

These pistols are Chinese manufactured copies of the original German design.

HAND-MADE MAUSER CHINESE MARKED AND OTHERS — very poorly made Mauser copies, many thousands made.

	100%	98%	95%	90%	80%	70%	60%
	$650	$550	$475	$400	$300	$250	$235

HAND-MADE UNMARKED — poor quality.

	100%	98%	95%	90%	80%	70%	60%
	$650	$550	$475	$400	$300	$250	$235

ASIATIC FLATSIDE UNMARKED — better quality, not exceedingly rare.

	100%	98%	95%	90%	80%	70%	60%
	$1,200	$950	$740	$680	$600	$500	$400

TAKU-NAVAL DOCKYARD FLATSIDE — machine-made, better quality, not exceedingly rare, approx. 6,000 mfg.

	100%	98%	95%	90%	80%	70%	60%
	$1,500	$1,100	$740	$680	$600	$500	$400

Add 30% with correct stock.
Add 5% if with holster.

SHANSI ARSENAL .45 CAL. — .45 ACP cal., approx. 8,500 mfg., scarce and desirable in excellent condition.

	100%	98%	95%	90%	80%	70%	60%
	$5,500	$4,500	$3,500	$2,100	$1,700	$1,600	$1,475

SPANISH COPIES OF MAUSER BROOMHANDLES

VERY EARLY ASTRA-900 — Bolo grips, frame has single-line address, approx. 1,200 mfg.

	100%	98%	95%	90%	80%	70%	60%
	$2,750	$2,500	$2,200	$2,000	$1,750	$1,600	$1,475

EARLY ASTRA-900 — single-line address, approx. ser. range 1,200-12,000.

	100%	98%	95%	90%	80%	70%	60%
	$2,500	$2,000	$1,350	$850	$700	$525	$425

LATE ASTRA-900 — two and three-line address, two-line address ser. range is approx. 12,000-20,000, three-line address ser. range is approx. 20,000-34,400.

	100%	98%	95%	90%	80%	70%	60%
	$2,350	$1,850	$1,350	$850	$700	$525	$425

Add 20% for Japanese character variation in the 27,000 serial range or if in Nazi procurement range.

ROYAL SEMI-AUTO — early Royals are mostly seen in semi-auto with round bolts.

	100%	98%	95%	90%	80%	70%	60%
	$3,000	$2,450	$1,900	$1,300	$850	$700	$600

There were many variations of the Royals and above values assume standard variation.

ROYAL SELECTIVE FIRE — 7.63mm, most of approx. 25,000 Royals manufactured were selective fire, several variations, transferable only. Add 20% if detachable mag., 100% if equipped with pneumatic rate retarder.

Class III	100%	98%	95%	90%	80%	70%	60%
	$2,500	$2,200	$2,000	$1,800	$1,700	$1,600	$1,475

This model had either a fixed mag., detachable mag., or pneumatic rate retarder.

MILITARY RIFLES

Deduct 30% if bolt is not matching or contract crests have been removed.

Grading	100%	98%	95%	90%	80%	70%	60%
CZECH MODEL 1924 SHORT — 7.92mm, 23.23 in. barrel.							
	$395	$350	$275	$250	$195	$165	$140
MODEL 1935 FN							
	$440	$375	$300	$220	$160	$140	$120
KAR 98 POLISH CREST — 7.92mm.							
	$325	$260	$200	$150	$125	$100	$80
SWISS CALVARY CARBINE — K31.							
	$1,150	$950	$800	$675	$525	$450	$350
GREEK FN							
	$395	$320	$275	$220	$190	$175	$140
GERMAN G 33/40-MOUNTAIN CARBINE, 1940-1943 DATES							
	$750	$575	$475	$400	$350	$300	$260
GERMAN G 98/40-MOUNTAIN CARBINE							
	$950	$875	$750	$650	$575	$500	$425
G 41 SEMI-AUTO							
Mauser mfg. (G 41M)							
	$1,400	$1,200	$900	$700	$650	$600	$550
Walther mfg. (G 41W)							
	$950	$900	$850	$700	$600	$500	$450
G 43 OR K 43 SNIPER RIFLE — add $500 if with scope, Nazi issue.							
	$990	$880	$770	$650	$600	$485	$400
KAR 98 ERFURT ROYAL ARSENAL							
	$180	$140	$120	$100	$90	$85	$65
GERMAN M98 — WWI Gewehr 98 (Mauser, Simson, Danzig, Amberg, Erfurt).							
	$295	$250	$195	$155	$140	$110	$90
KAR 98 GERMAN WWII — (K 98 K), dated 1936-1945, coded manufacturers, deduct 20% for 1943-1945 dates. Add 100% for K date S/42. Add 50% for G date S/42.							
	$395	$325	$250	$165	$145	$120	$100
RADOM MAUSER MODEL 29 — 7.92mm.							
	$395	$320	$275	$220	$190	$175	$140
K98K PORTUGUESE CONTRACT							
	$525	$440	$330	$275	$250	$220	$165
TURKISH M1888							
	$185	$140	$115	$90	$70	$55	$40
SWEDISH CONTRACT M98							
	$200	$175	$135	$110	$90	$75	$60
CZECH M98 VZ24 — 7.92mm.							
	$340	$275	$240	$210	$170	$140	$110

Grading	100%	98%	95%	90%	80%	70%	60%
YUGOSLAVIAN M24	$250	$200	$150	$120	$110	$100	$85
DANISH 1889 - 10	$250	$200	$165	$155	$140	$110	$90
CHILEAN MODEL 1895 RIFLE — 7mm, 29.06 in. barrel.	$285	$220	$185	$165	$140	$110	$100
CHILEAN MODEL 1898 CARBINE	$350	$325	$280	$250	$220	$185	$165
98K FRENCH OCCUPATION	$285	$220	$180	$165	$140	$110	$100
MODEL 98 COLUMBIAN — .30-06.	$285	$220	$175	$155	$110	$90	$85
SIAMESE MAUSER RIFLE — 29.13 in. barrel, 8 x 50R.	$165	$125	$110	$90	$75	$60	$50
SIAMESE MAUSER CARBINE — 8 x 50R.	$165	$125	$110	$90	$75	$60	$50
SPANDAU MODEL 1915 — 8 X 57mm, mfg. in Spandau, Germany.	$250	$210	$165	$140	$120	$100	$85
SCHILLING MODEL 1916 — 8 x 57mm, mfg. in Suhl, Germany.	$225	$190	$155	$130	$110	$100	$95
IRANIAN MODEL 98/29 — long rifle.	$250	$210	$165	$140	$120	$100	$85
IRANIAN MODEL 98/29 — 7.92mm, 17.91 in. barrel, short.	$270	$220	$195	$165	$145	$120	$100
SWEDISH MODEL 94 — 6.5mm, 17.38 in. barrel carbine.	$225	$190	$155	$130	$110	$100	$95
SPANISH MODEL 93 — 7mm, 29.06 in. barrel.	$185	$150	$120	$110	$90	$85	$65
SPANISH MODEL 43 SHORT — 7.9mm, 23.62 in. barrel.	$200	$160	$125	$100	$90	$85	$75
SOUTH AMERICAN G.E.W. M98 — 7.92mm.	$175	$145	$100	$90	$85	$70	$55
VZ24 ROMANIAN CREST	$325	$250	$220	$200	$180	$165	$140
BRAZILIAN M1908 — 7 x 57mm.	$350	$300	$240	$180	$110	$95	$65

MAUSER cont.

Grading	100%	98%	95%	90%	80%	70%	60%
ARGENTINE M1909 — 7.65mm.							
	$275	$225	$165	$140	$110	$95	$85
ARGENTINE M1891 — 7.65mm.							
	$300	$225	$165	$140	$110	$95	$85
1935 CHILIAN MAUSER BANNER — 7 x 57 Mauser.							
	$500	$450	$400	$325	$275	$225	$150
PERUVIAN M1935 SHORT — .30-06, 23 in. barrel.							
	$225	$190	$150	$120	$110	$100	$85
PERUVIAN CREST M98							
	$250	$185	$120	$110	$100	$90	$85
1934 MAUSER BANNER — 7.92mm. Characterized by side sling and turn down bolt handle.							
	$500	$450	$425	$350	$250	$200	$165
ITALIAN MAUSER — 7.92mm, 1,000 mfg. for Germany.							
	$250	$210	$160	$120	$110	$95	$85
GERMAN M71/84 — 11mm, 33.56 in. barrel. Add 60% if M 71 (without tubular mag.).							
	$250	$225	$200	$180	$160	$140	$125
CZ VZ-24 rebarreled to .308 Win. by I.M.I./I.D.F. in Israel.							
	$325	$275	$240	$210	$185	$160	$135

MAUSER OBERNDORF SPORTERS

Approx. 125,000 commercial sporting Mausers were built between 1898 and 1946. Three action lengths; overall measurements: Short (Kurz) 81/4 in., Standard 8³⁄4 in., and Magnum 9¹⁄4 in. Optional squarebridge receiver rings for custom sight mounting. Innumerable variations of triggers, barrels, sights and checkering.

Add $350-$550 for conversion unit.
Add 50% for single squarebridge action.
Add 100% for double squarebridge action.
Add 100% for Short (Kurz) action, except on Type K below.
Add 100% for Magnum action, except on African Type below.

SPECIAL RIFLE, TYPE A — expressly made for English market, superior finish, with round tapered barrel, silver-bead front sight on sleeved-on block with matted surface, hinged floorplate, pear shaped bolt knob, horn forend tip and PG cap, sling eyes.

	100%	98%	95%	90%	80%	70%	60%
	$3,000	$2,400	$2,000	$1,500	$1,000	$750	$575

NORMAL RIFLE, TYPE B — 24 in. barrel, steel-capped PG, Schnabel forend, sling swivels, pear shaped bolt knob, hinged floorplate.

	100%	98%	95%	90%	80%	70%	60%
	$2,000	$1,600	$1,400	$1,200	$900	$600	$475

Grading	100%	98%	95%	90%	80%	70%	60%

LIGHT SHORT RIFLE, TYPE K — 6.5 x 54 Mauser, 8 x 51, or .250-300 Savage, 22 in. barrel, steel PG cap, sling swivels, pear shaped bolt knob, hinged floorplate, hard rubber buttplate.

	$4,000	$3,500	$3,000	$2,500	$1,500	$1,000	$725

CARBINE, TYPE S — 20 or 24 in. barrel stocked to muzzle, steel PG cap, horn buttplate, sling swivels, pear shaped bolt knob, hinged floorplate.

	$2,500	$2,000	$1,750	$1,400	$1,000	$750	$575

CARBINE, TYPE M — 20 in. barrel stocked to muzzle with steel forend cap, steel PG cap, trapdoor steel buttplate holding sectional cleaning rod, butterknife bolt handle, hinged floorplate.

	$2,500	$2,000	$1,750	$1,400	$1,000	$750	$575

MILITARY SPORTING RIFLE, TYPE C — stepped round barrel, round bolt knob, half grip, banner Mauser imprint in side of buttstock.

	$750	$600	$500	$450	$400	$350	$295

AFRICAN TYPE — 28 in. round barrel, stocked to 4 in. from muzzle, Magnum action, pear shaped bolt knob.

	$5,000	$4,000	$3,000	$2,500	$2,250	$2,000	$1,700

RIFLES: RECENT MANUFACTURE

All long arms manufactured by Mauser-Werke are currently being imported exclusively by Precision Imports, Inc. located in San Antonio, TX. More information pertaining to current Mauser-Werke long arms can be obtained by contacting Precision Imports, Inc. directly.

Previous importation of Mauser-Werke rifles was by KDF, Inc. located in Seguin, TX until 1989.

MODEL 225 — available in 13 cals. between .243 Win. and .300 Wby. Mag., bolt action, 60 degree bolt lift with 3 locking lugs, ultra fast lock time, adj. trigger, 24 or 26 (Mag. only) in. barrel, 3 or 5 shot mag., no sights, guaranteed ½ in. accuracy at 100 yards, many stock options available at extra cost. Left-handed action available in certain cals. at the same price as Mag. cals. (Model 226).

Deluxe Standard Sporter — standard model available in 6 regular cals. and 9 Mag. cals. Importation disc. 1989.

	$1,275	$1,000	$875	$750	$625	$550	$495

Add $90 for Mag. cals.
This model was formerly the KDF Model K-15.
Last Mfg.'s Sug. Retail was $1,400.

MODEL 66A — similar to Model 66S except has American configured laminate stock (wood grain), cals., action, and features are the same as the Model 66S. Imported 1988-89 only.

Standard Calibers

	$1,900	$1,425	$1,150	$925	$800	$700	$650

Add $630 per interchangeable barrel.
The A suffix on this model denotes American.
Last Mfg.'s Sug. Retail was $2,100.

Magnum Calibers — includes Weatherby Mag. cals. also.

	$2,050	$1,500	$1,200	$975	$825	$700	$650

Add $670 per interchangeable barrel.
Last Mfg.'s Sug. Retail was $2,270.

Grading	100%	98%	95%	90%	80%	70%	60%

Big Game Calibers — includes most popular Mag. cals. up to .458 Win. Mag.

	100%	98%	95%	90%	80%	70%	60%
	$2,350	$1,900	$1,425	$1,150	$950	$825	$750

Last Mfg.'s Sug. Retail was $2,700.

MODEL 66S
— telescoping short action, 5.6 x 57mm, 6.5 x 57mm, 7 x 57mm Mauser (disc. 1992), 7 x 64mm, 9.3 x 62mm, .243 Win., .270 Win., .30-06, or .308 Win. cal., 24 in. barrel, standard interchangeable barrels, single or double set triggers, adj. and detachable sights, Monte Carlo walnut stock with checkering, swivels, new safety, rosewood tipped forearm and pistol grip, rubber recoil pad, 7½ lbs. Mfg. 1974-present.

Mfg.'s Sug. Retail	$1,783	$1,525	$1,175	$975	$875	$775	$695	$625

Magnum Model — 28 in. barrel, 6.5 x 68mm, 8 x 68mm S, 9.3 x 64mm, 7mm Rem. Mag., .300 Win. Mag., or .300 Wby. Mag. cal., 7.9 lbs.

Mfg.'s Sug. Retail	$1,873	$1,600	$1,225	$1,000	$900	$795	$695	$625

Stutzen-Mannlicher Model — 21 in. barrel, full-stock (Mannlicher only) and half-stock (disc. in 1989), double or single triggers, same cals. as Model 66S, 7.5 lbs.

Mfg.'s Sug. Retail	$1,873	$1,600	$1,225	$1,000	$900	$795	$695	$625

This model was available in a half-stock "Ultra" variation until 1989. Values are similar to those listed above.

Safari Model — .375 H&H Mag. or .458 Win. Mag. cal., single trigger, 9.3 lbs.

Mfg.'s Sug. Retail	$2,079	$1,825	$1,600	$1,250	$1,025	$875	$775	$650

MODEL 66 SM
— telescoping short action, .243 Win., .270 Win., 7 x 57mm Mauser, 7 x 64, .308 Win., .30-06, or 6.5 x 57 cal., 24 in. barrel, standard interchangeable barrels, set trigger on tang, adj. and detachable sights, Monte Carlo walnut stock with checkering, swivels, new safety, anatomical gripped select walnut stock with Mauser-nose, cocking lever on tang, rubber recoil pad, 7¼ lbs. Imported 1981-89.

	$1,550	$1,260	$1,075	$875	$730	$620	$520

Last Mfg.'s Sug. Retail was $1,801.

Model 66 SM Ultra — all standard cals., 21 in. barrel, 7¼ lbs.

	$1,625	$1,325	$1,140	$920	$760	$650	$550

Last Mfg.'s Sug. Retail was $1,903.

Magnum Calibers — similar to Model 66 S, 26 in. barrel, 8.4 lbs.

	$1,625	$1,325	$1,140	$920	$760	$650	$550

Last Mfg.'s Sug. Retail was $1,903.

Mannlicher type full stock — all standard cals., 21 in. barrel, 7 lbs.

	$1,625	$1,325	$1,140	$920	$760	$650	$550

Last Mfg.'s Sug. Retail was $1,903.

These models were previously available on a custom order only basis through KDF, Inc. located in Seguin, TX.

MODEL 66 SL
— similar to Model 66 SM, except features extra select walnut with special graining, 7¼ lbs. Disc. 1985.

	$1,370	$1,275	$890	$720	$580	$475	$420

Last Mfg.'s Sug. Retail was $1,470.

Model 66 SL Ultra — 7 x 64 or .30-06 cal., 21 in. barrel, 7¼ lbs. Disc. 1985.

	$1,475	$1,325	$940	$750	$600	$450	$400

Last Mfg.'s Sug. Retail was $1,520.

Grading	100%	98%	95%	90%	80%	70%	60%

Magnum Calibers — similar to Model 66 S, 8.4 lbs. Disc. 1985.

| | $1,475 | $1,325 | $940 | $750 | $600 | $450 | $400 |

Last Mfg.'s Sug. Retail was $1,520.

Mannlicher Type Full Stock — 21 in. barrel, 7 lbs. Disc. 1985.

| | $1,475 | $1,325 | $940 | $750 | $600 | $450 | $400 |

Last Mfg.'s Sug. Retail was $1,520.

MODEL 66SL DIPLOMAT — same specifications as Model 66 SM, except includes selected walnut and special engraving including deer and wild boar game scenes.
Add $93 for Mannlicher full-stock (21 in. barrel).
Add $387 for Mag. Cal.'s.
This model was available on an individual custom order basis only. The last published retail price (1988) for a standard model without options was $3,167.

MODEL 660 — U.S. designation of 66S. Imported 1971-1973.

| | $925 | $820 | $720 | $600 | $500 | $450 | $400 |

MODEL 66S DELUXE — special order engraved and inlaid, select wood. Priced per individual customer order. All guns are custom made only. Prices usually start in the $2,500 range.

MODEL 66SP SUPER MATCH — telescoping short action, .308 Win., 27½ in. heavy barrel with muzzle brake, no sights match trigger, 3 shot mag., select European walnut stock with stippling and thumbhole, adj. cheek piece and butt plate, includes premium scope, 12 lbs. Disc. 1990.

| | $7,375 | $6,200 | $5,500 | $4,800 | $4,300 | $3,900 | $3,500 |

Last Mfg.'s Sug. Retail was $8,160.

MODEL 77 — .243 Win., .270 Win., 6.5 x 57, 7 x 64, .308 Win., or .30-06 cal., 24 in. barrel, set trigger on tang, adj. and detachable sights, walnut stock with European cheek piece and hand checkering, swivels, new safety, steel detachable box mag., rubber recoil pad, 7¼ lbs. Disc.

| | $1,130 | $950 | $875 | $810 | $750 | $675 | $595 |

Last Mfg.'s Sug. Retail was $1,331.

Model 77 Ultra — 6.5 x 57, 7 x 64 or .30-06 cal., 20 in. barrel, 7.7 lbs. Disc.

| | $1,175 | $975 | $895 | $835 | $760 | $675 | $595 |

Last Mfg.'s Sug. Retail was $1,394.

Magnum Calibers — similar to Model 66S, 8⅛ lbs. Disc.

| | $1,175 | $975 | $895 | $835 | $760 | $675 | $595 |

Last Mfg.'s Sug. Retail was $1,394.

Mannlicher type full stock — 20 in. barrel, Mauser-set trigger, 7.7 lbs. Disc.

| | $1,175 | $975 | $895 | $835 | $760 | $675 | $595 |

Last Mfg.'s Sug. Retail was $1,394.

Big Game Model — .375 H&H Mag. cal., 26 in. barrel, 8⅛ lbs. Disc.

| | $1,075 | $1,000 | $900 | $795 | $675 | $575 | $475 |

Last Mfg.'s Sug. Retail was $1,150.

MODEL 77 SPORTSMAN — .243 or .308 Win. cal., sports version of the Model 77, set trigger on the tang, no sights, 24 in. barrel, 9 lbs. Disc.

| | $1,495 | $1,230 | $1,075 | $985 | $895 | $820 | $740 |

Add $430 for Zeiss 2½-10X scope and mounts.
Last Mfg.'s Sug. Retail was $1,754.

Grading	100%	98%	95%	90%	80%	70%	60%

MODEL 83 MATCH SINGLE SHOT — .308 Win. cals. only, cylinder locking action with 3 locking lugs in rear, match trigger, anatomical match stock with select walnut, adj. comb and butt plate. Disc.

	100%	98%	95%	90%	80%	70%	60%
	$2,170	$1,815	$1,660	$1,545	$1,400	$1,195	$925

This model is a UIT standard rifle at 300 meters.
Last Mfg.'s Sug. Retail was $2,594.

MODEL 83 MATCH UIT FREE RIFLE — .308 Win. cals. only, cylinder locking action with 3 locking lugs in rear, match trigger, anatomical match stock with select walnut, adj. comb and butt plate. Disc.

	100%	98%	95%	90%	80%	70%	60%
	$2,320	$1,940	$1,760	$1,600	$1,430	$1,195	$925

Last Mfg.'s Sug. Retail was $2,771.

MODEL 83 STANDARD RIFLE — similar to Model 83 Match, except has removable 10 shot steel mag., 26 in. barrel. Disc.

	100%	98%	95%	90%	80%	70%	60%
	$2,320	$1,950	$1,800	$1,625	$1,460	$1,250	$1,000

Last Mfg.'s Sug. Retail was $2,766.

MODEL 86-SR — .308 cal., updated version of the Model 83 action, 25.6 in. fluted barrel with muzzle brake, laminate wood stock with rail in forearm, adj. trigger, 9 shot detachable mag., cased, 10.8 lbs. Importation began 1989.

Mfg.'s Sug. Retail	$3,921		$3,575	$3,100	$2,700	$2,100	$1,775	$1,450	$1,200

Add $224 for match thumbhole wood stock.

Many other special order options are available on this model. Contact Precision Imports, Inc. directly for pricing information.

MODEL 99 — 5.6 x 57mm, 6.5 x 57mm, 7 x 57mm, 7 x 64mm, .243 Win., .25-06, .270 Win., .30-06 or .308 Win. cal., bolt action with 60 degree throw, 24 in. free-floating barrel, jeweled bolt, available in either hand-rubbed oil or high-luster lacquer finish for stock, mini-claw extractor, adj. single stage trigger, 4 shot detachable mag., no sights, 8 lbs. Importation began 1989.

⚐ **Classic Lacquer Finish** — high-luster lacquer finish for stock.

Mfg.'s Sug. Retail	$1,272		$1,100	$925	$850	$775	$700	$625	$550

This model is available with either a Schnabel forearm with regular stock or rosewood capped forearm with American Monte Carlo stock.
High luster stocks will no longer be available once inventory is depleted.

⚐ **Classic Oil Finish** — hand-rubbed oil finish for stock.

Mfg.'s Sug. Retail	$1,130		$995	$875	$775	$700	$625	$550	$495

This model is available with either a Schnabel forearm with regular stock or rosewood capped forearm with American Monte Carlo stock.

MODEL 99 MAGNUM — 8 x 68S, 9.3 x 64mm, 7mm Rem. Mag., .257 Wby., .270 Wby., .300 Wby., .300 Win. Mag., .338 Win. Mag., or .375 H&H cal., similar specifications as Model 99, except has 26 in. barrel and 3 shot mag. Importation began 1989.

⚐ **Classic Lacquer Finish** — high-luster lacquer finish for stock.

Mfg.'s Sug. Retail	$1,322		$1,135	$950	$875	$775	$700	$625	$550

This model is available with either a Schnabel forearm with regular stock or rosewood capped forearm with American Monte Carlo stock.
High luster stocks will no longer be available once inventory is depleted.

⚐ **Classic Oil Finish** — hand-rubbed oil finish for stock.

Mfg.'s Sug. Retail	$1,180		$1,025	$895	$795	$725	$625	$550	$495

This model is available with either a Schnabel forearm with regular stock or rosewood capped forearm with American Monte Carlo stock.

Grading	100%	98%	95%	90%	80%	70%	60%

MODEL 2000 BOLT ACTION — .270 Win., .308 Win., or .30-06 cal., 5 shot mag., 24 in. barrel, leaf rear sight, checkered walnut stock. Mfg. by F.W. Heym for Mauser, 1969-1971.

	100%	98%	95%	90%	80%	70%	60%
	$305	$290	$275	$220	$175	$155	$140

MODEL 3000 — bolt action, .243 Win., .270 Win., .308 Win., or .30-06 cal., 5 shot mag., 22 in. barrel, no sights, walnut Monte Carlo style stock, rosewood forearm and pistol grip, skipline checkering, recoil pad and swivels. Mfg. 1971-1974.

	$500	$450	$425	$400	$375	$325	$275

MODEL 3000 MAGNUM — similar to 3000, except 7mm Rem. Mag., .300 Win. Mag., or .375 H&H Mag. cal., 3 shot mag., 26 in. barrel.

	$550	$500	$450	$425	$375	$350	$325

This model was mfg. by Heym for Mauser.

MODEL 4000 VARMINT RIFLE — similar to 3000, except smaller action, .222 Rem. or .223 Rem. cal., folding leaf rear sight, rubber butt plate.

	$425	$400	$375	$350	$300	$260	$225

This model was mfg. by Heym for Mauser.

RIFLES: .22 CAL. SPORTING

MODEL 107 STANDARD — .22 LR only, bolt action, 19½ in. barrel, 5 shot clip mag., adj. iron sights, 6 lbs. Imported 1988-89, reintroduced 1993.

Mfg.'s Sug. Retail	$330	$290	$255	$215	$185	$170	$155	$140

This model is the same as KDF's previous Model 2107 mfg. by Voere.

Model 107 Deluxe — .22 LR or .22 Mag. cal., similar to Model 2107, except has deluxe checkered walnut. Imported 1988-89 only.

	$290	$240	$210	$175	$150	$135	$120

Add $90 for .22 Mag. cal.
Last Mfg.'s Sug. Retail was $320.
This model is the same as KDF's previous Model 2107 Deluxe mfg. by Voere.

MODEL 201 — .22 LR or .22 Mag. cal., bolt action, free-floating 21 in. barrel, clip 5 shot mag., adj. trigger, scaled-down version of the K-15, unusual action incorporates two front-located locking lugs on bolt face that engage Stellite inserts on the front receiver portion, blue only, no sights, beechwood stock with cheek piece, 6½ lbs.

Mfg.'s Sug. Retail	$472	$425	$365	$315	$260	$210	$175	$150

Add $19 for sights (disc. when inventory depleted).
Add $43 for .22 Mag. cal. (Model 201-SM).
This model is the same as KDF's disc. Model K-22 mfg. by Voere. Before 1989, this model came standard with a walnut stock.

Model 201 Luxus — similar to the Model 201 except has walnut stock with rosewood forend.

Mfg.'s Sug. Retail	$621	$550	$485	$425	$360	$310	$265	$225

Add $27 for sights (disc. when inventory depleted).
Add $50 for .22 Mag. cal.
This model is the same as KDF's previous Model K-22 Deluxe mfg. by Voere.

MODEL DSM34 — .22 LR, 25 in. barrel. "Deutches Sportmodell" lightweight trainer, side sling, no bayonet lug.

	$425	$375	$325	$300	$260	$225	$200

MODEL MS 420B — .22 LR Sporter, pre-war, 5 shot clip mag.

	$850	$725	$650	$550	$495	$450	$395

Add 15%-25% for double set triggers (rare).

Grading	100%	98%	95%	90%	80%	70%	60%

MODEL ES340 — .22 LR, single shot, bolt action, 25½ in. barrel, adj. sights, checkered pistol grip, grooved forearm, pre-1935.

	$500	$425	$350	$325	$295	$260	$230

MODEL ES350 — .22 LR, single shot, bolt action, 27½ in. barrel, championship rifle, micrometer rear sight, ramp front sight, checkered full target stock, swivels, pre-1935.

	$625	$550	$500	$460	$430	$400	$375

Add 15%-25% for double set triggers (rare).

MODEL M410 — .22 LR, bolt action, repeating, 5 shot detachable mag., 23½ in. barrel, adj. sights, sporter stock, checkered pistol grip, swivels, pre-1935.

	$850	$725	$650	$550	$495	$450	$395

Add 15%-25% for double set triggers (rare).

MODEL M420 — .22 LR, bolt action, repeating, 5 shot detachable mag., 25½ in. barrel, adj. sights, sporter stock, checkered pistol grip, swivels, pre-1935.

	$850	$725	$650	$550	$495	$450	$395

Add 15%-25% for double set triggers (rare).

MODEL EN310 — .22 LR, single shot, bolt action, 19¾ in. barrel, fixed sights, plain pistol grip stock, pre-1935.

	$425	$365	$315	$280	$260	$225	$200

MODEL EL320 — .22 LR, single shot, bolt action, 23½ in. barrel, fixed sights, checkered pistol grip stock.

	$475	$395	$330	$295	$275	$250	$225

MODEL KKW — .22 LR, single shot, bolt action, target, 26 in. barrel, tangent rear sight, military style stock with bayonet lug. This weapon was also produced by Walther, Gustloff, and Anschutz. It was used as a training rifle in addition to commercial sales. Deduct 15% for 4mm KKW Models.

	$425	$375	$325	$300	$260	$225	$200

MODEL MS350B — .22 LR, bolt action, repeating, 5 shot mag., 26¾ in. barrel, grooved receiver for scope or sight, micrometer rear sight, ramp front sight, target stock, checkered pistol grip and forearm, swivels.

	$850	$725	$650	$550	$495	$450	$395

MODEL ES350B — .22 LR, bolt action, single shot, 5 shot mag., 26¾ in. barrel, grooved receiver for scope or sight, micrometer rear sight, ramp front sight, target stock, checkered pistol grip and forearm, swivels.

	$500	$425	$350	$325	$295	$260	$230

MODEL ES340B — .22 LR, bolt action, single shot, 26¾ in. barrel, adj. sight, plain pistol grip stock.

	$425	$375	$325	$300	$260	$225	$200

MODEL MM410BN — .22 LR, bolt action sporter, 5 shot mag., 23½ in. barrel, adj. sights, lightweight stock, checkered pistol grip, swivels.

	$750	$650	$575	$500	$450	$400	$365

MODEL MS420B — .22 LR, bolt action target, 5 shot mag., 26¾ in. barrel, adj. sights, target style stock, checkered pistol grip, swivels.

	$750	$650	$575	$500	$450	$400	$365

SHOTGUNS

Mauser shotguns were sub-contracted to various European firms and were made in various O/U (including field and target), SxS (both boxlock and sidelock), and single shot configurations. While they are relatively rare (these shotguns had limited importation into the U.S. by Bauer located in Michigan - models included the 496 single shot, 496 SxS, 580 SxS, 610 O/U, 620 O/U, 71E O/U, and others), collectability to date has been minimal. Values will depend on the grade, configuration, features, engraving, and overall desirability. Most of these shotguns have been priced in the $395-$1,350 range, depending on the configuration's desirability.

MARK X SPORTING RIFLE

Currently imported by Interarms. Consult the Interarms Mark X section.

MAVERICK ARMS, INC.

Currently manufactured by Mossberg located in North Haven, CT. Previously manufactured (pre-1992) by Maverick Arms, Inc. located in Eagle Pass, TX. Distributor sales only.

SHOTGUNS

Beginning 1992, all Maverick slide action shotguns incorporate twin slide rails in the operating mechanism.

Grading	100%	98%	95%	90%	80%	70%	60%
MODEL 60 SEMI-AUTO — 12 ga. only, 2¾ or 3 in. (depending on barrel) chamber, semi-auto action, 18½ plain cyl. bore or 28 in. VR barrel with 1 choke tube, safety on receiver top, black synthetic stock and forearm. New 1993.							
Mfg.'s Sug. Retail $279	$230	$200	$175	$150	$125	$115	$110

Subtract $15 for 18½ in. non-Mag. cyl. bore barrel.
Add $33 for combo package (includes 18½ in. cyl. bore barrel).

⚐ **Model 60 Turkey/Deer** — 12 ga. only, features 24 in. Mag. barrel with ghost ring sighting system. New 1993.							
Mfg.'s Sug. Retail $324	$285	$235	$200	$175	$150	$125	$115

MODEL 88 SLIDE ACTION — 12 ga. only, 3 in. chamber, slide-action, 24 (Deer Model with iron sights), 28, or 30 in. plain or VR barrel, wood (mfg. 1992 only) or black synthetic stock and forearm with recoil pad, fixed choke, aluminum alloy receiver, crossbolt safety, approx. 7¼ lbs. New 1989.

Mfg.'s Sug. Retail $205	$175	$140	$125	$115	$110	$105	$100

Add $7 for VR.
Add $31 for wood stock and forearm (mfg. 1992 only).
Add $10 for Deer Model (24 in. cyl. bore barrel).
Add $14 for choked tube barrel (full choke supplied).

⚐ **Model 88 Combos** — includes various combinations of extra Deer barrels with rifle sights, 28 in. plain or VR barrel, or extra 18½ in. cyl. bore barrel. New in 1990.

Mfg.'s Sug. Retail $230	$200	$175	$150	$125	$115	$110	$105

Add $8 for VR barrel.
Add $29 for wood stock and forearm (mfg. 1992 only).

⚐ **Model 88 Security** — 12 or .410 ga., 18½ in. barrel with cyl. bore or spreader (.410 ga. only) choke, regular or pistol grip synthetic stock, plain or pistol grip synthetic forearm, muzzle brake on .410 ga. New 1993.

Mfg.'s Sug. Retail $199	$180	$160	$130	$115	$100	$90	$80

Add $27 for .410 ga. (Model HS410).
Add $167 for laser sights on .410 ga.
Add $98 for Bullpup configuration.

Grading		100%	98%	95%	90%	80%	70%	60%

Model 88 Combat — 12 ga. only, combat design featuring pistol grip stock and forearm, black synthetic stock is extension of receiver, 18½ in. cyl. bore barrel with vented shroud with built-in carrying handle, open sights. Mfg. 1990-92.

		100%	98%	95%	90%	80%	70%	60%
		$240	$215	$190	$175	$160	$150	$140

Last Mfg.'s Sug. Retail was $282.

MODEL 91 SLIDE ACTION — 12 ga. only, 3½ in. chamber, 28 in. plain or VR barrel with 1 choke tube, otherwise similar to Model 88. New in 1991.

		100%	98%	95%	90%	80%	70%	60%
Mfg.'s Sug. Retail	$226	$205	$185	$170	$160	$150	$140	$130

Add $8 for VR barrel (new 1992).

McMILLAN, G. & CO. INC.
Manufacturer located in Phoenix, AZ. Dealer sales only.

In addition to the high quality firearms listed below, McMillan also manufactures fiberglass synthetic stocks in a wide variety of configurations and styles (including many camouflaged models). More information can be obtained on McMillan's fiberglass stocks by contacting the company directly.

HANDGUNS

WOLVERINE — available in 9mm Para., 10mm, .38 Super, .38 Wad Cutter, .45 ACP, or .45 Italian cal., interchangeable barrels, competition ready handgun patterned after the Colt 1911. Importation began 1992.

Combat Wolverine — combat features including 5½ in. compensated barrel.

		100%	98%	95%	90%	80%	70%	60%
Mfg.'s Sug. Retail	$1,700	$1,600	$1,350	$1,025	$875	$750	$625	$550

Competition Match Wolverine — competition features including 6 in. non-compensated barrel.

		100%	98%	95%	90%	80%	70%	60%
Mfg.'s Sug. Retail	$1,700	$1,600	$1,350	$1,025	$875	$750	$625	$550

SIGNATURE JR. BOLT ACTION — available in a variety of cals., utilizes Signature bench rest short action, choice of stainless steel barrel lengths, right or left hand action, single shot or repeater, McMillan design fiberglass stock, choice of electroless nickel or teflon finish, 5 lbs. New 1992.

		100%	98%	95%	90%	80%	70%	60%
Mfg.'s Sug. Retail	$2,400	$2,175	$1,775	$1,350	$995	$895	$800	$700

This model is also available in all titanium.

RIFLES: BOLT ACTION

The models listed below are also available with custom wood stocks at varying prices. McMillan will also manufacture a custom rifle from a supplied action - features include new barreling, a fiberglass stock, matte black finish, and range testing to guarantee ¾ M.O.A. Prices start at $1,400.

Add $150 for stainless steel receiver on most models listed below.

TALON SPORTER — available in various cals. between .22-250 and .416 Rem., receiver available in either 4340 chrome molybdenum or 17-4 stainless steel, drilled and tapped, match grade barrel. New 1992.

		100%	98%	95%	90%	80%	70%	60%
Mfg.'s Sug. Retail	$2,600	$2,375	$1,950	$1,650	$1,325	$1,000	$895	$800

The Talon action is patterned after the Winchester pre-64 Model 70. It features a cone breech, controlled feed, claw extractor, and 3 position safety.

SIGNATURE CLASSIC SPORTER — various cals. available between .22-250 and .416 Rem., premium wood stock, matte metal finish, buttoning used on rifling for 22 or 24 in. stainless steel barrel, McMillan action made from 4340 chrome moly steel (either left or right-handed), 3 or 4 shot mag. supplied with 5 shot test target. New 1988.

		100%	98%	95%	90%	80%	70%	60%
Mfg.'s Sug. Retail	$2,400	$2,250	$1,850	$1,350	$950	$850	$750	$675

Grading	100%	98%	95%	90%	80%	70%	60%

SIGNATURE VARMINTER — similar to Signature Model, except is available in 10 cals. between .22-250 and .350 Rem. Mag., hand bedded fiberglass stock, adj. trigger, 26 in. heavily contoured barrel. New 1988.

Mfg.'s Sug. Retail	$2,400	$2,250	$1,850	$1,350	$995	$895	$800	$700

SIGNATURE TITANIUM MOUNTAIN RIFLE — .270 Win., .280 Rem., .30-06, .300 Win. Mag., .338 Win. Mag., or 7mm Rem. Mag. cal., lighter weight variation with shorter barrel. New 1990.

Mfg.'s Sug. Retail	$3,000	$2,750	$2,195	$1,850	$1,450	$1,100	$925	$825

Add $605 for titanium alloy light contour match grade barrel.

SIGNATURE ALASKAN — available in 11 cals. between .270 Win. and .416 Rem. New 1990.

Mfg.'s Sug. Retail	$3,300	$3,050	$2,475	$2,100	$1,575	$1,200	$1,000	$900

TALON SAFARI — available in 15 cals. between .300 Win. Mag. and .460 Weatherby, hand bedded fiberglass stock, 4 shot mag., 24 in. stainless steel barrel, matte black finish, 9 ½ lbs. New 1988.

Mfg.'s Sug. Retail	$3,600	$3,275	$2,675	$2,300	$1,675	$1,300	$1,100	$950

Add $600 for .300 Phoenix, .338 Lapua, .378 Wby., .416 Wby. or Rigby, or .460 Wby. cal. The Talon action is patterned after the Winchester pre-64 Model 70. It features a cone breech, controlled feed, claw extractor, and 3 position safety. Older Signature action rifles do not have this new Talon action.

M-40 SNIPER RIFLE — .308 Win., Remington action with McMillan match grade heavy contour barrel, fiberglass stock with recoil pad, 4 shot mag., 9 lbs. New 1990.

Mfg.'s Sug. Retail	$1,800	$1,675	$1,375	$1,050	$895	$800	$700	$600

M-86 SNIPER RIFLE — .300 Phoenix, .30-06 (new 1989), .300 Win. Mag. or .308 cal., fiberglass stock, variety of optical sights. New 1988.

Mfg.'s Sug. Retail	$1,900	$1,725	$1,400	$1,075	$925	$825	$725	$625

Add $550 for .300 Phoenix cal.
Add $200 for takedown feature (new 1993).

M-86 Sniper System — includes Model 86 Sniper Rifle, bipod, Ultra scope, rings, and bases. Cased. Mfg. 1988-92.

		$2,460	$2,050	$1,825	$1,600	$1,350	$1,100	$950

Last Mfg.'s Sug. Retail was $2,665.

M-87 LONG RANGE SNIPER RIFLE — .50 BMG, stainless steel bolt action, 29 in. barrel with muzzle brake, single shot, camo synthetic stock, accurate to 1500 meters, 21 lbs. New 1988.

Mfg.'s Sug. Retail	$3,735	$3,350	$2,750	$2,350	$2,000	$1,850	$1,700	$1,575

M-87 Sniper System — includes Model 87 Sniper Rifle, bipod, 20X Ultra scope, rings, and bases. Cased. Mfg. 1988-92.

		$3,950	$3,400	$3,000	$2,750	$2,450	$2,200	$2,000

Last Mfg.'s Sug. Retail was $4,200.

M-87R — same specs. as Model 87, except has 5 shot fixed box mag. New 1990.

Mfg.'s Sug. Retail	$4,000	$3,750	$2,950	$2,550	$2,200	$2,000	$1,850	$1,700

Add $300 for Combo option.

M-89 SNIPER RIFLE — .308 Win., 28 in. barrel with suppressor (also available without), fiberglass stock adj. for length and recoil pad, 15¼ lbs. New 1990.

Mfg.'s Sug. Retail	$2,300	$2,075	$1,675	$1,375	$1,050	$895	$800	$700

Add $425 for muzzle suppressor.

Grading	100%	98%	95%	90%	80%	70%	60%

M-92 BULL PUP — .50 BMG cal., bullpup configuration with shorter barrel. New 1993.

Mfg.'s Sug. Retail	$4,000	$3,750	$2,950	$2,550	$2,200	$2,000	$1,850	$1,700

M-93SN — .50 BMG cal., similar to M-87, except has folding stock and detachable 5 or 10 shot box mag. New 1993.

Mfg.'s Sug. Retail	$4,300	$3,950	$3,250	$2,750	$2,300	$2,000	$1,850	$1,700

.300 PHOENIX LONG RANGE RIFLE — .300 Phoenix cal., special fiberglass stock featuring adj. cheek pieces to accommodate night vision optics, adj. buttplate, 29 in. barrel, conventional box mag., 12½ lbs. Mfg. 1992 only.

	$2,700	$2,195	$1,850	$1,450	$1,100	$925	$825

.300 Phoenix is a new cartridge developed to function at ranges in excess of 800 yards. It produces muzzle velocities of 3100 ft. per second with a 250 grain bullet. Last Mfg.'s Sug. Retail was $3,000.

COMPETITION MODELS — available in Metallic Silhouette (.308 or 7mm/08 cal. - disc. 1989), National Match (.308 cal. only), Long Range (.300 Win. Mag. only), or Bench Rest (shooter's choice). Each model made specifically for individual competition events. New 1988.

Mfg.'s Sug. Retail	$2,600	$2,325	$1,775	$1,450	$1,100	$895	$800	$700

Add $200 for Benchrest Model.
Subtract $300 for Metallic Silhouette model (disc. 1989).

MENZ, AUGUST
Previous manufacturer located in Suhl, Germany.
Please refer to listings in the Liliput section of this text.

MERCURY
Previous importer of Spanish mfg. shotguns.

MAGNUM DOUBLE BARREL — 10, 12, or 20 ga. Mag., 28 and 32 in. barrels, full and mod., boxlock, extractors, double triggers, engraved frame, checkered pistol grip stock.

	$300	$275	$250	$225	$200	$180	$150
10 gauge	$400	$375	$325	$300	$275	$225	$200

MERCURY
Previous manufacturer located in Belgium.

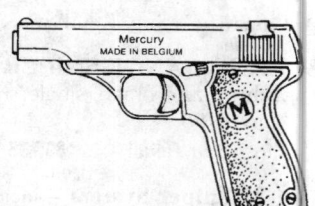

MERCURY SEMI-AUTO — .22 LR, 7 shot mag., steel frame, fixed sights.

	$400	$375	$325	$300	$275	$225	$200

MERKEL, GEBRUDER
Manufacturer located in Suhl, Germany since 1535. Currently imported exclusively by GSI, Inc. located in Trussville, AL. Previously imported (until 1992) by Armes de Chasse located in Chadds Ford, PA, 19317.

For many years Merkel shotguns had a unfair disadvantage in this country because of the politics of importing firearms from communist bloc countries (goods were subject to a 65% non-favored nation tax). With the re-unification of Germany in 1991, this trademark has become more competitive domestically.

Grading	100%	98%	95%	90%	80%	70%	60%

DRILLINGS

Current importation of this configuration into the U.S. has been limited during the past few decades. New mfg. includes a choice of 12, 16, or 20 ga. for the shotgun barrels with the rifle barrel being bored in most popular U.S. and metric cals. between .22 Hornet and 9.3 x 74 R. All current models are boxlocks with extractors. Currently, there are six Drilling models available (Models 90, 90S, 90K, 95, 95S, and 95K) ranging in value from $6,895 (Model 90) to $8,595 (Model 95K). Models differ in amount of engraving, cocking systems, and quality of wood - please contact the importer for more information on these individual models.

MERKEL ANSON DRILLING — usually 2 shotguns over rifle, although 2 rifles over shotgun have been noted, 12, 16, or 20 ga., calibers 7 x 57R, 8 x 57JR, and 9.3 x 74R cals. most common, others noted, 25.6 in. or 21.6 in. barrels, boxlock, Anson & Deeley system, double triggers, extractors, checkered pistol grip stock, pre-WWII.

MODEL 142 — engraved.

	100%	98%	95%	90%	80%	70%	60%
	$5,000	$4,000	$3,000	$2,750	$2,500	$2,200	$2,000

MODEL 142 — less ornamentation.

	100%	98%	95%	90%	80%	70%	60%
	$4,000	$3,500	$3,000	$2,500	$2,250	$2,100	$2,000

MODEL 145 — least ornamentation.

	100%	98%	95%	90%	80%	70%	60%
	$3,000	$2,800	$2,700	$2,600	$2,500	$2,100	$1,900

RIFLES AND COMBINATION GUNS

Models and values listed below reflect 1993 information (with the economic integration of previous Eastern bloc countries into the free marketplace, Merkel is once again manufacturing in more complete line-up of firearms).

O/U COMBINATION GUN — 12, 16, or 20 ga., over 5.6 x 50R, 5.6 x 52R, 6.5 x 55, 6.5 x 57R, 7 x 57R, 7 x 65R, 8 x 57JRS, 9.3 x 74R, .22 Hornet, .222 Rem., .243 Win., .30-06, .308 Win., or .375 H&H Mag. cal., 25.6 in. barrels, various chokes.

Model 210E

Mfg.'s Sug. Retail	$6,195	$5,700	$4,600	$3,700	$3,150	$2,600	$2,100	$1,800

Model 211E

Mfg.'s Sug. Retail	$7,895	$7,000	$4,850	$3,950	$3,350	$2,775	$2,275	$1,925

Model 213E

Mfg.'s Sug. Retail	$14,695	$13,250	$10,750	$8,100	$6,950	$5,725	$4,600	$3,550

Model 313E

Mfg.'s Sug. Retail	$23,395	$19,750	$15,000	$12,000	$9,750	$8,250	$7,000	$5,800

SxS COMBINATION GUN — similar gauges and cals. to O/U Combination Gun, boxlock models include 8EI and 9EI, 10EI is a sidelock, boxlock models range in price from $5,500-$7,000 and the Model 10EI is $9,500. Importation disc. 1990.

O/U DOUBLE RIFLE — same cals. as the O/U Combination Gun, various actions, engraving options, and other special orders.

Model 220E Boxlock — boxlock blitz action, scroll engraved case hardened receiver, DTs, pistol grip with cheekpiece.

Mfg.'s Sug. Retail	$10,795	$9,575	$8,250	$7,150	$6,100	$5,100	$4,250	$3,500

Grading	100%	98%	95%	90%	80%	70%	60%

Model 221E Boxlock — similar to 220E, except has silver grayed receiver with hunting scene engraving.

Mfg.'s Sug. Retail	$12,295	$11,000	$9,750	$8,350	$7,350	$6,250	$5,100	$4,250

Model 223E Sidelock — sidelock action with arabesque engraving featuring large scrolls, sideplates removed without tools.

Mfg.'s Sug. Retail	$18,395	$16,950	$13,250	$11,000	$9,750	$8,350	$7,350	$6,250

Model 323E Sidelock — similar to 223E Sidelock, except has medium scrollwork engraving, top-of-the-line O/U double rifle.

Mfg.'s Sug. Retail	$27,595	$23,750	$19,950	$16,950	$13,250	$11,000	$9,750	$8,350

SxS DOUBLE RIFLE — same cals. as listed for the O/U Combination Gun.

Model 160 — sidelock action with Greener crossbolt featuring hunting scenes, H&H ejectors, DTs, pistol grip stock with cheekpiece.

Mfg.'s Sug. Retail	$10,995	$9,725	$8,300	$7,175	$6,100	$5,100	$4,250	$3,500

SHOTGUNS: DISCONTINUED

MODEL 100 O/U — 12, 16, or 20 ga., various barrel lengths and chokes, boxlock, Greener cross bolt, double triggers, extractors, checkered pistol grip or English style stock, pre-WWII.

	100%	98%	95%	90%	80%	70%	60%
Plain	$1,450	$1,250	$1,000	$925	$850	$675	$550
Ribbed	$1,550	$1,300	$1,050	$950	$875	$700	$575

MODEL 101 — similar to 100, except selective extractors, rib barrel, some English style scroll engraving, pre-WWII.

	$1,600	$1,325	$1,100	$1,000	$900	$750	$600

MODEL 101E — similar to 100, except auto ejectors, pre-WWII.

	$1,750	$1,425	$1,250	$1,150	$1,000	$875	$750

MODEL 400 — similar to 101, except arabesque engraving and Kersten double cross bolt, pre-WWII.

	$1,650	$1,350	$1,200	$1,100	$975	$825	$675

MODEL 400E — similar to 400, except auto ejector, pre-WWII.

	$1,800	$1,450	$1,325	$1,175	$1,025	$925	$775

MODEL 410 — similar to 400, except more engraving and fancier wood, pre-WWII.

	$1,750	$1,425	$1,250	$1,150	$1,000	$875	$750

MODEL 410E — similar to 410, except auto ejectors, pre-WWII.

	$1,900	$1,600	$1,450	$1,225	$1,100	$995	$875

MODEL 200 O/U — 12, 16, 20, 24, 28, or 32 ga., ribbed barrels in various lengths, Kersten double cross bolt, scalloped frame, boxlock, double triggers, extractors, cocking indicators, either pistol grip or English style checkered stock.

	$1,700	$1,350	$1,100	$990	$770	$660	$635

MODEL 210 — similar to 200, except engraved and better grade wood, pre-WWII.

	$1,900	$1,500	$1,300	$1,075	$895	$800	$725

Grading	100%	98%	95%	90%	80%	70%	60%

MODEL 201 O/U — 12, 16, or 20 ga., Greener crossbolt, hunting engraving or fine arabesque, dark walnut.

	$2,000	$1,600	$1,425	$1,200	$995	$900	$800

MODEL 201E — similar to 201, except with auto ejectors, pre-WWII.

	$2,400	$1,825	$1,600	$1,400	$1,200	$1,075	$950

MODEL 202 — similar to 201, except with false sideplates, higher quality wood, more profuse engraving, pre-WWII.

	$2,800	$2,400	$2,035	$1,700	$1,450	$1,200	$1,050

MODEL 202E — similar to 202, with auto ejectors, pre-WWII.

	$3,200	$2,800	$2,485	$2,050	$1,700	$1,425	$1,200

MODEL 203E O/U — similar to 202E except better engraving and wood.

	$4,000	$3,400	$2,900	$2,500	$2,100	$1,800	$1,425

MODEL 204E O/U — similar to 203E, but fine English scroll engraving and Merkel sidelocks, ejectors, pre-WWII.

	$5,650	$4,900	$4,300	$3,850	$3,300	$2,750	$2,100

MODEL 300 O/U — 12, 16, 20, 24, 28, or 32 ga., various lengths and choke ribbed barrels, Merkel-Anson boxlock, Kersten double cross bolt, two underlugs, scalloped frame, either English or pistol grip style stock, cocking indicators, pre-WWII.

	$2,100	$1,900	$1,700	$1,550	$1,375	$1,200	$1,050

This model is usually encountered without engraving and has standard wood.

MODEL 300E — similar to 300, with auto ejectors, pre-WWII.

	$2,500	$2,250	$1,900	$1,750	$1,500	$1,350	$1,175

This model is usually encountered without engraving and has standard wood.

MODEL 301 — similar to 300, but more profusely engraved and better grade wood pre-WWII.

	$5,250	$4,250	$3,995	$3,500	$3,000	$2,600	$2,150

MODEL 310E — similar to 300, with auto ejectors, pre-WWII.

	$6,250	$5,300	$4,450	$3,900	$3,400	$3,000	$2,550

MODEL 302 — similar to 301, but has auto ejectors and more elaborate ornamentation, false sideplates and better grade wood.

	$10,500	$8,500	$6,500	$5,750	$4,900	$4,150	$3,400

MODEL 304E O/U — special order version of 303E, higher quality and more ornamentation, top of Merkel O/U line.

	$16,500	$12,000	$10,500	$8,750	$7,500	$6,250	$5,000

MODEL 130 SxS — all standard gauges, barrel lengths and chokes, Anson & Deeley action with false side plates, boxlock, auto ejectors, English style or pistol grip stock, elaborate game scenes and arabesque engraving, pre-WWII.

	$12,000	$9,500	$7,500	$6,350	$5,400	$4,600	$3,950

MODEL 127 SxS — all standard gauges, barrel lengths and chokes, H&H style hand detachable sidelocks, auto ejectors, double triggers, pistol or English style stock elaborately engraved, this is a best grade gun, pre-WWII.

	$21,500	$16,500	$12,500	$10,000	$8,800	$7,000	$5,750

Grading	100%	98%	95%	90%	80%	70%	60%

SHOTGUNS: SxS RECENT IMPORTATION

Imported exclusively by Armes de Chasse located in Chadds Ford, PA, 19317.

Prices below reflect the recent devaluation of the U.S. dollar against the German Deutschmarke. While the manufacturer's suggested retails have gone up considerably, prices for used specimens (98% or less original condition) have not increased proportionately, and in some cases, have changed very little.

MODEL 8 — 12, 16 (disc.), or 20 ga., case hardened scalloped boxlock action with light engraving, Greener crossbolt with chopper lump extension, extractors, SST (current) or DT, standard walnut with checkering, pistol grip or English style stock, sling swivels (disc. 1992).

Mfg.'s Sug. Retail	$1,295	$1,100	$950	$795	$700	$625	$550	$475

MODEL 47E — 12, 16, or 20 ga., case hardened scalloped boxlock action with chopper lump extension and Greener crossbolt, 26 (disc.), 26¾, or 28 in. barrels, SST (current) or DT, ejectors, deluxe checkered walnut, pistol grip or English style stock, sling swivels (disc. 1992), 6-7 lbs.

Mfg.'s Sug. Retail	$1,595	$1,325	$1,100	$950	$850	$750	$650	$550

MODEL 76E — top-of-the-line boxlock shotgun. Importation disc. 1992.

	$2,600	$2,100	$1,850	$1,600	$1,325	$995	$775

Last Mfg.'s Sug. Retail was $3,500.

MODEL 147 — 12, 16, or 20 ga., 26¾ or 28 in. barrels, Anson & Deeley boxlock, any choke, SST (current) or DT, extractors, straight or pistol grip stock, hunting scene engraved.

Mfg.'s Sug. Retail	$1,795	$1,525	$1,225	$1,000	$875	$750	$650	$550

Add $200 for H&H style auto ejectors (Model 147E).

MODEL 122 — 12, 16, or 20 ga., Anson & Deeley boxlock action with silver grayed false sideplates, H&H ejectors, SST or DT, fine hunting scenes with arabesque engraving, pistol grip or English style stock. Importation began 1993.

Mfg.'s Sug. Retail	$3,195	$2,725	$2,300	$1,995	$1,700	$1,400	$1,100	$995

MODEL 122E — 12, 16, or 20 ga., coin finished sidelock action with Greener crossbolt and chopper lump extension, cocking indicators, ejectors, DTs, deluxe game scene engraving. Importation disc. 1991.

	$3,200	$2,800	$2,250	$1,950	$1,650	$1,375	$995

Last Mfg.'s Sug. Retail was $3,500.

MODEL 147S — 12, 16, 20, 28 (disc.), or .410 (disc.) ga., coin finished sidelock action with Greener crossbolt and chopper lump extension, 25½ (disc.), 26 (disc.), 26¾, or 28 in. barrels, ejectors, ST (current) or DT, deluxe game scene engraving, 6-7 lbs.

Mfg.'s Sug. Retail	$5,195	$4,675	$3,950	$3,450	$3,000	$2,500	$2,100	$1,800

Add $995 for 28 or .410 ga. (mfg. 1992 only).

MODEL 247S — 12, 16, or 20 ga., similar to Model 147S, except has deluxe scroll engraving. Importation disc. 1991, resumed 1993.

Mfg.'s Sug. Retail	$6,895	$6,375	$4,450	$3,650	$3,150	$2,625	$2,175	$1,850

MODEL 347S — 12, 16, or 20 ga., similar to Model 247S, except has more elaborate engraving and better walnut. Importation disc. 1991, resumed 1993.

Mfg.'s Sug. Retail	$7,895	$7,000	$4,850	$3,950	$3,350	$2,775	$2,275	$1,925

MODEL 447S — similar to Model 347S, except has smaller type of scroll engraving. Importation disc. 1991, resumed 1993.

Mfg.'s Sug. Retail	$8,995	$7,750	$5,350	$4,250	$3,550	$2,900	$2,400	$2,000

Grading	100%	98%	95%	90%	80%	70%	60%

MODEL 47S — 12, 16, 20, 28 (disc.), or .410 (disc.) ga., coin finished sidelock action with scroll engraving, Greener crossbolt, ST (current) or DT, deluxe walnut stock (with cheek piece) and forearm, sling swivels (disc. 1992).

Mfg.'s Sug. Retail	$4,195	$3,675	$3,200	$2,700	$2,300	$1,975	$1,625	$1,475

Add $995 for 28 or .410 ga. (mfg. 1992 only).

SHOTGUNS: O/U CURRENT IMPORTATION

MODEL 200E BOXLOCK — 12, 16, or 20 ga., case hardened scalloped boxlock action with minor scroll engraving, 26 (disc.), 26¾, or 28 in. barrels, checkered European walnut stock and forearm, ejectors, SST or DT, pistol grip or English style stock, solid rib, 6-7 lbs.

Mfg.'s Sug. Retail	$3,395	$3,000	$2,500	$2,050	$1,850	$1,600	$1,300	$1,100

⚔ **Model 200ES Skeet** — 12 ga. only, 26¾ in. VR barrels bored skeet/skeet. Importation began 1993.

Mfg.'s Sug. Retail	$4,995	$4,550	$3,950	$3,500	$3,000	$2,500	$2,100	$1,625

⚔ **Model 200ET Trap** — 12 ga. only, 30 in. VR barrels bored full/full (other choke configurations available upon request).

Mfg.'s Sug. Retail	$4,775	$4,350	$3,750	$3,300	$2,800	$2,300	$2,000	$1,550

MODEL 201E — similar to Model 200E, except has coin finished action with light game scene engraving.

Mfg.'s Sug. Retail	$4,195	$3,650	$3,000	$2,400	$2,100	$1,775	$1,425	$1,200

⚔ **Model 201ES Skeet** — 12 ga. only, 26¾ in. VR barrels bored skeet/skeet. Importation began 1993.

Mfg.'s Sug. Retail	$5,595	$5,050	$4,550	$3,850	$3,350	$2,850	$2,250	$1,650

⚔ **Model 201ET Trap** — 12 ga. only, 30 in. VR barrels bored full/full (other choke configurations available upon request).

Mfg.'s Sug. Retail	$5,395	$4,875	$4,350	$3,750	$3,300	$2,800	$2,200	$1,600

MODEL 202E — similar to 201E, except has fine hunting scenes with arabesque engraving on silver false sideplates. Importation began 1993.

Mfg.'s Sug. Retail	$7,995	$7,225	$6,250	$5,100	$4,300	$3,700	$3,350	$2,850

⚔ **Model 200ES Skeet** — 12 ga. only, 26¾ in. VR barrels bored skeet/skeet. Importation began 1993.

Mfg.'s Sug. Retail	$4,995	$4,550	$3,950	$3,500	$3,000	$2,500	$2,100	$1,625

⚔ **Model 200ET Trap** — 12 ga. only, 30 in. VR barrels bored full/full (other choke configurations available upon request).

Mfg.'s Sug. Retail	$4,775	$4,350	$3,750	$3,300	$2,800	$2,300	$2,000	$1,550

MODEL 203E SIDELOCK — 12, 16, or 20 ga. (24, 28, and 32 ga.'s were once available but are now disc.), 26 (disc.), 26¾, or 28 in. barrels, VR, H&H ejectors, SST (current) or DT, elaborate scroll engraving on coin finished receiver, sidelock screws are H&H style but the removable sidelocks are not, choice of English or pistol grip stock, 6-7 lbs.

Mfg.'s Sug. Retail	$9,695	$8,250	$5,650	$4,500	$3,650	$3,000	$2,500	$2,150

⚔ **Model 203ES Skeet** — 12 ga. only, 26¾ in. VR barrels bored skeet/skeet. Importation began 1993.

Mfg.'s Sug. Retail	$9,795	$8,325	$5,700	$4,525	$3,650	$3,000	$2,500	$2,150

Grading	100%	98%	95%	90%	80%	70%	60%

Model 203ET Trap — 12 ga. only, 30 in. VR barrels bored full/full (other choke configurations available upon request).

Mfg.'s Sug. Retail	$9,795	$8,325	$5,700	$4,525	$3,650	$3,000	$2,500	$2,150

MODEL 303E — similar to 203E, except H&H type with hidden thumbnail detachable sidelocks, double underlugs, more ornamentation and better wood.

Mfg.'s Sug. Retail	$21,295	$17,750	$15,000	$12,000	$9,750	$8,250	$7,000	$5,800

MODEL 304E (LUXUS GRADE) — available in SXS, O/U, Drilling, or Combo configuration, top-of-the-line Merkel with extensive engraving and typically stock carving (with or without inlays).

Values generally start at $16,500 and go up according to engraving and stock work.

Luxus variations are also encountered in the 201 and 203 series in addition to older pre-war models.

SHOTGUNS: SPORTING CLAYS COMPETITION

MODEL 47LSC SxS SPORTING CLAYS — 12 ga. only, features Anson & Deeley boxlock action with scroll engraved case hardened receiver, 28 in. barrels with Briley screw-in chokes, H&H style ejectors, SST adj. for length of pull, select grade checkered walnut stock with pistol grip and beavertail forearm, competition recoil pad.

Mfg.'s Sug. Retail	$2,995	$2,725	$2,400	$2,050	$1,725	$1,450	$1,125	$925

MERRILL

SPORTSMAN SINGLE-SHOT PISTOL — .22 S, L, or LR, .22 WMR, .22 Rem. Jet., .22 Hornet, 30 Herrett, .38 Spl., .357 Mag., .256 Win. Mag., .45 Colt, .44 Mag., or .30-30 cal., 9 in. barrel, hinged break open available, smooth walnut grips.

	$650	$575	$525	$450	$395	$350	$300

Add $70 for interchangeable barrels.
Add $25 for wrist support.

MERWIN HULBERT & CO.

Headquarters located in New York, NY from 1874-1891. Manufactured by Hopkins & Allen Manufacturing Co.

Merwin Hulbert & Co. were designers and promoters who created a revolver that had such advanced features as an automatic ejection system, streamlined appearance, and ease of shooting.

Grading	100%	95%	80%	50%	20%	Traces	Grey

REVOLVERS

FIRST MODEL — .44-40 cal. various barrel lengths.

	$2,000	$1,600	$1,200	$900	$700	$600	$450

ENGRAVED .44-40 cals.

	$7,000	$6,000	$5,000	$4,000	$3,000	$2,000	$1,000

SECOND MODEL

	$1,800	$1,400	$1,000	$800	$600	$500	$450

ENGRAVED

	$7,000	$6,000	$5,000	$4,000	$3,000	$2,000	$1,000

Grading	100%	95%	80%	50%	20%	Traces	Grey
THIRD MODEL S.A.	$1,500	$1,200	$900	$700	$600	$500	$450
THIRD MODEL D.A.	$1,400	$1,100	$800	$600	$500	$400	$400
ENGRAVED	$6,000	$5,500	$4,500	$3,500	$2,500	$1,500	$1,000

This model is rare and only infrequently encountered.

FOURTH MODEL S.A. — 7 in. barrel.

	100%	95%	80%	50%	20%	Traces	Grey
	$10,000	$8,000	$6,000	$4,000	$3,000	$2,000	$1,000

This model is rare and only infrequently encountered.

FOURTH MODEL S.A. — 5½ in. barrel.

	100%	95%	80%	50%	20%	Traces	Grey
	$4,000	$3,200	$2,500	$2,000	$1,500	$1,100	$800

This model is rare and only infrequently encountered.

FOURTH MODEL D.A. — 5½ in. barrel.

	100%	95%	80%	50%	20%	Traces	Grey
	$3,000	$2,500	$2,000	$1,500	$1,000	$800	$600

This model is rare and only infrequently encountered.

FOURTH MODEL D.A. — 7 in. barrel.

	100%	95%	80%	50%	20%	Traces	Grey
	$9,000	$7,500	$5,500	$3,500	$2,500	$1,000	$800

This model is rare and only infrequently encountered.

FOURTH MODEL S.A. — 3½ in. barrel.

	100%	95%	80%	50%	20%	Traces	Grey
	$10,000	$8,000	$6,000	$4,000	$3,000	$2,000	$1,000

This model is rare and only infrequently encountered.

FOURTH MODEL D.A. — 3½ in. barrel.

	100%	95%	80%	50%	20%	Traces	Grey
	$9,000	$7,500	$5,500	$3,500	$2,500	$1,500	$800

This model is rare and only infrequently encountered.

POCKET PISTOLS

Add 25% for blued finish.
Add 25% for extra matching barrel.
Add $300 for pearl, ivory, or mottled grips.

POCKET ARMY S.A. THIRD MODEL

	100%	95%	80%	50%	20%	Traces	Grey
	$1,800	$1,400	$1,000	$800	$600	$500	$450

POCKET ARMY D.A.

	100%	95%	80%	50%	20%	Traces	Grey
	$1,500	$1,200	$900	$750	$550	$450	$400

POCKET ARMY FOURTH MODEL

	100%	95%	80%	50%	20%	Traces	Grey
	$9,000	$7,500	$5,500	$3,500	$2,500	$1,500	$800

This model is rare and only infrequently encountered.

.38 BIRD'S HEAD GRIP

	100%	95%	80%	50%	20%	Traces	Grey
	$1,000	$800	$600	$500	$450	$350	$300

This model is rare and only infrequently encountered.

Grading	100%	95%	80%	50%	20%	Traces	Grey
.38 SAW HANDLE							
	$800	$600	$500	$400	$300	$250	$200
.38 SINGLE ACTION							
	$2,000	$1,700	$1,400	$1,000	$700	$500	$300

This model is rare and only infrequently encountered.

1ST MODEL .38 CAL. 5 SHOT

	100%	95%	80%	50%	20%	Traces	Grey
⚔ Spur Trigger Bird's Head							
	$1,000	$800	$600	$500	$450	$350	$300

This model is rare and only infrequently encountered.

	100%	95%	80%	50%	20%	Traces	Grey
⚔ Spur Trigger Saw Handle							
	$800	$600	$500	$400	$300	$250	$200

2ND AND 3RD MODELS .38 CAL. 5 SHOT

	100%	95%	80%	50%	20%	Traces	Grey
⚔ Bird's Head Grips							
	$1,000	$800	$600	$500	$450	$350	$300

This model is rare and only infrequently encountered.

	100%	95%	80%	50%	20%	Traces	Grey
⚔ Saw Handle Double Action							
	$800	$600	$500	$400	$300	$250	$200

.32 CAL. LONG ON .38 CAL. FRAME 7 SHOT

	100%	95%	80%	50%	20%	Traces	Grey
	$1,200	$1,000	$900	$800	$700	$500	$400

This model is rare and only infrequently encountered.

.32 S&W 5 SHOT

	100%	95%	80%	50%	20%	Traces	Grey
	$600	$550	$400	$350	$300	$250	$200

.22 CAL. 7 SHOT

	100%	95%	80%	50%	20%	Traces	Grey
	$500	$450	$350	$250	$200	$150	$100

Add approx. 200% for engraved model.

FOREIGN S.A. .44 CAL.

	100%	95%	80%	50%	20%	Traces	Grey
⚔ Frontier Army							
	$1,800	$1,400	$1,000	$800	$600	$400	$300
⚔ Frontier Army D.A.							
	$1,600	$1,200	$900	$700	$500	$400	$300

FOREIGN S.A. .44 CAL. 7 IN.

	100%	95%	80%	50%	20%	Traces	Grey
	$1,500	$1,200	$800	$600	$500	$450	$400

FOREIGN S.A. .44 CAL. 3½ IN.

	100%	95%	80%	50%	20%	Traces	Grey
	$1,100	$700	$500	$400	$300	$250	$200

POCKET ARMY D.A.

	100%	95%	80%	50%	20%	Traces	Grey
	$1,300	$1,000	$600	$400	$300	$250	$200

MIIDA

Manufacturer located in Japan.

Grading	100%	98%	95%	90%	80%	70%	60%

MODEL 612 — O/U shotgun, 12 ga., 26 or 28 in. barrels, VR, various chokes, boxlock, auto ejectors, single selective trigger, checkered pistol grip stock. Mfg. 1972-1974.

	100%	98%	95%	90%	80%	70%	60%
	$880	$745	$660	$605	$550	$495	$440

MODEL 612 SKEET GUN — similar to 612, with 27 in. VR, skeet bore barrel, more elaborate engraving. Mfg. 1972-1974.

	100%	98%	95%	90%	80%	70%	60%
	$990	$855	$770	$715	$660	$605	$550

MODEL 2200T TRAP GUN — similar to 612, with 29¾ in. imp. mod. and full choke barrel, wide VR, 60% engraved coverage and select wood. Mfg. 1972-1974.

	100%	98%	95%	90%	80%	70%	60%
	$1,100	$935	$880	$825	$770	$715	$660

MODEL 2200S SKEET GUN — similar to 2200T, with 27 in. skeet bore barrel.

	100%	98%	95%	90%	80%	70%	60%
	$1,100	$935	$880	$825	$770	$715	$660

MODEL 2300 SERIES TRAP OR SKEET — similar to 2200, with more engraving. Mfg. 1972-1974.

	100%	98%	95%	90%	80%	70%	60%
	$1,320	$1,100	$990	$935	$880	$825	$715

MODEL GRT GRANDEE TRAP GUN — 12 ga., 29 in. full choke barrels, single selective trigger, auto ejector, sidelock with side plates, receiver fully engraved as well as breech ends of barrel, trigger guard and locking lever, gold inlaid, high grade select walnut stock. Mfg. 1972-1974.

	100%	98%	95%	90%	80%	70%	60%
	$3,150	$2,750	$2,250	$1,900	$1,675	$1,400	$1,175

MODEL GRS GRANDEE SKEET GUN — similar to GRT, with 27 in. skeet bored barrels.

	100%	98%	95%	90%	80%	70%	60%
	$3,300	$2,875	$2,350	$1,950	$1,725	$1,425	$1,200

MILLER, DAVID CO.

Custom rifle manufacturer located in Tucson, AZ since 1973.

The David Miller Co. is a custom rifle maker fabricating best quality bolt action rifles only. All guns are essentially built per individual custom order and the company should be contacted directly for more information and price quotations. Currently manufactured D. Miller rifles feature the new Winchester Model 70 Super Grade action. Used rifles have to be appraised one-at-a-time to ascertain up-to-date values. Several of Mr. Miller's rifles have sold for over $100,000, and almost any feature(s) can be special ordered to produce a truly one-of-a-kind firearm.

MIROKU SHOTGUNS

Manufacturer located in Miroku, Japan.

Shotguns marked Miroku only without another trademark listing represent that period of manufacture before Miroku began manufacturing shotguns for other companies (i.e. Charles Daly, SKB, Browning, and others). Most guns marked Miroku only were made on a limited basis and although somewhat rare, collector desirability to date has been minimal. Since model notations were not specified in most instances (many shotguns were made to test market demand), a model rundown is virtually impossible. Values can be approx. ascertained by comparing a Miroku shotgun of similar gauge, features, engraving/wood, and condition to an equivalent Japanese Charles Daly model.

Mitchell Arms, Inc.

MITCHELL ARMS, INC.

Manufacturer, importer and distributor located in Santa Ana, CA.
Distributor sales only.

PISTOLS

Grading	100%	98%	95%	90%	80%	70%	60%
AMERICAN EAGLE LUGER — 9mm Para., 4 in. barrel, stainless steel with toggle action, checkered American walnut grips, American Eagle version, contoured front grip strap.							
Mfg.'s Sug. Retail $695	$590	$475	$400	$350	$300	$260	$230
ROLLING BLOCK PISTOL — .22 LR, .22 Mag., .223, .357 Mag., or .45 LC cal., reproduction of the Remington Rolling Block design, 10 in. barrel. Mfg. 1991-92 only.							
	$340	$285	$240	$210	$185	$170	$150

Last Mfg.'s Sug. Retail was $395.

PISTOLS: HIGH STANDARD

Mitchell Arms began manufacturing High Standard pistols in 1993. All guns feature push button barrel takedown and usually, a choice between stainless steel or royal blue steel construction. Mitchell Arms is not responsible, nor do they have spare parts, for the older High Standard pistols manufactured in New Haven and East Hartford, CT.

CITATION II — .22 LR, 5½ or 7¼ in. fluted barrel, frame mounted bridge rear sight, checkered walnut grips with thumb rest, push button take down, stippled front and rear grip straps, adj. trigger, travel, and weight. Available in stainless or royal blue steel. Mfg. began 1993.							
Mfg.'s Sug. Retail $454	$375	$280	$245	$215	$190	$170	$150
OLYMPIC I.S.U. — .22 S, military grip style, 6¾ in. special barrel with internal stabilizer, adj. barrel weights, other features similar to Citation II, stainless steel or blue finish. Mfg. began 1993.							
Mfg.'s Sug. Retail $599	$500	$425	$375	$325	$275	$225	$195
SHARPSHOOTER II — .22 LR, 5½ in. bull barrel, standard trigger, adj. rear sight, smooth grip frame, stainless steel or blue finish. Mfg. began 1993.							
Mfg.'s Sug. Retail $364	$295	$270	$240	$210	$185	$160	$135
SPORT KING II — .22 LR, 4½ or 6¾ in. tapered barrel, military black checkered plastic grips, stainless steel only, adj. rear sight. Mfg. began 1993.							
Mfg.'s Sug. Retail $299	$250	$210	$185	$160	$135	$120	$110
TROPHY II — .22 LR, 5½ or 7¼ in. fluted barrel, military grips with full checkering and thumb rest, bridge rear sight, gold plated trigger safety and mag. release, stippled front and rear grip straps, stainless steel or royal blue finish. New 1993.							
Mfg.'s Sug. Retail $479	$390	$295	$260	$220	$190	$170	$150
VICTOR II — .22 LR, 4½ or 5½ in. full length VR barrel, checkered walnut grips with thumb rest, gold plated trigger, safety, mag. release, and side lock, rib mounted sights. New 1993.							
Mfg.'s Sug. Retail $554	$460	$395	$340	$295	$260	$230	$195

Add $40 for full length dove tail rib (5½ in. barrel only).
Add $79 for Weaver style base built into VR.

Grading	100%	98%	95%	90%	80%	70%	60%

PISTOLS: TOKAREV DESIGN

The models listed below are imported from Yugoslavia.

MODEL 57A — .30 Mauser, single action semi-auto, 9 shot mag., hammer block and mag. safety, all steel construction. Imported 1990 only.

	$240	$215	$180	$160	$145	$135	$120

Last Mfg.'s Sug. Retail was $280.

MODEL 70A — 9mm Para., otherwise similar to Model 57A. Imported 1990 only.

	$240	$215	$180	$160	$145	$135	$120

Last Mfg.'s Sug. Retail was $280.

88A OFFICERS MODEL — 9mm Para., newer slenderized variation issued to the Officers Corps., short slide and frame, finger extension mag. Imported 1990 only.

	$255	$225	$190	$165	$145	$135	$120

Last Mfg.'s Sug. Retail was $300.

SKORPION — .32 ACP only, single action, 4⅝ in. barrel, 20 or 30 shot mag., blue finish only. Mfg. Yugoslavia. Imported 1990 only.

	$615	$520	$480	$440	$395	$360	$330

Last Mfg.'s Sug. Retail was $740.

SPECTRE — 9mm, single action, 8 in. shrouded barrel, unique frame/barrel cooling system, 30 or 50 shot mag., approx. 4 lbs. Imported 1987-1988 only.

	$610	$515	$475	$440	$395	$360	$330

Last Mfg.'s Sug. Retail was $670.

⚮ **Spectre Carbine** — 9mm, carbine model with folding butt stock. Imported 1988 only.

	$610	$520	$480	$440	$395	$360	$330

Last Mfg.'s Sug. Retail was $680.

REVOLVERS

SINGLE ACTION ARMY — .22 LR (disc.), .357 Mag., .44 Mag. (disc.), .45 ACP (disc.), or .45 LC cal., 4¾, 5½, 6 (disc. 1993), or 7½ in. barrel lengths, hammer block safety mechanism, steel construction, case hardened frame, one piece walnut stock. Add $20 for adj. sights on some older models. New 1986.

⚮ **Cowboy Model** — .357 Mag., .44-40 (disc.), .45 ACP (disc.), or .45 LC cal., 4¾ in. barrel.

Mfg.'s Sug. Retail	$399	$300	$230	$195	$170	$155	$145	$135

Add $40 for nickel finish.
Add $50 for adj. rear sight (disc.).
Add $95 for steel back strap and trigger guard.
Add $150 for dual cylinder (includes either 9mm Para. or .45 ACP extra cylinder).

⚮ **U.S. Army Model** — similar to Cowboy Model, except has 5½ in. barrel.

Mfg.'s Sug. Retail	$399	$300	$230	$195	$170	$155	$145	$135

Add $40 for nickel finish.

⚮ **U.S. Cavalry Model** — similar to Cowboy Model, except has 7½ in. barrel.

Mfg.'s Sug. Retail	$399	$300	$230	$195	$170	$155	$145	$135

Add $40 for nickel finish.

⚮ **.44 Mag.** — .44 Mag. cal., fully adj. target sights. Disc. 1992.

	$425	$350	$295	$250	$200	$180	$165

Last Mfg.'s Sug. Retail was $495.

Grading	100%	98%	95%	90%	80%	70%	60%

⚎ **Rimfire Model** — .22 LR cal. Importation disc. 1989.

	100%	98%	95%	90%	80%	70%	60%
	$230	$200	$180	$160	$145	$130	$120

Add $30 for adj. rear sight.
Last Mfg.'s Sug. Retail was $280.

⚎ **Silhouette Model** — available with 10, 12, or 18 in. barrel in .44 Mag. or .45 LC cal. Importation disc. 1991.

	100%	98%	95%	90%	80%	70%	60%
	$395	$325	$260	$220	$195	$170	$155

Add $175 for shoulder stock (available with 18 in. barrel only).
Last Mfg.'s Sug. Retail was $450.
The shoulder stock is available with .44 Mag./.44-40 cals. only.

⚎ **Dual Cylinder** — available in either .22 LR/.22 Mag. (disc.), .22 LR/.22 Mag. stainless (disc. 1988), .357 Mag./9mm Para., .44 Mag./.44-40 (disc. 1991), or .45 LC/.45 ACP (new 1990). New 1986.

	Mfg.'s Sug. Retail	98%	95%	90%	80%	70%	60%
Mfg.'s Sug. Retail	$549	$475	$415	$365	$335	$300	$275	$250

Add $50 for adj. rear sight (disc.).
Add $39 for nickel finish.

⚎ **Stainless Model** — available in .22 LR or .357 Mag. (disc. 1987) only, adj. sights. Imported 1986-1988 only.

	100%	98%	95%
	$260	$225	$195

Add $25 for .357 Mag.
Last Mfg.'s Sug. Retail was $301.

BAT MASTERSON MODEL — .45 LC cal., 4¾ , 5½ or 7½ in. barrel with full ejector rod housing, nickel plated, one piece walnut stocks, hammer-block safety, rear sight is square notch in frame, two piece backstrap. Importation began 1989.

Mfg.'s Sug. Retail	$439	$375	$285	$240	$210	$185	$170	$150

Add $149 for extra .45 ACP cylinder.

MODEL 1875 REMINGTON — .357 Mag. or .45 LC cal., royal blue finish with color case hardened frame, walnut grips. Imported 1990-91.

		$345	$285	$245	$210	$185	$170	$150

Add $76 for nickel finish.
Add $51 for extra convertible .45 ACP cylinder.
Last Mfg.'s Sug. Retail was $399.

RIFLES: MODERN

M-16A1 — .22 LR, .22 Mag. (disc. 1987), or .32 ACP cal., patterned after Colt's AR-15. New 1987.

Mfg.'s Sug. Retail	$359	$280	$225	$185	$160	$150	$140	$130

Add $75 for .22 Mag. cal. or .32 ACP (disc. 1988).

CAR-15/22 — .22 LR, carbine variation of M-16 with shorter barrel and collapsible stock. New 1990.

Mfg.'s Sug. Retail	$359	$285	$240	$195	$160	$150	$140	$130

GALIL — .22 LR or .22 Mag. cal., patterned after Galil semi-auto paramilitary design rifle, choice of wood stock or folding stock (new 1992). New 1987.

Mfg.'s Sug. Retail	$359	$285	$240	$195	$160	$150	$140	$130

MAS — .22 LR or .22 Mag. cal., patterned after French MAS rifle. New 1987.

Mfg.'s Sug. Retail	$359	$285	$240	$195	$160	$150	$140	$130

Add $75 for .22 Mag. cal. (disc. 1988).

Grading	100%	98%	95%	90%	80%	70%	60%

PPS-50 — .22 LR cal., patterned after the Russian WWII PPS military rifle, full length barrel shroud, 20 shot banana clip, adj. rear sight, walnut stock. New 1989.

Mfg.'s Sug. Retail	$359	$285	$240	$195	$160	$150	$140	$130

Add $100 for 50 shot drum magazine.

AK-22 — .22 LR or .22 Mag. (new 1988) cal., copy of the famous Russian AK-47, fully adj. sights, built in cleaning rod, high quality European walnut stock, 20 shot clip mag. New 1985.

Mfg.'s Sug. Retail	$359	$285	$240	$195	$160	$150	$140	$130

AK-47 — 7.62 x 39 cal., copy of the original SKS AK-47, semi-auto, teak stock and forend, 30 shot steel mag., last shot hold open. Mfg. Yugoslavia. Imported 1986-1989.

	$595	$550	$495	$450	$400	$360	$310

Add $23 for steel folding butt stock.
Add $150 for 75 shot steel drum mag.
Last Mfg.'s Sug. Retail was $675.

.308 NATO AK-47 (M77B1) — .308 (7.62 NATO) cal., milled receiver, adj. gas port, otherwise similar to AK-47 except has scope rail, day/night Tritium sights, and 20 shot mag. Imported 1989 only.

	$900	$800	$700	$595	$525	$475	$425

Add $600 for military issue sniper scope and rings.
Last Mfg.'s Sug. Retail was $775.

M76 — similar to AK-47, except is 7.9mm cal. and has longer barrel and frame set up for scope mount, counter sniper design, 10 shot mag., mfg. to mil. specs. Imported 1986-1989.

	$1,725	$1,535	$1,350	$1,100	$900	$820	$760

Last Mfg.'s Sug. Retail was $1,995.

SKS-M59 — 7.62 x 39 cal., copy of the SKS-M59 standard rifle, full walnut stock, fully adj. sights, gas operated. Mfg. in Yugoslavia. Imported 1986-1989.

	$610	$525	$465	$410	$360	$315	$260

Last Mfg.'s Sug. Retail was $699.

R.P.K. — 7.62 x 39mm or .308 Win. cal., forged heavy barrel with cooling fins, teak stock, detachable bipod, mil. specs. Importation disc. 1992.

Mfg.'s Sug. Retail	$1,150	$1,050	$875	$725	$650	$575	$525	$475

Add $845 for .308 Win. cal.
Once inventory is depleted in this model, there will be no further importation.

MODEL M-90 — 7.62 x 39mm or .308 Win. cal., AK-47 type action, in various configurations (heavy barrel, folding or fixed stock, finned barrel, etc.), plastic thumbhole stock, 5 shot mag., limited importation from Yugoslavia 1991-92.

Mfg.'s Sug. Retail	$829	$750	$650	$550	$495	$450	$395	$350

Add $31 for folding stock.
Add $69 for .308 Win. cal. (wood stock only).
Once inventory is depleted in this model, there will be no further importation.

RIFLES: REPRODUCTIONS

HENRY RIFLE — .44-40 cal., polished brass frame, octagonal barrel, original loading system. Importation began 1990.

Mfg.'s Sug. Retail	$999	$840	$650	$585	$520	$465	$415	$375

Iron frame also available at extra charge.

Grading	100%	98%	95%	90%	80%	70%	60%

MODEL 1866 — .22 LR (disc.), .38 Spl. (disc.), or .44-40 cal., patterned after the Winchester Model 1866 rifle, solid brass frame, octagon barrel. Importation began 1990.

Mfg.'s Sug. Retail	$829	$715	$535	$465	$415	$375	$335	$295

This model is also available in a carbine variation.

MODEL 1873 — .22 LR (disc.), .38 Spl.(disc), .357 Mag. (disc.), .44-40 (disc.), or .45 LC cal., patterned after the Winchester 1873 rifle, octagon barrel, solid steel frame. Importation began 1990.

Mfg.'s Sug. Retail	$950	$810	$640	$550	$515	$465	$415	$375

This model was also available in a carbine variation until 1992.

MONTANA ARMORY, INC.

Manufacturer located in Big Timber, MT specializing in C. Sharps reproductions.

The Montana Armory, Inc. is currently manufacturing replicas of C. Sharps rifles/carbines and the Winchester Model 1885 single shot. They are available as black powder cartridge rifles. Most models are available in the following cals.: .40-50, .40-70, .40-90, .45-70, .45-90, .45-100, .45-110, .45-120, .50-70, .50-100, and .50-140. All models are authentically reproduced and high quality.

RIFLES: BLACK POWDER CARTRIDGE

MODEL 1874 LONG RANGE EXPRESS

Mfg.'s Sug. Retail	$995	$895	$800	$650	$550	$475	$410	$350

NEW MODEL 1874 SPORTING

Mfg.'s Sug. Retail	$995	$895	$800	$650	$550	$475	$410	$350

In addition to the 1874 Sporting Model, a custom long range target rifle or Scheutzen short range target rifle is available in this model.

NEW MODEL 1874 BOSS — features 34 in. No. 1 heavy tapered octagon barrel, vernier tang sight, straight grip stock with cheekrest and steel shotgun butt.
Please contact the factory to obtain a custom quotation on this model.

NEW MODEL 1875 SPORTING RIFLE — similar to New Model 1875 Classic, except has receiver with round crown.

Mfg.'s Sug. Retail	$850	$795	$725	$650	$575	$495	$325	$250

NEW MODEL 1875 CLASSIC RIFLE — receiver with octagon top, 26, 28, or 30 in. tapered full octagon barrel, straight grip stock with steel toe plate, 9½ lbs. New 1992.

Mfg.'s Sug. Retail	$1,075	$950	$825	$675	$550	$475	$410	$350

NEW MODEL 1875 SADDLE RIFLE — receiver with octagon crown, 26 in. barrel only.

Mfg.'s Sug. Retail	$825	$750	$675	$575	$475	$400	$350	$300

NEW MODEL 1875 BUSINSES RIFLE — receiver with round crown, 28 in. heavy tapered round barrel.

Mfg.'s Sug. Retail	$725	$650	$575	$500	$450	$375	$325	$275

Add $50 for barrel sights.

NEW MODEL 1885 HIGHWALL — .22 LR, .22 Hornet, .219 Zipper, .30-40 Craig, .32-40, .38-55, .40-65, or .45-70 cal., patterned after the Winchester Model 1885 single shot, falling block action, case colored receiver and small parts, 26-30 in. octagon barrel. New 1992.

Mfg.'s Sug. Retail	$1,095	$950	$825	$675	$550	$475	$410	$350

MONTGOMERY WARD

Catalog sales/retailer that has subcontracted various domestic and international manufacturers to private label various brand names under the Montgomery Ward conglomerate.

Montgomery Ward shotguns and rifles have appeared under various labels and endorsers, including Western Field, Ted Williams, and others. There have literally been hundreds of various models (shotguns and rifles) sold through the Montgomery Ward retail network. Most of these models were manufactured through subcontracts with both domestic and international firearms manufacturers. Typically, they were "spec." guns made to sell at a specific price to undersell the competition. Most of these models were derivatives of existing factory models with less expensive wood and perhaps missing the features found on those models from which they were derived.

To date, there has been very little interest in collecting Montgomery Ward guns, regardless of rarity. Rather than list Montgomery Ward models, a general guideline is that values generally are under those of their "1st generation relatives". As a result, prices are ascertained by the shooting value of the gun, rather than its collector value.

MORINI

Target Pistol Manufacturer located in Italy. Currently imported by Mandall Shooting Supplies located in Scottsdale, AZ. Previously imported and distributed by Osborne's, located in Cheboygan, MI.

PISTOLS: COMPETITION

Grading	100%	98%	95%	90%	80%	70%	60%

CM-80 STANDARD — .22 LR only, single shot, adj. grips, frame, and sights. Add $50 for left-hand model. Importation disc. 1989.

	100%	98%	95%	90%	80%	70%	60%
	$925	$825	$725	$650	$585	$520	$465

Last Mfg.'s Sug. Retail was $1,015.

⚡ **CM-80 Super Competition** — similar to CM-80 Standard, except has deluxe finish, and unique plexiglass front sighting system. Add $50 for left-hand model. Importation disc. 1989.

	100%	98%	95%	90%	80%	70%	60%
	$1,085	$920	$800	$690	$590	$520	$450

Last Mfg.'s Sug. Retail was $1,196.

MODEL CM-102 — .22 LR cal., advanced rapid fire competition pistol featuring updated ergonomic grips and flared triggerguard. New 1992.

		100%	98%	95%	90%	80%	70%	60%
Mfg.'s Sug. Retail	$1,695	$1,525	$1,250	$995	$895	$795	$695	$595

MOSSBERG, O.F. & SONS, INC.

Manufactured 1919-1966 in New Haven, CT, 1966-present in North Haven, CT. Oscar Mossberg developed an early reputation as a designer and inventor for the Iver Johnson, Marlin-Rockwell, Stevens and Shattuck Arms companies. In 1915, he began producing a 4-shot, .22 palm pistol known as the "Novelty," with revolving firing pin. After producing approx. 600 of these pistols, he sold the patent to C. S. Shattuck, which continued to manufacture under the name  "Unique." The first 600 had no markings except serial numbers, and were destined for export to South America. Very few of these original "Novelty" pistols survived in this country, and are extremely rare specimens.

Since 1985, O.F. Mossberg & Sons, Inc. has produced only shotguns and accessories. The publisher wishes to express thanks for the valuable Mossberg contributions provided by Victor and Cheryl Havlin, founders of the National Mossberg Collectors Association, and NMCA director Joseph S. Eisenlauer (specializing in .22 smoothbore rifles).

More information about the NMCA (including membership info.) can be found in the Firearms Associations section of this text.

Grading	100%	98%	95%	90%	80%	70%	60%

PISTOLS: DISC.

BROWNIE — .22 long rifle, top break open action, rotating firing pin, 4-bbl. derringer, double action, 4-shot, approx. 32,000 mfg. 1919-1932.

	100%	98%	95%	90%	80%	70%	60%
	$450	$300	$275	$250	$205	$175	$150

RIFLES: DISC.

MODEL K — .22 S, L and LR, tube mag., hammerless, 22 in. bbl., takedown, open sights, plain straight stock. Mfg. 1922-1931.

	$250	$225	$200	$175	$150	$100	$85

MODEL M — similar to Model K, except has 24 in. octagonal bbl. Mfg. 1928-1931.

	$285	$250	$200	$175	$150	$100	$85

MODEL S — similar to Model K, except has shorter mag. tube and 19¾ in. bbl., very rare. Mfg. 1927-1931.

	$350	$275	$225	$200	$175	$150	$135

MODEL L — .22 S, L and LR, falling block action, single shot, 24 in. takedown bbl., open sights, pistol grip stock. Mfg. 1929-1932.

	$450	$350	$300	$275	$200	$185	$165

MODEL L-1 — rare target version of Model L with Lyman 2A tang sight and factory sling.
Add $50 to Model L values.

MODEL R — .22 S, L and LR, bolt action, 24 in. round bbl., first tube feed, ivory bead front sight, open sporting bbl. sight. Mfg. 1930-1932.

	$250	$225	$200	$175	$150	$100	$85

MODEL B — .22 S, L and LR single shot, bolt action, 22 in. round tapered bbl. Mfg. 1930-1932.

	$165	$125	$100	$75	$60	$50	$35

MODEL C — .22 S, L and LR single shot, 24 in. bbl., ivory bead front sight, open sporting rear sight. Mfg. 1931-1932.

	$165	$125	$100	$75	$60	$50	$35

MODEL C-1 — target version of Model C, Lyman front and rear sights, leather sling and swivels, special walnut stock, rare.
Add $50 to Model C values.

MODELS 10, 14, 20, 21, 25, 25A, 125 — .22 S, L and LR, single shot models. Mfg. 1933-1938.

	$165	$125	$100	$75	$60	$50	$35

Add 25% to prices above for models equipped with aperture sights.

MODEL 26B — .22 S, L and LR, entirely new design in single shot rifles, easily identified by bolt handle at extreme rear of bolt, 26 in. tapered bbl., hooded ramp front sight, No. 4 rear peep, open bbl. sight, swivels. Mfg. 1938-1941.

	$165	$125	$100	$75	$60	$50	$35

MODEL 26-C — similar to Model 26B with less expensive sights. Mfg. 1938-1941.

	$140	$100	$85	$70	$55	$45	$35

MODEL 26M (OR B26M) — rare version of 26 series model with two-piece Mannlicher-style stock. Mfg. 1938.

	$185	$140	$125	$100	$85	$70	$55

Grading	100%	98%	95%	90%	80%	70%	60%

MODEL 30 — .22 S, L and LR, single shot, 24 in. bbl., rear peep and ramp front sights, swivels. Mfg. 1933-1935.

	100%	98%	95%	90%	80%	70%	60%
	$140	$100	$90	$75	$65	$55	$45

MODEL 34 — similar to Model 30, except with heavy stock, target style. Mfg. 1934-1935.

	$150	$110	$100	$85	$70	$55	$45

MODEL 35 — .22 single shot, first full target model, 26 in. heavy target bbl., walnut stock, hooded front ramp, No. 4 rear peep with adj. aperture, approx. 9½ lbs. Mfg. 1935-1937.

	$275	$225	$200	$175	$150	$125	$90

MODEL 35A — revised version of Model 35, with all-new "master action," approx. 8¼ lbs. Mfg. 1937.

	$275	$235	$210	$185	$160	$135	$110

Add 25% for Model 35A-LS with Lyman sights.

MODEL 40 — .22 caliber tubular repeater, 16 shot, 24 in. bbl., No. 3 Mossberg aperture sight, hooded ramp front sight, swivels, approx. 5 lbs. Mfg. 1933-1935.

	$125	$100	$90	$80	$70	$65	$60

MODEL 44 — similar to Model 40, but with heavier target stock, approx. 6 lbs. Mfg. 1934-1935.

	$150	$125	$100	$90	$80	$70	$65

MODEL 42 — .22 S, L and LR, first model with 7 rd. magazine, 24 in. bbl., front ramp, sporting bbl., rear aperture sights, 42 in. overall length, approx. 5 lbs. Mfg. 1935-1937.

	$125	$100	$90	$80	$70	$65	$60

MODEL 42A — redesign of Model 42, new master action with shorter bolt and receiver. Mfg. 1937-1938.

	$150	$125	$100	$90	$80	$70	$65

MODEL 42B — same basic specs. as Model 42A, approx. 6 lbs. Mfg. 1938-1941.

	$150	$125	$100	$90	$80	$70	$65

MODEL 42C — similar to Model 42B, with open bbl. and bead front sights. Mfg. 1938-1941.

	$110	$100	$90	$80	$65	$55	$45

MODEL 42M — .22 S, L and LR, 7-shot magazine, bolt action, two-piece Mannlicher-style stock, 23 in. bbl., 40 in. overall length, 6¾ lb., front ramp, open bbl., receiver aperture sights, trapdoor buttplate for extra mag. in butt stock. Mfg. 1940-1944.

	$175	$150	$135	$110	$100	$75	$50

Add $40 for extra magazine in butt stock.

MODEL 42M(a), 42M(b), 42M(c) — similar to Model 42M with minor changes in extractors and sights. Mfg. 1944-1950.

	$175	$150	$135	$110	$100	$75	$50

MODEL 42MB — military version of the Model 42M, approx. 50,000 mfg. for US and British troops as a training rifle. US Property marked with serial number, usually found w/o bbl. sight. Mfg. 1942-1943.

	$200	$175	$150	$135	$110	$100	$75

Add $50 for Lend-Lease models with British proofs.

MODEL L42A — left-handed version of Model 42A with true left handed aperture sight, walnut stock, 1¼ in. swivels. Mfg. 1937-1938.

	$225	$200	$175	$150	$135	$125	$100

Grading	100%	98%	95%	90%	80%	70%	60%

MODEL 43 — .22 S, L and LR, target rifle, 7-round magazine, external trigger adjustment, barrel 13/16 in., 26 in. long walnut stock with four-position 1¼ in. swivels in front, Lyman 17A front sight, Lyman 57 MS receiver peep sight, rare. Mfg. 1937-1938.

	$250	$225	$200	$185	$175	$150	$135

MODEL L43 — left-handed version of Model 43 target rifle with left-handed Lyman 57 MS rear aperture sight, rare. Mfg. 1937-1938.

	$350	$335	$300	$275	$250	$225	$200

Add $75 for models with true left-handed Mossberg scope.

MODEL 44B — .22 cal. target model, clip fed, 26 in. heavy bbl., 43 in. overall length, approx. 8 lbs., front ramp and No. 4 receiver aperture sights, four-position front swivels, walnut stock. Mfg. 1938-1941.

	$250	$225	$200	$185	$175	$150	$135

MODEL 44US — .22 cal. target model, 7 round magazine, bolt action, 26 in. heavy bbl., overall length 43 in., approx. 8½ lbs., ramp front sight with hood, rear aperture sight, detachable swivels. Mfg. 1943-45.

	$200	$185	$175	$165	$150	$135	$125

MODEL 44US (US PROPERTY MARKED) — used by all branches of military for target training, approx. 53,000 mfg. 1943-1944.

Add $60 to above values.

MODEL 44US(a), 44US(b), 44US(c), 44US(d) — same rifle as 44US with minor changes in sights and extractors. Mfg. 1944-1949.

	$200	$185	$175	$165	$150	$135	$125

MODEL 45 — .22 cal. S, L and LR, tube fed, bolt action, 24 in. heavy target bbl., overall length 42½ in., approx. 6¾ lbs., hooded front sight, sporting bbl. sight, receiver aperture sight. Mfg. 1935-1937.

	$175	$150	$135	$125	$100	$85	$65

MODEL 45-A — similar to Model 45 with newer, master action. Mfg. 1937-38.

	$175	$150	$135	$125	$100	$85	$65

MODEL L45-A — similar to Model 45-A, true left handed version. Mfg. 1937-1938.

	$225	$200	$175	$150	$135	$125	$100

MODEL 46 — .22 S, L and LR, tube fed, bolt action, 26 in. heavy bbl., overall 44½ in., beavertail walnut stock, hooded ramp front, rear aperture sight, 7½ lbs. Mfg. 1935-1937.

	$175	$150	$135	$125	$100	$85	$65

MODEL 46T — similar to Model 46 with heavier bbl. and stock. Mfg. 1936-1937.

	$200	$175	$150	$135	$125	$100	$75

MODEL 46A — similar to Model 46 with master action. Mfg. 1937-1938.

	$175	$150	$135	$125	$100	$85	$65

MODEL 46-ALS — similar to Model 46-A with Lyman 17A front sight and 57-MS rear aperture, rare. Mfg. 1937-1938.

	$225	$200	$175	$150	$125	$110	$100

MODEL L46-ALS — similar to Model 46-ALS with true left handed action and left-handed Lyman rear sight, very rare. Mfg. 1937-1938.

	$325	$300	$275	$250	$225	$200	$175

Grading	100%	98%	95%	90%	80%	70%	60%

MODEL 46B — .22 S, L and LR, tube fed, new streamlined design, 43⅓ in. overall, walnut stock, 7 lbs. Mfg. 1938-1945.

| | $150 | $135 | $110 | $100 | $85 | $75 | $65 |

MODEL 46B-T — heavy barrel and stock, target version of Model 46-B, rare. Mfg. 1938.

| | $200 | $175 | $150 | $135 | $110 | $95 | $85 |

MODEL 46M — .22 S, L and LR, bolt action, tube fed, with two-piece Mannlicher-style walnut stock, 23 in. bbl., overall 40 in., hooded front, sporting bbl., rear aperture sight, 7 lbs. Mfg. 1940-1945.

| | $185 | $150 | $135 | $125 | $110 | $95 | $80 |

MODEL 46M(a), 46M(b) — similar to Model 46M with minor changes in sights. Mfg. 1945-1952.

| | $185 | $150 | $135 | $125 | $110 | $95 | $80 |

MODEL 50 — .22 cal. semi-auto, tube fed through butt stock, 24 in. bbl., overall 43¾ in., hooded front sight, open bbl. sight, no swivels, 6¾ lbs. Mfg. 1939-1942.

| | $165 | $150 | $135 | $125 | $110 | $85 | $65 |

MODEL 51 — similar to Model 50 with receiver aperture sight, heavier, beavertail stock, q.d. swivels, 7¼ lbs. Mfg. 1939.

| | $165 | $150 | $135 | $125 | $110 | $85 | $65 |

MODEL 51M — similar to Model 51 with two-piece Mannlicher style walnut stock, 20 in. bbl, 40 in. overall, front ramp, rear aperture, sporting bbl. sights, 7 lbs. Mfg. 1939-1946.

| | $185 | $150 | $135 | $125 | $110 | $95 | $80 |

MODEL 140B — .22 S, L and LR, bolt action, clip fed, 24½ in. bbl., 42 in. overall, walnut stock, front ramp, sporting bbl., rear aperture sight, 5¾ lbs. Mfg. 1957-1958.

| | $165 | $150 | $135 | $125 | $110 | $85 | $65 |

MODEL 140K — similar to Model 140B with post front and no aperture sight. Mfg. 1955-1958.

| | $135 | $100 | $90 | $80 | $70 | $60 | $50 |

MODEL 142A — .22 S, L and LR, bolt action, 7 round clip, carbine model with fold down forearm, walnut stock with sling, 18 in. bbl., 27 in. overall length, rear aperture sight and military front sight, no bbl. sight, early models had "T" shaped bolt handles and wood forearms, later models had round knob bolt handle and black plastic forearm, 5 lbs. Mfg. 1949-1957.

| | $165 | $150 | $135 | $125 | $110 | $85 | $65 |

MODEL 142K — similar to Model 142A with less expensive sights, sporting barrel and post front type. No aperture sight. Mfg. 1953-1957.

| | $125 | $110 | $100 | $90 | $80 | $75 | $55 |

Grading	100%	98%	95%	90%	80%	70%	60%

MODEL 144 — .22 caliber, full target rifle, heavy 26 in. bbl., 43 in. overall length, 8 lbs., q.d. swivels, four-position front swivels, rear aperture, front ramp sights, "T" shaped bolt handle. Mfg. 1949-1954.

	$200	$185	$165	$150	$135	$125	$110

MODEL 144LS — similar to Model 144, with round knob handle, Lyman 57-MS aperture and 17-A front sight. Mfg. 1954-1960.

	$250	$235	$220	$200	$185	$165	$150

MODEL 144LS-A — similar to Model 144LS, with Mossberg S-130 rear aperture in place of Lyman 57-MS. Mfg. 1960-1979.

	$200	$185	$165	$150	$135	$125	$110

MODEL 144LS-B — last generation of 144 series, 27 in. bbl., 15/16 in. diameter, 44 in. overall length, new Mossberg S-331 aperture, Lyman 17-A front sight, 8½ lbs. Mfg. 1979-1985.

	$275	$250	$235	$210	$190	$175	$165

MODEL 146-B — .22 S, L and LR, bolt action, tube fed, capacity of 30S, 23L, 20LR, 26 in. bbl., overall length 43¼ in., ramp front sight, leaf bbl. and rear aperture sight, walnut Monte Carlo stock with cheek piece, QD swivels, adj. trigger, Schnabel forend, 7 lbs. Mfg. 1949-1954.

	$180	$150	$135	$125	$100	$85	$65

MODEL 146B-A — similar to Model 146-B, with different bbl. sight. Mfg. 1954-1958.

	$180	$150	$135	$125	$100	$85	$65

MODEL 151-K — .22 caliber semi-auto, butt fed, 24 in. bbl., overall 44 in., open sights, walnut Monte Carlo stock with cheek piece and Schnabel forend, 6 lbs. Mfg. 1950-1951.

	$160	$135	$110	$90	$80	$70	$60

MODEL 151(M) — .22 caliber semi-auto butt fed, capacity 15LR, 20 in. bbl., overall 40 in., two-piece Mannlicher-style walnut stock, QD swivels, steel butt plate, hooded ramp front, sporting rear, micro-click aperture sights, 7 lbs. Mfg. 1946-1947.

	$175	$150	$135	$125	$100	$85	$65

MODELS 151M(a), 151M(b), 151M(c) — similar to Model 151M with minor changes in butt plate and sights. Mfg. 1947-1958.

	$175	$150	$135	$125	$100	$85	$65

MODEL 152 — .22 caliber semi-auto, clip fed with 7 round capacity, carbine model with hinged, fold-down forend, Monte Carlo stock with adj. sling, 18 in. bbl., 27 in. overall, receiver aperture and military post front sights, 5 lbs. Mfg. 1948-1952.

	$175	$150	$135	$125	$100	$85	$65

MODEL 152K — similar to Model 152 with open sights. Mfg. 1950-1957.

	$150	$125	$110	$100	$90	$75	$50

MODEL 320B — .22 caliber single shot, junior target model, bolt action, new closed breech design, 24 in. bbl., overall 43½ in., 5¾ lbs., walnut finish Monte Carlo stock with swivels and pistol grip, front ramp, rear aperture and sporting bbl. sights. Mfg. 1960-1971.

	$165	$140	$125	$110	$85	$75	$55

MODELS 320K, 320K-A — similar to Model 320B with open sights, no swivels, later models marked 321, 321K. Mfg. 1960-1980.

	$105	$95	$80	$70	$60	$55	$50

Grading	100%	98%	95%	90%	80%	70%	60%

MODELS 340B, 340B-A — .22 S, L, LR, bolt action, 7 round clip magazine, 24 in. bbl., 43½ in. overall length, walnut, Monte Carlo stock with cheek piece and pistol grip, front ramp, sporting bbl., rear aperture sights, 6½ lbs. Mfg. 1958-1980.

	$165	$140	$125	$110	$85	$75	$55

MODELS 340K, 340K-A — similar to Model 340B with open sights, later models marked 341. Mfg. 1958-1980.

	$105	$95	$80	$70	$60	$55	$50

MODEL 340M — .22 caliber bolt action, clip fed, same operating design as other 340 series, with one-piece, walnut Mannlicher-style Monte Carlo stock with pistol grip and swivels, 18½ in. bbl., 38½ in. overall, open rear and bead front sights, rare, 5¼ lbs. Mfg. 1970-1972.

	$250	$235	$210	$200	$185	$175	$165

MODEL 342 — .22 S, L and LR, bolt action, clip fed, carbine model with hinged, black plastic, fold-down forend, walnut Monte Carlo stock with swivels and sling, 18 in. bbl., 38 in. overall, military post front and rear aperture sight, 5 lbs. Mfg. 1957-1959.

	$165	$140	$125	$110	$85	$75	$55

MODELS 342K, 342K-A — similar to Model 342 with open sights. Mfg. 1958-1971.

	$105	$95	$80	$70	$60	$55	$50

MODEL 344, 344K — .22 caliber bolt action, clip fed, walnut finish, checkered stock, 344K is carbine length. Mfg. 1985.

	$165	$140	$125	$110	$85	$75	$55

MODEL 346B — .22 S, L, and LR, bolt action tube feed, closed-breech design, walnut Monte Carlo stock with cheek piece, QD swivels, capacity 25S, 20L, 18LR, 24 in. bbl., 42½ in. overall, rear aperture, sporting bbl., hooded front ramp sights, 6½ lbs. Mfg. 1958-1960.

	$165	$140	$125	$110	$85	$75	$55

MODEL 346K, 346K-A — similar to Model 346B w/ open sights. Mfg. 1958-1968.

	$135	$120	$110	$100	$80	$70	$55

MODEL 350K — .22 caliber semi-auto, LR only, clip fed, walnut Monte Carlo stock with pistol grip and cheek piece, 23½ in. bbl., overall 43½ in., open sights, 6 lbs. Mfg. 1958-1960.

	$95	$85	$75	$65	$60	$50	$40

MODEL 350 K-A — similar to Model 350K with dovetail bbl. sight. Mfg. 1960-1968.

	$95	$85	$75	$65	$60	$50	$40

MODEL 351K — .22 LR semi-auto, tube fed through stock, walnut, Monte Carlo stock with pistol grip, 24 in. bbl., 43 in. overall, 6 lbs. Mfg. 1958-1960.

	$95	$85	$75	$65	$60	$50	$40

MODEL 351K-A — similar to Model 351K with dovetail bbl. sight. Mfg. 1960-68.

	$95	$85	$75	$65	$60	$50	$40

MODEL 352 — .22 LR, clip fed, carbine model with fold-down black plastic forend, walnut Monte Carlo stock, pistol grip, swivels, web strap, 18 in. bbl., overall 38 in., rear peep, post front sights, 5 lbs. Mfg. 1957-1959.

	$135	$120	$100	$85	$75	$65	$55

Grading	100%	98%	95%	90%	80%	70%	60%

MODELS 352K, 352 K-A, 352K-B — similar to Model 352 with open sights. Mfg. 1960-1971.

	100%	98%	95%	90%	80%	70%	60%
	$110	$95	$85	$75	$70	$65	$55

MODEL 377, "PLINKSTER" — .22 LR, semi auto, tube fed, synthetic stock with "thumb hole," capacity 15 rds., 20 in. bbl., overall 40 in., 6.25 lbs., equipped with 4X scope. Mfg. 1977-1979.

	$175	$150	$135	$100	$85	$75	$65

MODELS 380, 380S — same basic design as Model 377, only with solid, wood stock, open sights. Model 480 same in 1985. Mfg. 1980-1985.

	$135	$115	$100	$85	$75	$65	$55

MODEL 400 "PALAMINO" — .22 S, L and LR, lever action, tube fed, walnut, beaver tail stock and forearm, cross bolt safety, 24 in. bbl., overall length, 41 in., bead front, open rear sights, 5½ lbs. Mfg. 1959-1964.

	$225	$195	$170	$150	$135	$100	$85

Model 400-A similar to above in specs and value, dovetail.

MODEL 402 — carbine version of Model 400, bbl. 20 in. Mfg. 1961-1971.

	$225	$195	$170	$150	$135	$100	$85

MODEL 430 — .22 LR semi-auto, tubular mag. under bbl. with capacity of 18 LR, walnut checkered Monte Carlo stock and checkered forend, 24 in. bbl., overall length 43½ in., open sights, 6.25 lbs. Mfg. 1970-1971.

	$135	$115	$100	$85	$75	$65	$55

MODEL 432 — similar to Model 430 above with 20 in. bbl., straight grip, smooth stock and forend, walnut finish. Mfg. 1970-1971.

	$115	$100	$85	$75	$65	$60	$50

MODEL 472 — .30-30 or .35 Rem. cal., lever action carbine, 20 in. barrel, open sights, pistol grip or straight stock, saddle ring on straight model. Mfg. 1972-disc.

	$180	$155	$145	$130	$120	$110	$90

MODEL 472 RIFLE — similar to Carbine, except 24 in. barrel, pistol grip stock. Mfg. 1974-1976.

	$195	$165	$155	$145	$130	$120	$100

MODEL 472 BRUSH GUN — similar to Carbine, except 18 in. barrel, straight stock only. Mfg. 1974-1976.

	$195	$165	$155	$145	$130	$120	$100

MODEL 472 ONE IN FIVE THOUSAND — similar to Brush Gun, except Indian scene etched on receiver, brass butt plate, saddle ring and barrel bands, select stock, only 5,000 mfg., 1974.

	$415	$210	$195	$175	$165	$145	$120

MODEL 479 PCA — .30-30 lever action, 20 in. barrel, 6 shot capacity.

	$195	$135	$120	$110	$95	$85	$75

MODEL 479 RR — limited edition "Roy Rodgers" signature model, gold trigger, barrel bands, 5,000 total mfg. New 1983.

	$350	$275	$215				

Grading	100%	98%	95%	90%	80%	70%	60%

MODEL 479 — .30-30 cal. only, lever action, 6 shot tube mag., 20 in. barrel with adj. sights, 7 lbs. Mfg. 1985 only.

| | $190 | $175 | $160 | $150 | $145 | $140 | $135 |

Last Mfg.'s Sug. Retail was $232.

Mossberg also has made several .22 bolt action and semi-auto sporters that are in the $115 - $130 price range. While they are good shooting models, they are not covered in this section as they are not collectible.

MODEL 620K — .22 WMR Magnum, single shot, bolt action, walnut Monte Carlo stock, pistol grip, cheek piece, sling swivels, 24 in. bbl., overall 44¾ in., open rear, post front sights, 6 lbs. Mfg. 1959-1960.

| | $150 | $135 | $115 | $100 | $85 | $75 | $65 |

MODEL 620K-A — similar to Model 620K with change in bbl. sight. Mfg. 1960-1968.

| | $150 | $135 | $115 | $100 | $85 | $75 | $65 |

MODELS 640K, 640K-S — similar to 620 series, but 5 shot clip repeater. Mfg. 1959-1984.

| | $195 | $150 | $135 | $125 | $105 | $90 | $75 |

MODEL 640KS — similar to Model 640K with deluxe checkered stock and gold trigger. Mfg. 1960-1968.

| | $225 | $200 | $185 | $150 | $135 | $120 | $110 |

MODEL 640M — full length, Mannlicher-styled stock, version of 640, checkered stock, Monte Carlo, cheek piece, pistol grip, swivels and leather strap, heavy receiver, jeweled bolt, 20 in. bbl., overall 40¾ in., open rear sights, bead front, 6 lbs. Mfg. 1971.

| | $250 | $225 | $200 | $185 | $175 | $165 | $150 |

MODEL 642K — .22 mag. WMR, carbine style, bolt action, 5 rd. clip, fold-down forend, walnut stock with web sling, 18 in. bbl., overall 38¼ in., open bbl. and bead front sights, 5 lbs. Mfg. 1960-1968.

| | $225 | $200 | $185 | $150 | $135 | $120 | $110 |

MODEL 800 — .222, .22-250, .243, or .308 cal., bolt action, 22 in. barrel, folding sight, checkered pistol grip stock. Mfg. 1967-disc.

| | $220 | $195 | $165 | $110 | $85 | $55 | $45 |

MODEL 800VT — similar to 800, except .222, .22-250, or .243 cal., 24 in. heavy barrel, no sights. Mfg. 1968-disc.

| | $220 | $195 | $165 | $110 | $85 | $55 | $45 |

MODEL 800M — similar to 800, except 20 in. barrel, full length stock, spoon bolt handle. Mfg. 1969-1972.

| | $275 | $240 | $220 | $205 | $175 | $160 | $145 |

MODEL 800D — similar to 800, with roll-over combination and cheek piece, checkered stock with rosewood forearm tip and pistol cap, no .222 available. Mfg. 1970-1973.

| | $290 | $265 | $230 | $195 | $175 | $165 | $140 |

MODEL 810 — .270, .30-06, 8mm Rem. Mag., or .338 Win. Mag. cal., bolt action, 22 or 24 in. barrel, leaf sight, checkered Monte Carlo stock. Mfg. 1970-disc.

| | $285 | $260 | $220 | $175 | $160 | $150 | $130 |

Grading	100%	98%	95%	90%	80%	70%	60%

RIFLES: RECENT MFG.

In 1985, Mossberg purchased the parts inventory and importing rights for those rifles that Smith & Wesson imported from Howa of Japan. These new models were identical to those models which S&W disc.

MODEL 1500 MOUNTAINEER GRADE I — .223, .243, .270, 30-06, or 7mm Mag. cal., bolt action, 22 or 24 (7mm Mag. only) in. barrel, 5 or 6 shot mag., available with or without sights, hardwood stock is satin finished, blued finish, about 7 lbs. 10 oz. Imported 1986-87 only. Add $15 for 7mm Rem. Mag. cal., $25 for iron sights.

	$285	$250	$225	$195	$180	$165	$150

Last Mfg.'s Sug. Retail was $335.

Model 1500 Varmint — .22-250, .223, or .308 cal., similar to Model 1500 Grade I, except has 24 in. heavy barrel only, Monte Carlo stock. Imported 1986-87 only. Add $10 for parkerized finish (oil finished stock with swivels — not available in .22-250 cal.).

	$360	$300	$270	$235	$205	$190	$175

Last Mfg.'s Sug. Retail was $457.
Blued finish and high gloss wood finish available with .22-250 or .223 cal. only. Parkerized variation is available in .223 or .308 cal. only (matte wood finish, includes swivels).

MODEL 1500 MOUNTAINEER GRADE II — similar to Grade I Mountaineer, except has select checkered American walnut stock. Also available in .300 or .338 Win. Mag. cal. Imported 1986-87 only.

	$315	$270	$235	$205	$190	$175	$160

Add $15 for Mag. cals.
Add $25 for iron sights.
Last Mfg.'s Sug. Retail was $368.

MODEL 1550 — similar to Model 1500, except has detachable mag. and available in standard cals. (.243, .270, or .30-06), with or without sights. Imported 1986-87 only. Add $24 for iron sights.

	$330	$280	$245	$210	$190	$175	$160

Last Mfg.'s Sug. Retail was $391.

MODEL 1700 LS — .243, .270, or .30-06 cal., no sights, jeweled bolt body and knurled bolt handle, detachable mag., Schnabel forend, deluxe checkering, 7 lbs. Imported 1986-87 only.

	$405	$365	$310	$275	$240	$205	$190

Last Mfg.'s Sug. Retail was $492.

"TARGO" SHOTGUN/RIFLES

These dual-purpose smoothbore rifles were designed to fire both .22 RF bullets and shotshell ammunition. Targo barrels are threaded either externally (Models 26T, 42TR, 42T, B42T) or internally (Models 320TR, 340TR) at the muzzle for attachment of rifled and smoothbore adapters which enable the shooter to use the gun as a standard rifle, or (with the smoothbore adapter installed) as a miniature shotgun. Mossberg produced a line of Targo accessories including a barrel-mounted miniature clay target launcher, a hand trap, a target carrier, clay targets, and a target catching net. The presence of one or more of these accessories augments the value of any model Targo gun. Prices quoted below are for guns with all the listed features and accessories present.

MODEL 26-T SINGLE SHOT — single-shot, bolt action, safety thumb lever located at rear of bolt, black plastic buttplate and contoured black plastic trigger guard, rifle-style ("U" notch) rear sight with screw adjustments for windage and elevation, high-posted shotgun-style front bead sight with removable sight hood, smoothbore and rifled screw-on barrel adapters and spanner wrench for adapter removal and installation, stock provided with sling swivels, takedown screw has retaining bail to facilitate removal by hand. The scarcest of all Targo guns mfg. 1940-1942 (only 873 mfg.).

	$600	$450	$375	$335	$280	$245	$220

100% price is estimated since an example would be extremely rare.

Grading	100%	98%	95%	90%	80%	70%	60%

MODEL 42TR BOLT ACTION REPEATER — box magazine (7-round) fitted with adapter screw to enable firing of .22 Short cartridges, same features as Model 26T except stock lacks sling swivels, produced during the early and late 1940's. Early (pre-War) guns had the bolt knob nickeled and the forend necks down toward muzzle. Later (post- War) guns often have blued bolt knobs. Also, the takedown screw is slotted and lacks retracting bail, a blued metal magazine plate is installed on underside of forend, and the forend is shorter than on pre- War guns and does not neck down toward the muzzle. The most common of all Targo guns. Both early and late versions of this model are comparably priced.

	$415	$345	$295	$280	$245	$190	$175

MODEL 42T BOLT ACTION REPEATER — identical to the Model 42TR, except was not supplied originally with rifled adapter, rear sight, or front sight hood, apparently produced only in the late 1940's, less frequently encountered than the Model 42TR. Examples in 95%+ condition are uncommon.

	$440	$325	$310	$295	$260	$235	$200

MODEL B42T BOLT ACTION REPEATER — identical to the Model 42TR, except has stock sling swivels and metal buttplate with trapdoor for magazine storage. Also, the gun was supplied with 15-round box magazine in addition to the standard 7-round clip. A comparatively scarce model marketed exclusively through mail order stores (e.g., Spiegel) during the late 1940s.

	$465	$385	$350	$325	$285	$250	$210

MODEL 320TR SINGLE SHOT BOLT ACTION — automatic safety with thumb lever located on right side of receiver, black plastic buttplate and contoured black plastic trigger guard. Rifle-style ("U" notch) rear sight adjustable for elevation (via sliding wedge) and windage (by deflecting sight arm laterally by hand). Sporting type vertical blade front sight. Gun supplied with rifled and smoothbore screw-in barrel adapters. A hand thrower for launching miniature clay targets as well as a wire target carrier were included with each gun. Marketed during 1961-1962 only (including Model 340TR mfg.). Some post-1962 dealer orders apparently were filled using guns assembled from existing parts. This model is rarer than the 340TR.

	$320	$240	$225	$190	$150	$135	$115

MODEL 340TR BOLT ACTION REPEATER — box magazine (7-round) features adjustable top bar to enable feeding of .22 S, L, and LR cartridges. Other features identical to Model 320TR.

	$345	$265	$240	$215	$165	$145	$125

SHOTGUNS

In 1985, Mossberg purchased the parts inventory and manufacturing rights for the shotguns that Smith & Wesson discontinued in 1984. These new models (manufactured in Japan) are identical to those models which S&W discontinued. Parts and warranties are not interchangeable.

MODEL 200K — slide action shotgun, 12 ga., 28 in., select choke, plain pistol grip stock, black nylon slide handle. Mfg. 1955-1959.

	$130	$110	$100	$90	$65	$55	$40

MODEL 200D — similar to 200K, except interchangeable choke tubes (2). Mfg. 1955-1959.

	$130	$110	$100	$90	$65	$55	$40

Grading	100%	98%	95%	90%	80%	70%	60%

BOLT ACTION MODELS — 12, 20, or .410 ga., 3 shot mag., 26, 28, or 38 in. barrel.

	100%	98%	95%	90%	80%	70%	60%
	$125	$110	$100	$90	$75	$65	$55

Add $20 for 38 in. barrel.
Add 25% for .410 ga. (disc. 1985).
Models include the 500, 590, 595 (2 shot mag.), and others.
Last Mfg.'s Sug. Retail was $135.

HOME SECURITY .410 — .410 ga. only, 18½ in. barrel with spreader choke, Model 500 slide-action, matte beaded metal finish, synthetic field stock with pistol grip forearm, 6¼ lbs. New 1990.

Mfg.'s Sug. Retail	$253	$225	$200	$185	$165	$145	$125	$110

⅟ **Laser Home Security .410** — includes laser sighting device in right front of forearm. New 1990.

Mfg.'s Sug. Retail	$451	$400	$350	$315	$280	$250	$225	$195

MODEL 500 REGAL SERIES — 12 or 20 ga., slide action, 26 or 28 in. barrel, select checkered walnut, VR. Add $19 for Accu-choke. Importation disc. 1987.

	100%	98%	95%	90%	80%	70%	60%
	$240	$195	$175	$165	$155	$145	$135

Add $39 for Combo pack (includes 1 extra 24 in. slugster barrel).
Last Mfg.'s Sug. Retail was $286.

MODEL 500 FIELD GRADE — 12, 20, or .410 ga., slide action, 24 in. (with rifle sights) or 20-28 in. barrel (with various chokes), upper receiver slide safety, C Lect (disc.) & Accu choke(s), checkered hardwood pistol grip stock after 1973. Mfg. 1962-present.

Mfg.'s Sug. Retail	$253	$215	$180	$155	$135	$120	$110	$100

Add $6 for .410 ga.
Subtract $30 if without VR (disc.).
Add $10 for C Lect (disc.).
Add $21 for Accu II chokes (VR barrel only).
Subtract $7 for fixed choke barrel.

⅟ **Model 500 Slugster** — 12 or 20 ga., 24 in. cyl. or rifled bore barrel, choice of sights, walnut finished hardwood stock and forearm.

Mfg.'s Sug. Retail	$266	$220	$185	$155	$135	$120	$110	$100

Add $34 for rifled bore barrel.
Add $61 for rifled bore barrel with scope base and dual comb stock.

⅟ **Model 500 Bantam** — 20 or .410 ga. (new 1991) only, 22 in. (20 ga.), 24 in. fixed choke barrel (.410 ga.), or 26 in. VR barrel with Accu-choke(s), blue or blue matte (Bantam Jake with Realtree Camo finish in 20 ga./22 in. VR barrel only), 20 ga. has walnut finish stock and .410 ga. has synthetic stock (both stocks are tailored for youth dimensions), 6.9 lbs. New 1990.

Mfg.'s Sug. Retail	$274	$225	$185	$155	$135	$120	$110	$100

Subtract $16 for .410 ga.
Add $44 for Bantam Jake configuration.
Subtract $21 if with only one Accu-choke.

⅟ **Model 500 Camo** — 12 ga. only, parkerized camo (OFM Camo became standard late 1991) metal and stock finish, 24-30 in. VR barrel (choice of cylinder bore with rifle sights or Accu-II chokes), includes swivels, camo sling, and drilled and tapped receiver, older Speedfeed stock (disc. 1990) holds 4 extra shells. New 1986.

Mfg.'s Sug. Retail	$299	$250	$195	$150				

Subtract $20 if without Accu-II choke system.
Add $30 for speedfeed in synthetic stock (disc. 1990).
Add approx. $54 for Camo Combo (includes extra 24 in. slug barrel).
Add $54 for Turkey Model with 24 in. VR barrel with Ghost Ring Sight.
Accu-chokes became standard in 1991.

Grading	100%	98%	95%	90%	80%	70%	60%

Model 500 Combo — includes a wide variety of extra barrel combinations including slug barrel options, prices vary slightly depending on the configuration (gauge/barrel/choke set-up). Values listed below are approximations since there are nine different combinations available.

Mfg.'s Sug. Retail	$306	$265	$235	$200	$175	$155	$145	$135

Subtract approx. $25-$30 if without VR.
Add $23-$53 for rifled bore slug barrel with integral scope base.

Model 500 Muzzleloader Combo— 12 ga. only, includes 24 in. (rifled bore only, new 1993) or 28 in. VR Accu-choke barrel and additional 24 in. .50 cal. muzzleloader conversion barrel with rifled bore and iron sights, walnut finished hardwood stock and forearm, 7.2 lbs. New 1991.

Mfg.'s Sug. Retail	$399	$325	$275	$240	$215	$185	$170	$155

Model 500 Quail Unlimited — 20 ga. only, 26 in. VR barrel with Accu-II chokes (3), engraved receiver and hand selected stock and forearm, 3,500 mfg. in 1991 to commemorate the 10th anniversary of Quail Unlimited.

			$295	$240	$195

Last Mfg.'s Sug. Retail was $359.

Model 500 Sporting Steel Shot — 12 ga. only, 3 in. chamber, 28 in. VR multi-choke barrel capable of shooting steel shot. Mfg. 1987-90.

	$250	$200	$175	$165	$155	$145	$135

Add $29 for camo stock (disc. 1989).
This model was phased out of production in 1990 since all Mossberg shotguns currently manufactured are capable of shooting steel shot safely. The last mfg.'s sug. retail was $295.

MODEL 500 SPECIAL PURPOSE/PERSUADER — similar to 500L, except 12 ga. only, 6 or 8 shot, 18½ or 20 in. plain barrel, optional rifle sights (12 ga./20 in. cyl. bore barrel only), blue or parkerized (12 ga. only) finish, optional bayonet lug, plain pistol grip wood or synthetic stock.

Mfg.'s Sug. Retail	$251	$220	$180	$160	$145	$130	$115	$100

Add $21 for rifle sights.
Add $23 for parkerized finish (includes synthetic stock and forearm).
Add $15 for pistol grip (disc.).
Add $17 for speedfeed stock (disc. 1990).
Add $40 for combo with pistol grip (disc.).

Night Persuader Special Edition — 12 ga. only, includes synthetic stock and factory installed Mepro-Light night sight bead sight, only 300 mfg. for Lew Horton Distributing in 1990 only.

			$295	$250	$200	$175	$150	$130	$115

Last Mfg.'s Sug. Retail was $296.

MODEL 500 MARINER — 12 ga. only, 18½ or 20 in. barrel, Marinecote finish on all metal parts (more durable than stainless steel), synthetic stock and forearm, 6 or 9 shot.

Mfg.'s Sug. Retail	$353	$310	$250	$200

Add $15 for 8 shot mag. (disc.).
Add $15 for pistol grip adapter (mini-combo - disc.).
Add $23 for speedfeed stock (mini-combo only - disc.).

MODEL 500 CAMPER — 12, 20, or .410 ga. only, 18½ in. barrel, synthetic pistol grip (no stock), camo carrying case optional, blued finish. Mfg. 1986-90 only.

	$235	$190	$175	$165	$155	$145	$135

Add $25 for .410 ga.
Add $30 for camo case.
Last Mfg.'s Sug. Retail was $276.

Grading	100%	98%	95%	90%	80%	70%	60%

MODEL 500 CRUISER — 12, 20, or .410 (new 1993) ga., 18½ or 20 in. cylinder bore barrel with shroud, 6 or 8 shot (12 ga. only) mag., pistol grip only. New 1989.

Mfg.'s Sug. Retail	$242	$190	$175	$165	$155	$145	$135	$120

Add $6 for .410 ga.
Add $22-$32 for camper case (new 1993).

MODEL 500 HI-RIB TRAP — 12 ga. only, high post trap rib, 28 or 30 in. barrel. Add $20 for Accu-choke. Disc. 1986.

	$285	$250	$230	$200	$175	$155	$140

Last Mfg.'s Sug. Retail was $334.

MODEL 500 SUPER GRADE — similar to Field, except VR and checkered, no 16 ga. Mfg. 1965-1976.

	$250	$215	$180	$170	$160	$140	$130

MODEL 500 ATR SUPER GRADE — similar to Field, except 12 ga., VR, 30 in. full, checkered Monte Carlo. Mfg. 1968-1971.

	$295	$260	$230	$200	$175	$155	$140

MODEL 500 PIGEON GRADE — similar to 500 Super Grade, except etched and scroll engraving, select wood, floating VR. Mfg. 1971-1975.

	$385	$330	$305	$250	$210	$185	$165

MODEL 500 APTR PIGEON GRADE TRAP — similar to 500 ATR, except trap style stock. Mfg. 1971-1975.

	$440	$415	$330	$250	$220	$200	$175

MODEL 500 DSPR DUCK STAMP COMMERCIAL — similar to Pigeon Grade, except wood duck etching. 1,000 mfg. 1975.

	$525	$330	$310	$285	$260	$220	$195

MODEL 500L SERIES — similar to 500 Field Grade, except no 16 ga., etched receiver, new style stock and slide. Mfg. 1977-1983.

	$250	$220	$210	$200	$175	$165	$140

MODEL 500 BULLPUP — 12 ga. only, 18½ or 20 in. barrel, bullpup configuration, 6 shot mag., includes shrouded barrel, carrying handle, ejection port in stock, employs high impact materials. Mfg. 1986-90 only.

	$350	$300	$255				

Add $15 for 8 shot mag. (disc.).
Last Mfg.'s Sug. Retail was $425.

MODEL 500 GHOST RING SIGHT — 12 ga. only, 3 in. chamber, 18½ or 20 in. cyl. bore barrel, 6 or 9 shot tube mag., blue or parkerized finish, synthetic field stock, includes ghost ring sighting device. New 1990.

Mfg.'s Sug. Retail	$300	$250	$215	$180	$160	$150	$140	$130

Add $48 for parkerized finish.
Add $59 for 9 shot mag. (20 in. barrel only).

MODEL 500/590 INTIMIDATOR LASER — 12 ga. only, 3 in. chamber, 18½ (Model 500) or 20 (Model 590) in. cyl. bore barrel, 6 (Model 500) or 9 (Model 590) shot tube mag., blue or parkerized finish, synthetic field stock, includes laser sighting device. New 1990.

✥ **Model 500 Intimidator**

Mfg.'s Sug. Retail	$505	$440	$375	$340	$295	$260	$230	$195

Add $22 for parkerized finish.

Grading	100%	98%	95%	90%	80%	70%	60%

Model 590 Intimidator
| Mfg.'s Sug. Retail $556 | $495 | $440 | $375 | $340 | $295 | $260 | $230 |

Add $45 for parkerized finish.

SPECIAL PURPOSE 590 — similar to Model 500, except has 9 shot mag., 20 in. cyl. bore barrel with ¾ shroud, and bayonet lug, blued or parkerized finish. New 1987.
| Mfg.'s Sug. Retail $305 | $275 | $235 | $200 | $185 | $165 | $145 | $125 |

Add $46 for parkerized finish.
Add $14 for speedfeed stock.

Model 590 Mariner — similar to Model 500 Mariner except is 9 shot and has 20 in. barrel. New 1989.
| Mfg.'s Sug. Retail $353 | $310 | $250 | $200 | $185 | $165 | $145 | $125 |

Add $17 for speedfeed stock (disc. 1990).
Add $15 for pistol grip adapter (mini combo - disc.).

Model 590 Bullpup — similar to Model 500 Bullpup except is 9 shot and has 20 in. barrel. Mfg. 1989-90 only.
| | $425 | $360 | $300 | $250 | $225 | $195 | $175 |

Last Mfg.'s Sug. Retail was $497.

MODEL 600 — 12 ga. only, 2¾ or 3 in. chamber 28 in. VR barrel with Accu-choke, economical model with walnut finish stock, blue finish, 7.7 lbs. New 1993.
| Mfg.'s Sug. Retail $321 | $280 | $240 | $215 | $200 | $185 | $165 | $145 |

MODEL 712 — 12 ga. only, semi-auto, gas operated, shoots 2¾ and 3 in. shells interchangeably, plain barrel or VR, top of receiver safety, checkered hardwood stock, rubber recoil pad, fixed or Accu Choke II choking. Imported 1986-1988 only.
| | $285 | $250 | $220 | $200 | $190 | $175 | $160 |

Subtract $25 without Accu II choking.
Add $90 for combo pack (includes 1 extra 24 in. slugster barrel.
Last Mfg.'s Sug. Retail was $345.

Model 712 Steel Shot — similar to Model 712, except has Accu-Steel choking system for steel shot, 28 in. VR barrel. Imported 1988 only.
| | $290 | $250 | $220 | $200 | $190 | $175 | $160 |

Last Mfg.'s Sug. Retail was $349.

Model 712 Camo/Speedfeed — 12 ga. only, similar to Model 712, except has camo finished metal parts, stock, and forearm, 24 or 28 in. barrel. Add $20 for Accu II choke. Imported 1986-87 only.
| | $340 | $295 | $240 | | | | |

Last Mfg.'s Sug. Retail was $390.

MODEL 712 REGAL — 12 or 20 ga., action same as Model 712, special bright bluing, VR only, deluxe checkered walnut stock and forearm, gold trigger, inlaid medallion on receiver, top of receiver safety. Add $20 for Accu II choke. Imported 1986-87 only.
| | $310 | $280 | $250 | $225 | $200 | $185 | $170 |

Last Mfg.'s Sug. Retail was $366.

NEW HAVEN BRAND — similar to previous models, except plainer finish. Disc.
Values are 20% less per model.

Grading	100%	98%	95%	90%	80%	70%	60%

MODEL 835 ULTI-MAG — 12 ga. with 3½ in. chamber (new 1988), slide action, 24 (Turkey Model - new 1990) or 28 in. VR barrel with Accu-Mag choke tubes, 6 shot mag., safety on top rear of receiver, choice of camo synthetic or checkered hardwood stock. Introduced late 1988, disc. 1991.

		$375	**$310**	**$265**	**$220**	**$190**	**$165**	**$150**

Add $30 for synthetic camo field stock.
Last Mfg.'s Sug. Retail was $430.
Various Combo packages were available in this model with prices ranging from $469-$534 depending on barrel chokings and scope base options.
This model was followed by the 835 Regal Series introduced in late 1991.

ULTI-MAG 835 FIELD GRADE — 12 ga. only, 3½ in. chamber, 24 in. cyl. bore, 24 in. VR (Turkey Special), or 28 in. VR barrel with 1 Accu-Mag choke, walnut finish stock and forearm, blued finish, approx. 7½ lbs.

Mfg.'s Sug. Retail	**$284**	**$240**	**$215**	**$200**	**$185**	**$165**	**$145**	**$125**

Add $37 for combo package (includes extra slug barrel with choice of sights).

MODEL 835 CAMO — 12 ga. only, 3½ in. chamber, OFM Camo (all-purpose camo) or Realtree (new 1993) finish, 28 in. VR barrel with 6 choke tubes, dual comb stock, 7.7 lbs. New 1991.

Mfg.'s Sug. Retail	**$407**	**$350**	**$295**	**$260**	**$230**	**$200**	**$175**	**$160**

Add $29 for Realtree Camo finish.
Add $78 for combo package (includes 24 in. rifled barrel with rifle sights).

MODEL 835 REGAL ULTI-MAG — 12 ga., 3½ in. chamber, 28 in. VR barrel with Accu-Mag chokes or 24 in. rifled slug barrel, single (new 1993) or dual comb (2 comb inserts are provided for the stock affording different shooting positions), aluminum receiver, back-bored barrel, double slide bars, high gloss walnut stock with recoil pad, approx. 7½ lbs. New late 1991.

Mfg.'s Sug. Retail	**$381**	**$330**	**$285**	**$260**	**$230**	**$200**	**$175**	**$160**

Add $19 for 24 in. slug barrel with trophy scope base.
Add $48-$54 for combo package (includes extra slug barrel with choice of sights).
Subtract $7 for single comb stock (new 1993).

MODEL 835 WILD TURKEY FED. LIMITED EDITION — 12 ga. with 3½ in. chamber, 24 in. VR barrel with Accu-Mag. chokes, camo finish, includes camo sling, medallion in stock, and 10-pack of Federal Turkey loads. Mfg. 1989 only.

		$425	**$360**	**$295**				

Last Mfg.'s Sug. Retail was $477.

MODEL 835 NWTF SPECIAL EDITION — 12 ga. only, 24 in. VR barrel with Accu-Mag chokes, features Realtree camo finish, drilled and tapped receiver, 7½ lbs. Mfg. 1991 only to commemorate the National Wild Turkey Federation.

Mfg.'s Sug. Retail	**$436**	**$380**	**$300**	**$225**				

MODEL 835 WATERFOWL LIMITED EDITION — 12 ga. with 3½ in. chamber, 28 in. VR barrel with Accu-Mag. chokes, camo finish, synthetic stock, camo sling. Mfg. 1990 only.

		$425	**$360**	**$295**				

Last Mfg.'s Sug. Retail was $480.

Grading	100%	98%	95%	90%	80%	70%	60%

MODEL 1000 — 12 or 20 ga., gas semi-auto, 2¾ in. chamber, scroll engraved aluminum alloy receiver, plain or VR barrel, also available in trap and skeet configuration, checkered walnut stock and forearm. Imported 1986-87 only. Vent. rib became standard in 1987.

| | $410 | $345 | $300 | $270 | $245 | $220 | $200 |

Add $28 for multi-choke II.
Deduct $50 if without VR.
Last Mfg.'s Sug. Retail was $472.
Model 1000 barrels are not interchangeable with Model 1000 Super barrels.

Model 1000 Junior — similar to Model 1000, except 20 ga. only, shortened stock, and 22 in. VR multi-choke barrel. Imported 1986-87 only.

| | $425 | $355 | $310 | $275 | $250 | $220 | $200 |

Last Mfg.'s Sug. Retail was $499.

Model 1000 Slug — 12 or 20 ga., 22 in. barrel with rifle sights, recoil pad. Imported 1986-87 only.

| | $405 | $340 | $295 | $270 | $245 | $220 | $200 |

Last Mfg.'s Sug. Retail was $464.

Model 1000 Skeet — 12 or 20 ga., steel receiver, 26 in. VR barrel bored skeet. Mfg. 1986 only.

| | $395 | $335 | $295 | $270 | $245 | $220 | $200 |

Last Mfg.'s Sug. Retail was $439.

MODEL 1000 SUPER — 12 or 20(Super 20) ga., gas semi-auto, 3 in. chambers, shoots 2¾ and 3 in. shells interchangeably, steel receiver, vent. recoil pad, select checkered walnut stock and forearm, multi-choke II is standard (except on slug barrel). Slug models are approx. the same price as values listed directly below. Imported 1986-87 only.

| | $495 | $405 | $365 | $330 | $295 | $270 | $245 |

Last Mfg.'s Sug. Retail was $577.
Model 1000 Super barrels are not interchangeable with Model 1000 barrels.

Model 1000 Super Waterfowler — 12 ga. only, matte finished wood and metal, includes swivels and camouflaged sling, 28 in. multi-choke barrel. Imported 1986-87 only.

| | $510 | $430 | $370 |

Last Mfg.'s Sug. Retail was $605.

Model 1000 Super Skeet — 12 or 20 ga., 25 in. barrel, jug choking. Imported 1986-87 only.

| | $575 | $495 | $450 | $410 | $375 | $330 | $295 |

Last Mfg.'s Sug. Retail was $658.

Model 1000 Super Trap — 12 ga. only, 30 in. multi-choke II barrel with high vent. rib, Monte Carlo stock, recoil pad. Mfg. 1986 only.

| | $470 | $380 | $345 | $320 | $285 | $270 | $250 |

Last Mfg.'s Sug. Retail was $560.

MODEL 3000 — 12 or 20 ga. only, 3 in. chamber, slide action, steel receiver, double action bars, various chokes and VR barrel lengths, checkered walnut stock and forearm, vent. recoil pad. Add $25 for multi-choke II. This model was introduced in 1986 and the field version was disc. in 1987. Law enforcement variations are still available.

| | $325 | $275 | $250 | $220 | $200 | $185 | $170 |

Last Mfg.'s Sug. Retail was $360.

Grading	100%	98%	95%	90%	80%	70%	60%

Model 3000 Waterfowler — 12 ga. only, similar to Model 3000, except has dull matte finish on wood and metal, includes swivels and camouflaged sling, VR only. Add $30 for multi-choke II option, $70 for camo/speedfeed stock. Mfg. 1986 only.

	$340	$295	$265				

Last Mfg.'s Sug. Retail was $386.

Model 3000 Law Enforcement — 12 or 20 ga. only, 18½ or 20 in. cylinder bore only, rifle or bead sights. Imported 1986-87 only.

	$325	$275	$250	$220	$200	$185	$170

Add $25 for rifle sights.
Add $33 for black speedfeed stock.
Last Mfg.'s Sug. Retail was $362.

MODEL 5500 SEMI-AUTO — 12 ga., 2¾ or 3 in. mag., gas operated, 18½ - 30 in. barrels. Add $20 for VR. Disc. 1985.

	$250	$235	$205	$185	$170	$155	$140

Last Mfg.'s Sug. Retail was $307.

Model 5500 Mag. — 12 ga. only, 3 in. chamber, 30 in. VR barrel. Disc. 1985.

	$275	$250	$225	$205	$190	$175	$160

Last Mfg.'s Sug. Retail was $325.

MODEL 5500 MKII — 12 ga. only, supplied with 2 VR barrels - 26 in./2¾ in. chamber or 28 in./3 in. chamber VR barrel, includes choice of Accu-II choke tubes (lead shot only) or Accu-Steel choke tubes, blue or camo finish (new 1990), checkered hardwood stock and forearm, top receiver safety, recoil pad, 7½ lbs. Mfg. 1989-92.

	$260	$225	$200	$180	$160	$140	$125

Add $10 for 24 in. rifled bore barrel.
Add $43 for camo metal finish and synthetic stock.
Add $30 for Turkey Model (24 in. barrel, camo finish, and synthetic stock).
This model is also available with different Combo options. Prices vary between $463-$484, depending on configuration of barrel choking.
Last Mfg.'s Sug. Retail was $294.

Model 5500 U.S. Shooting Team — 2¾ in. chamber, 26 in. non-Mag. barrel with VR and Accu-II chokes, blue finish, checkered walnut stock and forearm, 7½ lbs. Mfg. 1991-92.

	$325	$250	$225	$200	$185	$170	$160

Last Mfg.'s Sug. Retail was $376.

NWTF Special Edition — 12 ga. only, 3 in. chamber, 24 in. VR barrel with 1 choke tube, Mossy Oak Camo finish with synthetic stock and forearm, 7.3 lbs. Mfg. 1991-92.

	$365	$300	$265	$235	$200	$175	$160

Last Mfg.'s Sug. Retail was $428.

MODEL 9200 — 12 ga. only, 3 in. chamber, gas operated semi-auto, shoots any shell interchangeably, 24 in. rifled, 24 (Turkey), 26 (U.S. Shooting Team variation, new 1993), or 28 in. VR barrel with 3 Accu-chokes, engraved aluminum receiver, walnut stained hardwood stock and forearm, top tang safety, approx. 7½ lbs. New 1992.

Mfg.'s Sug. Retail	$374	$325	$250	$225	$200	$185	$170	$160

Add $19 for 24 in. rifled bore barrel with trophy scope base.
Add $59-$67 for combo pack (includes extra 24 in. rifled bore barrel).

Model 9200 Camo — similar to Model 9200, except is supplied with OFM Camo finish and 28 in. VR barrel. New 1992.

Mfg.'s Sug. Retail	$393	$340	$265	$235	$210	$190	$170	$160

Add $63 for combo pack (includes extra 24 in. rifled bore barrel).

MUSGRAVE

Manufacturer located in the Republic of South Africa since 1951.

Currently, this manufacturer has no importation into the U.S. (due to Federal regulations) and listings below represent older models. Newer models manufactured by Musgrave (imported into Austria and Switzerland) include the Model 90 (features Musgrave action) Standard Rifle, Model 90 Light Rifle, Mini-90, Model 90 Varmint, Model 90 De Luxe Rifle, Magnum Rifle in addition to the same series in the Mauser 98 action. More information can be obtained (including prices and availability) by writing this manufacturer directly at: MUSGRAVE MANUFACTURERS & DISTRIBUTORS LTD., P.O. Box 183, Bloemfontein 9300, Jagersfontein Road, Republic of South Africa.

Grading	100%	98%	95%	90%	80%	70%	60%

VALIANT BOLT ACTION RIFLE — .243, .270, .30-06, .308, or 7mm Mag. cal., 24 in. barrel, leaf sight, skip checkered straight stock, pistol grip. Mfg. 1971-1976.

	100%	98%	95%	90%	80%	70%	60%
	$375	$325	$275	$250	$220	$195	$175

PREMIER — similar to Valiant, with 26 in. barrel, select Monte Carlo stock, rosewood pistol grip cap and forearm tip.

	100%	98%	95%	90%	80%	70%	60%
	$425	$365	$315	$275	$250	$225	$200

RSA SINGLE SHOT TARGET RIFLE — .308 cal. only, 26 in. heavy barrel, target sights and stock. Mfg. 1971-1976.

	100%	98%	95%	90%	80%	70%	60%
	$425	$365	$315	$275	$250	$225	$200

MUSKETEER RIFLES

Firearms International Company, Washington, D.C.

SPORTER — .243, .25-06, .270, .265 Mag., .308, .30-06, 7mm Mag., or .300 Win. Mag. cal., bolt action, FN Mauser action, 24 in. barrel, no sights, checkered Monte Carlo stock. Mfg. 1963-1972.

	100%	98%	95%	90%	80%	70%	60%
	$375	$325	$275	$250	$220	$195	$175

SPORTER DELUXE — adj. trigger, select wood, tear drop pistol grip, skipline checkering.

	100%	98%	95%	90%	80%	70%	60%
	$425	$365	$315	$275	$250	$225	$200

CARBINE — similar to Sporter, except 20 in. barrel.

	100%	98%	95%	90%	80%	70%	60%
	$375	$325	$275	$250	$220	$195	$175

N section

NAMBU PISTOLS

Manufacturer located in Japan for the Japanese Military between 1902-1945.

Grading	100%	98%	95%	90%	80%	70%	60%

TYPE 14 — 8mm, semi-auto pistol, recoil operated, 4.7 in. barrel, blued, wood grips, 8 shot mag., a simply designed pistol used by Japanese armed forces from 1925-1945.

Type 14 Nambus have a 3-digit number just forward of the lanyard ring on the right side of frame (on back of grip). To determine year and month of manufacture add "1925" to the first two digits and the last number will indicate the month (i.e. code 13.3 indicates a gun built in March of 1938).

Add 10% for matching mag. on models listed below.

⚐ **1925-1930 Mfg.**

	$475	$420	$360	$320	$295	$260	$230

⚐ **1930-1935 Mfg.** — small trigger guard.

	$375	$320	$260	$220	$200	$180	$165

⚐ **1935-1945 Mfg.** — large trigger guard.

	$295	$260	$215	$195	$180	$165	$150

Add 10% for strawed trigger and safety.

TYPE 94 — 8mm, semi-auto, recoil operated, 3.8 in. barrel, blued, and bakelite wood grips, 6 shot mag. Mfg. 1934-1945.

	$275	$225	$185	$160	$150	$135	$120

Add 20% for pre-WWII commercial.
Add 10% for late square bolt.

BABY NAMBU — 7mm Nambu, semi-auto, 3¼ in. barrel, blued, wood grips, grip safety, one of the most desirable Japanese handguns.

	$2,300	$2,000	$1,800	$1,600	$1,475	$1,300	$1,050

Add 10% for matching mag.
Add 50% for chamber marked "TGE" (Tokyo Gas & Electric).

PAPA NAMBU (MODEL 1904) — 8mm, semi-auto, 4.7 in. barrel, wood grips, grip safety, 8 shot mag., essentially the same action as the Baby, but a larger version. Mfg. 1904-1925.

	$1,450	$1,250	$1,100	$900	$700	$600	$500

Add 10% for matching mag.
Add 50% for chamber marked "TGE" (Tokyo Gas & Electric).

GRANDPA NAMBU — 8mm, similar to Papa Nambu, except has smaller trigger guard and fixed lanyard ring, cherry wood based mag., issued with 2 matching mags. Early Tokyo arsenal or later Thai issue, all Grandpa framers are slotted, original stocks are rare and expensive (selling in the $2,500-$3,250 range).

	$4,000	$3,500	$2,950	$2,600	$2,150	$1,850	$1,500

Add 100% for matching shoulder stock.
Add 10% for second matching mag.

1893 REVOLVER (MODEL 26) — 9mm, double action only, 4.7 in. barrel, blued, wood grips. Mfg. 1893-1925.

	$300	$250	$210	$170	$150	$135	$120

NAVY ARMS COMPANY

Importers since 1958 located in Ridgefield, NJ. Navy Arms firearms are fabricated by various manufacturers including the Italian companies Davide Pedersoli & Co., Pietta & Co., and Uberti & Co.

PISTOLS

Grading	100%	98%	95%	90%	80%	70%	60%

TU-711 MAUSER — 9mm Para. cal., patterned after Mauser 711 (semi-auto version of the Model 712 Schnellfeuer), 5¼ in. barrel, 712 upper receiver that has been converted to 9mm Para. and mounted on new lower receiver, supplied with 10 and 20 shot detachable mag., mfg. in China, 2 lbs. 11 oz. Imported 1992 only.

| | | $575 | $475 | $425 | $375 | $325 | $295 | $275 |

Last Mfg.'s Sug. Retail was $650.

TT-OLYMPIA — .22 LR cal., patterned after the Walther Olympia that won 1936 Olympics, 4⅝ in. barrel, checkered walnut grips, mfg. in China, 27 oz. Importation began 1992.

| Mfg.'s Sug. Retail | $300 | $265 | $225 | $195 | $175 | $160 | $150 | $140 |

TU-90 PISTOL — .30 Tokarev or 9mm Para. cal., patterned after the rare Tokagypt variation (improved TT-33 Tokarev), 4½ in. barrel, single action, wraparound synthetic grips, unique forward motion safety, mfg. in China, 30 oz. Importation began 1992.

| Mfg.'s Sug. Retail | $130 | $115 | $100 | $90 | $80 | $70 | $60 | $50 |

Add $15 for 9mm Para. cal.
Add $40 for pistol combo (includes both cals.).

U.S. GOVT. MODEL PISTOL — .45 ACP cal., standard G.I. issue, this model is used in good to very good condition. New 1993.

| Mfg.'s Sug. Retail | $350 | $300 | $240 | $215 | $190 | $165 | $145 | $130 |

HIGH POWER PISTOL — 9mm Para. cal., older FN manufacture with black plastic grips, this model is used in good to very good condition. New 1993.

| Mfg.'s Sug. Retail | $350 | $300 | $240 | $215 | $190 | $165 | $145 | $130 |

LUGER MODEL — .22 LR cal. only, 10 shot mag., Luger toggle type action, available in blued or matte finish, 4, 6, or 8 in. barrel, checkered walnut stocks. Mfg. in U.S. 1986-87 only.

| | | $140 | $120 | $95 | $85 | $75 | $70 | $65 |

Last Mfg.'s Sug. Retail was $165.

GRAND PRIX SILHOUETTE — .30-30, 7mm Spl., .44 Mag., or .45-70 cal., 13¾ in. barrel, non-glare matte blue finish, walnut forearm and grips, adj. heat dispersing aluminum rib, adj. target sights, 4 lbs. Mfg. 1985 only.

| | | $320 | $280 | $240 | $220 | $195 | $175 | $150 |

Last Mfg.'s Sug. Retail was $375.

REVOLVERS: RECENT MFG.

1873 SINGLE ACTION ARMY — .44-40 or .45 LC cal., reproduction of the Colt SAA, case hardened frame with blue or nickel finish, 3 (Sheriff's Model - new 1992), 4¾, 5½, or 7½ in. barrel, approx. 36 oz.

| Mfg.'s Sug. Retail | $370 | $315 | $260 | $210 | $180 | $160 | $145 | $130 |

Add $65 for nickel finish.
Subtract $20 for brass trigger guard and backstrap.

1873 SAA Economy — .44-40 or .45 LC cal., 3, 4¾, 5½ or 7½ in. barrel, brass trigger guard and backstrap, 2-piece walnut grips. New 1993.

| Mfg.'s Sug. Retail | $320 | $285 | $225 | $185 | $160 | $145 | $130 | $120 |

Grading	100%	98%	95%	90%	80%	70%	60%

⚔ **1873 SAA Cavalry Model** — .45 LC only, exact replica of the original U.S. Government issue SAA, 7½ in. barrel, arsenal stampings, inspector's cartouche on walnut stocks.

Mfg.'s Sug. Retail	$455	$410	$340	$295	$260	$230	$200	$175

⚔ **1895 SAA Artillery Model** — similar specifications to the Cavalry Model, except has 5½ in. barrel.

Mfg.'s Sug. Retail	$455	$410	$340	$295	$260	$230	$200	$175

1875 REMINGTON REVOLVER — .44-40 or .45 LC cal., reproduction of the 1875 Remington revolver, 7½ in. barrel, case colored frame, 41 oz. Importation disc. 1991.

	$410	$350	$295	$260	$230	$200	$175

Last Mfg.'s Sug. Retail was $470.

1890 REMINGTON REVOLVER — .44-40 LC cal., reproduction of the 1890 Remington revolver, 5½ in. barrel, brass trigger guard and lanyard loop, 39 oz. Importation disc. 1991.

	$405	$350	$295	$260	$230	$200	$175

Last Mfg.'s Sug. Retail was $465.

RIFLES: REPLICA MANUFACTURE

MODEL 1873 RIFLE — .22 LR, .357 Mag., or .44-40 cal., lever action replica of 1873 Winchester, case hardened receiver, 24 in. barrel. Mfg. 1972-1984.

	$305	$275	$250	$220	$165	$140	$110

⚔ **Model 1873 1 of 1,000** — only 1,000 mfg., deluxe wood, special engraving.

	$1,000	$775	$550

MODEL 1873 CARBINE — .44-40 cal., blue receiver, 19 in. round barrel.

	$260	$220	$195	$165	$140	$110	$100

MODEL 1873 TRAPPER — .44-40 cal., similar to Carbine, with 16½ in. barrel.

	$260	$220	$195	$165	$140	$110	$100

YELLOWBOY — .38 Spl., or .44-40 cal., lever action replica of Winchester 1866, 24 in. octagon barrel. Mfg. 1966-1984.

	$330	$275	$220	$195	$165	$140	$110

YELLOWBOY CARBINE — .44-40 cal., 19 in. round barrel.

	$215	$180	$165	$150	$140	$110	$85

YELLOWBOY TRAPPER — .44-40 cal., 16½ in. barrel.

	$215	$180	$165	$150	$140	$110	$85

REVOLVING CARBINE — .357 Mag., .44-40, or .45 Colt cal., 6 shot cylinder, 20 in. barrel, case hardened frame, straight stock. Mfg. 1968-1984.

	$250	$210	$180	$160	$150	$140	$120

REMINGTON ROLLING BLOCK BUFFALO RIFLE — .444 Marlin (disc.), .45-70, or .50-70 (disc.), replica of Remington Rolling Block, 26 or 30 in. heavy octagon or ½ round/½ oct. barrel, open sight, straight grip stock. Mfg. 1971-present.

Mfg.'s Sug. Retail	$510	$400	$325	$275	$230	$180	$160	$140

Add approx. $45 for long or short Creedmoor sight.
Add $55 for 50 x 3¼ Sharps cal. (disc.).

Grading	100%	98%	95%	90%	80%	70%	60%

BUFFALO CARBINE — similar to Rifle, with 18 in. barrel. Disc. 1985.

		100%	98%	95%	90%	80%	70%	60%
		$325	$280	$230	$180	$160	$140	$120

Last Mfg.'s Sug. Retail was $375.

ROLLING BLOCK BABY CARBINE — .22 LR, .22 Hornet, .357 Mag., or .44-40 cal., replica of small frame Remington, 20 in. octagon or 22 in. round barrel, open sight, straight stock. Mfg. 1968-1984.

	100%	98%	95%	90%	80%	70%	60%
	$160	$130	$110	$90	$65	$55	$40

ROLLING BLOCK CREEDMOOR TARGET — similar to Buffalo Rifle, in .45-70 or .50-70 (disc.) cal., with Creedmoor tang sight, color case hardened receiver, checkered walnut.

Mfg.'s Sug. Retail	$675	$545	$450	$350	$250	$195	$175	$150

SHARPS RIFLE/CARBINE — .45-70 or .54 (blackpowder) cal., reproduction of Sharps sporting rifle and carbine, 22 or 28½ (rifle) in. barrel, case colored frame and hammer, fixed rear sight.

Mfg.'s Sug. Retail	$715	$565	$450	$350	$250	$195	$175	$150

MODEL 1866 CARBINE/RIFLE — .44-40 cal. only, choice of rifle (24 in. octagon barrel) or carbine (19 in. round barrel), replica of the Winchester Model 1866.

Mfg.'s Sug. Retail	$685	$545	$450	$350	$250	$195	$175	$150

Add $25 for rifle variation.

MODEL 1873 — .44-40 or .45 LC cal., choice of rifle (24 in. octagon barrel) or carbine (19 in. round barrel), replica of the Winchester Model 1873.

Mfg.'s Sug. Retail	$815	$685	$550	$425	$300	$250	$220	$180

Add $25 for rifle variation.

⚔ **Model 1873 Deluxe Sporting Rifle** — deluxe variation of the Model 1873 featuring case hardened receiver, checkered pistol grip stock, and choice of 24 or 30 in. barrel, 8 lbs. 14 oz. New 1992.

Mfg.'s Sug. Retail	$895	$795	$685	$550	$425	$325	$275	$225

HENRY RIFLE — .44-40 or .44 Rem. (disc. 1989) cal., reproduction of Winchester's famous Henry Rifle, brass or iron frame. New for 1985.
Add $370 for "A" pattern engraving (25% coverage).
Add $585 for "B" pattern engraving (35% coverage).
Add $975 for "C" pattern engraving (50% coverage).
The above special order engraving patterns usually require 30-60 days.

⚔ **Military Rifle** — 24 in. barrel, brass frame, blued barrel, walnut stock, original style sling swivels, 9¼ lbs. New for 1985.

Mfg.'s Sug. Retail	$875	$685	$535	$450	$350	$275	$225	$195

⚔ **Union Pacific Railroad Commemorative** — .44-40, only 100 mfg.

	100%	98%	95%
	$795	$575	$475

Last Mfg.'s Sug. Retail was $695.

⚔ **Engraved Rifle** — limited mfg., extensive engraving on brass frame. Disc. 1988.

	100%	98%	95%	90%	80%	70%	60%
	$1,510	$1,275	$1,100	$900	$750	$650	$550

Add $100 for steel frame.
Last Mfg.'s Sug. Retail was $1,850.

⚔ **Carbine** — 24 in. barrel, limited edition of 1,000 units including 50 engraved specimens, no swivels, 8¼ lbs.

Mfg.'s Sug. Retail	$875	$685	$535	$450	$350	$275	$225	$195

Grading	100%	98%	95%	90%	80%	70%	60%

⚔ **Engraved Carbine** — limited production, only 50 mfg. Disc. 1988.

| | | $1,450 | $1,225 | $1,075 | $900 | $750 | $650 | $550 |

Last Mfg.'s Sug. Retail was $1,750.

⚔ **Trapper Model** — 16½ in. barrel, 7¼ lbs., 34¼ in. overall length.

| Mfg.'s Sug. Retail | $875 | $685 | $535 | $450 | $350 | $275 | $225 | $195 |

⚔ **Iron Frame Model** — with iron frame and butt plate, 24 in. blued barrel, select walnut, 9¼ lbs.

| Mfg.'s Sug. Retail | $895 | $725 | $640 | $550 | $480 | $430 | $360 | $295 |

This model is available with either blued or color case hardened receiver.

RIFLES: MODERN MFG.

In addition to the models listed below, Navy Arms in late 1990 purchased the manufacturing rights to the English firm, Parker-Hale. In 1991, Navy Arms built a manufacturing facility located in Martinsburg, WV to produce these rifles domestically. The name of this new company is Gibbs Rifle Co. and their section should be consulted for current models and values.

TU-KKW TRAINING RIFLE — .22 LR, replica of the German "KKW" Gewehr training rifle, full sized Mauser 98K action with military sights, 26 in. barrel, detachable 5 shot mag., mfg. in China, 8 lbs. Importation began 1992.

| Mfg.'s Sug. Retail | $210 | $180 | $150 | $135 | $120 | $105 | $90 | $75 |

Add $275 for 2¾ Type 89 quick mount scope (Sniper Trainer).

TU-33/40 CARBINE — .22 LR or 7.62 x 39mm K. cal., based on WWII Mauser G33/40 mountain carbine, 20¾ in. barrel, includes sling, adj. rear sight, mfg. in China, 7 lbs. 7 oz. Importation began 1992.

| Mfg.'s Sug. Retail | $210 | $180 | $150 | $135 | $120 | $105 | $90 | $75 |

7.62 x 39mm cal. is POR from Navy Arms in this model.

JW-15 RIFLE — .22 LR, sporter bolt action based on Brno Model 5 action, 24 in. barrel, detachable 5 shot mag., receiver top is dove-tailed, mfg. in China, 5 lbs. 12 oz. Importation began 1992.

| Mfg.'s Sug. Retail | $100 | $85 | $70 | $60 | $50 | $40 | $35 | $30 |

MARTINI TARGET RIFLE — .444, or .45-70 cal., single shot, 26 or 30 in. octagon barrel, tang sight, pistol grip stock. Mfg. 1972-1984.

| | | $480 | $420 | $350 | $250 | $195 | $175 | $150 |

RPKS-74 — .223 or 7.62 X 39mm (new 1989) cal., semi-automatic version of the Chinese RPK Squad Automatic Weapon, Kalashnikov action, 19 in. barrel, integral folding bipod, 9½ lbs. Imported 1988-1989 only.

| | | $525 | $445 | $350 | $250 | $195 | $175 | $150 |

Last Mfg.'s Sug. Retail was $649.

USED MILITARY FIREARMS

Navy Arms sells a wide variety of original military firearms in used condition. Handguns include the Mauser Broomhandle, Japanese Nambu, Colt 1911 Government Model, Tokarev, Browning Hi-Power, S & W Model 1917, and others. Rifles include Mauser contract models, Japanese Type 38s, Enfields, FNs, Nagants, M1 Carbines, M1 Garands, Chinese SKSs, Egyptian Rashids, French MAS Model 1936s, among others. Most of these firearms are priced in the $75-$500 price range depending on desirability of model and condition. Navy Arms should be contacted directly regarding specific prices for these models.

Grading	100%	98%	95%	90%	80%	70%	60%

SHOTGUNS: RECENT IMPORTATION

Importation of the models listed below was disc. in 1990.

MODEL 83 O/U — 12 or 20 ga., manufactured in Italy by R. Luciano, 3 in. chambers, extractors, double triggers, engraved chrome receiver, vent. barrels (bored M/F or IC/M) and rib. New 1985.

	100%	98%	95%	90%	80%	70%	60%
	$280	$240	$215	$195	$170	$160	$150

Last Mfg.'s Sug. Retail was $320.

MODEL 93 O/U — 12 or 20 ga., manufactured in Italy by R. Luciano, 3 in. chambers, ejectors, double triggers, engraved chrome receiver, vent. barrels (bored M/F or IC/M) and rib. New 1985.

	100%	98%	95%	90%	80%	70%	60%
	$325	$285	$250	$220	$200	$185	$160

Last Mfg.'s Sug. Retail was $380.

MODEL 95 O/U — similar to Model 93, except with single trigger and multi-chokes (includes 5 tubes), extractors.

	100%	98%	95%	90%	80%	70%	60%
	$375	$330	$295	$265	$235	$210	$190

Last Mfg.'s Sug. Retail was $420.

MODEL 96 SPORTSMAN O/U — 12 ga. only, 3 in. chambers, vent. barrels and rib, engraved chrome receiver, gold plated receiver, multi-choked with 5 choke tubes, ejectors. New 1985.

	100%	98%	95%	90%	80%	70%	60%
	$470	$425	$375	$330	$295	$260	$230

Last Mfg.'s Sug. Retail was $530.

MODEL 100 O/U — 12, 20, 28, or .410 ga., 3 in. chambers, 26 in. VR barrels, photo-engraved hard chrome receiver, single trigger, extractors, checkered walnut stock and forearm, approx. 6¼ lbs. New 1985.

	100%	98%	95%	90%	80%	70%	60%
	$225	$205	$190	$170	$160	$150	$140

Last Mfg.'s Sug. Retail was $250.

MODEL 100 SXS — 12 or 20 ga., 3 in. chambers, 27½ in. barrels, checkered European walnut, double triggers, extractors, 6½ or 7 lbs. Imported 1985-1987 only.

	100%	98%	95%	90%	80%	70%	60%
	$380	$330	$290	$260	$230	$200	$170

Last Mfg.'s Sug. Retail was $475.

MODEL 150 SXS — similar to Model 100, except with ejectors. Imported 1985-1987 only.

	100%	98%	95%	90%	80%	70%	60%
	$455	$395	$350	$310	$280	$250	$220

Last Mfg.'s Sug. Retail was $574.

MODEL 105 SINGLE BARREL — 12, 20, or .410 ga., 26 or 28 in. full choke barrel only, folding action, engraved chrome receiver, checkered hardwood stock and forearm. New 1985.

	100%	98%	95%	90%	80%	70%	60%
	$80	$70	$65	$60	$55	$50	$45

This model was designated the Model 600 before 1988.
Last Mfg.'s Sug. Retail was $90.

Model 105 Deluxe — similar to Model 105, except has European walnut stock and VR.

	100%	98%	95%	90%	80%	70%	60%
	$95	$85	$75	$65	$60	$55	$50

This model was designated the Model 600 Deluxe before 1988.
Last Mfg.'s Sug. Retail was $105.

NEW DETONICS MANUFACTURING CORPORATION

Previous manufacturer located in Phoenix, AZ 1989 -1992. Formerly named Detonics Firearms Industries (previous manufacturer located in Bellevue, WA 1976-1988). Detonics was sold in early 1988 to the New Detonics Manufacturing Corporation, a wholly owned subsidiary of "1045 Investors Group Limited".

PISTOLS: STAINLESS STEEL

Grading	100%	98%	95%	90%	80%	70%	60%
MARK I — .45 ACP, matte blue. Disc. 1981.	$550	$450	$395				
MARK II — .45 ACP, satin nickel finish. Disc. 1979.	$495	$375	$300				
MARK III — .45 ACP, hard chrome finish. Disc. 1979.	$520	$390	$325				
MARK IV — .45 ACP, polished blue. Disc. 1981.	$539	$410	$360				

COMBATMASTER MC1 (FORMERLY MARK I) — .45 ACP, 9mm, or .38 Super cal., 3½ in. barrel, two-tone (slide is non-glare blue and frame is matte stainless) finish, 6 shot mag., fixed sights, 28 oz. Disc. 1992.

	100%	98%	95%
	$775	$575	$450

Add $15 for OM-3 model (polished slide - disc. 1983).
Add $100 for 9mm or .38 Super cal. (disc. 1990).
This model was originally the MC1, then changed to the Mark I, then changed back to the MC1.
Last Mfg.'s Sug. Retail was $920.

COMBATMASTER MARK V — .45 ACP, 9mm, or .38 Super cal., matte stainless finish, fixed sights, 6 shot mag. in .45 ACP, 7 shot in 9mm and .38 Super, 3½ in. barrel, 29 oz. empty. This model was disc. 1985.

	100%	98%	95%
	$620	$550	$495

Add $100 for 9mm or .38 Super cal.
Last Mfg.'s Sug. Retail was $689.

COMBATMASTER MARK VI — .45 ACP, 9mm, or .38 Super cal., 3½ in. barrel, 6 shot mag., adj. sights and polished stainless slide sides. Disc. 1989.

	100%	98%	95%
	$685	$575	$450

Add $100 for 9mm or .38 Super cal.
Last Mfg.'s Sug. Retail was $795.

.451 Detonics Mag. Cal. — limited mfg. 1,000. Disc. 1985.

	100%	98%	95%
	$1,000	$900	$775

Last Mfg.'s Sug. Retail was $1,165.

COMBATMASTER MARK VII — similar to Mark VI, only no sights, special order only, 25 oz.

	100%	98%	95%
	$895	$775	$600

Add $100 for 9mm or .38 Super cal.
Add $350 for .451 Detonics Mag., (disc. 1982).

MILITARY COMBAT MC2 — .45 ACP, 9mm, or .38 Super cal., dull, non-glare combat finish, fixed sights. Add $55 for 9mm or .38 Super. Comes with camouflaged pile-lined wallet, and Pachmayr grips. Disc. 1984.

	100%	98%	95%
	$621	$560	$500

Grading	100%	98%	95%	90%	80%	70%	60%

O.S. MODEL — .45 ACP only, emergency backup pistol, similar to Combatmaster, 6 shot mag., choice of satin stainless or all black finish. Mfg. 1991-92 only.

$775 $550 $425

Last Mfg.'s Sug. Retail was $895.

SCOREMASTER — .45 ACP or .451 Mag. cal., match gun with closer tolerances, 5 or 6 in. barrel. Millett adj. sights, grip safety, 7 or 8 shot mag., 42 oz. Disc. 1992.

$995 $850 $695

Add $40 for 6 in. barrel.
Last Mfg.'s Sug. Retail was $1,178.

COMPMASTER — .45 ACP only, similar to Scoremaster, except is fully compensated. Mfg. 1988-92.

$1,375 $1,200 $950

This model was called the Janus Competition Scoremaster in 1988-1989.
Last Mfg.'s Sug. Retail was $1,550.

COMPETITION MASTER T.F. — .45 ACP cal., competition model with dual port compensator, rotational torque compensating vents, patented cone barrel system, hand tuned trigger, includes all competition modifications. Disc. 1992.

$1,375 $1,200 $950

Last Mfg.'s Sug. Retail was $1,550.

SERVICEMASTER — .45 ACP only, shortened version of the Scoremaster, non-glare combat finish, 4 1/4 in. barrel, coned barrel system, 8 shot mag., interchangeable front and adj. rear sights, 39 oz. Disc. 1986.

$625 $555 $495

Last Mfg.'s Sug. Retail was $686.

Servicemaster II — similar to Servicemaster, except has polished stainless steel finish. Mfg. 1986-92.

$810 $685 $595

Last Mfg.'s Sug. Retail was $998.

LADIES ESCORT SERIES

This series is designed specifically to suit a woman's shooting requirements.

ROYAL ESCORT — .45 ACP cal., action similar to Combatmaster, 3 1/2 in. barrel, 6 shot mag., black frame, slide and grips are iridescent purple, hammer and trigger are 24 Kt. gold plated. Mfg. 1990-92.

$860 $675 $525

Last Mfg.'s Sug. Retail was $990.

MIDNIGHT ESCORT — similar to Royal Escort, except is stainless with a black slide and smooth black grips. Mfg. 1990-92.

$965 $725 $580

Last Mfg.'s Sug. Retail was $1,090.

JADE ESCORT — similar to Midnight Escort, except has stainless frame, jade colored slide and grips. Mfg. 1990 only.

$825 $650 $525

Last Mfg.'s Sug. Retail was $918. Less than 25 of this color were mfg.

Grading	100%	98%	95%	90%	80%	70%	60%

POCKET 9 — 9mm, double action, 3 in. barrel, 6 shot mag., soft matte sheen finish, 26 oz. Mfg. 1985-86 only.

	$425	$385	$325				

Last Mfg.'s Sug. Retail was $458.
The entire Pocket 9 series was disc. 1986.

⚄ **Pocket 9 LS** — similar to Pocket 9, except has 4 in. barrel. Mfg. 1986 only.

	$410	$370	$325				

Last Mfg.'s Sug. Retail was $458.

⚄ **Pocket .380** — similar to Pocket 9, except is .380 ACP cal., 23 oz. Mfg. 1986 only.

	$410	$370	$325				

Last Mfg.'s Sug. Retail was $458.

POWER 9 — 9mm, similar to Pocket 9, except has polished slide sides and is supplied with 2 mag.'s. Disc. 1986.

	$455	$410	$350				

Last Mfg.'s Sug. Retail was $509.

NEW ENGLAND ARMS CO.
Importer/distributor/retailer located in Kittery Point, ME.

New England Arms Co. imports, distributes, or retails the following trademarks: Beretta Premium Grades, Bertuzzi, Carlo Casartelli, Americo Cosmi, Henri Dumoulin, Ferlib, Lebeau Courally, Westley Richards, Rizzini, Fabio Zanotti, and Webley & Scott. These trademarks may be found under their own headings in this text. For further information regarding any one of these manufacturers, please contact New England Arms, Co. directly. New England Arms also offers quality restoration services on best quality shotguns and rifles executed by trained European craftsmen, in addition to performing firearms appraisals and evaluation work.

NEW ENGLAND FIREARMS
Manufacturer located in Gardner, MA. Distributor sales only.

REVOLVERS: D/A

Ultra Models listed below are available in blue finish only.
Beginning 1993, all Ultra's include lockable storage case.

MODEL R92 — .22 LR cal., 9 shot, swing out cylinder, 2½, 4, or 6 (Ultra Model only) in. barrel, blue or nickel finish, hardwood stocks, fixed rear sight, 25-32 oz. New 1988.

Mfg.'s Sug. Retail	$120	$105	$95	$80	$70	$60	$55	$40

Add $10 for nickel finish (2½ or 4 in. barrel only).
Add $30 for Ultra Model (includes adj. rear sight, blued, 4 or 6 in. barrel only).

MODEL R22 ULTRA — .22 Mag. cal., 6 shot, 6 (Ultra Model only) in. barrel, adj. rear sight, blue or nickel finish, 25-28 oz. New 1988.

Mfg.'s Sug. Retail	$150	$130	$110	$95	$80	$70	$60	$55

MODEL R73 - .32 H&R MAG. — .32 H&R Mag. cal., 5 shot, 2½ or 4 in. barrel, blue or nickel finish, fixed sights, 23-26 oz. New 1988.

Mfg.'s Sug. Retail	$115	$100	$85	$75	$70	$60	$55	$40

Add $15 for nickel finish (2½ in. barrel only).
Add $43 for adj. rear sight (Ultra Model - 4 (disc.) or 6 in. barrel only).

690

New England Firearms, cont.

Grading	100%	98%	95%	90%	80%	70%	60%

LADY ULTRA — .32 H&R Mag. cal., swing out cylinder, 5 shot, blue finish, 3 in. barrel with rib, adj. sights. New 1991.

Mfg.'s Sug. Retail	$150	$130	$110	$95	$80	$70	$60	$55

New England Firearms Co. also manufactures blank starter revolvers (.22 or .32 cal.) which are variations of this model.

SHOTGUNS/COMBINATION GUNS

PARDNER — 12, 16 (new 1989), 20, 28 (new 1991), or .410 ga., single shot, break open action, safety transfer bar mechanism on hammer, side lever release, color case hardened receiver, 24 (disc.), 26, or 28 in. barrel, extractor, walnut stock and forearm. New 1987.

Mfg.'s Sug. Retail	$100	$90	$80	$70	$60	$50	$45	$40

Add $5 for Youth Gun (20 or .410 ga. - shorter dimension stock).
Add $25 for rifle sights (12 or 20 ga. - 24 in. cyl. barrel only).
Add $30 for 24 in. rifled bore slug gun.

Pardner Turkey and Goose — 10 ga. only, 3½ in. chamber, 28 in. barrel, blue or camo paint finish, recoil pad, 10 lbs. New 1988.

Mfg.'s Sug. Retail	$150	$130	$110	$90	$75	$65	$55	$45

Add $10 for camo finish, swivels, and swing.

National Wild Turkey Federation (NWTF) — 10 or 20 (new 1993) ga., Mag. chamber, 22 (20 ga. only) or 24 in. barrel with full screw-in choke, full mossy oak camo treatment, includes swivels and sling. New 1992.

Mfg.'s Sug. Retail	$200	$175	$150	$130	$110	$95	$80	$70

This model has been drilled and tapped for scope mounts.

PARDNER SURVIVAL SERIES — 12 or 20 ga., 3 in. chamber, 22 in. barrel with Mod. choke, blue or electroless nickel finish, synthetic thumbhole designed hollow stock with pistol grip, sling swivels, and black nylon sling. New 1992.

Mfg.'s Sug. Retail	$130	$110	$90	$75	$65	$55	$50	$45

TRACKER SLUG MODEL — 12 or 20 ga., 24 in. cyl. bore or rifled barrel, includes recoil pad and adj. sights. New 1992.

Mfg.'s Sug. Retail	$125	$105	$85	$70	$60	$50	$45	$40

RIFLES

HANDI-RIFLE — .22 Hornet, .22-250 Rem. (new 1992), .223 Rem., .243 Win. (new 1992), .270 Win. (new 1993), .30-30, .30-06 (new 1992) or .45-70 cal., 22 in. barrel, blued receiver, stained hardwood stock, scope mount rail or ramp front and adj. folding rear sights, sling swivels, 7 lbs. New 1989.

Mfg.'s Sug. Retail	$190	$165	$130	$110	$95	$80	$70	$60

Add $10 for .243 Rem. or .30-06 cal.
This model in .22-250 Rem. or .223 Rem. cal. is supplied with scope mount and no sights.

NEWTON ARMS CO.

Previous manufacturer located in Buffalo, NY 1913-1932. Also named Charles Newton Rifle Corp. and Buffalo Newton Rifle Co.

NEWTON-MAUSER RIFLE — Oberndorf bolt action, .256 Newton cal., 24 in. barrel, double set triggers, checkered pistol grip stock. Pre-WWI mfg.

	$800	$650	$550	$440	$385	$330	$275

Grading	100%	98%	95%	90%	80%	70%	60%

FIRST TYPE STANDARD RIFLE — Newton bolt action, .22, .256, .280, .30, .33, .35 Newton, and .30-06 cals., 24 in. barrel, double set triggers, open or aperture sights, checkered pistol grip stock. Mfg. 1916-1918 by Newton Arms.

	$1,150	$925	$750	$625	$500	$440	$385

SECOND TYPE STANDARD RIFLE — improved Newton action, has Enfield type bolt handle, .256, .30, .35 Newton, and .30-06 cals., open sights, checkered pistol grip stock. Mfg. post-WWI by Charles Newton Rifle Corporation.

	$1,000	$825	$660	$600	$500	$440	$385

BUFFALO NEWTON RIFLE — similar to Second Type. Mfg. 1922-1932 by Buffalo Newton Rifle company.

	$1,000	$825	$660	$600	$500	$440	$385

SPRINGFIELD NEWTON — kit consisting of a Newton barrel and sporter stock, barrels were chambered for Newton calibers, kits were available to adapt Springfield rifles into Newton calibers in the 1920's when the NRA made the Springfields available to its membership.

	$595	$540	$495	$450	$410	$375	$330

NIKKO FIREARMS CO. LTD.

Previous manufacturer located in Tochigi, Japan circa 1958-1989.

Publisher wishes to thank the Golden Eagle Collectors Association located at 11144 Slate Creek Road, Grass Valley, CA 95945 for providing this publication with the information listed below. Please refer to the Golden Eagle heading in this text for information on Nikko manufactured Golden Eagle firearms.

Both Nikko Firearms Co., Ltd. and Nikko Arms Co., Ltd. were trade names used by the Kodensha Co., Ltd. of Tochigi, Japan on products they manufactured and distributed worldwide. Nikko is the name of the Prefecture, or district, in which Tochigi City is located, about 50 miles north of Tokyo. The word Nikko translates to English as "sunshine". Kodensha first manufactured or distributed under the Nikko name in April 1955, and exported out of Japan beginning in August 1958. Nothing is known of the origin of the Kodensha Co.

Kodensha first approached the American shotgun market in about 1958 or 59 using the Japanese export marketing firm of Kyowa-Boeki-Bussan. They contacted various US distributors, and in about 1959 or 60, Continental Arms Co. of New York City began importing the Nikko "Grade 5". Continental imported these Nikko over/unders, in various models and configurations, until about 1972.

In 1962, the Kodensha Co. Ltd. formed a joint venture with Olin/Winchester of New Haven, CT to produce the Winchester Model 101 over/under shotgun. This venture was known as the Olin-Kodensha Co. Ltd. Added a little later was the side-by-side Model 23, and the Model 96 Xpert (a budget priced 101). The "pre-Olin" Kodensha factory was considerably outdated, and the joint venture began a complete modernization process, with the financial and technical assistance of Olin. Millions of dollars of machinery and technology were brought in, and the entire manufacturing process was upgraded to the then current standards.

One of the conditions of the joint venture was the Kodensha restrict their own products (made in the same factory, but recorded separately from the joint venture) to sale in Japan only. At the outset of the 25 years that the joint venture existed, Kodensha was probably amenable to this, as they were reaping huge financial and technical benefits from Olin. But, by the mid '60s, when the factory was in place and running smoothly, Kodensha essentially ignored that condition of the agreement, leaving Olin at somewhat of a disadvantage, not wanting to jeopardize their investment or production source. Additionally, Olin/Winchester was allowed only 2 permanent personnel, hardly enough to monitor the activities of a factory which employed up to 400 people. As an example, when walnut stock blanks arrived from France, Kodensha took first pick, and Olin got what was left over.

Grading	100%	98%	95%	90%	80%	70%	60%

Kodensha converted an existing building near the manufacturing plant into an assembly area for Nikko, and other brands of guns. This building was probably the "true" Nikko Firearms Co. Ltd. Manufactured components from the Olin-Kodensha factory were carted to the Nikko plant for final assembly and fitting. This "dual-factory" arrangement continued until the mid-1980s. In 1981, for an unknown reason, the Olin-Kodensha name was changed to OK Firearms Co. Ltd. In October 1987, Olin/Winchester sold their interest in OK Firearms to Classic Doubles International, which continued making the 101 style shotgun under their own name. For reasons unknown, Classic Doubles went out of business in December 1988. Shortly thereafter, the entire factory was torn down, and all that remains today is a vacant lot.

During the "dual-factory" days, Nikko produced firearms for the following distributors or retailers: 1) Kanematsu Gosho of Arlington Heights, IL approx. 1974-1982 - distributed Nikko brand shotguns, Golden Eagle brand shotguns and rifles (1975 through March 1977 only); 2) Golden Eagle Firearms, Houston, TX March 1977 through early 1981 - Golden Eagle shotguns and rifles; 3) Tradewinds, Inc. of Tacoma, WA exported from Japan by Caspoll International, Tokyo January 1971 through December 1972 - Shadow Seven; Shadow Indy (Model 707); Gold, Silver, and Black Shadow over/under shotguns; 4) Marubeni America, Inc. of New York City 1972-1974 - Miida brand over/under shotguns; 5) Winchester GMBH of West Germany, manufactured by Olin-Kodensha (dates unknown - early '80s) - Winchester Model 777 rifle (Golden Eagle look-alike); 6) Parker Reproduction shotguns, distributed in the US by Reagent Chemical & Research, Inc. 1984-1988; 7) International Star Commerce Corp. (ISCC) of Salt Lake City, Utah approx. 1982 - distributor of Nikko brand shotguns; 8) Moore Supply Co. of Salt Lake City, UT beginning mid-1981 - distributor of Nikko brand shotguns; 9) USA Nikko, Inc. of Los Angeles, CA (factory reps and distributors of Nikko shotguns), initial date unknown, through December 1981; 10) Weatherby, Inc. of Los Angeles, CA May 1972 to 1981. Centurion semi-auto and Patrician pump shotguns, some Mark 22 rifles. Olympian O/U shotgun and possibly other O/Us from 1978-81. Model 82 semi-auto and Model 92 pump shotguns; 11) Savage Industries of Hamden, CT 1981-1982 - Savage/Fox FA-1 and FP-1 shotguns; 12) Charles Daly. "Automatic" distributed by Sloan's (Japanese made only) mid-1980s; 13) Sears, Roebuck Co. Ted Williams Model 400 and possibly others; 14) Churchill semi-auto, imported by Kassnar mid-1980s; 15) High Standard of Hamden, CT 1974-75 - Supermatic Shadow Indy (Model 707, an O/U), Supermatic Shadow Seven (also O/U), and Supermatic Shadow semi-auto.

NOTE: ALL of the semi-auto shotguns used essentially the same design. Each distributor may have made a few cosmetic or dimensional embellishments to differentiate their gun. Differences exist in barrel/breech fit, magazine caps, pistol grip caps, checkering pattern, piston size, ejector location, fluted bolt. Use caution if interchanging parts. Generally, the same statement can be made about the pump versions also.

NORINCO

Manufacturer located in China. Various importers include: Century International Arms, Inc. located in St. Albans, VT; China Sports, Inc. located in Ontario, CA; Interarms located in Alexandria, VA; KBI, Inc. located in Harrisburg, PA; and others. Distributor sales only.

Norinco pistols, rifles, and shotguns are manufactured in the People's Republic of China by Northern China Industries Corp. (Norinco - with over 100 factories). Various other new models will be imported in the near future and China Sports, Inc. should be contacted to find out current availability and prices on these upcoming models.

PISTOLS

MODEL 213 — 9mm Para., single action, satin blue finish. Imported 1988 only.

	100%	98%	95%	90%	80%	70%	60%
	$185	$150	$135	$125	$115	$105	$100

Last Mfg.'s Sug. Retail was $200.

TYPE 54-1 TOKAREV STANDARD — 7.62 X 25mm or .38 Super cal., single action semi-auto, 4.5 in. barrel, 8 shot mag., fixed sights, blue finish, 29 oz. Importation began 1989.

Mfg.'s Sug. Retail	$145	$125	$100	$80	$70	$65	$60	$55

Type 54-1 Double Column — similar to Standard Model, except is also available in 9mm Para. cal. and has 13 shot mag., 35 oz. Importation began late 1991.

Mfg.'s Sug. Retail	$185	$155	$135	$120	$110	$100	$90	$80

Grading	100%	98%	95%	90%	80%	70%	60%

Type 54-1 Compact — .38 Super, 9mm Para., or 7.62 X 25mm cal., 3.8 in. barrel, 8 shot mag., 27 oz. Importation began late 1991.

Mfg.'s Sug. Retail	$185	$155	$135	$120	$110	$100	$90	$80

TYPE 59 MAKAROV — 9 X 18mm Makarov or .380 ACP, double action semi-auto, 3.5 in. barrel, 8 shot bottom release mag., checkered plastic grips, PPK design with additional features, adj. rear sight, 24 oz. Importation began 1989.

Mfg.'s Sug. Retail	$185	$150	$135	$125	$115	$95	$85	$75

TYPE 77B — 9mm Para. cal., semi-auto single action, action patterned after the older German Lignose (unique design permits one handed operation utilizing "trigger guard cocking" enabling the slide to be moved backward cocking the hammer), 5 in. barrel, 8 shot mag., adj. rear sight, 34 oz. Importation began 1991.

Mfg.'s Sug. Retail	$285	$235	$200	$180	$160	$140	$120	$100

MODEL 1911 A1 — .45 ACP only, patterned after the Colt 1911 A1, 5 in. barrel, 7 shot mag., fixed sights, blue or parkerized finish, wood grips, 39 oz. Importation began 1991.

Mfg.'s Sug. Retail	$320	$275	$245	$220	$195	$180	$165	$150

PARAMILITARY DESIGN CARBINES & RIFLES

Due to 1989 Federal legislation, values on paramilitary configuration firearms have been volatile. Initially (spring of 1989), prices escalated dramatically (many values doubled literally overnight), but gone down recently and become more stable and predictable. Since this is a specialized market, regional demand could lower the values listed below. If further legislation occurs, prices will probably rise again due to the increased demand created when the potential consumer fears that this could be his/her last chance once again to purchase this configuration of firearm.

TYPE 84S AK RIFLE — .223 cal., semi-auto Kalashnikov action, 16.34 in. barrel, hardwood stock and pistol grip, 30 shot mag., 1,000 meter adj. rear sight, includes bayonet and sheath, 8.87 lbs. Imported 1988-1989 only.

	$495	$450	$400	$360	$330	$300	$285

Last Mfg.'s Sug. Retail was $350.

Type 84S-1 — similar to Type 84S AK except has under-folding metal stock. Imported 1989 only.

	$525	$475	$425	$385	$350	$325	$300

Last Mfg.'s Sug. Retail was $350.

Type 84S-3 — similar to Type 84S AK except has composite fiber stock (1½ in. longer than wood stock). Imported 1989 only.

	$550	$500	$450	$400	$375	$350	$325

Last Mfg.'s Sug. Retail was $365.

Type 84S-5 — similar to Type 84S AK except has side-folding metal stock. Imported 1989 only.

	$525	$475	$425	$385	$350	$325	$300

Last Mfg.'s Sug. Retail was $350.

AK-47 THUMBHOLE — .223 Rem. or 7.62 x 39mm cal., features new thumbhole stock for legalized import, 5 shot mag. Importation began 1991.

Mfg.'s Sug. Retail	$375	$330	$285	$250	$225	$200	$185	$170

Add $8 for .223 Rem. cal.

R.P.K. RIFLE — 7.62mm cal., includes bipod.

Mfg.'s Sug. Retail	$600	$495	$425	$375	$325	$275	$250	$225

Grading	100%	98%	95%	90%	80%	70%	60%

TYPE SKS — .223 or 7.62 X 39mm cal., SKS action, 20.47 in. barrel, 30 shot clip mag., 1,000 meter adj. rear sight, hardwood stock, new design accepts standard AK mag., folding bayonet included, 8.8 lbs. Imported 1988-1989, re-introduced 1992 with Sporter configuration stock.

Mfg.'s Sug. Retail	**$154**	$125	$110	$100	$90	$80	$75	$70

Add $100 for synthetic stock and bayonet.
Subtract $20 if refinished.

TYPE 81S AK RIFLE — 7.62 x 39mm cal., semi-auto Kalashnikov action, 17.5 in. barrel, 5, 30, or 40 shot clip mag., 500 meter adj. rear sight, fixed wood stock, hold open device after last shot, 8 lbs. Imported 1988-1989.

	$495	$450	$400	$360	$330	$300	$285

Last Mfg.'s Sug. Retail was $385.

Type 81S-1 — similar to Type 81S AK except has under-folding metal stock. Imported 1988-1989.

	$525	$475	$425	$385	$350	$325	$300

Last Mfg.'s Sug. Retail was $385.

TYPE 56S-2 — 7.62 X 39mm cal., older Kalashnikov design with side-folding metal stock. Importation disc. 1989.

	$495	$450	$400	$360	$330	$300	$285

Last Mfg.'s Sug. Retail was $350.

TYPE 86S-7 RPK RIFLE — 7.62 X 39mm cal., AK action, 23.27 in. heavy barrel with built-in bipod, in-line butt stock, 11.02 lbs. Imported 1988-1989.

	$850	$775	$700	$640	$595	$550	$500

Last Mfg.'s Sug. Retail was $425.

TYPE 86S BULLPUP RIFLE — 7.62 X 39mm cal., bullpup configuration with AK action, under-folding metal stock, 17¼ in. barrel, ambidextrous cocking design, folding front handle, 7 lbs. Imported 1989 only.

	$725	$650	$575	$525	$460	$410	$350

Last Mfg.'s Sug. Retail was $400.

DRAGUNOV (MODEL 350 NDM-86 OR SVD) — 7.62 x 54mm, sniper variation of the AK-47, features 24 in. barrel with muzzle brake, special laminated skeletonized wood stock with vent. forearm, detachable 10 shot mag., 8 lbs. 9 oz.

Mfg.'s Sug. Retail	**$3,080**	$2,775	$2,350	$1,925	$1,575	$1,275	$1,050	$900

This model is also imported by Gibbs Rifle Co. located in Martinsburg, WV.

OFFICERS NINE — 9mm, 16.1 in. barrel, action patterned after the IMI Uzi, 32 shot mag., black military finish, 8.4 lbs. Imported 1988-1989.

	$550	$475	$415	$375	$335	$300	$275

This model was imported exclusively by Pacific International Merchandising Corporation located in Sacramento, CA.
Last Mfg.'s Sug. Retail was $450.

SPORTING RIFLES

MODEL EM-321 — .22 LR, slide action, 19.5 in. barrel, 10 shot tube mag., hardwood stock and forearm, fixed sights, 6 lbs. Importation began 1989-90 only.

	$100	$80	$70	$60	$55	$50	$45

Last estimated retail was $125.

Grading	100%	98%	95%	90%	80%	70%	60%

TYPE EM-332 — .22 LR cal., bolt action, 18½ in. barrel with adj. rear sight, mag. holder on stock holds two extra 5 shot mag.'s, Monte Carlo stock with cheek piece and recoil pad, 4½ lbs. Importation began 1991.

No Mfg.'s Retail	$250	$220	$180	$160	$140	$120	$95

NHM-90 SPORT AK — 7.62 X 39K cal., sporterized Kalashnikov action featuring American walnut thumb hole stock, 16.34 in. barrel, 5 shot mag., 9 lbs. Importation began 1990.

No Mfg.'s Retail	$400	$350	$300	$265	$225	$200	$185

Each Model NHM-90 is supplied with three 5 shot mag.'s, sling, and cleaning kit.

SHOTGUNS

TYPE HL12-203 O/U — 12 ga. only, 2¾ in. chambers, boxlock action, ejectors, 30 in. vent. barrels and rib, single trigger, multi-chokes, checkered stock and forearm, 7½ lbs. Importation began 1989.

No Mfg.'s Retail	$400	$350	$300	$265	$225	$200	$185

TYPE HL12-102 PUMP — 12 ga. only, 2¾ in. chamber, 28.4 in. barrel, 3 shot mag., crossbolt safety on rear trigger guard, fixed chokes, 9.3 lbs. Importation began 1989.

No Mfg.'s Retail	$230	$200	$175	$165	$150	$135	$120

NORTH AMERICAN ARMS

Manufactured by North American Arms located in Spanish Fork, UT. This company is owned by Teleflex Defense Systems, also located in Spanish Fork, UT. Distributor and dealer sales.

MINI REVOLVERS

All mini revolvers are manufactured to highest quality control standards and have half-way notches cut on the front cylinder face allowing the hammer to lock up the cylinder between cartridges. This allows the gun to be carried fully loaded without the danger of accidental discharge.

NAA .22 LR — .22 LR cal., 5 shot, single action, spur trigger, 1⅛, 1⅝, or 2½ (disc.) in. barrel, stainless steel, plastic (disc.) or laminated rosewood grips, approx. 4½ oz. Mfg. 1975-present.

Mfg.'s Sug. Retail	$165		$135	$105	$85

Add $15 for 2½ in. barrel (disc.).
Add $31 for holster grip accessory.
The optional holster grip allows the pistol to fold forward allowing concealability, safety, and a clip which allows it to be attached to a belt.

✗ **Viper Belt Buckle Option** — belt buckle with built in 1⅛ or 1⅝ in. barrel revolver (LR cal.), disc. 1990, reintroduced 1993.

Mfg.'s Sug. Retail	$198		$170	$145	$125

NAA .22 MAGNUM — similar to .22 LR, except in .22 Mag. cal.

Mfg.'s Sug. Retail	$185		$160	$125	$100

Add $18 for 2½ in. barrel (disc.).

NAA .22 MAGNUM CONVERTIBLE — similar to NAA .22 Mag., except has extra LR cylinder in pouch.

Mfg.'s Sug. Retail	$220		$190	$155	$125

Add $18 for 2½ in. barrel (disc.).

Grading	100%	98%	95%	90%	80%	70%	60%

MINI-MASTER TARGET REVOLVER — .22 LR or .22 Mag., 5 shot, 4 in. heavy vent. barrel, unfluted bull cylinder, spur trigger, fixed or adj. white outline rear sight, oversize black rubber Mini-master grip, 10.7 oz. New 1990.

Mfg.'s Sug. Retail	$258	$225	$190	$170

Add $35 for extra combo cylinder.
Add $10 for adj. rear sight (elevation only).
This model is also available in hot fuschia colored oversized grips.

MINI-MASTER BLACK WIDOW — .22 LR or .22 Mag. cal., 2 in. heavy VR barrel, full size black rubber grip, fixed or adj. rear sight, unfluted cylinder, 8.8 oz. New 1991.

Mfg.'s Sug. Retail	$226	$195	$160	$130

Add $35 for extra combo cylinder.
Add $10 for adj. rear sight (elevation only).
This model is also available in hot fuschia colored oversized grips.

NAA STANDARD SET — 3 gun set (.22 Short, .22 LR, and .22 Mag.) in walnut display case with matching serial numbers, high polish finish with matte contours.

Mfg.'s Sug. Retail	$724	$630	$480	$375

NAA DELUXE SET — 3 gun set (.22 Short, .22 LR, and .22 Mag.) in walnut display case with matching serial numbers, high polish finish on entire gun.

Mfg.'s Sug. Retail	$781	$675	$560	$450

CASED .22 MAG. — includes .22 Mag. model in walnut display case with high polish finish with matte contours.

Mfg.'s Sug. Retail	$343	$290	$225	$185

REVOLVERS

NAA SINGLE ACTION REVOLVER — .45 Win. Mag. or .450 Mag. Express, polished stainless steel, transfer bar safety inside the hammer, 5 shot, 7½ in. barrel, walnut grips, includes presentation case.

Matte finish	$1,200	$950	$700
High polish finish	$1,400	$1,100	$850
Both cylinders	$1,650	$1,275	$975

Last Mfg.'s Sug. Retail was $650.
Also available by special order with 10½ in. barrel and optional scope. Extra cylinders are also available at $75-$100 extra and must be fitted to the gun. A set including 2 cylinders can also be ordered.

NORTH AMERICAN SAFARI EXPRESS

Trademark for those rifles (side by side) assembled by A. Francotte of Belgium for exclusive importation by Armes De Chasse located in Chadds Ford, PA.

O section

O.D.I. (OMEGA DEFENSIVE INDUSTRIES)

Previously manufactured in Midland Park, NJ from approximately 1981-1982. Oak's Wholesale, Inc. located in Rockledge, FL has acquired the remaining O.D.I. Viking Inventory of the Double Action .45 ACP Pistols. Previously, Randco Manufacturing located in Monrovia, CA., was providing service (and had parts) for these older O.D.I. Pistols.

Grading	100%	98%	95%	90%	80%	70%	60%

VIKING & VIKING COMBAT — .45 ACP or 9mm, Viking Model is Government size and the Combat Model is Commander size. All stainless steel construction, the design utilizes the Seecamp double action, teakwood grips. 9mm advertised but never saw production. 5 in. barrel on the Viking Model and 4 1/4 in. barrel on the Viking Combat Model, 7 shot mag., 39 oz. Approx. 200-300 Viking Combat Models were made from kits.

$475 $375 $295

Last Mfg.'s Retail was $579.

OBREGON

Manufactured previously by Fabrica de Armas Mexico located in Mexico City, Mexico.

OBREGON — 11.35mm cal., patterned somewhat after the Colt Model 1911A1, features tubular slide and Savage/Steyr type action, limited mfg. in Mexico for commercial sale during and after WWII, slide marked "Sistema Obregon Cal 11.35mm".

$650 $550 $475 $400 $350 $300 $275

This model is not frequently encountered domestically.

OLD-WEST GUN CO.

Importer and distributor that took over the inventory of Allen Firearms after they went out of business in early 1987. Old-West Gun Co. in late 1987 changed their name to Cimarron Arms. Refer to Cimarron Arms in this text for approximate prices on similar models from Old-West Gun Co.

OLYMPIC ARMS, INC.

Manufacturer located in Olympia, WA. Dealer direct sales.

In late 1987, Olympic Arms, Inc. acquired Safari Arms of Phoenix, AZ.

RIFLES

ULTRAMATCH — .223 cal., AR-15 action with modifications, 20 or 24 in. match stainless steel barrel, handle removed, Williams set trigger, scope mounts. New 1988.

Mfg.'s Sug. Retail $1,153 $1,025 $800 $700 $600 $550 $500 $460
Add $130 for custom aperture sights.

INTERCONTINENTAL — .223 cal., features synthetic wood-grained thumbhole butt stock and aluminum handguard, 20 in. ultra match barrel (free floating). New 1992.

Mfg.'s Sug. Retail $1,371 $1,240 $1,050 $875 $750 $600 $550 $500

INTERNATIONAL MATCH — .223 cal., similar to Ultramatch, except has custom aperture sights. New 1991.

Mfg.'s Sug. Retail $1,240 $1,080 $800 $700 $600 $550 $500 $460

SERVICE MATCH RIFLE — .223 cal., AR-15 action with modifications, ultra match barrel, standard trigger, choice of A1 or A2 flash suppressor.

Mfg.'s Sug. Retail $902 $825 $725 $650 $575 $530 $495 $450

Grading	100%	98%	95%	90%	80%	70%	60%

MULTIMATCH — .223 cal., tactical short range rifle, 16 in. Ultramatch barrel, stealth vortex flash suppressor. New 1991.

Mfg.'s Sug. Retail	$917	$835	$725	$650	$575	$530	$495	$450

AR-15 — .223 cal., patterned after the AR-15 with 20 in. barrel and solid stock.

Mfg.'s Sug. Retail	$710	$620	$530	$475	$450	$425	$395	$375

CAR-15 — .223 cal., modified AR-15 with choice of 11½ or 16 in. barrel, stow-away pistol grip and collapsible stock.

Mfg.'s Sug. Retail	$665	$595	$500	$475	$450	$425	$395	$375

COUNTER SNIPER RIFLE — .308 cal., bolt action utilizing M-14 mag.'s, 26 in. heavy barrel, camo-fiberglass stock, 10½ lbs. Disc. 1987.

	$1,100	$900	$775	$695	$550	$440	$410

Last Mfg.'s Sug. Retail was $1,225.

SURVIVOR I CONVERSION UNIT — .223 or .45 ACP cal., converts M1911 variations into carbine, bolt action, collapsible stock, 16¼ in. barrel, 5 lbs.

	$275	$225	$195

This kit is also available for S&W and Browning Hi-Power models.

OMEGA
Maker: Armero Specialistas Reunidas, Eibar, Spain, 1920's.

SEMI AUTOMATIC PISTOL — "Eibar" type, marked Omega on slide, 6 shot mag.

	100%	98%	95%	90%	80%	70%	60%
6.35 cal.	$125	$115	$100	$80	$70	$55	$40
7.65 cal.	$130	$120	$105	$90	$80	$70	$55

OMEGA FIREARMS
Previously manufactured in Flower Mound, TX.

SINGLE SHOT BOLT ACTION RIFLE — various cals., premium walnut. Disc. late 1960's.

	$775	$650	$575	$495	$425	$360	$295

OMEGA PISTOL
Previously manufactured and distributed by Springfield Armory located in Geneseo, IL.

PISTOLS: SEMI-AUTO

OMEGA — .38 Super, 10mm Norma, or .45 ACP cal., single action, ported slide, 5 or 6 in. interchangeable ported or unported barrel with Polygon rifling, special lock-up system eliminates normal barrel link and bushing, Pachmayr grips, dual extractors, adj. rear sight. Mfg. 1987-90.

	$625	$560	$495	$425	$360	$295	$265

Add $663 for interchangeable conversion units.
Each conversion unit includes an entire slide assembly, one mag., 5 or 6 in barrel, recoil spring guide mechanism assembly, and factory fitting.
Add $336 for interchangeable 5 or 6 in. barrel (including factory installation).
Last Mfg.'s Sug. Retail was $849.

OMEGA SHOTGUNS
Omega is the trademark of select shotguns imported by K.B.I., Inc. located in Harrisburg, PA.
Other K.B.I. imported shotguns (Kassnar trademark) can be found under the K.B.I. heading in this text.

SHOTGUNS

Grading	100%	98%	95%	90%	80%	70%	60%
STANDARD O/U — 12, 20 (disc.), 28 (disc.), or .410 (disc) ga., boxlock action, folding design, SNT, 26 or 28 in. VR barrels, extractors, checkered walnut stock and forearm, 5½-7 lbs.							
No Mfg.'s Retail	$495	$330	$295	$260	$230	$200	$180
Deluxe O/U — 12 ga. only, similar to Standard Model except has better walnut. Importation disc. 1990.	$335	$290	$255	$220	$185	$160	$140

Last Mfg.'s Sug. Retail was $379.

	100%	98%	95%	90%	80%	70%	60%
STANDARD SXS — 20, 28, or .410 ga., boxlock action, folding design, double triggers, hardwood stock and forearm, 26 in. barrels, extractors, 5½ lbs. Disc. 1989.	$190	$165	$140	$120	$110	$100	$90

Add $40 for 28 or .410 ga.
Last Mfg.'s Sug. Retail was $229.

	100%	98%	95%	90%	80%	70%	60%
Deluxe SXS — .410 ga. only, similar to Standard Model except has better walnut. Disc. 1989.	$200	$185	$170	$155	$140	$130	$120

Last Mfg.'s Sug. Retail was $249.

	100%	98%	95%	90%	80%	70%	60%
SINGLE BARREL — 12, 20, or .410 ga., various barrel lengths, matte blue finish, extractor. Importation disc. 1987.	$85	$75	$65	$55	$45	$40	$35

Last Mfg.'s Sug. Retail was $95.

	100%	98%	95%	90%	80%	70%	60%
STANDARD FOLDING SINGLE BARREL — 12, 16, 20, 28, or .410 ga., 28 or 30 in. barrel, checkered hardwood stock, matte chrome receiver, approx. 5½ lbs. Importation disc. 1987.	$160	$135	$115	$100	$85	$70	$65

Last Mfg.'s Sug. Retail was $180.

	100%	98%	95%	90%	80%	70%	60%
DELUXE FOLDING SINGLE BARREL — 12, 16, 20, 28, or .410 ga., similar to Standard Model, except has checkered walnut stock and forearm, blued receiver. Importation disc. 1987.	$195	$160	$135	$115	$100	$85	$70

Last Mfg.'s Sug. Retail was $220.

OPUS SPORTING ARMS, INC.
Previously manufactured by Opus Sporting Arms, Inc. located in Long Beach, CA.

	100%	98%	95%	90%	80%	70%	60%
OPUS ONE — .243, .270, or .30-06 cal., U.S.R.A. Co. Model 70 action, 24 in. barrel, deluxe checkered walnut stock with ebony forend cap, guaranteed 100 yard accuracy, 6¾ lbs., Halliburton cased. Mfg. 1987-1988 only.	$2,350	$1,995	$1,675	$1,250	$1,000	$875	$795

Last Mfg.'s Sug. Retail was $2,700.

	100%	98%	95%	90%	80%	70%	60%
OPUS TWO — similar to Opus One, except in 7mm Rem. Mag. or .300 Win. Mag. cal., 7¼ lbs., cased. Mfg. 1987-1988 only.	$2,350	$2,050	$1,705	$1,300	$1,000	$875	$795

Last Mfg.'s Sug. Retail was $2,700.

Grading	100%	98%	95%	90%	80%	70%	60%

OPUS THREE — similar to Opus Two, except in .375 H&H or .458 Win. Mag. cal., 10¼ lbs., cased. Mfg. 1987-1988 only.

	$2,600	$2,275	$1,800	$1,375	$1,050	$900	$825

Last Mfg.'s Sug. Retail was $2,850.

ORTGIES PISTOLS
Previously manufactured by Deutsche Werke A.G. located in Erfurt, Germany.

VEST POCKET AUTOMATIC — .25 ACP cal., 6 shot, 2¾ in. barrel, blue or nickel finish, fixed sights, wood grips, post-WWI.

	$225	$190	$165	$145	$125	$110	$100

POCKET AUTOMATIC — .32 ACP cal. (8 shot) or .380 ACP cal. (7 shot), 3¼ in. barrel, blue or nickel finish, fixed sights, wood grips.

	$250	$215	$175	$150	$130	$115	$105

Add 10% for .380 ACP cal.

ORVIS
Retailer/importer of private label subcontracted rifles/shotguns located in Dallas, Houston, TX and many other locations.

Orvis imports various rifles and shotguns under subcontract with various international manufacturers. Typical custom order delivery time is 6-8 months. Most of these private label models will approximate the values of the equivalent model manufactured by the subcontractor unless there are additional features and/or options which will add to the value.

SHOTGUNS: OVER/UNDER

UPLANDER SERIES — 12, 20, or 28 ga., boxlock action, 26 in. barrels with choke tubes (except 28 ga.), SST, straight grip, select European walnut with 24 LPI checkering, 6-7 lbs. Mfg. by P. Beretta of Italy.

Mfg.'s Sug. Retail	$2,750	$2,750	$2,200	$1,850	$1,500	$1,175	$995	$875

WATERFOWLER/SPORTING CLAYS — 12 ga. only, 3 in. chambers, matte metal finish, 28 in. barrels with choke tubes, 7½ lbs. Mfg. by P. Beretta of Italy.

Mfg.'s Sug. Retail	$2,750	$2,750	$2,200	$1,850	$1,500	$1,175	$995	$875

RUGER/ORVIS MODEL — 12 or 20 ga., 3 in. chambers, Red Label Ruger action with customized Orvis features including blued receiver and straight grip English checkered stock.

Mfg.'s Sug. Retail	$1,295	$1,295	$975	$850	$725	$600	$495	$450

SHOTGUNS: SxS

WATERFOWLER — 12 ga. only, 3 in. chambers, matte metal finish, 28 in. barrels with choke tubes, 7¾ lbs. Mfg. by P. Beretta of Italy.

Mfg.'s Sug. Retail	$1,950	$1,950	$1,725	$1,475	$1,125	$950	$825	$700

Grading	100%	98%	95%	90%	80%	70%	60%

CUSTOM UPLANDER — 12 - .410 ga., custom ordered gun, 25 or 27 in. barrels only, boxlock action, DT, mfg. by Arrieta located in Spain.

Mfg.'s Sug. Retail $3,300	$3,300	$2,650	$2,225	$1,800	$1,400	$995	$725

Add $950 for SNT.
Add $1,200 for extra set of barrels (same ga.).

FINE GRADE — 12 - .410 ga., custom ordered gun, 25 or 28 in. barrels only, boxlock action, DT, mfg. by Arrieta located in Spain.

Mfg.'s Sug. Retail $4,550	$4,550	$3,750	$3,150	$2,500	$1,995	$1,500	$1,150

Add $950 for SNT.
Add $1,950 for extra set of barrels (same ga.).

ROUND ACTION — similar to Fine Grade, except boxlock action has rounded corners, mfg. by Arrieta located in Spain.

Mfg.'s Sug. Retail $6,200	$6,200	$4,825	$3,975	$3,300	$2,550	$1,995	$1,500

P section

P.A.F.
Petoria Arms Company. Previous manufacturer located in S. Africa.

Grading	100%	98%	95%	90%	80%	70%	60%

.25 ACP PISTOL — .25 ACP cal., patterned after the Baby Browning, blued finish. Approx. 10,000 mfg.

	100%	98%	95%	90%	80%	70%	60%
	$375	$300	$275	$250	$225	$200	$180

P.A.W.S., INC.
Manufacturer located in the U.S. Distributed by Sile Distributors Inc. located in New York, NY.

ZX6/ZX8 CARBINE — 9mm Para. or .45 ACP cal., semi-auto paramilitary design carbine, 16 in. barrel, 10 or 32 shot mag., folding metal stock, matte black finish, aperture rear sight, partial barrel shroud, 7½ lbs. New 1989.

Mfg.'s Sug. Retail	$565	$500	$450	$400	$360	$330	$295	$275

The ZX6 is chambered for 9mm Para., while the ZX8 is chambered for .45 ACP.

P.S.M.G. GUN COMPANY
Previous manufacturer located in Arlington, MA.

SIX IN ONE SUPREME — .22 LR, .30 Luger, .38 Super, .38 Spl., 9mm, or .45 ACP cal., single action semi-auto, 3¼, 5, or 7½ in. barrel with solid cooling rib, adj. rear sight, limited mfg. Mfg. 1988-89.

	$700	$600	$500	$450	$400	$365	$330

Add $20-$55 for caliber options.
Add $25 for 7½ in. barrel.
Add $35 for satin nickel plating.
Add $225 per extra barrel.
Add $450 per individual conversion unit.
Last Mfg.'s Sug. Retail was $895

PTK INTERNATIONAL, INC.
Distributor located in Atlanta, GA.
Please refer to listing under Poly-Technologies in this section.

P.38s
Standard German military 9mm handgun beginning 1938. On older WWII German mfg., please refer to the German WWII Military Pistols section of this text.

P.38: JOHN MARTZ CONVERSIONS

Baby P.38 — 9mm Para., shortened barrel (3 in.), grip, and 7-shot mag., 43 mfg.

	$2,500	$2,000	$1,500

P.38 — .38 Super or .45 ACP cal., various barrel lengths.

	$4,500	$3,250	$2,500

P.38 Carbine — 9mm, 16 in. barrel, adj. rear sight, 26 mfg.

	$5,000	$3,950	$3,250

PARAMOUNT

Manufactured by Imperial Gun Co., Ltd. located in Surrey, England.

Imperial manufactures top quality competition rifles utilizing their own action. Each rifle is hand checked before leaving the factory. For additional information regarding this trademark, please refer to the Trademark Index in this text.

Grading	100%	98%	95%	90%	80%	70%	60%

THE IMPERIAL — .308 cal., single shot target rifle featuring thumbhole stock and CPE aperture rear sight, fully adj. trigger, vent. forearm.

RANGEMASTER — various cals., single shot design, steel frame, contoured walnut grips, satin chrome finish, 8½ lbs. Importation began 1992.

	100%	98%	95%	90%	80%	70%	60%
Mfg.'s Sug. Retail $1,800	$1,800	$1,600	$1,400	$1,200	$995	$895	$795

PARA-ORDNANCE MFG. INC.

Manufacturer located in Scarborough, Ontario, Canada. Distributed domestically by Para-Ordnance located in Fort Lauderdale, FL. Distributor sales only.

Para-Ordnance also manufactures the Model 85 full or semi-auto paint-shell carbine (styled after the Ingram). This model retails for $300.

P14 — .45 ACP cal., patterned after the Colt Model 1911A1 except has choice of alloy, steel, or stainless steel frame that has been widened slightly for extra shot capacity (13 shot), single action, 3 dot sight system, rounded combat hammer, 5 in. ramped barrel, 38 oz. with steel frame or 28 oz. with alloy frame. Introduced 1990.

	100%	98%	95%	90%	80%	70%	60%
Mfg.'s Sug. Retail $595	$525	$450	$400	$365	$335	$300	$275

Add $121 for steel frame.

P13 — similar to P14, except has 12 shot mag., 4¼ in. barrel, and satin nickel finished slide, 35 oz. with steel frame or 25 oz. with alloy frame. New 1993.

	100%	98%	95%	90%	80%	70%	60%
Mfg.'s Sug. Retail $716	$660	$575	$525	$475	$435	$400	$360

P12 — compact variation of the P14 featuring 11 shot mag. and 3½ in. barrel, 33 oz. with steel frame or 24 oz. with alloy frame. New 1990.

	100%	98%	95%	90%	80%	70%	60%
Mfg.'s Sug. Retail $650	$575	$475	$425	$385	$350	$325	$295

Add $59 for steel frame.

PARDINI

Manufacturer located in Lu, Italy. Currently imported by Mo's Competitor Supplies & Range, Inc. located in Brookfield, CT. Previously imported and distributed by Fiocchi of America, Inc., located in Ozark, MO until 1992.

PISTOLS

Pardini pistols have always been known for their technological improvements developed from ongoing design research. Air pistols may be found in the Airgun section of this text.

STANDARD PISTOL — .22 LR only, target grips, adj. sights, 4.92 in. barrel, interchangeable grips, detachable mag. New 1986.

	100%	98%	95%	90%	80%	70%	60%
Mfg.'s Sug. Retail $981	$875	$700	$575	$475	$425	$395	$375

LADIES PISTOL — similar to Standard Pistol, except grips are suitable for smaller hands. Imported 1986-90 only.

100%	98%	95%	90%	80%	70%	60%
$850	$700	$600	$520	$460	$410	$380

This variation is imported in limited quantities only.
Last Mfg.'s Sug. Retail was $955.

Grading		100%	98%	95%	90%	80%	70%	60%

RAPID FIRE PISTOL — .22 Short, features enclosed style grip assembly, adj. sights, 5.12 in. barrel. New 1986.

Mfg.'s Sug. Retail	$1,101		$975	$775	$650	$525	$460	$420	$395

CENTERFIRE PISTOL — .32 S&W Long cal., otherwise similar to Standard Pistol, 4.92 in. barrel. New 1986.

Mfg.'s Sug. Retail	$1,151		$1,000	$800	$675	$550	$480	$440	$415

FREE PISTOL — .22 LR, single shot, sliding rotating bolt, 9.06 in. barrel, tilted anatomical grip, top-of-the-line match pistol.

Mfg.'s Sug. Retail	$1,052		$925	$725	$625	$500	$450	$400	$375

PARKER PISTOLS

Refer to the Wyoming Arms section in this text.

PARKER BROTHERS

Originally manufactured in Meriden, CT from 1866-1934. Remington took over production in 1934, and in 1938, the plant was moved to Ilion, NY. Over 4,500 "Transition Guns" (exhibiting Meriden and Ilion characteristics) were produced in Meriden between 1934-1937 and about 4,500 Parkers were manufactured at the Ilion location before production stopped. Total production reached approx. 242,387.

SHOTGUNS: DAMASCUS BARRELS – HAMMER MODELS

Parker damascus or hammer shotguns are very collectible if original condition is high. Specimens in 90% or better condition with strong case colors can approximate values of the steel barrel models if the bores are in excellent condition also (no pitting). Values for under 90% specimens fall off rapidly and are no longer comparable to steel barrel guns. As an example, a steel "D" Grade (without ejectors) might range from $1,500 to $7,000 (10%-100%) with a rather even downward progression of values in between the high and low values. A 100% damascus "D" Grade might range from $1,500 to $2,000, with the 70% and lower conditions being from $295 up to $800 — not much of a spread. REMEMBER — MOST OF THESE GUNS ARE NOT RARE, BUT THEIR ORIGINAL CONDITION IS.

SHOTGUNS: FLUID STEEL BARRELS

Values listed below in the 95%-100% condition columns can vary immensely as there is almost no supply for these high demand items, always a prerequisite for unpredictable prices. 95% OF THE ORIGINAL PARKERS BOUGHT AND SOLD EACH YEAR ARE IN 30% OR LESS CONDITION (REFERRING TO ORIGINAL CASE COLORS).

Note: Values are for non-ejector guns through the CH grade, ejectors assumed on BHE and better models. Add 15% - 30% for vent. ribs. Skeet model has beavertail forearm and single selective trigger valued at approx. 50%-75% higher than values shown. Higher grade guns typically had ejectors, and will not make as much difference percentage-wise in the overall value as those lower grades with ejectors. Ejectors typically will add 50% more value to a Parker in common grades. Also, lower condition high grade models sometimes have their values established by the potential gain in refurbishing these specimens.

Due to the extremely high value of Parker Guns, extreme care should be taken in their purchase. There are many upgraded and refinished guns represented as original; expert advice should always be sought. Many collectors would rather own a specimen with 30% original case colors than a refinished gun that is 100% (regardless who did the work). Many advanced collectors will discount a refinished Parker's value 40%-60% of the price for an original gun. Misrepresentation of refinished or upgraded Parkers is rampant today - especially case colors. In other words, do your homework, be careful, shop carefully, and above all, get a receipt for exactly what you are purchasing.

Parker Brothers, cont.

Frame size on Parker shotguns is determined by the number on the bottom of the barrel lug on breech. Frame sizes (from largest to smallest) include 7, 6, 5, 4, 3, 2, 1½, 1, 0, 00, and 000. 8 ga. guns typically are framed 5, 6, or 7. 10 ga. guns typically are 3 or 4. 12 ga. guns typically range from 2 through 1. 20 and 16 ga.'s range from 2 through 0. 28 ga. guns are either 0 or 00. .410 ga. shotguns are 0, 00, or 000 (most common and most desirable).

The grade on Parker shotguns is a number or initials located on the water table of the frame. An alphabetical designation would indicate the grade immediately. For numerals, a "2" would indicate a GH, while an "8" would specify an A-1 Special. Interpolate for the others (numbers 3 through 7).

A note about Parker condition: Percentages of condition indicate the amount of original case colors remaining on the frame. A Parker IS NOT 60% if the barrel bluing and stock/forearm varnish are 60% but case colors are only 10%. Typically, a 60% case color Parker shotgun will have 90%+ blue and varnish, yet this does not mean the gun is 90% overall. Similarly, a 20% case color Parker will probably have 90% barrel bluing remaining.

STRONG, ORIGINAL CASE COLORS ARE THE KEY IN DETERMINING PARKER CONDITION AND SUBSEQUENT VALUES.

♯ PREMIUMS FOR PARKER SHOTGUNS:
Add 50% for ejectors (except AAH).
Add 20% for SST.
Add 20% for beavertail forearm.
Add 20%-50% for VR (rare on smaller gauges).
Add 20% for straight English stock.
Add 20% for skeleton steel butt plate.
Add 20% for short barrels (26 in. with open chokes).

100%	98%	95%	90%	80%	70%	60%	50%	40%	30%	20%	10%

TROJAN — Parker's lowest-priced gun, single or double triggers, but no auto ejectors available, very rarely found in mint condition because they were used a lot, a genuine utility gun, introduced 1912-13 with approx. 48,000 total mfg.

♯ **12 ga.**

100%	98%	95%	90%	80%	70%	60%	50%	40%	30%	20%	10%
$2,000	$1,600	$1,325	$1,075	$895	$775	$650	$575	$495	$450	$425	$395

♯ **16 ga.**

100%	98%	95%	90%	80%	70%	60%	50%	40%	30%	20%	10%
$3,000	$2,500	$2,000	$1,500	$1,250	$1,000	$850	$700	$600	$525	$475	$425

♯ **20 ga.**

100%	98%	95%	90%	80%	70%	60%	50%	40%	30%	20%	10%
$3,000	$2,500	$2,000	$1,500	$1,250	$1,025	$895	$775	$675	$600	$550	$500

VH — Parker's biggest selling model, offered with all options, the most commonly found Parker. Approx. 60,000 mfg. 10 ga. is very rare in this model.
Add 50% for ejectors (VHE Model).

♯ **12 ga.**

100%	98%	95%	90%	80%	70%	60%	50%	40%	30%	20%	10%
$3,250	$2,750	$2,200	$1,750	$1,450	$1,200	$1,000	$900	$825	$750	$675	$600

♯ **16 ga.**

100%	98%	95%	90%	80%	70%	60%	50%	40%	30%	20%	10%
$3,250	$2,750	$2,200	$1,750	$1,450	$1,200	$1,000	$900	$825	$750	$675	$600

♯ **20 ga.**

100%	98%	95%	90%	80%	70%	60%	50%	40%	30%	20%	10%
$3,950	$3,750	$3,500	$3,200	$3,000	$2,800	$2,400	$2,200	$2,000	$1,800	$1,600	$1,400

	100%	98%	95%	90%	80%	70%	60%	50%	40%	30%	20%	10%

28 ga.

100%	98%	95%	90%	80%	70%	60%	50%	40%	30%	20%	10%
$6,500	$6,250	$5,750	$5,150	$4,600	$3,900	$3,220	$2,875	$2,645	$2,300	$2,075	$1,900

.410 ga.

100%	98%	95%	90%	80%	70%	60%	50%	40%	30%	20%	10%
$18,500	$16,100	$14,000	$12,250	$10,000	$8,750	$7,900	$6,900	$6,250	$5,750	$5,350	$4,775

PH — offered for a very short time, most had damascus barrels, prices here are for fluid steel barrels only. Approx. 8,500 mfg. A very few .410 ga.'s were mfg. 10 ga. is very rare in this model.
Add 50% for ejectors (PHE Model).

12 ga.

100%	98%	95%	90%	80%	70%	60%	50%	40%	30%	20%	10%
$3,150	$2,850	$2,600	$2,350	$2,100	$1,850	$1,625	$1,400	$1,150	$995	$900	$825

16 ga.

100%	98%	95%	90%	80%	70%	60%	50%	40%	30%	20%	10%
$3,150	$2,850	$2,600	$2,350	$2,100	$1,850	$1,625	$1,400	$1,150	$995	$900	$825

20 ga.

100%	98%	95%	90%	80%	70%	60%	50%	40%	30%	20%	10%
$4,600	$4,300	$4,000	$3,750	$3,350	$2,950	$2,600	$2,350	$2,175	$1,900	$1,650	$1,400

28 ga.

100%	98%	95%	90%	80%	70%	60%	50%	40%	30%	20%	10%
$8,100	$7,800	$7,400	$7,000	$6,500	$6,000	$5,750	$5,500	$5,000	$4,500	$3,750	$3,000

GH — very popular model, barrels marked Parker, special steel, engraved moderately with all options available. Approx. 28,500 mfg. 10 ga. is very rare in this model.
Add 50% for ejectors (GHE Model).

12 ga.

100%	98%	95%	90%	80%	70%	60%	50%	40%	30%	20%	10%
$3,950	$3,500	$3,150	$2,475	$1,850	$1,625	$1,400	$1,150	$950	$795	$695	$595

16 ga.

100%	98%	95%	90%	80%	70%	60%	50%	40%	30%	20%	10%
$4,250	$3,750	$3,350	$2,600	$2,175	$1,850	$1,575	$1,250	$950	$795	$695	$595

20 ga.

100%	98%	95%	90%	80%	70%	60%	50%	40%	30%	20%	10%
$4,600	$4,000	$3,350	$2,600	$2,175	$1,850	$1,625	$1,400	$1,150	$995	$875	$750

28 ga.

100%	98%	95%	90%	80%	70%	60%	50%	40%	30%	20%	10%
$7,000	$6,375	$5,750	$5,125	$4,550	$3,925	$3,375	$2,875	$2,645	$2,300	$2,075	$1,750

.410 ga.

100%	98%	95%	90%	80%	70%	60%	50%	40%	30%	20%	10%
$20,000	$17,250	$15,350	$12,850	$10,500	$8,525	$7,375	$6,600	$5,950	$5,300	$4,500	$3,850

DH — the most popular higher grade gun, very tastefully engraved and flawlessly finished. Approx. 48,000 mfg. 10 ga. is very rare in this model.
Add 40% for ejectors (DHE Model).

12 ga.

100%	98%	95%	90%	80%	70%	60%	50%	40%	30%	20%	10%
$5,500	$4,850	$4,100	$3,450	$2,675	$2,175	$1,850	$1,625	$1,400	$1,125	$925	$795

16 ga.

100%	98%	95%	90%	80%	70%	60%	50%	40%	30%	20%	10%
$5,800	$4,925	$4,200	$3,500	$2,675	$2,175	$1,850	$1,625	$1,400	$1,125	$925	$795

20 ga.

100%	98%	95%	90%	80%	70%	60%	50%	40%	30%	20%	10%
$6,375	$5,750	$5,125	$4,550	$3,925	$3,375	$2,875	$2,400	$2,075	$1,750	$1,350	$950

28 ga.

100%	98%	95%	90%	80%	70%	60%	50%	40%	30%	20%	10%
$10,500	$9,250	$8,175	$7,000	$6,375	$5,750	$5,125	$4,550	$3,925	$3,375	$2,875	$2,375

.410 ga.

100%	98%	95%	90%	80%	70%	60%	50%	40%	30%	20%	10%
$40,500	$35,250	$28,250	$22,000	$18,950	$16,350	$14,000	$12,750	$10,650	$9,100	$8,000	$7,250

	100%	98%	95%	90%	80%	70%	60%	50%	40%	30%	20%	10%

CHE — scarce because they were only slightly more decorative than the DHE, Acme steel barrels. Approx. 5,000 mfg. 10 ga. is very rare in this model.
Add 33% for ejectors (CHE Model).

12 ga.

100%	98%	95%	90%	80%	70%	60%	50%	40%	30%	20%	10%
$6,250	$5,575	$4,775	$4,000	$3,350	$2,600	$2,175	$1,850	$1,450	$1,100	$875	$750

16 ga.

100%	98%	95%	90%	80%	70%	60%	50%	40%	30%	20%	10%
$6,575	$5,700	$4,850	$4,050	$3,350	$2,600	$2,175	$1,850	$1,450	$1,100	$875	$750

20 ga.

100%	98%	95%	90%	80%	70%	60%	50%	40%	30%	20%	10%
$8,450	$7,425	$6,375	$5,550	$4,950	$4,300	$3,750	$3,100	$2,650	$2,175	$1,675	$1,000

28 ga.

100%	98%	95%	90%	80%	70%	60%	50%	40%	30%	20%	10%
$21,000	$17,500	$13,850	$10,500	$9,250	$8,175	$7,000	$6,375	$5,750	$5,125	$4,550	$3,895

.410 ga. — very rare, approx. 6 are known to exist.

100%	98%	95%	90%	80%	70%	60%	50%	40%	30%	20%	10%
$49,500	$40,500	$35,250	$28,250	$23,250	$19,950	$17,250	$14,450	$12,950	$11,000	$9,950	$8,950

BH — quite popular and decorative, 4 styles of engraving available, Acme steel barrels. Approx. 13,000 mfg. 10 ga. is very rare in this model.
Add 25% for ejectors (BHE Model).

12 ga.

100%	98%	95%	90%	80%	70%	60%	50%	40%	30%	20%	10%
$9,500	$8,450	$7,425	$6,375	$5,550	$4,950	$4,300	$3,750	$3,100	$2,650	$2,075	$1,575

16 ga.

100%	98%	95%	90%	80%	70%	60%	50%	40%	30%	20%	10%
$9,950	$8,650	$7,600	$6,400	$5,550	$4,950	$4,300	$3,750	$3,100	$2,650	$2,075	$1,575

20 ga.

100%	98%	95%	90%	80%	70%	60%	50%	40%	30%	20%	10%
$17,500	$14,500	$12,000	$10,250	$9,300	$8,275	$7,100	$6,375	$5,650	$5,000	$4,550	$3,650

28 ga.

100%	98%	95%	90%	80%	70%	60%	50%	40%	30%	20%	10%
$32,500	$27,650	$21,000	$17,500	$13,850	$10,500	$9,250	$8,175	$7,000	$6,275	$5,350	$4,550

.410 ga. — only 2 guns are known in this gauge, the BHE .410 is also the highest grade .410 ga. known to have been made. Extreme rarity precludes accurate price evaluation, but will be VERY expensive.

AHE — a scarce gun, extremely decorative and flawlessly executed, Acme steel barrels. Approx. 5,500 mfg. 10 ga. is very rare in this model.
Subtract 25% if without ejectors (AH Model).

12 ga.

100%	98%	95%	90%	80%	70%	60%	50%	40%	30%	20%	10%
$23,000	$19,550	$16,100	$12,250	$9,250	$8,000	$7,150	$6,250	$5,600	$4,950	$4,175	$3,450

16 ga.

100%	98%	95%	90%	80%	70%	60%	50%	40%	30%	20%	10%
$26,000	$21,000	$17,000	$13,000	$9,375	$8,100	$7,150	$6,250	$5,600	$4,950	$4,175	$3,450

20 ga.

100%	98%	95%	90%	80%	70%	60%	50%	40%	30%	20%	10%
$32,500	$27,650	$21,000	$17,500	$13,850	$10,500	$9,250	$8,175	$7,000	$6,400	$5,700	$5,100

28 ga.

100%	98%	95%	90%	80%	70%	60%	50%	40%	30%	20%	10%
$57,500	$49,750	$40,250	$31,500	$23,750	$18,975	$16,000	$14,000	$12,250	$10,750	$9,000	$8,250

.410 ga. — no original guns known to exist.

100%	98%	95%	90%	80%	70%	60%	50%	40%	30%	20%	10%

AAHE — very elaborate model, early AAs have Whitworth barrels, late ones have Peerless. Approx. 340 mfg.
    Subtract 20% if without ejectors (AAH Model).

⌐ **12 ga.**

100%	98%	95%	90%	80%	70%	60%	50%	40%	30%	20%	10%
$35,000	$32,000	$28,500	$26,000	$23,000	$21,000	$19,000	$17,000	$15,500	$13,750	$12,000	$10,500

⌐ **16 ga.**

100%	98%	95%	90%	80%	70%	60%	50%	40%	30%	20%	10%
$39,000	$35,000	$32,000	$28,500	$26,000	$23,000	$21,000	$19,000	$17,000	$15,500	$13,750	$12,000

⌐ **20 ga.**

100%	98%	95%	90%	80%	70%	60%	50%	40%	30%	20%	10%
$57,500	$54,000	$50,000	$45,000	$40,250	$35,000	$31,050	$28,000	$24,750	$21,000	$19,550	$17,250

⌐ **28 ga.**

100%	98%	95%	90%	80%	70%	60%	50%	40%	30%	20%	10%
$86,250	$79,000	$74,750	$68,500	$63,250	$58,750	$53,475	$46,000	$39,500	$33,925	$28,175	$25,875

A-1 SPECIAL GRADE — 100% engraved, all were special ordered, each one inspected by the company president before being shipped. Approx. 320 mfg.

⌐ **12 ga.**

100%	98%	95%	90%	80%	70%	60%	50%	40%	30%	20%	10%
$75,000	$67,500	$61,000	$57,000	$51,750	$46,250	$40,250	$36,175	$31,050	$28,500	$26,450	$22,000

⌐ **16 ga.**

100%	98%	95%	90%	80%	70%	60%	50%	40%	30%	20%	10%
$75,000	$67,500	$61,000	$57,000	$51,750	$46,250	$40,250	$36,175	$31,050	$28,500	$26,450	$22,000

⌐ **20 ga.**

100%	98%	95%	90%	80%	70%	60%	50%	40%	30%	20%	10%
$125,000	$112,500	$100,000	$90,000	$82,000	$76,000	$70,000	$64,000	$57,500	$53,000	$46,500	$40,000

⌐ **28 ga.** — extreme rarity and desirability factors preclude accurate price evaluation by condition factors. 70% original condition A-1 Specials HAVE sold for over $90,000.

SINGLE BARREL TRAP GUNS

12 ga. only, 26, 28, 30, 32, and 34 in. barrels, any boring is available, as is stock configuration, boxlock, auto ejector. The grades differ only in engraving, checkering and wood finish.

It should be noted that single barrel trap guns cannot be compared to the SxS models as they are not as desirable even though they are rarer. Most side by side collectors are not that interested in single barrel trap models and very few collectors specialize in single barrels.

S.C. GRADE

100%	98%	95%	90%	80%	70%	60%	50%	40%	30%	20%	10%
$2,275	$1,850	$1,625	$1,400	$1,150	$995	$900	$825	$750	$675	$600	$475

S.B. GRADE

100%	98%	95%	90%	80%	70%	60%	50%	40%	30%	20%	10%
$3,400	$3,050	$2,675	$2,275	$1,700	$1,425	$1,100	$950	$850	$750	$650	$500

S.A. GRADE

100%	98%	95%	90%	80%	70%	60%	50%	40%	30%	20%	10%
$4,750	$3,875	$3,050	$2,675	$2,275	$1,700	$1,425	$1,100	$950	$850	$750	$650

S.A.A. GRADE

100%	98%	95%	90%	80%	70%	60%	50%	40%	30%	20%	10%
$6,950	$5,800	$4,750	$3,875	$3,050	$2,675	$2,275	$1,700	$1,425	$1,100	$875	$750

S.A.-1 SPECIAL GRADE

100%	98%	95%	90%	80%	70%	60%	50%	40%	30%	20%	10%
$20,000	$18,000	$15,500	$13,000	$10,000	$9,150	$8,350	$7,425	$6,375	$5,550	$4,950	$4,300

PARKER REPRODUCTIONS

Previously imported by the Parker Reproduction Division of Reagent Chemical & Research, Inc., located in Middlesex, NJ. Distributed by Parker Reproductions located in Webb City, MO. These shotguns were manufactured in Japan to original Parker specifications by Winchester until the factory closed in January, 1989.

In 1984 Winchester was contracted by Reagent Chemical & Research, Inc. to manufacture a new Parker shotgun. The new SxS was a DHE model, available in 20 and 28 ga. initially. These models were fabricated in Japan to original Parker specifications, and the reproduction is so authentic that most parts are interchangeable with original Parker guns. Mfg. 1984-89. In 1993, a 16/20 ga. combo was introduced in some models.

SHOTGUNS: SIDE BY SIDE

Models listed below with Mfg.'s Sug. Retail indicates limited existing inventory as this edition goes to press. Because of the high quality and limited mfg. of these reproductions, they are becoming quite collectible.

Grading	100%	98%	95%	90%	80%	70%	60%

DHE GRADE — 12 (new 1986), 20, or 28 (new 1984) ga., boxlock action, ejectors, single selective or double triggers, beavertail or splinter forend, straight or pistol grip stock, skeleton steel butt plate, engraving in original DH style, case hardened frame, rust blued barrels. Supplied with leather trunk case, canvas and leather cover, and snap caps.

	100%	98%	95%	90%	80%	70%	60%
Mfg.'s Sug. Retail $3,370	$3,370	$2,995	$2,850	$2,100	$1,850	$1,650	$1,500

Add $1,000 for extra set of barrels.
Add $150 for beavertail forend.
Add $1,000 for internal screw chokes (sold out—original retail was $150 extra).

DHE SMALL GAUGE COMBO — available as a 28/.410 ga. combo with 2 barrels and 2 forends. Less than 160 mfg.

	100%	98%	95%	90%	80%	70%	60%
	$6,500	$5,750	$4,500	$4,000	$3,625	$3,150	$2,900

Last Mfg.'s Sug. Retail was $4,970.

3-Barrel Set — includes 28, and .410 ga. barrels. Cased.

	100%	98%	95%	90%	80%	70%	60%
	$7,700	$6,850	$5,300	$4,750	$4,325	$3,900	$3,400

Last Mfg.'s Sug. Retail was $5,970.

DHE STEEL SHOT SPECIAL — similar to 12 ga. D Grade, except has strengthened No. 1½ barrels, 3 in. chambers, and 28 in. chrome lined barrels, 7¼-7½ lbs. Very limited mfg. 1987-89.

	100%	98%	95%	90%	80%	70%	60%
	$4,250	$3,850	$3,100	$2,800	$2,500	$2,250	$2,000

Add $100 for beavertail forend.
Last Mfg.'s Sug. Retail was $3,120.

BHE GRADE LIMITED EDITION — 12, 20, or 28 ga., original Parker BH specifications, single selective or double trigger(s), straight or pistol grip stock, engraved skeleton butt plate, bank note scroll engraving around game scenes, cased. Only 100 manufactured in each gauge — mfg. began late 1987-89.

	100%	98%	95%	90%	80%	70%	60%
	$5,000	$4,500	$3,950	$2,650	$2,150	$1,800	$1,500

Add $4,000 for 28 or .410 ga.
Add $1,000 for extra set of barrels.
Add $150 for beavertail forend.
Last Mfg.'s Sug. Retail was $3,970.
A 28/.410 ga. combo was also available with 2 forends. Only seven 28 ga.'s were mfg. in this model.

Grading	100%	98%	95%	90%	80%	70%	60%

A-1 SPECIAL — 12, 20, or 28 (sold out) ga., original Parker A-1 specifications, single selective or double trigger(s), fine scroll engraving with game scenes, 32 lines/in. checkering, cased with accessories. Limited mfg. 1988-89.

Mfg.'s Sug. Retail	$11,200	$11,200	$8,500	$7,250	$6,000	$5,475	$4,800	$4,350

Add $3,000+ for 28 ga. (sold out).
Add $1,000 for extra set of barrels.
Add $200 for beavertail forend.

⚔ **A-1 Special Custom Engraved** — custom (per individual special order) engraving, available with two sets of barrels only, cased with accessories. Limited mfg. 1988-89. Prices start at $11,000 and go up according to individualized special features.

⚔ **Federal Duck Stamp Collector's Series** — available in 12 or 20 ga., A-1 Special specifications, authorized by U.S. Department of Interior. Mfg. was limited to 10 per year in 1988-89 only.

Mfg.'s Sug. Retail	$14,000	$14,000	$10,000	$8,000

This model includes special case and 2 barrels per buyer's specifications.

PARKER-HALE LIMITED

Manufacturer located in Birmingham, England. Rifles were manufactured in England until 1991 when Navy Arms purchased the manufacturing rights and built a plant in West Virginia for fabrication. This new company is called Gibbs Rifle Company and currently manufactured models are very similar to older Parker-Hale rifles (see Gibbs Rifle Company section in this text for a complete model listing). Shotguns are mfg. in Spain to Parker-Hale specifications and are currently being imported by Precision Sports, a Division of Cortland Line Company, Inc. located in Cortland, NY.

RIFLES: BOLT ACTION

All Parker rifle importation was discontinued in 1991. Parker-Hale bolt action rifles utilize the Mauser K-98 action and were offered in a variety of configurations. A single set trigger option was introduced in 1984 on most models which allows either "hair trigger" or conventional single stage operation - add $85.

MODEL 81 CLASSIC — available in 11 cals. between .22-250 and 7mm Rem. Mag., 24 in. barrel, open sights, 4 shot mag., select checkered walnut with sling swivels, $7\frac{3}{4}$ lbs. New 1985.

	$715	$565	$475	$395	$340	$300	$280

Last Mfg.'s Sug. Retail was $860.

⚔ **Model 81 African** — .375 H&H or 9.3 x 62mm cal., similar specifications as Model 81 Classic and has engraved action. New 1986.

	$875	$700	$600	$500	$425	$360	$330

Last Mfg.'s Sug. Retail was $1,110.

MODEL 84 TARGET — 7.62mm, match rifle with special sights, adj. cheek piece on stock. Importation disc. 1990.

	$1,080	$875	$760	$680	$610	$530	$465

Last Mfg.'s Sug. Retail was $1,300.

MODEL 85 SNIPER RIFLE — .308 cal., bolt action, extended heavy barrel, 10 shot mag., camo green synthetic stock with stippling, built in adj. bipod, enlarged contoured bolt, adj. recoil pad. Importation began 1989.

	$1,750	$1,425	$1,275	$1,050	$875	$750	$625

Last Mfg.'s Sug. Retail was $1,975.

Grading	100%	98%	95%	90%	80%	70%	60%

MODEL 86 TARGET — 7.62mm, 27½ in. barrel, 5 shot mag., stippled stock and forend, aperture front and rear sights, 11¼ lbs. Distributed 1986 only by North American Precision.

	$980	$830	$760	$690	$610	$530	$465

Last Mfg.'s Sug. Retail was $1,149.

MODEL 87 TARGET — .243, 6.5 x 55, .308, .30-06, or .300 Win. Mag. cal., target stock, aperture sights. Importation began 1987.

	$1,375	$1,100	$900	$775	$650	$550	$495

Last Mfg.'s Sug. Retail was $1,525.

MODEL 1000 STANDARD — available in 9 cals. between .22-250 and .308 Win., 22 in. barrel, 4 shot mag., walnut stock with cheek piece, 7¼ lbs. Disc. 1988.

	$400	$330	$285	$255	$230	$215	$195

Last Mfg.'s Sug. Retail was $500.

MODEL 1100 LIGHTWEIGHT — available in 9 cals. between .22-250 and .30-06, 22 in. barrel, open sights, 4 shot mag., 6½ lbs. New 1985.

	$495	$400	$350	$325	$285	$270	$255

Last Mfg.'s Sug. Retail was $595.

⚔ **Model 1100M African** — .375 H&H, .404 Jeffery, or .458 Win. Mag. cal., 24 in. barrel, 4 shot mag., 9½ lbs.

	$800	$650	$575	$500	$450	$425	$400

Last Mfg.'s Sug. Retail was $960.

MODEL 1200 SUPER — bolt action, Mauser type action, .22-250, .243, 6mm, .25-06, .270, .30-06, .300 Win. Mag., 7mm Rem., or .308 cal., 24 in. barrel, folding sight, skip checkered walnut stock, pad swivels, rosewood pistol grip cap and forend tip. Mfg. 1968-present.

	$540	$450	$375	$330	$295	$275	$260

This model in Magnum cals. is called the 1200 M Super Magnum.
Last Mfg.'s Sug. Retail was $680.

⚔ **Model 1200 C (Super Clip)** — similar to Model 1200 Super, except has detachable 4 shot box mag.

	$590	$500	$400	$350	$300	$280	$265

Last Mfg.'s Sug. Retail was $740.

MODEL 1200P PRESENTATION — similar to 1200, except .243 or .30-06 cal., scroll engraved, no sights. Mfg. 1969-1975.

	$495	$425	$395	$340	$315	$305	$275

MODEL 1200 SUPER VARMINT — similar to 1200, except .22-250, 6mm, .25-06, or .243 cal., 24 in. heavy barrel, no sights. Disc. 1988.

	$525	$425	$365	$325	$285	$270	$255

Last Mfg.'s Sug. Retail was $660.

MODEL 1300 C SCOUT — shorter barrel variation.

	$695	$550	$450	$385	$330	$300	$275

Last Mfg.'s Sug. Retail was $785.

MODEL 2100 MIDLAND (HYBRID ACTION) — available in 11 cals. between .22-250 or .300 Win. Mag. cal., 22 in. barrel, 4 shot mag., open sights, 7 lbs.

	$325	$270	$230	$200	$190	$180	$170

Last Mfg.'s Sug. Retail was $365.

Grading	100%	98%	95%	90%	80%	70%	60%

Model 2100 Midland Magnum — .300 Win. Mag., or 7mm Rem. Mag. cal., 24 in. barrel, 4 shot mag., 9½ lbs. Imported 1989-90 only.

| | $380 | $325 | $295 | $270 | $260 | $250 | $240 |

Last Mfg.'s Sug. Retail was $430.

MODEL 2600 MIDLAND SPECIAL — .243 Win., .270 Win., .308 Win., or .30-06 cal., Midland Gun Co. action, iron sights. New 1989.

| | $295 | $250 | $225 | $200 | $190 | $180 | $170 |

Last Mfg.'s Sug. Retail was $330.

MIDLAND 2700 LIGHTWEIGHT — lightweight variation of the Model 2600.

| | $340 | $285 | $240 | $200 | $190 | $180 | $170 |

Last Mfg.'s Sug. Retail was $390.

SHOTGUNS: SxS

MODEL 630 — 12 ga. only, 3 in. chambers, boxlock action with color case hardening, extractors, DTs, 26 or 28 in. barrels with fixed chokes, checkered English grip stock and forearm, includes deluxe shotgun case. New 1993.

| Mfg.'s Sug. Retail | $699 | $625 | $525 | $450 | $400 | $365 | $330 | $295 |

This model is available in limited quantities only from Ugartechea in Spain.

MODEL 640E (ENGLISH) — 12, 16, 20, 28, or .410 ga., boxlock action, double triggers, straight grip stock, splinter forend, concave rib, extractors, silver finished receiver. New 1986.

| Mfg.'s Sug. Retail | $850 | $750 | $595 | $540 | $475 | $415 | $350 | $295 |

Add $90 for 28 or $120 for .410 ga.
The "E" suffix in this model designates English configuration.

Model 640A (AMERICAN) — same ga.'s as 640E, except has non-selective single trigger, pistol grip, beavertail forend, and raised matted rib. New 1986.

| Mfg.'s Sug. Retail | $970 | $840 | $700 | $630 | $560 | $475 | $400 | $350 |

Add $110 for 28 or $130 for .410 ga.
The "A" suffix in this model designates American configuration (pistol grip stock and single trigger).

MODEL 640M (MAGNUM) — 10 ga., 3½ in. chambers, 26, 30, or 32 in. barrels bored full and full, DTs, recoil pad. New 1989.

| Mfg.'s Sug. Retail | $1,000 | $860 | $725 | $650 | $575 | $495 | $415 | $365 |

In this model, the 26 in. barrels are referred to as the Turkey Gun, the 30 in. is Big Ten, and the 32 in. is Goose Gun.

MODEL 640 SLUG GUN — 12 ga. only, 25 in. barrels bored IC/IC. New 1991.

| Mfg.'s Sug. Retail | $1,120 | $995 | $850 | $725 | $650 | $575 | $495 | $415 |

MODEL 645E (ENGLISH) — 12, 16, 20, 28 or .410 ga., boxlock action, double triggers, straight grip stock, moderate engraving, splinter forend, concave rib, ejectors, silver finished receiver. New 1986.

| Mfg.'s Sug. Retail | $1,090 | $940 | $775 | $675 | $595 | $500 | $415 | $365 |

Add $60 for 28 or $110 for .410 ga.

Model 645E-XXV — available in all ga.'s, 25 in. barrels only, ejectors, Churchill rib, moderately engraved, silver finished receiver. New 1986.

| Mfg.'s Sug. Retail | $1,100 | $940 | $775 | $675 | $595 | $500 | $415 | $365 |

Add $100 for 28 or $130 for .410 ga.

Grading	100%	98%	95%	90%	80%	70%	60%

⋇ **Model 645E Bi-Gauge** — 2 barrel set available in either 20/28 ga. or 28/.410 ga. combination. Mfg. 1988-92.

	$1,475	$1,175	$950	$800	$700	$600	$550

Add $150 for 28/.410 ga. combo. (disc. 1991).
Last Mfg.'s Sug. Retail was $1,620.

MODEL 645A (AMERICAN) — same ga.'s as 645E, except has non-selective single trigger, pistol grip, beavertail forend, and raised matted rib. New 1986.

Mfg.'s Sug. Retail	$1,200	$1,025	$825	$700	$615	$515	$440	$400

Add $110 for 28 or $150 for .410 ga.

⋇ **Model 645A Bi-Gauge** — 2 barrel set available in either 20/28 ga. or 28/.410 ga. combination. Mfg. 1988-92.

	$1,600	$1,325	$995	$850	$750	$625	$575

Add $150 for 28/.410 ga. combo. (disc. 1991).
Last Mfg.'s Sug. Retail was $1,750.

MODEL 650 ENGLISH OR AMERICAN — 12 ga. only, 28 in. barrels with IC/M choke tubes, extractors, choice of English (DT and straight grip stock) or American (SNT, pistol grip stock, and beavertail forend), silver frame finish. Importation began 1992.

Mfg.'s Sug. Retail	$920	$825	$700	$630	$560	$475	$400	$350

Add $120 for Model 650 American option.

MODEL 655 ENGLISH OR AMERICAN — 12 ga. only, 28 in. barrels with IC/M choke tubes, ejectors, choice of English (DT and straight grip stock) or American (SNT, pistol grip stock, and beavertail forend), silver frame finish. Importation began 1992.

Mfg.'s Sug. Retail	$1,150	$925	$825	$700	$630	$560	$475	$400

Add $110 for Model 655 American option.

MODEL 670E (ENGLISH) — 12, 16, or 20 ga., sidelock action, 26, 27, or 28 in. barrels, ejectors, engraved silver finished receiver, double triggers, straight grip. Imported 1986-91.

	$3,700	$2,975	$2,450	$1,850	$1,550	$1,375	$1,200

Add $770 for 28 or .410 ga.
This model was available by custom order only.
Last Mfg.'s Sug. Retail was $4,270.

MODEL 680E-XXV (ENGLISH) — similar to Model 670E, except has color case hardened sideplates and 25 in. barrels only.

	$3,500	$2,800	$2,300	$1,700	$1,475	$1,300	$1,175

Add $400 for 28 or .410 ga.
This model was available by custom order only.
Last Mfg.'s Sug. Retail was $4,070.

BILL HANUS BIRDGUN — 16, 20, or 28 ga., boxlock action, 26 in. barrels bored SK1/SK2, Churchill raised rib, SNT, ejectors, case colored receiver, checkered straight grip walnut stock and semi-beavertail forend, oil finish, lifetime warranty, 5¼-6½ lbs. New 1991.

Mfg.'s Sug. Retail	$1,270	$1,060	$835	$700	$615	$515	$440	$400

Add $130 for 28 ga.
Add $325 with hard case and accessories.

PAUZA SPECIALTIES

Manufactured by Pauza Specialties since 1991. Distributed by California Armory, Inc. located in San Bruno, CA. Dealer or distributor sales.

Grading	100%	98%	95%	90%	80%	70%	60%

RIFLES

P50 SEMI-AUTO — .50 BMG cal., semi-auto, 24 (carbine) or 29 (rifle) in. match grade barrel, 5 shot detachable mag., one-piece receiver, 3-stage gas system, takedown action, all exterior parts Teflon coated, with aluminum bipod, 25 or 30 lbs. New 1992.

	100%	98%	95%	90%	80%	70%	60%
Mfg.'s Sug. Retail $5,995	$5,500	$5,000	$4,500	$4,000	$3,600	$3,200	$2,800

PEDERSEN CUSTOM GUNS

Previously a division of O.F. Mossberg, North Haven, CT. Manufactured between 1973-1975.

RIFLES

MODEL 3000 — bolt action rifle, Mossberg Model 810 action, .270, .30-06, 7mm Mag., or .338 Mag. cal., 22 and 24 in. barrel, open sight, checkered Monte Carlo stock.

Grade III — no engraving.

	100%	98%	95%	90%	80%	70%	60%
	$550	$495	$470	$440	$420	$385	$330

Grade II — moderately engraved.

	$660	$580	$525	$495	$440	$420	$385

Grade I — heavily engraved and inlaid, with select wood.

	$990	$770	$745	$690	$635	$560	$495

Presentation Model — top-of-the-line model.

	$1,250	$1,000	$895	$800	$745	$690	$635

MODEL 4700 — custom deluxe lever action, (Model 472 Mossberg), .30-30 or .35 Rem. cal., 5 shot, tube mag., 24 in. barrel, open sight, black walnut stock.

	$250	$195	$165	$155	$145	$130	$120

SHOTGUNS

MODEL 4000 SLIDE ACTION SHOTGUN — custom Mossberg Model 500, 12, 20, or .410 ga., 3 in. chamber, 26 in. imp. cyl. or skeet, 28 in. full or mod., 30 in. full, vent. rib, floral engraved, checkered select walnut stock. Mfg. 1975.

	$460	$375	$330	$305	$265	$230	$220

MODEL 4000 TRAP — similar to 4000, except 12 ga., 30 in. full, Monte Carlo trap stock and pad. Mfg. 1975.

	$485	$395	$350	$325	$285	$255	$240

MODEL 4500 — similar to 4000, less engraving.

	$420	$330	$305	$275	$240	$200	$175

MODEL 4500 TRAP — similar to 4000 Trap, less engraving.

	$440	$350	$310	$280	$240	$210	$200

MODEL 1500 O/U HUNTING GUN — 12 ga., 2¾ or 3 in. chambers, 26 in. imp. cyl. and mod., 28 in. mod. and full, 30 in. mod. and full, boxlock, auto ejectors, selective or non-selective single trigger, checkered pistol grip stock. Mfg. 1973-1975.

	$700	$575	$500	$440	$415	$385	$365

MODEL 1500 SKEET — similar to Hunting Gun, except 27 in. skeet, skeet stock. Mfg. 1973-1975.

	$725	$600	$525	$450	$425	$400	$385

Grading	100%	98%	95%	90%	80%	70%	60%

MODEL 1500 TRAP — similar to Hunting Gun, except 30 and 32 in. full barrels, trap Monte Carlo stock. Mfg. 1973-1975.

	100%	98%	95%	90%	80%	70%	60%
	$650	$550	$475	$435	$410	$375	$350

MODEL 1000 O/U HUNTING GUN — 12 or 20 ga., 26, 28, or 30 in. barrels, various chokes, boxlock, auto ejectors, SST, checkered select walnut stock, silver inlays, more engraving. Mfg. 1973-1975.

	100%	98%	95%	90%	80%	70%	60%
Grade I	$2,200	$1,980	$1,870	$1,700	$1,540	$1,460	$1,375
Grade II	$1,815	$1,540	$1,430	$1,265	$1,185	$1,100	$1,045

MODEL 1000 TRAP GUN — similar to Hunting Gun, but 12 ga., 30 or 32 in. mod. and full barrels, Monte Carlo trap stock. Mfg. 1973-1975.

	100%	98%	95%	90%	80%	70%	60%
Grade I	$2,100	$1,800	$1,650	$1,500	$1,350	$1,200	$995
Grade II	$1,650	$1,500	$1,375	$1,200	$1,050	$900	$725

MODEL 1000 SKEET — similar to Hunting Gun, except 26 or 28 in. barrels, bored skeet. Mfg. 1973-1975.

	100%	98%	95%	90%	80%	70%	60%
Grade I	$2,255	$2,145	$2,035	$1,870	$1,705	$1,625	$1,540
Grade II	$1,980	$1,705	$1,595	$1,430	$1,350	$1,265	$1,210

MODEL 200 S X S — 12 or 20 ga., 26 in. imp. cyl. and mod., 28 in. mod. and full, 30 in. mod. and full, boxlock, auto ejectors, SST. Mfg. 1973-1974.

	100%	98%	95%	90%	80%	70%	60%
Grade I	$2,420	$2,175	$2,090	$1,955	$1,790	$1,705	$1,625
Grade II	$2,200	$1,955	$1,815	$1,735	$1,625	$1,540	$1,485

MODEL 2500 DOUBLE BARREL — 12 or 20 ga., 26 in. imp. cyl. and mod., 28 in. mod. and full, auto ejectors, boxlock, checkered pistol grip stock and forearm.

	100%	98%	95%	90%	80%	70%	60%
	$470	$385	$360	$305	$275	$260	$240

PENTHENY de PENTHENY

Current manufacturer and gunsmith located in Santa Rosa, CA. established In 1987.

RIFLES

The rifles listed below include ebony forend tips, old English style black recoil pads, steel skeleton grip caps, four panels of 22 LPI checkering, and other custom features. These models are built on a U.S.R.A. company Model 70 action.

THE INVADER — small and medium bore cals., classic styled Claro walnut stock, blued finish, includes Buehler rings and bases.

		100%	98%	95%	90%	80%	70%	60%
Mfg.'s Sug. Retail	$3,400	$3,400	$2,800	$2,350	$1,950	$1,500	$1,150	$875

THE NORMAN — Mag. cals., classic styled English walnut stock, blued finish, includes Buehler rings and bases.

		100%	98%	95%	90%	80%	70%	60%
Mfg.'s Sug. Retail	$3,400	$3,400	$2,800	$2,350	$1,950	$1,500	$1,150	$875

THE CONQUEROR — large bore cals., classic styled English walnut stock, blued finish, rifle has secondary recoil lug, dual steel reinforcing bolts, and express sights including fixed and folding leaves.

		100%	98%	95%	90%	80%	70%	60%
Mfg.'s Sug. Retail	$4,200	$4,200	$3,350	$2,850	$2,350	$1,950	$1,500	$1,150

PEDERSOLI, DAVIDE & C.

Manufacturer of blackpowder and older historically significant firearms located in Brescia, Italy.

D. Pedersoli manufactures top quality blackpowder replicas and other high quality reproductions. Most of their production domestically is subcontracted by other U.S. firms.

PERAZZI

Manufacturer located in Brescia, Italy. Imported and distributed by Perazzi USA, Inc. located in Monrovia, CA (previously located in Rome, NY).

Note: Previously, Perazzi shotguns were imported by both Winchester and Ithaca during the 1960's and 1970's. The company now has its own distribution network and its current model line-up is extensive. Perazzi shotguns are well known for their quality control standards and reliability in clay target championships and in-field conditions.

Because of the devaluation of the U.S. dollar since 1984, Perazzi shotguns have gone up in value substantially.

SHOTGUNS: DISCONTINUED

Perazzi shotguns have incorporated many improvements during their manufacture. One of the most important changes has been the modification of the forearm design. Basically, there have been 4 different types: Type 1 has a serial range of 30,000 - 33,250, Type 2 is serial numbered 33,251 - 35,450, Type 3 has a range of 35,451 - 51,242, Type 4 started at 51,243 and is still current as of this writing. Differences include changes in the forearm iron and barrel lug attachment. Because of these forearm changes (and other parts modifications), the desirability factor on a Type 4 forearm shotgun as opposed to a Type 1 is much greater. Competition shooters prefer Types 3 or 4 as they are the current design. If a Type 1 or 2 competition gun develops problems, they are automatically retrofitted to the Type 4 design - and these modifications are expensive. For these reasons, the serial number of a Perazzi competition gun will determine its type. Since Types 1 through 3 are discontinued, Types 1 and 2 will be less desirable (and less expensive) than the values listed below for Type 3.

As a final note on older Perazzi shotguns, the most collectable models will be those specimens which exhibit the highest quality and are equally rare. Older SCO grades on small frames with older style "V" springs are at the top for desirability. Also, any older SPECIAL GUNS were all custom made - usually engraved by master engravers with Angelo Galeazzi being considered the best. These models are exceedingly rare, with prices going over the $40,000 level in today's marketplace.

Grading	100%	98%	95%	90%	80%	70%	60%
COMPETITION ONE TRAP GRADE — single shot, 12 ga., auto ejector, VR, cased.							
	$2,500	$2,150	$1,875	$1,650	$1,450	$1,300	$1,175
COMPETITION ONE O/U TRAP — similar to Competition, except O/U double.							
	$3,950	$3,500	$3,000	$2,500	$2,150	$1,850	$1,650
COMPETITION ONE SKEET							
	$4,250	$3,750	$3,200	$2,700	$2,350	$2,000	$1,750
SINGLE BARREL TRAP — 12 ga., 34 in. VR, full choke barrel, boxlock, auto ejector, checkered pistol grip stock, recoil pad. Mfg. 1971-1972.							
	$2,350	$2,050	$1,800	$1,600	$1,450	$1,300	$1,175
LIGHT GAME MODEL O/U FIELD — 12 ga., 27½ in. VR barrels, mod. and full or imp. cyl. and mod., boxlock, auto ejectors, field stock. Mfg. 1972-1974.							
	$4,500	$3,900	$3,300	$2,800	$2,400	$2,050	$1,800
MT-6 GRADE — 12 ga., VR, auto ejector, cased, five interchangeable choke tubes. Disc. 1983.							
	$4,250	$3,750	$3,250	$2,800	$2,500	$2,200	$1,900

This model was also manufactured in DHO and SHO models as well. Please refer to those models listed in the current manufacture section for approximate values.

CURRENTLY MANUFACTURED TRAP, SKEET, AND HUNTING SHOTGUNS

Not until 1988 did most single barrel trap guns have a "Special" option package which includes an adjustable trigger group (designated P4). This P4 trigger is now standard. Non-adj. trigger is a special order. Values below assume shotguns with the "Special" designation (became standard in 1988).

Models listed in the following sections assume a Type 4 forearm attachment design and are serial numbered 51,243 and above. Models that are serial numbered below 51,243 are an older design and will be priced less than the newer Type 4 models (see explanation under SHOTGUNS: DISCONTINUED).

Rather than describe all the following models individually, descriptions will appear only once and are listed below. Because the various grades have similar features and engraving (i.e.: an SCO Grade Sideplate in American Skeet would appear similar to an American Trap SCO Grade Sideplate, except for stock dimensions of course).

Older SHO (Type 3s) and DHO models with rebounding hammers (disc.) are perhaps the most collectable Perazzi shotguns currently.

PERAZZI GRADES WITH DESCRIPTIONS

⚞ **Special Model** — introductory level model with high polished blue on barrels and receiver, normally listing model name on lower frame sides in gold letters and numerals. Checkered walnut stock (interchangeable) and forearm, all have adjustable trigger assembly.

⚞ **Gold Outline Model** — similar to Standard Model, except has gold line engraving around perimeter of frame, also features better grade of walnut. This configuration is very rare.

⚞ **SC3 Model** — features coined finished receiver with two different styles of scroll engraving and four different patterns of game scene engraving (snipe, grouse, pointing bird dog, or woodcock). Better grade of walnut than the Gold Outline Model.

⚞ **SCO Model** — more elaborate than SC3 Model in that it features two different styles of scroll engraving (deep relief "gargoyles" or fine English scroll) and four different game scene engraving patterns (two different styles of ducks, grouse, or woodcock). Again, a better grade of walnut (in addition to finer checkering) is utilized.

⚞ **SCO Gold Grade Model** — differentiated from SCO Model in that it has six engraving patterns featuring multiple gold inlays on receiver sides (including two different duck scenes, two separate grouse scenes, one woodcock, and one deep relief "gargoyle").

⚞ **SCO Grade Sideplate Model** — includes coined finished receiver with game scene engraved sideplates (with boxlock action). Game scene engraving choices include three different duck scenes, one grouse, one "Chisel" relief scroll, and a Diana Goddess of the Hunt pattern.

⚞ **SCO Gold Grade Sideplate Model** — similar to SCO Grade Sideplate Model, except has game figures on sideplates in relief gold. Patterns include three different grouse scenes, two separate ducks patterns, and dogs flushing upland game. This model can also be ordered with detachment lever for sideplates.

⚞ **Extra Grade Model** — denoted by top-of-the-line fine bank note style game scene engraving with elaborate scroll and relief work on metal perimeters. Game scene choices include two different dog scenes, one grouse, and one duck. Top quality Circassian walnut finely checkered.

⚞ **Extra Gold Grade Model** — top-of-the-line boxlock model that differs from Extra Grade Model in that birds/dogs are in gold relief. This model can also be ordered with detachment lever for sideplates.

⚞ **SHO Over & Under Model** — features sidelock action with coined finished receiver and intricate bank note game scene engraving with choices including three different duck patterns and one pheasant. Top quality walnut and checkering. Type One SHOs have non-rebounding firing pins, while Type Two guns have rebounding firing pins (since 1985).
This model is individually hand made per customer's specifications. Currently, no orders are being taken for this series.

⚡ **SHO Gold Over & Under Model** — similar to SHO Over & Under Model, except features game scene of wildlife in relief gold. This model is the best sidelock special order grade that Perazzi currently offers for sale.

This model is individually hand made per customer's specifications. Currently, no orders are being taken for this series.

⚡ **DHO Side-by-Side Models** — top-of-the-line sidelock model in 12 ga. only for DHO and DHO Gold grades. DHO Extra and DHO Gold Extra grades have similar engraving to Extra Grade and Extra Gold Grade models and are available in all gauges. The DHO Gold Extra is the most elaborate, highly finished side-by-side shotgun (and expensive - current retail is $82,000) that an individual can currently special order from any company. The DHO model is exceedingly rare, and specimens should be appraised individually.

This model is entirely hand made per customer's specifications. Currently, no orders are being taken for this series.

Some descriptions on the Standard Models listed below have not been duplicated into the other Perazzi sections because of space consideration.

AMERICAN TRAP SHOTGUNS: SINGLE BARREL

12 ga. only, 32 or 34 in. barrel, high post rib, select walnut, more expensive models vary in the amount of engraving, grade of walnut, and other special order features.

NOTE: Combination guns (Combo Models) listed below include either a 32 or 34 in. single barrel and a set of either 29½ or 31½ barrels.
Subtract $600 for shotguns without the "Special" model designation (pre-1988).

Grading	100%	98%	95%	90%	80%	70%	60%

STANDARD GRADE MODELS
Add 35%-43% for Combo Models depending on model variation.

⚡ **TM1 Special** — features normal trap rib.

Mfg.'s Sug. Retail	$5,750	$4,950	$3,600	$3,100	$2,350	$2,150	$1,850	$1,675

⚡ **TMX Special** — features high post trap rib.

Mfg.'s Sug. Retail	$5,950	$5,100	$3,700	$3,150	$2,400	$2,150	$1,850	$1,675

⚡ **MX3 Special** — features rib similar to TM1 Special. Disc. 1992.

	$5,200	$3,700	$3,250	$2,450	$2,200	$1,900	$1,700

Last Mfg.'s Sug. Retail was $6,150.

⚡ **MX8 Special** — has tapered stepped rib and adj. trigger.

Mfg.'s Sug. Retail	$7,300	$6,175	$4,350	$3,600	$3,200	$2,875	$2,600	$2,375

Add $2,750 for Gold Outline engraving.

⚡ **MX9** — 12 ga., 32 or 34 in. barrel with choke tubes, unique VR on vent. barrel features removable center inserts significantly changing the point of shot pattern impact, fully adj. cheekpiece. New 1993.

Mfg.'s Sug. Retail	$9,200	$7,500	$6,200	$4,400	$3,700	$3,250	$2,900	$2,625

⚡ **MX9 Combo** — includes a set O/U barrels and top single trap barrel, features new rib design with interchangeable middle bead inserts to change point of impact. Importation began 1992.

Mfg.'s Sug. Retail	$12,800	$11,750	$9,995	$8,750	$7,600	$6,500	$5,600	$4,500

This model is available with or without choke tubes. Choke tubes include 5 chokes and 5 rib inserts (3 in. pattern per insert).

⚡ **MX10** — 12 ga., 32 or 34 in. barrel featuring center-pivoting VR allowing for adj. point of impact, fixed chokes, fully adj. cheekpiece, removable trigger. New 1993.

Mfg.'s Sug. Retail	$9,450	$7,650	$6,300	$4,400	$3,700	$3,250	$2,900	$2,625

Grading	100%	98%	95%	90%	80%	70%	60%

⚞ **Grand American 88 Special** — features MX3 high ramped rib and grooved forearm. Mfg. 1988-92.

	100%	98%	95%	90%	80%	70%	60%
	$6,000	$4,250	$3,600	$3,200	$2,875	$2,600	$2,375

Add $2,750 for Gold Outline engraving.
Last Mfg.'s Sug. Retail was $7,000.

⚞ **DB81 Special** — features ultra high ramped rib.

		100%	98%	95%	90%	80%	70%	60%
Mfg.'s Sug. Retail	$7,600	$6,375	$4,500	$3,700	$3,250	$2,900	$2,625	$2,400

Add $2,750 for Gold Outline engraving.

SC3 GRADE MODELS
Add approx. 31% for Combo Models.

⚞ **MX 3 Special**

	100%	98%	95%	90%	80%	70%	60%
	$12,500	$9,950	$7,450	$5,800	$4,560	$4,175	$3,800

Last Mfg.'s Sug. Retail was $13,750.

⚞ **MX 8 Special**

		100%	98%	95%	90%	80%	70%	60%
Mfg.'s Sug. Retail	$12,500	$10,300	$7,850	$6,350	$5,500	$4,950	$4,200	$3,800

⚞ **MX 9**

		100%	98%	95%	90%	80%	70%	60%
Mfg.'s Sug. Retail	$14,400	$12,875	$10,050	$7,450	$5,800	$4,560	$4,175	$3,800

⚞ **MX 10**

		100%	98%	95%	90%	80%	70%	60%
Mfg.'s Sug. Retail	$14,650	$13,000	$10,100	$7,450	$5,800	$4,560	$4,175	$3,800

⚞ **Grand American 88 Special**

	100%	98%	95%	90%	80%	70%	60%
	$10,000	$7,750	$6,300	$5,500	$4,950	$4,200	$3,800

Last Mfg.'s Sug. Retail was $12,000.

⚞ **DB81 Special**

		100%	98%	95%	90%	80%	70%	60%
Mfg.'s Sug. Retail	$12,800	$10,450	$7,950	$6,375	$5,500	$4,950	$4,200	$3,800

SC0 GRADE MODELS
Add approx. 23% for Combo Models.

⚞ **TM1 Special**

		100%	98%	95%	90%	80%	70%	60%
Mfg.'s Sug. Retail	$16,850	$14,350	$10,250	$8,400	$7,555	$6,600	$6,100	$5,550

⚞ **TMX Special**

		100%	98%	95%	90%	80%	70%	60%
Mfg.'s Sug. Retail	$17,050	$14,450	$10,325	$8,450	$7,555	$6,600	$6,100	$5,550

⚞ **MX3 Special**

	100%	98%	95%	90%	80%	70%	60%
	$16,250	$11,650	$9,300	$8,500	$7,600	$7,000	$6,300

Last Mfg.'s Sug. Retail was $18,650.

⚞ **MX8 Special**

		100%	98%	95%	90%	80%	70%	60%
Mfg.'s Sug. Retail	$21,050	$17,750	$13,650	$10,800	$9,250	$8,500	$7,900	$6,850

⚞ **MX9**

		100%	98%	95%	90%	80%	70%	60%
Mfg.'s Sug. Retail	$22,950	$18,950	$14,250	$11,000	$9,300	$8,500	$7,900	$6,850

⚞ **MX10**

		100%	98%	95%	90%	80%	70%	60%
Mfg.'s Sug. Retail	$23,200	$19,050	$14,325	$11,000	$9,300	$8,500	$7,900	$6,850

⚞ **Grand American 88 Special**

	100%	98%	95%	90%	80%	70%	60%
	$17,350	$13,500	$10,800	$9,250	$8,500	$7,900	$6,850

Last Mfg.'s Sug. Retail was $20,250.

Grading		100%	98%	95%	90%	80%	70%	60%
DB81 Special								
Mfg.'s Sug. Retail	$21,400	$17,900	$13,750	$10,850	$9,250	$8,500	$7,900	$6,850

GOLD GRADE MODELS
Add approx. 24% for Combo Models.

		100%	98%	95%	90%	80%	70%	60%
TM1 Special								
Mfg.'s Sug. Retail	$18,800	$16,450	$11,525	$9,200	$8,500	$7,600	$7,000	$6,300
TMX Special								
Mfg.'s Sug. Retail	$19,000	$16,500	$11,550	$9,200	$8,500	$7,600	$7,000	$6,300
MX3 Special								
		$18,000	$13,750	$10,825	$9,250	$8,500	$7,900	$6,850

Last Mfg.'s Sug. Retail was $20,900.

		100%	98%	95%	90%	80%	70%	60%
MX8 Special								
Mfg.'s Sug. Retail	$23,250	$19,750	$14,375	$11,400	$9,650	$8,700	$8,100	$6,950
MX9								
Mfg.'s Sug. Retail	$25,150	$20,900	$14,950	$11,650	$9,750	$8,725	$8,100	$7,000
MX10								
Mfg.'s Sug. Retail	$25,400	$21,050	$15,000	$11,850	$9,750	$8,725	$8,100	$7,000
Grand American 88 Special								
		$19,250	$14,250	$11,350	$9,650	$8,700	$8,100	$6,950

Last Mfg.'s Sug. Retail was $22,350.

		100%	98%	95%	90%	80%	70%	60%
DB81 Special								
Mfg.'s Sug. Retail	$23,550	$19,900	$14,450	$11,450	$9,700	$8,725	$8,100	$7,000

SCO GRADE SIDEPLATES MODELS
Add approx. 15% for Combo Models.

		100%	98%	95%	90%	80%	70%	60%
MX8 Special								
Mfg.'s Sug. Retail	$32,600	$27,750	$19,000	$16,000	$13,250	$11,750	$10,250	$9,000
MX9								
Mfg.'s Sug. Retail	$34,500	$28,900	$19,650	$16,150	$13,300	$11,750	$10,250	$9,000
MX10								
Mfg.'s Sug. Retail	$34,750	$29,050	$19,725	$16,200	$13,300	$11,750	$10,250	$9,000
Grand American 88 Special								
		$27,250	$18,750	$16,000	$13,250	$11,750	$10,250	$9,000

Last Mfg.'s Sug. Retail was $31,350.

		100%	98%	95%	90%	80%	70%	60%
DB81 Special								
Mfg.'s Sug. Retail	$32,900	$27,875	$19,125	$16,100	$13,300	$11,750	$10,250	$9,000

GOLD GRADE SIDEPLATES MODELS
Add approx. 13%-15% for Combo Models depending on the model variation.

		100%	98%	95%	90%	80%	70%	60%
MX8 Special								
Mfg.'s Sug. Retail	$37,450	$31,250	$21,500	$17,500	$14,750	$12,250	$10,250	$9,000

Grading		100%	98%	95%	90%	80%	70%	60%
MX9								
Mfg.'s Sug. Retail	$39,350	$32,500	$22,250	$18,000	$15,000	$12,500	$10,500	$9,250
MX10								
Mfg.'s Sug. Retail	$39,600	$32,650	$22,300	$18,000	$15,000	$12,500	$10,500	$9,250
Grand American 88 Special		$33,000	$24,500	$21,000	$19,000	$15,250	$13,000	$11,250

Last Mfg.'s Sug. Retail was $40,500.

		100%	98%	95%	90%	80%	70%	60%
DB81 Special								
Mfg.'s Sug. Retail	$37,750	$31,400	$21,625	$17,600	$14,750	$12,250	$10,250	$9,000

EXTRA GRADE MODELS — the MX8 Special, Grand American 88 Special, and DB81 Special were disc. in this grade during 1992.

	98%	95%	90%	80%	70%	60%
$51,750	$36,000	$29,950	$25,000	$20,000	$17,000	$14,500

Last Mfg.'s Sug. Retail was $63,200.
Add 10% for Combo Model.

EXTRA GOLD GRADE MODELS — the MX8 Special, Grand American 88 Special, and DB81 Special were disc. in this grade during 1992.

	98%	95%	90%	80%	70%	60%
$57,250	$38,750	$32,500	$26,500	$21,250	$18,000	$15,500

Last Mfg.'s Sug. Retail was $68,850.
Add 11% for Combo Model.

INTERNATIONAL/OLYMPIC TRAP SHOTGUNS: O/U

12 ga. only, unless indicated otherwise.

STANDARD GRADE MODELS

The MX2/MX2L configuration is available mainly for the European marketplace. Values for this model represent recent pricing - Perazzi U.S.A. should be contacted directly for an up-to-date price quotation.

Models with "Special" nomenclature feature Perazzi's new, adjustable (4 positions) trigger group introduced on certain models beginning 1988.

MX3 Special — includes 6.4mm high ramped rib and separated barrels. Disc. 1992.

	100%	98%	95%	90%	80%	70%	60%
	$5,525	$4,050	$3,400	$2,950	$2,675	$2,350	$1,975

Add $380 for MX3C Model (includes choke tubes).
Last Mfg.'s Sug. Retail was $6,500.

MX7C — 29½ or 31½ in. barrels, features fixed coil spring trigger mechanism, safety incorporates selector switch, non-removable trigger group. New 1993.

		100%	98%	95%	90%	80%	70%	60%
Mfg.'s Sug. Retail	$6,100	$5,700	$4,950	$4,250	$3,550	$2,950	$2,625	$2,300

Mirage MX8 — denoted by low profile rib, vent. barrels and grooved forearm.

		100%	98%	95%	90%	80%	70%	60%
Mfg.'s Sug. Retail	$7,300	$6,100	$4,325	$3,600	$3,200	$2,875	$2,600	$2,375

Add $380 for choke tubes (Model Mirage C - MX8 C).
Add $2,450 for Gold Outline engraving.
This model is also available with standard triggers.

MX8 Special — similar to MX8, except four position adj. trigger (P4S).

		100%	98%	95%	90%	80%	70%	60%
Mfg.'s Sug. Retail	$7,700	$6,375	$4,450	$3,700	$3,250	$2,900	$2,625	$2,400

Add $2,850 for Gold Outline engraving.

MX8/20 — 20 ga., 29½ in. barrels with fixed chokes, flat VR with removable trigger group. New 1993.

		100%	98%	95%	90%	80%	70%	60%
Mfg.'s Sug. Retail	$7,300	$6,075	$4,250	$3,500	$3,050	$2,700	$2,500	$2,300

Grading	100%	98%	95%	90%	80%	70%	60%

⚜ **MX9** – 29½ or 31½ in. barrels with choke tubes, unique VR on vent. barrels features removable center inserts significantly changing the point of shot pattern impact, fully adj. cheekpiece, removable trigger. New 1993.

Mfg.'s Sug. Retail	$9,600	$7,825	$6,350	$5,500	$4,950	$4,200	$3,800	$3,650

⚜ **MX10** – 29½ in. barrels featuring center-pivoting VR allowing for adj. point of impact, fixed chokes, fully adj. cheekpiece, removable trigger. New 1993.

Mfg.'s Sug. Retail	$10,000	$8,350	$7,400	$6,400	$5,500	$4,950	$4,200	$3,800

⚜ **Grand American 88 Special** – features high ramped rib, separated barrels, and grooved forearm. Disc. 1992.

	$6,225	$4,400	$3,700	$3,250	$2,900	$2,625	$2,400

Add $2,850 for Gold Outline engraving.
Last Mfg.'s Sug. Retail was $7,400.

⚜ **DB81 Special** – features ultra high ramped rib and vent. barrels.

Mfg.'s Sug. Retail	$8,800	$7,100	$4,775	$3,875	$3,350	$2,950	$2,650	$2,450

Add $2,850 for Gold Outline engraving.

⚜ **MX2/MX2L** – denoted by 8.2mm high rib, Monte Carlo stock, and vented side ribs. Model MX2L designates light weight model and has no side ribs. Disc. 1992.

	$4,550	$3,700	$3,400	$3,050	$2,750	$2,500	$2,275

Add $2,750 for Gold Outline engraving.
Last Mfg.'s Sug. Retail was $5,510.

SC3 GRADE MODELS

⚜ **SC3** – 29½ or 31½ in. barrels, adj. trigger. New 1993.

Mfg.'s Sug. Retail	$12,450	$10,300	$7,850	$6,350	$5,500	$4,950	$4,200	$3,800

⚜ **MX3 Special**

	$9,200	$6,650	$5,300	$4,560	$4,175	$3,800	$3,350

Add $380 for MX3C Model (includes choke tubes).
Last Mfg.'s Sug. Retail was $10,850.

⚜ **Mirage MX8**

	$10,250	$7,775	$6,300	$5,500	$4,950	$4,200	$3,800

Last Mfg.'s Sug. Retail was $11,950.

⚜ **MX8 Special**

	$10,550	$7,800	$6,300	$5,500	$4,950	$4,200	$3,800

Last Mfg.'s Sug. Retail was $12,350.

⚜ **MX9**

Mfg.'s Sug. Retail	$14,750	$13,050	$10,100	$7,450	$5,800	$4,560	$4,175	$3,800

⚜ **MX10**

Mfg.'s Sug. Retail	$15,150	$13,250	$10,200	$7,500	$5,800	$4,560	$4,175	$3,800

⚜ **Grand American 88 Special**

	$10,550	$7,800	$6,300	$5,500	$4,950	$4,200	$3,800

Last Mfg.'s Sug. Retail was $12,350.

⚜ **DB81 Special**

Mfg.'s Sug. Retail	$13,150	$11,000	$9,875	$7,950	$6,300	$5,500	$4,950	$4,200

Grading	100%	98%	95%	90%	80%	70%	60%

MX2/MX2L

	$7,750	$6,300	$5,500	$4,950	$4,200	$3,800	$3,650

Last Mfg.'s Sug. Retail was $9,420.

SCO GRADE MODELS

SCO — 29½ or 31½ in. barrels, adj. trigger. New 1993.

Mfg.'s Sug. Retail $21,200	$18,250	$13,750	$10,900	$9,250	$8,500	$7,900	$6,850

MX3 Special

	$16,250	$11,800	$9,400	$8,500	$7,600	$7,000	$6,300

Add $380 for MX3C Special (includes choke tubes).
Last Mfg.'s Sug. Retail was $18,650.

Mirage MX8

	$17,650	$13,500	$10,770	$9,250	$8,500	$7,900	$6,850

Add $380 for choke tubes (Mirage C - MX8 C).
Last Mfg.'s Sug. Retail was $20,400.

MX8 Special

	$18,000	$13,600	$10,800	$9,250	$8,500	$7,900	$6,850

Last Mfg.'s Sug. Retail was $20,800.

MX9

Mfg.'s Sug. Retail $23,500	$20,050	$14,400	$11,450	$9,650	$8,700	$8,100	$6,950

MX10

Mfg.'s Sug. Retail $23,900	$20,250	$14,550	$11,500	$9,650	$8,700	$8,100	$6,950

Grand American 88 Special

	$18,000	$13,600	$10,800	$9,250	$8,500	$7,900	$6,850

Last Mfg.'s Sug. Retail was $20,800.

DB81 Special

Mfg.'s Sug. Retail $22,000	$18,600	$14,000	$11,000	$9,250	$8,500	$7,900	$6,850

MX2/MX2L

	$13,500	$10,770	$9,250	$8,500	$8,000	$7,400	$6,750

Last Mfg.'s Sug. Retail was $15,860.

GOLD GRADE MODELS

SCO

Mfg.'s Sug. Retail $23,920	$20,425	$14,600	$11,550	$9,650	$8,700	$8,100	$6,950

MX3 Special

	$18,150	$13,950	$11,000	$9,350	$8,500	$7,900	$6,850

Add $380 for MX3C Special (includes choke tubes).
Last Mfg.'s Sug. Retail was $21,050.

Mirage MX8

	$19,750	$14,250	$11,350	$9,650	$8,700	$7,900	$6,850

Last Mfg.'s Sug. Retail was $23,000.

MX8 Special

	$20,000	$14,400	$11,450	$9,650	$8,700	$8,100	$6,950

Last Mfg.'s Sug. Retail was $23,400.

Grading	100%	98%	95%	90%	80%	70%	60%
MX9							
Mfg.'s Sug. Retail $25,600	$21,400	$15,450	$12,000	$9,850	$8,700	$8,100	$6,950
MX10							
Mfg.'s Sug. Retail $26,620	$21,900	$15,750	$12,000	$9,850	$8,700	$8,100	$6,950
Grand American 88 Special							
	$20,000	$14,400	$11,450	$9,650	$8,700	$8,100	$6,950
Last Mfg.'s Sug. Retail was $23,400.							
DB81 Special							
Mfg.'s Sug. Retail $24,650	$20,875	$14,950	$11,700	$9,700	$8,700	$8,100	$6,950
MX2/MX2L							
	$14,145	$11,950	$9,750	$8,500	$8,000	$7,400	$6,750
Last Mfg.'s Sug. Retail was $17,610							

SCO GRADE SIDEPLATES MODELS

Grading	100%	98%	95%	90%	80%	70%	60%
SCO							
Mfg.'s Sug. Retail $32,550	$27,800	$19,150	$16,200	$13,250	$11,750	$10,250	$9,000
Mirage MX8							
	$27,000	$18,750	$16,000	$13,250	$11,750	$10,250	$9,000
Last Mfg.'s Sug. Retail was $31,300.							
MX8 Special							
	$27,300	$18,900	$16,100	$13,250	$11,750	$10,250	$9,000
Last Mfg.'s Sug. Retail was $31,700.							
MX9							
Mfg.'s Sug. Retail $34,850	$29,250	$20,650	$16,950	$13,250	$11,750	$10,250	$9,000
MX10							
Mfg.'s Sug. Retail $35,250	$29,450	$20,775	$17,000	$13,250	$11,750	$10,250	$9,000
Grand American 88 Special							
	$27,300	$18,900	$16,100	$13,250	$11,750	$10,250	$9,000
Last Mfg.'s Sug. Retail was $31,700.							
DB81 Special							
Mfg.'s Sug. Retail $33,300	$28,250	$19,650	$16,275	$13,250	$11,750	$10,250	$9,000
MX2/MX2L							
	$20,000	$18,000	$16,000	$13,250	$11,750	$10,500	$9,250
Last Mfg.'s Sug. Retail was $23,480.							

GOLD GRADE SIDEPLATES MODELS

Grading	100%	98%	95%	90%	80%	70%	60%
SCO							
Mfg.'s Sug. Retail $37,800	$33,000	$23,650	$20,750	$17,500	$15,250	$13,000	$11,250
Mirage MX8							
	$30,475	$22,150	$20,100	$17,500	$15,250	$13,000	$11,250

Add $380 for choke tubes (Model Mirage C - MX8 C).
Last Mfg.'s Sug. Retail was $36,350.

Grading	100%	98%	95%	90%	80%	70%	60%

❄ MX8 Special

	$30,775	$22,300	$20,200	$17,500	$15,250	$13,000	$11,250

Last Mfg.'s Sug. Retail was $36,750.

❄ MX9

Mfg.'s Sug. Retail $40,100	$34,500	$24,500	$21,250	$17,500	$15,250	$13,000	$11,250

❄ MX10

Mfg.'s Sug. Retail $40,500	$34,700	$24,600	$21,300	$17,500	$15,250	$13,000	$11,250

❄ Grand American 88 Special

	$30,775	$22,300	$20,200	$17,500	$15,250	$13,000	$11,250

Last Mfg.'s Sug. Retail was $36,750.

❄ DB81 Special

Mfg.'s Sug. Retail $38,550	$33,500	$23,950	$20,800	$17,500	$15,250	$13,000	$11,250

❄ MX2/MX2L

	$23,000	$20,250	$17,500	$15,250	$13,000	$11,800	$10,750

Last Mfg.'s Sug. Retail was $27,300.

EXTRA GRADE MODELS — the models Mirage MX8, MX8 Special, Grand American 88 Special, DB81 Special, and MX2/MX2L were all disc. 1992.

	$50,850	$35,150	$30,150	$25,000	$20,000	$17,000	$14,500

Subtract approx. 25% for MX2/MX2L model.
Add $380 for for choke tubes (Model Mirage C - MX8 C).
Last Mfg.'s Sug. Retail was $58,700.

❄ Extra Model — 29½ or 31½ in. barrels, removable trigger group. New 1993.

Mfg.'s Sug. Retail $60,600	$52,000	$36,250	$31,150	$25,000	$20,000	$17,000	$14,500

EXTRA GOLD GRADE MODELS — the models Mirage MX8, MX8 Special, Grand American 88 Special, DB81 Special, and MX2/MX2L were all disc. 1992.

	$54,550	$37,950	$31,950	$26,500	$21,250	$18,000	$15,500

Subtract approx. 25% for MX2/MX2L model.
Add $380 for for choke tubes (Model Mirage C - MX8 C).
Last Mfg.'s Sug. Retail was $63,000.

❄ Extra Model — 29½ or 31½ in. barrels, removable trigger group. New 1993.

Mfg.'s Sug. Retail $65,350	$55,450	$38,000	$32,750	$26,000	$20,500	$17,000	$14,500

OVER/UNDER SIDELOCK MODELS — older models without rebounding hammers are not as desirable. The most desirable configurations in this model are the Skeet, Pigeon, and Sporting variations (pricing follows new SHO Gold values). All SHO sidelock models were disc. 1992.

❄ SHO Older Mfg.

	$19,950	$16,750	$12,250	$9,500	$8,500	$7,600	$6,800

❄ SHO New Mfg.

	$30,000	$27,750	$25,750	$23,750	$21,750	$19,750	$17,750

Last Mfg.'s Sug. Retail was $43,000.

❄ SHO Gold Older Mfg.

	$40,000	$36,000	$31,000	$26,000	$21,000	$18,000	$15,000

Grading	100%	98%	95%	90%	80%	70%	60%

⚰ SHO Gold New Mfg.

		100%	98%	95%	90%	80%	70%	60%
		$60,000	$55,000	$49,500	$45,500	$40,000	$35,500	$30,000

Last Mfg.'s Sug. Retail was $48,000.

⚰ SHO Extra — while advertised, none were sold.
Last Mfg.'s Sug. Retail was $80,000.

⚰ SHO Gold Extra — while advertised, none were sold.
Last Mfg.'s Sug. Retail was $86,000.

AMERICAN SKEET SHOTGUNS: O/U

12 ga. only, 26, 27⅝ (standard and most common), or 28⅜ in. separated barrels, select walnut, more expensive models vary in the amount of engraving, grade of walnut, and other special order features.

STANDARD GRADE MODELS

⚰ MX3 Special — introductory skeet model, detachable and adj. four position P4S trigger, flat rib. Barrel lockup is same as MX8. Disc. 1992.

	100%	98%	95%	90%	80%	70%	60%
	$5,400	$4,100	$3,400	$2,950	$2,675	$2,350	$1,975

Previous to 1988, this model was designated the MX3. It did not have the P4 adj. selective trigger group.
Last Mfg.'s Sug. Retail was $6,500.

⚰ MX7C — 27⅝ or 28⅜ in. barrels with choke tubes, features fixed coil spring trigger mechanism, safety incorporates selector switch, non-removable trigger group. New 1993.

Mfg.'s Sug. Retail	$6,100		98%	95%	90%	80%	70%	60%
			$5,700	$4,950	$4,250	$3,550	$2,950	$2,625	$2,300

⚰ MX8/20 ga. — 20 ga., 27⅝ in. barrels bored SK/SK, flat VR with removable trigger group. New 1993.

Mfg.'s Sug. Retail	$7,300		$6,075	$4,250	$3,500	$3,050	$2,700	$2,500	$2,300

⚰ Mirage Special — evolved from Olympic Skeet Model, features detachable and adj. four position trigger.

Mfg.'s Sug. Retail	$7,700		$6,375	$4,450	$3,700	$3,250	$2,900	$2,625	$2,400

Add $2,850 for Gold Outline engraving.

SC3 GRADE MODELS

⚰ MX3 Special

	$9,200	$6,650	$5,300	$4,560	$4,175	$3,800	$3,350

Last Mfg.'s Sug. Retail was $10,580.

⚰ MX8/20 ga.

Mfg.'s Sug. Retail	$12,450		$10,575	$7,850	$6,350	$5,500	$4,950	$4,200	$3,800

⚰ Mirage Special

	$10,500	$7,775	$6,300	$5,500	$4,950	$4,200	$3,800

Last Mfg.'s Sug. Retail was $12,350.

SCO GRADE MODELS

⚰ MX3 Special

	$16,250	$11,800	$9,400	$8,500	$7,600	$7,000	$6,300

Last Mfg.'s Sug. Retail was $18,650.

Perazzi cont.

Grading	100%	98%	95%	90%	80%	70%	60%
MX8/20 ga.							
Mfg.'s Sug. Retail $21,200	$18,000	$13,725	$10,900	$9,250	$8,500	$7,900	$6,850
Mirage Special							
	$17,800	$13,600	$10,800	$9,250	$8,500	$7,900	$6,850

Last Mfg.'s Sug. Retail was $20,800.

GOLD GRADE MODELS

	100%	98%	95%	90%	80%	70%	60%
MX3 Special							
	$18,000	$13,950	$11,000	$9,350	$8,500	$7,900	$6,850

Last Mfg.'s Sug. Retail was $21,050.

	100%	98%	95%	90%	80%	70%	60%
MX8/20 ga.							
Mfg.'s Sug. Retail $23,920	$20,425	$14,600	$11,550	$9,650	$8,700	$8,100	$6,950
Mirage Special							
	$19,500	$14,400	$11,450	$9,650	$8,700	$8,100	$6,950

Last Mfg.'s Sug. Retail was $23,400.

SCO GRADE SIDEPLATES MODELS

	100%	98%	95%	90%	80%	70%	60%
MX8/20 ga.							
Mfg.'s Sug. Retail $32,550	$27,800	$19,150	$16,200	$13,250	$11,750	$10,250	$9,000
Mirage Special							
	$26,300	$18,900	$16,100	$13,250	$11,750	$10,250	$9,000

Last Mfg.'s Sug. Retail was $31,700.

GOLD GRADE SIDEPLATES MODELS

	100%	98%	95%	90%	80%	70%	60%
MX8/20 ga.							
Mfg.'s Sug. Retail $37,800	$33,000	$23,650	$20,750	$17,500	$15,250	$13,000	$11,250
Mirage Special							
	$30,775	$22,300	$20,200	$17,500	$15,250	$13,000	$11,250

Last Mfg.'s Sug. Retail was $36,750.

EXTRA GRADE MODELS

	100%	98%	95%	90%	80%	70%	60%
MX8/20 ga.							
Mfg.'s Sug. Retail $60,600	$52,000	$36,250	$31,150	$25,000	$20,000	$17,000	$14,500
Mirage Special							
	$50,850	$35,150	$30,150	$25,000	$20,000	$17,000	$14,500

Last Mfg.'s Sug. Retail was $58,700.

EXTRA GOLD GRADE MODELS

	100%	98%	95%	90%	80%	70%	60%
MX8/20 ga.							
Mfg.'s Sug. Retail $65,350	$55,450	$38,000	$32,750	$26,000	$20,500	$17,000	$14,500
Mirage Special							
	$54,550	$37,950	$31,950	$26,500	$21,250	$18,000	$15,500

Last Mfg.'s Sug. Retail was $63,250.

Grading	100%	98%	95%	90%	80%	70%	60%

AMERICAN SKEET O/U SHOTGUNS: 4-GAUGE SETS

STANDARD GRADE MODELS

⚞ **MX3 Special**

	100%	98%	95%	90%	80%	70%	60%
	$13,600	$10,500	$9,150	$8,230	$7,500	$6,750	$6,000

Last Mfg.'s Sug. Retail was $15,400.

⚞ **Mirage Special**

Mfg.'s Sug. Retail	$17,500						
	$14,800	$11,250	$9,750	$8,275	$7,500	$6,750	$6,000

Add $6,700 for Gold Outline engraving.

SC3 GRADE MODELS

⚞ **MX3 Special**

	$19,300	$14,850	$12,450	$10,250	$9,000	$8,000	$7,000

Last Mfg.'s Sug. Retail was $22,350.

⚞ **Mirage Special**

Mfg.'s Sug. Retail	$26,100						
	$21,995	$17,000	$14,000	$11,750	$11,000	$9,500	$8,500

SCO GRADE MODELS

⚞ **MX3 Special**

	$26,550	$22,500	$18,000	$15,000	$12,875	$11,500	$10,000

Last Mfg.'s Sug. Retail was $30,800.

⚞ **Mirage Special**

Mfg.'s Sug. Retail	$35,000						
	$29,950	$24,250	$19,250	$16,500	$13,750	$12,250	$10,750

GOLD GRADE MODELS

⚞ **MX3 Special**

	$29,750	$23,800	$19,000	$16,500	$13,750	$12,250	$10,750

Last Mfg.'s Sug. Retail was $33,450.

⚞ **Mirage Special**

Mfg.'s Sug. Retail	$37,800						
	$32,650	$25,000	$19,750	$16,500	$13,750	$12,250	$10,750

SCO GRADE SIDEPLATES MODELS

⚞ **Mirage Special**

Mfg.'s Sug. Retail	$51,200						
	$43,000	$33,000	$28,500	$24,000	$19,250	$16,500	$12,500

GOLD GRADE SIDEPLATES MODELS

⚞ **Mirage Special**

Mfg.'s Sug. Retail	$55,600						
	$46,500	$34,950	$29,000	$24,500	$19,250	$16,500	$12,500

EXTRA GRADE MODELS

⚞ **Mirage Special**

	$75,000	$64,450	$51,000	$41,000	$31,500	$25,000	$21,500

Last Mfg.'s Sug. Retail was $85,000.

Grading	100%	98%	95%	90%	80%	70%	60%

EXTRA GOLD GRADE MODELS

⚼ **Mirage Special**

	100%	98%	95%	90%	80%	70%	60%
	$78,800	$68,250	$54,950	$43,000	$33,000	$26,000	$22,000

Last Mfg.'s Sug. Retail was $91,500.

INTERNATIONAL/OLYMPIC SKEET SHOTGUNS: O/U

Available in 12 ga. only. Usually supplied with 29½ in. barrels.

Since the international skeet variations are similar to the American skeet models, rather than duplicating these models (with the exception of the Mirage MX8), please refer to pricing in the American Skeet Shotguns section for corresponding values and information. Only the Model MX8 remains below, since there is no similar American model.

STANDARD GRADE MODELS

Older Mirage Models (without the "Special" designation) do not have the adjustable 4 position trigger. Subtract $250-$500 on values listed below for these older variations.

⚼ **Mirage MX8** – developed especially for Olympic Skeet Competition featuring vent. barrels with optional muzzle brakes on sides, grooved forearm, interchangeable trigger groupings with non-adj. trigger.

	100%	98%	95%	90%	80%	70%	60%
Mfg.'s Sug. Retail $7,300		$6,100	$4,300	$3,600	$3,200	$2,875	$2,600	$2,375

Add $380 for choke tubes (Mirage C - MX8 C).
Add $2,750 for Gold Outline engraving.

SC3 GRADE MODELS — MX8 Special approximates the Mirage Special for values.

SCO GRADE MODELS — Mirage MX8 approximates the Mirage Special for values.

GOLD GRADE MODELS — Mirage MX8 approximates the Mirage Special for values.

SCO GRADE SIDEPLATES MODELS — Mirage MX8 approximates the Mirage Special for values.

GOLD GRADE SIDEPLATES MODELS — Mirage MX8 approximates the Mirage Special for values.

EXTRA GRADE MODELS — Mirage MX8 approximates the Mirage Special for values.

EXTRA GOLD GRADE MODELS — Mirage MX8 approximates the Mirage Special for values.

OVER/UNDER SIDELOCK MODELS — older models without rebounding hammers are not as desirable.

⚼ **SHO Older Mfg.**

	100%	98%	95%	90%	80%	70%	60%
	$18,000	$15,750	$12,000	$9,500	$8,500	$7,600	$6,800

⚼ **SHO New Mfg.**

	100%	98%	95%	90%	80%	70%	60%
	$35,850	$30,000	$25,000	$20,000	$17,000	$14,500	$12,750

Last Mfg.'s Sug. Retail was $43,000.

⚼ **SHO Gold Older Mfg.**

	100%	98%	95%	90%	80%	70%	60%
	$18,000	$15,750	$12,000	$9,500	$8,500	$7,600	$6,800

⚼ **SHO Gold New Mfg.**

	100%	98%	95%	90%	80%	70%	60%
	$39,000	$29,750	$25,000	$22,000	$18,500	$15,950	$13,750

Last Mfg.'s Sug. Retail was $48,000.

Grading	100%	98%	95%	90%	80%	70%	60%

SHO Extra — imported 1985-1992.

| | $68,750 | $54,700 | $38,100 | $32,000 | $26,500 | $21,250 | $18,000 |

Last Mfg.'s Sug. Retail was $80,000.

SHO Gold Extra — similar to SHO Extra, except has gold inlays. Imported 1992 only.

| | $72,750 | $56,500 | $39,500 | $33,000 | $27,000 | $22,000 | $18,500 |

Last Mfg.'s Sug. Retail was $86,000.

COMPETITION SPORTING/PIGEON SHOTGUNS: O/U

12 ga. only, unless indicated otherwise, designed for live pigeon or sporting clays competition.
The Mirage Sporting Classic Models listed below replace the Mirage Special Sporting and incorporate several new improvements.

STANDARD GRADE MODELS

The MX1/MX1B configuration is available mainly for the European marketplace. Values for this model represent recent pricing - Perazzi U.S.A. should be contacted directly for an up-to-date price quotation.

Choke tubes became standard on Perazzi's Sporting shotguns beginning in 1992. Subtract $400 - $500 for older variations without choke tubes (Models without the "C" suffix nomenclature). Older specimens without the "Special" designation do not have adjustable 4 position trigger group - subtract $400 from values below without this feature.

MX3C Special Sporting — features VR and barrels, includes adj. four position trigger, and 5 interchangeable choke tubes. Disc. 1992.

| | $5,875 | $4,275 | $3,600 | $3,200 | $2,875 | $2,600 | $2,375 |

Last Mfg.'s Sug. Retail was $6,880.

MX7C Sporting — Sporting or Pigeon configuration, includes 5 choke tubes. Importation began 1992.

| Mfg.'s Sug. Retail | $6,100 | | $5,700 | $4,950 | $4,250 | $3,550 | $2,950 | $2,625 | $2,300 |

MX8/20 ga. — 20 ga., 27 5/8, 28 3/8, or 29 1/2 in. barrels with fixed or screw-in chokes. New 1993.

| Mfg.'s Sug. Retail | $7,300 | | $6,100 | $4,300 | $3,600 | $3,200 | $2,875 | $2,600 | $2,375 |

MX10 — 12 or 20 ga., 27 5/8 in. barrels with fixed chokes, pigeon configuration. New 1993.

| Mfg.'s Sug. Retail | $10,000 | | $8,350 | $7,400 | $6,400 | $5,500 | $4,950 | $4,200 | $3,800 |

Mirage Special Sporting — 28 3/8 in. barrels with choke tubes, external SST (non-adj.), special sporting dimension stock and forend, Schnabel forearm.

| Mfg.'s Sug. Retail | $8,100 | | $6,675 | $4,500 | $3,700 | $3,250 | $2,900 | $2,625 | $2,400 |

Add $3,500 for Gold Outline engraving.

Mirage Special Sporting Classic — similar to Mirage Sporting, except has engraving package, SC3 quality wood, and SST.

| Mfg.'s Sug. Retail | $9,150 | | $7,700 | $5,600 | $4,250 | $3,650 | $3,150 | $2,900 | $2,600 |

MX1/MX1B Sporting — 12 ga. only, MX1 has high tapered ramped rib and separated barrels. MX1B has lower profile flat rib.

| | $4,550 | $3,700 | $3,400 | $3,050 | $2,750 | $2,500 | $2,275 |

Last Mfg.'s Sug. Retail was $5,510.

SC3 GRADE MODELS

MX3C Special Sporting

| | $9,650 | $7,900 | $6,350 | $5,500 | $4,950 | $4,200 | $3,800 |

Last Mfg.'s Sug. Retail was $11,230.

Perazzi cont.

Grading		100%	98%	95%	90%	80%	70%	60%
Mirage Special Sporting		$10,750	$8,500	$6,850	$5,900	$5,200	$4,300	$3,850

Last Mfg.'s Sug. Retail was $12,730.

MX1/MX1B Sporting		$7,750	$6,300	$5,500	$4,950	$4,200	$3,800	$3,650

Last Mfg.'s Sug. Retail was $9,420.

MX8/20 ga. Mfg.'s Sug. Retail $12,450	$10,575	$7,850	$6,350	$5,500	$4,950	$4,200	$3,800
MX10 Mfg.'s Sug. Retail $15,150	$13,250	$10,200	$7,500	$5,800	$4,560	$4,175	$3,800

SCO GRADE MODELS

MX3C Special Sporting	$16,525	$13,700	$10,850	$9,250	$8,500	$7,900	$6,850

Last Mfg.'s Sug. Retail was $19,030.

Mirage Special Sporting	$18,125	$14,550	$11,550	$9,650	$8,700	$8,100	$6,950

Last Mfg.'s Sug. Retail was $21,180.

MX1/MX1B Sporting	$13,500	$10,770	$9,250	$8,500	$8,000	$7,400	$6,750

Last Mfg.'s Sug. Retail was $15,860.

MX8/20 ga. Mfg.'s Sug. Retail $21,200	$18,000	$13,725	$10,900	$9,250	$8,500	$7,900	$6,850
MX10 Mfg.'s Sug. Retail $23,900	$20,250	$14,550	$11,500	$9,650	$8,700	$8,100	$6,950

GOLD GRADE MODELS

MX3C Special Sporting	$18,300	$14,550	$11,550	$9,650	$8,700	$8,100	$6,950

Last Mfg.'s Sug. Retail was $21,430.

Mirage Special Sporting	$20,225	$18,000	$16,000	$13,250	$11,750	$10,500	$9,250

Last Mfg.'s Sug. Retail was $23,780.

MX1/MX1B Sporting	$14,145	$11,950	$9,750	$8,500	$8,000	$7,400	$6,750

Last Mfg.'s Sug. Retail was $17,610.

MX8/20 ga. Mfg.'s Sug. Retail $23,920	$20,425	$14,600	$11,550	$9,650	$8,700	$8,100	$6,950
MX10 Mfg.'s Sug. Retail $26,620	$21,900	$15,750	$12,000	$9,850	$8,700	$8,100	$6,950

Grading	100%	98%	95%	90%	80%	70%	60%

SCO GRADE SIDEPLATES MODELS

⚞ Mirage Special Sporting

	100%	98%	95%	90%	80%	70%	60%
	$27,600	$22,450	$20,300	$17,500	$15,250	$13,000	$11,250

Last Mfg.'s Sug. Retail was $32,080.

⚞ MX1/MX1B Sporting

	100%	98%	95%	90%	80%	70%	60%
	$20,000	$18,000	$16,000	$13,250	$11,750	$10,500	$9,250

Last Mfg.'s Sug. Retail was $23,480.

⚞ MX8/20 ga.

Mfg.'s Sug. Retail	$32,550	$27,800	$19,150	$16,200	$13,250	$11,750	$10,250	$9,000

⚞ MX10

Mfg.'s Sug. Retail	$35,250	$29,450	$20,775	$17,000	$13,250	$11,750	$10,250	$9,000

GOLD GRADE SIDEPLATES MODELS

⚞ Mirage Special Sporting

	100%	98%	95%	90%	80%	70%	60%
	$32,550	$25,250	$22,000	$18,900	$16,500	$13,250	$10,000

Last Mfg.'s Sug. Retail was $37,130.

⚞ MX1/MX1B Sporting

	100%	98%	95%	90%	80%	70%	60%
	$23,000	$20,250	$17,500	$15,250	$13,000	$11,750	$10,000

Last Mfg.'s Sug. Retail was $27,300.

⚞ MX8/20 ga.

Mfg.'s Sug. Retail	$37,800	$32,650	$25,000	$19,750	$16,500	$13,750	$12,250	$10,750

⚞ MX10

Mfg.'s Sug. Retail	$40,500	$34,700	$24,600	$21,300	$17,500	$15,250	$13,000	$11,250

EXTRA GRADE MODELS

⚞ Mirage Special Sporting

	100%	98%	95%	90%	80%	70%	60%
	$51,150	$35,150	$30,150	$25,000	$20,000	$17,000	$14,500

Last Mfg.'s Sug. Retail was $59,080.

⚞ MX1/MX1B Sporting

	100%	98%	95%	90%	80%	70%	60%
	$35,950	$29,950	$25,000	$20,000	$17,000	$14,500	$12,750

Last Mfg.'s Sug. Retail was $43,670.

⚞ MX8/20 ga.

Mfg.'s Sug. Retail	$60,600	$52,000	$36,250	$31,150	$25,000	$20,000	$17,000	$14,500

EXTRA GOLD GRADE MODELS

⚞ Mirage Special Sporting

	100%	98%	95%	90%	80%	70%	60%
	$54,875	$37,950	$31,950	$26,500	$21,250	$18,000	$15,500

Last Mfg.'s Sug. Retail was $63,630.

⚞ MX1/MX1B Sporting

	100%	98%	95%	90%	80%	70%	60%
	$38,000	$31,500	$26,500	$21,250	$18,000	$15,500	$13,750

Last Mfg.'s Sug. Retail was $47,170.

⚞ MX8/20 ga.

Mfg.'s Sug. Retail	$65,350	$55,450	$38,000	$32,750	$26,000	$20,500	$17,000	$14,500

HUNTING SHOTGUNS: O/U BOXLOCK ACTION

12, 20, 28, or .410 ga., 26, 26⅜, or 27⅝ in. barrels only, choice of chokes. These small frame shotguns are available in 20, 28, or .410 ga. but choke tubes (MX20C designation) are optional only in 20 ga.

STANDARD GRADE MODELS

⚞ **MX8/20 ga.** — 20 ga., small frame, removable trigger group, 26 or 27⅝ in. separated barrels with fixed or screw-in chokes. New 1993.

Mfg.'s Sug. Retail $7,300 $6,150 $4,500 $3,700 $3,250 $2,900 $2,625 $2,400
Add $400 for five choke tubes (MX8/20C).

⚞ **MX12** — 12 ga. only, 2¾ in. chambers only, 26 or 27⅝ in. separated barrels with VR, coil springs, SST (fixed trigger group), Schnabel forearm, light receiver border engraving.

Mfg.'s Sug. Retail $7,300 $6,150 $4,500 $3,700 $3,250 $2,900 $2,625 $2,400
Add $400 for five choke tubes (MX12C).
Add $2,750 for Gold Outline engraving.
Vented side rib guns with flushed chokes are available beginning 1993.

⚞ **MX20** — similar to MX12, except 20, 28, or .410 ga. on smaller frame, 2¾ or 3 in. chambers, 26 or 27⅝ in. barrels.

Mfg.'s Sug. Retail $7,650 $6,400 $4,575 $3,800 $3,350 $2,950 $2,625 $2,400
Add $400 for five choke tubes (MX20C).
Add $2,950 for Gold Outline engraving.

⚞ **MX28/MX410** — 28 or .410 ga., small frame, 3 in. chambers on .410 ga., 26 in. flat VR barrels with fixed chokes, fixed trigger, straight grip, satin nickel receiver. New 1993.

Mfg.'s Sug. Retail $14,600 $12,950 $10,000 $7,450 $5,800 $4,560 $4,175 $3,800

SC3 GRADE MODELS

⚞ **MX8/20 ga.**

Mfg.'s Sug. Retail $12,450 $10,475 $8,350 $6,500 $5,500 $4,950 $4,200 $3,800
Add $400 for MX8/20C (includes 5 interchangeable choke tubes).

⚞ **MX12**

Mfg.'s Sug. Retail $12,450 $10,475 $8,350 $6,500 $5,500 $4,950 $4,200 $3,800
Add $400 for MX12C Model (includes 5 interchangeable choke tubes).

⚞ **MX20/SC3**

Mfg.'s Sug. Retail $13,200 $11,000 $8,800 $6,750 $5,750 $5,000 $4,200 $3,800
Add $400 for MX20C/SC3C (the SC3 Model replaced the MX20 in 1993) Model (includes 5 interchangeable choke tubes).

SCO GRADE MODELS

Add 200% for early smaller frame MX20s.

⚞ **MX8/20 ga.**

Mfg.'s Sug. Retail $21,250 $18,000 $14,450 $11,350 $9,650 $8,700 $7,900 $6,850
Add $350 for MX8/20C (includes 5 interchangeable choke tubes).

⚞ **MX12**

Mfg.'s Sug. Retail $21,250 $18,000 $14,450 $11,350 $9,650 $8,700 $7,900 $6,850
Add $350 for MX12C Model (includes 5 interchangeable choke tubes).

⚞ **MX20/SCO**

Mfg.'s Sug. Retail $21,750 $18,225 $14,500 $11,350 $9,650 $8,700 $7,900 $6,850
Add $400 for MX20C/SCOC Model (includes 5 interchangeable choke tubes).
Earlier small frame SCO 20 ga. variations are serialized below 10,100. These guns also have better engraving than later specimens.

Grading		100%	98%	95%	90%	80%	70%	60%
⚞ MX28/MX410								
Mfg.'s Sug. Retail	$28,550	$24,050	$20,400	$18,000	$16,000	$13,250	$11,750	$10,500

GOLD GRADE MODELS

		100%	98%	95%	90%	80%	70%	60%
⚞ MX8/20 ga.								
Mfg.'s Sug. Retail	$23,950	$20,100	$17,875	$16,000	$13,250	$11,750	$10,500	$9,250

Add $350 for MX8/20C Model (includes 5 interchangeable choke tubes).

		100%	98%	95%	90%	80%	70%	60%
⚞ MX12 Gold								
Mfg.'s Sug. Retail	$23,950	$20,100	$17,875	$16,000	$13,250	$11,750	$10,500	$9,250

Add $350 for MX12C Model (includes 5 interchangeable choke tubes).

		100%	98%	95%	90%	80%	70%	60%
⚞ MX20/SCO Gold								
Mfg.'s Sug. Retail	$25,000	$20,600	$18,150	$16,200	$13,250	$11,750	$10,500	$9,250

Add $400 for MX20C/SCOC Model (includes 5 interchangeable choke tubes).

		100%	98%	95%	90%	80%	70%	60%
⚞ MX20/MX410								
Mfg.'s Sug. Retail	$31,250	$26,000	$20,000	$17,550	$14,250	$12,250	$11,000	$10,000

SCO GRADE SIDEPLATES MODELS

		100%	98%	95%	90%	80%	70%	60%
⚞ MX8/20 ga.								
Mfg.'s Sug. Retail	$32,550	$27,750	$20,750	$18,000	$14,500	$12,500	$11,000	$10,000

Add $400 for MX8/20C Model (includes 5 interchangeable choke tubes).

		100%	98%	95%	90%	80%	70%	60%
⚞ MX12								
Mfg.'s Sug. Retail	$32,550	$27,750	$20,750	$18,000	$14,500	$12,500	$11,000	$10,000

Add $400 for MX12C Model (includes 5 interchangeable choke tubes).

		100%	98%	95%	90%	80%	70%	60%
⚞ MX20/SCO								
Mfg.'s Sug. Retail	$35,600	$30,350	$22,750	$19,000	$15,250	$13,500	$12,000	$10,750

Add $400 for MX20C/SCOC Model (includes 5 interchangeable choke tubes).

		100%	98%	95%	90%	80%	70%	60%
⚞ MX28/MX410								
Mfg.'s Sug. Retail	$39,850	$33,000	$24,550	$20,250	$16,000	$14,000	$12,000	$10,750

GOLD GRADE SIDEPLATES MODELS

		100%	98%	95%	90%	80%	70%	60%
⚞ MX8/20 ga.								
Mfg.'s Sug. Retail	$37,800	$33,000	$26,250	$22,750	$18,950	$16,500	$13,250	$10,000

Add $400 for MX8/20C Model (includes 5 interchangeable choke tubes).

		100%	98%	95%	90%	80%	70%	60%
⚞ MX12								
Mfg.'s Sug. Retail	$37,800	$33,000	$26,250	$22,750	$18,950	$16,500	$13,250	$10,000

Add $400 for MX12C Model (includes 5 interchangeable choke tubes).

		100%	98%	95%	90%	80%	70%	60%
⚞ MX20/SCO								
Mfg.'s Sug. Retail	$42,650	$36,750	$29,250	$25,250	$22,000	$18,500	$15,750	$13,700

Add $350 for MX20C/SCOC Model (includes 5 interchangeable choke tubes).

		100%	98%	95%	90%	80%	70%	60%
⚞ MX28/MX410								
Mfg.'s Sug. Retail	$45,100	$38,250	$30,750	$26,000	$22,250	$18,750	$15,750	$13,700

Grading	100%	98%	95%	90%	80%	70%	60%

EXTRA GRADE MODELS

MX12/Extra — 12 or 20 ga., 20 ga. has choice or removable (new 1993) or non-removable trigger group assembly.

Mfg.'s Sug. Retail	$60,600	$52,750	$38,750	$31,500	$25,750	$21,000	$18,000	$15,000

Add $400 for MX12C Model (includes 5 interchangeable choke tubes - disc. 1992).

EXTRA GOLD GRADE MODELS

Extra Gold — 12 or 20 ga., 20 ga. has choice or removable (new 1993) or non-removable trigger group assembly.

Mfg.'s Sug. Retail	$65,350	$56,000	$41,250	$33,250	$27,250	$23,000	$20,000	$17,000

Add $400 for Extra C Gold Model (includes 5 interchangeable choke tubes - disc. 1992).

Extra Gold Small Gauge — 20, 28, or .410 ga. Importation disc. 1992.

	$48,150	$37,850	$31,950	$26,500	$21,250	$18,000	$15,500

Add $350 for Extra C Gold Model (includes 5 interchangeable choke tubes).
Last Mfg.'s Sug. Retail was $54,700.

HUNTING SHOTGUNS: O/U SIDELOCK MODELS

All SHO models were disc. in 1992 (they were available through special order only).

SHO Older Mfg. — older models without rebounding hammers are not as desirable.

	$18,000	$15,750	$12,000	$9,500	$8,500	$7,600	$6,800

SHO Newer Mfg. — 12 ga. only, introductory sidelock O/U model with bank note game scene engraving on coin finished receiver.

	$35,500	$29,950	$25,000	$20,000	$17,000	$14,500	$12,750

Last Mfg.'s Sug. Retail was $43,000.

SHO Gold Older Mfg. — older models without rebounding hammers are not as desirable.

	$18,000	$15,750	$12,000	$9,500	$8,500	$7,600	$6,800

SHO Gold Newer Mfg. — similar to SHO, except has game scenes in gold relief.

	$38,650	$31,500	$26,500	$21,250	$18,000	$15,500	$13,750

Last Mfg.'s Sug. Retail was $48,000.

SHO Extra — importation began 1992.

	$68,750	$54,700	$38,100	$32,000	$26,500	$21,250	$18,000

Last Mfg.'s Sug. Retail was $80,000.

SHO Gold Extra — similar to SHO Extra, except has gold inlays. Importation began 1992.

	$72,750	$56,500	$39,500	$33,000	$27,000	$22,000	$18,500

Last Mfg.'s Sug. Retail was $86,000.

HUNTING SHOTGUNS: SIDE-BY-SIDE SIDELOCK MODELS

Deduct 40% without rebounding hammers on older DHO models.

DHO — 12 ga. only, extensive sidelock scroll engraving on coin finished receiver. Limited production-special order only.

Mfg.'s Sug. Retail	$45,000	$31,000	$25,000	$20,000	$17,000	$14,500	$12,750	$10,000

DHO Gold — 12 ga. only, extensive sidelock game scene engraving on coin finished receiver with multiple gold inlays.

Mfg.'s Sug. Retail	$50,300	$42,000	$33,000	$26,000	$22,000	$18,500	$15,950	$13,750

Grading	100%	98%	95%	90%	80%	70%	60%

DHO Extra — similar engraving to Extra Grade model. Importation disc. 1991.

	$89,500	$79,500	$69,500	$57,000	$45,000	$35,000	$22,500

Last Mfg.'s Sug. Retail was $77,500.

DHO Gold Extra — top of the line SXS, special order only, any gauge, rare. Perhaps the most expensive recently manufactured shotgun in the world. Importation disc. 1991.

	$89,500	$79,500	$69,500	$57,000	$45,000	$35,000	$22,500

Last Mfg.'s Sug. Retail was $82,000.

PEREGRINE INDUSTRIES, INC.

Manufacturer located in Huntington Beach, CA beginning 1991. Dealer direct sales only.

PISTOLS

FALCON — .40 S&W, 10mm, or .45 ACP cal., semi-auto with selective double/single action, ambidextrous thumb safety, 5 in. barrel, decocking lever, tri-square sighting system, two-tone metal finish with black Zytel grips. New 1991.

Mfg.'s Sug. Retail	$795	$700	$575	$525	$475	$425	$395	$360

While advertised, this model has yet to be made in any quantity for consumers.

PERUGINI-VISINI

Manufacturer located in Brescia, Italy. Rifles were previously imported and distributed until 1992 by W.L. Moore, located in Westlake Village, CA. All other models listed below were previously imported and distributed by Armes De Chasse located in Chadds Ford, PA until 1988.

As this edition went to press, Perugini-Visini did not have an importer for the U.S.

RIFLES

STANDARD MODEL: BOLT ACTION — available in most U.S. and metric cals., Mauser 98K action, 24 or 26 in. barrel, 3 shot mag.(non-detachable), matte finished European walnut, high polish bluing, no sights. Importation disc. 1987.

	$4,250	$3,800	$3,400	$2,950	$2,500	$2,000	$1,800

Last Mfg.'s Sug. Retail was $4,250.

DELUXE MODEL: BOLT ACTION — similar to Standard Model, except has finely checkered oil finished walnut stock, sights, knurled bolt handle, and is cased. Importation disc. 1987.

	$4,250	$3,800	$3,400	$2,950	$2,500	$2,000	$1,800

Last Mfg.'s Sug. Retail was $4,250.

MODEL EAGLE: SINGLE SHOT — available in most U.S. and metric cals., Anson & Deeley type action, ejector, sights, adj. trigger, oil finished finely checkered European walnut stock, 24 or 26 in. Hammerli barrel. Importation disc. 1987.

	$5,255	$4,500	$3,800	$3,400	$2,950	$2,500	$2,000

Last Mfg.'s Sug. Retail was $5,255.

MODEL VICTORIA M SxS — .30-06 (disc.), 7 x 57R, 7 x 65R, or 9.3 x 74R cal., Anson & Deeley type boxlock action, border engraving, ejectors, folding leaf rear sight, DTs, 24 or 26 in. monobloc barrels with chopper lumps, leather cased. Importation disc. 1992.

	$7,000	$5,700	$4,600	$3,500	$2,950	$2,500	$2,000

Last Mfg.'s Sug. Retail was $7,900.

Grading	100%	98%	95%	90%	80%	70%	60%

⚁ **Model Victoria D Mag. SxS** — similar to Model Victoria, except in .375 H&H, .458 Win., .470 NE, or .500-3 in. NE cal., demi-bloc barrels, and has elaborate engraving. Importation disc. 1992.

| | $10,950 | $9,150 | $8,200 | $7,400 | $6,600 | $5,800 | $5,100 |

Last Mfg.'s Sug. Retail was $13,750.

MODEL SELOUS SxS — 9.3 x 74R, 375 H&H, .458 Win. Mag., .470 NE, or .500 3 in. NE cal., H&H style detachable sidelock action, ejectors, folding leaf rear sight, border engraving with best quality checkered walnut, top-of-the-line model, leather cased. Importation disc. 1992.

| | $23,000 | $18,500 | $15,000 | $12,000 | $10,000 | $9,000 | $8,150 |

Last Mfg.'s Sug. Retail was $26,000.

BOXLOCK EXPRESS SxS — .444 Marlin or 9.3 x 74R cal., Anson & Deeley boxlock action, ejectors, color case hardened frame, iron sights. Importation disc. 1989.

| | $3,150 | $2,800 | $2,500 | $2,200 | $1,950 | $1,700 | $1,475 |

Last Mfg.'s Sug. Retail was $3,500.

BOXLOCK MAGNUM O/U — .270 Win., .375 H&H, or .458 Win. Mag. cal., Anson & Deeley boxlock action, ejectors, monobloc barrels, select walnut. Importation disc. 1989.

| | $5,500 | $4,900 | $4,300 | $3,750 | $3,100 | $2,600 | $2,200 |

Last Mfg.'s Sug. Retail was $6,100.

SIDELOCK SUPER EXPRESS SxS — choice of 9 different cals. including .470 Nitro Express, H&H patterned sidelocks, chopper lump barrels, third lever fastener, multi-leaf express sights, coin finished or case hardened receiver, engraving patterns optional. Importation disc. 1989.

| | $9,500 | $8,400 | $7,400 | $6,850 | $6,100 | $5,600 | $5,000 |

Last Mfg.'s Sug. Retail was $10,500.

SHOTGUNS

LIBERTY MODEL — 12, 20, 28, or .410 ga., Anson & Deeley type engraved action, 28 in. chopper lump barrels, double Purdey-type lock, ejectors, leather cased. Importation disc. 1989.

| | $5,255 | $4,500 | $3,800 | $3,400 | $2,950 | $2,500 | $2,000 |

Last Mfg.'s Sug. Retail was $5,255.

CLASSIC MODEL — 12 or 20 ga., H&H style scroll engraved sidelock action, 28 in. chopper lump barrels, double Purdey-type lock, best quality checkered walnut stock and forearm, top-of-the-line model, leather cased. Importation disc. 1989.

| | $10,970 | $8,650 | $7,500 | $6,925 | $6,200 | $5,675 | $5,050 |

Last Mfg.'s Sug. Retail was $10,970.

PETERS STAHL GmbH

Manufacturer located in Paderborn, Germany. Currently imported by McMillan Gunworks, Inc. and Safari Arms located in Olympia, WA.

Peters Stahl manufactures high quality semi-auto pistols based on the Model 1911 design.

PHELPS MFG. CO.

Current manufacturer located in Evansville, IN.

Phelps Manufacturing Company began shipping guns in early 1978. Phelps guns are investment-cast in 4140 steel, with basic single-action simplicity, using a transfer bar in the action.

Grading	100%	98%	95%	90%	80%	70%	60%

HERITAGE I — .45-70 cal., single action revolver, incorporates transfer bar hammer safety, blue finish (standard), nickel (optional), adj. rear sight, 8 in. barrel standard, other barrel lengths up to 20 in. available, 6 lbs.

Mfg.'s Sug. Retail	$1,085		$995	$825	$625		

Add $20 for each additional in. of barrel.

EAGLE I — .444 Marlin cal., single action revolver, blue finish, adj. rear sight, barrel options same as Heritage I, 6 lbs.

Mfg.'s Sug. Retail	$1,085		$995	$825	$625		

GRIZZLY .50-70 — .50-70 cal., otherwise similar to Heritage I. New 1992.

Mfg.'s Sug. Retail	$1,550		$1,375	$1,050	$850		

Add $20 for each additional in. of barrel.

PHILLIPS & ROGERS, INC.
Manufacturer located in Conroe, TX since 1992. Dealer direct sales.

MEDUSA MODEL 47 REVOLVER — over 25 cals. in the .355 - .380 diameter range (including .357 Mag., .38 Super, .38 Spl., 9mm Para., etc.), unique design utilizes no half-moon clips or cylinder/barrel changes, 6 shot, double action, Pachmayr or Trausch checkered walnut grips. New 1993.

No Mfg.'s Retail	$750	$675	$595	$550	$495	$450	$395

PHOENIX ARMS
Manufacturer located in Ontario, CA since 1992. Distributor sales only.

RAVEN — .25 ACP cal., single action semi auto, $2^7/_{16}$ in. barrel, 6 shot mag., alloy frame, choice of finishes and grips.

Mfg.'s Sug. Retail	$70	$60	$50	$45	$40	$35	$30	$25

This model is supplied with a magazine disconnect lock.

HP-22 — .22 LR cal., single action semi auto, VR barrel, 11 shot mag., alloy frame, adj. rear sight, high polish finish, mag. lock, 20 oz. New 1993.

Mfg.'s Sug. Retail	$95	$85	$65	$50	$45	$40	$35	$30

PHOENIX ARMS CO.
Previous importer located in Lowell, MA.

PHOENIX — .25 ACP cal., Belgian semi-auto, previously manufactured by Robar et DeKerkhove located in Liege, Belgium.
This trademark is rarely encountered - values would start at $350 and go up according to original condition.

PIETTA, F.LLI
Manufacturer located in Gussago, Italy.

Pietta manufactures blackpowder and modern firearms reproductions in many configurations for various American companies including Navy Arms, Dixie Gun Works, Mitchell Arms, K.B.I., and others. Please refer to the individual company headings in the Black Powder section of this text for more information on Pietta manufactured firearms, or contact the factory direcly for a comprehensive catalog listing of the wide assortment of firearms this company manufactures (see Trademark Index).

PIOTTI

Manufacturer located in Brescia, Italy. Currently imported and distributed exclusively by W.L. Moore & Co. located in Westlake Village, CA.

Fratelli Piotti is one of Italy's premier gunmakers. These shotguns meet the highest British standards of craftsmanship and are made to customer specifications. Variety of gauges, engraving, styles, chokes, etc.

For the following models — add $1,400 for single trigger, $650 for hand-detachable locks, approx. $1,100 for leather case, $650 for 16 or 20 ga., $1,000-$2,000 for 28 or .410 ga. (depending on if boxlock or sidelock).

SHOTGUNS

Grading	100%	98%	95%	90%	80%	70%	60%

PIUMA — 12, 16, 20, 28, or .410 ga., Anson & Deeley boxlock ejector double with chopper double barrels, level file-cut rib, light scroll and rosette engraving, scalloped frame.

	100%	98%	95%	90%	80%	70%	60%
Mfg.'s Sug. Retail $11,900	$9,500	$8,650	$7,700	$6,700	$5,600	$4,500	$3,400

WESTLAKE — 12, 16, 20, 28, or .410 ga., H&H sidelock action, moderate scroll engraving. Mfg. disc. 1989.

	100%	98%	95%	90%	80%	70%	60%
	$8,500	$7,500	$6,050	$5,300	$4,700	$4,200	$3,750

Last Mfg.'s Sug. Retail was $8,400.

MONTE CARLO — 12, 16, 20, 28, or .410 ga., best-quality H&H pattern sidelock ejector double with chopper lump barrels, Purdey style scroll and rosette engraving. Importation disc. 1990.

	100%	98%	95%	90%	80%	70%	60%
	$10,500	$9,250	$8,200	$7,100	$6,000	$5,000	$4,500

Last Mfg.'s Sug. Retail was $11,400.

KING NUMBER 1 — 12, 16, 20, 28, or .410 ga., best-quality H&H pattern sidelock ejector double with chopper lump barrels, level file-cut rib, very fine, full coverage scroll engraving with small floral bouquets, gold crest in forearm, gold crown in top lever, name in gold and finely figured wood.

	100%	98%	95%	90%	80%	70%	60%
Mfg.'s Sug. Retail $19,900	$16,000	$14,250	$11,500	$9,250	$7,650	$6,600	$5,500

LUNIK — 12, 16, 20, 28, or .410 ga., best-quality H&H pattern sidelock ejector double with lump (demi-bloc) barrels, level, file-cut rib, Renaissance style large scroll engraving in relief, gold crown in top lever, gold name, and gold crest in forearm, finely figured wood.

	100%	98%	95%	90%	80%	70%	60%
Mfg.'s Sug. Retail $21,500	$17,200	$14,950	$12,000	$9,400	$8,000	$6,900	$5,850

KING EXTRA — 12, 16, 20, 28, or .410 ga., best-quality H&H pattern sidelock ejector double with chopper lump barrels, level file-cut rib, choice of either bulino game scene engraving or game scene engraving with gold inlays, engraved and signed by a master engraver, exhibition grade wood.

	100%	98%	95%	90%	80%	70%	60%
Mfg.'s Sug. Retail $30,000	$24,000	$20,000	$16,750	$14,000	$11,750	$9,950	$8,450

MONACO NUMBER 1 OR 2 — 12, 16, 20, 28, or .410 ga., best-quality H&H pattern sidelock ejector double with lump (demi-bloc) barrels, level, file-cut rib, Renaissance style large scroll engraving in relief, gold crown in top lever, gold name, and gold crest in forearm, finely figured wood.

	100%	98%	95%	90%	80%	70%	60%
Mfg.'s Sug. Retail $28,600	$22,900	$19,250	$16,000	$13,750	$11,750	$9,950	$8,450

MONACO NUMBER 4 — top-of-the-line model with every refinement incorporated. Custom order only and extremely rare.

	100%	98%	95%	90%	80%	70%	60%
Mfg.'s Sug. Retail $37,000	$29,600	$25,000	$21,000	$17,500	$14,000	$11,750	$9,950

BOSS O/U — 12 or 20 ga. New 1992.

	100%	98%	95%	90%	80%	70%	60%
Mfg.'s Sug. Retail $34,000	$27,000	$22,500	$18,500	$15,750	$12,750	$10,000	$9,100

PIRANHA

While manufacture was supposed to be by Amprospec, Inc. (located in Phoenix, AZ), this trademark was never produced. This handgun was designed to have 85% less recoil, but financial difficulty precluded its manufacture.

POLY TECHNOLOGIES, INC.

Distributed by PTK International, Inc. located in Atlanta, GA. Imported by Keng's Firearms Specialty, Inc., located in Riverdale, GA. Manufactured in China by Poly Technologies, Inc.

Poly Technologies commercial firearms are made to Chinese military specifications and have excellent quality control.

These models have been banned from domestic importation due to 1989 Federal legislation.

Grading	100%	98%	95%	90%	80%	70%	60%

POLY TECH AKS-762 — 7.62 x 39mm K or .223 Rem. cal., 16¼ in. barrel, semi-auto version of the Chinese AKM (Type 56) paramilitary design rifle, 8.4 lbs., wood stock. Imported 1988-89.

	100%	98%	95%	90%	80%	70%	60%
	$525	$460	$415	$365	$300	$250	$230

Add $25 for side-fold plastic stock.
This model was also available with a downward folding stock at no extra charge.
Last Mfg.'s Sug. Retail was $400.

CHINESE SKS — 7.62 x 39mm Soviet military, 20⁹⁄₂₀ in. barrel, full wood stock, machine steel parts to Chinese military specifications, 7.9 lbs. Imported 1988-89.

	100%	98%	95%	90%	80%	70%	60%
	$295	$270	$230	$200	$175	$140	$130

Last Mfg.'s Sug. Retail was $200.

RUSSIAN AK-47/S (LEGEND) — 7.62 x 39mm Soviet military, 16⅜ in. barrel, semi-auto configuration of the original AK-47, 8.2 lbs. Imported 1988-89.

	100%	98%	95%	90%	80%	70%	60%
	$575	$500	$450	$410	$385	$350	$325

The S suffix in this variation designates third model specifications.
Last Mfg.'s Sug. Retail was $550.

National Match Legend — utilizes match parts in fabrication.

	100%	98%	95%	90%	80%	70%	60%
	$725	$650	$525	$450	$400	$350	$325

U.S. M-14/S — .308 cal., semi-auto, 22 in. barrel, forged receiver, quality reproduction of the famous M-14, 9.2 lbs. Imported 1988-89.

	100%	98%	95%	90%	80%	70%	60%
	$675	$625	$550	$495	$420	$385	$360

Last Mfg.'s Sug. Retail was $700.

POWELL, WILLIAM & SON LTD.

Manufacturer located in Birmingham, England since 1866. Currently imported by Bells Legendary Countrywear located in New York, NY. The Heritage Series was introduced into the U.S. in 1984.

SHOTGUNS: SxS

Values listed below do not include import duty or U.S. taxes.
Add $1,155 for 28 or .410 ga. in Heritage Series only.

NO. 1 SIDELOCK EJECTOR — 12, 16, 20, or .410 (disc.) ga., chopper lump barrels, extra choice French walnut, DTs, many special orders available. Gold inlays, deep relief carved action fences, can be obtained in self opener.

Mfg.'s Sug. Retail	$34,046	$34,046	$26,750	$22,250	$17,500	$14,750	$12,000	$10,000

Add $3,030 for assisted opening action.
Add $2,275 for SNT.

Grading	100%	98%	95%	90%	80%	70%	60%

NO. 3 BOXLOCK EJECTOR — 12, 16, 20, or .410 (disc.) ga., chopper lump barrels, scalloped boxlock action, extra choice French walnut, many special orders available.

Mfg.'s Sug. Retail	$15,310	$15,310	$12,500	$10,250	$8,700	$7,500	$6,250	$5,000

⚓ **Model 4 Boxlock Ejector** — similar to Number 3, but has dovetail lump barrels and less engraving.

Mfg.'s Sug. Retail	$13,260	$13,260	$11,000	$9,100	$7,800	$6,600	$5,400	$4,500

Add $2,050 for SNT.

⚓ **Model 6 Boxlock Ejector**

	$2,750	$2,450	$2,050	$1,700	$1,400	$1,150	$900

HERITAGE NO. 1 SIDELOCK EJECTOR — 12 or 20 ga., 2¾ in. chambers, chopper lump barrels, choice of game scene or bouquet and scroll engraving, DTs. New 1984.

Mfg.'s Sug. Retail	$17,360	$17,360	$14,950	$12,500	$10,250	$8,500	$7,250	$5,950

HERITAGE NO. 2 EASY OPENING SIDELOCK — similar to Heritage No. 1, except has less engraving and lesser grade walnut, easy opening action.

Mfg.'s Sug. Retail	$10,730	$10,730	$9,100	$7,950	$6,850	$5,850	$4,850	$3,750

HERITAGE DE LUXE BOXLOCK DETACHABLE LOCK — features detachable locks, choice of traditional scroll or game scene engraving, ejectors.

Mfg.'s Sug. Retail	$17,360	$17,360	$14,950	$12,500	$10,250	$8,500	$7,250	$5,950

HERITAGE ROUND ACTION EJECTOR — features unscalloped, rounded boxlock action with fine English scroll work throughout, DTs.

Mfg.'s Sug. Retail	$13,335	$13,335	$11,000	$9,100	$7,800	$6,600	$5,400	$4,500

PRANDELLI-GASPERINI

Previous manufacturer located in Brescia, Italy. Previously imported by Richland Arms located in Blissfield, MI.

Prandelli-Gasperini made both O/U and S X S shotguns in either sidelock or boxlock. Currently, older boxlock models start at approx. $1,250 (assuming 80% or better original condition). Sidelock models in similar condition usually start at $2,500, depending on gauge, embellishments, and condition.

Approx. 250 specimens of this trademark were imported during Richland Arms importation.

PREMIER

Previously manufactured in Italy and Spain.

SHOTGUNS: SIDE-BY-SIDE

REGENT DOUBLE BARREL SHOTGUN — 12, 16, 20, 28, or .410 ga., 26, 28, or 30 in. barrels, various chokes, checkered pistol grip stock and beavertail forearm. Mfg. 1955-disc.

	$275	$250	$220	$195	$140	$110	$100

REGENT MAGNUM EXPRESS — 12 ga., 3 in. chambers only, 30 in. full, recoil pad. Mfg. 1957-disc.

	$305	$275	$250	$220	$165	$140	$110

REGENT 10 GAUGE MAGNUM — similar to 12 ga. Mag., but 10 ga., 3½ in. chamber, 32 in. full and full. Mfg. 1975-disc.

	$330	$305	$275	$250	$195	$165	$140

Grading	100%	98%	95%	90%	80%	70%	60%

BRUSH KING — 12 or 20 ga., 22 in. imp. cyl. and mod. barrels, straight grip stock. Mfg. 1959-disc.

	$275	$250	$220	$195	$140	$110	$100

MONARCH SUPREME GRADE — 12 or 20 ga., 26 or 28 in. barrels, various chokes, boxlock, auto ejectors, select stock. Mfg. 1959-disc.

	$440	$385	$360	$330	$275	$250	$200

PRESENTATION CUSTOM GRADE — custom made, gold and silver game scene. Mfg. 1959-disc.

	$1,100	$990	$880	$825	$715	$605	$495

AMBASSADOR MODEL — 12, 16, 20, or .410 ga., 26 or 28 in. barrels, mod. and full choke, checkered pistol grip stock. Mfg. 1957-disc.

	$385	$360	$330	$305	$250	$220	$195

Note: The Premier is a trade name for guns that have been produced in both Spain and Italy for various importers.

PRINZ

Manufacturer of bolt action rifles, single shot rifles, and combination guns. Previously imported and distributed by Helmut Hofmann Inc. located in Placitas, NM.

Prinz rifles are now designated "Bavarian" and are currently imported by H & S, Inc. located in Durham, CT. Prinz rifles were imported 1989 only.

GRADE 1 BOLT ACTION — .243 Win., .30-06, .308 Win., .300 Win. Mag. or 7mm Rem. Mag. cal., single or double set trigger(s), oil finished walnut stock.

	$495	$440	$385	$360	$330	$275	$250

Grade 1 Carbine — similar to Grade 1 except has carbine barrel.

	$570	$495	$435	$390	$360	$330	$275

GRADE 2 BOLT ACTION — similar to Grade 1 except has rosewood forend cap.

	$545	$485	$425	$385	$360	$330	$275

TIP UP RIFLE — available in 8 cals. between .222 Rem. and .30-06, high quality and limited mfg. Importation began 1989.

	$2,175	$1,900	$1,675	$1,375	$1,100	$950	$775

PRINCESS MODEL 85 — combination gun available in 12 ga. (2¾ in. chamber) and choice of 8 cals. between .222 Rem. and .30-06.

	$1,450	$1,275	$1,100	$925	$800	$775	$650

This model comes standard with a leather case.

PURDEY, JAMES & SONS, LTD.

Manufacturer located in London, England. Purdey has been making top quality firearms since 1814.

Purdey guns have long been regarded as among the finest in the world. They were often custom made to customer specifications and as such should be regarded on an individual basis for purposes of evaluation. Value varies with gauge, barrel length, chamber length and age. We shall list the modern models and approximate values for reference purposes, but strongly recommend professional appraisal if purchase or sale is contemplated.

Grading		100%	98%	95%	90%	80%	70%	60%

RIFLES

PURDEY DOUBLE RIFLE — various English Nitro Express cals., 25½ in. barrels, folding leaf sight, checkered pistol grip stock, recoil pad, sidelock, auto ejectors. Mfg. pre-WWII and post-war.

⚒ **Large calibers.**

		100%	98%	95%	90%	80%	70%	60%
Mfg.'s Sug. Retail	$67,500	$67,500	$57,500	$42,500	$32,000	$27,500	$22,500	$17,500

⚒ **Smaller calibers.**

		100%	98%	95%	90%	80%	70%	60%
Mfg.'s Sug. Retail	$60,000	$60,000	$52,500	$40,000	$30,000	$26,500	$21,500	$16,950

The above values represent guidelines only for this trademark. Since each Purdey is basically a special order, new gun pricing is calculated per individual customer work order.

MAGAZINE RIFLE — Mauser type bolt action, 7 x 57mm, .300 H&H Mag., or 10.75 x 73mm cal., 24 in. barrel, folding leaf sight, checkered pistol grip stock.

	100%	98%	95%	90%	80%	70%	60%
	$6,875	$5,750	$4,500	$3,800	$3,500	$3,000	$2,500

Add a premium for large cals.

SHOTGUNS

BEST QUALITY GAME GUN SxS — 12, 16, or 20 ga., 26-30 in. barrels, any choke and style of rib, checkered straight or pistol grip stock. Mfg. 1880-present, auto ejector gun, best quality only.

		100%	98%	95%	90%	80%	70%	60%
Mfg.'s Sug. Retail	$37,875	$37,875	$32,500	$27,500	$23,000	$18,750	$15,000	$12,250

Add $2,625 for 28 or .410 ga. on new mfg.
Add $9,000 - $9,375 for extra set of barrels depending on gauge.

⚒ **Older mfg.**

	100%	98%	95%	90%	80%	70%	60%
Game gun	$23,450	$19,000	$15,750	$13,500	$11,000	$9,500	$8,750
Heavy Duck gun	$20,500	$17,000	$14,000	$11,000	$9,500	$8,750	$8,000

Add 50% for 20 ga.
Add 35%-50% for 28 or .410 ga.
Deduct 10% if not cased with accessories.
Add $1,000 for SST.

O/U GUN — 12, 16, 20, or 28 ga., 26-30 in. barrel, any choke, sidelock, auto ejectors, ST, checkered straight or pistol grip stock. Since WWII, Purdey has taken over the Woodward Company, and later guns have the Woodward O/U action. Very few early actions; early guns — ⅓ less.

		100%	98%	95%	90%	80%	70%	60%
Mfg.'s Sug. Retail	$44,250	$44,250	$37,750	$32,000	$26,000	$21,500	$17,750	$15,000

Add $13,500 for extra set of barrels.

⚒ **Older mfg.**

	100%	98%	95%	90%	80%	70%	60%
	$37,500	$33,000	$30,000	$26,000	$21,500	$17,750	$15,000

Add $3,000 for Woodward action.
Add 25% for 20 ga.
Add 60%+ for 28 ga.
Add 10% for SST.

SINGLE BARREL TRAP GUN — 12 ga. Purdey action only, similar to O/U specifications. Mfg. prior to WWII.

	100%	98%	95%	90%	80%	70%	60%
	$11,250	$10,000	$8,750	$7,900	$7,200	$6,750	$5,950

Q section

QFI (QUALITY FIREARMS INC.)
Previous manufacturer located in Opa Locka, FL December, 1990 -1992.

PISTOLS: SEMI-AUTO

Grading	100%	98%	95%	90%	80%	70%	60%

MODEL LA380 — .380 ACP cal., single action semi-auto, 6-shot, magazine disconnect, hammer, trigger, and firing pin block safety, 3¼ in. barrel, blue or chrome finish. Mfg. 1991-1992.

	100%	98%	95%	90%	80%	70%	60%
	$125	$100	$90	$80	$70	$60	$55

Add $23 for chrome finish.
Last Mfg.'s Sug. Retail was $147.

⚖ **Model LA380SS** — stainless steel variation of the Model LA380. Mfg. 1992 only.

	$195	$165	$135

Last Mfg.'s Sug. Retail was $220.

MODEL SA 25 — .25 ACP cal., semi-auto single action, 2½ in. barrel, 6-shot, includes inertial firing pin, external exposed hammer with half cock, and trigger blocking thumb safety, blue, dynachrome, or blue/gold finish, smooth walnut grips. Mfg. 1991 only.

	$55	$45	$40	$35	$30	$25	$25

Add $50 for blue/gold finish.
Add $10 for chrome finish with pearlite plastic grips.
Last Mfg.'s Sug. Retail was $55.

TIGRESS MODEL — .25 ACP or .380 ACP cal., semi-auto single action, 2½ (.25 ACP) or 3¼ (.380 ACP) in. barrel, blue frame with gold plated slide, 6-shot with finger extension on mag., white polymer grips with a red rose scrimshawed on both sides, designed for women, supplied with zippered gold pouch, 14 or 25 oz. Mfg. 1991 only.

	$130	$100	$90	$80	$70	$60	$55

Add $85 for .380 ACP cal.
Last Mfg.'s Sug. Retail was $155.

REVOLVERS: DOUBLE ACTION

All pistols under this heading are 6-shot.

RP SERIES STANDARD REVOLVER — .22 LR, .22 Mag., .32 S&W Long, .32 Mag. or .38 Spl., 2 or 4 in. barrel, blued or chrome finish, fixed sights, hammer block safety, without ejector assembly, composition grips. Mfg. in U.S. starting 1990.

Mfg.'s Sug. Retail	$105	$85	$70	$65	$60	$55	$50	$45

Add $15-20 for chrome finish.
Add approx. $5 for 4 in. barrel.

MODEL SO 38 — .38 Spl., swing out cylinder, 6-shot, 2 in. SR or 4 in. VR barrel, hammer block safety, composition grips. Mfg. 1991 only.

	$175	$135	$115	$95	$80	$75	$65

Last Mfg.'s Sug. Retail was $175.

Grading	100%	98%	95%	90%	80%	70%	60%

REVOLVERS: SINGLE ACTION

SAA WESTERN RANGER — .22 LR cal., 6-shot, 3, 4 (disc. 1991), $4\frac{3}{4}$ (new 1992), 6 (disc. 1991), $6\frac{1}{2}$ (new 1992), 7 (disc. 1991), or 9 in. barrel, blue finish with gold accenting, walnut grips. Mfg. 1991-1992.

	$85	$70	$65	$60	$55	$50	$45

Add approx. $5 for 7 (disc.) or $7 for 9 in. barrel.
Add approx. $15-35 for .22 Mag. extra cylinder (combo).
Last Mfg.'s Sug. Retail was $105.

SAA PLAINS RIDER — similar to Western Ranger, except has black composition grips and no gold accenting. Mfg. 1991-1992.

	$80	$65	$55	$50	$45	$40	$35

Add $11 for 9 in. barrel.
Add approx. $26 for .22 Mag. extra cylinder (combo).
Last Mfg.'s Sug. Retail was $100.

SAA HORSEMAN SERIES — .357 Mag., .44 Mag., or .45 LC cal., 6-shot, $6\frac{1}{2}$ or $7\frac{1}{2}$ in. barrel, color case hardened or blue (Dark Horseman only) finish, walnut or black composition grips, hammer block safety. Mfg. 1991 only.

	$250	$220	$190	$170	$150	$130	$115

The Dark Horseman has an extended grip frame with black composition grips and an adj. rear sight.
Last Mfg.'s Sug. Retail was $250.

QUALITY ARMS, INC.
Importer and sales agent located in Houston, TX.

Quality Arms currently imports Arrieta and Ferlib shotguns in addition to other quality European trademarks. They will also act as an import agent for those individuals who would like to special order a non-domestic trademark with a minimum of dealer mark-up. See the Trademark Index for more information.

QUALITY PARTS CO./BUSHMASTER
A division of Bushmaster Firearms, Inc. located in Windham, ME that manufactures paramilitary rifles patterned after the AR-15. Distributor and dealer sales.
Add $50 for the EM Series rifles.

XM15-E2S RIFLE — .223 cal., semi-auto patterned after the Colt AR-15, 20, 24, or 26 in. Govt. spec. match grade chrome lined barrel, manganese phosphate barrel finish, rear sight adj. for windage and elevation, Cage flash suppressor, mfg. started in 1989 in U.S.

Mfg.'s Sug. Retail	$895	$825	$725	$650	$600	$550	$500	$450

Add $40 for 24 or 26 in. barrel.

XM15-E2S Carbine — similar to above, except with telescoping buttstock and $11\frac{1}{2}$, 14, or 16 in. barrel and suppressor, mfg. started in 1989.

Mfg.'s Sug. Retail	$850	$775	$700	$625	$550	$500	$450	$395

This model does not have the target rear sight system of the XM15-E2S rifle.

IBUS M17S BULLPUP — .223 Rem. cal., semi-auto bullpup configuration featuring gas operated rotating bolt, 30 shot mag., 22 in. barrel with flash-hider, glass composites and aluminum materials, phosphate coating, 30 shot mag. New 1992.

Mfg.'s Sug. Retail	$999	$850	$775	$700	$625	$550	$500	$450

R section

R.G. INDUSTRIES

Importers located in Miami, FL. Operations ceased in January of 1986.

HANDGUNS

R.G. Industries manufactured and imported plain utilitarian revolvers and semi-auto pistols. Unfortunately, because of the current product liability situation, R.G. Industries was litigated out of business. Whereas their models represent good values, they are not collectible, and a generalized listing is provided below.

Grading	100%	98%	95%	90%	80%	70%	60%

RG 14 S, RG 23, RG 31 — prices vary from $61 to $100 retail.

RG 40, RG 74, & HIGHNOON S.A. — prices vary from $125 to $150 retail.

RG 26 SEMI-AUTO — .25 auto, 6 shot mag., 2¼ in. barrel, plastic grips, single action, 12 oz.

	$65	$55	$50	$40	$35	$30	$25

    Last Mfg.'s Sug. Retail was $66.

RWS

RWS is a trademark of Dynamit Nobel which has been manufacturing firearms in Nuremberg Stadeln, Germany since 1865. RWS is currently being imported by Dynamit Nobel of America, Inc. located in Northvale, NJ. Other trademarks currently being distributed by Dynamit Nobel can be located under individual heading names in this text.

RIFLES: MATCH TARGET

MODEL 820 L — .22 LR only, 24 (disc.) or 26 in. barrel, no. 100 aperture sight, oil polished stock for 3 position match, stippled pistol grip and forearm, recoil pad, adj. trigger, 10.6 lbs.

Mfg.'s Sug. Retail	$1,500	$1,275	$1,000	$850	$700	$575	$475	$400

Previous to 1986 this model was designated the 820 S and was supplied with a no. 75 aperture rear sight.

  Model 820 S — with Model 82 aperture sight.

	$1,100	$895	$795	$650	$560	$480	$420

    Last Mfg.'s Sug. Retail was $995.

MODEL 820 F MATCH — similar to Model 820 L, except has heavy match barrel, 15.4 lbs.

Mfg.'s Sug. Retail	$2,000	$1,750	$1,400	$1,275	$1,000	$850	$700	$575

  Model 820 SF — with Model 82 aperture sight. Disc.

	$1,125	$900	$795	$650	$560	$480	$420

    Last Mfg.'s Sug. Retail was $1,010.

MODEL 820 K — .22 LR only, made for running boar competition, 24 in. barrel, stock similar to Model 820 SF, no sights, 9½ lbs. without barrel weight or scope. Importation disc. 1986.

	$900	$775	$695	$615	$540	$470	$420

    Last Mfg.'s Sug. Retail was $870.

RADOM
Polish Arsenal, located in Radom, Poland.

Grading	100%	98%	95%	90%	80%	70%	60%

P-35 AUTOMATIC — 9mm, 8 shot, 4¾ in. barrel, blue, fixed sights, plastic grips. Mfg. 1935-WWII.

⚔ **Polish Eagle** — dated 1936, 1937, 1938, 1939.

	$1,750	$1,350	$1,000	$700	$500	$400	$300

⚔ **Polish Eagle Nazi Capture**

	$2,000	$1,600	$1,200	$900	$700	$600	$500

⚔ **Nazi Type I Slotted**

	$550	$450	$350	$295	$230	$180	$150

⚔ **Nazi Type II No Slot w/Takedown Lever**

	$400	$325	$275	$225	$200	$185	$150

⚔ **Nazi Type III No Slot, No Takedown Lever**

	$315	$275	$240	$200	$180	$160	$140

⚔ **Nazi Type III** — parkerized with wood grips, small parts blued.

	$600	$475	$350	$295	$230	$200	$175

Note: Certain Radoms with German acceptance marks will bring a premium.

RAM-LINE, INC.
Manufacturer located in Wheat Ridge, CO.

EXACTOR PISTOL — .22 LR cal., single action semi-auto, aircraft alloy receiver with 5½ in. polymer VR barrel and steel liner, unique two-motion safety featuring blocks on hammer, trigger, and sear, 15 shot mag., matte finish, easy disassembly, injected molded grip, fixed sight, 20.3 oz., supplied with case. New in 1990, limited quantities will be available 1993.

Mfg.'s Sug. Retail	$225	$195	$165	$135

⚔ **Target Exactor** — similar to above, except has 7½ in. barrel, 23 oz.

Mfg.'s Sug. Retail	$300	$265	$230	$195

RANDALL FIREARMS COMPANY
Previously manufactured in Sun Valley, CA. Manufactured between June 7, 1983 and December 15, 1984 - final plant closing was June 15, 1985.

Before manufacturing ceased in May of 1985, 24 models with 12 variations in 3 different calibers had been produced. In some instances, production on certain models was very limited and premiums for these low volume niches are starting to develop. Between June of 1983 and May of 1985, 9,968 handguns were manufactured with 75% of all 9mm cals. being exported to Europe, and 35% of 9mm production employing a 10 groove barrel. Models manufactured after 1984 came equipped with an extended slide stop, long trigger and beavertail grip safety. Production ser. no.'s started at 02000 for right hand models and 02100 for left hand models. All but the first 200 (approx.) serial numbers started with "RF" and ended with "C" or "W". A few rare mis-marks are in circulation. Total mfg. for all models and variations was 9,968. Randall prototype serialization starts with a "T" — less than 45 were manufactured and these specimens command up to a 50% premium. In addition, 78 serial numbers under 2,000 were manufactured by special order.

Models below are generally described with values per specific variations listed afterward.

It is advisable to procure a Randall research & factory letter when buying or selling many of the rarer Randall pistols. To take advantage of this service, call/FAX your name and address, Randall model name, serial number, and contact: Blue Book Publications, Inc., Attn: Randall Research, One Appletree Square, Minneapolis, MN 55425; phone number: 612-854-5229 or FAX number: 612-853-1486. The charge is $25 per serial number. Also available is a list of parts guns serial numbers for $15. Inclusion in print-out of the Randall Collector's Network is also available for $15 and is updated at least two times a year. Please allow adequate time for proper response.

COMBAT MODEL — same size as Service Model, ribbed top fixed sight slide, Pachmayr grips on right hand model only, left hand models had Herrett walnut grips. While this model was advertised as having a flat mainspring housing, it was never produced. The brochures of the time quoted $549 for mfg.'s sug. retail.

RAIDER/SERVICE MODEL-C — 9mm or .45 ACP cal., Colt Commander Model design, 4¼ in. barrel, 36 oz., total stainless steel construction. Add $130 for adj. sights/ribbed slide, available in either right-hand or left-hand (only 2 mfg.) model. Roll-marked Service Model-C in 1983 and Raider in 1984.
Last Mfg.'s Sug. Retail was $460.

⚡ **Raider/Service Model-C Featherweight** — .45 ACP only, alloy receiver, stainless steel slide, roll-marked Service Model-C, T-type serial numbers, 29 oz. Disc. 1984, only 4 mfg.

FULL SIZE SERVICE MODEL — .38 Super, 9mm, or .45 ACP cal., Colt Model 1911 A1 design, 5 in. barrel, total stainless steel construction, 38 oz. Available in either right-hand or left-hand model. Add $130 for adj. sights and rib top slide.
Last Mfg.'s Sug. Retail was $460.

CURTIS E. LEMAY 4-STAR MODEL — 9mm or .45 ACP cal., Gen. Curtis E. LeMay design, 4¼ in. barrel, 6 (.45 ACP) or 7 (9mm) shot mag., total stainless steel construction, 35 oz. Available in either right-hand or left-hand model, left hand models are a true mirror image with over 17 major parts changes. Add $10 for 9mm. Add $90 for adj. sight/ribbed top slide.
Last Mfg.'s Sug. Retail was $533.
This model was ½ in. shorter in magazine well and had a cast, squared off trigger guard compared to the Colt 1911A1 design.

⚡ **Curtis E. LeMay Featherweight Model** — .45 ACP cal. only, alloy receiver, stainless steel slide, T-type serial numbers, 28 oz. Disc. 1984 (only one mfg.).

RANDALL MATCHED SETS — .45 ACP cal. only, each set consisted of a right-hand and a left-hand Service Model with matching serial numbers. Only 4 sets were mfg. on a special order basis. A111/B111 model configuration.
Last Mfg.'s Sug. Retail was $1,250.

RANDALL VARIATIONS
IDENTIFYING RANDALL MODELS:
Randall pistols are denoted by a four-character model notation, starting with an alphabetical prefix followed by three digits. The alphabetical prefix will be either A, B, or C — A designates right-hand configuration only, B designates left-hand configuration only, and C designates right-hand lightweight model. The first digit will be 1, 2, or 3 — 1 denotes Service Model, 2 denotes Service Model-C or Raider, 3 represents the C.E. LeMay Model. The second digit again will be either 1, 2, or 3 — 1 designates round top and fixed sight slide, 2 denotes flat top fixed sight slide, and 3 represents adj. sights, flat top frame. The third digit again, is either 1, 2, or 3 — 1 denotes .45 ACP cal., 2 designates 9mm Para., and 3 represents .38 Super. Hence, if you had a left-hand Randall in the service model size with a flat top adj. sight slide, and in .45 ACP cal., your model would be a B131. These model codes are not marked on the pistols.

Randall Firearms Company, cont.

The following is a complete listing for Randall Firearms variations including production statistics. Values shown below represent recent aftermarket prices, but it should be noted regional interest can change these prices significantly. After only 8 years of discontinuance, Randall pistols are enjoying good demand.

All original Randall pistols had no blued parts. Only the front and rear sights were finished in black oxide.

Add 10%-20% for original factory boxes and paperwork.
Add 50% for prototypes with "T" serial numbers.

Grading	100%	98%	95%	90%	80%	70%	60%
A111 — 3,421 mfg.							
	$680	$595	$510	$465			

Five A111s were mfg. with Austrian proof marks with premiums existing (one NIB specimen recently sold for $3,000).

A112 — 301 mfg.							
	$895	$795	$650	$525			
A121 — 1067 mfg.							
	$700	$625	$510	$465			
A122 — 19 mfg.							
	$1,275	$1,125	$940	$795			
A131 — 2083 mfg.							
	$725	$640	$535	$495			
A211 — 992 mfg.							
	$750	$660	$535	$480			
A212 — 76 mfg.							
	$925	$815	$600	$500			
A231 — 574 mfg.							
	$850	$750	$535	$505			
A232 — 5 mfg.							
	$1,500	$1,075	$990	$775			
A311 — 361 mfg.							
	$1,100	$950	$725	$575			

Most LeMay models (4¼ in. barrel) were shipped in gunrugs without a factory box. Original factory LeMay boxes are rare — add 10% premium. Beware of Randall LeMay and service model pistols made from parts kits. There were 226 LeMay receivers and 322 service model receivers (all right hand) sold that could be parts guns. Accordingly, values are less for parts guns. A parts gun listing is available for $20.

A312 — 1 mfg.							

Too rare to evaluate.

A331 — 293 mfg.							
	$1,200	$1,075	$700	$595			

The note that appears for the Model A311 also applies to this variation.

A332 — 9 mfg.							
	$1,450	$1,275	$975	$825			
B111 — 297 mfg.							
	$1,250	$1,100	$850	$750			

Grading	100%	98%	95%	90%	80%	70%	60%

⚔ **B121** — 110 mfg.

	$1,500	$1,325	$1,075	$895			

⚔ **B122** — 2 mfg.
Extreme rarity precludes accurate price evaluation, but an NIB specimen would probably be priced at approx. $2,995.

⚔ **B123** — 2 mfg.
Extreme rarity precludes accurate price evaluation, but an NIB specimen would probably be priced at approx. $2,995.

⚔ **B131** — 225 mfg.

	$1,400	$1,250	$925	$775			

⚔ **B311** — 52 mfg.

	$1,495	$1,325	$895	$750			

⚔ **B312 w/.45 ACP factory conversion** — 1 mfg.
Rarity precludes accurate price evaluation.

⚔ **B312** — 9 mfg.

	$2,600	$2,300	$1,800	$1,550			

⚔ **B321** — 1 mfg.
Rarity precludes accurate price evaluation. The B321 was the only factory 3-slide set. It was fitted with the 3 different LH LeMay slides available (B311, B321, & B331). This model was mirror polished, engraved, and had ivory grips with the Randall logo.

⚔ **B331** — 45 mfg.

	$1,695	$1,495	$1,050	$875			

⚔ **B2/321** — 1 mfg.
Rarity precludes accurate price evaluation. This was the only factory model variation to leave Randall Firearms. This was a Left-hand Raider with the C.E. LeMay slide.

⚔ **C211** — 5 mfg.

	$1,375	$1,175	$1,000	$825			

⚔ **C331** — 1 mfg.
Too rare to evaluate.

⚔ **C332** — 4 mfg.

	$1,375	$1,175	$1,000	$850			

⚔ **Matched Sets** — large premiums exist for different models with the same serial number if NIB condition. Only 4 were mfg.

RAVELL

Manufacturer located in Barcelona, Spain. Currently, Ravell has no single U.S. importer and values below represent guns purchased directly from Spain without import duty/shipping.

MAXIM DOUBLE RIFLE — .375 H&H or 9.3 X 74R cal., H&H type sidelock action with automatic ejectors, Purdey scroll engraving, 23 in. barrels, deluxe walnut with full pistol grip and rubber butt plate, double articulated triggers.

	Mfg.'s Sug. Retail	$7,000	$6,600	$6,100	$5,000	$4,000	$3,500	$2,950	$2,600

Add $460 for .375 H&H Mag. cal.

RAVEN ARMS

Previous manufacturer located in Industry, CA 1970-1991. Approximately 2 million were mfg.

Grading	100%	98%	95%	90%	80%	70%	60%

P-25 — .25 cal., single action semi-auto, $2\frac{7}{16}$ in. barrel, 6 shot mag., walnut grips, available in nickel, blue, or chrome finish, 15 oz. Disc. 1984.

	$70	$60	$50	$40	$30	$25	$25

MP-25 — similar to Model P-25, except die-cast slide serrations are slightly different. Disc. 1992.

	$60	$50	$45	$40	$35	$30	$25

Walnut, slotted plastic, or ivory colored grips are available for this model. In 1987, a new sear-block safety was incorporated into manufacture.
Last Mfg.'s Sug. Retail was $70.

RECORD-MATCH
Manufactured by Anschutz, located in Zella-Mehlis, Germany.

MODEL 210 FREE PISTOL — .22 LR, Martini action, 11 in. barrel, single shot, blue, carved and checkered walnut grips and forearm, set trigger (button release), micrometer rear sight, deluxe target pistol, pre-WWII.

	$1,320	$1,265	$1,210	$1,100	$880	$745	$550

MODEL 210A — similar to 210, but alloy frame.

	$1,265	$1,210	$1,155	$1,045	$825	$690	$495

MODEL 200 FREE PISTOL — similar to 210, but less deluxe features and spur trigger guard, pre-WWII.

	$990	$935	$770	$660	$525	$440	$360

REISING ARMS COMPANY
Manufacturer originally located in New York, NY and later in Hartford, CT.

TARGET AUTOMATIC PISTOL — .22 LR, 12 shot, $6\frac{1}{2}$ in. barrel, blue, hard rubber grips, hinged frame, outside hammer. Mfg. 1921-1924.

	$385	$370	$340	$315	$265	$220	$195

This model was mfg. in New York, NY from serial number 1,001-4,000. The Hartford, CT address occurs in the serial range 10,000-12,000.
Warning: This pistol's slide may crack if modern high speed .22 ammo is used.

REMINGTON ARMS COMPANY

Remington®

Originally E. Remington, Litchfield, Herkimer County, NY 1816-1828; moved to Ilion, NY in 1828. Manufactured in Ilion, NY to date.

REMINGTON TRADEMARKS - 1816-PRESENT
　　　1816-1847 — Remington (mostly barrel and lock markings)
　　　1847-1856 — E. Remington & Son
　　　1856-1888 — E. Remington & Sons
　　　1888-1910 — Remington Arms Company
　　　1910-1920 — Remington Arms U.M.C. Company
　　　1920 to date — Remington Arms Company, Inc.

HANDGUNS: 1857-1945 MFG.

100%	98%	95%	90%	80%	70%	60%	50%	40%	30%	20%	10%

BEALS' FIRST MODEL POCKET REVOLVER — percussion .31 cal., 5 shot, smooth cylinder, 3 in. octagon barrel, blue finish, 1-piece Gutta Percha grips, brass or iron trigger guard. Approx. 5,000 produced, 1857-1858.

100%	98%	95%	90%	80%	70%	60%	50%	40%	30%	20%	10%
$975	$825	$795	$700	$635	$585	$535	$500	$475	$450	$425	$395

BEALS' SECOND MODEL POCKET REVOLVER — percussion .31 cal., 5 shot, smooth cylinder, 3 in. octagon barrel, blue finish, 2-piece Gutta Percha grips, spur trigger. Approx. 1,000 produced 1858-1860.

100%	98%	95%	90%	80%	70%	60%	50%	40%	30%	20%	10%
$6,250	$5,550	$5,000	$4,500	$4,050	$3,650	$3,250	$2,850	$2,500	$2,250	$2,000	$1,850

BEALS' THIRD MODEL POCKET REVOLVER — percussion .31 cal., 5 shot, smooth cylinder, 4 in. octagon barrel, blue finish, 2-piece Gutta Percha grips, spur trigger, first Remington revolver with loading lever. Approx. 1,000 produced.

100%	98%	95%	90%	80%	70%	60%	50%	40%	30%	20%	10%
$1,350	$1,225	$1,125	$1,025	$925	$850	$775	$700	$625	$550	$500	$450

BEALS' NAVY REVOLVER — percussion .36 cal., 6 shot, smooth cylinder, 7½ in. octagon barrel, blue finish, 2-piece walnut grips, some martially marked with inspector's initials and cartouche on grips. Approx. 15,000 produced, 1860-1862. Barrel address is "Beals' Patent, Sept. 14, 1858 - Manufactured by Remingtons', Ilion, N.Y.".

Commercial Model — single wing base pin (very rare), less than 400 mfg. Serial range under 200.

100%	98%	95%	90%	80%	70%	60%	50%	40%	30%	20%	10%
$4,350	$3,675	$3,175	$2,850	$2,550	$2,250	$2,000	$1,825	$1,675	$1,550	$1,450	$1,375

Commercial Model — several variations with serialization 1-15,500, most were purchased by military but were not inspected.

100%	98%	95%	90%	80%	70%	60%	50%	40%	30%	20%	10%
$3,375	$2,850	$2,500	$2,250	$2,025	$1,800	$1,575	$1,350	$1,150	$950	$750	$575

Deduct 20% for cartridge conversion.

Martially marked — serial range 13,500-15,500.

100%	98%	95%	90%	80%	70%	60%	50%	40%	30%	20%	10%
$4,100	$3,350	$2,800	$2,450	$2,100	$1,900	$1,750	$1,625	$1,500	$1,375	$1,250	$1,150

BEALS' ARMY REVOLVER — percussion .44 cal., 6 shot, smooth cylinder, 8 in. octagon barrel, blue finish, 2-piece walnut grips. Barrel address is "Beals' Patent, Sept. 14, 1858 - Manufactured by Remingtons', Ilion, N.Y.".

100%	98%	95%	90%	80%	70%	60%	50%	40%	30%	20%	10%
$3,750	$3,100	$2,800	$2,550	$2,325	$2,125	$1,900	$1,700	$1,500	$1,300	$1,100	$975

Deduct 20% for cartridge conversions.

Martially marked — serial range is 850-1,900 inspected by "WAT" or "CGC".

100%	98%	95%	90%	80%	70%	60%	50%	40%	30%	20%	10%
$8,000	$6,850	$5,850	$5,000	$4,350	$3,750	$3,250	$2,850	$2,500	$2,150	$1,800	$1,450

RIDER'S DOUBLE-ACTION POCKET REVOLVER — percussion .31 cal., 5 shot, unusual "mushroom-shaped" cylinder, 3 in. octagon barrel, blue finish, 2-piece Gutta Percha grips, brass trigger guard, no loading lever. One of the earliest double-action handguns produced. Approx. 20,000 produced, 1860-1888.

100%	98%	95%	90%	80%	70%	60%	50%	40%	30%	20%	10%
$1,050	$850	$725	$625	$575	$525	$485	$450	$425	$400	$375	$350

Deduct 30% for cartridge conversion.

RIDER'S SINGLE-SHOT DERRINGER — percussion .17 cal., all brass construction, grips included. Less than 1,000 produced, 1860-1863. MANY FAKES, caveat emptor.

100%	98%	95%	90%	80%	70%	60%	50%	40%	30%	20%	10%
$6,750	$5,900	$5,150	$4,600	$4,150	$3,750	$3,400	$3,100	$2,800	$2,500	$2,300	$2,100

100%	98%	95%	90%	80%	70%	60%	50%	40%	30%	20%	10%

MODEL OF 1861 NAVY REVOLVER — percussion .36 cal., 6 shot, unfluted cylinder, $7\frac{1}{2}$ in. octagon barrel, blue finish, 2-piece walnut grips. Loading lever has slot allowing cylinder pin to be pulled forward without lowering lever. Approx. 6,000 produced 1862-1863 in serial range 15,000-21,000. Barrel address "Patented Dec. 17, 1861, 1858 - Manufactured by Remingtons', Ilion, N.Y.".

⁂ **Commercial Model**

$2,500	$2,200	$1,950	$1,700	$1,450	$1,250	$1,050	$950	$825	$725	$600	$500

Deduct 30% for cartridge conversion.

⁂ **Martially Marked** — over 4,000 martially inspected "CGC".

$3,000	$2,700	$2,450	$2,200	$1,950	$1,700	$1,450	$1,200	$1,000	$850	$700	$575

MODEL OF 1861 ARMY REVOLVER — percussion .44 cal., 6 shot, unfluted cylinder, 8 in. octagon barrel, blue finish, 2-piece walnut grips. Majority are martially inspected "CGC". Loading lever has slot allowing cylinder pin to be pulled forward without lowering lever. Approx. 10,000 produced 1862-1863 in serial range 1,900-12,000. Barrel address "Patented Dec. 17, 1861, 1858 - Manufactured by Remingtons', Ilion, N.Y.".

$2,800	$2,500	$2,250	$2,000	$1,750	$1,500	$1,250	$1,050	$900	$800	$675	$550

Deduct 30% for cartridge conversion.

NEW MODEL ARMY REVOLVER — percussion .44 cal., 6 shot, unfluted cylinder, 8 in. octagon barrel, blue finish, 2-piece walnut grips. Approx. 135,000 produced 1863-1888 in serial range 12,000-148,000. Barrel address "Patented Sept. 14, 1858 - Manufactured by Remingtons', Ilion, N.Y. - New Model". Early models lack "New Model" markings on barrel and have transition features from "1861" model.

$1,800	$1,550	$1,400	$1,250	$1,100	$1,000	$900	$800	$700	$600	$500	$425

Deduct 20% for cartridge conversion.
Add 25% for martially inspected.

NEW MODEL NAVY REVOLVER — percussion .36 cal., 6 shot, unfluted cylinder, $7\frac{1}{2}$ in. octagon barrel, blue finish, 2-piece walnut grips. Approx. 18,000 produced in percussion from 1863-1878 with serial range 21,000-48,000. None were martially marked at time of mfg. Approx. 4,000 were purchased by U.S. Navy during 1863-1865 in serial range 21,000-32,000. Barrel address "Patented Sept. 14, 1858 - Manufactured by Remingtons', Ilion, N.Y. - New Model". Early specimens lack "New Model" markings on barrel and have transition features from "1861" model.

$3,200	$2,850	$2,550	$2,250	$1,950	$1,650	$1,350	$1,125	$975	$825	$675	$550

Deduct 20% for cartridge conversion if in 50%+ original condition.
No premium for martial markings.

NEW MODEL BELT REVOLVER, SINGLE ACTION — percussion .36 cal., 6 shot, unfluted or fluted cylinder, $6\frac{1}{2}$ in. octagon barrel, blue or nickel finish, 2-piece walnut grips. Approx. 5,000 produced 1863-1888.

$1,825	$1,525	$1,325	$1,150	$1,000	$900	$800	$725	$650	$575	$525	$475

Add 50% for fluted cylinder (cylinder numbered to the gun).
Deduct 30% for cartridge conversion.

NEW MODEL BELT REVOLVER, DOUBLE ACTION — percussion .36 cal., 6 shot, smooth or fluted cylinder, $6\frac{1}{2}$ in. octagon barrel, blue or nickel finish, 2-piece walnut grips. Approx. 2,500 produced 1863-1888.

$1,475	$1,225	$1,025	$900	$800	$700	$625	$575	$525	$475	$425	$400

Add 50% for fluted cylinder (most not numbered to the gun).
Deduct 30% for cartridge conversion.

100%	98%	95%	90%	80%	70%	60%	50%	40%	30%	20%	10%

NEW MODEL POLICE REVOLVER — percussion .36 cal., 5 shot, smooth cylinder, 3 to 6½ in. octagon barrels, blue or nickel finish, 2-piece walnut grips. Approx. 18,000 produced 1863-1888.

| $1,200 | $1,050 | $950 | $875 | $815 | $750 | $700 | $650 | $600 | $550 | $510 | $475 |

Add 10% for 6½ in. barrel.
Deduct 40% for cartridge conversion.

NEW MODEL POCKET REVOLVER — percussion .31 cal., 5 shot, smooth cylinder, spur trigger, 3 to 4½ in. octagon barrel, blue or nickel finish, 2-piece walnut grips. Approx. 25,000 produced, 1863-1888.

| $1,100 | $1,000 | $900 | $825 | $750 | $700 | $650 | $600 | $550 | $475 | $425 | $390 |

Add 25%-50% for brass frame and/or trigger sheath.
Deduct 40% for cartridge conversion.

ZIG-ZAG DERRINGER — cartridge .22 cal., 6 shot, 6 barrel cluster (rotating), ring trigger, 3 in. barrel cluster, blue finish, 2-piece hard rubber grips. Less than 1,000 produced, 1861-1863. Reputed to be Remington's first cartridge handgun.

| $2,850 | $2,575 | $2,275 | $2,025 | $1,775 | $1,525 | $1,325 | $1,175 | $1,050 | $950 | $850 | $765 |

ELLIOT'S FIVE SHOT DERRINGER — cartridge .22 cal., 5 shot, 5 barrel cluster (fixed), 3 in. barrel cluster, blue and/or nickel finish, 2-piece hard rubber, walnut, ivory or pearl grips, ring trigger. Approx. 25,000 produced (combined production total with .32 cal.).

| $1,475 | $1,350 | $1,250 | $1,125 | $1,025 | $900 | $800 | $700 | $600 | $525 | $475 | $425 |

ELLIOT'S FOUR SHOT DERRINGER — cartridge .32 cal., 4 shot, 4 barrel cluster (fixed), ring trigger, 3⅜ in. barrel cluster, blue and/or nickel finish, 2-piece hard rubber, walnut, ivory or pearl grips. Approx. 25,000 produced (combined production with .22 cal.).

| $1,150 | $1,050 | $950 | $850 | $775 | $700 | $625 | $575 | $515 | $455 | $400 | $365 |

VEST POCKET DERRINGER — cartridge .22, .30, .32, or .41 cal., single shot, various barrel lengths, blue or nickel finish, 2-piece walnut grips, spur trigger.

⚔ **.22 Rimfire** — approx. 25,000 produced, 1865-1888.

| $975 | $875 | $765 | $685 | $635 | $575 | $525 | $475 | $425 | $375 | $325 | $275 |

Deduct 25% for guns lacking company name.

⚔ **.30 or .32 Rimfire** — number produced unknown, 1865-1888.

| $1,300 | $1,175 | $1,050 | $950 | $850 | $725 | $600 | $550 | $500 | $450 | $400 | $350 |

⚔ **.41 Rimfire** — approx. 25,000 produced, 1865-1888.

| $1,250 | $1,075 | $950 | $850 | $750 | $650 | $575 | $525 | $475 | $425 | $375 | $325 |

OVER AND UNDER DERRINGER — cartridge .41 Rimfire cal., 2 shot, 3 in. superimposed barrels, oscillating firing pin, spur trigger, blue and/or nickel finish, hard rubber, walnut, ivory or pearl 2-piece grips. Approx. 150,000 produced, 1866-1934. A.K.A. Double Derringer or Model 95.

⚔ **Type One, Early Variation** — maker's name and patent data stamped between the barrels, made without extractor. 1866-1888.

| $1,575 | $1,400 | $1,250 | $1,150 | $1,025 | $900 | $800 | $700 | $625 | $550 | $475 | $425 |

⚔ **Type One, Late Variation** — maker's name and patent data stamped between the barrels, made with extractor. 1866-1888.

| $1,750 | $1,500 | $1,325 | $1,200 | $1,100 | $1,025 | $950 | $875 | $800 | $750 | $700 | $650 |

100%	98%	95%	90%	80%	70%	60%	50%	40%	30%	20%	10%

⅜ **Type Two** — two line markings atop barrels, maker's name and patent data. 1866-1888.

100%	98%	95%	90%	80%	70%	60%	50%	40%	30%	20%	10%
$1,150	$925	$775	$650	$575	$525	$475	$425	$375	$325	$275	$225

⅜ **Type Three** — marked on top of barrel, single line, "REMINGTON ARMS CO., ILION, N.Y.". 1888-1911.

100%	98%	95%	90%	80%	70%	60%	50%	40%	30%	20%	10%
$975	$850	$750	$650	$525	$450	$400	$350	$300	$250	$225	$200

⅜ **Type Four** — marked on top of barrel, single line, "REMINGTON ARMS-U.M.C. CO. ILION, N.Y.".

100%	98%	95%	90%	80%	70%	60%	50%	40%	30%	20%	10%
$875	$725	$650	$575	$500	$425	$375	$325	$290	$255	$225	$195

MODEL 1866 NAVY ROLLING BLOCK PISTOL — cartridge .50 Rimfire cal., single shot, 8½ in. round barrel, spur trigger, walnut grip and forearm, blue finish. Approx. 6,500 produced, 1866-1875. Erroneously designated as, "Model of 1865 Navy".

⅜ **Martially Marked**

100%	98%	95%	90%	80%	70%	60%	50%	40%	30%	20%	10%
$4,650	$3,750	$3,100	$2,600	$2,350	$2,150	$1,950	$1,750	$1,550	$1,400	$1,275	$1,175

Subtract 30% if not martially marked (Commercial Model mfg. 1866-1875).
Deduct 15% for centerfire breech block.
Less than 150 remain in original condition.

MODEL 1870 NAVY ROLLING BLOCK PISTOL — cartridge .50 Centerfire cal., single shot, 7 in. round barrel, standard trigger with trigger guard, walnut grip and forearm, blue finish. Approx. 6,400 produced 1870-1875. Modified by Remington for the Navy from the Model 1866.

100%	98%	95%	90%	80%	70%	60%	50%	40%	30%	20%	10%
$2,375	$2,000	$1,750	$1,550	$1,350	$1,200	$1,075	$975	$875	$800	$725	$750

Add approx. 20% for 8 in. commercial version (approx. 200-400 mfg.) without inspector's marks.

MODEL 1871 ARMY ROLLING BLOCK PISTOL — cartridge .50 Centerfire cal., single shot, 8 in. round barrel, standard trigger with trigger guard, walnut grip and forearm, blue finish. Approx. 5,000 produced, 1871-1872.

100%	98%	95%	90%	80%	70%	60%	50%	40%	30%	20%	10%
$2,175	$1,825	$1,575	$1,375	$1,200	$1,075	$975	$875	$775	$675	$600	$550

Deduct 10% for Commercial Model.
Pistols produced between 1871-1872 are martially marked.

MODEL 1887 TARGET ROLLING BLOCK PISTOL — cartridge .22, .25 Rimfire and .32, .50 Centerfire cals., single shot, 8 in. round barrel, standard trigger with trigger guard, walnut grip and forearm, blue finish. Approx. 900 produced 1887-1891. A.K.A. "Plinker Model of 1887".

100%	98%	95%	90%	80%	70%	60%	50%	40%	30%	20%	10%
$2,050	$1,770	$1,535	$1,325	$1,175	$1,050	$950	$850	$750	$650	$575	$525

Add 10% for Navy framed.
Navy framed 1887s are discernible by military proofs on right side of frame, Remington altered from original Navy Model 1870. Estimated mfg. of 100.

MODEL 1891 TARGET MODEL ROLLING BLOCK PISTOL — cartridge .22, .25 Rimfire and .32 Centerfire cals., single shot, 10 in. part octagon, part round barrel, standard trigger with trigger guard, smooth walnut grip and forearm, blue finish. Approx. 100 produced 1891-1900.

100%	98%	95%	90%	80%	70%	60%	50%	40%	30%	20%	10%
$2,375	$2,000	$1,750	$1,535	$1,325	$1,175	$1,050	$950	$850	$750	$675	$625

MODEL 1901 TARGET ROLLING BLOCK PISTOL — cartridge .22 S and L, .25 Rimfire, .32 Centerfire, or .44 S&W Russian cal., single shot, 10 in. part octagon, part round barrel, standard trigger with trigger guard, checkered walnut grip and forearm, blue finish. Approx. 800 produced 1900-1909.

100%	98%	95%	90%	80%	70%	60%	50%	40%	30%	20%	10%
$2,375	$2,000	$1,750	$1,535	$1,325	$1,175	$1,050	$950	$850	$750	$675	$625

Add $100 for S&W Russian.

100%	98%	95%	90%	80%	70%	60%	50%	40%	30%	20%	10%

RIDER'S MAGAZINE PISTOL — cartridge .32 cal., 5 shot, 3 in. octagon barrel, spur trigger, walnut, rosewood, ivory or pearl grips. Approx. 10,000 produced, 1871-1888.

100%	98%	95%	90%	80%	70%	60%	50%	40%	30%	20%	10%
$1,725	$1,475	$1,325	$1,225	$1,100	$1,000	$900	$800	$700	$625	$575	$525

ELLIOT'S SINGLE SHOT DERRINGER — cartridge .41 Rimfire cal., single shot, 2½ in. round barrel, spur trigger, walnut 2-piece grips, blue and/or nickel finish. Approx. 10,000 produced, 1867-1888. A.K.A. "Mississippi Derringer".

100%	98%	95%	90%	80%	70%	60%	50%	40%	30%	20%	10%
$1,450	$1,200	$1,000	$875	$775	$675	$600	$550	$500	$450	$400	$350

NUMBER ONE (SMOOT PATENT) REVOLVER — cartridge .30 Rimfire cal., 5 shot, 2¾ in. octagon barrel, spur trigger, walnut, hard rubber, pearl or ivory 2-piece grips. Number produced debatable, 1873-1888.

100%	98%	95%	90%	80%	70%	60%	50%	40%	30%	20%	10%
$545	$500	$465	$430	$395	$360	$325	$290	$265	$240	$215	$190

Add 100% on early #1s with revolving recoil shield.
On Number One through Number Four Revolvers, ivory grips refer to Remington Celluloid, not genuine ivory. Only in rare instances does ivory appear.

NUMBER TWO (SMOOT PATENT) REVOLVER — cartridge .30 or .32 Rimfire cal., 5 shot, 2¾ in. octagon barrel, spur trigger, hard rubber, pearl or ivory 2-piece grips. Number produced debatable, 1873-1888.

100%	98%	95%	90%	80%	70%	60%	50%	40%	30%	20%	10%
$500	$475	$450	$425	$400	$375	$350	$300	$275	$250	$225	$200

NUMBER THREE (SMOOT PATENT) REVOLVER — cartridge .38 Rimfire or .38 Centerfire cal., 3¾ in. octagon barrel with or without barrel rib, spur trigger, hard rubber, ivory or pearl 2-piece grips, "Bird-Head and SawHandle" grip frame with Remington logo "R" on the "saw-handle" hard rubber grips, Bird-Head referred to models with or without a barrel rib. Number produced debatable, 1875-1888.

100%	98%	95%	90%	80%	70%	60%	50%	40%	30%	20%	10%
$550	$525	$500	$475	$450	$425	$400	$350	$325	$300	$275	$250

Add small premiums on Centerfire Number 3s.

NUMBER FOUR REVOLVER — cartridge .38 and .41 Rimfire or .38 and .41 Centerfire cals., 5 shot, 2½ in. round barrel, hard rubber, pearl or ivory 2-piece grips. Number produced debatable, 1877-1888.

100%	98%	95%	90%	80%	70%	60%	50%	40%	30%	20%	10%
$600	$575	$550	$525	$500	$475	$450	$400	$375	$350	$325	$300

Add small premiums on Centerfire Number 4's.

IROQUOIS REVOLVER — cartridge .22 Rimfire cal., 7 shot, 2¼ in. round barrel, spur trigger, hard rubber, pearl or ivory 2-piece grips, fluted or non-fluted cylinder. Approx. 10,000 produced between, 1878-1888.

100%	98%	95%	90%	80%	70%	60%	50%	40%	30%	20%	10%
$600	$575	$550	$525	$500	$475	$450	$400	$375	$350	$325	$300

Deduct 33% if unmarked.
Note: fluted or non-fluted cylinder does not seem to affect valuation.

MODEL 1875 SINGLE ACTION REVOLVER — cartridge .44 or .45 Centerfire cal., 6 shot, 7½ or 5¾ in. round barrel, standard trigger with trigger guard, walnut, ivory or pearl 2-piece grips. Approx. 25,000 produced, 1875-1888.

100%	98%	95%	90%	80%	70%	60%	50%	40%	30%	20%	10%
$3,750	$3,000	$2,800	$2,500	$2,200	$2,000	$1,750	$1,500	$1,250	$1,000	$850	$700

Add 10% for government markings.
Add 50% for .45 cal.
There is some debate over originality of the 5¾ in. barrel.

MODEL 1890 TRANSITIONAL SINGLE ACTION REVOLVER — cartridge .44 Centerfire cal., resembles 1890 SA, has "E. Remington & Sons" barrel address, 5¾ in. barrel, nickel finish with walnut grips, perhaps mfg. during Remington's period of bankruptcy and receivership (circa late 1880s).

100%	98%	95%	90%	80%	70%	60%	50%	40%	30%	20%	10%
$2,450	$2,050	$1,750	$1,535	$1,325	$1,175	$1,050	$950	$850	$750	$675	$625

100%	98%	95%	90%	80%	70%	60%	50%	40%	30%	20%	10%

MODEL 1890 SINGLE ACTION REVOLVER — cartridge .44 Centerfire cal., 6 shot, $7\frac{1}{2}$ or $5\frac{3}{4}$ in. round barrel, standard trigger with trigger guard, hard rubber 2-piece grips with Remington monogram, ivory or pearl grips on special order, blue or nickel finish. Approx. 2,000 produced, 1891-1894.

100%	98%	95%	90%	80%	70%	60%	50%	40%	30%	20%	10%
$4,500	$4,300	$4,000	$3,700	$3,500	$3,000	$2,500	$2,000	$1,500	$1,000	$800	$700

Subtract 35% for nickel finish.

MODEL 51 SEMI-AUTO — cartridge .32 or .380 Centerfire cal., 8 shot (7 in mag., 1 in chamber), hard rubber 2-piece grips with company's name. Approx. 65,000 produced, 1918-1943.

100%	98%	95%	90%	80%	70%	60%	50%	40%	30%	20%	10%
$600	$525	$500	$475	$450	$425	$400	$350	$325	$300	$275	$250

Note: .380 cal. much more numerous than .32 cal., but valued equally.

MODEL 1911 SEMI-AUTO MILITARY — .45 ACP cal., 8 shot (7 in mag., 1 in chamber), checkered walnut 2-piece grips. 21,676 produced, 1918-1919.

100%	98%	95%	90%	80%	70%	60%	50%	40%	30%	20%	10%
$2,250	$1,500	$1,000	$750	$600	$550	$500	$475	$425	$375	$325	$275

The serial range for this variation is 1-21,676. The cut-off serial number for 1918 mfg. is 13,152.

Note: Model 1911 is marked Remington-U.M.C.

MARK III SIGNAL PISTOL — 10 ga., single shot, brass frame, 9 in. round steel barrel, spur trigger, walnut 2-piece grips. Approx. 25,000 produced, 1915-1918.

100%	98%	95%	90%	80%	70%	60%	50%	40%	30%	20%	10%
$550	$525	$475	$450	$400	$450	$400	$350	$325	$300	$250	$200

HANDGUNS: POST-WWII MFG.

Grading	100%	98%	95%	90%	80%	70%	60%

MODEL XP-100 VARMINT SPECIAL — single shot bolt action pistol, .221 Rem. Fireball (disc. 1985-$10\frac{1}{2}$ in. barrel) or .223 Rem. (new 1986) cal., $14\frac{1}{2}$ in. barrel, adj. sights (.221 cal. only), drilled and tapped for scope, one-piece pistol grip nylon stock, $4\frac{3}{8}$ lbs. Mfg. 1963-1992.

Grading	100%	98%	95%	90%	80%	70%	60%
		$335	$295	$230	$195	$165	$150	$140

Last Mfg.'s Sug. Retail was $419.

XP-SILHOUETTE — .35 Rem. (new 1987) or 7mm BR cal., bench rest model, $10\frac{1}{2}$ (new 1993) or $14\frac{1}{2}$ (disc. 1992) in. barrel, target sights became standard 1993, older models had no sights but were drilled and tapped, nylon (disc. 1992) or walnut (new 1993) stock, $4\frac{1}{8}$ lbs.

Mfg.'s Sug. Retail	$613	$525	$450	$400	$360	$330	$270	$220

Add $14 for .35 Rem. cal.

MODEL XP-100 HUNTER — .223 Rem., 7mm BR Rem., 7mm-.08 Rem., or .35 Rem. cal., $14\frac{1}{2}$ in. barrel, no sights, laminated wood stock, $4\frac{3}{4}$ lbs. New 1993.

Mfg.'s Sug. Retail	$532	$450	$375	$330	$270	$220	$200	$180

XP-100R KS — .22-250 (new 1992), .223 Rem., .250 Savage, 7mm-08 Rem., .308 (new 1992), .35 Rem., or .350 Rem. Mag. cal., repeater variation, Kevlar synthetic stock, right hand action only, $4\frac{1}{8}$ lbs.

Mfg.'s Sug. Retail	$840	$735	$600	$540	$495	$450	$400	$365

Remington. cont.

Grading	100%	98%	95%	90%	80%	70%	60%

XP-100 CUSTOM — .22-250 (new 1992), .223 Rem. standard or HB (heavy barrel-new 1987), .250 Savage standard or HB (new 1989), 6mm BR standard or HB (new 1989), 7mm BR standard or HB (new 1989), .308 (new 1992), .35 Rem. (standard barrel only), or 7mm-08 Rem. (HB new 1989) cal., available through custom gun shop only, choice of right or left hand action, wood stock with contoured pistol grip, regular or shrouded barrel, ramp front sight. New 1986.

Mfg.'s Sug. Retail	$945	$825	$735	$660	$575	$525	$450	$400

Also available, on special order only, is the .458 x 2 in. caliber.

RIFLES: DISC. MFG.

100%	98%	95%	90%	80%	70%	60%	50%	40%	30%	20%	10%

REVOLVING PERCUSSION RIFLE — .36 or .44 cal., 6 shot unfluted cylinder, 24 or 28 in. octagon barrel, walnut stock with crescent butt, scroll trigger guard, blue with case hardened frame. Less than 1,000 mfg., 1866-1879.

.36 Caliber

$3,500	$3,200	$2,900	$2,640	$2,475	$2,310	$2,200	$2,090	$1,980	$1,925	$1,815	$1,760

.44 Caliber — very rare.

$4,250	$3,850	$3,400	$3,150	$2,925	$2,650	$2,530	$2,420	$2,310	$2,200	$2,035	$1,925

MODEL 1862 "ZOUAVE RIFLE" — .58 cal., muzzle loading percussion, 33 in. round barrel, two barrel bands, blue barrel, case hardened lock, brass furniture. Mfg. 12,501, 1862-1865.

$3,200	$2,900	$2,650	$2,400	$2,150	$1,800	$1,575	$1,300	$1,050	$850	$650	$450

U.S. NAVY ROLLING BLOCK CARBINE — .50-70 cal., 23¼ in. barrel, open sight, blue with case hardened frame, bar and ring on frame, walnut straight grip stock. Mfg. 5,000, 1868-1869.

$1,400	$1,250	$1,075	$925	$795	$660	$635	$580	$525	$495	$440	$385

LONG RANGE "CREEDMOOR" — rolling block, .44-90, .44-100, .44-70, .50-45, or .50-70 cal., barrel ½ octagon, long range tang sight, globe front sight, checkered pistol grip stock, blue. Approx. 2,000 mfg., 1873-1890.

$3,250	$2,700	$2,400	$1,750	$1,375	$1,100	$990	$880	$770	$715	$605	$550

NO. 1 SPORTING RIFLE — rolling block, .40-50, .40-70, .44-70, .44-77, .45-70, .50-45, or .50-70 centerfire or .46 rimfire cal., 28 or 30 in. octagon barrels, folding leaf sight, straight grip stock. Several thousand mfg., 1868-1902.

$1,050	$950	$850	$775	$680	$560	$440	$385	$360	$330	$275	$220

Subtract 15% for rimfire cals.
Add 10% for .44-77, .45-70, or .50-70 cal. (primary buffalo hunting cals.).

NO. 1½ SPORTING RIFLE — .22, .25 Stevens, .25 Long, .32, and .38 Long & Extra Long rimfire, also in .32-20, .38-40, and .44-40 in centerfire, 24-28 in. octagon medium weight barrel, straight grip walnut stock, standard No. 1 frame - but somewhat lighter than the No. 1 Sporting. Several thousand mfg., 1888-1897.

$850	$775	$680	$560	$440	$385	$360	$330	$275	$220	$195	$175

NO. 2 SPORTING RIFLE — available in many rimfire cals. between .22 and .38 as well as centerfire cals. between .22 to .38-40, blued finish with case hardened frame, perch belly style walnut stock, many special orders available, smaller size action than the No.1 and rear of frame is curved, mfg. 1873-1909.

$550	$515	$480	$440	$400	$350	$300	$260	$230	$200	$165	$130

100%	98%	95%	90%	80%	70%	60%	50%	40%	30%	20%	10%

LIGHT BABY CARBINE — rolling block, .44-40 cal., 20 in. lightweight round barrel with band, straight stock. Few thousand mfg., 1892-1902.

100%	98%	95%	90%	80%	70%	60%	50%	40%	30%	20%	10%
$3,650	$3,100	$2,500	$2,000	$1,650	$1,375	$1,500	$895	$775	$700	$640	$575

REMINGTON — HEPBURN NO. 3 — falling block, single shot, side lever actuated, blue barrel, case hardened actions, patented 1879, first introduced 1880, many custom features were offered, variations as follows:

NO. 3 SPORTING & TARGET — various cals. from .22 Win. to .50-90 Sharps, 26, 28, or 30 in. round or octagon barrel, open sight, semi-pistol grip stock. Mfg. 1883-1907.

100%	98%	95%	90%	80%	70%	60%	50%	40%	30%	20%	10%
$1,550	$1,300	$1,150	$1,045	$935	$880	$770	$660	$550	$495	$440	$385

NO. 3 MATCH RIFLE A QUALITY — similar to Sporting and Target, with target match sights (tang), and Schuetzen stock. Less than 1,000 mfg., 1883-1907.

100%	98%	95%	90%	80%	70%	60%	50%	40%	30%	20%	10%
$1,700	$1,550	$1,400	$1,150	$1,045	$960	$880	$825	$715	$605	$550	$495

B Quality — select grade wood.

100%	98%	95%	90%	80%	70%	60%	50%	40%	30%	20%	10%
$2,150	$1,975	$1,825	$1,525	$1,200	$1,045	$935	$880	$770	$715	$605	$550

NO. 3 LONG RANGE CREEDMOOR — .44 cal., 32 or 34 in. octagon barrel, tang sight, otherwise similar to Target Model. A few hundred mfg., 1880-1907.

100%	98%	95%	90%	80%	70%	60%	50%	40%	30%	20%	10%
$2,500	$2,225	$1,950	$1,675	$1,400	$1,225	$1,100	$1,045	$935	$880	$770	$715

NO. 3 MID RANGE CREEDMOOR — similar to Long Range, in .40-65 cal., 28 in. barrel.

100%	98%	95%	90%	80%	70%	60%	50%	40%	30%	20%	10%
$2,150	$1,975	$1,825	$1,525	$1,200	$1,045	$935	$880	$770	$715	$660	$605

NO. 3 LONG RANGE MILITARY — similar to Creedmoor, with 34 in. full musket stock, in .44-75-520 Rem. cal., military sights, 1880's.

100%	98%	95%	90%	80%	70%	60%	50%	40%	30%	20%	10%
$3,375	$2,950	$2,625	$2,250	$1,925	$1,700	$1,540	$1,430	$1,320	$1,100	$990	$825

NO. 3 SCHUETZEN MATCH — under lever actuated, 30 or 32 in. barrel, tang sight, palm rest, target stock, very few known, perhaps the rarest single shot American rifle.

100%	98%	95%	90%	80%	70%	60%	50%	40%	30%	20%	10%
$5,500	$5,000	$4,600	$4,000	$3,500	$2,850	$2,420	$2,200	$2,145	$2,035	$1,925	$1,815

With False Muzzle

100%	98%	95%	90%	80%	70%	60%	50%	40%	30%	20%	10%
$6,100	$5,400	$4,900	$4,300	$3,875	$3,200	$2,850	$2,600	$2,300	$2,100	$2,000	$1,900

NO. 4 ROLLING BLOCK RIFLE — .22 S-L-LR, .25 Stevens (barrels marked "25-10"), or .32 Short or Long cal., 22½ octagon barrel standard with round barrels available late in the series, blued finish with case hardened frame, solid frame initially followed by takedown in 2 different types (lever - most common, or knob), this model was Remington's smallest rolling block. Approx. 50,000 mfg. 1890-1933.

100%	98%	95%	90%	80%	70%	60%	50%	40%	30%	20%	10%
$440	$400	$375	$335	$300	$260	$230	$200	$165	$130	$100	$90

Solid frame variations will command a premium, especially if over 50% original condition.

100%	98%	95%	90%	80%	70%	60%	50%	40%	30%	20%	10%

Model 4-S "Boy Scout" — .22 S-L-LR, either marked "MILITARY MODEL" (most common) or "AMERICAN BOY SCOUT" (rare), 28 in. round barrel with musket type forend (1 barrel band), thought to have been used by military academies to train their young cadets.

100%	98%	95%	90%	80%	70%	60%	50%	40%	30%	20%	10%
$750	$695	$625	$550	$515	$480	$440	$400	$350	$300	$260	$230

Bayonets are an extremely rare accessory for this model.

NO. 6 ROLLING BLOCK RIFLE — .22 S-L-LR or .32 Short or Long rimfire cal., 20 in. round barrel, boy's gun with small dimensions, takedown action, case hardened (early mfg.) or blue finish, also available in smooth bore, many thousands mfg. 1902-1933.

$350	$300	$280	$260	$240	$220	$200	$180	$160	$140	$120	$100

Original case colors will bring a premium on this model.

REMINGTON KEENE MAGAZINE BOLT RIFLE — .45-70 Govt., .40, or .43 cal. Mfg. 1880-1888. Approx. 5,000 mfg.,

Frontier Model — made for U.S. Dept. of Interior (Indian Police), marked U.S.I.D.

$1,325	$1,100	$900	$800	$725	$650	$575	$500	$425	$350	$275	$200

Carbine Model — 22 in. full stock.

$1,100	$950	$850	$750	$650	$550	$475	$400	$325	$275	$225	$175

Army Rifle — 32½ in. barrel, full stock.

$1,100	$950	$850	$750	$650	$550	$475	$400	$325	$275	$225	$175

Sporter Rifle — ½ oct. barrel, full or "BUTTON" mag. Add for pistol grip and select wood variations.

$1,100	$950	$850	$750	$650	$550	$475	$400	$325	$275	$225	$175

Navy Rifle — 29½ in. barrel, full stock.

$1,100	$950	$850	$750	$650	$550	$475	$400	$325	$275	$225	$175

RIFLES: CENTERFIRE - SEMI-AUTO & SLIDE ACTION

The models below have been listed in numerical sequence for quick reference.

Grading	100%	98%	95%	90%	80%	70%	60%

MODEL FOUR SEMI-AUTO — 6mm Rem., .243 Win., .270 Win., .280 Rem., .30-06, or .308 Win. (disc. 1984) cal., gas operation with metering system, 22 in. barrel, 4 shot detachable mag., deluxe Monte Carlo stock and forend, detachable sights. Mfg. 1982-1987.

			$395	$360	$325	$275	$250	$225	$195

Last Mfg.'s Sug. Retail was $475.

Model Four Diamond Anniversary — .30-06 only, 1,500 mfg. in 1981 to commemorate 75th anniversary of the Model 8, custom shop engraved with premium checkered walnut stock and forearm.

			$950	$795	$600

D Peerless Grade

			$1,975	$1,870	$1,200

Last Mfg.'s Sug. Retail was $2,291.

F Premier Grade

			$4,150	$3,835	$2,650

Last Mfg.'s Sug. Retail was $4,720.

F Premier Gold Grade — with gold inlays.

			$6,420	$5,735	$4,000

Last Mfg.'s Sug. Retail was $7,079.

Grading	100%	98%	95%	90%	80%	70%	60%

MODEL SIX SLIDE ACTION — 6mm Rem. (disc. 1984), 243 Win., 270 Win., .30-06, or 308 Win. (disc. 1984) cal., pump action, detachable sights, 4 shot mag. Mfg. 1981-1987.

	100%	98%	95%	90%	80%	70%	60%
	$400	$360	$290	$265	$235	$215	$195

Last Mfg.'s Sug. Retail was $439.

⚒ **D Peerless Grade**

	$1,975	$1,870	$1,200				

Last Mfg.'s Sug. Retail was $2,291.

⚒ **F Premier Grade**

	$4,150	$3,835	$2,650				

Last Mfg.'s Sug. Retail was $4,720.

⚒ **F Premier Gold Grade** — with gold inlays.

	$6,420	$5,735	$4,000				

Last Mfg.'s Sug. Retail was $7,079.

MODEL 8 AUTOLOADING RIFLE — .25, .30, .32, or .35 Rem. cal., 22 in. barrel, open sights, 5 shot non-detachable box mag., plain stock. Approx. 60,000 mfg. 1906-1936. Also made in higher grades C through F — add premiums.

	$400	$320	$270	$220	$195	$165	$140

MODEL 14/14A SLIDE ACTION — .25, .30, .32, or .35 cal., 22 in. barrel, open sight, plain pistol grip stock. Mfg. 1912-1935.

	$350	$285	$230	$195	$165	$130	$110

MODEL 14R CARBINE — similar to 14A, with 18½ in. barrel, straight grip stock.

	$400	$325	$285	$260	$220	$195	$165

MODEL 14½ RIFLE — similar to 14A, with 22½ in. barrel, .38-40 or .44-40 cal. Mfg. 1912-1934.

	$600	$550	$475	$425	$350	$300	$275

Quantities mfg. of this model are unknown as serial numbers were intermixed with the Model 14.

MODEL 14½R CARBINE — similar to 14½ Rifle, with 18½ in. barrel.

	$675	$600	$525	$475	$425	$375	$325

MODEL 25/25A SLIDE ACTION — .25-20 or .32-20 cal., 24 in. barrel, open sight, tube mag., plain pistol grip stock. Mfg. 1923-1936.

	$350	$300	$275	$250	$200	$175	$150

MODEL 25R CARBINE — similar to 25A, with 18 in. barrel and straight stock.

	$450	$400	$350	$275	$225	$200	$175

MODEL 74 SPORTSMAN SEMI-AUTO — .30-06 only, 22 in. barrel, 4 shot mag., unchecked hardwood stock and forearm, open sights, 7½ lbs. Mfg. 1985-1987.

	$295	$260	$235	$210	$190	$175	$160

Last Mfg.'s Sug. Retail was $353.

MODEL 76 SPORTSMAN SLIDE ACTION — .30-06 cal. only, 22 in. barrel, 4 shot mag., unchecked hardwood stock and forearm, open sights, 7½ lbs. Mfg. 1985-1987.

	$255	$225	$195	$180	$170	$160	$150

Last Mfg.'s Sug. Retail was $319.

Grading	100%	98%	95%	90%	80%	70%	60%

MODEL 81 "WOODSMASTER" SEMI-AUTO

— .30, .32, .35 Rem., or .300 Savage cal., semi-auto, takedown action, 5 shot, non-detachable box mag., 22 in. round barrel, notched elevator rear sight. An improvement of the Model 8 is available in 5 grades. Better grades bring higher prices. 55,581 mfg. 1936-1950.

	100%	98%	95%	90%	80%	70%	60%
	$400	$350	$300	$250	$200	$175	$150

Add 10% for .25 cal.

The .32 Rem. cal. was dropped after WWII and the .300 Savage was added in 1940. While a few specimens have been observed in .25 cal., it is probably the result of part swapping as the Remington Co. cannot verify this cal.

MODEL 141/141A SLIDE ACTION

— .30, .32, or .35 Rem. cal., 24 in. barrel, takedown, open sight, plain pistol grip stock. Mfg. 1936-1950.

	100%	98%	95%	90%	80%	70%	60%
	$395	$305	$250	$220	$195	$165	$140

MODEL 740 & 740A AUTOLOADER

— .30-06 or .308 cal., 22 in. barrel, open sight, box mag., gas operated, plain pistol grip stock. Mfg. 1955-1960.

	100%	98%	95%	90%	80%	70%	60%
.30-06 cal.	$335	$295	$275	$250	$225	$200	$180
.308 cal.	$425	$375	$325	$295	$275	$250	$225

Add 15% for carbine version.

MODEL 740ADL

— similar to 740A, with checkered stock, grip cap and swivels. Mfg. 1955-1960.

	100%	98%	95%	90%	80%	70%	60%
.30-06 cal.	$375	$325	$280	$250	$225	$200	$180
.308 cal.	$450	$400	$350	$300	$275	$250	$225

Add 15% for carbine version.

MODEL 740BDL

— similar to 740ADL, with select wood.

	100%	98%	95%	90%	80%	70%	60%
.30-06 cal.	$395	$340	$295	$250	$225	$200	$180
.308 cal.	$475	$415	$350	$300	$275	$250	$225

Add 15% for carbine version.

MODEL 742A "WOODSMASTER" SEMI-AUTO

— 6mm Rem., .243, .280, .30-06, or .308 cal., 22 in. barrel, open sights, 4 shot box mag., gas operated, checkered pistol grip stock. Mfg. 1960-1980.

	100%	98%	95%	90%	80%	70%	60%
	$325	$290	$275	$250	$235	$210	$185

Add 10% for .280 Rem. cal.

MODEL 742ADL DELUXE

— similar to the Model 742A, except has fine checkering, sling swivels and engraved game scenes on receiver.

	100%	98%	95%	90%	80%	70%	60%
	$350	$300	$275	$260	$235	$215	$195

MODEL 742 CARBINE

— similar to 742, except .30-06 or .308 cal. only, 18½ in. barrel. Mfg. 1961-1980.

	100%	98%	95%	90%	80%	70%	60%
	$350	$300	$275	$260	$235	$215	$195

MODEL 742BDL

— similar to 742, except .30-06 or .308 cal. only, Monte Carlo basket weave stock and forend, black pistol grip cap and forend tip. Mfg. 1966-1980.

	100%	98%	95%	90%	80%	70%	60%
	$350	$300	$275	$260	$235	$215	$195

MODEL 742D PEERLESS GRADE

— similar to 742, with scroll engraving and fancy wood. Mfg. 1961-1980.

	100%	98%	95%
	$2,000	$1,870	$1,200

MODEL 742F PREMIER GRADE

— similar to 742, with extensive game scenes and scroll engraving, best grade wood.

	100%	98%	95%
	$4,200	$3,860	$2,650

Remington. cont.

Grading	100%	98%	95%	90%	80%	70%	60%

MODEL 742F PREMIER GRADE (WITH INLAYS) — gold inlaid model.

	$6,500	$5,785	$4,180				

MODEL 742 150TH YEAR ANNIVERSARY — .30-06 only. Mfg. 1966 only.

	$375	$340	$300				

MODEL 742 CANADIAN CENTENNIAL — 1,000 mfg. in 1967. Issue price was $200.

	$395	$340	$300				

REMINGTON/RUGER CANADIAN CENTENNIAL SET — please refer to the Sturm, Ruger section later in this text.

MODEL 742 BICENTENNIAL — similar to 742, with inscription on receiver. Mfg. 1976 only.

	$375	$340	$300	$275	$225	$200	$185

MODEL 760 SLIDE ACTION "GAMEMASTER" RIFLE — .222, .223, 6mm, .243, .257 Roberts, .270, .280, .30-06, .300 Sav., .308 or .35 Rem. cal., 22 in. barrel, detachable mag., uncheckered pistol grip stock. Mfg. 1952-1982.

	100%	98%	95%	90%	80%	70%	60%
	$375	$325	$275	$250	$225	$200	$175
.222 cal.	$1,150	$900	$800	$725	$650	$575	$500
.223 cal.	$1,350	$995	$850	$775	$700	$625	$575
.257 R cal.	$795	$700	$600	$450	$400	$350	$300

Add 10% for .300 Savage or .35 Rem. cal.
The Model 760 seems to have regional pricing differences in the rare calibers. Values in the Eastern U.S. seem to be quite a bit higher than prices encountered in the Midwest and West. Hence, values on the .222, .223, and .257 R cals. reflect a nationalized average rather than one region's high or another's low. A few Model 760s were also mfg. in .244 cal. (before going to 6mm) — very rare with pricing unpredictable.

MODEL 760 CARBINE — .270, .280, .30-06, .308, or .35 Rem. cal., 18½ in. barrel.

	$425	$350	$300	$275	$240	$225	$200

MODEL 760D PEERLESS GRADE — similar to 760, with engraving and fancy wood. Mfg. 1953-1982.

	$1,100	$935	$825	$770	$690	$605	$525

MODEL 760F — similar to 760, with extensive engraved game scenes, best grade wood.

	$2,420	$1,980	$1,760	$1,650	$1,485	$1,375	$1,100

⚜ **Gold Inlaid Model**

	$5,500	$4,675	$4,180	$3,960	$3,300	$2,750	$2,200

MODEL 760 150 YEAR ANNIVERSARY — .30-06 only. Mfg. 1966 only.

	$375	$340	$300	$275	$225	$200	$185

MODEL 760 BICENTENNIAL — similar to 760, with commemorative inscription engraved on receiver. Mfg. 1976 only.

	$375	$340	$300	$275	$225	$200	$185

MODEL 760ADL — similar to 760, except with checkered pistol grip deluxe wood and sling swivels. Mfg. 1953-1963.

	$395	$350	$325	$300	$275	$250	$225

Grading	100%	98%	95%	90%	80%	70%	60%

MODEL 760BDL — similar to 760, except .270, .30-06, or .308 cal. only, basket weave checkering pattern became standard mid-'70s, Monte Carlo stock, black pistol grip and forend tip. Mfg. 1953-1982.

	$300	$275	$250	$225	$210	$200	$175

MODEL 7400 SEMI-AUTO RIFLE — 6mm Rem. (disc. 1987), .243 Win., .270 Win., .280 Rem., .30-06, .308 Win., or .35 Whelen cal., same action as 742, gas operation, 22 in. barrel, 4 shot detachable mag., pressed checkered walnut stock, 7½ lbs. Mfg. 1982 to date.

Mfg.'s Sug. Retail	$503	$425	$365	$300	$255	$230	$210	$185

Beginning in 1990, a high gloss wood finish became available in cals. .270 and .30-06 (Model 7400 gloss). In 1993, a non-reflective matte finish was applied to both the wood and metalwork (Model 7400 SP, cals. .270 and .30-06 only).

Model 7400 Carbine — .30-06 cal. only, similar to Model 7400 Rifle, except has 18½ in. barrel, 7¼ lbs. New 1988.

Mfg.'s Sug. Retail	$503	$425	$365	$300	$255	$230	$210	$185

Model 7400 175th Anniversary — .30-06 cal. only, Anniversary Model with light engraving and high gloss finish. Mfg. in 1991 only.

	$435	$365	$300

Last Mfg.'s Sug. Retail was $515.

Model 7400 Engraved — the below listed engraved Model 7400s were introduced 1988.

D Peerless Grade

Mfg.'s Sug. Retail	$2,509	$2,075	$1,650	$1,200

F Premier Grade

Mfg.'s Sug. Retail	$5,169	$4,375	$3,495	$2,500

F Premier Gold Grade — with gold inlays.

Mfg.'s Sug. Retail	$7,752	$6,900	$3,975	$3,000

MODEL 7600 SLIDE ACTION RIFLE — 6mm Rem. (disc. 1984), .243 Win., .270 Win., .280 Rem. (new 1988), .30-06, .308 Win., or .35 Whelen (new 1988) cal., modified 760 action, 22 in. barrel, detachable mag., pressed checkered pistol grip stock and forearm, 7½ lbs. Mfg. 1981 to date.

Mfg.'s Sug. Retail	$480	$410	$355	$280	$230	$205	$185	$165

Beginning in 1990, a high gloss wood finish became available in cals. .270 and .30-06 (Model 7600 gloss). In 1993, a non-reflective matte finish was applied to both the wood and metalwork (Model 7600 SP, cals. .270 and .30-06 only).

Model 7600 Carbine — .30-06 cal. only, similar to Model 7600 Rifle, except has 18½ in. barrel, 7¼ lbs.

Mfg.'s Sug. Retail	$480	$410	$355	$280	$230	$205	$185	$165

Model 7600 Engraved — the below listed engraved Model 7600s were introduced 1988.

D Peerless Grade

Mfg.'s Sug. Retail	$2,509	$2,075	$1,650	$1,200

F Premier Grade

Mfg.'s Sug. Retail	$5,169	$4,375	$3,495	$2,500

F Premier Gold Grade — with gold inlays.

Mfg.'s Sug. Retail	$7,752	$6,900	$3,975	$3,000

Grading	100%	98%	95%	90%	80%	70%	60%

RIFLES: RIMFIRE

From 1930-1960 Remington produced a number of bolt action .22 cal. Rimfire rifles, both single shot and repeaters. They were good quality, serviceable weapons with many slight variations upon a basic design.

	100%	98%	95%	90%	80%	70%	60%
Model 33	$135	$120	$90	$80	$70	$60	$50
Model 33 NRA	$195	$150	$110	$95	$85	$75	$65

263,557 of the Model 33 were mfg. 1932-1935.

Model 34	$135	$120	$90	$80	$70	$60	$50
Model 34 NRA	$195	$150	$110	$95	$85	$75	$65

162,941 of the Model 34 were mfg. 1932-1936.

Model 341 A	$110	$90	$75	$70	$65	$55	$50
Model 341 P	$110	$90	$75	$70	$65	$55	$50
Model 341 SB	$195	$175	$160	$140	$125	$110	$90

131,604 of the Model 341 "Sportsmaster" were mfg. 1936-1940.

Model 41 A	$110	$90	$75	$65	$60	$55	$50
Model 41 AS	$175	$160	$150	$140	$125	$110	$100
Model 41 P	$110	$90	$75	$65	$60	$55	$50
Model 41 SB	$195	$175	$160	$140	$125	$110	$100
Model 411	$350	$300	$250	$210	$200	$185	$175

306,880 of the Model 41 "Targetmaster" were produced 1936-1940.
The Model 411 is similar to the Model 41 single shot, but in CB Cap or .22 Short and without safety on rear of bolt. Eye screw for gallery use. 1,316 mfg. 1937- 1939 (although never cataloged).

Model 510 A	$100	$90	$75	$65	$60	$55	$50
Model 510 C (Carbine)	$115	$95	$85	$75	$65	$60	$55
Model 510 P	$100	$90	$75	$65	$60	$55	$50
Model 510 Routledge	$145	$130	$125	$120	$110	$100	$90
Model 510 SB	$145	$130	$125	$120	$110	$100	$90

These models were mfg. 1939-1962.

Model 511 A	$120	$110	$90	$75	$65	$60	$55
Model 511 P	$130	$115	$95	$80	$70	$65	$60

These models were mfg. 1939-1962.

Model 512 A	$120	$110	$100	$90	$80	$75	$70
Model 512 P	$130	$115	$95	$80	$70	$65	$60

These models were mfg. 1940-1962.

Model 510-X	$125	$110	$90	$80	$70	$60	$50
Model 511-X	$135	$125	$110	$100	$90	$80	$70
Model 512-X	$135	$125	$110	$100	$90	$80	$70

These models were mfg. 1964-1966.

Model 514 (1948-1970)	$110	$90	$75	$65	$55	$40	$30
Model 514 C (Carbine)	$115	$95	$80	$70	$60	$45	$35
Model 514 P (disc. 1971)	$175	$165	$145	$120	$85	$75	$60
Model 514 BC (disc. 1971)	$135	$120	$100	$85	$75	$65	$50
Model 514 Routledge	$145	$130	$120	$110	$100	$90	$80
Model 514 SB	$145	$130	$120	$110	$100	$90	$80

Grading	100%	98%	95%	90%	80%	70%	60%

MODEL 12A SLIDE ACTION RIFLE — .22 S, L, and LR, hammerless, 22 in. barrel, open sights, tube mag., plain grip stock. Mfg. 1909-1936.

| | $350 | $300 | $250 | $200 | $120 | $95 | $85 |

Originally designated Model 12.

MODEL 12B (GALLERY SPECIAL) — similar to 12C, except .22 Short, all had octagon barrels.

| | $400 | $350 | $300 | $200 | $120 | $95 | $85 |

MODEL 12C — similar to 12A, except 24 in. octagon barrel. Also mfg. in grades D, E, and F — add premiums.

| | $450 | $400 | $325 | $250 | $185 | $140 | $110 |

MODEL 12C NRA TARGET — limited manufacture.

| | $600 | $500 | $400 | $350 | $300 | $220 | $140 |

MODEL 12CS — similar to 12C, chambered for .22 Rem. Spl. (.22 WRF).

| | $450 | $400 | $300 | $200 | $120 | $95 | $85 |

MODEL 16/16A AUTOLOADING RIFLE — .22 autoloading cal., 22 in. barrel, open sight, tube mag. in butt stock, straight stock. Mfg. 1914-1928. Also mfg. in grades C, D, and F — add premiums.

| | $295 | $230 | $195 | $170 | $140 | $110 | $90 |

MODEL 24/24A AUTOLOADING RIFLE — .22 S or LR, 19 in. barrel, open sights, Browning semi-auto design, bottom ejection, tube mag. through butt stock, takedown, plain pistol grip stock. Mfg. 1922-1935.

| | $325 | $240 | $210 | $170 | $140 | $110 | $90 |

MODEL 37 "RANGEMASTER" BOLT ACTION — .22 LR, 5 shot with single shot adapter, 28 in. barrel, target sight and scope bases, target stock. Mfg. 1937-1940.

| | $495 | $450 | $400 | $350 | $300 | $250 | $225 |

MODEL 37 - 1940 — improved trigger and stock design. Mfg. 1940-1954.

| | $440 | $360 | $330 | $305 | $275 | $220 | $195 |

Total manufacture of the Model 37 was 12,198.

MODEL 121A SLIDE ACTION RIFLE — hammerless, .22 S, L, or LR, 24 in. round barrel, tube mag., plain pistol grip stock. Mfg. 1936-1954.

| | $350 | $285 | $225 | $195 | $165 | $140 | $110 |

Originally designated Model 121.

MODEL 121S — similar to 121A, except chambered for .22 Rem. Spl. (rare).

| | $450 | $375 | $315 | $260 | $215 | $175 | $140 |

MODEL 121SB/ROUTLEDGE — similar to 121A, except smooth bore for .22 shot. 5 different chamberings and barrel markings.

| | $500 | $400 | $350 | $275 | $240 | $200 | $165 |

MODEL 241/241A SPEEDMASTER — .22 S or LR, 24 in. barrel, replaced the Model 24, open sights, takedown, tube mag. through stock, non-checkered walnut stock and forearm. Approx. 56,000 mfg. 1935-1949.

| | $360 | $275 | $250 | $195 | $150 | $120 | $100 |

This model was also available in a Special, Peerless, Expert, and Premier Grade - add premiums.

Remington cont.

Grading	100%	98%	95%	90%	80%	70%	60%

MODEL 513TR "MATCHMASTER" BOLT ACTION — .22 LR, 27 in. barrel, Redfield aperture sight, target stock, 6 shot, sling swivels. Mfg. 1940-1969.

	100%	98%	95%	90%	80%	70%	60%
	$295	$250	$220	$180	$140	$115	$95

MODEL 513S — similar to 513TR, with Marbles open sight and checkered sporter stock. Mfg. 1941-1956.

	100%	98%	95%	90%	80%	70%	60%
	$400	$350	$320	$290	$260	$230	$210

MODEL 521TL JR. BOLT ACTION — .22 LR, 25 in. barrel, Lyman target sights, takedown, 6 shot mag., target stock. Mfg. 1947-1969.

	100%	98%	95%	90%	80%	70%	60%
	$225	$190	$160	$140	$120	$100	$90

MODEL 522 VIPER — .22 LR, semi-auto blowback action, 20 in. barrel, full-length black synthetic resin stock with beavertail fore-end, 10 shot mag., cocking indicator, adj. rear sight, grooved synthetic receiver, $4\frac{5}{8}$ lbs. New 1993.

	Mfg.'s Sug. Retail	$159	98%	95%	90%	80%	70%	60%
			$140	$120	$100	$90	$80	$70	$60

MODEL 541S CUSTOM — .22 S, L, or LR, bolt action, 24 in. barrel, no sights, 5 shot, scroll engraved receiver and trigger guard, checkered walnut stock with rosewood pistol grip cap and forend tip. Mfg. 1972-1984.

	100%	98%	95%	90%	80%	70%	60%
	$400	$350	$300	$275	$250	$225	$200

MODEL 541T — .22 LR only, 5 shot clip mag., 24 in. standard or heavy (new 1993) barrel, checkered American walnut stock with satin finish, barrel is drilled and tapped, $5\frac{7}{8}$ lbs. New 1986.

Mfg.'s Sug. Retail $371

		98%	95%	90%	80%	70%	60%
	$320	$265	$225	$200	$180	$165	$150

Add $26 for heavy barrel.

MODEL 550A AUTOLOADER — .22 S, L, or LR interchangeably, 24 in. barrel, open sight, shell deflector, 2 extractors, tube mag., plain one piece pistol stock. Approx. 220,000 mfg., 1941-1946.

	100%	98%	95%	90%	80%	70%	60%
	$150	$125	$110	$90	$80	$70	$60

This model replaced the Model 241.

MODEL 550-I — similar to 550A, except has single extractor, mfg. 1946-1971.

	100%	98%	95%	90%	80%	70%	60%
	$135	$115	$100	$85	$75	$65	$55

MODEL 550P — similar to 550A, with aperture sight.

	100%	98%	95%	90%	80%	70%	60%
	$190	$150	$125	$105	$85	$75	$65

MODEL 550-2G — similar to 550A, except 22 in. barrel and eye screw for counter chain in shooting gallery.

	100%	98%	95%	90%	80%	70%	60%
	$200	$175	$150	$130	$110	$100	$85

MODEL 552A SPEEDMASTER — .22 S, L, or LR, 23 in. barrel, semi-auto open sight, tube mag., pistol grip stock. Mfg. 1957-disc.

	100%	98%	95%	90%	80%	70%	60%
	$160	$135	$120	$100	$85	$75	$65

This model was also mfg. in a 150th Anniversary Model (1966 only). Slight premiums are being asked if condition is 98% or better.

MODEL 552C — similar to 552A, with 21 in. barrel. Mfg. 1961-1977.

	100%	98%	95%	90%	80%	70%	60%
	$170	$145	$130	$110	$95	$85	$75

Model 552 BDL Deluxe Speedmaster — similar to Model 552, except checkered walnut stock and forearm. Mfg. 1966 to date.

	Mfg.'s Sug. Retail	$256	98%	95%	90%	80%	70%	60%
			$210	$170	$140	$125	$105	$90	$75

Grading	100%	98%	95%	90%	80%	70%	60%

MODEL 572(A) LIGHTWEIGHT — anodized alloy receiver and barrel, steel sleeved, 3 colors: tan, blue, and black. Mfg. 1958-1962.

	100%	98%	95%	90%	80%	70%	60%
	$250	$210	$190	$170	$140	$125	$100

Add 50% for black or 100% for blue color receiver if in 98%+ condition.

MODEL 572SB/ROUTLEDGE — similar to 572A, except smooth bore.

	100%	98%	95%	90%	80%	70%	60%
	$350	$275	$225	$175	$140	$120	$100

MODEL 572(A) FIELDMASTER — .22 S, L, or LR, slide action, 21 in. barrel, walnut stock and forearm, tube mag., 5½ lbs. Mfg. 1955-1988.

	100%	98%	95%	90%	80%	70%	60%
	$160	$145	$125	$105	$90	$75	$65

Last Mfg.'s Sug. Retail was $176.
This model was also mfg. in a 150th Anniversary Model (1966 only). Slight premiums are being asked if condition is 98% or better.

‡ **Model 572 BDL Deluxe Fieldmaster** — similar to Model 572, except with checkered walnut stock and forearm. Mfg. 1966 to date.

	Mfg.'s Sug. Retail	$269	98%	95%	90%	80%	70%	60%
			$215	$175	$150	$125	$105	$90	$75

‡ **Model 572SB/Routledge** — similar to 572A, except smooth bore.

	100%	98%	95%	90%	80%	70%	60%
	$350	$275	$225	$175	$140	$120	$100

MODEL 580 SINGLE SHOT — .22 S, L or LR, bolt action, 24 in. barrel, open sights, Monte Carlo stock. Mfg. 1968-1978.

	100%	98%	95%	90%	80%	70%	60%
	$125	$115	$105	$100	$90	$80	$75

MODEL 580BR — Boy's Model, 1 in. shorter stock. Mfg. 1971-1978.

	100%	98%	95%	90%	80%	70%	60%
	$135	$120	$100	$85	$70	$65	$50

MODEL 581 — .22 LR cal., bolt action, 6 shot clip mag., converts to single shot. Mfg. 1967-1983.

	100%	98%	95%	90%	80%	70%	60%
	$150	$115	$110	$100	$90	$70	$60

MODEL 581 SPORTSMAN — .22 LR cal., bolt action, 5 shot clip mag., 24 in. barrel, hardwood uncheckered stock, 4¾ lbs. New 1986.

	Mfg.'s Sug. Retail	$204	98%	95%	90%	80%	70%	60%
			$185	$160	$145	$125	$105	$90	$75

MODEL 582 — similar to 581, with tube mag. Mfg. 1967-1983.

	100%	98%	95%	90%	80%	70%	60%
	$150	$110	$100	$90	$70	$65	$60

MODEL 591 BOLT ACTION — 5mm Rimfire Mag., 24 in. barrel, open sight, 5 shot clip mag., Monte Carlo stock. Approx. 25,000 mfg. 1970-1974.

	100%	98%	95%	90%	80%	70%	60%
	$195	$175	$140	$125	$100	$85	$75

5mm Rimfire ammo has been disc. for some time, and as a result, collectability on this model is mostly for 100% condition since there is no shooter utility in lower conditions. Original 5mm ammo is selling for $35-$50 per box.

MODEL 592 — similar to 591, with tube mag. Approx. 25,000 mfg. 1970-1974.

	100%	98%	95%	90%	80%	70%	60%
	$195	$175	$140	$125	$100	$85	$75

RIFLES: RIMFIRE - "NYLON SERIES"

NYLON 10 SINGLE SHOT — .22 S, L, or LR, bolt action. Mfg. 1962-1964.

	100%	98%	95%	90%	80%	70%	60%
	$125	$100	$80	$70	$60	$50	$40

Remington cont.

Grading	100%	98%	95%	90%	80%	70%	60%

Nylon 10-SB — similar to Nylon 10, except smooth bore barrel used for .22 shot cartridges.

	$300	$250	$200	$175	$150	$140	$125

This model is only infrequently encountered.

MODEL 10-C — similar to Model 77, renamed after changing to a 10 shot mag. Mfg. 1971-1978.

	$100	$85	$70	$65	$60	$55	$50

MODEL 11 NYLON — bolt action repeater, clip fed, 6 or 10 shot mag., 4½ lbs. Mfg. 1962-1964.

	$125	$100	$80	$70	$60	$50	$40

MODEL 12 NYLON — similar to 11, with tube mag. Mfg. 1962-1964.

	$125	$100	$80	$70	$60	$50	$40

NYLON 66 AUTOLOADER — .22 LR, $19\frac{5}{8}$ in. barrel, open sights, butt stock tube mag. holds 14 shells, 4 lbs. Stock made from Zytel plastic in black, brown, or green. Mfg. 1959-1987.

	$110	$95	$85	$70	$60	$55	$50

Add 20% for Black Diamond.
Add 15% for Apache black.
Add 25% for Seneca green.
Last Mfg.'s Sug. Retail was $124.

NYLON 66 150TH ANNIVERSARY — mfg. in 1966 only with 150th Anniversary Remington logo on receiver.

	$200	$185	$150	$100	$85	$70	$60

NYLON 66 BICENTENNIAL — inscription on receiver. Mfg. 1976 only, brown nylon stock only.

	$200	$185	$150	$100	$85	$70	$60

NYLON 76 LEVER ACTION — similar appearance to Nylon 66 with brown or black stock, short throw lever action. Mfg. 1962-1964 only.

	$150	$125	$95	$80	$70	$60	$55

The Nylon 76 "Trail Rider" is the only lever action repeating rifle ever mfg. by Remington.

NYLON 77 — similar to Nylon 66, except with 5 shot clip mag. Mfg. 1970-1971 only.

	$120	$100	$90	$75	$65	$55	$45

NYLON APACHE 77 — similar to Model 10-C, but bright green stock. Mfg. for K-Mart in 1987.

	$100	$85	$65	$55	$50	$45	$40

RIFLES: BOLT ACTION CENTERFIRE

The models in this section have been listed in numerical sequence for quick reference.

MODEL SEVEN BOLT ACTION — compact bolt action available in .17 Rem. (new 1993), .222 Rem., .223 Rem., .243 Win., 6mm Rem., 7mm-08 Rem., or .308 Win. cal., 18½ in. barrel, 6¼ lbs., 4 or 5 shot mag., individually test fired, oil finished American walnut, 1982-present.

Mfg.'s Sug. Retail	$524	$440	$350	$275	$225	$205	$180	$165

Add 10% for .222 Rem. cal.

All steel Model Sevens (including floor plate and trigger guard) are currently commanding a small premium.

Grading	100%	98%	95%	90%	80%	70%	60%

Model Seven Youth — .243 Win., 6mm Rem., or .308 Win. cal., uncheckered hardwood stock, stock shortened 1 in., 6 lbs. New 1993.

Mfg.'s Sug. Retail	$425	$355	$315	$275	$225	$205	$180	$165

Model Seven FS — .243 Win., 7mm-08 Rem., or .308 Win. cal., 18½ in. parkerized blue barrel, gray or gray camo Kevlar fiberglass stock, adj. rear sight, 5¼ lbs. Mfg. 1987-89 only.

		$525	$455	$415	$375	$335	$310	$285

Last Mfg.'s Sug. Retail was $600.

Model Seven Custom KS — .223 Rem. (new 1989), 7mm BR (new 1989), 7mm-08 Rem. (new 1989), .308 Win. (new 1991), .35 Rem. or .350 Rem. Mag., 20 in. barrel, synthetic Kevlar stock with solid recoil pad. New 1987.

Mfg.'s Sug. Retail	$997	$875	$695	$530	$475	$425	$385	$340

This model is available from the Custom Shop only (special order).

MODEL 30A BOLT ACTION RIFLE — Enfield M/1917 type action, 7mm, .30-06, .25, .30, .32, or .35 Rem. cal., 22 in. barrel, checkered pistol grip stock. Mfg. 1921-1940.

	$495	$450	$400	$350	$300	$260	$200

MODEL 30R CARBINE — similar to 30A, with 20 in. barrel.

	$550	$500	$450	$375	$325	$275	$225

MODEL 30S — deluxe version of Model 30A, .257 Robts., 7mm, or .30-06 cal., 24 in. barrel, Lyman receiver sight, special stock. Mfg. 1930-1940.

	$625	$550	$500	$450	$375	$300	$250

MODEL 78 SPORTSMAN BOLT ACTION — .223 Rem., .243 Win., .270 Win., .30-06, or .308 Win. cal., 22 in. barrel, 4 shot mag., uncheckered hardwood stock, open sights, 7 lbs. Mfg. 1985-89.

	$270	$235	$210	$190	$170	$160	$150

Last Mfg.'s Sug. Retail was $333.

MODEL 600 BOLT ACTION — .222, .223 (very rare), 6mm, .243, .308, or .35 Rem. cal., 18½ in. VR barrel, dog leg bolt handle, checkered pistol grip stock. 94,086 were mfg. 1964-1968.

Reg. cals.	$375	$295	$250	$210	$195	$175	$155
.35 Rem.	$450	$395	$350	$320	$295	$270	$250
.222 cal.	$450	$395	$350	$320	$295	$270	$250
.223 cal.	$800	$700	$600	$500	$400	$350	$325

315 Model 600s in .223 cal. were mfg.

Model 600 Montana Centennial — 6mm Rem., 1,020 mfg. in 1964 only.

	$650	$550	$375

Last Mfg.'s Sug. Retail was $125.

MODEL 600 MAGNUM — 6.5mm Rem. Mag. or .350 Rem. Mag. cal., laminated walnut/beech stock with recoil pad. Mfg. 1965-1968.

	$695	$625	$550	$500	$460	$440	$420

MODEL 600 MOHAWK — .222 Rem., 6mm Rem. (only 14,000 mfg.), .243 Win., or .308 Win. cal., this variation was a promotional model, 18½ in. barrel with no rib. 94,920 were mfg. in 1971-1980.

	$325	$300	$285	$265	$240	$225	$200

Add 50% for 6mm Rem. cal.

Remington. cont.

Grading	100%	98%	95%	90%	80%	70%	60%

MODEL 660 BOLT ACTION — .222, 6mm, .243, or .308 cal., 20 in. barrel, open sight, dog leg bolt handle, checkered pistol grip stock, black pistol grip cap and forend tip. 50,536 were mfg. 1968-1971.

	100%	98%	95%	90%	80%	70%	60%
	$595	$550	$500	$460	$440	$420	$350

Add 10% for .222 Rem. cal.

.223 cal. — 227 total mfg. This cal. was never listed in a Remington catalog.

	100%	98%	95%	90%	80%	70%	60%
	$1,100	$875	$725	$600	$500	$400	$350

MODEL 660 MAGNUM — 6.5 Mag. or .350 Mag. cal., laminated stock and recoil pad.

	100%	98%	95%	90%	80%	70%	60%
	$650	$575	$500	$450	$400	$350	$300

MODEL 720A BOLT ACTION — Enfield type action, .257 Robts., .270, or .30-06 cal., 22 in. barrel, open sights, 5 shot, checkered pistol grip stock, 2,500 mfg. 1941-1944.

	100%	98%	95%	90%	80%	70%	60%
	$1,150	$975	$850	$700	$600	$500	$400

Add 50%+ for .270 Win. cal.
Add 100%+ for .257 Robts. cal.
Most of the Model 720As were purchased by the military and used as trophies - these are discernible by crossed cannon proofs on wood.
Most of this model was chambered for .30-06 cal. Approx. 100 were chambered for .270 Win. and 20 or less were chambered for the .257 Robts.

MODEL 720R — similar to 720A, except with 20 in. barrel.

	100%	98%	95%	90%	80%	70%	60%
	$1,250	$1,050	$900	$750	$650	$550	$450

This is the rarest variation in the Model 720 Series.

MODEL 720S — similar to 720A, except with 24 in. barrel.

	100%	98%	95%	90%	80%	70%	60%
	$1,200	$1,000	$850	$700	$600	$500	$400

MODEL 721(A) BOLT ACTION — .264 Win. Mag., .270 Win., .280 Rem., .30-06, or .300 H&H cal., 24 in. barrel, open sights, 4 shot, plain pistol grip stock. Mfg. 1948-1962.

	100%	98%	95%	90%	80%	70%	60%
	$300	$260	$220	$195	$165	$155	$145

.280 Rem. (688 mfg.) and .264 Win. Mag. (1,115 mfg.) are rare in this model. 100% values on these calibers could bring $600+.

MODEL 721ADL — similar to Model 721A, except has deluxe checkered stock.

	100%	98%	95%	90%	80%	70%	60%
	$415	$375	$350	$300	$250	$200	$175

The above model suffix does not appear on the gun. ADL features will determine the model.

MODEL 721BDL — similar to 721 ADL, except has extra select wood.

	100%	98%	95%	90%	80%	70%	60%
	$550	$500	$425	$375	$325	$300	$275

The above model suffix does not appear on the gun. BDL features will determine the model.

MODEL 721A MAGNUM — .300 H&H, 26 in. heavy barrel, recoil pad, 3 shot mag., 8¼ lbs.

	100%	98%	95%	90%	80%	70%	60%
	$450	$400	$360	$320	$295	$275	$260

MODEL 721ADL MAGNUM — similar to 721A Mag., checkered.

	100%	98%	95%	90%	80%	70%	60%
	$495	$450	$400	$350	$315	$290	$275

MODEL 721BDL MAGNUM — similar to 721ADL Mag., select wood.

	100%	98%	95%	90%	80%	70%	60%
	$595	$540	$465	$425	$385	$360	$330

Grading	100%	98%	95%	90%	80%	70%	60%

MODEL 722(A) — short action version of 721A, .222 Rem., .222 Rem. Mag., .243 Win., .244 Rem., .257 Roberts, .264 Win. Mag., .300 Savage, or .308 cal., 7 lbs. Mfg. 1948-1962.

	100%	98%	95%	90%	80%	70%	60%
	$325	$265	$220	$200	$165	$155	$145

Deduct 10% for .300 Savage cal.
Add 10% for .257 Roberts cal.
.222 Rem. Mag. (3,803 mfg.) and .243 Win. (2,186 mfg.) are rare in this model. Add approx. 25% to above values for these cals.

MODEL 722ADL — similar to Model 722A, except with deluxe checkered wood.

	100%	98%	95%	90%	80%	70%	60%
	$400	$375	$350	$300	$250	$200	$175

The above model suffix does not appear on the gun. ADL features will determine the model.

MODEL 722BDL — similar to Model 722ADL, except features extra select wood.

	100%	98%	95%	90%	80%	70%	60%
	$475	$425	$375	$325	$280	$265	$245

The above model suffix does not appear on the gun. BDL features will determine the model.

MODEL 725ADL BOLT ACTION —.222, .243, .244, .270,, .280, or .30-06 cal., 22 in. barrel, open sights, 4 shot, checkered Monte Carlo stock. 16,635 mfg. 1958-1961.

	100%	98%	95%	90%	80%	70%	60%
.30-06 cal.	$475	$425	$375	$350	$325	$300	$280
.270 Win.	$550	$500	$450	$400	$375	$350	$325
.280 Rem.	$650	$575	$500	$450	$400	$350	$325
.222 Rem.	$600	$525	$475	$425	$375	$350	$325
.244 Rem.	$600	$525	$475	$425	$375	$350	$325
.243 Win.	$600	$525	$475	$425	$375	$350	$325

Caliber mfg. breakdown is as follows: 7,657 in .30-06; 2,784 in .280 Rem.; 2,818 in .270 Win.; 840 in .244 Rem.; 1,478 in .222 Rem.; 998 in .243 Win.

MODEL 725 KODIAK — .375 H&H Mag. or .458 Win. Mag. cal., 26 in. barrel, 3 shot, recoil reducer in muzzle, deluxe checkered Monte Carlo stock, black pistol grip cap and forend tip. 52 mfg. 1961 only.

	100%	98%	95%	90%	80%	70%	60%
	$3,000	$2,700	$2,500	$2,250	$2,000	$1,800	$1,650

Only 24 rifles in .458 Win. Mag. were mfg. and 28 rifles in .375 H&H Mag.

MODEL 788 BOLT ACTION — .222, .22-250, .223, 6mm, .243, .308, .30-30, 7mm-08, or .44 Mag. cal., 22 or 24 in. barrel, open sight, plain pistol grip Monte Carlo stock. Mfg. 1967-1984.

	100%	98%	95%	90%	80%	70%	60%
Rifle	$325	$275	$225	$200	$185	$175	$160
Carbine (18 in. barrel)	$325	$275	$225	$200	$185	$175	$160

Add 10% for .44 Mag. cal.

RIFLES: MODEL 700 & VARIATIONS

MODEL 700ADL DELUXE BOLT ACTION — .22-250 (disc. 1991), .222 Rem. Mag. (disc.), .25-06 (disc. 1991), 6mm (disc.), .243, .270, .30-06, .308, or 7mm Mag. cal., 20 (carbine), 22 and 24 in. barrel, open sights, 4 shot mag., checkered Monte Carlo stock or brown laminated stock (new 1988). Mfg. 1962-present.

		100%	98%	95%	90%	80%	70%	60%
Mfg.'s Sug. Retail	$439	$360	$310	$260	$210	$175	$165	$155

Add $26 for 7mm Rem. Mag. cal.
Add 20% for 20 in. carbine model.
Add 50% for .222 Rem. Mag. or .280 Rem. cal. in carbine variation.
Add 15% for 7mm Rem. Mag., .264 Win. Mag., or .300 Win. Mag. cal. with stainless steel barrel (mfg. 1962-1970).
Remington, in 1987-89, introduced a Model 700 Gun Kit that enabled the owner to assemble the stock to the barreled action. All metal work is completely finished and wood finishing is all that is required. This kit was available in most popular cals. - last mfg.'s sug. retail price was $333 (1989). Add $20 for 7mm Rem. Mag. cal.

Grading	100%	98%	95%	90%	80%	70%	60%

Model 700ADL/LS — .243 Win. (new 1989), .270 Win. (new 1989), .30-06, or 7mm Rem. Mag. cal., brown laminate stock with checkering. New 1988.

Mfg.'s Sug. Retail $485	$400	$345	$275	$230	$210	$195	$165

Add $27 for 7mm Rem. Mag. cal.

MODEL 700BDL CUSTOM DELUXE — similar to 700ADL Deluxe, except with hinged floorplate, cut skipline checkering, black pistol grip cap and forend tip, .17 Rem., .22-250, .222 Rem., .223 Rem., .243 Win., .25-06, .264 Mag. (disc.), .270 Win., .280 Rem. (new 1992), .300 Savage (mfg. 1992 only), .30-06, .308 Win., .35 Whelen (new 1989), 6mm Rem., 7mm Rem. Mag., 7mm-08 Rem., .300 Win. Mag., .338 Win. Mag. (new 1988), or 8mm Mag. (disc.) cal.

Mfg.'s Sug. Retail $524	$440	$375	$325	$280	$250	$220	$195
.222 Rem. Mag.	$495	$450	$400	$340	$300	$280	$260
.350 Rem. Mag.	$595	$495	$425	$350	$325	$300	$275
6.5mm Rem. Mag.	$595	$495	$425	$350	$325	$300	$275

Add $24 for left-hand model (available in certain cals. only).
Add $27 for .17 Rem., 7mm Rem. Mag., .300 Win. Mag., .35 Whelen or .338 Win. Mag. cal.
Add 15% for 7mm Rem. Mag., .264 Win. Mag., or .300 Win. Mag. cal. with stainless steel barrel (mfg. 1962-1970).
Remington mfg. the Model 700BDL in .350 Rem. Mag. and 6.5mm Rem. Mag. Approx. 1,500 were assembled in 1969 only. The .350 Rem. Mag. mfg. in 1969 is 3 times rarer than the 1985 Model 700 Classic chambered for .350 Rem. Mag.

Model 700BDL Lew Horton Special Edition — .257 Roberts cal., 500 mfg. in 1990 only, first time the 700BDL has been offered in .257 Roberts cal.

		$575	$525	$450	$395	$360	$325	$280

Last Mfg.'s Sug. Retail was $580.

MODEL 700BDL EUROPEAN — .243 Win., .270 Win., .280 Rem., 7mm-08 Rem., 7mm Rem. Mag., .30-06, or .308 cal., Monte Carlo stock with hand-rubbed oil finish, 22 or 24 (Mag. cals. only) in. barrel, hinge floorplate, iron sights, approx. 7¼ lbs.

Mfg.'s Sug. Retail $524	$440	$375	$325	$280	$250	$220	$195

Add $27 for 7mm Rem. Mag. cal.

MODEL 700BDL MOUNTAIN RIFLE — .243 Win. (new 1988), .25-06 (new 1992), .257 Roberts (new 1991), .270 Win., 7mm-08 Rem. (new 1988), .280 Rem., .30-06, .308 (new 1988), or 7 x 57mm Mauser (new 1990) cal., 22 in. tapered barrel, checkered satin finished American walnut stock with cheek piece and ebony forend, 4 shot mag., without sights, 6¾ lbs. New 1986.

Mfg.'s Sug. Retail $524	$440	$380	$315	$275	$250	$220	$195

Model 700BDL Mountain Stainless — .25-06, .270 Win., .280 Rem., or .30-06 cal., 22 in. barrel, black synthetic stock with pressed checkering, blind mag., 7¼ lbs. New 1993.

Mfg.'s Sug. Retail $532	$450	$385	$315				

MODEL 700 CUSTOM KS MOUNTAIN RIFLE — .270 Win., .280 Rem., .300 Win. Mag., .300 Wby. Mag. (new 1989), .30-06, .338 Win. Mag. (new 1986), .35 Whelen (new 1989), 7mm Rem. Mag., 8mm Rem. Mag. (new 1986), or .375 H&H Mag. cal., 22 in. barrel, features extra lightweight Kevlar fiber-reinforced stock — available in either right or left-hand action. New 1986.

Mfg.'s Sug. Retail $997	$825	$725	$550	$460	$415	$385	$350

Add $98 for left hand action.
This model is available from the Custom Shop only (special order).

Grading	100%	98%	95%	90%	80%	70%	60%

MODEL 700BDL CAMO SYNTHETIC — .22-250, .243 Win., .270 Win., .280 Rem., 7mm-08 Rem., 7mm Rem. Mag., .30-06, .308, or .300 Wby. Mag. cal., 22 or 24 (Mag. only) in. barrel, features synthetic stock and is fully camouflaged in Mossy Oak Bottomland pattern, iron sights, approx. 7¼ lbs. New 1992.

Mfg.'s Sug. Retail	$568	$480	$420	$350	$315	$285	$265	$250

Add $27 for Mag. cals.

MODEL 700BDL STAINLESS SYNTHETIC — .223 Rem. (new 1993), .243 Win. (new 1993), .25-06, .270 Win., .280 Rem., .30-06, .308, 6mm Rem. (new 1993), 7mm-08 Rem. (new 1993), .300 Win. Mag. (new 1993), .300 Wby Mag. (new 1993), .338 Win. Mag. (new 1993), 7mm Rem. Mag., or 7mm Wby. Mag. cal., features matte finished 416 stainless steel barrel, receiver, and bolt, black synthetic stock with checkering, drilled and tapped, blind mag., 24 in. barrel, no sights, 6¼ - 7 lbs. New 1992.

Mfg.'s Sug. Retail	$585	$490	$410	$340

Add $27 for Mag. cals.

MODEL 700BDL VARMINT SPECIAL — .22-250, .222, .223, .25-06 (disc.), 6mm, .243, .308 Win., or 7mm-08 cal., 24 in. heavy barrel, checkered walnut stock, no sights. Mfg. 1967-present.

Mfg.'s Sug. Retail	$557	$475	$415	$350	$315	$285	$265	$250

Model 700BDL Varmint Synthetic — .220 Swift, .22-250, .223 Rem., or .308 cal., composite, textured black and gray synthetic stock features Kevlar, fiberglass, and graphite, matte metal finish. New 1992.

Mfg.'s Sug. Retail	$632	$530	$450	$395	$325	$295	$265	$250

MODEL 700BDL SAFARI GRADE — heavier 700BDL, in .375 H&H, 8mm Rem. Mag. (new 1986), .416 Rem. Mag. (new 1989), or .458 Win. Mag. cal., 3 shot mag., 24 in. barrel, available with either Classic or Monte Carlo stock configuration, 9 lbs. Mfg. 1962-present.

Mfg.'s Sug. Retail	$1,001	$850	$725	$550	$440	$415	$385	$330

Add $62 for left-hand stock (Classic style only).

Model 700BDL Custom KS Safari Grade — 8mm Rem. Mag., .375 H&H, .416 Rem. Mag., or .458 Win. Mag., stock made from extra lightweight Kevlar fiber, 24 in. barrel. New 1989.

Mfg.'s Sug. Retail	$1,153	$1,025	$850	$700	$625	$550	$485	$430

Add $62 for left-hand stock.
Add $134 for stainless steel barreled action (new 1993).

Model 700 Mountain Rifle Custom KS Wood Grained Kevlar — similar to Model 700 Custom KS Safari Grade, except has wood grained Kevlar stock. New 1992.

Mfg.'s Sug. Retail	$1,109	$1,000	$875	$750	$650	$550	$485	$430

Add $63 for left-hand action.

MODEL 700BDL LIMITED CLASSIC — similar to 700BDL, except classic straight stock, high polish bluing, has been offered in .220 Swift, .222 Rem., .22-250, .250 Savage (250/3000), 6mm, 7 x 57 Mauser, .243, .25-06 Rem., .257 Roberts, .264 Win. Mag., .270, .300 Wby. Mag., .30-06, 7mm Wby. Mag., .338 Win. Mag., .350 Rem. Mag., .35 Whelen, .300 H&H, or .375 H&H cal.

Mfg.'s Sug. Retail	$524	$450	$365	$300	$265	$250	$220	$195

This model is produced in limited quantities of a different caliber each year. Add premiums for several older calibers in N.I.B. condition only (including 7 x 57 Mauser, .257 Roberts, .300 H&H, and .375 H&H).

The following is a partial list of calibers offered previously and year of manufacture: 7 x 57mm (1981), .257 Roberts (1982), .300 H&H (1983), .250 Savage (1984), .350 Rem. Mag. (1985), .264 Win. Mag. (1986), .338 Win. Mag. (1987), .35 Whelen (1988), .300 Wby. Mag. (1989), .25-06 Rem. (1990), 7mm Wby. Mag. (1991), .220 Swift (1992), and .222 Rem. (1993).

Grading	100%	98%	95%	90%	80%	70%	60%

MODEL 700C GRADE — from custom shop, no engraving, deluxe checkered wood with rosewood forearm cap.

	$850	$775	$695	$635	$510	$440	$400

MODEL 700D PEERLESS GRADE — scroll engraving, best wood.

	$1,650	$1,400	$1,200	$1,000	$880	$825	$690

MODEL 700F PREMIER GRADE — elaborate engraving, best wood.

	$3,250	$2,750	$2,420	$2,200	$2,035	$1,870	$1,760

MODEL 700 AS — .22-250, .243 Win., .270 Win., .280 Rem., .30-06, .308 Win., 7mm Rem. Mag., or .300 Wby. Mag. cal., synthetic stock is made from Arylon resin, matte black finished stock and metal, 22 or 24 in. barrel, 6½ lbs. Mfg. 1989-91 only.

	$445	$370	$310	$275	$250	$220	$195

Last Mfg.'s Sug. Retail was $528.
Add $21 for 7mm Rem. Mag. or .300 Wby. Mag. cal.

MODEL 700 RS — .270 Win., .280 Rem., or .30-06 cal., 22 in. polished blue barrel, gray or gray camo DuPont Rynite synthetic stock with smooth cheek piece and solid recoil pad, iron sights, 7¼ lbs. Mfg. 1987-1988 only.

	$490	$440	$405	$370	$335	$310	$285

Add 10% for .280 Rem. cal.
In 1987 approx. 1,000 rifles were dual barrel marked - 7mm EXP REM .280 REM. These specimens will command a 20-40% premium.
Last Mfg.'s Sug. Retail was $547.

MODEL 700 FS — .243 Win., .270 Win., .30-06, .308 Win., or 7mm Rem. Mag. cal., 22 in. polished blue barrel, gray or gray camo Kevlar fiberglass stock with solid recoil pad, iron sights, 6¼ lbs. Mfg. 1987-1988 only.

	$530	$460	$415	$375	$335	$310	$285

Add $20 for 7mm Rem. Mag. cal. (24 in. barrel).
Last Mfg.'s Sug. Retail was $613.

MODEL 700 CUSTOM RIFLE — the Remington Custom Shop should be contacted directly (see Trademark Index) for current information regarding this model. New 1992.

Mfg.'s Sug. Retail	$2,296	$1,925	$1,650	$1,200

Beginning 1992, Remington stopped Custom Grade Model designations in favor of individualized quotations per work order. The Custom Shop should be contacted directly regarding special order pricing (see Trademark Index).

MODEL 700 CUSTOM GRADE — special order only, grades differ in amount of engraving and type of walnut. Available as a custom order only through Remington. Values below reflect 1991 information. The Remington Custom Shop should be contacted for a current price quotation and the availability of options.

Special order Model 700s mfg. between early '60s - 1982 were designated C Grade, D Grade, or F Grade. Values will approximate Custom Grade Models I-III listed below. In 1991, Remington discontinued Custom Grade Model designations.

Custom Grade Model I — mfg. 1983-1991.

	$1,100	$925	$795

Last Mfg.'s Sug. Retail was $1,314.

Custom Grade Model II — mfg. 1983-1991.

	$1,995	$1,675	$1,295

Last Mfg.'s Sug. Retail was $2,335.

Grading	100%	98%	95%	90%	80%	70%	60%

☆ Custom Grade Model III — mfg. 1983-1991.

	$2,900	$2,150	$1,750

Last Mfg.'s Sug. Retail was $3,650.

☆ Custom Grade Model IV — mfg. 1983-1991.

	$4,875	$4,100	$2,950

Last Mfg.'s Sug. Retail was $5,695.

RIFLES: TARGET BOLT ACTION

MODEL 40X SPORTER — .22 LR only, sporterized version of the 40X Target Rifle, 5 shot clip, custom 700 stock, a special order only gun from the factory. Rare, less than 700 mfg. 1969-1977, parts clean-up to 1980.

$1,650	$1,325	$925	$800	$720	$650	$595

This model was last listed in the 1977 Remington catalog — retail was $525.

MODEL 40X TARGET RIFLE — bolt action single shot, .22 LR, 28 in. heavy barrel, Redfield Olympic sights, scope bases, target stock, rubber butt, 12¾ lbs. Mfg. 1955-1964.

	$495	$395	$325	$260	$220	$190	$175
No sights	$450	$360	$295	$240	$200	$180	$165

MODEL 40X STANDARD BARREL — similar to 40X Target Rifle, with lighter barrel, 10¾ lbs.

	$475	$380	$310	$250	$220	$190	$175
No sights	$450	$360	$295	$240	$200	$180	$165

MODEL 40X CENTERFIRE — similar to Model 40X Rim Fire, except in .222, .222 Mag., .30-06, or .308 cal. Mfg. 1961-1964.

	$475	$380	$310	$250	$220	$190	$175
No sights	$450	$360	$295	$240	$200	$180	$165

MODEL 40XB RANGEMASTER RIMFIRE — .22 LR, bolt action single shot, 28 in. light or heavy barrel, no sights, target stock with guide rail, rubber butt. Mfg. 1964-1974.

	$525	$420	$335	$275	$220	$195	$165

Add a premium for this model equipped with a mag.

MODEL 40XB RANGEMASTER CENTERFIRE — over 12 cals., custom made, 27½ in. barrel (current model is stainless), walnut stock, test fired. Mfg. 1964-present.

Mfg.'s Sug. Retail	$1,109	$950	$825	$625	$500	$410	$370	$315

Add $92 for repeater model.
Add $155 for 2 oz. trigger.
Add $62 for left-hand action.
An International Free Rifle was also offered - only 107 were mfg. with premiums being paid.

MODEL 40XB KEVLAR STOCKED — .220 Swift, 27¼ in. bright finished stainless steel barrel, single shot, black finish Kevlar stock, no sights, 9¾ lbs. New 1987.

Mfg.'s Sug. Retail	$1,265	$1,095	$875	$680

Add $80 for bench rest model (Model 40XBBR-KS).
Add $92 for repeater model.
Add $155 for 2 oz. trigger.

Grading	100%	98%	95%	90%	80%	70%	60%

MODEL 40XB REPEATER — similar to 40XB Centerfire, with 5 shot mag. Disc.

	100%	98%	95%	90%	80%	70%	60%
	$870	$770	$625	$500	$420	$370	$315

MODEL 40XC-KS — 7.62 Nato, National Match Course rifle, adj. trigger pull, wood (disc. 1989) or Kevlar (standard 1990) stock.

Mfg.'s Sug. Retail $1,345 $1,150 $940 $700
Subtract $120 for wood stock.

MODEL 40XR-KS RIMFIRE — .22 LR, single shot bolt action, 24 in. heavy barrel, no sights, adj. butt plate and palm stop, target wood (disc. 1989) or Kevlar (standard 1990) stock. Mfg. 1974-present.

Mfg.'s Sug. Retail $1,265 $1,095 $850 $680
Subtract $120 for wood stock.

MODEL 40XR CUSTOM SPORTER — the Remington Custom Shop should be contacted directly (see Trademark Index) for current information on this model.

Mfg.'s Sug. Retail $2,296 $1,925 $1,650 $1,200

Beginning 1992, Remington stopped Custom Grade Model designations in favor of individualized quotations per work order. The Custom Shop should be contacted directly regarding special order pricing (see Trademark Index).

MODEL 40XR CUSTOM SPORTER — .22 cal. only, single shot, available on special order from Remington's Custom Shop only, Grades I-IV (disc. 1991) increase by amount of engraving, quality of wood, and other special order options/features. Mfg. 1986-1991. Values for Custom Grades listed below reflect 1991 (the year of discontinuance) price information. The Remington Custom Shop should be contacted directly regarding current values and options.

⚞ **Custom Grade Model I** — mfg. 1986-1991.

$1,100 $925 $795

Last Mfg.'s Sug. Retail was $1,314.

⚞ **Custom Grade Model II** — mfg. 1986-1991.

$1,995 $1,675 $1,295

Last Mfg.'s Sug. Retail was $2,335.

⚞ **Custom Grade Model III** — mfg. 1986-1991.

$2,900 $2,150 $1,750

Last Mfg.'s Sug. Retail was $3,650.

⚞ **Custom Grade Model IV** — mfg. 1986-1991.

$4,875 $4,100 $2,950

Last Mfg.'s Sug. Retail was $5,695.

MODEL 540X RIMFIRE — .22 LR, single shot bolt action, 26 in. heavy barrel, no sights, target stock, adj. butt. Mfg. 1969-1974.

	100%	98%	95%	90%	80%	70%	60%
	$325	$285	$250	$225	$200	$175	$150

MODEL 540XR — similar to 540X, with large position style stock with adj. butt plate. Mfg. 1974-1983.

	100%	98%	95%	90%	80%	70%	60%
	$350	$300	$275	$225	$200	$185	$175

SHOTGUNS: SxS

100%	98%	95%	90%	80%	70%	60%	50%	40%	30%	20%	10%

MODEL 1873 SxS HAMMER — includes models 1876 and 1878, also known as Whitmore Hammer Lifter or Whitmore Lifter, 10 or 12 ga., 28 or 30 in. decarbonized or damascus barrels, top "thumb-lever" action activated by pushing upward on opening lever, rib top marked "E. REMINGTON & SONS, ILION. N.Y.", patented "AUG.8.1871, APRIL 16.1872", made in various models and grades, high grade models are damascus barreled, pistol grip was optional. Approx. 13,000 mfg. of all Whitmore models combined, mfg. 1873-1882.

100%	98%	95%	90%	80%	70%	60%	50%	40%	30%	20%	10%
$1,350	$1,100	$995	$895	$825	$750	$675	$600	$525	$450	$350	$275

There were also a very few double rifles and combination guns (shotgun/rifle barrel) made in this model - they are very rare. Above values represent standard model without extra options.

MODEL 1882 SxS HAMMER — includes the rare Model 1883, 10 or 12 ga., 28, 30, or 32 in. decarbonized, twist, or damascus steel barrels, rib marked "E.REMINGTON & SONS, ILION, N.Y.", checkered pistol grip stock, decarbonized steel barrels were lowest grade, higher grade examples are damascus barreled and will bring premiums. Approx. 13,750 Model 1882s were mfg. and 1,300 Model 1883s were mfg., overall mfg. 1882-1888.

⚑ **Damascus Barrels**

100%	98%	95%	90%	80%	70%	60%	50%	40%	30%	20%	10%
$1,150	$1,025	$950	$875	$795	$700	$600	$500	$400	$300	$250	$195

⚑ **Steel Barrels**

100%	98%	95%	90%	80%	70%	60%	50%	40%	30%	20%	10%
$1,275	$1,075	$995	$895	$825	$725	$625	$525	$425	$325	$275	$225

Add 15% for Model 1883 variation to above values.
Add $15 for optional auxiliary rifle barrel inserts.

MODEL 1885/1887 SxS HAMMER — 10, 12, or 16 ga., slightly improved variation of the Model 1882, 28, 30, or 32 in. decarbonized, twist, or damascus steel barrels, top of rib marked "E.REMINGTON & SONS, ILION, N.Y.", higher grades are damascus barreled and bring premiums, approx. 6,500 mfg. 1885-1889.

⚑ **Damascus Barrels**

100%	98%	95%	90%	80%	70%	60%	50%	40%	30%	20%	10%
$1,400	$1,200	$1,050	$975	$875	$795	$700	$600	$500	$400	$300	$250

⚑ **Steel Barrels**

100%	98%	95%	90%	80%	70%	60%	50%	40%	30%	20%	10%
$1,550	$1,300	$1,075	$995	$895	$825	$725	$625	$525	$425	$325	$275

MODEL 1889 SxS HAMMER — 10, 12 or 16 ga., 28, 30, or 32 in. decarbonized, twist, or damascus barrels, exposed "circular" hammers, rib top marked "REMINGTON ARMS CO. ILION N.Y. U.S.A.", checkered pistol grip stock, grade number is stamped on water table, higher grades are damascus barreled and will bring premiums. Approx. 134,200 mfg. 1889-1909.

⚑ **Twist Steel Barrels**

100%	98%	95%	90%	80%	70%	60%	50%	40%	30%	20%	10%
$1,250	$1,050	$950	$895	$835	$775	$625	$525	$425	$350	$275	$195

⚑ **Decarbonized Steel Barrels**

100%	98%	95%	90%	80%	70%	60%	50%	40%	30%	20%	10%
$1,450	$1,200	$1,000	$925	$850	$795	$650	$550	$450	$375	$295	$225

Grades range from No. 1 - No. 7, No. 7 being the highest. Values above assume No. 1 or 2 grade.

MODEL 1894 SxS HAMMERLESS — 10, 12, or 16 ga., 26-32 in. "Remington", "Ordnance", or damascus steel barrels, auto ejectors, hammerless, boxlock, double triggers, checkered pistol grip stock. 41,194 mfg. 1894-1910 in the 100,000 block serial range.

100%	98%	95%	90%	80%	70%	60%	50%	40%	30%	20%	10%
$895	$775	$675	$600	$550	$525	$475	$435	$395	$350	$325	$295

Grades offered range from "A" (lowest) to "E" and "Special" (highest). Large premiums exist for higher grade models in excellent condition. Trap model was named either "F.E." or "C.E.O.". Values above assume "A" model (most frequently encountered specimen).

100%	98%	95%	90%	80%	70%	60%	50%	40%	30%	20%	10%

MODEL 1900 SxS HAMMERLESS — 12 or 16 ga., 28 or 30 in. Remington or damascus steel barrels, lower priced to meet market competition, quality is a cut below the Model 1894. 98,475 mfg. 1900-1910 in the 300,000 block serial range.

$825	$725	$625	$550	$500	$465	$435	$400	$350	$300	$250	$195

Grades ranged from "K", "K.E.", or damascus "K.D." and "K.E.D.". Both steel and damascus barrels were guaranteed for nitro powder, mechanically the same as Model 1894.

PARKER AHE — while advertised, the Remington re-issue of the original Parker AHE Model was never mfg. due to product liability considerations. Older Remington manufactured Parkers may be found in the Parker section of this text.

SHOTGUNS: SLIDE ACTION & SEMI-AUTO

Grading	100%	98%	95%	90%	80%	70%	60%

MODEL 1908 SLIDE ACTION — 12 ga., hammerless, bottom ejection, takedown, plain barrel only, blue finish, sight notch on receiver top, marked "REMINGTON ARMS CO." with February 3rd, 1903 and May 18th, 1905 patent dates, walnut pistol grip stock and short forearm, hard rubber buttplate, 7½ lbs., approx. 10,000 mfg. 1908-1910.

			$475	$400	$350	$295	$250	$200	$150

There were 7 grades of this model (No.'s 0-6) that were originally priced from $27 to approx. $140. This model was renamed the Model 10 in 1911.

MODEL 10A SLIDE ACTION — 12 ga., 26-32 in. barrels, various chokes, takedown, plain pistol grip stock. Mfg. 1907-1929. Add 10% for 32 in. full choke 0barrel.

			$350	$300	$260	$215	$175	$150	$135

MODEL 11A AUTOLOADER 5-SHOT — 12, 16, or 20 ga., 26-32 in. barrels, takedown, various chokes, Browning type, checkered pistol stock. Approx. 300,000 mfg., 1911-1948.

	$295	$240	$215	$185	$165	$150	$120
Solid rib	$395	$315	$235	$200	$185	$165	$140
Vent. rib	$440	$360	$335	$305	$275	$220	$165

This model was mfg. under "A - 5" patent agreements (including royalties) with Fabrique Nationale in Herstal, Belgium.

MODEL 11R RIOT GUN — similar to Standard 11A, with 20 in. barrel.

$330	$250	$220	$195	$165	$150	$120

MODEL 11B SPECIAL — higher grade wood, engraved.

$525	$440	$385	$360	$305	$250	$195

MODEL 11D TOURNAMENT

$950	$850	$725	$550	$495	$470	$440

MODEL 11E EXPERT

$1,175	$975	$875	$775	$675	$595	$525

Grading	100%	98%	95%	90%	80%	70%	60%

MODEL 11F PREMIER

	$1,850	$1,550	$1,375	$1,100	$975	$850	$750

Note: Grades differ in quality, grade of wood, and amount of engraving.

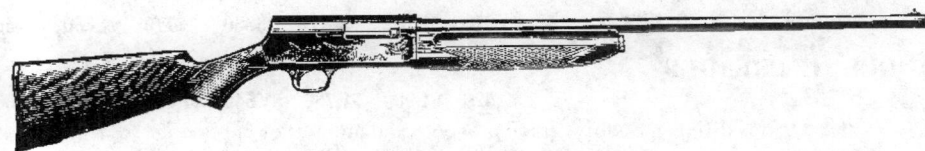

SPORTSMAN MODEL — 12, 16, or 20 ga., 26 in. barrel, skeet choke, beavertail forend. Mfg. 1931-1949.

	$340	$275	$250	$195	$165	$140	$120
Solid rib	$425	$375	$300	$250	$200	$180	$150
Vent. rib	$470	$415	$360	$330	$275	$250	$220

This model was manufactured in Field, Riot, and Skeet configurations.

MODEL 17A SLIDE ACTION — 20 ga., 26-32 in. barrels, various chokes, takedown, bottom ejection, 4 shot mag., plain grip stock. Approx. 48,000 mfg., 1917-1933.

Plain barrel	$330	$250	$220	$195	$165	$140	$110
Vent. rib	$495	$440	$380	$335	$290	$250	$210

Grades range from A - F in suffix form, F being the highest. Large premiums are paid for mint condition, higher grade models.

MODEL 29A SLIDE ACTION — 12 ga., 26-32 in. barrels, bottom ejection, various chokes, takedown, 5 shot mag., checkered pistol grip stock. Approx. 24,000 mfg., 1929-1933. Add 15% for solid rib, 25% for VR.

	$305	$220	$195	$165	$150	$120	$100

30 and 32 in. barrels

	$525	$475	$425	$350	$250	$200	$180

Grades range from A - C and TA - TF, lowest to highest. Premiums exist for finer condition upper grades. The Model 29 was similar in appearance to the Model 10.

MODEL 29S — "Trap Special" with trap style straight grip stock, matted rib.

	$450	$425	$400	$375	$350	$325	$300

MODEL 31A SLIDE ACTION — 12, 16, or 20 ga., side ejection, 2 or 4 shot mag., 26-32 in. barrels, various chokes, takedown, pistol grip stock. Approx. 160,000 mfg., 1931-1949.

	$395	$345	$300	$265	$225	$185	$150
Solid rib	$455	$385	$345	$300	$270	$230	$190
Vent. rib	$475	$415	$375	$320	$290	$250	$210

Grades range from A - F suffixes. Higher grades will bring considerable premiums in excellent condition. TC suffix is Target Model. A Model 31L (lightweight) was mfg. 1948-1950 and while rare, demand dictates to subtract 10% for this variation. Early models will command a small premium in this model.

MODEL 31R RIOT GUN — similar to 31A, with 20 in. barrel.

	$330	$250	$200	$175	$150	$130	$110

MODEL 31 SPECIAL — higher grade wood and engraving.

	$650	$550	$440	$385	$360	$305	$275

Grading	100%	98%	95%	90%	80%	70%	60%

MODEL 31 TOURNAMENT

	100%	98%	95%	90%	80%	70%	60%
	$1,100	$880	$715	$580	$525	$495	$470

MODEL 31E EXPERT

	100%	98%	95%	90%	80%	70%	60%
	$1,320	$1,100	$935	$880	$770	$660	$605

MODEL 31F PREMIER

	100%	98%	95%	90%	80%	70%	60%
	$2,420	$1,980	$1,760	$1,540	$1,320	$1,100	$880

Note: Grades differ in quality, grade of wood, and amount of engraving.

MODEL 31TC TRAP — similar to 31A, with 12 ga. only, 30 or 32 in. barrel, vent. rib, full choke, trap stock and beavertail forend, pad.

	100%	98%	95%	90%	80%	70%	60%
	$660	$550	$495	$470	$415	$385	$305

Subtract 10% for lightweight receiver.

MODEL 31S TRAP — solid rib barrel, plainer wood.

	100%	98%	95%	90%	80%	70%	60%
	$495	$415	$385	$330	$275	$250	$220

MODEL 31H HUNTER — similar to 31S, with sporter stock.

	100%	98%	95%	90%	80%	70%	60%
	$470	$385	$360	$305	$250	$220	$195

MODEL 31 SKEET — similar to 31A, with 26 in. skeet bored barrel, standard solid rib, beavertail forend.

	100%	98%	95%	90%	80%	70%	60%
	$495	$415	$385	$330	$275	$250	$220
Vent. rib	$605	$495	$445	$415	$360	$305	$275

Subtract 10% for lightweight receiver.

SHOTGUNS: MODEL 870 & VARIATIONS

3 in. shells (12 or 20 ga.) may be shot in Magnum receivers only regardless of what the barrel markings may indicate (the ejection port is larger in these Magnum models with M suffix serialization).

MODEL 870AP SLIDE ACTION — "Wingmaster", 12, 16, or 20 ga., 26, 28, or 30 in. barrel, 5 shot, various chokes, plain pistol grip stock. Mfg. 1950-1963.

	100%	98%	95%	90%	80%	70%	60%
	$220	$195	$175	$165	$140	$120	$110
Matted top barrel	$230	$205	$185	$175	$150	$130	$120
Vent. rib	$250	$220	$200	$195	$165	$150	$140

In 1959 "Sun Grain" blonde wood became an option.

MODEL 870DL — deluxe checkered version of 870AP. Mfg. 1950-1963.

	100%	98%	95%	90%	80%	70%	60%
	$250	$220	$200	$180	$165	$140	$120
Vent. rib	$275	$250	$220	$210	$195	$165	$140

MODEL 870BDL — select walnut stock.

	100%	98%	95%	90%	80%	70%	60%
	$275	$250	$220	$200	$180	$165	$140
Vent. rib	$305	$275	$250	$220	$210	$195	$165

SPORTSMAN 12 PUMP — 12 ga. only (3 in. chamber), 28 or 30 in. barrel, recoil pad, VR standard, hardwood stock and forearm, Model 870 type action, $7\frac{1}{2}$ lbs. Mfg. 1985-86 only.

	100%	98%	95%	90%	80%	70%	60%
	$225	$195	$180	$165	$150	$140	$130

Add $35 for Rem. chokes
Last Mfg.'s Sug. Retail was $270.

Grading	100%	98%	95%	90%	80%	70%	60%

MODEL 870 EXPRESS — 12, 20 (new 1991), or .410 (new 1992) ga., 3 in. chamber, 20, 21, 25 (.410 only), 26, or 28 in. VR Rem. choked (12 or 20 ga., supplied with Mod. Rem. choke) barrel, parkerized metal, matte finished hardwood stock and forearm, solid recoil pad, 7 1/4 lbs. New 1987.

Mfg.'s Sug. Retail	$277	$230	$190	$165	$150	$140	$130	$125

Add $15 for .410 ga.
Add $99 for Combo package (extra 20 in. IC barrel, 20 or 12 ga.).

⚡ **Model 870 Express Deer Gun** — 12 ga. only, 20 in. IC choked barrel or fully rifled barrel with rifle sights, Monte Carlo stock. Introduced in 1991.

Mfg.'s Sug. Retail	$273	$225	$190	$165	$150	$140	$130	$125

Add $31 for fully rifled deer barrel.
Add $78 for cantilever scope system and IC Rem. choke (disc. 1991).

⚡ **Model 870 Youth** — 20 ga. only, 21 in. VR barrel with Rem. choke, 13 in. LOP with recoil pad, 6 lbs.

Mfg.'s Sug. Retail	$277	$230	$190	$165	$150	$140	$130	$125

⚡ **Model 870 Express Security** — 12 ga. only, 18 in. cyl. choked barrel with bead sights. Introduced 1991.

Mfg.'s Sug. Retail	$273	$225	$190	$165	$150	$140	$130	$125

MODEL 870 FIELD WINGMASTER — 12, 20, 28, or .410 ga., various barrel lengths, incorporates twin slide rails, 3 in. chambers became standard in 1985, Rem. chokes became standard in 1987, checkered walnut stock and forearm, a choice of high gloss or satin wood finish became available in 1991. Mfg. 1964-present.

Plain barrel		$250	$225	$205	$190	$175	$160	$150

⚡ **Vent. rib** — became standard in 1985.

Mfg.'s Sug. Retail	$469	$350	$275	$240	$200	$185	$170	$160

Subtract $9 for 20 ga.
Subtract $45 without Rem. chokes.
Add $60 for left-hand model (12 ga. only).
Add $60 for 20 in. fully rifled Cantilever deer barrel (new 1992).

⚡ **Small Gauge Model 870** — scaled down 870, in 28 or .410 ga., 25 in. barrel, 6-6 1/2 lbs. Mfg. 1969-present. Vent. rib became standard 1984.

Mfg.'s Sug. Retail	$504	$395	$340	$285	$240	$200	$185	$170

Subtract $40 without VR.

MODEL 870 MAGNUM DUCK GUN — 3 in. chamber, 12 or 20 ga., 26, 28, or 30 in. full or mod. barrel, recoil pad. Mfg. 1964-present. 3 in. chambers became standard on all Model 870s starting in 1985. Rem. chokes became standard 1987 (introduced 1986 as $40 option).

Mfg.'s Sug. Retail	$469	$350	$275	$240	$200	$185	$170	$160

Subtract $45 without Rem. chokes.

MODEL 870 SPECIAL PURPOSE — 12 ga. only, differs only in that metal parts are sand blasted, choice of Mossy Oak Camo (new 1992), black synthetic, or checkered wood stock with low luster finish, 21 (Turkey barrel), 26, or 28 in. VR barrel. Rem. chokes were introduced 1986.

Mfg.'s Sug. Retail	$367	$300	$265	$225	$200	$170	$150	$130

Add $66 for Mossy Oak Camo finish on metal and wood.
Add $26 for Turkey gun (all black).
Add $92 for wood stock and forearm (disc. 1992).
Subtract $45 without Rem. chokes.

Grading	100%	98%	95%	90%	80%	70%	60%

⚔ **Model 870 Special Purpose Deer Gun** — 12 ga. only, 3 in. chamber, 20 in. Rem. choke barrel (disc. 1992) or fully rifled barrel with iron sights (new 1993), satin finished (disc. 1992) or black synthetic (new 1993) stock and forearm, matte black metal, 7¼ lbs. New 1989.

Mfg.'s Sug. Retail	$385	$310	$265	$225	$195	$175	$160	$145

Add $65 for Cantilever scope mount system (disc. 1992).

MODEL 870 LIGHTWEIGHT — 20 ga. only, lighter and shorter mahogany stock than model listed below, 23 in. barrel. Mfg. 1972-1983.

	$270	$230	$210	$190	$175	$165	$155

Add $30 for VR.

MODEL 870 LIGHTWEIGHT (MAGNUM) — 20 ga., 3 in. chamber, 26 or 28 in. barrel, 6 lbs. Mfg. 1972-present. Rem. chokes became standard 1987.

Mfg.'s Sug. Retail	$460	$365	$320	$260	$225	$200	$175	$160

Subtract $45 without Rem. chokes.
Subtract $40 without VR.

MODEL 870 SPECIAL FIELD — 12 or 20 ga., lighter straight grip stock with solid recoil pad, 21 in. VR barrel, 6¼ or 7 lbs. New 1984. Rem. chokes became standard 1987 (introduced 1986 as $40 option).

Mfg.'s Sug. Retail	$460	$370	$315	$265	$230	$210	$190	$175

Subtract $45 without Rem. chokes.

MODEL 870 MARINE — 12 ga. only, 18 in. barrel, features electroless nickel plating on all metal parts, supplied with 7 shot mag., sling swivels and Cordura sling, 7½ lbs.

Mfg.'s Sug. Retail	$447	$355	$310	$255	$225	$200	$175	$160

MODEL 870 RIOT — 12 ga. only, 18 or 20 in. barrel, choice of blue or parkerized metal finish. Disc. 1991.

	$295	$265	$225	$200	$170	$150	$130

Last Mfg.'s Sug. Retail was $355.
Add $19 for police rifle sights (20 in. barrel only).

MODEL 870 BRUSHMASTER — 12 or 20 ga., 20 in. imp. cyl. with rifle sights, 3 in. chamber standard for 1985, normal bluing with satin finished wood.

	$350	$300	$255	$225	$195	$180	$165

Subtract $27 for 20 ga.
Add $56 for left-hand model.
Add $32 for 20 in. fully rifled barrel.
Add $58 for Cantilever scope mount system, sling, and swivels.
Last Mfg.'s Sug. Retail was $439.

MODEL 870 D-GRADE (TOURNAMENT) — custom order only, any gauge. Mfg. 1950-present.

Mfg.'s Sug. Retail	$2,509		$2,075	$1,650	$1,200

MODEL 870 F-GRADE (PREMIER) — custom order only, any gauge. Mfg. 1950-present.

Mfg.'s Sug. Retail	$5,169		$4,375	$3,495	$2,500

MODEL 870 F-GRADE W/GOLD (GOLD PREMIER) — with gold inlays, custom order only. Mfg. 1950-present.

Mfg.'s Sug. Retail	$7,752		$6,900	$3,975	$3,000

Note: Grades differ in quality, grade of wood, and amount of engraving.

Grading	100%	98%	95%	90%	80%	70%	60%

MODEL 870 DUCKS UNLIMITED — "DU" in serial number, disc.

	$335	$270	$195				

Remington has offered many variations of the Model 870 specifically manufactured according to individual DU chapter specifications. The price of a DU 870 varies substantially from the "DU point of purchase" to real market conditions. When contemplating a DU gun it is always important to know how many of that particular variation were manufactured. The Remington factory normally has this information unless the special DU work was subcontracted elsewhere. While most DU guns are good vehicles for fund raising, their collectability to date has been minimal. Actual market conditions indicate that unless production is truly limited, most DU firearms sell very close to the model it was derived from. Also, any collectability that does exist is for 100% guns new in the box with warranty papers. Used DU guns have values comparable to the standard model from which they are derived.

In addition to regular DU guns, Remington has also produced special editions including the 1982 Mississippi Edition (dinner gun) and a 1974 DU (dinner gun — first 500 mfg.). These were rarer DU shotguns, and current values could vary significantly.

MODEL 870 BICENTENNIAL — 12 ga. only, configurations include Trap, Skeet, and Trade, mfg. to commemorate U.S. Bicentennial (1776-1976).

	100%	98%	95%	90%	80%	70%	60%
Trap or Skeet	$425	$350	$295				
Trade	$375	$295	$225				

In 1976, the 870 Bicentennial Trap retailed for $255 (add $10 for Monte Carlo stock), and the Skeet retailed for $220.

MODEL 870 SKEET — 12, 20, 28, or .410 ga., 26 in. VR skeet bore barrel. Mfg. 1950-1981.

$295	$260	$230	$215	$200	$185	$170

MODEL 870 SKEET MATCHED PAIR — .410 or 28 ga., 1,503 cased sets mfg. 1969 only.

$995	$850	$700	$650	$620	$575	$530

MODEL 870TA TRAP — 12 ga. trap model, deluxe walnut, VR. Add $15 for Monte Carlo stock. Disc. 1986.

$365	$345	$280	$240	$220	$200	$180

Last Mfg.'s Sug. Retail was $430.

MODEL 870TB TRAP — similar to 870, with 28 or 30 in. VR full choke barrel, trap stock, recoil pad. Mfg. 1950-1981.

$395	$355	$285	$245	$220	$200	$185

MODEL 870TC TRAP — higher grade walnut and special VR, Rem. chokes became standard 1987.

Mfg.'s Sug. Retail	$613	$565	$450	$350	$275	$240	$220	$200

Add $15 for Monte Carlo stock.
Early Model 870TC Trap guns had hand cut checkering.

COMPETITION TRAP — 12 ga. competition model, reduced recoil, special checkered walnut, VR. Disc. 1986.

$575	$545	$390	$320	$280	$240	$210

Last Mfg.'s Sug. Retail was $680.

MODEL 870 ALL AMERICAN TRAP — 30 in. full choke barrel, engraved receiver, trigger guard and barrel, deluxe trap stock. Approx. 1,000 mfg., 1972-1976.

$795	$700	$650	$605	$495	$440	$385

Remington. cont.

Grading	100%	98%	95%	90%	80%	70%	60%

SHOTGUNS: SEMI-AUTO

MODEL 48 SPORTSMAN SEMI-AUTO — 12, 16, or 20 ga., 26, 28, or 32 in. barrels, 3 shot, mechanical (solid breech) ejection system, various chokes, rounded receiver, checkered pistol grip stock. Approx. 275,000 mfg., 1949-1959.

	100%	98%	95%	90%	80%	70%	60%
	$310	$250	$220	$200	$175	$165	$140
Matted top barrel	$325	$255	$220	$200	$175	$165	$140

Differs from Model 11-48 in that forearm sides have longitudinal grooves and also has capped grips.

MODEL 48B SELECT

	100%	98%	95%	90%	80%	70%	60%
	$420	$360	$310	$290	$245	$220	$195

MODEL 48D TOURNAMENT

	100%	98%	95%	90%	80%	70%	60%
	$1,100	$825	$715	$660	$605	$440	$415

MODEL 48F PREMIER

	100%	98%	95%	90%	80%	70%	60%
	$2,420	$2,035	$1,540	$1,210	$990	$770	$715

MODEL 48A RIOT GUN — 12 ga. only, 20 in. plain barrel.

	100%	98%	95%	90%	80%	70%	60%
	$275	$220	$195	$165	$150	$140	$110

MODEL 48SA SKEET — 26 in. barrel, skeet bore, ivory bead. Mfg. 1949-1960.

	100%	98%	95%	90%	80%	70%	60%
	$305	$275	$255	$230	$210	$195	$165
With VR	$360	$310	$285	$260	$230	$210	$195

MODEL 48SC TARGET

	100%	98%	95%	90%	80%	70%	60%
	$385	$360	$330	$305	$275	$250	$220

MODEL 48SD TOURNAMENT

	100%	98%	95%	90%	80%	70%	60%
	$1,100	$825	$715	$660	$605	$440	$415

MODEL 48SF PREMIER

	100%	98%	95%	90%	80%	70%	60%
	$2,200	$1,925	$1,650	$1,210	$990	$770	$715

MODEL 11-48 SEMI-AUTO — 12, 16, 20, 28 (introduced 1952), or .410 (introduced 1954) ga., recoil operated action, walnut stock. Approx. 429,000 mfg., 1949-1968.

	100%	98%	95%	90%	80%	70%	60%
	$310	$250	$220	$200	$175	$165	$140

Add 15% - 40% for 28 and .410 ga.'s, $40 for VR.

MODEL 58ADL "SPORTSMAN - 58" SEMI-AUTO — 12, 16, or 20 ga., 26, 28, or 30 in. barrel, gas operation, various chokes, 3 shot, checkered pistol grip stock, scroll game scene engraved. Approx. 271,000 mfg., 1956-1963.

	100%	98%	95%	90%	80%	70%	60%
	$275	$250	$220	$195	$140	$120	$110
With VR	$360	$305	$275	$250	$220	$165	$140

MODEL 58BDL — similar to 58ADL, with select wood.

	100%	98%	95%	90%	80%	70%	60%
	$360	$330	$305	$275	$220	$195	$165
With VR	$415	$360	$330	$305	$275	$220	$195

MODEL 58SA SKEET GUN — similar to 58ADL, with 26 in. skeet bore VR barrel, skeet stock.

	100%	98%	95%	90%	80%	70%	60%
	$360	$330	$305	$275	$220	$195	$165

MODEL 58SC TARGET

	100%	98%	95%	90%	80%	70%	60%
	$495	$440	$415	$385	$330	$305	$275

Grading	100%	98%	95%	90%	80%	70%	60%

MODEL 58D TOURNAMENT

	$825	$715	$635	$580	$525	$470	$440

MODEL 58SF PREMIER

	$1,650	$1,375	$1,210	$1,045	$965	$880	$800

Note: Models differ in grade of wood, and amount of engraving.

MODEL 878A "AUTOMASTER" — 12 ga. gas operated semi-auto, 26, 28, or 30 in. barrels, action similar to Model 58. Approx. 62,000 mfg., 1959-1962. Add 15% for VR.

	$250	$220	$195	$170	$160	$150	$135

Barrels on this model are interchangeable with those on the Model 58.

MODEL SP-10 — 10 ga., 3½ in. chamber, semi-auto stainless steel gas system operation, lighter recoil than most 12 ga. Mag.'s, 23 (new 1993), 26 or 30 in. barrel with ⅜ in. VR and Rem. chokes (2), checkered stock and forearm with choice of low gloss satin or Mossy Oak Bottomland Camo (23 in. barrel only) finish, metal is either matte or Camo finished, crossbolt safety, recoil pad, supplied with camo sling, approx. 11 lbs. Introduced 1989.

Mfg.'s Sug. Retail	$966	$850	$740	$650	$595	$525	$450	$395

Add $84 for Mossy Oak Bottomland Camo finish.
The first 5,000 SP-10s were assigned special serialization (LE89 prefix) and will no doubt command premiums shortly.
This model is NOT a re-designed Ithaca Mag-10 and the parts are NOT interchangeable. The SP-10 is a new design.

⚒ **Model SP-10 Turkey Combo** — includes choice of either 26 or 30 VR regular barrel and extra 22 in. deer barrel with rifle sights. New in 1991.

Mfg.'s Sug. Retail	$1,104	$980	$860	$750	$675	$625	$550	$475

SHOTGUNS: MODEL 1100 & VARIATIONS

3 in. shells (12 or 20 ga.) may be shot in Magnum receivers only, regardless of what the barrel markings may indicate (the ejection port is larger in these Magnum models with M suffix serialization).

MODEL 1100 SEMI-AUTO FIELD — 12 (disc. 1987), 16 (disc.), or 20 ga., 26, 28, or 30 in. barrels, various chokes, gas operated, checkered pistol grip stock. Mfg. 1963-1988. Rem. chokes became standard 1987 (introduced 1986 as $40 option). In 1985, VRs became standard on this model. Prices below assume VR and Rem. chokes. Mfg. 1963-1988.

	$325	$280	$250	$220	$200	$180	$165

Subtract $40 if without VR.
Subtract $45 if without Rem. chokes.
Last Mfg.'s Sug. Retail was $545.
This model is currently produced only in a Lightweight or Mag. 20 (3 in. chamber), 28, or .410 ga., since the release of the Model 11-87.

SPORTSMAN 12 AUTO — 12 ga. only, 2¾ in. chamber, 28 or 30 in. barrel, similar to Model 1100 action, VR standard, hardwood stock and forearm, 7¾ lbs. Mfg. 1985-86 only. Add $40 for Rem. chokes (new 1986).

	$300	$260	$220	$195	$170	$160	$150

Last Mfg.'s Sug. Retail was $405.

MODEL 1100 SPECIAL FIELD — 12 or 20 ga., 21 in. VR barrel, various chokes, gas operated, checkered straight grip stock, VR standard, a high gloss wood finish was available 1991 only. New 1984. Rem. chokes became standard in 1987.

Mfg.'s Sug. Retail	$589	$455	$385	$325	$265	$230	$210	$180

Subtract $45 if without Rem. chokes.

Grading	100%	98%	95%	90%	80%	70%	60%

MODEL 1100 SMALL GAUGE — 28 or .410 ga., 25 in. barrel, scaled down receiver, skeet and field chokes, VR standard. Mfg. 1969-present.

Mfg.'s Sug. Retail	$633	$495	$400	$350	$285	$250	$225	$200

MODEL 1100 LT-20 (LIGHTWEIGHT) — similar to 1100, 20 ga. only, with mahogany stock and lightened receiver, 21, 26, or 28 in. barrel, VR became standard 1985, 6½ lbs.

Mfg.'s Sug. Retail	$589	$455	$385	$325	$265	$225	$200	$180

Subtract $40 if without VR.
This model is offered in either a satin or gloss wood finish.

Model 1100 Youth — similar to Model 1100 Lightweight, except stock is 1 in. shorter and 21 in. barrel only.

Mfg.'s Sug. Retail	$576	$440	$365	$300	$255	$220	$200	$180

MODEL 1100 LIGHTWEIGHT (MAGNUM) — chambered for 3 in. 20 ga. Mag., VR standard, Rem. chokes became standard 1987.

Mfg.'s Sug. Retail	$589	$455	$385	$325	$265	$225	$200	$180

Subtract $40 if without VR.

MODEL 1100 MAGNUM DUCK GUN — similar to 1100, in 12 (disc. 1987) or 20 ga., 3 in. chamber, recoil pad, VR became standard 1984. Mfg. 1963-1988. Rem. chokes became standard 1987.

	$400	$325	$280	$260	$220	$200	$180

Add $80 for left-hand model (disc. 1986).
Subtract $40 if without VR.
Subtract $45 if without Rem. chokes.
Last Mfg.'s Sug. Retail was $533.

Model 1100 Magnum Special Purpose (SP) — 12 ga. only, low luster finish on stock and forearm, sand blasted metal parts. Mfg. 1985-86 only. Add $40 for Rem. chokes (new 1986).

	$365	$300	$275	$255	$220	$200	$180

Last Mfg.'s Sug. Retail was $550.

MODEL 1100 "1 OF 3,000" FIELD — 12 ga. only, limited edition, serial numbered 1-3,000, deluxe walnut, gold washed etched hunting scenes on receiver, 28 in. modified VR barrel. Mfg. 1980.

	$1,100	$900	$600	$500	$425	$350	$300

MODEL 1100 DEER GUN — 12 (disc. 1987) or 20 ga., 20 (disc.), 21 in. (20 ga. only) or 22 (disc.) in. imp. cyl. barrel with rifle sights.

Mfg.'s Sug. Retail	$532	$400	$330	$270	$225	$200	$185	$165

Add $80 for left-hand model (disc. 1986).

Model 1100 Special Purpose Deer (SP) — similar to Model 1100 Deer Gun, except has low luster finish on stock and forearm, sandblasted metal parts. Mfg. 1986 only.

	$335	$295	$275	$255	$220	$200	$180

Last Mfg.'s Sug. Retail was $495.

MODEL 1100 LT-20 (TOURNAMENT SKEET) — 12 (disc. 1987) or 20 ga., 26 in. skeet bored barrel, optional Cutts Compensator. Mfg. 1963-present.

Mfg.'s Sug. Retail	$670	$495	$425	$375	$325	$275	$225	$200

Add $40 for left-hand model (disc.1986).

MODEL 1100 SMALL GAUGE SKEET — 20, 28 or .410 ga., 25 or 26 (disc.) in. VR barrel, 6½-7¼ lbs. Mfg. 1969-present.

Mfg.'s Sug. Retail	$670	$495	$425	$375	$325	$275	$225	$200

2½ in. chamber is standard on the .410 ga.

Grading	100%	98%	95%	90%	80%	70%	60%

MODEL 1100 SKEET MATCHED PAIR — 28 and .410 ga.'s, walnut stock and forearm.
5,067 cased Skeet sets were mfg. 1969 and 1970 only.

	$1,125	$950	$800	$725	$675	$630	$600

MODEL 1100 150TH ANNIVERSARY — limited mfg. in 1966 only.

	$400	$340	$290				

MODEL 1100 BICENTENNIAL — 12 ga. only, configurations include Trap, Skeet, and Trade, mfg. to commemorate U.S. Bicentennial (1776-1976).

	100%	98%	95%
Trap or Skeet	$425	$350	$295
Trade	$375	$295	$225

In 1976, the 1100 Bicentennial Trap retailed for $320 (add $10 for Monte Carlo stock), the Skeet retailed for $285, and the Trade retailed for $270.

MODEL 1100TA TRAP — 12 ga., 30 in. barrel, recoil pad on regular stock, available in left or right-hand. Mfg. 1979-86.

	$410	$330	$295	$270	$230	$210	$190

Last Mfg.'s Sug. Retail was $570.
Add $15 for Monte Carlo stock.
Add $50 for left-hand model.

MODEL 1100TB TRAP — 12 ga., 30 in. VR full choke barrel, special trap stock, select wood. Mfg. 1963-1981.

	$435	$350	$300	$270	$230	$210	$190
Monte Carlo stock	$450	$360	$310	$280	$235	$220	$195

MODEL 1100 TOURNAMENT TRAP — 12 ga., 30 in. VR full choke barrel, special trap stock, extra select wood. Mfg. 1979-86.

	$540	$480	$390	$345	$295	$255	$210

Last Mfg.'s Sug. Retail was $675.
Add $15 for Monte Carlo stock.

MODEL 1100 DUCKS UNLIMITED — "DU" in serial number.

Remington has offered many variations of the Model 1100 specifically manufactured according to individual DU chapter specifications. The price of a DU 1100 varies substantially from the "DU point of purchase" to real market conditions. When contemplating a DU gun it is always important to know how many of that particular variation were manufactured. The Remington factory normally has this information unless the special DU work was subcontracted elsewhere. While most DU guns are good vehicles for fund raising, their collectability to date has been minimal. Actual market conditions indicate that unless production is truly limited, most DU firearms sell very close to the model it was derived from. Also, any collectability that does exist is for 100% guns new in the box with warranty papers. Used DU guns have values comparable to the standard model from which they are derived.

In addition to regular DU guns, Remington has also produced special editions including the 1982 Atlantic Flyway (dinner gun) and a 1981 DU Lt. 20 ga. and 12 ga. (dinner gun — 2,400 mfg. each), and a 1973 dinner gun (600 mfg.). These were rarer DU shotguns, and current values could vary significantly.

MODEL 1100 D-GRADE (TOURNAMENT) — custom order only, any gauge. Mfg. 1963-present.

Mfg.'s Sug. Retail	$2,509		$2,075	$1,650	$1,200		

MODEL 1100 F-GRADE (PREMIER) — custom order only, any gauge. Mfg. 1963-present.

Mfg.'s Sug. Retail	$5,169		$4,375	$3,495	$2,500		

MODEL 1100 F-GRADE W/GOLD (GOLD PREMIER) — with gold inlay, custom order only. Mfg. 1963-present.

Mfg.'s Sug. Retail	$7,752	$6,900	$3,975	$3,000

Note: Grades differ in quality, grade of wood, and amount of engraving.

SHOTGUNS: MODEL 11-87 & VARIATIONS

MODEL 11-87 PREMIER — 12 ga. only (3 in. chamber), 26, 28, or 32 in. VR Rem. choked barrel, successor to Model 1100, gas compensating action adaptable to all loads, stainless steel magazine tube, polished blue finish, satin finished and checkered walnut stock and forearm, a high gloss wood finish option became available in 1991 at N/C, solid recoil pad, 8⅛-8⅜ lbs. Introduced 1987.

Mfg.'s Sug. Retail	$637	$515	$420	$335	$285	$240	$220	$200

Add $62 for left-hand action.

Note: Model 11-87 Premier barrels are not interchangeable with Model 1100 barrels.

MODEL 11-87 SPECIAL PURPOSE — 12 ga. only (3 in. chamber), 26, 28, or 30 (disc.) in. VR Rem. choked barrel, parkerized metal with matte finish wood stock and forearm, vent recoil pad, includes camouflaged nylon sling, 8¼ lbs. New 1987.

Mfg.'s Sug. Retail	$619	$500	$415	$335	$285	$240	$220	$200

MODEL 11-87 SPECIAL PURPOSE SYNTHETIC — 12 ga. only, 21, 26, or 28 in. VR Rem-choke barrel, choice of Mossy Oak Camo metal and wood (new 1992) or matte finished synthetic stock and forearm. Introduced in 1991.

Mfg.'s Sug. Retail	$619	$500	$415	$335	$285	$240	$220	$200

Add $13 for 21 in. Turkey barrel.
Add $81 for Mossy Oak Greenleaf Camo finish with 21 in. barrel.
Add $68 for Mossy Oak Camo finish with rifle sights on 21 in. barrel.
Add $79 for NWTF variation with brown tree bark finish on wood and metal (disc. 1992).

MODEL 11-87 SPECIAL PURPOSE DEER GUN — 12 ga. only (3 in. chamber), 21 in. IC or Rem. choked (new 1989) or fully rifled (new 1993) barrel with iron sights, parkerized metal with matte finished wood or black synthetic (new 1993) stock and forearm, vent recoil pad, includes camouflaged nylon sling, 7¼ lbs. New 1987.

Mfg.'s Sug. Retail	$599	$480	$395	$320	$270	$240	$220	$200

Add $54 for Cantilever scope mount system.
Add $26 for black synthetic stock and forearm.
Subtract $40 for fixed choke barrel.

Rem. chokes became standard on this model in 1989.

MODEL 11-87 SPORTING CLAYS — 12 ga. only, 26 or 28 in. VR barrel with extended Rem. chokes (knurled extension chokes allow for no-wrench field changes), specially balanced, top metal surfaces have been fine matte finished, radiused recoil pad, twin bead sights on 5/16 wide VR, 7½ lbs. New 1992.

Mfg.'s Sug. Retail	$725	$625	$525	$425	$375	$325	$295	$260

MODEL 11-87 PREMIER SKEET — 12 ga. only, 26 in. VR Rem. choked barrel, deluxe walnut with quality cut checkering, 7¾ lbs. New 1987.

Mfg.'s Sug. Retail	$669	$525	$440	$350	$295	$250	$225	$200

Add $66 for left-hand action.
Subtract $40 if without Rem. chokes.

Grading	100%	98%	95%	90%	80%	70%	60%

MODEL 11-87 PREMIER TRAP — 12 ga. only, 30 in. raised VR Rem. choked barrel, deluxe walnut with quality cut checkering, 8¼ lbs. New 1987.

Mfg.'s Sug. Retail	$677	$525	$400	$325	$285	$240	$215	$195

Add $68 for left-hand action.
Add $15 for Monte Carlo stock.
Subtract $40 if without Rem. chokes.

MODEL 11-87 175TH ANNIVERSARY — 12 ga. only, 28 in. barrel with Rem-chokes, 175th Anniversary Model (1816-1991) with light engraving and high gloss wood finish. 1991 mfg. only.

		$515	$425	$335

Last Mfg.'s Sug. Retail was $618.

MODEL 11-87 D-GRADE (TOURNAMENT) — custom order only, any gauge. Mfg. 1963-present.

Mfg.'s Sug. Retail	$2,509		$2,075	$1,650	$1,200

MODEL 11-87 F-GRADE (PREMIER) — custom order only, any gauge. Mfg. 1963-present.

Mfg.'s Sug. Retail	$5,169		$4,375	$3,495	$2,500

MODEL 11-87 F-GRADE W/GOLD (GOLD PREMIER) — with gold inlay, custom order only. Mfg. 1963-present.

Mfg.'s Sug. Retail	$7,752		$6,900	$3,975	$3,000

Note: Grades differ in quality, grade of wood, and amount of engraving.

SHOTGUNS: SINGLE BARREL

100%	98%	95%	90%	80%	70%	60%	50%	40%	30%	20%	10%

MODEL NO. 3 RIDER SINGLE BARREL — 10, 12, 16, 20, 24, or 28 ga., single barrel, 30 or 32 in. barrels, top lever break open, plain pistol grip stock. Approx. 25,000 mfg. 1893-1905.

$325	$290	$260	$230	$200	$170	$140	$110	$85	$65	$50	$35

MODEL NO. 9 RIDER SINGLE BARREL — similar to No. 3, with auto ejector. Mfg. 1902-1910.

$375	$325	$290	$260	$230	$200	$170	$140	$110	$85	$65	$50

Grading	100%	98%	95%	90%	80%	70%	60%

MODEL 90-T (TRAP) — 12 ga., 32 or 34 in. full choke VR barrel, matte black receiver and wood around tang area, deluxe checkered stock and forearm, short throw top-lever release, elongated forcing cone, approx. 8¾ lbs. New 1992.

Mfg.'s Sug. Retail	$2,995	$2,650	$2,300	$1,975	$1,650	$1,375	$1,150	$975

MODEL 310 SKEET — .32 Rimfire case loaded with No. 12 leadshot, breakopen single shot, .310 bore shotgun mfg. at Remington's Brazilian plant, used in conjunction with a self-operated trap set which threw half-size clay targets, entire set-up included gun, shooting booth, ammunition, and trap thrower, 5½ lbs., mfg. circa late '50s - early '60s.

Gun only			$375	$325	$275	$225	$195	$175	$150

Add 25%-75% depending on the amount of original accessories included.
This model was never mass produced, but test marketed for approx. 5 years in CT, NJ, and TX primarly at amusement parks. It failed commercially due to lack of sales.

Remington. cont.

Grading	100%	98%	95%	90%	80%	70%	60%

SHOTGUNS: O/U

MODEL 32 — 12 ga., double lock action, SST, separated barrels, 26, 28, or 30 in. barrels without rib, SR, or VR. Approx. 6,050 mfg. (ser. range approx. 0001-6,053) 1931-1947. There is a discrepancy as to when serialization started on this model.

	100%	98%	95%	90%	80%	70%	60%
	$1,925	$1,650	$1,400	$1,200	$1,000	$900	$800

Add 10% for SST.
Add 10% for vent. or solid rib.
Add 20% for VR on 28 in. barrels.
MODEL 32 SERIALIZATION IS AS FOLLOWS: 1931 - 0001-1,009; 1932 - 1,010-1,903; 1933 - 1,904-1,948; 1934 - 1,949-2,727; 1935 - 2,728-3,610; 1936 - 3,611-4,259; 1937 - 4,260-4,755; 1938 - 4,756-4,958; 1939 - 4,959-5,202; 1940 - 5,203-5,425; 1941 - 5,426-5,741; 1942 - 5,742-6,020; 1943 - 6,021-6,031; 1944 - 6,032-6,049; 1945 to 1947 - 6,050-6,053.

MODEL 32D TOURNAMENT

	100%	98%	95%	90%	80%	70%	60%
	$3,500	$2,950	$2,400	$2,100	$1,750	$1,400	$1,175

MODEL 32E EXPERT — less than 35 mfg.

	100%	98%	95%	90%	80%	70%	60%
	$5,000	$4,450	$3,850	$3,350	$2,650	$2,200	$1,875

MODEL 32F PREMIER

	100%	98%	95%	90%	80%	70%	60%
	$6,500	$5,750	$5,000	$4,400	$3,520	$2,750	$2,300

Note: Grades differ in quality, grade of wood, and amount of engraving.

MODEL 32 SKEET — similar to 32A, with 26-28 in. skeet bored barrel, SST. Mfg. 1932-1942.

	100%	98%	95%	90%	80%	70%	60%
	$2,350	$1,900	$1,650	$1,400	$1,200	$1,100	$995

Add 10% for VR.
Add 20% for VR on 28 in. barrels.

MODEL 32TC TARGET — similar to 32A, with 30-32 in. VR, full choke barrels, trap style stock. Mfg. 1932-1942.

	100%	98%	95%	90%	80%	70%	60%
	$3,500	$3,000	$2,500	$2,000	$1,750	$1,525	$1,325

Add 10% for 30 in. VR barrels.

MODEL 3200 FIELD — 12 ga., 26, 28, or 30 in. barrels, VR, various chokes, boxlock, auto ejectors, single selective trigger, checkered pistol grip stock, separated barrels. Mfg. 1972-1984.

	100%	98%	95%	90%	80%	70%	60%
	$1,050	$925	$825	$750	$680	$640	$560

Model 3200s with shorter barrels (26 or 28 in.) and open choking are more desirable than 30 in. tubes bored F/M.
MODEL 3200 SERIALIZATION IS AS FOLLOWS: 1973 - 4,200-16,667; 1974 - 16,668-27,393; 1975 - 27,394-35,303; 1976 - 35,304-39,216; 1977 - 39,217-41,432; 1978 - 41,433-42,813; 1979 - 42,814-44,278; 1980 - 44,279-45,504; 1981 - 45,505-45,974; 1982 - 45,975-47,200; 1983 - 47,201-47,308.

MODEL 3200 MAGNUM — 12 ga., 3 in. chambers, 30 in. heavy wall barrels (steel shot compatible), less than 1,000 mfg. 1975-1980.

	100%	98%	95%	90%	80%	70%	60%
	$1,250	$1,000	$875	$750	$680	$640	$560

MODEL 3200 SKEET — similar to 3200 Field, with 26 or 28 in. skeet bored barrels, skeet style stock. Mfg. 1973-1980.

	100%	98%	95%	90%	80%	70%	60%
	$1,100	$995	$900	$825	$750	$680	$640

28 in. barrels will command a premium on this model.
This model was also mfg. in a 28 in. IM/F configuration with gold pigeon on bottom for live pigeon shooting. Since less than 300 were mfg., prices in the $2,300 range are being asked if NIB condition.

Grading	100%	98%	95%	90%	80%	70%	60%

Model 3200 Four Ga. Set — includes 12, 20, 28, or .410 ga., cased.

| | $4,750 | $4,000 | $3,650 | $3,400 | $3,200 | $2,950 | $2,750 |

28 in. barrels will command a premium on this model.

MODEL 3200 COMPETITION SKEET — similar to 3200 Skeet, with scroll engraved frame and trigger guard, select wood. Mfg. 1973-1983.

| | $1,275 | $1,075 | $975 | $895 | $825 | $750 | $700 |

Add 20% for 28 in. VR barrels.

MODEL 3200 TRAP — similar as 3200 Field, with 30 or 32 in. barrels, trap stock. Mfg. 1973-1980.

| | $1,100 | $975 | $850 | $795 | $740 | $680 | $640 |

MODEL 3200 SPECIAL TRAP — similar to 3200 Trap, except fancy wood. Mfg. 1973-1981.

| | $1,295 | $1,050 | $900 | $825 | $775 | $700 | $650 |

MODEL 3200 COMPETITION TRAP — similar to 3200 Trap, with scroll engraving. Mfg. 1973-1981.

| | $1,650 | $1,450 | $1,250 | $995 | $800 | $700 | $650 |

MODEL 3200 PREMIER — 12 ga., sold through Remington's International Division, 500 mfg. 1975 only, patterned after "One of 1000" series, regular or Monte Carlo stock, 116 were engraved in Belgium — add 25%+.

| | $2,650 | $2,200 | $1,800 | $1,600 | $1,400 | $1,250 | $1,100 |

MODEL 3200 "ONE OF 1000" — limited edition, elaborate engraving, fancy wood, supplied with hard case, made in both skeet and trap models. Mfg. 1,000 each model mfg. 1973 (Trap) and 1974 (Skeet).

| Trap | $1,995 | $1,650 | $1,475 | $1,300 | $1,200 | $1,100 | $875 |
| Skeet | $1,995 | $1,650 | $1,475 | $1,300 | $1,200 | $1,100 | $875 |

Add 20% for 28 in. barrels on the Skeet Model.

PEERLESS MODEL — 12 ga. only, 26, 28, or 30 in. VR barrel, boxlock with engraved sideplates, SST, ejectors, checkered walnut stock and forearm with vent. recoil pad, 3.28 milliseconds lock time, blued metal, approx. 7½ lbs. New 1993.

| Mfg.'s Sug. Retail | $1,105 | $995 | $875 | $750 | $675 | $600 | $550 | $495 |

This model is an entirely new design not sharing any parts with either the Models 32 or 3200.

RENETTE, GASTINE
Please refer to the "G" section of this text.

RHODE ISLAND ARMS COMPANY
Previous manufacturer located in Hope Valley, RI.

MORRONE O/U — 12 or 20 ga., 26 or 28 in. plain barrels, boxlock, extractors, single trigger, checkered straight or pistol grip stock. Mfg. 1949-1953, only 500 of these guns were mfg., 450 in 12 ga., and 50 in 20 ga., very few with VR, they are quite rare although collector interest is not overwhelming.

| | $1,100 | $880 | $770 | $660 | $550 | $495 | $440 |

Add 20% for 20 gauge.
Add 20% for VR.

RICHLAND ARMS COMPANY

Previous importer (until 1986) located in Blissfield, MI. Below listed shotguns were Spanish and Italian manufactured.

SHOTGUNS

Grading	100%	98%	95%	90%	80%	70%	60%

MODEL 80 LS SINGLE SHOT — 12, 20, or .410 ga., 26 or 28 in. full choke barrel. Mfg. 1986 only.

	100%	98%	95%	90%	80%	70%	60%
	$140	$120	$110	$100	$90	$80	$70

Last Mfg.'s Sug. Retail was $162.

MODEL 711 MAGNUM SXS — 10 ga., 3½ in. chamber, 12 ga., 3 in. chamber, 32 in. full and full, 30 in. full and full, 20, 28, and .410 ga.'s also available on special order, hammerless, boxlock, extractors, checkered, walnut stock, recoil pad. Mfg. 1963-1985 in Spain.

	100%	98%	95%	90%	80%	70%	60%
10 gauge	$400	$325	$275	$250	$230	$210	$190
12 gauge	$340	$295	$265	$250	$230	$210	$190
20 gauge	$450	$340	$295	$260	$230	$210	$195

MODEL 707 DELUXE SXS — 12 or 20 ga., 3 in. chambers, 26, 28, or 30 in. barrels, various chokes, boxlock, extractors, double triggers, checkered stock and forend. Mfg. 1963-1972 in Spain.

	100%	98%	95%	90%	80%	70%	60%
	$330	$305	$290	$275	$250	$230	$210

MODEL 200 FIELD GRADE SXS — 12, 16, 20, 28, or .410 ga., 22, 26, and 28 in. barrels, various chokes, Anson & Deeley boxlock, extractors, double triggers, checkered stock, 6 lbs. 2 oz. - 7 lbs. 4 oz. Mfg. 1963-1985 in Spain.

	100%	98%	95%	90%	80%	70%	60%
	$320	$285	$255	$225	$195	$175	$150

Last Mfg.'s Sug. Retail was $379.

MODEL 202 ALL PURPOSE — similar to Field, except 2 sets of barrels, 12 and 20 ga. only. Mfg. 1963-disc. in Spain.

	100%	98%	95%	90%	80%	70%	60%
	$305	$260	$230	$220	$195	$165	$150

MODEL 41 ULTRA O/U — 20, 28, or .410 ga., 3 in. chambers (.410 ga. only), single non-selective trigger, 26 or 28 in. barrels, extractors, VR, engraved silver finished receiver, select checkered walnut stock and forearm, 6 lbs. 2 oz. Importation disc. 1986.

	100%	98%	95%	90%	80%	70%	60%
	$265	$220	$210	$200	$190	$180	$170

Last Mfg.'s Sug. Retail was $298.

MODEL 747 O/U — 20 ga. only, 3 in. chambers, boxlock action, VR and barrels, SST, extractors. Importation disc. 1986.

	100%	98%	95%	90%	80%	70%	60%
	$420	$350	$325	$310	$295	$280	$265

Last Mfg.'s Sug. Retail was $464.

MODEL 757 O/U — 12 ga., 3 in. chambers, boxlock action with Greener crossbolt, vent. barrels and rib, double triggers, extractors, walnut stock and forearm, 7 lbs. 4 oz. New 1986. Add $70 for multi-chokes (Model 7570). Importation disc. 1986.

	100%	98%	95%	90%	80%	70%	60%
	$290	$260	$230	$215	$200	$185	$170

Last Mfg.'s Sug. Retail was $325.

MODEL 787 O/U — 12 ga. only, 3 in. chambers, boxlock action with silver finish, single trigger, vent. barrels and rib, extractors, walnut stock with recoil pad, is supplied with 5 interchangeable choke tubes, 7¼ lbs. Made 1986 only.

	100%	98%	95%	90%	80%	70%	60%
	$435	$375	$340	$310	$295	$280	$265

Last Mfg.'s Sug. Retail was $471.

Grading	100%	98%	95%	90%	80%	70%	60%

MODEL 808 O/U — 12 ga., 26, 28, or 30 in. barrels, various chokes, boxlock, extractors, checkered stock. Mfg. 1963-1968 in Italy.

	100%	98%	95%	90%	80%	70%	60%
	$420	$360	$330	$315	$290	$270	$230

MODEL 810 O/U — 10 ga., 3½ in. chambers, ST, extractors.

	100%	98%	95%	90%	80%	70%	60%
	$600	$550	$500	$460	$430	$395	$360

MODEL 828 O/U — 20 ga., single non-selective trigger, extractors, engraved, only 250 imported.

	100%	98%	95%	90%	80%	70%	60%
	$550	$500	$450	$400	$350	$325	$300

RIEDL RIFLE COMPANY

SINGLE SHOT RIFLE — available in any caliber, 22-30 in. barrel, rack and pinion action, lever trigger guard activated, fully adj. trigger, select walnut stock, basically custom made.

	100%	98%	95%	90%	80%	70%	60%
	$495	$470	$440	$415	$385	$330	$305

⚞ **Stainless barrel**

	100%	98%	95%	90%	80%	70%	60%
	$560	$535	$505	$480	$450	$395	$370

RIGBY, JOHN & CO. (GUNMAKERS), LTD.

Manufacture began in Dublin, Ireland in 1735. Current manufacture is in London, England. Griffin & Howe is the U.S. agent/importer for J. Rigby (see Trademark Index).

The first London Branch of J. Rigby was opened in 1865 and the Dublin Premises were closed during 1895. The firm became a company in 1900, and has been responsible for many of the large caliber developments in both rifles and ammunition.

Rigby is one of the world's finest weapons makers. A good portion of the guns they manufacture were custom built to customer specifications. They were chambered for the large black powder express cartridges used for dangerous game in Africa and Asia. The modern Rigby guns follow this same tradition.

We will list the modern Rigby Guns with approximate values but strongly urge that if purchase or sale is contemplated, professional appraisal be utilized.

RIFLES: BOLT ACTION & SIDE BY SIDE

RIGBY MAGAZINE RIFLE — Mauser action (pre-1939), bolt action, various standard cals. including .243 Win., .270, .275 Rigby, 7mm x 57mm, .30-06, .300 H&H, .300 Win. Mag., .308, 7mm Rem. Mag., or .375 H&H, 3-5 shot mag., 20-25 in. barrel, checkered half pistol grip stock, includes non-detachable scope mounts.
New Rigby Magazine rifles range in price from $7,200-$12,000.
Add $500 for .375 H&H, .404 Rigby, or .458 Win. Mag. cal.
Add $1,920 for express sights.
Add approx. $500 for Mag. cals.
Above values are minimums for the Standard Rigby bolt action rifle. The factory quotes a price range of $5,760-$11,520 depending on alternate type of action (Brno, Dumoulin, Heym, or Mauser Magnum), the grade of wood, engraving, telescopic sight, case, or other details.

LIGHTWEIGHT MAGAZINE RIFLE — similar to Standard, with 24 in. barrel.
New Lightweight Rigby Magazine rifles range in price from $7,200-$12,000.
Add $500 for .375 H&H, .404 Rigby, or .458 Win. Mag. cal.

.416 RIGBY BIG GAME MAGAZINE RIFLE — similar to Standard Rigby rifle, except is available in .375 H&H, .404 (disc.), .416 Rigby, .416 Rem. Mag., .458 Win. Mag., or .505 cal. only, modified Brno square bridge magnum action, 4 shot mag., 21-24 in. barrel, approx. 10 lbs.
New .416 Rigby Magazine rifles start at $10,500, depending on options.
Add $680 for .505 cal.

Grading	100%	98%	95%	90%	80%	70%	60%

⅓ **.416 Rigby Deluxe Model** — same cals. as Big Game Rifle, includes extra quality wood and special engraving.
New .416 Rigby Magazine rifles start at $12,000, depending on options.

.350 MAGNUM MAGAZINE RIFLE — .350 Magnum cal.

	100%	98%	95%	90%	80%	70%	60%
	$3,995	$3,400	$2,950	$2,600	$2,300	$2,000	$1,700

Values assume out of production models.

SINGLE SHOT FALLING BLOCK — Farquharson lever actuated action, various English and European cals., 24 in. barrel, ejector, checkered pistol grip stock, deluxe finish and engraving.

	100%	98%	95%	90%	80%	70%	60%
	$4,100	$3,400	$2,800	$2,400	$2,000	$1,600	$1,250

BEST QUALITY SIDELOCK EJECTOR DOUBLE RIFLE — .22 LR, .275 Mag., .350 Mag., .416, .458 Win. Mag., .465, or .470 Nitro Express cal., 24-28 in. barrels, sidelocks, folding express rear sight, checkered pistol grip stock, deluxe finish and engraving.

Mfg.'s Sug. Retail	$57,600	$57,600	$47,500	$38,000	$29,000	$24,000	$20,000	$17,500

Add $9,600 for .577 cal.
Subtract 35% without ejectors.
Rigby sidelock double rifles can instantly be recognized by their contoured sideplates. John Rigby & Co. will also build a .600 Nitro Express — price available by quotation only.

SECOND QUALITY BOXLOCK EJECTOR DOUBLE RIFLE — .470 cal., 22-26 in. barrel, similar to Best Quality, except has boxlock action.

New 2nd Quality Double Rifles start at $18,200, depending on options.
Subtract 35% without ejectors.
Values above are for larger calibers, smaller cals. could have less value than listed.

THIRD QUALITY BOXLOCK EJECTOR DOUBLE RIFLE — similar to Second Quality, with plainer wood and less engraving.

	100%	98%	95%	90%	80%	70%	60%
	$12,750	$10,750	$9,750	$8,750	$7,350	$6,350	$5,000

Subtract 35% without ejectors.
Values above are for larger calibers, smaller cals. could have less value than listed.

SHOTGUNS: SxS

The sidelock models listed below have an approximate delivery period of 1 - 2½ years.

BEST QUALITY SIDELOCK — 12 or 20 ga. only, features DTs, elaborate fine English scroll engraving with border scroll on frame. Values below do not include value added tax (VAT) from England.

Mfg.'s Sug. Retail	$27,565	$27,565	$22,000	$18,500	$14,000	$11,000	$8,750	$7,500

Add $2,235 for self-opening system.

⅓ **Sidelock Matched Pair**

Mfg.'s Sug. Retail	$56,620	$56,620	$48,000	$40,000	$33,000	$26,000	$21,000	$15,750

Add $4,470 for self-opening system.

BOXLOCK DOUBLE BARREL SHOTGUN — all ga.'s, barrel lengths and chokes to order, checkered stock to order, auto ejectors, double triggers.

⅓ **Chatsworth Grade**

	100%	98%	95%	90%	80%	70%	60%
	$4,500	$3,500	$3,000	$2,500	$2,000	$1,600	$1,200

⅓ **Sackville Grade** — deluxe engraved.

	100%	98%	95%	90%	80%	70%	60%
	$5,900	$5,000	$4,500	$3,750	$3,100	$2,650	$2,200

Add 20% for 20 ga.
Add 40% for 28 ga.
Add 60% for .410 ga.

Grading	100%	98%	95%	90%	80%	70%	60%

⚞ **Boxlock Game Gun** — 12, 20, or 28 ga., traditional deep scroll engraving, current mfg. This is John Rigby's only current production boxlock shotgun. The factory should be contacted directly (see Trademark Index) for a price quotation on this model.

SIDELOCK DOUBLE BARREL SHOTGUN — all ga.'s, barrel lengths and chokes to specifications, double triggers, auto ejectors stocked to order.

⚞ **Sandringham Grade**

	$9,500	$7,500	$6,000	$5,000	$4,450	$3,775	$2,950

⚞ **Regal Grade** — deluxe engraved.

	$12,500	$10,000	$8,750	$7,500	$6,400	$5,250	$4,250

Add 20% for 20 ga.
Add 40% for 28 ga.
Add 60% for .410 ga.

⚞ **Sidelock Game Gun** — 12 or 20 ga., engraving similar to Best Quality SxS rifle, current mfg. New Sidelock Game Guns start at $35,500, depending on options.
Add $3,225 for self-opening system.
A matched pair of the Sidelock Game Guns starts at $73,000.

RIPAMONTI, GUY
While advertised, this trademark does not exist.

RIZZINI, BATTISTA
Manufacturer located in Marcheno, Italy since 1965. Imported exclusively in the U.S. by Lou Alessandri & Son starting 1992 located in Rehoboth, MA.

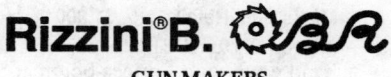

RIFLES: O/U

EXPRESS 90 — various cals., ST, ejectors, deluxe wood and features.

	Mfg.'s Sug. Retail						
	$4,464	$3,995	$3,600	$3,200	$2,750	$2,300	$1,950	$1,600

Add $430 for upgraded wood (Model Express 90 L).

EXPRESS 92 — similar to Express 90, except has sideplates with more elaborate engraving.

	Mfg.'s Sug. Retail						
	$5,342	$4,875	$4,150	$3,650	$3,200	$2,800	$2,250	$1,875

SHOTGUNS

780 FIELD SERIES O/U — 10, 12, or 16 ga., boxlock action, DTs, extractors, checkered walnut stock and forearm.

	Mfg.'s Sug. Retail						
	$1,100	$995	$875	$750	$675	$595	$525	$450

Add $550 for 10 ga.
Add $150 for ejectors (Model S780 E).
Add $200 for SST with ejectors (Model S780 EM).
Add $350 for SST, ejectors, and upgraded wood (Model S780 EML).
A Model S780 EMEL is also available that is entirely hand finished and engraved for $7,100.

⚞ **780 Competition Series** — includes Skeet, Trap, and Sporting Clays configuration.

	Mfg.'s Sug. Retail						
	$1,450	$1,295	$1,050	$925	$825	$700	$650	$595

⚞ **780 Small Gauge Series** — includes 20, 28, or 36 ga., DTs, ejectors.

	Mfg.'s Sug. Retail						
	$1,350	$1,195	$975	$875	$800	$725	$675	$625

Add $50 for SST (Model 780 EM).

Grading	100%	98%	95%	90%	80%	70%	60%

782 EM FIELD SERIES O/U — 12 or 16 ga., boxlock action with sideplates, SST ejectors, extractors, checkered walnut stock and forearm.

Mfg.'s Sug. Retail	$1,550		$1,375	$1,125	$995	$875	$750	$675	$595

Add $450 for Slug variation (Model 782 EM Slug).
Add $350 for better engraving and wood (Model 782 EML).
A Model S7820 EMEL is also available that is entirely hand finished and engraved for $12,000.

790 SERIES O/U COMPETITION — 12 or 20 ga., choice of Trap, Skeet, or Sporting Clays configuration, features black frame outlined with gold line engraving.

Mfg.'s Sug. Retail	$2,050		$1,875	$1,550	$1,300	$1,050	$925	$825	$695

Subtract $150 for 20 ga. Trap.
Subtract $50 for 20 ga. Skeet.
Add $1,050 for 20 ga. Sporting (includes sideplates and quick detachable stock).
A Model 790 Trap EL is also available that is entirely hand finished with 18 Kt. gold and hand engraving - prices begin at $5,650 in 12 ga., $5,200 in 20 ga.

790 Small Gauge Series — similar to 790 Competition Series, except in 20, 28, or 36 ga., SST and ejectors standard.

Mfg.'s Sug. Retail	$1,600		$1,425	$1,150	$995	$875	$750	$675	$595

A Model 790 EMEL is also available that is entirely hand finished with 18 Kt. gold and hand engraving - prices begin at $8,600.

792 SMALL GAUGE MAG. SERIES O/U — 20, 28, or 36 ga., Mag. chambers, SST, ejectors, includes engraved sideplates.

Mfg.'s Sug. Retail	$1,800		$1,575	$1,250	$1,050	$895	$750	$675	$595

A Model 792 EMEL is also available that is entirely hand finished with 18 Kt. gold and hand engraving - prices begin at $7,600.

MODEL 2000 O/U TRAP — 12 ga. only, includes nickel finished receiver with sideplates, gold trigger, VR barrels and rib.

Mfg.'s Sug. Retail	$2,000		$1,775	$1,375	$1,150	$950	$825	$725	$650

A Model 2000 Trap EL is also available that is entirely hand finished with 18 Kt. gold and hand engraving - prices begin at $5,290.

MODEL MC SINGLE BARREL — 12, 16, 20, 24, 28, 32, 36, or .410 ga., 27½ in. single barrel with VR, sling swivels, checkered hardwood stock.

Mfg.'s Sug. Retail	$400		$350	$275	$240	$200	$175	$160	$145

RIZZINI, F.LLI

Manufacturer located in Magno di Gardone V.T., Italy. Currently imported and distributed by W.L. Moore & Co. located in West Lake Village, CA and New England Arms, Co. located in Kittery Point, ME.

In the past, this manufacturer collaborated with Antonio Zoli to make "spec" guns that were usually imported by Abercrombie & Fitch or Von Lengerke & Detmold. These guns are normally marked on the water table "Zoli-Rizzini" or "F.lli Rizzini" (in the latter case, most of the time these guns have the Abercrombie & Fitch, etc. logo as well). These guns are not to be confused with the quality of current Rizzini F.lli mfg. Normally, these older Field Grade models (non-ejector, boxlock actions in 12, 16, 20, 28, or .410 ga.) sell in the $395-$800 range, with a 25% premium for 28 or .410 ga. Deluxe Field Models with a scalloped boxlock action and ejectors are currently valued in the $600-$1,200 range, with a 25% premium for 28 or .410 ga. The Extra Lusso Model (top-of-the-line) currently sell in the $1,200-$2,500 range, with a 25% premium for 28 or .410 ga.

Rizzini shotguns are made to individual custom order only (about 25 are made a year). Prices below do not include engraving (prices range from $8,700-$21,700) and are subject to fluctuation in exchange rates.

Grading	100%		98%	95%	90%	80%	70%	60%

SHOTGUNS

BOXLOCK EJECTOR — 12, 16, or 20 ga., select walnut, detachable bottom inspection plate, various barrel lengths.

Mfg.'s Sug. Retail	$23,000		$18,500	$14,250	$11,800	$9,700	$8,850	$7,100	$6,200

28 or .410 ga. — otherwise similar to above.

Mfg.'s Sug. Retail	$25,500		$20,500	$15,750	$12,250	$9,995	$8,950	$7,300	$6,300

SIDELOCK EJECTOR — 12, 16, or 20 ga., H&H patterned sidelocks, select Circassian walnut, various barrel lengths.

Mfg.'s Sug. Retail	$40,000		$32,500	$24,000	$18,750	$15,700	$12,500	$10,400	$9,150

28 or .410 ga. — otherwise similar to above.

Mfg.'s Sug. Retail	$46,000		$37,000	$29,500	$22,500	$16,750	$13,250	$11,200	$9,875

RIZZINI, ARMI TECNICHE OF EMILIO
Manufacturer located in Brescia, Italy.

Please refer to the Armi Tecniche of Emilio Rizzini in the A section.

ROCKY MOUNTAIN ARMS, INC.
Manufacturer located in Long Mount, CO since 1990.

Rocky Mountain Arms is a quality specialty manufacturer of rifles and pistols. All firearms are finished in Dupont Teflon-S industrial coatings. Direct sales only (see listing in Trademark Index for more information).

PISTOLS

1911A1-LH — .40 S&W or .45 ACP cal., specifically designed for left handed shooters, featuring left side ejection port and right side controls, gold cup size, stainless steel construction, hand fitted parts, integral ramp barrel, Millett adj. sights, test target. New 1991.

Mfg.'s Sug. Retail	$1,395		$1,295	$995	$750

Add $100 for Bomar sights.

22K PISTOLS — .22 LR, AR style pistols featuring 7 in. barrel, choice of matte black or NATO Green Teflon-S finish, will use Colt conversion kit, choice of carrying handle or flat-top upper receiver, 10 or 30 shot mag., includes black nylon case. New 1993.

Mfg.'s Sug. Retail	$525		$475	$425	$375	$350	$325	$295	$275

Add $50 for flat-top receiver with Weaver style bases.

PATRIOT PISTOL — .223 Rem. cal., AR style pistol featuring 7 in. barrel with integral Max Dynamic muzzle brake, 21 in. overall, flat-top receiver with Weaver style bases, accepts standard AR-15 mag.'s. New 1993.

Mfg.'s Sug. Retail	$1,095		$995	$895	$750	$650	$550	$495	$450

BAP (BOLT ACTION PISTOL) — .308 Win., 7.62 x 39mm, or 10mm Rocky Mountain Thunderer (10 x 51mm) cal., features 14 in. heavy fluted Douglas Match barrel, Kevlar/graphite pistol grip stock, supplied with Harris bi-pod and black nylon case. New 1993.

Mfg.'s Sug. Retail	$1,595		$1,425	$1,275	$1,100	$950	$825	$700	$575

Grading	100%	98%	95%	90%	80%	70%	60%

RIFLES: BOLT ACTION

PROFESSIONAL SERIES — .223 Rem., .30-06, .308 Win., or .300 Win. Mag. cal., bolt action rifle utilizing modified Mauser action, fluted 26 in. Douglas premium heavy match barrel with integral muzzle brake, custom Kevlar-Graphite stock with off-set thumb hole, test target. New 1991.

Mfg.'s Sug. Retail	$1,995	$1,850	$1,550	$1,250	$995	$850	$725	$600

Add $100 for .300 Win. Mag. cal.
Add $300 for left handed action.

POLICE MARKSMAN — .308 Win. or .300 Win. Mag. cal., similar to Professional Series, except has 40X-C stock featuring adj. cheekpiece and buttplate, target rail, Buehler micro-dial scope mounting system. New 1991.

Mfg.'s Sug. Retail	$2,395	$2,250	$1,950	$1,650	$1,325	$1,100	$900	$700

Add $100 for .300 Win. Mag. cal.
Add $400 for left handed action.
Add $400 for illuminated dot scope (4X-12X x 56mm).

NINJA SCOUT RIFLE — .22 Mag., takedown rifle based on Marlin action, black stock, 16½ in. match grade crowned barrel, forward mounted Weaver style scope base, adj. rear sight, 7 shot mag. New 1991.

Mfg.'s Sug. Retail	$595	$550	$440	$395	$350	$295	$260	$220

Add $200 for illuminated dot scope (1.5X-4X) w/ extended eye relief.

SCOUT SEMI-AUTO — .22 Mag., patterned after Marlin action. New 1993.

Mfg.'s Sug. Retail	$725	$650	$575	$495	$395	$350	$295	$260

Add $200 for illuminated dot scope (1.5X-4X) w/ extended eye relief.

M-SHORTEEN — .308 Win. cal., compact highly modified M1-A featuring 17" match crowned barrel, custom front sight, mod. gas system, hand honed action & trigger, custom muzzle brake. New 1991.

Mfg.'s Sug. Retail	$1,895	$1,725	$1,500	$1,250	$995	$850	$725	$600

Add $200 for Woodland/Desert camo.

VARMINTER — .223 Rem. cal. only, AR-15 styled rifle with 20 in. fluted heavy match barrel, flat-top receiver with Weaver style bases, round metal National Match hand guard with floating barrel, choice of NATO green or matte black Teflon-S finish, supplied with case and factory test target (sub-MOA). Mfg. began 1993.

Mfg.'s Sug. Retail	$1,295	$1,100	$995	$875	$750	$675	$595	$525

ROGAK

Please refer to the L E S Incorporated listing in this text for more information on the Rogak Pistol.

ROHM

Manufacturer located in Sontheim, Germany. Limited importation into the U.S.

DERRINGER — .22 LR, blued, copy of Remington O/U derringer. Excellently made, but half-cock safety is old design and could fail if dropped. No longer imported.

	$150	$115	$95	$85	$75	$65	$55

ROSS RIFLE COMPANY

Quebec, Canada.

CANADIAN 1907 MARK II — .303 Brit. cal., bolt action, straight pull, 28 in. barrel, pre-WWII.

	$295	$250	$200	$180	$160	$140	$120

Grading	100%	98%	95%	90%	80%	70%	60%

MODEL 1910 SPORTING RIFLE — similar action as 1907, .280 Ross or .303 Brit. cal., checkered Sporter stock, leaf sights. Mfg. 1910-1920.

	$275	$225	$200	$180	$160	$140	$120

Note: Many experts state this rifle is unsafe to fire.

ROSSI

Manufactured by Amade Rossi S.A., located in S. Leopoldo, Brazil. Currently imported by Interarms, located in Alexandria, VA.

REVOLVERS: DOUBLE ACTION

MODEL 31 — .38 Spl., 5 shot, 4 in. medium barrel, target trigger and hammer, 22 oz. Disc. 1985. Add $5 for nickel.

	$120	$105	$95	$85	$75	$70	$65

Last Mfg.'s Sug. Retail was $139.

MODEL 51 — .22 LR, 6 shot, 6 in. barrel, blue only, adj. sights. Disc. 1985.

	$125	$110	$100	$90	$85	$80	$75

Last Mfg.'s Sug. Retail was $149.

⁂ **Sportsman 511 Stainless** — .22 LR only, stainless steel, 4 in. barrel, with matted rib, adj. rear sight, 6 shot, hardwood stocks, 30 oz. Imported 1986-90 only.

	$190	$160	$125				

Last Mfg.'s Sug. Retail was $235.

MODEL 68 — .38 Spl., 5 shot, 2 or 3 in. barrel, choice of wood or rubber grips with 2 in. barrel.

Mfg.'s Sug. Retail	$227	$170	$130	$100	$90	$80	$70	$65

Add $5 for nickel (3 in. barrel only).
Add $11 for 2 in. barrel.

MODEL 69 — .32 S&W, 6 shot, 3 in. barrel, walnut grips. Disc. 1985. Add $5 for nickel.

	$120	$105	$95	$85	$75	$70	$65

Last Mfg.'s Sug. Retail was $139.

MODEL 70 — .22 cal, 6 shot, 3 in. barrel. Disc. 1985. Add $5 for nickel.

	$120	$105	$95	$85	$75	$70	$65

Last Mfg.'s Sug. Retail was $139.

MODEL 84 STAINLESS — .38 Spl., 6 shot, 3 or 4 in. solid raised rib barrel, standard service sights, checkered hardwood grips, 27½ oz. Imported 1985-86 only.

	$190	$155	$125				

Last Mfg.'s Sug. Retail was $205.

MODEL 515(M) STAINLESS — .22 LR or .22 Mag. (Model 515M) cal., double action, 6 shot, classic kit gun design, stainless steel with shrouded ejector rod, adj. rear sights, checkered custom wood grips, 4 in. barrel, 30 oz. Imported 1992 only.

	$195	$145	$110				

Last Mfg.'s Sug. Retail was $248.

MODEL 720 STAINLESS — .44 Spl. cal., 3 in. ribbed barrel, double action, 5 shot with unfluted cylinder, full ejector rod shroud, adj. rear sight, rubber combat grips, stainless, 27½ oz. Importation began 1992.

Mfg.'s Sug. Retail	$332	$250	$195	$165			

Rossi, cont.

Grading	100%	98%	95%	90%	80%	70%	60%

MODEL 851 STAINLESS — .38 Spl., 3 or 4 in. VR barrel, 6 shot, walnut grips, adj. rear sight, 27½ oz. New 1985.

Mfg.'s Sug. Retail	$280		$220	$165	$135		

This model was previously the Model 85 Stainless.

MODEL 88 STAINLESS — .38 Spl., 5 shot, stainless steel construction, 2 or 3 in. barrel, hardwood or rubber (2 in. barrel only) grips, 21 oz.

Mfg.'s Sug. Retail	$262		$195	$140	$110		

Add $13 for 2 in. barrel.

MODEL 89 STAINLESS — .32 S&W cal. only, 6 shot, 3 in. barrel. Imported 1985-86. Reintroduced 1989-90.

			$175	$135	$115		

Last Mfg.'s Sug. Retail was $215.

MODEL 94 — .38 Spl., 6 shot, 3 or 4 in. barrel, blued finish only, 27½ oz. Imported 1985-1988.

			$160	$140	$120	$110	$95	$85	$75

Last Mfg.'s Sug. Retail was $185.

MODEL 951 — .38 Spl., 6 shot, 3 or 4 in. VR barrel, blued finish only, 27½ oz. Imported 1985-90.

			$190	$155	$135	$120	$110	$100	$90

Last Mfg.'s Sug. Retail was $233.
This model was previously designated the Model 95.

MODEL 971 — .357 Mag., 4 in. solid rib barrel with internal ejector shroud, 6 shot, adj. rear sight, blue only, hardwood grips, 36 oz. Importation began 1988.

Mfg.'s Sug. Retail	$280		$215	$165	$145	$135	$125	$115	$105

Model 971 Stainless — .357 Mag., 2½ (new 1992), 4 or 6 in. solid rib barrel with full shroud, 6 shot, combat style rubber grips, adj. rear sight, 35.4 - 40.5 oz. Importation began 1989.

Mfg.'s Sug. Retail	$315		$240	$190	$160		

Add $5 for 2½ in. barrel.

Model 971 Competition — .357 Mag. cal., stainless steel, 3¼ in. compensated barrel, 32 oz. Importation began 1993.

Mfg.'s Sug. Retail	$320		$245	$190	$160		

RIFLES

MODEL 92 SRC LEVER ACTION — .38 Spl./.357 Mag, .44 Spl., .44 Mag, or .44-40 cal., copy of Win. Model 92, 16 (Model 92 SRS) or 20 in. round barrel, 5-5¾ lbs. Also available in matte blue finish at no extra charge.

Mfg.'s Sug. Retail	$350		$275	$215	$165	$125	$110	$100	$90

Add $17 for .44 Spl., .44 Mag., or .44-40 (disc.) cal.
.44 Spl., .44-40, or .44 Mag. cal. are Model 65 SRCs.

Blue Engraved — with etched engraving and special wood. Disc. 1989.

			$275	$225	$175		

Last Mfg.'s Sug. Retail was $327.

Gold or Chrome Engraved — either gold (disc. 1987) or chrome (disc.) finish with special wood.

			$280	$230	$185	$150	$130	$120	$110

Last Mfg.'s Sug. Retail was $330.

Grading	100%	98%	95%	90%	80%	70%	60%

MODEL 62 SA SLIDE ACTION — .22 LR cal., copy of Win. 1890 "gallery" model, rifle (23 in. barrel) or carbine (16½ in. barrel) available, takedown action, round or octagonal barrel, 12 or 13 shot tube mag.

Mfg.'s Sug. Retail	$227	$175	$140	$115	$95	$85	$80	$75

Add $18 for nickel finish.
Add $25 for octagonal barrel.

⚭ **Model 62 SA Carbine (C)** — similar to Model 62 SA, except has 16½ in. carbine barrel with full length mag. tube (12 shot), 4¼ lbs. Importation began 1988.

Mfg.'s Sug. Retail	$227	$175	$140	$115	$95	$85	$80	$75

Add $18 for nickel finish.

⚭ **Model 62 SA Stainless** — similar to regular model, except is stainless steel. Imported 1986 only.

			100%	98%	95%
			$165	$145	$120

Last Mfg.'s Sug. Retail was $192.

MODEL 59 — .22 Mag. version of Model 62 SA, 10 shot mag., 5.5 lbs.

Mfg.'s Sug. Retail	$280	$220	$165	$130	$120	$110	$100	$90

MODEL 65 SRC — .44 Spl./.44 Mag. cal., lever action carbine, 20 in. barrel, full tube mag. holding 10 rounds, iron sights, 5¾ lbs. Importation began 1989.

Mfg.'s Sug. Retail	$367	$280	$200	$170	$150	$135	$125	$115

SHOTGUNS

OVERLUND SxS — 12, 20, or .410 ga., exposed hammers, 20 (Coach Model), 26, or 28 in. barrels, double triggers. Importation disc. 1988.

			$275	$230	$185	$155	$140	$125	$115

Add $5 for .410 ga.
Last Mfg.'s Sug. Retail was $332.

SQUIRE SxS — 12, 20, or .410 ga., hammerless, 20, 26 or 28 in. barrels, double triggers, raised matted rib, beavertail forearm, pistol grip, hardwood stock, 3 in. chambers. Imported 1985-90.

			$300	$245	$195	$160	$150	$140	$130

Add $10 for .410 ga.
Last Mfg.'s Sug. Retail was $350.

ROTTWEIL

Manufacturer located in Rottweil, Germany. Currently imported by Dynamit Nobel of America located in Northvale, NJ.

SHOTGUNS

PARAGON — 12 ga. only, new design featuring boxlock action, 11 different stock configurations, detachable and interchangeable trigger action, trigger and sear safety, ejectors (switchable to extractors), various barrel lengths and rib combinations, cased. Importation began 1993.

Mfg.'s Sug. Retail	$6,995	$6,500	$5,750	$4,850	$3,950	$3,000	$2,500	$2,250

MODEL 650 FIELD O/U — 12 ga. only, 28 in. barrels with VR, ejectors, single trigger, select checkered walnut, multi-choked with 6 choke tubes, lightly engraved, coin finished receiver. Importation disc. 1986.

			$750	$650	$595	$550	$500	$460	$435

Last Mfg.'s Sug. Retail was $850.

Grading	100%	98%	95%	90%	80%	70%	60%

MODEL 72 FIELD O/U — 12 ga. only, 28 in. vent. barrels and rib, sand blasted receiver, select walnut with checkered stock and forearm, single trigger, ejectors. Importation disc. 1987.

	$1,850	$1,650	$1,450	$1,200	$1,000	$850	$700

Last Mfg.'s Sug. Retail was $2,295.

MODEL 72 AMERICAN SKEET O/U — 12 ga. only, 26¾ in. barrels, VR, ejectors, select French walnut, marginal engraving on sand blasted receiver, single trigger, 7½ lbs. Importation disc. 1987.

	$1,850	$1,650	$1,450	$1,200	$1,000	$850	$700

Last Mfg.'s Sug. Retail was $2,295.
This model was distributed exclusively by Paxton Arms, located in Dallas, TX.

MODEL 72 AAT SINGLE BARREL TRAP — 12 ga. only, adj. American trap (AAT), barrel features adj. point of impact, 34 in. barrel bored full, high VR. Importation disc. 1986.

	$1,400	$1,200	$1,000	$850	$700	$650	$600

Last Mfg.'s Sug. Retail was $2,295.

MODEL 72 AT O/U — 12 ga. only, 32 in. IM & F barrels, VR and barrels, sand blasted receiver, checkered select walnut stock and forearm, non-adj. point of impact, single trigger ejectors. Importation disc. 1987.

	$1,850	$1,650	$1,450	$1,200	$1,000	$850	$700

Last Mfg.'s Sug. Retail was $2,295.

MODEL 72 AAT COMBINATION — 12 ga. only, comes with 2 single barrels (32 and 34 in.) that have adj. impacts. Importation disc. 1986.

	$2,450	$2,100	$1,850	$1,600	$1,450	$1,250	$995

Last Mfg.'s Sug. Retail was $2,850.

72 AAT Combination — supplied with 1 single adj. barrel and 32 in. O/U barrels.

	$2,450	$2,100	$1,850	$1,600	$1,450	$1,250	$995

Last Mfg.'s Sug. Retail was $2,850.

MODEL 72 AAT 3-BARREL SET — 12 ga. only, supplied with 2 single barrels (32 and 34 in.) with adj. impact and 1 set of 32 in. O/U barrels bored IM & F. Importation disc. 1986.

	$2,850	$2,600	$2,300	$2,000	$1,800	$1,600	$1,400

Last Mfg.'s Sug. Retail was $3,250.

MODEL 72 INTERNATIONAL TRAP — 12 ga. only, O/U 30 in. barrels bored IM & F with extra high rib. Importation disc. 1987.

	$1,850	$1,650	$1,450	$1,200	$1,000	$850	$700

Last Mfg.'s Sug. Retail was $2,295.

MODEL 72 INTERNATIONAL SKEET — 12 ga. only, 26¾ in. barrels, VR, select walnut stock and forearm. Importation disc. 1987.

	$1,850	$1,650	$1,450	$1,200	$1,000	$850	$700

Last Mfg.'s Sug. Retail was $2,295.

ROYAL AMERICAN SHOTGUNS
Previously imported by Royal Arms International, located in Woodland Hills, CA.

SHOTGUNS

Grading	100%	98%	95%	90%	80%	70%	60%

MODEL 100 O/U — 12 or 20 ga., 2¾ in. chambers, double triggers, extractors, vent. rib and barrels. Imported 1985-87 only.

	100%	98%	95%	90%	80%	70%	60%
	$325	$265	$240	$220	$200	$180	$170

Add $40 for above model with 3 in. chambers, single trigger, and auto ejectors.
Last Mfg.'s Sug. Retail was $390.

MODEL 600 BOXLOCK SxS — 12, 20, 28, or .410 ga., sideplates, silver finished receiver, 3 in. chambers, single trigger, auto ejectors. Imported 1985-87 only.

	100%	98%	95%	90%	80%	70%	60%
	$365	$295	$265	$235	$210	$195	$180

Deduct 25% for double triggers and 2¾ in. chambers.
Last Mfg.'s Sug. Retail was $420.

MODEL 800 SIDELOCK SxS — 12, 20, 28, or .410 ga., sidelocks with sideplates, silver finished receiver, 3 in. chambers, single trigger, checkered straight grip stock with select walnut, auto ejectors. Imported 1985-87 only.

	100%	98%	95%	90%	80%	70%	60%
	$775	$650	$595	$550	$500	$460	$435

Last Mfg.'s Sug. Retail was $899.

RUBY
Manufacturer located in Eibar, Spain.

MILITARY TYPE — trade name for Spanish auto pistol fashioned after Colt's M1903, cal. 7.65mm, mag. release at bottom of grip, fixed sights. No longer mfg.

	100%	98%	95%	90%	80%	70%	60%
	$200	$150	$100	$75	$70	$65	$60

RUGER
See Sturm, Ruger, & Co. section in this text.

RUKO PRODUCTS, INC.
Importer located in Buffalo, NY since 1990. Ruko Products, Inc. firearms are manufactured by the Arms Corporation of the Philippines. Dealer direct sales.

Arms Corp. of the Philippines firearms imported before 1991 may be located under that listing in this text. In 1991, Ruko Products, Inc. became the exclusive domestic importer for arms manufactured by Arms Corp. of the Philippines. These firearms are marked "Ruko-Armscor" on the barrels.

RIFLES

MODEL M14P — .22 LR, bolt action, 10 shot mag., 23 in. barrel, open sights, 6 lbs.

	Mfg.'s Sug. Retail	100%	98%	95%	90%	80%	70%	60%
	$119	$95	$75	$60	$50	$45	$40	$35

MODEL M14D — .22 LR, bolt action, similar to Model 14P, except has adj. rear sight and rear checkered mahogany stock.

	Mfg.'s Sug. Retail	100%	98%	95%	90%	80%	70%	60%
	$129	$100	$85	$70	$60	$50	$45	$40

Grading	100%	98%	95%	90%	80%	70%	60%

MODEL M1400LW — .22 LR, similar action to Model 14P, except has checkered stock and Schnabel forend, 10 shot mag., hard rubber pad, 6 lbs. Imported 1990-92.

	$185	$165	$150	$135	$120	$105	$95

Last Mfg.'s Sug. Retail was $219.

MODEL M1400SC (SUPER CLASSIC) — .22 LR, otherwise similar to Model M1500SC, except has 10 shot mag. and 23 in. barrel, 6 lbs. Imported 1990-92.

	$245	$215	$190	$175	$155	$135	$120

Last Mfg.'s Sug. Retail was $289.

MODEL M1500 — .22 Mag., deluxe bolt action, 5 shot mag., $21\frac{1}{2}$ in. barrel, checkered mahogany stock, open sights, $6\frac{1}{2}$ lbs.

Mfg.'s Sug. Retail	$189	$150	$115	$95	$75	$65	$55	$50

Model 1500LW (Lightweight) — similar to Model M1500, except has lightweight classic European styled stock made of checkered American Walnut, with butt pad. Imported 1990-92.

	$190	$170	$150	$135	$120	$105	$95

Last Mfg.'s Sug. Retail was $229.

Model 1500SC (Super Classic) — checkered American Walnut stock with hard rubber pad and Monte Carlo cheek piece, hardwood forend tip, engine turned bolt, $6\frac{1}{2}$ lbs. New 1990.

	$240	$195	$160	$130	$110	$95	$85

Last Mfg.'s Sug. Retail was $299.

MODEL M1600 — .22 LR, semi-auto, 15 shot mag., 18 in. barrel, copy of the Armalite M16, ebony stock, $5\frac{1}{4}$ lbs.

Mfg.'s Sug. Retail	$189	$150	$115	$95	$75	$65	$55	$50

M1600R — similar to M1600, except has stainless steel retractable butt stock and vent. barrel hood, $7\frac{1}{4}$ lbs.

Mfg.'s Sug. Retail	$189	$150	$115	$95	$75	$65	$55	$50

MODEL M20P — .22 LR, semi-auto, 15 shot mag., $20\frac{3}{4}$ in. barrel, open sights, $5\frac{1}{2}$ lbs.

Mfg.'s Sug. Retail	$119	$95	$75	$60	$50	$45	$40	$35

MODEL M20C — similar to Model M20P, except has carbine style stock, barrel band, and curved steel buttplate, $16\frac{1}{2}$ in. barrel, $5\frac{1}{4}$ lbs.

Mfg.'s Sug. Retail	$149	$115	$95	$80	$65	$50	$45	$40

MODEL M2000 — same specifications as Model M20P, except has checkered mahogany stock and adj. rear sight.

Mfg.'s Sug. Retail	$129	$105	$90	$75	$60	$55	$50	$45

Model M2000SC (Super Classic) — similar to Model M2000, except has checkered American Walnut stock with cheek piece and hardwood forend tip, engine turned bolt, 6 lbs. Imported 1990-92.

	$235	$205	$185	$170	$150	$135	$120

Last Mfg.'s Sug. Retail was $279.

MODEL M-50 S — .22 LR, semi-auto design, $16\frac{1}{2}$ in. shrouded barrel, 25 or 30 shot mag., uncheckered mahogany stock, $6\frac{1}{2}$ lbs.

Mfg.'s Sug. Retail	$199	$150	$115	$95	$75	$65	$50	$45

Ruko Products, Inc., cont.

Grading	100%	98%	95%	90%	80%	70%	60%

MODEL AK22 S — .22 LR, semi-auto, copy of the famous Russian Kalashnikov AK-47 rifle, 18½ in. barrel, 15 shot mag., mahogany stock and forearm, 7 lbs.

Mfg.'s Sug. Retail	$259	$195	$160	$135	$110	$90	$75	$65

Model AK22 F — similar to Model AK22, except has metal folding stock, and 30 shot mag.

Mfg.'s Sug. Retail	$289	$230	$185	$160	$130	$100	$90	$80

SHOTGUNS

Ruko also imports a Model 700 boxlock SxS and Model 900 sidelock SxS shotgun. More information can be obtained by contacting the importer directly (see Trademark Index).

MODEL M30 D/IC (INTERCHANGEABLE CHOKES) — 12 ga. only, 28 in. plain barrel with 3 choke tubes, 5 shot mag., uncheckered stock and forearm. Importation disc.

		$195	$170	$145	$120	$100	$90	$80

Last Mfg.'s Sug. Retail was $239.

Model M30 D/IC (Deluxe) — similar to Model M30 IC, except has checkered walnut stock. Importation disc.

		$235	$195	$160	$130	$110	$95	$85

Last Mfg.'s Sug. Retail was $289.

MODEL M30 DG (DEER GUN) — 12 ga. only, law enforcement version of Model M30, 20 in. plain barrel, iron sights, 7 shot mag., about 7 lbs.

Mfg.'s Sug. Retail	$259	$195	$160	$135	$110	$90	$75	$65

MODEL M30 R (RIOT) — 12 ga. only, similar to Model M30DG, except has front bead sight only, 8 shot mag.

Mfg.'s Sug. Retail	$259	$195	$160	$135	$110	$90	$75	$65

MODEL M30 C (COMBO) — 12 ga., 20 in. barrel, 5 shot mag., unique detachable black synthetic butt stock that separates allowing pistol grip only operation.

Mfg.'s Sug. Retail	$269	$200	$170	$145	$120	$100	$90	$80

MODEL M30 RP (COMBO) — 12 ga. only, same action as M30 DG, interchangeable black pistol grip, 18¼ in. plain barrel w/front bead sight, 6¼ lbs.

Mfg.'s Sug. Retail	$269	$200	$170	$145	$120	$100	$90	$80

RUSSIAN SERVICE PISTOL AND RIFLE
Tula Arsenal.

MODEL TT30 & TT33 TOKAREV AUTOMATIC — design borrowed from Colt 1911 Petter-type unitized trigger/hammer assembly, 7.62mm Russian, 8 shot, 4½ in. barrel, blue. Mfg. 1930-1954. Add 20% for TT30 model.

		$325	$290	$250	$225	$165	$145	$110
M.244ADL		$295	$250	$200	$150	$120	$95	$80

Values listed above assume original condition - no recent imports.

NAGANT REVOLVER — 7 shot, cylinder comes forward to seal barrel. Add 10% for pre-communist Imperial marked.

		$260	$225	$185	$165	$135	$115	$100

MAKAROV MD — 9mm, clip fed double action, post-war manufacture.

		$1,075	$950	$850	$800	$750	$700	$650

Grading	100%	98%	95%	90%	80%	70%	60%

TOKAREV M38 & M40 RIFLE — semi-auto Russian issue bolt action. Add 20% for M38, 100% for scoped sniper.

	100%	98%	95%	90%	80%	70%	60%
	$365	$310	$270	$250	$230	$210	$195

S section

S.A.C.M.
Cholet, France.

Grading	100%	98%	95%	90%	80%	70%	60%

FRENCH MODEL 1935A — semi-auto, 7.65mm long, 8 shot, 4.3 in. barrel, blue, fixed sights, checkered stocks, used by French troops in WWII and Indo-China 1945-1954. Mfg. 1935-1945.

	$250	$220	$205	$180	$165	$150	$140

Add 50% for Nazi WWII mfg. (Waffenamt proofed).

SAE
Spain America Enterprises Inc. (SAE) Previous importer of Felix Sarasqueta Shotguns from Spain. SAE was located in Miami, FL.

SHOTGUNS: O/U

MODEL 70 — 12 or 20 ga., 3 in. chambers, boxlock action, single trigger, ejectors, 26 in. VR barrel, European checkered walnut stock and forearm, standard finish is blue, Model 70 multi-choke has silver finished action with Florentine engraving and low gloss stock finish. Imported 1988 only.

	$400	$275	$260	$245	$230	$215	$195

Add $120 for multi-chokes (27 in. barrel).
Last Mfg.'s Sug. Retail was $598.

MODEL 66C — 12 ga. only, 26 in. Skeet or 30 in. F&M VR barrels, boxlock with engraved sideplates including 24Kt. inlays, Monte Carlo deluxe stock and beavertail forearm. Imported 1988 only.

	$950	$725	$650	$575	$495	$450	$395

Last Mfg.'s Sug. Retail was $1,544.

SHOTGUNS: SxS

MODEL 210S — 12, 20, or .410 ga., 3 in. chambers, boxlock action, double triggers, extractors, silver finished receiver with light engraving, approx. 7 lbs. Imported 1988 only.

	$420	$280	$260	$245	$230	$215	$195

Last Mfg.'s Sug. Retail was $638.

MODEL 340X — 12 or 20 ga., sidelock action, 26 in. barrels with 2¾ in. chambers, H&H boxlock action, case hardened finish with moderate scroll engraving, straight grip select walnut stock and forearm with high gloss finish. Imported 1988 only.

	$700	$550	$495	$460	$430	$395	$375

Last Mfg.'s Sug. Retail was $1,170.

MODEL 209E — 12, 20, or .410 ga., H&H type sidelock action, 26 or 28 in. barrels with 2¾ in. chambers, hand engraved coin finished receiver, select checkered walnut stock and forearm, double triggers. Imported 1988 only.

	$925	$700	$650	$575	$495	$450	$395

Last Mfg.'s Sug. Retail was $1,490.

S K B ARMS COMPANY

Manufacturer located in Tokyo, Japan by the new S K B Arms Company. Currently imported and distributed by G.U. Inc. located in Omaha, NE. SKB has been manufacturing firearms since 1855. Distributor and dealer sales.

Formerly imported by Ithaca. In 1987, importation resumed on most SKB models. While the model numbers have changed, quality is similar to those models imported previously by Ithaca. In most cases, the newer models are derived closely from their previous counterparts. Listings below will differentiate older disc. models from currently imported models.

SHOTGUNS: O/U AND SINGLE SHOT

Grading	100%	98%	95%	90%	80%	70%	60%

MODEL 500 — 12, 20, 28, or .410 ga., field grade, VR, selective ejector, 26 in. imp. cyl. and mod., 28 in. full and mod., and 30 in. full and mod., checkered stock. Mfg. in Japan by SKB 1966-1979.

	100%	98%	95%	90%	80%	70%	60%
	$525	$440	$395	$365	$330	$300	$275

Add 15% for 20 ga.
Add 25% for 28 or .410 ga.

Model 500 Magnum — 12 ga., 3 in. Mag., field grade, similar to 500, except 3 in. Mag. chambers.

	100%	98%	95%	90%	80%	70%	60%
	$625	$455	$410	$385	$355	$320	$290

MODEL 505 DELUXE FIELD O/U — 12, 20, or 28 ga., silver nitride engraved receiver, 3 in. chambers, 26 or 28 in. barrels (supplied with choke tubes), single selective trigger, ejectors, checkered walnut stock with recoil pad and forearm. Importation disc. 1992.

	100%	98%	95%	90%	80%	70%	60%
	$875	$750	$675	$575	$500	$460	$420

Add $500 for combo package.
The combo package includes either 12/20 ga. barrels with inter-chokes or 28/.410 ga. barrels.
Last Mfg.'s Sug. Retail was $995.

Model 505 Trap — 12 ga., 30 or 32 in. choke tube barrels with or without Monte Carlo stock, high rib.

	100%	98%	95%	90%	80%	70%	60%
	$875	$725	$650	$525	$475	$430	$395

Add $400 for O/U Trap Combo.
The above Combo includes one set of O/U Trap barrels and a top single Trap barrel.
Last Mfg.'s Sug. Retail was $995.

Model 505 Trap Single Barrel — 12 ga., 32 or 34 in. barrel with multi-chokes, regular or Monte Carlo stock.

	100%	98%	95%	90%	80%	70%	60%
	$875	$725	$650	$525	$475	$430	$395

Last Mfg.'s Sug. Retail was $995.

Model 505 Skeet — 12, 20, 28, or .410 ga., 28 in. barrels with multi-chokes.

	100%	98%	95%	90%	80%	70%	60%
	$875	$725	$650	$525	$475	$430	$395

Last Mfg.'s Sug. Retail was $995.

Model 505 3-Ga. Skeet Set — includes 20, 28, and .410 ga. extra Skeet barrels, aluminum case.

	100%	98%	95%	90%	80%	70%	60%
	$1,925	$1,575	$1,350	$1,200	$1,125	$950	$875

Last Mfg.'s Sug. Retail was $2,195.

Model 505 Sporting Clay — 28 or 30 in. multi-choke barrels, dimensioned for Sporting Clay competition.

	100%	98%	95%	90%	80%	70%	60%
	$885	$725	$650	$525	$475	$430	$395

Last Mfg.'s Sug. Retail was $1,045.

Grading	100%	98%	95%	90%	80%	70%	60%

MODEL 585 DELUXE FIELD O/U — 12, 20, or 28 ga., silver nitride engraved receiver, 3 in. chambers, 26 or 28 in. barrels (supplied with choke tubes), similar to 505 Series, except has .735 diameter bore on 12 ga. models and includes lengthened forcing cones with extended length "Competition Series" Inter-Choke System designed to improve shot patterns and reduce recoil, single selective trigger, ejectors, checkered walnut stock with recoil pad and forearm, 6 lbs. 10 oz. - 7 lbs. 11 oz. Importation began 1992.

	Mfg.'s Sug. Retail	$995	$875	$750	$675	$575	$500	$460	$420

The combo package includes either 12/20 ga. barrels with inter-chokes or 28/.410 ga. barrels.
Add $500 for combo package (Field Set).

Model 585 Trap — 12 ga., 30 or 32 in. choke tube barrels with or without Monte Carlo stock, high rib.

	Mfg.'s Sug. Retail	$1,095	$950	$775	$675	$525	$475	$430	$395

Add $500 for O/U Trap Combo.
The above Combo includes one set of O/U Trap barrels and a top single Trap barrel.

Model 585 Skeet — 12, 20, 28, or .410 ga., 28 in. barrels with multi-chokes.

	Mfg.'s Sug. Retail	$1,095	$950	$775	$675	$525	$475	$430	$395

Model 585 3-Ga. Skeet Set — includes 20, 28, and .410 ga. extra Skeet barrels, aluminum case.

	Mfg.'s Sug. Retail	$2,495	$2,195	$1,925	$1,725	$1,575	$1,475	$1,375	$1,275

Model 585 Sporting Clay — 28 or 30 in. multi-choke barrels, dimensioned for Sporting Clay competition.

	Mfg.'s Sug. Retail	$1,095	$950	$775	$675	$525	$475	$430	$395

MODEL 600 FIELD GRADE — similar to 500, except silver plated frame and select wood.

	$700	$495	$465	$440	$375	$345	$325

Add 20% for 20 ga.
An unknown quantity of Model 600s was mfg. with blued receivers - a small premium may be asked.

MODEL 600 MAGNUM — similar to 600 Field, except chambered for 3 in. Mag., 12 ga. Mfg. 1969-1972 by SKB.

	$720	$510	$480	$455	$415	$390	$355

MODEL 600 TRAP GRADE — similar to 600, except 12 ga. only, trap stock, recoil pad, select wood.

	$675	$555	$520	$485	$445	$410	$385

MODEL 600 DOUBLES GUN — similar to 600 Trap, except choked for 21 yd. and 30 yd. targets. Mfg. 1973-1975.

	$675	$555	$520	$485	$445	$410	$385

MODEL 600 SKEET GRADE — 12, 20, 28, or .410 ga., 26 or 28 in. barrels, bored S&S, otherwise similar to 600 Trap.

	$700	$540	$510	$475	$430	$400	$370

28 or .410 ga.

	$850	$740	$620	$560	$485	$440	$420

MODEL 600 SKEET GRADE COMBO SET — similar to 600 Skeet, except fitted with matched set of 20, 28, and .410 ga. barrels, in fitted case.

	$2,000	$1,430	$1,265	$1,155	$935	$770	$660

Grading	100%	98%	95%	90%	80%	70%	60%

MODEL 605 FIELD O/U — similar to Model 505 except has silver finished engraved receiver with better walnut. Importation disc. 1992.

	$1,075	$850	$750	$675	$575	$500	$450

Add $500 for extra set of barrels (Combo).
Last Mfg.'s Sug. Retail was $1,195.

✁ **Model 605 Trap** — 12 ga., 30 or 32 in. choke tube barrel with or without Monte Carlo stock, high rib.

	$1,075	$850	$750	$675	$575	$500	$450

Add $400 for O/U Trap Combo.
The above Combo includes one set of O/U Trap barrels and a top single Trap barrel.
Last Mfg.'s Sug. Retail was $1,195.

✁ **Model 605 Trap Single Barrel** — 12 ga., 32 or 34 in. barrel with multi-chokes.

	$1,075	$850	$750	$675	$575	$500	$450

Last Mfg.'s Sug. Retail was $1,195.

✁ **Model 605 Skeet** — 12, 20, 28, or .410 ga., 28 in. barrels with multi-chokes.

	$1,100	$850	$750	$675	$575	$500	$450

Last Mfg.'s Sug. Retail was $1,195.

✁ **Model 605 3-Ga. Skeet Set** — includes 20, 28, and .410 ga. extra Skeet barrels, aluminum case.

	$2,175	$1,650	$1,400	$1,250	$1,125	$950	$875

Last Mfg.'s Sug. Retail was $2,395.

✁ **Model 605 Sporting Clay** — 28 or 30 in. multi-choke barrels, dimensioned for Sporting Clay competition.

	$1,110	$850	$750	$675	$575	$500	$450

Last Mfg.'s Sug. Retail was $1,245.

✁ **Model 605 DU Sponsor Gun** — mfg. for DU chapters - dinner auction gun, 850 mfg. in 12 ga. (1990) and 850 mfg. in 20 ga. (1991). Features gold inlays and presentation case.
DU sponsor gun values are usually hard to ascertain in the secondary marketplace. Currently, prices seem to range between $1,200-$1,700.

MODEL 685 FIELD O/U — similar to Model 585, except has silver finished engraved receiver with gold inlays and better walnut, engine turned interior metal parts.

Mfg.'s Sug. Retail	$1,295	$1,150	$895	$775	$675	$575	$500	$450

Add $600 for extra set of barrels (Combo - Field Set).

✁ **Model 685 Trap** — 12 ga., 30 or 32 in. choke tube barrel with or without Monte Carlo stock, high rib.

Mfg.'s Sug. Retail	$1,395	$1,225	$925	$800	$700	$600	$525	$450

Add $600 for O/U Trap Combo.
The above Combo includes one set of O/U Trap barrels and a top single Trap barrel.

✁ **Model 685 Skeet** — 12, 20, 28, or .410 ga., 28 in. barrels with multi-chokes.

Mfg.'s Sug. Retail	$1,395	$1,225	$925	$800	$700	$600	$525	$450

✁ **Model 685 3-Ga. Skeet Set** — includes 20, 28, and .410 ga. extra Skeet barrels, aluminum case.

Mfg.'s Sug. Retail	$2,895	$2,525	$2,175	$1,875	$1,675	$1,450	$1,275	$1,125

✁ **Model 685 Sporting Clay** — 28 or 30 in. multi-choke barrels, dimensioned for Sporting Clay competition.

Mfg.'s Sug. Retail	$1,395	$1,225	$925	$800	$700	$600	$525	$450

Grading	100%	98%	95%	90%	80%	70%	60%

Model 685 DU Sponsor Gun — mfg. for DU chapters - dinner auction gun, 850 mfg. in 12 ga. (1990) and 850 mfg. in 20 ga. (1991). Features gold inlays and presentation case.
DU sponsor gun values are usually hard to ascertain in the secondary marketplace. Currently, prices seem to range between $1,200-$1,700.

MODEL 680 ENGLISH — similar to 600 Field, except English style stock, select walnut and fine scroll engraving. Mfg. 1973-1976.

		100%	98%	95%	90%	80%	70%	60%
		$725	$640	$600	$555	$520	$495	$445

Add 20% for 20 ga.

MODEL 700 TRAP GRADE — 12 ga., similar to 600 Trap, except more engraving, better grade wood, wide rib. Mfg. 1969-1975.

	$820	$770	$740	$685	$630	$595	$565

MODEL 700 DOUBLES GUN — 12 ga., similar to 700 Trap, except choked for 21 yd. and 30 yd. targets. Mfg. 1973-1975.

	$795	$770	$740	$685	$630	$595	$565

MODEL 700 SKEET GRADE — 12 ga., similar to 700 Doubles, only bored S&S, available in 12 or 20 ga.

	$840	$770	$740	$685	$620	$585	$555

MODEL 800 TRAP GRADE — 12 ga., similar to 700 Trap, except more engraving, better grade wood, wide rib. Mfg. 1969-1975.

	$1,150	$875	$775	$675	$575	$500	$425

MODEL 800 SKEET GRADE — 12 or 20 ga., skeet chokes. Mfg. 1969-1975.

	$1,200	$1,000	$895	$795	$680	$595	$565

MODEL 880 CROWN GRADE — 12, 20, 28, or .410 ga., coin finish receiver, extensively engraved with sideplates, SST, ejectors, select walnut with fleur-de-lis scroll style checkering, double cross bolt action. Disc. 1980.

	$1,650	$1,300	$1,150	$975	$890	$835	$750

Add 25% for 28 or .410 ga.

MODEL 885 O/U — available in either Field, Skeet, or Trap configuration, coin finished receiver featuring fine scroll engraving with game scenes, boxlock action with sideplates, beginning 1992, the Model 885 Series in 12 ga. features lengthened forcing cones, .735 bore, and a competition series of extended length multi-chokes. Importation started 1988.

Model 885 Field — 12, 20, 28, or .410 ga., field dimensions, barrels include choke tubes. Importation started 1989.

		100%	98%	95%	90%	80%	70%	60%
Mfg.'s Sug. Retail	$1,695	$1,450	$1,125	$950	$825	$725	$650	$595

Add $700 for combo package (Field Set).
The combo package includes either 12/20 ga. barrels with inter-chokes or 28/.410 ga. barrels.

Model 885 Trap — 12 ga., 30 or 32 in. barrels with multi-chokes.

		100%	98%	95%	90%	80%	70%	60%
Mfg.'s Sug. Retail	$1,795	$1,550	$1,175	$975	$850	$750	$650	$595

Add $700 for O/U Trap Combo.
The above Combo includes one set of O/U Trap barrels and a top single Trap barrel.

Model 885 Skeet — 12, 20, 28, or .410 ga., 28 in. barrels with multi-chokes.

		100%	98%	95%	90%	80%	70%	60%
Mfg.'s Sug. Retail	$1,795	$1,550	$1,175	$975	$850	$750	$650	$595

Model 885 3-Ga. Skeet Set — includes 20, 28, and .410 ga. extra Skeet barrels, aluminum case.

		100%	98%	95%	90%	80%	70%	60%
Mfg.'s Sug. Retail	$3,295	$2,995	$2,600	$2,250	$1,975	$1,725	$1,500	$1,400

Grading	100%	98%	95%	90%	80%	70%	60%

Model 885 Sporting Clay — 28 and 30 in. multi-choke barrels, dimensioned for Sporting Clay competition.

Mfg.'s Sug. Retail	$1,795	$1,550	$1,175	$975	$850	$750	$650	$595

MODEL 5600 — 12 ga. only, available as Trap or Skeet model only, vent. rib (Trap only) and barrels (Skeet only), no engraving, select walnut. Disc. 1980.

	$575	$495	$450	$420	$390	$360	$330

Model 5700 — available as Trap or Skeet model only, light engraving, select walnut, VR. Disc. 1980.

	$750	$625	$540	$495	$460	$430	$400

Model 5800 — available as Trap or Skeet model only, more deluxe engraving, select walnut. Disc. 1980.

	$950	$800	$695	$595	$500	$450	$425

SHOTGUNS: SIDE-BY-SIDE

Models 100, 150, 200, 280, 300, 400, 480 — 12 and 20 ga. only, 25-30 in. barrels, all boxlock actions, more expensive models differ in the amount of engraving, grade of walnut, and style of checkering, beavertail forend, 6¼ - 7 lbs. Disc. 1980.

MODEL 100 — 12 or 20 ga., Mag. model also, SST, AE, blue only.

	$485	$425	$380	$340	$310	$275	$250

MODEL 150 — similar to 100, except scroll engraving, beavertail forearm. Mfg. 1972-1974 by SKB.

	$520	$435	$385	$345	$310	$275	$250

MODEL 200 — 12 or 20 ga., Mag. model also, SST, AE, boxlock, scalloped frame, lightly engraved coin finish receiver.

	$550	$475	$410	$375	$340	$310	$280

MODEL 200 (NEW MFG.) — similar to original Model 200, SST, ejectors, recoil pad. Imported 1987-1988 only.

	$725	$525	$425	$420	$375	$345	$325

Last Mfg.'s Sug. Retail was $895.

Model 200E (English) — similar to New Model 200, except has straight grip stock. Importation disc. 1988.

	$725	$525	$425	$420	$375	$345	$325

Last Mfg.'s Sug. Retail was $895.

MODEL 280 ENGLISH — 12 or 20 ga., Mag. model also, SST, AE, lightly engraved blue receiver, straight grip.

	$850	$775	$625	$525	$440	$410	$375

MODEL 300 — 12 or 20 ga., Mag. model also, SST, AE, lightly engraved coin finish receiver.

	$750	$650	$575	$485	$440	$410	$375

MODEL 385 — 12 or 28 ga., boxlock action with silver nitride receiver, engraved scroll and game scene designs, SST, ejectors, automatic safety, semi-fancy American walnut and pistol grip stock, limited quantities mfg. Importation began 1992.

Mfg.'s Sug. Retail	$1,395	$1,225	$925	$800	$700	$600	$525	$450

Grading	100%	98%	95%	90%	80%	70%	60%

Model 385 DU — features gold inlaid mallards on both receiver sides and gold inlaid DU duck head on receiver bottom, includes hard shell case, and signed letter from SKB president, DU proofmarks, limited mfg. - 200 sets in 1992.

Mfg.'s Sug. Retail	$5,000	$4,500	$3,650	$2,800			

MODEL 400 — 12 or 20 ga., Mag. model also, boxlock, SST, AE, moderately engraved coin finish receiver with sideplates.

		$695	$600	$510	$460	$430	$410	$385

MODEL 400 (NEW MFG.) — similar to original Model 400, SST, ejectors, recoil pad. Imported 1987-1988 only.

		$975	$850	$780	$690	$595	$525	$475

Last Mfg.'s Sug. Retail was $1,195.

Model 400E (English) — similar to New Model 400, except has engraved sideplates and straight grip stock. Importation disc. 1989.

		$975	$850	$780	$690	$595	$525	$475

Last Mfg.'s Sug. Retail was $1,195.

MODEL 480 ENGLISH — 12 or 20 ga., Mag. model also, SST, AE, moderately engraved coin finish receiver, straight grip.

	$1,250	$1,000	$825	$725	$625	$525	$475

SHOTGUNS: SEMI-AUTO

MODEL 300 STANDARD — 12 or 20 ga., 3 in. chamber, 26 in. imp. cyl., 28 in. mod. or full, 30 in. full, recoil operated, autoloading, checkered pistol grip stock. Mfg. 1968-1972.

		$295	$255	$205	$165	$155	$145	$140
Vent. rib model		$320	$275	$220	$195	$165	$155	$150

MODEL 1300 UPLAND — 12 or 20 ga., 3 in. chamber, 22, 26, or 28 in. VR barrel with multi-chokes, matte black receiver, checkered walnut stock and forearm. Importation resumed 1988.

Mfg.'s Sug. Retail	$495	$450	$385	$340	$300	$270	$240	$210

This model was previously designated the Model 300. The new Model 1300 is also available in Slug configuration with 22 in. barrel/iron sights at no extra charge. New Model 1300s have a magazine cutoff system on front left side of frame.

XL 900 MR — 12 ga. only, gas operated semi-auto, 26-30 in. barrels, 5 shot, alloy receiver, etched game bird scroll work on receiver, shoots both 2¾ and 3 in. shells by interchanging barrels. Disc. 1980.

		$325	$280	$260	$240	$225	$190	$175

XL 900 — similar to XL 900, only in 20 ga. and no recoil pad, 6¼ lbs.

		$360	$315	$275	$250	$230	$190	$175

XL 900 TRAP GRADE — similar to XL 900, 12 ga. only, scroll engraved black chrome receiver, 30 in. imp. mod. or full, trap style stock, straight or Monte Carlo, recoil pad. Mfg. 1972-present.

		$395	$350	$320	$305	$275	$265	$260

XL 900 SKEET GRADE — similar to XL 900, except scroll engraved black chrome receiver, 26 in. barrel, skeet stock. Mfg. 1972-disc.

		$400	$350	$320	$305	$275	$265	$260

Grading	100%	98%	95%	90%	80%	70%	60%

XL 900 SLUG GUN — similar to XL 900, except 24 in. slug barrel, rifle sights, no rib. Mfg. 1972-disc.

	100%	98%	95%	90%	80%	70%	60%
	$350	$310	$280	$265	$250	$220	$200

MODEL 1900 — 12 or 20 ga., 3 in. chamber, 22, 26, or 28 in. VR barrel with multi-chokes, deluxe outdoor field scene etched on receiver, gold trigger, approx. 1,000-2,000 mfg. per year.

Mfg.'s Sug. Retail	$545	$485	$430	$395	$360	$330	$295	$260

This model was previously designated the Model 900. The new Model 1900 is also available in Slug configuration with 22 in. barrel and iron sights or Trap Model at no extra charge. New Model 1900s have a magazine cutoff system on front left side of frame.

MODEL 3000 — 12 or 20 ga., 3 in. chamber, gas semi-auto (shoots both 2¾ and 3 in. shells interchangeably) with semi-squareback styling, elaborate game scenes etched on both sides of receiver, deluxe checkered walnut stock and forearm. Imported 1988-90.

	100%	98%	95%	90%	80%	70%	60%
	$545	$475	$415	$380	$350	$315	$285

Add $125 for Trap model (2¾ in. chamber).
This model has not previously been imported in this configuration.
Last Mfg.'s Sug. Retail was $597.

SHOTGUNS: SLIDE ACTION

MODEL 7300 — 12 or 20 ga., 2¾ or 3 in. chambers, blue only, French walnut stock-hand checkered, twin action slide bars. Disc. 1980.

	100%	98%	95%	90%	80%	70%	60%
	$295	$250	$225	$200	$180	$165	$150

MODEL 7900 — trap or skeet variation of the Model 7300.

	100%	98%	95%	90%	80%	70%	60%
	$350	$310	$265	$235	$200	$180	$160

SKS
Manufactured in Russia, China, Yugoslavia, and other countries.
Over 600 million SKS models have been manufactured in China alone.

SKS — semi-auto rifle, 7.62 x 39mm Russian, Soviet designed, gas operated weapon, 10 shot fixed mag., wood stock, permanently attached folding bayonet, tangent rear and hooded front sight.
Please refer to this model under those importers/distributors who import this model and are listed in this text. Values typically range between $95-$225.

SSK INDUSTRIES
Class II manufacturer located in Wintersville, OH.

SSK Industries uses Thompson Center flatside frames and applies an industrial hard chrome finish. Most SSK handguns and rifles are extensively customized in exotic calibers, finishes, and various engraving options. Receivers and barrels may be purchased separately—values below are for a complete assembled pistol.

SSK has also manufactured various limited editions including the Handgun Hunters International (HHI) Models 1, 2, and 3. Issue price on these guns was $1,100 (Model 3), $1,200 (Model 2), and $1,300 (Model 1). Only 50 were mfg. total in 1987. SSK also customizes a Ruger Super Redhawk (.44 Mag. or .45 LC cal.). This variation comes with either a scoped 7½ in. octagon barrel (Beauty Model) or a 6 in. bull barrel with muzzle brake (Beast Model). Prices start at $1,430 - add $245 for .45 LC cal.

Grading	100%	98%	95%	90%	80%	70%	60%

PISTOLS

Values listed below are for basic models with no options or special features.

SSK-CONTENDER — over 150 cals. available from .17 Bee to .50-70, various custom barrels available, basically, this is a custom order gun only.

Mfg.'s Sug. Retail	$1,100	$1,100	$875	$795	$675	$600	$550	$495

Individual barrels are available starting at $248.
An arrestor muzzle brake is available on special order.
This model includes barrel, frame, stocks, and sights as standard equipment.

SSK-XP100 — various cals. between .17 and .50, includes TSOB mount and rings.

Mfg.'s Sug. Retail	$1,200	$1,200	$975	$850	$725	$650	$575	$500

The .50 cal. XP100 (12.9 X 50.8 JDJ) comes with SSK muzzle brake, scope, dies and new reinforced fiberglass stock - retail price is $1,700.

RIFLES

Values listed below are for basic models with no options or special features. In addition, SSK also custom manufactures a bolt action rifle available in almost any caliber and configuration - prices start at $1,800 and can go as high as $6,000, depending on the customer's individual special orders.

SSK TCR 87 — .17 through .50 cals., certain Nitro Express cals. are also available, features Thompson Center TRC 87 receiver, and SSK custom barrels, muzzle brakes and exotic finishes are available at extra cost.

Mfg.'s Sug. Retail	$1,000	$1,000	$850	$700	$600	$550	$500	$450

SSK RUGER NO. 1 — many cals. including .577 NE (optional), custom order rifle based on a Ruger No. 1 frame.

Mfg.'s Sug. Retail	$1,400	$1,400	$1,125	$850	$725	$650	$575	$500

Add $700 for .577 NE

S.W.D., INC.

Manufactured in Atlanta, GA. Similar models have previously been manufactured by R.P.B. Industries, Inc. (1979-82), and were met with B.A.T.F. disapproval because of convertibility into fully automatic operation. "Cobray" is a trademark for the M11/9 semi-automatic pistol. Dealer sales.

COBRAY PISTOLS

M-11/NINE mm SEMI-AUTO PISTOL — 9mm, fires from closed bolt, 3rd generation design, stamped steel frame, 32 shot mag., parkerized finish, similar in appearance to Ingram Mac 10.

No Mfg.'s Retail	$215	$175	$160	$150	$140	$135	$125

This model is also available in a fully-auto variation, class III transferable only.

CARBINES

SEMI-AUTO CARBINE — 9mm, same mechanism as M11, 16¼ in. shrouded barrel, telescoping stock, various Mag.'s.

No Mfg.'s Retail	$265	$230	$195	$170	$160	$150	$140

REVOLVERS

LADIES HOME COMPANION — .45-70 cal., double action design utilizing spring wound 12 shot rotary mag., 12 in. barrel, steel barrel and frame, 9 lbs. 6 oz. New 1990.

No Mfg.'s Retail	$525	$400	$360	$335	$310	$290	$270

Grading	100%	98%	95%	90%	80%	70%	60%

SHOTGUNS

TERMINATOR — 12 or 20 ga., single shot paramilitary design shotgun with 18 in. cylinder bore barrel, parkerized finish, ejector. Mfg. 1986-1988 only.

| | | $95 | $80 | $70 | $60 | $55 | $50 | $45 |

Last Mfg.'s Sug. Retail was $110.

SAFARI ARMS

Manufacturer/customizer located in Olympia, WA. M-S Safari Arms was started in 1978 and was a division of M-S Safari Outfitters. In 1987, Safari Arms was absorbed by Olympic Arms located in Olympia, WA.

Safari Arms manufactures single action, semi-auto pistols derived from the Browning M1911 design with modifications.

DEFENSE PISTOLS

ENFORCER — .45 ACP, 3.8 in. barrel, 6 shot mag., shortened grip, available with max hard finish aluminum frame, parkerized, electroless nickel or lightweight anodized finishes, flat or arched mainspring housing, adj. sights, ambidextrous safety, neoprene or checkered walnut grips, 27 oz. (lightweight model).

| Mfg.'s Sug. Retail | $709 | | $650 | $545 | $495 | $450 | $425 | $400 | $375 |

⚐ **MatchMaster** — similar to the Enforcer, except has 5 in. barrel and 7 shot mag., 40 oz.

| Mfg.'s Sug. Retail | $685 | | $625 | $525 | $485 | $450 | $425 | $400 | $375 |

Safari Arms also has made the Phoenix, Special Forces, Camp Perry, and Royal Order of Jesters commemoratives in various configurations and quantities. Prices average in the $1,500 range except for the Royal Order of Jesters ($2,000).

GI SAFARI — .45 ACP cal., patterned after the Colt Model 1911 A1, Safari frame, beavertail grip safety and commander hammer. New 1991.

| Mfg.'s Sug. Retail | $425 | | $375 | $315 | $275 | $250 | $230 | $210 | $190 |

BLACK WIDOW — .45 ACP, 3.9 in. barrel, hand-contoured front grip strap, schrimshawed ivory Micarta grips with black widow emblem, 6 shot mag., 27 oz. Inventory was depleted 1988.

| | | $565 | $510 | $460 | $430 | $400 | $375 | $350 |

Last Mfg.'s Sug. Retail was $595.

BILL OF RIGHTS BICENTENNIAL MATCHED SET—includes the MatchMaster Pistol and ServiceMatch Rifle, features beryllium receivers and special engraving.

| Mfg.'s Sug. Retail | $7,400 | | $6,950 | $5,250 | $3,950 |

TARGET PISTOLS

MODEL 81 — .38 Spl. or .45 ACP, 5 in. barrel, hand-contoured front grip strap, 2 lbs. 10 oz. Disc. 1987.

| | | $775 | $695 | $550 | $440 | $410 | $375 | $350 |

Add $50 for Deluxe Model (with Herrett adj. grips).
Last Mfg.'s Sug. Retail was $875.

⚐ **Model 81L** — .38 Spl. or .45 ACP, 6 in. barrel, 2 lbs. 13 oz. Disc. 1987.

| | | $850 | $775 | $695 | $550 | $440 | $410 | $375 |

Add $50 for Deluxe Model (with Herrett adj. grips).
Last Mfg.'s Sug. Retail was $975.

Grading	100%	98%	95%	90%	80%	70%	60%

Model 81 NM — .38 Spl. or .45 ACP, similar frame as Model 81, except has flat front grip strap, 5 in. barrel, 2 lbs. 5 oz. Disc. 1987.

	$775	$695	$550	$440	$410	$375	$350

Last Mfg.'s Sug. Retail was $875.

Model 81BP — .38 Spl. or .45 ACP, 6 in barrel, contoured front grip strap, faster cycle time, 2 lbs. 9 oz. Disc. 1987.

	$875	$775	$695	$550	$440	$410	$375

Last Mfg.'s Sug. Retail was $995.

Silueta — .45 ACP or .38/.45 Wildcat, 10 in. extended barrel, designed for silhouette shooting, 2 lbs. 14 oz. Disc. 1987.

	$875	$775	$695	$550	$440	$410	$375

Last Mfg.'s Sug. Retail was $1,050.

ULTIMATE/UNLIMITED — various cals., bolt action target pistol, single shot, $14\frac{15}{16}$ in. barrel, black finished metal, laminate stock. Disc. 1987.

	$850	$775	$695	$550	$440	$410	$375

Last Mfg.'s Sug. Retail was $975.

SAKO

Manufacturer located in Riihimaki, Finland. Current models are presently being imported by Stoeger Industries located in South Hackensack, NJ.

Note: Prices below are for pre-1972 rifles unless stated otherwise. Post-1972 models will sell for approx. 25% less.

≡ SAKO

RIFLES: DISC.

DELUXE — various cals., Monte Carlo stock, skipline checkering, long, medium, or short actions, contrasting P.G. Cap & Forearm, engraved floorplate.

	$850	$775	$695	$550	$440	$410	$375

STANDARD SPORTER — long, medium, and short actions.

	$695	$625	$550	$475	$440	$410	$375

HEAVY BARREL MODEL — long, medium, and short actions.

	$695	$625	$550	$475	$440	$410	$375

FULL STOCK MODELS — 20 in. carbine barrel (all actions), $23\frac{1}{2}$ in. barrel on rifle (short & medium actions).

Finnbear — long action.

	$675	$595	$525	$475	$425	$375	$350

Forester — medium action.

	$675	$595	$525	$475	$425	$375	$350

Vixen — short action.

	$675	$595	$525	$475	$425	$375	$350

Early short action pre-Vixen Sakos had detachable mags.

MAUSER ACTION (FN) — .270 Win. or .30-06 cal., long action. Mfg. 1950-1957.

	$550	$500	$400	$345	$310	$280	$260

MAGNUM MAUSER (FN) — 8 x 60S, 8.2 x 57mm, .300 H&H, or .375 H&H cal.

	$695	$635	$580	$495	$450	$410	$375

Grading	100%	98%	95%	90%	80%	70%	60%

MODEL 74 — various cals.

| | $560 | $495 | $440 | $375 | $340 | $320 | $290 |

FINNWOLF — lever action, various cals., 4 shot clip early model, 3 shot clip later model. Mfg. 1962-1974.

| | $725 | $650 | $550 | $500 | $440 | $410 | $375 |

ANNIVERSARY MODEL — 7mm Rem. Mag. only, 1,000 made.

| | $1,500 | $995 | $850 |

RIFLES: RECENT MFG.

All Sako left-handed models are available in medium or long action only.

HUNTER LIGHTWEIGHT RIFLE — available in short action (AI) in .17 Rem., .222 Rem., or .223 Rem. cal., medium action (AII) in .22-250, .243 Win., .308 Win., or 7mm-08 cal., or long action (AIII) in .25-06 Rem., .270 Win., .280 Rem., .30-06, 7mm Rem. Mag., .300 Win. Mag., .300 Wby. Mag., .338 Win. Mag., .375 H&H, or .416 Rem. Mag. (new 1991) cal., 21¼, 21¾, or 22 in. barrel, classic styled stock with choice of oil or lacquer finish, finely checkered French walnut.

| Mfg.'s Sug. Retail | $975 | $795 | $650 | $550 | $490 | $460 | $430 | $410 |

Add $25 for long action.
Add $45-$60 for Mag. cals.
Add $80-$140 for left-hand action (available in medium or long action only).

Hunter Carbine (Handy) — available in medium action in .22-250 (disc. 1990), .243 Win. (new 1991), .308 (new 1991) cal. or long action in .25-06 (disc. 1990), Rem., 7mm Rem. Mag. (disc. 1990), .338 Win. Mag. cal., or .375 H&H Mag. (new 1990) cal., 18½ in. barrel with iron sights, oil or lacquer finished deluxe walnut stock with checkering, approx. 7 lbs. Mfg. 1986-91.

| | $775 | $635 | $550 | $490 | $460 | $430 | $410 |

Add $50-$65 for long action (Mag. cals.).
Last Mfg.'s Sug. Retail was $945.

FIBERCLASS MODEL — available in medium action (disc. 1992) in .22-250, .243 Win., .308 Win., or 7mm-08 cal., or long action in .25-06 Rem., .270 Win., .280 Rem., .30-06, 7mm Rem. Mag., .300 Win. Mag., .338 Win. Mag., .375 H&H, or .416 Rem. Mag. (new 1991) cal., has black fiberglass stock.

| Mfg.'s Sug. Retail | $1,310 | $1,125 | $900 | $775 | $725 | $630 | $560 | $510 |

Add $15-$30 for Mag. cals.
Subtract $40 for medium action cals. (disc. 1992).
Add $80 for left-hand action (disc. 1989).

FiberClass Carbine (Handy) — available in medium action in .243 Win. or .308 Win. cal. and long action in .25-06 Rem. (disc.), .270 Win. (disc.), .30-06, 7mm Rem. Mag. (disc.), .300 Win. Mag. (disc.), .338 Win. Mag., or .375 H&H (new 1991) cal., 18½ in. barrel with fiberglass stock. Mfg. 1986-91.

| | $1,100 | $895 | $775 | $725 | $630 | $560 | $510 |

Add $50-$65 for Mag. cals.
Last Mfg.'s Sug. Retail was $1,239.

LAMINATED RIFLE — available in short action (disc. 1989), medium action in .22-250 Rem., .243 Win., .308 Win., or 7mm-08 cal., or long action in .25-06 Rem., .270 Win., .280 Rem., .30-06, 7mm Rem. Mag., .300 Win. Mag., .338 Win. Mag., .375 H&H, or .416 Rem. (new 1991) cal., features laminated wood stock. New 1988.

| Mfg.'s Sug. Retail | $1,190 | $975 | $785 | $625 | $550 | $495 | $460 | $430 |

Add $35 for short action.
Subtract $35 for long action.   Subtract $15-$25 for Mag. cals.
Add approx. $100 for left-hand action (disc.).
The left-handed action was available in .270 Win., .280 Rem., .30-06, 7mm Rem. Mag., 300 Win. Mag., 338 Win. Mag., .375 H&H, or .416 Rem. Mag. cal.

Grading	100%	98%	95%	90%	80%	70%	60%

MODEL TRG-21 — .308 Win. cal., bolt action, 25¾ in. barrel, new design features modular synthetic stock construction with adj. cheekpiece and buttplate, stainless steel barrel, cold hammer forged receiver, and resistance free bolt, 10 shot detachable mag., 10½ lbs. Importation began 1993.

Mfg.'s Sug. Retail $3,075	$2,650	$2,250	$1,750	$1,450	$1,250	$1,050	$900

MODEL TRG-S — available in medium action in .243 Win. or 7mm-08 cal., or long action in .270 Win., .30-06, 7mm Rem. Mag., .300 Win. Mag., .338 Win. Mag., or .375 H&H Mag. cal., Sporter variation derived from the Model TRG-21, 22 or 24 (Mag. cals. only) in. barrel, 5 shot detachable mag., fully adj. trigger, 60 degree bolt-lift, matte finish, 7¾ lbs. Importation began 1993.

Mfg.'s Sug. Retail $730	$650	$550	$490	$460	$430	$410	$380

Add $35 for Mag. cals.

MANNLICHER CARBINE — available in short action (disc. 1989), medium action in .243 Win. or .308 Win. cal., or long action in .25-06 Rem. (disc. 1991), .270 Win., .30-06, 7mm Rem. Mag. (disc. 1991), .300 Win. Mag. (disc. 1991), .338 Win. Mag., or .375 H&H cal., 18½ in. barrel, two-piece full Mannlicher style stock, open sights.

Mfg.'s Sug. Retail $1,130	$935	$750	$600	$545	$495	$465	$440

Add $35 for long action.
Add $50-$70 for Mag. cals.

PPC MODEL — 22 PPC or 6 PPC cal., 21¾ or 23¾ (Benchrest Model) in. barrel, single shot in Benchrest Model, 4 shot mag. in Hunter or Deluxe Model, checkered walnut stock, Deluxe Model has rosewood pistol grip and forearm caps plus skip line checkering, matte lacquer finish on Hunter and Deluxe, oiled finish on Benchrest, 6¼ or 8¾ (Benchrest Model with heavy barrel) lbs. Importation began 1989.

Mfg.'s Sug. Retail $1,330	$1,095	$875	$700	$650	$590	$540	$500

Add $320 for Deluxe Hunter Model.
Add $85 for Benchrest Model.

VARMINT RIFLE — available in short action (AI) in .17 Rem., .222 Rem., or .223 Rem., and medium action (AII) .22-250 Rem., .243 Win., .308 Win., or 7mm-08 cal., 22¾ in. heavy barrel, no sights.

Mfg.'s Sug. Retail $1,110	$925	$750	$600	$545	$475	$430	$400

Also available in single shot configuration (6mm PPC or .22 PPC only) — subtract $110 (disc. 1989).

CLASSIC GRADE — currently available in .243 Win., .270 Win., .30-06, or 7mm Rem. Mag. cal., short (AI, disc. 1992), medium (AII), or long (AIII) action, .17-7mm Mag. cals., classic styled stock, finely checkered French walnut. Disc. 1985, reintroduced 1992.

Mfg.'s Sug. Retail $975	$850	$725	$595	$545	$475	$430	$400

Add $45 for Mag. cals.
Add $25 for long action.
Add $110-$125 for left hand action (.270 Win. or 7mm Rem. Mag cal. only).
In 1992, the Classic Grade was once again imported into the U.S. in .243 Win., .270 Win., .30-06, 7mm Rem. Mag. cal.

DELUXE LIGHTWEIGHT RIFLE — available in short action (AI) in .17 Rem., .222 Rem., or .223 Rem. cal., medium action (AII) in .22-250 Rem., .243 Win., .308 Win., or 7mm-08 cal., or long action (AIII) in .25-06 Rem., .270 Win., .280 Rem., .30-06, 7mm Rem. Mag., .300 Win. Mag., .300 Wby. Mag., .338 Win. Mag., .375 H&H, or .416 Rem. Mag. (new 1991) cal., 21¼, 21¾, or 22 in. barrel, deluxe quality skipline checkered walnut stock with rosewood forend tip.

Mfg.'s Sug. Retail $1,325	$1,095	$900	$725	$650	$595	$540	$500

Add $40 for long action.
Add $55-$70 for Mag. cals.
Add approx. $105-$135 for left-hand action (available in long action only).

Grading	100%	98%	95%	90%	80%	70%	60%

SAFARI GRADE — available in long (AIII) action only, .300 Win. Mag. (disc. 1989), .338 Win. Mag., .375 H&H Mag., or .416 Rem. Mag. (new 1991) cal., deluxe walnut with sculptured cheek piece, 22 in. barrel, 4 shot mag., open sights, sling swivels.

Mfg.'s Sug. Retail	$2,625	$2,125	$1,750	$1,450	$1,250	$1,050	$900	$795

SUPER DELUXE — a limited edition rifle available on special order only, various cals. are available in the short (AI), medium (AII), and long (AIII) actions, presentation grade walnut with both checkering and carving, rosewood forend tip.

Mfg.'s Sug. Retail	$2,790	$2,200	$1,750	$1,450	$1,250	$1,050	$900	$795

MODEL 78 — .22 LR and .22 Hornet, clip mag., same size as short action Standard Model. Importation disc. 1986.

	$480	$395	$340	$310	$280	$265	$250

Add $30 for .22 Hornet cal.
Last Mfg.'s Sug. Retail was $647.

FINSPORT MODEL 2700 — available in long (AIII) action only, .270 - .300 Win. Mag. cals., select checkered walnut. Disc. 1985.

	$795	$680	$600	$560	$510	$475	$430

Last Mfg.'s Sug. Retail was $910.

PISTOLS

Less than 200 Triace pistols were imported into the United States.

TRIACE — .22 Short, .22 LR or .32 S&W wadcutter cals., target pistol incorporating unique action, competition walnut grips with thumb rest and adj. heel, blued finish with chrome accents. Imported 1985-86 only.

	$1,300	$1,150	$950	$825	$700	$600	$500

Last Mfg.'s Sug. Retail was $1,395.

Triace Pistol Kit — consists of Triace frame, .22 Short, .22 LR, and .32 S&W barrels. Cased with accessories. Imported 1985-86 only.

	$2,300	$1,975	$1,700	$1,450	$1,300	$1,175	$1,025

Last Mfg.'s Sug. Retail was $2,385.

SAMCO GLOBAL ARMS, INC.
Importer/distributor located in Miami, FL. Dealer sales.

Samco Global Arms currently imports a variety of foreign and domestic surplus military rifles (including various contract Mausers, Loewe, Steyr, Czech, Lee Enfield, etc.). Most of these guns are in the $60-$250 range and they offer excellent values to both shooters and collectors. Samco also sells newly remanufactured sporting rifles (German or Spanish) in .308 Win. or 7 x 57mm cal. These sporters range in value from approx. $195-$250.

SARDIUS
Manufacturer located in Israel. Previously imported and distributed by Armscorp of America, Inc. located in Baltimore, MD.

SD-9 — 9mm Para., semi-auto double action, compact design, 3.07 in. barrel, matte black finish, 6 shot mag., 3 dot sighting system, 1.54 lbs. Imported 1988-90 only.

	$315	$280	$260	$240	$220	$200	$185

Last Mfg.'s Sug. Retail was $350.

SARASQUETA, FELIX

Manufacturer located in Eibar, Spain. Previously imported and distributed by SAE (Spain America Enterprises), Inc. located in Miami, FL.

SHOTGUNS

Grading	100%	98%	95%	90%	80%	70%	60%

MODEL MERKE O/U — 12 ga. only, boxlock action, 22 or 27 in. separated barrels, single non-selective trigger, blue only, extractors, recoil pad. Imported 1986 only.

	100%	98%	95%	90%	80%	70%	60%
	$255	$215	$200	$190	$180	$170	$160

Last Mfg.'s Sug. Retail was $291.

SARASQUETA, J.J.

Manufacturer located in Eibar, Spain. Imported until 1984 by American Arms, Inc. located in Overland Park, KS.

SHOTGUNS: SIDE-BY-SIDE

MODEL 107 E — 12, 16, or 20 ga., ejectors, various barrel lengths, checkered walnut stock and forearm, double triggers.

	100%	98%	95%	90%	80%	70%	60%
	$360	$290	$270	$255	$240	$215	$200

Last Mfg.'s Sug. Retail was $435.

MODELS 119E-132E-1882E — more deluxe versions of Model 107E.

	100%	98%	95%	90%	80%	70%	60%
	$470	$375	$340	$315	$285	$255	$230

Last Mfg.'s Sug. Retail was $570.

MODEL 130 E — more deluxe version of Model 119 E.

	100%	98%	95%	90%	80%	70%	60%
	$800	$635	$590	$555	$515	$480	$450

Last Mfg.'s Sug. Retail was $960.

MODEL 131 E — action similar to Model 107 E, except has deluxe engraving.

	100%	98%	95%	90%	80%	70%	60%
	$1,050	$845	$770	$710	$665	$620	$585

Last Mfg.'s Sug. Retail was $1,250.

MODEL 1882 E LUXE — double triggers, moderate engraving, otherwise similar to Model 107 E.

	100%	98%	95%	90%	80%	70%	60%
	$825	$660	$615	$565	$520	$480	$450

Last Mfg.'s Sug. Retail was $990.

Model 1882 E Luxe w/gold inlays — SST, extensive engraving.

	100%	98%	95%	90%	80%	70%	60%
	$1,120	$920	$850	$790	$740	$695	$650

Last Mfg.'s Sug. Retail was $1,320.

Model 1882 E Luxe w/silver inlays — SST, extensive engraving.

	100%	98%	95%	90%	80%	70%	60%
	$1,055	$855	$795	$740	$700	$660	$630

Last Mfg.'s Sug. Retail was $1,260.

MODEL 150 E — 12 or 16 ga., single trigger, ejectors, select walnut and extensive engraving.

	100%	98%	95%	90%	80%	70%	60%
	$1,285	$1,035	$960	$895	$835	$770	$695

Last Mfg.'s Sug. Retail was $1,500.

Model 150 E Trap — similar to Model 150 E, except trap dimensions on stock.

	100%	98%	95%	90%	80%	70%	60%
	$1,360	$1,125	$1,010	$940	$875	$790	$720

Last Mfg.'s Sug. Retail was $1,600.

Grading	100%	98%	95%	90%	80%	70%	60%

SARASQUETA, VICTOR

Previous manufacturer located in Eibar, Spain. Trademark is currently owned by Diarm S.A.

SHOTGUNS

MODEL 3 SXS — 12, 16, or 20 ga., all standard barrel lengths and chokes, boxlock, double triggers, checkered English style stock and forend.

Auto ejectors

	100%	98%	95%	90%	80%	70%	60%
	$580	$505	$480	$440	$380	$365	$345

HAMMERLESS SIDELOCK — 12, 16, or 20 ga., s x s, barrel length and choke to order, straight English style stock, models differ as to amount of engraving, grade of wood, and overall quality as follows:

MODEL 4 — extractors.

	100%	98%	95%	90%	80%	70%	60%
	$620	$550	$525	$495	$450	$415	$360

MODEL 4E — auto ejectors.

	$680	$605	$580	$550	$505	$470	$415

MODEL 203 — extractors.

	$650	$570	$545	$515	$475	$435	$380

MODEL 203E — auto ejectors.

	$710	$625	$600	$570	$530	$490	$435

MODEL 6E

	$800	$715	$690	$660	$615	$580	$525

MODEL 7E

	$855	$770	$745	$715	$670	$635	$580

MODEL 10E

	$1,735	$1,595	$1,485	$1,405	$1,320	$1,240	$1,100

MODEL 11E

	$1,870	$1,680	$1,595	$1,515	$1,430	$1,350	$1,265

MODEL 12E

	$2,145	$1,900	$1,790	$1,705	$1,570	$1,430	$1,375

SARRIUGARTE, FRANCISO S.A.

Manufacturer located in Elgoibar, Spain. Previously part of the Diarm S.A. Group which was imported and distributed by American Arms, Inc. located in North Kansas City, MO.

SAUER, J.P. & SOHN

Manufactured since 1751 in Germany (originally Prussia). Previously located in Suhl - currently headquartered in Eckernforde, W. Germany. Bolt action rifles (Model's 90 Lux, 90 Supreme, and 3000 Drilling) are currently being imported and distributed by G.U. Inc. located in Omaha, NE. In 1972, J.P. Sauer & Sohn formed a cooperation with the Sig Swiss Industrial Company which is presently the parent house of Sauer & Sohn.

Grading	100%	98%	95%	90%	80%	70%	60%

PISTOLS

MODEL 1913 POCKET AUTOMATIC — .32 auto, 7 shot, 3 in. barrel, fixed sights, blue, black rubber grips. Mfg. 1913-1930.

	$250	$220	$185	$165	$155	$145	$135

MODEL 1913 25 AUTOMATIC — .25 auto, 7 shot, 2½ in. barrel, fixed sights, blue, black rubber grips. Mfg. 1913-1930.

	$275	$240	$200	$175	$150	$140	$135

MODEL 28 — .25 ACP, 7 shot, 3 in. barrel, fixed sights, blue, black rubber grips. Mfg. 1930-1938.

	$300	$240	$185	$170	$155	$145	$135

BEHORDEN (SERVICE) MODEL — .32 ACP, 3 in. barrel, blue only, black plastic grips.

	$325	$240	$200	$175	$150	$145	$135

MODEL 38 H DOUBLE ACTION

AUTOMATIC — .22 LR (extremely rare), .32 ACP, or .380 ACP (rare) cal., 3¼ in. barrel, fixed sights, blue, plastic grips. Mfg. 1938-1945.

	100%	98%	95%	90%	80%	70%	60%
.32 ACP	$365	$300	$240	$205	$185	$165	$150
.380 ACP	$1,500	$1,250	$995	$875	$750	$625	$575
.22 LR	$2,500	$2,200	$1,850	$1,550	$1,250	$995	$775

Add 10% for Waffenamt proofing.
Add 60% for alloy frame.

RIFLES: BOLT ACTION

The Model 200 Bolt Action listed below is available by special order only beginning 1992. In Europe, Models 200 Europa and Europa Lux are available. Values assume standard rifle with no options.

GRADE 380

	$4,500	$4,000	$3,500	$3,000	$2,500	$2,200	$1,500

GRADE F-40

Rarity factory precludes accurate price evaluation.

MODEL F-45

	$12,000	$10,500	$9,000	$8,000	$6,500	$5,000	$3,200

MODEL F-60

	$23,000	$20,000	$17,000	$14,000	$12,000	$9,000	$5,000

SAUER PRE-WWII BOLT ACTION RIFLE — most popular European cals. and .30-06, 22 or 24 in. barrel, raised solid rib, Krupp steel, double set triggers, folding 3 leaf express sight, checkered sporter stock. Mfg. pre-WWII.

	$715	$550	$495	$440	$360	$330	$305

Grading	100%	98%	95%	90%	80%	70%	60%

MODEL 200 BOLT ACTION — available in 15 cals. between .243 Win. and .375 H&H Mag., short and medium actions only, 23.62 in. unique interchangeable barrels, 6 lug bolt, easily detachable stock and forearm, optional set trigger, detachable mag. with hidden release button, 7.7 lbs.

Mfg.'s Sug. Retail	$1,395	$1,225	$925	$800	$700	$600	$525	$450

Add $100 for 7mm Rem. Mag. or .300 Win. Mag. cal.
Add $300 for extra interchangeable barrel.

⅜ **Model 200 Lightweight** — similar to Model 200, only with alloy receiver, 6.6 lbs.

Mfg.'s Sug. Retail	$1,395	$1,225	$925	$800	$700	$600	$525	$450

Add $150 for left-hand version.

⅜ **Model 200 Lux** — similar to Model 200, except has deluxe walnut, rosewood forend tip and pistol grip cap, marmorized bolt and gold trigger.

Mfg.'s Sug. Retail	$1,595	$1,395	$1,175	$925	$800	$700	$600	$525

⅜ **American 200 Lux** — similar to Model 200 Lux, except has high gloss Monte Carlo stock, 24 in. barrel, jeweled bolt, and gold trigger.

Mfg.'s Sug. Retail	$1,595	$1,395	$1,175	$925	$800	$700	$600	$525

Add $150 for left-hand version.

⅜ **European 200 Lux** — similar to Model 200 Lux, except has European configured stock with Schnabel forearm, 26 in. barrel.

Mfg.'s Sug. Retail	$1,595	$1,395	$1,175	$925	$800	$700	$600	$525

Add $95 for left-hand version.

⅜ **Model 200 Carbon Fiber** — similar to Model 200, except has carbon fiber stock. Imported 1987-88 only.

		$800	$700	$625	$565	$500	$465	$430

Last Mfg.'s Sug. Retail was $1,200.

MODEL 90 BOLT ACTION — available in 16 cals. between .222 Rem. and .458 Win. Mag., short, medium and long actions, 22.44 or 26 in. barrel, 3 or 4 shot detachable mag., deluxe checkered walnut stock, approx. 7½ lbs. (except .458 Win. Mag.). Importation disc. 1989.

		$775	$675	$600	$550	$500	$465	$430

Last Mfg.'s Sug. Retail was $1,175.

⅜ **Model 90 Stutzen** — Mannlicher style full stock, not available in European or Mag. cals. Importation disc. 1989.

		$800	$700	$600	$550	$500	$465	$430

Last Mfg.'s Sug. Retail was $1,225.

⅜ **Safari Model** — .458 Win. Mag, 23.62 in. barrel, 10½ lbs. Imported 1986-1988 only.

		$1,250	$950	$850	$750	$650	$575	$500

Last Mfg.'s Sug. Retail was $1,675.

MODEL 90 LUX — .300 Win. Mag., .300 Wby., .338 Win. Mag, or .375 H&H cal., similar to Model 90, except has deluxe oil finished walnut stock with rosewood forearm tip and pistol grip cap, recoil pad, gold trigger.

Mfg.'s Sug. Retail	$1,495	$1,300	$1,025	$900	$795	$585	$465	$430

⅜ **Model 90 Stutzen Lux** — Mannlicher style full stock, not available in European or Mag. cals. Importation disc. 1990.

		$1,200	$1,020	$900	$795	$585	$465	$430

Last Mfg.'s Sug. Retail was $1,325.

Grading	100%	98%	95%	90%	80%	70%	60%

⚔ **Safari Model Lux** — .458 Win. Mag., 23.62 in. barrel, 10½ lbs., Bugina oil finished stock, rosewood forearm and pistol grip cap, William sights, recoil pad, gold trigger.

	$1,650	$1,400	$1,100	$940	$775	$680	$600

Last Mfg.'s Sug. Retail was $1,995.

MODEL 90 SUPREME — 25-06, .270 Win., .30-06, .300 Win. Mag., .300 Wby., 7mm Rem. Mag., .338 Win. Mag., or .375 H&H cal., similar to Model 90 Lux, except has high gloss lacquer stock with Monte Carlo cheek piece, jeweled bolt, and gold trigger. New 1987.

Mfg.'s Sug. Retail	$1,495	$1,300	$1,025	$900	$795	$585	$465	$430

On Models 90 Lux and Supreme add 69% for Grade I engraving, 105% for Grade II, 128% for Grade III, and 164% for Grade IV.

RIFLES: DRILLINGS – O/U COMBINATION GUNS

SAUER MODEL 3000 DRILLING — available in either 16 ga./.30-06, 6.5 x 57R, 7 x 57R, 7 x 65R or 12 ga./.222 Rem. (disc.), .243 Win., .30-06, 6.5 x 57R, 7 x 57R, 7 x 65R, 9.3 x 74R, Greener cross-bolt and double barrel lug locking, cocking indicators, front set trigger, automatic sight, walnut pistol grip stock with hog-back and cheek piece, grade III scroll engraving, 7¼ lbs.

Mfg.'s Sug. Retail	$6,450	$5,950	$2,950	$2,500	$2,100	$1,800	$1,500	$1,250

⚔ **Luxury Grade** — similar to Model 3000 standard, except select root timber and extensive engraving featuring two animals.

Mfg.'s Sug. Retail	$7,350	$6,800	$3,500	$2,850	$2,400	$1,975	$1,650	$1,350

COMBO BBF 54 O/U — standard grade combination gun, 16 ga./.222 Rem., .243 Win., 6.5 x 57R, 7 x 57R, 7 x 65R, and .30-06 cals., ejectors, double triggers with front set trigger, moderate engraving on coin finished receiver, Greener cross-bolt with double barrel lugs, 6 lbs. Importation disc. 1986.

	$2,200	$2,060	$1,760	$1,565	$1,380	$1,250	$1,125

Last Mfg.'s Sug. Retail was $2,495.
This model was still available in 1987 from the distributor in limited quantities.

⚔ **Luxury Grade** — similar to BBF 54, except game scene engraved and deluxe crotch walnut.

	$2,450	$2,200	$2,000	$1,785	$1,600	$1,475	$1,300

Last Mfg.'s Sug. Retail was $2,745.

LUFTWAFFE SURVIVAL DRILLING — 12 or 16 ga. (65mm) SxS over 9.3 x 74 R, 28 in. barrels, large eagle swastika on stock and breech end of right barrel. Originally mfg. for Luftwaffe pilots during WWII.

	$4,500	$4,000	$3,600	$3,200	$2,600	$2,400	$2,200

Add 20% for original aluminum case and accessories.

SAUER MODEL 3000E DRILLING — see listing under Colt Sauer Drilling.

SNIPER RIFLE — very accurate, special order only Sniper Rifle, built to customer specifications.

	$4,845	$3,655	$3,200	$2,850	$2,500	$2,275	$2,000

SHOTGUNS

MODEL 60 — various ga.'s, boxlock action, DT, extractors, checkered walnut stock and forearm, this model was the standard model of its period.

	$975	$875	$750	$650	$550	$450	$395

Add 20% for 20 ga.

Grading	100%	98%	95%	90%	80%	70%	60%

ROYAL DOUBLE BARREL SHOTGUN — 12, 16 or 20 ga., 26, 28, or 30 in. barrels, various chokes, boxlock, scalloped engraved frame, cocking indicators, SST, auto ejectors, Krupp steel barrel, checkered pistol grip stock. Mfg. 1955-1977.

	$1,650	$1,375	$1,210	$1,100	$880	$770	$660

Add 20% for 20 ga.

ARTEMIS — 12 ga., 28 in. barrels, mod. and full choke, H&H type sidelock, SST, auto ejector, Krupp steel, checkered pistol grip stock. Mfg. 1966-1977.

⚔ **Grade I** — fine line engraved.

	$5,500	$4,620	$3,850	$3,520	$3,080	$2,640	$2,200

⚔ **Grade II** — extensive engraving.

	$6,600	$5,500	$4,840	$4,235	$3,850	$3,300	$3,080

MODEL 66 O/U FIELD GUN — 12 ga., 28 in. mod. and full, Krupp steel barrels, H&H type sidelocks, SST, auto ejectors, checkered pistol grip stock, available in three grades of engraving. Mfg. 1966-1975.

	100%	98%	95%	90%	80%	70%	60%
Grade I	$2,200	$1,760	$1,540	$1,320	$1,100	$880	$770
Grade II	$3,080	$2,420	$1,980	$1,650	$1,430	$1,210	$990
Grade III	$3,850	$3,300	$2,860	$2,420	$1,980	$1,650	$1,320

MODEL 66 O/U SKEET GUN — similar to Field Gun, with 26 in. VR skeet bored barrel and vent. forearm. Mfg. 1966-1975.

MODEL 66 O/U TRAP GUN — similar to 66 Skeet, with 30 in. barrels, full and full, or mod. and full choke, trap style stock.

	100%	98%	95%	90%	80%	70%	60%
Grade I	$2,090	$1,760	$1,540	$1,320	$1,100	$880	$770
Grade II	$3,080	$2,420	$1,980	$1,650	$1,430	$1,210	$880
Grade III	$3,850	$3,300	$2,860	$2,420	$1,980	$1,650	$1,320

SAUER/FRANCHI STANDARD GRADE O/U — 12 ga. only, double triggers, checkered walnut stock and forearm, SST, blued finish only, sling swivels, VR. Importation disc. 1986.

	$375	$340	$315	$290	$275	$260	$245

Last Mfg.'s Sug. Retail was $785.

⚔ **Regent Grade** — similar to Standard grade, except has single trigger and lightly engraved silver finished receiver. Importation disc. 1986.

	$475	$395	$350	$310	$290	$275	$265

Last Mfg.'s Sug. Retail was $825.

⚔ **Favorit Grade** — similar to Regent Grade, except has elaborate scroll engraving on coin finished receiver, gold plated trigger. Importation disc. 1986.

	$550	$495	$450	$420	$385	$350	$300

Last Mfg.'s Sug. Retail was $875.

⚔ **Diplomat Grade** — similar to Favorit Grade, except has more elaborate scroll engraving and with model name gold filled on receiver sides and barrel, extra grain French walnut, cased.

	$875	$750	$625	$550	$495	$460	$435

Last Mfg.'s Sug. Retail was $1,520.

SAUER/FRANCHI SPORTING S O/U — 12 ga. only, 28 in. barrels, ejectors, SST, select European walnut with checkered stock and forearm, 10mm VR, plain silver finished receiver with model name gold filled on both sides. Importation disc. 1986.

	$800	$700	$600	$500	$450	$420	$395

Last Mfg.'s Sug. Retail was $1,375.

Grading	100%	98%	95%	90%	80%	70%	60%

SAUER/FRANCHI MODEL TRAP O/U — similar to Sporting S, except has 29 in. barrels, trap chokes and stock dimensions. Importation disc. 1986.

	$875	$750	$625	$550	$495	$460	$435

Last Mfg.'s Sug. Retail was $1,375.

SAUER/FRANCHI MODEL SKEET O/U — similar to Sporting S, except has skeet chokes. Importation disc. 1986.

	$875	$750	$625	$550	$495	$460	$435

Last Mfg.'s Sug. Retail was $1,375.

SAVAGE ARMS, INC.

Initially manufactured in Utica, NY. Later manufacture was in Chicopee Falls, MA. Currently manufactured in Westfield, MA since 1959. Distributor sales only.

This company originally started in Utica, NY in 1895. The Model 1895 was initially manufactured by Marlin between 1895-1899. The company was renamed Savage Arms Co. in 1899. After WWI, the name was again changed to the Savage Arms Corporation. Savage moved to Chicopee Falls, MA circa 1946 (to its J. Stevens Arms Co. plants). In the mid-1960s the company became The Savage Arms Division of American Hardware Corp., which later became The Emhart Corporation. This division was sold in September 1981, and became Savage Industries, Inc. located in Westfield, MA (since the move in circa 1959). On November 1, 1989, Savage Arms Inc. acquired the majority of assets of Savage Industries, Inc.

Savage Arms, Inc. will offer service and parts on their current line of firearms only (those manufactured after Nov. 1, 1989). These models include the 24, 99, and 110 plus the importation of the Model 312. Warranty and repair claims for products not acquired by Savage Arms, Inc. will remain the responsibility of Savage Industries. For information regarding the repair and/or parts of Savage Industries firearms, please refer to the Trademark Index in the back of this text. Parts for pre-1981 Savage Industries firearms may be obtained by containing the Gun Parts Corporation located in West Hurley, NY (listed in Trademark Index). Savage Arms, Inc. has older records/info. on the Model 24, Model 99, and Model 110 only.

SAVAGE HAS NOT PUBLISHED RETAIL PRICES SINCE 1988.

PISTOLS

MODEL 1907 AUTO PISTOL — .32 auto, 10 shot, .380 auto, 9 shot, $3^{13}/_{16}$ (.32 ACP) or $4^5/_{16}$ (.380 ACP) in. barrel, blue, fixed sights, hard rubber grips, exposed hammer. Mfg. 1910-1917.

	$350	$220	$175	$150	$125	$115	$100

Add 80% for factory nickel finish (rare).
Add 15% for .380.

MODEL 1915 HAMMERLESS — similar to 1907, with grip safety and no visible hammer. Mfg. 1915-1917.

	$325	$290	$210	$190	$170	$150	$130

Add 15% for .380.

MODEL 1917 AUTOMATIC — similar to 1907, with spur hammer and trapezoidal grips. Mfg. 1920-1928.

	$250	$225	$175	$145	$130	$110	$100

Add 15 for .380.

Grading	100%	98%	95%	90%	80%	70%	60%

U.S. ARMY TEST TRIAL .45 ACP — .45 ACP, large version of 1910, exposed hammer. Approx. 400 mfg. 1907-1910 for military trials.

	$4,500	$3,800	$3,300	$2,800	$2,400	$2,000	$1,800

Most pistols were repurchased from the government, reconditioned (many reblued), and resold to the public as commercial models. Add 100% if in original condition.

MODEL 101 SINGLE SHOT — single action, .22 cal., 5½ in. barrel, adj. sight, swing out barrel, blue, wood grips. Mfg. 1960-1968.

	$150	$120	$95	$80	$70	$60	$50

RIFLES

Savage made a wide variety of inexpensive, utilitarian rifles that to date have attracted mostly shooting interest, but little collector interest. A listing of these models may be found in the back of this text under "Serialization".

MODEL 1895 — .303 Savage only, lever action, mfg. in either carbine (22 in.), rifle (26 in.), or musket (30 in.) variations, round (scarce) or octagon barrel that has Marlin proofmark under the forend, closed top, solid breech, side ejecting, 5 shot rotating box mag., unfired shots indicator. Originally mfg. by Marlin, marked "Savage Repeating Arms Co. Utica, N.Y. U.S.A. Pat. Feb. 7, 1893.", approx. 6,000 mfg. 1895-1899, early models had hole in top of bolt — latter ones were smooth.

	$1,500	$1,250	$995	$880	$770	$660	$495

Values assume rifle configuration — add premiums for the carbine (rare) and musket.

MODEL 1899 — .25-35, .30-30, .303 Savage, .32-40, or .38-55 cal., improvement of Model 1895, 20 in. round (carbine), 22 in. (round), or 26 in. (round, half-oct. or full oct.) barrel marked "Savage Arms Company, Utica, N.Y. Pat. Feb. 7.1893.", over 75,000 mfg. 1899-1917, approx. 7½ lbs. Older "perch-belly stocks" and high-gloss bluing will command a 10%-15% premium on this variation.

	$695	$575	$500	$450	$375	$300	$225

Add 25% for takedown (added 1909).
Add 10% for .25-35, .32-40, or .38-55 cal.
In 1905 Savage broadened the variety of this model and added the 1899A2, CD, BC, AB, Excelsior, Leader, Crescent, Victor, Rival, Premier, and Monarch (top-of-the-line model). Prices at the time ranged from $21 to $250 — quite a range of prices. Any factory engraved Savage 99 is rare (less than 1,000 mfg. to date) with values having to be computed one gun at a time. Recently, a collection of older, engraved Model 99s was sold with prices ranging from $2,000 to over $40,000. Because of this, the above values assume standard rifle with no engraving options (Grades A through G).
All Model 99s fall within the domain of Savage Arms, Inc.

MODEL 99A — .30-30, .250-3000, .300 Sav. .303 Sav., or .375 Win. cal., lever action, 24 in. barrel, open sight, hammerless, straight grip stock, crescent butt. Mfg. 1920-1936.

	$550	$440	$330	$275	$180	$165	$150

MODEL 99A RECENT — similar to original, with .243, .250 Sav., .300 Sav., or .308 Win. cal., 20 or 22 in. barrel, tang safety, conventional butt. Mfg. 1971-1981.

	$375	$340	$310	$275	$250	$225	$200

MODEL 99B — takedown version of original 99A. Mfg. 1920-1936.

	$880	$770	$660	$495	$330	$250	$195

MODEL 99C — .243 Win. or .308 Win. cal., 22 in. barrel, 4 shot detachable mag., checkered American walnut stock and forearm, adj. rear sight, drilled and tapped, 7¾ lbs. New 1992.

No Mfg.'s Retail	$635	$495	$450	$395	$360	$330	$300

Grading	100%	98%	95%	90%	80%	70%	60%

MODEL 99H CARBINE — .250-3000, .30-30, or .300 Sav. cal., solid frame, carbine type stock. Mfg. 1931-1942.

	100%	98%	95%	90%	80%	70%	60%
	$440	$330	$275	$220	$180	$165	$150

MODEL 99E — .22 Hi Power, .250-3000, .30-30, .300 Sav., or .303 Sav. cal., 22 in. barrel. Mfg. 1920-1936.

	$475	$350	$275	$220	$180	$165	$150

MODEL 99E CARBINE — .243, .250 Sav., .300 Sav., or .308 Win. cal., 22 in. barrel, checkered pistol grip stock, 5 shot rotary mag. Mfg. 1960-1982.

	$320	$260	$230	$200	$180	$165	$150

Last Mfg.'s Sug. Retail was $343.

MODEL 99F FEATHERWEIGHT — similar to pre-war 99E, except takedown and ½ pound lighter. Mfg. 1920-1942.

	$440	$330	$275	$220	$195	$175	$160

MODEL 99F — .243, .250-3000, .284 Win., .300 Sav., .308 Win., or .358 Win. cal., solid frame, checkered pistol grip stock. Disc. 1970.

	$350	$310	$285	$260	$230	$210	$190

Add 10% for .358 Win. cal.
Add 15% for .284 Win. cal.
This model had the receiver marked "99M".

MODEL 99G — similar to 99E pre-war, with checkered stock and takedown. Mfg. 1920-1942.

	$660	$550	$440	$275	$220	$165	$150

MODEL 99EG — similar to 99G, with solid frame and no checkering. Mfg. 1936-1941.

	$550	$440	$330	$260	$230	$210	$190

MODEL 99EG POST-WAR — .243, .250 Sav., .300 Sav., .308, or .358 cal., checkered stock. Mfg. 1946-1960.

	$350	$310	$285	$260	$230	$210	$190

MODEL 99R PRE-WAR — .250-3000 or .300 Sav. cal., 22 or 24 in. barrel, large pistol grip stock and forearm. Mfg. 1936-1942.

	$495	$440	$305	$275	$250	$220	$195

MODEL 99R POST-WAR — similar to Pre-War, .300 Sav., .308, .358, or .243 cal., 24 in. barrel only, swivel studs. Mfg. 1946-1960.

	$350	$310	$285	$260	$230	$210	$190

MODEL 99RS PRE-WAR — similar to 99R Pre-War, with Lyman aperture sight, swivels and sling. Mfg. 1936-1942.

	$605	$550	$440	$330	$275	$250	$220

MODEL 99RS POST-WAR — similar to 99R Post-War, with Redfield receiver sight. Mfg. 1946-1958.

	$350	$330	$285	$250	$225	$200	$180

Savage Arms, Inc., cont.

Grading	100%	98%	95%	90%	80%	70%	60%

MODEL 99T — 20 or 22 in. barrel, solid frame, lightweight, checkered pistol grip stock. Mfg. 1936-1942.

	100%	98%	95%	90%	80%	70%	60%
	$440	$330	$275	$205	$180	$165	$150

MODEL 99K — engraved receiver and fancy wood stock, Lyman aperture sight and folding middle sight. Mfg. 1931-1942.

	100%	98%	95%	90%	80%	70%	60%
	$2,200	$1,870	$1,210	$880	$770	$550	$440

MODEL 99DL — .243, .250-3000, .284 Win., .300 Savage, .308 Win., or .358 Win. cal., Monte Carlo stock and sling swivels. Post-war mfg. 1960-1973.

	100%	98%	95%	90%	80%	70%	60%
	$350	$310	$285	$260	$230	$210	$185

MODEL 99C — similar to 99F Post-War, available in .22-250 (rare), .243 Win., .284 Win. (disc.), 7mm-08 (disc.), or .308 Win. cal., 22 in. barrel, Monte Carlo stock with cut checkering and recoil pad, top tang safety, cocking indicator, open sights, detachable 4 shot mag., 8 lbs. Mfg. 1965-present.

	100%	98%	95%	90%	80%	70%	60%
No Mfg.'s Retail	$525	$430	$365	$300	$260	$230	$200

Add 10% for .22-250 cal.

MODEL 99CD — similar to 99C, with Monte Carlo cheek piece stock. Mfg. 1980-1981.

	100%	98%	95%	90%	80%	70%	60%
	$525	$450	$375	$325	$295	$260	$230

MODEL 99-358 — .358 Win. cal., recoil pad. Mfg. 1977-1980.

	100%	98%	95%	90%	80%	70%	60%
	$450	$400	$350	$325	$295	$260	$230

MODEL 99PE — elaborately engraved and plated receiver, tang, and lever, fancy wood with hand cut checkering. Mfg. 1966-1970.

	100%	98%	95%	90%	80%	70%	60%
	$1,320	$990	$740	$500	$375	$300	$260

This model had the receiver marked "99M".

MODEL 99DE CITATION — similar to Model 99PE, except with less engraving and pressed checkering. Mfg. 1968-1970.

	100%	98%	95%	90%	80%	70%	60%
	$885	$660	$495	$330	$250	$220	$195

This model had the receiver marked "99M".

MODEL 99M — while the receivers on models 99F, 99PE, and 99DE were marked "99M" this is not a model designation. Rather, the "M" barrel designation indicated Monte Carlo stock.

SAVAGE 1895 ANNIVERSARY — a replica of the original M1895, .308 cal., 24 in. octagon barrel, engraved receiver, brass plated lever, straight stock, Schnabel forend, medallion in stock, brass crescent butt plate. Mfg. 9,999 in 1970 only, to commemorate Savage's 75th year.

	100%	98%	95%
	$450	$350	$275

Last Mfg.'s Sug. Retail was $195 and mfg. by Savage Industries, Inc.

MODEL 1903 SLIDE ACTION — .22 S, L, or LR, 24 in. barrel, open sights, box mag., pistol grip stock. Mfg. 1903-1921.

	100%	98%	95%	90%	80%	70%	60%
	$275	$220	$110	$90	$75	$65	$45

MODEL 1909 SLIDE ACTION — similar to 1903, with 20 in. round barrel. Mfg. 1909-1915.

	100%	98%	95%	90%	80%	70%	60%
	$220	$140	$110	$90	$75	$65	$45

MODEL 1904 SINGLE SHOT — .22 S, L, or LR, bolt action, 18 in. barrel, straight stock. Mfg. 1904-1917.

	100%	98%	95%	90%	80%	70%	60%
	$140	$85	$55	$45	$35	$30	$30

Grading	100%	98%	95%	90%	80%	70%	60%

MODEL 1905 SINGLE SHOT — similar to 1904, except 24 in. barrel, takedown. Mfg. 1905-1919.

	100%	98%	95%	90%	80%	70%	60%
	$140	$85	$55	$45	$35	$30	$30

MODEL 1912 AUTOLOADER — .22 LR, 20 in. barrel, takedown, straight stock. Mfg. 1912-1916.

	$330	$275	$195	$110	$90	$75	$65

MODEL 1914 SLIDE ACTION — .22 S, L, and LR, 24 in. octagon barrel, plain pistol grip stock. Mfg. 1914-1924.

	$275	$250	$195	$110	$90	$75	$65

MODEL 19 NRA BOLT ACTION — .22 LR, 25 in. barrel, adj. aperture sight, 5 shot military stock. Approx. 50,000 mfg. 1919-1937.

	$220	$140	$110	$100	$90	$75	$65

Between 1943-1945 approx. 6,000 Model 19s were made under military contract — add 15%.

MODEL 10 BOLT ACTION TARGET — .22 LR, 25 in. barrel, speed lock, adj. aperture sight, target stock. Mfg. 1933-1946.

	$250	$165	$140	$110	$100	$90	$70

MODEL 19L — similar to 19, with Lyman receiver sight. Mfg. 1933-1942.

	$330	$275	$195	$140	$120	$110	$100

MODEL 19M — similar to 19, with 28 in. heavy barrel and scope bases. Mfg. 1933-1942.

	$330	$275	$195	$165	$140	$120	$110

MODEL 19H — similar to 19, except .22 Hornet. Mfg. 1933-1942.

	$550	$495	$330	$220	$175	$165	$155

MODEL 1920 BOLT ACTION — Mauser type action, .250-3000 or .300 Sav. cal., 22 or 24 in. barrel, open sights, 5 shot, checkered pistol grip, Schnabel forend. Mfg. 1920-1926.

	$330	$250	$220	$200	$175	$165	$155

Add 10% for .250-3000 cal.

MODEL 1920-1926 — similar to 1920, with 24 in. barrel, Lyman aperture sight, Mfg. 1926-1927.

	$330	$250	$220	$200	$175	$165	$155

MODEL 23A BOLT ACTION RIFLE — .22 LR, 23 in. barrel, open sights, plain pistol grip stock, Schnabel forend. Mfg. 1923-1933.

	$220	$165	$140	$110	$95	$85	$70

MODEL 23AA — improved version of 23A, with speedlock and checkered stock. Mfg. 1933-1942.

	$275	$195	$165	$130	$110	$100	$85

MODEL 23B — same configuration as 23A, with .25-20 cal., 25 in. barrel, full forearm. Mfg. 1923-1942.

	$220	$140	$110	$100	$90	$75	$65

MODEL 23C — similar to 23B, with .32-20. Mfg. 1923-1942.

	$220	$140	$110	$100	$90	$75	$65

Grading	100%	98%	95%	90%	80%	70%	60%

MODEL 23D — similar to 23B, with .22 Hornet. Mfg. 1933-1947.

	100%	98%	95%	90%	80%	70%	60%
	$305	$250	$220	$195	$165	$140	$110

MODEL 25 SLIDE ACTION — .22 S, L, or LR, 24 in. octagon barrel, open sight, takedown, hammerless, tube mag., plain pistol grip stock. Mfg. 1925-1929.

	$330	$275	$220	$140	$110	$75	$65

MODEL 40 BOLT ACTION RIFLE — .250-3000, .300 Sav., .30-30, or .30-06 cal., 22 or 24 in. barrel, open sight, 4 shot mag., plain pistol grip stock, Schnabel forend. Mfg. 1928-1940.

	$330	$220	$195	$165	$155	$140	$120

Add 10% for .250-3000 cal.

MODEL 45 SUPER — similar to 40, with Lyman receiver sight and checkered stock. Mfg. 1928-1940.

	$385	$275	$250	$200	$175	$165	$140

MODEL 29 SLIDE ACTION — .22 S, L, or LR, 22 in. barrel, octagon until 1940, round on post-WWII, open sights, checkered pistol grip stock on pre-war, plain on late model. Mfg. 1929-1967.

	$275	$220	$165	$100	$90	$75	$65
Pre-war	$330	$275	$195	$120	$110	$100	$90

MODEL 3 SINGLE SHOT — .22 S, L, or LR, bolt action, 26 in. barrel, 24 in. barrel on post-war, open sights, plain grip stock. Mfg. 1933-1952.

	$85	$65	$55	$40	$30	$30	$30

MODEL 3S — similar to 3, with aperture sight. Mfg. 1933-1942.

	$100	$85	$70	$55	$40	$30	$30

MODEL 3ST — similar to 3S, with swivels and sling. Mfg. 1933-1942.

	$110	$90	$85	$70	$45	$35	$30

MODEL 4 BOLT ACTION REPEATER — .22 S, L, or LR, 24 in. barrel, open sight, takedown, 5 shot, checkered pistol grip stock on pre-war, plain stock on post-war. Mfg. 1933-1965.

	$110	$85	$70	$55	$40	$30	$30
Pre-war	$120	$95	$85	$65	$50	$40	$30

MODEL 4S — similar to 4, with aperture sight. Mfg. 1933-1942.

	$120	$90	$75	$65	$55	$40	$30

MODEL 4M — similar to 4, except .22 WRM.

	$110	$85	$70	$55	$45	$30	$30

MODEL 5 — similar to 4, with tubular mag. Mfg. 1936-1961.

	$110	$85	$70	$55	$45	$30	$30

MODEL 5S — similar to 5, with aperture sight. Mfg. 1936-1942.

	$120	$95	$85	$65	$55	$40	$30

Grading	100%	98%	95%	90%	80%	70%	60%

MODEL 6 AUTOLOADER — .22 S, L, or LR, 24 in. barrel, tubular mag., takedown, checkered pistol grip stock on pre-war, plain stock on post-war. Mfg. 1938-1968.

	100%	98%	95%	90%	80%	70%	60%
	$140	$110	$95	$85	$65	$55	$40
Pre-war	$150	$120	$105	$95	$75	$65	$50

MODEL 6S — similar to 6, with aperture sight. Mfg. 1938-1942.

	100%	98%	95%	90%	80%	70%	60%
	$150	$120	$105	$95	$75	$65	$45

MODEL 7 AUTOLOADER — similar to 6, with box mag. Mfg. 1939-1951.

	100%	98%	95%	90%	80%	70%	60%
	$140	$110	$95	$65	$55	$55	$40
Pre-war	$150	$120	$105	$95	$75	$65	$50

MODEL 7S — similar to 7, with aperture sight. Mfg. 1938-1942.

	100%	98%	95%	90%	80%	70%	60%
	$150	$120	$105	$95	$75	$65	$45

MODEL 60 AUTOLOADER — .22 LR, 20 in. barrel, leaf sight, tubular mag., checkered Monte Carlo stock. Mfg. 1969-1972.

100%	98%	95%	90%	80%	70%	60%
$95	$85	$70	$55	$45	$35	$30

MODEL 90 AUTOLOADING CARBINE — similar to 60, with 16½ in. barrel, plain carbine stock, with barrel band.

100%	98%	95%	90%	80%	70%	60%
$95	$85	$70	$55	$45	$35	$30

MODEL 88 AUTOLOADER — similar to 60, except has walnut finished hardwood stock. Mfg. 1969-1972.

100%	98%	95%	90%	80%	70%	60%
$85	$65	$55	$45	$40	$35	$30

MODEL 63K SINGLE SHOT — .22 S, L, or LR, bolt action, 18 in. barrel, open sights, trigger locks with key, full length pistol grip stock. Mfg. 1970-1972.

100%	98%	95%	90%	80%	70%	60%
$80	$65	$55	$45	$40	$35	$30

MODEL 63KM — similar to 63K, except .22 WRM.

100%	98%	95%	90%	80%	70%	60%
$90	$70	$65	$55	$45	$40	$35

MODEL 219 SINGLE SHOT — .22 Hornet, .25-20, .32-20, or .30-30 cal., 26 in. barrel, open sight, hammerless, break open, top lever, plain pistol grip stock. Mfg. 1938-1965.

	100%	98%	95%	90%	80%	70%	60%
.30-30 cal.	$140	$125	$110	$100	$90	$80	$70

Add 15% for all other cals.

MODEL 219L — similar to 219, with side lever. Mfg. 1965-1967.

100%	98%	95%	90%	80%	70%	60%
$100	$85	$70	$55	$45	$35	$30

MODELS 221, 222, 223, 227, 228, AND 229 — single barrel, similar to 219, only supplied with additional shotgun barrel, interchangeable, different model numbers are for different cals., ga.'s, and barrel lengths, all have been disc.

100%	98%	95%	90%	80%	70%	60%
$130	$100	$85	$65	$55	$45	$30

SAVAGE/STEVENS MODEL 65 — please refer to listing under Stevens section.

MODEL 34M — similar to 34, chambered for .22 WRM. Mfg. 1969-1973.

100%	98%	95%	90%	80%	70%	60%
$90	$70	$55	$45	$35	$30	$30

Grading	100%	98%	95%	90%	80%	70%	60%

MODEL 35 — .22 LR, bolt action, 22 in. barrel, 5 shot clip mag., open sights, hardwood Monte Carlo stock. Disc. 1985.

| | $90 | $80 | $65 | $50 | $35 | $30 | $30 |

Last Mfg.'s Sug. Retail was $100.

MODEL 46 — similar to 34, with tubular mag. Mfg. 1969-1973.

| | $90 | $70 | $55 | $45 | $35 | $30 | $30 |

MODEL 65M — similar to 65, in .22 WRM.

| | $95 | $75 | $65 | $55 | $45 | $35 | $30 |

SAVAGE/STEVENS MODEL 72 "CRACKSHOT" — please refer to listing under Stevens section.

SAVAGE/STEVENS MODEL 89 SINGLE SHOT — please refer to listing under Stevens section.

MODEL 340 BOLT ACTION — .22 Hornet, .222 Rem., .223 Win., or .30-30 cal., 22 and 24 in. barrel, open sights, 4 or 5 shot mag., 7½ lbs., plain pistol grip stock. Mfg. 1950-1985.

| | $225 | $195 | $170 | $160 | $150 | $140 | $130 |

Last Mfg.'s Sug. Retail was $257.

EL 340C — similar to 340, with aperture sight, checkered stock and sling swivels. Mfg. 1952-1960.

| | $235 | $205 | $180 | $165 | $155 | $145 | $135 |

MODEL 340V — .225 Win., varmint configuration, 24 in. barrel. Limited mfg. in late 1960s.

| | $295 | $265 | $235 | $205 | $180 | $165 | $150 |

MODEL 340S DELUXE — similar to 340, with aperture sight, checkered stock, sling swivels. Mfg. 1952-1960.

| | $260 | $225 | $205 | $190 | $175 | $160 | $150 |

MODEL 342 AND 342S — similar to 340, .22 Hornet designation. Mfg. 1950-1955.

| | $250 | $215 | $200 | $185 | $170 | $160 | $150 |

RIFLES: MODEL 110 SERIES

Beginning in 1992, Savage Arms, Inc. began supplying this model with a master trigger lock, earmuffs, shooting glasses (disc. 1992), and test target.

MODEL 110 SPORTER — .243, .270, .308, or .30-06 cal., 22 in. barrel, open sight, 4 shot, checkered pistol grip stock. Mfg. 1958-1963.

| | $175 | $145 | $120 | $110 | $95 | $85 | $55 |

MODEL 110-MC — similar to 110, with Monte Carlo stock. Mfg. 1959-1969.

| | $195 | $160 | $140 | $120 | $110 | $95 | $85 |

MODEL 110-M — similar to 110MC, except 7mm Mag., .264 Mag., .300 Win. Mag., or .338 Mag. cal., recoil pad. Mfg. 1963-1969.

| | $275 | $220 | $195 | $150 | $140 | $125 | $110 |

MODEL 110-C/CL — various cals., push-button detachable mag., walnut stock. Mfg. 1966-disc.

| | $300 | $265 | $230 | $200 | $185 | $170 | $160 |

Grading	100%	98%	95%	90%	80%	70%	60%

MODEL 110-D — .22-250 (disc.), .223, .243, .25-06 (disc.), .270, .308 (disc.), .30-06, 7mm Mag., .300 Win. Mag. (disc.), or .338 Win. Mag. cal., similar to Model 110B, hinged floorplate, checkered walnut stock, removable and adj. rear sight, 7½ lbs. Mfg. 1966-1988.

| | $340 | $290 | $260 | $240 | $215 | $190 | $170 |

Add $80 for left-hand version.
Last Mfg.'s Sug. Retail was $409.

MODEL 110-E — .22-250, .223, .243, .270, 7mm Rem. Mag., .308 Win., or .30-06 cal., 22 or 24 (Mag. only) in. barrel, open sights, unchecked hardwood Monte Carlo stock, blind internal floorplate, 7 lbs. Mfg. 1963-1988.

| | $260 | $230 | $190 | $175 | $165 | $155 | $145 |

Subtract $16 without sights.
Last Mfg.'s Sug. Retail was $325.

MODEL 110-F — .22-250, .223 Rem., .243 Win., .250 Sav. (new 1993), .25-06 (new 1993), .308 Win., .30-06, .270 Win., 7mm-08 Rem. (new 1993), 7mm Rem. Mag., .300 Sav. (new 1993), .300 Win. Mag., .338 Win. Mag. (new 1991) cal., 22 or 24 (Magnum) in. barrel, black DuPont Rynite stock with swivel studs and recoil pad, adj. rear sight, drilled and tapped for scope mounts, 4 or 5 shot mag., 6¾ lbs. New 1989.

| No Mfg.'s Retail | $395 | $300 | $265 | $235 | $210 | $195 | $180 |

All Model 110 mfg. is in the domain of Savage Arms, Inc.

Model 110-FNS — similar to Model 110-F, except has no sights. New 1991.

| No Mfg.'s Retail | $380 | $285 | $250 | $225 | $200 | $190 | $175 |

Model 110-FXP3 — .22-250 (new 1992), .223 Rem. (new 1992), .243 Win., .270 Win., .30-06, .308 Win. (new 1992), 7mm Rem. Mag., or .300 Win. Mag. cal., similar to Model 110-F except is without sights and has integral Weaver type scope bases. New 1989.

| No Mfg.'s Retail | $460 | $370 | $325 | $285 | $250 | $225 | $195 |

MODEL 110-CY — .223 Rem. (new 1993), .243 Win. or .300 Savage cal., youth/ladies variation with shortened classic stock. New 1991.

| No Mfg.'s Retail | $360 | $265 | $225 | $200 | $180 | $165 | $150 |

MODEL 110-WLE — .250-3000 Savage, .300 Savage, or 7x57mm Mauser cal. New 1991.

| No Mfg.'s Retail | $475 | $395 | $360 | $320 | $280 | $250 | $225 |

1,000 of each cal. will be mfg. in this model.

Model 110-WLE 1 of 1,000 — 7x57mm Mauser, features select walnut stock with Monte Carlo cheekpiece, high luster blue finish with laser etched Savage logo on bolt body, drilled and tapped, 1,000 mfg. beginning 1992, 7¾ lbs. New 1992.

| No Mfg.'s Retail | $460 | $370 | $325 | $285 | $250 | $225 | $195 |

MODEL 110-FP POLICE RIFLE — .223 Rem. or .308 Win. cal., 24 in. heavy barrel, all metal parts are non-reflective, 4 shot internal mag., black Dupont Rynite stock, tapped for scope mounts, 8 lbs. New 1990.

| No Mfg.'s Retail | $410 | $325 | $275 | $240 | $210 | $180 | $165 |

MODEL 110-G — .22-250, .223 Rem., .243 Win., .250 Sav. (new 1992), .25-06 (new 1992), .300 Sav. (new 1993), .308 Win., .30-06, .270 Win., 7mm-08 Rem. (new 1992), 7mm Rem. Mag., or .300 Win. Mag. cal., top loading internal box mag., 22 or 24 in. barrel, adj. iron sights, checkered hardwood stock, approx. 7 lbs. New 1989.

| No Mfg.'s Retail | $360 | $265 | $225 | $200 | $180 | $165 | $150 |

Subtract $10-$20 if without sights (Model 110-GNS).

Savage Arms, Inc., cont.

Grading	100%	98%	95%	90%	80%	70%	60%

Model 110-GC — .270 Win., .30-06, 7mm Rem. Mag., or .300 Win. Mag. cal., features detachable 3 or 4 shot mag., 22 or 24 in. barrel, checkered hardwood stock, adj. sights, 6¾ lbs. New 1992.

No Mfg.'s Retail	$410	$325	$275	$240	$210	$180	$165

Add $20 for Mag. cals.

Model 110-GXP3 — .22-250 Rem., .223 Rem., .243 Win., .270 Win., .30-06, .308, 7mm Rem. Mag., or .300 Win. Mag. cal., similar to Model 110-G, except has no sights and includes integral Weaver type scope bases. New 1989.

No Mfg.'s Retail	$445	$345	$290	$250	$215	$180	$165

Model 110-GLXP3 — .270 Win., .30-06, or 7mm Rem. Mag. cal., internal mag., supplied with scope, rings, and base, is bore sighted.

No Mfg.'s Retail	$510	$425	$345	$290	$250	$215	$180

Model 110-GCXP3 — .270 Win., .30-06, .300 Win. Mag., or 7mm Rem. Mag. cal., detachable mag.

No Mfg.'s Retail	$510	$425	$345	$290	$250	$215	$180

Model 110-GL — .30-06, .270 Win., or 7mm Rem. Mag. cal., left hand variation of the Model 110-G.

No Mfg.'s Retail	$360	$265	$225	$200	$180	$165	$150

Model 110-GLNS — similar to Model 110-GL, except has no sights. New 1991.

No Mfg.'s Retail	$350	$260	$220	$200	$180	$165	$150

MODEL 110-K — .243, .270, or .30-06 cal., incorporates laminated camouflage stock. Mfg. 1986-1988.

	$335	$280	$240				

Last Mfg.'s Sug. Retail was $399.

MODEL 110-S — .308 Win. & 7mm-08 Rem. (disc.) cals., silhouette model, 22 in. heavy barrel, Wundhammer swell pistol grip with stippling, no sights, 4 shot mag., 8 lbs. 10 oz. Disc. 1985.

	$340	$290	$255	$225	$205	$190	$175

Last Mfg.'s Sug. Retail was $385.

MODEL 110-V — .22-250 or .223 cal. only, varmint model, 26 in. heavy barrel, no sights, 5 shot mag., stippled walnut Wundhammer pistol grip stock, 9¼ lbs. Disc. 1989.

	$370	$315	$265	$230	$205	$190	$175

Last Mfg.'s Sug. Retail was $439.

MODEL 110-GV — .22-250 or .223 Rem. cal., varmint variation, 24 in. medium barrel, no sights, checkered hardwood stock with rubber rifle pad, drilled and tapped for scope, 8¼ lbs. New 1989.

No Mfg.'s Retail	$380	$285	$250	$225	$200	$190	$175

MODEL 110-B — similar to 110E, select stock and pistol grip cap on previous manufacture. Mfg. 1976-1979. Reintroduced 1989 with laminate stock (Model 110-B Laminate).

	$360	$300	$265	$235	$205	$190	$175

MODEL 110-B LAMINATE — similar to Model 110-B, except is available in .300 Win. Mag. or .338 Win. Mag. also, has brown laminate hardwood stock with iron sights, approx. 7½ lbs. Mfg. 1989-91.

	$385	$310	$250	$225	$200	$190	$180

Last Mfg.'s Sug. Retail was $477.

Grading	100%	98%	95%	90%	80%	70%	60%

MODEL 110-P PREMIER GRADE — similar to 110B, with select French walnut stock, skip checkered, rosewood forend and pistol grip cap, sling swivels, 7mm Mag. has recoil pad. Mfg. 1964-1970.

	100%	98%	95%	90%	80%	70%	60%
	$440	$330	$310	$275	$250	$220	$195
7mm Mag.	$460	$350	$330	$305	$275	$240	$220

MODEL 110-PE PRESENTATION GRADE — similar to 110P, with engraved receiver, floorplate and trigger guard. Mfg. 1968-1970.

	100%	98%	95%	90%	80%	70%	60%
	$660	$550	$525	$470	$440	$415	$385
7mm Mag.	$690	$580	$550	$495	$470	$440	$415

MODEL 111 CHIEFTAIN ACTION — .243, .270, 7 x 57mm, 7mm Mag., or .30-06 cal., 22 in. barrel, 24 in. barrel on Mag., leaf sight, 4 shot detachable mag., checkered walnut Monte Carlo stock, pistol grip cap, sling swivels. Mfg. 1974-1978.

	100%	98%	95%	90%	80%	70%	60%
	$330	$275	$240	$220	$195	$165	$155
Magnum	$315	$285	$265	$240	$220	$195	$165

MODEL 112V VARMINT RIFLE — .220 Swift, .222 Rem., .223 Rem., .225 Win., .22-250, .243, or .25-06 cal., single shot, bolt action, 26 in. heavy barrel, no sights, heavy select walnut stock, checkered, swivels. Mfg. 1975-1978.

100%	98%	95%	90%	80%	70%	60%
$350	$325	$300	$275	$250	$235	$225

MODEL 112 R — .22-250, .25-06, or .243 cal., similar to Model 112V, except has 4 shot mag. Disc. 1980.

100%	98%	95%	90%	80%	70%	60%
$340	$305	$275	$250	$230	$210	$175

Model 112-BV — .22-250 Rem. or .223 Rem. cal., alloy steel construction, 26 in. barrel with recessed muzzle, 4 shot mag., brown laminate stock with ambidextrous Wundhammer style pistol grip, 9½ lbs. New 1993.

No Mfg.'s Retail	$525	$430	$365	$315	$285	$250	$215

MODEL 112-FV — .22-250 Rem. or .223 Rem. cal., varmint variation with 26 in. heavy barrel, with or without iron sights, 4-shot mag., black Rynite synthetic stock with recoil pad, 9 lbs. New 1991.

No Mfg.'s Retail	$400	$310	$265	$235	$210	$195	$180

Model 112-FVS — similar to Model 112-FV, except is single shot with solid bottom receiver and is available in .220 Swift (new 1993) cal. New 1992.

No Mfg.'s Retail	$400	$310	$265	$235	$210	$195	$180

Model 112-FVSS — .22-250 Rem. or .223 Rem. cal., alloy receiver with 26 in. stainless steel barrel, 4 shot mag., black synthetic sporter stock, no sights, 9 lbs. New 1993.

No Mfg.'s Retail	$525	$430	$365	$315	$285	$250	$215

MODEL 114-CU CLASSIC ULTRA — .270 Win., .30-06, .300 Win. Mag., or 7mm Rem. Mag. cal., 22 or 24 in. barrel, features high gloss classic American black walnut stock with cut checkering, fitted grip cap, and recoil pad, removable 3 or 4 shot staggered box mag., deluxe adj. sights, approx. 7½ lbs. New 1991.

No Mfg.'s Retail	$515	$400	$350	$300	$265	$230	$200

MODEL 116-FSS — .22-250 Rem. (mfg. 1992 only), .223 Rem. (new 1992), .243 Win. (new 1993), .270 Win., .30-06, 7mm Rem. Mag., .300 Win. Mag., or .338 Win. Mag., features black Dupont Rynite synthetic stock, stainless steel metal parts, drilled and tapped for scope mounting, 22 or 24 in. barrel, 3 or 4 shot mag., 7½ lbs. New 1991.

No Mfg.'s Retail	$495	$390	$340	$300	$265	$230	$200

Grading	100%	98%	95%	90%	80%	70%	60%

Model 116-FCS — .270 Win., .30-06, 7mm Rem. Mag., or .300 Win. Mag. cal., otherwise similar to Model 116-FSS, except has removable 3 or 4 shot mag. with recessed push button release. New 1992.

No Mfg.'s Retail $590 $490 $440 $395 $360 $330 $295

Model 116-FSK (Kodiak) — .338 Win. Mag. cal., stainless steel construction, 22 in. barrel with recoil arrester, cocking indicator, 3 shot mag., black synthetic sporter stock, no sights, 7 lbs. New 1993.

No Mfg.'s Retail $590 $490 $440 $395 $360 $330 $295

MODEL 170 PUMP RIFLE — .30-30 or .35 Rem. cal., 22 in. barrel, folding leaf sight, 3 shot tube mag., checkered pistol grip stock. Mfg. 1970-1981.

$180 $155 $140 $110 $90 $65 $55

This model was mfg. by Savage Industries, Inc.

MODEL 170C — similar to 170, .30-30 only, 18½ in. barrel. Mfg. 1974-1981.

COMBINATION GUNS

All Model 24s are under the domain of Savage Arms, Inc.

MODEL 24 O/U COMBINATION GUN — .22 over .410, 24 in. separated barrels, open rifle sight, visible hammer, break open, plain pistol grip stock. Mfg. 1950-1965.

$160 $130 $110 $100 $85 $70 $55

MODEL 24S — similar to 24, with 20 ga. or .410 barrel, sidelever, dovetail for scope. Mfg. 1965-1971.

$185 $155 $135 $120 $100 $90 $80

MODEL 24MS — similar to 24S, with .22 WRM barrel. Mfg. 1965-1971.

$170 $140 $120 $110 $90 $85 $70

MODEL 24DL — similar to 24S, with top lever, satin chrome frame and checkered stock. Mfg. 1965-1969.

$170 $140 $120 $110 $90 $85 $70

MODEL 24MDL — similar to 24DL, with .22 WRM barrel. Mfg. 1965-1969.

$175 $145 $125 $115 $95 $85 $70

MODEL 24FG — similar to 24S, with top lever. Mfg. 1972-disc.

$165 $130 $110 $90 $85 $65 $55

MODEL 24 FIELD — .22 LR or .22 Mag. over 20 or .410 ga., lightweight field version, 24 in. separated barrels, 3 in. chambers, 6¾ lbs. Disc. 1989.

$185 $150 $120 $100 $85 $80 $70

Last Mfg.'s Sug. Retail was $209.

MODEL 24F — choice of .22 LR, .22 Hornet, .222 Rem. (disc. 1989), .223 Rem., or .30-30 cal. over 12 or 20 ga., 3 in. chamber, stocked in wood or matte black Dupont Rynite synthetic, hammer block safety, DTs, approx. 8 lbs. New 1989.

No Mfg.'s Retail $410 $325 $275 $240 $210 $180 $165

Add $7 for shotgun choke tube.
Add $30 for Camo Rynite stock (Model 12-T, Turkey Model-12 ga./.22 Hornet or .223 Rem. only).
The .22 LR cal. is available with 20 ga. barrel only.

MODEL 24V — similar to 24, with .22 Hornet (disc. 1984), .222, .223, .30-30, .357 Max., or .357 Mag.(disc.), over 24 in. 20 ga. (3 in.) barrel, single trigger, 7 lbs. Mfg. 1971-89.

$300 $265 $230 $200 $175 $150 $130

Grading	100%	98%	95%	90%	80%	70%	60%

MODEL 24D — .22 LR or .22 Mag. over .410 or 20 ga., black or case hardened frame, game scene decoration was eliminated in 1974, forearm not checkered after 1976.

| | $250 | $220 | $185 | $150 | $130 | $115 | $105 |

MODEL 24C CAMPER'S COMPANION — nickel finish, .22 LR over 20 ga., 20 in. barrel cylinder bore, buttplate opens to store ten .22 LR cartridges and one 20 ga. shell in buttstock, carrying case, 5¾ lbs. Mfg. 1972-1988.

| | $200 | $165 | $130 | $115 | $105 | $95 | $80 |

Add 10% for nickel finish (Model 24CS - shipped with pistol grip stock also).
Last Mfg.'s Sug. Retail was $239.

MODEL 24 VS — similar to 24CS, only .357 Mag. over 20 ga., nickel finish, accessory pistol grip stock is included.

| | $250 | $210 | $185 | $160 | $145 | $135 | $120 |

MODEL 389 — 12 ga. with 3 in. chamber over choice of .308 Win. or .222 Rem., choke tubes standard, hammerless, double triggers, checkered walnut stock and forearm with recoil pad. Mfg. 1988-90 only.

| | $800 | $640 | $550 | $495 | $435 | $365 | $300 |

Last Mfg.'s Sug. Retail was $919.

SHOTGUNS

Most Savage shotguns (except the Model 312 Series) fall under the domain of Savage Industries, Inc.

Savage made a wide variety of inexpensive, utilitarian shotguns that to date have attracted mostly shooting interest, but little collector interest. A listing of these models may be found in the back of this text under "Serialization".

MODEL 420 O/U — 12, 16, or 20 ga., 26-30 in. barrel, various chokes, boxlock, double trigger, extractors, plain pistol grip stock. Mfg. 1938-1942.

| | $385 | $305 | $275 | $250 | $210 | $195 | $155 |
| Single trigger | $440 | $360 | $330 | $305 | $265 | $220 | $195 |

MODEL 430 — similar to 420, with checkered stock and solid rib, recoil pad.

| | $440 | $360 | $305 | $275 | $240 | $220 | $195 |
| Single trigger | $495 | $415 | $360 | $320 | $285 | $265 | $220 |

MODEL 220 SINGLE BARREL — 12, 16, 20, 28 or .410 ga., 26-32 in. barrel, various chokes, hammerless, plain pistol grip stock. Mfg. 1938-1965.

| | $90 | $65 | $55 | $45 | $35 | $30 | $30 |

MODEL 220P — similar to 220, with poly choke, not made in .410.

| | $90 | $65 | $55 | $45 | $35 | $30 | $30 |

MODEL 220 AC — similar to 220, with Savage adj. choke.

| | $100 | $85 | $65 | $55 | $45 | $35 | $30 |

MODEL 220L — similar to 220, with sidelever. Mfg. 1965-1972.

| | $90 | $65 | $55 | $45 | $35 | $30 | $30 |

MODEL 720 AUTOLOADER STANDARD — 12 or 16 ga., Browning A-5 style action, 26-32 in. barrels, various chokes, checkered pistol grip stock. Mfg. 1930-1949.

| | $275 | $195 | $165 | $155 | $140 | $120 | $110 |

Grading	100%	98%	95%	90%	80%	70%	60%

MODEL 720 RIOT — see the "Trench/Riot Shotgun" category in the T section for more information and prices.

MODEL 726 UPLAND SPORTER — similar to 720, except 2 shell mag. Mfg. 1931-1949.

	$275	$195	$165	$155	$140	$120	$110

MODEL 740C SKEET GUN — similar to 726, with Cutts Compensator and skeet stock, 24½ in. barrel. Mfg. 1936-1949.

	$305	$230	$200	$175	$155	$140	$120

MODEL 745 LIGHTWEIGHT — similar to 720, with alloy receiver, 12 ga. only, 28 in. barrel. Mfg. 1940-1949.

	$275	$195	$165	$155	$140	$120	$110

MODEL 755 STANDARD SEMI-AUTO — 12 or 16 ga., 26, 28, or 30 in. barrel, various chokes, rounded off receiver, checkered pistol grip stock. Mfg. 1949-1958.

	$265	$180	$160	$150	$140	$120	$110

MODEL 755SC — similar to 755, with Savage Super Choke.

	$275	$195	$165	$155	$140	$120	$110

MODEL 775 LIGHTWEIGHT — similar to 755, with alloy receiver. Mfg. 1950-1965.

	$275	$195	$180	$165	$150	$140	$120

MODEL 775SC — similar to 775, with Savage Super Choke.

	$285	$205	$195	$175	$160	$150	$130

MODEL 750 SEMI-AUTO — 12 ga., Browning patterned semi-auto, 26 or 28 in. barrels, various chokes, checkered pistol grip stock. Mfg. 1960-1967.

	$275	$195	$165	$155	$140	$120	$110

MODEL 750SC — similar to 750, with Savage Super Choke.

	$285	$205	$175	$165	$150	$130	$120

MODEL 750AC — similar to 750, with poly choke.

	$285	$205	$175	$165	$150	$130	$120

MODEL 30 SLIDE ACTION — 12, 16, 20, or .410 ga., 26, 28, or 30 in. barrels, various chokes, VR, plain pistol grip stock. Mfg. 1958-1970.

	$220	$175	$155	$140	$120	$100	$85

Checkered Late Model

	$230	$185	$165	$150	$130	$110	$95

MODEL 30AC — similar to 30, with adj. choke, 12 ga. only. Mfg. 1959-1970.

Checkered.

	$240	$200	$175	$160	$145	$120	$100

MODEL 30T TRAP AND DUCK GUN — similar to 30, with 30 in. full, 12 ga. only, Monte Carlo stock and pad. Mfg. 1963-1970.

	$230	$185	$165	$150	$130	$110	$90

MODEL 30FG TAKEDOWN ACTION — 12, 20, or .410 ga., 26, 28, or 30 in., barrel, various chokes, checkered pistol grip stock. Mfg. 1970-1975.

	$175	$155	$130	$110	$95	$85	$70

Grading	100%	98%	95%	90%	80%	70%	60%

MODEL 30T TAKEDOWN TRAP — 12 ga. only, 30 in. full, Monte Carlo stock with pad. Mfg. 1970-1973.

| | $195 | $175 | $155 | $140 | $110 | $100 | $85 |

MODEL 30AC TAKEDOWN — similar to 30FG, with adj. choke, 12 or 20 ga., 26 in. barrel. Mfg. 1971-1972.

| | $200 | $180 | $165 | $150 | $120 | $110 | $90 |

MODEL 30 TAKEDOWN SLUG GUN — similar to 30FG, with 32 in. cylinder bore barrel, rifle sights. Mfg. 1971-disc.

| | $195 | $175 | $160 | $140 | $110 | $100 | $85 |

MODEL 30D TAKEDOWN — similar to 30FG, with VR, engraved receiver and pad. Mfg. 1971-disc.

| | $200 | $180 | $165 | $150 | $120 | $110 | $90 |

MODEL 67 SLIDE ACTION — see listing under Stevens Section.

MODEL 69R/69N/69RXL RIOT GUNS — see listing under Trench/Riot Guns in this text.

FOX MODELS B, B-SE, AND STEVENS 311 — see listing under Stevens Section.

MODEL 242 O/U — .410 ga., single exposed hammer, single trigger, barrel selector lever, full chokes. Mfg. 1977-1981.

| | $350 | $300 | $260 | $230 | $200 | $175 | $150 |

MODEL 440 O/U — 12 or 20 ga., 26, 28, or 30 in. barrels, various chokes, boxlock, SST, extractors, checkered pistol grip stock, VR. Imported from Italy 1968-1972.

| | $495 | $440 | $415 | $385 | $330 | $305 | $250 |

MODEL 440T — similar to Model 440, 12 ga., 30 in. only, imp mod. or full choke, wide VR, trap style stock, pad. Mfg. 1969-1972.

| | $550 | $470 | $440 | $415 | $385 | $360 | $330 |

MODEL 444 DELUXE — similar to Model 440, with auto ejectors, select walnut. Mfg. 1969-1972.

| | $550 | $470 | $440 | $415 | $385 | $360 | $330 |

MODEL 550 SXS — 12 or 20 ga., 26, 28, or 30 in. barrels, various chokes, boxlock, auto ejectors, single trigger, checkered pistol grip stock. Mfg. 1971-1973.

| | $275 | $220 | $195 | $165 | $150 | $130 | $110 |

MODEL 312 SERIES O/U — 12 ga. only, boxlock action, 3 in. chambers, vent. barrels, satin chrome finished receiver, checkered walnut stock and forearm, SST, choke tubes, approx. 7 lbs. New 1990.
The Model 312 Series falls under the domain of Savage Arms, Inc.

312 Field — 26 or 28 in. VR barrels with choke tubes.

| No Mfg.'s Retail | $675 | $520 | $485 | $435 | $395 | $360 | $330 |

312 Trap — 30 in. barrels only, Monte Carlo stock with recoil pad.

| No Mfg.'s Retail | $715 | $550 | $500 | $460 | $415 | $375 | $330 |

312 Sporting Clays — 28 in. barrels only with 7 choke tubes provided, recoil pad.

| No Mfg.'s Retail | $685 | $530 | $485 | $435 | $395 | $360 | $320 |

Grading	100%	98%	95%	90%	80%	70%	60%

MODEL 320 FIELD — 20 ga., 3 in. chambers, 26 in. VR barrels with choke tubes, same action as Model 312, high gloss wood finish, DT, ejectors, 6¾ lbs. New 1991.
As this edition goes to press, prices have yet to be established on this model.

MODEL 330 O/U — 12 or 20 ga., 26, 28, or 30 in. barrels, various chokes, boxlock, SST, extractors, checkered pistol grip stock. Mfg. by Valmet between 1969-1980.

	$495	$440	$385	$335	$275	$250	$220

MODEL 333T — similar to 330, with 30 in. VR, imp. mod. and full choke, trap stock with pad. Mfg. by Valmet between 1972-1980.

	$550	$470	$415	$385	$360	$305	$275

MODEL 333 O/U — 12 or 20 ga., 26, 28, or 30 in. barrels, various chokes, boxlock, SST, auto ejectors, checkered pistol grip stock. Mfg. by Valmet between 1973-1980.

	$580	$525	$470	$440	$400	$375	$330

MODEL 2400 O/U COMBINATION GUN — 12 ga. full choke barrel over .222 or .308 rifle barrel, 23½ in. barrels, folding leaf sight, solid rib, dovetailed for scope mount, checkered Monte Carlo stock. Mfg. by Valmet between 1975-1980.

	$605	$550	$525	$495	$440	$415	$385

SCATTERGUN TECHNOLOGIES INC. (S.G.T.)

Manufacturer located in Nashville, TN since 1991. Distributor, dealer, and consumer sales.

S.G.T. manufactures practical defense and combat shotguns in 12 ga. only, utilizing Remington Models 870 and 11-87 actions in various configurations as listed below. All shotguns feature 3 in. chamber capacity and parkerized finish.

SHOTGUNS: SLIDE ACTION

STANDARD MODEL — 18 in. barrel, adj. ghost ring rear sight, 7 shot mag. tube, parkerized finish, synthetic buttstock and forearm with 11,000 CP flashlight.

Mfg.'s Sug. Retail	$695	$625	$500	$395

PROFESSIONAL MODEL — similar to Standard Model, except has 14 in. barrel and 6 shot mag.

Mfg.'s Sug. Retail	$695	$625	$500	$395

ENTRY MODEL — 12½ in. barrel with fixed choke, 5 shot mag., adj. ghost ring rear sight, synthetic buttstock and nylon strap assisted forearm with 5,000 CP flashlight.

Mfg.'s Sug. Retail	$695	$625	$500	$395

F.B.I.MODEL — similar to Standard Model, except has 5 shot mag.

Mfg.'s Sug. Retail	$665	$600	$480	$380

PATROL MODEL — similar to Standard Model, except has normal grooved synthetic forearm and 5 shot mag.

Mfg.'s Sug. Retail	$525	$475	$395	$295

BORDER PATROL MODEL 20 — similar to Patrol Model, except has 7 shot mag.

Mfg.'s Sug. Retail	$555	$495	$415	$315

BORDER PATROL MODEL 21 — similar to Border Patrol Model 20, except has 6 shot mag.

Mfg.'s Sug. Retail	$555	$495	$415	$315

Grading	100%	98%	95%	90%	80%	70%	60%

CONCEALMENT MODEL 00 — 12½ in. barrel with fixed choke, 5 shot mag., bead sight, grooved synthetic forearm and pistol grip.

Mfg.'s Sug. Retail	$495	$450	$375	$275			

BREACHING MODEL — similar to Concealment Model 00, except has slotted barrel with choke and standoff device.

Mfg.'s Sug. Retail	$450	$400	$350	$275			

CONCEALMENT MODEL 01 — 12½ in. barrel with fixed choke, 5 shot mag., bead sight, synthetic finger-grooved combat forearm and pistol grip.

Mfg.'s Sug. Retail	$525	$475	$395	$295			

CONCEALMENT MODEL 02 — similar to Concealment Model 00, except has Pachmayr forearm and pistol grip.

Mfg.'s Sug. Retail	$555	$495	$415	$315			

CONCEALMENT MODEL 03 — similar to Concealment Model 01, except has synthetic nylon strap assisted forearm with 5,000 CP flashlight.

Mfg.'s Sug. Retail	$625	$550	$455	$350			

SHOTGUNS: SEMI-AUTO

K-9 MODEL — 18 in. barrel, 7 shot mag., synthetic buttstock stock and forearm, adj. ghost ring rear sight.

Mfg.'s Sug. Retail	$755	$675	$550	$450			

SWAT MODEL — 14 in. barrel, synthetic buttstock and forearm with 11,000 CP flashlight.

Mfg.'s Sug. Retail	$895	$795	$650	$525			

URBAN SNIPER MODEL — features 18 in. rifled barrel and scout optics.

Mfg.'s Sug. Retail	$1,095	$950	$775	$525			

SCHALL

Previous manufacturer located in Hartford, CT.

REPEATING HANDGUN — .22 LR only, target pistol, mag. fed manual repeating action. Unusual.

		$425	$360	$320	$270	$220	$180	$150

SCHELLER - SPEZIALWAFFEN

Manufacturer located in Suhl, Germany specializing in bolt action rifles.

For more information regarding this manufacturer (including current model information and U.S. prices) please contact this company directly (see Trademark Index).

SCHULTZ & LARSEN

Manufacturer located in Otterup, Denmark since 1911.

NO. 47 MATCH RIFLE — .22 LR, bolt action, single shot, 28 in. heavy barrel, target sights, set trigger, free rifle stock.

	$660	$550	$495	$440	$385	$360	$330

M61 MATCH RIFLE — .22 LR, bolt action, single shot, 28 in. heavy barrel, target sights, set trigger, free rifle stock, palm rest.

	$895	$825	$740	$680	$600	$550	$500

Grading	100%	98%	95%	90%	80%	70%	60%

M62 MATCH RIFLE — various cals., bolt action, single shot, 28 in. heavy barrel, target sights, set trigger, free rifle stock, palm rest.

	100%	98%	95%	90%	80%	70%	60%
	$995	$875	$780	$700	$620	$550	$500

MODEL 54 FREE RIFLE — any American centerfire standard caliber, plus 6.5 x 55mm, 27 in. heavy barrel, target sights, free rifle stock.

	$825	$745	$690	$605	$550	$495	$440

MODEL 54J SPORTING RIFLE — .270, .30-06, 7 x 61 Sharpe and Hart cal., bolt action, 3 shot, 24 in. barrel, checkered Monte Carlo stock, no sights.

	$650	$550	$470	$415	$360	$330	$300

MODEL 68 DL — .22-250, .243 Win., 6mm Rem., .264 Win. Mag., .270, .30-06, .308 Win., 7 x 61 S&H, 7 mm Rem. Mag., 8 x 57 JS, 300 Win. Mag., .308 Norma Mag., .338 Win. Mag., .358 Norma Mag., or .458 Win. Mag. cal., bolt action, 24 in. barrel, Bofors Steel receiver, bolt has 4 rear locking lugs, select French walnut, adj. trigger, no sights except for .458 Mag.

	$725	$650	$575	$525	$495	$460	$430

SCHUETZEN RIFLES

A Schuetzen Rifle is a special single shot target rifle. During the time span 1875-1945 this target configuration rifle was very popular for competition shooters. Many of these guns had elaborate locking systems, top quality sights, double set triggers, heavy barrels, palm and thumb rests, sculptured cheek piece, Swiss style butt plate, etc. Rather than list all the various domestic and European makers (there are hundreds), it should be noted that since there are so many combinations of options for this configuration that most guns have to be examined and appraised individually. Most non-major trademarks sell in the $550-$1,500 range, depending on features and condition. Schuetzen Rifles are a field in themselves and a knowledgeable dealer/collector should be consulted before buying or selling one of these guns.

SCOTT, W.C., LTD.

Established in 1834 by William Scott, located in Birmingham, England, and remained in the family until 1897. At this time, Scott merged with P. Webley & Son to form Webley & Scott Revolver and Arms Co., Ltd. (later changed to Webley & Scott Ltd.). Even though Scott family members were no longer associated with this new company, the Scott gun-line was continued with the trademark intact until 1935. Thereafter, only a few guns were marked Scott. In 1979, Webley & Scott ceased manufacture of all firearms. A new company, W. & C. Scott, was formed in 1980 utilizing mostly employees of Webley & Scott. W. & C. Scott remained part of its parent company, Harris & Sheldon (also had controlling interest in Hardy and Churchill trademarks), until 1985 when Scott was purchased by Holland & Holland. Manufacture of Scott guns decreased substantially after the merger, and in September 1991, W. & C. Scott ceased operation all together. During its 157 years of production, Scott and Webley & Scott produced approximately, 150,00 double guns, 10,000 rifles (either double or bolt-action) and thousands of single guns and single rifles.

SHOTGUNS: SxS

All W.C. Scott Shotguns were discontinued in 1990. W.C. Scott also manufactured many hammer guns that vary in price from $250-$2,500, depending on grade and original condition.

KINMOUNT — 12, 16, 20, or 28 ga., double barrel boxlock action, ejectors, deluxe checkered walnut, scroll engraving.

	$6,500	$5,750	$5,000	$4,500	$4,000	$3,000	$2,500

Add 20% for 28 or .410 ga.
Add 10% for SNT.
Last Mfg.'s Sug. Retail was $11,000.

Grading	100%	98%	95%	90%	80%	70%	60%

BOWOOD — 12, 16, 20, or 28 ga., double barrel boxlock action, ejectors, deluxe checkered walnut, extensive scroll engraving.

	$7,500	$6,500	$5,750	$5,000	$4,500	$4,000	$3,500

Add 20% for 28 or .410 ga.
Add 10% for SNT.
Last Mfg.'s Sug. Retail was $12,500.

CHATSWORTH — 12, 16, 20, or 28 ga., top-of-the-line boxlock action, ejectors, deluxe checkered walnut, extensive scroll engraving.

	$8,750	$7,500	$6,500	$5,750	$5,000	$4,500	$4,000

Add 20% for 28 or .410 ga.
Add 10% for SNT.
Last Mfg.'s Sug. Retail was $14,000.

BLENHEIM — 12 bore only, upgraded models, custom made to individual specifications, originally priced per individual order.
Specimen rarity precludes percentage grading pricing. Individual appraisals have to be secured on this model.

SECURITY INDUSTRIES
Previous manufacturer located in Little Ferry, NJ.

MODEL PSS 38 DOUBLE ACTION — .38 Spl. 5 shot cylinder, 2 in. barrel, stainless steel, fixed sights, wood grips. Mfg. 1973-1978.

	$175	$150	$140	$130	$125	$110	$100

MODEL PM357 — similar to PSS 38, except .357 Mag., 2½ in. barrel. Mfg. 1975-disc.

	$225	$175	$165	$150	$140	$125	$110

MODEL PPM 357 — .357 Mag., 5 shot, 2 in. barrel, spurless hammer until 1977, new models have spur. Mfg. 1965-disc.

	$225	$175	$165	$150	$140	$125	$110

SEDCO INDUSTRIES, INC.
Previous manufacturer located in Lake Elsinore, CA until 1991.

MODEL SP-22 — .22 LR cal., semi-auto single action, 2½ in. barrel, rotary safety, serrated slide, nickel, satin nickel (new 1990), or black metal finish, simulated pearl grips in white, blue, gray, or pink, 11 oz. Mfg. 1989-90 only.

	$60	$55	$50	$45	$40	$35	$35

Last Mfg.'s Sug. Retail was $69.

SEDGLEY, R.F., INC.
Previous manufacturer located in Philadelphia, PA.

SPRINGFIELD SPORTING RIFLE — '03 Springfield bolt action, .220 Swift, .218 Bee, .22-3000, .22-4000, .22 Hornet, .25-35, .250-3000, .257 Roberts, .270, 7mm, or .30-06 cal., 24 in. barrel, Lyman receiver sight, checkered pistol grip stock, pre-WWII.

	$550	$470	$415	$360	$315	$275	$250

SPRINGFIELD CARBINE SPORTER — similar to Rifle, with 20 in. barrel, and full length stock.

	$605	$525	$470	$415	$360	$330	$295

Seecamp, L.W. Co., Inc.

SEECAMP, L.W. CO., INC.

Manufacturer located in Milford, CT. Dealer direct sales only.

All Seecamp pistols are hand machined and hand fitted from stainless steel. Manufacture has always emphasized quality over quantity - this explains why values often exceed the company's retail prices. There is simply more demand than supply. Currently, approx. 100 pistols (LWS 32 Model) per month are being fabricated.

Grading	100%	98%	95%	90%	80%	70%	60%

LWS .25 ACP MODEL — .25 ACP, double action, semi-auto, 2 in. barrel, 7 shot mag., stainless steel, matte finish, 12 oz. Approx. 5,000 mfg. 1982-1985.

		$340	$295	$260	$235	$220	$210	$200

Last Mfg.'s Sug. Retail was $275.

LWS 32 MODEL — .32 ACP Silvertip, double action, semi-auto, 2 in. barrel, stainless steel, 6 shot mag., 12½ oz. Limited mfg.

Mfg.'s Sug. Retail	$350		$440	$385	$360	$330	$310	$295	$280

This model is available in either a matte or polished finish. The polished finish carries a slight premium.

MATCHED PAIR — includes both .25 ACP and .32 ACP pistols with the same serial number, approx. 200 sets were mfg. before the BATF stopped this practice.

		$950	$800	$700

This set contains a matte finished .25 ACP and a polished .32 ACP.

SEITZ

SINGLE BARREL TRAP GUN — 12 ga. only, single barrel, various barrel lengths, pull or release trigger, only 45 guns mfg.

	$13,000	$10,000	$8,500	$7,700	$6,950	$6,200	$5,400

SEMMERLING

Manufactured by American Derringer Corp. located in Waco, TX.

Less than 600 LM-4 pistols have been mfg. since 1978.

LM-4 PISTOL — 9mm (new 1986) or .45 ACP cal., 2 in. barrel, blue, smallest .45 ACP repeater available, slide is worked manually with thumb on serrated slide-top, extremely high quality, hand fitted and finished, a special purpose weapon, very limited production with 14-24 month waiting period.

Mfg.'s Sug. Retail	$1,750		$1,600	$1,250	$1,100	$1,000	$895	$795	$695

The original U.S. Army contract pistol sold for $5,000. Earlier mfg. by Lichtman will also command a premium over values listed above.

⚔ **Stainless Steel** — matte finish stainless steel variation of the LM-4, combat gray, satin, high polish finish, rosewood grips. Limited mfg. (approx. 100 guns per year). New 1986.

Mfg.'s Sug. Retail	$1,875		$1,775	$1,350	$1,125

Add $100-$150 for satin or high polish finish.

SHARPS, CHRISTIAN

Manufactured in Windsor, VT under Sharps Rifle Manufacturing Company between 1851-1855. Manufactured in Hartford, CT under same name between 1855-1874. Reorganized as Sharps Rifle Company in 1876 with production resuming in Hartford (1876 only) and Bridgeport, CT. from 1877-1881.

REVOLVER, PERCUSSION — made 1850s in Philadelphia, production about 2000, 3 in. octagonal tip-up barrel with rib, .25 caliber, 6 shot.

		$900	$850	$800	$750	$675	$600	$500

Grading	100%	98%	95%	90%	80%	70%	60%

PEPPERBOX PISTOL — also marked Sharps and Hankins, 4-shot breech-loading, .32, .30, or .22 rimfire cal., firing pin rotates, brass frame with silver plating, or case-hardening on iron frame.

⚞ **First model** — 5 variations. Scarcer variations can be worth up to 150% more.

	$375	$350	$300	$250	$200	$175	$125

⚞ **Second model** — 5 variations. Scarcer variations can be worth up to 150% more.

	$425	$400	$375	$325	$250	$200	$150

⚞ **Third model** — Sharps and Hankins markings, .32 rimfire short, 4 variations. Premium for scarcer variations.

	$375	$350	$325	$275	$225	$175	$150

⚞ **Fourth model** — 4 variations, bird's-head grip, .32 rimfire long. Premium for scarcer variations.

	$385	$360	$330	$275	$220	$195	$140

RIFLES: BREECH LOADING

The Model 1863 Carbine was one of the highest production rifles of the Civil War with production totaling over 100,000. During a period after the Civil War, the Model 1874 was loosely dubbed "Buffalo Rifle" because of its involvement on the western plains.

MODEL 1851 CARBINE — .52-caliber percussion, breech-loading, Maynard tape primer, U.S. military markings. Deduct 40% for non-martial sporting rifle version.

	$3,000	$2,650	$2,500	$2,000	$1,500	$1,350	$1,000

MODEL 1852 CARBINE — slanting breech, approx. 4500 mfg. 1853-1855, caliber .52 with Sharps' patented pellet primer built into lockplate. Add 50% for U.S. martial markings. Also sporting rifles in .52, .44, or .36 cal.

	$925	$900	$850	$750	$650	$550	$425

MODEL 1853 CARBINE — mfg. 1854-1858 in quantity of some 10,350, caliber .52 with Sharps' patented pellet primer feed. Deduct 10% for sporting-rifle version.

	$900	$850	$800	$750	$700	$625	$500

MODEL 1855 CARBINE — U.S. martial model in .52 caliber, breech-loading, Maynard tape primer system, sling ring is mounted on left side.

	$1,750	$1,675	$1,600	$1,500	$1,200	$1,000	$800

STRAIGHT-BREECH RIFLES AND CARBINES, 1859, 1863, 1865. — breech-loading caliber .52 with Sharps' patented pellet-priming system in lockplate. (Prices listed are for models that are original and have not been converted). The Model 1859 is worth a slight premium.

	$1,200	$1,150	$1,100	$1,000	$800	$650	$400

Over 32,000 carbines (majority) and rifles were converted to .50-70 centerfire. Can be detected by additional "DFC" ribbon cartouche on left center of stock. These converted specimens (mostly Model 1863s) are worth approx. 50% of values listed above.

COFFEE-MILL MODEL — built-in coffee-grinding mill in stock for cavalry use. Easy to fake.

	$8,500	$8,000	$7,500	$6,000	$5,000	$4,500	$4,000

MODEL 1874 RIFLE — mfg. from 1871 until 1881, known as the "Buffalo Rifle" in its day. Many variations, cals., and accessories. Research should be done before purchasing.

Grading	100%	98%	95%	90%	80%	70%	60%

SPORTING RIFLE — .50, .45, .44, or .40 cal. Heavier barrels are worth more. Approx. 6,500 mfg.

	$2,000	$1,800	$1,600	$1,250	$1,000	$900	$800

MILITARY RIFLE — mostly in .50-70 or .45-70 cal., 30 in. barrel with three bands. Approx. 1700 mfg.

	$1,400	$1,300	$1,200	$1,000	$850	$750	$650

MILITARY CARBINE — mostly .50-70 cal. Fewer than 500 mfg.

	$1,750	$1,650	$1,500	$1,150	$850	$750	$675

CREEDMOOR, MID-RANGE, LONG-RANGE, AND BUSINESS RIFLE — these have a basically common look, though there are many differences and variations among them. (Price range is quite general).

	$2,500	$2,350	$2,000	$1,600	$1,350	$1,000	$750

SCHUETZEN RIFLE — .40-50 cal., 30 in. octagonal barrel. Only 70 mfg.

	$2,255	$2,000	$1,800	$1,500	$1,250	$1,000	$900

SHERIDAN PRODUCTS INCORPORATED
Previous manufacturer located in Racine, WI.

PISTOL

KNOCKABOUT — .22 S or L, single shot, 5 in. barrel, checkered plastic grips, fixed sights. Mfg. 1953-1960.

	$110	$100	$85	$75	$60	$50	$40

SHILEN RIFLES, INCORPORATED
Previous manufacturer located in Enis, TX.

RIFLES: BOLT ACTION

DGA SPORTER — .17 Rem., .223 Rem., .22-250, .220 Swift, 6mm Rem., .243 Win., .250 Savage, .257 Roberts, .284 Win., .308 Win., or .358 Win. cal., 3 shot mag., 24 in. barrel, no sights, claro walnut stock.

	$800	$775	$750	$700	$600	$500	$400

DGA VARMINTER — similar to Sporter, except 25 in. medium heavy barrel.

	$640	$580	$530	$495	$440	$415	$385

DGA SILHOUETTE RIFLE — similar to Varminter, .308 only.

	$580	$540	$495	$440	$415	$385	$365

DGA BENCHREST RIFLE — single shot, choice of cals., 26 in. heavy barrel or medium barrel, no sights, choice of fiberglass or walnut stock, thumbhole available.

	$690	$670	$635	$580	$525	$475	$430

SHILOH RIFLE MFG. CO.
Manufacturer located in Big Timber, MT. Dealer direct sales.

The Shiloh Rifle Mfg. Company is currently manufacturing replicas of Sharps rifles and carbines. They are available as black powder cartridge rifles. Most models are available in the following cals.: .40-50, .40-65 Win., .40-70, .40-90, .45-70, .45-90, .45-100, .45-110, .45-120, .50-70, .50-90 (disc.), .50-100, and .50-140 (disc.). Percussion Rifles also are available in .54 cal. and are breech loading. All models are authentically reproduced and are high quality.

RIFLES: BLACK POWDER CARTRIDGE

Currently, many of the models listed below are back ordered, with some orders taking up to 2 years to fill. In this type of market (when demand is sometimes greater than supply), premiums may exist.

Grading	100%	98%	95%	90%	80%	70%	60%
MODEL 1874 LONG RANGE EXPRESS							
Mfg.'s Sug. Retail $995	$895	$800	$650	$550	$475	$410	$350
MODEL 1874 NO. 1 SPORTING							
Mfg.'s Sug. Retail $970	$860	$775	$625	$525	$450	$395	$325
MODEL 1874 NO. 2 SPORTING							
	$605	$520	$440	$380	$320	$285	$270
MODEL 1874 NO. 3 SPORTING							
Mfg.'s Sug. Retail $870	$775	$675	$535	$450	$380	$320	$295
MODEL 1874 BUSINESS RIFLE							
Mfg.'s Sug. Retail $875	$780	$675	$535	$450	$380	$320	$295
MODEL 1874 HUNTER'S RIFLE							
	$480	$440	$400	$340	$300	$280	$260
MODEL 1874 HARTFORD — features Hartford collar between receiver and barrel assembly. New 1989.							
Mfg.'s Sug. Retail $1,033	$925	$825	$675	$550	$475	$410	$350
MODEL 1874 MILITARY RIFLE							
Mfg.'s Sug. Retail $995	$895	$800	$650	$550	$475	$410	$350
MODEL 1874 MILITARY CARBINE							
Mfg.'s Sug. Retail $925	$815	$700	$575	$450	$380	$320	$295
MODEL 1874 CARBINE "CIVILIAN"							
Mfg.'s Sug. Retail $895	$790	$675	$535	$450	$380	$320	$295
MODEL 1874 SADDLE RIFLE							
Mfg.'s Sug. Retail $925	$815	$700	$575	$450	$380	$320	$295
MODEL 1874 ROUGHRIDER							
Mfg.'s Sug. Retail $870	$765	$675	$535	$450	$380	$320	$295
Add $80 for semi-fancy walnut.							
MODEL 1874 JAEGER HUNTING RIFLE — hunting rifle with lightweight half-octagon/half-round barrel. Mfg. 1987-92.							
	$720	$570	$450	$380	$320	$295	$270

Last Mfg.'s Sug. Retail was $835.

Shiloh Rifle Mfg., Co., cont.

Grading	100%	98%	95%	90%	80%	70%	60%

CUSTOM SHARPS BUFFALO RIFLE — .45-70 or .45-110 cal., 34 in. heavy barrel, military stock with patch box, vernier aperture rear sight with globe front, mfg. for the motion picture "Quigley Down Under", approx. 13 lbs. New 1990.

	100%	98%	95%	90%
Mfg.'s Sug. Retail	$2,650	$2,450	$2,000	$1,500

RIFLES: PERCUSSION-BREECH LOADING

Models 1863 Sporting, 1863 Military Rifle and Carbine models listed below have prices available through special request only. Last retail prices shown below indicate 1992 information.

MODEL 1863 SPORTING

100%	98%	95%	90%	80%	70%	60%
$685	$550	$450	$380	$320	$295	$270

Last Mfg.'s Sug. Retail was $785.

MODEL 1863 NO. 2 SPORTING

100%	98%	95%	90%	80%	70%	60%
$550	$470	$415	$360	$300	$275	$250

MODEL 1863 NO. 3 SPORTING

100%	98%	95%	90%	80%	70%	60%
$525	$440	$385	$340	$290	$270	$250

MODEL 1863 MILITARY RIFLE

100%	98%	95%	90%	80%	70%	60%
$800	$650	$550	$475	$410	$350	$320

Last Mfg.'s Sug. Retail was $895.

MODEL 1863 MILITARY CARBINE

100%	98%	95%	90%	80%	70%	60%
$690	$550	$450	$380	$320	$295	$270

Last Mfg.'s Sug. Retail was $795.

MODEL 1859 MILITARY CARBINE

100%	98%	95%	90%	80%	70%	60%
$440	$360	$305	$275	$220	$165	$140

MODEL 1862 ROBINSON CONFEDERATE CARBINE

100%	98%	95%	90%	80%	70%	60%
$805	$650	$550	$475	$410	$350	$320

Last Mfg.'s Sug. Retail was $915.

MONTANA CENTENNIAL RIFLE SERIES — mfg. to commemorate Montana's 100th Centennial (1889-1989), limited manufacture. Mfg. 1988-90.

⚹ **Creedmoor Rifle** — .45-70 cal., extra fancy rifle with engraving, 32 in. barrel, walnut cased. 100 mfg. only ser. numbered 1-101.

100%	98%	95%
$3,750	$2,500	$1,950

Last Mfg.'s Sug. Retail was $3,750.

⚹ **Hartford Rifle** — .45-70 cal, 30 in. barrel, case colored receiver, 12 lbs. Serial numbered 102-902.

100%	98%	95%
$1,375	$995	$750

Last Mfg.'s Sug. Retail was $1,375.

⚹ **Bridgeport Rifle** — .45-70, 30 in. barrel, similar to Hartford rifle without Pewter forearm cap, 12 lbs.

100%	98%	95%
$1,075	$775	$575

Last Mfg.'s Sug. Retail was $1,075.

SIDEWINDER

Manufactured by D-Max, Inc. located in Bagley, MN beginning 1993. Dealer or consumer sales.

Grading	100%	98%	95%	90%	80%	70%	60%

SIDEWINDER — .45 LC or 2½/3 in. .410 shotshells/slugs, 6 shot, stainless steel construction, 6½ or 7½ in. bull barrel (muzzle end bored for choke), Pachmayr grips, hammer bar safety, adj. rear sight, unique design permits one cylinder to shoot above listed loads, cased with choke tube, 3.8 lbs. New 1993.

Mfg.'s Sug. Retail	**$675**		**$650**	**$575**	**$475**		

SIG

Manufactured by Sig Swiss Industrial Company since 1860 in Neuhausen, Switzerland. Previously imported and distributed by Sigarms Located in Herndon, VA.

PISTOLS

Mandall Shooting Supplies, Inc. located in Scottsdale, AZ still has limited quantities of the 210-1, 210-2, 210-5, and 210-6.

P 210 — 9mm or 7.65 Para., single action, 4¾ in. barrel, 8 shot mag., standard weapon of the Swiss Army, 2 lbs.

Originally mfg. in 1947, this pistol was first designated the SP 47/8 and became the standard military pistol of the Swiss Army in 1949. Later designated the P 210, this handgun has been mfg. continuously for over 40 years.

P 210-1 — polished finish, walnut grips, special hammer, fixed sights. Importation disc. 1986.

	$1,950	$1,675	$1,400	$1,195	$975	$850	$750

Last Mfg.'s Sug. Retail was $1,861.

P 210-2 — matte finish, field sights, plastic grips. Importation disc. 1987.

	$1,575	$1,225	$1,000	$875	$750	$625	$550

Last Mfg.'s Sug. Retail was $1,350.

P 210-5 — matte finish, micrometer sights, 150mm or 180mm (rare) extended barrel, hard rubber grips, special order only, very limited mfg. Importation disc. 1987.

	$1,850	$1,475	$1,325	$1,150	$950	$825	$725

Last Mfg.'s Sug. Retail was $1,795.

P 210-6 — matte finish, micrometer sights, 120mm barrel, hard rubber grips. Importation disc. 1987.

	$1,675	$1,335	$1,100	$925	$775	$650	$575

Last Mfg.'s Sug. Retail was $1,595.

P 210 Deluxe Models — various models differ in the amount of engraving, gold inlays, carved wooden grips, presentation cases, and other special order features available from the factory. Prices start at $3,500 and can go up to $5,500, depending on the amount of special orders executed.

Conversion kits can be special ordered converting to either 7.65 Luger or .22 LR cal. Add $630 for conversion kit with field sights or $781 for conversion kit with fixed sights standard (adj. by special order).

Sig, cont.

Grading	100%	98%	95%	90%	80%	70%	60%

RIFLES

While SIG rifles have not been imported in quantity since 1988, Mandall Shooting Supplies, Inc. still has these models left in limited quantities. 1993 retail prices are as follows: PE-57 is $4,400, the AMT is $4,400, and the SG 550/551 is $4,000.

PE-57 — 7.5 Swiss cal. only, semi-auto version of the Swiss military rifle, 24 in. barrel, includes 24 shot mag., leather sling, bipod and maintenance kit. Importation disc. 1988.

	100%	98%	95%	90%	80%	70%	60%
	$2,000	$1,800	$1,675	$1,445	$1,325	$1,150	$950

The PE-57 was previously distributed in limited quantities by Osborne's located in Cheboygan, MI.
Last Mfg.'s Sug. Retail was $1,745.

SIG-AMT SEMI-AUTO RIFLE — semi-auto version of SG510-4 auto paramilitary design rifle, roller delayed blowback action, .308 Win., 5, 10, or 20 shot mag., 18¾ in. barrel, wood stock, folding bipod. Mfg. 1960-present. Importation disc. 1988.

	100%	98%	95%	90%	80%	70%	60%
	$2,500	$2,250	$2,000	$1,850	$1,700	$1,550	$1,400

This model is available in very limited quantities through Osborne's located in Cheboygan, MI.
Last Mfg.'s Sug. Retail was $1,795.

SG 550/551 — .223 cal. with heavier bullet, Swiss Army's semi-auto version of its newest paramilitary design rifle (SIG 90), 20.8 (SG 550) or 16 in. (SG 551 Carbine) barrel, some synthetics used to save weight, 20 shot mag., diopter night sights, built-in folding bipod, 7.7 or 9 lbs.

	100%	98%	95%	90%	80%	70%	60%
	$3,250	$2,700	$2,400	$2,150	$1,900	$1,700	$1,500

Add $250 for case.
Last Mfg.'s Sug. Retail was $1,950.
This model has been banned from domestic importation due to 1989 Federal legislation.

SIG-HAMMERLI

Manufactured by Hammerli Ltd. in Lenzburg, Switzerland. Previously imported by Osborne's located in Cheboygan, MI.

P240 TARGET PISTOL — .32 S&W Long wadcutter or .38 (disc.) cal., single action, 5 shot mag., 5.9 in. barrel, blued finish, thumb rest walnut grips, adj. sights and trigger, 3 lbs. Add $100 for Morini adj. grips. Importation disc. 1986.

	100%	98%	95%	90%	80%	70%	60%
	$1,250	$1,100	$985	$870	$770	$715	$660

Last Mfg.'s Sug. Retail was $1,350.
.38 Mid-range cal. is very desirable in this model - healthy premiums (and inconsistent) are being asked currently.

.22 CONVERSION UNIT

	100%	98%	95%
	$550	$495	$400

Last Mfg.'s Sug. Retail was $595.

SIG SAUER

Manufacturer located in Germany. Currently imported and distributed by Sigarms located in Exeter, NH.

Grading	100%	98%	95%	90%	80%	70%	60%

PISTOLS: SEMI-AUTO

MODEL P210 — refer to listing under SIG pistols.

MODEL P220 — double action, .22 LR (disc.), .38 Super, 7.65mm (disc.), 9mm Luger (disc 1991), or .45 ACP cal., 7 (.45 ACP) or 9 shot mag., 4.4 in. barrel, decocking lever safety, matte blue, lightweight alloy frame, black plastic grips, (action is same as Browning BDA), values are for .45 ACP cal. and assume American side mag. release (standard 1986), 28.2 oz. Mfg. 1976-present.

Mfg.'s Sug. Retail	$780	$680	$600	$495	$440	$395	$350	$310

Add $100 for Siglite night sights.
Add $70 for factory K-Kote finish.
Add $25 for nickel finished slide (new 1992).
Add $70 for electroless nickel finish (disc. 1991).
Add $680 for .22 LR conversion kit (disc.).
Subtract 10% for "European" Model (bottom mag. release - includes 9mm and .38 Super cals.).

MODEL P225 — 9mm Para., double action, similar to P220, shorter dimensions, 3.85 in. barrel, 8 shot, thumb actuated button release mag., fully adj. sights, 28.8 oz.

Mfg.'s Sug. Retail	$775	$675	$600	$500	$450	$400	$350	$310

Add $70 for factory K-Kote finish.
Add $100 for Siglite night sights.
Add $25 for nickel finished slide (new 1992).
Add $70 for electroless nickel finish (disc. 1991).

MODEL P226 — 9mm Para., compact variation, choice of traditional double action or double action only (new 1992) operation, 15 or 20 shot mag., 4.4 in. barrel, alloy frame, high contrast sights, 29.9 oz. New 1983.

Mfg.'s Sug. Retail	$805	$725	$625	$525	$475	$415	$360	$310

Add $100 for Siglite night sights.
Add $70 for K-Kote (Polymer) finish.
Add $25 for nickel finished slide (new 1992).
Add $70 for electroless nickel finish (disc. 1991).
This model is also available in double action only (all finishes) at no extra charge.

MODEL P228 — 9mm Para., choice of traditional double action or double action only (new 1992) operation, compact design, 4.41 in. barrel, 13 shot mag., automatic firing pin lock safety, 3 dot sighting system, alloy frame, choice of blue, nickel slide (new 1991), or K-Kote finish, 29.3 oz. New 1990.

Mfg.'s Sug. Retail	$805	$725	$625	$525	$475	$415	$360	$310

Add $100 for Siglite night sights.
Add $70 for K-Kote (Polymer) finish.
Add $25 for nickel finished slide (new 1992).
Add $70 for electroless nickel finish (disc. 1991).
This model is also available in double action only (all finishes) at no extra charge.

MODEL P229 — .40 S&W cal., similar to Model P228, except has blue stainless steel slide with aluminum alloy frame, 12 shot mag., includes lockable carrying case, 30½oz. New 1991.

Mfg.'s Sug. Retail	$875	$775	$650	$550	$475	$415	$360	$310

Add $100 for Siglite night sights.
This model is also available in double action only at no extra charge.

MODEL P230 — double action, .22 LR (disc.)-10 shot, .32 ACP-8 shot (disc.), .380 ACP, and 9mm Ultra (disc.)-7 shot, 3.6 in. barrel, blue, wood grips. Mfg. 1976-present, 17.6 oz.

Mfg.'s Sug. Retail	$510	$425	$375	$300	$270	$240	$215	$190

Grading	100%	98%	95%	90%	80%	70%	60%

Model P230 SL Stainless — similar to Model P230, except stainless steel construction, 22.4 oz.

Mfg.'s Sug. Retail	$595	$480	$425	$350			

RIFLES

MODEL SSG 2000 — available in .223, 7.5mm Swiss, .300 Wby. Mag., or .308 (standard) cal., bolt action, 4 shot mag., no sights, deluxe sniper rifle featuring thumbhole style walnut stock with stippling and thumbwheel adj. cheek piece, 13 lbs. Importation disc. 1986.

	$2,480	$2,260	$1,950	$1,700	$1,500	$1,300	$1,100

This model was available in .223, .300 Wby. Mag., or 7.5mm cal. by special order only. Last Mfg.'s Sug. Retail was $2,850.

SILE DISTRIBUTORS
Distributor/importer/manufacturer located in New York, NY.

In addition to distributing a wide variety of firearms and related accessories (including the mfg. of stocks and grips), Sile Distributors also has some handguns "private labeled" to their specifications. These pistols may be found under the Sphinx heading in the S section of this text.

SILMA SPORTING GUNS
Manufacturer located in Brescia, Italy since 1949. Currently, Silma does not have a domestic importer. To date, there has been limited importation into the U.S. All Silma Shotguns are high quality and utilize premium materials in their manufacture.

Rather than list the various shotgun models and options separately, the following information will help you in ascertaining correct values. Models 70 and 80 are O/U hunting models available in either 12, 20, or .410 ga. They are available with double triggers standard, extractors or ejectors (extra cost), with or without sideplates, or in superlight configuration - retail values range between $500-$1,000. Competition models (including T.J. 70, T.S. 81, Cobra T1, T2, or T3) are also available for trap, skeet, or sporting clays events. Values range between $1,000-$6,200 (with T.J. 70 being the least expensive, and Cobra T2 the most expensive). Two side by side models (AS/70 N and AS/70 EJ) are also available.

For further information regarding Silma's current model line-up, please contact either the Blue Book of Gun Values or the factory. To order a shotgun directly from the manufacturer, please contact them by FAX (refer to the Trademark Index) for more information and a firm price quotation.

SIRKIS INDUSTRIES, LTD.
Manufacturer located in Ramat-Gan, Israel. Previously imported and distributed by Armscorp of America, Inc. located in Baltimore, MD.

PISTOLS: SEMI-AUTO

S.D. 9 — 9mm Para., double action mechanism, frame is constructed mostly of heavy gauge sheet metal stampings, 3.07 in. barrel, parkerized finish, loaded chamber indicator, 7 shot mag., plastic grips, 24½ oz. Imported under this trademark between 1986-1988.

	$300	$250	$225	$200	$190	$180	$170

Last Mfg.'s Sug. Retail was $330.
This pistol is now listed under the Sardius heading in this section.

RIFLES

MODEL 35 MATCH RIFLE — .22 LR only, single shot bolt action, 26 in. full floating barrel, select walnut, match trigger, micrometer sights. Disc. 1985.

	$650	$625	$595	$550	$510	$460	$420

Last Mfg.'s Sug. Retail was $690.

Grading	100%	98%	95%	90%	80%	70%	60%

MODEL 36 SNIPER RIFLE — 7.62mm only, gas operated action, carbon fiber stock, 22 in. barrel, flash suppressor, free range sights. Disc. 1985.

	100%	98%	95%	90%	80%	70%	60%
	$670	$580	$520	$475	$430	$390	$350

Last Mfg.'s Sug. Retail was $760.

SKORPION

Please refer to Armitage International, Ltd. in the "A" section of this text.

SMITH, L.C.

Manufactured from 1880-1888 in Syracuse, NY. Manufactured in Fulton, NY 1890-1945 by Hunter Arms Company.

The L.C. Smith shotgun was made from 1890-1945 by the Hunter Arms Company in Fulton, New York. In 1946, the company was acquired by Marlin Firearms Company. Production continued until 1951 when it ceased for a period of 17 years. In 1968, Marlin brought the L.C. Smith back to life for a period of 5 years. Production stopped in 1973. The L.C. Smith is one of the finest American made shotguns and collector interest is very high. All values shown are for hammerless shotguns.

HAMMERLESS SHOTGUNS 1890-1913

All prices listed below are for guns with fluid steel barrels (except A-1 grade).

    It is important to note that damascus barreled guns with hammers in 90% original condition or better are very collectible and values can approximate those of steel barrel models if the bore is excellent with no pitting. Damascus specimens below 90% condition are not as collectible, however, and values fall off rapidly if under 90%. Prices shown below for 90% and up condition are very difficult to evaluate and are meant as a guide only. L.C. Smith shotguns are rare and hard to evaluate if over 95% condition in the higher grades.

100%	98%	95%	90%	80%	70%	60%	50%	40%	30%	20%	10%

OO GRADE — 12, 16, or 20 ga. Approx. 60,000 mfg.

100%	98%	95%	90%	80%	70%	60%	50%	40%	30%	20%	10%
$1,500	$1,200	$800	$600	$500	$465	$430	$395	$375	$350	$325	$295

Add 33% for auto ejectors.
Add 50% for 20 ga.

O GRADE — 10, 12, 16, or 20 ga. Approx. 30,000 mfg.

100%	98%	95%	90%	80%	70%	60%	50%	40%	30%	20%	10%
$1,600	$1,400	$1,000	$775	$675	$600	$550	$515	$460	$400	$350	$300

Add 50% for 20 ga.

NO. 1 GRADE — 10, 12, 16, or 20 ga. Approx. 10,000 mfg.

100%	98%	95%	90%	80%	70%	60%	50%	40%	30%	20%	10%
$2,400	$1,950	$1,425	$995	$850	$750	$700	$625	$550	$495	$450	$400

Add 33% for auto ejectors.
Add 50% for 20 ga.
Add $200 for SST.

NO. 2 GRADE — 10, 12, 16, or 20 ga. Approx. 13,000 mfg.

100%	98%	95%	90%	80%	70%	60%	50%	40%	30%	20%	10%
$2,900	$2,275	$1,700	$1,400	$1,200	$1,000	$825	$750	$675	$600	$550	$500

Add 33% for auto ejectors.
Add 75% for 20 ga.
Add $200 for SST.

NO. 3 GRADE — 10, 12, 16, or 20 ga. Approx. 4,000 mfg.

100%	98%	95%	90%	80%	70%	60%	50%	40%	30%	20%	10%
$3,475	$2,950	$2,400	$1,850	$1,500	$1,300	$1,100	$995	$875	$775	$625	$500

Add 25% for auto ejectors.
Add 75% for 20 ga.
Add $200 for SST.

	100%	98%	95%	90%	80%	70%	60%	50%	40%	30%	20%	10%

PIGEON GRADE — 10, 12, 16, or 20 ga. Approx. 1,200 mfg.

$3,475	$2,950	$2,400	$1,850	$1,500	$1,300	$1,100	$995	$875	$775	$625	$500

Add 25% for auto ejectors.
Add 75% for 20 ga.
Add $200 for SST.

NO. 4 GRADE — 10, 12, 16, or 20 ga. Approx. 500 mfg., seldomly encountered.

$10,000	$8,000	$5,750	$4,500	$3,500	$2,650	$2,000	$1,775	$1,500	$1,375	$1,200	$1,095

Add 25% for auto ejectors.
Add 75% for 20 ga.
Add $200 for SST.

A-1 GRADE — 10, 12, or 16 ga. Approx. 700 mfg. Damascus barrels only.

$4,850	$3,700	$3,000	$2,200	$1,850	$1,725	$1,425	$1,175	$995	$800	$700	$600

Auto ejectors standard.
Add $200 for SST.

NO. 5 GRADE — 10, 12, 16, or 20 ga. Approx. 500 mfg.

$9,000	$7,000	$4,950	$4,500	$4,000	$3,500	$3,150	$2,700	$2,450	$2,200	$1,995	$1,800

Auto ejectors standard.
Add $200 for SST.
Add 75% for 20 ga., extremely rare.

MONOGRAM GRADE — 10, 12, 16, or 20 ga. Approx. 100 mfg.

$10,750	$9,475	$7,400	$6,000	$5,500	$5,000	$4,600	$4,100	$3,800	$3,500	$3,250	$3,000

Auto ejectors standard.
Add 50% for 20 ga., extremely rare.

A-2 GRADE — 10, 12, 16, or 20 ga. Approx. 200 mfg.

$15,000	$11,000	$8,000	$7,000	$6,000	$5,200	$4,700	$4,200	$3,850	$3,500	$3,250	$3,000

Auto ejectors standard.
20 ga. — only 6 mfg.

A-3 GRADE — 10, 12, 16, or 20 ga. Approx. 20 mfg. Rarity precludes accurate pricing on this model.
Auto ejectors standard.
20 ga. — only 2 mfg.

SHOTGUNS: 1914-1951 MFG.

Fulton trademarked shotguns mfg. by Hunter Arms Co. were inexpensive, utilitarian shotguns designed for a price point rather than quality. Models Fulton and Fulton Special were supplied in 12, 16, 20, or .410 ga. (rare). When encountered today, values usually are in the $100-$300 range. The Hunter Special, although not an L.C. Smith shotgun, did employ the rotary locking bolt system. This was also a low priced gun in its day and prices today are usually in the $125-$350 range. These models had nothing in common with the L.C. Smith shotguns of that time.

L.C. SMITH DOUBLE BARREL SHOTGUN — 12, 16, 20, or .410 ga., any choke, side-lock, auto ejectors standard from Crown Grade up, extractors on lower grades, double or single triggers, straight, 1/2 pistol grip, or pistol grip stock, grade specifications differ in grade of wood, degree of engraving, and overall quality.

STANDARD FIELD GRADE

$1,250	$1,000	$775	$675	$600	$500	$465	$435	$395	$375	$340	$295

Add 33% for auto ejectors.
Add $200 for SST.
Add 30% for 20 ga.
Add 300% for .410 ga.

100%	98%	95%	90%	80%	70%	60%	50%	40%	30%	20%	10%

IDEAL GRADE STANDARD

100%	98%	95%	90%	80%	70%	60%	50%	40%	30%	20%	10%
$1,600	$1,400	$1,100	$900	$825	$750	$700	$650	$595	$550	$530	$495

Add 33% for auto ejectors.
Add $200 for SST.
Add 30% for 20 ga.
Add 400% for .410 ga.

TRAP GRADE

100%	98%	95%	90%	80%	70%	60%	50%	40%	30%	20%	10%
$2,000	$1,500	$1,200	$1,100	$1,000	$925	$850	$775	$675	$600	$550	$500

Auto ejectors — add 33%.
Add $200 for SST.
Add 50% for 20 ga.
Add 400% for .410 ga.

SPECIALTY GRADE

100%	98%	95%	90%	80%	70%	60%	50%	40%	30%	20%	10%
$2,950	$2,450	$1,800	$1,375	$1,100	$1,000	$925	$875	$825	$775	$695	$625

Add $200 for SST.
Add 50% for 20 ga.
Add 400% for .410 ga.
Add 33% for auto ejectors.

EAGLE GRADE

100%	98%	95%	90%	80%	70%	60%	50%	40%	30%	20%	10%
$4,750	$4,250	$3,500	$2,900	$2,350	$1,850	$1,500	$1,400	$1,300	$1,200	$1,100	$1,000

Add $200 for SST.
Add 50% for 20 ga.

SKEET SPECIAL GRADE

100%	98%	95%	90%	80%	70%	60%	50%	40%	30%	20%	10%
$3,100	$2,600	$1,650	$1,200	$1,100	$925	$875	$825	$775	$725	$675	$600

Add $200 for SST.
Add 50% for 20 ga.
Add 400% for .410 ga.
Add 33% for auto ejectors.

PREMIER SKEET GRADE

100%	98%	95%	90%	80%	70%	60%	50%	40%	30%	20%	10%
$3,100	$2,600	$1,650	$1,200	$1,100	$925	$875	$825	$775	$725	$675	$600

Add $200 for SST.
Add 50% for 20 ga.
Add 400% for .410 ga.
Add 33% for auto ejectors.

CROWN GRADE

100%	98%	95%	90%	80%	70%	60%	50%	40%	30%	20%	10%
$5,750	$4,950	$4,250	$4,000	$3,500	$3,100	$2,700	$2,450	$2,225	$2,000	$1,900	$1,800

Add $200 for SST.
20 gauge — very rare.
.410 — rare and very expensive, only 6 mfg.

MONOGRAM GRADE

100%	98%	95%	90%	80%	70%	60%	50%	40%	30%	20%	10%
$12,000	$9,750	$7,750	$6,400	$5,650	$5,100	$4,650	$4,150	$3,775	$3,500	$3,250	$3,000

Add 50% for 20 ga.

PREMIER GRADE — very limited mfg., rarity precludes accurate pricing on this model.

DELUXE GRADE — very limited mfg., rarity precludes accurate pricing on this model.

SINGLE BARREL TRAP GUN — 12 ga. only, 32 or 34 in. VR barrel, boxlock, auto ejector, checkered pistol grip stock, recoil pad. Approx. 2,650 mfg. 1917-1951.

⚔ Olympic Grade

100%	98%	95%	90%	80%	70%	60%	50%	40%	30%	20%	10%
$1,650	$1,400	$1,200	$1,100	$1,000	$900	$800	$725	$675	$625	$575	$550

	100%	98%	95%	90%	80%	70%	60%	50%	40%	30%	20%	10%

⇥ Specialty Grade

| $1,950 | $1,700 | $1,500 | $1,400 | $1,300 | $1,200 | $1,125 | $1,075 | $1,000 | $925 | $875 | $800 |

⇥ Crown Grade

| $3,450 | $3,125 | $2,750 | $2,350 | $2,100 | $2,000 | $1,900 | $1,800 | $1,700 | $1,600 | $1,500 | $1,400 |

⇥ Monogram Grade

| $6,000 | $5,000 | $4,250 | $3,700 | $3,150 | $2,750 | $2,400 | $2,150 | $2,000 | $1,850 | $1,700 | $1,525 |

⇥ Premier Grade

| $9,750 | $8,350 | $6,400 | $5,275 | $3,850 | $3,300 | $2,900 | $2,600 | $2,350 | $2,100 | $1,900 | $1,750 |

⇥ Deluxe Grade

| $13,950 | $12,000 | $9,995 | $7,850 | $6,000 | $5,000 | $4,500 | $3,995 | $3,375 | $2,900 | $2,500 | $2,150 |

1968-1973 MFG.

Grading	100%	98%	95%	90%	80%	70%	60%

1968 SXS MODEL — 12 ga., 28 in. VR barrel, full and mod. choke, sidelock, extractors, double triggers, checkered pistol grip stock. Mfg. 1968-1973 by Marlin.

| | | | $725 | $600 | $550 | $495 | $425 | $350 | $275 |

1968 SXS DELUXE MODEL — similar to Standard, with Simmons floating rib, beavertail forearm. Mfg. 1971-1973 by Marlin.

| | | | $995 | $825 | $725 | $600 | $495 | $400 | $350 |

Smith & Wesson

Manufacturer located in Springfield, MA 1857 to date. S & W became a subsidiary of Bangor-Punta from 1957-1983. Between 1983 -1987 Smith & Wesson was owned by the Lear Siegler Co. On May 22, 1987 Smith & Wesson was sold to Tompkins, an English holding company.

REVOLVERS: EARLY MODELS

	100%	98%	95%	90%	80%	70%	60%	50%	40%	30%	20%	10%

MODEL NO. 1 FIRST ISSUE — .22 Short, single action, 7 shot non-fluted cylinder, $3\frac{3}{16}$ in. octagon barrel, bottom break, spur trigger, silver plated brass frame, blue barrel and cylinder, square rosewood grips. 11,671 mfg. 1857-1860.

⇥ First Type — serial range approx. 1-200.

| $5,250 | $4,750 | $4,450 | $4,150 | $3,875 | $3,625 | $3,275 | $2,925 | $2,500 | $1,950 | $1,650 | $1,275 |

⇥ Second Type — serial range approx. 200-1130.

| $3,350 | $2,850 | $2,550 | $2,300 | $2,100 | $1,900 | $1,750 | $1,600 | $1,450 | $1,300 | $1,150 | $1,050 |

⇥ Third Type — serial range approx. 1130-3000.

| $2,650 | $2,275 | $2,050 | $1,900 | $1,750 | $1,600 | $1,500 | $1,400 | $1,300 | $1,200 | $1,100 | $1,025 |

⇥ Fourth Type — serial range approx. 3000-4200.

| $2,300 | $1,850 | $1,700 | $1,600 | $1,450 | $1,300 | $1,200 | $1,125 | $1,050 | $975 | $925 | $900 |

⇥ Fifth Type — serial range approx. 4200-5500.

| $2,300 | $1,950 | $1,700 | $1,600 | $1,450 | $1,300 | $1,200 | $1,125 | $1,050 | $975 | $925 | $900 |

	100%	98%	95%	90%	80%	70%	60%	50%	40%	30%	20%	10%

⚔ Sixth Type — serial range approx. 5500-11,671.

	100%	98%	95%	90%	80%	70%	60%	50%	40%	30%	20%	10%
	$2,150	$1,800	$1,550	$1,450	$1,300	$1,175	$1,075	$1,000	$925	$875	8215	$800

MODEL NO. 1 SECOND ISSUE — similar to First Issue, except flat sided frame and irregular shaped sideplate. 117,000 mfg. 1860-1868. Serial range approx. 11,672- approx. 128,000.

	100%	98%	95%	90%	80%	70%	60%	50%	40%	30%	20%	10%
	$950	$875	$825	$795	$755	$700	$625	$575	$525	$475	$425	$390

⚔ Second Quality — is marked on approx. 4,402 revolvers.

	100%	98%	95%	90%	80%	70%	60%	50%	40%	30%	20%	10%
	$1,250	$1,100	$1,000	$925	$850	$775	$700	$625	$575	$525	$475	$435

MODEL NO. 1 THIRD ISSUE — similar to Second Issue, except fluted cylinder and birds head grip. 131,163 mfg. 1868-1881. This model has its own serial range no. 1-131,163.

⚔ $3^3/16$ in. barrel Model. — will have markings on top of barrel.

	100%	98%	95%	90%	80%	70%	60%	50%	40%	30%	20%	10%
	$475	$435	$400	$375	$350	$325	$300	$275	$250	$225	$200	$175

⚔ $2^{11}/16$ in. barrel Model. — will have markings on side of barrel.

	100%	98%	95%	90%	80%	70%	60%	50%	40%	30%	20%	10%
	$650	$610	$575	$550	$525	$500	$475	$450	$375	$350	$325	$300

.22/32 HAND EJECTOR (ALSO KNOWN AS .22/32 BEKEART MODEL) — .22 LR cal., 6 shot fluted cylinder, 6 in. barrel, blued, checkered walnut grips with "S&W" medallions, extension square butt style, there were several hundred thousand of the standard .22/.32 Hand Ejector mfg., but only those guns with a separate identification number are on the bottom of the wooden grips are classified as true Bekeart Models.

⚔ True Bekeart Model — will be found with separate identification number on bottom of wooden grip. Serial range for true Bekeart Model is 138,226-139,275.

	100%	98%	95%	90%	80%	70%	60%	50%	40%	30%	20%	10%
	$1,075	$875	$750	$650	$550	$450	$350	$275	$200	$150	$135	$110

This model was specifically mfg. for a San Francisco retailer, Phil Bekeart. Originally, Mr. Bekeart ordered 1,000 guns to his specifications, S&W mfg. 3,000, but only 292 were delivered.

⚔ Standard .22/.32 Hand Ejector Model — over 100,000 mfg. between approx. 1913-1953.

	100%	98%	95%	90%	80%	70%	60%	50%	40%	30%	20%	10%
	$850	$675	$550	$450	$375	$325	$275	$225	$175	$135	$115	$100

LADYSMITH (MODEL M HAND EJECTOR) — originally chambered for .22 S&W (same as .22 Long), 7 shot fluted cylinder, small frame, available in blue or nickel finish, dubbed "Ladysmith" because many women (including Ladies of the Night) liked them as a personal defense weapon due to the diminutive size. Over 26,000 mfg. between 1902-1921.

⚔ First Model — .22 L, 3, or $3^1/2$ in. barrel length, serial numbered 1-4,575, checkered hard rubber grips, round butt. 4,575 mfg. 1902-1906. Serial range 1-4,575. Identifiable by frame mounted cylinder release lever.

	100%	98%	95%	90%	80%	70%	60%	50%	40%	30%	20%	10%
	$1,575	$1,350	$1,150	$1,000	$850	$750	$650	$550	$475	$400	$350	$315

⚔ Second Model — .22 L, 3, or $3^1/2$ in. barrel, distinguishable from first model in that cylinder locking device was placed on barrel bottom, locking both ends. 9,400 mfg. 1906-1910. S.N. 4,576-13,950.

	100%	98%	95%	90%	80%	70%	60%	50%	40%	30%	20%	10%
	$1,500	$1,300	$1,100	$950	$800	$700	$600	$500	$425	$350	$300	$275

⚔ Third Model — .22 L, $2^1/2$, 3, $3^1/2$, or 6 in. barrel, smooth walnut grips with S&W medallion inlays, square butt. Ivory or pearl grips will command a premium. 12,200 mfg. 1910-1921. Serial range 13,951-26,154.

	100%	98%	95%	90%	80%	70%	60%	50%	40%	30%	20%	10%
	$1,450	$1,225	$1,050	$900	$750	$650	$550	$450	$375	$325	$285	$260

Add 85% for 6 in. barrel with target sights.
Add 95% for 6 in. barrel with plain sights.

100%	98%	95%	90%	80%	70%	60%	50%	40%	30%	20%	10%

MODEL NO. 1½ FIRST ISSUE — .32 rimfire, single action, 3½ or 4 (rare) in. octagon barrel, 5 shot non-fluted cylinder, bottom break, spur trigger, blue or nickel, rosewood grips. 26,300 mfg. 1865-1868. Serial range 1- approx. 26,300.

100%	98%	95%	90%	80%	70%	60%	50%	40%	30%	20%	10%
$575	$500	$435	$375	$325	$300	$275	$250	$225	$210	$195	$185

4 in. barrel

100%	98%	95%	90%	80%	70%	60%	50%	40%	30%	20%	10%
$3,500	$3,150	$2,750	$2,300	$1,950	$1,650	$1,450	1,250	$1,050	$900	$775	$650

Watch for fakes (i.e. stretched barrels).

MODEL NO. 1½ SECOND ISSUE — similar to First Issue, with birds head grips and round barrel. 100,700 mfg. 1868-1875. Serial range 26,301-127,100.

2½ in. barrel model — barrel markings on side, length varies from 2½-2¾ in.

100%	98%	95%	90%	80%	70%	60%	50%	40%	30%	20%	10%
$575	$500	$435	$385	$365	$335	$305	$275	$250	$225	$200	$185

3½ in. barrel model

100%	98%	95%	90%	80%	70%	60%	50%	40%	30%	20%	10%
$425	$385	$335	$300	$275	$250	$225	$200	$180	$165	$150	$135

Transitional Model — octagon barrel with birdshead grips, serial range 27,200-28,800.

100%	98%	95%	90%	80%	70%	60%	50%	40%	30%	20%	10%
$1,750	$1,625	$1,525	$1,425	$1,350	$1,275	$1,200	$1,125	$1,050	$975	$900	$835

MODEL NO. 2 ARMY — .32 rimfire long, similar in appearance to No. 1½ First Issue, except 6 shot cylinder, different barrel lengths, used as a sidearm during Civil War. 77,155 mfg. 1861-1874. Serial number range 1-77,155.

5 or 6 in. Early Model — referred to as 2-pin variation, serial range 1-3,000.

100%	98%	95%	90%	80%	70%	60%	50%	40%	30%	20%	10%
$1,550	$1,375	$1,225	$1,125	$1,025	$925	$825	$750	$675	$600	$550	$500

5 or 6 in. Standard Model — remainder of serial range.

100%	98%	95%	90%	80%	70%	60%	50%	40%	30%	20%	10%
$1,375	$1,225	$1,100	$1,000	$900	$800	$700	$625	$525	$450	$400	$375

4 in. barrel Model

100%	98%	95%	90%	80%	70%	60%	50%	40%	30%	20%	10%
$2,275	$2,000	$1,800	$1,750	$1,650	$1,550	$1,450	$1,350	$1,250	$1,100	$975	$875

Note: Watch for fakes on 4 in. model.

.32 SINGLE ACTION — .32 S&W, spur trigger, top break, rebounding hammer, auto extraction. 97,574 mfg. 1878-1892. Serial range 1-97,574.

Early Model — without strain screw, serial range 1-6,500.

100%	98%	95%	90%	80%	70%	60%	50%	40%	30%	20%	10%
$435	$390	$350	$315	$285	$255	$225	$195	$170	$145	$125	$110

Later Model — with strain screw, remainder of serial range.

100%	98%	95%	90%	80%	70%	60%	50%	40%	30%	20%	10%
$375	$330	$295	$265	$230	$205	$180	$155	$135	$125	$115	$100

8 or 10 in. barrel model.

100%	98%	95%	90%	80%	70%	60%	50%	40%	30%	20%	10%
$925	$775	$675	$600	$540	$490	$440	$390	$350	$300	$260	$235

REVOLVERS: DOUBLE ACTION

On the models listed below, target variations of all models command various levels of premiums, especially on the First Model and other rarer configurations (depending on rarity, prices may range from $995-2,500, if condition is over 50%).

.32 DOUBLE ACTION FIRST MODEL — .32 S&W, 5 shot fluted cylinder, 3 in. round barrel, blue or nickel finish, black rubber grips, one of the rarest of all S&Ws. Only 30 mfg. 1880. Serial range 1-30.

100%	98%	95%	90%	80%	70%	60%	50%	40%	30%	20%	10%
$4,250	$3,800	$3,400	$3,100	$2,800	$2,500	$2,200	$1,900	$1,600	$1,300	$1,050	$850

100%	98%	95%	90%	80%	70%	60%	50%	40%	30%	20%	10%

.32 DOUBLE ACTION SECOND MODEL — similar to First Model, except irregular shaped sideplate, 3, 3¼, 4, 5, or 6 in. barrel, 22,142 mfg. 1880-1882. Serial range 31-22,172.

| $475 | $425 | $380 | $340 | $300 | $260 | $220 | $180 | $150 | $120 | $100 | $90 |

.32 DOUBLE ACTION THIRD MODEL — similar to Second Model, except without groove around cylinder. 22,232 mfg. 1882-1883. Serial range 22,173-43,405.

| $475 | $425 | $380 | $340 | $300 | $260 | $220 | $180 | $150 | $120 | $100 | $90 |

.32 DOUBLE ACTION FOURTH MODEL — similar to Third Model, except rounded trigger guard. 239,600 mfg. 1883-1909. Serial range 43,406-approx. 282,999.

| $345 | $305 | $270 | $240 | $210 | $185 | $160 | $135 | $115 | $100 | $90 | $85 |

An 8 or 10 in. on this model will command a premium.

.32 DOUBLE ACTION FIFTH MODEL — similar to Fourth Model, except integral front sight. 44,641 mfg. 1909-1919. Serial range approx. 28,300-327,641.

| $375 | $335 | $300 | $270 | $240 | $215 | $190 | $165 | $135 | $120 | $105 | $90 |

.32 SAFETY HAMMERLESS FIRST MODEL (LEMON SQUEEZER) — .32 S&W cal., 5 shot fluted cylinder, 2, 3 (most common), 3½, or 6 (rare) in. round barrel, blue or nickel, black rubber grips. This model was dubbed New Departure at the time. 91,417 mfg. 1888-1902. Serial range 1-91,417.

⚰ Standard Model — 3, or 3½ in. barrel.

| $350 | $295 | $255 | $220 | $195 | $180 | $165 | $155 | $145 | $135 | $120 | $110 |

⚰ 2 in. Barrel Model — markings on side of barrel, dubbed the "Bicycle Model".

| $635 | $575 | $525 | $500 | $475 | $450 | $425 | $400 | $375 | $350 | $325 | $295 |

.32 SAFETY HAMMERLESS SECOND MODEL — 2, 3, 3½, or 6 in. barrel. 78,500 mfg. 1902-1909. Serial range 91,418-170,000.

⚰ Standard Model — 3 or 3½ in. barrel.

| $310 | $265 | $230 | $195 | $180 | $165 | $155 | $145 | $135 | $125 | $110 | $95 |

Add 30% for 6 in. barrel.

⚰ 2 in. Barrel Model — markings on side of barrel, this model was also referred to as the "Bicycle Model".

| $565 | $510 | $465 | $425 | $400 | $375 | $350 | $325 | $300 | $275 | $250 | $235 |

.32 SAFETY HAMMERLESS THIRD MODEL — 2, 3, or 3½ in. barrel. 73,000 mfg. 1909-1937. Serial range 163,082-175,772 (with some overlap from the Second Model).

⚰ Standard Model

| $310 | $265 | $230 | $200 | $180 | $165 | $155 | $145 | $135 | $125 | $110 | $95 |

⚰ 2 in. Barrel Model

| $550 | $500 | $455 | $415 | $390 | $365 | $340 | $315 | $290 | $265 | $240 | $255 |

.32 HAND EJECTOR FIRST MODEL (MODEL OF 1896) — .32 S&W long cal., 6 shot fluted cylinder, 3¼, 4¼ or 6 in. barrel, blue or nickel, black rubber grips, round or square butt extension target grip. 19,712 mfg. 1896-1903. Serial range 1-19,712.

| $535 | $475 | $425 | $375 | $335 | $300 | $275 | $250 | $225 | $200 | $175 | $165 |

.32 HAND EJECTOR (MODEL OF 1903) .32 S&W long cal., 6 shot fluted cylinder, 3¼, 4¼ or 6 in. barrel, blue or nickel, black rubber grips. 19,425 mfg. 1903-1904. Serial range 1-19,425.

| $400 | $340 | $300 | $275 | $250 | $225 | $200 | $175 | $150 | $130 | $115 | $100 |

100%	98%	95%	90%	80%	70%	60%	50%	40%	30%	20%	10%

.32 Hand Ejector - Model of 1903 1st Change — rubber or walnut grips. 31,700 mfg. 1904-1906. Serial range 19,426-51,126.

| $395 | $340 | $300 | $275 | $250 | $225 | $200 | $175 | $150 | $130 | $115 | $100 |

.32 Hand Ejector - Model of 1903 2nd Change — rubber or walnut grips. 44,373 mfg. 1906-1909. Serial range 51,127-95,500.

| $395 | $340 | $300 | $275 | $250 | $225 | $200 | $175 | $150 | $130 | $115 | $100 |

.32 Hand Ejector - Model of 1903 3rd Change — rubber or walnut grips. 624 mfg. 1909-1910. Serial range 95,501-96,125.

| $525 | $475 | $420 | $385 | $350 | $320 | $290 | $265 | $240 | $220 | $205 | $190 |

.32 Hand Ejector - Model of 1903 4th Change — rubber or walnut grips. 6,374 mfg. 1910. Serial range 96,126-102,500.

| $400 | $340 | $300 | $275 | $250 | $225 | $200 | $175 | $150 | $130 | $115 | $100 |

.32 Hand Ejector - Model of 1903 5th Change — rubber or walnut grips.

| $355 | $315 | $280 | $250 | $225 | $200 | $175 | $150 | $125 | $110 | $100 | $90 |

.32 HAND EJECTOR THIRD MODEL — .32 S&W long caliber, 6 shot fluted cylinder, 3¼, 4¼ or 6 in. barrel, blue or nickel finish, grips of checkered hard rubber with "S&W" monogram, round butt. 271,531 mfg. 1911-1942. Serial range approx. 263,001-534,532.

| $350 | $310 | $275 | $250 | $225 | $200 | $175 | $150 | $125 | $110 | $100 | $90 |

.32-20 Hand Ejector First Model — .32-20 Winchester caliber, 6 shot fluted cylinder, 4, 5, 6, or 6½ in. barrel, blue or nickel, case hardened trigger and hammer, grips of hard rubber with "S&W" monogram or walnut, round butt style.

| $650 | $575 | $520 | $475 | $450 | $425 | $400 | $375 | $350 | $325 | $305 | $290 |

.32/20 HAND EJECTOR SECOND MODEL (MODEL OF 1902) — .32-20 caliber, 6 shot fluted cylinder, 4, 5, or 6½ in. barrel, blue or nickel, grips of hard rubber with "S&W" monogram or walnut, round butt style. 4,499 mfg. 1902-1905. Serial range 5,312-9,811.

| $725 | $575 | $475 | $400 | $350 | $300 | $250 | $200 | $150 | $125 | $110 | $95 |

.32-20 Hand Ejector Second Model (Model of 1902 - 1st Change) — grip also available in checkered walnut with square butt. 8,313 mfg. 1903-1905. Serial range 9,812-18,125.

| $710 | $565 | $465 | $390 | $340 | $290 | $240 | $190 | $140 | $120 | $105 | $90 |

.32/20 HAND EJECTOR (MODEL OF 1905) — caliber, cylinder, barrel and grip specifications same as above. 4,300 mfg. 1905-1906. Serial range 18,126-22,426.

| $725 | $575 | $475 | $400 | $350 | $300 | $250 | $200 | $150 | $125 | $110 | $95 |

.32-20 Hand Ejector (Model of 1905 - 1st Change) — 4, 5, 6, or 6½ barrel, blue or nickel, grips same as above, round or square butt. 11,073 mfg. 1906-1907. Serial range 22,427 to approx. 33,500.

| $710 | $565 | $465 | $390 | $340 | $290 | $240 | $190 | $140 | $120 | $105 | $90 |

.32-20 Hand Ejector (Model of 1905 - 2nd Change) — caliber, cylinder, barrel and grip specifications same as above. 11,699 mfg. 1906-1907. Serial range 33,501-45,200.

| $710 | $565 | $465 | $390 | $340 | $290 | $240 | $190 | $140 | $120 | $105 | $90 |

.32-20 Hand Ejector (Model of 1905 - 3rd Change) — caliber and cylinder same as above, 4 or 6 in. barrel, finish and grips same as above. 20,499 mfg. 1909-1915. Serial range approx. 45,201-65,700.

| $700 | $550 | $455 | $380 | $330 | $280 | $230 | $180 | $140 | $120 | $105 | $90 |

100%	98%	95%	90%	80%	70%	60%	50%	40%	30%	20%	10%

⊰ **.32-20 Hand Ejector (Model of 1905 - 4th Change)** — caliber and cylinder same as above, 4, 5, or 6 in. barrel, finish and grips same as above. 78,983 mfg. 1915-1940. Serial range 65,701-144,684.

| $575 | $450 | $375 | $325 | $280 | $235 | $200 | $175 | $135 | $115 | $100 | $85 |

.38 SINGLE ACTION FIRST MODEL (BABY RUSSIAN) — .38 S&W cal., 5 shot fluted cylinder, 3¼ or 4 in. barrel, blue with wood grips, nickel with "S&W" monogram hard rubber grips. 25,548 mfg. 1876-1877. Serial range 1-25,548.

⊰ **Standard Model**

| $625 | $525 | $450 | $400 | $365 | $330 | $295 | $260 | $235 | $200 | $185 | $175 |

⊰ **Very Early Model** — with early hammer style safety latch (up to approx. ser. no. 100).

| $2,500 | $2,250 | $2,000 | $1,750 | $1,450 | $1,150 | $950 | $800 | $700 | $600 | $500 | $400 |

This type of hammer configuration is called the "Aldrich" model.

⊰ **Early Model** — having two screws to hold side plate (up to approx. ser. no. 2,550).

| $735 | $625 | $550 | $500 | $465 | $425 | $390 | $355 | $320 | $285 | $250 | $235 |

.38 SINGLE ACTION SECOND MODEL — cal. and cylinder same as above, 3¼, 4, 5, 6, 8, or 10 in. barrel, grips same as above. 108,225 mfg. 1877-1891. Serial range 1-108,255.

⊰ **Standard Model**

| $335 | $275 | $235 | $200 | $185 | $160 | $150 | $140 | $130 | $125 | $120 | $115 |

⊰ **8 or 10 in. Barrel**

| $1,825 | $1,575 | $1,375 | $1,200 | $1,050 | $925 | $825 | $750 | $675 | $625 | $590 | $565 |

.38 SINGLE ACTION THIRD MODEL (MODEL OF 1891) — cal. and cylinder same as above, except also accepts the single shot barrel, 3½, 4, 5, or 6 in. barrel, blue or nickel finish with "S&W" monogram, hard rubber grips. 26,850 mfg. 1891-1911. Serial range 1-28,107 which also includes the serial number range of the Single Shot First Model in .38 S&W cal. and the .38 S.A. Mexican Model described below.

| $1,235 | $1,075 | $950 | $850 | $775 | $700 | $625 | $550 | $475 | $425 | $375 | $335 |

Add 35% for single shot barrel with matching serial number.

.38 SINGLE ACTION MEXICAN MODEL — .38 S&W cal., 5 shot fluted cylinder, 3¼, 4, 5, or 6 in. barrel, blue or nickel finish, "S&W" monogram checkered hard rubber or walnut grips. Features unique to this model are flat sided hammer half cock notch and "inserted" spur trigger assembly (not integral with frame). This model would also accept the single shot barrel, limited mfg. 1891-1911. Serial range described above.

| $2,875 | $2,550 | $2,250 | $2,000 | $1,750 | $1,550 | $1,400 | $1,250 | $1,150 | $1,050 | $975 | $950 |

Add 35% for single shot barrel with matching serial number.

.38 DOUBLE ACTION FIRST MODEL — .38 S&W cal., 5 shot fluted cylinder, 3¼ or 4 in. barrel, blue or nickel finish, "S&W" monogram checkered hard rubber grips. 4,000 mfg. 1880. Serial range 1-4,000.

| $1,250 | $1,125 | $975 | $850 | $750 | $650 | $550 | $440 | $350 | $275 | $200 | $150 |

An 8 or 10 in. barrel commands a premium on this model and the other .38 cal. models listed below.

.38 DOUBLE ACTION SECOND MODEL — cal. and cylinder same as above, 3¼, 4, 5, or 6 in. barrel, blue or nickel finish, "S&W" monogram checkered hard rubber grips in black or red. 115,000 mfg. 1880-1884. Serial range approx. 4,001-11,900.

| $350 | $275 | $235 | $200 | $175 | $155 | $135 | $120 | $110 | $100 | $90 | $85 |

100%	98%	95%	90%	80%	70%	60%	50%	40%	30%	20%	10%

.38 DOUBLE ACTION THIRD MODEL
— cal. and cylinder same as above, 3¼, 4, 5, 6, 8, or 10 in. barrel, blue or nickel finish, "S&W" monogram hard rubber grips. 203,700 mfg. 1884-1895. Serial range approx. 119,001-322,700.

100%	98%	95%	90%	80%	70%	60%	50%	40%	30%	20%	10%
$325	$265	$225	$190	$170	$150	$135	$120	$110	$100	$90	$85

⅜ 8 or 10 in. Barrel

100%	98%	95%	90%	80%	70%	60%	50%	40%	30%	20%	10%
$2,150	$1,850	$1,600	$1,400	$1,250	$1,125	$1,000	$900	$800	$700	$600	$535

.38 DOUBLE ACTION FOURTH MODEL
— cal. and cylinder same as above, 3¼, 4, 5, or 6 in. barrel, blue or nickel finish, "S&W" monogram checkered hard rubber grips, also offered in an extended square butt target style. 216,300 mfg. 1895-1901. Serial range 322,701-539,000.

100%	98%	95%	90%	80%	70%	60%	50%	40%	30%	20%	10%
$325	$270	$230	$200	$175	$155	$135	$120	$110	$100	$90	$85

.38 DOUBLE ACTION FIFTH MODEL
— cal., cylinder, barrel, and grip specifications same as above with the additional availability of an extended square butt target style walnut grip as an option. 15,000 mfg. 1909-1911. Serial range approx. 539,001-554,077.

100%	98%	95%	90%	80%	70%	60%	50%	40%	30%	20%	10%
$600	$525	$465	$425	$375	$325	$285	$250	$225	$205	$190	$175

.38 DOUBLE ACTION PERFECTED MODEL
— cal., cylinder, barrel and grip specifications same as above, trigger guard is integral part of frame, and side plate is on right side - not left side. The last of the S&W break open revolvers. 59,400 mfg. 1909-1920. Serial range 1-59,400.

100%	98%	95%	90%	80%	70%	60%	50%	40%	30%	20%	10%
$650	$545	$465	$400	$350	$300	$275	$240	$215	$200	$185	$170

This model was mfg. from the .32 solid frame with 2 latches (side latch and top latch).

⅜ .38 Double Action Perfected Model Top Latch Only
— as above, except no side latch.

100%	98%	95%	90%	80%	70%	60%	50%	40%	30%	20%	10%
$1,250	$1,125	$975	$850	$750	$650	$550	$440	$350	$275	$200	$150

.38 SAFETY HAMMERLESS FIRST MODEL (.38 NEW DEPARTURE)
— .38 S&W cal., 5 shot fluted cylinder, 3¼, 4, 5, or 6 in. barrel, blue or nickel finish, "S&W" monogram checkered hard rubber grips. Approx. 5,125 mfg. in 1887. Serial range 1-5,250 which reflects an overlap with the .38 Safety Second Model D.A.

100%	98%	95%	90%	80%	70%	60%	50%	40%	30%	20%	10%
$900	$785	$685	$600	$525	$450	$375	$325	$275	$250	$225	$200

Add 25% for blue finish.

⅜ 6 in. Barrel

100%	98%	95%	90%	80%	70%	60%	50%	40%	30%	20%	10%
$1,450	$1,200	$1,025	$900	$790	$675	$565	$490	$425	$375	$340	$310

.38 SAFETY HAMMERLESS SECOND MODEL
— cal. and cylinder same as above, 3¼, 4, or 5 in. barrel, finish and grips same as above. 37,350 mfg. 1887-1890. Serial range approx. 5,001-42,483 which reflects some overlap from the First Model listed above.

100%	98%	95%	90%	80%	70%	60%	50%	40%	30%	20%	10%
$600	$495	$415	$350	$300	$250	$200	$150	$125	$110	$100	$90

U.S. MARTIALLY MARKED
— 100 purchased by Gov.'t in 1890, serial range 41,333-41,470.

100%	98%	95%	90%	80%	70%	60%	50%	40%	30%	20%	10%
$4,500	$4,100	$3,750	$3,500	$3,250	$3,000	$2,750	$2,500	$2,300	$2,200	$2,150	$2,100

Beware of fakes!

.38 SAFETY HAMMERLESS THIRD MODEL
— cal. and cylinder same as above, 3¼, 4, 5, or 6 in. barrel, finish and grips same as above. 73,500 mfg. 1890-1898. Serial range 24,284-116,002.

100%	98%	95%	90%	80%	70%	60%	50%	40%	30%	20%	10%
$435	$375	$330	$300	$275	$250	$225	$200	$175	$150	$135	$125

100%	98%	95%	90%	80%	70%	60%	50%	40%	30%	20%	10%

.38 SAFETY HAMMERLESS FOURTH MODEL — cal., cylinder, barrel lengths, finishes and grips same as above. 104,000 mfg. 1898-1907. Serial range 116,003 to approx. 220,000 reflecting some overlap with the Fifth Model from approx. 216,500- 223,100.

100%	98%	95%	90%	80%	70%	60%	50%	40%	30%	20%	10%
$340	$280	$240	$205	$190	$165	$155	$145	$135	$125	$120	$115

A 2 in. barrel in this variation is rare (Bicycle Model).

.38 SAFETY HAMMERLESS FIFTH MODEL — cal. and cylinder same as above, 2, 3¼, 4, 5, or 6 in. barrel, blue or nickel finish, "S&W" monogram checkered hard rubber or checkered walnut grips. 41,500 mfg. 1907-1940. Serial range 220,000-261,493 reflecting some overlap with Fourth Model listed above from 216,500-223,100.

100%	98%	95%	90%	80%	70%	60%	50%	40%	30%	20%	10%
$355	$320	$290	$265	$240	$225	$210	$200	$190	$180	$170	$165

⚔ 2 in. Barrel

100%	98%	95%	90%	80%	70%	60%	50%	40%	30%	20%	10%
$825	$750	$670	$635	$575	$540	$505	$480	$455	$432	$410	$390

.38 MILITARY & POLICE FIRST MODEL (MODEL OF 1899) —.38 L Colt or .38 S&W Special cal., these models are also referred to as .38 Hand Ejectors, 6 shot fluted cylinder, 4, 5, 6, or 6½ in. barrel, blue or nickel finish, "S&W" monogram checkered hard rubber or checkered walnut grips with walnut grips exhibiting an impressed circle at top, left plain for civilian issue, marked with inspector's initials for military issue. 20,975 mfg. 1899-1902. Serial range 1-20,975.

On these models, fixed sights are referred to as Military & Police models while target sights are referred to as .38 Hand Ejectors.

⚔ Standard Model - Civilian Issue

100%	98%	95%	90%	80%	70%	60%	50%	40%	30%	20%	10%
$650	$550	$475	$425	$375	$325	$275	$240	$205	$190	$180	$170

⚔ U.S. Navy Model — 1,000 revolvers in .38 L Colt cal. with 6 in. barrel, blued, checkered walnut grips, delivered in 1900. Stamped on butt "U.S.N." with an anchor and inspector's initials. All in S&W serial range 5,001-6,000. U.S. Navy serial range 1-1,000.

100%	98%	95%	90%	80%	70%	60%	50%	40%	30%	20%	10%
$1,900	$1,600	$1,375	$1,200	$1,050	$925	$825	$725	$625	$525	$435	$375

⚔ U.S. Army Model — 1,000 revolvers in .38 L Colt cal. with 6 in. barrel, blued, checkered walnut grips, inspector's initials "K.S.M. " on right grip panel with "J.T.T.1901" on left grip panel. Stamped on butt "U.S. ARMY/MODEL 1899". S&W serial range 13,001-14,000.

.38 MILITARY & POLICE SECOND MODEL (MODEL OF 1902) — .38 S&W Special and .38 L Colt cal., 6 shot fluted cylinder, 4, 5, 6, and 6½ in. barrels, blue or nickel, "S&W" monogram checkered hard rubber or checkered walnut grips. 12,827 mfg. 1902-1903. Serial range 20,976-33,803.

⚔ Standard Model — civilian issue, all in .38 S&W Special cal. (barrel is marked .38 Military and .38 Special).

100%	98%	95%	90%	80%	70%	60%	50%	40%	30%	20%	10%
$545	$470	$425	$390	$335	$320	$290	$260	$235	$210	$200	$185

⚔ U.S. Navy Model — 1,000 revolvers in .38 L Colt caliber with 6 in. barrel, delivered in 1902. Stamped on butt "U.S.N." with "J.A.B.", anchor, and arrow through horizontal "S" and "No." (Naval Ser. No. designation).

100%	98%	95%	90%	80%	70%	60%	50%	40%	30%	20%	10%
$1,800	$1,575	$1,400	$1,250	$1,125	$1,000	$900	$800	$750	$700	$650	$610

.38 MILITARY & POLICE SECOND MODEL - 1ST CHANGE — .38 S&W Special cal., 6 shot fluted cylinder, 4, 5, or 6½ in. barrel, blue or nickel, "S&W" monogram checkered hard rubber or checkered walnut grips, rounded butt style, checkered walnut grips of square butt style available after the 58,000 serial range. 28,645 mfg. 1903-1905. Serial range 33,804-62,449.

⚔ Standard Model — hard rubber or round walnut butt grips.

100%	98%	95%	90%	80%	70%	60%	50%	40%	30%	20%	10%
$395	$345	$310	$275	$250	$210	$175	$150	$135	$125	$115	$100

100%	98%	95%	90%	80%	70%	60%	50%	40%	30%	20%	10%

Standard Model — checkered walnut grips or square butt and square butt to frame style. All will have serial numbers over the 58,000 range.

| $410 | $355 | $335 | $300 | $275 | $235 | $200 | $175 | $160 | $145 | $130 | $115 |

.38 MILITARY & POLICE (MODEL OF 1905) — .38 S&W Special cal., 6 shot fluted cylinder, 4, 5, or 6½ in. barrel, blue or nickel finish, "S&W" monogram checkered hard rubber or checkered walnut grips available in round or square butt style. 10,800 mfg. 1905-1906. Serial range 62,450-73,250.

| $440 | $385 | $345 | $310 | $275 | $240 | $205 | $175 | $150 | $125 | $110 | $100 |

.38 MILITARY & POLICE (MODEL OF 1905) - 1ST CHANGE — .38 S&W Special cal., 6 shot fluted cylinder, 4, 5, 6, or 6½ in. barrel, blue or nickel finish, grips same as above. 73,648 mfg. (including Model 1905 2nd change), exact quantity of both models has not been determined. The first change mfg. in 1906-1908. Serial range 73,251-unknown.

| $310 | $275 | $250 | $225 | $200 | $175 | $155 | $135 | $115 | $100 | $90 | $80 |

.38 MILITARY & POLICE (MODEL OF 1905) - 2ND CHANGE — cal., cylinder barrel lengths, finishes and grip styles same as above. 73,648 (including Model 1905 1st change) mfg. Exact quantity unknown. The second change mfg. in 1908-1909. Serial range unknown-146,899.

| $310 | $275 | $250 | $225 | $200 | $175 | $155 | $135 | $115 | $100 | $90 | $80 |

.38 MILITARY & POLICE (MODEL OF 1905) - 3RD CHANGE — .38 S&W Special cal., 6 shot fluted cylinder, 4, 5, or 6 in. barrel, finishes and grip styles same as above. 94,803 mfg. 1909-1915. Serial range 146,900-241,703.

| $310 | $275 | $250 | $225 | $200 | $175 | $155 | $135 | $115 | $100 | $90 | $80 |

.38 MILITARY & POLICE (MODEL OF 1905) - 4TH CHANGE — .38 S&W Special cal., 6 shot fluted cylinder, 2, 4, 5, or 6 in. barrel, finishes and grip styles same as above. 458,296 mfg. 1915-1942. Serial range 241,704 - approx. 700,000.

| $295 | $255 | $230 | $205 | $180 | $165 | $140 | $125 | $110 | $100 | $90 | $80 |

REVOLVERS: MODEL 3/NEW MODEL NO. 3 & VARIATIONS

On a few of the models listed below, shoulder stocks were available as a factory option. This rare configuration should be factory cut on the rear and bottom of grip strap to accept a shoulder stock. Healthy premiums exist for these "cut" models - the key is to determine whether the machining is factory or otherwise (many have been cut recently to enhance the value of a standard model).

MODEL 3 AMERICAN FIRST MODEL — .44 S&W or .44 rimfire Henry cal., single action, 6 shot fluted cylinder, 6, 7, or 8 in. round barrel, blue or nickel finish, walnut grips. 8,000 mfg. 1870-1872. Serial range 1-approx. 8,000.

Standard Model — vent. hole in extractor housing, first 1,500 mfg.

| $4,250 | $3,750 | $3,350 | $3,000 | $2,750 | $2,500 | $2,250 | $2,000 | $1,750 | $1,500 | $1,250 | $1,000 |

Standard Model — without hole in extractor.

| $2,850 | $2,500 | $2,250 | $2,150 | $1,850 | $1,650 | $1,450 | $1,250 | $1,050 | $925 | $825 | $750 |

Transitional Model — includes locking notch on hammer, shorter cylinder, serial range 6,700-8,000.

| $3,100 | $2,750 | $2,500 | $2,300 | $2,100 | $1,900 | $1,700 | $1,500 | $1,300 | $1,150 | $1,150 | $900 |

.44 Rim Fire Henry — 100 mfg.

| $4,850 | $4,350 | $4,000 | $3,750 | $3,500 | $3,250 | $3,000 | $2,750 | $2,500 | $2,250 | $2,000 | $1,850 |

	100%	98%	95%	90%	80%	70%	60%	50%	40%	30%	20%	10%

⚒ **U.S. Marked** — approx. 1,000 mfg.

100%	98%	95%	90%	80%	70%	60%	50%	40%	30%	20%	10%
$8,750	$7,750	$7,000	$6,500	$6,000	$5,500	$5,000	$4,750	$4,500	$4,250	$4,000	$3,750

⚒ **Nashville Police** — very rare, only 32 manufactured. Scarcity precludes accurate pricing.

MODEL 3 AMERICAN SECOND MODEL — .44 S&W or .44 rimfire Henry cal., single action, 6 shot fluted cylinder, 5½, 6, 6½, 7, or 8 in. barrel, blue or nickel, walnut grips. 20,735 mfg. 1872-1874, serial range approx. 8,000-32,800 which includes commercial version of Model 3 Russian First Model.

⚒ **Standard Model** — .44 S&W, American cal., 8 in. barrel.

100%	98%	95%	90%	80%	70%	60%	50%	40%	30%	20%	10%
$2,850	$2,550	$2,300	$2,050	$1,850	$1,650	$1,450	$1,250	$1,050	$850	$650	$550

Add 35% for 5½, 6, 6½, or 7 in. barrel.

⚒ **Standard Model .44 Rimfire Henry** — 6, 7, or 8 in. barrel, 3,014 mfg.

100%	98%	95%	90%	80%	70%	60%	50%	40%	30%	20%	10%
$3,550	$3,200	$2,950	$2,700	$2,500	$2,300	$2,100	$1,900	$1,700	$1,500	$1,300	$1,150

MODEL 3 RUSSIAN FIRST MODEL (OLD OLD RUSSIAN) — .44 S&W Russian, 5½, 6, 7, or 8 in. barrel, Russian contract 8 in., blue or nickel finish, walnut grips, looks similar to First and Second Model American. 5,165 mfg. 1871-1874 for commercial sale and 20,014 for Russian Contract. Serial range 6,000-32,800, see No. 3 Second Model American.

⚒ **Commercial Version** — 4,665 mfg.

100%	98%	95%	90%	80%	70%	60%	50%	40%	30%	20%	10%
$2,050	$1,850	$1,700	$1,600	$1,500	$1,400	$1,300	$1,200	$1,100	$1,000	$900	$800

⚒ **Reject Russian Contract** — 500 mfg. Serial range 1-approx. 2,000.

100%	98%	95%	90%	80%	70%	60%	50%	40%	30%	20%	10%
$2,800	$2,400	$2,100	$1,850	$1,750	$1,650	$1,550	$1,450	$1,350	$1,250	$1,150	$1,075

⚒ **Russian Contract** — 20,014 mfg., rare, most sent to Russia, cryllic marked. Serial range 1-approx. 20,014.

100%	98%	95%	90%	80%	70%	60%	50%	40%	30%	20%	10%
$4,250	$3,750	$3,350	$3,000	$2,750	$2,500	$2,250	$2,000	$1,750	$1,500	$1,250	$1,000

MODEL 3 AMERICAN SECOND MODEL — similar to First Model, except hump on bottom of frame and steel front sight instead of German silver, locking notch on hammer, 20,735 mfg. between 1872-1874.

⚒ **Standard Model**

100%	98%	95%	90%	80%	70%	60%	50%	40%	30%	20%	10%
$2,475	$2,000	$1,675	$1,485	$1,275	$1,100	$990	$880	$770	$660	$550	$500

MODEL 3 AMERICAN SECOND MODEL — .44 Rimfire Henry, 3,014 mfg.

100%	98%	95%	90%	80%	70%	60%	50%	40%	30%	20%	10%
$3,245	$2,750	$2,300	$1,925	$1,815	$1,650	$1,485	$1,210	$1,045	$825	$715	$650

MODEL 3 RUSSIAN SECOND MODEL (OLD RUSSIAN) — 2nd and 3rd Model Russians have an extreme knuckle at the top of backstrap and trigger guard spur, 85,200 mfg. in all variations between 1873-78.

⚒ **Commercial Version** — 6,200 mfg.

100%	98%	95%	90%	80%	70%	60%	50%	40%	30%	20%	10%
$1,600	$1,475	$1,350	$1,225	$1,100	$1,000	$900	$800	$700	$600	$525	$450

⚒ **.44 Rimfire Henry** — approx. 500 mfg.

100%	98%	95%	90%	80%	70%	60%	50%	40%	30%	20%	10%
$2,900	$2,625	$2,475	$2,300	$2,150	$2,000	$1,850	$1,700	$1,550	$1,400	$1,250	$1,000

⚒ **Russian Contract** — approx. 70,000 mfg., cryllic marked, rare in U.S.

100%	98%	95%	90%	80%	70%	60%	50%	40%	30%	20%	10%
$2,700	$2,475	$2,275	$2,100	$1,950	$1,800	$1,650	$1,500	$1,350	$1,100	$950	$750

⚒ **Turkish Model** — 1,000 mfg. in their own serial number range in .44 Rimfire. This is probably the rarest and most valuable variation.

100%	98%	95%	90%	80%	70%	60%	50%	40%	30%	20%	10%
$4,000	$3,650	$3,300	$3,000	$2,750	$2,500	$2,250	$2,000	$1,750	$1,500	$1,250	$1,000

100%	98%	95%	90%	80%	70%	60%	50%	40%	30%	20%	10%

⁂ **Japanese Contract** — 1,000 mfg., marked with an anchor on butt.

| $2,050 | $1,825 | $1,650 | $1,500 | $1,375 | $1,250 | $1,175 | $1,000 | $875 | $750 | $650 | $550 |

MODEL 3 RUSSIAN THIRD MODEL — commonly called the "New Model Russian" and is similar to old model, except has shorter extractor housing, approx. 60,600 mfg. between 1874 and 1878. Values are similar to old model for comparable variations.

⁂ **Commercial Version** — approx. 13,500 mfg.

| $1,650 | $1,450 | $1,275 | $1,125 | $1,000 | $900 | $800 | $700 | $600 | $500 | $425 | $375 |

⁂ **.44 Rimfire Henry**

| $3,350 | $3,000 | $2,700 | $2,450 | $2,250 | $2,050 | $1,850 | $1,650 | $1,450 | $1,250 | $1,050 | $875 |

⁂ **Russian Contract** — 41,138 mfg. Cyrillic lettering.

| $3,300 | $2,950 | $2,650 | $2,400 | $2,200 | $2,000 | $1,800 | $1,600 | $1,400 | $1,200 | $1,000 | $850 |

⁂ **Ludwig & Lowe, & Tula Copies** — copies mfg. for the Russian government.

| $2,000 | $1,850 | $1,625 | $1,475 | 1,3505 | $1,225 | $1,100 | $975 | $850 | $725 | $625 | $525 |

⁂ **Turkish Contract** — 5,000 mfg.

| $3,850 | $3,500 | $3,150 | $2,850 | $2,600 | $2,350 | $2,100 | $1,850 | $1,600 | $1,350 | $1,100 | $900 |

⁂ **Japanese Contract** — 1,000 made.

| $2,050 | $1,825 | $1,650 | $1,500 | $1,375 | $1,250 | $1,175 | $1,000 | $875 | $750 | $650 | $550 |

NEW MODEL NO. 3 — features very short extractor housing under the barrel, knuckle on backstrap is less pronounced than 2nd and 3rd Models, 35,796 mfg. between 1878-1912.

⁂ **Commercial Version** — 3½, 4, 5, 6, 6½, 7, or 8 in. barrel, .44 Russian cal.

| $1,875 | $1,675 | $1,500 | $1,350 | $1,200 | $1,050 | $900 | $750 | $600 | $500 | $445 | $400 |

   Add $200 if cut for shoulder stock.
   Early model has rack and gear extractor and will bring a premium over the later mfg. Also, premiums do exist for the 3½, 7, or 8 in. barrel lengths.

⁂ **Japanese Navy Model** — anchor on butt.

| $2,150 | $1,900 | $1,750 | $1,550 | $1,375 | $1,150 | $1,000 | $825 | $775 | $675 | $575 | $495 |

⁂ **Australian Model** — 7 in. barrel, detachable stock, for Australian Colonial Police, broad arrow marking, 200 mfg.

| $3,100 | $2,825 | $2,575 | $2,350 | $2,250 | $2,150 | $2,050 | $1,950 | $1,850 | $1,750 | $1,650 | $1,575 |

⁂ **Argentine Model** — 2,000 mfg., marked "Ejercito Argentina".

| $2,500 | $2,225 | $2,075 | $1,900 | $1,750 | $1,600 | $1,450 | $1,300 | $1,150 | $1,000 | $900 | $800 |

⁂ **State of Maryland Model** — U.S. marked, serial number range 7,126-7,405.

| $4,125 | $3,850 | $3,500 | $3,250 | $3,000 | $2,750 | $2,500 | $2,250 | $2,000 | $1,750 | $1,550 | $1,375 |

NEW MODEL NO. 3 FRONTIER — .44-40 cal., single action, 4, 5, or 6½ in. barrel, blue or nickel finish, walnut or hard rubber grips. 2,072 mfg. 1885-1908.

⁂ **Japanese Purchase** — 786 converted to .44 Russian cal., cylinder should measure 1⁹⁄₁₆ in., in the Frontier serial range of 1-2,072.

| $2,500 | $2,200 | $1,100 | $1,750 | $1,550 | $1,350 | $1,150 | $950 | $800 | $675 | $575 | $500 |

⁂ **Standard Model** — .44-40.

| $3,100 | $2,725 | $2,500 | $2,250 | $2,000 | $1,750 | $1,500 | $1,250 | $1,000 | $850 | $775 | $700 |

100%	98%	95%	90%	80%	70%	60%	50%	40%	30%	20%	10%

NEW MODEL NO. 3 - .38 WIN. — separate ser. range, only 74 mfg., ser. no. 1-74.

$4,125	$3,850	$3,500	$3,250	$3,000	$2,750	$2,500	$2,250	$2,000	$1,750	$1,550	$1,375

NEW MODEL NO. 3 TARGET MODEL — .32-44 S&W or .38-44 S&W, 4,333 mfg. between 1887-1910.

$2,450	$2,175	$1,925	$1,700	$1,500	$1,300	$1,100	$900	$700	$550	$475	$400

NEW MODEL NO. 3 TURKISH — .44 rimfire, 5,461 mfg. between 1879-1888, in separate serial number series.

$5,400	$5,025	$4,675	$4,350	$4,050	$3,750	$3,450	$3,150	$2,850	$2,550	$2,275	$1,950

MODEL 3 SCHOFIELD FIRST MODEL — .45 S&W, single action, 7 in. barrel, 6 shot fluted cylinder, blue finish only, walnut grips, 3,035 mfg. 1875.

⚔ **U.S. Issue** — 3,000 mfg.

$4,700	$4,325	$3,875	$3,650	$3,350	$3,050	$2,750	$2,450	$2,150	$1,850	$1,600	$1,425

⚔ **Commercial Model (not U.S. marked)** — 35 were produced without U.S. markings, very rare - beware of fakes - there could be more phony ones than real ones.

$7,900	$7,500	$7,125	$4,750	$4,400	$4,250	$3,700	$3,350	$3,000	$2,650	$2,325	$2,050

⚔ **Wells Fargo and Company**

$3,475	$3,200	$2,950	$2,700	$2,475	$2,250	$2,025	$1,800	$1,575	$1,350	$1,175	$1,000

Beware of fakes, there could be more phony ones than real ones.

MODEL 3 SCHOFIELD SECOND MODEL — improved version of First Model.

⚔ **Standard Model** — U.S. on butt.

$4,250	$3,875	$3,525	$3,250	$3,000	$2,750	$2,500	$2,250	$2,000	$1,750	$1,550	$1,385

⚔ **Commercial Model** — blue or nickel finish, U.S. only available in blue, 650 mfg.

$4,350	$4,025	$3,725	$3,400	$3,150	$2,900	$2,650	$2,400	$2,150	$1,900	$1,650	$1,480

⚔ **Wells Fargo and Company**

$3,475	$3,250	$2,950	$2,700	$2,475	$2,250	$2,025	$1,800	$1,575	$1,350	$1,175	$1,000

Beware of fakes!

.44 DOUBLE ACTION FIRST MODEL — .44 S&W Russian cal. 6 shot fluted cylinder, 4, 5, 6, or 6½ in. barrel, blue or nickel finish, "S&W" monogram checkered hard rubber or walnut grips. Walnut grips with "S&W" inlays will be found after 1900. 53,668 mfg. 1881-1913. Serial range 1-54,668.

⚔ **Standard Model** — all barrel lengths and 1⁷/₁₆ in. cylinder.

$1,050	$925	$800	$700	$625	$500	$475	$350	$275	$225	$150	$100

⚔ **Standard Model** — similar to above, except has 1⁹/₁₆ in. late production cylinder.

$1,150	$975	$850	$750	$650	$550	$525	$425	$325	$250	$200	$150

⚔ **.44 Double Action Wesson Favorite** — as standard model above but in 5 in. barrel only, blue or nickel finish. Approx. 1,000 mfg. 1882-1883. Serial range included with .44 Double Action First Model, between approx. 8,900-10,100.

$7,600	$6,670	$5,995	$5,360	$4,750	$4,170	$3,590	$3,360	$2,780	$2,200	$1,650	$1,100

Add 30-40% for blue finish.

100%	98%	95%	90%	80%	70%	60%	50%	40%	30%	20%	10%

.38 WIN. DOUBLE ACTION — .38-40 cal., 4, 5, 6, or 6½ in. barrel, only 276 mfg. in separate ser. range 1-276.

| $3,550 | $3,155 | $2,780 | $2,200 | $1,970 | $1,825 | $1,575 | $1,325 | $1,200 | $1,100 | $1,025 | $900 |

.44 DOUBLE ACTION FRONTIER — .44-40 cal., 4, 5, 6, or 6½ in. barrel, only 15,340 mfg. in separate ser. range 1-15,340.

| $1,650 | $1,425 | $1,225 | $1,050 | $900 | $750 | $550 | $400 | $350 | $275 | $225 | $175 |

.44 HAND EJECTOR FIRST MODEL (.44 HAND EJECTOR NEW CENTURY OR .44 TRIPLE LOCK) — .44 S&W Special cal. (standard), .44-40 W.C.F., .44 S&W Russian, .45 LC, .450 Eley, or .455 Mark II cal., 4, 5, 6½, or 7½ in. barrel, checkered walnut grips and square butt, gold monogram inlay on later production walnut grips. 15,375 mfg. 1908-1915. Serial range 1-5,375 (with respect to .455 Mark II).

 Standard Model — in .44 Russian, .44-40 S&W Special, .45 LC, or .450 Eley cal.

| $1,875 | $1,650 | $1,450 | $1,275 | $1,130 | $985 | $840 | $695 | $550 | $365 | $315 | $290 |

 Conversion Model — .455 Mark II cal.

| $885 | $765 | $675 | $600 | $540 | $480 | $420 | $360 | $300 | $250 | $235 | $225 |

 Standard Model — .44 S&W Special cal.

| $1,182 | $1,037 | $910 | $800 | $715 | $630 | $545 | $460 | $375 | $310 | $225 | $215 |

.44 HAND EJECTOR 2ND MODEL — .44 S&W Special cal. as standard, .38-40, .44-40, or .45 LC cal., 4, 5, 6, or 6½ in. barrel, blue or nickel finish, checkered walnut grips of square butt style, with or without "S&W" monogram inlays. 34,624 mfg. 1915-1937. Serial range 15,376-approx. 50,000.

 Standard Model — .44 S&W cal.

| $675 | $595 | $530 | $475 | $430 | $385 | $340 | $295 | $250 | $210 | $175 | $145 |

 Standard Model — .44-40 or .45 LC cal.

| $2,450 | $2,150 | $1,800 | $1,600 | $1,400 | $1,200 | $1,000 | $895 | $795 | $700 | $575 | $475 |

.44 HAND EJECTOR THIRD MODEL (MODEL 1926 HAND EJECTOR THIRD MODEL) — .44 S&W Special cal., very rare in .44-40 or .45 LC cal., 6 shot fluted cylinder, 4, 5, or 6½ in. barrel, finishes and grips same as above. Approx. 33,054 mfg. 1926-1950. Serial range 28,358-61,412.

 Standard Model — .44 S&W Special cal.

| $825 | $715 | $625 | $550 | $490 | $430 | $370 | $310 | $225 | $175 | $150 | $125 |

 Model .44 Hand Ejector 1926 Target — target sight, blue only, otherwise same as above. Mfg. 1926-1941.

| $1,400 | $1,250 | $1,100 | $975 | $875 | $800 | $700 | $600 | $500 | $425 | $350 | $295 |

 .455 Hand Ejector First Model — .455 Mark II cal., serial range 1-5,000 in its own range, English or Canadian proofed.

| $885 | $765 | $675 | $600 | $540 | $480 | $420 | $360 | $300 | $250 | $235 | $225 |

 .455 Hand Ejector Second Model — serial no. range 5,001-74,755, generally British or Canadian proofed.

| $550 | $480 | $420 | $360 | $300 | $250 | $235 | $225 | $215 | $200 | $185 | $150 |

PISTOLS: SINGLE SHOT - EARLY MODELS

FIRST MODEL — .22 LR, .32 S&W, or .38 S&W cal., 6, 8, or 10 in. barrel, blue or nickel, hard rubber grips. 1,251 mfg. 1893-1905, serial range (same as Third Model 38 Single Action) 1-28,107.

	100%	98%	95%	90%	80%	70%	60%	50%	40%	30%	20%	10%

.22 LR — 862 mfg.

$800	$700	$625	$575	$525	$475	$425	$375	$350	$325	$300	$285

.32 S&W — 229 mfg.

$950	$850	$775	$700	$650	$600	$550	$500	$450	$400	$350	$335

.38 S&W — 160 mfg.

$1,075	$950	$850	$775	$725	$675	$625	$575	$525	$475	$425	$395

SECOND MODEL .22 LR — similar to First Model, but will not accommodate a revolver cylinder, flatsided frame (does not have recoil shield) 10 in. barrel only, 4,617 mfg. 1905-1909. Serial range 1-4,617.

$750	$675	$625	$575	$525	$475	$425	$375	$325	$280	$250	$225

THIRD MODEL .22 LR — similar to Second Model, except is built on "I" solid frame with integral trigger guard, side plate on right side, made both single or double action. 6,949 mfg. 1909-1923. Serial range 4,618-11,641.

$725	$650	$600	$550	$500	$450	$400	$350	$300	$265	$235	$210

STRAIGHT LINE TARGET SINGLE SHOT —.22 LR, single shot, 10 in. barrel, sideswing barrel, blue, target sights, smooth walnut grips, shaped like an autoloader. 1,870 mfg. 1925-1936. Serial range 1-1,870. Values below assume case.

$1,275	$1,100	$950	$850	$750	$650	$550	$450	$415	$350	$355	$335

Deduct 30% without case.

REVOLVERS: MODERN DISCONTINUED

Grading	100%	98%	95%	90%	80%	70%	60%

.32 HAND EJECTOR (MODEL 30) — .32 S&W Long, 6 shot, 2, 3, 4, or 6 in. barrel, blue or nickel, fixed sights, walnut or rubber grips. Mfg. 1908-1976.

	$275	$220	$165	$140	$110	$105	$100

This model was designated Model 30 after 1958.

.45 HAND EJECTOR MODEL OF 1917 — .45 Auto Rim or .45 ACP in half moon clip, 6 shot, 5½ in. barrel, fixed sights, satin blue on military - high gloss blue on commercial, smooth walnut on military, checkered walnut on commercial.

Military — 175,000 mfg., 1917-1919.

	$360	$340	$320	$275	$220	$195	$165

Commercial — mfg. 1919-1941.

	$440	$420	$395	$370	$320	$285	$230

Brazilian Contract of 1937 — Brazilian shield on right side, 14,000 recently imported.

	$175	$150	$125	$110	$100	$90	$80

REGULATION POLICE TARGET — similar to Regulation Police, but target sight, .32 S&W, 6 in. barrel only, blue. Mfg. 1917-1940.

	$300	$250	$195	$165	$130	$110	$90

REGULATION POLICE (MODEL 31) — .32 S&W, 6 shot, .38 S&W, 5 shot, 2, 3, 4, or 6 in. barrel in .32 cal., 4 in. barrel in .38 cal. (Model 33), square butt, walnut grips, fixed sights, blue or nickel. Mfg. 1917-present.

Pre-1958 Manufacture	$325	$275	$225	$170	$145	$135	$125
Model 31-1	$275	$220	$180	$160	$130	$110	$85

Grading	100%	98%	95%	90%	80%	70%	60%

⊀ Regulation Police Target — features adj. sights.

| | $440 | $420 | $395 | $370 | $320 | $285 | $230 |

MODEL 35

| | $300 | $250 | $195 | $165 | $130 | $110 | $90 |

MODEL .22 MILITARY & POLICE — .22 LR only, originally mfg. as training gun between 1931-1957, also mfg. 500 in 1963 (Model 45).

| Pre-War | $1,300 | $1,100 | $925 | $775 | $625 | $525 | $475 |
| Post-War | $650 | $550 | $450 | $375 | $300 | $280 | $270 |

.38/44 HEAVY DUTY — .38 cal., 6 shot, 4, 5, or 6½ in. barrel lengths, fixed sights, walnut grips, blue or nickel, walnut grips. Mfg. 1930-1941 and re-introduced 1946 (with S prefix starting at serial 62,940). The 38/44 Heavy Duty became the Model 20 in 1957.

| | $595 | $490 | $450 | $415 | $385 | $340 | $300 |

MODEL 20 — .38 Spl. or .44 cal., 6 shot, 4, 5, or 6½ in. barrel, fixed sights, blue or nickel, checkered walnut grips. Mfg. 1957-1967.

| | $350 | $285 | $260 | $220 | $195 | $145 | $125 |

.38/44 OUTDOORSMAN (MODEL 23) — .38 Spl., similar to Model 20 in .38 Spl., except with adj. sights, blue only, pre-war guns had plain barrels, post-war mfg. featured ribbed barrels. Mfg. 1930-1967.

| | $650 | $550 | $450 | $375 | $300 | $280 | $270 |

Add approx. 50% for older 5 screw model.
The 44 in this model's nomenclature refers to the size frame, not the caliber. This variation became designated the Model 23 after 1958.

.44 HAND EJECTOR FOURTH MODEL - MODEL OF 1950 MILITARY (MODEL 21) — .44 S&W, 6 shot, 4, 5, or 6½ in. large frame, blue, walnut grips, fixed sights. Mfg. 1926-1941.

| | $490 | $400 | $360 | $300 | $275 | $250 | $225 |

VICTORY MODEL — .38 Spl. cal., mfg. in accordance to British/American lend-lease agreement of WWII, parkerized finish, mfg. 1942-1944.

| | $425 | $375 | $325 | $275 | $225 | $200 | $175 |

MODEL 51 — .22 Mag. only, .22/32 kit gun, 3 in. barrel, 6 shot, adj. rear sight, blue or nickel, walnut stocks. Disc.

| | $400 | $350 | $300 | $275 | $250 | $225 | $200 |

.38 TERRIER (MODEL 32) — .38 S&W, 5 shot, 2 in. barrel, walnut or rubber grips, blue or nickel, fixed sights, built on .32 frame. Mfg. 1936-1974.

| | $330 | $220 | $175 | $150 | $135 | $125 | $115 |

This variation was designated the Model 32 after 1958.

K-22 OUTDOORSMAN — K frame, .22 LR, 6 shot, 6 in. round barrel, blue, adj. target sights, walnut grips. Mfg. 1931-1940.

| | $575 | $500 | $450 | $375 | $330 | $285 | $250 |

Early pre-war manufacture do not have a "K" prefix in this model.

K-22 MASTERPIECE — similar to K-22 Outdoorsman, but has micro click rear sight, short action. Approx. 1,000 mfg. in 1940 only.

| | $1,200 | $1,050 | $875 | $750 | $675 | $600 | $550 |

K-22 MASTERPIECE POST-WAR MODEL 17 — see listing in revolvers: recent production section.

Grading	100%	98%	95%	90%	80%	70%	60%

K-32 MODEL 16 — .32 S&W long, 6 in. barrel, adj. sights, checkered walnut, blue. Only 3630 mfg., 1947-1974.

	$1,350	$1,150	$995	$875	$750	$625	$525

⚞ Pre-War K-32 Model 16 — only 104 mfg. pre-war, scarce.

	$2,250	$1,950	$1,700	$1,475	$1,250	$1,050	$875

.22/32 KIT GUN — similar to .22/32 Target, except has 2 or 4 in. barrels, round or square butt. Mfg. 1935-1953.

	$800	$700	$575	$500	$450	$400	$350

Pre-war mfg. commands a premium.

.22/32 KIT GUN AIRWEIGHT (MODEL 43) — .22 LR, 3½ in. barrel, round or square butt, adj. sights, aluminum frame and cylinder, mfg. 1955-1974.

	$425	$350	$275	$240	$185	$165	$150

U.S. AIR FORCE MODEL 13 LIGHTWEIGHT — .38 Spl., aluminum cylinder and frame. Most were destroyed by the Government.

	$800	$725	$675	$525	$475	$425	$350

This model is S&Ws .38 Military & Police Airway (later became the Model 12).

.44 HAND EJECTOR FOURTH MODEL - 1950 TARGET (MODEL 24) — post-war 1926 Model .44 Target, redesigned hammer, ribbed barrel, micrometer sights. Mfg. 1950-1967.

	$695	$575	$500	$400	$375	$350	$320

.45 HAND EJECTOR MODEL OF 1950 MILITARY (MODEL 22) — .45 auto rim or .45 ACP, same specifications as 1917 Army, except redesigned hammer, fixed sights. Approx. 1,200 mfg. 1950-1964.

	$1,500	$1,275	$1,050	$875	$725	$650	$525

.45 HAND EJECTOR MODEL OF 1950 TARGET (MODEL 26) — adj. sights, thin ribbed barrel.

	$770	$660	$550	$440	$275	$200	$150

MODEL 29 (5 SCREW) — .44 Mag. 5 screw, 4 exposed screws on right sideplate, 1 in front of the trigger guard. Approx. 6,500 mfg. during 1956-1957. Disc.

	$850	$750	$650	$575	$500	$450	$400

Subtract $100 if no box.
100% value assumes new gun with box, papers, and tools.

MODEL 29 (4 SCREW) — .44 Mag., 4 screw, 3 exposed screws on right sideplate (eliminated top screw on sideplate). Mfg. began 1957 after approx. ser. no. S175,000.

	$695	$650	$600	$550	$475	$425	$375

MODEL 29 (3 SCREW) — .44 mag, 4, 6½, or 8⅜ in. barrel, eliminated top screw on sideplate and 1 screw in front of triggerguard. Disc.

	$650	$550	$500	$400	$300	$275	$250

Subtract $40 if without case.
The S serial number prefix was used on this model until 1968, at which time the law required a new numbering system, and the serial number prefix was changed to N. The S prefix designates the hammer block safety.
A rare variation in this model is a 5 in. barrel. Only 500 were mfg. in 1956-57 with bright blue finish, diamond target stocks, and wood case. In N.I.B. condition the value is $2,800 - add 25% for nickel finish.

⚞ 4 in. barrel — 500 mfg. in 1957-58 only.

	$1,800	$1,600	$1,395

Grading	100%	98%	95%	90%	80%	70%	60%

CENTENNIAL MODEL 40 — .38 Spl., 2 in. barrel double action only, hammerless, grip safety, checkered walnut grips, blue or nickel. Mfg. 1953-1974.

	$475	$425	$345	$290	$260	$240	$220

This model commands a premium for the first series with no letter prefix.

CENTENNIAL AIRWEIGHT MODEL 42 — .38 S&W Spl., aluminum variation of Model 40 Centennial, mfg. began 1953. Disc.

Blue	$475	$425	$395	$325	$300	$265	$240
Nickel	$1,100	$950	$875	$775	$675	$550	$475

.38 CHIEF SPECIAL TARGET (MODEL 50) — Chief Special Target, .38 Spl., mfg. from 1955 in 2 or 3 (mfg. began mid '70s) in. barrels, target sights, most were unmarked for model number, approx. 1,100 mfg. The other variation was designated Model 36.

	$795	$700	$625	$550	$475	$400	$350

MODEL 53 .22 REM. JET — .22 S, L, or LR inserts, 6 shot, 4, 6, or 8⅜ in. barrel, blue, walnut grips, adj. sights. Mfg. 1960-1974.

	$735	$650	$550	$470	$385	$360	$330

Add 10% for 8⅜ in. barrel.

MODEL 58 — .41 Mag, M&P, fixed sights, 4 in. barrel, blue or nickel finish. Disc.

	$495	$450	$385	$340	$315	$290	$260

Add $25 for nickel finish or "S" serial number prefix.

.22/32 TARGET MODEL OF 1953 (MODEL 35) — similar to .22-32 Target, except micrometer rear sight, magna target grips. Mfg. 1953-1974.

	$425	$300	$265	$230	$200	$180	$160

MODEL 520 — .357 mag., 4 in. barrel, fixed sights, N frame, originally ordered for N.Y. State Police but never purchased. Approx. 3,000 mfg. with "N.Y.S.P." on frame.

	$325	$275	$240	$210	$185	$175	$165

.357 MAGNUM FACTORY REGISTERED — This model was mfg. 1935-1938. It could be custom ordered with any barrel length from 3½ - 8¾ in., adj. sights, checkered walnut grips. The gun was hand fitted and registered to the buyer by a number found on the inside of the yoke. This practice was disc. 1938 (approx. 5,500 were mfg.) due to the tremendous demand for the .357 Mag. revolver.

	$1,150	$995	$850	$675	$575	$500	$450

.357 MAGNUM PRE-WAR NON-REGISTERED — similar to above, but not registered. 1,142 mfg. 1938-1941.

	$775	$725	$660	$525	$470	$385	$330

ENGRAVING OPTIONS FOR CURRENT MFG. HANDGUNS

The prices listed below are for original factory finished guns with no extra engraving. The listings below show 1993 factory engraving costs. These prices should be added to the cost of each engraved production gun to determine the correct value.

CLASS "C" ENGRAVING—1/3 METAL COVERAGE
Pistols — add $975.
For J Frame — add $772.
10⅝ in. N Frame — add $1,183.
2-5 in. K, L, or N Frame — add $995.
6-8⅜ in. K, L, or N Frame — add $1,131.

CLASS "B" ENGRAVING — ⅔ METAL COVERAGE
Pistols — add $1,276.
For J Frame — add $1,259.
10⅝ in. N Frames — add $1,472.
2-5 in. K, L, or N Frame — add $1,301.
6-8⅜ in. K, L, or N Frame — add $1,408.

CLASS "A" ENGRAVING — FULL COVERAGE
Pistols — add $1,552.
For J Frame — add $1,322.
2-5 in. K, L, or N Frame — add $1,598.
6-8⅜ in. K, L, or N Frame — add $1,690.
10⅝ in. N Frame — add $1,767.

SPECIAL ENGRAVING — Also available: inlays, seals, game scenes, lettering, prices quoted on request.

LASERSMITH ENGRAVING — laser etching was available 1989-1990 only. This process involved a digitally controlled laser producing a variety of designs, logos, commemorative messages, or autograph on the metal surface(s). Some of these designs were made exclusively for major firearms distributors. Others were custom designed for clubs or organizations. Retail prices started at just under $18 and can go as high as $150+, depending on the amount and complexity of the laser etching. To date, premiums are not being paid for these "rarer" variations.

REVOLVERS: RECENT PRODUCTION

SMITH & WESSON DID NOT ASSIGN MODEL NUMBERS UNTIL 1958.

To determine which variation a particular revolver is in the following section, simply swing the cylinder out to the loading position and notice the model number inside the yoke. A two digit number followed by a dash and another number designates which engineering change was underway when the gun was manufactured. Hence, a 48-3 is a Model 48 in its 3rd improvement (i.e. 3rd engineering update). Usually, earlier variations are the most desirable to collectors unless a particular improvement is rare. The same rule applies to semi-auto pistols and the model designation is usually marked on the outside of the gun.

SMITH & WESSON COMMEMORATIVES/SPECIAL EDITIONS:

During the course of a year, I receive many phone calls and letters on special editions and limited editions that do not appear in this section. It should be noted that a commemorative issue is a gun that has been manufactured, marketed, and sold through the auspices of the specific trademark (in this case S&W). During the past several decades, hundreds of limited editions have been ordered through various police agencies, state highway patrol units, and other law enforcement organizations. Many of these variations do not have the special suffix serialization (and may not have had a retail price when issued). Since most of these special editions/commemoratives were made for a specific organization, regional demand has a lot to do with determining values (a Model 66 Montana HP Commemorative will not sell for a premium in Alabama). For this reason, most of these guns will not appear in this section and you should contact the factory to learn more about the provenance of these special editions. Remember - values on these models can vary A LOT from one region to another and an averaged "national" single price is almost impossible. While these guns do have special interest, they do not have the collectability or desirability of many of the standard models listed below.

The variations listed below represent the only five factory S&W Commemoratives manufactured to date. Anything else will be a special or limited edition made for a organization, company, or special event.

Grading	100%	Issue Price	Qty. made
MODEL 19 TEXAS RANGER — .357 Mag., with or without knife, approx. 8,000 with knife, approx. 2,000 without, cased. Mfg. 1973 only.			
	$595	$250	10,000
⚞ **Model 19 Texas Ranger Deluxe** — approx. 50 mfg. with a serial numbers divisible by 10, cased.			
	N/A	N/A	50

Grading	100%	Issue Price	Qty. made

125TH ANNIVERSARY COMMEMORATIVE — .45 LC cal., plain variation was called Model 25-3, 10,000 mfg. total in 1977, cased with nickel silver medallion, and Roy Jinks book, "125th Anniversary of Smith & Wesson".

	$450	$350	10,000

⚝ **125th Anniversary Commemorative Deluxe** — Model 25-4, approx. 50 mfg. with S&W prefix serial numbers divisible by 10, cased, sterling silver medallion, and a leather bound "History of Smith & Wesson" book by Roy Jinks.

	N/A	N/A	50

MODEL 29 ELMER KEITH COMMEMORATIVE — .44 Mag. cal., 4 in. barrel, standard and deluxe editions, approx. 2,000 total mfg.

	$850	N/A	2,000

50TH ANNIVERSARY OF THE .357 MAGNUM — Model 27, both standard and deluxe editions, 1987 mfg.

	$450	N/A	N/A

MODEL 544 TEXAS WAGON TRAIN COMMEMORATIVE — .44-40 cal. only, 6 shot, 5 in. barrel, bright blue finish, adj. sights, 7,800 mfg. 1986 to commemorate the Texas Sesquicentennial (1836-1986). Special markings on frame and barrel, smooth Goncalo commemorative grips, ser. no. TWT001 - TWT7800 (estimated). Made 1986 only.

	$450	N/A	7,800

In this section, the stainless steel variations have been placed next to the standard models from which they are derived for convenience. For a sequential numerical listing, please refer to the section: REVOLVERS: STAINLESS STEEL (following this section).
ADD 10%-15% FOR THOSE MODELS LISTED BELOW THAT ARE PINNED AND RE-CESSED (PRE-1981 MFG.).

Grading	100%	98%	95%	90%	80%	70%	60%

MODEL 10 M & P — .38 Spl., 6 shot, round or square butt (4 in. bbl. only starting 1992), fixed sights, 2, 3 (disc.), 4, 5 (disc.), or 6 (disc.) in. barrels.

Mfg.'s Sug. Retail	$361	$275	$215	$160	$140	$130	$115	$100

Add $12 for nickel finish - disc. 1991 (4 in. only).
The Model 10 is currently available in 2 or 4 in. barrel only (a 4 in. heavy barrel nickel square butt variation was disc. in 1992).

MODEL 12 M & P AIRWEIGHT — similar to Model 10, only alloy frame, 2 or 4 in. barrel. Disc. 1986.

	$280	$245	$210	$200	$185	$175	$150

Add $40 for nickel finish (disc.).
Last Mfg.'s Sug. Retail was $320.

MODEL 13 M & P — .357 Mag., heavy barrel, fixed sights, 3 (round butt) or 4 (square butt) in. barrel.

Mfg.'s Sug. Retail	$367	$280	$220	$165	$145	$135	$125	$120

Add $20 for nickel finish (disc. 1986).

⚝ **Model 13 - N.Y. State Police** — .357 Mag., 4 in. barrel, blued, fixed sights, 1200 were mfg. for the N.Y. State Police and are so marked. All 1200 were recalled by S&W and exchanged for Model 28s).

	$375	$300	$250	$200	$175	$150	$140

Grading	100%	98%	95%	90%	80%	70%	60%

MODEL 13 LIGHTWEIGHT, USAF — .38 Spl., aluminum cylinder and frame, 6 shot, only 14⅜ oz. Most were destroyed by the Government.

		$800	$750	$675			

This model was purchased in large quantities during 1953 and early 1954 only. While S&W never assigned a model number to this variation, M 13 is marked on the top strap and thus retains the Model 13 designation. In 1954, a conventional steel cylinder replaced the aluminum cylinder because of cracking.

MODEL 14 K-38 — .38 Spl., target model, blue only. Disc. 1981.

		$300	$250	$215	$200	$185	$175	$160

Add $20 for 6 in. barrels single action.

⚞ **Model 14 K-38 Masterpiece**—.38 Spl., 6 in. full lug barrel, adj. rear sight, combat style Morado wood square butt grips, blue finish, 47 oz. 2,000 mfg. in 1991 only.

Mfg.'s Sug. Retail	$442	$350	$300	$255	$225	$200	$185	$165

MODEL 15 COMBAT MASTERPIECE — .38 Spl., adj. sights, 6 shot, 2 (disc.), 4, 6 (disc. 1991), or 8⅜ (disc.) in. barrel (6 and 8⅜ new 1986).

Mfg.'s Sug. Retail	$391	$300	$245	$210	$190	$180	$160	$150

Add $31 for TT or TH (disc. 1991).
Add $11 for 8⅜ in. barrel (disc.).
Add $20 for nickel finish (disc. 1987).

MODEL 16 — .32 cal./.32 Mag., 6 shot, 4 (mfg. 1990-91 only), 6, or 8⅜ (disc. 1991) in. barrel, square butt, blue finish only, TH and TT. Mfg. 1990-92.

		$335	$280	$225	$210	$200	$190	$180

Add 5%-10% for 8⅜ in. barrel.
Last Mfg.'s Sug. Retail was $419.

MODEL 17 K-22 MASTERPIECE — .22 LR, blue only, 4 (new 1986), 6, or 8⅜ (disc. 1992) in. barrel.

Mfg.'s Sug. Retail	$410	$315	$265	$235	$215	$200	$185	$175

Add $39 for full lug 6 in. long barrel (w/TT & TH).
Add $50 for full lug 8⅜ in. long barrel (w/TT & TH) (disc. 1992).

MODEL 18 .22 COMBAT MASTERPIECE — .22 LR, combat style adj. sights, 4 in. barrel, blue only. Disc. 1985.

		$305	$270	$225	$200	$180	$175	$165

Add $30 for TT and TH.
Last Mfg.'s Sug. Retail was $352.

MODEL 19 .357 COMBAT MAGNUM — K frame, .357 Mag., adj. sights, 2½, 4, or 6 in. barrel, bright blue or nickel (disc. 1992) finish.

Mfg.'s Sug. Retail	$388	$305	$250	$205	$190	$180	$170	$160

Add $9 for 4 or 6 in. barrel.
Add $32 for white outline rear sight.
Add $20 for nickel finish - disc. 1991 (4 or 6 in. only).
Add $60 for TS, TT, TH, RR, and WO - disc. 1991 (6 in. barrel only).
This model is supplied with a round butt on 2½ in. barrel. Nickel finish is available with a 4 or 6 in. barrel only. The 2½ and 6 in. barrels (blue finish) were disc. in 1991 along with the 4 and 6 in. nickel variations.

Smith&Wesson cont.

Grading	100%	98%	95%	90%	80%	70%	60%

Model 19 Oregon State Police Commemorative — boxed with belt buckle.

	100%	98%	95%	90%	80%	70%	60%
	$895	$750	$650				

Model 19 Texas Ranger Commemorative

	100%	98%	95%	90%	80%	70%	60%
	$750	$625	$495				

MODEL 24 — 44 Spl., 4 or 6½ in. barrel, blue finish only. Mfg. 1983 and 1984 only.

	100%	98%	95%	90%	80%	70%	60%
	$300	$275	$240	$225	$205	$190	$175

Add $30 for TS, TT, and TH.
Last Mfg.'s Sug. Retail was $359.

Model 24-3 Lew Horton Special — .44 Spl., 3 in. barrel, round butt, adj. sights, blue finish, includes special fitted holster.

	100%	98%	95%	90%	80%	70%	60%
	$380	$325	$250				

Deduct 10% without holster.

MODEL 25-2 .45 ACP — N frame, blue or nickel, target grips, 4, 6, 6½, or 8⅜ in. barrel. Disc.

	100%	98%	95%	90%	80%	70%	60%
	$450	$400	$350	$300	$235	$200	$190

Add $14 for nickel finish.
Add $150 for 6½ in. barrel (older mfg. with pinned barrel).
Last Mfg.'s Sug. Retail was $347.

Model 25-3 Lew Horton Special — .45 ACP, 3 in. barrel, adj. sights, blue finish, only 100 mfg.

	100%	98%	95%	90%	80%	70%	60%
	$500	$450	$375				

MODEL 25-5 — .45 Long Colt cal., 4, 6, or 8⅜ in. barrel, blue or nickel finish (no extra charge - disc. 1987). Disc. 1991.

	100%	98%	95%	90%	80%	70%	60%
	$340	$285	$225	$210	$200	$190	$180

Add 5%-10% for 8⅜ in. barrel.
Last Mfg.'s Sug. Retail was $429.

Model 25-5 125th Anniversary — .45 LC, presentation cased.

	100%	98%	95%	90%	80%	70%	60%
	$450	$300	$250				

MODEL 27 — .357 Mag., N frame, 3½ (disc.), 4 (disc. 1991), 5 (disc.), 6, or 8⅜ (disc. 1991) in. barrel, blue or nickel (disc. 1987) finish.

		100%	98%	95%	90%	80%	70%	60%
Mfg.'s Sug. Retail	$462	$365	$295	$235	$220	$205	$190	$180

Add $28 for white outlined rear sight -(disc. 1991).
Add $8 for 8⅜ in. barrel - (disc. 1991).
Add 20% for 3½ or 5 in. barrel (disc.).

3½ and 5 in. barrel — disc.

	100%	98%	95%	90%	80%	70%	60%
	$425	$365	$275	$265	$240	$230	$180

50th Year .357 Mag. Commemorative — presentation cased.

	100%	98%	95%	90%	80%	70%	60%
	$400	$275	$225				

MODEL 28 HIGHWAY PATROLMAN — .357 Mag., "Highway Patrol" utility model, dull finish, adj. sights, standard grips, blue only, 4 or 6 in. barrel. Disc. 1986.

	100%	98%	95%	90%	80%	70%	60%
	$270	$235	$210	$200	$190	$180	$150

Add $20 for TS.
Last Mfg.'s Sug. Retail was $306.

Grading	100%	98%	95%	90%	80%	70%	60%

MODEL 29 — .44 Mag., 6 shot, similar to Model 25-5, except .44 Mag., 4 (disc. 1992), 6, or 8⅜ in. barrel, blue or nickel (disc. 1991) finish.

| Mfg.'s Sug. Retail | $526 | $375 | $320 | $285 | $265 | $255 | $245 | $210 |

Add $11 for nickel finish (disc. 1991).
Add $45 for combat grips with scope mount - disc. 1991 (8⅜ in. barrel only).
Note: It must be noted that collectors will often pay a 50% premium for the older 5 screw versions of these current production guns. First year production of Model 29 can bring $1500 if condition warrants. Original boxes are extremely desirable! When examining S&Ws for purchase, be aware of these factors.
Older Model 29 mfg. will appear under the previous subheading: "REVOLVERS: MODERN, OUT OF PRODUCTION".

Model 29-3 Lew Horton Special — similar to Model 29, except has 3 in. barrel, round butt, adj. sights.

| | | | | $425 | $350 | $295 |

MODEL 29 CLASSIC — .44 Mag., 5, 6½, or 8⅜ in. full lug barrel, blue only, square butt with Hogue combat grips, interchangeable front sights with white outline rear sight, frame is drilled and tapped to accept scope mounts, blue finish only. New in 1990.

| Mfg.'s Sug. Retail | $567 | $460 | $370 | $295 | $280 | $260 | $240 | $225 |

Add $9 for 8⅜ in. barrel.

MODEL 29 SILHOUETTE — .44 Mag., 10⅝ in. barrel, adj. front and rear sights, bright blue only, Goncalo Alves target stocks. Mfg. 1983-91.

| | | $445 | $370 | $300 | $280 | $260 | $240 | $225 |

Last Mfg.'s Sug. Retail was $536.

MODEL 29 MAGNACLASSIC — .44 Mag., 7½ full lug, ported barrel, high bright bluing, round butt, interchangeable front sight, supplied with cherry wood display case mfg. in England, 3,000 mfg. in 1990 only.

| | | $850 | $725 | $600 | $500 | $450 | $395 | $360 |

Last Mfg.'s Sug. Retail was $999.

MODEL 31 REGULATION POLICE — .32 S&W Long, fixed sights, 2, 3 or 4 (disc.) in. barrel, blue only. Disc. 1991.

| | | $290 | $235 | $195 | $185 | $175 | $165 | $150 |

Add 25% for early flatlatch models.
Last Mfg.'s Sug. Retail was $365.

MODEL 34 - 1953 .22/32 KIT GUN — .22 LR or .32 cal. (disc.), adj. sights, J frame, 6 shot, 2 or 4 in. barrel, round or square butt, blue or nickel (disc. 1986). Disc. 1991. This model was re-issued for 2-3 years.

| | | $300 | $235 | $195 | $185 | $175 | $165 | $150 |

Add $25 for nickel finish.
Add 25% for early flatlatch models.
Last Mfg.'s Sug. Retail was $366.

MODEL 36 CHIEF'S SPECIAL — .38 Spl., 5 shot, J frame, round or square (disc. 1991) butt, 2 in. regular or 3 in. (heavy) barrel, blue or nickel (disc. 1992) finish.

| Mfg.'s Sug. Retail | $366 | $270 | $220 | $175 | $165 | $155 | $150 | $145 |

Add $12 for nickel finish (round butt - 2 in. barrel only).
Note: 1st models with high polish blue and diamond grips will bring premiums when mint in original box.

Grading	100%	98%	95%	90%	80%	70%	60%

MODEL 36 LADYSMITH — .38 S&W Special, 5 shot, 2 in. regular or 3 (disc. 1991) in. heavy barrel, blue finish only, grips are anatomically designed for women (round butt on 2 in., wood combat grips on 3 in.), fixed sights, redesigned double action, 20-23 oz., Morocco grained (disc. 1991) or soft side case. New 1990.

Mfg.'s Sug. Retail	$399	$310	$235	$195	$185	$175	$165	$150

MODEL 37 CHIEF'S SPECIAL AIRWEIGHT — similar to 36 Chief's Special, except alloy frame and 2 in. barrel only, blue or nickel finish.

Mfg.'s Sug. Retail	$394	$305	$235	$195	$185	$175	$165	$150

Add $16 for nickel finish.

MODEL 38 BODYGUARD AIRWEIGHT — .38 S&W Spl., 5 shot, alloy frame, round butt, shrouded hammer, 2 in. barrel, blue or nickel finish.

Mfg.'s Sug. Retail	$418	$320	$250	$205	$190	$180	$170	$150

Add $15 for nickel finish.

MODEL 48 K-22 MASTERPIECE — .22 Mag, 4, 6 or 8⅜ in. barrel, blue only. Disc. 1986.

		$275	$245	$200	$185	$175	$165	$150

Add $15 for 8⅜ in. barrel.
Add $15 for TT, TH, and TS (disc.).
Last Mfg.'s Sug. Retail was $320.

MODEL 49 BODYGUARD — similar to Model 38, only steel frame, 2 in. barrel, blue or nickel (disc.) finish.

Mfg.'s Sug. Retail	$389	$290	$255	$180	$170	$160	$150	$145

Add $25 for nickel finish (disc.).

MODEL 57 — .41 Mag., similar to Model 29, except for cal., 4 (disc. 1991), 6 or 8⅜ (disc. 1991) in. barrel, blue or nickel (disc.) finish.

Mfg.'s Sug. Retail	$466	$350	$255	$225	$205	$190	$175	$165

Add 10% for nickel finish if NIB.
Add $20 for 8⅜ in. barrel.

MODEL 58 — .41 Mag., M&P, fixed sights, 4 in. barrel, blue or nickel finish. Disc.

		$350	$315	$290	$260	$220	$200	$180

Add $25 for nickel finish.

MODEL 442 CENTENNIAL AIRWEIGHT — .38 S&W Spl. cal., 2 in. barrel only, blue or nickel finish, round butt. New 1993.

Mfg.'s Sug. Retail	$418	$320	$250	$205	$190	$180	$170	$150

Add $15 for nickel finish.

MODEL 547 M & P — 9mm, 3 or 4 in. heavy barrel, 6 shot, round (3 in. barrel) or square (4 in. barrel) butt, blue only, 32 oz. Disc. 1985.

		$295	$265	$240	$210	$195	$185	$175

Last Mfg.'s Sug. Retail was $317.

MODEL 581 — .357 Mag., L-Frame, 4 in. barrel, 6 shot, blue or nickel finish, 38 oz. Disc. 1992.

		$275	$225	$180	$170	$160	$150	$145

Add $20 for nickel (disc. 1987).
This model was disc. 1985-86, and reintroduced 1987-92.
Last Mfg.'s Sug. Retail was $335.

Grading	100%	98%	95%	90%	80%	70%	60%

MODEL 586 — .357 Mag., L-Frame, 4, 6, or 8⅜ (disc. 1991) in. barrel, fixed or adj. sights, blue or nickel (disc. 1991) finish.

Mfg.'s Sug. Retail	$439		$335	$270	$210	$195	$185	$175	$165

Add 5%-10% for nickel finish.
Add $4 for white outlined rear sight.
Add $22 for 8⅜ in. barrel (disc. 1991).
Add $35 for adj. front sight - disc. 1991 (6 in. barrel only, new 1986).

1985 Model 586 Iowa Highway State Patrol — mfg. to commemorate 50th anniversary, gold etching, 4 in. barrel. Mfg. 1985 only.

$375 $250 $225

MODEL 1989 SERIES — there are a variety of models and calibers in this series, research is underway to gather more information on this series.

REVOLVERS: STAINLESS STEEL

MODEL 60 CHIEF'S SPECIAL — .38 Spl., stainless version of Chief's Special, 2 or 3 in. barrel.

Mfg.'s Sug. Retail $417 $315 $240 $195

Add $26 for 3 in. full lug barrel and combat grips.
The full lug barrel option began in 1990 with limited mfg. It has been tested for +P+ ammo and features an adj. rear sight - 24½ oz.

MODEL 60 LADYSMITH — .38 S&W Special, 5 shot, 2 in. regular or 3 in. heavy barrel (disc. 1991), frosted stainless steel finish, grips are anatomically designed for women (round butt on 2 in., wood combat grips on 3 in.), fixed sights, redesigned double action, 20-23 oz, Morocco grained (disc. 1991) or soft side case. New 1990.

Mfg.'s Sug. Retail $450 $345 $245 $195

MODEL 63 .22/32 KIT GUN — .22 LR/.32, stainless kit gun, 2 or 4 in. barrel, 19 oz.

Mfg.'s Sug. Retail $435 $335 $240 $195

MODEL 64 M & P — .38 S&W, stainless Model 10, has 2, 3, or 4 in. barrel. 3 (square butt disc. 1992) 4 in. (square butt only) barrels are heavy.

Mfg.'s Sug. Retail $402 $300 $215 $185

MODEL 65 — .357 Mag., stainless version of Model 13, has 3 (round butt) or 4 (square butt) in. heavy barrels.

Mfg.'s Sug. Retail $402 $300 $215 $185

Add $35 for TT, TH, and TS (disc.).

MODEL 65 LADYSMITH — .357 Mag., 3 in. barrel with round butt, glass beaded stainless finish, soft side case. New 1992.

Mfg.'s Sug. Retail $450 $345 $245 $195

MODEL 66 — .357 Mag., stainless version of model 19, has 2½, 4, or 6 in. barrel.

Mfg.'s Sug. Retail $437 $355 $260 $195

Add $6 for 4 or 6 in. barrel.
Add $5 for white outlined rear sight.
Add $48 for TH and TT with 4 (disc. 1991) or 6 in. barrel only.
Note: Several models of the Model 66 were made — such features as an all-stainless steel rear sight and a recessed cylinder will bring a slight premium if N.I.B.

Model 66 Missouri Highway Patrol Commemorative — cased, with Bowie knife and badge. Disc.

$850 $600 $500

⚰ **Model 66 Montana Highway Patrol Commemorative** — 4 in. barrel, commemorates 44 years of service, 213 mfg.

	$650	$525	$425

⚰ **Model 66-1 Chicago Police Commemorative** — 4 in. barrel, presentation cased.

	$375	$300	$260

⚰ **Model 66 Border Patrol** — .357 Mag., includes Goncalo Alves hand carved grips, border patrol badge etched on right side of frame, 50th anniversary (1924-1974), USBP serialization prefix.

	$650	$525	$425

MODEL 67 COMBAT MASTERPIECE — .38 S&W, stainless version of Model 15, has 4 in. barrel. Disc. 1988, reintroduced 1991.

Mfg.'s Sug. Retail	$443	$335	$245	$195

1991 mfg. includes square butt and red ramp front sight insert.

MODEL 68 — .38 Spl. cal., similar in appearance to the Model 66, except is in .38 Spl. cal., 4 or 6 in. barrel, approx. 7,500 mfg.

	$375	$300	$250

MODEL 610 — 10mm cal., 6 shot, 5 or 6$\frac{1}{2}$ in. full lug barrel, round butt, target hammer optional, approx. 5,000 mfg. 1990 only.

	$550	$450	$375

Last Mfg.'s Sug. Retail was $510.

MODEL 617 — .22 LR cal., stainless steel variation of the Model 17, 6 shot, 4, 6, or 8$\frac{3}{8}$ in. barrel, straight backstrap grip, combat trigger and grips, semi-target. New 1990.

Mfg.'s Sug. Retail	$432	$330	$245	$195

Add $34 for 6 in. barrel with TT and TH.
Add $44 for 8$\frac{3}{8}$ in. barrel with TT and TH.

MODEL 624 .44 TARGET — .44 S&W Spl., 6 shot, 4 or 6$\frac{1}{2}$ in. barrel, 42 oz. Mfg. 1986-87 only.

	$340	$250	$225

Add $14 for 6$\frac{1}{2}$ in. barrel.
Last Mfg.'s Sug. Retail was $449.

⚰ **Model 624-2 Lew Horton Special** — .44 Spl., 3 in. barrel with round butt, adj. sights, includes special fitted holster.

	$395	$350	$295

Deduct 10% if without holster.

MODEL 625 — .45 ACP, stainless variation of the Model 25-2, 6 shot, 3 (disc. 1991), 4 (disc. 1991), or 5 in. barrel, round butt, full lug barrel, Pachmayr grips. New 1988.

Mfg.'s Sug. Retail	$562	$465	$380	$300

This variation has the frame stamped "625-2", roll engraved barrel with ".45 CAL MODEL OF 1988" barrel inscription.

MODEL 629 — .44 Mag., similar to Model 29. Available with 4, 6, or 8$\frac{3}{8}$ in. barrel.

Mfg.'s Sug. Retail	$557	$465	$380	$300

Add $18 for 8$\frac{3}{8}$ in. barrel.
Add $52 for combat grips with scope mount - disc. 1991 (8$\frac{3}{8}$ in. barrel only).
During 1978, approx. 100 revolvers were made with pinned barrels and recessed cylinders, serial range is 629,XXX-629,XXX, includes wood box. Prices range from $650-$750, depending on condition.

Grading	100%	98%	95%	90%	80%	70%	60%

⚔ **Model 629 Classic** — stainless steel variation of the Model 29 Classic. New in 1990.
Mfg.'s Sug. Retail $598 $485 $395 $315
Add $19 for 8⅜ in. barrel.

⚔ **Model 629 Classic DX** — .44 Mag., similar to Classic, except is supplied with 2 sets of grips (Hogue combat square and Morado wood round butt stocks), 5 interchangeable front sights, numbered test target, 51-54 oz. New 1992.
Mfg.'s Sug. Retail $786 $645 $560 $480
Add $25 for 8⅜ in. barrel.

⚔ **Model 629 Magna Classic** — .44 Mag., similar to Model 29, 3,000 mfg. during 1990 only.
                   $900 $825 $750
Last Mfg.'s Sug. Retail was $999.

⚔ **Model 629-3 Lew Horton Special** — .44 Mag., 3 in. barrel with round butt, adj. sights.
                   $400 $350 $295

MODEL 631 — .32 Mag., 6 shot, 2 or 4 in. barrel, combat stocks, round butt only, approx. 5,500 mfg. 1990-92.
                   $340 $275 $200
Last Mfg.'s Sug. Retail was $386.

⚔ **631 Ladysmith** — 2 in. barrel only, rose stocks.
                   $365 $295 $225
Last Mfg.'s Sug. Retail was $400.

MODEL 632 CENTENNIAL — .32 Mag., 2 or 3 (disc. 1991) in. barrel, stainless/alloy construction, fully concealed hammer, small frame, Santoprene combat grips, fixed sights, 15.5 oz. Mfg. 1991-1992.
                   $315 $240 $195
Last Mfg.'s Sug. Retail was $410.

MODEL 637 CHIEF'S SPECIAL AIRWEIGHT — .38 S&W Spl., 5 shot, alloy frame, 2 in. barrel, stainless steel cylinder and barrel. 560 mfg. during 1991 only.
                   $305 $250 $200
Last Mfg.'s Sug. Retail was $390.

MODEL 638 BODYGUARD AIRWEIGHT — .38 S&W Spl., 5 shot, alloy frame, 2 in. barrel, shrouded hammer, round butt, stainless steel barrel and cylinder, 1,200 mfg. during 1990 only.
                   $310 $250 $210
Last Mfg.'s Sug. Retail was $395.

MODEL 640 CENTENNIAL — .38 S&W, 5 shot, 2 (new 1991) or 3 (disc. 1992) in. barrel, fully concealed hammer, round butt, tested for +P+ ammo, 22½ oz. New in 1991.
Mfg.'s Sug. Retail $441 $335 $245 $195

MODEL 642 CENTENNIAL AIRWEIGHT — .38 Spl, 5 shot, 2 or 3 (disc. 1991) in. barrel, alloy frame with stainless steel cylinder and barrel, combat grips, concealed hammer, fixed rear sight, approx. 16 oz. Mfg. 1990-1992.
                   $325 $240 $195
Last Mfg.'s Sug. Retail was $426.

MODEL 648 — .22 Mag., 6 in. full lug barrel, combat grips, square butt, combat trigger, semi-target hammer. New in 1990.
Mfg.'s Sug. Retail $437 $335 $240 $195

Grading	100%	98%	95%	90%	80%	70%	60%

MODEL 649 BODYGUARD — similar to Model 49 Bodyguard, except in stainless steel, 2 in. barrel. New 1986.

Mfg.'s Sug. Retail	$441		$335	$245	$195		

MODEL 650 — .22 Mag., service kit gun, 3 in. heavy barrel, J-Frame, fixed sights. Mfg. 1983-87.

			$250	$200	$185		

Last Mfg.'s Sug. Retail was $305.

MODEL 651 KIT GUN — .22 Mag., target kit gun, 4 in. barrel, J-Frame, adj. sights (same as old Model 51). Mfg. 1983-87, re-released in late 1990.

Mfg.'s Sug. Retail	$428		$330	$240	$195		

This model could be ordered with a factory fitted optional .22 LR cylinder until 1987 (last mfg. sug. retail was $295 for the cylinder alone). This variation with the extra cylinder is very desirable.

MODEL 657 — .41 Mag., 4 (disc.), 6, or 8⅜ (disc. 1992) in. barrel. New 1986.

Mfg.'s Sug. Retail	$497		$395	$310	$260		

Add $17 for 8⅜ in. barrel (disc. 1992).

⚐ **Model 657-3 Lew Horton Special** — .41 Mag., 3 in. barrel with round butt, adj. sights.

			$410	$360	$300		

MODEL 681 DISTINGUISHED SERVICE — .357 Mag., 4 in. barrel, L-Frame. Disc. 1988, reintroduced 1991-1992.

			$320	$235	$195		

1991 mfg. includes square butt.
Last Mfg.'s Sug. Retail was $412.

MODEL 686 DISTINGUISHED COMBAT — .357 Mag., similar to Model 586, except 2½ (new 1990), 4, 6, or 8⅜ in. barrel, adj. sights, L-Frame.

Mfg.'s Sug. Retail	$447		$365	$255	$225		

Add $10 for 4 or 6 in. barrel.
Add $32 for 8⅜ in. barrel.
Add $14 for white outline rear sight.
Add $40 for adj. front sight with 6 or 8⅜ (disc. 1991) in. barrel only - new 1986.

⚐ **1984 Model 686 Lew Horton Edition** — 2½ in. barrel only, limited mfg.

			$450	$275	$225		

MODEL 940 CENTENNIAL — 9mm Para. cal., fully concealed hammer, 2 or 3 (disc. 1992) in. barrel, fixed rear sight, Santoprene combat grips, 23-25 oz. New 1991.

Mfg.'s Sug. Retail	$446		$360	$250	$220		

PISTOLS: SEMI-AUTO - PRE-WWII MFG.

The following models have been arranged in a numerical model format to allow faster indexing.

100%	98%	95%	90%	80%	70%	60%	50%	40%	30%	20%	10%

.32 AUTOMATIC PISTOL — .32 ACP cal., 7 shot mag., 3½ in. barrel, blued with "S&W" monogram inlayed plain walnut grip. 957 mfg. 1924-1936. Serial range starting with S.N. 1.

100%	98%	95%	90%	80%	70%	60%	50%	40%	30%	20%	10%
$3,250	$2,800	$2,500	$2,250	$2,000	$1,750	$1,500	$1,250	$1,100	$1,000	$950	$900

	100%	98%	95%	90%	80%	70%	60%	50%	40%	30%	20%	10%

.35 AUTOMATIC PISTOL (MODEL 1913)

.35 AUTOMATIC PISTOL (MODEL 1913) — .35 S&W Auto. cal., 7 shot mag., 3½ in. barrel, blue or nickel w/"S&W" monogram inlayed in plain walnut grips. 8,350 mfg. 1913-1921. Serial range starting with No. 1.

100%	98%	95%	90%	80%	70%	60%	50%	40%	30%	20%	10%
$775	$625	$525	$450	$375	$325	$275	$235	$200	$185	$175	$165

A slight premium might exist for the first model (up to ser. no. 3,125).

PISTOLS: SEMI-AUTO - RECENT MFG.

Grading	100%	98%	95%	90%	80%	70%	60%

MODEL 39 EARLY STEEL FRAME — 9mm Para., 8 shot, 4 in. barrel, walnut stocks, blue, adj. rear windage only sight, double action M41 without the fine finish and walnut grips. Mfg. 927 pistols, 1954-1966.

100%	98%	95%	90%	80%	70%	60%
$1,100	$875	$775	$675	$600	$500	$425

First commercially mfg. 9mm double action semi-auto in the U.S.

MODEL 39 ALLOY FRAME — 9mm, double action, 8 shot mag., 4 in. barrel, checkered walnut grips, adj. sight, alloy frame. Disc. 1982.

100%	98%	95%	90%	80%	70%	60%
$360	$325	$260	$240	$220	$200	$195

Add $35 for nickel finish.

MODEL 44 — 9mm Para. cal., single action design, S&W's rarest semi-auto pistol, approx. 10 mfg. Extreme rarity precludes accurate price evaluation. However, mint specimens in this variation have recently been priced in the $12,000-$15,000 range.

MODEL 46 — .22 LR, 5, 5½, or 7 in. barrel, blue, nylon grips, adj. sights. Mfg. 4000, 1957-1966.

100%	98%	95%	90%	80%	70%	60%
$450	$335	$300	$260	$225	$200	$195

This model is the same as a Model 41 without high polish bluing.

MODEL 52-A — .38 Spl., similar action to Model 39, 5 in. barrel. Originally mfg. for U.S. Army Marksman Training Unit, 87 mfg.

100%	98%	95%	90%	80%	70%	60%
$3,000	$2,500	$2,200	$1,950	$1,600	$1,300	$1,000

MODEL 52 — .38 Spl. wadcutter only, similar action to Model 39, except incorporates a set screw locking out the double action, 5 in. barrel, 5 shot mag. Approx. 3,500 mfg. 1961-1963.

100%	98%	95%	90%	80%	70%	60%
$875	$775	$675	$575	$475	$395	$360

MODEL 52-1 — .38 Spl. wadcutter only, 5 shot mag., 5 in. barrel, single action trigger and hammer, bright blue only. Mfg. 1963-1971.

100%	98%	95%	90%	80%	70%	60%
$500	$460	$385	$350	$325	$300	$295

MODEL 52-2 — .38 Spl. Mid Range Wad Cutter only, single action semi-auto, 5 in. barrel, adj. sights, checkered walnut grips, blue only, 5 shot mag. Mfg. 1971-present.

Mfg.'s Sug. Retail	$908	98%	95%	90%	80%	70%	60%
		$675	$556	$450	$400	$350	$295	$265

MODEL 59 — similar to Model 39, except has 14 shot mag., black nylon grips. Disc. 1981.

100%	98%	95%	90%	80%	70%	60%
$385	$340	$270	$250	$225	$215	$200

Add $35 for nickel finish.

MODEL 61 ESCORT POCKET — .22 LR, 5 shot, semi-auto, blue or nickel, 2½ in. barrel, plastic grips, mfg. 1970-1974.

	100%	98%	95%	90%	80%	70%	60%
Blue finish	$250	$210	$165	$150	$140	$110	$95
Nickel finish	$275	$230	$165	$150	$140	$110	$95

MODEL 147-A — 9mm Para., 14 shot, steel frame, 4 in. barrel, black plastic grips, adj. sights for windage only, similar to Model 59, except has steel frame, 112 mfg. in 1979 only.

100%	98%	95%	90%	80%	70%	60%
$1,050	$875	$800	$725	$650	$575	$495

Grading	100%	98%	95%	90%	80%	70%	60%

MODEL 439 — 9mm, double action, 4 in. barrel, blue or nickel finish, alloy frame, 8 shot mag., checkered walnut grips, 30 oz. Disc. 1988.

	$385	$315	$255	$240	$225	$210	$200

Add $34 for nickel finish (disc. 1986).
Add $26 for adj. sights.
Last Mfg.'s Sug. Retail was $472.

MODEL 459 — 9mm, 14 shot version of Model 439, checkered nylon stocks. Disc. 1988.

	$410	$345	$290	$270	$255	$240	$210

Add $26 for adj. sights.
Add $44 for nickel finish (disc. 1986).
Last Mfg.'s Sug. Retail was $501.

⚹ **Model 459 "FBI" Variation** — 9mm Para., 14 shot, 4 in. barrel, dull finish, fixed sights, special grips made to F.B.I. or Police specs., 803 mfg.

	$650	$600	$550	$440	$385	$330	$300

MODEL 469 "MINI" — 9mm, double action, alloy frame, 12 shot finger extension mag., short frame, bobbed hammer, 3½ in. barrel, sandblast blue finish, ambidextrous safety standard (1986), molded Delrin black Grips, 26 oz. Disc. 1988.

	$370	$320	$265	$250	$235	$220	$210

Last Mfg.'s Sug. Retail was $478.

MODEL 539 — 9mm, double action, steel frame, 8 shot, 4 in. barrel, blue or nickel. Disc. 1983.

	$450	$395	$375	$350	$325	$300	$275

Add $35 for nickel finish.
Add $30 for adj. rear sight.

MODEL 559 — 9mm, double action, steel frame, 12 shot, 4 in. barrel, blue or nickel. Disc. 1983.

	$485	$435	$375	$275	$250	$225	$200

Add $35 for nickel finish.
Add $30 for adj. rear sight.

MODEL 639 STAINLESS — 9mm, similar to Model 439-only stainless steel, 8 shot mag., ambidextrous safety became standard 1986, 36 oz. Disc. 1988.

	$420	$300	$275				

Add $27 for adj. sights.
Last Mfg.'s Sug. Retail was $523.

MODEL 645 STAINLESS — .45 ACP only, 5 in. barrel, 8 shot mag., squared off trigger guard, black molded nylon grips, ambidextrous safety, fixed sights, 37½ oz. New 1986. Disc. 1988.

	$475	$365	$300				

Add $27 for adj. sight.
Last Mfg.'s Sug. Retail was $622.
Approx. 150 Model 645 "Interim" pistols were mfg. in 1988 only. Add $120 to values listed above.

MODEL 659 STAINLESS — 9mm, similar to Model 459-only stainless steel, 14 shot mag., ambidextrous safety became standard 1986, 39½ oz. Disc. 1988.

	$445	$335	$300				

Add $27 for adj. sights.
Last Mfg.'s Sug. Retail was $553.
Approx. 150 Model 659 "Interim" pistols were mfg. in 1988 only. Add $150 to values listed above.

Grading	100%	98%	95%	90%	80%	70%	60%

MODEL 669 STAINLESS — 9mm, smaller version of Model 659 with 12 shot finger extension mag., 3½ in. barrel, fixed sights, molded Delrin grips, ambidextrous safety standard, 26 oz. Mfg. 1986-1988 only.

				$425	$305	$275	

Last Mfg.'s Sug. Retail was $522.
Approx. 150 Model 669 "Interim" pistols were mfg. in 1988 only. Add $150 to values listed above.

MODEL 745 IPSC — .45 ACP, single action, 5 in. barrel, stainless steel frame with steel slide hammer and trigger, checkered walnut stocks, fixed rear sight, 38¾ oz. Mfg. 1987-90.

			$575	$440	$335		

Last Mfg.'s Sug. Retail was $699.
Add $45 for "IPSC" markings on left side of slide (N.I.B. only).

PISTOLS: SEMI-AUTO - 3RD GENERATION CURRENT MFG.

To understand S&W 3rd generation model nomenclature, the following rules apply. The first two digits (of the four digit model number) specify caliber. Numbers 39, 59, and 69 refer to 9mm Para. cal. The third digit refers to the model type. 0 means standard model, 1 is for compact, 2 is for standard model with decocking lever, 3 is for compact variation with decocking lever, 4 is for standard with double action only, 5 designates a compact model in double action only, 6 indicates a non-standard barrel length, 7 is a non standard barrel length with decocking lever, 8 refers to non-standard barrel length in double action only. The fourth digit refers to the material(s) used in the fabrication of the pistol. 3 refers to an aluminum alloy frame with stainless steel slide, 4 designates an aluminum alloy frame with carbon steel slide, 5 is for carbon steel frame and slide, 6 is a stainless steel frame and slide, and 7 refers to a stainless steel frame and carbon steel slide. Hence, a Model 4053 refers to a pistol in .40 S&W cal. configured in compact version with double action only and fabricated with an aluminum alloy frame and stainless steel slide. This model nomenclature does not apply to 2 or 3 digit model numbers (i.e., Rimfire Models and the Model 52).

MODEL 41 RIMFIRE — .22 LR, match target pistol, single action, 10 shot mag., adj. sights, walnut grips, 5½ or 7 in. heavy barrel, blue only. Mfg. 1957-present.

Mfg.'s Sug. Retail	$753	$535	$465	$375	$300	$260	$240	$220

Add $60 for 5 or 5½ in. barrel with extended sight (disc.).
Add $35 for 7⅜ in. barrel with muzzle brake (disc.).
Add 125% for .22 Short cal. with counterweight and muzzle brake.
Earlier variations (A series guns with cocking indicator, Model 41-1, etc.) will command substantial premiums over values listed above.
Note: there are several disc. barrels on the Model 41. They are the 5 in. standard weight w/extended sight, 7⅜ in. with muzzle brake, and 5½ in. heavy barrel with extended sight.

MODEL 11 — .40 S&W cal., 4 in. barrel, 11 shot mag., fixed sights, blue finish, aluminum alloy frame, manual safety. New 1993.

Mfg.'s Sug. Retail	$525		$440	$375	$335	$310	$295	$280	$265

MODEL 422 RIMFIRE FIELD — .22 LR, single action, 4½ or 6 in. barrel, aluminum frame with steel slide, 10 shot mag., fixed sights, black plastic or wood grips, matte blue finish, 22 oz. New 1987.

Mfg.'s Sug. Retail	$225		$180	$145	$115	$110	$105	$100	$95

Model 422 Target — .22 LR, single action, 4½ or 6 in. barrel, aluminum frame with steel slide, 10 shot mag., adj. rear sight, checkered walnut grips, matte blue finish, 22 oz. New 1987.

Mfg.'s Sug. Retail	$278		$220	$170	$140	$115	$110	$105	$95

Grading	100%	98%	95%	90%	80%	70%	60%

MODEL 622 RIMFIRE FIELD — .22 LR, single action, 4½ or 6 in. barrel, stainless/ alloy construction, 10 shot mag., fixed sights, black plastic grips, 21½ or 23½ oz. New 1990.

Mfg.'s Sug. Retail	$272	$215	$185	$160

Model 622 Target — .22 LR, single action, 4½ or 6 in. barrel, stainless steel construction, 10 shot mag., adj. rear sight, checkered walnut grips, 21½ or 23½ oz. New 1990.

Mfg.'s Sug. Retail	$324	$265	$220	$175

MODEL 915 — 9mm Para. cal., 4 in. barrel, fixed sights, 15 shot mag., manual safety, aluminum alloy frame, blue finish. New 1993.

Mfg.'s Sug. Retail	$467	$350	$255	$225	$205	$190	$175	$165

MODEL 1006 STAINLESS — 10mm, double action semi-auto, stainless steel construction, 5 in. barrel, exposed hammer, 9 shot mag., fixed or adj. sights, ambidextrous safety. New 1990.

Mfg.'s Sug. Retail	$769	$635	$530	$400

Add $27 for adj. rear sight.

MODEL 1026 STAINLESS — 10mm, 5 in. barrel, traditional double action, features frame mounted decocking lever, 9 shot mag., straight backstrap. Mfg. 1990-91 only.

	$630	$525	$400

Last Mfg.'s Sug. Retail was $755.

MODEL 1046 STAINLESS — 10mm, 5 in. barrel, fixed sights, double action only, 9 shot mag., straight backstrap. Mfg. 1991 only.

	$620	$515	$400

Last Mfg.'s Sug. Retail was $747.

MODEL 1066 STAINLESS — 10mm, 4¼ in. barrel, 9 shot mag., straight backstrap, ambidextrous safety, traditional double action, fixed sights. Mfg. 1990-1992.

	$610	$515	$395

Add $40 for Tritium night sights - disc. 1991 (Model 1066-NS).
Only 1,000 Model 1066-NSs were manufactured.
Last Mfg.'s Sug. Retail was $730.

MODEL 1076 STAINLESS — similar to Model 1026 Stainless, except has 4¼ in. barrel. New in 1990.

Mfg.'s Sug. Retail	$778	$645	$530	$400

MODEL 1086 STAINLESS — similar to Model 1066 Stainless, except is double action only.

Mfg.'s Sug. Retail	$730	$610	$515	$395

MODEL 2206 STAINLESS RIMFIRE — .22 LR cal., similar to Model 622 Field, except is all stainless steel with black plastic grips, 35 or 39 oz. New 1990.

Mfg.'s Sug. Retail	$314	$240	$200	$165

Add $56 for adj. sights.

MODEL 2213 STAINLESS RIMFIRE "SPORTSMAN" — .22 LR cal., single action, 3 in. barrel, alloy frame with stainless steel slide, 8 shot mag., 2 dot fixed rear sight, black plastic molded grips, 18 oz., includes holster/carry case. New 1992.

Mfg.'s Sug. Retail	$302	$230	$195	$160

MODEL 2214 RIMFIRE "SPORTSMAN" — .22 LR cal., similar to Model 2213, except has alloy frame with blue carbon steel slide with matte black finish, and no case. New in 1991.

Mfg.'s Sug. Retail	$258	$205	$175	$160	$150	$140	$130	$120

Grading	100%	98%	95%	90%	80%	70%	60%

MODEL 3904 — 9mm Para., double action semi-auto, aluminum alloy frame, 4 in. barrel with fixed bushing, 8 shot mag., Delrin one piece wraparound grips, exposed hammer, ambidextrous safety, beveled magazine well, extended squared off trigger guard, adj. or fixed rear sight, 3 dot sighting system, 28 oz. Mfg. 1989-91.

	$450	$385	$350	$325	$300	$280	$265

Add $25 for adj. rear sight.
Last Mfg.'s Sug. Retail was $541.

MODEL 3906 STAINLESS — stainless steel variation of the Model 3904, 35½ oz. Mfg. 1989-91.

	$510	$435	$375

Add $28 for adj. rear sight.
Last Mfg.'s Sug. Retail was $604.

MODEL 3913 COMPACT STAINLESS — stainless steel variation of the Model 3914, 25 oz. New 1990.

Mfg.'s Sug. Retail	$597	$495	$420	$365

Model 3913NL — similar to Model 3913 Ladysmith, except does not have Ladysmith on the slide.

Mfg.'s Sug. Retail	$597	$495	$420	$365

Model 3913 LadySmith — similar to Model 3913 Stainless, except has white Delrin grips and mag. does not have finger extension, 25 oz. New in 1990.

Mfg.'s Sug. Retail	$615	$515	$430	$365

MODEL 3914 COMPACT — 9mm Para., double action semi-auto, aluminum alloy frame, 3½ in. barrel, hammerless, 8 shot finger extension mag., fixed sights only, ambidextrous safety, blue finish, straight backstrap grip, 25 oz. New 1990.

Mfg.'s Sug. Retail	$539	$450	$380	$340	$320	$295	$280	$265

This model is also available with a single side manual safety at no extra charge - disc. 1991 (Model 3914NL).

Model 3914 LadySmith — similar to Model 3914, except has Delrin grips, 25 oz. Mfg. 1990-91 only.

	$485	$415	$365

Last Mfg.'s Sug. Retail was $568.

MODEL 3953 COMPACT STAINLESS — 9mm Para., double action only, aluminum alloy frame with stainless steel slide, compact model with 3½ in. barrel, 8 shot mag. New in 1990.

Mfg.'s Sug. Retail	$597	$495	$420	$365

MODEL 3954 — similar to Model 3953, except has blue steel slide. Mfg. 1990-1992.

	$445	$380	$340	$320	$295	$280	$265

Last Mfg.'s Sug. Retail was $528.

MODEL 4003 STAINLESS — .40 S&W cal., traditional double action, 4 in. barrel, 11 shot mag., white dot fixed sights, ambidextrous safety, aluminum alloy frame with stainless steel slide, one piece Xenoy wraparound grips, straight gripstrap, 28 oz. New 1991.

Mfg.'s Sug. Retail	$698	$585	$495	$395

MODEL 4004 — .40 S&W cal., similar to Model 4003, except has aluminum alloy frame with blue carbon steel slide. Mfg. 1991-1992.

	$540	$460	$375	$325	$295	$280	$265

Last Mfg.'s Sug. Retail was $643.

Smith&Wesson cont.

Grading	100%	98%	95%	90%	80%	70%	60%

MODEL 4006 STAINLESS — .40 S&W cal., 4 in. barrel, 11 shot mag., satin stainless finish, exposed hammer, Delrin one piece wraparound grips, 3 dot sights, 38½ oz. New in 1990.

Mfg.'s Sug. Retail	$715	$605	$515	$400			

Add $28 for adj. rear sight.
Add $105 for fixed Tritium night sights (new 1992).
The bobbed hammer option on this model was disc. in 1991.

MODEL 4013 COMPACT STAINLESS — .40 S&W cal., semi-auto, standard double action, 3½ in. barrel, 8 shot mag., fixed sights, ambidextrous safety, alloy frame. New 1991.

Mfg.'s Sug. Retail	$693	$575	$480	$380	$330	$295	$280	$265

MODEL 4014 COMPACT — similar to Model 4013, except is steel with blue finish. New 1991.

Mfg.'s Sug. Retail	$635	$510	$425	$375	$330	$300	$275	$250

MODEL 4026 STAINLESS — .40 S&W cal., traditional double action with frame mounted decocking lever, 11 shot mag., fixed sights, curved backstrap, 36 oz. New 1991.

Mfg.'s Sug. Retail	$731	$620	$520	$400			

MODEL 4043 STAINLESS — .40 S&W cal., double action only, aluminum alloy frame with stainless steel slide, 11 shot mag., one piece Xenoy wraparound grips, straight backstrap, white dot fixed sights, 30 oz. New 1991.

Mfg.'s Sug. Retail	$698	$580	$480	$380			

MODEL 4044 — .40 S&W cal., similar to Model 4043, except has carbon steel slide. Mfg. 1991-1992.

		$540	$460	$375	$325	$295	$280	$265

Last Mfg.'s Sug. Retail was $643.

MODEL 4046 STAINLESS — similar to Model 4006 Stainless, except is double action only. New in 1991.

Mfg.'s Sug. Retail	$715	$605	$515	$400			

Add $105 for Tritium night sights (new 1992).

MODEL 4053 COMPACT STAINLESS — double action only variation of the Model 4013. New 1991.

Mfg.'s Sug. Retail	$693	$580	$480	$380			

MODEL 4054 — double action only variation of the Model 4014. Mfg. 1991-1992.

		$510	$425	$375			

Last Mfg.'s Sug. Retail was $629.

MODEL 4505 — .45 ACP, carbon steel variation of the Model 4506. Mfg. 1990-91 only. More research is underway regarding this model.

MODEL 4506 STAINLESS — .45 ACP, 5 in. barrel, 8 shot mag., combat trigger guard, exposed hammer, fixed or adj. rear sight, straight backstrap (curved is optional), Delrin one-piece grips, 38½ oz. New in 1990.

Mfg.'s Sug. Retail	$742	$625	$520	$400			

Add $31 for adj. rear sight.
Approx. 100 Model 4506s left the factory mismarked Model 645 on the frame. In N.I.B. condition they are worth $700.

MODEL 4516 COMPACT STAINLESS — .45 ACP, hammerless compact variation of the Model 4506, 3¾ in. barrel, 7 shot mag., fixed rear sight only, 34½ oz. Mfg. 1990-1992.

		$620	$520	$400			

Last Mfg.'s Sug. Retail was $735.

Grading	100%	98%	95%	90%	80%	70%	60%

MODEL 4526 STAINLESS — similar to Model 4506 Stainless, except has frame mounted decocking lever. Mfg. 1990-91 only.

		$635	$530	$400			

Last Mfg.'s Sug. Retail was $762.

MODEL 4536 STAINLESS — similar to Model 4516 Compact, except has frame mounted decocking lever only. Mfg. 1990-91 only.

		$635	$530	$400			

Last Mfg.'s Sug. Retail was $762.

MODEL 4546 STAINLESS — similar to Model 4506, except is double action only. Mfg. 1990-91 only.

		$620	$520	$400			

Last Mfg.'s Sug. Retail was $735.

MODEL 4556 STAINLESS — .45 ACP, features double action only, $3\frac{3}{4}$ in. barrel, 7 shot mag., fixed sights. Mfg. 1991 only.

		$620	$520	$400			

Last Mfg.'s Sug. Retail was $735.

MODEL 4566 STAINLESS — .45 ACP, traditional double action with ambidextrous safety, $4\frac{1}{4}$ in. barrel, 8 shot mag. New in 1990.

Mfg.'s Sug. Retail	$742	$620	$520	$400			

MODEL 4567-NS STAINLESS — similar to Model 4566 Stainless, except has Tritium night sights, stainless steel frame and carbon steel slide. 2,500 mfg. in 1991 only.

		$620	$520	$400			

Last Mfg.'s Sug. Retail was $735.

MODEL 4576 STAINLESS — .45 ACP, features $4\frac{1}{4}$ in. barrel, frame mounted decocking lever, fixed sights. Mfg. 1990-1992.

		$635	$535	$410			

Last Mfg.'s Sug. Retail was $762.

MODEL 4586 STAINLESS — .45 ACP, $4\frac{1}{4}$ in. barrel, double action only, 8 shot mag. New in 1990.

Mfg.'s Sug. Retail	$742	$620	$520	$400			

MODEL 5903 — 9mm Para., double action semi-auto, 4 in. barrel, exposed hammer, 15 shot mag., adj. or fixed rear sight, ambidextrous safety. New 1990.

Mfg.'s Sug. Retail	$662	$555	$465	$395	$365	$325	$300	$285

Add $32 for adj. rear sight.

MODEL 5904 — similar to Model 5903, except has steel slide and blue finish, $26\frac{1}{2}$ oz. New 1989.

Mfg.'s Sug. Retail	$616	$505	$435	$360	$330	$300	$280	$265

Add $29 for adj. rear sight.

MODEL 5905 — 9mm Para., similar to Model 5904, except has carbon steel frame and slide. Mfg. 1990-91 only.
More research is underway regarding this model.

MODEL 5906 STAINLESS — stainless steel variation of the Model 5904, $37\frac{1}{2}$ oz. New 1989.

Mfg.'s Sug. Retail	$679	$570	$470	$395			

Add $32 for adj. rear sight.
Add $105 for Tritium night sights.

Grading	100%	98%	95%	90%	80%	70%	60%

MODEL 5924 — 9mm Para., 4 in. barrel, features frame mounted decocking lever, 15 shot mag., 37½ oz. Mfg. 1990-91 only.

	$515	$440	$365	$330	$300	$280	$265

Last Mfg.'s Sug. Retail was $635.

MODEL 5926 STAINLESS — stainless variation of the Model 5924. Disc. 1992.

	$580	$480	$395

Last Mfg.'s Sug. Retail was $697.

MODEL 5943 STAINLESS — 9mm Para., double action only, 4 in. barrel, aluminum alloy frame with stainless steel slide, straight backstrap, 15 shot mag. Mfg. 1990-91 only.

	$550	$465	$390

Last Mfg.'s Sug. Retail was $655.

Model 5943-SSV Stainless — similar to Model 5943 Stainless, except has 3½ in. barrel, Tritium night sights. Mfg. 1990-91 only.

	$580	$485	$395

Last Mfg.'s Sug. Retail was $690.

MODEL 5944 — similar to Model 5943, except has blue finish slide. Mfg. 1990-91 only.

	$510	$435	$360	$330	$300	$280	$265

Last Mfg.'s Sug. Retail was $610.

MODEL 5946 STAINLESS — double action only, one piece Xenoy wraparound grips, all stainless steel variation of the Model 5943, 39½ oz. New in 1990.

Mfg.'s Sug. Retail	$679		$570	$470	$390

MODEL 6904 COMPACT — compact variation of the Model 5904, 3½ in. barrel, 12 shot finger extension mag., fixed rear sight, 26½ oz. New 1989.

Mfg.'s Sug. Retail	$590		$485	$400	$350	$325	$300	$280	$265

MODEL 6906 COMPACT STAINLESS — stainless steel variation of the Model 6904, 26½ oz. New 1989.

Mfg.'s Sug. Retail	$650		$540	$450	$375

Add $106 for Tritium night sights (new 1992).

MODEL 6926 STAINLESS — 9mm Para., 3½ in. barrel, standard double action, features frame mounted decocking lever, aluminum alloy frame with stainless slide, 12 shot mag. Mfg. 1990-91 only.

	$550	$455	$375

Last Mfg.'s Sug. Retail was $663.

MODEL 6944 — 9mm Para., double action only, 3½ in. barrel, 12 shot mag., aluminum alloy frame with blue steel slide. Mfg. 1990-91 only.

	$480	$400	$350	$325	$300	$280	$265

Last Mfg.'s Sug. Retail was $578.

MODEL 6946 STAINLESS — similar to Model 6944, except has stainless steel slide, semi-bobbed hammer, 26½ oz. New in 1990.

Mfg.'s Sug. Retail	$650		$535	$445	$375

RIFLES

S&W in 1984 disc. importation of all Howa manufactured rifles. Mossberg continued importation utilizing both leftover S&W parts in addition to fabricating their own.

100%	98%	95%	90%	80%	70%	60%	50%	40%	30%	20%	10%

MODEL 320 REVOLVING RIFLE — .320 S&W, 6 shot cylinder, 16, 18, or 20 in. round barrel, hard rubber grips, detachable shoulder stock, blue or nickel (rare, add a premium) finish. 977 mfg. 1879-1887.

16 or 20 in. barrel Model — 239 mfg. with 16 in., and 224 with 20 in. barrel.

100%	98%	95%	90%	80%	70%	60%	50%	40%	30%	20%	10%
$6,550	$5,550	$4,850	$4,350	$3,850	$3,400	$3,000	$2,750	$2,550	$2,350	$2,150	$1,950

18 in. barrel Model — 514 mfg.

100%	98%	95%	90%	80%	70%	60%	50%	40%	30%	20%	10%
$6,200	$5,200	$4,500	$4,100	$3,600	$3,150	$2,750	$2,500	$2,300	$2,100	$1,925	$1,775

Grading	100%	98%	95%	90%	80%	70%	60%

MODEL A BOLT ACTION RIFLE — .22-250, .243, .270, .308, .30-06, 7mm Mag., or .300 Win. Mag. cal., 23¾ in. barrel, folding leaf sight, checkered Monte Carlo stock with rosewood forend tip and pistol grip cap. Mfg. 1969-1972.

	100%	98%	95%	90%	80%	70%	60%
	$385	$330	$305	$275	$220	$195	$165

MODEL B — similar to A, in .243, .270, or .30-06 cal., 20¾ in. barrel, Schnabel forend.

	100%	98%	95%	90%	80%	70%	60%
	$425	$305	$275	$250	$195	$165	$140

MODEL C — similar to B, with cheek piece.

	100%	98%	95%	90%	80%	70%	60%
	$425	$305	$275	$250	$195	$165	$140

MODEL D — similar to C, with full length stock.

	100%	98%	95%	90%	80%	70%	60%
	$550	$385	$360	$305	$250	$220	$195

MODEL E — similar to D, with no cheek piece.

	100%	98%	95%	90%	80%	70%	60%
	$550	$385	$360	$305	$250	$220	$195

Note: These rifles were made for S&W by Husqvarna in Sweden.

MODEL 1500 MOUNTAINEER — .222 Rem., .22-250, 223 Rem, .243 Win, .25-06 Rem, .270 Win, .30-06, or .308 Win. cal., bolt action, 22 in. barrel 5-6 shot mag., no sights, walnut stock and forend, approx. 7 lbs. 10 oz. New 1983.

	100%	98%	95%	90%	80%	70%	60%
	$300	$250	$245	$210	$195	$175	$160

Add $27 for sights.

Model 1500 Mountaineer Magnum — 7mm Rem. Mag. or .300 Win. Mag. cal.

	100%	98%	95%	90%	80%	70%	60%
	$325	$275	$260	$225	$200	$180	$160

MODEL 1500 DELUXE — same cals. as standard 1500, Monte Carlo stock, skip-line checkering, select walnut, no sights. New 1983.

	100%	98%	95%	90%	80%	70%	60%
	$350	$300	$260	$220	$200	$180	$160

Add $20 for 7mm Mag. and .300 Win. Mag.

MODEL 1500 DELUXE VARMINT — .222 Rem, .22-250, or .223 Rem. cal., heavy 24 in. barrel, skip-line checkering, no sights. New 1983.

	100%	98%	95%	90%	80%	70%	60%
	$350	$275	$315	$275	$215	$195	$170

Add $15 for parkerized finish.

MODEL 1700 LS "CLASSIC HUNTER" — .243 Win, 270 Win, or .30-06 cal., 22 in. barrel, removable 5 shot mag., solid recoil pad, no sights, Schnabel forend, finely checkered. New 1983.

	100%	98%	95%	90%	80%	70%	60%
	$400	$350	$315	$265	$240	$220	$195

SHOTGUNS

S&W in 1984 disc. importation of all Howa manufactured shotguns. Mossberg continued importation utilizing both leftover S&W parts in addition to fabricating their own.

Grading	100%	98%	95%	90%	80%	70%	60%

MODEL 916 SLIDE ACTION SHOTGUN — 12, 16, or 20 ga., 20, 26, 28, or 30 in. barrels, various chokes, plain pistol grip stock, solid frame. Mfg. 1972-disc.

	$175	$150	$140	$130	$120	$110	$100

⚔ **Vent. rib and pad**

	$200	$175	$155	$145	$135	$130	$120

MODEL 916T SLIDE ACTION — similar to 916, except barrels can be interchanged.

	$195	$170	$155	$145	$135	$130	$125

⚔ **Vent. rib and pad**

	$225	$200	$180	$170	$155	$145	$135

MODEL 96 SLIDE ACTION — various cals., ga.'s, disc.

	$125	$110	$100	$90	$75	$70	$65

MODEL 1000 P SLIDE ACTION — 12 ga, various barrel lengths, chokes, VR.

	$350	$305	$270	$230	$210	$190	$170

This model is the same as the Model 3000.

MODEL 3000 SLIDE ACTION — 12 or 20 ga., 3 in. chambers, 22-30 in. barrels, walnut stock and forend, 6¼-7½ lbs.

	$350	$305	$270	$230	$210	$190	$170

Add $30 for multi-choke insertion tubes.
Subtract $40 for slug gun (rifle sights on 22 in. barrel).
This model was also available in a "Waterfowler" variation - values are approx. the same as listed above.

MODEL 3000 POLICE — 12 ga. only, blue or parkerized finish, many combinations of finishes, stock types, and other combat accessories were available for this model, 18 or 20 in. barrel.

	$332	$255	$215	$185	$170	$155	$140

Add $70 for folding stock.

MODEL 1000 AUTOLOADER — 12 or 20 ga., 22-30 in. barrels, various chokes, gas operated, vent rib, engraved alloy receiver, checkered pistol grip stock. Mfg. 1972-1984.

	$350	$325	$295	$260	$240	$220	$200

Add $30 for multi-choke tubes.

⚔ **12 and 20 gauge** — Magnum 28 or 30 in. barrel, multi chokes, steel receiver, "M" suffix.

	$375	$340	$310	$275	$255	$235	$215

⚔ **Model 1000 Super 12** — handles all loads interchangeably, top-of-the-line model during its time.

	$500	$450	$400	$360	$330	$300	$280

Add $50 for multi-choke.

MODEL 1000 TARGET — 12 or 20 ga., skeet, super skeet and trap models available. Super skeet has 15 barrel muzzle vents to reduce recoil. Trap model has multi-choke tubes, Monte Carlo select walnut stock and forend. Both alloy and steel receivers available in Skeet model, Trap is steel only.

	100%	98%	95%	90%	80%	70%	60%
Skeet (Model 1000S)	$400	$390	$335	$260	$235	$215	$190
Super skeet-steel frame	$450	$535	$460	$390	$355	$320	$285
Trap (Model 1000T)	$450	$460	$370	$310	$285	$255	$225

Note: Shotguns made for S&W by Howa Machinery, Ltd., Japan.

SNAKE CHARMER

Manufactured by Sporting Arms Manufacturing, Inc. located in Littlefield, TX. Distributor sales only.

Grading	100%	98%	95%	90%	80%	70%	60%

SNAKE CHARMER II — .410 ga. only, stainless steel, break open single shot, molded plastic stock and forend, shell holder in stock, 3½ lbs. Also available as Night Charmer (disc. 1988) and Sea Charmer (disc. 1988).

Mfg.'s Sug. Retail	$149		$125	$100	$85

Add $10 for Night Charmer.
Add $18 for Sea Charmer.
Subtract $10 for black carbon steel barrel (New Generation Model).

SOCIETA SIDERURGICA GLISENTI

Manufacturer located in Brescia, Italy.

GLISENTI MODEL 1910 — 9mm Glisenti, 7 shot, 4 in. barrel, fixed sights, blue, checkered wood, rubber or plastic grips, Italian service pistol. Mfg. 1910-WWII.
Warning: While some Glisentis may chamber and fire the 9mm Luger cartridge, it is extremely dangerous to do so.

$210	$200	$180	$170	$140	$125	$100

SODIA, FRANZ

Manufacturer located in Ferlach, Austria.

Sodia arms are superb and are often excellently engraved and inlaid. Professional appraisal should be sought before purchase, since prices are high. Sodia is famous for double-barrel shotguns as well as two- and three-barrel combinations of rifles and shotguns.

BOCHDRILLING — various cals., top quality workmanship.

$7,000	$6,500	$6,000	$5,000	$4,000	$3,000	$2,500

DOPPLEBUSCHE — various cals., top quality workmanship.

$5,000	$4,500	$4,000	$3,000	$2,000	$1,800	$1,600

RIFLE, OVER/UNDER — various cals., top quality workmanship.

$4,500	$4,250	$4,000	$3,500	$3,000	$2,000	$1,800

TRAP SHOTGUN — 12 ga. only, boxlock action, various degrees of engraving and ornamentation.

$2,500	$1,850	$1,475	$1,100	$900	$750	$600

SOKOLOVSKY CORPORATION SPORT ARMS (SCSA)

Previous manufacturer until 1990 located in Sunnyvale, CA.

SOKOLOVSKY .45 AUTOMASTER — .45 ACP only, stainless steel, single action, 6 in. barrel, 6 shot mag., adj. Millet sights, unique action, is free of external devices, 55 oz. Mfg. 1984-90.

$2,700	$2,200	$1,850

Total production on this model is 50 pistols.
Last Mfg.'s Sug. Retail was $3,300.

SPHINX

Manufactured by Sphinx Engineering S.A. located in Switzerland. Currently imported exclusively by Sile Distributors located in New York, NY.

Grading	100%	98%	95%	90%	80%	70%	60%

PISTOLS

MODEL AT-380 — .380 ACP cal., semi-auto double action only, 3.27 in. barrel, stainless steel fabrication, two-tone finish, 10 shot mag. with finger extension, checkered walnut grips.

Mfg.'s Sug. Retail	$572	$515	$450	$415	$375	$350	$325	$295

Add $58 for N/Pall finish.

MODEL AT-2000S STANDARD — 9mm Para. or .40 S&W (new 1993) cal., semi-auto in standard double action or double action only, 4.53 in. barrel, stainless steel fabrication, 15 (9mm Para.) or 11 (.40 S&W) shot mag., checkered walnut grips, fixed sights, 35 oz. This model was originally derived from the Action Arms Model AT-88.

Mfg.'s Sug. Retail	$903	$795	$675	$575	$475	$440	$410	$375

Add $9 for .40 S&W cal.
Add $87 for N/Pall finish.

⚔ **Model AT-2000PS Police Special** — similar to AT-2000S, except has compact slide and 3.66 in. barrel.

Mfg.'s Sug. Retail	$859	$750	$575	$475	$440	$410	$380	$350

Add $9 for .40 S&W cal.
Add $87 for N/Pall finish.

⚔ **Model AT-2000P Compact** — similar to Model AT-2000 Standard, except has 3.66 in. barrel and 13 shot mag., 31 oz.

Mfg.'s Sug. Retail	$859	$750	$575	$475	$440	$410	$380	$350

Add $9 for .40 S&W cal.
Add $87 for N/Pall finish.

⚔ **Model AT-2000H Sub-Compact** — similar to Model AT-2000 Compact, except has 3.34 in. barrel and 10 shot mag., 26 oz.

Mfg.'s Sug. Retail	$859	$750	$575	$475	$440	$410	$380	$350

Add $9 for .40 S&W cal.
Add $87 for N/Pall finish.

Model AT-2000CS Competitor — 9mm Para., 9x21mm, or .40 S&W cal., single or double action, competition model featuring many shooting improvements including 5.3 in. compensated barrel, 11 (.40 S&W) or 15 shot mag., Bo-Mar adj. sights, two-tone finish. Importation began 1993.

Mfg.'s Sug. Retail	$1,902	$1,795	$1,500	$1,250	$1,050	$895	$775	$650

Add $287 for Model AT-2000C (includes Sphinx scope mount).

Model AT-2000GMS Grand Master — similar to Model AT-2000 Competitor, except is SA only and includes more advance competitive shooting features, Bo-Mar sights, top-of-the-line competition model. Importation began 1993.

Mfg.'s Sug. Retail	$2,894	$2,475	$1,995	$1,795	$1,500	$1,250	$1,050	$895

Add $78 for Model AT-2000GM (includes Sphinx scope mount).

SPITFIRE

See listing under JSL (Hereford) in this text.

SPRINGFIELD ARMORY

America's first federal armory located in Springfield, MA. Production began in 1795 and an Act of Congress made it an official federal arsenal in 1872. Not associated with the private firm of the same name located in Geneseo, IL.

In recent years, collectors have realized that military specimens in 98%-100% original condition are very rare and desirable in most cases. Since the supply of these guns is so limited, values listed below for these condition factors may not be indicative of current market conditions. As always, many collectors agree that it is hard to overpay for a mint, original, military specimen.

Grading	100%	98%	95%	90%	80%	70%	60%

MODEL 1870 ROLLING-BLOCK RIFLE, U.S.N. — .50 cal. centerfire, 32⅝ in. barrel, not serial numbered, 22,013 mfg.

| | $1,600 | $1,300 | $1,050 | $900 | $775 | $650 | $600 |

MODEL 1871 ROLLING-BLOCK RIFLE, U.S.A. — .50 cal. centerfire, 36 in. barrel, not serial numbered, 10,001 mfg.

| | $1,600 | $1,300 | $1,050 | $900 | $775 | $650 | $600 |

MODEL 1873 RIFLE "TRAPDOOR" — .45-70, 32⅝ in. barrel, 2 bands. Approx. 73,000 mfg. between 1873-1877. Deduct 20% if stock cartouche faint or absent.

| | $1,500 | $1,200 | $900 | $775 | $650 | $495 | $395 |

MODEL 1884 RIFLE "TRAPDOOR" — .45-70, 32⅝ in. barrel, 2 bands. Approx. 232,000 mfg. between 1885-1890. Deduct 20% if stock cartouche faint or absent.

| | $1,250 | $950 | $725 | $625 | $525 | $425 | $360 |

MODEL 1873 CARBINE — 22 in. barrel, half stock, single barrel band/stacking swivel, 20,000 made, but semi-scarce. Pre-Custer serial numbers made below 43,700, add up to 50%. (Pre-1876 mfg.).

| | $2,350 | $1,950 | $1,750 | $1,595 | $1,400 | $1,150 | $900 |

MODEL 1873 CADET RIFLE — 29½ in. barrel, stacking swivel, no sling swivels. Deduct $100 for variation with sling-swivels.

| | $1,600 | $1,300 | $1,050 | $900 | $775 | $650 | $600 |

Deduct 25-35% if restocked with butt plate and hole drilled for cleaning tools.

MODEL 1875 OFFICER'S RIFLE FIRST TYPE — mfg. 477 between 1875 and 1886, 26 in. barrel, single barrel band. Not serial numbered, some dated, non-issue.

| | $7,750 | $6,800 | $5,750 | $5,500 | $5,000 | $4,500 | $4,000 |

Deduct 15-20% for types 2 and 3.
Approx. 25 rifles were mfg. prior to the standardization of this model.

MODEL 1877 RIFLE — mfg. 3943.

| | $1,450 | $1,200 | $900 | $800 | $700 | $600 | $550 |

MODEL 1877 CARBINE — 22 in. barrel, "C" rear sight to 1,200 yards. Mfg. 2946.

| | $2,750 | $2,400 | $2,000 | $1,900 | $1,800 | $1,600 | $1,300 |

MODEL 1877 CADET RIFLE — 29½ in. barrel. Mfg. 1,050.

| | $1,475 | $1,200 | $1,000 | $950 | $900 | $800 | $700 |

MODEL 1879 RIFLE — mfg. approx. 140,000.

| | $795 | $650 | $500 | $450 | $400 | $350 | $300 |

MODEL 1879 CARBINE — no stacking swivel. Approx. 15,000 mfg.

| | $1,100 | $900 | $800 | $700 | $650 | $550 | $500 |

MODEL 1879 CADET RIFLE — stacking swivel but no sling swivels. Mfg. 5,000.

| | $850 | $775 | $650 | $550 | $475 | $425 | $375 |

MODEL 1880 — combination triangular, sliding type, bayonet-ramrod. Mfg. 1,001.

| | $1,400 | $1,200 | $1,000 | $895 | $800 | $700 | $600 |

MODEL 1881 FORAGER — 20 ga., 1,376 mfg. 1881-1885. Be cautious when purchasing.

| | $2,250 | $1,950 | $1,700 | $1,500 | $1,250 | $1,000 | $875 |

Grading	100%	98%	95%	90%	80%	70%	60%

U.S. MODEL 1892-1895-1896-1898 KRAG JORGENSEN — .30-40 Krag, bolt action. Mfg. until 1904.

	100%	98%	95%	90%	80%	70%	60%
	$650	$550	$450	$395	$320	$280	$240

1898 CARBINE — similar to 1898 Krag Jorgensen, with 22 in. barrel.

	$750	$625	$595	$525	$460	$420	$385

Add 20% for Model 1899 Carbine.

1898 KRAG NRA CARBINE — Carbine stock and hardware, shortened rifle (22 in.) barreled action, identifiable by full band front sight.

	$725	$600	$525	$450	$360	$330	$250

U.S. MODEL 1903 SPRINGFIELD — .30-06, bolt action, 24 in. barrel. Mfg. 1903-1930.

☆ **Pre-WWI Mfg.** — values below represent original rifles - deduct 80% if reworked.

	$1,750	$1,500	$1,250	$995	$750	$675	$600

☆ **Serialized 800,000 - 1,275,767** — double heat treated receiver.

	$395	$350	$275	$220	$195	$165	$140

☆ **Serialized 1,275,768+** — nickel steel receiver.

	$450	$395	$330	$275	$250	$220	$180

U.S. MODEL 1903 MARK I — similar to 1903, except altered for the Pedersen device, a slot is milled into the left side of receiver to act as an ejection port for use of the semi-auto bolt insert, value without device.

	$450	$395	$330	$275	$250	$220	$180

1903-A1 — similar to 1903, except type C pistol grip stock. Mfg. 1930-1939. In 1941 Remington mfg. approx. 350,000.

	$450	$395	$350	$300	$260	$230	$195

☆ **Remington produced**

	$395	$350	$295	$250	$210	$180	$155

1903-A1 NATIONAL MATCH

	$1,200	$1,050	$895	$750	$625	$500	$395

1903-A3 — similar to 1903, with production modifications, aperture rear sight, no finger groove in forestock, lower quality finish, stamped floorplate and barrel band. Mfg. WWII by Remington and Smith Corona.

	$450	$420	$390	$360	$330	$300	$275

1903-A3 NATIONAL MATCH — 200 mfg., known as the "unmatched" match rifle.

	$1,500	$1,300	$1,000	$850	$750	$675	$600

1903-A4 SNIPER — .30-06 with M73B1 or M84 scope in Redfield mount, no front sight.

	$1,250	$1,000	$775	$675	$575	$500	$450

1903 NRA SPORTING RIFLE — over 4,000 mfg.

	$695	$625	$550	$495	$450	$375	$295

1903 NRA NATIONAL MATCH — similar to 1903, with hand selected and custom fit parts, produced for target shooting. "NRA" and flaming bomb proofed on trigger guard. 1915 date.

	$1,250	$1,000	$775	$675	$575	$500	$450

Grading	100%	98%	95%	90%	80%	70%	60%

1903 SPORTER — similar to National Match, with sporter stock and Lyman sight.

	100%	98%	95%	90%	80%	70%	60%
	$1,200	$1,000	$825	$750	$625	$525	$470

1903 MATCH STYLE T — similar to Sporter, with heavy barrel, globe sight, target bases, 26, 28, or 30 in. barrel.

	$1,500	$1,275	$1,000	$825	$725	$635	$580

1903 FREE RIFLE TYPE A — similar to Type T, with 28 in. barrel, and Swiss hook butt.

	$1,650	$1,475	$1,300	$1,150	$995	$895	$775

1903 FREE RIFLE TYPE B — similar to Type A, with double set triggers, cheek piece stock, modified firing pin.

	$2,250	$1,900	$1,600	$1,300	$1,075	$950	$825

MODEL 1922-M1 — .22 Target Rifle or .22 LR, 5 shot mag., 24 in. barrel, modified 1903, Lyman receiver sight, sporter stock, issued 1927.

	$950	$875	$795	$695	$595	$540	$495

M2 .22 TARGET RIFLE — similar to 1922 M1, except improved lock time, adj. head space, bolt design.

	$1,000	$900	$800	$700	$600	$550	$500

SPRINGFIELD, INC.

Private manufacturer/importer located in Geneseo, IL. Until 1992, this company was named Springfield Armory, Geneseo, IL.

The Springfield Armory manufactures commercial reproductions of older military handguns and rifles. Prices shown below are for current manufactured models.

COMBINATION GUNS

M6 SCOUT — .22 LR, .22 Mag. (disc.), or .22 Hornet (disc.)/.410 O/U Survival Gun, 14 (legal transfer needed) or 18 ½ in. barrels, 4½ lbs.

Mfg.'s Sug. Retail	$199	$175	$150	$135	$120	$110	$100	$95

Add $20 for .22 Hornet cal.

PISTOLS

M6 PISTOL — .22 cal. over .45 LC cal. (also shoots .410 ga. shotshells), 16 in. barrels. Mfg. Aug. 1991 - 1992.

	$200	$185	$165	$150	$135	$120	$110

Last Mfg.'s Sug. Retail was $226.

OMEGA PISTOL — .38 Super, 10mm Norma, or .45 ACP cal., single action, ported slide, 5 or 6 in. interchangeable ported or unported barrel with Polygon rifling, special lock-up system eliminates normal barrel link and bushing, Pachmayr grips, dual extractors, adj. rear sight. Mfg. 1987-90.

	$775	$650	$575	$495	$425	$360	$295

Add $663 for interchangeable conversion units.
Each conversion unit includes an entire slide assembly, one mag., 5 or 6 in barrel, recoil spring guide mechanism assembly, and factory fitting.
Add $336 for interchangeable 5 or 6 in. barrel (including factory installation).
Last Mfg.'s Sug. Retail was $849.

Grading	100%	98%	95%	90%	80%	70%	60%

OMEGA MATCH — same cals. as Omega, except has low profile combat sights, 8 shot mag., and beveled mag. well. Mfg. 1991-1992.

	$925	$775	$660	$535	$460	$420	$385

Last Mfg.'s Sug. Retail was $1,103.

PISTOLS: P9 SERIES

MODEL P9 — 9mm Para., 9 x 21mm (new 1991) .40 S&W (new 1991), or .45 ACP cal., patterned after the Czech CZ-75, selective double action design, blue (standard beginning 1993), parkerized (standard until 1992), or duotone finish, various barrel lengths, checkered walnut grips. Mfg. in U.S. starting 1990.

P9 Standard — 4.72 in. barrel, 15 shot (9mm Para.), 11 shot (.40 S&W), or 10 shot (.45 ACP) mag., parkerized finish standard until 1992 - blued finish beginning 1993, 32.16 oz.

Mfg.'s Sug. Retail	$518	$430	$375	$335	$295	$275	$215	$225

Add $61 for .45 ACP cal.
Add $182 for duotone finish (disc. 1992).
Subtract $40 for parkerized finish.
In 1992, Springfield added a redesigned stainless steel trigger, patented sear safety which disengages the trigger from the double action mechanism when the safety is on, lengthened the beavertail grip area offering less "pinch", and added a two piece slide stop design.

P9 Stainless — similar to P9 Standard, except is constructed from stainless steel, 35.3 oz. New 1991.

Mfg.'s Sug. Retail	$589	$475	$425	$350

Add $50 for .45 ACP cal.

P9 Compact — 9mm Para. or .40 S&W cal., 3.66 in. barrel, 13 shot (9mm Para.) or 10 shot (.40 S&W) mag., shorter slide and frame, rounded trigger guard, 30 ½ oz. Disc. 1992.

	$395	$350	$300	$275	$250	$225	$200

Add $20 for .40 S&W cal.
Add $20-$30 for blue finish depending on cal.
Add $78 for duotone finish.
Last Mfg.'s Sug. Retail was $499.

P9 Sub-Compact — 9mm Para. or .40 S&W cal., smaller frame than the P9 Compact, 3.66 in. barrel, 12 shot (9mm Para.) or 9 shot (.40 S&W) finger extension mag., squared off trigger guard, 30.1 oz. Disc. 1992.

	$395	$350	$300	$275	$250	$225	$200

Add $20 for .40 S&W cal.
Add $20-$30 for blue finish depending on cal.
Last Mfg.'s Sug. Retail was $499.

P9 Factory Comp — 9mm Para., .40 S&W, or .45 ACP cal., 5 ½ in. barrel (with compensator attached), extended sear safety and mag. release, adj. rear sight, slim competition checkered wood grips, choice of all stainless (disc. 1992) or stainless bi-tone (matte black slide), dual port compensated, 15 shot (9mm Para.), 11 shot (.40 S&W), or 10 shot (.45 ACP) mag., 33.9 oz. New 1992.

Mfg.'s Sug. Retail	$699	$595	$525	$450	$420	$390	$360	$330

Add $36 for .45 ACP cal.
Add $75-$100 for all stainless finish.

Grading	100%	98%	95%	90%	80%	70%	60%

P9 Ultra IPSC (LSP) — competition model with 5.03 in. barrel (long slide ported), adj. rear sight, choice of parkerized (standard finish until 1992 when disc.), blued (disc. 1992), bi-tone (became standard 1993), or stainless steel (disc. 1992) finish, extended thumb safety, and rubberized competition (9mm Para. and .40 S&W cals. only) or checkered walnut (.45 ACP cal. only) grips, 15 shot (9mm Para.), 11 shot (.40 S&W), or 10 shot (.45 ACP) mag., 34.6 oz.

Mfg.'s Sug. Retail $649	$555	$475	$415	$350	$300	$275	$250

Add $30 for .45 ACP cal.

P9 Ultra LSP Stainless — stainless steel variation of the P9 Ultra LSP. Mfg. 1991-92.

	$675	$525	$425

Add $30 for .40 S&W cal.
Add $90 for .45 ACP cal.
Last Mfg.'s Sug. Retail was $769.

P9 World Cup — see listing under 1911-A1 Custom Models heading.

R-SERIES PISTOLS

PANTHER MODEL — 9mm Para., .40 S&W, or .45 ACP cal., semi-auto single or double action, 3.8 in. barrel, hammer drop or firing pin safety, 15 shot (9mm Para.), 11 shot (.40 S&W), or 9 shot (.45 ACP) mag., Commander hammer, frame mounted slide stop, narrow profile, non-glare blue finish only, walnut grips, squared off trigger guard, 29 oz. Mfg. 1992 only.

	$535	$450	$395	$350	$300	$275	$250

Last Mfg.'s Sug. Retail was $609.

FIRECAT MODEL — 9mm Para. or .40 S&W cal., single action, 3.5 in. barrel, 3 dot low profile sights, all steel mfg., firing pin block and frame mounted ambidextrous safety, 8 shot (9mm Para.) or 7 shot (.40 S&W) mag., checkered combat style trigger guard and front/rear grip straps, non-glare blue finish, 35 3/4 oz. New 1992.

Mfg.'s Sug. Retail $569	$495	$425	$375	$330	$295	$275	$250

BOBCAT MODEL — .380 ACP cal. only, patterned after PPK, double action, 13 shot mag., low profile windage adj. sights, slide mounted ambidextrous hammer lowering safety (decocker), special black molded target grips, Commander hammer, matte blue finish, 21.9 oz. New 1992.

Mfg.'s Sug. Retail $449	$375	$325	$295	$275	$250	$225	$200

LINX MODEL — .25 ACP cal., single action, all steel, 3 dot windage adj. low profile sights, 2.23 in. barrel, black checkered composite grips, mag. and frame mounted safety, non-glare blue finish, 7 shot mag., 10 1/2 oz. Mfg. 1992 only.

	$230	$185	$165	$150	$135	$120	$100

Last Mfg.'s Sug. Retail was $269.

1911-A2 S.A.S.S. SINGLE SHOT

1911-A2 S.A.S.S. — various cals., single shot breakopen action featuring interchangeable barrels, Pachmayr grips, adj. front and rear sights, blue finish only, various weights. Mfg. 1990-1992.

10.7 in. barrel — .22 LR, 7mm BR, .243 Win., .357 Mag., or .44 Mag. cal.

	$650	$560	$495	$450	$420	$390	$360

Add $399 per interchangeable conversion unit (includes barrel).
Last Mfg.'s Sug. Retail was $749.

Grading	100%	98%	95%	90%	80%	70%	60%

14.9 in. barrel — .22 LR, .223 Rem., .243 Rem. (new 1991), 7mm BR, 7mm-08 Rem., .308 Win., or .358 Win. cal.

	$650	$560	$495	$450	$420	$390	$360

Add $399 per interchangeable conversion unit (includes barrel).
Last Mfg.'s Sug. Retail was $749.

PISTOLS: DISC. 1911-A1 MODELS

MODEL 1911-A1 STANDARD MODEL — .38 Super, 9mm Para., 10mm (new 1990), or .45 ACP cal., patterned after the Colt M1911-A1, 5.04 (Standard) or 3.63 (Commander or Compact Model) in. barrel, 7 shot (Compact), 8 shot (.45 ACP), 9 shot (10mm), or 10 shot (9mm Para. and .38 Super) mag., walnut grips, parkerized, blue, or duotone finish. Mfg. 1985-1990.

	$400	$360	$330	$300	$280	$260	$240

Add $35 for blued finish.
Add $80 for duotone finish.
This model is also available with a .45 ACP to 9mm Para. conversion kit for $170 in parkerized finish, or $175 in blued finish.
Last Mfg.'s Sug. Retail was $454.

Defender Model — .45 ACP only, similar to Standard 1911-A1 Model, except has fixed combat sights, beveled mag. well, extended thumb safety, bobbed hammer, flared ejection port, walnut grips, factory serrated front strap and two stainless steel magazines, parkerized or blued finish. Mfg. 1988-90.

	$485	$435	$375	$340	$300	$280	$260

Add $35 for blued finish.
Last Mfg.'s Sug. Retail was $567.

Commander Model — .45 ACP cal. only, similar to Standard 1911-A1 Model, except has 3.63 in. barrel, shortened slide, Commander hammer, low profile 3-dot sights, walnut grips, parkerized, blued, or duotone finish. Mfg. in 1990 only.

	$450	$415	$350	$325	$285	$260	$245

Add $30 for blued finish.
Add $80 for duotone finish.
Last Mfg.'s Sug. Retail was $514.

Combat Commander Model — .45 ACP cal. only, 4¼ in. barrel, bobbed hammer, walnut grips. Mfg. 1988-89.

	$435	$385	$325	$295	$275	$250	$230

Add $20 for blued finish.

Compact Model — .45 ACP cal. only, compact variation featuring shortened Commander barrel and slide, reduced M1911 straight grip strap frame, checkered walnut grips, low profile 3-dot sights, extended slide stop, combat hammer, parkerized, blued, or duotone finish. Mfg. 1990 only.

	$450	$415	$350	$325	$285	$260	$245

Add $30 for blued finish.
Add $80 for duotone finish.
Last Mfg.'s Sug. Retail was $514.

Custom Carry Gun — .38 Super (special order only), 9mm, 10mm (new 1990), or .45 ACP cal., similar to Defender Model, except has tuned trigger pull, heavy recoil spring, extended thumb safety, and other features. New 1988.

	$860	$725	$660	$535	$460	$420	$385

Add $130 for .38 Super Ramped, 10mm was POR.
Last Mfg.'s Sug. Retail was $969.

Grading	100%	98%	95%	90%	80%	70%	60%

National Match Hardball Model — .38 Super (disc.), 9mm (disc.), or .45 ACP cal., National Match barrel and bushing, specially fitted frame and slide, BoMar adj. rear sight, Herrett walnut grips, plastic cased. Mfg. 1988-90.

	$780	$650	$565	$515	$460	$415	$385

This model is made specifically for DCM competition shooting.
Last Mfg.'s Sug. Retail was $897.

Bullseye Wadcutter Model — .45 ACP cal. only, designed for wadcutter loads only, 5 or 6 (ported or unported) in. barrel, BoMar rib mounted on slide, checkered grip straps, match trigger, beavertail grip safety, polished feed ramp and throated barrel. New 1989.

	$1,415	$1,200	$1,025	$925	$825	$750	$675

Add $25 for 6 in. barrel.
Add $80 for 6 in. ported barrel.
Last Mfg.'s Sug. Retail was $1,599.

Trophy Master Competition Pistol — .38 Super, 9mm (disc.), 10mm (new 1990), or .45 ACP cal., competition model which includes low profile combat sights, ambidextrous safety, long match trigger, bobbed hammer, Pachmayr wraparound grips. Mfg. 1988-90.

	$1,300	$1,100	$950	$875	$800	$730	$660

Add $130 for .38 Super with supported chamber, 10mm was POR.
Last Mfg.'s Sug. Retail was $1,443.

Trophy Master Competition Expert Model — .38 Super, 9mm (disc.), 10mm (new 1990), or .45 ACP cal., mfg. for IPSC competition shooting, dual chamber compensator system on match barrel, blued finish, ambidextrous thumb safety, beveled and polished mag. well, lowered and flared ejection port, wraparound Pachmayr grips, shock buffer, includes 2 mag.'s and plastic carrying case. Mfg. 1988-90.

	$1,664	$1,450	$1,225	$1,025	$950	$890	$850

Add $130 for .38 Super with supported chamber, 10mm was POR.
This model is an improved variation of the Master Grade Competition Pistol "A".
Last Mfg.'s Sug. Retail was $1,664.

Trophy Master Competition Distinguished Model — similar to Expert Model, except has brushed hard chrome finish, checkered grip straps and trigger guard, top-of-the-line competition model. Mfg. 1988-90.

	$2,000	$1,675	$1,450	$1,225	$1,025	$950	$875

Add $130 for .38 Super with supported chamber, 10mm was POR.
Subtract $130 for "B" Model.
This model is an improved variation of the Master Grade Competition Pistol "B-1".
Last Mfg.'s Sug. Retail was $2,275.

MODEL 1911-A1 90s EDITION PISTOLS

MODEL 1911-A1 90s EDITION — .38 Super, 9mm Para., 10mm (disc. 1991), .40 S&W, or .45 ACP cal., patterned after the Colt M1911-A1, except has linkless operating system, 5.04 (Standard) or 4 (Champion or Compact Model) in. barrel, 7 shot (Compact), 8 shot (.40 S&W or .45 ACP Standard), 9 shot (9mm Para. or 10mm), or 10 shot (.38 Super) mag., checkered walnut grips, parkerized (.45 ACP only beginning 1993), blue, or duotone (disc. 1992) finish. New 1991.

Basic Model

Mfg.'s Sug. Retail	$449	$400	$350	$325	$295	$275	$250	$225

Add $40-$60 for 9mm Para. or .38 Super cal. (blued finish only beginning 1993).
Add $40 for blued finish.

Stainless Standard Model — .45 ACP only, 8 shot mag., wraparound rubber grips, beveled mag. well, 39.2 oz. New 1991.

Mfg.'s Sug. Retail	$532	$450	$395	$350

Springfield, Inc., cont.

Grading	100%	98%	95%	90%	80%	70%	60%

Factory Comp — .38 Super or .45 ACP cal. only, entry level IPSC gun, featuring 5 5/8 in. barrel with compensator attached, adj. rear sight, Videki speed trigger, checkered walnut grips, beveled mag. well, 10 shot (.38 Super) or 8 shot (.45 ACP) mag., blued finish only, 40 oz. New 1991.

Mfg.'s Sug. Retail	$869	$740	$635	$550	$495	$450	$420	$390

Add $30 for .38 Super cal.

Defender Model — .40 S&W (disc. 1992) or .45 ACP cal., similar to Standard Model, except has fixed combat sights, beveled mag. well, extended thumb safety, flared ejection port, walnut (disc.) or 2 piece rubber grips, Commander style hammer, parkerized (disc. 1992), duotone (bi-tone), or blued (disc. 1993) finish. Mfg. began 1991.

Mfg.'s Sug. Retail	$959	$825	$725	$625	$550	$495	$450	$425

Commander Model — .45 ACP cal. only, similar to Standard 1911-A1 Model, except has 3.63 in. barrel, shortened slide, Commander hammer, low profile 3-dot sights, walnut grips, parkerized, blued, or duotone finish. Mfg. 1991-92.

		$425	$365	$330	$300	$275	$250	$225

Combat Commander Model — .45 ACP cal. only, 4 1/4 in. barrel, bobbed hammer, walnut grips. Mfg. 1991 only.

		$425	$365	$330	$300	$275	$250	$225

Champion Model — .45 ACP cal., similar to Standard Model, except has 4 in. barrel and shortened slide, blue finish only, Commander hammer, checkered walnut grips, 3 dot sights, 8 shot mag., 33 1/2 oz. New 1992.

Mfg.'s Sug. Retail	$513	$450	$395	$350	$300	$275	$250	$225

Stainless Champion Model — stainless steel variation of the Champion Model. New 1992.

Mfg.'s Sug. Retail	$558	$475	$415	$350				

Champion Comp — compensated version of the Champion Model, blue. New 1993.

Mfg.'s Sug. Retail	$829	$750	$675	$600	$550	$500	$450	$395

Compact Model — .45 ACP cal. only, compact variation featuring shortened 4 in. barrel and slide, reduced M1911-A1 curved grip strap frame, checkered walnut grips, low profile 3-dot sights, extended slide stop, combat hammer, parkerized (disc. 1992), blued, or duotone (disc. 1992) finish. New 1991.

Mfg.'s Sug. Retail	$509	$450	$395	$350	$300	$275	$250	$225

Stainless Compact Model — stainless steel variation of the Compact Model. New 1991.

Mfg.'s Sug. Retail	$558	$475	$415	$350				

Compact Comp — compensated version of the Compact Model, bi-tone finish only. New 1993.

Mfg.'s Sug. Retail	$829	$750	$675	$600	$550	$500	$450	$395

Gulf Victory Special Edition — .45 ACP cal., special edition featuring presentation grade blued finish, gold etching on slide and other gold plated small parts, includes specially padded and embroidered storage case with jacket patch, window decal, and cloisonne medallion honoring all U.S. Armed Forces. Mfg. 1991-1992.

		$750	$600	$475				

Last Mfg.'s Sug. Retail was $869.

High Capacity Model — .45 ACP or 9 x 21mm cal., features widened frame for high capacity mag., blued finish only. New 1993.

Mfg.'s Sug. Retail	$799	$725	$650	$595	$550	$500	$450	$395

High Capacity Factory Compensated — .45 ACP cal. only, blued finish. New 1993.

Mfg.'s Sug. Retail	$999	$875	$750	$650	$575	$500	$450	$395

Grading	100%	98%	95%	90%	80%	70%	60%

1911-A1 CUSTOM MODELS

Because many of these guns had limited manufacture (1991-1992 only), model descriptions on the variations listed below have been intentionally shortened. Please refer to the 13th Edition for complete model descriptions.

⇥ **Custom Carry Gun** — .38 Super (special order only), 9mm Para., 9mm x 21, 10mm, .40 S&W, or .45 ACP cal., similar to Defender Model, except has tuned trigger pull, heavy recoil spring, extended thumb safety, available in blue or phosphate finish. Mfg. 1991-92.

	$925	$750	$675	$550	$475	$425	$385

Add $240 for 10mm or .40 S&W cal.
Add $131 for 9mm Para., .38 Super or 9x21 cal.
This model features supported chamber in all cals. except .45 ACP. Last Mfg.'s Sug. Retail was $1,069.

⇥ **1911-A1 Custom Compact** — .45 ACP cal. only, carry or lady's model with shortened slide and frame, compensated, fixed 3 dot sights, Commander style hammer, Herrett walnut grips, other custom features, blue only.

	$1,615	$1,325	$1,100	$950	$850	$750	$675

Last Mfg.'s Sug. Retail was $1,815.

⇥ **1911-A1 Custom Champion** — similar to Custom Compact, except is based on Champion model with full size frame and shortened slide.

	$1,615	$1,325	$1,100	$950	$850	$750	$675

Last Mfg.'s Sug. Retail was $1,815.

⇥ **National Match Hardball** — .45 ACP cal. only, National Match barrel and bushing, specially fitted frame and slide, blue only, BoMar adj. rear sight, Herrett walnut grips, plastic cased.

	$875	$725	$650	$550	$475	$425	$385

This model is made specifically for DCM competition shooting. Last Mfg.'s Sug. Retail was $1,000.

⇥ **Bullseye Wadcutter** — .38 Super, .40 S&W, 10mm, or .45 ACP cal., specifically designed for wadcutter loads, BoMar rib mounted on slide top, 5 or 6 in. barrel.

	$1,475	$1,200	$995	$850	$750	$650	$575

Add $24-$29 for 6 in. barrel. Add $200 for .38 Super cal. Add $349 for 10mm or .40 S&W cal. Add $80 for ported 6 in. barrel in .45 ACP cal.
This model features supported chamber in all cals. except .45 ACP. Last Mfg.'s Sug. Retail was $1,640.

⇥ **Entry Level Wadcutter** — .38 Super, .40 S&W, 10mm, or .45 ACP cal., 5 in. barrel, standard competition features.

	$925	$800	$700	$600	$550	$475	$425

Add $200 for .38 Super cal. Add $391 for 10mm or .40 S&W cal.
This model features supported chamber in all cals. except .45 ACP. Last Mfg.'s Sug. Retail was $1,049.

⇥ **Trophy Master "Competition"** — .38 Super, 9mm x 21, 10mm, .40 S&W, or .45 ACP cal., competition model which includes low profile combat sights, ambidextrous safety, long match trigger, bobbed hammer, Pachmayr wraparound grips.

	$1,400	$1,125	$950	$875	$800	$725	$650

Add $266 for 10mm or .40 S&W cal. Add $131 for .38 Super or 9mm x 21 cal.
Last Mfg.'s Sug. Retail was $1,569.

⇥ **Trophy Master "Expert"** — .38 Super, 9mm x 21, 10mm, .40 S&W, or .45 ACP cal., mfg. for IPSC competition shooting, dual chamber compensator system on match barrel, duotone finish.

	$1,625	$1,325	$1,100	$950	$850	$750	$675

Add $266 for 10mm or .40 S&W cal. Add $131 for .38 Super or 9mm x 21 cal.
This model is an improved variation of the Trophy Master Competition Model. Last Mfg.'s Sug. Retail was $1,829.

Springfield, Inc., cont.

Grading	100%	98%	95%	90%	80%	70%	60%

Trophy Master "Distinguished" — similar to Expert Model, except has brushed hard chrome finish, checkered grip straps and trigger guard, top-of-the-line competition model.

	$2,275	$1,875	$1,500	$1,200	$975	$850	$750

Add $300 for 10mm or .40 S&W cal.   **Add $180 for .38 Super or 9mm x 21 cal.**
Last Mfg.'s Sug. Retail was $2,569.

P9 World Cup — 9mm x 21 or .40 S&W cal., state-of-the-art competition pistol, based on factory P9 Racegun, hard chrome finish only.

	$2,550	$2,100	$1,775	$1,500	$1,250	$975	$795

Last Mfg.'s Sug. Retail was $2,935.

RIFLES: MILITARY DESIGN

The M1 Garand and variations listed below were temporarily discontinued in 1991, with production resuming in 1993. The factory should be contacted directly for prices and availability of M1A parts and other rifle related accessories.

M1 GARAND AND VARIATIONS — .30-06 Springfield (disc.), .270 (disc. 1987), or .308 Win. cal., semi-auto, 24 in. barrel, gas operated, 8 shot mag., adj. sights, 9½ lbs.

Standard Model — supplied standard with camo GI fiberglass stock. Temporarily disc. in 1990.

	$725	$650	$575	$525	$485	$450	$425

Subtract $65 if with GI stock.
Last Mfg.'s Sug. Retail was $761.

National Match — walnut stock, match barrel and sights.

	$850	$775	$700	$650	$600	$550	$495

Add $240 for Kevlar stock (disc.).
Last Mfg.'s Sug. Retail was $897.

Ultra Match — match barrel and sights, glass bedded stock, walnut stock standard. Temporarily disc. in 1990.

	$950	$850	$725	$675	$610	$550	$500

Add $240 for Kevlar stock (disc.).
Last Mfg.'s Sug. Retail was $1,033.

M1-D Sniper Rifle — limited quantities, with original M84 scope, prong type flash suppressor, leather cheek pad and slings, .30-06 only.

	$950	$850	$725	$675	$610	$550	$500

Last Mfg.'s Sug. Retail was $1,033.

Tanker Rifle — similar to T-26 authorized by Gen. MacArthur at the end of WWII, 18¼ in. barrel, .30-06 or .308 cal., GI stock standard.

	$725	$675	$600	$525	$460	$380	$335

Add $23 for walnut full stock.
Last Mfg.'s Sug. Retail was $797.

BM 59 — .308 Win. cal., mfg. in Italy and machined and assembled in the Springfield Armory factory, 19.32 in. barrel, 20 shot box mag., 9½ lbs.

Standard Italian Rifle — with grenade launcher, winter trigger, tri-compensator, and bipod.

	$1,750	$1,400	$1,200	$1,000	$895	$850	$800

Last Mfg.'s Sug. Retail was $1,950.

Alpine Rifle — with Beretta pistol grip type stock.

	$2,025	$1,625	$1,350	$1,150	$1,000	$925	$850

This model is also available in a Paratrooper configuration with folding stock at no extra charge.
Last Mfg.'s Sug. Retail was $2,275.

Grading	100%	98%	95%	90%	80%	70%	60%

⚞ Nigerian Rifle — similar to BM 59, except has Beretta pistol grip type stock.

| | $2,075 | $1,650 | $1,375 | $1,150 | $1,000 | $925 | $850 |

Last Mfg.'s Sug. Retail was $2,340.

⚞ E Model Rifle

| | $1,975 | $1,595 | $1,325 | $1,125 | $975 | $900 | $825 |

Last Mfg.'s Sug. Retail was $2,210.

BM 59 M-1 GARAND — with original Beretta M1 receiver, only 200 imported into the U.S.

| | $1,850 | $1,475 | $1,250 | $1,000 | $895 | $850 | $800 |

Last Mfg.'s Sug. Retail was $2,080.

M1A RIFLES — .243 Win. (disc.), .308 Win., or 7mm08 (1991 mfg. only) cal., patterned after the original Springfield M14 - except semi-auto, walnut or fiberglass stock, 22 in. barrel, fiberglass handguard, 9 lbs.

⚞ Standard Model — above specifications, choice of new walnut (standard stock beginning 1993), camo fiberglass (disc. 1992), or GI wood (disc. 1992) stock.

| Mfg.'s Sug. Retail | $1,239 | $1,050 | $850 | $750 | $625 | $550 | $495 | $450 |

Subtract $174 for black fiberglass stock.

⚞ M1A E-2 — standard stock is birch. Disc.

| | $745 | $650 | $590 | $550 | $495 | $505 | $460 |

Add $30 for walnut stock.
Add $120 for Shaw stock with Harris bi-pod.
Last Mfg.'s Sug. Retail was $842.

⚞ National Match — National Match sights, barrel, mainspring guide, flash suppressor, and gas cylinder, special glass bedded oil finished match stock, tuned trigger, walnut stock became standard in 1991, 9 lbs.

| Mfg.'s Sug. Retail | $1,539 | $1,350 | $995 | $825 | $725 | $650 | $575 | $525 |

Add $155 for heavy composition stock (disc.).
Add $250 for either fiberglass or fancy burl wood stock (disc.).
.243 Win. and 7mm-08 cals. are also available at no extra charge (disc.).

⚞ Super Match — similar to National Match, except has air-gauged Douglas or Hart heavy barrel, oversized walnut super match stock, and modified operating rod guide, approx. 10 lbs.

| Mfg.'s Sug. Retail | $1,849 | $1,575 | $1,150 | $925 | $800 | $700 | $625 | $575 |

Add approx. $200 for fiberglass or fancy burl walnut stock (disc.).
.243 and 7mm-08 cals. are also available at no extra charge (disc.).

⚞ Law Enforcement Rifle — .308 Win. cal., law enforcement variation of the M1A mfg. with match grade parts giving superior accuracy. Mfg. 1990-1992.

| | $1,875 | $1,525 | $1,340 | $1,100 | $925 | $800 | $700 |

Last Mfg.'s Sug. Retail was $2,163.

M1A "GOLD SERIES" — .308 Win. cal., heavy walnut competition stock, gold medal grade heavy Douglas barrel. Add $126 for Kevlar stock, add $390 for special Hart stainless steel barrel, add $516 for Hart stainless steel barrel with Kevlar stock. Mfg. 1987 only.

| | $1,944 | $1,750 | $1,375 | $1,150 | $975 | $850 | $740 | $650 |

Last Mfg.'s Sug. Retail was $1,944.

M1A-A1 RIFLE — .308 Win. cal., features new walnut stock. New 1993.

| Mfg.'s Sug. Retail | $1,249 | $1,050 | $850 | $750 | $625 | $550 | $495 | $450 |

Add $150 for folding stock.

Grading	100%	98%	95%	90%	80%	70%	60%

M1A-A1 Bush Rifle — .308 Win. cal., 18¼ in. shrouded barrel, 8 lbs. 12 oz., choice of walnut or camo GI fiberglass stock. Disc. 1992.

	$1,100	$875	$775	$675	$575	$500	$450

Add $235 for National Match variation (disc.).
Add $525 for Super Match variation (disc.).
Last Mfg.'s Sug. Retail was $1,229.

SAR-8 — .308 Win. cal., patterned after the H & K Model 91, recoil operated delayed roller lock action, fluted chamber, rotary adj. rear aperture sight, 18 in. barrel, supplied with walnut thumbhole sporter stock, 20 shot detachable mag., 8.7 lbs. Mfg. in U.S. starting 1990.

	$995	$825	$750	$675	$600	$550	$500

Add $254 for compact accurizing package (includes retractable stock).
SAR-8 parts are interchangeable with both SAR-3 and HK-91 parts.
Last Mfg.'s Sug. Retail was $1,164.

SAR-48/SAR-4800 SPORTER MODEL — .308 Win. cal., authentic model of the Belgian semi-auto FAL/LAR rifle, 21 in. barrel, adj. gas operation, 20 shot mag., adj. sights, supplied with two 20 shot mag.'s, sling, and mag. loader. New 1985.

	$1,125	$925	$795	$695	$640	$595	$550

Add $70 for Paratrooper model with folding stock (disc.).
Add $17 for Compact Sporter Model.
The SAR-48 was disc. in 1989 and reintroduced as the Model SAR-4800 in 1990. The SAR-4800 comes standard with a walnut thumbhole sporter stock. All SAR-4800 parts are interchangeable with both SAR-48 and FN/FAL parts. This model is an updated variation of the pre-WWII FN Model 49.
Last Mfg.'s Sug. Retail was $1,286.

SAR-48/SAR-4800 Bush Rifle Sporter Model — similar to standard model, except has 18 in. barrel.

	$1,085	$900	$795	$695	$640	$595	$550

Last Mfg.'s Sug. Retail was $1,216.

SAR-48 .22 Cal. — .22 LR variation of the Sporter Model. Disc. 1989.

	$725	$660	$595	$540	$495	$450	$400

Last Mfg.'s Sug. Retail was $760.

DR-200 SPORTER RIFLE — while advertised, this model was never mfg. ($687 was planned MSR).

RIFLES: SPORTING

MAUSER M98 — 7 x 57mm, surplus rifles with standard military dimensions and features. Importation disc. 1989.

Hunting/Utility Grade

	$70	$50	$45	$45	$40	$40	$35

Last Mfg.'s Sug. Retail was $75.

Collector Grade

	$105	$90	$80	$70	$60	$50	$40

Last Mfg.'s Sug. Retail was $116.

Premium Grade

	$170	$150	$130	$115	$100	$90	$80

Last Mfg.'s Sug. Retail was $194.

STALLARD ARMS

Manufacturer located in Mansfield, OH since 1991. Distributed by MKS Supply, Inc. located in Mansfield, OH.

Please refer to the Hi-Point listing in this text.

STANDARD ARMS COMPANY

Wilmington, DE.

Grading	100%	98%	95%	90%	80%	70%	60%

MODEL G AUTOLOADER — .25-35, .30-30, .25 Rem., .30 Rem., or .35 Rem. cal., bottom loading box mag., 22 in. barrel, open sight, straight stock. This was the first gas operated rifle in U.S.A. Gas port can be closed and gun will function as a slide action, mfg. 1910.

	$400	$300	$275	$250	$225	$175	$150

A variation that was slide action only (Model M) also was mfg. — subtract 35% from values listed above.

STAR, BONIFACIO ECHEVERRIA

Manufactured in Eibar, Spain. Currently imported by Interarms located in Alexandria, VA.

PISTOLS: SEMI-AUTO

MODEL I — .32 ACP, 9 shot, 4¾ in. barrel, blue, fixed sights, plastic grips. Mfg. 1934-1936.

	$275	$215	$160	$120	$100	$85	$70

MODEL IN — similar to Model I, except .380 ACP, 8 shot, 4¾ in. barrel, blue.

	$295	$225	$170	$125	$105	$90	$75

MODEL HN — .380 auto, 6 shot, 2¾ in. barrel, blue, fixed sights, plastic grips. Mfg. 1934-1941.

	$250	$195	$140	$120	$100	$90	$75

MODEL H — similar to HN, except 7.65mm, 7 shot.

	$225	$180	$140	$120	$100	$90	$75

MODEL 1920 — 9mm BB or .38 Super cal., easily identified by unusual safety located on left rear slide.

	$425	$350	$295	$240	$185	$150	$120

MODEL 1921 — 9mm BB or .38 Super cal., predecessor to the later Model A, this model was fitted with a grip safety that was later dropped when standardizing the Model A production.

	$400	$325	$240	$215	$180	$145	$115

MODEL 1922 — designation for the early Model A.

	$325	$285	$240	$215	$180	$145	$115

MODEL A — modified Government Colt, .38 Super, 5 in. barrel, no grip safety, blue, checkered wood grips. Mfg. 1934-present but not currently imported.

	$275	$230	$200	$165	$145	$130	$110

MODEL A CARBINE — usually 7.63mm, unusual variation, slotted with tangent rear sight and extended barrel.

	$1,750	$1,350	$1,050	$825	$700	$575	$450

Add $500 for original stock (different from MB and MMS stock).

MODEL B — similar to Model A, but 9mm Luger. Mfg. 1934-1975.

	$295	$250	$205	$170	$150	$140	$115

Add 150% if Waffen proofed.

Grading	100%	98%	95%	90%	80%	70%	60%

MODEL M (MILITARY) — similar to Model A, except has large frame, available in 9mm Bergman, 9mm Luger, or .38 Super cal., 8 shot, and .45 ACP, 7 shot, 5 in. barrel, blue, fixed sights, checkered wood grips.

	$295	$250	$200	$165	$150	$140	$120

MODEL P — .45 ACP cal. only, similar to Model A, except has large frame, 7 shot mag. Mfg. 1934-1975.

	$325	$275	$210	$175	$155	$145	$120

MODELS SUPER A, M, & P — similar to Models A, M, & P, except has loaded chamber indicator, mag. safety and easier takedown feature. Mfg. 1946-1989.

	$395	$325	$215	$180	$160	$145	$125

Add 50% for Super P.
Last Mfg.'s Sug. Retail was $340. The Super A was a Spanish Service pistol.

MODELS SUPER B — 9mm Para., similar to Models A, M, & P, except has loaded chamber indicator, mag. safety and easier takedown feature, choice of blue or Starvel finish on Model B. Importation disc. in 1990.

	$270	$240	$210	$185	$160	$140	$120

Add $30 for Starvel finish.
Last Mfg.'s Sug. Retail was $330.

SUPER STAR TARGET MODEL — similar to Super Star, but target sights, extended trigger guard.

	$1,250	$950	$800	$700	$600	$500	$400

MODEL MB — 9mm Para., late production Model M cut for shoulder stock, mag. safety. Add $300 for shoulder stock.

	$1,295	$975	$675	$565	$450	$365	$250

MODEL MMS — 7.63mm, late production Model M cut for shoulder stock, mag. safety. Add $300 for original stock.

	$900	$675	$460	$400	$325	$260	$200

MODEL SI — .32 ACP, 8 shot, 4 in. barrel, blue, without grip safety, small version of Government .45 in appearance, plastic grips. Mfg. 1941-1965.

	$200	$190	$160	$135	$115	$100	$80

MODEL S — similar to S1, except .380 ACP cal., 9 shot, mfg. 1941-1965. Importation of these Police contract models was disc. 1991.

	$195	$170	$145	$125	$110	$95	$85

Add $30 for Starvel finish.
Last Mfg.'s Sug. Retail was $237.
Beginning in 1989, Interarms started importing factory reconditioned used Spanish Police Contract Model S pistols - these guns are available in either blue or Starvel finish and are supplied with a plastic box with accessories.

MODELS SUPER SI AND S — similar to S, with Super Star improvements. Mfg. 1946-1972.

	$240	$230	$210	$195	$165	$140	$120

MODEL SUPER SM — similar to Super S, except adjustable sight and wood grips. Mfg. 1973-1981.

	$250	$235	$220	$200	$175	$145	$125

MODEL CO POCKET — .25 auto, 2¾ in. barrel, blue, fixed sights, plastic grips. Mfg. 1941-1957.

	$225	$180	$165	$145	$120	$110	$90

Grading	100%	98%	95%	90%	80%	70%	60%

MODEL CU STARLET — .25 auto, 2⅜ in. barrel, alloy frame, fixed sights, plastic grips, blue, or chrome slide, frame anodized in black, blue, green, gray, or gold. Mfg. 1957-present, no longer imported as of 1968 due to Federal GCA legislation.

	$235	$200	$165	$145	$120	$110	$90

MODEL DK (STARFIRE) — .380 auto, 3⅛ in. barrel, fixed sights, plastic stocks, finished in same color availability as Model CU. Mfg. 1957-present, U.S. import ceased as of 1968 due to Federal GCA legislation.

	$400	$350	$295	$255	$225	$180	$155

MODEL HK LANCER — similar to Starfire, except .22 LR. Mfg. 1955-1968.

	$225	$200	$180	$160	$140	$120	$110

MODEL F — .22 LR, 10 shot, 4 in. barrel, fixed sights, blue, plastic grips. Mfg. 1942-1967.

	$250	$195	$140	$110	$95	$85	$55

MODEL FS — similar to F, except 6 in. barrel, adj. sights. Mfg. 1942-1967.

	$250	$195	$150	$120	$100	$90	$65

MODEL F OLYMPIC RAPID FIRE — .22 Short, 9 shot, 7 in. barrel, adj. sight, aluminum slide, barrel weights and muzzle brake, blue, plastic grips. Mfg. 1942-1967.

	$275	$235	$210	$175	$155	$140	$130

MODEL FR — restyled Model F, adj. sight and slide stop. Mfg. 1967-1972.

	$250	$195	$150	$120	$100	$90	$65

MODEL FRS — similar to FR, only 6 in. barrel, available in chrome. Mfg. 1967-present.

	$250	$195	$150	$120	$100	$90	$65

MODEL FM — similar to FR, except heavier frame, web ahead of trigger guard, 4½ in. barrel. Mfg. 1972-present.

	$235	$180	$150	$120	$100	$90	$65

MODEL BKS STARLIGHT — 9mm Para., 8 shot, 4¼ in. barrel, plastic grips. Mfg. 1970-1981.

	100%	98%	95%	90%	80%	70%	60%
Blue	$265	$230	$210	$180	$160	$145	$130
Chrome	$295	$240	$220	$195	$170	$155	$145

MODEL BM SEMI-AUTO — 9mm, single action, 8 shot mag., 4 in. barrel, steel frame, Colt 1911 action, blue, chrome (disc. 1989), or Starvel (new 1990) finish, plastic grips, 35 oz. Importation disc. 1991.

	$285	$245	$205	$180	$165	$155	$145

Add $30 for Starvel or chrome (disc. 1990) finish.
Last Mfg.'s Sug. Retail was $415.

MODEL BKM — similar to BM, except lightweight duraluminum frame, blued finish only, 26 oz. Importation disc. 1991.

	$285	$250	$215	$190	$170	$160	$150

Last Mfg.'s Sug. Retail was $415.

MODEL PD — .45 ACP, 6 shot mag., single action, 4 in. barrel, adj. rear sight, blue or Starvel (new 1990) finish only, walnut grips, alloy frame, 25 oz. Mfg. 1975-present. Importation disc. 1991.

	$345	$290	$250	$215	$195	$170	$160

Add $20 for Starvel finish (new 1990).
Last Mfg.'s Sug. Retail was $475.

Grading	100%	98%	95%	90%	80%	70%	60%

MODEL 28 — 9mm, double action, 15 shot mag., 4¼ in. barrel, blue finish only, advanced design, 40 oz. Mfg. 1983 and 1984 only.

	$375	$310	$325	$275	$250	$225	$200

Note: Model 28 is interesting since no screws are used in its manufacture. Hammer assembly (including spring, cocking lever, sear, disconnector and ejector) is housed under removable backstrap.

MODEL 30M — 9mm Para. only, successor to the Model 28, double action, 4.33 in. barrel, 15 shot mag., blued finish only, adj. rear sight, checkered wrap around plastic grips, steel frame, 40 oz. New 1985. Importation disc. 1991.

	$400	$340	$315	$295	$270	$250	$225

Last Mfg.'s Sug. Retail was $495.

MODEL 30/31 PK STARFIRE DURAL — similar to Model 30M, except duraluminum frame, 3.86 in. barrel, 30 oz.

Mfg.'s Sug. Retail	$580	$455	$360	$315	$295	$270	$250	$225

The Model 30 PK was discontinued in 1989 and the Model 31 PK was introduced in 1990.

MODEL 31P STARFIRE — 9mm Para. or .40 S&W (new 1990) cal., compact variation utilizing double action, features Acculine barrel (3.86 in.) similar to Firestar Model, 14 shot mag., ambidextrous safety with decocking lever, blue or Starvel finish, all steel construction, 39.4 oz. New 1990.

Mfg.'s Sug. Retail	$580	$455	$360	$315	$295	$270	$250	$225

Add $63 for .40 S&W cal.
Add $32 for Starvel finish.

MODEL M40/M43 FIRESTAR — 9mm Para. (M43) or .40 S&W (M40, new 1990) cal., single action, 7 shot mag., 3.39 in. Acculine barrel, checkered rubber grips, compact design utilizing all steel construction, 3 dot sighting system with adjustable rear sight, blue or Starvel finish, 30.35 oz. New 1990.

Mfg.'s Sug. Retail	$460	$335	$280	$255	$225	$200	$180	$165

Add $28 for .40 S&W cal.
Add $32 for Starvel finish.

MODEL M45 FIRESTAR — .45 ACP, single action, ultra compact design featuring 4 barrel lugs, steel frame and slide, 3.6 in. reverse taper Acculine barrel, 6 shot mag., black synthetic grips, blue or starvel finish, 35 oz. New 1992.

Mfg.'s Sug. Retail	$525	$420	$335	$280	$250	$225	$200	$180

Add $28 for Starvel finish.

MEGASTAR — 10mm or .45 ACP cal., larger variation of the Firestar featuring 4½ in. barrel and 12 shot mag., 47.6 oz. New 1992.

Mfg.'s Sug. Retail	$693	$600	$410	$350	$325	$295	$275	$250

Add $32 for Starvel finish.

STEEL CITY ARMS, INC.

Manufacturer located in Pittsburgh, PA until 1990. In 1991, Desert Industries, Inc. acquired Steel City Arms, Inc. and moved the manufacture to Las Vegas, NV. To date, only the Steel City Arms, Inc. logo has appeared on newly mfg. Desert Industries, Inc. guns.

DOUBLE DEUCE — .22 LR only, double action semi-auto, matte finish stainless steel, 2½ in. barrel, 7 shot mag., uncheckered rosewood grips, 18 oz. Mfg. 1984-90.

	$265	$230	$200

Various select hardwood stocks were also available at extra cost ($20-100).
Last Mfg.'s Sug. Retail was $290.

STERLING
Previous manufacturer located in Gasport, NY. Disc. 1983.

PISTOLS

Rather than list individual models, the following generalizations will help in ascertaining values for this trademark. Models 300, 302 and 402 will average between $75 and $150 if in 70%+ condition, Models 283, 284, 285 (Husky), and 286 (Trapper) are semi-auto .22 cal. pistols with various barrel lengths — values will range between $90-$150. Models 400 (.380 ACP), PPL (.380 ACP short barrel), and 450 (.45 ACP) usually range in the $150-$275 range.

STERLING ARMAMENT, LTD.
Manufacturer located in England since 1900. Previously imported and distributed by Cassi Inc. located in Colorado Springs, CO until 1990.

CARBINES

Grading	100%	98%	95%	90%	80%	70%	60%

AR-180 — .223 Rem. cal., patterned after the AR-15, disc.

	100%	98%	95%	90%	80%	70%	60%
	$775	$700	$625	$550	$495	$450	$400

STERLING MK 6 — 9mm Para., blowback semi-auto with floating firing pin, shrouded 16.1 in. barrel, side mounted mag., folding stock, 7½ lbs.

	100%	98%	95%	90%	80%	70%	60%
	$565	$495	$450	$410	$375	$340	$310

Last Mfg.'s Sug. Retail was $650.

PISTOLS

PARAPISTOL MK 7 C4 — 9mm Para., 4 in. barrel, semi-auto paramilitary design pistol, crinkle finish, same action as MK. 6 Carbine, fires from closed bolt, 10, 15, 20, 30, 34 or 68 shot mag., 5 lbs.

	100%	98%	95%	90%	80%	70%	60%
	$500	$435	$375	$350	$325	$295	$265

Last Mfg.'s Sug. Retail was $600.

PARAPISTOL MK 7 C8 — 9mm, similar to C4, except has 7.8 in. barrel, 5¼ lbs.

	100%	98%	95%	90%	80%	70%	60%
	$525	$450	$390	$365	$330	$300	$275

Last Mfg.'s Sug. Retail was $620.

STEVENS, J., ARMS COMPANY
J. Stevens Arms Company was founded in 1864 at Chicopee Falls, MA as J. Stevens & Co. In 1866 the name was changed to J. Stevens Arms and Tool Co. In 1916, the plant became New England Westinghouse, and tooled up for both Browning machine guns and Moisin-Nagant Rifles. In 1920, the plant was sold to the Savage Arms Corp. and manufactured guns were marked "J. Stevens Arms Co.". This designation was dropped in the late 1940's, and only the name "Stevens" has been used up to the present date.

In 1990, Savage Arms discontinued the manufacture of all firearms (rifles and shotguns) bearing the Stevens trademark. All guns manufactured by Savage Arms now bear the Savage trademark only.

PISTOLS

NO. 10 TARGET SINGLE SHOT — .22 LR, 8 in. barrel, blue, adj. sights, rubber grips, squared off like an automatic pistol, tip up action. Mfg. 1919-1939.

	100%	98%	95%	90%	80%	70%	60%
	$220	$200	$185	$165	$140	$120	$100

NO. 35 TARGET SINGLE SHOT — .22 LR, 6, 8, 10, or 12¼ in. barrel, blue, walnut grips. Mfg. 1907-1939.

	100%	98%	95%	90%	80%	70%	60%
	$350	$300	$265	$220	$200	$185	$165

Grading	100%	98%	95%	90%	80%	70%	60%

NO. 35 "OFFHAND" AUTOSHOT — .410 (actually a pistol-length shotgun). Class Three — must be registered with BATF. Introduced 1931, disc. 1935.

	$300	$250	$200	$150	$100	$75	$60

RIFLES

Stevens made a wide variety of inexpensive, utilitarian rifles that to date have attracted mostly shooting interest, but little collector interest. A listing of these models may be found in the back of this text under "Serialization".

MODEL 44 IDEAL SINGLE SHOT — .22 LR through .44-40 cals., rolling block, lever action, takedown, 24 or 26 in. barrels, straight grip stock and forearm. Mfg. 1894-1932.

	$600	$550	$500	$425	$325	$300	$275

MODEL 44½ IDEAL SINGLE SHOT — similar to Model 44, except .22 LR through .44-40 cals., falling block, lever action, takedown, 24 or 26 in. barrels, straight grip stock and forearm, action redesigned 1903. Mfg. 1903-1916.

	$850	$775	$675	$575	$500	$425	$350

MODELS 45-54 SINGLE SHOTS — .22 LR through .44-40 cals., rolling and falling block receivers, lever action, takedown, deluxe versions of the Models 44 and 44½, many special order features, including double set triggers, types of finish, engraving, length and weight of barrels, stock configuration could be special ordered. The higher grade Schuetzens and Stevens-Pope are very collectible and command premiums. These models have to be taken one at a time for determining value. Therefore, no prices are shown. Mfg. 1896-1916.

NO. 414 ARMORY MODEL — .22 LR or .22 Short only, lever action, 26 in. barrel, single shot, Lyman aperture sight. Mfg. 1912-1932.

	$450	$400	$375	$330	$290	$250	$220

MODEL 416 — bolt action, .22 LR, 25 in. medium barrel, 5 shot mag. Disc.

	$140	$120	$110	$100	$90	$80	$70

This model was also mfg. as a U.S. military training rifle. Can be denoted by "U.S. Property" on rear of bolt housing. Healthy premiums exist for this variation.

NO. 417 WALNUT HILL MODEL — .22 LR, .22 Short, and .22 Hornet, lever action, 28 or 29 in. extra heavy barrel, target stock with full pistol grip, beavertail forend, made in 0-3 suffix variations (different sights). Mfg. 1932-1947.

	$700	$600	$525	$475	$440	$395	$360

NO. 417½ WALNUT HILL MODEL — similar to No. 417, except available in .25 rimfire also. Mfg. 1932-1940.

	$700	$600	$525	$475	$440	$395	$360

NO. 418 WALNUT HILL MODEL — .22 LR or .22 Short only, 26 in. barrel, pistol grip stock, semi beavertail forearm. Mfg. 1932-1940.

	$375	$330	$290	$260	$230	$200	$180

STEVENS' FAVORITE NO.'S 17-29 — .22 LR, .25 RF or .32 RF cal., 24 in. barrel most common, other lengths available, Rocky Mountain front sight, straight grip stock, small tapered forearm. Mfg. 1894-1935. Octagonal barrels command a 33% premium.

	$225	$175	$150	$130	$115	$100	$90

STEVENS' MODEL 65 — bolt action, 20 in. barrel, open sights, 5 shot mag., checkered walnut stock. Mfg. 1969-disc.

	$90	$70	$55	$45	$35	$30	$30

Grading	100%	98%	95%	90%	80%	70%	60%

NO. 70 "VISIBLE LOADING" SLIDE ACTION RIFLE — .22 LR-L-S, exposed hammer, 22 in. barrel, open sights, straight grip stock, tube mag., grooved slide handle. Other variations with different barrel lengths and sights will command slight premiums.

	$250	$175	$150	$130	$115	$100	$90

MODEL 71 "STEVENS' FAVORITE" COMMEMORATIVE — replica of original, .22 LR, 22 in. octagon barrel, plain straight stock, medallion inlaid, crescent butt. 1,000 mfg. in 1971.

	$250	$195	$150

Last Mfg.'s Sug. Retail was $75.

MODEL 72 CRACKSHOT — single shot falling block action, .22 cal., 22 in. octagon barrel, open sights, color case hardened frame, straight stock. Mfg. 1972-89.

	$125	$105	$85	$70	$60	$50	$40

Last Mfg.'s Sug. Retail was $165.

MODEL 987 — .22 LR only, semi-auto, 15 shot tube mag., 20 in. barrel, hardwood Monte Carlo stock, adj. rear sight, 6 lbs. Disc. 1989.

	$95	$80	$70	$60	$50	$40	$45

Last Mfg.'s Sug. Retail was $119.

MODEL 89 LEVER ACTION — .22 LR, single shot, 18½ in. barrel, Martini type action, Western style lever, straight stock. Mfg. 1976-disc.

	$85	$65	$60	$50	$45	$40	$35

SHOTGUNS

Stevens made a wide variety of inexpensive, utilitarian shotguns that to date have attracted mostly shooting interest, but little collector interest. A listing of these models may be found in the back of this text under "Serialization".

MODEL 520 PUMP

	$190	$180	$150	$125	$95	$85	$75

MODEL 520-30 TRENCH/RIOT — see the "Trench/Riot Shotgun" category in the T section for more information and prices.

MODEL 620 — an improved version of the Model 520 with streamlined receiver.

	$325	$290	$250	$225	$175	$150	$100

MODEL 620A TRENCH/RIOT — see the "Trench/Riot Shotgun" category in the T section for more information and prices.

MODEL 77 (F, M, & SC) SLIDE ACTION — 12, 16, or 20 ga., "M" suffix is 12 ga. Mag., "SC" designate Super Choke, "F" refers to 16 ga.

	$175	$160	$140	$120	$100	$80	$60

MODEL 77E RIOT — see the "Trench/Riot Shotgun" category in the T section for more information and prices.

Stevens, J., Arms Company, cont.

Grading	100%	98%	95%	90%	80%	70%	60%

MODEL 67 SLIDE ACTION — 12, 20, or .410 ga., all are 3 in. chambered, steel receiver, 5 shot, upper receiver safety, 6¼ - 7½ lbs. Recent mfg. by Stevens. Disc. 1989.

	$200	$180	$170	$155	$145	$135	$125

Add $30 for choke tubes (with VR).
Add $10 for VR only.
Last Mfg.'s Sug. Retail was $229.

⚔ **Model 67 VTR-K Camo** — 12 or 20 ga., 28 in. VR barrel with choke tubes, laminated camo stock. Mfg. 1986-1988.

	$250	$220	$190	$170	$155	$145	$135

Last Mfg.'s Sug. Retail was $295.

⚔ **Slug Model** — 12 ga. only, 21 in. barrel, rifle sights. Disc. 1989.

	$200	$165	$140	$110	$100	$90	$80

Last Mfg.'s Sug. Retail was $245.

⚔ **Model 67 VRT-Y** — 20 ga. only, 22 in. VR barrel with choke tubes, youth model with smaller stock dimensions. Mfg. 1987-1988.

	$205	$170	$140	$110	$100	$90	$80

Last Mfg.'s Sug. Retail was $259.

MODEL 675 — 12 ga. only, 24 in. VR multi-choked barrel with iron sights (including removable rear ramp), hardwood stock with recoil pad, 6½ lbs. Mfg. 1987-1988.

	$250	$220	$190	$170	$155	$145	$135

Last Mfg.'s Sug. Retail was $295.

MODEL 240 O/U — .410 ga.

	$350	$300	$250	$220	$190	$170	$155

MODEL 69-RXL — 12 ga. only, slide action law enforcement version of the Model 67, 18¼ in. cylinder bore barrel with recoil pad, 6½ lbs. Disc. 1989.

	$200	$165	$140	$110	$100	$90	$80

Last Mfg.'s Sug. Retail was $245.

MODEL 311 — 12, 16, 20, or .410 ga., 3 in. chambers, double triggers, extractors, VR. Disc. 1989.

	$245	$205	$185	$150	$140	$125	$115

Last Mfg.'s Sug. Retail was $309.

⚔ **Model 311-R** — 12 ga. only, similar to Model 311, except has 18¼ in. cylinder bore barrels for law enforcement use, 3 in. chambers, 6¾ lbs. Disc. 1989.

	$245	$205	$185	$150	$140	$125	$115

Last Mfg.'s Sug. Retail was $309.

FOX/STEVENS MODEL B — 12, 20 or .410 ga., double triggers, VR, extractors, 26, 28, or 30 in. barrels, 7 lbs. Disc. 1986.

	$315	$280	$240	$220	$200	$180	$160

Add 25% for BDE Model (with ejectors).
Last Mfg.'s Sug. Retail was $369.

FOX/STEVENS MODEL B-SE — 12, 20, or .410 ga., single trigger, selective ejectors, VR, beavertail forend, select walnut. Disc. 1989.

	$415	$370	$325	$280	$240	$210	$180

Add 20% for .410 ga.
Last Mfg.'s Sug. Retail was $525.

Grading	100%	98%	95%	90%	80%	70%	60%

MODEL 94 — 12, 16, 20, or .410 ga., single shot breakopen, inertia firing pin design, open hammer, 6¼ lbs. Mfg. 1939-1937.

	$80	$70	$65	$55	$50	$45	$40

Last Mfg.'s Sug. Retail was $92.

STEYR AUSTRIAN MILITARY
Manufacturer located in Steyr, Austria.

MODEL 95 RIFLE — straight pull bolt action, 8 x 50R Mannlicher, 30 in. barrel, adj. sights, military full stock.

	$140	$110	$100	$85	$65	$55	$40

MODEL 90 CARBINE — similar to Model 95, except 19½ in. barrel.

	$155	$125	$110	$95	$85	$65	$45

STEYR DAIMLER PUCH A.G.
Steyr, Austria. 1911 to date.

COMMERCIAL MODEL 1901

	$1,850	$1,500	$1,200	$900	$600	$500	$400

COMMERCIAL MODEL 1905

	$1,250	$950	$700	$500	$400	$350	$300

ARGENTINE MODEL 1905 — 7.65mm, Argentine crest on left panel is usually machined off. Values assume matching numbers but removed crest.

	$400	$350	$300	$255	$220	$185	$150

POCKET AUTO — .25 ACP or .32 cal., tip up barrel, mag. fed. Disc.

	$325	$265	$200	$150	$140	$130	$120

ROTH STEYR AUTO (MODEL 1907) — 8mm Steyr cal.

	$600	$500	$400	$350	$300	$250	$200

Add 30% for "Budapest" markings.

STEYR-HAHN MODEL 1911 AUTOMATIC — 9mm Steyr, 8 shot, 5.1 in. barrel, fixed magazine top loaded by stripper clip, blue, checkered wood grips. Mfg. 1911-1919. In 1938, the Germans confiscated and converted about 250,000 Steyr Hahns to 9mm Para., "08" was stamped on the left side of these guns.

	$425	$375	$325	$275	$225	$195	$175

Add 100% if marked "08" or with Rumanian Crest.

MODEL SP — .32 ACP, semi-auto, trigger cocking mechanism, very rare - mfg. in 1959 only.

	$650	$595	$540	$495	$450	$400	$350

STEYR MANNLICHER
Manufactured by Steyr-Daimler-Puch in Austria. Founded by Ferdinand Ritter Von Mannlicher and Otto Schoenauer in 1903. Currently imported and distributed by Gun South, Inc. located in Trussville, AL.

Note: also see Mannlicher Schoenauer in the M section for pre-WWII models.

Grading	100%	98%	95%	90%	80%	70%	60%

PISTOLS

MODEL GB — 9mm, double action, 18 shot mag, gas delayed blowback action, non-glare checkered plastic grips, 5¼ in. barrel with Polygon rifling, matte finish, steel construction, 2 lbs. 6 oz. Importation disc. 1988.

	100%	98%	95%	90%	80%	70%	60%
Commercial	$525	$475	$425	$375	$335	$300	$280
Military	$450	$395	$350	$300	$280	$260	$240

Last Mfg.'s Sug. Retail was $514.

In 1987, Steyr mfg. a military variation of the Model GB featuring a phosphate finish - only 937 were imported into the U.S.

MODEL SPP — 9mm Para., single action semi-auto, delayed blow back system with rotating 5.9 in. barrel, 15 or 30 shot mag., utilizes synthetic materials and advanced ergonomics, adj. sights, grooved receiver for scope mounting, matte black finish, 44 oz. Importation began 1992.

	100%	98%	95%	90%	80%	70%	60%
Mfg.'s Sug. Retail $895	$800	$675	$600	$550	$495	$450	$400

RIFLES: RECENT MFG.

Current production guns are now called Steyr-Mannlicher models. For models manufactured 1903-1971, please refer to the Mannlicher Schoenauer Sporting Rifles section in this text.

In the past several years, the manufacturer's suggested retails have gone up considerably. Prices for used specimens (98% or less original condition) have not increased proportionately, and in some cases, have changed very little.

The below listed models have 4 different action lengths and model designations stand for the following: SL=Super Light, L=Light, M=Medium, S=Magnum, S/T=Magnum with heavy barrel. All sporting rifles are available with left-hand stock - add $109 and with either single set or double set triggers - add $159.

MODEL M72 L/M RIFLE — M72 bolt action, .243, .308, .270, .30-06, 7 x 57, and 7 x 64 cals., 23 in. barrel, single or double set triggers. Mfg. 1972-1980.

	100%	98%	95%	90%	80%	70%	60%
	$795	$725	$650	$575	$500	$460	$420

MODEL SL — .222 Rem. and Mag., .223 Rem., .22-250 Rem. (disc. 1992), or 5.6 x 50mm (disc. 1991) cal., bolt action, 23.6 in. barrel, double set triggers, rotary mag. Available in full-stock (Carbine), half stock (rifle), or varmint version (vent square forearm).

	100%	98%	95%	90%	80%	70%	60%
Mfg.'s Sug. Retail $2,023	$1,725	$1,225	$925	$775	$675	$600	$540

⚡ **Carbine Model (Full Stock)** — skipline checkered full stock, 20 in. barrel.

	100%	98%	95%	90%	80%	70%	60%
Mfg.'s Sug. Retail $2,179	$1,825	$1,275	$975	$795	$675	$600	$540

⚡ **Varmint Rifle** — .222 Rem., .223 Rem. (new 1993), or .22-250 (disc. 1992) cal., 26 in. heavy barrel, stippled pistol grip, vent. forearm, no sights.

	100%	98%	95%	90%	80%	70%	60%
Mfg.'s Sug. Retail $2,179	$1,825	$1,275	$975	$795	$675	$600	$540

MODEL L — 5.6 x 57mm (disc. 1991), .243 Win., or .308 Win. cals., available in .22-250 and 6mm Rem. on special order only, otherwise same general specifications as Model SL.

	100%	98%	95%	90%	80%	70%	60%
Mfg.'s Sug. Retail $2,023	$1,725	$1,225	$925	$775	$675	$600	$540

⚡ **Carbine Model (Full Stock)** — skip-line checkered full stock, 20 in. barrel.

	100%	98%	95%	90%	80%	70%	60%
Mfg.'s Sug. Retail $2,179	$1,825	$1,275	$975	$795	$675	$600	$540

⚡ **Varmint Rifle** — .222 Rem. (disc. 1991), .22-250 (special order), .243 Win., or .308 Win. cals., 26 in. heavy barrel, stippled pistol grip, vent. forearm, no sights.

	100%	98%	95%	90%	80%	70%	60%
Mfg.'s Sug. Retail $2,179	$1,825	$1,275	$975	$795	$675	$600	$540

⚡ **Model L Luxus** — 5.6 x 57mm, .243 Win., or .308 Win. cals., full or half stock only, .22-250 and 6mm Rem. available on special order, 3 shot mag.

	100%	98%	95%	90%	80%	70%	60%
Mfg.'s Sug. Retail $2,648	$2,275	$1,625	$1,275	$975	$775	$700	$650

Grading		100%	98%	95%	90%	80%	70%	60%

Model L Luxus Carbine — similar to L Luxus rifle, except has full stock and 20 in. barrel.

Mfg.'s Sug. Retail	$2,804	$2,375	$1,700	$1,300	$995	$800	$725	$660

MODEL M — 6.5 x 57mm, 7 x 64mm, .270 Win., .30-06, or 9.3 x 62mm cal., bolt action, full stock or half stock, rotary mag., double set triggers.

Mfg.'s Sug. Retail	$2,023	$1,725	$1,225	$925	$775	$675	$600	$540

Carbine Model (Full Stock) — skipline checkered full stock, 20 in. barrel.

Mfg.'s Sug. Retail	$2,179	$1,825	$1,275	$975	$795	$675	$600	$540

Professional Rifle — .270 Win., 7 x 57mm (disc. 1991), 7 x 64mm, .30-06, or 9.3 x 62mm cal., 23.6 in. barrel, Cycolac synthetic stock, 7½ lbs.

Mfg.'s Sug. Retail	$1,710	$1,500	$1,025	$850	$700	$600	$540	$495

Add $469 for left hand action with half stock (rifle).
Add $625 for left hand action with full stock (carbine).
This variation is also available in .270 Win. or .30-06 cal. with half stock and 20 in. barrel (carbine).

Model M Luxus — 6.5 x 57, 7 x 64, .270 Win., and .30-06 cals., special order in 6.5 x 55 and 7.5 Swiss.

Mfg.'s Sug. Retail	$2,648	$2,275	$1,625	$1,275	$975	$775	$700	$650

Model M Luxus Carbine — similar to Model M Luxus, except with full stock and 20 in. barrel.

Mfg.'s Sug. Retail	$2,804	$2,375	$1,700	$1,300	$995	$800	$725	$660

Carbine - 1000 Year Commemorative — 1984 only, .30-06 cal.

		$4,200	$3,620	$2,835				

MODEL S (MAGNUM) — 6.5 x 68, 8 x 68S, .300 Win. Mag., .338 Win. Mag. (disc. 1992), .375 H&H Mag., 7mm Rem. Mag. cals., half-stock, 26 in. barrel, bolt action.

Mfg.'s Sug. Retail	$2,179	$1,825	$1,275	$975	$795	$675	$600	$540

MODEL S/T — available in 9.3 x 64 (disc. 1992), .375 H&H Mag., or .458 Win. Mag. cal., 26 in. heavy barrel.

Mfg.'s Sug. Retail	$2,335	$1,950	$1,350	$1,000	$850	$725	$625	$550

Tropical Rifle — .375 H&H and .458 Win. Mag. cals., 26 in. heavy barrel. Disc. 1985.

		$1,150	$900	$810	$730	$660	$600	$550

Last Mfg.'s Sug. Retail was $1,332.

Luxus S — available in 6.5 x 68, 8 x 68S, 7mm Mag., .300 Win. Mag. cals., 26 in. barrel, half stock only, 3 shot mag., 8 lbs.

Mfg.'s Sug. Retail	$2,804	$2,375	$1,700	$1,300	$995	$800	$725	$660

MODEL SSG — .243 Win. (PII Sniper only) or .308 Win cal., for competition or law-enforcement use. Marksman has regular sights, rotary mag., teflon coated bolt with heavy duty locking lugs, synthetic stock has removable spacers, parkerized finish. Match version has heavier target barrel and "match" bolt carrier, can be used as single shot. Extremely accurate.

PI Rifle — 26 in. barrel, 3 shot mag., black or green ABS Cycolac synthetic stock.

Mfg.'s Sug. Retail	$2,043	$1,735	$1,225	$925	$775	$675	$600	$540

Add $448 for walnut stock (disc. 1992).

PII Sniper Rifle — .243 or .308 Win. cal., 26 in. heavy barrel, no sights, green or black synthetic Cycolac stock, modified bolt handle, choice of single or set triggers.

Mfg.'s Sug. Retail	$2,229	$1,860	$1,285	$975	$795	$675	$600	$540

Add $448 for walnut stock (disc. 1992).

Grading	100%	98%	95%	90%	80%	70%	60%

⚔ **PIII Rifle** — .308 Win. cal., 26 in. heavy barrel with diopter match sight bases, H-S Precision Pro-Series stock in black only. Importation began 1991.

Mfg.'s Sug. Retail	$3,162	$2,600	$1,875	$1,425	$1,050	$825	$700	$600

⚔ **PIV Urban Rifle** — .308 Win. cal., carbine variation with 16½ in. heavy barrel and flash hider, ABS Cycolac synthetic stock in green or black. Importation began 1991.

Mfg.'s Sug. Retail	$2,603	$2,250	$1,600	$1,275	$975	$775	$700	$650

⚔ **Jagd Match** — .222 Rem., .243 Win., or .308 Win. cal., hunting rifle that features checkered wood laminate stock, 23.6 in. barrel, Mannlicher sights, double set triggers, supplied with test target. Mfg. 1991-92.

	$1,550	$1,050	$950	$800	$675	$600	$540

Last Mfg.'s Sug. Retail was $1,550.

⚔ **Match Rifle** — .308 Win. only, 26 in. heavy barrel, brown ABS Cycolac stock, Walther Diopter sights, 8.6 lbs. Mfg. disc. 1992.

	$2,000	$1,500	$1,225	$925	$800	$700	$600

Add $437 for walnut stock.
Last Mfg.'s Sug. Retail was $2,306.

⚔ **Model SPG-T** — .308 Win. cal., Target model. New 1993.

Mfg.'s Sug. Retail	$3,695	$3,225	$2,850	$2,550	$2,200	$1,850	$1,500	$1,200

⚔ **Model SPG-CISM** — .308 Win. cal. New 1993.

Mfg.'s Sug. Retail	$4,295	$3,850	$3,275	$2,850	$2,450	$2,050	$1,700	$1,400

⚔ **Match UIT** — .308 Win. only, 10 shot steel mag., special single set trigger, free floating barrel, Diopter sights, raked bolt handle, 10.8 lbs.

Mfg.'s Sug. Retail	$3,995	$3,600	$3,150	$2,750	$2,400	$2,050	$1,700	$1,400

UIT stands for Union Internationale de Tir.

AUG S.A. — .223 Rem./5.56mm, semi-auto paramilitary design rifle, design incorporates use of advanced plastics, integral Swarovski scope, 20 in. barrel, bullpup configuration, 7.9 lbs.

Mfg.'s Sug. Retail	$1,375	$1,100	$900	$800	$725	$650	$575	$525

Add $595 for special receiver mfg. with Stanag.
This model is now available in limited quantities only to law enforcement agencies due to 1989 Federal legislation banning the importation for commercial sales.

⚔ **AUG S.A. Commercial** — similar to above, except values reflect price increases due to consumer demand after Federal legislation banned the commercial importation in 1989.

	$2,500	$2,150	$1,900	$1,700	$1,500	$1,250	$1,000

Last Mfg.'s Sug. Retail was $1,362 (1989).

MODEL MAADI AKM — 7.62 x 39 Russian, semi-auto, copy of Soviet AKM paramilitary design rifle, 30 shot mag., open sights.

	$1,500	$1,300	$1,150	$995	$850	$775	$700

STOCK, FRANZ
Germany.

SEMI-AUTO PISTOL — .22 LR. Mfg. in Germany 1920-1940.

	$275	$250	$225	$175	$125	$100	$75

SEMI-AUTO PISTOL — .25 ACP, .32 ACP. Mfg. in Germany 1920-1940.

	$275	$225	$175	$150	$100	$90	$80

STOEGER ARMS CORP.
Importer located in New York, NY.

Stoeger has imported a wide variety of firearms during the past seven decades. Most of these guns were good quality and came from known makers in Europe (some were private labeled). Stoeger carried an extensive firearms inventory of both house brand and famous European trademarks - many of which were finely made with beautiful engraving, stock work, and other popular special order features. As a general rule, values for Stoeger rifles and shotguns may be ascertained by comparing them with a known trademark of equal quality and cal./ga. Certain configurations will be more desirable than others (i.e. a Stoeger .22 caliber Mannlicher with double set triggers and detachable mag. will be worth considerably more than a single shot target rifle).

Perhaps the best reference works available on these older Stoeger firearms (not to mention the other trademarks of that time) are the older Stoeger catalogs themselves - quite collectible in their own right. It is advised to purchase these older catalogs if more information is needed on not only older Stoeger models, but the other firearms being sold at that time.

STONER RIFLE
Manufactured by Knight's Manufacturing Company located in Vero Beach, FL. Dealer and consumer direct sales.

Grading	100%	98%	95%	90%	80%	70%	60%

SR-25 STANDARD — 7.62 x 51mm cal., 20 in. barrel, AR-15 configuration, 5 or 20 shot detachable mag., less than 2 MOA guaranteed, non-glare finish, 8.8 lbs. New 1993.

Mfg.'s Sug. Retail	$2,495	$2,250	$1,900	$1,600	$1,300	$1,000	$850	$695

SR-25 Match — similar to SR-25 Standard, except has 24 in. free floating match barrel and flattop receiver, less than 1 MOA guaranteed, 10¾ lbs. New 1993.

Mfg.'s Sug. Retail	$2,495	$2,250	$1,900	$1,600	$1,300	$1,000	$850	$695

STREET SWEEPER
Manufactured by Sales of Georgia, Inc. located in Atlanta, GA.

STREET SWEEPER — 12 ga. only, 12 shot rotary mag., paramilitary configuration with 18 in. barrel, double action, folding stock, 9¾ lbs. New 1989.

No Mfg.'s Retail	$525	$450	$395	$365	$335	$300	$275

STURM, RUGER, & COMPANY
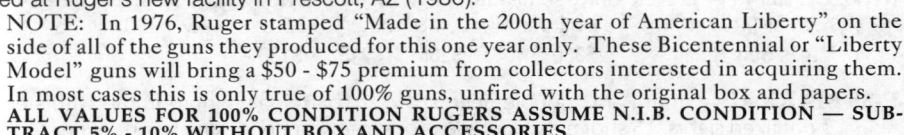

Manufactured in Southport, CT 1949 to date. "P" Series centerfire pistols and .22 Mark II pistols are being manufactured at Ruger's new facility in Prescott, AZ (1986).

NOTE: In 1976, Ruger stamped "Made in the 200th year of American Liberty" on the side of all of the guns they produced for this one year only. These Bicentennial or "Liberty Model" guns will bring a $50 - $75 premium from collectors interested in acquiring them. In most cases this is only true of 100% guns, unfired with the original box and papers. **ALL VALUES FOR 100% CONDITION RUGERS ASSUME N.I.B. CONDITION — SUBTRACT 5% - 10% WITHOUT BOX AND ACCESSORIES.**

PISTOLS: SEMI-AUTO

STANDARD MODEL — .22 LR, 9 shot, 4¾ in. or 6 in. barrel, blue, fixed sights, checkered wood or rubber grips. Mfg. 1951-1982.

	$140	$125	$115	$105	$95	$85	$75

Variations marked "Hencho En Mexico" are rare. NIB specimens have sold for $750. Standard Model was also available in a refined version called the Mark I. Barrel lengths were 5¼, 5½, and 6⅞ in. - add 10%.

Stainless Steel 1 of 5,000

	$450	$390	$325

Grading	100%	98%	95%	90%	80%	70%	60%

"RED EAGLE" — approx. 25,600 mfg. 1949-1952, most production occurred prior to Alexander Sturm's death (1951).

		100%	98%	95%	90%	80%	70%	60%
		$550	$500	$450	$375	$325	$275	$225

Distinguishable by recessed red enamel eagle in grips. Produced until early 1952. Serialized approx. 001 - 30,000 with Mark I Auto occupying blocks from 15,000 - 17,000 and 25,000 - 30,000.

MARK I TARGET — similar to Standard, but $5\frac{1}{2}$ in. heavy barrel, or 7 in. heavy tapered barrel, adj. rear sights, target sight. Mfg. 1951-1982.

	100%	98%	95%	90%	80%	70%	60%
	$190	$175	$160	$150	$140	$130	$120

Add 200%-300% if U.S. marked.
Add $100 for factory installed muzzle brake.

MARK II STANDARD — .22 LR, $4\frac{3}{4}$ or 6 in. barrel, checkered black Delrin synthetic grips, blue finish, 10 shot mag., approx. $2\frac{1}{4}$ lbs. Mfg. 1982 to date.

	100%	98%	95%	90%	80%	70%	60%
Mfg.'s Sug. Retail $252	$195	$155	$125	$115	$110	$100	$95

⚄ **Stainless Steel** — variation of the Mark II Standard.

	100%	98%	95%
Mfg.'s Sug. Retail $330	$260	$195	$165

Serial numbers start approx. at 18-00001.

MARK II TARGET — .22 LR, $5\frac{1}{4}$, $5\frac{1}{2}$ bull, $6\frac{7}{8}$ standard, or 10 in. bull barrel, single action, $2\frac{5}{8}$ - $3\frac{1}{4}$ lbs. depending on barrel.

	100%	98%	95%	90%	80%	70%	60%
Mfg.'s Sug. Retail $311	$240	$185	$150	$135	$120	$110	$100

Subtract $16 for 10 in. bull barrel.

⚄ **Stainless Steel** — stainless variation of the Mark II Target, includes choice of $6\frac{7}{8}$ bull, $6\frac{7}{8}$ slab side bull, or 10 in. bull barrel.

	100%	98%	95%
Mfg.'s Sug. Retail $389	$300	$245	$185

Subtract $16 for 10 in. bull barrel.

GOVERNMENT TARGET MODEL (MK678G) — commercial variation of the government training model without "U.S." markings, $6\frac{7}{8}$ in. bull barrel, adj. rear sight, blue finish, black plastic grips, 46 oz., individually test targeted. New 1987.

	100%	98%	95%	90%	80%	70%	60%
Mfg.'s Sug. Retail $357	$285	$240	$190	$170	$155	$140	$125

⚄ **Stainless Government Target Model** — $6\frac{7}{8}$ in. bull barrel only. New 1993.

	100%	98%	95%
Mfg.'s Sug. Retail $427	$340	$275	$215

Add $14 for $6\frac{7}{8}$ slab side bull barrel with scope rings and base.

MODEL 22/45 — .22 LR only, semi-auto single action, Zytel frame, stainless steel, $4\frac{3}{4}$, $5\frac{1}{4}$ regular (Target), or $5\frac{1}{2}$ bull barrel, 10 shot mag., 28-35 oz. New 1993.

	100%	98%	95%
Mfg.'s Sug. Retail $330	$265	$215	$185

P-85 MARK II — 9mm Para., double action, $4\frac{1}{2}$ in. barrel, aluminum frame with steel slide, 3-dot fixed sights, 15 shot mag., ambidextrous safety or decocking levers, oversized trigger, synthetic Xenoy grips, matte black finish, 2 lbs. Mfg. 1987-92.

	100%	98%	95%	90%	80%	70%	60%
	$335	$295	$265	$235	$215	$200	$185

Subtract $30 if without case and extra mag.
Last Mfg.'s Sug. Retail was $410.
A variation (P-89DAC) can be ordered in a decocking or double action only (P-89DAO) version at no extra charge.

⚄ **KP-85 Mark II Stainless Steel** — stainless variation of the P-85. Mfg. 1990-92.

	100%	98%	95%
	$350	$315	$280

Subtract $30 if without case and extra mag.
Last Mfg.'s Sug. Retail was $452.
A variation (P-89) can be ordered in a decocking or double action only version at no extra charge.

Grading	100%	98%	95%	90%	80%	70%	60%

P-89 — 9mm Para., improved variation of the P-85 Mark II, ambidextrous safety or decocker, blued finish. New 1992.

Mfg.'s Sug. Retail	$410	$335	$295	$265	$235	$215	$200	$185

P-89 Stainless — stainless variation of the P-89, also available in double action only. New 1992.

Mfg.'s Sug. Retail	$452	$375	$325	$295

MODEL K-P90 STAINLESS — .45 ACP cal., double action, 4½ in. barrel, oversized trigger, aluminum frame with stainless steel slide, 7 shot single column mag., decocking lever, with or without ambidextrous external safety, Xenoy grips, 3 dot fixed sights. New 1991.

Mfg.'s Sug. Retail	$489	$385	$335	$295

Available in a decocking (K-P90D) or double action version (K-P90C, disc. 1992) at no extra charge.

MODEL K-P91 STAINLESS — .40 S&W cal., similar to Model K-P90 Stainless, except is not available with external safety and has 11 shot double column mag. New 1992.

Mfg.'s Sug. Retail	$489	$385	$335	$295

This model is available in a decocking variation (K-P91D) or double action only (K-P91DAO).

REVOLVERS: OLD MODELS · SINGLE ACTION

Note: Some of the following Rugers are known as "Old Models" (mfg. 1963 - late 1972) and are instantly recognized by the three screws through the frame and the four clicks emitted upon cocking. They are now actively sought by collectors and some shooters who desire the smoother operation they afford.

SINGLE SIX REVOLVER — .22 LR, 4⅝, 5½, 6½, or 9½ in. barrel, fixed sights, rubber or wood grips, blue. Mfg. 1953-1972.

	$265	$195	$175	$130	$120	$110	$100

This model will command a premium with either a 4⅝ in. or 9½ in. barrel.

Flat loading gate — 5½ in. barrel only, approx. 61,000 mfg. from 1953-1957. Four variations.

	$300	$250	$200	$175	$165	$160	$150

.22 Mag. — 6½ in. barrel only, mfg. only three years, serial numbered between 300,000 - 342,000. Frame stamped Mag. only.

	$300	$250	$200	$175	$165	$160	$150

Add 40% for extra .22 LR cylinder.

Approx. 250 factory cased, engraved Single Six models have been mfg. Seldom seen and among the rarest of Ruger revolvers, prices have been reported at over $3,000 - $6,000.

SINGLE SIX CONVERTIBLE — similar to Single Six, except .22 LR and .22 WMR interchangeable cylinders, 4⅝, 5½, and 6½ in. barrels with 4⅝ in. being the rarest.

	$275	$200	$175	$150	$140	$115	$100

LIGHTWEIGHT SINGLE SIX — similar to Single Six, except alloy frame, 4⅝ in. barrel, made 1956-1958. 200,000 - 212,000 serial range, can have alloy or steel cylinder.

	$300	$250	$175	$170	$165	$160	$150

Add 100% if all blue with blue alloy cyl.

SUPER SINGLE SIX CONVERTIBLE — similar to Single Six Convertible, except adj. sights. Mfg. 1964-1972.

	$275	$250	$200	$155	$140	$120	$105

This model in 4⅝ in. barrel is the rarest with prices ranging between $1,500-$1,800 in blue finish, nickel finish specimens are trading for $2,000-$2,500.

Grading	100%	98%	95%	90%	80%	70%	60%

BLACKHAWK SINGLE ACTION — .357 Mag., .41 Mag., or .45 LC cals., this model is the 1962 variation, hooded rear sight, 4⅝ or 6½ in barrel.

	$350	$300	$250	$215	$180	$160	$140

Add $150 for brass grip frame (rare).
This model was also available in .30 carbine with a 7½ in. barrel — add 10%. Beware of non-factory brass grip frames on this model.

BLACKHAWK SINGLE ACTION "FLAT-TOP" — .357 Mag., 6 shot, 4⅝, 6½, and 10 in. barrel, flat top cylinder strap, adj. sight, blue, black rubber or walnut grips. Approx. 43,000 mfg. between 1955-1963.

	$400	$350	$300	$250	$210	$200	$175

Add 50% for 6½ in. barrel.
Add 150% for 10 in. barrel.

BLACKHAWK CONVERTIBLE — similar to Blackhawk, with extra cylinder, .357 and 9mm, and .45 Colt and .45 ACP cals.

	$395	$350	$295	$250	$225	$195	$175

Add $50 for .45 LC/.45 ACP combination.

Buckeye Special — .32-20/.32 H&R Mag., 6½ in. barrel.

	$425	$350	$295	$250	$220	$200	$180

BLACKHAWK FLAT-TOP .44 MAGNUM — similar to Blackhawk Flat-Top, except heavier frame and cylinder, .44 Mag., 6½, 7½, and 10 in. barrels. Approx. 28,000 mfg. between 1956-1963.

	$550	$485	$415	$360	$305	$230	$210

Add 100% for 7½ in. barrel.
Add 100% for 10 in. barrel.
Distinguishable by fluted cylinder and rounded trigger guard.

SUPER BLACKHAWK — .44 Mag., 6½ (rare) or 7½ in. barrel, larger frame and improved trigger guard, unfluted cylinder, adj. sights, walnut grips. Mfg. 1959-1972.

	$300	$250	$200	$195	$190	$185	$175

Rare early models in wood case will command 200-300% premium. White cardboard boxed (rarer) Super Blackhawks will command a 300-400% premium. 6½ in. barrel will command a 50%+ premium.

BEARCAT — .22 cal., 6 shot, 4 in. barrel, alloy frame, brass trigger guard, blue, wood grips with medallion, 17 oz. Mfg. 1958-1973.

	$300	$265	$225	$195	$180	$165	$150

Numerous variations exist within this model incorporating production changes.

SUPER BEARCAT — similar to Bearcat, except steel frame, made with brass trigger guard (early model), or blued steel guard, 25 oz. Mfg. 1971-1973.

	$330	$290	$250	$225	$200	$180	$165

HAWKEYE SINGLE SHOT — .256 Mag., single shot, cylinder replaced by rotating breech block, 8½ in. barrel, blue, walnut grips, adj. sight, very rare, approx. 3,300 mfg. Mfg. 1963-1964.

	$1,175	$1,000	$875	$700	$580	$475	$400

REVOLVERS: NEW MODELS - SINGLE ACTION

The following single actions are known as "New Models". They have 2 pins through the frame and cock without the clicks associated with the single action. The change over occurred as a result of desire for safety features. The "New Models" have a transfer bar similar to those found on modern double action revolvers and do not accidentally discharge if dropped. Manufacture started 1973.

Grading	100%	98%	95%	90%	80%	70%	60%

During certain years of manufacture, Ruger's changes in production on certain models (cals., barrel markings, barrel lengths, etc.) have created rare variations that are now considered premium niches. These areas of low manufacture will add premiums to the values listed below on standard models.

SUPER SINGLE SIX CONVERTIBLE — .22 LR, includes interchangeable .22 WMR cylinder, $4\frac{5}{8}$, $5\frac{1}{2}$, $6\frac{1}{2}$, or $9\frac{1}{2}$ in. barrel, similar to old Super Single Six, except has new interlocking safety mechanism previously described, adj. rear sight. Mfg. 1973-present.

Mfg.'s Sug. Retail	$281	$220	$180	$150	$130	$120	$110	$100

Subtract 15% if without extra .22 Mag. cylinder.

* **Stainless Steel** — similar to Super Single Six, except stainless steel construction, $4\frac{5}{8}$ (disc. 1992), $9\frac{1}{2}$ (disc.-rare), $5\frac{1}{2}$, or $6\frac{1}{2}$ in. barrel.

Mfg.'s Sug. Retail	$354	$280	$230	$180

Values for $4\frac{5}{8}$ or $9\frac{1}{2}$ in. barrel are approx. $575 if N.I.B.

* **Colorado Centennial Super Single Six** — 15,000 mfg. 1975 only, includes walnut case with medallion insert, stainless steel grip frame, $6\frac{1}{2}$ in. barrel, issue price was $250.

	$295	$245	$200

This model also was a U.S. Bicentennial gun as well as the Colorado Centennial Pistol. Most specimens do not have the Bicentennial statement on the barrel and are rarer with that stamping.

SINGLE SIX SSM — .32 H&R Mag. cal., $4\frac{5}{8}$, $5\frac{1}{2}$, $6\frac{1}{2}$ or $9\frac{1}{2}$ in. barrel, blue only, 32 oz. with $5\frac{1}{2}$ in. barrel.

Mfg.'s Sug. Retail	$281	$220	$170	$145	$135	$125	$115	$105

BLACKHAWK — .30 Carbine, .357 Mag., .41 Mag., and .45 LC cals., similar to old Model Blackhawk, with new interlocking safety mechanism, $4\frac{5}{8}$, $6\frac{1}{2}$, or $7\frac{1}{2}$ in. (.30 Carbine and .45 LC only) barrel. Mfg. 1973-present.

Mfg.'s Sug. Retail	$328	$255	$200	$170	$155	$145	$135	$125

Add $76 for .45 LC cal. with $4\frac{5}{8}$ or $7\frac{1}{2}$ in. barrel.

* **Blackhawk Convertible** — similar to New Model Blackhawk, except interchangeable cylinders, .357 Mag./9mm (current), .44 Mag./.44-40 (disc.), or .45 LC/.45 ACP (disc. 1985), $4\frac{5}{8}$ or $6\frac{1}{2}$ in. barrel only.

Mfg.'s Sug. Retail	$344	$270	$215	$185	$170	$160	$150	$140

* **Stainless Steel** — .357 Mag. or .45 LC (new 1993) cal., $4\frac{5}{8}$ or $6\frac{1}{2}$ in. barrel.

Mfg.'s Sug. Retail	$404	$335	$250	$210

300 Convertible pistols were made in this model - NIB prices have ranged $750-$850. New Model Blackhawks are serial numbered 32-00001 on up.

BLACKHAWK-SRM — similar to New Model Blackhawk, except is chambered for .357 Rem. MAXIMUM, $7\frac{1}{2}$ or $10\frac{1}{2}$ in. barrels available, target sights, 53 oz., 14,000 mfg. 1984 only - production suspended due to unresolvable engineering problems.

	$395	$360	$310	$275	$250	$225	$200

SUPER BLACKHAWK — .44 Mag., $5\frac{1}{2}$ (new 1987), $7\frac{1}{2}$ or $10\frac{1}{2}$ in. barrel, blued finish, walnut grips, similar to old model in appearance, but has new action. Mfg. 1973-present. The new model started with serial number 81-00001.

Mfg.'s Sug. Retail	$379	$290	$235	$200	$180	$170	$160	$150

* **Stainless Steel** — version of the Super Blackhawk.

Mfg.'s Sug. Retail	$414	$345	$280	$220

* **Stainless Hunter** — $7\frac{1}{2}$ in. ribbed barrel only, laminated wood grips, includes scope rings. New 1992.

Mfg.'s Sug. Retail	$480	$395	$300	$245

Grading	100%	98%	95%	90%	80%	70%	60%

VAQUERO — .45 LC only, 4⅝, 5½, or 7l/2 in barrel, color case hardened frame, blued steel grip frame, barrel, and cylinder, hammer block safety, patterned after the Colt SAA, fixed sights. New 1993.

Mfg.'s Sug. Retail $394	$325	$260	$230	$210	$190	$170	$160

BISLEY MODEL — .22 LR, .32 H&R Mag., .357 Mag., .41 Mag., .44 Mag., and .45 LC cals., incorporates Bisley features (flat-top frame, raked hammer, longer grip frame), 6½ (.22 LR or .32 H&R Mag. only) or 7½ in. barrel, fixed (disc. 1992) or adj. sights, available with fluted/unfluted or roll-marked/unmarked (disc.) cylinders, satin blue finish only, Goncalo Alves smooth grips. New 1986.

Rimfire Model

Mfg.'s Sug. Retail $329	$270	$215	$180	$170	$160	$150	$140

Centerfire Model

Mfg.'s Sug. Retail $391	$325	$285	$250	$225	$200	$180	$160

OLD ARMY PERCUSSION — .44 cal., black powder, 6 shot, 7½ in. barrel, single action, blued finish, walnut grips.

Mfg.'s Sug. Retail $379	$300	$220	$170	$150	$135	$120	$110

Add $100 for brass frame (disc.).
This model may have limited supply in 1993 since the manufacturer is temporarily out of stock.

Stainless Steel

Mfg.'s Sug. Retail $428	$340	$275	$210

This model may have limited supply in 1993 since the manufacturer is temporarily out of stock.

REVOLVERS: DOUBLE ACTION

During certain years of manufacture, Ruger's changes in production on certain models (cals., barrel markings, barrel lengths, etc.) have created rare variations that are now considered premium niches. These areas of low manufacture will add premiums to the values listed below on standard models.

SPEED SIX (MODELS 207, 208 and 209) — .38 Spl., .357 Mag., or 9mm cals., 2¾ or 4 in. barrel, fixed sights, checkered walnut grips, round butt, blued finish, some guns have factory speed hammer (no hammer spur). Mfg. 1973-present. Model 207 and 208 disc. 1988.

	$220	$205	$190	$170	$160	$150	$140

Add $40 for 9mm (Model 209 disc. 1984).
Last Mfg.'s Sug. Retail was $292.

Models 737 and 738 — stainless steel versions of Models 207 and 208, .357 Mag and .38 Spl. cals., 2¾ or 4 in. barrel. Disc. 1988.

	$280	$245	$220

Last Mfg.'s Sug. Retail was $320.

Model 739 — stainless steel, 9mm. Disc. 1984.

	$300	$250	$230

SECURITY SIX MODEL 117 — .357 Mag. cal., 6 shot, 2¾, 4 (heavy), or 6 in. barrel, adj. sights, checkered walnut grips, square butt. Mfg. 1970-1985.

	$250	$225	$195	$185	$160	$150	$140

Add $15 for target grips.
Last Mfg.'s Sug. Retail was $309.
500 of this model were mfg. for the California Highway Patrol during 1983 (.38 Spl. cal.) in stainless steel only. They are distinguishable by a C.H.P. marking. Premiums might exist in certain regions for this derivative.

Grading	100%	98%	95%	90%	80%	70%	60%

Model 717 — stainless steel version of Model 117. Disc. 1985.

	100%	98%	95%				
	$295	$255	$230				

Last Mfg.'s Sug. Retail was $338.

POLICE SERVICE SIX — .357 Mag, .38 Spl., and 9mm cals., blued finish only, square butt, fixed sights, checkered walnut grips.

Model 107 — .357 Mag, 2¾ or 4 in. barrel, fixed sights. Disc. 1988.

	100%	98%	95%	90%	80%	70%	60%
	$250	$220	$200	$190	$180	$170	$165

Last Mfg.'s Sug. Retail was $287.

Model 108 — .38 Spl., 4 in. barrel, fixed sights. Disc. 1988.

	100%	98%	95%	90%	80%	70%	60%
	$250	$220	$200	$190	$180	$170	$165

Last Mfg.'s Sug. Retail was $287.

Model 109 — 9mm, 4 in. barrel, fixed sights. Disc. 1984.

	100%	98%	95%	90%	80%	70%	60%
	$275	$230	$205	$195	$185	$180	$175

POLICE SERVICE SIX STAINLESS — stainless construction, 4 in. barrel only, fixed sights, checkered walnut grips.

Model 707 — .357 Mag., square butt. Disc. 1988.

	100%	98%	95%				
	$270	$235	$210				

Last Mfg.'s Sug. Retail was $310.

Model 708 — .38 Spl., square butt. Disc. 1988.

	100%	98%	95%				
	$270	$235	$210				

Last Mfg.'s Sug. Retail was $310.

GP-100 — .357 Mag. or .38 Spl. cal., 3 (new 1990), 4, or 6 (.357 Mag. only) in. standard or heavy barrel, strengthened design intended for constant use with all .357 Mag. ammunition, rubber cushioned grip panels with polished Goncalo Alves wood inserts, fixed (.38 Spl. only) or adj. sights with white outlined rear and interchangeable front, 6 shot, 35 - 46 oz. depending on barrel configuration. New 1986.

	Mfg.'s Sug. Retail	100%	98%	95%	90%	80%	70%	60%
	$397	$335	$275	$240	$220	$200	$185	$170

Add $17 for adj. rear sight (.357 Mag. cal., 4 or 6 in. barrel only).

GP-100 Stainless — similar to GP-100, except is stainless steel. New 1987.

	Mfg.'s Sug. Retail	100%	98%	95%				
	$430	$360	$290	$250				

Add $17 for adj. rear sight (.357 Mag. cal. only).

SP-101 STAINLESS — .22 LR (6 shot - new 1990), .22 Mag. (6 shot - mfg. 1992 only), .32 H&R (6 shot - new 1991), .38 Spl.(5 shot), 9mm Para. (5 shot - new 1991), or .357 Mag. (5 shot - new 1991) cal., 2¼, 3¹⁄₁₆, or 4 (new 1990) in. barrel, small frame variation of the GP-100 Stainless, fixed sights, approx. 27 oz. New 1989.

	Mfg.'s Sug. Retail	100%	98%	95%				
	$408	$340	$270	$240				

In 1993, Ruger introduced a .357 Mag./2¼ in. configuration featuring a spurless hammer, double action only.

SP-101 barrel lengths are as follows: .22 cal. is available in 2¼ or 4 in. standard or heavy barrel, .32 H&R is available in 3¹⁄₁₆ only, .38 Spl. is available in 2¼ or 3¹⁄₁₆ in. length only, 9mm Para. is available in 2¼ (new 1992) or 3¹⁄₁₆ in. only, and .357 Mag. is available in 2¼ or 3¹⁄₁₆ in. only.

Grading	100%	98%	95%	90%	80%	70%	60%

REDHAWK — .357 Mag. (disc. 1985), .41 Mag. (disc. 1992), or .44 Mag. cal., this is a redesigned stainless steel, large frame handgun, 5½ and 7½ in. barrel only, square butt, smooth hardwood grips, 52 oz.

	100%	98%	95%	90%	80%	70%	60%
Mfg.'s Sug. Retail $459	$385	$320	$285	$240	$215	$180	$165

Add $38 for scope rings.

⚮ **Redhawk Stainless** — stainless steel construction.

	100%	98%	95%	90%
Mfg.'s Sug. Retail $517	$430	$360	$300	

Add $41 for stainless scope rings.

SUPER REDHAWK STAINLESS — .44 Mag., 7½ or 9½ barrel, adj. rear sight, cushioned grip panels (GP-100 style), stainless steel scope rings, 53 oz. Delivery began in late 1987.

	100%	98%	95%	90%
Mfg.'s Sug. Retail $589	$490	$375	$285	

RIFLES: SEMI-AUTO

During certain years of manufacture, Ruger's changes in production on certain models (cals., barrel markings, barrel lengths, etc.) have created rare variations that are now considered premium niches. These areas of low manufacture will add premiums to the values listed below on standard models.

The Model 10/22 has been mfg. in a variety of limited production models including a multi-colored or green laminate wood stock variation (1986), a brown laminate stock (1988), a Kittery Trading Post Commemorative (1988), a smoke or tree bark laminate stock (1989), a Chief AJ Model, Wal-Mart (stainless with black laminated hardwood stock - 1990), etc. These limited editions will command premiums over the standard models listed below, depending on the desirability of the special edition.

10/22 STANDARD CARBINE — .22 LR, 10 shot rotary mag., 18½ in. barrel, birch or deluxe hand checkered walnut stock, folding rear sight. Mfg. 1964-present.

	100%	98%	95%	90%	80%	70%	60%
Mfg.'s Sug. Retail $202	$160	$135	$100	$80	$70	$60	$55

Add $20 for uncheckered walnut stock (mfg. 1987-1989).
Add $53 for deluxe checkered walnut stock.

⚮ **10/22 Standard Carbine Stainless** — similar to Standard Carbine, except has stainless barrel and birch stock. New 1992.

	100%	98%	95%
Mfg.'s Sug. Retail $236	$180	$150	$115

Only infrequently encountered, the G & G Special Edition (10/22 Deluxe Sporter Stainless) is priced in the $225 range.

10/22 SPORTER — similar to Standard, except Monte Carlo stock and beavertail forearm. Mfg. 1964-1971.

	98%	95%	90%	80%	70%	60%
	$170	$150	$140	$130	$120	$110	$100

10/22 CANADIAN CENTENNIAL — 2,000 mfg. in 1967.

	100%	98%	95%
	$375	$295	$225

Last Mfg.'s Sug. Retail was $100.

RUGER/REMINGTON CANADIAN CENTENNIAL MATCHED NO. 3 SET — includes a Remington Model 742 in .308 Win. cal. and a Ruger 10/22 Sporter with special commemoratice appointments, cased. 1,900 sets mfg. 1967 only.

	100%	98%	95%
	$650	$495	$425

⚮ **Ruger Canadian Centennial Matched No. 2 Set** — 70 sets mfg. 1967 only.

	100%	98%	95%
	$850	$695	$550

⚮ **Ruger Canadian Centennial Matched No. 1 Special Deluxe Set** — 30 sets mfg. 1967 only.

	100%	98%	95%
	$1,050	$895	$675

Grading	100%	98%	95%	90%	80%	70%	60%

10/22 INTERNATIONAL — similar to Standard, except full stock Mannlicher style. Mfg. 1964-1971.

	100%	98%	95%	90%	80%	70%	60%
	$475	$425	$350	$330	$300	$250	$225

MODEL 44 STANDARD CARBINE — .44 Mag., 4 shot mag., 18½ in. barrel, gas operated, folding sight, curved butt. Mfg. 1961-1985.

	100%	98%	95%	90%	80%	70%	60%
	$395	$350	$325	$295	$275	$250	$225

Last Mfg.'s Sug. Retail was $332.

※ **Deerstalker Model** — approx. 2,000 mfg. with "Deerstalker" marked on rifle until Ithaca lawsuit disc. manufacture (1962).

	100%	98%	95%	90%	80%	70%	60%
	$475	$425	$350	$285	$250	$220	$195

※ **25th Year Anniversary Model** — mfg. 1985 only, limited production, engraved.

	100%	98%	95%
	$450	$395	$350

Last Mfg.'s Sug. Retail was $495.

MODEL 44RS — similar to 44, but has aperture sight and swivels.

	100%	98%	95%	90%	80%	70%	60%
	$450	$395	$350	$295	$275	$250	$230

MODEL 44 SPORTER DELUXE — stocked version of 44 Standard. Mfg. until 1971.

	100%	98%	95%	90%	80%	70%	60%
	$475	$425	$365	$300	$275	$250	$230

MODEL 44 INTERNATIONAL — similar to Standard, except full length Mannlicher style stock. Mfg. until 1971.

	100%	98%	95%	90%	80%	70%	60%
	$750	$625	$500	$400	$350	$300	$275

MINI-14 — .223 Rem. or .222 (disc.) cals., 5 (standard mag. starting in 1989), 10, or 20 shot detachable mag., 18½ in. barrel, gas operated, aperture rear sight, military style stock, 6½ lbs. Mfg. 1976-present.

	100%	98%	95%	90%	80%	70%	60%
Mfg.'s Sug. Retail	$492	$410	$365	$335	$300	$265	$240	$215

Add $85 for folding stock (disc. 1989).
Due to 1989 Federal legislation and public sentiment, the Mini-14 is now being shipped with a 5 shot detachable mag. only.

※ **Mini 14 Stainless** — mini stainless steel version.

	100%	98%	95%	90%
Mfg.'s Sug. Retail	$542	$440	$375	$340

Add $85 for folding stock (disc. 1990).
Due to 1989 Federal legislation and public sentiment, the K Mini-14 is now being shipped with a 5 shot detachable mag. only.

MINI-14 RANCH RIFLE — .223 cal., 18½ in. barrel, folding rear sight, receiver cut for factory rings, similar to Mini-14, supplied with scope rings, approx. 6 lbs. 5 oz.

	100%	98%	95%	90%	80%	70%	60%
Mfg.'s Sug. Retail	$530	$430	$375	$340	$325	$300	$265	$240

Due to 1989 Federal legislation and public sentiment, the Mini-14 Ranch Rifle is now being shipped with a 5 shot detachable mag. only.

※ **Stainless Ranch Rifle** — stainless steel construction. New 1986.

	100%	98%	95%	90%
Mfg.'s Sug. Retail	$580	$460	$395	$350

Add $85 for folding stock (disc. 1990).
Due to 1989 Federal legislation and public sentiment, the Mini-14 Ranch Rifle is now being shipped with a 5 shot detachable mag. only.

MINI-THIRTY — 7.62 x 39mm Russian, 18½ in. barrel, 5 shot detachable mag., hardwood stock, includes scope rings, 7 lbs. 3 oz. New 1987.

	100%	98%	95%	90%	80%	70%	60%
Mfg.'s Sug. Retail	$530	$430	$375	$340	$325	$300	$265	$240

Grading	100%	98%	95%	90%	80%	70%	60%

Mini-Thirty Stainless — steel variation of the Mini-Thirty, new 1990.

Mfg.'s Sug. Retail	$580	$460	$395	$350			

XGI — .243 Win. or .308 Win. cal., similar to Mini-14, except has 20 in. barrel with vent. handguard over barrel, 5 shot mag., adj. folding aperture rear sight, 8 lbs. Mfg. 1985-1986 only.

		$495	$425	$375	$350	$325	$300	$285

Last Mfg.'s Sug. Retail was $425.

RIFLES: SINGLE SHOT

Note: All Ruger Rifles, except Stainless Mini-14, were made during 1976 in a "Liberty" version. Add $50 - $75 when in 100% in the original box condition.

During certain years of manufacture, Ruger's changes in production on certain models (cals., barrel markings, barrel lengths, etc.) have created rare variations that are now considered premium niches. These areas of low manufacture will add premiums to the values listed below on standard models.

NO. 1-A LIGHT SPORTER — similar to Standard, .243, .270, 7x57mm, .30-06 cals., 22 in. barrel, folding sight on quarter rib, ramp front sight, no rings, Alexander Henry forearm, front swivel in barrel band, 7¼ lbs. Mfg. 1966-present.

Mfg.'s Sug. Retail	$634	$450	$385	$325	$300	$275	$245	$215

The "A" suffix designates an Alexander Henry classic forearm with light barrel.

NO. 1-B STANDARD — falling block action with curved Farquharson lever, popular cals. include .218 Bee (limited mfg. 1993), .22 Hornet (special production 1993, limited mfg. beginning 1988), .22-250, .220 Swift, .223, .257 Roberts, .243, 6mm, .25-06, .270, .280, .30-06, 7mm Mag., .270 Wby. Mag. (new 1990), .300 Wby. Mag. (new in 1990), .300 Win. Mag., or .338 Win. Mag., 22 or 26 in. barrel, quarter rib with integral scope bases, supplied with rings and no sights, checkered stock and semi beavertail forearm. Mfg. 1966-present.

Mfg.'s Sug. Retail	$634	$475	$395	$335	$295	$260	$230	$200

The "B" suffix designates semi beavertail forearm with medium barrel and is available in all cals. under .375 H&H except 7x57mm.

NO. 1-RSI — .243 Win., .270 Win., 7x57mm, or .30-06 cal., features 20 in. barrel with full length Mannlicher stock, includes swivels and open sights, 7¼ lbs.

Mfg.'s Sug. Retail	$656	$485	$400	$330	$300	$270	$240	$210

NO. 1-V VARMINT — similar to No. 1-B Standard, except .22 PPC (limited mfg. 1993), .22-250, .220 Swift, .223, .243 (disc.), .25-06, 6mm, 6mm PPC (limited mfg. 1993), or .280 (disc.) cal., 24 or 26 (.220 Swift only) in. heavy barrel, without rib, target scope blocks, 9 lbs. Mfg. 1966-present.

Mfg.'s Sug. Retail	$634	$475	$395	$330	$300	$275	$245	$215

NO. 1-S MEDIUM SPORTER — similar to Light Sporter, only 218 Bee (limited mfg. 1993), 7mm, .45-70, .300 Win. Mag. and .338 Win. Mag. cals., 22 (.45-70 cal. only) or 26 in. medium barrel, open sights, 7¼ - 8 lbs.

Mfg.'s Sug. Retail	$634	$450	$385	$325	$300	$275	$245	$215

NO. 1-H TROPICAL RIFLE — similar to Medium Sporter, except .375 H&H, .404 Jeffery (limited mfg. 1993), .416 Rem. (limited mfg. 1993), .416 Rigby (new 1991), or .458 Win. Mag. cal., 24 in. heavy barrel, open sights, approx. 9 lbs.

Mfg.'s Sug. Retail	$634	$525	$450	$395	$360	$320	$290	$260

NO. 1 INTERNATIONAL — .243 Win., .30-06, .270 Win., and 7 x 57mm cals., lightweight 20 in. barrel, Mannlicher style forearm. Disc.

		$595	$525	$450	$400	$360	$320	$290

Grading	100%	98%	95%	90%	80%	70%	60%

NO. 3 CARBINE — same basic action as No. 1, except simpler lever design, stock uncheckered and very similar to .44 Carbine, made in .22 Hornet, .30-40 Krag, .45-70 (only cal. available 1986), .223, .44 Mag., and .375 Win. cals., 22 in. barrel, folding sight. Mfg. 1972-1987.

	100%	98%	95%	90%	80%	70%	60%
	$250	$215	$200	$180	$165	$145	$130

Add 25-35% for .223 cal.
Last Mfg.'s Sug. Retail was $284.

RIFLES: BOLT ACTION

Note: All Ruger Rifles, except Stainless Mini-14, were made during 1976 in a "Liberty" version. Add $50 - $75 when in 100% in the original box condition.

During certain years of manufacture, Ruger's changes in production on certain models (cals., barrel markings, barrel lengths, etc.) have created rare variations that are now considered premium niches. These areas of low manufacture will add premiums to the values listed below on standard models.

Earlier flat-bolt models (pre-1972) are desirable in the rarer cals. and will command premiums if 98%+ condition.

MODEL 77/22 — .22 LR only, 10 shot rotary mag., 20 in. barrel, all steel construction, 3 position safety, checkered walnut stock, blue finish, non-adj. trigger, available with either iron sights or plain barrel (no sights) with scope rings, 2.7 millisecond lock time on trigger, 6 lbs. 2 oz. New 1984.

Mfg.'s Sug. Retail	$402	$330	$295	$250	$230	$210	$190	$175

Add $22 for scope rings and iron sights.

⚞ **Model 77/22 Synthetic Stock** — similar to Model 77/22 except has matte black synthetic stock, approx. 6 lbs. New 1989.

Mfg.'s Sug. Retail	$353	$290	$235	$200	$185	$175	$165	$155

Add $22 for scope rings.

⚞ **Model 77/22 All-Weather Stainless** — similar to Model 77/22 except has stainless steel metal with matte black DuPont Zytel synthetic stock affording the lowest shooter maintenance, 5 lbs. 14 oz. New 1989.

Mfg.'s Sug. Retail	$397	$325	$295	$250

Add $22 for scope rings.

MODEL 77/.22 MAG. — similar to Model 77/22, except in .22 Win. Mag. cal., blue finish, checkered walnut stock. New 1990.

Mfg.'s Sug. Retail	$402	$330	$295	$250	$230	$210	$190	$175

Add $22 for scope rings.

⚞ **Model 77/.22 Mag. All-Weather Stainless** — similar to Model 77/.22 All-Weather Stainless, except in .22 Win. Mag. cal. New 1990.

Mfg.'s Sug. Retail	$419	$340	$295	$250

Add $26 for scope rings.

⚞ **Model 77/.22 Mag. Laminated** — similar to Model 77/.22 Mag., stainless steel, 9 shot mag., heavy barrel.

Mfg.'s Sug. Retail	$485	$385	$325	$275

MODEL 77R — .22-250, .220 Swift, 6mm (disc.), .243 (disc.), .257 Roberts, .25-06, .270, 7x57mm, 7mm-08 (disc.), 6.5 Rem. Mag. (scarce), 7mm Rem. Mag., .280 Rem., .308 (disc.), .30-06, .300 Win. Mag., or .338 Win Mag. cal., long or short action, blue finish, 5 shot mag., 3 shot in Mag. cals., 22 or 24 in. barrel, available with integral bases or round top, some models supplied with sights, stock is checkered walnut with red rubber butt plate, approx. 7 lbs. Mfg. 1968-1992.

	100%	98%	95%	90%	80%	70%	60%
	$420	$350	$295	$265	$245	$200	$200

Add 10-15% for .284 cal.
This model is encountered with or without the "R" suffix.
Last Mfg.'s Sug. Retail was $558.

Grading	100%	98%	95%	90%	80%	70%	60%

Model 77 RL — .22-250 (disc.), .257 Roberts, .270, or .30-06 cal., ultra light variation weighing 6 lbs., black forearm tip. Disc. 1992.

	$445	$375	$300	$270	$250	$225	$205

Last Mfg.'s Sug. Retail was $592.

Model 77 RS — .25-06 (disc.), 270, .30-06, 7mm Rem. Mag., 300 Win. Mag., .338 Win. Mag, .35 Whelen, or .358 Win. cal., similar to Model 77R, except has open sights. Disc. 1992.

	$460	$395	$315	$285	$265	$230	$210

Last Mfg.'s Sug. Retail was $616.

Model 77V Varmint — .22-250, .220 Swift, .243 (disc.), 6mm (disc.), .25-06, or .308 cal., 24 in. heavy barrel (26 in. on .220 Swift), drilled and tapped for target bases, approx. 9 lbs. Mfg. 1968-92.

	$430	$365	$300	$265	$245	$210	$200

Last Mfg.'s Sug. Retail was $574.

Model 77 RS African — similar to Model 77R, except in .458 Win. Mag. cal. Disc. 1991.

	$550	$475	$400	$365	$335	$315	$300

This model is supplied standard with a steel trigger guard and steel floor plate.
Last Mfg.'s Sug. Retail was $680.

Model 77 RSC — similar to Model 77 RS African, except has fiddleback walnut stock (C suffix), circa 1982.

	$675	$575	$500	$450	$400	$365	$335

Model 77 RLS — .243 (disc. 1989), .270, .30-06, and .308 cal. (disc. 1989), ultra light, 18½ in. barrel, open sights, 6 lbs. Mfg. 1987-92.

	$445	$375	$310	$280	$260	$230	$210

Last Mfg.'s Sug. Retail was $592.

Model 77 RSI — .22-250 (disc. 1991), .250-3000 (reintroduced 1990), .270, .30-06, .308 (disc. 1991), or 7mm-08 cal., international Mannlicher (full length stock) with 18½ in. barrel and open sights (includes scope rings), approx. 7 lbs. Disc. 1992.

	$470	$400	$325	$295	$265	$230	$210

Last Mfg.'s Sug. Retail was $623.

MODEL 77R MARK II SERIES — various cals. as listed below, evolutionary design of the Ruger Model 77R featuring slenderized proportioning, 3 position swing-back safety, new trigger, trigger guard and floor plate latch, stainless steel bolt with Mauser extractor design, 20 in. barrel, integral base receiver, hand checkered American walnut stock, approx. 6 lbs. 7 oz. New 1989.

Model 77R — .22-250 (new 1993), .223 (new 1992), .243 Win., .25-06 (new 1993), .257 Roberts (new 1993), .270 Win. (new 1993), .280 Rem. (new 1993), 6mm, 6.5 x 55 Swedish (limited mfg. 1993), 7 x 57mm (new 1993), .30-06 (new 1993), .308 Win., 7mm Rem. Mag. (new 1993), .300 Win. Mag. (new 1993), or .338 Win. Mag. (new 1993) cal., standard model of the new Mark II Series.

Mfg.'s Sug. Retail	$558	$445	$350	$295	$265	$245	$200	$200

Model 77 RL — .223, .243, .257 Roberts (new 1993), .270 Win. (new 1993), .30-06 (new 1993), or .308 cal., ultra light variation weighing approx. 6 lbs., black forearm tip. New 1990.

Mfg.'s Sug. Retail	$592	$475	$395	$300	$270	$250	$225	$205

Grading	100%	98%	95%	90%	80%	70%	60%

Model 77 RS — 6mm (disc.), .243, .25-06 (new 1993), .270 Win. (new 1993), .30-06 (new 1993), .308, 7mm Rem. Mag. (new 1993), .300 Win. Mag. (new 1993), or .338 Win Mag. (new 1993) cal., similar to Model 77R, except has open sights. New 1990.

Mfg.'s Sug. Retail	$617	$495	$415	$325	$285	$265	$230	$210

Model 77 RSI — .243 Win., .270 Win., .30-06, or .308 cal., international Mannlicher (full length stock) with 18½ in. barrel and open sights (includes scope rings), approx. 7 lbs. New 1993.

Mfg.'s Sug. Retail	$623	$500	$415	$325	$285	$265	$230	$210

Model 77 RLS — .243 or .308 cal., ultra light, 18½ in. barrel, open sights.   Mfg. 1990 only.

		$460	$375	$310	$280	$260	$230	$210

Last Mfg.'s Sug. Retail was $564.

Model K77 RP All-Weather Stainless — .223, .243, .270, .280 Rem. (new 1993), .30-06, .308, 7mm Rem. Mag., .300 Win. Mag., or .338 Win. Mag. (new 1992) cal., similar to Model 77R Mark II except has stainless steel metal with matte black DuPont Zytel synthetic stock affording the lowest shooter maintenance. New 1990.

Mfg.'s Sug. Retail	$558	$450	$360	$295				

Model K77VBZ — .22 PPC, .220 Swift, .22-250 Rem., .223 Rem., .243 Win., .25-06, .308 Win., or 6mm PPC cal., features laminated stock and heavy steel barrel. New 1993.

Mfg.'s Sug. Retail	$665	$530	$425	$325				

Model 77LR — .270 Win., .30-06, .300 Win. Mag., or 7mm Rem. Mag. cal., left hand variation of the Model 77R. New 1991.

Mfg.'s Sug. Retail	$558	$450	$360	$295	$265	$245	$200	$200

Model 77 RSM — .375 H&H or .416 Rigby cal., premium grade wood with hand cut checkering and ebony forend tip, integral barrel and sighting rib. New 1990.

Mfg.'s Sug. Retail	$1,550	$1,375	$1,100	$950	$825	$750	$675	$595

Model 77RS Express — .270 Win., .30-06, 7mm Rem. Mag., or .300 Win. Mag. cal., similar construction to Model 77RSM with premium grade wood and other materials. New 1991.

Mfg.'s Sug. Retail	$1,550	$1,375	$1,100	$950	$825	$750	$675	$595

SHOTGUNS

RED LABEL O/U — 12 or 20 ga., 3 in. chambers, various barrel lengths and choke (including skeet) combinations, boxlock, SST, 26 or 28 in. VR barrels, auto ejectors, choice of checkered pistol grip or English straight grip (new 1992) stock, stainless steel frame became standard on 12 ga. 1985 (not available in 20 ga.). Choke tubes became optional in 1988, standard 1990. Mfg. 1977-present.

Mfg.'s Sug. Retail	$1,158	$875	$725	$650	$595	$550	$500	$450

Subtract 15%-20% without choke tubes.
Earlier all-steel 12 ga. models (approx. 500 mfg.) with short field tubes could command 10%-15% premiums over values listed above to collectors interested in acquiring this variation. 20 ga. models are blue only.

Red Label English Field — similar to Red Label, except has English style straight grip stock. New 1992.

Mfg.'s Sug. Retail	$1,158	$875	$725	$650	$595	$550	$500	$450

Red Label Sporting Clays — 12 ga. only, features 30 in. separated barrels, Briley chokes with bores back bored to .744 in., ⅜ in. VR with middle bead, sporting clays recoil pad. New 1992.

Mfg.'s Sug. Retail	$1,285	$950	$795	$700	$625	$550	$500	$450

Sundance Industries, Inc.

SUNDANCE INDUSTRIES, INC.
Manufacturer located in Valencia, CA. Distributor sales only.

Grading	100%	98%	95%	90%	80%	70%	60%

MODEL A-25 SEMI-AUTO PISTOL — .25 ACP cal., semi-auto single action design, 2$^7/_{16}$ in. barrel, 7 shot mag., rotary safety, lower grip push button mag. release, satin nickel (disc.), bright chrome, or black teflon finish, choice of simulated pearl with different colors or grooved black grips, serrated slide. New 1989.

Mfg.'s Sug. Retail	$80	$65	$55	$45	$40	$35	$30	$25

MODEL BOA — similar to Model A-25, except has patented squeeze grip safety. New in 1990.

Mfg.'s Sug. Retail	$95	$75	$60	$50	$45	$40	$35	$30

MODEL D-22M DERRINGER — .22 LR cal., O/U design, double action, 3 in. barrels, black matte finish, 8 oz. Mfg. late 1993.
As this edition went to press, prices had yet to be established.

SURVIVAL ARMS, INC.
Manufacturer since 1990 located in Cocoa, FL. Distributor and dealer sales.

In 1990, Survival Arms, Inc. took over the manufacture of AR-7 Explorer rifles from Charter Arms located in Stratford, CT.

RIFLES

AR-7 EXPLORER RIFLE — .22 LR cal., takedown or normal wood stock, takedown barreled action stores in Cycolac synthetic stock, 8 shot mag., adj. sights, 16 in. barrel, black matte finish on AR-7, silvertone on AR-7S, camouflage finish on AR-7C.

Mfg.'s Sug. Retail	$150	$120	$100	$85	$75	$65	$55	$50

AR-25 — .22 LR cal., 16 in. barrel, black rifle with choice of wood (disc. 1992) or metal folding stock (includes 25 shot mag.).

Mfg.'s Sug. Retail	$200	$155	$120	$95	$80	$70	$60	$55

SVENDSEN, ERL, F.A. MFG. CO.
Previous manufacturer located in Itasca, IL.

DERRINGERS

LITTLE ACE — .22 S cal., patterned after the Ethan Allen "HIDE-A-WAY", bronze frame, blued steel barrel with case hardened hammer and spur trigger.

	$85	$75	$70	$65	$60	$55	$50

4-ACES — .22 S cal., 4 barrel derringer with rotating firing pin and spur trigger, bronze frame with blued rifled steel barrels and case hardened parts.

	$175	$150	$135	$120	$105	$90	$75

SYMES & WRIGHT LTD.
Manufacturer located in London, England. Direct sales only.

Symes & Wright Ltd. manufactures approx. 25 best quality shotguns and double rifles annually. This manufacturer should be contacted directly (see listing in Trademark Index) for more information, including a price quotation based on an individual special order.

T section

TALON

While advertised, a presidential import ban and related government actions prohibited importation of the Talon MKI Model (suggested retail was planned at $495).

TANNER, ANDRE

Manufacturer located in Switzerland. Currently imported and distributed by Mandall Shooting Supplies, Inc. located in Scottsdale, AZ. Previously imported by Osborne's located in Cheboygan, MI.

Tanner rifles are noted for their superior accuracy and limited production - less than 150 are mfg. each year.

Prices below reflect the recent devaluation of the U.S. dollar against some foreign currencies. While the manufacturer's suggested retails have gone up considerably, prices for used specimens (98% or less original condition) have not increased proportionately, and in some cases, have changed very little.

Grading	100%	98%	95%	90%	80%	70%	60%

300 METER MATCH RIFLE — 7.5 Swiss (special order) or 7.62mm cal. only, single shot, top-of-the-line 300 meter match rifle incorporating all match shooting features including deluxe palm rest, aperture sights.

Mfg.'s Sug. Retail	$4,900	$4,650	$3,995	$3,400	$2,775	$2,250	$1,900	$1,600

Subtract $190 for repeating model with similar features.
Add $100 for adj. cheek piece.

300 Meter UIT Standard — similar to Model 300 F, except is without palm rest and adj. Swiss butt plate, 10 shot mag., aperture sights.

Mfg.'s Sug. Retail	$4,700	$4,450	$3,850	$3,350	$2,750	$2,225	$1,925	$1,600

Add $100 for adj. cheek piece.

SUPERMATCH MODEL 50 M — .22 LR only, 50 meter free rifle, deluxe palm rest, adj. butt plate, thumbhole stock. Add $100 for adj. cheek piece.

Mfg.'s Sug. Retail	$3,900	$3,600	$3,200	$2,850	$2,450	$2,050	$1,800	$1,600

Add $100 for adj. cheek piece.

TAR-HUNT CUSTOM RIFLES, INC.

Custom rifled shotgun manufacturer located in Bloomsburg, PA. Direct sales only.

RSG-12/20 — 12 (RSG-12) or 20 (RSG-20, disc. 1992) ga., 2¾ in. chamber, bolt action shotgun featuring 21½ in. Shaw rifled slug barrel, 2 shot box mag., matte black finish, McMillan fiberglass stock with Pachmayr Decelerator rifle pad, receiver equipped for a top mounted scope, various options (including muzzle brake), 7¾ lbs. New 1991.

Mfg.'s Sug. Retail	$1,195	$1,175	$1,000	$875	$800	$750	$700	$650

Add $100 for muzzle brake.

RSG-SNIPER — 12 ga. only, similar to RSG-12, except has M-86 McMillan fiberglass black sniper stock with Pachmayr Decelerator pad.

Mfg.'s Sug. Retail	$1,595	$1,495	$1,250	$995	$875	$750	$700	$650

TAURUS INTERNATIONAL FIREARMS

Manufacturer located in Porto Alegre, Brazil. Currently imported by Taurus International Firearms located in Miami, FL since 1982. Distributor sales only.

Previous to 1990, this company's name was Taurus International Manufacturing, Inc. All Taurus products are backed by a lifetime repair policy.

Grading	100%	98%	95%	90%	80%	70%	60%

REVOLVERS: CURRENT MANUFACTURE

From 1990-1992, certain models became available with a Laser Aim LA1 sighting system that included mounts, rings (in matching finish), 110 volt AC recharging unit, 9 volt DC field charger, and high impact custom case.

MODEL 431 — .44 Spl. cal., 5 shot, 3 or 4 in. barrel, blue only, fixed sights. New 1993.

Mfg.'s Sug. Retail	$281	$220	$165	$135	$125	$115	$100	$90

‡ **Model 431 Stainlesss** — similar to Model 431, except stainless steel. New 1993.

Mfg.'s Sug. Retail	$351	$285	$215	$180

MODEL 441 — similar to Model 431, except also has 6 in. barrel, adj. sights. New 1993.

Mfg.'s Sug. Retail	$307	$235	$170	$140	$125	$115	$100	$90

‡ **Model 441 Stainless** — similar to Model 441, except is stainless steel. New 1993.

Mfg.'s Sug. Retail	$386	$315	$230	$190

MODEL 65 — .357 Mag./.38 Spl. cal., double action, 6 shot, 2½ (new 1993), 3 (disc. 1992) or 4 in. barrel, blue finish, checkered walnut grips, 34 oz.

Mfg.'s Sug. Retail	$264	$210	$155	$125	$115	$100	$90	$85

Add $15 for satin nickel finish (disc.).

‡ **Model 65 Stainless** — similar to Model 65, except in stainless steel. New 1993.

Mfg.'s Sug. Retail	$338	$275	$215	$185

MODEL 66 — .357 Mag./.38 Spl. cal., double action, 6 shot, 3 (disc. 1992), 2½ (new 1993), 4, or 6 in. barrel, checkered walnut grips, blue finish, adj. sights, 35 oz.

Mfg.'s Sug. Retail	$290	$225	$165	$135	$125	$115	$100	$90

Add $9 for 4 or 6 in. compensated (66CP) barrel (new 1993).
Add $15 for satin nickel finish (disc.).

‡ **Model 66 Stainless** — similar to Model 66, but in stainless steel. New 1987.

Mfg.'s Sug. Retail	$368	$295	$220	$185

Add $7 for 4 or 6 in. compensated (66CP) barrel (new 1993).

MODEL 669 — similar to Model 66 except has fully shrouded barrel, 4 or 6 in. barrel, blue finish, 37 oz.

Mfg.'s Sug. Retail	$301	$235	$175	$145	$125	$115	$100	$90

Add $10 for VR barrel (mfg. 1989-1992).
Add $400 for Laser Aim Sight (offered 1990-1992).
Add $7 for compensated (669PC) barrel (new 1993).

‡ **Model 669 Stainless** — similar to Model 669, but in stainless steel.

Mfg.'s Sug. Retail	$379	$310	$230	$190

Add $7 for compensated (669PC) barrel (new 1993).

MODEL 689 — similar to Model 669, except has VR.

Mfg.'s Sug. Retail	$313	$240	$180	$145	$125	$115	$100	$90

Add $400 for Laser Aim Sight (mfg. 1990-91 only).

‡ **Model 689 Stainless** — similar to Model 669, but in stainless steel.

Mfg.'s Sug. Retail	$392	$315	$235	$190

MODEL 73 — .32 Long cal. only, double action, 6 shot, 3 in. heavy barrel only, checkered walnut grips, 20 oz. Disc. 1992.

	$175	$150	$125	$115	$105	$95	$85

Add $20 for satin nickel finish.
Last Mfg.'s Sug. Retail was $223.

Grading		100%	98%	95%	90%	80%	70%	60%

MODEL 76 — .32 H&R cal., double action, 6 shot, 6 in. heavy barrel with solid rib, fully adj. rear sight, transfer bar safety, checkered hard wood grips, blue only, 34 oz. New 1991.

		100%	98%	95%	90%	80%	70%	60%
		$240	$190	$155	$130	$115	$100	$90

Last Mfg.'s Sug. Retail was $308.

MODEL 741 — .32 H&R Mag. cal., 6 shot, 3 or 4 in. barrel, blue only, adj. sights. New 1993.

Mfg.'s Sug. Retail	$254	$205	$155	$125	$115	$100	$90	$85

⚔ **Model 741 Stainless** — similar to Model 741, except is stainless steel. New 1993.

Mfg.'s Sug. Retail	$342	$275	$215	$185				

MODEL 761 — .32 H&R Mag. cal., 6 shot, 6 in. barrel, blue only, adj. sights. New 1993.

Mfg.'s Sug. Retail	$326	$250	$185	$145	$125	$115	$100	$90

MODEL 80 — .38 Spl. cal. only, double action, 6 shot, 3 or 4 in. barrel, checkered walnut grips, 30 oz.

Mfg.'s Sug. Retail	$229	$175	$135	$115	$105	$95	$85	$80

Add $15 for satin nickel finish (disc. 1992).

⚔ **Model 80 Stainless** — similar to Model 80, except stainless steel. New 1993.

Mfg.'s Sug. Retail	$282	$225	$165	$135				

MODEL 82 — .38 Spl. cal. only, double action, 6 shot, 3 or 4 in. heavy barrel, checkered walnut grips, 34 oz.

Mfg.'s Sug. Retail	$229	$175	$135	$115	$105	$95	$85	$80

Add $15 for satin nickel finish (disc.).

⚔ **Model 82 Stainless** — similar to Model 82, except stainless steel. New 1993.

Mfg.'s Sug. Retail	$282	$225	$165	$135				

MODEL 83 — .38 Spl. cal. only, double action, 6 shot, 4 in. heavy barrel, checkered walnut grips, adj. sights, 34½ oz.

Mfg.'s Sug. Retail	$241	$185	$140	$125	$115	$105	$95	$80

Add $13 for satin nickel finish (disc.).

⚔ **Model 83 Stainless** — similar to Model 83, except stainless steel. New 1993.

Mfg.'s Sug. Retail	$292	$230	$170	$135				

MODEL 85 — .38 Spl. cal. only, double action, 5 shot, 2 or 3 in. heavy barrel, checkered walnut grips, 21 oz.

Mfg.'s Sug. Retail	$251	$195	$150	$125	$115	$105	$95	$85

Add $20 for satin nickel finish (3 in. barrel only, disc. 1992).

⚔ **Model 85CH** — similar to Model 85, except has Brazilian hardwood combat grips and spurless hammer that fits flush with the frame, 2 in. barrel, double action only, 21 oz. New 1992.

Mfg.'s Sug. Retail	$251	$195	$150	$125	$115	$105	$95	$85

Add $64 for stainless steel variation.

⚔ **Model 85 Stainless** — version of Model 85.

Mfg.'s Sug. Retail	$315	$245	$190	$150				

MODEL 86 CUSTOM TARGET — .38 Spl. cal. only, double action target model, 6 shot, 6 in. barrel, specially contoured smooth walnut grips, adj. rear sight, blue only, 34 oz.

Mfg.'s Sug. Retail	$326	$255	$195	$160	$150	$140	$130	$120

This model is available in either single or double action with adj. counterweight and interchangeable front sight inserts.

Grading	100%	98%	95%	90%	80%	70%	60%

MODEL 94 — .22 LR cal., double action, 9 shot, 3 (new 1991) or 4 in. barrel, blue finish, adj. rear sight, target features, 25 oz. New 1989.

Mfg.'s Sug. Retail	$264	$200	$155	$135	$120	$105	$95	$85

⚹ **Model 94 Stainless** — version of Model 94. New 1990.

Mfg.'s Sug. Retail	$314	$250	$195	$150

MODEL 941 — .22 Mag. cal., 8 shot, 3 or 4 in. barrel, blue only, adj. sights. New 1993.

Mfg.'s Sug. Retail	$290	$225	$170	$140	$120	$105	$95	$85

⚹ **Model 941 Stainless** — similar to Model 941, except is stainless steel. New 1993.

Mfg.'s Sug. Retail	$346	$260	$195	$145

MODEL 96 TARGET SCOUT — .22 LR cal. only, double action, 6 shot, 6 in. barrel, checkered walnut grips, same features as Model 86, 34 oz.

Mfg.'s Sug. Retail	$326	$250	$190	$160	$150	$140	$130	$120

PISTOLS: SEMI-AUTO

From 1990-1992, certain models became available with a Laser Aim LA1 sighting system that included mounts, rings (in matching finish), 110 volt AC recharging unit, 9 volt DC field charger, and high impact custom case.

Add approx. $30 for the Deluxe Shooter's Pack option (includes extra mag. and custom case) on the 92, 99, 100, and 101 Series.

PT-22 — .22 LR cal., single or double action operation, tip-up 2¾ in. barrel, 9 shot mag., fixed sights, ambidextrous safety, blue finish, smooth hardwood grips, 12.3 oz. New 1992.

Mfg.'s Sug. Retail	$182	$150	$125	$110	$100	$90	$80	$70

PT-25 — .25 ACP cal., similar to PT-22, except has 8 shot mag. New 1992.

Mfg.'s Sug. Retail	$182	$150	$125	$110	$100	$90	$80	$70

PT-58 — .380 ACP, similar to PT-99AF, except in .380 ACP cal., 4 in. barrel, 12 shot mag. New 1988.

Mfg.'s Sug. Retail	$423	$330	$270	$235	$215	$200	$190	$180

Add $31 for satin nickel finish.

⚹ **PT-58 Stainless** — similar to PT-58, except is stainless steel. New 1992.

Mfg.'s Sug. Retail	$481	$390	$305	$265

PT-91AF — .41 Action Express cal., action similar to PT-92AF, except is in .41 AE cal., 10 shot mag., 34 oz. Imported 1990 only.

		$365	$300	$250	$225	$200	$190	$180

Add $36 for satin nickel finish.
Add $25 for shooter's pack (includes custom case and extra mag.).
Last Mfg.'s Sug. Retail was $446.

PT-92AF — 9mm Para., semi-auto double action, design similar to Beretta Model 92 SB-F, exposed hammer, 5 in. barrel, 15 shot mag., smooth Brazilian walnut grips, blue or nickel finish, fixed sights, 34 oz.

Mfg.'s Sug. Retail	$473	$385	$300	$250	$225	$200	$190	$180

Add $38 for satin nickel finish.
Add $415 for Laser Aim Sight (disc. 1991).
Add $28 for shooter's pack (includes custom case and extra mag.).

⚹ **PT-92SS (Stainless Steel)** — similar to PT-92AF, except is fabricated from stainless steel. New 1992.

Mfg.'s Sug. Retail	$538	$435	$350	$295

Grading	100%	98%	95%	90%	80%	70%	60%

⚔ **PT-92AFC** — compact variation of the Model PT-92AF, 4 in. barrel, 13 shot mag., fixed sights.

Mfg.'s Sug. Retail	$473	$385	$300	$250	$225	$200	$190	$180

Add $38 for satin nickel finish.

⚔ **PT-92AFC Stainless** — similar to PT-92AFC, except stainless steel. New 1993.

Mfg.'s Sug. Retail	$538	$435	$350	$295

⚔ **PT-92AF Lew Horton Special Edition** — 9mm Para., matte satin finished frame with high polish stainless steel slide, blue barrel, hammer, trigger, mag. release, safety, and slide release. 250 mfg. in 1990 only.

	$395	$350	$295	$250	$225	$210	$190

Last Mfg.'s Sug. Retail was $454.

PT-99AF — similar to Model PT-92AF, except has adj. rear sight.

Mfg.'s Sug. Retail	$512	$400	$325	$270	$235	$210	$200	$190

Add $42 for satin nickel finish.
Add $28 for shooter's pack (includes custom case and extra mag.).
This action is similar to the Beretta Model 92SB-F.

⚔ **PT-99SS (Stainless Steel)** — similar to PT-99AF, except is fabricated from stainless steel. New 1992.

Mfg.'s Sug. Retail	$582	$475	$395	$325

PT-908 — 9mm Para., compact version of the PT-92 with 3.8 in. barrel and 8 shot mag., fixed sights, blue or nickel finish. New 1993.

Mfg.'s Sug. Retail	$473	$385	$295	$250	$225	$200	$190	$180

⚔ **Model PT-908 Stainless** — similar to Model PT-908, except is stainless steel. New 1993.

Mfg.'s Sug. Retail	$538	$445	$375	$300

PT-100 — .40 S&W cal., semi-auto, standard double action, 5 in. barrel, 11 shot mag., safeties include ambidextrous manual, hammer drop, inertia firing pin, and chamber loaded indicator, choice of blue, satin nickel or stainless steel finish, smooth Brazilian hard wood stocks, 34 oz. New 1992.

Mfg.'s Sug. Retail	$482	$390	$300	$250	$225	$200	$190	$180

Add $39 for satin nickel finish.

⚔ **PT-100SS (Stainless Steel)** — similar to PT-100, except is fabricated from stainless steel. New 1992.

Mfg.'s Sug. Retail	$547	$450	$375	$300

PT-101 — similar to PT-100, except has adj. sights. New 1992.

Mfg.'s Sug. Retail	$522	$420	$320	$265	$235	$200	$190	$180

Add $42 for satin nickel finish.
Add $70 for stainless steel variation.

TECHNI-MEC

Manufacturer located in Brescia, Italy (owned by Isidoro Rizzini). Limited current importation and distribution by Mandall Shooting Supplies, Inc. located in Scottsdale, AZ.

SHOTGUNS

Techni-Mec manufactures a wide variety of shotguns including O/Us and single shots in assorted models. Most models, however, are not being imported into the U.S. at this time. The models listed below are exclusively imported by Mandall Shooting Supplies, Inc. For more information on the complete Techni-Mec model line-up, please contact the factory in Italy directly (please refer to the Trademark Index in the back of this text).

Grading	100%	98%	95%	90%	80%	70%	60%

MODEL S 610 — 10 ga., 3$\frac{1}{2}$ in. Mag., O/U boxlock action, double underlug blocking, 32 in. VR barrels, SST, ejectors, checkered walnut stock and forearm. Importation began 1991.

Mfg.'s Sug. Retail	$1,000	$925	$825	$750	$675	$595	$525	$450

MODEL SPL 640 — 12, 16, 20, 28, or .410 ga., folding O/U design, DT, 26 in. VR barrels.

Mfg.'s Sug. Retail	$500	$465	$390	$325	$260	$215	$180	$160

TERRIER ONE
Previously distributed by Serrifile located in Lancaster, CA.

TERRIER ONE — .32 S&W cal. revolver, double action, 2$\frac{1}{4}$ in. barrel, 5 shot, nickel plated, 17 oz. Mfg. 1984-87.

		$45	$35	$30	$25	$25	$25	$25

Last Mfg.'s Sug. Retail was $55.

TEXAS GUNFIGHTERS
Importer located in Irving, TX.

SHOOTIST EDITION SINGLE ACTION — .45 LC cal., patterned after the Colt SAA, 4$\frac{3}{4}$ in. barrel, nickel plated blackpowder frame, one piece walnut grips, mfg. by A. Uberti of Italy. New 1988.

⚁ **Standard Model** — 1,000 total mfg., cased.

Mfg.'s Sug. Retail	$649	$649	$525	$440

⚁ **1 of 100 Edition** — 100 total mfg., fully engraved, genuine mother-of-pearl one piece grips, cased.

Mfg.'s Sug. Retail	$1,395	$1,395	$1,050	$775

This model is also supplied with an extra set of walnut grips.

TEXAS LONGHORN ARMS, INC.
Manufacturer located in Richmond, TX.

REVOLVERS

SINGLE-ACTION — various cals., patterned after Colt's S.A.A., except the ejection port has been moved to left side of frame enabling left-hand loading, mfg. from 4140 steel, Pope rifled barrels, 1 piece grips, adj. trigger, case-hardened and blued, entirely hand-made, supplied with lifetime warranty. Mfg. 1,000 of each model.

⚁ **Texas Border Special** — .44 Spl. or .45 LC cal., 3$\frac{1}{2}$ (disc.) or 4 in. barrel, 1-piece birdshead grip.

Mfg.'s Sug. Retail	$1,500	$1,500	$1,300	$1,000

⚁ **South Texas Army** — .357 Mag., .44 Spl., or .45 LC cal., 4$\frac{3}{4}$ in. barrel, 1 piece regular walnut stock.

Mfg.'s Sug. Retail	$1,500	$1,500	$1,300	$1,000

⚁ **Texas Flattop Target** — .32-20, .357 Mag., .44 Mag./Spl., or .45 LC cal., flat top frame, 7$\frac{1}{2}$ in. barrel.

Mfg.'s Sug. Retail	$1,500	$1,500	$1,300	$1,000

⚁ **Grover's Improved Number Five** — .44 Mag. or .45 LC cal., 5$\frac{1}{2}$ in. target barrel, 1,200 mfg. serial numbered K1-K1200. This variation incorporates Elmer Keith's 1926 designs including No. 5 lockwork, base pin and latch, and grip straps. New 1988.

Mfg.'s Sug. Retail	$985	$985	$725	$595

Grading	100%	98%	95%	90%	80%	70%	60%

SPECIAL EDITIONS — in addition to the models listed above, Texas Longhorn Arms also manufactures various special editions, including a Standard Model Set (3 guns, 1 of each above) retailing at $5,750, an Engraved Special Edition Set (3 gun set) retailing for $7,650, a Texas Sesquecentennial Commemorative retailing for $2,500, and a Mason Commemorative retailing for $1,500. For more information on these limited editions, please contact the manufacturer directly (see Trademark Index).

PISTOLS

JEZEBEL MODEL — .22 LR or .22 Mag. cal., single shot, tip-up action, stainless steel, 6 in. barrel, walnut stock and forearm, right or left hand action, 17 oz. Mfg. 1987-1992.

	$200	$160	$135				

Last Mfg.'s Sug. Retail was $200.

THOMAS
Manufactured by Alexander James Ordnance, Inc. located in Covina, CA.

THOMAS SEMI-AUTO PISTOL — .45 ACP cal., semi-auto, double action only - hammerless, 3½ in. barrel, 6 shot mag., chrome or high polish blue finish, checkered synthetic grips, 36 oz. Mfg. circa late '70s.

	$750	$695	$625	$550	$495	$450	$395

Last Mfg.'s Sug. Retail (circa 1979) was $375 blue, $425 chrome.

THOMPSON CARBINES
See Auto Ordnance section of this book.

THOMPSON/CENTER ARMS
Manufacturer located in Rochester, NH from 1967 to date.

PISTOL: SINGLE SHOT

Caution: older and newer TC components do not interchange safely. Although parts will fit, they may not function properly. Special ordering of barrels, frames, and calibers started in 1988.

CONTENDER — .22 LR, .22 WMR, 5mm Rem., .218 Bee, .22 Hornet, .22 Jet, .221 Fireball, .222, .25-35, .256 Mag., .30 Carb., .30-30, .38 Spl., .357 Mag., .17 Ackley Bee, .17 Bumblebee, .17 Hornet, .17K Hornet, .17 Rem., .30 Herrett, .357 Herrett, .357-44 B&D, 7 x 30 Waters, .32 H&R Mag., .32-20 Win., 6mm TCU, 6.5mm TCU, or 9mm Para. cal., barrels are interchangeable, 8¾ (disc.), 10, or 14 in. barrel, hinged break open, trigger guard, action lever, blue, 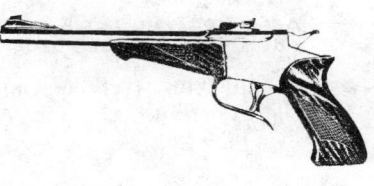 .44, .357 Mag., and .45 Colt available with detachable choke for hot shot cartridges, VR, 10 in. barrel available, 10 in. bull barrel, adj. sights, checkered walnut grip and forearm. The Contender action is in its third variation and a wide variety of changes have been made to grips, stocks, sights, etc. since 1967. These production variances do not necessarily add premiums to values listed below.

⚡ **Stainless Steel** — various cals., 10 in. bull barrel. New 1993.

	Mfg.'s Sug. Retail	$445	$340	$270	$200			

Add $5 for .45/.410 with adj. sights, $10 for same with VR.

⚡ **Octagon Barrel** — .22 LR, .22 Mag., .22 Hornet, .22K Hornet, .222 Rem., or .357 Mag. cal., 10 in. barrel.

	Mfg.'s Sug. Retail	$415	$320	$245	$195	$180	$170	$160	$150

Thompson/ Center Arms, cont.

Grading	100%	98%	95%	90%	80%	70%	60%

⁑ **Match Grade Barrel** — .22 LR cal. only, choice of 10 or 14 in. match barrel. New 1992.

Mfg.'s Sug. Retail	$425	$325	$250	$195	$180	$170	$160	$150

Add $10 for 14 in. barrel.

⁑ **Bull Barrel** — available in 15 cals. between .22 LR and .45 Win. Mag., 10 in. round barrel only.

Mfg.'s Sug. Retail	$415	$320	$245	$195	$180	$170	$160	$150

Add $5 for .44 Mag/.45 Colt with internal chokes.

⁑ **Armour Alloy II Bull Barrel** — 7 cals. between .22 LR and .30-30, similar to regular Bull Barrel, except has Armour Alloy II satin finish which is harder than stainless steel. Mfg. 1986-89.

		$320	$285	$230			

Add $5 for .45 Colt/.410 ga. internal choke.
Last Mfg.'s Sug. Retail was $415.

⁑ **Vent. Rib** — .357 Mag.(disc.), .44 Mag.(disc.) or .45 Colt/.410 cal., 10 in. VR barrel only, adj. front and flip up rear sight, internal choke became standard in 1985.

Mfg.'s Sug. Retail	$435	$335	$260	$200	$190	$180	$165	$155

Extra barrels (14 available) without VR — $205, or with VR — $225.

⁑ **Armour Alloy Vent. Rib** — .45/.410 internal choke, has Armour Alloy II satin finish which is harder than stainless steel. New 1986.

		$350	$295	$230			

Last Mfg.'s Sug. Retail was $435.

CONTENDER SUPER — 13 cals. available from .17 Rem. - .45 Win. Mag. (disc.), 14 or 16 in. bull barrel only, special grips, beavertail forearm, adj. sight, 3½ lbs.

Mfg.'s Sug. Retail	$425	$325	$250	$200	$190	$180	$165	$155

Add $5 for 16 in. barrel.
Add $30 for .17 Rem. cal. (new 1992).
Add $25 for .45-70 cal. in 16 in. barrel only with muzzle brake (new 1992).
Add approx. $210 per extra barrel.
Add $30 for VR barrel (.45 ACP/.410 ga. only).
Thompson Center will also make special order guns in different cals. other than those listed above. If factory work, these pistols will be worth a premium.

⁑ **Stainless Contender Super** — various cals., choice of 14 or 16 in. barrel. New 1993.

Mfg.'s Sug. Retail	$455	$345	$260	$210			

Add $5 for 16 in. barrel.
Add $20 for .45-70 bull barrel with Muzzle Tamer.

⁑ **Armour Alloy II Super Contender** — 5 cals. between .22 LR and 7mm, similar to regular Super Contender, except has Armour Alloy II satin finish which is harder than stainless steel. Mfg. 1986-89.

		$355	$295	$240			

Extra Armour Alloy II Bull Barrels were available for $195+.
Last Mfg.'s Sug. Retail was $425.

CONTENDER HUNTER — .223 Rem., .7-30 Waters, .30-30, .35 Rem., .357 Rem. Max., .375 Win. Mag. (new 1992), .44 Mag., or .45-70 cal., special 12 or 14 (new 1992) in. barrel with muzzle brake, 2.5X power scope with lighted recticle, walnut grip has nonslip rubber insert to cushion recoil, includes studs, swivels, sling, and deluxe carrying case, approx. 4 lbs. New 1990.

Mfg.'s Sug. Retail	$615	$600	$525	$465	$410	$360	$315	$275

This model is also available in a Hunter Package (14 in. barrel only) - add $10.

Grading	100%	98%	95%	90%	80%	70%	60%

CONTENDER 25TH ANNIVERSARY — .22 LR cal. only, 10 in. octagon barrel, laser etched anniversary logo on receiver sides and barrel, checkered stock and forearm, limited mfg. in 1992 only.

	100%	98%	95%	90%	80%	70%	60%
	$610	$535	$465	$410	$360	$315	$275

Last Mfg.'s Sug. Retail was $700.

⚔ **Contender 25th Anniversary Cased Set** — cased set with 4 barrels including .22 LR, .22 Mag., .22 Jet, .22 Hornet, and .38 Spl., 50 sets mfg. 1992 only.

	100%	98%	95%	90%	80%	70%	60%
	$1,850	$1,550	$1,225	$1,050	$900	$775	$650

Last Mfg.'s Sug. Retail was $1,975.

RIFLES

CONTENDER CARBINE — available in 15 cals. between .17 Rem. and .44 Rem. Mag., also .410 ga. (3 in.), Contender action with pistol grip full stock and forearm, 21 in. interchangeable barrel, drilled for scope mounts, iron sights standard. New 1986.

	100%	98%	95%	90%	80%	70%	60%
Mfg.'s Sug. Retail $460	$365	$295	$245	$215	$190	$175	$160

Add $30 for .17 Rem. cal.
Add $20 for .410 ga. barrel.
Add approx. $205 per extra barrel.
Add $10 for match grade .22 LR barrel.
Subtract $35 for Youth Model (16¼ in. barrel w/o VR).
Add $175 for Survival Carbine System (includes Rynite stock, 16¼ .223 Rem. barrel, extra .45 Colt/.410 barrel, and soft camo cordura case).

⚔ **Rynite Contender Carbine** — similar to above, except has Rynite stock and forend. New 1990.

	100%	98%	95%	90%	80%	70%	60%
Mfg.'s Sug. Retail $425	$335	$270	$220	$195	$180	$165	$155

Add $30 for .17 Rem. cal.
Add $10 for match grade barrel.
Add $25 for 21 in. VR smooth bore .410 ga. barrel.

⚔ **Thompson Carbine Stainless** — various cals., 21 in. barrel, choice of walnut or Rynite stock. New 1993.

	100%	98%	95%	90%	80%	70%	60%
Mfg.'s Sug. Retail $455	$355	$280	$225				

Add $35 for walnut stock.
Add $20 for .10 smooth bore barrel with screw-in full choke.
This model is also available in a Youth Model with walnut stock at no extra charge.

HUNTER RIFLE MODEL — single shot, top lever break open action w/interchangeable barrels, .22 Hornet, .223, .22-250, .243, .270, 7mm, .30-06, .308 Win. .375 H&H (new 1992), or .416 Rem. Mag. (new 1992) cal., 23 in. barrel, 6 lbs. 14 oz., checkered walnut stock, choice of medium or light sporter weight barrel. New 1983 and improved in 1987. Available in left-hand at no extra charge. Disc. 1992.

	100%	98%	95%	90%	80%	70%	60%
	$500	$415	$350	$295	$265	$240	$220

Add $20 for .375 H&H or .416 Rem. Mag. cal.
Add approx. $275 per extra rifle barrel.
Last Mfg.'s Sug. Retail was $595.

⚔ **Hunter Deluxe Rifle Model** — similar to Hunter Model, except features double triggers and upgraded walnut stock and forearm. Mfg. 1992 only.

	100%	98%	95%	90%	80%	70%	60%
	$550	$450	$375	$325	$285	$250	$225

Add $20 for .375 H&H or .416 Rem. Mag. cal.
Last Mfg.'s Sug. Retail was $675.

Grading	100%	98%	95%	90%	80%	70%	60%

Hunter Shotgun Model — same action as Hunter Rifle, except is supplied with 12 ga. barrel (field choke with 3½ in. chamber or slug with 3 in. chamber and iron sights) or 10 ga. barrel (3½ in. chamber). Disc. 1992.

| | | $500 | $415 | $350 | $295 | $265 | $240 | $220 |

Add $275 per additional shotgun barrel.
Last Mfg.'s Sug. Retail was $595.

TCR '83 ARISTOCRAT — similar to Hunter Model, except stock has cheek piece and forearm is checkered, stainless steel double set triggers. Disc. 1986.

| | | $425 | $370 | $345 | $320 | $300 | $280 | $260 |

Add $175 for each additional barrel(s) (including 12 ga. slug).
Last Mfg.'s Sug. Retail was $475.

THUNDER-FIVE
Shotgun revolver mfg. by Mil, Inc. located in Piney Flats, TN. Distributed by C.L. Reedy & Associates, Inc. located in Melbourne, FL. Dealer and direct consumer sales.
While previously advertised as the Spectre Five (not mfg.), this firearm has been re-named the Thunder Five.

THUNDER-FIVE — .45 LC cal./.410 ga. with 3 in. chamber, double action, unique 5 shot revolver design (double action) permits shooting .45 LC or .410 shotshells interchangeably, 2 in. rifled barrel, phosphate finish, external ambidextrous hammer block safety, internal draw bar safety, combat sights, hammer, trigger, and trigger guard, Pachmayr grips, includes padded plastic carrying case, 48 oz., serialization starts at 1,101. New 1992.

| Mfg.'s Sug. Retail | $499 | $450 | $400 | $375 | $350 | $325 | $300 | $275 |

TIKKA
O/U shotguns are currently manufactured by Armi Marocchi located in Italy. Rifles are currently manufactured by Sako, Ltd. located in Riihimaki, Finland. Previously manufactured by Oy Tikkakoski Ab, of Tikkakoski Finland (pre-1989). Currently imported by Stoeger Industries located in South Hackensack, NJ.
Also see listings under Ithaca LSA for older models.

RIFLES: BOLT ACTION

NEW GENERATION RIFLE — .22-250 Rem., .223 Rem., .243 Win., .270 Win., .30-06, .308 Win., 7mm Rem. Mag., .300 Win. Mag., or .338 Win Mag. cal., 22½ (non-Mag.) or 24½ (Mag. cals.) in. barrel, detachable 3 (standard) or 5 (optional) shot mag., forged and milled action in two lengths, checkered walnut stock, 7-7 ½ lbs. Sako mfg. began in 1989.

| Mfg.'s Sug. Retail | $835 | $725 | $600 | $550 | $500 | $450 | $400 | $360 |

Add $25 for Mag. cals.
Cal.'s .22-250 Rem., .308 Win., and .300 Win. Mag. were introduced in late 1989.

PREMIUM GRADE RIFLE — same cals. as New Generation Rifle, stock is select walnut with roll-over cheek-piece and rosewood pistol grip cap and forend tip, high polished barrel blue. Importation began 1989.

| Mfg.'s Sug. Retail | $1,030 | $860 | $715 | $600 | $550 | $500 | $450 | $400 |

Add $40 for Mag. cals.

VARMINT RIFLE — .22-250, .223, .243 Win., or .308 Win. cal., 24½ in. heavy barrel, no sights. New in 1991.

| Mfg.'s Sug. Retail | $1,090 | $895 | $750 | $625 | $550 | $500 | $450 | $400 |

WHITETAIL/BATTUE RIFLE — .270 Win., .30-06, .308 Win., 7mm Rem. Mag., .300 Win. Mag., or .338 Win. Mag. cal., 20½ in. barrel, open sights on raised rib. New in 1991.

| Mfg.'s Sug. Retail | $860 | $745 | $625 | $575 | $500 | $450 | $400 | $360 |

Add $35 for Mag. cals.

Grading	100%	98%	95%	90%	80%	70%	60%

O/U COMBINATIONS (MODEL 412S)

Previously manufactured in Jyvaskyla, Finland. In 1989, under a joint venture agreement made in Italy, the 412 O/U shooting system is now being manufactured in Italy. Older models may be found in the Valmet trademark section of this text.

When current inventory levels are depleted, the Model 412 will no longer be imported.

MODEL 412S O/U SHOOTING SYSTEM — interchangeable barrel assemblies permit a double rifle, shotgun/rifle, and O&U shotgun configuration, user installed interchangeable barrels, monobloc locking, rifle barrel positioning by adjustment, SST, extractors or ejectors, checkered walnut stock and forend, cocking indicators, blued finish.

Model 412S Field Grade — 12 ga. only, 3 in. chambers, auto ejectors, screw-in choke tubes (includes 5), 26 or 28 in. barrels, matte nickel finish. New 1986.

Mfg.'s Sug. Retail	$1,155		$950	$725	$575	$550	$475	$440	$400

Model 412ST Trap — 12 ga., Monte Carlo stock, 30 in. barrels, screw-in chokes standard.

	$1,125	$925	$725	$650	$580	$540	$475

This variation was made by Valmet in Finland and only small quantities remain. Last Mfg.'s Sug. Retail was $1,325.

Model 412ST Premium Grade Trap — similar to Model 412ST Trap, except has better walnut and checkering.

	$1,425	$1,000	$875	$750	$625	$580	$515

This variation was made by Valmet in Finland and only small quantities remain. Last Mfg.'s Sug. Retail was $1,665.

Model 412S Sporting Clays — 12 ga. only, sporting clays configuration with 28 in. VR barrels and choke tubes. Importation began 1992.

Mfg.'s Sug. Retail	$1,270		$1,100	$925	$725	$650	$580	$540	$475

Model 412S Combination Gun — combination rifle/shotgun, 12 ga, 3 in. chambers, 24 in. barrels, under rifle barrel has choice of .222 or .308 cal., extractors.

Mfg.'s Sug. Retail	$1,255		$1,060	$875	$700	$600	$550	$475	$440

Model 412S Double Rifle — 9.3 x 74R cal., 24 in. barrels, extractors.

Mfg.'s Sug. Retail	$1,470		$1,150	$975	$775	$700	$625	$550	$475

Extra Barrel Assemblies (Model 412S O/U) — $635 each for shotgun (includes screw-in chokes), $720 each for shotgun/rifle combo, $935 each for double rifle.

TIMBERWOLF

Manufactured by I.M.I. Industries located in Israel. Currently imported and distributed by Action Arms located in Philadelphia, PA.

RIFLE

TIMBERWOLF — .357 Mag. or .44 Mag. (disc.) cal., slide action, straight grip shotgun style stock with adj. drop, blue or satin chrome finish, takedown, 18½ in. barrel, 10 shot tube mag., pushbutton trigger guard, sear locking and firing pin safeties, integral scope base, approx. 5½ lbs. New 1989.

Mfg.'s Sug. Retail	$299		$260	$230	$195	$180	$160	$145	$130

Add $80 for satin chrome finish.
Add $110 for .44 Mag. cal. (disc., blue finish only).
Springfield Armory imported 1,000 .44 Mag. Timberwolf models during 1990-1991.

TIPPMAN ARMS CO.

Previous manufacturer located in Fort Wayne, IN.

Tippman Arms manufactured 1/2 scale semi-auto working models of famous machine guns. All models were available with an optional hardwood case, extra ammo cans, and other accessories. Mfg. 1986-1987 only.

Grading	100%	98%	95%	90%	80%	70%	60%

MODEL 1919 A-4 — .22 LR cal. only, copy of Browning 1919 A-4 Model, belt fed, closed bolt operation, 11 in. barrel, includes tripod, 10 lbs.

	100%	98%	95%	90%	80%	70%	60%
	$1,195	$1,045	$950	$870	$800	$750	$695

Last Mfg.'s Sug. Retail was $1,325.

MODEL 1917 — .22 LR cal. only, copy of Browning M1917, watercooled, belt fed, closed bolt operation, 11 in. barrel, includes tripod, 10 lbs.

	100%	98%	95%	90%	80%	70%	60%
	$1,650	$1,445	$1,285	$1,140	$995	$895	$795

Last Mfg.'s Sug. Retail was $1,830.

MODEL .50 HB — .22 Mag. cal. only, copy of Browning .50 cal. machine gun, belt fed, closed bolt operation, 18¼ in. barrel, includes tripod, 13 lbs.

	100%	98%	95%	90%	80%	70%	60%
	$1,750	$1,525	$1,350	$1,200	$1,050	$950	$850

Last Mfg.'s Sug. Retail was $1,929.

TOKAREV

See Russian Military heading.

TRADEWINDS

Tacoma, WA Importers.

HUSKY MODEL 5000 — .22-250, .243, .270, .308, or .30-06 cal., bolt action, 23¾ in. barrel, adj. sight, removable mag., hand checkered walnut stock.

	100%	98%	95%	90%	80%	70%	60%
	$325	$310	$290	$250	$225	$200	$175

MODEL 311-A — .22 LR cal., bolt action, 5 shot, 22½ in. barrel, folding leaf rear sight, walnut checkered stock.

	100%	98%	95%	90%	80%	70%	60%
	$180	$170	$150	$130	$120	$100	$85

MODEL 260-A — .22 LR cal., semi-auto, 5 shot, 22½ in. barrel, 3 leaf folding sight, checkered walnut stock.

	100%	98%	95%	90%	80%	70%	60%
	$200	$190	$175	$150	$130	$120	$100

MODEL H-170 — 12 ga., auto shotgun, 2¾ in. chamber, 26 in. mod. or 28 in. full, recoil operated action, alloy receiver, 5 shot, tube mag., VR, checkered walnut stock.

	100%	98%	95%	90%	80%	70%	60%
	$275	$265	$250	$225	$200	$180	$150

TRENCH/RIOT SHOTGUNS

The following is an alphabetical listing of the various U.S. commercial Riot and military Trench and Riot shotguns mfg. to date in chronological order.

The publisher wishes to express thanks to Pat Redmond and Rick Crosier for the information in this section, much of which has been not been published previously. 100% values have been intentionally omitted in this section as they are seldom seen or sold.

Grading	100%	98%	95%	90%	80%	70%	60%

COMMERCIAL RIOT GUNS

Models listed below are the variations that were commercially available to the consumer from the various domestic manufacturers. For military trench/riot guns, please refer to the various listings later in this section.

ITHACA MODEL 37 RIOT

	100%	98%	95%	90%	80%	70%	60%
Early WWII blued	$350	$315	$275	$240	$205	$165	$125
'60s mfg. parkerized	$250	$225	$195	$175	$150	$125	$100

REMINGTON MODEL 10 RIOT

	100%	98%	95%	90%	80%	70%	60%
	$500	$450	$395	$340	$285	$235	$175

REMINGTON MODEL 11R

While this model was advertised in the 1936 Remington catalog, rarity precludes accurate price evaluation.

REMINGTON MODEL 31 RIOT

	100%	98%	95%	90%	80%	70%	60%
	$500	$450	$395	$340	$285	$235	$175

STEVENS MODEL 520/530 RIOT

	100%	98%	95%	90%	80%	70%	60%
	$200	$185	$160	$145	$130	$115	$95

STEVENS MODEL 620 RIOT

	100%	98%	95%	90%	80%	70%	60%
	$200	$185	$160	$145	$130	$115	$95

STEVENS MODEL 77E LEVER ACTION RIOT

	100%	98%	95%	90%	80%	70%	60%
	$125	$110	$100	$90	$80	$70	$60

WINCHESTER MODEL 97 RIOT

	100%	98%	95%	90%	80%	70%	60%
Takedown frame	$600	$550	$450	$395	$350	$295	$240
Solid frame	$1,200	$1,050	$875	$750	$625	$550	$500

WINCHESTER MODEL 12 RIOT

	100%	98%	95%	90%	80%	70%	60%
	$600	$550	$450	$395	$350	$295	$240

ITHACA MILITARY TRENCH AND RIOT GUNS

WWII MODEL 37 MILITARY TRENCH GUN — rarest of all trench guns, high polish commercial blue finish, R.L.B. and ordnance bomb on left side of receiver, Ordnance bomb on barrel, stocks not proofed, blued vent. handguard for bayonet attachment, only 1,420 Ithaca trench guns were ordered by the military in 1941 and are found in the ser. range 58,000-62,000.

	100%	98%	95%	90%	80%	70%	60%
	N/A	$2,500	$1,800	$1,500	$1,200	$1,000	$800

WWII MODEL 37 MILITARY RIOT GUN — riot configuration, ser. range 23,630-63,137 (shared with Model 37 Military Trench Gun).

	100%	98%	95%	90%	80%	70%	60%
	N/A	$1,800	$1,500	$1,200	$1,000	$800	$600

VIETNAM MODEL 37 TRENCH AND RIOT GUN — used during the Vietnam War, ser. range approx. 600,000-900,000.

	100%	98%	95%	90%	80%	70%	60%
Riot	N/A	$500	$450	$400	$350	$300	$275
Trench	N/A	$800	$600	$500	$450	$400	$350

Trench/Riot Shotguns, cont.

Grading	100%	98%	95%	90%	80%	70%	60%

REMINGTON MILITARY TRENCH AND RIOT GUNS

WWI MODEL 10 MILITARY TRENCH GUN — commercial blue finish with wood handguard on top of barrel, separate bayonet adaptor attaches to front of barrel, U.S. and flaming bomb marked on left side of receiver, stock is unmarked. Extremely rare trench gun and hard to find complete and in original condition. Trench gun barrel length is 22 in. as compared to 20 in. riot gun.

	N/A	$3,500	$2,500	$1,800	$1,400	$1,000	$900

WWI MODEL 10 MILITARY RIOT GUN — riot configuration.

	N/A	$1,200	$1,000	$800	$700	$600	$400

WWII MODEL 11 MILITARY RIOT GUN — semi-auto, 3 and 5 shot, 20 in. riot guns are the most common of all U.S. military WWII marked shotguns. High polish commercial blue finish found with engraved game scene and plain receivers, military markings found on left side of receiver and barrel, stocks can be fancy checkered or plain and have inspector initials and ordnance wheel on left side. Many of these guns sold as surplus after WWII, ser. range 455,273-499,431, also 701,669-711,086.

	N/A	$500	$400	$350	$325	$300	$250

WWII MODEL 31 MILITARY RIOT GUN — riot configuration, ser. range 51,111-63,218.

	N/A	$1,000	$850	$700	$600	$500	$400

SAVAGE MILITARY RIOT GUNS

WWII MODEL 720 MILITARY RIOT GUN — riot configuration, ser. range 68,540-88,210.

	N/A	$1,600	$1,200	$1,000	$800	$650	$500

STEVENS MILITARY TRENCH AND RIOT GUNS

WWII MODEL 520-30 MILITARY TRENCH GUN — blue finish with purple colored vent. handguard for bayonet attachment, U.S., ordnance bomb and "P" proofs on left side of receiver, barrel proofed with ordnance bomb and "P", stocks are not marked. This is the most common WWII trench gun used by the military, ser. range 37,941-69,985 (shared with riot gun).

	N/A	$700	$500	$450	$400	$375	$300

WWII MODEL 520-30 MILITARY RIOT GUN — riot configuration, ser. range (shared with trench gun).

	N/A	$700	$500	$450	$400	$375	$300

WWII MODEL 620 MILITARY TRENCH GUN — blue finish with purple colored vent. handguard for bayonet attachment, U.S., ordnance bomb and "P" proofs on left side of receiver, barrel proofed with ordnance bomb and "P", stocks are not marked. This model preceded the Stevens 520-30 trench gun and is a much scarcer variation, ser. range 7,192-9,108 and 16,939-32,433 (shared with riot gun).

	N/A	$850	$600	$500	$450	$400	$350

WWII MODEL 620 MILITARY RIOT GUN — riot configuration, ser. range (shared with trench gun).

	N/A	$850	$600	$500	$450	$400	$350

VIETNAM MODEL 77E MILITARY RIOT GUN — riot configuration, used during Vietnam War.

	N/A	$650	$500	$450	$375	$300	$275

Grading		100%	98%	95%	90%	80%	70%	60%

WINCHESTER MILITARY TRENCH AND RIOT GUNS

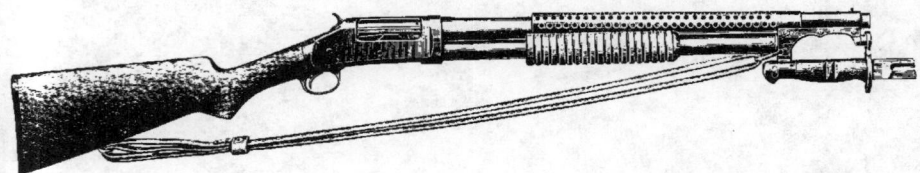

WWI MODEL 1897 MILITARY TRENCH GUN — high polish commercial blue finish, solid frame with vent. handguard for bayonet attachment, used by U.S. Army for trench warfare in WWI, ser. range 650,000-700,000, U.S. and ordnance bomb stamped on right side of receiver.

		N/A	$2,500	$1,500	$1,000	$800	$600	$500

WWI MODEL 1897 MILITARY RIOT GUN — riot configuration, ser. range E566,857-E707,577 (shared with trench gun).

		N/A	$1,200	$800	$600	$500	$450	$400

WWII MODEL 1897 MILITARY TRENCH GUN — high polish commercial blue finish, takedown model, U.S. Army issue during WWII, vent. handguard for bayonet attachment, U.S. with or without ordnance bomb machine marked on left side of receiver, ordnance bomb on barrel, later finger grooved stock has inspector initials and ordnance wheel on left side of stock, ser. range 915,825-956,146.

		N/A	$1,800	$1,400	$900	$700	$600	$500

WWII MODEL 12 MILITARY TRENCH GUN — takedown model with vent. handguard for bayonet attachment, high polish commercial blue finish models in ser. range 980,000-1,029,000, factory parkerized examples are in ser. range 1,030,000-1,040,000. U.S. and ordnance bomb machined on right side of receiver, barrel is ordnance bomb marked and stock is marked on left side with inspector initials and ordnance wheel.

		100%	98%	95%	90%	80%	70%	60%
Blued		N/A	$1,500	$1,200	$900	$700	$600	$500
Parkerized		N/A	$1,800	$1,400	$900	$700	$600	$500

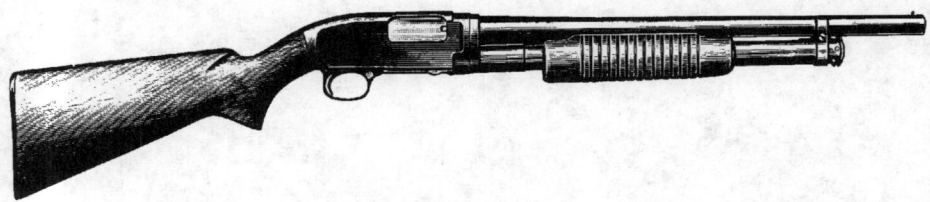

WWII MODEL 12 MILITARY RIOT GUN — high polish commercial blue finish, model in ser. range 980,000-1,029,000, U.S. and ordnance bomb machined on right side of receiver, barrel is ordnance bomb marked, stock is marked on left side with inspector initials and ordnance wheel and has no sling swivel.

		N/A	$1,200	$800	$700	$600	$450	$400

U section

USAS 12

Currently manufactured by Internationale Ordnance Corporation located in Nashville, TN beginning 1992. Previously manufactured (1990-91) by Ramo Mfg., Inc. located in Nashville, TN because of BATF ruling. Currently distributed by Kiesler's Wholesale located in Jeffersonville, IN. Originally designed and previously distributed in the U.S by Gilbert Equipment Co., Inc. located in Mobile, AL. Previously manufactured under license by Daewoo Precision Industries, Ltd. located in South Korea.

Grading	100%	98%	95%	90%	80%	70%	60%

USAS 12 — 12 ga. only, gas operated action available in either semi or fully auto versions, 18¼ in. cylinder bore barrel, closed bolt, synthetic stock, pistol grip, and forearm, carrying handle, 10 round box or 20 drum (disc.) mag., 2¾ in. chamber only, parkerized finish, 12 lbs. New 1987.

	100%	98%	95%	90%	80%	70%	60%
Mfg.'s Sug. Retail $1,199	$1,125	$925	$825	$725	$625	$550	$495

Add $150 for extra 20 shot drum magazine (banned by the BATF).
Values above are for a semi-auto model. Add $50 for fully auto version (Class III only). This model currently is saleable to only military or law enforcement agencies because of BATF rulings.

U.S. ARMS COMPANY

Previous manufacturer located in Riverhead, NY.

REVOLVERS: SINGLE ACTION

ABILENE .357 MAG. — 6 shot, 4⅝, 5½, or 6½ in. barrel, adj. sights, transfer bar ignition, smooth walnut grips, blue finish only. Mfg. 1976-1983.

$275	$240	$200	$185	$170	$155	$140

ABILENE .357 MAG. STAINLESS STEEL — similar to Abilene, only in stainless steel.

$325	$275	$225

ABILENE .44 MAG. — 7½ and 8½ in. barrel, unfluted cylinder blue finish only, otherwise similar to .357 Mag.

$325	$265	$240	$220	$200	$165	$150

ABILENE .44 MAG. STAINLESS STEEL — similar to Abilene .44 Mag., only stainless steel.

$375	$330	$290

UBERTI USA, INC.

Importer and distributor located in Lakeville, CT. Both Black Powder and Modern firearms are imported by Uberti USA, Inc. and are manufactured by Aldo Uberti of Ponte Zanano, Italy.
Other firms have imported Uberti guns under various names in the past.

REVOLVERS & CARBINES: SINGLE ACTION REPRODUCTIONS

These guns can be ordered with either black powder or modern configured frames. Factory engraving and other embellishments or finishes (including antique charcoal blue, white steel, nickel, etc.) can be special ordered by contacting the importer directly.
Add $500 for standard hand engraving pattern on Cattleman variations.
Add $30 for antique charcoal blue finish on all Cattleman variations.

CATTLEMAN VARIATIONS — available in .22 LR (disc. 1990), .22 Mag. (disc. 1990), .357 Mag., .38 Spl., .38-40 (new 1989), .44 S&W Spl., .44-40, or .45 LC cal., 4¾, 5½, and 7½ in. barrel lengths, brass or steel backstraps and trigger guard.

Grading	100%	98%	95%	90%	80%	70%	60%

⚔ **Quick Draw Model**
Mfg.'s Sug. Retail $415 $345 $265 $210 $175 $160 $150 | $135
Add $60 for convertible cylinder (.45 LC/.45 ACP).
Add $64 for stainless steel construction (disc. 1989).

⚔ **Sheriff's Model** — .44-40 or .45 LC cal., 3 in. barrel, brass backstrap.
Mfg.'s Sug. Retail $415 $345 $265 $210 $175 $160 $150 | $135

⚔ **Target Model** — similar to standard Cattleman model, only fully adj. rear blade sight, brass backstrap. Importation disc. 1990.
$315 $245 $200 $185 $170 $150 | $135
Add $25 for steel backstrap and trigger guard.
Add $60 for stainless steel construction (disc.).
Last Mfg.'s Sug. Retail was $335.

CATTLEMAN BUNTLINE — .357 Mag., .44-40, or .45 LC cal., 18 in. barrel, steel backstrap cut for shoulder stock. Importation disc. 1989, re-introduced 1993.
Mfg.'s Sug. Retail $450 $375 $295 $235 $195 $175 $160 | $150

⚔ **Buntline Carbine** — similar to Cattleman Buntline, 18 in. barrel, includes non-detachable shoulder stock with brass hardware and lanyard ring. Importation disc. 1989, re-introduced 1993.
Mfg.'s Sug. Retail $475 $390 $310 $245 $200 $175 $160 | $150
Add $34 for target sights.
Add $34 for .22 LR/.22 Mag. combo. (disc. 1989).
Add $175 for detachable shoulder stock.

BUCKHORN — .44 Mag., .44 Spl., or .44-40 cal., various barrel lengths, brass or steel backstrap, Buntline and revolving carbine models also available in the Buckhorn series — add approx. $65.

⚔ **Quick Draw Model** — importation disc. 1989, resumed 1992.
Mfg.'s Sug. Retail $445 $375 $295 $235 $195 $175 $160 | $150
Add $50 for convertible cylinder.
Add $40 for Target Model.

⚔ **Buckhorn Carbine** — .44-40 or .44 Mag. cal., 18 in. barrel, includes non-detachable shoulder stock with brass hardware and lanyard ring. Importation disc. 1989.
$360 $285 $230 $200 $185 $180 | $175
Add $34 for target sights.
Add $40 for extra .44-40 cylinder combo.
Add $122 for detachable shoulder stock.
Last Mfg.'s Sug. Retail was $450.

STALLION 1873 COLT — .22 LR/.22 Mag. cal. combo only, 4¾, 5½, or 6½ in. barrel, case hardened frame, 1-piece walnut grip, 2.4 lbs. Importation disc. 1989.
$300 $210 $195 $170 $155 $140 | $120
Add $27 for steel backstrap and trigger guard.
Add $26 for Target Model.
Last Mfg.'s Sug. Retail was $325.

⚔ **Stainless Stallion** — similar to standard Stallion, except is stainless steel. Importation disc. 1989.
$370 $275 $225 $200 $185 $180 | $175
Last Mfg.'s Sug. Retail was $425.

"OUTLAW" 1875 REMINGTON — .357 Mag., .44-40, .45 ACP (new 1992), or .45 LC cal., 7½ barrel, brass or steel (new 1993) trigger guard.
Mfg.'s Sug. Retail $415 $345 $265 $210 $175 $160 $150 | $135
Add $50 for nickel plating.
Add $50 for convertible cylinder (.45 LC/.45 ACP).

Grading	100%	98%	95%	90%	80%	70%	60%

Model 1875 Carbine — same cals. as Outlaw 1875, 18 in. barrel, includes non-detachable shoulder stock with brass hardware and lanyard ring. Importation disc. 1989.

	$425	$285	$230	$200	$185	$180	$175

Add $110 for nickel plating.
Last Mfg.'s Sug. Retail was $440.

1890 REMINGTON — .357 Mag., .44-40, .45 ACP (new 1993), or .45 LC cal., 5½ barrel, brass or steel (new 1993) trigger guard.

Mfg.'s Sug. Retail	$420	$365	$275	$215	$175	$160	$150	$135

Add $50 for nickel plating.
Add $50 for convertible cylinder (.45 LC/.45 ACP).

PHANTOM MODEL — .357 or .44 Mag. cal. only, 10½ in. barrel for silhouette use. Imported 1985-89.

	$475	$395	$325	$290	$260	$230	$215

Last Mfg.'s Sug. Retail was $509.

REVOLVERS: DOUBLE ACTION

INSPECTOR MODEL — .32 S&W or .38 Spl. cal., 3, 4, or 6 in. barrels, double action, blued or chrome finish. Imported 1985-89.

	$390	$295	$245	$210	$170	$145	$125

Add $35 for target sights.   Add $25 for chrome plating.
Last Mfg.'s Sug. Retail was $406.

TARGET PISTOLS

1871 ROLLING BLOCK TARGET PISTOL — available in .22 LR, .22 Mag., .22 Hornet, .357 Mag. or .45 LC (Navy Model with open sights only, new 1992) cal., 9½ in. barrel.

Mfg.'s Sug. Retail	$450	$375	$295	$235	$195	$175	$155	$135

Add $100 for carbine model (22 in. barrel - not available in .45 LC cal).

RIFLES: REPRODUCTIONS

HENRY RIFLE/CARBINE — .44-40 or .45 LC (rifle only) cal., brass or steel (.44-40 only) frame, 24½ in. barrel on rifle, 22½ in. barrel on carbine, available in modern gun blue, charcoal blue, white, or chrome finish.

Mfg.'s Sug. Retail	$900	$810	$625	$515	$425	$360	$320	$260

Add $25 for carbine model.
Add $500 for standard hand engraving.
The carbine was disc. in 1989, re-introduced 1992.

Henry Trapper — similar to above, except has 16½ or 18½ in. barrel. Limited importation began 1990.

Mfg.'s Sug. Retail	$1,000	$885	$650	$525	$425	$360	$320	$260

Henry 1 of 1,000 — disc. several years ago.

	$1,450	$1,150	$975	$850	$700	$575	$425

1866 CARBINE — .22 Mag. (disc. 1989), .22 LR (disc. 1989), .38 Spl., or .44-40 cal., brass receiver, 19 in. round barrel.

Mfg.'s Sug. Retail	$720	$640	$550	$450	$375	$320	$260	$215

Last Mfg.'s Sug. Retail was $587 for .22 Mag. or .22 LR (disc. 1989).

1866 Trapper Carbine — .22 LR, .38 Spl., or .44-40 cal., 16 in. barrel. Importation disc. 1989.

	$650	$475	$395	$340	$285	$260	$235

Last Mfg.'s Sug. Retail was $686.

Uberti USA, Inc., cont.

Grading	100%	98%	95%	90%	80%	70%	60%

1866 Yellowboy Indian Carbine — .22 LR (disc. 1989), .22 Mag. (disc. 1989), .38 Spl., or .44-40 cal., 19 in. barrel. Limited importation.

Mfg.'s Sug. Retail $720	$640	$525	$425	$360	$310	$275	$240

Subtract $50 without brass tacks.

Red Cloud Commemorative Carbine — same cals., special engraving and brass tacks in forearm and stock. Importation officially disc. 1989, but still available through special order.

Mfg.'s Sug. Retail $850	$720	$600	$475	$400	$350	$330	$300

1866 RIFLE — .38 Spl. or .44-40 cal., brass receiver, 24¼ in. round (new 1993) or octagonal barrel.

Mfg.'s Sug. Retail $780	$700	$560	$475	$385	$300	$260	$235

Add $500 for standard hand engraving.

1866 Yellowboy Indian Rifle — .22 LR (disc. 1989), .22 Mag. (disc. 1989), .38 Spl., or .44-40 cal., 24¼ in. barrel. Importation disc. 1989, reintroduced 1993.

Mfg.'s Sug. Retail $800	$700	$560	$475	$385	$300	$260	$235

1873 CARBINE — .22 LR (disc. 1991), .22 Mag. (disc. 1991), .357 Mag., .38 Spl. (disc. 1991) .44-40, or .45 LC (new 1992) cal., steel receiver, 19 in. round barrel.

Mfg.'s Sug. Retail $900	$800	$600	$500	$425	$360	$320	$280

Add $95 for nickel plating (disc.).

1873 Trapper Carbine — .357 Mag., .44-40, or .45 LC cal. only, 16⅛ in. barrel. Importation disc. 1990.

		$695	$550	$475	$400	$360	$320	$280

Last Mfg.'s Sug. Retail was $750.

1873 SPORTING RIFLE — .45 LC cal., case hardened receiver, 20 in. octagon (new 1990), 24¼ in. octagon or round, or 30 (new 1990) in. octagonal barrel, can be drilled and tapped for Uberti rear tang aperture sight (new 1993).

Mfg.'s Sug. Retail $900	$800	$625	$515	$425	$360	$320	$260

Add $50 for 30 in. octagonal barrel.
Add $500 for standard hand engraving.
Add $800 for "1 of 1,000" engraving pattern.
Add $100 for hand checkered pistol grip stock.
The 20 or 30 in. barrel is available in .44-40 or .45 LC cal. only.

UGARTECHEA, IGNACIO

Manufacturer located in Eibar, Spain. Currently imported by Precision Sports, Inc. located in Cortland, NY. Direct and dealer sales only.

Please refer to the Parker-Hale listing in this text for the 600 Series SxS shotguns.

ULTIMATE

Please refer to Camex-Blaser USA in the C section of this text.

ULTRA LIGHT ARMS, INC.

Manufacturer located in Granville, WV. Dealer direct sales only.

RIFLES: BOLT ACTION

ULTRA LIGHT RIFLE — caliber to customer specs., various actions, stock 2 position lever safety, Timney trigger, Douglas 22 or 24 in. barrel, no sights, graphite reinforced stock with recoil pad, matte finish standard, other finishes at extra cost. Many special order features and services are available on these models - contact the manufacturer for prices, 4¾-5¾ lbs. New 1985.

Grading	100%	98%	95%	90%	80%	70%	60%

Model 20 RF — .22 LR cal., convertible from repeater to single shot, 22 in. Douglas premium barrel, DuPont composite stock with Imron paint (some color options available), no sights, drilled and tapped, 5½ lbs. Mfg. 1983-1992.

		$750	$650	$550	$475	$400	$350	$300

The first 100 pre-production rifles in this model are marked "1-of-100" consecutively, with owner's initials.
Last Mfg.'s Sug. Retail was $800.

Model 20 — 18 cals. available between .17 Rem. and .358 Win. Mag., short action, Kevlar stock.

Mfg.'s Sug. Retail	**$2,400**	$2,150	$1,650	$1,225	$950	$800	$700	$640

Add $100 for left-hand action.

Model 24 — .25-06, .270 Win., .280 Rem. (mfg. 1992 only), .30-06, or 7mm Exp. cal., long action, Kevlar stock, 5¼ lbs.

Mfg.'s Sug. Retail	**$2,500**	$2,250	$1,750	$1,300	$995	$825	$700	$640

Add $100 for left-hand action.

Model 28 Magnum — .264 Win. Mag., .300 Win. Mag., .338 Win. Mag., 7mm Rem. Mag., or .416 Rigby (mfg. 1992 only) cal., Kevlar stock, 5¾ lbs.

Mfg.'s Sug. Retail	**$2,900**	$2,625	$1,975	$1,550	$1,225	$950	$700	$600

Add $100 for left-hand action.

MODEL 40 MAGNUM — .300 Wby. Mag. or .416 Rigby cal., otherwise similar to Model 28 Series. New 1993.

Mfg.'s Sug. Retail	**$2,900**	$2,625	$1,975	$1,550	$1,225	$950	$700	$600

Add $100 for left-hand action.

PISTOLS: BOLT-ACTION

MODEL 20 HUNTERS PISTOL — various cals., 14 in. Douglas heavy barrel, 5-shot mag., Kevlar graphite reinforced stock in choice of 4 colors, Timney trigger, left-hand or right-hand bolt, approx. 4 lbs. Mfg. 1987-89.

		$1,175	$1,000	$900	$800	$700	$640	$575

Last Mfg.'s Sug. Retail was $1,300.

UNIQUE

Manufacturer located in Hendaye, France. Imported by Nygord Precision Products located in La Crescenta, CA and Beeman Arms located in Santa Rosa, CA.

PISTOLS: SEMI-AUTO

All currently manufactured Unique pistols are supplied with leatherette case, weights are additional.

KREIGS MODEL L — 7.65mm, 9 shot, 3.2 in. barrel, blue, plastic grips, fixed sights. Mfg. 1940-1945, during German occupation of France, has German acceptance marks.

	$325	$250	$220	$200	$180	$160	$140

MODEL RR — post-war commercial version of Kreigsmodell, higher quality finish. Mfg. 1951-disc. Add 15% for .22 LR cal.

	$180	$170	$155	$130	$120	$110	$90

MODEL B/CF — 7.65mm, 9 shot, or .380 auto cal., 8 shot, 4 in. barrel, blue, plastic thumbrest grips. Mfg. 1954-disc.

	$205	$195	$175	$155	$145	$130	$110

Grading	100%	98%	95%	90%	80%	70%	60%

MODEL D6 — .22 LR cal., 10 shot, 6 in. barrel, adj. sights, blue, plastic grips. Mfg. 1954-disc.

	100%	98%	95%	90%	80%	70%	60%
	$300	$250	$200	$160	$145	$135	$120

MODEL D2 — similar to D6, except 4½ in. barrel.

	100%	98%	95%	90%	80%	70%	60%
	$300	$250	$200	$160	$145	$135	$120

MODEL L — .22 LR cal., 10 shot, 7.65mm, 7 shot, and .380 auto cal., 6 shot, 3.3 in. barrel, fixed sights, steel and alloy frame offered, plastic grips. Mfg. 1955-disc.

	100%	98%	95%	90%	80%	70%	60%
	$250	$200	$150	$130	$115	$100	$90

MODEL MIKROS POCKET — .22 Short and .25 auto cal., 6 shot, fixed sights, blue, plastic grips, steel or alloy frame. Mfg. 1957-disc.

	100%	98%	95%	90%	80%	70%	60%
	$200	$155	$140	$120	$100	$90	$75

MODEL DES/32U — .32 S&W L Wadcutter, 5.9 in. barrel, dry firing device, ergonomically designed French walnut grips with adj. hand rest, 5 or 6 shot mag., 40.2 oz.

	100%	98%	95%	90%	80%	70%	60%
Mfg.'s Sug. Retail $1,295	$1,225	$1,025	$900	$775	$625	$500	$450

MODEL DES/69U STANDARD MATCH — .22 LR cal., 5 shot mag., 5.9 in. barrel, adj. rear sight, adj. target, stippled stocks, blue finish only. Importation began 1969.

	100%	98%	95%	90%	80%	70%	60%
Mfg.'s Sug. Retail $1,195	$1,150	$995	$875	$750	$625	$500	$450

Add $30 for left-hand model.

MODEL DES/823-U RAPID FIRE MATCH — .22 Short cal., 5 shot, 6 in. barrel, adj. sight, adj. trigger, adj. walnut target grips, squared barrel assembly, dry fire mechanism. Imported 1974-1988.

	100%	98%	95%	90%	80%	70%	60%
	$1,100	$850	$725	$625	$550	$490	$445

Add $60 for left-hand model.
Last Mfg.'s Sug. Retail was $1,300.

MODEL DES/2000-U — .22 LR cal. target pistol, wrap around grips, adj. features. Imported 1986-1988.

	100%	98%	95%	90%	80%	70%	60%
	$995	$850	$725	$625	$550	$490	$445

Add $62 for left-hand model.
Last Mfg.'s Sug. Retail was $1,198.

MODEL 2000-U — .22 Short cal. only, specifically designed for rapid fire U.I.T. competition, 5.9 in. barrel, ergonomic styled grips with adj. hand rest, 5 shot mag. (inserted in top), 43.4 oz.

	100%	98%	95%	90%	80%	70%	60%
Mfg.'s Sug. Retail $1,350	$1,250	$1,050	$925	$775	$625	$500	$450

Add $30 for left-hand model.

RIFLES

T66 MATCH RIFLE — .22 LR cal., single shot, bolt action, 25½ in. barrel, micro rear globe front, full target stock. Mfg. 1966-disc.

	100%	98%	95%	90%	80%	70%	60%
	$425	$410	$390	$350	$300	$280	$250

MODEL F 11 — .22 LR cal., military trainer, adj. sights, target walnut stock. Limited importation.

	100%	98%	95%	90%	80%	70%	60%
	$560	$435	$350	$285	$260	$240	$220

Last Mfg.'s Sug. Retail was $695.

MODEL T DIOPTRA — .22 LR or .22 Mag. cal., bolt action Sporter with 23.6 in. barrel and adj. rear sight, 5 (.22 Mag. only) or 10 shot mag., grooved receiver for scope, checkered French walnut Monte Carlo stock, approx. 6.4 lbs.

	100%	98%	95%	90%	80%	70%	60%
Mfg.'s Sug. Retail $890	$795	$700	$600	$525	$450	$375	$300

Grading	100%	98%	95%	90%	80%	70%	60%

MODEL T/SM — .22 LR or .22 Mag cal., bolt action Target variation with 20½ in. barrel, no sights, 5 (.22 Mag. only) or 10 shot mag., stippled pistol grip stock and forend, right or left-hand action, 6.6 lbs.

Mfg.'s Sug. Retail $960	$850	$735	$625	$525	$450	$375	$300

Add $50 for left-hand action.

MODEL T/STANDARD UIT — .22 LR cal., designed for UIT competition, single shot, aperture sights, adj. cheekpiece and buttplate on stippled walnut stock, right or left-hand action, 10.8 lbs.

Mfg.'s Sug. Retail $1,450	$1,350	$1,125	$975	$850	$725	$625	$525

Add $50 for left-hand action.

MODEL T/LIBRE UIT FREE RIFLE — .22 LR cal., Free Rifle variation of the Model T/Standard UIT.
Nygord Precision should be contacted directly for pricing on this model.

UNITED SPORTING ARMS, INC.

Previous manufacturer located in Tucson, AZ. Manufacture ceased in early 1986.
All the below models were disc. in early 1986.

SEVILLE — .357 Mag., .41 Mag., .44 Mag., or .45 Colt cal., single action revolver, 4⅝, 5½, 6½, or 7½ in. barrels, adj. sights, smooth walnut grips.

$395	$350	$315	$280	$260	$240	$220

Last Mfg.'s Sug. Retail was $435.

* **Stainless steel** — version of the Seville.

$395	$350	$315

Last Mfg.'s Sug. Retail was $435.

* **Silver Seville** — similar to Seville, except has blue barrel, and high polish stainless steel grip frame.

$425	$370	$330

Last Mfg.'s Sug. Retail was $460.

* **Stainless .357 Maxi** — available in 5½ or 7½ in. barrel only.

$575	$475	$395

Last Mfg.'s Sug. Retail was $465.

* **Stainless .375 USA** — only in 7½ in. barrel.

$625	$525	$425

Last Mfg.'s Sug. Retail was $490.

* **Stainless .454 Mag.** — only in 7½ in. barrel, 5 shot.

$700	$600	$500

Last Mfg.'s Sug. Retail was $595.
Note: In late 1986, some .454 Mag.'s were made up from parts purchased from the manufacturer. Unfortunately, while the exterior appearance might seem normal, they were not involved with any type of factory quality control program. As a result, shooting these non-factory revolvers could be dangerous, and careful inspection should be made before purchasing/shooting this particular specimen.

* **Eldorado Stainless** — .44 Mag., 10½ in. barrel, adj. sights.

$700	$600	$500

SILVER SEVILLE SILHOUETTE — .357 Mag., .41 Mag., or .44 Mag. cal., single action revolver, 10½ in. barrel, adj. sights, Pachmayr grips, blued barrel finish with stainless grip frame.

$445	$370	$330	$295	$270	$250	$230

Last Mfg.'s Sug. Retail was $485.

Grading	100%	98%	95%	90%	80%	70%	60%

⚔ **Stainless steel** — version of the Silver Seville Silhouette.

	100%	98%	95%
	$425	$370	$330

Last Mfg.'s Sug. Retail was $460.

⚔ **Stainless .357 Maxi** — available in 10½ in. barrel only.

	100%	98%	95%
	$575	$475	$395

Last Mfg.'s Sug. Retail was $480.

⚔ **Stainless .375 USA** — available in 10½ in. barrel only.

	100%	98%	95%
	$625	$525	$425

Last Mfg.'s Sug. Retail was $515.

⚔ **Stainless .454 Mag.** — available in 10½ in. barrel only, 5 shot.

	100%	98%	95%
	$700	$600	$500

Last Mfg.'s Sug. Retail was $620.
Note: In late 1986, some .454 Mag.'s were made up from parts purchased from the manufacturer. Unfortunately, while the exterior appearance might seem normal, they were not involved with any type of factory quality control program. As a result, shooting these non-factory revolvers could be dangerous, and careful inspection should be made before purchasing/shooting this particular specimen.

SHERIFF MODEL — .357 Mag., .38 Spl., .44 Spl., .44 Mag., or .45 Colt cal., single action revolver, 3½ in. barrel, adj. sights, smooth walnut grips.

	100%	98%	95%	90%	80%	70%	60%
	$395	$350	$315	$280	$260	$240	$220

Last Mfg.'s Sug. Retail was $435.

⚔ **Stainless steel** — version of the Sheriff Model.

	100%	98%	95%
	$395	$350	$315

Last Mfg.'s Sug. Retail was $435.

UNITED STATES HISTORICAL SOCIETY

An organization which markets Historically Significant Firearms Reproductions. Located in Richmond, VA. Most firearms are manufactured by the Williamsburg Firearms Manufactory and the Virginia Firearms Manufactory.

PISTOLS

ANDREW JACKSON

⚔ **Silver Edition** — 2,500 mfg.

	100%	98%	95%
	$2,100	$1,750	$1,400

Issue price was $2,100.

⚔ **Gold Edition** — 100 mfg.

	100%	98%	95%
	$5,500	$3,995	$2,750

Issue price was $5,500.

PITCAIRN — 900 mfg.

	100%	98%	95%
	$2,950	$2,300	$1,750

Issue price was $2,950.

THOMAS JEFFERSON — 1,000 mfg., issue price was $1,900.

	100%	98%	95%
	$3,500	$2,750	$1,995

Grading	100%	98%	95%	90%	80%	70%	60%

HAMILTON — BURR DUELING PISTOLS — 1,200 mfg., issue price was $2,995 in 1981.

$3,500 $2,750 $1,995

WASHINGTON AND LEE FLINTLOCK PISTOLS — .69 cal., flintlock pistols with 9$^{15}/_{16}$ in. barrels, burl walnut stocks with sterling silver fittings, engraved silver plated lock plates, trigger guard, and side plate, firing capability, cased with accessories, limited issue of 1,000 in 1989.

Mfg.'s Sug. Retail $2,700 $2,700 $2,150 $1,650

GEORGE WASHINGTON — includes pair of flintlocks, 975 mfg. 1976, cased, issue price was initially $3,000, and ended at $3,500.

$4,250 $3,400 $2,450

H. DERINGER PISTOL SET — .41 cal., percussion, reproduction of H. Deringer's famous pistol. Available with sterling silver mounts (1,000 pair manufactured — issue price $1,900), 14Kt. gold mounted (100 pair mfg.-$2,700 issue price), precious gem stone mounted (only 5 pair mfg. — $25,000 issue price). Mfg. 1978.

⊰ **Silver mounted**

$2,500 $1,750 $1,000

⊰ **14Kt. gold mounted**

$7,500 $5,000 $3,000

⊰ **18Kt. jewel mounted** — too limited a supply for price evaluation.

TEXAS PATERSON EDITION — reproduction of the famous Colt folding trigger model mfg. in Paterson, NJ, engraved, cased. 1,000 mfg. starting in 1988. Cased with accessories.

Mfg.'s Sug. Retail $2,500 $2,500 $1,900 $1,450

This model is an exact reproduction of the original Colt Paterson ser. no. 755, Model 5.

SAM HOUSTON WALKER — .44 cal., reproduction of the Colt Walker, 9 in. barrel, extensive gold etching on highly polished blued surface, smooth walnut stocks with S. Houston medallions, cased with accessories. 2,500 mfg.

$2,300 $2,000 $1,575

Issue price was $2,300

TEXAS RANGER DRAGOON — .44 cal., features silver plated cylinder, trigger guard, and gripstraps, color case hardened frame and loading lever, multiple 24 Kt. etchings on barrel and frame front, cased with accessories, 66 oz. 1,000 mfg. in 1990 only.

Mfg.'s Sug. Retail $1,585 $1,585 $1,050 $795

TOWER OF LONDON COL. SAM COLT DRAGOON — .44 cal., exact reproduction of the Second Model Dragoon, 7$^1/_2$ in. barrel, hand engraved, Texas ranger cylinder scene, one piece walnut grip with inscribed sterling silver plaque, casehardened frame, hammer, loading lever and rammer, cased with accessories, limited issue of 1,000 in 1989.

Mfg.'s Sug. Retail $2,450 $2,450 $1,950 $1,500

ROBERT E. LEE MODEL 1851 NAVY — .36 cal. only, reproduction of the 1851 Navy Colt, extensive gold etching, cylinder scene portrays historical Civil War events, walnut stocks with Robert E. Lee medallion, cased with accessories, 41 oz. 2,500 mfg. during 1984.

$2,100 $1,900 $1,450

Issue price is $2,100.

Grading	100%	98%	95%	90%	80%	70%	60%

MONITOR AND VIRGINIA MODEL 1851 NAVY REVOLVER — .44 cal., issued to commemorate the Civil War naval battle between the USS Monitor and Confederate Virginia, features gold etchings on barrel, frame, and Monitor/Virginia battle scene on cylinder, cased, 41 oz. 1.000 mfg. in 1991.

Mfg.'s Sug. Retail $1,250 $1,250 $875 $500

STONEWALL JACKSON MODEL 1851 REVOLVER — .36 cal., reproduction of Colt's Model 1851 Navy, elaborate gold etching on frame and barrel, walnut grip with medallion, cased with sterling medallion and silver plated powder flask. 1988 release. 2,500 total mfg.

Mfg.'s Sug. Retail $2,100 $2,100 $1,650 $1,250

JEFFERSON DAVIS 1851 NAVY REVOLVER — .36 cal., extensive Nimschke style engraving on barrel, loading lever, frame, and trigger, case hardened frame with silver plated brass backstrap and trigger guard, includes engraved, silver plated detachable shoulder stock, cased with accessories, 41 oz. 1,000 mfg. in 1990 only.

Mfg.'s Sug. Retail $2,750 $2,750 $1,850 $1,250

MODEL 1851 U.S. NAVY REVOLVER — .36 cal., 7½ in. octagon barrel, features gold etched cylinder and other embellishments, brass trigger guard and backstrap plated with 24 Kt. gold, 41 oz. 1,000 mfg. in 1988 only.

Mfg.'s Sug. Retail $1,250 $1,250 $875 $500

U.S. CAVALRY MODEL 1860 ARMY — .44 cal., reproduction of the Colt Model 1860, stag grips, gold etched cylinder scene, cased with brass buckle. 975 manufactured starting in 1988.

Mfg.'s Sug. Retail $1,450 $1,450 $1,050 $800

FREDERIC REMINGTON MODEL 1860 ARMY REVOLVER — .44 cal., issued to commemorate Frederic Remington's 100th anniversary as an associate of the National Academy of Design, features gold etched barrel, cylinder (with 5 panels), trigger, frame, and gripstraps, cased with accessories, 42 oz. 1,000 mfg. in 1990 only.

Mfg.'s Sug. Retail $1,500 $1,500 $1,000 $775

BUFFALO BILL CENTENNIAL MODEL 1860 ARMY — .44 cal., reproduction of the Colt Model 1860, bonded ivory stocks, extensive gold etchings portraying various wild west scenes, bonded ivory powder flask, brass accessories, cased. 2,500 mfg. 1983.

        $1,950 $1,450 $1,100

Issue price is $1,950.

BAT MASTERSON MODEL 1860 ARMY — .44 cal., original roll engraved pattern on cylinder, walnut grips, blued barrel decorated in 24 Kt. gold. 2,500 mfg. beginning 1991.

Mfg.'s Sug. Retail $1,250 $1,250 $875 $500

SECRET SERVICE MUSEUM EDITION — 500 mfg. starting 1988.

Mfg.'s Sug. Retail $2,750 $2,750 $2,000 $1,600

Secret Service Investigator's Edition — 1,000 mfg. starting 1988.

Mfg.'s Sug. Retail $1,250 $1,250 $875 $500

ROY ROGERS COWBOY EDITION SAA — .45 LC cal., SAA revolver, 4¾ in. barrel, features gold plated cylinder and other 24 Kt. etchings on barrel, frame and gripstrap, hand fitted stag grips, made to commemorate Roy Rogers 50th Anniversary (1940-1990), cased. 2,500 mfg. in 1990 only.

Mfg.'s Sug. Retail $1,350 $1,350 $900 $550

Grading	100%	98%	95%	90%	80%	70%	60%

⚊ **Roy Premier Edition SAA** — similar to Cowboy Edition, except has elaborate inlays and engraving. 250 mfg. in 1990 only.

Mfg.'s Sug. Retail $4,500 $4,500 $2,950 $1,750

U.S. MARSHALS WYATT EARP SAA — .45 LC cal., 4¾ in. blued barrel, select walnut grips, case hardened frame and hammer, Marshal's etched 24 Kt. badge inset in grip. 2,500 mfg. beginning 1991.

Mfg.'s Sug. Retail $1,250 $1,250 $875 $500

NATIONAL COWBOY HALL OF FAME SAA — .45 LC cal., 4¾ in. barrel, 24 Kt. filigree on barrel and gold symbols of the American cowboy on cylinder, staghorn grips, velvet lined display case with glass lid. 1,000 mfg. beginning 1992.

Mfg.'s Sug. Retail $1,600 $1,600 $1,125 $825

INTERPOL COLT SAA — .45 LC cal., 4¾ in. barrel, hand engraving based on Kornbrath Interpol Model, silver-plated faux ivory eagle grips, display cased in luxurious leather (designed like a book), 154 mfg. beginning 1991.

Mfg.'s Sug. Retail $4,500 $4,500 $2,950 $1,750

MINIATURE REVOLVER SERIES

1847 WALKER PRESIDENTIAL EDITION — miniature reproduction of 1847 Colt Walker, color case hardened receiver, all parts operational, sterling silver grips, full coverage engraving, cased. 1,500 mfg. starting 1990.

Mfg.'s Sug. Retail $1,575 $1,575 $1,100 $825

⚊ **1847 Walker Classic Edition** — similar to Presidential Edition, except has walnut grips and frame is not engraved, cased. 1,500 mfg. starting 1990.

Mfg.'s Sug. Retail $625 $625 $450 $325

1851 NAVY PRESIDENTIAL EDITION — miniature reproduction of 1851 Navy Colt, color case hardened receiver, all parts operational, mother-of-pearl grips, full coverage engraving, cased. 1,500 mfg. starting 1988.

Mfg.'s Sug. Retail $1,575 $1,575 $1,100 $825

⚊ **1851 Classic Edition** — similar to Presidential Edition, except has walnut grips and cylinder is roll-engraved, cased. 3,500 mfg. starting 1986.

Mfg.'s Sug. Retail $525 $525 $400 $295

1860 ARMY PRESIDENTIAL EDITION — miniature reproduction of 1860 Army Colt, color case hardened engraved receiver and barrel, roll-engraved cylinder scene, all parts operational, ivory grips, cherry cased. 1,500 mfg. starting 1988.

Mfg.'s Sug. Retail $1,575 $1,575 $1,200 $875

⚊ **1860 Classic Edition** — similar to Presidential Edition without engraving, except has rosewood grips, cased. 3,500 mfg. starting 1988.

Mfg.'s Sug. Retail $525 $525 $400 $295

1861 NAVY PRESIDENTIAL EDITION — miniature reproduction of 1861 Navy Colt, color case hardened engraved receiver and barrel, roll-engraved cylinder scene, all parts operational, includes detachable shoulder stock, cased. 1,500 mfg. starting 1990.

Mfg.'s Sug. Retail $1,500 $1,500 $1,150 $850

⚊ **1861 Navy Classic Edition** — similar to Presidential Edition without engraving, cased. 1,500 mfg. starting 1990.

Mfg.'s Sug. Retail $750 $750 $550 $395

Grading	100%	98%	95%	90%	80%	70%	60%

SA ARMY PRESIDENTIAL EDITION — miniature reproduction of 1873 SAA Colt, nickel plated receiver and barrel with scroll engraving, gold plated cylinder, hammer, trigger, and ejector rod housing, one piece ivory grips, cherry cased. 1,500 mfg. starting 1988.

Mfg.'s Sug. Retail $1,550 $1,550 $1,100 $825

This miniature is an exact replica of Serial No. 114 SAA (earliest known gold engraved SAA). All features are the same, only on a miniature basis.

⚔ **SA Army Classic Edition** — similar to Presidential Edition without engraving, except has color case hardened receiver and blued metal parts, one piece rosewood grips. 1,500 mfg. starting 1988.

Mfg.'s Sug. Retail $575 $575 $425 $300

The Classic Edition is miniaturized, exact reproduction of Colt Serial No. 1 (includes pinched frame, slanted barrel address marking, donut ejector rod head, knurled hammer spur, etc.). All are serial numbered 1.

RIFLES

CONFEDERATE COMMEMORATIVE RIFLE — replicates Cook & Brother original 1861 Model Carbine, 1,500 mfg. during 1986, includes wood wall mount and velvet sleeved bag, 24 Kt. gold plating and accenting.

$1,750 $1,450 $995

Issue price was $1,900.

SHOTGUNS

CHUCK YEAGER SHOTGUN — 12 ga. only, O/U boxlock action with engraved silver finished sideplates depicting Gen. Yeager and his P-51 Mustang, SST, 28 in. VR barrels with choke tubes, cased with accessories. 100 mfg. in 1989 only.

Mfg.'s Sug. Retail $12,500 $12,500 $9,000 $6,250

This model was mfg. by Bertuzzi located in Brescia, Italy. Over 120 hours were required to engrave each gun.

ARNOLD PALMER SHOTGUN — 20 ga., SxS boxlock with engraved sideplates depicting Arnold Palmer in 24 Kt. gold as well as other inlays, 26 in. barrels, 6 lbs. 6 oz. 100 mfg. in 1990 only.

Mfg.'s Sug. Retail $9,750 $9,750 $6,250 $3,995

CHRISTOPHER COLUMBUS SHOTGUN — 20 ga., O/U boxlock action featuring engraved silver-plated sideplate depicting various scenes in 24 Kt. gold, 25.4 in. barrels with choke tubes, cased with accessories. 200 mfg. beginning 1991.

Mfg.'s Sug. Retail $12,500 $12,500 $9,000 $6,250

EISENHOWER .45 AUTO PISTOL — .45 ACP cal., 1911 Govt. Model mfg. by Springfield Armory, 7 shot mag., 5 in. barrel, checkered walnut grips inset with 2 bronze medallions, blued steel slide decorated in 24 Kt. gold, Eisenhower's signature etched on velvet-lined walnut display case, comes with framed portrait of D. Eisenhower, signed by his son, John Eisenhower. 1,000 mfg. beginning 1992.

Mfg.'s Sug. Retail $1,675 $1,675 $1,150 $825

"DON'T GIVE UP THE SHIP" MODEL — .45 ACP cal., 1911 Colt Govt. Model, 7 shot mag., 5 in. barrel, rosewood grips, blue steel decorated with 24 Kt. gold, velvet-lined solid oak case with symbol of U.S. Navy carved into top of lid. 1,997 mfg. starting 1993.

Mfg.'s Sug. Retail $1,485 $1,485 $1,075 $825

Grading	100%	98%	95%	90%	80%	70%	60%

HOPALONG CASSIDY COWBOY EDITION SAA REVOLVER — .45 LC cal., 5½ in. barrel, blue steel with silver decorations on cylinder, barrel, and frame, hand fitted genuine black horn grips, velvet lined cherry display case. 950 mfg. starting 1993.

Mfg.'s Sug. Retail	$1,675	$1,675	$1,150	$825

HOPALONG PREMIER COLT EDITION SAA REVOLVER — .45 LC cal., 5½ in. barrel, silver-plated, deep hand engraving, 18 Kt. gold inlays, hand fitted genuine black buffalo horn inset with William Boyd's monogram in sterling silver, gold-embossed leather display case lined in velvet. 100 mfg. starting 1993.

Mfg.'s Sug. Retail	$4,500	$4,500	$3,500	$2,450

RICHARD PETTY SILVER EDITION SAA REVOLVER — .45 LC cal., 5½ in. barrel, blue steel with silver decoration, hand fitted faux ivory grips, Petty's signature carved on velvet lined cherry display case, comes with signed Richard Petty portrait and numbered to match gun. 1,000 mfg. starting 1992.

Mfg.'s Sug. Retail	$1,675	$1,675	$1,150	$825

MEL TORME COLT SAA REVOLVER — .45 LC cal., 5½ in. barrel, elaborate silver engraving with 24 Kt. gold highlights, mother-of-pearl grips, leather display case with Mel Torme's signature in gold. 100 mfg. starting 1992.

Mfg.'s Sug. Retail	$4,500	$4,500	$3,500	$2,950

UNIVERSAL FIREARMS

Universal Firearms became a division of Iver Johnson's Arms, Inc. in 1982. Formerly imported out of Hialeah, FL. Currently manufactured in Jacksonville, AR.

RIFLES: SEMI-AUTO CARBINE

1000 MILITARY — .30 cal., "G.I." copy, satin blue, birch stock, 18 in. barrel. Disc.

	$229	$180	$170	$160	$150	$135	$125

MODEL 1003 — 16, 18, or 20 in. barrel, .30 M1 copy, blued finish, adj. sight, birch stock, 5½ lbs. Add $45 for 4X scope. See current listing under Iver Johnson. Disc.

	$180	$160	$140	$120	$110	$100	$85

Last Mfg.'s Sug. Retail was $203.

⚐ **Model 1010** — nickel finish, disc.

	$299	$265	$240	$210	$180	$155	$120

⚐ **Model 1015** — gold electroplated, disc.

	$325	$275	$250	$215	$185	$160	$130

1005 DELUXE — .30 cal., custom Monte Carlo walnut stock, high polish blue, oil finish on wood.

	$246	$200	$180	$170	$150	$140	$130

1006 STAINLESS — .30 cal., stainless steel construction, birch stock, 18 in. barrel, 6 lbs. Disc.

	$205	$190	$170

Last Mfg.'s Sug. Retail was $234.

1020 TEFLON — .30 cal., Dupont Teflon-S finish on metal parts, black or gray color, Monte Carlo stock.

	$279	$259	$240

Universal Firearms, cont.

Grading	100%	98%	95%	90%	80%	70%	60%

1256 "FERRET" — .256 Win. Mag. cal., M1 Action, satin blue, birch stock, 18 in. barrel, 5½ lbs. Disc.

	$200	$175	$165	$155	$145	$135	$125

Last Mfg.'s Sug. Retail was $219.

2200 LEATHERNECK — .22 cal., recoil operated action, birch stock, satin blue, 18 in. barrel, 5½ lbs.

	$240	$190	$180	$170	$160	$145	$135

MODEL 3000 ENFORCER PISTOL — 11¼ in. barrel, .30 cal. M1 Carbine, walnut stock, 17¾ in. overall, 15, and 30 shot. Mfg. 1964-1983. Add $50 for Teflon-S finish. See current listing under Iver Johnson.

	100%	98%	95%	90%	80%	70%	60%
Blued finish	$235	$200	$185	$170	$160	$150	$140
Nickel plated	$289	$235	$220	$200	$185	$165	$145
Gold plated	$328	$235	$220	$200	$185	$165	$145
Stainless	$312	$280	$260				

5000 PARATROOPER — .30 cal., metal folding extension, walnut stock, 16 or 18 in. barrel. Disc. See current listing under Iver Johnson.

	$215	$185	$170	$160	$150	$140	$130

Last Mfg.'s Sug. Retail was $234.

5006 PARATROOPER STAINLESS — similar to 5000, only stainless with 18 in. barrel only. Disc.

	$255	$235	$205

Last Mfg.'s Sug. Retail was $281.

1981 COMMEMORATIVE CARBINE — .30 cal., "G.I Military" model, cased with accessories. Mfg. for 40th Anniversary 1941-1981.

	$650	$490	$400

SHOTGUNS

All Universal shotguns were disc. after 1982.

MODEL 7312 O/U — 12 ga., 30 in. full and mod., VR barrel, boxlock, vent. barrel spacer, SST, auto ejectors, barrels ported to reduce recoil, engraved, color case hardened receiver, trap or skeet style, checkered select stock.

	$1,650	$1,540	$1,485	$1,430	$1,320	$1,210	$1,045

MODEL 7412 O/U — similar to 7312, without ejectors, blue and silver receiver.

	$1,430	$1,210	$1,155	$1,100	$9,900	$880	$825

MODEL 7712 O/U — 12 ga., 26 or 28 in. barrel, VR, non-selective single trigger, extractors, light engraving, checkered pistol grip stock.

	$440	$415	$385	$360	$330	$275	$220

MODEL 7812 O/U — similar to 7712, with auto ejectors and more engraving.

	$605	$580	$550	$525	$470	$415	$385

MODEL 7912 O/U — similar to 7812, with selective single trigger and gold damascene engraving.

	$1,210	$1,155	$1,100	$1,045	$965	$880	$825

Grading	100%	98%	95%	90%	80%	70%	60%

MODEL 7112 DOUBLE BARREL — 12 ga., 26 or 28 in. barrels, various chokes, boxlock, extractors, engraved case hardened frame, checkered pistol grip stock.

	$330	$305	$275	$250	$195	$165	$140

DOUBLE WING — 10, 12, 20, or .410 ga., 26, 28, or 30 in. barrels, various chokes, double triggers, boxlock, extractors, checkered pistol grip stock.

	$330	$305	$275	$250	$195	$165	$140
10 gauge.	$385	$360	$330	$305	$250	$220	$165

MODEL 7212 SINGLE BARREL TRAP — 12 ga., 30 in. full, Simmons type VR, engraved case colored frame, vent. barrel to reduce recoil, boxlock, auto ejector, select checkered trap style stock.

	$1,100	$990	$935	$880	$770	$715	$605

U.S. MILITARY
See listings under Colt, Springfield Armory, and Winchester. U.S. Military Trench and Riot guns may be found under the "Trench/Riot Shotguns" category in the T section of this text.

U.S. M1 CARBINE
Various makers.

U.S. M1 CARBINE — semi-auto, .30 cal., 18 in. barrel, 15 or 30 shot box mag., wood stocked, two or four position aperture rear, blade front sight with protective ears, with or without bayonet lug. This weapon was designed by Winchester for the U.S. government, over 6 million were produced by 10 different companies. It is a gas operated lightweight carbine that was also used by other countries' armed forces. Makers and values as follows. Values are for original, unmodified carbines, with proper parts makers and stock cartouches. Deduct 10% - 20% if modified for bayonet or adj. rear sight.

Values below are for original mfg. only, not recent imports.

	100%	98%	95%	90%	80%	70%	60%
Underwood	$650	$575	$495	$400	$350	$300	$275
S.G. Saginaw	$625	$550	$475	$400	$350	$300	$275
Quality Hardware	$650	$575	$495	$415	$370	$325	$295
Nat'l Postal Meter	$725	$625	$525	$425	$375	$325	$295
IBM	$725	$625	$525	$425	$370	$325	$295
Standard Products	$650	$575	$495	$415	$370	$325	$295
Inland (round or square butt)	$650	$575	$495	$415	$370	$325	$295
SG Grand Rapids	$725	$625	$525	$425	$375	$325	$295
Winchester	$875	$800	$675	$525	$425	$350	$325
Irwin Pedersen	$1,350	$1,150	$950	$850	$775	$675	$580
Rockola	$875	$800	$675	$525	$425	$350	$325
Plainfield	$195	$175	$160	$150	$140	$130	$120

M1 A1 PARATROOPER CARBINE — .30 cal., mfg. by Inland — WWII production, folding stock, crossed cannon proofed on bottom, 110,000 mfg. between 1942-1945. Stock folds to 26½ in. overall.

	$675	$600	$525	$450	$400	$350	$300

M1 GARAND — .30-06 cal., semi-auto, 8 shot en bloc clip fed, gas operated, adj. aperture sight, wooden stock. Made 1937-1957 by Springfield, Winchester, H&R, and International Harvester. Add 10% for WWII date, deduct 40% if rewelded, 20% if mismatched.

	$850	$700	$525	$475	$430	$400	$375

Grading	100%	98%	95%	90%	80%	70%	60%
M1-C or M1-D Sniper — with scope and mounts (be wary of fakes and rewelds).							
	$1,650	$1,455	$1,200	$1,060	$900	$780	$650
M1 NATIONAL MATCH — target version of the Garand, using National Match barrel and sights, glass bedding, etc. Should have serialized N.M. paperwork for premium.							
	$1,250	$1,000	$900	$700	$500	$460	$425
U.S. MODEL 1917 ENFIELD RIFLE — .30-06 cal., bolt action, 5 shot, 26 in. barrel, adj. sights, military stock, derived from English P14 Enfield, over two million produced in 1917 and 1918.							
	$450	$400	$350	$300	$275	$250	$225

UZI

Manufactured by Israel Military Industries (IMI). Currently imported by Action Arms, Ltd., located in Philadelphia, PA.

Serial number prefixes used on Uzi Firearms are as follows: "SA" on all 9mm Para. semi-auto carbines Models A and B; "45 SA" on all .45 ACP Model B carbines; "41 SA" on all .41 AE Model B carbines; "MC" on all 9mm (only cal. made) semi-auto mini-carbines; "UP" on all 9mm Para. semi-auto Uzi pistols; "45 UP" on all .45 semi-auto Uzi pistols (disc. 1989). There are also prototypes or experimental Uzis with either "AA" or "AAL" prefixes - these are rare and will command premiums over values listed below.

CARBINE MODEL A — 9mm Para., semi-auto, 16.1 in. barrel, parkerized finish, mfg. by IMI 1980-1983 and serial range is SA01001-SA037000.

	$1,050	$950	$825	$725	$650	$600	$550

Approx. 100 Model As were mfg. with a nickel finish. These are rare and command considerable premiums over values listed above.

CARBINE MODEL B — 9mm, .41 Action Express (new 1987), or .45 ACP (new 1987) cal., semi-auto carbine, 16.1 in. barrel, baked enamel black finish over phosphated (parkerized) base finish, 20 or 25 shot mag., metal folding stock, includes molded case and carrying sling, 8.4 lbs. Mfg. 1983 - until Federal legislation disc. importation 1989 and serial range is 037001-SA073544.

	$925	$875	$825	$725	$650	$600	$550

Last Mfg.'s Sug. Retail was $698.
Add $150 for .22 cal. conversion kit (new 1987).
Add $215 for .45 ACP to 9mm/.41 AE conversion kit.
Add $150 for 9mm to .41 AE (or vice-versa) conversion kit.
Add $215 for 9mm to .45 ACP conversion kit.

MINI CARBINE — 9mm or .45 ACP cal., similar to Carbine except has 19¾ in. barrel, swing-away metal stock, scaled down version of the regular carbine, 7.2 lbs. New 1987. Federal legislation disc. importation 1989.

	$1,050	$950	$825	$725	$650	$600	$550

Last Mfg.'s Sug. Retail was $698.

PISTOL — 9mm or .45 ACP cal. (disc.), semi-auto pistol, 4½ in. barrel, parkerized finish, 20 shot mag., supplied with molded carrying case, sight adj. key and mag. loading tool, 3.8 lbs.

Mfg.'s Sug. Retail	$695	$550	$450	$395	$360	$330	$300	$280

Add $285 for .45 ACP to 9mm/.41 AE conversion kit.
Add $100 for 9mm to .41 AE conversion kit.

V section

VALMET, INC.

Manufacturer located in Jyvaskyla, Finland. Previously imported by Stoeger Industries, Inc. located in South Hackensack, NJ.

The Valmet line was discontinued in 1989 and replaced by Tikka (please refer to the Tikka section in this text) in 1990. All models below have been discontinued and values reflect older mfg.

Grading	100%	98%	95%	90%	80%	70%	60%

LION O/U SHOTGUN — 12 ga., 26, 28, or 30 in. barrels, various chokes, boxlock, SST, checkered stock. Mfg. 1947-1968.

	100%	98%	95%	90%	80%	70%	60%
	$415	$370	$340	$320	$305	$275	$240

M-625 PARAMILITARY DESIGN RIFLE — semi-auto version of Finn M-62, 7.62 x 39 Russian, 15 or 30 shot mag., $16\frac{5}{8}$ in. barrel, gas operated, rotary bolt, adj. rear sight, tube steel or wood stock. Mfg. 1962-disc.

	100%	98%	95%	90%	80%	70%	60%
	$770	$715	$635	$605	$550	$530	$495

Add $50 for wood stock.

M-715 — similar to M-625, except .223, reinforced resin or wood stock.

	100%	98%	95%	90%	80%	70%	60%
	$635	$550	$415	$385	$370	$340	$325

Add $50 for wood stock.

PRE-1989 MFG.

MODEL 412 O/U SHOOTING SYSTEM — interchangeable barrel assemblies permit a double rifle, shotgun/rifle, and O&U shotgun configuration, user installed interchangeable barrels, monobloc locking, rifle barrel positioning by adjustment, SST, extractors or ejectors checkered walnut stock and forend, cocking indicators, blued finish. Importation on all models was disc. 1989.
Add $100 for synthetic stock on all 412 models.

⚔ **Model 412S Field Grade** — 12 ga. only, auto ejectors, screw-in choke tubes, matte nickel finish. New 1986.

	100%	98%	95%	90%	80%	70%	60%
	$855	$670	$580	$540	$475	$440	$400

Last Mfg.'s Sug. Retail was $999.

⚔ **Model 412S Field and Target** — 12 ga. only, $2\frac{3}{4}$ and 3 in. chambers, ejectors. Disc. 1988.

	100%	98%	95%	90%	80%	70%	60%
	$775	$660	$580	$540	$475	$440	$400

Last Mfg.'s Sug. Retail was $874.

⚔ **Model 412ST Trap and Skeet** — 12 ga., Monte Carlo stock on Trap model, 28 in. barrels on Skeet model, screw-in chokes standard.

	100%	98%	95%	90%	80%	70%	60%
	$1,040	$875	$695	$650	$580	$540	$475

Last Mfg.'s Sug. Retail was $1,215.

⚔ **Model 412ST Premium Grade Target** — similar to Model 412ST Trap and Skeet, except has better walnut and checkering. New 1987.

	100%	98%	95%	90%	80%	70%	60%
	$1,355	$1,050	$865	$750	$640	$580	$515

Last Mfg.'s Sug. Retail was $1,550.

Grading	100%	98%	95%	90%	80%	70%	60%

Model 412S Combination Gun — combination, 12 ga, 3 in. chamber over choice of .222, .223, .243, .30-06, or .308 cal., extractors.

	$1,025	$850	$675	$600	$550	$475	$440

Last Mfg.'s Sug. Retail was $1,615.

Model 412S Double Rifle — .243 (disc. 1987), .30-06, .308 (disc. 1987), .375 H&H (disc. 1987), or 9.3 x 73 R cal., extractors, 24 in. barrels.

	$1,060	$895	$725	$650	$580	$540	$475

Add $100 for 9.3 x 74 R cal. or .375 H&H cal.
This model in .30-06 cal. has extractors only while in 9.3 x 74 R cal. ejectors are standard.
Last Mfg.'s Sug. Retail was $1,275.

Model 412K Double Rifle — .30-06 or .308 cal. only, 24 in. separated barrels, extractors. Importation disc. 1986.

	$800	$660	$580	$540	$475	$440	$400

Last Mfg.'s Sug. Retail was $899.

Model 412 Engraved — satin finish, receiver extensively bank note engraved in choice of 4 patterns, select Triple-X wood hand checkered — choice of field or target, available in any Valmet model. Add $85 for shotgun rifle, $320 for double rifle.
This model has limited availability and prices are on request from the manufacturer. Last Mfg.'s Sug. retail was $2,499.

Extra Barrel Assemblies (Model 412 O/U) — $505 - $605 each for shotgun (includes screw-in chokes), $579 each for shotgun/rifle combo, $660 each for double rifle (add $100 for ejectors).

RIFLES

HUNTER MODEL — .223, .243, or .308 cal., gas operated semi-auto, Kalashnikov action, 20½ in. barrel, checkered walnut stock and forearm, matte finished metal, 5, 9, or 20 shot mag., 8 lbs. New 1986, Federal legislation disc. importation 1989.

	$795	$700	$625	$550	$500	$450	$420

Last Mfg.'s Sug. Retail was $795.

MODEL 76 — .223, 7.62 x 39mm, or .308 cal., gas operated semi-auto paramilitary design rifle, 16¾ in. or 20½ (.308 only) in. barrel, 15 or 30 (7.62 x 39mm only) shot mag., parkerized finish. Federal legislation disc. importation 1989.

	$750	$675	$600	$525	$475	$450	$420

Add $95-$125 for synthetic or folding stock.
Last Mfg.'s Sug. Retail was $740.

MODEL 78 — .308 cal. only, similar to Model 76, except has 24½ in. barrel, wood stock and forearm, and barrel bipod, 11 lbs. New 1987. Federal legislation disc. importation 1989.

	$1,100	$925	$800	$700	$600	$530	$475

Last Mfg.'s Sug. Retail was $1,060.

VARNER SPORTING ARMS, INC.

Manufacturer previously located in Marietta, GA until approximately 1989.

VARNER FAVORITE HUNTER — .22 LR cal., patterned after J. Stevens Favorite Model, ½ round - ½ octagon 21½ in. takedown barrel, blued frame, walnut stock and forearm, aperture rear sight, 5 lbs. Mfg. 1988-89.

	$325	$270	$220	$185	$150	$130	$110

Last Mfg.'s Sug. Retail was $369.

Grading	100%	98%	95%	90%	80%	70%	60%

⁂ **Hunter Deluxe** — similar to Field Grade, except has case colored frame and lever, and deluxe walnut. Mfg. 1988-89.

	$450	$375	$285	$225	$175	$150	$135

Last Mfg.'s Sug. Retail was $500.

⁂ **Presentation Grade** — includes target hammer and trigger, AAA quality checkered stock and forearm, includes takedown case. Mfg. 1988-89.

	$480	$400	$310	$250	$195	$170	$155

Last Mfg.'s Sug. Retail was $569.

PRESENTATION ENGRAVED — available in a No. 1 Grade for $649, a No. 2 for $779, or a No. 3 for $1,099.

VERNEY-CARRON
Ventura Imports.

O/U SHOTGUN — 12 ga., 26 or 28 in. VR barrel, boxlock, auto ejectors, SST, choked to specifications, checkered French walnut straight or pistol grip stock. Mfg. 1978-disc.

	$990	$880	$825	$770	$715	$660	$605

SKEET GUN — 12 ga., similar to Field, with 28 in. skeet and skeet barrel, skeet style pistol grip stock.

	$1,045	$935	$880	$825	$770	$715	$660

VICKERS LIMITED
Manufacturer located in Crayford/Kent, England.

JUBILEE SINGLE SHOT TARGET RIFLE — Martini type action, .22 LR cal., 28 in. heavy barrel, target sights, one piece pistol grip, target stock, pre-WWII.

	$440	$330	$305	$275	$250	$220	$165

EMPIRE MODEL — similar to Jubilee, with 27 or 30 in. barrel, straight grip stock.

	$415	$310	$285	$260	$220	$195	$150

VICTORY ARMS CO. LIMITED
Previously manufactured in prototype format only by Modern Manufacturing Company located in Phoenix, AZ.

PISTOL: SEMI-AUTO

MODEL MC5 — while a few prototypes were mfg. for trade shows (circa 1991-92), this model was never commercially manufactured. Last advertised retail was $465.

VIERLINGS
Four Barrel Long Arm Configuration mostly mfg. previously in Germany or Austria.

This configuration of long arm has four barrels, typically with a .22 caliber barrel incorporated in the center rib or stacked below two SxS shotgun barrels and a lower, larger caliber rifle barrel. Vierlings typically have two triggers, both single set. Barrel selectors are usually on the top tang. This unusual configuration is mostly of German mfg., although there are a few Austrian specimens also (the gunmakers of Ferlach still custom make this model). All Vierlings are mfg. one at a time, with fabrication being very complicated, lengthy, and expensive. As a result, every Vierling must be appraised individually - most specimens, however, are priced approx. $2,750-$6,500+.

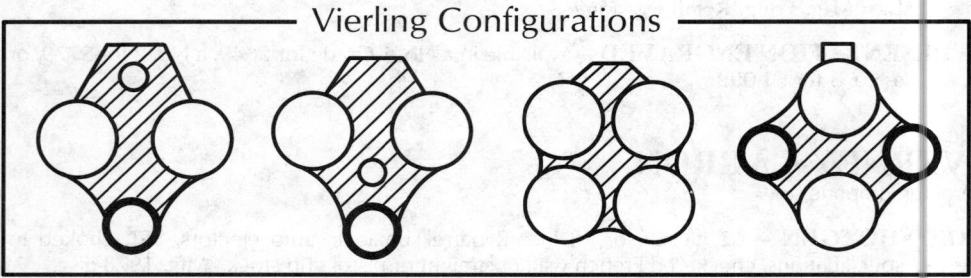

Vierling Configurations

VIRGINIAN
This trademark can be located under the Interarms section in this text.

VOERE
Manufacturer located in Kufstein, Austria since 1965. Currently imported by Mandall Shooting Supplies located in Scottsdale, AZ. To date, Voere has had little distribution in the U.S. Rahn Gun Works, Inc. located in Hastings, MI has imported this trademark on a limited basis in the past.

Voere of Austria has nothing to do with the Voere trademark of Germany that was taken over by Mauser-Werke after going bankrupt.

Voere manufactures a complete line of quality rimfire semi-auto and centerfire bolt-action/semi-auto rifles. Their new caseless ammunition released in 1991 is a bold step and will have to hold up to the performance and reliability of its cased relatives. More information on this trademark can be obtained by writing/FAXing Mandall Shooting Supplies or Voere directly (see Trademark Index for information).

RIFLES

Grading	100%	98%	95%	90%	80%	70%	60%

MODEL VEC 91 BOLT ACTION — 5.7 x 26 UCC caseless ammo, unique ignition system requires electrical impulse to activate semi-conducting primer that ignites propellant (2 small batteries are housed in the pistol grip capable of igniting 5,000 shots), 5 shot detachable mag., 20 in. free floating barrel, twin forward locking lugs, 2 stage electrical trigger adj. from $\frac{1}{2}$ oz. to 7 lbs, 55 grain bullet achieves 3,300 fps with no loss in accuracy over normal mechanical primer ignited cartridges, 6 lbs. New late 1992.

Please contact the distributor directly to obtain pricing and import information on this new, unique model.

MODEL 2185 MATCH SEMI-AUTO — .308 Win. cal., gas operated, free floating barrel, 5 shot detachable mag., manual safety, iron sights, laminate wood, 11 lbs.

Mfg.'s Sug. Retail	$4,495	$4,495	$3,950	$3,500	$3,000	$2,500	$2,000	$1,500

Other calibers are available on special order only.

Grading	100%	98%	95%	90%	80%	70%	60%

MODEL 2185 HUNTING RIFLE — 9.3 x 62mm, other cals. available upon special request, checkered stock and forend, iron sights.

Mfg.'s Sug. Retail	$1,895	$1,895	$1,550	$1,275	$1,000	$850	$725	$600

BOLT-ACTION MODEL — various cals., no longer imported.

	$325	$250	$225	$200	$175	$125	$100

.22 SEMI-AUTO — .22 LR cal., open or closed bolt design, clip mag., checkered hardwood stock, adj. rear sight.

	$225	$195	$165	$145	$130	$120	$95

VOLUNTEER ENTERPRISES

Previous manufacturer located in Knoxville, TN.

Volunteer Enterprises became Commando Arms after 1978.

COMMANDO MARK III CARBINE — semi-auto, blowback action, .45 ACP cal., 16½ in. barrel, aperture sight, stock styled after "Tommy Gun". Mfg. 1969-1976.

	$425	$365	$315	$280	$225	$195	$160

COMMANDO MARK III CARBINE

Vertical grip	$440	$365	$320	$280	$225	$195	$160

COMMANDO MARK 9 — similar to Mark III in 9mm.

	$440	$375	$325	$285	$230	$195	$160
Vertical grip	$440	$365	$320	$280	$225	$195	$160

VOUZELAUD

Previous manufacturer located in France. Previously imported by Waverly Arms Co. located in Suffolk, VA.

SHOTGUNS: SIDE-BY-SIDE

MODEL 315 E — 12, 16 or 20 ga., boxlock, 28 in. barrels, auto ejectors, straight grip French walnut stock, double triggers, case colored receiver, light engraving. Importation disc. 1987.
Values generally range between $1,350-$2,000 for this model.

MODEL 315 EL — similar to Model 315 E, except has satin finish receiver engraved with bouquets of fine English scroll work, trigger guard and forearm also engraved. Importation disc. 1987.
Values generally range between $1,475-$2,250 for this model.
This model was also available by special order in 28 or .410 ga. (Model 315 EL-S) - add $600.

MODEL 315 EGL — 12, 16 or 20 ga., sidelock, 28 in. barrels, selective ejectors, double triggers, extensive scroll engraving on coin finish receiver, English style stock of extra fancy French walnut. Importation disc. 1987.
Values generally range between $1,750-$2,750 for this model.

MODEL 315 EGL-S — same general features as the Model 315 EGL, except monobloc barrel construction, extensive game scene engraving, and grand deluxe walnut stock and forearm with extra fine hand checkering. Importation disc. 1987.
Values generally range between $1,950-$2,950 for this model.
Last Mfg.'s Sug. Retail was $5,895.

W section

WAFFEN VERATSCHNIG
Manufacturer located in Ferlach, Austria.

Waffen Veratschnig manufactures a variety of high grade, made to individual special order, rifles, shotguns, combination guns, drillings, and vierlings. A wide variety of engraving scenes, wood carvings, and other special features are available at extra cost. Currently, they do not have a U.S. importer and for more information, please contact them directly (see Trademark Index).

WALTHER
Previously manufactured in Zella-Mehlis (now Suhl, Germany) 1886 to 1945. Current production is in Ulm, Germany, 1953 to date. Currently imported and distributed by Interarms located in Alexandria, VA.

The calibers listed in the Walther Pistol sections are listed in American caliber designations. The German metric conversion is as follows: .22 LR - same, .25 ACP - 6.35mm, .32 ACP - 7.65mm, .380 ACP - 9mm Kurz. The metric caliber designations in most cases will be indicated on the left slide legend for German mfg. pistols listed in the Walther section.

SEMI-AUTO PISTOLS, PRE-WAR

Grading	100%	98%	95%	90%	80%	70%	60%

MODEL 1 — .25 ACP, 2.1 in. barrel, fixed sights, blue, checkered hard rubber grips, pre-WWI. Mfg. 1908.

	100%	98%	95%	90%	80%	70%	60%
	$500	$400	$350	$250	$200	$150	$125

MODEL 2 — .25 ACP, 2.1 in. barrel, fixed sights, blue, rubber grips, pop-up rear sight on early models, fixed on late models. Mfg. 1909.

	$425	$390	$325	$225	$175	$120	$100

This model can usually be distinguished by its knurled barrel ring.

⚶ **Early Model** — differentiated by its pop-up rear sight.

	$1,100	$950	$875	$750	$675	$550	$400

MODEL 3 — .32 ACP, 2.6 in. barrel, blue, fixed sights, rubber grips, ejection port on left side. Mfg. 1910.

	$1,500	$1,250	$1,100	$800	$550	$500	$400

MODEL 4 — .32 ACP, 8 shot, 3½ in. barrel, blue, rubber grips, ejection port on left side. Mfg. 1910-1918.

	$375	$300	$250	$200	$125	$100	$80

Add 10% for WWI "Eagle" proofs.

MODEL 5 — better quality version of 2, fixed rear sight. Mfg. 1913.

	$300	$350	$275	$200	$145	$115	$100

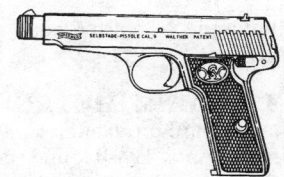

MODEL 6 — 9mm Para., 4¾ in. barrel, blue, hard rubber grips, ejection port on right side. Mfg. 1915-1917. Some are Imperial proofed.

	$5,500	$4,500	$3,000	$2,300	$1,500	$1,050	$800

Grading	100%	98%	95%	90%	80%	70%	60%

MODEL 7 — .25 ACP, 3 in. barrel, blue, fixed sights, rubber grips, ejector port on right side. Mfg. 1917-1918.

	$625	$475	$400	$325	$250	$200	$125

MODEL 8 — .25 ACP, 2⅞ in. barrel, blue, fixed sights, plastic grips. Mfg. 1920-1945. Add 25% for engraved slide.

	$425	$375	$325	$265	$200	$150	$125

Add 10% for "Eagle N" proofing.

MODEL 9 VEST POCKET — .25 ACP, engineering revision of Model 1, 2 in. barrel, blued finish standard, upward ejection, 6 shot bottom release mag., fixed sights, black checkered plastic grips with oval medallions, safety lever on left frame side behind trigger, 9 oz. Mfg. 1921-1945.

	$475	$425	$350	$275	$200	$160	$140

Add 40% for engraved slide, 20% for nickel, 100% for gold engraved.

MODEL PP DOUBLE ACTION AUTOMATIC "POLICE PISTOL" — .22 LR, .25 ACP, .32 ACP, or .380 ACP cal., 3⅞ in. barrel, blue, fixed sights, plastic grips. Mfg. 1929-1945. Crown N proof until 1939. Eagle N Nazi commercial proof until 1945.

	100%	98%	95%	90%	80%	70%	60%
.22 LR cal.	$895	$775	$675	$600	$525	$450	$375
.25 ACP cal.	$3,450	$3,100	$2,650	$2,000	$1,500	$1,200	$1,000
.32 ACP cal.	$450	$395	$375	$350	$275	$225	$200
.380 ACP cal.	$895	$825	$750	$675	$600	$550	$500

Add 15% for alloy frame.

Original nickel finished Model PPs are very rare; this precludes accurate price evaluation.

Values above assume original guns without import markings. Recently imported WWII/surplus Police used guns are stamped on the frame or receiver, indicating the current importer and address - deduct 20%-30% from values listed above for these recent imports.

.32 ACP Bottom Release Magazine — 90 degree safety

	$800	$700	$625	$600	$525	$425	$395

.380 ACP Bottom Release Magazine — 90 degree safety.

	$1,050	$950	$875	$800	$700	$600	$500

Pre-War Persian proofed — 9mm Kurz BMR.

	$2,000	$1,800	$1,600	$1,450	$1,250	$995	$825

Pre-War Verchromt .32 ACP cal. — add 50% for .380 ACP cal.

	$1,450	$1,250	$800	$750	$675	$485	$395

Pre-War Stoeger — .32 ACP cal. only.

	$1,200	$1,050	$925	$800	$600	$425	$325

Nairobi — Chas. Heyer.

	$1,200	$1,000	$850	$725	$575	$400	$300

Aluminum frame — 90 degree safety.

	$650	$600	$500	$400	$275	$235	$200

Allemagne — French Comm.

	$1,050	$950	$825	$720	$600	$425	$325

MODEL PP WARTIME PRODUCTION — mfg. 1940-1945, "Eagle N" Proof (Nazi commercial nitro proof after April 1940) or "Crown N" proof (German commercial proof mark used to April, 1940) found on pre-WWII military production. Variations are listed either by proof marks or frame/slide markings.

Grading	100%	98%	95%	90%	80%	70%	60%

⚔ **"Waffenamt" Proofed** — .32 ACP or .380 ACP cal., "Eagle N", military acceptance marking.

.32 ACP cal.	$500	$400	$350	$300	$250	$220	$200
.380 ACP cal.	$800	$725	$650	$600	$550	$500	$450

Original nickel finished Model PP's are very rare; this precludes accurate price evaluation. Late war PPs are sometimes encountered with Walther marked walnut grips - add 20% if Waffenamt proofed.

⚔ **Eagle N Proofed** — .22 LR or .32 ACP cal., with lanyard loop.

.32 ACP cal.	$450	$395	$350	$300	$250	$200	$150
.22 LR cal.	$750	$700	$625	$550	$495	$450	$395

After WWII the French added a lanyard to the left side of the grip. Deduct 25% for this alteration.

⚔ **Eagle C & F Marked (Nazi Police)** — .32 ACP cal., "Eagle N or C" proofed on left side of frame.

	$700	$650	$600	$500	$450	$380	$300

Add 50% if Eagle C marked.

⚔ **RFV Marked** — .32 ACP cal., "Crown N". Mfg. for Reich Finance Administration.

	$700	$650	$600	$500	$400	$325	$225

⚔ **RJ Marked** — .32 ACP cal., "Crown N". Mfg. for Reich Justice Ministry.

	$750	$675	$600	$525	$450	$325	$225

⚔ **SA Marked** — .22 LR or .32 ACP cal., "Crown N". Mfg. for SA (Sturm Abteilung - storm troops) of the Nazi party.

	$1,450	$1,350	$1,050	$925	$725	$600	$425

Add 10% for .22 LR.
Rare SA markings may bring as much as 50% more over values listed above.

⚔ **NSKK Marked** — .32 ACP cal., "Crown N or Eagle N" proofed. Mfg. for Nazi Party Transport Corps, rare.

	$2,500	$2,000	$1,500	$1,025	$875	$700	$550

⚔ **RRZ proofed** — .32 ACP cal., "Reich Rundfunk Zenhale", for German Radio Broadcasting - only 3 known.

	$3,500	$3,000	$2,500				

⚔ **PDM Marked** — .32 ACP cal., "Crown N", Munich Police Department.

	$850	$775	$700	$625	$525	$450	$360

⚔ **AC Marked** — .32 ACP cal., replaced Walther Banner during 1945, "Eagle N".

	$300	$275	$250	$225	$175	$150	$125

⚔ **Czech. Contract** — stamped Rampant Lion.

	$950	$850	$825	$700	$600	$500	$400

⚔ **Panagraphed**

	$825	$750	$695	$630	$550	$385	$275

⚔ **Danish Rplt.**

	$975	$925	$825	$775	$700	$625	$400

MODEL PP LIGHTWEIGHT — aluminum alloy version.
Add 20% to Standard Model prices.
Add 20%-40% for original nickel finish (very rare).

Grading	100%	98%	95%	90%	80%	70%	60%

MODEL PPK PRE-WAR PRODUCTION

— .22 LR, .25 ACP, .32 ACP, or .380 ACP cal., PPK designates Police Pistol Kriminal, 3¼ in. barrel, blue, fixed sights, plastic grips. Mfg. 1931-1940.

	100%	98%	95%	90%	80%	70%	60%
.22 LR cal.	$1,100	$925	$750	$700	$650	$525	$400
.25 ACP cal.	$5,000	$4,475	$3,800	$3,400	$2,800	$2,100	$1,475
.32 ACP cal.	$550	$500	$425	$350	$300	$250	$225
.380 ACP cal.	$2,000	$1,725	$1,500	$1,100	$800	$600	$500

Add 60% for bottom release Mag (.32 ACP cal.).

MODEL PPK WARTIME PRODUCTION

— mfg. 1940-1945, "Eagle N" proofed after April 1940, "Crown N" proofs appear on pre-1940 production with frame/slide markings. Variations are listed either by proof marks, frame/slide markings, or type of finish.

⚞ **Commercial "Eagle N" Proofed** — .22 LR, .32 ACP, or .380 ACP cal., Nazi Eagle over N (standard Nazi commercial acceptance proof).

	100%	98%	95%	90%	80%	70%	60%
.22 LR cal.	$1,100	$850	$675	$595	$525	$460	$420
.32 ACP cal.	$495	$425	$350	$300	$200	$180	$160
.380 ACP cal.	$1,100	$900	$800	$700	$600	$500	$400

This variation is normally encountered with semi-polished, exterior metal showing milling marks to a various degree.

⚞ **Waffenamt Proofed With High Polish**

100%	98%	95%	90%	80%	70%	60%
$850	$650	$575	$500	$425	$330	$275

⚞ **Eagle C Marked** — .32 ACP cal., "Crown N - Eagle C", mfg. for Nazi Police.

100%	98%	95%	90%	80%	70%	60%
$650	$525	$450	$400	$315	$260	$200

Add 25% for high polish finish.

⚞ **Eagle F Marked** — .32 ACP cal., "Crown N - Eagle F", Nazi Police.

100%	98%	95%	90%	80%	70%	60%
$800	$700	$600	$475	$375	$300	$250

⚞ **RZM Marked** — .32 ACP cal., "Crown N", proof marking for Nazi Party Purchasing Office.

100%	98%	95%	90%	80%	70%	60%
$875	$800	$765	$600	$350	$275	$225

⚞ **Party Leader** — .32 ACP cal., named because grips (brown or black plastic) have the German Eagle holding a Swastika, "Crown N" proofed, honor weapon awarded 3rd Reich political leaders, rare. Be very wary of fake grips (especially black color) as reproductions have been made recently. Unfortunately, the grips on a Party Leader (in correct serial range) are the only distinguishing feature on this very desirable configuration.

100%	98%	95%	90%	80%	70%	60%
$2,500	$2,250	$1,800	$1,500	$1,200	$1,100	$1,000

⚞ **RZM Party Leader** — .32 ACP cal., RZM marked, "Crown N" proofed.

100%	98%	95%	90%	80%	70%	60%
$3,200	$2,950	$2,650	$2,200	$1,300	$1,200	$1,100

⚞ **NSKK Marked** — perhaps the rarest of the WWII military PPK variations. Rarity makes accurate price evaluation unpredictable - however, an original specimen could be in the $6,000-$11,000 range, depending on original condition.

⚞ **RFV Marked** — .32 ACP cal., "Crown N". Mfg. for Reich Finance Administration.

100%	98%	95%	90%	80%	70%	60%
$975	$900	$825	$750	$800	$700	$675

⚞ **PDM Marked** — .32 ACP cal., "Crown N". Mfg. for Police Dept. Munich.

100%	98%	95%	90%	80%	70%	60%
$975	$900	$825	$750	$600	$500	$395

⚞ **POM** — aluminum frame — BMR.

100%	98%	95%	90%	80%	70%	60%
$900	$825	$750	$650	$525	$500	$475

Grading	100%	98%	95%	90%	80%	70%	60%
DRP Marked — .32 ACP cal., "Crown N". Mfg. for Postal Service.							
	$850	$750	$675	$525	$420	$350	$260
Panagraph Slide							
	$850	$750	$675	$525	$450	$375	$300
Verchromt — .32 ACP or 380 ACP cal., differentiated by dull silver satin type finish.							
	$2,000	$1,600	$1,300	$1,000	$800	$650	$500
Add 25% for .380 ACP cal.							
"K" suffix — "K" beneath ser. no.							
	$625	$525	$475	$375	$300	$275	$250
"W" suffix — .32 ACP cal., "Crown N" proofed, W-suffix ser. no.							
	$725	$650	$575	$525	$475	$450	$375
Early 90 degree safety							
	$650	$575	$475	$425	$325	$260	$195
Early bottom release Mag.							
	$950	$850	$750	$650	$500	$475	$375
PPK Marked PP							
	$2,500	$2,150	$1,850	$1,600	$1,400	$1,180	$900
7-digit ser. no.							
	$725	$700	$650	$600	$550	$400	$300
Dural frame — .22 LR, .32 ACP, or .380 ACP cal., chrome finish (very rare), "Eagle N".							
	$650	$600	$575	$525	$400	$325	$275
Add 25% for .380 ACP or .22 LR cal.							
Stoeger Contract — .32 ACP cal., marked "A. F. Stoeger Inc. New York" on left center of slide.							
	$1,200	$900	$700	$500	$350	$225	$200
Heyer Contract — .32 ACP cal., marked "Chas. A. Heyer and Co., Nairobi" on top left of slide.							
	$1,200	$1,050	$900	$775	$675	$550	$400
Czech. Contract — Rampant Lion stamped.							
	$950	$875	$750	$625	$550	$425	$325
Danish Rplt.							
	$950	$875	$750	$625	$550	$425	$325
Allemagne — French Commercial — rare.							
	$950	$875	$750	$625	$550	$425	$325

MODEL PPK LIGHTWEIGHT — aluminum alloy version.
Add 20% to Standard Model pricing.

SPORT MODEL 1926 — .22 S and LR (known as Standard Model in Germany) cals.

	100%	98%	95%	90%	80%	70%	60%
	$1,050	$900	$800	$675	$595	$550	$495

1932 OLYMPIA MODEL — .22 S or LR, 10 shot, 6 or 9 in. barrel, target sights, one piece grip, introduced in 1928 and used in 1932 Olympics. Marketed by Stoeger and Chas. Heyer-Nairobi.

	100%	98%	95%	90%	80%	70%	60%
	$1,050	$850	$750	$575	$495	$440	$395

Grading	100%	98%	95%	90%	80%	70%	60%

OLYMPIA SPORT MODEL — .22 LR, 4 in. barrel, adj. target sights, blue, wood grips, 4 barrel weights available. Mfg. 1936-1940.

	$925	$800	$700	$600	$475	$420	$375

Add 20% for weight set.

1936 OLYMPIA "JAGERSCHAFTS" HUNTING MODEL — similar to Sport, with 4 in. barrel. Mfg. 1936-1940. Also seen with Eagle N proofs.

	$850	$750	$675	$550	$495	$440	$360

OLYMPIA RAPID FIRE MODEL — .22 Short only, 7.4 in. barrel, blue, adj. sight, wood grip, has alloy slide. Mfg. 1936-1940.

	$950	$850	$785	$600	$520	$460	$380

1936 OLYMPIA FUNFKAMPF MODEL — .22 Short or LR, $9\frac{1}{4}$ in. barrel, blue, adj. sight, wood grips, barrel weights, circa 1936.

	$1,250	$1,000	$850	$775	$575	$500	$440

MODEL HP COMMERCIAL DOUBLE ACTION — pre-war version of P-38, 9mm, 5 in. barrel, fixed sight, blue, wood or plastic grips. Mfg. 1937-1944. Many variations, including several different finishes.
See German WWII Military Pistols for values on this model.

PISTOLS: SEMI-AUTO, POST-WAR

In 1983, Carl Walther from West Germany announced the discontinuance of models PP and PPK/S from the American market. These guns are attracting more collector interest as their production records are now complete. Manurhin of France no longer imports into the U.S. and guns imported between 1984-86 will not have the Interarms logo or Walther trademark.

Prices below reflect the recent devaluation of the U.S. dollar against some foreign currencies. While the manufacturer's suggested retails have gone up considerably, prices for used specimens (98% or less original condition) have not increased proportionally, and in some cases, have changed very little.

MODEL PP DOUBLE ACTION — .22 LR, .32 ACP, or .380 ACP cal., specifications similar to pre-war PP, $3\frac{7}{8}$ in. barrel. Imported 1963-present. W. German manufacture.

⚟ **.380 ACP cal.** — 6 shot mag.

Mfg.'s Sug. Retail	$1,492	$1,250	$495	$395	$330	$300	$275	$250

⚟ **.32 ACP cal.** — 6 shot mag.

Mfg.'s Sug. Retail	$1,448	$1,250	$425	$350	$295	$275	$250	$225

⚟ **.22 LR cal.** — 7 shot mag., disc. 1989, reintroduced 1992.

Mfg.'s Sug. Retail	$948	$825	$450	$375	$350	$325	$300	$275

⚟ **Blue Engraved** — .22 LR (disc.) or .380 ACP (disc. 1991) cal.

	$1,350	$1,100	$950

Last Mfg.'s Sug. Retail was $1,650.00
Add 5% for .22 LR cal.

⚟ **Chrome Engraved** — .22 LR or .380 ACP cal. Disc. 1990.

	$1,350	$1,100	$950

Add $50 for .22 LR cal.
Last Mfg.'s Sug. Retail was $1,600.

Grading	100%	98%	95%	90%	80%	70%	60%
⚰ **Silver Engraved** — .22 LR or .380 ACP (disc. 1990) cal.							
Mfg.'s Sug. Retail $1,948	$1,575	$1,150	$1,000				
⚰ **Gold Engraved** — .22 LR or .380 ACP (disc. 1989) cal.							
Mfg.'s Sug. Retail $2,053	$1,725	$1,350	$1,150				
⚰ **Manurhin PP** — .22 LR, .32 ACP, or .380 ACP cal.							
	$350	$310	$285	$225	$180	$165	$150
Add 10% for .380 ACP cal.							

⚰ **Model PP 50th Anniversary Commemorative** — .22 LR or .380 ACP cal., gold-plated parts, hand carved grips, presentation case. 500 imported to U.S. 1979.

	100%	98%	95%
	$1,000	$800	$600

Add $100 for .22 LR cal.
Last Mfg.'s Sug. Retail was $1,700.

PP SPORT — double action, thumbrest grips, round hammer with spur, adj. rear sight, long barrel. Mfg. 1953-1970.

	100%	98%	95%	90%	80%	70%	60%
Manurhin manufacture	$650	$625	$600	$525	$475	$400	$325
Mark II (mfg. 1955-1957)	$725	$680	$625	$575	$520	$480	$425
Walther manufacture	$775	$725	$700	$575	$520	$475	$400

Deduct 10% if not marked.
Note: Add $75 for barrel weight, $100 for factory case, 20% for factory nickel, 5% for single action.

⚰ **PP Sport "C" Model C** — mfg. for competition shooting, single action, 7⅝ in. barrel, spur hammer.

	100%	98%	95%	90%	80%	70%	60%
	$750	$725	$675	$625	$525	$475	$400

MODEL PPK — similar to pre-war PPK, .22 LR, .32 ACP, or .380 ACP cal., 3.31 in. barrel. Mfg. 1963-present, U.S. import stopped by GCA 68 on W. German and French production.

	100%	98%	95%	90%	80%	70%	60%
.32 ACP cal.	$525	$450	$375	$325	$295	$270	$250
.22 LR cal.	$725	$625	$550	$500	$425	$350	$300
.380 ACP cal.	$650	$575	$500	$450	$400	$325	$275
Blue engraved	$1,600	$1,300	$950				
Silver engraved	$1,850	$1,400	$1,000				
Gold engraved	$2,200	$1,675	$1,250				

100% column assumes NIB condition - deduct 15% if not boxed.

MODEL PPK LIGHTWEIGHT — similar to Standard, with dural frame, .22 LR or .32 ACP cal.

	100%	98%	95%	90%	80%	70%	60%
	$445	$400	$365	$325	$295	$270	$250

Add 20% for .22 LR cal.

MODEL PPK-1986 U.S. MFG. — .380 ACP cal. only, 3.2 in. barrel, similar specifications as previous W. German and French manufacture, 6 shot finger extension mag., black plastic grips, 21 oz. Made in the U.S. Introduced 1986.

	100%	98%	95%	90%	80%	70%	60%
Mfg.'s Sug. Retail $627	$495	$395	$340	$310	$290	$275	$260

Manufacture in the U.S. is under an exclusive licensing agreement with Walther of W. Germany.

Grading	100%	98%	95%	90%	80%	70%	60%
PPK Stainless — stainless steel construction. New 1986.							
Mfg.'s Sug. Retail $627	$495	$395	$340				

MODEL PPK/S — .22 LR, .32 ACP, or .380 ACP cal., similar to PPK, except has larger PP frame to meet import requirements of 1968, 3¼ in. barrel, production in W. Germany (now disc.), Manurhin of France (disc. 1986), and in the U.S. (mfg. under license from Walther by Interarms). 7 or 8 shot, double action, fixed sights.

	100%	98%	95%	90%	80%	70%	60%
American PPK/S — .380 ACP cal. only, blue finish, 7 shot finger extension mag.							
Mfg.'s Sug. Retail $627	$495	$395	$340	$310	$290	$275	$260
Stainless PPK/S — .380 ACP cal. only, American manufacture, introduction July of 1983.							
Mfg.'s Sug. Retail $627	$495	$395	$340				
W. German PPK/S — .22 LR, .32 ACP, or .380 ACP cal. Disc. 1982.							
.32 ACP cal.	$495	$425	$350	$325	$295	$270	$250
.22 LR cal.	$650	$575	$525	$425	$350	$300	$275
.380 ACP cal.	$600	$525	$475	$375	$300	$275	$250
American PPK/S — blue engraved. Disc. 1985.							
	$875	$850	$800				
Last Mfg.'s Sug. Retail was $990.							
American PPK/S Gold-Engraved Commemorative — 500 total mfg. Disc. 1987.							
	$1,000	$850	$675				
Last Mfg.'s Sug. Retail was $1,200.							
American PPK/S Gold-Engraved — disc. 1985.							
	$975	$800	$675				
Last Mfg.'s Sug. Retail was $1,070.							
W. German PPK/S Blue Engraved — all quantities became out of stock in 1990.							
	$1,395	$1,050	$850				
Last Mfg.'s Sug. Retail was $1,550.							
W. German PPK/S Chrome Engraved — importation disc. 1991.							
	$1,450	$1,075	$950				
Last Mfg.'s Sug. Retail was $1,700.							
W. German PPK/S Silver Engraved — disc. 1988.							
	$1,595	$1,150	$975				
Last Mfg.'s Sug. Retail was $1,700.							
W. German PPK/S Gold Engraved — disc. 1985.							
	$1,850	$1,250	$1,000				
Last Mfg.'s Sug. Retail was $1,800.							
PPK/S Durgarde (Manurhin mfg.) — similar to above, only with bonded brushed chrome finish.							
Under Walther license	$395	$310	$290	$265	$245	$210	$195
Add $25 for .22 LR cal.							

MANURHIN PPK/S — see listings under Manurhin section.

Grading	100%	98%	95%	90%	80%	70%	60%

MODEL PP SUPER — 9 x 18mm, (Police) or .380 ACP cal., 3.6 in. barrel, fixed sights, plastic grips, blue. Mfg. 1975-1981.

	$600	$525	$400	$345	$275	$250	$235

Deduct 25% if in 9 x 18mm cal.

⚮ **PP Super-Cutaway**

	$650	$600	$550

MODEL TP — .22 LR or .25 ACP cal., updated version of Model 9, concealed hammer. Mfg. 1962-1970.

	100%	98%	95%	90%	80%	70%	60%
.22 LR cal.	$675	$600	$435	$350	$300	$260	$210
.25 ACP cal.	$495	$425	$360	$300	$250	$220	$185

MODEL TPH — .22 LR or .25 ACP cal., double action 2.8 in. barrel, alloy frame, blue, fixed sights, plastic grips. Mfg. 1969-present in W. Germany, U.S. import stopped by GCA of 1968.

	100%	98%	95%	90%	80%	70%	60%
.22 LR cal.	$600	$550	$495	$425	$300	$275	$220
.25 ACP cal.	$650	$600	$550	$475	$350	$300	$250

Deduct 10% on the 100% values if not boxed with all accessories.
100% price assumes NIB condition.

AMERICAN MODEL TPH — .22 LR or .25 ACP (new 1992) cal., blued finish or stainless steel, double action, black plastic grips, 6 shot mag., 2¼ in. barrel, 14 oz. Introduced 1987.

Mfg.'s Sug. Retail	$473	$390	$325	$250

⚮ **American Model TPH Stainless** — stainless steel fabrication.

Mfg.'s Sug. Retail	$473	$390	$325	$250

MODEL P.38 — Post-war version of P.38 Military, .22 LR, .30 Luger (disc.), or 9mm Para. cal., 5 in. barrel, alloy frame, matte black finish, 28 oz. W. German manufacture. See German WWII Military Pistols for wartime listings.
Note: Due to the release of large numbers of W. German Police and Army trade-ins of P.38 9mm and PP .32 ACP cal. models, the actual value of these models has only recently gone down. The two models most affected are the P-1 variation of the P.38, and the German PP in .32 ACP cal.

Mfg.'s Sug. Retail	$1,000	$750	$525	$425	$350	$295	$245	$190

⚮ **Steel Frame P.38** — 9mm Para., similar to regular P.38, except has steel frame, 34 oz. Imported 1987-1989 only.

	$975	$850	$650	$550	$400	$295	$245

Last Mfg.'s Sug. Retail was $1,400.

⚮ **P.38 in .22 LR cal.** — disc. 1989.

	$850	$700	$550	$450	$350	$300	$200

Last Mfg.'s Sug. Retail was $1,050.

MODEL P.38 SPECIAL EDITIONS/ENGRAVED

⚮ **P.38 100th Year Commemorative** — alloy frame, presentation engraved with deluxe walnut presentation case. Introduced 1987, inventory depleted 1992.

	$750	$550	$450

Last Mfg.'s Sug. Retail was $950.

Grading	100%	98%	95%	90%	80%	70%	60%

⚔ Blue Engraved — 9mm Para. cal. Importation disc. 1991.

	$1,850	$1,325	$1,125	$900			

Last Mfg.'s Sug. Retail was $1,850.

⚔ Chrome Engraved — 9mm Para. cal. Importation disc. 1991.

	$1,475	$1,175	$925				

Last Mfg.'s Sug. Retail was $2,125.

⚔ Silver Engraved — 9mm Para. cal. Importation disc. 1991.

	$1,450	$1,175	$925				

Last Mfg.'s Sug. Retail was $2,100.

⚔ Gold Engraved — 9mm Para. cal. Disc. 1987.

	$1,800	$1,500	$1,000				

Last Mfg.'s Sug. Retail was $2,050.

MODEL P1 — 9mm Para., post-war commercial variation of the P.38 with steel slide and alloy frame, 5 in. barrel, 8 shot mag., black plastic grips, Disc.

	$575	$500	$425	$350	$300	$250	$200

MODEL P.38 IV — 9mm Para. cal., modernized variation of the original P.38, 4½ in. barrel, 8 shot mag., updates include reinforced steel slide and alloy frame, includes decocking lever and automatic safeties, adj. rear sight, 29 oz. Importation disc. 1982.

	$595	$525	$450	$350	$300	$250	$200

MODEL P.38K — 9mm Para. cal., shortened 2.8 in. barrel variation of P.38, front sight on slide. Mfg. 1974-1980.

	$850	$750	$500	$400	$300	$250	$200

MODEL P-5 — 9mm Para. cal., double action, alloy frame, frame mounted decocking lever, 3½ in. barrel, adj. rear sight, blue finish only, 8 shot mag., auto safeties, 28 oz.

Mfg.'s Sug. Retail	$1,257	$940	$650	$550	$495	$465	$425	$380

⚔ P-5 Compact — compact variation of P-5.

Mfg.'s Sug. Retail	$1,257	$940	$650	$550	$495	$465	$425	$380

⚔ P-5 100th Year Commemorative — elaborate engraving with presentation walnut case. Importation 1987-91.

	$2,100	$1,425	$1,025				

Last Mfg.'s Sug. Retail was $2,890.

MODEL P-88 — 9mm Para. cal., double action, alloy frame, 4 in. barrel, 15 shot side release mag., ambidextrous decocking lever, matte finish, adj. rear sight, internal safeties, loaded chamber indicator, black synthetic grips, 31½ oz. New 1987.

Mfg.'s Sug. Retail	$1,200	$950	$750	$625	$575	$490	$450	$400

TARGET PISTOLS

Add 10% to the values listed below for left-hand stocks (available on most models).

MODEL GSP TARGET — .22 LR cal., 4½ in. barrel, single action, 5 shot mag., adj. sights, blue finish, walnut target grips, supplied with carrying case, 49.4 oz.

Mfg.'s Sug. Retail	$1,843	$1,495	$1,250	$1,000	$750	$600	$500	$425

Grading		100%	98%	95%	90%	80%	70%	60%

Model GSP Junior – similar to GSP Target, except has slimmer barrel design, smaller walnut grips, less weight. Importation disc. 1992.

		$1,400	$1,100	$925	$750	$600	$500	$425

Last Mfg.'s Sug. Retail was $1,810.

Model GSP-C – similar to Model GSP Target, except in .32 S&W Wadcutter, 42.3 oz.

Mfg.'s Sug. Retail	$2,545	$1,895	$1,300	$995	$800	$650	$550	$475

Add $1,495 for GSP-C .22 Short conversion unit.
Add $1,053 for GSP-C .22 LR cal. conversion unit.
Add $1,400 for GSP-C .32 S&W Wadcutter converison unit.

MODEL OSP RAPID FIRE – similar to GSP, in .22 Short. Mfg. 1968-present, for international competition (meets ISU and NRA regs.), 4½ in. barrel, 44.4 oz., supplied with case.

Mfg.'s Sug. Retail	$2,275	$1,795	$1,275	$950	$800	$650	$550	$475

FREE PISTOL – .22 LR cal., single shot, electronic trigger, 11.7 in. heavy barrel, advanced target design with fully adj. grips and sights, 48 oz. Importation disc. 1991.

		$1,600	$1,200	$1,000	$850	$675	$575	$500

Last Mfg.'s Sug. Retail was $2,140.

P.38 WWII MILITARY MFG. – see German Military for breakdown.

HAMMERLI-WALTHER – see Hammerli.

RIFLES: DISCONTINUED

MODEL B – .30-06 bolt action, post-war mfg., 22 in. barrel. Add 20% for double set triggers. Disc.

$450	$420	$380	$340	$300	$275	$250

OLYMPIC SINGLE SHOT – .22 LR cal., bolt action, 26 in. heavy barrel, target sights, checkered pistol grip, full beavertail forearm, palm rest, adj. butt, pre-war.

$935	$825	$770	$715	$605	$550	$440

MODEL 1 – Carbine model, clip fed.

$395	$350	$310	$295	$270	$250	$200

MODEL 2 AUTOLOADING – may be used as bolt action, autoloader or single shot, .22 LR cal., 24½ in. barrel, tangent sight, checkered sporter stock, pre-war.

$495	$440	$385	$330	$275	$220	$165

MODEL 2 LIGHTWEIGHT – 20 in. barrel, lighter stock.

$495	$440	$385	$330	$275	$220	$165

MODEL V SINGLE SHOT – .22 LR cal., bolt action, 26 in. barrel, open sight, plain pistol grip stock, pre-war.

$385	$360	$330	$305	$275	$250	$195

MODEL V CHAMPION – similar to Standard, with micrometer adj. sight and checkered pistol grip stock.

$470	$440	$415	$385	$330	$305	$250

MODEL KKM INTERNATIONAL MATCH – .22 LR cal., single shot bolt action, 28 in. heavy barrel, adj. aperture sight, adj. hook butt, thumbhole stock, accessory rail, post-war mfg.

$880	$770	$715	$660	$550	$495	$440

Grading	100%	98%	95%	90%	80%	70%	60%

MODEL KKM-S — similar to KKM, with adj. cheek piece.

	100%	98%	95%	90%	80%	70%	60%
	$935	$825	$770	$715	$605	$550	$495

MODEL KKJ SPORTER — .22 LR cal., bolt action, 5 shot, 22½ in. barrel, open sight, checkered sporter stock, post-war.

	100%	98%	95%	90%	80%	70%	60%
	$595	$500	$450	$385	$330	$250	$200

Add 20% for double set triggers.

MODEL KKW — .22 LR cal., single shot, military stock, tangent sight, pre-war mfg.

	100%	98%	95%	90%	80%	70%	60%
	$540	$490	$420	$300	$260	$220	$195

MODEL KKJ-MA — .22 WMR cal.

	100%	98%	95%	90%	80%	70%	60%
	$550	$495	$440	$385	$305	$250	$220

MODEL KKJ-HO — .22 Hornet cal.

	100%	98%	95%	90%	80%	70%	60%
	$725	$675	$625	$580	$540	$480	$440

Add 20% for double set triggers.

MODEL SSV VARMINT — .22 LR cal., single shot bolt action, 25½ in. barrel, no sights, Monte Carlo pistol grip stock, post-war mfg.

	100%	98%	95%	90%	80%	70%	60%
	$605	$550	$525	$495	$415	$360	$330
.22 Hornet	$660	$605	$580	$550	$470	$415	$385

MODEL PRONE 400 — similar to UIT Match, with Prone style competitive stock and no sights. Disc.

	100%	98%	95%	90%	80%	70%	60%
	$750	$635	$580	$525	$415	$360	$305

RIFLES: RECENT MFG.

Prices below reflect the recent devaluation of the U.S. dollar against some foreign currencies. While the manufacturer's suggested retails have gone up considerably, prices for used specimens (98% or less original condition) have not increased proportionally, and in some cases, have changed very little.

MODEL UIT BV UNIVERSAL — .22 LR cal., single shot bolt action, 25½ in. heavy barrel, adj. aperture sight, target stock with palm rest, adj. butt, meets ISU regs., 16 lbs. Disc. 1990.

	100%	98%	95%	90%	80%	70%	60%
	$1,325	$1,050	$850	$700	$635	$580	$530

Last Mfg.'s Sug. Retail was $1,700. This model was previously known as the Model UIT Special.

MODEL UIT MATCH — similar to UIT Special, except with improved stock design which includes fully stippled lower forearm and pistol grip, 13 lbs.

		100%	98%	95%	90%	80%	70%	60%
Mfg.'s Sug. Retail	$1,400	$1,125	$925	$800	$660	$610	$555	$510

Model UIT-E — electronic trigger, 25½ in. barrel, 9 lbs. Disc. 1986.

	100%	98%	95%	90%	80%	70%	60%
	$1,350	$940	$860	$770	$670	$630	$560

Last Mfg.'s Sug. Retail was $1,250.

GX-1 — similar to UIT Match, 25½ in. barrel with fully adj. free rifle stock, all accessories included, 16½ lbs. Importation disc. 1991.

	100%	98%	95%	90%	80%	70%	60%
	$1,895	$1,375	$1,125	$985	$860	$775	$680

Last Mfg.'s Sug. Retail was $2,350.

Grading	100%	98%	95%	90%	80%	70%	60%

MODEL KK/MS SILHOUETTE — .22 LR cal. only, designed for silhouette shooting with no sights, thumbhole stock with adj. butt, fully stippled forend and stock grip, front barrel weight, 25½ in. barrel, 8¾ lbs. Imported 1984-91.

	$975	$795	$625	$560	$495	$435	$395

Last Mfg.'s Sug. Retail was $1,175.

RUNNING BOAR MODEL 500 — similar to KK/MS, no sights, thumbhole stock with adj. butt and cheek piece, 23½ in. barrel, 10¼ lbs. Disc. 1990.

	$1,025	$825	$640	$570	$500	$435	$395

Last Mfg.'s Sug. Retail was $1,300.

MODEL WA-2000 — .300 Win. Mag. or .308 cal., ultra-deluxe bolt action, special order only. Disc. 1988.

	$6,400	$4,800	$4,500	$4,000	$3,500	$3,000	$2,500

SHOTGUNS: SIDE-BY-SIDE

MODEL SF — 12 or 16 ga., double barrel, checkered walnut stock, double triggers, boxlock, sling swivels. Disc.

	$500	$450	$395	$325	$275	$240	$200

MODEL SFD — 12 or 16 ga., double barrel, cheek piece, checkered walnut stock, double triggers, boxlock, sling swivels. Disc.

	$625	$575	$500	$425	$375	$340	$300

WALTHER, FRENCH-MADE BY MANURHIN

Manufactured in Mulhouse, France. Previously imported 1984-86 by Matra-Manurhin International, Inc., Alexandria, VA.

PISTOLS: SEMI-AUTO

Manufacture of these Walther pistols commenced in France in 1951. They were marked MANURHIN on slide until 1954. Since then they were designated Walther MKII. They were imported into the USA by Interarms up to 1983. In 1984, Manurhin was imported directly with no Interarms logo or Walther trademark appearing on Models PP and PPK/S. Importation disc. 1986.

MODEL PP — .22 LR, .32 ACP, or .380 ACP cal., 3⅞ in. barrel, 10 shot mag.-.22 LR, 8 shot mag.-.32 ACP, 7 shot mag.-.380 ACP, blue only, all steel construction, double action with positive steel block safety, 24 oz.

	$360	$320	$275	$230	$205	$185	$170

Add $10 for .22 LR cal.
Add $46 for Durgarde finish.
Last Mfg.'s Sug. Retail was $419.

⚞ **Collector Model** — blue finish, special engraving. New 1986.

	$465	$415	$350

Last Mfg.'s Sug. Retail was $529.

⚞ **Presentation Model** — blue finish, special ornamentation. New 1986.

	$720	$650	$500

Last Mfg.'s Sug. Retail was $819.
Also available with various engraving options in either blue, nickel, or gold finish - prices range from $222 - $540.

Interarms import	$350	$325	$285	$230	$205	$180	$160

Grading	100%	98%	95%	90%	80%	70%	60%

PP SPORT — .22 LR cal. only, double action, 6.1 or 8.1 in. barrel, blue finish only, precision adj. sights, contoured plastic grips with thumb rest, 25 oz. New Manurhin design for 1985.

	$545	$485	$430	$385	$325	$290	$270

Last Mfg.'s Sug. Retail was $635.

⚮ **PP Sport-C** — similar to PP Sport, except is single action.

	$540	$475	$415	$370	$310	$280	$260

Last Mfg.'s Sug. Retail was $635.

MODEL PPK — .22 LR, .32 ACP, or .380 ACP cal., 3¼ in. barrel, 10 shot mag.-.22 LR, 8 shot mag.-.32 ACP, 7 shot mag.-.380 ACP, blue only, all steel construction, double action with positive steel block safety, 23 oz.

	$600	$495	$425	$375	$350	$325	$300

Add 10% for .22 LR cal.

MODEL PPK/S — .22 LR, .32 ACP, or .380 ACP cal., 3¼ in. barrel, 10 shot mag.-.22 LR, 8 shot mag.-.32 ACP, 7 shot mag.-.380 ACP, blue only, all steel construction, double action with positive steel block safety, 23 oz.

	$360	$320	$275	$230	$205	$185	$170

Add 10% for .22 LR cal.
Last Mfg.'s Sug. Retail was $419.

⚮ **PPK/S Durgarde** — similar to above, only with bonded brushed chrome finish.

	$410	$365	$325	$290	$265	$250	$240

Add 10% for .22 LR cal.
Last Mfg.'s Sug. Retail was $465.

⚮ **Collector Model** — blue finish, special engraving. New 1986.

	$465	$415	$350

Last Mfg.'s Sug. Retail was $529.

⚮ **Presentation Model** — blue finish, special ornamentation. New 1986.

	$720	$650	$500

Last Mfg.'s Sug. Retail was $819.

Interarms import

	$395	$340	$300	$275	$250	$235	$210

Also available with various engraving options in either blue, nickel, or gold finish — prices range from $222 - $540.

WARNER ARMS CORPORATION
Norwich, CT.

INFALLIBLE POCKET AUTO PISTOL — .32 auto cal., 7 shot, 3 in. barrel, fixed sights, rubber grips. Mfg. 1917-1919.

	$450	$350	$250	$150	$125	$100	$90

WEATHERBY
Manufacturer/importer located in South Gate, CA, 1945 to date.

Weatherby is an importer of long arms. Earlier production was from Germany and Italy, and German mfg. is usually what is collectible. Current production is from Japan. Workmanship in all instances is quite good. Weatherby is well known for their high-velocity proprietary rifle calibers.

Weatherby®

Early Weatherby rifles used a Mathieu Arms action in the 1950s - primarily since it was available in left hand action. Right handed actions were normally mfg. from the FN Mauser type.

Grading	100%	98%	95%	90%	80%	70%	60%

SILHOUETTE PISTOL

WEATHERBY SILHOUETTE PISTOL — .22-250 or .308 cal., mfg. in Japan during late 1970s, 14½ in. barrel, Lyman or Williams sights, fitted case. Only 50 were mfg. in .22-250 and 150 in .308 cal.

	100%	98%	95%	90%	80%	70%	60%
	$3,750	$3,300	$2,750	$2,450	$2,100	$1,850	$1,650

RIFLES - MARK V BOLT ACTION

For German rifle manufacture, add 15% to 25% for calibers under .35. In 1992, 24 in. barrels were disc. on most calibers of .300 or greater (including Models Mark V Deluxe, Fibermark, Lazermark, and Euromark).

MARK V DELUXE — .240 Wby. Mag., .257 Wby. Mag., .270 Wby. Mag., 7mm Wby. Mag., .30-06, .300 Wby. Mag., or .375 H&H Mag. (new 1993) cal., bolt action, 3-5 shot mag., 24 or 26 in. barrel, deluxe skip line checkered pistol grip walnut stock with rosewood tipped forearm and pistol grip, no sights, 8 lbs. Left-hand actions available at no extra charge.

Mfg.'s Sug. Retail	$1,225	$1,025	$750	$625	$525	$475	$450	$410

Add $14 for 26 in. barrel.
Add $181 for .375 H&H Mag. cal.

⚔ **Mark V .300 or .340 Wby. Mag.** — 26 in. barrel only, 8½ lbs.

Mfg.'s Sug. Retail	$1,270	$1,075	$775	$625	$525	$475	$450	$410

⚔ **Mark V .378 Wby. Mag.** — 26 in. barrel only, 8½ lbs.

Mfg.'s Sug. Retail	$1,305	$1,100	$800	$700	$600	$525	$475	$425
German mfg.		$1,600	$1,400	$1,250	$1,000	$900.	$825	$750

German mfg. in this model used the .375 Wby. Mag. cal.

⚔ **Mark V .416 Wby. Mag.** — first new caliber (introduced 1989) since the .240 Mag. was released 1965.

Mfg.'s Sug. Retail	$1,346	$1,125	$825	$700	$600	$525	$475	$425

⚔ **Mark V .460 Wby. Mag.** — 24 or 26 in. barrel, includes custom stock, integral muzzle brake, 10 lbs. No extra charge for left-hand.

Mfg.'s Sug. Retail	$1,660	$1,400	$1,100	$925	$775	$650	$600	$550
German mfg.		$1,750	$1,500	$1,350	$1,100	$1,000	$925	$850

CLASSICMARK I — available in 9 Wby. Mag. cals. in addition to .270 Win., 7mm Rem. Mag., .30-06, or .375 H&H Mag. cal., oil finished American Claro walnut stock with no cheekpiece and ebony forend cap, 1 in. solid recoil pad, panel point checkering. New 1992.

Mfg.'s Sug. Retail	$1,295	$1,075	$750	$625	$525	$475	$450	$410

Add $15 for 26 in. barrel.
Add $130 for .375 H&H Mag. cal.

⚔ **.300 or .340 Wby. Mag.** — 26 in. barrel only, right or left-hand action, 8½ lbs.

Mfg.'s Sug. Retail	$1,323	$1,095	$775	$625	$525	$475	$450	$410

⚔ **.378 Wby. Mag.** — 26 in. barrel only, right or left-hand action, 8½ lbs.

Mfg.'s Sug. Retail	$1,356	$1,125	$795	$625	$525	$475	$450	$410

⚔ **.416 Wby. Mag.** — 26 in. barrel only, right or left-hand action.

Mfg.'s Sug. Retail	$1,411	$1,150	$825	$650	$550	$495	$460	$430

⚔ **.460 Wby. Mag.** — 26 in. barrel only, includes custom stock, integral muzzle brake, 10 lbs. No extra charge for left-hand.

Mfg.'s Sug. Retail	$1,573	$1,250	$900	$675	$575	$525	$475	$430

Grading	100%	98%	95%	90%	80%	70%	60%

CLASSICMARK II — available in 9 Wby. Mag. cals. in addition .270 Win., 7mm Rem. Mag., or .30-06, similar to Classicmark I, except has deluxe American walnut with 22 LPI multiple point checkering, steel grip cap, satin finished wood and metal, guaranteed 1½ in. or less 3 shot grouping at 100 yards, right hand action only. Mfg. 1992 only.

	$1,525	$1,175	$975	$800	$650	$600	$550

Add $28 for 26 in. barrel.
Last Mfg.'s Sug. Retail was $1,775.

.300 or .340 Wby. Mag. — 26 in. barrel only.

	$1,550	$1,175	$975	$800	$650	$600	$550

Last Mfg.'s Sug. Retail was $1,803.

.378 Wby. Mag. — 26 in. barrel only.

	$1,700	$1,250	$1,000	$800	$650	$600	$550

Last Mfg.'s Sug. Retail was $1,976.

.416 Wby. Mag. — 26 in. barrel only.

	$1,875	$1,375	$1,050	$825	$650	$600	$550

Last Mfg.'s Sug. Retail was $2,128.

.460 Wby. Mag. — 26 in. barrel only, includes custom stock, integral muzzle brake, 10 lbs.

	$1,925	$1,400	$1,050	$825	$650	$600	$550

Last Mfg.'s Sug. Retail was $2,207.

Safari Classic — .375 H&H cal., 24 in. barrel only, right-hand action, limited edition featuring custom action, quarter rib express and front ramp sights, barrel band swivel and engraved floor plate, stock similar to Classicmark II. Mfg. 1992 only.

	$2,300	$1,850	$1,650	$1,450	$1,300	$1,175	$995

Last Mfg.'s Sug. Retail was $2,693.

MARK V ULTRAMARK — .240 Wby. Mag., .257 Wby. Mag., .270 Wby. Mag., .30-06, 7mm Wby. Mag., .300 Wby. Mag., .378 Wby. Mag. (mfg. 1989 only), or .416 Wby. Mag. (mfg. 1989 only) cal., fancy American walnut, individually hand-bedded, high lustre finish, customized action, 24 or 26 in. barrel, basket weave checkering (including pistol grip). Imported 1989-90 only.

	$1,125	$925	$800	$700	$630	$590	$550

Add $25 for 26 in. barrel.
Add $220 for .378 Wby. Mag. cal. (26 in. barrel only).
Add $325 for .416 Wby. Mag. cal. (26 in. barrel only).
Last Mfg.'s Sug. Retail was $1,315.

WEATHERMARK — available in various Wby. Mag. cals. from .257 to .340 and .257 Roberts, .270 Win., 7mm Rem. Mag., .300 Win. Mag., .30-06, .338 Win. Mag., and .375 H&H Mag. cal., similar design as the Classicmark II, except is fitted with black checkered composite stock, satin finish black metal, 22 (.270 Win. or .30-06 only), 24, or 26 in. barrel, right-hand only, 7½ lbs. New 1992.

Mfg.'s Sug. Retail	$599	$525	$475	$425	$395	$360	$330	$300

Add $26 for Wby. Mag. cals.
Add $112 for .375 H&H Mag. cal.

SPORTER — cals. similar to Weathermark, except not available in .257, .270, and 7mm Wby. Mag. cals., similar features to the Mark V, except has checkered walnut stock without forearm or pistol grip caps, low luster metalwork, vent. recoil pad, no sights. New 1993.

Mfg.'s Sug. Retail	$732	$650	$575	$525	$475	$425	$395	$350

Add $48 for Wby. Mag. cals.
Add $101 for .375 H&H Mag. cal.

Grading	100%	98%	95%	90%	80%	70%	60%

WHITETAIL — .257 Savage cal., limited edition features deluxe high grade Claro walnut, hand checkered bolt knob and engraved floorplate, 22 in. #1 contoured barrel, 6 lbs. New 1993.

Mfg.'s Sug. Retail	$1,366	$1,150	$925	$775			

ALASKAN MODEL — same cals. as Weathermark, similar to Weathermark, except has non-glare electroless nickel plated metal parts, right or left-hand (mfg. 1992 only) action. New 1992.

Mfg.'s Sug. Retail	$799	$700	$625	$550	$495	$450	$400	$360

Add $34 for Wby. Mag. cals.
Add $150 for .375 H&H Mag. cal.
Add $375 for left-hand action (disc.).

MARK V VARMINTMASTER — .22-250 or .224 Varmintmaster cal., 24 (disc. 1991) or 26 in. barrel, 6½ lbs.

Mfg.'s Sug. Retail	$1,196	$1,025	$750	$625	$525	$475	$450	$410

Not available in left-hand action.

MARK V EUROMARK — available in all cals., except .22-250 and .224 Varmintmaster, differs from Mark V in that it has an oil finished, hand checkered, deluxe American claro walnut pistol grip cap stock with ebony forend tip, low lustre bluing, and solid black recoil pad. Mfg. 1986-92.

		$1,075	$775	$625	$525	$475	$450	$410

Add $28 for 26 in. barrel.
Last Mfg.'s Sug. Retail was $1,257.

.300 or .340 Wby. Mag. — 26 in. barrel only.

		$1,100	$795	$625	$525	$475	$450	$410

Last Mfg.'s Sug. Retail was $1,285.

.378 Wby. Mag. — 26 in. barrel only.

		$1,225	$975	$825	$700	$600	$550	$500

Last Mfg.'s Sug. Retail was $1,469.

.416 Wby. Mag. — first new caliber (introduced 1989) since the .240 Mag. was released in 1965, includes muzzle brake.

		$1,375	$1,050	$875	$750	$625	$575	$525

Last Mfg.'s Sug. Retail was $1,631.

.460 Wby. Mag. — 24 or 26 in. barrel, includes custom stock, internal muzzle brake, no extra charge for left-hand.

		$1,450	$1,100	$925	$775	$650	$600	$550

Last Mfg.'s Sug. Retail was $1,708.

MARK V LAZERMARK — available in the same cals. (except for .375 H&H Mag.) and barrel lengths as the Mark V Deluxe, differs only in that stock and forearm have been laser carved. New 1985.

Mfg.'s Sug. Retail	$1,355	$1,175	$850	$700	$600	$525	$475	$450

Add $13 for 26 in. barrel.

.300 or .340 Wby. Mag. — 26 in. barrel only.

Mfg.'s Sug. Retail	$1,403	$1,200	$875	$725	$600	$525	$475	$450

.378 Wby. Mag. — 26 in. barrel only.

Mfg.'s Sug. Retail	$1,443	$1,250	$900	$825	$725	$625	$575	$525

Weatherby. **cont.**

Grading		100%	98%	95%	90%	80%	70%	60%

.416 Wby. Mag. — first new caliber (introduced 1989) since the .240 Mag. was released 1965, includes muzzle brake.

Mfg.'s Sug. Retail $1,489 $1,275 $925 $850 $725 $625 $575 $525

.460 Wby. Mag. — 24 or 26 in. barrel, includes custom stock, internal muzzle brake, no extra charge for left-hand.

Mfg.'s Sug. Retail $1,844 $1,575 $1,200 $995 $800 $650 $600 $550

Varmintmaster — .22-250 or .224 Varmintmaster cal., 24 or 26 in. barrel. Disc. 1991.

     $1,085 $815 $675 $575 $500 $460 $425

Add $25 for 26 in. barrel.
Not available in left-hand action.
Last Mfg.'s Sug. Retail was $675.

MARK V FIBERMARK — available in .240 Wby. Mag., .257 Wby. Mag., .270 Wby. Mag., .30-06, 7mm Wby. Mag., .300 Wby. Mag., or .340 Wby. Mag. cal., black non-glare fiberglass with wrinkle finish stock, metal has non-glare matte finish, 24 or 26 in. barrel, available in right (disc. 1991) or left-hand action, 7¼ lbs. Mfg. disc. 1992.

     $1,195 $875 $725 $600 $525 $475 $450

Add $118 for .300 or .340 Mag. cal.
This model was available in left-hand action (22 in. barrel) in .270 Win. or .30-06 cal. only.
Last Mfg.'s Sug. Retail was $1,376.

1976 BICENTENNIAL MARK V — .257 Wby. Mag., .270 Wby. Mag., 7mm Wby. Mag., or .300 Wby Mag. cal., 1,000 mfg. in 1976 only.

     $1,495 $1,150 $895

Last Mfg.'s Sug. Retail was $2,000.

1984 MARK V OLYMPIC COMMEMORATIVE — .257 Wby. Mag., .270 Wby Mag., 7mm Wby. Mag., or .300 Wby. Mag. cal., special gold accenting, extra-fancy walnut stock with "star in motion" inlay. Mfg. 1,000 1984 only at $2,000 retail.

     $1,000 $895 $700

MARK V 35TH ANNIVERSARY COMMEMORATIVE — .257 Wby. Mag., .270 Wby. Mag., 7mm Wby. Mag., or .300 Wby. Mag. cal., limited mfg. 1980, 1,000 produced total.

     $1,000 $895 $700

SAFARI GRADE CUSTOM — .300 Wby. Mag., .340 Wby. Mag., .378 Wby. Mag., .416 Wby Mag., or .460 Wby. Mag. cal., custom order only, various options available, 8-10 month delivery.

Mfg.'s Sug. Retail $3,301 $2,875 $2,275 $1,875 $1,600 $1,450 $1,300 $1,175

Add approx. $180 - $273 for .378 and larger cals.

CROWN MODEL CUSTOM — custom order only, engraved barrel receiver and scope mount, top-of-the-line model.

Mfg.'s Sug. Retail $4,933 $4,475 $3,450 $2,750 $2,300 $1,850 $1,550 $1,350

Subtract $1,400 without Crown engraving option.

RIFLES - VANGUARD SERIES BOLT ACTION

VANGUARD CLASSIC I — .223 Rem., .243 Win., .270 Win., 7mm/08 Rem., 7mm Rem. Mag., .30-06 or .308 Win. cal., checkered walnut stock with satin finish, black butt pad, 24 in. barrel, 3 (7mm Rem. Mag.) or 5 shot mag., No. 1 barrel contour, approx. 7 lbs. 5 oz. New 1989.

Mfg.'s Sug. Retail $549 $480 $375 $325 $295 $260 $230 $200

This model is the replacement for the Vanguard VGS and VGL.

Grading	100%	98%	95%	90%	80%	70%	60%

VANGUARD CLASSIC II — .22-250, .243 Win., .270 Wby. Mag., .270 Win., 7mm Rem. Mag., .30-06, .300 Win. Mag., .300 Wby. Mag., or .338 Win. Mag. cal., 24 in. No. 2 barrel contour, 3 or 5 shot mag., custom checkered deluxe walnut stock with pistol grip cap and black forend cap, solid black recoil pad, matte finished metal, approx. 7¾ lbs. Mfg. 1989-92.

	$675	$550	$475	$425	$395	$360	$330

This model is also available in a No. 3 barrel contour in .22-250 Rem. cal. only.
Last Mfg.'s Sug. Retail was $750.

VANGUARD VGX — .22-250, .243 Win., .25-06, .270 Win., 7mm Rem. Mag., .30-06, or 300 Win. Mag. cal., bolt action, checkered deluxe walnut stock with rosewood tip forearm and pistol grip, 24 in. barrel, no sights, 5 shot mag.(except 3 shot for .300 Win. Mag.), high luster bluing, about 8 lbs. Disc. 1988.

	$525	$425	$365	$330	$300	$275	$255

Not available in left-hand action.
Last Mfg.'s Sug. Retail was $600.

VANGUARD VGX DELUXE — .22-250, .243 Win., .270 Win., .270 Wby. Mag., .300 Win. Mag., .300 Wby. Mag., .30-06, .338 Win. Mag., or 7mm Rem. Mag. cal., 24 in. barrel, Monte Carlo stock with skipline checkering, high gloss wood and metal, rosewood forend cap. New 1989.

Mfg.'s Sug. Retail	$699	$625	$550	$475	$425	$395	$360	$330

VANGUARD VGS — same cals. as Vanguard VGX, bolt action, checkered satin finished walnut stock, 24 in. barrel, no sights, approx. 8 lbs. Disc. 1988.

	$415	$355	$295	$265	$245	$220	$200

Not available in left-hand action.
Last Mfg.'s Sug. Retail was $467.

VANGUARD VGL — .223 Rem., .243 Win., .270 Win., 7mm Rem. Mag., .30-06, or 308 Win. cal., lightweight bolt action, checkered walnut stock, 5 shot mag.(6 on .223 Rem.), 20 in. barrel, no sights, 6½ lbs. Disc. 1988.

	$415	$355	$295	$265	$245	$220	$200

Not available in left-hand action.
Last Mfg.'s Sug. Retail was $467.

VANGUARD WEATHERGUARD — same cals. as Classic I, replacement for Fiberguard, wrinkle black finished synthetic stock, entry level Weatherby, similar specs. as Classic I, approx. 8 lbs. New 1989.

Mfg.'s Sug. Retail	$499	$440	$350	$320	$290	$260	$230	$200

VANGUARD ALASKAN — same cals. as Classic I, features electroless nickel metal plating, no sights. New 1993.

Mfg.'s Sug. Retail	$699	$625	$550	$475	$425	$395	$360	$330

VANGUARD FIBERGUARD — .223 Rem., .243 Win., .270 Win., 7 mm Rem Mag., .30-06, or 308 Win. cal., 20 in. barrel, green fiberglass stock, 3 to 6 shot mag.'s, no sights, blued metal parts, approx. 6½ lbs. Disc. 1988.

	$500	$450	$395	$355	$285	$255	$220

Not available in left-hand action.
Last Mfg.'s Sug. Retail was $560.

Grading	100%	98%	95%	90%	80%	70%	60%

RIFLES - .22 LR BOLT ACTION

ACCUMARK CLASSIC & DELUXE — while these models were advertised in 1990 ($635 retail), they were never manufactured.

RIFLES - .22 LR SEMI-AUTO

MARK XXII CLIP MAG — .22 LR cal., mag. feed, skipline checkered walnut stock with rosewood forearm and pistol grip caps, 10 shot detachable mag., 24 in. barrel, open sights, 6 lbs. Disc. 1989.

	100%	98%	95%	90%	80%	70%	60%
	$395	$320	$265	$245	$215	$195	$180

Last Mfg.'s Sug. Retail was $454.
The Mark XXII clip mag. was originally mfg. in Italy - a slight premium might be asked. This model featured a receiver slide-switch that allowed semi-auto operation to be converted to single shot mode.

MARK XXII TUBE MAG — .22 LR cal., same general specifications as above model, except tube-feed, 15 shot, 6 lbs. Disc. 1989.

	100%	98%	95%	90%	80%	70%	60%
	$395	$320	$265	$245	$215	$195	$180

Last Mfg.'s Sug. Retail was $454.

SHOTGUNS: OVER AND UNDER

REGENCY FIELD GRADE — 20 ga. Mag. or 12 ga., checkered stock, VR, engraved side plates, SST, early importation beginning in 1972 was from Italy, later mfg. was switched to Japan.

	100%	98%	95%	90%	80%	70%	60%
	$900	$800	$700	$600	$550	$500	$475

Add 10-15% for early Italian mfg. (note proof marks).

REGENCY TRAP GRADE — 12 ga., checkered trap stock, engraved, VR, SST. Imported from Italy.

	100%	98%	95%	90%	80%	70%	60%
	$900	$800	$700	$600	$550	$500	$475

OLYMPIAN STANDARD — 12 and 20 ga., lightly engraved sideplates. Disc. 1980.

	100%	98%	95%	90%	80%	70%	60%
	$850	$775	$725	$625	$525	$450	$400

OLYMPIAN SKEET — 26 or 28 in. barrel.

	100%	98%	95%	90%	80%	70%	60%
	$885	$775	$725	$625	$525	$450	$400

OLYMPIAN TRAP — 30 or 32 in. barrel, VR.

	100%	98%	95%	90%	80%	70%	60%
	$850	$775	$725	$625	$525	$440	$400

ATHENA GRADE IV — 12, 20, 28 (new 1989), or .410 (new 1989) ga., 3 in. chambers, boxlock with Greener Crossbolt, SST, ejectors, high luster finish on hand checkered claro walnut, engraved sideplates with satin nickel finish, vent. barrels and rib, multi-chokes became standard (except .410 ga.) 1986 and 1992 (28 ga.), 7-8½lbs. Introduced 1982.

	100%	98%	95%	90%	80%	70%	60%
Mfg.'s Sug. Retail $1,950		$1,675	$1,275	$1,000	$875	$725	$600	$525

Subtract $150 if without choke tubes.
This model was redesignated the Grade IV in 1989.

Skeet & Trap Models — 12 (Trap only) or 20 ga., special stock dimensions, target sights. Disc. 1992.

	100%	98%	95%	90%	80%	70%	60%
	$1,675	$1,275	$1,000	$875	$725	$600	$525

Add $10 for Trap Model.
Skeet models are available in fixed choke only.
Last Mfg.'s Sug. Retail was $1,965.

Grading	100%	98%	95%	90%	80%	70%	60%

Single Trap Model — 12 ga., 32 or 34 in. barrel with multi-choke feature. Disc. 1992.

		100%	98%	95%	90%	80%	70%	60%
		$1,675	$1,275	$1,000	$875	$725	$600	$525

Last Mfg.'s Sug. Retail was $1,975.

Trap Combo — 12 ga., includes a set of O/U barrels and oversingle barrel with multi-choke feature. Disc. 1992.

	100%	98%	95%	90%	80%	70%	60%
	$2,300	$1,900	$1,605	$1,300	$995	$800	$675

Last Mfg.'s Sug. Retail was $2,616.

Master Skeet Set — 12 ga., includes 6 fitted full length Briley tubes with integral extractors (20, 28, and .410 ga.), cased. Imported 1988-91.

	100%	98%	95%	90%	80%	70%	60%
	$3,100	$2,650	$2,150	$1,900	$1,775	$1,625	$1,525

ATHENA GRADE V — 12 or 20 ga., 3 in. chambers, similar to Grade IV, except has more elaborate engraving and better walnut. New 1989.

	100%		98%	95%	90%	80%	70%	60%
Mfg.'s Sug. Retail	$2,450		$2,100	$1,700	$1,375	$1,150	$900	$775	$675

In 1993, Weatherby changed the styling of the gun to incorporate European shooting features including an oil finished, round knob stock and slim forearm, tight rose-and-scroll engraving, and matte VR.

ORION GRADE I — 12 or 20 ga., 3 in. chambers, 26, 28, or 30 (12 ga. only) in. VR barrels with multi-chokes, SST, ejectors, entry level O/U with no engraving, checkered walnut stock and forearm. New 1989.

	100%	98%	95%	90%	80%	70%	60%
Mfg.'s Sug. Retail	$1,050	$895	$775	$675	$550	$495	$450	$400

ORION GRADE II — 12, 20, 28, or .410 ga., 3 in. chambers (except 28 ga.), boxlock with Greener Crossbolt, SST, ejectors, walnut with high-gloss finish, blue only, light engraving. Multi-chokes became standard 1986.

	100%	98%	95%	90%	80%	70%	60%
Mfg.'s Sug. Retail	$1,207	$1,075	$875	$750	$625	$550	$500	$450

Subtract 10% without choke tubes on older models.
Subtract $14 for Skeet grade (12 and 20 ga., fixed chokes only).
This model was redesignated Grade II in 1989. In 1993, the Standard Field Models in this variation were discontinued (Classic Grade took its place) - only Trap, Skeet, and Sporting Clays variations are now available.

Orion Grade II Classic Field — 12, 20, or 28 ga., multi-choked barrels, features rounded pistol grip stock and oil finished Claro walnut stock and forearm, waterfowl scene on silver grey nitride finish, matted VR. New 1993.

	100%	98%	95%	90%	80%	70%	60%
Mfg.'s Sug. Retail	$1,150	$1,000	$850	$725	$625	$550	$500	$450

Orion Grade II Sporting Clays — 12 ga. only, Sporting Clays configuration, early mfg. was blue finish, current mfg. is silver nitride finish, acid etched engraving, rounded recoil pad, matte finish VR, lengthened forcing cones. New 1991.

	100%	98%	95%	90%	80%	70%	60%
Mfg.'s Sug. Retail	$1,249	$1,050	$875	$750	$625	$550	$500	$450

Ducks Unlimited Orion — 12 ga. (sponsor gun in 1986) or 20 ga. (sponsor gun in 1987), deluxe walnut with gold duck scenes, blue receiver, multi-chokes, includes presentation case.

	100%	98%	95%
	$1,395	$1,100	$875

ORION GRADE III FIELD — 12 or 20 ga. only, similar to Grade II, except has silver grey receiver with custom engraving including mallard and pheasant game scenes, multi-chokes standard. New 1989.

	100%	98%	95%	90%	80%	70%	60%
Mfg.'s Sug. Retail	$1,350	$1,150	$925	$775	$650	$575	$500	$450

Orion Grade III Classic Field — 12 or 20 ga., multi-choked barrels, features rounded pistol grip stock and oil finished Claro walnut stock and forearm, extensive engraving on silver grey nitride finish, matted VR. New 1993.

	100%	98%	95%	90%	80%	70%	60%
Mfg.'s Sug. Retail	$1,350	$1,150	$925	$775	$650	$575	$500	$450

Grading	100%	98%	95%	90%	80%	70%	60%

SHOTGUNS: SEMI-AUTO

CENTURION FIELD GRADE — 12 ga., VR, checkered stock, gas operation, walnut full pistol grip stock. Mfg. 1972-1981.

	100%	98%	95%	90%	80%	70%	60%
	$300	$280	$250	$240	$230	$210	$190

CENTURION TRAP GRADE — 12 ga., checkered stock, VR.

	$335	$300	$250	$240	$230	$210	$190

CENTURION DE LUXE — 12 ga., VR, checkered stock, lightly engraved, fancy wood ($200-250).

	$375	$350	$310	$275	$250	$235	$210

⚔ **Centurion DU** — mfg. 1980 for DU chapters.

	$550	$375	$325				

MODEL 82 — 12 ga. only, 2¾ or 3 in. chamber, gas operation, alloy receiver, VR, deluxe walnut, multi-chokes became standard in 1985, Trap Grade was disc. 1984. Mfg. 1983-89.

	$395	$350	$315	$280	$250	$235	$210

Subtract $30 without multi-chokes.
Subtract $35 for Trap Grade (disc. 1984).
Last Mfg.'s Sug. Retail was $500.

⚔ **Model 82 Buckmaster** — 22 in. barrel choked skeet, rifle sights, 7½ lbs. Disc. 1989.

	$395	$350	$315	$280	$250	$235	$210

Last Mfg.'s Sug. Retail was $500.

SHOTGUNS: SLIDE ACTION

PATRICIAN FIELD GRADE — 12 ga., checkered stock, VR. Mfg. 1972-1981.

	$275	$230	$210	$190	$180	$160	$140

PATRICIAN TRAP GRADE — 12 ga., checkered stock, VR.

	$295	$250	$225	$200	$185	$175	$165

PATRICIAN DE LUXE — 12 ga., checkered stock, lightly engraved, fancy wood, VR.

	$325	$275	$250	$215	$195	$175	$165

MODEL 92 — 12 ga. only, 2¾ and 3 in. chambers, ultra-short slide action w/twin rails, 26-30 in. VR barrels, engraved black alloy receiver, checkered pistol grip walnut stock and forearm. New 1983. Subtract $30 for Trap grade (disc. 1984), $20 if fixed choke (multi-chokes became standard 1985) barrel. Disc. 1987.

	$325	$275	$250	$225	$200	$185	$175

Last Mfg.'s Sug. Retail was $400.

⚔ **Model 92 Buckmaster** — 22 in. skeet bore barrel rifle sights, 7½ lbs. Disc. 1987.

	$345	$285	$260	$240	$220	$200	$185

Last Mfg.'s Sug. Retail was $400.

WEAVER ARMS CORPORATION
Previous manufacturer located in Escondido, CA from 1984-1990.

Grading	100%	98%	95%	90%	80%	70%	60%

NIGHTHAWK CARBINE — 9mm Para., closed bolt semi-auto paramilitary design carbine, fires from closed bolt, 16.1 in. barrel, retractable shoulder stock, 25, 32, 40, or 50 shot mag. (interchangeable with Uzi), ambidextrous safety, parkerized finish, 6½ lbs.

	$440	$360	$330	$300	$275	$250	$230

Last Mfg.'s Sug. Retail was $575.

NIGHTHAWK PISTOL — 9mm Para., closed bolt semi-auto, 10 or 12 in. barrel, alloy upper receiver, ambidextrous safety, black finish, 5 lbs. New 1987.

	$410	$340	$320	$295	$275	$250	$230

Last Mfg.'s Sug. Retail was $475.

WEBLEY & SCOTT, LIMITED

Firearms manufacturer located in Birmingham, England 1898 to 1979. Beginning 1980, Webley & Scott, Ltd. began manufacturing high quality weapons only. More information may be obtained by contacting the factory directly (see Trademark Index).

Webley & Scott, Ltd. had the shotgun business re-established as a separate company named W & C Scott (Gunmakers) Ltd. in 1979. This new company was acquired by Holland & Holland and all inquiries should be directed to H&H regarding W & C Scott guns.

PISTOLS

MARK III M&P REVOLVER — .32 S&W, .320 S&W, or .38 S&W cal., single/double action, 6 shot, 3 in. and 4 in. barrel, hinged top break, blue, fixed sights, wood service or competition grips. Mfg. 1896-1939.

	$350	$295	$255	$220	$195	$165	$140

Some Mark III revolvers were fitted with a manual safe.

Mark III Target Model — .38 S&W cal., similar to above, except was also available with 6 - 10 in. barrel with adj. sights.

	$450	$375	$325	$275	$250	$225	$200

MARK IV M&P REVOLVER — similar to Mark III, except 3 in., 4 in., or 5 in. barrel, improved hammer and grip design. Mfg. 1929-1979.

	$350	$295	$255	$220	$195	$165	$140

This was the last of the Webley series of revolvers.

MARK IV .22 TARGET REVOLVER — similar to Mark IV, except .22 LR, 6 in. barrel, target sights, mfg. 1931-1967.

	$450	$385	$330	$285	$235	$200	$165

MARK IV SERVICE REVOLVER — .455 cal., single/double action, 4 or 6 in. barrel, top break, blue, fixed sights, known as the Boer War Model and is not to be confused with the smaller, later Mark IV introduced in 1929. Mfg. 1899-1914.

	$375	$325	$275	$225	$175	$140	$110

NO. 1 MARK VI BRITISH SERVICE REVOLVER — .45 LC, .45 ACP, or .455 Webley cal., single/double action, 4, 6, or 7½ in. barrel, top break, blue, fixed sights, wood service or competition grips. Mfg. 1914-1939.

	$300	$250	$225	$195	$165	$135	$110

Grading	100%	98%	95%	90%	80%	70%	60%

MARK VI .22 TARGET REVOLVER — similar to Mark VI, except .22 LR, target sights, mfg. until 1945.

	$300	$250	$225	$195	$165	$135	$110

Bayonet and should stock attachments were also available for this model. These accessories are rare and command considerable premiums over values listed above.

MARK V REVOLVER — .455 cal., single/double action. Many were military-modified for .45 Colt or .45 ACP, many were civilian-modified, round butt, top break. Mfg. 1914-1915 only.

	$375	$325	$275	$225	$175	$150	$125

BULLDOG OR RIC MODEL — available in .320 - .476 cals. (.455 Webley most common), 5 shot, 2⅛ - 4½ in. barrel, solid frame, blue, fixed sights. Mfg. 1867-1939 for Royal Irish Constabulary.

	$295	$250	$225	$175	$140	$110	$90

WEBLEY-FOSBERY AUTOMATIC REVOLVER — .455 Webley cal., 6 shot, top break, recoil revolves cylinder and cocks hammer, walnut or hard rubber grips. Mfg. 1901-1939.

A small number of Webley-Fosbery pistols were chambered for .38 Colt Auto Cartridge, usually found in 13xx range, features 8 shot cylinder.
Add $1,000 for .38 cal.

✠ **1901 Model** — large frame, early features.

	$3,500	$3,000	$2,500	$2,250	$1,800	$1,350	$900

Add 20% for Target Model (adj. rear sight).

✠ **1902 Model** — large frame, late features.

	$2,750	$2,350	$2,000	$1,750	$1,500	$1,200	$900

Add 20% for Target Model (adj. rear sight).

✠ **1904 Model** — small frame, late features.

	$2,750	$2,350	$2,000	$1,750	$1,500	$1,200	$900

Add 20% for Target Model (adj. rear sight).

HAMMER MODEL .25 AUTOMATIC — .25 auto cal., 6 shot mag., 2 in. barrel, no sights, blue, composition grips. Mfg. 1906-1940.

	$275	$225	$175	$150	$135	$125	$115

HAMMERLESS MODEL .25 — .25 auto cal., similar to Hammer Model .25, except no exposed hammer and fixed sights. Mfg. 1909-1940.

	$275	$225	$175	$150	$135	$125	$115

SINGLE SHOT TARGET PISTOL — .22 LR, .32 (special order), or .38 (special order) cal., 10 in. barrel, top break, blue, fixed sights on early models. Mfg. 1909-1964.

	$250	$195	$120	$110	$100	$90	$75

METROPOLITAN POLICE AUTOMATIC — .32 auto or .380 auto cal., 7 or 8 shot, 3½ in. barrel, blue, fixed sights, composition grips. Mfg. 1906-1940.

	$850	$750	$650	$600	$550	$475	$400

SEMI-AUTO SINGLE SHOT — .22 long, 4¼ and 9 in. barrel, adj. sights, blue, composition grips, empty case is ejected and hammer cocked as in a semi-auto, then it is loaded singly and slide closed. Mfg. 1911-1927.

	$330	$275	$165	$120	$110	$100	$85

Grading	100%	98%	95%	90%	80%	70%	60%

9MM M&P AUTOMATIC — 9mm Browning Long, 8 shot, 5 in. barrel, blue, fixed sights. Mfg. 1909-1930.

	$950	$850	$750	$650	$550	$475	$400

HAMMERLESS MODEL 1913 — .38 cal., high velocity, approx. 1,000 mfg.

	$1,650	$1,250	$1,000	$800	$700	$600	$500

MARK I .455 AUTO PISTOL — .455 Webley cal., 7 shot, 5 in. barrel, blue, fixed sights. Mfg. 1912-1945.

	$1,500	$1,150	$900	$750	$600	$500	$400

MARK I NO. 2 — similar to Mark I, except adj. sights, modified safety, and cut for shoulder stock.

	$2,750	$2,250	$1,800	$1,500	$1,200	$900	$600

The shoulder stock is an extremely rare accessory for this variation.

SHOTGUNS

MODEL 700 SIDE-BY-SIDE DOUBLE BARREL — 12 or 20 ga.'s, boxlock, case hardened receiver, minimum engraving, single trigger. Deduct $50 for double trigger. Mfg. 1949-1980.

	$1,700	$1,625	$1,500	$1,250	$1,000	$750	$600

MODEL 701 — similar to 700 but fanciest walnut, most engraving. Deduct $100 for double trigger. Mfg. 1949-1980.

	$3,150	$2,500	$2,100	$1,800	$1,400	$1,150	$925

MODEL 702 — similar to 700 but middle grade. Deduct $75 for double trigger. Mfg. 1949-1980.

	$2,650	$2,200	$1,800	$1,500	$1,250	$950	$750

MODEL 710 — same action as the Model 700, except is 28 ga. and designed specifically for the American market, only 40 were mfg. 1966-1968.

	$2,750	$2,400	$2,050	$1,775	$1,525	$1,300	$1,100

MODEL 712 — 12 ga., specifically designed for the American market.

	$1,700	$1,625	$1,500	$1,250	$1,000	$750	$600

MODEL 720 — 20 ga.

	$2,100	$1,700	$1,625	$1,500	$1,250	$1,000	$750

WEIHRAUCH, HANS-HERMANN

Manufacturer located in Mellrichstadt, Germany. Exclusive factory authorized U.S. distributor is European American Armory, located in Hialeah, FL.

MODEL HW 60 TARGET — .22 LR cal., target rifle featuring adj. sights, 26¾ in. barrel, single shot, match walnut stock, and other match features, aperture sights, 10.8 lbs.

Mfg.'s Sug. Retail	$995	$750	$650	$550	$450	$395	$350	$295

Add $220 for lefthand action.

MODEL HW 60J — .22 LR or .222 Rem. cal., sporter model with checkered walnut stock. Importation disc. 1992.

	$525	$465	$435	$395	$345	$300	$260

Add $304 for .222 Rem. cal.
Last Mfg.'s Sug. Retail was $585.

Grading	100%	98%	95%	90%	80%	70%	60%

MODEL HW 66 RIFLE — .22 Hornet or .222 Rem. cal., match grade bolt action rifle. Imported 1989-90 only.

	$575	$495	$395	$325	$285	$250	$215

Add $78 for double set triggers.
Add $55 for stainless steel barrel (.22 Hornet).
Last Mfg.'s Sug. Retail was $688.

MODEL HW 660 MATCH — .22 LR cal., match rifle variation featuring adj. stock comb with vent. fore-end, aperture sights, 10.8 lbs. Importation began 1991.

Mfg.'s Sug. Retail $1,195	$895	$775	$650	$550	$450	$375	$300

WESSON FIREARMS CO. INC.

Manufacturer located in Palmer, MA. In late 1990, ownership of Dan Wesson Arms changed (within the family), and the new company has been renamed Wesson Firearms Co., Inc.

REVOLVERS: DOUBLE ACTION

MODEL 11 — .357 Mag.cal., 6 shot, 2½, 4, or 6 in. interchangeable barrels, fixed sights, blue, interchangeable grips, exposed barrel nut. Mfg. 1970-1971.

	$200	$175	$160	$150	$140	$130	$120

Add $60 per extra barrel.

MODEL 12 — similar to 11, with adj. sights. Mfg. 1970-1971.

	$245	$200	$175	$160	$150	$140	$130

MODEL 14 — similar to 11, with recessed barrel nut. Mfg. 1971-1975.

	$225	$185	$170	$160	$150	$140	$130

MODEL 8 — similar to 14, except .38 Spl. cal.

	$200	$170	$155	$145	$135	$125	$115

MODEL 15 — similar to 14, with adj. sights. Mfg. 1971-1975.

	$245	$200	$155	$145	$135	$125	$115

MODEL 9 — similar to 15, except .38 Spl. cal. Mfg. 1971-1975.

	$245	$200	$155	$145	$135	$125	$115

REVOLVERS: CURRENT MANUFACTURE

As a guideline, the following information is provided on Wesson Firearms frames. The smallest frames are Models 738P and 38P. Small frame models include 22, 722, 22M, 722M, 32, 732, 322, 7322, 8-2, 708, 9-2, 709, 14-2, 714, 15-2, and 715-2. Large frames include 41, 741, 44, 744, 45, and 745. SuperMag frame models include 40, 740, 375, 445, and 7445. Small frames are sideplate design, while large frames are solid frame construction. Current models listed below assume interchangeable barrels unless otherwise specified.

Dan Wesson revolvers are mfg. with solid rib barrels as standard equipment.

MODEL 22 — .22 LR cal., double action, 6 shot, adj. sights, 2½, 4, 6, 8, or 10 in. (disc. 1987) barrel, current production. Add $21 for VR, $48 for heavy VR, $8-$11 for each additional longer barrel length.

Mfg.'s Sug. Retail $338	$280	$225	$200	$190	$180	$170	$160

Model 22 Pistol Pac — includes 2½, 4, 6, and 8 in. barrel assemblies, extra grip, 4 additional front sight blades, and aluminum case.

Mfg.'s Sug. Retail $637	$510	$400	$360	$330	$300	$275	$260

Add $101 for full shroud VR barrels.
Add $191 for heavy full shroud VR barrels.

Grading	100%	98%	95%	90%	80%	70%	60%

Model 22 Silhouette — .22 LR cal., choice of 10 in. vent. or heavy vent. barrel, single action only, combat style grip, narrow rear sight blade and patridge front. New 1992.

Mfg.'s Sug. Retail	$430	$365	$315	$295	$275	$260	$245	$230

Add $18 for vent. heavy barrel.

MODEL 22M — .22 Mag. cal., otherwise similar to Model 22.

Mfg.'s Sug. Retail	$349	$290	$230	$200	$190	$180	$170	$160

Model 22M Pistol Pac — includes 2½, 4, 6, and 8 in. barrel assemblies, extra grip, 4 additional front sight blades, and aluminum case.

Mfg.'s Sug. Retail	$637	$500	$400	$360	$330	$300	$275	$260

Add $101 for full shroud VR barrels.
Add $191 for heavy full shroud VR barrels.

MODEL 32 — .32 H&R Mag. cal., 2½, 4, 6, or 8 in. barrel, adj. rear sight, interchangeable colored front sight blades, blue finish, checkered target grips. New 1986. Add $21 for VR barrel shroud (Model 32-V), add $48 for VR heavy barrel shroud (Model 32-VH). Also add approx. $8-$11 for each additional barrel length over 2½ in.

Mfg.'s Sug. Retail	$338	$280	$225	$200	$190	$180	$170	$160

Model 32 Pistol Pac — includes 2½, 4, 6, and 8 in. barrel assemblies, extra grip, 4 additional front sight blades, and aluminum case.

Mfg.'s Sug. Retail	$615	$495	$395	$360	$330	$300	$275	$260

Add $101 for full shroud VR barrels.
Add $190 for heavy full shroud VR barrels.

MODEL 38P — .38+P cal., 5 shot, 6½ in. barrel, fixed sights, wood or rubber grips, 24.6 oz. New 1992.

Mfg.'s Sug. Retail	$270	$225	$190	$170	$150	$135	$120	$110

MODEL 322 — .32-20 cal., 2½, 4, 6, or 8 in. barrel, adj. rear sight, interchangeable colored front sight blades, blue finish, checkered target grips. New 1986. Add $21 for VR barrel shroud (Model 322-V), add $48 for VR heavy barrel shroud (Model 322-VH). Also add approx. $8-$11 for each additional barrel length over 2½ in. New 1991.

Mfg.'s Sug. Retail	$338	$280	$225	$200	$190	$180	$170	$160

Model 322 Pistol Pac — includes 2½, 4, 6, and 8 in. barrel assemblies, extra grip, 4 additional front sight blades, and aluminum case.

Mfg.'s Sug. Retail	$615	$495	$395	$360	$330	$300	$275	$260

Add $101 for full shroud VR barrels.
Add $190 for heavy full shroud VR barrels.

MODEL 14-2 — .357 Mag. cal., 4, 6, or 8 in. interchangeable barrels, fixed sights, blue. Mfg. 1975-present. Add $7 for each additional longer barrel length.

Mfg.'s Sug. Retail	$267	$215	$170	$150	$140	$130	$120	$110

Model 14-2 Pistol Pac — includes 2½, 4, and 6 in. barrel assemblies, extra grip and aluminum case.

Mfg.'s Sug. Retail	$456	$385	$325	$300	$275	$260	$245	$230

Model 14-2 PPC — .357 Mag. cal., extra heavy 6 in. bull shroud barrel with removable underweight, Hogue Gripper grips, Aristocrat sights. New 1992.

Mfg.'s Sug. Retail	$780	$675	$550	$450	$375	$330	$300	$275

MODEL 14 FIXED BARREL — .357 Mag., 2½ or 4 in. (fixed sight Service Model) barrel, satin blue finish. New 1993.

Mfg.'s Sug. Retail	$240	$195	$165	$150	$140	$130	$120	$110

Add $6 for 4 in. barrel.

Grading	100%	98%	95%	90%	80%	70%	60%

MODEL 8-2 — similar to 14-2, except .38 Spl. cal.

Mfg.'s Sug. Retail	$267	$215	$170	$150	$140	$130	$120	$110

This model is also available in a Pistol Pac - same specifications and values as the Model 14-2 Pistol Pac.

Model 8-2 PPC — .38 Spl. cal., extra heavy 6 in. bull shroud barrel with removable underweight, Hogue Gripper grips, Aristocrat sights. New 1992.

Mfg.'s Sug. Retail	$780	$675	$550	$450	$375	$330	$300	$275

MODEL 15-2 — similar to 14-2, except adj. sights, available with 2, 4, 6, 8, 10, 12, or 15 in. barrels. Add approx. $9-$11 for each additional barrel length over 2 inches, $21 for VR barrel (Model 15-2V), or $48 for VR heavy barrel shroud (Model 15-2HV).

2 in. barrel

Mfg.'s Sug. Retail	$338	$280	$225	$200	$190	$180	$170	$160

Model 15-2 Pistol Pac — includes 2½, 4, 6, and 8 in. barrel assemblies, extra grip, 4 additional front sight blades, and aluminum case.

Mfg.'s Sug. Retail	$615	$495	$395	$360	$330	$300	$275	$260

Add $101 for full shroud VR barrels.
Add $190 for heavy full shroud VR barrels.

MODEL 15 FIXED BARREL — .357 Mag. cal., 3 or 5 in. (adj. rear sight Target Model) barrel, brushed stainless steel or high bright blue finish. New 1993.

Mfg.'s Sug. Retail	$248	$215	$180	$160	$140	$130	$115	$100

Add $8 for 5 in. barrel.

MODEL 15 GOLD SERIES — .357 Mag. cal., 6 or 8 in. VR heavy slotted barrel, "Gold" stamped shroud with Dan Wesson signature, smoother action (8 lb. double action pull), 18 kt. gold plated trigger, white triangle rear sight with orange dot patridge front sight, exotic hardwood grips. Mfg. 1989-present.

Mfg.'s Sug. Retail	$544	$425	$380	$340	$300	$260	$225	$185

MODEL 9-2 — similar to 15-2, except .38 Spl. cal. Use same add-ons as in Model 15-2.

Mfg.'s Sug. Retail	$338	$280	$225	$200	$190	$180	$170	$160

This model is also available in a Pistol Pac - same specifications and values as the Model 9-2 Pistol Pac.

MODEL 375V SUPERMAG — .375 Super Mag. cal., 4, 6, 8, or 10 in. VR barrel, adj. rear sight, interchangeable front and rear sight blades, bright blue finish, smooth target grips. New 1986. Add approx. $15 for each barrel length after 6 in., $39 for slotted shroud (Model 375-V8S, 8 in. barrel only), $10-$12 for VR heavy shroud (Model 375 -VH).

Mfg.'s Sug. Retail	$498	$410	$335	$285	$260	$240	$230	$225

MODEL 40V (.357 SUPERMAG) — .357 Super Mag. cal. (.357 Max.), double action, 6 shot, 4, 6, 8, or 10 in. barrel VR. Add $39 for slotted barrel shroud (8 in. barrel only), $16-$32 for heavy VR barrel, $15 for each additional barrel length.

Mfg.'s Sug. Retail	$488	$405	$335	$285	$260	$240	$230	$225

MODEL 41V — .41 Mag. cal., double action, 6 shot, 4, 6, 8, or 10 in. barrel VR. Add $23 for heavy barrel, $11 for each additional barrel length.

Mfg.'s Sug. Retail	$413	$345	$290	$270	$255	$240	$230	$225

Model 41V Pistol Pac — includes 6 and 8 in. VR barrel assemblies, extra grip, 2 additional front sight blades, and aluminum case.

Mfg.'s Sug. Retail	$624	$495	$395	$360	$330	$300	$275	$260

Add $48 for full shroud VR barrels.

Grading		100%	98%	95%	90%	80%	70%	60%

MODEL 44V — .44 Mag. cal., double action, similar to Model 41V, adj. sights. Add $23 for heavy barrel, $11 for each additional barrel length.

Mfg.'s Sug. Retail	$431	$365	$300	$265	$250	$230	$215	$200

⚵ **Model 44V Pistol Pac** — includes 6 and 8 in. VR barrel assemblies, extra grip, 4 additional front sight blades, and aluminum case.

Mfg.'s Sug. Retail	$708	$585	$425	$380	$330	$300	$275	$260

Add $50 for full shroud VR barrels.

MODEL 45V — .45 Long Colt cal., 4, 6, 8, or 10 in. VR barrel, same frame as Model 44V, blued finish. Add $23 for heavy barrel, $11 for each additional barrel length. New 1988.

Mfg.'s Sug. Retail	$431	$365	$300	$265	$250	$230	$215	$200

⚵ **Model 45V Pistol Pac** — includes 6 and 8 in. VR barrel assemblies, extra grip, 2 additional front sight blades, and aluminum case.

Mfg.'s Sug. Retail	$708	$585	$425	$380	$330	$300	$275	$260

Add $50 for full shroud VR barrels.

MODEL .45 PIN GUN — .45 ACP cal., competition pin gun model with 5 in. vent. or heavy vent barrel configuration, blued steel, two stage Taylor forcing cone, 54 oz. New 1993.

Mfg.'s Sug. Retail	$654	$575	$495	$440	$395	$350	$300	$250

Add $9 for VR heavy shroud barrel.

MODEL .445 SUPERMAG — .445 Super Mag. cal., 4, 6, 8, or 10 in. VR barrel, adj. rear sight, interchangeable front and rear sight blades (optional), bright blue finish, smooth target grips. New 1991. Add approx. $18 for each barrel length after 6 in., $30 for slotted shroud (Model 445-V8S, 8 in. barrel only). Add approx. $17 for VR heavy rib shroud, approx. $90 for VR heavy shroud and interchangeable sights (Model 445-VH).

Mfg.'s Sug. Retail	$516	$425	$335	$290	$275	$250	$230	$225

REVOLVERS: STAINLESS STEEL

MODEL 722 — stainless version of Model 22, use same add-ons for various barrel options.

Mfg.'s Sug. Retail	$366	$315	$250	$205

This model is also available in a Pistol Pac including 2½, 4, 6, and 8 in. solid rib barrel assemblies, extra grip, 4 additional sight blades, and fitted carrying case - Mfg.'s Suggested Retail is $724. Add $101 for VR barrels, $199 for full shroud heavy VR barrels.

⚵ **Model 722 Silhouette** — .22 LR cal., choice of 10 in. vent. or heavy vent. barrel, single action only, combat style grip, narrow rear sight blade and patridge front. New 1992.

Mfg.'s Sug. Retail	$458	$380	$325	$295

MODEL 722M — .22 Mag cal., otherwise similar to Model 722, use same add-ons for various barrel options.

Mfg.'s Sug. Retail	$391	$320	$270	$230

This model is also available in a Pistol Pac including 2½, 4, 6, and 8 in. solid rib barrel assemblies, extra grip, 4 additional sight blades, and fitted carrying case. Mfg.'s Suggested Retail is $724. Add $101 for VR barrels, $199 for full shroud heavy VR barrels.

MODEL 708 — .38 Spl cal.., similar to Model 8-2. Add $6 for each additional barrel length.

Mfg.'s Sug. Retail	$311	$260	$200	$170

This model is also available in a Pistol Pac including 2½, 4, and 6 in. solid rib barrel assemblies, extra grip and fitted carrying case. Mfg.'s Suggested Retail is $517.

Grading	100%	98%	95%	90%	80%	70%	60%

⚔ **Model 708 Action Cup/PPC** — .38 Spl. cal., extra heavy 6 in. bull shroud barrel with removable underweight, Hogue Gripper grips, mounted Tasco Pro Point II on Action Cup, Aristocrat sights on PPC. New 1992.

Mfg.'s Sug. Retail $857 $725 $650 $550
Add $56 for Action Cup Model with Tasco Scope.

MODEL 709 — .38 Spl. cal., target revolver, adj. sights. Add $9 for each additional longer barrel length, $22 for VR, $50 for heavy vent. rib. Also available in special order 10, 12 (disc.), or 15 (disc.) in. barrel lengths (add approx. $50 for 10 in.).

Mfg.'s Sug. Retail $366 $305 $250 $205

This model is also available in a Pistol Pac including 2½, 4, 6, and 8 in. solid rib barrel assemblies, extra grip, 4 additional sight blades, and fitted carrying case. Mfg.'s Suggested Retail is $689. Add $101 for VR barrels, $199 for full shroud heavy VR barrels.

MODEL 714 FIXED BARREL — .357 Mag. cal., 2½ and 4 in. (fixed sight Service Model) barrel, brushed stainless steel. New 1993.

Mfg.'s Sug. Retail $253 $220 $185 $160
Add $6 for 4 in. barrel.

MODEL 714 — .357 Mag. cal., similar to Model 14-2. Add $7 for each additional barrel length.

Mfg.'s Sug. Retail $311 $260 $200 $170

This model is also available in a Pistol Pac including 2½, 4, and 6 in. solid rib barrel assemblies, extra grip and fitted carrying case. Mfg.'s Suggested Retail is $517.

⚔ **Model 714 Action Cup/PPC** — .357 Mag. cal., extra heavy 6 in. bull shroud barrel with removable underweight, Hogue Gripper grips, mounted Tasco Pro Point II on Action Cup, Aristocrat sights on PPC. New 1992.

Mfg.'s Sug. Retail $857 $725 $650 $550
Add $56 for Action Cup Model with Tasco Scope.

MODEL 715 FIXED BARREL — .357 Mag cal.., 3 or 5 in. (adj. rear sight Target Model) barrel, brushed stainless steel. New 1993.

Mfg.'s Sug. Retail $260 $225 $185 $160
Add $8 for 5 in. barrel.

MODEL 715 — .357 Mag. cal., target revolver, adj. sights. Add $22 for vent. rib, $48 for heavy VR.

Mfg.'s Sug. Retail $366 $305 $250 $205

This model is also available in a Pistol Pac including 2½, 4, 6, and 8 in. solid rib barrel assemblies, extra grip, 4 additional sight blades, and fitted carrying case. Mfg.'s Suggested Retail is $689. Add $101 for VR barrels, $199 for full shroud heavy VR barrels.

MODEL 732 — .32 H&R Mag. cal., similar to Model 32, except is stainless steel. New 1986. Add $22 for VR barrel shroud (Model 732-V), $48 for VR heavy barrel shroud (Model 732-VH). Also add approx. $9 for each additional barrel length over 2½ in.

Mfg.'s Sug. Retail $366 $305 $250 $205

This model is also available in a Pistol Pac including 2½, 4, 6, and 8 in. solid rib barrel assemblies, extra grip, 4 additional sight blades, and fitted carrying case. Mfg.'s Suggested Retail is $689. Add $101 for VR barrels, $199 for full shroud heavy VR barrels.

MODEL 738P — .38+P cal., 5 shot, 6½ in. barrel, fixed sights, wood or rubber grips, 24.6 oz. New 1992.

Mfg.'s Sug. Retail $270 $225 $190 $170

Wesson Firearms Co. Inc., cont.

Grading	100%	98%	95%	90%	80%	70%	60%

MODEL 7322 — .32-20 cal., similar to Model 322, except is stainless steel. New 1991. Add $22 for VR barrel shroud (Model 7322-V), $48 for VR heavy barrel shroud (Model 7322-VH). Also add approx. $9 for each additional barrel length over 2½ in.

Mfg.'s Sug. Retail	$366	$305	$250	$205

This model is also available in a Pistol Pac including 2½, 4, 6, and 8 in. solid rib barrel assemblies, extra grip, 4 additional sight blades, and fitted carrying case. Mfg.'s Suggested Retail is $689. Add $101 for VR barrels, $199 for full shroud heavy VR barrels.

MODEL 740V - .357 SUPERMAG — .357 Max. cal., 4, 6, 8, or 10 in. barrel, adj. rear sight with interchangeable front and rear blades, high polished finish, smooth target grips. New 1986. Add approx. $20 for each additional barrel length after 6 in., $45 for slotted shroud (only avail. with 8 in. barrel), $20 for VR heavy barrel shroud (Model 740-VH).

Mfg.'s Sug. Retail	$550	$455	$350	$315

MODEL 741V — .41 Mag. cal., similar to Model 41V. Add $23 for heavy VR, $11 for each barrel length over 4 in.

Mfg.'s Sug. Retail	$462	$385	$315	$270

This model is also available in a Pistol Pac including 6 and 8 in. VR barrel assemblies, extra grip, 2 additional sight blades, and fitted carrying case. Mfg.'s Suggested Retail is $690. Add $49 for full shroud VR barrels.

MODEL 744V — .44 Mag. cal., similar to Model 44V. Add $23 for heavy VR, $11 for each barrel length over 4 in.

Mfg.'s Sug. Retail	$507	$420	$340	$285

This model is also available in a Pistol Pac including 6 and 8 in. VR barrel assemblies, extra grip, 2 additional sight blades, and fitted carrying case. Mfg.'s Suggested Retail is $814. Add $53 for full shroud VR barrels.

Model 744 Commemorative — limited mfg.

	$595	$475	$325

MODEL 745V — .45 Long Colt cal., similar to Model 45V, except in stainless steel. Add $23 for heavy full shroud VR barrels, $11 for each additional barrel length.

Mfg.'s Sug. Retail	$507	$420	$340	$285

This model is also available in a Pistol Pac including 6 and 8 in. VR barrel assemblies, extra grip, 2 additional sight blades, and fitted carrying case. Mfg.'s Suggested Retail is $814. Add $53 for full shroud VR barrels.

MODEL .45 PIN GUN — .45 ACP cal., similar to model described previously, except is stainless steel. New 1993.

Mfg.'s Sug. Retail	$713	$625	$525	$425

Add $49 for VR heavy rib shroud.

MODEL 7445 SUPERMAG — .445 Super Mag. cal., 4, 6, 8, or 10 in. VR barrel, adj. rear sight, interchangeable front and rear sight blades (optional), high polished finish, smooth target grips. New 1991. Add approx. $17 for each barrel length after 6 in., $40 for slotted shroud (Model 7445-V8S, 8 in. barrel only). Add approx. $17 for VR heavy rib shroud, approx. $65 for VR heavy shroud and interchangeable sights (Model 7445-VH).

Mfg.'s Sug. Retail	$592	$460	$350	$300

WESSON, FRANK

Worcester, MA 1854 to 1865, Springfield, MA 1865-1875.

100%	98%	95%	90%	80%	70%	60%	50%	40%	30%	20%	10%

PISTOLS: SINGLE SHOT

SMALL FRAME FIRST MODEL — .22 cal., tip up action, 3½ in. ½ octagon barrel, brass frame, spur trigger, rosewood grips, round frame, irregular sideplate. Mfg. 2500, 1859-1862.

| $605 | $550 | $495 | $440 | $385 | $330 | $275 | $220 | $195 | $165 | $140 | $110 |

SMALL FRAME SECOND MODEL — similar to First Model, with flat sided frame and circular sideplate. Mfg. 12,000, 1862-1880.

| $550 | $495 | $440 | $385 | $330 | $305 | $250 | $195 | $165 | $110 | $105 | $85 |

MEDIUM FRAME FIRST MODEL — .30 S or L, .32 S rimfires cal., 4 in. ½ octagon barrel, iron frame, same as Small Frame in other respects, narrow hinge and short trigger. Mfg. 1000, 1859-1862.

| $525 | $470 | $415 | $360 | $305 | $275 | $220 | $195 | $165 | $110 | $105 | $85 |

MEDIUM FRAME SECOND MODEL — similar to First Model, with wider hinge and longer trigger. Mfg. 1000, 1862-1870.

| $495 | $440 | $385 | $330 | $275 | $250 | $220 | $195 | $165 | $110 | $105 | $85 |

RIFLES

NO. 1 LONG RANGE — side hammer, falling block lever actuated, .44-100 and .45-100 standard cal., 34 in. octagon barrel, tang. sight, select checkered pistol grip stock. Less than 50 mfg., circa 1870-1880.

| $4,950 | $4,675 | $4,400 | $3,850 | $3,575 | $3,080 | $2,860 | $2,475 | $2,200 | $2,035 | $1,760 | $1,540 |

NO. 2 HUNTING RIFLE — similar to No. 1, with finger loop lever. Less than 100 mfg.

| $4,400 | $4,180 | $3,850 | $3,520 | $3,025 | $2,750 | $2,420 | $2,255 | $2,035 | $1,925 | $1,760 | $1,540 |

NO. 1 SPORTING RIFLE — similar to No. 2, with center hammer, .38-100, .40-100, .45-100. Less than 25 mfg.

| $4,400 | $4,180 | $3,850 | $3,520 | $3,025 | $2,750 | $2,420 | $2,255 | $2,035 | $1,925 | $1,760 | $1,540 |

POCKET RIFLES

SMALL FRAME TIP UP — .22 rimfire cal., 6 in. ½ octagon barrel, brass frame, spur trigger, rosewood grips. Approx. 500 mfg., 1865-1875.

| $605 | $550 | $525 | $495 | $470 | $440 | $415 | $360 | $330 | $275 | $220 | $165 |

If without stock - deduct 25%.

MEDIUM FRAME TIP UP — .22, .30, or .32 rimfire cal.s, 10 or 12 in. barrel, same as small frame, with exceptions noted and larger frame. Approx. 1000 mfg., 1862-1870.

| $605 | $550 | $525 | $495 | $470 | $440 | $415 | $360 | $330 | $275 | $220 | $165 |

If without stock - deduct 25%.

MODEL 1870 SMALL FRAME FIRST TYPE — similar to Small Frame Tip Up, except barrel rotates on its axis to load, detachable stock. Approx. 3000 mfg., 1870-1890.

| $550 | $495 | $470 | $440 | $415 | $385 | $360 | $305 | $275 | $220 | $195 | $165 |

If without stock - deduct 25%.

MODEL 1870 SMALL FRAME SECOND TYPE — full octagon barrel.

| $525 | $470 | $440 | $415 | $385 | $360 | $330 | $275 | $250 | $195 | $165 | $140 |

MODEL 1870 SMALL FRAME THIRD TYPE — iron frame, push button ½ cock.

| $495 | $440 | $415 | $385 | $360 | $330 | $305 | $250 | $220 | $165 | $140 | $110 |

100%	98%	95%	90%	80%	70%	60%	50%	40%	30%	20%	10%

MODEL 1870 MEDIUM FRAME FIRST TYPE — similar to Small Frame, except in size and availability of .32 cal. Approx. 5000 mfg., 1870-1893.

| $525 | $495 | $470 | $440 | $415 | $385 | $360 | $305 | $275 | $250 | $195 | $165 |

Deduct 25% if without stock.

MODEL 1870 MEDIUM FRAME SECOND TYPE — external push-button half cock and iron frame.

| $440 | $415 | $385 | $330 | $305 | $275 | $220 | $195 | $165 | $140 | $110 | $90 |

Deduct 25% if without stock.

MODEL 1870 MEDIUM FRAME THIRD TYPE — has three screws in frame, iron frame.

| $440 | $415 | $385 | $330 | $305 | $275 | $220 | $195 | $165 | $140 | $110 | $90 |

Deduct 25% if without stock.

MODEL 1870 LARGE FRAME FIRST TYPE — .32, .38, .42, or .44 rimfire cal., 15-24 in. barrels, similar to smaller frame models, auto extractor. Approx. 500 mfg., 1870-1880.

| $825 | $770 | $715 | $660 | $605 | $550 | $525 | $495 | $440 | $385 | $305 | $275 |

If without stock — deduct 25%.

MODEL 1870 LARGE FRAME SECOND TYPE — similar to First Type, with standard sliding extractor.

| $825 | $770 | $715 | $660 | $605 | $550 | $525 | $495 | $440 | $385 | $305 | $275 |

Deduct 25% if without stock.

WESTERN ARMS COMPANY
Ithaca, NY.

Grading	100%	98%	95%	90%	80%	70%	60%

WESTERN LONG RANGE DOUBLE BARREL SHOTGUN — 12, 16, 20, or .410 ga., 26-32 in. barrels, mod. and full choke, boxlock, extractors, double or single trigger, plain pistol grip stock, Western Arms Co. was a division of Ithaca Gun. Mfg. 1929-1946.

| | $275 | $225 | $200 | $175 | $150 | $125 | $100 |

Single trigger

| | $325 | $275 | $250 | $225 | $200 | $150 | $125 |

WESTERN FIELD
Trademark used on Montgomery Ward rifles and shotguns.

The Western Field trademark has appeared literally on hundreds of various models (shotguns and rifles) sold through the Montgomery Ward retail network. Most of these models were manufactured through subcontracts with both domestic and international firearms manufacturers. Typically, they were "spec." guns made to sell at a specific price to undersell the competition. Most of these models were derivatives of existing factory models with less expensive wood and perhaps missing the features found on those models from which they were derived. To date, there has been very little interest in collecting Western Field guns, regardless of rarity. Rather than list J.C. Higgins models, a general guideline is that values generally are under those of their "1st generation relatives". As a result, prices are ascertained by the shooting value of the gun, rather than its collector value.

WESTLEY RICHARDS & CO. LTD.
Originally William Westley Richards was located in Birmingham, England. Currently manufactured by Westley Richards and Co., Ltd. located on 40 Grange Road, Birmingham, England (B296AR). Manufactured 1812 to date. Currently imported exclusively in the U.S. by The Sporting Field, Inc. located in North Salem, NY.

There seems to be a lot of confusion regarding W. Richards, W. R. Richards, William Richards, and other generic derivatives of the famous English gunmaker, Westley Richards. Part of the problem is that there are seventeen registered firms in England, including several in London, who have made guns by the name of Richards. A genuine Westley Richards gun never has the first name abbreviated, and the London address is usually found on the rib panel. Further compounding the problem, a previous Belgian gunmaker identifiable by W. Richards on the locks or rib, had many shotguns exported into the United States and are commonly confused with the real London maker. These Belgian guns are commonly hammer guns with damascus twist barrels most frequently encountered in either 10, 12, or 16 ga. The easiest way to determine this maker is recognize the Liege proofmarks on the barrel flats and chamber length given in millimeters. Most of these Belgian guns sell in the $100-$400 range, depending on condition and configuration.

Note: Westley Richards guns are essentially custom ordered - only 25-30 guns are made annually. They make many weapons that are impossible to list and evaluate, except on an individual basis. Professional appraisal is necessary upon purchase or sale.

To obtain a quotation for a new Westley Richards shotgun, an inquiry should be submitted to the manufacturer or importer (see Trademark Index for addresses).

SHOTGUNS

Grading	100%	98%	95%	90%	80%	70%	60%
OVUNDO O/U — 12 ga., barrel length and choke to order, hand detachable boxlock with dummy sideplates, SST, checkered straight or pistol grip stock, pre-WWII.							
	$18,000	$15,000	$13,000	$11,000	$9,750	$8,500	$7,250
MODEL E SxS — 12, 16, or 20 ga., barrel length and choke to order, boxlock, extractors, double triggers, checkered pistol grip or straight stock. Disc. 1992.							
	$4,100	$3,600	$3,100	$2,700	$2,300	$1,950	$1,600

Add 20% for 20 gauge.
Add 50% for auto ejectors.
Last Mfg.'s Sug. Retail was $4,545.

CONNAUGHT MODEL SxS — 12, 20, or 28 ga., Anson & Deeley scalloped boxlock action, scroll engraving, 26 or 28 in. barrels, ejectors, about 6½ lbs.							
Mfg.'s Sug. Retail $10,900	$10,900	$8,000	$6,600	$5,600	$4,800	$4,000	$3,400

Add $325 for 20 or 28 ga.

BEST QUALITY BOXLOCK SxS — 12, 16, 20, 28, or .410 ga., barrel lengths and chokes to order, detachable locks with hinged cover, checkered straight or pistol grip stock, auto ejectors.							
Mfg.'s Sug. Retail $15,900	$15,900	$11,250	$8,850	$7,000	$5,500	$4,400	$3,700

Add 30%-40% for 28 ga.
Add 20% for 20 ga.
Add $1,000 for SST.
Only 6 .410 Best Quality Boxlocks have been mfg. to date - values for mint condition specimens can exceed $30,000.

BEST QUALITY SIDELOCK — 12, 16, 20, 28, or .410 ga., barrel length and choke to order, hand detachable sidelocks, auto ejectors, checkered straight or pistol grip stock.							
Mfg.'s Sug. Retail $25,000	$25,000	$18,950	$14,000	$10,750	$8,750	$7,600	$6,400

Add 20% for 20 ga.
Add 40% for 28 ga.
Add 60% for .410 ga.
Add $1,000 for SST.
Most specimens in this model were custom ordered, and as a result, each gun has to be evaluated individually.

WILLIAM BISHOP SIDELOCK MODEL — current mfg., best quality sidelock, made to individual customer specifications.							
Mfg.'s Sug. Retail $30,000	$30,000	$24,000	$18,750	$15,000	$11,750	$9,500	$8,250

Add $145 - $295 for 20 or 28 ga.

Grading	100%	98%	95%	90%	80%	70%	60%

CARLTON DETACHABLE LOCK — 12 or 20 ga., current mfg., detachable sidelocks, top of the line shotgun custom made per customer specifications, elaborate game scene engraving. Many options upon request - values below are for base gun only.

Mfg.'s Sug. Retail	$34,075	$34,075	$26,500	$21,750	$17,250	$13,750	$10,500	$9,000

RIFLES

BEST QUALITY DOUBLE RIFLE — .300, .375 H&H, .470 NE, .577 NE, or .600 NE cal., auto ejectors, boxlock, hammerless, folding leaf rear sight, hooded front sight, engraved with quality French walnut stock, horn forend tip. Values will vary according to caliber.

Mfg.'s Sug. Retail	$45,400	$45,400	$35,750	$30,000	$25,000	$21,000	$18,750	$16,000

Values will vary greatly on this model depending on caliber and type/style of engraving. Values above are for .577 Nitro Express.

DETACHABLE LOCK DOUBLE RIFLE — available in most cals., boxlock with detachable locks, ejectors, colored case hardened frame, cased.

Mfg.'s Sug. Retail	$52,250	$52,250	$42,500	$35,750	$30,000	$25,000	$22,000	$18,250

STALKER MAGAZINE RIFLE — .243 Win., .270 Win., .30-06, .300 H&H, .375 H&H, or .458 Win. Mag. cal., bolt action, Mauser action, 22, 24, or 25 in. barrel, leaf rear and hooded front sight, engraved with French walnut stock, horn forend tip. Current mfg.

Mfg.'s Sug. Retail	$10,250	$10,250	$8,000	$6,950	$5,750	$4,750	$4,000	$3,300

Add approx. $380 for mag. cals.

WHITNEY FIREARMS COMPANY
Manufactured between 1956-1959 in Hartford, CT.

PISTOL: SEMI-AUTO

WOLVERINE OR LIGHTNING — .22 auto cal., unique futuristic appearance, 10 shot, 4⅝ in. barrel, plastic grips, aluminum alloy frame and barrel shroud, blue model is more common (approx. 13,000 mfg.), nickel is rare (approx. 900 mfg.). Mfg. 1955-1962.

	100%	98%	95%	90%	80%	70%	60%
Blue finish	$425	$350	$300	$260	$230	$200	$175
Nickel finish	$550	$450	$375	$300	$260	$230	$200

WHITWORTH
This trademark can be found in the Interarms section of this text.

WICHITA ARMS, INC.
Manufacturer located in Wichita, KS.

PISTOLS

WICHITA INTERNATIONAL PISTOL (WIP) — available in 8 cals. between .22 LR and .357 Mag., single shot, break open action, stainless steel, adj. sights, 10½ or 14 in. barrel, adj. sights or scope mounts, smooth walnut stocks and forearm.

Mfg.'s Sug. Retail	$550	$495	$400	$350

WICHITA CLASSIC PISTOL — assorted cals. to .308 Win., 11¼ in. barrel, action has left-hand bolt for shooting with right-hand, deluxe walnut, custom made, 3 lbs. 15 oz.

Mfg.'s Sug. Retail	$2,950	$2,950	$2,400	$2,100	$1,850	$1,575	$1,265	$1,000

Grading	100%	98%	95%	90%	80%	70%	60%

✣ **Wichita Classic Engraved** — similar to Wichita Classic, except is extensively engraved.

	100%	98%	95%	90%	80%	70%	60%
Mfg.'s Sug. Retail $4,850	$4,850	$3,500	$2,750				

WICHITA SILHOUETTE PISTOL (WSP) — .308 Win. or 7mm/IHMSA cal., adj. trigger and sights, 14^{15}/$_{16}$ in. barrel, center grip walnut stock, 4½ lbs. Left-hand action for shooting with right-hand.

	100%	98%	95%	90%	80%	70%	60%
Mfg.'s Sug. Retail $1,100	$1,100	$900	$750	$600	$525	$460	$400

WICHITA MK40 — .308 Win. or 7mm/IHMSA, fiberthane (disc. 1987) or walnut (new 1988) stock, 13 in. barrel, adj. trigger, multi-range sights, 4½ lbs.

	100%	98%	95%	90%	80%	70%	60%
Mfg.'s Sug. Retail $1,100	$1,100	$900	$750	$600	$525	$460	$400

Add $225 for stainless steel barrel.

RIFLES

WICHITA CLASSIC RIFLE (WCR) — 17-222, 17-222 Mag., .222 Rem, 222 Mag., 223 Rem., 6x47, and other cals. up to and including .308 cal., bolt action, single shot, select walnut, 21 in. octagon barrel, Canjar trigger, no sights, 7 lbs.

	100%	98%	95%	90%	80%	70%	60%
Mfg.'s Sug. Retail $2,950	$2,950	$2,400	$2,100	$1,850	$1,575	$1,265	$1,000

Add P.O.R. for blind box mag.
Add $175 for left-hand action.

✣ **Wichita Varmint Rifle (WVR)** — similar to WCR, except available only in Varmint cals. (up to and including .308) and round barrel.

	100%	98%	95%	90%	80%	70%	60%
Mfg.'s Sug. Retail $2,150	$2,075	$1,650	$1,325	$1,100	$950	$800	$750

Add P.O.R. for blind box mag.
Add $175 for left-hand action.

✣ **Wichita Silhouette Rifle (WSR)** — available in most cals., gray fiberthane stock, 24 in. match grade barrel, 2 oz Canjar trigger, no sights, 9 lbs.

	100%	98%	95%	90%	80%	70%	60%
Mfg.'s Sug. Retail $2,150	$2,150	$1,700	$1,375	$1,140	$975	$825	$750

Add $175 for left-hand action.

✣ **Wichita Magnum** — Mag. cals. Disc. 1984.

	100%	98%	95%	90%	80%	70%	60%
	$1,725	$1,300	$1,175	$1,100	$1,000	$925	$875

WICKLIFFE RIFLES

Previous mfg. by Triple S Development located in Wickliffe, OH.

RIFLES - SINGLE SHOT

MODEL 76 STANDARD — falling block action, most popular cals., 22 or 26 in. barrel, no sights, select walnut pistol grip, 2 piece stock. Mfg. 1976-disc.

	100%	98%	95%	90%	80%	70%	60%
	$395	$350	$325	$300	$275	$250	$225

MODEL 76 DELUXE GRADE — similar to Standard, in .30-06 cal. only, 22 in. barrel, fancy wood, silver pistol grip cap.

	100%	98%	95%	90%	80%	70%	60%
	$460	$415	$385	$360	$320	$290	$250

MODEL 76 COMMEMORATIVE — similar to Deluxe, except etched receiver, U.S. silver dollar inlaid in stock, presentation case. Mfg. 100, 1976.

	100%	98%	95%	90%	80%	70%	60%
	$1,100	$825	$550	$495	$440	$330	$305

Grading	100%	98%	95%	90%	80%	70%	60%

STINGER — similar to 76, .22 Hornet or .223 cal., lightweight 22 in. barrel.

	$395	$350	$325	$300	$275	$250	$225

STINGER DELUXE — similar to 76 Deluxe, in .22 Hornet or .223 cal., lightweight 22 in. barrel.

	$460	$415	$385	$360	$325	$290	$250

TRADITIONALIST — similar to Standard 76, in .30-06 or .45-70 cal., 24 in. barrel.

	$395	$350	$325	$300	$275	$250	$225

KODIAK COMMEMORATIVE — similar to Deluxe, .338 Mag. cal., 26 in. barrel, etched receiver.

	$650	$550	$475	$425	$375	$325	$275

WILDEY, INC.

Originally manufactured in Cheshire, CT. Current manufacture is in New Melford, CT. Distributor and direct sales.

PISTOLS

Wildey has announced they will introduce 3 new proprietary cartridges during 1993. They are the .30 WM, 10mm WM, and 11mm WM based on the .475 Wildey Mag. necked down to respective cartridge dimensions. Norma, located in Sweden, produces the .475 WM brass.

WILDEY AUTO PISTOL — .45 Win. Mag., .357 Peterbilt (limited mfg.), or .475 Wildey Mag., gas operated, 5, 6, 7, 8, 10, or 14 in. VR barrel, selective single shot or semi-auto, 3 lug rotary bolt, fixed barrel (interchangeable), stainless steel construction, 7 shot, double action, adj. sights, smooth wood grips, designed to fire proprietary new cartridges specifically for this gun including the .45 Win. Mag. cal., 64 oz. with 5 in. barrel.
Add $475-$590 per interchangeable barrel.

Survivor Model — .45 Win. Mag., 11mm Wildey Mag., or .475 Wildey Mag. cal., 5, 6, 7, 8, 10, or 12 in. barrel only. New 1990.
Mfg.'s Sug. Retail $1,295 $1,125 $875 $725
Add $100 for 12 in. barrel.
Add $21 for 8 or 10 in. barrel.
Add $50 for new model VR (8, 10, or 12 in. barrel only).
The .475 Wildey cal. is derived from the .284 Win. case. This cal. is available in 8 or 10 in. barrel only.

Survivor Guardsman — similar to Survivor Model, except has squared off trigger guard. New 1990.
Mfg.'s Sug. Retail $1,295 $1,125 $885 $725
Add $100 for 12 in. barrel.
Add $21 for 8 or 10 in. barrel.
Add $46 for new model VR (8, 10, or 12 in. barrel only).

Hunter Model — .45 Win. Mag. or .475 Wildey Mag. cal., 5, 6, 7, 8, 10, or 12 in. barrel, matte finish on all metal parts, adj. sights. New 1990.
Mfg.'s Sug. Retail $1,413 $1,200 $975 $825
Add $36 for 12 in. barrel.
.475 Wildey Mag. is available in 8, 10, or 12 in. barrel only.

Hunter Guardsman — similar to Hunter Model, except has squared off trigger guard. New 1990.
Mfg.'s Sug. Retail $1,413 $1,200 $975 $850
Add $36 for 12 in. barrel.

Grading	100%	98%	95%	90%	80%	70%	60%

⊰ **Older Mfg.** — .45 Win. Mag. or .475 Wildey Mag. cal., Cheshire, CT addressed, serial numbered 1-2,489 with 3 character prefix, priced by serialization, 7, 8, or 10 in. barrel is most desirable. These pistols are older mfg. and Wildey should be contacted directly to find out which models are still remaining (address can be found in the Trademark Index in the back of this text). **Add $413-$513 per interchangeable barrel.**

.475 Wildey Mag. cal. is available in 8 or 10 in. barrel only.

SERIAL NO. 1-200.

Mfg.'s Sug. Retail	$2,180	$1,900	$1,700	$1,550			

Add $20 for 8 or 10 in. barrel.

SERIAL NO. 201-400.

Mfg.'s Sug. Retail	$1,980	$1,750	$1,550	$1,400			

Add $20 for 8 or 10 in. barrel.

SERIAL NO. 401-600.

Mfg.'s Sug. Retail	$1,780	$1,650	$1,375	$1,250			

Add $20 for 8 or 10 in. barrel.

SERIAL NO. 601-800.

Mfg.'s Sug. Retail	$1,580	$1,450	$1,200	$1,000			

Add $20 for 8 or 10 in. barrel.

SERIAL NO. 801-1,000.

Mfg.'s Sug. Retail	$1,275	$1,100	$925	$800			

Add $25 for 8 or 10 in. barrel.

SERIAL NO. 1,001-2,489.

Mfg.'s Sug. Retail	$1,175	$1,025	$850	$750			

Add $20 for 8 or 10 in. barrel.

⊰ **Presentation Model** — same specifications as above model, except is engraved with hand checkered stocks.

			$2,500	$2,000	$1,600		

Last Mfg.'s Sug. Retail was $2,000.

WILKINSON ARMS

Previous manufacturer located in Porma, ID.

DIANE AUTOMATIC PISTOL — .25 ACP cal., 6 shot, 2 1/8 in. barrel, fixed sight, matte blue, plastic grips.

	$125	$110	$90	$80	$65	$55	$50

LINDA PISTOL — 9mm Para., blowback action firing from closed bolt, 8.3 in. barrel, 31 shot mag., PVC pistol grip, maple forearm, Williams adj. rear sight.

	$325	$295	$260	$230	$200	$180	$165

A conversion unit was also available enabling conversion of the Linda Pistol to the Terry Carbine.

"TERRY" CARBINE — blowback action, 9mm Para., 30 shot mag., 16 3/16 in. barrel, closed breech, adj. sights.

	100%	98%	95%	90%	80%	70%	60%
With black P.V.C. stock	$325	$310	$300	$275	$230	$210	$180
With maple stock	$350	$340	$325	$300	$260	$230	$200

WINCHESTER

Manufactured in New Haven, CT from 1866 to date. Also includes U.S. Repeating Arms formed in 1981 with licensing agreement from Olin Corp. to manufacture shotguns and rifles domestically using the Winchester Trademark. Olin Corp. previously mfg. shotguns and rifles bearing the Winchester Hallmark at the Olin Kodensha Plant (closed 1989) located in Tochigi, Japan and also in European Countries. In 1992, U.S. Repeating Arms was acquired by Giat located in France.

WINCHESTER OVERVIEW

Note: Winchester Rifles are a field in themselves. Models Henry, 1866, 1873, 1876, 1885, 1886, 1892, 1894, and 1895 all were produced with a multitude of special order options. Special orders included front and rear special sights, half or ⅔ magazines, takedown, various barrel lengths, configurations, and weights, special metal finishes, deluxe wood (either checkered or carved) in a variety of finishes, an impressive range of engraving options, different butt plates, etc. All of these special orders act independently and interdependently to determine the correct value of a particular Winchester. Some of the finest rifles ever made are special order Winchesters engraved by the Ulrichs, G. Young, L.D. Nimschke, and others. For these reasons a Model 92 Winchester can range in price from $200 to over $250,000 - quite a price range for one model alone! When contemplating a purchase on the higher dollar range, qualified and professional opinions should be secured, preferably from at least 2 sources. Unfortunately many fakes and upgraded (non-original) guns have surfaced in the last 10 years with the sudden increase in prices. Winchesters shown in this section are priced assuming a standard model with no special orders. Any special orders will further add to the prices shown. Caliber rarities must also be considered. Many of the early Winchesters are broken down by year of manufacture. Refer to the "Model Serialization" section in this book.

A factory letter specifying original shipping information by serial number will certainly help solidify values shown on older out of production Winchester rifles and shotguns. A listing has been provided below by model number with serialization range which can be historically researched by the Winchester Museum now located in Cody, WY. To use this outstanding service, make sure the model and its serial number fall within the range listed below. If so, send $25 per serial number needing research payable to the Buffalo Bill Historical Center, P.O. Box 1000 in Cody, WY, 82414. Information received back will include specimen caliber, barrel length, any special orders or finishes, return(s) to the factory, as well as any additional provenance contained within Winchesters' factory shipping ledgers. I would recommend a trip to the Buffalo Bill Historical Center as it contains the most comprehensive collection of projectile arms (including Chinese specimens that date back 2,000 years) and Americana housed under one roof in this country.

A NOTE ON WINCHESTER FINISHES: It is very important to understand that there is a big value difference between a Model 1873 with 90% bright blue as opposed to a gun that has 90% patina finish (turning brown). Even though it is true that both guns are 90%, the bright blue specimen might be worth 50%+ more because it is closer to the way it originally left the factory — with bright bluing. For this reason, the type of finish remaining becomes as important as the amount of finish. "Brown" guns are simply not as desirable as bright guns that show little discoloration, even though many surviving original specimens are typically encountered in either grayish patina or somewhat brown finish. Because of this, much consideration must be given as to what type of finish a specimen has, and if shiny or mostly brown, value has to be taken away from prices listed below accordingly.

With the recent price appreciation on most upper condition Winchester rifles, excellent original condition has become so expensive that the many special order features Winchester offered do not cost that much more currently. However, on lesser condition guns that are much less expensive, these same special order features will cost more percentage-wise since the condition factor did not cost a premium.

PLEASE REFER TO THE 32-PAGE PHOTO PERCENTAGE GRADING SYSTEM IN THE FRONT OF THIS TEXT (PAGES 33-64) TO LEARN MORE ABOUT THE VARIOUS CONDITION FACTORS ENCOUNTERED ON WINCHESTER RIFLES AND SHOTGUNS.

Model 1866 Lever Action Rifle — ser. no. range 124,995-170,101.

Model 1873 Lever Action Rifle — ser. no. range 1-720,496.

Model 1876 Lever Action Rifle — ser. no. range 1-63,871.

Model 1883 Bolt Action Rifle (Hotchkiss Repeater) — ser. no. range 1-84,555.

Model 1885 Single Shot Rifle or Shotgun — ser. no. range 1-109,999.

Model 1886 Lever Action Rifle — ser. no. range 1-156,599.

Model 1887 & 1901 Lever Action Shotguns — ser. no. range 1-72,999.

Model 1890 Slide Action Rifle — ser. no. range 1-329,999.

Model 1892 Lever Action Rifle — ser. no. range 1-379,999.

Model 1893 Slide Action Shotgun — ser. no. range 1-34,050.

Model 1894 Lever Action Rifle — ser. no. range 1-353,999.

Model 1895 Lever Action Rifle — ser. no. range 1-59,999.

Model "Lee" Bolt Action Rifle — ser. no. range 1-19,999.

Model 1897 Lever Action Shotgun — ser. no. range 34,051-377,999.

Model 1903 Semi-Auto .22 Cal. Rifle — ser. no. range 1-39,999.

Model 1905 Semi-Auto Rifle — ser. no. range 1-29,078.

Model 1906 Semi-Auto Rifle — ser. no. range 1-79,999.

Model 1907 Semi-Auto Rifle — ser. no. range 1-9,999.

    Winchester factory data on models produced between approx. 1907-1961 is almost non-existent (except Custom Shop mfg.) since there was a fire at the Winchester factory in 1961.

RIFLES: LEVER ACTIONS – 1860-1964

    A new grading system has been designed exclusively for this section to assist the reader ascertain the value of a particular specimen more accurately. Hopefully, we have eliminated the guesswork of trying to figure out what percentage condition a gun is in when types of metal/wood finish are different (there is a drastic value difference between 50% bright blue and 50% dull patina on older Winchesters. Instead, three value ranges have been created to encompass most of the specimens commonly encountered.

Models found in above average condition may have a premium notation listed after the price groupings.

The three groupings include "Below Average Price Range", "Average Price Range", and "Above Average Price Range" (note the new grading line underneath specifying these condition factors). These ranges indicate the following:

    "Below Average Price Range" - a specimen with no finish remaining, perhaps some parts have been replaced, deteriorated metal may be lightly pitted with faint barrel/frame markings, rounded edges of wood and metal, wood showing much wear with possible repairs or cracks, must be in working order. (Please refer to Photo No. 12 on page 40 for visual identification.)

    "Average Price Range" - a specimen with all original parts, exhibits gun metal patina finish, metal mostly smooth (perhaps lightly pitted), principle lettering and markings legible throughout, wood showing honest wear with little finish remaining (may have small cracks and other imperfections), good working order. (Please refer to Photos No. 10 and 11 on pages 39 and 40 for visual identification).

    "Above Average Price Range" - a specimen featuring unpolished brass (on Henry's and Model 1866s) or plum brown patina with traces of bluing in protected areas (on all steel frame models), sharp corners, crisp barrel markings, traces of original finish remaining, metal should exhibit nice patina or older flaking finish, wood should have some original stock varnish remaining and minor handling marks and dings, good bore, perfect working order with no replacement parts. (Please refer to Photos No. 8 and 9 on pages 38 and 39 for visual identification).

	Below Average	Average	Above Average

HENRY RIFLE — .44 rimfire, 15 shot, 24 in. barrel with integral slotted tube mag. and loading lever, blued barrel, brass frame. Approx. 13,000 total production, mfg. 1860-1866. Because almost all Henrys have little or no original finish left, values below are in ranges rather than in separate condition factors.
Add 50%-75% for engraving (these specimens should have fancy wood).

⚔ **Iron Frame Model** — frame made of iron, round type butt plate, no lever latch, adj. sporting type rear leaf sight, serial numbers are in three digits only. Total production is believed to be less than 300.
    $9,000 - $12,000 $12,000 - $17,500 $17,500 - $22,500

⚔ **First Model** — approx. 3,500 mfg., generally serialized below 3,500, with or without lever latch, perch belly stock and slotted receiver for rear sight.
    $6,250 - $7,500 $7,500 - $10,000 $10,000 - $15,000

⚔ **Martial Marked** — contracted by U.S. military for Civil War use, denoted by "C.G.C." inspector markings on upper barrel breech and stock, approx. 1,900 with serialization scattered.
    $7,000 - $8,250 $8,250 - $11,500 $11,500 - $17,500

This rifle was the most revolutionary shoulder weapon introduced in the Civil War.

	Below Average	Average	Above Average

⚹ **Late Model** — similar to first model, except butt plate heel has pointed profile, lever latch became standard and receiver is not slotted for rear sight, serial number over approx. 3,500, most commonly encountered Henry with approx. 8,000 mfg.

	$4,500 - $6,000	$6,000 - $8,000	$8,000 - $9,995

MODEL 1866 LEVER ACTION — .44 rimfire or centerfire (4th Model only), 24 in. barrel, blued barrel with brass frame, differs from Henry in that it has a wood forearm, frame cartridge loading port (King's improvement), and separate tube mag. Total production reached 170,101 for all models, mfg. 1866-1898.

⚹ **Model 1866 First Model Rifle** — "Improved Henry" action, .44 cal. rimfire, no forend cap, serialization is concealed on lower tang inside butt stock, serial range is from mid 12,000 to mid 15,000 (in Henry serial range sequence).

	$2,000 - $4,000	$4,000 - $8,000	$8,000 - $12,000

⚹ **Model 1866 Carbine First Model** — same action as Rifle, only with 20 in. barrel, 2 barrel bands and saddle ring.

	$1,000 - $2,000	$2,000 - $3,000	$3,000 - $5,000

⚹ **Model 1866 Rifle Second Model** — "New Model" with redesigned frame, with Henry barrel markings, serial numbered outside lower tang beneath lever (approx. after serial number 20,000).

	$1,500 - $2,500	$2,500 - $4,000	$4,000 - $6,000

⚹ **Model 1866 Carbine Second Model** — frame and other changes similar to Second Model Rifle.

	$1,000 - $1,750	$1,750 - $2,750	$2,750 - $4,500

⚹ **Model 1866 Rifle Third Model** — block style serial numbers usually located behind trigger, improved frame. Serial numbered approx. 25,000-149,000.

	$1,250 - $1,750	$1,750 - $2,500	$2,500 - $4,000

Add 20% for brass forend cap and buttplate.

⚹ **Model 1866 Carbine Third Model** — same changes as Model 1866 Third Model Rifle, 20 in. barrel with 2 bands.

	$1,000 - $1,500	$1,500 - $2,500	$2,500 - $4,000

⚹ **Model 1866 Musket Third Model** — 27 in. round barrel, 24 in. magazine, 3 barrel bands.

	$1,250 - $1,750	$1,750 - $2,500	$2,500 - $3,500

⚹ **Model 1866 Rifle/Carbine/Musket Fourth Model** — .44 cal., twin rimfire and centerfire, script style serial number on lower tang near lever latch, improved frame, serial range approx. 149,000-170,101.

Values for these models are the same as for equivalent Third Model 1866s.

MODEL 1873 LEVER ACTION — .32-20, .38-40, or .44-40 centerfire cal., iron frame (changed to steel 1884) with sideplates, frame loading port, 24 in. round or octagon barrel, tube mag., blued finish with case hardened parts, oil finished stock, serial numbered on lower tang, 720,610 mfg. between 1873-1919, guns produced after serial number 525,923 are modern firearms.

Deluxe Models 1873 with color case hardened frames will add at least 50% to the values listed below for standard models.

	Below Average	Average	Above Average

Model 1873 First Model Rifle — ser. #'s approx. 1 - 30,000, sliding thumbprint dust cover on 2 guides that are integral part of upper frame, absence of any cal. marking.
$400 - $800 $800 - $1,200 $1,200 - $1,700
98% bright bluing (Photo No. 2, pg. 35) commands $5,000 - $6,000.

Model 1873 Carbine First Model — 20 in. round barrel with 2 bands. Distinctive curved butt plate, with saddle ring.
$500 - $900 $900 - $1,400 $1,400 - $2,000

Model 1873 Musket First Model — 30 in. round barrel, 27 in. mag. with 3 barrel bands, approx. 500 mfg.
$750 - $1,250 $1,250 - $1,800 $1,800 - $2,500
98% bright bluing (Photo No. 2, pg. 35) commands $6,000 - $8,000.

Model 1873 Rifle Second Model — improved dust cover featuring slides on center rail on rear section of frame top which is held in place by 2 screws, serial range 31,000 - 90,000.
$300 - $400 $400 - $600 $600 - $1,000
98% bright bluing (Photo No. 2, pg. 35) commands $3,000 - $4,000.

Model 1873 Carbine Second Model — changes similar to 1873 Second Model Rifle, with 20 in. round barrel and 2 barrel bands.
$400 - $600 $600 - $1,000 $1,000 - $1,500
98% bright bluing (Photo No. 2, pg. 35) commands $4,000 - $6,000.

Model 1873 Musket Second Model — changes similar to 1873 Second Model Rifle, with 30 in. barrel and 3 barrel bands.
$500 - $800 $800 - $1,200 $1,200 - $1,500

Model 1873 Rifle Third Model — dust cover rail integral with frame, improved action with rear frame screws (2), serial 90,000-end of production.
$300 - $400 $400 - $500 $500 - $750
Add 20% for octagon barrel, 30% for .44-40 cal.
98% bright bluing (Photo No. 2, pg. 35) commands $3,000 - $4,000.
80% bright bluing (Photo No. 5, pg. 37) commands $1,250 - $1,500.

Model 1873 Carbine Third Model — changes similar to 1873 Rifle Third Model, with 20 in. barrel and 2 barrel bands.
$400 - $600 $600 - $800 $800 - $1,250
Add 30% for .32-20 cal.
98% bright bluing (Photo No. 2, pg. 35) commands $7,500 - $8,500.

Model 1873 Musket Third Model — changes similar to 1873 Rifle Third Model, with 30 in. round barrel and 3 barrel bands.
$400 - $600 $600 - $800 $800 - $1,000
98% bright bluing (Photo No. 2, pg. 35) commands $2,500 - $3,500.

Model 1873 .22 Rim Fire Rifle — .22 S, L, or Extra L (very rare) cal., 24 in. barrel, no loading gate, the first .22 caliber repeater, 19,552 produced, mfg. 1884-1904. Made in rifle configuration only.
$500 - $700 $700 - $900 $900 - $1,200
50% bright bluing (Photo No. 8, pg. 38) commands $1,500 - $2,000.

Model 1873 "One of One Thousand" — special care taken in manufacture to guarantee better accuracy, markings on top of breech designate model, deluxe walnut, extremely rare, barrel marked "One of One Thousand" in most cases, 136 mfg. Original cost was $100.
Values can range from $25,000 - $75,000, depending on condition. A factory letter is a must for any "One of One Thousand" Winchester. Believe it or not, watch for fake letters.
Note: Rarity of the "One of One Thousand" and the "One of One Hundred" models makes upgrading to this model fairly common. Use extreme caution in purchasing.

WINCHESTER. cont.

⚔ **Model 1873 "*One of One Hundred*"** — similar to "One of One Thousand" only rarer, 8 mfg. Sold new for $20 over the list price of a similarly equipped Model 1873.
Values can range from $30,000 - $75,000, depending on condition. A factory letter is a must for any "One of One Hundred" Winchester. Believe it or not, watch for fake letters.

MODEL 1876 LEVER ACTION — .40-60, .45-60, .45-75 (first caliber offered), or .50-95
Express cal., 26 or 28 in. round or octagon barrel, similar but larger frame than Model 1873, tube mag., crescent butt, blued finish, straight grip stock, 63,871 mfg. between 1876-1897. The Model 1876 was also called the Centennial Model since its introduction coincided with the U.S. Centennial Exposition held in Philadelphia, PA in 1876. Popularity for this model decreased ten years later when the more powerful and advanced Model 1886 was introduced.
Deluxe Model 1876 with color case hardened frames will add at least 50% to the values listed below for standard models. Deluxe Models 1876 with 90%+ original case colors are rare.

	Below Average	Average	Above Average

⚔ **Model 1876 Rifle First Model** — serial numbered approx. 1-3,000, distinguishable by no dust cover on frame top.

| | $600 - $800 | $800 - $1,200 | $1,200 - $1,800 |

20% dull bluing (Photo No. 10, pg. 39) commands $2,500 - $3,000.
98% bright bluing (Photo No. 2, pg. 35) commands $8,000 - $9,000.

⚔ **Model 1876 Carbine First Model** — 22 in. round barrel, one barrel band, saddle ring, full length forearm giving a musket appearance .

| | $700 - $1,000 | $1,000 - $1,500 | $1,500 - $2,000 |

⚔ **Model 1876 Musket First Model** — 32 in. round barrel with 1 band, scarce model because no foreign military contracts.

| | $1,500 - $2,500 | $2,500 - $4,000 | $4,000 - $6,000 |

⚔ **Model 1876 Rifle Second Model** — "Thumbprint" dust cover rail held on by screw, serial range 3,000-30,000.

| | $500 - $700 | $700 - $900 | $900 - $1,200 |

98% bright bluing (Photo No. 2, pg. 35) commands $4,500 - $5,500.

⚔ **Model 1876 Carbine Second Model** — changes similar to Model 1876 Rifle Early Second Model, with 22 in. round barrel and full length forearm giving a musket appearance.

| | $600 - $900 | $900 - $1,200 | $1,200 - $1,750 |

⚔ **Model 1876 Musket Second Model** — changes similar to Model 1876 Rifle Early Second Model, with 32 in. round barrel and carbine forend tip.

| | $1,250 - $1,750 | $1,750 - $3,000 | $3,000 - $5,000 |

⚔ **Model 1876 Rifle Third Model** — dust cover rail integral with frame, serial range 30,000-end of production.

| | $500 - $700 | $700 - $900 | $900 - $1,200 |

98% bright bluing (Photo No. 2, pg. 35) commands $4,500 - $5,500.

⚔ **Model 1876 Carbine Third Model** — frame similar to Model 1876 Rifle Third Model, with 22 in. round barrel and full length forearm giving a musket appearance.

| | $600 - $900 | $900 - $1,200 | $1,200 - $1,750 |

⚔ **Model 1876 Musket Third Model** — frame similar to Model 1876 Rifle Third Model, with 32 in. round barrel.

| | $1,250 - $1,750 | $1,750 - $3,000 | $3,000 - $5,000 |

	Below Average	Average	Above Average

🛠 **Model 1876** *"One of One Thousand"* — special care taken in manufacture to guarantee better accuracy, markings on top of breech designate model, deluxe walnut, extremely rare, 54 mfg. Original cost was $100.
Values can range from $25,000 - $70,000, depending on condition. A factory letter is a must for any "One of One Thousand" Winchester. Believe it or not, watch for fake letters.
Values are not listed because too few original specimens are bought or sold to accurately establish pricing. A factory letter is a must for any "One of One Thousand" Winchester. Note: Rarity of the "One of One Thousand" & the "One of One Hundred" models makes unethical upgrading to this model fairly common. Use extreme caution in purchasing.

🛠 **Model 1876** *"One of One Hundred"* — similar to "One of One Thousand" only rarer, 8 mfg. Sold new for $20 over the list price of a similarly equipped Model 1876.
Values can range from $30,000 - $70,000, depending on condition. A factory letter is a must for any "One of One Hundred" Winchester. Believe it or not, watch for fake letters.
Values are not listed because too few original specimens are bought or sold to accurately establish pricing. A factory letter is a must for any "One of One Hundred" Winchester.

🛠 **Model 1876 Northwest Mounted Police Carbine** — .45-75 cal. only, 22 in. barrel, "NWMP" stamped on butt stock.

	$1,000 - $1,500	$1,500 - $2,500	$2,500 - $3,500

Above average specimens in this model should have traces of blue and excellent stock cartouche.

MODEL 1886 LEVER ACTION — .33 WCF, .38-56 WCF, .38-70 WCF, .40-65 WCF, .40-70 WCF, .40-82 WCF, .45-70, .45-90, .50-110 Express, or .50-100-450 cal. available, Browning's first high power lever action design distinguishable by vertical locking bars, .45-70 most popular cal., 26 in. round or octagon barrel, tube mag., steel forend cap, straight grip stock. Approx. 159,990 mfg. between 1886-1935.
The Model 1886 had case hardening standard on the frame, butt plate, and forend cap until 1901 (approx. 122,000 serial range) when the standard finish became blue.
On the Model 1886 variations listed below, add the following percentages for special order features.
Add 10% for octagon barrel.
Add 20% premium for Takedown Model.
Add 30% for .45-70 or .45-90 cal.
Add 100% for .50/110 cal.
Add 100% for Deluxe Model (pistol grip checkered walnut stock).

🛠 **Model 1886 Rifle** — similar to above.

	$500 - $700	$700 - $900	$900 - $1,250

70% case colors (Photo No. 6, pg. 37) command $2,000 - $2,500.

🛠 **Model 1886 Carbine** — same general specifications as Rifle, except 22 in. round barrel and saddle ring, solid frame only.

	$700 - $1,000	$1,000 - $1,600	$1,600 - $2,250

Add 35% for full stock carbine (extended forend).
70% case colors (Photo No. 6, pg. 37) command $4,500 - $5,000.

🛠 **Model 1886 Musket** — 30 in. round barrel, one barrel band, military sights, only 350 mfg., very rare.

	$2,500 - $4,000	$4,000 - $6,000	$6,000 - $9,000

Most specimens encountered in this variation are in very good condition - a pitted musket is almost never encountered.

🛠 **Model 1886 Lightweight Rifle** — .45-70 or .33 WCF cal. only, 22 (.45-70 cal.) or 24 (.33 WCF cal.) in. round nickel steel tapered barrel, half mag., rubber shotgun butt plate.

🛠 **.33 caliber**

	$400 - $550	$550 - $700	$700 - $1,000

98% bright bluing (Photo No. 2, pg. 35) commands $1,500 - $1,750.

Below Average	Average	Above Average

⚑ **.45-70 caliber**

$700 - $900	$900 - $1,250	$1,250 - $1,750

98% bright bluing (Photo No. 2, pg. 35) commands $2,500 - $3,000.

Since lightweight rifles were fairly late production, all specimens are blue and in very good condition usually.

100%	98%	95%	90%	80%	70%	60%	50%	40%	30%	20%	10%

MODEL 1892 RIFLE — .218 Bee, .25-20, .32-20, .38-40, or .44-40 cal., 24 in. round or octagon barrel, blue, tube mag., forend cap, crescent butt. Mfg. 1,004,067 between 1892-1941.

N/A	N/A	$1,775	$1,300	$1,100	$995	$875	$775	$675	$550	$450	$350

Add 25% for .44-40.
Add 25% for Takedown Model.
Add 10% for early mfg. featuring case colored lever and hammer.
.218 Bee is extremely rare in this model. Most specimens are re-barreled rather than being original.

MODEL 1892 CARBINE — 20 in. round barrel, two bands and saddle ring.

N/A	N/A	$1,775	$1,300	$1,100	$995	$875	$775	$675	$550	$450	$350

Add 15% for .44-40.

MODEL 1892 TRAPPER'S CARBINE — similar to Carbine, with 12, 14, 15, 16, or 18 in. barrels. So called because was handy for trappers who had to carry a powerful but lightweight repeating rifle.

N/A	N/A	$3,500	$3,100	$2,600	$2,200	$1,700	$1,400	$1,100	$900	$775	$650

Most 1892 Trapper's Carbines are in the 15 in., .44-40 cal. configuration. Most of the 1892 Trapper's Carbine were shipped to South America or Australia. This variation is almost never encountered over 30% condition - most are brown guns.

MODEL 1892 MUSKET — 30 in. round barrel, 3 barrel bands, military sights. Modified shotgun style butt plate.

N/A	N/A	$17,500	$16,000	$12,500	$10,000	$7,500	$6,000	$4,750	$3,500	$2,500	$1,750

MODEL 1894 RIFLE — .25-35, .30-30 (.30 WCF), .32-40, .32 Spl., or .38-55 cal., most common (and popular) is .30-30 cal., tube mag., 26 in. octagon barrel, blue, straight grip stock. Over 5,000,000 produced to date, mfg. 1894-present, currently available - see Modern Section.

⚑ **Antique Model** — ser. no.'s before approx. 148,000.

N/A	N/A	$1,775	$1,300	$1,100	$995	$875	$775	$675	$550	$450	$350

Add 10% for early mfg. featuring case colored lever and hammer.

100%	98%	95%	90%	80%	70%	60%	50%	40%	30%	20%	10%

1899-1936 Mfg. — model 94s built post 1898-1936.

| N/A | $1,675 | $1,450 | $1,150 | $925 | $850 | $725 | $650 | $575 | $500 | $425 | $350 |

The Model 1894 Winchester has the distinction of being the world's most popular rifle. Deluxe models or takedown variations will command substantial premiums over values listed above.

Model 1894 Takedown Rifle — magazine unscrews at frame allowing barrel/magazine takedown.
Add 20%+ premium.

MODEL 1894 TRAPPER'S CARBINE — similar to Carbine, with 14, 15 (common), 16, 17 (rare) or 18 in. barrel.

| N/A | N/A | N/A | $3,000 | $2,700 | $2,400 | $2,150 | $1,825 | $1,625 | $1,475 | $1,250 | $1,050 |

The large majority of this variation are encountered in .30-30 cal. with 15 in. barrel. Any other caliber or barrel length will constitute a premium. Most of these carbines are brown and rusty.

Note: Check federal laws on legality of 14 in. barrel. 70%-100% specimens are almost never encountered in this model. Shorter barrels than 14 in. have not been encountered on this model.

MODEL 1894 SADDLE RING CARBINE — 20 in. round barrel.

| N/A | N/A | $1,300 | $1,100 | $995 | $875 | $775 | $675 | $550 | $450 | $350 | $295 |

Add 30% for Antique Model.
Add 25% for any cal. other than .30-30 or .32 Spl.

Without saddle ring — mfg. early '30s - WWII.

| $875 | $725 | $650 | $550 | $450 | $375 | $350 | $325 | $300 | $275 | $250 | $225 |

Eastern Carbine — features long forearm, early stock design, early style carbine post front sight, and without saddle ring, mfg. late '20s - mid-'30s.

| N/A | N/A | $1,000 | $900 | $800 | $700 | $625 | $550 | $495 | $450 | $395 | $350 |

MODEL 1894 1940-1964 MFG. CARBINE — 1940-1964 mfg. without saddle ring.

| $450 | $395 | $375 | $350 | $325 | $300 | $275 | $250 | $220 | $195 | $175 | $150 |

Add 40% for .25-35 cal.
Some WWII carbines with special U.S. markings will bring a premium over prices listed above.

MODEL 1895 RIFLE — .30-03, .30-06, .30-40 Krag, .303 Brit., .35 Win., .38-72, .40-72, .405 Win., or .762 Russian cal., 24-28 in. barrel, blued action, box mag., straight grip stock, 425,881 mfg. from 1896-1931.

| $2,050 | $1,375 | $1,100 | $935 | $825 | $675 | $600 | $525 | $475 | $450 | $425 | $375 |

Add 50% for Deluxe Models.
Add 50% for octagon barrel.
Add 50% for .405 Win. cal.
Add 15% for Takedown Model.
The Model 1895 was a Browning design incorporating the first box type mag. in a lever action repeating rifle. A large Russian military contract was secured in 1915 with chambering for the 7.62mm Russian cartridge (over 293,000 mfg. or over 66% of total production). A very few were made with color case hardened frames (Winchesters last large frame rifle to have case colors) and are very rare and expensive.

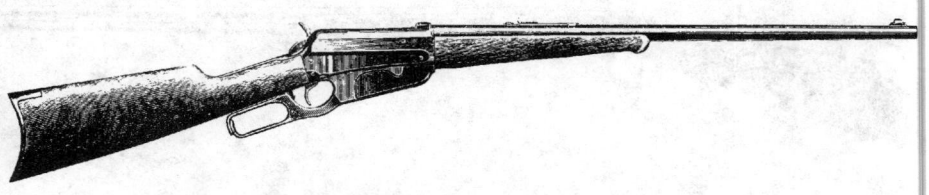

100%	98%	95%	90%	80%	70%	60%	50%	40%	30%	20%	10%

MODEL 1895 RIFLE FLATSIDE — early model, distinguishable in that frame does not have fluting or ridge contouring, serial range approx. 1-5000.

| N/A | N/A | $1,950 | $1,725 | $1,525 | $1,275 | $1,000 | $825 | $695 | $575 | $475 | $425 |

MODEL 1895 CARBINE — .30 US (.30/40 Krag Army - most common cal.), .30-03, .30-06, or .303 Brit. cal., 22 in. round barrel, one barrel band, with or without saddle ring, escalloped frame sides.

| $2,500 | $2,150 | $1,850 | $1,600 | $1,400 | $1,200 | $1,000 | $875 | $750 | $625 | $500 | $375 |

◄ **Model 1895 Government Carbine** — with government markings.

| $4,000 | $3,600 | $3,200 | $2,700 | $2,300 | $2,000 | $1,700 | $1,400 | $1,100 | $900 | $700 | $500 |

MODEL 1895 FLATSIDE MUSKET — early models have serial range under 5,000, no flutes on frame, .30-40 Krag only.

Rarity on this variation means only a few specimens in several museums.

MODEL 1895 MUSKET — .30-03, .30-06, or .30-40 Krag cal., 24 (.30-03 or .30-06 cal.) or 28 (.30/40 Krag only) in. round barrel, two bands, hand guard over barrel, military sights.

| N/A | N/A | $1,850 | $1,600 | $1,400 | $1,200 | $1,000 | $875 | $750 | $625 | $500 | $375 |

Add 10%-15% if U.S. Govt. marked.

MODEL 1895 NRA MUSKET — similar to Standard, with 30 in. barrel, 1901 Krag, rear sight. NRA approved for official NRA competition.

| N/A | N/A | $2,500 | $2,150 | $1,850 | $1,600 | $1,400 | $1,200 | $1,075 | $975 | $875 | $750 |

Also available in Models 1903 and 1906 which designated .30-30 and .30-06 cals. respectively.

MODEL 1895 RUSSIAN MUSKET — 7.62mm Russian cal., over 293,000 mfg. for Imperial Russian Govt., mfg. 1915-1916, various Russian Ordnance stamps should be present.

| N/A | N/A | $1,900 | $1,600 | $1,400 | $1,200 | $1,025 | $900 | $800 | $700 | $600 | $500 |

MODEL 53 RIFLE — .25-20, .32-20, or .44-40 cal., 22 in. round barrel, ½ tube mag. holding 6 cartridges, blued finish, pistol grip or straight grip stock. Mfg. 24,916 between 1924-1932.

| N/A | N/A | $1,650 | $1,375 | $1,075 | $950 | $875 | $800 | $725 | $650 | $575 | $525 |

Add 50% for .44-40 cal.
Add 15% for Takedown Model.

MODEL 65 RIFLE — .218 Bee (introduced 1939), .25-20, or .32-20 cal., 22 in. round barrel (except .218 Bee - 24 in.), ½ tube mag. holding 7 cartridges, blue with pistol grip stock. Mfg. 5704 between 1933-1947.

| $2,500 | $2,200 | $1,875 | $1,650 | $1,475 | $1,325 | $1,150 | $1,050 | $950 | $875 | $800 | $750 |

While the .25-20 cal. is the rarest, the .218 Bee has the most demand.
The Model 65 was a design evolved from the Model 53. The Model 65 was not tapped on receiver side for scope mounts. As a rule, most specimens are in either pretty nice or refinished condition.

MODEL 55 RIFLE — .25-35, .30-30, or .32 Win. Spl. cal., lever action designed, solid frame and takedown, 24 in. round barrel, shotgun style butt stock with checkered steel butt plate, tube mag., holds 3 cartridges. Approx. 20,500 mfg. between 1924-1932. Serial numbered independently to approx. 2,865, then serialized with Model 1894 production on underside of receiver. Simply could not compete with the Model 1894.

| $1,325 | $1,100 | $900 | $825 | $750 | $675 | $600 | $525 | $475 | $425 | $375 | $325 |

Add 50% for .25-35 cal.

100%	98%	95%	90%	80%	70%	60%	50%	40%	30%	20%	10%

MODEL 71 RIFLE STANDARD — .348 Win. cal., ⅔ tube mag. holding 4 cartridges, improved Model 1886 frame, blued metal with pistol grip stock, 20 or 24 in. barrel, short or long tang. Mfg. 47,254 between 1935-1957.

| $950 | $875 | $795 | $750 | $700 | $650 | $600 | $550 | $515 | $475 | $425 | $395 |

Add 25% for pre-war long tang.

⚹ **Model 71 — 20 in. barrel** — disc. in 1938, earlier models had long tangs only.

| N/A | $2,950 | $2,650 | $2,400 | $2,200 | $2,000 | $1,800 | $1,650 | $1,475 | $1,350 | $1,250 | $1,000 |

MODEL 71 RIFLE DELUXE — similar to Standard, with checkered stock and sling swivels.

| $1,375 | $1,100 | $950 | $875 | $800 | $775 | $750 | $725 | $700 | $675 | $650 | $625 |

Add 40% for pre-war long tang.

MODEL 64 RIFLE — .219 Zipper, .25-35, .30-30, or .32 Win. Spl. cal., 20, 24, or 26 (standard on .219 Zipper cal.) in. round barrel, blued metal, pistol grip stock, revamped Model 55 action with increased mag. capacity, 66,783 mfg. between 1933-1957 and 1972-1973 (over 8,250 mfg. in .30-30 cal. only - these last two years with minor changes).

| $600 | $560 | $530 | $495 | $470 | $440 | $410 | $370 | $340 | $295 | $260 | $215 |

Add 100% for Deluxe Model.
Add 30% for .25-30 cal.

⚹ **.219 Zipper cal.** — mfg. 1938-1941 only.

| $1,400 | $1,300 | $1,200 | $1,100 | $1,000 | $925 | $850 | $775 | $700 | $650 | $595 | $550 |

Many of this variation now have extra holes drilled on the top of the receiver to accept scope mounts - deduct 50% for this alteration. The Model 64 is usually found in excellent condition.
Model 64 1972-1973 mfg. may be found in the post-'64 section.

⚹ **.25-35 Cal.**

| $1,400 | $1,300 | $1,200 | $1,100 | $1,000 | $925 | $850 | $775 | $700 | $650 | $595 | $550 |

MODEL 88 RIFLE AND CARBINE — see listing under "Rifles: Lever Action - Post-1964 Mfg." section.

RIFLES: SINGLE SHOT

MODEL 1885 — most popular cals. available from .22-.50, falling block trigger guard activated action, John Browning's first high power single shot rifle design, many variations were made and we will list the standard types. Over 139,725 mfg. between 1885-1920.
This design was originally mfg. as the Model 1878 by the Browning Brothers in Ogden, UT in the early 1880s. Fewer than 600 were mfg. - see the Browning section for values.

⚹ **Sporting Rifle Low Wall** — 28 in. round or octagon barrel, open sights, solid frame, standard trigger.

| N/A | N/A | $950 | $875 | $800 | $750 | $700 | $650 | $600 | $550 | $500 | $450 |

Add 20% for centerfire cal.

⚹ **Sporting Rifle High Wall** — 30 in. barrel, standard trigger, open sights, solid frame. Available in various size and weight barrels numbered (in front of forearm) from numeric 1, 2, 3, 3½ (introduced 1910), 4, and 5, lightest to heaviest. Case hardened frames standard until 1901 when bluing became standard, three different frames depending on caliber. Heavier barrels in rare calibers will bring a premium.

⚹ **Blued finish**

| N/A | N/A | $1,500 | $1,350 | $1,200 | $1,075 | $975 | $900 | $825 | $750 | $675 | $595 |

100%	98%	95%	90%	80%	70%	60%	50%	40%	30%	20%	10%

⚔ Case colored frame

100%	98%	95%	90%	80%	70%	60%	50%	40%	30%	20%	10%
N/A	N/A	$2,250	$1,900	$1,600	$1,400	$1,200	$1,050	$900	$800	$700	$600

Add 30% for Takedown frame.
Add 25% for #5 barrel.
Add 25% for .45-70 or .45-90 cal.

⚔ 20 ga. High Wall Shotgun — chambered for 3 in., 26 in. full choke nickel steel barrel standard, receiver has matting on top. Also available with matted ribs (rare). Solid frame or takedown. Introduced 1914.

100%	98%	95%	90%	80%	70%	60%	50%	40%	30%	20%	10%
N/A	N/A	$2,150	$1,800	$1,550	$1,350	$1,200	$1,050	$900	$775	$650	$600

⚔ Deluxe Grade High Wall — similar to Standard, with fancy walnut and checkering.

100%	98%	95%	90%	80%	70%	60%	50%	40%	30%	20%	10%
N/A	N/A	$2,850	$2,550	$2,275	$2,000	$1,800	$1,650	$1,450	$1,300	$1,200	$1,125

⚔ Schuetzen Rifle — high wall, 30 in. octagon barrel, double set triggers, spur lever, aperture sight, Schuetzen style stock, adj. palm rest and butt plate.

100%	98%	95%	90%	80%	70%	60%	50%	40%	30%	20%	10%
$5,100	$4,600	$4,250	$3,950	$3,750	$3,500	$3,250	$3,000	$2,750	$2,500	$2,250	$2,100

Add 20% for Takedown frame.
This model had many shooting alterations performed by various aftermarket suppliers of its time. Perhaps only 10% of remaining specimens are unaltered (or 100% factory).

⚔ Winder Musket — low wall, 3rd model, .22 Short or LR, 28 in. barrel, standard trigger and lever, military style stock and sights, grooved forearm, one barrel band.

100%	98%	95%	90%	80%	70%	60%	50%	40%	30%	20%	10%
$850	$775	$700	$650	$600	$550	$500	$450	$400	$365	$335	$300

Add 20% for Takedown frame.

RIFLES: BOLT ACTION

MODEL 1883 (HOTCHKISS REPEATER) — .45-70 cal., designed by Benjamin D. Hotchkiss, unique tube mag. located in butt stock attached to receiver, up-turn/pull-back bolt action, 26 in. round or octagon barrel standard on rifle. Over 84,000 mfg. between 1879-1889. Also available in carbine configuration (24 in. round barrel with one band), and musket (32 in. round barrel with cleaning rod and two barrel bands) — subtract 25%. Carbine extremely rare in Third Model (20 in. barrel).

⚔ First Style — approx. 6,419 mfg. with magazine cut off and safety control incorporated into one unit.

100%	98%	95%	90%	80%	70%	60%	50%	40%	30%	20%	10%
$1,650	$1,450	$1,250	$1,100	$1,100	$950	$900	$850	$800	$765	$735	$710

⚔ Second Style — approx. 16,102 mfg., magazine cut off on right receiver top, safety on left side.

100%	98%	95%	90%	80%	70%	60%	50%	40%	30%	20%	10%
$1,450	$1,250	$1,050	$900	$800	$750	$700	$650	$600	$565	$535	$510

⚔ Third Style — most commonly encountered Hotchkiss, 2-piece stock, approx. 62,034 mfg. 1883-1899.

100%	98%	95%	90%	80%	70%	60%	50%	40%	30%	20%	10%
$1,650	$1,425	$1,250	$1,100	$900	$825	$750	$675	$625	$565	$525	$480

The Model 1883 Hotchkiss was the first bolt action designed for the U.S. military .45-70 cartridge. On the First and Second models inspect wood directly below bolt and left frame side for cracks, breaks or older repairs as it is frequently encountered on these early models with thin wrists.

LEE STRAIGHT PULL RIFLE — 6mm Lee (.236 U.S.N. cal.), 5 shot non-detachable box mag., 24 (Sporting Rifle) or 28 (Musket) in. barrel, folding leaf sight, blue metal, military style full stock, mfg. 1897-1902, Navy Issue Model is the Musket with "236 U.S.N." on barrels. Approx. 20,000 mfg. (including 15,000 Muskets for the U.S. Navy military contract) between 1895-1902 with parts clean up occurring in 1916.

⚔ U.S.N. Military Musket

100%	98%	95%	90%	80%	70%	60%	50%	40%	30%	20%	10%
$1,475	$1,300	$1,150	$1,000	$900	$800	$700	$625	$550	$500	$450	$425

100%	98%	95%	90%	80%	70%	60%	50%	40%	30%	20%	10%

⚡ Lee Sporting Rifle — similar to Musket, with 24 in, barrel, sporter style stock. Approx. 1,700 mfg. 1897-1902.

100%	98%	95%	90%	80%	70%	60%	50%	40%	30%	20%	10%
$1,475	$1,300	$1,150	$1,000	$900	$800	$700	$625	$550	$500	$450	$425

This design was originally patented by James Paris Lee and assigned to the Lee Arms Company. Winchester obtained manufacturing rights to produce this model for the U.S Navy military contract 1895-1902.

MODEL 1900 SINGLE SHOT — .22 S and L cal., 18 in. round barrel, blued metal, open sights, one-piece straight grip gumwood stock without fitted butt plate, takedown, not serial numbered. Approx. 105,000 mfg. between 1899-1902.

100%	98%	95%	90%	80%	70%	60%	50%	40%	30%	20%	10%
N/A	N/A	$350	$330	$310	$290	$270	$250	$220	$185	$140	$110

This model is usually encountered with flaked frames.

MODEL 1902 SINGLE SHOT — similar to 1900, with minor improvements. Distinguishable by special shaped extended trigger guard. Not serial numbered. Approx. 640,299 mfg. between 1902-1931.

100%	98%	95%	90%	80%	70%	60%	50%	40%	30%	20%	10%
N/A	N/A	$175	$150	$135	$120	$100	$90	$80	$75	$65	$60

Chambering included .22 cal. Extra Long in 1914 (interchangeable with S&L).

THUMB TRIGGER MODEL 99 — similar to 1902, with button behind cocking piece used to fire with thumb instead of trigger, not serial numbered. Approx. 75,433 were mfg. between 1904-1923.

100%	98%	95%	90%	80%	70%	60%	50%	40%	30%	20%	10%
N/A	N/A	$425	$375	$325	$275	$235	$195	$175	$150	$135	$120

MODEL 1904 SINGLE SHOT — improved version of 1902, 21 in. round barrel, chambering included .22 Extra Long in 1914, not serial numbered. Approx. 302,859 mfg. between 1904-1931.

100%	98%	95%	90%	80%	70%	60%	50%	40%	30%	20%	10%
$235	$200	$175	$160	$150	$140	$130	$120	$110	$100	$90	$80

⚡ Model 1904-A — introduced 1927 with new sear bar and chambered for .22 LR.

100%	98%	95%	90%	80%	70%	60%	50%	40%	30%	20%	10%
$250	$215	$190	$175	$165	$155	$145	$135	$125	$115	$105	$95

MODEL 43 — .218 Bee, .22 Hornet, .25-20, or .32-20 cal., dubbed "Poor Man's Model 70", 24 in. round tapered barrel, box type mag. Approx. 62,617 mfg. between 1949-1957.

100%	98%	95%	90%	80%	70%	60%	50%	40%	30%	20%	10%
$695	$595	$535	$475	$440	$400	$360	$320	$290	$260	$240	$220

Add 10% for Deluxe Model.
Add $50 for Special Grade.
Premiums exist (in order of rarity) for .32-20, .25-20, or .218 Bee cals.
Subtract 50% if non-factory drilled and tapped (early models).

Grading	100%	98%	95%	90%	80%	70%	60%

On Models 52, 54, 56, 57, 58, 59, 60, 60A, 67, 677, 68, 69, 69A, 697, and 70 values in 50% or less original condition have been omitted since values in those conditions will approximate the 60% price. This reflects the fact that while these lower condition specimens are not as desirable to collectors, they are still sought after as shooters.

MODEL 47 — .22 S, L, or LR cal., single shot bolt action with unique bolt, 25 in. round barrel, uncheckered walnut stock, 5¼ lbs., approx. 43,000 (not serialed) mfg. during 1948-1954.

		100%	98%	95%	90%	80%	70%	60%
		$395	$350	$250	$175	$150	$125	$100

MODEL 52 TARGET — .22 S (rare) or LR cal., 5 shot mag., 28 in. standard or heavy barrel, target sights and target style stock, speedlock trigger feature was introduced in 1929. Approx. 125,233 Model 52s in all variations were mfg. between 1919-1979.

	100%	98%	95%	90%	80%	70%	60%
	$440	$415	$375	$345	$315	$290	$265
With speedlock	$495	$470	$415	$375	$335	$310	$290

Barrel drilling and tapping for scope blocks was not standard on the first Model 52's, but became more apparent approx. 1926.

Grading	100%	98%	95%	90%	80%	70%	60%

⚔ **Model 52A Target** — similar to Model 52, except all A-suffix Model 52's have a speedlock trigger. Values are similar to above. In scarcity, it seems the E suffix is probably the scarcest (also the most poorly mfg.), followed by the A suffix variation.

MODEL 52A HEAVY BARREL — similar to Standard Target, with heavy barrel.

	$660	$605	$550	$525	$470	$415	$330

MODEL 52-B TARGET — extensively redesigned action, improved stock design, offered with a variety of sights. Approx. mfg. 1940-1947.

	$605	$550	$495	$470	$415	$360	$305

MODEL 52-B HEAVY BARREL — similar to 52-B, with heavy barrel.

	$660	$605	$550	$525	$470	$415	$330

MODEL 52-B BULL GUN — extra heavy weight barrel.

	$690	$635	$580	$550	$495	$440	$360

MODEL 52 SPORTER (SPORTING RIFLE) — 24 in. round lightweight barrel with front sight cover, sporting type select walnut stock with cheek piece, hard rubber pistol grip cap, black plastic tipped forearm, checkered steel butt plate, about 7¼ lbs. Mfg. 1934-1958. There is some controversy whether any of the Model 52 Sporters were drilled and tapped per factory worksmanship. Be cautious of "factory" drilled and tapped receivers on all model 52s, as there are many "gunsmith" Sporters that have been made with turned down, shortened target barrels.

⚔ **Model 52** — advertised approx. 1936.

	$2,350	$1,875	$1,500	$1,400	$1,275	$1,150	$975

⚔ **Model 52A** — introduced approx. 1937, receiver and locking lug were strengthened.

	$2,350	$1,875	$1,500	$1,400	$1,275	$1,150	$950

⚔ **Model 52B** — introduced approx. 1940, 5 shot detachable mag., with adj. sling swivel assembly and single shot adapter.

	$2,350	$1,700	$1,400	$1,200	$1,100	$1,000	$900

⚔ **Model 52B (1993 Re-issue)** — .22 LR cal., patterned after the original Model 52B and includes steel buttplate, forearm adjusting screw, and B-style stock with small cheekpiece, 6,250 mfg. beginning 1993.

Mfg.'s Sug. Retail	$576	$500	$395	$325			

⚔ **Model 52C** — introduced 1947 with adj. Micro Motion trigger, less than 100 mfg., 2 screws in trigger guard.

	$2,950	$2,450	$1,950	$1,650	$1,275	$1,150	$950

A few Model 52 Sporters & Targets were mfg. with stainless steel barrels (17,XXX-27,XXX serial range) - these guns will command a premium over values shown above.

MODEL 52-C STANDARD TARGET — "Micro Motion" trigger and "Marksman" stock, single shot adaptor, 5 or 10 shot mag. was avail., standard barrel, otherwise similar to 52-B. Mfg. 1947-1961.

	$700	$625	$550	$525	$470	$415	$330

MODEL 52-C HEAVY TARGET — similar to Standard Target, with heavy sporter barrel.

	$625	$550	$490	$470	$415	$360	$305

MODEL 52-C BULL TARGET — extra heavy (bull) barrel model of Heavy Target 52-C. Mfg. 1952-1961.

	$775	$675	$580	$550	$495	$440	$360

Grading	100%	98%	95%	90%	80%	70%	60%

MODEL 52-D TARGET — improved version of 52-C with free floating standard or heavy barrel and adj. bedding device, all 52-D's were single shot. Mfg. 1961- approx. 1969.

	$625	$550	$495	$440	$385	$360	$275

MODEL 52-D & -E INTERNATIONAL MATCH — similar to 52-D, with free rifle stock, accessory rail. Mfg. 1969-disc.

	$750	$675	$605	$550	$495	$470	$385

Previous Model 52's with A, B, C, and D had serial suffixes following the ser. no., but after approx. 1969, rifles started appearing with an E serial prefix. Both Model 52 International and Prone could have factory stocks that were not Winchester mfg.

MODEL 52-D & -E INTERNATIONAL PRONE — similar to International Match, with prone style stock. Mfg. 1975-disc.

	$750	$675	$605	$550	$495	$470	$385

MODEL 54 HIGH POWER SPORTER — .270, 7 x 57mm, .30-30, or .30-06 cal., 5 shot mag., 24 in. barrel, open sights, checkered pistol grip stock. Mfg. 1925-1930. Approx. 50,145 Model 54s were mfg. in all variations between 1925-1936.

	$675	$595	$525	$450	$385	$330	$305

Rare cals. will add premiums to the values listed above. This model was also mfg. with a stainless steel barrel during the late 1920s - early '30s with premiums also being asked.

MODEL 54 CARBINE — introduced 1927, similar to Rifle, with 20 in. barrel, plain stock.

	$750	$675	$595	$525	$475	$385	$360

MODEL 54 IMPROVED SPORTER — .22 Hornet, .220 Swift, .250-3000, .257 Robts., .270, 7 x 57mm, or .30-06 cal., 5 shot mag., 24 or 26 in. barrel, one piece firing pin, checkered pistol grip stock. Mfg. 1930-1936.

	$675	$595	$525	$450	$385	$330	$305

Rare cals. will add premiums to the values listed above.

MODEL 54 CARBINE IMPROVED — similar to Rifle, with 20 in. barrel.

	$750	$675	$595	$525	$475	$385	$360

MODEL 54 SUPER GRADE — introduced 1934, similar to Sporter, with better wood and black forend tip and pistol grip cap.

	$950	$850	$775	$695	$625	$550	$525

Rare calibers will command considerable premiums (i.e. this variation in 7 x 57mm cal. will sell for $2,500 in mint condition).

MODEL 54 SPORTING SNIPER'S RIFLE — introduced 1929, similar to Sporter, with 26 in. heavy barrel, .30-06 only, aperture sight.

	$1,000	$875	$775	$695	$625	$550	$525

MODEL 54 NATIONAL MATCH — introduced 1935, similar to Standard, with Lyman sights and Marksman stock.

	$1,000	$875	$775	$695	$625	$550	$525

MODEL 56 SPORTER — .22 S or LR cal., 5 or 10 shot box mag., 22 in. round barrel, open sights, plain pistol grip stock. Approx. 8,297 mfg. between 1926-1929.

	$600	$525	$460	$400	$350	$300	$250

The .22 cal. Short was disc. 1929.

MODEL 57 TARGET — similar to Model 56, except with aperture sight and heavier target stock. Approx. 18,600 were mfg. between 1926-1936.

	$595	$525	$450	$375	$300	$260	$220

Grading	100%	98%	95%	90%	80%	70%	60%

MODEL 58 SINGLE SHOT — similar to Models 1902 and 1904, .22 LR cal., 18 in. round barrel, open sights, takedown. Approx. 38,992 mfg. between 1928-1931.

	$375	$295	$240	$185	$160	$130	$120

MODEL 59 SINGLE SHOT — improved Model 58 with 23 in. round barrel and pistol grip stock with butt plate. Approx. 9,200 mfg. between 1930-1931.

	$450	$425	$400	$350	$300	$250	$200

This model was disc. due to lack of sales.

MODEL 60 — improved Model 59, 23 in. round barrel increased to 27 in. 1933. Approx. 160,754 mfg. between 1930-1934.

	$395	$350	$300	$225	$175	$150	$125

MODEL 60A TARGET — similar to Model 60 with Lyman 55W aperture rear sight, heavier target stock, and 27 in. round tapered barrel. Approx. 6,118 mfg. between 1932-1939.

	$575	$475	$400	$325	$275	$235	$200

MODEL 67 — .22 LR or .22 WRF (authorized 1935) cal., 20 in. (Junior Rifle), 24 (miniature target boring), and 27 in. (sporting or smooth bore) round barrels, same basic action as the Model 60, not serial numbered. Approx. 383,000 mfg. between 1934-1963.

	$175	$130	$95	$80	$70	$60	$50

MODEL 677 — same basic specifications as Model 67, except no iron sights or sight cuts in barrel, not serial numbered. Approx. 2,240 mfg. between 1937-1939.

	$400	$350	$320	$250	$200	$150	$100
In .22 WRF cal. (rare)	$1,200	$1,000	$800	$600	$400	$300	$250

MODEL 68 — .22 LR or .22 WRF cal., bolt action single shot, similar to Model 67, walnut stock. Approx. 100,000 mfg. between 1934-1946 no ser. no.'s on gun.

	$175	$130	$95	$80	$70	$60	$50

MODEL 69 & 69A — .22 LR or RF cal., 5 or 10 shot repeater, 25 in. barrel, aperture or open rear sight, not serial numbered. Approx. 355,000 mfg. between 1935-1963. Add $50 for Target version.

	$200	$150	$110	$95	$85	$75	$70

The Model 69 was cocked by the closing motion of the bolt and had a non-swept back bolt handle, whereas the 69A was cocked by the opening motion of the bolt and had a swept back bolt handle. Number 97B rear aperture sight and 80A hooded front target sights and standard open sights were offered on both the Model 69 and 69A. Late 69As had "grooved" receiver for "tip-off" scope mounts - add 20%-25% for this feature.

MODEL 72/72A — .22 LR and Gallery Model (.22 short only), tube mag., bolt action, 25 in. round, tapered barrel, aperture or open rear sight, not serial numbered. Over 161,000 mfg. between 1938-1959. Add $50 for Target version.

	$200	$150	$110	$95	$85	$75	$70

Add 50% for Gallery Model (mfg. 1939-1942) - rare.

The Model 72 and 72A both cocked on opening. The Model 72A has a swept back bolt handle and some minor internal mechanical improvements. Same open sight options as Models 69/69A. Late 72As had "grooved" receiver for "tip-off" scope mounts - add 20%-25% for this feature.

MODEL 75 TARGET — .22 LR, 5 or 10 shot mag., 28 in. barrel, target sights, slight variation used by Government in WWII. Approx. 88,715 Model 75 Target and Model 75s were mfg. between 1938-1958.

	$300	$275	$250	$225	$200	$175	$150

Add up to 10% for original Winchester leather sling.

Grading	100%	98%	95%	90%	80%	70%	60%

MODEL 75 SPORTER — similar to Target, except 24 in. tapered barrel, clip feed, non-target sights and select checkered walnut.

	100%	98%	95%	90%	80%	70%	60%
	$795	$725	$650	$575	$475	$400	$325

Late 75 Sporters had "grooved" receiver for "tip-off" scope mounts - add 10%-15% for this feature.

MODEL 697 — same general specifications as the Model 69, except no iron sights or sight cuts in barrel and no ramp or sight cover. Telescope bases attached to barrel were standard.

	100%	98%	95%	90%	80%	70%	60%
	$425	$395	$375	$300	$250	$200	$150
.22 WRF cal.	$550	$495	$450	$400	$350	$300	$250

MODEL 777 — .30-06 cal., bolt action, 4 shot mag., mfg. by Nikko in Japan during 1979-80 for sale to Winchester subsidiaries in Australia, Germany, Italy, and Scandinavia, only 3 were shipped to the U.S., checkered Monte Carlo stock with Wundhammer swell grip, lightweight barrel, engraved action, "Winchester" is cast on the left side of the receiver near the top, approx. 1,000 mfg. with 250 in .30-06 cal. - 750 mfg. in different cal. and sold elsewhere, 8½ lbs.

Extreme rarity factor precludes accurate price evaluation. Some specimens have been reported as sold in the $1,850+ range.

RIFLES: MODEL 70 BOLT ACTION

The Pre-'64 Model 70 Bolt Action Rifle (advertised by Winchester throughout much of its production history as "The Rifleman's Rifle") was produced from 1936 through 1963. Collectors recognize three major manufacturing periods: "Pre-War" (1936-1941); "Transition" (1942-1948); and "Latter" (1949-1963). There were only eighteen (18) original chamberings, these are: .22 Hornet, .220 Swift, .243 Win., .250 Savage (.250-3000), .257 Roberts, .264 Win. Mag., .270 Win., 7 x 57mm Mauser, .300 Savage, .300 H&H Mag., .300 Win. Mag., .30-06 (.30 Govt. '06) Springfield, .308 Win. (standard in Featherweight Style only), .338 Win. Mag., .35 Rem., .358 Win. (in Featherweight Style only), .375 H&H Mag., and .458 Win. Mag. (in Super Grade AFRICAN Style only). It is important to note that every caliber was not available during each manufacturing period. Any other caliber encountered (including 7.65mm Argentine and 9mm Mauser) may be regarded as either special ordered or non-original. Magazine capacities are as follows: "Standard Calibers" (including .22 Hornet) five (5) rounds; "H&H Magnums" (.300 & .375) four (4) rounds; and "Winchester Short Magnums" (.264, .300, .338, .458) three (3) rounds. The rifle was produced in a myriad of styles and variations – most of which are covered below individually. Unfortunately, a veritable "cottage industry" has developed involving the alteration, "upgrading" and/or outright faking of these guns. Be careful when contemplating a purchase of any rare Model 70 (and get a receipt describing the purchase accurately).

MODEL 70 PRE-WWII MFG. STANDARD GRADE — 12 standard cals., 5 shot mag., 4 shot mag. on Magnums, 24, 25, or 26 in. barrels, open sights, checkered walnut pistol grip stock, ser. range is 1-31,675. Mfg. 1937-1941.

Values listed below assume original, unaltered specimens — modifications/alterations to either the metal or wood surfaces can reduce prices by large amounts. All pre-war Model 70s have only 2 holes drilled in the front of the receiver (none in the back). An extra set of "holes" can decrease value as much as 50%. Some pre-WWII Model 70s have a "D" suffix indicating a doubled up serial number - this variation will command a premium because of its rarity. The Model 70 is one gun that caliber ranks before condition in terms of desirability. Specimens encountered in under 60% condition will not decrease in price substantially since almost any shooter is worth $600-$650.

	100%	98%	95%	90%	80%	70%	60%
Standard Cals.	$1,100	$900	$800	$725	$675	$600	$550
.22 Hornet	$1,750	$1,500	$1,200	$995	$875	$775	$675
.220 Swift	$1,500	$1,275	$1,050	$895	$775	$675	$575
.257 Roberts	$1,750	$1,500	$1,200	$995	$875	$775	$675
.270 Win.	$1,250	$1,075	$925	$800	$695	$625	$550
.300 H&H	$1,600	$1,275	$1,050	$895	$775	$675	$575

Grading	100%	98%	95%	90%	80%	70%	60%
.375 H&H	$2,950	$2,500	$2,100	$1,750	$1,450	$1,150	$995
7 x 57mm Mauser	N/A	N/A	N/A	$1,600	$1,350	$1,125	$895
.250-3000 Savage	N/A	N/A	N/A	$1,325	$1,100	$925	$775

Add approx. 80% for carbine variations (mfg. 1936-1946 with 20 in. barrel in .22 Hornet, .250-3000, .257 Roberts, .270, 7mm, and .30-06).

There are more fakes than legitimate specimens in cals. 7 x 57mm and .250-3000 Savage! Rare cals. such as the .300 Savage, .35 Rem., 7.65mm, and 9mm are seldomly encountered and their scarcity precludes accurate price evaluation. Cals. 7.65mm and 9mm were special order only and made up from left-over Model 54 barrels. Also, the original factory box, papers, and hanging tag will add 25%-30% to the values listed above.

MODEL 70 CARBINE (MFG. 1936-1946) — available in most cals. during its period, 20 in. barrel, short rifle variation of the Pre-'64 Model 70 (Winchester never officially used the "Carbine" terminology). If original, front sight base will be an integral part of the barrel. All carbines were disc. shortly after WWII. Beware of fakes.
Model 70 Carbine values will bring an approximate 50% premium over Standard Rifles of identical chambering.

MODEL 70 TRANSITION (MFG. 1946-1948) — several of the post-war Model 70s mfg. between 1946-1948 exhibit the pre-war receiver characteristics and have a transition safety. This variation is more rare than normal models, with asking prices 10%-20% higher. On this Transitional Model, the receiver bride may or may not be factory drilled.

MODEL 70 1946-1963 MFG. STANDARD GRADE — 18 standard cals. including .22 Hornet, .220 Swift, .243 Win., .250 Savage (.250-3000), .257 Roberts, .264 Win. Mag., .270 Win., 7x57mm Mauser, .300 Savage, .300 H&H Mag., .300 Win. Mag., .30-06, .308 Win., .338 Win. Mag., .35 Rem., .358 Win., and .375 H&H Mag., 5 shot mag., 4 shot mag. on Magnums, 24, 25, or 26 in. barrels, open sights, checkered walnut pistol grip stock, ser. range is 52,549-581,471. Mfg. 1946-1963.
Values listed below assume original, unaltered specimens — modifications/alterations to either the metal or wood surfaces can reduce prices by large amounts. Most post war Model 70s are drilled on top of the receiver (2 holes in front and 2 holes in back) to accept scope mounts (except early .300 & .375 H&H cals.). Pre-1952 mfg. Model 70s are desirable since Winchester implemented manufacturing techniques that lowered the quality in 1953.

	100%	98%	95%	90%	80%	70%	60%
.22 Hornet	$1,175	$950	$875	$825	$700	$500	$400
.220 Swift	$950	$900	$800	$750	$650	$500	$400
.243 Win.	$995	$850	$700	$650	$575	$500	$400
.257 Roberts	$1,150	$995	$875	$775	$625	$525	$450
.264 Win. Mag.	$875	$750	$675	$625	$595	$500	$400
.270 Win.	$775	$675	$625	$595	$525	$475	$400
.30-06 cal.	$725	$600	$550	$500	$450	$425	$400
.300 H&H	$1,150	$925	$875	$825	$700	$600	$525
.300 Win. Mag.	$1,500	$1,295	$1,050	$900	$800	$700	$625
.338 Win. Mag.	$2,150	$1,850	$1,600	$1,250	$900	$800	$700
.375 H&H	$2,150	$1,850	$1,400	$1,000	$850	$775	$700

Rare cals. such as the .250-3000, .300 Savage, .308 Win. (extremely rare and watch for fakes), .35 Rem., and 7 x 57mm Mauser are seldomly seen or sold. Premiums depend on the rarity of the caliber and original condition.

Grading	100%	98%	95%	90%	80%	70%	60%

MODEL 70 SUPER GRADE — similar to Standard Model, except has deluxe wood, black pistol grip cap and forend tip, all Super Grades have a raised cheekpiece with deluxe wrap-around checkering. Disc. 1960.
A general rule for Super Grades is that if you add 100% to the standard grade in similar cals., values should be rather close. For .375 H&H Mag. cal., values are listed below.

.375 H&H	$2,750	$2,350	$1,950	$1,675	$1,450	$1,200	$1,000

Later Model 70 Super Grades have jeweled action components.

MODEL 70 SUPER GRADE FEATHERWEIGHT — .243 Win., .270 Win., .30-06, or .308 Win. cal. only, because of inconsistencies of Super Grade action component jeweling (i.e., engine turning), a simple stock and hinged floorplate change can create an "instant" Super Grade Featherweight (check stock carefully for wood filling near area of Standard Super Grade rear sight "boss" in barrel channel), all Super Grades have a raised cheekpiece with wrap-around "fish tail" checkering, less than 1,000 mfg.
Original S.G. Featherweights will command 4 times the value of a Standard Featherweight Model. Perhaps the rarest variation of the Pre-'64 Model 70 - beware of fakes.

MODEL 70 SUPER GRADE AFRICAN — .458 Win. Mag. only, front swivel base relocated and attached to bottom of barrel, nearly all possess one or two visible stock crossbolts (usually covered with Bakelite). Most have all action components (bolt body, extractor, extractor ring and magazine follower) jeweled (i.e., engine turned). 1,226 mfg. 1956-1963.

	$3,750	$3,500	$3,250	$3,000	$2,750	$2,500	$2,250

While other Super Grades were disc. approx. 1960, the "AFRICAN" continued in that style until the end of all production. Normal attrition and collectors owning more than one contribute to extreme rarity. Retains considerable "shooter" value in lesser external conditions.

MODEL 70 FEATHERWEIGHT — lightened version of Standard, .243 Win., .264 Win. Mag. (Westerner), .270 Win., .308 Win., .30-06, or .358 Win. cal., 22 in. barrel, aluminum trigger guard and floorplate, ser. range is 206,626-581,471. Mfg. 1952-1963.

	100%	98%	95%	90%	80%	70%	60%
.243 W., .270 W., .30-06	$825	$750	$675	$600	$550	$500	$450
.264 Win. Mag. (Westerner)	$1,575	$1,300	$1,100	$900	$800	$700	$600
.308 Win.	$695	$575	$525	$475	$450	$425	$400
.358 Win.	$1,775	$1,475	$1,250	$950	$825	$750	$675

Add 300% for Super Grade Models.
The .358 Win. cal. is rare because Winchester had problems with this cal. Many of them were exchanged for other calibers, and the result is that original guns are rare in this cal.

MODEL 70 NATIONAL MATCH — similar to Standard, with target stock and scope bases, .30-06 only. Disc. 1960.

	$1,450	$1,200	$995	$895	$775	$700	$660

MODEL 70 TARGET — similar to Model 70 Standard, in .243 or .30-06 cal. (mfg. 1955-1963), earlier pre-'51 Target guns were available in virtually any cal. (i.e., .22 Hornet, .220 Swift, etc.), 24 in. medium weight barrel and target stock. Disc. 1963.
Rather than list prices, add 80%-100% over standard values if condition is over 90%. 60% condition will be priced the same.

MODEL 70 BULL GUN — similar to Standard Model 70, with 28 in. heavy barrel, .300 H & H or .30-06 cal. only.
Add 300% to Standard Model values.

MODEL 70 VARMINT — similar to Standard Model 70, in .220 Swift or .243 cal., 26 in. heavy barrel, scope bases, varmint style stock. Mfg. 1956-1963.

	$1,250	$995	$925	$850	$750	$675	$600

Less than 900 were mfg. in .220 Swift cal. stainless steel barrels are also encountered in this model with 3 different types of finishes.

Grading	100%	98%	95%	90%	80%	70%	60%

MODEL 70 ALASKAN — similar to Standard Model 70, in .300 Win. Mag. (mfg. 1963 only with 24 in. barrel - known as Westerner-Alaskan), .338 Win. Mag., or .375 H&H Mag. cal., 25 in. barrel, recoil pad. Mfg. 1960-1963.

	$2,150	$1,850	$1,600	$1,400	$1,200	$995	$875

RIFLES: SEMI-AUTO, DISC.

100%	98%	95%	90%	80%	70%	60%	50%	40%	30%	20%	10%

MODEL 1903 — .22 Win. Auto rimfire, 10 shot tube mag., 20 in. round barrel, open sights, straight grip stock cut out for partial magazine filling. Approx. 126,000 mfg. between 1903-1932.

100%	98%	95%	90%	80%	70%	60%	50%	40%	30%	20%	10%
$450	$400	$365	$330	$300	$275	$250	$225	$195	$175	$150	$125

First U.S. semi-auto rifle designed for .22 rimfire cartridges.

MODEL 1905 — .32 Win. or .35 Win. cal., 5 or 10 shot box mag., 22 in. round barrel, open sights, plain pistol grip stock. Approx. 29,113 mfg. between 1905-1920.

100%	98%	95%	90%	80%	70%	60%	50%	40%	30%	20%	10%
$650	$575	$525	$465	$400	$365	$330	$300	$275	$250	$225	$195

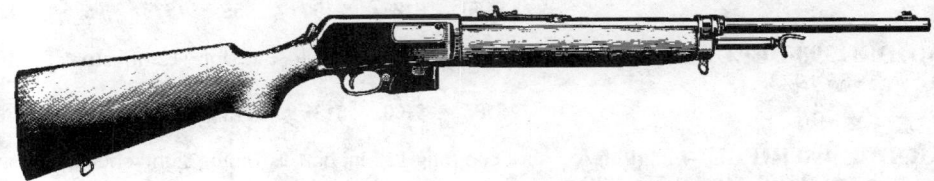

MODEL 1907 — .351 Win., 5 or 10 shot box mag., 20 in. round barrel, open sights, plain pistol grip stock, an improved version of the Model 1905. Approx. 58,490 mfg. between 1907-1957.

100%	98%	95%	90%	80%	70%	60%	50%	40%	30%	20%	10%
$475	$425	$375	$330	$300	$275	$250	$225	$195	$175	$160	$145

MODEL 1910 — .401 Win., 4 shot box mag., 20 in. barrel, open sight, plain pistol grip stock. Mfg. 20,786 between 1910-1936.

100%	98%	95%	90%	80%	70%	60%	50%	40%	30%	20%	10%
$625	$550	$500	$450	$400	$365	$330	$300	$275	$250	$225	$195

Add 10-15% for Fancy Sporting Rifle (special checkered walnut).

MODEL 55 — .22 cal. only, top loading single shot, bottom ejection, 22 in. round barrel, open sporting sights, not serial numbered. Over 45,000 mfg. between 1958-1961.

100%	98%	95%	90%	80%	70%	60%	50%	40%	30%	20%	10%
$225	$175	$150	$135	$125	$115	$105	$95	$85	$75	$70	$65

MODEL 63 — .22 LR, styling similar to Model 1903, 10 shot tube mag., 20 (disc. 1936) or 23 in. barrel, open sights, plain pistol grip stock. Approx. 174,692 mfg. between 1933-1958.

100%	98%	95%	90%	80%	70%	60%	50%	40%	30%	20%	10%
$600	$495	$450	$395	$350	$300	$265	$235	$215	$190	$175	$160

Add 50%-100% for 20 in barrel depending on condition.
The Model 63 was introduced to take advantage of the new .22 LR cartridge, which the older Model 1903 couldn't chamber. Add a slight premium for grooved receiver variation.

MODEL 74 — .22 Short or LR, tubular mag. in stock, pop-out bolt assembly. Approx. 406,574 mfg. between 1939-1955. Distinguishable by squared off rear receiver.

100%	98%	95%	90%	80%	70%	60%	50%	40%	30%	20%	10%
$195	$175	$150	$125	$110	$100	$95	$90	$85	$80	$75	$70

Add 10% for .22 Short.

MODEL 77 — .22 rimfire, detachable box mag. or tubular mag. under barrel. Over 217,000 mfg. between 1955-1962. Add $15 for tubular mag.

100%	98%	95%	90%	80%	70%	60%	50%	40%	30%	20%	10%
$195	$175	$150	$125	$110	$100	$95	$90	$85	$80	$75	$70

Grading	100%	98%	95%	90%	80%	70%	60%

MODEL 100 RIFLE — .243, .284, or .308 cal., 4 shot detachable mag., 22 in. round barrel with open sights, gas operated, one piece basket weave stock, pistol grip cap. Over 262,000 mfg. 1961-1973.

	100%	98%	95%	90%	80%	70%	60%
	$375	$320	$285	$265	$240	$220	$200

⚰ **Pre-1964 production**
    Add $25 for .243 cal.
    Add $50 for .284 cal.

MODEL 100 CARBINE — similar to rifle, with 19 in. barrel, plain pistol grip stock, barrel band. Mfg. 1967-1973.

	100%	98%	95%	90%	80%	70%	60%
	$475	$375	$300	$260	$235	$215	$200

    Add $25 for .243 cal.
    Add $50 for .284 cal.

MODEL 190 RIFLE — .22 S, L, or LR cal., semi-auto, 15 shot LR tube mag., alloy receiver, uncheckered walnut finished hardwood stock, 20½ (Carbine Model) or 24 (Rifle Model) in. barrel, approx. 2,150,000 (including the Model 290 listed below also) during 1967-1980.

	100%	98%	95%	90%	80%	70%	60%
	$150	$125	$100	$85	$75	$65	$55

MODEL 290 DELUXE RIFLE — similar to 290, with select Monte Carlo stock. Mfg. 1965-1973.

	100%	98%	95%	90%	80%	70%	60%
	$185	$160	$135	$115	$100	$90	$80

MODEL 490 RIFLE — .22 rimfire, 5 shot clip mag., 22 in. barrel, folding sight, checkered one piece stock. Mfg. 1975-1980.

	100%	98%	95%	90%	80%	70%	60%
	$250	$215	$185	$155	$145	$130	$110

RIFLES: SLIDE ACTION, DISC.

100%	98%	95%	90%	80%	70%	60%	50%	40%	30%	20%	10%

MODEL 1890 SLIDE ACTION — .22 S, L, LR, or WRF rimfire, cals. were non-interchangeable, visible hammer, solid-frame (first 15,000) or takedown, 24 in. octagonal barrel, case hardened receivers until 1901. Approx. 849,000 mfg. between 1890-1932.

⚰ **Blued Finish** — post-1901 manufacture.

100%	98%	95%	90%	80%	70%	60%	50%	40%	30%	20%	10%
N/A	N/A	$675	$625	$550	$495	$450	$400	$350	$300	$250	$200

    Add 20% premium for .22 LR cal.

⚰ **Color casehardened receiver** — disc. 1901, takedown feature was added in 1892 after over 15,000 solid frames had been made.
    Add 25%-200% for color case hardening, depending on original condition.
    Deluxe models or solid frames will bring premiums over values listed above. There were also a limited amount of guns mfg. with stainless steel barrels which will add to values of post-1901 mfg.
    The Model 1890 was Winchester's first slide action repeating rifle. It replaced the Model 1873 .22 cal. It was an excellent and inexpensive .22 rifle that rapidly became the universal firearm used in shooting galleries. Even though production reached approx. 849,000 units, most guns were heavily used and specimens existing today in 98%+ condition are rare. Check carefully for rebarreling (notice proofmarks on barrel).

100%	98%	95%	90%	80%	70%	60%	50%	40%	30%	20%	10%

MODEL 1906 — .22 S, L, or LR, 20 in. round barrel, tube mag., visible hammer, open sights, straight stock with shotgun butt plate. Approx. 848,000 mfg. between 1906-1932.

100%	98%	95%	90%	80%	70%	60%	50%	40%	30%	20%	10%
N/A	$700	$600	$500	$400	$325	$250	$225	$175	$150	$125	$100

This model is seldom encountered in over 90% original condition.

⚔ **Model 1906 Expert** — similar to Model 1906, except has a pistol grip stock and different shaped slide handle, finish choices included blue, nickel trimmed receiver, guard, and bolt, or full nickel trimmed, mfg. 1917-1925.

100%	98%	95%	90%	80%	70%	60%	50%	40%	30%	20%	10%
$1,650	$1,350	$1,100	$900	$850	$775	$700	$655	$600	$550	$515	$475

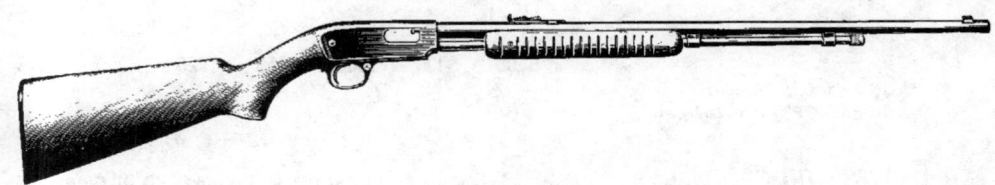

MODEL 61 HAMMERLESS — .22 S, L, LR, or WRF cal., 24 in. round or octagonal barrel, tube mag., open sights, plain grip stock. Approx. 342,000 mfg. between 1932-1963.

100%	98%	95%	90%	80%	70%	60%	50%	40%	30%	20%	10%
$550	$500	$450	$400	$365	$330	$300	$275	$250	$225	$195	$180

Add 15% for single cal. barrel marking.
Pre-war manufacture has small forearm. Pre-war octagon barrel in S or L cals. will command a 100% premium. "WRF" marked round barrel is rare - front of receiver must be marked "W.R.F.".

⚔ **Model 61 Octagon** — .22 S, L, or LR cal., octagon barrel variation of the Model 61. Disc. approx. 1943.

100%	98%	95%	90%	80%	70%	60%	50%	40%	30%	20%	10%
$1,395	$1,100	$900	$850	$775	$700	$655	$600	$550	$500	$450	$395

⚔ **Model 61 Magnum** — similar to Standard 61, but chambered for .22 Win. Mag. Mfg. 1960-1963.

100%	98%	95%	90%	80%	70%	60%	50%	40%	30%	20%	10%
$725	$625	$550	$500	$450	$400	$365	$330	$300	$275	$250	$225

MODEL 62 — 62A VISIBLE HAMMER — modern version of 1890, 23 in. round tapered barrel. Over 409,000 mfg. between 1932-1958.

100%	98%	95%	90%	80%	70%	60%	50%	40%	30%	20%	10%
$475	$425	$375	$330	$300	$275	$250	$225	$195	$175	$160	$145

Add 30% for pre-war Model 62.
Pre-war model is 62, distinguishable by small forearm. The Model 62-A was introduced 1940 at serial number 99,200 with minor changes. Model 62A single cal. barrel markings do not add premiums. Gallery variations of these models will command a large premium.

Grading	100%	98%	95%	90%	80%	70%	60%

MODEL 270 SLIDE ACTION — .22 rimfire, tube mag., 20½ in. barrel, checkered pistol grip stock. Mfg. 1963-1973.

100%	98%	95%	90%	80%	70%	60%
$115	$90	$75	$60	$50	$40	$35

⚔ **Plastic stock version**

100%	98%	95%	90%	80%	70%	60%
$85	$75	$50	$40	$30	$20	$20

⚔ **Model 270 Deluxe** — similar to 270, with select wood, Monte Carlo stock. Mfg. 1965-1973.

100%	98%	95%	90%	80%	70%	60%
$135	$110	$90	$80	$70	$60	$50

MODEL 275 — similar to 270, in .22 WMR.

100%	98%	95%	90%	80%	70%	60%
$135	$110	$100	$90	$80	$70	$65

Grading	100%	98%	95%	90%	80%	70%	60%

Model 275 Deluxe — similar to 270 Deluxe, in .22 WMR.

	100%	98%	95%	90%	80%	70%	60%
	$165	$140	$110	$90	$80	$70	$60

RIFLES: LEVER ACTION - POST 1964 MFG.

Beginning in 1992, all Model 94s and variations (not including the 9422 models) received an engineering change utilizing a cross-bolt in the upper rear of the receiver that prevents the hammer from contacting the firing pin.

MODEL 88 LEVER ACTION CARBINE — .243, .284, or .308 cal., 19 in. barrel, pistol gripped, one piece stock, barrel band. Mfg. 1968-1973.

.308 cal.

	100%	98%	95%	90%	80%	70%	60%
	$500	$400	$300	$250	$225	$200	$175

Add 25% for .243 cal.
Add 50%-75% for .284 cal.

MODEL 88 RIFLE — .243, .284, .308, or .358 cal., 22 in. barrel, basket weave or diamond cut checkering, no barrel band. Approx. 284,000 mfg. 1955-1973.

	100%	98%	95%	90%	80%	70%	60%
.308 cal.	$375	$325	$300	$250	$225	$200	$175
.243 cal.	$450	$380	$350	$325	$275	$250	$225
Pre-1964 production — add $50.							
.284 cal.	$700	$585	$500	$450	$400	$300	$200
Pre-1964 production — add 50%.							
.358 cal.	$850	$775	$700	$500	$400	$300	$250

Available between 1956-1962 only.

MODEL 94 STANDARD RIFLE — lever action, .30-30, .32 Win. Spl. (new 1992), 7-30 Waters (new 1989), or .44 Mag. (mfg. 1984 and 1985 only) cal., 6 or 7 (24 in. barrel only) shot tube mag., 20 or 24 (mfg. 1987-88 only) in. round barrel, open sights, straight walnut stock, barrel band on forearm. Mfg. 1964-present. Angled ejection became standard 1982, 6½ lbs.

		100%	98%	95%	90%	80%	70%	60%
Mfg.'s Sug. Retail	$335	$260	$215	$180	$165	$150	$140	$135

Add $15 for 24 in. barrel (disc. 1990).
Add $16 for .44 Mag. cal. (disc. 1986).

Model 94 Deluxe — .30-30 only, similar to Standard Rifle, except has checkered walnut stock and forearm. New 1988.

		100%	98%	95%	90%	80%	70%	60%
Mfg.'s Sug. Retail	$362	$280	$220	$180	$165	$150	$140	$135

Add $50 for 1.5 - 4.5X scope with low mounts (disc.).

Model 94 Ranger — .30-30 only, 20 in. barrel, uncheckered hardwood stock and forearm, 5 shot mag., 6½ lbs. New for 1985.

		100%	98%	95%	90%	80%	70%	60%
Mfg.'s Sug. Retail	$296	$235	$190	$160	$150	$140	$130	$120

Add $52 for 4x32 scope with see-through mounts.

Model 94 Wrangler Large Loop — .30-30 or .44 Mag. cal., 16 in. barrel, has large loop lever, uncheckered walnut stock and forearm, blued finish, open sights, 6 lbs. New 1992.

		100%	98%	95%	90%	80%	70%	60%
Mfg.'s Sug. Retail	$354	$275	$215	$175	$165	$150	$140	$135

Add $20 for .44 Mag. cal.

Win-Tuff Rifle — similar to Model 94 Rifle, except has laminated hardwood stock and forearm with checkering. Drilled and tapped for scope mounts. New 1987.

		100%	98%	95%	90%	80%	70%	60%
Mfg.'s Sug. Retail	$374	$285	$225	$180	$165	$150	$140	$135

Grading	100%	98%	95%	90%	80%	70%	60%

MODEL 94 XTR — .30-30 or 7-30 Waters (new 1985) cal., 20 or 24 (7-30 Waters only) in. barrel, checkered select walnut, hooded front sight (except 7-30 Waters which has dovetailed front blade), 6½ lbs. Disc. 1988.

	$260	$225	$205	$185	$160	$150	$140

Add $26 for 7-30 Waters cal. rifle.
Last Mfg.'s Sug. Retail was $285.

⚮ **Model 94 XTR Deluxe** — .30-30 cal. only, deluxe American walnut stock and lengthened forearm with fancy checkering, 20 in. barrel with deluxe script, rubber butt pad. Mfg. 1987-1988 only.

	$370	$310	$270	$235	$210	$190	$160

Last Mfg.'s Sug. Retail was $426.

MODEL 94 TRAPPER — .30-30, .357 Mag. (new 1992), .45 Colt (new 1985), or .44 Mag./.44 Spl. cal., 16 in. barrel, side ejection, walnut stock, 5 or 9 shot tube mag., blue finish, dovetailed front sight, 6 lbs.

Mfg.'s Sug. Retail	$335	$275	$220	$180	$160	$150	$140	$130

Add $19 for .357 Mag., .45 Colt, or .44 Mag. cal.
The .44 Mag. cal. was introduced 1985.

MODEL 94 .44 MAG. S.R.C. — .44 Mag., top eject, 20 in. barrel, SRC. Mfg. 1967-72.

	$325	$275	$250	$225	$200	$175	$150

MODEL 94 CLASSIC SERIES — .30-30 cal., 20 or 26 in. barrel. Approx. 47,000 mfg. 1967-70.

	$325	$285	$235	$200	$185	$160	$150

MODEL 94 ANTIQUE CARBINE — similar to Standard, with scroll on receiver, case hardened, gold-plated saddle ring. Mfg. 1964-1983.

	$250	$225	$200	$175	$160	$150	$140

MODEL 94 WRANGLER — .32 Win. Special, top ejection, only 7,947 mfg. Disc.

	$350	$310	$270	$235	$210	$190	$160

MODEL 94 WRANGLER II — .32 Win. Special (disc. 1984) or .38-55 Win. cal., angle ejection, 16 in. barrel, oversized hoop-shaped lever, roll-engraved receiver, 5 shot mag., 6⅛ lbs. Made 1983-1985 only.

	$245	$220	$200	$185	$165	$150	$140

Last Mfg.'s Sug. Retail was $275.

MODEL 94 BIG BORE — .307 Win., .356 Win., or .375 (disc. 1987) Win. cal., angled ejection port provides scope mounting, checkered walnut Monte Carlo stock with recoil pad, 20 in. barrel, 6 shot mag., sling swivels, 6½ lbs. New 1983.

Mfg.'s Sug. Retail	$374	$295	$225	$195	$175	$160	$150	$140

Also mfg. in a top eject (pre-USRA).
This model had an "XTR" suffix until 1989.

MODEL 9422 STANDARD — .22 LR or Mag., takedown, 20½ in. round barrel, 15 shot (LR) mag., grooved forged steel receiver, checkered straight grip, checkered high gloss (disc.) or satin weather resistant finish (new 1988) walnut stock and forearm, sights, 6¼ lbs. Mfg. 1972-present.

Mfg.'s Sug. Retail	$376	$300	$250	$210	$190	$175	$160	$145

This model had an "XTR" suffix until 1989. Earlier mfg. including pre-XTR and early XTR rifles had no checkering - these guns will command slight premiums over values listed above.

Grading	100%	98%	95%	90%	80%	70%	60%

⚡ **.22 Mag. cal.** — 11 shot mag., 6¼ lbs.

| Mfg.'s Sug. Retail | $393 | | $315 | $265 | $225 | $200 | $185 | $175 | $165 |

⚡ **Model 9422 Win-Cam** — .22 Win. Mag. only, similar to 9422 XTR Standard, except has checkered greenish laminated hardwood stock and forearm. New 1987.

| Mfg.'s Sug. Retail | $393 | | $315 | $265 | $225 | $200 | $185 | $175 | $165 |

⚡ **Model 9422 Win-Tuff** — .22 LR or .22 Mag., checkered laminated brown hardwood stock and forearm. New 1988.

| Mfg.'s Sug. Retail | $376 | | $300 | $250 | $210 | $190 | $175 | $160 | $145 |

Add $17 for .22 Mag. cal.

MODEL 9422 XTR CLASSIC — same general specifications as Model 9422 XTR Standard, except has 22½ in. barrel and non-checkered, satin finished, pistol grip walnut stock and extended forearm, stock also has fluted comb with crescent steel butt plate, curved finger lever, 6½ lbs. Mfg. 1985-1987.

| | | $315 | $285 | $255 | $230 | $205 | $185 | $175 |

Last Mfg.'s Sug. Retail was $301.

MODEL 64 1972-1974 MODEL — .30-30, lever action, 5 shot, ⅔ tube mag., 24 in. barrel, open sight, plain pistol grip stock. Mfg. 1972-1974.

| | | $220 | $195 | $165 | $140 | $110 | $90 | $70 |

MODEL 250 LEVER ACTION — .22 rimfire, 20½ in. barrel, tube mag., hammerless, checkered pistol grip stock. Mfg. 1963-1973.

| | | $125 | $110 | $95 | $70 | $60 | $50 | $40 |

⚡ **Model 250 Deluxe** — similar to Model 250, with select wood and sling swivels. Mfg. 1965-1971.

| | | $150 | $125 | $90 | $75 | $60 | $50 | $45 |

MODEL 255 — .22 WMR, otherwise similar to Model 250. Mfg. 1964-1970.

| | | $150 | $135 | $115 | $90 | $70 | $60 | $50 |

⚡ **Model 255 Deluxe** — .22 WMR, with select wood and swivels. Mfg. 1965-1973.

| | | $195 | $175 | $140 | $110 | $90 | $80 | $70 |

RIFLES: BOLT ACTION - POST 1964 MFG.

MODEL 52D BOLT ACTION TARGET RIFLE — .22 LR, single shot, free floating standard or heavy barrel, scope bases, target stock with palm stop. Mfg. 1961-1980. Total production on all variations is approx. 125,233.

| | | $475 | $435 | $415 | $385 | $360 | $305 | $275 |

MODEL 52 INTERNATIONAL MATCH — similar to 52-D Heavy Barrel, with special free rifle stock, hooked butt.

| | | $495 | $470 | $440 | $415 | $330 | $305 | $250 |

MODEL 52 INTERNATIONAL PRONE — similar to 52-D, with prone stock, removable roll over cheek piece. Mfg. 1975-1980.

| | | $495 | $470 | $440 | $415 | $330 | $305 | $250 |

MODEL 70 STANDARD — .22-250, .222, .225, .242, .270, .308, or .30-06 cal., 5 shot, 22 in. barrel, open sight, Monte Carlo stock, swivels. Mfg. 1972-1980.

| | | $350 | $330 | $310 | $285 | $220 | $200 | $175 |

Grading	100%	98%	95%	90%	80%	70%	60%

MODEL 70 MAGNUM — .264 Win. Mag., 7mm Rem. Mag., .300 H&H Mag., .300 Win. Mag., .338 Win. Mag., .375 H&H Mag., or .458 Win. Mag. cal., 24 in. barrel.

		$400	$350	$330	$310	$285	$220	$200

Add 25-35% for .375 H&H Mag. or .458 Win. Mag. cal.

MODEL 70 FEATHERWEIGHT — .22-250, .223 Rem., .243 Win., .25-06, .257 Robts. (disc.), .270 Win., .280 Rem., 6.5 x 55mm Swedish (new 1991), 7mm Mauser (disc.), .30-06, .308, 7mm-08 Rem. (new 1992), 7mm Rem. Mag. (mfg. 1991-92 only), or .300 Win. Mag. (mfg. 1991-92 only) cal., bolt action, both short and medium action, 5 shot mag., 22 in. barrel (24 in. with .300 Win. Mag.), checkered walnut stock, no sights, approx. 6½ lbs. New 1981.

Mfg.'s Sug. Retail	$562	$435	$380	$325	$300	$280	$260	$240

In 1981, during U.S.R.A. takeover transition, guns were built distinguishable by the U.S.R.A. trademark on the recoil pad. Some collectors will pay a premium for Win. marked pads. Cal.'s .257 Robts. and 7mm Mauser were disc. 1985.
This model had an "XTR" suffix until 1989.

⚒ **Model 70 Featherweight Classic** — .270 Win., .280 Rem., or .30-06 cal., 22 in. barrel, features claw-controlled round feeding action bedded into standard grade walnut stock, includes rings and bases, 6¾ lbs. New 1992.

Mfg.'s Sug. Retail	$749	$650	$550	$475	$425	$375	$330	$295

⚒ **Model 70 Win-Tuff Featherweight Rifle** — .22-250, .223 Rem., .243 Win., .270 Win., .30-06, or .308 Win. cal., features brown laminated, checkered stock with Schnabel forend, includes base and rings, pistol grip cap, 7 lbs., new 1988 - reintroduced 1992.

Mfg.'s Sug. Retail	$572	$445	$385	$325	$300	$280	$260	$240

This model was originally introduced in 1988 - it was discontinued in 1989 and reintroduced in 1992.

MODEL 70 XTR EUROPEAN FEATHERWEIGHT — 6.5 x 55 Swedish Mauser cal., 22 in. barrel, 5 shot mag., rifle sights, 6¾ lbs. Made 1986 only.

		$390	$365	$330	$305	$280	$260	$240

Last Mfg.'s Sug. Retail was $460.

MODEL 70 LIGHTWEIGHT CARBINE — .22-250, .223 Rem., .243 Win., .250 Savage (new 1986), .308 Win., .270 Win., or .30-06 cal., bolt action, 5 shot mag., both short and medium action, 20 in. barrel, checkered walnut stock, no sights, approx. 6 lbs. Mfg. 1984-86. Add $15 for open sights.

		$355	$320	$285	$255	$230	$210	$190

Last Mfg.'s Sug. Retail was $395.

MODEL 70 LIGHTWEIGHT RIFLE — .22-250 (disc. 1992), .223 Rem., .243 Win., .270 Win., .280 Rem. (mfg. 1988-92), .30-06, or .308 Win. cal., 22 in. barrel, checkered walnut stock, no sights, 6½ lbs. New 1987.

Mfg.'s Sug. Retail	$485	$400	$330	$290	$255	$230	$210	$190

⚒ **Model 70 Win-Tuff Lightweight Rifle** — .22-250 (mfg. 1988-89), .223 (new 1989), .243 Win. (new 1988), .270 Win. .30-06 or .308 Win. (new 1989) cal., similar to Model 70 Lightweight Rifle, except has laminated brown hardwood stock with checkering. Mfg. 1987-92.

		$395	$330	$290	$255	$230	$210	$190

Last Mfg.'s Sug. Retail was $471.

⚒ **Model 70 Win-Cam Lightweight Rifle** — .270 Win. or .30-06 cal., greenish laminated hardwood stock with checkering, 22 in. barrel. New 1987.

		$395	$330	$290	$255	$230	$210	$190

This model was previously desigated Featherweight before 1989.
Last Mfg.'s Sug. Retail was $471.

Grading	100%	98%	95%	90%	80%	70%	60%

MODEL 70 SPORTER — .22-250 (new 1989), .223 (new 1989), .243 (new 1989), .25-06 Rem. (mfg. 1985-87 and reintroduced 1990), .270 Win., .30-06, or .308 Win. (mfg. 1986-89) cal., 24 in. barrel, 5 shot mag., custom Sporter styling, Monte Carlo cheek piece, detachable sling swivels, 7¾ lbs.

Mfg.'s Sug. Retail	$556	$435	$375	$325	$300	$280	$260	$240

This model had an "XTR" suffix until 1989. Before 1989, iron sights cost $15 additionally - for 1990, prices became the same for choice of either iron sights or base and rings in .243 Win., .270 Win., or .30-06 cal.

Sporter Win-Tuff — .270 Win., .30-06, 7mm Rem. Mag., .300 Win. Mag., .300 Wby. Mag., or .338 Win. Mag., similar to Model 70 Sporter, except has checkered brown laminate stock with sling swivels, solid recoil pad, 24 in. barrel, approx. 7¾ lbs. Mfg. 1992 only.

		$445	$380	$325	$300	$280	$260	$240

Last Mfg.'s Sug. Retail was $572.

MODEL 70 SPORTER MAGNUM — same general specifications as standard Sporter, 7mm Rem. Mag., .264 Win. Mag., .270 Wby. Mag. (new 1988), .300 Wby. Mag. (new 1989), .300 Win. Mag., .300 H&H (mfg. 1989-92), or .338 Win. Mag. cal., reinforced stock, 3 shot mag., 24 in. barrel, 7¾ lbs. Mfg. 1972-present.

Mfg.'s Sug. Retail	$556	$435	$375	$325	$300	$280	$260	$240

This model had an "XTR" suffix until 1989. Before 1989, iron sights cost $15 additionally - for 1990, prices became the same for either iron sights or base and rings in 7mm Rem. Mag., .300 Win. Mag., or .338 Win. Mag. cal.

Model 70 Super Express Mag. — .375 H&H or .458 Win. Mag. cal., 3 shot mag., claw extractor controlled round feeding (new 1993), open sights, 22 or 24 in. (.375 H&H only) barrel, 8½ lbs.

Mfg.'s Sug. Retail	$816	$700	$575	$525	$495	$460	$430	$400

This model had an "XTR" suffix until 1989.

MODEL 70 DBM (DETACHABLE BOX MAGAZINE) — .22-250 Rem. (new 1993), .223 Rem. (new 1993), .243 Win. (new 1993), .270 Win., .30-06, .308 Win. (new 1993), 7mm Rem. Mag., or .300 Win. Mag. cal., checkered walnut stock and forend, features 3 shot detachable box mag., 24 in. barrel with or without sights, includes bases and rings or choice of iron sights (new 1993) in all cals. except .22-250 Rem. and .223 Rem., 7¾ lbs. New 1992.

Mfg.'s Sug. Retail	$598	$465	$390	$330	$300	$280	$260	$240

Model 70 DBM-S — similar to Model 70 DBM, except has black synthetic stock. New 1993.

Mfg.'s Sug. Retail	$618	$475	$395	$330	$300	$280	$260	$240

MODEL 70 STAINLESS — .270 Win., .30-06, 7mm Rem. Mag., .300 Win. Mag., or .338 Win. Mag., features matte finished stainless steel receiver barrel and bolt, black, synthetic, composite stock, 22 (.270 or .30-06 only, disc. 1992) or 24 in. barrel, approx. 6¾ lbs. New 1992.

Mfg.'s Sug. Retail	$604	$465	$390	$330	$300	$280	$260	$240

MODEL 70 SM (SYNTHETIC MATTE) — .22-250 Rem. (new 1993), .223 Rem. (new 1993), .243 Win. (new 1993), .270 Win., .30-06, .308 Win. (new 1993), 7mm Rem. Mag., .300 Win. Mag., .338 Win. Mag., or .375 H&H Mag. (new 1993) cal., features black composite stock with checkering and sling swivels, 22 (.22-250, .223, .243, or .308 only, new 1993) or 24 in. barrel with matte metal finish, approx. 7½ lbs. New 1992.

Mfg.'s Sug. Retail	$576	$440	$385	$325	$300	$280	$260	$240

Add $28 for .375 H&H Mag. cal.
Until 1993, this model was called the Model 70 SSM.

Grading	100%	98%	95%	90%	80%	70%	60%

MODEL 70 VARMINT — same general specifications as standard Sporter, .22-250 Rem., .223 Rem., .225 Win., .243 Win., or .308 Win. cal., 26 in. heavy barrel with cold hammer forged rifling and counter-bored at muzzle, no sights, 5 shot mag., target scope bases, 7¾ lbs. Mfg. 1964-present.

| Mfg.'s Sug. Retail | $580 | $470 | $375 | $325 | $295 | $280 | $260 | $240 |

This model had an "XTR" suffix 1978-89.

Model 70 Heavy Varmint — .22-250 Rem., .223 Rem., .243 Win., or .308 Win. cal., 26 in. barrel (countersunk muzzle) without sights, features black synthetic beavertail H&S precision stock with aluminum bedding block. New 1993.

| Mfg.'s Sug. Retail | $580 | $470 | $375 | $325 | $295 | $280 | $260 | $240 |

1,500 guns were mfg. in this variation 1993 only.

MODEL 70 SHB (SYNTHETIC HEAVY BARREL) — .308 Win. cal., features checkered black composite stock, 26 in. barrel with matte metal finish, jeweled bolt, 9 lbs. Mfg. 1992 only.

| | | $460 | $375 | $325 | $300 | $280 | $260 | $240 |

Last Mfg.'s Sug. Retail was $563.

MODEL 70 WINLIGHT — .25-06, .270, .280 Rem. (new 1987), .30-06, 7mm Rem. Mag., .300 Win. Mag., .300 Wby. Mag., or .338 Win. Mag. cal., McMillan fiberglass stock, thermoplastic receiver bedding, blued metal parts, 22 or 24 (Mag. cals. only) in. barrel, 3 or 4 shot mag., no sights, approx. 6½ lbs. Mfg. 1986-90.

| | | $555 | $490 | $440 | $395 | $350 | $310 | $280 |

Last Mfg.'s Sug. Retail was $637.

MODEL 70 50TH ANNIVERSARY MODEL — .300 Win. Mag., 24 in. barrel, deluxe walnut stock, engraving and special motifs on metal surfaces, serial numbered 50 ANV 1 - 50 ANV 500, 7¾ lbs. 500 mfg. 1987 only.

| | $1,000 | $840 | $725 |

Last Mfg.'s Sug. Retail was $939.

MODEL 70 CUSTOM GRADE — various cals., old style Model 70 action, semi-fancy American walnut checkered stock, engine turned bolt and follower, hand honed internal parts. Mfg. 1988-89 only.

| | $1,100 | $875 | $700 |

Last Mfg.'s Sug. Retail was $1,172.

MODEL 70 SUPER GRADE — .270 Win. (new 1991), .30-06 (new 1991), 7mm Rem. Mag., .300 Win. Mag., or .338 Win. Mag. cal., 24 in. barrel, 3 shot mag., jeweled bolt, stainless steel extractor for true claw controlled round feeding and ejecting, three-position safety, checkered satin finish walnut stock with wood cheek piece, bases and rings included, 7¾ lbs. New 1990.

| Mfg.'s Sug. Retail | $997 | | $925 | $795 | $625 |

MODEL 70 CUSTOM GRADE — .270 Win., .30-06, 7mm Rem. Mag., .300 Win. Mag., or .338 Win. Mag. cal., similar to Model 70 Super Grade, but must be special ordered through the Custom Gun Shop and includes many custom features including semi-fancy walnut with satin finish and hand-honed internal parts. New 1990.

| Mfg.'s Sug. Retail | $1,695 | | $1,695 | $1,250 | $995 |

A Model 70 Collector Grade is also a variation of this model that is mfg. in the Custom Gun Shop - this model is priced on request only.

Grading	100%	98%	95%	90%	80%	70%	60%

Model 70 Custom Grade Featherweight — .270 Win., .280 Rem., or .30-06 cal., 22 in. barrel, includes Featherweight features, controlled round feeding, higher grade wood. New 1992.

Mfg.'s Sug. Retail	$1,695		$1,695	$1,250	$995		

Model 70 Custom Sharpshooter — .22-250 Rem. (new 1993), .223 Rem. (new 1993), .308 Win., or .300 Win. Mag. cal., includes specially designed McMillan A-2 stock, and Schneider 24 (.308 cal. only) or 26 in. barrel. New 1992.

Mfg.'s Sug. Retail	$1,650		$1,650	$1,125	$895		

Model 70 Custom Sporting Sharpshooter — .270 Win., 7mm STW, or .300 Win. Mag. cal., ½-minute of angle sporting version of the Custom Sharpshooter, custom shop only. New 1993.

Mfg.'s Sug. Retail	$1,595		$1,595	$1,100	$875		

Model 70 Custom Grade Express — .375 H&H Mag., .375 JRS (new 1992), 7mm STW (new 1993), .416 Rem. Mag., .458 Win. Mag. cal., or .470 Capstick, 24 in. (22 in. on .458 Win. Mag.) barrel, features claw controlled round feeding, deluxe walnut with satin finish and checkering, 3-leaf express rear sight, high luster metal finish, bolt and follower are engine turned, available by special order through the custom gun shop only. New 1990.

Mfg.'s Sug. Retail	$2,125		$2,125	$1,500	$1,175		

Add $240 for .375 JRS or .470 Capstick cal.
Subtract $130 for 7mm STW cal.

MODEL 70 COLLECTOR GRADE — various cals., this variation must be special ordered through the Winchester Custom Shop and prices vary individually per quotation.

MODEL 70 CUSTOM BUILT — various cals., this variation must be special ordered through the Winchester Custom Shop and prices vary individually per quotation.

MODEL 70 EXHIBITION GRADE — various cals., fancy checkered American walnut stock with hardwood forend tip. Mfg. 1988-89 only.

			$1,995	$1,575	$1,000		

Last Mfg.'s Sug. Retail was $2,192.

MODEL 70 XTR FEATHERWEIGHT ULTRA GRADE "1 OF 1,000" — .270 Win., bolt action, extensively engraved, finely checkered deluxe French walnut, with mahogany presentation case.

			$1,800	$1,450	$950		

Last Mfg.'s Sug. Retail was $5,000.

RANGER RIFLE — .223 Rem. (new 1992), .243 Win. (new 1991), .270 Win., .30-06, or 7mm Rem. Mag. (disc. 1985) cal., 22 or 24 (disc. 1992) in. barrel, 3 (7mm Rem. Mag.) or 4 shot mag., plain hardwood stock without checkering, open sights, 7⅛ lbs.

Mfg.'s Sug. Retail	$440		$335	$270	$215	$200	$180	$165	$155

RANGER YOUTH/LADIES CARBINE — .223 Rem. (disc. 1989), .243 Win., or .308 Win. (new 1991), cal., 20 (disc. 1992) or 22 (new 1993) in. barrel, 4 or 5 (.223 Rem.) shot mag., shorter hardwood stock dimensions, open sights, 5¾ lbs.

Mfg.'s Sug. Retail	$465		$360	$285	$220	$200	$180	$165	$155

MODEL 70 DELUXE — .243, .270, .30-06, or .300 Win. Mag. cal., 22 in. barrel, open sight, hand checkered, black forend tip, became standard 1972. Mfg. 1964-1971.

			$475	$415	$360	$320	$285	$220	$180

MODEL 70 TARGET RIFLE 1964-1971 — .308 or .30-06 cal., 24 in. heavy barrel, no sights, target bases, heavy target style stock with hand stop. Mfg. 1972-disc.

			$630	$550	$495	$440	$360	$330	$275

Grading	100%	98%	95%	90%	80%	70%	60%

MODEL 70 INTERNATIONAL ARMY MATCH 1971 — .308 cal., 5 shot, 24 in. heavy barrel, no sights, adj. trigger, ISU stock with forearm, accessory rail, adj. butt. Mfg. 1973-disc.

	$715	$660	$605	$550	$470	$440	$385

MODEL 70 MANNLICHER 1969-1971 — .243, .270, .30-06, or .308 Win. cal., 19 in. barrel, open sight, full length Monte Carlo stock with steel forend cap. Disc. 1972.

	$550	$440	$385	$360	$305	$275	$250

MODEL 70A — economy version of 1972 type Model 70, same cals., no hinged floorplate or forend tip. Mfg. 1972-1978.

	$325	$285	$265	$230	$200	$165	$140

MODEL 70A MAGNUM — similar to Model 70A, except in Mag. cals. but not .375 H&H or .458. Mfg. 1972-1978.

	$340	$310	$275	$250	$220	$195	$165

MODEL 670 BOLT ACTION RIFLE — another economy version of the model 70, .225, .243, .270, .308, or .30-06 cal., 22 in. barrel, open sights, no hinged floorplate, pistol grip stock. Mfg. 1967-1973.

	$300	$250	$220	$195	$175	$165	$140

MODEL 670 CARBINE — similar to 670, with 19 in. barrel, not available in .308. Mfg. 1967-1970.

	$300	$250	$220	$195	$175	$165	$140

MODEL 670 MAGNUM — similar to 670, with reinforced stock, .264 Mag., 7mm Mag., or .300 Win. Mag. cal. Mfg. 1967-1970.

	$330	$275	$255	$220	$205	$195	$165

MODEL 770 BOLT ACTION — .22-250, .222, .243, .270, or .30-30 cal., 22 in. barrel, open sights, no floorplate or forend tip. Mfg. 1969-1971.

	$325	$285	$275	$260	$250	$220	$195

MODEL 770 MAGNUM — similar to Standard, in .264 Mag., 7mm Mag., or .300 Win. Mag. cal., recoil pad. Mfg. 1969-1971.

	$350	$310	$285	$275	$265	$250	$220

MODEL 121 SINGLE SHOT RIFLE — .22 rimfire, bolt action, $20\frac{3}{4}$ in. barrel, open sights, plain pistol grip stock. Mfg. 1967-1973.

	$115	$85	$70	$55	$45	$35	$30

MODEL 121Y SINGLE SHOT RIFLE — similar to 121, with shorter stock.

	$115	$85	$70	$55	$45	$35	$30

MODEL 121 DELUXE — similar to 121, with ramp front sight and sling swivels.

	$125	$90	$75	$60	$50	$40	$35

MODEL 131 REPEATING RIFLE — .22 rimfire, bolt action, 7 shot, $20\frac{3}{4}$ in. barrel, plain Monte Carlo stock. Mfg. 1967-1973.

	$160	$135	$100	$85	$70	$60	$50

MODEL 141 REPEATER — similar to 131, with tube mag. in butt stock. Mfg. 1967-1973.

	$160	$135	$100	$90	$75	$65	$55

Grading	100%	98%	95%	90%	80%	70%	60%

MODEL 310 SINGLE SHOT — .22 rimfire, bolt action, 22 in. barrel, open sights, checkered pistol grip stock, swivels. Mfg. 1972-1975.

	100%	98%	95%	90%	80%	70%	60%
	$200	$175	$140	$100	$80	$70	$60

MODEL 320 REPEATING RIFLE — similar to 310, with 5 shot clip. Mfg. 1972-1974.

	100%	98%	95%	90%	80%	70%	60%
	$375	$325	$275	$225	$165	$140	$100

RIFLES: O/U

DOUBLE EXPRESS RIFLE — .30-06, 7x65R, 9.3x74R, .257 Roberts, or .270 Win. cal., 23½ in. O/U barrels, iron sights with claw scope mounts, ejectors, fully engraved satin finish receiver with game scene engraving, walnut specially hand checkered, sling swivels, 8½ lbs. Mfg. 1984-1985 only.

	100%	98%	95%	90%	80%	70%	60%
	$2,500	$2,150	$1,850	$1,650	$1,450	$1,300	$1,200

Last Mfg.'s Sug. Retail was $2,995.
In 1984, Aero Marine located in Birmingham, AL special ordered 200 deluxe double rifles in 7 x 57mm Mauser cal. They featured better engraving and game scenes with bottom of receiver marked Jaeger. Of the 200, 100 were rifles with 90 being standard grade and 10 being deluxe. The other 100 were supplied with an extra set of O/U shotgun barrels. Sales were slow on these special guns and eventually they were liquidated to another wholesaler. Recently, prices are in the $2,250-$3,000 range for the rifle alone and $3,000-$3,750 for the Combo.

SHOTGUNS: 1879-1964

BREECH LOADING SxS — 10 or 12 ga., imported from England for sales through the Winchester New York City office only, exposed hammers, available in 5 grades ranging from Class D - Class A and Match gun (lowest to highest). Higher grades were mfg. by W.C. Scott & Sons, about 10,000 were imported between 1879-1884. Prices vary greatly due to condition and grade. Prices can range from $300 (poor condition Class D) to over $4,000 (95%+ condition specimen in Class A or Match gun).
This side by side model was the first shotgun bearing the Winchester name sold in the U.S. Identifiable by "Winchester Repeating Arms Co., New Haven, Connecticut, U.S.A." marking on barrel rib top.

100%	98%	95%	90%	80%	70%	60%	50%	40%	30%	20%	10%

MODEL 1887 LEVER ACTION — 10 or 12 ga., 4 shot tube mag., 30 or 32 in. full choke fluid steel barrels, plain pistol grip stock, first Browning patent shotgun mfg. by Winchester. Mfg. 1887-1901. Approx. 64,855 mfg.

100%	98%	95%	90%	80%	70%	60%	50%	40%	30%	20%	10%
$2,250	$1,850	$1,550	$1,275	$1,000	$875	$775	$675	$575	$475	$375	$275

Standard frame finish on this model was color case hardening. Premiums exist for original bright case colored specimens. 10 ga. began production with serial number 22148. Also mfg. in Riot configuration (20 in. cylinder bore barrel). Gauges were chambered for 2⅝ in. (12 ga.) and 2⅞ in. (10 ga.). First lever action repeating shotgun domestically mfg.

Model 1887 Deluxe — damascus barrel, checkered stock, and other special order features.

100%	98%	95%	90%	80%	70%	60%	50%	40%	30%	20%	10%
$3,000	$2,650	$2,300	$2,000	$1,750	$1,500	$1,275	$1,100	$950	$795	$650	$525

MODEL 1893 SLIDE ACTION — 12 ga., 30 (standard) and 32 in. barrel, black powder only. First Winchester shotgun with sliding forearm action, first Browning slide action patent, disc. 1897 after run of some 34,050. Note: chambered for 2⅝ shells only, damascus barrels were available at extra cost, as were fancy stocks.

100%	98%	95%	90%	80%	70%	60%	50%	40%	30%	20%	10%
$950	$850	$750	$675	$600	$525	$485	$425	$375	$325	$275	$225

This gun had limited sales because mechanical weaknesses developed when shooting smokeless powder.

100%	98%	95%	90%	80%	70%	60%	50%	40%	30%	20%	10%

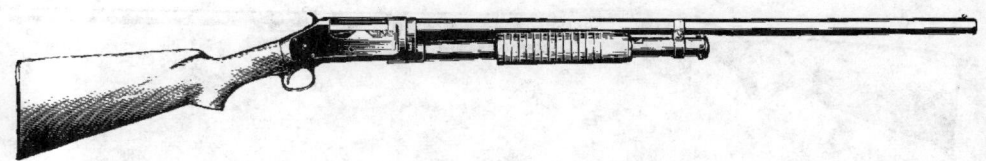

MODEL 1897 SLIDE ACTION — 12 or 16 ga. (introduced 1900), improved Model 1893 action, 26-32 in. barrels, visible hammer, various chokes, takedown or solid frame, plain pistol grip stock. Over 1,024,700 mfg. between 1897-1957.

$550	$450	$350	$325	$295	$275	$250	$225	$195	$175	$150	$125

First Winchester shotgun chambered for 2¾ in. smokeless ammunition.

MODEL 1897 RIOT GUNS — see the "Trench/Riot Shotgun" category in the T section for more information and prices.

MODEL 1897 TRENCH GUNS — see the "Trench/Riot Shotgun" category in the T section for more information and prices.
This model changed its stock configuration after WWI.

MODEL 1897 TRAP — higher grade version of Standard, checkered stock, could have black diamond inlay in stock until 1919 (Black Diamond Trap), breech block marked Trap until approx. 1926. Mfg. 1897-1931.

$925	$800	$675	$550	$450	$375	$325	$295	$275	$250	$225	$200

Model 1897 Black Diamond Trap — distinguishable by diamond ebony inlays in stock pistol grip.

$1,750	$1,500	$1,250	$1,075	$975	$850	$700	$575	$465	$385	$325	$295

MODEL 1897 PIGEON — higher grade version of Standard 97, should have engraved pigeon behind hammer on frame, breech block marked "Pigeon", most exhibit black diamond stock inlays until 1919. Mfg. 1897-1939.

$2,750	$2,450	$2,100	$1,850	$1,650	$1,450	$1,225	$1,000	$875	$725	$600	$525

MODEL 1901 — 10 ga. only, strengthened Model 1887 action to accept smokeless powder, lever action, standard barrel 32 in., blued barrel and frame, 5 shot mag. 13,500 mfg. between 1901-1920, starting with serial number 64,856.

$1,750	$1,500	$1,225	$1,000	$875	$775	$675	$575	$475	$375	$275	$225

Add 25% for Deluxe Grade (checkered wood).
This shotgun was chambered for 2⅞ in. smokeless powder ammunition.

MODEL 1911 SL AUTOLOADER — 12 ga., recoil operated, 26 or 28 in. barrel, various chokes, pistol grip laminated birch stock. Mfg. 1911-1925, 82,774 produced, action had design problems.

$525	$450	$375	$300	$275	$255	$235	$210	$195	$180	$165	$150

The Model 1911 was Winchester's first semi-auto shotgun. It did not prove to be satisfactory partly because the design had to be exclusive of the patents for Browning's famous A-5 model, interestingly enough a design which Winchester originally had helped Browning patent.

MODEL 36 SINGLE SHOT — 9mm long shot, short shot, and ball, 18 in. round barrel, single shot bolt action, guns were not serial numbered, one piece plain stock and forearm, special shaped trigger guard, 2¾ lbs. Approx. 20,000 mfg. between 1920-1927.

$695	$625	$550	$495	$450	$400	$360	$330	$300	$270	$240	$200

WINCHESTER. cont.

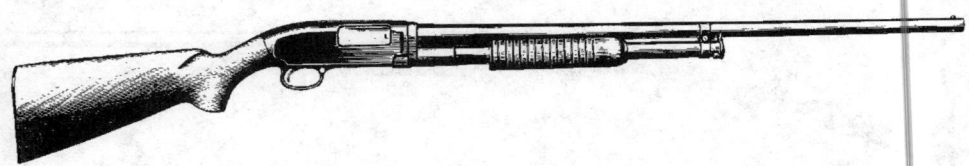

MODEL 12 SLIDE ACTION — 12, 16, 20, or 28 ga., 25-32 in. standard or nickel steel barrel, 6 shot, blued metal, various chokes, hammerless, plain pistol grip walnut stock. Mfg. 1912-1976. The following add-ons do not apply to the 28 ga.

Add $100 if in original unremarked box (N.I.B. only).

Add 20%-30% for Win. special VR (offset barrel proofmark).

Add 30%-40% for Win. solid rib.

Add 40%-50% for Win. milled VR.

Extra barrel(s) — add 50% of specimen's value/set.

Special order features on field guns have captured much collector interest in recent years. Combinations of these features can add a considerable percentage to the base values listed below. Rare special orders on rare variations are very desirable and prices can double and more if the combination is right. As is the case with most other collectible shotguns at this time, Model 12s with open choked barrels in shorter lengths are a lot more desirable (and expensive) than a specimen with a 30 in. full choke barrel (most common). Values listed below are for standard configuration (28 or 30 in. full choke barrel with no rib). For most Model 12s, values for condition factors less than 60% will approximate the 60% price, because of shooter demand. Premiums must be added for the rarer open choked barrels in shorter length on all gauges.

ORIGINAL GAUGE CAN BE DETERMINED BY REMOVING THE BUTT STOCK AND OBSERVING THE GAUGE MARKING ON THE STOCK SCREW BOSS.

	100%	98%	95%	90%	80%	70%	60%
12 ga.	$595	$500	$415	$365	$330	$295	$250
16 ga.	$675	$595	$550	$475	$400	$340	$315
20 ga.	$795	$675	$600	$525	$450	$395	$375
28 ga.	$3,500	$3,200	$2,750	$2,450	$2,000	$1,750	$1,500

Subtract 40% if with factory Cutts compensator.

In the past several years many non-original, re-stamped 28 ga. barrels have been added to 16 or 20 ga. frames "creating" a more desirable (and expensive) gun to unsuspecting buyers. Roll die markings are getting better and better so be very cautious when considering a non-Cutts 28 ga. (as in get a receipt specifying originality). The last observed ser. no. for an original 28 ga. is 1,586,817.

Editor's Note: The Model 12 Winchester was produced continuously from 1912-1980. Over 2,027,500 were produced both in standard and deluxe (Pigeon) grades. Pigeon grades were first listed in 1914 and disc. during the war (1941). Reintroduced in 1948, they were disc. permanently in 1964, after which the Super Pigeon Grade became available only on a custom order basis from Winchester's Custom Gun Shop. These guns are worth 50-300% premiums depending on gauge, barrel lengths, stock options, engraving patterns, etc. With an attrition rate of 33%, Model 12s with rare features 50 years ago will only be much rarer today (and expensive). 28 ga. guns were built between 1934 and 1960. Gauge rarity in increasing order is 12 ga, 16 ga, 20 ga, .410 (Model 42), and 28 ga. Serialization breakdown by year of manufacture is provided under the "Model Serialization" section of this book. When collecting Model 12s, ser. no.'s on the underside of receiver (forward end), should match ser. no. on bottom rear of Mag. tube. Stainless steel barrel Model 12s were mostly mfg. in the late 1920s - early 1930s (65X,XXX serial range). Values typically range between $1,000-$2,500.

"Y" prefix appears on Model 12s built 1964-1980 — see listing under Post-64 Models.

Grading	100%	98%	95%	90%	80%	70%	60%

MODEL 12 FEATHERWEIGHT — similar to Standard, with alloy guard. Mfg. 1959-1962. "F" suffix after ser. no.

	100%	98%	95%	90%	80%	70%	60%
	$495	$425	$365	$320	$275	$250	$200

MODEL 12 RIOT GUNS — see the "Trench/Riot Shotgun" category in the T section for more information and prices.

MODEL 12 MILITARY TRENCH GUNS — see the "Trench/Riot Shotgun" category in the T section for more information and prices.

MODEL 12 HEAVY DUCK GUN — 12 ga., 3 in. chamber, 30 or 32 in. barrel, solid rubber recoil pad, $\frac{1}{2}$ in. shorter pull than regular Model 12. Mfg. 1935-1963.

	100%	98%	95%	90%	80%	70%	60%
	$675	$525	$450	$400	$350	$325	$300

Add 25% for solid rib.

✷ **Vent. rib** — 2 different styles mfg. by Simmons, notice barrel proof marking - rare.
Add 15% for 32 in. barrel.

MODEL 12 SKEET GUN — 12, 16, 20, or 28 ga., 26 in. barrel, skeet choke, checkered pistol grip stock, pre-WWII. Mfg. 1933-1976.

	100%	98%	95%	90%	80%	70%	60%
	$695	$625	$550	$500	$450	$400	$350

Add 15% for solid rib.
Add 25% for Win. Special VR.
Add 30% for Win. milled VR.
Factory-Cuts compensator — subtract 50%.
16 gauge — rarity will command a premium.
Add 40% for 20 ga.
Add 400% for 28 ga.

MODEL 12 TRAP GUN — various ga.'s, full choke barrel, deluxe trap styled stock, solid recoil pad. Mfg. 1938-1964.

	100%	98%	95%	90%	80%	70%	60%
	$895	$795	$695	$650	$500	$435	$400

Add $100 for white or brown plastic Hydrocoil stock. While plain barrelled variation is rare, it is not as desirable.

MODEL 12 PIGEON GRADE — finer and more deluxe version of Model 12, many variations. Mfg. 1914-1941 and 1948-1964, usually with engraved pigeon on bottom rear of mag. tube. Add $500 or more if N.I.B.

	100%	98%	95%	90%	80%	70%	60%
	$1,900	$1,500	$1,175	$850	$800	$775	$700

Add 15%-20% for VR.
Add 100% for 20 or 28 ga.
Above values are for 12 ga. - smaller gauges with desirable features will command healthy premiums.

MODEL 20 — .410 bore, hammer, boxlock, 26 in. full choke, 6 pounds. Mfg. 23,616 between 1919-1924.

	100%	98%	95%	90%	80%	70%	60%
	$400	$300	$250	$175	$140	$110	$85

✷ **Winchester Junior Trap Shooting Outfit** — includes shotgun, midget hand trap, 150 .410 ga. shells, 100 clay targets and accessories, cased.

	100%	98%	95%	90%	80%	70%	60%
	$1,000	$900	$800	$700	$600	$500	$450

MODEL 21

Approx. 32,000 mfg. since 1931. Approx. 2,000 mfg. in Custom Grade to date.

The Winchester Model 21 is a boxlock side by side double barrelled shotgun. After years in the design stage, production began in 1929 with guns being shipped to the warehouse in 1930 and first offered in Winchester's 1931 price list. Regular production continued for thirty years, through 1959.

The early guns were plain, standard 12 gauge models with double triggers and extractors. Later in 1931, 16 and 20 gauge chamberings became available as did selective single triggers and automatic ejectors.

By the end of 1933 the Model 21 skeet gun had been introduced as had Tournament, Trap and Custom Built grades. By about this time options included fancier wood, beavertail or semi-beavertail fore-ends, checkered butts (standard on skeet guns) or skeleton steel butt plates, recoil pads and almost any variation the customers might desire. Metal finishes on a Model 21 are unusual in that they have salt blued frames and rust blued barrels — this explains the difference in coloration between these metal surfaces.

The Tournament Grade was dropped in 1936 and the Trap Grade in 1940. A Standard Grade Trap Gun was added in 1941. The early Custom Built Grade was dropped in 1942 and the Deluxe Grade was added. This grade included as standard many of the previously available extra cost options.

Relatively few guns were produced in chamberings smaller than 20 gauge. 28 gauge first appeared in the 1936 catalog, although a few were probably produced before that. Winchester records are unclear as to the total but it is generally believed that fewer than 100 original factory guns were made. In addition, a number of original 20 gauge guns have been modified at the factory or elsewhere with factory 28 gauge barrels. These latter guns are just as valuable if the conversion was done at the Winchester Custom Gun Shop. Authenticity of the original guns should be established by factory letter.

.410 bore guns were first listed in 1955 but again some had been produced earlier, one having been built for John Olin in 1950. Throughout Winchester history all the rules seem to have had exceptions and nowhere is this more apparent than with respect to the Model 21 which, after all, has been pretty much a custom gun from the very beginning. Factory records and tallies among dealers indicate the existence of from 40 to 50 original factory guns. As in the case of the 28 gauge, extra barrels were available and at least some of those have been added to original 20 gauge guns.

The 3 inch Magnum 12 gauge Duck gun (stamped "Duck" on floor plate) was offered in Winchester catalogs from 1940 through 1952. Selective single triggers and automatic ejectors were standard as were the solid red Winchester recoil pads and 30 in. or 32 in. barrels. Some cases of non-factory upgrading of 2¾ or 3 inch Magnum guns have been reported. If authenticity is important to the buyer, a factory letter should be requested.

With respect to such letters, in cases where records may be missing or incomplete, the resultant letters may be less conclusive than desired. In some instances, consultation with, or a written appraisal from an authoritative collector arms dealer might be helpful.

Six standard patterns of engraving and several stock checkering and carving styles evolved during the production years. Values added by these and other embellishments such as precious metal inlays are beyond the scope of this work.

The following retail prices are for a standard field gun with average wood, beavertail forearm, ejectors, and single selective trigger with no alterations.

Grading	100%	98%	95%	90%	80%	70%	60%
12 ga.							
	$3,250	$3,000	$2,700	$2,450	$2,250	$2,000	$1,800
16 ga.							
	$3,850	$3,350	$3,000	$2,700	$2,500	$2,250	$2,100
20 ga.							
	$4,850	$4,400	$4,050	$3,700	$3,400	$3,200	$3,000

Add $400-$550 for VR.
Double triggers w/extractors — deduct approx. 50%.
If double triggers with ejectors, subtract 10%-20%. Normally DT, extractor guns have splinter forearms.

⚜ **Skeet Gun** — available in Standard, Tournament, and Trap grades. Introduced 1933. Add 20-50% depending on grade.

⚜ **Trap Gun** — introduced 1940, Trap Grade disc. same year, unaltered specimens will bring premium — add 10-25%.

⚜ **3 Inch Duck Gun** — introduced 1940, must be so stamped (observe the 3 in. marking very carefully — no premium exists for this variation.

As can be seen, values are partly based on a certain interdependence between options. Higher grade guns, of course, will bring somewhat higher prices although much of their increased value results from many "options" being included as standard features.

Buyers or sellers with limited experience should always seek expert advice or appraisals in dealing with a Model 21. This is especially true with regard to higher grade guns and those with extra ornamentation.

.410 BORE:

Retail prices for original guns may be expected to range between $25,000 and $45,000 for mechanically sound guns depending on quality of finish. These prices take into consideration the reported sale of a plain standard gun in recent years for $37,000. Non-original guns with add-on factory barrels would probably be reduced by one-third.

28 GAUGE:

Factory original guns will probably bring from $11,500 to $17,000 and, as with the 410s, 20 gauge guns modified to 28 gauge with factory barrels would be worth approx. the same if done at the factory.

Refinishing or Restoration: There is disagreement as to the effects of refinishing a Model 21. Many shooters and at least some collectors prefer a well refinished gun to a badly worn one. Higher grade guns restored by a master craftsman may approach factory original guns in value.

Grading	100%	98%	95%	90%	80%	70%	60%

MODEL 21: RECENT MFG. — since 1960 Model 21 production has been limited to high grade, built from special order, U. S. Repeating Arms currently offers the Model 21 in 12, 16 or 20 ga. U.S.R.A. has disc. the mfg. of the Model 21 since 1988 as their Custom Gun Shop is backordered on many other projects. Values below reflect 1989 information. It is important to note that while advertised, U.S. Repeating Arms has not taken an order for approximately 3 years on any Model 21 Winchester.

Standard Custom guns (12 ga.) are currently trading in the $6,500 - $7,000 range if NIB.

⚜ **Custom Built** — standard model with no engraving.
Mfg.'s Sug. Retail $8,100 $8,100 $5,000 $3,750

⚜ **Custom Grade** — includes No. 6 engraved reciever and VR.
Mfg.'s Sug. Retail $11,080 $11,080 $7,250 $5,500

⚜ **Grand American Grade** — includes 2 sets of barrels with forearms, No. 6 engraved with gold inlays, cased.
Mfg.'s Sug. Retail $22,745 $22,745 $15,000 $11,500

⚜ **Grand American Small Gauge** — 28 or .410 ga.
Mfg.'s Sug. Retail $34,460 $34,460 $25,000 $17,500
Add 10% for 28/.410 ga. combo.

MODEL 24 DOUBLE-BARREL — 12, 16, or 20 ga., boxlock, hammerless, double triggers. Introduced 1940, disc. 1957 after approx. 116,280 mfg.

	$495	$425	$350	$300	$250	$200	$150

Add 20% for 20 ga.

MODEL 25 SLIDE ACTION — 12 ga. only, non-takedown version of the Model 12, 26 or 28 in. barrel. 87,937 mfg. between 1949-1954.

	$375	$295	$240	$215	$185	$160	$135

WINCHESTER. cont.

Grading	100%	98%	95%	90%	80%	70%	60%

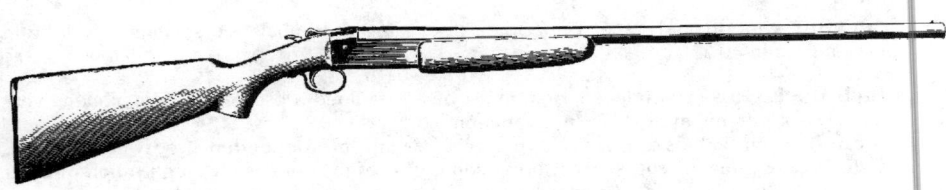

MODEL 37 SINGLE-SHOT — 12, 16, 20, 28 or .410 ga., .410 bore, top-lever break-open action. Not serial-numbered. Over 1,015,000 mfg. between 1936-1963.

	100%	98%	95%	90%	80%	70%	60%
12 gauge	$175	$145	$125	$100	$85	$75	$55
16 gauge	$175	$145	$125	$100	$85	$75	$55
20 gauge	$200	$150	$125	$105	$85	$75	$55
28 gauge	$875	$775	$650	$550	$450	$350	$250
.410 gauge	$250	$200	$175	$125	$95	$85	$75

"Red Letter" models will bring 10%+ premiums. Subtract 10-15% for post-64 models. Plain 28 ga. is most desirable since there are more "Red Letter" 28s than regular models.

MODEL 40 SEMI-AUTO — 12 ga. only, long recoil action, 28 or 30 in. barrel, walnut stock, skeet model also, poorly designed, many recalled by Winchester. Approx. 12,000 mfg. 1940-1941.

	100%	98%	95%	90%	80%	70%	60%
	$525	$450	$400	$350	$250	$200	$150

MODEL 41 BOLT ACTION — .410 ga., 2½ in. chamber until 1933 when it changed to 3 in., bolt action, single shot, 24 in. round barrel bored F, one-piece plain walnut stock and forearm, not serialized, approx. 22,145 were mfg. 1920-1934.

	100%	98%	95%	90%	80%	70%	60%
	N/A	N/A	$525	$450	$350	$250	$200

This model is rarely encountered with over 80% original condition.

MODEL 42 SLIDE ACTION — the first pump specifically made for the .410 ga., hammerless, 2½ (introduced 1935) or 3 in. chamber, 26 or 28 in. barrel, plain walnut pistol grip stock with circular grooved forearm (modified 1947). Approx. 160,000 mfg. between 1933-1963.

Special order features on field guns have captured much collector interest in recent years. Combinations of these features can add a considerable percentage to the base values listed below. Rare special orders on rare variations are very desirable and prices can double and more if the combination is right.

⧣ **Standard Grade**

	100%	98%	95%	90%	80%	70%	60%
	$900	$800	$700	$625	$550	$500	$450

Add 55% for solid rib.
Add 65% for Win. special VR.

⧣ **Skeet or Trap Grade** — has solid matted rib, fancy wood.

	100%	98%	95%	90%	80%	70%	60%
	$1,650	$1,450	$1,350	$1,100	$1,000	$900	$800

⧣ **Deluxe Grade** — fanciest grade, value is affected by wood and finish. Factory special orders can bring prices up to $10,000.

	100%	98%	95%	90%	80%	70%	60%
	$1,850	$1,650	$1,600	$1,500	$1,400	$1,200	$1,000

MODEL 42 HIGH GRADE LIMITED EDITION — .410 ga., 26 in. full choke VR barrel, features Grade V-VI wood with special scroll and gold border engraving, 850 mfg. beginning 1993.

	Mfg.'s Sug. Retail						
Mfg.'s Sug. Retail	$1,617		$1,400	$1,100	$895		

Grading	100%	98%	95%	90%	80%	70%	60%

MODEL 50 SEMI-AUTO — 12 or 20 ga., 3 shot, recoil-operated (non-recoiling barrel), 26-30 in. barrels, VR optional, feather weight model introduced 1958, all steel construction. Over 196,000 mfg. between 1954-1961, starting with serial number 1,000.

	$425	$360	$295	$280	$265	$240	$220

Add $50 for VR (Simmons installed).
Add $50 for 20 ga.
Add 15% for Trap & Skeet Model.
Add 200%-350% for Pigeon Grade.

MODEL 59 SEMI-AUTO — 12 ga. only, 3 shot, short recoil operation, Win-lite (steel and fiberglass) ribless barrels, 26-30 in. barrel lengths, alloy receiver inscribed with hunting scenes, Versalite (first interchangeable choke tubes) option introduced 1961, $6\frac{1}{2}$ lbs. 82,085 mfg. between 1960-1965.

	$450	$400	$335	$275	$225	$200	$165

Inspect carefully for either cracked receiver (by bolt handle cutout), or separating fiberglass on end of barrel.

✱ **Pigeon Grade** — mfg. 1962-1965, add 200-350% (rare).
Winchester also mfg. 20 and 14 ga.'s experimentally in this model, extremely rare and expensive.

SHOTGUNS: POST-1964

MODEL 370 SINGLE BARREL — 12, 16, 20, 28 or .410 ga., 28-32 in. full choke plain barrel, replaced the Model 37, top lever break open, exposed hammer, plain pistol grip stock. Approx. 221,578 mfg. between 1968-1973.

	$120	$100	$90	$85	$80	$75	$70

Add 20-60%+ for .28 ga. and .410 ga.
The Model 370 was mfg. in Winchester's Canadian plant in Cobourg, Ontario.

MODEL 370 YOUTH — similar to 370, with 26 in. barrel, $12\frac{1}{2}$ in. stock, with recoil pad.

	$145	$110	$95	$85	$80	$75	$70

MODEL 37A SINGLE BARREL — replaced the Model 370, roll engraved receiver, gold trigger. Approx. 391,168 mfg. between 1973-1980 in the Winchester plant in Cobourg, Ontario.

	$140	$110	$95	$85	$75	$65	$55

Add 10% for 36 in. goose barrel.
Add 30% for 28 ga. and 60% for .410 ga.

MODEL 37A YOUTH — similar to 37A, except 20 or .410 ga. with $12\frac{1}{2}$ in. pull stock.

	$175	$145	$100	$85	$70	$55	$40

MODEL 12 SUPER PIGEON GRADE — 12 ga., slide action, 26, 28, or 30 in. barrel, VR, any choke, hand honed action, engine turned breech block and loading flap, "B" checkering and No. 5 engraving, custom order grade walnut stock. Limited production between 1964-1972.

	$2,995	$2,500	$2,250	$2,100	$1,750	$1,500	$1,300

An additional 380 Super Pigeon Grades were mfg. 1984-85.

MODEL 12 FIELD GRADE — 12 ga., slide action, 26, 28, or 30 in. VR barrel, various chokes, jeweled bolt, hand checkered, checkered select walnut stock. Mfg. 1972-1976, "Y" Serial No. Prefix.

	$675	$550	$525	$495	$450	$400	$350

In 1984, Y series Model 12s were once again available through a private contract with U.S.R.A. Co. which included engraving on Grades 1A-1C, and 2-5. These guns were available in either Field, Trap, or Skeet configurations. Since there was no manufacturer's suggested retail, Model 12 values shown below are established by analyzing the sales of the two private contractors - no more of these variations are available.

≒ **Grades 1-A, 1-B, & 1-C** — light engraving depicting dogs or ducks. Disc.

	100%	98%	95%	90%	80%	70%	60%
	$1,300	$1,195	$1,000	$875	$785	$695	$600

Last Mfg.'s Sug. Retail was $1,375.

≒ **Grades 2 & 3** — engraving features large duck and dog game scenes on receiver flats. Disc.

	$1,600	$1,495	$1,295	$1,075	$950	$830	$725

Last Mfg.'s Sug. Retail was $1,695.

≒ **Grade 4** — more elaborate game scene engraving than Grades 2 & 3. Disc.

	$1,850	$1,695	$1,450	$1,225	$1,075	$950	$850

Last Mfg.'s Sug. Retail was $1,995.

≒ **Grade 5** — elaborate game scene engraving with style B checkering. Disc.

	$2,195	$1,995	$1,725	$1,500	$1,225	$1,095	$950

Also available with gold inlays - add $1,000 to values shown above. Last Mfg.'s Sug. Retail was $2,450.

≒ **3 Barrel Set** — grade 5 engraving with gold inlays and two extra barrels. Disc.

	$5,500	$4,995	$4,350	$3,750	$3,325	$2,750	$2,300

Last Mfg.'s Sug. Retail was $6,000.

MODEL 12 SKEET GRADE — similar to Field Grade, with 26 in. VR skeet bore barrel, skeet style stock, with recoil pad. Mfg. 1972-1975.

	$825	$750	$625	$550	$495	$450	$425

See listings under Model 12 Field Grade for engraved values.

MODEL 12 TRAP GRADE — similar to Field grade, with 30 in. VR full choke barrel, trap style stock, straight or Monte Carlo, recoil pad. Mfg. 1972-1980.

	$750	$675	$575	$525	$495	$450	$425

See listings under Model 12 Field Grade for engraved values.

MODEL 12 DU — limited mfg. for Ducks Unlimited Chapters.

	$1,200	$995	$825				

MODEL 12 LIMITED EDITION GRADE I — 20 ga. only, 26 in. VR barrel, exact reproduction of the original Model 12, Grade I wood with no engraving, 4,000 mfg. beginning 1993.

Mfg.'s Sug. Retail	$879		$795	$625	$495		

MODEL 12 LIMITED EDITION GRADE IV — similar to Limited Edition Grade I, except has Grade II-III wood and special Model 12 Grade IV engraving, 1,000 mfg. beginning 1993.

Mfg.'s Sug. Retail	$1,431		$1,200	$950	$750		

MODEL 1200 SLIDE ACTION FIELD GRADE — 12, 16, or 20 ga., 26, 28, or 30 in. barrel, alloy receiver, various chokes, checkered pistol grip stock, pad. Mfg. 1964-1981.

	100%	98%	95%	90%	80%	70%	60%
	$220	$200	$180	$165	$140	$110	$100
Vent. rib	$240	$220	$205	$195	$165	$140	$110
Winchoke	$260	$240	$215	$200	$190	$180	$160

Add 33% for Hydro-coil recoil system.

MODEL 1200 MAGNUM — similar to 1200, chambered for 12 or 20 ga., 3 in. magnum shells. Mfg. 1964-1980.

	$230	$200	$175	$165	$140	$110	$100
Vent. rib	$275	$225	$200	$185	$150	$140	$110

Grading	100%	98%	95%	90%	80%	70%	60%

MODEL 1200 SKEET GUN — similar to 1200, 12 or 20 ga., 26 in. VR barrel, skeet bore, 2 shot mag. and select style stock. Mfg. 1965-1974.

	100%	98%	95%	90%	80%	70%	60%
	$300	$275	$250	$220	$195	$165	$140

MODEL 1200 TRAP GUN — similar to 1200, with 12 ga., VR, 30 in. full choke barrel, select trap style stock. Mfg. 1965-1974.

	100%	98%	95%	90%	80%	70%	60%
	$300	$275	$250	$220	$195	$165	$140
Winchoke	$360	$330	$305	$275	$250	$220	$165

MODEL 1200 DEER GUN — similar to 1200, with 22 in. barrel, rifle sights, 12 ga. only. Mfg. 1965-1974.

	100%	98%	95%	90%	80%	70%	60%
	$220	$195	$165	$140	$110	$100	$85

MODEL 1200 POLICE STAINLESS — 12 ga. only, 18 in. barrel, 7 shot mag. Disc.

	100%	98%	95%
	$275	$225	$195

MODEL 1200 DEFENDER — 12 ga. only, 18 in. cylinder bore barrel, 7 shot mag., 6 lbs. Disc.

	100%	98%	95%	90%	80%	70%	60%
	$275	$225	$195	$170	$155	$140	$125

MODEL 1300 FEATHERWEIGHT SLIDE ACTION — 12 or 20 ga., 3 in. chamber, takedown, 26 (new 1991) or 28 in. barrel, 5 shot, plain or VR. (became standard 1990), Winchoke tubes, checkered walnut stock and grooved forearm, alloy frame, recoil pad, $6\frac{3}{4}$ - $7\frac{1}{8}$ lbs. Mfg. 1978-present.

Mfg.'s Sug. Retail	$374	$300	$260	$230	$195	$175	$160	$145

Subtract $30 without VR.

This model had an "XTR" suffix until 1989. Older Model 1300 Featherweights had roll-engraving but no premiums are being asked at this time.

MODEL 1300 CUSTOM HIGH GRADE — while advertised, this model was never mfg. Advertised retail was $1,395.

MODEL 1300 WATERFOWL — 12 ga. only, 3 in. chamber, 28 or 30 (disc.) in. VR barrel, matte finished metal, choice of low luster walnut finish or brown Win-Tuff wood, recoil pad, includes camo sling and swivels, Winchokes standard, 7 lbs. Mfg. 1984-91.

	100%	98%	95%	90%	80%	70%	60%
	$295	$260	$235	$200	$180	$165	$150

Last Mfg.'s Sug. Retail was $367.

MODEL 1300 TURKEY GUN — 12 ga. only, 3 in. chamber, 22 in. VR barrel, Winchoked, walnut stock and forearm with low luster finish, metal surfaces have matte finish, supplied with camouflaged fabric sling, $6\frac{3}{8}$ lbs. Mfg. 1985-1988 only.

	100%	98%	95%	90%	80%	70%	60%
	$290	$265	$235	$200	$180	$165	$150

Last Mfg.'s Sug. Retail was $348.

Model 1300 Win-Cam Turkey Gun — similar to Model 1300 Turkey Gun, except has greenish laminated hardwood stock and forearm. New 1987.

Mfg.'s Sug. Retail	$435	$350	$295	$250	$200	$180	$165	$150

Model 1300 Ladies-Youth Win-Cam Turkey Gun — 20 ga. only, 3 in. chamber, 22 in. VR barrel, green camo laminate shortened stock and forearm, includes sling and National Wild Turkey Federation engraving, 6 lbs. Mfg. 1992 only.

	100%	98%	95%	90%	80%	70%	60%
	$340	$295	$250	$200	$180	$165	$150

Last Mfg.'s Sug. Retail was $411.

Grading	100%	98%	95%	90%	80%	70%	60%

Model 1300 Win-Cam NWTF Series I-IV — 12 or 20 ga., Series I was released 1989 (12 ga. only) and included special receiver engraving featuring National Wild Turkey Federation motifs, Series II was released 1990 with a choice of either 12 (disc.) or 20 ga. Ladies/Youth model, Series III was released 1991-92, Series IV was released 1993.

Mfg.'s Sug. Retail $458	$365	$300	$250	$200	$180	$165	$150

MODEL 1300 COMBO PACK WIN-CAM — 12 ga., supplied with 22 and 30 in. VR non-glare finished barrels, greenish laminated hardwood stock and forearm, camo sling, matte finished metal. Mfg. 1987-1988 only.

$360	$320	$290	$260	$230	$200	$185

Last Mfg.'s Sug. Retail was $425.

MODEL 1300 LADIES-YOUTH — 20 ga. only, 3 in. chamber, 22 in. VR barrel, shortened stock dimensions, walnut stock with recoil pad and rear positioned, grooved forearm, 61/4 lbs. Mfg. 1992 only.

$315	$260	$220	$180	$165	$150	$135

Last Mfg.'s Sug. Retail was $355.

MODEL 1300 SLUG HUNTER — 12 ga. only, 3 in. chamber, 22 in. rifled or smooth bore barrel with iron sights, checkered stock and forearm, satin walnut finish or brown laminate stock (Win-Tuff). Supplied with camo fabric sling and rings and bases. New 1988.

Mfg.'s Sug. Retail $445	$360	$300	$250	$200	$180	$165	$150

Add $10 for smooth bore barrel with Sabot rifled tubes (disc. 1992).
Add $4 for "Whitetails Unlimited" Model (new 1991).

MODEL 1300 RANGER SLIDE ACTION — 12 or 20 ga., 3 in. chamber, 24⅛ (disc. deer barrel), 26 (new 1991), 28 or 30 (disc. 1992) in. plain or VR barrel, walnut finished hardwood stock, alloy receiver. New 1983.

Mfg.'s Sug. Retail $294	$235	$180	$150	$135	$120	$110	$95

Subtract $20 without VR or Winchokes.
Add $51 for 22 in. cyl. bore deer barrel.
Add $39 for 22 in. rifled bore deer barrel.
This model is also available in a deer combination package which includes a deer and regular Winchoke barrel in either 12 or 20 ga. — add approx. 20% to values listed above.

Ranger Youth Model — 20 ga. only, 3 in. chamber, 22 in. VR barrel, youth stock dimensions - 13 in. length of pull and rearward positioned forearm.

Mfg.'s Sug. Retail $312	$250	$200	$170	$150	$125	$110	$100

Subtract $35 if without Winchoke and VR.

MODEL 1300 DEFENDER — 12 or 20 ga., 3 in. chamber, available in Police (disc. 1989), Marine, and Defender variations, 18 in. cyl. bore barrel, 5, 7 (disc), or 8 shot mag., wood (high gloss), synthetic (matte finish), or pistol grip (matte finish) stock, 5½- 7 lbs.

Mfg.'s Sug. Retail $270	$220	$185	$150

Add $101 for Combo Package (includes extra 28 in. VR barrel).

Stainless Marine Defender — a new Sandstrom 9A phosphate coating was released late 1989 to give long lasting corrosion protection to all receiver and internal working parts, 7 shot mag., synthetic pistol grip or stock configuration, 6 - 7 lbs.

Mfg.'s Sug. Retail $436	$380	$330	$250

MODEL 1400 SEMI-AUTO — 12, 16, or 20 ga., 26, 28, or 30 in. barrels, alloy receiver, various chokes, gas operated, checkered pistol grip stock. Mfg. 1964-1981.

$275	$250	$220	$200	$175	$155	$140
Vent. rib $315	$265	$240	$220	$195	$165	$150

Add 33% for Hydro-coil recoil system.

Grading	100%	98%	95%	90%	80%	70%	60%

NEW MODEL 1400 WALNUT SEMI-AUTO — 12 or 20 ga., 2¾ in. chamber, 22 (disc.), 26 (new 1991), or 28 (12 ga. only) in. VR barrel, checkered walnut stock and forearm, Winchokes standard, 3 shot mag., rotary bolt system, 7-7½ lbs. New 1989.

Mfg.'s Sug. Retail $407 $340 $285 $260 $240 $220 $190 $165
Add $15 for limited mfg. 1993 Quail Unlimited Model (2,500 mfg. 1993).

MODEL 1400 CUSTOM HIGH GRADE — 12 ga. only, 28 in. VR Winchoke barrel, special order only through the Custom Gun Shop, features deluxe hand checkered walnut and special engraving. Mfg. 1991-1992.

$1,295 $995 $750

Last Mfg.'s Sug. Retail was $1,695.

MODEL 1400 SKEET GRADE — similar to 1400, 12 or 20 ga., with 26 in. VR barrel, skeet bore, select skeet style stock. Mfg. 1965-1973.

$360 $330 $305 $275 $220 $195 $165

MODEL 1400 TRAP GRADE — similar to 1400, with 30 in. full choke VR barrel, select trap style stock. Mfg. 1965-1973.

$360 $330 $305 $275 $220 $195 $165

MODEL 1400 DEER GUN — similar to 1400, with 22 in. barrel, rifle sights, 12 ga. only. Mfg. 1965-1974.

$265 $240 $220 $200 $175 $165 $140

Note: In 1968 the model 1400 series was modified. The action release was improved and the checkering redesigned. From 1968-1972, they were designated MKII, which was then dropped. The values for the later guns mfg. from 1968-1973 may run approx. 10% higher - values shown are for guns mfg. from 1965-1968.

MODEL 1400 SLUG HUNTER — 12 ga. only, 22 in. smooth bore cyl. or rifled Sabot choke-tubed barrel, drilled and tapped for scope, includes bases or iron sights, 7¼ lbs. Mfg. 1990-92.

$355 $310 $270 $250 $225 $195 $165

Last Mfg.'s Sug. Retail was $420.

MODEL 1500 XTR SEMI-AUTO — 12 or 20 ga., 2¾ inch only, 28 inch barrel, plain or VR, Winchoke tubes, gas operation. Mfg. 1978-1982.

$300 $260 $240 $220 $200 $180 $160

MODEL 1400 RANGER SEMI-AUTO — 12 or 20 ga., gas operation, alloy receiver, 22 cyl. deer, 26 (new 1991), or 28 in. Winchoke barrel, checkered walnut finished hardwood stock and forearm, VR became standard 1985, 7¼ lbs.

Mfg.'s Sug. Retail $367 $280 $230 $200 $180 $160 $140 $120
Add $56 for deer comb. (includes extra 22 in. cyl. bore barrel).
Subtract $30 without VR.

SUPER X MODEL 1 SEMI-AUTO — 12 ga., 26, 28, or 30 in. VR barrel, various chokes, steel receiver, gas operated - self compensating, checkered pistol grip stock and forearm. Mfg. 1974-1981.

$425 $365 $345 $315 $295 $275 $240

SUPER X MODEL 1 SKEET — similar to Standard, with 26 in. skeet bore barrel, select skeet style stock. Mfg. 1974-1981.

$550 $500 $475 $450 $425 $400 $350

Grading	100%	98%	95%	90%	80%	70%	60%

SUPER X MODEL 1 TRAP — similar to Standard, with 30 in. barrel, imp. mod. or full choke, select trap style stock.

	100%	98%	95%	90%	80%	70%	60%
	$475	$425	$400	$385	$330	$305	$275

SUPER X MODEL 1 CUSTOM TRAP OR SKEET — 12 ga. only, limited production from the Custom Shop, deluxe checkered walnut stock and forearm, extensive scroll engraving on receiver, built to custom order. Limited mfg. 1987-1992.

	100%	98%	95%
	$1,100	$850	$650

Add $700 for factory gold inlays (8 flying ducks).
Last Mfg.'s Sug. Retail was $1,295.

SHOTGUNS: RECENT MFG. OVER AND UNDER

Model 101 dates of manufacture and serialization data can be found in the SERIALIZATION section in the back of this text.

In November of 1987 Olin/Winchester disc. the Model 101. Classic Doubles (listed separately in this text) is now importing this model under their own trademark. With the discontinuance of the Model 101 and its many variations, both dealers and collectors have created a lot more demand for this model recently. As a result, prices have escalated and the scramble is on to try and pick off those rare and desirable variations. Since there have been a lot of limited editions and production changes in the 101 O/U series, it could very well be that this model might become very collectible in upcoming years (as in look what happened to the Model 12).

MODEL 101 FIELD GRADE O/U — 12, 20, or .410 ga., 26, 28, or 30 in. barrels, various chokes, boxlock, auto ejectors, SST, engraved receiver, checkered American walnut pistol grip stock. Mfg. 1963-1987. Values below assume Winchokes (standard since 1983) - subtract $60 if without.

Older production — checkered walnut stock and forearm, ejectors, SST, blued metal with light engraving on receiver.

	100%	98%	95%	90%	80%	70%	60%
	$750	$695	$650	$620	$585	$550	$500

Add 40% for 28 ga. or .410 ga.

Field Special — 12 or 20 ga., 3 in. chambers, VR, 27 in. barrels with Winchokes, blued receiver with scroll engraving ejectors, 7 lbs. Disc. 1987.

	100%	98%	95%	90%	80%	70%	60%
	$995	$840	$775	$695	$600	$500	$450

Last Mfg.'s Sug. Retail was $1,185.

Lightweight Field — 12 or 20 ga., similar to regular Field Grade, except has coin finished receiver, vent. barrels, and solid rubber recoil pad, 6½ - 7 lbs. Disc. 1987.

	100%	98%	95%	90%	80%	70%	60%
	$1,285	$1,030	$965	$895	$800	$700	$600

Last Mfg.'s Sug. Retail was $1,425.

Waterfowl Model — 12 ga. only, 3 in. chambers, 30 or 32(disc.) in. Winchoked barrels, VR, matte blued receiver with moderate engraving, low gloss walnut stock with vent. recoil pad, 7 ¾ lbs. Disc. 1987.

	100%	98%	95%	90%	80%	70%	60%
	$1,410	$1,175	$995	$895	$800	$700	$600

Last Mfg.'s Sug. Retail was $1,570.

Model 101 Field Grade 2 Barrel Hunting Set — 12 or 20 ga. barrels, both with Winchokes, 26 in. barrels - 20 ga., 28 in. barrels - 12 ga., scroll engraved, blued receiver with game scene engraving and borders, cased. Mfg. 1984-1987.

	100%	98%	95%	90%	80%	70%	60%
	$2,020	$1,825	$1,550	$1,375	$1,220	$1,050	$975

Last Mfg.'s Sug. Retail was $2,345.

Grading	100%	98%	95%	90%	80%	70%	60%

Quail Special — 12, 20 (disc.1984), 28 (new 1987) or .410 (new 1987) ga., 25½ in. Winchoke barrels, 6¾ lbs. - 12 ga., straight grip stock, vent. barrels and rib, coin finished receiver with game scene engraving, 500 of each ga. were mfg. Imported 1984-1986.

| | $1,695 | $1,475 | $1,245 | $1,100 | $1,000 | $900 | $825 |

Add 15% for 28 or .410 ga.
Last Mfg.'s Sug. Retail was $1,950.

National Wild Turkey Federation Commemorative — features golden turkeys on receiver sides, 27 in. VR barrels with choke tubes, only 300 mfg.

| | $1,350 | $1,100 | $950 |

Original issue price was $1,950.

American Flyer Live Bird — 12 ga. only, 28 or 29½ (new 1988) in. separated barrels with special competition VR, blued frame with gold wire borders and pigeon inlay, 8 - 8½ lbs. Imported 1987 only.

| | $2,595 | $2,275 | $1,950 | $1,775 | $1,600 | $1,425 | $1,300 |

Add $925 for Combo Model (extra set of 29½ in. barrels - 45 mfg.).
Add $265 for 29½ in. barrel with WT4 choke tubes.
Approx. 200 of this model were mfg.
Last Mfg.'s Sug. Retail was $2,910.

MODEL 101 MAGNUM O/U — similar to 101 Field, 12 or 20 ga., 3 in. Mag. chambering, recoil pad, 30 in. barrels, full and mod., or full and full choke. Mfg. 1966-1981.

| | $775 | $715 | $660 | $605 | $550 | $500 | $460 |

MODEL 101 SKEET GRADE — similar to 101 Field, with 26 in. skeet bored barrels, skeet style stock. Mfg. 1966-1984.

| | $1,000 | $825 | $770 | $700 | $650 | $595 | $540 |

MODEL 101 THREE GAUGE SKEET SET — similar to Skeet 101, with 20, 28, and .410 ga. barrels, cased. Mfg. 1974-1984.

| | $3,750 | $3,250 | $2,750 | $2,300 | $2,000 | $1,850 | $1,700 |

MODEL 101 TRAP GRADE — 12 ga. only, 30 or 32 in. barrels with normal or wide VR, imp. mod. and full or full and full choke, trap style stock. Mfg. 1966-1984.

| | $1,320 | $1,100 | $935 | $825 | $715 | $660 | $605 |

MODEL 101 SINGLE BARREL TRAP — similar to O/U Trap, with 32 or 34 in. full choke barrel, Monte Carlo trap style stock. Mfg. 1967-1971.

| | $880 | $660 | $550 | $495 | $385 | $360 | $330 |

MODEL 101 XTR PIGEON GRADE — 12, 20, 28 or .410 (disc. 1986) ga.,barrels are vented, deluxe engraved silver receiver version of 101, select checkered wood. Mfg. 1974-1987.

Lightweight Field Model — lightweight variation, Winchokes standard, 6½ - 7 lbs. Disc. 1987.

| | $1,500 | $1,375 | $1,120 | $940 | $785 | $675 | $600 |

Last Mfg.'s Sug. Retail was $1,950.
Deduct 5% if without Winchokes (available in all gauges).

Lightweight two barrel set — includes 28 and .410 ga. 27 in. barrels, 28 ga. has Winchokes; .410 ga. has fixed M/F chokes. Disc. 1986.

| | $2,275 | $1,950 | $1,775 | $1,600 | $1,425 | $1,300 | $1,100 |

Last Mfg.'s Sug. Retail was $2,500.

WINCHESTER cont.

Grading	100%	98%	95%	90%	80%	70%	60%

Featherweight — 12 or 20 ga., English straight stock, $25\frac{1}{2}$ in. barrels bored IC/IM, $6\frac{1}{2}$ - $6\frac{3}{4}$ lbs. Disc. 1987.

	100%	98%	95%	90%	80%	70%	60%
	$1,325	$1,175	$975	$850	$750	$675	$600

Last Mfg.'s Sug. Retail was $1,580.

Skeet Grade — 12, 20, 28, or .410 ga.

	100%	98%	95%	90%	80%	70%	60%
	$1,275	$1,100	$995	$880	$770	$715	$660

Trap Grade — 12 ga. only, vent. barrels and rib, coin finish receiver with fine scroll engraving, engraved pigeon on floorplate, Winchoke standard, $8\frac{1}{4}$ lbs. Disc. 1985.

	100%	98%	95%	90%	80%	70%	60%
	$1,300	$1,180	$990	$880	$770	$715	$660

Last Mfg.'s Sug. Retail was $1,475.

Super Pigeon Grade — 12 ga. only, blued receiver with elaborate engraving including multiple gold inlays, extra select walnut with fleur-de-lis checkering on stock and forearm, Winchoke standard, $7\frac{1}{2}$ lbs. Imported 1985-1987 only.

	100%	98%	95%	90%	80%	70%	60%
	$4,025	$3,625	$3,225	$2,835	$2,500	$2,150	$1,920

Last Mfg.'s Sug. Retail was $4,590.

101 DIAMOND GRADE — Trap or Skeet O/U, 12 (Trap only), 20, 28, or .410 ga., vent. barrels and rib, Winchoke standard on Trap — add $75 on Skeet model (disc.1986), select hand checkered walnut, engraved satin-finish receiver. Trap model has extra high VR. Skeet model has raised rib and muzzle vents.

Standard Trap — 12 ga. only, 30 or 32 in. vent. barrels, $8\frac{3}{4}$ - 9 lbs. Disc. 1987.

	100%	98%	95%	90%	80%	70%	60%
	$1,620	$1,440	$1,230	$1,075	$900	$780	$640

Last Mfg.'s Sug. Retail was $1,860.

Unsingle Trap — 12 ga. only, lower single barrel, 32 or 34 in. barrel, extended rib. Add $60 for Winchoke. Disc. 1986.

	100%	98%	95%	90%	80%	70%	60%
	$1,575	$1,430	$1,200	$995	$895	$830	$740

Last Mfg.'s Sug. Retail was $1,760.

Oversingle Trap — 12 ga. only, Winchokes, 34 in. upper barrel only, $8\frac{1}{2}$ lbs. Imported 1986-1987 only.

	100%	98%	95%	90%	80%	70%	60%
	$1,985	$1,695	$1,545	$1,395	$1,200	$995	$895

Last Mfg.'s Sug. Retail was $2,145.

Oversingle Combo — includes one set of O/U barrels and an oversingle barrel, cased. Imported 1987 only.

	100%	98%	95%	90%	80%	70%	60%
	$3,075	$2,750	$2,525	$2,300	$2,000	$1,750	$1,625

Last Mfg.'s Sug. Retail was $3,550.

Trap Combo — 12 ga. only, includes a set of 30 or 32 in. vent. O/U barrels and a 32 or 34 in. high ribbed unsingle (lower) barrel, standard or Monte Carlo stock, approx. 9 lbs. Disc. 1987.

	100%	98%	95%	90%	80%	70%	60%
	$2,570	$2,320	$1,975	$1,800	$1,600	$1,400	$1,200

Add $275 for ATA Trap set.
Last Mfg.'s Sug. Retail was $2,940.

Standard Skeet — 12, 20, 28, or .410 ga., $27\frac{1}{2}$ in. vent. barrels and competition rib, $6\frac{1}{2}$ - $7\frac{1}{4}$ lbs. Disc. 1987.

	100%	98%	95%	90%	80%	70%	60%
	$1,650	$1,465	$1,240	$1,075	$900	$780	$640

Last Mfg.'s Sug. Retail was $1,950.

Grading	100%	98%	95%	90%	80%	70%	60%

⚑ **Four gauge Skeet set** — includes 12, 20, 28, and .410 ga. 27½ in. separated barrel assemblies, cased. Imported 1985-1987 only.

	100%	98%	95%	90%	80%	70%	60%
	$4,600	$3,975	$3,600	$3,200	$2,800	$2,500	$2,150

Last Mfg.'s Sug. Retail was $5,025.

⚑ **Sporting Clays Grade** — 12 ga. only, 28 or 30 in. barrels with Winchokes, designed for Sporting Clay competition. Disc. 1987.

	100%	98%	95%	90%	80%	70%	60%
	$1,675	$1,475	$1,230	$1,075	$900	$780	$640

Last Mfg.'s Sug. Retail was $1,965.

501 GRAND EUROPEAN — Trap or Skeet, 12 or 20 (Skeet only) ga., 27, 30, or 32 in. barrels, extra select hand checkered walnut with oil finish, Schnabel forearm, entensive scroll engraving on satin-finished receiver, vent. barrels and rib. Mfg. 1981-86.

	100%	98%	95%	90%	80%	70%	60%
	$1,520	$1,385	$1,200	$1,050	$900	$780	$640

Last Mfg.'s Sug. Retail was $1,720.

⚑ **Grand European Featherweight** — 20 ga. only, straight grip stock, 25½ in. VR barrels, 5¾ lbs. Disc. 1986.

	100%	98%	95%	90%	80%	70%	60%
	$1,520	$1,385	$1,200	$1,050	$900	$780	$640

Last Mfg.'s Sug. Retail was $1,720.

MODEL 5500 — 12 ga. only.

	100%	98%	95%	90%	80%	70%	60%
	$1,550	$1,390	$1,200	$1,050	$900	$780	$640

MODEL 6500 SPORTER — 12 ga. only.

	100%	98%	95%	90%	80%	70%	60%
	$1,850	$1,550	$1,390	$1,200	$1,050	$900	$780

PRESENTATION GRADE — 12 ga. only, available in both Trap and Skeet models, blued action-extensively engraved with gold inlays, special crotch walnut, 27 (Skeet) or 30 in. vent. barrels, hand checkered, gold lining on perimeter of receiver. Imported 1984-1987 only.

	100%	98%	95%	90%	80%	70%	60%
	$3,475	$2,850	$2,510	$2,280	$1,950	$1,800	$1,600

Last Mfg.'s Sug. Retail was $3,840.

SHOTGUN/RIFLE COMBINATION — combination 12 ga./.30-06 O/U, 25 in. barrels, top barrel is Winchoked, Grand European engraving and finish, 8½ lbs. Mfg. 1983-1985.

	100%	98%	95%	90%	80%	70%	60%
	$1,750	$1,495	$1,250	$1,125	$1,000	$875	$750

Also available in limited quantities in .222 Rem., .223 Rem., or 9.3 x 74R cal. Last Mfg.'s Sug. Retail was $2,550.

DOUBLE EXPRESS RIFLE — .30-06, 7x65R, 9.3x74R, .257 Roberts, or .270 Win. cal., 23½ in. O/U barrels, iron sights with claw scope mounts, ejectors, fully engraved satin finish receiver with game scene engraving, walnut specially hand checkered, sling swivels, 8½ lbs. Mfg. 1984-1985 only.

	100%	98%	95%	90%	80%	70%	60%
	$2,500	$2,150	$1,850	$1,650	$1,450	$1,300	$1,200

Last Mfg.'s Sug. Retail was $2,995.

MODEL 91 O/U — 12 ga. only, mfg. by Laurona in Spain for international sales including Europe, SST, ejectors optional, VR, distinguishable by black chrome finish on metal parts. Disc. Prices hard to evaluate because of limited importation domestically. In some regions they are bought as medium priced field guns, while in others they are sold as a rare Winchester O&U.

MODEL 96 XPERT O/U FIELD GRADE — similar action to Model 101, 12 or 20 ga., auto ejectors, SST, various barrel lengths and chokes, action similar to 101, no engraving, checkered pistol grip stock and forearm. Mfg. 1976-1982.

	100%	98%	95%	90%	80%	70%	60%
	$650	$575	$500	$450	$410	$370	$330

Grading	100%	98%	95%	90%	80%	70%	60%

MODEL 96 XPERT SKEET GRADE — similar to Field Grade, with 27 in. skeet barrels, skeet style stock. Mfg. 1976-1982.

	100%	98%	95%	90%	80%	70%	60%
	$700	$625	$550	$500	$450	$410	$370

MODEL 96 XPERT TRAP GRADE — similar to Field, 12 ga. only, 30 in. imp. mod. and full or full and full choke, trap style stock. Mfg. 1976-1982.

	$650	$575	$525	$470	$430	$395	$360

Note: Model 101 and Model 96 Xpert guns were made by Olin Kodensha located in Tochigi, Japan.

MODEL 1001 FIELD GRADE — 12 ga. only, boxlock action, 28 in. VR (8mm) barrel with WinPlus chokes, blued metal featuring 40% engraving coverage, Grade I stock and forearm, high lustre finish, mfg. in Italy by Marocchi beginning 1993.

Mfg.'s Sug. Retail	$1,099	$975	$795	$725	$650	$595	$550	$495

MODEL 1001 SPORTING CLAYS — 12 ga. only, 28 or 30 in. VR (10mm) barrel with WinPlus chokes, full engraving (includes scroll and flying W with clay bird), silver nitrate receiver with remaining parts blue, Grade II-III stock and forearm, satin finish, mfg. in Italy by Marocchi beginning 1993.

Mfg.'s Sug. Retail	$1,253	$1,075	$925	$795	$725	$650	$595	$550

SHOTGUNS: RECENT MFG. SIDE-BY-SIDE

MODEL 21: RECENT MFG. — since 1960 Model 21 production has been limited to high grade, built from special order, U. S. Repeating Arms currently offers the Model 21 in 12, 16 or 20 ga. U.S.R.A. has disc. the mfg. of the Model 21 temporarily beginning in 1990 as their Custom Gun Shop is backordered on many other projects. Model 21 production has ceased since 1988. Values below reflect 1988 information. Standard Custom guns (12 ga.) are currently trading in the $6,000 range if NIB.

⚐ **Custom Built** — standard model with no engraving.

Mfg.'s Sug. Retail	$8,100	$8,100	$5,000	$3,750

⚐ **Custom Grade** — includes No. 6 engraved receiver and VR.

Mfg.'s Sug. Retail	$11,080	$11,080	$7,250	$5,500

⚐ **Grand American Grade** — includes 2 sets of barrels with forearms, No. 6 engraved with gold inlays, cased.

Mfg.'s Sug. Retail	$22,745	$22,745	$15,000	$11,500

⚐ **Grand American Small Gauge** — 28 or .410 ga.

Mfg.'s Sug. Retail	$34,460	$34,460	$25,000	$17,500

Add 10% for 28/.410 ga. combo.

⚐ **Grand American "1 of 8" set** — includes 20, 28, and .410 ga. VR barrels. Only 8 sets mfg.

Mfg.'s Sug. Retail	$55,000	$55,000	$39,500	$27,500

Note: See Model 21 listing also under Pre-64 shotguns.

MODEL 22 DOUBLE BARREL — 12 ga. only, subcontracted by Winchester and manufactured in Spain by Laurona circa 1975 for international sales including Europe, field configuration only with 28 in. barrels, DT, oil finished checkered walnut stock and semi-beavertail forearm, matted rib, black-chrome finish on metal parts, hand engraved receiver, limited mfg.

	$1,200	$995	$825	$700	$600	$525	$475

Grading	100%	98%	95%	90%	80%	70%	60%

MODEL 23 XTR — 12 or 20 ga., 3 in. chambers, 25½, 26, 28, or 30 in. barrels, various chokes, single trigger, VR, auto ejectors, scroll engraved, silver grey satin finish, blued barrel, checkered select walnut stock and forearm, first commercial gun to employ interchangeable chokes. Mfg. 1978-disc.

| Grade 1 (disc.) | $915 | $820 | $750 | $650 | $575 | $500 | $440 |

⚐ **Pigeon Grade** — standard weight model, 6½ - 7 lbs, coin finished receiver with scroll engraving. Winchoke option became standard in 1986. Subtract $150 without Winchokes. Disc. 1986.

| | $1,150 | $995 | $875 | $750 | $675 | $600 | $550 |

Last Mfg.'s Sug. Retail was $1,460.

⚐ **Pigeon Grade Lightweight** — 25½ in. barrels only, 6¼ - 6¾ lbs., coin finished receiver with scroll engraving. English stock, Winchoke not available. Disc. 1986.

| | $1,300 | $1,150 | $995 | $880 | $760 | $730 | $680 |

Last Mfg.'s Sug. Retail was $1,420.

⚐ **Pigeon Grade Ducks Unlimited** — only 500 mfg. 1981, "SPO" serial no. suffix, cased.

| | $1,450 | $1,200 | $995 | $880 | $760 | $730 | $680 |

⚐ **Golden Quail Model Series** — 12 ga. (1986), 20 ga. (1984), 28 ga. (1985), or .410 ga. (1987), 25½ in. barrels bored IC/M, beavertail forearm, straight grip English stock with recoil pad. Only 500 mfg. each year per gauge. Disc. 1987.

| | $1,450 | $1,150 | $995 | $875 | $780 | $700 | $640 |

Add $165 for .410 and earlier ga.'s.
This limited production series is now complete with the release of the .410 ga. 1987.
Last Mfg.'s Sug. Retail was $1,950.

⚐ **Model 23 Light Duck** — limited edition, 500 mfg., introduced 1985, blued receiver and barrels, select walnut, 20 ga., 28 in.- F&F, 8½ lbs.

| | $1,475 | $1,225 | $995 | $900 | $825 | $775 | $725 |

Last Mfg.'s Sug. Retail was $1,660.

⚐ **Model 23 Heavy Duck** — limited edition, 500 mfg. 1984 only, blued receiver and barrels, select walnut, 12 ga., 30 in.- F&F, 8½ lbs.

| | $1,500 | $1,265 | $1,025 | $920 | $840 | $785 | $730 |

⚐ **Custom 2 Barrel Set** — interchangeable 20 and 28 ga. 26 in. barrels, blue engraved receiver with gold inlays, "B" checkering on stock and forearm, leather cased with accessories, only 500 sets mfg. 1986. Disc. 1987.

| | $3,700 | $3,300 | $2,995 | $2,750 | $2,500 | $2,150 | $1,920 |

Last Mfg.'s Sug. Retail was $4,625.

MODEL 23 CUSTOM — 12 ga. only, 27 in. Winchoke barrels, high lustre bluing, no engraving, SST, ejectors, solid red rubber recoil pad, 7 lbs. Imported 1987 only.

| | $1,795 | $1,475 | $1,100 | $925 | $875 | $775 | $650 |

Last Mfg.'s Sug. Retail was $1,975.

MODEL 23 CLASSIC — 12, 20, 28, or .410 ga., 26 in. VR barrels, single trigger, deluxe hand checkered walnut stock and beavertail forearm, solid recoil pad, brass name plate, gold inlay on bottom of receiver, ebony inlay in forearm, 5¾ - 7 lbs. Imported 1986-1987 only.

| | $1,450 | $1,225 | $1,025 | $925 | $875 | $780 | $640 |

Add 10% for 28 or .410 ga.
The 28 and .410 ga.'s in this model feature a smaller frame.
Last Mfg.'s Sug. Retail was $1,975.

WINCHESTER® cont.

COMMEMORATIVES: U.S. PRODUCTION

Until recently, commemoratives in general have experienced poor liquidity because of oversupply versus consumer demand. Commemorative production in some trademarks has totalled well over 250,000 units, and some collectors are weighing the "limited production" factor on each model before paying a premium over the standard production model of that particular commemorative. The values below reflect actual prices paid recently in various areas of the U.S. In some regions it is possible to purchase a Winchester 94 commemorative made in substantial quantity for almost no premium over a standard production Winchester 94. Because of this, prices could fluctuate over 25% depending on the geographic location of purchase or sale. It is also important to remember that N.I.B. becomes especially important with commemoratives. Values below assume boxes, informational material, and warranty cards - subtract $75-$100 if without box and literature. Commemoratives having been shot as little as 3 times can only be classified as fancy hunting guns with little premium if any over the standard hunting model from which they were derived.

During the course of a year, I receive many phone calls and letters on special editions and limited editions that do not appear in this section. It should be noted that a commemorative issue is a gun that has been manufactured, marketed, and sold through the auspices of the specific trademark (in this case Winchester). Many "special interest" limited editions have been ordered through outside private contracts with Winchester (including General Motors, Dodge, Coca-Cola, etc.). These variations do not have the special suffix serialization (and may not have had a retail price when issued) and many times, the embellishments were subcontracted outside of the factory. While these guns do have special interest, they do not have the collectability or desirability of the below listed factory models. Typically, these limited editions sell in the $195-$350 range.

Many commemorative dealers have told me that recent changes in overseas currency rates have made domestic guns less expensive to own for Europeans especially. For this reason, many commemoratives are being sold overseas resulting in less supply for the domestic market. This secondary demand factor has strengthened commemorative prices. Desirability is the key to determining values on these firearms. More information on these special and limited editions not listed in the following pages can be obtained by contacting the factory.

A final note on commemoratives: As a rule, what determines the bottom of the market in commemoratives is the top of the market for their standard model production relatives. A problem with limited editions is that over the years of ownership, most of the original amount manufactured stays in the same N.I.B. condition. Thus, if supply always is constant and in one condition (NIB), demand has to increase before price appreciation can occur. Taking into consideration the inflation factor during the past 2 decades, many older, high manufacture commemoratives/Limited editions have not performed very well as investments. Yet, others have. After 24 years of special edition production, many models' performance record can be accurately analyzed and any appreciation (or depreciation) can be compared against other purchases of equal vintage. You be the judge.

Grading	100%	issue price	qty made
1964 WYOMING DIAMOND JUBILEE 94 CARBINE			
	$1,295	$100	1,501
1966 CENTENNIAL '66 RIFLE			
	$395	$125	
1966 CENTENNIAL '66 CARBINE — total mfg. of both the rifle and carbine was 102,309.			
	$395	$125	102,309
Add $50-$75 over individual prices for consecutively serial numbered rifle and carbine set.			
1966 NEBRASKA CENTENNIAL 94 RIFLE			
	$1,295	$100	2,500
1967 CANADIAN '67 CENTENNIAL RIFLE			
	$350	$125	

Grading	100%	issue price	qty made

1967 CANADIAN '67 CENTENNIAL CARBINE — total mfg. of both the rifle and carbine was 90,301.

	100%	issue price	qty made
	$350	$125	90,301

Add $50-$75 over individual prices for consecutively serial numbered rifle and carbine set.

1967 ALASKAN PURCHASE CENTENNIAL CARBINE

	$1,495	$125	1,501

1968 ILLINOIS SESQUICENTENNIAL 94 CARBINE

	$350	$110	37,468

1968 BUFFALO BILL RIFLE "1 OF 300" PRES.

	$1,995	$1,000	300

1968 BUFFALO BILL RIFLE

	$375	$130	

1968 BUFFALO BILL CARBINE — total mfg. of both the rifle and carbine was 112,923.

	$375	$130	112,923

Add $50-$75 over individual prices for consecutively serial numbered rifle and carbine set.

1969 GOLDEN SPIKE CARBINE

	$350	$120	69,996

1969 THEO. ROOSEVELT RIFLE

	$375	$135	

1969 THEO. ROOSEVELT CARBINE — total mfg. of both the rifle and carbine was 52,386.

	$375	$135	52,386

1970 COWBOY COMMEMORATIVE CARBINE

	$450	$125	27,549

1970 COWBOY CARBINE "1 OF 300"

	$2,350	$1,000	300

1970 LONE STAR RIFLE

	$425	$140	

1970 LONE STAR CARBINE — total mfg. of both the rifle and carbine was 38,385.

	$425	$140	38,385

1971 NRA CENTENNIAL MUSKET

	$350	$150	23,400

1971 NRA CENTENNIAL RIFLE

	$350	$150	21,000

1974 TEXAS RANGER CARBINE

	$695	$135	4,850

1974 TEXAS RANGER PRESENTATION

	$2,350	$1,000	150

1976 U.S. BICENTENNIAL CARBINE

	$595	$325	19,999

Grading	100%	issue price	qty made
1977 WELLS FARGO			
	$450	$350	19,999
1977 "LIMITED EDITION I"			
	$1,395	$1,500	1,500
1977 LEGENDARY LAWMEN			
	$450	$375	19,999
1978 ANTLERED GAME CARBINE			
	$450	$375	19,999
1979 LEGENDARY FRONTIERSMAN RIFLE			
	$450	$425	19,999
1979 "LIMITED EDITION II"			
	$1,395	$1,750	1,500
1979 MATCHED SET OF 1000			
	$2,250	$3,000	1,000
1980 BAT MASTERSON CARBINE			
	$695	$650	8,000
1980 "OLIVER WINCHESTER"			
	$550	$375	19,999
1981 U.S. BORDER PATROL			
	$550	$1,195	1,000
1981 U.S. BORDER PATROL — MEMBERS MODEL			
	$550	$695	800
1981 JOHN WAYNE			
	$795	$600	49,000

Optional accessories were also available for this model: the gun rack with leather insert is currently selling for approx. $40 and the leather scabbard is trading for $60.

Grading	100%	issue price	qty made
1981 "DUKE"			
	$2,950	$2,250	1,000
1981 JOHN WAYNE "1 OF 300" SET			
	$6,500	$10,000	300
1982 GREAT WESTERN ARTIST I			
	$1,195	$2,200	999
1982 GREAT WESTERN ARTIST II			
	$1,195	$2,200	999
1982 ANNIE OAKLEY			
	$650	$699	6,000
1982 OKLAHOMA DIAMOND JUBILEE			
	$1,395	$2,250	1,001

Grading	100%	issue price	qty made

1982 AMERICAN BALD EAGLE - SILVER

	$595	$895	2,800

1982 AMERICAN BALD EAGLE - GOLD

	$1,995	$2,950	200

1983 CHIEF CRAZY HORSE

	$450	$600	19,999

1984 WINCHESTER-COLT COMMEMORATIVE SET — 1 each of the Model 1894 Carbine and Colt Peacemaker, serial numbered 1 WC-4440 WC. .44-40 cal., elaborate gold etching, cased.

	$1,995	$3,995	2,300

Approx. 2,300 sets were actually put together in this combination. These sets have been split up with individual prices being discounted (Colt SAAs have been trading in the $700-$800 range).

1985 BOY SCOUTS 75TH ANNIVERSARY — Model 9422 action, .22 cal., rifle configuration, 6 1/4 lbs.

⚜ **Eagle Scout** — 1,000 mfg., serial numbered Eagle 1 - Eagle 1,000, receiver has triple level gold etching, select American walnut stock and forearm, gold plated lever, hammer, and forearm cap.

	$1,895	$1,710	1,000

⚜ **Boy Scout** — 15,000 mfg., serial numbered BSA 1 - BSA 15,000, roll engraved, antique pewter receiver, hooded front sight.

	$425	$495	15,000

1985 MODEL 94 TEXAS SESQUICENTENNIAL — .38-55 cal., available in carbine or rifle.

⚜ **Model 94 Rifle** — 24 in. round barrel, elaborate gold etching, includes Bowie knife, oak cased, 586 mfg.

	$2,400	$2,995	1,500

⚜ **Model 94 Carbine** — 18 1/2 in. round barrel, gold finished receiver and barrel bands, roll engraved receiver, 2,600 mfg., serial numbered TEX 1 and up.

	$550	$695	15,000

⚜ **Rifle/Carbine Set** — includes one each of the Model 94 rifle and carbine, Bowie knife, 150 mfg.

	$6,250	$7,995	150

1986 120TH ANNIVERSARY MODEL 94 CARBINE — .44-40 cal. only, 20 in. barrel, hoop-type finger lever, crescent butt plate, deluxe checkered walnut stock and forearm, extensive gold etching on barrel and framesides, 1,000 mfg. ser. no. WRA001-WRA1000.

	$850	$995	1,000

1986 STATUE OF LIBERTY MODEL 94 — Model 94 rifle in .30-30 cal. with octagon barrel, extensive C. Giovanelli scroll engraving with multiple 22Kt. gold inlays, deluxe walnut with fine checkering, also includes 29 in. hand carved wooden statue of the Statue of Liberty, serial numbered SL1-SL100.

	$6,500	$6,500	100

1986 MODEL 94 DU — .30-30 cal., approx. 2,800 rifles were mfg. in the U.S. Since each Model 94 DU was bid on for ownership, prices will vary from points of origin. An average bid price seems to be in the $700-$995 range with lower and completing set ser. no.'s selling at premiums. Serial numbered DU-86 0001 on up.

This model is not a factory commemorative, but rather a trade gun commissioned by Ducks Unlimited.

Grading	100%	issue price	qty made

1987 U.S. CONSTITUTION 200TH ANNIVERSARY

	$13,000	$12,000	8

1988 WINCHESTER ARMS COLLECTOR'S ASSOCIATION CASED SET — includes Colt SAA and Winchester Model 1894 in cased set, features special embellishments and W.A.C.A. emblems and medallions. 100 sets were advertised, but only 22 were sold.

	$2,995	$2,695	22 sets

1990 WYOMING CENTENNIAL .30-30

	$995	$895	500

1991 125TH ANNIVERSARY .30-30

	$4,995	$4,995	125

1992 KENTUCKY BICENTENNIAL .30-30 — Winchester Model 94 with true charcoal case coloring, engraving depicts important KY graphics, serial numbered KY001-KY500.

	$995	$995	500

This model is distributed exclusively by Cherry's located in Greensboro, NC.

1992 ARAPAHO .30-30 — features gold plated receiver with etched Indian scenes on both sides, checkered semi-fancy American walnut stock.

	$895	$895	500

WINCHESTER COMMEMORATIVES: NON-DOMESTIC – 1970 TO DATE

1970 NORTH WEST TERRITORIES (CANADIAN)

	$850	$150	2,500

1970 NORTHWEST TERRITORIES DELUXE (CANADIAN)

	$1,100	$250	500

1973 YELLOW BOY (SOLD IN EUROPE ONLY)

	$995	$150	4,903

1973 M.P.X. (MADE ESPECIALLY FOR A MOVIE)

	$9,995	$ 78	32

1973 R.C.M.P. (CANADIAN)

	$750	$190	9,500

1973 R.C.M.P. MEMBERS ISSUE (CANADIAN)

	$750	$190	4,850

1973 M.P. (MOUNTED POLICE) - (CANADIAN)

	$1,275	$190	5,100

1974 APACHE (CANADIAN)

	$750	$150	8,600

1975 KLONDIKE GOLD RUSH (CANADIAN)

	$750	$230	10,200

1975 K.G.R. (DAWSON CITY ISSUE) - (CANADIAN)

	$8,500	N/A	25

Grading	100%	issue price	qty made
1975 COMANCHE (CANADIAN)			
	$750	$230	11,511
1976 SIOUX (CANADIAN)			
	$750	$280	10,000
1976 LITTLE BIG HORN (CANADIAN)			
	$750	$230	11,000
1977 CHEYENNE (CANADIAN) — .44-40 Cal.			
	$750	$300	11,225
1977 CHEYENNE (CANADIAN) — .22 Cal.			
	$595	$320	5,000
1978 CHEROKEE (CANADIAN) — .30-30 Cal.			
	$750	$385	9,000
1978 CHEROKEE (CANADIAN) — .22 Cal.			
	$595	$385	3,950
1978 ONE OF ONE THOUSAND (SOLD IN EUROPE ONLY)			
	$7,995	$5,000	250
This model was not advertised in the U.S.			
1980 ALBERTA DIAMOND JUBILEE (CANADIAN)			
	$750	$650	2,700
1980 A.D.J. DELUXE PRESENTATION (CANADIAN)			
	$1,495	$1,900	300
1980 SASKATCHEWAN DIAMOND JUBILEE (CANADIAN)			
	$750	$695	2,700
1980 S.D.J. DELUXE PRESENTATION (CANADIAN)			
	$1,495	$1,995	300
1981 CALGARY STAMPEDE (CANADIAN)			
	$1,250	$2,200	1,000
1981 CANADIAN PACIFIC CENTENNIAL (CANADIAN)			
	$550	$800	2,700
1981 CANADIAN PACIFIC CENTENNIAL PRESENTATION (CANADIAN)			
	$1,100	$2,200	300
1981 CANADIAN PACIFIC (EMPL.) - (CANADIAN)			
	$550	$800	2,000
1981 JOHN WAYNE (CANADIAN)			
	$995	$995	1,000
1986 SECOND SERIES EUROPEAN 1 OF 1,000 — mfg. for European sales only 1986.			
	$6,500	$6,000	150

Grading	100%	issue price	qty made

1992 ONTARIO CONSERVATION — this model was marketed in Canada only.

	$1,195	$1,195	400

WINSLOW ARMS COMPANY
Camden, SC.

WINSLOW BOLT ACTION SPORTING RIFLE — offered with various actions, FN Supreme, Mark X Mauser, Rem. 700 and 788, Sako and Win. 70, offered in all popular calibers from .17 Rem. to .458 Mag., standard calibers have 24 in. barrels and 3 shot magazines, magnum calibers have 26 in. barrels and 2 shot magazines, two style stocks, "Bushmaster Conventional", slender pistol grip and beavertail forearm, "Plainsmaster", full curl, hooked pistol grip and flat wide forearm, both are Monte Carlo with cheek pieces, recoil pads and swivels, walnut, maple, and myrtle are used with rosewood forend tip and pistol grip cap, rifle comes in 8 basic grades, custom embellishments can increase values greatly, discretion must be used, values are for basic models.

Grading	100%	98%	95%	90%	80%	70%	60%
COMMANDER GRADE							
	$495	$475	$440	$385	$360	$330	$305
REGAL GRADE							
	$605	$590	$560	$525	$470	$440	$415
REGENT GRADE							
	$725	$700	$670	$640	$605	$550	$495
REGIMENTAL GRADE							
	$935	$890	$855	$800	$745	$660	$605
CROWN GRADE							
	$1,375	$1,265	$1,155	$990	$910	$825	$715
ROYAL GRADE							
	$1,540	$1,375	$1,210	$1,100	$1,020	$965	$825
IMPERIAL GRADE							
	$3,520	$3,080	$2,860	$2,475	$2,200	$1,925	$1,320
EMPEROR GRADE							
	$6,215	$5,500	$4,950	$4,400	$3,300	$2,750	$2,200

WISEMAN, BILL AND CO.
Custom rifle manufacturer/retailer located in College Station, TX.
Wiseman/McMillan also manufactures rifle barrels and custom stocks.

RIFLES

HUNTER MODEL — available in various cals., Sako action, stainless steel barrel by Wiseman/McMillan, laminate stock, teflon finished metal parts, Pachmayr decelerator pad, sling swivels, glass bedded action.

Mfg.'s Sug. Retail	$1,981	$1,981	$1,625	$1,300	$1,100	$900	$775	$675

HUNTER DELUXE — similar to Hunter Model except has custom checkering.

Mfg.'s Sug. Retail	$2,181	$2,181	$1,825	$1,500	$1,225	$995	$875	$775

Grading	100%		98%	95%	90%	80%	70%	60%

MAVERICK — similar to Hunter but with black fiberglass stock.

Mfg.'s Sug. Retail	$1,881		$1,881	$1,525	$1,200	$995	$875	$775	$675

VARMENTER — similar to Hunter but with thumbhole stock.

Mfg.'s Sug. Retail	$2,081		$2,081	$1,725	$1,400	$1,225	$995	$875	$775

SILHOUETTE PISTOL

SILHOUETTE PISTOL — various cals., Sako action, 14 in. Wiseman/McMillan fluted stainless barrel, 5 or 7 shot magazine, laminate pistol grip stock, no sights, 4½-5½ lbs. New 1989.

Mfg.'s Sug. Retail	$1,295		$1,295	$1,000	$900	$800	$750	$700	$650

WOODWARD, JAMES AND SONS

Previously mfg. in London, England. Acquired by James Purdey & Sons approx. 1935.

SHOTGUNS: DOUBLE AND SINGLE BARREL

Woodward made one of the world's finest shotguns. Prior to WWII, they were acquired by Purdey and Sons. Many of the weapons they made were custom built and grading and pricing should be done individually. We will list some of the general models with approximate values as a guideline, but strongly urge competent professional appraisal when contemplating purchase or sale.

BEST QUALITY DOUBLE BARREL SHOTGUN — custom built in all gauges, barrel lengths and chokes, sidelock, auto ejectors, stocked to specifications, pre-WWII.

$26,000 $23,000 $19,950 $17,000 $14,250 $12,000 $10,000

Add 20% for 20 ga.
Add 40% for 28 ga.
Add 60% for .410 ga.
Add $1,000 for SST.

BEST QUALITY O/U SHOTGUN — custom built in all gauges, barrel lengths, and chokes, VR, sidelock, auto ejectors, stocked to customer specifications, pre-WWII.

$29,500 $25,500 $21,500 $18,500 $15,750 $13,800 $12,000

Add 35% for 20 ga.
Add 75% for 28 ga.
.410 gauge — too rare to accurately predict.
Add $1,000 for ST.

BEST QUALITY SINGLE BARREL TRAP GUN — 12 ga. only, limited mfg. - pre-WWII only.

$12,750 $10,000 $8,950 $7,725 $6,500 $5,750 $4,900

WYOMING ARMS MFG. CORP.

Previous manufacturer located in Thermopolis, WY. Very small quantities of Parker pistols were mfg.

PARKER PISTOLS: STAINLESS STEEL

STANDARD PISTOL — 9mm Para., 10mm, .40 S&W, or .45 ACP cal., 3⅜, 5, or 7 in. barrel, 7 (.45 ACP), 8 (10mm & .40 S&W), or 9 (9mm Para.) shot mag., Millett adj. sights, grooved synthetic grips, 29-39 oz. Disc. 1992.

$350 $300 $250

Add $50 for 7 in. barrel.
Last Mfg.'s Sug. Retail was $399.

Grading	100%	98%	95%	90%	80%	70%	60%

.357 MAG. — .357 Mag. cal., single action semi-auto, 7 in. barrel, adj. sights, 8 shot mag., lifetime warranty, 44 oz. Disc. 1992.

| | | | $425 | $350 | $300 | | |

Last Mfg.'s Sug. Retail was $479.

Z section

Z-B RIFLE
Brno, Czechoslovakia.

Grading	100%	98%	95%	90%	80%	70%	60%

Z-B MAUSER VARMINT RIFLE — small Mauser bolt action, .22 Hornet, 23 in. barrel, double set triggers, 3 leaf sight, checkered pistol grip stock, (also known as Brno Hornet).

$825 $745 $690 $605 $550 $470 $415

ZABALA HERMANOS, S.A.
Manufacturer located in Eibar, Spain. Z. Hermanos has had limited importation to date (American Arms located in Kansas City is private labeling a few models).

Zabala Hermanos manufactures quality boxlock SxS or O/U shotguns and sidelock side-by-sides. For more information regarding this trademark, (including current models and prices) please contact the manufacturer directly (see Trademark Index).

ZANARDINI
Manufacturer located in Brescia, Italy since 1946. Currently, Zanardini does not have a U.S. importer. Several U.S. firms have stocked a few Zanardini models in the past, but not the complete line. For further information regarding this company, please contact them directly (see Trademark Index).

COMBINATION GUNS O/U

PRINCESS — super light variation.

$2,200 $1,925 $1,675 $1,400 $1,200 $1,000 $800

Last Mfg.'s Sug. Retail was $2,542.

BOXER MODEL — H&H styled sidelocks, top-quality engraving.

$5,750 $5,150 $4,600 $4,000 $3,550 $3,000 $2,650

Last Mfg.'s Sug. Retail was $6,246.

BOXER 4-LOCKS MODEL

$3,900 $3,400 $2,975 $2,625 $2,300 $2,050 $1,750

Last Mfg.'s Sug. Retail was $4,562.

402 STRAUSS — top-of-the-line combination gun with best quality engraving and wood.

$9,000 $8,000 $7,000 $6,000 $5,000 $4,000 $3,000

Last Mfg.'s Sug. Retail was $10,548.

RIFLES

403 OXFORD SxS — 9.3 x 74R and smaller cals.

$3,400 $3,000 $2,700 $2,425 $2,150 $1,875 $1,575

Last Mfg.'s Sug. Retail was $3,835.

Larger cals..375 H&H, .458 Win. Mag., or .470 Nitro cal.

$6,700 $6,000 $5,500 $5,000 $4,500 $3,950 $3,450

Add approx. 135% for .470 Nitro cal.
Last Mfg.'s Sug. Retail was $7,555.

Grading	100%	98%	95%	90%	80%	70%	60%

EXPRESS RIFLE SxS — .470 NE cal., boxlock action, ST, checkered walnut stock (with cheek piece), express sights. Other cals. available upon special order.

Mfg.'s Sug. Retail	$8,995	$8,400	$8,100	$7,450	$6,750	$6,000	$5,500	$5,000

This model is imported exclusively by Mandall Shooting Supplies, Inc. located in Scottsdale, AZ.

409 BRISTOL SxS — priced by individual request.

407 OXFORD SL SxS — sidelock action.

	$15,000	$13,250	$11,950	$10,000	$9,250	$8,500	$7,750

Last Mfg.'s Sug. Retail was $17,095.

MODEL 403 KOENIG O/U — 7.65R or 9.3 x 74R cal.

	$6,500	$5,850	$5,350	$4,850	$4,350	$3,800	$3,300

Last Mfg.'s Sug. Retail was $7,368.

MODEL 403 DELUXE O/U

	$3,650	$3,200	$2,875	$2,525	$2,250	$1,925	$1,600

Last Mfg.'s Sug. Retail was $4,188.

SHOTGUNS

HAMMER LONDON MODEL SxS — features external hammers.

	$9,150	$8,125	$7,100	$6,100	$5,050	$4,000	$3,050

Last Mfg.'s Sug. Retail was $10,735.

HAMMERLESS LONDON MODEL SxS

	$4,200	$3,700	$3,175	$2,825	$2,500	$2,100	$1,700

Last Mfg.'s Sug. Retail was $4,936.

DONAU STANDARD MODEL SxS — boxlock action.

	$9,000	$8,000	$7,000	$6,000	$5,000	$4,000	$3,000

Last Mfg.'s Sug. Retail was $10,548.

DONAU SIDELOCK SxS — H&H style sidelock action.

	$16,500	$14,750	$12,950	$11,000	$9,950	$9,000	$8,000

Last Mfg.'s Sug. Retail was $18,966.

PRESTIGE TRAP AND SKEET SxS

	$2,250	$1,950	$1,675	$1,400	$1,200	$1,000	$800

Last Mfg.'s Sug. Retail was $2,598.

HASE CACCIA MONTECATINI SxS — boxlock action, double set triggers, extractors.

	$900	$800	$700	$600	$550	$495	$450

Add 30% for ejectors.
Last Mfg.'s Sug. Retail was $1,027.

HORN MODEL SxS — boxlock action, double set triggers, extractors.

	$950	$850	$750	$625	$550	$495	$450

Add 40% for ejectors.
Last Mfg.'s Sug. Retail was $1,102.

ZANOTTI, FABIO

Manufacturer located in Brescia, Italy since 1625. Currently imported and distributed by New England Arms, Co. located in Kittery Point, ME. Fabio Zanotti became part of the Renato Gamba Group in 1985.

Fabio Zanotti is one of the world's oldest quality shotgun manufacturers. Current domestic importation is often times done on a custom order only basis. For more information on Zanotti models and their values, contact New England Arms Co.

SHOTGUNS: OVER/UNDER

Grading	100%	98%	95%	90%	80%	70%	60%

MODEL 725 — 28 or .410 ga. only, scalloped case hardened shallow frame, DT or ST, ejectors, game scene and scroll engraving, custom built to individual specifications.

	100%	98%	95%	90%	80%	70%	60%
Mfg.'s Sug. Retail $4,950	$4,550	$3,925	$3,450	$2,950	$2,450	$2,000	$1,875

CASSIANO — 12, 20, 28, or .410 ga., Boss style shallow action, best quality gun built to individual specifications. Prices start at $18,500 and go up accordingly.

SHOTGUNS: SIDE BY SIDE

Add $300 for ST.
Add $250 for beavertail forearm.
Add $450 for leather case.

MODEL 625 BOXLOCK

	100%	98%	95%	90%	80%	70%	60%
Mfg.'s Sug. Retail $4,500	$3,900	$3,300	$2,850	$2,500	$2,200	$1,900	$1,800

MODEL 626 BOXLOCK — scroll, game scene, or combination engraving.

	100%	98%	95%	90%	80%	70%	60%
Mfg.'s Sug. Retail $5,500	$5,100	$4,100	$3,650	$3,375	$3,100	$2,950	$2,600

MODEL GIACINTO — hammer gun.

	100%	98%	95%	90%	80%	70%	60%
Mfg.'s Sug. Retail $4,950	$4,600	$3,850	$3,175	$2,450	$2,000	$1,825	$1,430

MODEL MAXIM SIDELOCK

	100%	98%	95%	90%	80%	70%	60%
Mfg.'s Sug. Retail $8,000	$7,350	$6,100	$5,250	$4,600	$3,850	$3,175	$2,450

MODEL EDWARD SIDELOCK

	100%	98%	95%	90%	80%	70%	60%
Mfg.'s Sug. Retail $10,500	$9,875	$8,250	$7,000	$6,150	$5,250	$4,000	$3,575

MODEL CASSIANO I SIDELOCK

	100%	98%	95%	90%	80%	70%	60%
Mfg.'s Sug. Retail $12,000	$10,000	$8,750	$7,450	$6,450	$5,575	$4,700	$3,850

MODEL CASSIANO II

	100%	98%	95%	90%	80%	70%	60%
Mfg.'s Sug. Retail $14,000	$12,250	$10,250	$9,350	$8,150	$6,700	$5,900	$5,100

CASSIANO EXECUTIVE — prices vary per individual order, top-of-the-line model. Prices start at $15,000 and go up.

ZASTAVA ARMS

Manufacturer located in Yugoslavia. Because of a current trade embargo, Zastava Arms are not currently imported into the U.S. Previously imported by K.B.I., Inc. located in Harrisburg, PA and previously distributed by Nationwide Sports Distributors located in Southampton, PA.

Grading	100%	98%	95%	90%	80%	70%	60%

HANDGUNS: SEMI-AUTO

MODEL Z9 — 9mm Para., double action semi-auto, 15 shot, $4\frac{1}{4}$ in. barrel, short recoil, choice of mil. spec. black or commercial blue finish, Browning locking system, ambidextrous controls, 3-dot Tritium sighting system, alloy frame, firing pin block, chamber indicator, squared-off trigger guard, checkered dark gray polymer grips, 32 oz. Imported mid-1990-92.

	100%	98%	95%	90%	80%	70%	60%
	$450	$395	$365	$330	$300	$285	$265

Last Mfg.'s Sug. Retail was $495. Prior to 1991, this model was named the CZ-99.

MODEL Z40 — .40 S&W cal, although advertised, this model was never imported. Suggested retail was $495.

RIFLES

MODEL ZR 22 — .22 LR, .22 Mag., or .22 Hornet cal., although advertised, this model was never imported. Suggested retail was $275.

ZEPHYR

Manufacturer located in Spain, and imported by Stoegers 1930s-1972.

RIFLES

Stoeger's has imported a wide variety of bolt action rifles during the past 60 years. Rather than list the many models individually, each Zephyr rifle should be compared to a gun of equal caliber, quality, and features to ascertain an approximate value range.

SHOTGUNS: SxS OR SINGLE SHOT

WOODLANDER II DOUBLE BARREL SHOTGUN — 12 or 20 ga., various chokes, boxlock, double triggers, extractors, engraved, checkered pistol grip stock.

	100%	98%	95%	90%	80%	70%	60%
	$495	$440	$385	$360	$305	$275	$250

UPLANDER (4E) SXS — 12, 16, 20, 28, or .410 ga., sidelock action, double triggers, ejectors, engraved.

	100%	98%	95%	90%	80%	70%	60%
	$775	$695	$640	$585	$570	$480	$440

STERLINGWORTH II DOUBLE BARREL SHOTGUN — similar to Woodlander, with sidelock action.

	100%	98%	95%	90%	80%	70%	60%
	$825	$725	$660	$605	$580	$525	$495

UPLAND KING SXS — 12 or 16 ga., sidelock, single trigger, VR, ejectors, fully engraved.

	100%	98%	95%	90%	80%	70%	60%
	$1,000	$900	$800	$725	$650	$600	$550

THUNDERBIRD SXS — 10 ga. Mag, 32 in. barrels, double triggers, French walnut, engraved. Add $175 for ejectors.

	100%	98%	95%	90%	80%	70%	60%
	$850	$750	$625	$550	$510	$490	$475

HONKER — 10 ga. Mag, single shot, 36 in. VR barrel, lightly engraved.

	100%	98%	95%	90%	80%	70%	60%
	$500	$460	$420	$350	$310	$290	$270

VANDALIA — 12 ga. Trap Model, 32 in. barrel, engraved.

	100%	98%	95%	90%	80%	70%	60%
	$700	$620	$575	$525	$475	$425	$390

VICTOR SPECIAL DOUBLE BARREL SHOTGUN — 12 ga., 25, 28, or 30 in. barrels, various chokes, double triggers, extractors, checkered pistol grip stock.

	100%	98%	95%	90%	80%	70%	60%
	$440	$385	$330	$305	$250	$220	$195

ZOLI, ANGELO

Previous manufacturer located in Brescia, Italy. Previously imported and distributed exclusively by Angelo Zoli USA located in Addison, IL. Mfg. 1985-87.

Angelo Zoli went out of business in December, 1987 and was taken over by the Italian Bank of Brescia in 1989. Many people tend to confuse the shotguns of Angelo and Antonio Zoli (it is hard to determine which manufacturer made a gun marked "A. Zoli"). There is no correlation between these trademarks and Antonio Zoli DOES NOT have parts for these earlier Angelo Zoli long arms. Even though both trademarks may indicate "A. ZOLI" for a barrel address, they are mostly discernable by the model listings under both headings in this section.

Cape Outfitters (see Trademark Index under Angelo Zoli for address) has parts for most Angelo Zoli guns and should be contacted directly for availability and prices. All repairs are strictly non-warranty.

SHOTGUNS: OVER AND UNDER

Grading	100%	98%	95%	90%	80%	70%	60%
SNIPE	$230	$200	$185	$170	$155	$145	$135

SNIPE — .410 ga., 3 in. chambers, 26 or 28 in. barrels, single trigger. Disc. 1987.

Last Mfg.'s Sug. Retail was $265.

	100%	98%	95%	90%	80%	70%	60%
TEXAS	$250	$220	$200	$185	$170	$155	$145

TEXAS — all ga.'s, 26 or 28 in. barrels, double triggers, folding design, lever action. Disc. 1987.

Last Mfg.'s Sug. Retail was $291.

	100%	98%	95%	90%	80%	70%	60%
DOVE	$260	$230	$200	$185	$170	$155	$145

DOVE — .410 ga. only, 3 in. chambers, 26 or 28 in. barrels, single trigger. Disc. 1987.

Last Mfg.'s Sug. Retail was $306.

FIELD SPECIAL — 12, 20, or 28 ga., 3 in. chambers, various barrel lengths and chokings, single trigger. Disc. 1989.

	100%	98%	95%	90%	80%	70%	60%
	$450	$400	$360	$330	$300	$270	$240

Last Mfg.'s Sug. Retail was $699.

PIGEON MODEL — 12 or 20 ga., 3 in. chambers, various barrel lengths, single trigger. Disc. 1987.

	100%	98%	95%	90%	80%	70%	60%
	$350	$295	$270	$250	$220	$195	$175

Add $60 for 20 ga.
Last Mfg.'s Sug. Retail was $394.

STANDARD MODEL — 12 or 20 ga., 3 in. chambers, various barrel lengths and chokings, single trigger. Disc. 1987.

	100%	98%	95%	90%	80%	70%	60%
	$395	$345	$320	$300	$280	$260	$245

Last Mfg.'s Sug. Retail was $459.

SILVER SNIPE — 12 or 20 ga., 3 in. chambers on the 20 ga., single trigger, ejectors, light engraving. Disc. 1987.

	100%	98%	95%	90%	80%	70%	60%
	$675	$585	$530	$485	$440	$400	$375

Add $50 for multi-chokes (12 ga. only).
This model was distributed by Euroarms of America, Inc.
Last Mfg.'s Sug. Retail was $739.

CONDOR MODEL — 12 ga. skeet model, 28 in. barrels, SST, ejectors, wide VR, engraved silver finished receiver, recoil pad. Disc. 1987.

	100%	98%	95%	90%	80%	70%	60%
	$795	$700	$640	$585	$530	$485	$440

This model was distributed by Mandall Shooting Supplies, Inc.
Last Mfg.'s Sug. Retail was $895.

Grading	100%	98%	95%	90%	80%	70%	60%

TARGET MODEL 208 — 12 ga. only, available in either Trap, Skeet, or Monotrap configuration. Disc. 1987.

	$895	$775	$695	$620	$575	$500	$450

Add $494 for Monotrap II 208 Model.
Last Mfg.'s Sug. Retail was $996.

TARGET MODEL 308 — 12 ga. only, available in either Trap, Skeet, or Monotrap configuration. Disc. 1987.

	$1,375	$1,125	$950	$875	$795	$725	$650

Add $76 for multi-chokes.
Add $824 for Monotrap II 308 Model.
Last Mfg.'s Sug. Retail was $1,581.

SPECIAL MODEL — 12 ga. only, 3 in. chambers, various barrel lengths and chokings, SST. Disc. 1987.

	$465	$395	$355	$325	$290	$270	$250

Add $120 for multi-chokes.
Last Mfg.'s Sug. Retail was $528.

DELUXE MODEL — similar to Special Model, except better wood and engraving. Disc. 1987.

	$645	$550	$495	$450	$400	$360	$320

Add $80 for multi-chokes.
Last Mfg.'s Sug. Retail was $730.

PRESENTATION MODEL — 12 ga. only, includes sideplates. Disc. 1987.

	$740	$630	$575	$495	$450	$395	$350

Add $42 for multi-chokes.
Last Mfg.'s Sug. Retail was $842.

ANGEL MODEL — 12 ga. only, field grade, SST, ejectors, wide VR, engraved receiver, recoil pad. Disc.

	$850	$775	$700	$640	$585	$530	$485

This model was distributed by Mandall Shooting Supplies, Inc.

ST. GEORGE'S TARGET — 12 ga. only, trap or skeet gun, SST, fixed choke. Disc. 1987.

	$900	$730	$645	$550	$495	$450	$400

Last Mfg.'s Sug. Retail was $1,024.

St. George's Competition — 12 ga. only, includes 30 in. O/U barrels and single barrel multi-choke. Disc. 1989.

	$1,995	$1,750	$1,550	$1,250	$995	$875	$775

Last Mfg.'s Sug. Retail was $1,627.

PATRICIA MODEL — .410 ga. only, 3 in. chambers, 28 in. barrels, SST. Disc. 1987.

	$1,175	$1,010	$900	$895	$820	$740	$650

Add $121 for case.
Last Mfg.'s Sug. Retail was $1,345.

SHOTGUNS: SIDE-BY-SIDE

QUAIL SPECIAL — .410 ga., 3 in. chambers, single trigger, 28 in. barrels. Disc. 1987.

	$205	$185	$170	$150	$125	$110	$100

Last Mfg.'s Sug. Retail was $243.

Grading	100%	98%	95%	90%	80%	70%	60%

FALCON II — .410 ga., 3 in. chambers, 26 or 28 in. barrels, double triggers. Disc. 1987.

	$205	$185	$170	$150	$125	$110	$100

Last Mfg.'s Sug. Retail was $246.

SILVER HAWK — 12 or 20 ga., double trigger, engraved.

	$420	$395	$360	$330	$300	$280	$260

SILVER SNIPE — 12 or 20 ga., various barrel lengths, VR, single trigger, engraved.

	$485	$440	$400	$360	$330	$300	$280

PHEASANT — 12 ga. only, 3 in. chambers, 28 in. barrels only, single trigger. Disc. 1987.

	$370	$320	$300	$280	$260	$240	$220

Last Mfg.'s Sug. Retail was $428.

ALLEY CLEANER — 12 or 20 ga., 3 in. chambers, 20 in. barrels, riot configuration, SST. Disc. 1987.

	$575	$495	$460	$420	$390	$350	$310

Add $65 for multi-chokes.
Last Mfg.'s Sug. Retail was $649.

CLASSIC — 12 or 20 ga., 3 in. chambers, 26-30 in. barrels, ST. Disc. 1989.

	$995	$875	$750	$650	$550	$475	$400

Add $80 for multi-chokes.
Last Mfg.'s Sug. Retail was $706.

SHOTGUNS: SINGLE BARREL AND LEVER ACTION

DIANO I — 12, 20, or .410 ga., 3 in. chambers, top lever single barrel action, folding configuration, VR. Disc. 1987.

	$115	$95	$85	$80	$75	$70	$65

Last Mfg.'s Sug. Retail was $129.

DIANO II — similar to Diano I, except has bottom lever opening. Disc. 1987.

	$115	$95	$85	$80	$75	$70	$65

Last Mfg.'s Sug. Retail was $129.

LONER I — similar to Diano I. Disc. 1987.

	$95	$80	$75	$65	$55	$45	$35

Last Mfg.'s Sug. Retail was $109.

LONER II — similar to Diano II. Disc. 1987.

	$95	$80	$75	$65	$55	$45	$35

Last Mfg.'s Sug. Retail was $109.

APACHE — 12 ga. only, lever action, 3 in. chambers, 20 in. barrel, SST. Disc. 1987.

	$410	$355	$325	$300	$280	$260	$245

Add $80 for multi-chokes.
Last Mfg.'s Sug. Retail was $473.

Grading	100%	98%	95%	90%	80%	70%	60%

SHOTGUNS: SLIDE ACTION

PUMP ACTION — 12 ga. only, available in riot, field, or deer (slug) barrel configurations, 3 in. chamber, hunter model has multi-chokes standard. Disc. 1987.

	$290	$245	$205	$185	$170	$150	$125

Last Mfg.'s Sug. Retail was $329.

COMBINATION GUNS

AIRONE — 12 ga./.30-06 or .308 Win. cal., boxlock with false sideplates, double triggers, checkered walnut stock and forearm, swivels. Disc. 1987.

	$1,450	$1,275	$1,050	$900	$800	$700	$600

CONDOR — similar to Airone, except does not have false sideplates. Disc. 1987.

	$1,295	$1,050	$900	$800	$700	$600	$500

DOUBLE RIFLES

LEOPARD EXPRESS — .30-06, .308 Win., .375 H&H, or 7 x 65R cal., boxlock action, double triggers, checkered walnut stock and forearm. Disc. 1987.

	$1,325	$1,150	$975	$900	$840	$775	$725

Last Mfg.'s Sug. Retail was $1,529.

ZOLI, ANTONIO

Manufacturer located in Brescia, Italy. No current importation. Previously imported and distributed (1990-91 only) by European American Armory Corp. located in Hialeah, FL. Prior to 1990, A. Zoli was imported and distributed exclusively by Antonio Zoli U.S.A., Inc. located in Fort Wayne, IN.

Antonio Zoli firearms are totally unrelated to those guns of Angelo Zoli (guns marked "A. Zoli" make it hard to determine the correct manufacturer). Parts are not interchangeable and warranties from Antonio Zoli firearms DO NOT apply to Angelo Zoli guns.

RIFLES: O/U

The rifles listed below (including O/U, side by side, and bolt action) are imported exclusively by Euroarms of America.

EXPRESS — 7 x 65R, 7 x 57, .30-06, .308 Win. or 9.3 x 74R cal., 25.6 in. barrels, hand checkered walnut stock with cheekpiece, set trigger for bottom barrel, extractors. Importation disc. 1993.

	$3,875	$3,250	$2,900	$2,600	$2,200	$1,950	$1,650

Add $600 for E Model (with ejectors).
Last Mfg.'s Sug. Retail was $4,400.

EXPRESS EM — 7 x 65R, .30-06, .308 Win., or 9.3 x 74R cal., mechanical single trigger, ejectors. Importation disc. 1990, reintroduced 1992 only.

	$4,850	$3,975	$3,300	$2,900	$2,600	$2,200	$1,900

Add $2,395 for De Luxe Model (disc.).
Add $7,200 for E3 De Luxe Model (disc.).
The Express E3 De Luxe Model includes 2 extra sets of barrels - 1 set is shotgun (20 ga. - 2¾ or 3 in. chambers).
Last Mfg.'s Sug. Retail was $5,300.

Grading	100%	98%	95%	90%	80%	70%	60%

RIFLES: S X S

SAVANA E — 7 x 65R, .30-06, .308 Win. or 9.3 x 74R cal., boxlock action, ejectors. Importation disc. 1990.

	$5,850	$4,850	$3,975	$3,300	$2,800	$2,350	$2,000

Add $400 for Savana EM Model (single trigger).
Last Mfg.'s Sug. Retail was $6,600.

Savana Deluxe — similar to Savana E, except has elaborate game scene engraving. Importation disc. 1990.

	$7,750	$7,100	$6,500	$6,000	$5,500	$5,000	$4,600

Last Mfg.'s Sug. Retail was $8,295.

TROPHY MODEL — similar to Savana E, except is also available in .375 H&H cal., 25½ in. barrels, 8 lbs. Imported 1991 only.

	$5,275	$4,200	$3,600	$3,150	$2,750	$2,400	$2,050

Last Mfg.'s Sug. Retail was $5,895.

RIFLES: BOLT ACTION

AZ 1900C — .243 Win., .270 Win., 6.5 x 55, .30-06, .308 Win., 7mm Rem. Mag., or .300 Win. Mag. cal., 21 or 24 (Mag. cals.) in. barrel, checkered walnut stock with weatherproof stock finish, sling swivels, iron sights, 7.4 lbs. Importation disc. 1993.

	$1,100	$850	$740	$660	$585	$500	$450

Add approx. 10% for AZ 1900 Deluxe (better walnut).
Add 60% for AZ 1900 Super Deluxe (select walnut and moderate engraving).
Add approx. 10% for Model AZ 1900 DL (photo engraved receiver and floorplate).
Last Mfg.'s Sug. Retail was $1,295.

MODEL AZ 1900M — .243 Win., 6.5 x 55mm, .270 Win., .30-06, or .308 Win. cal., 21 in. barrel, composite stock is composed of fiberglass, Kevlar, and graphite and features baked on walnut wood grain finish with checkering, drilled and tapped receiver. Imported 1991 only.

	$725	$625	$550	$495	$450	$415	$375

Add approx. 10% for Model AZ 1900M DL (photo engraved receiver and floorplate).
Last Mfg.'s Sug. Retail was $840.

SHOTGUNS: CURRENT MFG. O/U

SILVER FALCON — 12 or 20 ga., 3 in. chambers, boxlock action, SST, ejectors, 26 or 28 in. barrels with multi-chokes, coin finished receiver with engraving, checkered Turkish walnut stock and forearm with weatherproof finish. Importation disc. 1991.

	$1,450	$700	$575	$500	$450	$400	$365

Last Mfg.'s Sug. Retail was $1,695.

WOODSMAN — 12 ga. only, 3 in. chambers, 23 in. vent. barrels are designed to shoot rifle slugs at 55 yards and to accept 5 interchangeable choke tubes, SST, ejectors, quarter rib on barrels with pop-up rifle sights, checkered Circassian walnut stock and forearm with swivels (waterproof finish).

	$1,650	$1,150	$950	$800	$700	$600	$500

Last Mfg.'s Sug. Retail was $1,895.

Woodsman Combo — includes 2 sets of barrels (3 in. chambers) with Zoli interchangeable choke system.

	$2,050	$1,700	$1,475	$1,200	$1,050	$925	$800

Last Mfg.'s Sug. Retail was $2,320.

Grading	100%	98%	95%	90%	80%	70%	60%

MODEL Z-90 TARGET MODEL — 12 ga. only, boxlock action, adj. SST, black competition receiver, deluxe checkered Turkish walnut stock with recoil pad and forearm, vent. barrels and rib, SST, ejectors.

⚹ **Trap Gun** — 29½ or 32 in. barrels with screw-in chokes and raised VR, Monte Carlo stock, blue finish. Importation disc. 1993.

	$2,150	$1,450	$1,200	$995	$850	$700	$600

Last Mfg.'s Sug. Retail was $2,495.

⚹ **Mono Trap Gun** — 32 or 34 in. barrel with screw-in chokes and raised VR, Monte Carlo stock. Importation disc. 1993.

	$2,150	$1,450	$1,200	$995	$850	$700	$600

Last Mfg.'s Sug. Retail was $2,495.

⚹ **Z-90 Combo Trap Set** — includes O/U trap barrels as well as Mono trap barrel on same receiver, available as 30/32 in. sets or 32/34 in. sets. Imported 1991-92.

	$2,350	$1,900	$1,650	$1,400	$1,150	$950	$825

Last Mfg.'s Sug. Retail was $2,700.

⚹ **Skeet Gun** — 28 in. barrels only with screw-in chokes. Importation disc. 1993.

	$2,150	$1,450	$1,200	$995	$850	$700	$600

Last Mfg.'s Sug. Retail was $2,495.

⚹ **Sporting Clays Gun** — 28 in. barrels with screw-in chokes, coin finished receiver with engraved sideplates, separated barrels, Schnabel forend, solid recoil pad. Importation disc. 1990.

	$2,150	$1,450	$1,200	$995	$850	$700	$600

Last Mfg.'s Sug. Retail was $2,495.

SHOTGUNS: DISC. MFG. O/U

GOLDEN SNIPE — 12 or 20 ga, various barrel lengths, VR, single trigger, ejectors, engraved.

	$560	$520	$475	$430	$395	$360	$330

DELFINO — 12 or 20 ga., 3 in. chambers, 26 or 28 in. barrels, ejectors, VR, single non-selective trigger, blued frame with delicate engraving, walnut pistol grip stock and forearm. Disc.

	$500	$425	$375	$325	$295	$280	$265

RITMO HUNTING — 12 ga. only, 3 in. chambers, 26 or 28 in. vent. barrels and rib, SST, ejectors, select checkered walnut, blued frame and barrels with moderate engraving, recoil pad, 7¼ lbs. Disc.

	$575	$510	$465	$410	$370	$350	$335

RITMO PIGEON GRADE IV — 12 ga. only, live pigeon gun, 28 in. barrels, SST, ejectors, superbly engraved silver finished receiver, extra fine checkering on deluxe walnut, vent. barrels and rib, cased, 7½ lbs. Disc.

	$1,600	$1,450	$1,200	$1,000	$875	$795	$725

M85 RITMO TRAP OR SKEET — 12 ga. only, 28 in. (Skeet only), 30, or 32 in. barrels, ejectors, SST, special stock dimensions, engraved blue receiver, select checkered walnut stock and forearm, cased, 7¾ lbs. Disc.

	$595	$500	$465	$440	$415	$395	$370

This model was also available in a single barrel trap model at no extra charge.

Grading	100%	98%	95%	90%	80%	70%	60%

✂ **M85 Ritmo Trap Combination** — 12 ga. only, supplied with O/U and single barrel sets, various barrel lengths, cased. Disc.

	$995	$895	$800	$700	$620	$575	$500

SHOTGUNS: CURRENT MFG. SIDE-BY-SIDE

UPLANDER — 12 or 20 ga., 3 in. chambers, 25 in. barrels with fixed chokes (IC/M), ST, ejectors, color case hardened receiver, English style checkered Circassian walnut stock and forearm with oil or polyurethane finish. Importation disc. 1990.

	$750	$625	$560	$520	$485	$450	$425

Last Mfg.'s Sug. Retail was $1,295.

SILVER FOX — 12 or 20 ga., 3 in. chambers, 26 or 28 (12 ga. only) in. barrels with fixed chokes, ST, ejectors, hand engraved silver finished receiver with "AZ" in gold, straight grip checkered Circassian walnut stock and forearm. Importation disc. 1990.

	$1,650	$1,425	$1,200	$995	$875	$750	$625

Last Mfg.'s Sug. Retail was $2,995.

SHOTGUNS: DISC. MFG. SIDE-BY-SIDE

ARIETE M3 — 12 ga. only, 26 or 28 in. barrels, matted rib, single non-selective trigger, ejectors, blued receiver with fine scroll engraving, cased. Disc.

	$550	$475	$400	$360	$330	$310	$285

EMPIRE — 12 or 20 ga. Mag., 27 or 28 in. barrels, moderate engraving, coin finished receiver. Disc.

	$1,425	$1,175	$975	$875	$795	$725	$650

Add $100 for 3 in. Mag. chambers.
This model was distributed by Euroarms of America, Inc.

VOLCANO RECORD — 12 ga. only, 28 in. barrels, H&H type sidelocks, ejectors, SST, treble Purdey locks, silver finished receiver with elaborate engraving, best quality fine checkered walnut, special order only. Disc.

	$5,300	$4,475	$3,950	$3,400	$2,950	$2,650	$2,300

✂ **Volcano Record ELM** — 12 ga. only, built to individual customer specifications, best quality H&H style sidelock. Discs.

	$13,250	$11,000	$9,750	$8,600	$7,400	$6,300	$5,450

This model was distributed by Euroarms of America, Inc.

CUSTOM SERIES — SxS, individual custom order only, every refinement is used in the construction of these extremely rare and expensive shotguns. These guns have to be appraised individually since their numbers are so few.

COMBINATION GUNS

COMBINATO — 12 or 20 ga. over .243 or .222 cal., boxlock action, game scene engraved receiver with silver finish, double triggers, folding rear sight, skipline checkering, with sling swivels. Importation disc. 1993.

	$1,750	$1,500	$1,300	$1,100	$950	$775	$600

Last Mfg.'s Sug. Retail was $1,995.

✂ **Combinato Set** — includes one set of either 20 or 12 ga. barrels and an additional rifle/shotgun barrel set, same cals. as Combinato, cased. Importation disc. 1993.

	$2,400	$2,150	$1,850	$1,600	$1,400	$1,200	$995

Last Mfg.'s Sug. Retail was $2,700.

Grading	100%	98%	95%	90%	80%	70%	60%

SAFARI DELUXE — similar to Combinato, except has sideplates with elaborate game scene engraving. Importation disc. 1993.

| | $4,850 | $4,400 | $3,950 | $3,550 | $3,175 | $2,800 | $2,400 |

Add approx. 50% for Safari Deluxe 2 (includes 2 sets of shotgun barrels).
Last Mfg.'s Sug. Retail was $5,200.

EXPRESS E3 SET — includes one set of .30-06 O/U barrels, one set of 20 ga./.243 cal. barrels, one set of 20 ga./20 ga. barrels, special order, elaborate game scene engraving, includes German claw mount 4X scope and case. Disc.

| | $2,750 | $2,400 | $2,100 | $1,850 | $1,650 | $1,500 | $1,375 |

MODERN AIRGUNS

While watching KARE 11 News the other night, I was pleased to hear, "with all the bad news associated with firearms in our society today, it's nice to bring you a story about the fun, recreational use of guns today." The story was called "It's All Air", a wonderful 3 to 5 minute piece on the recreational use of air rifles and pistols. The story covered a broad range of people and activities from a gentleman who shot targets in his basement for relaxation, to a woman who picked up the sport a few years ago (practicing in an upstairs hallway) and is now one of the best competitors in the midwest. It was really a thrill to see this on prime time news and I must thank KARE 11 News in Minneapolis, MN for running this great human interest story.

Another wonderful bit of recognition was given to the airgun industry at the 1993 SHOT Show in Houston, TX. Dr. Robert Beeman was presented the Lifetime Achievement Award by the National Alliance of Stocking Gun Dealers. This prestigious award has only been given four times before, placing Dr. Beeman in such elite company as John Browning, Bill Ruger and Ron Weatherby. Dr. Beeman has been and continues to be a driving force in pioneering and marketing of precision adult airguns worldwide. His company, Beeman Precision Arms, Inc. in Santa Rosa, CA, continues to expand their product line and have just opened a branch in Queensland, Australia. In a personal conversation with Dr. Beeman, he made reference to a lot of rumors floating around in 1992 regarding his personal health. His response was, "I feel wonderful and to paraphrase Mark Twain, the rumors of my death have been greatly exaggerated." Congratulations to Dr. Beeman on his personal award as well as the recognition he has brought the Airgun industry as a whole.

A note about Pricing: You can see this section, like Black Powder, only contains pricing down to 95% grading. Due to the mechanical complexity of Airguns, and the fact that most sophisticated Airguns are used solely for target practice (many have had several thousand rounds through them), guns under 95% condition retain very little of their original value. Most collector guns (i.e. old Benjamins, Crosman and Daisy) trade for under $100 with only a few 100% guns trading for more.

Medium priced airguns from large distributors, such as Marksman, RWS, Norica and Gamo are so heavily discounted to the Distributor/Dealer that many "new-in-the-box" guns can be purchased for the price of a 98% gun. Also, the lack of available parts for older collectibles and non-functioning airguns contribute to a reduced value. It should also be noted that prices in this section have to cover a broad range of vendors. Used guns purchased from factory importers with test facilities or from dealers with factory authorized repair centers will command a higher sales price.

AS WITH THE SECTION OF BLACK POWDER GUNS, AIRGUNS UNDER $100 ARE NOT SHOWN. ENGRAVED GUNS OR GUNS WITH FANCY WOOD SHOULD BE DISCOUNTED A MINIMUM OF 50% IF UNDER 95% CONDITION.

Sincerely,

Patrick M. Lucking
Modern Airguns Editor
Blue Book of Gun Values

ARS/FARCO

Manufactured in the Philippines. Imported by Air Rifle Specialists located in Elmira, NY. Guns available both through dealer and direct importer.

AIR RIFLES

Grading	100%	98%	95%

AR6 (6 SHOT REPEATING AIR RIFLE)—.22 CO_2 or compressed air powered, $23\frac{1}{4}$ in. barrel, capable of delivering 18 shots at 50 ft/lbs. power (1,000 FPS) using compressed air or up to 80 shots at 19-22 ft/lbs. power using CO_2 (single fill), checkered walnut stock, 6 lbs. 12 oz.

Mfg.'s Sug. Retail	$550	$490	$430	$320

Add $20 for extra 6 shot cylinder.
Add $50 for charging unit.

AIR SHOTGUNS

FARCO AIR SHOTGUN — 28 ga., CO_2 powered, 30 in. barrel, 100 FT/LBS. of energy (standard airgun has 12-14 lbs.), charged by refillable (and removable) 10 oz. cylinder, hardwood stock, 7 lbs. Importation began in 1988.

Mfg.'s Sug. Retail	$395	$360	$295	$235

AIR ARMS

Imported by Air Rifle Specialists located in Elmira, NY, Beeman Precision Arms, Inc. located in Santa Rosa, CA, and Dynamit Nobel-RWS, Inc. located in Closter, NJ. Available both through dealers and direct importer.

Editors note: These guns are filled from high pressure scuba tanks allowing many shots to be fired from one charge. This also allows one to adjust the power level of each shot. All guns are made with Walther barrels that float so that expansion or contraction of the air chamber will not affect its accuracy. Add $150 for Olympic trigger, $200 for regulator, and $50 for lever bolt.

SM100 — .177 or .22 cal. precharged pneumatic, 22 in. barrel, power can range from 12 to 19 ft/lbs. in .177 or 12 to 22 ft/lbs. in .22 cal, two stage trigger (adjustable), beech stock, 8 lbs. 8 oz.

Mfg.'s Sug. Retail	$870	$750	$630	$505

Add $60 for left hand.

XM100 — same as above but with quick release tank connector, and walnut stock, 8 lbs.

Mfg.'s Sug. Retail	$1,060	$940	$700	$630

Add $60 for left hand.

TM100 — same as above but with adj. cheek piece and shoulder pad, (target style stock), 8 lbs. 12 oz.

Mfg.'s Sug. Retail	$1,300	$1,170	$1,010	$800

Add $60 for left hand.

TX200 — .177 or .22 cal., underlever action, $15\frac{3}{4}$ in. barrel, 913/800 FPS, 9.3 lbs.

Mfg.'s Sug. Retail	$495	$425	N/A	N/A

NJR100 — same as above but with hand picked barrel for accuracy, adj. cheek piece, forearm and shoulder pad, designed by and named after Nick Jenkinson (one of England's top field target shooters), 10 lbs. 12 oz.

Mfg.'s Sug. Retail	$1,800	$1,670	$1,430	$1,045

Add $60 for left hand.

AIR LOGIC

Manufacturer/distributor located in Forest Row, Sussex, England. Available through dealers and used market.

Air Logic has limited importation into the U.S. More information can be obtained by contacting Air Logic directly at: Air Logic Limited, 3 Medway Bldgs., Lower Road Forest Row, East Sussex ENGLAND RH18 5HE.

Grading	100%	98%	95%

GENESIS — .22 cal., single stroke pneumatic, 630 FPS, unique bolt action sliding barrel (by L. Walther), recoilless, adj. trigger, side lever action, $9\frac{1}{2}$ lbs. New for 1988.

	$550	$400	$350

Last Mfg.'s Sug. Retail was $750.

AIR MATCH
Previously imported by Kendall International located in Paris, KY. No longer imported, used guns only.

Grading	100%	98%	95%

AIR MATCH MODEL 600 PISTOL — .177 cal., side lever action, adj. trigger, professional target model, 2 lbs.

	$395	$250	$185

AMERICAN ARMS, INC.
Manufacturer/importer located in North Kansas City, MO.

Even though American Arms, Inc. imports Norica airguns, they are listed in this section because of their private label status. Importation began in late 1988 and was discontinued in 1989.

RIFLES

JET RIFLE — .177 cal., barrel break action, 855 FPS, adj. double set triggers, hardwood stock, 7 lbs.

	$105	$90	$75

Last Mfg.'s Sug. Retail was $160.
Deduct $65 for Junior Model.

COMMANDO — .177 cal., barrel break action, 540 FPS, adj. sights, 5 lbs.

	$80	$60	$40

Last Mfg.'s Sug. Retail was $115.

PISTOLS

IDEAL — .177 cal., barrel break action, 400 FPS, adj. sights, 3 lbs.

	$80	$60	$40

Last Mfg.'s Sug. Retail was $105.

ANSCHUTZ
Manufactured in Ulm, Germany. Available through dealers and some models through Marksman direct. Models 2001 and 2002 imported by Precision Sales Intl. Inc. PO Box 1776, Westfield, MA 01086.

Models 333, 335, and 380 were previously imported by Crosman from 1986-1988. While discontinued, some dealers may still have remaining inventories of these models. Model 380 now imported by Marksman.

MODEL 333 — .177 cal., barrel cocking action, 700 FPS, adj. trigger, 18 in. barrel, 6¾ lbs.

	$160	$115	$85

Last Mfg.'s Sug. Retail was $175.

MODEL 335 — .177 cal., barrel cocking, 700 FPS, adj. trigger, 18½ in. barrel, 7½ lbs. Add $10 for 335 Mag. (20% higher velocity).

	$165	$130	$95

Last Mfg.'s Sug. Retail was $200.

MODEL 380 — .177 cal., under lever cocking, 600-640 FPS, professional match model, removable cheekpiece, adj. trigger, stippled walnut grips. Add $30 for left hand, $60 for moving target.

Mfg.'s Sug. Retail	$1,250	$1,000	$800	$575

MODEL 2001 — .177 cal., single stroke pneumatic, side lever action, exceptional target model, 10 lbs. 8 oz. Add $80 for left hand.

	$1,410	$920	$815

Add $80 for Running Target Model.
Last Mfg.'s Sug. Retail was $1,800.

Grading	100%	98%	95%

MODEL 2002 — .177 cal. single stroke pneumatic, side lever action, 26" barrel, this gun incorporates some of the latest technology used in air rifles, wt. 10½ lbs. New 1992. Add $40 for left hand.

Mfg.'s Sug. Retail	$2,000	$1,700	$1,445	$1,156

Add $80 for running target.

Model 2002 imported by Precision Sales, Westfield, Mass.

BRNO AERON

Manufactured in Czechoslovakia and imported by Century International Arms, Inc. located in St. Albans, VT. Available thru dealers.

RIFLES

TAU-200 — .177 cal., CO_2 powered professional target model, synthetic adj. stock.

No Mfg.'s Retail	$290	$250	N/A

PISTOLS

TAU FREE PISTOL — .177 cal., CO_2 powered professional target model, attache case, extra seals and counter weight.

No Mfg.'s Retail	$285	$240	N/A

B S A GUNS (U.K.), LTD.

Manufactured in Birmingham, England. Imported from January 1992 by Dynamit-Nobel RWS of North Vale, NJ, Air Rifle Specialists in Elmira, NY and Spot-on-Air Mpls, MN. Available both dealer and importer direct.

Add $100 for guns equipped with Theoben gas ram. (spring).

AIRSPORTER/AIRSPORTER SUPER: — .177 or .22 cal., under lever action, 700-550 FPS/825-600 FPS. (Super), 8 lbs. Add $50 for Super, $25 for Monte Carlo stock Stutzen Model.

	$140	$110	$85

CENTENNIAL COMMEMORATIVE — .177 or .22 cal., designed to commemorate BSA's 100th year.

	$225	$190	$125

Last Mfg.'s Sug. Retail was $650.

GOLDSTAR — .22 cal., under lever action, 625 FPS, 18½ in. barrel, two stage adjustable trigger, hardwood stock has10 shot rotary magazine (developed from the VS2000), 8½ lbs.

Mfg.'s Sug. Retail	$790	$500	$400	$320

MERCURY/MERCURY SUPER — .177 or .22 cal., barrel cocking action, 700-550 FPS/825-600 FPS (super), 7¼ lbs. Add $35 for Super.

	$120	$90	$70

MERCURY CHALLENGER — .177 or .22 cal., barrel cocking action, 850-625 FPS, 7 lbs. 4 oz. Disc. 1988.

	$120	$90	$70

Last Mfg.'s Sug. Retail was $205.

METEOR/METEOR SUPER — .177 or .22 cal., barrel cocking action, 650-500 FPS, 18½" barrel, 6 lbs. Add $15 for Super.

	$70	$45	$35

SUPER SPORT/SUPER SPORT CUSTOM — .177, .22 or .25 cal., barrel cocking action, (850/625/530 FPS), 18½" barrel approx. 7 lbs. Add $115 for custom model, $120 for guns equipped with Theoben gas ram (spring).

Mfg.'s Sug. Retail	$250	$210	$185	$160

Importation began in 1990.

Grading	100%	98%	95%

SUPERSTAR — .177, .22, or .25 cal., underlever action, (850/625/530 FPS), 18½ in. barrel, unique rotating breech for loading pellets directly into bore, checkered beech stock, maxi grip scope rail, two stage trigger, approx. 7¾ lbs.

Mfg.'s Sug. Retail	$435	$365	$315	$265

Add $120 for guns equipped with Theoben gas ram (spring).

STUTZEN — same as above with shorter overall length (39") (14" barrel) and Stutzen full length stock, 7 lbs. 4 oz.

Mfg.'s Sug. Retail	$490	$415	$355	$290

VS 2000 — .177 or .22 cal., 9 shot repeater, side lever action, 850-625 FPS, 9 lbs. Add $65 for custom model. Disc. 1988.

	$325	$230	$160

Last Mfg.'s Sug. Retail was $330.
Only 20 or so of this model ever made.

PISTOLS

SCORPION PISTOL — .177 or .22 cal., barrel-cocking action 510-380 FPS, 3.6 lbs. Add $50 for carbine stock, Shadow Model.

Mfg.'s Sug. Retail	$190	$170	$145	$90

B.S.F. (BAYERISCHE SPORTWAFFENFABRIK)

Manufactured in Germany. Previously imported by Kendell International located in Paris, KY and Beeman Precision Arms under the Wischo label. Available only on the used market.

B.S.F. tooling and machinery have been purchased by Weihrauch and is being utilized to manufacture older versions of B.S.F. Models for Marksman (Marksman Models 28, 40, 55, 56, 58, 59, 70, 71, 72 and 75).

RIFLES

BAVARIA MODEL 35 — .177 cal., barrel-cocking action, 500 FPS, 4½ lbs.

	$125	$100	$85

Last Mfg.'s Sug. Retail was $125.

BAVARIA MODEL 45 — .177 cal., barrel-cocking action, 700 FPS, 6 lbs.

	$135	$105	$80

Last Mfg.'s Sug. Retail was $125.

BAVARIA MODEL 50 — .177 cal., barrel-cocking action, 700 FPS, 6 lbs.

	$140	$105	$80

BAVARIA MODEL S54 — .177 or .22 cal., under lever action, 685/500 FPS, 8 lbs. Add $15 for Sport Model (discontinued 1986), $30 for M Model.

	$200	$160	$100

BAVARIA MODEL 55 — .177 or .22 cal., barrel-cocking action, 800/570 FPS, 6½ lbs. Add $15 for Deluxe Model, $30 for Special Model (both discontinued 1986).

	$155	$130	$100

BAVARIA MODEL S60 — .177 or .22 cal., barrel-cocking action, 800/570 FPS, 6½ lbs.

	$160	$135	$80

BAVARIA MODEL S70 — .177 or .22 cal., barrel-cocking action, 800/570 FPS, 7 lbs.

	$165	$140	$100

BAVARIA MODEL S80 — .177 or .22 cal., barrel-cocking action, 800/570 FPS, 8¼ lbs.

	$185	$150	$125

Last Mfg.'s Sug. Retail was $185.

BEEMAN PRECISION ARMS, INC.

Importers and distributors located in Santa Rosa, CA. Beeman has exclusive rights to any items marketed in the U.S. under the names Beeman, Feinwerkbau, Weihrauch and Webley.

Beeman imported Feinwerkbau and Weihrauch Airguns will appear under their respective headings in this section. Available through dealers and Beeman direct.

RIFLES

Grading	100%	98%	95%

BEEMAN R1—.177, .20, .22 or .25 cal., barrel-cocking action, 1000-610 FPS, 8.8 lbs. Add $300 for custom grade, $335 for custom fancy, $400 for X fancy, $50 for left-hand.

Mfg.'s Sug. Retail	$450	$345	$300	$230

Add $450 for Laser Model.
Add $160 for Field Target or Tyrolean Model.
Add $35 for blue/stainless steel version.
Add $100 for Tyrolean stock.
Add $75 for commemorative model.

BEEMAN R7 — .177, .20 cal., barrel-cocking action, 700 - 620 FPS, 6.1 lbs. Add $10 for .20 cal.

Mfg.'s Sug. Retail	$280	$205	$180	$145

BEEMAN R8 — .177 cal., barrel-cocking action, 720 FPS, 7.2 lbs.

Mfg.'s Sug. Retail	$350	$255	$220	$170

BEEMAN R10 — .177, .20, or .22 cal., barrel-cocking action, 1,000- 750 FPS, 7.9 lbs. Add $300 for custom grade, $335 for custom fancy, $400 for X fancy, $40 for left-hand, and $50 for deluxe, $10 for .20 cal.

Mfg.'s Sug. Retail	$360	$275	$240	$215

Add $20 for .20 cal.
Add $400 for Laser Model.

BEEMAN RX — .177, .20, .22, and .25 cal., Theoben gas spring, spring piston system (See Theoben), up to 1200 FPS/.177 cal., adj. velocity, (release delayed until summer 1991). Add $10 for .20 and .25 cal., $140 for Field Target, and $60 for left hand. Add $100 for commemorative model. Disc. 1992.

	$400	$330	$220

Last Mfg.'s Sug. Retail was $470.

BEEMAN RX-1 — improved version of Model RX above.

Mfg.'s Sug. Retail	$485	$395	N/A	N/A

Add $50 for right-hand.
Add $60 for commemorative model.

BEEMAN AIR WOLF — .177, .20, .22 and .25 cal. precharged pneumatic, 21" barrel, internal air chamber, manual safety. Wt. 5⅝ lbs. New in 1992.

Mfg.'s Sug. Retail	$600	$540	$450	$360

Add $20 for .20 cal.
Add $75 for charging adapter w/gauge.

BEEMAN CARBINE C1 — .177 or .22 cal., barrel-cocking action, 830-670 FPS, 6.2-6.3 lbs.

Mfg.'s Sug. Retail	$260	$180	$165	$130

BEEMAN CLASSIC MAGNUM — .177, .20, .22 and .25 cal., gas spring, barrel cocking action, 15" barrel, manual button safety, checkered walnut stock, 8⅝ lbs. New 1992.

Mfg.'s Sug. Retail	$895	$800	$700	$560

Add $80 for power adjustment pump.

BEEMAN CROW MAGNUM — .20, .22, and .25 cal., gas spring, barrel cocking action, 16" barrel, manual button safety, 8¼ lbs. New 1992.

Mfg.'s Sug. Retail	$1,095	$1,000	$900	$750

Add $80 for power adjustment pump.

Grading	100%	98%	95%

BEEMAN FALCON 1 & 2 — .177 cal., barrel-cocking action, 620-680 FPS/560-600 FPS, 6.7/5.9 lbs. Add $30 for Falcon 2. Discontinued in 1984.

	$105	$80	$60

Last Mfg.'s Sug. Retail was $110.

BEEMAN FX 1 & 2 — same as Beeman Falcon 1 & 2. Add $30 for FX 1. Disc. 1992.

	$110	$90	$75

Last Mfg.'s Sug. Retail was $140.

BEEMAN GAME KEEPER — .25 cal., precharged pneumatic, quick change gas cylinder (bottle), 15" barrel, manual lever safety, 7⅞-8¼ lbs. New 1992.

Mfg.'s Sug. Retail	$990	$890	$750	$600

Add $80 for extra quick change bottle.
Add $90 each for interchangeable barrels.
Add $100 for deluxe grade 2 walnut stock.

BEEMAN/HARPER AIR CANE — .22 or .25 cal., pneumatic (reuseable gas cartridge), 650 FPS, reproduction of 19th century Walking Cane Gun, 1 lb. Add $60 for decorative head piece.

	$595	$500	$400

Last Mfg.'s Sug. Retail was $595.
Only 50 of these models were ever imported into the U.S.

BEEMAN MANITOU FT — .177 cal. precharged pneumatic, internal air chamber, 21" barrel, 8¾ lbs. New 1992.

Mfg.'s Sug. Retail	$895	$820	$780	$625

Add $50 for left-hand.
Add $40 for High Power model.
Add $75 for charge adapter with gauge.

BEEMAN SUPER 7 — .22 precharged pneumatic, quick change gas cylinder (bottle), 19" barrel, checkered walnut stock, manual button safety, 7¼ lbs. New 1992.

Mfg.'s Sug. Retail	$1,560	$1,430	$1,200	$950

BEEMAN UL-7 — .22 cal., underlever action, gas spring, 12" barrel, manual button safety, 7 shot repeater with removable rotary magazine, checkered walnut stock. New 1992.

Mfg.'s Sug. Retail	$1,560	$1,400	$1,200	$950

Add $80 for power adjustment pump.

BEEMAN/WEBLEY OMEGA — .177 or .22 cal., barrel cocking action, 830-675 FPS, 7.8 lbs. Disc. 1992.

	$225	$190	$160

Last Mfg.'s Sug. Retail was $430.

BEEMAN/WEBLEY ECLIPSE — .177, .22 or .25 cal., underlever action, 990 FPS (in .177 cal.). New 1990.

Mfg.'s Sug. Retail	$460	$350	$290	$210

BEEMAN/WEBLEY KODIAK SUPER MAGNUM — .177, .22, or .25 cal., barrel cocking action, 820 FPS (.25 cal.), 17½ in. barrel, 8.9 lbs. New 1993.

Mfg.'s Sug. Retail	$550	$450	N/A	N/A

BEEMAN/WEBLEY VULCAN III AND VULCAN III DELUXE — .177 or .22 cal., barrel-cocking action, 830-675 FPS, 7.6-7.7 lbs. Add $60 for Deluxe.

Mfg.'s Sug. Retail	$260	$190	$165	$130

BEEMAN WOLF PUP — .20, .22, and .25 precharged pneumatic, internal cylinder, 13½" barrel, manual safety.

Mfg.'s Sug. Retail	$600	$540	N/A	N/A

Add $20 for .20 cal.
Add $75 for charging adaptor w/gauge.
Add $150 for Deluxe Model with thumbhole stock and match trigger.

Grading	100%	98%	95%

PISTOLS

BEEMAN ADDER — .20 and .25 cal. precharged pneumatic, internal air chamber, 7" barrel, manual safety, 2¾ lbs. New 1992.

Mfg.'s Sug. Retail	$480	$420	$350	N/A

BEEMAN/FAS 604 — .177 cal., top lever spring pneumatic action, 380 FPS, 2.3 lbs. Add $30 for left-hand. Disc. 1988.

	$460	$400	$240

Last Mfg.'s Sug. Retail was $495.

BEEMAN/HARPER CLASSIC PISTOL — .22 or .25 cal., similar to Harper Air Cane rifle action, 300 FPS, 4 oz. Add $10 for .25 cal., $35 for deluxe. Disc. 1989.

	$385	$320	$255

Add $210 if cased. Retail for a cased pair is $700.
Only 6 ever imported into U.S.
Last Mfg.'s Sug. Retail was $285.

BEEMAN/HARPER PEPPERBOX PISTOL — .22 cal., pneumatic (like above), 9.8 oz. Disc. 1989.

	$770	$620	$410

Only 3 of this model imported into U.S.
Last Mfg.'s Sug. Retail was $575.

BEEMAN P1 — .177, .20 or .22 cal. Mag., top cocking action, 600-350 FPS, dual power, walnut grips, Colt .45 look alike.

Mfg.'s Sug. Retail	$345	$270	$210	$175

Add $295 for gold plating.
Add $35 for stainless steel style or blue/stainless dual finish.
Add $60 for Commemorative Model.

BEEMAN P2 — .177 and .20 cal., single stroke pneumatic, similar to above but professional mid-priced match gun. New 1991.

Mfg.'s Sug. Retail	$385	$275	$245	$195

Add $15 for match grips.

BEEMAN/WEBLEY HURRICANE — .177 or .22 cal., barrel-cocking action, 470-400 FPS, 2.4 lbs. Add $40 for M20 scope combo.

Mfg.'s Sug. Retail	$200	$160	$135	$100

BEEMAN/WEBLEY TEMPEST — .177 or .22 cal., barrel-cocking action, 470-400 FPS, 2 lbs.

Mfg.'s Sug. Retail	$175	$135	$120	$90

BEEMAN WOLVERINE — .177, .20, .22, and .25 cal. precharged pneumatic, internal air chamber, 10½" barrel, manual safety, 3 lbs.

Mfg.'s Sug. Retail	$600	$535	$465	$370

BENJAMIN AIR RIFLE COMPANY

Manufacturer located in Racine, WI. Available both through dealers and factory direct. Purchased January 1992 by Crosman Air Guns located in E. Bloomfield, NY.

CENTENNIAL MODEL 87 — .177 or .22 cal., multi-stroke pneumatic, 750/650 FPS, polished brass barrel, all nickel trim, Williams aperture, built to commemorate the 100th anniversary, bronze medallion in stock, 6 lbs., 6,086 mfg.

	$205	$105	$70

Last Mfg.'s Sug. Retail was $250.

BENJAMIN MODEL 340, 342, AND 347 — BB, .177 or .22 cal., pneumatic pump action, 750-650 FPS, 4½ lbs., (340-BB), (342-.22), (347-.177). Add $15 for Williams sight, $30 for 4 x 15 scope.

	$85	$65	$50

Last Mfg.'s Sug. Retail was $110.

Grading	100%	98%	95%

BENJAMIN MODEL 392/397 — .177 and .22 cal. (392), CO_2 or pneumatic pump action, 750-700 FPS, $19\frac{3}{8}$ in. barrel, available in chrome or black matte finish, walnut stock, 5 lbs. 8 oz. New 1991.

Mfg.'s Sug. Retail	$125	$110	$95	$80

Add $5 for chrome.
Add $25 for Williams peepsight.
Subtract $10 for CO_2 (600-500 FPS). Denoted with "G" prefix.

PISTOLS

BENJAMIN AIR PISTOL MODEL 130, 132, AND 137 — .177 cal., pneumatic pump action, 380 FPS, 2 lbs.

	$70	$50	$35

Last Mfg.'s Sug. Retail was $85.

BENJAMIN AIR PISTOL MODEL 242, 247 — .177 and .22 cal., pneumatic pump action, 418/315 FPS, 2 lbs. 8 oz..

	$75	$65	$50

Last Mfg.'s Sug. Retail was $90.

BENJAMIN/SHERIDAN AIR PISTOL MODEL H/HB—.177, .20, and .22 cal., pneumatic pump action, 400 FPS, $9\frac{3}{8}$ in. barrel, available in chrome (H) or black matte finish (HB), walnut grips, 2 lbs. 8 oz. New in 1991. Add $5 for chrome.

Mfg.'s Sug. Retail	$110	$90	$75	$60

Model E/EB is CO_2 version of above. Deduct $10 for CO_2.

CROSMAN AIR GUNS

East Bloomfield, NY.

Other than the continued sale of the Model 84 and Skanaker, Crosman has dropped adult precision Airguns. The Crosman/Anschutz models listed below should be watched for collectors value due to their limited U.S. distribution using Crosman model numbers. Available both through dealers and factory direct.

MODEL 84 AIR RIFLE — .177 cal., CO_2 powered, match rifle, 0-720 FPS (fully adj.), adj. sights, walnut stock with adj. cheekplate and butt plate, 11 lbs. Disc. 1992.

	$800	$600	$500

Crosman Model 84 was the first U.S. made air rifle designed to compete with established European models. Unlike its competitors, it is CO_2 powered with a digital gauge mounted on the forearm to show remaining pressure.
Last Mfg.'s Sug. Retail was $1,295.

6500 (ANSCHUTZ MODEL 335) — .177 cal., barrel break action, 700 FPS, $18\frac{1}{2}$ in. barrel, 7 lbs. 10.5 oz. Disc. in 1989.

	$175	$125	$95

Last Mfg.'s Sug. Retail was $200.

6300 (ANSCHUTZ MODEL 333) — .177 cal., barrel break action, 700 FPS, $18\frac{1}{2}$ in. barrel, 6 lbs. 13 oz. Disc. in 1989.

	$170	$110	$85

Last Mfg.'s Sug. Retail was $175.

MODEL 6100 (MADE BY DIANAWERK) — .177 cal., barrel break action, 780/830 FPS, $20\frac{1}{2}$ in. barrel, 8 lbs. 6 oz. Disc. in 1989.

	$155	$115	$85

Last Mfg.'s Sug. Retail was $235.

Grading	100%	98%	95%

PISTOLS

SKANAKER PISTOL (AVAILABLE 1987) MODEL 88 — .177 cal., CO_2 powered, 550 FPS, professional target model. Add $65 for carrying case.

$400 $350 $300

As of Dec. 31, 1991 Crosman liquidated its supply of Skanaker pistols. This was due to the expiration of a contract allowing them to use the Skanaker name. All remaining pistols were sold to Air Rifle Specialists, Elmira, NY.
Last Mfg.'s Sug. Retail was $795.

DAISY MANUFACTURING CO., INC.
Manufactured and distributed in Rogers, AR.

Even though Daisy is one of the largest airgun manufacturers in the world, only 6 weapons would fall into the category of adult precision airguns - these are the Daisy 126 El Gamo, Model 128 Gamo Olympic, Model 953, Model 753, and their 2 target pistols (Models 747 and 777). The Daisy 126 El Gamo rifle and Model 128 Gamo Olympic are manufactured in Spain and assembled in the U.S. All 6 airguns have barrels made by Lothar Walther. Available through dealers only.

RIFLES

EL GAMO 126 SUPER MATCH TARGET RIFLE — .177 cal., single stroke pneumatic, 590 FPS, adj. sights, hardwood stock, 10 lbs. 9 oz.

Mfg.'s Sug. Retail	$620	$440	$350	$250

MODEL 128 GAMO OLYMPIC — same as above except with adj. cheek and butt piece, high quality European diopter sight.

	$490	$425	$350

Last Mfg.'s Sug. Retail was $735.

MODEL 130 — .177 cal., barrel cocking action, 800 FPS, adjustable micrometer sight, 5¾ lbs.

Mfg.'s Sug. Retail	$150	$120	$95	$60

MODEL 753 COMPETITION — .177 cal., single stroke pneumatic, 480 FPS, competition sights, 6lbs. 8 oz.

Mfg.'s Sug. Retail	$325	$230	$200	$145

953 TARGET — .177 cal., single stroke pneumatic, 480 FPS, Lothar Walther barrel, adj. sights, 5 lbs. 8 oz.

	$150	$125	$95

Last Mfg.'s Sug. Retail was $200.

853 TARGET — .177 cal., same as Model 953 which was being phased out in 1991.

Mfg.'s Sug. Retail	$200	$140	$120	$95

PISTOLS

MODEL 747 TARGET PISTOL — .177 cal., side lever action, single stroke pneumatic, 360 FPS, 3 lbs. 3 oz.

Mfg.'s Sug. Retail	$135	$95	$80	$55

MODEL 777 TARGET PISTOL — .177 cal., side lever action, single stroke pneumatic, 360 FPS, wood target style grips, 3 lbs. 3 oz.

Mfg.'s Sug. Retail	$275	$190	$165	$115

MODEL 91 — .177 cal., CO_2 powered, 425 FPS, 10¼ in. barrel, imported from Hungary, 2 lbs. 7 oz. New spring 1991.

Mfg.'s Sug. Retail	$525	$360	$320	$235

This is being imported by Daisy as an entry level professional target pistol, similar in design to Feinwerkbau or Crosman's Skanaker pistol.

DIANAWERK, MAYER AND GRAMMELSPACHER

Manufacturer located in Germany.

Dynamit Nobel RWS Inc. is the exclusive Dianawerk importer located in Closter, NJ. Available both from dealer and importer direct. Dynamit Nobel RWS, Inc. is also importing airguns manufactured by Air Arms, BSA, and Gamo. Please refer to their respective listings under this section for pricing.

RIFLES

Grading	100%	98%	95%

MODEL 24 — .177 or .22 cal., barrel-cocking action, 700/400 FPS, 17¼ in. barrel, 6 lbs. Deduct $25 for Model 24J. New in 1987.

Mfg.'s Sug. Retail	$185	$110	$95	$75

MODEL 25D — .177 or .22 cal., barrel-cocking action, 525/380 FPS, 15¾ in. barrel, 5¾ lbs. (sport). Disc. in 1987.

	$105	$80	$60

Last Mfg.'s Sug. Retail was $120.

MODEL 26 — .177 or .22 cal., barrel-cocking action, 750/500 FPS, 17¼ in. barrel, 6 lbs. 1 oz. Disc. 1992.

	$160	$130	$80

Last Mfg.'s Sug. Retail was $195.

MODEL 27 — .177 or .22 cal., barrel-cocking action, 550/415 FPS, 17¼ in. barrel, 6 lbs. (sport). Disc. in 1987.

	$150	$110	$90

Last Mfg.'s Sug. Retail was $150.

MODEL 28 — .177 or .22 cal., barrel-cocking action, 750/500 FPS, 15¾ in. barrel, 6 lbs. 12 oz. Disc. 1992.

	$135	$115	$90

Last Mfg.'s Sug. Retail was $205.

MODEL 30 — 4.4mm (RWS #7) round ball, original European gallery gun action, 17 in. barrel, 7¼ lbs. New 1993, limited production piece.

Mfg.'s Sug. Retail	$1,000	$600	N/A	N/A

MODEL 34 — .177 or .22 cal., barrel-cocking action, 950/700 FPS, 19½ in. barrel, 7 lbs. 6 oz. Add $10 for 100 year Diana Commemorative Model (new in 1990).

Mfg.'s Sug. Retail	$245	$160	$120	$95

MODEL 35 — .177 or .22 cal., barrel-cocking action, 665/540 FPS, 19 in. barrel, 8 lbs. (sport/target). Disc. in 1987.

	$105	$80	$60

Last Mfg.'s Sug. Retail was $160.

MODEL 36 AND 36 CARBINE — .177 or .22 cal., barrel brake action, 1000/700 FPS, 19½ in. barrel, 8 lbs. Add $40 for new S Model w/scope, deduct $10 for muzzle break model without factory sights.

Mfg.'s Sug. Retail	$345	$190	$135	$100

MODEL 38 — .177 or .22 cal., barrel break action, 1000/700 FPS, 19½ in. barrel, 8 lbs., walnut stock.

	$230	$180	$120

Model 38 is the deluxe version of the Model 36 listed above.
Last Mfg.'s Sug. Retail was $345.

MODEL 45 S/45 DELUXE — .177 or .22 cal., barrel-cocking action, 900/650 FPS, 20½ in. barrel, 7 lbs. 9 oz., S Model equipped w/factory sling and scope. Add $40 for deluxe, $70 for S model with scope.

Mfg.'s Sug. Retail	$280	$160	$125	$90

Grading	100%	98%	95%

MODEL 48 — .177 or .22 cal., side lever action, 1,100/780 FPS, 17 in. barrel, 8½ lbs.

Mfg.'s Sug. Retail	$400	$235	$160	$120

MODEL 50T/T01 — .177 or .22 cal., under lever action, 745/600 FPS, 18½ in. barrel, 8 lbs., (sport/target), parkerized finish. Add $20 for blue finish, $100 for T01 Model. Disc. 1988.

	$225	$180	$145

Last Mfg.'s Sug. Retail was $210.

MODEL 52 — .177 or .22 cal., side lever action, 1,100/780 FPS, 17 in. barrel, 8½ lbs.

Mfg.'s Sug. Retail	$450	$280	$200	$160

Add $150 for Deluxe version.

MODEL 54 — .177 or .22 cal., sidelever "recoilless" action, 1100/900 FPS, 17 in. barrel, 9 lbs.

Mfg.'s Sug. Retail	$635	$450	N/A	N/A

MODEL 70 — .177 cal., barrel cocking action, 450 FPS, 13½ in. barrel. This is a junior sized adult air rifle.

	$110	$90	$70

Last Mfg.'s Sug. Retail was $190.

MODEL 72 — .177 cal., same as above but with recoilless action.

Mfg.'s Sug. Retail	$340	$185	$150	$120

MODEL 75, 75 HV, 75U, 75K, 75S — .177 cal., side lever action, 580 FPS, 19 in. barrel (professional target), 11 lbs. Add $30 for left-hand, $165 for U, $100 for K, $90 for 75S with adj. cheek piece and micrometer sight. Model 75 HV and Model 75 U were disc. in 1989. Model K disc. 1990.

Mfg.'s Sug. Retail	$1,150	$600	$500	$400

MODEL 100 — .177 cal., single stroke pneumatic, 580 FPS, 19 in. barrel, adj. cheekpiece, professional target model, 11 lbs. New in 1989.

Mfg.'s Sug. Retail	$1,425	$650	$500	$390

MODEL 1000 — .177 cal., barrel-break action, unique colored plastic stocks (black, red, blue, white, and yellow). Disc. 1991.

	$120	$90	$75

Last Mfg.'s Sug. Retail was $215.
Model 1000 is the sport model of the standard Model 34.

PISTOLS

MODEL 5G/GS — .177 or .22 cal., barrel-cocking action, 450/300 FPS, 7 in. barrel, (sport) 2 lbs. 12 oz. GS Model equipped w/factory scope. Add $70 for GS.

Mfg.'s Sug. Retail	$200	$120	$95	$75

MODEL 6G/6M/6GS — .177 cal., barrel-cocking action, 450 FPS , 7 in. barrel, (professional target), 3 lbs. GS Model equipped with factory scope. Add $70 for GS model, $30 for left hand.

6G

Mfg.'s Sug. Retail	$350	$230	$150	$110

6M

Mfg.'s Sug. Retail	$475	$275	$185	$140

MODEL 10 — .177 cal., barrel-cocking action, 450 FPS, 7 in. barrel, (professional target) 3 lbs. 4 oz. Add $50 for cased model, $40 for left-hand.

	$380	$305	$260

Last Mfg.'s Sug. Retail was $670.

ENSIGN ARMS CO., LTD.

Previous international distributors for Saxby Palmer Airguns located in Newbury, England. Available only on the used market.

Ensign Arms previously distributed the Saxby Palmer line of airguns into the U.S. Please refer to the Saxby Palmer section for these guns. "Ensign" designated models were trademarked by Ensign Arms Co., Ltd. Marksman Products was the importer until 1988 located in Huntington Beach, CA.

FAMAS

Imported by Century International Arms, Inc. St. Albans, VT.

Grading	100%	98%	95%
FAMAS AIR RIFLE — .177 cal., CO_2 action, copy of French made MAS .223 semi-automatic, used for military training, true semi-auto clip fed air rifle.			
Mfg.'s Sug. Retail N/A	$240	$210	$170

F.A.S.

Previously imported by Beeman until 1988. Line now distributed by Nimbus Ltd., Winthrop, MA. Nygord Products, La Crescenta, CA. and Mandall Shooting Supplies, Scottsdale, AZ. Manufactured in Italy. Available through dealers and importer direct.

FAS 604—.177 cal., top lever spring, pneumatic action, $7\frac{1}{2}$ in. barrel, 380 FPS, 2 lbs. 6 oz.

Mfg.'s Sug. Retail $475 $460 $400 $240

FAS 606 — .177 top lever spring, pneumatic action, $7\frac{1}{2}$ in. barrel, professional target model, walnut grips, 2 lbs. 3 oz.

No Mfg.'s Retail $690 $600 $440

F.E.G.

Formerly imported by K.B.I. INC. (formerly Kassnar Imports). (Model GPM also imported as Daisy Model 91). Manufactured in Hungary. Available through dealers and used market.

RIFLES

CLG-462 — .177 or .22 cal., CO_2 cartridge or cylinder charge, 490-410 FPS, $16\frac{1}{2}$ in. barrel, (24 in. .22 cal.), 5 lbs. 8 oz.

$475 $400 $280

Last Mfg.'s Sug. Retail was $550.

CLG-468 — .177 or .22 cal., CO_2 cartridge or cylinder charge, 705-525 FPS, $26\frac{3}{4}$ in. barrel, 5 lbs. 12 oz.

$545 $435 $325

Last Mfg.'s Sug. Retail was $600.

PISTOLS

MODEL GPM-01.177 cal., CO_2 cartridge or cylinder charge, 425 FPS, $10\frac{1}{4}$ in. barrel, 2 lbs. 7 oz.

Mfg.'s Sug. Retail $525 $360 $300 $215

FEINWERKBAU

Manufactured in Oberndorf, Germany. Imported and distributed by Beeman Precision Arms Inc. located in Santa Rosa, CA. Available through dealers and Beeman direct.

Feinwerkbau has been responsible for developing many of the current technical innovations used in fabricating target Air Pistols and Rifles. In 1988, Feinwerkbau Airguns swept the Olympic competition in this newly formed Olympic sport. Feinwerkbau has always been a leader in Airgun technology. The Feinwerkbau trademark is now owned in the U.S. by Beeman Precision Arms, Inc.

Grading	100%	98%	95%

RIFLES

MODEL 124 — .177 cal., barrel-cocking action, 780-830 FPS, 7.2 lbs. Add $35 for deluxe, $20 for left-hand deluxe, $400 for custom select, $425 for custom fancy, $475 for custom extra fancy. Disc. 1989.

	$395	$340	$280

Add $250 for factory marked 5mm. Only 3 ever made.
Last Mfg.'s Sug. Retail was $490.

MODEL 127 — .22 cal., barrel-cocking action, 620-680 FPS, 6-7.1 lbs. Additions same as above. Disc. 1989.

	$395	$340	$280

Last Mfg.'s Sug. Retail was $490.

MODEL 300S — .177 cal., side lever action, 640 FPS, 8.8-10.8 lbs. Add $75 for left-hand (all styles), $60 for barrel sleeve.

Mfg.'s Sug. Retail	$1,095	$1,015	$875	$675

Add $200 for Tyrolean stock. Add $75 for Running Boar stock configuration or Universal Model.

MODEL 600 — .177 cal., sidelever action, single stroke pneumatic operation, top of the line match rifle with aperture sights, unique hardwood laminate stock, 585 FPS, 10½ lbs. Add $30 for left-hand. Disc. 1988.

	$980	$870	$760

Last Mfg.'s Sug. Retail was $900.
This model was also available in a Running Boar variation with extra-long barrel that unscrews for transporting.

MODEL 601 — .177 cal., side lever action, single stroke, pneumatic operation, replaces Model 600 (see above), 10 lbs. 8 oz. Add $110 for left hand. Deduct $45 for Running Target.

Mfg.'s Sug. Retail	$1,495	$1,300	$1,140	$800

MODEL C60 — .177 cal., CO_2 powered, 570 FPS, similar in style to Model 600/601 above, 9.2 to 10.6 lbs. Add $110 for left hand, deduct $30 for running target.

Mfg.'s Sug. Retail	$1,390	$1,160	$1,060	$700

C60 MINI — .177 cal., CO_2 powered, quick change cylinder (bottle) smaller version of C60 Match Rifle, 7¾ lbs. New 1991.

Mfg.'s Sug. Retail	$1,390	$1,250	$1,050	$800

PISTOLS

MODEL 65 MK I AND II — .177 cal., side lever action, 525 FPS, 2.6-2.9 lbs., short barrel Mark II only. Add $60 for left, $20 for adj. grips.

Mfg.'s Sug. Retail	$965	$850	$650	$450

MODEL 80 — .177 cal., side lever action, 475-525 FPS, 2.8-3.2 lbs. Discontinued in 1983. (Like Model 65 with stacking barrel weights and fine mechanical trigger).

	$745	$645	$540

Last Mfg.'s Sug. Retail was $625.

MODEL 90 — specifications same as above but with electric trigger. Add $45 for short barrel, $50 for left-hand. Disc. 1990.

	$830	$645	$510

Last Mfg.'s Sug. Retail was $1,155.

MODEL 100 — .177 cal., pneumatic action, 460 FPS, 2½ lbs. Disc. 1992.

	$750	$650	$550

Add $40 for left hand variation.
Last Mfg.'s Sug. Retail was $1,100.

Grading	100%	98%	95%

MODEL 102 —new version of Model 100 above (1992).

Mfg.'s Sug. Retail $1,200 $1,065 $900 $700

Add $60 for left hand variation.

MODEL C2 — .177 cal., CO$_2$ cylinder, 425-525 FPS, 2½ lbs. Add $40 for left, deduct $20 for mini. Disc. 1989.

$565 $460 $360

Last Mfg.'s Sug. Retail was $780.

MODEL C5 — .177 cal., CO$_2$ powered 5 shot rapid fire, 7⅓ in. barrel, 510 FPS, 2 lbs. 6 oz. New in 1991. Add $60 for left hand.

Mfg.'s Sug. Retail $1,350 $1,230 $1,050 $840

MODEL C 10 — .177 cal., CO$_2$ cartridge, 510 FPS, 2½ lbs. Disc. 1990.

$720 $620 $465

Last Mfg.'s Sug. Retail was $965.

Add $60 for left hand model.

MODEL C20—.177 cal., CO$_2$ powered, 510 FPS. Add $60 for left hand, 2 lbs. 8 oz. (replacement for the C2 and C10 new in 1991).

Mfg.'s Sug. Retail $1,025 $895 $740 $545

Add $50 for left hand model.

C-25 — .177 cal., CO$_2$ powered, 510 FPS, unique CO$_2$ ball placed directly below action (instead of standard long CO$_2$ cylinder), for better balance, 2½ lbs.

Mfg.'s Sug. Retail $1,100 $990 $820 $640

Add $50 for left hand.

GAMO

Previously imported by Stoeger Industries - importation discontinued in 1986. A few models are currently being imported by Daisy. Line now imported and distributed by Dynamit Nobel, RWS Inc., Northvale, NJ. Available through dealers and importer direct.

PISTOLS

AF-10 — .177 cal., pneumatic action, 430 FPS, 7" barrel, similar in style to Beeman P-1, 1¼ lbs.

Mfg.'s Sug. Retail $115 $75 $60 $45

CENTER — .177 cal., under barrel lever cocking, 400-435 FPS, 14 in. barrel, 2.8 lbs.

$90 $75 $55

PR-45 — .177 cal., pneumatic, 9¼ in. barrel, 1 lb 9 oz., looks similar to a Beeman P1.

Mfg.'s Sug. Retail $135 $100 $85 $70

COMPACT — .177 cal., pneumatic, 9¼ in. barrel, two stage trigger, walnut grips, adj. sights, target model, 2 lbs.

Mfg.'s Sug. Retail $210 $145 $120 $95

FALCON — .177 cal., underlever action, 430 FPS, 7" barrel. ABS plastic grips, 2⅞ lbs.

Mfg.'s Sug. Retail $105 $70 $55 $40

RIFLES

CF 20—.177 and .22 cal., underlever action, 790-625 FPS, 17¾ in. barrel, checkered stock, 6 lbs. 6 oz.

Mfg.'s Sug. Retail $190 $155 $125 $100

CADET—.177 cal., barrel break action, 570 FPS, beechwood stock, 5 lbs.

$70 $60 $50

Grading	100%	98%	95%

CONTEST — .177 cal., side lever action, 543 FPS, beechwood stock, 10.1 lbs.

	$100	$80	$60

CUSTOM 600—.177 or .22 cal., barrel break action, 690 FPS, 17¾ in. barrel, two stage adj. trigger, checkered stock, 6 lbs. 3 oz.

	$130	$105	$80

Last Mfg.'s Sug. Retail was $170.

DELTA — .177 cal., barrel break action, 525 FPS, 15¾ in. barrel, two stage trigger, automatic safety, adj. sights, plastic stock, 5 lbs. 5 oz.

Mfg.'s Sug. Retail	$115	$85	$70	$55

EXPO — .177 or .22 cal., barrel break action, 625 FPS, adj. trigger, special sights, 5 lbs. 8 oz.

Mfg.'s Sug. Retail	$135	$80	$65	$50

EXPOMATIC—.177 cal., repeating barrel break action, 575 FPS, adj. trigger, 5 lbs. 5 oz.

	$115	$95	$75

EXPO 2000 — .177 cal., barrel cocking action, 625 FPS, 17" barrel, Monte Carlo style stock, 5½ lbs. New 1992.

Mfg.'s Sug. Retail	$135	$95	$75	$50

GAMO 68 — .177 or .22 cal., barrel locking action, 600 FPS, 6 lbs. 8 oz.

	$80	$65	$50

GAMATIC 85 — .177 cal., barrel break action, 560 FPS, 17¾ in. barrel, two stage trigger, unique loading system for up to 25 pellets, pistol grip stock, 6 lbs. 3 oz.

	$125	$100	$80

Last Mfg.'s Sug. Retail was $160.

G-1200 — .177 cal., CO_2 cylinder, 560 FPS, 17¾ in. barrel, unique pump action loading system for up to 12 pellets (styled like a pump centerfire rifle), 6 lbs. 6 oz.

	$155	$125	$95

Last Mfg.'s Sug. Retail was $185.

HUNTER 440 — .177 cal., barrel cocking action, 1000 FPS, 18" barrel, Monte Carlo style stock, 6¾ lbs. New 1992.

Mfg.'s Sug. Retail	$210	$155	$120	$95

MAGNUM 2000 — .177 and .22 cal., barrel break action, 820-660 FPS, 17¾ in. barrel, adj. two stage trigger, checkered stock, 7 lbs. 2 oz.

	$155	$130	$100

Last Mfg.'s Sug. Retail was $200.

SUPER — .177 cal., side lever action, 593 FPS, 10 lbs. 8 oz.

	$140	$120	$100

HAENEL

Sold by Cape Outfitters, FL.

Unfortunately, no specifications were available at time of printing. The following models were current manufactured old models imported by Cape Outfitters. Products will be imported by G.S.I. 108 Morrow Ave., Trussville, AL 35173.

KI 101 (MLG 550) — .177 cal., match rifle.

Mfg.'s Sug. Retail	$695	$480	$405	$320

KI 102 (ML 311) — .177 cal. match rifle.

Mfg.'s Sug. Retail	$395	$270	$230	$180

KI 103 (ML308-8) — .177 cal. match rifle.

Mfg.'s Sug. Retail	$300	$170	$135	$100

Grading		100%	98%	95%

KI 104 (310-4) — .177 cal.

Mfg.'s Sug. Retail	$200	$130	$110	$80

KI 105 (303-4) — BB cal., BB clip fed.

Mfg.'s Sug. Retail	$190	$120	$100	$70

KI 106 (85) — .177 cal.

Mfg.'s Sug. Retail	$130	$90	$70	$50

MARKSMAN

Division of S/R Industries, Huntington Beach, CA. Available both through dealers and Marksman direct.

JUNIOR MODEL 28 — .177 cal., barrel cocking action, 600 FPS, 16¾ in. barrel, 6 lbs. Mfg. for Marksman by Weihrauch.

Mfg.'s Sug. Retail	$200	$160	$135	$95

MODEL 29/30 — .177 or .22 cal., barrel cocking action, 800/625 FPS, 18½ in. barrel, 6 lbs. Mfg. for Marksman by BSA. Disc. 1991.

		$170	$130	$85

Last Mfg.'s Sug. Retail was $200.

MODEL 40 — .177 cal., barrel cocking action, 720 FPS, 18⅜ in. barrel, 7 lbs. 5 oz.

Mfg.'s Sug. Retail	$225	$185	$140	$110

MODEL 45 — .177 cal., barrel cocking action, 900-930 FPS, 19⅛ in. barrel, 7.3 lbs. New 1993.

Mfg.'s Sug. Retail	$190	$160	N/A	N/A

MODEL 55 (RIFLE) & 59 CARBINE — .177 cal., barrel cocking action, 925 FPS, 19¾ (rifle) or 14 (carbine) in. barrel, 7 lbs. 8 oz. Mfg. for Marksman by Weihrauch.

Mfg.'s Sug. Retail	$280	$230	$170	$120

MODEL 56/56K — .177 cal., barrel cocking action, 925 FPS, 19⅝ in. barrel, adj. cheekpiece and trigger, 8 lbs. 11 oz.

Mfg.'s Sug. Retail	$450	$345	$275	$225

Add $180 for 56K Model with Marksman Model 6941 scope.
The Model 56/56K is manufactured for Marksman by Weihrauch.

MODEL 58/58K—.177 cal., barrel cocking action, 925 FPS, 16 in. heavy bull barrel, adj. trigger, designed for silhouette shooting, 8 lbs. 8 oz.

Mfg.'s Sug. Retail	$390	$280	$220	$175

Add $180 for 58K Model with Marksman Model 6941 scope.
The Model 58/58K is manufactured for Marksman by Weihrauch.

MODEL 60/61 CARBINE — .177 cal., under lever cocking action, 810-840 FPS, 8 lbs. 12 oz.

Mfg.'s Sug. Retail	$440	$350	$230	$170

Modified version of HW77 by Weihrauch.

MODEL 70, 71, 72 — .177, .20, or .22 cal., barrel cocking action, 925/760 FPS, 19¾ in. barrel, 8 lbs. Add $15 for .20 cal. Mfg. for Marksman by Weihrauch.

Mfg.'s Sug. Retail	$330	$265	$200	$130

The Model 72 is a .20 cal.

MAUSER

Mauser Airguns are subcontracted under license to use the Mauser trademark and are not manufactured by Mauser-Werke. Previously imported and distributed by Marksman located in Huntington Beach, CA. Available through dealers and used market.

RIFLES

MATCH 300SL/SLC — .177 cal., under-lever action, 550/450 FPS, adj. sights and hardwood stock, 8.8 lbs. Add $75 for SLC Model with diopter sights.

	100%	98%	95%
	$245	$205	$145

This model is mfg. in Hungary.
Last Mfg.'s Sug. Retail was $330.

PISTOLS

U90/U91 JUMBO AIR PISTOLS — .177 cal., barrel break action, 260 FPS, 2 lbs.

	100%	98%	95%
	$80	$65	$45

Add $15 for deluxe model U91 with adj. sights and checkered grips.
Last Mfg.'s Sug. Retail was $100.
This model was mfg. by Record.

NORICA

Imported by KBI (Kassnar) Imports located in Harrisburg, PA and American Arms, Inc. located in North Kansas City, MO. Previously imported by S.A.E. located in Miami, FL.

Norica airguns imported by American Arms, Inc. will appear under the American Arms, Inc. heading in this text.

Even though the dollar has fallen on international markets, the current lack of an importer has caused prices to remain flat. Available on used market only.

MODEL 47 — .177 cal., side lever action, 600 FPS, unique black pistol grip handle, 5½ lbs.

Mfg.'s Sug. Retail	$175	$125	$85	$65

MODEL 61C — .177 cal., barrel break action, 600 FPS, 5.8 lbs.

Mfg.'s Sug. Retail	$130	$90	$65	$45

MODEL 73 — .177 or .22 cal., barrel break action, 580/525 FPS, 6.4 lbs.

Mfg.'s Sug. Retail	$155	$110	$80	$50

MODEL 80G — .177 or .22 cal., barrel break action, 635/570 FPS, 7.2 lbs.

Mfg.'s Sug. Retail	$200	$140	$105	$70

MODEL 90 — .177 cal., barrel break action, 650 FPS, factory equipped with scope.

Mfg.'s Sug. Retail	$185	$130	$95	$65

MODEL 92 — .177 cal., side lever action, 650 FPS, 5.75 lbs.

Mfg.'s Sug. Retail	$175	$125	$90	$65

NORICA YOUNG — .177 cal., barrel break action, 600 FPS, unique colored stock.

Mfg.'s Sug. Retail	$120	$80	$60	$40

BLACK WIDOW — .177 or .22 cal., barrel break action, 500/450 FPS, unique black plastic stock, 5 lbs.

Mfg.'s Sug. Retail	$150	$120	$80	$55

PARDINI PISTOLS

Imported by MCS. Inc.

MODEL K58 — .177 cal., underlever pneumatic, 9 in. barrel, 2 lbs. 6 oz., professional target model.

Mfg.'s Sug. Retail	$900	$560	$490	$440

MODEL K60 — .177 cal., CO_2 cylinder charge, 9½ in. barrel, 2 lbs. 4 oz.

Mfg.'s Sug. Retail	$900	$560	$490	$440

Grading	100%	98%	95%

MODEL K90 — .177 cal. CO_2 powered junior model, 7¼" barrel, wt. 1⅞ lbs.

Mfg.'s Sug. Retail	$780	$460	N/A	N/A

MODEL P10 — .177 cal., underlever pneumatic, 7¾ in. barrel, 2 lbs. 3 oz., being phased out in 1990.

	$425	$355	$295

Last Mfg.'s Sug. Retail was $560.

R W S

Importers located in Northvale, NJ. See Dianawerk (earlier in this text).

S G S (SPORTING GUNS SELECTION)

Previously Imported by Kendell International. Available on used market only.

DUO 300AP — .177 or .22 cal., top cocking action, 455/430 FPS.

	$105	$70	$50

DUO 300AR — .177 or .22 cal., top cocking action, 455/430 FPS, with extra stock and barrel assembly to create a 3-in-1 gun.

	$180	$130	$80

SAXBY PALMER

Manufactured by Saxby Palmer located in Stratford-Upon-Avon, England. Previously imported/distributed by Marksman Products located in Huntington Beach, CA. Available on used market only.

Saxby Palmer has developed the world's first cartridge loading air rifle. This is not a CO_2 or other type of compressed gas gun. The cartridges are pressurized (2250 PSI) and reusable facilitating speed of loading and much greater velocities. New rifles are supplied with the table pump (for reloading brass or plastic cartridges) and 10 cartridges. You must have these accessories in order to operate air rifles or pistols. Deduct 50% for used guns without these accessories.

RIFLES: DISCONTINUED

ENSIGN ELITE — .177 or .22 cal., bolt action cartridge, 1000-800 FPS auto safety.

	$110	$90	$75

Last Mfg.'s Sug. Retail was $175.

ENSIGN ROYAL — .177 or .22 cal., bolt action cartridge, 1000-800 FPS auto safety, walnut stock.

	$120	$105	$80

Last Mfg.'s Sug. Retail was $275.

RIFLES

GALAXY — .177 or .22 cal., bolt action cartridge, 1,000/800 FPS, auto safety, walnut stain, hardwood stock 6½ lbs. Current mfg.

	$110	$90	$75

SATURN — .177 or .22 cal., bolt action cartridge, 1,000/800 FPS, auto safety, hi-strength black polymer stock 6½ lbs. Disc. in 1987.

	$110	$90	$75

Last Mfg.'s Sug. Retail was $175.

Grading	100%	98%	95%

REVOLVERS: DISCONTINUED

ORION AIR REVOLVER — .177 cal., 6 shot, compressed gas cartridges (reusable), 550 FPS, 6 in. barrel, 2 lbs. 3 oz. Disc. 1988.

$210 $165 $140

This model is manufactured by Weihrauch of Germany and includes a Slim Jim pump and 12 reuseable cartridges. It also came with a 30 grain 38 cal. zinc pellet to allow cartridges to be used in a .38 Special pistol for practice.

MODEL 54 — .177 cal., 5 shot, compressed gas cartridges (reusable), 4 in. barrel, 1 lb. 5 oz. Disc. 1988.

$135 $100 $75

This model is manufactured by Weihrauch of Germany and includes a Slim Jim pump and 12 reuseable cartridges.

SHARP
Japan (Imported By Beeman). Available on used market only.

SHARP INNOVA — .177 or .22 cal., pneumatic pump action, 920/720 FPS, 4 lbs. 6 oz. Disc. 1988.

$150 $130 $95

Last Mfg.'s Sug. Retail was $175.

SHARP ACE — .177 or .22 cal., pneumatic pump action, 920/750 FPS, 6 lbs. 4 oz. Disc. 1988.

$255 $220 $150

Last Mfg.'s Sug. Retail was $295.

SHERIDAN
Manufactured by Benjamin Air Rifle Co. located in Racine, WI. Available through dealers and Benjamin-Sheridan direct.

SHERIDAN BLUE STREAK/SILVER STREAK — .20 cal., pneumatic pump or CO_2 action, 700 FPS, 6 lbs. Add $5 for Silver Streak, $25 for Williams sight, $30 for 4 x 15 scope, $25 for paint pellet rifle. Deduct $15 for CO_2.

Mfg.'s Sug. Retail	$140		$120	$95	$70

SHERIDAN AIR PISTOL

Model E — .177, .20, or .22 cal., CO_2 cartridge, 400 FPS, 6⅜ in. barrel, 2 lbs. 4 oz. Add $40 for paint pellet pistol.

Mfg.'s Sug. Retail	$110		$85	$70	$45

SIG HAMMERLI
Imported by Mandall Shooting Supplies, Inc. located in Scottsdale, AZ. Available through dealers and importer direct.

Sig Hammerli Airguns are not mfg. by Sig in Switzerland, but rather subcontracted to other airgun manufacturers (including El Gamo), these models are German made. Prices may increase or decrease based on the value of dollar on international markets.

RIFLES

MODEL 403 — .177 cal., side lever action, 700 FPS, adj. sight target model, 9¼ lbs.

$275 $230 $160

Last Mfg.'s Sug. Retail was $400.

MODEL 420 — .177 cal., side lever action, 700 FPS, military style plastic stock, 7½ lbs.

$205 $170 $105

Last Mfg.'s Sug. Retail was $300.

SMITH & WESSON
Springfield, MA.

Smith & Wesson had a few air guns manufactured to their specifications for distribution in the U.S. Most guns trade for under $100 with a few models selling for $120 to $140.

STERLING
Manufactured by Benjamin Air Rifle Company located in Racine, WI. Available through dealers and Benjamin-Sheridan direct.

RIFLES

Grading	100%	98%	95%

HR 81—.177, 20, .22 cal., under lever cocking action, 700/660 FPS, adj. V type rear sight, 8½ lbs. Add $10 for .22 cal.

Mfg.'s Sug. Retail	$340	$270	$200	$135

Add $30 for original English markings.

HR 83—.177, .20 or .22 cal., under lever cocking action, 700/660 FPS, adj. Williams "FP" peep sight, walnut stock, 8½ lbs. Add $5 for .22 cal.

Mfg.'s Sug. Retail	$480	$380	$250	$180

Add $30 for original English markings.

STEYR
Manufactured by Steyr located in Austria. Imported and distributed by Guns South Inc. located in Trussville, AL and Nygord Precision Products, La Crescenta, CA. Available through dealers and importer direct.

RIFLES

MATCH 91 — .177 cal., CO_2 powered match rifle with precision receiver sight and adj. butt plate. New in 1988.

Mfg.'s Sug. Retail	$1,450	$1,350	$1,030	$650

Add $50 for left hand.
Add $100 for Running Target.

PISTOLS

LP-1 — .177 cal., CO_2 powered match pistol, 15 ⅓ in. overall, 2 lbs. 8 oz.

Mfg.'s Sug. Retail	$1,075	$915	$760	$495

LP-5 — .177 cal., CO_2 powered match pistol.

Mfg.'s Sug. Retail	$1,250	$1,150	N/A	N/A

THEOBEN ENGINEERING
Manufacturer located in England. Imported by Air Rifle Specialists located in Elmira, NY. Available both dealer and importer direct.

Beeman Precision Arms, Inc. began importing Theoben manufactured rifles in 1992. These guns differ enough from standard Thoeben arms that they are listed in the Beeman section of this text.

Add $75 for Theoben pump applicable to some models listed below.

SIROCCO COUNTRYMAN — .177 or .22 cal., Anschutz barrel break action, 1,100/800 FPS, unique precharged sealed gas system replaces the metal main springs used in most spring piston air rifles, not to be confused with a gas powered (CO_2) air rifle, includes scope rings, barrel weight, walnut stained beech stock, 7½ lbs. Importation disc. in 1987.

	$465	$350	$275

Last Mfg.'s Sug. Retail was $585.

Grading	100%	98%	95%

SIROCCO DELUXE — similar to Countryman, except has hand checkered walnut stock. Importation disc. in 1987.

	$650	$500	$300

Last Mfg.'s Sug. Retail was $650.

SIROCCO CLASSIC — similar to Sirocco Deluxe, except has updated floating inertia system in piston chamber and auto safety, variable power, 900/1100 FPS. New in 1987. Add $60 for left hand.

Mfg.'s Sug. Retail	$830	$795	$635	$550

This model is available with either a choked or unchoked Anschutz barrel as standard equipment.

SIROCCO GRAND PRIX — similar specifications to the Sirocco Classic, except has checkered walnut thumbhole stock.

Mfg.'s Sug. Retail	$940	$895	$760	$600

Add $60 for left hand.
Subtract 50% for older models without safety and new piston design.
In 1987, this model was updated with a floating inertia system in piston chamber and auto safety, variable power.
This model is available with either a choked or unchoked Anschutz barrel as standard equipment.

ELIMINATOR — .177 or .22 cal., barrel break action, 1100/1400 FPS, variable power, deluxe checkered thumb hole stock with cheekpiece and pad 9½ lbs. New in 1987.

Mfg.'s Sug. Retail	$1,500	$1,295	$700	$560

Add $60 for left hand.
This model incorporates an improved barrel design featuring pronounced rifling for the higher velocity pellets.

IMPERATOR — .22 cal., underlever action, 750 FPS, variable power, walnut hand checkered stock, auto safety. New in 1989.

Mfg.'s Sug. Retail	$1,500	$1,350	$1,150	$850

IMPERATOR SLR 88 — similar to above but with a 7 shot mag. Very limited importation, predecessor of Rapid 7.

Mfg.'s Sug. Retail	$1,680	$1,300	$1,000	$800

RAPID 7 — .22 cal. precharged pneumatic, variable power, 19" Anschutz barrel, stippled walnut stock, unique 7 shot bolt action design, cylinder charge lasts 160 shots, 6¾ lbs.

Mfg.'s Sug. Retail	$1,300	$1,295	$1,000	$750

Add $60 for left hand.
Add $120 for scuba tank adaptor.

VENOM ARMS CUSTOM GUNS
United Kingdom.

Venom Arms specializes in customizing Weihrauch firearms manufactured in Germany. A quick review of their latest pricing schedule for custom guns indicate prices may run nearly 100% over the initial cost of the uncustomized gun (see Weihrauch). Many of their airguns are available through MAC-1 Airgun Distributor, Inglewood, CA. Available only on used market.

WALTHER
Manufactured in Germany. Imported by Interarms located in Alexandria, VA. Available through dealers.

RIFLES

CG 90 — .177 cal., CO_2 powered, tilting block action, 18.9 in. barrel, 10 lbs. 2 oz. New in 1989.

Mfg.'s Sug. Retail	$1,750	$1,500	$1,270	$800

LG 90 — side lever action, single stroke pneumatic mechanism, professional target, 11 lbs.

Mfg.'s Sug. Retail	$1,320	$1,100	N/A	N/A

Grading	100%	98%	95%

LGM-1 — .177 cal., single stroke pneumatic, side lever action, 19" barrel, wt. approx. 10 lbs. New 1992.

Mfg.'s Sug. Retail	$1,890	$1,615	$1,300	$810

LGR RIFLE — .177 cal., side lever action, single stroke pneumatic mechanism, 580 FPS (professional target) 10.8 lbs. Add $100 for universal, 10% for left-hand. Disc. 1991.

	$1,120	$970	$580

Add $150 for Running Boar Model.
Last Mfg.'s Sug. Retail was $1,250.

PISTOLS

CPM — .177 cal., CO_2 powered professional target model. New 1993.

Mfg.'s Sug. Retail	$1,405	$1,200	N/A	N/A

CP 2 — .177 cal., CO_2 powered, 9 in. barrel, $2\frac{1}{2}$ lbs, professional target model. Disc. 1990.

	$655	$515	$410

Last Mfg.'s Sug. Retail was $850.

CP-3 — .177 cal., CO_2 powered, professional target model.

Mfg.'s Sug. Retail	$1,360	$1,100	$800	$500

CP-5 — .177 cal., CO_2 powered, professional target model. Disc. 1992.

	$1,320	$1,100	$600

Last Mfg.'s Sug. Retail was $1,650.

LP 3 AIR PISTOL — .177 cal., single stroke pneumatic action, 405 FPS, 2.8-3.0 lbs. Add $60 for match grade.

	$520	$450	$340

Add $50 for shaped barrel rather than round.

LP 53 — .177 cal.

	$395	$300	$200

Add $75 for blued receiver.

LGM-1 PISTOL — .177 cal. single stroke pneumatic, 10" barrel, $2\frac{1}{4}$ lbs. New 1992.

Mfg.'s Sug. Retail	$1,670	$1,365	$1,000	$700

WEIHRAUCH

Manufactured in Germany. Imported by Beeman Precision Arms Inc. located in Santa Rosa, CA. Available through dealers or Beeman direct.

RIFLES

MODEL 30 — .177 or .20 cal., barrel cocking action, 660 FPS/600 FPS, 17" barrel, 40 in. overall, 5.5 lbs. Add $5 for .20 cal.

Mfg.'s Sug. Retail	$180	$145	$125	$100

MODEL 35EB — .177 or .22 cal., barrel-cocking action, 755/660 FPS, 8 lbs. Add $50 for chrome, $10 for .22 cal. Deduct $20 for 35L. Disc. 1992.

	$275	$235	$170

Last Mfg.'s Sug. Retail was $450.

MODEL 50 — .177 cal., barrel cocking action, 705 FPS, 17" barrel, 43.1 in. overall, 6.9 lbs.

Mfg.'s Sug. Retail	$200	$160	$140	$110

MODEL 55 — .177 cal., barrel-cocking action, 660-700 FPS, 7.8 lbs. Add $40 for left-hand, $105 for Match, $105 for Tyrolean.

Mfg.'s Sug. Retail	$560	$420	$360	$270

Grading	100%	98%	95%

MODEL 77/77 CARBINE — .177, .20, or .22 cal., under lever cocking action, 830-710 FPS, 8.9 lbs. Add $30 for left-hand, $20 for .20 cal. (5mm) or .22 cal., $30 for Deluxe, $100 for tyrolean stock.

Mfg.'s Sug. Retail	$480	$340	$290	$230

PISTOLS

HW MODEL 70 — .177 cal., barrel-cocking action, 410 FPS, 2.4 lbs. Add $45 for chrome.

Mfg.'s Sug. Retail	$170	$135	$115	$90

WINCHESTER

Imported by Winchester from 1969 through 1974. Available through used market only.

Between 1969 and 1975 Winchester imported 8 rifle models and 2 pistols into the United States from a manufacturer in Germany. A total of 19,259 air guns were made and imported through 1973. Due to the $100 rule, only 6 guns will be listed in this section.

RIFLES

MODEL 427 — .22 cal., barrel cocking action, 660 FPS, micrometer rear and hooded front sight, 42" overall, 6 lbs.

	$145	$105	$90

MODEL 435 — .177 cal. barrel cocking action, 693 FPS, micrometer rear and interchangeable front sight, checkered stock and adjustable trigger, 44" overall, 6½ lbs.

	$175	$145	$115

MODEL 450 — .177 cal., under-lever cocking action, 693 FPS, micrometer rear and interchangeable front sight, 44½" overall dovetail base for scope, checkered Schutzen style stock, 7¾ lbs.

	$210	$175	$140

MODEL 333 — .177 cal., barrel cocking action, 576 FPS, diopter target sight, fully adjustable trigger, double piston recoilless action, walnut stock, checkered and stippled, 43½" overall, 9½ lbs.

	$435	$370	$295

PISTOLS

MODEL 353 — .177 and .22 cal., barrel cocking action, 378 FPS, plastic stock, 16" overall, 2¾ lbs.

	$100	$85	$70

MODEL 363 — .177 cal., barrel cocking action, 378 FPS, double piston recoilless design micrometer rear and interchangeable front sights, fully adjustable trigger, plastic stock, 16" overall, 3 lbs.

	$120	$100	$80

WISCHO

Previously imported by Beeman Precision Arms, Inc. located in Santa Rosa, CA. Manufactured by B.S.F. Available through used market only.

WISCHO AIR PISTOL MODEL S-20 STANDARD — .177 cal., barrel-cocking action, 450 FPS, 2.8 lbs. Disc. 1988.

	$100	$80	$45

Last Mfg.'s Sug. Retail was $130

MODEL CM — same as above but target style. Disc. in 1988.

	$115	$100	$70

Last Mfg.'s Sug. Retail was $160.

BLACK POWDER

MODERN BLACK POWDER GUNS

1993 should be the strongest year for Black Powder we have seen in some time. Prices have stabilized and buyers finally seem willing to accept that prices will never be as low as they were before the last major devaluation of the dollar several years ago. Another interesting aspect of the Black Powder marketplace is the change in inventories from the traditional flintlocks and percussion guns of the pioneer days to the more modern guns of the 1850s and beyond. This is particularly true of the Sharps rifle in both percussion and Black Powder cartridge. Some manufacturers such as Pedersoli have completely retooled to produce higher quality guns and other manufacturers like Shiloh report lead times on some models to be two years or more. Modern in-line-ignition muzzleloading rifles have also gained broad range acceptance with no less than 3 new models being introduced at this year's SHOT Show in Houston, TX. On a sad note, Col. Michael J. Powasnick, President of Trail Guns Armory (formerly of League City, TX) passed away unexpectedly shortly after this year's SHOT Show. Col. Mike was known for his marketing of Pedersoli Black Powder double rifles for use in big game hunting. His philosophy was simple, "If you're good, a second shot shouldn't be necessary, but, since anything can happen in the wild, your life may depend on a second chance." Col. Mike's presence will be greatly missed.

A note about pricing: The following section differs from the rest of the book in the number of pricing lines contained. You will notice guns under 95% are not listed and should be heavily scrutinized by the Buyer if one is presented to him (or her) at the trading table. Although many fine shooters exist under 95% condition, their value as collector pieces are negligible. This is due to limited demand for used guns and the relatively low price of many fine guns that are still in "new-in-the-box" condition.

Collectors and shooters wanting to enter the world of black powder guns would be far better off to buy a new gun that is being liquidated because of a blemish or overstock conditions, than to invest in the unknown mechanical condition of a less than 95% gun. Of course, if you find a gun in excellent mechanical shape under 95% condition feel free to buy it for pleasure but not as an investment.

The guns listed in this section are factory assembled, and kit guns are also available from many of the below listed manufacturers at substantial savings. They are not included in this section, however. Also, most Black Powder guns under $100 in value are not listed, and all prices are rounded to the nearest $5.

ALL ADD-ON'S FOR PRICING LISTED IN THIS SECTION ARE RETAIL WITHOUT DEALER DISCOUNTING. ENGRAVING PRICES ON LESS THAN 100% GUNS SHOULD BE DISCOUNTED BY A MINIMUM OF 50%.

Sincerely,

Patrick M. Lucking
Black Powder Editor
Blue Book of Gun Values

ALLEN FIREARMS

Previous importer located in Santa Fe, NM importing A. Uberti firearms until early in 1987. After Allen Firearms closed, Old-West Gun Co. (now called Cimarron Arms) located in Houston, TX purchased the remaining inventory. Since all guns sold by Allen Firearms were manufactured by A. Uberti (they even used the same catalog), please refer to the A. Uberti section at the end of this section.

Add the following amounts for engraving on handguns:
Add $350 for "A" style engraving (30% coverage).
Add $425 for "B" style engraving (50% coverage).
Add $750 for "C" style engraving (100% coverage).
Add $800 for "Texas Cattlebrands" engraving pattern.

AMERICAN ARMS, INC.

N. Kansas City, MO. Available through dealers. American Arms also imports a line of black powder revolvers manufactured by Armi San Marco. Please refer to the following section for pricing.

RIFLES

Grading	100%	98%	95%

HAWKEYE — .50 and .54 cal. percussion, in-line ignition, 22 in. round blued or stainless steel barrel, dual safety contemporary styled design,stock has rubber recoil pad.

Mfg.'s Sug. Retail	$275	$265	$220	$175

Add $120 for stainless steel.

ARMI SAN MARCO

Mfg. in Italy, currently imported by Denver Arms (formerly House of Muskets) located in Pagosa Springs, CO, Muzzle Loaders, Inc. located in Burke, VA, E.M.F., located in Santa Ana, CA, and Taylor's & Co. located in Winchester, VA. May be purchased through dealers and catalog houses.

PISTOLS

CHARLIEVILLE 1777 PISTOL — .69 cal. flintlock, 7½" white steel smooth bore barrel, brass furniture, belt hook, walnut stock, wt. 2¾ lbs.

	$215	$180	$125

REVOLVERS: PERCUSSION

WALKER MODEL 1847 — .44 cal., percussion, 9 in. barrel, color case hardened frame, loading lever and hammer, brass trigger guard and steel backstrap, 4½ lbs.

	$230	$200	$150

BABY DRAGOON — .31 cal., percussion, 5 in. octagonal barrel, 5 shot cylinder, color case hardened frame, hammer and load lever, silver plated brass backstrap and trigger guard.

	$185	$160	$120

1ST MODEL DRAGOON — .44 cal., percussion, 8 in. barrel, color case hardened frame, loading lever and hammer, silver plated brass backstrap and trigger guard.

	$275	$220	$140

2ND MODEL DRAGOON — same as 1st Model Dragoon, except 7½ in. barrel.

	$275	$220	$140

3RD MODEL DRAGOON — .44 cal., percussion, 7½ in. barrel, Western Model has silver plated brass backstrap, Military Model has steel backstrap - cut for stock, Texas Model has brass backstrap. Add $15 for Western Model.

	$275	$220	$140

1851 NAVY — .36 or .44 cal., percussion, 7½ in. octagonal barrel, engraved (roll) cylinder, color case hardened frame and load lever, silver plated brass backstrap and square back trigger guard. Sheriff's Model has 5 in. barrel, brass trigger guard and backstrap. Deduct $20 for brass back strap and trigger guard, $25 for brass frame.

	$125	$110	$95

1860 ARMY — .44 cal., percussion 8 in. round barrel, color case hardened frame, hammer and load lever, Sheriff's Model has 5 in. barrel, 2¾ lbs. Add $5 for Sheriff's Model. Add $35 for fluted cylinder model. Deduct $35 for brass frame.

	$140	$125	$105

1861 NAVY — .36 cal., percussion, 7½ in. round barrel, color case hardened frame, hammer and load lever, silver plated brass backstrap and trigger guard (very similar to 1860 Army, except cal. and shorter Navy grips).

	$145	$125	$100

Grading	100%	98%	95%

1858 REMINGTON ARMY — .44 cal percussion, 6 shot, 8" octagonal barrel, brass frame, trigger guard & backstrap, walnut grips, wt. 2⅜ lbs.

| | $140 | $120 | $95 |

Add $120 for stainless steel target model.

RIFLES

HAWKENS — .50 cal., percussion, 30 in. octagonal chrome lined barrel, brass patchbox, target sights, double set triggers, 8 lbs.

| | $350 | $250 | $180 |

ST. LOUIS HAWKEN — .50, .54, or .58 cal., percussion, color case hardened hammer and lock, 28 in. octagonal barrel, brass trim, 7 lbs. 15 oz. Add $65 for curly maple stock.

| | $400 | $350 | $260 |

ROCKY MOUNTAIN SHORT RIFLE — .50 cal., percussion, 24 in. octagonal barrel, brass furniture.

| | $225 | $200 | $140 |

ARMI SAN PAOLO

Mfg. in Italy. Armi San Paolo is a wholly owned subsidiary of Euroarms of Europe which also owns Euroarms of America. See Euroarms section for pricing. Previously imported by Kendall International located in Paris, KY and Muzzle Loaders, Inc. located in Burke, VA. May be purchased through dealers and catalog houses.

ARMSPORT

Importers located in Miami, FL. Available through dealers.

PISTOLS

CORSAIR PISTOL — .44 cal., percussion, double barrel, blued finish, color case hardened hammer and lock, brass trim.

| | $265 | $210 | $135 |

DUELING PISTOL — .45 cal., percussion, blued finish, color case hardened hammer and lock, brass trim.

| | $200 | $150 | $110 |

KENTUCKY PISTOL — .45 or .50 cal., percussion or flintlock, blued finish, color case hardened hammer and lock, brass trim. Add $10 for flint lock.

| | $175 | $140 | $110 |

REVOLVERS

MODEL 1847 COLT WALKER REVOLVER — .44 cal., percussion, color case hardened frame, hammer, and load lever, brass trigger guard, steel backstrap, 6 shot, 4½ lbs.

| Mfg.'s Sug. Retail | $290 | $245 | $210 | $165 |

MODEL 1851 COLT NAVY — .36 or .44 cal., percussion, brass or color case hardened frame, brass trigger guard and backstrap, 6 shot. Add $30 for color case hardened steel with engraved cylinders. Add $100 for engraved gold and nickel.

| Mfg.'s Sug. Retail | $145 | $130 | $105 | $80 |

MODEL 1860 COLT ARMY — .44 cal., percussion, brass frame, trigger guard, and backstrap, color case hardened hammer and load lever, 6 shot. Add $50 for color case hardened steel, $20 for Steel Sheriff Model, $160 for stainless steel, $115 for engraved gold and silver.

| Mfg.'s Sug. Retail | $150 | $125 | $105 | $80 |

Grading	100%	98%	95%

MODEL 1858 REMINGTON ARMY — .44 cal., percussion, blued frame, brass trigger guard, steel backstrap, 6 shot. Add $115 for stainless steel, $80 for engraved gold and silver, $25 for Target Model, $140 for stainless Target Model. Deduct $40 for brass frame, $30 for nickel plated brass.

Mfg.'s Sug. Retail	$210	$185	$160	$125

REMINGTON BUFFALO TARGET — .44 cal., percussion, 12 in. octagonal barrel, brass frame and trigger guard, adj. sights, based on 1858 Navy frame, 38 oz. Add $5 for nickel plated brass.

Mfg.'s Sug. Retail	$205	$175	$155	$110

REMINGTON POCKET — .31 cal. percussion, 5 shot 4" octagonal barrel, brass frame, 15 oz.

Mfg.'s Sug. Retail	$160	$115	$100	$75

RIFLES

BRISTOL KID RIFLE — .32 or .36 cal., percussion. Add $15 for standard version, $25 for deluxe. Discontinued in 1984.

	$195	$170	$125

HAWKEN RIFLE — .45, .50, .54 or .58 cal., percussion or flintlock, color case hardened hammer and lock, percussion cap holder in stock, chrome lined barrels. Add $25 for flintlock.

	$400	$350	$260

HAWKENTUCKY RIFLE — .36, or .50 cal., percussion or flintlock, color case hardened hammer and lock, percussion cap holder in stock, chrome lined barrels. Add $10 for flintlock.

	$330	$265	$180

KENTUCKY RIFLE — .36, .45, or .50, cal., percussion or flintlock, color case hardened hammer and lock, percussion cap holder in stock, chrome lined barrels, brass trim. Add $10 for flintlock, $55 for deluxe with engraved white steel hammer and lock.

	$330	$265	$180

SHARPS RIFLE/CARBINE — .45 and .54 cal., percussion, 28 in. barrel (22 in. carbine). New 1992.

Mfg.'s Sug. Retail	$780	$665	$575	$460

Subtract $20 for carbine.

TRYON TRAILBLAZER — .50 or .54 cal., percussion, color case hardened hammer and lock, cap holder in stock. Add $45 for deluxe engraved.

	$400	$335	$260

TRYON BACK ACTION RIFLE — .50 and .54 cal., percussion, 28 and 30 in. barrel. New 1992.

Mfg.'s Sug. Retail	$825	$690	$610	$490

Add $55 for silver finish.

BLACK POWDER CARTRIDGE

SHARPS RIFLE/CARBINE — .45/70 black powder cartridge, 28 in. round or octagonal barrel (22 in. on carbine). New 1992.

Mfg.'s Sug. Retail	$860	$745	$630	$500

Add $15 for octagonal barrel.
Deduct $25 for Carbine model.
Add $25 for double "set" triggers.
Add $75 for Deluxe Model w/28" octagonal browned bbl. and double "set" triggers.

SHOTGUNS

KENTUCKY RIFLE/SHOTGUN COMBO — .45 or .50 cal., 20 ga., percussion only, same as above.

	$360	$270	$190

DOUBLE BARREL SHOTGUN — 12 or 10 ga., percussion only, blued finish, color case hardened hammer and lock. Add $50 for 10 ga.

	$380	$330	$270

Grading	100%	98%	95%

CANNONS

BORDA CANNON — .50 cal. wick, nickel plated.

	$180	$160	$120

Last Mfg.'s Sug. Retail was $195.
Add $80 for gold plating.

NAPOLEON CANNON — .45, .69 or .75 wick, nickel plated. Deduct $230 for .45 cal. Add for gold plating .75 cal. $150, .45 $70, .69 $120.

Mfg.'s Sug. Retail	$525	$450	$390	$310

YORKTOWN CANNON — .50 cal. wick, nickel plated. Add $100 for gold plating.

	$180	$160	$120

Last Mfg.'s Sug. Retail was $195.

ASSOCIATION FOR THE PRESERVATION OF WESTERN ANTIQUITY

Distributed by William Benjamin Ltd. located in Ashville, NC.

1862 COLT NAVY — .36 cal., percussion, standard construction, roll engraved cylinder with 24Kt. gold inlay, only 100 revolvers made, sold in custom cameo art presentation case depicting a miner panning for gold, some sets may come with the addition of a seated Liberty silver dollar and a Double Eagle gold piece, coins value should be based on current numismatic value, present retail for entire set including gold pieces is $2,395.

Mfg.'s Sug. Retail	$995	$795	$695	$545

BENSON FIREARMS, LTD.

Previous importer/distributor of A. Uberti Firearms mfg. in Italy. Benson Firearms was located in Seattle, WA.

Benson Firearms was a recent importer (1987-1988) and imported A. Uberti firearms that were marked "Benson Firearms Seattle, WA". In 1989 Benson Firearms, Ltd. combined with Uberti USA, Inc. located in New Milford, CT.

All guns were manufactured to the same exact specifications as the originals. Crafted with an unmistakable fire blue finish. A. Uberti is one of the largest manufacturers of black powder firearms. See A. Uberti at the end of this section for pricing.

BERETTA

Manufacturer located in Brescia, Italy 1680-present. Available on the used market only.

SHOTGUNS

COMMEMORATIVE O/U MODEL M1000 — 12 ga., percussion, 30 in. barrel, limited production.

	$470	$410	$310

Last Mfg.'s Sug. Retail was $840.

BONDINI

Manufacturer located in Italy. Imported by Helmut Hofman, Inc. located in Placitas, NH. Previously imported by House Of Muskets located in Pagosa Lakes, CO. Some models now imported by Austin-Sheridan, USA Middlefield, CT. Available through dealers and catalog houses.

PISTOLS

ASHABELLA COOK UNDERHAMMER — .45 cal., unique underhammer design uses trigger guard as mainspring. Very accurate.

	$175	$150	$100

Grading	100%	98%	95%

WM. PARKER PISTOL — .45 cal., flintlock or percussion, 11 in. octagonal browned barrel, silver plated furniture, double set triggers. Add $10 for flintlock.

$300 $250 $200

F. ROCHATTE — .45 cal., percussion, round barrel, single set triggers, hand checkered stock.

$250 $210 $160

RIFLES

SANFTL SCHUETZEN RIFLE — .45 cal., percussion, 31 in. octagonal barrel, unique backward lock, both peep and open iron sights, Schuetzen style butt plate and trigger guard, brass furniture.

$570 $475 $385

SHOTGUNS

GALLYON SHOTGUN — 12 ga., percussion, blued barrel, single shot. Add $150 for extra 12 ga. barrel.

$305 $265 $210

BROWNING
Headquarters located in Morgan, UT. Available only on the used market.

RIFLES

JONATHAN BROWNING MOUNTAIN RIFLE — 50 cal., percussion, 30 in. octagonal barrel, single set trigger, engraved lock plate, select walnut stock, cased with medallion, 1,000 produced in 1978. Issue price — $650.

$525 $435 $300

MOUNTAIN RIFLE — same as Jonathan Browning Mountain Rifle, without Centennial embellishments, not cased. Also in .45 or .54 cal.

$260 $225 $180

CHARLES DALY
See Daly, Charles.

CHENEY RIFLE WORKS/LEMAN RIFLES
Owned and distributed by Mountain State Muzzle Loading Supplies, Williamstown, WV. Manufactured by Cheney Rifle Works located in Waldron, IN. Available from Mountain State or through dealers.

ELKHUNTER RIFLE — .50 or .54 cal. percussion, 32 in. octagonal browned barrel, browned furniture, hammer and lock, curly maple stock, double set triggers, adjustable buckhorn rear sight, wt. 9 lbs.

Mfg.'s Sug. Retail $495 $425 $375   N/A

MOUNTAINEER RIFLE — .36, .40, .45 or .50 cal. flintlock or percussion, 39 in. octagonal browned barrel, brass or browned furniture, hammer and lock, curly maple full stock, double set triggers, adjustable buckhorn rear sight, wt. 7¼ to 8 lbs.

Mfg.'s Sug. Retail $525 $425 $375   N/A
Add $20 for flintlock.

PLAINS RIFLE — .50 and .54 percussion, 32 in. octagonal barrel, fancy maple stock, furniture is brass or browned steel, single set double action trigger, 9 lbs.

Mfg.'s Sug. Retail $495 $425 $375 $310

PRAIRIE RIFLE — .36, .40, .45 and .50 cal., percussion, 32 in. barrel, furniture is brass or browned steel, double set triggers, fancy figure maple stock, wt. 8 lbs.

Mfg.'s Sug. Retail $495 $425 $375 $310

Grading	100%	98%	95%

SUMMIT RIFLE — .50 and .54 cal. percussion, 30 in. octagonal barrel, furniture is brass or browned steel, single set double action trigger, fancy figure maple stock, wt. 9 lbs.

Mfg.'s Sug. Retail	$495	$425	$375	$310

CIMARRON ARMS COMPANY

Importer/distributor of custom crafted A. Uberti Modern and Blackpowder Firearms. Cimarron Arms is located in Houston, TX. Available direct or through dealers.

Cimarron Arms was previously named Old-West Gun Company.

After years of research, Cimarron Arms Co. has contracted A. Uberti to manufacture the most authentic western firearms reproductions to date, including such exact modifications as changing the taper of the cylinder face to exactly match the original Colt's. Also, serial number location, cylinder scenes, stock configuration, etc. have all been carefully manufactured to duplicate the original. In 1992, Cimarron has started bringing in guns in white steel and having the bluing and color case hardening done in the U.S. to match the original colors.

Add the following amounts for engraving on handguns:
   Add $350 for "A" style engraving (30% coverage).
   Add $425 for "B" style engraving (50% coverage).
   Add $750 for "C" style engraving (100% coverage).
   Add $800 for "Texas Cattlebrands" engraving pattern.
   Add $100 for old style case hardened frame.

REVOLVERS

1847 WALKER — .44 cal., percussion, charcoal finish, color case hardened frame, hammer, and load lever, brass trim, engraved cylinder, 4.4 lbs.

Mfg.'s Sug. Retail	$300	$285	$250	$185

1848 BABY DRAGOON — .31 cal., percussion, 3, 4, or 5 in. barrel, 5 shot, color case hardened frame, hammer, no load lever, engraved cylinder, 1.4 lbs. Add $15 for silver straps and trigger guard.

Mfg.'s Sug. Retail	$270	$245	$215	$155

DRAGOON (1ST, 2ND, OR 3RD) — .44 cal., percussion, 6 shot, brass grip straps, color case hardened frame, hammer, and load lever, brass trim, 3.9 lbs. Add $20 for silver-plated straps, or cut for stock on 3rd Dragoon Model. Add $180 for stock.

Mfg.'s Sug. Retail	$285	$270	$235	$160

1849 WELLS FARGO — .31 cal., percussion, 3, 4, or 5 in. octagonal barrel, 5 shot, color case hardened frame, hammer, no load lever, brass trim, 1½ lbs. Add $15 for silver straps.

Mfg.'s Sug. Retail	$270	$245	$215	$155

1849 POCKET — .31 cal., percussion, with loading lever, 3, 4, or 5 in. barrel, 5 shot, color case hardened frame, hammer, and load lever, brass trim, 1½ lbs. Add $15 for silver straps and trigger guard.

Mfg.'s Sug. Retail	$270	$245	$215	$155

1851 NAVY — .36 cal., percussion, many styles, loading lever, 6 shot engraved cylinder, 2.8 lbs. Add $130 for stock, $45 for stainless steel, $15 for silver plated strap and trigger guard, or steel strap and trigger guard, for London model or cut for stock 3rd model.

Mfg.'s Sug. Retail	$250	$230	$200	$150

1860 ARMY — .44 cal., percussion, 8 in. barrel, 6 shot, loading lever, color case hardened frame, hammer, and load lever, all brass backstrap and trigger guard, or steel backstrap and brass trigger guard on fluted cylinder model, 2.6 lbs. Add $145 for stock, $15 for silver plated strap and trigger guard, $35 for cut for stock or $5 for fluted cylinder model, $30 for Civilian Model, $50 for stainless steel.

Mfg.'s Sug. Retail	$225	$205	$180	$140

Grading	100%	98%	95%

1861 NAVY — .36 cal., percussion, 5 in. barrel, many styles, brass backstrap or trigger guard, color case hardened frame, hammer, and load lever, 2½ lbs. Add $15 for silver plated strap and trigger guard, $15 for cut-for-stock or fluted military cylinder (except on civilian model), $50 for stainless steel, $145 for shoulder stock.

Mfg.'s Sug. Retail	$250	$230	$200	$160

PATERSON — .36 cal., percussion, 7½ in. octagonal barrel, standard hidden trigger design, blued steel hardware, no loading lever, 2½ lbs.

Mfg.'s Sug. Retail	$360	$325	$285	$210

Add $40 for loading lever.

1862 POLICE — .36 cal., percussion, 4½, 5½, or 6½ in. barrel, color case hardened frame, hammer, and load lever, cylinder, semi-fluted or engraved, 1.6 lbs. Add $15 for silver plated straps and trigger guard, $50 for stainless steel.

Mfg.'s Sug. Retail	$275	$250	$220	$165

1862 POCKET NAVY — .36 cal., percussion, 4½, 5½, or 6½ in. barrel, color case hardened frame, hammer, and load lever, cylinder, semi-fluted or engraved, 1.6 lbs. Add $15 for silver plated straps and trigger guard, $50 for stainless steel.

Mfg.'s Sug. Retail	$275	$250	$220	$165

AUGUSTA CONFEDERATE — .36 cal., percussion, 7½ in. octagonal barrel, color case hardened hammer and trigger, all brass frame, engraved cylinder, 2½-2¾ lbs.

Mfg.'s Sug. Retail	$210	$190	$165	$130

GRISWOLD AND GUNNISON CONFEDERATE — .36 or .44 cal., percussion, same as above except round barrel, forward of lug, does not have engraved cylinder.

	$190	$165	$130

Last Mfg.'s Sug. Retail was $150.

LEECH AND RIGDON CONFEDERATE — .36 cal., percussion, same as above except all steel frame.

Mfg.'s Sug. Retail	$260	$235	$205	$150

TEXAS CONFEDERATE DRAGOON — .44 cal., percussion, 7½ in. round barrel, color case hardened frame, hammer, and load lever, brass trim, "Tucker, Sherrard, and Co.", 4 lbs.

	$240	$200	$140

Last Mfg.'s Sug. Retail was $210.

1858 REMINGTON — .44 cal., percussion, 7½ in. barrel, 6 shot, blued steel, brass trigger guard, 2.6 lbs. Add $40 for adj. sights.

Mfg.'s Sug. Retail	$250	$230	$200	$160

1858 REMINGTON STAINLESS — same as above, has brass strap and trigger guard. Add $40 for adj. sights.

	$305	$265	$210

Last Mfg.'s Sug. Retail was $260.

1858 REMINGTON NEW NAVY — .36 cal., percussion, 6½ in. octagonal barrel, 6 shot, blue frame, 2½ lbs. Add $40 for adj. sights.

	$235	$195	$155

Last Mfg.'s Sug. Retail was $185.

1866 REVOLVING CARBINE — .44 cal., percussion, 18 in. barrel, 6 shot, blued steel, brass trigger guard, walnut stock, 4.6 lbs.

	$345	$300	$200

Last Mfg.'s Sug. Retail was $320.

Grading	100%	98%	95%

RIFLES: PERCUSSION

HAWKEN SANTA FE — .53 cal., single shot, 32 in. oct. barrel, damascened finish, double set triggers, 9½ lbs., walnut stock.

	$405	$355	$270

Last Mfg.'s Sug. Retail was $350.

JEREDIAH SMITH SANTA FE HAWKENS — .50 and .54 cal. percussion, similar to above. Add $35 for Flintlock.

Mfg.'s Sug. Retail	$450	$410	$360	$285

LEMAN TRADE RIFLE — .45, .50, .54, and .58 cal. percussion. Add $15 for .54 and .58 cal.

	$250	$220	$160

Last Mfg.'s Sug. Retail was $250.

ST. LOUIS RIFLE — .45, .50, .54, or .58 cal., flintlock and percussion, color case hardened hammer lock and trigger guard, octagonal barrel. Add $15 for .54 and .58 cal. percussion, $15 for flintlock, $30 for 50 cal. flintlock.

	$345	$280	$210

Last Mfg.'s Sug. Retail was $280.

BLACKPOWDER CARTRIDGE

ROLLING BLOCK SPORTING RIFLE — .45/.70 blackpowder cartridge, 30 in. barrel. Add $100 for deluxe sporting rifle.

	$380	$330	$265

Last Mfg.'s Sug. Retail was $620.

COLT'S FIREARMS

Hartford, CT. Colt subcontracted the manufacture of these black powder pistols to Aldo Uberti in Italy from 1979-1982. Parts were shipped into the U.S. and assembled stateside.

PERCUSSION REVOLVERS: 2ND GENERATION

See Colt Black Powder 2nd Generation Serialization section in the back of this text for more information. Last manufacturer's suggested retail values listed below are from the 1982 Colt factory catalog.

WALKER MODEL — .44 cal., 9 in. barrel, color case hardened frame, hammer, and loading lever, 73 oz., mfg. 1979-1982. Add $100 for cased Heritage Walker Commemorative Model.

	$895	$675	$495

Last Mfg.'s Sug. Retail was $562.

BABY DRAGOON — .31 cal., 4 in. barrel, unfluted straight cylinder, color case hardened frame, short frame.

	$450	$375	$275

Last Mfg.'s Sug. Retail was $405.

⚑ **"1 of 500" cased set**

	$675	$525	$400

Last Mfg.'s Sug. Retail was $900.

1ST MODEL DRAGOON — .44 cal., 7½ in. barrel, oval bolt cuts in cylinder, color case hardened frame, loading lever, plunger, and hammer, one piece stocks, 66 oz. Disc. 1982.

	$425	$325	$250

Last Mfg.'s Sug. Retail was $448.

Grading	100%	98%	95%

2ND MODEL DRAGOON — .44 cal., 7½ in. barrel, rectangular bolt cuts in cylinder, color case hardened frame, loading lever, plunger, and hammer, one piece stocks, 66 oz. Disc. 1982.

$425 $325 $250

Last Mfg.'s Sug. Retail was $448.

3RD MODEL DRAGOON — .44 cal., 7½ in. barrel, rectangular bolt cuts in cylinder, color case hardened frame, loading lever, plunger, and hammer, round trigger guard, one piece stocks, 66 oz. Disc. 1982. Add $275 for cased Giuseppe Garibaldi Commemorative Model.

$425 $325 $250

Last Mfg.'s Sug. Retail was $448.

1851 NAVY — .36 cal., 7½ in. octagonal barrel, color case hardened frame, loading lever, plunger, and hammer, square trigger guard, one piece stocks, 42 oz. Disc. 1982.

$450 $350 $275

Last Mfg.'s Sug. Retail was $420.

1851 Stainless Navy — stainless steel, only 498 mfg.

$695 $500 $395

Last Mfg.'s Sug. Retail was $473.

1860 ARMY — .44 cal., 8 in. round barrel, color case hardened frame, loading lever, plunger, and hammer, round trigger guard, one piece stocks, 42 oz. Discontinued in 1981. Two versions made, one has an engraved rebated cylinder and the other has a blued fluted cylinder.

Fluted Cylinder $625 $475 $300
Rebated Cylinder $595 $495 $325

Last Mfg.'s Sug. Retail was $431 (non-fluted), $456 (fluted).

1860 Army Stainless Unfluted — mfg. 1982.

$700 $550 $375

Last Mfg.'s Sug. Retail was $485.

1861 NAVY — .36 cal., 7½ in. round barrel, color case hardened frame, loading lever, plunger, and hammer, round trigger guard, one piece stocks, 42 oz. Disc. 1982.

$495 $375 $295

Last Mfg.'s Sug. Retail was $420.
Stainless variations of this model (only 3 or 4 are known to exist) are very desirable - 100% specimens would probably trade in the $2,000 range.
Last Mfg.'s Sug. Retail was $473.

1862 POCKET NAVY — .36 cal., 5½ in. octagonal barrel, color case hardened frame, loading lever, plunger, and hammer, round trigger guard, one piece stocks, 27 oz. Disc. 1982.

$395 $300 $250

Last Mfg.'s Sug. Retail was $394.

"1 of 500" cased set

$650 $525 $350

1862 POCKET POLICE — .36 cal., 5½ in. round barrel, color case hardened frame, loading lever, plunger, and hammer, fluted cylinder, one piece stocks, 25 oz. Disc. 1982.

$375 $250 $200

Last Mfg.'s Sug. Retail was $394.

"1 of 500" cased

$650 $525 $350

CONNECTICUT VALLEY ARMS
Distributed in Norcross, GA. Available through dealers and catalog houses.
All pistols have color case hardened finishes with solid brass trim.

Grading	100%	98%	95%

PISTOLS

COLONIAL PISTOL — .45 cal., percussion, 6¾ in. octagonal barrel, 31 oz. New in 1989.

Mfg.'s Sug. Retail	$115	$110	$95	$65

"HAWKEN" PISTOL — .50 cal., percussion or flintlock, 9¾ in. octagonal barrel, 50 oz. Add $10 for flintlock.

Mfg.'s Sug. Retail	$175	$150	$130	$95

STANDARD KENTUCKY PISTOL — .45 or .50 cal., percussion, 10¼ in. octagonal barrel, brass blade front sight, 40 oz.

Mfg.'s Sug. Retail	$160	$140	$120	$90

MOUNTAIN PISTOL — .45 or .50 cal., percussion, 9 in. octagonal barrel, German silver wedge plate with pewter cap, 40 oz.

	$125	$100	$80

PHILADELPHIA DERRINGER — .45 cal., percussion, 3¼ in. octagonal barrel, 16 oz.

Mfg.'s Sug. Retail	$90	$80	$65	$50

SIBER PISTOL — .45 cal., percussion, 10½ in. octagonal, white steel engraved barrel, lock also engraved white steel, checkered walnut grip, 38 oz.

Mfg.'s Sug. Retail	$440	$380	$330	$250

TOWER PISTOL — .45 cal., percussion, 9 in. octagonal barrel at breech tapers to round, antique brass trigger, 36 oz.

	$125	$100	$80

REVOLVERS

All revolvers have solid brass trim and walnut grips.

COLT WALKER MODEL — .44 cal., percussion, 9 in. barrel, color case hardened frame, hammer, and loading lever, 72 oz.

Mfg.'s Sug. Retail	$280	$240	$210	$170

3RD MODEL DRAGOON — .44 cal., 7½ in. barrel, rectangular bolt cuts in cylinder, color case hardened frame, loading lever, plunger, and hammer, round trigger guard, one piece stocks, 66 oz.

Mfg.'s Sug. Retail	$240	$205	$180	$145

WELLS FARGO — .31 cal., percussion, 3, 4, or 5 in. octagonal barrel, 5 shot, color case hardened frame, hammer, no load lever, brass trim, 1½ lbs. Add $65 for steel frame.

Mfg.'s Sug. Retail	$130	$115	$100	$75

1851 NAVY — .36 cal., percussion, 7½ in. octagonal barrel, brass frame, 38 oz. Add $50 for steel frame.

Mfg.'s Sug. Retail	$135	$100	$85	$70

CVA COLT POCKET POLICE — .36 cal., 5½ in. round barrel, color case hardened frame, loading lever, plunger, and hammer, round trigger guard, fluted cylinder, one piece stocks, 25 oz. Add $55 for steel frame.

Mfg.'s Sug. Retail	$140	$120	$105	$80

Add $15 for Sheriff's Model.
Add $65 for engraved, nickel plated Sheriff's Model w/matching powder flask.

1860 ARMY — .44 cal., percussion, 8 in. round barrel, 6 shot engraved cylinder, color case hardened frame, trigger, and load lever, 44 oz.

Mfg.'s Sug. Retail	$230	$185	$160	$130

Grading	100%	98%	95%

1861 NAVY — .36 or .44 cal., percussion, 7½ in. round barrel, 6 shot engraved cylinder, color case hardened frame, trigger, and load lever, or brass frame (.44 cal. only), 44 oz. Add $60 for color case hardened steel frame, $60 for presentation grade Sheriff's Model with matching powder flask (new in 1986).

Mfg.'s Sug. Retail	$130	$115	$100	$80

Add $10 for brass frame on Standard Sheriff Model.
Add $25 for steel frame on Standard Sheriff Model.

WAR AND PEACE — .36 cal., 1851 Navy and 1851 Sheriff's Model, heavily engraved in rosewood presentation case.

	$350	$300	$240

Last Mfg.'s Sug. Retail was $630.

1873 COLT SINGLE ACTION — .44 cal. percussion, 7 in. round barrel, brass backstrap and trigger guard, color case hardened frame and cylinder, new in 1991 (this is a ball and cap version of the 1873 Colt Cartridge gun).

	$280	$245	$200

Last Mfg.'s Sug. Retail was $350.

1858 REMINGTON ARMY — .44 cal., percussion, 8 in. octagonal barrel, color case hardened hammer, steel or brass frame, 38 oz. Add $60 for steel.

Mfg.'s Sug. Retail	$170	$140	$120	$90

REMINGTON BISON — .44 cal., percussion, 1858 Remington Army frame brass, 10¼ in. octagonal barrel, adj. sights, 3 lbs.

Mfg.'s Sug. Retail	$245	$195	$170	$135

REMINGTON POCKET — .31 cal., percussion, 5 shot, 4 in. octagonal barrel, brass frame, 15 oz. New in 1989.

Mfg.'s Sug. Retail	$130	$115	$100	$75

REMINGTON TARGET — .44 cal., percussion, 12 in. octagonal barrel, brass frame and trigger guard, adj. sights, based on 1858 Navy frame, 38 oz.

Mfg.'s Sug. Retail	$240	$200	$180	$140

OFFICER AND THE GENTLEMAN —matched set .44 cal., 1858 Rem. Army and .31 cal. Pocket Rem., heavily engraved in rosewood presentation case.

	$400	$300	$200

Last Mfg.'s Sug. Retail was $650.

RIFLES

APOLLO 90 RIFLE/CARBINE — .50 cal. percussion, straight-through ignition, 27 in. (22 in. carbine) round tapered barrel with chrome bore, slide bolt design, similar to Gonic Arms, Monte Carlo laminated stock, adj. sights, 7 lbs., 8 oz.

Mfg.'s Sug. Retail	$440	$240	$215	$150

Subtract $65 for standard stock.

APOLLO 90 SHADOW RIFLE — .50 and .54 cal. percussion, same as above but with epoxy coated hard wood stock. New 1992.

Mfg.'s Sug. Retail	$315	$260	$235	$180

Add $35 for New Model with carbelite stock and 25 in. bbl.

APOLLO SPORTER — same as Apollo Rifle above but with 25 in. tapered round barrel and standard (non-Monte Carlo) stock. 8½ lbs. New 1992.

Mfg.'s Sug. Retail	$225	$190	$165	$130

BLAZER RIFLE — .50 cal., percussion, straight ignition (like Percussion Revolver), 28 in. octagonal barrel, stainless steel nipple, brass tipped ramrod, 6 lbs., 12 oz. Deduct $10 for Blazer II.

	$130	$110	$90

Last Mfg.'s Sug. Retail was $210.

Grading	100%	98%	95%

BLUNDERBUSS — .69 cal., flintlock, 16 in. tapered to flared muzzle barrel, brass trim, available right or left-hand, 5 lbs. 5 oz.

	$240	$195	$155

Last Mfg.'s Sug. Retail was $255.

BUSHWACKER RIFLE — .50 cal., percussion, 26 in. octagonal barrel, color case hardened hammer, lock and nipple, blued furniture, 7½ lbs.

Mfg.'s Sug. Retail	$160	$140	$120	$95

EXPRESS RIFLE —.50 or .54 cal., percussion, double barrel, 28 in. tapered round barrel, color case hardened plate, hammers and trim, adj. sights. Add $375 for presentation grade (new in 1986).

Mfg.'s Sug. Retail	$525	$450	$390	$300

Add $160 for extra set of 12 ga. barrels.

FRONTIER RIFLE/CARBINE —.45, .50 & .54 cal., percussion or flintlock, 28 in. octagonal barrel, brass trim, right or left hand, 7 lbs. 15 oz. Add $15 for flintlock, $10 for left-hand, deduct $30 for carbine model.

Mfg.'s Sug. Retail	$255	$180	$155	$110

FRONTIER HUNTER CARBINE — .50 & .54 cal. percussion, 24 in. blued octagonal barrel, color case hardened hammer & lock, blued furniture, adj. sight (rear), wt. 7½ lbs.

Mfg.'s Sug. Retail	$205	$155	$130	$100

HAWKEN RIFLE/CARBINE —.50 or .54 cal., percussion or flintlock, 28 in. octagonal chrome bore barrel, brass trim, beaver tail select walnut stock, 7 lbs. 15 oz. Add $10 for flintlock.

	$250	$225	$165

Last Mfg.'s Sug. Retail was $390.

HAWKEN DEERSLAYER RIFLE/CARBINE — .50 cal., percussion, similar to above, 7½ lbs. New 1992.

	$200	$175	$130

Last Mfg.'s Sug. Retail was $250.

HUNTER HAWKEN RIFLE/CARBINE — .50 and .54 cal., percussion, 28 in. (24 in. carbine) octagonal barrel, color case hardened lock and nipple, sling swivels, adj. hunting sights. 8 lbs.

Mfg.'s Sug. Retail	$360	$190	$165	$130

Add $70 for premier grade (.50 cal. only).

KENTUCKY RIFLE/HUNTER — .45 or .50 cal., percussion or flintlock, 33½ in. octagonal barrel, color case hardened hammer and plate, antique brass trigger, 7 lbs. 4 oz. Add $10 for flintlock, or adj. hunting sights.

Mfg.'s Sug. Retail	$260	$225	$195	$150

MISSOURI HUNTER RIFLE — .50 cal. percussion, 28 in. octagonal barrel, adjustable hunting sights, color case hardened hammer and lock recoil pad, 9 lbs. 6 oz. New 1991.

	$190	$165	$130

Last Mfg.'s Sug. Retail was $300.

MISSOURI RANGER —.50 cal., percussion, 28 in. octagonal barrel, color case hardened trim, right or left hand, 7 lb. 8 oz.

	$180	$160	$120

MOUNTAIN RIFLE — .50 and .54 cal., percussion or flintlock, 32 in. octagonal barrel, German silver wedge plate and patch box, pewter or German silver nose cap, 7 lbs. 14 oz.

Mfg.'s Sug. Retail	$260	$240	$210	$170

Add $80 for premier grade (chrome bore and German silver trim).

OVER/UNDER DOUBLE BARREL CARBINE — .50 cal., percussion, O/U 26 in. octagonal tapering to round barrels, color case hardened lock, hammers, and triggers, checkered walnut stock, 8½ lbs.

	$480	$400	$320

Last Mfg.'s Sug. Retail was $800.

Grading	100%	98%	95%

PENNSYLVANIA LONG RIFLE — .50 cal., percussion or flintlock, 40 in. octagonal barrel, color case hardened hammers and plate, brass trim, 8 lbs. 3 oz.

Mfg.'s Sug. Retail	$455	$385	$335	$255

PLAINSMAN RIFLE — .50 cal., percussion, 26 in. octagonal barrel, color case hardened lock and nipple, 6 lbs. 9 oz.

Mfg.'s Sug. Retail	$140	$115	$100	$80

SIERRA STALKER RIFLE — .50 cal. percussion, 28 in. blued octagonal barrel, color case hardened hammer & lock, adj. sight (rear), wt. 7¼ lbs. New 1993.

Mfg.'s Sug. Retail	$190	$160	N/A	N/A

SQUIRREL RIFLE — .32 cal., percussion or flintlock, 25 in. octagonal barrel, color case hardened hammer and plate, brass trim, stainless steel nipple, 5 lbs. 12 oz. Add $10 for flintlock, $10 for left-hand.

	$190	$175	$140

Last Mfg.'s Sug. Retail was $250.

ST. LOUIS HAWKEN — .50, .54, or .58 cal., percussion or flintlock, 28 in. octagonal barrel, brass trim, 7 lbs. 13 oz. Add $40 for flintlock, $75 for 12 ga. combo. barrel, $70 for 1-48 twist extra .50 cal. barrel, $40 for left hand.

Mfg.'s Sug. Retail	$215	$185	$160	$125

STALKER RIFLE — .50 cal. percussion, 28 in. octagonal barrel, hunting style sight (click adjustable) color case hardened hammer and lock recoil pad, 7 lbs. 4 oz. New 1991.

Mfg.'s Sug. Retail	$220	$190	$165	$130

Add $100 for premier grade.
Add $20 for left hand.

TRACKER CARBINE — .50 cal., percussion, 21 in. blued half round, half octagonal barrel, color case hardened nipple, hammer and lock, 6½ lbs. New 1992.

Mfg.'s Sug. Retail	$255	$220	$190	$130

TROPHY CARBINE — .50 and .54 cal. percussion, 24 in. half round/half octagonal, similar to above with sling swivel mounts and dark stained Monte Carlo stock, 7½ lbs.

Mfg.'s Sug. Retail	$255	$220	$190	$130

VARMINT RIFLE — .32 cal. percussion, 24 in. octagonal, blued barrel, color case hardened hammer & lock, brass trigger guard and furniture, adj. rear sight, wt. 6¾ lbs. New 1993.

Mfg.'s Sug. Retail	$235	$200	N/A	N/A

ZOUAVE RIFLE — .58 cal., percussion, 32½ in. tapered barrel with bayonet mount, brass trim and lands, adj. sight, 9¾ lbs. New in 1989.

	$270	$235	$190

Last Mfg.'s Sug. Retail was $335.

SHOTGUNS

BRITTANY SHOTGUN — 12 ga., 28 in. double barrel, 7 lbs. 7 oz. Disc. after 1989.

	$255	$220	$170

Last Mfg.'s Sug. Retail was $295.

BRITTANY SHOTGUN II — .410 ga., 24 in. double barrel, 6 lbs. 4 oz. Disc. after 1989.

	$200	$170	$140

Last Mfg.'s Sug. Retail was $210.

SHOTGUN — 12 or .410 ga., percussion, 28 in. (24 in. on .410) double barrel, 6 lbs. 10 oz (6 lbs. 4 oz. on .410). Deduct $85 for .410 ga. New in 1987. Presentation grade side by side add $350. Disc. 1989.

	$255	$220	$170

Last Mfg.'s Sug. Retail was $275.

Grading	100%	98%	95%

TRAPPER SHOTGUN — 12 ga., 28 in. single barrel, color case hardened hammer and lock, blued barrel, 3 chokes, recoil pad ,5 lbs. 10 oz. New in 1988.

Mfg.'s Sug. Retail	$340	$280	$245	$190

Add $60 for extra 1-66 twist .50 cal. barrel combo.

CLASSIC TURKEY SXS — 12 ga., percussion, 28 in. round barrel, color casehardened lock, stainless steel nipple, recoil pad, 9 lbs.

Mfg.'s Sug. Retail	$405	$355	$300	$240

D.P. (DAVIDE PEDERSOLI and CO.)

Imported by Navy, E.M.F., House of Muskets, and Sile Distributors, and Taylors, Inc. In 1992, entire Pedersoli line now being imported by Beauchamp and Son, Inc./Flintlocks, ETC. Available through dealers and catalog houses.

Add approximately 25% for engraving, 200% for extra luxury engraving.

PISTOLS

BOUNTY — .44 or .50 cal., flintlock or percussion, 16½ in. octagonal barrel, white steel hammer and lock, brass furniture and trigger guard, walnut stock, 3 lbs.

Mfg.'s Sug. Retail	$200	$175	$150	$120

Add $10 for flintlock.
Add $35 for engraved model (hammer, lock and barrel).

ENGLISH DUELING PISTOL — .45 cal., percussion, 11 in. octagonal barrel, silver thimble and nosecap.

	$290	$240	$180

HARPERS FERRY 1806 — .58 cal., flintlock, 10 in. barrel, color case hardened lock, brass furniture, and inlaid butt cap, 2½ lbs. Add $100 for commemorative model with silver plated hardware and white steel barrel (stamped U.S. Army Commemorative).

Mfg.'s Sug. Retail	$275	$250	$210	$160

KENTUCKY PISTOL — .44 cal., flintlock or percussion, 10¼ octagonal barrel (steel or brass), walnut stock, brass furniture and trigger guard, 2¼ lbs. Add $10 for flintlock, $55 for deluxe engraved model w/German silver inlaid barrel, and color case hardened hammer and lock, $120 for silver star model with engraved white steel hammer and lock, German silver furniture, inlayed stock (star on forearm) and browned barrel.

Mfg.'s Sug. Retail	$195	$175	$140	$110

LEPAGE PISTOL — .31, .36, .44, and .45 cal., flintlock or percussion, 10½ in. browned octagonal barrel, white steel barrel percussion, white steel hammer, and lock, adj. triggers, 2 lbs. (cased set, gold trim, consecutive serial number).

Mfg.'s Sug. Retail	$480	$400	$325	$240

Add $40 for .31 cal., $110 for flintlock, $630 for deluxe engraved with skin case, $200 for mahogany case.

MANG TARGET PISTOL — .38 cal., percussion, 11½ in. octagonal browned barrel, color case hardened hammer and lock, fluted walnut stock, 2½ lbs.

Mfg.'s Sug. Retail	$820	$700	$600	$390

Add $1,750 for deluxe model with skin case.

CHARLES MOORE PISTOL — .36 and .45 cal., flintlock or percussion, 11 in. octagonal barrel, white steel hammer and lock (flintlock), color case hardened (percussion), brass furniture, adj. trigger, hand checkered walnut stock, 2½ lbs.

Mfg.'s Sug. Retail	$365	$330	$260	$200

Add $15 for flintlock.
Deduct $65 for .54 cal. Big Bore Model, deduct $20 for target model with removeable barrel.

Grading	100%	98%	95%

MOUNTAIN PISTOL — .44 or .50 cal., flintlock or percussion, 14½ in. octagonal barrel, color case hardened hammer and lock, brass furniture and trigger guard, hand checkered walnut stock, 2¼ lbs.

Mfg.'s Sug. Retail	$215	$190	$165	$130

Add $10 for flintlock.

PENNSYLVANIA PISTOL — .44 cal, percussion, 10 in. octagonal barrel, brass furniture, locks left in white.

	$150	$125	$100

QUEEN ANN PISTOL — .50 cal., flintlock, 7½ in. cannon shaped barrel (smooth bore), white steel hammer and lock, grotesque mask under buttstock, 2¼ lbs.

Mfg.'s Sug. Retail	$205	$190	$150	$120

Add $30 for silver plated or deluxe model.
Add $15 for flintlock.

SALOON PISTOL — .36 cal., percussion, straight through ignition, 8 in. rounded barrel, color case hardened hammer and frame, walnut stock, 1¾ lbs.

Mfg.'s Sug. Retail	$150	$135	$120	$95

UNDERHAMMER PISTOL — .36 cal. percussion, 8½ in. octagonal to round browned barrel, metal fittings are color case hardened, walnut stock, 2 lbs.

Mfg.'s Sug. Retail	$690	$625	$540	$430

ZIMMER PISTOL — .36 and 4.3 cal., percussion, 8 in. octagonal blued barrel, white steel hammer and frame, fluted walnut stock, 1⅝ lbs.

Mfg.'s Sug. Retail	$220	$195	$170	$135

Add $35 for 4.3 cal. (designed to shoot with cap alone no powder).
Add $30 for deluxe model either caliber.

REVOLVERS

PATERSON — .36 cal., percussion, 5 shot, 9 in. octagonal barrel, no loading lever, walnut stock, 2½ lbs.

Mfg.'s Sug. Retail	$310	$275	$240	$190

Add $450 for deluxe model with engraved cylinder, barrel, and frame with skin case.

ROGERS AND SPENCER FEINWERKBAU — .44 cal. percussion, 6 shot, 7½ in. octagonal barrel, walnut grips, 3 lbs.

Mfg.'s Sug. Retail	$1,525	$1,380	$1,200	$850

Manufactured by Feinwerkbau using the latest technology, molybdenum chrome steel frame, etc. Weight balanced for accurate firing.

RIFLES

ALAMO — .38, .45. or .50 cal., percussion or flintlock, 36 in. octagonal barrel with double set triggers, white steel hammer and lock, brass furniture, patchbox engraved with scenes of the period, walnut stock, 6½ lbs. Add $20 for flintlock.

Mfg.'s Sug. Retail	$405	$370	$315	$220

BRISTLEN MORGES — .44 cal. percussion, 29½ in. octagonal barrel, color case hardened hammer and lock, walnut ½ stock, palm rest professional target rifle, 16¾ lbs.

Mfg.'s Sug. Retail	$1,595	$1,465	$1,275	$950

Add $500 for deluxe version with engraved white steel hammer and lock.

BROWN BESS MUSKET/CARBINE — .75 cal., flintlock, 31½ or 42 in. smooth bore barrel, white steel hammer and lock, brass furniture, ¾ stock (walnut), 8¾ lbs. (7¾ carbine). Deduct $25 for carbine.

Mfg.'s Sug. Retail	$635	$610	$550	$400

Add $65 for bayonet.

Grading	100%	98%	95%

1777 CHARLEVILLE MUSKET — .69 cal., flintlock or percussion, 44⅝ in. white steel barrel, hammer, lock, and trim, 9¾ lbs. New in 1989.

Mfg.'s Sug. Retail	$750	$660	$550	$440

COUNTRY BOY — .32, .36, .45, and .50 cal., percussion, 26 in. octagonal barrel, color case hardened hammer and lock, unique mule ear hammer, blued furniture, adj. sights, walnut ½ stock, 5½ lbs.

Mfg.'s Sug. Retail	$240	$225	$195	$160

COUNTRY HUNTER — .50 cal., flintlock or percussion, 28¼ in. octagonal barrel, blued hardware, color case hardened hammer and lock, walnut ½ stock, 6 lbs.

Mfg.'s Sug. Retail	$220	$195	$170	$125

Add $20 for flintlock.

FREDERICKSBURG MUSKET — .75 cal., flintlock.

	$600	$500	$400

FRONTIER RIFLE/CARBINE — .36, .45 and .50 cal., flintlock or percussion, 39 in. octagonal browned barrel, color case hardened hammer and lock, brass furniture, walnut or birdseye maple full stock, 7¾ lbs. (7¼ lbs. .45 and .50 cal.).

Mfg.'s Sug. Retail	$420	$380	$330	$260

Add $20 for flintlock.
Add $150 for birdseye maple.

HAWKEN RIFLE — .54 cal. percussion, 32¼ in. octagonal browned barrel, color case hardened hammer, lock, and furniture, double set triggers, walnut or birdseye maple ½ stock, 8¾ lbs.

Mfg.'s Sug. Retail	$450	$400	$350	$260

Add $115 for birds eye maple stock.

JAPANESE RIFLE — .492 cal., matchlock 41½ in. octagonal browned barrel, brass matchlock and furniture, authentic reproduction of 16th century Tomonobu rifle.

Mfg.'s Sug. Retail	$1,075	$980	$850	$500

KENTUCKY — .32, .45, or .50 cal., percussion or flintlock, 35 in. barrel, color case hardened hammer and lock, brass furniture and patchbox, walnut full stock, 6½ lbs. Add $20 for flintlock, $65 for deluxe model with engraved white steel hammer, lock, and engraved brass patchbox and trigger guard, $300 for silver star model with engraved silver plated hammer, lock, trigger guard and patchbox, also has silver stars inlaid in stock.

Mfg.'s Sug. Retail	$330	$300	$265	$180

KODIAK — .50, .54, and .58 cal. percussion, double rifle (SxS), see Kodiak express combo below.

Mfg.'s Sug. Retail	$680	$635	$525	$410

MORTIMER/MORTIMER HUNTER RIFLE — .54 cal. Flintlock & percussion, 36¼ in. octagonal to round browned barrel, color case hardened hammer, lock and trigger guard, waterproof pan, 8⅞ lbs. Prices based on Mortimer Hunter.

Mfg.'s Sug. Retail	$425	$400	$325	$260

Add $345 for target model with target sights and checkered stock, $1,100 for extra deluxe engraved with engraved white steel hammer, lock, and hardware with gold inlays.
Add $250 for Std. Mortimer Rifle (flintlock or percussion).

1816 MT. WICKHAM RIFLE — similar to Charleville rifle above but with slightly shorter barrel.

Mfg.'s Sug. Retail	$750	$660	$550	$440

1816 SPRINGFIELD — .75 cal. flintlock. More information available from manufacturer.

Mfg.'s Sug. Retail	$750	$660	N/A	N/A

PENNSYLVANIA RIFLE — .32 and .45 cal., flintlock or percussion, 41½ in. barrel, brass trim, color case hardened or white steel lock, hammer, and double set trigger, walnut full stock, 8¼ lbs. New in 1989.

Mfg.'s Sug. Retail	$400	$365	$315	$230

Add $20 for flintlock.

Grading	100%	98%	95%

PLAINSMAN RIFLE — .38, .45. or .50 cal., flintlock or percussion, 37 in. octagonal barrel, white steel hammer and lock, brass furniture and patchbox, adj. sights and double set triggers, 6½ lbs.

Mfg.'s Sug. Retail	$435	$400	$345	$240

Add $20 for flintlock
$65 for engraved model.

SCOUT RIFLE — .32, .45, and .50 cal., flintlock or percussion, carbine version of Pennsylvania rifle listed above with 28¼ in. barrel, 6 lbs.

Mfg.'s Sug. Retail	$350	$315	$270	$200

Add $20 for flintlock.

SHARPS RIFLE — .45 and .54 cal., percussion, 22 or 28 in. octagonal or round barrel, color case hardened hammer, frame and butt plate, 7¾ lbs. Add $20 for octagonal barrel on civilian model, $55 for sporter model with hand checkered walnut stock.

Mfg.'s Sug. Retail	$665	$600	$520	$400

SPRINGFIELD RIFLE — .58 cal., percussion, 40 in. white steel barrel, color case hardened hammer and lock, white steel furniture, walnut full stock, 9¾ lbs.

Mfg.'s Sug. Retail	$550	$500	$440	$350

TRYON RIFLE — .45, .50, or .54 cal., percussion, 32¼ in. octagonal barrel, color case hardened hammer, lock, patchbox, and furniture, double set triggers, walnut ½ stock, 9½ lbs. Add $50 for engraved model with white steel hammer, lock, furniture and patchbox.

Mfg.'s Sug. Retail	$560	$400	$335	$260

TRYON CREEDMOOR — .45 cal., percussion, 32¾ in. barrel, all blued hardware, target version of above, 9½ lbs.

Mfg.'s Sug. Retail	$740	$685	$595	$440

WAADTLANDER RIFLE — .45 cal., percussion, 31 in. octagonal browned barrel, target sights, 14⅜ lbs. Target version of Bristlen Morges above. Add $500 for deluxe engraved model with white steel hardware and silver inlays.

Mfg.'s Sug. Retail	$1,595	$1,465	$1,275	$950

BLACK POWDER CARTRIDGE

KODIAK MARK IV — .45-70 cartridge, 24 in. SxS barrel, color case hardened hammer lock and trigger guard, double leaf adj. rear sights, copy of 19th century "Colt Double Rifle", hand checkered walnut stock, 10 lbs. Add $550 for extra 12 ga./.45/.70 barrel, $800 for engraved model with white steel engraved frame and hardware, browned barrels.

Mfg.'s Sug. Retail	$1,895	$1,600	$1,360	$950

REMINGTON ROLLING BLOCK REPRODUCTION — .45-70 cartridge, 19½, 24½, 26 and 30 in. octagonal blued barrel (octagonal to round on cavalry model), color case hardened frame and hammer, brass trigger guard and furniture, walnut stock, 9¾, 11½, 11⅞, and 13 lbs. respectively, (9⅜, 11, 11⅜, 12⅜ lbs. respectively on cavalry models). Add $45 for target model with adj. sights and white steel hammer and frame, $100 for Creedmore sights, $150 for Creedmoor Target with Creedmoor adj. sights and color case hardened trigger guard, $450 for engraved model with white steel engraved frame and brass trigger guard.

Mfg.'s Sug. Retail	$580	$515	$450	$320

SHARPS — .45-70 cartridge, 22 or 28 in. octagonal or round barrel, color case hardened hammer, frame and buttplate, 7¾-9 lbs. Add $20 for octagonal barrel on civilian model, $100 for Sporter model with hand checkered walnut stock. (Very improved 1993).

Mfg.'s Sug. Retail	$685	$600	$515	$400

Add $75 for target sights.

SHOTGUNS

CLASSIC TURKEY SXS — 12 ga., percussion, 28 in. round double barrel, color case hardened lock, stainless steel nipple, recoil pad, 9 lbs.

	$435	$370	$280

Grading	100%	98%	95%

KODIAK SXS SHOTGUN/EXPRESS/COMBO. — 10 or 12 ga. x .50, .12 x .58, or .50 x .58 cal., percussion, 28 in. double barrel, engraved white steel hammer and lock, blued furniture, checkered walnut ½ stock, 9 lbs. Add $50 for .10 ga., $300 for rifle or comb. barrels (extra set).

Mfg.'s Sug. Retail	$680	$635	$525	$410

SXS SHOTGUN — 10, 12, and 20 ga., percussion, 28 in. barrel, chrome bore, color case hardened hammer and lock, (engraved white steel on 10 ga.), checkered walnut stock, double triggers, 7½ lbs. Add $20 for 10 ga., $20 for cavalry model, $1,500 for extra deluxe with gold inlays.

Mfg.'s Sug. Retail	$485	$440	$350	$280

Add $200 for extra 12 ga. barrels, $240 for extra 10 ga. barrels.

MORTIMER SHOTGUN — 12 ga. flintlock or percussion, version of Mortimer Rifle above. Add $65 for flintlock.

Mfg.'s Sug. Retail	$690	$615	$525	$390

DALY, CHARLES

Previously distributed by Outdoor Sports, Hdqtrs., in Dayton, OH. Available only on the used market.

All rifles feature adj. sights, investment cast brass trim, patch boxes, color case hardened hammer and locks, octagonal rifle barrels, adj. double set triggers, and European hard wood stocks.

HAWKEN RIFLE — .45 cal., percussion, 28 in. barrel, right-hand only.

	$400	$300	$200

Last Mfg.'s Sug. Retail was $240.

HAWKEN RIFLE — .50 cal., percussion, 28 in. barrel, right and left-hand. Add $20 for left-hand.

	$400	$300	$200

Last Mfg.'s Sug. Retail was $240.

HAWKEN RIFLE — .50 cal., flintlock, 28 in. barrel, right and left-hand. Add $20 for left-hand.

	$410	$305	$210

Last Mfg.'s Sug. Retail was $280.

HAWKEN CARBINE — .50 cal., flintlock, 22 in. barrel.

	$400	$300	$200

Last Mfg.'s Sug. Retail was $240.

DEER CREEK MFG.

Manufacturer located in Waldron, IN. Sold exclusively by Mountain States Muzzle Loading in Williamstown, WV.

RIFLES

HIGHLANDER RIFLE — .50 or .54 cal. percussion, 32 in. browned octagonal barrel, browned furniture, hammer, lock & patchbox, maple half stock, wt. 7½ to 7¾ lbs.

Mfg.'s Sug. Retail	$280	$260	$220	N/A

J.P. MCCOY SQUIRREL RIFLE — .32 or .45 cal. flintlock or percussion, 42 in. browned barrel, browned hammer and lock, brass buttplate & trigger guard, full length select curly maple stock, wt. 7½ lbs.

Mfg.'s Sug. Retail	$590	$590	$520	N/A

Add $20 for flintlock.

ROUGHRIDER RIFLE — .45, .50 or .54 cal. percussion, 32 in. octagonal blued barrel, pewter nosecap, German silver, cap box and wedge plates, maple half stock, wt. 7½ to 7¾ lbs.

Mfg.'s Sug. Retail	$280	$260	$220	N/A

DIXIE GUN WORKS

Union City, TN — manufacturer and distributor. Available through dealers or from Dixie direct.

Short descriptions are for models of standard construction. Also, since 1986, many models are imported from Uberti (to eliminate duplications see Uberti, Aldo and Co.).

REVOLVERS: PERCUSSION

Grading	100%	98%	95%

WALKER — .44 cal., percussion, 9 in. barrel, 6 shot, color case hardened frame, hammer, and load lever, brass trim, 4½ lbs. Add $65 for Deluxe Uberti version.

Mfg.'s Sug. Retail	$225	$205	$180	$125

1ST MODEL DRAGOON — .44 cal., percussion, 6 shot, brass grip straps, color case hardened frame, hammer, and load lever, brass trim, 3.9 lbs. Add $15 for silver-plated straps, (Uberti version).

Mfg.'s Sug. Retail	$295	$265	$230	$150

2ND MODEL DRAGOON — .44 cal., percussion, 6 shot, brass grip straps, color case hardened frame, hammer, and load lever, brass trim, 3.9 lbs. Add $15 for silver-plated straps, (Uberti version).

Mfg.'s Sug. Retail	$295	$265	$230	$150

3RD MODEL DRAGOON — .45 cal., percussion, 7³⁄₈ in. barrel, color case hardened frame, hammer, and load lever, brass trigger guard and back strap. Add $75 for Deluxe Uberti version.

Mfg.'s Sug. Retail	$200	$175	$155	$120

BABY DRAGOON — .31 cal., 6 in. barrel, color case hardened frame. Add $55 for Deluxe Uberti version.

Mfg.'s Sug. Retail	$185	$165	$145	$110

MODEL 1849 POCKET — .31 cal., percussion, with loading lever, 3, 4, or 5 in. barrel, 5 shot, color case hardened frame, hammer, and load lever, brass trim, 1½ lbs. (Uberti version). Add $15 for silver straps and trigger guard.

Mfg.'s Sug. Retail	$255	$230	$200	$150

1851 NAVY — .36 cal., brass frame. Add $35 for engraved model, $40 for steel, $130 for Deluxe or London marked Uberti versions, or $35 for steel frame.

Mfg.'s Sug. Retail	$100	$85	$75	$60

TEXAS PATERSON HOLSTER PISTOL — .36 cal., percussion, 7½ or 9 in. barrel, has hidden trigger and no loading lever (Uberti version). Add $20 for 9 in. barrel.

Mfg.'s Sug. Retail	$310	$300	$260	$205

1860 ARMY — .44 cal., percussion, half-fluted cylinder, 8 in. barrel, color case hardened hammer, frame, and load lever, and brass trigger guard. Add $70 for Deluxe Uberti version, $20 for silver plated backstrap and trigger guard.

Mfg.'s Sug. Retail	$170	$155	$135	$100

MODEL 1861 NAVY REVOLVER — .36 cal., percussion, 5 in. barrel, many styles, brass back strap or trigger guard, color case hardened frame, hammer, and load lever, 2½ lbs. (Uberti version). Add $15 for silver plated strap and trigger guard, $15 for fluted military cylinder, $50 for stainless steel. Add $100 for shoulder stock.

Mfg.'s Sug. Retail	$255	$230	$200	$140

MODEL 1862 POLICE — .36 cal., percussion, 4½, 5½, or 6½ in. barrel, color case hardened frame, hammer, and load lever, cylinder, semi-fluted or engraved, 1.6 lbs. (Uberti version). Add $15 for silver plated straps and trigger guard, $50 for stainless steel.

Mfg.'s Sug. Retail	$260	$230	$200	$155

1858 REMINGTON — .44 cal., percussion, 8 in. octagonal barrel, blue finish. Add $60 for Deluxe Uberti version. Add $135 for stainless steel. Add $175 for new "Shooters" Revolver.

Mfg.'s Sug. Retail	$160	$145	$125	$80

Grading	100%	98%	95%

REMINGTON NAVY — .36 cal., percussion, 6¼ in. octagonal barrel, .36 cal. variation of the 1858 Remington, 2½ lbs. New in 1989. (Uberti version).

Mfg.'s Sug. Retail	$230	$205	$180	$135

LEECH and RIGDON — .36 cal., percussion, 7 in. round barrel, Confederate copy of the Colt Navy, 2¾ lbs. New in 1989. (Uberti version).

Mfg.'s Sug. Retail	$220	$200	$175	$140

SPILLER and BURR — .36 cal., percussion, octagonal barrel, color case hardened hammer and load lever, brass frame and trigger guard.

Mfg.'s Sug. Retail	$125	$115	$100	$65

WYATT EARP — .44 cal., percussion, 6 shot, 12 in. oct. barrel, brass frame.

Mfg.'s Sug. Retail	$130	$115	$100	$70

PISTOLS BLACK POWDER CARTRIDGE

CATTLEMAN S.A. REVOLVER — .44-40 cal., 4¾, 5½, 7½ in. barrel, color case hardened frame, brass trigger guard.

Mfg.'s Sug. Retail	$375	$365	$300	$240

1875 ARMY S.A. — .44-40 cal. cartridge, 7½ in. barrel, fluted cylinder, color case hardened frame, brass trigger guard. Add $50 for nickel.

Mfg.'s Sug. Retail	$325	$320	$270	$210

1890 ARMY — .44-40 cal., 6 shot, 5½ in. barrel, color case hardened frame. Add $40 for nickel.

Mfg.'s Sug. Retail	$350	$330	$290	$235

PISTOLS

This is an alphabetized listing.

ABILENE DERRINGER — .41 cal., percussion with case.

Mfg.'s Sug. Retail	$80	$75	$65	$40

BLACK WATCH SCOTTISH PISTOL — .577 cal., flintlock, 7 in. smooth bore barrel.

Mfg.'s Sug. Retail	$175	$160	$140	$95

BRASS FRAME DERRINGER — percussion. Add $20 for engraving.

Mfg.'s Sug. Retail	$70	$60	$55	$40

CHARLEVILLE PISTOL — .69 cal., flintlock, 7½ in. white steel barrel.

Mfg.'s Sug. Retail	$195	$170	$145	$100

ENGLISH DUELING PISTOL — .45 cal. percussion, 11 in. octagonal barrel, silver thimble and nose cap.

Mfg.'s Sug. Retail	$265	$240	$210	$165

HARPERS FERRY — .58 cal., flintlock, 10 in. barrel, color case hardened hammer and lock.

Mfg.'s Sug. Retail	$250	$230	$200	$150

KENTUCKY PISTOL — .44 cal. flintlock or percussion, 10¼" blued barrel, color case hardened hammer & lock, brass furniture, wt. 2¼ lbs.

Mfg.'s Sug. Retail	$150	$140	$120	$85

LEPAGE DELUXE TARGET PISTOL — .45 cal., percussion, 9¼ in. white steel barrel, adj. sights.

Mfg.'s Sug. Retail	$395	$360	$315	$240

LEPAGE DUELING PISTOL — .45 cal., percussion, 10 in. barrel.

Mfg.'s Sug. Retail	$260	$240	$205	$160

Grading	100%	98%	95%

LINCOLN DERRINGER — .41 cal., percussion, 2 in. barrel, with case.

Mfg.'s Sug. Retail	$285	$260	$225	$150

MANG TARGET PISTOL — .38 cal. percussion, $10^7/_{16}$ in. octagonal browned barrel, white steel hammer and lock.

Mfg.'s Sug. Retail	$750	$690	$550	$400

MOORE AND PATRICK PISTOL — .45 cal., flintlock, 10 in. browned octagonal barrel.

Mfg.'s Sug. Retail	$335	$310	$260	$200

MURDOCK SCOTTISH HIGHLANDERS PISTOL — .52 cal., flintlock, $7^3/_4$ in. white steel barrel, hammer, lock, and furniture, 4 lbs. Mfg. 1989-91 only.

Mfg.'s Sug. Retail	$300	$265	$230	$195

PENNSYLVANIA PISTOL — .44 cal., flintlock or percussion, 10 in. barrel, brass furniture, white steel hammer and lock. Add $5 for flintlock.

Mfg.'s Sug. Retail	$150	$130	$115	$85

PHILADELPHIA DERRINGER

	$40	$35	$30

Last Mfg.'s Sug. Retail was $45.

QUEEN ANNE PISTOL — .50 cal., flintlock, $7^1/_2$ in. bronzed steel barrel.

Mfg.'s Sug. Retail	$190	$170	$145	$100

TORNADO TARGET — .44 cal., percussion, 10 in. octagonal barrel. Built on Remington 1860 army frame.

Mfg.'s Sug. Retail	$215	$190	$165	$130

WILLIAM PARKER PISTOL — .45 cal., flintlock, 11 in. barrel, hand checkered half stock, 2 lbs. 8 oz.

Mfg.'s Sug. Retail	$310	$280	$245	$200

RIFLES

BROWN BESS MUSKET — .74 cal., flintlock, $41^1/_2$ in. barrel, 9 lbs. 8 oz. Add $100 for 2nd Model (1762).

Mfg.'s Sug. Retail	$495	$460	$400	$305

BUFFALO HUNTER — .58 cal., percussion, 26 in. barrel.

	$225	$190	$140

CHARLEVILLE MUSKET — .69 cal., flintlock, $44^5/_8$ in. white steel barrel, hammer, lock, and furniture, $8^3/_4$ lbs. New in 1989. Add $180 for 1777 French Model, (Pedersoli).

Mfg.'s Sug. Retail	$450	$400	$350	$260

DELUXE CUB RIFLE — .40 cal., flintlock or percussion, 28 in. octagonal barrel, color case hardened hammer, plate and triggers, brass trim and patch box, double set triggers. Add $80 for percussion.

Mfg.'s Sug. Retail	$250	$220	$190	$145

1858 2-BAND ENFIELD — .58 cal., percussion, 2 barrel bands, 9 lbs. 4 oz.

Mfg.'s Sug. Retail	$425	$380	$330	$260

1862 3-BAND ENFIELD — .58 cal., percussion, 3 barrel bands, 10 lbs. 8 oz.

Mfg.'s Sug. Retail	$485	$435	$380	$280

ENFIELD MUSKETOON LONDON ARMORY — .58 cal. percussion, 24 in. round barrel, color case hardened hammer and lock, brass buttplate, trigger guard and nose cap.

Mfg.'s Sug. Retail	$340	$340	$310	$235

Grading	100%	98%	95%

HAWKEN RIFLE — .45, .50, .54 or .58 cal., percussion, color case hardened hammer and lock, brass patch box.

Mfg.'s Sug. Retail	$250	$225	$195	$145

HARPERS FERRY RIFLE — .54 and .58 cal. Flintlock, 35½ in. octagonal to round barrel, color case hardened hammer and lock, brass trigger guard and patchbox.

Mfg.'s Sug. Retail	$595	$540	$475	$370

Subtract $75 for .58 cal.

INDIAN GUN — same as Brown Bess Musket except 31 in. barrel.

Mfg.'s Sug. Retail	$675	$600	$500	$400

J.P. MURRAY CARBINE — .58 cal. percussion, 23½ in. round barrel, color case hardened hammer and lock, brass buttplate trigger guard and barrel bands (2), factory sling swivels.

Mfg.'s Sug. Retail	$375	$360	$300	$220

KENTUCKIAN CARBINE — .45 cal., flintlock or percussion, 27½ in. barrel. Add $15 for flintlock.

Mfg.'s Sug. Retail	$270	$240	$210	$160

KENTUCKY RIFLE — .45 cal., flintlock or percussion, 33½ in. barrel, brass patchbox and furniture. Add $10 for flintlock.

Mfg.'s Sug. Retail	$250	$225	$195	$155

KODIAK DOUBLE RIFLE — .50, .54 and .58 (combo barrels 50x12 ga. and 58x12 ga.) cal. percussion, S x S, 28 in. barrels, hand checkered walnut stock, adjustable sights.

Mfg.'s Sug. Retail	$625	$600	$530	$420

KODIAK MKIII RIFLE SHOTGUN COMBO — same as above but with one 12 ga. barrel, .50 and .58 cal. percussion.

Mfg.'s Sug. Retail	$625	$600	$530	$420

LANCASTER COUNTY RIFLE — .45 cal., flintlock or percussion (same as Pennsylvania Rifle above, except less ornate trigger guard and patch box). Add $5 for flintlock.

	$190	$175	$160

MISSISSIPPI RIFLE — U.S. rifle model 1841, .58 cal., percussion, 33½ in. barrel, color case hardened hammer and lock, solid brass furniture, similar to Zouave with nose cap replacing front barrel band.

Mfg.'s Sug. Retail	$430	$400	$345	$250

MORTIMER RIFLE — .54 cal. Flintlock, 36¼ in. octagonal to round barrel, color case hardened hammer, lock and trigger guard, waterproof pan, 8⅞ lbs.

Mfg.'s Sug. Retail	$645	$620	$545	$435

PENNSYLVANIA RIFLE — .45 cal., flintlock or percussion, 41½ in. octagonal barrel, browned hammer, lock and barrel, brass patchbox and furniture walnut full stock, 8 lbs.

Mfg.'s Sug. Retail	$395	$360	$315	$230

SANFTL SCHUETZEN TARGET RIFLE — .45 cal., percussion, 29 in. barrel, adj. sights. Disc. 1991

	$570	$475	$385

Last Mfg.'s Sug. Retail was $595.

SHARPS RIFLE/CARBINE — .54 cal., percussion. 28 in. barrel. Deduct $30 for carbine. Disc. in 1987.

	$310	$280	$235

1861 SPRINGFIELD MUSKET — .58 cal., percussion, 40 in. round tapered barrel, white steel furniture, 9 lbs. 8 oz.

Mfg.'s Sug. Retail	$450	$425	$385	$275

1863 SPRINGFIELD MUSKET — .58 cal., percussion, 41½ in. barrel.

Mfg.'s Sug. Retail	$475	$420	$375	$275

Grading	100%	98%	95%

TENNESSEE MOUNTAIN/SQUIRREL RIFLE — .32 or .50 cal., percussion or flintlock, $41\frac{1}{2}$ in. browned barrel, browned furniture, cherry full stock, $8\frac{1}{2}$ and $9\frac{1}{2}$ lbs. respectively, (.32 cal. is a small cal. squirrel rifle), right or left hand.

Mfg.'s Sug. Retail	$495	$425	$370	$275

TRYON CREEDMOOR RIFLE — .50 cal., percussion, 32 in. octagonal all black barrel, matte finish furniture and patchbox adjustable Creedmoor sights, $9\frac{1}{2}$ lbs.

Mfg.'s Sug. Retail	$595	$580	$535	$400

TRYON RIFLE — .50 cal. percussion, 32 in. octagonal barrel, color case hardened furniture and patchbox, chrome bore, $9\frac{1}{2}$ lbs.

Mfg.'s Sug. Retail	$450	$400	$350	$270

WAADTLANDER RIFLE — .44 cal. percussion, 31 in. octagonal browned barrel, color case hardened hammer, lock and trigger guard and heavy butt plate, adj. sights, professional target model.

Mfg.'s Sug. Retail	$1,295	$1,260	$1,145	$920

WESSON RIFLE — .50 cal., percussion, 28 in. barrel, adj. sights.

	$385	$335	$260

Last Mfg.'s Sug. Retail was $395.

YORK COUNTY RIFLE — .45 cal., flintlock or percussion, 36 in. barrel. Add $15 for flintlock. Disc. in 1987.

	$210	$175	$140

Last Mfg.'s Sug. Retail was $210.

ZOUAVE RIFLE — .58 cal., percussion, $33\frac{1}{2}$ in. blued barrel, color case hardened hammer and lock. Deduct $35 for carbine barrel. Add $100 for Deluxe Model.

Mfg.'s Sug. Retail	$325	$290	$250	$150

BLACKPOWDER CARTRIDGE

HENRY RIFLE — .44-40 cal., brass frame, lever action, $24\frac{1}{2}$ in. barrel. Add $275 for engraving.

Mfg.'s Sug. Retail	$850	$775	$675	$495

1866 CARBINE — .44-40 cal., brass receiver, lever action, 19 in. round barrel.

Mfg.'s Sug. Retail	$645	$575	$500	$385

1873 SPORTING RIFLE — .44-40 cal., color case hardened steel receiver, lever action, $24\frac{1}{4}$ in. octagonal barrel. Also available with slight engraving. Add $160 for deluxe w/pistol grip stock, $400 for engraving (Uberti), add $220 for engraving (non-Uberti).

Mfg.'s Sug. Retail	$775	$690	$600	$475

1873 CARBINE — .44-40 cal., steel receiver, 19 in. round barrel (Uberti model). Add $160 for Deluxe, $255 for deluxe engraved with engraved blued receiver.

Mfg.'s Sug. Retail	$745	$690	$600	$475

CATTLEMAN REVOLVING CARBINE — .44-40 cal., 18 in. barrel, brass backstrap, with shoulder stock.

	$360	$300	$240

Last Mfg.'s Sug. Retail was $400.

SHOTGUNS

MAGNUM SxS SHOTGUN — 10 and 12 ga., percussion, 28 in. barrel, chrome bore, color case hardened hammer and lock. (Engraved white steel on 10 ga.), checkered walnut stock. $7\frac{1}{2}$ lbs. Add $60 for 10 ga., $1,500 for extra deluxe with gold inlays.

Mfg.'s Sug. Retail	$400	$380	$330	$270

MORTIMER SHOTGUN — 12 ga. Flintlock, similar to Mortimer Rifle listed in rifle section, 7 lbs.

Mfg.'s Sug. Retail	$625	$575	$500	$375

Grading	100%	98%	95%

DOUBLE BARREL: PERCUSSION — 10 and 12 ga., percussion, 28 in. barrel, chrome bore, color case hardened hammer and lock. (Engraved white steel on 10 ga.), checkered walnut stock. 7½ lbs. Add $60 for 10 ga., $1,500 for extra deluxe with gold inlays.

Mfg.'s Sug. Retail	$400	$380	$330	$270

NORTHWEST TRADE — 20 ga., flintlock, 36 in. octagonal tapering to round barrel, browned barrel and lock assembly, 11 lbs. New in 1989. Disc.1991.

	$425	$370	$295

Last Mfg.'s Sug. Retail was $495.

E.M.F. COMPANY

Manufactured and distributed in Santa Ana, CA. Available through dealers and from E.M.F. direct. *Most percussion revolvers are available in a cased presentation set. Add $100 for cased set.*

PISTOLS

1775 BLACK WATCH SCOTTISH PISTOL — .58 cal., flintlock, 7 in. smooth bore white steel barrel, brass frame, ram's horn grips with round ball trigger.

	$160	$140	$95

Last Mfg.'s Sug. Retail was $260.

CHARLES MOORE — .45 cal. flintlock, 10 in. octagonal barrel, 2 lbs.

	$325	$275	$220

Last Mfg.'s Sug. Retail was $400.

1777 CHARLEVILLE PISTOL — .69 cal., flintlock, 7½ in. white steel barrel, brass frame.

	$170	$145	$100

Last Mfg.'s Sug. Retail was $315.

CORSAIR PISTOL — .36 or .44 cal., percussion, double barrel, color case hardened hammer and lock, brass trim. Disc. in 1987.

	$300	$200	$130

Last Mfg.'s Sug. Retail was $160.

HARPERS FERRY — .58 cal., flintlock, brass mounted brown barrel.

	$250	$210	$160

Last Mfg.'s Sug. Retail was $405.

HAWKEN PISTOL — .54 cal. percussion, 9 in. octagonal barrel, adj. trigger, 2 lbs. 9 oz.

	$230	$195	$155

Last Mfg.'s Sug. Retail was $370.

KENTUCKY PISTOL — .44 cal., flintlock or percussion, available engraved or with brass barrel. Add $30 for flintlock, $20 for brass barrel, $25 for engraved percussion.

	$175	$140	$110

Last Mfg.'s Sug. Retail was $250.

LE PAGE PISTOL — .45 cal. percussion, 9 in. octagonal white steel barrel and trim, adj. sights, 2 lbs. 2 oz.

	$260	$220	$175

Last Mfg.'s Sug. Retail was $400.

REMINGTON STYLE TARGET PISTOL — .44 cal., percussion, 9 in. octagonal barrel, factory engraved, adj. sights (windage only), based on Rem. frame, 43 oz.

	$190	$165	$130

Last Mfg.'s Sug. Retail was $310.

Grading	100%	98%	95%

WM. PARKER PISTOL — .45 cal. percussion, 10 in. octagonal barrel, German silver lock and trim, adj. double set of triggers, 2 lbs. 8 oz.

| | $310 | $265 | $210 |

Last Mfg.'s Sug. Retail was $400.

REVOLVERS

All percussion revolvers are available in cased sets. Add $80 for cased set. In 1993 the Hartford line was introduced w/German silver plated backstrap & triggerguard. Guns trade at same prices listed.

1847 WALKER — .44 cal., percussion, 9 in. barrel, color case hardened frame and load lever, brass trim, 4 lbs. 8 oz. Add $75 for nickel plate, $135 for engraving.

| Mfg.'s Sug. Retail | $280 | $230 | $200 | $150 |

1ST MODEL DRAGOON — .44 cal., percussion, 7½ in. barrel, color case hardened frame, brass trim, engraved cylinder, 4 lbs. 2 oz.

| Mfg.'s Sug. Retail | $275 | $220 | $180 | $140 |

2ND MODEL DRAGOON — .44 cal., percussion, 7½ in. barrel, color case hardened frame, brass trim, engraved cylinder, 4 lbs.

| Mfg.'s Sug. Retail | $275 | $220 | $180 | $140 |

3RD MODEL DRAGOON — .44 cal., percussion, 7½ in. barrel, color case hardened frame and loading lever, brass trim, engraved cylinder, 4 lbs. 2 oz., adj. target sights. Add $25 for buntline model. Add $10 for Texas Dragoon Model (Tucker and Sherrard and Co., Confederate States, Texas Star engraved on cylinder, square brass trigger guard).

| Mfg.'s Sug. Retail | $275 | $220 | $180 | $140 |

BABY DRAGOON — .31 cal., percussion, 5 shot, 4 and 6 in. barrel, color case hardened frame and loading lever, brass trim, Add $20 for engraving, $30 for steel frame.

| | $185 | $160 | $120 |

WELLS FARGO MODEL 1849 — .31 cal., percussion, 5 shot, 5 in. barrel, no loading lever.

| | $185 | $160 | $120 |

1851 NAVY — .36 or .44 cal., percussion, 7½ in. barrel, brass frame, color case hardened hammer, and load lever, brass trim, engraved cylinder. Add $20 for engraving, brass, $140 for steel. Add $30 for steel frame, $25 for nickel plated brass (Mason Dixon Model), $70 for silver trimmed steel, $100 for 3 barrel set (.44 cal. only). Add $140 for commemorative issued with special grip, $100 for shoulder stock.

| Mfg.'s Sug. Retail | $140 | $100 | $84 | $70 |

1851 NAVY BALLISTER — .44 cal., percussion, same as above, except with 12 in. barrel.

| | $100 | $85 | $70 |

1851 NAVY SHERIFF'S MODEL — .36 or .44 cal., percussion, 5 in. round or octagonal barrel, (shorter barrel version of 1851 Navy), brass frame - add $35 for steel.

| Mfg.'s Sug. Retail | $140 | $100 | $85 | $70 |

The same add on's apply to this model as the 1851 Navy.

1851 GRISWOLD CONFEDERATE — .36 and .44 cal. percussion, 7½ in. round barrel, brass frame, 2 lbs. 12 oz.

| Mfg.'s Sug. Retail | $140 | $100 | $85 | $70 |

1860 ARMY — .44 cal., percussion, 8 in. barrel, brass frame, 2 lbs. 9 oz. Add $40 for steel frame, $150 for stainless steel, engraving, add $25 for brass, $150 for steel. Add $80 for steel Sheriff's Model, $90 for fluted cylinder (steel), $100 for shoulder stock, $145 for deluxe engraving.

| Mfg.'s Sug. Retail | $145 | $105 | $90 | $70 |

1861 NAVY — .36 cal., percussion, steel frame. Disc. in 1987.

| | $145 | $125 | $100 |

Last Mfg.'s Sug. Retail was $215.

Grading	100%	98%	95%

1862 POLICE — .36 cal., percussion, 5 shot, color case hardened frame. Add $50 for steel frame, $100 for engraved steel.

Mfg.'s Sug. Retail	$150	$115	$100	$80

1862 POCKET NAVY — .36 cal., percussion, 5 shot, color case hardened frame.

Mfg.'s Sug. Retail	$200	$140	$120	$95

NAVY SQUAREBACK — .36 or .44 cal., percussion, 7½ in. barrel, color case hardened frame and load lever, Dragoon style square back trigger guard.

	$100	$85	$70

Last Mfg.'s Sug. Retail was $130.
The same add on's apply to this model as the 1851 Navy.

1858 REMINGTON ARMY — .36 and .44 cal., percussion, 8 in. barrel, brass frame, blue finish, 2 lbs. 8 oz. For engraving, add $100 brass, $140 steel. Add $35 for steel frame, $140 for stainless steel, $100 for 12 in. Buffalo Model, $120 for Target Model w/adj. sights.

Mfg.'s Sug. Retail	$155	$115	$100	$80

RIFLES

BOSTONIAN — .45 cal., percussion. New in 1989.

Mfg.'s Sug. Retail	$285	$220	$190	$150

ALAMO COMMEMORATIVE — .45 cal., percussion, embellished to commemorate the anniversary of the Alamo. New in 1989.

	$370	$315	$220

Last Mfg.'s Sug. Retail was $435.

DELUXE BROWN BESS MUSKET — .75 cal., flintlock. Add $60 for bayonet.

	$610	$550	$400

Last Mfg.'s Sug. Retail was $850.

HAWKEN RIFLE — .50 cal., percussion, brass trim, color case hardened lock and hammer, adj. sights, and stainless steel nipple.

Mfg.'s Sug. Retail	$325	$245	$215	$160

KENTUCKY RIFLE — .36, .44, or .45 cal., percussion and flintlock, factory engraved, brass trim, color case hardened lock and hammer. Add $20 for flintlock, $30 for deluxe model, $50 for deluxe engraved.

	$300	$265	$180

"LONDON ARMORY" ENFIELD — .58 cal., percussion. Add $30 for 3 Band Model. Deduct $20 for Musketoon Model. Disc. in 1987.

	$345	$295	$235

Last Mfg.'s Sug. Retail was $285.

MINUTEMAN KENTUCKY RIFLE — .45 cal., flintlock or percussion, 36 in. octagonal barrel, brass blade front sight, brass trim, color case hardened lock, hammer, and trigger. Add $15 for engraving, $15 for flintlock.

	$260	$210	$170

PENNSYLVANIA KENTUCKY RIFLE — .50 cal., percussion, brass trim, color case hardened lock, hammer, and trigger.

	$315	$275	$200

Last Mfg.'s Sug. Retail was $440.

PLAINSMAN KENTUCKY RIFLE — .44 cal., percussion, shorter forearm than Pennsylvania with more ornate finish.

	$300	$250	$200

Last Mfg.'s Sug. Retail was $450.

Grading	100%	98%	95%

PURDEY DELUXE — .50 cal., percussion, half stock English style, select checkered walnut, color case hardened nose cap, lock, tang, butt plate and patch box, adj. sights, double set triggers. Carbine or rifles.

	$310	$260	$210

SAN FRANCISCO TO ST. LOUIS COMMEMORATIVE — .45 cal., Kentucky rifle, highly embellished, made to commemorate the 130th anniversary of the stage coach crossing "2,400 miles in 24 days". New in 1989. Disc. 1991.

	$350	$300	$220

Last Mfg.'s Sug. Retail was $395.

WESSON BERDAN RIFLE — .45 cal., percussion, engraved brass frame.

	$345	$305	$250

ZOUAVE RIFLE DELUXE — .58 cal., percussion, brass trim, color case hardened lock and hammer, blue finish, adj. "Sniper Sight".

Mfg.'s Sug. Retail	$500		$325	$275	$220

SHOTGUNS

SHOTGUN —.12 ga., S X S, percussion, based on early English design, brown barrel, color case hardened lock and hammer, imported from Italy.

	$380	$330	$270

Last Mfg.'s Sug. Retail was $535.

SHOTGUN O/U — 12 ga., percussion, O/U design. New in 1989. Disc. 1991.

	$470	$410	$310

Last Mfg.'s Sug. Retail was $640.

EASTERN MUZZLELOADERS SUPPLY

Importer/distributor located in Bear, Delaware. Available through dealers and catalog houses.

RIFLES

CRISTOFORO COLOMBO QUINCENTENARY MATCHLOCK — 1 of 500 made serial numbered CC 1492-CC 1992, classic matchlock styling of the period. The rear sight is a dolphin (a sign of good luck) the front sight, a stylized dolphin. The hammer is shaped like a sea monster (trigger being the tail), walnut stock, custom made by Pedersoli.

Mfg.'s Sug. Retail	$780		$745	N/A	N/A

We are not positive any of these guns actually made it to market.

FRENCH M1777 NAVY MUSKET — .69 cal. flintlock, 42½ in. white steel barrel, brass furniture, split ring iron center barrel band. non-corrosive brass priming pan, walnut stock, 8½ - 9½ lbs. (similar to Charleville Musket) custom manufactured by Pedersoli.

	$550	$475	$380

BLACKPOWDER CARTRIDGE

All models with the E.M.S. stamp are made by Uberti. See Uberti section at end of this section.

EUROARMS OF AMERICA

Manufacturer/importer, Winchester, VA. Available through dealers and catalog houses.

REVOLVERS

1851 NAVY "SCHNEIDER and GLASSICK" — .36 or .44 cal., percussion, 5 or 7 in. octagonal barrel, brass frame, 38-40 oz.

Mfg.'s Sug. Retail	$145		$125	$110	$85

Grading	100%	98%	95%

1851 NAVY "GRISWOLD and GUNNISON" — .36 or .44 cal., percussion, 7½ in. octagonal round barrel, brass frame, 39-41 oz. Disc. in 1987.

	$125	$110	$85

Last Mfg.'s Sug. Retail was $100.

1851 NAVY — .36 or .44 cal., percussion, 7½ in. barrel, steel frame, 39-43 oz. Add $10 for square back trigger, $25 for silver strap.

Mfg.'s Sug. Retail	$190	$160	$140	$105

1851 NAVY POLICE MODEL — .36 cal., percussion, 5 or 7½ in. octagonal barrel, steel frame, 5 shot fluted cylinder, 38-41 oz.

	$150	$130	$100

Last Mfg.'s Sug. Retail was $135.

1851 NAVY SHERIFF'S MODEL —.36 or .44 cal., percussion, 5 in. barrel, steel frame, 39 oz.

	$150	$130	$100

Last Mfg.'s Sug. Retail was $105.

1860 ARMY — .44 cal., percussion, 5 or 8 in. barrel, steel frame, 41 oz. Add $50 for steel, $75 for stainless steel, $50 for engraving. Deduct $40 for brass frame.

Mfg.'s Sug. Retail	$215	$190	$160	$120

1861 NAVY —.36 cal., percussion, 7½ in. barrel, steel frame, 42 oz.

Mfg.'s Sug. Retail	$245	$210	$185	$140

1862 POLICE — .36 cal., percussion, 7½ in. barrel, steel frame, 40 oz. Disc. in 1987.

	$150	$130	$100

Last Mfg.'s Sug. Retail was $135.

REMINGTON REPLICAS

1858 ARMY — .36 or .44 cal., percussion, 6½ and 8 in. octagonal barrel, 40 oz. Add $70 for engraving, $30 for stainless steel, $15 for target adj. sights, deduct $50 for brass frame.

Mfg.'s Sug. Retail	$260	$225	$195	$130

1858 NAVY — .36 cal., percussion, 6½ in. octagonal barrel, 40 oz. Disc. 1991.

Mfg.'s Sug. Retail	$260	$225	$195	$130

ROGERS and SPENCER — .44 cal., percussion, 7½ in. octagonal barrel, 47 oz. Add $15 for target sights, $25 for London gray finish, $75 for engraving.

Mfg.'s Sug. Retail	$275	$230	$200	$140

RIFLES

BROWN BESS MUSKET "TOWER FLINTLOCK" — .75 cal. flintlock, 41¾ in. barrel, smooth bore.

	$495	$410	$320

Last Mfg.'s Sug. Retail was $755.

BUFFALO CARBINE — .58 cal., percussion, 26 in. round barrel, color case hardened hammer and lock, brass patch box and furniture, 7¾ lbs. New in 1989.

Mfg.'s Sug. Retail	$515	$420	$365	$275

C.S. RICHMOND MUSKET — .58 cal. percussion, 40 in. round barrel, white steel hammer & lock, brass buttplate & nose cap, walnut stock, 10½ lbs.

Mfg.'s Sug. Retail	$645	$490	$410	$330

CAPE GUN RIFLE — .50 cal., percussion, 32 in. barrel, engraved with walnut stock. New in 1989. Disc. 1991.

Mfg.'s Sug. Retail	$515	$420	$365	$275

Grading	100%	98%	95%

COOK and BROTHER RIFLE/CARBINE — .58 cal., percussion, 24 in. barrel, adj. front sight (windage only), 2 barrel bands, walnut stock, 7½ lbs. Add $45 for rifle.

Mfg.'s Sug. Retail	$505	$325	$275	$230

ENFIELD RIFLE MUSKET (LONDON ARMORY CO.), 1853 — .58 cal., percussion, 39 in. barrel, adj. rear sight (windage only), 3 barrel bands, walnut stock, 9½ lbs. Add $30 for white steel barrel.

Mfg.'s Sug. Retail	$565	$385	$335	$250

ENFIELD RIFLE MUSKET (LONDON ARMORY CO.), 1858 — .58 cal., percussion, 33 in. barrel, adj. rear sight (windage only), 2 barrel bands, walnut stock, 8 lbs.

Mfg.'s Sug. Retail	$530	$340	$295	$230

ENFIELD MUSKETOON (LONDON ARMORY CO.), 1861 — .58 cal., percussion, 24 in. barrel, adj. rear sight (windage only), 2 barrel bands, walnut stock, 8 lbs.

Mfg.'s Sug. Retail	$495	$310	$275	$210

FRENCH MODEL 1777 MUSKET — .69 cal. flintlock, 44¾ in. white steel barrel, smooth bore.

	$450	$380	$310

Last Mfg.'s Sug. Retail was $835.

HARPER'S FERRY MODEL 1803 — .54 and .58 cal., flintlock, 35/33 in. browned barrel, walnut stock, 9 lbs.

Mfg.'s Sug. Retail	$650	$470	$420	$325

HAWKEN RIFLE — .58 cal., percussion, 28 in. octagonal barrel, double set triggers, target model, 9 lbs. 6 oz. Disc. in 1989.

	$240	$205	$165

Last Mfg.'s Sug. Retail was $295.

J.P. MURRAY MODEL 1863 — .58 cal., percussion, 23 in. barrel, 7 lbs. 9 oz.

Mfg.'s Sug. Retail	$495	$415	$360	$270

MISSISSIPPI RIFLE MODEL 1841 — .58 cal., percussion, 33 in. barrel, 9 lbs. 8 oz.

Mfg.'s Sug. Retail	$570	$400	$345	$300

PENNSYLVANIA RIFLE — .45 or .50 cal., flintlock or percussion, 36 in. barrel, adj. rear sight (windage only), walnut stock, 7 lbs. Add $30 for flintlock. Disc. in 1987.

	$300	$250	$200

Last Mfg.'s Sug. Retail was $285.

REMINGTON 1862 RIFLE — .58 cal., percussion, 33 in. barrel, 3 leaf folding rear sight, 3 barrel bands, beech stock, 9½ lbs. Disc. in 1987.

	$360	$315	$230

Last Mfg.'s Sug. Retail was $285.

SPRINGFIELD RIFLE MUSKET — .58 cal. percussion, 40 in. barrel with 3 bands.

Mfg.'s Sug. Retail	$645	$490	$410	$330

VOLUNTEER TARGET RIFLE (2 BAND) — .451 cal. percussion, 33 in. round barrel, color case hardened hammer & lock, two barrel bands, brass furniture, adj. rear and hooded front sights, walnut stock, wt. 9½ lbs. New 1993.

Mfg.'s Sug. Retail	$870	$620	N/A	N/A

VOLUNTEER TARGET RIFLE (3 BAND) — .451 cal. percussion, same as above except with 3 bbl. bands and longer barrel.

Mfg.'s Sug. Retail	$935	$665	N/A	N/A

ZOUAVE RIFLE — .58 cal., percussion, brass trim, color case hardened lock and hammer, blue finish, adj. sniper sight.

Mfg.'s Sug. Retail	$425	$365	$320	$250

Add $160 for "Range" grade Target Model.

Grading	100%	98%	95%

SHOTGUNS

MAGNUM CAPE SHOTGUN — 12 ga., percussion, 32 in. barrel, engraved with walnut stock, 5½ lbs.

Mfg.'s Sug. Retail	$515	$325	$275	$220

DUCK SHOTGUN — 8, 10, or 12 ga., percussion, 33 in. round barrel, color case hardened hammer and lock, brass patchbox and furniture, 8½ lbs. New in 1989. Disc. 1992.

	$300	$250	$200

Last Mfg.'s Sug. Retail was $455.

DOUBLE BARREL SHOTGUN —12 ga., percussion, 28 in. barrel, engraved with walnut stock, 6 lbs.

	$325	$275	$220

Last Mfg.'s Sug. Retail was $405.

FABER BROTHERS
Distributor located in Chicago, IL. Available through dealers.

Faber Brothers is currently marketing customized C.V.A. and InvestArms Hawken Rifles. These rifles come drilled and tapped for scope with offset hammers and chrome bores. Even though these rifles trade for prices equal to the C.V.A. Hawken, Faber Brothers could command a slight premium (see Connecticut Valley Arms).

FEDERAL ORDNANCE CORPORATION
Manufacturer/importer located in South El Monte, CA discontinued importation of Blackpowder Arms in 1990. Available only on the used market.

PISTOLS

DURS EGG SAW HANDLED PISTOL — .45 cal., flintlock or percussion, 9½ in. blued octagonal barrel, unique stock, hand checkered, German silver trim, white steel hammer and lock.

	$240	$210	$165

Last Mfg.'s Sug. Retail was $225.

F. ROCHATTE — .45 cal., percussion, single set triggers, hand checkered stock.

	$240	$210	$165

Last Mfg.'s Sug. Retail was $250.

KENTUCKY PISTOL — .45 cal., percussion, 10¼ in. octagonal barrel, brass blade front sight, 40 oz.

	$150	$125	$100

Last Mfg.'s Sug. Retail was $110.

WILLIAM MOORE PISTOL — .45 cal., flintlock or percussion, 10 in. octagonal barrel, white steel hammer and lock, silver plated trim, 2 lbs. Add $10 for flintlock.

	$300	$250	$190

Last Mfg.'s Sug. Retail was $230.

NAPOLEON LEPAGE PISTOL — .45 cal., percussion, 10 in. octagonal white steel barrel and lock, brass trim, adj. double set triggers, fluted grip, 2 lbs. 7 oz.

	$260	$220	$175

Last Mfg.'s Sug. Retail was $185.

WILLIAM PARKER PISTOL — .45 cal., flintlock or percussion, 11 in. octagonal browned barrel, silver plated furniture, double set triggers. Add $10 for flintlock.

	$310	$265	$210

Last Mfg.'s Sug. Retail was $200.

Grading	100%	98%	95%

REVOLVERS

1858 REMINGTON — .44 cal., percussion, 7½ in. octagonal barrel, 6 shot, brass frame and trigger guard, 2 lbs. 10 oz. Add $30 for steel, $135 for stainless steel frame.

	$115	$100	$80

Last Mfg.'s Sug. Retail was $110.
Add $75 for target model.

1860 ARMY — .44 cal., percussion, 8 in. barrel, 6 shot, color case hardened hammer, lock, and load lever, brass backstrap and trigger guard. Add $15 for Sheriff's Model, $75 for shoulder stock.

	$150	$120	$80

Last Mfg.'s Sug. Retail was $125.

1862 POCKET NAVY — .36 cal., percussion, 6½ in. barrel, color case hardened frame, hammer and load lever, cylinder semi-fluted, or engraved. 1 lb. 9 oz.

	$150	$130	$100

Last Mfg.'s Sug. Retail was $205.

ROGERS and SPENCER — .44 cal., percussion, 7½ in. octagonal barrel, blued steel, 3 lbs.

	$230	$200	$140

Last Mfg.'s Sug. Retail was $200.

RIFLES

1853 3-BAND ENFIELD — .58 cal., percussion, 39 in. round barrel, color case hardened hammer and lock, brass trim, blued bands, adj. rear sight, 9½ lbs.

	$385	$335	$250

Last Mfg.'s Sug. Retail was $400.

MODEL 1858 2-BAND ENFIELD — similar to P-1853 3-Band Enfield except has 33 in. round barrel, 10 lbs.

	$340	$295	$230

Last Mfg.'s Sug. Retail was $340.

ENFIELD MUSKETOON — .58 cal., percussion, 24 in. barrel, adj. rear sight (windage only), 2 barrel bands, walnut stock, 8 lbs.

	$340	$290	$230

Last Mfg.'s Sug. Retail was $480

HARPERS FERRY — .58 cal., flintlock, 35 in. round barrel, color case hardened hammer and lock, brass trim, 8½ lbs.

	$470	$410	$330

Last Mfg.'s Sug. Retail was $440.

HAWKENS RIFLE — .45 or .50 cal., flintlock or percussion, 28½ in. octagonal barrel, color case hardened hammer and lock, double set triggers, 7¾ lbs.

	$240	$205	$165

Last Mfg.'s Sug. Retail was $220.

KENTUCKY RIFLE — .45 cal., percussion, color case hardened hammer and lock, percussion cap holder in stock, brass trim.

	$225	$195	$155

Last Mfg.'s Sug. Retail was $210.

THE J.P. MURRAY CARBINE — .58 cal., percussion, 23½ in. browned round barrel, color case hardened hammer and lock, brass trim and bands, 7½ lbs.

	$375	$325	$160

Last Mfg.'s Sug. Retail was $370.

Grading	100%	98%	95%

MISSISSIPPI RIFLE — .58 cal., percussion, 33 in. browned round barrel, color case hardened hammer and lock, brass trim and bands, 9½ lbs.

	$400	$345	$300

Last Mfg.'s Sug. Retail was $410.

SANFTL SCHUETZEN RIFLE — .45 cal., percussion, 31 in. octagonal barrel, both peep and iron sights, Schuetzen style butt plate and trigger guard, brass furniture.

	$570	$475	$385

Last Mfg.'s Sug. Retail was $590.

ZOUAVE RIFLE — .58 cal., percussion, 32½ in. round barrel, color case hardened hammer, lock and trigger, brass trim, adj. rear sight, 9 lbs.

	$365	$320	$250

Last Mfg.'s Sug. Retail was $360.

FREEDOM ARMS

Manufactured and distributed in Freedom, WY. Available only on the used market.

REVOLVERS

STAINLESS MINI-REVOLVER — .22 cal., percussion, 5 shot, 1, 1¾, or 3 in. barrel, stainless steel. Add $15 for 3 in. barrel, $40 for brass buckle.

	$240	$200	$155

Last Mfg.'s Sug. Retail was $205.
Due to an increase in demand for Freedom Arms .454 Casull, the .22 cal. percussion pistol is temporarily out of production. It is unknown if production of this gun will ever begin again.

GIBBS RIFLE CO.

Manufacturer, Martinsburg, WV.

Founded in 1991, the Gibbs Rifle Company has purchased the rights to manufacture the Parker-Hale Enfield Black Powder replicas from Parker-Hale located in Birmingham, England. Navy Arms is still the only distributor of Parker-Hale Black Powder Replicas. See Navy Arms.

GONIC ARMS INC.

Manufacturer located in Gonic, NH. Available through dealers.

Gonic Arms has designed a true hunter's Black Powder rifle. Equipped with an ambidextrous safety, it eliminates the noisy "click" often associated with bringing a hammer back from half cock or setting the first of double set triggers. A specially designed firing pin and housing allow spent caps to blow out the bottom of the rifle, thus eliminating the need to "dig out" the spent cap from the breech. This combined with its modern appearance and newly designed loading system make it a true hunter's rifle without the problems associated with most Black Powder arms.

MODEL GA-87 RIFLE/CARBINE — .308 Spitfire, .38, .44, .458 Express, .50 cal. (rifle only), .54, and 20 ga., 26 in. round barrel, (24" carbine custom shop only) single stage trigger with left or right safety, cap is placed in breech, hand checkered walnut stock (deluxe model), 6 lbs. New in 1987.

Mfg.'s Sug. Retail	$495	$400	$340	$300

Add $30 for sights, $20 for Deluxe, $30 for laminated stock, $250 for 1-1,000 limited edition.

MODEL GA-93 CARBINE — .50 cal., 24 in. barrel, adj. trigger, tapped for scope bases, (26" custom shop only), open hunting sights, hardwood stock.

Mfg.'s Sug. Retail	$310	$295	N/A	N/A

Grading	100%	98%	95%

MODEL GA-90 PISTOL BARREL — .30, .38, .44 and .45 cal. percussion, 16 or 24 in. barrels, uniquely designed to fit into a Thompson contender frame, using either a #11 percussion cap or a 209 shotgun shell primer, standard Thompson forearm must also be replaced. Add $10 for #11 percussion ignition, $40 for open or peep sights, $50 for **required** forearm assembly, $80 for thumbhole rifle stock (not required), $85 for laminated thumbhole stock.

Mfg.'s Sug. Retail	$190	$150	$130	$100

Deduct $15 FOR 16" barrel.

HATFIELD RIFLE WORKS
Previously manufactured in St. Joseph, MO. Sold by Mountain State Muzzleloading Supplies.

MOUNTAIN RIFLE — .50 and .54 cal. percussion, 32 in. octagonal barrel, browned furniture, 1/2 stock, 9 lbs.

Mfg.'s Sug. Retail	$665	$575	$500	$360

Over the last two years extensive work has been done to all internal working parts to insure greater longevity for target or field use. All internal parts now U.S. made.

SQUIRREL RIFLE — .32, .36, .45, or .50 cal., flintlock or percussion, 39 in. barrel, adj. sights, double set triggers, brass trim, 7 1/2 lbs. Add $20 for flintlock.

Mfg.'s Sug. Retail	$600	$520	$450	$360

Add $65 for extra fancy maple Grade II.
Add $175 for hand selected fancy Grade III.
Custom guns could easily run 200% over standard.
This gun is a one-of-a-kind model with exceptional craftsmanship in both wood and metal.

HEGE
Uberlingen, Germany (imported by Beeman Precision Arms, Inc. Santa Rosa, CA).
This item is no longer stocked by Beeman, but can be special ordered. Price is set at time of order.

HEGE-MANTON — .44 cal., flintlock, 6 lbs. Add $100 for engraving.

	$1,610	$1,390	$990

Last Mfg.'s Sug. Retail was $1,695.

HEGE-SIBER PISTOL — .33 or .44 cal., percussion, 10 in. blue octagonal barrel, exceptional finish, world class target model, color case hardened hammer and lock.

	$990	$880	$550

Last Mfg.'s Sug. Retail was $1,000.

FRENCH STYLE HEGE-SIBER PISTOL — .33 or .44 cal. percussion, 10 in. blue octagonal barrel, exceptional finish, world class target model, London gray finish, 24 Kt. gold inlays, blue trigger guard.

	$1,720	$1,495	$1,100

Last Mfg.'s Sug. Retail was $1,795.

‡ **Matched set** — same serial number.

	$3,000	$2,650	$1,835

Last Mfg.'s Sug. Retail was $2,995.

IVER JOHNSON
Manufactured in Jackson, AR. Available only on the used market.

OVER/UNDER DOUBLE RIFLE MODEL BP50HB — .50 cal., percussion, double barrel, separate hammers and triggers, color case hardened hammer and furniture.

	$500	$425	$340

KBI
Harrisburg, PA. Available through dealers.

Grading	100%	98%	95%

PISTOLS

1851 NAVY — .44 cal., percussion, 7½ in. barrel, brass frame, 39-43 oz. Add $30 for engraving, or for Pony Express Sheriff Model.

Mfg.'s Sug. Retail	$150	$115	$100	$70

1860 ARMY — .44 cal., percussion, 5 or 8 in. barrel, steel frame, 41 oz.

	$165	$140	$100

Last Mfg.'s Sug. Retail was $240.

1858 REMINGTON ARMY — .36 or .44 cal., percussion, 6½ and 8 in. octagonal barrel, 40 oz. Add $25 for steel frame, $140 for stainless steel. Add $20 for 12 in. Buffalo Model.

Mfg.'s Sug. Retail	$170	$150	$130	$95

RIFLES

HAWKEN RIFLE — .45, .50, .54, or .58 cal., flintlock or percussion, 28 in. octagonal barrel, color case hardened hammer and lock, 9 lbs. Add $30 for flintlock and $10 for left hand.

Mfg.'s Sug. Retail	$300	$255	$220	$175

Deduct $45 for Field Grade.

KENTUCKY RIFLE — .50 cal. percussion, 35 in. octagonal barrel, color case hardened hammer and lock, brass furniture and trigger guard, 7 lbs.

	$350	$300	$240

Last Mfg.'s Sug. Retail was $420.

KAHNKE GUNWORKS
Manufacturer/retailer located in Redwood Falls, MN.

KAHNKE .54 CAL. MODEL — .54 cal., percussion, single-shot hunting pistol, adj. sights, unusual combination of utilizing both old and new technologies, straight through ignition system, 3½ lbs. New in 1988.

Mfg.'s Sug. Retail	$295	$285	$190	$140

This model is available direct from the factory only.

LOVEN-PIERSON INC.
Apalachin Arsenal - Apalachin, NY.

RIFLES: PERCUSSION

All rifles have a unique rotating over and under set of barrels to speed a 2nd shot. Available only through the used market.

LOVEN MODEL 10 — .45 cal., percussion swivel breech, 22 in. carbine or 28 in. rifle, octagonal or ½ in. round barrel, blued furniture, maple stock, 7¾ - 8½ lbs.

	$275	$225	$180

Last Mfg.'s Sug. Retail was $330.

LOVEN MODEL 13 — .45, .50 or .54 cal., percussion, same as Loven Model 10, except brass furniture and walnut stock.

	$340	$285	$220

Last Mfg.'s Sug. Retail was $440.

LOVEN MODEL 16 — .45, .50 or .54 cal., percussion, same as above except color case hardened lock and furniture, browned barrels and curly or bird's-eye maple or figured walnut stock.

	$650	$550	$440

Last Mfg.'s Sug. Retail was $880.

LYMAN GUNS
Middlefield, CT.

Discontinued models still sold by Dixie Gun Works, others available through Lyman or through dealers.

PISTOLS

Grading	100%	98%	95%

REMINGTON .44 ARMY — .44 cal., 6 shot, percussion. Discontinued.

	100%	98%	95%
	$130	$110	$90

Last Mfg.'s Sug. Retail was $170.

1851 NAVY — .36 cal., percussion. Discontinued.

	$110	$90	$75

Last Mfg.'s Sug. Retail was $165.

1860 ARMY — .44 cal., percussion. Discontinued.

	$145	$120	$95

Last Mfg.'s Sug. Retail was $170.

PLAINS PISTOL — .50 or .54 cal., percussion, color case hardened hammer and lock, brass trigger guard.

Mfg.'s Sug. Retail	$220	$195	$160	$125

RIFLES

GREAT PLAINS RIFLE — .50 or .54 cal., flintlock or percussion, color case hardened hammer and lock, blackened steel furniture, 32 in. octagonal barrel, 11 lbs. 6 oz. Add $25 for flintlock.

Mfg.'s Sug. Retail	$410	$345	$300	$230

TRADE RIFLE — .50 or .54 cal., percussion or flintlock, color case hardened hammer and lock, 11 lbs. Add $20 for flintlock.

Mfg.'s Sug. Retail	$310	$265	$230	$175

DEERSTALKER — .50 and .54 cal., flintlock or percussion, 24 in. octagonal barrel, color case hardened hammer and lock, sling swivels, adj. sights, 10 lbs. 6 oz. Add $20 for flintlock.

Mfg.'s Sug. Retail	$340	$295	$255	$190

Add $10 for Carbine Model w/21" stepped barrel.

MANDALL SHOOTING SUPPLIES, INC.
Importer and distributor located in Scottsdale, AZ. Available through dealers or Mandall direct.

FRENCH DUELING PISTOL — .44 cal., percussion, single trigger, classic fluted handle, sold with velvet lined display case and accessories.

	$260	$200	$160

Last Mfg.'s Sug. Retail was $295.

"NAPOLEON" CANNON — .69 ball, detailed scaled down model of the original used by both the Union and Confederacy during the Civil War, brass furniture, with carriage, 18 lbs.

	$395	$300	$210

Last Mfg.'s Sug. Retail was $290.

MICHIGAN ARMS CORPORATION
Manufactured in Troy, MI.

Michigan Arms made a long needed change for Black Powder enthusiasts. It is now possible with their 3 models — the Wolverine, the Friendship Special Match, and the Silver Wolf — to enjoy Black Powder shooting without the drawbacks commonly associated with it. Rather than using a percussion cap or flint, Michigan Arms designed an extremely accurate and reliable ignition system using a Model 209 Win. shotgun primer. It is unsure whether any of these guns were produced. Shortly after beginning production, an ATF ruling stated that the use of a primer rather than a percussion cap changed the

Grading	100%	98%	95%

classification of this from a Black Powder gun to a firearm, requiring a dealers license for purchase. Because of this, any gun that could be acquired would have a unique collectors value. Available only through used market.

WOLVERINE RIFLE — .45, .50 or .54 cal., positive ignition Win. Model 209 centerfire primer, 25¼ in. octagonal barrel, adj. sights, Dayton Traister rifle trigger with adj. pull, 8 lbs.

	$400	$340	$250

Last Mfg.'s Sug. Retail was $400.

FRIENDSHIP SPECIAL MATCH — .45, .50 or .54 cal., positive ignition Win. Model 209 centerfire primer, 25¼ in. octagonal barrel, fully adj. target sights with custom Maple stock, Dayton Traister rifle trigger with adj. pull, 8 lbs.

	$470	$390	$310

Last Mfg.'s Sug. Retail was $600.

SILVERWOLF — same as Wolverine, only available in stainless steel.

	$500	$425	$330

Last Mfg.'s Sug. Retail was $600.

MITCHELL ARMS

Manufacturer/importer, located in Santa Ana, CA. Available through dealers.

REVOLVERS

1851 NAVY — .36 and .44 cal., percussion, 7½ in. round barrel, many styles, 6 shot engraved cylinder, 2 lbs. 12 oz.

Mfg.'s Sug. Retail	$225	$130	$115	$90

Prices are equal on Sheriff's Model. Prices are equal for both brass and steel frame.

1860 ARMY — .44 cal., percussion, 7½ in. barrel, 6 shot rebated cylinder, color case hardened frame, hammer and load lever, all brass backstrap and trigger guard, 2 lbs. 9 oz.

Mfg.'s Sug. Retail	$225	$150	$130	$100

Also available with brass frame.

1861 NAVY — .36 and .44 cal., percussion, 7½ in. barrel, brass backstrap and trigger guard, color case hardened frame, hammer, and load lever, 2 lbs. 8 oz.

Mfg.'s Sug. Retail	$225	$130	$115	$90

1858 REMINGTON — .36 and .44 cal., percussion, 8 in. octagonal barrel, 6 shot, brass frame and trigger guard.

Mfg.'s Sug. Retail	$225	$130	$115	$90

1858 REMINGTON — same as above, has steel frame with brass backstrap and trigger guard.

Mfg.'s Sug. Retail	$225	$145	$125	$100

SPILLER and BURR — .36 cal., percussion, 7½ in. barrel, brass frame, color case hardened hammer and loading lever, 2 lbs. 8 oz.

Mfg.'s Sug. Retail	$225	$120	$105	$80

BLACKPOWDER CARTRIDGE

1858 HENRY RIFLE — .44-40 cal., 24½ in. barrel, brass frame.

Mfg.'s Sug. Retail	$1,000	$775	$675	$495

1866 WINCHESTER RIFLE/CARBINE — .44-40 cal., brass receiver, 24¼ in. octagonal barrel (19 in. round on carbine).

Mfg.'s Sug. Retail	$830	$575	$500	$385

Add $40 for rifle w/24¼" barrel.

Grading	100%	98%	95%

1873 WINCHESTER RIFLE — .44-40 cal., color case hardened steel receiver, 24 ¼ in. octagonal barrel.

Mfg.'s Sug. Retail	$950	$720	$625	$490

MODERN MUZZLE LOADING, INC.

Distributor located in Lancaster, MO. Available through dealers, catalog houses or Modern Muzzle Loading directly.

The Knight MK Series is the forerunner of the modern Black Powder rifle designed as a true hunting/sporting rifle. These Black Powder rifles feature a unique straight through sure-fire ignition system, double safety, in-line bolt assembly, and Timney deluxe trigger system. The Knight rifle is extremely accurate (especially with MMP Sabot bullets) and weighs under 7 lbs. New in 1988.

PISTOLS

R-K 88 HAWK — .45, .50 and .54 cal. percussion, same action as MK rifles, modern (swept back) black composite stock. Mfg. 1991-1992 only.

	$365	$290	$230

Last Mfg.'s Sug. Retail was $430.

RIFLES

BK-92 BLACK KNIGHT — .50 or .54 cal. percussion, 24 in. blued barrel, Monte Carlo, wood, epoxy coated wood or composite stock, double safety, under 7 lbs. New 1991.

Mfg.'s Sug. Retail	$350	$260	$220	$180

Add $40 for composite stock.

MK-85 BACK COUNTRY CARBINE — .45, .50, and .54 cal., percussion, 20 in. round barrel, Monte Carlo stock, double safety, 6 lbs. 10 oz. Add $60 for stainless steel. Disc. 1992.

	$420	$360	$295

Last Mfg.'s Sug. Retail was $520.

GRAND AMERICAN — .50 and .54 cal. percussion, hand selected deluxe model of MK-85 Hunter listed below. With thumbhole stock and gold inlaid barrel. New 1992.

Mfg.'s Sug. Retail	$995	$865	$735	$600

Add $100 for stainless steel.

KNIGHT MK85 KNIGHT HAWK — .50 & .54 cal. percussion, 24 in. blued barrel, synthetic thumbhole stock, tapped for scope, double safety system, wt. (6.75 lbs. stainless) 7.25 lbs. blued steel.

Mfg.'s Sug. Retail	$620	$550	$490	N/A

Add $65 for stainless.

KNIGHT MK-85 HUNTER — .45, .50 or .54 cal., percussion rifle, straight through ignition system, 24 in. round barrel drilled and tapped for scope, walnut stock, double safety system, under 7 lbs.

Mfg.'s Sug. Retail	$530	$450	$385	$310

KNIGHT MK-85 STALKER — .45, .50 or .54 cal., percussion, 22 in. round barrel, Monte Carlo stock, double safety system, under 7 lbs.

Mfg.'s Sug. Retail	$580	$500	$435	$350

KNIGHT MK-85 PREDATOR — .50 or .54 cal., percussion, 20 in. round barrel, black synthetic stock, double safety system, under 7 lbs.

Mfg.'s Sug. Retail	$650	$555	$470	$390

LIGHT KNIGHT MK-85 — .50 or .54 cal. percussion, 20 in. round barrel, walnut or black composite stock, lightweight version of MK-85 Hunter listed above. Add $20 for composite stock.

Mfg.'s Sug. Retail	$500	$420	$360	$295

Grading	100%	98%	95%

BK-89 SQUIRREL — .36 cal., percussion, 24 in. barrel, Monte Carlo stock, double safety, 5 lbs. 8 oz. Disc. 1992.

	$420	$370	$295

Last Mfg.'s Sug. Retail was $500.

T-5 WOODSMAN — .50 and .54 cal. percussion, 20 in. round barrel, hardwood stock, double safety, adj. sights, approx. 7 lbs. New in 1991. Disc. 1992.

	$215	$185	$150

Last Mfg.'s Sug. Retail was $230.

MK-85 GRIZZLY "PLB" — .54 cal. percussion, brown laminate stock, double safety. New in 1991. Disc. 1992.

	$450	$385	$310

Last Mfg.'s Sug. Retail was $650.
Add $100 for stainless steel.

MOWREY GUN WORKS, INC.

Currently manufactured in Waldren, IN, previously manufactured in Saginaw, TX. Distributed exclusively by Mountain State Muzzle Loaders Supply, Williamstown, WV. Available through dealers and Mountain State direct.

Mowrey Gun Works has recreated the guns designed by Ethan Allen and marketed under the name Allen and Thurber in the early and mid 1800s. The guns themselves are beautifully hand crafted with "cut rifled" browned barrels (each groove cut individually using as many as 20 passes) and actions using only 5 moving parts creating exceptional accuracy and reliability. The 1 in 30 inch rifling was designed specifically to stabilize conical bullets. Each gun is available with a number of features and options (listed below).

Standard: curly maple stocks and forearms, front blade-buckhorn rear and hand rubbed finish, brass or browned steel receivers.

Options: premium curly maple, cherry or walnut stock and forearm, barrel length from 22-40 in., primitive fixed sight, target sights, Scheutzen style butt plate. Add $38 for fancy Grade Curly Maple, $25 for other than standard barrel length or modern sights, $25 for brass forearm on Plains Rifle, $30 for fancy brass or steel Scheutzen butt plate.

RIFLES: PERCUSSION

1-N-30 CONICAL RIFLE — .45, .50 and .54 cal., percussion, 28 in. octagonal barrel, brass furniture, special 1-N-30 twist rifling for conical bullets, 8 lbs.

Mfg.'s Sug. Retail	$350	$315	$275	$200

PLAINS RIFLE — .50 or .54 cal., percussion, 28 or 32 in. full octagonal barrel, brass furniture, 10 lbs. Add $25 for brass forearm.

Mfg.'s Sug. Retail	$350	$315	$275	$200

ROCKY MOUNTAIN HUNTER — .50 or .54 cal., percussion, 28 in. full octagonal barrel, all browned steel furniture, 8 lbs.

Mfg.'s Sug. Retail	$350	$315	$275	$200

SILHOUETTE RIFLE — .40 cal., percussion, 28 or 32 in. octagonal barrel, brass furniture.

Mfg.'s Sug. Retail	$350	$315	$275	$200

SQUIRREL RIFLE — .32, .36 or .45 cal., percussion, 28 in. full octagonal barrel, brass furniture, 7 lbs., deduct $10 for all steel furniture.

Mfg.'s Sug. Retail	$350	$315	$275	$200

SHOTGUNS: PERCUSSION

12 GAUGE SHOTGUN — 12 ga., percussion, 32 in. full octagonal barrel, brass or steel furniture, 7½ lbs.

Mfg.'s Sug. Retail	$340	$310	$260	$200

Grading	100%	98%	95%

28 GAUGE SHOTGUN — 28 ga., percussion, 28 in. full octagonal barrel, brass or steel furniture, built on squirrel frame, 7½ lbs.

	$310	$260	$200

Last Mfg.'s Sug. Retail was $350.

MUZZLE LOADERS, INC.
Previous importer/distributor located in Burke, VA. Available only on used market.

REVOLVERS

1847 WALKER — .44 cal., percussion, charcoal finish, color case hardened frame, hammer, and load lever, brass trim, engraved cylinder. 4.4 lbs.

	$230	$200	$150

1848 1ST MODEL DRAGOON — .44 cal., percussion, 6 shot, brass grip straps, color case hardened frame, hammer, and load lever, brass trim, 3.9 lbs.

	$220	$180	$140

1850 2ND MODEL DRAGOON — .44 cal., percussion, 6 shot, brass grip straps, color case hardened frame, hammer, and load lever, brass trim, 3.9 lbs.

	$220	$180	$140

1851 3RD MODEL DRAGOON — .44 cal., percussion, 6 shot, brass grip straps, color case hardened frame, hammer, and load lever, brass trim, 3.9 lbs. Add $15 for silver-plated straps, or cut for stock, add $35 for Military Model.

	$220	$180	$140

1851 NAVY — .36 or .44 cal., percussion, 7½ in. octagonal barrel, engraved (roll) cylinder, color case hardened frame and load lever, silver plated brass backstrap and square back trigger guard. Sheriff's Model has 5 in. barrel, brass trigger guard and backstrap. Deduct $10 for Sheriff's Model, $20 for brass backstrap and trigger guard, $50 for brass frame.

	$150	$135	$120

1860 ARMY — .44 cal., percussion, 8 in round barrel, color case hardened frame, hammer and load lever, 2 lbs. 9 oz. Deduct $40 for brass frame.

	$145	$130	$110

1862 POLICE — .36 cal., 5½ in. round barrel, color case hardened frame, loading lever, plunger, and hammer, round trigger guard, fluted cylinder, one piece stocks, 25 oz.

	$115	$100	$80

1858 REMINGTON — .36 or .44 cal., percussion, blued frame, brass trigger guard, steel backstrap, 6 shot, 2 lbs. 7 oz. Add $35 for stainless, deduct $35 for brass frame.

	$150	$135	$115

ROGERS & SPENCER — .44 cal., percussion, 7½ in. octagonal barrel, 2 lbs. 15 oz. Add $15 for target sights, $25 for engraved London grey finish.

	$150	$135	$110

PISTOLS

DELUXE KENTUCKY PISTOL — .44 cal., percussion or flintlock, 10¼ in. octagonal barrel, brass blade front sight, 40 oz. Add $15 for flintlock.

	$175	$140	$110

RIFLES

1853 2-BAND ENFIELD — .58 cal., percussion, 33 in. barrel, 2 barrel bands.

	$385	$335	$250

Grading	100%	98%	95%

DELUXE HAWKEN RIFLE — .45 or .50 cal., percussion or flintlock, color case hardened hammer and lock, percussion cap holder in stock, chrome lined barrels.

	100%	98%	95%
	$240	$205	$165

DELUXE KENTUCKY RIFLE — .45 or .50 cal., percussion or flintlock, color case hardened hammer and lock, percussion cap holder in stock, chrome lined barrels, brass trim. Add $15 for flintlock.

	$300	$265	$180

ST. LOUIS HAWKENS — .50 cal., percussion, color case hardened hammer and lock, 28 in. octagonal barrel, brass trim, 7 lbs. 15 oz.

	$260	$220	$175

ZOUAVE RIFLE — .58 cal., percussion, brass trim, color case hardened hammer and lock, blue finish.

	$365	$320	$250

NAVY ARMS CO.

Manufacturer/importer/distributor located in Ridgefield, NJ. Available through dealers, catalog houses and from Navy direct.

PISTOLS: SINGLE SHOT

1775 BLACK WATCH SCOTTISH PISTOL — .58 cal., flintlock, 7 in. smooth bore white steel barrel, brass frame, ram's horn grip with round ball trigger.

	100%	98%	95%	
Mfg.'s Sug. Retail	$200	$160	$140	$95

BRITISH DRAGOON PISTOL — .614 cal., flintlock, white steel with brass trim, first 240 production models were used in Governor's palace restoration, Colonial Williamsburg. Add $100 for official Williamsburg crest.

	$360	$300	$240

Last Mfg.'s Sug. Retail was $395.

CHARLEVILLE 1777 PISTOL — .69 cal. flintlock, $7\frac{1}{2}$ in. white steel smooth bore barrel, brass furniture, belt hook, walnut stock, $2\frac{3}{4}$ lbs.

Mfg.'s Sug. Retail	$225	$170	$145	$100

DURS EGG SAW HANDLED PISTOL — .45 cal., flintlock, $9\frac{1}{2}$ in. blued octagonal barrel, unique stock, hand checkered, German silver trim, white steel hammer and lock.

	$210	$175	$140

Last Mfg.'s Sug. Retail was $235.

HARPERS FERRY MODEL 1806 — .58 cal., flintlock or percussion, $11\frac{3}{4}$ in. barrel, color case hardened lock and hammer, brass trim, 3 lbs. 14 oz. Add $40 for cased gun. Deduct $25 for percussion.

Mfg.'s Sug. Retail	$265	$240	$210	$140

J.S. HAWKINS PISTOL — .50 or .54 cal., percussion, 9 in. octagonal barrel, German silver trim, blued barrel, adj. trigger, 2 lbs. 9 oz.

	$195	$170	$120

Last Mfg.'s Sug. Retail was $200.

KENTUCKY PISTOL — .44 cal., flintlock or percussion, $10\frac{1}{8}$ in. barrel, color case hardened lock and hammer, brass trim, 2 lbs. Add $15 for brass barrel. Deduct $10 for percussion (each gun).

Mfg.'s Sug. Retail	$205	$195	$170	$125

⚐ **Cased**

Mfg.'s Sug. Retail	$300	$285	$250	$175

⚐ **Double cased set**

Mfg.'s Sug. Retail	$515	$480	$420	$300

Grading	100%	98%	95%

LEPAGE PISTOL — .45 cal., flintlock or percussion, 9 in. octagonal white steel barrel and trim, adj. sights, engraved spur type trigger guard, 2 lbs. 2 oz. Deduct $75 for percussion, $75 for percussion cased set, $150 for percussion cased pair. Values also apply to smooth bore model (flintlock only).

Mfg.'s Sug. Retail	$550	$525	$450	$360

⚛ **Cased**

Mfg.'s Sug. Retail	$760	$725	$630	$470

⚛ **Cased pair**

Mfg.'s Sug. Retail	$1,430	$1,270	$1,100	$700

⚛ **1985 cased set** — custom order only, gold trim, consecutive serial number.

	$1,800	$1,200	$1,000

Last Mfg.'s Sug. Retail was $1,975.

JOHN MANTON MATCH PISTOL — .45 cal., percussion, 10 in. white steel barrel and lock, brass trim, 2 lbs. 4 oz.

	$215	$185	$135

Last Mfg.'s Sug. Retail was $225.

MOORE AND PATRICK PISTOL — .45 cal., flintlock or percussion, 10 in. octagonal barrel, white steel hammer and lock, German silver trim, 2 lbs. Disc. in 1987.

	$330	$260	$200

Last Mfg.'s Sug. Retail was $295.

MOUNTAIN PISTOL — .50 cal., flintlock or percussion, 10 in. octagonal barrel, color case hardened hammer and lock, brass furniture, 2 lbs. 4 oz. Add $10 for flintlock.

Mfg.'s Sug. Retail	$215	$190	$165	$130

NAPOLEON LEPAGE PISTOL — .45 cal., percussion, 10 in. octagonal white steel barrel and lock, brass trim, adj. double set triggers, fluted grip, 2 lbs. 7 oz.

	$240	$205	$160

Last Mfg.'s Sug. Retail was $175.

W. PARKER PISTOL — .45 cal., percussion, 10 in. blued octagonal barrel, German silver lock and trim, adj. double set triggers, 2 lbs. 8 oz.

	$280	$245	$200

Last Mfg.'s Sug. Retail was $250.

QUEEN ANNE PISTOL — .50 cal., flintlock, 7½ in. smooth bore, unique cannon style bronzed steel barrel, 2 lbs. 4 oz.

Mfg.'s Sug. Retail	$200	$190	$150	$120

F. ROCHETTE PISTOL — .45 cal., percussion, 10 in. round barrel with flat top, white steel lock and trim, adj. double set triggers, 2 lbs. 8 oz.

	$275	$225	$190

Last Mfg.'s Sug. Retail was $250.

PISTOLS: DERRINGER STYLE

ELGIN CUTLAS — .44 cal., percussion, combination knife pistol, white steel hammer and barrel, brass trim, 2 lbs.

	$80	$65	$50

Last Mfg.'s Sug. Retail was $80.

PHILADELPHIA DERRINGER — .45 cal., percussion, 3 in. barrel, color case hardened lock and hammer, German silver trim, checkered stock, ¾ lb.

	$120	$100	$80

Last Mfg.'s Sug. Retail was $130.

Grading	100%	98%	95%

ENGRAVED "SNAKE EYES" PISTOL — .36 cal., percussion, $2\frac{5}{8}$ in. brass double barrel, double hammers, $1\frac{1}{2}$ lbs. Deduct $75 if not engraved.

	$145	$120	$95

REVOLVERS

1847 WALKER — .44 cal., percussion, 9 in. round barrel, color case hardened hammer, frame, and load lever, brass trim, engraved barrel and cylinder, 4 lbs. 11 oz. Add $90 for cased set, $220 for deluxe Uberti cased set.

Mfg.'s Sug. Retail	$260	$245	$210	$165

COLT 1851 NAVY - YANK — .36 or .44 cal., percussion, $7\frac{1}{2}$ in. octagonal barrel, color case hardened hammer, frame, and load lever, brass trim. Add $5 for silver plated back strap and trigger guard, $90 for shoulder stock.

Mfg.'s Sug. Retail	$145	$130	$115	$90

⚔ Cased set

Mfg.'s Sug. Retail	$245	$225	$195	$155

⚔ Double cased set

Mfg.'s Sug. Retail	$405	$385	$320	$245

AUGUSTA CONFEDERATE — .36 cal. percussion, 5 or $7\frac{1}{2}$ in. barrel, brass frame (confederate copy of 1851 Navy), walnut grips.

	$175	$150	$120

Last Mfg.'s Sug. Retail was $200.

1861 NAVY —.36 cal., percussion, $7\frac{1}{2}$ in. round barrel, cylinder engraved with navy scene, color case hardened hammer, frame, and load lever, brass trim, $2\frac{3}{4}$ lbs. Add $60 for shoulder stock. Also available in $5\frac{1}{2}$ in. barrel Sheriff's model.

	$130	$115	$90

Last Mfg.'s Sug. Retail was $140.

⚔ Cased set

	$225	$195	$155

Last Mfg.'s Sug. Retail was $230.

⚔ Double cased set

	$360	$300	$240

Last Mfg.'s Sug. Retail was $385.

1860 ARMY — .44 cal., percussion, 8 in. round barrel, color case hardened hammer, frame, and load lever, roll engraved or fluted cylinder, 2 lbs. 12 oz. Add $100 for shoulder stock. Deduct $40 for $5\frac{1}{2}$ in. barrel Sheriff's model for each gun in cased set (Sheriff's Model available in .36 or .44 cal.).

Mfg.'s Sug. Retail	$165	$150	$130	$100

⚔ Cased set

Mfg.'s Sug. Retail	$265	$240	$210	$160

⚔ Double cased set

Mfg.'s Sug. Retail	$430	$390	$340	$265

REB MODEL 1860 "GRISWOLD AND GUNNISON" — .36 or .44 cal., percussion, $7\frac{1}{2}$ in. round barrel, brass frame, color case hardened hammer and load lever, $5\frac{1}{2}$ in. barrel Sheriff's Model, 2 lbs. 12 oz.

Mfg.'s Sug. Retail	$110	$100	$85	$65

Due to overstock, several 1860 Reb revolvers were factory de-activated and cannot be re-activated. These guns can be used only as props — values currently are in the $55 range.

Grading	100%	98%	95%

⇥ **Cased set**
Mfg.'s Sug. Retail $205 $180 $155 $125

⇥ **Double cased set**
Mfg.'s Sug. Retail $335 $280 $245 $190

1862 POLICE — .36 cal., percussion, 5½ in. round to octagonal barrel, color case hardened hammer, frame, and load lever, brass trim, 1 lb. 10 oz. Add $65 for cased Law and Order set (book style presentation case).
Mfg.'s Sug. Retail $285 $265 $225 $170

COLT PATERSON — .36 cal., percussion, 7½ in. octagonal barrel, standard "hidden trigger" design, blued steel hardware, no loading lever, 2 lbs. 9 oz. Add $135 for engraved version.
Mfg.'s Sug. Retail $325 $285 $250 $200

LEECH and RIGDON — .36 cal., percussion, 7½ in. barrel, color case hardened hammer, frame, and load lever, brass trim, 2 lbs. 10 oz.
$120 $105 $80

LE MAT REVOLVER —.44 cal., percussion, 9 shot cylinder, plus 1 shot center barrel (maximum fire power for its day), 7⅝ in. octagonal barrel, white steel frame, 3 lbs. 7 oz. Add $375 for engraved Beauregard model, $160 for 18th Georgia engraved model.
Mfg.'s Sug. Retail $595 $570 $495 $380
Add $85 for single case, $110 for double case (not including guns).

REMINGTON 1858 NEW ARMY — .36. or .44 cal., percussion, 6½ in. barrel, brass trim. Add $40 for nickel or target model, $80 for stainless steel, $180 for Deluxe Uberti Model. Deduct $30 for brass frame (each gun in a cased set).
Mfg.'s Sug. Retail $160 $145 $125 $100

⇥ **Cased set**
Mfg.'s Sug. Retail $255 $230 $200 $160

⇥ **Double cased set**
Mfg.'s Sug. Retail $420 $375 $325 $260

ROGERS and SPENCER — .44 cal., percussion, 7½ in. octagonal barrel, blued trim, 3 lbs. Add $20 for satin finish (London Grey Model), $20 for Target Model.
Mfg.'s Sug. Retail $240 $215 $185 $140

SPILLER and BURR — .36. cal., percussion, 7 in. barrel, brass frame, color case hardened hammer and load lever, 2 lbs. 8 oz.
Mfg.'s Sug. Retail $135 $120 $105 $80

⇥ **Cased set**
Mfg.'s Sug. Retail $230 $205 $180 $140

⇥ **Double cased set**
Mfg.'s Sug. Retail $370 $325 $285 $220

RIFLES

BROWN BESS MUSKET — .75 cal., flintlock, 42 in. white steel barrel, hammer, and lock, brass trim, 9½ lbs. Add $100 for Colonial Williamsburg seal. Carbine model available in 30 in. barrel.
Mfg.'s Sug. Retail $635 $610 $550 $400

BROWN BESS MUSKET (ECONOMY MODEL) — same as above, all brass hardware.
Mfg.'s Sug. Retail $490 $460 $400 $320

BUFFALO HUNTER — .58 cal., percussion, 26 in. round barrel, color case hardened hammer and lock, brass trim, 8 lbs.
$240 $200 $160

Grading	100%	98%	95%

1763 CHARLEVILLE MUSKET — .69 cal., flintlock, 44⅝ in. white steel barrel, hammer, and lock, brass trim, 8¾ lbs. Add $125 for 1777 model, or 1816 Mt. Wickman model with steel ramrod and brass flash pan.

Mfg.'s Sug. Retail	$575	$520	$450	$350

COUNTRY BOY — .32, .36, .45 or .50 cal., percussion, 26 in. octagonal barrel, matte black metal "no glare" finish on all parts, based on mule ear percussion lock, adj. sights, 6 lbs. Add $60 each for extra barrels.

	$225	$195	$160

Last Mfg.'s Sug. Retail was $165.

CUB RIFLE — .36 cal., percussion, 26 in. octagonal barrel, adj. sights, color case hardened lock, walnut stock, 5 lbs. 12 oz. Add $60 for extra barrel.

	$200	$170	$135

Last Mfg.'s Sug. Retail was $185.

MODEL 1853 3 BAND ENFIELD — .58 cal., percussion, 39 in. round barrel, color case hardened hammer and lock, brass trim, blued bands, adj. rear sight, 9½ lbs. Add $80 for Parker Hale version.

Mfg.'s Sug. Retail	$480	$440	$375	$275

MODEL 1858 2 BAND ENFIELD — .58 cal., percussion, 33 in. round barrel, color case hardened hammer and lock, brass trim, blued bands, adj. rear sight, 10 lbs. Add $80 for Parker Hale version.

Mfg.'s Sug. Retail	$450	$410	$340	$250

MODEL 1861 ENFIELD MUSKETOON — .58 cal., percussion, 24 in. round barrel, color case hardened hammer and lock, brass trim, blued bands, adj. rear sight, 7 lbs. Add $50 for Parker Hale version.

Mfg.'s Sug. Retail	$370	$355	$310	$240

HAWKEN RIFLE — .50, .54, or .58 cal., flintlock and percussion, 28 in. octagonal barrel, double set triggers, brass trim, 8 lbs. 8 oz. Deduct $15 for percussion.

Mfg.'s Sug. Retail	$230	$215	$185	$140

HAWKEN MARK 1 RIFLE — .50 or .54 cal., flintlock or percussion. 26 in. octagonal barrel, adj. double set triggers and sights, brass trim, 9 lbs. Add $15 for flintlock, $140 for commemorative model.

	$220	$190	$150

Last Mfg.'s Sug. Retail was $260.

HUNTER RIFLE/CARBINE — .50, .54, or .58 cal., percussion, 28½ in. octagonal barrel, (22½ in. carbine), color case hardened hammer and lock, double set triggers, 7 lbs. 12 oz. (6 lbs. 12 oz. carbine).

Mfg.'s Sug. Retail	$250	$230	$200	$150

ITHACA-NAVY HAWKEN — .50 or .54 cal., flintlock or percussion, 26 in. octagonal barrel, adj. double set triggers and sights, brass trim, 9 lbs. Add $65 for flintlock. (Left hand version disc. in 1987).

Mfg.'s Sug. Retail	$400	$370	$325	$240

HARPERS FERRY 1803 RIFLE — .58 cal., flintlock, 35 in. round barrel, color case hardened hammer and lock, brass trim, 8 lbs. 8 oz.

Mfg.'s Sug. Retail	$555	$525	$450	$360

J.P. MURRAY ARTILLERY CARBINE — .58 cal., percussion, 23½ in. browned, round barrel, color case hardened hammer and lock, brass trim and bands, 7½ lbs.

Mfg.'s Sug. Retail	$380	$370	$300	$220

KENTUCKY RIFLE — .45 or .50 cal., percussion or flintlock, 35 in. barrel, color case hardened hammer and lock, brass trim, adj. brass rear sight (windage only), 6 lbs. 14 oz. Add $20 for flintlock or .45 cal. standard, $125 for .45 cal. deluxe.

Mfg.'s Sug. Retail	$330	$305	$250	$200

Grading		100%	98%	95%

KODIAK DOUBLE RIFLE — .50, .54, or .58 cal., percussion, 28 in. double barrel, white steel furniture. New in 1989.

Mfg.'s Sug. Retail	$680	$635	$540	$425

MISSISSIPPI RIFLE 1841 — .54 or .58 cal., percussion, 33 in. browned round barrel, color case hardened hammer and lock, brass trim and bands, $9\frac{1}{2}$ lbs.

Mfg.'s Sug. Retail	$450	$410	$350	$250

MORSE RIFLE — .50 cal., percussion, 26 in. octagonal barrel, brass trim and action, blued barrel and hammer, adj. rear sight, windage only, 6 lbs.

		$250	$215	$180

MORTIMER RIFLE — .54 cal., flintlock, 36 in. browned barrel, color case hardened furniture, waterproof flash pan, chrome lined bore, 9 lbs. New in 1989. Add $250 for extra 12 ga. barrel.

Mfg.'s Sug. Retail	$690	$660	$575	$430

MULE EAR MOUNTAIN MAN'S SQUIRREL RIFLE — .32, .36, or .45 cal., percussion, 26 in. octagonal barrel, brass trim, blued barrel, hammer, lock, and trigger, $5\frac{1}{2}$ lbs.

		$225	$195	$160

Last Mfg.'s Sug. Retail was $185.

PARKER HALE VOLUNTEER RIFLE (IMPORTED) —.451 cal., percussion, 32 in. barrel, brass trim, blued band, color case hardened hammer and lock, adj. sights, $9\frac{1}{2}$ lbs. Add $55 for 3-Band model.

Mfg.'s Sug. Retail	$750	$690	$600	$480

PARKER HALE WHITWORTH VOLUNTEER RIFLE (IMPORTED) — .45 cal., percussion, 36 in. barrel, brass trim, blued barrel and bands, color case hardened hammer and lock, adj. sights, detented lock hammer, long range accuracy app. 1000 yds., comes with accessories, $9\frac{1}{4}$ lbs. (Pricing same for Parker-Hale 3 Band Volunteer rifle).

Mfg.'s Sug. Retail	$815	$750	$650	$520

Add $180 for limited edition rifle w/4X scope of the period. Copy of a piece in the Confederate Museum in Richmond, VA.

PENNSYLVANIA HALF STOCK HUNTER — .50 cal., percussion, 30 in. octagonal barrel, white steel hammer and lock, brass patchbox and trim, walnut stock, 6 lbs. 4 oz.

		$190	$165	$130

Last Mfg.'s Sug. Retail was $220.

PENNSYLVANIA LONG RIFLE — .32 or .45 cal., flintlock or percussion, $40\frac{1}{2}$ in. octagonal barrel, color case hardened hammer and lock, brass patchbox and trim, walnut stock, 7 lbs. 8 oz. Deduct $15 for percussion.

Mfg.'s Sug. Retail	$410	$365	$315	$230

PIONEER RIFLE — .45 or .50 cal., flintlock, 30 in. octagonal barrel, color case hardened hammer and lock, walnut stock, 6 lbs. 4 oz.

		$155	$130	$100

Last Mfg.'s Sug. Retail was $200.

RIGBY STYLE TARGET —.451 cal., 32 in. round blued barrel, color case hardened hammer and lock, hand checkered walnut stock, very similar to a modern day firearm, adj. vernier sights, 7 lbs. 12 oz.

		$680	$570	$450

Last Mfg.'s Sug. Retail was $645.

1808/1835 SPRINGFIELD — .69 cal., flintlock, 44 in. round barrel, all white steel, walnut stock, 8 lbs. 12 oz.

Mfg.'s Sug. Retail	$625	$575	$500	$390

The Model 1835 Springfield is a more refined version of the Model 1808. This was the last flintlock issued by the U.S. Army.

Grading	100%	98%	95%

1863 SPRINGFIELD — .58 cal., percussion, 40 in. barrel, all white steel, 3 barrel bands, 9½ lbs. (1861 Springfield and 1862 C.S. Richmond Musket are both earlier models of the 1863 Springfield, values are equal).

Mfg.'s Sug. Retail	$550	$505	$440	$325

SMITH ARTILLERY/CAVALRY CARBINE — .54 cal., percussion, 20½ in. octagonal tapering to round barrel, white steel hammer and receiver. New in 1989.

Mfg.'s Sug. Retail	$600	$535	$475	$370

SWISS FEDERAL TARGET RIFLE — .45 cal., percussion, 32 in. octagonal barrel, color case hardened hammer, lock, and trim, double set triggers, classic Bristlen and Morges design, adj., sights, 13¼ lbs. Add $35 for palm rest. Imported from West Germany by Neumann Co.

	$1,080	$925	$745

Last Mfg.'s Sug. Retail was $1,200.

TRYON RIFLE — .45 cal., percussion, 34 in octagonal barrel, white steel hammer and engraved lock and patchbox, double set triggers, walnut stock, 9 lbs. 12 oz. Add $35 for target sights, $220 for Creedmoor Target Model.

Mfg.'s Sug. Retail	$455	$420	$365	$250

ZOUAVE RIFLE — .58 cal., percussion, 32½ in. round barrel, color case hardened hammer, lock, and trigger, brass trim, adj. rear sight, 9 lbs. Add $140 for deluxe.

Mfg.'s Sug. Retail	$450	$410	$355	$275

RIFLES: BLACK POWDER CARTRIDGE

CREEDMOOR TARGET — .45-70 rimfire, 30 in. tapered barrel, color case hardened action, beautiful reproduction, adj. sights, 9 lbs.

Mfg.'s Sug. Retail	$695	$670	$580	$460

IRON FRAME HENRY — .44-40, or .44 rimfire, 24 in. barrel, cast iron action, color case hardened receiver, lever and hammer, beautiful reproduction, adj. sights, 9¼ lbs. Add $10 for blued receiver.

Mfg.'s Sug. Retail	$895	$800	$695	$510

HENRY MILITARY/CARBINE RIFLE — .44-40, or .44 rimfire, 24 in. barrel, brass frame and trim, color case hardened lever and hammer, beautiful reproduction, military version has sling swivels, mounted on left side, adj. sights, 9¼ lbs.

Mfg.'s Sug. Retail	$875	$775	$675	$495

For engraving add $330 for 25%, $540 for 35%, $900 for 50%.

HENRY TRAPPER — .44-40, or .44 rimfire, 16½ in. barrel, brass frame and trim, color case hardened lever and hammer, beautiful reproduction, adj. sights, 7¼ lbs.

Mfg.'s Sug. Retail	$875	$775	$675	$495

For engraving add $330 for 25%, $540 for 35%, $900 for 50%.

ROLLING BLOCK BUFFALO RIFLE (REMINGTON STYLE) — .45-70 rimfire, 26 or 30 in. barrel length, ½ round or octagonal, color case hardened action, brass trigger guard, beautiful reproduction, adj. sights, approx. 9 lbs. Add $25 for Creedmoor Model.

Mfg.'s Sug. Retail	$510	$485	$425	$340

SHARPS PLAINS RIFLE/CAVALRY CARBINE — .45-70 rimfire, 28½ in. barrel, (22 in. barrel carbine), color case hardened hammer and receiver, walnut stock, 7 lbs. 12 oz.

Mfg.'s Sug. Retail	$715	$625	$540	$420

Cavalry Model also available in .50 or .54 cal. percussion. Deduct $35 for .50 cal.

WINCHESTER 1873 RIFLE/CARBINE — .44-40 cal. rimfire, 20 in. round barrel, 11 shot walnut stock, trapdoor buttplate for cleaning rod, 7 lbs. Add $20 for rifle, $80 for sporting rifle with 24 or 30 in. barrel.

Mfg.'s Sug. Retail	$815	$720	$625	$490

Grading	100%	98%	95%

1866 YELLOW BOY RIFLE/CARBINE — .44-40 cal. rimfire, 19 in. round barrel, walnut stock, 7½ lbs. Add $25 for rifle.

Mfg.'s Sug. Retail	$685	$605	$525	$420

REVOLVERS BLACK POWDER CARTRIDGE

1873 SAA REVOLVER — .44-40 cartridge, 3, 4¾, 5½ and 7½ in. barrel, color case hardened frame hammer and trigger guard (or brass backstrap and trigger guard), 2½ lbs.

Mfg.'s Sug. Retail	$370	$325	$280	$225

Add $50 for nickel finish.
Deduct $50 for brass backstrap and trigger guard.

1875 REMINGTON — .44-40 cartridge, 7½" barrel, color case hardened frame, brass trigger guard, wt. 2½ lbs.

Mfg.'s Sug. Retail	$365	$325	$280	$225

1890 REMINGTON — .44-40 cartridge, 5½" barrel, blued finish, brass trigger guard walnut grips w/lanyard loop, wt. 2½ lbs.

Mfg.'s Sug. Retail	$370	$325	$280	$225

SHOTGUNS

CLASSIC SXS — 12 or 10 ga., percussion, 28 in. barrel, color case hardened hammer, lock, and trim, 7¾ lbs. Add $20 for .10 ga. (10 ga. disc. in 1987). (12 ga. disc. 1993).

	$365	$305	$250

Last Mfg.'s Sug. Retail was $395.

FOWLER SHOTGUN — 10 or 12 ga., 28 in. barrel, color case hardened hammer and lock, 7 lbs. 6 oz.

Mfg.'s Sug. Retail	$325	$305	$265	$200

Add $150 for steel shot 10 ga. model.
Add $100 for extra 10 ga. barrel.

HUNTER SHOTGUN — 20 ga., 28½ in. barrel, round chrome lined color case hardened hammer and lock, double set triggers, 7 lbs. 12 oz. Disc. in 1989.

	$235	$200	$170

Last Mfg.'s Sug. Retail was $190.

MORSE SHOTGUN — .12 ga., percussion, 26 in. barrel, brass receiver and trim, blued hammer and butt plate, 5¾ lbs. Disc. in 1987.

	$250	$215	$180

Last Mfg.'s Sug. Retail was $165.

MORTIMER SHOTGUN — 12 ga., flintlock, 36 in. browned barrel, color case hardened furniture, walnut stock, waterproof pan and chrome bore. New in 1989.

Mfg.'s Sug. Retail	$670	$615	$535	$400

TURKEY AND TRAP — 12 ga., percussion s x s, 28 in. blued barrels, color case hardened locks and furniture, walnut stock.

Mfg.'s Sug. Retail	$480	$435	$370	$280

OLD-WEST GUN CO.

Importer and distributor that took over the inventory of Allen Firearms after they went out of business in early 1987. Old-West Gun Co. became Cimarron Arms Co. in 1987. Older guns marked Old West have the same values as those of Cimarron Arms Co. (Please refer to the Cimarron heading in this text). Available only on used market.

PIETTA, F. LLI

Manufacturer located in Brescia, Italy.

Grading	100%	98%	95%

1851 NAVY — .36 and .44 cal., percussion, 7½ in. round barrel, many styles, 6 shot engraved cylinder, 2 lbs. 12 oz.

$130 $115 $90

Prices are equal on Sheriff's Model. Prices are equal for both brass and steel frame.

1860 ARMY — .44 cal., percussion, 7½ in. barrel, 6 shot rebated cylinder, color case hardened frame, hammer and load lever, all brass backstrap and trigger guard, 2 lbs. 9 oz.

$150 $130 $100

Also available with brass frame.

1861 NAVY — .36 and .44 cal., percussion, 7½ in. barrel, brass backstrap and trigger guard, color case hardened frame, hammer, and load lever, 2 lbs. 8 oz.

$130 $115 $90

1862 POLICE — .36 cal., percussion, 5½ in. round to octagonal barrel, color case hardened hammer, frame, and load lever, brass trim, 1 lb. 10 oz.

$265 $225 $170

COLT PATERSON — .36 cal., percussion, 7½ in. octagonal barrel, standard "hidden trigger" design, blued steel hardware, no loading lever, 2 lbs. 9 oz. Add $135 for engraved version.

$285 $250 $200

LE MAT REVOLVER — .44 cal., percussion, 9 shot cylinder, plus 1 shot center barrel (maximum fire power for its day), 7⅝ in. octagonal barrel, white steel frame, 3 lbs. 7 oz. Add $375 for engraved Beauregard model, $160 for 18th Georgia engraved model.

$570 $495 $380

1858 REMINGTON — .36 and .44 cal., percussion, 8 in. octagonal barrel, 6 shot, brass frame and trigger guard.

$130 $115 $90

1858 REMINGTON — same as above, has steel frame with brass backstrap and trigger guard.

$145 $125 $100

SPILLER and BURR — .36 cal., percussion, 7½ in. barrel, brass frame, color case hardened hammer and loading lever, 2 lbs. 8 oz.

$120 $105 $80

RICHLAND ARMS
Previously distributed in Blissfield, MI. Available only on the used market.

PISTOLS

ANDREW TARGET — .32, .36. or .45 cal., percussion, 10 in. octagonal barrel, white steel hammer, barrel, frame, and sights, brass trigger guard, adj. trigger and sights, blued and engraved, 2 lbs. 10 oz. Add $55 for deluxe grade.

$220 $185 $150

Last Mfg.'s Sug. Retail was $150.

REVOLVERS

1860 ARMY — .44 cal., percussion, 8 in. barrel, color case hardened hammer, frame, trigger and load lever, brass trigger guard, engraved cylinder. Deduct $40 for brass frame.

$145 $130 $110

Last Mfg.'s Sug. Retail was $160.

3rd MODEL DRAGOON — .44 cal., percussion, 7½ in. barrel, color case hardened hammer, frame, trigger and load lever, engraved cylinder, 66 oz.

$220 $180 $140

Last Mfg.'s Sug. Retail was $165.

Grading	100%	98%	95%

1851 NAVY — .36 cal., percussion, 7½ in. octagonal barrel, color case hardened load lever and hammer, brass frame and trigger guard, 44 oz. Add $35 for steel frame.

$100 $85 $70

Last Mfg.'s Sug. Retail was $100.

WALKER — .44 cal., percussion, 9 in. round barrel, color case hardened hammer, frame, trigger and load lever, engraved cylinder, brass trigger guard, 73 oz.

$230 $200 $150

Last Mfg.'s Sug. Retail was $185.

REMINGTON REPLICAS

1858 ARMY — .44 cal., percussion, 8 in. octagonal barrel, brass frame and trigger guard, 44 oz. Add $35 for steel frame.

$155 $100 $80

Last Mfg.'s Sug. Retail was $125.

BUFFALO TARGET — .44 cal., percussion, 12 in. octagonal barrel, brass frame and trigger guard, adj. sights, based on 1858 Navy frame, 38 oz.

$215 $180 $140

Last Mfg.'s Sug. Retail was $150.

RIFLES

BRISTOL HUNTER — .50 or .54 cal., percussion, 28 in. octagonal barrel, color case hardened hammer and lock, rubber recoil pad, adj. rear sights, chrome plated bore, double set triggers.

$260 $200 $160

Last Mfg.'s Sug. Retail was $240.

HAWKEN RIFLE — .50 cal., percussion, 28 in. octagonal barrel, color case hardened hammer and lock, brass trim, adj. sights, double set triggers.

$260 $200 $160

Last Mfg.'s Sug. Retail was $225.

KODIAK DOUBLE BARREL RIFLE — .50 or .58 cal., percussion, 28 in. octagonal barrel. Add $280 for extra .12 ga. shotgun barrels.

$635 $525 $440

Last Mfg.'s Sug. Retail was $560.

SHOTGUNS

MUZZLE LOADING SHOTGUNS — .10 or .12 ga., percussion. Add $55 for .10 ga.

$280 $245 $190

Last Mfg.'s Sug. Retail was $320.

RUGER

Manufactured in Southport, CT. Available through dealers and catalog houses.

OLD ARMY — .44 cal., 6 shot, percussion, 7½ in. barrel, adj. rear sight, blue or stainless.

Mfg.'s Sug. Retail $380 $335 $280 $225

⚕ **Stainless Old Army** — stainless steel variation of the Old Army.

Mfg.'s Sug. Retail $430 $375 $325 $240

SILE DISTRIBUTORS

Previous importer and distributor of Invest Arms brand and D. Pedersoli brand, located in New York, NY. Available through dealers.

Grading	100%	98%	95%

REVOLVERS

1860 COLT ARMY — .44 cal., percussion, 8 in. blued round barrel, brass or color case hardened steel frame, brass trigger guard and back strap, color case hardened hammer, trigger, and load lever, 2 lbs. 11 oz. Deduct $15 for brass frame.

$180 $150 $110

1858 REMINGTON ARMY — .44 cal., percussion, 8 in. white octagonal barrel, white steel frame, brass trigger guard, 2 lbs. 9 oz. Add $50 for stainless steel, $75 for stainless steel target.

$155 $135 $110

RIFLES

BROWN BESS MUSKET — .75 cal., flintlock, 41¾ in. smooth bore barrel, brass furniture, white steel barrel, hammer, and lock, engraved lock, 9 lbs.

$495 $410 $320

Last Mfg.'s Sug. Retail was $565.

HAWKEN RIFLE — .45, .50 or .54 cal., flintlock or percussion (.50 cal. only in flintlock), 29 in. octagonal barrel, solid brass furniture, color case hardened engraved lock, coil spring mechanism with adj. set triggers, stainless steel nipple, chrome bore, brass patch box, adj. sights, 8 lbs. 10 oz. Add $35 for flintlock.

$220 $190 $155

Last Mfg.'s Sug. Retail was $230.

HAWKEN RIFLE CARBINE — .45, .50 or .54 cal., flintlock or percussion (.50 cal. only in flintlock), 22 in. octagonal barrel, solid brass furniture, color case hardened engraved lock, coil spring mechanism with adj. set triggers, stainless steel nipple, chrome bore, brass patch box, adj. sights, 7 lbs. Add $10 for flintlock.

$210 $185 $140

Last Mfg.'s Sug. Retail was $250.

HAWKEN HUNTER CARBINE — .45, .50 or .54 cal., flintlock or percussion (.50 cal. only in flintlock), 22 in. octagonal barrel, solid brass furniture, color case hardened engraved lock, coil spring mechanism with adj. set triggers, stainless steel nipple, chrome bore, brass patch box, adj. sights, 7 lbs. Add $10 for flintlock.

$190 $165 $130

Last Mfg.'s Sug. Retail was $225.

KENTUCKY RIFLE — .45 or .50 cal., flintlock or percussion, 32 in. blued octagonal barrel, solid brass furniture, color case hardened hammer and engraved lock, brass patch box, adj. rear sight, 7 lbs. 2 oz. Add $10 for flintlock.

$300 $265 $180

PENNSYLVANIAN SQUIRREL RIFLE — .32 cal., flintlock, 40½ in. browned octagonal barrel, adj. double set triggers, polished white steel hammer and lock, 9 lbs.

$365 $315 $230

SHOTGUNS

SXS DOUBLE BARREL — 10 or 12 ga., percussion, 28 in. double blued barrels, engraved furniture, color case hardened hammer and engraved lock, chrome lined bores, 7 lbs. 12 oz. (8 lbs. 12 oz. for 10 ga.). Add $45 for 10 ga.

$315 $275 $220

SOUTHWEST MUZZLE LOADERS SUPPLY
Located in Angleton, TX.

Importer of Uberti, Italian replicas. See Uberti.

Grading	100%	98%	95%

DANCE REVOLVER — .36 or .44 cal., exact reproduction of the original J.H. Dance and Brothers revolver manufactured in Dance, Texas, 500 total production, manufactured by Aldo Uberti and Co. from Brescia, Italy, cased. New in 1985.

$240 $210 $180

Last Mfg.'s Sug. Retail was $1,500.

TAYLOR'S and CO., INC.

Importer/distributor located in Winchester, VA. Available through dealers or from Taylor's direct.

PISTOLS: SINGLE SHOT

KENTUCKY PISTOL — .45 cal., percussion, $10\frac{1}{4}$ in. octagonal barrel, brass blade front sight, $2\frac{1}{2}$ lbs.

$150 $130 $105

Last Mfg.'s Sug. Retail was $170.

NAPOLEON LEPAGE PISTOL — .45 cal., percussion, 10 in. barrel, white steel barrel and lock, fixed sights with single barrel wedge, silver plated butt cap and trigger guard, double set triggers, 2 lbs. 7 oz.

$240 $210 $170

Last Mfg.'s Sug. Retail was $310.

F. ROCHATTE DUELING PISTOL — .45 cal., percussion, 10 in. round barrel with flat top, white steel lock and trim, adj. double set triggers, $2\frac{1}{2}$ lbs.

$275 $225 $190

Last Mfg.'s Sug. Retail was $395.

REVOLVERS

1847 WALKER — .44 cal., percussion, 9 in. blued barrel, color case hardened frame, hammer, and loading lever, brass trigger guard and steel backstrap, 4 lbs. 6 oz.

Mfg.'s Sug. Retail	$230	$215	$180	$140

DRAGOON (1ST, 2ND, OR 3RD) — .44 cal., percussion, $7\frac{1}{2}$ in. barrel, roll engraving cylinder, brass backstrap.

Mfg.'s Sug. Retail	$230	$215	$180	$140

1851 NAVY — .36 or .44 cal., percussion, $7\frac{1}{2}$ in. octagonal barrel, rolled cylinder scene, color case hardened frame, hammer, and loading lever, brass backstrap and trigger guard. Sheriff's Model has 5 in. barrel.

Mfg.'s Sug. Retail	$150	$140	$120	$95

Deduct $30 for brass frame.

1860 ARMY — .44 cal., percussion, 8 in. round barrel, color case hardened frame, hammer, and loading lever, $2\frac{3}{4}$ lbs.

Mfg.'s Sug. Retail	$165	$155	$135	$100

Deduct $30 for brass frame.

1862 POLICE — .44 cal., $5\frac{1}{2}$ in. barrel, color case hardened frame, hammer and loading lever.

$165 $145 $105

Last Mfg.'s Sug. Retail was $175.

1858 REMINGTON ARMY — .36 or .44 cal., percussion, $6\frac{1}{2}$ and 8 in. octagonal barrel, color case hardened hammer, steel or brass frame, 2 lbs. 6 oz.

Mfg.'s Sug. Retail	$170	$155	$135	$100

Deduct $40 for brass frame.

Grading	100%	98%	95%

RIFLES

BROWN BESS MUSKET — .75 cal. flintlock, 31½ in. or 42 in. smooth bore barrel, white steel barrel, hammer, lock and furniture, 8½ lbs.
Mfg.'s Sug. Retail $675 $640 $540 $410

C.S. RICHMOND MUSKET — .58 cal., percussion, white steel hammer and furniture, brass nosecap, similar to 1861 Springfield.
Mfg.'s Sug. Retail $440 $425 $370 $295

CHARLEVILLE 1777 MUSKET — .69 cal., flintlock, 44¾ in. smooth bore barrel, white steel lockplate, hammer, and ramrod, brass barrel bands, trigger guard, and buttplate, walnut stock.
Mfg.'s Sug. Retail $595 $540 $470 $340

ENFIELD 1853 "THREE BAND" — .58 cal. percussion, 39 in. round barrel, color case hardened hammer and lock, brass furniture, blued barrel bands, 9½ lbs.
Mfg.'s Sug. Retail $375 $370 $325 $250

DELUXE HAWKEN RIFLE — .50 cal., percussion, 30 in. octagonal chrome lined barrel, brass patchbox, target sights, double set triggers, 8 lbs.
Mfg.'s Sug. Retail $260 $245 $215 $160

HAWKEN HUNTER CARBINE — .50 cal., percussion, 24 in. octagonal chrome lined barrel, rubber recoil pad, sling swivels, double set triggers.
Mfg.'s Sug. Retail $260 $245 $215 $160

KENTUCKY RIFLE — .45 and .50 cal., percussion, 35 in. octagonal barrel, color case hardened lock, brass buttplate, trigger guard, patchbox, sideplates, thimbles and nosecap, walnut stock with large or small patchbox, rifle weighs 7½ lbs., carbine is 6 lbs.
Mfg.'s Sug. Retail $385 $300 $200 $160
Add $10 for large patchbox.

⚞ **Carbine Model** — .50 cal., percussion, chrome lined barrel.
Mfg.'s Sug. Retail $325 $300 $260 $200
Add $20 for large patchbox.

MORTIMER HUNTER RIFLE — .50 or .54 cal. percussion, 25 in. blued (matte finish) ½ octagonal, ½ round barrel, adj. sights (rear), wt. 8⅞ lbs.
Mfg.'s Sug. Retail $485 $400 $325 $260

PENNSYLVANIA RIFLE —.45 cal., percussion, octagonal barrel, color case hardened hammer and lock, small brass patchbox, approx. 7 lbs. Add $185 for new Pedersoli model.
Mfg.'s Sug. Retail $215 $190 $165 $130

1861 SPRINGFIELD — .58 cal., percussion, 40 in. round barrel, white steel barrel, hammer, lock, trigger, and trim, 10¼ lbs.
Mfg.'s Sug. Retail $425 $410 $355 $285

1863 SHARPS CARBINE — .54 cal. percussion, 22 in. round barrel, color case hardened hammer & receiver.
Mfg.'s Sug. Retail $575 $540 $460 $370

ST. LOUIS HAWKEN RIFLE — .50 cal., percussion, 30 in. octagonal barrel, all black steel furniture, adj. rear sight, double set triggers, approx. 8 lbs.
Mfg.'s Sug. Retail $260 $245 $215 $160

TRYON RIFLE — .50 or .54 cal. percussion, 32¼ in. octagonal barrel, all white steel, engraved lock and hammer, 9½ lbs.
Mfg.'s Sug. Retail $595 $435 $360 $310

1863 ZOUAVE RIFLE — .58 cal., percussion, 32½ in. round barrel, color case hardened hammer, lock, and trigger, brass patchbox, trigger guard, and barrel bands, 9 lbs.
Mfg.'s Sug. Retail $355 $325 $280 $200

Grading	100%	98%	95%

BLACKPOWDER CARTRIDGE

SHARPS RIFLE MODEL 1866 — .45-70 cal., 28 in. octagonal browned barrel, color case hardened hammer & receiver, double set triggers.

Mfg.'s Sug. Retail	$695	$645	$550	$440

THOMPSON/CENTER ARMS

U.S. manufacturer located in Rochester, NH. Available through dealers.

All Thompson/Center products are U.S. made.

PISTOLS

PATRIOT — .36 or .45 cal., percussion, 9 in. barrel, double set triggers, target stock, walnut, color case hardened hammer and lock. Disc. 1987.

	$240	$200	$145

Last Mfg.'s Sug. Retail was $235.

SCOUT PISTOL — .50 and .54 cal., percussion, 12 in. barrel, in-line ignition, walnut grips, 4 lbs. 6 oz.

Mfg.'s Sug. Retail	$315	$270	$230	$185

Similar in design to old style single shot Remington Target. Add $125 for extra barrel.

RIFLES

BIG BOAR — .58 cal. percussion, 26 in. octagonal barrel, color case hardened hammer and lock, single hunting style trigger, American walnut stock, recoil pad and swivels, 7 lbs. 12 oz.

Mfg.'s Sug. Retail	$340	$315	$275	$210

CHEROKEE — .32, .36 or .45 cal., percussion, 24 in. octagonal barrel, double set triggers, color case hardened hammer and lock, brass trim, American walnut. Add $105 for extra barrel.

	$295	$255	$200

Last Mfg.'s Sug. Retail was $320.

GREY HAWK — .50 cal. percussion, 24 in. round bbl., all stainless steel construction, rynite stock, 7 lbs. New 1993

Mfg.'s Sug. Retail	$275	$250	N/A	N/A

HAWKEN — .45, .50, or .54 cal., percussion or flintlock, 28 in. octagonal barrel, color case hardened hammer and lock, double set triggers, 8½ lbs. Add $10 for flintlock, add $105 for 12 ga. barrel.

Mfg.'s Sug. Retail	$375	$345	$300	$230

HAWKEN COUGAR — .45 or .50 cal., stainless steel version of Hawken, percussion only, select hardwood stock.

	$300	$250	$200

HIGH PLAINS SPORTER — .50 cal. percussion, 24 in. round blued barrel, blued furniture, sling swivels, walnut stock w/recoil pad, 7 lbs. New 1992.

Mfg.'s Sug. Retail	$340	$310	$270	$210

NEW ENGLANDER RIFLE — .50 and .54 cal., percussion, 24 and 28 in. barrel, brass furniture, walnut or rynite (new 1991) stock, 5 lbs. 2 oz. Add $105 for extra .50 cal. barrel, $15 for left hand.

Mfg.'s Sug. Retail	$270	$250	$215	$170

Also available with Rynite stock, deduct $15.

PENNSYLVANIA HUNTER — .50 cal., flintlock or percussion, 31 in. octagonal barrel, color case hardened hammer and lock, 7 lbs. 9 oz. Add $15 for left hand, $15 for flintlock, $135 for 21 in. extra carbine barrel.

Mfg.'s Sug. Retail	$320	$295	$255	$200

Grading	100%	98%	95%

RENEGADE —.50 or .54 cal., percussion or flintlock, 26 in. octagonal barrel, color case hardened hammer and lock, double set triggers, 8 lbs. Also in .56 cal.—smooth bore. Add $10 for flintlock, add $105 for 12 ga. barrel. Deduct $20 for single trigger Hunter Model (new in 1987).

Mfg.'s Sug. Retail	$335	$310	$270	$210

SCOUT RIFLE — .50 and .54 cal., percussion, 21 in. round barrel, in-line ignition, 7 lbs. 4 oz.

Mfg.'s Sug. Retail	$395	$360	$315	$250

Deduct $80 for rynite stock model (new 1993).
Similar in design to old style single shot Remington Target. Add $135 for extra barrels.

SENECA — .36 or .45 cal., percussion, 27 in. octagonal barrel, color case hardened hammer and lock, double set triggers, American walnut, 6 lbs. Disc. in 1987.

	$280	$245	$200

Last Mfg.'s Sug. Retail was $300.

THUNDER HAWK — .50 cal. cap lock percussion, in-line ignition 21 in. round blued bbl., adj. rear sight, walnut stock w/recoil pad, wt. 6¾ lbs. (This is a modern style muzzleloader). New 1993.

Mfg.'s Sug. Retail	$275	$250	N/A	N/A

TREE HAWK CARBINE — .50 cal. percussion, 21 in. round camo barrel, camo furniture, rynite camo stock, with swivels and sling, 6¾ lbs. Add $135 for extra 12 ga. barrel. New 1992.

Mfg.'s Sug. Retail	$340	$300	$270	$210

WHITE MOUNTAIN CARBINE — .50 cal., flintlock or percussion, 21 in. octagonal tapering to a round barrel, color case hardened furniture, single hunting trigger, walnut stock, 6½ lbs. New in 1989.Add $20 for flintlock.

Mfg.'s Sug. Retail	$335	$310	$270	$210

SHOTGUNS

NEW ENGLANDER SHOTGUN — 12 ga., percussion, 26 and 28 in. barrel, brass furniture, 5 lbs. 2 oz. Add $105 for extra .50 cal. barrel, $15 for left hand, $20 for full choke. Also available with Rynite stock, deduct $15.

Mfg.'s Sug. Retail	$290	$250	$215	$170

TREE HAWK SHOTGUN — 12 ga., same as Tree Hawk above. Add $130 for extra .50 cal. revolver.

Mfg.'s Sug. Retail	$345	$315	$270	$215

TRADITIONS, INC.
Deep River, CT. Available through dealers and catalog houses.

PISTOLS

BUCKSKINNER PISTOL —.50 cal. percussion, 10 in. octagonal blued barrel, color case hardened hammer & lock, black furniture, beech or laminated stock, 2½ lbs. New 1993.

Mfg.'s Sug. Retail	$155	$120	N/A	N/A

Add $25 for laminated stock.

PIONEER PISTOL — .45 or .50 cal. percussion, 9⅝ octagonal barrel, German silver furniture, blackened hardware, 2 lbs. 4 oz. New in 1991.

Mfg.'s Sug. Retail	$170	$130	$110	$90

TRAPPER PISTOL — .45 or .50 cal., percussion or 10 in. octagonal barrel, double set triggers, adj. sights, brass trim, 3 lbs. 4 oz.

Mfg.'s Sug. Retail	$170	$130	$110	$90

WILLIAM PARKER PISTOL — .45 or .50 cal., percussion, 10⅜ in. barrel, all white steel, double set triggers, 2 lbs. 8 oz.

Mfg.'s Sug. Retail	$265	$195	$170	$135

Grading	100%	98%	95%

REVOLVERS

1847 WALKER — .44 cal. percussion, 9" barrel, color case hardened hammer, frame and load lever, brass triggerguard, wt. 3.9 lbs.

Mfg.'s Sug. Retail	$280	$220	N/A	N/A

1851 NAVY .44 cal. percussion, 7½ octagonal barrel, color case hardened hammer and load lever, brass frame, cylinder has roll engraving.

Mfg.'s Sug. Retail	$130	$100	N/A	N/A

1860 ARMY — .44 cal. percussion, 8" barrel (round), color case hardened steel or brass frame, brass triggerguard.

Mfg.'s Sug. Retail	$140	$105	N/A	N/A

Add $60 for color case hardened steel frame.

1858 Remington — .44 cal. percussion, 8" octagonal barrel, brass frame & trigger guard.

Mfg.'s Sug. Retail	$165	$125	N/A	N/A

Add $120 for stainless steel model w/adj. target sights.

RIFLES

BUCKSKINNER CARBINE — .50 cal. flintlock or percussion, 21 in. octagonal to round barrel, German silver furniture, blackened hardware, 6 lbs. (New 1991).

Mfg.'s Sug. Retail	$275	$210	$180	$145

Add $10 for flintlock.
Add $10 for left hand, $35 for laminated stock.

DEERHUNTER RIFLE — .50 cal. flintlock or percussion, 26" octagonal bbl., color case hardened hammer & lock, single trigger, black furniture, wt. approx. 6 lbs.

Mfg.'s Sug. Retail	$165	$140	N/A	N/A

Add $15 for flintlock.

FRONTIER RIFLE/FRONTIER CARBINE — .45 or .50 cal., percussion or flintlock, 28 in. octagonal barrel (24 in. carbine), double set triggers, adj. sights, brass trim, 6 lbs. 14 oz (6 lbs. 8 oz. carbine). Add $15 for flintlock (.50 cal. only).

Mfg.'s Sug. Retail	$255	$190	$160	$125

FRONTIER SCOUT RIFLE — .36, .45 or .50 cal., flintlock or percussion, 26 in. octagonal barrel, double set triggers, adj. sights, brass trim, 5 lbs. 8 oz., lock has adj. sear. Add $10 for flintlock, $15 for carbine.

Mfg.'s Sug. Retail	$235	$180	$155	$120

HAWKEN RIFLE — .50, .54, or .58 cal., percussion or flintlock, 32¼ in. octagonal barrel, double set triggers, adj. sights, brass trim, 8 lbs. 2 oz. Add $10 for flintlock (.50 and .54 cal. only).

Mfg.'s Sug. Retail	$415	$310	$265	$210

A fiberglass ramrod and deluxe rear sight were introduced in 1989.

HAWKEN WOODSMAN RIFLE — .50 cal., percussion, 29 in. octagonal barrel, color case hardened hammer and lock, brass trim and patchbox, 7½ lbs. Add $15 for left hand.

Mfg.'s Sug. Retail	$290	$220	$190	$155

HUNTER RIFLE — .50 or .54 cal., percussion, 28 in. long octagonal barrel, double set triggers, adj. sights, black chrome brass trim with German silver wedge plates, lock has adj. sear, walnut stock, 8 lbs., 10 oz.

	$310	$265	$210

Last Mfg.'s Sug. Retail was $425.
A fiberglass ramrod and deluxe rear sight were introduced in 1989.

Grading	100%	98%	95%

KENTUCKY 2-PIECE RIFLE — .45 or .50 cal., percussion, 33½ in. octagonal barrel, color case hardened hammer and lock, unique full length two piece stock is joined with brass plate, 7 lbs. 4 oz. Disc. in 1989.

	$165	$140	$115

Last Mfg.'s Sug. Retail was $145.

KENTUCKY SCOUT RIFLE — .45 or .50 cal., percussion or 26 in. octagonal barrel, double set triggers, adj. sights, brass trim, full length stock, lock has adj. sear, 5 lbs. 8 oz. Add $10 for flintlock. Disc. 1989.

	$160	$140	$110

Last Mfg.'s Sug. Retail was $135.

PENNSYLVANIA RIFLE — .45 or .50 cal., flintlock or percussion, 40½ in. octagonal barrel, double set triggers, adj. sights, brass trim, 9 lbs. 13 oz. Add $25 for flintlock.

Mfg.'s Sug. Retail	$465	$350	$305	$245

PIONEER CARBINE/RIFLE — .50 or .54 cal., percussion, 27¼ in. (24" carbine), octagonal barrel, color case hardened hammer, lock and furniture, German silver blade front sight, recoil pad, carbine style stock.

Mfg.'s Sug. Retail	$225	$175	$130	$105

SHENANDOAH RIFLE — .45 or .50 cal., flintlock or percussion, color case hardened hammer and lock, 33½ in. long octagonal barrel, brass furniture, 7 lbs. 4 oz. Add $10 for flintlock.

	$185	$160	$130

Last Mfg.'s Sug. Retail was $185.

T93 CARBINE/RIFLE — .50 cal. percussion, in-line ignition, 28" (21" carbine) round barrel, adj. sights, black furniture, modern hunting rifle style, wt. approx. 8 lbs.

Mfg.'s Sug. Retail	$430	$330	N/A	N/A

Deduct $160 for Sporter Model.

TRAPPER RIFLE — .36, .45 and .50 cal., percussion, 25 in. octagonal barrel, color case hardened hammer and lock, brass trim, 5 lbs. Disc. 1989.

	$185	$160	$130

Last Mfg.'s Sug. Retail was $200.

TROPHY RIFLE — .50 or .54 cal., percussion, 27½ in. octagonal tapering to round barrel, adj. trigger, fiberglass ramrod, carbine style walnut stock, 7 lbs.

	$370	$320	$245

Last Mfg.'s Sug. Retail was $425.

WHITEAIL CARBINE/RIFLE — .50 or .54 flintlock or percussion, 26" (21" carbine) octagonal to round barrel, color case hardened hammer & lock, single trigger, adj. sights, wt. 5¾ lbs. New 1993.

Mfg.'s Sug. Retail	$255	$195	N/A	N/A

Add $10 for flintlock, $60 for synthetic stock and stainless steel bbl.

SHOTGUNS

SINGLE BARREL — 12 ga., percussion, 32 in. octagonal tapering to round barrel, German silver wedge plate, blued furniture, scroll engraving, and polished steel furniture on Deluxe version, 4 lbs. Add $85 for Deluxe.

	$260	$225	$180

Last Mfg.'s Sug. Retail was $315.

TRAIL GUNS ARMORY

Conroe, TX. (guns manufactured by D. Pedersoli Co. Italy). Available through dealers.

ALAMO LONG RIFLE — .45 or .50 cal., percussion or flintlock. Add $15 for flintlock.

Mfg.'s Sug. Retail	$450	$370	$315	$220

Grading		100%	98%	95%

KODIAK MK-I, MK-II and MK-III DOUBLE RIFLE — .50 and .58 cal., or 12 ga. percussion, 28 in. barrel, adj. sights. Add $300 for spare combo. barrels (.50 cal. x 12 ga.). $240 for 12 ga. barrels.

		100%	98%	95%
Mfg.'s Sug. Retail	$650	$635	$500	$410

TRYON PLAINS RIFLE — .50 or .54 cal., percussion, 31 in. browned octagonal barrel, browned furniture, white steel hammer and lock, 9 lbs. 6 oz.

		100%	98%	95%
Mfg.'s Sug. Retail	$490	$400	$335	$260
Mfg.'s Sug. Retail Deluxe	$555	$440	$375	$300

RIFLES: BLACK POWDER CARTRIDGE

CREEDMOOR DELUXE ROLLING BLOCK — .45-70 cal., rimfire, 30 in. tapered barrel, color case hardened, w/double set triggers, adj. sights, 9 lbs.

		100%	98%	95%
Mfg.'s Sug. Retail	$695	$615	$550	$420

REMINGTON SPORTING RIFLE — .45-70 cal. rimfire, same as above but without Creedmore sight, straight stock.

		100%	98%	95%
Mfg.'s Sug. Retail	$595	$515	$450	$320

KODIAK DOUBLE RIFLE —.45-70 cal. rimfire, 24 in. tapered round barrel, color case hardened hammer and lock, 2 piece high gloss walnut hand checkered stock, adj. twin sights, patterned after the very rare Colt SxS Double Rifle of the 1870's.

		100%	98%	95%
Mfg.'s Sug. Retail	$1,895	$1,600	$1,360	$950

SHARPS LONG RANGE RIFLE — .45-70 cal. rimfire, 28 in. octagonal barrel, color case hardened hammer and receiver, checkered walnut stock, 9 lbs.

		100%	98%	95%
Mfg.'s Sug. Retail	$725	$700	$615	$500

SHARPS CARBINE — .45-70 cal. rimfire, 22 in. octagonal barrel, color case hardened receiver and hammer, 8 lbs.

		100%	98%	95%
Mfg.'s Sug. Retail	$650	$600	$515	$400

SHOTGUNS

KODIAK 10 DOUBLE BARREL — 10 ga., percussion, goose gun barrels. Add $200 for spare barrel.

		100%	98%	95%
Mfg.'s Sug. Retail	$495	$460	$400	$300

UBERTI, ALDO and CO

Manufactured in Italy by Aldo Uberti and Co. Uberti guns are imported and distributed by various U.S. companies under both the Uberti trademark as well as a multitude of others (Uberti USA, Inc., Cimarron Arms Co., (formerly Old-West Gun Co.), Navy Arms, Dixie Gun Works, Etc.). Also previously imported by Allen Firearms and Benson Firearms Ltd. Available through dealers and catalog houses.

All guns are to the exact specifications of the original manufacture. Crafted with an unmistakable fire blue finish. A. Uberti is one of the largest manufacturers of black powder firearms.

Add the following amounts for engraving on handguns:

Add $325 for "A" style engraving (30% coverage).
Add $425 for "B" style engraving (50% coverage).
Add $750 for "C" style engraving (100% coverage).
Add $800 for "Texas Cattlebrands" engraving pattern.
Prices may fluctuate due to the recent devaluation of the U.S. dollar in international markets.

Grading	100%	98%	95%

REVOLVERS

PATERSON MODEL — .36 cal., 7$\frac{1}{2}$ in. octagon barrel, hidden trigger design, without loading lever, 2 lbs. 9 oz. New in 1988.

Mfg.'s Sug. Retail	$395	$315	$275	$220

Add $40 for load lever.

1847 WALKER — .44 cal., percussion, 9 in. barrel, charcoal finish, color case hardened frame, hammer, and load lever, brass trim, engraved cylinder, 4.4 lbs.

Mfg.'s Sug. Retail	$360	$290	$240	$195

1848 BABY DRAGOON — .31 cal., percussion, 3, 4, or 5 in. barrel, 5 shot, color case hardened frame, hammer, no load lever, engraved cylinder, 1.4 lbs. Add $15 for silver straps and trigger guard.

Mfg.'s Sug. Retail	$295	$240	$205	$165

DRAGOON (1ST, 2ND, OR 3RD) — .44 cal., percussion, 6 shot, brass grip straps, color case hardened frame, hammer, and load lever, brass trim, 3.9 lbs. Add $20 for silver-plated straps, $10 for cut stock on 3rd Model Dragoon, $170 for shoulder stock for 3rd Model Dragoon.

Mfg.'s Sug. Retail	$325	$260	$225	$180

1849 WELLS FARGO — .31 cal., percussion, 3, 4, or 5 in. octagonal barrel, 5 shot, color case hardened frame, hammer, no load lever, brass trim, 1$\frac{1}{2}$ lbs. Add $20 for silver straps.

Mfg.'s Sug. Retail	$300	$240	$210	$165

1849 POCKET — .31 cal., percussion, with loading lever, 3, 4, or 5 in. barrel, 5 shot, color case hardened frame, hammer, and load lever, brass trim, 1$\frac{1}{2}$ lbs. Add $15 for silver straps and trigger guard.

Mfg.'s Sug. Retail	$300	$240	$210	$165

1851 NAVY/NAVY SHERIFF — .36 cal., percussion, 5 (Sheriff's Model) or 7$\frac{1}{2}$ in. barrel, many styles, loading lever, 6 shot engraved cylinder, 2.8 lbs. Add $140 for stock, $50 for stainless steel, $15 for silver plated strap and trigger guard, or steel strap and trigger guard, $15 for "London" Model w/steel backstrap and trigger guard or if cut for stock (3rd Model Navy).

Mfg.'s Sug. Retail	$280	$225	$195	$155

1860 ARMY — .44 cal., percussion, 8 in. barrel, 6 shot, loading lever, color case hardened frame, hammer, and load lever, all brass back strap and trigger guard, or steel backstrap and brass trigger guard on fluted cylinder model, 2.6 lbs. Add $140 for stock, $15 for silver plated strap and trigger guard, $50 for stainless steel, $25 for steel backstrap.

Mfg.'s Sug. Retail	$265	$205	$180	$145

1861 NAVY — .36 cal., percussion, 7$\frac{1}{2}$ in. barrel, many styles, brass back strap or trigger guard, color case hardened frame, hammer, and load lever, 2$\frac{1}{2}$ lbs. Add $15 for silver plated strap and trigger guard, $15 for fluted military cylinder, $25 for cut stock w/steel backstrap and trigger guard, $50 for stainless steel, $140 for shoulder stock.

Mfg.'s Sug. Retail	$280	$225	$195	$160

1862 POCKET NAVY — .36 cal., percussion, 4$\frac{1}{2}$, 5$\frac{1}{2}$, or 6$\frac{1}{2}$ in. barrel, color case hardened frame, hammer, and load lever, cylinder, semi-fluted or engraved, 1.6 lbs. Add $15 for silver plated straps and trigger guard, $50 for stainless steel.

Mfg.'s Sug. Retail	$310	$250	$215	$165

1862 POLICE — .36 cal., percussion, 4$\frac{1}{2}$, 5$\frac{1}{2}$, or 6$\frac{1}{2}$ in. barrel, color case hardened frame, hammer, and load lever, cylinder, semi-fluted or engraved, 1.6 lbs. Add $15 for silver plated straps and trigger guard or fluted cylinder model, $50 for stainless steel.

Mfg.'s Sug. Retail	$300	$240	$210	$160

Grading	100%	98%	95%

AUGUSTA CONFEDERATE — .36 cal., percussion, $7\frac{1}{2}$ in. octagonal barrel, color case hardened hammer and trigger, all brass frame, engraved cylinder, $2\frac{1}{2}$-$2\frac{3}{4}$ lbs.

Mfg.'s Sug. Retail	$225	$185	$160	$130

GRISWOLD CONFEDERATE —.36 or .44 cal., $5\frac{1}{2}$ or $7\frac{1}{2}$ in. barrel, percussion, same as above except round barrel, forward of lug, does not have engraved cylinder.

		$185	$160	$130

Last Mfg.'s Sug. Retail was $220.

LEECH AND RIGDON CONFEDERATE — .36 cal., percussion, same as above except all steel frame.

Mfg.'s Sug. Retail	$300	$220	$190	$150

TEXAS CONFEDERATE DRAGOON — .44 cal., percussion, $7\frac{1}{2}$ in. round barrel, color case hardened frame, hammer, and load lever, brass trim, "Tucker, Sherrard, and Co.", 4 lbs. Add $35 for stainless steel.

		$250	$215	$170

Last Mfg.'s Sug. Retail was $235.

1858 REMINGTON — .44 cal., percussion, $7\frac{1}{2}$ in. barrel, 6 shot, blued steel, brass trigger guard, 2.6 lbs. Add $30 for adj. sights.

Mfg.'s Sug. Retail	$280	$225	$195	$155

1858 REMINGTON STAINLESS — same as above, has brass strap and trigger guard. Add $30 for adj. sights.

Mfg.'s Sug. Retail	$380	$305	$265	$210

1858 REMINGTON NEW NAVY — .36 cal., percussion, $6\frac{1}{2}$ in. octagonal barrel, 6 shot, blue frame, $2\frac{1}{2}$ lbs. Add $30 for adj. sights.

Mfg.'s Sug. Retail	$280	$235	$195	$155

1866 REVOLVING CARBINE — .44 cal., percussion, 18 in. barrel, 6 shot, blued steel, brass trigger guard, walnut stock, 4.6 lbs.

Mfg.'s Sug. Retail	$425	$345	$300	$200

RIFLES: PERCUSSION

HAWKEN RIFLE — .50 and .54 cal., 32 in. octagonal barrel, double set triggers, approx. 9 lbs.

		$405	$355	$270

Last Mfg.'s Sug. Retail was $535.

SANTA FE HAWKEN — .50 and .54 cal., percussion, single shot, 32 in. oct. barrel, damascened finish, double set triggers, $9\frac{1}{2}$ lbs., walnut stock.

Mfg.'s Sug. Retail	$495	$405	$355	$270

ST. LOUIS RIFLE — .45, .50, .54, or .58 cal., flintlock and percussion, color case hardened hammer lock and trigger guard, octagonal barrel. Add $25 for .54 and .58 cal. percussion, $15 for flintlock, $30 for 54 cal. flintlock.

		$345	$280	$210

Last Mfg.'s Sug. Retail was $265.

SQUIRREL RIFLE — .32 cal., percussion or flintlock, color case hardened hammer and lock, brass trigger guard, 28 in. octagonal barrel. Add $15 for flintlock.

		$280	$225	$160

BLACKPOWDER CARTRIDGE

Grading	100%	98%	95%

RIFLES REPRODUCTIONS

HENRY RIFLE/CARBINE — .44-40 cal., brass frame, 24½ in. barrel on rifle, 22½ in. barrel on carbine.

Mfg.'s Sug. Retail	$895	$775	$675	$495

Add $100 for steel frame.

Can also be special ordered with Grade A engraving ($385 extra), Grade B engraving ($500 extra), and Grade 3 (C) engraving ($800 extra).

⚞ **Henry 1 of 1,000** — discontinued several years ago, premiums are slightly higher than a C engraved gun.

1866 CARBINE — .44-40 cal., brass receiver, 19 in. round barrel. "Indian" model - add $40.

Mfg.'s Sug. Retail	$720	$575	$500	$385

⚞ **1866 Trapper Carbine** — .44-40 cal., 16 or 18½ in. barrel.

	$640	$560	$495

Last Mfg.'s Sug. Retail was $795.

⚞ **1866 Yellowboy Indian Carbine** — .44-40 cal., 19 in. barrel.

Mfg.'s Sug. Retail	$720	$605	$525	$420

Subtract $20 without brass tacks.

⚞ **Red Cloud Commemorative Carbine** — .44-40 cal., special engraving and brass tacks in forearm and stock.

	$640	$560	$420

Last Mfg.'s Sug. Retail was $720.

1866 RIFLE — .44-40 cal., brass receiver, 24¼ in. octagonal barrel.

Mfg.'s Sug. Retail	$780	$640	$560	$420

⚞ **Yellowboy Indian Rifle** — .44-40 cal., 19 in. rifle.

Mfg.'s Sug. Retail	$760	$640	$560	$420

This model comes without brass tacks.

1873 CARBINE — .44-40 cal., steel receiver, 19 in. round barrel.

Mfg.'s Sug. Retail	$890	$690	$600	$475

Add $95 for nickel plating.

⚞ **1873 Trapper Carbine** — .44-40 cal., 16 in. barrel.

Mfg.'s Sug. Retail	$890	$700	$620	$500

1873 RIFLE — .44-40 cal., case hardened receiver, 24¼ in. octagonal barrel. Add $40 for 30 in. barrel, also available in 20 in. barrel.

Mfg.'s Sug. Retail	$900	$720	$625	$490

Add $100 for pistol grip checkered stock.

ULTRA LIGHT ARMS

Manufacturer located in Granville, WV.

MODEL 90 — .45 or .50 cal., 28 in. button rifled barrel, adj. Timney trigger, in-line action, Kevlar/graphite stock with colors optional, Williams rear sight, 6 lbs., includes hard case.

Mfg.'s Sug. Retail	$950	$925	$805	$675

Grading	100%	98%	95%

U.S. HISTORICAL SOCIETY

Marketing organization which subcontracts special editions/commemoratives. Located in Richmond, VA. Available direct.

Please refer to listing in the Modern Firearms section of this text also.

WHITE MUZZLELOADING SYSTEMS, INC.

Manufacturer located in Roosevelt, Utah. Available through dealers and catalog houses. Modern rifle styling.

In conversations with the competition, this is the gun to try and beat in 1992. Quality construction and a true hunting style rifle.

RIFLES

BISON — .50 or .54 cal. percussion, 22" slightly tapered blued bull barrel, new G Series in-line ignition action, fully adjustable open hunting sights, drilled & tapped for scope, hardwood stock, wt. 6½ lbs. New 1993.

Mfg.'s Sug. Retail	$400	$275	N/A	N/A

ORIGINAL 68 — .45 or .50 cal. percussion, 24" round tapered blued barrel, W series in-line ignition action, fully adjustable hunting sights, drilled & tapped for scope, black composite stock, wt. 7¾ lbs. New 1993.

Mfg.'s Sug. Retail	$600	$400	N/A	N/A

SUPER 91 — .410, .451 and .504 caliber, percussion, 24 in. barrel, W Series in-line ignition, #416 stainless throughout, insta-fire stainless hardened nipple, cleans with soap and water, walnut or composite stock, approx. 7¾ lbs.

Mfg.'s Sug. Retail	$700	$475	$370	$300

WHITETAIL RIFLE — .401, .451, .504 or .54 cal. percussion, 22 in. bull barrel (blued) tapered (stainless), new G series action, insta-fire in-line ignition, beech stock (blued), composite stock (stainless), wt. 6½ lbs. New 1992.

Mfg.'s Sug. Retail	$450	$300	$240	$190

Add $100 for stainless steel.

TRADEMARK INDEX

The listings below represent manufacturers, trademarks, and related information (inlcuding importer and factory address for international makers) to assist you in obtaining additional firearms information from these companies.

As the 14th Edition goes to press, we feel confident that the information listed below is the most up-to-date and accurate listing that has ever been published on current manufacturers and/or related trademarks. If you should require additional assistance in "tracking" any of the firearms manufacturers, distributors, or importers listed in this publication who are currently engaged in the business of selling newly manufactured goods, please call or FAX us and we will try to help you regarding these specific requests.

AMAC, INC.
2202 Redmond Road
Jacksonville, AR 72076
Phone No.: 501-982-1633
FAX No.: 501-982-8075

AMT
Arcadia Machine & Tool
6226 Santos Diaz Street
Irwindale, CA 91702
FAX No.: 818-969-5247

ARS/FARCO
311 E. Water Street
Elmira, NY 14901

A-SQUARE
One Industrial Park
Bedford, KY 40006
Phone No.: 502-255-7456
FAX No.: 502-255-7657

AYA
Importer - See Armes De Chasse listing.
Factory - AYA
Edificio Aurrera
Urtzaile, 1-2
P.O. Box 45
20600 EIBAR (Guipuzcoa) SPAIN
FAX No.: (943) 11 01 33

ABBIATICO & SALVINELLI
Mr. Joe Bojalad - Exclusive U.S. Agent
P.O. Box 4523
Pittsburgh, PA 15238
Phone No.: 412-921-7737 (H)
Phone No.: 412-929-2125 (B)
FAX No.: 412-929-3011
Factory
Via Valtrompia
25063 Gardone, V.T. ITALY
FAX No.: 011-3930/8912122

ACCU-TEK
4525 Carter Court
Chino, CA 91710
FAX No.: 909-627-7817

ACTION ARMS, LTD.
P.O. Box 9573
Philadelphia, PA 19124-0573
FAX No.: 215-533-2188

AMERICAN ARMS, INC.
715 E. Armour Road
N. Kansas City, MO 64116
FAX No.: 816-474-1225

AMERICAN DERRINGER CORPORATION
127 N. Lacy Dr.
Waco, TX 76705
FAX No.: 817-799-7935

AMERICAN HISTORICAL FOUNDATION
1142 W. Grace St., #C175
Richmond, VA 23220
Phone No.: 804-353-1812
FAX No.: 804-359-4895

ANSCHUTZ
Importer - See Precision Sales Int'l listing.
Factory - Anschutz, J.G., GmbH
Daimlerstrabe 12
D-7900 Ulm-Donautal, Germany
FAX No.: 0731-4012-700

ARLINGTON ORDNANCE
39 Old Stage Coach Rd
Weston, CT 06883
Phone No.: 203-454-9747
FAX No.: 203-222-1275

ARMES DE CHASSE
P.O. Box No. 827
Chadds Ford, PA 19317
Phone No.: 215-388-1146

ARMI SAN PAOLO
3590 NW 49th Street
Miami, FL 33142
FAX No.: 305-633-2877

ARMI TECNICHE OF EMILIO RIZZINI
Armi Tecniche di Rizzini E. & C. S.N.C.
Via Localita Rovedolo
I-25060 Marcheno (Brescia) ITALY
Phone No.: 030/861-235
FAX No.: 011-3930-861-367

ARMS CORPORATION OF THE PHILIPPINES
Please refer to the Ruko listing.

ARMS RESEARCH ASSOCIATES
1800 Mannheim Rd.
Stone Park, IL 60165
Phone No.: 708-344-1155

ARMSCORP USA, INC.
4424 John Avenue
Baltimore, MD 21227
FAX No.: 410-247-6205

ARMSPORT, INC.
3590 NW 49th St.
Miami, FL 33142
FAX No.: 305-633-2877

ARRIETA, S.L.
Importer - See Quality Arms listing.
Importer - See New England Arms listing.
Importer - See Orvis listing.
Factory - Arrieta, Manufacturas, S.L.
C/.Morkaiko, 5 Barrio Urasandi
E-20870 Elgoibar (Guipuzcoa) SPAIN
FAX No.: 011-34-43-74-3154

ARRIZABLAGA
Importer - See New England Arms Co. listing.
Factory - Arrizabalaga, Pedro, S.A.
Errekatxu, 5
E-20600 Eibar (Guipuzcoa) SPAIN
FAX No.: 011-3443-11-1743

ASTRA
European American Armory
P.O. Box 3498
Bright Station
Hialea, FL 33013
FAX No.: 305-688-5656
Factory - Astra Unceta Y Cia S.A.
Guernica Vizcaya S-48300 Spain
FAX No.: 011-344-6255186

AUSTRALIAN AUTOMATIC ARMS PTY. LTD.
California Armory, Inc.
119 El Camino Real
San Bruno, CA 94066
Phone No.: 415-872-1010
FAX No.: 415-871-0713

AUTO-ORDNANCE CORP.
Williams Lane
West Hurley, NY 12491
FAX No.: 914-679-2698

BSA GUNS LTD. (AIRGUNS)
Armoury Rd., Small Heath
Birmingham, W. Mids, B11 2PX, ENG-LAND
FAX No.: 021-773-0845

BAFORD ARMS
C.L. Reedy & Associates, Inc.
2485 Grassmere Drive
Melbourne, FL 32904
Phone No.: 407-984-1719
FAX No.: 800-248-6745

BAIKAL
Importer - See K.B.I., Inc. listing.
Baikal Factory
Bogdan Khmelnitskij, 12
Moskau 107140/UdSSR
FAX No.: 0230/2363

BAILONS GUNMAKERS LTD.
Factory
94-95 Bath Street
Birmingham, England B4 6HG
Factory Phone No.: 011-44-21-236-7593
Factory FAX No.: 011-44-21-236-3396

BARRETT FIREARMS MANUFACTURING, INC.
P.O. Box 1077
Murfreesboro, TN 37133
FAX No.: 615-896-7313

BEEMAN PRECISION ARMS, INC.
3440 Airway Drive
Santa Rosa, CA 95403-2040
Phone No.: 707-578-7900
FAX No.: 707-578-4751

BENELLI
Importer (Handguns) - See European American Armory listing.
Importer (Handguns) - See Sile Distributors listing.
Importer (Shotguns) - See Heckler & Koch listing.
Factory - Benelli Armi S.p.A.
Via della Stazione, 50
I-61029 Urbino (PS) ITALY
FAX No.: 0722/327427

BENJAMIN AIR RIFLE COMPANY
2600 Chicory Rd
Racine, WI 53403
Phone No.: 414-554-7900

BERETTA, DR. FRANCO
Importer - Nevada Cartridge Co.
44 Montgomery St., Suite 500
San Francisco, CA 94104
Phone No.: 415-925-9394
FAX No.: 415-925-9396
Factory
Via Rossa, 4
I-25062 Concesio (BS) ITALY
FAX. No.: 011-3930-2180414

BERETTA, PIETRO
Importer - Beretta U.S.A. Corp
17601 Beretta Drive
Accokeek, MD 20607
FAX No.: 301-283-0435

BERNARDELLI, V.
Factory - Bernardelli, Vincenzo, S.p.A.
Via G. Matteotti, 125
I-25063 Gardone V.T. (Brescia) ITALY
FAX No.: 030-8910249

BERSA
Eagle Imports Inc.
1907 Hwy #35
Ocean, NJ 07712
FAX No.: 908-531-1520

BERTUZZI
Importer - See New England Arms Co. listing.
Importer - See W. L. Moore & Co. listing.
Factory - Bertuzzi, F.lli
Via Alessandro Volta, 65
I-25063 Gardone V.T. (BS) ITALY
FAX No.: 011-3930-837188

BIG BEAR (Tula Arsenal Shotguns)
2714 Fairmount Street
Dallas, TX 75201
Phone No.: 214-871-7061
FAX No.: 214-754-0449

BLAND, THOMAS & SONS GUNMAKERS LTD.
Woodcock Hill, INC.
P.O. Box 363
Benton, PA 17814
Phone No.: 717-864-3242
FAX No.: 717-864-3232

BLASER
Importer - Autumn Sales, Inc.
1320 Lake Street
Fort Worth, TX 76102
Phone No.: 817-335-1634
FAX No.: 817-338-0119
Factory - Blaser Jagdwaffen GmbH
Ziegelstadel 1
D-7972 Isny im Allgau, GERMANY
FAX No.: 011-4975-62702-43

BOSS & CO., LTD.
13 Dover St
London, ENGLAND W1X 3PH
Phone No.: 071-493-1127 & 0711

BOSWELL, CHARLES
Charles Boswell Gunmakers
Cape Horn Outfitters
1411 S. Tryon
Charlotte, NC 28203
Phone No.: 704-331-4837
FAX No.: 704-372-9656

BRETTON
Importer - See Mandall Shooting Supplies listing.

BRICKLEY TRADING CO.
1443 Potrero Ave.
South El Monte, CA 91733
Phone No.: 818-990-8284
FAX No.: 818-401-3299

BRITARMS
Importer - See Mandall Shooting Supplies listing.

BRNO AERON
Air Rifles
PO Box 714
St. Albans, VT 05478
FAX 802-527-0470

BRNO ARMS (some bolt action rifles)
Importer - See Action Arms Ltd. listing.
Importer - Bohemia Arms (some bolt action rifles, semi-auto & O/U rifles, shotguns)
17101 Los Modelos Street
Fountain Valley, CA 92708
Phone/FAX No.: 714-963-0809
Importer (Canada) - Pragotrade
307 Humberline Dr.
Rexdale, Ontario M9W 5V1 Canada
FAX No.: 416-675-4567
Factory - BRNO Arms
BRNO 656 17
Lazaretni 7, Czechoslovakia
FAX No.: 42-5571191

BROWN PRECISION, INC.
P.O. Box 270W
7786 Molinos Avenue
Los Molinos, CA 96055
Phone No.: 800-543-2506
FAX No.: 916-384-1638

BROWNING ARMS
Route 1
Morgan, UT 84050
FAX No.: 800-234-4155

BRUCHET
See Darne listing.

Trademark Index, cont.

BRYCO ARMS
Jennings Firearms, Inc.
3680 Research Way
Carson City, NV 89706
FAX No.: 702-882-3129

C Z (CESKA ZBROJOVKA)
Importer - See Action Arms Ltd. listing.
688 27 Uhersky Brod
CZECHOSLOVAKIA
FAX No.: 042-633-3665

CABANAS
Importer - See Mandall Shooting Supplies listing.
Factory - Industrias Cabanas, S.A.
Calz. de las Aguilas 815
Col. Aguilas
01710 Mexico, D.F. MEXICO
FAX No.: 664-34-92

CABELA'S INC.
812 13th Ave.
Sidney, NE 69160
Phone No.: 308-254-5505

CALICO
405 East 19th Street
Bakersfield, CA 93305
FAX No.: 805-323-7844

CASARTELLI, CARLO
Importer - See New England Arms Co. listing.

CASPIAN ARMS, LTD.
14 North Main Street
Hardwick, VT 05843
FAX No.: 802-472-6709

CENTURY GUN DIST., INC.
1467 Jason Road
Greenfield, IN 46140
Phone No.: 317-462-4524

CENTURY INTERNATIONAL ARMS, INC.
P.O. Box 714
St. Albans, VT 05478
FAX No.: 802-527-0470

CHAMPLIN FIREARMS, INC.
P.O. Box 3191
Enid, OK 73702
Phone No.: 405-237-7388
FAX No.: 405-233-1724

CHAPUIS ARMES
Importer - Chapuis USA
416 Business Park
Bedford, KY 40006

Factory - Chapuis Armes
Z.I. La Gravoux, B.P. 15
F-42380 St. Bonnet le Chateau, FRANCE
Phone No.: 011-3377/500696
FAX No.: 011-3377/501070

CHAPUIS, P. ARMES ET FILES
Factory
12, rue le Mont Mille
F-42380 St. Bonnet le Chateau FRANCE
FAX No.: 7750-1008

CHARTER ARMS
Manufacturer - Charco, Inc.
26 Beaver St.
Ansonia, CT 06401
Phone No.: 203-735-4686
FAX No.: 203-735-6569

CHENEY RIFLE WORKS/LEMAN RIFLES
MOUNTAIN STATES MUZZLELOADING SUPPLY
RT 2 Box 154-1
Williamstown, WV 26187
FAX No.: 304-375-3737

CHIPMUNK MANUFACTURING, INC.
Oregon Arms Co.
P.O. Box 1104
Medford, OR 97501
Phone No.: 503-664-5586

CHURCHILL, E.J., (GUNMAKERS) LTD.
Ockley Road, Beare Green, Dorking
Surrey, ENGLAND RH5 4PU
Phone No.: 0306-711435

CHURCHILL
Ellett Brothers
P.O. Box 128
Chapin, SC 29036
FAX No.: 803-345-1820

CIMARRON, F.A. MFG. CO.
1106-G Wisterwood
Houston, TX 77043
Phone No.: 713-468-2007
FAX No.: 713-461-8320

CLARIDGE HI-TECH, INC.
8946 Winnetka Ave.
Northridge, CA 91324
FAX No.: 818-700-0026

CLARK CUSTOM GUNS, INC.
11462 Keatchie Rd.
P.O. Box 530
Keithville, LA 71047
Phone No.: 318-925-0836
FAX No.: 318-925-9425

CLIFTON ARMS
P.O. Box 1471
Medina, TX 78055
FAX No.: 210-589-2661

COLT'S FIREARMS
P.O. Box 1868
Hartford, CT 06144
Phone No.: 203-236-6311
FAX No.: 203-244-1449

COMPETITOR
Competitor Corporation, Inc.
293 Townsend Rd.
P.O. Box 244
W. Groton, MA 01472
Phone No.: 508-448-3521

CONNECTICUT VALLEY ARMS, INC.
5988 Peachtree Corners E.
Norcross, GA 30071
FAX No.: 404-242-8546

CONNECTICUT VALLEY CLASSICS
P.O. Box 2068
12 Taylor Lane
Westport, CT 06880
FAX No.: 203-435-4600

COONAN ARMS, INC.
830 Hampden Ave.
St. Paul, MN 55114
FAX No.: 612-646-0902
Phone No.: 612-646-0902

COOPER ARMS
P.O. Box 114
Stevensville, MT 59870
Phone No.: 406-777-5534
FAX No.: 406-777-5228

COSMI, AMERICO & FIGLIO
Importer - See New England Arms Co. listing.
Factory - Cosmi Americo & Figlio S.n.c.
Via Flaminia, 307
I-60020 Torrette di Ancona, ITALY
FAX No.: 0039-71-887008

CROSMAN AIR GUNS
RTS 5 & 20
East Bloomfield, NY 14443
FAX No.: 716-657-5405

DAEWOO
Importer - See K.B.I., Inc. listing.
Firstshot, Inc.
P.O. Box 6099
Harrisburg, PA 17112
FAX No.: 717-238-2663

DAISY MANUFACTURING CO., INC.
P.O. Box 220
2111 S. 8th St.
Rodgers, AR 72756
FAX No.: 501-636-1601

DAKOTA ARMS, INC.
Whitewood Rd., HC55 Box 326
Sturgis, SD 57785
Phone No.: 605-347-4686
FAX No.: 605-347-4459

DAKOTA SINGLE ACTION REVOLVERS
Importer - See E.M.F. Company listing.

DALY, CHARLES: MODERN MFG.
Outdoor Sports Hdqtrs.
Attn: C. Daly Customer Service
967 Watertower Lane
Dayton, OH 45449
Phone No.: 800-444-6744
FAX No.: 513-865-5962

DARNE S.A.
Wes Gilpin
8139 San Benito Way
Dallas, TX 75218
Phone No.: 214-328-4000

D.P. (DAVIDE PEDERSOLI and CO.)
Flintlocks, Etc.
160 Rossiter Drive
Richmond, MA 01254
FAX 413-698-3866

DAVIS INDUSTRIES
11186 Venture Drive
Mira Loma, CA 91725

DESERT INDUSTRIES, INC.
3245 E. Patrick Lane, Suite H
La Vegas, NV 89120
Phone No.: 702-597-1066
FAX No.: 702-434-9495

DIANAWERK, MAYER AND GRAM-MERLSPACHER
81 RUCKMAN RD
Closter, NJ 07624
FAX No.: 201-767-1589

DIXIE GUN WORKS
Hwy. 51 South
Union City, TN 38261
FAX No.: 901-885-0440

DOMINO
Importer - See Mandall Shooting Supplies listing.

DUMOULIN, ERNEST
Factory
Rue Florent Boclinville, 8-10
4410 Votten-Herstal, BELGIUM
Phone No. 41/ 27 7892

DUMOULIN, HENRI & FILS
Importer - See New England Arms Co. listing.
Factory - Dumoulin, Henri & Fils
P.O. Box 30
Herstal 4400, BELGIUM
FAX No.: 011-31/493013255

DYNAMIT NOBEL OF AMERICA
105 Stonehurst Ct.
Northvale, NJ 07647
FAX No.: 201-767-1589

EGO ARMAS, S.A.
Victor Sarasqueta, 1
E-20600 Eibar (Guipuzcoa) SPAIN
FAX No.: 011-3443-120463

E.M.F. COMPANY
1900 E. Warner Ave., Suite 1-D
Santa Ana, CA 92705
FAX No.: 714-756-0133

EAGLE ARMS INC.
P.O. Box 457
131 E. 22nd Ave.
Coal Valley, IL 61240
Phone No.: 309-799-5619
FAX No.: 309-799-5150

ERMA-WERKE
Importer - See Precision Sales Int'l listing.
Importer - See Mandall Shooting Supplies listing.
Factory - Erma-Werke GmbH
Johann-Ziegler-Strabe 13-15
D-8060 Dachau GERMANY
FAX No.: 08131/2803-59

EUROARMS OF AMERICA
208 East Piccadilly Street
Winchester, VA 22601
FAX No.: 703-662-4464

EUROPEAN AMERICAN ARMORY CORP.
P.O. Box 3498, Bright Station
Hialeah, FL 33013
Phone No.: 305-688-4442
FAX No.: 305-688-5656

FAS
Importer - See Mandall Shooting Supplies listing.
Importer - Nygord Precision Products
P.O. Box 8394
La Crescenta, CA 91224-0394
Phone No.: 818-352-3027

FEG
Importer - See K.B.I., Inc. listing.

F.I.E. FIREARMS CORP. (repairs only)
Please refer to Quality Firearms, Inc.

FABARM
Factory - Fabarm/S.N.P.E.
Via G. Zola
33 Brescia, ITALY 25060
FAX No.: 011-3930-2004816

FABBRI, ARMI
Via Dante Alighieri, 29
25062 Concesio (BS) Italy
FAX No.: 030-275-2050

FABRIQUE NATIONALE
Factory - Browning S.A.
Fabrique Nationale Herstal SA
Parc Industriel des Hauts Sarts
3e Ave.
B-4040 Herstal, Belgium
FAX No.: 041/481490

FAMARS
Refer to listing under Abbiatico & Salvinelli

FAUSTI, STEFANO
Via Parte 33
25060 Marcheno V.T. ITALY
FAX No.: 011-3930/8610155

FEATHER INDUSTRIES, INC.
2300 Central Ave. Unit K
Boulder, CO 80301
FAX No.: 303-447-0944

FEINWERKBAU
Importer - See Beeman Precision Arms listing.
Factory - Feinwerkbau
Neckarstrabe 43
D-7238 Oberndorf/Neckar GERMANY
FAX No.: 07423/814-89

FERLACH GUNS
Exclusive Importer
Adler Arms ($10 for complete catalog)
268 Freeport Road, Suite 3006
Pittsburgh, PA 15238
Phone No.: 412-826-1232
FAX No.: 412-826-1232

Factory - Ferlach
Attn: Customer Service
Waagplatz, 6
A-9170 Ferlach, AUSTRIA
FAX No.: 011-434227/3714

FERLIB
Importer - See W. L. Moore & Co. listing.
Importer - See New England Arms Co. listing.
Importer - See Quality Arms, Inc. listing.
Factory - Ferlib & Cs.d.f
Via Costa 46, Gardone
1-25063 ITALY
FAX No. 01139-3089-12586

FIOCCHI OF AMERICA, INC.
Importer - Fiocchi of America, Inc.
Rt. 2, Box 90-8
Ozark, MO 65721
FAX No.: 417-725-1039
Factory - Fiocchi Munizioni S.P.A.
Via Santa Barbara, 4
22053 Lecco ITALY
FAX No.: 0341/281-171

FRANCHI, LUIGI
Importer - See American Arms, Inc. listing.
Factory - Franchi, Luigi, S.p.A.
Via del Serpente, 12
I-25131 Fornaci (Brescia) ITALY
FAX No.: 030-347415

FRANCOTTE, AUGUSTE & CIE. S.A.
Importer - See Armes De Chasse listing.
Factory - Auguste Francotte
Rue due Trois Juin, 109
B - 4040 Herstal BELGIUM
FAX No.: 011-3241-481179

FREEDOM ARMS
P.O. Box 1776
Freedom, WY 83120
FAX No.: 307-883-2005

FRIGON GUNS
627 West Crawford
Clay Center, KS 67432
Phone No.: 913-632-5607

GALIL
Importer - See Action Arms, Ltd. listing.

GAMBA, RENATO
Importer - Giacomo Sporting Inc.
Delta Plaza, Rt 26/N
Rome, NY 13440
Importer - See New England Arms Co. listing.

Factory - Renato Gamba
Via Artigiani, 91/93
25063 Gardone V.T. (Brescia), ITALY
FAX No.: 30-8912-180

GARBI
Importer - See W. L. Moore & Co. listing.
Factory - Armas Garbi
Urki, 12-14
20600 Eibar, SPAIN

GASTINNE RENETTE
39 Avenue Franklin D. Roosevelt
Paris, FRANCE 75008
FAX No.: 331-4256-2111

GATLING GUN COMPANY
Distributor - J & G Sales, Inc.
440 Miller Valley Rd.
Prescott, AZ 86304-0400
FAX No.: 602-445-9658
Phone No.: 602-445-9658

GAUCHER - Armes S.A.
Importer - See Mandall Shooting Supplies listing.
Factory
46, rue Desjoyaux
F-42000 Saint-Etienne
FAX No.: 77419572

GENTRY, DAVID
314 N. Hoffman
Belgrade, MT 59714
Phone No.: 406-388-GUNS

GIBBS RIFLE CO.
Rt. 2, Box 214 Hoffman Road
Cannon Hill Industrial Park
Martinsburg, WV 25401
Phone No.: 304-274-0458
FAX No.: 304-274-0078

GLOCK, INC.
6000 Highlands Pkwy.
Smyrna, GA 30082
FAX No.: 404-433-8719

GONIC ARMS INC.
134 Flagg Rd
Gonic, NH 03839
Phone No.: 603-332-8456

GRANGER, G.
66, Cours Fauriel
F-42100 Saint-Etienne, FRANCE
Phone No.: 77/25-1473

Trademark Index, cont.

GREENER, W. W.
Importer - Gibbs Rifle Co.
Rt. 2, Box 214 Hoffman Road
Cannon Hill Industrial Park
Martinsburg, WV 25401
Phone No.: 304-274-0458
FAX No.: 304-274-0078
Factory - W. W. Greener
One Belmont Row
GB-Birmingham, ENGLAND B4 7RE
FAX No.: 011-4421-359-4300

GRENDEL, INC.
P.O. Box 908
Rockledge, FL 32955
FAX No.: 407-633-6710

GRIFFIN & HOWE
36 West 44th Street, Suite 1011
New York, NY 10036
Phone No.: 212-921-0980
FAX No.: 908-766-1068 (NJ location)

GRULLA ARMAS
Avda Otaola, 12
E-20600 Eibar (Guipuzcoa) SPAIN
FAX No.: 011-3443/702133

GUN PARTS CORP.
Parts supplier only
Williams Lane
W. Hurley, NY 12491
Phone No.: 914-679-2417
FAX No.: 914-679-5849

GUN SOUTH, INC.
108 Morrow Avenue
Trussville, AL 35173
FAX No.: 205-655-7078

GUSTAF, CARL
Importer - See Precision Sales Int'l listing.
Factory - Winscan AB, c/o Carl Gustaf
P.O. Box 545
S-631 07 Eskilstuna SWEDEN
FAX No.: 16-120054

H & R 1871, INC.
Harrington & Richardson (post-1991 mfg. only)
60 Industrial Rowe
Gardner, MA 01440
FAX No.: 508-632-2300

H-S PRECISION, INC.
1301 Turbine Dr.
Rapid City, SD 57701
FAX No.: 605-342-8964

HAMBRUSCH JAGDWAFFEN GmbH
Gartengasse 4
A-9170 Ferlach, AUSTRIA
FAX No.: 011-4227/4106

HAMMERLI
Importer - See Mandall Shooting Supplies listing.
Importer - See Beeman Precision Arms listing.
Factory - Hammerli AG
Seoner Strabe
CH-5600 Lenzburg SWITZERLAND
FAX No.: 064/513827

HASKELL MFG. INC.
Refer to Hi-Point listing.

HATFIELD GUN CO., INC.
224 N 4th St.
St. Joseph, MO 64501
Phone No.: 816-279-8688
FAX No.: 816-279-2716

HECKLER & KOCH
Importer - Heckler & Koch
21480 Pacific Blvd.
Sterling, VA 20166-8903
FAX No.: 703-450-8160
Factory - Heckler & Koch GmbH
Postfach 1329
Oberndorf Neckar D-7238 Germany
FAX No.: 01149-7423-2539

HELWAN
Importer - See Interarms listing.
Importer - See Navy Arms Co. listing.

HEYM, FRIEDRICH WILH.
Factory - F. W. Heym
Coburger Strabe 8
D-8732 Munnerstadt GERMANY
FAX No.: 09733/63-49

HI-POINT FIREARMS
Distributor - MKS Supply, Inc.
174 S. Mulberry
Mansfield, OH 44902
Phone No.: 419-522-8330

HOFER-JAGDWAFFEN, PETER
Kirchgasse 24
A-9170 Ferlach, AUSTRIA
FAX No.: 011-434227/3683

HOLLAND & HOLLAND LTD.
Attn: Customer Service-BB
33 Bruton Street
London, ENGLAND W1X 8JS
Phone No.: 71-499 4411
FAX NO.: 71-499 4544
Telex No.: 011-4471-499-4544

I.A.B.
Factory - Industria Armi Brescaine
Via 1 Maggio, 39
Sarezzo Brescia 1-25068 Italy
FAX No.: 01139-3080-0313

IGA SHOTGUNS
Importer - See Stoeger Arms Corp. listing.

IBERIA FIREARMS
Refer to Hi-Point listing.

INTERARMS
10 Prince Street
Alexandria, VA 22314
FAX No.: 703-549-7826

INTRATEC
12405 SW 130th St.
Miami, FL 33186
FAX No.: 305-253-7207

IRWINDALE ARMS, INC.
See A M T listing.

ISRAEL ARMS LTD.
Importer - J.O. Arms, Inc.
5709 Hartsdale
Houston, TX 77036
FAX No.: 713-789-7513

ITHACA ACQUISITION CORP.
891 Route 348, P.O. Box 4
King Ferry, NY 13081
FAX No.: 315-364-5134

J.S.L. (HEREFORD) LTD.
Importer - Specialty Shooters Supply, Inc.
3325 Griffin Road, Suite 9MM
Fort Lauderdale, FL 33312
Phone No.: 305-792-2787
FAX No.: 305-964-4418
Factory
35 Church Street
Hereford, HR1 2LR, ENGLAND
FAX No.: 011-44432-355242

JARRETT RIFLES, INC.
383 Brown Rd.
Jackson, SC 29831
Phone No.: 803-471-3616
FAX No.: 803-471-9246

JENNINGS FIREARMS, INC.
Distributor - Jennings Firearms, Inc.
3680 Research Way, Ste.#1
Carson City, NV 89706
Phone/FAX No.: 702-882-4007

IVER JOHNSON
Refer to AMAC listing.

JURRAS
J & G Sales, Inc.
Attn: Mr. Jurras, Pistolsmith
440 Miller Valley Rd.
Prescott, AZ 86301
Phone No.: 602-455-9650
FAX No.: 602-455-9658

K.B.I., INC.
P.O. Box 6346
Harrisburg, PA 17112
Phone No.: 717-540-8518
FAX No.: 717-540-8567

KDF, INC.
2485 Highway 46 North
Seguin, TX 78155
Phone No.: 512-379-8141
FAX No.: 512-379-5420

KAHNKE GUNWORKS
206 West 11th
Redwood Falls, MN 56283
FAX No.: 507-637-2905

KEPPELER, DIETER
Riedheimer Strabe 6
D-7907 Langenau, GERMANY
FAX No.: 07345/3503

KEPPLINGER, ING. HANNES
Carl-Wagner-Strabe 1
A-6330 Kufstein, AUSTRIA
FAX No.: 05372/71887

KIMEL INDUSTRIES
Distributor
P.O. Box 335
Matthews, NC 28106
FAX No.: 704-821-6339
Factory - AAArms
4811 Persimmons Ct.
Monroe, NC 28110

Trademark Index, cont.

KLEINGUENTHER FIREARMS
1604 N. Heideke St.
Seguin, TX 78155
Phone No.: 512-372-5050
FAX No.: 512-557-5310

KORTH
*Importer - See Mandall Shooting Supplies
listing.*
Factory - Korth

Robert Bosch Strabe 4
D-2418 Ratzeburg, Germany
FAX No.: 011-49451/4993230

KRICO
*Importer - See Mandall Shooting Supplies
listing.*
Factory - A. Kriegeskorte GmbH
Kronacher Str. 63
8510 Furth-Stadeln, Germany
FAX No.: 0911-796074

KRIEGHOFF, H., GUN CO.
Importer - Krieghoff Intl., Inc.
P.O. Box 549
Ottsville, PA 18942
FAX No.: 215-847-8691
Factory - Krieghoff Int'l, Inc.
Boschstrasse 22
D-7900 Ulm, GERMANY
FAX No.: 731/40 18270

L.A.R. MANUFACTURING, INC.
4133 West Farm Road
West Jordan, UT 84084
FAX No.: 801-569-1972

LAKE FIELD ARMS LTD.
P.O. Box 129
Lakefield, Ontario
Canada K0L 2H0
FAX No.: 705-652-8431

LANBER
Lanber Armas, S.A.
Attn: Customer Service-BB
Zubiaurre, 5
E-Zaldibar, 48250 Vizcaya, SPAIN
FAX No.: 011-344-6827999

LASERARMS
Distributor - Emerging Technologies, Inc.
P.O. Box 3548
Little Rock, AR 72203
Phone No.: 501-375-2227
FAX No.: 501-372-1445

LAURONA ARMAS, S.A.
P.O. Box 260, Avda de Otaola, 25
Eibar (Guipuzcoa) SPAIN
Phone No.: 011-3443/700600
FAX No.: 011-3443/700616

LEBEAU-COURALLY
Importer - See New England Arms Co. listing.
Factory - Aug. Lebeau-Courally
386, rue Saint-Gilles
B-4000 Liege, Belgium
FAX No.: 3241-522008

LIBERTY ARMS WORKS, INC.
823 Lincoln Ave.
West Chester, PA 19380
Phone No.: 215-429-1114

LJUTIC INDUSTRIES, INC.
P.O. Box 2117
Yakima, WA 98907
Phone No.: 509-248-0476

LLAMA PISTOLS
Importer - See Stoeger Arms Corp. listing.

LORCIN ENGINEERING CO., INC.
10427 San Sevaine Way-A
Mira Loma, CA 91752
FAX No.: 714-360-0623

LUGER (New Mfg. Only)
Precision Imports, Inc.
5040 Space Center Drive
San Antonio, TX 78218
Phone No.: 512-666-3033
FAX No.: 512-666-2723

LYMAN GUNS
Lyman Products Corporation
Rt 147
Middlefield, CT 06455
FAX No.: 203-349-3586

MK ARMS
P.O. Box 16411
Irvina, CA 92713
Phone No.: 714-261-2767

MKE
*Importer - See Mandall Shooting Supplies,
Inc. listing.*

M.O.A. CORPORATION
2451 Old Camden Pike
Eaton, OH 45320
Phone No.: 513-456-3669

MAGNUM RESEARCH INC.

7110 University Ave. NE
Minneapolis, MN 55432
FAX No.: 612-574-0109

MAGTECH RECREATIONAL PRODUCTS, INC.

5030 Paradise Road, Suite C211
Las Vegas, NV 89119
Phone No.: 702-795-7191
FAX No.: 702-795-2769

MALIN, F.E.

Cape Horn International
1411 S. Tryon
Charlotte, NC 28203
Phone No.: 704-331-4837
FAX No.: 704-372-9656

MANDALL SHOOTING SUPPLIES

3616 N. Scottsdale Rd.
Scottsdale, AZ 85252
Phone No.: 602-945-2553
FAX No.: 602-949-0734

MANURHIN HANDGUNS

Importer - ABO Industries
6046 Cornerstone Ct. W., Suite 206
San Diego, CA 92121
FAX No.: 619-453-2133
Factory - Manurhin Equipment
15, rue de Quimper
F-68060 Mulhouse Gedex FRANCE
FAX No.: 011-3389-536311

MARKSMAN

5482 Argosy Drive
Huntington Beach, CA 92649
FAX No.: 714-891-0782

MARLIN FIREARMS

100 Kenna Drive
North Haven, CT 06473
FAX No.: 203-234-7991

MAROCCHI SHOTGUNS

Shotguns: Avanza Series
Precision Sales Int.'l Inc.
Attn: Avanza Customer Service
P.O. Box 1776
Westfield, MA 01086
FAX No.: 413-562-5056
Shotguns and Combo's
Importer - See Sile Distributors listing.
Factory - Marocchi di Stefano, F.lli, S.p.A.
Via Galileo Galilei, 6
I-25068 Sarezzo (Brescia) Italy
FAX No.: 030/890-0370

MAUSER-WERKE

Precision Imports, Inc.
5040 Space Center Drive
San Antonio, TX 78218
FAX No.: 512-666-2723
Factory - Mauser-Werke GmbH
Teckstrabe
D-7238 Oberndorf am Neckar, Germany
FAX No.: 07423/70-655

MAVERICK ARMS, INC.

7 Grasso Ave., P.O. Box 497
North Haven, CT 06473
FAX No.: 203-288-2404

McMILLAN GUNWORKS, INC.

302 W. Melinda Ln. Suites 1, 2, & 3
Phoenix, AZ 85027
FAX No.: 602-582-5178

MERKEL & GEBRUDER

Importer - See Gun South, Inc. listing.
FAX No.: 205-655-7078
Factory - Jagd-und Sportwaffen
Auenstrabe 5
Suhl, Germany 0-6000
FAX No.: 66-24-562

MILLER, DAVID

3131 E. Greenlee Rd.
Tucson, AZ 85716
FAX No.: 602-326-3117

MITCHELL ARMS, INC.

3400 I-West MacArthur Blvd.
Santa Ana, CA 92704
FAX No.: 714-957-5732

MODERN MUZZLE LOADING, INC.

PO Box 130-CAT
Centerville, IA 52544
FAX No.: 515-856-2628

MONTANA ARMORY, INC.

P.O. Box 885
Big Timber, MT 59011
Phone No.: 406-932-4353

MORINI

Importer - See Mandall Shooting Supplies, Inc. listing.
Factory - Morini Competition Arm SA
CH-6814 Lamone-Lugano, Italy

MOSSBERG

O.F. Mossberg & Sons, Inc.
7 Grasso Ave.
North Haven, CT 06473-9844
FAX No.: 203-288-2404

Trademark Index, cont.

MUSGRAVE
Musgrave Mfr.'s and Dist. Ltd.
Jagersfontein Road
Bloemfontein 9300, REPUBLIC OF S. AFRICA
FAX No.: 051/212-903

NAVY ARMS CO.
689 Bergen Blvd.
Ridgefield, NJ 07657
FAX No.: 201-945-6859

NEW ENGLAND ARMS CO.
Lawrence Lane - Box 278
Kittery Point, ME 03905
Phone No.: 207-439-0593
FAX No.: 207-439-6726

NEW ENGLAND FIREARMS
60 Industrial Rowe
Gardner, MA 01440
FAX No.: 508-632-2300

NORINCO
Importer - See Interarms listing.
Importer - See Century International Arms listing.
Importer - See K.B.I, Inc. listing.
Importer - China Sports, Inc.
2010 S. Lynx Place
P.O. Box 3250
Ontario, CA 91761
FAX No.: 714-923-0775

NORTH AMERICAN ARMS
1800 N. 300 W.
P.O. Box 707
Spanish Fork, UT 84660
FAX No.: 801-798-9418

OLYMPIC ARMS, INC.
624 Old Pacific Hwy. S.E.
Olympia, WA 98503
FAX No.: 206-491-3447

OMEGA SHOTGUNS
See K.B.I., Inc. listing.

ORVIS
5848 Westheimer
Houston, TX 77057
Phone No.: 713-783-2111

P.A.W.S., INC.
Distributor - See Sile Distributors listing.

P.S.M.G. GUN CO.
10 Park Avenue
Arlington, MA 02174
Phone No.: 617-646-1699
FAX No.: 617-648-7482

PARAMOUNT
Importer - O.K. Weber, Inc.
P.O. Box 7485
Eugene, OR 97401
Phone No.: 503-747-0458
FAX No.: 503-747-5927
Factory - Imperial Gun Co., Ltd.
Unite 1E, Threshold Way
Fairoaks Airport, Chobham
Surrey, England GU24 8HU
FAX No.: (0726) 856565

PARA-ORDNANCE MFG. INC.
3411 McNicoll Avenue #14
Scarborough, Ontario
CANADA M1V 2V6
FAX No.: 416-297-1289

PARDINI
Importer - Mo's Competitor Supplies & Range, Inc.
34 Delmar Dr.
Brookfield, CT 06804
Phone No.: 203-775-1013
FAX No.: 203-775-9462
Factory - Pardini Armi Commerciale
55043 Lido di Camaiore
Lu, Italy
FAX No.: 011-39584-90122

PARKER REPRODUCTIONS
Parker Reproduction Div.
124 River Road
Middlesex, NJ 08846
FAX No.: 908-469-9692

PARKER-HALE LTD.
Importer (Shotguns) - Precision Sports
3736 Kellogg Road
P.O. Box 5588
Cortland, NY 13045-5588
FAX No.: 607-753-8835
Factory (Rifles) - See Gibbs Rifle listing.

PAUZA SPECIALTIES
Distributor - California Armory, Inc.
881 W. San Bruno Ave.
San Bruno, CA 94066
Phone No.: 415-871-4885

PENTHENY de PENTHENY, INC.
2352 Baggett Ct.
Santa Rosa, CA 95401
Phone No.: 707-573-1390

PERAZZI
Importer - Perazzi USA, Inc.
1207 South Shamrock Ave.
Monrovia, CA 91016
Phone No.: 818-303-0068
FAX No.: 818-303-2081
Factory - Manifattura Armi Perazzi
Via Fontanelle, 1-3
25080 Botticino M. Brescia Italy
FAX No.: 011-3930-2692594

PEREGRINE INDUSTRIES, INC.
P.O. Box 1310
Huntington Beach, CA 92647-1310
Phone No.: 714-847-4700
FAX No.: 714-847-4141

PETERS STAHL GmbH
Importer - Safari Arms
624 Old Pacific Hwy. S.E.
Olympia, WA 98503
FAX No.: 206-491-3447
Importer - See McMillan Gunworks listing.
Factory
Stettiner Strabe 42
D-4790 Paderborn, GERMANY
FAX No.: 011-495251/75611

PHELPS MFG. CO.
P.O. Box 2266
Evansville, IN 47714
Phone No.: 812-423-8791

PHILLIPS & ROGERS, INC.
100 Hilbig, Suite C
Conroe, TX 77301
Phone No.: 409-756-1001

PHOENIX ARMS
1420 S. Archibald Ave.
Ontario, CA 91761
Phone No.: 714-947-4843

PIETTA, Flli s.n.c.
Via Briggia, 51
25064 Gussago (Brescia) ITALY
FAX No.: 011-3930/2521409

PIOTTI
Importer - See W. L. Moore & Co. listing.
Factory - Piorri, F.lli, S.n.c.
Via Cinelli, 10-12
I-25063 Gardone V.I. Brescia, Italy
FAX No.: 030-358-0652

POLY TECHNOLOGIES, INC.
Distributor - PTK International, Inc.
2814 New Spring Rd., 340
Atlanta, GA 30339
Phone No.: 404-233-2340
FAX No.: 404-438-7839

POWELL, WILLIAM & SON GUNMAKERS, LTD.
Importer - Bells Legendary Countrywear
22 Circle Dr.
Bellmore, NY 11710
Factory
35-37 Carrs Lane
Birmingham England B47SX
FAX No.: 011-4421-631-3504

PRECISION SALES INT'L, INC.
P.O. Box 1776
Westfield, MA 01086
FAX No.: 413-562-5056

PURDEY, JAMES, & SONS, LTD.
57-58 S Audley Street
London, ENGLAND W1Y 6ED
Phone No.: (44) 71-499-1801
FAX No.: 011-4471-355-3297

QUALITY ARMS, INC.
P.O. Box 19477
Houston, TX 77224
Phone No.: 713-870-8377
FAX No.: 713-870-8524

QUALITY PARTS CO.
Manufacturer - Bushmaster Firearms, Inc.
999 Roosevelt Trail Bldg. 3
Windham, ME 04062
FAX No.: 207-892-8068

RWS
Importer - See Dynamit Nobel of America listing.
105 Stonehurst Ct.
Northvale, NJ 07647
FAX No.: 201-767-1589

RAM-LINE, INC.
10601 West 48th Ave.
Wheat Ridge, CO 80033
FAX No.: 303-467-9833

RANDALL FIREARMS CO.
Blue Book Publications, Inc.
Attn: Older Randall Research
One Appletree Square
Minneapolis, MN 55425
Phone No.: 612-854-5229
FAX No.: 612-853-1486

RAVELL LTD.
289 Diputacion Street
08009 Barcelona, SPAIN
FAX No.: 011-343-488-1394

REMINGTON
Remington Arms Co., Inc.
Attn: Consumer Information
Brandywine Bldg. - 1007 Market Street
Wilmington, DE 19898
Phone no.: 302-773-5291
FAX No.: 302-774-5776
Remington Arms Co., Inc. (Repairs)
14 Hoefler Ave.
Ilion, NY 13357
Phone No.: 315-895-7791

RIGBY, JOHN & CO. (GUNMAKERS), LTD.
Importer - Griffin & Howe
36 West 44th Street, Suite 1011
New York, NY 10036
Phone No.: 212-921-0980
FAX No.: 908-766-1068 (NJ location)
Factory
66 Great Suffolk Street
London, England SE1 OBU
FAX No.: 011-4471-928-9205

RIZZINI B.
Importer - Lou Alessandri & Son
24 French St.
Rehoboth, MA 02769
Phone No.: 508-252-5590
FAX No.: 508-252-3436
Factory
Via 2 Giugno, 7/7 bis
25060 Marcheno
Marcheno (Brescia), ITALY
FAX No.: 011-3930/861319

RIZZINI, F.LLI
Importer - See W. L. Moore & Co. listing.
Importer - See New England Arms Co. listing.

ROCKY MOUNTAIN ARMS, INC.
600 S. Sunset, Unit C
Longmont, CO 80501
Phone No: 303-678-8522
FAX No.: 303-678-8766

ROSSI
Importer - See Interarms listing.

ROTTWEIL
Importer - See Dynamit Nobel of America listing.

RUKO PRODUCTS, INC.
P.O. Box 1181
Buffalo, NY 14240-1181
Phone No.: 416-826-9192
FAX No.: 416-826-1353

SKB ARMS CO.
G. U., Inc.
P.O. Box 37669
4325 S 120th Street
Omaha, NE 68137
FAX No.: 402-330-8029

SSK INDUSTRIES
721 Woodvue Lane
Wintersville, OH 43952
Phone No. 614-264-7317
FAX No. 614-264-2257

S.W.D., INC.
1872 Marietta Blvd.
Atlanta, GA 30318
Phone No. 404-355-2641
FAX No.: 404-350-9714

SAFARI ARMS
624 Old Pacific Hwy. S.E.
Olympia, WA 98503
FAX No.: 206-491-3447

SAKO
Importer - See Stoeger Arms Corp. listing.
Factory - Sako, Ltd.
P.O. Box 149, Sakonkatu 2
SF-11101 Riihimaki, FINLAND
FAX No.: 014/720446

SAMCO GLOBAL ARMS, INC.
6995 North W. 43rd St.
Miami, FL 33166
FAX No.: 305-477-1232

F. SARASQUETA
Factory - Industria de la Escopeta S.A.L.
P.O. Box 233
20600 Eibar, Guipuzcoa, SPAIN
FAX No.: 01134-4311-7210

SARDIUS
Previous Importer - Armscorp of America
4424 John Avenue
Baltimore, MD 21227
FAX No.: 301-247-6205

Trademark Index, cont.

SAUER, J.P. & SOHN
G. U., Inc.
P.O. Box 37669
4325 S. 120th Street
Omaha, NE 68137
FAX No.: 402-330-8029
Factory - Sauer, J.P. & Sohn GmbH
Postfach 1408, Sauerstrabe
D-2330 Eckernforde, Germany
FAX No.: 011-4943-511471-160

SAVAGE ARMS, INC.
Attn: David Tolly
Springfield Road
P.O. Box 1110
Westfield, MA 01085
FAX No.: 413-562-7764

SCATTERGUN TECHNOLOGIES
P.O. Box 24517
Nashville, TN 37202
Phone No.: 615-254-1441
FAX No.: 615-254-1449

SCHELLER - SPEZIALWAFFEN
Factory - Schiebsportzentrum
Postfach 405
Suhl, Germany O-6000

SCOTT, W. C., LTD.
Repair address
Holland & Holland, Ltd.
Attn: Mr. P. C. Chismon
33 Bruton St.
London W1X 8JS ENGLAND
FAX No.: 071/499-4544

SEECAMP, L.W. CO., INC.
301 Brewster Road
Milford, CT 06460
Phone No.: 203-877-3429

SEMMERLING
Manufacturer - American Derringer Corp.
127 N. Lacy Drive
Waco, TX 76705
FAX No.: 817-799-7935

SHILOH RIFLE MFG. CO.
P.O. Box 279, Ind. Park
Big Timber, MT 59011
Phone No.: 406-932-4454
FAX No.: 406-932-5627

SIDEWINDER
Manufacturer - D-Max, Inc.
RR 1, Box 473
Bagley, MN 56621
Phone No.: 218-785-2278

SIG SAUER
Importer - Sigarms, Inc.
Corporate Park Industrial Drive
Exeter, NH 03833
FAX No.: 603-772-9082
Factory - SIG - Schweizerische
CH-8212 Neuhausen am Rheinfall, Germany
FAX No.: 0153/216-601

SILE DISTRIBUTORS
7 Centre Market Place
New York, NY 10013
Phone No.: 212-925-4111
FAX No.: 212-925-3149

SILMA
Via 1- Maggio, 74
I-25060 Zanano di Sarezzo, (Brescia) ITALY
FAX No. 011-3930-801493

SMITH & WESSON
Attn: Mr. Roy Jinks, S&W Historian
2100 Roosevelt Avenue
Springfield, MA 01102-2208
Phone No.: 413-781-8300
FAX No.: 413-731-8980

SNAKE CHARMER
Sporting Arms Mfg. Inc.
P.O. Box 191
Littlefield, TX 79339
FAX No.: 806-385-3394

SPHINX
Importer - See Sile Distributors listing.
Factory - SPHINX ENGINEERING SA
Ch. des Grandes-Vies 2
CH-2900 Porrentruy
Switzerland
FAX No.: 041 66/66 30 90

SPRINGFIELD, INC.
25144 Ridge Rd.
Colona, IL 61241
Phone No.: 309-441-6002
FAX No.: 309-441-6003

STALLARD ARMS
Refer to Hi-Point listing.

STAR
Importer - See Interarms listing.
Factory - Star Bonifacio Echevarria S.A.
Torrekua 3
Eibar E-20600 Spain
FAX No.: 01134-4311-1524

STEYR - AIRGUNS ONLY
PO Box 8394
La Crescenta, CA 91224

STEYR MANNLICHER
Importer - See Gun South, Inc. listing.
Factory - Steyr Mannlicher A.G.
Box 1000, Mannlicher Str. 1
Steyr A-4400 Austria
FAX No.: 01143-7252-68621

STOEGER ARMS CORP.
55 Ruta Court
S. Hackensack, NJ 07606
FAX No.: 201-440-2707

STONER RIFLE
Factory - Knight's Manufacturing Co.
7750 - 9th St. SW
Vero Beach, FL 32968
FAX No.: 407-569-2955

STREET SWEEPER
Sales of Georgia
P.O. Box 94168
Atlanta, GA 30318
FAX No.: 404-350-9714

STURM, RUGER & CO.
Lacey Place
Southport, CT 06490
FAX No.: 203-259-2167

SUNDANCE INDUSTRIES
25163 W. Ave. Stanford
Valencia, CA 91355
FAX No.: 805-257-4891

SURVIVAL ARMS, INC.
4500 Pine Cone Place
Cocoa, FL 32922
Phone No.: 407-633-4880
FAX No.: 407-633-4975

SYMES & WRIGHT LTD.
8 Monmouth Place
London, ENGLAND W2 5SA
FAX No.: 011-71-221-1424

TANNER, ANDRE
Importer - See Mandall Shooting Supplies listing.

TAR-HUNT CUSTOM RIFLES, INC.
R.R. 3 Box 572
Bloomsburg, PA 17815-9351
Phone No.: 717-784-6368

TAURUS INTERNATIONAL FIREARMS
16175 NW 49th Ave
Miami, FL 33014-6314
Phone No.: 800-327-3776
FAX No.: 305-623-7506

TECNI-MEC
Importer - See Mandall Shooting Supplies listing.
Factory - Armi di Isidoro Rizzini
Via Gitti, Localita Rovedolo
I-25060 Marcheno (BS) ITALY
FAX No.: 011-3930-8610179

TEXAS LONGHORN ARMS, INC.
(Administrative Offices)
5959 West Loop South, Ste. 424
Bellaire, TX 77401
Phone No.: 713-660-6323
FAX No.: 713-660-0493

THOMPSON/CENTER ARMS
P.O. Box 5002
Farmington Road
Rochester, NH 03867
FAX No.: 603-332-5133

THUNDER FIVE
C.L. Reedy & Associates, Inc.
2485 Grassmere Drive
Melbourne, FL 32904
Phone No.: 407-984-1719
FAX No.: 800-248-6745

TIKKA
Importer - See Stoeger Arms Corp. listing.

TIMBERWOLF
Importer (.357 Mag. only) - See Action Arms Ltd. listing.

TRADITIONS, INC.
PO Box 235
Deep River, CT 06417
FAX No.: 203-526-4564

TRAIL GUN ARMORY
Route 22, Box 760
Conroe, TX 77303

U.S.A.S.
Distributor - Kiesler's Wholesale
3300 Industrial Parkway
Jeffersonville, IN 47130
FAX No.: 812-285-5095

UBERTI U.S.A., INC.
Importer
P.O. Box 469
362 Limerock Road
Lakeville, CT 06039
FAX No.: 203-435-2846
Factory - Aldo Uberti & C., S.r.l.
Via G. Carducci, 41
I-25068 Sarezzo (BS) Italy
FAX No.: 030-8911061

UGARTECHEA, IGNACIO
Importer - Precision Sports, Inc.
P.O. Box 708
Cortland, NY 13045
Phone No.: 607-756-2851
Factory - Ugartechea, Ignacio
P.O. Box 21
Eibar, SPAIN
FAX No.: 011-3443-121669

ULTRA LIGHT ARMS
P.O. Box 1270
214 Prince Street
Granville, WV 26534
FAX No.: 304-599-5687

UNIQUE
Importer - See Beeman Precision Arms listing.
Importer - Nygord Precision Products
P.O. Box 8394
La Crescenta, CA 91224-0394
Phone No.: 818-352-3027
Factory - Unique Manufacture d'Armes
10, Avenue des Allees
F-64700 Hendaye, FRANCE
FAX No.: 33-5920/5085

U.S. HISTORICAL SOCIETY
First & Main Streets
Richmond, VA 23219
FAX No.: 804-648-0002

UZI
Importer - See Action Arms Ltd. listing.

VOERE
Importer - See Mandall Shooting Supplies listing.
Factory - Voere Austria
Postfach 416
A-633 Kufstein, AUSTRIA
FAX No.: 05372/5752

WAFFEN VERATSHNIG
Factory
Niederdorfl 30
9173 St. Margareten I. Rosental
Ferlach, Austria
FAX No.: 011-4226-397

WALTHER
Importer - See Interarms listing.
Factory - Carl Walther, GmbH, Sportwaffenfabrik
Karlstrabe 33
D-7900 Ulm/Donau, Germany.
FAX No.: 0731-1539-170

WEATHERBY, INC.
2781 Firestone Blvd.
South Gate, CA 90280
FAX No.: 213-569-5025

WEBLEY & SCOTT LTD.
Shotguns - repair only
Holland & Holland
Attn: Customer Service-BB
33 Bruton Street
London, ENGLAND W1X 8JS
Phone No.: 71-499 4411
FAX NO.: 71-499 4544
Telex No.: 269021
Factory (airguns only)
Frankley Industrial Park
Tay Road, Rubery, Rednal
GB-Birmingham B45 OPA
Phone No.: 021/453-1864
FAX No.: 021/457-7846

WEIHRAUCH, HANS-HERMANN
Importer - See European American Armory listing.
Factory - H. Weihrauch, Sportwaffenfabrik
Industriestrabe 11
D-8744 Mellrichstadt, GERMANY
FAX No.: 09776/5532

WESSON FIREARMS CO., INC.
Maple Tree Industrial Ctr, Rt. 20
Wilbraham Road
Palmer, MA 01069
Phone No.: 413-267-4081
FAX No.: 413-267-3601

WESTLEY RICHARDS & CO., LTD.
Importer - The Sporting Field, Inc.
RD #1, Peach Lake Road
North Salem, NY 10560
FAX No.: 914-669-8962
Factory - Westley Richards & Co., Ltd.
40 Grange Road
Birmingham, ENGLAND B29 6AR
FAX No.: 021-472-1701
Telex. No.: 334049 DETACH

WHITE MUZZLE LOADING SYSTEMS, INC.
PO Box 190
Roosevelt, UT 84066
FAX No.: 801-722-3054

WICHITA ARMS, INC.
P.O. Box 11371
444 Ellis
Wichita, KS 67211
Phone No.: 316-265-0760
FAX No.: 316-265-0760

WILDEY, INC.
458 Danbury Rd., No. 6
New Milford, CT 06776
FAX No.: 203-354-7759

WILLIAM LARKIN MOORE & CO.
31360 Via Colinas, SE 109
Westlake Village, CA 91361
Phone No.: 818-889-4160

WINCHESTER (U.S.Repeating Arms)
U.S. Repeating Arms Co.
275 Winchester Avenue, P.O. Box 30-300
New Haven, CT 06511
FAX No.: 203-789-5071

WINCHESTER/OLIN
Models 101 & 23 only (Disc.)
Attn: Shotgun Customer Service
427 N. Shamrock Street
East Alton, IL 62024
FAX No.: 618-258-3393

WISEMAN, BILL & CO.
(Mailing Address)
P.O. Box 3427
Bryan, TX 77805
Phone No.: 409-690-3456
FAX No.: 409-690-0156

ZABALLA HERMANOS, S.A.
Lasao, 6
E-20690 Elgueta (Guipuzcoa), SPAIN
FAX No.: 011-3443-768201

ZANARDINI
Factory - Zanardini, P. & C., S.n.c.
Via C. Goldoni, 34
I-25063 Gardone v.T. (Brescia), ITALY
FAX No.: 011-3930-8910590

ZANOTTI, FABIO
Importer - See New England Arms Co. listing.
Factory - R. Gamba c/o Zanotti
Via Artigiani, 93
IO-25063 Gardone Val Trompia
Brescia, ITALY
FAX No.: 011-3930-837180

ZASTAVA ARMS
Factory - Zastava Arms
29 Novembra 12
YU-11000 Beograd, YUGOSLAVIA
11/184-007

ZOLI, ANGELO (discontinued)
Parts - Cape Outfitters
Rt. 2, Box 437-C
Cape Girardeau, MO 63701
Phone No.: 314-335-4103

ZOLI, ANTONIO
Not affiliated with Angelo Zoli.
Factory - Zoli Antonio S.p.A.
Via Zanardelli, 39
I-25063 Gardone V.T. (BS) ITALY
Phone No.: 030/891-21612
FAX No.: 030/891-1165

This section is included to identify year of manufacture dates on Brownings, Colts (including 3rd generation Colt S.A. model numbers), High Standard, Mauser broomhandles, Parker shotguns, Remington (manufacture dates), Savage/Stevens model information, Savage M-1899, and selected Winchesters. To use these tables, simply locate the Ser. No. of the above mentioned trademarks, locate the proper bracket it falls into by model, and refer to the adjacent year to determine the year of manufacture. In several cases, caliber rarity can also be determined.

BROWNING BELGIUM PRODUCTION

Year	Serial Number Beginning of Year	Serial Number at End of Year
A-5 (AUTOMATIC 5) SHOTGUN - approximate recapitulation - 12 ga.		
1924	1	3000
1925	3001	18000
1926	18001	33000
1927	33001	48000
1928	48001	63000
1929	63001	78000
1930	78001	93000
1931	93001	108000
1932	108001	123000
1933	123001	138000
1934	138001	153000
1935	153001	168000
1936	168001	183000
1937	183001	198000
1938	198001	213000
1939	213001	229000
1940 -		
1945	NO PRODUCTION	
1946	229001	237000
1947	237001	249000
1948	249001	270000
1949	270001	285000
1950	285001	315000
1952	346001	387000
1953	387001	438000
	Standard Model	
1954	H1	H39000
	Lightweight Model	
	L1	L42000
1955	**Standard Model**	
	H39001	H83000
	Lightweight Model	
	L42001	L83000
1956	**Standard Model**	
	H83001	H99000
	M1	M22000
	Lightweight Model	
	L83001	L99000
	G1	G23000
1957	**Standard Model**	
	M22001	M85000
	Lightweight Model	
	G23001	G85000
1958	**Standard Model**	
	M85001	M99000
	Lightweight Model	
	G85001	G99000

Year	Serial Number Beginning of Year	Serial Number at End of Year
1958- 1976	Ser. No. sequence changed to include a one or two digit numeral followed by an alpha character. "M" prefix designates standard models, "G" includes lightweight models, and "V" shows magnum models. To illustrate, an A-5 with a Ser. No. of 8G19264 would indicate a lightweight model manufactured in 1958. Ser. No. 71V24690 would specify a 3 inch magnum gun built in 1971.	
SUPERPOSED MODEL - O & U - 12 GA.		
1931	1	2000
1932	2001	4000
1933	4001	6000
1934	6001	8000
1935	8001	10000
1936	10001	12000
1937	12001	14000
1938	14001	17000
1939 -		
1947	NO PRODUCTION	
1948	17001	17200
1949	17201	20000
1950	20001	21000
1951	21001	27000
1952	27001	33000
1953	33001	37000
1954	37001	43000
1955	43001	48000
1956	48001	54000
1957	54001	59000
1958	59001	68500
1959	68501	76500
1960	76501	86500
1961	86501	96500
1962	96501	99999
1963	S3 suffix after Ser. No.	
1964	S4 suffix after Ser. No.	
1965	S5 suffix after Ser. No.	
1966	S6 suffix after Ser. No.	
1967	S7 suffix after Ser. No.	
1968	S8 suffix after Ser. No.	
1969	S69 suffix after Ser. No.	
1970	S70 suffix after Ser. No.	
1971	S71 suffix after Ser. No.	
1972	S72 suffix after Ser. No.	
1973	S73 suffix after Ser. No.	
1974	S74 suffix after Ser. No.	

Year	Serial Number Beginning of Year	Serial Number at End of Year
1975	S75 suffix after Ser. No.	
1976	S76 suffix after Ser. No.	
1976 to date	"P" or Presentation Models only	

LIEGE O & U -
Approximately 10,000 produced

1973	73J prefix before Ser. No.	
1974	74J prefix before Ser. No.	
1975	75J prefix before Ser. No.	

DOUBLE AUTOMATIC SHOTGUN

1952 - 1959	N/A	
1960 - 1971	1st or both digits indicate last 2 digits in year of manufacture (i.e. - OA1947 - 1960 mfg., 70A245671 - 1970 mfg.)	

HI-POWER (9mm) PISTOL

1955 - 1956	No records available	
1957	70000	80000
1958	80001	85267
1959	85268	89687
1960	89688	93027
1961	93028	109145
1962	109146	113548
1963	113549	115822
1964	115823	T136538
1965	T136569	T146372
1966	T146373	T173285
1967	T173286	T213999
1968	T214000	T258000
1969	69C prefix before Ser. No.	
1970	70C prefix before Ser. No.	
1971	71C prefix before Ser. No.	
1972	72C prefix before Ser. No.	
1973	73C prefix before Ser. No.	
1974	74C prefix before Ser. No.	
1975	75C prefix before Ser. No.	
1976	76C prefix before Ser. No.	
1977 to date	New style serialization	

BROWNING .380

1955 - 1964	No records exist	
1965	500000	598804
1966	598805	603890
1967	603891	619474
1968	619475	N/A
1969 - 1970	Discontinued due to GCA of 1968. New model has longer barrel, adj. rear sight, modified grip.	
1971	71N prefix before Ser. No.	
1972	72N prefix before Ser. No.	
1973	73N prefix before Ser. No.	
1974	74N prefix before Ser. No.	
1975	75N prefix before Ser. No.	

.25 CAL. BABY BROWNING PISTOL

Year	Serial Number Beginning of Year	Serial Number at End of Year
1955 - 1958	Records not available	
1959	181000	206349
1960	206350	230999
1961	231000	250999
1962	251000	278999
1963	279000	286099
1964	286100	308499
1965	308500	329999
1966	333000	367443
1967	367444	412999
1968	413000	479000
1969	Discontinued because of GCA of 1968	

.22 CAL. PISTOLS
(Nomad-Challenger-Medalist)

One or two digit suffix after single capital letter. "P" designates Nomad, "U" designates Challenger model, "T" designates Medalist model. "P5" suffix would indicate a Nomad built in 1965. "U71" suffix would indicate a Challenger built in 1971. Nomad models were manufactured from 1962 to 1973. Challenger and Medalist models were produced from 1962 to 1974.

BOLT ACTION RIFLES
(Safari, Medallion, & Olympian Models)

1959 - 1962	No prefix (numeral-letter) before Ser. No. (i.e., only digits)	
1963	3-single letter prefix or suffix by Ser. No.	
1964	4-single letter prefix or suffix by Ser. No.	
1965	5-single letter prefix or suffix by Ser. No.	
1966	6-single letter prefix or suffix by Ser. No.	
1967	7-single letter prefix or suffix by Ser. No.	
1968	8-single letter prefix or suffix by Ser. No.	
1969	Single letter (Y, Z, or L) followed by last 2 digits of year of mfg. Prefix only.	
1970	"Y70" prefix	
1971	"L71" prefix	
1972	"Z72" prefix	
1973	"Y73" prefix	
1974	"Z74" prefix	
1975	"L75" prefix	

B.A.R.

1967	"M7" suffix after Ser. No.	
1968	"M8" suffix after Ser. No.	
1969	"M69" suffix after Ser. No.	
1970	"M70" suffix after Ser. No.	
1971	"M71" suffix after Ser. No.	

Year	Serial Number Beginning of Year	Serial Number at End of Year
1972	"M72" suffix after Ser. No.	
1973	"M73" suffix after Ser. No.	
1974	"M74" suffix after Ser. No.	
1975	"M75" suffix after Ser. No.	
1976	"M76" suffix after Ser. No.	
1977 to date	New sequence with "RT" appearing in middle of Ser. No.	

.22 AUTO RIFLE (Grades I, II, and III)

Year	Serial Number Beginning of Year	Serial Number at End of Year
1956 - 1964	Numeric only - 5 digits or less	
1965	"5T" or "5E" prefix before Ser. No.	
1966	"6T" or "6E" prefix before Ser. No.	
1967	"7T" or "7E" prefix before Ser. No.	
1968	"8T" or "8E" prefix before Ser. No.	
1969	"69T" or "69E" prefix before Ser. No.	

Year	Serial Number Beginning of Year	Serial Number at End of Year1970
1970	"70T" or "70E" prefix before Ser. No.	
1971	"71T" or "71E" prefix before Ser. No.	
1972	"72T" or "72E" prefix before Ser. No.	
1973	Japan production	

T-BOLT RIFLE (T1 and T2)

Year	Serial	
1965	"X5" suffix after Ser. No.	
1966	"X6" suffix after Ser. No.	
1967	"X7" suffix after Ser. No.	
1968	"X8" suffix after Ser. No.	
1969	"X69" suffix after Ser. No.	
1970	"X70" suffix after Ser. No.	
1971	"X71" suffix after Ser. No.	
1972	"X72" suffix after Ser. No.	
1973	"X73" suffix after Ser. No.	
1974	"X74" suffix after Ser. No.	
1975	"X75" suffix after Ser. No.	

COLT'S FIREARMS

MODEL 1849 POCKET REVOLVER

Year	Serial Number Beginning of Year	Serial Number at End of Year	Total Guns Produced in Year
1849	1	11999	11,999
1850	12000	15999	3,999
1851	16000	24999	8,999
1852	25000	54999	29,999
1853	55000	84999	29,999
1854	85000	99999	14,999
1855	100000	109999	9,999
1856	110000	129999	19,999
1857	130000	139999	9,999
1858	140000	149999	9,999
1859	150000	159999	9,999
1860	160000	183999	23,999
1861	184000	196999	12,999
1862	197000	222999	25,999
1863	223000	249999	26,999
1864	250000	269999	16,999
1865	270000	279999	9,999
1866	280000	289999	9,999
1867	290000	299999	9,999
1868	300000	309999	9,999
1869	310000	319999	9,999
1870	320000	324999	4,999
1871	325000	329999	4,999
1872	330000	330999	999
1873	331000	340000	9,000

MODEL 1849 POCKET REVOLVER - LONDON BARREL ADDRESS

Year	Serial Number Beginning of Year	Serial Number at End of Year	Total Guns Produced in Year
1853	1	999	999
1854	1000	4999	3999
1855	5000	8999	3999
1856	9000	11000	2000

MODEL 1851 NAVY

Year	Serial Number Beginning of Year	Serial Number at End of Year	Total Guns Produced in Year
1850	1	2499	2499
1851	2500	9999	7499
1852	10000	19999	9999
1853	20000	34999	14,999
1854	35000	39999	4,999
1855	40000	44999	4,999
1856	45000	64999	19,999
1857	65000	84999	19,999
1858	85000	89999	4,999
1859	90000	92999	2,999
1860	93000	97999	4,999
1861	98000	117999	19,999
1862	118000	131999	13,999
1863	132000	174999	42,999
1864	175000	179999	4,999
1865	180000	184999	4,999
1866	185000	200000	14,999
1867	200000	203999	3,999
1868	204000	206999	2,999
1869	207000	209999	2,999
1870	210000	211999	1,999
1871	212000	213999	1,999
1872	214000	214999	999
1873	215000	215348	348

MODEL 1851 NAVY - LONDON BARREL ADDRESS

Year	Serial Number Beginning of Year	Serial Number at End of Year	Total Guns Produced in Year
1853	1	3999	3,999
1854	4000	14999	10,999
1855	15000	40999	25,999
1856	41000	42000	1,000

MODEL 1860 ARMY

Year	Serial Number Beginning of Year	Serial Number at End of Year	Total Guns Produced in Year
1860	1	1999	1,999
1861	2000	24999	22,999
1862	25000	84999	59,999
1863	85000	149999	64,999
1864	150000	152999	2,999
1865	153000	155999	2,999
1866	156000	161999	5,999
1867	162000	169999	7,999
1868	170000	176999	6,999
1869	177000	184999	7,999
1870	185000	189999	4,999
1871	190000	197999	7,999
1872	198000	198999	999
1873	199000	200500	1,500

MODEL 1861 NAVY

Year	Serial Number Beginning of Year	Serial Number at End of Year	Total Guns Produced in Year
1861	1	4599	4999
1862	4600	9999	53999
1863	1000	16999	6999
1864	17000	24999	7999
1865	25000	27999	2999
1866	28000	29999	1999
1867	30000	30999	999
1868	31000	32999	1,999
1869	33000	33999	999
1870	34000	34999	999
1871	35000	35999	999
1872	36000	36999	999
1873	37000	38843	1,843

MODEL 1862 POLICE

Year	Serial Number Beginning of Year	Serial Number at End of Year	Total Guns Produced in Year
1861	1	8499	84,999
1862	8500	14999	64,999
1863	15000	25999	10,999
1864	26000	28999	2,999
1865	29000	31999	2,999
1866	32000	34999	2,999
1867	35000	36999	1,999
1868	37000	39999	2,999
1869	40000	41999	1,999
1870	42000	43999	1,999
1871	44000	44999	999
1872	45000	45999	999
1873	46000	47000	1,000

MODEL 1873 - SINGLE ACTION ARMY (SAA) - PRE-WAR

Year	Caliber	Serial Number Beginning in Year
1873	.45 Colt Caliber, Standard	1
1874		200
1875	.44 Rimfire series (own serials, 1-1863 made through 1880)	1500
1876	.476 Eley introduced	22000
1877		
1878	.44-40 introduced in quantity	41000
1879		49000
1880		53000
1881		62000
1882	Sheriff's model introduced	73000
1883	.22 rimfire introduced	85000

Year	Caliber	Serial Number Beginning in Year
1884	.32-20 and .38-40 introduced	102000
1885	.41 Colt introduced	114000
1886	.38 Colt introduced	117000
1887	.32 Colt and .32 S&W introduced	119000
1888	Flattop Target S.A.A. began; no. 126530	125000
1889	.32 rimfire; ,32-44 S&W, .38 S&W; and .44 Russian introduced	128000
1890	.44 Smoothbore; .380 and .450 Eley; and .44 S&W introduced	130000
1891	.38-44 introduced	136000
1892	Transverse cylinder latch introduced, screw lock at front of frame dropped	144000
1893		
1894	Beginning of Bisley models	154000
1895		159000
1896		163000
1897		168000
1898		175000
1899		182000
1900	Revolvers built to handle smokeless powder	192000
1901		203000
1902		220000
1903		238000
1904		250000
1905		261000
1906		273000
1907		288000
1908		304000
1909		308000
1910		312000
1911		316000
1912	Discontinue Bisley model	321000
1913	.44 Russian and S&W Special introduced	325000
1914		328000
1915	Long flute cylinders; range no. 330001 to 331480	329500
1916		332000
1917		335000
1918		337000
1919		337200
1920		338000
1921		341000
1922		343000
1923		344500
1924	.45 ACP 33000 introduced, requiring special cylinders	346400
1925		347300
1926		348200
1927		349800
1928		351300
1929		352400

Year	Caliber	Serial Number Beginning in Year
1930	.38 Special introduced	353800
1931		354100
1932		354500
1933		354800
1934		355000
1935	.357 Magnum introduced	355200
1936		355300
1937		355400
1938		356100
1939		356600
1940	A few S.A.A. during and just after the war	357000 thru 357859

COLT SINGLE ACTION ARMY - POST-WAR PRODUCTION
"SA" suffix from 1956 to 1978, "SA" prefix 1978 to 1981

Year	Serial Number Beginning of Year	Serial Number at End of Year
1956	0001SA	8799SA
1957	8800SA	18499SA
1958	18500SA	23399SA
1959	23400SA	28499SA
1960	28500SA	33599SA
1961	33600SA	35649SA
1962	35650SA	37299SA
1963	37300SA	38499SA
1964	38500SA	39999SA
1965	40000SA	41499SA
1966	41500SA	43799SA
1967	43800SA	46299SA
1968	46300SA	48999SA
1969	49000SA	52599SA
1970	52600SA	59399SA
1971	59400SA	61699SA
1972	61700SA	64399SA
1973	64400SA	69399SA
1974	69400SA	73319SA
1975	NONE PRODUCED	
1976	80000SA	82000SA
	(start of 3rd generation of production)	
1977	82001SA	95999SA
1978	96000SA	99999SA
1978	Start of "SA" prefix on front of Ser. No.	
Mid-1978	SA01000	SA12999
1979	SA13000	
	Discontinuance in 1981	

NEW FRONTIER SINGLE ACTION ARMY

Year	Serial Number Beginning of Year	Serial Number at End of Year
1961	3000NF	3005NF
1962	3006NF	3849NF
1963	4325NF	4699NF
1964	4700NF	4974NF
1965	4975NF	5399NF
1966	5400NF	5674NF
1967	5675NF	5699NF
1968	5700NF	
1969	5701NF	5924NF
1970	5925NF	6874NF
1971	6875NF	7049NF
1972	7050NF	7074NF
1973	7075NF	7174NF
1974	7175NF	7264NF
1975	7265NF	7288NF
1978	7501NF	
	discontinuance in 1981	

COLT SINGLE ACTION ARMY - CALIBER BREAKDOWN

Caliber	S.A.A	Flattop Target	Bisley	Bisley Target
.22 Rimfire	107	93	0	0
.32 Rimfire	1	0	0	0
.32 Colt	192	24	160	44
.32 S&W	32	30	18	17
.32-44	2	9	14	17
.32-20	29,812	30	13,291	131
.38 Colt (through 1914)	1,011	122	412	96
.38 Colt (post-1922)	1,365	0	0	0
.38 S&W	9	39	10	5
.38 Colt Special	82	7	0	0
.38 S&W Special	25	0	2	0
.38-44	2	11	6	47
.357 Magnum	525	0	0	0
.380 Eley	1	3	0	0
.38-40	38,240	19	12,163	98
.41	16,402	91	3,159	24
.44 Smoothbore	15	0	1	0
.44 Rimfire	1,863	0	0	0
.44 German	59	0	0	0
.44 Russian	154	51	90	62
.44 S&W	24	51	29	64
.44 S&W Special	506	1	0	0
.44-40	64,489	21	6,803	78
.45	150,683	100	8,005	97
.45 Smoothbore	4	0	2	0
.45 ACP	44	0	0	0
.450 Boxer	729	89	0	0
.450 Eley	2,697	84	5	0
.455 Eley	1,150	37	180	196
.476 Eley	161	2	0	0
Total Quantities	310,386	914	44,350	976

MODEL 1911 AND 1911A1 -
Commercial production - Capital "C" prefix - .45 cal.

Year	Serial Number Beginning of Year	Serial Number at End of Year
1912	C1	C1899
1913	C1900	C5399
1914	C5400	C16599
1915	C16600	C27599
1916	C27600	C74999
1917	C75000	C98999

Year	Serial Number Beginning of Year	Serial Number at End of Year
1918	C99000	C105999
1919	C106000	C120999
1920	C120000	C126999
1921	C127000	C128999
1922	C129000	C133999
1923	C134000	C144999
1924	C135000	C150999
1925	C140000	C154999
1926	C145000	C155999
1927	C151000	C158999
1928	C152000	C154999
1929	C155000	C155999
1930	C156000	C158999
1931	C159000	C160999
1932	C161000	C164799
1933	C164800	C174599
1934	C174600	C177999
1935	C178000	C179799
1936	C179800	C183199
1937	C183200	C188699
1938	C188700	C189599
1939	C189600	C198899
1940	C198900	C199299
1941	C199300	C208799
1942	C208800	C215018
1943-1945:	Commercial production interrupted by WWII	
1946	C221001	C222000
1947	C222001	C231999
1948	C232000	C238500
1949	C238501	C240000
1950	C240000	247701C
	"C" SUFFIX STARTED WITH SER. NO. 240228	
1951	247701C	253179C
1952	253180C	259549C
1953	259550C	266349C
1954	266350C	270549C
1955	270550C	272549C
1956	272550C	276699C
1957	276700C	281999C
1958	282000C	283799C
1959	283800C	285799C
1960	285800C	287999C
1961	288000C	289849C
1962	289850C	291299C
1963	291300C	293799C
1964	293800C	295999C
1965	296000C	300299C
1966	300300C	308499C
1967	308500C	315599C
1968	315600C	324499C
1969	324500C	332649C
1970	332650C	336169C
New Range	70G01001	70G05550
1971	70G05551	70G18000
1972	70G18001	70G34400
1973	70G34401	70G43000
1974	70G43001	70G73000
1975	70G73001	70G88900
1976	70G88901	70G99999
New Range	01001G70	13900G70
1977	13901G70	45199G70
1978 TO DATE	45200G70	

MODEL 1911 AND 1911A1 MILITARY PRODUCTION

Year	Serial Number Beginning of Year	Serial Number at End of Year	Manufacturer
1912	1	500	COLT
	501	1000	COLT USN
	1001	1500	COLT
	1501	2000	COLT USN
	2001	2500	COLT
	2501	3500	COLT USN
	3501	3800	COLT USMC
	3801	4500	COLT
	4501	5500	COLT USN
	5501	6500	COLT
	6501	7500	COLT USN
	7501	8500	COLT
	8501	9500	COLT USN
	9501	10500	COLT
	10501	11500	COLT USN
	11501	12500	COLT
	12501	13500	COLT USN
	13501	17250	COLT USN
1913	17251	36400	COLT
	36401	37650	COLT USMC
	37651	38000	COLT
	38001	44000	COLT USN
	44001	60400	COLT
1914	60401	72570	COLT
	72571	83855	SPRINGFIELD -(THESE NUMBERS RESERVED SPRINGFIELD)
	83856	83900	COLT
	83901	84400	COLT USMC
	84401	96000	COLT
	96001	97537	COLT
	97538	102596	SPRINGFIELD -RESERVED FOR SPRINGFIELD
1915	107597	109500	COLT
	109501	110000	COLT USN
	110001	113496	COLT
	113497	120566	SPRINGFIELD -(RESERVED FOR SPRINGFIELD)
	120567	125566	COLT
	125567	133186	SPRINGFIELD -(RESERVED FOR SPRINGFIELD)
1916	133187	137400	COLT
1917	137401	151186	COLT
	151187	151986	COLT USMC
	151987	185800	COLT
	185801	186200	COLT USMC
	186201	209586	COLT
	209587	210386	COLT USMC

Year	Serial Number Beginning of Year	Serial Number at End of Year	Manu-facturer		Year	Serial Number Beginning of Year	Serial Number at End of Year	Manu-facturer
	210387	215386	COLT FRAMES (RESERVED FOR RECEIVERS)		1943	801001	958100	COLT
						958101	1088725	US&S
	215387	216186	COLT USMC			1088726	1208673	COLT
	216187	216586	COLT			1208674	1279673	ITHACA
	216587	216986	COLT USMC			1279674	1279698	RE NO AA
1918	216987	217386	COLT USMC			1279699	1441430	REMINGTON RAND
	217387	232000	COLT			1441431	1471430	ITHACA
	232001	233600	COLT USN			1471431	1609528	REMINGTON RAND
	233601	594000	COLT		1944	1609529	1743846	COLT
	1	13152	REM UMC			1743847	1890503	ITHACA
1919	13153	21676	REM UMC			1890504	2075103	REMINGTON RAND
	594001	629500	COLT		1945	2075104	2134403	ITHACA
	629501	700000	UNKNOWN			2134404	2244803	REMINGTON RAND
1924	700001	710000	COLT					
1937	710001	712349	COLT			2244804	2380013	COLT
1938	712350	713645	COLT			2380014	2619013	REMINGTON RAND
1939	713646	717281	COLT USN			2619014	2693613	ITHACA
1940	717282	721977	COLT					
1941	721978	756733	COLT					
1942	756734	800000	COLT					
	S800001	S800500	SINGER					
	800501	801000	THESE NUMBERS ASSIGNED TO H&R					

COLT SINGLE-ACTION MODEL NUMBERS

The author wishes to express thanks to Mr. Don Wilkerson for allowing the edited information published below from his 1986 **Post-War Single-Action Revolver, 1976-1986** publication.

A working knowledge of model numbers for the various Colt single-action revolvers is a must for even a novice collector. Since the mid-1970s Colt has placed the model number on the end label of the shipping cartons of virtually all their firearms. Many collectors and publications regularly use the model number to describe or differentiate between revolvers. Using the model number is an accurate and efficient method to dileneate a particular variation. Example: .45 caliber revolver with a $4^3/_4$ in. barrel, blue and casehardened finish and eagle stocks can be described as a simple "P-1840".

Each Colt model is specified by an alphabetical letter and 4 numerical digits. The basic model number as it pertains to single-action revolvers can be broken down as follows:

MODEL P — basic type of frame. The letter "P" is used to dileneate the single-action type of frame.

FIRST NUMERAL — "1" is the first model built on a particular type of frame. Numerals 2, 3, 4, etc. indicate later versions. These versions are not always numbered in numerical order and the same number has been used for different models at different times. A "1" denotes the basic standard single-action frame. A "2" denotes the new black powder frame available through the Colt Custom Gun Shop. A "3" has been used at various times to denote a non-standard frame or cylinder. The "4" is used to specify the New Frontier style of frame. Numbers such as "7" and "8" are frequently used to specify commemorative or special editions.

SECOND NUMERAL — specifies caliber. A "4" denotes .32-20, a "6" denotes .357 Magnum, a "7" denotes .44 Special, an "8" denotes .45 caliber, and a "9" specifies .44-40 caliber.*

THIRD NUMERAL — denotes barrel length. "3" is used to denote both a 3 inch and a 4 inch barrel. "4" is $4^3/_4$ inch or 5 inch, "5" is $5^1/_2$ inch, "7" is $7^1/_2$ inch, and "1" is 12 inch.*

FOURTH NUMERAL — is used to denote several different variations of the standard model. Some of the most common examples are: "1", "2", or "6" for nickel finish, "1" for full blue finish in the case of P-1871, and "2", "3", and "4" as used for the Sheriff's Model series to denote blue and casehardened finish, nickel finish, and Royal Blue and casehardened finish, respectively. The fourth numeral can also denote the type of stocks as in P-1673. The fourth numeral in the basic model designation must be used in conjunction with the preceding three numerals to determine its exact meaning. The fourth numeral is kind of a "catch-all" number. Many times this number serves only to differentiate a later model from a similar model assembled years earlier.

*The .32-20 caliber and the 5 inch barrel length are listed in the 1984 *Colt Buyer's Guide*, but as of this date (early 1986) neither have been produced.

STANDARD MODEL P REVOLVER

The primary model numbers used by Colt for Model P revolvers produced since 1976 are as follows:

P-1640 - .357 Magnum, 4¾ in. barrel, blue finish, eagle stocks.

P-1641 - .357 Magnum, 4¾ in. barrel, nickel finish, wood stocks.

P-1650 - .357 Magnum, 5½ in. barrel, blue finish, eagle stocks.

P-1656 - .357 Magnum, 5½ in. barrel, nickel finish, wood stocks.

P-1670 - .357 Magnum, 7½ in. barrel, blue finish, eagle stocks.

P-1673 - .357 Magnum, 7½ in. barrel, blue finish, wood stocks.

P-1676 - .357 Magnum, 7½ in. barrel, nickel finish, wood stocks.

P-1740 - .44 Special, 4¾ in. barrel, blue finish, eagle stocks.

P-1746 - .44 Special, 4¾ in. barrel, nickel finish, wood stocks.

P-1750 - .44 Special, 5½ in. barrel, blue finish, eagle stocks.

P-1756 - .44 Special, 5½ in. barrel, nickel finish, wood stocks.

P-1770 - .44 Special, 7½ in. barrel, blue finish, eagle stocks.

P-1776 - .44 Special, 7½ in. barrel, nickel finish, wood stocks.

P-1716 - .44 Special, 12 in. barrel, nickel finish, wood stocks.

P-1840 - .45 Colt, 4¾ in. barrel, blue finish, eagle stocks.

P-1841 - .45 Colt, 4¾ in. barrel, nickel finish, wood stocks.

P-1850 - .45 Colt, 5½ in. barrel, blue finish, eagle stocks.

P-1856 - .45 Colt, 5½ in. barrel, nickel finish, wood stocks.

P-1870 - .45 Colt, 7½ in. barrel, blue finish, eagle stocks.

P-1876 - .45 Colt, 7½ in. barrel, nickel finish, wood stocks.

P-1813 - .45 Colt, 12 in. barrel, blue finish, eagle stocks.

P-1816 - .45 Colt, 12 in. barrel, nickel finish, wood stocks.

P-1940 - .44-40 caliber, 4¾ in. barrel, blue finish, eagle stocks.

P-1941* - .44-40 caliber, 4¾ in. barrel, nickel finish, wood stocks.

P-1950 - .44-40 caliber, 5½ in. barrel, blue finish, eagle stocks.

P-1970 - .44-40 caliber, 7½ in. barrel, blue finish, eagle stocks.

P-1976* - .44-40 caliber, 7½ in. barrel, nickel finish, wood stocks.

P-1911 - .44-40 caliber, 12 in. barrel, nickel finish, wood stocks.

*These model numbers were used primarily for engraved or special ordered revolvers as the two models indicated were never produced as a regular model. "Blue finish" in the above chart denotes the standard blue finish, i.e., blue with casehardened frame.

NEW FRONTIER MODEL

P-4671 - .357 Magnum, 7½ in. barrel, nickel finish, wood stocks.

P-4750 - .44 Special, 5½ in. barrel, Royal Blue finish, wood stocks.

P-4770 - .44 Special, 7½ in. barrel, Royal Blue finish, wood stocks.

P-4840 - .45 Colt, 4¾ in. barrel, Royal Blue finish, wood stocks.

P-4850 - .45 Colt, 5½ in. barrel, Royal Blue finish, wood stocks.

P-4870 - .45 Colt, 7½ in. barrel, Royal Blue finish, wood stocks.

P-4940 - .44-40 caliber, 4¾ in. barrel, Royal Blue finish, wood stocks.

P-4970 - .44-40 caliber, 7½ in. barrel, Royal Blue finish, wood stocks.

Note: The term "Royal Blue" in the New Frontier chart denotes a revolver with a casehardened frame and a Royal (high polish) Blue finish on the other major components.

SHERIFF'S MODELS

P-1932 - .44-40 caliber, 3 in. barrel, blue finish, eagle stocks.

P-1933* - .44-40/.44 Special, 3 in. barrel, nickel finish, wood stocks.

P-1934* - .44-40/.44 Special, 3 in. barrel, Royal Blue finish, wood stocks.

*Circa 1984 all Sheriff's Models are listed as single calibers: .44-40 or .45 caliber.

REVOLVERS WITH FULL BLUE FRAMES

Some of the "full blue" models have had more than one model number assigned to the same variation. As a result, a particular model may have been identified by different model numbers at different times. Following the model numbers and descriptions in this chart will be an approximate time frame during which that particular model was in use. No date following the description indicates that only one model number for that particular variation is known to the author (Don Wilkerson).

P-1640 - FB - .357 Magnum, 4¾ in. barrel, fluted cylinder, eagle stocks.

P-1650 - FB - .357 Magnum, 5½ in. barrel, fluted cylinder, eagle stocks.

P-1740 - FB - .44 Special, 4¾ in. barrel, fluted cylinder, eagle stocks.

P-1750 - FB - .44 Special, 5½ in. barrel, fluted cylinder, eagle stocks.

P-1770 - FB - .44 Special, 7½ in. barrel, fluted cylinder, eagle stocks.

P-1770 - UB - .44 Special, 7½ in. barrel, unfluted cylinder, eagle stocks.

P-3840 - .45 Colt, 4¾ in. barrel, both fluted and unfluted cylinders, eagle stocks (early to mid-1982).

P-1840 - FB - .45 Colt, 4¾ in. barrel, fluted cylinder, eagle stocks (mid to late 1982 to date).

P-1840 - UB - .45 Colt, 4¾ in. barrel, unfluted cylinder, eagle stocks (mid to late 1982 to date).

P-1850 - FB - .45 Colt, 5½ in. barrel, fluted cylinder, eagle stocks.

P-1850 - UB - .45 Colt, 5½ in. barrel, unfluted cylinder, eagle stocks.

P-1871 - .45 Colt, 7½ in. barrel, fluted cylinder, wood stocks (1977 to 1979).

P-1870 - FB - .45 Colt, 7½ in. barrel, fluted cylinder, wood stocks (1982 to date).

P-1870 - UB - .45 Colt, 7½ in. barrel, unfluted cylinder, wood stocks (1982 to date).

P-1871 - FB - .45 Colt, 12 in. barrel, fluted cylinder, eagle stocks.

FULL BLUE NEW FRONTIERS

P-4770 - FB - .44 Special, 7½ in. barrel, fluted cylinder, wood stocks.

P-4870 - FB - .45 Colt, 7½ in. barrel, fluted cylinder, wood stocks.

P-4870 - UB - .45 Colt, 7½ in. barrel, unfluted cylinder, wood stocks.

MISCELLANEOUS MODEL NUMBERS

1750 - AA - .44 Special, 5½ in. barrel, blue finish with nickel cylinder, eagle stocks.

1750 - AB - .44 Special, 5½ in. barrel, blue finish with nickel cylinder with blue flutes, eagle stocks.

1840 - UC - .45 Colt, 4¾ in. barrel, blue finish, unfluted cylinder, eagle stocks.

1850 - UC - .45 Colt, 5½ in. barrel, blue finish, unfluted cylinder, eagle stocks.

1870 - UC - .45 Colt, 7½ in. barrel, blue finish, unfluted cylinder, eagle stocks.

Note: The term "blue finish" in this chart is the standard blue finish with a casehardened frame.

BLACK POWDER MODEL P REVOLVERS

P-2830 - .45 Colt, 3 in. barrel, blue finish.

P-2833 - .45 Colt, 3 in. barrel, nickel finish.

P-2834* - .45 Colt, 3 in. barrel, Royal Blue finish.

P-2836 - .45 Colt, 4 in. barrel, Royal Blue finish.

P-2837 - .45 Colt, 4 in. barrel, nickel finish.

P-2840 - .45 Colt, 4¾ in. barrel, blue finish.

P-2841 - .45 Colt, 4¾ in. barrel, nickel finish.

P-2847* - .45 Colt, 5 in. barrel, nickel finish.

P-2870 - .45 Colt, 7½ in. barrel, blue finish.

P-2871 - .45 Colt, 7½ in. barrel, nickel finish.

P-2940 - .44-40 caliber, 4¾ in. barrel, blue finish.

P-2941 - .44-40 caliber, 4¾ in. barrel, nickel finish.

P-2970 - .44-40 caliber, 7½ in. barrel, blue finish.

P-2971 - .44-40 caliber, 7½ in. barrel, nickel finish.

P-2437* - .32-20 caliber, 4 in. barrel, nickel finish.

P-2474* - .32-20 caliber, 7½ in. barrel, Royal Blue finish.

*As of this writing (early 1986) these calibers have not been produced. The terms "blue finish" and "Royal" in this chart refer to Colt's standard single-action finish, i.e., casehardened frame with all components finished in either standard blue or Royal Blue.

COLT BLACKPOWDER
2ND GENERATION SERIALIZATION

Model No.	Serial # Range		Total Prod.	Prod. Began	Prod. Ended
MODEL 1851 NAVY					
C-1121	4201	25100	20900	1971	1978
C-1122	As above but at higher range of numbers				
	Unk'n				1978
MODEL 1851 NAVY, R. E. LEE					
C-9001	251 REL	5000 REL	4750	—	1971
MODEL 1851 NAVY, U. S. GRANT					
C-9002	251 USG	5000 USG	4750	—	1971
MODEL 1851 GRANT-LEE PAIR					
C-9003	01 GLP	250 GLP	250	—	1971
3rd MODEL DRAGOON					
C-1770	20801	208	25	1974	1978
	Prototype				
	20901	24501	3601		
C-1770MN	S/N's As Above		20	1984	1984
MODEL 1851 NAVY					
F-1100	24900	29150	4250	5/80	10/81

Model No.	Serial # Range	Total Prod.	Prod. Began	Prod. Ended
F-1101	S/N's As Above	300	10/81	11/81
	W/Blank Cylinders			
F-1110	29151s 29640s	489	6/82	10/82
	Stainless Steel			
MODEL 1860 ARMY				
F-1200	201000 212835	7593	11/78	11/82
	Rebated Cylinder			
F-1200 EBO	S/N's As Above	500	1979	1979
	Butterfield			
F-1200 LNK	S/N's As Above	Unk'n	Unk'n	Unk'n
	Electroless Nickel			
F-1200MN	S/N's As Above	12	1984	1984
	Nickel/Ivory			
F-1202	S/N's As Above	500	1979	1979
	Limited Edition			
F-1203	207330 211250	2670	7/80	10/81
	Fluted Cylinder			
F-1210	211263s 212540s	1278	1/82	4/82
	Stainless Steel			
1861 NAVY				
F-1300	40000 43165	3166	9/80	10/81
1862 POCKET NAVY				
F-1400	48000 58850	5765	12/79	11/81
	and skip odd no's.			
F-1400MN	S/N's As Above	25	1984	1984
	Nickel/Ivory			
F-1401	S/N's As Above	500	1979	1980
	Limited Edition			

Model No.	Serial # Range	Total Prod.	Prod. Began	Prod. Ended
1862 POCKET POLICE				
F-1500	49000 57300	4801	1/80	9/81
	and skip even no's.			
F-1500MN	S/N's As Above	25	1984	1984
	Nickel/Ivory			
F-1501	S/N's As Above	500	1979	1980
	Limited Edition			
1847 WALKER				
F-1600	1200 4120	2573	6/80	4/82
	32256 32500	245	5/81	9/81
1st MODEL DRAGOON				
F-1700	25100 34500	3878	1/80	2/82
2nd MODEL DRAGOON				
F-172	S/N's As Above and Mix at Random for			
	1st, 2nd & 3rd 2676		1/80	2/82
3rd MODEL DRAGOON				
F-140	S/N's As Above and Mix at Random for			
	1st, 2nd & 3rd 2856		1/80	2/82
	31401 31450	50	10/81	11/81
F-1740EGA	Unk'n Unk'n	200	1982	1982
	(Garabaldi Model– "GCA" prefix)			
BABY DRAGOON				
F-1760	16000 17851	1852	2/81	4/81
F-1761	S/N's As Above	500	1979	1980
	Limited Edition			
1860 ARMY				
F-9005	US 001/001 US to			
	US 3025/3025 US	3025	9/77	1/80
	Cavalry Commemorative (Two Gun Set)			
HERITAGE WALKER				
F-9006	01 1853	1853	6/80	6/81

HIGH STANDARD SERIAL NUMBERS

Year Starting	Serial Number	Year Starting	Serial Number	Year Starting	Serial Number
1932	5,000	1941	70,600	1950	325,000
1933	5,050	1942	92,600	1951	330,000
1934	6,500	1943	103,600	1952	355,000
1935	8,300	1944	115,000	1953	400,000
1936	11,500	1945	134,700	1954	440,000
1937	18,500	1946	145,800	1955	480,000
1938	29,600	1947	174,200	1956	550,000
1939	39,200	1948	235,000	1957	640,000
1940	50,500	1949	299,000		

HIGH STANDARD AUTOMATIC PISTOL
1958- 1984

Year Starting	Serial Number	Year Starting	Serial Number
1958	8192XX	1969	21609XX
1959	9854XX	1970	21971XX
1962	12606XX	1971	22662XX
1963	12954XX	1972	22874XX
1965	14204XX	1972	23337XX
1965	15709XX	1973	23639XX
1966	16078XX	1973	24140XX
1967	17509XX	1974	24337XX
1967	18141XX	1975	ML15XXX
1968	18891XX	1976	ML19XXX
1968	19909XX	1977	ML23XXX
1969	20485XX	Feb.1981	ML71000

Year Starting	Serial Number	Year Starting	Serial Number
Apr.1981	ML84000	Feb. 1983	SH19000
May 1981	ML85000	Apr. 1983	SH21000
June 1981	ML86000	May 1983	SH23000
June 1981	SH10000	Oct. 1983	SH24000
Sept.1982	SH14000	Feb. 1984	SH25000
Oct. 1982	SH15000	Apr. 1984	SH26000
Nov. 1982	SH16000	May 1984	SH27000
Dec. 1982	SH17000	June 1984	SH29000
Jan. 1983	SH18000	Sept 1984	SH34000

MAUSER BROOMHANDLES
produced from 1896 to late '30's

Serial # Range	Date	Nature of Changes
before #25	1896	— The cone hammer used in place of spur hammer.
#50	1896	— "SYSTEM MAUSER" marked on top of the chamber.
before #200	1897	— The locking system changed from one to two lugs.
		— The barrel contour at the chamber is tapered instead of stepped.
#390	1897	— "WAFFENFABRIK MAUSER OBERNDORF A/N" marked on top of the chamber.
#975	1897	— The center section of the rear panel on the left side of the frame is not milled out (this feature appears earlier on a few 20-shot pistols). This area is sometimes used for special markings on contract pieces such as the Turkish and Persian.
#12,200 to #14,999	1898	— The large ring hammer replaces the cone hammer.
#21,000	1899	— There is no panel milling on either side of the frame.
		— A single lug bayonet type mount adopted for retaining the firing pin instead of the dovetail plate.
		— The trigger is mounted directly to the frame by two integral lugs rather than attached to a removable block.
		— The position of the serial number moved from the rear of the frame above the stock slot to the left side of the chamber.
#22,000	1900	— Two integral lugs used to mount the rear sight instead of a pin.
#29,000	1902	— Very shallow panels milled into the frame on both sides.*
#31,200	1903	— "WAFFENFABRIK MAUSER OBERNDORF A NECKAR" added to the right rear frame panel.*
#34,000	1904	— The depth of the frame panel milling increased.*
#35,000	1904	— The barrel extension side rails lengthened about a half inch.*
		— An additional lug for mounting the firing pin added.*
		— The hammer changed to the small ring pattern.*
		— The safety mechanism altered to require that the lever be pushed up to engaged it instead of down.*
		— The center of the safety lever knob is no longer milled out.*
#38,000	1905	— The short extractor with two ribs replaces the long thin extractor.*
#100,000	1910 to	— The rifling changed from four groove to six groove.
#130,000	1911	
#270,000	1915	— "NS" (Neues Sicherung or New Safety) appears on the back of the hammer. The hammer must be moved back beyond the cocked position to engage the safety.
#440,000	1921	— The lanyard ring stud is rotated 90 degrees.
#501,000	1923	— The Mauser "banner" appears on the left rear frame panel.
#800,000	1930	— The Mauser banner is enlarged.
		— A step is added to the barrel contour just ahead of the chamber.
		— The safety is changed to allow the hammer to be dropped from a cocked position, without danger, by pulling the trigger (called Universal Safety).
		— The front of the grip frame widened to equal the rear part where the stock slot is.
#850,000	1932	— "D.R.P.u.A.P." (Deutsches Reich Pattenten und Anderes Patenten) added below the inscription on the right rear frame panel.
#860,000	1932	— The lettering in the frame inscription is slanted forward.
#900,000	1934	— The serial number is moved to the rear of the barrel extension behind the sight.
		— The two grooves in each side of the barrel extension side rails are eliminated.

*These nine changes appear out of sequence (either early or late) on three small batches of guns (29,000 to 29,900, 40,000 to 41,000, and 42,600 to 43,900). Most of these pistols are of the "bolo" style, that is they have 3.9 inch barrels, small grips, six or 10-shot magazines and fixed or adjustable rear sights. A few of these pistols show non-standard barrel contours, barrel extension milling and hammer safety devices. Apparently the factory withheld these numbers from the regular production series and reissued them at later dates.

PARKER SHOTGUNS

Date	Number Serial	Date	Number Serial
1866-1868	0-6,800	1913	165,000
1868-1877	9,700	1914	168,200
1877-1879	15,700	1915	171,500
1880	17,600		*first year of Trojan grade*
1881	22,700	1916	173,450
1882	27,300	1917	175,650
1883	34,900		*first single barrel trap gun*
1884	36,000	1918	180,250
1885	46,450	1919	184,900
1886	48,125	1920	190,100
1887	56,650	1921	195,000
1889	59,500	1922	200,500
1890	61,350		*first Parker single trigger*
1891	66,800	1923	205,150
1892	71,600	1924	207,150
1893	77,000		*first beavertail forend*
1894	80,300	1925	214,400
1895	82,400	1926	218,050
1896	85,200		*first ventilated rib, first .410*
1897	86,450	1927	222,650
1898	89,350	1928	228,200
1899	92,450		*PH grade dropped*
1900	97,300	1929	230,700
1901	105,750	1930	234,200
1902	113,100	1931	235,950
1903	121,900	1932	236,100
1904	129,200	1933	236,300
1905	132,000	1934	236,650
1906	138,300		*first skeet guns,*
1907	144,250		*takeover of factory*
1908	148,250		*by Remington*
1910	153,000	1935	237,000
1911	157,050	1936	239,900
1912	157,800		*last regular catalog*
		1937	240,300
		1938-1942	242,385

REMINGTON
Firearms Serial Number Identification
(Code located on barrel, left side at frame)

Month of Manufacture
(Code letter corresponds to numeral underneath)

B	L	A	C	K	P	O	W	D	E	R	X
1	2	3	4	5	6	7	8	9	10	11	12

Year of Manufacture

1921	M	1932	A	1943	MM	1954	A	1965	M		
1922	N	1933	B	1944	NN	1955	B	1966	N		
1923	P	1934	C	1945	PP	1956	C	1967	P		
1924	R	1935	D	1946	RR	1957	D	1968	R		
1925	S	1936	E	1947	SS	1958	E	1969	S		
1926	T	1937	F	1948	TT	1959	F	1970	T		
1927	U	1938	G	1949	UU	1960	G	1971	U		
1928	W	1939	H	1950	WW	1961	H	1972	W		
1929	X	1940	J	1951	XX	1962	J				
1930	Y	1941	K	1952	YY	1963	K				
1931	Z	1942	L	1953	ZZ	1964	L				

SAVAGE/STEVENS PRODUCTION DATA

The information below represents a listing of most Savage/Stevens rifles and shotguns mfg. in the past (some data has been approximated). Rather than list these models separately, they have been provided in this section for quick reference. Values on many of the models listed below typically range between $ 50 - $175, depending on rarity and condition.

SAVAGE

MODEL	DATES	APPROX. GUNS
1903	1912-20	13,000
1904	1912-32	62,000
1905	1912-15	6,500
1909	1912-15	3,500
1911	1912-15	22,500
1912	1913-15	12,000
1914	1914-26	49,500
19	1933-45	16,000
1920	1920-32	12,000
1922	1922-25	16,000
'23A	1924-45	88,000
'23B	1924-45	16,500
'23C	1924-42	14,500
'23D	1932-45	15,000
3	1931-45	121,000
4	1933-45	38,000
5	1936-45	22,000
6	1938-45	45,500
7	1939-45	6,000
40	1928-42	16,000
45	1928-42	6,000
1925	1925-32	36,000
29	1933-45	23,500
CS22	1926-45	87,500
219	1938-45	12,500
220	1937-45	50,000
420	1937-42	13,500
430	1937-42	11.000
1921	1921-32	13,000
1928	1928-32	6,500
721	1930-32	12,000
FOX	1933-45	31,000
FX B	1940-45	20,000

STEVENS

MODEL	DATES	APPROX. GUNS
No. 12	1912-35	166,500
14-1/2	1912-41	592,500
Fav.	1912-42	462,000
No. 26	1912-45	501,500
44+414	1912-35	23,000
No. 70	1912-31	295,500
No. 71	1930-34	10,000
No. 75	1928-34	19,000
15+425	1912-17	11,500
No. 35	1912-19	12,500
No. 35	1923-42	43,000
41-43	1912-18	18,500
No. 10	1919-34	9,500
85-89	1912-42	38,500
No. 93	1912-19	12,500
No. 97	1912-19	16,000
No. 101	1914-20	5,000
No. 105	1912-45	221,500
No. 107	1912-45	443,500
106-08	1916-35	56,500
No. 115	1912-31	23,000

MODEL	DATES	APPROX. GUNS
No. 125	1912-23	5,000
180-85	1912-23	16,000
No. 958	1925-33	5,000
116-17	1926-35	5,000
946-48	1928-34	7,000
No. 215	1913-32	61,000
No. 235	1912-32	61,500
No. 315	1914-36	192,000
No. 335	1912-31	67,500
No. 345	1916-31	3,500
No. 311	1926-45	145,500
No. 330	1926-35	33,500
No. 335	1926-35	2,000
No. 520	1912-32	191,000
No. 521	1930-32	5,000
60&61	1930-34	6,500
620-21	1926-45	66,500
Mod. 30	1933-34	26,000
Mod. 31	1933-34	2,000
No. 15	1936-45	224,000
No. 11	1923-33	141,500
No. 95	1926-35	55,000
No. 52	1933-37	88,000
No. 55	1935-36	3,500
No. 54	1933-42	23,500
No. 56	1933-45	97,500
No. 57	1939-42	500
No. 58	1933-45	29,500
No. 37	1936-42	29,000
No. 38	1936-45	33,500
No. 39	1938-45	64,000
No. 59	1938-45	21,000
No. 76	1938-45	6,000
65-66	1929-45	174,000
No. 82	1936-37	35,500
No. 83	1936-42	159,000
No. 84	1936-45	99,500
No. 85	1939-43	14,000
No. 86	1936-43	82,500
No. 87	1938-45	200,000
No. 872	1940-42	3,500
NO. 89	1926-37	12,000
No. 94	1926-45	934,000
No. 96	1926-33	3,500
No. 416	1937-42	2,000
No. 417	1932-42	1,000
No. 418	1932-42	1,500
No. 419	1932-36	1,000
No. 237	1936-43	16,000
No. 254	1936-42	1,000
No. 238	1936-45	40,000
No. 258	1936-45	11,000
102-04	1936-42	500
No. 116	1936-42	1,000
No. 944	1936-42	1,500
No. 600	1936-42	5,500
No. 900	1936-42	2,000
No. 515	1936-42	500
No. 5151	1936-42	95,000

MODEL	DATES	APPROX. GUNS		MODEL	DATES	APPROX. GUNS
No. 530	1936-42	8,000		22-410	1939-45	105,000
No. 500	1936-42	500		M.240	1940-45	20,500

THE NINETY-NINE

Serial Numbers At Year End:			Serial Numbers At Year End:	
10,000	1899		256,000	1923
13,400	1900		270,000	1924
19,500	1901		280,000	1925
25,000	1902		292,500	1926
35,000	1903		305,000	1927
45,000	1904		317,000	1928
53,000	1905		324,500	1929
67,500	1906		334,500	1930
73,500	1907		338,500	1931
81,000	1908		341,000	1932
95,000	1909		344,500	1933
110,000	1910		345,800	1934
119,000	1911		350,800	1935
131,000	1912		359,800	1936
146,500	1913		-	1937
162,000	1914		381,351	1938
175,500	1915		388,640	1939
187,500	1916		398,400	1940
193,000	1917		416,000	1941
-	1918		438,000	1946
212,500	1919		464,000	1947
229,000	1920		494,000	1948
237,500	1921		528,000	1949
244,500	1922		566,000	1950

WINCHESTER RIFLES

The following Winchester serial numbers appear courtesy of U.S. Repeating Arms, New Haven, CT. I would like to thank U.S. Repeating Arms and Mr. Pardee for making these production figures available.

Records at the factory indicate the following serial numbers were assigned to guns at the end of the calendar year.

MODEL 1866

Year	Serial		Year	Serial		Year	Serial
1866 -	12476 to 14813		93 -	169007		93 -	466641
67 -	15578		94 -	169011		94 -	481826
68 -	19768		95 -	NONE		95 -	499308
69 -	29516		96 -	NONE		96 -	507545
70 -	52527		97 -	169015		97 -	513421
71 -	88184		98 -	170100		98 -	525922
72 -	109784		99 -	DISCONTINUED		99 -	541328
73 -	118401					1900 -	554128
74 -	125038		**MODEL 1873**			01 -	557236
75 -	125965		1873 -	1 to 126		02 -	564557
76 -	131907		74 -	2726		03 -	573957
77 -	148207		75 -	11325		04 -	588953
78 -	150493		76 -	23151		05 -	602557
79 -	152201		77 -	23628		06 -	613780
80 -	154379		78 -	27501		07 -	NONE
81 -	156107		79 -	41525		08 -	NONE
82 -	159513		80 -	63537		09 -	630385
83 -	162376		81 -	81620		10 -	656101
84 -	163649		82 -	109507		11 -	669324
85 -	163664		83 -	145503		12 -	678527
86 -	165071		84 -	175126		13 -	684419
87 -	165912		85 -	196221		14 -	686510
88 -	167155		86 -	222937		15 -	688431
89 -	167401		87 -	225922		16 -	694020
90 -	167702		88 -	284529		17 -	698617
91 -	169003		89 -	323220		18 -	700734
92 -	NONE		90 -	363220		19 -	702042
			91 -	405026		No last # available	
			92 -	441625		20, 21, 22, 23,	720609

MODEL 1876

Year	Serial
1876 -	1 to 1429
77 -	3579
78 -	7967
79 -	8971
80 -	14700
81 -	21759
82 -	32407
83 -	42410
84 -	54666
85 -	58714
86 -	60397
87 -	62420
88 -	63539
89 -	NONE
90 -	NONE
91 -	NONE
92 -	63561
93 -	63670
94 -	63678
95 -	NONE
96 -	63702
97 -	63869
98 -	63871

MODEL 1885 SINGLE SHOT

Year	Serial
1885 -	1 to 375
86 -	6841
87 -	18328
88 -	30571
89 -	45019
90 -	NONE
91 -	53700
92 -	60371
93 -	69534
94 -	NONE
95 -	73771
96 -	78253
97 -	78815
98 -	84700
99 -	85086
1900 -	88501
01 -	90424
02 -	92031
03 -	92359
04 -	92785
05 -	93611
06 -	94208
07 -	95743
08 -	96819
09 -	98097
10 -	98506
11 -	99012
12 -	NONE
13 -	100352

No further serial numbers were recorded until the end of 1923. Last No. known was: 139700

MODEL 1886

Year	Serial
1886 -	1 to 3211
87 -	14728
88 -	28577
89 -	38401
90 -	49723
91 -	63601
92 -	73816
93 -	83261
94 -	94543
95 -	103708

Year	Serial
96 -	109670
97 -	113997
98 -	119192
99 -	120571
1900 -	122834
01 -	125630
02 -	128942
03 -	132213
04 -	135524
05 -	138838
06 -	142249
07 -	145119
08 -	147322
09 -	148237
10 -	150129
11 -	151622
12 -	152943
13 -	152947
14 -	153859
15 -	154452
16 -	154979
17 -	155387
18 -	156219
19 -	156930
20 -	158716
21 -	159108
22 -	159337

No further serial numbers were recorded until the discontinuance of the model which was in 1935 - at - 159994

MODEL 1887

Year	Serial
1887 -	1 to 7431
88 -	22408
89 -	25673
90 -	29105
91 -	38541
92 -	49763
93 -	54367
94 -	56849
95 -	58289
96 -	60175
97 -	63952
98 -	64855

According to these records no guns were produced during the last few years of this model and it was therefore discontinued in 1901.

MODEL 1890

Records on the Model 1890 are somewhat incomplete. Our records indicate the following serial numbers were assigned to guns at the end of the calendar year beginning with 1908. Actual records on the firearms which were manufactured between 1890 and 1907 will be available from the "Winchester Museum", located at the **"Buffalo Bill Historical Center"** **Attn: Cody Firearms Museum P.O. Box 1000, Cody, WY 82414**

Year	Serial
1908 -	330000 to 363850
09 -	393427
10 -	423567
11 -	451264
12 -	478595
13 -	506936
14 -	531019
15 -	551290
16 -	570497
17 -	589204
18 -	603438
19 -	630801
20 -	NONE
21 -	634783
22 -	643304
23 -	654837
24 -	664613
25 -	675774
26 -	687049
27 -	698987
28 -	711354
29 -	722125
30 -	729015
31 -	733178
32 -	734454

The Model 1890 was discontinued in 1932, however, a clean up of the production run lasted another 8+ years and included another 14 to 15000 guns. Our figures indicate approximately 749,000 guns were made.

MODEL 1892

Year	Serial
1892 -	1 to 23701
93 -	35987
94 -	73508
95 -	106721
96 -	144935
97 -	159312
98 -	165431
99 -	171820
1900 -	183411
01 -	191787
02 -	208871
03 -	253935
04 -	278546
05 -	315425
06 -	376496
07 -	437919
08 -	476540
09 -	522162
10 -	586996
11 -	643483
12 -	694752
13 -	742675
14 -	771444
15 -	804622
16 -	830031
17 -	853819
18 -	870942
19 -	903649
20 -	906754
21 -	910476
22 -	917300
23 -	926329
24 -	938641
25 -	954997
26 -	973896
27 -	990883
28 -	996517
29 -	999238
30 -	999730

31 -	1000727
32 -	1001324

MODEL 94

Records at the factory, and in some years, estimates, indicate the following serial numbers were assigned to guns at the end of the calendar year.

1894 -	1 to 14579
95 -	44359
96 -	76464
97 -	111453
98 -	147684
99 -	183371
1900 -	204427
01 -	233975
02 -	273854
03 -	291506
04 -	311363
05 -	337557
06 -	378878
07 -	430985
08 -	474241
09 -	505831
10 -	553062
11 -	599263
12 -	646114
13 -	703701
14 -	756066
15 -	784052
16 -	807741
17 -	821972
18 -	838175
19 -	870762
20 -	880627
21 -	908318
22 -	919583
23 -	938539
24 -	953198
25 -	978523
26 -	997603
27 -	1027571
28 -	1054465
29 -	1077097
30 -	1081755
31 -	1084156
32 -	1087836
33 -	1089270
34 -	1091190
35 -	1099605
36 -	1100065
37 -	1100679
38 -	1100915
39 -	1101051
40 -	1142423
41 -	1191307
42 -	1221289
43 -	No Record Available
44 -	No Record Available
45 -	No Record Available
46 -	No Record Available
47 -	No Record Available
48 -	1500000
49 -	1626100
50 -	1724295
51 -	1724295
52 -	1910000
53 -	2000000
54 -	2071100
55 -	2145296
56 -	2225000
57 -	2290296
58 -	2365887
59 -	2410555
60 -	2469821
61 -	2500000
62 -	2551921
63 -	2586000
*1964	2700000 - 2797428
65 -	2894428
66 -	2991927
67 -	3088458
68 -	3185691
69 -	3284570
70 -	3381299
71 -	3557385
72 -	3806499
73 -	3929364
74 -	4111426
75 -	4277926
75 -	4463553
76 -	4463553
77 -	4565925
78 -	4662210
79 -	4826596
80 -	4892951
81 -	5024957
82 -	5103248

* The post-64 Model 94 began with serial number 2,700,000.

Serial number 1,000,000 was presented to President Calvin Coolidge in 1927.
Serial number 1,500,000 was presented to President Harry S. Truman in 1948.
Serial number 2,500,000 and 3,000,000 were presented to the Winchester Gun Museum, now located in Cody, Wyoming.
Serial number 3,500,000 was not constructed until 1979 and was sold as auction in Las Vegas, Nevada.
Serial number 4,000,000 - whereabouts unknown at this time.
Serial number 4,500,000 - shipped to Italy by Olin in 1978. Whereabouts unknown.
Serial number 5,000,000 - in New Haven, not constructed as of March 1983.

Records at the factory indicate the following serial numbers were assigned to guns at the end of the calendar year.

MODEL 1895

1895 -	1 to 287
96 -	5715
97 -	7814
98 -	19871
99 -	26434
1900 -	29817
01 -	31584
02 -	35601
03 -	42514
04 -	47805
05 -	54783
06 -	55011
07 -	57351
08 -	60002
09 -	60951
10 -	63771
11 -	65017
12 -	67331
13 -	70823
14 -	72082
15 -	174233
16 -	377411
17 -	389106
18 -	392731
19 -	397250
20 -	400463
21 -	404075
22 -	407200
23 -	410289
24 -	413276
25 -	417402
26 -	419533
27 -	421584
28 -	422676
29 -	423680
30 -	424181
31 -	425132
32 -	425825

MODEL 1903

1903 -	# Not Available
04 -	6944
05 -	14865
06 -	23097
07 -	31852
08 -	39105
09 -	46496
10 -	54298
11 -	61679
12 -	69586
13 -	76732
14 -	81776
15 -	84563
16 -	87148
17 -	89501
18 -	92617
19 -	96565
20 -	# Not Available
21 -	97650
22 -	99011
23 -	100452
24 -	101688
25 -	103075
26 -	104230
27 -	105537
28 -	107157
29 -	109414
30 -	111276
31 -	112533

32 - 112992

This model was discontinued in 1932, however, a clean up of parts was used for further production of approximately 2000 guns. Total production was stopped at serial number 114962... in 1936.

MODEL 1905

1905 -	1 to 5659
06 -	15288
07 -	19194
08 -	20385
09 -	21280
10 -	22423
11 -	23503
12 -	24602
13 -	25559
14 -	26110
15 -	26561
16 -	26910
17 -	27297
18 -	27585
19 -	28287
20 -	29113

MODEL 1906

1906 -	1 to 52278
07 -	89147
08 -	114138
09 -	165068
10 -	221189
11 -	273355
12 -	327955
13 -	381922
14 -	422734
15 -	453880
16 -	483805
17 -	517743
18 -	535540
19 -	593917
20 -	NONE
21 -	598691
22 -	608011
23 -	622601
24 -	636163
25 -	649952
26 -	665484
27 -	679892
28 -	695915
29 -	711202
30 -	720116
31 -	725978
32 -	727353

A clean up of production took place for the next few years with a record of production reaching approximately 729305.

MODEL 1907

1907 -	1 to 8657
08 -	14486
09 -	19707
10 -	23230
11 -	25523
12 -	27724
13 -	29607
14 -	30872
15 -	32272
16 -	36215
17 -	38235
18 -	39172
19 -	40448
20 -	No # Available
21 -	40784
22 -	41289
23 -	41658
24 -	42029
25 -	42360
26 -	42688
27 -	43226
28 -	43685
29 -	44046
30 -	44357
31 -	44572
32 -	44683
33 -	44806
34 -	44990
35 -	45203
36 -	45482
37 -	45920
38 -	46419
39 -	46758
40 -	47296
1941 -	47957
42 -	48275
43 -	NONE
44 -	NONE
45 -	48281
46 -	48395
47 -	48996
48 -	49684
**49 -	50662
**50 -	51640
**51 -	52618
**52 -	53596
**53 -	54574
**54 -	55552
**55 -	56530
**56 -	57508
**57 -	58486

** Actual records on serial numbers stops in 1948. The serial numbers ending each year from 1948 to 1957 were derived at by taking the last serial number recorded (58486) and the last number from 1948, (49684) and dividing the years of production (9), which relates to 978 guns each year for the nine year period.

MODEL 1910

1910 -	1 to 4766
11 -	7695
12 -	9712
13 -	11487
14 -	12311
15 -	13233
16 -	13788
17 -	14255
18 -	14625
19 -	15665
20 -	No # Available
21 -	15845
22 -	16347
23 -	16637
24 -	17030
25 -	17281
26 -	17696
27 -	18182
28 -	18469
29 -	18893
30 -	19065
31 -	19172
32 -	19232
33 -	19281
34 -	19338
35 -	19388
36 -	19445

A cleanup of production continued into 1937 when the total of the guns was completed at approximately 20786

MODEL 1911 S.L.

1911 -	1 to 3819
12 -	27659
13 -	36677
14 -	40105
15 -	43284
16 -	45391
17 -	49893
18 -	52895
19 -	57337
20 -	60719
21 -	64109
22 -	69132
23 -	73186
24 -	76199
25 -	78611

The Model 1911 was discontinued in 1925. However, guns were produced for three years after that date to clean up production and excess parts. When this practice ceased there were approximately 82774 guns produced.

MODEL 52

1920 -	None indicated
21 -	397
22 -	745
23 -	1394
24 -	2361
25 -	3513
26 -	6383
27 -	9436
28 -	12082
29 -	14594
30 -	17253
31 -	21954
32 -	24951
33 -	26725
34 -	29030
35 -	32448
36 -	36632
37 -	40419
38 -	43632
39 -	45460
40 -	47519
41 -	50317
42 -	52129
43 -	52553
44 -	52560
45 -	52718
46 -	56080
47 -	60158

Year	Serial
48 -	64265
49 -	68149
50 -	70766
51 -	73385
52 -	76000
53 -	79500
54 -	80693
55 -	81831
56 -	96869
57 -	97869
58 -	98599
59 -	98899
60 -	102200
61 -	106986
62 -	108718
63 -	113583
64 -	118447
65 -	120992
66 -	123537
67 -	123727
68 -	123917
69 -	E 124107
70 -	E 124297
71 -	E 124489
72 -	E 124574
73 -	E 124659
74 -	E 124744
75 -	E 124828
76 -	E 125019
77 -	E 125211
78 -	E 125315

This Model was discontinued in 1978. A small clean up of production was completed in 1979 with a total of - 125419.

MODEL 53

In the case of the Model 53 the following list pertains to the amount of guns produced each year rather than a serial number list. The Model 53 was serially numbered concurrently with the MODEL 92.

MODEL 53s PRODUCED

Year	Produced
1924 -	1488
25 -	2861
26 -	2531
27 -	2297
28 -	1958
29 -	1733
30 -	920
31 -	621
32 -	206

This Model was discontinued in 1932, however, a clean up of production continued for 9 more years with an additional 486 guns.

Total Production Approximately - 15100

Records at the factory indicate the following serial numbers were assigned to guns at the end of the calendar year.

MODEL 54

Year	Serial
1925 -	1 to 3140
26 -	8051
27 -	14176
28 -	19587
29 -	29104
30 -	32499
31 -	36731
32 -	38543
33 -	40722
34 -	43466
35 -	47125
36 -	50145

MODEL 55 CENTERFIRE

Year	Serial
1924 -	1 to 836
25 -	2783
26 -	4957
27 -	8021
28 -	10467
29 -	12258
30 -	17393
31 -	18198
32 -	19204
33 -	Clean up 20580

MODEL 61

Year	Serial
1932 -	1 to 3532
33 -	6008
34 -	8554
35 -	12379
36 -	20615
37 -	30334
38 -	36326
39 -	42610
40 -	49270
41 -	57493
42 -	59871
43 -	59872
44 -	59879
45 -	60512
46 -	71629
47 -	92297
48 -	115281
49 -	125461
50 -	135461
51 -	145821
52 -	156000
53 -	171000
54 -	186000
55 -	200962
56 -	216923
57 -	229457
58 -	242992
59 -	262793
60 -	282594
61 -	302395
62 -	322196
63 -	342001

This Model was discontinued in 1963. For some unknown reason there are no actual records available from 1949 through 1963. The serial number figures for these years are arrived at by taking the total production figure of 342001, subtracting the last known # of 115281, and di-

viding the difference equally by the amount of remaining years available, (15).

MODEL 62

Year	Serial
1932 -	1 to 7643
33 -	10695
34 -	14090
35 -	23924
36 -	42759
37 -	66059
38 -	80205
39 -	96534
40 -	116393
41 -	137379
42 -	155152
43 -	155422
44 -	155425
45 -	156073
46 -	183756
47 -	219085
48 -	252298
49 -	262473
50 -	272648
51 -	282823
52 -	293000
53 -	310500
54 -	328000
55 -	342776
56 -	357551
57 -	383513
58 -	409475

MODEL 63

Year	Serial
1933 -	1 to 2667
34 -	5361
35 -	9830
36 -	16781
37 -	25435
38 -	30934
39 -	36055
40 -	41456
41 -	47708
42 -	51258
43 -	51631
44 -	51656
45 -	53853
46 -	61607
47 -	71714
48 -	80519
49 -	88889
50 -	97259
51 -	105629
52 -	114000
53 -	120500
54 -	127000
55 -	138000
56 -	150000
57 -	162345
58 -	174692

MODEL 70

Year	Serial
1935 -	1 to 19
36 -	2238
37 -	11573
38 -	17844
39 -	23991
40 -	31675
41 -	41753
42 -	49206
43 -	49983
44 -	49997

45 -	50921			53 -	354348
46 -	58382			54 -	380460
47 -	75675			55 -	406574

MODEL 71

48 -	101680	1935 -	1 to 4
49 -	131580	36 -	7821
50 -	173150	37 -	12988
51 -	206625	38 -	14690

MODEL 88

Model 70		Model 71		Model 88	
45 -	50921			53 -	354348
46 -	58382	**MODEL 71**		54 -	380460
47 -	75675	1935 -	1 to 4	55 -	406574
48 -	101680	36 -	7821	**MODEL 88**	
49 -	131580	37 -	12988	1955 -	1 to 18378
50 -	173150	38 -	14690	56 -	36756
51 -	206625	39 -	16155	57 -	55134
52 -	238820	40 -	18267	58 -	73512
53 -	282735	41 -	20810	59 -	91890
54 -	323530	42 -	21959	60 -	110268
55 -	361025	43 -	22048	61 -	128651
56 -	393595	44 -	22051	62 -	139838
57 -	425283	45 -	22224	63 -	148858
58 -	440792	46 -	23534	64 -	160307
59 -	465040	47 -	25728	65 -	162699
60 -	504257	48 -	27900	66 -	192595
61 -	545446	49 -	29675	67 -	212416
62 -	565592	50 -	31450	68 -	230199
63 -	581471	51 -	33225	69 -	H239899
All post 64 Model 70s began with the serial number 700,000.		52 -	35000	70 -	H258229
		53 -	37500	71 -	H266784
64 -	740599	54 -	40770	72 -	H279014
65 -	809177	55 -	43306	73 -	H283718
66 -	833795	56 -	45843	**MODEL 100**	
67 -	869000	57 -	47254	1961 -	1 to 32189
68 -	925908	**MODEL 74**		62 -	60760
69 -	G941900	1939 -	1 to 30890	63 -	78863
70 -	G957995	40 -	67085	64 -	92016
71 -	G1018991	41 -	114355	65 -	135388
72 -	G1099257	42 -	128293	66 -	145239
73 -	G1128731	43 -	NONE	67 -	209498
74 -	G1175000	44 -	128295	68 -	210053
75 -	G1218700	45 -	128878	69 -	A210999
76 -	G1266000	46 -	145168	70 -	A229995
77 -	G1350000	47 -	173524	71 -	A242999
78 -	G1410000	48 -	223788	72 -	A258001
79 -	G1447000	49 -	249900	73 -	A262833
80 -	G1490709	50 -	276012		
81 -	G1537134	51 -	302124		
		52 -	328236		

WINCHESTER SHOTGUNS

Records at the factory indicate the following serial numbers were assigned to guns at the end of the calendar year.

MODEL 1897

1897 -	1 to 32335	21 -	700428	47 -	936682
98 -	64668	22 -	715902	48 -	944085
99 -	96999	23 -	732060	49 -	953042
1900 -	129332	24 -	744942	50 -	961999
01 -	161665	25 -	757629	51 -	970956
02 -	193998	26 -	770527	52 -	979913
03 -	226331	27 -	783574	53 -	988860
04 -	258664	28 -	769806	54 -	997827
05 -	296037	1929 -	807321	55 -	1006784
06 -	334059	30 -	812729	56 -	1015741
07 -	377999	31 -	830721	57 -	1024700
08 -	413618	32 -	833926	Records on this Model are incomplete. The above serial numbers are estimated from 1897 thru 1903 and again from 1949 thru 1957. The actual records are in existence from 1904 through 1949.	
09 -	446888	33 -	835637		
10 -	481062	34 -	837364		
11 -	512632	35 -	839728		
12 -	544313	36 -	848684		
13 -	575213	37 -	856729		
14 -	592732	38 -	860725		
15 -	607673	39 -	866938	**MODEL 1901 SHOTGUN**	
16 -	624537	40 -	875945	1904 -	64,856 to 64,860
17 -	646124	41 -	891190	05 -	66453
18 -	668383	42 -	910072	06 -	67486
19 -	691943	43 -	912265	07 -	68424
20 -	696183	44 -	912327		
		45 -	916472		
		46 -	926409		

08 -	69197
09 -	70009
10 -	70753
11 -	71441
12 -	72167
13 -	72764
14 -	73202
15 -	73509
16 -	73770
17 -	74027
18 -	74311
19 -	74872
20 -	77000

MODEL 12

1912 -	5308
13 -	32418
14 -	79765
15 -	109515
16 -	136412
17 -	159391
18 -	183461
19 -	219457
20 -	247458
21 -	267253
22 -	304314
23 -	346319
24 -	385196
25 -	423056
26 -	464564
27 -	510693
28 -	557850
29 -	600834
30 -	626996
31 -	651255
32 -	660110
33 -	664544
34 -	673994
35 -	686978
36 -	720316
37 -	754250
38 -	779455
39 -	814121
40 -	856499
41 -	907431
42 -	958303
43 -	975640

44 -	975727
45 -	990004
1946 -	1029152
47 -	1102371
48 -	1176055
49 -	1214041
50 -	1252028
51 -	1290015
52 -	1328002
53 -	1399996
54 -	1471990
55 -	1541929
56 -	1611868
57 -	1651435
58 -	1690999
59 -	1795500
60 -	1800000
61 -	1930999
62 -	1956990
63 -	1962001

A clean up of production took place from 64 through 66 with the ending serial # 1970875.

NEW STYLE M/12

1972 -	Y200 011-
	Y2006396
73 -	Y2015662
74 -	Y2022061
75 -	Y2024478
76 -	Y2025482
77 -	Y2025874
78 -	Y2026156
79 -	Y2026399

MODEL 24

1939 -	1 to 8118
40 -	21382
41 -	27045
42 -	33670
43 -	NONE RECORDED
44 -	33683
45 -	34965
46 -	45250
47 -	58940
48 -	64417

There were no records kept on this model from 1949 until its

discontinuance in 1958. The total production was approximately 116280.

MODEL 42

1933 -	1 to 9398
34 -	13963
35 -	17728
36 -	24849
37 -	30900
38 -	34659
39 -	38967
40 -	43348
41 -	48203
42 -	50818
43 -	50822
44 -	50828
45 -	51168
46 -	54256
47 -	64853
48 -	75142
49 -	81107
50 -	87071
51 -	93038
52 -	99000
53 -	108201
54 -	117200
55 -	121883
56 -	126566
57 -	131249
58 -	135932
59 -	140615
60 -	145298
61 -	149981
62 -	154664
63 -	159353

MODEL 50

1954 -	1 to 24550
55 -	49100
56 -	73650
57 -	98200
58 -	122750
59 -	147300
60 -	171850
61 -	196400

WINCHESTER MODEL 101 SERIALIZATION

Ser. No.	Mfg. Mo.	Year	Ser. No.	Mfg. Mo.	Year	Ser. No.	Mfg. Mo.	Year
50,000	10	1959	60,500	8	1963	71,000	8	1964
50,500	3	1960	61,000	8	1963	71,500	9	1964
51,000	5	1960	61,500	11	1963	72,000	9	1964
51,500	6	1960	62,000	11	1963	72,500	10	1964
52,000	9	1961	62,500	11	1963	73,000	10	1964
52,500	3	1962	63,000	12	1963	73,500	11	1964
53,000	4	1962	63,500	1	1964	74,000	11	1964
53,500	5	1962	64,000	1	1964	74,500	12	1964
54,000	8	1962	64,500	2	1964	75,000	12	1964
54,500	9	1962	65,000	3	1964	75,500	1	1965
55,000	10	1962	65,500	3	1964	76,000	2	1965
55,500	12	1962	66,000	3	1964	76,500	2	1965
56,000	1	1963	66,500	3	1964	77,000	3	1965
56,500	2	1963	67,000	5	1964	77,500	4	1965
57,000	3	1963	67,500	5	1964	78,000	4	1965
57,500	3	1963	68,000	5	1964	78,500	4	1965
58,000	4	1963	68,500	5	1964	79,000	4	1965
58,500	5	1963	69,000	6	1964	79,500	4	1965
59,000	6	1963	69,500	6	1964	80,000	5	1965
59,500	6	1963	70,000	7	1964	80,500	6	1965
60,000	7	1963	70,500	7	1964	81,000	6	1965

Ser. No.	Mfg. Mo.	Year	Ser. No.	Mfg. Mo.	Year	Ser. No.	Mfg. Mo.	Year
81,500	6	1965	113,500	4	1968	145,000	4	1971
82,000	6	1965	114,000	5	1968	145,500	5	1971
82,500	8	1965	114,500	5	1968	200,000	3	1966
83,000	8	1965	115,000	6	1968	200,500	3	1966
83,500	8	1965	115,500	6	1968	201,000	3	1966
84,000	9	1965	116,000	7	1968	201,500	3	1966
84,500	9	1965	116,500	7	1968	202,000	4	1966
85,000	10	1965	117,000	9	1968	202,500	4	1966
85,500	10	1965	117,500	10	1968	203,000	4	1966
86,000	10	1965	118,000	1	1969	203,500	5	1966
86,500	10	1965	118,500	1	1969	204,000	6	1966
87,000	10	1965	119,000	2	1969	204,500	6	1966
87,500	10	1965	119,500	3	1969	205,000	7	1966
88,000	11	1965	120,000	4	1969	205,500	8	1966
88,500	11	1965	120,500	4	1969	206,000	8	1966
89,000	11	1965	121,000	4	1969	206,500	8	1966
90,000	12	1965	121,500	4	1969	207,000	9	1966
90,500	12	1965	122,000	5	1969	207,500	9	1966
91,000	12	1965	122,500	6	1969	208,000	9	1966
91,500	1	1966	123,000	6	1969	208,500	12	1966
92,000	1	1966	123,500	6	1969	209,000	2	1967
92,500	2	1966	124,000	7	1969	209,500	7	1967
93,000	2	1966	124,500	7	1969	210,000	10	1967
93,500	2	1966	125,000	7	1969	210,500	12	1967
94,000	3	1966	125,500	8	1969	211,000	1	1968
94,500	3	1966	126,000	8	1969	211,500	1	1968
95,000	5	1966	126,500	9	1969	212,000	10	1968
95,500	5	1966	127,000	9	1969	212,500	10	1968
96,000	6	1966	127,500	10	1969	213,000	10	1968
96,500	7	1966	128,000	11	1969	213,500	11	1968
97,000	7	1966	128,500	11	1969	214,000	12	1968
97,500	7	1966	129,000	11	1969	214,500	12	1968
98,000	8	1966	129,500	2	1970	215,000	1	1969
98,500	8	1966	130,000	2	1970	215,500	2	1969
99,000	9	1966	130,500	3	1970	216,000	5	1969
99,500	9	1966	131,000	3	1970	216,500	6	1969
100,000	10	1966	131,500	4	1970	217,000	9	1969
100,500	10	1966	132,000	4	1970	217,500	10	1969
101,000	10	1966	132,500	4	1970	218,000	11	1969
101,500	11	1966	133,000	4	1970	218,500	12	1969
102,000	11	1966	133,500	5	1970	219,000	12	1969
102,500	12	1966	134,000	5	1970	219,500	12	1969
103,000	1	1967	134,500	5	1970	220,000	12	1969
103,500	1	1967	135,000	6	1970	220,500	1	1970
104,000	2	1967	135,500	6	1970	221,000	1	1970
104,500	3	1967	136,000	6	1970	221,500	2	1970
105,000	4	1967	136,500	8	1970	222,000	3	1970
105,500	5	1967	137,000	8	1970	222,500	7	1970
106,000	5	1967	137,500	8	1970	223,000	9	1970
106,500	5	1967	138,000	8	1970	223,500	9	1970
107,000	9	1967	138,500	11	1970	224,000	9	1970
107,500	10	1967	139,000	12	1970	224,500	9	1970
108,000	10	1967	139,500	12	1970	225,000	10	1970
108,500	11	1967	140,000	12	1970	225,500	10	1970
109,000	11	1967	140,500	1	1971	226,000	11	1970
109,500	11	1967	141,000	2	1971	226,500	11	1970
110,000	12	1967	141,500	2	1971	227,000	11	1970
110,500	1	1968	142,000	2	1971	227,500	12	1970
111,000	2	1968	142,500	3	1971	228,000	12	1970
111,500	3	1968	143,000	3	1971	228,500	4	1971
112,000	3	1968	143,500	4	1971	229,000	4	1971
112,500	3	1968	144,000	4	1971	229,500	4	1971
113,000	3	1968	144,500	4	1971			

PROOF MARKS

The proof marks shown below will assist in determining nationality of manufacturers when no other markings are evident. Since the U.S. has no proofing houses (as in England, France, Germany and other European countris), most U.S. built guns voluntarily proof their firearms with a specifed style of proofmark (i.e. the interlocked "WP" synonymous with the Winchester trademark can be fired using modern (smokeless powder) shells. Pre-1850 European firearms oftentimes do not exhibit any commercial proof marks and with the exception of an occasional barrel address, they represent the single hardest bracket of firearms I can research properly. Captured weapons from major wars occasionally show 2 different nationalities of proofmarks. This is acceptable since the gun was proofed in a national proof house after original manufacture and again when the gun was "exported" to a different country as a military acquisition.

AUSTRIAN PROOF MARKS

PROOF MARK	CIRCA	PROOF HOUSE	TYPE OF PROOF and GUN
	since 1891	Vienna	provisional proof for multi barrel guns
	since 1891	Ferlach	provisional proof for multi barrel guns
	1829-1958	Vienna	black powder proof for multi barrel guns
	1829-1958	Ferlach	black powder proof for multi barrel guns
BH	since 1891	Bundesheer	preliminary proof for multi barrel guns
NPB	1891-1928	Budapest	smokeless powder proof for parabellum pistols
NPF	1891 to date	Ferlach	smokeless powder proof for parabellum pistols
NPP	1891-1931	Ferlach	smokeless powder proof for parabellum pistols
NPV	since 1891	Vienna	smokeless powder proof for parabellum pistols
NPW	1891-1931	Weipert	smokeless powder proof for parabellum pistols

BELGIAN PROOF MARKS

PROOF MARK	CIRCA	PROOF HOUSE	TYPE OF PROOF and GUN
	since 1852	Belgian	provisional black powder proof for breech loading guns & rifled barrels

PROOF MARK	CIRCA	PROOF HOUSE	TYPE OF PROOF and GUN
	—	—	double proof marking for unfurnished barrels
	—	—	triple proof provisional marking for unfurnished barrels
	since 1893	—	definitive black powdr proof for breech loading guns, small bore guns & handguns
	since 1853	Perron	View stamp & inspectors mark for parabellum pistols
P.V	since 1924	—	Nitro proof for rifled barrel & parabellum pistols
R	since 1852	—	rifled arms defense for smokeless proof parabellum pistols
PV	—	—	Superior nitro proof

BRITISH PROOF MARKS - ENGLAND-

PROOF MARK	CIRCA	PROOF HOUSE	TYPE OF PROOF and GUN
	since 1856	London	provisional proof for barrels
	since 1856	Birmingham	provisional proof for barrels
	since 1637	London	definitive black powder proof for shotguns, muzzle loader barrels
NP	since 1904	London	definitive nitro proof for all guns - parabellum pistols
BNP	since 1954	Birmingham	definitive nitro proof for barrel & action
BP	since 1904	Birmingham	black powder proof only for parabellum pistols
	1868-1925	London	definitive special super power proof for parabellum pistols
SP	1868-1925	Birmingham	voluntary special black powder proof

PROOF MARKS: British, cont.

	1868-1925	London	reproof marking for black powder rifles
	1868-1925	Birmingham	reproof marking for black powder rifles
	1868-1925	Birmingham	definitive black powder proof for shotguns
	since 1904	Birmingham	definitive nitro proof for all guns
	since 1670	London	view mark
	since 1904	Birmingham	view mark

FRENCH PROOF MARKS

PARIS HOUSE	ST ETIENNE HOUSE	CIRCA	TYPE OF PROOF and GUN
		since 1897	provisional proof unfinished short barreled guns
	ST ETIENNE	1897	standard proof for finished guns
	ST ETIENNE	1897	double proof finished & joined barrels
N.A.	N.A. ST ETIENNE	1897	single barrel proof for non-assembled guns
	F	1897	finished black powder guns
	S	1897	special proof for finished guns
		1897	ordinary smokeless powder proof
	AR ST. ETIENNE	1897	superior smokeless powder proof

GERMAN PROOF MARKS

PROOF MARK	CIRCA	PROOF HOUSE	TYPE OF PROOF and GUN
	since 1952	Ulm	
	since 1968	Hannover	
	since 1968	Kiel (W. German)	
	since 1968	Munich	
	since 1968	Cologne (W. German)	
	since 1968	Belin (W. German)	
FB	since 1952	W. German	voluntary proof for Flobert rifle
J	since 1952	W. German	repair proof for major gun parts
M	since 1952	W. German	provisional black powder for shotgun & multi barreld rifles
N	since 1952	W. German	definitive nitro proof for all guns
SP	since 1952	W. German	definitive black powder for smokeless ammo guns
	since 1952	W. German	Flobert for special purpose guns signal, flare, gas, & stun guns
N	since 1945	E. German, Suhl	smokeless powder proof
G	since 1950	E. German, Suhl	1st black powder proof for rifled barrels
N	since 1950	E. German, Suhl	nitro powder proof

PROOF MARKS: German, cont.

PROOF MARK	since 1950	E. German, Suhl repair proof
	since 1950	E. German, Suhl 1st black powder proof for smooth bored barrels
	since 1950	E. German, Suhl inspection mark
	since 1950	E. German, Suhl choke-bore barrel mark

ITALIAN PROOF MARKS

PROOF MARK	CIRCA	PROOF HOUSE	TYPE OF PROOF and GUN
	since 1951	Brescia	provisional proof for all guns
	since 1951	Gardone	provisional proof for all guns
PSF	since 1951	Gardone & Brescia	definitive proof for guns with smokeless powder
PSF FINITO	since 1951	Gardone & Brescia	finish proof for firearms non saleable
P N	since 1951	Gardone & Brescia	1st black powder proof

SPANISH PROOF MARKS

PROOF MARK	CIRCA	PROOF HOUSE	TYPE OF PROOF and GUN
Pº	since 1910	Eibar	provisional black powder proof for shotguns
EX	since 1910	Eibar	temporary black powder proof for shotguns
NF	since 1910	Eibar	final black powder proof for breech loading shotguns
BV	since 1910	Eibar	final smokeless powder proof for breech loading shotguns
SCH	since 1910	Eibar	re-enforced smokeless powder proof for breech loading shotguns
	since 1910	Eibar	provisional proof for shotguns

	since 1910	Eibar	final black powder proof for breech loading shotgun
	since 1923	Eibar	final & single black powder proof for double barreled muzzle loading shotun
	since 1923	Eibar	final & single black powder proof for single barrel smooth bored breechloading guns
	since 1923	Eibar	final black powder proof for double barreled breechloading rifles
	since 1923	Eibar	final black powder proof for single barrel breechloading rifles
E	since 1923	Eibar	re-enforced voluntary proof for single proof for single & double barrel shotguns
	since 1923	Eibar	Final proof of military-style rifle
	since 1923	Eibar	single & final proof of non-self loading pistols
	since 1923	Eibar	single & final proof for self loading pistols & revolvers
	since 1929	Eibar	admission proof for guns with old marks
	since 1929	Eibar	proof used in Barcelona for guns with old marks
R	since 1929	Eibar	final proof for revolver
P	since 1929	Eibar	proof for semi-automatic pistols
FE	since 1929	Eibar	special manufacturer's mark for guns made for foreign sales
AXIII	since 1929	Eibar	smokeless proof for shotgun barrels
CH	since 1929	Eibar	re-inforced smokeless proof for shotgun barrels

Index of Manufacturers

A.A. ...87
A.A.A. ...87
A & R Sales ...87
A F C ...87
A.J. Ordnance ...87
AKS ...87
AMAC ...88
A M T. ...88
A-Square ...90
A T C S A. ...91
AYA (Aguirre Y Aranzabal). ...91
Abadie ...94
Abbey, George T. ...95
Abbey, F.J. & Company ...95
Abbiatico & Salvinelli ...95
Accu-Tek ...96
Acha ...97
Acme ...97
Acme Arms ...97
Acme Hammerless ...98
Action (M.S.) ...98
Action Arms, Ltd. ...98
Adams ...99
Adams, Joseph ...99
Adamy, Gebruder ...99
Adirondack Arms Company ...99
Adler ...100
Advantage Arms USA, Inc. ...100
Aetna ...100
Aetna Arms Company ...100
Agner ...101
Airguns, Modern ...1081
Air Match ...101
Ajax Army ...101
Akrill, E. ...101
Alamo Ranger ...101
Alaska ...101
Alaskan Commemoratives ...102
Aldazabal ...103
Alert ...103
Alexia ...103
Alfa ...103
Alkartasuna Fabrica De Armas, S.A. ...104
Allen & Thurber ...104
Allen Firearms ...104
Alpha Arms, Inc. ...104
American Arms ...104
American Arms Co. ...106
American Arms, Inc. ...106
American Barlock Wonder ...112
American Derringer Corp. ...112
American Firearms Manufacturing
    Company, Inc ...115
American Gun Co. ...116
American Historical Foundation, The ...116
American Industries ...121
American International ...121
Anciens Etablissements Pieper ...121
Anschutz ...121
Apache ...129
Arlington Ordnance ...129
Armalite Incorporated ...129
Armament Technology Corp. ...130
Armes De Chasse ...130
Armi Techniche of Emilio Rizzini ...130
Arminex Ltd. ...130
Arminius ...131
Armitage International, Ltd. ...131
Arms Corporation of the Philippines ...132
Arms Research Associates ...133
Armscorp USA, Inc. ...133
Armsport ...135
Arrieta, S.L. ...144
Arrizablaga ...145
ASP ...146
Astra ...146

Australian Automatic Arms Pty. Ltd ...150
Auto Mag ...151
Auto-Ordnance Corp. ...152
Auto Pointer ...153
BSA Guns Limited ...155
Baford Arms, Inc. ...157
Baikal ...157
Bailons Gunmakers Limited ...158
Baker Gun & Forging Co. ...158
Barrett Firearms Manufacturing, Inc. ...159
Bar-Sto ...160
Bauer Firearms Corporation ...160
Bayard ...160
Beeman Precision Arms, Inc. ...160
Beholla Pistol ...161
Benelli ...161
Benson Firearms, Ltd. ...165
Beretta, Dr. Franco ...165
Beretta, Pietro ...167
Beretta, Pietro, Handguns ...167
Beretta, Pietro, Rifles ...174
Beretta, Pietro, Shotguns ...176
Bergmann ...191
Bernardelli, Vincenzo ...192
Bersa ...200
Bertuzzi ...202
Big Bear ...202
Big Horn Arms Corp. ...203
Bighorn Rifle Co. ...203
Bingham, Ltd. ...203
Bittner ...204
Black Powder, Modern ...1105
Bland, Thomas & Sons Gunmakers Ltd. ...204
Blaser ...204
Boito ...206
Borchardt ...206
Boss & Company ...206
Boswell, Charles ...207
Breda, Ernesto ...208
Bren ...209
Bretton ...210
Britarms ...210
Brno Arms ...211
Bronco ...216
Brown Precision Inc. ...216
Browning Arms ...218
Browning Pistols ...219
Browning Single Shot Rifles ...225
Browning .22 Semi-Auto Rifles ...226
Browning BAR Rifles ...227
Browning FAL Rifles ...228
Browning Lever Action Rifles 229
Browning Bolt Action Rifles 231
Browning Slide Action Rifles ...234
Browning O/U Rifle ...234
Browning A-5 Shotguns 235
Browning O/U Superposed ...240
Browning Citori Shotguns 245
Browning Single Barrel Trap ...250
Browning SxS Shotguns ...252
Browning Slide Action Shotguns ...252
Browning Limited Edition Sets ...254
Browning Limited Edition Sets/Black-
powder ...254
Bruchet ...255
Bryco Arms ...255
Budischowsky ...256
Bushmaster Firearms Inc. ...256
Cetme ...257
C Z ...257
Cabanas ...261
Cabela's Inc. ...261
Calico ...262
Camex-Blaser USA, Inc. ...263
Cartridge Firearms ...263
Casartelli, Carlo ...263

Caspian Arms Ltd. 263
Century Gun Distributing, Inc. 264
Century International Arms, Inc. 264
Champlin Firearms 267
Chapuis Armes 267
Chapuis, P.Armes Et Fils 268
Charlin Arms 268
Charles Daly 269
Charter Arms 269
Chinese Firearms 271
Chipmunk Manufacturing, Inc. 271
Churchill, E.J., (Gunmakers) Limited 272
Churchill 274
Cimarron F.A. Mfg. Co. 276
Claridge Hi-Tec Inc. 280
Clark Custom Guns, Inc. 281
Classic Doubles 281
Clerke Products 283
Clifton Arms 283
Cobray Industries 283
Cogswell & Harrison, Limited 283
Colt's Manufacturing Co., Inc. 284
Colt's Percussion Revolvers 285
Colt's Derringers 292
Colt's Pocket Pistol 293
Colt's New Line Revolver 293
Colt's Percussion Conversions 294
Colt's Open Top Revolvers 294
Colt's SAA (1873-1940 mfg.) 294
Colt's SAA 2nd Gen (1956-75 mfg.) 297
Colt's SAA 3rd Gen. (1976-81 mfg.) 299
Colt's SAA Current Mfg. 302
Colt's Scout SAA 303
Colt's Gov.'t Model 1911 Commercial 306
Colt's Gov.'t Model 1911 .45 ACP 306
Colt's Gov.t Model 1911 A1 Variations 308
Colt's Gov.t Model 1911 A1 Military 309
Colt's Ace Models 310
Colt's Semi-Auto Pistol Centerfire 311
Colt's Semi-Auto Pistol Rimfire 317
Colt's Revolvers: Double Action 319
Colt's Rifles 327
Colt's Shotguns 332
Colt's Commemoratives 333
Commando Arms 345
Competitor 346
Connecticut Valley Arms, Inc. 346
Connecticut Valley Classics 346
Contento/Ventura 346
Continental Arms Corporation 347
Cooey Machine & Arms Co. Ltd. 347
Coonan Arms, Inc. 348
Cooper Arms 348
Cop 349
Cosmi, Americo & Figlio 349
Crescent Firearms Company 350
Custom Gun Guild 350
D W M 351
Daewoo 351
Daisy 351
Dakin Gun Co. 352
Dakota Arms, Inc. 353
Dakota S.A. Revolvers 353
Daly, Charles 356
Daly, Charles 1976 to Present 358
Daly, Charles - Prussian Mfg. 356
Dan Arms of America 360
Dardick 361
Darne S.A. 361
Davidson Firearms 363
Davis Industries 363
Demro 363
Desert Industries, Inc. 364
Detonics Firearms Industrie 364
Diarm S.A. 364
Dixie Gun Works 364
Domingo Acha 365
Domino IGI 365
Dreyse Pistol 365
Drillings 365
Dubiel Arms Company 367

Dumoulin, Ernest 368
Dumoulin, Henri & Fils 371
E.M.F. Co., Inc. 373
84 Gun Co. 375
Eagle Arms Inc. 376
Ego Armas, S.A. 376
Enfield 377
Enfield America, Inc. 378
ERA 378
Erma-Werke 378
European American Armory Corp. 380
Excam 384
Exel Arms of America, Inc. 388
F A S 391
FEG 391
F.I.E. 392
Fabarm 399
Fabbri, Armi 402
Fabrique Nationale 402
Falcon Firearms 405
Famars, A & S. 406
Fausti, Stefano 406
Feather Enterprises, Inc. 406
Federal Engineering Corporation 407
Federal Ordnance, Inc. 408
Feinwerkbau 410
Ferlach Guns 411
Femaru 411
Ferlib 412
Fiala Outfitters Incorporated 413
Fias 413
Finnish Lion 413
Fiocchi of America, Inc. 413
Firearms International (F I) 413
Fox, A.H. 414
Franchi, Luigi 417
Francotte, Auguste & CIE S.A. 423
Fraser, Danl. & Co. 425
Fraser Firearms Corp. 425
Freedom Arms 425
French Military 427
Frigon 428
Frommer Pistols 428
Furr Arms 428
Galef Shotguns 429
Galil 429
Gamba, Renato 430
Garbi 434
Gastinne Renette 436
Gatling Gun Company 437
Gaucher 438
Gavage 438
Gentry, David 438
German WWII Mil. Pistols (P.38's) 438
Gevarm 439
Gib 439
Gibbs Guns, Inc. 440
Gibbs Rifle Co. 440
Glock 442
Golden Eagle 443
Golden State Arms 443
Goncz Armament, Inc. 444
Granger, G. 444
Grant, Stephen 444
Great Western Arms Co. 444
Greener, W.W., Limited 445
Greifelt and Company 447
Grendel, Inc. 448
Griffin & Howe 449
Grulla Armas 450
Gunworks, Ltd. 450
Gustaf, Carl 450
Gyrojet 451
H.J.S. Industries, Inc. 453
H&R 1871, Inc. 453
H-S Precision, Inc. 454
HWP Industries 454
Haenel, C.G. 455
Hambrusch Jagdwaffen GmbH 455
Hammerli 455
Hammerli-Walther 458

Harrington & Richardson, Inc. 459
Harrington & Richardson Handguns 459
Harrington & Richardson Rifles 464
Harrington & Richardson Shotguns 466
Harrington & Richardson Commem.'s. ..468
Hartford Arms & Equipment Co. 469
Haskell Manufacturing 470
Hatfield Gun Co., Inc. 470
Hawes Firearms 471
Heckler & Koch 471
Helwan....................... 476
Henry Rifle 476
Herold Rifle 476
Herters 476
Heym, Friedrich Wilh 476
Hi-Point Firearms 480
Higgins, J. C. 480
High Standard 481
High Standard .22 LR Semi-Autos 481
High Standard Revolvers................... 492
High Standard Rifles...................... 495
High Standard Shotguns.................... 495
Hofer-Jagdwaffen P..................... 497
Holland & Holland, Ltd. 498
Holloway Arms Co. 502
Holmes Firearms 502
Hopkins & Allen Arms Co., 1902-1914........ 502
Howa..................................... 505
Hunter Arms Co. 505
Husqvarna 505
Hy-Hunter Inc. Firearms Mfg. Co. 506
Hyper.................................. 506
I A B Shotguns......................... 507
I A I.................................... 507
I G A Shotguns........................... 507
Iberia Firearms 508
Indian Arms.............................. 508
Industria Armi Galesi 508
Infallible.............................. 508
Inglis Hi-Powers 508
Ingram 509
Interarms 509
Interdynamic of America, Inc. 513
Intratec 514
Irwindale Arms, Inc. (IAI) 515
Israel Arms Ltd. 515
Israeli Military Industries (IMI) 516
Italian Military Arms..................... 516
Ithaca Gun 516
Ithaca Rifles........................... 516
Ithaca Shotguns: Side by Side 518
Ithaca Trap Guns 521
Ithaca SKB Shotguns..................... 522
Ithaca Single Barrel Trap 521
Ithaca Models 37 and 87 523
Ithaca Semi- Auto Shotguns.............. 526
JSL (Hereford)........................... 529
Jackson Hole Firearms 529
Jagd-Und Sportwaffen Suhl GmbH............ 529
Japanese Military Rifles 530
Jarrett Rifles, Inc. 530
Jeffery, W.J. & Co., Ltd 531
Jennings Firearms Inc. 531
Jericho 532
Johnson Automatics, Inc. 532
Iver Johnson Arms, Inc. 533
Iver Johnson Revolvers.................. 533
Iver Johnson Semi-Auto Pistols 535
Iver Johnson Rifles......................536
Iver Johnson Shotguns................... 538
Jurras.................................. 539
KBI Inc................................. 541
KDF Inc. (Kleinguenther) 542
K.F.C. 545
Kassnar Imports, Inc. 546
Keberst International................... 546
Kendall International..................... 546
Keppeler, Dieter 546
Kepplinger, I. Hannes 546
Kessler Arms Corporation 547
Kimball, J., Arms Co. 547

Kimber of Oregon, Inc. 547
Kimel 553
Kleinguenther Firearms Co................ 554
Kodiak Co............................... 554
Kolibri................................. 554
Korriphila.............................. 554
Korth 555
Krag-Jorgensen 556
Krico 557
H. Krieghoff Gun Co..................... 560
L.A.R. Manufacturing Inc................ 567
L E S Incorporated 567
Lahti Pistol 568
Lake Field Arms Ltd..................... 568
Lames................................... 568
Lanber Shotguns 569
Lasalle 570
Laurona 571
Law Enforcement Ordnance Corp. 575
Lebeau-Courally 575
Lefever Arms Company 576
Lefever, D.M. & Son..................... 578
Le Forgeron 579
Le Francais Pistols 579
Liberator............................... 580
Liberty Arms Works, Inc. 580
Liegeoise D' Armes 580
Lignose (Bergman)....................... 580
Liliput................................. 580
Ljungman 581
Ljutic Industries....................... 581
Llama Handguns 582
Lorcin Engineering Co., Inc. 584
Lugers with Variations.............. 585
Luger Toggle Identification............. 585
Lugers-1900 DWM Manufacture 588
Lugers-1902 DWM Manufacture 589
Lugers-1904 DWM Manufacture 589
Lugers-1906 DWM Manufacture 589
Lugers 1906-1918 DWM & Erfurt Mfg 590
Lugers 1920-1930 DWM Manufacture 592
Lugers-Kreighoff 594
Lugers-Mauser........................... 595
Luger-Reworks 596
Lugers-Simson 597
Lugers-Swiss Bern 597
Lugers-Interarms, Stoeger & Recent
  Importation........................... 597
Lugers-Special Interest 598
Lugers-Accessories 599
Luna.................................... 600
MAC 601
MAS 601
MBA Gyrojet 601
MK Arms, Inc 601
MKE 601
M.O.A. Corporation 602
Magnum Research, Inc.................... 602
Malin, F.E.............................. 604
Mag-Tech 604
Makarov................................. 604
Mamba 604
Mandall Shooting Supplies............... 604
Mannlicher Schoenauer
  Sporting Rifles....................... 606
Manufrance 608
Manurhin................................ 608
Marathon Products, Inc.................. 610
Marble's Game Getter 610
Margolin 611
Marlin Firearms Company 611
Marlin Antique Rifles 611
Marlin Modern Rifles 612
Marlin Single Shot Rifles 620
Marlin Shotguns 621
Marrochi............................... 624
Masquelier S.A. 625
Matiba.................................. 626
Matra-Manurhin Defense.................. 626
Mauser-Werke 626
Mauser-Werke Pistols.................... 626

Mauser-Werke Broomhandles 632
Mauser-Werke Military Rifles 633
Mauser-Werke Sporting Rifles....................... 636
Maverick Arms, Inc. 643
McMillan, G. & Co.. 644
Menz, August 646
Mercury 646
Mercury (Belgian)... 646
Merkel, Gebruder... 646
Merkel Drillings... 647
Merkel Rifles & Combination Guns.............. 647
Merkel Shotguns... 648
Merkel Shotguns SxS Recent 650
Merkel Shotguns O/U..................................... 651
Merrill 652
Merwin Hulbert & Co. 652
Miida.. 655
Miller, David Co. 655
Miroku Shotguns 655
Mitchell Arms Inc. 656
Montana Armory Inc....................................... 660
Montgomery Ward 661
Morini 661
Mossberg, O.F. & Sons, Inc. 661
Mossberg Pistols... 662
Mossberg Rifles... 662
Mossberg Targo Shotgun 670
Mossberg Shotguns 671
Musgrave.. 679
Musketeer Rifles 679
Nambu Pistol Japanese Military.................... 681
Navy Arms Company 682
New Detonics Mfg. Corp................................ 687
New England Arms Co.................................... 689
New England Firearms 689
Newton Arms Co... 690
Nikko Firearms Co. Ltd.................................. 691
Norinco.. 692
North American Arms 695
North American Safari Express 696
ODI... 697
Obregon... 697
Old-West Gun Co. 697
Olympic Arms Inc. 697
Omega.. 698
Omega Firearms 698
Omega Pistol 698
Omega Shotguns 699
Opus Sporting Arms, Inc. 699
Ortgies Pistols 700
Orvis... 700
P.A.F... 703
P.A.W.S., Inc. 703
P.S.M.G. Gun Co... 703
PTK International Inc. 703
Paramount Manufacturing Ltd. 704
Para-Ordnance Mfg. Inc................................. 704
Pardini 704
Parker Pistols... 705
Parker Brothers.. 705
Parker Reproductions 710
Parker-Hale Limited.. 711
Pauza Specialties 714
Pedersen Custom Guns 715
Pentheny de Pentheny, Inc. 716
Pedersoli, Davide & C. 716
Perazzi... 717
Peregrine Industries, Co. 737
Perugini-Visini 737
Peters Stahl GmbH 738
Phelps Mfg. Co. 738
Phillips & Rogers Inc....................................... 739
Phoenix Arms 739
Phoenix Arms Co. 739
Photo-Percentage Grading System.............. 33
Pietta, F.lli 739
Piotti.. 740
Piranha 741
Poly Technologies, Inc.................................... 741
Powell, William & Son Ltd............................. 741
Prandelli-Gasperini 742

Premier 742
Prinz 743
Purdey, James and Sons, Limited 743
QFI... 745
Quality Arms, Inc. 746
Quality Parts Co./Bushmaster 746
R.G. Industries 747
RWS 747
Radom.. 748
Ram-Line Inc.. 748
Randall Firearms Company 748
Ravell 751
Raven Arms 752
Record-Match 752
Reising Arms Company 752
Remington Arms Company 752
Remington Handguns...................................... 753
Remington Rifles Antique 759
Remington Rifles Centerfire 761
Remington Rifles Rimfire 766
Remington Shotguns 779
Renette, Gastine... 793
Rhode Island Arms Company......................... 793
Richland Arms Company 794
Riedl Rifle Company 795
Rigby, John and Company 795
Ripamonti, G... 797
Rizzini, Battista 797
Rizzini, F.lli 798
Rizzini, Armi Techniche of Emilio 799
Rocky Mountain Arms, Inc. 799
Rogak... 800
Rohm 800
Ross Rifle Company 800
Rossi.. 801
Rottweil.. 803
Royal American Shotguns 805
Ruby... 805
Ruger.. 805
Ruko Products, Inc. 805
Russian Service Pistol and Rifle 807
S.A.C.M. 807
S.A.E. 807
S K B Arms Company 810
SKS 816
SSK Industries 816
S.W.D., Inc. 817
Safari Arms 818
Sako... 819
Samco Global Arms 822
Sardius... 822
Sarriugarte, Francisco S.A. 823
Sarasqueta, Felix 823
Sarasqueta, J.J. 823
Sarasqueta, Victor 824
Sauer, J.P. & Sohn 824
Savage Arms Inc... 829
Savage Pistols 829
Savage Rifles... 830
Savage Combo. Guns...................................... 840
Savage Shotguns 841
Scattergun Technologies, Inc. 844
Schall 845
Scheller-Spezialwaffen 845
Schultz & Larsen 845
Schuetzen Rifles 846
Scott, W.C., Ltd. 846
Security Industries 847
Sedco Industries Inc. 847
Sedgley, R.F., Inc. 847
Seecamp, L.W. Co.,Inc. 848
Seitz... 848
Semmerling 848
Serialization Listings 1,027
Sharps, Christian... 848
Sheridan Products, Inc. 850
Shilen Rifles Incorporated.............................. 850
Shiloh Rifle Mfg. Co., Inc. 851
Sidewinder... 853
Sig.. 853
Sig-Hammerli.. 854

Sig Sauer ... 854
Sile Distributors ... 856
Silma Sporting Guns ... 856
Sirkis Industries, Ltd. ... 856
Skorpion ... 857
Smith, L.C. ... 857
Smith & Wesson ... 860
S & W Revolvers Early Models ... 860
S & W Revolvers Older Mfg. ... 862
S & W Revolvers Recent Mfg. ... 873
S & W Semi-Auto Pistols ... 886
S & W Rifles ... 894
S & W Shotguns ... 895
Snake Charmer ... 897
Societa Siderurgica Glisenti ... 897
Sodia, Franz ... 897
Sokolovsky Corporation Sport Arms (SCSA) 897
Sphinx ... 897
Spitfire ... 898
Springfield Armory ... 898
Springfield Inc. ... 804
Stallard Arms ... 911
Standard Arms Company ... 911
Star, Bonifacio Echeverria ... 911
Steel City Arms, Inc. ... 914
Sterling ... 915
Sterling Armament, Ltd. ... 915
Stevens, J., Arms Company ... 915
Stevens, J. Rifles ... 916
Stevens, J. Shotguns ... 917
Steyr Austrian Military ... 919
Steyr Daimler Puch A.G. ... 919
Steyr Mannlicher ... 919
Stock, Franz ... 922
Stoeger Arms Corp. ... 923
Stoner Rifle ... 923
Street Sweeper ... 923
Sturm, Ruger & Co. ... 923
Sturm, Ruger & Co. Pistols ... 923
Sturm, Ruger & Co. Revolvers ... 925
Sturm, Ruger & Co. Rifles ... 930
Sturm, Ruger & Co. Shotguns ... 935
Sundance Industries, Inc. ... 936
Survival Arms, Inc. ... 936
Svendsen, Erl, F. A. Mfg. Co. ... 936
Symes & Wright Ltd. ... 936
Talon ... 937
Tanner, Andre ... 937
Tar-Hunt Custom Rifles, Inc. ... 937
Taurus International Firearms ... 937
Techni-Mec ... 941
Terrier One ... 942
Texas Gunfighters ... 942
Texas Longhorn Arms, Inc. ... 942
Thomas ... 943
Thompson Carbines ... 943
Thompson/Center Arms ... 943
Thunder-Five ... 946
Tikka ... 946
Timberwolf ... 947
Tippman Arms Co. ... 948
Tokarev ... 948
Tradewinds ... 948
Trench/Riot Shotguns ... 948
USAS 12 ... 953
U.S. Arms Company ... 953
Uberti USA, Inc. ... 953
Ugartechea, Ignacio ... 956
Ultimate ... 956
Ultra Light Arms Co., Inc. ... 956
Unique ... 957
United Sporting Arms, Inc. ... 959
United States Historical Society ... 960
Universal Firearms ... 965
U.S. Military ... 967
U.S. M1 Carbine ... 967

UZI ... 968
Valmet, Inc. ... 969
Varner Sporting Arms, Inc. ... 970
Verney-Carron ... 971
Vickers Limited ... 971
Victory Arms Co. Ltd. ... 971
Vierlings ... 971
Virginian ... 972
Voere ... 972
Volunteer Enterprises ... 972
Vouzelaud ... 973
Walther ... 975
Walther Pre-War Pistols ... 975
Walther PP Wartime Mfg. ... 976
Walther PPK Wartime Mfg. ... 978
Walther Post-War Pistols 980
Walther PPK/S Pistols ... 982
Walther Post WWII P.38's ... 983
Walther Target Pistols ... 984
Walther Rifles ... 985
Walther Shotguns ... 987
Walther, Manurhin Mfg. ... 987
Warner Arms Corporation ... 988
Weatherby ... 988
Weatherby Rifles ... 992
Weatherby .22 LR Rifles ... 994
Weatherby Shotguns ... 994
Weaver Arms Corporation ... 996
Webley & Scott, Limited ... 997
Weihrauch, Hans-Hermann ... 999
Wesson, Firearms Co. Inc. (D. Wesson). ... 1000
Wesson, Frank ... 105
Western Arms Company ... 1007
Western Field ... 1007
Westley Richards & Co. Ltd ... 1007
Whitney Firearms Company ... 1009
Whitworth ... 1009
Wichita Arms, Inc. ... 1009
Wickliffe Rifles ... 1010
Wildey Firearms ... 1011
Wilkinson Arms ... 1012
Winchester ... 1012
Winchester Rifle Lever Actions 1860-95 ... 1014
Winchester Rifles: Single Shot ... 1022
Winchester Rifles: Bolt Action ... 1023
Winchester Rifles: Model 70 ... 1028
Winchester Rifles: Semi-Auto ... 1031
Winchester Rifles: Disc. Slide Action ... 1032
Winchester Rifles: Post-64 Lever Act. ... 1034
Winchester Rifles: Post-64 Bolt Act. ... 1036
Winchester Shotguns: 1879-1964 Mfg. ... 1042
Winchester Shotguns: Model 12 ... 1044
Winchester Shotguns: Model 21 ... 1045
Winchester Shotguns: Post-64 Mfg. ... 1049
Winchester Shotguns: Model 101 ... 1054
Winchester Shotguns: SXS Recent Mfg. ... 1058
Winchester U.S. Commemoratives ... 1060
Winchester Foreign Commem's ... 1064
Winslow Arms Company ... 1066
Wiseman, Bill & Co. ... 1066
Woodward, James and Sons ... 1067
Wyoming Arms Mfg. Corp. ... 1067
Z-B Rifle ... 1069
Zabala Hermanos ... 1069
Zanardini ... 1069
Zanotti, Fabio ... 1071
Zastava Arms ... 1071
Zephyr ... 1072
Zoli, Angelo (Disc.) ... 1073
Zoli, Antonio (Current Mfg.) ... 1076
Modern Airguns ... 1081
Modern Black Powder Firearms ... 1105
Trademark Index ... 1175
Serialization ... 1185
Proof Marks ... 1206
Index ... 1212